Handbook of
THE
BIOLOGY
OF AGING

THE HANDBOOKS OF AGING

Consisting of Three Volumes:

Critical comprehensive reviews of
research knowledge, theories,
concepts, and issues

Editor-in-Chief: **James E. Birren**

Handbook of the Biology of Aging

Edited by Caleb E. Finch and Edward L. Schneider

Handbook of the Psychology of Aging

Edited by James E. Birren and K. Warner Schaie

Handbook of Aging and the Social Sciences

Edited by Robert H. Binstock and Ethel Shanas

Handbook of
THE BIOLOGY OF AGING

Second Edition

Editors
Caleb E. Finch
Edward L. Schneider

With the assistance of Associate Editors

Richard C. Adelman
George M. Martin
Edward J. Masoro

VNR VAN NOSTRAND REINHOLD COMPANY
New York

Manufactured in the United States of America

Published by Van Nostrand Reinhold Company Inc.
135 West 50th Street
New York, New York 10020

Van Nostrand Reinhold Company Limited
Molly Millars Lane
Wokingham, Berkshire RG11 2PY, England

Van Nostrand Reinhold
480 Latrobe Street
Melbourne, Victoria 3000, Australia

Macmillan of Canada
Division of Gage Publishing Limited
164 Commander Boulevard
Agincourt, Ontario M1S 3C7, Canada

15   14   13   12   11   10   9   8   7   6   5   4   3   2   1

Library of Congress Cataloging in Publication Data
Maine entry under title:

Handbook of the biology of aging.

  (The Handbooks of aging)
  Includes indexes.
  1. Aging—Handbooks, manuals, etc.   I. Finch, Caleb
Ellicott.   II. Schneider, Edward L.   III. Series.
[DNLM: 1. Aging.   WT 104 H236]
QP86.H35   1985   574.3'72   84-27052
ISBN 0-442-22529-6

CONTRIBUTORS

Richard C. Adelman, Ph.D.
Institute of Gerontology, Univerity of Michigan, Ann Arbor, MI

Arthur K. Balin, M.D., Ph.D.
Rockefeller University, New York, N.Y.

Edwin L. Bierman, M.D.
Department of Medicine, University of Washington, School of Medicine, Seattle, WA

Floyd D. Bloom, Ph.D.
The Salk Institute, San Diego, CA

Dwight B. Brock, Ph.D.
Chief, Biometry Office, National Institute on Aging, Bethesda, MD. 20205

Jacob A. Brody, M.D.
National Institute on Aging, National Institutes of Health, Bethesda, MD

Ellsworth R. Buskirk, M.D.
Director, Laboratory for Human Performance Research, Pennsylvania State University, University Park, PA

Mary Carskadon, Ph.D.
Sleep Disorders & Research Center, Stanford University School of Medicine, Palo Alto, CA.

Carl Cotman, Ph.D.
University of California, Department of Physchobiology, Irvine, CA

Charles Czeisler,Ph.D.
Center for Health Policy, JFK School of Government, Harvard University, Boston, MA

Gary W. Dawson, Ph.D.
Associate Professor of Clinical Pharmacy, Idaho State University, College of Pharmacy, Pocatello, ID

William Dement, M.D., Ph.D.
Stanford University, School of Medicine, Stanford, CA

Ranjan Duara, M.D.
Laboratory of Neurosciences, National Institutes of Health, Bethesda, MD

A. N. Exton-Smith, M.D.
St. Pancras Hospital, Department of Geriatric Medicine, London, ENGLAND

Caleb E. Finch, Ph.D.
University of Southern California, Andrus Gerontology Center, Los Angeles, CA

Michael J. Getz, M.D.
Mayo Clinic, Department of Cell Biology, Rochester, MN

Gary L. Grove, Ph.D.
Skin Study Center, Philadelphia, PA

Yves Guigoz, M.D.
Research Department, Nestle Products, Technical Assistance Co., SWITZERLAND

S. Mitchell Harman, M.D., Ph.D.
National Institute on Aging, Gerontology Research Center, Baltimore City Hospitals, Baltimore, MD

David E. Harrison, Ph.D.
The Jackson Laboratory, Bar Harbor, ME

Perrie B. Hausman, Ph.D.
Division of Geriatrics and Gerontology, Department of Medicine, Cornell University Medical School, New York, NY

Vicky Holets, Ph.D.
Department of Psychobiology, University of California at Irvine, Irvine, CA

Lewis A. Jacobson, Ph.D.
Department of Biological Sciences, University of Pittsburgh, Pittsburgh, PA

William B. Kannel, M.D.
Chief, Section of Preventive Medicine and Epidemiology, Boston University Medical Center, School of Medicine, Boston, MA

Thomas B. L. Kirkwood, M.D.
National Institute of Biological Standards & Control, Hampstead, London, ENGLAND

Albert M. Kligman, M.D., Ph.D.
University of Pennsylvania, School of Medicine, Department of Dermatology, Philadelphia, PA

Daniel Kripke, Ph.D.
Department of Psychiatry, University of California, San Diego, La Jolla, CA

Edward G. Lakatta, M.D.
Gerontology Research Center, Cardiology Section, Laboratory of Clinical Physiology, Baltimore, MD

Philip W. Landfield, M.D.
Department of Physiology & Pharmacology, Bowman-Gray School of Medicine, Winston Salem, NC

F. A. Lints, M.D.
Laboratoire de Genetique, Faculte des Sciences Argonomique, Universite Catholique de Louvain, BELGIUM

Edythe London, Ph.D.
Laboratory of Neurosciences, National Institute on Aging, Gerontology Research Center, Baltimore City Hospitals, Baltimore, MD

George Martin, Ph.D.
Department of Pathology, University of Washington, Seattle, WA

Edward J. Masoro, Ph.D.
University of Texas, Department of Physiology, San Antonio, TX

Graydon S. Meneilly, M.D., F.R.C.P.
Harvard Medical School, Division of Aging, Boston, MA

Kenneth L. Minaker, M.D., F.R.C.P.
Beth Israel Hospital, Boston, MA; and Assistant Professor of Medicine, Division of Aging, Harvard Medical School, Boston, MA

Hamish N. Munro, M.B., D.S.D.
Human Nutrition Research Center on Aging, Tufts University, Boston, MA

Faramarz Naeim, M.D.
Department of Pathology, Center for the Health Sciences, University of California, Los Angeles, Los Angeles, CA

Larry D. Nooden, Ph.D.
University of Michigan, Department of Botony, Ann Arbor, MI

Thomas H. Norwood, M.D.
University of Washington, School of Medicine, Seattle, WA

Patricia Prinz, Ph.D.
Department of Psychiatry & Behavioral Science, University of Washington, Seattle, WA

Stanley I. Rapoport, M.D.
Gerontology Research Center, Baltimore City Hospitals, Baltimore, MD

John Reed, Ph.D.
National Institute on Aging, National Institutes of Health, Bethesda, MD

Mitchell E. Reff, Ph.D.
Smith, Kline, and Beckman Corp. Philadelphia, PA.

Gary Richardson, M.D.
Neuroendocrinology Laboratory, Fuller Pavillion, Brigham and Women's Hospital, Boston, MA

Joseph Rogers, Ph.D.
Department of Neurology, University of Massachusetts, Medical Center, Worcester, MA

John W. Rowe, M.D.
Division of Gerontology, Department of Medicine, Harvard Medical School, Beth Israel Hospital, Boston, MA

Richard L. Russell, Ph.D.
University of Pittsburgh, Department of Biology, Pittsburgh, PA

Edward L. Schneider, M.D.
Associate Director of Biomedical Research and Clinical Medicine National Institute of Aging, National Institutes of Health, Bethesda, MD

Nathan W. Schock, Ph.D.
Scientist Emeritus, National Institute on Aging, Baltimore City Hospitals, Baltimore, MD

Richard B. Setlow, M.D.
Brookhaven National Laboratory, Associated Universities, Inc., Upton, NY

James R. Smith, Ph.D.
Department of Virology & Epidemiology, Baylor College of Medicine, Houston, TX

Joan Smith-Sonneborn, Ph.D.
University of Wyoming, Department of Zoology, Laramie, WY

George B. Talbert, M.D.
Department of Anatomy, Downstate Medical Center, Brooklyn, NY

John E. Thompson, Ph.D.
Department of Biology, University of Waterloo, Waterloo, Ontario, Canada

Raymond R. Tice, M.D.
Brookhaven National Labs, Medical Department, Upton, NY

Robert E. Vestal, M.D.
Veterans Administrative Hospital, Division of Geriatrics, Boise, ID

Roy L. Walford, M.D.
Professor of Pathology, UCLA School of Medicine, Center for the Health Sciences, Los Angeles, CA

Marc E. Weksler, M.D.
Division of Geriatrics & Gerontology, Department of Medicine, Cornell University Medical School, New York, NY

PREFACE

The 2nd Edition of the *Handbook of the Biology of Aging* is intended to update and extend the 1st Edition, published seven years ago. This new edition has an almost completely different authorship and includes many new topics. Overall, the same editorial policies have been followed, particularly the ideal of writing for the general scientific audience as well as the specialist. Topics from geriatric medicine, an area that has only recently emerged, appear in a number of chapters. We believe that the pathobiology of aging in humans should be regarded as an important aspect of the intellectually important problems and puzzles of biogerontology. The basic and clinical aspects of aging presented here should encourage more attention to the interrelationships between aging and disease that will be of critical importance to the future of our societies. Regretfully, some thriving research areas can be mentioned only briefly in a volume of this size, but excellent reviews of some neglected topics are still available in the 1st Edition.

Finally, we wish to acknowledge our gratitude to our colleagues (listed below) who served as outside reviewers, and to Brooke Jacobson for patient and attentive editorial assistance.

R. Adelman	B. Gilchrest	H. McGill
B. Baum	I. Goldstein	E. McGuire
C. Baxter	J. Halter	T. McNeill
E. Bierman	P. Hanawalt	J. Meites
C. Blomquist	J. Holland	E. Miller
D. Bowden	J. Holloszy	R. Monnat
H. Brody	S. Horvath	A. Muggleton-Harris
W. Brown	K. Jeon	A. Ostfeld
R. Bruce	J. Johnson	M. Reff
D. Buetow	Z. Khachaturian	G. Reigle
A. Clark	D. Kalu	R. J. Shmookler-Reis
V. Cristofalo	A. Kenny	J. Roberts
K. Davis	E. Lakatta	M. Rose
W. Ershler	P. Landfield	M. Rothstein
J. Florini	A. Leopold	J. W. Rowe
I. Freedberg	B. Levy	D. R. Sanadi
D. Freeman	L. Libow	J. Siegle
I. Fridovich	M. Lieberman	C. Smith
J. Gallant	J. H. K. Lu	R. S. Sohal
D. Gershon	E. Masoro	R. Steffanus

G. Stein

M. Talal

J. Trosko

E. Vesell

R. L. Walford

W. Ward

M. E. Weksler

P. Wise

H. Woolhouse

V. Young

B. P. Yu

Editors-in-Chief

Caleb E. Finch

Edward L. Schneider

Associate Editors

Richard C. Adelman

George M. Martin

Edward J. Masoro

CONTENTS

PART TWO

Aging in Lower Systems

PART THREE

Molecular Biology

PART SIX

Neurobiology

PART SEVEN

Human Biology and Pathology

PART **1** PERSPECTIVES ON AGING AND MORTALITY

1
EPIDEMIOLOGIC AND STATISTICAL CHARACTERISTICS OF THE UNITED STATES ELDERLY POPULATION

Jacob A. Brody
and
Dwight B. Brock
Epidemiology, Demography, and Biometry Program
National Institute on Aging
National Institutes of Health

INTRODUCTION

In 1900 there were approximately 3.1 million people over age 65 in the United States. This number increased to 24.1 million in 1978 (U.S. Bureau of the Census, 1979c). While these figures show an absolute increase of eightfold in the total number of elderly persons, people over age 65 also represent a larger proportion of the total population— that number having risen from 4.1 percent in 1900 to 11 percent in 1978. Projections made on classic demographic and Census Bureau assumptions suggest that persons over age 65 will number at least 32 million, and constitute no less than 11.9 percent of the population, by the year 2000. This assumes that mortality rates will not change appreciably over time. These projections do not account for declining mortality rates and, hence, have tended to be underestimates of the actual size and proportion of the elderly population. If mortality rates continue to decline as they have since 1900, and certainly

since 1970, the number of people over age 65 could reach 38 million by the year 2000, or 13.6 percent of the total population (Rice, 1978). Further, there is accumulating evidence which questions the claim that declining mortality in the twentieth century is a phenomenon of lowered infant mortality and the control of infectious diseases. In fact, age-specific death rates have been declining for all ages for the better part of the twentieth century. While the numbers involved certainly give credence to the enormous impact of the effect on longevity of controlling infectious diseases of childhood, maternal mortality, etc., the declining mortalities in elderly age groups throughout the century are certainly having an impact on the accumulation of the very old and very vulnerable within our society (Brody, 1982c).

In terms of general health and well-being, as well as the problems of financing Medicare, Medicaid, and the retirement systems, it is useful to state some concerns which will be brought up related to mortality and morbidity in middle and late life. The proportion of the population over age 65 is 11.0 percent, while the mortality in this age group is 66.1 percent of the total (NCHS, 1980a). As can be seen in Table 1, the proportion of the population declines very particularly over age 75, while the percentage of total deaths rises rapidly. Thus, 2.3 percent of the total population is 80 years and over, but this age group accounts for 29.6 percent of the total mortality, while at age 85 and over 1.0 percent of the total population accounts for 16.8 percent of the total mortality. Through extension of life we place more people into the age group 85 and over. Here, very slight changes in total numbers associated with high mortality rates have already altered the basic pattern of diminishing mortality. Recently (NCHS, 1980b), provisional data suggested that the age-specific mortality rates for those 85 and over had risen. This trend will surely increase as we place more elderly into the group 85 and over. We anticipate more dramatic mortality shifts as the median age of individuals 85 and over rises. A further disquieting set of data compiled by the National Health Interview Survey (NHIS) which is conducted annually by the National Center for Health Statistics (NCHS) seems to indicate a general rise in morbidity for all age groups which, however, is particularly notable in middle life (Colvez and Blanchett, 1981). Thus while life expectancy is being prolonged, there is at least some evidence that disabilities may also be increasing. Since at present these data are not controverted or confirmed through any mechanism but self-reported surveys, the full extent of the problem cannot be appraised totally. However, the implications are that in recent years, the U.S. population either is, or considers itself to be, less healthy before entering into the age group 65 and over.

In this chapter we will discuss the characteristics of the elderly population principally as they relate to mortality trends and future implications. Some attention will be directed toward morbidity and mortality in later years. Questions relating to the emerging data on relatively long-term trends for diminished age-specific mortality even among the elderly, as well as a serious possibility of increasing morbidity and disability in these populations, will be alluded to.

It is obvious that the aging process is a continuum throughout an individual's life and a reflection of the impact of numerous exogenous and endogenous factors, and related medical, social, and inherent characteristics. The rate of aging cannot be accurately measured, but empirically it has been shown in some careful, limited studies that there is a great disparity in the age of different in-

TABLE 1. Estimates of the Population 65 Years and Over—by Race, Sex, and Age, 1978. Numbers in thousands. (Figures may not add to totals due to rounding.)

Sex and Race	65 and Over	AGE GROUP					
		65–69	70–74	75 and Over	75–79	80–84	85 and Over
All races	24,065	8,576	6,364	9,125	4,171	2,748	2,206
Male	9,782	3,803	2,687	3,292	1,631	973	688
Female	14,282	4,773	3,677	5,832	2,540	1,774	1,518
White	21,809	7,650	5,817	8,342	3,842	2,517	1,983
Male	8,819	3,398	2,442	2,979	1,487	882	610
Female	12,990	4,252	3,375	5,363	2,356	1,634	1,373
Other	2,256	926	547	783	329	231	223
Male	964	405	245	314	145	91	78
Female	1,292	521	302	469	184	140	145

SOURCE: U.S. Bureau of the Census, *Current Population Reports,* Series P-25, No. 870, 1979.

dividuals for different physiological parameters (Eisdorfer, 1977). There is undoubtedly a basic flaw in characterizing a person as elderly simply upon the attainment of a particular chronological age, but no mechanism has been suggested which gives a more consistently reliable appraisal than chronological age. The recognition that chronological age is a relatively weak indicator of physiological age is readily appreciated when one sees the wide range in health status among individuals of the same age. This, of course, provides maximum incentive for future research into the cause of these wide discrepancies in health status on an age-specific basis and also allows us to be optimistic that through better understanding and research we can place the majority of the population into the healthiest segment of a given chronological age.

POPULATION CHARACTERISTICS

Age, Sex, and Race

Age. Estimates for 1978 of the population over 65 by age, race, and sex are given in Table 1. As mentioned, this group of 24.1 million constituted 11 percent of the total U.S. population of approximately 218 million. A number of observations can be made on the basis of the estimates in this table. First, it has been noted in the past that the older population has itself been getting older and will continue to do so for some time (Siegel, 1980). Individuals over age 75 constituted 38 percent of the total population over age 65. By the year 2003, this proportion will increase to 47 percent (Rice, 1978). After age 75 or so, morbidity and mortality rates increase strikingly; the appearance of more than one chronic disease and the increased likelihood of presently poorly understood, but devastating illnesses such as the senile dementias become more prominent.

Sex. A second important factor shown in Table 1 is the ratio of males to females among the elderly population. For each successive age group, the female population

progressively outnumbered the male population by increasing margins. The number of men per 100 women decreased from 80 for the age group 65–69 to 45 for the population 85 and over. Siegel's (1980) projections showed that for the 65–69 age group, the corresponding ratio would rise to 82 in the year 2000 and to 83 in 2020, but for the 85-and-over segment, the ratio would fall to 39 in 2000 and slightly below 39 in 2020. These facts also have considerable significance for the medical care system since females have been heavier users of services than males. Female survival advantage is a phenomenon in all advanced human societies although few nations have differentials as large as the United States. It must be pointed out, however, that while the discrepancies between males and females are not as great in other nations, there are basic and fundamental questions posed by the fact that female survival seems to be one of the most pervasive findings within the animal kingdom. For virtually every species as far down the phylogenetic tree as can be studied (Hamilton, 1948), it has been documented that there is a female survival advantage. Thus, sex differences alone provide one of the most promising areas of research into health and longevity available to science.

Race. White persons constituted 87.9 percent of the population 65 and over, and 86.4 percent of the entire U.S. population. This, too, varied by age group, increasing from 87.9 percent for the 65–69 age group to a high of 91.4 percent among persons 75–79, and declining to 87.8 percent of those 85 and over. Cause-specific as well as age-specific mortality rates vary among ethnic groups, which provides a potentially useful tool for epidemiologic (specifically etiologic) research.

Geographic Distribution

In 1978 some 45 percent of persons 65 and over lived in the states of California, Florida, Illinois, New York, Ohio, Pennsylvania, and Texas (U.S. Bureau of the Census,

1979a). Of these seven states, both California and New York had elderly populations numbering over two million. The other five states each had elderly populations in excess of a million persons. Population figures by state are given in Table 2, along with the percent increase in population between 1970 and 1978.

Since 1970 six states had grown in elderly population by more than 40 percent: Nevada (79), Arizona (67), Florida (53), Hawaii (51), and Alaska and New Mexico (47 percent each). The 14 states with 12 percent or more of their total population in the 65-and-over age group included Florida (17.6 percent), Arkansas (13.4 percent), Iowa (13.1 percent), Missouri and South Dakota (13.0 percent each), Nebraska and Rhode Island (12.9 percent each), Kansas (12.6 percent), Oklahoma and Pennsylvania (12.4 percent each), Maine (12.2 percent), Massachusetts (12.1 percent), and North Dakota and West Virginia (12.0 percent each).

Interstate migration rates for elderly persons tended to be low, and the elderly often remained in rural areas or large urban centers. The high proportions of the elderly occurring in certain states were due more to the out-migration of younger people over a period of time than to the recent in-migration of older persons or to relatively low fertility rates (Rives and Serow, 1981). As shown in Table 3, most older persons resided in metropolitan areas. The proportion living in central cities was about the same as that living in other parts of the metropolitan area. There was little variation by age group or sex in these proportions.

Family Composition and Living Arrangements

Most persons 65 years and over live in families that consist of an elderly married couple with no children or other relatives residing in their homes. The difference in living arrangements between elderly men and women is striking, regardless of age or ethnicity (Table 4) (U.S. Bureau of the Census, 1979b). As shown in Figure 1, in 1978 a high proportion (78 percent) of males were married and living with their spouses, whereas only 37 percent of females over 65 were married

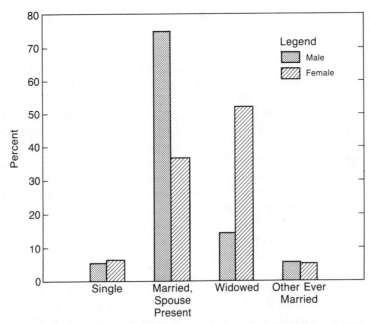

Figure 1. Percent of persons 65 years and over—by marital status and sex: March 1978. (Source: U.S. Bureau of the Census, *Current Population Reports,* Series P-23, No. 85, 1979.)

TABLE 2. Estimates of the Noninstitutionalized Population 65 and Over—by State: Provisional Figures for 1978.

State	Number (thousands)	Percent of Total Population	Percent Increase 1970–78	State	Number (thousands)	Percent of Total Population	Percent Increase 1970–78	State	Number (thousands)	Percent of Total Population	Percent Increase 1970–78
U.S. total	24,054	11.0	20.4	Kansas	297	12.6	11.9	North Carolina	550	9.9	33.6
Alabama	408	10.9	25.9	Kentucky	388	11.1	15.5	North Dakota	78	12.0	18.2
Alaska	10	2.5	46.7	Louisiana	370	9.3	21.5	Ohio	1,125	10.5	13.2
Arizona	269	11.4	66.7	Maine	133	12.2	16.3	Oklahoma	357	12.4	19.5
Arkansas	293	13.4	23.9	Maryland	370	8.9	24.0	Oregon	285	11.7	26.5
California	2,243	10.1	25.1	Massachusetts	700	12.1	10.5	Pennsylvania	1,461	12.4	15.3
Colorado	232	8.7	24.1	Michigan	867	9.4	15.7	Rhode Island	120	12.9	16.0
Connecticut	347	11.2	20.9	Minnesota	463	11.6	13.7	South Carolina	258	8.8	35.8
Delaware	55	9.5	26.2	Mississippi	269	11.2	21.6	South Dakota	89	13.0	11.3
District of Columbia	73	10.8	3.3	Missouri	629	13.0	12.7	Tennessee	478	11.0	25.1
Florida	1,510	17.6	53.2	Montana	81	10.3	18.5	Texas	1,264	9.7	28.0
Georgia	473	9.3	29.3	Nebraska	202	12.9	10.7	Utah	102	7.8	32.3
Hawaii	66	7.4	50.8	Nevada	55	8.4	79.4	Vermont	55	11.3	16.1
Idaho	87	9.9	29.5	New Hampshire	96	11.0	22.8	Virginia	468	9.1	27.4
Illinois	1,206	10.7	10.8	New Jersey	824	11.3	18.8	Washington	401	10.6	24.9
Indiana	564	10.5	14.6	New Mexico	104	8.5	47.4	West Virginia	223	12.0	14.9
Iowa	378	13.1	8.3	New York	2,095	11.8	7.3	Wisconsin	546	11.7	16.0
								Wyoming	36	8.4	18.3

SOURCE: U.S. Bureau of the Census, *Current Population Reports*, Series P-25, No. 794, 1979.

TABLE 3. Metropolitan-Nonmetropolitan Residence of Persons 55 Years and Over—by Sex and Age: March 1978. Numbers in thousands (noninstitutional population).

Residence	BOTH SEXES				MALE				FEMALE			
	Total, 55 Years and Over	55 to 64 Years	65 to 74 Years	75 Years and Over	Total, 55 Years and Over	55 to 64 Years	65 to 74 Years	75 Years and Over	Total, 55 Years and Over	55 to 64 Years	65 to 74 Years	75 Years and Over
NUMBER												
Total	42,977	20,509	14,269	8,199	18,939	9,769	6,080	3,090	24,038	10,740	8,189	5,109
Metropolitan	27,557	13,557	8,984	5,016	12,019	6,471	3,726	1,822	15,536	7,086	5,257	3,193
Central city	12,580	5,880	4,234	2,466	5,304	2,732	1,689	883	7,276	3,149	2,545	1,582
Outside central city	14,977	7,677	4,750	2,550	6,715	3,739	2,037	939	8,260	3,937	2,712	1,611
Nonmetropolitan	15,418	6,951	5,284	3,183	6,920	3,297	2,355	1,268	8,502	3,655	2,930	1,917
PERCENT												
Total	100.0	100.0	100.0	100.0	100.0	100.0	100.0	100.0	100.0	100.0	100.0	100.0
Metropolitan	64.1	66.1	63.0	61.2	63.5	66.2	61.3	59.0	64.6	66.0	64.2	62.5
Central city	29.3	28.7	29.7	30.1	28.0	28.0	27.8	28.6	30.3	29.3	31.1	31.0
Outside central city	34.8	37.4	33.3	31.1	35.5	38.3	33.5	30.4	34.4	36.7	33.1	31.5
Nonmetropolitan	35.9	33.9	37.0	38.8	36.5	33.7	38.7	41.0	35.4	34.0	35.8	37.5

SOURCE: U.S. Bureau of the Census, *Current Population Reports*, Series P-20, No. 331, 1979.

TABLE 4. Family Status of Persons 55 Years and Older—by Race, Age, and Sex: March 1978. (Noninstitutional population.)

Race and Family Status	55 YEARS AND OVER			55 TO 64 YEARS			65 TO 74 YEARS			75 YEARS AND OVER		
	Both Sexes	Male	Female	Both Sexes	Male	Female	Both Sexes	Male	Female	Both Sexes	Male	Female
ALL RACES												
Total, thousands	42,977	18,939	24,038	20,509	9,769	10,740	14,269	6,080	8,189	8,199	3,090	5,109
Percent	100.0	100.0	100.0	100.0	100.0	100.0	100.0	100.0	100.0	100.0	100.0	100.0
In families	75.6	85.7	67.6	84.5	89.1	80.3	71.7	84.9	61.9	60.0	76.6	50.0
Head of family	40.8	81.3	8.8	45.4	85.5	8.9	38.9	79.9	8.5	32.4	70.8	9.2
Wife of head	27.9	. . .	49.9	35.0	. . .	66.8	26.2	. . .	45.7	13.2	. . .	21.2
Other family member	6.9	4.4	8.8	4.1	3.6	4.6	6.6	5.0	7.7	14.4	5.8	19.6
Primary individual	23.0	12.6	31.3	14.1	9.1	18.6	26.8	13.3	36.9	38.9	22.1	49.1
Living alone	22.2	11.9	30.3	13.4	8.4	18.0	26.0	12.8	35.8	37.7	21.3	47.6
Secondary individual	1.4	1.7	1.1	1.5	1.8	1.2	1.5	1.7	1.3	1.1	1.3	0.9
In group quarters	0.3	0.2	0.4	0.3	0.2	0.4	0.4	0.2	0.5	0.2	0.3	0.2
WHITE												
Total, thousands	38,846	17,110	21,736	18,530	8,861	9,669	12,836	5,441	7,395	7,480	2,808	4,672
Percent	100.0	100.0	100.0	100.0	100.0	100.0	100.0	100.0	100.0	100.0	100.0	100.0
In families	76.1	87.0	67.5	85.2	90.1	80.7	72.2	86.5	61.6	60.0	77.8	49.3
Head of family	40.8	83.0	7.7	45.4	86.6	7.6	39.2	82.6	7.2	32.6	72.6	8.5
Wife of head	28.8	. . .	51.4	36.0	. . .	69.0	27.1	. . .	47.1	13.7	. . .	21.9
Other family member	6.4	4.0	8.4	3.9	3.6	4.2	5.9	4.0	7.2	13.7	5.2	18.9
Primary individual	22.8	11.8	31.4	13.4	8.2	18.2	26.8	12.6	37.2	39.2	21.7	49.8
Living alone	22.1	11.3	30.6	12.8	7.6	17.6	26.1	12.2	36.3	38.3	21.2	48.5
Secondary individual	1.2	1.2	1.1	1.4	1.7	1.1	1.1	0.9	1.2	0.8	0.5	0.9
In group quarters	0.3	0.1	0.4	0.3	0.2	0.5	0.3	0.1	0.5	0.2	0.2	0.2
BLACK												
Total, thousands	3,666	1,597	2,069	1,736	778	958	1,306	575	731	624	244	380
Percent	100.0	100.0	100.0	100.0	100.0	100.0	100.0	100.0	100.0	100.0	100.0	100.0
In families	69.7	72.7	67.4	75.5	76.2	74.8	66.8	71.0	63.5	59.9	65.6	56.3
Head of family	39.9	64.6	20.7	45.1	73.0	22.4	36.4	57.6	19.8	32.5	54.5	18.2
Wife of head	19.7	. . .	35.0	24.7	. . .	44.8	18.1	. . .	32.4	9.3	. . .	15.3
Other family member	10.1	8.1	11.7	5.6	3.2	7.6	12.2	13.4	11.2	18.1	11.1	22.9
Primary individual	26.5	20.7	31.0	22.0	20.2	23.5	28.1	19.8	34.5	35.9	24.6	43.2
Living alone	24.4	18.8	28.7	20.5	17.9	22.7	25.7	18.3	31.5	32.7	23.4	38.7
Secondary individual	3.7	6.6	1.6	2.5	3.6	1.8	5.1	9.2	2.1	4.2	9.8	0.5
In group quarters	0.5	1.0	(Z)	0.1	0.3	—	0.8	1.6	0.1	0.8	2.0	—

SOURCE: U. S. Bureau of the Census, *Current Population Reports,* Series P-20, No. 338, 1979.
NOTE: The symbol . . . indicates category not applicable.
   The symbol Z indicates a number which rounds to less than 0.05.
   The symbol — represents zero or rounds to zero.

and living with their husbands. By contrast, some 52 percent of females were widowed, whereas only 14 percent of males over 65 were widowed. If one considers the population 75 and over, half the female population was living alone in 1978, compared to about one-fifth of the male group. No fewer than 5.5 million women and 1.5 million men over age 65 lived alone. Thus, because the mortality rates for older men are much higher than for older women, fewer older women continue to live in a family setting in their old age.

Institutional Population

According to the 1970 census, some 5 percent of persons 65 years and over were residents of institutions, with the vast majority (estimated at 96 percent) of those residents being in nursing homes. These figures were essentially unchanged in 1976 (U.S. Bureau of the Census, 1979c). The estimates in Table 5 indicate that most residents of long-

term care facilities age 65 and over were white (94 percent) and that among whites, more than twice as many females as males were institutionalized (65 percent versus 29 percent of total), due largely to lower mortality rates among females. Considering that in the total population age 65 and over the comparable percentages were 90 percent white, and among whites 60 percent female and 40 percent male, we see that minorities and males tended to be underrepresented in nursing homes. Some 63 percent were over the age of 80 (Table 6). Approximately 20 percent of all people over age 65 will be institutionalized in a nursing home at some time (U.S. Bureau of the Census, 1979c).

MORTALITY

The average life span in the United States has increased remarkably in this century. In recent years, the death rate for people 65 years and over has declined considerably (Table 7). In particular, an age-specific decline in mor-

TABLE 5. Inmates of Long-Term Care Institutions—by Race, Sex, and Age: 1976.

Race and Sex	Total	65 to 99 Years	18 to 64 Years	Less than 18 Years	Age Not Reported
NUMBER					
All races	1,550,100	1,027,850	334,120	151,530	36,600
Male	596,820	322,530	182,420	85,410	6,450
Female	947,880	703,150	151,250	64,750	28,730
White	1,410,020	970,070	292,750	115,350	31,850
Male	524,850	299,040	158,210	63,580	4,010
Female	885,170	671,030	134,540	51,760	27,840
Other races	134,670	55,610	40,920	34,810	3,330
Male	71,970	23,490	24,210	21,820	2,440
Female	62,710	32,120	16,710	12,990	890
Not reported	5,410	2,170	450	1,380	1,420
PERCENT					
All races	100.0	100.0	100.0	100.0	100.0
Male	38.5	31.4	54.6	56.4	17.6
Female	61.1	68.4	45.3	42.7	78.5
White	91.0	94.4	87.6	76.1	87.0
Male	33.9	29.1	47.4	42.0	11.0
Female	57.1	65.3	40.3	34.2	76.1
Other races	8.7	5.4	12.2	23.0	9.1
Male	4.6	2.3	7.2	14.4	6.7
Female	4.0	3.1	5.0	8.6	2.4
Not reported	0.3	0.2	0.1	0.9	3.9

SOURCE: U.S. Bureau of the Census, *Current Population Reports,* Series P-23, No. 69, 1979.

TABLE 6. Inmates of Long-Term Care Institutions—by Type of Institution and Age: 1976.

| Type of Facility | Total[a] | 65 YEARS OLD AND OVER | | |
		Total	65 to 79 Years	80 Years and Over
NUMBER				
Total	1,550,100	1,027,850	390,720	637,130
Nursing homes	1,182,670	989,340	368,370	620,970
Physically handicapped	37,780	2,280	1,360	920
Psychiatric	65,400	4,540	3,890	650
Mentally handicapped	189,210	5,690	4,370	1,320
All other	75,060	26,010	12,740	13,270
PERCENT				
Total	100.0	100.0	100.0	100.0
Nursing homes	76.3	96.3	94.3	97.5
Physically handicapped	2.4	0.2	0.3	0.1
Psychiatric	4.2	0.4	1.0	0.1
Mentally handicapped	12.2	0.6	1.1	0.2
All other	4.8	2.5	3.3	2.1

SOURCE: U.S. Bureau of the Census, *Current Population Reports,* Series P-23, No. 69, 1979.
[a]Total includes persons who did not report on age.

tality from chronic diseases has been observed, largely due to decreases in cardiovascular disease (NIH, 1979). As a result, life expectancy among the elderly population has increased, as shown in Table 7. Mortality data based on official vital statistics, while far from perfect, are the most widely used indicators of the impact of specific diseases on human populations. In this section, we will examine mortality rates for the elderly population for some specific diseases and their distribution among various subgroups of the elderly. In addition, some trends will be presented.

Sex Differences

Earlier in this chapter, it was mentioned that the population over age 65 has considerably more females than males and that the total population over 85 was rapidly increasing. Age-specific mortality rates are consistently

TABLE 7. Death Rate for the Population 65 Years and Over (by Age) and Expectation of Life at Age 65 (by Sex and Color): 1940 to 1978.

Age	1940	1954	1968	1973	1978
	Death Rates per 1000 Population				
65–74 years	48.4	37.9	37.2	34.4	30.3
75–84 years	112.0	86.0	82.9	79.3	71.9
85 years and over	235.7	181.6	195.8	174.3	147.0
Total 65 years and over	72.2	58.6	61.4	58.7	52.9
	Expectation of Life at Age 65				
Total	12.8	14.4	14.6	15.3	16.3
White male	12.1	13.1	12.8	13.2	14.0
All other male	12.2	13.5	12.1	13.1	14.1
White female	13.6	15.7	16.4	17.3	18.4
All other female	13.9	15.7	15.1	16.2	18.0

SOURCE: National Center for Health Statistics, various annual volumes of *Vital Statistics of the United States* and various issues of *Monthly Vital Statistics Report.*

higher for males, while it is noteworthy that at birth, males outnumber females 105 to 100. By 1978 the difference in life expectancy at birth between females and males reached 7.7 years, whereas in 1940 it had been 4.5 years. A substantial portion of this difference is accounted for by the difference in life expectancy between females and males at age 65: 4.4 years (18.4 versus 14.0) in 1978, compared to 1.5 years (13.6 versus 12.1) in 1940 (Siegel, 1980; NCHS, 1980a). Explanations for these increasingly large male-female differences are not entirely satisfactory. Siegel (1980) lists several studies that offer numerous possible reasons, including social and environmental factors, as well as combinations and interactions of these factors with genetic and biological considerations.

Race Differences

Differences in life expectancy at birth between races (white and "all other") decreased substantially from 1940 to 1976 (Siegel, 1980). At age 65, however, the differences in life expectancy between races are small and have remained so for years (Table 7). In fact, the racial differences in life expectancy in Table 7 are so small that they are completely dominated by sex differences. In 1978, death rates for the "all other" population were higher than those for whites for all adult age groups up to age 75, but lower for persons over 75 years of age (NCHS, 1980a). This "crossover" effect occurred for both males and females, and has been observed both in previous years' mortality data and in other studies involving comparisons among races (Siegel, 1980).

Causes of Death

The ten leading causes of death of persons 65 years and over have not changed appreciably for the past several years, and the relationships among causes has remained essentially the same for this time period (Table 8). As reductions in death rates due to infectious and parasitic diseases have oc-

curred, chronic diseases and conditions have become the dominant causes of death. Currently, cardiovascular diseases and malignant neoplasms occupy four of the five top rankings among causes of death in 1978 and account for 77 percent of all deaths among the population 65 and over.

Cardiovascular Disease. The diseases most commonly occurring among elderly populations are diseases of the cardiovascular system. Three forms recognized by the International Classification of Diseases show up as major causes of death in the elderly. These include diseases of the heart, the number one cause which accounts for almost half of all deaths, cerebrovascular disease, and arteriosclerosis (Table 8). These three causes comprise 97 percent of all deaths due to cardiovascular disease (NCHS, 1980a). The influence of these conditions on mortality is so great that the major proportion (55 percent) of the decline in overall mortality between 1950 and 1975 was due to the decline in the death rate for heart disease alone during that period (Kovar, 1977). The age-specific death rates for 1978 given in Table 8 show an exponential increase in mortality with successive age groups for heart disease, stroke, and arteriosclerosis. As might be expected, these cardiovascular disease rates parallel the age-specific death rates for all causes, as shown dramatically in Figure 2. Thus, two effects are operating simultaneously with these data: the rise in age-specific mortality and the decline in mortality over time. Hence, caution should be exercised in the explanation and interpretation of these data, as will be described.

It has been pointed out (Patrick et al., 1982) that since 1965 each successive birth cohort has shown a decrease in heart disease mortality rates. At the same time, these cohorts continue to age and become more susceptible to dying from heart disease. This apparent paradox is due, at least in part, to the fact that age is itself dependent upon the passage of time. Age-specific plots of mortality rates as a function of year at death (period) are influenced by the year of birth

TABLE 8. Death Rates for the Ten Leading Causes of Death Among Persons 65 Years and Over—by 1978 Rank Order and by Age for 1978: 1970, 1975, and 1978. Rates per 100,000 population in age group.

Cause of Death and ICDA Code[a]	1970	1975	1978 65 and Over	1978 65–69	1978 70–74	1978 75–79	1978 80–84	1978 85 and Over
All causes	5,892.1	5,432.4	5,293.5	2,463.0	3,787.4	6,024.2	8,954.0	14,700.7
1. Diseases of heart 390–398,402,404,410–429	2,683.3	2,403.9	2,331.1	975.7	1,574.5	2,618.7	4,061.1	7,084.3
2. Malignant neoplasms including neoplasms of lymphatic and hematopoietic tissues 140–209	923.4	961.1	1,002.0	698.2	938.8	1,216.0	1,412.0	1,450.5
3. Cerebrovascular diseases 430–438	847.5	729.7	622.0	171.3	341.0	693.8	1,238.6	2,281.6
4. Influenza and pneumonia 470–474,480–486	200.4	187.1	193.2	47.2	90.8	189.1	372.9	839.8
5. Arteriosclerosis 440	149.7	123.0	115.0	14.9	37.0	93.6	220.2	638.4
6. Diabetes mellitus 250	131.4	112.9	101.3	51.4	82.0	128.4	171.5	211.9
7. Accidents E800–E949	135.9	109.6	100.3	53.7	70.2	107.7	162.4	276.8
Motor vehicle accidents E810–E823	36.2	25.3	24.5	19.6	24.1	30.5	32.2	24.0
All other accidents E800–E807,E825–E949	99.7	84.3	75.8	34.0	46.2	77.2	130.2	252.8
8. Bronchitis, emphysema, asthma 490–493	102.2	80.5	66.1	42.1	63.5	87.5	96.0	89.5
9. Cirrhosis of liver 571	37.1	36.6	36.3	44.1	38.2	34.5	25.2	18.0
10. Nephritis and nephrosis 580–584	23.7	23.2	25.6	11.9	19.4	31.1	44.3	62.6
All other causes Residual	657.5	664.9	700.6	352.5	532.0	823.8	1,149.8	1,747.3

SOURCE: National Center for Health Statistics: *Vital Statistics of the United States*, **2**, 1970 and 1975; 1978, unpublished tabulations.

[a]ICDA = International Classification of Diseases, Adapted, Eighth Revision, 1965.

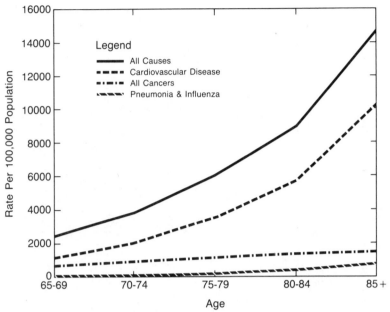

Figure 2. Mortality rates per 100,000 population for selected causes: United States, 1978. (Source: Unpublished tabulations from the National Center for Health Statistics.)

(cohort) of the people who died at the specified age in the years under consideration (Janis et al., 1981). It is difficult to separate these effects in order to study mortality trends as a function of each distinct variable adjusted for the others. Susser (1977) has carefully pointed out these problems in a discussion of the analysis of demographic and epidemiologic data on aging. We mention them here primarily as a cautionary remark so that misinterpretations of the mortality data being presented might be avoided. It is important to consider both periodic and cohort analyses when working with these data.

To return briefly to the work of Patrick et al. (1982), the declines in heart disease mortality have been observed for both males and females. However, it appears that the decline began much earlier for females than for males. In addition, mortality differentials between males and females have persisted, even though rates for both groups have decreased since 1965. It remains to be explained what factors are responsible for the decline (over time) in heart disease mortality and why the discrepancies between male and female patterns persist (NIH, 1979).

Cardiovascular disease is closely associated with aging, morbidity, and mortality. Table 9 contains figures obtained from the cause-of-death life tables prepared from 1969–71 mortality data and the 1970 census. Two-thirds of those reaching age 65 die of cardiovascular disease, while the next most frequent disease group—cancer—accounts for less than 15 percent of all deaths. If it were possible to eliminate cardiovascular disease as a cause of death, the implications for the future of the elderly population would be tremendous.

Cancer. The cancers rank second to cardiovascular disease as a cause of death among elderly U.S. residents and in 1978 accounted for 19 percent of the total death rate for persons 65 and over (Table 8). Patterns of mortality from cancer, however, have been somewhat different from those for cardiovascular disease. Whereas death rates from cardiovascular disease have shown substantial decreases since 1965, cancer mortality rates have risen modestly over the same period and at a different order of magnitude from the reduction in cardiovascular mor-

TABLE 9. Gain in Life Expectancy from Eliminating Specified Causes of Death and Chance of Eventually Dying from these Causes: 1969–71.

Cause of Death	GAIN IN LIFE EXPECTANCY (YEARS)		CHANCE OF EVENTUALLY DYING	
	At Birth	At Age 65	At Birth	At Age 65
Major cardiovascular-renal diseases	11.8	11.4	.588	.672
Diseases of the heart	5.9	5.1	.412	.460
Cerebrovascular diseases	1.2	1.2	.122	.149
Malignant neoplasms[a]	2.5	1.4	.163	.145
Motor vehicle accidents	.7	.1	.020	.006
All other accidents	.6	.1	.026	.018
Influenza and pneumonia	.5	.2	.034	.037
Diabetes mellitus	.2	.2	.020	.021
Infective and parasitic disease	.2	.1	.007	.005

SOURCE: National Center for Health Statistics, *U.S. Life Tables by Cause of Death: 1969–71,* by T.N.E. Greville; *U.S. Decennial Life Tables for 1969–71,* **1,** No. 5, 1976.
[a]Including neoplasms of lymphatic and hematopoietic tissues.

tality. In fact, recent provisional statistics from the National Center for Health Statistics (NCHS, 1980b) showed an observed slight decrease in the overall cancer mortality rate, as did Canadian data (Center for Disease Control, 1981). Even though this figure was based on a sample of deaths and is subject to inherent sampling variability, nevertheless it may mark the beginning of a slowdown in total mortality from cancer.

The data in Figure 2 deserve further mention at this point. As noted before, cardiovascular disease rises exponentially with age and has a curvature essentially parallel to the curve for total mortality. These features, which can actually be observed in Figure 2, have been seen also in the mortality data for 1973 and 1976 (Brody, 1982c). The cancer curve, on the other hand, shows a small linear rise from ages 65–69 up to 80–84 and continues to rise, but at an even slower rate, at 85 and over. Cancer is best considered to be several different diseases with different etiologies, and this is reflected by the fact that cancers for some sites continue to increase with age whereas others begin to decline at some point along the age scale (Tables 10 and 11). Cancer mortality declines with age relative to the total mortality or to cardiovascular mortality. Thus it is difficult to relate

cumulative endogenous or exogenous factors postulated to be associated with biological aging, such as radiation and deposition of toxic substances or declining immune capacity, progressive imperfections in DNA integrity and expression, and the "free radical theory" as having a simple linear role in the etiology of cancers. Apparently, cumulative factors become carcinogenic under specific, as yet poorly understood, circumstances.

Age-adjusted cancer mortality rates by site are shown in Table 10 for the period 1969–76. These data show increasing mortality rates for lung cancer, with females increasing at a significantly higher rate than males. Other sites with increasing rates include melanoma (males), colon (males), and prostate gland. Sites with decreasing mortality over time include stomach (both sexes), rectum (both sexes), cervix, corpus uteri, bladder (females), and leukemia (females).

A number of researchers have attempted to explain through various means the age distribution of cancer mortality. Barrett (1973) studied mortality data for cancer of the cervix in England and Wales by five-year age groups for 1951–70. Barrett's success came in explaining the separate effects for age, cohort, and time period, but he failed to account for the joint or interactive effects

TABLE 10. Age-Adjusted[a] Cancer Mortality Rates Per 100,000 Population for Selected Sites— by Sex and Year, Average Annual Percent Change, and 95% Confidence Interval for Percent Change: United States 1969-71 and 1973-76 (Whites).

Site	Sex	MORTALITY RATE PER 100,000 POPULATION							Average Annual Percent Change	95% Confidence Interval	
		1969	1970	1971	1973	1974	1975	1976			
All sites	M	195.0	199.5	204.0	203.6	206.5	206.6	210.2	0.9	0.60	1.20
	F	129.0	132.4	134.2	131.3	132.2	131.9	133.8	0.2	−0.20	0.60
Stomach	M	10.6	10.4	10.0	9.4	9.2	8.8	8.7	−2.9	−3.13	−2.67
	F	5.3	5.1	5.0	4.5	4.4	4.3	4.1	−3.6	−3.95	−3.25
Colon, excluding rectum	M	18.7	19.0	19.5	19.4	20.3	20.1	20.7	1.3	0.90	1.70
	F	16.2	16.8	16.7	16.5	16.6	16.2	16.5	0.0	−0.47	0.47
Rectum	M	6.9	6.7	6.6	6.0	5.9	5.8	5.6	−3.0	−3.37	−2.63
	F	3.9	3.9	3.9	3.5	3.4	3.3	3.2	−3.1	−3.75	−2.45
Pancreas	M	11.0	11.2	11.1	11.1	10.8	11.0	11.0	0.2	−0.14	0.54
	F	6.6	6.7	6.7	6.6	6.8	6.7	6.8	0.3	−0.03	0.63
Lung	M	55.0	57.6	60.2	61.9	63.6	64.8	66.7	2.6	2.20	3.00
	F	10.2	11.1	12.2	13.4	14.5	15.5	16.8	7.1	6.60	7.60
Melanoma	M	2.0	2.0	2.1	2.2	2.5	2.4	2.6	4.0	2.94	5.06
	F	1.4	1.4	1.5	1.4	1.4	1.4	1.6	0.8	−0.84	2.44
Breast	F	26.2	27.0	27.1	27.3	27.0	26.8	27.2	0.3	−0.09	0.69
Cervix	F	5.5	5.2	5.1	4.4	4.4	4.0	3.9	−4.9	−5.56	−4.24
Corpus + Uterus NOS[b]	F	4.6	4.6	4.6	4.4	4.3	4.1	4.2	−1.7	−2.26	−1.14
Ovary	F	8.9	9.0	9.0	8.6	8.8	8.8	8.9	−0.3	−0.79	0.19
Prostate gland	M	19.0	19.4	20.0	20.5	20.4	20.3	21.0	1.2	0.77	1.63
Bladder	M	7.1	7.5	7.2	7.4	7.5	7.5	7.5	0.6	0.05	1.15
	F	2.1	2.3	2.2	2.1	2.1	2.0	2.0	−1.4	−2.53	−0.27
Kidney	M	4.3	4.4	4.5	4.4	4.6	4.5	4.5	0.6	0.06	1.14
	F	2.0	2.0	2.0	2.0	2.0	2.1	2.1	0.7	0.17	1.23
Leukemia	M	9.4	9.2	9.4	9.1	9.0	9.1	9.2	−0.4	−0.82	0.02
	F	5.7	5.8	5.7	5.3	5.3	5.2	5.2	−1.7	−2.24	−1.16

SOURCE: From Pollack and Horm (1980).
[a] 1970 U.S. population was used as standard.
[b] Not otherwise specified.

of these factors because of the intervariable mixing which we mentioned earlier.

Breslow and Day (1975) constructed a simple multiplicative model to describe the relationship of age-specific mortality rates among several populations. However, as pointed out by Freeman and Holford (1980), models of this type must be extensively evaluated before they can be used with confidence.

Recent progress has been made, however, in the attempts to sort out these various factors by Moolgavkar et al. (1979) and by Manton et al. (1981). The models presented by these researchers are quite complicated

mathematically, and in order to make any persuasive commentary on their biologic relevance, they must be evaluated as to their applicability to the general problem of assessing age, period, and cohort effects on data sets other than those used by the researchers in their investigations.

Age-specific cancer mortality rates appear in Table 11 for 1976 for the sites and groups of sites which constitute some 87 percent of mortality from cancers among the population 65 and over. Those sites which exhibit an age-specific rise include digestive system, breast, prostate, urinary system, and leukemia. The remaining sites generally increase

TABLE 11. Cancer Mortality Rates—by Site and Age: 1976.

Site	AGE GROUP Rate per 100,000 Population in Age Group				
	65–69	70–74	75–79	80–84	85 and Over
Digestive system	184.2	272.5	373.6	458.6	518.9
Lung	187.3	222.7	229.3	192.4	139.8
Breast	51.8	63.4	77.4	88.8	112.6
Female genital system	70.9	86.5	103.9	115.4	106.4
Prostate	74.9	148.1	269.4	397.4	508.6
Urinary system	30.8	44.5	64.7	79.3	93.5
Leukemia	20.7	31.5	47.7	58.9	68.8
Lymphomas, male	36.4	51.3	66.2	73.2	61.6
All sites	685.3	927.8	1,185.0	1,343.1	1,441.5
	Percent of Total Cancer Mortality				
Digestive system	26.9	29.4	31.5	34.1	36.0
Lung	27.3	24.0	19.3	14.3	9.7
Breast	7.6	6.8	6.5	6.6	7.8
Female genital system[a]	5.8	5.4	5.3	5.5	5.0
Prostate[a]	4.8	6.8	8.9	10.7	11.3
Urinary system	4.5	4.8	5.5	5.9	6.5
Leukemia	3.0	3.4	4.0	4.4	4.8
Lymphomas	5.3	5.5	5.6	5.5	4.3

SOURCE: National Center for Health Statistics, *Vital Statistics of the United States, 2*, 1976.
[a]Denominators for these percentages adjusted for total population.

with age up to a point and begin to decline in the older age groups. As more and more people survive to ages 85 and over, it is likely that this phenomenon will become more prominent. Heretofore, the numbers of persons in the 85-and-over group have been too small to draw definitive conclusions regarding these mortality rates, but this is now changing since almost 20 percent of all deaths occur in the one percent of the population 85 years and over.

Pneumonia and Influenza. Pneumonia and influenza, the fourth leading cause of death among the elderly in 1978, accounted for almost 4 percent of all deaths among persons age 65 and over (Table 8). The death rates in the table showed considerable variability over time because of the strong influence of epidemics. A good example of the difficulties caused by seasonal variations and epidemics of influenza is given by Alling et al. (1981). They concluded that excess mortality occurred during at least three major outbreaks of influenza in the period 1968–76. In another study, Choi and Thacker (1981a, 1981b) presented forecasting methods for determining excess pneumonia and influenza deaths over time.

Despite the problems attendant upon trend analysis of pneumonia and influenza mortality, it is important to note the increased risk of mortality from these causes with rising age. In Table 8 and Figure 2, it can be seen that the rate of increase in mortality (by age) from pneumonia and influenza is essentially parallel to that of cardiovascular disease. If these curves had been plotted on logarithmic paper—which would have resulted in their appearing as straight lines—the slopes of the lines could be seen to be similar. While in 1978 there were 763,554 deaths from cardiovascular disease and 46,487 from influenza and pneumonia, the potential or actual efficacy of vaccines and antibiotics makes the rewards of intervention and prevention considerable.

Diabetes Mellitus. Diabetes mellitus, the sixth leading cause of death among the elderly in 1978, has experienced a modest decline in mortality from 1970 to 1978 (Table 8). For 1978, age-specific rates showed a fourfold increase from 51.4 for persons 65–69 years of age to 211.9 for those 85 and over. Problems of underreporting and inappropriate reporting prevent useful interpretation of these data.

Accidents. In 1978 accidents were the seventh leading cause of death for persons 65 years of age and over (Table 8). The trend data showed that mortality rates due to accidents (excluding motor vehicle accidents) continued a long-term decline, with a 25 percent drop from 99.7 deaths per 100,000 population in 1970 to 75.8 deaths per 100,000 in 1978. A one-third reduction in mortality from 167.7 in 1950 to 116.1 in 1965 has been reported (Kovar, 1977). Accidents involving motor vehicles also declined by about one-third during this period.

Age-specific mortality due to accidents rose with age, especially for non-motor-vehicle accidents. The death rate for the 65–69 age group in 1978 was 34.0, compared to a rate of 252.8 for those 85 years and over. Numerous concomitant factors in the elderly, such as sensory disabilities, other debilitating diseases, and drug effects, contribute to higher risks in more vulnerable individuals.

We are baffled at the steep decline over time in mortality from accidents. Better knowledge of this phenomenon might assist us in efforts to define the precipitating events in accidents in the older age groups where prevention may be possible.

MORBIDITY

We have seen that mortality data by cause of death are widely available and very useful for analysis of the impact of various diseases and conditions on the United States population. Furthermore, we have seen that declines in mortality have led to increased life expectancy in this century. Data on morbidity and disability, however, are sufficiently limited in their availability and specificity that making assessment of the functional and health status of the population is much more difficult. The data collected by such programs as the Framingham Heart Study, the Surveillance, Epidemiology, and End Results (SEER) program of the National Cancer Institute, the morbidity and mortality reporting system of the Centers for Disease Control, and others—valuable as they are—provide neither the national geographic coverage nor the comprehensive scope of illnesses and disabilities necessary to determine whether, in increasing life expectancy, we are also improving health status and the quality of life. The data systems most useful for such analyses are the national surveys conducted by the National Center for Health Statistics (NCHS), particularly the National Health Interview Survey (NHIS).

Conducted continuously since 1957, the NHIS presents long-term national morbidity estimates based on a probability sample of 120,000 of the U.S. civilian noninstitutionalized population (NCHS, 1979). Information gathered in household interviews includes self-reports of limitation of activity and physical mobility, specific acute and chronic conditions experienced by the respondents, and measures of utilization of medical services and facilities. Thus, with these data it is possible to examine the morbidity experienced by the population represented by these samples in somewhat the same way as the mortality experience for the entire population, subject to the limitations inherent in respondent-reported conditions.

Colvez and Blanchet (1981) have conducted a study of disability trends in the United States for the period 1966–76, using data from the NHIS. This process involved the examination of disability indicators concerning adverse changes in physical mobility, physical independence in the most basic actions, and the ability to carry on one's usual activities. Measurements obtained in the NHIS involve one or the other of these characteristics or a combination of them, the principal indicator being activity restriction.

Short-term disability is measured in terms of the number of restricted-activity days per 100 persons, whereas long-term disability is a prevalence measure (per 10,000 persons) categorized into four degrees of severity:

- Severe: unable to carry on major activity
- Moderate: limited in amount or kind of major activity
- Slight: not limited in major activity but otherwise limited
- Nil: not limited in activities

Note that major activity refers to the ability to work, keep house, or engage in school or preschool activities (NCHS, 1979). Table 12 contains estimates of the prevalence of short- and long-term disability in the United States for selected years between 1966 and 1976. As one can see from the table, substantial increases in both short- and long-term disability have occurred during this period, with the greatest increase in the more severe cases of long-term disability.

As Colvez and Blanchet point out in their analysis, the increases in disability cannot be accounted for by sampling variability, by changes in the NHIS methodology, or by the aging of the population. The latter point is apparent from the age-specific data given in Table 13. Here, increases over time are seen to have occurred in all age groups, with the largest increases taking place in the group 45–65 years of age. For those age 65 and over, the prevalence of limitation of activity was very high, but there was little change in this prevalence over the period. Sex differences appeared to favor females except for cases of moderate and slight limitation of activity.

Estimates of the prevalence and trend in limitation of activity caused by specific disease and medical conditions for three broad age categories are presented in Table 14. The principal diseases for which the largest changes in disability occurred in the group 45–64 years of age include the leading causes of death described in the previous section for the 65-and-over age group, the one exception being musculoskeletal disorders. Furthermore, disability due to these causes increased substantially between 1966 and 1974.

In the 65-and-over age group, there were important changes in the prevalence of disability due to three causes between 1966 and 1974. Mental and nervous conditions were reported to have decreased for both males and females during the period. On the other hand, there were increases in limitation of activity for both sexes due to diabetes and

TABLE 12. Evolution of Prevalence of Short-Term and Long-Term Disability in the United States Between 1966 and 1976.

Year	SHORT TERM (DAYS PER 100 INHABITANTS)		LONG TERM (PREVALENCE PER 10,000 INHABITANTS)	
	Bed Disability (days)	Other Restricted Activity (days)	Main Activity Impossible	Other Limitation
1966	6.3	9.3	213	935
1969	6.1	8.7	286	884
1972	6.5	10.2	295	972
1974	6.7	10.5	334	1079
1976	7.1	11.1	355	1078
Percent variation 1966–76	+13	+19	+67	+15

SOURCE: Adapted from Colvez and Blanchet (1981).

TABLE 13. Variation in the Prevalence[a] of Limitation of Activity in the United States Between 1966 and 1974—by Sex, Age, and Category of Limitation of Activity.

Limitation of Activity	< 17 Years		17–44 Years		45–64 Years		65+ Years	
	M	F	M	F	M	F	M	F
Severe: main activity impossible								
Prevalence 1974	25	17	143	67	937	214	2983	816
Variation 1966–74, %	+32	+21	+57	+76	+106	+78	+38	+6
Average: main activity restricted								
Prevalence 1974	187	150	402	511	1046	1595	1506	2718
Variation 1966–74, %	+148	+118	+12	+41	−12	+46	−44	+9
Slight: other types of restrictions								
Prevalence 1974	188	163	371	278	545	493	485	780
Variation 1966–74, %	+69	+66	+51	+2	+25	−13	+6	−3

SOURCE: Adapted from Colvez and Blanchet (1981).
[a]Prevalence per 10,000 inhabitants in 1974.

circulatory diseases (excluding heart conditions and hypertension).

One other morbidity data set useful for examining trends is the cancer registry data from the Surveillance, Epidemiology, and End Results (SEER) program of the National Cancer Institute. Using data from this system, Pollack and Horm (1980) have provided a comprehensive assembly of information on trends in cancer incidence by site for the period 1969–76. Some of their incidence data for whites are reproduced in Table 15. Among sites where incidence has been increasing the most are lung cancer (among females), melanoma (both sexes), corpus uteri, and prostate gland. Sites showing declines in incidence during this period include stomach, cervix uteri, and leukemia. While breast cancer incidence in females and lung cancer among males remained high over time, they showed only modest increases in incidence rates.

While all of the data presented in this section are subject to limitations in generalizability for one reason or another—the NHIS depends on respondent recall, for example, and the SEER data cover only a small number of geographic areas—they do seem to cast serious doubts relating to a steady, clearcut improvement in health status. Further, debilitating conditions such as the senile dementias, decubitus ulcer, hip fractures, etc.,

did not occur in sufficient numbers in these data to appear as major morbid events leading to disability and, ultimately, institutionalization. As the size of the elderly population increases and more data accumulate, the conditions will exert a greater influence on overall disabling pathology.

CONCLUSIONS

Gaps in Data

Data in this chapter have been presented in terms of demographic trends and cause-specific mortality, with some information relating to morbidity and disability. The principal source of data on mortality is death certificates. Morbidity is determined through various complicated and expensive national surveys. Except for demographic trends, none of these sources of data can be considered robust, hence, critical information is lacking or only partially reliable. While 67 percent of all deaths occur among people over age 65, the reliability of specific diagnoses in death certificates is open to serious question. In a classic review of cancer mortality in the United States, Doll and Peto (1981) confined their analysis of specific cancers to the population under age 65. While they suggested that the total number of deaths from cancer in those over age 65 was

TABLE 14. Variation in Prevalence[a] of Long-Term Disability Between 1966 and 1974 in the United States—by Sex, Age, and Type of Pathological Cause Declared.

Cause of Limitation of Activity (All Categories)	Prevalence per 10,000 Inhabitants		Cause of Limitation of Activity (All Categories)	Prevalence per 10,000 Inhabitants	
	Male	Female		Male	Female
(A) Age: under 45 years			Heart conditions		
Visual impairments			Prevalence 1974	612	359
Prevalence 1974	37	18	Variation 1966–74, %	+38	+21
Variation 1966–74, %	+95	+100	Hypertension without heart involvement		
Hearing impairments			Prevalence 1974	150	271
Prevalence 1974	28	15	Variation 1966–74, %	+85	+64
Variation 1966–74, %	+155	+150	Other circulatory disorders		
Asthma (and hay fever)			Prevalence 1974	173	157
Prevalence 1974	81	71	Variation 1966–74, %	+197	+224
Variation 1966–74, %	+99	+76	Musculoskeletal disorders (others: excluding arthritis and rheumatism)		
Musculoskeletal disorders (others: excluding arthritis and rheumatism)			Prevalence 1974	197	182
Prevalence 1974	46	38	Variation 1966–74, %	+89	+156
Variation 1966–74, %	+53	+111	*(C) Age: 65 and over*		
Impairments of locomotive system			Mental and nervous conditions		
Prevalence 1974	173	146	Prevalence 1974	149	162
Variation 1966–74, %	+8	+52	Variation 1966–74, %	−33	−46
(B) Age: 45–64 years			Diabetes		
Malignant neoplasm			Prevalence 1974	283	334
Prevalence 1974	62	89	Variation 1966–74, %	+127	+104
Variation 1966–74, %	+104	+158	Other circulatory disorders (not including heart disease and hypertension)		
Diabetes			Prevalence 1974	557	453
Prevalence 1974	136	142	Variation 1966–74, %	+167	+183
Variation 1966–74, %	+151	+144			

Source: Adapted from Colvez and Blanchet (1981).
[a] Prevalence per 10,000 inhabitants in 1974.

TABLE 15. Age-Adjusted[a] Cancer Incidence Rates Per 100,000 Population for Selected Sites, by Sex and Year, Average Annual Percent Change, and 95% Confidence Interval for Percent Change: TNCS[d] 1969-71 and Seer Areas 1973-76 (WHITES).

Site	Sex	INCIDENCE RATE PER 100,000 POPULATION							Average Annual Percent Change	95% Confidence Interval	
		1969	1970	1971	1973	1974	1975	1976			
All sites	M	346.6	343.7	337.2	355.5	365.3	365.8	374.0	1.3	0.74	1.86
	F	271.5	268.6	270.9	287.3	305.2	301.8	301.2	2.0	1.28	2.72
Stomach	M	15.4	14.1	13.4	13.8	13.1	12.7	12.6	−2.3	−3.34	−1.26
	F	7.1	7.0	6.3	6.1	5.9	5.4	5.6	−3.7	−4.70	−2.70
Colon, excluding rectum	M	34.5	33.2	32.4	34.2	37.3	35.5	36.9	1.5	0.29	2.71
	F	30.6	28.9	28.6	29.7	30.1	30.6	31.4	0.7	−0.22	1.62
Rectum	M	17.5	17.8	18.1	18.8	19.3	18.3	19.4	1.3	0.60	2.00
	F	11.1	10.6	10.6	11.3	11.2	12.0	11.4	1.2	0.18	2.22
Pancreas	M	12.1	12.1	12.3	12.7	11.2	12.5	11.5	−0.5	−1.96	0.96
	F	7.5	7.3	7.0	7.5	8.0	7.2	8.0	0.9	−0.61	2.41
Lung	M	70.6	71.5	70.0	72.3	74.5	76.4	77.8	1.4	0.87	1.93
	F	13.3	14.4	15.5	17.7	20.0	21.8	23.7	8.6	8.06	9.14
Melanoma	M	4.4	4.7	4.7	5.8	6.3	6.4	6.8	6.8	5.75	7.85
	F	4.1	4.2	4.8	5.1	5.5	6.0	6.1	6.2	5.32	7.08
Breast[b]	F	73.9	76.1	75.1	81.0	92.5	86.2	83.5	1.8	1.17	2.43
Cervix	F	16.0	14.5	14.3	12.6	11.5	10.7	10.6	−5.9	−6.67	−5.13
Corpus + Uterus NOS[c]	F	22.6	22.7	24.6	29.0	31.1	32.4	31.2	5.9	4.48	7.32
Ovary	F	14.9	14.2	13.6	14.2	14.9	14.2	13.6	−0.4	−1.61	0.81
Prostate gland	M	59.0	57.4	56.7	61.0	62.1	64.8	68.6	2.3	1.27	3.33
Bladder	M	23.8	23.3	23.4	25.5	27.1	25.8	26.4	2.3	1.31	3.29
	F	6.3	5.9	6.3	6.1	6.9	6.9	7.3	2.5	1.01	3.99
Kidney	M	9.0	8.7	8.2	9.4	9.1	9.0	9.6	1.2	−0.20	2.60
	F	4.3	4.0	3.8	4.4	4.1	4.0	4.8	1.3	−1.09	3.69
Leukemia	M	13.2	13.6	12.2	13.2	13.4	12.5	13.1	−0.2	−1.51	1.11
	F	8.0	7.6	7.2	7.8	7.5	7.3	7.1	−1.0	−2.14	−0.14

SOURCE: From Pollack and Horm (1980).
[a]1970 U.S. population was used as standard.
[b]1974 and 1975 were not included in the computation of trend for breast cancer.
[c]Not otherwise specified.
[d]TNCS = Third National Cancer Survey

probably reasonably accurate, they found unacceptable the reliability of specific cancer diagnosis in older age groups. Cardiovascular disease, which accounts for more than 50 percent of mortality, is also imprecise on death certificates, particularly in the older age groups. Lack of a specific terminal diagnosis, as well as apathy and fashion (Gittelsohn, 1982) in reporting, contribute to the problems in utilizing information from death certificates for cancer and cardiovascular disease which, when aggregated, account for 75 percent of all mortality.

Data concerning morbidity and disability are even more suspect on a national level, although we do believe that these data are useful for trend analysis and perhaps in some specific conditions. The greater gains in recent years noted in the life expectancy of adults relative to newborns (McGinnis, 1982) are both a triumph and still, in large part, a mystery. Surely this phenomenon "offers a challenge for us to apply our national resources effectively to capture the additional gains that are possible and to prepare for the demographic implications of increased life expectancy for adults" (McGinnis, 1982). Currently, however, the chief data collection and analysis components for the elderly are being constricted rather than expanded. There is surely no evidence of an improvement in correct certification of cause of death. Budgetary limitations have now made more thorough collection and analysis in the expanding elderly segment more difficult because of the shrinking size of the Bureau of the Census and the National Center for Health Statistics. At the National Institute on Aging, the demography program is currently nonexistent. Thus there is considerable pessimism concerning the availability of better data on morbidity, mortality, and disability in the foreseeable future. It is, of course, probable that data relating to health costs and utilization of health services will improve, but the information will probably not improve the accuracy of morbidity and mortality reporting. Thus, research on etiology and potential measures for prevention will suffer, while costs will be more closely accounted for and information about them will be more precise.

We are hardly the first to point out the inadequacies of diagnoses as they appear on death certificates and hospital discharge data. Only greater awareness of the need for accuracy will improve the quality of these data, particularly for the elderly.

Areas for Future Research

We have suggested mechanisms whereby mortality and morbidity data and their interrelationship could be more effectively developed and followed (Brody et al., 1981). While the data collection ability at a national level has diminished as stated, extremely valuable information is currently available which is not being linked or utilized at present. This results from a variety of causes such as Privacy Act regulations, lack of time or of research staff, and the fact that data are collected by different agencies with dissimilar mandates and research capabilities. We have suggested that in this modern age of computers, it would not be an overwhelming task to merge large data sets such as the entire Medicare-Medicaid files, Social Security, the Internal Revenue Service, and the National Death Index. The last is a recently developed data source whereby all deaths are centrally tabulated by specific identifiers including name and Social Security number. Creative utilization of these data would enable us to have an enormous amount of information on individuals collected over time and, of course, until death that would inform us of patterns and risks as well as their costs. While this is not possible at the present time, we believe that in the near future health costs will make it essential that a patient's entire medical history be made available to his physician. The patient rarely knows what conditions he had in the past or such things as what tests were performed and what the results were. It is not presently possible to secure these data because legislation now exists protecting the individual privacy of these records. That is, of course, a necessary safeguard, but even the concept of privacy is not a static one. If 100 years ago we had asked every citizen in every town in the United States to write down his name and address in a book that would be available to anyone who wished it, this would have been rejected as utter nonsense and a tremendous invasion of privacy. However, once Americans decided that they wanted telephones in their homes, all was changed and such books now exist. Thus, the day in which medical data will become available is near at hand. These data, however, must be combined with data from the other sources mentioned to inexpensively outline life events to the extent that they are available from existing records. Then with such data in hand, one can start making some of the critical associations that would almost surely be highly insightful and beneficial to the individual and to society. In the short run, we cannot afford to deny the physician and his patient access to previous health information. In the longer run, we cannot deny these data to researchers.

We find fault with those who claim that "the medical and social task of eliminating premature death is largely accomplished" (Fries, 1980) and whose "predictions suggest that the number of very old persons will not increase, that the average period of diminished vigor will decrease, that chronic disease will occupy a smaller proportion of the typical lifespan, and that the need for medical care in later life will decrease" (Fries, 1980). There is evidence which now suggests that the initial prediction of 3.3 million people age 85 and over in the year 2000 was a miscalculation, in view of the rapidly diminishing death rate of the elderly, and that by the year 2000 there may be as many as 6.7 million people in the United States age 85 and over (Kovar, 1980). The decline in mortality due to cardiovascular disease preceded the advent of important medical and social intervention. As Stallones suggested (Stallones, 1980; Weinblatt et al. 1982), it is important that we find out what actually did cause the declining mortality, rather than rushing to take credit for this phenomenon, so as to utilize that information and hopefully perpetuate the decline in mortality rates. We view with concern recent data, referred to earlier, from the National Health Interview Survey of the National Center for Health Statistics (Colvez and Blanchet, 1981) which indicate that morbidity and attending disability increased rapidly from 1966 through 1976 in the United States. This national survey, which reaches more than 100,000 people per year, includes questions about limitations and ability to perform normal activities as well as the presence of chronic diseases or conditions. A marked increase in morbidity and disability was noted for those age 45–64 years. A previous report suggested a slight decrease between 1959 and 1965–66 (Sullivan, 1971). While flaws, biases, and artifacts surely occur in surveys and the decline in mortality is unambiguous, we must temper our optimism about a prolonged healthy life in the face of these as yet uncontested data describing a rise in childhood and in middle- and late-life morbidity (Brody, 1982b). As Colvez and Blanchet (1981) state, "It is one of the only sources that can be used in trying to determine whether in increasing life expectancy we are also improving the quality of life."

Acceptance of the notion that "the med-ical and social task of eliminating premature death is largely accomplished" (Fries, 1980) is indeed sad and stultifying. In the face of the burgeoning number of old and very old people, we must admit to ourselves that scientific knowledge of the cause and prevention of most chronic diseases is limited. The etiology and pathogenesis of only a fraction of the cancers, heart diseases, strokes, neurologic diseases, and arthritides are understood, and we know virtually nothing about the causes and prevention of senile dementia which will inexorably afflict 20 percent of our population 80 years of age and older (Brody, 1982a). We believe that improvement in life-style, as well as the alteration of health behavior whereby people are involved more in self-care, is indeed to be encouraged. Health promotion at this level is inexpensive and of great appeal to many frustrated physicians and policy makers, and offers real benefits to the populace. We have, however, another obligation which involves admitting our ignorance of causation and our tendency to suggest mechanisms which create guilt and anxiety among the elderly in areas in which the benefits of specific interventions have not been scientifically documented. To quote from Lewis Thomas (1979),

How does one make plans for science policy with such a list? The quick and easy way is to conclude that these diseases, not yet mastered, are simply beyond our grasp. The thing to do is to settle down with today's versions of science and technology, and to make sure that our health-care system is equipped to do the best it can in an imperfect world. The trouble with this approach is that we cannot afford it. The costs are already too high, and they escalate higher each year. Moreover the measures available are simply not good enough. We cannot go on indefinitely trying to cope with heart disease by open-heart surgery, carried out at formidable expense after the disease has run its destructive course. Nor can we postpone such issues by oversimplifying the problems, which is what we do, in my opinion, by attributing so much of today's chronic and disabling disease to the environment, or to wrong ways of living. The plain fact of the matter is that we do not know enough about the facts of the matter, and we should be more open about our ignorance.

Health promotion must, of course, involve continued emphasis on the individual's participation and responsibility in fostering his well-being. We emphasize that basic research on chronic diseases is also most urgently needed if we are to promote health. We must learn why the U.S. population is surviving longer and why white females are doing so much better than the rest. Further elucidation of the recently reported increase in morbidity and disability at all ages is essential. If it is true, what are the implications concerning the quality of life as we increase life expectancy? Urgent priorities include understanding the basic biochemistry of nutrition and of estrogens and other hormones; the differences in body composition and lean body mass; the precursors of senile dementia; the prevention of chronic diseases; and the interrelationships of social support, lifestyle, and health.

REFERENCES

Alling, D. W., Blackwelder, W., and Stuart-Harris, C. H. 1981. A study of excess mortality during influenza epidemics in the United States, 1968–1976. *Am. J. Epidemiol.* 113: 30–43.

Barrett, J. C. 1973. Age, time and cohort factors in mortality from cancer of the cervix. *J. Hyg. Camb.* 71: 253–259.

Breslow, N. E. and Day, N. E. 1975. Indirect standardization and multiplicative models for rates, with reference to the age adjustment of cancer incidence and relative frequency data. *J. Chron. Dis.* 28: 289–303.

Brody, J. A. 1982a. An epidemiologist views senile dementia—facts and fragments. *Am. J. Epidemiol.* 115: 155–163.

Brody, J. A. 1982b. Life expectancy and the health of older persons. *J. Am. Geriatics Society,* pp. 681–683.

Brody, J. A. 1982c. Psychosocial influences on aging—declining age-specific mortality in the 20th century. *Proceedings of the Xth International Conference, International Social Gerontology Center, Deauville, France,* May 26–28, 1982 (in press).

Brody, J. A. 1983. Limited importance of cancer and of competing-risk theories in aging *J Clinical Experimental Gerontology,* 5(2), 141–151.

Brody, J. A., Cornoni-Huntley, J., and Patrick, C. H. 1981. Research epidemiology as a growth industry at the National Institute on Aging. *Public Health Reports,* 96: 269–273.

Center for Disease Control. 1981. *Morbidity and Mortality Weekly Report,* Vol. 30, No. 38, DHHS Publication No. (CDC) 81–8017.

Choi, K. and Thacker, S. B. 1981a. An evaluation of influenza mortality surveillance, 1962–1979. I. Time series forecasts of expected pneumonia and influenza deaths. *Am. J. Epidemiol.* 113: 215–226.

Choi, K. and Thacker, S. B. 1981b. An evaluation of influenza mortality surveillance, 1962–1979. II. Percentage of pneumonia and influenza deaths as an indicator of influenza activity. *Am. J. Epidemiol.* 113: 227–235.

Colvez, A. and Blanchet, M. 1981. Disability trends in the United States population 1966–76: analysis of reported causes. *Am. J. Public Health* 71: 464–471.

Doll, R. and Peto, R. 1981. The causes of cancer: quantitative estimates of avoidable risks of cancer in the United States today. *J. Natl. Cancer Inst.* 66: 1192–1308.

Eisdorfer, C. 1977. Some variables relating to longevity in humans. *In,* A. M. Ostfeld and D. C. Gibson (eds.), *Epidemiology of Aging,* pp. 97–108. DHEW Publication No. (NIH) 77–711.

Freeman, D. H. and Holford, T. R. 1980. Summary rates. *Biometrics* 36: 195–205.

Fries, J. F. 1980. Aging, natural death, and the compression of morbidity. *New Engl. J. Med.* 303: 130–135.

Gittelsohn, A. M. 1982. On the distribution of underlying causes of death. *Am. J. Public Health* 72: 133–140.

Hamilton, J. B. 1948. The role of testicular secretions as indicated by the effects of castration in man and the short lifespan associated with maleness. *Recent Progress in Hormone Research,* Vol. 3. New York: Academic Press.

Janis, J. M., Kupper, L. L., and Greenberg, B. G. 1981. Age-period-cohort analysis of lung cancer mortality data. Abstract, *Am. J. Epidemiol.* 114: 440.

Kovar, M. G. 1977. Elderly people: the population 65 years and over. *In, Health, United States, 1976–1977;* DHEW Publication No. (HRA) 77–1232. Hyattsville, Md.: National Center for Health Statistics.

Kovar, M. G. 1980. The elderly population: use of medical care services by men and women in their middle and later years. Presented at the 108th annual meeting of the American Public Health Association, Detroit.

Manton, K. G., Woodbury, M. A., and Stallard, E. 1981. A variance components approach to categorical data models with heterogeneous cell populations: analysis of spatial gradients in lung cancer mortality rates in North Carolina counties. *Biometrics* 37: 259–269.

McGinnis, J. M. 1982. Recent health gains for adults. *New Engl. J. Med.* 306:671–673.

Moolgavkar, S. H., Stevens, R. G., and Lee, J. A. H.

1979. Effect of age on incidence of breast cancer in females. *J. Natl. Cancer Inst.* 62: 493–501.

National Center for Health Statistics (NCHS). 1979. Current estimates from the Health Interview Survey: United States—1978. *Vital and Health Statistics,* Series 10, No. 130, DHEW Publication No. (PHS) 80–1551.

National Center for Health Statistics (NCHS). 1980a. Final mortality statistics, 1978. *Monthly Vital Statistics Report,* **29,** No. 6, Supplement (2); DHHS Publication No. (PHS) 80–1120.

National Center for Health Statistics (NCHS). 1980b. Annual summary for the United States, 1979. *Monthly Vital Statistics Report,* Vol. 28, No. 13. DHHS Publication No. (PHS) 81–1120.

National Institutes of Health (NIH). 1979. *Proceedings of the Conference on the Decline in Coronary Heart Disease Mortality;* NIH Publication No. 79–1610.

Patrick, C. H., Palesch, Y. Y., Feinleib, M., and Brody, J. A. 1982. Sex differences in declining cohort death rates from heart disease. *Am. J. Public Health* 72: 161–166.

Pollack, E. S. and Horm, J. W. 1980. Trends in cancer incidence and mortality in the United States, 1969–76. *J. Natl. Cancer Inst.* 64: 1091–1103.

Rice, D. P. 1978. Projection and analysis of health status trends. Presented at the 106th annual meeting of the American Public Health Association, Los Angeles.

Rives, N. W. and Serow, W. J. 1981. Interstate migration of the elderly: demographic aspects. *Research on Aging* 3: 259–278.

Siegel, J. S. 1980. Recent and prospective demographic trends for the elderly population and some implications for health care. *In,* S. G. Haynes and M. Feinleib (eds.), *Second Conference on the Epidemiology of Aging,* pp. 289–316; NIH Publication No. 80–969. Washington, D.C.: U.S. Government Printing Office.

Stallones, R. A. 1980. The rise and fall of ischemic heart disease. *Scientific American* 243: 53–59.

Sullivan, D. F. 1971. Disability components for an index of health. *Vital and Health Statistics,* Series 2, No. 42, Public Health Service Publication No. 1000.

Susser, M. 1977. Demography of aging—discussant's perspective. *In,* A. M. Ostfeld and D. C. Gibson (eds.), *Epidemiology of Aging,* pp. 83–96; DHEW Publication No. (NIH) 77–711. Washington, D.C.: U.S. Government Printing Office.

Thomas, L. 1979. *The Medusa and the Snail,* pp. 165–166. New York: Viking Press.

U.S. Bureau of the Census. 1979a. Estimates of the population of states by age: July 1, 1978. *Current Population Reports,* Series P-25, No. 794. Washington, D.C.: U.S. Government Printing Office.

U.S. Bureau of the Census. 1979b. Marital status and living arrangements: March, 1978. *Current Population Reports,* Series P-20, No. 338. Washington, D.C.: U.S. Government Printing Office.

U.S. Bureau of the Census. 1979c. Social and economic characteristics of the older population: 1978. *Current Population Reports,* Series P-23, No. 85. Washington, D.C.: U.S. Government Printing Office.

Weinblatt, E., Goldberg, J. D., Ruberman, W., et al. 1982. Mortality after first myocardial infarction. *J.A.M.A.* 247: 1576–1581.

2
COMPARATIVE AND EVOLUTIONARY ASPECTS OF LONGEVITY

Thomas B.L. Kirkwood

National Institute for Medical Research
London, U.K.

INTRODUCTION

The comparative study of longevity is made complex by the fact that life span is a trait which is strongly affected by chance. The proximate cause of death is usually some random hazard such as injury or disease, with the result that even individuals that are genetically identical may live to quite different ages. Nevertheless, when mortality statistics are gathered for populations of adequate size, it is found that the *distribution* of life spans in a given environment tends to be more or less reproducible and that the probability of death within a fixed period of time shows a dependency on age which is characteristic for the species. It is these systematic patterns of mortality which are the basis of comparative and evolutionary gerontology.

In this chapter, a review is made of the present state of knowledge on comparative aspects of longevity, and of the theories which have been advanced to explain the evolution of aging. For example, it has been observed among mammals that many species exhibit an exponential increase in age-specific mortality rates (Sacher and Staffeldt, 1972). This leads naturally to questions of whether

the mortality pattern may reveal an informative allometry with other physical and metabolic variables, and whether the theory of natural selection can suggest why, and perhaps even how, such mortality patterns have evolved. In contrast to the normal mammalian pattern, certain small marsupials of the genus *Antechinus* exhibit a striking life history plan in which males and, in some cases females, die abruptly after completing an annual cycle of reproduction (see Diamond, 1982). What is it about these marsupials, and about other species such as Pacific salmon which also undergo "once-only," or *semelparous,* reproduction, that distinguishes them from *iteroparous* species which reproduce repeatedly during the adult phase of their life span?

Before we attempt to answer these questions, it is necessary to define carefully what is to be understood by the terms "aging" and "longevity." In this chapter, longevity will be used to refer only to species or populations and will not be used to describe the life span of an individual. For the most part, longevity will be taken to mean the *maximum* life span reported for the species in question. This is because average life span, or any similar measure, is highly sensitive to environmental conditions and tends to be substantially lower for natural populations than for captive or protected ones. Maximum life span, by contrast, is largely unaffected by environment, provided that the sample of individuals is not too small. As an extreme value statistic, maximum life span is to some degree influenced by the size of the population, tending to be shorter in smaller populations than in larger ones even when the underlying distribution is the same (Gumbel, 1958). However, this is only a minor complication (Sacher, 1975) and usually can be safely ignored. [When necessary, a more stable statistic such as the 99 percentile (that is, the life span exceeded by only 1 percent of the sample) may be employed, but it is seldom the case that sufficiently detailed information on the distribution of life span is available.]

The definition of aging is more problematical, and the lack of an agreed, universally applicable definition has previously been held as proof of the immaturity of gerontological science (Medawar, 1955). While this view is less tenable today, it remains true that "aging" is still only loosely defined and that, as a result, confusion can easily arise when the term is used without proper qualification. Nowhere is the potential for confusion greater than when comparing species which differ in their life history plans. The next two sections of this chapter, therefore, set out to clarify this point.

SURVIVORSHIP AND THE DEFINITION OF AGING

The pattern of mortality experienced by human populations serves to illustrate what is most commonly understood by the term *aging*. Following the attainment of sexual maturity and a peak of vitality which occurs early in adulthood, a long period of progressive deterioration takes place during which individuals become increasingly likely to die. The effect of aging on a population may be examined using the actuarial device of a life table (see Sacher, 1977; Lamb,

1977), or it may be illustrated as a survival curve.

A survival curve for a typical industrialized human society is shown in Figure 1(a). Survivorship (l_x) plotted against age (x) shows a form, sometimes described as "rectangular," which is taken to be definitive of aging. Apart from an initial drop in infancy, survivorship remains nearly constant until about the fourth decade after which it declines rapidly, reaching zero around 110 years of age. The increase in mortality in older individuals is revealed strikingly in a plot of age-specific mortality rate (μ_x) against age [Figure 1(b)]. In particular, Figure 1(b) shows that although the survival curve seems to flatten out again at very high ages, the *death rate per survivor* goes on rising at an accelerating rate.

Figure 1 also shows, for comparison, the survivorship and mortality curves of a hypothetical population in which the individuals do not age in the sense defined above

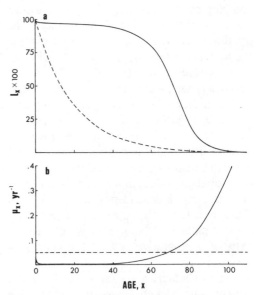

Figure 1. (a) Relationship between survivorship, l_x, and age, x, for a typical industrialized human population in the late twentieth century (continuous curve) and for a hypothetical population of organisms which do not age (broken curve). (b) Relationship between age-specific mortality rate, μ_x, and age, x, for the same populations as in (a).

but retain a constant death rate. Such individuals are potentially immortal in the limited sense that, whatever their current age, their survival prospects remain the same. However, as Figure 1(a) shows, the chance of surviving for a very long time may be extremely small.

As noted by Gompertz (1825), the form of the mortality curve in adult humans is closely approximated by a simple exponential

$$\mu_X = \mu_0 e^{\alpha X} \qquad (1)$$

and this relation is commonly called the Gompertz equation. The slope parameter, α, is a rate term, described by Sacher (1978) as the *actuarial aging rate,* which expresses how fast the force of mortality increases with age. μ_0 can be interpreted as a measure of "basal vulnerability." Note that while the Gompertz equation gives μ_0 as the force of mortality at age zero, the true mortality at birth is always greater than this. The Gompertz equation cannot be assumed to hold outside the adult age range over which it has been fitted.

The role of the Gompertz equation in the comparative study of aging and longevity has been considerably extended through studies by Sacher and Staffeldt (1972), who have shown it to hold for several species of mammal other than humans. The equation is also made more flexible through the addition of a further constant to give

$$\mu_X = \mu_0 e^{\alpha x} + \beta \qquad (2)$$

known as the Gompertz-Makeham equation (see Sacher, 1977 and Comfort, 1979). The importance of the additional constant β is that it represents age-independent mortality, such as may be experienced in a hazardous environment. Equation (2) has the attractive property that if fixed values are assumed for the "intrinsic" parameters μ_0 and α, but the "extrinsic" parameter β is allowed to vary, the same basic equation can approximate the mortality patterns of both wild and captive populations of a given species (Figure 2). When β is large enough, the presence of aging in a given species may be masked (Figure

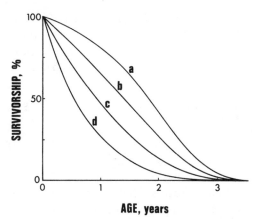

AGE, years

Figure 2. The curves illustrate the relationship between survivorship and age calculated using the Gompertz-Makeham equation with fixed values of basal vulnerability (μ_0) and actuarial aging rate (α), but with four different values of age-independent mortality (β). The values for μ_0 and α are those quoted by Sacher (1978) for *Mus musculus* (see Table 2), and the values of β are 0, $2\mu_0$, $5\mu_0$, and $10\mu_0$ for curves a, b, c, and d, respectively. No allowance is made for infant mortality.

2, curve c) or concealed altogether (Figure 2, curve d).

It would be unrealistic to conclude this section without pointing out the limitations of defining aging in terms of a particular pattern of survivorship (see also Medawar, 1955). Firstly, a definition of aging based on an increasing probability of death relates only to a subset of the time-dependent changes which occur after maturity of size, form, or function is attained. It is not necessarily the case that all age-related changes are deleterious in terms of survival (see Lamb 1977), although exceptions to this rule are admittedly rare. Secondly, the survival curve is highly susceptible to modification by extrinsic factors, so that many populations in the wild may show little or no sign of any intrinsic process of senescence (Lack 1954). Thirdly, a survivorship pattern suggestive of "normal" aging may arise artificially where individuals remain immune from a major cause of mortality until either a specific age or a specific size is attained. Such an effect may be caused, for example, by human interference such as occurs in commercial or

sport fisheries. It may also arise quite naturally in certain semelparous species where
death follows closely on the act of reproduction.

AGING AND ITS INTERACTION WITH LIFE HISTORY PLAN

The life history of an organism is the set of
co-adapted traits that together determine its
age-related pattern of reproduction and
mortality (Stearns, 1976). Although species
differ in the precise values of key life history
variables, most conform to a few easily recognizable basic plans. The two classifica-
tions of major importance here are (1)
between species which do and do not have a
clear distinction between germ line and somatic tissue, and (2) between species which
reproduce once only (semelparous) and those
which reproduce repeatedly (iteroparous).

Importance of the Soma in Relation to Aging

The relevance of a clearly defined soma in
relation to aging has been recognized for
more than a century, in fact ever since Weismann first proposed his theory of the "germ
plasm" (see Weismann, 1891; Kirkwood and
Cremer, 1982). Where there is no clear distinction between soma and germ line, the
problem of arriving at a satisfactory definition of aging is complex (Kirkwood, 1981;
Kirkwood and Cremer, 1982). For example,
in a unicellular organism, the soma and germ
line are essentially one and the same, and the
germ line must, in a certain sense, be immortal. However, it has been found that certain protozoa undergo a form of clonal
senescence unless sexual crossing occurs (see,
for example, Sonneborn, 1954); this phenomenon has been extensively studied as a
special instance of "aging" (Smith-Sonneborn 1979; see also Chapter 4). Among multicellular organisms, the majority of plant
species and numerous animal invertebrates
are capable of regenerating whole organisms
from almost any piece of tissue, provided a
suitable environment is supplied. In many
such species, senescence may occur in a part

like a leaf without affecting the vitality of
the organism as a whole (Woolhouse 1967;
see also Chapter 5). In the case of trees, mechanical constraints may eventually limit
survival, but even old, decrepit specimens
may be capable of unlimited vegetative propagation. Under these circumstances, the individual organism is sometimes rather
arbitrarily defined, and concepts of aging
and longevity are correspondingly imprecise.

A related distinction is whether reproduction occurs sexually or asexually. In obligate
sexual species, somatic tissue is clearly distinguished from the germ cells whose function is oriented specifically towards the
production of gametes. However, in many
lower organisms, sexual reproduction may
be employed only in certain circumstances,
and the relation between sex and aging may
be complex. One example of an interaction
between sex and aging has already been mentioned, namely the clonal senescence of protozoa such as *Paramecium* when restricted
only to asexual fission. Another is the interesting case of the flowering bamboos of the
family Poaceae (subfamily *Bambusoideae*).
These plants propagate asexually for considerable periods of time, as much as 60 years,
before all members of the resultant clone
flower simultaneously and die following the
production of seed. Examples like this are of
considerable interest for the questions they
raise about the diverse organization of life
histories and, in particular, about the factors
which govern survival patterns. Above all,
they show that concepts of aging and longevity derived from studies of higher animals
may need to be considerably qualified when
applied to species which can reproduce without sex.

Semelparous (Once Only) Reproduction

Species that always reproduce sexually are
divided into those that reproduce only once
in a lifetime and die (semelparous) and those
that reproduce repeatedly (iteroparous)
(Cole, 1954). In either case, the soma is distinct from the germ line, and although age-
related changes may arise within the germ

line (Kram and Schneider, 1978; Medvedev, 1981; see also Chapter 18), attention is restricted in this chapter to the aging of the soma alone.

Semelparous reproduction is most likely to evolve in species in which the chance of an adult surviving to breed a second time would, in any case, have been small (Charnov and Schaffer, 1973). Since parental care is usually precluded by death, semelparity tends to be associated with large numbers of progeny and with high infant mortality. Examples of semelparous animals include the Pacific salmon, octopus, many invertebrates, and the marsupial mice cited earlier.

The semelparous life history may be divided into two principal phases, the first consisting of growth and maturation and the second of reproduction. Following reproduction, death usually occurs rapidly, frequently in a highly deterministic fashion. Depending upon whether the signal to reproduce is synchronous within a population, as when reproduction follows a strict seasonal pattern, or contingent on some more variable process such as the attainment of a certain minimum body size, the survival curve may be either more or less rectangular (Figure 3).

During the growth phase of a semelparous life history, age-specific mortality is just as likely to decrease as to increase while the hazards of early life are passed and the acquisition of greater size confers a survival advantage. Semelparous organisms prevented from breeding, either by castration or by physical isolation, may live for periods considerably in excess of the normal life span (Calow, 1979; Diamond 1982), which suggests that death is a direct consequence of factors associated with the act of reproduction and is not, to any significant degree, due to an independent intrinsic process of aging. Hormonal changes have been shown to exert a controlling influence on postreproductive death in the octopus (Wodinsky, 1977) and in Pacific salmon (Robertson, 1961). Similar hormonal effects seem likely also to be involved in the (partial) semelparity of marsupial mice (Calaby and Taylor, 1981).

Iteroparous (Repeated) Reproduction

The comparative and evolutionary study of longevity takes on particular interest among iteroparous species, partly because our own species is iteroparous, but mainly because iteroparous life histories could, in principle,

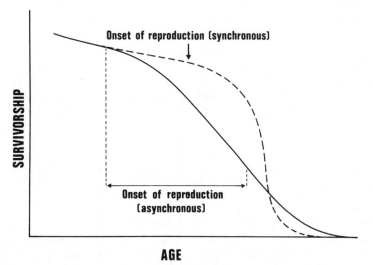

AGE

Figure 3. Relationship between survivorship and age in semelparous species which exhibit synchronous (broken curve) and asynchronous (continuous curve) onset of reproduction. Neither curve represents infant mortality, which in most cases is extremely high.

extend indefinitely. For an iteroparous organism, reproduction occurs repeatedly during adulthood and is not coincident with the end of the individual life cycle. Why, then, does the mortality rate increase with age? Does somatic aging occur within all iteroparous vertebrates, and what are the factors which determine a species' longevity? These questions are considered in detail in the following sections of this chapter.

DISTRIBUTION OF SENESCENCE AMONG ITEROPAROUS VERTEBRATES

In spite of the limitations inherent in a life table definition of aging, the survival curve remains the most useful diagnostic tool for examining whether senescence may be detected within any given species. However, the practical difficulties in obtaining a reliable set of data from which a survival curve can be constructed may be immense (Caughley, 1966). Firstly, in order that senescence is not concealed by too high a level of accidental mortality, the population must usually be maintained in a protected environment such as a laboratory or a zoo. Secondly, care must be taken that the artificial habitat does not introduce its own peculiarities which influence the survival curve. Thirdly, for all but the shortest-lived species the study may need to be prohibitively long. For these reasons, the life table data which are available are remarkably scant, and it is necessary to draw also on less precise sources of information. The most complete collection of information on the phylogenic distribution of senescence is to be found in the book by Comfort (1979).

Mammals

Survival curves for humans, laboratory mammals (Sacher and Staffeldt, 1972), and thoroughbred horses (Comfort 1958, 1959) show the clearest evidence of senescence. Less formal experience with domestic and agricultural species shows senescence to be present in all mammalian species well known to man. It is reasonably assumed that senescence is an attribute of all mammalian spe-

cies, although the fairly recent discovery of semelparity among male marsupial mice (Woolley 1966) cautions against the assumption that all mammals necessarily age in the same way.

Birds

Information on senescence in birds is confined largely to studies based on the ringing of populations in the wild, with the attendant statistical difficulties of constructing reliable estimates of survival curves (Seber, 1973; Buckland, 1980). For many small birds, natural mortality is so high that adult survival curves are close to exponential (Lack, 1954). However, studies of some larger species [e.g., *Fulmarus glacialis* (Dunnett and Ollason, 1978)] have reported evidence of increased mortality among older birds. For captive populations, survival curves of Japanese quail (*Coturnix coturnix japonica*) show clear evidence of senescence (Cherkin and Eckhardt, 1977), and the considerable, though anecdotal, experience of those who keep smaller birds as pets or in zoos suggests that senility and death occur at ages which are fairly constant for any given species. Despite the paucity of the evidence, it is generally believed that senescence comparable to that seen in mammals is to be found in all avian species.

Reptiles and Amphibians

Reptiles and amphibians may live for considerable periods of time, exceeding 100 years in the case of some species of tortoise (see Comfort, 1979). Life table data do not exist for populations in the wild, and records of survival in captivity, particularly for reptiles, are limited by the poor adaptation of many species to artificial conditions. On reviewing as much information as he could collect, Comfort (1979) concluded: "The high probability is that all reptiles and amphibians age if they live long enough; small forms (lizards, chameleons) appear to have limited lives, and the only question about published work on their pathology is whether the changes observed are in fact senile changes: in the larger forms the life-cycle is so easily modified by diapause, diet, temperature, and the like that individuals probably age at rates so different as to be beyond the access of actuarial statistics except in an experiment of intolerable length."

Fish

Studies on senescence in fish received particular impetus from the hypothesis of Bidder (1932) that senescence in vertebrates is linked to determinacy of size. Bidder suggested that aging was caused by the continued action of the growth mechanism after growth was stopped and that in those species of fish whose growth was indeterminate, senescence would not occur. Bidder's hypothesis was contradicted, however, by the observation of Gerking (1957) that many small teleosts undergo senescence even though growth in the female may continue throughout life. Also, Comfort (1960, 1961) showed that the growth of the guppy, *Lebistes reticulatus,* could be varied considerably by modifying its environment without significantly altering its typically senescent survival curve. A comprehensive review of data on the survival of fish in captivity and in the wild led Comfort (1979) to conclude for teleosts: "Some forms apparently resemble monocarpic plants, mortality being linked to reproduction. Some, in captivity, have a lifespan determined by senescence, their mortality increasing with age on a curve closely similar to that of mammals. Some forms, however, may conceivably have an effectively indeterminate lifespan, though this may well mean only that their determinate maximum, as in wild birds, comes so late in relation to mortality as never to be reached in practice."

COMPARATIVE ASPECTS OF LONGEVITY IN VERTEBRATES

Maximum longevities for a selected range of vertebrate species are shown in Table 1. From data like these, certain basic observations may be made: for example, large animals tend to be longer-lived than small ones, and birds on the whole live longer than comparably sized mammals. To take comparative analyses further, more detailed information is required.

Comparative Studies of Life History

Reasons commonly suggested for the greater longevity of larger species are that, in general, the gestation period is longer, the litter size smaller, and the time to maturation more extended than in smaller species. Thus, if a breeding population that is subject to natural mortality is to sustain itself, individuals may not be permitted to undergo senescence too soon, and hence a positive correlation between body size and longevity makes sense. On the other hand, larger species as a rule suffer less acutely from predation than smaller ones so the demand for replacement may not be as large.

Observations like these, although obviously true in part, fall well short of providing a satisfactory explanation of the observed differences in life span. For this, the detailed interactions of fecundity, natural mortality, growth, and senescence must be studied using the analytical tools of life history theory (Gadgil and Bossert, 1970; Taylor et al., 1974; Leon, 1976; Stearns, 1976, 1977; Charlesworth, 1980). However, these studies are at present largely formal, and in order to apply them in specific practical cases, it will be necessary both to develop the theory in greater depth and to expand the data base of information on natural populations.

Comparison of Survival Patterns among Mammals

In the selection of species for comparative research on the biology of aging, it may be relevant to consider the survival pattern as a whole. Evidence has been obtained that the survival of protected populations of several mammalian species can be described quite well by the Gompertz equation (Sacher and Staffeldt, 1972; Sacher 1978). Sacher (1978)

TABLE 1. Maximum Recorded Life Spans for Selected Mammals, Birds, Reptiles, and Amphibians.[a]

	Scientific Name	Common Name	Maximum Life Span (years)
Primates	Macaca mulatta	Rhesus monkey	29
	Pan troglodytes	Chimpanzee	44
	Gorilla gorilla	Gorilla	39
	Homo sapiens	Man	115
Carnivores	Felis catus	Domestic cat	28
	Canis familiaris	Domestic dog	20
	Ursus arctos	Brown bear	36
Ungulates	Ovis aries	Sheep	20
	Sus scrofa	Swine	27
	Equus caballus	Horse	46
	Elephas maximus	Indian elephant	70
Rodents	Mus musculus	House mouse	3
	Rattus rattus	Black rat	5
	Sciurus carolinensis	Gray squirrel	15
	Hystrix brachyura	Porcupine	27
Bats	Desmodus rotundus	Vampire bat	13
	Pteropus giganteus	Indian fruit bat	17
Birds	Streptopelia risoria	Domestic dove	30
	Larus argentatus	Herring gull	41
	Aquila chrysaëtos	Golden eagle	46
	Bubo bubo	Eagle owl	68
Reptiles	Eunectes murinus	Anaconda	29
	Macroclemys temmincki	Snapping turtle	58+
	Alligator sinensis	Chinese alligator	52
	Testudo elephantopus	Galapagos tortoise	100+
Amphibians	Xenopus laevis	African clawed toad	15
	Bufo bufo	Common toad	36
	Cynops pyrrhogaster	Japanese newt	25

[a]From data given by Altman and Dittmer (1972); Flower (1938); Comfort, (1979).

gave estimates for the slope (α) and intercept (μ_0) parameters of the Gompertz equation for captive populations of nine species of mammals drawn from five orders (Table 2). "Basal vulnerability" ranged over three orders of magnitude among these species, although part of this range may be attributed to differences in the quality of environmental conditions. "Actuarial aging rate," α, was less variable, covering approximately a 40-fold range. If the two extremes of this range are considered, the adult short-tailed shrew (*Blarina brevicauda*) experienced a doubling in mortality rate every 2.5 months, compared with a mortality rate doubling time for *Homo sapiens* of 8.5 years.

It is perhaps unwise to attach too much

significance to the values of these parameters, derived as they are from an entirely empirical function. Nevertheless, it is interesting in making detailed comparisons, such as have been carried out between the two muroid rodent species *Peromyscus leucopus* and *Mus musculus* (Sacher and Hart, 1978), to know in which of these two respects the survival curves may differ. In the case of *P. leucopus* and *M. musculus,* the 2.5-fold difference in life expectancy is attributable mostly to a twofold difference in the acutarial aging rate (α), although *M. musculus* also has a higher basal vulnerability (μ_0) [see Equation (1)]. When comparing *P. leucopus* with the shorter-lived *P. californicus,* however, it would appear that the one-year difference in

TABLE 2. Characteristics of the Gompertz Relationship Between Age-Specific Mortality Rate and Age for Nine Mammalian Species.[a,b]

Species		Life Expectancy (years)	Mortality Rate Doubling Time (years)	Basal Vulnerability (years^{-1})
Blarina brevicauda	(short-tailed shrew)	0.7	0.2	1.6×10^{-1}
Sigmodon hispidus	(cotton rat)	1.4	0.3	8.0×10^{-2}
Oryzomys palustris	(rice rat)	2.2	0.5	4.0×10^{-2}
Mus musculus	(house mouse)	1.6	0.6	1.1×10^{-1}
Peromyscus leucopus	(white-footed mouse)	4.0	1.2	4.4×10^{-2}
Peromyscus californicus	(Californian mouse)	3.0	1.2	8.8×10^{-2}
Canis familiaris	(dog, beagle)	9.9	2.2	9.9×10^{-3}
Equus caballus	(thoroughbred mare)	17.3	3.7	2.2×10^{-3}
Homo sapiens	(U.S. white female, 1969)	75.9	8.5	5.5×10^{-5}

[a]Adapted from Sacher (1978).
[b]*Mortality rate doubling time* ($\log_e 2/\alpha$) is an inverse measure of the actuarial aging rate, α (see text). *Basal vulnerability* is the intercept, μ_0, calculated by extrapolating the Gompertz equation to age zero. Also shown is the life expectancy, excluding deaths from birth to weaning in the cases of the rodents and the shrew (see Sacher 1978; maximum life spans were not given).

life expectancy is due solely to a twofold difference in basal vulnerability. Thus, for comparative research on factors which may govern the *rate* of aging, it is clearly preferable to compare *P. leucopus* with *M. musculus* than to compare the two *Peromyscus* species.

Relationship of Longevity to Other Physiological and Anatomical Variables

The existence of a simple mathematical relationship between two or more biological variables across a range of species may reveal a pattern or constraint which can throw light on how certain processes are organized. The analysis of such relationships, when one of the variables is body size, is termed *allometry,* and for brevity the same term will be used with more general meaning here. Because reliable data suitable for life table analysis are scarce, allometric studies on survivorship patterns have so far been carried out only with estimates of maximum longevity.

Using the technique of multiple regression, Sacher (1976) examined the dependence of maximum life span, L (years), on four anatomical and metabolic variables in 85 mammalian species. These variables were:

adult brain weight, E (grams); adult body weight, S (grams); specific metabolic rate, M (watts per gram body weight); deep body temperature, T (°C). The relation obtained was

$$\log L = 0.62 \log E - 0.41 \log S - 0.52 \log M + 0.026T + 0.9$$

where the logarithms are to base 10. Each regression coefficient was judged to be statistically significant, and the relationship accounted for 82 percent of the total variation in $\log L$ among the 85 species.

Defining $K_c = E \cdot S^{-2/3}$ as an index of cephalization and $K_m = M \times 10^{-0.05T}$ as a metabolic factor, Sacher formulated the allometric relationship as

$$L = 8K_c^{0.6} K_m^{-0.5}$$

The correlation of life span with the index of cephalization suggests an important, though *not necessarily causative,* association between survivorship and the brain-body relationship defined by K_c. It is interesting to note that although the separate regressions of $\log L$ on $\log E$ and $\log S$ indicated that longevity increased with either E or S (Sacher 1976), the negative coefficient of $\log S$ in the multiple regression shows that if brain weight is fixed, longevity *decreases* with body weight.

The dependence of L on K_m shows that longevity decreases as the inverse square root of the metabolic factor. A curious feature of this relationship, pointed out by Sacher (1976), is that at constant metabolic rate, a fall in deep body temperature results in decreased life span. This seems counter to intuition and, at first sight, contradictory to studies by Liu and Walford (1975) who showed that the life span of the annual fish *Cynolebias bellottii* was significantly greater when kept at 15°C than at 20°C. However, Liu and Walford's observation was of an *intraspecific* effect, and even though an interspecies allometry may sometimes be paralleled by a similar relationship within a given species [as in the inverse relation between longevity and metabolic rate for "shaker" mutants of *Drosophila melanogaster* (Trout and Kaplan, 1970)], there is no reason why this should generally be the case. Sacher (1976) speculated that the positive coefficient for the dependence of log L on T in the multiple regression could be why passerine birds frequently outlive mammals of comparable size by a considerable margin and have body temperatures 2–5°C higher (Altman and Dittmer, 1972). To confirm this, it will be necessary to measure the body temperatures and metabolic rates of birds and to demonstrate that the same allometry is true for birds as for mammals.

Sacher (1977) also suggested that the inverse relationship between life span and metabolic rate may explain why dietary restriction can markedly prolong the life spans of laboratory rats. However, Masoro et al. (1982) have recently shown that food-restricted rats consume a greater number of calories per gram body weight than rats fed *ad libitum,* which does not support the concept that food restriction slows the rate of aging by decreasing the metabolic rate (see Chapter 20).

THEORIES ON THE EVOLUTION OF AGING

In order to understand the diversity of survival patterns and, in particular, the apparent universality of aging in higher animals, it is relevant to ask how these patterns have evolved. One school of thought holds that aging is simply an inevitable attribute of complex metazoans and in itself requires no evolutionary explanation (see Sacher 1978; Cutler, 1978). The question, then, is not how aging originated, but merely how its rate of onset has been modified. However, the grounds for making this assumption *a priori* seem inadequate (Williams, 1957), and various theories to explain the origin, as well as the shaping, of senescence have been advanced.

Aging: Adaptive or Nonadaptive

Two sharply contrasting types of theory on the origin of aging may be distinguished. The first sees it as advantageous, or even essential, to set a finite limit to the life of the individual. Theories of this kind suggest that aging has been favored by natural selection as a positive adaptation in itself; they are termed *adaptive* theories. The second, *nonadaptive* kind of theory takes the view that senescence is detrimental to the fitness of the genotype which causes it or, at best, selectively neutral. Nonadaptive theories therefore have to explain the evolution of aging indirectly. The two main kinds of nonadaptive theory which will be described state that (a) the force of natural selection declines with age and is eventually too weak to prevent senescence or (b) senescence is a by-product of other adaptive traits.

The view that aging is adaptive is widely popular, although few attempts have been made to justify it explicitly. Two recurrent themes are (1) that aging is necessary to eliminate old individuals from the population to provide space and nutriment for their progeny and (2) that possession of a finite life span ensures a more rapid succession of generations and thus improves the chance of a species adapting to changes in its environment (see, for example, Woolhouse, 1967; von Weizsäcker, 1980). An attraction of the adaptive theory is that it permits aging to be seen as a programmed process under its own strict genetic control. Consequently, all that is required to understand, and perhaps alter, the aging process is to unravel the details of the program.

Two cogent arguments speak against general adaptive theories of aging. Firstly, accidental mortality is sufficiently high in most species that obvious senility is rarely seen in wild populations (Medawar, 1952; Lack, 1954). Thus, the "living space" argument does not hold up, and there is neither need for a mechanism specifically to terminate life nor opportunity for it to evolve. Secondly, for aging to have arisen as an adaptive trait would have required that selection for advantage to the species or group was more effective than selection among individuals within the group for the reproductive advantages of a longer life. Superiority of the former kind of selection over the latter is very seldom the case (Maynard Smith, 1976), and it is easy to show that if two genotypes A and B differ only in that A has a mechanism to terminate life at some fixed age, while B does not, then B is selectively fitter than A (Kirkwood, 1981). For these reasons, adaptive senescence is only to be expected where species demonstrably age in the wild, *and* where there is both scope and cause for effective group selection to favor it. Such stringent conditions will be satisfied only very rarely, with the result that aging is most plausibly explained in nonadaptive terms.

Late-acting Deleterious Genes

Medawar (1952; see also Haldane, 1941) suggested a nonadaptive theory of aging based on the observation that even without senescence already present, the cumulative effect of accidental mortality is to reduce progressively the fraction of individuals surviving to older and older ages. In consequence, mutations with late age-specific effects affect only the subsequent reproductive contributions of the small number of individuals surviving to that age; they are, therefore, subject to much weaker selection than equivalent mutations with early age-specific effects (Medawar, 1952; see also Williams, 1957; Hamilton, 1966; Edney and

Gill, 1968; Kirkwood and Holliday, 1979; Charlesworth, 1980). For this reason, Medawar (1952) suggested that senescence might, in fact, be nothing more than the result of random accumulation of deleterious mutations with late age-specific effects, since such mutations would encounter little or no negative selection in natural populations (senescence being seen only when accidental mortality is greatly reduced in protected environments).

Medawar's theory is clearly a nonadaptive one. Aging, although potentially deleterious, arises as a selectively neutral trait because the force of natural selection becomes negligible at the late end of an iteroparous life span. This principle lies at the core of all nonadaptive explanations of aging, although the ability of Medawar's particular version of the theory to explain the *origin* of senescence has been questioned since, in the absence of senescence, it is hard to see what would be the timing mechanism to determine "lateness" in a life history which potentially could continue forever (Kirkwood, 1977; Calow, 1978; Sacher, 1978; Kirkwood and Holliday, 1979). This difficulty is circumvented, however, in a later version of the late-acting deleterious gene hypothesis proposed by Williams (1957).

Williams (1957) similarly recognized that the force of natural selection declines with age (or, more precisely, with the remaining fraction of the total expectation of reproduction, which reduces with age; see Kirkwood and Holliday, 1979) but suggested that aging is attributable to pleiotropic genes that have good effects early in life, but become harmful later. As an example of such a gene, Williams cited the hypothetical case of a mutation which has a favorable effect on the calcification of bone during development but which subsequently results in the calcification of arteries. Provided the deleterious effects occur sufficiently late, negative selection against such pleiotropic genes will be outweighed by positive selection for their beneficial properties, and aging may thus evolve as a by-product of selection for other traits. It is important to note that although

Williams' theory regards senescence as resulting from adaptation, it is not seen as conferring *by itself* any selective advantage. Thus, Williams' theory is also a nonadaptive one.

Mathematical analyses of the rules governing selection of genes with age-specific effects on survivorship have supported Williams' hypothesis and placed particular emphasis on the interaction between the reproductive schedule of a population and the evolution of senescence within it (Hamilton, 1966; Charlesworth, 1980). Evidence that pleiotropic genes of the sort postulated by Williams may exist has been found in the flour-beetle *Tribolium* (Sokal, 1970; Mertz, 1975) and *Drosophila* (Wattiaux, 1968a, 1968b; Rose and Charlesworth, 1981a, 1981b). Rose and Charlesworth, whose experiments involved selection on life history components in *Drosophila melanogaster,* also found no evidence of the increase in additive genetic variance with age which is predicted by Medawar's version of the theory.

Disposable Soma Theory—Insufficiency of Repair

An alternative way to explain the evolution of aging is to consider how an iteroparous organism ought best to allocate its resources (primarily its intake of energy) among the various metabolic tasks it needs to perform. The organism may, in a sense, be viewed as an entity which transforms free energy from its environment into its progeny. Part of the energy input must, however, be used for activities such as growth, foraging, defense, and repair. As the following argument reveals, the optimum allocation of energy involves a smaller investment in somatic maintenance and repair than would be required for the soma to last indefinitely.

Given the continual hazard of accidental death, from which no species can be entirely immune, each individual soma can have only a finite expectation of life, even if it were not subject to senescence. When the soma dies, the resources invested in its maintenance are lost. Too low an investment in the prevention or repair of somatic damage is obviously unsatisfactory because then the soma may disintegrate before it can reproduce. However, too high an investment in these activities is also wasteful because there is no advantage in maintaining the soma better than is necessary for it to survive its expected lifetime in the wild environment in reasonably sound condition. Fitness in the latter case would actually be enhanced by reducing the investment in somatic maintenance and channeling the extra energy into, for example, more rapid growth or greater reproductive output. *Fitness is therefore maximized at a level of repair which is less than would be required for indefinite somatic survival* (see Figure 4). This argument, proposed originally in specific cellular form (Kirkwood, 1977; Kirkwood and Holliday, 1979) and recently developed more generally (Kirkwood, 1981), is termed the "disposable soma" theory.

The precise optimum level of investment in somatic maintenance will depend on the species' ecological niche. For example, a species subject to high accidental mortality will do better not to invest heavily in each individual soma, which will therefore age relatively soon, but should concentrate instead on more rapid and prolific reproduction. Conversely, a species which experiences low accidental mortality may profit by doing the reverse. Thus, the theory readily explains the well-known inverse correlation between longevity and fecundity. The theory also makes explicit predictions about the nature of the aging process. Firstly, it predicts that aging is the result of an accumulation of somatic damage. Secondly, it predicts that species with different longevities should exhibit corresponding differences in their levels of somatic maintenance and repair. Thirdly, it predicts that since damage cannot be permitted to accumulate progessively within the germ line, there may exist within germ cells special maintenance processes to prevent this (this last prediction is not, however, essential to the theory since other factors, such as the competitive elimination of defective gametes, may be sufficient).

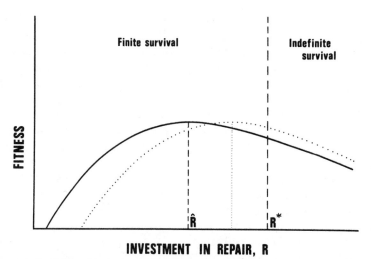

INVESTMENT IN REPAIR, R

Figure 4. Theoretical relationship between fitness and the level of investment of resources in somatic maintenance and repair for species which reproduce repeatedly during the life span. The disposable soma theory (see text) predicts that the optimum level of investment in repair (i.e., that which maximizes fitness) will be less than the minimum required for indefinite somatic survival. The exact optimum depends on a species' ecological niche and, particularly, on its rate of accidental mortality. For a species subject to high accidental mortality (continuous curve), the optimum will generally be lower than for a species subject to low mortality (dotted curve). (From Kirkwood and Cremer, 1982.)

It should be noted that the paradigm generated by the disposable soma theory also embraces a number of other views. Firstly, the theory can be related to Williams' pleiotropic gene hypothesis, the genes in question being those which control the levels of somatic maintenance. In this case, the good and bad effects of a reduced level of maintenance are, respectively, increased reproduction and earlier senescence. Secondly, the theory serves to unify several specific hypotheses which postulate particular kinds of somatic damage as the cause of aging [e.g., damage by free radicals (Harman, 1956); somatic mutation (Szilard, 1959); errors in protein synthesis (Orgel, 1963); macromolecular cross-linkage (Bjorksten, 1968); see also Kirkwood, 1981; Kirkwood and Cremer, 1982)]. Thirdly, the theory encompasses the evolutionary insights of Cutler (1978) into the nature of the senescence process, while going further in also explaining why higher metazoans have not followed an evolutionary path which might have permitted them indefinite survival. Finally, the theory offers a resolution in evolutionary terms of controversy over "wear and tear" theories of ag-

ing—senescence indeed being attributed to wear and tear, not however because wear and tear is inevitable but because it arises as the indirect result of optimizing the balance between somatic maintenance and reproduction.

EVOLUTION OF LONGEVITY—GENETIC DETERMINANTS OF AGING RATE

An important question on which evolutionary and comparative studies of longevity may throw light is how many genes are involved in the aging process in higher organisms. On the one hand, the senescent phenotype is highly variable, which suggests that many genes are involved. After surveying Mc-Kusick's (1975) catalogue of known human genetic loci, Martin (1978, 1979) concluded that as many as several thousand genes may have potential relevance for the pathobiology of aging. On the other hand, the fact that most mammalian species age qualitatively in very much the same manner, but at rates which vary over a 40-fold range, suggests that the genes controlling the *rate of aging* may be few (Cutler, 1975).

The short evolutionary time scale of mammalian evolution, and particularly of the hominid ancestral lineage, has been used to estimate rough upper bounds for the number of genes whose mutation can have been responsible for the present diversity of life span. Using an allometric relationship between longevity, brain, and body size for present-day species, Sacher (1975) has estimated the longevities of extinct hominid ancestors from measurements of cranial and skeletal fossils. Employing similar methods, Cutler (1975) showed that an apparent peak in the rate of increase in longevity occurred about 100,000 years ago. Cutler estimated that over a period as short as this, only 0.6 percent of the total functional genes (equivalent to about 250 genes on the assumption of 4×10^4 genes per genome) would have received base substitutions leading to one or more adaptive amino acid changes. Since only a fraction of these mutations would be likely to have been concerned with longevity, Cutler concluded that there exist primary aging processes in which only a few genetic changes are necessary to decrease uniformly the aging rate of many different physiological functions.

Cutler's argument can be criticized, however, on two major grounds. Firstly, his calculation was based on an estimate by Haldane of a mutation rate of one substitution per genome per 300 generations, and there is good reason to regard this as too low by as much as several orders of magnitude (Maynard Smith, 1968). Secondly, recent insights into the mode of genome evolution suggest that major genetic rearrangements may be more important than the slow accumulation of point mutations on which Cutler based his calculations (see, for example, Gillespie et al., 1982). Nevertheless, the general argument that aging rate is determined by comparatively few key genes remains fairly attractive. If the disposable soma theory is correct, major candidates for these genes are those which determine the levels of somatic maintenance and repair, particularly at the intracellular level. The

demonstration by Hart and Setlow (1974) and by Sacher and Hart (1978) of a positive correlation among mammals between longevity and the efficiency of DNA excision repair following ultraviolet irradiation is directly consistent with this view and suggests that further comparative research on fidelity assurance mechanisms for DNA replication, transcription, translation, and repair may be revealing (see also Cutler, 1977; Hart et al., 1979; Kirkwood, 1981).

POSTREPRODUCTIVE SURVIVAL

In most species, a decline in reproductive function occurs with age (Comfort, 1979). Usually this is a gradual process which may be regarded as a part of the general loss of function that characterizes senescence. However, in semelparous species and in women, reproduction ends in a more determinate fashion, and there may exist a distinct period of postreproductive survival. The postreproductive period is of evolutionary interest in that although the individual can make no further *direct* genetic contribution, it may yet affect the fitness of its progeny.

Postreproductive Survival in Semelparous Species

In semelparous life histories, the pattern of selective forces through the life span is quite different from that of iteroparous species. Selection operates with full force until reproduction begins and thereafter drops to zero unless the adult plays an active part in promoting survival of the young. Since all is risked on a single reproductive venture, a semelparous organism which has embarked on the reproductive phase of its life history should mobilize all its resources to maximize reproductive success, even if this is directly suicidal. In extreme cases, death of the adult is inseparably linked with the reproductive cycle, as in the mite *Adactylidium* where the young hatch inside the body of the female and eat their way out. In others such as *Oc-*

topus hummelincki, the female broods the eggs until they hatch, but eats less while caring for them and dies soon afterwards. Starvation enforced by brooding is clearly not the *primary* cause of death, since individuals do leave the eggs to catch prey but may then leave it uneaten. Instead, it appears that the modified feeding behavior is the result of secretions from the optic gland, since surgical removal of the gland leads to cessation of broodiness, resumption of feeding, increased growth, and greatly extended life span (Wodinsky, 1977).

Various alternative hypotheses could explain these observations in *Octopus,* and they serve to illustrate the potential diversity of postreproductive survival in semelparous species. Firstly, the inhibition of feeding may have zero effect on reproductive success and may simply be an endocrinological by-product of hormonal changes associated with the act of reproduction. Provided death does not occur before brooding is complete, selection against such an effect would be nonexistent once semelparity had become established. Secondly, by permitting more intensive care of the eggs, the inhibition of feeding while brooding may enhance survival of the progeny and, therefore, be under positive selection. In this case, selective control terminates when the eggs hatch, and the subsequent death of the adult again merely reflects the lack of selection to prevent it. Finally, it is conceivable that the actual death of the adult is of significant advantage to the young, perhaps through vacation of territory; thus selective control may operate right up to the point of death.

These three hypotheses differ progressively from each other in the extent to which the behavior of *Octopus* may be explained as the result of an adaptive genetic program. While it might be possible, in theory, to carry out selection experiments to discriminate among them, such studies would in practice be exceedingly difficult. In making comparison of postreproductive survival periods among semelparous species, it is important to recognize that this diversity may exist and

that observations relevant to one species may not be relevant to others.

Menopause

Although aging is accompanied by changes and increasing irregularity in reproductive cycles in all iteroparous mammals, the menopause appears to be unique, or very nearly so, to the human female (Butler, 1974; Jones, 1975). [For evidence that female chimpanzees and macaques may also exhibit a form of menopause, see Graham et al. (1979) and Gould et al., (1981). Menopause-like features are also reported in some inbred strains of mice, although they are not normally seen in outbred females (Holinka et al., 1979; Gosden et al., 1983).] Usually during the fifth decade of life, the menstrual cycle ceases altogether and there follows a period of postreproductive survival which may amount to approximately one-third of the total life span.

The best explanation for the evolution of the menopause is that humans are unique both in the very slow development of children and in the extent to which senescence occurs in the "wild" (Medawar, 1952). As a woman grows older, the hazards of a further pregnancy increase, and beyond 40–50 years of age, it may be more advantageous for a woman to cease reproduction while she is bringing up her later children. In many societies, postmenopausal women also play an active role in caring for their grandchildren, and this too will result in an increase in "inclusive fitness" (Hamilton, 1964). In prehistoric times, the proportion of women surviving to postmenopausal age must have been small, although Jones (1975) estimated from data quoted by Young (1971) that about 28 percent of medieval women reached menopausal age. It is probable, therefore, that in evolutionary terms the menopause is a comparatively recent innovation.

Despite a certain similarity between postmenopausal survival in women and postreproductive survival in semelparous species, it is important to recognize that the menopause and semelparous reproduction have fundamentally different biological significance. Although both are under endocrinological control, it is quite incorrect, therefore, to suggest that the "life cycles of humans and [semelparous] *Antechinus* species pose similar questions of aging, but on a different time-scale" (Diamond, 1982).

CONCLUSIONS

Research on aging differs from most areas of biology in two major respects. Firstly, it is difficult to define precisely what characterizes the aging process when species differ significantly in the qualitative features of their life histories. Secondly, many of the phenomena which may be observed are likely to be secondary, not primary, and it may be a hard task to determine which is which. Progress in both these areas is assisted by adopting a comparative or evolutionary approach.

The comparative study of survivorship patterns, although beset by numerous technical difficulties and as yet only in a fragmentary state, allows species to be classified according to whether or not they exhibit actuarial senescence. In most vertebrates, it seems that senescence does take place and that maximum life span is quite sharply determined. Allometric studies among mammals suggest that longevity is closely associated with two factors. The first is an index of cephalization describing the relationship of brain to body weight. The second is a metabolic factor combining metabolic rate and deep body temperature.

Theories on the evolution of aging suggest that iteroparous life spans are finite primarily because of a progressive diminution with age in the force of natural selection. In particular, the disposable soma theory suggests that natural selection favors the investment of resources in greater reproductive output at the expense of indefinite somatic longevity. The theory predicts that iteroparous species age through an accumulation of random somatic damage, and that evolution to greater or shorter longevity results from raising or lowering the levels of somatic maintenance and repair. This prediction is consistent with comparative observations on the efficiency of DNA excision repair (Hart and Setlow, 1974; Sacher and Hart, 1978), and it is to be hoped that similar studies will be made of other repair and maintenance mechanisms.

Finally, it is essential to stress that an organisms's life history must be taken into account when considering what is meant by the terms "aging" and "longevity." As emphasized by Kirkwood and Cremer (1982), the postreproductive life of a semelparous organism is very different from the later part of an iteroparous life span, and this is different again from the old age of a vegetatively reproducing plant or invertebrate. Progress in understanding the complex array of mechanisms by which living organisms regulate their duration of life will be seriously impeded unless these fundamental distinctions are kept firmly in mind.

REFERENCES

Altman, P.A. and Dittmer, D. S. (eds.) 1972. *Biology Data Book* Vol. 1, 2nd ed. Bethesda: Federation of American Societies for Experimental Biology.

Bidder, G. P. 1932. Senescence. *Br. Med. J.,* ii: 583–585.

Bjorksten, J. 1968. The crosslinkage theory of aging. *J. Am. Geriatrics Soc.* 16: 408–427.

Buckland, S. T. 1980. A modified analysis of the Jolly-Seber capture-recapture model. *Biometrics* 36: 419–435.

Butler, H. 1974. Evolutionary trends in primate sex cycles. *Contrib. Primat.* 3: 2–35.

Calaby, J. H. and Taylor, J. M. 1981. Reproduction in two marsupial mice, *Antechinus bellus* and *Antechinus bilarni* (Dasyuridae), of tropical Australia. *J. Mammal.* 62: 329–341.

Calow, P. 1978. Bidder's hypothesis revisited: solution to some key problems associated with general molecular theory of ageing. *Gerontology* 24: 448–458.

Calow, P. 1979. The cost of reproduction—a physiological approach. *Biol. Rev.* 54: 23–40.

Caughley, G. 1966. Mortality patterns in mammals. *Ecology* 47: 906–918.

Charlesworth, B. 1980. *Evolution in Age-structured Populations.* Cambridge: Cambridge University Press.

Charnov, E. L. and Schaffer, W. M. 1973. Life history consequences of natural selection: Cole's result revisited. *Am. Nat.* 107: 791–793.

Cherkin, A. and Eckhardt, M. J. 1977. Effects of dimethylaminoethanol upon life-span and behavior of aged Japanese quail. *J. Gerontol.* 32: 38–45.

Cole, L. C. 1954. The population consequences of life history phenomena. *Q. Rev. Biol.* 29: 103–137.

Comfort, A. 1959. Studies on the longevity and mortality of English thoroughbred horses. *In,* G. E. W. Wolstenholme and M. O'Connor (eds.), *Ciba Foundation Colloquia on Ageing,* Vol. 5, pp 35–54. London: Churchill.

Comfort, A. 1960. The effect of age on growth-resumption in fish (*Lebistes*) checked by food restriction. *Gerontologia* 4: 177–186.

Comfort, A. 1961. The longevity and mortality of a fish (*Lebistes reticulatus* Peters) in captivity. *Gerontologia* 5, 209–222.

Comfort, A. 1979. *The Biology of Senescence,* 3rd ed. Edinburgh: Churchill Livingstone.

Cutler, R. G. 1975. Evolution of human longevity and the genetic complexity governing aging rate. *Proc. Nat. Acad. Sci. USA,* 72: 4664–4668.

Cutler, R. G. 1977. Nature of aging and life maintenance processes. *Interdiscipl. Topics Geront.* 9: 83–133.

Cutler, R. G. 1978. Evolutionary biology of senescence. *In,* J. A. Behnke, C. E. Finch, and G. B. Moment (eds.), *The Biology of Aging.* New York: Plenum.

Diamond, J. M. 1982. Big-bang reproduction and ageing in male marsupial mice. *Nature* 298: 115–116.

Dunnett, G. M. and Ollason, J. C. 1978. The estimation of survival rate in the fulmar, *Fulmarus glacialis. J. Animal Ecol.* 47: 507–520.

Edney, E. B. and Gill, R. W. 1968. Evolution of senescence and specific longevity. *Nature* 220: 281–282.

Flower, S. S. 1938. Further notes on the duration of life in animals. IV. Birds. *Proc. Zool. Soc. (Lond.)* A: 195.

Gadgil, M. and Bossert, W. H. 1970. Life historical consequences of natural selection. *Am. Nat.* 104: 1–24.

Gerking, S. D. 1957. Evidence of aging in natural populations of fishes. *Gerontologia* 1: 287–305.

Gillespie, D., Donehower, L., and Strayer, D. 1982. Evolution of primate DNA organization. *In,* G. A. Dover and R. B. Flavell (eds.), *Genome Evolution,* pp. 113–133. London: Academic Press.

Gompertz, B. 1825. On the nature of the function expressive of the law of human mortality and on a new mode of determining life contingencies. *Phil. Trans. R. Soc. London* II: 513–585.

Gosden, R. G., Laing, S. C., Felicio, L. S., Nelson, J. F., and Finch, C. E. 1983. Imminent oocyte exhaustion and reduced follicular recruitment mark the transition to acyclicity in ageing C57BL/6J mice. *Biol. Reprod.* 28: 255–260.

Gould, K. G., Flint, M., and Graham, C. E. 1981. Chimpanzee reproductive senescence: a possible model for evolution of the menopause. *Maturitas* 3: 157–166.

Graham, C. E., Kling, O.R., and Steiner, R. A. 1979.

Reproductive senescence in female nonhuman primates. *In,* D. M. Bowden (ed.), *Aging in Non-Human Primates,* pp. 183–202. New York: Van Nostrand Reinhold.

Gumbel, E. J. 1958. *Statistics of Extremes.* New York: Columbia University Press.

Haldane, J. B. S. 1941. *New Paths in Genetics.* London: Allen and Unwin.

Hamilton, W. D. 1964. The genetical evolution of social behaviour. I. *J. Theor. Biol.* 7: 1–16.

Hamilton, W. D. 1966. The moulding of senescence by natural selection. *J. Theor. Biol.* 12: 12–45.

Harman, D., 1956. Aging: a theory based on free radical and radiation chemistry. *J. Gerontol.* 11: 298–300.

Hart, R. W., D'Ambrosio, S. M., Ng, K. J., and Modak, S. P. 1979. Longevity, stability and DNA repair. *Mech. Ageing Dev.* 9: 203–223.

Hart, R. W. and Setlow, R. B. 1974. Correlation between deoxyribonucleic acid excision-repair and life-span in a number of mammalian species. *Proc. Nat. Acad. Sci. USA* 71: 2169–2173.

Holinka, C. F., Tseng, Y.-C., and Finch, C. E. 1979. Reproductive aging in C57BL/6J mice: plasma progesterone, viable embryos and resorption frequency throughout pregnancy. *Biol. Reprod.* 20: 1201–1211.

Jones, E. C. 1975. The post-reproductive phase in mammals. *Front. Hormone Res.* 3: 1–19.

Kirkwood, T. B. L. 1977. Evolution of ageing. *Nature* 270: 301–304.

Kirkwood, T. B. L. 1981. Repair and its evolution: survival versus reproduction. *In,* C. R. Townsend and P. Calow (eds.), *Physiological Ecology: An Evolutionary Approach to Resource Use,* pp. 165–189. Oxford: Blackwell.

Kirkwood, T. B. L. and Cremer, T. 1982. Cytogerontology since 1881: a reappraisal of August Weismann and a review of modern progress. *Hum. Genet.* 60: 101–121.

Kirkwood, T. B. L. and Holliday, R. 1979. The evolution of ageing and longevity. *Proc. R. Soc. Lond. B* 205: 531–546.

Kram, D. and Schneider, E. L. 1978. Parental age effects: increased frequencies of genetically abnormal offspring. *In,* E. L. Schneider (ed.), *The Genetics of Aging,* pp. 225–260. New York: Plenum.

Lack, D. 1954. *The Natural Regulation of Animal Numbers.* Oxford: Clarendon Press.

Lamb, M. J. 1977. *Biology of Ageing.* London: Blackie.

Leon, J. A. 1976. Life histories as adaptive strategies. *J. Theor. Biol.* 60: 301–335.

Liu, R. K. and Walford, R. L. 1975. Mid-life temperature-transfer effects on life-span of annual fish. *J. Gerontol.* 30: 129–131.

Martin, G. M. 1978. Genetic syndromes in man with potential relevance to the pathobiology of aging. *In,* D. Bergsma and D. Harrison (eds.), *Birth Defects: Original Article Series,* Vol. 14, No. 1, pp. 5–39. New York: Alan R. Liss.

Martin, G. M. 1979. Genetic and evolutionary aspects of aging. *Fed. Proc.* 38: 1962–1967.

Masoro, E. J., Yu, B. P., and Bertrand, H. H. 1982. Action of food restriction in delaying the aging process. *Proc. Nat. Acad. Sci. USA* 79: 4239–4241.

Maynard Smith, J. 1968. "Haldane's dilemma" and the rate of evolution. *Nature* 219: 1114–1116.

Maynard Smith, J. 1976. Group selection. *Q. Rev. Biol.* 51: 277–283.

McKusick, V. A. 1975. *Mendelian Inheritance in Man,* 4th ed. Baltimore: Johns Hopkins University Press.

Medawar, P. B. 1952. *An Unsolved Problem in Biology.* London: H. K. Lewis. (Reprinted in *The Uniqueness of the Individual.* 1957. London: Methuen.)

Medawar, P. B. 1955. The definition and measurement of senescence. *In,* G. E. W. Wolstenholme and M. P. Cameron (eds.), *Ciba Foundation Colloquia on Ageing,* Vol. 1, pp. 4–15. London: Churchill.

Medvedev, Zh. A. 1981. Age changes and the rejuvenation processes related to reproduction. *Mech. Ageing. Dev.* 17: 331–359.

Mertz, D. B. 1975. Senescent decline in flour beetles selected for early adult fitness. *Physiol. Zool.* 48: 1–23.

Orgel, L. E. 1963. The maintenance of the accuracy of protein synthesis and its relevance to ageing. *Proc. Nat. Acad. Sci. USA* 49: 517–521.

Robertson, O. H. 1961. Prolongation of the life span of Kokanee salmon (*Oncorhynkus nerka kennerlyi*) by castration before beginning of gonad development. *Proc. Nat. Acad. Sci. USA* 47: 609–621.

Rose, M. R. and Charlesworth, B. 1981a. Genetics of life history in *Drosophila melanogaster.* I. Sib analysis of adult females. *Genetics* 97: 173–186.

Rose, M. R. and Charlesworth, B. 1981b. Genetics of life history in *Drosophila melanogaster.* II. Exploratory selection experiments. *Genetics* 97: 187–196.

Sacher, G. A. 1975. Maturation and longevity in relation to cranial capacity in hominid evolution. *In,* R. H. Tuttle (ed.), *Primates: Functional Morphology and Evolution,* pp. 417–441. The Hague: Mouton.

Sacher, G. A. 1976. Evaluation of the entropy and information terms governing mammalian longevity. *Interdiscipl. Topics Geront.* 9: 69–82.

Sacher, G. A. 1977. Life table modification and life prolongation. *In,* C. E. Finch and L. Hayflick (eds.), *Handbook of the Biology of Aging,* pp. 582–638. New York: Van Nostrand Reinhold.

Sacher, G. A. 1978. Evolution of longevity and survival characteristics in mammals. *In,* E. L. Schneider (ed.), *The Genetics of Aging,* pp. 151–167. New York: Plenum.

Sacher, G. A. and Hart, R. W. 1978. Longevity, aging and comparative cellular and molecular biology of the house mouse, *Mus musculus,* and the white-footed mouse, *Peromyscus leucopus. In,* D. Bergsma

and D. E. Harrison (eds.), *Genetic Effects on Aging.* New York: Alan Liss.

Sacher, G. A. and Staffeldt, E. 1972. Life tables of seven species of laboratory-reared rodents. *Gerontologist,* 12: 39.

Seber, G. A. F. 1973. *The Estimation of Animal Abundance and Related Parameters.* London: Griffin.

Smith-Sonneborn, J. 1979. DNA repair and longevity assurance in *Paramecium tetraurelia. Science,* 203: 1115–1117.

Sokal, R. R. 1970. Senescence and genetic load: evidence from *Tribolium. Science,* 167: 1733–1734.

Sonneborn, T. M. 1954. The relation of autogamy to senescence and rejuvenescence in *Paramecium aurelia. J. Protozool,* 1: 38–53.

Stearns, S. C. 1976. Life-history tactics: a review of the ideas. *Q. Rev. Biol.,* 51: 3–47.

Stearns, S. C. 1977. The evolution of life-history traits: a critique of the theory and a review of the data. *Ann. Rev. Ecol. Syst.,* 8: 145–171.

Szilard, L. 1959. On the nature of the aging process. *Proc. Nat. Acad. Sci. USA* 45: 30–45.

Taylor, H. M., Gourley, R. S., Lawrence, C. E., and Kaplan, R. S. 1974. Natural selection of life history attributes: an analytical approach. *Theoret. Pop. Biol.* 5: 104–122.

Trout, W. E. and Kaplan, W. D. 1970. A relation between longevity, metabolic rate and activity in shaker mutants of *Drosophila melanogaster. Exp. Gerontol.* 5: 83–92.

Wattiaux, J. M. 1968a. Parental age effects in *Drosophila pseudoobscura. Exp. Geront.* 3: 55–61.

Wattiaux, J. M. 1968b. Cumulative parental age effects in *Drosophila subobscura. Evolution* 22: 406–421.

Weismann, A. 1891. *Essays upon Heredity and Kindred Biological Problems,* 2nd ed., Vol. 1. Oxford: Clarendon Press.

Weizsacker, C. F. von. 1980. Ageing as a process of evolution. *In, Conference on Structural Pathology in DNA and the Biology of Ageing,* pp. 11–20. Bonn: Deutsche Forschungsgemeinschaft.

Williams, G. C. 1957. Pleiotropy, natural selection and the evolution of senescence. *Evolution* 11: 398–411.

Wodinsky, J. 1977. Hormonal inhibition of feeding and death in *Octopus:* control by optic gland secretion. *Science* 198: 948–951.

Woolhouse, H. W. 1967. The nature of senescence in plants. *In,* H. W. Woolhouse (ed.), *Aspects of the Biology of Ageing, Symposia of the Society for Experimental Biology,* No. XXI, pp. 179–213. Cambridge: Cambridge University Press.

Woolley, P. 1966. Reproduction in *Antechinus,* spp. and other dasyurid marsupials. *Symp. Zool. Soc. Lond.* 15: 281–294.

Young, J. Z. 1971. *An Introduction to the Study of Man.* Oxford: Clarendon Press.

3
MODULATIONS OF AGING PROCESSES

Edward L. Schneider
and
John D. Reed
National Institute on Aging
National Institutes of Health

INTRODUCTION

A frequent question that is asked of physicians is how to achieve a healthy, long life. Most responses deal with reducing risk factors. Epidemiologic studies suggest that not smoking and reducing blood pressure may delay the onset of certain diseases (Kannel, 1983), but is there a way to extend life span in a positive fashion, that is, in a way other than by reducing the impact of specific diseases?

To prolong life is one of man's oldest and most persistent dreams. One of the fundamentals of the ancient Taoist religion was to prolong life by various dietary, mental (meditation), athletic, and even sexual means. However, despite the long history of interest in the nature of aging processes, little intense scientific interest has been generated until the last decade.

Limitations of Human Life Span

While the achievement of human immortality has not been accomplished, we have made impressive gains in extending life expectancy from the 30- and 40-year average of the last centuries to almost 75 years today. However,

these impressive gains have not been matched with significant increases in maximal life span, which has remained relatively constant. Fries (1980) has postulated that we are rapidly approaching human maximum life expectancy at approximately 85 years. However, examination of actuarial data indicates that maximum life expectancy has been increasing and that these increases will not stop at an 85-year limit (Schneider and Brody, 1983). In fact, the most rapidly growing age group in America is the group aged 85 and above.

The competitive risk theory proposes that as one age-related disease is controlled, others will increase in frequency to negate any significant increase in life span. Examination of mortality trends in the last two decades does not support this contention. Cardiovascular mortality, the number one cause of death, has declined 12 percent in individuals over age 65 since 1965 (Kovar, 1977). However, deaths from cancer have shown only a modest 1 percent increase in this period (Brody and Brock, 1983). Thus, there has not been a compensatory increase in other diseases to fill the place of cardiovascular disease. Instead, individuals over age 65 have experienced an increase in life expectancy, and the absolute number of deaths after ages 65, 75, and even 85 is declining (Brody, 1982).

It has been suggested that there may be a genetically determined limit to life span in man (Fries, 1980). This argument was based on the observation that human fetal lung fibroblasts, when placed into tissue culture, have a finite number of cell replications (Hayflick and Moorhead, 1961). However, it has been demonstrated that replicating cell populations *in vivo* can survive well past the life span of the organism (Daniel and Young, 1971; Harrison, 1973). Thus, it is highly unlikely that the *in vivo* survival of the organism is related to the finite replicating ability of cells in tissue culture.

Enclaves of Longevity

Secrets to longer life span were thought to reside among certain primitive peoples who had mastered the art of longevity and were able to prevent the ravages of modern civilization from intruding into their lives. Leaf (1973) reported in the *National Geographic* magazine his colorful visits to enclaves of supposed longevity among the Hunzas in Pakistan, to Georgia in the Soviet Union, and to the village of Vilcambamba in Ecuador. However, careful analyses of birth records and successive yearly interviews with alleged centenarians have revealed that these groups do not appear to possess any significant increases in longevity (Medvedev, 1974; Mazess and Forman, 1979; Leaf, 1982).

BIOLOGICAL CONSIDERATIONS FOR EXTENDING LIFE SPAN

The "Magic Bullet." The remarkable achievements of modern medicine, such as the introduction of antibiotics and vaccines for the conquest of infectious diseases, have encouraged the hope of "magic bullets" for other diseases. Many of the theories proposed to explain aging have focused on a single mechanism, thus encouraging research to find a single "magic bullet" to arrest aging. Progress in cancer research, where a "magic bullet" has been sought intensively for decades, points toward multiple etiologies for various malignancies. Thus, it is becoming increasingly probable that multiple interventions will be necessary to prevent and/or cure various malignancies. Our current knowledge of the mechanisms of aging is clearly at an earlier stage than cancer research. In aging research as in cancer research, increasing knowledge should reveal multiple mechanisms underlying aging processes at the molecular, cellular, and organ levels. Therefore, we predict that it is equally unlikely that a single "magic bullet" will reverse or arrest all aging processes.

Global versus Segmental Interventions. While it is unlikely that a single global intervention will affect all aging processes, segmental interventions (defined as interventions which affect a single aging process) may be developed which have significant impact. An example would be the potential attempt to prevent or restore the decline in immune function that occurs with aging. Rejuvenation of the immune system might increase the ability of older individuals to combat infectious diseases, and this might lead to a significant increase in the quantity as well as the quality of life.

Potential Biological Risks of Interventions. The immune system also provides an example of potential risks of interventions to alter aging processes. The age-related decline in the function of the immune system may have evolved as a beneficial mechanism. Since an increase in autoimmune phenomena occurs with aging, the decline in immune function may protect us from the development of high levels of autoimmune diseases in old age. Restoring immune function to youthful levels might potentially increase the incidence of autoimmune diseases in older individuals. Fortunately, this possibility should be easy to assess in aging experimental animals. Any attempts to intervene in aging processes should consider the risks of potential adverse responses.

Ethical Considerations for Extending Life Span. Besides the biological considerations for life extension, there are also many ethical considerations. In the literature, attempts to alter life span have led to serious harm to the individual. Fictional characters have exchanged their souls for perpetual youth, with unfortunate consequences. Are the increases in life expectancy a mixed blessing? Will they produce more harm than good for the individual and society?

The addition of years of dependency, illness, and disability would certainly not be a blessing to the individual or to society. However, the vast majority of our older citizens enter their last decades without significant disability. The addition of healthy years to this group clearly would not be considered detrimental. Society should also benefit from the addition of productive, healthy years to its mature and elderly population. Therefore, interventions to increase longevity should be oriented toward the maintenance of health and vigor, rather than on the prolongation of terminal illnesses.

Interventions that modify aging processes may also contribute to changing the biases which exist in relation to aging. Many of the negative feelings about aging are derived from the concept that aging is the sum of irreversible, immutable losses of individual functions. Thus, many physicians conceive that their role is mostly supportive of the elderly while they experience these inevitable losses. Segmental interventions, which may arrest or even reverse the aging of certain organs, would demonstrate that some declines in function may not be inevitable and thus provide a positive stimulus for increasing the interest of physicians in caring for the elderly.

NUTRITION

Caloric restriction has been the most consistent method of extending life span in laboratory animals. The remarkable extension of life span attainable through "undernutrition" was first documented in detail by McCay and his coworkers (1935). They found that rats that were severely retarded in growth by being fed a nutritionally adequate and balanced, but calorically deficient, diet postweaning had much longer mean and maximum life spans than control animals fed *ad libitum*. Numerous studies have verified the life-prolonging effect of food restriction in rats (McCay et al., 1939, 1943; Berg and Simms, 1960; Nolen, 1972) and mice (Ball et al., 1947; Tucker, 1979). Recently, it has been shown that even in long-lived, barrier-reared and maintained rats, a significant increment in longevity is still achieved through dietary restriction (Yu et al., 1982). The vast literature on this subject can only be selectively reviewed here, but comprehensive reviews are available (Everitt and Porter, 1976; Young, 1978).

The effect of protein intake on longevity has also been extensively investigated. Miller and Payne (1968) demonstrated an increase in mean and maximum life span in rats fed a 12 percent protein diet when young (below 120 days) followed by a 4 percent protein diet thereafter. On the other hand, no effect of protein level (varied between 10 and 36 percent) was found on the longevity of rats when isocaloric diets were fed throughout postweaning life (Nakagawa et al., 1974). When rats were allowed to select their own diets, protein intake was found to correlate with longevity only during the periods before 50 days and after 300 days (Ross and Bras, 1975). Between 50 and 300 days, longevity correlated only with total food intake. Further, it was shown that protein intake correlated positively with longevity in early life and negatively in late life, in accord with the findings of Miller and Payne. Leto et al. (1976) reported that in mice, a 4 percent protein diet fed throughout life markedly increased both mean and maximum life span (as well as decreasing body temperature and increasing oxygen consumption) compared with a 26 percent protein, isocaloric diet. On the other hand, Stoltzner (1977) found that a similar low protein diet only slightly prolonged the life expectancy of mice. The different results of these two studies might be explained by the fact that a voluntary restriction in food intake and consequent weight loss occurred in the low protein intake group in the studies of Leto et al. (1976) when compared to controls. Thus, the marked increase in life span observed in this study may have been due to the effects of caloric restriction rather than to the effects of protein intake alone.

Segall and Timiras (1976) have shown that feeding a diet deficient in tryptophan, an essential amino acid, can prolong the life span of rats and produce many other effects similar to caloric restriction, including delayed fertility and decreased incidence of tumors. In addition, rats raised on tryptophan-deficient diets do not show the same loss of thermoregulatory capacity with aging as control rats (Segall and Timiras, 1975), which may indicate that this regimen can prevent certain age-related changes in the central nervous system. It is hypothesized that these effects are mediated through a modification of the central nervous system since tryptophan is the precursor of the important neurotransmitter serotonin. However, in the two preceding studies, rats raised on tryptophan-deficient diets showed marked diminution of weight gain. Thus, the observed effects may have been the result of simple caloric restriction. Restriction of a number of other amino acids appears to selectively inhibit tumor growth in mice (Theuer, 1971), but the effects on longevity have not been examined, to our knowledge.

The extremely retarded growth which results from severe caloric restriction makes this type of intervention unattractive. However, milder forms of food restriction (50–70 percent of *ad libitum*) instituted in early life can produce moderate life extension in rats, with only slight retardation of growth (Berg and Simms, 1960). Furthermore, Nolen (1972) has demonstrated that comparable effects on longevity could be attained regardless of whether caloric restriction was instituted immediately postweaning or after 12 weeks of *ad libitum* feeding. Thus, it appears that caloric restriction begun in early life can extend the mean life span of laboratory animals without gross developmental retardation. In terms of the application of caloric restriction to humans, it is important to determine whether caloric restriction begun in mid- or late-life can increase longevity. Employing a 50 percent level of caloric restriction, Barrows and Roeder (1969) found a slight decrease in life span of rats calorically restricted in adulthood, although they were able to achieve the usual large increase in life span with restriction begun after weaning. However, Ross (1972) showed that while limiting food intake to 6 g/day (beginning at 300 days) versus 20 g/day for controls decreased subsequent survival of rats, imposing milder food restriction (8 or 10 g/day) in later life could increase survival, and other reports have confirmed this (Deyl et al., 1975). An increase in both mean and maximum life span with caloric restriction (approximately 50 percent of *ad libitum* calories) instituted gradually at 1 year of age has been demonstrated recently (Weindruch and Walford, 1982) in mice (Figure 1). Interestingly, mild caloric restriction in the form of withholding winter feed supplements has been reported to increase the average life span of cattle (Pinney et al., 1972). Taken together, these studies suggest that mild caloric restriction begun in middle life can effectively extend the longevity of various animals.

Considerable effort has been expended to examine the mechanisms for the effects of dietary restriction on longevity. In many studies of dietary restriction, a decrease in the incidence of a number of chronic diseases was observed (McCay et al., 1943; Berg and Simms, 1960; Cheney et al., 1980). Tannenbaum (1940) reported a decreased incidence as well as a delayed appearance of a variety of spontaneous and induced tumors in several strains of mice subjected to caloric restriction. Many subsequent studies have confirmed this relationship between caloric intake and tumor incidence in mice (Tannenbaum, 1944; Tannenbaum and Silverstone, 1949; Fernandes et al., 1976; Tucker, 1979; Cheney et al., 1980) and rats (Saxton et al., 1948; Ross and Bras, 1965, 1971, 1973; Ross et al., 1970).

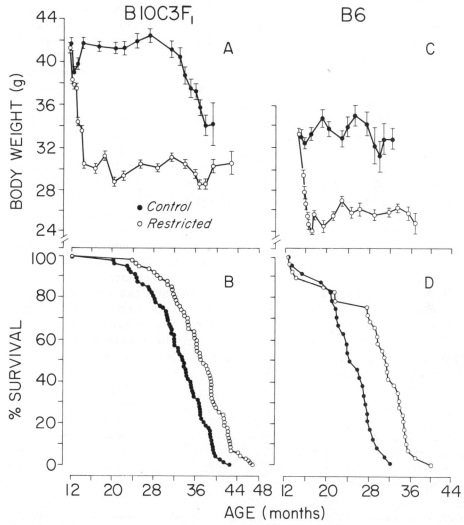

Figure 1. Body weights and survival of B10C3F$_1$ mice (A and B) and B6 mice (C and D) fed on control and restricted diets. Weights are plotted as means ± standard error for all mice alive at the indicated ages. Each point in the survival curves represents one mouse. (From Weindruch and Walford, 1982.)

In rats fed *ad libitum,* the incidence of tumors is proportional to the total caloric intake. In rats kept under food-restricted conditions, the tumor risk over the life span of the animal is similar to that of nonrestricted rats over their shorter life span and may be related to protein intake (Ross and Bras, 1965; Ross et al., 1970). Caloric restriction in early life, followed by *ad libitum* feeding thereafter, decreases subsequent tumor incidence (Ross and Bras, 1971). However, caloric restriction does not affect all

tumor types to an equal degree. Complex interrelationships exist among the level of caloric restriction, protein intake, time of onset and duration of restriction, tissue of origin, and type and degree of malignancy of the tumor (Ross and Bras, 1973; Tucker, 1979).

This antitumor effect of caloric restriction may reflect the effect of diet on the aging of key organ systems such as the immune system. The immunologic effects of caloric restriction are the subject of a recent review (Fernandes et al., 1979). Caloric restriction begun after weaning results in improved immunological responses later in life to T and B cell mitogens, to sheep red blood cells, and to skin allografts when compared to nonrestricted, age-matched controls (Walford et al., 1973–74; Gerbase-DeLima et al., 1975). This improvement in immune competence in later life may be related to delayed maturation of the immune system since caloric restriction depresses immunologic function prior to mid-life (Gerbase-DeLima et al., 1975). Improvement in immune responsiveness is also observed when caloric restriction is initiated in adulthood, at 12 and 17 months in mice (Weindruch et al., 1979; Weindruch et al., 1982). Caloric restriction in mid-life also produced decreased occurrence of autoantibodies (Weindruch et al., 1982). The effect of dietary restriction on the production of autoantibodies might explain the delayed development of immune-complex glomerulonephritis in strains of mice susceptible to "autoimmune" disease (Fernandes et al., 1976). While the mechanism(s) for the effect of dietary restriction on extending life span remain to be discerned, the effects of caloric restriction on rejuvenating immune responsiveness are clearly impressive.

Caloric restriction has also been reported to decrease the accumulation of liver collagen, and to increase both the seminal vesicle weight and the growth period in response to somatotropin treatment in rats (Hruza and Fabry, 1957). It has also been found to delay the physiological aging of tail tendon collagen (Hruza and Hlavackava, 1969) and to increase the fertility of female rats (Berg, 1960). Biochemical studies have demonstrated that caloric restriction in rats partially delays or prevents age-related (1) declines in lipolytic response of adipocytes to glucagon or epinephrine, (2) declines in post-absorptive serum free fatty acid levels, (3) increases in post-absorptive cholesterol levels (Masoro et al., 1980; Leipa et al., 1980), and (4) changes in isoproterenol-induced relaxation of rat aortic strips (Herlihy and Yu, 1980). Moreover, calorically restricted rats do not show the same increases with aging in serum triglyceride levels (Reaven and Reaven, 1981a), serum insulin levels, or pancreatic islet pathology as sedentary control rats (Reaven and Reaven, 1981a). In this last study, however, age-related changes in glucose-induced release of insulin by pancreatic islet cells *in vitro* were not altered in the calorie-restricted group.

Before recommending intense dieting to the reader, one should examine studies of the relationship between body weight and longevity in humans. Andres (1981) recently summarized a number of these studies which indicate that the heaviest and thinnest cohorts had the shortest survivals, while those slightly over the "ideal body weight" had the greatest survival. However, interpretation of these studies is limited by the definition of "ideal body weight," since the vast majority of individuals have weights over this restricted index. Of interest, "ideal body weight" figures have recently been revised upwards by insurance companies (*N.Y. Times,* March 2, 1983).

TEMPERATURE

It has been demonstrated in several poikilothermic (where body temperature is determined by ambient temperature) organisms that lowered body temperature results in increased longevity (Liu and Walford, 1966, 1970; Miquel et al., 1976). In hibernating homeothermic (where body temperature is regulated independently of ambient temperature) animals which are prevented from hibernation, life span is significantly reduced (Kayser, 1961). In certain poikilothermic organisms, developmental temperatures strongly influence life span (Burcombe and Hillingsworth, 1970; Lints, 1971; Lints and Lints, 1971). Liu and Walford (1975) performed an elegant experiment in which annual fish were transferred from high to low temperatures (and vice versa) at mid-life, they found that the longest life span occurs in those fish transferred from high to low temperature. Even in organisms comprised entirely of postmitotic cells, survival is inversely related to environmental temperature (Osanai, 1978).

Walford has suggested that this increase in longevity with decreased temperature may be related to decreased immune responsiveness (Liu and Walford, 1972). Decreasing the temperature of poikilotherms has been demonstrated to result in diminished cellular and humoral immune reponsiveness (Hildemann, 1957; Tait, 1969). If autoimmune responses contribute to age-related diseases and disorders, lowered temperature might serve a preventive function. It has been hypothesized that in homeotherms such as man, fever is an evolutionary mechanism for increasing the efficiency of the immune system to deal with external challenge, and that the immune system is normally operating at nonoptimum temperatures to suppress autoimmune responses (Sohnle and Gambert, 1982).

Drug-induced hypothermia in homeotherms has been shown to produce increased survival times in tumor bearing animals (Fondy et al., 1974). This effect was demonstrated to be related to hypothermia rather than to the drugs. If one considers the age-related exponential incidence of tumors, the effects of temperature on tumor retardation might be a potential mechanism for longevity.

Lowered temperature also appears to improve survival after irradiation of the small teleost fish *Oryzias Latipes* (Egami, 1980). In this organism, death from radiation is related to the inability of the fish to replace replicating intestinal cells. The effect of temperature appears to be through the reduction of cell cycle times (Egami, 1980), thereby prolonging the viability of this replicating cell population.

Most experiments related to longevity and hypothermia have been performed on poikilothermic organisms. Further research is clearly needed on homeotherms. Several compounds have been shown to induce hypothermia in homeotherms including chlorpromazine, L-DOPA, reserpine, parachlorophenylalanine, delta-8 and delta-9 tetrahydrocannabinol (THC), and 1-hydroxy-3-(1,2-dimethylheptyl)-6, 6, 9-trimethyl-7,8,9, 10-tetrahydro-6-dibenzopyran (DMHP), a THC analogue (Janoff and Rosenberg, 1978; Liu and Walford, 1972). Unfortunately, most of these compounds have central nervous system effects which might make interpretations of hypothermic studies difficult. In addition, tolerance can develop to the hypothermic effects of certain of these agents (Janoff and Rosenberg, 1978; Liu and Walford, 1972).

EXERCISE

Ever since the collapse and death of the Greek runner Pheidippides from the exertion of running from the battlefield at Marathon to Athens to report the Greek victory over the Persians, there has been concern over the effect of exercise on longevity. In the late nineteenth century, the popular belief was that vigorous exercise damaged the body and therefore decreased the longevity of athletes. Since crew rowing is an extremely strenuous form of exercise, there was concern that college oarsmen might have diminished life spans, and this group has since become a favorite subject of longevity studies relating to exercise. These studies, too numerous to mention here, are reviewed elsewhere (Polednak and Damon, 1970), and only a few of the most important ones will be discussed.

When the longevities of Oxford and Cambridge oarsmen were compared to mortality tables published by British actuaries, decreased mortality was observed in the oarsmen (Hartley and Llewellyn, 1939). However, when the longevities of Cambridge oarsmen and other athletes were compared with those of their classmates, no significant differences were observed (Rook, 1954). A similar study of college athletes at an American university revealed no significant difference in life expectancies between athletes and their nonathletic classmates (Montoye et al., 1956). More recently, Schnohr (1971) observed that before the age of 50, Danish athletic champions had a lower mortality rate when compared to mortality tables derived from the general population of Denmark, whereas after the age of 50, the mortality of the athletes was significantly higher than that of the general populace. Thus, there does not appear to be any clear relationship between history of athletic competition and longevity.

However, these studies do not address the issue of whether lifelong physical activity has an effect on longevity. To determine whether regular, vigorous exercise over many years would prolong the life span, Karvonen et al. (1974) examined the longevity of champion, Finnish cross-country skiers who purportedly have long competitive careers and tend to continue to ski as a hobby throughout life. The median life expectancy of the general male population was significantly shorter than that of the skiers. However, these results must be interpreted with caution. The general male population of Finland may be no more appropriate for comparison to cross-country skiers than the British population for Cambridge oarsmen.

While retrospective human studies fail to disclose a clear relationship between exercise and longevity, the effect of forced or voluntary exercise on the longevity of rats has been more consistent. Several studies have demonstrated an increase in mean (Retzlaff et al., 1966; Edington et al., 1972; Drori and Folman, 1976; Sperling et al., 1978) and maximum life span (Retzlaff et al., 1966) when exercise was begun early in life, at ages 30 to 120 days. Exercise begun late in life has been shown both to slightly increase (Goodrick, 1974) and to decrease (Edington et al., 1972) the survival of old rats. In these studies, weight loss did not appear to be a contributing factor to the increased life expectancy observed with exercise.

The effect of exercise on various physiological changes which occur with aging is extensively reviewed in Chapter 32 (Buskirk, 1984). In rats, regular exercise regimens have been reported to slow or prevent age-related (1) cross-linking of tail tendon collagen (Byrd, 1973), (2) decreases in myocardial actomyosin ATPase activity (Rockstein et al., 1981), (3) increases in serum triglyceride levels (Reaven and Reaven, 1981a), (4) changes in pancreatic islet pathology and increases in serum insulin levels (Reaven and Reaven,

1981b), and (5) improved cardiac contraction (Lakatta, 1983). No effect of chronic exercise was observed on age-associated accumulation of connective tissue in the hearts of rats (Tomanek et al., 1972). Decreases in serum lipids and insulin levels have also been demonstrated in physically well-trained, middle-aged men (Bjorntorp et al., 1972). Part of the improvement in serum insulin levels with exercise might be explained by the observation that insulin-induced glucose uptake increases with exercise in skeletal muscle (Mondon et al., 1980).

Studies in humans have revealed that the function of the cardiovascular and respiratory systems declines with aging, thus limiting physical performance (Astrand, 1968). For example, in the aging human heart there is left ventricular wall hypertrophy, decreased maximal heart rate, and slowed myocardial relaxation (Lakatta, 1979) which tend to limit cardiac output. These changes are perhaps reflected in the age-related decrease in aerobic power (i.e., maximum oxygen intake) that is observed in humans (Hodgson and Buskirk, 1977). It has been suggested that regular exercise or physical activity can delay or prevent these changes (Bortz, 1980). However, a longitudinal study has demonstrated that there was no difference in the decline in maximal aerobic capacity between active and sedentary groups of elderly women, although the active group had increased endurance on a treadmill test (Plowman, 1979). On the other hand, older women placed on a regular exercise regimen for three months showed significant decreases in resting heart rate and work capacity, though several other parameters were unaffected (Adams and deVries, 1973). These results suggest that physical conditioning in the aged is possible. Even if exercise does not slow all aging processes, it certainly may improve the function of certain aspects of the cardiopulmonary systems as well as provide an increased feeling of well-being.

Studies in humans have also examined the effects of exercise on certain age-related disorders such as osteoporosis. It is clear that total immobility leads to the development of osteoporosis even in young healthy adults (Donaldson et al., 1970). Longitudinal and cross-sectional studies indicate that the rate of bone mineral loss in postmenopausal women is greater in the 50- to 70-year age group than in the over-70 age group (D. Smith et al., 1976). The authors interpret these results as indicating that physical activity levels are not the main determinant of bone loss, since activity levels are clearly higher in the younger group. However, aged women on an exercise regimen had similar increases in bone mineral content (BMC) to women on supplemental vitamin D and calcium who were not exercising, while untreated controls experienced a decrease in BMC during the same period (E. Smith et al., 1981). These results would suggest that physical activity has an important influence on the rate of bone mineral loss. Clearly, longitudinal as well as cross-sectional studies on larger groups of older cohorts are necessary to carefully assess the effect of exercise in preventing or slowing the loss of bone with aging.

Several epidemiological studies have revealed an association between the level of exercise or physical activity and mortality rate, specifically mortality from cardiovascular diseases. Rose and Cohen (1977) examined 36 variables in a retrospective population study and found that off-job activity level was positively correlated with longevity. However, while this variable was a better predictor of longevity than about two-thirds of the other variables analyzed, there were a number of other variables that were much better predictors, such as education and occupation level. An examination of the Framingham cohort has revealed that in this generally sedentary group, the mortality from cardiovascular diseases is inversely correlated with physical activity level in men, while in women no statistically significant association is observed (Kannel and Sorlie, 1979). Furthermore, this protective effect appears to be due to a decreased mortality from myocardial infarctions rather than to a decrease in the incidence of myocardial infarction (Kannel et al., 1970). This suggests that physical activity may not necessarily prevent coronary atherosclerotic disease but may increase the ability of heart muscle to withstand an ischemic insult. Another longitudinal study, the Puerto Rico Study, demonstrates a small inverse correlation between physical activity and mortality from coronary heart disease in men (Costas et al., 1978). However, this association was found only in urban men. Rural men, with generally higher physical activity levels than urban men, did not display this relationship. Taken together, the Framingham and Puerto Rico studies suggest an important role for physical activity in preventing mortality from coronary heart disease.

ANTIOXIDANTS

The free radical theory of aging as first proposed by Harman (1956) hypothesizes that free radicals are produced during normal metabolism and that they subsequently react with important biological molecules. According to this theory, the accumulated damage due to free radicals would lead to an age-related decrease in function. The free radical theory has led to the testing of pharmacologic interventions through the use of chemically diverse antioxidants which are capable of interrupting free radical chain reactions.

In living cells, the most abundant free radicals are the superoxide anion and the free radicals derived from its interaction with other molecules (Figure 2). The superoxide radical is produced at a small, but not insignificant, percentage of the cellular respiratory chain oxygen utilization (Lippman, 1981; Noel and Hegner, 1978). Superoxide radicals are generated by a number of enzyme systems (Fridovich, 1975). The superoxide radical itself may not be immediately involved in free radical attack on biological molecules (it cannot abstract allelic hydrogen atoms, for instance). However, its conjugate acid, the hydroperoxyl radical (HOO·), is a much more potent oxidant. Moreover, superoxide can react with hydrogen peroxide and other hydroperoxides in the presence of metal ion complexes to form

Free Radical Reactions Involved in Lipid Peroxidation

I. Lipid Auto-oxidation:

1a. $R-H + O_2 \longrightarrow R\cdot + H-O-O\cdot$
1b. $R-H + X\cdot \longrightarrow R\cdot + X-H$
(where $X\cdot$ = any free radical, e.g., $R\cdot$, $HO\cdot$, $RO\cdot$, etc.)
2. $R\cdot + O_2 \longrightarrow R-O-O\cdot$ [$\rightarrow \rightarrow$ malondialdehyde]
3. $R-O-O\cdot + R'-H \longrightarrow R-O-O-H + R'\cdot$
4. repeat (2), (3), and (4).

II. Reactions of Superoxide Anion Radical:

1. $O_2^- + O_2^- + 2H^+ \longrightarrow H_2O_2 + O_2$
2. $O_2^- + R-O-O-H \longrightarrow RO\cdot + HO^- + O_2$
3. $O_2^- + H-O-O-H \longrightarrow HO\cdot + HO^- + O_2$

Figure 2. Summary of reactions involved in: I. the auto-oxidation of lipids by free radicals; II. the generation of free radicals and hydrogen peroxide from superoxide radical. (Adapted from Pryor, 1973; Pryor, 1978; and Fridovich, 1975.)

highly reactive alkoxyl and hydroxyl radicals as shown in Figure 2 (Pryor, 1978). In addition, other secondary radicals derived from attack by these radicals on organic molecules, from exogenous toxic substances (air pollutants, ozone, pesticides, drugs, etc.), or from radiation (Leibovitz and Siegel, 1975) may be involved in free radical damage to cells.

Among the deleterious free radical reactions which might occur, the peroxidation of lipids (Figure 2) has been proposed as a major source of damage to the integrity of cells (Tappel, 1970). Auto-oxidation of lipids by free radical pathway(s) leads to the formation of hydroperoxides (Figure 2), which may then decompose to a variety of products (e.g., alkanes and aldehydes) or form additional radicals capable of propagating the chain of free radical reactions. Polyunsaturated lipids may undergo multiple peroxidations and cyclizations to yield prostaglandin-like endoperoxides which then decompose to malondialdehyde as well as other products (Pryor, 1978). Measurement of the levels of malondialdehyde and various al-kanes permits the detection of the occurrence of lipid peroxidation (Tappel, 1978; Plaa and Witschi, 1976). In addition, malondialdehyde has been shown to form cross-links through Schiff base formation with the amino groups of biological macromolecules (e.g., proteins, DNA, RNA). The reaction of malondialdehyde with cellular proteins results in the production of a fluorescent chromophore, $R-N=CH-CH=CH-NH-R$, whose fluorescence spectrum is similar to that of lipofuscin or age pigments (Tappel, 1970). This has been offered as indirect evidence for the origin of such pigments from lipid peroxidation products (Tappel, 1973).

There are many examples of the protective action of antioxidants against free radicals in biological systems. Nordihydroguaiaretic acid (NDGA) has been shown to protect wild-type *Neurospora crassa* against the inhibition of growth produced by hydroperoxides added to the medium (Munkres and Colvin, 1976). It has been suggested that D-penicillamine, which has been used to protect premature infants from retrolental fibroplasia (an ophthalmologic disorder caused by oxygen toxicity) induced by protracted oxygen therapy, probably acts by scavenging free radicals and decreasing lipid peroxidation (Borkman and Lerman, 1977; Matkovics et al., 1981). Furthermore, alpha-tocopherol inhibits some of the effects of ozone exposure (Chow and Tappel, 1972). Finally, it has been demonstrated that several antioxidants can directly reduce the amount of free radicals detected by electron spin resonance spectroscopy (ESR) in rat muscle (Duchesne et al., 1975) or by chemiluminescence in isolated preparations of living human and rat mitochondria (Lippman, 1980; Lippman, 1981).

While it is generally accepted that free radical reactions and lipid peroxidation do occur to some extent in living cells, the degree to which these reactions may contribute to cell damage and to pathology and senescence remains to be determined. Organisms have evolved enzymatic and nonenzymatic systems for scavenging free radicals and destroying potentially harmful products before further damage can occur. The enzymatic system (Figure 3) consists largely of superoxide dismutase, catalase, and glutathione peroxidase which detoxify, respectively, superoxide radical, hydrogen peroxide, and lipid hydroperoxides (Leibovitz and Seigel, 1980). The nonenzymatic protection consists primarily of the free radical scavenging action of vitamins E and C, various sulfhydryl compounds such as cysteine and glutathione (Leibovitz and Seigel, 1980), and uric acid (Ames, 1981).

Harman (1957) first attempted to supplement these natural protective mechanisms and thus prolong the life span of an animal by the chronic administration of antioxidants. Three of five antioxidants tested (cysteine HCl, 2-mercaptoethylamine HCl, 2,2′-diaminodiethyl disulfide HCl) extended the half-survival time of the short-lived, leukemia-prone, AKR mouse strain, while none of these compounds had a discernible effect on the longer-lived C3H strain. Subsequent studies demonstrated that chronic administration of 2-mercaptoethylamine (2-MEA) or hydroxylamine could extend the mean life span of C3H mice (Harman 1961). However, the mice that he chose for these experiments had relatively short mean life spans (14.5 and 9.6 months for the C3H and AKR strains, respectively). None of the administered compounds prolonged the mean life span of Swiss mice, which was 22 months (Harman, 1961).

Harman (1968) also reported that administration of 2-MEA or BHT (butylated hydroxytoluene) extended the mean life span of longer-lived LAF_1 mice, and BHT has since been shown to increase survival times of long-lived BALB/c mice (Clapp et al., 1979). On the other hand, Kohn (1971) found no increase in life span with 2-MEA or BHT treatment in C57B1/6 mice when care was taken to ensure that the control animals lived as long as possible. Thus, it appears that antioxidant administration can extend the mean life span of mice but only when the animals have genetic predisposition to life-shortening diseases or exposure to environmental conditions which reduce survival.

Sacher has emphasized that most longevity-enhancing treatments act by reducing the age-independent death risk; only nutritional restriction in rats seems to reduce the more fundamental gerontologic parameter, the age-dependent mortality risk (Sacher, 1977). Unfortunately, many attempts to increase longevity were done on rodent populations with high (suboptimal) age-independent mortality risk. The suboptimum longevity of many rodent populations thus obscures interpretation of most studies.

Both the mean and the maximum life span of C3H mice have also been extended with chronic administration of another antioxidant ethoxyquin (Comfort et al., 1971). However, in this study it was noted that the treated animals experienced a significant weight loss. The maximum life spans of the treated group were within the range of life spans for that mouse strain, yet below those obtained in this strain under conditions of caloric restriction. Harman (1968) also noted a 10–20 percent decrease in food consumption in the LAF_1, mice treated with antioxidants, a level of food restriction known to increase life span in mice (Tucker, 1979). Unfortunately, Clapp et al., (1979) did not report weight changes in their report. Therefore, it appears that the unintentional food restriction which occurs during the administration of antioxidants may confound the interpretation of the results of these experiments.

While most of the antioxidant studies have been conducted in mice, other organisms

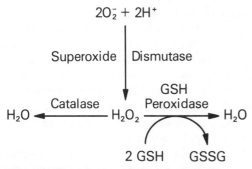

$$2O_2^- + 2H^+$$

Superoxide | Dismutase

$$H_2O \longleftarrow \underset{\text{Catalase}}{} H_2O_2 \overset{\text{GSH}}{\underset{\text{Peroxidase}}{\longrightarrow}} H_2O$$

2 GSH   GSSG

Figure 3. Enzymes involved in removal of superoxide radicals.

have been examined. In the rat, NDGA administration has been reported to extend life span (Buu-Hoi and Ratsimamanga, 1959). Injection of either cysteine or thiazolidine carboxylic acid has been reported to increase the life spans of both mice and guinea pigs, but not rats (Oeriu and Vochitu, 1965). Chronic large doses of ascorbic acid did not prolong the life span of guinea pigs (Davies et al., 1977). Vitamin E and NDGA have been shown to prolong the time before senescence and death of a natural-death mutant of *Neurospora crassa* (Munkres and Minssen, 1976). In *Drosophila,* administration of thiazolidine carboxylate salts (Miquel and Economos, 1979) and lactic and gluconic acids (Massie and Williams, 1979) has been reported to increase life span, whereas no effect on life span of diethylhydroxylamine (DEHA) administration has been observed (Massie and Williams, 1978). Only two of these studies addressed the question of weight loss: Miquel and Economos (1979) found no difference in the weights of control and treated fruit flies, whereas Massie and Williams (1979) mention a small (about 10 percent) decrease in the weights of treated flies.

A variety of antioxidant supplementations had no effect on age-related accumulation of chromosomal aberrations in liver tissue from LAF$_1$ mice (Harman et al., 1970).

Besides the direct administration of antioxidants to animals, other experimental approaches have been used to modulate the level of free radical reactions *in vivo*. Since it is known that polyunsaturated fatty acids are particularly vulnerable to peroxidation by free radicals, Harman (1971) varied the amount of unsaturated dietary fat in mice and rats. He found a significant decrease in mean life span of C3H mice with increasing unsaturation of dietary fat but no statistically significant effect on life span of Swiss mice or rats. Other studies of the effects of increasing the level of unsaturation of dietary fat have shown either a slight decrease in longevity (French et al., 1953) or no effect on longevity (Morin, 1967; Horn et al., 1979). Another method for reducing the generation of free radicals involves the administration of ethidium bromide to reduce oxygen consumption (i.e., reduce mitochondrial respiration). *Drosophila* administered this compound during development were found not only to have increased mean and maximum life spans but also to have prolonged development and decreased body weight (Fleming et al., 1981).

VITAMIN E

Vitamin E or alpha-tocopherol was first identified by Evans and Bishop (1922) as a fat soluble factor necessary for normal reproduction in rats. It has subsequently been reported to play a structural role in membranes (Lucy, 1972), to serve as a metabolic regulator (Hauswirth and Nair, 1972; Nair, 1972), and to have lipid antioxidant properties (Alfin-Slater, 1974; Tappel, 1962; Tappel, 1972). Unfortunately, the exact mechanisms for the antioxidant function of vitamin E have not yet been elucidated.

A number of investigators have administered varying amounts of vitamin E to mice (Tappel et al., 1973; Ledvina and Hodanova, 1980; Blackett and Hall, 1981a), rats (Berg, 1959; Porta et al., 1980a), *Drosophila melanogaster* (Miquel et al., 1973), rotifers (Enesco and Verdone-Smith, 1980), nematodes (Epstein and Gershon, 1972), and human cell cultures (Packer and Smith, 1974; Packer and Smith, 1977; Sakagami and Yamada, 1977) in an attempt to increase their longevity. The majority of these studies have revealed no significant increase in life span. Some of the studies have shown increases in mean life span or survival time (Porta et al., 1980a; Enesco and Verdone-Smith, 1980; Blackett and Hall, 1981a; Miquel et al., 1973). However, with the exception of the administration of vitamin E to *Drosophila* (Miquel et al., 1973) and nematodes (Epstein and Gershon, 1972), none of these studies revealed any increase in the maximum life span of the organism under study.

Since lipofuscin is considered to be the end stage of lipid peroxidation, several investigators have examined the effect of administration of vitamin E on the age-related accumulation of lipofuscin. Most of these studies have demonstrated that chronic vitamin E administration can decrease lipofuscin levels in mouse tissues: heart (Tappel et al., 1973; Blackett and Hall, 1981b), liver (Csallany et al., 1977), testes (Tappel et al., 1973), and brain (Freund, 1979). In rat brain, on the other hand, no effect of dietary vitamin E levels on lipofuscin content was observed (Porta et al., 1980b).

The accumulation of lipofuscin is an indirect means of assessing peroxidative damage to important cellular organelles, such as mitochondria, lysosomes, and endoplasmic reticulum. A few investigators have attempted to directly measure an effect of vitamin E on *in vitro* preparations of some subcellular organelles. Scott et al. (1974) found that hepatic mitochondrial and microsomal fractions from vitamin E-deficient chicks had higher levels of lipid peroxidation products than those from chicks that had been supplemented with vitamin E and selenium, but not with either agent alone. Grinna (1976) has reported that similar preparations from vitamin E-supplemented or deficient rats showed no differences in age-related membrane changes, including lipid peroxidation.

An important question is whether the lipid peroxidation products measured *in vitro* accurately reflect *in vivo* levels. Several investigators (Green et al., 1967; Bunyan et al., 1967, 1968) have demonstrated that manipulation of dietary vitamin E levels or of the degree of unsaturation of dietary lipids has no effect on the levels of lipid peroxides *in vivo*, except in adipose tissue. This could be related to the observation that radiolabeled vitamin E does not undergo decomposition *in vivo* in response to unsaturated fatty acids though it does *in vitro* (Green et al., 1967). These results reflect the caution that needs to be taken in extrapolating the effects of *in vitro* vitamin E adminstration to the *in vivo* situation.

Harman has suggested that vitamin E and other antioxidants may affect longevity by reducing the incidence of age-related diseases and disorders (Harman, 1981). Chronic vitamin E administration to mice resulted in a decreased accumulation of amyloid in their spleens (Harman et al., 1976). Studies of the effect of vitamin E administration on humoral and cell-mediated immunity have also suggested that this antioxidant can delay the loss of these immune functions with aging (Harman et al., 1977). However, other age-related pathological alterations do not appear to be affected by vitamin E administration. Degenerative changes occurring with aging in the neurons of the dorsal column nuclei of mice were not prevented by vitamin E administration (Johnson et al., 1975). Vitamin E administration also had no effect on age-related connective tissue changes in mice (Blackett and Hall, 1980).

A number of other vitamin supplements have been suggested as being beneficial for the promotion of good health in humans. As many as 50 percent of all adults are now consuming vitamin supplements. Despite this enormous level of consumption, there is little evidence of their benefit. Consumption of too high a level of certain vitamins can be detrimental. The toxic effects of vitamin A are well-known. Vitamin E toxicity has been reported in laboratory animals (Bieri, 1975; March et al., 1973), and minor complaints of nausea, intestinal distress, and fatigue have been noted in man (Bieri, 1975; Cohen, 1973). Population studies of vitamin consumption in a highly selected group of individuals over age 65 have also shown increased mortality in those individuals consuming very high levels of vitamin E, more than 1000 I.U./day (Enstrom and Pauling, 1982). In this same study, no dose-response relationship could be found between mortality and the levels of vitamin supplementation in this group (Enstrom and Pauling, 1982).

SUPEROXIDE DISMUTASE

McCord and Fridovich (1969) were the first to demonstrate the presence in eukaryotic cells of an enzyme superoxide dismutase, capable of converting superoxide radicals to hydrogen peroxide:

$$2O_2^- + 2H^+ \xrightarrow{\text{superoxide dismutase}} H_2O_2 + O_2$$

The hydrogen peroxide generated by superoxide dismutase is reduced to water and oxygen by the enzymes catalase and glutathione peroxidase.

Superoxide dismutase occurs in two forms in most eukaryotic cells, a cytosol enzyme which contains copper and zinc, and a mitochondrial form which contains manganese (Fridovich, 1975). Most studies of superoxide dismutase have involved examination of the cytosol enzyme. This cytosol enzyme is present in large amounts in cells, thus ensuring the rapid removal of superoxide radicals (Fridovich, 1975). The protective effect of this enzyme was demonstrated *in vivo* by the increased survival of x-irradiated Swiss mice injected with the enzyme over noninjected x-irradiated control animals (Petkau et al., 1975), and *in vitro* by the decrease in chromosome aberrations in cultured cells from patients with Fanconi's anemia (Nordensen, 1977a) and Werner's syndrome (Nordenson, 1977b).

Several investigators have examined the effect of aging on superoxide dismutase. Kellogg and Fridovich (1976) reported that superoxide dismutase levels did not change with aging in the brain and liver of Sprague-Dawley rats. Reiss and Gershon (1976a) isolated and purified superoxide dismutase from WF rat liver and reported a reduction in specific activity, the accumulation of antigenically cross-reacting material (CRM), and increased temperature sensitivity with aging. These authors extended their studies to demonstrate similar age-related findings in C57BL/6J mouse liver homogenates (Reiss and Gershon, 1976b). However, examination of homogenates of heart tissues revealed minimum reductions, and brain tissues showed no changes in superoxide dismutase specific activities with aging in both mice and rats (Reiss and Gershon, 1976b). However, in both tissues an accumulation of CRM with

age was found. Massie et al. (1979), on the other hand, found a decrease in superoxide dismutase activity in crude homogenates of mouse brain with aging. In *Drosophila melanogaster,* the fruit fly, total superoxide dismutase activities did not vary with aging (Massie et al., 1980).

Superoxide dismutase levels have also been reported to decline as a function of human erythrocyte aging (Bartosz et al., 1978a). However, superoxide dismutase levels in erythrocytes derived from young and old individuals do not appear to differ (Stevens et al., 1975; Joenje et al., 1978). On the other hand, Glass and Gershon (1981) have described a decline in superoxide dismutase activity in rat erythrocytes as a function of cell and, more significantly, of animal age. Also, Dourat and Gershon (1981) have described a considerable decline of superoxide dismutase activity in the rat ocular lens. In both cases, a concomitant age-associated accumulation of enzyme CRM was observed. Age-related changes in superoxide dismutase levels were not found in human and rhesus monkey heart, brain, and liver tissues (Tolmasoff et al., 1980). Finally, superoxide dismutase levels did not change in cultured fetal lung fibroblasts as a function of *in vitro* serial passage (*in vitro* aging) (Yamanaka and Deamer, 1974) or as a function of human donor age in skin fibroblast cultures (Duncan et al., 1979). Thus, with the exception of the findings of Reiss and Gershon (1976a, 1976b), Glass and Gershon (1981), and Dourat and Gershon (1981) with purified superoxide dismutase in mice and rat liver tissues, there is no consistent pattern of change in superoxide dismutase activities as a function of aging.

Comparative aging studies of superoxide dismutase have been more positive. Kellogg and Fridovich (1976) first showed that superoxide dismutase activities were higher in relatively long-lived, LP/J mice than in short-lived, A/J mice. Bartosz and coworkers (1978a) also found that superoxide dismutase activities were lower in vestigial *Drosophila melanogaster* than in the longer-lived wild type. A wide number of different animal species were surveyed by Tolmasoff and coworkers (1980) who found that the longest-lived species, man, also had the highest superoxide dismutase levels. There appeared to be a rough correlation between species life span and superoxide dismutase levels in liver, heart, and brain tissues. In an attempt to improve this correlation, these authors created a ratio of superoxide dismutase activity to the specific metabolic rate of the tissue or organism, and found a linear relationship between this ratio and species maximal life span. The results of the three studies suggest, therefore, that superoxide dismutase activities may have contributed to the evolution of increased life span.

It should be noted that Tolmasoff did not make adjustments for the proportion of superoxide dismutase activity contributed by the mitochondrial form which varies widely between species. In rodents, for instance, it is only 8 percent of total superoxide dismutase activity, but in man it is approximately 50 percent. This mitochondrial form is probably the adaptive enzymatic form, at least in the lungs (Autor and Stevens, 1980). The proposal that superoxide dismutase levels relate to species life span may be too simplistic, as there is no obvious correlation between the levels of oxygen consumption of a tissue and its superoxide dismutase levels (Glass et al., 1982). However, the most compelling argument which makes Tolmasoff's hypothesis unlikely is the fact that the cell is equipped with an arsenal of protective factors against oxygen free radicals (not only superoxide but singlet oxygen and hydroxyl radical) and peroxides. There are also efficient means of maintaining the redox state of cells. Among these are catalase, glutathione peroxidase, glutathione reductase (and G-GPD, which generates NADPH necessary for the regeneration of reduced glutathione), and the whole glutathione synthesizing enzymatic apparatus. Different cell types contain a variety of antioxidants such as vitamins E and C. Also, serum contains high levels of ceruloplasmin which supposedly confers dismutating protection on various tissues. Thus, it is difficult to conclude that superoxide dismutase levels are specifically important for the evolution of longevity.

DIMETHYLAMINOETHYL PARA-CHLORO-PHENOXYACETATE (CENTROPHENOXINE, CLOFENOXINE, MECLOFENOXATE, LUCIDRIL, HELFERGIN, ANP 235)

Most studies of centrophenoxine have involved its effect on the deposition of lipofuscin pigments. Lipofuscin has been shown to accumulate with aging in a number of organisms (Toth, 1968). It has been postulated that lipofuscin pigments are composed of heterogeneous lipoprotein polymerization products of lipid peroxidation (Wolman, 1980) which may represent the residual bodies of autophagic, lysosomal degradation of organelle membranes. Of particular interest are reports that the rate of lipofuscin deposition is accelerated in short-lived, high activity houseflies and is diminished in houseflies whose life has been extended by decreasing their flight activity (Sohal and Donato, 1979; Sohal, 1981), which indicates perhaps that lipofuscin accumulation is related to the functional activity of cells rather than to their chronological age.

Dimethylaminoethyl *p*-chlorophenoxyacetate or centrophenoxine was first synthesized by Thuillier in an attempt to improve the action of dimethylaminoethanol (a precursor of choline) through esterification with several analogues of the plant trophic factor auxin (1959). In various clinical studies, centrophenoxine was employed in attempts to treat memory disturbances, confusional states, apathy, agitation, and dementia in older patients (Delay et al., 1960; Houillon et al., 1963).

Nandy demonstrated that centrophenoxine treatment could decrease the accumulation of lipofuscin pigment in the neurons of aging guinea pigs (Nandy and Bourne, 1966; Nandy, 1968). Further electron-microscopic and histochemical studies have confirmed the effect of this compound on the removal of lipofuscin in guinea pig brain (Hasan et al., 1974a, 1974b), myocardium (Spoerri et al., 1974), and liver (Glees and Spoerri, 1975).

The removal of lipofuscin by centrophenoxine has also been demonstrated in rats (Riga and Riga, 1974), mice (Nandy, 1978a), and torpedos (Totaro and Pisanti, 1980). This effect appears to be specific for aging animals since administration of centrophenoxine to 1-month-old mice did not appear to retard the accumulation of lipofuscin pigment (Nandy, 1978a). It has also been demonstrated that centrophenoxine can reduce the accumulation of lipofuscin pigment in cultured neuroblastoma cells (Nandy et al., 1978).

Centrophenoxine has been reported to reverse several other aging parameters. In Wistar rats, centrophenoxine treatment of older animals resulted in the restoration of surface densities and total length of the cerebellar glomerulus synaptic contact zones to levels observed in young animals (Giuli et al., 1980). In CPH rats, administration of centrophenoxine reversed the age-related accumulation of water insoluble proteins in brain and liver tissues (Zs.-Nagy and Nagy, 1980; Zs.-Nagy et al., 1981). These investigators postulated that the dimethylaminoethanol component of centrophenoxine acted to scavenge free radicals and prevent them from cross-linking proteins. Nandy (1978b) demonstrated that chronic centrophenoxine administration could reduce the time necessary for maze learning in 11- to 12-month-old C57B1/6 mice. In tissue culture, centrophenoxine was reported to lengthen the *in vitro* life span of cultured diploid human glial cells (Rodemann and Bayreuther, 1979).

Chronic centrophenoxine administration has been reported to increase both mean and maximum life span of *Drosophila melanogaster* (Hochschild, 1971) and of male Swiss Webster Albino mice (Hochschild, 1973a). In the latter study, the treated mice weighed 25 percent less than controls. In the histological studies of the effects of centrophenoxine on lipofuscin deposition, no reference was made regarding the weights of the treated and control animals. However, in one study, a comment was made that all of the treated animals experienced weight loss (Hasan et al., 1974a). In a clinical trial, Schmid and Schlick (1979) found that centrophenoxine treatment reduced fasting blood glucose levels and increased maximum oxygen consumption, but again the patients experienced a significant loss of weight. If centrophenoxine causes weight loss, many of the observed effects could be related to caloric restriction rather than to direct actions of the compound.

Hochschild (1973b) also reported that the metabolite of centrophenoxine, dimethylaminoethanol (DMAE), could prolong the life span of A/J mice though without the concomitant weight loss. DMAE has been utilized as a treatment for tardive dyskinesias (Miller, 1974) and may also act as a neuronal stimulant (Pfeiffer et al., 1957). It is of interest that dimethylaminoethanol resembles the major metabolite (diethylaminoethanol) of Gerovital-H_3 and is also, as mentioned earlier, a precursor of choline. In addition, chlorpromazine, which contains the dimethylaminoethanol moiety, has been shown to decrease the deposition of lipofuscin in mouse brain (Samorajski and Rolsten, 1976).

Despite the large number of histological reports of the effects of centrophenoxine, there has been a dearth of studies of the pharmacology of this compound. Furthermore, while the action of this compound in arresting lipofuscin deposition is impressive, there is little evidence that lipofuscin *per se* is damaging to the function of cells or the organism. For example, the neurons of the inferior olivary nucleus of humans accumulate such large amounts of lipofuscin that their cell nuclei are displaced (Monagle and Brody, 1974), yet neuronal loss is not detected even into the 90s (Monagle, 1968).

L-DOPA

The rationale for the use of L-DOPA as an intervention in aging processes is twofold. Studies in both humans and animals have suggested that deficiencies in brain aminergic transmitters occur with aging (Rogers and Bloom, 1983). In addition, the administration of L-DOPA has been effective in reducing the symptoms and slowing the progression of the common age-related disorder Parkinson's disease (Rinne et al., 1970; Joseph, 1978).

L-DOPA administered over the life span produced a significant increase in survivorship in male Swiss albino mice receiving near toxic levels (40 mg/g food) of this compound (Cotzias et al., 1974). However, the treated mice also exhibited diminished weights when compared to controls, and the life span of the control mice was rather short. Using a longer-living cohort of both male and female Swiss albino mice, Cotzias et al. (1977) demonstrated a significant increase in mean and maximum longevity at these high doses of L-DOPA. Again, a significant loss of weight was observed in the treated group. L-DOPA at lower doses did not seem to have any life-extending properties (Cotzias et al., 1974; Cotzias et al., 1977; Dilman and Anisimov, 1980). Papavasiliou et al. (1981) have recently confirmed the increased longevity and decreased weight produced by the high concentration of L-DOPA employed by Cotzias and coworkers in male Swiss albino mice. It is also noteworthy that the usual increase with aging in brain monoamine oxidase levels was found not to occur in the mice receiving chronic L-DOPA administration (Papavasiliou et al., 1981).

Studies of mortality of patients with Parkinson's disease who received long-term treatment with L-DOPA indicate increased survival of these patients when compared to untreated patients (Marttila et al., 1977; Joseph et al., 1978). However, these individuals still had reduced longevities when compared to the population at large.

HYPOPHYSECTOMY

Most of the interventions discussed in this chapter relate to the addition of a factor intended to lengthen life span or slow aging processes. Another approach is to remove negative factors which might have important aging effects. A number of investigators have suggested that hormones play a significant role in aging and that the pituitary is a major source of such hormones (Everitt, 1973;

Denkla, 1974). The presence of these aging hormones can be assessed by hypophysectomy coupled with specific hormone replacement therapies.

Everitt and coworkers were the first to demonstrate that hypophysectomy can retard certain age-related changes. Utilizing the breaking time of tail tendon fibers, an assay which reflects the degree of collagen cross-linking, these authors demonstrated that collagen ages more slowly in hypophysectomized rats than in normal controls (Olsen and Everitt, 1965; Everitt and Cavanaugh, 1965). This finding was further expanded by Verzar and Spichtin (1966) who found that the aging of collagen in the skin of hypophysectomized rats is markedly retarded (as demonstrated by a higher level of soluble hydroxyproline or "labile" collagen). Studies of hypophysectomized animals have also revealed diminished proteinuria associated with the common chronic kidney disease of laboratory rodents (Everitt and Cavanaugh, 1965), decreased aortic wall thickness and diminished numbers of tumors (Everitt et al., 1980), increased ability to reject xenografts (Bilder and Denckla, 1977), and prevention of, or restoration of, the loss of minimal oxygen capacity (Denckla, 1974). It is not clear whether this last measure is an accurate biomarker of aging.

Hypophysectomy of Wistar rats in early life (at age 70 days), in combination with cortisone supplementation, has been shown to substantially increase maximum life span (Everitt et al., 1980). However, hypophysectomy of these animals in middle life (400 days) had a life-shortening effect, despite cortisone therapy (Everitt et al., 1980). Denckla has proposed that these effects are due to the removal of a purported "DECO" factor, a putative pituitary hormone responsible for the decreasing oxygen consumption observed with aging (Bilder and Denckla, 1977).

The life-extending effects of hypophysectomy have to be interpreted with caution in rat strains, such as the Wistar, which have significant (26 percent) prevalence of pituitary tumors (Everitt et al., 1980). Hypophysectomized animals have significant early life mortality and significantly reduced weights when compared to control animals (Olsen and Everitt, 1965; Everitt and Cavanaugh, 1965). In fact, many of the observed changes with hypophysectomy resemble those of food restriction. Everitt compared these two treatments and found only one significant difference in both physiologic and pathologic changes between the two approaches: animals started on food restriction in middle life had no change in collagen aging (determined by tail tendon breakage time), while animals that were hypophysectomized had diminished aging of collagen (Everitt et al., 1980). It has also been reported that food restriction can lead to pituitary atrophy and diminished blood levels of pituitary hormones (Mulinos and Pomerantz, 1940; Sorrentino, 1971), as well as decreased hypothalamic function (Nisbett, 1972). This similarity between food restriction and hypophysectomy is intriguing and should be pursued.

IMMUNOLOGICAL INTERVENTIONS

It is well established that a general decline in immune competence occurs with aging, and this has been attributed to alterations in the functional capacity of both T and B cell populations (Segre and Segre, 1977; Freidman and Globerson, 1978a, 1978b). This age-related decline in immune function is believed to be an important contributor to senescence and to the development of chronic diseases and disorders (Burnet, 1974). A variety of approaches have been devised to prevent or restore this loss of immune responsiveness (Walford et al., 1977; Makinodan, 1979).

Two approaches to immune manipulation have been discussed in preceding sections—hypothermia and dietary restriction. Another approach to immunological rejuvenation of aging animals is to transplant histocompatible immune cells from young donors into old recipients. Teague and Friou (1969) demonstrated that injection of thymus cells from young mice could reduce or eliminate anti-deoxyribonucleoprotein (anti-

DNP) antibodies in old mice. Furthermore, they found that such thymus cell injections in 36-week-old mice could prevent the subsequent development of anti-DNP antibodies, even when the mice were specifically immunized with DNP. Injections of lymph node lymphocytes from young normal mice markedly prolonged the survival of short-lived dwarf mice, a strain which purportedly exhibits signs of precocious aging (Fabris et al., 1972). Finally, Perkins et al. (1972) have reported that survival of old mice following injections of *Salmonella typhimurium* was substantially increased by administration of spleen cells from specifically immunized young mice. The converse experiments have also been performed and have revealed that transplantation of spleen cells from old mice into young mice induces the formation of autoantibodies in the young mice (Teague and Friou, 1969) and markedly decreases survival of irradiated young mice compared to irradiated mice receiving young spleen cells or no spleen cells (Albright et al., 1969). Since it was found in this last study that spleen cells from old mice had a life-shortening effect on young mice, the effect of splenectomy on the survival of mice was also examined. Mice splenectomized at 97 weeks of age had a significantly prolonged life span when compared to sham-operated or untreated control mice (Albright et al., 1969).

Transplantation of syngeneic thymus or bone marrow grafts is another approach to immunological rejuvenation. Kysela and Steinberg (1973) have shown that multiple thymus grafts from young donors produced a slight increase in survival of NZB/W mice, a strain prone to autoimmune disease. This technique has also been tried in a long-lived strain of mice. Although longevity was not assessed in this study, combined bone marrow and thymus grafts from young mice were found to substantially improve the response of spleen cells from old mice to sheep erythrocytes and mitogens (Hirokawa et al., 1976).

In the last decade it has become increasingly clear that thymic factors modulate a variety of immune functions. Weksler et al.

(1978) demonstrated that thymectomy could accelerate the immune deficiencies observed with aging. Goldstein et al. (1970) have shown that administration of a thymic extract can restore cellular immune function (skin allograft rejection) in neonatally thymectomized mice but has little effect on the humoral responses in these mice. Incubation of thymosin *in vitro* with sheep erythrocytes and lymphocytes from patients with cellular immunodeficiencies resulted in an increase in the formation of T cell rosettes (Wara et al., 1975). Aged mice spleen cells incubated with thymic factors regain their graft-versus-host reactivity (Friedman et al., 1974), their generation of IgG plaque-forming cells (PFC), and the generation of PFC that have high affinity for antigen (Weksler et al., 1978). In a clinical trial, thymosin treatment was found to improve cellular immune function in a patient with cellular immunodeficiency and thymic hypoplasia (Wara et al., 1975). In addition, thymosin administration has been shown to prevent abnormal thymocyte proliferation in autoimmunity-susceptible NZB mice and was marginally effective in delaying the formation of anti–nucleic acid antibodies (Talal et al., 1975). The National Institute on Aging is now supporting a cross-sectional as well as longitudinal trial of several thymic preparations in several long-lived mouse strains to examine the effects of these preparations on age-related declines in immune function and on longevity.

It has been proposed that the involution of the immune system may be partially dependent on a deficiency of coenzyme Q, a group of closely related quinone compounds which participate in the mitochondrial electron transport chain (Bliznakov, 1979). Coenzyme Q (specifically, coenzyme Q_{10}) levels have been reported to decline with aging in several organs, most notably the thymus (Bliznakov et al., 1978; Pignatti et al., 1980). Bliznakov (1978) administered coenzyme Q_{10} to 22-month-old mice and found that a single injection partially restored the age-associated decline in humoral response to sheep erythrocytes. Coenzyme Q_{10} administration has also been reported to increase survival of mice infected with Friend leukemia virus, and to reduce both the size of tumors and the percentage of mice acquiring tumors in response to dibenzpyrene (Bliznakov, 1973). While these effects of coenzyme Q are promising, most have been conducted in a single laboratory. Clearly, more studies of coenzyme Q are needed before conclusions regardings its immunorejuvenative effects can be made.

Another chemical approach to restore age-related diminished immune function was tried by Makinodan and Albright (1979), who administered 2-mercaptoethanol *in vitro* to cultured spleen cells and obtained enhanced primary antibody responsiveness.

Finally, as our knowledge of immunology increases, it is becoming clear that there are many subtypes of immune cells. These subtypes may have different quantitative and qualitative responses to aging. For example, it appears that T suppressor cell function may increase with aging (Segre, 1982). Thus, attempts to restore immune function may need to focus on specific immune cell populations.

GEROVITAL-H$_3$

Gerovital-H$_3$ (GH) has been promoted by Aslan for over 30 years as a treatment for aging as well as for a variety of age-related disorders (Aslan, 1956; Aslan, 1974). Initially, Aslan administered procaine to older patients with purported favorable results for peripheral vascular disorders (Aslan, 1974). In an attempt to stabilize procaine which is rapidly broken down into para-aminobenzoic acid (PABA) and diethylaminoethanol (DEAE), Aslan added benzoic acid and metabisulfite to solutions of procaine, and named the preparation Gerovital-H$_3$.

Since its introduction, Gerovital-H$_3$ has been promoted as an effective agent for the treatment of a wide range of disorders. It also has been reported to have effects on generalized aging processes. The extensive literature on this drug was expertly summarized by Ostfeld et al. (1977). The only consistent effect of Gerovital-H$_3$ has been as a mild antidepressant (Zung et al., 1974; Sakalis et al., 1974; Cohen and Ditman, 1974). However, even this effect has been challenged (Olsen et al., 1978). If Gerovital-H_3 has an antidepressant effect, it is probably related to the effects of procaine as a weak, reversible, competitive monoamine oxidase inhibitor *in vitro* (MacFarlane and Bresbis, 1974; Yau, 1974; MacFarlane, 1975) and possibly *in vivo* (Fuller and Roush, 1977). The antidepressant effects of Gerovital-H_3 may also account for the many subjective reports of anti-aging effects of this compound.

While Aslan and coworkers have reported that chronic Gerovital-H_3 administration to rats increases their life span (Aslan and David, 1957; Aslan et al., 1959), other studies have not found any significant effect of this drug on longevity (Verzar, 1959).

DEHYDROEPIANDROSTERONE

Dehydroepiandrosterone (DHEA) is a weak androgenic steroid which is present in high concentration in human serum, mostly as the inactive form conjugated to sulfate (DHEA-S) (Baulieu et al., 1965). The blood levels of DHEA-S are high in the fetus, decline to near zero after birth, rise again at puberty, reach their maximal value sometime in the second decade, and then begin to fall gradually again so that by the seventh decade there is scarcely any DHEA-S detectable in the blood (Yamaji and Ibayashi, 1969; Migeon et al., 1975; Orentreich, 1982). A wide variety of effects have been attributed to DHEA (Sonka, 1976), but the precise function of this steroid, except as a precursor for other steroids, is uncertain.

The extremely high concentrations of DHEA in the blood of young adults and its dramatic early decline with aging have led to the speculation that DHEA may play a role in aging processes. Schwartz (1979, 1982) has administered DHEA to C3H mice and observed an increased survival, primarily due to a decrease in the incidence of spontaneous breast cancer to which this strain is susceptible. DHEA administration to autoimmune prone NZB mice has resulted in a delayed onset of immune dysfunction and an increased survival of this mouse strain.

Treated mice had substantially reduced weight compared to control animals although their food consumption was reported to be similar to that of controls (Schwartz, 1979). Thus, it has been proposed that in inhibiting tumor growth and retarding loss of immune function in mice, DHEA may be acting through a mechanism similar to that of caloric restriction. Since DHEA is an effective competitive inhibitor of glucose-6-phosphate dehydrogenase, some of its actions may be related to its effect on inhibiting the production of reduced coenzymes necessary for fat synthesis.

The crucial experiment—that is, the administration of DHEA to mice that are not tumor prone, are not immune deficient, and have a normal life span—has not yet been performed. However, the mouse may not be a good model for the effect of DHEA in man since DHEA levels do not appear to decline with aging in the mouse. In addition, the distribution of DHEA between sulfated and nonsulfated forms is quite different in mice and men.

DISCUSSION

It is clear from the preceding sections that a wide range of environmental, chemical, hormonal, and pharmacological interventions have been examined for their ability to extend life span and to arrest aging processes in a variety of organisms. The intervention that has most consistently been demonstrated to increase longevity and to affect the largest range of aging processes is caloric restriction. Of particular interest is the observation that this intervention can be successful even if commenced at mid-life. Detractors of this intervention have suggested that caloric restriction is the natural state of most organisms that feed on an irregular schedule. They suggest that the caged, *ad libitum* fed laboratory rodent, which has been used for most studies of caloric restriction, is an overweight animal with an abnormal feeding schedule. This argument is unresolvable since comparative life span studies on wild mice and rats could not be conducted in their natural environment which is filled with predators. It is of interest that many of the other interventions that have been reported to increase life span produce weight loss. In Table 1, the presence or absence of weight loss is listed for those interventions that have been claimed to increase mean or maximum life span. These include L-DOPA, antioxidants, vitamin E, centrophenoxine, Gerovital, hypophysectomy, and DHEA. The vast majority of the interventions which resulted in increased mean or maximum life span produced weight loss in the treated animals. It should be noted that many studies did not report the weight of the animals used in their studies. Thus, the proposed life-extending properties of many of these interventions may be related to caloric restriction.

Most of the studies on interventions have examined life span as their end point. This focus on life span was related to the global approach of these interventions. However, if there are multiple etiologies for aging processes, future emphasis should be on "segmental interventions." These segmental interventions can best be assessed through the measurements of specific biomarkers of aging. The reader is referred to the proceedings of a recent conference which examined various segmental interventions in rodents and humans (Reff and Schneider, 1982).

Successful segmental interventions have already been accomplished in the brain regions which control the functions of the female reproductive system. Mature female rats experience regular estrous cycles until a certain age, at which time the cycles become irregular and eventually cease. The cessation of estrous cycles follows altered patterns of gonadotrophin secretion by the anterior pituitary which may be secondary to alterations in hypothalamic aminergic systems (Meites et al., 1979). Quadri et al. (1973) have demonstrated that regular estrous cycles can be reinitiated in old constant estrous female rats through the administration of drugs which increase brain catecholamine levels (epinephrine, L-DOPA, or iproniazid).

Forman et al. (1980) demonstrated a restoration of estrous cycles in 16 of 19 aging female rats with L-DOPA administration, while no control rats experienced estrous cycles. In addition, it has been demonstrated that electrical stimulation of specific hypothalamic regions can also reinstate normal estrous cycling in old female rats (Clemens et al., 1969). These studies suggest that modification of brain neurotransmitter systems can restore to some extent the normal youthful functioning of the hypothalamic-hypophyseal-gonadal system in aged laboratory animals.

Future segmental interventions may focus on cholinergic neurons. The proposed cholinergic deficit that accompanies aging has recently been summarized in an extensive review (Bartus, 1982). This decline in cholinergic activity may be associated with age-related memory changes. Bartus (1982) has demonstrated that administration of choline can reverse the age-related decline in memory observed in laboratory rodents.

An accelerated decline in cholinergic function has also been postulated to be involved in senile dementia of the Alzheimer's type (Bartus, 1982). Pharmacologic interventions to restore cholinergic function could involve administration of acetylcholine precursors, cholinergic agonists, and acetylcholinesterase inhibitors. This approach has been successful in Parkinson's disease, which features a loss of dopaminergic neurons in the substantia nigra. Oral administration of L-DOPA, a precursor of dopamine, has been effective in diminishing the symptoms of this disorder (Rinne et al., 1970).

Another promising approach is through the transplantation of cholinergic neurons to brain areas that have lost significant numbers of cholinergic neurons. The brain is a good site for transplantation since blood-brain barriers may slow or reduce immune rejection of the transplanted tissues. Several investigators have demonstrated that transplanted fetal brain tissue can function effectively in the adult recipient brain (Kreiger, 1982).

In assessing interventions, the choice of

TABLE 1. Relation Between Weight Loss and Effects of Various Interventions on Life Span and Age-Related Changes.

Intervention	Prolongs Life Span	Prevents or Delays Age-related Changes	Weight Reduction	References
L-DOPA				
	yes	yes	yes	Cotzias et al., 1974
	yes	yes	yes	Cotzias et al., 1977
	yes	yes	yes	Papavasiliou et al., 1981
	no	—	—	Dilman and Anisimov, 1980
Antioxidants				
	yes	—	yes	Comfort et al., 1971
	yes	—	yes	Massie and Williams, 1979
	yes	—	yes	Harman, 1968
	yes	—	no	Clapp et al., 1979
	yes	—	no	Harman, 1961
	yes	—	no	Harman, 1957
	yes	—	no	Miquel and Economos, 1979
	yes	—	—	Massie and Williams, 1978
	yes	—	—	Oeriu and Vochitu, 1965
	yes	—	—	Buu-Hoi and Ratsimamanga, 1959
	no	—	yes	Kohn, 1971
Vitamin E				
	yes	yes	yes	Porta et al., 1980
	yes	yes	—	Epstein and Gershon, 1972
	yes	yes	—	Blackett and Hall, 1981a
	yes	—	—	Enesco and Verdone-Smith, 1980
	no	—	no	Ledvina and Hodanova, 1980
	no	yes	—	Blackett and Hall, 1981b
	no	no	—	Berg, 1959
	no	yes	no	Tappel et al., 1973
	—	yes	no	Csallany et al., 1977
	—	yes	no	Harman et al., 1976
	—	yes	no	Harman et al., 1977
	—	no	—	Blackett and Hall, 1980
Centrophenoxine				
	yes	yes	yes	Hochschild, 1973
	yes	—	—	Hochschild, 1971
	—	yes	yes	Hasan et al., 1974
	—	yes	yes	Schmid and Schlick, 1979
	—	yes	—	Nandy and Bourne, 1966 (and many others)
Gerovital-H$_3$				
	yes	?	?	Aslan et al., 1959
	no	no	no	Verzar, 1959
Hypophysectomy				
	yes	yes	yes	Everitt et al., 1980
	no	yes	yes	Everitt and Cavanaugh, 1965
	no	yes	yes	Verzar and Spichtin, 1966
	—	yes	yes	Olsen and Everitt, 1965
	—	yes	—	Bilder and Denckla, 1977
	—	yes	—	Denckla, 1974
DHEA				
	yes	—	yes	Schwartz, 1979
	yes	yes	—	Schwartz, 1982

experimental animals is crucial. Since interventions are oriented toward the improvement of health in humans, the experimental animals selected for examining specific interventions should display age-related changes which resemble those observed in humans. Many of the rodent models used in the studies discussed in this chapter had life expectancies well below those of the longer-lived strains. Increases in longevity achieved by interventions in these experimental animals may, therefore, not have any effect on aging processes but rather may delay the onset of specific disorders. In humans, the administration of insulin will certainly prolong the life of insulin-dependent diabetics. However, this would not be interpreted as a modulation of an aging process but rather as the modulation of a specific disease. Therefore, it is advisable in all studies of interventions that the strain selected for testing an intervention have a life span which is close to the maximum life span for that species. In addition, if an intervention is being tested on a specific organ system, the strain should not have significant pathology involving that organ. An example would be the inappropriate use of a mouse strain which features tumors of the immune system to test an intervention which is targeted toward the modulation of aging of the immune system. One of the commonly employed mouse strains for studies of the immunology of aging is the C57B1/6 mouse strain. However, at autopsy, most mice aged 2 years or older have lymphomas (Hurvitz, 1979), which may well interfere with the assessment of immunologic interventions in this strain.

Other factors that need close examination in assessing interventions are diets and caging conditions. Common laboratory diets may have significant differences in nutrient composition, and caging conditions can affect the obesity of the housed animals.

It must be reemphasized at this point that although a wide number of interventions have been examined in humans and in experimental animals, none has shown significant modulations of longevity with the exception of caloric restriction. While the effects of caloric restriction are impressive in rodents, it is certainly too early to suggest this approach as a possible intervention in man. The caged *ad libitum* fed mouse may not be an appropriate model for the free living human population. In addition, review of the data accumulated by life insurance companies suggests that being overweight (above their definition of "ideal body weight") rather than underweight may be correlated with increased life span (Andres, 1981). However, the definition of ideal body weight used for these studies has subsequently been redefined (*N.Y. Times,* March 2, 1983). Therefore, at this time there is little advice that can be given to individuals concerning the optimum caloric intake for longevity. However, there are risk factors which can be effectively reduced to increase longevity, such as stopping cigarette smoking and the reduction of diastolic blood pressure. In addition, there are effective segmental interventions such as estrogen and exercise which can retard the age-related loss of bone in older women.

Application of many interventions may have to wait for the state of the art of gerontologic research to progress to the point where logical applications are possible. Aging research, while one of the oldest areas of research interest, has only had substantial financial support in the last ten years. Therefore, it is not surprising that we know relatively little about the basic mechanisms of aging at the molecular, cellular, and organ levels. Until our knowledge of these areas is more complete, formulation of effective interventions may be very difficult, if not impossible. It is, therefore, vital that our major efforts remain focused on basic research to elucidate the mechanisms of aging processes.

The future for the modulation of segmental aging processes is extremely bright, particularly if a substantial increase in our understanding of aging processes occurs. The exciting developments in molecular biology, immunology, endocrinology, and the neurosciences might then provide effective segmental interventions. These interventions will need to be rigorously tested with standardized biomarkers of aging in appropriate animal models and then examined in carefully designed, well-controlled human clinical studies. Until then, caution will need to be exercised in dealing with claims for the rejuvenating properties of various agents or regimens.

ACKNOWLEDGMENTS

We thank Drs. C. Finch, I. Fridovich, W. Kachadorian, E. Lakatta, E. Masoro, E. A. McGuire, D. Gershon, R. Walford, A. Ostfeld, L. Libow, K. Davis, G. Reigle, and W. Ershler for their editorial assistance; Ms. L. Alexander for her professional assistance; and Dr. E. Hadley for his suggestions.

REFERENCES

Adams, G. M. and deVries, H. A. 1973. Physiological effects of an exercise training regimen upon women aged 52 to 79. *J. Gerontol.* 28: 50–55.

Albright, J. F., Makinodan, T., and Deitchman, J. W. 1969. Presence of life-shortening factors in spleens of aged mice and extension of life expectancy by splenectomy. *Exp. Geront.* 4: 267–276.

Alfin-Slater, R. B. 1974. Vitamin E: fact and speculation. *In,* T. T. Craig (ed.), *The Medical Aspects of Sports.* Chicago: American Medical Association.

Ames, B. N., Cathcart, R., Schwiers, E., and Hochstein, P. 1981. Uric acid provides an antioxidant defense against oxidant- and radical-caused aging and cancer: a hypothesis. *Proc. Nat. Acad. Sci. USA* 78: 6858–6862.

Andres, R. 1981. Aging, diabetes, and obesity: standards of normality. *Mt. Sinai J. Med.* 48: 489–495.

Aslan, A. 1956. A new method for the prophylaxis and treatment of aging with Novocain-eutrophic and rejuvenating effects. *Therapiewoche* 7: 14–22.

Aslan, A. 1974. Theoretical and practical aspects of chemotherapeutic techniques in the retardation of the aging process. *In,* Rockstein et al. (eds.), *Theoretical Aspects of Aging,* pp. 145–156. New York: Academic Press.

Aslan, A. and David, N. 1957. Ergebnisse der Novokain-Behandlung bei dysmetabolischen Arthropathien. *Therapiewoche* 8: 1–14.

Aslan, A., David, C., Nicolae, D., and Ispas, I. 1959. L'aspect de la maladie ulcereuse et les resultats therapeutiques par decades d'age. *L'Inform Med. Roumanie* 2: 94–95.

Aslan, A., Vrabiescu, A., Domilescu, C., Cimpeanu, L., Costiniu, M., and Stanescu, S. 1965. Long-term treatment with procaine (Gerovital H_3) in Albino rats. *J. Gerontol.* 20: 1–8.

Astrand, P. 1968. Physical performance as a function of age. *J.A.M.A.* 205: 729–733.

Autor, A. P. and Stevens, J. B. 1980. Regulation of mitochondrial SOD by mitochondrially produced superoxide anions and hydrogen peroxide in a higher eukaryote. *In,* J. V. Bannister and H. A. O. Hill

(eds.), *Chemical and Biochemical Aspects of Superoxide and SOD,* pp. 104–115. New York, Amsterdam, Oxford: Elsevier.

Ball, Z. B., Barnes, R. H., and Visscher, M. B. 1947. The effects of dietary caloric restriction on maturity and senescence with particular reference to fertility and longevity. *Am. J. Physiol.* 150: 511–519.

Barrows, C. H. and Roeder, L. M. 1969. The effect of reduced dietary intake on enzymatic activities and life span of rats. *J. Gerontol.* 20: 69–71.

Bartosz, G., Leyko, W., and Fried R. 1978a. Superoxide dismutase and life span of *Drosophila melanogaster. Experentia* 35: 5.

Bartosz, G., Tannert, C., Fried, R., and Leyko, W. 1978b. Superoxide dismutase activity decreases during erythrocyte aging. *Experentia* 34: 1464.

Bartus, T. R., Dean, R. L., III, Beer, B., and Lippa, A. S. 1982. The cholinergic hypothesis of geriatric memory dysfunction. *Science* 217: 408–417.

Baulieu, E. E., Corpechot, C., Dray, F., *et al.* 1965. An adrenal-secreted "androgen:" dehydroisoandrosterone sulfate. Its metabolism and a tentative generalization on the metabolism of other steroid conjugates in man. *Rec. Progr. Horm. Res.,* 21, 411–500.

Berg, B. N. 1959. Study of vitamin E supplements in relation to muscular dystrophy and other diseases in aging rats. *J. Gerontol.* 14: 174–180.

Berg, B. N. 1960. Nutrition and longevity in the rat. I. Food intake in relation to size, health, and fertility. *J. Nutr.* 71: 242–254.

Berg, B. N. and Simms, H. S. 1960. Nutrition and longevity in the rat: II. Longevity and onset of disease with different levels of food intake. *J. Nutr.* 71: 255–263.

Bieri, J. G. 1975. Vitamin E. *Nutr. Rev.* 33: 161–167.

Bilder, G. E. and Denckla, W. D. 1977. Restoration of ability to reject xenografts and clear carbon after hypophysectomy of adult rats. *Mech. Ageing Dev.* 6: 153–163.

Bjorntorp, P., Fahlen, M., Grimby, G., Gustafson, A., Holm, J., Renstrom, P., and Schersten, T. 1972. Carbohydrate and lipid metabolism in middle-aged, physically well-trained men. *Metab.* 21: 1037–1044.

Blackett, A. D. and Hall, D. A. 1980. The action of vitamin E on the ageing of connective tissues in the mouse. *Mech. Ageing Dev.* 14: 305–316.

Blackett, A. D. and Hall, D. A. 1981a. Vitamine E—its significance in mouse ageing. *Age and Ageing* 10: 191–195.

Blackett, A. D. and Hall, D. A. 1981b. Tissue vitamin E levels and lipofuscin accumulation with age in the mouse. *J. Gerontol.* 36: 529–533.

Bliznakov, E. G. 1973. Effect of stimulation of the host defense system by coenzyme Q_{10} on dibenzpyrene-induced tumors and infection with Friend leukemia virus in mice. *Proc. Nat. Acad. Sci. USA* 70: 390–394.

Bliznakov, E. G. 1978. Immunological senescence in mice and its reversal by coenzyme Q_{10}. *Mech. Ageing Dev.* 7: 189–197.

Bliznakov, E. G. 1979. Suppression of immunological responsiveness in aged mice and its relationship with coenzyme Q deficiency. *Adv. Exp. Med. Biol.* 121: 361–369.

Bliznakov, E. G., Watanabe, T., Seisuke, S., and Folkers, K. 1978. Coenzyme Q deficiency in aged mice. *J. Med.* 9: 337–346.

Borkman, R. F. and Lerman, S. 1977. Evidence for a free radical mechanism in aging and UV-irradiated ocular lenses. *Exp. Eye Res.* 25: 303–309.

Bortz, W. M. 1980. Effect of exercise on aging—effect of aging on exercise. *J. Am. Geriat. Soc.* 28: 49–51.

Brody, J. A. and Brock, D. B. 1984. Epidemiologic and statistical characterizations of the United States elderly population. *In,* C. Finch and E. L. Schneider (eds.), *Handbook of the Biology of Aging,* pp. 3–26. New York: Van Nostrand Reinhold.

Bunyan, J., Green, J., Murrell, E. A., Diplock, A. T., and Cawthorne, M. A. 1968. On the postulated peroxidation of unsaturated lipids in the tissues of vitamin E-deficient rats. *Brit. J. Nutr.* 22: 97–110.

Bunyan, J., Murrell, E. A., Green, J., and Diplock, A. T. 1967. On the existence and significance of lipid peroxides in vitamin E-deficient animals. *Brit. J. Nutr.* 21: 475–495.

Burcombe, J. V. and Hollingswirth, M. J. 1970. The relationship between developmental temperature and longevity in *Drosophila. Gerontologia* 16: 172–181.

Burnet, M. 1974. *Intrinsic Mutagenesis: A Genetic Approach to Ageing.* New York: John Wiley & Sons.

Buskirk, E. R. 1983. Exercise. *In,* C. Finch and E. L. Schneider (eds.), Handbook of the Biology of Aging, pp. 894–931. New York: Van Nostrand Reinhold.

Buu-Hoi, N. P. and Ratsimamanga, A. R. 1959. Action retardante de l'acide norhydroguaretique sur le vieillissement chez le rat. *C. R. Soc. Biol.* 153: 1180–1182.

Byrd, R. J. 1973. The effect of controlled, mild exercise on the rate of physiological ageing of rats. *J. Med. Phys. Fitness* 13: 1–3.

Cheney, K. E., Liu, R. K., Smith, G. S., Leung, R. E., Mickey, M. R., and Walford, R. L. 1980. Survival and disease patterns in C57B1/6J mice subjected to undernutrition. *Exp. Geront.* 15: 237–258.

Chow, C. K. and Tappel, A. L. 1972. An enzymatic protective mechanism against lipid peroxidation damage to lungs of ozone-exposed rats. *Lipids* 7: 518–524.

Clapp, N. K., Satterfield, L. C., and Bowles, N. D. 1979. Effects of the antioxidant butylated hydroxytoluene (BHT) on mortality in BALB/c mice. *J. Gerontol.* 34: 497–501.

Clemens, J. A., Amenomori, Y., Jenkins, T., and Meites, J. 1969. Effects of hypothalamic stimulation, hormones, and drugs on ovarian function in old female rats (34260). *Proc. Soc. Exp. Biol. Med.,* 132: 561–563.

Cohen, H. M. 1973. Fatigue caused by vitamin E? *Calif. Med.,* 119, 72.

Cohen, S. and Ditman, K. S. 1974. Gerovital H3 in the treatment of the depressed aging patient. *Psychosomatics* 15: 15–19.

Comfort, A., Youhotsky-Gore, I., and Pathmanathan, K. 1971. Effect of ethoxyquin on the longevity of C3H mice. Nature 229: 254–255.

Costas, R., Jr., Garcia-Palmieri, M. R., Nazario, E., and Sorlie, P. D. 1978. Relation of lipids, weight and physical activity to incidence of coronary heart disease: the Puerto Rico heart study. *Am. J. Cardiology* 42: 653–658.

Cotzias, G. C., Miller, S. T., Nicholson, A. R., Jr., Maston, W. H., and Tang, L. C. 1974. Prolongation of the life span in mice adapted to large amounts of L-dopa. *Proc. Nat. Acad. Sci. USA* 71: 2466–2469.

Cotzias, G. C., Miller, S. T., Tang, L. C., and Papa-

vasiliou, P. S. 1977. Levodopa, fertility and longevity. *Science* 196: 549–551.

Csallany, A. S., Ayaz, L. K., and Su, L. 1977. Effect of dietary vitamin E and aging on tissue lipofuscin pigment concentration in mice. *J. Nutr.* 107: 1792–1799.

Daniel, C. W. and Young, L. J. T. 1971. Influence of cell division on an aging process. Life span of mouse mammary epithelium during serial propagation *in vivo. Exp. Cell Res.* 65: 27–32.

Davies, J. E. W., Ellery, P. M., and Hughes, R. E. 1977. Dietary ascorbic acid and life span of guinea-pigs. *Exp. Geront.* 12: 215–216.

Delay, J., Thuillier, J., Pichot, P., Lemperiere, T., and Brion, M. S. 1960. Premiers resultats en clinique psychiatrique du para-chlorophenoxy-acetate de dimethylaminoethyle (A.N.P. 235). *Ann. Med. Psych.* 118: 133–144.

Denckla, W. D. 1974. Role of the pituitary and thyroid glands in the decline of minimal O_2 consumption with age. *J. Clin. Invest.* 53: 572–581.

Deyl, Z., Juricova, M., and Stuchlikova, E. 1975. The effect of nutritional regimes upon collagen concentration and survival of rats. *Adv. Exp. Med. Biol.* 53: 359–369.

Dilman, V. M. and Anisimov, V. N. 1980. Effect of treatment with phenformin, diphenylhydantoin or L-dopa on life span and tumor incidence in C3H/Sn mice. *Gerontology* 26: 241–246.

Dourat, A. and Gershon, D. 1981. Rat lens superoxide dismutase and glucose-6-phosphate dehydrogenase: studies of the catalytic activity and the fate of enzyme antigen as a function of age. *Exp. Eye Res.* 33: 655–661.

Drori, D. and Folman, Y. 1976. Environmental effects on longevity in the male rat: exercise, mating, castration and restricted feeding. *Exp. Geront.* 11: 25–32.

Duchesne, J., Gilles, R., and Mosora, F. 1975. Effet de substances anti-oxidantes sur le taux de radicaux libres organiques naturellement présents dans le diaphragme du rat. C. R. Acad. Sc. Paris 281: 945–947.

Duncan, M. R., Dell'orco, R. T., and Kirk, K. D. 1979. Superoxide dismutase specific activity in cultured human diploid cells of various donor ages. *J. Cell Physiol.* 98: 437–442.

Edington, D. W., Cosmas, A. C., and McCafferty, W. B. 1972. Exercise and longevity: evidence for a threshold age. *J. Gerontol.* 27: 341–343.

Egami, N. 1980. Environment and aging: an approach to the analysis of aging mechanisms using poikilothermic vertebrates. *Adv. Exp. Med. Biol.* 129: 249–259.

Enesco, H. E. and Verdone-Smith, C. 1980. alpha-Tocopherol increases lifespan in the rotifer *Philodina. Exp. Geront.* 15: 335–338.

Enstrom, J. E. and Pauling, L. 1982. Mortality among health-conscious elderly Californians. *Proc. Nat. Acad. Sci USA* 79: 6023–6027.

Epstein, J., Himmelhoch, S., and Gershon, D. 1972. Studies on ageing in nematodes. III: Electronmicroscopical studies on age-associated cellular damage. *Mech. Ageing Dev.* 1: 245–255.

Evans, H. M. and Bishop, K. S. 1922. On the relation between fertility and nutrition. II. The ovulation rhythm in the rat on inadequate nutritional regimes. *J. Metab. Res.* 1: 335–356.

Everitt, A. V. 1973. The hypothalamic-pituitary control of ageing and age-related pathology. *Exp. Geront.* 8: 265–277.

Everitt, A. V. and Cavanagh, L. M. 1965. The ageing process in hypophysectomized rat. *Gerontologia* 11: 198–207.

Everitt, A. V. and Porter, B. 1976. Nutrition and aging. *In*, A. V. Everitt and J. A. Burgess (eds.), *Hypothalamus, Pituitary and Aging*, p. 570. Springfield, Ill.: Charles C. Thomas.

Everitt, A. V., Seedsman, N. J., and Jones, F. 1980. The effects of hypophysectomy and continuous food restriction, begun at ages 70 and 400 days, on collagen aging, proteinuria, incidence of pathology and longevity in the male rat. *Mech. Ageing Dev.* 12: 161–172.

Fabris, N., Pierpaoli, W., Sorkin, E. 1972. Lymphocytes, hormones and ageing. *Nature* 240: 557–559.

Fernandes, G., West, A., and Good, R. A. 1979. Nutrition, immunity and cancer—a review. Part III: Effects of diet on the diseases of aging. *Clin. Bull.* 9: 91–106.

Fernandes, G., Yunis, E. J., and Good, R. A. 1976a. Influence of diet on survival of mice. *Proc. Nat. Acad. Sci. USA* 73: 1279–1283.

Fernandes, G., Yunis, E. J., and Good, R. A. 1976b. Suppression of adenocarcinoma by the immunological consequences of calorie restriction. *Nature* 263: 504–506.

Fleming, J. E., Leon, H. A., and Miquel, J. 1981. Effects of ethidium bromide on development and aging of *Drosophila:* implications for the free radical theory of aging. *Exp. Geront.* 16: 287–293.

Fondy, T. P., Karker, K. L., Calcagnino, C., and Emlich, C. A. 1974. Effect of reserpine (NSC-59272)-induced hypothermia on lifespan in mouse L1210 leukemia. *Cancer Chemother. Rep.* 58: 317–332.

Forman, L. J., Sonntag, W. E., Miki, N., and Meites, J. 1980. Maintenance by L-dopa treatment of estrous cycles and LH response to estrogen in aging female rats. *Exp. Ageing Res.* 6: 549–554.

French, C. E., Ingram, R. H., Uram, J. A., Barron, J. P., and Swift, R. W. 1953. The influence of dietary fat and carbohydrate on growth and longevity in rats. *J. Nutr.* 51: 329–339.

Freund, G. 1979. The effects of chronic alcohol and vitamin E consumption on aging pigments and learning performance in mice. *Life Sciences* 24: 145–152.

Fridovich, I. 1975. Superoxide dismutases. *Ann. Rev. Biochem.* 44: 147–159.

Friedman, D. and Globerson, A. 1978a. Immune reactivity during aging. I. T-helper dependent and independent antibody responses to different antigens, *in vivo* and *in vitro. Mech. Ageing Dev.* 7: 289–298.

Friedman, D. and Globerson, A. 1978b. Immune reactivity during aging. II. Analysis of the cellular mechanisms involved in the deficient antibody response in old mice. *Mech. Ageing Dev.* 7: 299–307.

Friedman, E., Keiser, V., and Globerson, A. 1974. Reactivation of immunocompetence in spleen cells of aged mice. *Nature* 251: 545–547.

Fries, J. F. 1980. Aging, natural death, and the compression of morbidity. *New Engl. J. Med.* 303: 130–135.

Fuller, R. W. and Roush, B. W. 1977. Procaine hydrochloride as a monoamine oxidase inhibitor: implications for geriatic therapy. *J. Am. Geriat. Soc.* 25: 90–93.

Gerbase-Delima, M., Liu, R. K., Cheney, K. E., Mickey, R., and Walford, R. L. 1975. Immune function and survival in a long-lived strain subjected to undernutrition. *Gerontologia* 21: 184–202.

Glass, G. A. and Gershon, D. 1981. Enzymatic changes in rat erythrocytes with increasing cell and donor age: loss of superoxide dismutase activity associated with increases in catalytically defective forms. *Biochem. Biophys. Res. Comm.* 103: 1245–1253.

Glass, G. A., Lavie, L., Dourat, A., Shpund, S., and Gershon, D. 1982. Further studies on SOD function and properties in different tissues of animals of various ages. *In*, R. A. Greenwald and G. Cohen (eds.), *Oxyradicals and Their Scavenger Systems. II.*, pp. 1–10. New York: Elsevier, North Holland.

Glees, V. P. and induzierter Abbau und Abtransport von Lipofuszin (Eine elektronenmikroskopische Studie). *Arzneim.-Forsch.* 25: 1543–1548.

Goldstein, A. L., Asanuma, Y., Battisto, J. R., Hardy, M. A., Quint, J., and White, A. 1970. Influence of thymosin on cell-mediated and humoral immune responses in normal and in immunologically deficient mice. *J. Immunol.* 104: 359–366.

Goodrick, C. I. 1974. The effects of exercise on longevity and behavior of hybrid mice which differ in coat color. *J. Gerontol.* 29: 129–133.

Green, J., Diplock, A. T., Bunyan, J., McHale, D., and Muthy, I. R. 1967. Vitamin E and stress: I. Dietary unsaturated fatty acid stress and the metabolism of alpha-tocopherol in the rat. *Br. J. Nutr.* 21: 69–101.

Grinna, L. S. 1976. Effect of dietary alpha-tocopherol on liver microsomes and mitochondria of aging rats. *J. Nutr.* 106: 918–929.

Guili, C., Bertoni-Freddari, C., and Pieri, C. 1980. Morphometric studies on synapses of the cerebellar glomerulus: the effect of centrophenoxine treatment in old rats. *Mech. Ageing Dev.* 14: 265–271.

Harman, D. 1956. Aging: a theory based on free radical and radiation chemistry. *J. Gerontol.* 11: 298–300.

Harman, D. 1957. Prolongation of the normal life span by radiation protection chemicals. *J. Gerontol.* 12: 257–263.

Harman, D. 1961. Prolongation of the normal lifespan and inhibition of spontaneous cancer by antioxidants. *J. Gerontol.* 16: 247–254.

Harman, D. 1968. Free radical theory of aging: effect of free radical reaction inhibitors on the mortality rate of male LAF1 mice. *J. Gerontol.* 23: 476–482.

Harman, D. 1971. Free radical theory of aging: effect of the amount and degree of unsaturation of dietary fat on mortality rate. *J. Gerontol.* 26: 451–457.

Harman, D. 1981. The aging process. *Proc. Nat. Acad. Sci. USA* 78: 7124–7128.

Harman, D., Curtis, H. J., and Tilley, J. 1970. Chromosomal aberrations in liver cells of mice fed free radical inhibitors. *J. Gerontol.* 25: 17–19.

Harman, D., Eddy, D. E., and Noffsinger, J. 1976. Free radical theory of aging: inhibition of amyloidosis in mice by antioxidants; possible mechanism. *J. Am. Geriat. Soc.* 24: 203–210.

Harman, D., Heindrick, M. L., and Eddy, D. E. 1977. Free radical theory of aging: effect of free-radical-reaction inhibitors on the immune response. *J. Am. Geriat. Soc.* 25: 400–407.

Harrison, D. E. 1973. Normal production of erythrocytes by mouse marrow continuous for 73 months. *Proc. Nat. Acad. Sci. USA* 11: 3184–3188.

Hartley, P. H. and Llewellyn, G. F. 1939. The longevity of oarsmen. A study of those who rowed in the Oxford and Cambridge boat race from 1829–1928. *Br. Med. J.* 1: 657–662.

Hasan, M., Glees, P., and Spoerri, P. E. 1974a. Dissolution and removal of neuronal lipofuscin following dimethylaminoethyl *p*-chlorophenoxyacetate administration to guinea pigs. *Cell Tissue Res.* 150: 369–375.

Hasan, M., Glees, P., and El-Ghazzawi, E. 1974b. Age-associated changes in the hypothalamus of the guinea pig: effect of dimethylaminoethyl *p*-chlorophenoxyacetate. An electronmicroscopic and histochemical study. *Exp. Geront.* 9: 153–159.

Hauswirth, J. W. and Nair, P. P. 1972. Some aspects of vitamin E in the expression of biological information. Ann. N. Y. Acad. Sci. 203: 111–122.

Hayflick, L. and Moorhead, P. S. 1961. The serial cultivation of human diploid cell strains. *Exp. Cell Res.* 25: 585–621.

Herlihy, J. T. and Yu, B. P. 1980. Dietary manipulation of age-related decline in vascular smooth muscle function. *Am. J. Physiol.* 238 (Heart Circ. Physiol. 7),H652–H655.

Hildemann, W. H., 1957. Scale homotransplantation in goldfish (*Carassius auratus*). *Ann. N.Y. Acad. Sci.* 64: 775–791.

Hirokawa, K., Albright, J. W., and Makinodan, T. 1976. Restoration of impaired immune functions in aging animals: I. Effect of syngeneic thymus and bone marrow grafts. *Clin. Immun. Immunopath.* 5: 371–376.

Hochschild, R. 1971. Effect of membrane stabilizing drugs on mortality in *Drosophila melanogaster*. *Exp. Geront.* 6: 133–151.

Hochschild, R. 1973a. Effect of dimethylaminoethyl *p*-chlorophenoxyacetate on the lifespan of male Swiss Webster albino mice. *Exp. Geront.* 8: 177–183.

Hochschild, R. 1973b. Effect of dimethylaminoethanol on the lifespan of senile male A/J mice. *Exp. Geront.* 8: 185–191.

Hodgson, J. L. and Buskirk, E. R. 1977. Physical fitness and age, with emphasis on cardiovascular function in the elderly. *J. Am. Geriat. Soc.* 25: 358–392.

Horn, P. L., Laver, J. J., Fogerty, A. C., and Johnson, A. R. 1979. Effects of life-span feeding of ruminant-derived human diets to rats. *J. Nutr.* 109: 1234–1243.

Houillon, M. M., Salles, Y. and Selin, A. R. 1963. Considerations sur l'emploi de la centrophenoxine en cure hospitaliere et ambulatoire. *Ann. Med. Psych.* 121(2): 63–69.

Hruza, Z. and Fabry, P. 1957. Some metabolic and endocrine changes due to long lasting caloric undernutrition. *Gerontologia* 1: 279–287.

Hruza, Z. and Hlavackova, V. 1969. Effect of environmental temperature and undernutrition on collagen aging. *Exp. Gerontol.,* 4: 169–175.

Hurvitz, A. L. 1979. Neoplasia in C57B1/6, DBA/2 and B6D2F1 hybrids. *In,* D. C. Gibson, R. C. Adelman, and C. E. Finch (eds.), *Development of the Rodent as a Model System of Aging,* DHEW Pub. NIH-79-161.

Janoff, A. S. and Rosenberg, B. 1978. Chemically evoked hypothermia in the mouse: towards a method for investigating thermodynamic parameters of aging and death in mammals. *Mech. Ageing Dev.* 3: 335–349.

Joenje, H., Frants, R. R., Arwert, F., and Eriksson, A.

W. 1978. Specific activity of human erythrocyte superoxide dismutase as a function of donor age. A brief note. *Mech. Ageing Dev.* 8: 265–267.

Johnson, J. E., Jr., Mehler, W. R., and Miquel, J. 1975. A fine structural study of degenerative changes in the dorsal column nuclei of aging mice. Lack of protection by vitamin E. *J. Gerontol.* 30: 395–411.

Jose, D. G. and Good, R. A. 1971. Absence of enhancing antibody in cell mediated immunity to tumor heterografts in protein deficient rats. *Nature* 231 323–325.

Joseph, C. Chassan, J. B., and Koch, M. 1978. Levodopa in Parkinson's disease: A long-term appraisal of mortality. *Ann. Neurol.* 3: 116–118.

Kannel, W. B. 1983. Hypertension and aging. *In,* C. Finch and E. L. Schneider (eds.), *Handbook of the Biology of Aging,* pp.   –   . New York: Van Nostrand Reinhold.

Kannel, W. B. and Sorlie, P. 1979. Some health benefits of physical activity. The Framingham study. *Arch. Int. Med.* 139: 857–861.

Kannel, W. B., Sorlie, P., and McNamara, P. 1970. The relation of physical activity to risk of coronary heart disease: the Framingham study. *In,* O. A. Larsen and R. O. Malmburg (eds.), Coronary Heart Disease and Physical Fitness (Proceedings of a Symposium held in Copenhagen, Sept. 2–5, 1970), pp. 256–260. Copenhagen: Munksgaard.

Karvonen, M. J., Klemola, H., Virkajarvi, J., and Kekkonen, A. 1974. Longevity of endurance skiers. *Med. Science Sports* 6: 49–51.

Kayser, C. 1961. *The Physiology of Natural Hibernation,* p. 299. New York: Pergamon Press.

Kellogg, E. W., III, and Fridovich, I. 1976. Superoxide dismutase in the rat and mouse as a function of age and longevity. *J. Gerontol.* 31: 405–408.

Kohn, R. R. 1971. Effect of antioxidants on life-span of C5781 mice. *J. Gerontol.* 26: 378–380.

Kovar, M. G. 1977. Elderly people: the population 65 years and over. *In, Health, United States, 1976–1977.* DHEW Publication No. (HRA) 77-1232. Hyattsville, Md.: National Center for Health Statistics.

Krieger, D. T., Perlow, M. J., Gibson, M. J., Davies, T. F., Zimmerman, E. A., Ferin, M., and Charlton, H. M. 1982. Brain grafts reverse hypogonadism of gonadotropin releasing hormone deficiency. *Nature* 298: 468–471.

Kysela, S. and Steinberg, A. D. 1973. Increased survival of NZB/W mice given multiple syngeneic young thymus grafts. *Clin. Immun. Immunopath.* 2: 133–136.

Lakatta, E. G. 1979. Alterations in the cardiovascular system that occur with advanced age. *Fed. Proc.* 38: 163–167.

Lakatta, E. G. 1984. Heart and circulation. *In,* C. E. Finch and E. L. Schneider (eds.), *The Handbook of the Biology of Aging,* pp. 377–413. New York: Van Nostrand Reinhold.

Leaf, A. 1982. Long-lived populations: extreme old age. *J. Am. Geriat. Soc.* 30: 485–487.

Leaf, A. and Lannois, J. 1973. Search for the oldest people. *Nat. Geographic* 143: 93–119.

Ledvina, M. and Hodanova, M. 1980. The effect of simultaneous administration of tocopherol and sunflower oil on the life-span of female mice. *Exp. Geront.* 15: 67–71.

Leibovitz, B. E. and Siegel, B. V. 1980. Aspects of free radical reactions in biological systems: aging. J. Gerontol. 35: 45–56.

Leto, S., Kokkonen, G. C., and Barrows, C. H., Jr. 1976. Dietary protein, life-span and physiological variables in female mice. *J. Gerontol.* 31: 149–154.

Liepa, G. U., Masoro, E. J., Bertrand, H. A., and Yu, B. P. 1980. Food restriction as a modulator of age-related changes in serum lipids. *Am. J. Physiol.* 238 (Endocrinol. Metab. 1),E253–E257.

Lints, F. A. 1971. Life span in Drosophila. *Gerontologia,* 17: 33–51.

Lints, F. A. and Lints, C. V. 1971. Relationship between growth and ageing in Drosophila. *Nature N.B.* 229: 86–87.

Lippman, R. D. 1980. Chemiluminescent measurement of free radicals and antioxidant molecular protection inside living rat-mitochondria. *Exp. Geront.* 15: 339–351.

Lippman, R. D. 1981. The prolongation of life: A comparison of antioxidants and geroprotectors versus superoxide in human mitochondria. *J. Gerontol.* 36: 550–557.

Liu, R. K. and Walford, R. L. 1966. Increased growth and life-span with lowered ambient temperature in the annual fish Cynolebias adloffi. *Nature* 212: 1277–1278.

Liu, R. K. and Walford, R. L. 1970. Observations on the lifespans of several species of annual fishes and of the world's smallest fishes. *Exp. Geront.* 5: 241–246.

Liu, R. K. and Walford, R. L. 1972. The effect of lowered body temperature on lifespan and immune and non-immune processes. *Gerontologia* 18: 363–388.

Liu, R. K. and Walford, R. L. 1975. Mid-life temperature transfer effects on life-span of annual fish. *J. Gerontol.* 30: 129–131.

Lucy, J. A. 1972. Functional and structural aspects of biological membranes: a suggested role for vitamin E in the control of membrane permeability and stability. *Ann. N.Y. Acad. Sci.* 203: 4–11.

MacFarlane, M. D. 1975. Procaine HCl (Gerovital-H₃): a weak, reversible, fully competitive inhibitor of monoamine oxidase. *Fed. Proc.* 34: 108–110.

MacFarlane, M. D. and Bresbis, H. 1974. Procaine (Gerovital H₃) therapy: mechanism of inhibition of monoamine oxidase. *J. Am. Geriat. Soc.* 22: 365–371.

Makinodan, T. 1979. Control of immunologic abnormalities associated with aging. *Mech. Ageing Dev.* 9: 7–17.

Makinodan, T. and Albright, J. W. 1979. Restoration of impaired immune functions in aging animals. II. Effect of mercaptoethanol in enhancing the reduced primary antibody responsiveness *in vitro. Mech. Ageing Dev.* 10: 325–340.

March, B. E., Wong, E., Seier, L., Sim, J., and Biely, J. 1973. Hypervitaminosis E in the chick. *J. Nutr.* 103: 371–377.

Marttila, R. J., Rinne, U. K., Siirtola, T., and Sonninen, V. 1977. Mortality of patients with Parkinson's disease treated with levodopa. *J. Neurol.* 216: 147–153.

Masoro, E. J., Yu, B. P., Bertrand, H. A., and Lynd, F. T. 1980. Nutritional probe of the aging process. *Fed. Proc.* 39: 3178–3182.

Massie, H. R., Aiello, V. R., and Iodice, A. A. 1979. Changes with age in copper and superoxide dismutase levels in brains of C57B1/6J mice. *Mech. Ageing Dev.* 10: 93–99.

Massie, H. R., Aiello, V. R., and Williams, T. R. 1980. Changes in superoxide dismutase activity and copper during development and ageing in the fruit fly Drosophila melanogaster. *Mech. Ageing Dev.* 12: 279–286.

Massie, H. R. and Williams, T. R. 1978. Invariance of longevity for Drosophila fed N,N¹-diethylhydroxylamine. *Toxicology* 10: 203–204.

Massie, H. R. and Williams, T. R. 1979. Increased longevity of Drosophila melanogaster with lactic and gluconic acids. *Exp. Geront.* 14: 109–115.

Matkovics, B., Lakatos, L., Szabo, L., and Karmazsin, L. 1981. Effects of D-penicillamine on some oxidative enzymes of rat organs *in vivo. Experientia* 37: 79–80.

Maynard Smith, J. 1962. Review lectures on senescence: I. The causes of ageing. *Proc. Roy. Soc. Br.* 157: 115–127.

Mazess, R. B. and Forman, S. H. 1979. Longevity and age exaggeration in Vilcabamba, Ecuador. *J. Gerontol.* 34: 94–98.

McCay, C. M., Crowell, M. F., and Maynard, L. A. 1935. The effect of retarded growth upon the length of life span and upon the ultimate body size. *J. Nutr.* 10: 63–79.

McCay, C. M., Maynard, L. A., Sperling, G., and Barnes, L. L. 1939. Retarded growth, life span, ultimate body size and age changes in the albino rat after feeding diets restricted in calories. *J. Nutr.* 18: 1–13.

McCay, C. M., Sperling, G., and Barnes, L. L. 1943. Growth, ageing, chronic diseases and life span in rats. *Arch. Biochem.* 2: 469–479.

McCord, J. M. and Fridovich, I. 1969. Superoxide dismutase. an enzymatic function for erythrocuprein (hemocuprein). *J. Biol. Chem.* 244: 6049–6055.

Medvedev, Z. A. 1974. Caucasus and Altay longevity: a biological or social problem? *Gerontologist* 14: 381–387.

Meites, J., Simpkins, J. W., and Huang, H. H. 1979. The relation of hypothalamic biogenic amines to secretion of gonadotropins and prolactin in the aging rat. *In,* A. Cherkin *et al.* (eds.), *Physiology and Cell Biology of Aging (Aging, Volume 8),* pp. 87–94. New York: Raven Press.

Migeon, C. J., Keller, A. R., Lawrence, B. and Shepard, T. H. 1957. Dehydroepiandrosterone and androsterone levels in human plasma. Effect of age and sex, day-to-day and diurnal variations. *J. Clin. Endocrinol. Metab.,* 7: 1051–1062.

Miller, D. S. and Payne, P. R. 1968. Longevity and protein intake. *Exp. Geront.* 3: 231–234.

Miller, E. 1974. Deanol in the treatment of levodopa-induced dyskinesias. *Neurology* 24: 116–119.

Miquel, J., Binnard, R., and Howard, W. H. 1973. Effects of DL-alpha-tocopherol on the lifespan of Drosophila melanogaster. *Gerontologist* 3: 37.

Miquel, J. and Economos, A. C. 1979. Favorable effects of the antioxidants sodium and magnesium thiazolidine carboxylate on the viability and life span of Drosophila and mice. *Exp. Geront.* 14: 279–285.

Miquel, J., Lundgren, P. R., Bensch, K. G., and Atlan, H. 1976. Effects of temperature on the life span, vitality and fine structure of Drosophila melanogaster. *Mech. Ageing Dev.* 5: 347–370.

Monagle, D. R. 1968. Aging of the human inferior olive. Ph.D. thesis. State Univ. of New York.

Monagle, D. R. and Brody, H. 1974. The effects of age upon the main nucleus of the inferior olive in the human. *J. Comp. Neurol.,* 155: 61–66.

Mondon, C. E., Dolkas, C. B., and Reaven, G. M. 1980. Site of enhanced insulin sensitivity in exercise-trained rats at rest. *Am. J. Physiol.* 239: (Endocrin. Metab. 2), E169–E177.

Montoye, H. J., Van Huss, W. D., Olson, H., Hudec, A., and Mahoney, E. 1956. Study of the longevity and morbidity of college athletes. *J.A.M.A.* 162: 1132–1134.

Morin, R. J. 1967. Longevity, hepatic lipid peroxidation and hepatic fatty acid composition of mice fed saturated or unsaturated fat-supplemented diets. *Experientia* 23: 1003–1004.

Mulinos, M. G. and Pomerantz, L. 1940. Pseudo-hypophysectomy. A condition resembling hypophysectomy produced by malnutrition. *J. Nutr.* 19: 493–504.

Munkres, K. D. and Colvin, H. J. 1976. Ageing of *Neurospora crassa:* II. Organic hydroperoxide toxicity and the protective role of antioxidants and the antioxygenic enzymes. *Mech. Ageing Dev.* 5: 99–107.

Munkres, K. D. and Minssen, M. 1976. Ageing of *Neurospora crassa:* I. Evidence for the free radical theory of ageing from studies of a natural-death mutant. *Mech. Ageing Dev.* 5: 79–98.

Nair, P. P. 1972. Vitamin E and metabolic regulation. *Ann. N.Y. Acad. Sci.* 203:53–61.

Nakagawa, I., Sasaki, A., Kajimoto, M., Fukuyama, T., Suzuki, T., and Yamada, E. 1974. Effect of protein nutrition on growth, longevity and incidence of lesions in the rat. *J. Nutr.* 104: 1576–1583.

Nandy, K. 1968. Further studies on the effects of centrophenoxine on the lipofuscin pigment in the neurons of senile guinea pigs. *J. Gerontol.* 23: 82–92.

Nandy, K. 1978a. Lipofuscinogenesis in mice early treated with centrophenoxine. *Mech. Ageing Dev.* 8: 131–138.

Nandy, K. 1978b. Centrophenoxine: effects on aging mammalian brain. *J. Am. Geriat. Soc.* 26: 74–81.

Nandy, K., Baste, C., and Schneider, F. H. 1978. Further studies on the effects of centrophenoxine on lipofuscin pigment in neuroblastoma cells in culture. An electron microscopic study. *Exp. Geront.* 13: 311–322.

Nandy, K. and Bourne, G. H. 1966. Effect of centrophenoxine on the lipofuscin pigments in the neurones of senile guinea-pigs. *Nature* 210: 313–314.

Nisbett, R. E. 1972. Hunger, obesity, and the ventromedial hypothalamus. *Psychol. Rev.* 79: 433–453.

Nohl, H. and Hegner, D. 1978. Do mitochondria produce oxygen radicals *in vivo? Eur. J. Biochem.,* 82, 563–567.

Nolen, G. A. 1972. Effect of various restricted dietary regimens on the growth, health and longevity of albino rats. *J. Nutr.* 102: 1477–1494.

Nordenson, I. 1977a. Effect of superoxide dismutase and catalase on spontaneously occurring chromosome breaks in patients with Fanconi's anemia. *Hereditas* 86: 147–150.

Nordenson, I. 1977b. Chromosome breaks in Werner's syndrome and their prevention *in vitro* by radical-scavenging enzymes. *Hereditas* 87: 151–154.

Oeriu, S. and Vochitu, E. 1965. The effect of the administration of compounds which contain sulfhy-dryl groups on the survival of mice, rats and guinea pigs. *J. Gerontol.* 20: 417–419.

Olsen, E. J., Bank, L., and Jarvik, L. F. 1978. Gerovital-H₃: a clinical trial as an antidepressant. *J. Gerontol.* 33: 514–520.

Olsen, G. G. and Everitt, A. V. 1965. Retardation of the ageing process in collagen fibres from the tail tendon of the old hypophysectomized rat. *Nature* 206: 307–308.

Orentreich, N. 1982. Orentreich Foundation Annual Report.

Osanai, M. 1978. Longevity and body weight loss of silkworm, *Bombyx mori,* varied by different temperature treatments. *Exp. Geront.* 13: 375–388.

Ostfeld, A., Smith, C. M., and Stotsky, B. A. 1977. The systemic use of procaine in the treatment of the elderly: a review. *J. Am. Geriat. Soc.* 25: 1–19.

Packer, L. and Smith, J. R. 1974. Extension of the lifespan of cultured normal human diploid cells by vitamin E. *Proc. Nat. Acad. Sci. USA* 71: 4763–4767.

Packer, L. and Smith, J. R. 1977. Extension of the lifespan of cultured normal human diploid cells by vitamin E. A reevaluation. *Proc. Nat. Acad. Sci. USA* 74: 1640–1641.

Papavasiliou, P. S., Miller, S. T., Thal, L. J., Nerder, L. J., Houlihan, G., Rao, S. N., and Stevens, J. M. 1981. Age-related motor and catecholamine alterations in mice on levodopa supplemented diet. *Life Sciences* 28: 2945–2952.

Perkins, E. H., Makinodan, T., and Seibert, C. 1972. Model approach to immunological rejuvenation of the aged. *Infect. Immun.* 6: 518–524.

Petkau, A. Chelack, W. S., Pleskach, S. D., Meeker, B. E., and Brady, C. M. 1975. Radioprotection of mice by superoxide dismutase. *Biochem. Biophys. Res. Comm.* 65: 886–893.

Pfeiffer, C. C., Jenney, E. H., Gallagher, W., Smith, R. P., Bevan, W., Jr., Killiam, E. K., and Blackmore, W. 1957. Stimulant effect of 2-dimethylaminoethanol—possible precursor of brain acetylcholine. *Science* 126: 610–611.

Pignatti, C., Cocchi, M., and Weiss, H. 1980. Coenzyme Q levels in rat heart of different age. *Biochem. Exp. Biol.* 16: 39–42.

Pinney, D. O., Stephens, D. F., and Pope, L. S. 1972. Lifetime effects of winter supplemental feed level and age of first parturition on range beef cows. *J. Animal Science* 34: 1067–1074.

Plaa, G. L. and Witschi, H. 1976. Chemicals, drugs and lipid peroxidation. *Ann. Rev. Pharm.* 16: 125–141.

Plowman, S. A., Drinkwater, B. L., and Harvath, S. M. 1979. Age and aerobic power in women: a longitudinal study. *J. Gerontol.* 34: 512–520.

Polednak, A. P. and Damon, A. 1970. College athletics, longevity and cause of death. *Human Bio.* 42: 28–46.

Porta, E. A., Joun, N. S., and Nitta, R. T. 1980a. Effects of the type of dietary fat at two levels of vitamin E in Wistar male rats during development and aging. I. Life span, serum biochemical parameters and pathological changes. *Mech. Ageing Dev.* 13: 1–39.

Porta, E. A., Nitta, R. T., Kia, L., Joun, N. S., and Nguyen, L. 1980b. Effects of the type of dietary fat at two levels of vitamin E in Wistar male rats during development and aging. II. Biochemical and morphometric parameters of the brain. *Mech. Aging Dev.* 13: 319–355.

Pradhan, S. N. 1980. Minireview. Central neurotransmitters and aging. *Life Sciences* 26: 1643–1656.

Pryor, W. A. 1973. Free radical reaction and their importance in biochemical systems. *Fed. Proc.* 32: 1862–1869.

Pryor, W. A. 1978. The formation of free radicals and the consequences of their reactions *in vivo*. *Photochem. Photobiol.* 28: 787–801.

Quadri, S. K., Kledzik, G. S., and Meites, J. 1973. Reinitiation of estrous cycles in old constant estrous rats by central-acting drugs. *Neuroendocrinology* 11: 248–255.

Reaven, E. P. and Reaven, G. M. 1981b. Structure and function changes in the endrocrine pancreas of aging rats with reference to the modulating effects of exercise and caloric restriction. *J. Clin. Invest.* 68: 75–84.

Reaven, G. M. and Reaven, E. P. 1981a. Prevention of age-related hypertriglyceridemia by caloric restriction and exercise training in the rat. *Metabolism* 30: 982–986.

Reff, M. E. and Schneider, E. L. 1982. *Biological Markers of Aging*, U.S. Health and Human Services Publication No. 82-2221, Washington, D.C.

Reiss, U. and Gershon, D. 1976a. Rat-liver superoxide dismutase, purification and age-related modifications. *Eur. J. Biochem.* 63: 617–623.

Reiss, U. and Gershon, D. 1976b. Comparison of cytoplasmic superoxide dismutase in liver, heart and brain of aging rats and mice. *Biochem. Biophys. Res. Comm.* 73: 255–261.

Retzlaff, E., Fontaine, J., and Furuta, W. 1966. Effect of daily exercise on life-span of albino rats. *Geriatrics* 21: 171–177.

Riga, S. and Riga, D. 1974. Effects of centrophenoxine on the lipofuscin pigments in the nervous system of old rats. *Brain Res.* 72: 265–275.

Rinne, U. K., Sonninen, V., and Siirtola, T. 1972. Treatment of Parkinson's disease with L-DOPA and a decarboxylase inhibitor. *J. Neurol.* 202:1–20.

Rockstein, M., Chesky, J. A., and Lopez, T. 1981. Effects of exercise on the biochemical aging of mammalian myocardium. I. Actomyosin ATPase. *J. Gerontol.* 36: 294–297.

Rodemann, Von H. P. and Bayreuther, K. 1979. Verlangerung der mitotischen Lebensspanne menschlicher Glia-Zellen in einen quantitativen Zellkultursysten durch centrophenoxin. *Arzneim.-Forsch.* 29: 124–129.

Rogers, J. and Bloom, F. E. 1983. Neurotransmitter metabolism and function in te aging central nervous system. *In*, C. E. Finch and E. L. Schneider (eds.), *Handbook of the Biology of Aging*, pp. 645–691. New York: Van Nostrand Reinhold.

Rook, A. 1954. An investigation into the longevity of Cambridge sportsmen. *Br. Med. J.* 1: 773–777.

Rose, C. L. and Cohen, M. L. 1977. Relative importance of physical activity for longevity. *Ann. N.Y. Acad. Sci.* 31: 671–697.

Ross, M. H. 1972. Length of life and caloric intake. *Am. J. Clin. Nutr.* 25: 834–838.

Ross, M. H. and Bras, G. 1965. Tumor incidence patterns and nutrition in the rat. *J. Nutr.* 87: 245–260.

Ross, M. H. and Bras, G. 1971. Lasting influence of early caloric restriction on prevalence of neoplasms in the rat. *J. Natl. Cancer Inst.* 47: 1095–1113.

Ross, M. H. and Bras, G. 1973. Influence of protein under- and overnutrition on spontaneous tumor prevalence in the rat. *J. Nutr.* 103: 944–963.

Ross, M. H. and Bras, G. 1975. Food preference and length of life. *Science* 190: 165–167.

Ross, M. H., Bras, G., and Ragbeer, M. S. 1970. Influence of protein and caloric intake upon spontaneous tumor incidence of the anterior pituitary gland of the rat. *J. Nutr.* 100: 177–189.

Sacher, G. A. 1977. Life table modification and life prolongation. *In*, C. E. Finch and L. Hayflick (eds.), *Handbook of the Biology of Aging*, pp. 582–628. New York: Van Nostrand Reinhold.

Sakagami, H. and Yamada, M. 1977. Failure of vitamin E to extend the life span of a human diploid cell line in culture. *Cell Struct. Function* 2: 219–227.

Sakalis, G., Oh, D., Gershon, S., and Shopsin, B. 1974. A trial of Gerovital in depression during senility. *Curr. Therap. Res.* 16: 59–63.

Samorajski, T. and Rolsten, C. 1976. Chlorpromazine and aging in the brain. *Exp. Geront.* 11: 141–147.

Sapadnjuk, W. I., Kuprasch, L. P., Strishowa-Salowa, N. I., Saika, M. U., Fenshin, K. M. and Oranskaja, S. A. 1974. Der pharmakodymamische Effekt komplexer polyvitaminpraparate bei alten Tieren. *Z. Alternsforsch.* 28: 211–214.

Saxton, J. A., Sperling, G. A., Barnes, L. L., and McCay, C. M. 1948. The influence of nutrition upon the incidence of spontaneous tumors of the albino rat. *Acta Int. Canc.* 6: 423–430.

Schmid, P. and Schlick, W. 1979. Influence of centrophenoxine administered for one year in high dose on maximal oxygen consumption in aged persons. *Akt. Gerontol.* 9: 125–131.

Schneider, E. L. and Brody, J. 1983. Aging, natural death and the compression of morbidity: another view. *N.E.J.M.* 309:854–856.

Schnohr, P. 1971. Longevity and causes of death in male athletic champions. *Lancet* 11: 1364–1366.

Schwartz, A. G. 1979. Inhibition of spontaneous breast cancer formation in female C3H (A^{vy}/a) mice by long-term treatment with dehydroepiandrosterone. *Cancer Res.,* 39, 1129–1132.

Scott, M. L., Noguchi, T., and Coombs, G. F., Jr. 1974. New evidence concerning mechanisms of action of vitamin E and selenium. *Vit. Horm.* 32: 429–444.

Segall, P. E. and Timiras, P. S. 1975. Age-related changes in thermoregulatory capacity of tryptophan-deficient rats. *Fed. Proc.* 34: 83–85.

Segall, P. E. and Timiras, P. S. 1976. Patho-physiologic findings after chronic tryptophan deficiency in rats: a model for delayed growth and aging. *Mech. Ageing Dev.* 5: 109–124.

Segre, D. and Segre, M. 1977. Age-related changes in B and T lymphocytes and decline of humoral immune responsiveness in aged mice. *Mech. Ageing Dev.* 6: 115–129.

Smith, D. M., Khairi, M. R. A., Norton, J., and Johnston, C. C., Jr. 1976. Age and activity effects on rate of bone mineral loss. *J. Clin. Invest.* 58: 716–721.

Smith, E. L., Jr., Reddan, W., and Smith, P. E. 1981. Physical activity and calcium modalities for bone mineral increase in aged women. *Med. Science Sports Exer.* 13: 60–64.

Sohal, R. S. 1981. Relationship between metabolic rate, lipofuscin accumulation and lysomal enzyme activity during aging in the adult housefly, *Musca domestica*. *Exp. Geront.* 16: 347–355.

Sohal, R. S. and Donato, H., Jr. 1979. Effect of experimental prolongation of life span on lipofuscin content and lysosomal enzyme activity in the brain of the housefly, *Musca domestica. J. Gerontol.* 34: 489–496.

Sohnle, P. G. and Gambert, S. R. 1982. Thermoneutrality: an evolutionary advantage against ageing? *Lancet* ii: 1099–1100.

Sonka, J. 1976. Dehydroepiandrosterone metabolic effects. *Acta Univ. Carol.* 71: 1–137, 146–171.

Sorrentino, S. J. R., Reiter, R. J., and Schalch, D. S. 1971. Interactions of the pineal gland, blinding, and underfeeding on reproductive organ size and radioimmunoassayable growth hormone. *Neuroendocrinology* 7: 105–115.

Sperling, G. A., Loosli, J. K., Lupien, P., and McCay, C. M. 1978. Effect of sulfamerazine and exercise on life span of rats and hamsters. *Gerontology* 24: 220–224.

Spoerri, P. E., Glees, P., and El-Ghazzawi, E. 1974. Accumulation of lipofuscin in the myocardium of senile guinea pigs: dissolution and removal of lipofuscin following dimethylaminoethyl *p*-chlorophenoxyacetate administration. An electron microscopic study. *Mech. Ageing Dev.* 3: 311–321.

Stevens, C., Goldblatt, M. J., and Freedman, J. C. 1975. Lack of erythrocyte superoxide dismutase change during human senescence. *Mech. Ageing Dev.* 4: 415–421.

Stoltzner, G. 1977. Effects of life-long dietary protein restriction on mortality, growth, organ weights, blood counts, liver aldolase, and kidney catalase in BALB/c mice. *Growth* 41: 337–348.

Talal, N., Dauphinee, M., Pillarisetty, R., and Goldblum, R. 1975. Effect of thymosin on thymocyte proliferation and autoimmunity in NZB mice. *Ann. N.Y. Acad. Sci.* 249: 438–449.

Tait, N. N. 1969. The effect of temperature on the immune response in cold-blooded vertebrates. *Physiol. Zool.* 42: 29–35.

Tannen, R. H. and Schwartz, A. G. 1982. Reduced weight gain and delay of Coomb's positive hemolytic anemia in NZB mice treated with dehydroepiandrosterone (DHEA). *Fed. Proc.,* 41, 463. Abstract.

Tannenbaum, A. 1940. The initiation and growth of tumors: I. Effects of underfeeding. *Am. J. Cancer* 38: 335–350.

Tannenbaum, A. 1944. The dependence of the genesis of induced skin tumors on the caloric intake during different stages of carcinogenesis. *Cancer Res.* 4: 673–677.

Tannenbaum, A. and Silverstone, H. 1949. The influence of the degree of caloric restriction on the formation of skin tumors and hepatomas in mice. *Cancer Res.* 9: 724–727.

Tappel, A. L. 1962. Vitamin E as the biological lipid antioxidant. *Vit. Hormones* 20: 493–510.

Tappel, A. L. 1970. Biological antioxidant protection against lipid peroxidation damage. *Am. J. Clin. Nutr.* 23: 1137–1139.

Tappel, A. L. 1972. Vitamin E and free radical peroxidation of lipids. *Ann. N.Y. Acad. Sci.* 203: 12–28.

Tappel, A. L. 1973. Lipid peroxidation damage to cell components. *Fed. Proc.* 32: 1870–1874.

Tappel, A. L. 1978. Protection against free radical lipid peroxidation reactions. *Adv. Exp. Med. Biol.* 97: 111–131.

Tappel, A. L., Fletcher, B., and Deamer, D. 1973. Effect of antioxidants and nutrients on lipid peroxidation fluorescent products and aging parameters in the mouse. *J. Gerontol.* 28: 415–424.

Teague, P. O. and Friou, G. J. 1969. Antinuclear antibodies in mice. II. Transmission with spleen cells; inhibition or prevention with thymus or spleen cells. *Immunology* 17: 665–675.

Theuer, R. C. 1971. Effect of essential amino acid restriction on the growth of female C57B1 mice and their implanted BW10232 adenocarcinomas. *J. Nutr.* 101: 223–232.

Thuillier, G., Rumpe, P., and Thuillier, J. 1959. Preparation et etude pharmacologique preliminaire des esters dimethylaminoethyliques de divers acides agissant comme regulateurs de croissance des vegetaux. *C.R. Acad. Sci.* (Paris), 249: 2081–2083.

Tolmasoff, J. M., Ono, T., and Cutler, R. G. 1980. Superoxide dismutase: correlation with life-span and specific metabolic rate in primate species. *Proc. Nat. Acad. Sci. USA* 77: 2777–2781.

Tomanek, R. J., Taunton, C. A., and Liskop, K. S. 1972. Relationship between age, chronic exercise, and connective tissue of the heart. *J. Gerontol.* 27: 33–38.

Totaro, E. A. and Pisanti, F. A. 1980. Biological bases and prospects of the lipofuscinolytic activity of meclofenoxate: a study of Torpedo M. neurons. *Acta Neurol.* 35: 79–85.

Toth, S. E. 1968. The origin of lipofuscin age pigments. *Exp. Geront.* 3: 19–30.

Tucker, M. J. 1979. The effect of long-term food restriction on tumors in rodents. *Am. J. Cancer* 23: 803–807.

Verzar, F. 1959. Note on the influence of procaine (Novocain), para-aminobenzoic acid or dimethylethanolamine on the ageing of rats. *Gerontologia* 3: 351–358.

Verzar, F. and Spichtin, H. 1966. The role of the pituitary in the aging of collagen. *Gerontologia* 12: 48–56.

Walford, R. L., Liu, R. K., Gerbase-Delima, M., Mathies, M., and Smith, G. S. 1973–74. Long-term dietary restriction and immune function in mice: response to sheep red blood cells and mitogenic agents. *Mech. Ageing Dev.* 2: 447–454.

Walford, R. L., Meredith, P. J., and Cheney, K. E. 1977. Immunoengineering: prospects for correction of age-related immunodeficiency states. *In,* T. Makinodan and E. Yunis (eds.), *Immunology and Aging,* pp. 183–201. New York: Plenum Medical Book Co.

Wara, M. D., Goldstein, S. L., Doyle, N. E., and Ammann, A. J. 1975. Thymosin activity in patients with cellular immunodeficiency. *N.E.J.M.* 292: 70–74.

Weindruch, R., Gottesman, S. R. S., and Walford, R. L. 1982. Modification of age-related immune decline in mice dietarily restricted from or after mid-adulthood. *Proc. Nat. Acad. Sci. USA* 79: 898–902.

Weindruch, R. H., Kristie, J. A., Cheney, K. E., and Walford, R. L. 1979. Influence of controlled dietary restriction on immunologic function and aging. *Fed. Proc.* 38: 2007–2016.

Weindruch, R. and Walford, R. L. 1982. Dietary restriction in mice beginning at 1 year of age: effect on life-span and spontaneous cancer incidence. *Science* 215: 1415–1418.

Weksler, M. E., Innes, J. B., and Goldstein, G. 1978.

Immunological studies of aging. IV. The contribution of thymic involution to the immune deficiencies of aging mice and reversal with thymopoietin. *J. Exp. Med.* 148: 996–1006.

Wolman, M. 1980. Lipid pigments (chromolipids): their origin, nature and significance. *Pathobiol. Annual* 10: 253–267.

Yamaji, J. and Ibayashi, H. 1969. Plasma dehydroepiandrosterone sulfate in normal and pathological conditions. *J. Clin. Endocrinol. Metab.,* 29: 273–278.

Yamanaka, N. and Deamer, D. 1974. Superoxide dismutase activity in WI-38 cell cultures: effects of age, trypsinization and SV-40 transformation. *Physiol. Chem. Physics* 6: 95–106.

Yau, T. M. 1974. Gerovital-H3, monoamine oxidases, and brain monoamines. *In,* M. Rockstein, M. L. Sussman, and J. Chesky (eds.), *Theoretical Aspects of Aging,* pp. 157–165. New York: Academic Press.

Young, V. R. 1978. Nutrition and aging. *In,* J. Roberts, R. C. Adelman, an V. J. Cristofalo (eds.), *Phar-*

macological Intervention in the Aging Process, p. 85. New York: Plenum Press.

Yu, B. P., Masoro, E. J., Murata, I., Bertrand, H. A., and Lynd, F. T. 1982. Life span of SPF Fischer 344 male rats fed *ad libitum* or restricted diets: longevity, growth, lean body mass and disease. *J. Gerontol* 37: 130–141.

Zs.-Nagy, I. and Nagy, K. 1980. On the role of crosslinking of cellular proteins in aging. *Mech. Ageing Dev.* 14: 245–251.

Zs.-Nagy, I., Nagy, K., Zs.-Nagy, V., Kalmar, A., and Nagy, E. 1981. Alterations in total content and solubility characteristics of proteins in rat brain and liver during ageing and centrophenoxine treatment. *Exp. Geront.* 16: 229–240.

Zung, W. W. K., Gianturco, D., Pfeiffer, E., Wang, H., Whanger, A., Bridge, T. P., and Potkin, S. G. 1974. Pharmacology of depression in the aged: evaluation of Gerovital-H3 as an antidepressant drug. *Psychosomatics* 14: 127–131.

PART 2 AGING IN LOWER SYSTEMS

4
AGING IN UNICELLULAR ORGANISMS

Joan Smith-Sonneborn

Zoology and Physiology Department
University of Wyoming

BACTERIA

Aging can be defined as a species-specific predictable chronological loss of function during the life span of the organism. Physiological dysfunctions which might contribute to loss of vitality can be studied in simple model systems. The fidelity of macromolecular synthesis and degradation is fruitfully investigated using simple life forms. Bacteria exhibit apparent infinite capacity for cell replication under appropriate growth conditions. The loss of function, typical of aging higher (eukaryotic) cells, though not observed in normal bacterial cells, has been found in certain mutants which produce "minicells," or tiny daughter cells which lack a genome, after unequal cell partitioning during division of the parent cell (Reeve, 1979, 1981).

Since cell septation in certain mutant cells occurs abnormally close to one pole of the parent cell, the small cell produced is enucleate or lacks a genome, such enucleated cells cannot direct the synthesis of new enzymes, are nondividing, and eventually deteriorate. Minicells exhibit all the activities of bacterial cells which do not require the direct participation of the DNA template, i.e., intermediary metabolism, motility, active transport, and cell envelope biosynthesis. Such activity is continued for 24–48 hours at 37°C in the minicell, but eventually cell function ceases. The fidelity of protein synthesis in the "aging" minicell can be assayed by the ability of the minicells to produce correct proteins when infected with DNA viruses. Since the DNA of the virus does not age, the ability of the minicell to carry out transcription and translation as a function of minicell age can be determined. Radiochemically labeled viral proteins synthesized in infected minicells are examined for the presence of incorrectly incorporated amino acids. Bacterial viruses whose regulation of gene expression is well characterized, such as lambda T7, can be used to assay the effect of "age" on viral gene expression.

Minicell strains have been genetically constructed to have different physiological composition such as ribosomal defects and the absence of proteases. Minicells can also be used to determine the effect of toxic environments on the rate of "aging" as assayed by proteins produced as a function of age after viral infection. Although the minicell model system cannot be directly extrapolated to aging in multicellular systems, the fidelity of cell function as cell components age can be determined.

PROTOZOA

Introduction

The protozoa exhibit a spectrum of finite life span from days to apparent immortality, i.e., unlimited multiplication of a clone (Sonneborn, 1960). The infinite life span of certain protozoa has been found to be a precarious state subject to conversion to mortality by environmental and genetic changes. A universal aging mechanism is not a prerequisite for relevance of studies of aging in protozoa to man. The similarity, though not identity, of structure and function shared by all eukaryotic cells suggests some commonality in regulatory mechanisms in single celled and multicellular organisms. Regulatory mechanisms involved in cellular aging should be more apparent in single celled than multicelled organisms where tissue-tissue interactions could mask the fundamental processes. The diverse strategies employed by different protozoans to maintain and regulate life processes may be operative in higher organisms in different cell types in the same organism, and/or meshed in unique ways to carry out the same or different biological processes. The varieties of protozoa offer varied eukaryotic models to illuminate regulatory processes which may impinge directly or indirectly on the quality and length of our life. Although unicellularity is a dominant feature among protozoans, multicellular forms occur among ameba, flagellates, and ciliates.

Immortality is a feature of cells or cell types among ameba and flagellates. Ciliates show species-specific life spans ranging from several days in one species of *Paramecium,* or 15 years in another, to infinite life span in another ciliate (Table 1). The diversity in life span may reflect enormous differences in evolutionary time, since single celled organisms which look alike are not necessarily closely related by molecular comparisons. Unicellular organisms show morphological similarity and molecular diversity, in contrast with multicellular organisms which

TABLE 1. Clonal Aging in Ciliates: Life Span Duration.[a]

Organism	LIFE SPAN		References
	Fissions	Days	
Spathidium musciocola	134		Williams (1980)
Euplotes woodruffi (fresh water)	208		Kosaka (1970, 1972, 1974)
Paramecium tetraurelia	244	(40–60)	Sonneborn (1954, 1957); Smith-Sonneborn et al. (1974)
Paramecium biaurelia	286	(162)	Sonneborn (1954, 1957)
Stylonychia pustula	316	(133)	Jennings (1929)
Paramecium primaurelia	340	(120)	Sonneborn (1954, 1957)
Euplotes woodruffi (marine)	339	(181)	Kosaka (1974); Frankel (1973)
Spathidium spathula	658		Williams (1980)
Paramecium caudatum	600–700	(205)	Takagi and Yoshida (1980)
Tokophrya lemnarum (clonal)	800		Colgin-Bukovsan (1979)
Stylonychia mytilus	1000		Lipps et al. (1978)
Oxytricha bifaria		(900)	Siegel (1956)
Euplotes crassus	1000		Heckmann (1967)
Euplotes patella (diploid)	1300	(1900)	Katashima (1961, 1971)
Tetrahymena (inbreeding-induced mortality)	40–1500		Nanney (1957, 1974); Allen (1967)
Paramecium bursaria		2585	Jennings (1944a)
Paramecium multimicronucleatum		5400	Sonneborn (1957)
Tetrahymena thermophila		Immortal	Nanney (1974)

[a]The median life span or range reported in cell divisions or the number of fissions since fertilization (or sporulation in *Spathidium*) until death of representative members of the clone is given. Variation in life span can be expected as a result of strain differences and variations in the methodology of the investigators.

show molecular similarity and morphological diversity. Species of *Tetrahymena,* for example, which are morphologically similar, exhibit from 25 to 33 percent G + C composition (Suyama, 1966) and scarcely show any molecular homologies (Nanney and McCoy, 1976). Also, the similar-looking 14 species in the *P. aurelia* complex are separated by their ability to produce viable hybrids (Sonneborn, 1974) and by enzyme electrophoretic patterns (Tait, 1970; Allen and Gibson, 1971; Allen et al., 1971, 1973). Progressive deterioration of dividing cells and individual cells can occur in a constant external environment (intrinsic aging), or it can be induced by altered culture environment (extrinsic aging).

Clonal Aging

A clone is a multicellular unit derived from a single cell. Clonal aging refers to the decreased probability that a cell will give rise to viable progeny at the next cell division as time increases since the last fertilization (Jennings, 1929; Sonneborn, 1954). In ciliates, fertilization can occur by conjugation (mating), autogamy (self-fertilization), or selfing (mating with a clone). The products of mating (conjugation) or of self-fertilization processes are the cells whose subsequent asexual cell divisions comprise the clone or "multicells" separated in space. The members of the clone pass through developmental periods of immaturity (when cells cannot mate), maturity (when cells can mate), senescence (when the probability that a viable cell will be produced at the next cell division is reduced), and finally death. The different developmental periods are found at a species-specific number of cell divisions postfertilization. A specific cytoplasmic protein, immaturin, represses sexual activity in *Paramecium* (Haga and Hiwatashi, 1981; Miwa et al., 1975).

A prerequisite for clonal aging studies is thorough investigation of the life cycle under consideration. Serious errors have been made. The "*Paramecium* Methuselah" strain, once thought to be immortal (Wood-

ruff, 1932), was later shown to be a succession of clones undergoing autogamy or self-fertilization (Sonneborn, 1954). Without fertilization, the clone undergoes progressive deterioration and death of all members of the clone follows.

In general, the ciliates contain two kinds of nuclei—the micronucleus, or germ line, and the macronucleus, or somatic line. The micronuclei represent a repository of the genetic information for the next generation after fertilization and show little transcriptional activity during the asexual (binary cell division) cycle (Sonneborn, 1946, 1954; Nobili, 1962; Pasternak, 1967; Gorovsky and Woodard, 1969; Murti and Prescott, 1970; Klass, 1974). The micronuclei form gametes which fuse to form the zygote for differentiation of new nuclei in typical ciliate fertilization processes.

During conjugation in the ciliate *Paramecium,* for example, cells come together side by side and eventually exchange nuclear gametes through a temporary transfer organelle. Like the gametic nuclei in higher organisms, the micronuclei undergo meiosis to generate gametes which function during fertilization. In true conjugation, the two members of a mating pair become genetically identical, each with one half from its own duplicated haploid complement and one half from its partner's. The details of the developmental events after fertilization differ with species, but normally the zygote undergoes differentiation of a new micro- and macronucleus for progeny cells. In autogamy, fertilization occurs in a single cell. After meiosis, one haploid gamete is retained and duplicated into two identical gametes which fuse to form a homozygous diploid gamete (for review of ciliate genetics, see Preer, 1968).

If the genotype of the two gametes is denoted "A" and "A" in one mate and "a" and "a" in its partner, then after mutual exchange of gametes both members of the pair become Aa. In autogamy, the two identical gametes fuse in a single cell, yielding either AA or aa from an Aa parent cell; ½ AA and ½ aa progeny result from a population of hybrid parents. After conjugation or autogamy, the zygote nucleus (the synkaryon) divides mitotically twice to form four genotypically identical diploid nuclei. In *Tetrahymena,* one disintegrates, one stays a micronucleus, and the remaining two develop into macronuclei (for review, see Sonneborn, 1977). The position of the synkaryon products within the cell can determine which nuclear differentiation is favored (Nanney, 1953; Sonneborn, 1954a). In the cell division which follows, the micronuclei divide but the macronuclei pass without division to each daughter cell, producing two sister caryonides. (A subclone derived from one of the macronuclei of the fertilized cell is called a caryonide.) Macronuclear development proceeds by several rounds of DNA replication with half or more occurring in the first cell division and the rest in the second to provide a *Paramecium* macronucleus with 800 times the DNA content of the haploid micronucleus. The ancestral macronucleus can function during the development of the new filial macronucleus (Berger, 1973, 1974, 1976). The RNA produced by the ancestral macronucleus represents a maternal cytoplasmic environment reminiscent of the stored RNA in oocyte cytoplasm in higher organisms. If the new macronucleus fails to form, the ancestral macronucleus can persist (*Tetrahymena*), or fragments or the ancestral macronucleus can regenerate (*Paramecium*); these are termed macronuclear retention and regeneration, respectively.

The methodologies used to study clonal aging vary with investigators, but in general, cells after fertilization are placed in growth medium and transferred daily or at regular intervals. The total number of cell divisions (or buds in *Tokophrya*) from the origin of the clone at fertilization to death represents the life span. Daily isolations of several sublines (representatives) of a clone allow observation of the number of cells produced by each single cell ($\log_2$ of that number is the daily fission rate) each day after fertilization. A single cell from a population of cells produced in the previous 24 hours in a subline is reisolated on successive days, and the sum of the fissions per day is the age of the clone. When an isolated cell fails to survive on any day, the sum of the number of cell divisions or days since fertilization represents the life span of that subline. The mean life span is the average clonal age for all sublines in a control or experimental group. Maximal life span is the highest number of cell divisions or days attained by any subline within an experimental or control group.

Clonal aging has been documented in certain species of *Paramecium, Euplotes, Stylonychia, Tokophrya,* and *Spathidium,* and it can be induced by inbreeding in *Tetrahymena* (Williams, 1980; for reviews, see Nanney, 1974; Smith-Sonneborn, 1981).

Cultural Aging

In contrast to the intrinsic clonal aging seen in ciliates, morphological and physiological changes, followed by cell death, can be induced by starvation or "cultural aging." This is distinctly different from naturally occurring aging in a constant environment. Abnormalities are inflicted on cells due to unfavorable environmental conditions rather than sequentially expressed under constant external environmental conditions as in clonal aging (Sonneborn, 1954). When starved, dinoflagellates have been found with fused chromatin in the nucleus (Sousa e Silva, 1977), *Euglena* cytoplasm contained heavily pigmented bodies and membrane fragments (Gomez et al., 1973), *Tetrahymena* cytoplasm was vacuolized and showed increased numbers of mitochondria and lipid droplets (Eliott and Bak, 1964), and *Ochromonas* cytoplasm was characterized by increased lysosome activity, lipid vacuoles, and disorganization (Grusky and Aaronson, 1969). In *Paramecium caudatum,* decrease in digestive vacuoles was concomitant with an increase of lysosomes, autophagosomes, and lipofuscin-like or age-pigment granules (Fok and Allen, 1981).

Variations in temperature, oxygen tension, and the culture age used to inoculate fresh axenic medium, all influenced the bio-chemical, physiological, and ultrastructural relationships (Fok et al., 1981). The ability of some small proportions of cells in early death phase to exclude accumulated wastes and return to a healthy state when trans-ferred to fresh medium is of interest to un-derstanding both (1) the regulation of phagosome-lysosome systems of cells (Fok et al., 1981) and (2) the recovery potential from starvation as a function of clonal age.

Some morphological changes seen in ex-ogenously starved cells mimicked the struc-tural changes seen in aged *Paramecium, Euplotes,* and *Tokophrya* adults. The mor-phological changes in the macronuclei of aged paramecia (Sundararaman and Cum-mings 1976) have also been noted in young starved cells (Heifetz and Smith-Sonneborn, 1981). Aged paramecia, even in the presence of excess food, can show few or no food vac-uoles (Smith-Sonneborn and Rodermel, 1976). Starvation may not be a cause of ag-ing, but it appears to be a proximal cause of death. Autolytic processes, stimulated at the termination of cell life, mimic those of young cells when starved.

Colonial Flagellates

Colonial aging is a loss of function of indi-vidual cell types when the cells are united into a colony. In certain *Volvox* colonies, more than 99 percent of the cells are somatic and undergo synchronous programmed senes-cence and cell death every generation (Hagen and Kochert, 1980). A small number of re-productive cells survive to produce the next generation. The potential reproductive cells are set aside at a particular stage by unequal cell division (Kochert, 1968; Starr, 1969). The electrophoretic pattern of polypeptides changes at the onset of senescent character-istics in somatic cells (Hagen and Kochert, 1980).

In the terminally differentiated somatic cells of the colonial green algae *Volvox car-teria,* they are age-related disorganizations of chloroplast structure, decreases in cyto-plasmic ribosomes, and accumulations of cy-toplasmic lipid bodies. Since these changes are typical of those noted in starved cells, there may be an inability to take up or utilize nutrients which causes or contributes to se-nescence in terminally differentiated somatic cells (Pommerville and Kochert, 1981).

Colonies can be propagated indefinitely by vegetative reproduction in haploid (one rep-resentative of each chromosome) colonial green flagellates. The only diploid (two chro-mosomes of each type and one from each mate) stage in the life cycle is the zygote which, like the spores of bacteria, can re-main dormant and genetically preserved for years. [Similarly, lotus seeds can be germi-nated after prolonged dormancy, docu-mented in one case for 400 years (Priestly and Posthumas, 1982).] Examples of colonial flagelletes are seen in Figure 1.

The colonial flagellates represent the an-tithesis of cellular aging by production of certain cell types which can apparently mul-tiply endlessly with no symptoms of deteri-oration. The colonial green flagellates pro-vide a model system for regulation of cell proliferation potential. Mutants in *Volvox* are available which fail to segregate repli-cating and nonreplicating cells. The array of mutants found suggests that proliferative ca-pacity involves several regulatory genes (Ses-soms and Huskey, 1973).

Amoeba

The apparent immortality of *Amoeba* seen when these cells are grown exponentially is a precarious state. Growth of *Amoeba proteus* or *A. discoides* (see Figure 2) in a mainte-nance diet induces a finite life span, and the "life spanning or aging" phenomenon in the free living protozoa *A. proteus* was reported (Muggleton and Danielli, 1958, 1959). When cells were exposed for 2–9 weeks to a main-tenance diet, they had a defined life span, which varied from 4 to 30 weeks. The cells with defined life span show two major forms of behavior. Type A cells produced one vi-able and one nonviable produce (died within

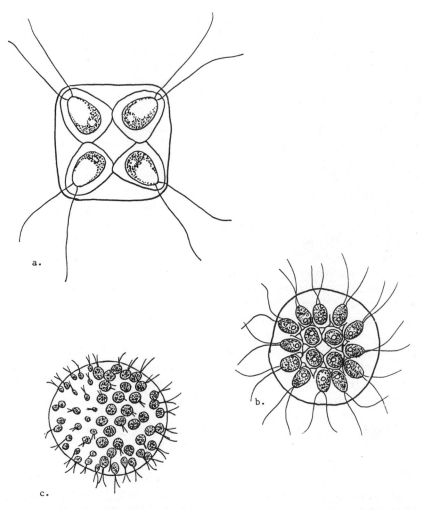

Figure 1. (a) The colonial flagellate *Gonium sociale* and (b) *Gonium pectorale* ($\times 670$). (From Kudo, R. R., *Protozoology,* 5th ed., 1977, p. 343. Courtesy of Charles C. Thomas, Publisher, Springfield, Illinois.) (c) *Pleodorina california.* (From Grell, K. G., *Protozoology,* 1973, p. 160. Courtesy of Springer-Verlag, New York.) Redrawn by C. Nunamaker.

a day or two after cell division) until eventually both daughter cells died. Type B cells produced cells upon division which were equally viable until the time when all cells in the clone died.

Transfer of a normal (immortal) nucleus to cytoplasm of Type A or B cells resulted in all Type B recipients. Transfer of the nucleus from a Type B cell to normal cytoplasm produced Type A cells. Transfer of Type A nucleus to normal cytoplasm produced Type A cells. This behavior suggested that the spanned cytoplasm carried Type B behavior while the spanned nucleus carried the Type A behavior. Therefore, both Type A and Type B cells possess an A nucleus and a B cytoplasm. The Type A nucleus in Type B cells could be expressed only in normal cytoplasm. Injection of "spanned" cytoplasm to normal cells then induced finite life spans in normal cells (Muggleton and Danielli, 1968). Expression of the spanned phenotype (prior transfer of cells exposed to maintenance diet to nutritive food diet) was not a prerequisite for imposition of spanned phenotype on normal cells as shown by nuclear and

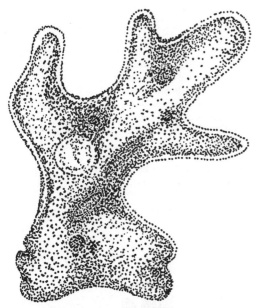

Figure 2. *Amoeba discoides.* (From Kudo, R. R., *Protozoology,* 5th ed., 1977, p. 521. Courtesy of Charles C. Thomas, Publisher, Springfield, Illinois.) Redrawn by C. Nunamaker.

cytoplasmic transfer (Widdus et al., 1978). The results of nuclear and cytoplasmic microsurgical transfers between normal and "spanned" cells indicate that both the nucleus and the cytoplasm contribute to the spanning phenomenon (Muggleton and Danielli, 1968; Muggleton-Harris, 1979).

Paramecium

In the *Paramecium aurelia* complex, the life spans of species 1, 2, and 4 are between 200 and 350 cell divisions, or about 60 days post-fertilization (Sonneborn, 1954; Smith-Sonneborn, 1981). These organisms (Figure 3a) must experience successive fertilizations to escape species extinction by forming continuums of generations. Note the morphological similarity of the different species of *Paramecium* (Figure 3) and the diversity of life span duration (Table 1); i.e., *P. aurelia* complex, 60 days; *P. caudatum,* 200 days; *P. bursaria,* 3000 days; and *P. multimicronucleatum,* 5400 days (Sonneborn, 1957). Age-related changes in *Paramecium* can be seen in Table 2.

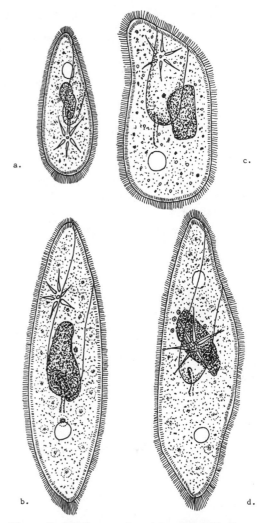

Figure 3. (a) *Paramecium tetraurelia,* (b) *Paramecium caudatum,* (c) *Paramecium bursaria,* and (d) *Paramecium multimicronucleatum.* (From Kudo, R. R., *Protozoology,* 5th ed., 1977, p. 904. Courtesy of Charles C. Thomas, Publisher, Springfield, Illinois.) Redrawn by C. Nunamaker.

The capacity for fertilization to provide fully vigorous rejuvenated offspring declines with increased parental age (Pierson, 1938; Raffel, 1932; Sonneborn and Schneller, 1955; Mitchison, 1955; Smith-Sonneborn et al., 1974; Jennings, 1944a, 1944b, 1944c, 1945). The onset of maturity is shortened in progeny of older parents (Siegel, 1961). An increase in micronuclear damage with age (Sonneborn and Schneller, 1960; Rodermel and Smith-Sonneborn, 1977) could contrib-

TABLE 2. Age-related Changes in *Paramecium*.

Age-associated Morphological Characteristics	References
Variable number of micronuclei	Mitchison (1955); Sonneborn and Dippell (1960)
Micronuclear chromosomal aberration	Sonneborn (1954); Sonneborn and Schneller (1960); Dippell (1955); Sonneborn and Dippell (1960); Rodermel and Smith-Sonneborn (1977); Fukushima (1975)
Fused macronuclear chromatin	Sundararaman and Cummings (1976)
Abnormal macronuclear appearance	Siegel (1967); Sundararaman and Cummings (1976); Schwartz and Meister (1973)
Increased	
Number of food vacuoles	Smith-Sonneborn and Rodermel (1976)
Abnormal mitochondria	Sundararaman and Cummings (1976a)
Age pigments	Sundararaman and Cummings (1976a)
Nucleolar volume	Heifetz and Smith-Sonneborn (1981)
Functional Changes in Aged Cells	
Decreased	
Fission rate	Sonneborn (1954); Smith-Sonneborn et al. (1974); Takagi and Yoshida (1980)
DNA synthesis	Smith-Sonneborn and Klass (1974)
RNA synthesis	Klass and Smith-Sonneborn (1976)
DNA transcription	Klass and Smith-Sonneborn (1976)
Progeny viabililty	Sonneborn and Schneller (1960); Williams and Smith-Sonneborn (1980); Pierson, (1938); Smith-Sonneborn et al. (1974); Sonneborn and Schneller (1955, 1955a, 1960); Sonneborn (1954)
Increased	
UV sensitivity	Smith-Sonneborn (1971, 1979)
Lysosomal activity	Sundararaman and Cummings (1976, 1976a)
Cytoplasmic toxicity	Williams and Smith-Sonneborn (1980); Sonneborn and Schneller (1960, 1960a)
Quantitative Aspects of Aged Cells	
Decreased	
Total amount of DNA	Klass and Smith-Sonneborn (1976); Schwartz and Meister (1973, 1975)
No change	
Copper sensitivity	Nyberg (1978)
DNA polymerase activity	Williams and Smith-Sonneborn (1980)

ute to decreased longevity in the progeny from older parent cells after autogamy (self-fertilization). In general, progeny from older parents show greater variations in vitality than offspring from young parents. Fertilization, if delayed too long, does not necessarily rejuvenate the clone; some cells will not survive the process (Sonneborn, 1954; Smith-Sonneborn et al., 1974). Lethality after fertilization in an old cell may be due to micronuclear abnormalities (Dippell, 1955) as well as cytoplasmic incompatibility. The absence of an expected delay in gene expression (phenotypic lag) for recessive le-

thal mutations among some of the progeny of old parents implies that death is not due solely to micronuclear mutations (Mitchison, 1955). In old-young crosses, some lethality results from age-correlated micronuclear damage (Sonneborn and Schneller, 1960), though old-young cytoplasmic incompatibility is also indicated by the observation that abnormalities in the young mate are induced prior to nuclear transfer (Chen, 1946). The toxicity of aged cytoplasm was also seen in "merogones" (old cells whose nuclei fail to function but which receive the young nuclear complement). Usually, merogones do not survive, which indicates the toxic nature of aged cytoplasm. The occurrence of death without phenotypic lag (Mitchison, 1955) in *P. primaurelia* implies dominant lesions or cytoplasmic toxicity. Evidence for the ability of a young nucleus to rejuvenate an old cytoplasm was provided by merogones; occasionally, if the young nucleus survived the crisis, vigorous progeny could be obtained (Sonneborn and Schneller, 1960). Evidence for the ability of a young cytoplasm to rejuvenate an old nucleus was provided in *P. caudatum*. Micronuclei transferred from aged cells to young cells produced more viable offspring than observed when the aged nuclei remained in the aged line. In very old cells, a point of "no return" was found when transfer of the old nucleus to a young cytoplasm had no beneficial effect (Karino and Hiwatashi, 1981). It is possible that (1) the old nucleus which could be "rejuvenated" in young cytoplasm was not damaged but became injured only when development occurred in aged cytoplasm or (2) the old micronucleus was damaged and could be repaired in young cytoplasm. In any case, to function to produce many vigorous offspring, the old nucleus needed the young cytoplasm.

The increase in micronuclear damage with age may reflect the age-related loss in DNA repair capacity. Presumptive evidence of loss of excision repair includes: (1) sensitivity to UV irradiation increases with clonal age, suggesting loss of excision repair ability (Smith-Sonneborn, 1971); (2) life span is modulated by the amount of UV-induced damage and repair (Smith-Sonneborn, 1979); (3) UV-induced lethality after autogamy is increased by treating young cells with novobiocin (Lipetz and Smith-Sonneborn, 1980), a drug which can reduce DNA negative superhelicity, interfere with repair of UV-induced damage, and reduce normal replicative DNA synthesis; and (4) in old-young crosses, the old member of the pair shows greater F_2 lethality than the young despite their genetic identity after mutual exchange of gametes (Williams, 1980), which suggests that the young mate may have cytoplasmic repair capacity not available to the old mate and/or that the old cytoplasm is simply toxic in the old mate.

In addition to age-related cytoplasmic and nuclear damage in *Paramecium,* organellar damage can contribute to intraclonal variation in vigor. The division products of asexually dividing cells are not equal, since in the formation of organelles to produce two daughters from one cell, the anterior cell (the proter) retains the old, but the posterior cell (the opisthe) receives the new oral apparatus. Studies of successive lineages showed that the fission rate was higher for the posterior line with the new oral apparatus (Siegel, 1970). The hypothesis advanced was that the old gullet could not be repaired should accidental damage occur, which thereby reduces the viability of these individuals in the clone and contributes to variation in vigor within the clone. Thus nuclear, cytoplasmic, and organellar functions contribute to longevity.

Euplotes and Other Hypotrichs

The life spans and general morphology of some of these ciliates can be found in Table 1 and Figure 4. In *E. crassus,* age-related loss of dominance is found in regulation of the expression of a mating-type gene. In this species, mating type is determined directly and uniquely by the genotype. Five different alleles of a single mating-type locus are revealed by cross-breeding analyses. The five alleles each showed serial dominance over all those below in the hierarchy. In any combination of two alleles, the higher index dominates (Heckmann, 1964). Heterozygous clones which had been phenotypically stable for long periods suddenly showed selfing conjugation after 500 cell divisions. The appearance of selfing in old age implies that a loss of rigid dominance replaced by oscillation of expression between mutually exclusive types then allows cells within a clone to express complementary mating types. Exceptional heterozygous clones were found which did not self even after 800 consecutive cell divisions. A genetic block against mating-type instability explains the exceptional non-

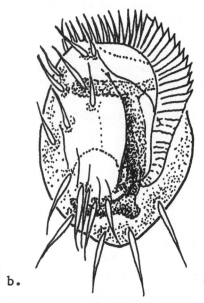

Figure 4. (a) *Euplotes patella* and (b) *Eupotes woodruffi*). (From Kudo, R. R., *Protozoology,* 5th ed., 1977, p. 1005. Courtesy of Charles C. Thomas, Publisher, Springfield, Illinois.) Redrawn by C. Nunamaker.

selfing heterozygous old clones, and implies that mating-type instability in old age is not an accidental event but an actively triggered process under genic control (Heckmann, 1967). Selfing in aged clones is seen also in *P. bursaria* (Jennings, 1941) and, like autogamy in the *P. aurelia* complex, provides a mechanism for fertilization if the members of the aging clone have failed to find a mate. Selfing, like autogamy, initiates a new life cycle (Heckmann, 1967). In old-young

crosses of both *E. woodruffi* (Kosaka, 1974) and *E. patella,* both members of the mating pair showed abnormalities, i.e., the aged phenotype was dominant. Since abnormalities occurred prior to nuclear exchange in *E. patella,* the dominance of the aged phenotype was at least partly cytoplasmically determined (Katashima, 1971). The old mate was unable to undergo normal nuclear development and was unable to form a normal mouth.

Evidence for age-dependent change in surface organelle function has been documented in *Euplotes*. Activity of the ciliary ampules (surface organelles which are probably secretory in nature) increases with age. The morphology of the ampules characteristic of "ripe" or functional organelles increased from 2 percent in immature cells to 25 percent in organisms which were fully sexually mature (Verni et al., 1981).

Recent studies in *E. aediculatus* indicate that normal macronuclear development is essential for normal life span. Two distinct developmental "hurdles" must be passed, one early (a few hours after separation of pairs) and one late (34–37 hours after pair separation). The late crisis occurs when the peak number of chromosomes have been replicated. After this time, these ciliates degenerate certain chromosomes. The possibility that, at this late crisis period, chromosomes function "only this once in a life time" and are then eliminated has been suggested (Kloetzel, 1981). The genes which must function in these ciliates are related to cortical or surface morphogenesis of mouth parts. Clearly, if cytoplasmic conditions in an old cell do not favor expression of genes at this critical time, normal function is not possible.

There is general agreement that most DNA sequences in the micronuclear zygote are lost during differentiation to the final somatic macronucleus in *Euplotes* and other hypotrichs like *Stylonychia mytilus* and *Oxytricha* (Ammermann et al., 1974; Lauth et al., 1976), in contrast to both *Paramecium* and *Tetrahymena* which keep most of the micronuclear sequences in the macronucleus (Yao and Gorovsky, 1974; Yao and Gall,

1979; Cummings, 1975; Doerder and De-bault, 1975; Berger, 1973). *Stylonychia* and *Oxytricha* may have developmental hurdles like those of *Euplotes.* The recent studies also provide a rationale for the micronucleus carrying more genes than are incorporated into the macronucleus: i.e., certain genes need to function only early in development. Once this function is performed, these genes do not need to be carried in the somatic macronucleus and can be preserved for the next generation in the relatively transcriptionally inert micronucleus.

Tokophrya

The study of clonal aging in *Tokophrya lemnarum* (Colgin-Bukovsan, 1979) was possible after the discovery of mating types in this species (Colgin-Bukovsan, 1976). Senescence is noted by decreased survival after conjugation and by complete fusion of some pairs. The immaturity period is 0–60 cell divisions, and maturity lasts at least 800 fissions. *Tokophrya,* since it reproduces by budding and exhibits striking differences between the parent cell and its progeny (Figure 5), as well as among adolescent, young adult, and old cells (Figures 6 and 7), offers an opportunity to monitor the life span of nondividing individuals within the clone (Rudzinska, 1951, 1955, 1961a, & 1961b, 1962; Colgin-Bukovsan, 1979). The mature *Tokophrya* produces a swimming bud which metamorphoses into the stalked adult. The adult lives ten days in *T. infusionum* (Rudzinska, 1961a) and 16 days in *T. lemnarum* (Colgin-Bukovsan, 1979). After formation of the adult, there is a short immaturity period in which buds are not produced, a mature period of bud pro-

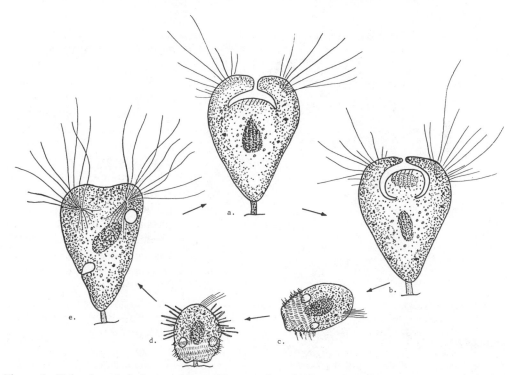

Figure 5. *Tokophrya infusionum:* (a) trophic suctorian, (b) formation of broad chamber and beginning of the bud, (c) young swimming suctorian, (d) a young attached adult, and (e) the mature adult. (and d From Kudo, R. R., *Protozoology,* 5th ed., 1977, p. 1037. Courtesy of Charles C. Thomas, Publisher, Springfield, Illinois.) Life cycle (From Mackinnon, D. L. and Hawes, R. S. J., *An Introduction to the Study of Protozoa,* 1961, p. 247. Courtesy of Oxford University Press, Oxford, England.) Redrawn by C. Nunamaker.

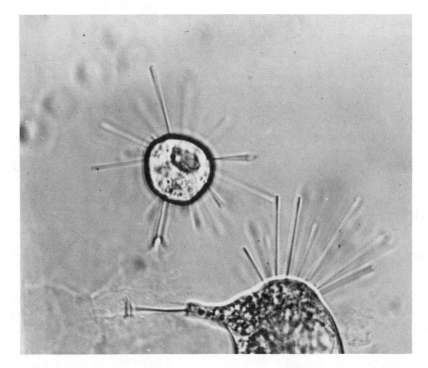

(a)

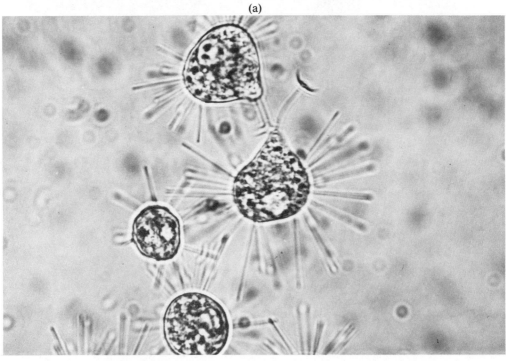

(b)

Figure 6. *Tokophrya infusionum:* (a) adolescent with tentacles, (b) young adult with tentacles, and (c) old adult with only a few short tentacles. (Courtesy of M. Rudzinska.)

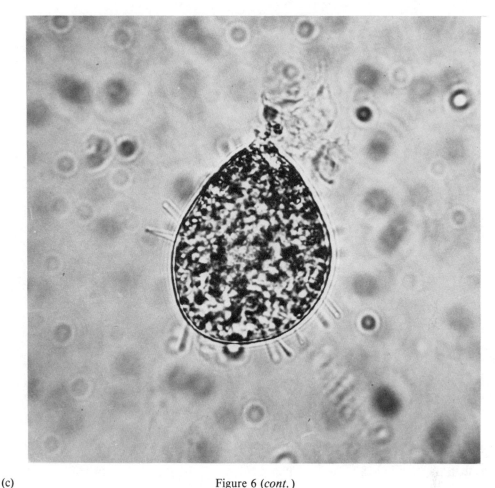

(c)   Figure 6 (*cont.*)

duction, and a "senescent" period in which no buds can be formed. *Tokophrya* feeds on living prey by sucking the contents through long slender tubes (tentacles). The sessile *Tokophrya* must come into chance contact with the prey and then seems to paralyze the victim. Although 2–5 tentacles are usually attached to one prey (*Tetrahymena*), one tentacle will suffice. When given excess food, however, a *Tokophrya* can feed simultaneously with all 50 tentacles. The young gluttonous *Tokophrya* at the age of 4 days resembles a normal organism twice that age and can assume giant proportions (120 times normal). The adult *Tokophrya* does not have an organelle for excretion of solid wastes; the

opening to the outside is for release of buds (Rudzinska, 1962). The adult *Tokophrya* serves as a model system for effects of accumulated digestive wastes in nondividing cell survival. As might be predicted in these adults with defective excretory capacity, overfeeding shortens life, and so does intermittent starvation since proper nutrition is unavailable (Rudzinska, 1951, 1955, 1961a). The senescent changes in adult *Tokophrya* can be seen in Table 3.

Tetrahymena

The ciliate *Tetrahymena* (Figure 8) can exhibit an infinite or finite life span, and dif-

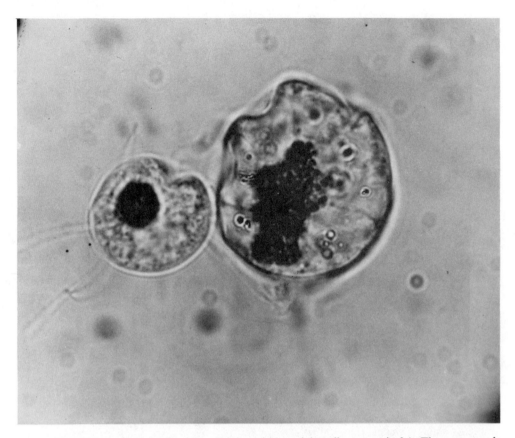

Figure 7. Young and old *Tokophrya* (small left and large right cells, respectively). The macronucleus of the young cell is spherical while the old wrinkled cell shows an irregular lobated nucleus. (Courtesy of M. Rudzinska.)

ferent species appear widely separated in evolutionary time (for review, see Nanney, 1974). Of the eight strains of *Tetrahymena* examined for the probability that a cell line would terminate at successive transfers when followed for over 800 generations, most maintained a relatively constant rate of production of defective lines which did not in-

TABLE 3. Age-related Changes in Adult *Tokophrya*.

Morphological changes
   Reduction in
      Tentacles from 50 to 5
      Microvilli number
      Mitochondrial number
      Endoplasmic reticulum number
   Increase in
      Age pigments
      Macronuclear diameter ($5 \rightarrow 15$–20 microns)
      Body size
      Chromatin bodies (50–100)
Functional change
   Reduction in bud production ($12 \rightarrow 0$–2 per day)

[a]From Rudzinska (1961a, 1961b).

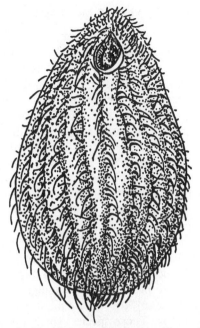

Figure 8. *Tetrahymena pyriformis*. (From Grell, K. G., *Protozoology*, 1973, p. 454. Courtesy of Springer-Verlag, New York.) Redrawn by C. Nunamaker.

crease with age. However, the one exception showed an increase with age in the probability of producing defective lines. Both "constant ageless" and "aging" strains were detected (Nanney, 1959). If a particular micronucleated strain produced an amicronucleated one, the newly arisen amicronucleate was usually dead within 1–10 transfers. This is in sharp contrast with the immortality of amicronucleated strains of *Tetrahymena* which may have independent evolutionary origins (Nanney, 1974). When long-lived strains are inbred, detrimental effects include: (1) exconjugants which die within the first fission or within ten fissions postconjugation; (2) nonconjugants in which a new macronucleus does not develop (the old macronucleus is retained); or (3) accelerated onset of micronuclear anomalies showing "inbreeding deterioration" normally observed 500–1500 fissions after conjugation, though anomalous micronuclei may appear as early as 13 fissions or, more commonly, 40–100 fissions after fertilization (Nanney,

1957; Allen, 1967). The micronuclear spindle is often displaced in organisms with micronuclear anomalies (Nanney, 1957). Age-related micronuclear erosion is found in some but not all species of *Tetrahymena,* and the onset of mutations appears to be random, not programmed to increase with age (Simon and Nanney, 1979). Senescent-like changes induced by inbreeding include severe disorganization of cell division, asynchrony of division of micro- and macronuclei, and abnormalities in micronuclear structure. Successive inbreeding and stringent selection eventually produce viable progeny (Nanney, 1957). Micronuclei, like the germ line cells of higher organisms, are shielded from natural selection during vegetative growth since the micronuclear genome is expressed only after fertilization. Selective pressures can be exerted only in the somatic cycle. It is, therefore, not surprising that micronuclear damage can occur at a rate which precedes the somatic death of the ciliates since accumulated damage in the micronucleus is "silent." The genetically inbred and conditioned short-lived variants in *Tetrahymena* may represent the expression of micronuclear genetic accidents allowed to become homozygous by laboratory inbreeding of strains or chromosomal aberrations. Inbreeding is not natural for *Tetrahymena* in the wild.

When cells with defective micronuclei are crossed with normal cells, full vigor can be restored to the senescent clone (Weindruch and Doerder, 1975). In the cross, replacement of the abnormal micronucleus occurs, but the ancestral macronucleus can be retained, thereby producing heterokaryons. If new macronuclei are formed, the anlage appear to undergo autolysis and eventually the cells die (Doerder and Shabatura, 1980). The rejuvenated heterokaryon clones show signs of senescence, which implies ancestral macronuclear regulation of onset of premature micronuclear abnormalities, and the interval for timing of senescence is dependent on the strain (Weindruch and Doerder, 1975).

Age-associated changes in the micronuclear cycle of *Tetrahymena thermophila* were investigated by a cross between A*III, a severely aneuploid clone, and a normal clone. The abnormal mate essentially receives a micronuclear transplant since the new normal nucleus is placed in the cell with the A*III macronucleus and cytoplasm, producing a heterokaryon. The micronuclear cycle of the A*III heterokaryons changed with increased clonal age. Autoradiography and cytofluorimetric studies suggest that alterations may be due to loss of late replicating sequences or changes in timing of micronuclear division with respect to cell division (Shabatura and Doerder, 1981).

Tetrahymena, which does not normally manifest age-related somatic decline or timing of onset of germ line abnormalities, exhibits other well-ordered aspects of its life cycle, i.e., the ordered onset of maturity, the timing of expression of antigenic types and various enzymes. Thus, *Tetrahymena* display a separation of differentiation and aging.

The structure of the macronucleus in any ciliate is still an unsolved problem. All macronuclei are compound in that they contain multiple copies of some or all the genetic elements. The organization of this macronucleus which determines phenotype, and therefore presumably the rate of aging, is considered to be of critical importance in the aging process. Since the expression of different phenotypes in *Tetrahymena* diverges from that seen in *Euplotes* and *Paramecium,* the organization of the *Tetrahymena* macronucleus could be expected to be substantially different. For example, hybrids for the H immobilization locus segregate clones which express one or the other allele. The macronucleus behaves in a manner consistent with haploid subunits. The micronuclei of the cells which have assorted the alternative alleles have been shown to be still heterozygous (Nanney and Dubert, 1960). Several other loci behave in a similar manner, and phenotypes can be arrayed into a calendar of timed events (Bleyman, 1971; Nanney, 1974). The organization of the macronucleus can be expected to impact on longevity, which will be discussed.

IMMORTALITY VERSUS MORTALITY

For species survival, some part of the "whole" capable of producing the entire organism, or the whole organism itself, must be immortal. In humans, the germ line is set aside for transfer to the successive generation; in ciliates, the germ line micronucleus is the immortal transfer organelle. In unicellular and multicellular organisms, the integrity of the germ line DNA is preserved if fertilization occurs prior to the onset of age or environmentally induced genetic damage. Some repair of genetic damage may be possible during fertilization. The germ line then must bear all the longevity assurance loci for potential immortality, but regulatory gene level of function will be adjusted during development to provide a long enough individual life span for subsequent fruitful fertilizations. Those species which survived have maintenance of sufficient levels of DNA integrity or regulation of longevity assurance genes to provide long enough life to produce successive generations. In those haploid organisms which do not separate germ and somatic nuclei, the "whole" proliferative cell is immortal.

Haploids and Diploids

Sonneborn (1978) has pointed out that aging arose after the advent of, and within, the diploids. Haploid unicellular species are immortal, and since they possess only one chromosome of each kind, they can accumulate mutations only very slowly and precariously. Deleterious mutations will be expressed and eliminated by death or selection against the less vigorous cells which bear the mutation. A consideration of the role of haploidy and diploidy in the onset of aging has of necessity some speculative aspects. It should be stressed that haploidy *per se* will not result in immortality or long life since: (1) forward and backward mutation rates must be genetically adjusted relative to the reproductive rate to assure survival of some members of the species, and (2) increased longevity in haploids includes the opportunity for continuous selective pressure for more vigorous or rapidly dividing cells. This approach to immortality demands that the cells are dividing to permit overgrowth of the most fit types. Diploids, on the other hand, can carry recessive mutations of all kinds covered by the normal allele. Optimal genetic adaptation potential involves assortment of different mutations in the same individual since most mutations are harmful and may be favorable only in combination. Diploidy, sex, fertilization, and recombination allow accumulated mutations to be assorted in all possible combinations including some combinations in which both genes of a pair are mutant and can be expressed. The different combinations can be subject to the changed environment for their adaptive advantage, and natural selection can preserve the beneficial combinations. Mutations which assure a program for a limited period of fruitful fertilization followed by aging and death were selected (or there was no selection against those combinations), and fertilization ceased to be optional and became mandatory for species survival (Sonneborn, 1978). The immortality of haploid organisms could be considered, at least in part, a consequence of selective elimination of individuals with harmful mutations, and the price of adaptation and fertilization in diploids was inadvertently the evolution of aging. With the onset of diploidy came both a greater possibility for assortment of mutant genes in all combinations and longer life spans. The opportunity for assortment of different mutations among diploids depends on the breeding behavior: inbreeding versus outbreeding.

The various ciliates can be classified with respect to their commitment to inbreeding or outbreeding (see Sonneborn, 1957). Outbreeders tend to mate with "strangers" and, therefore, tend to accumulate genetic variety. To favor outbreeding, these organisms have multiple mating types (increasing the chance that an encountered stranger will be of a mating type different from itself and, therefore, will be suitable as a sexual partner), long immaturity periods (allowing spatial separation between closely related individuals before mating can occur), and the inability to undergo self-fertilization (discouraging homozygosity). The option for genetic assortment in outbreeders is greater than in inbreeders since mutations will become homozygous at a much slower rate after fertilization (therefore in the outbreeders, detrimental mutations, favorable only in certain genetic backgrounds, will not be "prematurely" eliminated). Inbreeders can undergo self-fertilization, have only two mating types, and have short immaturity periods. Spontaneous recessive mutations quickly become homozygous after autogamy, and if they are nonadaptive in that genetic and environmental background, the possessor of that mutation may die or be overpowered by neighbors, which reduces genetic variety. The opportunity for assortment of different combinations of mutations is less among the inbreeders then, since a single mutation is "prematurely" eliminated, i.e., prior to the chance to be combined with another which is beneficial only in combination. It might be expected from the smaller reservoir of genetic variety that inbreeders are less resistant to environmental stress and fluctuation than are outbreeders, and such a correlation has been found (Nyberg, 1974). Outbreeding organisms may require a lower mutation rate than inbreeders to achieve comparable genetic variety (Nanney, 1974), and their repair systems may be evolutionarily adjusted for their respective genetic strategies (Sonneborn, 1978).

Ciliates can be arrayed in a linear series of relative duration of immaturity (Sonneborn, 1957; Smith-Sonneborn, 1981). Length of immaturity and life span are correlated both in ciliates and in multicellular organisms (Rockstein et al., 1977; Cutler, 1978), though in ciliates, immaturity and longevity are measured in cell divisions, not days, since fertilization (Kroll and Barnett, 1968; Miwa and Hiwatashi, 1970; Takagi, 1970, 1974; Smith-Sonneborn and Reed, 1976; Takagi and Yoshida, 1980), and outbreeders are the longest lived among the diploids.

Although an outbreeding species like *Tetrahymena* would be expected to have a longer life span than in inbreeding *Paramecium aurelia,* the "immortality" of the *Tetrahymena* is an apparent violation of the onset of aging with diploidy. Vegetative or somatic immortality of ciliates may depend not only on the genetic variation contributed by the germ line, as mentioned, but also on the organization of the macronucleus into diploid or haploid subunits.

Although the macronuclear structure of any ciliate is still not understood (for review, see Berger, 1977; Nanney and Preparata, 1979), hybrid *Tetrahymena* exhibit the atypical ability to assort loci during somatic reproduction. Thus sublines of the same clone express alternative alleles; the nucleus behaves as a homozygote or a functional haploid. The organization of the macronucleus then appears to be haploid subunits which can assort to different cells so that the cells contain one or the other haploid chromosome of the diploid pair. If macronuclear damage accumulated with age were to be assorted also, then the subunit with age damage would be expressed and possibly eliminated by selective growth of the more vigorous nonmutated sublines. A "phenotypic homozygote" is equivalent to a haploid since mutant genes can be expressed, i.e., no wild-type allele masks their expression. *Tetrahymena* may be able to utilize the "haploid" mechanism of elimination of harmful mutations from the population by expression and selection against them during somatic growth to achieve immortality, and "purification" of the macronucleus during vegetative growth could occur by segregation and elimination of cells which carry harmful mutations (Pitts, 1979). On the other hand, *Paramecium* and *Euplotes* do not show any similar phenotypic assortment. Selfing in old age *Euplotes* and in *P. bursaria* shows an oscillation between expression of alternative alleles, rather than segregation of the alleles to subline cells of the population. Therefore, these ciliates, which cannot segregate and express harmful macronuclear mutations, would accumulate damage and age. Although this attractive hypothesis would help explain the difference in longevity between *Tetrahymena* and some other ciliates, experimental approaches have not yet been possible to test its validity.

Thus, the prediction is that the immortal *Tetrahymena* macronucleus has a haploid subunit organization, while finite life span organisms have diploid subunit (or nonhaploid) organization. Haploids allow selective elimination of detrimental mutations, thereby "purifying" the genetic organelle, the macronucleus. Among diploids (which accumulate mutations), the greater the potential for storing and recombination, the greater is the longevity. This assortment occurs during fertilization, which became a requisite, not an option, for survival. *Tetrahymena,* as a "closet haploid," no longer needs fertilization for survival. The whole cell, not a part of the cell, is immortal due, theoretically, to haploid subunits subject to selection, as well as the ability to renew surface structure during somatic growth. *Tetrahymena* can repair its gullet without undergoing mating, while certain obligate breeders in *Paramecium* require fertilization for gullet replacement (Frankel, 1970; Sonneborn, 1978). *Paramecium* and *Euplotes* may have cortical or surface repair possibly only during fertilization when old parts can be replaced. The value of fertilization rests to some extent on the ability of the cells to replace and repair damaged parts. If this renewal can occur during vegetative growth, fertilization is not a stringent requirement for species survival. If certain repair or renewal processes can occur only during the fertilization cycle, the sexual phase is not an option, but a requirement for species survival. Fertilization, in addition to its role in recombination of genetic material, represents then a unique period for replacement of cell parts for certain species.

ENVIRONMENTAL MODULATION OF LONGEVITY

The diverse predictable life spans of ciliates suggest genetic control of longevity. The genetic system, however, must be broad enough to include: (1) the primary sequence of nucleotides in DNA; (2) the conformation of the DNA, its interactions with chromosomal proteins at various levels of organization, and its response to cell surface, cytoplasmic, and environmental cues; and (3) the heritability of cytoplasmic and surface organelles. The precarious nature of immortality seen both in *Tetrahymena* after inbreeding and in *Amoeba* by alteration in the nutritional environment emphasized that longevity can be a heritable response to changes in genetic composition, and to nuclear and cytoplasmic "states." The determination of gene function is the critical variable for both development and aging. The ciliated protozoans can be viewed as developmental genetic cells both (1) during the "sensitive period," the interval from zygote formation until the end of the second postfertilization cell division when determination of alternative alleles and different loci can be made, and (2) during the asexual cell cycle when changes in gene function are expressed. Some of the determinations in the sensitive period are made early, some late, but the heritable nuclear determinations are subject to intra- and extracellular conditions (Sonneborn, 1977; Sonneborn and Schneller, 1979). Temperature, nutrition, and ion concentrations during the sensitive period can alter nuclear differentiation and can prejudice the resulting phenotype both in the *P. aurelia* complex and in *Tetrahymena* (for reviews, see Sonneborn, 1977; Nanney, 1976; Nanney and Meyer, 1977). Dauer modifications (or enduring modifications) have been induced by exposure of cells to agents during the sensitive period (Jollos, 1921) and can be inherited as stable determinations (Genermont, 1961, 1966). Examples of stable nuclear differentiations which occur during the sensitive period include the choice of a particular ciliary antigen (Preer et al., 1963) and the phase of the circadian rhythm of mating-type change in *Paramecium multimicronucleatum* (Barnett, 1966). Protozoa offer a research resource to prove mechanisms of determination of gene function. Mating type in *P. bursaria* follows the progression that

immature cells lack mating-type substance, adolescent cells form a single substance, and mature cells form two substances. The temporal sequence is under genetic control; the B locus directs not only the production of B mating-type substance but also the production of A at a nonallelic locus (Siegel, 1967). The loss of the ability to maintain the determined state with increased clonal age has been observed in *Paramecium bursaria* (Jennings, 1941) and *Euplotes* (Heckmann, 1967).

The cytoplasmic environment can also impact on longevity: an aged or spanned cytoplasm can induce detrimental effects on the young or normal nucleus in *Amoeba, Euplotes,* and *Paramecium,* while a young cytoplasm can be beneficial to an old nucleus in *Paramecium* as cited earlier. Cell surface changes are also known to modulate gene expression and are altered with age. Structural changes in the cell cortex of the ciliate *Stentor* and invertebrate eggs can modulate intracellular events and interfere with normal nuclear division (for review, see deTerra, 1967, 1970, 1974). Temporal correlation of cortical morphogenesis with micronuclear and macronuclear events was observed in *Euplotes eurystomus* (Rufallo, 1980; Kloetzel, 1981). Since cell surface changes must be coordinated with intracellular events for maintenance of self-reproducibility, changes in cell surface could impact on longevity. The decline of gullet function in cell lineages with the old gullet represents organelle-mediated loss of vigor in even young sublines and contributes to intraclonal variation (Siegel, 1970). Cell surface changes with age also have been observed in *Euplotes* (Katashima, 1971; Frankel, 1973; Verni et al., 1981). Since replacement of these organelles in *Paramecium* and *Euplotes* occurs only during fertilization, fertilization represents a necessary process for survival of these species.

Physical and chemical agents have been tested for their impact on longevity and sensitivity as age increased: x-ray administered by repeated fractionated doses for a total irradiation of 138,000 R during the asexual cycle reduced life span and accelerated the decline in fission rate (Fukushima, 1974).

The effects of very low doses of ionizing radiation on clonal life span in *Paramecium tetraurelia* were investigated. Longevity was determined under conditions of culture with (1) control chamber with radiopermeable walls, (2) a shielding device with lead walls 10 cm thick, and (3) a similar shielding device with ^{60}Co source giving a dose of 760 mR per year at the culture level (Tixador et al., 1981). Decreased longevity was found in the shielded-irradiated cultures relative to controls. These studies could not unequivocally exclude the occurrence of autogamy in their life span lines. Unless autogamy or self-fertilization was favored by a given condition, the environment-induced alterations in longevity should be valid. The range in life span was greatest for representatives of the clone in the shielded-irradiated group. The shielded-irradiated cells started to die younger than representatives in the other groups, but the "survivors" lived as long or longer than the controls. It is surprising that a chronic dose of only 760 R could effect life span, when acute doses of x-irradiation from 100 to several thousand roentgens were used to detect a shortened life span of the same species (Fukushima, 1974). Irradiation with 80,000 R at the two anlage stage of autogamy (when induced mutations should be amplified by several rounds of DNA replication) did not accelerate aging (Kimball and Gaither, 1954). The different results may reflect differences in cell cycle timing of x-ray administration when repair may differ and the dosages used by various investigators and radiation source.

Carcinogen-induced life span extension in *P. multimicronucleatum* has been reported (Spencer and Melroy, 1949), but unfortunately selfing in the respective control and treated populations was not monitored. *Paramecium* and *Spathidum* show increased sensitivity to ultraviolet irradiation with age (Smith-Sonneborn, 1971; Williams and Williams, 1965).

Ultraviolet irradiation reduced the life span of *Paramecium tetraurelia* but not if the damage was enzymatically repaired by exposure to photoreactivation repair (Smith-Sonneborn, 1979). The cumulative effect of two cycles of irradiation followed by photoreactivation repair increased the mean and maximal life spans (Smith-Sonneborn, 1979). Although clones show increased sensitivity to UV irradiation with age (Smith-Sonneborn, 1971), those cells pretreated with ultraviolet light and then photoreactivated responded like young cells. It is not known whether the beneficial effect represents a decelerated rate of aging or that the cells were rejuvenated with respect to this age-correlated trait (decreased sensitivity to ultraviolet relative to clonal age). The UV dose correlates with length of life. If the UV-induced damage exceeds the capacity of the cells to repair the damage, reduced life span results; if the damage does not saturate the repair system, increased repair capacity also might facilitate correction of some age-correlated damage. Should some age damage be repaired, the putative age clock would be reset to some extent, but if repair of new damage is facilitated, the rate of aging may be retarded.

Since DNA polymerase activity does not decline with age (Williams and Smith-Sonneborn, 1980), other enzymes or variables may contribute to the beneficial effects of the ultraviolet and photoreactivation treatment. For example, UV-altered modulation of gene expression, greater accessibility of DNA to repair, and increase in repair and/or removal of age-induced damage contained within patches of UV-induced damage may be responsible for the increased longevity observed after UV irradiation and photoreactivation cycles. Evidence for radiation-increased repair is found, in addition to paramecia, in insects (Ducoff, 1976), mammals (Calkins and Greenlaw, 1971), and aging chicken and human fibroblasts (Kontermann et al., 1981). Beneficial effects of radiation under restricted conditions of total lymphoid radiation (TLR) have also been found to prevent rejection of grafts (King et al., 1981) and to reduce inflammation in arthritic rats (Schurman et al., 1981). The increase in tumor blocking factors (Voisin et al., 1968; Hellstrom et al., 1973) and the stimulation of suppressor cell activity induced by x-rays (Dorsch and Roser, 1977; Hilgert et al., 1979) may contribute to the observed inhibition of graft rejection by TLR.

Ultraviolet treatment in prokaryotes is known to initiate a complex induction process culminating in derepression of a group of metabolically diverse but coordinated functions which could promote survival (Witkin, 1976) or long life. DNA damage and repair have been correlated with longevity in mammals (for review, see Hart et al., 1978). Age-induced DNA damage and loss of repair are found in some aging human cells, though experimental design and cell type influence the results obtained (for review, see Tice, 1978; Williams and Dearfield, 1981). Loss of repair in aged paramecia is suggested by increased sensitivity to ultraviolet with increased age (Smith-Sonneborn, 1971). The effect of reduction in DNA repair on longevity could be conjectured to be due to preferential damage to regulatory regions of chromatin. Regulatory sites on chromatin have an altered conformation (Kolata, 1981) which may affect their susceptibility to DNA damage and/or repair. Since such regions may not be transcribed, abnormal proteins would not be detected; rather the amount of quality proteins produced may change.

DNA conformational changes need not be the primary event, but rather an integral part of a cascade of events, in aging. Regulation of superhelical DNA coiling may be a critical intermediate step in the expression of several age-related pathologies (Lipetz, 1981). It is intriguing that the antibiotic novobiocin increased sensitivity to UV irradiation decreased the longevity of *Paramecium* (Smith-Sonneborn, 1981; Lipetz et al., 1981). The number of DNA supercoils is reduced by novobiocin treatment in mammalian cells and *Paramecium* (Mattern and Painter, 1979; Lipetz and Smith-Sonneborn, 1980). Thus, drugs which can alter DNA conformation can alter DNA repair and longevity.

Nucleocytoplasmic interactions can alter the rate of aging of the cell and its parts

(Shabatura and Doerder, 1981; Karino and Hiwatashi, 1981) as has been noted previously (for reviews, see Muggleton-Harris, 1979; Smith-Sonneborn, 1981).

CONCLUSION

Age-related changes in food uptake and utilization may represent terminal stages in senescence which mimic ultrastructural changes seen in young starved cells. Continued growth in the deprived culture is required for the extrinsic cultural aging.

Nutritional changes can also induce heritable changes in phenotype in both ameba and paramecia at critical developmental periods, i.e., an extrinsic agent can induce intrinsic changes. Radiation-induced changes in gene expression, DNA repair capacity, and replication of certain cell types have been observed as radiation offers a tool to be used cautiously for implementation of beneficial effects of a usually noxious physical agent.

The biological system is viewed here as a complex unit involving an interaction of the genetic blueprint with its external environment. Both alteration of the blueprint and alteration of its function by environmental factors can be used to potentially extend the vitality and longevity of organisms.

REFERENCES

Allen, S. L. 1967. Cytogenetics of genomic exclusion in *Tetrahymena. Genetics* 55: 797–822.

Allen, S. L., Bryne, B. C., and Cronkite, D. L. 1971. Intersyngenic variations in the esterases of bacterized *Paramecium aurelia. Biochem. Genet.* 5: 135–150.

Allen, S. L., Farrow, S. W., and Golembiewsky, P. A. 1973. Esterase variations between the 14 syngens of *Paramecium aurelia* under axenic growth. *Genetics* 73: 561–573.

Allen, S. L. and Gibson, I. 1971. Intersyngenic variations in the esterases of axenic stocks of *Paramecium aurelia. Biochem. Genet.* 5: 161–181.

Ammermann, D., Steinbruck, G., van Berger, L., and Hennig, W. 1974. The development of the macronucleus in the ciliated protozoan *Stylonychia mytilus. Chromosoma* 45: 401–430.

Barnett, A. 1966. A circadian rhythm of mating type reversals in *Paramecium multimicronucleatum,* syngen 2, and its genetic control. *J. Cell Physiol.* 67: No. 2, 239–270.

Benham, C. J. 1979. Torsional stress and local denaturation in supercoiled DNA. *Proc. Natl. Acad. Sci. U.S.A.* 76: 3870–3874.

Berger, J. D. 1973. Nuclear differentiation and nucleic acid synthesis in well-fed exconjugants of *Paramecium aurelia. Chromosoma* 42: 247–268.

Berger, J. D. 1974. Selective autolysis of nuclei as a source of DNA precursors in *Paramecium aurelia* exconjugants. *J. Protozool.* 21: 145–152.

Berger, J. D. 1976. Gene expression and phenotype change in *Paramecium* exconjugants. *Genet. Res.* 27: 123–134.

Berger, J. 1977. Organization and expression of the nuclear genetic material; Round Table No. 15. *5th International Congress of Protozoology,* 113–123.

Bleyman, L. 1971. Temporal patterns in the ciliated protozoan in developmental aspects of the cell cycle. *In,* I. L. Cameron, G. M. Padilla, and A. M. Zimmerman (eds.), *Developmental Aspects of the Cell Cycle,* pp. 67–91. New York: Academic Press.

Botchan, P., Wang, J. C., and Echols, H. 1973. Effect of circularity and superhelicity on transcription from bacteriophage λ DNA. *Proc. Natl. Acad. Sci. U.S.A.* 70: 3077–3081.

Calkins, J. and Greenlaw, R. H. 1971. Activated repair of skin: a damage induced radiation repair system. *Radiology* 100: 389–395.

Chen, T. T. 1946. Conjugation in *Paramecium bursaria.* II. Nuclear phenomena in lethal conjugation between varieties. *J. Morphol.* 79: 125–262.

Coleman, A. 1979. Sexuality in colonial green flagellates. *In,* M. Levandowsky and S. B. Hutner (eds.), *Biochemistry and Physiology of Protozoa,* 2nd ed. pp. 307–340. New York: Academic Press.

Colgin-Bukovsan, L. A. 1976. The genetics of mating types in the Suctoria *Tokophrya lemnarum. Genet. Res.* 27: 303–314.

Colgin-Bukovsan, L. A. 1979. Life cycles and conditions for conjugation in the Suctoria *Tokophrya lemnarum. Arch. Prostistenk.* 121: 223–237.

Collins, C. and Johnson, R. 1979. Novobiocin: an inhibitor of the repair of UV induced but not X-ray-induced damage in mammalian cells. *Nuc. Acid. Res.* 7: No. 5., 1311–1320.

Cook, P. R. and Brazell, I. A. 1975. Supercoils in human DNA. *J. Cell Sci.* 19: 261–279.

Cook, P. R., Brazell, I. A., and Jost, E. 1976. Characterization of nuclear structures containing superhelical DNA. *J. Cell Sci.* 22: 303–324.

Cummings, D. J. 1975. Studies on macronuclear DNA from *Paramecium aurelia. Chromosoma* (Berl.) 53: 191–208.

Cutler, R. G. 1978. The biology of aging. *In,* J. A. Behnke, C. E. Finch, and G. B. Moment (eds.), *Evolutionary Biology of Senescence,* pp. 311–336. New York: Plenum Press.

Danielli, J. F. and Muggleton, A. L. 1959. Some alternative states of amoeba, with special reference to lifespan. *Gerontologia* 3: 76–90.

deTerra, N. 1967. Macronuclear DNA synthesis in *Stentor:* regulation by a cytoplasmic initiator. *Proc. Natl. Acad. Sci. U.S.A.* 57: 607–614.

deTerra, N. 1970. *Cytoplasmic Control of Macronuclear Events in the Cell of Stentor,* pp. 345–368. London: Cambridge University Press.

deTerra, N. 1974. Cortical control of cell division. *Science* 184: 530–537.

DeWyngaert, M. A. and Hinkle, D. 1979. Involvement of DNA gyrase in replication and transcription of bacteriophage T7 DNA. *J. Virol.* 29: 529–535.

Dippell, R. V. 1955. Some cytological aspects of aging in a variety of *Paramecium aurelia. J. Protozool.* 2 (Suppl.): 7.

Doerder, F. P. and Debault, L. E. 1975. Cytofluorimetric analysis of DNA during meiosis, fertilization and macronuclear development in the ciliate *Tetrahymena pyriformis,* syngen 1. *J. Cell Sci.* 17: 471–493.

Doerder, F. P. and Shabatura, S. K. 1980. Genomic exclusion in *Tetrahymena thermophila:* a cytogenetic and cytofluorimetric study. *Devel. Genet.* 1: 205–218.

Dorsch, S. and Roser, B. 1977. Recirculating suppressor T cells in transplantation tolerance. *J. Exp. Med.* 145: 1144–1157.

Ducoff, H. S. 1976. Radiation-induced increase in lifespan of insects. *In, Biological and Environmental Effects of Low Level Radiation,* Vol. 1, pp. 103–109. Vienna: International Atomic Energy Agency.

Elliot, A. M. and Bak, I. J. 1964. The fate of mitochondria during aging in *Tetrahymena pyriformis. J. Cell Biol.* 20: 113–129.

Fok, A. and Allen, R. 1981. Axenic *Paramecium caudatum.* II. Changes in fine structure with culture age. *Eur. J. Cell Biol.* 25: 182–192.

Fok, A. K., Allen, R. D., and Kaneshiro, E. S. 1981. Axenic *Paramecium caudatum.* III. Biochemical and physiological changes with culture age. *Eur. J. Cell Biol.* 25: 193–201.

Frankel, J. 1970. The synchronization of oral development without cell division in *Tetrahymena pyriformis* GL-C[1]. *J. Exp. Zool.* 173: 79–100.

Frankel, J. 1973. Dimensions of control of cortical patterns in *Euplotes:* the role of pre-existing structure, the clonal life cycle, and the genotype. *J. Exp. Zool.* 183: 71–91.

Fukushima, S. 1974. Effect of x-irradiations on the clonal life-span and fission rate in *Paramecium aurelia. Exp. Cell Res.* 84: 267–270.

Fukushima, S. 1975. Clonal age and the proportion of defective progeny after autogamy in *Paramecium aurelia. Genetics* 79: 377–381.

Génermont, J. 1961. Determinants genetiques macronucleaires et cytoplasmiques controlant la resistance au chlorure de calcium chez *Paramecium aurelia* (souche 90, variete 1). *Ann. Genet.* 3: G1–G8.

Génermont, J. 1966. Recherches sur les modifications durables et le determinisme genetique de certains caracteres quantitatifs chez *Paramecium aurelia.* These, Faculte des Sciences de Paris.

Generoso, W. M., Cain, K. T., Krishna, M., and Huff,

S. W. 1979. Genetic lesions induced by chemicals in spermatozoa and spermatids of mice are repaired in the egg. *Proc. Natl. Acad. Sci. U.S.A.* 76: 435–437.

Gomez, M. P., Harris, J. B., and Walne, P. L. 1973. Ultrastructural cytochemistry of *Euglena gracilis* Z: from aging cultures. *J. Protozool.* 20: 515–516.

Gorovsky, M. A., Pleger, G. L., Keevert, J. B., and Johmann, C. A. 1973. Studies on histone fraction F2A1 in macro-and micronuclei of *Tetrahymena pyriformis. J. Cell Biol.* 57: 773–781.

Gorovsky, M. A. and Woodard, J. 1969. Studies in the nuclear structure and function in *Tetrahymena pyriformis.* I. RNA synthesis in macro and micronuclei. *J. Cell Biol.* 42: 673–682.

Grell, K. G. 1973. *Protozoology.* New York: Springer-Verlag.

Grusky, G. E. and Aaronson, S. 1969. Cytochemical changes in aging *Ochromonas:* evidence for an alkaline phosphatase. *J. Protozool.* 16: 686–689.

Haga, N. and Hiwatashi, K. 1981. A protein called immaturin controlling sexual immaturity in *Paramecium. Nature* 289: 177–179.

Hagen, G. and Kochert, G. 1980. Protein synthesis in a new system for the study of senescence. *Exp. Cell Res.* 127: 451–457.

Hart, R. W., Hall, K. Y., and Daniel, F. B. 1978. DNA repair and mutagenesis in mammalian cells. *Photochem. Photobiol.* 28: 131–155.

Heckmann, K. 1964. Experimentelle Untersuchungen an *Euplotes crassus.* I. Paarungsystem, Konjugation und Determination der paarungstypen. *Z. Verebungsl.* 95: 114–141.

Heckmann, K. 1967. Age-dependent intraclonal conjugation in *Euplotes crassus. J. Exp. Zool.* No. 2, 165: 269–278.

Heifetz, S. and Smith-Sonneborn, J. 1981. Nucleolar changes in aging and autogamous *Paramecium tetraurelia. Mech. Age. Dev.* 16: 255–263.

Hellstrom, I. Hellstrom, K. E., and Trentin, J. J. 1973. Cellular immunity and blocking serum activity in chimeric mice. *Cell Immunol.* 7: 73–84.

Hilgert, I., Rieger, M., Kristofova, H., Vlachou, K., and Singh, S. K. 1979. Possible manipulations of allograft tolerance by suppressor cells. *Transplant. Proc.* 11: 887–890.

Jennings, H. S. 1929. Genetics of the Protozoa. *Bibliographic Genetics* 5: 105–330.

Jennings, H. S. 1941. Genetics of *P. bursaria.* II. Self-differentiation and self-fertilization of clones. *Proc. Am. Philos. Soc.* 85: 25–48.

Jennings, H. S. 1944. *Paramecium bursaria:* life history. I. Immaturity, maturity and age. *Biol. Bull.* 86: 131–145.

Jennings, H. S. 1944a. *Paramecium bursaria:* life history. II. Age and death of clones in relation to the results of conjugation. *J. Exp. Zool.* 96: 17–52.

Jennings, H. S. 1944b. *Paramecium bursaria:* life history. III. Repeated conjugations in the same stock at different ages, with and without inbreeding, in re-

lation to mortality at conjugation. *J. Exp. Zool.* 96: 243–273.

Jennings, H. S. 1944c. *Paramecium bursaria:* life history. IV. Relation of inbreeding to mortality of exconjugant clones. *J. Exp. Zool.* 97: 165–197.

Jennings, H. S 1945. *Paramecium bursaria:* life history. V. Some relations of external conditions, past or present, to aging and to mortality of exconjugants, with summary of conclusions in age and death. *J. Exp. Zool.* 99: 15–31.

Jollos, V. 1921. Experimentelle Protistenstudien. I. Untersuchunger uber Variabilitat und Vererbilitat und Vererbeing bei Infusoreen. *Arch. Protistenk.* 43: 1–122.

Karino, S. and Hiwatashi, K. 1981. Analysis of germinal aging in *Paramecium caudatum* by micronuclear transplantation. *Exp. Cell Res.* 136: 407–415.

Katashima, R. 1961. Breeding systems in *Euplotes patella. Jpn. J. Zool.* 13: 39–61.

Katashima, R. 1971. Several features of aged cells in *Euplotes patella,* syngen 1. *J. Sci. Hiroshima Univ.,* Ser. B., Div. 1: 23: 59–93.

Kimball, R. F. and Gaither, N. 1954. Lack of an effect of a high dose of x-rays on aging in *Paramecium aurelia,* Variety I. *Genetics* 37: 977.

King, D. P., Stober, S., and Kaplou, H. S. 1981. Suppression of the mixed leukocyte response and of graft-vs-host disease by spleen cells following total lymphical irradiation (TLI). *J. Immunol.* 26: 1140–1145.

Klass, M. 1974. DNA template activity of ethanol-fixed micronuclei of *Paramecium aurelia,* Ph.D. Thesis, University of Wyoming, Laramie.

Klass, M. and Smith-Sonneborn, J. 1976. Studies in DNA content, RNA synthesis and DNA template activity in aging cells of *Paramecium aurelia. Exp. Cell Res.* 98: 63–72.

Kloetzel, J. A. 1981. Nuclear roles in postconjugant development of the ciliated protozoan *Euplotes aediculatus. Dev. Biol.* 83: 20–32.

Kochert, G. 1968. Differentiation of reproductive cells in *Volvox carteri. J. Protozool.* 15: 438–452.

Kolata, C. B. 1981. Genes regulated through chromatin structure. *Science* 214: 775–776.

Kontermann, K., Hommel, A., and Bayreuther, K. 1981. UV irradiation induced DNA repair in aging chicken and human fibroblasts. Vol. 2, p. 126. *XII Int. Congr. Gerontol., July 12–17, Hamburg, Germany.*

Kosaka, T. 1970. Autogamy in fresh water *Euplotes woodruffi,* (Ciliata). *Zool. Mag.* 79: 302–308.

Kosaka, T. 1972. Effect of autogamy on clonal aging in *Euplotes woodruffi,* (Ciliata). *Zool. Mag.* 81: 302–308.

Kosaka, T. 1974. Age-dependent monsters or macronuclear abnormalities, the length of life, and a change in the fission rate with clonal aging in marine *Euplotes woodruffi. J. Sci. Hiroshima Univ., Ser B., Div. 1,* 25: 173–189.

Kroll, R. J. and Barnett, A. 1968. The effect of different fission rates on the onset of maturity in *Paramecium multimicronucleatum*. *J. Protozool.* 15: 10.

Kudo, R. R. 1977. *Protozoology,* 5th ed. Springfield, Ill.: Charles C. Thomas.

Lauth, M. R., Spear, B. B., Heumann, J. M., and Prescott, D. M. 1976. DNA of ciliated protozoa: DNA sequence diminution during macronuclear development of *Oxytricha*. *Cell* 7: 67–74.

Lipetz, P. D. 1981. DNA superstructure differentiation and aging. *In,* R. T. Schimke (ed.), *Biological Mechanisms of Aging,* pp. 290–314. N81-2194, Bethesda: U.S. Department of Health and Human Services.

Lipetz, P. D. and Smith-Sonneborn J. 1980. Biology of aging. August, Gordon Conference, Laconia, N.H.

Lipetz, P. D., Stephens, R. E., and Smith-Sonneborn, J. 1981. Altered DNA superhelicity and novobiocin sensitivity with age. *Int. Congr. Gerontology, July 12–17, Hamburg, Germany.*

Lipps, H. J., Nock, A., Riewe, M., and Steinbruck, G. 1978. Chromatin structure in the macronucleus of the ciliate *Stylonychia mytilus*. *Nuc. Acid Res.* 5: 4699–4709.

Mackinnon, D. L. and Hawes, R. S. J. 1961. *An Introduction to the Study of Protozoa.* Oxford: Clarendon Press.

Mattern, M. R. and Painter, R. B. 1979. Dependence of mammalian DNA replication on DNA supercoiling. II. Effect of novobiocin on DNA synthesis in Chinese hamster ovary cells. *Biochim. Biophys. Acta.* 563: 306–312.

Mitchison, M. A. 1955. Evidence against micronuclear mutations as the sole bases for death at fertilization in aged, and in the progeny of ultraviolet irradiated *Paramecium aurelia*. *Genetics* 40: 61–75.

Miwa, I. and Hiwatashi, K. 1970. Effect of mitomycin C on the expression of mating ability in *Paramecium caudatum*. *Jap. J. Genet.* 45: 269–275.

Miwa, I., Haga, N., and Hiwatashi, K. 1975. Immaturity substances: material basis for immaturity in *Paramecium*. *J. Cell Sci.* 19: 360–378.

Muggleton, A. and Danielli, J. F. 1958. Aging of *Amoeba proteus* and *A. discoides* cells. *Nature,* 181: 1783.

Muggleton, A. and Danielli, J. F. 1968. Inheritance of the "life-spanning" phenomenon in *Amoeba proteus*. *Exp. Cell Res.* 49: 116–120.

Muggleton-Harris, A. L. 1979. Reassembly of cellular components for the study of aging and finite life span. *Int. Rev. Cytol.* 9 (Suppl.): 279–301.

Murti, K. G. and Prescott, D. M. 1970. Macronuclear ribonucleic acid in *Tetrahymena pyriformis*. *J. Cell Biol.* 47: 460–467.

Nanney, D. L. 1953. Nucleo-cytoplasmic interaction during conjugation in *Tetrahymena*. *Biol. Bull.* 105: 133–148.

Nanney, D. L. 1957. Inbreeding degeneration in *Tetrahymena*. *Genetics* 42: 137–146.

Nanney, D. L. 1959. Vegetative mutants and clonal senility in *Tetrahymena*. *J. Protozool.* 6: 171–177.

Nanney, D. L. 1974. Aging and long term temporal reg-

ulation in ciliated protozoa. A critical review. Mech. Ageing Dev. 3: 81–105.

Nanney, D. L. 1976. Calcium chloride effects on nuclear development in *Tetrahymena*. *Genet. Res. (Camb.)* 27: 297–302.

Nanney, D. L. and Dubert, J. M. 1960. The genetics of the H serotype system in variety 1 of *Tetrahymena pyriformis*. *Genetics* 45: 1335–1358.

Nanney, D. L. and McCoy, W. 1976. Characterization of the species of the *Tetrahymena pyriformis* complex. *Trans. Am. Micros. Soc.* 95: 664–682.

Nanney, D. L. and Meyer, E. B., 1977. Traumatic induction of early maturity in *Tetrahymena*. *Genetics* 86: 103–112.

Nanney, D. L. and Preparata, R. M. 1979. Genetic evidence concerning the structure of the *Tetrahymena thermophila* macronucleus. *J. Protozool.* 26: 2–9.

Nobili, R. 1962. I. Dimorfismo nucleare die Ciliate: inerzia vegetativa del micronucleo. *Accad. Nazi. Lincei Rend. Class Sci. Fisiche Mat. Nat. Ser.* 8 (32): 392–396.

Nyberg, D. 1974. Breeding systems and resistance to environmental stress. *Evol.* 28: 367–380.

Nyberg, D. 1978. Copper tolerance and segregation distortion in aged *Paramecium*. *Exp. Gerontol.* 13: 431–437.

Pasternak, J. 1967. Differential genic activity in *Paramecium aurelia*. *J. Exp. Zool.* 165: 395–418.

Pierson, B. F. 1938. The relation of mortality after endomixis to the prior interendomictic interval in *Paramecium aurelia*. *Biol. Bull.* 74: 235–243.

Pitts, R. A. 1979. Age associated micronuclear defects of *Tetrahymena thermophila:* genetic and cytogenetic studies. Masters Thesis, University of Pittsburgh.

Pommerville, J. C. and Kochert, G. D. 1981. Changes in somatic cell structure during senescence of *Volvox carteri*. *European J. Cell Biol.* 24: 236–243.

Preer, J. R., Jr., 1968. Genetics of the protozoa. *In,* T. T. Chen (ed.), *Research in Protozoology,* Vol. 3, pp. 139–288. New York: Pergamon Press.

Preer, J. R., Jr., Bray, M., and Koizumi, S. 1963. The role of cytoplasm and nucleus in the determination of serotype in *Paramecium*. *Proc. XIth Intern. Congr. Gen., The Hague* 1: 189.

Priestley, D. A. and Posthumas, M. A. 1982. Extreme longevity of lotus seeds from Pulantien. *Nature* 229: 148–149.

Raffel, D. 1932. The occurrence of gene mutations in *Paramecium aurelia*. *J. Exp. Zool.* 63: 371–412.

Reeve, J. 1979. Use of minicells for bacteriophage-directed polypeptide synthesis. *Methods of Enzymology* 68: 493–503.

Reeve, J. 1981. Ohio State University, Personal Communication.

Richardson, J. P. 1975. Initiation of transcription by *Escherichia coli* RNA from supercoiled and non-supercoiled bacteriophage PM2 DNA. *J. Mol. Biol.* 91: 477–487.

Rockstein, M., Chesky, J., and Sussman, M. 1977.

Comparative biology and evolution of aging. *In*, C. E. Finch and L. Hayflick (eds.), *Biology of Aging* pp. 1034. New York: Van Nostrand Reinhold.

Rodermel, S. R. and Smith-Sonneborn, J. 1977. Age-correlated changes in expression of micronuclear damage and repair in *Paramecium tetraurelia*. *Genetics* 87: 259–274.

Rudzinska, M. A. 1951. The influence of amount of food in the reproduction rate and longevity of suctorian *Tokophrya infusionum*. *Science* 113: 10–11.

Rudzinska, M. A. 1955. The differences between young and old organisms in *Tokophrya infusionum*. *J. Gerontol.* 10: 469.

Rudzinska, M. A. 1961a. The use of a protozoan for studies on ageing. I. Differences between young and old organisms of *Tokophrya infusionum* as revealed by light and electron microscopy. *J. Gerontol.* 16: 213–223.

Rudzinska, M. A. 1961b. The use of a protozoan for studies on ageing. II. Macronucleus in young and old organisms of *Tokophrya infusionum:* light and electron microscopy. *J. Gerontol.* 16: 326–334.

Rudzinska, M. A. 1962. The use of protozoan for studies on ageing. III. Similarities between young overfed and old normally fed *Tokophrya infusionum:* a light and electron microscope study. *Gerontologia* 6: 206–226.

Ruffalo, J. J. Jr., 1980. Cell cycle analysis of *Euplotes*. *J. Cell Biol.* 87: 3a.

Schurman, D. J., Hirshman, H. P., and Strober, S. 1981. *Arthritis Rheum.* 24: 38–44.

Schwartz, V. and Meister, H. 1973. Eine alterveranderung des makronucleus von *Paramecium*. *Z. Naturforsch. Sect. B.* 28c: 232.

Schwartz, V. and Meister, H. 1975. Aging in *Paramecium* several quantitative aspects. *Arch. Protistenk. Biol.* 117: 5, 85–109.

Sessoms, A. H. and Huskey, R. J. 1973. Genetic control of development in *Volvox:* isolation and characterization of morphogenetic mutants. *Proc. Natl. Acad. Sci. U.S.A.* 70: 1335–1338.

Shabatura, S. K. and Doerder, D. P. 1981. Age-associated changes in the micronuclear cycle of *Tetrahymena thermophila* A*III heterokaryons. A brief note. *Mech. Ageing Devel.* 15: 235–238.

Siegel, R. W. 1956. Mating types in *Oxytricha* and the significance of mating type systems in ciliates. *Biol. Bull.* 110: 352–357.

Siegel, R. W. 1961. Nuclear differentiation and transitional cellular phenotypes in the life cycle of *Paramecium Exp. Cell Res.* 24: 6–20.

Siegel, R. W. 1963. New results on the genetics of mating types in *Paramecium bursaria*. *Genet. Res.* 4: 132–142.

Siegel, R. W. 1967. Genetics of ageing and the life cycle in Ciliates. *Symp. Soc. Exp. Biol.* 21: 127–148.

Siegel, R. W. 1970. Organellar damage as a possible basis for intraclonal variation in *Paramecium*. *Genetics* 66: 305–314.

Simon, E. M. and Nanney, D. L. 1979. Germinal aging in *Tetrahymena thermophila*. *Mech. Ageing Dev.* 11: 253–268.

Smith-Sonneborn, J. 1971. Age correlated sensitivity to ultraviolet radiation in *Paramecium*. *Radiat. Res.* 46: 64–69.

Smith-Sonneborn, J. 1979. DNA repair and longevity assurance in *Paramecium tetraurelia*. *Science,* 203: 1115–1117.

Smith-Sonneborn, J. 1981. Genetics and aging in protozoa. *Int. Rev. Cytol.* 73: 319–354.

Smith-Sonneborn, J. and Klass, M. 1974. Changes in the DNA synthesis pattern of *Paramecium* with increased clonal age and interfission time. *J. Cell Biol.* 61: 591–598.

Smith-Sonneborn, J., Klass, M., and Cotton, D. 1974. Parental age and life span versus progeny life span in *Paramecium J. Cell Sci.,* 14: 691–699.

Smith-Sonneborn, J. and Reed, J. C. 1976. Calendar life-span versus fission life-span of *Paramecium aurelia*. *J. Gerontol.* 31: 2–7.

Smith-Sonneborn, J. and Rodermel, S. R. 1976. Loss of endocytic capacity in aging *Paramecium:* the importance of cytoplasmic organelles. *J. Cell Biol.* 71: 575–588.

Sonneborn, T. M. 1946. Inert nuclei: inactivity of micronuclear genes in variety 4 of *Paramecium aurelia*. *Genetics* 31: 231 (abstract).

Sonneborn, T. M. 1947. Recent advances in the genetics of *Paramecium* and *Euplotes*. *Adv. Genet.* 1: 263–358.

Sonneborn, T. M. 1954. The relation of autogamy to senescence and rejuvenescence in *Paramecium aurelia*. *J. Protozool.* 1: 38–53.

Sonneborn, T. M. 1954a. Patterns of nucleocytoplasmic interactions in *Paramecium*. *Caryologia* 6: 307–325.

Sonneborn, T. M. 1957. Breeding systems, reproductive methods, and species problems in protozoa. *In*, E. Mayr (ed.), *The Species Problem*. Washington: American Association for the Advancement of Science.

Sonneborn, T. M. 1960. Enormous differences in length of life of closely related ciliates and their significance. *In*, B. L. Strehler (ed.), *The Biology of Aging*, pp. 289, American Institute of Biological Sciences Symposium 6. Baltimore: Waverly Press.

Sonneborn, T. M. 1974. *Paramecium aurelia. In*, R. C. King (ed.), *Handbook of Genetics,* Vol. 3, pp. 469–594. New York and London: Plenum Press.

Sonneborn, T. M. 1977. Genetics of cellular differentiation: stable nuclear differentiation in eucaryote unicells. *Annu. Rev. Genet.* 11: 349–367.

Sonneborn, T. M. 1978. The origin, evolution, nature and causes of aging. *In*, J. S. Behnke, C. E. Finch, and G. B. Moment (eds.), *The Biology of Aging*, pp. 361–374. New York: Plenum Press.

Sonneborn, T. M. and Dippell, R. V. 1960. Cellular changes with age in *Paramecium*. *In*, B. L. Strehler (ed.), *The Biology of Aging*, p. 285, American Institute of Biological Science Symposium 6. Baltimore: Waverly Press.

Sonneborn, T. M. and Schneller, M. V. 1955. Are there cumulative effects of parental age transmissible through sexual reproduction in variety 4 of *Paramecium aurelia? J. Protozool.,* 2 (suppl.), 6.

Sonneborn, T. M. and Schneller, M. V. 1955a. The basis of aging in variety 4 *Paramecium aurelia. J. Protozool.* 2: 6.

Sonneborn, T. M. and Schneller, M. V. 1960. Age-induced mutations in *Paramecium. In,* B. L. Strehler (ed.), *The Biology of Aging,* pp. 286–287. American Institute of Biological Sciences Symposium 6. Baltimore: Waverly Press.

Sonneborn, T. M. and Schneller, M. V. 1960a. Measures of the rate and amount of aging on the cellular level. *In,* B. L. Strehler (ed.), *The Biology of Aging,* pp. 290–291. American Institute of Biological Sciences, Symposium 6, Baltimore: Waverly Press.

Sonneborn, T. M. and Schneller, M. V. 1979. A genetic system for alternative stable characteristics in genomically identical homozygous clones. *Dev. Genetics* 1: 21–46.

Sousa e Silva, E. 1977. Ultrastructural variations of the nucleus in dinoflagellates throughout the life cycle. *Acta Protozool.* 31: 277–288.

Spencer, R. R. and Melroy, M. P. 1949. Studies of survival of unicellular species. I. Variations in life expectance of a *Paramecium* under laboratory conditions. *J. Nat. Cancer Inst.* 10: 1–10.

Starr, R. C. 1969. Structure, reproduction, and differentiation in *Volvox carteri* f. nargariensis Iyengar, strains HK 9 and 10. *Arch. Protistenk.* 3: 204.

Sundararaman, V. and Cummings, D. J. 1976. Morphological changes in aging cell lines of *Paramecium aurelia.* II. Macronuclear alterations. *Mech. Ageing Dev.* 5: 325–338.

Sundararaman, V. and Cummings, D. J. 1976a. Morphological changes in aging cell lines of *Paramecium aurelia.* I. Alterations in the cytoplasm. *Mech. Ageing Dev.* 5: 139–154.

Suyama, Y. 1966. Mitochondrial deoxyribonucleic acid of *Tetrahymena,* its partial physical characterization. *Biochem.* 5: 2214–2221.

Tait, A. 1970. Enzyme variation between syngens in *Paramecium aurelia. Biochem. Gen.* 4: 461–470.

Takagi, Y. 1970. Expression of the mating type trait in the clonal life history after conjugation in *Paramecium multimicronucleatum* and *Paramecium caudatum. Jpn. J. Genet.* 45: 11–21.

Takagi, Y. 1974. The effect of ultraviolet irradiation on the period of immaturity in *Paramecium caudatum. Zool. Mag.* 83: 96–98.

Takagi, Y. and Yoshida, M. 1980. Clonal death coupled with the number of fissions in *Paramecium caudatum. J. Cell Sci.* 41: 177–191.

Tice, R. R. 1978. Aging and DNA repair capability. *In,* E. L. Schneider (ed.), *The Genetics of Aging,* pp. 53–90. New York: Plenum Press.

Tixador, R., Richoilley, G., Monrozies, E., Planel, H., and Tap, G. 1981. Effects of very low doses of ionizing radiation on the clonal life-span in *Paramecium tetraurelia. Int. J. Radiat. Biol.* 39: (1), 47–54.

Verni, F., Rosati, G., and Luporini, P. 1981. Activity of the ciliary ampules through successive ages of the ciliate *Euplotes crasus. Experienta* 37: 42–44.

Voisin, G. A., Kinsky, R., and Maillard, Y. 1968. Protection against homologous disease in hybrid mice by passive and active immunological enhancement facilitation. *Transplanatation* 6: 187–202.

Weindruch, R. H. and Doerder, F. P. 1975. Age-dependent micronuclear deterioration in *Tetrahymena pyriformis,* syngen 1. *Mech. Ageing Dev.* 4: 263–279.

Weise, L. M. 1976. Genetic aspects of sexuality in *Volvocoles. In,* R. A. Lewin *(ed.), The Genetics of Algae,* pp. 174–197. Berkeley: University of California Press.

Widdus, R., Tayler, M., Powers, L., and Danielli, J. R. 1978. Characteristics of the "life spanning" phenomenon in *Amoeba proteus. Gerontologia,* 24, 208–219.

Williams, D. B. 1980. Clonal aging in two species of *Spathidium* (Ciliophora: Gymnostomatida). *J. Protozool.* 27: (2), 212–215.

Williams, D. B. and Williams, E. L. 1965. Aging and its relationship to ultraviolet light sensitivity in the ciliate *Spathidium spathula. In,* R. A. Neal (ed.), *Progress in Protozoology,* Proc. 2nd Int. Conf. Protozool., London, Excerpta Medica Found; Amsterdam, *Intern. Congr. Ser. No. 91,* 231–232.

Williams, J. R. and Dearfield, K. L. 1981. DNA damage and repair in aging mammals, CRC (in press).

Williams T. 1980. Determination of clonal lifespan in *P. tetraurelia.* Ph.D. Thesis, University of Wyoming, Laramie.

Williams, T. J. 1980. Induction of DNA polymerase activity after ultraviolet irradiation of *Paramecium tetraurelia.* Ph.D. Thesis, University of Wyoming, Laramie.

Witkin, E. M. 1976. Ultraviolet mutagenesis and inducible DNA repair in *Escherichia coli. Bacteriol. Rev.* 40: 869–907.

Woodruff, L. L. 1932. *Paramecium aurelia* in pedigree culture for twenty-five years. *Trans. Am. Microsc. Soc.* 51: 196–198.

Yang, H. L., Heller, K., Gellert, M., and Zubay, G. 1979. Differential sensitivity of gene expression *in vitro* to inhibitors of DNA gyrase. *Proc. Natl. Acad. Sci. U.S.A.* 76: 3304–3308.

Yao, M. C. and Gall, J. G. 1979. Alteration of the *Tetrahymena* genome during nuclear differentiation. *J. Protozool.* 26: 10–13.

Yao, M. C. and Gorovsky, M. A. 1974. Comparison of the sequence of macro and micronuclei on DNA of *Tetrahymena pyriformis. Chromosoma* 48: 1–18.

5
AGING AND SENESCENCE IN PLANTS

Larry D. Noodén
University of Michigan
and
John E. Thompson
University of Waterloo

This review is aimed primarily toward gerontologists outside of plant physiology. Owing to the vastness of the literature on aging and senescence in plants, this chapter can only summarize this field (up to June, 1982) and not review it in depth. Likewise, the literature citations will favor reviews rather than original papers; detailed reviews of subtopics and extensive listings of publications can be found in the references cited. Readers of this volume should also be aware that this field of plant biology has developed almost totally independently of animal gerontology.

INTRODUCTION

While senescence in different tissues may seem similar at the cellular level, it performs diverse functions in the life cycle of an organism. In addition, the factors controlling senescence appear to be different among tissues; these controls are endogenous (from within the organism) as opposed to exogenous (e.g., wear and tear) but can apparently be triggered by environmental cues. Senescence, then, is an active degenerative process leading to death and is internally controlled; it marks the end of a developmental sequence and is not strictly time (age) dependent, though it may progress with time (Leopold, 1961; Noodén and Leopold, 1978). Aging is distinguishable from senescence, the former being caused more directly by external factors, being passive, and being more time dependent. At present, the distinction between aging and senescence is mostly conceptual, but as our knowledge of these processes becomes more complete, more precise (biochemical) definitions should be possible.

Senescence is intimately associated with many phases of plant development (Figure 1) (Leopold, 1961, 1980; Noodén and Leopold, 1978) both in monocarpic plants (e.g., soybean) which have one reproductive phase followed by abrupt death and in polycarpic plants (e.g., apple) with repeated reproductive phases. Senescence probably has more varied, pervasive, and distinct roles in the life cycle of plants than of animals. The process occurs at all levels from cells (e.g., certain cells such as the water-conducting xylem cells, the proplasts autolyze and empty as they mature) and organs (leaves, petals, stamens, and other flower parts, shoot apices, and even branches) to whole plants (exemplified by monocarpic senescence which is degeneration of the organism at the end of the reproductive phase). Although senescence has been studied more extensively in higher plants, it is also important in the lives of lower plants, especially in cell differentiation but also in degeneration of the whole organism, e.g., liquefication of inky cap mushrooms. Following harvest, vegetables and fruits senesce and eventually lose their food quality; this (postharvest physiology) may be of considerable economic importance, among other senescence processes (Willis et al., 1981; Burton, 1982).

A transmissible "senescence" factor in fungi (Fencl, 1978; Esser and Tudzynski, 1980) seems to be a virus and will not be considered further here, just as disease-induced death is mostly omitted. Readers of the plant literature will find frequent reference to "aging" of certain excised tissues (e.g., potato or artichoke tuber tissue) which have been cut on all surfaces; these phenomena reflect mainly wounding recovery reactions (van Steveninck, 1975) rather than aging or senescence.

FUNDAMENTAL QUESTIONS

Senescence versus Aging?

Can death be an internally programmed event? Numerous examples in both annual and perennial plants (Figure 1) support an affirmative answer. During development from seeds, the various parts of annual plants such as the soybean show different patterns of senescence, including monocarpic senescence which causes death of the plant. Likewise, many parts of trees (e.g. leaves) senesce on an annual cycle. By contrast, when seeds are stored in a cool, dry environment, their entire developmental program is blocked—"suspended animation"—and they (especially seeds of annuals) usually live much longer (Molisch, 1938). Usually, the senescence process in plants is quite abrupt, a few hours for the petals of some flowers or a few days for monocarpic senescence as in soybeans (although it may last a year in some long-lived bamboos) (Molisch, 1938; Noodén, 1980b).

Similarly, the petals and certain other flower parts, which play a role in attracting pollinators in some orchids with specialized and infrequent pollinators, may persist for up to 1½ years until the flower is pollinated, after which they degenerate rapidly (Faegri and van der Piel, 1979; Dressler, 1981). Thus, age *per se* is only indirectly connected with senescence.

Although the seeds of some species can last a very long time in storage (at least 460 years, Osborne, 1980; Priestley and Posthumus, 1982), they gradually lose their viability at a rate which is greatly influenced by environmental conditions (a cool, dry environment favors longevity). This gradual loss of viability (especially in dry seeds during storage, but also in moistened seeds buried in soil) represents a different type of phenomenon, normally termed aging (Leopold, 1961; Noodén and Leopold, 1978). Thus, even if their developmental senescence program is halted by preventing germination, seeds do not remain viable indefinitely. This degeneration may be due to the gradual, time-dependent accumulation of lesions in DNA, the protein-synthesizing apparatus, membranes, and probably other components of the cell (Osborne, 1980; Villiers, 1980). There is reason to believe that these lesions are induced directly or indirectly by free radicals, reactive ions, and ionizing radiation, factors which occur naturally in our environment (Pryor, 1976).

To What Extent Do Environmental Factors Alter Aging and Senescence?

The external environment can exert a very substantial influence on the senescence and aging of cells, organs, and organisms. A commonly held view is that organisms deteriorate and die due to "wear and tear" or a gradual accumulation of environmentally induced lesions. Drought, cold, heat, light deficiency, and mineral nutrient deficiencies can promote senescence of plant parts (especially lower, older leaves or detached leaves), but the importance of such factors in senescence of the whole plant is less clear.

By contrast, a massive trauma (e.g., sudden and complete water deprivation) usually stops the senescence process; chlorophyll degradation, leaf abscission, etc., are halted, and the resulting dead plant will have attached, dry, green-gray leaves. Similarly, the leaves on a branch torn from a tree by a storm in midsummer do not senesce or abscise, but instead dry up and die.

Thus, environmental stress does not necessarily accelerate senescence (particularly that of whole plants). In fact, mildly adverse environmental conditions may actually increase longevity (Noodén, 1980b), as do low temperature or nitrogen deficiency in duckweed (Wangermann and Lacey, 1955), or unidentified adversities probably including drought in bristlecone pine (LaMarche, 1969). An unfavorable environment may delay senescence by postponing the entire developmental program, as in the "suspended animation" of seeds discussed earlier. Environmental stress, however, seems to trigger a reallocation of resources within a plant; most often, this is represented by accelerated senescence of certain leaves (especially the lowest one) and the withdrawal of nutrients invested in them.

Does a Cell Die Because It Is Specifically Targeted to Die or Because of Its Position in an Organ or Organism Which Is Deteriorating?

Individuals of each plant species have a fairly well-defined maximum longevity which may range from a few weeks for those which complete their life cycle during the very brief favorable periods found in deserts to more than 4000 years in bristlecone pines (Hildebrand, 1881; Molisch, 1938; Wangermann, 1965; Noodén, 1980b). Thus, it appears that longevity is genetically determined, but does a plant degenerate and die because its individual cells die or because the integrity of the organized unit declines? Even though the physiology of whole plant senescence may differ between monocarps and polycarps, the answer to this question may be similar for both. It has long been known that cuttings made from an old plant can produce vigorous, young plants which can live long beyond the parent (Noodén, 1980b). The gradual loss of vigor observed in some clones (e.g., sugarcane) seems to be due to a buildup of viruses with a low level of pathogenicity (Frost, 1952; Trippi, 1976; Noodén, 1980b). However, subculturing plants from meristems (which tend to remain virus free) can be used to restore a clone's vigor (Sharp et al., 1979). Cultivars have been propagated vegetatively with a retention of vigor and identity for very long periods: Reine Claude plum about 400 years (Westing, 1964) and Cabernet Sauvignon grape for over 1000 years (Dion, 1959; Penning-Roswell, 1971). Thus, a part of the organism, which would be destined to die if left in place, can live much longer if excised from the larger, "parent" unit and can be used to initiate a new organism (vegetative propagation). The same is often true for individual organs such as leaves, and especially roots, when they are excised and cultured (DeVries, 1890; White, 1934; Molisch, 1938), but the effect of excision is most pronounced when small pieces (or even single cells) are explanted and cultured on rich media to form disorganized, relatively undifferentiated masses known as callus. These callus tissues appear to be in a perpetual "embryonic" state and capable of growing indefinitely (Gautheret, 1939; White, 1939; Noodén, 1980b), although they sometimes lose their ability to regenerate whole plants (Murashige, 1974). This applies equally to monocarpic and polycarpic plants.

Clearly, many cells and organs die as an indirect result of the deterioration of the larger unit to which they belong. It is equally clear that individual cells or small numbers of cells may be targeted to die as part of their normal differentiation (e.g., xylem differentiation discussed earlier); however, even these are influenced by their position within a larger organized unit.

Is Senescence a Global or a System Failure?

This question (Rosen, 1978) can be applied to all levels of senescence within a plant, and the answer probably differs depending on the specific case. Does the organism (or cell) degenerate due to failure of one single key component (system) on which other parts depend, or do a large number of interdependent systems (global) decline together until, like Oliver Wendell Holmes' one horse shay, the whole falls apart in a great calamity. Unfortunately, we usually do not have enough data to answer this rarely posed type of question. In the case of monocarpic senescence of the soybean, it does appear that the plant dies because the leaves degenerate (Noodén, 1980a); therefore, death here involves a system failure.

What Is the Upper Limit on Life?

Although the life spans of biological units and their components vary a great deal, all are finite. In general, the more complex the unit, the greater is its longevity (Leopold, 1980). Expressed in a different way: a larger, more complex unit (e.g., an organism) will last longer than its components (e.g., cells). The same can be said for cells and their substructures. As mentioned, seeds in nongerminating conditions can survive for centuries. Some plants, such as bristlecone pines, seem to be able to live for over 4000 years (Noodén, 1980b). In North America, clones of creosote bush (Vasek, 1980) and aspen (Stebbins, 1957) appear to have endured since the Wisconsin glacial period, over 11,000 years ago. Since there is continuous turnover and renewal of the cells and organs, one can question whether or not the organism has really survived; the distinction then becomes philosophical.

When the question of longevity is applied to cells, some very notable examples do exist. The pith parenchyma cells of an Australian grass tree appear to stay alive for more than 400 years (Lamont, 1980). No doubt, the issue of cell longevity in seeds and other structures will be considered further in the future.

Epilogue to Fundamental Questions

Many fundamental questions regarding aging and senescence are only starting to be formulated and investigated, much less answered. It seems valid to make a distinction between aging and senescence even in the absence of biochemical specifics. While aging is linked with chronological age, senescence clearly is not; instead, it is tied to developmental stage. Nonetheless, genes may determine the rates of both aging and senescence.

To some extent, the enormous longevity of individuals of some plant species is a function of their unique ability to maintain embryonic regions (meristems) in various parts of their bodies, but it may not be correct to ascribe their extreme longevity only to this factor.

Given the clear internal control of senescence in plants, the reader must wonder how it is actually accomplished. The problem of how senescence is controlled and executed will be addressed in the following section and then summarized in our conclusions. We will then use this background to examine the broader problem of the function(s) of senescence at the end of the chapter.

THE PHYSIOLOGY OF SENESCENCE

Introduction and Overview

As shown in Figure 1, senescence occurs in all phases of plant development, and it serves many different functions. Clearly, the process has evolved independently many times; even superficially similar processes such as monocarpic senescence must have evolved separately in different taxonomic groups (Noodén, 1980b). Therefore, it is not surprising that the senescence processes in different cells, organs, and species show some differences in their controls, particularly hormonal controls, though their biochemical steps need not differ (Noodén and Leopold, 1978).

Most studies on plant senescence have focused on particular organs rather than processes; leaves have been most extensively studied, followed by flowers and fruits. Recently, interest in whole plant senescence, particularly monocarpic senescence, has increased, but this is much more complex since several organs which interact are involved (reviewed in Noodén, 1980b, 1984).

The selectivity of the senescence process is

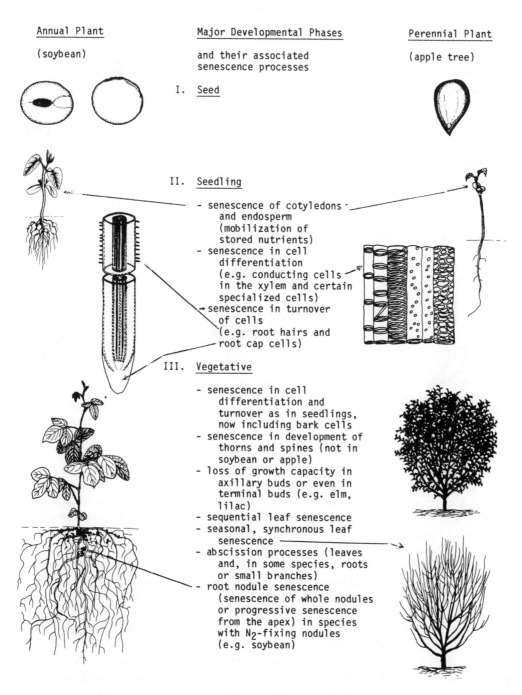

Annual Plant

(soybean)

Major Developmental Phases

and their associated
senescence processes

I. Seed

Perennial Plant

(apple tree)

II. Seedling

- senescence of cotyledons
  and endosperm
  (mobilization of
  stored nutrients)
- senescence in cell
  differentiation
  (e.g. conducting cells
  in the xylem and certain
  specialized cells)
- senescence in turnover
  of cells
  (e.g. root hairs and
  root cap cells)

III. Vegetative

- senescence in cell
  differentiation and
  turnover as in seedlings,
  now including bark cells
- senescence in development of
  thorns and spines (not in
  soybean or apple)
- loss of growth capacity in
  axillary buds or even in
  terminal buds (e.g. elm,
  lilac)
- sequential leaf senescence
- seasonal, synchronous leaf
  senescence
- abscission processes (leaves
  and, in some species, roots
  or small branches)
- root nodule senescence
  (senescence of whole nodules
  or progressive senescence
  from the apex) in species
  with N_2-fixing nodules
  (e.g. soybean)

Figure 1. Senescence in the life cycle of seed plants.

shown in Figure 1. Different organs right next to one another in the flower will follow very different courses. Even specific cells may be targeted for senescence, while their neighbors are not (e.g., regenerating xylem versus neighboring pith cells in coleus stems; Shininger, 1979).

In the past, senescence has been considered to be a collapse of order within a living system. As we learn more about the process,

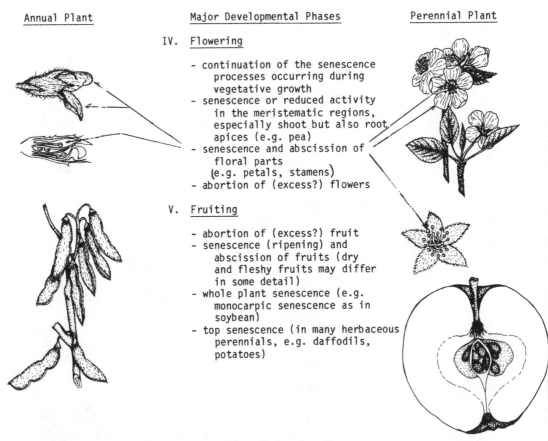

Annual Plant   Major Developmental Phases   Perennial Plant

IV. Flowering

- continuation of the senescence
  processes occurring during
  vegetative growth
- senescence or reduced activity
  in the meristematic regions,
  especially shoot but also root
  apices (e.g. pea)
- senescence and abscission of
  floral parts
  (e.g. petals, stamens)
- abortion of (excess?) flowers

V. Fruiting

- abortion of (excess?) fruit
- senescence (ripening) and
  abscission of fruits (dry
  and fleshy fruits may differ
  in some detail)
- whole plant senescence (e.g.
  monocarpic senescence as in
  soybean)
- top senescence (in many herbaceous
  perennials, e.g. daffodils,
  potatoes)

Figure 1. (continued)

it appears to be a carefully orchestrated retreat, rather than a plunge into chaos (Noodén and Leopold, 1978). The target selectivity mentioned points in this direction, but similar selectivity can be seen at the subcellular level, where chloroplasts and ribosomes show some of the first symptoms of deterioration, while mitochondria and nuclei change later, and the cell and vacuolar membranes last of all. Since new proteins must be synthesized during senescence (evidenced by the action of selective protein synthesis inhibitors, by enucleation experiments, and by the rise in activity of certain enzymes; Noodén and Leopold, 1978; Thomas and Stoddart, 1980), the nucleus may play a guiding role in senescence. Similarly, inhibition of energy production interferes with senescence (Noodén and Leopold, 1978); thus, continued mitochondrial activity is

needed to support the senescence process and these organelles must be kept functioning until fairly late in the process. The final collapse seems to be breakdown of (a) the vacuolar membrane, releasing the degradative enzymes and the toxic contents of the vacuole, and (b) the cell membrane which isolates the cell from its external environment and maintains homeostasis.

Degradation seems to be a common, if not pervasive, feature of senescence. Most visible and very important among these breakdown processes is chlorophyll loss (yellowing), but many tissues (e.g., petals) lack chlorophyll from the start and a few may remain green throughout senescence. Proteolysis also appears to be a key and more general feature of plant senescence. Probably, these degradative processes contribute significantly to the death of senescing tissues; however, a more important function is the release and redistribution of nutrients invested in the senescing tissues.

Correlative Controls

Very often, a specific cell or an organ is induced to senesce by a signal from other parts of the plant rather than by factors within itself. These controls, which originate outside the target cells but within the organism, are termed correlative controls and coordinate the activities of the different parts of the organism or tissue. Hormones appear to play an important, if not dominant, role. Nutrient fluxes may also be significant (Leopold and Noodén, 1984).

In the past, the sites of correlative control were identified primarily by excising the source (Molisch, 1938). For example, removal of reproductive structures (e.g., seeds in soybeans) usually prevents monocarpic senescence (Noodén, 1980b). In the case of soybean, the target of this influence (the senescence signal) is the leaves (Noodén, 1980a). In flowers, pollination (fertilization) triggers senescence of the petals and male reproductive structures, which are subsequently no longer needed, and emasculation or other methods of preventing pollination will delay senescence of these structures (Fitting, 1911; Halevy and Mayak, 1979, 1981). Healthy leaf blades prevent complete development (senescence) of the abscission zone and shedding of the leaves (Mai, 1934; Addicott and Lyon, 1973; Noodén and Leopold, 1978; Addicott, 1982). Similarly, healthy growing shoot apices with young leaves induce senescence of the lower (older) leaves; decapitation (removal of the younger leaves and apex) can prevent this senescence of the older leaves and even rejuvenates them (Noodén, 1980b). Young leaf blades can also induce the regeneration of xylem tissue connections in the pith tissue around cut vascular bundles (Shininger, 1979). Unfortunately, the studies on correlative controls (source-target) are limited and are not yet well integrated into the more extensive studies on the biochemistry of senescence including hormonal controls.

Hormonal Influences

Small quantities of plant hormones, particularly the cytokinins and ethylene, exert dramatic effects on senescence in many tissues by poorly understood mechanisms. It also seems likely that new hormones will be implicated in senescence. Because of the substantial differences in the hormonal controls of senescence in different organs, this section will be organized around the controls in the three best-studied organs.

Leaf Senescence. A variety of experimental approaches has provided compelling evidence that cytokinins can delay or even reverse senescence in excised organs, particularly leaves, and these observations have strongly supported the contention that a reduction in the endogenous titer of cytokinins in leaves is an important factor in the initiation of their senescence (Richmond and Lang, 1957; Kende, 1971; Noodén and Leopold, 1978; Noodén, 1980b). The effectiveness of exogenous cytokinin treatments on attached leaves is less clear, although cytokinin, especially in combination with auxin, can inhibit the seed-induced senescence of the leaves on intact soybean plants (Noodén et al., 1979; Noodén, 1980a, 1980b). Moreover, while foliar cytokinin levels generally decrease prior to or during senescence, there are notable exceptions (Lorenzi et al., 1975; Davey and van Staden, 1978; Noodén and Leopold, 1978; Noodén, 1980b). It is of interest that cytokinin may affect different senescence-related processes (chlorophyll breakdown and phosphate loss) independently, which suggests that cytokinin may prevent leaf senescence through multiple actions (Sabater et al., 1981). Auxin and gibberellins apparently also retard foliar senescence in some but not all species (Brian et al., 1959; Osborne and Hallaway, 1960; Noodén and Leopold, 1978; Thimann, 1980); however, the data are limited. It is significant that auxin exerts exactly the opposite effect, promotion of senescence, during induction of xylem formation (Shininger, 1979).

Much of the cytokinin in a plant is synthesized in the root tips and transported to the leaves through the xylem as water is pulled into the leaves (Letham, 1978; van Staden and Davey, 1979). This root-produced cytokinin is a major factor in sustaining the foliage (Kulaeva, 1962; Kende, 1971; Skene, 1975; Noodén, 1980b). The longevity of excised leaves is long known to be greatly extended by the formation of roots on these leaves (Molisch, 1938; Chibnall, 1939). Similarly, environmental stress effects on the roots or partial (or complete) root removal causes a foliar yellowing, which may be relieved by applications of cytokinin (Burrows and Carr, 1969; Noodén, 1980b; Neumann et al., 1983). The flux of cytokinins from the roots is relatively high during vegetative growth and relatively low during late reproductive phase (van Staden and Davey, 1979; Noodén, 1980b).

Abscisic acid (ABA) was implicated as a senescence-promoting hormone in leaves because of its ability to promote senescence in detached leaves (El-Antably et al., 1969; Milborrow, 1974; Noodén and Leopold, 1978; Walton, 1980; Noodén, 1980b; Thimann, 1980). Some studies link rising ABA levels with senescence of leaves and petals. In soybean leaves, for example, there is a rise in ABA-like activity (Lindoo and Noodén, 1978) or ABA (Samet and Sinclair, 1980) at the time when the developing seeds induce the final phase of senescence. On the other hand, there are also some striking cases of noncorrelation: for example, younger leaves may have higher ABA levels than older leaves (Raschke and Zeevaart, 1976; Noodén, 1980b). Environmental stress, especially drought, greatly increases ABA levels, which causes the guard cells to close the main gas exchange routes (stomata) in the leaves and thereby curtails further water loss (Walton, 1980). Recent evidence (Gepstein and Thimann, 1980; Satler and Thimann, 1980) suggests that ABA could exert some of its influence on foliar senescence through induction of stomatal closure. In any case, control of water loss is crucial even in the later phases of foliar senescence; hence, the guard cells at these openings are among the

last to degenerate (Heath and Mansfield, 1969). In summary, ABA seems to be a factor in leaf senescence though perhaps not a primary trigger (senescence signal). ABA probably is not the only senescence-promoting substance even in foliage. Other possible foliar senescence-inducing hormones include ethylene (Crocker, 1948; Aharoni and Lieberman, 1979) and some as yet unidentified substances (Noodén and Leopold, 1978). Ethylene, however, may not be a primary control in leaves (Noodén and Leopold, 1978; Thimann, 1980). A decline in senescence-retarding hormones (discussed earlier) also plays a role in foliar senescence; therefore, expectations that senescence must correlate perfectly with endogenous levels of a single factor may not be warranted. Rather, hormone balances are likely to regulate senescence, as they do many other processes (Leopold and Noodén, 1984).

In most cases, foliar senescence results in abscission (Kozlowski, 1973; Sexton and Roberts, 1982; Addicott, 1982); grasses are exceptions. Foliar abscission may occur at the upper and/or lower end of the petiole (leaf stalk) and is often facilitated by an abscission or fracture zone, which minimizes damage and facilitates healing. The continuing flux of auxin from the healthy leaf blade prevents abscission, and its loss promotes (or allows) abscission (La Rue, 1936; Noodén and Leopold, 1978; Addicott, 1982). ABA appears to promote abscission, although its role may be less important than that of ethylene. Ethylene not only promotes the formation of cell wall-softening enzymes, which allow fracturing of the abscission zone (Horton and Osborne, 1967; Abeles, 1969) but also appears to interfere with the abscission-retarding flux of auxin from the leaf blade (Morgan and Gausman, 1966), thereby further promoting abscission. In spite of its abscission-promoting effects in older leaves, ethylene usually does not promote senescence and abscission of healthy, young leaves (Noodén and Leopold, 1978; Thimann, 1980). Again, this probably reflects the participation of other factors and a need for the petioles to develop to a responsive state.

Petal Senescence. Senescence of petals and other flower parts seems to respond to a different set of controls than leaves. Ethylene appears to be the primary inducer of flower senescence (Crocker and Knight, 1908; Fischer, 1950; Halevy and Mayak, 1979, 1981; Mayak and Halevy, 1980). Generally, flower parts are so sensitive to ethylene that even very small amounts (1–2 ppm) can destroy shipments of cut flowers. For this reason, flower arrangers do not mix ripe fruit (known to generate large amounts of ethylene) with cut flowers. Treatments such as high CO_2 and low air pressure, which counteract the effects of ethylene, have been extremely useful in cut flower preservation. In intact flowers, the ovary or associated parts seem to generate the ethylene which triggers a cascade of ethylene production and senescence of peripheral flower parts (Burg and Dijkman, 1967; Gillissen, 1976). Cytokinin and even ABA have been implicated in senescence of flower parts, but their roles are less clear (Halevy and Mayak, 1979, 1981).

Fruit Senescence. Because of their economic importance, fruit ripening and senescence have been studied extensively (Hulme, 1970, 1971; Rhodes, 1980a). During the maturation process, both the dry and the fleshy tissues surrounding the seeds senesce. Before and during senescence, the fleshy tissues also undergo complex changes that make them look, taste, and smell better to animals, which eat the fruit and disperse the seeds (Hulme, 1970, 1971; Rhodes, 1980a). Ethylene plays a central role in promoting fruit ripening, particularly in fleshy fruits, but the details differ somewhat for climacteric (a large burst of respiration during ripening) and nonclimacteric fruit (Rhodes, 1980a, 1980b). Both types of fruit produce relatively low levels of ethylene during early ripening; however, climacteric fruit show a large, temporary rise in ethylene production, which may precede or follow the respiratory peak. Exogenous ethylene (0.1 ppm and upwards) can hasten ripening in both climacteric and nonclimacteric fruits, while treatments known to counteract ethylene delay ripening

in both. This knowledge is used commercially both for induction of ripening in fruit picked and shipped "green" and for retardation of ripening to prolong the storage life of fruits.

Increased levels of ABA also seem to be involved in fruit ripening (McGlasson et al., 1978). ABA translocated from soybean foliage into the pods (Noodén and Obermeyer, 1981; Setter et al., 1981) may control certain aspects of pod maturation. The roles of other hormones such as auxin and cytokinin in fruit senescence are obscure (McGlasson et al., 1978). The senescence of many fruits is delayed while they are attached to the parent plant (Hulme, 1970, 1971; Rhodes, 1980a), and this could involve senescence-retarding hormones.

Nutrient Distribution

The redistribution of nutrients seems important in senescence of organs and whole plants (Halevy and Mayak, 1979, 1980; Noodén, 1980b). Movement of amino acids occurs from petals and stamens to the developing ovary, from the pod wall to seeds, from foliage to the growing fruit, from older leaves to younger leaves, from tree leaves in autumn to the bark and roots, and from senescing shoots to underground parts such as bulbs (Miller, 1938; Loehwing, 1951; Lonergan et al., 1976; Halevy and Mayak, 1979, 1981; Noodén, 1980b). Not only are nitrogenous compounds redistributed in this way, but other carbon compounds (e.g., sugars) and certain minerals (e.g., phosphate) are as well. Since the transport forms of these compounds may differ from their immediate breakdown products, specialized metabolic systems are needed to make the necessary conversions. The efficiency of reclamation is usually high, even in whole plant (monocarpic) senescence, for example more than 90% from soybean leaves (Derman et al., 1978). In nature, the selective advantage conferred by an ability to reclaim scarce or energetically "expensive" nutrients must be very great, but the domestication of plants has also inadvertently favored it. Given the importance of nutrient redistribution, it is not surprising that the phloem (the vascular tissue involved in export from most organs) is the last tissue to senesce in an organ (Matile and Winkenbach, 1971).

The massive redistribution of resources from vegetative to reproductive parts led early workers to conclude that developing fruit induce monocarpic senescence by withdrawal of nutrients from the rest of the plant; the process was actually called "exhaustion death" (Molisch, 1938). Not only are old assimilates withdrawn from senescing tissues and reallocated, but new assimilates are translocated elsewhere than to the senescing tissues (nutrient diversion). For example, products of photosynthesis travel to the seeds instead of going to the vegetative growing tissues in soybeans and wheat (Thrower, 1967; Wardlaw, 1968; Noodén, 1980b). In fact, a deficient supply of photosynthate to the roots may impair their function and contribute to the decline of the whole plant (Crowther, 1934; Herridge and Pate, 1973; Hume and Criswell, 1973). Likewise, fixed nitrogen and minerals taken up by the roots tend to move to the seeds; however, assimilation of nitrogen and other minerals decreases during the reproductive phase (Loehwing, 1951; Noodén, 1980b).

The nutrient withdrawal theory of senescence has, however, been questioned for some time (Leopold et al., 1959; Noodén et al., 1978; Noodén and Leopold, 1978; Noodén, 1980b). For example, male flowers with very low nutrient demands are able to induce senescence of spinach plants (Leopold et al., 1959). Moreover, soybean pods can still induce senescence of the leaves even when nutrient withdrawal from the leaves is blocked (Noodén and Murray, 1982). Similar arguments plus some additional points can be made against the nutrient diversion theory (Noodén 1980a,b, 1984). Although it seems that the flux of root assimilates (minerals and cytokinins) up through the xylem into the leaves could be controlled by stomatal appertures, this does not seem to be a causal factor in monocarpic senescence of soybean (Noodén, 1984). In fact, the pods

cause monocarpic senescence in soybean independently of the mineral or cytokinin flux (Neumann et al., 1983). Furthermore, treatments such as phloem blockage or depodding which are known to increase stomatal resistance to gas exchange do not cause foliar senescence and may even counteract it (Leopold et al., 1959; Koller and Thorne, 1978; Setter et al., 1980; Noodén and Murray, 1982).

In addition, detached leaves and other parts usually senesce even when they have been disconnected from sinks (Noodén, 1980b). Furthermore, the fleshy tissues in fruit senesce even though they appear to be laden with nutrients (though deficiencies of single, critical nutrients cannot be ruled out).

The exact role of nutrient deficiency in senescence, whether by withdrawal or diversion, is not clear. Though it can be argued that nutrient deprivation is not a primary trigger of whole plant senescence, at least in soybean, nutrient deficiencies are probably important secondary factors (Noodén, 1980b, 1984; Noodén and Murray, 1982).

The mechanism by which the developing fruit cause monocarpic senescence in soybean or any plant is unknown. The soybean pods exert an influence (senescence signal) very late in their development. The simplest explanation is that the pods produce some senescence-inducing hormone; however, there is no direct evidence for this (Noodén, 1980b; 1984).

Apex senescence, a somewhat related phenomenon which causes cessation of growth in peas, also seems not to be due to a nutrient deficiency induced by the pods and may be induced by a decrease in certain gibberellins (Proebsting et al., 1978).

Metabolic Changes

Fine Structural Changes in Senescing Leaves. Deteriorative changes during senescence are best understood in the context of the pattern of fine structural changes within the leaf cells, especially the chloroplasts (Table 1). Shaw and Manocha (1965) made early studies of the time course for the various ul-

TABLE 1. Degeneration of Organelles in the Mesophyll Cells of Excised Wheat Leaves Senescing on Water.[a]

	DAYS ON WATER				
	Color and Condition				
	2	3	4	5–6	7–8
	Green, turgid	Green, turgid	Pale green, turgid	Yellow, flaccid	Gray, flaccid
ER and ribosomes	Normal	Vesiculation of ER	Absent after fourth or fifth day	—	—
Mitochondria	Normal	Normal	Swelling Cristae degenerating	Formation of vesicles	Separation of double membranes[b]
Chloroplasts	Loss of parallel alignment of grana Swelling of thylakoids Loss of ribosomes from stroma and appearance of lipid droplets	—	Collapse of grana vesicles in intergrana lamellae	Formation of vesicles	Absent or greatly modified[b]
Nucleus	Normal	Normal	Shrinkage and condensation of dense regions Membrane crenated	—	Absent or greatly modified[b]
Vacuole	Normal	Normal	Vacuolar contraction and fragmentation	—	Vacuole not distinguishable[b]
Tonoplast	Normal	Normal	Breakdown following vacuolar contraction		
Plasma membrane	Normal	Normal	Normal	Usually normal	Breakdown and formation of vesicles[b]

[a]Adapted from Shaw and Manocha (1965) and subsequent literature.
[b]Except in cells associated with veins where senescence is slower.

trastructural changes in senescing leaf cells, and their overall sequence still applies. In fact, the same general sequence (minus chloroplasts) holds for nongreen tissues as well. Among the earliest changes (earlier than shown in Table 1) is a swelling of the chloroplast thylakoid membranes and the appearance of lipid droplets in the immediate vicinity of these membranes. As the thylakoid membranes shrink, lipid droplets start to appear around them. Chloroplast and cytoplasmic ribosomes also become less abundant early in senescence (Oota and Takata, 1959; Butler, 1967; Butler and Simon, 1971; Noodén and Leopold, 1978). As senescence intensifies, a variety of other fine structural alterations become apparent including vesiculation of endoplasmic reticulum and a decreased abundance of Golgi membranes, but it is not clear if these contribute to the senescence or are simply a side effect of it. Substantial structural changes in the mitochondria do not occur until later. Aside from a decrease in nucleolar size or subtle modifications such as "textural changes", the nucleus also does not show marked deterioration until fairly late. As leaf senescence progresses, the chloroplasts shrink and, depending upon the species, may at various stages become engulfed in the vacuole (Wittenbach et al., 1982). Visible disintegration of the vacuole occurs very late and releases large amounts of acids, other toxic substances, and some degradative enzymes. Lastly, the plasma membrane disintegrates, and the cell's homeostatic ability is lost. While it does appear that senescence may be manifested at the subcellular level as a series of steps, some observations show that organelles may become engulfed within a vacuole, producing a more abrupt loss of function.

Loss of Photosynthetic Capability. Perhaps the most visible symptom of leaf senescence is a change in color from green to yellow. This reflects loss of chlorophyll or, more specifically, a more rapid breakdown of chlorophyll than of the yellow carotenoids, plus formation of new types of carotenoids and even anthocyanins in some leaves (Willstätter and Stoll, 1918; Goodwin, 1958).

The loss of chlorophyll is, of course, accompanied by a decrease in photosynthesis (Šestak and Catsky, 1967). However, the two do not necessarily decline precisely together, because total photosynthetic competency is dependent upon the concerted actions both of the energy-converting "light reactions," in which chlorophyll plays a pivotal role, and of the "dark reactions" of CO_2 fixation. Usually, photosynthetic rate declines ahead of chlorophyll (Šestak and Catsky, 1967), but numerous exceptions exist.

Chloroplast membranes show some of the earliest signs of senescence in leaves (Butler and Simon, 1971; Adler et al., 1979). In addition, ribosomes are decreased at a very early stage in chloroplasts and in the cytoplasm. Chloroplast deterioration is of particular significance in that it represents a loss of the plant's primary productive capacity. In intact plants (e.g., monocarpic senescence of soybean; Noodén, 1980a), this loss of photosynthetic capacity probably causes death of the whole plant.

In many crop plants, photosynthetic capacity declines at a time when it appears to be needed most to support seed growth (Noodén, 1980b). When "demand" by the reproductive structures exceeds the plant's assimilatory capacity, the assimilatory "machinery" and other life-sustaining cell components, as well as stored nutrients, are catabolized and the resulting metabolites are mobilized to support seed growth. This, of course, leads to death of the plant. Assimilatory demand *per se* does not, however, cause a decline in photosynthesis; on the contrary, it may actually stimulate photosynthesis (Noodén, 1980b). The arguments made earlier against nutrient exhaustion as a primary cause of senescence can be applied here.

A large proportion of the total resources within a plant (e.g., 75 percent of the total nitrogen in a hydroponically grown soybean plant at early pod growth; Derman et al., 1978) is invested in the leaves. Within the leaves, a large proportion of the nitrogen (and other resources) is in turn tied up in the chloroplast, especially in the photosynthetic CO_2-fixing enzyme, ribulose 1, 5–diphosphate (RuDP) carboxylase (Dorner et al., 1957; Thomas and Stoddart, 1980). Thus, mobilization of the nutrients invested in the vegetative tissues to meet the "demands" of the growing seeds must be at the expense of the photosynthetic apparatus. However, since it can be argued (as above) that nutrient deficiency is not the primary cause of senescence, one must wonder whether it is necessary to mobilize the nutrients tied up in the leaves, especially the photosynthetic apparatus, to support seed growth. In fact, when photosynthetic and other assimilatory capabilities are maintained in the soybean, the seed's requirements can be met by current assimilation without breaking down the life- supporting metabolic machinery of the plant (Abu-Shakra et al., 1978; Noodén et al., 1978, 1979; Noodén, 1980b). An argument can, however, be made for the centrality of chloroplast breakdown in leaf senescence and for its economic implications as well. Nonetheless, loss of chloroplast function does not contribute directly to senescence of petals, fruit, and xylem cells; therefore, other metabolic changes must also be important and perhaps more basic to senescence, even in leaves.

The rate of photosynthesis is largely determined by the activities of the CO_2-fixing enzymes or the ATP-forming reactions, etc., in the chloroplast, but the influx of CO_2 into the leaves can also greatly influence the rate of photosynthesis. In fact, this influence is likely to predominate when the guard cells close the stomatal openings. As senescence progresses, the stomatal resistance to CO_2 diffusion increases (reflecting stomatal closure), which also means that the rate of water loss (transpiration) is reduced; however, this can be a relatively late event (Noodén, 1980b, 1984). The decrease in photosynthesis is usually not due to increased stomatal resistance (Noodén, 1980b).

Changes in CO_2 Fixation and Photosynthetic Electron Transport. Leaf maturation is commonly characterized by a gradual loss of photosynthetic capability followed by a much more rapid decline during which there is also extensive loss of chlorophyll, increased hydrolytic activity, and accelerated catabolism of macromolecules. Whether the initial gradual decline is actually part of the senescence sequence is not certain, but the rapid decrease seems to be. Foliar senescence involves loss of the CO_2-fixing enzymes and associated enzymes of carbon metabolism (Thimann, 1980; Thomas and Stoddart, 1980).

RuDP carboxylase (a CO_2-fixing enzyme and the predominant soluble protein in many leaves) is lost at a faster rate than is total protein during senescence (Wittenbach, 1979). Moreover, the rate of decrease in RuDP carboxylase activity may exceed the net decline in photosynthesis (Hall et al., 1978), which suggests that CO_2 fixation is not the rate-limiting step of photosynthesis during senescence. The breakdown of RuDP carboxylase presumably reflects the concerted action of several proteases, and the impact of this degradation is accentuated by the fact that synthesis of the enzyme seems also to be curtailed (Peterson et al., 1973).

The rapid decline in photosynthetic competency during leaf senescence also results from impairment of photosynthetic electron transport (Adler et al., 1979; Thomas and Stoddart, 1980). In bean leaves, there is an 80 percent decrease in noncyclic electron transport with advancing senescence under conditions in which photophosphorylation remains tightly coupled (Jenkins and Woolhouse, 1981a). Of particular interest is the small (30 percent) decline in photosystems I and II over the same period, which indicates that the much larger decline in total noncyclic electron transport may reflect an impairment of electron transfer between the two photosystems (Jenkins and Woolhouse, 1981b).

During senescence, the unique galacto- and sulfolipids of chloroplasts also undergo a striking decrease, and this generally parallels chlorophyll loss (Draper, 1969; Harwood, 1980).

Changes in Respiratory Activity. In general, it has been observed that mitochondrial integrity and respiratory activity are maintained until the later stages of senescence (Beevers, 1976; Noodén and Leopold, 1978; Rhodes, 1980b), presumably because there is a need for energy to synthesize catabolic enzymes and to export the resulting metabolites from senescing tissues. Indeed, senescence (in fruits and flowers particularly and leaves to a lesser extent) is often marked by a dramatic upsurge in respiration (Kidd and West, 1925; Rhodes, 1980a, 1980b; Thimann, 1980) known as the "respiratory climacteric," which appears to be induced by ethylene. The respiratory climacteric is in turn associated with a rise in protein synthesis during which a new complement of hydrolytic enzymes is formed (Lieberman, 1979).

The climacteric rise in respiration does not result from an uncoupling of electron transport and oxidative phosphorylation in fruit or leaves (Rhodes, 1980b; Malik and Thimann, 1980). One remarkable feature of the respiratory climacteric in fruits is its insensitivity to cyanide (Solomos and Laties, 1976). This implies that electrons are shunted through an alternate oxidase that is cyanide insensitive, rather than through the cytochrome oxidase of the respiratory chain.

Changes in Nucleic Acid Levels and Synthesis. Senescence of plant tissues is characterized by a progressive decline in cellular RNA (Böttger and Wollgiehn, 1958; Beevers, 1976; Noodén and Leopold, 1978; Thimann, 1980; Thomas and Stoddart, 1980). By contrast, DNA decreases very late, and redundant ribosomal DNA is not preferentially eliminated (Keegan and Timmis, 1981). The various types of RNA do not all decline at the same time or rate; for example, rRNA falls off before tRNA, and some fractions of tRNA increase while others decrease (Pillay and Cherry, 1974). Chloroplast rRNA normally declines ahead of cytoplasmic rRNA (but some exceptions have been noted), and chloroplast protein synthesis decreases ahead of cytoplasmic protein synthesis (Callow et al., 1972; Noodén and Leopold, 1978; Keegan and Timmis, 1981). The presence of polysomes in the cytoplasm of senescent tissues implies that mRNA is still present, but changes in the nature of the translatable mRNAs were noted during the early stages of senescence (Watanabe and Imaseki, 1982). The relative contributions of decreased synthesis and increased degradation to the decline in RNA remain to be determined. RNA synthesis decreases, especially in the chloroplasts. The unique DNA-dependent RNA polymerase present in chloroplasts becomes virtually inactive in senescent leaves (Ness and Woolhouse, 1980). Similarly, the activity of RNA-degrading enzymes may increase, yet in some cases, there seems to be no parallel between nuclease activity and the changes in RNA levels (Noodén and Leopold, 1978). Thus compartmentation and accessibility of the enzymes to the nucleic acids seems crucial. In fact, there appears to be enough nuclease activity present in a normal cell to degrade all of its RNA rather quickly without some sort of compartmentation.

Changes in Protein Levels and Synthesis. The breakdown of protein components, especially the soluble proteins, in senescing tissues was observed long ago (Meyer, 1918; Molisch, 1918; Wood and Cruickshank, 1944) and is now recognized as a common, almost universal, feature of senescence (Beevers, 1976; Noodén and Leopold, 1978; Noodén, 1980). As with RNA, it is difficult to evaluate the relative contributions of decreased protein synthesis and increased breakdown to this decline.

Both the shutdown in RNA synthesis and the net loss of RNA during senescence could be expected to result in decreased protein synthesis, and this is, indeed, the case (Böttger and Wollgiehn, 1958; Beevers, 1976; Noodén and Leopold, 1978). However, protein synthesis continues during senescence, and presumably unique proteins needed to carry out senescence are synthesized. In leaves, the chloroplasts (especially the soluble or stromal proteins) show the largest decrease in protein, and there is also less synthesis of protein in chloroplasts than in the cytoplasm.

Protein hydrolysis during senescence appears to be attributable to a variety of proteases, particularly carboxyl proteases, whose activities do not always increase with advancing age of the tissue (Frith and Dalling, 1980; Thimann, 1980). As with nucleases above, compartmentation is necessary to contain the high levels of protease activity normally present (Storey and Beevers, 1977). The nature of the lytic compartment in plant cells is uncertain. Some evidence supports the existence of structures comparable to the secondary lysosomes of animal cells (Matile, 1975), but the large vacuole, which predominates in most plant cells, may well be a lytic compartment. The vacuolar interior tends to be acidic; many of the suspected degradative enzymes have acidic pH optima (Boller and Kende, 1979; Lin and Wittenbach, 1981; Nishimura and Beevers, 1978).

On the Role of RNA and Protein Synthesis in Senescence. Senescence is an active process requiring energy and protein synthesis. Thus, even though there is a net degradation of protein and RNA, there is still sufficient macromolecular synthesis to allow formation of a new complement of enzymes. Many of these enzymes are hydrolytic in nature (nucleases, proteases, polysaccharidases) and can mediate the degradation of a variety of macromolecules. Chlorophyll, protein, RNA, and membrane lipids are all broken down during senescence, and in most instances, the products of this catabolism are exported to other parts of the plant where they are utilized. The need for protein synthesis during senescence has been demonstrated through the use of protein synthesis inhibitors in fruits, flowers, and detached leaves (Mayak and Halevy, 1980; Rhodes, 1980a; Thimann, 1980; Thomas and Stoddart, 1980). Agents acting mainly on 80s ribosomes (cycloheximide) are generally more effective than agents working mainly on 70s ribosomes (chloramphenicol) (Martin and Thimann, 1972; Thomas and Stoddart, 1980). This suggests that cytoplasmic protein synthesis is more important in promoting senescence than chloroplastic protein synthesis is.

The role of the nucleus in senescence is less clear. On the one hand, enucleation can block senescence (Yoshida, 1961), and there are nuclear mutations which, on the surface at least, seem to block such important steps in senescence as chlorophyll breakdown (Kahanak et al., 1978; Abu-Shakra et al., 1978; Thomas and Stoddart, 1980). However, on the other hand, the senescence process in leaves is not inhibited by actinomycin D (Knypl, 1970; von Abrams, 1974; Noodén and Leopold, 1978; Thomas and Stoddart, 1980). This discrepancy might be due to the failure of the large actinomycin D molecules to penetrate the treated tissues. Cordycepin, which inhibits post-transcriptional adenylation of mRNA, does inhibit leaf senescence (Takegami and Yoshida, 1975), while rifampicin which would act on chloroplastic or mitochondrial RNA polymerase does not (Thomas and Stoddart, 1980).

Membrane Deterioration

One of the most characteristic features of a senescing tissue is the onset of membrane leakiness. With advancing age, membranes invariably become leaky to the point where they can no longer compartmentalize, and this leads to release of essential substrates and cofactors, loss of ion gradients, and an unleashing of sequestered digestive enzymes. Increased leakage in senescing plant tissues is accompanied by a striking decline in phospholipid, which presumably contributes to the loss of membrane integrity (Simon, 1977). During senescence, the phase properties of membrane lipids undergo a pronounced change which is detectable by wide angle x-ray diffraction. Specifically, portions of the membrane lipid undergo a phase transition, forming a gel phase in which the fatty acid side chains are essentially immobilized. Thus, the membranes of a senescent tissue contain a mixture of discrete domains of gel phase (solid) lipid and liquid-crystalline (fluid) lipid, whereas nonsenescent membranes are exclusively liquid-crystalline (McKersie et al., 1976; McKersie and Thompson, 1977, 1978, 1979). Electron spin resonance and fluorescence depolarization studies of protoplasts and isolated membranes from senescing tissues have also provided evidence for a decrease in lipid fluidity with advancing age (Borochov et al., 1978; McKersie et al., 1978; Thompson et al., 1982; see also Chapter 11).

Liposomes prepared from total lipid extracts of senescing membranes also contain a mixture of liquid-crystalline and gel phase lipid, which implies that formation of the gel phase is attributable to chemical changes in the lipids themselves (McKersie and Thompson, 1979). There is no overt increase in the fatty acid saturation of membrane lipid during senescence; any changes are insufficient to account for the presence of gel phase lipid (McKersie et al., 1978).

There are important physiological consequences of these lipid phase changes in membranes. Of particular significance is the fact that the mixture of phases renders the lipid bilayers highly permeable (Barber and Thompson, 1980) and presumably contributes to the leakiness of senescing tissues. In addition, membrane proteins are squeezed laterally out of forming gel phase domains into adjacent areas of liquid-crystalline lipid (Shechter et al., 1974), thus altering the whole pattern of protein organization over the surface of the membrane. This could certainly contribute to loss of receptor activity and membrane-bound enzyme activity. For some senescing tissues, there is a close temporal correlation between loss of membrane-bound enzyme activity and the initiation of gel phase lipid formation (McKersie and Thompson, 1977).

The pronounced loss of fatty acids from membranes during senescence gives rise to a large increase in the sterol to phospholipid (or sterol to fatty acid) ratio (Beutelmann and Kende, 1977; McKersie et al., 1978; Borochov et al., 1978; Chia et al., 1981). Concurrently, there is a decrease in membrane fluidity, an observation consistent with the known ability of sterols to rigidify membrane lipids. The limited qualitative changes in fatty acid composition or phospholipid composition during this dismantling of membranes (Beutelmann and Kende, 1977; McKersie et al., 1978) implies that most lipids are equally prone to de-esterification.

Such an extensive loss of lipid implies increased phospholipase activity, yet actual measurements of phospholipase in senescing tissues have not borne this out. It is, however, also possible that senescence-related changes in membrane structure render the phospholipids increasingly prone to phospholipase attack. In addition, the decreased capability for fatty acid esterification (Beutelmann and Kende, 1977) could result in net loss of fatty acids from the membranes even if there were no increase in de-esterification.

Role of Lipid Peroxidation and Free Radicals.

Free radical reactions may contribute to tissue aging in many organisms (Baker et al., 1977; Harman, 1981; Leshem, 1981). The generation of free radicals is virtually ubiquitous in cells, and for enzymic reactions involving oxygen, the superoxide anion (O_2^-) is the radical species most often formed. Superoxide is not stable and spontaneously dismutates to give H_2O_2 and oxygen, which can in turn react to form the hydroxyl radical (OH·). This latter reaction is probably catalyzed *in vivo* by complexes of iron or other transition metals, since pure H_2O_2 and O_2 do not react together at significant rates (Czapski and Ilan, 1978). Because the hydroxyl radical is the most potent oxidant known, it may well be the prime mediator of oxygen toxicity.

Three key enzymes—superoxide dismutase, catalase, and peroxidase—function in plant cells to prevent the buildup of reactive oxygen species. Antioxidants such as tocopherols may act as a second line of defense (Pryor, 1976). In addition, protection against singlet oxygen is afforded by quenchers such as carotene or by the photooxidation of tocopherol (Fragata and Bellemare, 1980).

It is hypothesized that despite these several lines of defense, free radicals do accumulate in aging tissues (Baker et al., 1977; Harman, 1981). Superoxide dismutase activity does not increase with advancing senescence, at least in fruits (Baker, 1976). Significantly, senescence of a variety of plant tissues including fruits, flower petals, and leaves can be delayed by treatment with radical scavengers (Baker et al., 1977). A deleterious consequence of the accumulation of reactive oxygen species is the initiation of lipid peroxidation in the hydrophobic interior of membranes. Malondialdehyde and lipofuscin, products of lipid peroxidation, are known to accumulate in aging plant tissues (Chia et al., 1981). Moreover, *in vitro* experiments have demonstrated that treatment of isolated membranes with free radicals induces the formation of gel phase lipid (Pauls and Thompson, 1981). Lipid peroxidation and symptoms such as the appearance of gel phase membrane lipid and the loss of fatty acids can also be induced by treatment of attached leaves with paraquat, a herbicide that short-circuits photosynthesis to form O_2^- (Chia et al., 1981). Such observations tend to suggest that membrane deterioration during senescence may, in part, be mediated by free radicals.

There is also evidence that the susceptibility of membranes to free radical attack is regulated by the degree of molecular order at the bilayer surface. For example, Ca^{+2} delays senescence, in particular the onset of lipid peroxidation, in a manner that can be correlated with its ability to rigidify the surfaces of lipid bilayers by acting as a divalent ligand (Legge et al., 1982). Polyamines are also known to stabilize membranes, presumably by acting as polyvalent ligands, and this may account for their apparent ability to delay dark-induced senescence in detached leaves and leaf disks (Cohen et al., 1979).

CONCLUSIONS

Is the senescence process a single sequence of events which is similar in all tissues? Perhaps, but parallel, interconnected sequences are likely at the whole plant level (Noodén, 1984). Extensive ultrastructural studies on senescing cells show many differences between tissues, yet some changes (and their sequence) seem to occur in all senescing tissues. Thus, one can speculate that certain changes

are central to the senescence process, while others are peripheral (the latter might include most of the tissue-specific changes). The loss of ribosomes and protein synthesis in the cytoplasm and the chloroplast seems important, as do the membrane changes which alter permeability and eventually cause a breakdown in homeostasis. Senescence is an active process under nuclear control and involves synthesis of new proteins. The single most visible and important difference among senescing tissues is the presence or absence of chloroplasts. Since chloroplasts are not present in all senescing tissues, can the degeneration of chloroplasts be part of the central sequence? We have argued that the loss of photosynthetic capacity is an important, even a key aspect of monocarpic senescence in soybean. Nevertheless, studies with inhibitors of protein synthesis indicate that senescence is imposed on the chloroplasts by factors from the cytoplasm. It seems premature, therefore, to try to identify a primary or central sequence(s) in this summary.

The rapidity and the orderly efficiency of the senescence process (self-destruction) in plants are very striking. It was mentioned earlier that there is no single purpose for senescence; its function is multifaceted. The role of senescence in cell differentiation (as in the lysis of the protoplast from xylem cells to increase water conductivity) is quite different from its roles in organ senescence and whole plant (monocarpic) senescence. Usually, organ senescence followed by abscission disposes of excess structures (e.g., flowers, fruits, and twigs), removes damaged, diseased, or "worn out" structures (especially leaves), or eliminates structures that have served their purpose and are no longer needed (e.g., peripheral flower parts such as petals). Apparently, as part of the frugal economy of life, resource retrieval (e.g., mineral nutrients) from structures destined to die confers a big advantage on the organism. In times of stress, senescence and adjustment of body size or reproductive load through partial senescence presumably enable the organism to cope more effectively.

Senescence (autumnal leaf shedding and top senescence of many herbaceous perennials) plays a major role in the plant's preparation for an adverse season by disposing of vulnerable parts. Senescence also aids in combating disease; the isolation of diseased areas by the "hyperimmune reaction" (Klement and Goodman, 1967; Bell, 1981) and the shedding of diseased parts (Kefford, 1976; Addicott, 1982) may reduce spreading of the disease.

Localized cell death may also play a role in shaping the early development of certain plant organs, particularly leaves (Melville and Wrigley, 1969). Synchronized senescence of the entire plant may represent a sacrifice of the parent plant (often destined to be killed by adverse weather in any case) to produce more seeds, and/or it may be part of a natural turnover process in the community where older, less vigorous individuals are replaced by younger, more vigorous individuals (Harper, 1977; Leopold, 1980). Both strategies are risky, for seedlings must compete anew to regain even the site occupied by their parent. In the case of monocarpic crops, a sharp transition from vegetative to reproductive growth, followed by rapid and synchronous defoliation and drydown, probably was selected by humans over many centuries to optimize yield and to increase harvestability (Denholm, 1975; Noodén, 1980b). The concept of turnover as an essential process can be applied at all levels of biology from molecules through organelles, cells, organs, and organisms, to species and entire floras (Leopold, 1980). Thus, future examinations of the biochemistry and physiology of senescence should be integrated with broader efforts to analyze its role at higher levels of biological organization.

REFERENCES

Abu-Shakra, S. S., Phillips, D. A., and Huffaker, R. C. 1978. Nitrogen fixation and delayed leaf senescence in soybeans. Science 199: 973–975.

Addicott, F. T. 1982. Abscission. Berkeley: University of California Press.

Addicott, F. T. and Lyon, J. T. 1973. Physiological ecology of abscission. In, T. T. Kozlowski (ed.), Shedding of Plant Parts, pp. 85–124. New York: Academic Press.

Adler, K., Brecht, E., Meister, A., Schmidt, O. and Süss, K.-H. 1979. Die Chloroplasten-thylakoid Membran: Biogenese, Pigmentorganisation, Protein-funktionsbezichungen und Degeneration während der Seneszenz. Eine Übersicht. Kulturpflanze 27: 13–48.

Aharoni, N. and Lieberman, M. 1979. Patterns of ethylene production in senescing leaves. Plant Physiol. 64: 796–800.

Baker, J. E. 1976. Superoxide dismutase in ripening fruits. Plant Physiol. 58: 644–647.

Baker, J. E., Wang, C. Y., Lieberman, M., and Hardenburg, R. 1977. Delay of senescence in carnations Dianthus caryophyllus by a rhizobitoxine analog and sodium benzoate. HortScience 12: 38–39.

Beevers, L. 1976. Senescence. In, J. Bonner and J. E. Varner (eds.), Plant Biochemistry, 3rd ed., pp. 771–794. New York: Academic Press.

Bell, A. A. 1981. Biochemical mechanisms of disease resistance. Ann. Rev. Plant Physiol. 32: 21–81.

Beutelmann, P. and Kende, H. 1977. Membrane lipids in senescing flower tissue of Ipomoea tricolor. Plant Physiol. 59: 888–893.

Boller, T. and Kende, H. 1979. Hydrolytic enzymes in the central vacuole of plant cells. Plant Physiol. 63: 1123–1132.

Borochov, A., Halevy, A. H., Borochov, H., and Shinitzky, M. 1978. Microviscosity of plasmalemmas in rose petals as affected by age and environmental factors. Plant Physiol. 61: 812–815.

Böttger, I. and Wollgiehn, R. 1958. Untersuchungen über Zusammenhang zwischen Nucleinsaure und Eiweisstoffwechsel in grünen Blättern. Flora 146: 302–320.

Brian, P. W., Petty, J. H. P., and Richmond, P. T. 1959. Effects of gibberellic acid on development of autumn color and leaf fall of deciduous woody plants. Nature 183: 58–59.

Burg, S. P. and Dijkman, M. J. 1967. Ethylene and auxin participation in pollen induced fading of Vanda orchid blossoms. Plant Physiol. 42: 1648–1650.

Burrows, W. J. and Carr, D. J. 1969. Effects of flooding on the root system of sunflower plants on the cytokinin content in the xylem sap. Physiol. Plant. 22: 1105–1112.

Burton, W. G. 1982. Post-harvest Physiology of Food Crops. London: Longman.

Butler, R. D. 1967. The fine structure of senescing cotyledons of cucumber. J. Exp. Bot. 18: 535–543.

Butler, R. D. and Simon, E. W. 1971. Ultrastructural aspects of senescence in plants. Adv. Gerontol. Res. 3: 73–129.

Callow, J. A., Callow, M. E., and Woolhouse, H. W. 1972. In vitro protein synthesis, RNA and polyribosomes in senescing leaves of Perilla. Cell Differ. 1: 79–90.

Chia, L. S., Thompson, J. E., and Dumbroff, E. B. 1981. Simulation of the effects of leaf senescence on membranes by treatment with paraquat. *Plant Physiol.* 67: 415–420.

Chibnall, A. C. 1939. *Protein Metabolism in the Plant.* New Haven: Yale University Press.

Cohen, A. S., Popovic, R. B., and Zalik, S. 1979. Effects of polyamines on chlorophyll and protein content, photochemical activity and chloroplast ultrastructure of barley, *Hordeum vulgare,* leaf discs during senescence. *Plant Physiol.* 64: 717–720.

Crocker, W. 1948. *Growth of Plants.* New York: Van Nostrand Reinhold.

Crocker, W. C. and Knight, L. I. 1908. Effect of illuminating gas and ethylene upon flowering carnations. *Bot. Gaz.* 46: 259–276.

Crowther, F. 1935. Studies in growth analysis of cotton plant under irrigation in the Sudan. I. The effects of different combinations of nitrogen applications and water supply. *Ann. Bot.* 48: 897–913.

Czapski, G. and Ilan, Y. A. 1978. On the generation of the hydroxylation agent from superoxide radical. Can the Haber-Weiss reaction be the source of OH· radicals? *Photochem. Photobiol.* 28: 651–653.

Davey, J. E. and van Staden, J. 1978. Cytokinin activity in *Lupinus albus.* II. Distribution in fruiting plants. *Physiol. Plant.* 43: 82–86.

Denholm, J. V. 1975. Necessary condition for maximum yield in a senescing two-phase plant. *J. Theor. Biol.* 52: 251–254.

Derman, B. D., Rupp, D. C., and Noodén, L. D. 1978. Mineral distribution in relation to fruit development and monocarpic senescence in Anoka soybeans. *Am. J. Bot.* 65: 205–213.

DeVries, H. 1890. Über abnormale Entstehung secundärer Gewebe. *Jahrb. Wiss. Bot.* 22: 35–72.

Dion, R. 1959. In *Historie de la Vigne et du Vinen France,* pp. 118–126 *des Origines aux XIXe Siècle.* Paris: Collège de France.

Dorner, R. W., Kahn, A., and Wildman, S. G. 1957. Synthesis and decay of the cytoplasmic proteins during the life of the tobacco leaf. *J. Biol. Chem.* 229: 945–952.

Draper, S. R. 1969. Lipid changes in senescing cucumber cotyledons. *Phytochemistry* 8: 1641–1647.

Dressler, R. L. 1981. *The Orchids.* Cambridge: Harvard University Press.

El-Antably, H. M. M., Wareing, P. F., and Hillman, J. 1967. Some physiological responses to D, L-abscisin (dormin). *Planta* 73: 74–90.

Esser, K. and Tudzynski, P. 1980. Senescence in fungi. *In,* K. V. Thimann (ed.), *Senescence in Plants,* pp. 67–83. Boca Raton, Fla.: CRC Press.

Faegri, K. and van der Pijl, K. 1979. *The Principles of Pollination Ecology,* 3rd ed. Oxford: Pergamon Press.

Farkas, G. L. 1978. Senescence and plant disease. *In,* J. Horsfall and E. Cowling (eds.), *Plant Disease: An Advanced Treatise,* Vol. 3, pp. 391–412. New York: Academic Press.

Fencl, Z. 1978. Cell aging and autolysis. *In,* J. E. Smith and D. R. Berry (eds.), *The Filamentous Fungi,* Vol.

3: *Developmental Mycology,* pp. 389–405. New York: Halsted Press/Wiley.

Fischer, C. W. 1950. Ethylene gas a problem in cut flower storage. *N. Y. State Flower Growers Bull.,* **61,** 1.

Fitting, H. 1911. Untersuchungen über die vorzeitige Entblätterung von Blüten. *Jahrb. Wiss. Bot.* 49: 187–263.

Fragata, M. and Bellemare, F. 1980. Model of singlet oxygen scavenging by α-tocopherol in biomembranes. *Chem. Phys. Lipids* 27: 93–99.

Frith, G. J. T. and Dalling, M. J. 1980. The role of peptide hydrolases in leaf senescence. *In,* K. V. Thimann (ed.), *Senescence in Plants,* pp. 117–130. Boca Raton, Fla.: CRC Press.

Frost, H. B. 1952. Characteristics in the nursery of *Citrus* budlings of young nucellar-seedling lines and parental old lines. *Proc. Amer. Soc. Hort. Sci.* 60: 247–254.

Gautheret, R. J. 1939. Sur la possibilité de réaliser la culture indéfinie des tissus de tubercules de Carrote. *C. R. Acad. Sci., Paris* 208: 118–120.

Gepstein, S. and Thimann, K. V. 1980. Changes in the abscisic acid content of oat leaves during senescence. *Proc. Nat. Acad. Sci.* 77: 2050–2053.

Gillissen, L. J. W. 1976. The role of the style as a sense-organ in relation to wilting of the flower. *Planta* 131: 201–202.

Goldschmidt, E. E. 1980. Pigment changes associated with fruit maturation and their control. *In,* K. V. Thimann (ed.), *Senescence in Plants,* pp. 207–217. Boca Raton, Fla.: CRC Press.

Goodwin, T. W. 1958. Studies in carotegenesis 24. The changes in carotenoid and chlorophyll pigments in the leaves of deciduous trees during autumn necrosis. *Biochem. J.* 68: 503–511.

Goormaghtigh, E., Van Campenhoud, M., and Ruysschaert, J. M. 1981. Lipid phase separation mediates binding of porcine pancreatic phospholipase A_2 to its substrate. *Biochem. Biophys. Res. Commun.* 101: 1410–1418.

Halevy, A. H. and Mayak, S. 1979. Senescence and postharvest physiology of cut flowers, part 1. *Horticult. Revs.* 1: 204–236.

Halevy, A. H. and Mayak, S. 1981. Senescence and postharvest physiology of cut flowers, part 2. *Horticult. Revs.* 3: 59–143.

Hall, N. P., Keys, A. J., and Merrett, M. J. 1978. Ribulose-1, 5-diphosphate carboxylase protein during flag leaf senescence. *J. Exp. Bot.* 29: 31–37.

Harman, D. 1981. The aging process. *Proc. Nat. Acad. Sci.* 78: 7124–7128.

Harper, J. L. 1977. *Population Biology of Plants.* London: Academic Press.

Harwood, J. L. 1980. Plant acyl lipids: structure, distribution and analysis. *In,* P. K. Stumpf (ed.), *The Biochemistry of Plants,* Vol. 4: *Lipids: Structure and Function,* pp. 1–55. New York: Academic Press.

Heath, O. V. S. and Mansfield, T. A. 1969. The movements of stomata. *In,* M. B. Wilkins (ed.), *The Phys-*

iology of Plant Growth and Development, pp. 301–332. New York: McGraw-Hill.

Herridge, D. F. and Pate, J. S. 1977. Utilization of net photosynthate for nitrogen fixation and protein production of an annual legume. *Plant Physiol.* 60: 759–764.

Hildebrand, F. 1881. Die Lebensdauer und Vegetationsweise der Pflanzen, ihre Ursache und ihre Entwicklung. *Bot. Jahrb.* 2: 51–135.

Horton, R. F. and Osborne, D. J. 1967. Senescence, abscission and cellulose activity in *Phaseolus vulgaris. Nature* 214: 1086–1088.

Hulme, A. C. (ed.) 1970. *The Biochemistry of Fruits and their Products,* Vol. 1. London: Academic Press.

Hulme, A. C. (ed.) 1971. *The Biochemistry of Fruits and Their Products.* Vol. 2. London: Academic Press.

Hume, D. J. and Criswell, J. G. 1973. Distribution and utilization of ^{14}C-labelled assimilates in soybeans. *Crop Sci.* 13: 519–524.

Jenkins, G. I. and Woolhouse, H. W. 1981a. Photosynthetic electron transport during senescence of the primary leaves of *Phaseolus vulgaris* L. I. Noncyclic electron transport. *J. Exp. Bot.* 32: 467–478.

Jenkins, G. I. and Woolhouse, H. W. 1981b. Photosynthetic electron transport during senescence of the primary leaves of *Phaseolus vulgaris* L. II. The activity of photosystems one and two, and a note on the site of reduction of ferricyanide. *J. Exp. Bot.* 32: 989–997.

Kahanak, G. M., Okatan, Y., Rupp, D. C., and Noodén, L. D. 1978. Hormonal and genetic alteration of monocarpic senescence in soybeans. *Plant Physiol.* 61 (Suppl.): 26.

Keegan, L. P. and Timmis, J. N. 1982. Ribosomal RNA gene redundancy and aging in radish (*Raphanus sativus*) cotyledons. *J. Life Sci. R. Dublin Soc.* 2: 171–179.

Kende, H. 1971. The cytokinins. *Int. Rev. Cytol.* 31: 301–338.

Kidd, F. and West, C. 1925. The course of respiratory activity throughout the life of an apple. *Rep. Food Invest. Bd., London,* pp. 27–34.

Klement, A. and R. N. Goodman. 1967. The hypersensitive reaction to infection by bacterial plant pathogens. *Ann. Rev. Phytopath.* 5: 17–44.

Koller, H. R. and Thorne, J. H. 1978. Soybean pod removal alters leaf diffusion resistance and leaflet orientation. Crop. Sci. 18: 305–307.

Kozlowski, T. T. (ed.) 1973. *Shedding of Plant Parts.* New York: Academic Press.

Kulaeva, O. N. 1962. The effect of roots on leaf metabolism in relation to the action of kinetin on leaves. *Fiziol. Rast.* (English transl.) 9: 182–189.

LaMarche, V. C. 1969. Environment in relation to age of bristlecone pines. *Ecology* 50: 53–59.

Lamont, B. B. 1980. Tissue longevity of the arborescent monocotyledon *Kingia australis* (Xanthorrhoeaceae). *Am. J. Bot.* 67: 1262–1264.

LaRue, C. D. 1936. Effect of auxin on abscission of petioles. *Proc. Nat. Acad. Sci.*

Legge, R. L., Thompson, J. E., Baker, J. E., and Lieberman, M. 1982. The effect of calcium on the fluidity and phase properties of microsomal membranes isolated from postclimacteric golden delicious apples. *Plant Cell Physiol.* 23:161–169.

Leopold, A. C. 1961. Senescence in plant development. *Science* 134: 1727–1732.

Leopold, A. C. 1980. Aging and senescence in plant development. *In,* K. V. Thimann (ed.), *Senescence in Plants,* pp. 1–12. Boca Raton, Fla.: CRC Press.

Leopold, A. C., Niedergang-Kamien, E., and Janick, J. 1959. Experimental modification of plant senescence. *Plant Physiol.* 34: 570–573.

Leopold, A. C. and Noodén, L. D. 1984. Hormonal regulatory systems in plants. *In,* T. K. Scott (ed.), *Encyclopedia of Plant Physiology,* Vol. 10: *Hormonal Regulation of Plant Development* II, pp. 4–21. New York: Springer-Verlag.

Leshem, Y. 1981. Oxy free radicals and plant senescence. *What's New in Plant Physiology* 12: 1–4.

Lieberman, M. 1979. Biosynthesis and action of ethylene. *Ann. Rev. Plant Physiol.* 30: 533–591.

Lindoo, S. J. and Noodén, L. D. 1978. Correlations of cytokinins and abscisic acid with monocarpic senescence in soybean. *Plant Cell Physiol.* 19: 977–1006.

Linn, W. and Wittenbach, V. A. 1981. Subcellular localization of proteases in wheat and corn mesophyll protoplasts. *Plant Physiol.* 67: 969–972.

Loehwing, F. W. 1951. Mineral nutrition in relation to ontogeny of plants. *In,* E. Troug (ed.), *Mineral Nutrition in Plants,* pp. 343–358. Madison: University of Wisconsin Press.

Loneragan, J. F., Snowball, K., and Robson, A. D. 1976. Remobilization of nutrients and its significance in plant nutrition. *In,* J. F. Wardlaw and J. B. Passioura (eds.), *Transport and Transfer Processes in Plants,* pp. 463–469. New York: Academic Press.

Lorenzi, R., Horgan, R., and Wareing, P. F. 1975. Cytokinins in *Picea sitchensis* Carriere: identification and relation to growth. *Bioch. Physiol. Pflanzen* 168: 333–339.

Mai, G. 1934. Korrelationsuntersuchungen an entspreiteten Blattstielen mittels lebender Orchideenpollinien als Wuchsstoffquelle. *Jahrb. Wiss. Bot.* 79: 681–713.

Martin, C. and Thimann, K. V. 1972. The role of protein synthesis in the senescence of leaves. I: The formation of protease. *Plant Physiol.,* 49: 64–71.

Matile, P. 1975. *The Lytic Compartment of Plant Cells.* New York: Springer-Verlag.

Matile, P. and Winkenbach, F. 1971. Functions of lysosomes and lysosomal enzymes in the senescing corolla of the Morning Glory (*Ipomoea purpurea*). *J. Exp. Bot.* 22: 759–771.

Mayak, S. and Halevy, A. H. 1980. Flower senescence. *In,* K. V. Thimann (ed.), *Senescence in Plants,* pp. 131–156. Boca Raton, Fla.: CRC Press.

McGlasson, W. B., Wade, D. L., and Adato, I. 1978.

Phytohormones and fruit ripening. *In,* D. S. Letham, P. B. Goodwin, and T. J. V. Higgins (eds.), *Phytohormones and Related Compounds,* Vol. II: *Phytohormones and Development of Higher Plants,* pp. 447–493. Amsterdam: Elsevier/North Holland Biomedical Press.

McKersie, B. D., Lepock, J. R., Kruuv, J., and Thompson, J. E. 1978. The effects of cotyledon senescence on the physical properties of membrane lipid. *Biochim. Biophys. Acta* 508: 197–212.

McKersie, B. D. and Thompson, J. E. 1977. Lipid crystallization in senescent membranes from cotyledons. *Plant Physiol.* 59: 803–807.

McKersie, B. D. and Thompson, J. E. 1978. Phase behaviour of chloroplast and microsomal membranes during leaf senescence. *Plant Physiol.* 61: 639–643.

McKersie, B. D. and Thompson, J. E. 1979. Phase properties of senescing plant membranes. Role of neutral lipids. *Biochim. Biophys. Acta* 500: 48–58.

McKersie, B. D., Thompson, J. E., and Brandon, J. K. 1976. X-ray diffraction evidence for decreased lipid fluidity in senescent membranes from cotyledons. *Can. J. Bot.* 54: 1074–1078.

Melville, R. and Wrigley, F. A. 1969. Fenestration in the leaves of *Monstera* and its bearing on the morphogenesis and colour patterns of leaves. *J. Linn. Soc. Bot.* 62: 1–16.

Meyer, A. 1918. Eiweisstoffwechsel und Vergilben der Laubblätter von *Tropaeolum majus. Flora* 111: 85–127.

Milborrow, B. V. 1974. The chemistry and physiology of abscisic acid. *Ann. Rev. Plant Physiol.* 25: 259–307.

Miller, E. C. 1938. *Plant Physiology.* New York: McGraw-Hill.

Molisch, H. 1918. Über die Vergilbung der Blätter. *Sitz.-ber. Akad. Wiss. Wien Math.-Nat.* 127: 3–34.

Molisch, H. 1938. *The Longevity of Plants* (H. Fulling, Transl.). Lancaster, Pa.: Science Press.

Morgan, P. W. and Gausman, H. W. 1966. Effects of ethylene on auxin transport. *Plant Physiol.* 41: 45–52.

Murashige, T. 1974. Plant propagation through tissue cultures. *Ann. Rev. Plant Physiol.* 25: 135–166.

Ness, P. J. and Woolhouse, H. W. 1980. RNA synthesis in *Phaseolus* chloroplasts. II. Ribonucleic acid synthesis in chloroplasts from developing and senescing leaves. *J. Exp. Bot.* 31: 235–245.

Neumann, P., Tucker, T., and Noodén, L. D. 1983. Characterization of leaf senescence and pod development in soybean explants. *Plant Physiol.* 72:182–185.

Nishimura, M. and H. Beevers. 1978. Hydrolases in vacuoles from castor bean endosperm. *Plant Physiol.* 62: 44–48.

Noodén, L. D. 1980a. Regulation of senescence. *In,* F. T. Corbin (ed.), *World Soybean Research Conference II. Proceedings,* pp. 139–152. Boulder, Colo.: Westview Press.

Noodén, L. D. 1980b. Senescence in the whole plant. *In,* K. V. Thimann (ed.), *Senescence in Plants,* pp. 219–258. Boca Raton, Fla.: CRC Press.

Noodén, L. D. 1984. Integration of soybean pod development and monocarpic senescence. A minireview. *Physiol. Plant.* in press.

Noodén, L. D., Kahanak, G. M., and Okatan, Y. 1979. Prevention of monocarpic senescence in soybeans with auxin and cytokinin antidote for self-destruction. *Science* 206: 841–843.

Noodén, L. D. and Leopold, A. C. 1978. Phytohormones and the endogenous regulation of senescence and abscission. *In,* D. S. Letham, P. B. Goodwin, and T. J. V. Higgins (eds.), *Phytohormones and Related Compounds—A Comprehensive Treatise,* Vol. II: *Phytohormones and the Development of Higher Plants,* Amsterdam: Elsevier/North Holland Biomedical Press.

Noodén, L. D. and Murray, B. J. 1982. Transmission of the monocarpic senescence signal via the xylem in soybean. *Plant Physiol.* 69: 754–756.

Noodén, L. D. and Obermeyer, W. R. 1981. Changes in abscisic acid translocation during pod development and senescence in soybeans. *Biochem. Physiol. Pflanzen* 176: 859–868.

Noodén, L. D., Rupp, D. C., and Derman, B. D. 1978. Separation of seed development from monocarpic senescence in soybeans. *Nature* 271: 354–357.

Osborne, D. J. 1980. Senescence in seeds. *In,* K. V. Thimann (ed.), *Senescence in Plants,* pp. 13–37. Boca Raton, Fla.: CRC Press.

Osborne, D. J. and Hallaway, H. M. 1960. Auxin control of protein levels in detached autumn leaves. *Nature* 188: 240–241.

Pauls, K. P. and Thompson, J. E. 1981. Effects of *in vitro* treatment with ozone on the physical and chemical properties of membranes. *Physiol. Plant.* 53: 255–262.

Penning-Roswell, E. 1971. *The Wines of Bordeaux.* London: International Wine and Food Publishing Co.

Peterson, L. W., Kleinkopf, G. E., and Huffaker, R. C. 1973. Evidence for lack of turnover of ribulose 1,5-diphosphate carboxylase in barley leaves Plant Physiol. 51:1042–1045.

Pillay, D. T. N. and Cherry, J. H. 1974. Changes in leucyl, seryl and tyrosyl transfer RNAs in aging soybean cotyledons. *Can. J. Bot.* 52: 2499–2504.

Priestley, D. A. and Posthumus, M. A. 1982. Extreme longevity of lotus seeds from Pulantien. *Nature* 299: 148–149.

Proebsting, W. M., Davies, P. J., and Marx, G. A. 1978. Photoperiod-induced changes in gibberellin metabolism in relation to apical growth and senescence in genetic lines of peas (*Pisum Sativum* L.). Planta 141:231–238.

Pryor, W. A. 1976. *In,* W. A. Pryor (ed.), *Free Radicals in Biology,* Vol. 1, pp. 1–49. New York: Academic Press.

Raschke, K. and Zeevaart, J. A. D. 1976. Abscisic acid content, transpiration, and stomatal conductance as related to leaf age in plants of *Xanthium strumarium* L. *Plant Physiol.* 58: 169–174.

Rhodes, M. J. C. 1980a. The maturation and ripening of fruits. *In,* K. V. Thimann (ed.), *Senescence in Plants,* pp. 157–205. Boca Raton, Fla.: CRC Press.

Rhodes, M. J. C. 1980b. Respiration and senescence of plant organs. *In,* D. D. Davies (ed.), *The Biochemistry of Plants,* Vol. 2: *Metabolism and Respiration,* pp. 419–462. New York: Academic Press.

Richmond, A. E. and Lang, A. 1957. Effect of kinetin on protein content and survival of detached *Xanthium* leaves. *Science* 125: 650–651.

Richter, O. 1915. Über das Erhaltenbleiben des Chlorophylls in herbstlich verfärbten und abgefallenen Blättern durch Tiere. *Z. Pflanzenkr.,* 25: 385–392.

Rosen, R. 1978. Feed forwards and global system failure: a general mechanism for senescence. *J. Theor. Biol.* 74: 579–590.

Sabater, B., Rodriguez, M. T., and Zamorano, A. 1981. Effects and interactions of gibberellic acid and cytokinins on the retention of cholorphyll and phosphate in barley leaf segments. *Physiol. Plant.* 51: 361–364.

Samet, J. S. and Sinclair, T. R. 1980. Leaf senescence and abscisic acid in leaves of field grown soybean. *Plant Physiol.* 66: 1164–1168.

Satler, S. O. and Thimann, K. V. 1980. The influence of aliphatic alcohols on leaf senescence. *Plant Physiol.* 66: 395–399.

Šestak, Z. and Catsky, J. 1967. Sur les Relations entre le Contenu en Chlorophylle et l'Activité Photosynthetique pendant la Croissance et le Vieillissement des Feuilles. *In,* C. Sironval (ed.), *Le Chloroplaste, Croissance et Vieillissement,* pp. 213–262. Paris: Mason.

Setter, T. L., Brun, W. A., and Brenner, M. L. 1980. Effect of obstructed translocation on leaf abscisic acid, and associated stomatal closure and photosynthesis decline. *Plant Physiol.* 65: 1111–1115.

Sexton, R. and Roberts, J. A. 1982. Cell biology of abscission. *Ann. Rev. Plant Physiol.* 33: 133–162.

Sharp, W. R., Larsen, P. O., Paddock, E. F., and Raghavan, V. (eds.) 1979. *Plant Cell and Tissue Culture. Principles and Applications.* Columbus: Ohio State University Press.

Shaw, M. and Manocha, M. S. 1965. Fine structure in detached, senescing wheat leaves. *Can. J. Bot.* 43: 747–755.

Shechter, E., Letellier, L., and Gulik-Kuzywiki, T. 1974. Relations between structure and function in cytoplasmic membrane vesicles isolated from an *E. coli* fatty acid auxotroph. *Eur. J. Biochem.* 49: 61–76.

Shininger, T. L. 1979. The control of vascular development. *Ann. Rev. Plant Physiol.* 30: 313–337.

Skene, K. G. M. 1975. Cytokinin production by roots as a factor in the control of plant growth. *In,* J. G. Torrey and D. T. Clarkson (eds.), *The Development and Function of Roots,* pp. 365–396. London: Academic Press.

Stebbins, G. L. 1957. *Variation and Evolution in Plants.* New York: Columbia University Press.

Storey, R. L. and Beevers, L. 1977. Proteolytic activity in relationship to senescence and cotyledonary development in *Pisum sativum* L. *Planta* 137: 37–44.

Takegami, T. and Yoshida, Y. 1975. Remarkable retardation of the senescence of tobacco leaf discs by cordycepin, an inhibitor of RNA polyadenylation. *Plant Cell Physiol.* 16: 1163–1166.

Thimann, K. V. 1980. The senescence of leaves. *In,* K. V. Thimann (ed.), *Senescence in Plants,* pp. 85–115. Boca Raton, Fla.: CRC Press.

Thomas, H. and Stoddart, J. L. 1980. Leaf senescence. *Ann. Rev. Plant Physiol.* 31: 83–111.

Thompson, J. E., Mayak, S., Shinitzky, M., and Halevy, A. H. 1982. Acceleration of membrane senescence in cut carnation flowers by treatment with ethylene. *Plant Physiol.* 69: 859–863.

Trippi, V. S. 1976. Dégénérescence des clones. *In,* R. Jacques (ed.), *En Etudes de Biologie Vegetale "Homage au Professeur Chouard,"* pp. 143–150. Paris.

Trippi, V. and Montaldi, E. 1960. The aging of sugar cane clones. *Phyton* 14: 79–91.

Ueda, J. and Kato, J. 1980. Isolation and identification of a senescence-promoting substance from wormwood (*Artemisia absinthium* L). *Plant Physiol.* 66: 246–249.

van Staden, J. and Davey, J. E. 1979. The synthesis, transport and metabolism of endogenous cytokinins. *Plant, Cell and Environment* 2: 93–116.

van Steveninck, R. F. M. 1975. The "washing" or "aging" phenomenon in plant tissues. *Ann. Rev. Plant. Physiol.* 26: 237–258.

Vasek, F. C. 1980. Creosote bush: long-lived clones in the Mojave desert. *Am. J. Bot.* 67: 246–255.

Villers, T. A. 1980. Ultrastructural changes in seed dormancy and senescence. *In,* K. V. Thimann (ed.), *Senescence in Plants,* pp. 39–66. Boca Raton, Fla.: CRC Press.

Von Abrams, G. J. 1974. An effect of ornithine on degradation of chlorophyll and protein in excised leaf tissue. *Z. Pflanzenphysiol.* 72: 410–421.

Walton, D. C. 1980. Biochemistry and physiology of abscisic acid. *Ann. Rev. Plant Physiol.* 31: 453–489.

Wangermann, E. 1965. Longevity and ageing in plants and plant organs. *In,* W. Ruhland (ed.), *Handbuch der Pflanzenphysiologie,* Vol. 15/2, pp. 1026–1057. Berlin: Springer-Verlag.

Wangermann, E. and Lacey, H. J. 1955. Studies on the morphogenesis of leaves. X. Preliminary experiments on the relation between nitrogen nutrition, rate of respiration and rate of ageing of fronds of *Lemna minor.* *New Physiol.* 54: 182–198.

Watanabe, A. and H. Imaseki. 1982. Changes in translatable mRNA in senescing wheat leaves. *Plant and Cell Physiol.* 23: 489–497.

Westing, A. H. 1964. The longevity and aging of trees. *Gerontologist* 4: 10–15.

White, P. R. 1934. Potentially unlimited growth of excised tomato root tips in a liquid medium. *Plant Physiol.* 9: 585–600.

White, P. R. 1939. Potentially unlimited growth of excised plant callus in an artificial nutrient. *Am. J. Bot.* 26: 59–64.

Willis, R. H. H., Lee, T. H, Graham, D., McGlasson W. B., and Hall, E. G. 1981. *Postharvest.* Westport, Conn.: Avi Publishing Co.

Willstätter, R. and Stoll, A. 1918. *Untersuchungen über die Assimilation der Kohlensäure.* Berlin: Springer-Verlag.

Wittenbach, V. A. 1979. Ribulose bisphosphate carboxylase and proteolytic activity in wheat leaves from anthesis through senescence. *Plant Physiol.* 64: 884–887.

Wittenbach, V. A., Lin, W., and Hebert, R. R. 1982. Vacuolar localization of proteases and degradation of chloroplasts in mesophyll protoplasts from senescing primary wheat leaves. *Plant Physiol.* 69: 98–102.

Wood, J. G. and Cruickshank, D. H. 1944. The metabolism of starving leaves. 5. Changes in amounts of some amino acids during starvation of grass leaves; and their bearing on the nature of the relationship between proteins and amino acids. *Aust. J. Exp. Biol. Med. Sci.* 22: 111–123.

Woodward, R. G. and Rawson, H. M. 1976. Photosynthesis and transpiration in dicotyledonous plants. II. Expanding and senescing leaves of soybean. *Austral. J. Plant Physiol.* 3:257–267.

Yoshida, Y. 1961. Nuclear control of chloroplast activity in *Elodea* leaf cells. *Protoplasma* 54: 476–492.

6
SOME ASPECTS OF AGING CAN BE STUDIED EASILY IN NEMATODES

Richard L. Russell*
and
Lewis A. Jacobson
Department of Biological Sciences
University of Pittsburgh

INTRODUCTION

Studies of aging in nematodes are based largely on the hope that there are some general mechanisms of aging which can be expeditiously revealed in simple multicellular organisms. Although differing greatly from mammals in size, body plan, and some organ systems, nematodes nonetheless strongly resemble other metazoans at the cellular, subcellular, and biochemical levels. Moreover, nematodes do exhibit some rather widespread aging phenomena, such as nutritional prolongation of life span, accumulation of age pigments, and enzyme alterations, and their short life span, cellular simplicity, and genetic manipulability can be real advantages in studying the mechanisms underlying these phenomena.

*Our own work described herein has been supported by grants from the U. S. Public Health Service (AG 01154, AG 02655). We thank Kathryn Ambrose and Mary Simon for technical assistance, and L. Barnett, M. Bolanowski, S. Brenner, D. B. Dusenbery, E. M. Hedgecock, L. Jen-Jacobson, T. E. Johnson, C. M. Link, J. B. Rand, E. Schierenberg, J. E. Sulston, N. Thomson, and J. G. White for permission to cite results before publication.

EXPERIMENTAL ADVANTAGES AND DISADVANTAGES OF NEMATODES FOR AGING STUDIES

Aging studies of nematodes have concentrated on a few species, notably the vinegar eel worm *Turbatrix aceti,* the free-living soil species *Caenorhabditis briggsae,* and recently, the free-living soil species *Caenorhabditis elegans.* Because of the recent attention focussed on *C. elegans* as a model organism for eukaryotic developmental genetics (Edgar and Wood, 1977; Sulston and Hodgkin, 1979), we will concentrate on it, noting similarities and differences of the other two species as necessary.

Advantages

Short Life Span. As *C. elegans* is frequently cultured, at 20°C on agar-containing Petri dishes with a lawn of *Escherichia coli* as food source, it has a median life span of 11.5–15.0 days and a maximum life span of 18.6–20.0 days (Klass, 1977; Mitchell et al., 1979, Bolanowski, et al., 1981). For *C. briggsae* and *T. aceti,* usually grown under different conditions, median life spans are only slightly longer, 34 and 18–26 days, respectively (Gershon, 1970; Epstein and Gershon, 1972; Epstein et al., 1972; Reiss and Rothstein, 1975; Gupta and Rothstein, 1976b; Reznick and Gershon, 1979). An obvious advantage of these short life spans is that many longitudinal aging experiments can be done quickly.

Ease of Maintaining Large Populations. All three commonly studied species are small sized, and large numbers can be maintained in a limited space. For *C. elegans,* a standard 100 × 15 mm Petri dish, seeded with a lawn of *E. coli* strain OP50 (Brenner, 1974) can support the full life cycle of at least 200 individuals (our unpublished observations). For large-scale biochemical purposes *C. elegans* can also be grown in aerated liquid cultures (50,000–100,000 individuals/ml). *C. briggsae* and *T. aceti* are typically grown in liquid cultures, at densities of up to 250,000 individuals/ml (Rothstein, 1974; Rothstein and Coppens, 1978). Given methods for initiating and maintaining age-synchrony (to be discussed), it is thus possible to maintain large, age-synchronous cohorts so that statistically and biochemically adequate samples can be obtained throughout the life span.

Freedom from Disease. Recognized nematode diseases are rare (Loewenberg et al., 1959; Bird, 1971). The three commonly studied species do not, to our knowledge, have any infectious diseases (bacterial, viral, or otherwise) or any neoplastic diseases. Thus, in aging studies one need not be concerned with avoidable, erratic diseases, and differential mortality due to different unavoidable diseases under different conditions does not occur.

Cellular Simplicity. For *C. elegans,* the cell number in each organ system is known exactly. For many systems, the cell number is quite small (e.g., 95 longitudinal body muscle cells, 302 neurons), and in all organ systems the cell number is invariant, or nearly so. Complete cell-lineage charts exist for all

adult somatic cells (Sulston, 1976; Sulston and Horvitz, 1977; Deppe et al., 1976; Krieg et al., 1978; Kimble and Hirsh, 1979; Sulston et al., 1983). Each somatic cell can be uniquely recognized, and the divisional histories also appear almost totally invariant (Kimble et al., 1979; Sulston and White, 1980; von Ehrenstein and Schierenberg, 1980; Kimble and White, 1981). For aging studies, there are two important consequences. First, because adults are relatively transparent, many of the identified cells may be observed directly using Nomarski optics, thus making it possible to follow age-related changes, longitudinally and noninvasively, in single identified cells. Second, all somatic cell divisions cease before early adulthood, so that aging occurs without the introduction of "new" cells into an old organism.

Manipulative Genetics. *Turbatrix aceti* is a dioecious species and has distinct males and females (Peters, 1928). *C. briggsae* and *C. elegans,* on the other hand, are self-fertilizing hermaphrodites (Nigon, 1943, 1949; Brenner, 1974), a property which opens up the possibility of extensive genetic exploitation because it facilitates mutant isolation. In brief, induced mutations, which are usually recessive, are difficult to detect in dioecious species because there is no simple method for producing mutant homozygotes. In a self-fertilizing species, however, induced mutant heterozygotes automatically produce such mutant homozygotes as one-fourth of their progeny. In *C. elegans,* this property has been extensively exploited; over 2000 independently isolated mutant strains are available (Brenner, 1974; Herman and Horvitz, 1980; Riddle, 1980; Siddiqui and von Ehrenstein, 1980). Fortunately, mutant strains can be easily stored in liquid nitrogen and successfully recovered. Mapping and complementation testing of these mutants are made possible through the rare occurrence of males (XO), by chromosomal nondisjunction from hermaphrodites (XX); over 240 genes have been mapped on six chromosomes (Herman et al., 1980). For aging studies, this library of available mutants has two important consequences. First, for about half a dozen genes the primary product of the affected gene is now known with reasonable certainty (Sulston, 1976; McLeod et al., 1977; Waterson et al., 1977; Baillie and Rosenbluth, 1977; Siddiqui and Babu, 1980; Bhat and Babu, 1980; Johnson et al., 1981; Culotti et al., 1981; Rand and Russell, 1984); in these cases, the mutants become a highly specific and unambiguous tool for testing the involvement of those gene products in aging. Second, even when the primary product of the affected gene is not known, mutants can serve to discredit potential causes of aging; thus, a mutant defective in a given process can, if it ages normally, rule out any hypothesis in which that process is necessary for normal aging.

Two other advantages for aging studies derive from the self-fertilizing mode of reproduction of C. elegans and C. briggsae. The first is that inbreeding is easy, indeed probably the prevalent form of reproduction in the wild. Thus, laboratory individuals and even most wild isolates are likely to be homozygous at virtually all loci. Since animals can be maintained clonally, aging studies can be carried out on populations with an extremely high degree of genetic uniformity. Second, it may be possible to isolate mutants with specific and rather central effects on aging (Mitchell, 1976; Klass, 1977; see discussion of prospects at the end of this chapter).

A Nonaging Developmental Variant. All three commonly studied species can, under appropriate conditions, have an arrested developmental form known as a dauerlarva (Peters, 1928; Yarwood and Hansen, 1969; Cassada and Russell, 1975). Probably specialized as a survival or dispersal stage, the dauerlarva is induced by harsh conditions, including (for C. elegans) at least starvation and crowding (Cassada and Russell, 1975; Albert et al., 1981; Swanson and Riddle, 1981); dauerlarvae can be made to reenter the normal developmental pathway by return to favorable conditions. Dauerlarvae can live for very long times, up to 60 days, and as judged by their subsequent life spans upon recovery,

they do not appear to age detectably while in the dauerlarva state (Klass and Hirsh, 1976). For aging studies, the dauerlarva can sometimes serve as a useful control, although its differences from the normal developmental stages are manifold and clearly not confined to aging rate alone (Hedgecock and Russell, 1975; Anderson, 1976). Also, C. elegans mutants affecting dauerlarva formation exist (Cassada and Russell, 1975; Riddle et al., 1981; Albert and Riddle, 1980).

Disadvantages

Limited Tissue Separation. Because of small size, individual dissection not only is technically infeasible but would yield very small amounts of material. Mass treatments of populations generally run afoul of the fact that operations sufficiently harsh to disrupt the tough external cuticle usually damage internal structures. Some success has, however, been achieved for sperm (Argon and Ward, 1980; Klass and Hirsh, 1981) and the cuticle itself (Cox, Staprans, and Edgar, 1981; Cox, Kusch, and Edgar, 1981).

No Tissue Sampling. Nematodes lack a dispensable circulating fluid like mammalian blood, and because the sampling techniques would be very tedious, it is not practical to obtain repeated tissue samples from a given individual in a longitudinal study. For some purposes, this disadvantage may be offset by the extreme genetic uniformity of the population.

No Cell Culture. In contrast with mammals, nematodes have not yet, despite serious efforts yielded viable cell cultures. The absence of cell culture methods means that aging phenomena observed in the intact organism cannot be pursued during cell culture *in vitro*.

Causes of Death Uncertain. Autopsies of dead individuals, either by dissection or by visual observation, appear technically infeasible and are complicated by a relatively rapid degeneration following death. Consequently, the cause of death is uncertain, and the importance ascribed to this uncertainty depends on the importance accorded to death as an aging phenomenon. In our view, death should not be accorded the special place which it has occupied in many previous studies of aging. Instead, we argue that aging should be assessed by measuring multiple parameters, whose concomitant changes with time give a more accurate measure of the aging process.

METHODOLOGICAL CONSIDERATIONS

Culture Conditions

The three commonly studied species can be grown either axenically (without other organisms) or monoxenically (with one additional organism, usually the bacterium *Escherichia coli;* see Vanfleteren, 1980). Fully defined axenic media now exist to support growth and reproduction of all three species, but because the resulting growth is slow, a common alternative is the use of axenic media with one or a few undefined supplements, such as soy peptone or yeast extract.

The axenic mode avoids any possible (but as yet undemonstrated) deleterious effects of excreted bacterial metabolites on nematode growth and allows nematode extracts to be made without possible bacterial contamination. In the monoxenic mode, the food is much more nearly like the normal particulate food consumed in the wild, and faster rates of growth and development are obtained (Klass, 1977; Mitchell et al., 1979; Zuckerman and Himmelhoch, 1980). For nutritional restriction studies, the monoxenic mode is probably to be preferred, to ensure that the well-fed animals which will be compared with the restricted ones are indeed optimally fed. Monoxenic conditions may indeed be best for any studies in which animals must be well-fed and healthy. On the other hand, for studies of enzyme alteration, where the phenomenology is hopefully independent of nutritional status, axenic conditions may be preferable because they facilitate enzyme purification with minimal contamination and degradation (Rothstein, 1980).

A related issue is that of genetic divergence under different maintenance conditions. In the past, different laboratories focusing on different growth modes have maintained their stocks by serial transfer in the chosen growth mode. Recent experience with *C. elegans* suggest that even as little as 2–3 years of separate maintenance under axenic and monoxenic conditions can lead to discernible variations in development and behavior, presumably reflecting different selective pressures (Mitchell et al., 1979). Lest this divergence become a source of confusion, we urge (1) that frozen canonical stocks be established for each species and maintained in a central location (all three species are kept by the Caenorhabditis Genetics Center, 110 Tucker Hall, University of Missouri, Columbia MO 65211, USA); (2) that new investigators obtain their starting stocks from this location and that all investigators periodically check their stocks against samples from a standardized source; (3) that existing variants, e.g., long-term axenically maintained strains which may have acquired better axenic growth properties over time, also be stored frozen as soon as possible as a benchmark against further selective change; and (4) that wherever possible, the use of the less natural, axenic growth mode be carried out by axenizing, for the purpose, stocks which are maintained in the more natural monoxenic mode.

Initiation and Maintenance of Age Synchrony

Age-synchronous populations of all three species can be initiated easily, since eggs, newly hatched juveniles, and adults can be separated from one another by a number of physical properties and/or resistances to potentially lethal treatments. Maintaining a synchronous cohort free of progeny animals is more difficult, however, because the number of progeny produced is large (e.g., about 280 for each adult *C. elegans* in monoxenic culture) and the generation time is short relative to the life span. In choosing among available methods, an important consideration has been the number (or mass) of synchronous nematodes needed. In general, studies with biochemical objectives have employed large cohorts, grown axenically in liquid medium, whereas those with more descriptive objectives have employed smaller cohorts, grown monoxenically.

Initiation. Small age-synchronous populations to be grown monoxenically on agar are usually initiated by hand-picking gravid adults to fresh plates and removing them several hours later, leaving fertilized eggs behind on the surface. Significantly improved synchrony, at a moderate cost in yield, has been obtained by taking advantage of the selective adherence of eggs to the agar surface (Byerly et al., 1976; Mitchell et al., 1979); if the egg-containing plate is gently rinsed at hourly intervals around the time of hatching (9–12 hours after egg deposit), each rinse contains only juveniles hatching in the previous hour.

Much larger-scale cohorts, usually used for axenic growth, can be initiated from eggs obtained by treating either an asynchronous population or a population consisting mostly of gravid adults with either glutaraldehyde (Brenner, 1974; Mitchell et al., 1979) or alkaline hypochlorite (Patel and McFadden, 1978; Khan and McFadden, 1980). Both treatments kill adults, juveniles, and any bacteria which may be present, but leave eggs intact. If obtained from inside gravid adults by the alkaline hypochlorite method, the resulting eggs hatch quite synchronously (between 9 and 12 hours after treatment; Khan and McFadden, 1980). Alternatively, when the parental population is axenically grown and partially synchronized by development from dauerlarvae, extruded eggs can be harvested by flotation as large floccules, containing thousands of aggregated eggs each; juveniles emerging from these eggs over any chosen synchrony period can be separated from the eggs by filtration through a narrow mesh (9–12 μm) wire screen (Gandhi et al., 1980). This method has been used to obtain cohorts containing $\sim 10^6$ individuals whose eggs were synchronous to within 6 hours.

Even larger synchronous populations have been initiated with young juveniles obtained by percolation through a column of small glass beads (Gershon, 1970; Zeelon et al., 1973), by filtration through glass wool (Vogel, 1974; Gandhi et al., 1980), or by screening with fine mesh screens of nylon (Bollinger and Willett, 1980) or stainless steel (Tilby and Moses, 1975; Hieb and Rothstein, 1975; Bolla and Brot, 1975; Rothstein and Sharma, 1978). These methods are most useful when less precisely synchronized animals are needed, and have been used to generate cohorts of as many as 10^7 individuals.

Maintenance. Two strategies are available for maintaining an age-synchronous culture. Either reproduction must be prevented, or the members of the original cohort must be repeatedly separated from their progeny.

For small scale experiments it is possible to repeatedly transfer individual adult nematodes away from their smaller progeny until reproduction ceases (Zuckerman et al., 1971; Epstein et al., 1972; Kisiel et al., 1974; Searcy et al., 1976; Himmelhoch et al., 1977; Klass, 1977; Croll et al., 1977a, 1977b; Mitchell et al., 1979; Willett et al., 1980; Bolanowski et al., 1981). This method has been used both for liquid axenic culture and for monoxenic culture on agar plates, but it is far too laborious when more than a few hundred animals are required.

Larger scale methods for physical separation of large adults from smaller progeny include differential sieving, either on a continuous basis (Tilby and Moses, 1975) or intermittently (Rothstein and Sharma, 1978; Bollinger and Willett, 1980), and differential sedimentation (Klass, 1977; Bollinger and Willett, 1980). These methods are readily adaptable to cultivation in liquid media and can be used to maintain quite large cohorts. Their principal disadvantages are that they involve significant effort, that they may involve unintended losses of the adults, that they subject the aging animals to manipulations which may affect their survival, and in the case of sieving, that the size of the maintainable cohort is limited by the need to maintain a sizable screen surface area.

Several techniques are used to inhibit reproduction. The oldest and most controversial involves DNA synthesis inhibitors such as 5-fluorodeoxyuridine (FUdR), aminopterin, or hydroxyurea (Gershon, 1970). To minimize pathological effects on postembryonic development, inhibitors should be administered to young adult nematodes just before the onset of reproduction (Mitchell et al., 1979). Survival curves may be unaffected by this treatment, but even so, the high concentrations of FUdR usually used produce anatomical and behavioral abnormalities (Kisiel et al., 1972; Mitchell et al., 1979; Bolanowski et al., 1981). Lower concentrations of FUdR, as described in one report (Gandhi et al., 1980), may be able to achieve adequate inhibition of reproduction without major drug-induced abnormalities; this method warrants further examination.

Reproduction can also be inhibited by using mutants of *C. elegans* with temperature-sensitive defects. Klass (1977) used a mutant strain (DH26) defective in spermatogenesis at 25.5°C, but there are mutants defective in gonadogenesis or fertilization and also a large number of early embryonic *ts* lethals which might be used in analogous ways (Hirsh and Vanderslice, 1976; Miwa et al., 1980; Schierenberg et al., 1980). A possible disadvantage of such mutants is that they might be altered in processes other than reproduction, either because the primary mutant lesion has pleiotropic consequences or because the customary backcrossing of new mutants to wild type may by chance have failed to remove secondary mutations induced in the original mutagenesis (see Brenner, 1974).

In *T. aceti,* reproduction can be blocked in two other ways. The first is to conduct studies at 36°C, instead of 30°C, since reproduction is blocked for unknown reasons at the higher temperature (Hieb and Rothstein, 1975). However, this higher temperature clearly affects growth as well as reproduction, and at 37°C, only one degree

higher, *T. aceti* dies quite rapidly (Rothstein, 1980). The second method, which applies to the dioecious *T. aceti* but not to *C. elegans* and *C. briggsae,* is individual isolation to prevent mating (Gershon, 1970; Vogel, 1974; Kisiel and Zuckerman, 1974). While involving somewhat less effort than the repeated manual removal of progeny, this method is still limited to relatively small cohorts.

Measures of Senescence

In any aging study, aging must be defined and measured. The simplest choice, often taken, is to use mortality or survival in a population as the sole measure of aging. We believe that this is probably an unwise choice, primarily because survival can be perturbed in a number of irrelevant ways. For work with nematodes, the choice of survival as a sole criterion poses several special problems.

The first, albeit relatively minor, problem is standardizing the definition of death. The absence of spontaneous body movement or pharyngeal pumping, while sometimes used as a criterion (Hieb and Rothstein, 1975; Patel and McFadden, 1978), is not sufficient to identify dead nematodes; in our experience, many old nematodes initiate body movement only after direct tactile stimulation. (However, since nematodes appear to be strongly stimulated to move when suspended in liquid, the absence of self-initiated motion may be a sufficient criterion of death for nematodes in liquid medium.) The absence of movement after stimulation is more commonly used as a criterion (Mitchell et al., 1979; Gandhi et al., 1980; Bolanowski et al., 1981; Johnson and Wood, 1982). Other criteria used are significant deterioration of internal anatomy (Bolanowski et al., 1981) and lack of osmotic turgor, assessed (destructively) by cutting and observing for extrusion of internal contents (Johnson and Wood, 1982). As a standard set of criteria for adoption in future work we recommend:

1. The absence of self-initiated movement of body muscle or pharynx

2. The failure to respond to direct tactile stimulation
3. Significant deterioration of internal anatomy

The second problem is that survival statistics can be badly in error when even very low levels of reproduction occur in experimental populations. For *C. elegans,* the normal brood size is about 280 for each adult hermaphrodite, so that even if reproduction were limited to a level 1000-fold lower than normal (i.e., about one progeny animal for each three members of the original cohort), errors of 50 percent or more might accrue in determining surviving fractions late in the life span. For this reason, scrupulous maintenance of age synchrony is essential if survival is to be used as a measure of aging.

The third problem is that of premature death due to causes other than senescence. Occasionally, an unusual wave of deaths occurs around the reproductive period, especially in nutritionally poor media (Tilby and Moses, 1975; Gandhi et al., 1980). Because *C. elegans* tends to retain eggs under poor nutritional conditions (Croll, 1975), death may result from internal hatching, after which the newly hatched larvae devour the parent from within (*"endotokia matricida"*). Internal hatching should not present a serious problem when reproduction is suppressed by genetic or pharmacologic means, but it must be observed carefully when progeny animals are removed by physical means.

As an alternative to the use of survival as the sole measure of aging, many laboratories are characterizing quantitative changes which occur with chronological age. Some of these changes have been studied in sufficient detail to serve as useful "markers" of senescent processes.

In general, the rate of nematode movement declines with age. Pai (1928) observed a general slowing in aging *T. aceti,* and in *C. elegans* both the frequency of self-initiated movement (Croll, 1975) and the rate of sinusoidal body wave formation (Croll et al., 1977a; Hosono, 1978; Hosono et al., 1980; Bolanowski et al., 1981) decline with age.

Although the mechanism of this decreased mobility is not known, it probably does not reflect a decline in the enzymes of acetylcholine metabolism, since both acetylcholinesterase and choline acetyltransferase levels change little with age (Bolanowski et al., 1983). Some alterations in muscle structure have been observed in old *C. briggsae* (Zuckerman et al., 1971) and *T. aceti* (Kisiel et al., 1975), but it is not clear what role, if any, these changes play in declining movement rates. Age-related declines in pharyngeal bulb pulsation rate in *C. elegans* were observed by Mitchell et al. (1979), but no consistent changes were observed by Croll et al. (1977b). The frequency of defecations declines with age (Croll et al., 1977b; Bolanowski et al., 1981), although the reported temporal details of the decline vary; there was some indication of differences between axenic and monoxenic cultures in the former report.

A greater osmotic fragility of old *C. briggsae* has been reported for animals grown axenically (Zuckerman et al., 1971), but monoxenically grown *C. elegans* do not exhibit this property (Zuckerman and Himmelhoch, 1980; Bolanowski et al., 1981). An increasing specific gravity with age has been noted in *C. briggsae* (Zuckerman et al., 1972) but not in *T. aceti* (Kisiel and Zuckerman, 1974). An increased permeability of the cuticular surface, as measured by the exchange of ^3H_2O, was reported for axenically grown *C. elegans* (Searcy et al., 1976) but was absent in monoxenically grown *C. elegans* (Bolanowski et al., 1981). Ultrastructural cuticle changes, although not very convenient as aging markers, have been described for *C. briggsae* (Epstein et al., 1971; Zuckerman et al., 1972, 1973; Himmelhoch et al., 1977).

The use of biochemical changes as markers of senescence in nematodes is still relatively undeveloped. Erlanger and Gershon (1970) noted age-related changes in the levels of several enzymes in *T. aceti*. Bolanowski et al. (1983) showed that in *C. elegans* the activities of six lysosomal hydrolases (acid phosphatase, β-N-acetyl-hexosaminidase, β-glucosidase, β-galactosidase, β-glucuronidase, and α-mannosidase) increase quite strongly with age, whereas acetylcholinesterase, choline acetyltransferase, and α-glucosidase levels are nearly invariant with age. Both acid phosphatase and β-glucosidase have multiple chromatographic forms whose age dependencies are not equal. The activity of lysosomal cathepsin D is also strongly age dependent, but unlike the other lysosomal hydrolases, its activity declines from about the middle of the reproductive period (Jen-Jacobson and Jacobson, unpublished results). For most of these enzymes, sensitive fluorometric or radiometric assays permit reproducible measurements using 1–10 animals.

Attempts to combine several such aging markers into a useful index were made by Bolanowski et al. (1981). They observed that two behavioral parameters (movement rate and defecation frequency), which were very highly correlated with chronological age both in individuals and in populations, were nonetheless poor predictors of longevity for individuals. Furthermore, the variance between individuals in rates of changes in these measures was large, despite the genetic homogeneity of the populations. Bolanowski et al. (1981) raised the possibility that the peripheral symptoms of senescence might be only stochastically coupled to a hypothetical "central timer" and suggested that an index which was composed of many such symptomatic measures might permit better estimation of the position of the "central timer" than any one measure alone. As had been previously attempted for humans (Hollingsworth et al., 1965), Bolanowski et al. (1981) constructed a primitive multiparametric index of "physiological age" by combining three quantitative age-dependent measures, using multiple linear regression. This index correlated encouragingly well with chronological age, but it needs both statistical refinement and practical testing. An important test will be whether the index responds in the expected ways to environmental manipulations (e.g., altered temperatures and nutritional regimens) which affect life span (Klass, 1977).

SOME RELATIVELY WELL—STUDIED PHENOMENA IN NEMATODE AGING

Accumulation of Altered Enzymes

The occurrence of catalytically or structurally altered enzyme molecules in aging organisms is the best-known example of an aging phenomenon first discovered in nematodes and only later demonstrated in mammals. Probably prompted by the "error-catastrophe" hypothesis of Orgel (1963, 1970), Gershon and Gershon (1970) found that the isocitrate lyase of old *Turbatrix aceti* consisted of both active and inactive molecules. This conclusion, based upon the reduced precipitation of enzyme activity from crude homogenates with a given amount of antibody, was later extended to the fructose-1, 6–diphosphate aldolase of old mouse liver (Gershon and Gershon, 1973) and many other enzymes (see Chapter 9). Purified isocitrate lyase from old *T. aceti* was later shown to have a 60 percent lower specific activity than the pure enzyme from young animals (Reiss and Rothstein, 1975). This reduction in specific activity was associated with increased heat-lability for two of five isoenzymes (Reiss and Rothstein, 1974), and it was inferred that "old" isocitrate lyase consisted of a mixture of fully active and partially active molecules. It is now generally accepted that the unambiguous demonstration of enzyme alteration requires measurement of the catalytic and/or structural properties of pure enzyme. One possible artifactual origin for the alteration, namely, miscoding produced by the FUdR used to maintain age synchrony, was laid to rest by Rothstein and Sharma (1978), who showed that the age-related decline in specific activity of *T. aceti* isocitrate lyase, phosphoglycerate kinase, and enolase was the same in animals synchronized by repetitive physical screening as in animals treated with FUdR. While several alterations have been demonstrated, there is no evidence indicating functional importance for any of them. A summary of some of the properties of altered enzymes from old nematodes is given in Table 1.

TABLE 1. Properties of Altered Enzymes from *T. Aceti*.

Enzyme	Altered Specific Activity	Altered K_m	Electrophoresis Change	Antigenic Difference	Immunological Cross-reaction	Altered Heat Stability	Reference
Isocitrate lyase	Yes	No	[a]	No	Yes	Yes	Reiss and Rothstein, 1974, 1975
Enolase	Yes	Yes?	No	Yes	Yes	Yes	Sharma and Rothstein, 1978a, 1978b; Sharma, Gupta, and Rothstein, 1976; Sharma and Rothstein, 1980
Fructose-1,6-diphosphate aldolase	Yes	No?	No	No	Yes	Yes	Reznick and Gershon, 1977; Goren et al., 1977; Zeelon et al., 1973
Phosphoglycerate kinase	Yes	Yes?	No	—	—	No	Gupta and Rothstein, 1976a
Elongation factor, EF-1	Yes	—	—	—	Yes	—	Bolla and Brot, 1975

[a]Change in relative quantities of isozymes. All isozymes have altered specific activity.

Several kinds of observations on altered nematode enzymes indicate that they do not arise through transcriptional or translational errors of the type envisioned by Orgel (1963, 1970). First, "young" and "old" enzymes generally do not differ in isoelectric point or electrophoretic behavior, whereas random errors in transcription or translation should produce such changes. In the case of enolase from *T. aceti,* the evidence is compelling that the age-related decline in specific activity of pure enzyme results from an altered tertiary structure rather than from primary sequence errors or covalent post-translational modification (Sharma and Rothstein, 1980). Second, some unaltered enzymes (e.g., triosephosphate isomerase; Gupta and Rothstein, 1976b) coexist in old nematodes with altered forms of other enzymes, and it is difficult to imagine how a high error rate in protein synthesis might exempt some gene products from primary sequence errors. (The flaw in this argument is that the examination of pure enzymes, albeit essential to the rigorous demonstration of altered forms, necessarily limits consideration to those molecules with properties not very different from those of the "normal" species. This is true whether conventional purification methods, affinity methods, or immunological cross-reactivity are employed to obtain the "altered" species. Though it appears unlikely, the most abnormal variants might be missed entirely if their properties were sufficiently different from those of the "normal" protein.)

As an alternative to the accrual of errors during synthesis, a failure of protein turnover in old nematodes is now under consideration to explain the accumulation of altered enzymes. Goldberg and St. John (1976) first pointed out that a reduced rate of catabolism of altered or damaged proteins might also lead to an "error catastrophe." Rothstein (1977) extended this argument to the accumulation of proteins altered post-translationally. In *T. aceti,* the half-life of total soluble protein may increase severalfold during aging, although there are disconcerting discrepancies both in the measured half-lives and in the magnitude of the aging-

related change (Sharma et al., 1979; Reznick and Gershon, 1979; Prasanna and Lane, 1979). Whether this descreased rate of protein turnover derives from changes in the amounts of proteolytic enzymes, changes in the nature of the target proteins, or changes in the accessibility of the target proteins to degradative compartments (e.g., lysosomes) is not clear.

One important issue in the etiology of altered enzymes has not yet been addressed: Do the altered enzyme molecules in old animals represent "young" (newly synthesized) or "old" molecules? Clearly, the postsynthetic "error" hypotheses predict that alteration would be more prevalent in those molecules which had persisted from youth to old age. Density-shift experiments using heavy isotopes (Hu et al., 1962) might permit physical separation of "young" and "old" molecules in order to answer this question. Nematodes seem well suited to this kind of experiment.

Nutritional Restriction and Life Span

Extension of life span by nutritional restriction has been known in rodents since the pioneering work of McCay and coworkers (McCay et al., 1935, 1939, 1943). In general, the greatest differences observed in rodents are on the order of a 50 percent increase in median life span (Stuchlikova et al., 1975).

In nematodes, the range of life spans obtainable by manipulating the nutritional regimen may be at least as great. For example, Klass (1977) reported a median life span of 14.5 ± 2 days for *C. elegans* cultured monoxenically on "lawns" of live *E. coli* at 20°C, whereas Tilby and Moses (1975) observed a median life span of about 58 days in axenic cultures at 20°C in a chemically defined liquid medium. The latter is by far the most extreme longevity reported for this species. More typical comparisons are those of Croll et al. (1977a), who reported 12.3 days for monoxenic cultures of *C. elegans* at 20°C and 17.6 days for axenic cultures in liquid, chemically undefined medium.

A possible objection to the interpretation of these results as representing "nutritional restriction" was raised by Croll et al. (1977a) and by Zuckerman and Himmelhoch (1980). Basing their argument on microscopically observed abnormalities and on abrupt changes in survival, pharyngeal bulb pulsation rate, and defecation rate, these authors suggested that monoxenically grown *C. elegans* may suffer pathological damage by live *E. coli*. We believe this suggestion is probably incorrect for several reasons. First, other workers have observed no abrupt changes in monoxenic cultures in survival (Klass, 1977; Bolanowski et al., 1981), in defecation frequency or movement rate (Bolanowski et al., 1981), or in fluorescent pigment accumulation (Klass, 1977). Second, experiments in our laboratories (Russell and Jacobson, unpublished results) have shown that *C. elegans* grown in liquid medium on killed, metabolically inert *E. coli* show growth rates and population survival curves nearly indistinguishable from those obtained on live *E. coli* on agar lawns. Third, by varying only the concentration of live *E. coli* cells used as food in liquid suspensions, Klass (1977) achieved significantly different life spans for *C. elegans* (16 ± 1.9 days at 10^9 cells/ml; 25.9 ± 4.7 days at 10^8 cell/ml). Nematodes whose diet was restricted beginning in the growth phase (one day after hatching at $25.5°C$) showed the greatest extension of life span (50 percent over nonrestricted controls), but even when dietary restriction was begun in the early postreproductive phase (day 6), mean life span was increased by 20 percent (Klass, 1977). These results strongly parallel those obtained with rodents (Ross, 1972; Weindruch and Walford, 1982) and suggest that nematodes may be valid models in which to study the putatively general mechanisms underlying such nutritional restriction effects.

Age Pigment Accumulation

Like essentially all other animals examined, nematodes accumulate autofluorescent pigments as a function of age. In all three species, these accumulations can be seen directly in the living animal as a pronounced dark-ening of the intestinal cells. In axenically maintained *C. briggsae* (mean life span 34 days), the intestinal cells of young (7 days) animals contain only spherical, relatively electron-lucent inclusions, which are assumed to be lipid droplets, whereas the intestinal cells of old (28 days) animals are nearly filled with qualitatively different inclusions, which are much more electron dense and usually not spherical (Epstein et al., 1972). The latter inclusions appear to be membrane limited, and their contents often appear torn, which suggests that they may not be fixed and/or embedded as well as other cellular constituents. Because a single inclusion sometimes has two well-demarcated zones, one relatively electron lucent and often central, the other relatively electron dense and peripheral, the electron-dense inclusions predominating in other animals are inferred to be formed in some way from the electron-lucent (putatively lipid) inclusions seen in younger animals. That lysosomes might be involved in such a process is inferred because the inclusions apparently stain positively for acid phosphatase.

In both *C. elegans* and *T. aceti,* similar electron-dense inclusions have been observed, which are more prevalent in older animals (Himmelhoch et al., 1973; Kisiel et al., 1980; O. J. Bashor, L. A. Jacobson, and R. L. Russell, unpublished results). In all three species, the electron-dense inclusions are more prevalent in the anterior portions of the intestine. In all three species also, some electron-dense deposits appear with age outside the intestinal cells, in the pseudocoelom (body cavity). These extracellular deposits appear to be somewhat less electron dense than those in the intestinal cells, are overall less pronounced than the intestinal inclusions, and are usually more irregularly shaped, as if compressed by the contours of the surrounding cells.

Because the intestinal inclusions are electron dense and accumulate with age, they resemble the lipofuscin inclusions of other organisms. The inclusions have not been purified to determine whether they harbor lipofuscins, but extracts of whole nematodes contain lipid-extractable fluorescent substances which resemble the lipofuscins of other systems. Such extracts contain three principal classes of fluorescent substances, distinguishable by excitation and emission spectra (Buecher and Hansen, 1974; Zuckerman et al., 1978; Klass, 1977; Davis et al., 1982; Link et al., 1984). One class represents protein tryptophanyl residues (excitation maximum, 290 nm/emission maximum, 350 nm), and a second class (280, 380, 470/510 nm) represents flavin. The third class resembles lipofuscins from other sources, both in its fluorescence properties (330–345/405–420 nm) and in its extractability in the commonly used chloroform-method procedure of Fletcher et al. (1973). Age-dependent increases of 3–5 fold have been reported for both the flavin fluroescence and the ''lipofuscin'' fluorescence in *C. elegans* (Klass, 1977; Davis et al., 1982; Link et al., 1984). Quantitative microspectrofluorometry on whole mounts of *C. elegans* indicates that the lipofuscin fluorescence is localized in intestinal cell granules; these are presumably the inclusions seen by electron microscopy (Link et al., 1984).

The chemical nature of the lipofuscin(s) remains inknown. In *C. elegans* lipid extractability is markedly improved by base hydrolysis followed by acidification for extraction, which suggests that the fluorophore(s) might initially be linked to larger, hydrophilic molecules (Link et al., 1984). As with other organisms, the observed excitation and emission maxima are at least broadly consistent with the notion that the fluorophore is a Schiff base formed by the reaction of malondialdehyde with amino groups (Tappel, 1975). It is also remotely possible that the lipofuscin fluorescence could be due to tryptophan catabolites, since Babu and his colleagues have provided evidence for localization of such catabolites to the intestine (Babu, 1974; Siddiqui and Babu, 1980; Bhat and Babu, 1980). However, even though some such catabolies have approximately correct fluorescence properties, none of a sizable number examined directly has the right combination of such properties and ex-

tractability to account for the lipofuscin fluorescence (J. Anistranski and R. L. Russell, unpublished results).

PROSPECTS

Among the three commonly studied species, as we see it, the prospects for aging research appear brightest for *C. elegans* because of the extensive effort being devoted to the development, genetics, and molecular biology of this species. This effort has already generated, and will no doubt continue to generate, tools for aging research which are unique not just among nematodes but indeed among metazoan animals generally. Among these tools, the most important would seem to be the extensive library of existing mutants, the relative ease with which new mutants can be isolated, and the unparalleled information available on development in general and cell lineages in particular.

For these tools to be maximally useful in aging research, they must be applied toward understanding the mechanisms of general aging phenomena shared by other organisms. As noted, some such phenomena have already been identified in *C. elegans,* namely, effects of nutritional restriction and accumulation of age pigments. However, several others have not yet been investigated in *C. elegans.* For instance, qualitative enzyme alterations have not yet been sought, little has yet been done to characterize DNA repair and its potential involvement in aging, and there is still very little information on the several protective enzymes (superoxide dismutase, catalase, peroxidases) and related free radical intermediates posited to have important effects on aging in other systems (Tappel, 1975; Liebovitz and Siegel, 1980). To us, these uninvestigated phenomena represent areas of opportunity in which new investigators might make novel and useful contributions, and we hope to see developments in these directions.

Another development which we encourage is the adoption of standards in two important areas, culture conditions and criteria of senescence. In our view, past results have too often been compromised by culture differences (particularly between monoxenic and axenic cultures). While selection and adoption of a standard culture condition must be voluntary, we believe it would be of significant benefit. Similarly, rather than to rely solely on survival as has often been done in the past, it seems preferable to use a composite aging index based on a few reliable and relatively easily measured parameters.

Among possible approaches using the advantages of *C. elegans,* the use of mutations to perturb the aging rate is attractive because it offers the prospect that specific, identifiable gene products might be causally associable with aging. If the primary product of a gene is known, an aging effect due to a mutation in that gene necessarily implies a causal relationship of some sort between that gene's product and aging. Among the few *C. elegans* genes whose products are known with reasonable certainty, there are some whose mutant effects on aging, if any, could be revealing. These include *ace-1* and *ace-2,* two genes for separable classes of acetylcholinesterase (Johnson et al., 1981; Culotti et al., 1981); *cha-1,* a gene for choline acetyltransferase (Rand and Russell, 1984); *nuc-1,* a gene for a major endonuclease involved in digesting nuclear DNA after embryonic cell death (Sulston, 1976); and *flu-1* and *flu-2,* genes for the tryptophan catabolic enzymes kynurenine hydroxylase and kynureninase, respectively (Babu, 1974; Siddiqui and Babu, 1980; Bhat and Babu, 1980). Mutants in these genes can and should be used to test directly the involvement of the corresponding gene products in aging. In our view, it would be particularly valuable to add to this list structural genes for superoxide dismutase, catalase, peroxidase, and DNA repair enzymes whose possible involvement in aging is of considerable interest.

Available mutants in the very much larger number of genes whose products are not known can also be useful, either to suggest relationships that can be tested in other ways or to rule out the involvement of some processes in aging. Among existing mutants, for instance, those of the genes *ced-1* and *ced-2,* because they do not exhibit normal embryonic and postembryonic cell death (Hedgecock and Sulston, 1982), could serve either to suggest an association between such cell death and aging or to rule it out depending on whether they affect aging rates. Likewise, existing mutants with altered radiation sensitivity (Hartman and Herman, 1982), if they turn out to have DNA repair deficiencies as in other organisms, could act similarly for the possible relationship between DNA repair and aging. Among future mutants which might be isolated for this sort of application, those affecting lipofuscin accumulation or, if it exists in *C. elegans,* the qualitative age-dependent alteration of enzymes, could be quite useful.

Another potential use of the genetic advantages of *C. elegans* is for the isolation of mutants or other genetic variants with altered life spans. Klass has isolated three mutants with increased life spans (Klass, 1977), and Johnson and Wood (1982) have generated several recombinant inbred lines, varying over an almost 3-fold range of life spans, from F_2 progeny between two *C. elegans* strains, Bristol and Bergerac. Such variants serve to demonstrate the relatively high heritability of life span, and could also prove useful for demonstrating correlations between life span and other aging-related variables. As with available mutants affecting unknown gene products, interpretation of aging effects in such variants must be made with care. Klass, for instance, noted that two of his mutants had behavioral defects which apparently limited food intake, while the third produced dauerlarvae spontaneously without starvation. Thus, in all three cases, the extended life spans could be most directly ascribed to nutritional effects already known to affect life span. Hopefully, new mutants isolated by different strategies, or perhaps major aging genes identified by analysis of the recombinant inbred lines, will prove to affect aging in less predictable ways that will shed light on underlying mechanisms.

A major feature of *C. elegans* which has as yet been little exploited is the apparent suspension of senescent changes in the dauerlarva state (Klass and Hirsh, 1976; Bolanowski et al., 1983). The dauerlarva is not in any sense in "suspended animation" even though it has ceased development and has acquired increased environmental resistance (Cassada and Russell, 1975). The dauerlarva remains sensitive to both chemical and mechanical stimulation and is capable of movement upon stimulation. Beyond the simple observation that the dauerlarva has ceased eating because it has ceased pharyngeal pumping, little is known about the changes which may have occurred in metabolic processes or in "damage surveillance" systems (e.g., DNA repair, protein turnover, free radical scavenging; Yeargers, 1981). It seems unlikely that the absence of feeding alone can account for the extraordinary longevity of dauerlarvae, inasmuch as extreme starvation of nematodes for which the dauerlarva state is developmentally inaccessible shortens life rather than prolonging it. We believe that an attempt to identify the unique biochemical properties of dauerlarvae is well justified. It also seems that available mutants, blocked at various stages in the process by which a starvation signal leads to dauerlarva formation, could serve to determine whether the same signal is important for nutritional effects on aging.

Finally, the ability to generate large numbers of genetically identical individual nematodes might allow an investigator to study differences in the rates of senescent changes among individuals in the absence of genetic diversity as an obscuring factor. A preliminary analysis (Bolanowski et al., 1981) indicates that the rates of specific age-related changes, although consistent for any one individual, may vary markedly from animal to animal. What is not yet clear is whether an individual that shows particularly rapid aging changes in one property also "ages rapidly" with respect to all properties, which would suggest that each individual has a "clock" that runs at a specific rate, or whether the various outputs of a hypothetical and perhaps quite constant-rate "central clock" are stochastically related to each other. In no other group of metazoans are such questions presently open to quite such rigorous experimentation.

REFERENCES

Albert, P. S., Brown, S. J., and Riddle, D. L. 1981. Sensory control of dauer larva formation in *Caenorhabditis elegans*. *J. Comp. Neurol.* 198: 435–451.

Albert, P. S. and Riddle, D. L. 1980. Abnormal sensory ultrastructure in mutants of *Caenorhabditis elegans* unable to form dauer larvae. *J. Nematol.* 12: 213.

Anderson, G. L. 1976. Responses of dauer larvae of *Caenorhabditis elegans* (Nematoda Rhabditidae) to thermal stress and oxygen deprivation. *Can. J. Zool.* 56: 1786–1791.

Argon, Y. and Ward, S. 1980. *Caenorhabditis elegans* fertilization-defective mutants with abnormal sperm. *Genetics* 96: 413–433.

Babu, P. 1974. Biochemical genetics of *Caenorhabditis elegans*. *Mol. Gen. Genet.* 135: 39–44.

Baillie, D. L. and Rosenbluth, R. 1977. Selection and characterization of alcohol dehydrogenase mutants in *Caenorhabditis elegans*. *J. Supramol. Struc. Suppl.* 1: 66.

Bhat, S. G. and Babu, P. 1980. Mutagen Sensitivity of kynureninase mutants of the nematode *Caenorhabditis elegans*. *Mol. Gen. Genet.* 180: 635–638.

Bird, A. F. 1971. *The Structure of Nematodes.* New York: Academic Press.

Bolanowski, M. A., Russell, R. L., and Jacobson, L. A. 1981. Quantitative measures of aging in the nematode *Caenorhabditis elegans*. I. Populational and longitudinal studies of two behavioral parameters. *Mech. Ageing Dev.* 15: 279–295.

Bolanoswki, M. A., Jacobson, L. A., and Russell, R. L. 1983. Quantitative measures of aging in the nematode *Caenorhabditis elegans*. II. Lysosomal hydrolases as markers of senescence. *Mech. Ageing Dev.* 21: 295–319.

Bolla, R. and Brot, N. 1975. Age-dependent changes in enzymes involved in macromolecular synthesis in *Turbatrix aceti*. *Arch. Biochem. Biophys.* 169: 227–236.

Bollinger, J. A. and Willett, J. D. 1980. A method for synchrony of adult *Caenorhabditis elegans*. *Nematologica* 26: 491–492.

Brenner, S. 1974. The genetics of *Caenorhabditis elegans*. *Genetics,* 77: 71–94.

Buecher, E. and Hansen, E. 1974. Fluorescent pigments of *Caenorhabditis briggsae*. *IRCS Libr. Compend.* 2: 1595.

Byerly, L., Cassada, R. C., and Russell, R. L. 1976. The life cycle of the nematode *Caenorhabditis elegans*. I. Wild type growth and reproduction. *Dev. Biol.* 51: 23–33.

Cassada, R. C. and Russell, R. L. 1975. The dauerlarva, a post-embryonic developmental variant of the nematode *Caenorhabditis elegans. Dev. Biol.,* 46: 326–342.

Cox, G. N., Kusch, M., and Edgar, R. S. 1981. Cuticle of *Caenorhabditis elegans*: its isolation and partial characterization. *J. Cell. Biol.* 90: 7–17.

Cox, G. N., Staprans, S., and Edgar, R. S. 1981. The cuticle of *Caenorhabditis elegans.* II. Stage specific changes in ultrastructure and protein composition during post-embryonic development. *Dev. Biol.* 86: 456–470.

Croll, N. A. 1975. Indolealkylamines in the coordination of nematode behavioral activities. *Can. J. Zool.* 53: 894–903.

Croll, N. A., Smith, J. M., and Zuckerman, B. M. 1977a. Behavioral parameters in the aging of *Caenorhabditis elegans. J. Nematol.* 9: 266–267.

Croll, N. A., Smith, J. M., and Zuckerman, B. M. 1977b. The aging process of the nematode *Caenorhabditis elegans* in bacterial and axenic culture. *Exp. Aging Res.* 3: 175–199.

Culotti, J. G., von Ehrenstein, G., Culotti, M. R., and Russell, R. L. 1981. A second class of acetylcholinesterase-deficient mutants of the nematode *Caenorhabditis elegans. Genetics* 97: 281–305.

Davis, B. O., Anderson, G. L., and Dusenbury, D. B. 1982. Total luminescence spectroscopy of fluorescence changes during aging in *Caenorhabditis elegans. Biochemistry* 21: 4089–4095.

Deppe, A., Schierenberg, E., Cole, T., Krieg, C., Schmitt, D., Yoder, B., and von Ehrenstein, G. 1976. Cell lineages of the embryo of the nematode *Caenorhabditis elegans. Proc. Nat. Acad. Sci. USA* 75: 376–380.

Edgar, R. S. and Wood, W. B. 1977. The nematode *Caenorhabditis elegans*, a new organism for intensive biological study. *Science* 198: 1285–1286.

Epstein, J., Castillo, J., Himmelhoch, S., and Zuckerman, B. M. 1971. Ultrastructural studies on *Caenorhabditis briggsae. J. Nematol.* 3: 69–78.

Epstein, J. and Gershon, D. 1972. Studies on ageing in nematodes. IV. The effect of anti-oxidants on cellular damage and lifespan. *Mech. Ageing. Dev.* 1: 257–264.

Epstein, J., Himmelhoch, S., and Gershon, D. 1972. Studies on ageing in nematodes. III. Electronmicroscopical studies on age-associated cellular damage. *Mech. Ageing Dev.* 1: 245–255.

Erlanger, M. and Gershon, D. 1970. Studies on aging in nematodes. II. Studies of the activities of several enzymes as a function of age. *Exp. Gerontol.* 5: 13–19.

Fletcher, B. L., Dillard, C. J., and Tappel, A. L. 1973. Measurement of fluorescent lipid peroxidation products in biological systems and tissues. *Anal. Biochem.* 52: 1–9.

Gandhi, S., Santelli, J., Mitchell, D. H., Stiles, J. W., and Sanadi, D. R. 1980. A simple method for maintaining large, aging populations of *Caenorhabditis elegans. Mech. Ageing. Dev.* 12: 137–150.

Gershon, D. 1970. Studies on aging in nematodes. I. The nematode as a model organism for aging research. *Exp. Gerontol.* 5: 7–12.

Gershon, H. and Gershon, D. 1970. Detection of inactive enzyme molecules in aging organisms. *Nature* 227: 1214–1217.

Gershon, H. and Gershon, D. 1973. Inactive enzymes in aging mice: liver aldolase. *Proc. Nat. Acad. Sci. USA* 70: 909–913.

Goldberg, A. L. and St. John, A. C. 1976. Intracellular protein degradation in mammalian and bacterial cells. Part II. *Ann. Rev. Biochem.* 45: 747–803.

Goren, P., Reznick, A. Z., Reiss, U., and Gershon, D. 1977 Isoelectric properties of nematode aldolase and rat liver superoxide dismutase from young and old animals. *Fed. Eur. Biochem. Soc. Lett.* 84: 83–86.

Gupta, S. K., and Rothstein, M. 1976a Phosphoglycerate kinase from young and old *Turbatrix aceti. Biochim. Biophys. Acta* 445: 632–644.

Gupta, S. K. and Rothstein, M. 1976b. Triosephosphate isomerase from young and old *Turbatrix aceti. Arch. Biochem. Biophys.* 174: 333–338.

Hartman, P. S. and Herman, R. K. 1982. Radiation sensitive mutants of *Caenorhabditis elegans. Genetics* 102: 159–178.

Hedgecock, E. M. and Russell, R. L. 1975. Normal and mutant thermotaxis in the nematode *Caenorhabditis elegans. Proc. Nat. Acad. Sci. USA* 72: 4061–4065.

Herman, R. K. and Horvitz, H. R. 1980. Genetic Analyses of *Caenorhabditis elegans. In,* B. M. Zuckerman (ed.), *Nematodes as Biological Models,* Vol. 1: *Behavioral and Developmental Models,* pp. 228–261. New York: Academic Press.

Herman, R. K., Horvitz, H. R., and Riddle, D. L. 1980. The nematode *Caenorhabditis elegans. Genetic Maps* 1: 183–193.

Hieb, W. F. and Rothstein, M. 1975. Aging in the free-living nematode *Turbatrix aceti.* Techniques for synchronization and aging of large-scale axenic cultures. *Exp. Gerontol.* 10: 145–153.

Himmelhoch, S., Kisiel, M., Lavimoniere, J., and Zuckerman, B. M. 1973. Fine structure of young adult *Turbatrix aceti. Nematologica* 19: 449–454.

Himmelhoch, S., Kisiel, M. J., and Zuckerman, B. M. 1977. *Caenorhabditis briggsae.* Electron microscope analysis of changes in negative surface charge density of the outer cuticle membrane. *Exp. Parasitol.* 41: 118–123.

Hirsh, D. and Vanderslice, R. 1976. Temperature-sensitive developmental mutants of *Caenorhabditis elegans. Dev. Biol.* 49: 220–235.

Hollingsworth, J. W., Hashizume, A., and Jablon, S. 1965. Correlations between tests of aging of Hiroshima subjects—an attempt to define "physiological age." *Yale J. Biol. Med.* 38: 11–26.

Hosono, R. 1978. Age-dependent changes in the behavior of *Caenorhabditis elegans* on attraction to *Escherichia coli. Exp. Gerontol.* 13: 31–36.

Hosono, R., Sato, Y., Argawa, S., and Mitsui, Y. 1980. Age-dependent changes in mobility and separation of the nematode *Caenorhabditis elegans*. *Exp. Gerontol.* 15: 285–289.

Hu, A. S. L., Bock, R. M., and Halvorson, H. O. 1962. Separation of labeled from unlabeled proteins by equilibrium density gradient centrifugation. *Anal. Biochem.* 4: 489–504.

Johnson, C. D., Duckett, J. G., Culotti, J. G., Herman, R. K., Meneely, P. M., and Russell, R. L. 1981. An acetylcholinesterase-deficient mutant of the nematode *Caenorhabditis elegans*. *Genetics* 97: 261–279.

Johnson, T. E. and Wood, W. B. 1982. Genetic analysis of lifespan in *Caenorhabditis elegans*. *Proc. Nat. Acad. Sci. USA* 79: 6603–6607.

Khan, F. R. and McFadden, B. A. 1980. A rapid method of synchronizing developmental stages of *Caenorhabditis elegans*. *Nematol.* 26: 280–282.

Kimble, J. and Hirsh, D. 1979. Post-embryonic cell lineages of the hermaphrodite and male gonads in *Caenorhabditis elegans*. *Dev. Biol.* 70: 396–417.

Kimble, J., Sulston, J., and White, J. 1979. Regulative development in the post-embryonic lineages of *Caenorhabditis elegans*. *In* N. LeDouarin (ed.), *Cell Lineage, Stem Cells, and Cell Determinations*, pp. 59–68. New York: Elsevier.

Kimble, J. E., and White, J. G. 1981. On the control of germ cell development in *Caenorhabditis elegans*. *Dev. Biol.* 81: 208–219.

Kisiel, M. J., Castillo, J. M., Zuckerman, L. S., Zuckerman, B. M., and Himmelhoch, S. 1975. Studies on aging in *Turbatrix aceti*. *Mech. Ageing. Dev.* 4: 81–88.

Kisiel, M. J., Himmelhoch, S., and Zuckerman, B. M. 1974. *Caenorhabditis briggsae*: effects of aminopterin. *Exp. Parasitol.* 36: 430–438.

Kisiel, M., Nelson, B., and Zuckerman, B. M. 1972. Effects of DNA synthesis inhibitors on *Caenorhabditis briggsae* and *Turbatrix aceti*. *Nematol.* 18: 373–384.

Kisiel, M. J. and Zuckerman, B. M. 1974. Studies on aging of *Turbatrix aceti*. *Nematol.* 20: 277–282.

Klass, M. R. 1977. Aging in the nematode *Caenorhabditis elegans*: major biological and environmental factors influencing lifespan. *Mech. Ageing. Dev.* 6: 413–429.

Klass, M. R. and Hirsh, D. 1976. Nonaging developmental variant of *Caenorhabditis elegans*. *Nature* 260: 523–525.

Klass, M. R. and Hirsh, D. 1981. Sperm isolation and biochemical analysis of the major sperm protein from *Caenorhabditis elegans*. *Dev. Biol.* 84: 299–312.

Krieg, C., Cole, T., Deppe, A., Schierenberg, E., Schmitt, D., Yoder, B., and von Ehrenstein, G. 1978. The cellular anatomy of embryos of the nematode *Caenorhabditis elegans*. Analysis and reconstruction of serial section electron micrographs. *Dev. Biol.* 65: 193–215.

Liebovitz, B. E. and Siegel, B. V. 1980. Aspects of free radical reactions in biological systems: aging. *J. Gerontol.* 35: 45–56.

Link, C. M., Jacobson, L. A., and Russell, R. L. 1984.

Age-related fluorescent pigments in the nematode *Caenorhabditis elegans*: extraction, quantitation, anatomical localization, and some chemical properties. *Mech. Ageing Dev.* (submitted).

Loewenberg, J. R., Sullivan, T., and Schuster, M. L. 1959. A virus disease of *Meliodogyne incognita incognita,* the Southern root knot nematode. *Nature* 184: 1896.

MacLeod, A. R., Waterston, R. H., Fishpool, R. M., and Brenner, S. 1977. Identification of the structural gene for myosin heavy chain in *Caenorhabditis elegans*. *J. Mol. Biol.* 114: 133–140.

McCay, C. M., Crowell, M. F., and Maynard, L. A. 1935. The effect of retarded growth upon the length of lifespan and upon the ultimate body size. *J. Nutrit.* 10: 63–79.

McCay, C. M., Maynard, L. A., Sperling, G., and Barnes, L. L. 1939. Retarded growth, lifespan, ultimate body size and age changes in the albino rat after feeding diets restricted in calories. *J. Nutrit.* 18: 1–13.

McCay, C. M., Sperling, G., and Barnes, L. L. 1943. Growth, ageing, chronic diseases and lifespan in rats. *Arch. Biochem.* 2: 469–479.

Mitchell, D. H. 1976. A nematode variant with increased lifespan. *J. Cell Biol.* 70: 97.

Mitchell, D. H., Stiles, J. W., Santelli, J., and Sanadi, D. R. 1979. Synchronous growth and aging of *Caenorhabditis elegans* in the presence of fluorodeoxyuridine. *J. Gerontol.* 34: 28–36.

Miwa, J., Schierenberg, E., Miwa, S., and von Ehrenstein, G. 1980. Genetics and mode of expression of temperature sensitive mutations arresting embryonic development in *Caenorhabditis elegans*. *Dev. Biol.* 76: 160–174.

Nigon, V. 1943. Le determinisme du sexe chez un nematode libre hermaphrodit, *Rhabditis elegans* Maupas. *Comptes Rendus Soc. Biol.* 137: 40–41.

Nigon, V. 1949. Les modalites de la reproduction et le determinisme du sexe chez quelques nematodes libres. *Ann. Sci. Nat. Zool.* 11: 1–132.

Orgel, L. E. 1963. The maintenance of the accuracy of protein synthesis and its relevance to ageing. *Proc. Nat. Acad. Sci. USA* 49: 517–521.

Orgel, L. E. 1970. The maintenance of the accuracy of protein synthesis and its relevance to ageing: a correction. *Proc. Nat. Acad. Sci. USA* 67: 1476.

Pai, S. 1928. Lebenszyklus der *Anguillula aceti.* Ehrbg. *Zool. Anzeiger* 74: 257–270.

Patel, T. R. and McFadden, B. A. 1978. Axenic and synchronous cultures of *Caenorhabditis elegans*. *Nematologica* 24: 51–62.

Peters, B. G. 1928. On the bionomics of the vinegar eelworm. *J. Helminthol.* 6: 1–38.

Prasanna, H. R. and Lane, R. S. 1979. Protein degradation in aged nematodes (*Turbatrix aceti*). *Biochem. Biophys. Res. Commun.* 86: 552–559.

Rand, J. B. and Russell, R. L. 1984. Choline acetyltransferase-deficient mutants of the nematode *Caenorhabditis elegans*. *Genetics* 106: 227–248.

Reiss, U. and Rothstein, M. 1974. Heat-labile isozymes of isocitrate lyase from aging *Turbatrix aceti. Biochem. Biophys. Res. Commun.* 61: 1012–1016.

Reiss, U. and Rothstein, M. 1975. Age-related changes in isocitrate lyase from the free-living nematode, *Turbatrix aceti. J. Biol. Chem.* 250: 826–830.

Reznick, A. Z., and Gershon, D. 1977 Age-related alterations in purified fructose-1, 6-diphosphate aldolase from the nematode *Turbatrix aceti. Mech. Ageing Dev.* 6: 345–353.

Reznick, A. Z. and Gershon, D. 1979. The effect of age on the protein degradation system in the nematode *Turbatrix aceti. Mech. Ageing Dev.* 11: 403–415.

Riddle, D. L. 1980. Developmental genetics of *Caenorhabditis elegans. In,* B. M. Zuckerman (ed.), *Nematodes as Biological Models,* Vol 1. *Behavioral and Developmental Models,* pp. 263–283. New York: Academic Press.

Riddle, D. L., Swanson, M. M., and Albert, P. S. 1981. Interacting genes in nematode dauerlarva formation. *Nature* 290: 668–671.

Ross, M. H. 1972. Length of life and caloric intake. *Am. J. Clin. Nutrit.* 25: 834–838.

Rothstein, M. 1974. Practical methods for the axenic culture of the free-living nematodes *Turbatrix aceti* and *Caenorhabditis briggsae. Comp. Biochem. Physiol.* 49B: 669–678.

Rothstein, M. 1977. Recent developments in the age-related alteration of enzymes: a review. *Mech. Ageing Dev.* 6: 241–257.

Rothstein, M. 1980. Effects of aging on enzymes. *In* B. M. Zuckerman (ed.), *Nematodes as Biological Models,* Vol. 2: *Aging and Other Model Systems,* pp. 29–46. New York: Academic Press.

Rothstein, M. and Coppens, M. 1978. Nutritional factors and conditions for the axenic culture of free-living nematodes. *Comp. Biochem. Physiol.* 618: 99–104.

Rothstein, M. and Sharma, H. K. 1978. Altered enzymes in the free-living nematode *Turbatrix aceti* aged in the absence of fluorodeoxyuridine. *Mech. Ageing Dev.* 8: 175–180.

Schierenberg, E., Miwa, J., and von Ehrenstein, G. 1980. Cell lineages and developmental defects of temperature sensitive embryonic arrest mutants in *Caenorhabditis elegans. Dev. Biol.* 76: 141–159.

Searcy, D. G., Kisiel, M. J., and Zuckerman, B. M. 1976. Age-related increase of cuticle permeability in the nematode *Caenorhabditis briggsae. Exp. Aging Res.* 2: 293–301.

Sharma, H. K., Gupta, S. K., and Rothstein, M. 1976 Age-related alteration of enolase in the free-living nematode, *Turbatrix aceti, Arch. Biochem. Biophys.* 194: 324–332.

Sharma, H. K., Prasanna, H. R., Lane, R. S., and Rothstein, M. 1979. The effect of age on enolase turnover in the free-living nematode *Turbatrix aceti. Arch. Biochem. Biophys.* 194: 275–282.

Sharma, H. K., and Rothstein, M. 1978a Age related changes in the properties of enolase from *Turbatrix aceti Biochem.* 17: 2869–2876.

Sharma, H. K., and Rothstein, M. 1978b Serological evidence for the alteration of enolase during aging. *Mech. Ageing Dev.* 8: 341–354.

Sharma, H. K. and Rothstein, M. 1980. Altered enolase in aged *Turbatrix aceti* results from conformational changes in the enzyme. *Proc. Nat. Acad. Sci. USA* 77: 5865–5868.

Siddiqui, S. S. and Babu, P. 1980. Kynurenine hydroxylase mutants of the nematode *Caenorhabditis elegans. Mol. Gen. Genet.* 179: 21–24.

Siddiqui, S. S. and von Ehrenstein, G. 1980. Biochemical genetics of *Caenorhabditis elegans. In,* B. M. Zuckerman (ed.), *Nematodes as Biological Models,* Vol. 1. *Behavioral and Developmental Models,* pp. 284–304. New York: Academic Press.

Stuchlikova, E., Juricova-Horakova, M., and Deyl, Z. 1975. New aspects of the dietary effect of life prolongation in rodents. What is the role of obesity in aging? *Exp. Gerontol.* 10: 141–144.

Sulston, J. E. 1976. Postembryonic development in the ventral cord of *Caenorhabditis elegans. Phil. Trans. Roy. Soc. London* B275: 287–298.

Sulston, J. E., and Hodgkin, J. 1979. A diet of worms. *Nature* 279: 758–759.

Sulston, J. E. and Horvitz, H. R. 1977. Post-embryonic cell lineages of the nematode *Caenorhabditis elegans. Dev. Biol.* 56: 110–156.

Sulston, J. E., Schierenberg, E., White, J. G., and Thomson, J. N. 1983 The embryonic cell lineage of the nematode *Caenorhabditis elegans. Dev. Biol.* 100: 64–119.

Sulston, J. E. and White, J. G. 1980. Regulation and cell autonomy during postembryonic development of *Caenorhabditis elegans. Dev. Biol.* 78: 577–597.

Swanson, M. M. and Riddle, D. L. 1981. Critical periods in the development of the *Caenorhabditis elegans* duaerlarva. *Dev. Biol.* 84: 27–40.

Tappel, A. L. 1975. Lipid peroxidation and fluorescent molecular damage to membranes. *In,* B. F. Trump and A. U. Arstila (eds.), *Pathobiology of Cell Membranes,* Vol. 1, pp. 145–170. New York: Academic Press.

Tilby, M. J. and Moses, V. 1975. Nematode ageing. Automatic maintenance of age synchrony without inhibitors. *Exp. Gerontol.* 10: 213–223.

Vanfleteren, J. R. 1980. Nematodes as nutritional models. *In,* B. M. Zuckerman (ed.), *Nematodes as Biological Models,* Vol. 2: *Aging and Other Model Systems,* pp. 47–79. New York: Academic Press.

Vogel, K. G. 1974. Temperature and length of life in *Turbatrix aceti. Nematologica* 20: 361–362.

von Ehrenstein, G. and Schierenberg, E. 1980. Cell lineages and development of *Caenorhabditis elegans* and other nematodes. *In,* B. M. Zuckerman (ed.), *Nematodes as Biological Models,* Vol. 1. *Behavioral and Developmental Models,* pp. 1–71. New York: Academic Press.

Waterston, R. H., Fishpool, R. M., and Brenner, S. 1977. Mutants affecting paramyosin in *Caenorhabditis elegans*. *J. Mol. Biol.* 117: 679–698.

Weindruch, R., and Walford, R. L. 1982. Dietary restriction in mice beginning at 1 year of age. Effect on lifespan and spontaneous cancer incidence. *Science* 215: 1415–1418.

Willett, J. D., Rahim, I., Geist, M., and Zuckerman, B. M. 1980. Cyclic nucleotide exudation by nematodes and the effects on nematode growth, development and longevity. *Age* 3: 82–87.

Yarwood, E. A. and Hansen, E. L. 1969. Dauerlarvae of *Caenorhabditis briggsae* in axenic culture. *J. Nematol.* 1: 184–189.

Yeargers, E. 1981. Effect of γ-radiation on dauerlarvae of *Caenorhabditis elegans*. *J. Nematol.* 13: 235–237.

Zeelon, P., Gershon, H., and Gershon, D. 1973. Inactive enzyme molecules in aging organisms. Nematode fructose-1,6-diphosphate aldolase. *Biochem.* 12: 1743–1750.

Zuckerman, B. M., Fagerson, I. S., and Kisiel, M. J. 1978. Age pigment studies on the nematode *Caenorhabditis briggsae*. *Age* 1: 26–27.

Zuckerman, B. M. and Himmelhoch, S. 1980. Nematodes as models to study aging. *In,* B. M. Zuckerman (ed.), *Nematodes as Biological Models,* Vol. 2: *Aging and Other Model Systems,* pp. 3–28. New York: Academic Press.

Zuckerman, B. M., Himmelhoch, S., and Kisiel, M. 1972. Age related changes in the fine structure of the cuticle in *Caenorhabditis briggsae*. *J. Nematol.* 4: 237–238.

Zuckerman, B. M., Himmelhoch, S., and Kisiel, M. 1973. Fine structure changes in the cuticle of adult *Caenorhabditis briggsae* with age. *Nematologica* 19: 109–112.

Zuckerman, B. M., Himmelhoch, S., Nelson, B., Epstein, J., and Kisiel, M. 1971. Aging in *Caenorhabditis briggsae*. *Nematol.* 17: 478–487.

Zuckerman, B. M., Nelson, B., and Kisiel, M. 1972. Specific gravity increase of *Caenorhabditis briggsae* with age. *J. Nematol.* 4: 261–262.

7
INSECTS

F. A. Lints

Laboratoire de Génétique
Université de Louvain
Louvain-la-Neuve, Belgium

INTRODUCTION

Insects include an estimated 800,000–900,000 species, and offer a marvelous tool for research on aging and longevity. The insect life span is usually short, and many generations may be observed in a few months. In general, insects are cheap and relatively easy to breed and may, therefore, be raised in very large numbers. Their physiology and biochemistry, though complex, are—for some species—relatively well known. A disadvantage, however, is that insects are poikilotherms; therefore, any extrapolation to homeotherms, and singularly to mammals, of the results obtained with insects should be made with great caution.

Surprisingly, very few species of insects have been studied in relation to aging: two or three species of *Drosophila*—*D. melanogaster, D. pseudoobscura, D. subobscura*—and a few others, *Tribolium castaneum, Musca domestica, Habrobracon serinopae, Aedes stimulans*. Among them, *Drosophila*, next to man, is probably the metazoan whose biology is the best understood and remains a favorite laboratory model for gerontologists. As early as 1921, Pearl and Parker observed that *Drosophila* was in different ways the ideal animal for studies of longevity and aging: "This organism has the great advantage over any other which could be used, that

its genetic behavior and potentialities are more thoroughly understood than those of any other animal, thanks to the epoch-making researches of Morgan and his students." This has remained true. Besides the well-known advantages of using *Drosophila* in biological research—reproductive capacity, generation time, size, conditions of culture, plasticity, short life span, and so on—there are also an amenability to sophisticated genetic manipulations and the availability of many chromosomal and gene mutations (In 1976, Soliman and Lints published an indexed bibliography on longevity and aging in *Drosophila* which counted 451 titles; that list was certainly not exhaustive.) All this may explain—and justify?—why, in some respects, the present review might appear to be biased in favor of *Drosophila*.

The reader may also consider two excellent and less personalized reviews on the aging of insects which have been published by Rockstein and Miquel (1973) and, for *Drosophila* only, by Lamb (1978). For review of enzymes and aging, see Wilson (1973).

PHENOMENOLOGY OF AGING AND LONGEVITY

Life span tables for a few insect species have been published by Rockstein and Miquel (1973), while tables of maximum recorded longevities have been published by Comfort (1979). Insects, apparently, have a very wide range of life spans. The life span of adult mayflies (Ephemeroptera) is only a day or so and may be as short as 1 hour, while some termites, *Neotermes castaneus,* for instance, may live as long as 25 years (Howard 1939). The life span of the insect imago is usually of the order of days or weeks, rather than months or years. An interesting exception concerns the order Coleoptera in which life spans of 1–2 years are not exceptional. A maximum longevity of over 4 years has been reported for *Akis bacarozzo,* over 7 years for *Prionotheca coronata* (Flower manuscript at the London Zoo, quoted by Comfort, 1979), and over 10 years for *Blaps gigas* (Labitte, 1916).

These life span data must however, for different reasons, be considered *cum grano salis.* Indeed the life spans of insects in the wild remain almost totally *terra incognita.* Most, if not all, published data concern either observations and experimental results obtained under laboratory conditions, or observations made on animals kept in captivity (Labitte, 1916). Furthermore, and with a few exceptions, life span data for insects pertain to the imaginal stage. Yet in insects that metamorphose, the larval life span mainly depends on the physical factors of the environment and the availability of proper sources of food. The length of the larval and pupal stages which may represent either a large or a small proportion of the imaginal life (or may even be many times larger than that part of life) is not usually taken into account. In *Drosophila* grown at 25°C, the preimaginal period lasts for 10 days while the imago may live for 40–50 days. By contrast, in most species of mayflies which survive only a few hours as imago, the nymphal period is usually 6–12 months and sometimes 2 or more years.

In general, we know more about the maximum recorded longevity within a given species or within a particular strain than about the mean life span of that species or strain. This last estimate depends effectively on the day-to-day recording of the number of

deaths in a population, the so-called life tables: for example, *Drosophila melanogaster* by Pearl and Parker (1921), *Musca vicina* by Feldman-Muhsam and Muhsam (1945), and *Musca domestica* by Rockstein and Lieberman (1959).

A review of the factors which affect the life span of insects will show how large that number of factors is and to how extreme an extent they may influence life span. Therefore, we suspect that all published results are only snapshots of what the life span is for a well-defined strain of a given species, at a given moment, and under a very precise set of environmental conditions, including the age of the parents, the physical environment during the developmental period, and the physical and biological environment during the imaginal period. Unfortunately, too many factors which have or may have an influence on the imaginal life span of insects are partially or completely neglected, or even ignored, by experimentalists (Lints, 1971). Next to nothing is known about the life span of insects in the wild.

To illustrate the snapshot nature of most published results we surveyed the papers published in *Experimental Gerontology* from its origin (1964) until 1979, pertaining to the life span of a widely used laboratory wild strain of *Drosophila melanogaster,* namely, Oregon. Only observations made at 25°C for both males and females were taken into consideration; seven papers were thus analyzed (Lints et al., 1983). The minimal mean life spans observed are 38 days for males and 42 days for females (Biscardi and Webster, 1977); the maximal, 85 days for males and 79 days for females (Gould and Clark, 1977), roughly a 100 percent difference.

The laboratory ecology of the most widely used species, even *Drosophila,* remains largely unknown. One suspects that gerontological studies of various physical, biological, and genetic factors acting on life span will only be fully useful when the potential life span of a given strain or species can be measured under standardized conditions. Too many published mean life spans of given strains or species are obviously only means of anticipated accidental deaths and of senescent deaths; the senescent deaths are, in a first analysis, the only ones which are of interest to the gerontologist. Only when experimentalists are able to reduce the anticipated deaths to a strict minimum will the study of the effects on life span of various manipulations of the environment yield some new insights into the analysis of aging.

Two last points may be emphasized in relation to that rapid survey of life span in the insect species. Structural, physiological, and biochemical changes linked to aging are almost exclusively studied in the single species *Drosophila*. The fact that some orders of insects appear to have life spans radically different from most other orders then prompts us to develop interorder comparative studies. The fact that some imagoes (adults) of insects, e.g., *Zabrotes subfasciatus, Callosobrachus maculatus* (Coleoptera), do not feed suggests a new field of research, encompassing a comparison of the structural, physiological, and biochemical variations, as a function both of the chronological and the physiological time, in species which die from simple nutrient exhaustion and in species which die from aging.

FACTORS AFFECTING LIFE SPAN

Extrinsic Factors

Some extrinsic factors induce variations of the imaginal aging and life span through influences which act on the preimaginal stages of the life cycle; most, however, act directly during and on the imaginal stage of the life cycle.

Preimaginal Factors. It is now well accepted that the conditions to which insects are submitted during their preimaginal life profoundly affect their imaginal aging and life span. Alpatov and Pearl (1929) grew *Drosophila* at 18 and 28°C; they found that flies grown at low temperature had a larger size and a longer duration of development; more importantly, these flies had, at all temperatures, a longer life span than flies grown at 28°C. Miller and Thomas (1958) were the first to show the influence of larval density

in *Drosophila*; high larval densities result in extended developmental period, smaller size, and increased longevity. Lints and Lints (1971a) confirmed the results of Alpatov and Pearl and of Miller and Thomas, and showed that the prolongation of imaginal life span was a direct function of the decrease in preimaginal growth rate (also see "Life Span and Development" later in this chapter).

Increased longevity was accompanied by a decrease in mean daily egg production, an increased period of egg laying—the mean total fecundity remained constant—, an increase in the postreproductive period, a delay in the age at which egg production was maximal, and a decrease in the maximum number of eggs laid in a 24-hour period (Lints and Lints, 1971a).

Some other data (reviewed in Lamb, 1978) do not fit the disclosed relation between life span and traits related to development. This could be because both in earlier studies and in more recent ones, insufficient attention was given to the conditions in which the preimaginal stages were grown. A second explanation concerns the choice of the strain; for instance, if a wild strain, genetically heterogeneous, is used in such studies, the individuals surviving in the extreme environments (extreme temperatures, high larval densities) might constitute a small part of the original population, selected on the basis of its genotype. In such studies, care should be taken to use strains of a uniform genotype, such as inbred or hybrid strains.

However, a study by Clark and Kidwell (1967) with the wasp *Mormoniella vitripennis* (a parasite of the pupa of the flesh fly *Sarcophaga bullata*) shows that the relation between growth rate and life span should be further analysed; these authors do find a relation clearly opposite to the one disclosed in *Drosophila melanogaster*. Indeed, in *Mormoniella vitripennis* a higher temperature during the preimaginal stages is associated, at all imaginal temperatures, with a *longer* adult life span.

Imaginal Factors. The most important extrinsic factor affecting aging and life span in insects, a poikilothermic organism, is temperature. Although less important, ionizing radiation has been abundantly studied. The influence of food and nutrition is not perfectly understood. Of the experimental conditions which may affect life span, population density, sexual activity, and light variations are among the most important. Other, more or less peripheral influences have been studied from time to time, for example oxygen tension, toxic agents, membrane stabilizers, magnetic fields, and so on. We feel, however, that our knowledge of these last factors is too incomplete and will, therefore, not review them.

Temperature. Much evidence shows that the life span of insects decreases when the environmental temperature increases. Lamb (1978) has reviewed a large number of papers which study the influence of temperature (20 different temperatures between 3 and 37°C) on the life span of a hybrid strain of *Drosophila subobscura:* the flies survive 224 days at 3°C, 83 days at 20°C, 39 days at 30°C, 75 minutes at 35°C, and 13 minutes at 37°C (see also Samis et al., 1973). Importantly, when survival times are plotted on a logarithmic scale, there is a sudden change in the slope of the curve at about 29°C. This change in slope suggests that the causes of death at high temperature are different from those at low temperature.

Concerning the effects of temperature within a normal physiological range, two theories deal with the temperature-dependent survival time of insects (and, eventually, of other poikilotherms). The rate-of-living theory of Pearl (1928) considers that aging is due to the loss of something which is necessary to maintain life or to the accumulation of undesirable by-products of biochemical reactions. It further assumes that higher temperatures accelerate aging because they accelerate metabolic rate. The classic study of Loeb and Northrop (1917) described how high temperature decreased the life span of *Drosophila melanogaster* and found that the temperature coefficient for longevity was similar to that for chemical reactions, i.e., the Q^{10} was 2–3.

An alternative and opposite theory relat-

ing temperature and life span was developed in 1961, by Clarke and Maynard Smith: it is known as the threshold theory of aging and proposes that there are two phases in the aging phenomenon—a temperature-independent aging phase, followed by a temperature-dependent dying phase. *Drosophila subobscura* were kept at 30°C for periods of up to half their expected life at that temperature and were then transferred to 20°C. If the rate-of-living theory is correct, these flies should have died before those kept at the low temperature throughout life; however, contrary to the predictions of the theory, they had similar mean life spans to those kept continuously at 20°C. In another experiment, flies were first kept at low temperature (20°C) for various periods and then transferred to a higher temperature (26°C); during the early part of the life span, for every day spent at 20°C the life span at 26°C was reduced by one day, but this was not true for flies which had spent more than 24 days at the low temperature. For these older flies, the survival times at 26°C were about 16 days and declined only slightly with the increasing age at transfer. The authors suggested that by 24 days of age, the vitality of the flies had fallen below the threshold needed for survival at 26°C; the dying process began immediately after the flies had been transferred to 26°C. Dying, at 26°C, took 16 days. Other experiments showed that the length of the dying phase was shorter at high temperatures. Therefore, Clarke and Maynard Smith suggested that the rate of aging or the rate of loss of vitality is independent of temperature. What determines the different longevities found at different temperatures is the ''level of vitality'' necessary to maintain life; dying begins when vitality falls below a threshold and this threshold is higher at high temperatures than at low temperatures. Furthermore, if the initial aging phase is temperature independent, the second phase, called the dying phase, is temperature dependent.

Pearl's rate-of-living theory, and Clarke and Maynard Smith's threshold theory, were given many experimental tests, by observing the life span of insects transferred during their imaginal life from one temperature to the other. The outcomes of these studies are ambiguous, favoring both theories. Some authors (Lamb, 1968; Hollingsworth, 1969) obtained results which were incompatible with either the threshold or the rate-of-living theory. (Reviews, with differences in opinion, appear in Lints, 1971; Sohal, 1976; Lamb, 1977, 1978.)

A direct experimental test of the rate-of-living theory was made by observing the rate of oxygen consumption of *Drosophila melanogaster* at various temperatures (Miquel et al., 1976). The oxygen consumption increased sharply with temperature; life span, of course, decreased as temperature increased (18°C: mean life span 130 days, oxygen consumption 38 μl/fly per 24 hours; 21°C: 86 days and 54 μl; 27°C: 43 days and 92 μl). The authors state that their "respiration data are in agreement with the inverse relationship between life span and a . . . mean value of the rate-of-living at a given temperature. . . . The ratio of life span at 18°C to life span at 21°C = 1.5 is nearly identical with that of oxygen utilization at 21°C to oxygen utilization at 18°C = 1.4." (For 21°C/27°C, the ratio of life spans equals 2 and that of oxygen utilization equals 1.7.)

On the other hand, there is detailed evidence which is hard to reconcile with the rate-of-living theory (Lints and Lints, 1968). At 25°C, the oxygen consumption was measured in a hybrid obtained from a cross between the Gabarros 4 and the Abeele inbred *Drosophila* lines; measurements were made on individual females, and age, size, and weight were considered. The particularity of their experiment was that two groups of larvae, of an identical genotype, were grown in standard vials grouped either by 30 or by 240. The latter cultures gave rise to flies with a prolonged development and a smaller size at emergence; these flies also had a considerably prolonged imaginal life span. However, the rate of oxygen consumption of the two groups of flies was *not* different (Hybrid G♀A♂ 30: 3.7 ± 0.1 μl O_2/mg fresh weight per hour; AG 30: 3.4 ± 0.1; GA 240: 3.7 ±

0.1, AG 240: 3.5 ± 0.1) although the life span was prolonged by more than 26 percent in the GA 240 hybrids and by more than 35 percent in the AG 240 hybrids. Even more interesting are the results obtained for total oxygen consumption per life. Expressed in μl/mg$_2$ fresh weight/life they are equal to 4.1, 3.6, 5.1 and 4.9; in μl/individual/life to 5.3, 4.7, 4.5 and 4.6 for the hybrids GA 30, AG 30, GA 240 and AG 240, respectively. It is noteworthy that the small fly respires as much as the large one; in other words, per unit of weight, the small flies appear to respire more than the large ones.

The study of Clark and Kidwell (1967) on the wasp *Mormoniella vitripennis* is also pertinent. The imaginal life span depended greatly on the preimaginal temperature. They concluded that there is *not* a fixed quantity of material which is used up at different rates at different temperatures, thus negating the postulates of the rate-of-living theory.

The evidence cited does not confirm the rate-of-living theory, at least under the simple form of a direct relationship among life span, rate of living (as measured by oxygen consumption), and temperature (see also discussion of sexual and physical activity under "Imaginal Factors: Experimental Conditions").

Sacher (1967), in an extensive review of the published data on the temperature dependence of longevity, metabolic rate, and so on in insects, concluded that aging was not a consequence of metabolic activity *per se* but "rather of the production of entropy concomitant with metabolic activity." He suggested that entropy increases on either side of a temperature *optimum* because of the heterogeneity of activation energies of enzyme-catalyzed reactions. Therefore, longevity does depend on temperature because temperature determines the rate of living, but Sacher adds that "aging can no longer be considered as simply a question of *how much* metabolic work; it is also a function of *how well* the work is done, in thermodynamic and informational terms." Hollingsworth (1969) and Atlan et al. (1976) reached the same conclusion.

Ionizing Radiation. The influence of ionizing radiation on aging and longevity of insects, mainly of Diptera, Coleoptera, and Hymenoptera, yielded literature with many contradictory results. Adult insects are much more resistant to the life-shortening effects of radiation than vertebrates, for instance, presumably because of the low level of mitotic activity in the imago. There is, however, no clear relationship between the dose of radiation and the life span shortening. Lamb (1978) noted that this may be because of at least three distinct effects of ionizing radiation on longevity: the effect of relatively low doses which increase the life span; the delayed life-shortening effect found after doses in the range 20–100 krad; and an acute effect resulting in death within a few days of irradiation with very high doses.

Furthermore, it is of prime importance whether radiation is administered as single or fractionated doses; in general, the effect is less detrimental when the dose is fractionated, even at intervals as low as 1½ hours (Wharton and Wharton, 1959). In *Drosophila* the detrimental effect of radiations depends also on gender, males being sometimes more and sometimes less sensitive than females (see Giess and Planel, 1977). There is no agreement about the influence of the age of the treated insects on the susceptibility to irradiation; some find that the radiosensitivity of different insect species is greater when irradiated in the mature stage, or less when irradiated early during imaginal life; others find that radiation-induced death is solely dependent on the absorbed dose and has no connection with the age of the animals (see Giess, 1980). However, it is almost impossible to compare the many experimental results because the sources of ionizing radiations, the doses used, the age at irradiation, the sex(es) studied, the way the irradiated animals are maintained (number of animals per vial, sexes separated or not), the genotypes used, and so on are so diverse from one experiment to the other.

How, then, does the exposure to ionizing radiation generally result in a decrease in life span? Is there any relation between natural aging and "aging" induced by irradiation? On the basis of observations made on irradiated *Drosophila,* three types of explanation have been expressed. Lamb (1966) and Lamb and Maynard Smith (1969) favor the hypothesis that radiation accelerates the natural aging process. Baxter and Blair (1967) hold that radiation injury does not accelerate the aging process, but simply adds an equivalent of natural aging. Finally, Atlan et al. (1969) consider that death caused by irradiation is the outcome of a radiation syndrome totally different from that of natural aging; support for this view is given by electron microscopic studies showing that the degenerative changes visible in the tissues of old flies are different from those shown by irradiated imagoes (Miquel et al., 1972). This is in agreement with the opinion expressed by Muller (1963) that permanent alterations in genes are not involved in natural aging and that the radiation-induced modification of life span, which results from damage to the nuclear genetic material, is not comparable to the spontaneous aging process (see also "The Mutation Theory of Aging" in this chapter).

Food and Nutrition. It must be admitted that very little is known about the feeding habits of most insect species or about their ecology relevant to nutrition. The only exception concerns the nutritional requirements of *Drosophila melanogaster.* Sang (1978) published a remarkable review of that problem; he also pointed out some sparse information about the nutritional requirements of half a dozen other *Drosophila* species, which shows that the differences between *Drosophila* species are most likely quantitative, rather than qualitative. Furthermore, except for insects adapted to very specialized environments which might be expected to select for particular nutritional requirements, the nutritional requirements of *Drosophila* are quite similar to those of other insects (see also House, 1974). However, when refined analyses are made, such as the study of Sang (1964) on inbred lines and hybrid crosses of *Drosophila melanogaster,* each line and each cross show their own optimal nutritional environment and their particular reactions to departure from this.

From a review of the influence of nutrition on the duration of life of the adult insect, Rockstein and Miquel (1973) suggested that four generalizations could be made. First, the nutritional levels required for optimal growth and development during the preimaginal stages are different from those required for the adult. Second, inadequate diets lengthen the preimaginal stages, whereas they shorten the imaginal duration of life. Third, the lengthening of the preimaginal stages by inadequate diets does not necessarily result in a lengthened adult life span. Fourth, males and females may have different nutritional requirements; it is therefore not impossible that some differences in life span between males and females are the result of metabolic differences provoked by nutritional influences.

To what extent could the use of auxotrophic mutants of insects, and more specifically of *Drosophila melanogaster,* assist in solving some problems related to aging? The use of mutant auxotrophs may aid in understanding the unique, as well as the general, biochemical features of aging. The first auxotroph reported was an adenine-requiring strain of *Drosophila melanogaster,* recorded as the first clear-cut case in animals of the inheritance of the basic biochemical difference involving a nutritional deficiency (Hinton et al., 1951). A few more have been reported since, and techniques have been devised to improve their production and isolation (review in Falk and Nash, 1974).

Light. Northrop (1925) reported that high light intensities reduce life span in *Drosophila melanogaster.* Similarly, *Musca domestica* kept in total darkness have a longer life span than flies kept in constant light (Greenberg, 1960). Although such a difference could be due to the decreased activity of the flies kept in darkness, that suggestion is probably wrong, since the life spans of *Drosophila melanogaster* kept in permanent light, in a 12-hour-light–12-hour-dark cycle, or in darkness for 95 percent of the time, were similar (Allemand et al., 1973); however, flies kept in permanent darkness lived significantly longer than any of the preceding groups, including the one in which flies were kept in darkness for 95 percent of the time. The increase in life span was not due to some effect of darkness on reproduction, since *Drosophila melanogaster* readily mates in the dark.

Experimental Conditions. The extraordinary diversity of experimental conditions is extremely frustrating, since it renders almost impossible the comparison of published results. Indeed the population density, the rhythm of change of food, the presence or absence of the opposite sex, the possibility or impossibility of physical activity, etc., all have important influences on aging. We do not yet know how to better standardize the experimental conditions.

Population Density—Staling Media. The influence on aging and life span of the number of imagoes present in vials of a given volume has received little attention. Depending on the population density of imagoes, the life span of *Drosophila* could be multiplied by a factor of four (Pearl et al., 1927); the relation between life span and imaginal crowding is *not* linear; and finally, a minimal population density is not optimal for longevity.

Jones et al. (1975) reported that the adult corn earworm, *Heliothis zea,* lived longer and mated more frequently when held at lower population densities. For the milkweed bug, *Oncopeltus fasciatus,* and the cotton stainer, *Dysdercus fasciatus,* Dingle (1968) reported no sex difference in the mortality rate in uncrowded cultures; however, under conditions of crowding the female mortality increased. In adult caged *Musca domestica,* the median longevity, the maximal longevity, and the number of flies exhibiting complete wing retention at death increased as the number of individuals per cage decreased from 240 to 10 flies per cage

(Rockstein et al., 1981). Under conditions of individual confinement, the life expectancy of females was not greater than that of males, and was similar to that of flies maintained at densities of 10 or 20 per cage.

These last observations could be at variance with some results of Bourgois (unpublished data). *Drosophila melanogaster* were kept, at 28°C, in standard 50 ml vials in groups constituted by 1, 5, 10, 20, or 40 pairs. Small differences in life span were observed for the groups of 5 to 40 pairs. However the life span of flies kept by pairs was extremely reduced; moreover, when flies kept in groups of 20 pairs were transferred as single pairs, the number of deaths increased sharply and soon reached the level of the death curve proper to the flies maintained as single pairs (Figure 1).

The shorter life span of insects at high densities could be due to the fact that in such conditions the animals show more activity, dispose of less room for feeding and are more

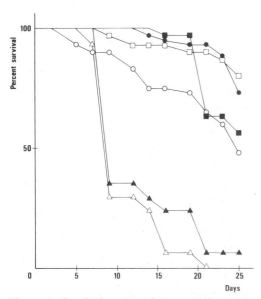

Figure 1. Survival curves of *Drosophila melanogaster* kept in standard vials in groups constituted by 1 (△), 5(■), 10 (□), 20 (●), or 40 (○) pairs, at 28°C. Flies first kept in groups of 20 pairs (▲) and then redistributed in groups of 1 pair die as flies kept continuously by single pairs. Females.

or less undernourished. The shorter life span found at low densities is more difficult to understand, and as far as we know, no satisfactory hypothesis has yet been proposed. It is not impossible that the reduced amount of some excretion product could have some influence on life span, but no clear evidence has been presented in favor of that hypothesis. However, for *Drosophila melanogaster*, staling medium decreases life expectancy and has complex influences on various quantitative traits including fecundity (David, 1961); it may be deduced that a normal medium becomes stale after 24 hours.

Sexual (and Physical) Activity. Beetles of the genus *Carabus* do not live as long when they reproduce, as when they are prevented from reproducing (Krumbiegel, 1930). Bilewicz (1953) found that in *Drosophila melanogaster*, virgin females lived approximately twice as long as mated ones; unmated males lived longer than mated ones, but the difference was smaller than for females. Maynard Smith (1958) confirmed those data for *Drosophila subobscura* and further showed that the unmated state of the females has as a consequence a lower rate of egg laying. Ragland and Sohal (1973), by varying the population composition (i.e., the ratio of males to females) in *Musca domestica,* have shown that the life span of males decreased as their mating (and physical) activities increased. Elimination of mating *and* severe restriction of physical activity, by confining flies individually, doubles the mean and maximum life spans of males, and increases slightly these values for females; under these conditions, mean and maximum life spans of males and females become equal. (Females normally outlive males.) Unfortunately, Ragland and Sohal's experimental protocol does not allow one to clearly separate the effects of mating activity from those of physical activity. (More precisely, data for flies with high mating and physical activities, with a high physical activity, and with no mating and no physical activities are provided. No data are given for flies with mating activity and no or low physical activity.) Thus, the relative importance of both of these activities cannot be estimated.

More recently, Buchan and Sohal (1981) studied the effects of both temperature and different sex ratios on the physical activity and life span of *Musca domestica*. The life spans of the flies were longer at 18°C than at 28°C. Female flies lived longer than males. Populations with female flies only exhibited lower levels of physical activity compared to populations of male flies only. Male flies with a high male-to-female ratio had the highest level of walking and flying activities, and lived a shorter period than their counterparts without any females. The authors estimate that the "variations in life span seem to be related to differences in the level of physical activity of the flies"; they add that "the life spans of the flies were thus inversely related to the level of physical activity." Finally, they conclude that the results of their study "support the concept that the rate of metabolic expenditure has a strong influence on lifespan."

Buchan and Sohal (1981) measured the level of physical activity—walking and flying activities—by means of a radar-Doppler system, from 16 to 28°C. Physical activity increases regularly between 16 and ~25°C, and then remains practically stable up to 28°C. Their conclusions could have been strengthened if, instead of measuring life span at 18° and 28°C only, it had been measured at 25°C also. If their hypothesis relating life span to physical activity is true, then the life spans observed at 25 and 28°C should be similar. If it is not true, then the comparison of data for life spans at 25 and 28°C could allow one to estimate—at least partially—the relative importance of physical activity and temperature in the control of life span.

Thus, the problem of the influence of physical activity and rate of metabolic expenditure on life span remains to be analyzed further (see also "Imaginal Factors: Temperature").

Intrinsic Factors

Among the intrinsic (organismic) factors having an influence, not yet clearly understood, on aging and longevity are factors linked to the genetic constitution of the individual or population analyzed and factors linked in an unknown way to the age of the parents.

Genetic Factors. Gerontologists have repeatedly affirmed that longevity is a genetically determined trait. What does that assertion mean exactly? That interspecific, intraspecific, or both the inter- and the intraspecific, differences are under genetic control?

If one considers the respective sizes of the mayfly and the elephant, one may claim that because these sizes are so different, they are genetically determined. However, does one, by that claim, really gain any insight into the mechanism of the genetic control of size in mayflies and in elephants? For an individual to reach the normal life span characteristic of the species to which he belongs, implies a proper development of the zygote and of the embryo, a harmonious growth, and once the adult stage is reached, accurately balanced maintenance activities. All these phases of development, growth, and life maintenance may be affected by genetic accidents which will eventually result in a premature death. Such accidental deaths, although due to genetic causes, have no relation whatsoever to the normal life span of, say, *Drosophila*. They do not demonstrate that *Drosophila* life span is under genetic control or that the difference in life span between *Drosophila* and *Tribolium,* for instance, is under genetic control. Ignorance about the eventual genetic basis of the interspecific differences in life spans is great. Such a gap in our knowledge will only be bridged after a clear answer has been given to the question of the control of intraspecific differences in life span. Even then the answer will not be obvious. Indeed, geneticists have repeatedly demonstrated that a difference in the average phenotypes of two populations (or species) need not have a genetic basis, even though similar phenotypic variations within either or both populations are largely genetic in origin (Wallace, 1975).

Intraspecific Differences. A genetically controlled trait is essentially the advanced stage, sometimes the end point, of a developmental sequence whose individual steps are controlled by one or numerous genes. Discontinuous or qualitative traits are primarily controlled by one or a few genes, the so-called major genes, each of which makes a large contribution to the process of character formation. On the contrary, continuous or quantitative traits are supposed (and sometimes have been shown) to be controlled by many genes, the so-called minor genes or polygenes, with small individual contributions.

Considered as a phenotypic character, longevity may appear as a peculiar trait. It could indeed constitute the most advanced stage, the real end point, of innumerable developmental sequences. Any interference with any biosynthetic pathway at any stage of life could have some effect on longevity. The question of the genetic control of life span could therefore be spurious. In other words, does any specific gene (or genes) exert some sort of control on longevity, or does the entire genome do so? The data concerning the influence of both the major and the minor genes on intraspecific differences should be considered.

Major Genes. In *Drosophila*, many studies show that longevity can be affected by major genes. Gonzales (1923), a student of Pearl, measured, under constant environmental conditions, the life spans of a wild strain of *Drosophila melanogaster,* of the carriers of five mutations located on chromosome II, of eight double, six triple, three quadruple, and the quintuple combination of these genes. Large differences were observed, but the life span of flies with various gene combinations was only rarely the average of the single mutations entering it. Sixty years after the work of Gonzales, the numerous studies on the influence of major genes on life span have added little more to what Gonzales has shown. Three criticisms may be leveled at such studies. Firstly, it is by no means certain that the comparison of the life span of the so-called laboratory wild strain with that of a mutant strain is indicative of the influence on life span of the mutant gene only.

This would be true only if the genetic backgrounds of both strains were identical, except for the mutant gene. [See, for instance the work of Clark and Gould (1970) who, in *Drosophila melanogaster*, investigated the effect on longevity of the vestigial mutant on the genetic background of both a short-lived and a long-lived wild strain. Their results clearly show that the effect of the mutant gene on life span is related to both sex and genetic background. On some genetic backgrounds the mutant gene has a life-shortening effect; on others, it has no effect. Furthermore, comparison of the average life spans of various Oregon strains of *Drosophila melanogaster* used in different laboratories has shown that divergences—due to mutation, selection linked to breeding techniques, random drift, and so on—among strains are extremely common.] A uniformity in genetic background may be obtained by repeated backcrosses of the wild strain to the mutant strain, for instance; however, that technique is used extremely rarely. Secondly, the major genes studied are all genes which mainly affect morphological traits. If one accepts that there are good reasons to consider aging as the ultimate expression of development, then, obviously, major genes with effects on traits linked to development should be analyzed. In *Drosophila* such genes have never been studied. Finally, it seems significant that all the major gene mutations analyzed shorten life span. We, therefore, feel that the evidence resulting from the analysis of major genes is not conclusive in favor of specific longevity genes, but rather indicates totally nonspecific mutations with lethal or sublethal effects. Such mutations pertain to genetic accidents, not to the genetic control of life span.

Minor Genes with Additive Action. What about minor genes? At the onset, it must be noted that gerontologists are not always sensitive to the distinction between the additive and the nonadditive action of minor genes. The study of both these aspects of polygenic action requires, of course, different approaches. To make the point, it may be useful to quote from a recent book on the genetics of aging (Schneider, 1978) which contains two interesting studies on the genetics of aging in man. The first of these studies (Murphy, 1978), originated by Pearl and Pearl (1934), investigates the relationship between the life spans of a large group of parents and offspring, thus analyzing essentially the action of minor genes with additive action. The author shows that there is a positive but small correlation between parent and offspring life spans. However, a careful analysis of his data leads him to the unequivocal conclusion that "there is no clear evidence to suggest whether . . . [the] clear and almost uniform parental component in the length of life is due to genetic factors . . . or to purely cultural and environmental factors." The second of these studies (Bank and Jarvik, 1978) concerns a longitudinal study of aging in human twins, originally started by Kallman and Sander (1948). That type of analysis includes the consideration of both the additive and the nonadditive action of minor genes. The conclusion of the authors is also unequivocal: "There is strong support of the hypothesis that heredity is a significant factor in determining the human life span."

The continuous variation exhibited in a definite species or population suggests that like other continuously varying traits, life span could be controlled by an array of minor genes with additive action. The existence of such a genetic control might be demonstrated either by a response to selection or by the existence of a significant degree of heritability. We know of no experimental results showing a successful selection for a prolonged life span. (The much-quoted work of Strong (1936) on selection for life span in mice, as shown by Lints (1978), does not stand up to a critical reading of the original paper.) Lints et al. (1979) selected towards a higher longevity for eight successive generations in a wild strain of *Drosophila melanogaster*. Absolutely no response to selection could be observed. Using a different method of analysis, Flanagan (1980) recently claimed to have confirmed these results. It thus appears that the large phenotypic variability displayed by life span in a wild strain of *Drosophila melanogaster* does not depend on a precise set of polygenes with additive action.

Minor Genes with Epistatic Action. Do these results mean that the entire phenotypic variance in longevity exhibited by a particular strain of insects is entirely of nongenetic origin, i.e., environmental and intangible? In fact, a part of the variance could be the result of nonadditive genetic variance, i.e., variance due to the epistatic interactions between genes. Indeed longevity has been shown to be a trait exhibiting both inbreeding depression and heterosis. Clear results are provided by Maynard Smith (1959; see also Clarke and Maynard Smith, 1955): he reciprocally crossed two inbred lines of *Drosophila subobscura* whose life spans were approximately 30 days and obtained two hybrid strains which survived for more than 60 days (reviews in Lamb, 1978; Lints, 1978).

The precise causes of inbreeding depression and heterosis are not perfectly understood. However, it is generally assumed that inbreeding depression is due either to increased homozygosity for deleterious genes or to the break up of balanced polygenic systems. On the other hand, heterosis is assumed to be the phenotypic result of gene interaction in heterozygotes. Thus, a trait exhibiting either inbreeding depression or heterosis is clearly under some type of genetic control. However, both these phenomena imply the totality of the phenotype and thus, probably, the entire genome. That evidence, therefore, is not totally conclusive; indeed, it may not be unequivocally concluded that specific genes for life span, rather than the entire genome, are affected by increased homozygosity or heterozygosity.

Another approach to the problem of the existence of epistatic genetic variance in natural populations could be developed through the analysis of subpopulations issued from a definite strain and submitted for a certain period of time to different environments. Such subpopulations should adaptively diverge through genome remodeling and subsequent selection. Such an experiment has been in progress in my laboratory for the last two years. Three subpopulations of the Oregon strain of *Drosophila melanogaster* have been kept in cage populations in three different environments. Gradual and significant divergences in life span have been observed in these subpopulations. Appropriate crosses between them demonstrate that the divergences are genetic in origin (Bourgois and Lints, 1982).

Sex. Many authors have claimed that in insects, and eventually in most animals, the male sex is the shorter lived (Clark and Rockstein, 1964; Lints, 1971; Rockstein and Miquel, 1973; Smith, 1978; Comfort, 1979). For exceptions, see Lamb (1977) and Lints (1978).

The most common argument to explain the postulated longer life span of females relates to the difference in chromosome number or structure between males and females and, more specifically, to the fact that in a great number of animal orders the male is heterogametic and the female homogametic. If this were true, then in Lepidoptera, where the female is heterogametic and the male homogametic, the latter should have a longer life span. MacArthur and Baillie (1932) reviewed the evidence pertaining to the life span of 13 species of Lepidoptera: with a single exception, all 13 species show a longer life span for females. In Hymenoptera, there are apparently no special sex chromosomes but ploidy differences may exist in which the male is usually haploid and the female diploid. In a few species, for example, *Habrobracon juglandis* and *H. serinopae,* both haploid and diploid males may be obtained. In *H. serinopae,* Clark and Rubin (1961) observed that the life spans of both haploid and diploid males were identical. These life spans were, however, shorter by 50 percent than that of diploid females. The available data do not substantiate the hypothetical influence of chromosome number and/or heterosomal differences on life span.

Comfort (1979) argued that the true explanation for the claimed longer life span of females is immunological. Females, he said, may be more prone to, but less hurt by, autoimmune effects by reason of being pro-grammed to live with half a foreign fetus. As insects do not have an immune system, that explanation cannot hold for these species. Rockstein and Miquel (1973) reviewed the possible influence of differences in metabolic rate between the sexes and concluded that there is little, if any, basis to explain differences in sex-related longevity in terms of metabolic rate or other metabolic differences. As far as we know, no one has ever tried to interpret sex-related longevity differences in terms of sexual hormones.

The first question that should be asked is: in insects, are females really longer lived than males? In a recent study of life span in *Tribolium castaneum* by Soliman and Lints (1982), the females outlived the males in only 4 cases out of 20. We then decided to look systematically at the published data concerning *Drosophila melanogaster*, the insect for which we most probably have the largest number of observations. In order to reduce any bias, we considered all papers published in *Experimental Gerontology* from its origin in 1964 up to 1981, i.e., 18 years. A few experiments were discarded in which the influence of various more or less toxic drugs had been analyzed; 18 papers were thus considered in which 228 comparisons between male and female life spans could be made. In 128 cases (56 percent; $\chi^2 = 3.44$; $0.05 < P < 0.10$), males outlived females! When one experiment (Lints and Hoste, 1974) with 105 possible comparisons (males outlived females in 73 cases) was discarded, males still outlived females in 55 cases out of 123 (45 percent; $\chi^2 = 1.38$; $P < 0.25$). At 25°C, the longest mean life span recorded for females equals 86.1 ± 1.6 days for a sample of 100 flies of the F_1 of a cross between the Oregon wild strain and a triple sex-linked mutant *w*, *m*, *f*—white, miniature, forked (Unlü and Bozcuk, 1979). For males (Bozcuk, 1978), the longest mean life spans equal 90.0 ± 2.5 and 90.1 ± 1.4 days for two samples of 88 and 99 flies, respectively, of the F_1 reciprocal hybrids between two mutant strains, vestigial and white.

At 25°C, the largest absolute sex difference in mean life span occurred for the artificial wild strain CUGO (♀ 30 ± 4.3 days;

♂ 61 ± 4.0; difference 31 days or 68 percent of the average life span), but on a relatively small sample of ten females and ten males only (Lints and Hoste, 1974). In a Swedish C-nipped strain (Clark and Gould, 1970), the difference amounted to 29 days (♀ 22 ± 2.2; ♂ 51 ± 2.9; difference 29 days or 77 percent; sample size 54 ♀ and 53 ♂). In a F_1 hybrid between a wild strain Champetières and the mutant vestigial (Allemand et al., 1973), the difference between sexes equaled 25 days, but in the opposite direction ♀ 80 ± 3.1 days; ♂ 55 ± 4; difference 25 days or 37 percent; sample size 85 ♀ and 77 ♂).

Do females really outlive males? More studies, taking into account one or more variables eventually related to and influencing life span (growth components?), are absolutely necessary before that question can be answered and, more essentially, before an answer can be found to the question of the determinism of eventual sex-related life span differences. (Lints et al., 1983)

Parental Age and Lansing Effects. For a detailed review of parental age and Lansing effects in man, insects, and other organisms, see Lints (1978). Parental age effects are the observable outcome, transmissible or not, produced in first generation offspring by one or a series of biological factors directly related to the age of the parents. Lansing effects are transmissible, cumulative parental age effects due to the reproduction at a given time of the life cycle through successive parental generations. Lansing effects may reverse either spontaneously or when the reproductive pattern is modified. The analysis of Lansing effects requires the analysis of successive generations of descendants (Soliman and Lints, 1976). Lansing effects were first demonstrated in the rotifers *Philodina citrina* and *Euchlanis triquetra* (Lansing, 1947, 1954). Parental age effects have been observed in a few organisms. The question of their permanence and transmissibility is only rarely addressed. Indeed successive generations have only occasionally been bred and observed although a clear distinction between the characteristics of first generation progeny, and the ability of such progeny to transmit a distinctive pattern to successive generations must be made. Clark (1964) stressed that distinction in relation to the longevity of first generation offspring of young and old parents.

Many reports describe subtle differences in growth, development, longevity, and various other quantitative traits between the offspring of young and old parents (reviews in Strong, 1954; Parsons, 1964; Lints, 1978; partial reviews in Lints and Hoste, 1974, 1977). Such evidence, however, is difficult to interpret because the progeny of aging parents were observed only at a few moments of the parental lifetime. This follows from an *a priori* belief, which closely follows the interpretation of Lansing (1954), that parental age effects are a linear function of parental age, i.e., that they are absent when the parents are young, and that they appear and increase as the parents grow older. However, it is clear in a certain number of cases, at least in insects, that when a given trait is measured in all successive daily progenies of aging pairs, the trait appears to vary in a cyclic, rather than in a linear, way. Examples, in *Drosophila melanogaster* are, for instance: variations in the size of the egg (David, 1959; Parsons, 1962; Delcour, 1969), in the number of abdominal bristles (Wattiaux and Heuts, 1963), in the sternopleural chaeta number asymmetry (Parsons, 1962), in wing size (Delcour and Heuts, 1968), in the sum of percentages of recombination for seven loci of chromosome III (Bridges, 1927), in the DNA and RNA content of virgin eggs (Tsien and Wattiaux, 1971), and so on.

Thus, the offspring of young and old parents may differ for many quantitative characters. One hypothesis is that offspring from old parents are offspring from a selected long-living, and thus possibly genetically different, component of the base population. Such a hypothesis can in general hardly be rejected on the basis of the published data. Indeed some authors use different groups of adults to yield offspring from young and old parents, while others do not identify the relationship between young and old parents. A few experiments are not subject to such criticism and indeed show that parental age effects are due to aging. Examples are experiments in which the young and old parents are identical (Lints and Hoste, 1974, 1977) and experiments in which the successive daily offspring of aging single pairs are observed. The number of abdominal bristles (Wattiaux and Heuts, 1963), the wing size (Delcour and Heuts, 1968), and the cell size and cell number of the wing (Delcour, 1969) of *Drosophila melanogaster* were observed in the successive progenies of single pairs of flies. All these traits were shown to vary cyclically rather than linearly as a function of parental age. In the case of age-dependent cyclic variations in wing size, the curves of variations of single pairs have been shown to be synchronous when the data were plotted as a function of relative maternal age (Delcour and Heuts, 1968).

What is the known influence of parental age on the life span of the F_1 offspring? Comfort (1953), in *Drosophila subobscura,* found no such influence. In 1959, Rockstein showed that the life span of the offspring females (not the males) in *Musca domestica* was reduced as parental age increased from 4 to 27 days. Butz and Hayden (1962), in *Drosophila melanogaster*, and Kiritani and Kimura (1967), in the Heteroptera *Nezara viridula,* demonstrated essentially the same. Lints and Hoste (1974) in two independent experiments, each of them replicated thrice, could not demonstrate any consistent relationship between parental age and F_1 progeny life span in *Drosophila melanogaster*.

The correct interpretation of much research on the cumulative effects of parental age in successive generations is extremely difficult. This is due to the fact that most experimentalists, closely following the interpretation of Lansing, *a priori* believed (1) that the effects of parental age were cumulative and, when present, culminated necessarily in the extinction of the strain, and (2) that they were strictly a positive function of parental age, i.e., that they were absent when

the parents were young and that they appeared and increased as the parents grew older.

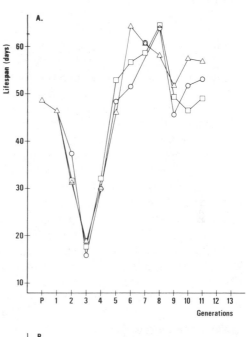

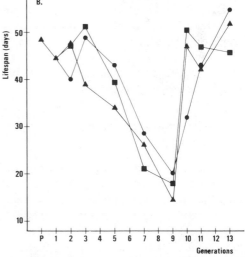

Figure 2. Mean life span of successive generations of *Drosophila melanogaster* reproduced at an old age for 11 generations (A) and at a young age for 13 generations (B). The three lines in each series refer to three replicates, one of which was selected for high bristle number, another for low bristle number; the third one is a control. Females. (Redrawn from Lints and Hoste, 1974).

Lints and Hoste (1974, 1977) conducted two independent experiments measuring life span and other quantitative traits: in the first experiment, during 13 successive generations; in the second, during 11 generations. In both experiments, three lines were reproduced at a young parental age and three other lines at an old parental age (Figure 2). Their results parallel those of Lansing on three main points: (1) the age of the parents at reproduction affects the mean longevity of the offspring; (2) that effect is cumulative; and (3) that effect is due neither to genic nor to environmental factors. Their results, however, differ in three fundamental aspects: (1) constant reproduction at *both* a young and an old age decreases the mean longevity of the offspring; (2) as in Lansing's experiments, the effects are cumulative; the accumulation, however, does not culminate in the extinction of the lines but only goes up to a certain point at which the evolutionary trend is reversed; (3) the reversibility is not induced by a change in the age at which reproduction occurs but by a feedback mechanism present in the strain itself. The authors proposed an explanatory hypothesis of the mechanism of Lansing effects in terms of the effects in time and space of the cellular composition and configuration of the ova of a given generation on the phenotypic expressions of the following generation (see also "The Evolutionary Theory of Senescence").

THEORIES OF AGING TESTED WITH INSECTS

Different theories of aging have been tested with insects. The rate-of-aging and the threshold theories of aging which concern the relation between environmental temperature and life span were reviewed earlier (see the discussion of temperature under "Extrinsic Factors: Imaginal Factors"). In 1973, von Hahn convincingly argued that hypotheses on the primary mechanisms of aging could be classified into two groups, the stochastic or error-accumulation group, and the genetic or aging program group. Among the first group, the mutation theory and a modern version of it, the error-catastrophe the-

ory, are the subject of many studies with insects. Theories relating aging to organelles, lysosomes, ribosomes, or mitochondria (this last organelle containing its own genetic information) constitute a special case. The sparse evidence in favor of a classical genetic control of aging was reviewed earlier (see "Intrinsic Factors: Genetic Factors"). The developmental theory of aging, which analyses the causes of aging considered as a developmental trait, may be said to be epigenetic as defined by Waddington (1940). Finally, a few experimental tests have been made in order to ascertain the evolutionary theories of senescence, i.e., those theories which try to understand how the mechanisms of evolution are at the origin of the various manifestations of postmaturation decline in survivorship and fecundity that accompanies advancing age.

Stochastic Theories

The Mutation Theory of Aging. Among others, Curtis and Gebhard (1958) proposed that aging and death were due to the accumulation of a certain number of somatic mutations. Says Curtis (1966): "According to this theory, the somatic cells of the body develop spontaneous mutations in the same way as do the germ cells. Once a mutation has been formed, subsequent cell divisions will perpetuate it. As more and more cells develop mutations, the time comes where an appreciable fraction of the cells is mutated. Practically all mutations are deleterious, so the cells carrying mutations are less well able to perform their functions. The organs become inefficient and senescent." The major argument in favor of the theory apparently was the supposed parallelism between aging and the damages produced by x-irradiation, since radiation, at least in mammals, results in various chromosomal damages and induces or, at least, accelerates the development of degenerative diseases (see chapter 8).

In insects, the major objection to the mutation theory of aging came from elegant experimental evidence on the wasp *Habrobracon serinopae,* which produces both haploid and diploid males (Clark and Rubin,

1961; Clark et al., 1963). When haploid and diploid males are treated by x-rays, the decrease of life span observed is related to chromosomal damage brought about by irradiation; the decrease observed in haploids is larger than that observed in diploids. Now the somatic mutation theory implies that in nonirradiated animals, haploid males should have a shorter life span than diploids simply because the haploids lack the genetic redundancy of the diploids. In fact, nonirradiated haploid and diploid males have identical life spans.

The Error-Catastrophe Theory. A modern version of the mutation theory, which also rests on random events, was proposed in 1963 by Orgel and became rapidly famous under the name of protein-error or error-catastrophe theory: "The basic idea is a simple one, namely that the ability of a cell to produce its complement of functional proteins depends not only on the correct specification of the various polypeptide sequences, but also on the competence of the protein-synthetic apparatus. A cell inherits, in addition to its genetic DNA, the enzymes necessary for the transcription of that material into polypeptide sequences. . . . A cell may deteriorate through a progressive decrease in the adequacy of its transcription mechanism, just as it may through the accumulation of somatic mutations."

Harrison and Holliday (1967) tested the error-catastrophe theory by feeding various amino acid analogues to third instar larvae of *Drosophila melanogaster* and observed a decrease in life span of the emerged imagoes. This confirms, at first view, one of the predictions of the theory since agents which are expected to increase the number of errors in protein synthesis shorten life span. Two other hypotheses were considered. One may assume that amino acid analogues are, prior to metamorphosis, incorporated in proteins which last throughout the life of the adult flies. Indeed, about 80 percent of the proteins of *Drosophila* adults do not turn over during adult life and only 20 percent turn over with a half-life approximately equal to 10 days. Such proteins with incorporated

amino acid analogues could be functionally defective and, therefore, shorten life span because of a lowering of the metabolic efficiency. Also, the toxicity of the treatment could destroy or damage cells just prior to or during metamorphosis; consequently, some relatively nonvisible morphological abnormalities could shorten adult life span.

To distinguish between these two possibilities and Orgel's hypothesis, Dingley and Maynard Smith (1969) fed various amino acid analogues, but principally *p*-fluoro-phenylalanine (*p*-FPA), to young adult male *Drosophila subobscura* and measured their effects on subsequent longevity of the flies surviving the treatment. First, *p*-FPA is effectively incorporated into the proteins of adult flies. Second, flies kept continuously on *p*-FPA die almost as quickly as flies in which almost all protein synthesis has been stopped by treatment with cycloheximide. If errors in protein synthesis may provoke a catastrophe, then the treatment with *p*-FPA must be expected to reduce life span. Yet, feeding sublethal doses of *p*-FPA to young adults produces *no* shortening of life, and in one experiment, a small increase in life span of the treated flies was observed. This makes it unlikely that the mechanism suggested by the error-catastrophe theory is an important cause of death in *Drosophila*. These results have been fully confirmed by Bozcuk (1976). Other criticisms, based on observations of the normal life span of diploid cell cultures grown in sublethal doses of amino acid analogues and on observations of the identity of viruses grown either in young or in old fibroblasts, have been made of the error-catastrophe theory (review in Lints, 1978; see also Morrow and Garner, 1979; see however Holliday, 1975; Kirkwood and Holliday, 1979).

Organelles

Mitochondria. The hypothesis has been defended that senescence linked to fixed post-mitotic cell aging might be due to irreversible injury to the mitochondrial DNA, which could play a role as essential as that of the nuclear genome in programming the phenotypic manifestations of senescence. The arguments in favor of the idea are mostly indirect (review in Miquel et al., 1980). Miquel claims that the mitochondrial DNA is closely associated with the inner mitochondrial membrane, thus allowing chemical interaction among the free radical generating system in the electron transport chain, the easily peroxidizable lipids of the membrane, and the mitochondrial genome; in contrast to nuclear DNA which is protected against oxidative and cross-linking inactivation by histones, the mitochondrial DNA is not surrounded by histones, and the repair mechanisms of mitochondrial DNA could be less effective than those of the nuclear genome.

What are the implications of the idea that the primary injury resulting in mitochondrial senescence (e.g., fine structural and biochemical alterations of the mitochondria and decrease in their total number) is linked with the disorganizing effect of free radicals formed in the inner mitochondrial membrane during the course of normal respiration? A first implication is that in insects, the amount of oxygen consumed during a lifetime should be independent of the temperature at which the insects are maintained; this is, in fact, exactly what the rate-of-living theory affirms. As shown before (see "Imaginal Factors: Temperature"), there is no definite evidence in favor of that theory.

Furthermore, the rate of respiration generally declines with advancing age (see Chapter 20); it was however shown that, depending on the preimaginal environment in which *Drosophila melanogaster* were grown, the rate of respiration could either decline or remain perfectly constant during the life of the imagoes (Lints and Lints, 1969).

A recent study by Massie et al. (1981b) concerns the level of total and mitochondrial superoxide dismutase (SOD) in two strains of *Drosophila melanogaster*, Oregon R and Swedish C whose life spans differ by 40 percent. SOD, the scavenger enzyme of O_2 free radicals could be expected, if the free radical hypothesis of aging is correct, to have a higher activity level in longer-living flies. Massie and his coworkers were unable to demonstrate any difference in either mitochondrial or total SOD activity level and concluded that SOD enzyme concentrations are probably not a determining factor in the senescence of *Drosophila melanogaster*. They remind us, however, that Bartosz et al. (1979), studying a wild type and a vestigial mutant, showed that total SOD activity level could be a determining factor; their own results, according to Massie and his coworkers, indicate that this is not a general phenomenon.

Lysosomes. Brunk and Ericsson (1972) argued that various elements of the endoplasmic reticulum and of the lysosomal apparatus were implicated in the formation of age-pigment granules (lipofuscin). An increase with age in the activity of some lysosomal enzymes was observed in some instances, although in other cases a decrease in activity with age has also been observed (see, for instance, Wilson, 1973); furthermore, the expression of different lysosomal enzymes during aging appears to have an independent and species-specific pattern. In *Musca domestica,* Sohal and McCarthy (1973) showed that acid phosphatase, a lysosome-associated enzyme, increases with age in most of the male house fly's tissues, indicating that lysosomes could be significantly involved in cellular aging processes. However, a careful study (Sohal and Donato, 1979) of relationships involving the rate of lipofuscin accumulation, the rate of lysosomal enzyme activity, and aging in *Musca domestica* indicated that there is still room for doubt concerning the role of lysosomal enzymes in aging. The idea of that last experiment was to compare the rates of lipofuscin accumulation and the activity of lysosomal enzymes (β-glycerophosphatase and β-acetyl glucosaminidase) in short-lived, high-activity and in long-lived, low-activity flies; or, in other words, to eventually demonstrate the relationship of a time-related alteration to the physiological, rather than the chronological, age of the organism. The results support the view that lipofuscin accumulation represents an integral aspect of aging and may be used as a cellular marker for physiological age, whereas the lysosomal enzyme activities observed, which do increase with chronological age, do not appear to be directly related to the physiological age or, in other words, to the rate of aging.

Ribosomes. Miquel and Johnson (1979) surveyed the extensive literature pertaining to ribosomal changes in relation to aging, and concluded that the data on ribosomal changes in dividing cells both *in vivo* and *in vitro* are not yet clear-cut (e.g., for insects, in *Drosophila* and *Musca*). However, the authors contend that there is strong histological and biochemical evidence in favor of some degree of quantitative loss in fixed postmitotic cells. They further claim that these decreases in ribosomes could represent a universal manifestation of cytoplasmic senescence in certain types of fixed postmitotic animal cells. However, a decrease in the rate of protein synthesis with age is certainly not a universal phenomenon (Wilson, 1973; see Chapter 9); furthermore, as was also shown, there are now good reasons to admit that Orgel's error-catastrophe theory does not constitute an adequate theory of aging.

Life Span and Development

In 1963, Lints from an experimental approach and Muller from a review of the mechanisms of life span shortening, drew attention to the relations between development and life span. Muller (1963) argued that development is a continuous process of which senescence forms the last stage or, in other words, that aging is a built-in consequence of differentiation. Clark (1964) came to the same conclusion and suggested that the problem of senescence, exactly like the study of ontogeny, should be approached studying the pattern of gene action, "the most important and at the same time the least understood chain of events leading to senescence and death." Considered from these points of view, life span appears as an epigenetically controlled trait, i.e., a trait whose expression is linked to the regulation of gene function,

of differentiation, or of the topographic distribution and function of proteins.

In homeotherms, a few instances demonstrate a close link between life span and development (review in Lints, 1980) and suggest a genetic correlation between these two traits, i.e., that some genes affect pleiotropically both traits or that genes affecting both characters are closely linked.

Insects appear to be more suitable than homeotherms to test a developmental theory of aging, simply because their early developmental mechanisms are not strictly regulated. Lints and Lints (1971a, 1971b) manipulated the conditions—temperature and larval crowding—in which the preimaginal life of hybrid *Drosophila melanogaster* was spent. In *Drosophila*, the duration of development can be prolonged either by decreasing the temperature at which development occurs or by increasing the larval population density. Decreasing the preimaginal temperature prolongs the duration of development, increases adult size, and increases imaginal life span. Increasing the preimaginal population density results in prolonged duration of development, a smaller size, and an increase in life span. More essential, however, is the fact that there is a strong negative correlation between growth rate—estimated as a function of the ratio of thoracic size and duration of development—and life span. Recently, the same relation was confirmed for two natural populations, two selected strains, and two mutant strains of *Tribolium castaneum* (Soliman and Lints, 1982). Cohet (1976) confirmed the relation between preimaginal temperature and imaginal life span for temperatures between 17 and 32°C; however, for temperatures of 12, 13, and 14°C, the relation was inverse. These last results confirm the idea of Sacher (1967) about the efficacy of metabolic work.

The Evolutionary Theory of Senescence

Medawar (1952) defined the evolutionary theory of senescence in the following terms: "If hereditary factors achieve their overt expression at some intermediate age; if the age of overt expression is variable; and if these variations are themselves inheritable: then natural selection will so act as to enforce the postponement of the age of the expression of those factors that are unfavourable and, correspondingly, to expedite the effects of those that are favourable. . . . " Different authors have reformulated and somewhat refined Medawar's theory. Williams (1957) suggested that senescence could have evolved by selection of genes which have different effects on fitness at different ages and, more precisely, of pleiotropic genes with beneficial effects in the first stages of life history and with deleterious effects later on. This is sometimes called the pleiotropy theory. Edney and Gill (1968) assumed that the hazard factor (i.e., the chances of accidental death) added to the effects of extrinsically caused senescence sets a specific limit to the longevity of a given species. As a consequence, a load of deleterious random mutations and gene interactions, applicable only in later life, would be allowed to accumulate, thus permitting intrinsic senescence to develop. This is referred to as to the mutation-accumulation theory.

Recently, Rose and Charlesworth (1980) contended that selection experiments in *Drosophila* (Wattiaux, 1968a) and *Tribolium* (Sokal, 1970) support the pleiotropy theory, but allowed that another experiment with *Tribolium* (Mertz, 1975) gave only marginal results. These claims deserve some critical evaluation, and various misinterpreted or neglected results merit some attention.

Rose and Charlesworth (1980), in *Drosophila melanogaster,* compared two populations: the first one reproduced at a young age (3–4 days; E population); the second one reproduced at an old age (21 days; L population). Both populations were bred for 12 generations. Subsequently, the total egg laying of the L population was smaller in the first five days of life and higher in the later periods. The life span of the L population was larger, and the rate of egg laying for the whole life span higher, than the corresponding values of the E population. Wattiaux

(1968a) studied the fecundity of two lines of *Drosophila subobscura* after reproduction, either by young parents for 21 generations (Y line) or by old parents for 7 generations (O line). He claimed that the fecundity of the offspring of the O line was higher than that of the Y line. In a study of the effects of parental age on longevity in *Drosophila pseudoobscura,* Wattiaux (1968b) concluded that flies used from lines repeatedly reproduced from old parents live longer than flies from young parental descent. The author compared single generations of descendants of young and old lines—the F_3 of an old line with the F_9 of a young line, for instance. Sokal (1970) studied the longevity of a wild-type and a mutant black strain of *Tribolium castaneum* after 40 generations of reproduction at a very young age, 1–3 days after emergence. Selected wild-type females and black males lived significantly less than the nonselected stock cultures, while selected wild-type males and black females did not show any significant difference from the nonselected stocks.

Taken together, the evidence is not conclusive. Other experiments (review in Lints, 1978), including the experiments of Lansing himself, either provide results which point in the other direction or have not been able to detect any parental age effects. Yet all these experiments suffer the same basic defect. Indeed parental age effects due to reproduction at a young or at an old age have been shown to be both cumulative and spontaneously *reversible* (Figure 2). Likewise the rate at which cumulation and reversibility occur was shown to depend on the age of reproduction. Therefore, a large number of *successive* generations must be observed in order to circumscribe the phenomenon correctly. Also, it will be extremely difficult to reach an unequivocal conclusion about the effects of selection for William's or Edney and Gill's type of genes before the mode of action of parental age effects is really understood. Indeed, as shown by Lints and Hoste (1977), the reversibility of the parental age effects depends on some reequilibration mechanism present in the strain itself, which, in *Drosophila*, tends to modify the speed of oogenesis. Similar spontaneous reequilibration mechanisms are not totally unknown, although hardly understood, and were described in *Aspergillus nidulans* (Jinks, 1956), *Aspergillus glaucus* (Mather and Jinks, 1958), vegetatively reproducing *Lemna minor* (Ashby and Wangermann, 1954), and *Drosophila melanogaster* (Lints and Gruwez, 1972). We believe that the mechanism for such a reequilibration implies modifications in the relative rates of synthesis of different constituents of the ovocyte. [See the work of De Robertis and Gurdon (1977) in *Xenopus laevis* and *Pleurodeles waltlii*, which demonstrates the paramount importance for development and for the control of genic action of molecules present in the ovocyte, i.e., before fertilization of the egg.] A rarely quoted experiment of Murphy and Davidoff (1972) gives some ground to that idea: these authors were able to demonstrate the existence of Lansing effects in the parthenogenetic crustacean *Moina macrocopa*. In the present respect, the important observation is that these effects could be modified and partly prevented by varying the environment in which *Moina* was grown and, more precisely, by exposing the animals to inositol or liver infusion.

CONCLUSION

Aging is an extraordinarily complex phenomenon, since all functions and components of organisms are inexorably impaired as time passes. This may explain to a certain extent why progress in our understanding of the primary cause(s) of aging in insects, and other organisms as well, has been so slow, as it may be perceived by any observer of gerontological studies. However, there are probably some other reasons for that very difficult progress in our knowledge. First of all, aging and longevity studies, even in insects, are long and tedious and in no way spectacular. In our day of generalized desire for rapid success and shattering discoveries, it is clear that only a relatively small number of scientists will be attracted to the field of

gerontology. Secondly, most authors develop their own methods of observing aging populations of insects and of breeding, feeding, or keeping them, and this renders useful comparison of results particularly difficult and sometimes impossible. Thirdly, for most insect species analyzed, insufficient care is given to the development of techniques and methods which would allow us to eliminate the maximum number of anticipated accidental deaths and thus to observe the maximum number of senescent deaths. Fourthly, not enough attention is paid to the genotypes of the strains studied; in a certain number of cases, insects of a uniform genotype, inbred lines or hybrid strains, should be used. Fifthly, in too many cases the comparison of young and old populations is made on different groups of insects; wherever possible, longitudinal studies should be preferred to cross-sectional analyses. Finally, the influences of the preimaginal environment and of the parental age are largely ignored or falsely understood and, therefore, not properly taken into account.

What are the prospective lines of research in gerontological studies with insects? We still do not know to what extent aging and death are genetically controlled. More studies should be made in relation to that problem, taking into account the different types of genes—and their mode of action—which could eventually play a role in the control of aging. There appears to be a link, the nature of which is hardly understood, between development and aging; mutations affecting traits linked to development—size, duration of development, growth rate, and so on— should be searched for and analyzed. Careful studies testing the evolutionary theories of senescence are needed. These studies could be made in only a few species provided their genetics is well known and their laboratory ecology well understood.

Interorder studies should also be undertaken on the behavior, rate of aging, biochemistry, ultrastructure, and physiology of long-lived and short-lived species. Comparisons should also be made between species which do not feed during their imaginal life, and thus probably die from exhaustion, and species which do feed and probably die from senescence. Finally, some sort of collaboration should be developed between students of aging in organisms and students of cell aging. In holometabolous insects, in which there are no mitotic divisions after emergence, the death of the organism could to some extent coincide with cellular death. The relationship of cell size, cell number, cell alteration, and cell death to the death of the insect should be analyzed.

ACKNOWLEDGMENT

This work was supported by U.S. NIH grant AG 02087. The collaboration of C. V. Lints is gratefully acknowledged.

REFERENCES

Allemand, R., Cohet, Y., and David, J. 1973. Increase in the longevity of adult *Drosophila melanogaster* kept in permanent darkness. *Exp. Geront.* 8: 279–283.

Alpatov, W. W. and Pearl, R. 1929. Experimental studies on the duration of life. XII. Influence of temperature during the larval period and adult life on the duration of the life of the imago of *Drosophila melanogaster*. *Am. Nat.* 63: 37–67.

Ashby, E. and Wangermann, E. 1954. The effects of meristem aging on the morphology and behavior of fronds in *Lemna minor*. *Ann. N.Y. Acad. Sci.* 57: 476–483.

Atlan, H., Miquel, J., and Binnard, R. 1969. Differences between radiation-induced life shortening and natural aging in *Drosophila melanogaster*. *J. Geront.* 24: 1–4.

Atlan, H., Miquel, J., Helmle, L. C. and Dolkas, C. B. 1976. Thermodynamics of aging in *Drosophila melanogaster*. *Mech. Ageing Dev.* 5: 371–387.

Bank, L. and Jarvik, L. F. 1978. A longitudinal study of aging human twins. *In*, E. L. Schneider (ed.), *The Genetics of Aging,* pp. 303–333. New York: Plenum Press.

Bartosz, G., Leyko, W., and Fried, R. 1979. Superoxide dismutase and lifespan of *Drosophila melanogaster*. *Experientia* 35: 1193.

Baxter, R. C. and Blair, H. A. 1967. Kinetics of aging as revealed by x-ray-dose-lethality in *Drosophila*. *Radiat. Res.* 30: 48–70.

Bilewicz, S. 1953. Experiments on the effect of reproductive functions on the length of life of *Drosophila melanogaster* (in Polish, with English summary). *Folia Biol., Krakow* 1: 177–194.

Biscardi, H. M. and Webster, G. C. 1977. Accumulation of fluorescent age pigments in different genetic strains of *Drosophila melanogaster*. *Exp. Geront.* 12: 201–205.

Bourgois, M. and Lints, F. A. 1982. Evolutionary divergence of growth components and life span in subpopulations of *Drosophila melanogaster* raised in different environments. *In*, S. Lakovaara (ed.), *Advances in Genetics, Development, and Evolution of Drosophila,* pp. 211–226.

Bozcuk, A. N. 1976. Testing the protein error hypothesis of ageing in *Drosophila*. *Exp. Geront.* 11: 103–112.

Bozcuk, A. N. 1978. The effect of some genotypes on the longevity of adult *Drosophila*. *Exp. Geront.* 13: 279–285.

Bridges, C. B. 1927. The relation of the age of the female to crossing-over in the third chromosome of *Drosophila melanogaster*. *J. Gen. Physiol.* 8: 689–700.

Brunk, U. and Ericsson, J. L. 1972. Electron microscopical studies on rat brain neurons. Localization of acid phosphatase and mode of formation of lipofuscin bodies. *J. Ultrastruct. Res.* 38: 1–15.

Buchan, P.B. and Sohal, R. S. 1981. Effect of temperature and different sex ratios on physical activity and lifespan in the adult housefly, *Musca domestica*. *Exp. Geront.* 16: 223–228.

Butz, A. and Hayden, P. 1962. The effects of age of male and female parents on the life cycle of *Drosophila melanogaster*. *Ann. Entom. Soc. Am.* 55: 617–618.

Clark, A. M. 1964. Genetic factors associated with ageing. *In*, B. L. Strehler (ed.), *Advances in Gerontological Research,* Vol. 1, pp. 207–255. New York: Academic Press.

Clark, A. M., Bertrand, H. A., and Smith, R. E. 1963. Life-span differences between haploid and diploid males of *Habrobracon serinopae* after exposure as adults to x-rays. *Am. Nat.* 97: 203–208.

Clark, A. M. and Gould, A. B. 1970. Genetic control of adult life-span in *Drosophila melanogaster*. *Exp. Geront.* 5: 157–162.

Clark, A. M. and Kidwell, R. N. 1967. Effects of developmental temperature on the adult life span of *Mormoniella vitripennis* females. *Exp. Geront.* 2: 79–84.

Clark, A. M. and Rockstein, M. 1964. Aging in insects. *In*, M. Rockstein (ed.), *Physiology of Insecta,* 1st ed., Vol. 1, pp. 227–281. New York: Academic Press.

Clark, A. M. and Rubin, M. A. 1961. The modification of x-irradiation of the life-span of haploids and diploids *Habrobracon* sp. *Radiat. Res.* 15: 244–253.

Clarke, J. M. and Maynard Smith, J. 1955. The genetics and cytology of *Drosophila subobscura*. XI. Hybrid vigour and longevity. *J. Genet.* 53: 172–180.

Clarke, J. M. and Maynard Smith, J. 1961. Two phases of ageing in *Drosophila subobscura*. *J. Exp. Biol.* 38: 679–684.

Cohet, Y. 1976. Epigenetic influences on the lifespan of the *Drosophila:* existence of an optimal growth temperature for adult longevity. *Exp. Geront.* 10: 181–184.

Comfort, A. 1953. Absence of a Lansing effect in *Drosophila subobscura. Nature* 172: 83.

Comfort, A. 1979. *The Biology of Senescence,* 3rd ed. Edinburgh and London: Churchill Livingstone.

Curtis, H. J. 1966. *Biological Mechanisms of Aging.* Springfield, Ill.: Charles C. Thomas.

Curtis, H. J. and Gebhard, K. L. 1958. Radiation induced aging in mice. *Proc. of the Second International Conference on Peaceful Uses of Atomic Energy* 22: 53–57.

David J. 1959. Influence de l'âge de la femelle sur la dimension des oeufs de *Drosophila melanogaster. C. R. hebd. Séances Acad. Sci. Paris Sér. D. Sci. Nat.* 249: 1145–1147.

David, J. 1961. Influence de l'état physiologique des parents sur les caractères des descendants. Etude chez *Drosophila melanogaster. Ann. Génét.* 3: 1–77.

Delcour, J. 1969. Influence de l'âge parental sur la dimension des oeufs, la durée de développement et la taille thoracique chez *Drosophila melanogaster. J. Insect Physiol.* 15: 1999–2011.

Delcour, J. and Heuts, M. J. 1968. Cyclic variation in wing size related to parental aging in *Drosophila melanogaster. Exp. Geront.* 3: 45–53.

De Robertis, E. M. and Gurdon, J. B. 1977. Gene activation in somatic nuclei after injection into amphibian oocytes. *Proc. Natl. Acad. Sci. U.S.A.* 74: 2470–2474.

Dingle, H. 1968. The effect of population density on mortality and sex-ratio in the milkweed bug, *Oncopeltus* and the cotton stainer, *Dysdercus* (Heteroptera). *Am. Nat.* 100: 465–470.

Dingley, F. and Maynard Smith, J. 1969. Absence of a life-shortening effect of amino-acid analogues on adult *Drosophila. Exp. Geront.* 4: 145–149.

Edney, E. B. and Gill, R. W. 1968. Evolution of senescence and specific longevity. *Nature* 220: 281–282.

Falk, D. R. and Nash, D. 1974. Sex-linked auxotrophic and putative auxotrophic mutants of *Drosophila melanogaster. Genetics* 76: 755–766.

Feldman-Muhsam, B. and Muhsam, H. V. 1945. Life tables for *Musca vicina* and *Calliphora erythrocephala. Proc. Zool. Soc. London* 115: 296–305.

Flanagan, J. R. 1980. Detecting early-life components in the determination of the age of death. *Mech. Ageing Dev.* 13: 41–62.

Giess, M. C. 1980. Differences between natural ageing and radio-induced shortening of the life expectancy in *Drosophila melanogaster. Gerontology* 26: 301–310.

Giess, M. C. and Planel, H. 1977. Influence of sex on the radiation-induced lifespan modifications in *Drosophila melanogaster. Gerontology* 23: 325–333.

Gonzales, B. M. 1923. Experimental studies on the duration of life. VIII. The influence upon duration of life of certain mutant genes of *Drosophila melanogaster. Am. Nat.* 57: 289–325.

Gould, A. B. and Clark, A. M. 1977. X-ray induced

mutations causing adult life-shortening in *Drosophila melanogaster. Exp. Geront.* 12: 107–112.

Greenberg, B. 1960. House fly nutrition. II. Comparative survival values of sucrose and water. *Ann. Entom. Soc. America* 53: 125–128.

Hahn, H. P. von. 1973. Primary causes of ageing: a brief review of some modern theories and concepts. *Mech. Ageing Dev.* 2: 245–250.

Harrison, B. J. and Holliday, R. 1967. Senescence and the fidelity of protein synthesis in *Drosophila. Nature,* 213: 990–992.

Hinton, T., Noyes, D. T., and Ellis, J. F. 1951. Amino acids and growth factors in a chemically defined medium for *Drosophila. Physiol. Zool.* 24: 335–353.

Holliday, R. 1975. Testing the protein error theory of ageing. A reply to Baird, Samis, Massie and Zimmerman. *Gerontology* 21: 64–68.

Hollingsworth, M. J. 1969. Temperature and length of life in *Drosophila. Exp. Geront.* 4: 49–55.

House, H. L. 1974. Nutrition. *In,* M. Rockstein (ed.), *The Physiology of Insecta,* 2nd ed., Vol. 5, pp. 1–62. New York: Academic Press.

Howard, L. O. 1939. Ageing in insects. *In,* E. V. Cowdry (ed.), *Problems of Ageing.* London: Baillière, Trudall and Cox.

Jinks, J. L. 1956. Naturally occurring cytoplasmic changes in fungi. *C. R. Trav. Lab. Carlsberg* 26: 183–203.

Jones, R., Perkins, W., and Sparks, A. 1975. *Heliottis zea:* effect of population density and a marker dye in the laboratory. *J. Econ. Entomol.* 68: 349–350.

Kallman, F. J. and Sander, G. 1948. Twin studies on aging and longevity. *J. Hered.* 39: 349–357.

Kiritani, K. and Kimura, K. 1967. Effects of parental age on the life cycle of the southern green stink bug, *Nezara viridula* L. (Heteroptera: Pentatomidae). *Appl. Entomol. Zool.* 2: 69–78.

Kirkwood, T. B. L. and Holliday, R. 1979. The evolution of ageing and longevity. *Proc. Roy. Soc. Edinburgh, Sect. B.* 205: 531–546.

Krumbiegel, I. 1930. Die Einwirkung der Fortpflanzung auf Altern und Lebensdauer Insekten. *Forschungen und Fortschritte* 6: 85–86.

Labitte, A. 1916. Longévité de quelques insectes en captivité. *Bull. Mus. Natl. Hist. Nat. (Paris)* 22: 105–113.

Lamb, M. J. 1966. The relationship between age at irradiation and life-shortening in adult *Drosophila. In,* P. J. Lindop and G. A. Sacher (eds.), *Radiation and Ageing,* pp. 163–174. London: Taylor and Francis.

Lamb, M. J. 1968. Temperature and life-span in *Drosophila. Nature* 220: 808–809.

Lamb, M. J. 1977. *Biology of Ageing.* Glasgow and London: Blackie.

Lamb, M. J. 1978. Ageing. *In,* M. Ashburner and T. R. F. Wright (eds.), *The Genetics and Biology of Drosophila,* Vol. 2c, pp. 43–104. London and New York: Academic Press.

Lamb, M. J. and Maynard Smith, J. 1969. Radiation-induced life-shortening in *Drosophila. Radiat. Res.* 40: 450-464.

Lansing, A. I. 1947. A transmissible, cumulative and reversible factor in aging. *J. Geront.* 2: 228-239.

Lansing, A. I. 1954. A nongenic factor in the longevity of rotifers. *Ann. N.Y. Acad. Sci.* 57: 455-464.

Lints, F. A. 1963. De l'influence de la formule caryo-cytoplasmique et du milieu sur les relations entre lon-gévité et vitesse de croissance chez *Drosophila me-lanogaster. Bull. Biol. Fr. Belg.* 97: 605-626.

Lints, F. A. 1971. Life-span in *Drosophila. Geronto-logia* 17: 33-51.

Lints, F. A. 1978. *Genetics and Ageing.* Basel: Karger.

Lints, F. A. 1980. *Drosophila* and the future of research in the genetics of ageing. *Genetika* 12: 187-200.

Lints, F. A., Bourgois, M., Delalieux, A., Stoll, J., and Lints, C. V. 1983. Does the female life span exceed that of the male? *Gerontology 29:* 336-352.

Lints, F. A. and Gruwez, G. 1972. What determines the duration of development in *Drosophila melanogas-ter? Mech. Ageing Dev.* 1: 285-297.

Lints, F. A. and Hoste, C. 1974. The Lansing effect revisited. I. Life-span. *Exp. Geront.* 9: 51-69.

Lints, F. A. and Hoste, C. 1977. The Lansing effect revisited. II. Cumulative and spontaneously reversi-ble parental age effects on fecundity in *Drosophila melanogaster. Evolution* 31: 387-404.

Lints, F. A. and Lints, C. V. 1968. Respiration in *Dro-sophila.* II. Respiration in relation to age by wild, inbred and hybrid *Drosophila melanogaster* imagos. *Exp. Geront.* 3: 341-349.

Lints, F. A. and Lints, C. V. 1969. Respiration in *Dro-sophila.* III. Influence of preimaginal environment on respiration and ageing in *Drosophila melanogas-ter* hybrids. *Exp. Geront.* 4: 81-94.

Lints, F. A. and Lints, C. V. 1971a. Influence of pre-imaginal environment on fecundity and ageing in *Drosophila melanogaster* hybrids. III. Develop-mental speed and life-span. *Exp. Geront.* 6: 427-445.

Lints, F. A. and Lints, C. V. 1971b. Relationship be-tween growth and ageing in *Drosophila. Nature New Biol.* 229: 86-88.

Lints, F. A., Stoll, J., Gruwez, G., and Lints, C. V. 1979. An attempt to select for increased longevity in *Drosophila melanogaster. Gerontology* 25: 192-204.

Loeb, J. and Northrop, J. H. 1917. On the influence of food and temperature upon the duration of life. *J. Biol. Chem.* 32: 103-121.

MacArthur, J. W. and Baillie, W. H. T. 1932. Sex dif-ferences of mortality in *Abraxas*-type species. *Quart. Rev. Biol.* 7: 313-325.

Massie, H. R., Williams, T. R., and Aiello, V. R. 1981b. Superoxide dismutase activity in two different wild-type strains of *Drosophila melanogaster. Gerontol-ogy* 27: 205-208.

Mather, K. and Jinks, J. L. 1958. Cytoplasm in sexual reproduction. *Nature* 182: 1188-1190.

Maynard Smith, J. 1958. The effects of temperature and of egg-laying on the longevity of *Drosophila subob-scura. J. Exp. Biol.* 35: 832-842.

Maynard Smith, J. 1959. The role of ageing in *Droso-phila subobscura. In,* G. E. W. Wolstenholme and M. O'Connor (eds.), *The Lifespan of Animals,* Vol. 5, pp. 269-285. London: Ciba Foundation Sympos-ium.

Medawar, P. B. 1952. *An Unsolved Problem of Biol-ogy.* London: Lewis.

Mertz, D. B. 1975. Senescent decline in flour beetle strains selected for early adult fitness. *Physiol. Zool.* 48: 1-23.

Miller, R. S. and Thomas, J. L. 1958. The effects of larval crowding and body size on the longevity of adult *Drosophila melanogaster. Ecology* 39: 118-125.

Miquel, J., Bensch, K. G., Philpott, D. E., and Atlan, H. 1972. Natural aging and radiation reduced life-shortening in *Drosophila melanogaster. Mech. Age-ing Dev.* 1: 71-97.

Miquel, J., Economos, A. C., Fleming, J., and John-son, J. E. 1980. Mitochondrial role in cell aging. *Exp. Geront.* 15: 575-591.

Miquel, J. and Johnson, J. E. 1979. Senescent changes in the ribosomes of animal cells *in vivo* and *in vitro. Mech. Ageing Dev.* 9: 247-266.

Miquel, J., Lundgren, P. R., Bensch, K. G. and Atlan, H. 1976. Effects of temperature on the life span, vi-tality and fine structure of *Drosophila melanogaster. Mech. Ageing Dev.* 5: 347-370.

Morrow, J. and Garner, C. 1979. An evaluation of some theories of the mechanism of aging. *Gerontology* 25: 136-144.

Muller, H. J. 1963. Mechanisms of life-shortening. *In,* R. J. C. Harris (ed.), *Cellular Basis and Aetiology of Late Somatic Effects of Ionizing Radiation,* pp. 235-245. New York: Academic Press.

Murphy, E. A. 1978. Genetics of longevity in man. *In,* E. L. Schneider (ed.), *The Genetics of Aging,* pp. 261-301. New York: Plenum Press.

Murphy, J. S. and Davidoff, M. 1972. The result of improved nutrition on the Lansing effect in *Moina macrocopa. Biol. Bull.* 142: 302-309.

Northrop, J. H. 1925. The influence of the intensity of light on the rate of growth and duration of life of *Drosophila. J. Gen. Physiol.* 9: 81-86.

Orgel, L. E. 1963. The maintenance of the accuracy of protein synthesis and its relevance to ageing. *Proc. Natl. Acad. Sci. U.S.A.* 49: 517-521.

Parsons, P. A. 1962. Maternal age and developmental variability. *J. Exp. Biol.* 39: 251-260.

Parsons, P. A. 1964. Parental age and the offspring. *Quart. Rev. Biol.* 39: 258-275.

Pearl, R. 1928. *The Rate of Living.* London: University of London Press.

Pearl, R., Miner, J. R., and Parker, S. L. 1927. Ex-perimental studies on the duration of life. XI. Den-sity of population and life duration in *Drosophila. Am. Nat.* 61: 289-318.

Pearl, R. and Parker, S. L. 1921. Experimental studies on the duration of life. I. Introductory discussion on the duration of life in *Drosophila. Am. Nat.* 55: 481-509.

Pearl, R. and Pearl, R. D. 1934. *The Ancestry of the Long-lived.* Baltimore: Johns Hopkins University Press.

Ragland, S. S. and Sohal, R. S. 1973. Mating behavior, physical activity and aging in the housefly, *Musca domestica. Exp. Geront.* 8: 135–145.

Rockstein, M. 1959. The biology of ageing in insects. *In,* G. E. W. Wolstenholme and M. O'Connor (eds.), *The Lifespan of Animals,* Vol. 5, pp. 247–264. London: Ciba Foundation Symposium.

Rockstein, M., Chesky, J. A., Levy, M. H., and Yore, L. 1981. Effect of population density upon life expectancy and wing retention in the common house fly, *Musca domestica* L. *Gerontology* 27: 13–19.

Rockstein, M. and Lieberman, H. M. 1959. A life table for the common house fly, *Musca domestica. Gerontologia* 3: 23–26.

Rockstein, M. and Miquel, J. 1973. Aging in insects. *In,* M. Rockstein (ed.), *The Physiology of Insecta,* 2nd ed. Vol. 1, pp. 371–478. New York: Academic Press.

Rose, M. and Charlesworth, B. 1980. A test of evolutionary theories of senescence. *Nature* 287: 141–142.

Sacher, G. A. 1967. The complementarity of entropy terms for the temperature-dependence of development and aging. *Ann. N.Y. Acad. Sci.* 138: 680–712.

Samis, H. V., Baird, M. B., and Lints, F. A. 1973. Lifespan and temperature: insects. *In,* P. L. Altman and D. S. Dittmer (eds.), *Biology Data Book,* 2nd ed., Vol. 2, p. 873. Bethesda, Md.: Federation of American Societies for Experimental Biology.

Sang, J. H. 1964. Nutritional requirements of inbred lines and crosses of *Drosophila melanogaster. Genet. Res.* 5: 50–67.

Sang, J. H. 1978. The nutritional requirements of *Drosophila. In,* M. Ashburner and T. R. F. Wright (eds.), *The Genetics and Biology of Drosophila,* Vol. 2a, pp. 159–189. London: Academic Press.

Schneider, E. L. (ed.) 1978. *The Genetics of Aging.* New York: Plenum Press.

Smith, J. R. 1978. Genetics of aging in lower forms. *In,* E. L. Schneider (ed.), *The Genetics of Aging,* pp. 137–149. New York: Plenum Press.

Sohal, R. S. 1976. Metabolic rate and life-span. *In,* R. G. Cutler (ed.), *Cellular Ageing: Concepts and Mechanisms.* Part I. *Interdisciplinary Topics in Gerontology,* Vol. 9, pp. 25–40. Basel: Karger.

Sohal, R. S. and Donato, H. 1979. Effect of experimental prolongation of life-span on lipofuscin content and lysosomal enzyme activity in the brain of the house fly, *Musca domestica. J. Geront.* 34: 489–496.

Sohal, R. S. and McCarthy, J. L. 1973. Age-related changes in acid phosphatase activity in adult male house fly, *Musca domestica.* A histochemical and biochemical study. *Exp. Geront.* 8: 223–227.

Sokal, R. R. 1970. Senescence and genetic load: evidence from *Tribolium. Science* 167: 1733–1734.

Soliman, M. H. and Lints, F. A. 1976. Bibliography on longevity, ageing and parental age effects in *Drosophila. Gerontology* 22: 380–410.

Soliman, M. H. and Lints, F. A. 1982. Influence of preimaginal constant and alternating temperatures on growth-rate and longevity of adults of five genotypes in *Tribolium castaneum. Mech. Ageing Dev.* 18: 19–31.

Strong, L. C. 1936. Production of the CBA strain of inbred mice: long life associated with low tumour incidence. *British J. Exp. Pathol.* 17: 60–63.

Strong, L. C. (ed.) 1954. *Parental Age and the Characteristics of the Offspring.* New York: N.Y. Academy of Science.

Tsien, H. C. and Wattiaux, J. M. 1971. Effect of maternal age on DNA and RNA content of *Drosophila* eggs. *Nature New Biol.* 230: 147–148.

Unlü, H. and Bozcuk, A. N. 1979. Genetics of longevity in *Drosophila.* I. The effects of *w, m,* and *f* mutant genes in various genotype combinations. *Exp. Geront.* 14: 117–124.

Waddington, C. H. 1957. *The Strategy of the Genes.* Allen and Unwin: London.

Wallace, B. 1975. Genetics and the great IQ controversy. *Am. Biol. Teacher* 37: 12–19.

Wattiaux, J. M. 1968a. Cumulative parental age effects in *Drosophila subobscura. Evolution* 22: 406–421.

Wattiaux, J. M. 1968b. Parental age effects in *Drosophila pseudoobscura. Exp. Geront.* 3: 55–61.

Wattiaux, J. M. and Heuts, M. J. 1963. Cyclic variation of bristle number with parental age in *Drosophila melanogaster. Proceedings 11th International Congress of Genetics,* 1: 168.

Wharton, D. R. A. and Wharton, M. L. 1959. The effect of radiation on the longevity of the cockroach, *Periplaneta americana* as affected by dose, age, sex and food intake. *Radiat. Res.* 11: 600–615.

Williams, G. C. 1957. Pleiotropy, natural selection and the evolution of senescence. *Evolution* 11: 398–411.

Wilson, P. D. 1973. Enzyme changes in ageing mammals. *Gerontologia* 19: 79–125.

PART 3 MOLECULAR BIOLOGY

8
DNA REPAIR AND REPLICATION IN AGING ORGANISMS AND CELLS

Raymond R. Tice
and
Richard B. Setlow

Medical Department and Biology Department
*Brookhaven National Laboratory**

INTRODUCTION

The integrity of DNA is essential for the well-being of cells and of organisms. The maintenance of that integrity is the central element of several theories on aging (Samis, 1966; Alexander, 1967; Yielding, 1974; Smith, 1976). Not only is the faithful replication of DNA important for cell division, but its transcription into RNA and the subsequent translation of RNA into protein determine the functional capability of the cell. Thus, even in nondividing cells, the maintenance of DNA is critical. For such cells, DNA repair maintains the template for RNA synthesis, and the efficacy of DNA repair will depend upon its reliability and rate compared to the rate of RNA synthesis. For dividing cells, because the faithful replication of DNA is also important, the time and the rate at which DNA repair take place relative to the onset and rate of DNA synthesis are also crucial.

There are other, less general reasons for us

to be concerned with DNA replication and repair. A number of mammalian tissues (e.g., skin and the lining of the small intestine) are in a steady state process of cell renewal. If renewal is faulty, the tissue will cease to function correctly and the organism will deteriorate. Moreover, all organisms are exposed to deleterious environmental agents, such as background levels of ionizing radiation, ultraviolet radiation (UV), and chemicals like polycyclic aromatic hydrocarbons, aflatoxins, and nitrosamines. Furthermore, endogenous metabolic processes and reactions occurring at normal thermal conditions can also affect DNA. The amount of damage introduced by endogenous or exogenous reactions is not trivial. For example, Table 1 gives estimated numbers of damages per cell per hour to the DNA of mammalian cells. It is obvious that the numbers of damages are appreciable. If DNA repair mechanisms did not exist, the accumulation of damage over one year's time would be so large (for example, $\sim 2 \times 10^7$ single-strand breaks per genome of 6×10^9 base pairs) that such cells could not replicate or transcribe their DNA. Thus, from numbers alone, DNA repair is

*Brookhaven National Laboratory is operated by Associated Universities, Inc., for the Department of Energy.

173

TABLE 1. Rate of Appearance of Damage in 6×10^{12} Daltons of Double-Stranded DNA[a] AT 37°C.

Damage	Events per/hour	Reference[b]
Depurination	580	1
Depyrimidination	29	1
Deamination of cytosine	8	1
Single-strand breaks (ssb)	2300	1
ssb after depurination	580	1
O^6-methylguanine	130	2
Pyrimidine dimers in skin (noon Texas sun)	5×10^4	3

[a]The amount in a mammalian cell.
[b]The values given are estimates from data on (1) DNA in solution (Shapiro, 1982); (2) alkylation of DNA by S-adenosylmethionine (Barrows and Magee, 1982); and (3) UV dosimetry from the inactivation of bacteria corrected for the transmission of skin (Harm, 1969; Setlow, 1982).

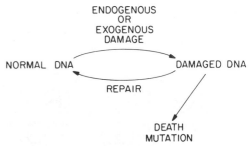

Figure 1. A schematic representation indicating that the level of damaged DNA depends upon the relative rates of input of damage and repair.

necessary. The rate of DNA repair must be sufficient to cope with the production of DNA damage or such damage will accumulate. Most of the types of damage which we know of, and the only ones we will discuss in detail, are those for which known DNA repair mechanisms exist. Damages that are not repaired by such mechanisms will accumulate. Thus, cells and organisms are in a delicate balance between the production of damage and its repair. If the production of damage accelerates, or if the level and the accuracy of repair decline, a new steady state condition for DNA damage will exist. It is important to realize that even with efficient DNA repair systems, there always will be some damage existing in DNA. The level of this damage depends upon its relative rates of production and of repair (Figure 1).

We can investigate the possible relations of DNA repair, DNA replication, and aging from six points of view.

1. Examine the frequency of DNA damage and the competency of DNA synthesis and repair in cells aging *in vitro* (for a description of *in vitro* senescence, see p. 237). These experiments assume, of course, that there is some relation between aging in culture and aging of organisms.

2. Examine the DNA metabolic activities of cells from old and young animals of the same species. Are there differences in the rates of replication and of repair, and more importantly, is there any indication that damage has accumulated in the cells of old animals?

3. Examine DNA repair in cells of the same age from organisms with completely different life spans. If life span is a function of DNA repair competency, then cells from longer-lived animals should have greater repair capacity.

4. Examine the rate of the aging process in cells or organisms stressed by exposure to agents known to damage DNA. If aging is due to an accumulation of DNA damage, then more damage per unit time should accelerate the aging process.

5. Examine DNA repair and replication in cells from individuals with disorders that appear to accelerate the aging process. If such syndromes are good mimics of normal aging, one would expect to observe deficiencies in DNA synthesis and/or DNA repair if a cause-effect situation exists.

We shall examine the data available for each of these experimental systems. Several other reviews (Little, 1976; Hart and Trosko, 1976; Williams, 1976; Cutler, 1976c; Tice, 1978; Hart et al., 1979a; Gensler and Bernstein, 1981; Setlow, 1982), which assess many of these same points, but possibly with a different interpretation, are also available to the reader for comparison. However, it is first necessary to know something about normal DNA synthesis and repair: what are their characteristics and what are the procedures by which they are measured?

DNA REPAIR PROCESSES AND THEIR DETECTION

There are six repair systems that have been characterized reasonably well (Setlow and Setlow, 1972; Hanawalt et al., 1979; Friedberg et al., 1979; Seeberg and Kleppe, 1981). The reader, however, should not infer that all of the enzymological details of these repair systems are known or that these systems are completely independent of each other. The repair systems to be considered briefly are:

1. Repair of single-strand breaks
2. Repair of double-strand breaks
3. Nucleotide excision repair
4. Base excision repair
5. Photoreactivation
6. Postreplication repair

These systems repair different types of damages produced by a variety of exogenous or endogenous sources.

Single-strand Break Repair. As indicated in Table 1, large numbers of single-strand breaks are induced in cells, in part from unknown metabolic reactions (e.g., oxidative processes) and in part probably as a result of enzymological actions near depurinated regions of the DNA—regions that accumulate as a result of existence at 37°C. When such breaks are introduced into cells by ionizing radiation (endogenous breaks do not arise in significant numbers from background ionizing radiation), they are quickly repaired. Thus, as indicated in Table 2, mammalian cells are capable of repairing about 200,000 single-strand breaks per hour. Such repair measurements are made by two general techniques. In both, the cells can be labeled with radioactivity so as to detect the DNA in sub-

TABLE 2. Approximate Numbers of Products that could be Repaired Per Hour Per Human Cell.

Damage	Numbers	Reference[a]
Single-strand breaks	2×10^5	1
Pyrimidine dimers		
Normal cells	5×10^4	1
Xeroderma pigmentosum group C cells	5×10^3	1
O^6-methylguanine	10^4–10^5	2

[a]*References:* (1) Setlow (1982) and (2) Waldstein et al. (1982).

sequent analytical steps or the DNA can be detected by fluorescence after absorption of a fluorescent dye. The cells are lysed in alkali, which causes the DNA to unwind. The rate of unwinding depends upon the number of single-strand nicks in the DNA since the unwinding of the DNA duplex starts at such breaks. In one technique—sedimentation in alkali—the unwinding reaction is allowed to go to completion, and the molecular weight distribution of the resulting DNA is determined by sedimentation in alkali. From the number average molecular weight, one can calculate the number of single-strand nicks in the DNA as the reciprocal of the number average molecular weight. In a second technique, the reaction is stopped part way through the unwinding by neutralizing the solution, and the fraction of DNA that has reformed the double helix is determined either by chromatographic techniques or by resistance to digestion by a single-strand nuclease. In a third technique, alkaline elution, cells are lysed on filters, and the DNA is eluted with mild alkali to give an estimate of the rate of DNA unwinding. The alkaline sucrose technique, although very easy to do, can only measure breaks at the levels of several in 10^8 daltons, whereas the other techniques have sensitivities in the neighborhood of several in 10^{10} daltons. Measurements made at different times after the introduction of single-strand breaks indicate that the breaks disappear rapidly, and it is from this rapid disappearance that the numbers given in Table 2 are derived. The techniques are described in detail in a laboratory manual edited by Friedberg and Hanawalt (1981). As a practical matter, sedimentation in alkali is only a useful technique for cells that have accumulated single-strand breaks resulting from the equivalent of 5000 rads or more, whereas the techniques that depend upon the rate of unwinding may be used in the biological range of several hundred rads.

Double-strand Break Repair. Double strand breaks are rare events compared to single-strand ones. They may arise from ionizing radiation, from the action of certain chemicals (e.g., bleomycin), or from a combination of single-strand nicks plus endonucleolytic attack on the strand opposite the nick. Such breaks also are readily repaired in mammalian cells but perhaps less readily than single-strand breaks. They can be measured by sedimentation in neutral gradients or by elution from filters after cell lysis at a pH in the neighborhood of 9.

Nucleotide Excision. This is one of the better-studied DNA repair pathways. The prototype damage is represented by pyrimidine dimers resulting from UV irradiation. The irradiation produces dimers between adjacent pyrimidines in the same strand, and such lesions are recognized by specific endonucleases or glycosylases that initiate a rather complicated series of reactions (illustrated in Figure 2) which result in the removal of the damaged section of DNA and its replacement by normal nucleotides using the opposite unaltered strand as a template. In mammalian cells, the average size of the repaired section is large—25–100 nucleotides depending on the method used and the laboratory reporting—and seems independent of species. This type of repair may be measured in a number of ways, each of which has its virtues and experimental difficulties. If particular products such as pyrimidine dimers are known, it is possible to measure their loss from DNA by radiochromato-

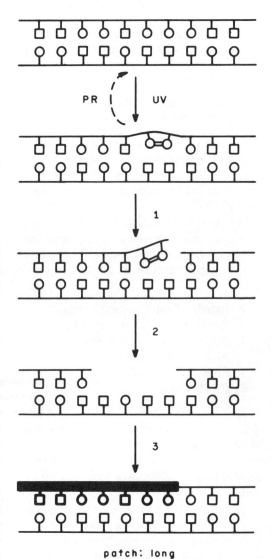

Nucleotide excision repair

patch: long

Figure 2. A schematic diagram showing the process of nucleotide excision repair of pyrimidine dimers. The dimers (which can be reversed by photoreactivation, PR) are acted upon by a combination of endonucleolytic and exonucleolytic attacks followed by polymerization using the opposite unaltered strand as a template. This repolymerization, represented by the solid dark line, represents for mammalian cells about 100 nucleotides and is a relatively long patch. It is estimated by experiments measuring repair replication or unscheduled DNA synthesis. Circles represent pyrimidines; squares, purines.

graphic procedures or, in an assay that can measure smaller numbers of lesions per unit length, by the loss of sites sensitive to damage-specific endonucleases. The endonuclease introduces single-strand nicks into the DNA, and the nicks are quantified by sedimentation in alkali. A variation of the latter procedure is to render cells permeable so that an exogenous endonuclease can be introduced to probe for the regions sensitive to enzymic action. This technique, in conjunction with experiments on purified DNA, would measure the accessibility of the lesions in chromatin to nucleases.

It should be clear from Figure 2 that during the process of nucleotide excision repair, there is an increase followed by a subsequent decrease in the number of single-strand nicks in cellular DNA. Such nicks can also be measured by sedimentation in alkali. A commonly used way of measuring repair is to determine the incorporation of an isotope such as ^{3}H-dThd into parental DNA. The repaired DNA, indicated by the thick line in Figure 2, represents so-called unscheduled DNA synthesis (UDS; i.e., synthesis during the non–S phase of the cell cycle). Such measurements are usually made in one of two ways, either as the radioactivity incorporated per microgram of DNA or, by radioautography, as the number of grains per nucleus. Complications in the quantitative interpretation of such measurements arise because the specific activity of the radioisotope may not be known, since there may well be unlabeled thymidine in the growth medium, or because the cells may have an endogenous pool of thymidine metabolites that competes with the exogenous label. The latter can be minimized by shutting off the endogenous pathway for DNA synthesis by use of the inhibitor fluorodeoxyuridine (FdUrd). The interpretation of UDS can be further complicated by the presence of cells undergoing "normal" DNA synthesis. The scheduled incorporation of radioactive label may far outweigh the unscheduled. Hence, it is customary to inhibit scheduled synthesis by antimetabolic agents such as hydroxyurea

with the hope that this inhibitor will not affect unscheduled DNA synthesis. In actual practice, too low a concentration of inhibitor permits too much scheduled DNA synthesis and too high a concentration of inhibitor tends to inhibit unscheduled DNA synthesis. The optimum concentration between these two extremes is usually not known. Thus, it is better to avoid the use of inhibitors and measure UDS by radioautography since this technique permits the unique identification of cells doing scheduled synthesis and allows them to be eliminated from the computation. Some examples of this technique are given in the following sections.

Measurements of UDS do not provide direct evidence that the incorporated label is going into parental DNA as was illustrated in Figure 2. The measurements of repair replication in which cells are permitted to repair in the presence of a radioactive dense isotope such as tritium-labeled bromodeoxyuridine (BrdUrd) avoids this difficulty. By isopycnic sedimentation, replicated DNA can be separated from unreplicated and the amount of incorporation into parental DNA measured uniquely. A variation on this latter technique uses the photochemical sensitivity of BrdUrd incorporated into DNA (light of wavelength 313 nm specifically makes single-strand nicks in DNA containing BrdUrd) to measure both the number and, in many cases, the patch size of the repaired regions. It is this type of measurement that gives most of the estimates of patch sizes quoted in this chapter.

A completely different way of measuring DNA repair, and one that is essentially applicable to all repair pathways, is host cell reactivation of DNA-containing viruses. If viruses are inactivated by a DNA-damaging agent, the level of inactivation depends upon the ability of the host cells on which they will be grown to repair damage to the viral DNA. Cells proficient in repair show much higher viral survival than cells deficient in repair. The technique is important not only because of its sensitivity but because its use eliminates the possibility that differences in chemical metabolism and/or transport may be responsible for an apparent change in cellular sensitivity to specific chemical agents.

Base Excision Repair. Nucleotide excision involves an initial attack on the polynucleotide backbone; base excision repair does not. Three major subdivisions of this repair scheme are illustrated in Figure 3. Alkylation damage and, in particular, 0^6-alkylguanine products may be repaired by direct dealkylation through transfer of the alkyl group to an acceptor protein, which converts the DNA to its original unaffected form. This repair *cannot* be measured by UDS or by repair replication. A second base excision repair pathway involves the removal of the affected base itself without touching the polynucleotide strand. Two possibilities for the completion of this repair are illustrated in Figure 3. In the first, a new base is inserted in place of the old one, while in the second, there is an endonuclease attack on the apurinic site.

Either the patch size is one (since the inserted base is usually a purine, UDS using ^{3}H-dThd would measure a patch of zero), or the patch size will be short. Hence, UDS is not a good measure of base excision repair especially since 0^6-alkylguanine, the major mutational product, is repaired with zero patch size.

Photoreactivation. Photoreactivation repair (Sutherland, 1981), also illustrated in Figure 1, is specific for pyrimidine dimers. It involves binding of enzyme to the damaged DNA, absorption of visible light by the enzyme-DNA complex, monomerization of the dimer, and dissociation of the enzyme from what is now unaltered DNA. The repair system is useful analytically because it gives one an indication of the fraction of UV damage that may be ascribed to dimers.

Postreplication Repair. If one of the repair systems just discussed has not completed re-

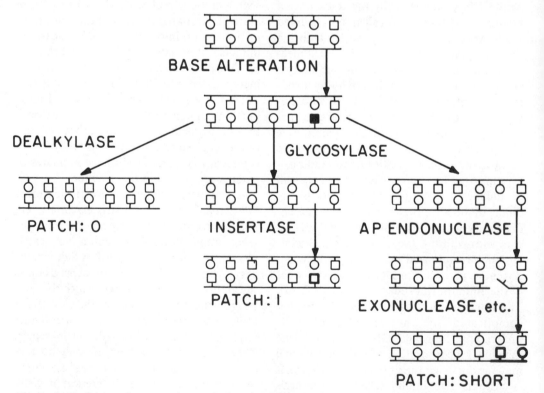

Figure 3. Various pathways and steps in base excision repair. It is assumed that a purine has been altered. The various pathways give rise to various patch sizes. Circles represent pyrimidines; squares, purines.

pair before DNA synthesis, replication may be attempted on a damaged template. If the changes in DNA are small, (e.g., the presence of an O^6-alkylguanine or an apurinic site), miscoding may take place. If the changes are bulky ones, (e.g., a pyrimidine dimer), then the replication fork may stop, at least temporarily, near the site of damage. If the fork passes the damage, a gap is left in that Okazaki fragment that is blocked, which leaves a gap in the newly synthesized strand. The gaps are eventually filled in by mechanisms called postreplication repair which are not clearly understood for eukaryotic systems. Postreplication repair is usually measured by pulse labeling the newly synthesized DNA and determining the distribution of its molecular weight in alkaline sucrose gradients. Such distributions permit one to determine whether the newly synthesized DNA is chased into parental size material as rapidly as that made on a normal template. They also allow one to determine if replicon initiation is inhibited, because if it is, a pulse label will only add on to large replicating DNA and have a high sedimentation rate.

CELLS OF DIFFERENT AGES IN CULTURE

The obvious limitations inherent in large scale *in vivo* experimentation have prompted the development of *in vitro* mammalian models of aging. One *in vitro* system frequently utilized for aging studies employs the characteristic pattern of growth of fibroblast cells derived from human embryonic lung as a correlate for aging *in vivo* (Hayflick, 1975). After a period of rapid, sustained growth (known as Phase I), these cells with successive passages enter a period of gradually decreasing proliferation (Phase II) followed by complete cessation of growth (Phase III) (Hayflick, 1965). Whether or not this *in vitro* model of aging is a valid one (for instance, see Mitusi and Schneider, 1978), a number of studies have assessed different types of DNA repair competency and/or the accumulation of unrepaired damage in these cells as a function of passage number.

Chromosomal Aberrations

Frequency of Spontaneous Aberrations. As an indicator of age-related DNA repair capacity, several investigators have examined the "spontaneous" level of chromosomal aberrations in metaphase cells of mammalian cultures as a function of *in vitro* passage level. Chromosomal aberrations can result from the presence of unrepaired DNA lesions (Parrington et al., 1971; Sasaki, 1973), and many types of DNA lesions can induce the same general classes of aberrations (Bender et al., 1973a, 1973b; 1974). Consequently, a decline in the efficiency of any DNA repair process may give rise to an increase in the level of spontaneous aberrations. A decrease in DNA repair capability is not, however, the only possible mechanism by which increased levels of spontaneous aberrations could arise. Chromosomal aberrations could also occur as a result of interference with normal DNA synthesis (Kihlman, 1966) and, by extrapolation, as a result of a decline in the competency of DNA synthesis.

Several investigators have detected an increase in the frequency of spontaneous chromosomal aberrations in human fibroblasts aging *in vitro* (Sax and Passano, 1961; Saksela and Moorehead, 1963; Thompson and Holliday, 1975; Benn, 1976; Miller et al., 1977), while others have not observed such increases (Kadanka et al., 1973; Chen and Ruddle, 1974; Reis and Goldstein, 1980) (see Table 3). Where an increase in the frequency of chromosomal aberrations was observed, the aberration type largely involved an increased incidence of dicentric chromosomes. An increase in dicentric chromosomes could result from a delay in single-strand break rejoining, which offers a greater opportunity for open breaks to interact, or from an increase in the number of breaks formed due to more damage and/or to better repair recognition of existing damage. The increased occurrence of chromosomal aberrations in senescent cells has also been suggested to be a consequence of defective proteins and not a major cause of senescence (Thompson and Holliday, 1975).

TABLE 3. Frequency of Spontaneous Chromosomal Aberrations in Aging Cells *In Vitro*.

Cell Strain[a]	Species	Age-related Response	Reference[b]
Fibroblast (emb. lung)	Human	Increase	1
Fibroblast (emb. lung)	Human	Increase	2
Fibroblast (emb. lung)	Human	No change	3
Fibroblast (emb. lung)	Human	No change	4
Fibroblast (emb. lung)	Human	No change	5
Fibroblast (emb. lung)	Human	Increase	6
Fibroblast (emb. lung)	Human	Increase	7
Fibroblast (emb. lung)	Human	Increase	8
Fibroblast (emb. lung)	Human	No change	9

[a]*Abbreviation:* emb. = embryonic.
[b]*References:* (1) Sax and Passano (1961); (2) Saksela and Moorhead (1963); (3) Goodman et al (1969); (4) Kadanka et al. (1973); (5) Chen and Ruddle (1974); (6) Thompson and Holliday (1975); (7) Benn (1976); (8) Miller et al. (1977); (9) Reis and Goldstein (1980).

The spontaneous frequency of sister chromatid exchanges (SCE), another cytogenetic phenomenon with possible relevance to the existence of DNA lesions and/or to DNA repair competency, is discussed in Chapter 14.

Frequency of Induced Aberrations. No studies in the induction of chromosomal aberrations in mammalian cell strains as a function of *in vitro* life span have been reported. The reader is directed to Chapter 14 for a review of the age-related induction of other cytogenetic phenomena *in vitro*.

Cross-linking

Several investigators have attempted to assess the presence of cross-linking between DNA strands and/or between DNA and some other cellular constituent. Cross-linking could result in repressed gene activity, leading to a loss of cellular function and/or in cell death. Few assays directly assess cross-linking. However, assays for thermal stability (i.e., the temperature at which complementary DNA strands separate), protein-DNA binding, and DNA template activity for exogenous RNA polymerases can provide inferential evidence for the existence of cross-linking (see Table 4).

Direct Cross-linking. Bradley et al. (1976) used alkaline elution techniques to directly assess levels of DNA-DNA and DNA-protein cross-links in WI–38 cells. No alteration in the occurrence of either type of cross-link was observed throughout their *in vitro* lifespan.

Thermal Stability. An increase in cross-linking between complementary DNA strands and/or between DNA strands and the chromosomal proteins (histone and nonhistone) should increase the melting temperature (T_m) at which the DNA strands separate. Comings and Vance (1971) detected a constant T_m for DNA and chromatin isolated from quiescent human embryonic lung fibroblasts as a

TABLE 4. Accumulation of DNA Cross-Links in Aging Cells *In Vitro.*

Cell Type[a]	Species	Assay	Age-related Response	Reference[b]
Fibroblast (emb. lung)	Human	Thermal stability	No change	1
Fibroblast (emb. lung)	Human	Template activity	Decrease in activity[c]	2
Fibroblast (embryonic)	Chick	Template activity	No change	3
Fibroblast (emb. lung)	Human	Template activity	No change	4
Fibroblast (emb. lung)	Human	Template activity	Decrease in activity	5
Fibroblast (emb. lung)	Human	Alkaline elution	No change	6
Fibroblast (emb. lung)	Human	Template activity	Decrease in activity[c]	7
Fibroblast (emb. lung)	Human	Template activity	Decrease in activity[c]	8

[a]*Abbreviation:* emb. = embryonic.
[b]*References:* (1) Comings and Vance (1971); (2) Srivastava (1973); (3) Curtois (1974); (4) Stein and Stein (1976); (5) Ryan and Cristofalo (1975); (6) Bradley et al. (1976); (7) Hill et al. (1978); (8) Whatley and Hill (1980).
[c]Decline occurred after initiation of *in vitro* senescence.

function of increasing passage level, which suggests a lack of cross-linking.

Protein Binding. No published studies, to our knowledge, have assessed the degree or extent of protein binding to DNA *in vitro* as a function of passage level.

Template Activity. DNA template activity *in vitro* is thought to reflect the accessibility of the DNA to the RNA polymerase and, therefore, the amount and degree of binding of chromosomal proteins (Cutler, 1976a; Whatley and Hill, 1980). Thus, a decrease in template accessibility to an exogenous RNA polymerase (generally *E. coli* in origin) could indicate an increase in cross-linking. In aging WI–38 cells, different investigators have observed: (1) a significant decline in chromatin template activity but only in very late passage (Phase III) cells (Srivastava, 1973; Hill et al., 1978; Whatley and Hill, 1979), (2) a significant decline in template active in mid-passage (Phase II) cells (Ryan and Cristofalo, 1975), or (3) a constant level of template activity throughout their *in vitro* life span (Stein and Stein, 1976). A constant level in template activity was also observed by Courtois (1974) in quiescent chick embryo cells sampled at different passage levels.

The inconsistency of these results leaves us unable to make a sound conclusion as to whether DNA-DNA or DNA-protein cross-linking does increase in cells senescing in culture and, if such bonds do occur, whether they increase in frequency prior to, or after, senescence has begun.

DNA Strand Breakage

Accumulation of Unrepaired Damage. DNA damage, as measured by single-strand breaks and estimated by alkaline elution techniques, accumulated in human fibroblasts cells aging *in vitro,* but the accumulation was only appreciable at passages close to senescence (Suzuki et al., 1980) (see Table 5A). In agreement with this observation in human cells, Icard et al. (1979) detected an increase in single-strand breaks (measured by alkaline

TABLE 5A.   DNA Strand Breaks in Aging Cells: Accumulation of Spontaneous Strand Breaks.[a]

Cell Strain	Species	Lesion	Assay	Age-related Response	Reference[b]
Fibroblast (emb. lung)	Human	S–S	ASGS	Increase in late passage cells	1
Fibroblast (emb. lung)	Human	D–S	NGS	No change	1
Fibroblast (emb. lung)	Human	S–S	AE	Increase in late passage cells	2
Fibroblast	Mouse	S–S	ASGS	Increase	3

[a]*Abbreviations:* emb. = embryonic; S–S = single-strand breaks; D–S = double-strand breaks; AE = alkaline elution; ASGS = alkaline sucrose gradient sedimentation; NGS = neutral gradient sedimentation.
[b]*References:* (1) Icard et al. (1979); (2) Suzuki et al. (1980); (3) Beupain et al. (1980).

sucrose gradient centrifugation) but not of double- strand breaks (measured by neutral gradient centrifugation) in late passage fibroblasts. Qualitatively similar results—an accumulation of single-strand breaks at late passage levels—have also been obtained in mouse cell strains *in vitro* (Beupain et al., 1980).

Repair of Induced Breakage. The rate of rejoining of induced breakage has been extensively examined in human fibroblast cells at different *in vitro* passage levels (see Table 5B). Clarkson and Painter (1974) examined x-ray-induced single-strand break rejoining in aging human embryonic lung fibroblast cells (WI–38) using alkaline sucrose gradient centrifugation. The rate of repair remained constant throughout the *in vitro* life span of the cell strain. Normal rates of single-strand break rejoining for WI–38 cells were also reported by Bradley et al. (1976) using alkaline elution and alkaline sedimentation techniques. Suzuki et al. (1980) observed normal

TABLE 5B.   DNA Strand Breaks in Aging Cells: Repair of Induced Strand Breaks.[a]

Cell Line	Species	Agent	Assay	Result	Reference[b]
Fibroblasts (emb. lung)	Human	X-ray	ASGS	No change	1
Fibroblasts (emb. lung)	Human	X-ray	AE	No change	2
Fibroblasts (emb. lung)	Human	X-ray	AE	Decline at end of life span	3
Fibroblasts (skin)	Human	X-ray	ASGS	Decline	4
Fibroblasts (skin)	Human	X-ray	ASGS	Decline	5
Fibroblasts (embryonic)	Hamster	X-ray	ASGS	Decline	6
Fibroblasts (emb. lung)	Human	X-ray	CS	No change	7
Fibroblasts (emb. lung)	Human	Neutron	CS	No change	8

[a]*Abbreviations:* emb. = embryonic; ASGS = alkaline sucrose gradient sedimentation; AE = alkaline elution; CS = cell survival.
[b]*References:* (1) Clarkson and Painter (1974); (2) Bradley et al. (1976); (3) Suzuki et al (1980); (4) Epstein et al. (1973, 1974); (5) Little et al. (1975); (6) Williams and Little (1975); (7) Ban et al. (1980); (8) Ban et al. (1981).

rates of break rejoining until the fibroblast cultures had reached very near the end of their *in vitro* life span where a slight decrease was observed. Furthermore, cell survival, a measure of strand break rejoining capacity in combination with other repair systems, remained unaltered during the *in vitro* life span of these cells after exposure to x-rays (Ban et al., 1980) and neutrons (Ban et al., 1981).

In human skin fibroblasts, Epstein et al. (1973, 1974) and Little et al. (1975) observed a decline in the rate of strand rejoining measured by alkaline sucrose gradient centrifugation as the cells approached senescence. While this decline in DNA repair capacity was more marked in cells at the end of their *in vitro* life span, it appeared to commence prior to any indication of terminal senescence (Little, 1976). This decline in single-strand break rejoining in midpassage (Phase II) cells was also observed in primary hamster embryo cultures (Williams and Little, 1975).

DNA Synthetic Capability

A few investigators have assessed DNA synthetic activity as another indicator of cellular competency. Such studies are, of course, limited to proliferating tissues, and care must be taken to avoid confounding effects which arise from a cessation of DNA synthetic capability during cellular differentiation. Alterations in DNA synthesis could result from DNA-DNA or DNA-protein cross-linking, from changes in DNA polymerase(s) activity, from alterations in the production and utilization of nucleotide precursors, or from a large number of other, interrelated cellular processes.

In vitro, the proportion of cells synthesizing DNA per unit time declines with increasing passage level (Macieira-Coelho et al., 1966; Cristofalo and Sharf, 1974; Vincent and Huang, 1976; Cristofalo, 1976; Matsumura et al., 1979; reviewed in Macieira-Coelho and Taboury, 1982) (see Table 6). Concomitant with the decreased replicative capability is a prolongation of the average duration of the cell cycle (Macieira-

Coelho et al., 1966; Absher et al., 1974; Kapp and Klevecz, 1976). This prolongation is generally due to an increase in the length of G_1 and, to a lesser extent, of G_2; the lengths of S and cytokinesis remaining constant (Macieira-Coelho et al., 1966; Macieira-Coelho, 1973; Petes et al., 1974; Grove and Mitchell, 1974; Yanishevsky et al., 1974; Macieira-Coelho, 1977; Grove and Cristofalo, 1977; Sisken and Bonner, 1979; Macieira-Coelho and Taboury, 1982). However, using fibroblasts obtained from the black-tailed wallaby, Moore (1971) detected an increase in the length of S with increasing *in vitro* passage level. The increase in S phase was primarily due to the time taken by the cells to synthesize the first 50 percent, and especially the first 10 percent, of their DNA.

Only one study has directly examined the transcriptional function of DNA polymerase in aging cells in culture. Petes et al. (1974) detected a 20 percent decrease in the rate of DNA chain elongation in senescing human fibroblasts. The distance between initiation sites remained constant, suggesting that the ability of the polymerase(s) to recognize such sites remained unaltered. As the authors mentioned, a decrease of this magnitude may not have delayed the total duration of the cell cycle or the length of S.

Consequently, the majority of *in vitro* experimentation indicates an unaltered capability of mammalian cells senescing *in vitro* to complete normal DNA synthesis. Any significant alteration in cell cycle duration can be attributed primarily to a change in the length of G_1. The decrease in the number of cells capable of proliferating may be due not to a decline in DNA polymerase activity and/or DNA template accessibility but rather to a loss in the ability to initiate cell division.

Excision Repair

Excision repair can only be assessed by using genotoxic agents to induce DNA damage. The principal agent for assessing nucleotide excision repair competency has been UV (see Table 7). In proliferating human fibroblast cultures, excision repair capacity as mea-

TABLE 6. DNA Synthetic Capability in Aging Cells *In Vitro*.

Cell Strain[a]	Species	Assay	Age-related Result	Reference[b]
Fibroblast (emb. lung)	Human	DNA chain elongation	Decline	1
		Length of S phase	Constant	
Fibroblast (emb. lung)	Human	Length of S phase	Constant	2
		Cell cycle duration	Increase	
		Cells synthesizing DNA	Decline	
Fibroblast (emb. lung)	Human	Cells synthesizing DNA	Decline	3
Fibroblast (skin)	Human	Cells synthesizing DNA	Decline	4
Fibroblast (emb. lung)	Human	Cells synthesizing DNA	Decline	5
Fibroblast (emb. lung)	Human	Cells synthesizing DNA	Decline	6
Fibroblast (emb. lung)	Human	Cell cycle duration	Increase	7
Fibroblast (emb. lung)	Human	Cell cycle duration	Increase	8
Fibroblast (emb. lung)	Human	Length of S phase	Constant	9
Fibroblast (emb. lung)	Human	Length of S phase	Constant	10
Fibroblast (emb. lung)	Human	Length of S phase	Constant	11
Fibroblast (emb. lung)	Human	Length of S phase	Constant	12
Fibroblast (skin)	Wallaby	Length of S phase	Increase	13

[a]*Abbreviation:* emb. = embryonic.
[b]*References:* (1) Petes et al. (1974); (2) Macieira-Coelho et al. (1966); (3) Cristofalo and Sharf (1974); (4) Vincent and Huang (1976); (5) Cristofalo (1976); (6) Matsumura et al. (1979); (7) Absher et al. (1974); (8) Kapp and Klevecz (1976); (9) Grove and Mitchell (1974); (10) Yanishevsky et al. (1974); (11) Macieira-Coelho (1977); (12) Grove and Cristofalo (1977); (13) Moore (1971).

sured by UDS declined at late passages (Goldstein, 1971; Painter et al., 1973; Bowman et al., 1976). However, in confluent cultures, UDS was observed to be independent of age (Dell'Orco and Whittle, 1978; Dell'Orco and Anderson, 1981), and Smith and Hanawalt (1976)—assessing repair replication in senescing cultures of WI-38 cells exposed to UV light—observed no dose-dependent differences in repair rates between mid- and late passage cells. A problem with the interpretation of the experiments involving proliferating cells lies in the heterogeneity of the repair response among cells at late passages (Hart and Setlow, 1976). Figure 4 shows a typical grain distribution in radioautographs to illustrate this point. At later pas-

sages, not all cells are equally competent in UDS. As a rough rule, it was found that as the amount of scheduled synthesis of the culture decreased, so did the amount of UDS following UV irradiation. To determine if this correlation at the culture level also held at the cell level, the experiment illustrated in Figure 5 was completed. The idea was to measure by double-label radioautography the amount of both scheduled and unscheduled synthesis in the same cell. The results of such an experiment are shown in Figure 6. These results indicate that there are two broad classes of cells at later passages: those that undergo a considerable degree of scheduled and unscheduled synthesis, and those that undergo very little scheduled or unscheduled

TABLE 7. Excision Repair and Postreplication Competency in Aging Cells *In Vitro*.[a]

Cell Line	Species	Agent	Assay	Age-related Result	Reference[b]
Fibroblast (skin)	Human	UV	UDS	Decline at late passages	1
Fibroblast (emb. lung)	Human	UV	UDS	Decline at late passages	2
Fibroblast (emb. lung)	Human	UV	UDS	Decline at late passages	3
Fibroblast (emb. lung)	Human	UV	RR	No change	4
Fibroblast (newborn for.)	Human	UV	UDS	No change in confluent cells	5
Fibroblast (skin)	Human	UV	UDS	No change in confluent cells	6
Fibroblast (skin)	Human	UV	UDS	Decline in nondividing cells at late passages	7
Fibroblast (skin)	Human	UV	PDR	No change	8
Fibroblast (skin)	Human	UV	ESS	No change	9
Fibroblast (skin)	Human	X-ray	ddTR	Complete loss in late passage cells	10
Fibroblast (skin)	Human	UV	CS	No change	11
Fibroblast (embryonic)	Mouse	UV	UDS PDR	Decline at late passages	12
Fibroblast (embryonic)	Mouse	UV	UDS	Decline at late passages	13
Fibroblast (embryonic)	Hamster	UV, X-ray	UDS	Decline at late passages	14
Fibroblast (embryonic)	Chick	UV	UDS	Decline at middle passages	15
Fibroblast (kidney)	African green monkey	UV	HCR	Increase to passage 60 and then decline	16
Fibroblast (embryonic)	Rat	4NQO	ASGS	Decline at middle passages	17

[a]*Abbreviations:* emb. = embryonic; for. = foreskin; 4NQO = 4-nitroquinoline-1-oxide; ASGS = alkaline sucrose gradient sedimentation; CS = cell survival; ddTR = removal of 5,6-dihydroxydihydrothymine; ESS = thymidine dimer-specific endonuclease sensitive sites; HCR = host cell reactivation; PDR = pyrimidine dimer removal; RR = repair replication; UDS = unscheduled DNA synthesis.

[b]*References:* (1) Goldstein (1971); (2) Painter et al. (1973); (3) Bowman et al. (1976); (4) Smith and Hanawalt (1976); (5) Dell'Orco and Whittle (1978); (6) Dell'Orco and Anderson (1981); (7) Hart and Setlow (1976); (8) Cooke and Harris (1981); (9) Dell'Orco and Whittle (1981); (10) Mattern and Cerutti (1981); (11) Kantor et al. (1978); (12) Ben-Ishai and Peleg (1975); (13) Meek et al. (1980); (14) Williams and Little (1975); (15) Paterson et al. (1974); (16) Moore and Coohill (1979); (17) Chan and Walker (1977).

synthesis. Such data make it difficult to conclude that the failure of DNA repair is a cause of aging; rather they suggest that DNA synthesis and nucleotide excision repair decline coordinately.

Although several studies with human cells *in vitro* have indicated a decline in UV-induced UDS (a measure of the resynthesis step of the excision repair process) with passage level, several investigators have not detected a corresponding decline in the removal of pyrimidine dimers measured either chro-

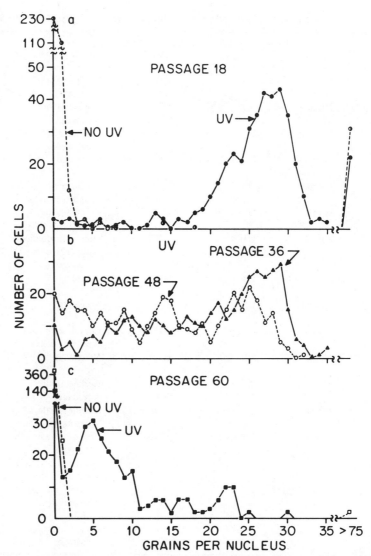

Figure 4. The distribution of grains among cells of WI–38 exposed to 10 J/m² of 254 nm UV and then incubated in ³H-dThd so as to measure unscheduled synthesis. The three panels represent different passages, and the heterogeneity in the unscheduled synthesis response is apparent at the later passages (Hart and Setlow, 1976).

matographically (Cooke and Harris, 1981) or by the number of UV-specific endonuclease sensitive sites (Dell'Orco and Whittle, 1981). In measuring excision repair com-

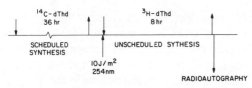

Figure 5. The labeling procedure used in attempts to correlate scheduled and unscheduled synthesis in treated cells.

petency coupled with the involvement of other DNA repair systems, Kantor et al. (1978) observed no difference in the survival of multiply UV-irradiated human embryonic lung fibroblasts as a function of *in vitro* passage level, an observation consistent with the preceding results. Another type of lesion, however, does not appear to be removed at all in late passage cells. Mattern and Cerutti (1975) examined aging WI–38 cell nuclei and nuclear sonicates for their ability to specifically excise osmium tetroxide– or γ-ray-induced 5,6-dihydroxydihydrothymine resi-

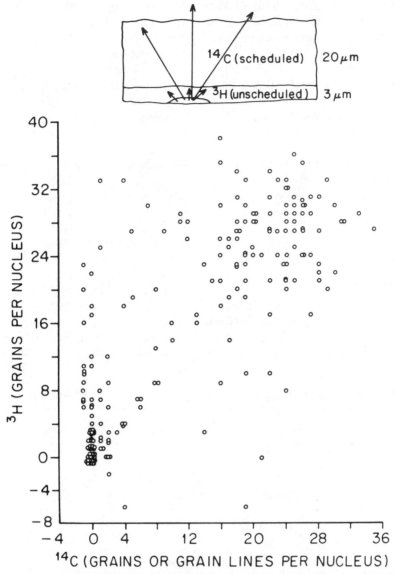

Figure 6. The results of the double-labeling experiment shown in Figure 5. Each point represents one cell (Hart and Setlow, 1976).

dues. Late passage cells exhibited a complete loss in their ability to excise this specific type of DNA lesion, and this loss in repair occurred prior to complete cessation in growth.

Examination of nonhuman cellular systems for DNA repair capability during their *in vitro* life span has been largely limited to rodent fetal fibroblasts. In mouse embryo fibroblast cultures, UV-induced UDS (Ben-Ishai and Peleg, 1975; Meek et al., 1980) and pyrimidine dimer release (Ben-Ishai and Peleg, 1975) declined only in terminally senescent cultures. These changes were reversed

by spontaneous transformation of the cultures. However, primary rat fibroblasts underwent a loss in 4-nitroquinoline-1-oxide-induced repair synthesis and in the formation and repair of excision repair–related single-strand breaks by the third subculture (Chan and Walker, 1977).

Williams and Little (1975) investigated UV- and γ-induced UDS in primary hamster embryo cultures. In agreement with the results observed in mouse embryo cells, active UV- and γ-induced UDS was present throughout their *in vitro* life span, ceasing only in terminally senescent cultures. Also, transformed cells retained both the UDS activity and the single-strand break rejoining rates of early passage cells. Using host cell reactivation, Moore and Coohill (1979) detected an increase in reactivation of UV-treated herpes simplex virus in UV-pretreated African green monkey kidney cells until passage 60, followed by a decline in reactivation. Finally, in a chick fibroblast system, Paterson et al. (1974) observed a decline in UV-induced UDS in middle and late passage cells in comparison with early passage populations.

CELLS FROM OLD AND YOUNG ANIMALS

Chromosomal Aberrations

Frequency of Spontaneous Aberrations. *In vivo,* three cellular systems have been examined for spontaneous chromosomal aberrations as a function of age (see Table 8). Two of the systems involve tissues which are normally quiescent—liver and peripheral lymphocytes—but which can be forced into active mitosis under the appropriate stimulus. The liver system was initially chosen because it offered an opportunity to examine a tissue that would have the potential of accumulating DNA lesions without their loss due to normal cellular turnover (Curtis, 1963). This system involves the partial destruction of the liver either by subcutaneous injections of carbon tetrachloride (Stevenson and Curtis, 1961) or by partial hepatectomy (Brooks et al., 1973). While the liver is subsequently undergoing regeneration, metaphase or anaphase cells can be examined for chromosomal aberrations.

Several investigators have observed an age-dependent increase in chromosomal aberrations in the liver of mice (Stevenson and Curtis, 1961), dogs (Curtis et al., 1966), guinea pigs (Curtis and Miller, 1971), and Chinese hamsters (Brooks et al., 1973). This age-

TABLE 8A. Chromosomal Aberrations in Aging Cells *In Vivo*: Spontaneous Frequency.

Tissue[a]	Species	Age-related Response	Reference[b]
Bone marrow	Rat	Increase	1
	Rat	No change	2
	Mouse	No change	2
Liver	Chinese hamster	Increase	3
(regenerating)	Dog	Increase	4
	Guinea pig	Increase	5
	Mouse	Increase	6
	Mouse	Increase	7
Lymphocytes	Human	Increase	8
(PHA stimulated)	Human	Increase	9
	Human	Increase	10
	Swine	Increase	11
	Human	Increase	12
	Human	Increase	13
	Human	No change	14
	Human	No change	15
	Human	No change	16
	Human	No change	17
	Human	No change	18

[a]*Abbreviation:* PHA = phytohemagglutinin.
[b]*References:* (1) Chlebovsky et al. (1966); (2) Curtis and Tilley (1971); (3) Brooks et al. (1963); (4) Curtis et al. (1966); (5) Curtis and Miller (1971); (6) Stevenson and Curtis (1961); (7) Crowley and Curtis (1963); (8) Court Brown et al. (1966); (9) McFee et al. (1970); (10) Tough et al. (1970); (11) Jarvick and Kato (1970); (12) Liniecke et al. (1971); (13) Ayme et al. (1976); (14) Jacobs and Court Brown (1966); (15) Sandberg et al. (1967); (16) Bochkov et al. (1968); (17) Goodman et al. (1969); (18) Bochkov (1972).

TABLE 8B. Chromosomal Aberrations in Aging Cells *In Vivo:* Induced Frequency.

Tissue	Species	Agent[a]	Age-related Response	Reference[b]
Bone marrow	Mouse	X-ray	No change	1
Fibroblast	Human	X-ray	Increase	2
(skin)	Human	MMC	Increase	3
Lymphocytes	Human	X-ray	Increase in dicentrics	4
(PHA stimulated)	Human	X-ray	Increase	5
	Swine	X-ray	Increase in chromatid-type aberrations	6
	Human	Thio-tepa, Degranol	Increase	7
	Human	MMC	Increase	8

[a]*Abbreviation:* MMC = mitomycin C.
[b]*References:* (1) Curtis and Tilley (1971); (2) Bourgeois et al. (1981); (3) Schneider and Gilman (1979); (4) Liniecki et al. (1971); (5) Deknudt and Leonard (1977); (6) McFee et al. (1970); (7) Bochkov and Kuleshov (1971, 1972); (8) Tice et al. (1982).

dependent increase was inversely proportional to life span, increasing at a faster rate in inbred mouse strains with shorter life spans than in inbred mouse strains with longer life spans (Crowley and Curtis, 1963). While this proportionality also held true for mice, guinea pigs, and dogs, Chinese hamsters appeared to be an exception (Brooks et al., 1973). This discrepancy, however, could have been due to differences in the method of ascertainment.

In another *in vivo* cellular system, peripheral lymphocytes obtained from donors of different ages are stimulated to divide with a mitogen, generally phytohemagglutinin (PHA). After a specific time interval, metaphase cells are then examined for chromosomal aberrations. In man, Court Brown et al. (1966), Tough et al. (1970), Jarvik and Kato (1970), Liniecki et al. (1971), and Ayme et al. (1976) have observed a slight to moderate increase in the spontaneous frequency of aberrations in aged populations. However, Jacobs and Court Brown (1966), Sandberg et al. (1967), Bochkov et al. (1968), Goodman et al. (1969), and Bochkov (1972) have not detected any alteration in the spontaneous frequency of chromosomal aberrations with increasing donor age. In swine, a marginal increase in chromosome deletions was observed with increasing age, all other types of aberrations remaining constant in frequency (McFee et al., 1970). The periph-

eral blood lymphocyte system is extremely complex, however, and there are significant differences between the replicative rates of stimulated cells obtained from young and aged donors (Tice et al., 1979). Consequently, differences in spontaneous aberration frequencies might be attributable to proliferative differences and not to the presence of unrepaired lesions in DNA.

In normally proliferating cellular populations, the data are similarly inconsistent. Chlebovsky et al. (1966) reported a dramatic increase in the frequency of chromosomal aberrations in extremely aged rat bone marrow cells, while Curtis and Tilley (1971) observed a contant level of aberrations in bone marrow cells sampled from either aging mice or rats.

Frequency of Induced Aberrations. Examination of the induction of chromosomal aberrations in humans as a function of age has been limited to two cellular systems: skin fibroblast cultures and mitogen-stimulated peripheral lymphocyte cultures. Because of their greater accessibility, cultured lymphocytes have been examined more often. Liniecki et al. (1971) examined G_1 x-ray-induced chromosomal aberration yields in PHA-stimulated lymphocytes from donors ranging in age from 0 to 72 years. No differences were observed between young and aged donors in the yields of acentric fragments, rings, or intercalary deletions. Dicentric frequencies appeared to decrease as a function of age. However, in a more recent study also involving ionizing radiation, an increase in aberration yields in peripheral blood lymphocytes from aged humans was observed by Deknudt and Leonard (1977). Also, in a comparative approach, adult lung fibroblast contained more chromosomal aberrations after x-ray and neutron exposure *in vitro* than did comparably exposed embryonic lung fibroblasts (Bourgeois et al., 1981).

The induction of chromosomal aberrations in lymphocyte cultures from young and aged persons by chemical agents has also been examined. Bochkov and Kuleshov (1971, 1972) exposed stimulated lymphocytes to Thio-tepa and Degranol, and observed that the frequency of induced aberrations increased significantly in the aged population. One confounding variable inherent in this system is the difficulty of ensuring that metaphase cell populations with identical replicative histories are scored for chromosomal aberrations. Chromosomal aberration yields vary in metaphase cells depending on the number of generations completed since cessation of the damaging treatment. Because peripheral blood lymphocytes from young and aged donor are stimulated and subsequently cycle at different rates (Tice et al., 1979), apparent differences in chromosomal aberration yields could be explained trivially by the differences in growth characteristics. In experiments primarily directed at assessing the frequency of mitomycin C–induced sister chromatid exchanges (SCE) in human peripheral blood lymphocytes (Tice, unpublished data) and in fibroblasts (Schneider and Gilman, 1979) as a function of donor age (see Chapter 14), a greater incidence of chromosomal aberrations was observed in first generation metaphase cells in cultures obtained from aged individuals ($\sim$75 years) than in cultures obtained from young ones ($\sim$25 years). Whether the result is due to greater chemical damage (Pero et al., 1978) or to decreased repair capability is not known.

In γ-ray-irradiated lymphocyte cultures from young and aged swine, the level of chromosome-type aberrations (e.g., fragments, rings, or dicentrics) did not change, while chromatid-type aberrations (i.e., breaks or achromatic lesions) increased in number (McFee et al., 1970).

To assess DNA repair in an actively proliferating cellular population *in vivo,* Curtis and Tilley (1971) irradiated mice and examined chromosomal aberration frequencies in bone marrow in metaphase cells. Not only was there no difference between young and aged mice in induced aberration yields, but the aberration frequencies also declined with time at the same rates.

Cross-linking

Direct Cross-linking. Direct measurements of cross-linking *in vivo* have been exceedingly few (see Table 9). Acharya (1972) fed pregnant rats tritium, and examined brain and liver of their offspring at different ages for cross-linked products. With age, not only was there an increase in the frequency of DNA-protein-RNA complexes, but also their molecular size increased. Since some of these substances retained tritium activity, it appeared as though they had remained fixed in the cells from birth and were, therefore, presumably immune to normal DNA repair processes. In a similar investigation, Cutler (1976b) observed an accumulation of DNA-protein cross-links with age in liver tissue at a rate approximately inversely proportional to life span potential in two rodent species.

Thermal Stability. DNA preparations from rat liver exhibited an age-related increase in thermal stability, depending on the amount of bound protein remaining after various extraction processes (von Hahn and Fritz, 1966). No increase in T_m was observed for relatively "pure" DNA preparations. DNA-protein complexes isolated from young (8 weeks) and aged ($>$10 years) bovine thymus (Phytila and Sherman, 1968) and from liver in aging mice (Russell et al., 1970) exhibited the same pattern of thermal stability as did

TABLE 9. Accumulation of DNA Cross-Links in Aging Cells *In Vivo*.

Tissue	Species	Assay	Age-related Response	Reference[a]
Brain	Mouse	Thermal stability	Decrease in T_m from 3 to 13 mo. of age	1
			Increase in T_m from 13 to 30 mo. of age	
	Mouse	Cross-linked species	Increase	2
	Mouse	Thermal stability	Increase in T_m	3
	Mouse	Protein binding	Decrease in protein extractabililty	4
		Template activity	Decrease in activity	
	Mouse	Thermal stability	No change	5
Heart	Dog	Template activity	No change	6
Intestine	Rat	Protein binding	Increase in protein extractability	7
Kidney	Rat	Protein binding	Decrease in protein extractability	7
	Mouse	Protein binding	Decrease in protein extractability	4
		Template activity	Decrease in *E. coli* RNA polymerase but not for endogenous RNA polymerase	
	Mouse	Thermal stability	No change	5
	Mouse	Cross-linked species	Increase	2
Liver	Rat	Thermal stability	Increase in T_m depending on protein content	8
	Rat	Protein binding	No change	9
		Template activity	No change	
	Rat	Template activity	No change	10
	Mouse	Thermal stability	Increase in T_m depending on protein content	11
	Mouse	Protein binding	Decrease in protein extractabililty	12
		Template activity	Decrease in activity	
	Rat	Protein binding	No change	7
	Rat	Protein binding	Decrease in protein extractability	13
		Template activity	Decrease in activity	
		Thermal stability	Increase in T_m	
	Mouse	Protein binding	Decrease in protein extractability	2
	Rat	Template activity	No change	14
	Rat	Free sulfhydryl groups	Decrease in number in chromatin	15
	Mouse	Cross-linked species	Increase	16
	Mouse	Protein binding	Decrease in protein extractability	4
		Template activity	Decrease in activity	
	Mouse	Thermal stability	No change	17
Spleen	Rat	Protein binding	Decrease in protein extractability	7
	Mouse	Thermal stability	No change	5
Submandib-ular gland	Rat	Protein binding	Increase in protein extractability	15
		Template activity	Increase in activity	
Thymus	Cow	Template activity	Decrease in activity depending on protein content	18
		Thermal stability	Increase in T_m	
	Rat	Protein binding	Decrease in protein extractability	19

[a]*References:* (1) Kurtz and Sinex (1967); (2) Acharya (1972); (3) Kurtz et al. (1974); (4) Hill (1976); (5) Gaubatz and Cutler (1978); (6) Shirey and Sobel (1972); (7) Salser and Balis (1972); (8) von Hahn and Fritz (1966); (9) Samis et al. (1968); (10) Samis and Wulff (1969); (11) Russell et al. (1970); (12) O'Meara and Hermann (1972); (13) Berdyshev and Zhelabovskaya (1972); Berdyshev (1976); (14) Stein et al. (1973); Stein and Stein (1976); (15) Tas (1976); (16) Cutler (1976b); (17) Dean and Cutler (1978); (18) Phytila and Sherman (1968); (19) Bojanovic et al. (1970).

rat liver: DNA-protein complexes from aged animals exhibited an increased thermal stability which was dependent on the amount of the unextracted protein. Similar results have been reported for mouse liver DNA-protein fractions by Berdyshev and Zhelabovskaya (1972) and Berdyshev (1976), and for mouse brain chromatin isolated from middle-aged and old animals by Kurtz and Sinex (1967) and Kurtz et al. (1974). Using a technique which results in highly purified DNA, investigators have reported a constant thermal stability with increasing animal age for mouse brain, kidney, and spleen (Gaubatz and Cutler, 1978) and for mouse liver (Dean and Cutler, 1978).

The studies by Kurtz and Sinex (1967) and by Kurtz et al. (1974) with mouse brain chromatin are especially interesting. Thermal stability in this tissue steadily declined in mice between the ages of 3 and 13 months. From 13 to 20 months of age, the T_m increased to a level higher than that observed for a 3-month-old animal. Thus, depending on the ages of the animals being compared, thermal stability decreased, increased, or remained constant. These results emphasize the importance of comparative investigations which involve the entire life span of the organism being studied, rather than a select group of "young" versus "aged" animals.

Protein Binding. Thermal stability depends on the amount and nature of the protein fractions remaining bound to DNA during the extraction process. As another approach for assessing cross-linking and/or gene function in aging mammals, several investigators have examined protein extractability from DNA as a function of animal age. Samis et al. (1968) detected no age-related differences in protein binding to rat liver DNA. Bojanovec et al. (1970) observed a decrease in protein extractability in rat thymus DNA obtained from older animals (75 days) when compared with similarly treated DNA from 10-day-old animals. Although 75-day-old animals are not "old," the inclusion of these data in an aging study may be justified in

that the involution of the thymus is occurring around this time (Cutler, 1976a).

Salser and Balis (1972) examined the amount of DNA-bound protein after extensive extraction procedures in several different tissues of aging rats (weanlings to 30 months). While observing no change in total bound protein in liver, in agreement with Samis et al. (1968), these investigators did observe a shift from acid and basic amino acids to neutral ones. These alterations were not mimicked in other tissues. Total bound protein increased in spleen and kidney, while decreasing in intestinal tissue, as a function of animal age. The composition of the protein in these tissues did not change in the same manner or to the same extent as it did for liver.

O'Meara and Hermann (1972) observed an age-related decrease in protein extractability at high ionic strengths in mouse liver, a finding also observed in the aging rat liver (Berdyshev and Zhelabovskaya, 1972; Berdyshev, 1976). Hill (1976) also detected a decrease with age in protein extractability in mouse brain, kidney, and liver. However, this decrease was not observed in 20-month-old but only in 31-month-old animals, animals at the end of their life span. Finally, in support of an age-related decrease in protein extractability, Tas (1976) found that with aging, the chromatin proteins of rat liver entered a more compact stage, a compactness due in part to an increased number of disulfide bonds in older chromatin.

Template Activity. *In vitro,* template activity has been examined in DNA or chromatin from aging animals by a number of investigators, often with conflicting results. Phytila and Sherman (1968) measured the template activity of DNA and of chromatin extracted from the thymus of cows either 8 weeks old or over 10 years of age. Template activity remained the same for purified DNA between the two ages, while chromatin suffered a 20 percent decrease in activity in the older animals. Samis et al. (1968) and Samis and Wulf (1969) reported that the age of the adult rat from which liver chromatin was extracted did not influence template activity. Dog heart chromatin also retained its template activity throughout the life span of the animals (Shirey and Sobal, 1972). However, Berdyshev and Zhelabovshaya (1972) and Berdyshev (1976) reported a significant decline in template activity in rat liver chromatin isolated from animals 30 months old when compared to chromatin isolated from animals up to 12 months of age.

Hill (1976) indicated the possible confounding effect on the interpretation of the data of the *E. coli* RNA polymerase normally used in such studies. Using this enzyme, Hill detected a decrease in template activity of chromatin isolated from brain, liver, and kidney of aging mice. This decline resulted from fewer sites of active RNA synthesis and not from shorter RNA chains. However, when homologous RNA polymerase extracted from identical cells was used,

template activity remained constant throughout the life span of the animals. These experimental data make interpretation of positive or negative results difficult.

DNA Strand Breakage

Accumulation of Unrepaired Damage. While many types of unrepaired damages may be present in DNA, most *in vivo* investigations have been largely concerned with assessing the presence of single- or double-strand breaks (see Table 10A). The first strong evidence that there might be an accumulation of DNA damage in the cells of older animals came from the work of Price et al. (1971) and Modak and Price (1971) on liver, heart, and brain cells from old and young mice. In these studies, the template activity of isolated nuclei for calf thymus DNA polymerase was tested with and without acid denaturation of cells fixed on slides. Single-

TABLE 10A. DNA Strand Breaks in Aging Cells *In Vivo*: Accumulation of Spontaneous Strand Breaks.

Organ	Species	Assay[a]	Response	Reference[b]
Brain	Mouse	CTDT	Increase	1
	Dog	AZC	Increase	2
	Mouse	ASGS	No change	3
	Mouse	ASGS	Increase	4
	Mouse	S_1N	Increase	4
	Mouse	CCGS	No change	5
Heart	Mouse	CTDT	Increase after acid denaturation	6
	Mouse	S_1N	Increase	7
Kidney	Mouse	CCGS	No change	5
Liver	Mouse	CTDT	Increase after acid denaturation	6
	Rat	HM	Increase over first third of life span	8
	Mouse	S_1N	Increase	9
	Mouse	ASGS	Increase over first third of life span	3
	Mouse	S_1N	No change	5
	Mouse	IGS	No change	5
Muscle	Rat	ASGS	Increase	10
Spleen	Mouse	ASGS	No change	3
	Mouse	CCGS	No change	5
Thymus	Mouse	ASGS	No change	3

[a]*Abbreviations:* ASGS = alkaline sucrose gradient sedimentation; AZC = alkaline zonal centrifugation; CCGS = cesium chloride gradient sedimentation; CTDT = calf thymus DNA polymerase template activity; IGS = isopycnic gradient sedimentation; HM = hydrodynamic measurement; S_1N = S_1 nuclease sensitivity.
[b]*References:* (1) Modak and Price (1971); (2) Wheeler and Lett (1974); (3) Ono et al. (1976); (4) Chetsanga et al. (1977); (5) Dean and Cutler (1978); (6) Price et al. (1971); (7) Chetsanga et al. (1976); (8) Massie et al. (1972); (9) Chetsanga et al. (1975); (10) Karran and Ormerod (1973).

TABLE 10B. DNA Strand Breaks in Aging Cells In Vivo: Repair of Induced Strand Breaks.

Tissue	Species	Agent	Assay[a]	Age-related result	Reference[b]
Cerebellar	Mouse	X-ray	AZC	No change	1
Colon	Mouse	X-ray	CS	No change	2
Liver	Mouse	X-ray	ASGS	No change	1
	Rat	Bleomycin	UDS	Decline	3
Lymphocytes	Human	X-ray	CS	Decline	4
Muscle	Rat	X-ray	ASGS	Decline	5
Neural	Dog	X-ray	ASGS	No change	6
Photoreceptor cells	Rabbit	X-ray	ASGS	No change	7

[a]*Abbreviations:* ASGS = alkaline sucrose gradient sedimentation; AZC = alkaline zonal centrifugations; CS = cell survival; UDS = unscheduled DNA synthesis.
[b]*References:* (1) Ono and Okada (1978); (2) Hamilton and Franks (1980); (3) Ove and Coetzee (1978); (4) Kutlaca et al. (1982); (5) Karran and Ormerod (1973); (6) Wheeler and Lett (1974); (7) Lett (1978).

strand DNA breaks could act as initiation points for DNA synthesis detected radioautographically by the incorporation of tritium-labeled triphosphate into acid insoluble material. Acid denaturation was used to possibly enhance the expression of such breaks. Table 11 shows a summary of these data. Denaturation increased the template activity in cells from both young and old animals but appreciably more so in cells from old ones. The accumulation of the putative single-strand nicks under denaturation conditions in the cells of older animals was independent of the type of cell investigated. Without denaturation, only brain cells exhibited an age-related increase in polymerase activity. These experiments stimulated much of the subsequent research directed at assessing the accumulation of DNA damage in aging systems and its relation to DNA repair.

Massie et al. (1972) hydrodynamically measured the molecular weight of both single- and double-stranded DNA isolated from rat liver cells as a function of animal age. Average molecular weight decreased approximately tenfold with increasing age, demonstrating an increase in single- and double-strand breaks. While this result might appear to be indicative of a decline in strand break repair with age, it is interesting to note that the largest decrease in molecular weight took place in the first third of the animal's life span.

The alkaline sucrose sedimentation technique was used by Karran and Ormerod (1973) to detect the accumulation of single-strand breaks in aging animals. Strand breaks accumulated in the muscle cells of older (i.e., 28 days versus 1 day) rats and in the red blood cells of older chickens. As Kar-

TABLE 11. Template Activity with Calf Thymus DNA Polymerase of Ethanol-Fixed Mouse Cells.[a]

Cell Type	YOUNG ANIMALS (3–4 MO.)		OLD ANIMALS (30–35 MO.)	
	Not Denatured	Acid Denatured	Not Denatured	Acid Denatured
Neurons/Astroctyes (200)	9	30	22	>90
Kupffer cells (50)	2	5	6	14
Cardiac muscle	1	2	3	9

[a]Net grains per nucleus. Data from Price et al. (1971).

ran and Omerod (1973) suggested, this apparent increase in single-strand breaks might have reflected developmental changes or been the result of the preparative procedure and may not reflect *in vivo* aging. Wheeler and Lett (1974) used zonal centrifugation in alkali to investigate DNA from young and old dog neurons. With age, the DNA was found to have a decreased molecular weight, indicative of a possible accumulation of unrepaired single-strand breaks. More recently, Ono et al. (1976) used alkaline sucrose gradient centrifugation to examine DNA isolated from aging mouse liver, spleen, thymus, and cerebellum for strand breakage. Only hepatic DNA was observed to decrease in molecular weight with age. This decrease in molecular weight occurred, however, in mice between 1–2 and 14 months old. There was no further significant decrease in molecular weight after 14 months of age.

Other experiments (Chetsanga et al., 1975) showed that the DNA isolated from the liver of older mice acted as if it had many more single-stranded regions than the DNA from the liver of younger animals. The single-stranded regions were detected by the ability of a single-strand nuclease—S_1—to digest the DNA from older animals more rapidly than that from younger ones. The difficulty with such experiments on bulk DNA, rather than radioautographic investigations, is the inability to determine whether the changes in DNA are intrinsic to almost all cells or whether the single-strand regions arise from a small fraction of nonviable cells. Nevertheless, in these experiments, the amount of single-stranded DNA increased in the liver of older animals (i.e., after one-half of their life span) to as much as 25 percent of the total, making it improbable that this finding could result from only a small fraction of dead cells. Chetsanga and his colleagues subsequently also examined the S_1 nuclease sensitivity of DNA from heart (Chetsanga et al., 1976) and brain (Chetsanga et al., 1977) of aging mice. DNA from both organs exhibited an age-related increased sensitivity to S_1 digestion, but to a lesser extent than that observed for liver (Chetsanga et al., 1975). The

increased S_1 sensitivity in aged mouse brain DNA correlated with a decrease in molecular weight detected by alkaline sucrose gradient centrifugation (Chetsanga et al., 1977). These results by Chetsanga et al. (1975, 1976, 1977) were not confirmed by Dean and Cutler (1978). These investigators observed a constant level of S_1 nuclease sensitivity and the same molecular weight in DNA obtained from liver, brain, spleen, and kidney of aging mice: discrepant data which remain unresolved.

Repair of Induced Breakage. Most cells, whether proliferating or quiescent, rejoin x-ray-induced single-strand breaks readily (Karran and Ormerod, 1973), and observations suggesting an age-related decline *in vivo* are not very convincing (see Table 10B). Rat muscle cells from older animals were slower at such repair than cells from younger animals, and there was no single-strand break repair in chicken red blood cells (Karran and Ormerod, 1973). However, it is not easy to generalize from such data because several other studies indicate normal levels of such repair throughout the life span. Careful experiments on rabbit photoreceptor cells irradiated *in vivo* showed repair of single-strand breaks at rates independent of the animal's age, from a few days to 7 years, provided that the dose used was not great enough to affect the electrophysiological response of the cells (Lett et al., 1978). Neuronal tissue in old beagles also retained its capacity to repair single-strand breaks induced by x-rays (Wheeler and Lett, 1974). Moreover, there was no difference in single-strand break repair in cerebellar, splenic, or hepatic cells obtained from mice 2 or 22 months old (Ono and Okada, 1978). In agreement with these results, the repair of strand breaks in hepatic DNA from young and aged rats treated with bleomycin is the same (Ove and Coetzee, 1978), and the survival of x-ray-exposed colonic cells in young (6 months) and old (24 months) mice is identical (Hamilton and Franks, 1980). Finally, in a study involving the survival of x-irradiated human lymphocytes obtained from donors of different ages, lymphocytes from aged individuals (60–90 years) were approximately twice as sensitive as lymphocytes from young individuals (17–40 years) (Kutlaca et al., 1982).

DNA Synthetic Capability

As animals approach senescence, normally proliferating cell populations (e.g., bone marrow, intestinal crypt cells) frequently undergo a lengthening of the cell cycle (Buetow, 1971) (see Table 12). In the small intestine, this increase in cell cycle duration is accompanied by an increase in the length of S (Lesher et al., 1961; Lesher and Sacher, 1968), while in colonic epithelium and esophageal epithelium, the duration of S remains constant (Thrasher, 1967, 1971).

Several normally quiescent cell populations have also been examined for alterations in growth following an appropriate stimulus. Isoproterenol induces DNA synthesis and cell growth in salivary gland tissue. With increasing age of the animal, fewer cells respond and the initiation of DNA synthesis is delayed (Adelman et al., 1972; Piatanelli et al., 1978). A similar response is observed during liver (Bucher and Glinos, 1950) and kidney (Phillips and Leong, 1967) regeneration and in the PHA stimulation of lymphocytes from young and aged humans (Tice et al., 1979). In the latter study, although average cell cycle duration increased in the aged population, some cells retained the same rate of proliferation observed for cells obtained from young donors. In a study involving the estrogenic stimulation of growth in the vaginal epithelium of castrated mice, the initiation of DNA synthesis remained constant with age (de Maertalaer et al., 1981). No studies in the rate of DNA chain elongation and/or initiation have utilized tissue obtained from aging animals.

Although the data are extremely limited, they are consistent with the in vitro data and suggest that a decrease in DNA synthetic capability per se is not responsible for the observed changes in cell cycle duration. Rather, it seems more likely that with age, (i) cells become more refractory to the initiation of DNA synthesis due to a decline in some regulatory signal necessary during the G_1 phase of the cell cycle, or (ii) cells produce a repressor substance which inhibits this stimulatory response. Experimental data consistent with the latter possibility come from the heterokaryon studies of Norwood (1978) who found that the fusion of senescent fibroblasts (i.e., late passage level cells) with young fibroblasts (i.e., early passage level cells) prevented the young fibroblast cells from entering S phase. These studies suggested the existence of a repressor molecule capable of stopping the initiation of S even in the presence of normal polymerase capbility.

Excision and Postreplication Repair

In animal studies (see Table 13), myocardial cells isolated from newborn and adult rats were among the first cell types to be compared for UV-induced UDS. The adult cell exhibited a complete loss of repair capability (Lampidis and Schaiberger, 1975). However,

TABLE 12. DNA Synthetic Capability in Aging Cells In Vivo.

Tissue	Species	Assay	Age-related response	Reference[a]
Bone marrow	Mouse	Cell cycle duration	Increase	1
Colon	Mouse	S phase duration	No change	2
Esophagus	Mouse	S phase duration	No change	3
Intestine	Mouse	Cell cycle duration	Increase	1
	Mouse	S phase duration	Increase	4
Lymphocytes	Human	Cell cycle duration	Increase	5

[a]References: (1) Buetow (1971); (2) Thrasher (1967); (3) Thrasher (1971); (4) Lesher et al. (1961); Lesher and Sacher (1968); (5) Tice et al. (1979).

TABLE 13. Excision Repair Capability in Aging Cells *In Vivo*.[a]

Tissue	Species	Agent	Assay	Age-related Response	Reference[b]
Bone	Human	UV	UDS	No change	1
(Chondro-			ESS	No change	2
cytes)					
	Rabbit	UV	UDS	No change	1
			ESS	No change	2
Brain	Hamster	UV	UDS	Decrease at early ages	3
Colon mucosa	Rat	Alkylators	ASGS	Decrease	4
Heart	Rat	UV	UDS	Decrease	5
Kidney	Hamster	UV	UDS	Decrease at early ages	3
Lens	Rat	UV	UDS	No change	6
epithelium					
Liver	Hamster	UV	UDS	Decrease at early ages	3
	Rat	Alkylators	UDS	Decrease	7
Lung	Hamster	UV	UDS	Decrease at early ages	3
Lymphocytes	Human	DMBA, AAAF	UDS	Increase	8
	Human	UV	UDS	Decrease at ages >60 yr	9
	Human	UV	UDS	Decrease	10
	Human		O⁶Methyl- guanine repair protein	No change up to <60 yr	11
	Human	UV	CS	No change	12
Retina	Chick	UV	UDS	Decrease	13
	Rat	DMBA	UDS	No change	14
Skin	Human	UV	CS	No change	15
(fibroblast)	Rat	ENU	AE	Decrease	16
	Human	UV	UDS	No change	17
	Human	UV	CS	No change	18
		UV,MMS, TPS	HCR		
Skin	Human	UV	RR	No change	19
(keratinocytes)					
Spermatocyte	Human	UV	UDS	No change	20

[a]*Abbreviations:* AAAF = N-acetoxyacetylaminofluorene; DMBA = dimethylbenz[a]anthracene; ENU = ethyl nitrosourea EES = thymidine dimer-specific endonuclease sensitive sites; MMS = methyl methanesulfonate; RR = repair replication; TPS = trimethylpsoralen plus light; UV = ultraviolet light; AE = alkaline elution; ASGS = alkaline sucrose gradient sedimentation; CS = cell survival; HCR = host cell reactivation; UDS = unscheduled DNA synthesis.

[b]*References:* (1) Krystal et al. (1983); (2) Setlow et al. (1983); (3) Gensler (1981); (4) Kanagalingam and Balis (1975); (5) Lampidis and Schaiberger (1975); (6) Treton and Courtois (1981); (7) Prodi et al. (1977); (8) Pero et al. (1978); (9) Lambert et al. (1979); (10) Lezhava et al. (1979); (11) Waldstein et al. (1982); (12) Kutlaca et al. (1982); (13) Karran et al. (1977); (14) Ishikawa et al. (1978); (15) Goldstein (1971); (16) Fort and Cerutti (1981); (17) Hennis et al. (1981); (18) Hall et al. (1982); (19) Liu et al. (1982); (20) Chandley and Kofman-Alfaro (1971).

because the newborn rat myocardial cells still evidenced some normal DNA synthesis, this observation could be attributed to the normal process of differentiation and not to aging. Similarly, in retinal cells of chicken embryos, there was a rapid decrease in UV-induced UDS from day 8 to day 15, and the decrease qualitatively paralleled the decrease in replicative synthesis (Karran et al., 1977). It is of interest that in cells from earlier embryos, the amount of repair from the alkylating agent methyl methanesulfonate (MMS) (which induces short patch repair, see Figure 3) and the carcinogen N-acetoxyacetylaminofluorene (AAAF) (a long patch repair agent that mimics UV damage) both decreased with age. However, the connection between UDS and replication is not unique because if the retinal cells are stimulated to divide by trypsinization, there is a burst of DNA synthesis but not of UDS. As a general rule, embryonic chicken cells are not very proficient in nucleotide excision repair (Paterson et al., 1974).

Decreases in repair after alkylation treatment have been observed in colonic mucosal cells of aging rats (Kanagalingam and Balis, 1975) and in the liver cells from newborn and adult rats (Prodi et al., 1977). However, since the measures of repair were alkaline sucrose gradients in the former study and UDS in the latter, and since one of the most important alkylation products—0^6-methylguanine—gives no strand breakage or unscheduled synthesis upon repair, the significance of these observations is not apparent. Perhaps, the assays measure steps subsequent to the depurination of the alkylated DNA as a result of other methylation products (see Figure 3).

A different result was obtained with rat retinal ganglion cells treated in organ culture with a number of chemical carcinogens and then assayed for UDS. There was no significant age-associated change in repair measured radioautographically (Ishikawa et al., 1978). Lens epithelial cells in rats also retained their UDS capacity throughout the life span of the animal (Treton and Courtois, 1981). Using primary fibroblast cultures obtained from 3-week-old and 2-year-old Fischer 344 rats, Fort and Cerutti (1981) concluded that the excision repair of ethylnitrosourea-induced DNA damage was more competent in young animals than in old animals. These investigators observed, by the alkaline elution technique, that shortly after chemical treatment there were fewer breaks in the DNA of cells from older animals. These results suggest probably that a rate of repair resulting from depurination was slower and, therefore, the steady state appearance of single-strand nicks was less.

UDS, measured radioautographically, has been followed in the brain, liver, lung, and kidney cells of hamsters of different ages

(Gensler, 1981). There were no significant changes between 8 and 520 days of age, but there were large changes between days 4 and 6. During that time, there was almost a threefold increase in the percentage of cells labeled by UDS and a 20 percent increase in the amount of radioactivity per labeled cell. The reasons for the large change in the fraction of cells labeled at early ages are not known. However, even at the older ages, only about 30 percent of the cells were labeled, indicating that the population was either heterogeneous in its repair capability or heterogeneous in its exposure to UV radiation.

In human lymphocytes exposed to chemical agents such as AAAF and dimethylbenzanthracene, UDS tended to increase with donor age (Pero et al., 1978). The investigators interpreted their results as indicating greater damage but not greater repair in the lymphocytes from older individuals. On the other hand, there seems to be an age-related decrease in UDS in human leukocytes (at least in subjects over 60) exposed to UV (Lambert et al., 1979). The correlation appeared to be a clear one, but the most impressive observation about these experiments on almost 60 individuals was the wide variation in UDS levels among individuals independent of age. Such experiments were carried out in the presence of hydroxyurea and were done on a heterogeneous population of cells in which the estimate of UDS was made by scintillation counting. This experimental design would not permit the detection of wide variations among cell types. Similar results consistent with a decline in UDS capacity in humans with increasing subject age have been also reported by Lezhava et al. (1979). The relationship between age and UDS in human peripheral blood lymphocytes after UV or after a UV mimetic chemical is complicated in that there seem to be two kinetic components of UDS. One of the components correlates positively with age, the other negatively (Pero and Ostlund, 1980). The wide variation in DNA repair capacity among lymphocytes indicates that there are parameters other than age or sex that are the major determinants of repair measured by UDS. Also, the levels of UV-induced excision repair in this system depend on the degree and extent of lymphocyte stimulation (Darzynkiewicz, 1971). Consequently, these results might be artifactual and not reflect the true state of DNA repair capacity. Furthermore, cell survival of UV-exposed lymphocytes from aged individuals (60–90 years) appeared to equal the survival of comparably exposed lymphocytes from young individuals (17–40 years) (Kutlaca et al., 1982).

Using an assay system to measure the activity of the methyl acceptor protein specific for the repair of 0^6-methylguanine damage, a process not capable of eliciting UDS, Waldstein et al. (1982) detected comparable levels of activity in extracts of lymphocytes from individuals 60 years or younger. Older individuals have not yet been included in the study.

Goldstein (1971) has published data in which DNA repair levels were compared in skin fibroblast cultures derived from young and aged donors. He examined cell survival after UV exposure to early passage cultures of fetal, newborn, young, and aged origins and observed no significant differences in UV sensitivity. In agreement, Hall et al. (1982) observed similar levels of colony forming ability in skin fibroblast cultures from young (3 days to 3 years) and old (84–94 years) donors exposed *in vitro* in UV. These investigators also observed an equal ability to reactivate UV, MMS, or 4,5', 8-trimethylpsoralen plus light treated herpes simplex virus among these young and aged fibroblast cultures. Hennes et al. (1981) detected similar levels of UV-induced UDS in early passage skin fibroblasts obtained from humans of different ages. In a limited study, no differences in UV-induced UDS were detected in late zygotene–early pachytene spermatocytes obtained from a small group of young and old male subjects (Chandley and Kofman-Alfaro, 1971). Finally, in limited studies involving epidermal keratinocyte cultures established from a newborn and from aged adults (72 and 90 years of age), no sig-

nificant differences in UV-induced rates of repair replication were detected (Liu et al., 1982), and no significant differences were found in UV-induced UDS in cultures of chondrocytes derived from 23-, 43-, or 63-year-old adults or between chondrocytes from 3-month-old and 2-year-old rabbits (Krystal et al., 1983), although the rabbit chondrocytes were less proficient in UV repair than were human ones (Setlow et al., 1983).

ACCELERATION OF THE AGING PROCESS BY EXPOSURE TO DNA-DAMAGING AGENTS

The acceleration of the aging process by ionizing radiation has long been held as a fundamental proof for the involvement of DNA repair in aging (Yielding, 1974). If aging is the consequence of an accumulation of unrepaired DNA lesions, then exposure of animals to a greater than normal level of agents capable of damaging DNA should accelerate the aging process. Early evidence suggested that radiation-induced life shortening was mechanistically related to normal aging. Exposure of animals to ionizing radiation appeared to age their physical appearance prematurely, to advance the incidence of age-related biochemical changes, and to increase the mortality rate by accelerating the time of onset for many diseases (Alexander, 1957; Upton, 1957; Lindop and Rotblat, 1961a, 1961b; Casarett, 1964; Storer et al., 1979).

Extensive reassessment of all phases of radiation-induced life shortening has suggested that this phenomenon is substantially different from the normal aging process (Alexander, 1967; Walburg, 1975). While high radiation doses accelerated the appearance of nonneoplastic diseases such as nephrosclerosis, anemia, and sterility (Upton et al., 1960), no evidence for such effects has been found after single, acute exposures below 300 rads when corrections for competing probabilities of death are made (Walburg, 1975). Yet, these exposure levels caused significant life shortening in irradiated populations (Walburg, 1975). Exposure of animals to ionizing radiation appears to increase the incidence of cancer in most organs, resulting in premature death. However, when survivor data are analyzed with the deaths from neoplasia removed, there are no differences between the life expectancy of the treated animals and that of the controls (Hoel and Walburg, 1972). Moreover, many of the morphological and physiological manifestations of the normal aging process in animals (Berech and Curtis, 1964) or in man (Conard et al., 1966; Hollingworth et al., 1969) do not appear to be proportionally advanced in time. Classic senescent events such as alterations in collagen, pigment accumulation, and neuromuscular function appear to be refractory to irradiation (Walburg, 1975).

The possible effects of chemical mutagens on life shortening and aging have also been examined. Alexander and Connell (1960) observed that chlorambucil (a nitrogen mustard compound) and Myleran (an alkylating agent) shortened the life span of mice, but did not hasten the onset of any typical aging manifestations. Conklin et al. (1963) concluded that midlethal doses of nitrogen mustard shortened life span and that although it was not the result of an increase in neoplasia, the process was still not equivalent to normal aging. Curtis (1963) and Stevenson and Curtis (1961) subjected mice to either a generalized or an acute stress with nitrogen mustard or typhoid toxoid. In both instances, the life expectancy of the mice were not significantly altered. Finally, Alexander (1967) exposed mice to ethyl methanesulfonate (EMS), a known mutagen, without any evidence for life shortening. Thus, while some mutagenic compounds can cause life shortening, accelerated aging does not appear to be involved.

Radiation appears to accelerate aging at the cellular level in some *in vitro* systems. Lima et al. (1972) examined the long-term effects of cobalt-60 on the growth potential of chick embryo fibroblasts, cells that normally have a limited division potential *in vitro* and which attain lower cellular densities at confluence as a function of passage level. The effect of radiation exposure was both ir-

reversible and cumulative—shortening the *in vitro* life span while decreasing saturation densities. Macieira-Coelho et al. (1976) concluded that exposure to ionizing radiation not only shortened the *in vitro* life span of many cell types, but also concurrently accelerated the acquisition of an infinite growth potential (transformation) in those cells capable of such a process. However, early passage human embryonic lung fibroblasts cells exposed to ionizing radiation at low dose rates exhibited the same cell density at confluence and the same *in vitro* life span as the unexposed control populations (Macieira-Coelho et al., 1977; Macieira-Coelho et al., 1978; Icard et al., 1979). This lack of an effect is largely dependent upon the passage level of the human cells being exposed. Midpassage embryonic lung fibroblast cells and early passage adult skin fibroblast cells exposed to the same dose rate of radiation exhibited a decline in the cell density reached at confluence but not in the total number of passage levels attained (Macieira-Coelho et al., 1978; Icard et al., 1979). At high dose rates, human embryonic lung fibroblast cells exposed to ionizing radiation (x-rays and neutrons) exhibited a shortened *in vitro* life span (Ban et al., 1980; 1981). The decrease in life span was greater in exposed early and late passage cultures than in midpassage ones. Thus, exposure to ionizing radiation, under certain circumstances and in some cells, has accelerated at least two normal *in vitro* aging parameters, but the possible relationship between these *in vitro* observations and *in vivo* studies has not been explored.

With nonionizing radiation, Kantor et al. (1978) chronically exposed human embryonic lung fibroblasts to UV and detected no alteration in their *in vitro* life span. However, when Gilchrest (1980) biopsied UV-exposed and non-UV-exposed regions of human skin, a shorter *in vitro* life span was observed for the UV-exposed regions. Finally, exposure to two known mutagens—EMS and N-methyl-N'-nitro-N-nitrosoguanidine did not diminish the number of passage levels attained by human fetal lung fibroblasts, in spite of inducing significant numbers of diptheria toxin resistant mutants (Gupta, 1980).

Life shortening induced by ionizing radiation or mutagenic compounds appears to differ both quantitatively and qualitatively from the normal process of aging. The life shortening observed after exposure of animals to agents capable of inducing DNA damage is generally a consequence of increased frequencies of neoplasia. Furthermore, the conclusion that many of the normal aging parameters are not present during this life-shortening process suggests that the accumulation of mutational events is not fundamental to the aging process. It suggests as well, however, that certain age-related components, such as the observed increase in neoplasia, might be a consequence of the presence of unrepaired DNA lesions. Perhaps this is an indication that different tissues in an organism not only age at different rates but also age for different reasons.

CELLS FROM ANIMALS OF DIFFERENT LIFE SPANS

If aging is a consequence of the accumulation of damage to DNA, animals with long life spans should have more efficient DNA repair systems. Hence, a number of experiments have been carried out in attempts to correlate life span with DNA repair proficiency. As a matter of fact, wide differences have been reported in the ability of cells from animals with different life spans to repair UV damage to their DNA. The usual measure of such repair has been UDS. UV has been used as the damaging agent in most studies for historical reasons: it was the first repair system to be carefully analyzed, the level of damage does not depend on metabolic activation, and the repair of this damage by nucleotide excision results in long patches of repair synthesis, thus making the amount of repair easy to estimate by UDS. However, repair measured by radioautographic detection or scintillation counting of incorporated ^{3}H-dThd depends on the endogenous nucleo-

tide pool sizes, the average patch size, and the number of repaired regions per cell. The available data indicate that the patch size does not vary significantly from species to species (Hart et al., 1979b; Francis et al., 1981). Hence, properly made UDS measurements probably represent the number of repaired regions per cell. UV repair has both fast and slow components, probably because portions of DNA in chromatin are more or less accessible to repair enzymes. It is not known how the proportion of these putative regions varies with species, but it is reasonable to assume that the variation is nowhere nearly as large as the variation observed in UDS.

Despite the fact that there have been many experiments attempting to correlate UDS after UV irradiation with life span, UV is probably a poor model for such studies since it is not a stress on existing species. Even in humans, skin cancer is a disease of old age, and it is hard to see how proficiency in UV repair would have any selective reproductive advantage. However, one could argue that the nucleotide excision repair elicited by UV damage is typical of that detected after many of the damages induced by chemicals such as polycyclic aromatic hydrocarbons (Setlow, 1978). A high level of UV repair would also imply a high level of repair of the DNA adducts induced by chemical compounds. These UV mimetic adducts could affect cells in tissues other than skin; therefore, an efficient repair system of this type could have a selective advantage. On the other hand, the available epidemiological data on humans deficient in UV repair—xeroderma pigmentosum individuals—do *not* indicate that they have large numbers of internal cancers (Cairns, 1981). The implication is that UV mimetics are not important sources of cancer among these individuals and, therefore, that such chemicals are not important at present for cancer in the average repair-proficient population. Thus, depending on an explicit relation between cancer and aging, the theoretical basis for a correlation between life span and UV repair may or may not exist. Also in this same context, it is intriguing to note that there is an inverse correlation between life span and the ability of fibroblasts from animals with different life spans to metabolize polycyclic aromatic hydrocarbons (Moore and Schwartz, 1978; Schwartz and Moore, 1977). Typical data are shown in Figure 7. Based on the data in Figure 7, short-lived animals would probably suffer from more DNA damage as a result of exposure to exogenous UV mimetic chemicals requiring metabolic activation. Cells from these animals would also be less efficient in the repair of such damage, as shown in the following material.

The first experiment showing a correlation between UV excision repair and life span was by Hart and Setlow (1974). Excision repair, measured by UDS, increased with life span among seven fibroblast strains from different mammalian species with maximum life spans ranging from 1.5 years (shrew) to 100 years (human) (Figure 8). The correlation was a striking one and stimulated a number of other experimenters to extend these results. The low excision repair of mouse compared to human not only is a property of fibroblasts *in vitro* but is also observed in skin (Ley et al., 1977; Sutherland et al.,

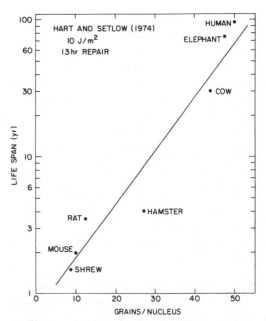

Figure 8. A correlation between life span and the ability of fibroblasts from various mammalian species to do unscheduled synthesis represented by the average number of grains per nucleus.

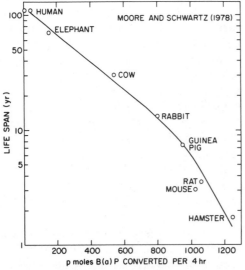

Figure 7. The results of Moore and Schwartz (1978) on the abilities of fibroblast cultures from various mammals to convert benzo[a]pyrene to watersoluble form.

1980). Paffenholz (1978) showed that fibroblasts from three inbred mouse strains ranging in life span from 300 to 900 days showed UDS increasing with life span at a rate approximately consistent with the data in Figure 8. On the other hand, there was no observed difference in the amount of UV excision repair between embryonic cells from congeneic mouse strains differing by 30–40 percent in life span (Collier et al., 1982). However, as judged from UDS measurements on lymphocytes, there may well be an interrelationship among three quantities—the histocompatibility complex, repair of UV damage, and life span (Hall et al., 1981)—which could obscure a simple relationship between two of them. Hart et al. (1979b) showed that there was a large difference in UDS after UV irradiation in fibroblasts from *Mus* (3.4 years) and *Peromyscus* (8.2 years), the latter having about 2.5-fold more UDS than the former. Moreover, the patch size for repair in the two sets of cells was the same, which indicated that there was probably a real difference in the numbers of UV photoproducts excised per cell. No difference was found between the two species in their ability to repair single-strand breaks introduced by gamma rays.

Three other extensive experiments have been completed which support the association between excision repair of UV damage and life span. One study was by Hart and Daniel (1980) who measured repair among a number of primate species (Figure 9). The data showed an excellent correlation with life span. However, the correlation for this group of primates does not fall along the curve indicated in Figure 8.

Francis et al. (1981) examined carefully the amount of excision repair from cells, usually fibroblasts, of 21 different species. They used the BrdUrd photolysis technique to measure both the number of repaired regions per 10^8 daltons of DNA and the patch size. Their data are also shown in Figure 9. Again, there was a correlation between the number of repaired regions (called sites in the figure) and the life span. A comparison of the two parts of Figure 9 indicates that the data of Francis

et al. (1981) give a good correlation on linear scales whereas the data of Hart and Daniel (1980) for primates give a good relation between the logarithm of the life span and repair. Moreover, it should be clear that a second difference between these experiments is the numbers chosen for life span: Hart and Daniel used 100 years as the life span of humans; Francis et al. used 80 years. Note also that the two studies give significantly different values for the repair by gorilla compared to human.

A third series of measurements, shown in Figure 10, measured UDS in epithelial cells of the lens of five species (Treton and Courtois, 1982). The correlation is excellent.

There are two large experimental exceptions to the correlations shown in Figures 8, 9, and 10. The first exception involves the extensive data of Kato et al. (1980) in which UV-induced UDS was investigated in fibroblast cells from 34 species representing 11 orders. Most of the cells investigated were derived from lung tissue explants obtained from animals of unknown ages. Their data

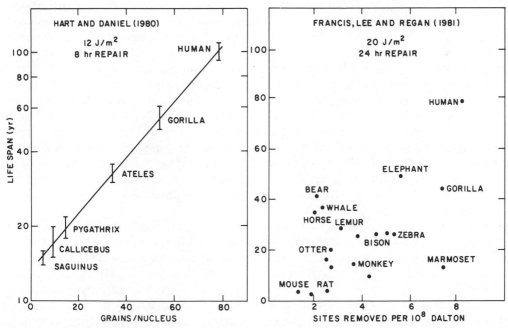

Figure 9. Other correlations between the ability to repair ultraviolet damage to fibroblasts and the life span of mammalian species. The left panel shows data on primates. The right panel shows data on the number of pyrimidine dimers removed (sites per 10^8 daltons) as a function of life span. The left panel is on log-linear coordinates; the right panel is on linear coordinates.

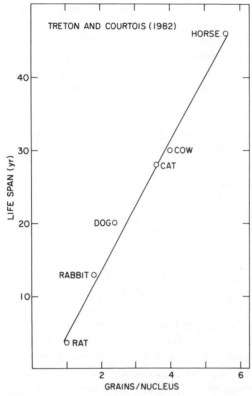

Figure 10. A correlation between unscheduled synthesis in lens epithelial cells from various mammalian species and life span.

box turtle (Woodhead et al., 1980). Despite the 100-year life span of the box turtle, its excision repair is less than that of the mouse.

The lower vertebrates, despite their negligible levels of excision repair of UV damage, have high levels of photoreactivating activity. For fish cells in culture derived from closely related species, there is fivefold more photo-reactivating activity in cells from the species with the fivefold greater life span (Regan et al., 1982a). This kind of repair is specific for pyrimidine dimers in DNA and, at least as far as humans and mice are concerned, also conforms to the correlation observed for excision repair. Humans have high levels of such activity in their skin (Sutherland et al., 1980; D'Ambrosio et al., 1981), but the level of this activity in mouse skin is negligible (Ley et al., 1978). Such experiments cannot easily be done on human cells in culture because the photoreactivating activity in such systems seems to depend markedly on factors as yet unidentified in the growth medium (Sutherland and Oliver, 1976).

It is unfortunate that there are no systematic data on the repair of the kinds of damages that arise from endogenous reactions in cells such as indicated in Table 1. In one example, the level of repair activity of 0^6-methyl-guanine activity in human liver is about tenfold greater than that in rat liver (Montesano et al., 1982). Thus, this repair system also conforms to the correlation between life span and repair. However, before generalizing these data to a correlation between life span and repair, the levels of endogenous reactions involved in alkylating DNA in humans and rats should also be known.

on all 34 species are shown in Figure 11. Obviously, there is no correlation between UDS and life span. Two orders of species destroy any correlation that might exist. These are the Primates—which have a short life span and a high UDS, in contradistinction to the data of Hart and Daniel (1980) shown in Figure 9—and Chiroptera. Cells from the latter animals with long life spans have low UDS. The bats have a very different metabolic regime than the other animals. If Chiroptera and Primates are omitted from the data of Kato et al., there is a reasonable correlation between UDS and life span as indicated in Figure 12.

The hint that the apparent correlation between life span and repair of UV damage should not be generalized over disparate species is futher indicated by measurements of the amount of excision repair in cells of the

Consequently, provided one does not go over too broad a range of mammalian species, there can be a close correlation between the excision repair of UV damage and life span. Although it is attractive to think that this correlation may have some causal relationship to aging, no good theoretical or experimental reasons have been advanced to support this point of view. It could be that many different types of repair activities are

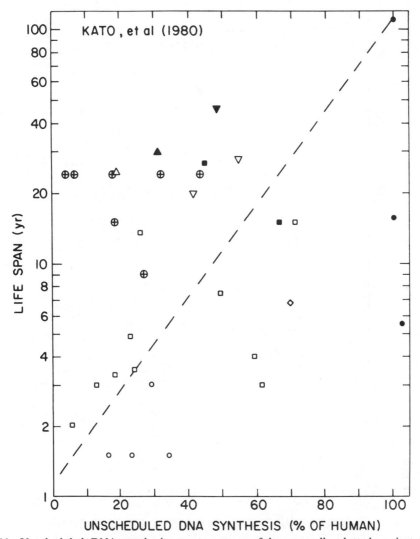

Figure 11. Unscheduled DNA synthesis as percentage of human cells plotted against life span for a number of mammalian species. The points represent the following: Insectivora, o; Primates, •; Edentata, △; Lagomorpha, ◇; Rodentia, □; Cetacea, ▲; Carnivora, ▽; Equus, ▼; Artiodactyla, ■; Chiroptera ○. There is no good correlation between unscheduled synthesis and life span. The dashed line has a slope similar to that of the left-hand panel in Figure 9.

coordinately expressed and that the findings for UV repair are only an indication that other, presumably more important, repair systems for living are correlated with life span.

HUMAN GENETIC SYNDROME STUDIES

If aging is causally related to DNA repair competency, then it would be expected that human genetic syndromes exhibiting accelerated or delayed aging would have intrinsically lower or higher levels of DNA repair, respectively. Conversely, it would follow that human genetic syndromes exhibiting decreased levels of DNA repair would also express characteristics of accelerated aging. The role of accelerated aging in these latter genetic syndromes will not be discussed in this chapter (see Tice, 1978).

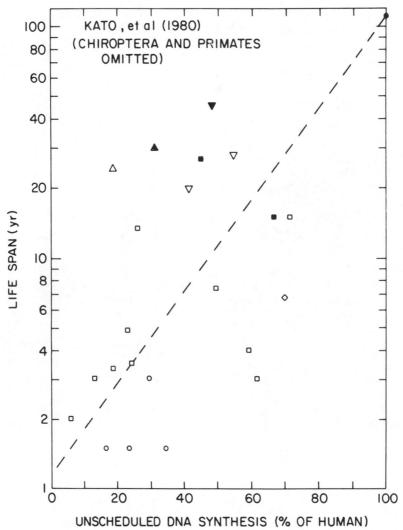

Figure 12. The same data as in Figure 11, but the points for Primates, other than human, and Chiroptera have been omitted. A correlation between unscheduled DNA synthesis and life span is now apparent.

Disorders Which Exhibit Features of Accelerated Aging

Although a genetic syndrome which exhibits a lengthened life span is not known, a number of inherited diseases shorten life span. Martin (1977) exhaustively analyzed the genetic disorders listed in McKusick's catalogue of Mendelian inheritance in man for 21 "symptoms" of accelerated aging [see Goldstein (1978) for a more extensive discussion of the work]. These symptoms included such alterations as an increased frequency of chromosomal aberrations, premature graying of hair, presenile dementia, autoimmunity, cataracts, and increased neoplasia. Martin concluded that although a "global progeria" syndrome did not exist, many diseases exhibited some aspect of premature aging. He next ranked ten syndromes exhibiting the greatest degree of premature senescence. The syndromes, in decreasing order of accelerated aging, are: Down syndrome; Werner syndrome; Cockayne syndrome; Hutchinson-Gilford syndrome (progeria); ataxia-telangiectasia; cervical lipodysplasia, familial; Serp syndrome; Klinefelter syndrome; Turner syndrome; and myotonic dystrophy. The genetic syndromes progeria, Down syndrome, and Werner syndrome for which the greatest amount of aging-related data are available are discussed below.

Progeria. Progeria, or the Hutchinson-Gilford syndrome, is a relatively rare, possible genetically heterogeneous disease with some suggestion of having an autosomal recessive mode of inheritance. The syndrome displays a number of clinical symptoms suggestive of accelerated aging. Mean life span is dramatically shortend (~ 13 years of age), and death is generally a consequence of severe atherosclerosis with cardiac and cerebral involvement (DeBusk, 1972; Goldstein, 1978; Brown, 1979). While thinning of the skin, atherosclerosis, and the loss of subcutaneous fat (DeBusk, 1972) are representative of accelerated aging, other features are not. These nonrepresentative features include delayed dentition, presbyopia, articular cartilage destruction, no increased incidence of tumors (DeBusk, 1972), and no elevated tissue lipofuscin levels (Spence and Herman, 1973).

In vitro, progeric skin fibroblast cultures have been reported to undergo significantly fewer population doublings than control cells (Goldstein, 1969; Singal and Goldstein, 1973; Goldstein and Moerman, 1976). Other investigations, however, have indicated relatively normal *in vitro* life spans (Martin et al., 1970; Danes, 1971). Goldstein and Moerman (1976) observed significant increases in altered enzyme levels in progeric fibroblast cells, levels in excess of those normally observed in senescent fibroblasts *in vitro* (Holliday and Tarrant, 1972). There does not appear to be any corresponding increase in the altered morphology (Danes, 1971) normally observed in aging fibroblast cultures (Robbins et al., 1970; Lipetz and Cristofalo, 1972).

Although these observations suggest that

there are quantitative and qualitative differences between normal aging and the presumed accelerated aging observed in progeria, several investigators have used progeric cell lines to assess possible parameters of aging (Epstein et al., 1973; Goldstein and Moerman, 1976). Epstein and his colleagues (1973) proposed that progeric fibroblasts are deficient in their ability to repair x-ray-induced single-strand breaks. Brown et al. (1976) detected a decrease in the repair of radiation-induced single-strand breaks in midpassage fibroblasts from two progerics. This deficiency in repair was corrected by cultivating these two cell lines with normal cells or with each other. Rainbow and Howes (1977a), using host cell reactivation of x-ray-inactivated adenovirus, also reported that progeric cells were deficient in the repair of x-ray damage. These observations of a decreased DNA repair capability have not been confirmed by other investigators. Regan and Setlow (1974), Epstein et al. (1974), and Bradley et al. (1976) report normal single-strand break rejoining capability in progeric cell lines. In addition, Bender and Rary (1974) have reported normal levels of induced chromosomal aberrations in x-irradiated cultured lymphocytes from the progeric individual examined by Epstein et al. (1973).

The evidence suggests that progerics suffer not from an intrinsic defect in DNA repair (Brown et al., 1980), but rather from a loss in homeostatic capability as a consequence of abnormal metabolism and/or some type of genetic repression. This interpretation would be consistent with the finding that SV40 transformation of progeric cells restores normal ability to rejoin single-strand breaks (Little et al., 1975).

The Werner Syndrome (WS). This syndrome, which is inherited as an autosomal recessive trait, has its onset in persons between the ages of 15 and 20 (Epstein et al., 1966; Zucker-Franklin et al., 1968). Some of the clinical features that resemble premature or accelerated aging include marked lymphoid depletion, glucose intolerance, cataracts, graying of the hair, increased incidence of neoplasms, and arteriosclerosis (Epstein et al., 1966; Zucker-Franklin et al., 1968; Fleischmajer and Nedwich, 1973; Goldstein, 1978). As in progeria, however, there are clinical features that are qualitatively and quantitatively different from those observed in the elderly, such as delayed sexual maturity (Epstein et al., 1966).

In vitro, WS fibroblast cultures routinely exhibit poor growth, decreased life span, and accelerated morphological alterations similar to those observed in senescent normal fibroblast cultures (Epstein et al., 1966; Martin et al., 1970; Stecker and Gardner, 1970; Danes, 1971; Nienhaus et al., 1971; Fujiwara et al. 1977, Higashikawa and Fujiwara, 1978). Increased levels of altered enzymes and an increase in concanavalin A–mediated red blood cell adsorption have also been reported for WS fibroblast cell lines, consistent with the notion of premature aging (Holliday et al., 1974; Goldstein and Singal, 1974; Goldstein and Moerman, 1976; Aizawa et al., 1980).

Studies on DNA repair capability and/or DNA synthetic activity in WS are limited. Fujiwara et al. (1977) investigated the DNA repair capacity and the rate of DNA replication in skin fibroblasts from eight individuals afflicted with this syndrome. These cells exhibited normal levels of sensitivity toward x-ray and UV killing, normal levels of repair of x-ray-induced single-strand breaks, and normal levels of UV-induced UDS. However, DNA chain elongation was slower in these cells. A decrease in DNA chain elongation in WS fibroblasts was not observed by Takeuchi et al. (1982); however, an increase in the distance between initiation sites along the DNA was detected. These conflicting results have not been resolved. More extensive studies on the levels of UV-induced UDS in seven WS cell lines have also indicated normal DNA repair levels (Higashikawa and Fujiwara, 1978).

Down Syndrome. Down syndrome (DS), or trisomy for chromosome 21, originates through a process of meiotic nondisjunction which is generally maternal in origin (re-

viewed in Kram and Schneider, 1978). The life span of these patients is markedly reduced, with only 20 percent surviving past 30 years of age, 8 percent past 40, and 2.6 percent past 50 (Forrsman and Akesson, 1965). DS has been ranked by Martin (1977) as the disorder which most typifies accelerated aging. At a relatively early age, individuals with this syndrome exhibit an increased incidence of neoplasms (Miller, 1970) and autoimmunity diseases (Fialkow, 1970), both age-related conditions. The most striking clinical finding is the early onset of senile dementia in DS. Postmortem neuropathological examination of brain tissue from these patients has revealed a degree of neuronal degeneration usually observed only in the very elderly (Jervis, 1970; Ellis et al., 1974).

Individuals affected with DS often exhibit short stature, degenerative vascular disease, hyperglycemia and/or insulin resistance, osteoporosis, osteoarthritis, cataracts, skin atrophy, hair loss and/or graying, hypogonadism, amyloid deposition, and deposition of lipofuscin at an early age—all indicators of accelerated aging (Martin, 1977; Goldstein, 1978). Several investigators have also demonstrated a decreased response of DS lymphocytes to phytohemagglutinin (PHA) stimulation (Rigas et al., 1970; Agarwal et al., 1970; Serra et al., 1978). Decreased lymphocyte response to PHA is a well-documented age-related phenomenon (Pisciotta et al., 1967).

Schneider and Epstein (1972) observed a significantly decreased *in vitro* life span of DS fibroblasts when compared to cultures derived from age-matched controls. Several investigators have also observed a decreased growth rate in fibroblast cultures derived from patients with DS as compared to control cultures (Kaback and Bernstein, 1970; Schneider and Epstein, 1972; Segal and McCoy, 1974; Kaina et al., 1977). The slower rate of growth is generally attributed to a longer S and/or G_2 phase of the cell cycle (Kukharenko et al., 1974; Paton et al., 1974). However, DNA chain elongation in these same cells appears to be faster than normal (Yurov, 1978). In spite of the apparently decreased PHA response in DS, trisomy 21 lymphocytes have been reported to have either normal cell cycle kinetics (Kishi, 1977) or faster than normal growth rates (Yanagisawa, 1978). Tice (unpublished data), using the bromodeoxyuridine staining technique to assess proliferation kinetics in PHA-stimulated peripheral blood cultures, also observed normal stimulation kinetics and normal cell cycle duration in three DS individuals when compared with age- matched controls.

Trisomy 21 cells are more susceptible to transformation by SV40 virus than are normal fibroblasts (Todaro and Martin, 1967) and demonstrate increased sensitivity to chromosomal damage induced by x-irradiation (Higurashi and Conen, 1972; Sasaki et al., 1970; Preston 1981), MMC (Banerjee et al., 1974; Banerjee et al., 1977), methylnitrosourea (Kaina et al., 1977), Trenimon (Aldenhoff et al., 1980), UV (Lambert et al., 1976), DMBA (O'Brien et al., 1971), and measles virus (Higurashi et al., 1973). Baseline frequencies of SCE are normal in DS lymphocytes (Yu and Borgoankar, 1977; Lezana et al., 1977; Yanagisawa, 1978), but Trenimon-induced SCE frequencies are greater than normal (Aldenhoff et al., 1980). However, UV- and 4-nitroquinoline-l-oxide-induced UDS levels (O'Brien et al., 1971) and strand break repair after exposure to ionizing radiation (Treton et al., 1978) are normal in DS cells. Data obtained by Preston (1981) suggest that, if anything, repair of x-ray-induced damage is more rapid in trisomy 21 lymphocytes.

DISCUSSION

The expectation of a causal relationship between DNA repair capability and aging is based on the assumption that aging is a direct consequence of the detrimental accumulation of unrepaired DNA lesions. The number of DNA damages introduced by endogenous and exogenous processes is not trivial. Presumably, when the frequency of DNA lesions reaches a certain level and/or specific genes become inactive, a loss in cellular function ensues. As the proportion of such cells increases in various tissues, the organism "ages." If this assumption is valid, then the more effective a cell is in preventing or repairing DNA damage, the slower is the aging process.

It is possible to envision two separate, but not mutually exclusive, mechanisms by which unrepaired DNA lesions could accumulate with time. First, a certain proportion of DNA lesions might escape detection and repair. If we assume that both repair capabilities and environmental conditions do not vary significantly with time, unrepaired DNA lesions should accumulate in a cell at a fairly constant rate. The second mechanism also assumes that there is no significant alteration in the number of potential lesions induced, but rather that the proportion of successful repair events diminishes with time as a consequence of a declining DNA repair capability. In this event, unrepaired DNA lesions should increase in substantially faster rates as the level of repair capability becomes more inefficient with advancing age. Both mechanisms would give rise to levels of DNA lesions capable of killing or incapacitating cells. However, the former mechanism suggests that the life span is related to the intrinsic capacity of the cells in an organism to repair DNA damage and that different organisms with different repair capabilities should have different life spans. The latter mechanism, while not negating the former, suggests that life spans could be longer except for the decline in DNA repair capability.

Investigations concerned with determining frequencies of unrepaired DNA lesions have generally compared tissues derived from animals at the two extremes of their natural life span. A further difficulty arises from the rather limited types of tissues examined. However, some conclusions can be drawn concerning both the occurrence and the rate of accumulation of unrepaired DNA lesions in different tissues. The only *in vivo* tissue that has been clearly demonstrated to undergo an age-related increase in unrepaired DNA lesions is the liver. All investigations into other tissues, *in vitro* as well as *in vivo,* have given results either routinely negative or inconsistently positive. The frequency of cross-linked DNA-DNA and/or DNA-protein molecules and of chromosomal aberrations in the liver appears to accumulate steadily at a rate inversely proportional to the animal's life span, and not to increase abruptly near the end (Stevenson and Curtis, 1961; Curtis et al., 1966; Curtis and Miller, 1971; Cutler, 1976a). The increase in strand breakage observed in liver cells occurs more significantly in the early portion of an animal's life span than near the end of life (Massie et al., 1972; Ono et al., 1976). This observation suggests that a decline in DNA repair competency is not critical for aging. Rather, a certain proportion or type of DNA lesions escapes repair and accumulates within a cell, perhaps with irreparable damage to cellular function. This increase in unrepaired lesions in the liver might be tissue specific, however, and not reflect general *in vivo* conditions during aging.

The results on cross-linking are probably not as inconsistent as they may appear. Thermal stability and template activity depend upon the method of DNA extraction: highly purified DNA (i.e., DNA containing very little bound protein) retains the same T_m and template activity regardless of the age of the donor animal or the passage level of the culture (Phytila and Sherman, 1967; Russell et al., 1970; Comings and Vance, 1971; Kurtz et al., 1974). Thus, there is little evidence from thermal stability or template activity studies to suggest an age-related increase in DNA-DNA cross-linking. However, in cruder DNA preparations (i.e., those containing more bound protein) or in isolated chromatin, an age-related increase in thermal stability and a decrease in template activity are generally observed (e.g., Russell et al., 1970). These data are suggestive of an increase in DNA-protein cross-links with increasing donor age. However, not only are template activity and thermal stability dependent upon the amount of protein remaining bound to DNA after a particular extraction process, they are also dependent upon the nature of the bound protein (see Cutler, 1976c). With increasing age, the histone: nonhistone ratio in many tissues changes (e.g., Berdyshev, 1976; Cutler, 1976c), a change which may be responsible for the decrease in protein extractability, the increase in T_m, and the decrease in template activity (e.g., Phytila and Sherman, 1967; Russell et al., 1970; Hill, 1976; O'Meara and Hermann, 1972). Whether this change in chromatin protein results from an increase in cross-linking between protein and DNA or from the normal process of cellular differentiation remains unsolved. However, either process may lead to repressed gene activity.

As mentioned, the only cellular system to consistently exhibit an increase in DNA lesions with age is liver tissue *in vivo.* DNA strand breaks, DNA cross-linking, and spontaneous chromosomal aberrations increase in frequency in liver tissue beginning early in the animal's life span. The importance of the conclusion that the increase in DNA lesions in liver cells is inversely proportional to the animal's life span (Cutler, 1976b) must be examined, however, in terms of a general aging process. It is extremely difficult to demonstrate an age-related loss in liver function (Thompson and Williams, 1965; Thung and Hollander, 1967), and liver failure is generally not a cause of death in the aged animal (Kohn, 1966). The conclusion that life span does not depend on either the number or the percentage of altered liver cells suggests that the general accumulation of DNA lesions might rather be a consequence of liver-specific metabolic processes. In this context, it is interesting to note that a strong correlation exists between life span and the ability of cultured fibroblasts to metabolize DMBA to its mutagenic metabolites (Schwartz and Moore, 1977; Moore and Schwartz, 1978). Consequently, the rate of accumulation of DNA lesions in liver cells might reflect metabolic enzyme levels and not life span–specific DNA repair capabilities.

The lack of correlation between aging of the liver and age-related mortality suggests that other tissues might be of greater importance to the aging process. Aging does not appear to be a consequence of a decline in tissues that normally proliferate (e.g., bone marrow) or in tissues that retain the capacity to proliferate in response to a specific stress situation (e.g., liver) (Kohn, 1975; Franks, 1974; Cutler, 1976a). Aging appears to be more conspicuous in terminally differentiated postmitotic tissues such as neural or muscle tissue (Aune, 1976). In fact, a significant proportion of natural deaths can be attributed to degenerative age-associated alterations in the central nervous system (Burnett, 1974). Tissue-dependent aging appears to be the result not of an actual loss in cell number (Kohn, 1975; Cameron and Thrasher, 1976) but rather of a continuous decline in functional capacity (Aune, 1976).

The aforementioned observations on the accumulation of DNA lesions suggest a constant rate of DNA repair with age, and broadly speaking, investigations concerned with assessing DNA repair capability are in accord. *In vivo*, retinal cells from aging rabbits (Lett, 1978), neurons from aging beagles (Wheeler and Lett, 1974), and cerebellar, splenic, and hepatic cells from aging mice (Ono and Okada, 1978) are equally capable of rejoining γ-ray-induced single-strand breaks, while skin fibroblasts from aged donors exhibit the same sensitivity to UV light as measured by cell killing (Goldstein, 1971; Hall et al., 1982). Reports have appeared, however, of a decline in UV-induced UDS (Lambert et al., 1976) and of an increase in chemically induced chromosomal aberrations in lymphocytes from aged donors (Bochkov and Kuleshov, 1971, 1972). While UV-induced UDS is decreased in these cells, cell survival is not (Kutlaca et al., 1982). It is also difficult to interpret the findings of studies involving chemical agents. The apparent differences in yields of chromosomal aberrations could be the result of differences in mutagen metabolism or they could be due to differences in the proliferative rate of the cultures. *In vitro* investigations concerned with the efficiency of DNA strand break rejoining have resulted in conflicting conclusions. Some investigations have observed a constant level of this type of repair ability

until *in vitro* senescence has already begun (Clarkson and Painter, 1974; Bradley et al., 1976; Suzuki et al., 1980), while others have reported a decline prior to senescence (Epstein et al., 1973, 1974; Little et al., 1975; Williams and Little, 1975). Excision repair appears to decline after the onset of *in vitro* senescence and to correlate with a loss in replicative ability (Hart and Setlow, 1976; Bowman et al., 1976).

The results of the investigations on DNA repair capability during the *in vitro* life spans of explants derived from human and animal tissues often conflict. However, it is difficult to compare results on rodent cells quantitatively with those on human cells. Rodent cells in culture or in animals (Ley et al., 1977) are much less proficient at nucleotide excision than are human cells (Setlow, 1978). It has been suggested that the low level of excision repair in mouse cells is a developmental phenomenon because cells from young BALB/c embryos are very proficient at the excision of UV damage, a proficiency which is lost with growth *in vitro* or *in vivo* (Peleg et al., 1976). However, other investigators have not been able to obtain these same results using a different strain of mice (Regan et al., 1982b) or the same mouse strain (Tice and Setlow, unpublished). Cells from both young and old embryos were severely deficient in nucleotide excision repair even when the analysis involved the use of the most sensitive assay for the number of pyrimidine dimers remaining in DNA—the dimer-specific endonuclease technique.

The accumulated data do not firmly support an age-related decline in DNA repair capability. A large variety of cellular systems exhibit a constant level of unrepaired DNA lesions and a constant level of DNA repair capability with age. One of the difficulties with making clear-cut interpretations of the excision repair data is that most of the results have been obtained on tissues that are relatively low in excision repair compared to the very excision-proficient human cells. Recall that rodent cells are much less proficient at excision repair than are human cells and that when UDS levels are compared they are close to being the analogues of the repair-deficient humans affected with xeroderma pigmentosum. However, it is also important to remember that rodent cells and human cells exhibit similar survivals after exposure to the same UV doses. What are needed are careful studies of the amount of repair versus age in human cells rather than in rodent cells. An appropriate approach would be to compare both stimulated and unstimulated lymphocytes with fibroblasts from the same individual. There seem to be good indications that stimulated lymphocytes are close to fibroblasts in their level of DNA repair.

Also, the assessment of DNA repair as a function of age through the use of various chemicals is often complicated by the requirement of metabolically activating them to reactive forms before they can interact with cellular macromolecules. For example, the activation of polycyclic aromatic hydrocarbons to metabolites mutagenic in short-term bacterial tests was greater when activation was by liver homogenates from senescent rats rather than from young ones Birnbaum, 1979). Thus, it should be clear that what is needed for a comparison of DNA repair capacity in old and young tissues is the amount of repair for equal amounts of damage to DNA.

In general, there seems to be an association between a decrease in repair and cellular differentiation. Several investigations have suggested that nonproliferating, terminally differentiated cells undergo a loss in DNA repair capacity in comparison with proliferating precursor cells. Rat or embryonic chicken skeletal muscle cells suffer a significant loss in UDS induced by UV (Stockdale, 1971; Stockdale and O'Neill, 1972), MMS (Hahn et al., 1971), and x-rays or 4-nitro-quinoline-1-oxide (Chan et al., 1976) as they fuse in vitro into multinucleated cells and myotubes. The loss of UDS activity in myotube cells was due in part to a complete cessation in the recognization and repair of alkali sensitive lesions (Chan et al., 1976). In one study, UDS following UV radiation seemed to be maintained during the differ-

entiation from myoblasts to myotubes (Koval and Kaufman, 1981). However, these experiments were carried out in very high concentrations of hydroxyurea—75 mM—and, at least in human fibroblasts, such concentrations inhibit DNA repair by at least tenfold (Francis et al., 1979). Developing chick retinoblasts also undergo a loss in UV-induced UDS capacity (Strauss, 1976), and mouse neuroblastoma cells also become increasingly sensitive to UV exposure during differentiation (McCombe et al., 1976). In one cellular system, the loss in UDS activity with differentiation did not coincide with a loss in the ability to rejoin single-strand breaks (Chan et al., 1976). This loss in DNA excision repair capability with differentiation appears to be reversible. The mouse neuroblastoma cell system of McCombe et al. (1976) is capable of undergoing reversible differentiation in vitro depending on serum concentration. With dedifferentiation, these cells regain normal levels of repair after UV radiation, but not until after completion of the first mitosis.

This correlation between proliferative activity and excision repair competence also occurs in peripheral lymphocytes. These cells exhibit dramatic increases in their ability to remove AAAF-induced damage (Strauss, 1976; Scudiero et al., 1976) and to undergo UV-induced UDS (Darzynkiewicz, 1971) after mitogen stimulation. Although not equal in magnitude, this increase in repair competence occurs in parallel with increasing levels of DNA polymerase activity (Scudiero et al., 1976). The loss in DNA repair capacity with differentiation is also observed in comparative tissue studies. Examinations of UV-induced UDS revealed that peripheral lymphocytes have a greater capacity to repair than peripheral granulocytes (Darzynkiewicz, 1971) and that fibroblasts have a greater capacity to repair than pulsating cardiac cells from the same rat organ (Lampidis and Little, 1971). In agreement with a retention of normal break rejoining capacity with differentiation in vitro, cultured bovine lens epithelial cells and lung fibroblast cells from the same animal have equal capacities for repairing x-ray-induced single-strand scissions (Treton and Courtois, 1976).

Thus, the process of differentiation results in a decreased ability to repair DNA. This decreased repair competency could have a trivial explanation. Repair seems to be accomplished by a complex of enzymes. If one of the components, such as the polymerase, is lacking from differentiated cells, then the whole complex may cease to function. Alternatively, the levels of nucleoside triphosphates necessary for DNA polymerization may be too low to accommodate repair.

Whether or not a positive correlation exists between DNA polymerase activity and DNA excision repair capability, different tissues vary qualitatively and quantitatively in their abilities to repair specific DNA lesions. These differences correlate strongly with proliferative activity. The loss of excision repair capacity concomitant with a loss in proliferation during differentiation suggests that perhaps some of the apparent decline in DNA repair capability observed in some proliferating cellular systems as they approach senescence (e.g., WI–38) could be due directly to a loss in proliferative activity. If DNA repair capability is critical to the aging process, and since not all tissues are equally repair competent, then some variation in the aging rate might be expected to occur between different tissues. Because differentiated tissues exhibit the lowest repair capability, tissues such as neuronal or muscular should age fastest. In fact, *in vivo* aging does appear to be more conspicuous in certain tissues and particularly in those involving differentiated postmitotic cells (Franks, 1974; Aune, 1976).

A possible significant correlation with differences in tissue-specific aging rates in an organism would be corresponding tissue differences in DNA repair capability. The ability of any tissue to monitor and repair DNA damage depends not only on the extent, nature, and location of the induced lesion(s) (Hart and Trosko, 1976; Trosko and Hart, 1976) but also on the proliferative state of the cellular population (i.e., replicating, quiescent, or postmitotic). Postmitotic cells not only lack postreplication repair but also exhibit a significant decrease in excision repair capability in comparison with proliferating cells from the same organism. This difference in DNA repair competency suggests that since postmitotic cells may accumulate more lesions with time than proliferating tissues, they may also age at a faster rate. That they do is supported by aging studies *in vivo,* suggesting that a positive correlation may exist between DNA repair capability and life span.

If this correlation is to be considered a strong one, then agents that induce extensive DNA damage should also accelerate the aging process. Early investigators concluded that exposure to ionizing radiation did accelerate the normal rate of aging. More recent extensive reassessments of the accumulated data, however, have suggested both quantitative and qualitative differences from the normal aging process (Walburg, 1975). It is apparent that exposure to ionizing radiation primarily increases the incidence of neoplasia, resulting in premature death and a shortened life span. Investigations based on treatments with chemical mutagens have been equally negative in obtaining an acceleration of the normal aging process (Alexander and Connell, 1960; Curtis, 1963; Stevenson and Curtis, 1961). *In vitro,* the chronic exposure of animal cells to ionizing radiation, UV, and chemical mutagens shortened the life span of some culture systems (Lima et al., 1972; Ban et al., 1980, 1981; Gilchrest, 1980) while not affecting the life span of others (Macieira- Coelho et al., 1978; Icard et al., 1979; Gupta, 1980). These findings suggest that DNA damage is not fundamental to the aging process. It is possible, however, that aging is normally a consequence of changes in a relatively few critical tissues, and extensive exposures to DNA-damaging agents may mask these important alterations.

The data on DNA synthetic capability also do not appear to indicate a cause-effect relationship with aging. DNA synthetic capability (i.e., the rate of DNA chain elongation) declined in aged cells (Petes et al., 1974). However, this decline does not appear to be responsible for a delay in the length of S *in vitro* (e.g., Macieira-Coelho et al., 1966; Grove and Cristofalo, 1977; Macieira-Coelho and Taboury, 1982) or *in vivo* (Thrasher, 1967; 1971). Rather, the lengthening of the cell cycle and the decline in the number of proliferating cells (Buetow, 1971; Adelman et al., 1972; Cristofalo and Sharf, 1974; Macieira-Coelho and Taboury, 1982) appear related to some alteration(s) in G_1 (e.g., Tice et al., 1979; Macieira-Coelho and Taboury, 1982). Thus, DNA synthetic capability in proliferating cells also does not appear to be related to the aging process.

Of equal importance to a correlation between life span and DNA repair capability is the expression of accelerated aging in genetic syndromes with a demonstrable decrease in DNA repair capability and, conversely, a decrease in the ability to repair DNA in genetic syndromes which exhibit accelerated aging. The results obtained from such studies are far from conclusive.

Martin (1977) has rated Down syndrome (DS) as the disorder which best exemplifies accelerated aging. Other diseases highly rated by Martin include Werner syndrome (WS), and progeria. Of these "accelerated" aging disorders, DS cells exhibit increased sensitivity to aklylating agents and/or to radiation although the defect(s) in DNA repair has not been elucidated. Progeria was suggested to involve a defect in DNA strand break rejoining capability (Epstein et al., 1973b), but subsequent investigations have demonstrated normal repair levels in some progeric patients (Epstein et al., 1974; Regan and Setlow, 1974; Bradley et al., 1976). Possibly, the repair loss in some progeric cell lines was a result of gene repression and/or of altered metabolism but not of an intrinsic defect in DNA repair (Little, 1976). WS cells have not been observed to be deficient in any aspect of DNA repair. At least one known DNA repair deficiency syndrome, ataxia-telangiec-

tasia (AT), expresses signs of accelerated aging (Martin, 1977; discussed by Tice, 1978). AT is deficient in the repair of damage induced by ionizing radiation (e.g., Paterson and Smith, 1979). Thus, some syndromes considered to express symptoms of accelerated aging are DNA repair defective while others are not. Xeroderma pigmentosum (XP) and Fanconi's anemia (FA), the two human diseases other than AT which are demonstrably DNA repair defective, are usually not considered to express many general signs of accelerated aging (Tice, 1978). The only possible correlation between defective DNA repair and aging occurs in XP, where the more severe the loss in excision repair capability, the greater are the indications of premature aging of the skin and neural tissues (Robbins et al., 1974; Robbins, 1977).

This lack of a consistent correlation between DNA repair deficiency and premature aging suggests that the two processes are not necessarily related. One of the difficulties in making this conclusion, however, is that it assumes that all DNA repair processes are equally important. This statement is obviously false, since persons affected with the variant form of XP, involving a deficiency in postreplication repair, exhibit milder clinical manifestations than those with the excision repair–deficient form (Cleaver and Bootsma, 1975). This finding might be expected, since postmitotic cells have no need for that particular repair process.

The strongest observations in support of a correlation between life span and DNA repair capacity are in the numerous experiments (Figures 7, 8, 9, 10, and 12) relating high levels of UV-induced UDS to long life span. We indicated, however, that UV is of relatively low environmental impact to be associated with aging. Moreover, the correlation may not be a direct one because there is an indication from measurements on stimulated lymphocytes that the magnitude of UV repair in mice may not only be related to life span but to the H–2 histocompatibility type (Hall et al., 1981) as well. Also, aging does not appear to be a consequence of a decline in cellular systems capable of proliferation. It has been proposed that life span is controlled by small groups of essential, post-mitotic cells in critical organs and tissues such as the brain or the neuroendocrine system (Franks, 1974). If true, then a comparison of DNA repair in these cells among different species is of primary importance.

CONCLUSION

Aging does not appear to be the direct consequence of a decline in DNA repair capability. Neither can it be attributed to a change in DNA synthetic activity. The possibility remains that differences in life span among the various animal species are a direct result of different levels of DNA repair capability. Current experimental support for this hypothesis, however, remains inconclusive. Also, it has yet to be proved that unrepaired DNA lesions accumulate with age in tissues more critical to aging. While it is expected that DNA damage certainly contributes to the aging process, it is difficult to conclude that all aging is a consequence of the accumulation of DNA lesions. Other factors may play an equally critical role, such as the degree of genetic redundancy for vital functions within the genome (Hart and Trosko, 1976) or the extent of cellular redundancy within organs. This review should by no means discourage research directed at the possible relationship between DNA repair and aging; the current state of understanding concerning both these processes is still in its infancy. Rather, it should indicate the areas of interest in which research ought to be encouraged because of presently conflicting results and/or a lack of information.

ACKNOWLEDGMENTS

R. B. Setlow and R. R. Tice are supported by the U.S. Department of Energy.

The library research assistance of Ms. A. Giovannelli and Ms. D. Smith, and the heroic labor of Ms. K. Kissel in typing this manuscript are very gratefully appreciated.

REFERENCES

Absher, P. M., Absher, R. G., and Barnes, W. D. 1974. Genealogies of clones of diploid fibroblasts. Cine-microphotographic observations of cell division patterns in relation to population age. *Exp. Cell Res.* 88: 95–104.

Acharya, P. V. N. 1972. The isolation and partial characterization of age-correlated oligodeoxyribo-ribonucleotide with covalently linked aspartyl-glutamyl-polypeptides. *John Hopkins Med. J. Suppl.* 1: 254–260.

Adelman, R. C., Stein, G., Roth, G. S., and Englander, D. 1972. Age-dependent regulation of mammalian DNA synthesis and cell proliferation *in vivo*. *Mech. Age. Dev.* 1: 49–59.

Agarwal, S. S., Blumberg, B. S., Gerstley, B. J. S., London, W. I., Sutnick, A. I., and Loeb, L. A. 1970. DNA polymerase activity as an index of lymphocyte stimulation: studies in Down's syndrome. *J. Clin. Invest.* 48: 161–169.

Aizawa, S., Mitsui, Y., Kurimoto, F., and Matsuoka, K. 1980. Cell-surface changes accompanying aging in human diploid fibroblasts: effects of tissue, donor age and genotype. *Mech. Age. Develop.* 13: 297–306.

Aldenhoff, P., Wegner, R.-D., and Sperling, K. 1980. Different sensitivity of diploid and trisomic cells from patients with Down syndrome mosaic after treatment with the trifunctional alkylating agent Trenimon. *Hum. Genet.* 56: 123–125.

Alexander, P. 1957. Accelerated ageing—a long term effect of exposure to ionizing radiations. *Gerontologia* 1: 174–193.

Alexander, P. 1967. The role of DNA lesions in the processes leading to ageing in mice. *Symp. Soc. Exp. Biol.* 21: 29–50.

Alexander, P. and Connell, D. I. 1960. Shortening of the life span of mice by irradiation with x-rays and treatment with radiomimetic chemicals. *Radiat. Res.* 12: 36–48.

Aune, J. 1976. Ultrastructure changes with age. *Interdiscip. Top. Gerontol.* 10: 44–61.

Ayme, S., Mattei, J. F., Mattei, M. G., Aurran, Y., and Giraud, F. 1976. Nonrandom distribution of chromosome breaks in cultured lymphocytes of normal subjects. *Hum. Genet.* 31: 161–176.

Ban, S., Ikushima, T., and Sugahara, T. 1981. Reduction in proliferative life span of human diploid cells after exposure to a reactor radiation beam. *Radiat. Res.* 87: 1–9.

Ban, S., Nikaido, O., and Sugahara, T. 1980. Acute and late effects of a single exposure of ionizing radiation on cultured human diploid cell populations. *Radiat. Res.* 81: 120–130.

Banerjee, A., Huang, C. C., and Fiel, R. J. 1974. Differential sensitivity of mitomycin C to the hematopoietic cell lines from normal individuals and patients with Down's syndrome. *Proc. Am. Cancer Res.* 15: 141–152.

Banerjee, A., Jung, O., and Huang, C. C. 1977. Response of hematopoietic cell lines derived from patients with Down's syndrome and from normal individuals to mitomycin C and caffeine. *J. Natl. Cancer Inst.* 59: 37–39.

Barrows, L. R. and Magee, P. N. 1982. Nonenzymatic methylation of DNA by S-adenosylmethionine *in vitro*. *Carcinogenesis* 3: 349–351.

Bartram, C. R., Koske-Westphal, T., and Passarge, E. 1976. Chromatid exchanges in ataxia telangiectasia, Bloom syndrome, Werner syndrome and xeroderma pigmentosum. *Ann. Hum. Genet.* 40: 79–86.

Bender, M. A., Bedford, J. S., and Mitchell, J. B. 1973b. Mechanism of chromosomal aberration production. II. Aberrations induced by 5-bromodeoxyuridine and visible light. *Mutat. Res.* 20: 403–416.

Bender, M. A., Griggs, H. G., and Bedford, J. S. 1974. Mechanism of chromosomal aberration. III. Chemicals and ionizing radiation. *Mutat. Res.* 23: 197–212.

Bender, M. A., Griggs, H. G., and Walker, P. L. 1973a. Mechanism of chromosomal aberration production. I. Aberration induction by ultra-violet light. *Mutat. Res.* 20: 387–402.

Bender, M. A. and Rary, J. M. 1974. Spontaneous and x-ray-induced chromosomal aberrations in progeria. *Radiat. Res.* 59: 181a.

Ben-Ishai, R. and Peleg, L. 1975. Excision-repair in primary cultures of mouse embryo cells and its decline in progressive passages and established cell lines. *In,* P. Hanawalt and R. Setlow (eds.), *Molecular Mechanisms for Repair of DNA,* pp. 607–610. New York: Plenum Press.

Benn, P. A. 1976. Specific chromosome aberrations in senescent fibroblast cell lines derived from human embryos. *Amer. J. Hum. Genet.* 28: 465–473.

Berdyshev, G. D. 1976. Age-dependent changes of *in vitro* transcription activities of animals. *Interdiscipl. Topics Geront.* 10: 70–82.

Berdyshev, G. D. and Zhelabovskaya, S. M. 1972. Composition, template properties and thermostability of liver chromatin from rats of various age at deproteinization by NaCl solutions. *Exp. Geront.* 7: 321–330.

Berech, J. and Curtis, H. J. 1964. The role of age and x-irradiation on kidney function in the mouse. *Radiat. Res.* 22: 95–105.

Beupain, B., Icard, C., and Macieira-Coelho, A. 1980. Changes in DNA alkali-sensitive sites during senescence and establishment of fibroblasts *in vitro*. *Biochim. Biophys. Acta* 606: 251–261.

Birnbaum, L. S. 1979. Increased production of mutagenic metabolites of carcinogens by tissues of senescent rodents. *Cancer Res.* 39: 4752–4755.

Bochkov, N. P. 1972. Spontaneous chromosome aberrations in human somatic cells. *Humanagentik* 16: 159–165.

Bochkov, N. P., Kozlov, V. M., Pilosov, P. A., and Sevankaev, A. V. 1968. Spontaneous level of chromosome aberrations in cultures of human leukocytes. *Genetika* 4: 93.

Bochkov, N. P. and Kuleshov, N. P. 1971. Dependence of the intensity of the chemical mutagenesis in human cells on sex and age of individuals. *Genetika* 7: 132–136.

Bochkov, N. P. and Kuleshov, N. P. 1972. Age sensitivity of human chromosomes to alkylating agents. *Mutat. Res.* 14: 345–353.

Bojanovic, J. J., Jevtovic, A. D., Pantic, V. S., Dugandzic, S. M., and Jovanovic, D. S. 1970. Thymus nucleoproteins. Thymus histones in young and adult rats. *Gerontologia* 16: 304–312.

Bourgeois, C. A., Raynaud, N., Diatloff-Zito, C., and Macieira-Coelho, A. 1981. Effect of low dose rate ionizing radiation on the division potential of cells *in vitro*. VIII. Cytogenetic analysis of human fibroblasts. *Mech. Age. Develop.* 17: 225–235.

Bradley, M. O., Erickson, L. C., and Kohn, K. W. 1976. Normal DNA strand rejoining and absence of DNA crosslinking in progeroid and aging human cells. *Mutat. Res.* 37: 279–292.

Brooks, A. L., Mead, D. K., and Peters, R. F. 1973. Effect of ageing on the frequency of metaphase chromosome aberrations in the liver of the Chinese hamster. *J. Gerontol.* 28: 452–454.

Brown, W. T. 1979. Human mutations affecting aging—a review. *Mech. Age. Develop.* 9: 325–336.

Brown, W. T., Epstein, J., and Little, J. B. 1976. Progeria cells are stimulated to repair DNA by cocultivation with normal cells. *Exp. Cell Res.* 97: 291–296.

Brown, W. T., Ford, J. P., and Gershey, E. L. 1980. Variation of DNA repair capacity in progeria cells unrelated to growth condition. *Biochem. Biophys. Res. Commun.* 97: 347–353.

Bucher, N. L. R. and Glinos, A. D. 1950. The effect of age on regeneration of rat liver. *Cancer Res.* 10: 324–332.

Buetow, D. E. 1971. Cellular content and cellular proliferation changes in the tissues and organs of the aging mammal. *In,* I. L. Cameron, J. D. Thrasher (eds.), *Cellular and Molecular Renewal in the Mammalian Body,* pp. 87–106. New York: Academic Press.

Burnett, F. M. 1974. *Intrinsic Mutagenesis: A Genetic Approach to Ageing.* New York: John Wiley & Sons.

Cairns, J. 1981. The origin of human cancers. *Nature* 289: 353–357.

Cameron, I. L. and Thrasher, J. D. 1976. Cell renewal and cell loss in the tissues of aging mammals. *Interdiscip. Top. Gerontol.* 10: 108–129.

Casarett, G. W. 1964. Similarities and contrasts between radiation and time pathology. *Adv. Gerontol. Res.* 1: 109–163.

Chan, A. C. and Walker, I. G. 1977. Loss of DNA repair capacity during successive subcultures of primary rat fibroblasts. *J. Cell. Biol.* 74: 365–370.

Chan, A. C., Ng, S. K. C., and Walker, I. G. 1976. Reduced DNA repair during differentiation of a myogenic cell line. *J. Cell. Biol.* 70, 685–691.

Chandley, A. C. and Kofman-Alfaro, S. 1971. "Unscheduled'' DNA synthesis in human germ cells following UV irradiation. *Exp. Cell Res.* 69: 45-48.

Chen, T. R. and Ruddle, F. H. 1974. Chromosome changes revealed by the Q-band staining method during cell senescence of WI-38. *Proc. Soc. Exp. Biol. Med.* 147: 533-536.

Chetsanga, C. J., Boyd, V., Peterson, L., and Rushlow, K. 1975. Single-stranded regions in DNA of old mice. *Nature* 253: 130-131.

Chetsanga, C. J., Tuttle, M., and Jacoboni, A. 1976. Changes in structural integrity of heart DNA from aging mice. *Life Sciences* 18: 1405-1412.

Chetsanga, C. J., Tuttle, M., Jacoboni, A., and Johnson, C. 1977. Age-associated structural alterations in senescent mouse brain DNA. *Biochim. Biophys. Acta* 474: 180-187.

Chlebovsky, O., Praslicka, M., and Horak, J. 1966. Chromosome aberrations: increased incidence in bone marrow of continuously irradiated rats. *Science* 153: 195-196.

Clarkson, J. M. and Painter, R. B. 1974. Repair of x-ray damage in ageing WI-38 cells. *Mutat. Res.* 23: 107-112.

Cleaver, J. E. and Bootsma, D. 1975. Xeroderma pigmentosum: biochemical and genetic characteristics. *Annu. Rev. Genet.* 9: 19-38.

Collier, I. E., Popp, D. M., Lee, W. H., and Regan, J. D. 1982. DNA repair in a congeneic repair of mice with different longevities. *Mech. Age. Develop.* 19: 141-146.

Comings, D. E. and Vance, C. K. 1971. Thermal denaturation of DNA and chromatin of early and late passage human fibroblasts. *Gerontologia* 17: 116-121.

Conard, R. A., Lowrey, A., Eicher, M., Thompson, K., and Scoot, W. A. 1966. Aging studies in a Marshallese population exposed to radioactive fallout in 1954. *In*, P. J. Lindop and G. A. Sacher (eds.), *Radiation and Ageing*, pp. 345-360. London: Taylor and Frances.

Conklin, J. W., Upton, A. C., Christenberry, K. W., and McDonald, T. P. 1963. Comparative late somatic effects of some radiomimetic agents and x-rays. *Radiat. Res.* 19: 156-179.

Cooke, A. and Harris, W. J. 1981. Pyrimidine dimer excision in ageing human cells in tissue culture. *Radiat. Biol.* 39: 223-226.

Court Brown, W. M., Buckton, K. E., Jacobs, P. A. Tough, I. M., Kuenseberg, E. V., and Knox, J. D. E. 1966. Chromosome studies on adults. *Eugen. Lab. Mem.* 42: 1-14.

Courtois, Y. G. C. 1974. Chromatin modification of chick embryo cells during *in vitro* senescence. *Mech. Age. Develop.* 3: 51-63.

Cristofalo, V. J. 1976. Thymidine labelling index as a criterion of aging *in vitro. Gerontology* 22: 9-27.

Cristofalo, V. J. and Sharf, B. B. 1973. Cellular senescence and DNA synthesis: thymidine incorporation as a measure of population age in human diploid cells. *Exp. Cell Res.* 76: 419-427.

Crowley, C. and Curtis, H. J. 1963. The development of somatic mutations in mice with age. *Proc. Natl. Acad. Sci. U.S.A.* 49: 626-628.

Curtis, H. J. 1963. Biological mechanisms underlying the aging process. *Science* 141: 686-694.

Curtis, H. J., Leith, J., and Tilley, J. 1966. Chromosome aberrations in liver cells of dogs of different ages. *J. Gerontol.* 21: 268-270.

Curtis, H. J. and Tilley, J. 1971. The life-span of dividing mammalian cells *in vivo. J. Geront.* 26: 1-7.

Curtis, H. J. and Miller, K. 1971. Chromosome aberrations in liver cells of guinea pigs. *J. Gerontol* 26: 292-293.

Cutler, R. G. 1976a. Nature of aging and life maintenance processes. *Interdiscip. Top. Gerontol.* 9: 83-133.

Cutler, R. G. 1976b. Alteration of chromatin as a function of age in *Mus* and *Peromyscus* rodent species. Abstract, 29th Annual Meeting Gerontological Society, New York.

Cutler, R. G. 1976c. Cross-linking hypothesis of aging; DNA adducts in chromatin as a primary aging process. *In*, K. C. Smith (ed.), *Aging, Carcinogenesis and Radiation Biology. The Role of Nucleic Acid Addition Reactions*, pp. 443-492. New York: Plenum Press.

D'Ambrosio, S. M., Slazinski, L., Whetstone, J. W., and Lowney, E. 1981. Photorepair of pyrimidine dimers in human skin *in vivo. Photochem. Photobiol.* 34: 461-464.

Danes, S. B. 1971. Progeria: a cell culture study in aging. *J. Clin. Invest.* 50: 2000-2003.

Darzynkiewicz, Z. 1971. Radiation induced DNA synthesis in normal and stimulated human lymphocytes. *Exp. Cell. Res.* 69: 356-360.

Dean, R. G. and Cutler, R. G. 1978. Absence of significant age-dependent increase of single-stranded DNA extracted from mouse liver nuclei. *Exp. Geront.* 13: 287-292.

DeBusk, F. L. 1972. The Hutchinson-Gilford progeria syndrome. *J. Pediat.* 80: 697-724.

Deknudt, G. and Leonard, A. 1977. Aging and radiosensitivity of human somatic chromosomes. *Exp. Geront.* 12: 237-240.

Dell'Orco, R. T. and Anderson, L. E. 1981. Unscheduled DNA synthesis in human diploid cells of different donor ages. *Cell Biol.—Intern. Rep.* 5: 359-364.

Dell'Orco, R. T. and Whittle, W. L. 1978. Unscheduled DNA synthesis in confluent and mitotically arrested populations of aging human diploid fibroblasts. *Mech. Age. Develop.* 8: 269-279.

Dell'Orco, R. T. and Whittle, W. L. 1981. Evidence for an increased level on DNA damage in high doubling level human diploid cells in culture. *Mech. Age. Develop.* 15: 141-152.

de Maertelaer, V., Authelet, M., and Neve, P. 1981. Effect of aging on the proliferative activity of renewing cell populations after a specific stimulus. *IRCS Medical Science* 9: 548-549.

Ellis, W. G., McCulloch, J. R., and Corley, C. L. 1974.

Presenile dementia in Down's syndrome. *Neurology, Minneap.* 24: 101–106.

Epstein, C. J., Martin, G. M., Schultz, A. L. and Motulsky, A. 1966. Werner's syndrome. *Medicine, Baltimore* 45: 177–221.

Epstein, J., Williams, J. R., and Little, J. B. 1973. Deficient DNA repair in human progeriod cells. *Proc. Natl. Acad. Sci. U.S.A.* 70: 977–981.

Epstein, J., Williams, J. R., and Little, J. B. 1974. Role of DNA repair in progeric and normal human fibroblasts. *Biochem. Biophys. Res. Commun.* 59: 850–857.

Fialkow, P. J. 1970. Thyroid autoimmunity and Down's syndrome. *Ann. N.Y. Acad. Sci.* 71: 500–511.

Fleischmajer, R. and Nedwich, A. 1973. Werner's syndrome. *Amer. J. Med.* 54: 111–118.

Forrsman, H. and Akesson, H. O. 1965. Mortality in patients with Down's syndrome. *J. Ment. Defic. Res.* 9: 146–149.

Fort, F. L. and Cerutti, P. A. 1981. Altered DNA repair in fibroblasts from aged rats. *Gerontol.* 27: 306–312.

Francis, A. A., Blevins, R. D., Carrier, W. L., Smith, D. P., and Regan, J. D. 1979. Inhibition of DNA repair in ultraviolet-irradiated human cells by hydroxyurea. *Biochim. Biophys. Acta* 563: 385–392.

Francis, A. A., Lee, W. H., and Regan, J. D. 1981. The relationship of DNA excision repair of ultraviolet induced lesions to the maximum life span of mammals. *Mech. Age Develop.* 16: 181–189.

Franks, L. M. 1974. Aging in differentiated cells. *Gerontologia* 20: 51–62.

Friedberg, E. C. and Hanawalt, P. C. (eds.) 1981. *DNA Repair: A Laboratory Manual of Research Procedures.* New York: Marcel Dekker.

Fujiwara, Y., Higashikawa, T., and Tatsumi, M. 1977. A retarded rate of DNA replication and normal level of DNA repair in Werner's syndrome fibroblasts in culture. *J. Cell. Physiol.* 92: 365–374.

Gaubatz, J. W. and Cutler, R. G. 1978. Age-related differences in the number of ribosomal RNA genes of mouse tissue. *Gerontology* 24: 179–207.

Gensler, H. L. 1981. The effect of hamster age on U.V.-induced unscheduled DNA synthesis in freshly isolated lung and kidney cells. *Exp. Geront.* 16: 59–68.

Gensler, H. L. and Bernstein, H. 1981. DNA damage as the primary cause of aging. *Quart. Rev. Biol.* 56: 279–303.

Gilchrest, B. A. 1980. Prior chronic sun exposure decreases the lifespan of human skin fibroblasts in vitro. *J. Gerontol.* 35: 537–541.

Goldstein, S. 1969. Lifespan of cultured cells in progeria. *Lancet*, 1, 424.

Goldstein, S. 1971. The role of DNA repair in aging of cultured fibroblasts from xeroderma pigmentosum and normals. *Proc. Soc. Exp. Biol. Med.* 137: 730–734.

Goldstein, S. 1978. Human genetic disorders that feature premature onset and accelerated progression of biological aging. *In,* E. L. Schneider (ed.), *The Genetics of Aging*, pp. 171–224. New York, Plenum Press.

Goldstein, S. and Moerman, E. J. 1976. Defective proteins in normal and abnormal human fibroblasts during ageing *in vitro. Interdiscip. Top. Gerontol.* 10: 24–43.

Goldstein, S. and Singal, D. P. 1974. Alteration of fibroblast gene products *in vitro* from a subject with Werner's syndrome. *Nature* 251: 719–721.

Goodman, R. M., Fechheimer, N. S., Miller, F., Miller, R., and Zartman, D. 1969. Chromosome alterations in three age groups of human females. *Amer. J. Med. Sci.* 258: 26–34.

Grove, G. L. and Cristofalo, V. J. 1977. Characterization of the cell cycle of cultured human diploid cells: effects of aging and hydrocortisone. *J. Cell. Physiol.* 90: 415–422.

Grove, G. L. and Mitchell, R. B. 1974. DNA microdensitometry as a measure of cycling-non-cycling activity in aged human diploid cells in culture. *Mech. Age. Dev.* 3: 235–240.

Gupta, R. S. 1980. Senescence of cultured human diploid fibroblasts. Are mutations responsible? *J. Cell. Physiol.* 103: 209–216.

Hahn, G. M., King, D., and Yang, S. J. 1971. Quantitative changes in unscheduled DNA synthesis in rat muscle cells after differentiation. *Nature New Biol.* 230: 242–244.

Hall, J. D., Almy, R. E., and Scherer, K. L. 1982. DNA repair in cultured human fibroblasts does not decline with donor age. *Exp. Cell Res.* 139: 351–359.

Hall, K. Y., Bergman, K., and Walford, R. L. 1981. DNA repair, H–2, and aging in NZB and CBA mice. *Tissue Antigens* 16: 104–110.

Hamilton, E. and Franks, L. M. 1980. Cell proliferation and ageing in mouse colon. II. Late effects of repeated x-irradiation in young and old mice. *Europ. J. Cancer* 16: 663–669.

Hanawalt, P. C., Cooper, P. K., Ganesan, A. K., and Smith, C. A. 1979. DNA repair in bacteria and mammalian cells. *Ann. Rev. Biochem.* 48: 783–836.

Harm, W. 1969. Biological determination of the germicidal activity of sunlight. *Radiat. Res.* 40: 63–69.

Hart, R. and Setlow, R. B. 1974. Correlation between deoxyribonucleic acid excision-repair and life-span in a number of mammalian species. *Proc. Natl. Acad. Sci. U.S.A.* 71: 2169–2173.

Hart, R. W., D'Ambrosio, S. M., Ng, K. J., and Modak, S. P. 1979a. Longevity, stability and DNA repair. *Mech. Age. Develop.* 9: 203–223.

Hart, R. W. and Daniel, F. B. 1980. Genetic stability *in vitro* and *in vivo. Adv. Pathobiol.* 7: 123–141.

Hart, R. W., Sacher, G. A., and Hoskins, T. L. 1979b. DNA repair in a short- and a long-lived rodent species. *J. Gerontol.* 34: 808–817.

Hart, R. W. and Setlow, R. B. 1976. DNA repair in late-passage human cells. *Mech. Age. Develop.* 5: 67–77.

Hart, R. W. and Trosko, J. E. 1976. DNA repair processes in mammals. *Interdiscip. Top. Gerontol.* 9: 134–167.

Hayflick, L. 1965. The limited *in vitro* lifespan of human diploid cell strains. *Exp. Cell. Res.* 37: 614–635.

Hayflick, L. 1975. Current theories of biological ageing. *Fed. Proc. Fed. Am. Soc. Exp. Biol.* 34: 9–13.

Hennis, H. L., III, Braid, H. L., and Vincent, R. A., Jr. 1981. Unscheduled DNA synthesis in cells of different shape in fibroblast cultures from donors of various ages. *Mech. Age. Develop.* 16: 355–361.

Higashikawa, T. and Fujiwara, Y. 1978. Normal level of unscheduled DNA synthesis in Werner's syndrome fibroblasts in culture. *Exp. Cell Res.* 113: 438–441.

Higurashi, M. and Conen, P. E. 1971. Comparison of chromosomal behavior in cultured lymphocytes and fibroblasts from patients with chromosomal disorders and controls. *Cytogenetics* 10, 273–285.

Higurashi, M. and Conen, P. E. 1972. *In vitro* chromosomal radiosensitivity in patients and in carriers with abnormal non-Down's syndrome karyotypes. *Pediat. Res.* 6: 514–520.

Higurashi, M., Tamura, T., and Nakatake, T. 1973. Cytogenetic observations in cultured lymphocytes from patients with Down's syndrome and measles. *Pediat. Res.* 7: 582–587.

Hill, B. T. 1976. Influence of age on chromatin transcription in murine tissues using an heterologous and an homologous RNA polymerase. *Gerontology* 22: 111–123.

Hill, B. T., Whelan, R. D. H., and Whatley, S. 1978. Evidence that transcription changes in ageing cultures are terminal events occurring after the expression of a reduced replicative potential. *Mech. Age. Develop.* 8: 85–95.

Hoel, D. G. and Walburg, H. E. 1972. Statistical analysis of survival experiments. *J. Natl. Cancer Inst.* 49: 361.

Holliday, R., Porterfield, J. S., and Gibbs, D. D. 1974. Werner's syndrome: premature aging in vivo and in vitro. *Nature* 248: 762–763.

Holliday, R. and Tarrant, G. M. 1972. Altered enzymes in aging human fibroblasts. *Nature* 238: 26–30.

Hollingworth, D. R., Hollingworth, J. W., Bogitch, S., and Keehn, R. J. 1969. Neuromuscular tests of aging Hiroshima subjects. *J. Gerontol.* 24: 276–291.

Icard, C., Beaupain, R., Diatloff, C., and Macieira-Coelho, A. 1979. Effects of low dose rate irradiation on the division potential of cells *in vitro*. VI. Changes in DNA and in radiosensitivity during aging of human fibroblasts. *Mech. Age. Develop.* 11: 269–278.

Ishikawa, T., Takayama, S., and Kitagawa, T. 1978. DNA repair synthesis in rat retinal ganglion cells treated with chemical carcinogens or ultraviolet light *in vitro* with special reference to aging and repair level. *J. Natl. Cancer Inst.* 61: 1101–1105.

Jacobs, P. A. and Court Brown, W. M. 1966. Age and chromosomes. *Nature* 212: 823–824.

Jarvik, L. F. and Kato, T. 1970. Chromosome examinations in aged twins. *Amer. J. Hum. Genet.* 22: 562–573.

Jervis, G. A. 1970. Premature senility in Down's syndrome. *Ann. N.Y. Acad. Sci* 171: 559–561.

Kaback, M. M. and Bernstein, L. H. 1970. Metabolic studies of trisomic cells growing *in vitro*. *Ann. N.Y. Acad. Sci.* 171: 526–536.

Kadanka, Z. K., Sparkes, J. D., and Macmorine, H. G. 1973. A study of the cytogenetics of the human cell strain WI-38. *In Vitro* 8: 353–361.

Kaina, B., Waller, H., Waller, M., and Rieger, R. 1977. The action of N-methyl-N-nitrosourea on non-established human cell lines *in vitro*. I. Cell cycle inhibition and aberration induction in diploid and Down's fibroblasts. *Mutat. Res.* 43: 387–400.

Kanagalingam, K. and Balis, M. E. 1975. *In vivo* repair of rat intestinal DNA damage by alkylating agents. *Cancer* 36: 2364–2372.

Kantor, G. J., Mulkie, J. R., and Hull, D. R. 1978. A study of the effect of ultraviolet light on the division potential of human diploid fibroblasts. *Exp. Cell. Res.* 113: 283–294.

Kapp, L. N. and Klevecz, R. R. 1976. The cell cycle of low passage and high passage human diploid fibroblasts. *Exp. Cell. Res.* 101: 154–158.

Karran, P., Moscona, A. and Strauss, B. 1977. Developmental decline in DNA repair in neural retina cells of chick embryos. *J. Cell. Biol.* 74: 274–286.

Karran, P. and Ormerod, M. G. 1973. Is the ability to repair damages to DNA related to the proliferative capacity of a cell? The rejoining of x-ray-produced strand breaks. *Biochim. Biophys. Acta* 229: 54–64.

Kato, H., Harada, M., Tsuchiya, K., and Moriwaki, K. 1980. Absence of correlation between DNA repair in ultraviolet irradiated mammalian cells and life span of the donor species. *Jap. J. Genet.* 55: 99–108.

Kihlman, B. A. 1966. *Actions of Chemicals on Dividing Cells.* Englewood Cliffs, N. J.: Prentice Hall.

Kishi, K. 1977. Cell cycle analysis and properties of two sub-populations in PHA responding lymphocytes: a comparison of 21-trisomic and normal cells. *Jap. J. Human Genet.* 22: 17–26.

Kohn, R. R. 1966. A possible final common pathway for natural ageing and radiation-induced life-shortening. *In*, P. J. Lindop and G. A. Sacher (eds.), *Radiation and Ageing*, pp. 373–392. London: Taylor and Frances.

Kohn, R. R. 1975. Intrinsic aging of postmitotic cells. *In, International Symposium on Aging Gametes, Seattle*, pp. 1–18. Basel: Karger.

Koval, T. M. and Kaufman, S. J. 1981. Maintenance of DNA repair capacity in differentiating rat muscle cells *in vitro*. *Photochem. Photobiol.* 33: 403–405.

Kram, D. and Schneider, E. L. 1978. Parental-age effects: increased frequencies of genetically abnormal offspring. *In*, E. L. Schneider (ed.), *The Genetics of Aging*, pp. 225–260. New York: Plenum Press.

Krystal, G., Morris, G. M., Lipman, J. M., and Sokoloff, L. 1983. DNA repair in articular chondrocytes. I. Unscheduled DNA synthesis following ultraviolet irradiation in monolayer culture. *Mech. Age. Develop.* 21: 83–96.

Kukharenko, V. I., Kuliev, A. M., Brinberg, K. N., and Terskikh, V. V. 1974. Cell cycles in human diploid and aneuploid strains. *Humangenetik,* 24: 285–296.

Kurtz, D. I., Russell, A. P., and Sinex, F. M. 1974. Multiple peaks in the derivative melting curve of chromatin from animals of varying age. *Mech. Age. Develop.* 3: 37–49.

Kurtz, D. I. and Sinex, F. M. 1967. Age related differences in the association of brain DNA and nuclear protein. *Biochim. Biophys. Acta* 145: 840–842.

Kutlaca, R., Seshadri, R., and Mosley, A. A. 1982. Effect of age on sensitivity of human lymphocytes to radiation. A brief note. *Mech. Age. Develop.* 19: 97–101.

Lambert, B., Hansson, K., Bui, T. H., Funes-Cravioto, F., Lindsten, J., Holmberg, M., and Straumanis, R. 1976. DNA repair and frequency of x-ray and UV-light induced chromosome aberrations in leukocytes from patients with Down's syndrome. *Ann. Hum. Genet. Lond.* 39: 293–303.

Lambert, B., Ringborg, U., and Skoog, L. 1979. Age-related decrease of ultraviolet light-induced DNA repair synthesis in human peripheral leukocytes. *Cancer Res.* 39: 2792–2795.

Lampidis, T. J. and Little, J. B. 1971. Unscheduled DNA synthesis in fibroblasts and pulsating myocardial cells isolated from newborn rat heart. *Radiat. Res.* 67: 621 (Abstract).

Lampidis, T. J. and Shaiberger, G. E. 1975. Age-related loss of DNA repair synthesis in isolated rat myocardial cells. *Expt. Cell. Res.* 96: 412–416.

Lesher, S., Fry, R., and Kohn, H. 1961. Aging and the generation time of the mouse duodenal epithelial cell. *Exp. Cell. Res.* 24: 334–343.

Lesher, S. and Sacher, G. 1968. Effects of age on cell proliferation in mouse duodenal crypts. *Exp. Gerontol.* 3: 211–217.

Lett, J. T., Keng, P. C., and Sun, C. 1978. Rejoining of DNA strand breaks in nondividing cells irradiated *in situ. In,* P. C. Hanawalt, E. C. Friedberg, C. F. Fox (eds.), *DNA Repair Mechanisms,* pp. 481–484. New York: Academic Press.

Ley, R. D., Sedita, B. A., and Grube, D. D. 1978. Absence of photoreactivation of pyrimidine dimers in the epidermis of hairless mice following exposure to ultraviolet light. *Photochem. Photobiol.* 27: 483–485.

Ley, R. D., Sedita, B. A., Grube, D. D., and Fry, R. J. M. 1977. Induction and persistence of pyrimidine dimers in the epidermal DNA of two strains of hairless mice. *Cancer Res.* 37: 3243–3248.

Lezana, E. A., Bianchi, N. O., Bianchi, M. S., and Zabala-Suarez, J. E. 1977. Sister chromatid exchanges in Down syndromes and normal human beings. *Mutat. Res.* 45: 85–90.

Lezhava, T. A., Prokofjeva, V. V., and Mikhelson, V. M. 1979. Reduction in UV-induced unscheduled DNA synthesis in human lymphocytes at an extreme age. *Tsitologica* 11: 1360–1363.

Lima, L., Malaise, E., and Macieira-Coelho, A. 1972. Aging *in vitro:* effect of low dose-rate irradiation on the division potential of chick embryonic fibroblasts. *Exp. Cell. Res.* 73: 345–350.

Lindop, P. and Rotblat, J. 1961a. Long-term effects of a single whole-body exposure of mice to ionizing radiations. I. Life-shortening. *Proc. R. Soc. London Ser. B* 154: 332–349.

Lindop, P. and Rotblat, J. 1961b. Long-term effects of a single whole-body exposure of mice to ionizing radiations. II. Cause of death. *Proc. R. Soc. London Ser. B* 154: 350–368.

Liniecki, J., Bajerska, A., and Andryszek, C. 1971. Chromosomal aberrations in human lymphocytes irradiated *in vitro* from donors (males-females) of varying age. *Int. J. Radiat. Biol.* 19: 349–360.

Lipetz, J. and Cristofalo, V. J. 1972. Ultrastructure changes accompanying the aging of human diploid cells in culture. *J. Ultrastruct Res.* 39: 43–56.

Little, J. B. 1976. Relationship between DNA repair capacity and cellular aging. *Gerontology* 22: 28–55.

Little, J. B., Epstein, J., and Williams, J. R. 1975. Repair of DNA strand breaks in progeric fibroblasts and aging human diploid cells. *In,* P. C. Hanawalt and R. R. Setlow (eds.), *Molecular Mechanisms for Repair of DNA,* pp. 793–800. New York: Plenum Press.

Liu, S. C. C., Parsons, C. S., and Hanawalt, P. C. 1982. DNA repair response in human epidermal keratinocytes from donors of different ages. *J. Invest. Dermatol.* 79: 330–335.

Macieira-Coelho, A. 1973. Aging and cell division. *Front. Matrix Biol.* 1: 46–77.

Macieira-Coelho, A. 1977. Kinetics of the proliferation of human fibroblasts during their lifespan *in vitro. Mech. Age. Dev.* 6: 341–343.

Macieira-Coelho, A., Diatloff, C., Billard, M., Fertil, B., Malaise, E., and Fries, D. 1978. Effect of low dose rate irradiation on the division potential of cells *in vitro.* IV. Embryonic and adult human lung fibroblast-like cells. *J. Cell. Physiol.* 95: 235–238.

Macieira-Coelho, A., Diatloff, C., Billardon, C., Bourgeois, C. A., and Malaise, E. 1977. Effect of low dose rate ionizing radiation on the division potential of cells in vitro. *Exp. Cell Res.* 104: 215–221.

Macieira-Coelho, A., Diatloff, C., and Malaise, E. 1976. Doubling potential of fibroblasts from different species after ionizing radiation. *Nature* 261: 586–588.

Macieira-Coelho, A., Ponten, J., and Philipson, L. 1966. The division cycle and RNA-synthesis in diploid human cells at different passage levels *in vitro. Exp. Cell Res.* 42: 673–684.

Macieira-Coelho, A. and Taboury, F. 1982. A re-evaluation of the changes in proliferation in human fibroblasts during ageing *in vitro. Cell Tissue Kinet.* 15: 213–224.

Martin, G. M. 1977. Genetic syndromes in man with

potential relevance to the pathobiology of aging. *In,* D. Bergsma and D. E. Harrison (eds.), *Genetic Effects on Aging, Birth Defects, Orig. Artic. Ser.* New York: The National Foundation March of Dimes.

Martin, G. M., Sprague, C. A., and Epstein, C. J. 1970. Replicative life-span of cultivated human cells: effects of donor's age, tissue, and genotype. *Lab. Invest.* 23: 86–92.

Massie, H. R., Baird, M. B., Nicolosi, R. J., and Samis, H. V. 1972. Changes in the structure of rat liver DNA in relation to age. *Arch. Biochem. Biophys.* 153: 736–741.

Matsumura, T., Pfendt, E. A., and Hayflick, L. 1979. DNA synthesis in the human diploid cell strain WI-38 during *in vitro* aging: an autoradiography study. *J. Geront.* 34: 323–327.

Mattern, M. R. and Cerutti, P. A. 1975. Age-dependent excision repair of damaged thymine from γ-irradiated DNA by isolated nuclei from human fibroblasts. *Nature* 254: 450–452.

McCombe, P., Lavin, M., and Kidson, C. 1976. Control of DNA repair linked to neuroblastoma differentiation. *Int. J. Radiat. Biol.* 29: 523–531.

McFee, A. F., Banner, M. W., and Sherill, M. N. 1970. Influence of animal age on radiation-induced chromosome aberrations in swine leukocytes. *Radiat. Res.* 41: 425–435.

McKusick, V. A. 1975. *Mendelian Inheritance in Man—Catalogs of Autosomal Dominant, Autosomal Recessive and X-linked Phenotypes.* Baltimore: Johns Hopkins University Press.

Meek, R. L., Rebeiro, T., and Daniel, C. W. 1980. Patterns of unscheduled DNA synthesis in mouse embryo cells associated with *in vitro* aging and with spontaneous transformation to a continuous cell line. *Exp. Cell. Res.* 129: 265–271.

Miller, R. C., Nichols, W. W., Pottash, J., and Aronson, M. M. 1977. *In vitro* aging. Cytogenetic comparison of diploid human fibroblasts and epithelial cell lines. *Exp. Cell Res.* 110: 63–74.

Miller, R. W. 1970. Neoplasia and Down's syndrome. *Ann. N.Y. Acad. Sci.* 171: 637–644.

Modak, S. P. and Price, G. B. 1971. Exogenous DNA polymerase-catalyzed incorporation of deoxyribonucleotide monophosphates in nuclei of fixed mousebrain cells. *Exp. Cell Res.* 65: 289–296.

Montesano, R., Bresil, H., Likhachev, A., vonBahr, C., Roberfroid, M., and Pegg, A. E. 1982. Removal from DNA of O^6-methylguanine (O^6-MeG) by human liver fractions. *Proc. Amer. Assoc. Cancer Res.* 23: 11.

Moore, C. J. and Schwartz, A. G. 1978. Inverse correlation between species life span and capacity of cultured fibroblasts to convert benzo[a]pyrene to water-soluble metabolites. *Exp. Cell. Res.* 116: 359–364.

Moore, R. C. 1971. Changes in the DNA synthetic period during the phase of rapid growth in cultured diploid fibroblastic cells. *Cell Tissue Kinet.* 4: 491–500.

Moore, S. P. and Coohill, T. P. 1979. An effect of cell-culture passage on ultraviolet-enhanced viral reactivation by mammalian cells. *Mutat. Res.* 62: 417–423.

Nienhaus, A. J., Dejong, B., and Ten Kate, L. P. 1971. Fibroblast culture in Werner's syndrome. *Humangenetik* 13: 244–246.

Norwood, T. H. 1978. Somatic cell genetics in the analysis of *in vitro* senescence. *In,* E. L. Schneider (ed.), *The Genetics of Aging.* New York: Plenum Press.

O'Brien, R. L., Poon, P., Kline, E., and Parker, J. W. 1971. Susceptibility of chromosomes from patients with Down's syndrome to 7,12-dimethylbenz[a]-anthracene-induced aberrations *in vitro. Int. J. Cancer* 8: 202–210.

O'Meara, A. R. and Herrmann, R. L. 1972. A modified mouse liver chromatin preparation displaying age-related differences in salt dissociation and template ability. *Biochim. Biophys. Acta* 269: 419–427.

Ono, T. and Okada, S. 1978. Does the capacity to rejoin radiation-induced DNA breaks decline in senescent mice? *Int. J. Radiat. Biol.* 33: 403–407.

Ono, T., Okada, S., and Sugahara, T. 1976. Comparative studies of DNA size in various tissues of mice during the aging process. *Exp. Gerontol.* 11: 127–132.

Ove, P. and Coetzee, M. L. 1978. A difference in bleomycin-induced DNA synthesis between liver nuclei from mature and old rats. *Mech. Age Develop.* 8: 363–375.

Paffenholz, V. 1978. Correlation between DNA repair of embryonic fibroblasts and different life span of 3 inbred mouse strains. *Mech. Age. Develop.* 7: 131–150.

Painter, R. B., Clarkson, J. M., and Young, B. R. 1973. Ultraviolet-induced repair replication in aging diploid human cells. *Radiat. Res.* 56: 560–564.

Paterson, M. C., Lohman, P. H. M., and deWeerd-Kastelein, E. A. 1974. Photoreactivation and excision repair of ultraviolet radiation-injured DNA in primary embryonic chick cells. *Biophys. J.* 14: 454–466.

Paterson, M. C. and Smith, P. J. 1979. Ataxia telangiectasia: an inherited disorder involving hypersensitivity to ionizing radiation and related DNA-damaging chemicals. *Ann. Rev. Genet.* 13: 291–318.

Paton, G. R., Silver, M. F., and Allison, A. C. 1974. Comparison of cell cycle time in normal and trisomic cells. *Humangenetik* 23: 173–182.

Peleg, L., Raz, E., and Ben-Ishai, R. 1976. Changing capacity for DNA excision repair in mouse embryonic cells *in vitro. Expt. Cell. Res.* 104: 301–307.

Pero, R. W., Bryngelsson, C., Mitelman, F., Kornfalt, R., Thulin, J., and Norden, A. 1978. Interindividual variation in the responses of cultured human lymphocytes to exposure from DNA damaging chemical agents. *Mutat. Res.* 53: 327–341.

Pero, R. W. and Ostlund, C. 1980. Direct comparison in human resting lymphocytes of the inter-individual variations in unscheduled DNA synthesis induced by

N-acetoxy-2-acetylaminofluorene and ultraviolet radiation. *Mutat. Res.* 73: 349–361.

Petes, T. D., Farber, R. A., Tarrant, G. M., and Holliday, R. 1974. Altered rate of DNA replication in ageing human fibroblast cultures. *Nature* 251: 434–436.

Phillips, T. L. and Leong, G. F. 1967. Kidney cell proliferation after unilateral nephrectomy as related to age. *Cancer Res.* 27: 286.

Phytila, M. J. and Sherman, F. G. 1968. Age-associated studies on thermal stability and template effectiveness of DNA and nucleoproteins from beef thymus. *Biochem. Biophys. Res. Commun.* 31: 340–344.

Piantanelli, L., Brogli, R., Bevilacqua, P., and Fabris, N. 1978. Age-dependence of isoproterenol-induced DNA synthesis in submandibular glands of BALB/c mice. *Mech. Age Develop.* 7: 163–169.

Pisciotta, A. V., Westring, D. W., Deprey, C., and Walsh, B. 1967. Mitogenic effect of phytohemagglutinin at different ages. *Nature* 215: 193–194.

Preston, R. J. 1981. X-ray-induced chromsome aberrations in Down lymphocytes: an explanation of their increased sensitivity. *Environ. Mutagen.* 3: 85–89.

Price, G. B., Modak, S. P., and Makinodan, T. 1971. Age-associated changes in the DNA of mouse tissue. *Science* 171: 917–920.

Prodi, G., Arfellini, G., and Grilli, S. 1977. DNA repair in newborns. *Proc. Perugia Quadren. Int. Conf. Cancer,* 803–810.

Rainbow, A. J. and Howes, M. 1977a. Decreased repair of gamma ray damaged DNA in progeria. *Biochem. Biophys. Res. Commun.* 74: 714–719.

Regan, J. D., Carrier, W. L., Samet, C., and Olla, B. L. 1982a. Photoreactivation in two closely related marine fishes having different longevities. *Mech. Age. Develop.* 18: 59–66.

Regan, J. D., Francis, A. A., and Carrier, W. L. 1982b. Capacity of mouse embryonic cells to perform excision repair of ultraviolet damage. *Amer. Soc. Photobiol. Abstracts,* 167.

Regan, J. D. and Setlow, R. B. 1974. DNA repair in progeroid cells. *Biochem. Biophys. Res. Commun.* 59: 858–864.

Reis, R. J. S. and Goldstein, S. 1980. Loss of reiterated DNA sequences during serial passage of human diploid fibroblasts. *Cell* 21: 739–749.

Rigas, D. A., Elsasser, P., and Hecht, F. 1970. Impaired *in vitro* response of circulating lymphocytes to phytohemagglutinin in Down's syndrome: dose-and-time response curves and relation to cellular immunity. *Int. Archs. Allergy Appl. Immun.* 39: 587–608.

Robbins, E., Levine, E. M., and Eagle, H. 1970. Morphological changes accompanying senescence of cultured human diploid cells. *J. Exp. Med.* 131: 1211–1222.

Robbins, J. H. 1978. Significance of repair of human DNA: evidence from studies of xeroderma pigmentosum. *J. Natl. Cancer Inst.* 61: 645–656.

Robbins, J. H., Kraemer, K. H., Lutzner, M. D., Fes-

toff, B. W., and Coon, H. G. 1974. Xeroderma pigmentosum: an inherited disease with sun sensitivity, multiple cutaneous neoplasms, and with abnormal DNA repair. *Ann. Intern. Med.* 80: 221–248.

Russell, A. P., Dowling, L. E., and Herrmann, R. L. 1970. Age-related differences in mouse liver DNA melting and hydroxylapatite fractionation. *Gerontologia* 16: 159–171.

Ryan, J. M. and Cristofalo, V. J. 1975. Chromatin template activity during ageing in WI38 cells. *Exptl. Cell. Res.* 90: 456–458.

Saksela, E. and Moorhead, P. S. 1963. Aneuploidy in the degenerative phase of serial cultivation of human cell strains. *Proc. Natl. Acad. Sci. U.S.A.* 50: 390–395.

Salser, J. S. and Balis, M. E. 1972. Alterations in deoxyribonucleic acid-bound amino acids with age and sex. *J. Gerontol.* 27: 1–9.

Samis, H. V., Jr. 1966. A concept of biological ageing: the role of compensatory processes. *J. Theor. Biol.* 13: 236.

Samis, H. V., Poccia, D. L., and Wulff, V. J. 1968. The effect of salt extraction and heat-denaturation on the behavior of rat liver chromatin. *Biochim. Biophys. Acta* 166: 410–418.

Samis, H. V., Jr. and Wulff, V. J. 1969. The template activity of rat liver chromatin. *Exp. Geront.* 4: 111–117.

Sandberg, A. A., Cohen, M. M., Rimon, A. A., and Levin, M. L. 1967. Aneuploidy and age in a population survey. *Amer. J. Hum. Genet.* 19: 633.

Sasaki, M. S., Tonomura, A., and Matsubara, S. 1970. Chromosomal constitution and its bearing on the chromosomal radiosensitivity in man. *Mutat. Res.* 10: 617–633.

Sax, H. J. and Passano, K. N. 1961. Spontaneous chromosome aberrations in human tissue cells. *Amer. Nat.* 95: 97–109.

Schneider, E. L. and Epstein, C. J. 1972. Replication rate and lifespan of cultured fibroblasts in Down's syndrome. *Proc. Soc. Exp. Biol. Med.* 141: 1092–1094.

Schneider, E. L. and Gilman, B. 1979. Sister chromatid exchanges and aging: III. The effect of donor age on mutagen induced sister chromatid exchanges in human diploid fibroblasts. *Hum. Genet.* 46: 57–63.

Schneider, E. L. and Mitsui, Y. 1976. The relationship between *in vitro* cellular aging and *in vivo* human age. *Proc. Natl. Acad. Sci. U.S.A.* 73: 3584–3588.

Schwartz, A. G. and Moore, C. J. 1977. Inverse correlation between species life span and capacity of cultured fibroblasts to bind 7,12-dimethylbenz[a] anthracene to DNA. *Exp. Cell Res.* 109: 448–450.

Scudiero, D., Norin, A., Karran, P., and Strauss, B. 1976. DNA excision-repair deficiency of human peripheral blood lymphocytes treated with chemical carcinogens. *Cancer Res.* 36: 1397–1403.

Seeberg, E. and Kleppe, K. (eds.) 1981. *Chromosome Damage and Repair.* New York: Plenum Press.

Segal, D. J. and McCoy, E. E. 1974. Studies on Down's

syndrome in tissue culture: growth rate and protein contents of fibroblast cultures. *J. Cell. Comp. Physiol.* 83: 95–90.

Serra, A., Arpain, E., and Bova, R. 1978. Kinetics of 21-trisomic lymphocytes. *Hum. Genet.* 41: 157–167.

Setlow, R. B. 1978. Repair-deficient human disorders and cancer. *Nature* 271: 713–717.

Setlow, R. B. 1982. DNA repair, aging, and cancer. *Natl. Cancer Inst. Monogr.* 60: 249–255.

Setlow, R. B., Lipman, J. M., and Sokoloff, L. 1983. DNA repair by articular chondrocytes. II. Direct measurements of repair of ultraviolet and x-ray damage in monolayer cultures. *Mech. Age. Develop.* (in 21: 97–103.

Setlow, R. B., Regan, J. D., German, J., and Carrier, W. L. 1969. Evidence that xeroderma pigmentosum cells do not perform the first step in the repair of ultraviolet damage to their DNA. *Proc. Natl. Acad. Sci. U.S.A.* 64: 1035–1041.

Setlow, R. B. and Setlow, J. K. 1972. Effects of radiation on polynucleotides. *Ann. Rev. Biophys. Bioengineer.* 1: 293–346.

Shapiro, R. 1981. Damage to DNA caused by hydrolysis. *In,* E. Seeberg and K. Kleppe (eds.), *Chromosome Damage and Repair,* pp. 3–18. New York: Plenum Press.

Shirey, T. L. and Sobel, H. 1972. Compositional and transcriptional properties of chromatins isolated from cardiac muscles of young-mature and old dogs. *Exp. Gerontol.* 7: 15–29.

Singal, D. P. and Goldstein, S. 1973. Absence of detectable HL-A antigens on cultured fibroblasts in progeria. *J. Clin. Invest.* 52: 2259–2263.

Sisken, J. E. and Bonner, S. V. 1979. On the duration of mitotic stages in senescing human fibroblasts in culture. *Mech. Age. Dev.* 11: 191–197.

Smith, C. A. and Hanawalt, P. C. 1976. Repair replication in cultured normal and transformed human fibroblasts. *Biochim. Biophys. Acta* 447: 121–132.

Smith, K. C. 1976. Chemical adducts to deoxyribonucleic acid: their importance to the genetic alteration theory of aging. *Interdiscip. Top. Gerontol.* 9: 16–24.

Spence, A. M. and Herman, M. M. 1973. Critical reexamination of the premature aging concept in progeria: a light and electron microscopic study. *Mech. Aging Dev.* 2: 211–227.

Srivastava, B. I. S. 1973. Changes in enzyme activity during cultivation of human cells *in vitro. Exp. Cell Res.* 80: 305–312.

Stecker, E. and Gardner, H. A. 1970. Werner's syndrome. *Lancet* ii: 1317.

Stein, G. S. and Stein, J. L. 1976. *In vitro* studies of transcription as a function of age in mammalian cells. *Interdiscipl. Topics Geront.* 10: 83–99.

Stevenson, K. G. and Curtis, H. J. 1961. Chromosome aberrations in irradiated and nitrogen mustard treated mice. *Radiat. Res.* 15: 774–784.

Stockdale, F. E. 1971. DNA synthesis in differentiating

skeletal muscle cells: initiation by ultraviolet light. *Science* 171: 1145–1147.

Stockdale, F. E. and O'Neill, M. D. 1972. Repair DNA synthesis in differentiated embryonic muscle cells. *J. Cell Biol.* 52: 589–597.

Storer, J. B., Serrano, L. J., Darden, E. B., Jr., Jernigan, M. C., and Ullrich, R. L. 1979. Life shortening in RFM and BALB/c mice as a function of radiation quality, dose and dose rate. *Radiat. Res.* 78: 122–161.

Strauss, B. 1976. Non-genetic factors affecting the quantitative repair capability of cells (abstract). *Second International Workshop on DNA Repair Mechanisms in Mammalian Cells.* The Netherlands: Noordwijkerhout.

Sutherland, B. M. 1981. Photoreactivating enzymes. *The Enzymes* 14: 481–515.

Sutherland, B. M., Harber, L. C., and Kochevar, I. E. 1980. Pyrimidine dimer formation and repair in human skin. *Cancer Res.* 40: 3181–3185.

Sutherland, B. M. and Oliver, R. 1976. Culture conditions affect photoreactivating enzyme levels in human fibroblasts. *Biochim. Biophys. Acta.* 442: 358–367.

Suzuki, F., Watanabe, E., and Horikawa, M. 1980. Repair of x-ray-induced DNA damage in aging human diploid cells. *Exp. Cell. Res.* 127: 299–307.

Takeuchi, F., Hanaoke, F., Goto, M., Akaoka, I., Hori, T., Yamada, M., and Miyamoto, T. 1982. Altered frequency of initiation sites of DNA replication in Werner's syndrome cells. *Hum. Genet.* 60: 365–368.

Tas, S. 1976. Disulfide bonding in chromatin proteins with age and a suggested mechanism for ageing and neoplasia. *Exp. Geront.* 11: 17–24.

Thompson, E. N. and Williams, R. 1965. Effect of age on liver function with particular reference to Bromosulphalein excretion. *Gut.* 6: 266–279.

Thompson, K. V. A. and Holliday, R. 1975. Chromosome changes during the *in vitro* ageing of MRC-5 human fibroblasts. *Exp. Cell Res.* 96: 1–6.

Thrasher, J. D. 1967. Age and the cell cycle of the mouse colonic epithelium. *Anat. Rec.* 157: 621–626.

Thrasher, J. D. 1971. Age and the cell cycle of the mouse esophageal epithelium. *Exp. Geront.* 6: 19–24.

Thung, P. J. and Hollander, C. F. 1967. Regenerative growth and accelerated aging. *Symp. Soc. Exp. Biol.* 21: 455–462.

Tice, R. R. 1978. Aging and DNA-repair capability. *In,* E. L. Schneider (ed.), *The Genetics of Aging,* pp. 53–89. New York: Plenum.

Tice, R. R., Schneider, E. L., Kram, D., and Thorne, P. 1979. Cytokinetic analysis of the impaired proliferative response of peripheral lymphocytes from aged humans to phytohemagglutinin. *J. Exp. Med.* 1029–1041.

Todaro, G. J. and Martin, G. M. 1967. Increased susceptibility of Down's syndrome fibroblasts to transformation by SV40. *Proc. Soc. Exp. Biol. Med.* 124: 1232–1236.

Tough, J. M., Smith, P. G., Brown, C., and Harden, D. G. 1970. Chromosome studies on workers exposed to atmospheric benzenes. The possible influence of age. *Eur. J. Cancer,* 6: 49–55.

Treton, J. A. and Courtois, Y. 1976. A comparison of DNA repair in cultured bovine lens epithelial cells and lung fibroblast cells. *Exp. Cell Res.* 102: 419–422.

Treton, J. A. and Courtois, Y. 1982. Correlation between DNA excision repair and mammalian lifespan in lens epithelial cells. *Cell Biol. Internat. Rpts.* 6: 253–260.

Treton, J., Boucays, A., Dersakissian, H., Boue, A., and Courtois, Y. 1978. The repair of DNA single strand breaks in human cells with genetical disorders. *Cell Biology International Reports* 2: 403–410.

Trosko, J. E. and Hart, R. W. 1976. DNA mutation frequencies in mammals. *Interdiscip. Top. Gerontol.* 9: 168–197.

Upton, A. C. 1957. Ionizing radiation and the aging process—a review. *J. Gerontol.* 12: 306–313.

Upton, A. C., Kimball, A. W., Furth, J., Christenberry, K. W., and Benedict, W. H. 1960. Some delayed effects of atom-bomb radiations in mice. *Cancer Res.,* 20 (Suppl. 8, Part 2), 1.

Vincent, R. A., Jr. and Huang, P. C. 1976. The proportion of cells labeled with tritiated thymidine as a function of population doubling level in cultures of fetal, adult, mutant and tumor orgin. *Exp. Cell Res.* 102: 31–42.

von Hahn, H. P. and Fritz, E. 1966. Age-related alterations in the structure of DNA. III. Thermal stability of rat liver DNA, related to age, histone content and ionic strength. *Gerontologia* 12: 237–250.

Walburg, H. E., Jr. 1975. Radiation-induced life-shortening and premature aging. *Adv. Radiat. Biol.* 5: 145.

Waldstein, E. A., Cao, E.-H., Bender, M. A., and Setlow, R. B. 1982. Abilities of extracts of human lymphocytes to remove 0^6-methylguanine from DNA. *Mutat. Res.* 95: 405–416.

Whatley, S. A. and Hill, B. T. 1980. Influence of growth state on relationship between nuclear template activity and *in vitro* "ageing." *Gerontology* 26: 129–137.

Wheeler, K. T. and Lett, J. T. 1974. On the possibility that DNA repair is related to age in non-dividing cells. *Proc. Natl. Acad. Sci. U.S.A.* 71: 1862–1865.

Williams, J. R. 1976. Role of DNA repair in cell inactivation, aging, and transformation: a selective review, a speculative model. *In,* S. T. Lett and H. Adler (eds.), *Advanced Radiation Biology,* Vol. 6, pp. 161–210. New York: Academic Press.

Williams, J. R. and Little, J. B. 1975. Correlation of DNA repair and *in vitro* growth potential in hamster embryo cells; cited in Little (1976).

Woodhead, A. D., Setlow, R. B., and Grist, E. 1980. DNA repair and longevity in three species of cold-blooded vertebrates. *Exp. Gerontol.* 15: 301–304.

Yanagisawa, S. 1978. Sister chromatid exchanges and the cell cycle in peripheral blood lymphocytes of Down syndrome. *Proc. Japan Acad.* 54: Ser. B., 173–178.

Yanishevsky, R., Mendelsohn, M. L., Mayall, B. H., and Cristofalo, V. J. 1974. Proliferative capacity and DNA content of aging human diploid cells in culture: a cytophotometric and autoradiographic analysis. *J. Cell. Physiol.* 84: 165–170.

Yielding, E. L. 1974. A model for aging based on differential repair of somatic mutational damage. *Perspect. Biol. Med.* 17: 201–208.

Yu, C. W. and Borgaonkar, D. S. 1977. Normal rate of sister chromatid exchange in Down syndrome. *Clinical Genetics* 11: 397–401.

Yurov, Yu, B. 1978. Replication of chromosomal DNA in cultured abnormal human cells. *Hum. Genet.* 43: 47–52.

Zucker-Franklin, D., Rifkin, H., and Jacobson, H. G. 1968. Werner's syndrome. An analysis of ten cases. *Geriatrics* 23: 123–135.

9
RNA AND PROTEIN METABOLISM

Mitchell Elliot Reff
National Cancer Institute

INTRODUCTION

The appearance of altered proteins in aging organisms and a decline in the rate of protein synthesis are the most prominent signs of aging in this area of molecular biology. The physiological significance of these changes to the function of aging organisms, and a review of age-associated changes in the metabolism of RNA and protein, are the topics of this chapter.

Other chapters concerned with macromolecules include the synthesis and repair of DNA (Chapter 8); the synthesis and degradation of collagen, elastin, glycosaminoglycans, and other components of the extracellular matrix (Chapter 9); the synthesis and degradation of membranes (Chapter 11); and the synthesis and degradation of carbohydrates and fats (Chapter 20). In this chapter, macromolecules will refer solely to RNA and protein.

It should be emphasized that the origins and significance of macromolecular changes found in aging organisms as diverse as insects, nematodes, and mammals may be totally different. Macromolecular aging may differ in postmitotic cells versus constantly replicating cell populations. For example, age changes might be similar in postmitotic cells such as somatic cells of insects and nematodes, and muscle and nerve cells of mammals, but different in epithelial or hematopoietic cells that continue to replicate.

There have been many studies of the changes in proteins in anucleate erythrocytes. The terminal differentiation of erythrocytes, sometimes referred to as red cell "aging," is not a contributing component to organismal aging and will not be discussed in this chapter.

Another potential area of confusion is the relationship between the behavior of mammalian fibroblasts in tissue culture and aging. Macromolecular alterations that occur with the *in vitro* passage of cells are covered in the chapters on cell biology and will not be reviewed here. An exception is made for macromolecular studies that compare cells of similar passage from young and old donors.

A final note of caution to the reader is that there has been a great deal of contradictory material published in this field. Much of this is due to inappropriate or insufficient choice of ages of organisms, to inappropriate controls or lack thereof, or to deficiencies in experimental design. These deficiencies tend to make studies either uninterpretable or meaningless. Examples include the use of *E. coli* RNA polymerase to measure the transcriptional activity of eukaryotic chromatin, or the *in vivo* or intracellular measurement of protein synthesis using radioactive amino acids without measuring the specific activity of the aminoacyl-tRNAs.

PHYSIOLOGICAL SIGNIFICANCE OF CHANGES IN RNA AND PROTEIN METABOLISM TO THE AGING ORGANISM

Altered proteins might contribute to the age-related decline in function of all cells and organs since they are integral components of all cellular functions. Proteins are involved, both as enzymes and as structural components, in the processes of macromolecular synthesis and degradation, cellular respiration and energy metabolism, intercellular communication, and cellular shape and locomotion. The process of macromolecular synthesis involves proteins which are enzymes (RNA polymerases, aminoacyl-tRNA synthetases, initiation factors, elongation factors) and structural components (histones, nonhistone chromosomal proteins, ribosomal proteins). Errors in the synthesis of proteins which are then involved in macromolecular synthesis could have a feedback effect, creating more errors, until the cell accumulates so many altered proteins that it is unable to function. This is the basis of the error catastrophe theory of Orgel (1963, 1970). This theory suggests a central role in the aging process for macromolecular synthesis inaccuracy.

The majority of accumulated data suggests that the accuracy of macromolecular synthesis does not decline with age. Similarly, there is little evidence to suggest that changes in the DNA (mutations) are responsible for the appearance of altered proteins in aging organisms.

Most, if not all, of the altered proteins which have been identified in aging animals are probably created by posttranslational modifications. Since most proteins turn over rapidly compared to the life span of the organism, accumulation of altered proteins in aging organisms is generally subtle. Posttranslational alterations can be grouped into two major types. The first is a charge or size alteration due to enzymatic processing or nonenzymatic chemical reactions such as deamidation. These alterations are charac-terized by electrophoretic variations of purified proteins that change with age. The second type appears to be a change in conformation, rather than a covalent alteration, since purified enzymes show no changes in molecular weight or charge. Altered proteins of the latter type are usually identified by an age-related decline in the ratio of a specific enzyme's activity to its antigenic reactivity. This indicates the presence in older organisms of an inactive or less active cross-reacting protein component. Changes in the thermal inactivation of enzymes also identify an altered enzyme component which is usually more heat labile. Many proteins appear to be unaltered by age according to any of these criteria.

If there is a subtle accumulation with age of some altered proteins, a general decline in the rate of protein synthesis with age may be the culprit. A slowed rate of protein synthesis, along with a compensatory slowed rate of degradation, could maintain a fixed intracellular level of protein but would also mean that the protein present in the cell has a longer half-life. The longer any protein is present, the more susceptible it may be to posttranslational modification. Thus the key to the unspectacular appearance of altered proteins in aging organisms may be the unexplained slowdown in protein synthesis.

Obviously, proteins that turn over very slowly, such as dentine (teeth) or crystallins (eye lens), are subject to much more extensive posttranslational modifications than proteins that turn over rapidly. The crystallins are subject to both enzymatic degradation and nonenzymatic processes of deamidation and racemization (Van Kleff et al., 1975; Masters et al., 1978). There is a relationship between the degree of racemization in high molecular weight aggregates of α-crystallins and senile cataracts (Masters et al., 1977). Posttranslational modifications of components of the extracellular matrix that turn over very slowly may also have a physiological impact.

Although a slowly increasing population of nonfunctional proteins may not produce a cellular crisis, it may create subtle changes in cellular function. A possible example of this would be the effect of an increase in the number of modified cellular membrane receptors. There are indications that receptor concentrations, but not affinity for hormones, decrease with increasing age (reviewed by Roth, 1979). A population of modified membrane receptors with no hormone affinity could account for these observations. Another possibility is that altered hormone receptors are rapidly removed from the membrane. Two examples of physiological changes that may be caused by receptor changes are as follows. The decrease in glucose metabolism that occurs with age in humans is accompanied by a decline in tissue responsiveness to insulin (DeFronzo, 1981). Although the mechanism of this decline is not known, an increase in modified insulin receptors could explain the phenomenon. Similarly, one of the causal theories of the age-associated pathology atherosclerosis involves an increase in defective cellular membrane receptors for cholesterol (Martin, 1981). The genetic disorder hypercholesteremia, which is due to the absence or production of a defective receptor for cholesterol, results in extensive atherosclerosis of the aorta, coronary, cerebral, and peripheral arteries, without involving the peripheral venous system (Goldstein, 1977). This is essentially the same pattern that accompanies "normal" aging.

The slowdown in the rate of cellular protein synthesis should have other effects on organ function that are not due to the creation of populations of altered protein. The slowdown is another example of an aging phenomenon at the molecular level which may not impair everyday cellular function, but which would contribute to the organism's inability to respond to a stressful situation that required maximal function.

The age-associated disorder senile dementia of the Alzheimer's type (SDAT) is characterized by the accumulation of neurofibrillary tangles in affected areas of the brain. Neurofibrillary proteins are apparently synthesized by the neurons in these areas, which show an uncharacteristic increase in RNA content with age (Uemura and Hartman, 1979). However, it is unknown whether or not the increase in RNA is related to the synthesis of a neurofibrillary protein. In general there do not appear to be major qualitative changes in RNA synthesis with aging. Total RNA synthesis probably slows down in most aging organisms and tissues. Besides possibly contributing to the slowdown in protein synthesis, the physiological importance of a decline in total RNA synthesis is not known.

THE ACCURACY OF MACROMOLECULAR SYNTHESIS IN AGING ORGANISMS

Indirect evidence for the accuracy of macromolecular synthesis with aging is the presence of unaltered proteins in the tissues of older organisms. Those proteins which do appear altered with age are probably modified postsynthetically, rather than missynthesized. This will be discussed in detail in the section on posttranslational modification and aging. Finally, both indirect and direct attempts to measure missynthesis of proteins have shown that the level of missynthesis is very low and does not change with the age of the organism or species.

Reports of unaltered proteins with age are summarized in Table 1. Investigators have found no change in the ratio of enzymatic activity to antigenic reactivity of crude cellular extracts as a function of age (i.e., no indication of inactive cross-reacting material) for the following enzymes: lactate dehydrogenase of mouse muscle (Oliveria and Pfuderer, 1973) and human granulocytes (Rubinson et al., 1976); triosephosphate isomerase of nematode (Gupta and Rothstein, 1976); creatine kinase of human muscle (Steinhagen-Thiessen and Hilz, 1976); aldolase A of human muscle (Steinhagen-Thiessen and Hilz, 1976) and human lymphocytes (Steinhagen-Thiessen and Hilz, 1979); aldolase B of rat liver (Weber et al., 1976) and mouse and dog liver (Burrows and Davidson, 1980); ornithine decarboxylase of rat liver and prostate (Obenrader and Prouty, 1977); and superoxide dismutase of human erythrocytes (Joenje et al., 1978) and dog liver (Burrows and Davidson, 1980). The studies of Rubinson et al. (1976) are partic-

TABLE 1. Unaltered Proteins in Aging Organisms.[a]

Enzyme	Tissue, Species	Characteristics Not Altered with Age	Reference
1. Triosephosphate isomerase	Nematode	R, S, E, H, Km Aa	Gupta and Rothstein (1976)
2. Aldolase A	Muscle, human	R, Hc	Steinhagen-Thiessen and Hilz (1976)
	Lymphocytes, human	R	Steinhagen-Thiessen and Hilz (1979)
	Muscle, dog	S, E	Burrows and Davidson (1980)
	Muscle, mouse	S	Burrows and Davidson (1980)
3. Aldolase B	Liver, dog	R, S, E	Burrows and Davidson (1980)
	Liver, mouse	R, S	Burrows and Davidson (1980)
	Liver, rat	R, Hc	Weber et al. (1976)
	Liver, rat	Rx	Anderson (1976)
	Liver, mouse	S, E, Ec	Petell and Lebherz (1979)
4. Ornithine decarboxylase	Liver, rat	R	Obenrader and Prouty (1977)
	Prostate, rat	R	Obenrader and Prouty (1977)
5. Lactate dehydrogenase	Muscle, mouse	R	Oliveira and Pfuderer (1973)
	Granulocytes, human	R	Rubinson et al. (1976)
6. Creatine Kinase	Muscle, human	R, Hc	Steinhagen-Thiessen and Hilz (1976)
7. Superoxide dismutase	Liver, dog	R, S, E	Burrows and Davidson (1980)
	Liver, mouse	S	Burrows and Davidson (1980)
	Erythrocytes, human, age of donor	R	Joenje et al. (1978)
8. Glucose 6-phosphate dehydrogenase	Granulocytes, human	R	Rubinson et al. (1976)
9. Pyruvate kinase	Granulocytes, human	R	Rubinson et al. (1976)
10. 6-Phosphogluconate dehydrogenase	Granulocytes, human	R	Rubinson et al. (1976)
11. Glucose G-phosphate isomerase	Granulocytes, human	R	Rubinson et al. (1976)
12. α-Mannosidase	Granulocytes, human	R	Rubinson et al. (1976)
13. β-Glucuronidase	Granulocytes, human	R	Rubinson et al. (1976)
14. α-Amylase	Parotid, human	L, Hc	Helfman and Price (1974)

[a]*Abbreviations:*
Aa   = amino acid composition
E   = electrophoretic mobility of purified protein on polyacrylamide SDS gels, molecular weight of subunits
Ec   = electrophoretic mobility on cellulose acetate
H   = heat inactivation kinetics of purified protein
Hc   = heat inactivation kinetics of crude extract
Km   = *Km* value, Michaelis constant
L   = ratio of enzyme activity to mg total protein in saliva
R   = ratio of enzyme activity to antigenic reactivity in crude extracts
Rx   = ratio of enzyme activity to amount of specific polypeptide in crude extracts
S   = specific activity of purified protein

ularly interesting. In addition to lactate dehydrogenase, they investigated six other enzymes from human granulocytes of newborn, young (20–30 years), and old (over 80 years) individuals, and found no evidence for an accumulation of cross-reacting material with age. Granulocytes were chosen because they have a short life span, so posttranslational modifications of proteins should be minimal. A slightly different technique was utilized by Anderson (1976), who showed that the ratio of enzymatic activity to the amount of a specific and unique carboxymethylated polypeptide in crude extracts did not change with age for the rat liver aldolase enzyme, thus confirming the immunological titrations of Weber et al. (1976).

Helfman and Price (1974) reported no change in the activity of α-amylase per unit total protein in the saliva of humans with age. In addition, the heat inactivation kinetics of saliva α-amylase showed no age-related alterations. The heat inactivation kinetics of saliva α-amylase were monophasic. Since α-amylase is a secretory protein, it is possible that altered proteins are synthesized but not secreted. Heat inactivation kinetics were also measured in crude extracts for the proteins aldolase A and creatine kinase of human muscle (Steinhagen-Thiessen and Hilz, 1976) and aldolase B of rat liver (Weber et al., 1976). No age-related changes were observed. The young and old heat inactivation kinetics of creatine kinase were monophasic, while those of the aldolases were biphasic. This biphasic heat inactivation character of aldolases is probably due to the presence of deamidated subunits (Lai et al., 1970). Since no cross-reacting material was detected in these studies, deamidation does not seem to contribute to enzyme inactivation in this case. In rabbit muscle where inactive cross-reacting material to aldolase A has been identified in older animals, there also is no correlation between the deamidated isozymes and the appearance of cross-reacting material (Mennecier and Dreyfus, 1974; Orlovska et al., 1980). Heat inactivation of enzyme activity in crude extracts must be treated with caution, because other investigators have shown that the apparent identity in heat inactivation kinetics of young and old disappears upon enzyme purification (Reznick and Gershon, 1977).

Purified aldolases A and B and superoxide dimutase from young and old mice have identical specific activities (Burrows and Davidson, 1980). Aldolase B has also been purified from mouse liver by Petell and Lebhertz (1979) who report identical specific activities and electrophoretic mobilities on cellulose acetate and SDS polyacrylamide gels. Purified aldolases A and B, and superoxide dismutase from the dog, have identical specific activities and electrophoretic mobil-

ities (Burrows and Davidson, 1980). Purified triosephosphate isomerases from young and old nematodes have identical specific activity, electrophoretic mobility, K_m, and monophasic heat inactivation kinetics (Gupta and Rothstein, 1976).

Both specific and general criticisms have been stated about these reports of unaltered proteins in aging organisms. The study on ornithine decarboxylase (an inducible liver enzyme) measured antigenic reactivity and enzymatic activity at the same time point (18 hours) following induction by thioacetimide in young and old rats (Obenrader and Prouty, 1977). Since induction of this enzyme by thioacetimide is delayed in old mice, and an increase in the half-life of this enzyme is found to occur during the peak of induction (Jacobus and Gershon, 1980), it is possible that cross-reacting material might be found at the peak of induction in older rats.

None of the above studies using the ratio of enzyme activity to antigenic reactivity would detect an altered protein that was modified in a way that it lost its recognizable antigenic sites. It is also possible that altered proteins may not copurify with unaltered protein and may be missed in the analysis of purified proteins. However, since cross-reacting material does copurify in all the cases in which it has been detected, this does not seem likely. Finally, an altered protein that was very rapidly degraded would not be detected. The presence of a significant population of rapidly degraded altered proteins in aging cells does not seem likely. If rapid degradation was common, it would place a burden on cells by forcing them to increase the rate of protein synthesis and protein degradation in order to eliminate missynthesized proteins and maintain a fixed level of active protein. All of the evidence seems to point, however, to a slowdown in both protein synthesis and degradation in older organisms.

It should be pointed out that the accumulation of cross-reacting material with aging has been detected in many of the same proteins reported to be unaltered (see Table 2). With the exception of aldolase A and B and superoxide dimutase of mouse (Burrows and Davidson, 1980; Petell and Lebherz,

TABLE 2. Altered Proteins in Aging Organisms: Changes in Conformation.[a]

Enzyme	Tissue, Species	Characteristics Altered with Age	Characteristics Not Altered with Age	Reference
1. Isocitrate lyase	Nematode	R		Gershon and Gershon (1970)
		H		Reiss and Rothstein (1974a)
		R,S,Id	Km, Mw, E, In	Reiss and Rothstein (1974b)
				Reiss and Rothstein (1975)
2. Enolase	Nematode	S,H	Km, Mwc, Ki, En,	Sharma et al. (1976)
			If	Sharma and Rothstein (1978)
		Cd	Sh, Aa	Sharma and Rothstein (1980a)
3. Phosphoglycerate kinase	Nematode	S	Mwc, En, H, Km	Gupta and Rothstein (1976b)
	Muscle, rat	H, Cd, RI	S, Km, If	Sharma and Rothstein (1980b)
4. Elongation factor 1	Nematode	R		Bolla and Brut (1975)
5. Aldolase	Nematode	R	Ec	Zeelon et al. (1973)
		S, H	Mwu, E, Km	Resnick and Gershon (1977)
			If	Goren et al. (1977)
6. Adolase A	Muscle, mouse	R	Ec, Mwu, Km	Gershon and Gershon (1973a)
	Muscle and heart, mouse	S	Km	Chetsanga and Liskiwskyi (1977)
	Muscle, rabbit	R		Mennecier (1970)
	Muscle, rabbit	S, Km	Id, En	Orlovska et al. (1980)
7. Adolase B	Liver, mice	R	Km, Ec	Reznick et al. (1981)
	Liver, rabbit	R, S		Gershon and Gershon (1973b)
		Rx		Anderson (1974)
	Liver, mice	S, H		Tan and Makinodan (1975)
8. Superoxide dismutase	Liver, mice and rats	R		Reiss and Gershon (1976a)
	Heart, mice and rats	R		Reiss and Gershon (1976a)
	Brain, mice and rats	R		Reiss and Gershon (1976a)
	Liver, rats	R, S, H	Mwc, Id, Mwu, En,	Reiss and Gershon (1976b)
			Ki	
	Liver, rats		If	Goren et al. (1977)

9. Lactate dehydrogenase	Liver, rats	R		Schapira et al. (1975)
10. Tyrosine aminotransferase	Liver, mouse, uninduced	R, Hc		Jacobus and Gershon (1980)
	Liver, rat, induced	R, T	Hc, If, Km	Weber et al. (1980)
11. Ornithine decarboxylase	Liver, mouse	Hc		Jacobus and Gershon (1980)
12. Glutathione peroxidase	Lens, bovine	Hc		Ohrloff et al. (1980)
13. Glutathione reductase	Lens, bovine	Hc		Ohrloff et al. (1980)
14. Albumin	Serum, mouse	Hcd	En, E, If, Aa, Cd	Schofield (1980a,b)

[a]*Abbreviations:*

Aa = amino acid composition
Cd = circular dichroism
E   = electrophoretic mobility of purified protein on denaturing polyacrylamide SDS gels, molecular weight of subunits
Ec = electrophoretic mobility on cellulose acetate membrane gel filtration
En = electrophoretic mobility on nondenaturing polyacrylamide gel
H   = heat inactivation kinetics of purified proteins
Hc = heat inactivation kinetics of crude extract
Hcd = heat inactivation kinetics studies with circular dichroism
Id = distribution of isozymes
If = isoelectric focusing
In = behavior towards inhibitors
Ki = K_i value, inhibition constant
Km = K_m value, Michaelis constant
Mwc = molecular weight determined by chromatography
Mwu = molecular weight determined by analytical ultracentrifugation
R   = ratio of enzyme activity to antigenic reactivity in crude extracts
RI = ratio of enzyme activity to antigenic activity of purified protein
Rx = ratio of enzyme activity to amount of specific polypeptide in crude extracts
S   = specific activity of purified protein
Sh = sulfhydryl groups oxidized or reduced
T   = sensitivity to trypsin

1979; Gershon and Gershon, 1973a, 1973b; Tan and Makinodan, 1975; Chetsanga and Lickiwshyii, 1977; Reznick et al., 1981; Reiss and Gershon, 1976a, 1976b), the discrepancies could be explained by the enzymes in question having been studied in different species. Although these enzymes may be altered in some cases, the modifications are thought to be postsynthetic alterations rather than errors in synthesis. The species differences could be due to differences in the rates of turnover of specific proteins. In the case of aldolase B from mice, Petell and Lebherz (1979) report that the altered protein that has been detected by others may arise from an artifact that occurs in storage. During storage, the carboxy terminal amino acid tyrosine is cleaved, giving rise to an immunologically identical but less active molecule. By use of protease inhibitors to prevent this cleavage, aldolase B from old mice has been shown to be identical to aldolase B from young mice. However, when Reznick et al. (1981) repeated their isolation of aldolase B, both with and without protease inhibitors, they still found evidence for age-related increases in cross-reacting inactive molecules. Whatever the reasons for the discrepancy, the turnover of each individual protein reported to be unaltered in aging organisms should be studied in detail.

Burns and Kaulenas (1979) used isoelectric focusing to examine the secretory proteins produced by the male accessory gland of the cricket. No age-related differences were seen. As pointed out previously, it is possible that altered proteins are present in the gland but not secreted.

The accuracy of protein synthesis was indirectly examined with two-dimensional gel electrophoresis of total *Drosophila melanogaster* proteins. This technique separates proteins by size in one direction and by charge in the second dimension. There were no detectable changes with age, indicating a substitution frequency of less than 4×10^{-4}/codon (Parker et al., 1976).

The fidelity of translation *in vitro* has been measured by looking for misincorporation of leucine in place of phenylalanine (Mori et al., 1979). The investigators utilized a cell free assay with ribosomes purified from the livers of young and old mice and a synthetic poly(U) template. No age changes were observed even when the system was stressed with high magnesium to increase the infidelity level to about 2 percent from a background of less than 0.2 percent. It should be pointed out that this *in vitro* reaction is only measuring the fidelity of polypeptide chain elongation and not possible alterations with age in the initiation or termination of translation. A similar result was obtained by Butzow et al. (1981) with ribosomes prepared from young and old rat livers. However when the aminoglycoside paromomycin was used to stress the system to increase the infidelity level to about 12–14 percent, a small but statistically significant increase in error frequency (~9 percent) was observed in the ribosomes isolated from old rat livers. The authors questioned whether this result had any physiological significance. Ekstrom et al. (1980) and Hardwick et al. (1981) also found no age-related changes in the infidelity of poly(U) translation using purified ribosomes from the brain and kidney, respectively, of young, adult, and old rats.

The most direct measurements of the accuracy of macromolecular synthesis come from amino acid analysis of a purified globin chain which does not normally contain the amino acid isoleucine (Popp et al., 1976). The frequency of substitution of isoleucine is a combination of both mutation in the DNA and errors in macromolecular synthesis. The frequency of substitution observed per amino acid residue was $3.2 \pm 1.5 \times 10^{-5}$ for humans aged 20 to 51, and there was no significant increase in substitution with age (Popp et al., 1976). It should be noted that, if all amino acids are similarly substituted at this frequency, about 2 percent of the average protein of 100 residues (10^{-5}/residue $\times$ 20 amino acids $\times$ 100 residues) would contain an error, i.e., a wrong amino acid.

In another study, the incorporation of a radioactive amino acid analogue was used to measure the frequency of error of aminoacyl-tRNA synthetase in various tissues of young and old mice. The ratio of incorporated radioactive aminoisobutyric acid (AIDA), a leucine analogue, to incorporated radioactive leucine showed no statistically significant change with age in proteins isolated from the brain, heart, kidney, liver, or serum (Hirsch et al., 1976).

Finally, a comparative life span study was performed using purified globins from rabbits, marmosets, pigs, sheep, cows, and humans which do not normally contain isoleucine. The study showed there was no correlation between substitution frequency of isoleucine and species life span; i.e., longer-lived species did not have a lower frequency of error substitution (Hirsch et al., 1980). Isoleucine substitution was similar when measured by amino acid analysis of purified globin (chemical quantitation) or incorporation of radioactive isoleucine into globin. If inaccurate proteins containing isoleucine were being synthesized and preferentially degraded, the latter method should have shown a higher level of substitution, since it measures newly synthesized proteins. Of course a very rapidly degraded inaccurate protein would not be detected.

By sequencing a protein that does not normally contain a specific amino acid and determining the substitution frequency of the amino acid at each residue, one can distinguish between mutation and errors of synthesis if the DNA sequence of the protein is known. This is done by assuming that a single base change is the most likely mutation. Therefore, only codons that would require a single base change to code for the specific amino acid being examined should show an increased substitution due to mutations. Analysis of the amino acids at the amino terminus of sheep globin shows that there is no difference in radioactive isoleucine substitution at codons that could or could not mutate to code for isoleucine (Hirsch et al., 1980). This apparently indicates that the contribution from mutation is significantly less than the frequency of missynthesis (approximately 5×10^{-5} isoleucine substitution at each amino acid residue in this case). Unfortunately, the probability of detecting mutations is decreased in this experiment because all of the globin chains being synthesized during the experiment (from billions of reticulocytes) may have derived from a very small number of active stem cells. Mutations should be detectable by this technique because a measurable increase in total isoleucine substitution in globin protein which normally does not contain this amino acid has been observed in humans who were subjected to radiation (Popp et al., 1976). This same substitution procedure should be used to distinguish between the synthetic error frequency and mutation rate in a protein that can be purified from a post-mitotic tissue or organism, where the DNA sequence coding for the protein is known.

In summation, there is no good evidence to support the concept that an increase in missynthesis of proteins occurs with age. A large amount of data is now available which documents the accuracy of macromolecular synthesis in old organisms.

RNA METABOLISM

RNA metabolism is an area that is relatively unexplored in terms of aging research. There may be a general decline in RNA synthesis with age, and there is preliminary evidence for some quantitative age changes in the metabolism of individual RNA species. This section will consider HnRNA (heterogeneous nuclear RNA) and mRNA. Ribosomal RNA and tRNA will be discussed in detail in the section on protein metabolism.

Many of the recent advances in knowledge in molecular biology are in the field of post-transcriptional processing of HnRNA. The methodology currently exists to follow an individual RNA species from transcription in the nucleus, through its processing and transport to the cytoplasm, and its eventual turnover. Aging studies are just beginning in this area. 5' (5 prime) capping, splicing, and 3' polyadenylation have not yet been adequately studied in terms of aging.

In vitro systems utilizing chromatin and purified RNA polymerase III (Marzluff and Huang, 1975), and more recently DNA, soluble cell extracts, and purified RNA polymerase III (Birkenmeier et al., 1978), accurately transcribe various 5S RNA, tRNA, and viral RNA species. *In vitro* systems using nucleolar chromatin and purified RNA polymerase I accurately transcribe rRNA (Ballal et al., 1977). Most recently, an *in vitro* system using purified DNA, soluble cell extract, and purified RNA polymerase II has been shown to transcribe a viral gene accurately (Weil et al., 1979). RNA polymerase II is the enzyme in eukaryotes responsible for transcription of single copy genes. None of these valuable systems has been employed in the field of aging. Many transcription studies have used *E. coli* RNA polymerase to assess changes in chromatin with age. Because *E. coli* RNA polymerase does not initiate or terminate correctly on eukaryotic chromatin and can copy from endogenous RNA as well as DNA, these studies are uninterpretable.

Some investigators have used isolated nuclei to study transcription and aging. This system is not without problems, such as age changes in pools of intranuclear nucleotides (Bolla and Miller, 1980).

Alterations in the structure of chromatin isolated from aging organisms have been reported, but the significance of these observations in terms of changes in transcription is unknown. An example is the increase in thermal stability with aging of chromatin isolated from mouse brain (Kurtz et al., 1974). The authors suggest that the increased stability is caused by changes in the nonhistone chromosomal protein (NHCP) content of chromatin with age.

Digestion of chromatin by various DNA endonucleases correlates both with the observed nucleosome structure and transcriptional activity. Micrococcal nuclease cleaves DNA between nucleosomes to generate a series of DNA fragments which are multiples of 180 to 200 base pairs (Noll and Kornberg, 1977). DNAse I differentiates between active and inactive genes, preferentially digesting active genes (Weintraub and Groudine, 1976). Using chromatin isolated from the liver and heart tissues of mice, Gaubatz et al. (1979) were unable to find any major age

changes in the digestive patterns of etiher micrococcal nuclesae or DNAse I. There was an indication, based on DNA fragment size distribution, that micrococcal nuclease cut less frequently between the nucleosomes of chromatin isolated from old mouse brain tissue than young. These results indicate that age-associated chromatin structure changes are small and the fraction of active chromatin remains relatively constant with age.

Contrasting results have been obtained by Tas et al. (1980). The investigators used micrococcal nuclease digestion of mouse liver nuclei to separate chromatin into three fractions: one supposedly enriched in active genes, one supposedly enriched in inactive genes, and a fraction resistant to digestion (Bloom and Anderson, 1978). An age-related increase in the ratio of the fraction enriched in inactive genes to the fraction enriched in active genes was observed. The fraction resistant to digestion with nuclease and isolated from old animals was found to be denser than the corresponding young fraction. Because β-mercaptoethanol eliminated this density difference, the age-related creation of additional disulfide bands between chromosomal proteins was suggested. It is unclear how these relatively gross structural age-related changes in chromatin relate to changes in gene expression.

Because the nature of the involvement of chromosomal proteins (histones and NHCP) in gene expression is not understood, the significance of reported age changes in these DNA binding proteins is unclear. Histones, which are involved in nucleosome structure, are conserved among tissues and species. NHCP shows both species and tissue specific patterns. Chromatin reconstitution experiments have been reported which have apparently shown stage or tissue specific gene expression to be associated with the NHCP fraction (Gadski and Chae, 1978). Unfortunately, these experiments have all used *E. coli* RNA polymerase to transcribe the reconstituted chromatin. One of the artifacts of *E. coli* RNA polymerase is its apparent ability to copy from RNA as well as DNA under certain *in vitro* conditions (Zasloff and

Felsenfeld, 1977). Since the NHCP fraction is always contaminated with endogenous RNA, *E. coli* RNA polymerase will produce an *in vitro* antistrand copy of the endogenous RNA. This newly synthesized antistrand will hybridize to the cDNA that is used to assay for the tissue specific gene expression. There have been no reports of modulation of gene expression by NHCP in any of the new *in vitro* systems that show accurate transcription.

Medvedev et al. (1979) reported age changes in the patterns of NHCP from the livers of mice and rats.

Histone acetylation undergoes an age-related decrease in rat liver, probably due to an increase in the activity of histone deacetylase with age (O'Meara and Pochron, 1979). There have been reports that the level of histone acetylation correlates with the level of RNA synthesis from chromatin, but as all of these reports used *E. coli* RNA polymerase, they are open to question.

Sodium butyrate increases histone acetylation by inhibiting histone deacetylase (Boffa et al., 1978). A study by Kanungo and Thakur (1979) showed that sodium butyrate stimulated histone acetylation in brain slices from young but not old rats. Nuclei were then isolated from the brain slices in an attempt to correlate histone acetylation with transcription. An increase in radioactive UTP incorporated into RNA was observed in nuclei isolated from brain slices and preincubated with sodium butyrate in the case of young rats, but not old rats. There was also an age-related decline in radioactive RNA in nuclei isolated from brain slices that had not been preincubated with sodium butyrate. Because the specific activity of the intranuclear UTP pools was not measured in these experiments, other interpretations besides a correlation between histone acetylation and transcriptional activity are possible.

Histone H_3 has a cysteine that, if oxidized, could participate in cross-linking by forming H_3-H_3 disulfide bridges in the nucleosome or H_3-NHCP disulfide bridges. The effects that cross-linking would have on transcription are unknown. Carter (1979) reported there was no age-dependent oxidation of histone H_3 in rats.

Other indications that the qualitative patterns of actively transcribed genes do not change dramatically with age come from studies of RNA complexity. Complexity is a measure of the total amount of unique sequences present in a population of DNA or RNA molecules. Colman et al. (1980) measured the complexity of the total poly(A)-RNA (polyadenylated HnRNA and mRNA) and the polysomal poly(A)RNA (polyadenylated mRNA) isolated from the brains of Fischer and Sprague-Dawley rats of various ages. No age differences in complexities were found in either strain. RNA mixture experiments indicated that most of the polysomal poly(A)RNAs were present at all ages. It was estimated that the maximum possible limit of age changes was about 10 percent of the polysomal poly(A)RNA complexity. This was less than the differences in polysomal poly(A)RNA complexity between the two strains of rat.

These studies suggest that there are no global qualitative differences in RNA transcription with age. However, there do appear to be age differences in the quantitative aspects of transcription, processing, or turnover of individual RNA species. Some of the quantitative heterogeneity of enzyme activities with age (Finch, 1972) is undoubtedly due to quantitative variations with age in the metabolism of individual RNA species.

A small (twofold) increase in the amount of globin HnRNA and cytoplasmic globin RNA in the brain and liver cells of old mice has been detected by hybridization analysis of isolated RNA to globin cDNA (Ono and Cutler, 1978). *In vitro* translation of isolated rat liver mRNA reveals age-dependent changes in three major RNA species, measured by quantitative changes in three undefined translation products (Chatterjee et al., 1981). As suggested earlier, further investigation of individual RNA species is necessary to determine at which stages of transcription, processing, or turnover, age-related alterations occur.

There is a small body of evidence that suggests a decline in total RNA synthesis with age, but the reason for this change is not clear. There is some decline in RNA polymerase activity with age, but most studies suggest that changes in the chromatin template are responsible. Bolla and Brut (1975) found a decline with age of total RNA polymerase activity in the nematode. All of the decline could be accounted for by a decline in RNA polymerase II activity.

Chen et al. (1980) examined RNA synthesis in intact human fibroblasts isolated from donors of various ages and made permeable to nucleotides with detergent to eliminate the problem of measuring intracellular nucleotide pools. The use of permeable cells also avoids losses of chromatin bound polymerase that can occur with nuclei isolation. A 30-40 percent decline with age was observed in RNA synthesis using this system. All of the decline was associated with RNA polymerase II (α-amanitin sensitive). It was suggested that the decline was due either to a loss of RNA polymerase II activity or to a change in the chromatin template.

Benson and Harker (1978), using partially purified RNA polymerase from the liver and brains of mice, found a small (but not statistically significant) decline in the activities of all three RNA polymerases with age.

A 37 percent decrease in RNA synthesis with age was observed in hepatocytes isolated from rats of various ages, in which the intracellular nucleotide pools were measured (Kreamer et al., 1978). Maximum RNA synthesis occurred at 12 months. RNA synthesis by hepatocytes isolated from 18- and 30-month-old rats was 70 percent and 63 percent, respectively, of that observed in hepatocytes from 12-month-old rats. It was suggested that a reported *increase* in protein synthesis (primarily albumin) in old age, which is peculiar to the liver, may be responsible for the very small decline in RNA synthesis between 18 and 30 months.

This reported decline in RNA synthesis in rat hepatocytes is in agreement with most of the early literature on RNA synthesis in isolated rat nuclei. Early studies showed a decline in RNA synthesis with donor age in

nuclei isolated from mouse liver and muscle (Britton et al., 1972) and from mouse liver and prostate (Mainwaring, 1968). Britton et al. (1972) used α-amanitin sensitivity to show that the decline in RNA synthesis in nuclei occurred with both mRNA and rRNA. However, they suggested that the decline was not due to the activity of the endogenous RNA polymerases, because solubilized RNA polymerase from the isolated nuclei did not exhibit a major decline in activity.

Castle et al. (1978) also reported a decline in RNA synthesis in nuclei isolated from young and old rat liver. They also reported small changes in the size distribution of isolated nuclear RNA with age. The significance of this size change is presently unclear.

Recently, Bolla and Miller (1980) characterized isolated liver nuclei from young and old rats. They found that a decrease in endogenous nucleotide concentration occurred with age. When the incorporation of proteins into nuclei was measured, no age difference was found in the rate of uptake or in the total amount of incorporation of specific proteins (such as RNA polymerase).

In another study by this group (Miller et al., 1980), the rate of initiation of RNA synthesis, as determined by the incorporation of $[\alpha-{}^{32}P]$ ATP and GTP, declined with age in isolated liver nuclei.

There is some evidence that polyadenylation of HnRNA is altered in senescent animals. A tract of about 50–200 AMP residues is added to the 3' end of HnRNA posttranscriptionally. The poly(A) is thought to be involved in transport from the nucleus to the cytoplasm and in RNA stability, though these have not been proven. The poly(A) is added by the enzyme poly(A) polymerase, and is specifically degraded by the enzymes endoribonuclease IV and a 5' exonuclease (Muller et al., 1976, 1977).

All of the studies on changes of poly(A) with age have been done by a single laboratory. Studies on polyadenylation of oviduct from mature (70 days) and senescent (950 days) quails found that poly(A) polymerase and endoribonuclease IV activities are unaltered with age, but 5' exonuclease activity is increased in senescent quail oviduct (Muller et al., 1979).

Induction of quail oviduct with progesterone leads to a decrease in the 5' exonuclease activity in mature quail and an increase in 5' exonuclease activity in senescent quail (Muller et al., 1979).

Physical measurement of the poly(A) tails of RNA in quail oviduct revealed an increase in shorter tails in senescent animals (Arendes et al., 1980). The authors believe that the decrease in the size of poly(A) tails of the RNA may be responsible for the general decline with age in protein synthesis in quail oviduct, as well as the specific decline that occurs with age in the induction of the avidin protein with progesterone. Measurement of both the amount and the turnover rate of avidin nuclear RNA by hybridization analysis and the demonstration that the avidin nuclear RNA from older animals had shorter poly(A) tails would make this hypothesis convincing.

Total RNA synthesis probably declines with age. Changes in the structure of chromatin have been implicated as the most likely cause. Age-related changes in NHCP, acetylation of histone, and chromatin thermal stability, have been reported, though the relationship of these changes to changes in transcription is unclear. Chromatin digestion studies and hybridization data suggest that there are only small changes in the qualitative aspects of transcription. There are some quantitative changes with age in individual RNA species. Poly(A) metabolism appears to be altered with age.

PROTEIN METABOLISM

Although the fidelity of macromolecular synthesis does not decline with age, there is substantial evidence for a slowdown, especially of protein synthesis, in older organisms. The reasons for the slowdown are unclear. While it is not true that there are as many theories of why protein synthesis slows down as there are theories of aging, the reader should keep in mind the cautions expounded in the introduction. It is entirely reasonable that the slowdown has multiple causes, and that these vary in different tissues and different organisms. All of the cellular components necessary for protein synthesis, including the RNAs, the proteins, and the membrane structure have been implicated. There appears to be an age-related decline in ribosomal DNA (rDNA) in postmitotic tissues (Johnson and Strehler, 1972). Ribosomal DNA genes are multicopy and tandemly repeated. They are amplified in certain specific cases, probably as a mechanism to allow a very high rate of protein synthesis. A loss of a rDNA might result in a lowered amount of rRNA being transcribed in the nucleus. This could create a decline in rRNA in the cytoplasm and a subsequent decline in protein synthesis due to lack of a sufficient number of ribosomes.

Studies in young and old beagles showed a decline in the hybridizable rDNA in DNA isolated from heart, skeletal muscle, and brain, but not liver, kidney, or spleen (Johnson and Strehler, 1972; Johnson et al., 1972). The concept that a loss of rDNA may lead to a decline in protein synthesis in postmitotic tissues is supported by the reports of age-related declines in total cytoplasmic RNA (mostly consisting of rRNA) in human brain tissue (Mann et al., 1978), total brain protein synthesis in rats (Dwyer et al., 1980), and protein synthesis in a cell free system isolated from rat brain (Ekstrom et al., 1980). However, since an age-related decline in the rate of protein synthesis ocurrs in liver cells of rats (Van Bezooijen et al., 1977; Ricca et al., 1978; Coniglio et al., 1979) and in cell free systems isolated from kidney (Hardwick et al., 1981), the availability of rRNA could not be the only factor involved in an age-related decline in protein synthesis. Subsequent studies from Strehler's laboratory have shown a decline in hybridizable rDNA from human myocardium and human cerebral cortex (Strehler and Chang, 1979; Strehler et al., 1979). It is interesting that the reported rate of loss of rDNA was sevenfold lower in humans than beagles, a ratio consistent with their relative longevities.

These results need to be confirmed in other

laboratories. The single attempt to confirm loss of rDNA in mouse and human liver and brain tissue was negative (Gaubatz et al., 1976). Although no change with age was found, the authors did find a wide individual range of hybridizable rDNA in human tissues of the same age, from 140 to 280 copies per haploid genome.

More direct evidence of the loss of rDNA could be derived from *in vitro* transcription studies using purified RNA polymerase I on chromatin isolated from these tissues; this system has been shown to accurately transcribe rRNA *in vitro* (Ballal et al., 1977). It is possible that rDNA is being lost without any loss of total rRNA synthesis, since many of the rDNA genes normally may not be functional.

There is a report that 18S rRNA accumulates relative to 28S rRNA during aging in the mouse (Mori et al., 1978). Further investigation found that there was an excess of 40S subunits to 60S subunits in the cytoplasm of mouse liver, and this excess was greater in older animals (Mori et al., 1979). It is unclear whether this excess has anything to do with the reported decrease in protein synthesis in this tissue, because polysomes purified from the same tissue have an equimolar ratio of large and small subunits.

Silver staining of nucleolar organizer regions (NOR), DNA regions that code for 18S and 28S rRNAs, on metaphase chromosomes is believed to be an indication of the activity of rRNA synthesis. Evidence for this comes from studies on somatic cell hybrids between mouse and human cells. In these hybrid cells, synthesis of either mouse or human rRNA is suppressed, and the corresponding mouse or human NOR containing chromosomes will not stain with silver (D. A. Miller, et al., 1976; O. J. Miller, et al., 1976). There are ten chromosomes in humans that contain these regions of tandemly repeated rDNA.

An examination of the total number of identifiable silver staining NORs in isolated human lymphocytes shows that there is a small age-related decline in females but not in males (Denton et al., 1981). An earlier study by Buys et al. (1979) found a small, but significant, decrease in the number of silver stained NORs in lymphocytes obtained from children less than 1 year old compared with individuals greater than 80 years old. A much larger decrease was observed in silver stained NORs in metaphase fibroblasts from boys less than 1 year old compared with men aged 69 to 83 years (Buys et al., 1979). While these studies suggest that an age-related decline in rRNA synthesis occurs, direct evidence is lacking. There may not be a correlation between the total number of active NORs and the total synthesis of rRNA.

There are structural changes in nucleolar organization with age in rat liver (Adamstone and Taylor, 1979) and kidney (Adamstone and Taylor, 1977). The pattern of nucleolar changes in kidney and liver is indistinguishable from those seen in the 48-hour life span of the intestinal epithelial cell (Adamstone and Taylor, 1972). In all of these studies, the RNA protein complex of the nucleolus separates from the DNA of the nucleolar organizer region. The consequences of this morphological separation on ribosome synthesis are unclear.

Loss of rough cytoplasmic endoplasmic reticulum has been observed by electron microscopy in cells from stomach epithelium of aged rotifers (Lansing, 1964). Loss of ribosomes and rough endoplasmic reticulum in *Drosophila* has been observed by electron microscopy in the cytoplasm of cells in the digestive canal and Malpighian tubules, but not in muscle cells (Miquel et al., 1972; Miquel and Johnson, 1979). When ribosomes are isolated from whole *Drosophila,* there is a numerical decrease with age that has been reported to be 23 percent by Baker and Schmidt (1976) and 6 percent by Webster and Webster (1979). Webster et al. (1981) report a large decrease in polyribosome (polysome) levels in *Drosophila* with age. Wallach and Gershon (1974) found no changes in the total number of ribosomes isolated from nematodes, but did observe a significant decrease in the percentage of ribosomes found in polysomes.

Age-related ribosome loss and disorganization of the rough endoplasmic reticulum have been seen in electron microscopic studies of various mammalian nerve cells (Miquel and Johnson, 1979). The physiological significance of these findings is unclear, since nerve cell death occurs with age in the mammalian brain and these observations may have been made on dead or dying cells. The contribution of nerve cell death to changes in neuronal function is controversial.

Liver cells from old Wistar rats (24 months) show a loss of rough endoplasmic reticulum that is not reversed by regeneration following hepatectomy (Pieri et al., 1975). However, a study by Moudgil et al. (1979) showed that the proportion of ribosomes active in protein synthesis in the microsomal fraction of Wistar rat liver does not decline with age when comparing 10–13 month to 24–30 month rats. In addition, there is a small increase in the amount of membrane bound polysomes in older rats (Cook and Buetow, 1981). The reason for this discrepancy between observation in the electron microscope and quantitation is not entirely clear. However, caution must be used in interpreting studies of protein synthesis in rat liver, especially as regards the age of the old animals, because it has been observed that protein synthesis measured in isolated liver parenchymal cells declines from 3 to 24 months and then increases slowly until 36 months (Van Bezooijen et al., 1977; Coniglio et al., 1979).

The important unanswered question is: does the age-related loss of polysomes and rough endoplasmic reticulum observed in some tissues cause a decline in protein synthesis, or does a decline in protein synthesis cause the loss of rough endoplasmic reticulum and polysomes?

The thermal stability of ribosomes isolated from nematodes (Wallach and Gershon, 1974) and *Drosophila* (Baker et al., 1979) declines with age. However, Mori et al. (1979) have reported there are no age changes in the thermal stability of ribosomes isolated from old mouse liver. Baker and Schmidt (1976) also found that the amount of protein dissociated in high salt from the ribosomes isolated from old *Drosophila* was increased significantly. Two-dimensional gel electrophoresis of high salt proteins revealed no differences with age (Schmidt and Baker, 1979). This is in agreement with the observations of Ogrodnik et al. (1975) who found that there were no age differences in ribosomal proteins of mouse liver on one-dimensional SDS polyacrylamide gels. Since the ribosomal proteins appear unaltered with age, an investigation of rRNA was performed. Zschunke et al. (1978) found a decrease in reassociation upon cooling in isolated rRNA of older *Drosophila*. It was suggested that undermethylation of the rRNA may be important to the stability of isolated ribosomes. The relationships of the age changes in ribosome thermal stability and high salt ribosomal protein dissociation to changes in protein synthesis are not clear.

Changes in tRNAs have been reported with age, including differences in the hyper modified bases present in tRNAs, changes in the isoacceptor populations of tRNAs, a decreased ability of tRNAs isolated from older animals to be acylated by aminoacyl-tRNA synthetases, and a decreased ability of aminoacyl-tRNA synthetases isolated from older animals to acylate tRNA.

Changes in the isoacceptor patterns of the mosquito *Aedis aegypti* were identified by changes in the ratios of tRNA peaks for valine, methionine, leucine, threonine, and tyrosine isoacceptors (Hoffman, 1972). The isoacceptor patterns of alanine, lysine, and phenylalanine were unchanged. An investigation of isoacceptor ratios in nematodes by Reitz and Sanadi (1970) showed that alterations occurred in the tRNAs for arginine and tyrosine, but not for 13 other amino acids. Frazer and Yang (1972) report no changes in the isoacceptor patterns of liver (9 tRNAs) and brain (6 tRNAs) in young and old mice. This finding is questioned by Mays et al. (1979), who believes that small changes in glutamine, histidine, and lysine tRNAs were overlooked. Mays et al. (1979) report age changes in the isoacceptor patterns of tRNAs for lysine, serine, and possibly phenylalanine in rats.

There are indications that the modified bases found in tRNAs of mice and mosquitoes do not change with age (Hoffman and McCoy, 1974). Similarly, an investigation of tRNA methylase from the brain of adult and old mice did not reveal any changes with age (Weber et al., 1979). However, changes in hypermodified bases do occur, and they may account for some of the observed changes in isoacceptor patterns. A study by Hosbach and Kubli (1979b), reported major isoacceptor changes in the tRNAs for aspartic acid, asparagine, histidine, and tyrosine, all tRNAs that contain the hypermodified base queuine (Q, a guanine derivative). The isoacceptor patterns of the tRNAs for alanine, leucine, methionine, and serine, which do not contain hypermodified bases, were all unchanged with age. It has been shown by Singhal et al. (1981) that the degree of guanine to queuine modification declines with age in rats after nine months. Owensby et al. (1979), have reported that the changes in isoacceptor patterns in two strains of *Drosophila* in tRNAs for tyrosine, histidine, and asparagine are due to an increase in the ratio of Q/non-Q isoacceptors. However, *in vitro* protein synthesis in a cell free system dependent on tRNA showed there was no effect of using Q enriched or Q deficient tRNAs (Owensby et al., 1979).

The acylation capacity of tRNAs (for nine different amino acids) isolated from mouse liver showed an age-related decline, but the same tRNAs isolated from mouse brain had an increased acylation capacity with age (Frazier and Yang, 1972). Reitz and Sanadi (1972) showed that tRNA isolated from old nematodes had only about one-half the acylation capacity for 15 different amino acids. Comolli (1973) found that the liver aminoacyl-tRNA synthetases assayed as a crude extract from young and old rats had four- to fivefold lower activities than those of adult rats. These observations have been extended by the studies in *Drosophila* of Hosbach and Kubli (1979a). They used an *in vitro* system containing isolated tRNAs from young (5 days), mature (22 days), or old (35 days) *Drosophila* in a nine-way cross for nine different amino acids. The tRNA synthetases for glycine, isoleucine, threonine, and valine did not show age changes in their ability to acylate. The tRNA synthetases for proline showed a small decline, and the tRNA synthetases for alanine, arginine, serine, and leucine showed a large decline (> 50 percent) in their ability to acylate. The tRNAs for all nine amino acids showed a decreased ability to be acylated with age, which ranged from less than 10 percent to greater than 50 percent.

An inhibitor of aminoacyl-tRNA synthetases in microsomal fractions from the liver of old rats has been suggested by *in vitro* protein synthesis studies of Goswami (1977). However, the major age change in this system was due to an unidentified activator of protein synthesis present in the young microsome fractions.

An interesting study by Mays et al. (1979) shows that the tRNAs isolated from homogenates of old rat liver have a reduced acylation capacity (17 different amino acids, greater than 50 percent for most), but tRNAs isolated from a high speed supernatant of the same tissue are primarily unchanged. The authors hypothesize, based on some preliminary data, that there may be a defective population of tRNAs bound to the ribosomes.

The direct approach to the effect that alterations in tRNAs have on protein synthesis is to test isolated tRNAs in a cell free system. In an elegant series of experiments, Foote and Stulberg (1980) used tRNAs isolated from the heart, kidney, liver, and spleen of mature (10–12 months) and aged (29 months) mice to translate encephalomyocarditis viral RNA in a cell free system derived from mouse ascites tumor cells. SDS gel electrophoresis and isoelectric focusing were used to examine the fidelity of the viral polypeptides. No significant differences in either the rate or the fidelity of translation were seen. This is good evidence that alterations in tRNA are not responsible for the slowdown in protein synthesis observed in heart, kidney, and liver, as well as another example of the large amount of evidence which suggests there are no changes in the accuracy of macromolecular synthesis with aging.

An excellent review of the literature on the effect of aging on protein synthesis was recently written by Richardson (1981). Most of the studies report a decline in protein synthesis with age. These include studies done *in vivo,* in perfused tissue, in cultured cells, and in cell free systems. Experiments have been performed in plants, invertebrates, rodents, and man. Although almost all the studies have used the incorporation of radioactive amino acids into acid insoluble material, very few until recently have measured the specific activity of the aminoacyl-tRNA. Studies by Florini et al. (1976) in perfused mouse heart indicated that neither the extracellular nor the intracellular leucine pool size is an accurate measure of the specific activity of leucyl-tRNA. The presence of a pool of inactive but acylated leucyl-tRNA was suggested to account for the difference in the intracellular leucine pool and the tRNA pool. This observation leaves the interpretation of most of the synthesis studies done *in vivo,* in tissue, or in cultured cells difficult.

Another problem common to many of the studies on protein synthesis is the choice of ages compared. Florini et al. (1975) showed that the rate of protein synthesis in perfused mouse heart muscle increased from young to adult and then declined in old animals. Van Bezooijen et al. (1977) and Coniglio et al. (1979) have both found a decline in protein synthesis in isolated liver parenchymal cells from rats aged 3½ to 24 months, followed by an increase in protein synthesis to 36 months. Experiments which only measured two ages (i.e., young and old) may have found no differences in protein synthesis in either of these two systems.

A general criticism of the rat liver studies is that increased synthesis with age of a single protein, albumin, may obscure other changes in protein synthesis (Laidlaw and Moldave, 1981). Using immunochemical detection, Van Bezooijan et al. (1976) compared albumin synthesis in hepatocytes from 3-, 12-, and 36-month-old rats. They found a 100 percent increase in the albumin synthesis from the 36-month compared to the 12-month animals.

To avoid isotope dilution problems and to clarify the nature of the slowdown in protein synthesis, many investigators have turned to cell free systems of protein synthesis. Several problems with these systems must be kept in mind. The rate of cell free protein synthesis by the liver is generally only 1 percent of the rate observed *in vivo* (Waterlow, 1975). Many of the cell free systems used in aging studies are not capable of translation of exogenous natural mRNAs and depend on the translation of endogenous mRNAs or on an exogenous synthetic template such as poly(U). These systems are probably measuring only the elongation of polypeptide chains, rather than the entire correct initiation, elongation, and correct termination process.

With these criticisms in mind, a short review of the effects of aging on protein synthesis will be presented. It will concentrate on those studies prior to 1978 that do not appear to have serious flaws which make interpretation difficult and on studies from 1979 to 1981. Unless otherwise stated, all of the following synthesis studies that have been done in cells or tissues and used radioactive amino acids to quantitate protein synthesis have also measured the intracellular amino acid pools.

Both the rate of amino acid turnover and the incorporation of amino acids into proteins have been observed to decline with age in *Drosophila* (Bauman and Chen, 1969) and in the blowfly *Phormia regina* (Levenbook and Krishna, 1971). The rates of protein synthesis in the male accessory gland of the cricket do not appear to change with age, although the uptake of tritiated leucine into the total intracellular leucine (acid soluble counts) does decline with age (Burns and Kaulenas, 1979).

Cell free protein synthesis by microsomal preparations of *Drosophila* utilizing endogenous mRNA shows a large decline in activity (Webster and Webster, 1979) when isolated from insects aged 1 to 14 days (70 percent), and thereafter a small decline in activity. This decline in synthesis (which is probably elongation) does not seem to be due to a loss of ribosomes with age, which decline only 6 percent during the 70 percent decline in *in vitro* protein synthesis. Also, the level of polysome bound message declines only 13 percent during the same period. An added synthetic template shows a similar pattern of decline of synthesis (elongation) as does the endogenous activity. Therefore, the decline in synthesis is probably due to some factor other than the number of ribosomes or amount of mRNA.

A follow-up investigation by the same group showed that the age-related decrease in microsomal protein synthesis differs greatly in different *Drosophila* cells (Webster et al., 1980). Microsomal preparations from the head and abdomen of *Drosophila* show declines of 15 percent and 33 percent with age, while protein synthesis from the thorax was decreased by greater than 95 percent.

Recently, Webster et al. (1981) reported that there was a major age-related decline in polyribosomes in their microsomal preparation. However, using different techniques to isolate ribosomes (and ribosomal subunits), they showed that the binding of methionyl-tRNA to ribosomal subunits in the presence of the initiation codon AUG did not change significantly with age (< 12 percent). Therefore, loss of the ability to initiate protein synthesis does not appear to be the reason for the age-related decline in polyribosomes found in *Drosophila*.

Sharma et al. (1979) report that in nematodes, under conditions where there are no age-related changes in the uptake of amino acid precursors, the synthesis of total soluble protein declines with age, and the synthesis of the specific protein enolase declines with age.

There are only two reports on whole body protein synthesis in humans. Young et al. (1975) and Winterer et al. (1976) both report a decline in age, although only in the first study was it statistically significant. The decline of protein synthesis is corroborated by

the experiments of Chen et al. (1980) that found a decline in protein synthesis in fibroblasts derived from older human donors.

Rodents have been the most intensively studied species in terms of aging, and there is no exception for studies of protein synthesis. A decline in protein synthesis with age has been reported in skeletal muscle (mice, cell free microsomal endogenous mRNA: Britton and Sherman, 1975), cardiac muscle (mice, perfused hearts: Florini et al., 1977), liver (rats, parenchymal cell: Van Bezooijen et al., 1977; Coniglio et al., 1979), brain (rats, cell free microsomal endogenous mRNA: Ekstrom et al., 1980; rats, *in vivo:* Dwyer et al., 1980), testes (rats, cell free microsomal endogenous mRNA: Liu et al., 1978), kidney (rats, cell free microsomal endogenous mRNA: Hardwick et al., 1981), and parotid gland (rats, tissue slices: Kim et al., 1980).

Investigations of the factors responsible for this decline in protein synthesis have been primarily carried out in cell free systems isolated from rat liver. This is unfortunate because of the previously described down-and-up nature of rat liver protein synthesis.

A study by Moudgil et al. (1979) showed that the proportion of ribosomes active in protein synthesis and the content of polyribosomal poly(A)RNA did not decline with age in the Wistar rat. This is in agreement with the previously cited study in *Drosophila* by Webster and Webster (1979). An earlier report by Mainwaring (1969) of an increase with age in free ribosomes (i.e., decrease in mRNA) in mouse liver may have been due to an increased RNAse activity with age (Mainwaring, 1968).

A cell free *in vitro* system including purified tRNAs and aminoacyl-tRNA synthetases used by Cook and Buetow (1981) showed that the decline in protein synthesis with age was related to a decline in tRNA synthetase activity and the acylation capacity of tRNAs, but was primarily due to age changes in the polysomes. Free polysomes did not show a decline in protein synthesis, but membrane bound polysomes showed a decrease in protein synthesis and accounted for a large proportion of the total polysomes.

One of the most detailed investigations to date of cell free protein synthesis from the rat liver and brain was performed by Moldave et al. (1979) using a polysome free cell extract containing ribosomes, ribosomal subunits, tRNAs, aminoacyl-tRNA synthetases, and factors; exogenous mRNA [reticulocyte poly(A)RNA]; GTP; and an energy generating system. The results showed that there was a decrease in protein synthesizing activity with age and a corresponding decrease in elongation factor 1 (EF-1) activity with age. This is especially interesting in light of the experiments of Bolla and Brut (1975), who found both a conversion of EF-1 from high to low molecular weight and the presence of inactive or partially active EF-1 molecules (cross-reacting material) in aging nematodes. Both these studies suggest that chain elongation is impaired. This is also in agreement with the studies of Webster et al. (1981), who found no loss of initiation in an *in vitro* system from *Drosophila,* but rather a decline in elongation (Webster and Webster, 1979).

Moldalve et al. (1979) also found there was no age-related decline in the rate of peptide synthesis of purified rat ribosomes performing chain elongation on a poly(U) template when incubated with a control extract containing elongation factors. This study can be contrasted with that of Ekstrom et al. (1980) who showed that there was a decline with age in the rate of peptide chain elongation by purified rat brain ribosomes on a poly(U) template incubated with a control cell sap. Similarly, Mori et al. (1979) have reported a decline with age in the rate of peptide chain elongation by purified rat liver ribosomes and polysomes on a poly(U) template incubated with rabbit reticulocyte translational factors. The reasons for these discrepancies are not clear.

In summary, the decline of protein synthesis with age, which is universal in eukaryotes and has been identified in numerous tissues, is not completely explained. A decline in the number of ribosomes or in the availability of mRNA does not seem to be responsible. Initiation does not seem to be impaired. Alterations in the aminoacyl-tRNA synthetases, the acylation ability of tRNAs, ribosome structure, polyribosome structure, and the activity of EF-1 may all contribute to the observed decline, which is apparently due to a decrease in the elongation rate.

POSTTRANSLATION MODIFICATION OF PROTEINS

Many recent reviews of posttranslation modification of proteins have appeared, including Gershon (1979), Rothstein (1979), McKerrow (1979), and Dreyfus et al. (1978). This section will be discussed in three parts. The first involves proteins in which the age-related posttranslational modification is a conformational change. Most age-related altered proteins appear to be of this type. Accumulation with age of proteins altered in conformation is probably dependent on the slowdown of protein synthesis and a concomitant slowdown of protein degradation which leads to an increase in the half-life of the protein in the cell.

The second part involves proteins with changes in charge or size. The most common reason for a change in charge of a protein appears to be nonenzymatic deamidation. Deamidated proteins appear in many tissues, but the only tissue in which deamidated proteins apparently increase with age is the lens of the eye, where protein synthesis is minimal or nonexistent. Deamidated proteins also accumulate during the life span of the postsynthetic erythrocyte, but the accumulation of deamidated proteins in erythrocytes does not change throughout the life span of the organism.

The final part will be a discussion of racemization of protein, another nonenzymatic chemical process. Racemization is only measurable in proteins that turn over very slowly or not at all, such as dentine (teeth) and the crystallin proteins of the eye lens.

Conformation, an Historical Account

Since the first independent reports of Mennecier (1970) and Gershon and Gershon (1970) that cross-reacting material (i.e., protein that is antigenically reactive but has little or no enzymatic activity) was present respectively in old rabbit muscle (aldolase A) and whole nematodes (isocitrate lyase), many proteins altered in conformation have been identified (see Table 2). In both of these cases, crude extracts showed that a decline in the ratio of enzymatic activity to immunologic reactivity occurred with age. This was at first thought to be evidence for an increase in the missynthesis of protein with age, but subsequent experiments have virtually ruled out this possibility.

Reports from Gershon's laboratory using the same method identified the presence in crude extracts from older organisms of cross-reacting material to nematode aldolase (Zeelon et al., 1973), mouse muscle aldolase A (Gershon and Gershon, 1973a), and mouse liver aldolase B (Gershon and Gershon, 1973b). The electrophoretic mobility of the nematode aldolase on cellulose acetate was unaltered with age. Purified mouse liver aldolase from older animals showed a decline in specific activity, indicative of an inactive or partially active component, but the K_m and the electrophoretic mobility of the protein on cellulose acetate showed no age-related alterations (Gershon and Gershon, 1973b). Similarly, mouse muscle aldolase A showed no age alterations in either molecular weight (determined by analytical ultracentrifugation), K_m, or electrophoretic mobility on cellulose acetate (Gershon and Gershon, 1973a). Mennecier and Dreyfus (1974) were unable to find any correlation between deamidation of rabbit muscle aldolase, which occurred but did not change with age, and the age-related appearance of cross-reacting material.

At this time, Anderson (1974) confirmed the presence of altered liver aldolase B in crude extracts from old rabbits, by using a different technique. He showed that the ratio of aldolase B enzymatic activity to the amount of a carboxymethylated polypeptide fragment specific only to aldolase B declined with age.

Reiss and Rothstein (1974) found that the heat inactivation curves of the purified isocitrate lyase differed when isolated from young and old nematodes. The enzyme isolated from old nematodes showed the presence of a heat labile component that was not present in enzyme isolated from young nematodes. The heat labile component was found in two of the three major isozymes of isocitrate lyase. The concept that a decline with age in protein turnover might be responsible for the age-related accumulation of altered proteins was first suggested in this paper. In further experiments, Reiss and Rothstein (1975) confirmed the accumulation of cross-reacting material in crude homogenates by antibody titration and demonstrated that the specific activity of the protein purified from older animals was lower. There were also changes in the distribution of isocitrate lyase isozymes with age. However, no age changes were seen in the K_m, the total molecular weight, the molecular weight of the subunits as determined by SDS polyacrylamide gel electrophoresis, or the behavior of the enzyme towards inhibitors. The presence of an altered but partially active enzyme was suggested.

Bolla and Brut (1975) reported a progressive accumulation of inactive or partially active EF-1 molecules in nematode with age. Rat liver lactate dehydrogenase was the next altered protein identified in older animals, as demonstrated by a decline in the ratio of its enzyme activity to its immunological reactivity (Schapira et al., 1975).

At this point, a break is necessary to reiterate that not all proteins appear altered with age (see Table 1). Oliviera and Pfuderer (1973) were unable to find any accumulation of cross-reacting material with age to lactate dehydrogenase of mouse muscle. Thus the identical protein in a different species (rat versus mouse) and tissue (liver versus muscle) appears altered with age in one case but not in the other. Tissue and/or species specific rates of turnover may account for these differences.

Reiss and Gershon (1976b) added another age-altered protein to the list when they found that mouse and rat superoxide dismutase, assayed in crude cellular extracts from liver, heart, or brain, all showed an age-related decline in the ratio of enzyme activity to antigenic activity. The total activity of superoxide dismutase declined in liver with age parallel to the appearance of cross-reacting material, but showed only a very small decline in heart with age and no change with age in the brain. The authors suggest that elevated synthesis of superoxide dimutase in cardiac muscle and brain compensates for the appearance of altered proteins with age in these tissues.

Purified superoxide dismutase from rat liver showed a decline in specific activity, as well as an alteration in its heat inactivation kinetics (Reiss and Gershon, 1976a). Both "young" and "old" superoxide dismutase had biphasic curves, but the "old" superoxide dismutase was much more rapidly inactivated. No differences were found in the electrophoretic mobility on nondenaturing gels, the molecular weight as determined both by gel filtration chromatography and by analytical ultracentrifugation, the distribution of isozymes, and the K_I (inhibition constant). Purified nematode aldolase showed similar results (Reznick and Gershon, 1977). The purified enzyme from old nematodes had lower specific activity. Heat inactivation curves were both biphasic, but the "old" enzyme was much more rapidly inactivated. On the other hand, the molecular weight as determined by analytical ultracentrifugation, the subunit molecular weight (SDS polyacrylamide gel electrophoresis), and the K_m were not significantly changed. Using high resolution isoelectric focusing gels, Goren et al. (1977) were unable to find any evidence of charge differences with age in rat liver superoxide dismutase or in nematode aldolase.

Gupta and Rothstein (1976) purified phos-phoglycerate kinase from nematodes and found an age-related decline in its specific activity. The heat inactivation kinetics were identical, as were the molecular weight determined by gel filtration chromatography, the K_m, and the electrophoretic behavior on nondenaturing gels at three different pHs. It was suggested that altered proteins identified by the presence of cross-reacting material might be classified into two groups. Those in which the heat inactivation kinetics of purified protein from young and old are different might consist of a population of active and partially active molecules, and those in which the heat inactivation kinetics do not change with age might consist of a population of active and inactive molecules. Only phosphoglycerate kinase from nematode fits the latter criterion.

An initial report that there was no change in heat inactivation kinetics with age of nematode aldolase (crude extract: Zeelon et al., 1973) was later found to be in error, since purified aldolase did show age changes in heat inactivation (Reznick and Gershon, 1977).

Another nematode protein purified by Rothstein's group, enolase, fits all of the criteria of a conformational alteration with age (Sharma et al., 1976). The purified protein from old nematodes shows a loss in specific activity and an alteration in heat inactivation kinetics, but no changes in molecular weight, K_m, K_I, or electrophoretic mobility on nondenaturing gels. In addition, high resolution isoelectric focusing shows that there are no alterations in charge with age.

Sharma and Rothstein (1980) purified rat muscle phosphoglycerate kinase and showed that the ratio of enzyme activity to immune reactivity declined with age and that the heat inactivation kinetics were altered. K_m was identical with age, as was the mobility on isoelectrofocusing gels. However, unlike other conformationally altered enzymes, the enzyme from old muscle was more thermostable, and the specific activity was unaltered. Therefore, the decline in the ratio of enzyme activity to immunological activity is due not to the presence of inactive or partially active enzyme molecules in this case, but to a population of antibody (raised to enzyme from young animal) that does not recognize the conformationally altered, but still active, enzyme from old rats.

A protein recently reported to be altered with age (cross-reacting material in crude extracts) is tyrosine aminotransferase from mouse liver (Jacobus and Gershon, 1980). This is interesting because it is an inducible enzyme. Cross-reacting material and an age-related alteration in heat inactivation kinetics (crude extract) were found only for the basal level of the enzyme. Induction was time delayed in older animals, but the specific activity (enzyme activity per milligram of protein in crude extract) of the induced enzyme at the peak of induction was identical for young and old animals. These results provide indirect evidence for newly synthesized (i.e., induced) proteins being unaltered in aging cells, as opposed to the proteins that are present all the time. Proteins that are always present may be subject to more posttranslational modification in older cells because of an increase in half-life.

Studies done with rat liver tyrosine aminotransferase gave very different results (Weber et al., 1980). In these studies, cross-reacting material was found in old animals only following induction. Isoelectric focusing, heat inactivation kinetics, and the K_m were unaltered for the induced enzyme from old animals, but it was more susceptible to trypsin digestion. The appearance of cross-reacting material following induction was blocked by the simultaneous addition of the serine protease inhibitor tosylphenylalanine chloromethyl ketone. The authors suggest that the induced enzyme of old rats undergoes a conformational change, which makes it more susceptible to proteolytic attack. Several important differences exist between the studies of Jacobus and Gershon (1980) and Weber et al. (1980). Jacobus and Gershon (1980) compared 4-month-old mice to 24-month-old mice, and looked at the induced enzyme at the peak of induction in both young and old animals. Weber et al. (1980) compared 3- to 6-month-old rats with 27- to 31-month-old rats, and looked at the induced enzyme at the same time following induction in both young and old animals. Thus the presence (or absence) of cross-reacting material with age in the uninduced liver may be due to species differences in the uninduced rate of degradation of tyrosine aminotransferase. The presence (or absence) of cross-reacting material with age in the induced liver may depend on the time period observed following induction.

Jacobus and Gershon (1980) report an age change in the heat inactivation kinetics of induced ornithine decarboxylase (crude extracts) coupled with an apparent increase in half-life of the induced enzyme at its peak of induction. However, heat inactivation kinetics of crude enzyme preparations are not very reliable because they are subject to artifacts. Therefore, this observation, and the report by Ohrloff et al. (1980) of altered glutathione peroxidase and glutathione reductase in aging bovine lens, based solely on heat inactivation kinetics of crude extracts, should be confirmed by other methods.

Orlovska et al. (1980) confirm and extend the observation of altered aldolase A in rabbit muscle (Mennicier, 1970; Mennicier and Dreyfus, 1974). Purified aldolase from older muscle has a lower specific activity. The isozyme distribution is unaltered with age, which again indicates that there is no correlation between deamidation and loss of activity. The electrophoretic mobility of nondenatured protein is unaltered. Although the authors report a significant change in the K_m of "young" and "old" enzyme, it is an extremely small difference.

Although most of these studies indicate the presence of partially active proteins with age and imply (because of lack of alterations in size or charge) that the partially active protein is probably a conformational change, it is only recently that direct attempts to measure conformation have been made.

Sharma and Rothstein (1978) examined enolase purified from young and old nematodes in detail (see previous discussion of enolase). They found that an extra tryptophan residue was detectable by titration with Nbromosuccinimide in undenatured "old" protein, but the same number of residues were detectable in protein denatured with urea. Circular dichroism spectra showed differences in secondary structure in both far UV and near UV. The differences in near UV disappeared when the proteins were denatured in guanidine hydrochloride. In addition, the number of sulfhydryl groups was identical, and they were all reduced, indicating that the conformational change was not due to either the breaking or the creating of disulfide bridges. Heat inactivation kinetics of purfied proteins, as well as changes in activity of purified "young" and "old" enzyme following column chromatography, suggest that at least three separate stages of changes in conformation may occur. Thus enolase could be described in four states: "young active," "stable old, partially active," "unstable old, partially active," and "inactive."

Sharma and Rothstein (1980) further showed that when purified enolase from young and old nematodes was denatured in guanidine hydrochloride and allowed to renature, the renatured enzymes appeared to be identical as determined by circular dichroism, heat inactivation kinetics, sensitivity to bacterial protease, and immunotitration.

Schofield (1980a, 1980b) also provides direct evidence that there may be age-related changes in the conformation of proteins in older animals. He examined purified serum albumin (produced by liver) from adult and old mice. Its amino acid composition and its electrophoretic mobility in native or denatured state were unaltered with age. There were very slight differences in the immunoelectrophoresis and isoelectric focusing properties, the "old" enzyme being more diffuse in both cases. The significance of this is not known, but it should be pointed out that deamidation of a single amino acid is easily detectable by isoelectric focusing as a separate band in the case of aldolase and α-crystallin. Far and near UV circular dichroism spectra were basically similar (slight differences), indicating a basically identical secondary structure with age. These results seem to show that albumin is unaltered with age (Schofield, 1980a). However, thermal denaturation of the purified protein, studied with circular dichroism, indicates that albumin isolated from old mice shows a greater conformational change at high temperature than does albumin isolated from adult mice. Although the reasons for this are unknown, one possibility is that albumin from old mice contains a population of molecules with a very small conformational change ("stable, old") which, upon heating to high temperatures, is more readily denatured.

Charge and Size

Deamidation of the amino acids asparagine and glutamine to aspartic acid and glutamic acid is a nonenzymatic process that is influenced by the surrounding amino acids (McKerrow, 1979). Deamidated forms of proteins, usually identified as anodic isozymes in isoelectric focusing gels, have been identified for cytochrome C (Flatmark, 1967), aldolase A (Lai et al., 1971), glucose 6-phosphate isomerase (Skala-Rubinson et al., 1976), triosephosphate isomerase (Skala-Rubinson et al., 1976; Yuan et al., 1981), nucleoside phosphorylase (Skala-Rubinson et al., 1976), and α-crystallin (Van Kleef et al., 1975). Although an increase in the half-life of proteins with age would be expected to increase the amount of deamidated proteins present in cells, this apparently is not the case. As previously mentioned, the accumulation of cross-reacting material of rabbit muscle aldolase in older cells does not correlate with its deamidated isozymes, which remain unaltered with age (Mennecier and Dreyfus, 1974; Orlaska et al., 1980). The reason for this may be that the half-life of the most rapid deamidation under physiological conditions is about 6 days, and the average is on the order of months (McKerrow, 1979). Even in older cells in which protein synthesis and protein degradation may be slowed down, the half-life of the average protein may not exceed two weeks (see section on protein degradation). In fact, the only tissue in which deamidated forms of proteins accumulate with increasing age of the organisms is the eye lens, where there is no protein synthesis. Similarly, deamidated forms of proteins accumulate during the "life span" of the erythrocyte. This anucleated cell has no protein synthesis and lasts for a number of months before it is destroyed.

The relationship between the deamidation of α-crystallin in the eye lens and any physiological change in vision with age is not known. α-Crystallin also undergoes a series of stepwise degradations with age, which are probably the result of nonenzymatic breaks of susceptible bonds (Van Kleef et al., 1975).

Changes with age in isocitrate lyase isozymes have been reported (Reiss and Rothstein, 1975). These isozyme changes do not correlate with the decline in specific activity of the purified protein, since all the isozymes of older animals have a lowered specific activity. The differences in these isozymes are unknown.

Sleyster and Knook (1980) report an increased appearance of multiple forms of acid phosphatase in long-lived parenchymal liver cells of old rats. In contrast, there is no change in the isozymes of acid phosphatase in the short-lived Kupffer liver cells. The relationship of these isozymes to the increase in specific activity of acid phosphatase (crude extracts) in old cells is not clear. The differences in these isozymes are unknown.

The enzyme arginyl-tRNA transferase catalyzes a posttransational change in other enzymes. It transfers an arginine from tRNA to the amino terminus of specific acceptor proteins which contain either an aspartic or glutamic at their amino terminus (Soffer, 1971). The physiological significance of this posttranslational modification is unknown. Laman and Kaji (1980) demonstrated that the activity of this enzyme declined in aging rat liver and kidney preparations but not in brain.

Other posttranslational modifications of proteins that would produce charge changes such as ADP-ribosylation or glycosylation have not yet been studied in terms of aging.

Racemization

If protein deamidation is a turtle, racemization is a slug. Racemization is the spontaneous chemical conversion of a natural L form amino acid to its mirror image D form. D-Aspartic acid has been shown to accumulate with age in human tooth enamel and dentine at a rate of about 0.1 percent per year (Helfman and Bada, 1975, 1976). It has been suggested that racemization is an excellent biological marker for estimation of chronological age (Masters, 1981). Racemization may have physiological significance in the crystallins of the human lens, where the water insoluble fraction of aging lens and cataracts has a high D/L ratio (Masters et al., 1977, 1978).

PROTEIN DEGRADATION, THE HALF-LIFE OF PROTEIN IN OLDER ORGANISMS

The decline in protein synthesis in older organisms and the expected corresponding decline in protein degradation should increase in half-life of proteins in older cells, rendering them subject to more posttranslational modifications.

Protein degradation is an area that should receive much attention in the future. As previously mentioned, the degradation and half-lives of specific proteins that appear to be either unaltered or altered in old organisms should be studied in detail.

Most of the studies on changes in half-life with age have been done in nematodes. Zeelon et al. (1973) found that the half-life of nematode aldolase, measured by the decay of activity following blockage of protein sythesis by cycloheximide, was increased in older organisms from about 25 to about 200 hours. This correlates with the appearance of cross-reacting aldolase that is partially active.

Sharma et al. (1979) used isotope dilution to show that the half-life of enolase and the half-life of total soluble proteins in nematodes increased two- to threefold with age between maturity and old age.

Prasanna and Lane (1979) reported that

the half-life of total proteins of nematodes increased from 25 hours (6 days old) to 269 hours (20 days old), when measured by using tritiated leucine pulse labeling. Since the total amount of cellular protein does not change, a decrease in protein synthesis must be accompanied by a decrease in protein degradation.

Reznick and Gershon (1979), using ^{14}C-labeled sodium bicarbonate, measured a fourfold increase with age in the half-life of total soluble proteins of nematodes. Sodium bicarbonate enters arginine and is irreversibly converted to urea.

Using amino acid analogues, Reznick and Gershon (1979) showed that older nematodes were less able to dispose of altered proteins then young nematodes. Therefore, a system for preferential degradation of abnormal molecules does not appear to be active in older nematodes. Because the analogues killed young nematodes (which correlated with the appearance of altered proteins), the authors hypothesized that the accumulation of altered proteins in older organisms may directly contribute to nematode senescence. Because it is not clear that the increase in half-life of total nematode proteins results in the accumulation of altered forms of all or even most proteins in the cell (see triosephosphate isomerase, Gupta and Rothstein, 1976), this hypothesis is premature.

Unfortunately, there are very few studies of changes in the half-life of specific proteins in higher organisms with age (or studies of changes in protein degradation with age). This is an area that obviously needs more attention.

Menzies and Gold (1971) reported no change in the half-life of mitochondrial protein in either liver, testes, heart, brain, intestine, kidney, or lung of rats aged 12 to 24 months.

Jacobus and Gershon (1980) report that the half-life of induced liver ornithinine decarboxylase, studied after cycloheximide administration, increased from 15 minutes in 3-to 4-month-old mice to 30 minutes in 24-month-old mice.

Recently, Reznick et al. (1981) reported that the half-life of liver aldolase B increased from 25 hours in 4-month-old mice to 37 hours in 25-month-old mice. They used a double-labeling technique, employing an initial injection of [^{32}S] methionine followed 24 hours later by [^{3}H] methionine. This increase in half-life could explain the appearance of altered aldolase B in livers of older mice (Gershon and Gershon, 1973).

SUMMARY

There does not appear to be any loss of accuracy of macromolecular synthesis with age. There do not appear to be major age-related changes in RNA transcription. Poly(A) metabolism may be altered with age, possibly leading to some loss of mRNA stability. Protein synthesis slows down with age. Multiple reasons for this decline in protein synthesis have been presented; some or all of them may be responsible in different tissues and different organisms. The slowdown in protein synthesis may be responsible for an increase in the half-lives of most proteins in older cells. Many proteins may be subject to time dependent changes in conformation that result in a decline or loss of activity. Therefore, accumulation of altered proteins in older organisms is probably primarily a result of an increase in protein half-life leading to conformationally altered and partially inactive forms. The physiological significance of altered proteins in aging cells is unclear, especially because not all proteins appear to be altered with age. The alteration in the nematode, of EF-1, a protein factor necessary for elongation of protein synthesis, is at least one example of the feedback nature of aging phenomena.

REFERENCES

Adamstone, F. B. and Taylor, A. B. 1972. Nucleolar reorganization in epithelial cells of the jejunum of the rat. *J. Morph.* 136: 131–152.

Adamstone, F. B. and Taylor, A. B. 1977. Nucleolar reorganization in cells of the kidney of the rat and its relation to aging. *J. Morph.* 154: 459–477.

Adamstone, F. B. and Taylor, A. B. 1979. Nucleolar

reorganization in liver cells of the aging rat. *J. Morph.* 161: 211–220.

Anderson, P. J. 1974. Aging effects on the liver aldolase of rabbits. *Biochem. J.* 140: 341–343.

Anderson, P. J. 1976. The specific activity of aldolase in the livers of old and young rats. *Can. J. Biochem.* 54: 194–196.

Arendes, J., Zahn, R. K., and Müller, W. E. G. 1980. Age-dependent gene induction in quail oviduct. XI. Alterations on the post-transcriptional liver (analytical aspect). *Mech. Ageing Dev.* 14: 49–57.

Baker, G. T. and Schmidt, T. 1976. Changes in 80S ribosomes from *Drosophila melangaster* with age. *Experientia* 32: 1505–1506.

Baker, G. T., Zschunke, R. E., and Podgorski, E. M. Jr. 1979. Alteration in thermal stability of ribosomes from *Drosophila melanogaster* with age. *Experientia* 35: 1053–1054.

Ballal, N. R., Choi, Y. C., Mouche, R., and Busch, H. 1977. Fidelity of synthesis of preribosomal RNA in isolated nucleoli and nucleolar chromatin. *Proc. Natl. Acad. Sci. USA* 74: 246–2450.

Bauman, P. and Chen, P. S. 1969. Alterung und proteinsynthese bei *Drosophila melanogaster*. *Rev. Suisse Zool.* 75: 1051–1055.

Benson, R. W. and Harker, C. W. 1978. RNA polymerase activities in liver and brain tissue of aging mice. *J. Geront.* 33: 323–328.

Birkenmeier, E. H., Brown, D. D., and Jordan, E. 1978. A nuclear extract of *Xenopus laevis* oocytes that accurately transcribes 5S RNA genes. *Cell* 15: 1077–1086.

Boffa, L. C., Vidali, G., Mann, R. S., and ALlfrey, V. G. 1978. Suppression of histone deacetylation *in vivo* and *in vitro* by sodium butyrate. *J. Biol. Chem.* 253: 3364–3366.

Bolla, R. and Brut, N. 1975. Age dependant changes in enzymes involved in macromolecular synthesis in *Turbatrix aceti*. *Arch. Biochem. Biophys.* 169: 227–236.

Bolla, R. and Miller, J. K. 1980. Endogenous nucleotide pools and protein incorporation into liver nuclei from young and old rats. 1980. *Mech. Ageing Dev.* 12: 107–118.

Britton, G. W. and Sherman, F. G. 1975. Altered regulation of protein synthesis during aging as determined by in vitro ribosomal assays. *Exp. Geront.* 10: 67–77.

Britton, V. J., Sherman, F. G., and Florini, J. R. 1972. Effect of age on RNA synthesis by nuclei and soluble RNA polymerases from liver and muscle of C57BL/6J mice. *J. Geront.* 27: 188–192.

Burns, A. L. and Kaulenas, M. S. 1979. Analysis of the translational capacity of the male accessory gland during aging in *Acheta domasticus*. *Mech. Ageing Dev.* 11: 153–169.

Burrows, R. B. and Davidson, P. F. 1980. Comparison of specific activities of enzymes from young and old dogs and mice. *Mech. Ageing Dev.* 13: 307–317.

Butzow, J. J., McCool, M. G., and Eichhorn, G. L.

1981. Does the capacity of ribosomes to control translation of fidelity change with age? *Mech. Ageing Dev.* 15: 203–216.

Buys, C. H. C. M., Osinga, J., and Anders, G. J. P. A. 1979. Age-dependent variability of ribosomal RNA-gene activity in man as determined from frequencies of silver staining nucleolus organizer regions on metaphase chromosomes of lymphocytes and fibroblasts. *Mech. Ageing Dev.* 11: 55–75.

Carter, D. B. 1979. No age-dependent oxidation of H3 histone. *Exp. Geront.* 14: 101–107.

Castle, T., Katz, A., and Richardson, A. 1978. Comparison of RNA synthesis by liver nulcei from rats of various ages. *Mech. Ageing Dev.* 8: 383–395.

Chatterjee, B., Nath, T. S., and Rey, A. K. 1981. Differential regulation of the messenger RNA for three major senescence marker proteins in male rat liver. *J. Biol. Chem.* 256: 5939–5941.

Chen, J-J., Brot, N., and Weissbach, H. 1980. RNA and protein synthesis in cultured human fibroblasts derived from donors of various ages. *Mech. Ageing. Dev.* 13: 285–295.

Chetsanga, C. J. and Liskiwskyi, M. 1977. Decrease in specific activity of heart and muscle aldolase in old mice. *Eur. J. Biochem.* 8: 753–756.

Colman, P. D., Kaplan, B. B., Osterburg, H. H., and Finch, C. E. 1980. Brain poly(A) RNA during aging: stability of yield and sequence complexity in two rat strains. *J. Neurochem.* 34: 335–345.

Comolli, R. 1972. Polyamine effects of ^{14}C-leucine transfer to microsomal protein in a rat liver cell free system during ageing. *Exp. Geront.* 8: 307–313.

Coniglio, J. J., Liu, D. S. H., and Richardson, A. 1979. A comparison of protein synthesis by liver parenchymal cells isolated from Fischer F344 rats of various ages. *Mech. Ageing Dev.* 11: 77–90.

Cook, J. R. and Buetow, D. E. 1981. Decreased protein synthesis by polysomes, tRNA, and aminoacyl-tRNA synthetases isolated from senescent rat liver. *Mech. Ageing Dev.* 17: 41–52.

DeFronzo, R. A. 1981. Glucose intolerance and aging. *In*, M. E. Reff and E. L. Schneider (eds.), *Biological Markers of Aging Conference*, pp. 97–118. Bethesda, Md.: National Institute of Aging.

Dreyfus, J-C., Kahn, A., and Schapira, F. 1978. Posttranslational modifications of enzymes. *Cur. Topics Cell. Reg.* 14: 243–297.

Dwyer, B. E., Fando, J. L., and Wasterlain, C. G. 1980. Rat brain protein synthesis declines during post-developmental aging. *J. Neurochem.* 35: 746–749.

Ekstrom, R., Liu, D. S. H., and Richardson, A. 1980. Changes in brain protein synthesis during the life span of male Fischer rats. *Geront.* 26: 121–128.

Finch, C. E. 1972. Enzyme activities, gene function and aging in mammals (review). *Exp. Geront.* 7: 53–67.

Flatmark, T. 1967. Multiple molecular forms of bovine heart cytochrome c. V. A comparative study of their physiochemical properties and their reactions in biological systems. *J. Biol. Chem.* 242: 2454–2459.

Florini, J. R., Geary, S., Saito, Y., Manowitz, E. J.,

and Sorrention, R. S. 1975. Changes in protein synthesis in heart. *Adv. Exp. Med. Biol.* 61: 149–162.

Foote, R. S. and Stulberg, M. P. 1980. Efficienty and fidelty of cell-free protein synthesis by transfer RNA from aged mice. *Mech. Ageing Dev.* 13: 93–104.

Frazer, J. M. and Yang, W-K. 1972. Isoaccepting transfer ribonucleic acids in liver and brain of young and old BC3F₁ mice. *Arch. Biochem. Biophys.* 153: 610–618.

Gadski, R. A. and Chae, C-B. 1978. Mode of chromatin reconstitution. Elements controlling globin gene transcription. *Biochem.* 17: 869–874.

Gaubatz, J., Prashad, N., and Cutler, R. G. 1976. Ribosomal RNA gene dosage as a function of tissue and age of mouse and human. *Biochim. Biophys. Acta* 418: 358–375.

Gershon, D. 1979. Current status of age altered enzymes: alternative mechanisms. *Mech. Ageing Dev.* 9: 189–196.

Gershon, H. and Gershon, V. 1970. Detection of inactive enzyme molecules in ageing organisms. *Nature* 227: 1214–1217.

Gershon H. and Gershon, D. 1973a. Altered enzyme molecules in senescent organisms: mouse muscle aldolase. *Mech. Ageing Dev.* 2: 33–41.

Gershon H. and Gershon, D. 1973b. Inactive enzyme molecules in aging mice: liver aldolase. *Proc. Natl. Acad. Sci. USA* 70: 909–913.

Goldstein, J. L., Brown, M. S., and Stone, N. J. 1977. Genetics of the LDL receptor: evidence that the mutations affecting binding and internalization are allelic. *Cell* 12: 629–641.

Goren, P., Reznick, A. Z., Reiss, U., and Gershon, D. 1977. Isoelectric properties of nematode aldolase and rat liver superoxide dismutase for young and old animals. *FEBS Lett.* 84: 83–86.

Goswami, M. N. D. 1977. Age-dependent change in the ability of protein synthesis by rat liver microsomes—significance of 2 associated factors. *Experientia* 33: 469–470.

Gupta, S. K. and Rothstein, M. 1976a. Triosephosphate isomerase from young and old *Turbatrix aceti*. *Arch. Biochem. Biophys.* 174: 333–338.

Gupta, S. K. and Rothstein, M. 1976b. Phosphoglycerate kinase from young and old *Turbatrix aceti*. *Biochim. Biophys. Acta* 445: 632–644.

Hardwick, J., Hsieh, W-H., Liu, D. S. H., and Richardson, A. 1981. Cell-free protein synthesis by kidney from the aging female Fischer 344 rat. *Biochim. Biophys. Acta* 652: 204–217.

Helfman, P. M. and Bada, J. L. 1976. Aspartic acid racemization in dentine as a measure of ageing. *Nature* 262: 279–281.

Helfman, P. M. and Price, P. A. 1974. Human parotid α-amylase—a test of the error theory of aging. *Exp. Geront.* 9: 209–214.

Hirsch, G., Grunder, P., and Popp, R. 1976. Error analysis by amino acid analog incorporation in tissues of aging mice. *Interdiscipl. Topics Geront.* 10: 1–10.

Hirsh, G. P., Popp, R. A., Francis, M. C., Bradshaw, B. S., and Bailiff, E. G. 1980. Species comparison of protein synthesis activity. *Adv. Pathobio.* 7: 142–159.

Hoffman, J. L. 1972. Quantitative and qualitative changes in mosquito tRNA as a function of age. *Fed. Proc.* 31: 866.

Hoffman, J. L. and McCoy, M. T. 1974. Stability of nucleoside composition of tRNA during biological ageing of mice and mosquitoes. *Nature* 249: 558–559.

Hosbach, H. A. and Kubli, E. 1979a. Transfer RNA in ageing *Drosophila*. I. Extent of aminoacylation. *Mech. Ageing Dev.* 10: 131–140.

Hosbach, H. A. and Kubli, E. 1979b. Transfer RNA in ageing *Drosophila*. II. Isoacceptor patterns. *Mech. Ageing Dev.* 10: 141–149.

Jacobus, S. and Gershon, D. 1980. Age-related changes in inducible mouse liver enzymes: ornithine decarboxylase and tyrosine amino transferase. *Mech. Ageing Dev.* 12: 311–322.

Joenje, H., Frants, R. R., Arewert, F., and Eriksson, A. W. 1978. Specific activity of human erythrocyte superoxide dismutase as a function of donor age. A brief note. *Mech. Ageing Dev.* 8: 265–267.

Johnson, R., Chrisp, C., and Strehler, B. L. 1972. Selective loss of ribosomal RNA genes during the aging of post-mitotic tissues. *Mech. Ageing Dev.* 1: 183–198.

Johnson, R. and Strehler, B. L. 1972. Loss of genes coding for ribosomal RNA in ageing brain cells. *Nature* 240: 412.

Kanungo, M. S. and Thakur, M. K. 1979. Modulation of acetylation of histones and transcription of chromatin by butyric acid and 17 β-estradiol in the brain of rats of various ages. *Biochem. Biophys. Res. Commun.* 87: 26–271.

Kim, S. K., Weinhold, P. A., Han, S. S., and Wagner, D. J. 1980. Age-related decline in protein synthesis in the rat parotid gland. *Exp. Geront.* 15: 77–85.

Kreamer, W., Zorich, N., Liu, D. S. H., and Richardson, A. 1979. Effect on age on RNA synthesis by rat hepatocytes. *Exp. Geront.* 14: 27–36.

Kurtz, D. I., Russell, A. P., and Sinex, F. M. 1974. Multiple peaks in the derivative melting curve of chromatin from animals of varying age. *Mech. Ageing Dev.* 3: 37–49.

Lai, C. Y., Chen, C., and Horecker, B. L. 1970. Primary structure of two COOH-terminal hexapeptides from rabbit muscle aldolase: a difference in the structure of the α and β subunits. *Biochem. Biophys. Res. Commun.* 40: 461–468.

Laidlaw, S. A. and Moldave, K. 1981. Protein synthesis and aging. *In*, R. T. Schimke (ed.), *Biological Mechanisms in Aging*, pp. 326–338. Washington, D.C.: U.S. Government Printing Office.

Lamon, K. D. and Hideko, K. 1980. Arginyl-tRNA transferase activity as a marker of cellular aging in peripheral rat tissues. *Exp. Geront.* 15: 53–64.

Lansing, A. L. 1964. Age variations in cortical membranes of rotifers. *J. Cell. Biol.* 23: 403–420.

Levenbook, L. and Krishna, I. 1971. Effect of aging on amino acid turnover and rate of protein synthesis in the blowfly *Phormia regina. J. Insect. Physiol.* 17: 9–12.

Liu, D. S. H., Ekstrom, R., Spicer, J. W., and Richardson, A. 1978. Age-related changes in protein, RNA and DNA content and protein synthesis in rat testes. *Exp. Geront.* 13: 197–205.

Mainwaring, W. I. P. 1968. Changes in the ribonucleic acid metabolism of aging mouse tissues with particular reference to the prostate gland. *Biochem. J.* 110: 79–86.

Mainwaring, W. I. P. 1969. The effect of age on protein synthesis in mouse liver. *Biochem. J.* 113: 869–878.

Mann, D. M. A., Yates, P. O., and Stamp, J. E. 1978. The relationship between lipofuscin and ageing in the human nervous system. *J. Neuro. Sci.* 37: 83–93.

Martin, G. M. 1981. Genetic heterogeneity: implications for the pathobiology of aging in man. *In,* R. T. Schimke (ed.), *Biological Mechanisms in Aging,* pp. 4–28. Washington, D.C.: U.S. Government Printing Office.

Marzluff, W. F., Jr. and Huang, R. C. C. 1975. Chromatin directed transcription of 5S and tRNA genes. *Proc. Natl. Acad. Sci. USA* 72: 1082–1086.

Masters, P. M. 1981. Amino acid racemization in structural proteins. *In,* M. E. Reff and E. L. Schneider (eds.), *Biological Markers of Aging Conference,* pp. 119–142. Bethesda, Md.: National Institute of Aging.

Masters, P. M., Bada, J. L., and Zigler, J. S. Jr. 1977. Aspartic acid racemization in the human lens during ageing and in cataract formation. *Nature* 268: 71–73.

Masters, P. M., Banda, J. L., and Zigler, J. S. Jr. 1978. Aspartic acid racemization in heavy molecular weight crystallins and water-insoluble protein from normal human lenses and cataracts. *Proc. Natl. Acad. Sci. USA* 75: 1204–1208.

Mays, L. L., Lawrence, A. E., Ho, R. W., and Ackley, S. 1979. Age-related changes in function of transfer ribonucleic acid of rat livers. *Fed. Proc.* 38: 1984–1988.

McKerrow, J. H. 1979. Non-enzymatic, posttranslational, amino acid modifications in ageing. A brief review. *Mech. Ageing Dev.* 10: 371–377.

Medvedev, Zh.A., Medvedeva, M. N., and Robson, L. 1979. Age-related changes of the pattern of non-histone chromatin proteins from rat and mouse liver chromatin. *Geront.* 25: 219–227.

Mennecier, F. 1970. Mise en evidence d'un material a reaction immunologique croisee (CPM) de l'aldolase dans les hemolysate de globules rouges et de reticulocytes de lupin. *C. R. Acad. Sci. Paris Series D* 270, 742–745.

Mennicier, F. and Dreyfus, J-C. 1974. Molecular aging of fructose-biphosphate aldolase in tissue of rabbit and man. *Biochim. Biophys. Acta* 364: 320–326.

Menzies, R. A. and Gold, P. H. 1971. The turnover of mitochondria in a variety of tissues of young adult and aged rats. *J. Biol. Chem.* 246: 2425–2429.

Miller, D. A., Dev, V. G., Tantravahi, R., and Miller,

O. J. 1976. Suppression of human nucleolus organizer activity in mouse-human somatic hybrid cells. *Exp. Cell Res.* 101: 235–243.

Miller, J. K., Bolla, R., and Devekla, W. D. 1980. Age-associated changes in initiation of ribonucleic acid synthesis in isolated rat liver nuclei. *Biochem. J.* 188: 55–60.

Miller, O. J., Miller, D. A., Dev, V. G., Tantravahi, R., and Croce, C. M. 1976. Expression of human and suppression of mouse nucleolus organizer activity in mouse-human somatic cell hybrids. *Proc. Natl. Acad. Sci. USA* 73: 4531–4535.

Miquel, J., Bensch, K. G., Philpott, D. E., and Atlan, H. 1972. Natural aging and radiation shortening induced life shortening in *Drosophila melanogaster. Mech. Ageing Dev.* 1: 71–97.

Miquel, J. and Johnson, J. E. Jr. 1979. Senescent changes in the ribosomes of animal cells *in vivo* and *in vitro. Mech. Ageing Dev.* 9: 247–266.

Moldave, K., Harris, J., Sabo, W., and Sadnik, I. 1979. Protein synthesis and aging: studies with cell free mammalian systems. *Fed. Proc.,* 38: 1979–1983.

Mori, N., Mizuno, D., and Goto, S. 1978. Increase in the ratio of 18S RNA to 28S RNA in the cytoplasm of mouse tissues during aging. *Mech. Ageing Dev.* 8: 285–297.

Mori, N., Mizuno, D., and Gato, S. 1979. Conservation of ribosomal fidelity during ageing. *Mech. Ageing Dev.* 10: 379–398.

Moudgil, P. G., Cook, J. R., and Buetow, D. E. 1979. The proporation of ribosomes active in protein synthesis and the content of poly(A)-containing RNA in adult and senescent rat livers. *Geront.* 25: 322–326.

Muller, W. E. G., Schröder, H. C., Arendes, J., Staffen, R, Zahn, R. K., and Dose, K. 1977. Alterations of activities of ribonucleases and polyadenylate polymerase in synchronized mouse L-cells. *Eur. J. Biochem.* 76: 531–540.

Muller, W. E. G., Seibert, G., Steffen, R., and Zahn, R. K. 1976. Endoribonuclease IV. 2. Further investigations on the specificity. *Eur. J. Biochem.* 70: 249–258.

Muller, W. E. G., Zahn, R. K., Schröder, C. H., and Arendes, J. 1979. Age-dependent enzymatic poly(A) metabolism in quail oviduct. *Geront.* 25: 61–68.

Noll, M. and Kornberg, R. 1977. Action of micrococcal nuclease on chromatin and the location of histone H1. *J. Mol. Biol.* 109: 393–404.

Obenrader, M. F. and Prouty, W. F. 1977. Production of monospecific antibodies to rat liver ornithine decarboxylase and their use in turnover studies. *J. Biol. Chem.* 252: 2866–2872.

Ogrodnik, J. P., Wulf, J. H., and Cutler, R.G. 1975. Altered protein hypothesis of mammalian ageing processes. II. Discrimination ratio of methionine vs ethionine in the synthesis of ribosomal protein and RNA of C57B1/6J mouse liver. *Exp. Geront.* 10: 119–136.

Ohrloff, C., Lange, G., and Hockwin, O. 1980. Postsynthetic changes of glutathione peroxidase (EC 1.11.1.9) and glutathione reductase (EC 1.6.4.2) in the ageing bovine lens. *Mech. Ageing Dev.* 14: 453–458.

Oliveira, R. J. and Pfuderer, P. 1973. Test for missynthesis of lactate dehydrogenase in aging mice by use of monospecific antibody. *Exp. Geront.* 8: 193–198.

O'Meara, A. R. and Pochron, S. F. 1979. Age-related effects on the incorporation of acetate into rat liver histones. *Biochim. Biophys. Acta* 586: 391–401.

Ono, T. and Cutler, R. G. 1978. Age-dependent relaxation of gene expression: increase of endogenous murine leukemia virus-related and globin-related RNA in brain and liver of mice. *Proc. Natl. Acad. Sci. USA* 75: 4431–4435.

Orgel, L. E. 1963. The maintenance of the accuracy of protein synthesis and its relevance to ageing. *Proc. Natl. Acad. Sci. USA* 49: 517–521.

Orgel, L. E., 1970. The maintenance of the accuracy of protein synthesis and its relevance to ageing. *Proc. Natl. Acad. Sci. USA* 67: 1476.

Orlovska, N. N., Demcheko, A. P., and Veselovska, L. D. 1980. Age-dependent changes of protein structure. 1. Tissue-specific, electrophoretic and catalytical properties of muscle aldolase of old rabbits. *Exp. Geront.* 15: 611–617.

Owenby, R. K., Stulberg, M. P., and Jacobson, K. B. 1979. Alteration of the Q family of transfer RNAs in adult *Drosophila melanogaster* as a function of age, nutrition, and genotype. *Mech. Ageing Dev.* 11: 91–103.

Parker, J., Flanagan, J., Murphy, J., and Gallant, J. 1981. On the accuracy of protein synthesis in *Drosophila melanogaster*. *Mech. Ageing Dev.* 16: 127–139.

Petell, J. K. and Lebherz, H. G. 1979. Properties and metabolism of fructose diphosphate aldolase in liver of "old" and "young" mice. *J. Biol. Chem.* 254: 8179–8184.

Pieri, C., Nagy, I. Zs., Giuli, C., and Mazzufferi, G. 1975. The aging of rat liver as revealed by electron microscopic morphometry. II. Parameters of regenerated old liver. *Exp. Geront.* 10: 341–349.

Popp, R. A., Bailiff, E. G., Hirsch, G. P., and Conrad, R. A. 1976. Errors in human hemoglobin as a function of age. *Interdiscipl. Topics Geront.* 9: 209–218.

Prasanna, H. R. and Lane, R. S. 1979. Protein degradation in aged nematodes (*Turbatrix aceti*). *Biochem. Biophys. Res. Commun.* 86: 552–559.

Reiss, U. and Gershon, D. 1976a. Comparison of cytoplasmic superoxide dismutase in liver, heart, and brain of aging rats and mice. *Biochem. Biophys. Res. Commun.* 73: 255–262.

Reiss, U. and Gershon, D. 1976b. Rat-liver superoxide dismutase purification and age related modifications. *Eur. J. Biochem.* 63: 617–623.

Reiss, U. and Rothstein, M. 1974a. Heat-labile enzymes of isocitrate lyase from aging *Turbatrix aceti*. *Biochem. Biophys. Res. Commun.* 61: 1012–1016.

Reiss, U. and Rothstein, M. 1974b. Isocitrate lyase from the free-living nematode *Turbatrix aceti:* purification and properties. *Biochem.* 13: 1796–1800.

Reiss, U. and Rothstein, M. 1975. Age-related changes in isocitrate lyase from the free living nematode, *Turbatrix aceti*. *J. Biol. Chem.* 250: 826–830.

Reitz, M. S. and Sandai, D. R. 1972. An aspect of translational control of protein synthesis in aging: changes in the isoaccepting forms of tRNA in *Turbatrix aceti*. *Exp. Geront.* 7: 119–129.

Reznick, A. Z. and Gershon, D. 1977. Age related alterations in purified fructose-1, 6,-diphosphate aldolase from the nematode *Turbatrix aceti*. *Mech. Ageing Dev.* 6: 345–353.

Reznick, A. Z. and Gershon, D. 1979. The effect of age on the protein degradation system in the nematode *Turbatrix aceti*. *Mech. Ageing Dev.* 11: 403–415.

Reznick, A. Z., Lavie, L., Gershon, H., and Gershon, D. 1981. Age-associated accumulation of altered FDP aldolase B in mice. *FEBS Lett.* 128: 221–224.

Ricca, G. S., Liu, D. S. H., Coniglio, J. J., and Richardson, A. 1978. Rates of protein synthesis by hepatocytes isolated from rats of various ages. *J. Cell. Physiol.* 97: 137–146.

Richardson, A. 1981. A comprehensive review of the scientific literature on the effect of aging on protein synthesis. *In*, R. T. Schimke (ed.), *Biological Mechanisms in Aging*, pp. 39–358. Washington, D.C.: U.S. Government Printing Office.

Roth, G. S. 1979. Hormone receptor changes during adulthood and senescence: significance for aging research. *Fed. Proc.* 38: 1910–1914.

Rothstein, M. 1979. The formation of altered enzymes in aging animals. *Mech. Ageing Dev.* 9: 197–202.

Rubinson, H., Kahn, A., Boivin, P., Schapira, F., Gregori, C., and Dreyfus, J-C. 1976. Aging and accuracy of protein synthesis in man: search for inactive enzymatic cross-reacting material in granulocytes of aged people. *Geront.* 22: 438–448.

Schapira, F., Weber, A., and Gregori, C. 1975. Vieillissement de la lacticodeshydrogenase hepatique du rat et renouvellement cellulaire. *C. R. Acad. Sci. Paris Series D* 280: 1161–1163.

Schmidt, T. and Baker, G. T. 1979. Analysis of ribosomal proteins from adult *Drosophila melanogaster* in relation to age. *Mech. Ageing Dev.* 11: 105–112.

Schofield, J. D. 1980a. Altered proteins in ageing organisms—purification and properties of serum albumin from adult and ageing C57BL mice. *Exp. Geront.* 15: 443–455.

Schofield, J. D. 1980b. Altered proteins in ageing organisms—application of circular dichroism spectroscopy to study the thermal denaturation of purified serum albumin from adult and ageing C57BL mice. *Exp. Geront.* 15: 533–538.

Sharma, H. K., Gupta, S. K., and Rothstein, M. 1976. Age-related alteration of enolase in the free-living nematode, *Turbatrix aceti*. *Arch. Biochem. Biophys.* 174: 324–332.

Sharma, H. K., Prasanna, H. R., Lane, R. S., and Rothstein, M. 1979. The effect of age on enolase turnover in the free-living nematode, *Turbatrix aceti*. *Arch. Biochem. Biophys.* 194: 275–282.

Sharma, H. K. and Rothstein, M. 1978. Age-related

changes in the properties of enolase from *Turbatrix aceti*. *Biochem.* 17: 2869–2876.

Sharma, H. K. and Rothstein, M. 1980a. Altered enolase in aged *Turbatrix aceti* results from conformational changes in the enzyme. *Proc. Natl. Acad. Sci. USA* 77: 5865–5868.

Sharma, H. K. and Rothstein, M. 1980b. Altered phosphoglycerate kinase in aging rats. *J. Biol. Chem.* 255: 5043–5050.

Singhal, R. P., Kopper, R. A., Nishimura, S., and Shindo-Okada, N. 1981. Modification of guanine to queuine in transfer RNAs during development and aging. *Biochem. Biophys. Res. Commun.* 99: 120–126.

Skala-Rubinson, H., Vibert, M., and Dreyfus, J-C. 1976. Elecrophoretic modifications of three enzymes of human and bovine lens. Posttranslational "ageing" of lens enzymes. *Clin. Chim. Acta.* 70: 385–390.

Sleyster, E. C. and Knook, D. L. 1980. Aging and multiple forms of acid phosphatase in isolated rat liver cells. *Mech. Ageing Dev.* 14: 443–452.

Soffer, R. L. 1971. Enzymatic modification of proteins. V. Protein acceptor specificity in the arginine-transfer reaction. *J. Biol. Chem.* 246: 1602–1606.

Steinhagen-Thiesen, E. and Hilz, H. 1976. The age-dependent decrease in creatine kinase and aldolase activities in human striated muscle is not caused by an accumulation of faulty proteins. *Mech. Ageing Dev.* 5: 447–457.

Steinhagen-Thiesen, E. and Hilz, H. 1979. Aldolase activity and cross-reacting material in lymphocytes of aged animals. *Geront.* 25: 132–135.

Strehler, B. L. and Chang, M-P. 1979. Loss of hybridizable ribosomal DNA from human post mitotic tissues during aging. II. Age-dependent loss in human cerebral cortex—hippocampal and somatosensory cortex comparison. *Mech. Ageing Dev.* 11: 379–382.

Strehler, B. L., Chang, M-P., and Johnson, L. K. 1979. Loss of hybridizable ribosomal DNA from human postmitotic tissues during aging. I. Age-dependent loss in human myocardium. *Mech. Ageing Dev.* 11: 371–378.

Tan, C. and Makinodan, T. 1975. The etiology of altered aldolase in aging rodents. *Fed. Proc.* 34: 278.

Tas, S., Tam, C. F., and Walford, R. L. 1980. Disulfide bonds and the structure of the chromatin complex in relation to aging. *Mech. Ageing Dev.* 12: 65–80.

Uemura, E. and Hartman, H. A. 1979. RNA content and volume of nerve cell bodies in human brain. II. Subiculum in aging normal patients. *Exp. Neurol.* 65: 107–117.

Van Bezooijen, C. F. A., Grell, T., and Knook, D. L. 1976. Albumin synthesis by liver parenchymal cells isolated from young, adult and old rats. *Biochem. Biophys. Res. Commun.* 71: 513–519.

Van Bezooijen, C. F. A., Grell, T., and Knook, D. L. 1977. The effect of age on protein synthesis by isolated liver parenchymal cells. *Mech. Ageing Dev.* 6: 293–304.

Van Kleef, F. S. M., De Jong, W. W., and Hoender, H. J. 1975. Stepwise degradations and deamidation of the eye lens protein α-crystallin in ageing. *Nature* 258: 264–266.

Wallach, Z. and Gershon, D. 1974. Altered ribosomes particles in senescent nematodes. *Mech. Ageing Dev.* 3: 225–234.

Waterlow, J. C. 1975. Protein turnover in the whole body. *Nature* 253: 157.

Weber, A., Gregori, C., and Schapira, F. 1976. Aldolase B in the liver of senescent rats. *Biochim. Biophys. Acta* 444: 810–815.

Weber, A., Szajnert, M-F., and Beck, G. 1980. Age-related changes of liver tyrosine aminotransferase in senescent rats. *Biochim. Biophys. Acta* 631: 412–419.

Weber, G., Margetan, J., Finch, C. E., and Mays, L. L. 1979. Brain transfer ribonucleic acid methytransferases in young adult and old mice. *Exp. Geront.* 14: 157–160.

Webster, G. C., Beachell, V. T., and Webster, S. L. 1980. Differential decrease in protein synthesis by microsomes from aging *Drosophila melanogaster*. *Exp. Geront.* 15: 485–487.

Webster, G. C. and Webster, S. L. 1979. Decreased protein synthesis by microsomes from aging. *Drosophila melanogaster*. *Exp. Geront.* 14: 343–348.

Webster, G. C., Webster, S. L., and Landis, W. A. 1981. The effect of age on the initiation of protein synthesis in *Drosophila melanogaster*. *Mech. Ageing Dev.* 16: 71–79.

Weil, P. A., Luse, D. S., Segall, J., and Roeder, R. G. 1979. Selective and accurate initiation of transcription at the Ad2 major late promoter in a soluble system dependent on purified RNA polymerase II and DNA. *Cell* 18: 469–484.

Weintraub, H. and Groudine, M. 1976. Chromosomal subunits in active genes have an altered conformation. *Science* 193: 848–856.

Winterer, J. C., Steffee, W. P., Davy, W., Perea, A., Uauy, R., Scrimshaw, N. S., and Young, V. R. 1976. Whole body protein turnover in aging man. *Exp. Geront.* 11: 79–87.

Young, V. R., Steffee, W. P., Pencharz, P. B., Winterer, J. C., and Scrimshaw, N. S. 1975. Total human body protein synthesis in relation to protein requirements at various ages. *Nature* 253: 192–194.

Yuan, P. M., Talent, J. M., and Gracy, R. W. 1981. Molecular basis for the accumulation of acidic isozymes of triosephosphate isomerase on aging. *Mech. Ageing Dev.* 17: 151–162.

Zasloff, M. and Felsenfeld, G. 1977. Use of mercury-substituted ribonuclease triphosphates can lead to artefacts in the analysis of *in vitro* chromatin transcripts. *Biochem. Biophys. Res. Commun.* 75: 598–603.

Zeelon, P., Gershon, H., and Gershon, D. 1973. Inactive enzyme molecules in aging organisms. Nematode fructose-1, 6,-diphosphate aldolase. *Biochem.* 12: 1743–1750.

Zschunke, R. F., Podgorski, E. M. Jr., Kubli, E., and Baker, G. T. 1978. Physiochemical characteristics of ribosomes from *Drosophila melanogaster* with age. *Fed. Proc.* 37: 365.

10
MOLECULAR MECHANISMS FOR AGE-RELATED VIRUS EXPRESSION

Michael J. Getz
Department of Cell Biology
Mayo Clinic/Foundation

INTRODUCTION

General Scope

The subject of virus expression and aging is broad and impinges upon a variety of clinical and basic science disciplines. It is not the intent of this review to cover all areas but rather to focus on one area which has received comparatively little attention, the molecular biology of age-related virus expression. It should be understood that this choice is reflective of both the author's personal preference and the general theme of this section of the *Handbook* and in no way implies that other areas are less deserving of attention. A number of these areas are touched upon at the outset, and where appropriate, the reader is referred to other reviews.

Until quite recently, a review dealing with the subject of virus expression and aging could not have been approached in the context of modern molecular biology. The major reason for this is a paucity of knowledge regarding the physical nature of the infectious agents associated with many diseases commonly conceived as being age related. Such diseases, often termed "slow virus" diseases, may be characterized by a long latency period between acquisition of the infectious agent and the onset of disease.

In 1954, Sigurdsson listed several examples of slow virus disease which included scrapie, visna, maedi, and infectious adenomatosis in sheep and "Gross" leukemia and mammary carcinoma in mice. Today several human diseases including kuru, Creutzfeldt-Jakob disease (CJD), delayed onset parkinsonism, progressive multifocal leukoencephalopathy (PML), and subacute sclerosing panencephalitis (SSPE) are usually considered to be examples of slow virus disease (Duvoisin and Vahr, 1965; Kimberlin, 1976; Marsh, 1977). It must be emphasized, however, that this listing represents an extremely heterogeneous group of diseases, and its composition will vary according to the author. In addition, the assignment of a virus as the etiological agent is often tenuous and can be based almost solely on the transmission of the disease by an "ultrafilterable" agent.

Unconventional Viruses

This precautionary note is particularly true with respect to a group of related disorders termed the subacute spongiform virus encephalopathies (SSVE) (Gibbs and Gajdusek, 1969). These disorders include scrapie in sheep, transmissible mink encephalopathy (TME), kuru, and CJD. All of these diseases exhibit similar features which are microscopic in nature and confined to the central nervous system. Morphologically, the major lesions are found in the gray matter of the brain and consist of spongiform degeneration, astrocyte hypertrophy, and neuronal degeneration (Marsh, 1976). Unlike other diseases of clear viral etiology, SSVE produce little or no evidence of an immune response. Indeed, no virus-like agent has been positively identified in ultrastructural studies, although virus-like structures have been reported in affected tissues of mice experimentally inoculated with scrapie (David-Ferreira et al., 1968), in natural scrapie (Bignami and Parry, 1971), and in experimental CJD (Lampert et al., 1971). Typically, these structures appear roughly circular, measure approximately 35 nm in diameter, and appear more like lipid rather than nucleoprotein as would be expected of a conventional virus. Attempts to isolate infectious nucleic acids have also been largely negative (Marsh et al., 1974; Ward, et al., 1974). Nevertheless, circumstantial evidence exists which implicates virus-like agents in SSVE (Gajdusek and Gibbs, 1973).

An excellent review of the current knowledge regarding the properties of one of these agents, scrapie, has recently been provided by Prusiner (1982). Briefly, the infectious scrapie agent appears to be a hydrophobic proteinaceous particle which, when subjected to disaggregating conditions, exhibits an apparent molecular weight of 50,000 daltons or less. Since the infectivity of scrapie particles is dependent upon the integrity of the protein structure, Prusiner has coined the term "prion" (proteinaceous infectious particle) to distinguish these agents from conventional viruses and viroids. Perhaps the most enigmatic yet intriguing aspect of the scrapie agent concerns the molecular basis of its replication. Prusiner has shown that a variety of agents which modify nucleic acid structure fail to inactivate scrapie particles. This observation is subject to at least two interpretations: either scrapie particles contain a nucleic acid core buried deep within the protein structure in such a manner as to be inaccessible to all nucleic acid modifying agents yet tried, or alternatively, scrapie particles lack a nucleic acid component and replicate by as yet undefined, protein-based

mechanisms. Recently, Rohwer (1984) concluded that the reported insensitivity of the scrapie agent to inactivating agents may be limited to a small subpopulation of the total scrapie activity. Furthermore, control experiments using other conventional viruses suggested that the scrapie agent may, in fact, be a small conventional virus rather than the proteinaceous particle proposed by Prusiner. Although prudence would seem to favor the former alternative, the latter possibility is perhaps not as heretical as it initially appears. Several mechanisms other than protein-directed protein synthesis can be envisioned. Perhaps the most plausible is that the information specifying the synthesis of prion protein resides in the host genome rather than in the prion particle itself. Thus, prion protein(s) might function to activate cellular genes encoding its own synthesis. While strictly hypothetical, such a mechanism might explain the aformentioned paucity of an immunological response against scrapie infection. Regardless, it is quite clear that scrapie and perhaps other agents of SSVE represent an exciting new molecular biological challenge with potentially profound physiological, regulatory, and perhaps evolutionary significance. If it turns out that these agents are in fact "conventional" in the broad sense of containing or being comprised of a nucleic acid (DNA or RNA) genome, it will be a relatively simple matter to assess their genetic relatedness by molecular hybridization, restriction enzyme mapping, and nucleic acid sequencing techniques. Similar techniques may also be applied to determine if their genomes exist extrachromosomally in infected cells or whether they possess the ability to integrate themselves in the host chromosomes. Such information is fundamental to elucidating the mechanisms which regulate both their expression and their particular mode(s) of host cell interactions.

Conventional Viruses

In common usage, "conventional" viruses refer to viral particles with identifiable nucleic acid genomes. Many such viruses are clearly involved in diseases of the aged, although the details of such interactions are often as scanty as those of the "unconventional" agents just discussed.

In 1975, Tamm classified viral-cell interactions into three categories: cytocidal, moderate, or oncogenic. Each type of interaction is characterized by a distinctive pattern of events, some of which clearly relate to the aging process and some of which probably do not. In terms of the molecular biology of aging, the moderate and oncogenic categories are probably of greatest interest, although age-related susceptibility to acute virus infection is clearly a major health problem.

In contrast to acute infections such as poliovirus, moderate viral-cell interactions usually do not lead to cytopathic events but can produce chronic cellular dysfunctions and resulting disease which often reoccur in an unpredictable fashion. Such persistent expression may result from the virus remaining in the host following the initial infection. Examples of such persistence are seen in adenovirus and hepatitis virus infections.

It should be noted that there are a number of diseases of the aged in which conventional viruses are likely to be involved but in which their role is unclear and, hence, cannot be easily classified. Among these diseases are Parkinson's disease and some senile dementias. Although a viral etiology has been specifically implicated in postencephalitic Parkinson's disease (Duvoisin and Yahr, 1965), it is not clear whether it is an example of a moderate type of virus-cell interaction in which a latent virus remains in the cells of the host. Indeed, the nature of the viral agent itself remains unknown. What is known is that, following the pandemic of Von Economo's disease (encephalitis lethargica) which occurred mainly in 1919–1926, many of the survivors developed parkinsonism (Duvoisin and Yahr, 1965; Poskanzer and Schwab, 1961), usually in the second or third decade of life. A viral etiology was suggested mainly on clinical and pathological evidence, although attempts to transmit Parkinson's disease to primates by inoculating brain extracts of Parkinson patients have proven negative

(Gibbs and Gajdusek, 1971). Recently, however, studies on a large number of patients with Parkinson's disease detected a significantly higher herpes simplex complement-fixing antibody level in sera than in carefully matched healthy controls (Marttila et al., 1977). Since disturbed cerebral dopamine metabolism is a central feature of Parkinson's disease, it is pertinent that changes in brain monoamine metabolism can be induced by herpes simplex virus infection in experimental animals (Lycke et al., 1970). If herpes simplex virus is in fact an etiological agent of Parkinson's disease (and this remains to be proven), then molecular virological studies of this age-related disorder are clearly possible since the molecular biology of the herpes viruses is well advanced. For a review, see that by Seman and Dmochowski (1977).

Oncogenic Virus-Cell Interactions

Although Sigurdsson (1954) originally included several oncogenic virus-induced neoplasias in the category of "slow virus" disease, they are usually not characterized as such today. Instead, most authors prefer to classify such neoplasias as resulting from "latent" infections since the oncogenic agent itself is usually integrated within the host chromosomes. In the opinion of the author, such distinctions are somewhat arbitrary and are of limited use in a molecular biology context. Visna, for example, is usually classified as a "slow virus" disease, yet it is caused by an RNA virus which shares many properties of oncogenic retroviruses possibly including the capacity to integrate a DNA copy of itself within host chromosomes (Clements et al., 1979). Murine leukemia and avian leukosis viruses are usually considered "oncogenic" agents yet lack direct transforming ability and induce disease only after a prolonged latency period. It is perhaps ironic, therefore, that such viruses are the most well understood in terms of their structure, the molecular mechanisms underlying their age-dependent patterns of expression, and the requirement for a prolonged latency period preceding the onset of disease. Most, if not all, of our current understanding of the disease states induced by these viruses is due primarily to two major factors. First, the viruses involved are extremely well characterized biochemically, and their nucleic acid genomes are well mapped and amenable to dissection and manipulation. Secondly, in the case of murine leukemia, the existence of many genetically defined inbred strains of host animals has allowed the identification of host genetic factors which influence both virus expression and disease progression. The remainder of this review will be devoted to the molecular biology of these agents and the age-dependent mechanisms by which they induce neoplasia. The rather surprising findings which have emerged from these studies may provide a useful conceptual framework for elucidating the mechanisms of action of some of the less well-understood agents.

ENDOGENOUS C-TYPE RETROVIRUSES OF LABORATORY MICE

A considerable amount of insight has accumulated into the age-dependent patterns of endogenous C-type retrovirus gene expression in inbred strains of laboratory mice. Initially, such viruses were identified in leukemic mice, but it is now known that type C genetic information is present in the germ line DNA of all mouse strains studied to date. The DNA forms of these viruses (proviruses) are covalently integrated into the host chromosomes and can be transmitted from parent to progeny in strict Mendelian fashion. Such viruses, therefore, may function both as classical infectious agents and as integrated genes under normal host regulatory mechanisms. Such viruses are variously referred to as murine leukemia viruses (MuLV), oncornaviruses, type C viruses, or retroviruses. Although oncornavirus and retrovirus are generalized terms referring to oncogenic and reverse transcriptase containing viruses of either the type C, A, B, or D varieties, the reader is apt to encounter all of these terms used interchangeably to describe endogenous or exogenous RNA viruses which replicate by means of a reverse transcriptase synthesized DNA intermediate.

All murine type C retroviruses have a similar chemical composition and morphology. An excellent review has recently been published (Pincus, 1980). Briefly, such viruses are composed of a central RNA core surrounded by viral proteins containing both group- and type-specific viral antigens. The internal antigens are derived from proteolytic cleavage of a precursor polypeptide (the product of the *gag* gene) and are classified according to their molecular weights as p30, p15, p12, and p10 (Baltimore, 1975). The viral *pol* gene encodes the RNA-dependent DNA polymerase (reverse transcriptase) which is located within the core and which makes a DNA copy of the RNA genome following exogenous infection (Baltimore, 1970; Temin and Mizutani, 1970). The major envelope glycoprotein, termed gp70, is encoded by the viral *env* gene and is the major determinant of the host range, interference, and neutralization properties of the virus (Elder et al., 1977b).

Type C retroviruses contain a genome composed of a high molecular weight RNA which sediments in a neutral sucrose gradient at 60–70S. This RNA is actually composed of two identical 35S RNA subunits of molecular weight $3–3.5 \times 10^6$ daltons (King, 1976). A variety of biochemical and immunological evidence suggests that the various viral genes are arranged within MuLV subunit RNA in the order 5'-*gag* (p15-p12-p30-p10)-*pol*-*env*-3' (Barbacid et al., 1976; Reynolds and Stephenson, 1977). In addition to the viral replicative genes, each subunit also contains a short terminally redundant sequence (repeated at both 3' and 5' ends) and two other sequences, one of which is unique to the 3' end (U3') and one of which is unique to the 5' end (U5').

Integrated Proviral DNA

Figure 1 illustrates generalized structures for murine C-type retrovirus 35S RNA and the corresponding integrated form of proviral DNA (for a recent review, see Varmus,

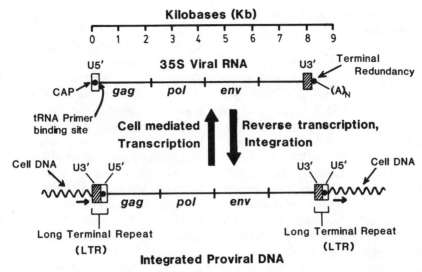

Figure 1. Generalized structures for C-type retroviral RNA and integrated provirus DNA.

1982). Following infection, the viral-encoded reverse transcriptase initiates at the site designated "tRNA primer binding site" and proceeds to the 5' end. The short complementary DNA (cDNA) is then believed to dissociate from the 5' end and hybridize to the terminally redundant sequence located at the 3' end of the molecule (Van Beveren et al., 1980). Synthesis then proceeds back towards the 5' end of the RNA, resulting in the synthesis of a composite DNA sequence designated U3'U5'. By a mechanism not completely understood, synthesis of the second DNA strand results in a double-stranded proviral DNA containing two such U3'U5' composite sequences. In addition to the linear form illustrated, covalently closed circular proviral DNAs are also found in the nucleus of infected cells. When integrated into the host chromosome, the U3'U5' composite sequences flank the viral replicative genes, form the junction points with cellular DNA sequences, and are referred to as long terminal repeats (LTRs). It has been shown in several types of proviral DNAs that LTR sequences contain both promoter sequences for the initiation of viral RNA synthesis ("TATA" boxes) and polyadenylation signals (Benz et al., 1980; Van Beveren et al.,

1980; Swanstrom et al., 1981); thus, the integrated provirus contains sequences which are involved in regulating its own transcription to yield viral messenger RNA.

Host Range Classes of Endogenous C-type Mouse Retroviruses

Three major classes of mouse C-type retroviruses have been identified on the basis of their host range. *Ecotropic* viruses (sometimes referred to as mouse-tropic) infect and grow well only in mouse cells and do not generally replicate in the cells of other species, while *xenotropic* viruses, in contrast, propagate only in cells of foreign hosts. A third class of viruses has also been isolated from feral mice in California, which replicates in both mouse cells and foreign cells (Gardner, 1978). These dual host range viruses are referred to as *amphotropic*. In addition, another group of dual host range viruses is associated with mouse leukemia (actually spontaneous lymphomas) and has been shown to consist of true genetic recombinants between ecotropic and xenotropic viruses (Hartley et al., 1977). These *polytropic* viruses are quite important and will be discussed in a later section.

Genetic Relatedness of Endogenous Mouse Retroviruses

Ecotropic mouse viruses have been most extensively studied in association with mouse leukemia, e.g., the Gross AKR virus. The high leukemia strain AKR mouse contains two independently segregating genetic loci for inducibility of this virus, termed Akv-1 and Akv-2 (Rowe, 1972); a third locus Akv-3 was also reported (Ihle and Joseph, 1978), although its functional status is not entirely clear. The Akv loci represent integrated ecotropic proviral genomes and are indistinguishable by molecular hybridization analysis (Chattopadhyay et al., 1974).

Recently, Steffen et al. (1980) demonstrated that all of the endogenous ecotropic proviruses of American laboratory mice share a common set of restriction endonuclease cleavage sites with the ecotropic virus of AKR mice and are thus closely related if not identical. For convenience, the term AKV will therefore be used to describe all such ecotropic proviruses.

An extremely important point is that all mice contain multiple copies of xenotropic proviral genomes which are related to the AKV-type provirus but which do not share the common set of restriction endonuclease sites. Such xenotropic viruses do share group-specific and reverse transcriptase antigenic determinants and, hence, a considerable amount of nucleotide sequence homology with the ecotropic AKV provirus. This genetic relatedness between ecotropic and xenotropic proviruses has been a serious impediment to the molecular analysis of age-dependent patterns of expression which are clearly different for ecotropic and xenotropic mouse viruses. The expression of xenotropic viruses appears to occur throughout the life span of mice, including embryogenesis (Huebner et al., 1970; Levy et al., 1975), while ecotropic virus production exhibits a much more pronounced age-dependent pattern of occurrence (Rowe et al., 1970). Molecular hybridization analyses using either reverse transcriptase synthesized cDNA from the AKV virus or even cloned AKV proviral genomes, however, cannot readily distinguish between ecotropic and xenotropic proviruses or their RNA transcripts.

Figure 2, lane A illustrates an agarose gel electrophoresis pattern of mouse DNA *Eco*RI restriction fragments which contain sequences related to the ecotropic AKV provirus. This pattern was obtained by transferring the gel-separated total mouse DNA to a nitrocellulose filter and hybridizing with a ^{32}P-labeled cloned AKV provirus genome. Far more bands are detected than would be expected based on the number of Akv loci (2-3), and these extra bands represent genetically related xenotropic provirus genomes. It is apparent that such lack of probe specificity prevents meaningful analysis of age-dependent patterns of expression on a molecular level. Recently, however, an important development has overcome this problem. Two groups have identified a short region in the *env* gene which contains sequences unique to ecotropic proviruses (Chan et al., 1980; Chattopadhyay et al., 1980). This ecotropic-specific region can be subcloned and used as a hybridization probe which will detect only ecotropic proviruses or their specific RNA transcripts. This is illustrated in Figure 2, lanes B and C. The top band in lane C is a doublet containing the Akv-1 and Akv-2 loci of AKR mouse DNA, while the lower band corresponds to the presumptive Akv-3 locus. Lane B contains C3H DNA which has been shown genetically to contain a single AKV-type provirus. Accordingly, only a single band is readily apparent.

Genetic and Age-dependent Factors in the Regulation of Endogenous Ecotropic Virus Expression

Inbred strains of laboratory mice can be classified on the basis of their naturally occurring, age-dependent frequency of production of ecotropic type C retroviruses (Rowe et al., 1970). High virus strains such as AKR and C58 exhibit high levels of viral antigens and high titers of infectious virus production commencing shortly after birth. In contrast,

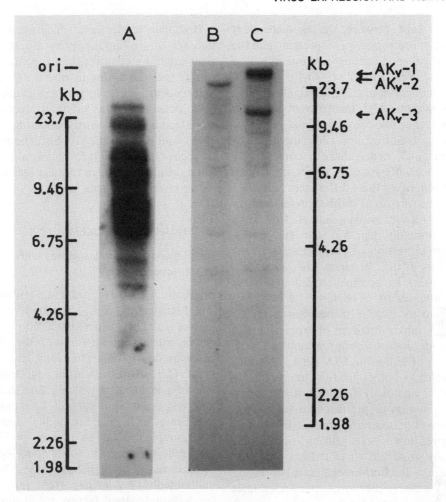

Figure 2. Ecotropic MuLV proviruses and related xenotropic proviruses in mouse DNA. Aliquots of either AKR (lanes A and C) or C3H (lane B) DNAs were digested with the restriction endonuclease *Eco*RI and electrophoresed in 0.8 percent agarose gels. Following electrophoresis, the DNAs were transferred to nitrocellulose paper and hybridized to either ^{32}P-labeled cloned AKR-MuLV proviral DNA (lane A) or to a ^{32}P-labeled ecotropic-specific fragment derived from the *env* gene of AKR-MuLV proviral DNA (lanes B and C). Bands corresponding to these probes were visualized by autoradiography. Fragment lengths in kilobases (Kb) were determined by parallel electrophoresis of a *Hin*d III digest of bacteriophage lambda DNA. (C. P. Giri and M. J. Getz, unpublished data.)

low virus strains such as C57BL/6J, BALB/c, DBA/2, and RF/J exhibit low levels of ecotropic virus antigens, with actual virus production occurring in a generally small subgroup of older mice. Some strains such as NIH-Swiss, C57/J, and 129J have never yielded infectious ecotropic retroviruses, but do exhibit some gs antigen production (Huebner et al., 1970). Comparison of these observations with analysis of integrated AKV-type proviral DNA genomes (Chattopadhyay et al., 1974; Steffen et al., 1980) reveals that high virus strains contain several copies (2–3) of the AKV provirus genome, low virus strains contain a single copy, and nonvirus strains lack a portion of this genome. As mentioned earlier, all strains contain multiple copies of related xenotropic proviruses.

An extremely important point is that correlations exist between the age-dependent patterns of ecotropic virus expression and the incidence of spontaneous leukemia in inbred strains of mice (Russell, 1966; Rowe, 1973; Chattopadhyay et al., 1974). Highly viremic strains exhibit a high incidence of leukemia and consequently are short-lived, whereas low virus strains exhibit a low incidence of leukemia and, hence, have a considerably longer mean life span. A major etiological factor underlying these differences (although not an exclusive one) is the expression of integrated AKV provirus genomes. Low virus strains normally maintain stringent control over the expression of AKV genes until the latter part of their life span when such control appears to become eroded and virus expression occurs. The term "eroded" is used here to distinguish between a genetically programmed pattern of expression and an age-dependent, nonprogrammed accumulation of lesions in AKV gene regulatory mechanisms. Although this interpretation cannot be rigorously defended, it seems reasonable in view of the fact that such relaxation does not occur uniformly in all animals of a given low virus strain but occurs in a generally small and variable fraction of the population. In contrast, the early expression of AKV genes in high virus strain AKR mice is clearly mandated by the genetic composition of the strain, since virtually 100 percent of AKR mice are highly viremic from birth.

The genetic factors which are responsible for strain-specific patterns of endogenous C-type viral gene expression are complex and poorly understood. They are known, however, to include both viral and host genomic elements. Broadly speaking, two main classes of regulatory elements exist, those which are responsible for virus inducibility *per se* and those which are responsible for regulating the spread of infectious virus. The former are better understood than the latter and were elucidated primarily by classical genetic studies involving crosses of high virus strain AKR mice with low virus strains (Rowe, 1973). These studies clearly demonstrate that AKR mice carry two dominant, independently segregating loci (*Akv*-1 and *Akv*-2) for virus inducibility.

Host genetic elements which are responsible for controlling the spread of infectious virus are more complex than the viral inducibility genes and may involve a number of independent genetic loci. These include the *Fv*-1 locus which was originally recognized as affecting Friend virus infection (Lilly, 1970), and perhaps the H-2 histocompatibility locus (Rowe, 1973; Strand et al., 1974). For a detailed treatment of these loci, see the recent review by Pincus (1980).

MECHANISMS OF LEUKEMOGENESIS

Long Latency Period Associated with MuLV Action

In accordance with Sigurdsson's (1954) original classification, viral-associated leukemia in mice may be considered as a "slow virus" disease since the induction of the disease generally occurs only after long latency periods. This is true even in the high leukemia strain AKR mouse in which actual leukemia does not occur until some 8–12 months of age. Since AKR mice are highly viremic at birth, simple production of ecotropic viruses cannot in itself account for the development of leukemia. Although host genetic factors undoubtedly play an important role, other less well-understood factors are also important. In order to understand the molecular mechanisms underlying the long latency period of MuLV-associated neoplasia, it is necessary to first consider the nature of C-type retroviruses which can directly induce tumors in susceptible hosts after only a short latency period.

The Oncogene Hypothesis

In the 1960s, the realization that type C genetic information was integrated into host chromosomes gave rise to the notion that information specifying malignant transformation was a normal component of the structural gene set of an organism. Normally in a genetically silent state, such information might be activated in response to environmental or physiological stimuli, thereby resulting in cell transformation and the development of neoplasia (Huebner and To-daro, 1969; Temin, 1971). Recent develop-ments in molecular virology now lend substantial credence to the concept that cell transformation can result from the increase in the expression or activity of a normal cel-lular product. The growing acceptance of this idea derives largely from elucidation of the molecular nature of C-type retroviral trans-forming genes.

Viral Oncogenes

Various C-type retroviruses have been iso-lated from naturally occurring or induced tu-mors which cause rapid tumor formation in animals and induce transformation in appro-priate tissue culture cells (Hanafusa, 1977; Fischinger, 1980). A common feature of all such viruses appears to be the presence of a specific nucleotide sequence which is not re-quired for viral replication but whose expres-sion leads to rapid transformation of the target cell. These transformation-specific se-quences are generally referred to as *onc* genes and, in all studied instances, are closely re-lated to sequences which are present in the genome of the uninfected host organisms as well as in the DNA of distantly related spe-cies (Coffin, 1980). These cellular homo-logues of viral *onc* genes are not linked to endogenous retrovirus information and are apparently of cellular, rather than viral, or-igin. A number of different *onc* genes have been identified in various viral isolates (for review, see Coffin et al., 1981), and it is thought that the transforming viruses bear-ing these genes arose by a mechanism in-volving genetic recombination between virus and cellular information.

A major issue is whether the transforming potential of these cell-derived viral *onc* genes is due to subtle differences with their cellular homologues, or whether viral-mediated overproduction of a normal gene product is sufficient to induce cell transformation. Al-though a formal resolution of this issue is not yet possible, available evidence suggests that both alternatives may occur. Oskarsson et al. (1980) joined the normal cellular homologue of a murine sarcoma virus oncogene with a

region of proviral DNA which included a copy of the long terminal repeat (LTR); as described earlier, proviral LTRs contain se-quences involved in regulating the expression of adjacent viral genes. Transfection of tar-get cells using this recombinant DNA re-sulted in transformed foci. Thus, the placing of the cellular gene under the control of viral regulatory sequences was sufficient to induce the transformation of recipient cells. It should be noted, however, that a single point mutation has also been shown to confer transforming potential upon a normal cel-lular gene (Reddy et al., 1982; Tabin et al., 1982). Thus, overexpression is not the only mechanism leading to oncogene-induced transformation. Nevertheless, it appears that a number of different types of viral onco-gene homologues exist in cells and that some may code for lineage-specific proteins which may be normally involved in the control of cell differentiation and/or proliferation. For example, defective avian leukemia viruses have been identified which transform either erythroblasts, myeloblasts, or macrophage-like cells (Graf and Beug, 1978); the speci-ficity of such transformation appears to de-pend on which particular type of oncogene is carried by the virus.

The implications arising from the study of viral oncogenes are therefore twofold. First, normal genes when abnormally expressed might result in neoplastic transformation; second, such abnormal expression could arise from a variety of causes and may represent a mechanism for the induction of a common neoplasia by diverse chemical, physical, or viral agents. These points have considerable significance in considering the mechanisms underlying the long latency period associated with virally induced leukemia in mice.

Murine Leukemia Viruses Lack Cell-derived Oncogenes

With the exception of one specialized case, all known murine leukemia viruses lack the ability to transform cells *in vitro* and do not contain any cell-derived sequences. Yet, the actual onset of leukemia clearly depends upon a state of prolonged virus production by the host organism. Aside from important host genetic factors already mentioned, other factors are important in the development of leukemia following a long latency period. These are: (1) the regulation of endogenous provirus genes themselves, (2) the necessity to generate recombinant polytropic viruses with an expanded host range, and (3) a much less well-understood mechanism whereby the target cells are actually transformed. These factors will now be considered in some detail.

Strain and Age-dependent Patterns of Regulation of Endogenous Provirus Gene Expression

As summarized earlier, the incidence of spontaneous leukemia in laboratory mice closely parallels the ecotropic virus phenotype (high or low) of the parent strain. Since the patterns of ecotropic virus expression are clearly age-dependent (early in high virus strains, late in low virus strains), knowledge of the molecular mechanisms underlying these strain and age-dependent patterns of expression is important to understanding the initial events leading to leukemia development.

Although the manifestation of endogenous provirus expression involves the appearance of certain viral antigens (p30, gp70) and/or the production of intact virus particles, changes at the level of the regulation of endogenous provirus genomes must necessarily precede the phenotypic appearance of intact virus or viral antigens. Several possibilities exist which might account for the strain-specific patterns of expression: (1) a simple gene dosage effect since high virus strains contain multiple AKV-type genomes; (2) differences in factors governing the transcription of provirus genomes; or (3) differences in the processing, transport, or utilization of viral-specific messenger RNA. Obviously these possibilities are not mutually exclusive.

Although AKV provirus gene dosage is closely correlated with the virus phenotype of the parent strain, it is difficult to say whether this factor alone can account for the strain-specific variations in virus expression. It is possible that a more important factor than gene dosage *per se* is the particular chromosomal locus at which an AKV provirus is integrated. Transfection experiments have suggested that the particular mouse genomic sequences which flank integrated MuLV proviruses may be important in regulating provirus expression (Copeland and Cooper, 1979). The data of Figure 2 (lanes B and C) demonstrate that AKV-type provirus genomes are present on different restriction nuclease fragments of AKR and C3H DNA and, therefore, occupy different sites in their respective genomes. Thus, it is quite possible that flanking sequence differences may account, in part, for strain-specific patterns of expression. The single AKV-type provirus genome in low virus strains may be integrated at a chromosomal site which is restrictive for transcription, while one or more of the same proviruses in high virus strains may occupy a site which is permissive due to its immediate flanking sequence environment.

Studies from our own laboratory have suggested that the stringency of transcriptional control over endogenous ecotropic provirus genomes is less in embryonic cell lines derived from high virus mouse strains than in low virus strains (Getz et al., 1979). AKR-2B cells are a fibroblast-like cell line derived from high virus strain AKR mouse embryos while C3H/10T½ cells are a similar line derived from low virus strain C3H embryos. Neither cell line produces intact virus particles, although AKR-2B cells can easily be induced to do so (Getz et al., 1977). Examination of nuclear- and polyribosome-associated MuLV-related RNA transcripts in these cell lines revealed that low levels of MuLV-related RNA were present in spite of the fact that no viruses were being produced. In the polysomes of both cell lines, as well as in the nucleus of the C3H-derived line, these viral-specific RNAs did not correspond to full-length transcripts of a complete provirus genome, but rather appeared to represent partial transcripts probably corresponding to a 21S envelope glycoprotein messenger RNA. Hybrid thermal denaturation analyses have since suggested that these "partial" transcripts probably originated from endogenous xenotropic rather than ecotropic proviruses (M. J. Getz and P. K. Elder, unpublished data). In contrast to these findings, nuclear RNA of AKR-2B cells was found to contain transcripts representative of a complete MuLV-related provirus genome. These full-length transcripts appeared to be of ecotropic origin, although this point remains to be firmly established. These results suggest that transcriptional controls over proviral RNA synthesis are somewhat "leaky" in the high virus strain derived cell line and that this may account, in part, for the ease by which virus production is activated in these cells.

Similar studies using liver and brain RNA from low virus strain C57BL/6J mice of increasing age have suggested that the stringent control over provirus transcription in these animals becomes less stringent, i.e., "leaky" as a function of age (Florine et al., 1980). Young mice (6 months) exhibited low levels of "partial" provirus RNA transcripts in both nucleus and cytoplasm in a manner identical to that of the C3H/10T½ cell line. In contrast, middle age (18 months) and old animals (27 months) were found to increasingly mimic the pattern displayed by the high virus strain AKR-2B cell line, i.e., an increasingly larger fraction of a provirus genome became represented in brain nuclear RNA, although cytoplasmic transcripts remained unchanged (Figure 3). Together, the data suggest that both transcriptional and

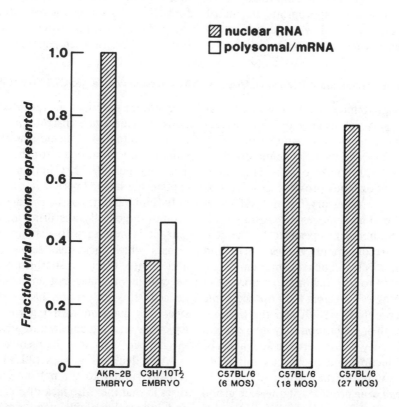

Figure 3. Strain and age-dependent patterns of AKR-MuLV related sequences in nuclear and polysomal RNA of AKR and C3H-derived embryonic cell lines and brain tissue of C57BL/6J mice of increasing age. (Data compiled from Getz et al., 1979 and from Florine et al., 1980.)

posttranscriptional mechanisms are important in regulating provirus expression, but that transcriptional controls are more subject to age-related lesions. Although this conclusion is presently based on limited data and may require modification, it is suggestive of a stepwise decline in the stringency of genetically determined patterns of provirus gene expression. It may be speculated that the rate of such decline plays some role in determining the age at which viremia and, hence, preleukemic changes occur. Most importantly, these experiments define a system which can be analyzed on a fine molecular level using recombinant DNA and molecular cloning techniques. For example, it should be possible to determine whether the age-dependent relaxation of control over MuLV expression in low virus strain mice is due to changes in chromosomal protein organization, or to DNA modifications such as methylation, rearrangement, or amplification. In addition, the use of appropriate strains of congenic mice might allow the identification of host genes which may also be involved.

Formation of Recombinant Polytropic Viruses

Although AKR mice are highly viremic at birth, they do not usually develop preleukemic changes in the thymus until 5–6 months of age, and overt leukemia does not occur until 8–12 months of age. Thus, activation of endogenous provirus gene expression may be a necessary but not sufficient prerequisite to leukemogenesis. A major additional requirement appears to be the generation of recombinants between eco- and xenotropic viruses. Such recombinants are now believed to be much more important in the induction of leukemia than the ecotropic AKV (Rowe et al., 1979), and the time required for their generation may help explain the long latency period between activation of virus production and overt leukemia. Biochemical studies of the gp70, p30, and p15 *env* and *gag* gene products of one such group of polytropic viruses have now provided convincing evidence that these viruses are the result of genetic recombination within the

envelope glycoprotein (*env*) gene, while the *gag* gene is of ecotropic origin (Elder et al., 1977a). This particular class of viruses has been designated mink cell focus-forming (MCF) and is further characterized by considerable heterogeneity among the various isolates.

Direct evidence for the importance of recombinant polytropic viruses in tumor formation has been provided by recent studies of integrated provirus genomes in normal and tumor tissue of a variety of AKR mouse substrains (Quint et al., 1981). Virus-induced tumors contained a pattern of newly acquired integrated proviruses which were unique for each individual animal, suggesting a monoclonal origin for the tumors. Most importantly, restriction enzyme mapping of these proviral genomes demonstrated that they were of the recombinant MCF type rather than the ecotropic AKV type. Thus, tumor formation itself may depend upon the formation of such genetic recombinants, followed by a horizontal spread and reintegration into the target cell genome.

Mechanisms of Target Cell Transformation

The studies described in the preceding sections provide some insight into the initial events leading to leukemogenesis and provide, in part, a rationale for the existence of a latency period. They may not, however, explain the latency period *in toto* and offer only minimal clues as to the actual mechanism of target cell transformation. In particular, it is necessary to explain how retroviruses which lack identifiable oncogenes, and hence direct transforming activity, nevertheless manage to transform their target cells. It is not yet possible to formally answer this question with regards to murine leukemia viruses, but certain aspects of the mechanisms may soon be resolved.

Avian leukosis viruses (ALV) are functionally similar to the murine leukemia viruses in that they also lack discrete *onc* genes and induce lymphatic neoplasms of B-cell lineage only after a prolonged latency period of 4–12 months. ALV proviruses, when covalently integrated into target cell DNA, can activate the expression of cellular genetic information located in the near vicinity of the integration site (Neel et al., 1981; Payne et al., 1981) by the priming of cellular DNA transcription by the viral promoter sequence located in an LTR region. The insertion of the viral promoter directs the initiation of RNA synthesis, which then proceeds into the adjacent cellular DNA, resulting in the transcription of a hybrid RNA containing both viral LTR and cell-specific sequences. Alternatively, adjacent cellular genes can also be activated by a poorly understood mechanism(s) which does not require the synthesis of a hybrid RNA (Payne et al., 1982). Since ALV, like other proviruses, integrates somewhat randomly within the host genome, most such integration events may have little consequence in terms of cell transformation. Occasionally, however, an integration event may occur adjacent to a cellular homologue of a viral oncogene. When this happens, enhanced expression of the oncogene may result in cell transformation. Hayward et al. (1981) have recently demonstrated that the insertion of an ALV provirus activates the cellular homologue of one such viral oncogene designated c-*myc*. Hybrid RNA transcripts were subsequently identified that contained c-*myc* information at up to 100-fold higher levels than that found in a normal cell.

These findings have potentially great importance, since they strongly suggest that nontransforming viruses may cause leukemia by inserting next to, and altering the expression of, a normal cellular gene. While many integration events occur in a population of potential target cells, the long latency period preceding the actual onset of the disease may be due to the low frequency with which such an event occurs by chance adjacent to the appropriate cellular counterpart of a viral oncogene. Whether recombinant polytropic murine leukemia viruses transform cells by similar mechanisms remains to be seen. It would be surprising, however, if a similar mechanism were not operative in at least certain cases.

Summary of MuLV-associated Leukemogenesis

Although many important aspects still remain unknown, we now have a broad picture of some major steps in the age-dependent development of viral-associated leukemia. Several of these have been described here in some detail; others, particularly those dealing with immunological aspects of host response, have not been dealt with. Host genetic factors regulating the spread of infectious virus are complex, poorly understood, but play an important role. In addition, other host factors such as the immediate chromosomal environment of endogenous proviruses may be important in regulating the actual expression of provirus genetic information. The expression of provirus genes, both ecotropic and xenotropic, appears to be required, possibly due to the necessity of generating recombinant viruses with an expanded host range. Although recombination could occur on the DNA level, recombination could also occur by inappropriate template switching during the reverse transcription of ecotropic and xenotropic viral RNA transcripts. Xenotropic viruses are in general expressed throughout the life span, while ecotropic virus expression is much more age-dependent and is a major determining factor in leukemia incidence.

The long latency period preceding the onset of overt leukemia is in part explicable by the time required to generate recombinant polytropic viruses. An extremely interesting additional factor may be the requirement for such a polytropic virus to integrate by chance next to an appropriate cellular oncogene. Such chance events may, in turn, result in overproduction of the normal cell product and, hence, target cell transformation.

PERSPECTIVE ON VIRUSES AND AGING

A major reason for current interest in viruses and aging stems from the etiological role of viruses in neural and proliferative diseases of the aged. The possibility merits attention that the study of the molecular biology of certain viruses or virus-like elements may ultimately allow insight (albeit indirectly) into the mechanisms of the aging process itself. This is not to suggest that viruses cause aging, but that the formation and mechanism of action of certain viruses reflect basic cellular processes which may also be important to cellular aging. For example, many type C retroviruses are the products of genetic recombination events. Such events can occur between different viruses as evidenced by polytropic MuLV formation or between viral and cellular genetic information leading to the formation of the strongly transforming classes of avian and murine sarcoma viruses. Indeed, as Temin has proposed (1980), C-type retroviruses may have evolved in the first place by rearrangements and duplications of cellular genetic elements, possibly analogous to the transposable genetic elements found in prokaryotes and some eukaryotes.

It is now clear that genetic rearrangements are not restricted to retroviruses but reflect widespread processes of rearrangements, duplications, and transpositions which appear to occur with alarming regularity in the genomes of higher organisms (Lewin, 1981). Most such genetic "gymnastics" appear to involve the duplication and dispersal of repetitive sequence elements which also may occur as a function of age (Shmookler Reis et al., 1983). However, expressed structural genes can also undergo programmed rearrangements as evidenced by immunoglobulin gene differentiation.

It is reasonable to ask whether the majority of such events have functional significance. In cases such as the differentiation of immunoglobulin-producing cells, the answer is obviously yes. Other examples are far less clear. Primary sequence analysis of the major class of dispersed repetitive sequence elements in the human and other mammalian genomes suggests that such elements, comprising up to 5–6 percent of the total genome, arose by the duplication and dispersal of an ancestral sequence throughout the genome (Haynes et al., 1981). Whether these repetitive sequences must necessarily have a function in the genome is currently the subject of considerable debate (Doolittle and Sapienza, 1980; Orgel and Crick, 1980).

While little direct evidence exists to support a role for genetic rearrangements in normal cellular regulation (the immunoglobulin system being a prominent exception), considerable evidence is accumulating to suggest that such rearrangements may play an important role in the etiology of many cancers (Cairns, 1981; Klein, 1981). The proviral-insertion model described earlier is only one example of how genetic rearrangements within the cell can lead to neoplasia. It is highly significant, however, in that it suggests that normal cells contain genes whose alteration or overexpression can lead to neoplastic transformation. Moreover, the underexpression of similar genes might lead to the functionally opposite process of cell senescence. Indeed, the proper regulation of cellular proliferative capacity may be a finely tuned process in which relatively small changes in gene dosage or activity can tip the scales in favor of either uncontrolled cellular proliferation on one hand or greatly diminished proliferative capacity on the other. This latter effect could easily result from insertions or rearrangements at crucial genetic loci which might inactivate cellular promoter sequences or disrupt the integrity of protein encoding sequences themselves.

While such speculation must be made cautiously, it is noteworthy that elucidation of the nature of retrovirus-associated oncogenes has led to the identification of a conserved family of genes which may function in regulating the proliferative capacity of cells. This gene family may ultimately prove quite large and already appears to encompass members whose activity is lineage specific. Many members may exist which have never recombined with retroviruses and thus must be identified by other means. The identification of such genes and the elucidation of their mechanism of action may prove to be of common interest in the study of both cancer and aging.

REFERENCES

Baltimore, D. 1970. Viral RNA-dependent DNA polymerase. *Nature* 226: 1209–1211.

Baltimore, D. 1974. Tumor viruses: 1974. *Cold Spring Harbor Symp. Quant. Biol.* 39: 1187–1200.

Barbacid, M., Stephenson, J. R., and Aaronson, S. A. 1976. *gag* gene of mammalian type-C RNA tumour viruses. *Nature* 262: 554–559.

Benz, E. W., Jr., Wyndro, R. M., Nadal-Ginard, B., and Dina, D. 1980. Moloney murine sarcoma proviral DNA is a transcriptional unit. *Nature* 288: 665–669.

Bignami, A. and Parry, H. B. 1971. Aggregations of 35-nanometer particles associated with neuronal cytopathic changes in natural scrapie. *Science* 171: 389–390.

Cairns, J. 1981. The origin of human cancers. *Nature* 289: 353–357.

Chan, H. W., Bryan, T., Moore, J. L., Staal, S. P., Rowe, W. P., and Martin, M. A. 1980. Identification of ecotropic proviral sequences in inbred mouse strains with a cloned subgenomic DNA fragment. *Proc. Natl. Acad. Sci. USA* 77: 5779–5783.

Chattopadhyay, S. K., Lander, M. R., Rands, E., and Lowy, D. R. 1980. Structure of endogenous murine leukemia virus DNA in mouse genomes. *Proc. Natl. Acad. Sci. USA* 77: 5774–5778.

Chattopadhyay, S. K., Lowy, D. R., Teich, N. M., Levine, A. S., and Rowe, W. P. 1974. Qualitative and quantitative studies of AKR-type murine leukemia virus sequences in mouse DNA. *Cold Spring Harbor Symp. Quant. Biol.* 39: 1085–1101.

Clements, J. E., Narayan, O., Griffin, D. E., and Johnson, R. T. 1979. The synthesis and structure of visna virus DNA. *Virology* 93: 377–386.

Coffin, J. M. *In,* J. R. Stephenson (ed.), *Molecular Biology of RNA Tumor Viruses,* p. 199. New York: Academic Press.

Coffin, J. M., Varmus, H. E., Bishop, J. M., Essex, M., Hardy, W. D., Jr., Martin, G. S., Rosenberg, N. E., Scolnick, E. M., Weinberg, R. A., and Vogt, P. K. 1981. Proposal for naming host cell-derived inserts in retrovirus genomes. *J. Virol.* 40: 953–957.

Copeland, N. G. and Cooper, G. M. 1979. Transfection by exogenous and endogenous murine retrovirus DNAs. *Cell,* 16: 347–356.

David-Ferreira, J. F., David-Ferreira, K. L., Gibbs, C. J., and Morris, J. A. 1968. Scrapie in mice: ultrastructural observations in the cerebral cortex. *Proc. Soc. Exp. Biol. Med.* 127: 313–300.

Doolittle, W. F. and Sapienza, C. 1980. Selfish genes, the phenotype paradigm and genome evolution. *Nature* 284: 601–603.

Duvoisin, R. C. and Yahr, M. D. 1965. Encephalitis and parkinsonism. *Arch. Neurol.* 12: 227–239.

Elder, J. H., Gautsch, J. W., Jensen, F. C., Lerner, R. A., Hartley, J. W., and Rowe, W. P. 1977a. Biochemical evidence that MCF murine leukemia viruses are envelope (*env*) gene recombinants. *Proc. Natl. Acad. Sci. USA* 74: 4676–4680.

Elder, J. H., Jensen, F. C., Bryant, M. L., and Lerner, R. A. 1977b. Polymorphism of the major envelope glycoprotein (gp70) of murine C-type viruses: virion associated and differentiation antigens encoded by a multi-gene family. *Nature* 267: 23–28.

Fischinger, P. J. 1980. *In,* J. R. Stephenson (ed.), *Mo-lecular Biology of RNA Tumor Viruses,* p. 163. New York: Academic Press.

Florine, D. L., Ono, T., Cutler, R. G., and Getz, M. J. 1980. Regulation of endogenous murine leukemia virus-related nuclear and cytoplasmic RNA complexity in C57BL/6J mice of increasing age. *Cancer Res.,* 40: 519–523.

Gajdusek, D. C. and Gibbs, C. J., Jr. 1973. Subacute and chronic diseases caused by atypical infections with unconventional viruses in aberrant hosts. *Perspect. Virol.* 8: 279–311.

Gardner, M. B. 1978. Type C viruses of wild mice: characterization and natural history of amphotropic, ecotropic, and xenotropic MuLV. *Curr. Top. Microbiol. Immunol.* 79: 215–259.

Getz, M. J., Elder, P. K., and Moses, H. L. 1979. Complexity and abundance of murine leukemia virus-related nuclear and messenger RNA sequences in mouse embryo cell lines which are differentially sensitive to carcinogen-induced virus activation. *Cancer Res.* 39: 321–327.

Getz, M. J., Reiman, H. M., Siegal, G. P., Quinlan, T. J., Proper, J., Elder, P. K., and Moses, H. L. 1977. Gene expression in chemically transformed mouse embryo cells: selective enhancement of the expression of C-type RNA tumor virus genes. *Cell* 11: 909–921.

Gibbs, C. J., Jr. and Gajdusek, D. C. 1969. Infection as the etiology of spongiform encephalopathy (Creutzfeldt-Jakob disease). *Science,* 165: 1023–1025.

Gibbs, C. J., Jr. and Gajdusek, D. C. 1971. Amyotrophic lateral sclerosis, Parkinson's disease, and the parkinsonism-dementia complex on Guam: a review and summary of attempts to demonstrate infection as the aetiology. *J. Clin. Path.,* 25: 132–140.

Graf, T. and Beug, H. 1978. Avian leukemia viruses' interaction with their target cells *in vivo* and *in vitro*. *Biochim. Biophys. Acta,* 516: 269–299.

Hanafusa, H. 1977. *In,* H. Fraenkel-Conrat and R. R. Wagner (eds.), *Comprehensive Virology,* Vol. 10, p. 401. New York: Plenum.

Hartley, J. W., Wolford, N. K., Old, L. J., and Rowe, W. P. 1977. A new class of murine leukemia virus associated with development of spontaneous lymphomas. *Proc. Natl. Acad. Sci. USA* 74: 789–792.

Haynes, S. R., Toomey, T. P., Leinward, L., and Jelinek, W. R. 1981. The Chinese hamster *Alu*-equivalent sequence; a conserved, highly repetitious, interspersed deoxyribonucleic acid sequence in mammals has a structure suggestive of a transposable element. *Molec. Cell. Biol.* 1: 573–583.

Hayward, W. S., Neel, B. G., and Astrin, S. M. 1981. Activation of a cellular *onc* gene by promoter insertion in ALV-induced lymphoid leukosis. *Nature* 290: 475–480.

Huebner, R. J., Kelloff, G. J., Sarma, P. S., Lane, W. T., Turner, H. C., Gilden, R. V., Oroszlan, S., Meier, H., Myers, D. D., and Peters, R. L. 1970. Group-specific antigen expression during embryogenesis of the genome of the C-type RNA tumor virus: implications for ontogenesis and oncogenesis. *Proc. Natl. Acad. Sci. USA* 67: 366–376.

Huebner, R. J. and Todaro, G. J. 1969. Oncogenes of RNA tumor viruses as determinants of cancer. *Proc. Natl. Acad. Sci. USA* 64: 1087–1094.

Ihle, J. N. and Joseph, D. R. 1978. Serological and virological analysis of NIH (NIH × AKR) mice: evidence for three AKR murine leukemia virus loci. *Virology* 87: 287–297.

Kimberlin, R. H. 1976. *In,* R. H. Kimberlin (ed.), *Slow Virus Diseases of Animals and Man,* p. 3. Amsterdam: Elsevier.

King, A. M. 1976. High molecular weight RNAs from Rous sarcoma virus and Moloney murine leukemia virus contain two subunits. *J. Biol. Chem.* 251: 141–149.

Klein, G. 1981. The role of gene dosage and genetic transpositions in carcinogenesis. *Nature* 294: 313–318.

Lampert, P. W., Gajdusek, D. C., and Gibbs, C. J., Jr. 1971. Experimental spongiform encephalopathy (Creutzfeldt-Jakob disease) in chimpanzees. Electron microscopic studies. *J. Neuropathol. Exp. Neurol.* 30: 20–32.

Levy, J. A., Kazan, P., Varnier, O., and Kleiman, H. 1975. Murine xenotropic type C viruses. I. Distribution and further characterization of the virus in NZB mice. *J. Virol.* 16: 844–853.

Lewin, R. 1981. Do jumping genes make evolutionary leaps? *Science,* 213: 634–636.

Lilly, F. 1970. Fv-2: identification and location of a second gene governing the spleen focus response to Friend leukemia virus in mice. *J. Natl. Cancer Inst.* 45: 163–169.

Lycke, E., Modigh, K., and Roos, B. E. 1970. The monoamine metabolism in viral encephalitis of the mouse. I. Virological and biochemical results. *Brain Res.* 23: 235–246.

Marsh, R. F. 1976. *In,* R. H. Kimberlin, (ed.), *Slow Virus Diseases of Animals and Man,* p. 359. Amsterdam: Elsevier.

Marsh, R. F. 1977. *In,* E. Kurstak and C. Kurstak (eds.), *Comparative Diagnosis of Viral Diseases,* Vol. 2, p. 87. New York: Academic Press.

Marsh, R. F., Semancik, J. S., Medappa, K. C., Hanson, R. P., and Rueckert, R. R. 1974. Scrapie and transmissible mink encephalopathy: search for infectious nucleic acid. *J. Virol.* 13: 993–996.

Marttila, R. J., Arstila, P., Nikoskelainen, J., Halonen, P. E., and Rinne, U. K. 1977. Viral antibodies in the sera from patients with Parkinson disease. *Eur. Neurol.* 15: 25–33.

Neel, B. G., Hayward, W. S., Robinson, H. L., Fang, J., and Astrin, S. M. 1981. Avian leukosis virus-induced tumors have common proviral integration sites and synthesize discrete new RNAs: oncogenesis by promoter insertion. *Cell* 23: 323–334.

Orgel, L. E. and Crick, F. H. C. 1980. Selfish DNA: the ultimate parasite. *Nature* 284: 604–607.

Oskarsson, M., McClements, W. L., Blair, D. G., Mai-

zel, J. V., and Vande Woude, G. F. 1980. Properties of a normal mouse cell DNA sequence (sarc) homologous to the src sequence of Moloney sarcoma virus. *Science* 207: 1222–1224.

Payne, G. S., Bishop, J. M., and Varmus, H. E. 1982. Multiple arrangements of viral DNA and an activated host oncogene in bursal lymphomas. *Nature* 295: 209–214.

Payne, G. S., Courtneidge, S. A., Crittenden, L. B., Fadly, A. M., Bishop, J. M., and Varmus, H. E. 1981. Analysis of avian leukosis virus DNA and RNA in bursal tumours: viral gene expression is not required for maintenance of the tumor state. *Cell* 23: 311–322.

Pincus, T. 1980. *In,* J. F. Stephenson (ed.), *Molecular Biology of RNA Tumor Viruses,* p. 77. New York: Academic Press.

Poskanzer, D. C. and Schwab, R. S. 1961. Studies in the epidemiology of Parkinson's disease predicting its disappearance as a major clinical entity by 1980. *Trans. Am. Neurol. Assoc.* 86: 234–235.

Prusiner, S. B. 1982. Novel proteinaceous infectious particles cause scrapie. *Science* 216: 136–144.

Quint, W., Quax, W., van der Putten, H., and Berns, A. 1981. Characterization of AKR murine leukemia virus sequences in AKR mouse substrains and structure of integrated recombinant genomes in tumor tissues. *J. Virol.* 39: 1–10.

Reddy, E. P., Reynolds, R. K., Santos, E., and Barbacid, M. 1982. A point mutation is responsible for the acquisition of transforming properties by the T24 human bladder carcinoma oncogene. *Nature* 300: 149.

Reynolds, R. K. and Stephenson, J. R. 1977. Intracistronic mapping of the murine type C viral *gag* gene by use of conditional lethal replication mutants. *Virology* 81: 328–340.

Rohwer, R. G. 1984. Scrapie infectious agent is virus-like in size and susceptibility to inactivation. *Nature* 308: 658–662.

Rowe, W. P. 1972. Studies of genetic transmission of murine leukemia virus by AKR mice. I. Cross with FV-1n strains of mice. *J. Exptl. Med.* 136: 1272–1285.

Rowe, W. P. 1973. Genetic factors in the natural history of murine leukemia virus infection: G. H. A. Clowes Memorial Lecture. *Cancer Res.* 33: 3061–3068.

Rowe, W. P., Cloyd, M. W., and Hartley, J. W. 1979. Status of the association of mink cell focus-forming viruses with leukemogenesis. *Cold Spring Harb. Symp. Quant. Biol.* 44: 1265–1268.

Rowe, W. P., Pugh, W. E., and Hartley, J. W. 1970. Plaque assay techniques for murine leukemia viruses. *Virology* 42: 1136–1139.

Russell, E. S. 1966. *In,* E. L. Green (ed.), *Biology of the Laboratory Mouse,* p. 511. New York: McGraw-Hill.

Seman, G. and Dmochowski, L. 1977. *In,* E. Kurstak and C. Kurstak (eds.), *Comparative Diagnosis of Viral Diseases,* Vol. 2, p. 167. New York: Academic Press.

Shmookler Reis, R. J., Lumpkin, C. K., Jr., McGill, J. R., Riabowol, K. T., and Goldstein, S. 1983. Extrachromosomal circular copies of an 'inter-alu' unstable sequence in human DNA are amplified during *in vitro* and *in vivo* aging. *Nature* 301: 394–398.

Sigurdsson, B. 1954. Rida, a chronic encephalitis of sheep. *Br. Vet. J.* 110: 341–354.

Steffen, D. L., Bird, S., and Weinberg, R. A. 1980. Evidence for the Asiatic origin of endogenous AKR-type murine leukemia proviruses. *J. Virol.* 35: 824–835.

Strand, M., Lilly, F., and August, J. T. 1974. Host control of endogenous murine leukemia virus gene expression: concentrations of viral proteins in high and low leukemia mouse strains. *Proc. Natl. Acad. Sci. USA* 71: 3682–3686.

Swanstrom, R., DeLorbe, W. J., Bishop, J. M., and Varmus, H. E. 1981. Nucleotide sequence of cloned unintegrated avian sarcoma virus DNA: viral DNA contains direct and inverted repeats similar to those in transposable elements. *Proc. Natl. Acad. Sci. USA* 78: 124–128.

Tabin, C. J., Bradley, S. M., Bargmann, C. I., Weinberg, R. A., Papageorge, A. G., Scolnick, E. M., Dhar, R., Lowy, D. R., and Chang, E. H. 1982. Mechanism of activation of a human oncogene. *Nature 300*: 143.

Tamm, I. 1975. Cell injury with viruses. *Am. J. Pathol.* 81: 163–178.

Temin, H. M. 1971. The protovirus hypothesis: speculations on the significance of RNA-directed DNA synthesis for normal development and for carcinogenesis. *J. Natl. Cancer Inst.* 46: 3–7.

Temin, H. M. 1980. Origin of retroviruses from cellular moveable genetic elements. *Cell* 21: 599–600.

Temin, H. M. and Mizutani, S. 1970. RNA-dependent DNA polymerase in virions of Rous sarcoma virus. *Nature* 266: 1211–1213.

Van Beveren, C., Goddard, J. G., Berns, A., and Verma, I. M. 1980. Structure of the Moloney murine leukemia viral DNA: nucleotide sequence of the 5' long terminal repeat and adjacent cellular sequences. *Proc. Natl. Acad. Sci. USA* 77: 3307–3311.

Varmus, H. E. 1982. Form and function of retroviral proviruses. *Science* 216: 812–820.

Ward, R. L., Porter, D. D., and Stevens, J. G. 1974. Nature of the scrapie agent: evidence against a viroid. *J. Virol.* 14: 1099–1103.

11

AGING AND CELL MEMBRANE COMPLEXES: THE LIPID BILAYER, INTEGRAL PROTEINS, AND CYTOSKELETON

Faramarz Naeim
and
Roy L. Walford
Department of Pathology
University of California

INTRODUCTION

Cell membranes are predominantly lipid structures with embedded proteins. The proteins possess enzyme, transport, or receptor activity. Intimately related to certain aspects of membrane structure are the cytoskeletal elements of the cell. To some degree, these several structures function together, and age-related changes may concern all three.

In living cells, contact between intracellular activities and the external environment generally involves the surface membrane. This membrane receives signals from the outside and relays information to interior cellular subunits. It plays an important role in recognition of self and nonself, in proliferation, in differentiation, and in adaptation and response. Ionic exchange between the cell and the surrounding environment, pinocytosis, phagocytosis, the release of cellular products, and response to ligands such as hormones, antibodies, and lectins are all phenomena in which the cell membrane, and in some instances the cytoskeleton, are in-

volved. Other membranous structures, of mitochondria, microsomes, lysosomes, and endoplasmic reticulum, serve to compartmentalize the interior architecture and economize functional requirements of the cell.

In this chapter, selected changes in membrane structures and functions and in the cytoskeleton are discussed as these may relate to the process of aging and, to some extent, to the "diseases of aging." Our emphasis includes, but is broader than, the customary "membranology" review, but at the same time is limited to subject matter which has been actually studied in relation to aging.

CELL MEMBRANE STRUCTURE AND FLUIDITY

Membranes are asymmetric enclosed bilayer structures consisting predominantly of lipids and embedded proteins. The lipid components are composed of phospholipids (phosphoglycerides and sphingomyelin), glycolipids, and neutral lipids with fatty acids of varying chain length and number of saturated bonds. Usually, phosphoglycerides from biological membranes consist of one saturated and one unsaturated fatty acid (Quinn and Chapman, 1980). Numerous studies have described variations in lipid composition in membranes of different species, cell types, and cellular organelles (Rouser et al., 1968; Law and Synder, 1972; Ness, 1974). For example, cholesterol is found much more abundantly in plasma membranes than in mitochondrial, Golgi or nuclear membranes, and is generally more highly concentrated toward the outside of the plasma membrane (Martin, 1981). Characteristic phospholipid classes are represented in each particular membrane, and the plasma membrane exhibits large variations in composition between different cell types (Rouser et al., 1968).

Membrane proteins are divisible into two general groups according to the degree of stabilization onto the membrane lipid bilayer. Those of the predominant group span the entire transverse distance of the bilayer; they are globular in shape, amphipathic, and made up of two hydrophilic ends separated by an intervening hydrophobic region. Distributed asymmetrically across the membrane bilayer (Martin, 1981), these so-called integral proteins play a major role in membrane function (Singer and Nicolson, 1972; Nicolson, 1976a, 1976b). They generally possess enzyme, transport, or receptor activity. The second group, the "peripheral membrane proteins," are hydrophilic, relatively soluble in aqueous media, and not essential to the integrity of the membrane; their removal does not result in destruction of the membrane (Singer and Nicolson, 1972).

In the "fluid mosaic model," membrane components are able to diffuse laterally within the plane of the membrane (Singer and Nicolson, 1972; Nicolson, 1976a, 1976b; and Edidin, 1974). This diffusion offers a potential mechanism for directed changes in the topography of specific membrane components (Nicolson and Poste, 1976a). Lateral diffusion of integral proteins and lipids has been observed. Proteins diffuse to a

greater degree than lipids (Edidin, 1974; Edelman et al., 1973), although certain proteins may be relatively immobile (Nicolson and Painter, 1973; Edelman, 1976).

The distinct differences in mobility of the membrane components suggest that the cell may possess a control mechanism for topography whereby the macromolecules can be redistributed (Nicolson and Poste, 1976a, 1976b). Topographic molecular patterns could play an important role in mechanisms of cell contact and recognition, cell-to-cell interactions, and modulation of cell surface properties after interaction with mitogens, antibodies, hormones, lectins, etc. (Nicolson and Poste, 1976a, 1976b).

In biological membranes at physiological temperatures, the lipid hydrocarbon chains are relatively fluid and the bulk of the lipids are in a liquid-crystalline state (Oldfield and Chapman, 1972; Chapman, 1975; Hegner, 1980). This state, which is to be distinguished from a gel phase in which hydrocarbon chains are rigid and closely packed, is an essential condition for maintaining membrane functions, and is affected by the following factors.

Natural Fatty Acid Residues

The degree of unsaturation of the phospholipid acyl chains is a prominent determinant of membrane fluidity. Unsaturated fatty acids are associated with greater fluidity (Hegner, 1980). Lecithin and sphingomyelin constitute more than 50 percent of the phospholipids in mammalian membranes, and the highly saturated sphingomyelin forms liposomes of a lower fluidity than lecithin (Shinitzky and Barenholz, 1974). The saturation/unsaturation ratio of fatty acids is modulated by intracellular metabolism, and is considered the major mechanism for regulating membrane fluidity and adaptation to temperature changes, or to metabolic and nutritional disorders.

Cholesterol

Cholesterol acts as an important modulator of the state of fluidity in the cell membrane

(Martin, 1981). In eukaryotic systems increased cholesterol decreases acyl chain mobility above the solid to liquid-crystalline transition, while decreased levels increase acyl chain mobility below the solid to liquid-crystalline transition (Sinensky, 1980): thus, if fluidity is less, cholesterol tends to make it more; if it is more, cholesterol makes it less.

Proteins

The fluidity and functional properties of biological membranes are achieved in part by collaboration between proteins and lipids (Nicolson, 1976a, 1976b). Proteins decrease membrane fluidity, especially in membranes with a low cholesterol/phospholipid ratio. A decline in protein solubilization in the lipid bilayer of the membrane will displace the vertical position of proteins (Borochov and Shinitzky, 1976). These changes probably play a significant role in modulation of membrane receptors (Shinitzky and Barenholz, 1978) and may explain some of the phenomena of aging (Heron et al., 1980).

Temperature

At physiological temperature, the bulk of the lipids in mammalian biological membranes are in the liquid-crystalline phase, in which the hydrocarbon chains are relatively fluid (Hegner, 1980). An increase in temperature induces a change in fatty acyl chains from a jell all-*trans* state with close molecular packing to a fluid liquid-crystalline *cis-trans* state with decreased packing and, therefore, increased molecular motion (Hegner, 1980). Living organisms are able to adapt themselves to some extent to changes in environmental temperature if the changes are gradual. The alterations associated with temperature acclimatization may be regulated by isoenzymes which display different affinities for their substrates at various temperatures and alter the physical properties of membranes (Quinn and Chapman, 1980). Studies by Thompson and Nazawa (1976) of a thermotolerant strain of the protozoan *Tetra-*

hymena pyriformis showed that the organism responds to various temperatures by altering both the degree of unsaturation of membrane phospholipids and the relative proportions of the different phospholipid classes in order to control membrane fluidity. Poikilothermic and heterothermic organisms acclimatize better to variations in environmental temperature than homeothermic animals. Studies on cold-adapted microorganisms suggest that to preserve the membrane in the fluid condition necessary to sustain activity of membrane-associated enzymes, the proportion of unsaturated fatty acyl residues in membrane lipids increases as temperature decreases (Quin and Chapman, 1980). The possible role of adaptive membrane changes in the longer life spans of poikilotherms maintained at reduced temperatures has not been explored (Liu and Walford, 1972).

AGE-ASSOCIATED ALTERATIONS IN MEMBRANE STRUCTURE AND FLUIDITY

Experimental evidence points to a broad spectrum of age-associated changes in the structures and functions of cell membranes, including plasma membranes, membranes of the intracellular organelles, and membrane-related structures.

Plasma Membrane

Studies on rat liver cells and the cultured human fibroblast WI-38 have demonstrated an increase in the surface area and cell volume during aging (Le Guilly et al., 1973; Pieri et al., 1977; Schmucker, 1976; Bowman and Daniel, 1975; Mitsui and Schneider, 1976). The number of fibroblasts making cell-to-cell contact and their degree of cellular mobility decrease with passage number (Bowman and Daniel, 1975). Increases in microvilli and blebs have been reported in late passage ("senescent") human diploid fibroblasts (Crusberg et al., 1979; Johnson, 1979; Wolosewick and Porter, 1977).

Age-associated changes in cell composition, especially in the lipid components, may vary between different tissues or the same tissue from different species. For example, total lipid or phospholipid decreased with animal age in rat and mouse liver (Grinna and Barber, 1972, 1973; Carlson et al., 1968) and in rat kidney and pancreas (Grinna and Barber, 1973; Prasannan, 1973), but remained constant with age in membranes from mouse and human brains (Fillerup and Mead, 1967; Sun and Samorajski, 1972), and from rat heart, skeletal muscle and, red blood cells (Carlson et al., 1968; Malhotra and Kritchivsky, 1975).

Composition of the individual lipid components of membranes has also been examined (reviewed by Grinna, 1977). Phosphatidylcholine, a predominant membrane phospholipid, decreased whereas phosphatidylethanolamine increased in red blood cells from aged humans (Gold and Altschuler, 1972). Hegner et al. (1979) found the phospholipid content in human red cell membranes to be significantly lower in older than in younger individuals, but Araki and Rifkind (1980) detected no significant changes. Reports on cholesterol changes with age are not uniform: increases are reported in rat liver and skeletal muscle (Carlson et al., 1968) and in mouse brain (Sun and Samorajski, 1972), and no change or decreases in rat liver (Rubin et al., 1973; Prasannan, 1972) and heart (Carlson et al., 1968).

The cholesterol/phospholipid ratio in the plasma membrane and other membranes increases during aging (Carlson et al., 1968; Grinna and Barber, 1975; Malhotra and Kritchivsky, 1975; Hegner et al., 1979; Araki and Rifkind, 1980). Despite the different expressions of results, this increase is evident for the representative data of Table 1. Investigations by Rivnay et al. (1978, 1979) on membrane fluidity by means of fluorescence polarization techniques showed a direct correlation between the cholesterol/phospholipid ratio in the serum and the microviscosity of peripheral blood lymphocyte membranes, both of which increased with age. The age-associated increase in microviscosity is accompanied by a decrease in response of the lymphocytes to stimulation by concanavalin A (Rivnay et al., 1980).

Microviscosity is defined as the intermolecular frictional force which opposes flow in biological membranes (Shinitzky and Barenholz, 1974). It should be noted that in "fluidity" measurements for determining microviscosity, the possible role of membrane heterogeneity has not always received adequate attention (Owicki and McConnell, 1980). Binary mixtures of cholesterol and phosphatidylcholines may consist of alternating "ridges" of pure phosphatidylcholine and "plains" containing cholesterol. Inhomogeneities in lipid composition, and therefore in "fluidity," in biological membranes

TABLE 1. Cholesterol/Phospholipid Ratios in Cell Membranes in Relation to Age.

Tissue	Age	Cholesterol		Phospholipid		Ratio	Reference
Red blood cells (human)	y (<30 yr)	2.79 n mol/mg		363 n mol/mg		0.77	Hegner et al. (1979)
	o (>70 yr)	2.79 n mol/mg		297 n mol/mg		0.94	
Red blood cells (rat)	y (1.5 mo.)	0.334	% of total lipid	0.077	% of total lipid	4.34	Malhorta and Kritchevsky (1975)
	o (1–2 yr)	0.598		0.077		7.72	
Plasma membrane (rat liver)	y (80 days)	6.6	% of total lipid	50	% of total lipid	0.13	Hegner and Platt (1975)
	o (780 days)	9.7		40		0.24	
Microsomal membrane (rat liver)	y (6 mo.)	—		—		0.22	Grinna and Barber (1976)
	o (24 mo.)	—		—		0.39	
Mitochondrial membrane (rat liver)	y (6 mo.)	—		—		0.082	Grinna and Barber (1976)
	o (24 mo.)	—		—		0.130	

are clearly demonstrated in at least a few instances (Owicki and McConnell, 1980). Recent studies by Karnovsky and associates (Karnovsky, 1979; Karnovsky et al., 1981; Klausner et al., 1980) indicate a considerable degree of heterogeneity of lipid components of the plasma membrane.

Fluidity of membranes may affect receptor binding sites. According to Heron et al. (1980), fluidization of membrane lipids by treatment with lecithin or linoleic acid causes a decline in binding sites for serotonin to mouse membranes, while up to a fivefold increase in serotonin binding may be noted when synaptic membranes are incubated with either cholesteryl hemisuccinate or stearic acid (both agents decrease membrane fluidity). An increase in the lipid viscosity of synaptic membranes from the brains of old compared to young animals has been observed (Heron et al., 1980), as well as an increased number of serotonin binding sites in brains from old humans (Shih and Young, 1978, Heron et al., 1980).

As illustrated in Table 2, the fatty acid composition of plasma membranes becomes more saturated with age (Gold and Altschuler, 1972; Grinna and Barber, 1975; Haw-

croft and Martin, 1974; Sun and Samorajski, 1973; Hubbard and Garratt, 1980; Hegner, 1980). A high cholesterol/phospholipid ratio and elevated levels of saturated fatty acids would be expected to affect the liquid-crystalline fluid state of the membrane, with a decline in its fluidity.

Other age-associated changes in plasma membrane components include quantitative alterations in glycoproteins, proteins, and the activities of membrane-bound enzymes. Sialic acid and galactosamine contents of the membranes of red blood cells decrease with age (Balduini et al., 1974; Hegner et al., 1979). The extrinisic proteins of human red blood cells are reported to increase with age, due to absorption of serum proteins onto surface membranes (Kadlubowski and Harris, 1974; Kay, 1975). In aged rats, the ratio of the number of exofacial sulfhydryl groups to exofacial sulfhydryl plus disulfide groups may be significantly decreased in the plasma membranes of adipocytes (Hughes et al., 1980). In the plasma membranes of rat liver, three classes of integral proteins were found to change relative to one another with age (Barclay et al., 1972).

The responsiveness of a variety of tissues to stimulation by hormones, neurotransmitters, antigens, and mitogens may decrease with age (Frolkis et al., 1973; Walker and Walker, 1973; Miller and Allen, 1973; Walford et al., 1981). These alterations in cell adaptation and responsiveness could in part result from changes in the structure or density of membrane receptors, or from disturbances in the redistribution and mobility of the receptors due either to changes in cell membrane fluidity or to alterations in cytoskeletal structure, function, or both.

The activity of Na^+, K^+-ATPase in human red blood cells decreases with age of the cells (Kadlubowski and Agutter, 1977; Hegner et al., 1979; Platt and Norwig, 1980). This enzyme is greatly influenced by the membrane fluidity, and the increase in the cholesterol/phospholipid ratio which occurs with age lowers the transport activities of the enzyme (Kimelberg and Papahadjopaulos, 1972; Stahl, 1973). The age-dependent phos-

TABLE 2. Fatty Acid Composition of Lecithin in Rat Liver Plasma Membranes of Young and Old Rats.

Saturated fatty acids (18.0) are increased and unsaturated fatty acids (18.2 and 20.4) decreased; however, the polyunsaturated fatty acid 22.6 is increased (adapted from Hegner, 1980).

Lecithin Fatty Acids (% of total)	Age of Animal	
	3 mo.	24 mo.
16	22.1	24.4
18	18.4	22.2
18.1	7.6	10.0
18.2	16.8	14.7
20.4	20.2	18.5
22.6	2.61	5.93
unsat./sat.	1.19	1.06

pholipid decline may reflect a loss of phosphatidylserine, considered to be the activator of ouabain-sensitive ATPase (Zwaal et al., 1973). Unlike the situation in human red cells, Na^+, K^+-ATPase has been reported to increase in hepatocyte membranes of aging rats (Hegner, 1976). Reiss and Sackton (1982) observed a decline in the specific activities of membrane-bound maltase in isolated brush border membranes of renal tissue in senescent rats.

Aging may also be associated with alterations in ionic permeability of the plasma membrane. The resting potassium permeability of the membrane decreases in liver and nerve cells of aging rats (Pieri et al., 1977; Zs-Nagy, 1978, 1979), resulting in an increase in concentration of intracellular potassium (Zs-Nagy, 1978, 1979).

Intracellular Membranes

Ultrastructural studies of rat, mouse, and human liver and rat and mouse heart showed an age-related decrease in the numbers of mitochondria (Frolkis and Bogatskaya, 1968; Huemer et al., 1971; Herbener, 1976; Tate and Herbener, 1976; Tauchi et al., 1974; Wilson and Franks, 1975). In the majority of studies, this decrease was accompanied by increases in mitochondrial size or volume (Tauchi et al., 1974; Wilson and Franks, 1975). Pieri et al. (1975) noted increases in mitochondrial size and number in the hepatocytes of old rats. Other investigations did not detect changes in mitochondrial size with age (Herbener, 1976; Tate and Herbener, 1976). In early passage, chick embryo cells display oval regular mitochondria with transverse cristae, while many of the mitochondria in late passage cells are kidney shaped, and the cristae are sometimes longitudinally oriented (Brock and Hay, 1971). Lipid peroxidation increases in mitochondrial membranes of aged animals (Hegner, 1980). The ratio of cholesterol to phospholipid phosphorus in membrane-associated elements of hepatic mitochondria increases with age in rats (Vorbeck et al., 1981).

Aging human fibroblasts in culture accumulate glycogen and lysosomes, and display a decrease in polyribosomes (Lipetz and Cristofalo, 1972). The Golgi system reveals some alterations in older cell populations: the cisternae are swollen and surrounded by numerous vacuoles (Lipetz and Cristofalo, 1972).

Accumulation of lipofuscins in various tissues in aged animals constitutes a morphologic hallmark of cellular aging (Strehler et al., 1959; Samorajski et al., 1964). Lipofuscins (age pigments), which are precipitated in lysosomes (residual bodies), are derived from peroxidation of subcellular membranes containing polyunsaturated lipids (Casselman, 1951; Chio et al., 1969; Brunk and Burn, 1972; Toth, 1968; Brunk and Collins, 1981). Lipofuscin has also been demonstrated in conditions other than aging, including hypoxia, vitamin E deficiency, acetanilide administration, stress, and cellular atrophy (Sulkin and Srivary, 1960; Wolman and Zaidel, 1962). Certain lysosomal enzymes, including acid phosphatase and β-glucuronidase, increase with age (Cristofalo, 1970). According to Hochschild (1971), cellular aging may be associated with the ''congestive engorgement'' of lysosomes, with leakage of lytic enzymes into the cytoplasm and damage to cellular organelles.

The surface area of smooth endoplasmic reticulum of rat and mouse liver cells increases with age, while that of rough endoplasmic reticulum decreases (Schmucker, 1976; Pieri et al., 1975). In aged animals, the smooth muscle cells of rat and rabbit aortas become irregular, show a decrease in endoplasmic reticulum, and appear rich in plasmalemmal vesicles (Eisenberg et al., 1969).

Biochemical changes occur in the membranes of cytoplasmic organelles of aging cells which are mostly similar to those occurring in the plasma membrane. Grinna and Barber (1972) demonstrated a decline of phospholipid/protein ratios in the microsomes of rat liver and kidney cells from old (24 months) compared to young (6 months) rats. In mouse liver microsomes, total phospholipid content decreases with age (Hawcroft and Martin, 1974) (Figure 1A); this

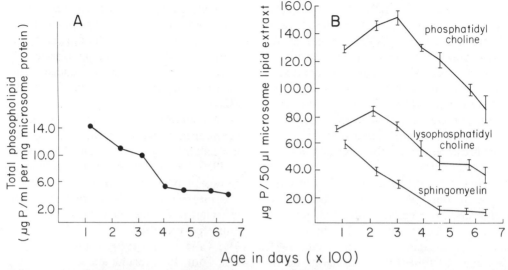

Figure 1. The relation between age and lipid content of mouse liver microsomes. A: total phospholipid content. B: content of phosphatidyl choline, lysophosphatidyl choline, and sphingomyelin (adapted from Hawcroft and Martin, 1974).

change may be noteworthy since phospholipids seem functionally the most important of the lipid complement of mammalian cells. With some variation, an age-related decline also occurs in microsomal phosphatidylcholine, lysophosphatidylcholine, and sphingomyelin (Fig. 1B), along with a decrease in glycolipid content (Hawcroft and Martin, 1974). In rat muscle, sarcoplasmic reticulum phosphatidylethanolamine was found to decrease with age (Bertrand et al., 1975).

The activities of many membrane-bound enzymes in organelles change with age. The specific activity of microsomal glucose-6-phosphatase is reduced in the liver and kidney of aged animals (Gold and Windell, 1974; Grinna and Barber, 1972, 1975). Some studies suggest that the decline in enzyme activity results from an age-related increase in enzyme inhibitors with age (Grinna and Barber, 1975). The specific activity of mitochondrial β-hydroxybutyrate dehydrogenase declines in the liver and kidney, while mitochondrial cytochrome C reductase increases in the liver and decreases in the kidney of aged rats (Grinna and Barber, 1972). Mitochondrial alanine aminotransferase activity decreases, but mitochondrial

malate dehydrogenase activity increases during aging (Kanugo and Gandhi, 1972; Patnaik and Kanugo, 1974).

Other Membrane-related Structures

Fibronectin, a glycoprotein present on the cell membrane and in the intercellular matrix, plays an important role in cell adhesions (Yamada and Olden, 1978). Recent studies by Chandrasekhar and Millis (1980) demonstrated an age-associated alteration in the adhesive potency of fibronectin released by human fibroblasts in culture. Fibronectin derived from senescent fibroblasts was less effective in causing cell spreading and in supporting cell-substrate adhesion. Fibronectin is present also in soluble form in plasma and other body fluids (Mosesson and Umfleet, 1970; Kuusela et al., 1978). Labat-Robert et al. (1981) have shown an age-dependent increase of fibronectin in human plasma.

Increased thickness of capillary basement membranes occurs in both aged individuals and diabetic patients (Siperstein et al., 1968; Bloodworth et al., 1969; Kilo et al., 1972; Xi et al., 1982). This basement membrane thickening appears segmental and does not involve the entire length of the capillary. Similar age-associated changes have been observed in glomerular, seminiferous tubular, and pulmonary epithelial basement membranes (Jorgensen and Bentzon, 1968; Adamson, 1968; Xi et al., 1982; Taylor and Price, 1982). Age-related thickening of glomerular and capillary basement membranes is associated with biochemical alterations (Smalley, 1980a, 1980b; Langeveld et al., 1981). The glomerular basement membranes of diabetic patients and aged individuals display significant increases in mannose, galactose, hydroxylysine, proline, and glycine, and decreases in sialic acid, glucose, lysine, histidine, and leucine (De Bats et al., 1982). The rat glomerular basement membrane becomes progressively less soluble in sodium dodecylsulfate and 2-mercaptoethanol with age (Taylor and Price, 1982).

Myelin undergoes age-related changes (see review by Sun and Sun, 1979). Investigations by Sun and Samorajski (1972) of 3-, 8-, and 24-month-old female mice revealed a threefold increase in protein and major lipid components in isolated myelin fractions from the old mice: the cholesterol/phospholipid ratio increased, whereas the galactolipid/phospholipid ratio decreased. Increase in myelin content of neural tissues with age has also been reported in aged mice (Morell et al., 1972).

Etiology of Cell Membrane Changes in Aging

Free radicals such as superoxide, hydroxyl radicals, and singlet oxygen initiate a series of chain reactions resulting in lipid peroxidation and the production of terminal aldehydes, with damage to cell membranes (Packer et al., 1967; Raynolds, 1977; Leibovitz and Siegel, 1980). The unsaturated fatty acids of phospholipids are extremely susceptible to oxidation: since the fatty acids of most subcellular organelles such as microsomal, mitochondrial, and lysosomal membranes tend to be highly unsaturated, the organelles are primary targets for free radical attack. According to Hegner (1980), age-associated changes in lipid composition, in

lipid-dependent enzyme activities, and in transport capacities of membranes result from lipid peroxidation secondary to increased production of superoxide radicals in aging. The result of the continuing lipid peroxidation is an age-dependent decrease of unsaturated fatty acids and an increase in saturated fatty acids. Damage to lysosomal membranes due to chronic exposure to lipid peroxidation was proposed by Hochschild (1971) to be fundamentally involved in aging, with leakage of lysosomal enzymes, DNases, RNases, and proteases into cytoplasmic and extracellular spaces.

Lipid peroxidation can be generated endogenously by intracellular enzymes such as TPNH oxidase, which increases peroxidation of microsomal lipids (Hochstein and Ernster, 1963). Peroxidation can also be generated by exposure to exogenous agents such as carbon tetrachloride, alcohols, ionizing radiation, and ultraviolet light (Boag, 1968; Gordis, 1969; Copeland, 1972; Reknagel and Glende, 1973; DiLuzio, 1973). Peroxidation may be decreased by various substances such as superoxide dismutase, catalase, reduced glutathione, ascorbic acid, butylated hydroxyanisole, and some metals such as calcium, barium, magnesium, and copper (see review by Robert, 1977), and by administration of "essential" phospholipids (Hegner and Platt, 1975).

Another interpretation of cell membrane damage in aging was proposed by Zs-Nagy (1978, 1979): that the membrane undergoes physicochemical changes during aging which result in increased rigidity, decreased potassium conductance, and an increase in intracellular potassium content. The increased intracellular ionic strength slows enzymatic reactions and chromatin functions such as transcription. These changes lead to retardation of protein synthesis, which in turn further adversely affects repair of membrane alterations.

SELF-RECOGNITION AND ADAPTATION

Self-recognition and adaptation are fundamental biologic phenomena associated with the control of many types of developmental and differentiation processes (Katz, 1981). Cell-cell interactions in immune reactions, in differentiation events, and in embryology are mediated by cell membrane receptors (Loor, 1980). Among these receptors, histocompatibility antigens stand out as playing a critical role in many cell responses. These antigens are transmembrane cell-surface glycoproteins which are products of the major histocompatibility complex of genes (MHC). The MHCs in all vertebrate species so far investigated are strikingly homologous and influence a wide array of biological activities, including allograft survival, immune responsiveness, and susceptibility to a number of diseases. The mouse MHC, the H-2 system (on chromosome 17), has been more completely mapped than the corresponding HLA system in man (on chromosome 6), largely because of the availability of congenic strains differing only in the MHC region.

Major Histocompatibity Complex (MHC) and Aging

The MHC is one of the best studied systems determining surface markers on cells. The MHC antigens reveal quantitative and perhaps qualitative alterations with age. More significantly, the MHC and associated gene systems are involved in the genetic basis for aging.

MHC Surface Antigens on Aging Cells. Autoimmune reactions in aging could represent an abnormal response to "self" antigens or a normal response to new antigenic determinants on old cells. Gozes et al. (1978) demonstrated that a syngeneic graft-versus-host response can be induced in lymph nodes of young mice by foot pad injection of syngeneic spleen cells from old donors: this would correspond to a qualitative difference with age in surface recognition markers. Studies by Callard and Basten (1979), using spleen cells from syngeneic young and old mice of the same sex in one-way mixed lymphocyte reactions, revealed a positive young-versus-old syngeneic re-

sponse. No response was obtained in young-to-young and old-to-old combinations.

Further evidence for age-related qualitative differences was the demonstration that macrophages from old mice are abnormal in their ability to function as stimulator cells in an allogeneic mixed lymphocyte reaction (Callard, 1978). Analyzing spleen cells from young and old Lewis rats, Woda et al. (1979) observed a decline in density and mobility of membrane Ia antigens with age. In fluorescence photobleach recovery experiments, the fluidity of the lymphocyte membrane from old rats was decreased. An age-associated decrease in theta antigen receptors on mouse T-lymphocytes was reported by Brennan and Jaroslow (1975).

Altered antigenic determinants in aging cells might have arisen in several ways. Changes in the cholesterol/phospholipid ratio of the cell membrane, which alters membrane fluidity, might expose hidden antigenic determinants (Rivnay et al., 1979); or somatic mutation with insertion of altered protein into the cell membrane (Burnet, 1970, 1974) might occur.

Studies on lymphoblast cultures obtained from patients with diseases associated with the "accelerated aging" have yielded somewhat conflicting results. Using the complement-dependent cytotoxicity assay, Goldstein et al. (1974) reported a marked reduction in expression of HLA antigens on progeria fibroblasts. Similar results were obtained on fibroblast cultures from patients with Werner's syndrome (an adult onset progeria) (Goldstein and Singal, 1974). However, recent studies by Milunsky and Tsung (1979) and by Brown et al. (1980) failed to demonstrate significant changes in HLA expression on fibroblast cultures from progeria patients.

Influence of the Major Histocompatibility Gene Complex on Aging. Direct evidence for an effect of the MHC on maximum life span was provided by Smith and Walford (1977): in different strains of congenic mice, both mean and maximum life spans were strongly influenced by alleles of the MHC. Studies in

MHC-typed F_1 hybrid mice by Yunis's group (Williams et al., 1981) confirmed and extended these findings. Popp (1978, 1981) demonstrated that life span segregates with H-2 in F_2 hybrids from congenic parental mice.

An important feature of mammalian aging is a severe decline in immune functional capacity, particularly thymus-dependent immunity, accompanied by an increase in the incidence of anti-self reactivity (see Chapter 16; see also Gottesman and Walford, 1982). These phenomena are greatly influenced by the MHC genotype.

Other, nonimmune phenomena which seem prominently involved in aging may also be linked to, or influenced by, the MHC (Walford, 1983). These may include the level of DNA repair capacity (Hall et al., 1981), cyclic nucleotide metabolism, the amounts of certain free-radical scavenging agents in cells, and possibly other enzyme systems important in aging. Cyclic nucleotides function as "second messengers" in carrying information from hormone surface receptors to the nucleus. In mice, two MHC-linked genes may control or influence the level of cAMP (Lafuse et al., 1979). The biological origin of free radical scavengers probably stems from the transition in remote geologic time from anaerobic to aerobic life forms. In mammals, superoxide dismutase is to be regulated by genes linked to the MHC (Novak et al., 1980), and kidney catalase may be similarly regulated. It has been suggested that a primitive gene or gene complex concerned with free radical scavenging and with aging was the ancestor of the MHC, which indeed still retains many of its original antibiosenescent properties (Walford, 1981, 1983; Gottesman et al., 1982). Recent studies in H-2 congenic mice suggest that genes governing levels of the p-450 mixed function oxidase system may also be MHC-linked (Imamura et al., 1983).

Other Immune Surface Markers in Relation to Aging

Woda and Feldman (1979) demonstrated a decline in density of surface membrane im-munoglobulin on the B-lymphocytes of aged rats. An age-related decline in Fc receptor-mediated immunoregulators was demonstrated in mouse lymphoid systems by Scribner et al. (1978). According to Woda et al. (1979), the density of AgB, Ia, and Fc receptors diminishes on the surface of cells from old rats. Kay (1981) presented evidence that the emergence of new surface receptors (e.g., the senescent cell antigens) on the aging cell initiates the generation of autoimmune antibodies, which results in the removal of the cells.

Whereas a substantial decline exists in response to the mitogen PHA (phytohemag-glutinin) with age (Mathies et al., 1973; Inkeles et al., 1977), other studies did not reveal any age-related alterations in PHA receptors at the lymphocyte cell surface (Hung et al., 1975). The affinity for sheep erythrocytes does not appear to be significantly different in lymphocytes from young compared to old individuals (Brohee et al., 1980).

MEMBRANE-ASSOCIATED CYTOSKELETAL STRUCTURES

In the "fluid mosaic model" of plasma membrane structure proposed by Singer and Nicolson (1972), integral membrane glycoproteins and proteins are able to diffuse and move laterally within the membrane lipid bilayer (Bretschen, 1973; Robbins and Nicolson, 1975). As noted earlier, this diffusion may be influenced by heterogeneity within intrinsic components of the lipid bilayer (Karnovsky, 1979; Owicki and McConnell, 1980); in addition, binding of multivalent ligands such as antibodies and lectins to surface receptors may cause redistribution of receptor-ligand complexes into "clusters," larger "patches," or "caps" on the cell surface (Nicolson and Poste, 1976a). Patching precedes capping in that patches distributed over the surface are brought together at one pole to become a cap. However, unlike patching, capping is a temperature-dependent, energy requiring process.

The mobility and topography of certain ligand receptor complexes may be controlled by membrane-associated cytoskeletal elements such as microtubules and microfilaments (Robbins and Nicolson, 1975; Nicolson, 1976a). Evidence for direct association between membrane receptors and cytoskeletal elements is that, in the process of capping, cross-linked surface immunoglobulin becomes attached to actin (Flanagan and Koch, 1978); in patching, cross-linkage of membrane receptors is postulated as the crucial step in the attachment of cell membrane receptors to actin. Similar investigations by Bourguignon and Singer (1977) and by Koch and Smith (1978) suggested that the mouse MHC antigens form a stable association with the microfilament protein actin. Studies by Portugal (1979) indicated that movement of MHC antigens in the plasma membrane is associated with the movement of cytoskeletal elements.

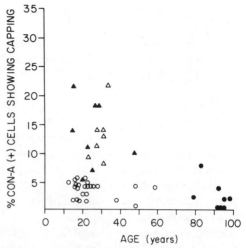

Figure 2. Percentage of Con-A capping according to age in 4 groups of individuals: normal staff members △; non-DS patients ▲; DS patients ○; and aged persons ●.

Disturbance of Membrane Receptor Mobility in Aging and in Diseases Associated with Accelerated Aging

Cell membrane receptors play an important role in cell recognition and adaptation. Their kinetics and redistribution influence or are affected by the process of aging. In studies by Naeim and Walford (1980), the percentage of cells showing capping of surface membrane immunoglobulin and Con-A receptor sites was significantly lower in aged persons (over 85 years) and in patients with Down's syndrome compared to age-matched institutional and normal controls (Figure 2). The finding of a lower degree of capping in Down's syndrome supports its status as a condition manifesting accelerated aging.

Colchicine, an inhibitor of tubulin assembly, significantly enhanced capping in lymphocytes (Figure 3), suggesting that an excess of polymerized tubulin (microtubules) may occur in lymphocytes during normal or accelerated aging (Naeim et al., 1981). Similar changes occurred in lymphocytes of Lewis rats (Woda and Feldman, 1979; Woda et al., 1979). Analysis of spleen cell populations from young (3–4 months) and old (>24

months) rats indicated a drop in capping percentage of surface membrane immunoglobulin, Ia, AgB, and Fc receptors in lymphoid cells of the old rats. The density of the membrane markers was also diminished on the surface of cells from old rats. By the fluorescence photobleach recovery technique, the fluidity of the lymphocyte membrane from old rats was diminished and the lateral diffusion of AgB was decreased. Thus, alterations both in plasma membrane fluidity and in cytoskeletal function contribute to the differences between old and young rat lymphocytes.

Possible Role of Cytoskeletal Structures in Cellular Aging (Cytoskeletal Hypothesis of Aging)

The cytoskeletal system plays an important role in cell recognition and adaptation by regulating redistribution of membrane receptors and cell-cell interactions, and by conveying functional and growth regulatory information from cell membrane to intracellular components (Puck, 1977). A considerable proportion of the age-associated changes at the cellular level may in part re-

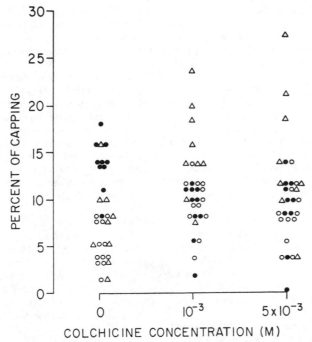

Figure 3. Effect of Colchicine on the capping of Concanavalin A (Con A) receptor sites in lymphoid cells obtained from controls (●) aged individuals (○), and patients with Down's syndrome (△).

flect defects of the cytoskeletal system in the conveyance of information from cell membrane to intracellular components, including decrease in the response of lymphoid cells to mitogens, in the mixed lymphocyte reaction (see Chapter 16), defects in neutrophil chemotactic responsiveness and transmembrane mobility (Walford et al., 1981; Naeim and Walford, 1980; Woda and Feldman, 1979), changes in size and contents of lysosomal granules and frequency of residual bodies (Lipetz and Cristofalo, 1972; Brunk and Brun, 1972; Brunk and Collins, 1981), alteration in cyclic GMP and AMP levels (Tam and Walford, 1978), changes in RNA and DNA content (Cristofalo and Kritchevsky, 1969; Hay and Strehler, 1967), and variations in numbers of cells in the proliferating pool in *in vitro* cultures (Merz and Ross 1969; Cristofalo and Sharf, 1973; Smith and Hayflick, 1974). Thus an age-related disequilibrium between polymer and monomer forms of tubulin, and disorganization of the cytoskeletal structures might be a common de-

nominator underlying some of the phenomena of aging.

CONCLUSION

"Membranology" generally lays heaviest emphasis on the lipid bilayer of cell membranes, giving less consideration to the embedded proteins, to those materials which, as it were, float in the lipid bilayer. In addition, the cytoskeleton is in fact intimately responsible for certain membrane events. In this chapter, we reviewed selected age-related changes in these three components of an interactive system. Alterations in lipid components, in membrane fluidity (and the consequences thereof in terms of receptors and membrane-bound enzymes), and in redistribution of surface receptors complexed to ligands stand ᶠᵒrth as among the most striking age-related changes in the system. Among surface markers, those of the major histocompatibility complex may be particularly significant for aging studies.

REFERENCES

Adamson, J. S. 1968. An electron microscopic comparison of the connective tissue from the lungs of young and elderly subjects. *Am. Rev. Resp. Dis.* 98: 399–406.

Araki, K. and Rifkind, J. 1980. Erythrocyte membrane cholesterol: an explanation of the aging effect on the rate of hemolysis. *Life Sciences* 26: 2223–2230.

Balduini, C., Balduini, C. L., and Ascari, E., 1974. Membrane glycopeptides from old and young human erythrocytes. *Biochem. J.* 140: 537–560.

Barclay, M., Skipski, V. P., and Terebus-Kekish, O. 1972. Alterations in lipoprotein pattern in liver plasma membranes from rats of different ages. *Mech. Age. Dev.* 1: 357–365.

Bertrand, H. A., Yu, B. P., and Masoro, E. J. 1975. The effect of rat age on the composition and functional activities of skeletal muscle sacroplasmic reticulum preparations. *Mech. Age. Dev.* 4: 7–17.

Bloodworth, J. M., Engerman, R. L., and Powers, K. L. 1969. Experimental diabetic microangiopathy. 1. Basement membrane statistics in the dog. *Diabetes* 18: 455–458.

Boag, J. W. 1968. Overlapping effects of ultraviolet and ionizing radiations. *Brit. J. Radiol.* 41: 879–881.

Borochov, H. and Shinitzky, M. 1976. Vertical displacement of membrane proteins mediated by changes in microviscosity. *Proc. Natl. Acad. Sci. USA* 73: 4526–4530.

Bourguignon, L. Y. W. and Singer, S. J. 1977. Transmembrane interactions and the mechanism of capping of surface receptors by their specific ligands. *Proc. Natl. Acad. Sci. USA* 74: 5031–5035.

Bowman, P. D. and Daniel, C. W. 1975. Aging of human fibroblasts in vitro: surface features and behavior of aging WI-38 cells. *Mech. Age. Dev.* 4: 147–158.

Brennan, P. C. and Jaroslow, B. M. 1975. Age-associated decline in theta antigen on spleen thymus-derived lymphocytes of BGCF₁ mice. *Cell Immunol.* 15: 51–56.

Bretschen, M. S. 1973. Membrane structure. Some general principles. *Science* 181: 622–629.

Brock, M. A. and Hay, R. J. 1971. Comparative ultrastructure of chick fibroblasts in vitro at early and late stages during their growth span. *J. Ultrastructure Res.* 36: 291–311.

Brohee, D., Kennes, B., Hubert, C., and Neve, P. 1980. Human lymphocyte affinity for sheep erythrocytes in young and aged healthy subjects. *Clin. Exp. Immunol.* 42: 399–401.

Brown, W. T., Darlington, G. J., Arnold A., and Fotino M. 1980. Detection of HLA antigens on progeria syndrome fibroblasts. *Clinic, Genet.* 17: 213–219.

Brunk, U. and Brun, A. 1972. The effect of aging on lysosomal permeability in nerve cells of the central nervous system, an enzyme histochemical study in rat. *Histochemic* 30: 315–324.

Brunk, U. T. and Collins, V. P. 1981. Cultured cells, lysomes and aging. *XII International Congress of Gerontology.*

Burnet, F. M. 1970. An immunogical approach to aging. *Lancet* 2: 358–360.

Burnet, F. M. 1974. Intrinsic mutagenesis: genetic basis of aging. *Pathology* 6: 1–11.

Callard, R. E. 1978. Immune function in aged mice. III. Role of macrophages and effect of 2-mercaptoethanol in the response of spleen cells from old mice to PHA, lipopolysaccharide and allogeneic cells. *Eur. J. Immun.* 8: 697–705.

Callard, R. E. and Basten, A. 1979. Loss of immune competence with age may be due to a qualitative abnormality in lymphocyte membranes. *Nature,* 281: 218–220.

Carlson, L. A., Froberg, S. O., and Nye, E. R. 1968. Effect of age on blood and tissue lipid levels in the male rat. *Gerontologia,* 14: 65–79.

Casselman, W. G. B. 1951. The in vitro preparation and histochemical properties of substances resembling ceroid. *J. Exp. Med.* 94: 549–562.

Chandrasekhar, S. and Millis, A. J. T. 1980. Aged human fibroblasts produce defective fibronectin. *J. Cell Biol.* 87, 85a.

Chapman, D. 1975. Phase transitions and fluidity characteristics of lipids and cell membranes. *Q. Rev. Biopsv,* 8: 185–235.

Chio, K. S., Reiss, U., Fletcher, B., and Tappel, A. L. 1969. Peroxidation of subcellular organelles, formation of lipofuscin like fluorescent pigments. *Science* 166: 1535–1536.

Copeland, E. S. 1972. Electron spin resonance studies in radiation biology. *In,* Swartz HM, Bolton TB, and Borg G (eds.), *Biological Aspects of Electron Spin Resonance,* pp. 449. New York: Wiley-Interscience.

Cristofalo, V. J. 1970. *In,* E. Holleckova and V. J. Cristofalo (eds.), *Aging in Cell and Tissue Culture,* pp. 83. New York: Plenum Press.

Cristofalo, V. J. and Kritchevsky, D. 1969. Cell size and nucleic acid content in the diploid human cell line WI-38 during aging. *Medicina Experimentalis* 19: 313–320.

Cristofalo, V. J. and Sharf, B. B. 1973. Cellular senescence and DNA synthesis: thymidine incorporation as a measure of population age in human diploid cells. *Exp. Cell. Res.* 76: 419–427.

Crusberg, T. C., Hoskins, B. B., and Widdus, R. 1979. Spreading behavior and surface characteristics of young and senescent WI-38 fibroblasts revealed by scanning electron microscopy. *Exp. Cell. Res.* 118: 39–46.

De Bats, A., Rhodes, E. L., Gordon, A. H., and Parke, D. V. 1982. Biochemical differences in human glomerular basement membrane related to diabetes and age. *Ann. Clin. Biochem.* 19: 17–21.

DiLuzio, N. R. 1973. Antioxidants, lipid peroxidation, and chemical-induced liver injury. *Fed. Proc. Am. Socs. Exp. Biol.* 32: 1875–1881.

Edelman, G. M., 1976. Surface modulation in cell recognition and cell growth, *Science* 192: 218–226.

Edelman, G. M., Yahara, I., and Wang, J. L. 1973. Receptor mobility and receptor cytoplasmic interactions in lymphocytes. *Proc. Natl. Acad. Sci. USA* 70: 1442–1446.

Edidin, M. 1974. Rational and translational diffusion membranes. *Ann. Rev. Biophys. Bioeng.* 3: 179–201.

Eisenberg, S., Stein, Y., and Stein, O. 1969. Phospholipase in arterial tissue. IV. The role of phosphatide acyl hydrolase, lysophosphatide acyl hydrolase, and sphingomyelin phospholipid composition in the normal human aorta with age. *J. Clin. Invest.* 48: 2320–2329.

Fillerup, D. L. and Mead, J. F. 1967. The lipids of the aging human brain. *Lipids* 2: 1–4.

Flanagan, J., and Koch, G. L. E. 1978. Cross-linked surface Ig attaches to actin. *Nature* 273: 278–281.

Frolkis, V. V., Bezrukov, V. V., Duplenko, Y. L., Shchegoleva, I. V., Shevchuk, V. G., and Verkhratsky, N. S. 1973. Acetylcholine metabolism and cholinergic regulation of functions in aging. *Gerontologia* 19: 45–57.

Frolkis, V. V. and Bogatskaya, L. N. 1968. The energy metabolism of myocardium and its regulation in animals of various ages. *Exp. Geront.* 7: 185–194.

Gold, G. and Windell, C. C. 1974. Reversal of age related changes in microsomal enzyme activities following the administration of triamcinolone, triiodothyronine and phenobarbital. *Biochim. Biophys. Acta* 334: 75–78.

Gold, M. and Altschuler, H. 1972. Red blood cells and plasma phospholipids in aged humans. *J. Geront.,* 27: 444–450.

Goldstein, S., Lin, C. C., and Singal, D. P. 1974. Immunological selections of HLA variants of cultured progeric fibroblasts and their identification by quinacrine fluorescence. *Exptl. Cell. Res.* 89: 451–454.

Goldstein, S. and Singal, D. P. 1974. Alteration of fibroblast gene products *in vitro* from a subject with Werner's syndrome. *Nature* 251: 719–721.

Gordis, E. 1969. Lipid metabolites of carbon tetrachloride. *J. Clin. Invest.* 48: 203–209.

Gottesman, S., Hall, D. Y., and Walford, R. L. 1982. A thesis of genetic linkage of immune regulation and aging: the major histocompatibility complex as a supergene system. *In,* E. L. Cooper (ed.), *Developmental Immunology: Clinical Problems and Aging.* New York: Academic Press.

Gottesman, S. and Walford, R. L., 1982. Autoimmunity theories and aging. Testing the theories of aging. *In,* R. C. Adelman and C. S. Roth (eds.), *The CRC Uniscience Series Methods in Aging Research.* : CRC Press. Pp. 233–279.

Gozes, Y., Umiel, T., Meshorer, A., and Trainin, N. 1978. Syngenic GVH induced in popliteal lymph nodes by spleen cells of old C57B1/6 mice. *J. Immunol.* 121: 2199–2204.

Grinna, L. S. 1977. Changes in cell membrane during aging. *Gerontology* 23: 452–464.

Grinna, L. S. and Barber, A. A. 1972. Age related changes in membrane lipid content and enzyme activities. *Biochim. Biophys. Acta* 288: 347–353.

Grinna, L. S. and Barber, A. A. 1973. Lipid peroxidation in liver and kidneys from young and old rats. *Biochem. Biophys. Res. Commun.* 55: 773–779.

Grinna, L. S. and Barber, A. A. 1976. Lipid changes in the microsomal and mitochondrial membranes of rat liver during aging. *Fed. Proc.* 35: 1425.

Hall, K. Y., Bergman, K., and Walford, R. L. 1981. DNA repair, H-2 and aging in NZB and CBA mice. *Tissue Antigens,* 17: 104–110.

Hawcroft, D. W. and Martin, P. A. 1974. Studies on age related changes in the lipids of mouse liver microsomes. *Mech. Age. Dev.* 3: 121–130.

Hay, R. J. and Strehler, B. L. 1967. The limited growth span of cell stains isolated from the chick embryo. *Exp. Geront.* 2: 123–135.

Hegner, D. 1976. *In,* D. Platt (ed.), *Alternstheorien,* pp. 171–177. Stuttgart/New York: Schattauer Verlag.

Hegner, D. 1980. Age-dependence of molecular and functional changes in biological membrane properties. *Mech. Aging. Dev.* 14: 101–118.

Hegner, D. and Platt, D. 1975. Effect of essential phospholipids on the properties of ATPase of isolated rat liver plasma membranes of young and old animals. *Mech. Aging Dev.* 4: 191–200.

Hegner, D., Platt, D., Heckers, H., Schloeder, U., and Breuninger, V. 1979. Age-dependent physiological and biochemical studies of human red cell membranes. *Mech. Aging Dev.* 10: 117–130.

Herbener, G. H. 1976. A morphometric study of age-dependent changes in mitochondrial populations of mouse liver and heart. *J. Geront.* 31: 8–12.

Heron, D. S., Shinitzky, M., Hershkowitz, M., and Samuel, D. 1980. Lipid fluidity markedly modulates the binding of serotonin to mouse brain membrane. *Proc. Natl. Acad. Sci. USA* 77: 7463–7467.

Hochschild, R. 1971. Lysosomes, membranes and aging. *Exp. Geront.* 6: 153–166.

Hochstein, P., and Ernster, L. 1963. ADP-activated lipid oxidation coupled to the TRNH oxidase system of microsomes. *Biochem. Biophys Res. Commun.* 12: 388–394.

Hubbard, R. E. and Garratt, C. J. 1980. The composition and fluidity of adipocyte membranes prepared from young and adult rats. *Biochim. Biophys. Acta* 600: 701–704.

Huemer, R. P., Bickert, C., Lee, K. O., and Reeves, A. E. 1971. Mitochondrial studies in senescent mice. 1. Turnover of brain mitochondrial lipids. *Expl. Gerontol.* 6: 259–265.

Hughes, B. A., Roth, G. S., and Pitha, J. 1980. Age-related decrease in repair of oxidative damage to surface sulfhydryl groups on rat adipocytes. *J. Cell. Physiol.* 103: 349–353.

Hung, C. Y., Parkins, E. H., and Yang, W. K. 1975. Age-related refractoriness of PHA-induced lymphocyte transformation. II. ^{125}I-PHA binding to spleen cells from young and old mice. *Mech. Age. Dev.* 4: 103–112.

Imamura, T., Devens, B., Weindruch, R., and Walford, R. 1983. Correlation of drug metabolizing capability, immune function, and H-2 genetic locus. *Fed. Proc.,* 42: 1295.

Inkeles, B., Innes, J. B., Kuntz, M. M., Kadish, A. S., and Weksler, M. E. 1977. Immunological studies of aging. III. Cytokinetic basis for the impaired response of lymphocytes from aged humans to plant lectins. *J. Exp. Med.* 145: 1176.

Johnson, J. E. 1979. Fine structure of IMR-90 cells in culture as examined by scanning and transmission electron microscopy. *Mech. Age. Dev.* 10: 405–443.

Jorgensen, F. and Bentzon, M. W. 1968. The ultrastructure of the normal human glomerolus. Thickness of glomerular basement membrane. *Lab. Invest.* 18: 42–48.

Kadlubowski, M. and Agutter, P. S. 1977. Changes in the activities of some membrane-associated enzymes during *in vivo* aging of the normal human erythrocyte. *Br. J. Haematol.* 37: 111–125.

Kadlubowski, M. and Harris, J. R. 1974. The appearance of a protein in the human erythrocyte membrane during aging. *FEBS Lett.* 47: 252–254.

Kanugo, M. S. and Gandhi, G. S. 1972. Induction of malate dehydrogenase enzymes in livers of young and old rats. *Proc. Natl. Acad. Sci. USA* 69: 2035–2038.

Karnovsky, M. J. 1979. Lipid domains in biological membranes. *Am. J. Pathol.* 97: 212–221.

Karnovsky, M. J., Hoover, R. L., MacIntyre, D. E., and Salzman, E. W. 1981. Effects of free fatty acids on the aggregation of human platelets. *J. Cell Biol.* 91: 1029.

Katz, D. H. 1981. New thoughts on the control of self-recognition, cell interactions, and immune responsiveness by major histocompatibility complex genes. *In,* R. A. Resifeld and S. Ferrone (eds.), *Current Trends in Histocompatibility,* Vol. 2, pp. 81. New York: Plenum Press.

Kay, M. 1981. Immunology of aging. *XII International Congress of Gerontology.*

Kay, M. M. B. 1975. Mechanism of removal of senescent cells by human macrophages *in situ. Proc. Natl. Acad. Sci. USA* 72: 3521–3523.

Kilo, C., Vogler, N., and Williamson, J. R. 1972. Muscle capillary basement membrane changes related to aging and to diabetes mellitus. *Diabetes* 21: 811–905.

Kimelberg, H. K. and Papahajopoulos, D. 1972. Phospholipid requirements of $Na^+ K^+$-ATPase activity: head-group specificity and fatty acid fluidity. *Biochim. Biophys. Acta.* 282: 277–292.

Klausner, R. D., Bhalla, D. K., Dragsten, P., Hoover, R. L., and Karnovsky, M. J. 1980. Model for capping derived from inhibition of surface receptor capping by free fatty acids. *Proc. Natl. Acad. Sci. USA* 77: 437–441.

Koch, G. L. E. and Smith, J. J. 1978. An association between actin and the major histocompatibility antigen H-2. *Nature* 273: 274–278.

Kuusela, P., Vaheria, A., Palo, J., and Ruoslahti, E. 1978. Demonstration of fibronectin in human cerebrospinal fluid. *J. Lab. Clin. Med.* 92: 595–601.

Labat-Robert, J., Potazman, J. P., Deroutelle, J. C., and Robert, L. 1981. Age-dependent increase of human plasma fibronectin. *Cell Biol. Intern. Rep.* 5: 969–973.

Lafuse, W., Meruelo, D., and Edidin, M. 1979. The genetic control of liver cAMP levels in mice. *Immunogenetics,* 9: 57–65.

Langeveld, J. P., Veerkamp, J. H., Duyf, C. M., and Monnens, L. H. 1981. Chemical characterization of glomerular and tubular basement membranes of men of different age. *Kidney Int.* 20: 104–114.

Law, J. H. and Synder, W. R. 1972. *In,* C. F. Fox and L. Manson (eds.), *Membrane Lipids in Membrane Molecular Biology,* pp. 159. New York: Plenum Press.

Le Guilly, Y., Simon, M., Lenoir, P., and Bourel, M. 1973. Long term culture of human adult liver cells: morphological changes related to *in vitro* senescence and effect of donor's age on growth potential. *Gerontologica* 19: 303–313.

Leibovitz, B. E. and Siegel, B. V. 1980. Aspects of free radical reactions in biological systems: ageing. *J. Gerontol.* 35: 45–56.

Lipetz, J. and Cristofalo, V. J. 1972. Ultrastructural changes accompanying the aging of human diploid cells in culture. *J. Ultrastruct. Res.* 39: 43–56.

Liu, R. K. and Walford, R. L. 1972. The effect of lowered body temperature on life span and immune and non-immune processes. *Gerontologia,* 18: 363–388.

Loor, F. 1980. Plasma membrane and cell cortex interactions in lymphocyte functions. *Adv. Immunol.* 30: 1–120.

Malhotra, S. and Kritchevsky, D. 1975. Cholesterol exchange between the red blood cells and plasma of young and old rats. *Mech. Age. Dev.* 4: 137–145.

Martin, D. W. 1981. *In,* D. W. Martin, P. A. Maye, and V. W. Rodwell (eds.), *Harper's Review of Biochemistry,* pp. 412–427. Los Altos, Calif.: Lang Medical Pub.

Mathies, M., Lipps, L., Smith, G. S., and Walford, R. L., 1973: Age-related decline in response to PHA pokeweed mitogen by spleen cells from hamsters and a long-lived mouse strain. *J. Geront.* 28: 425–430.

Merz, G. S. and Ross, J. D. 1969. Viability of human diploid cells as a function of *in vitro* age. *J. Cellular Geront.* 3: 129–134.

Miller, E. A. and Allen, D. O. 1973. Hormone-stimulated lipolysis in isolated fat cells from young and old rats. *J. Lipid Res.* 14: 331–336.

Milunsky, A. and Tsung, Y. K. 1979. Cell culture studies in progeria. I. Establishment and partial characterization of a lymphoblastoid cell line. *Mech. Age. Dev.* 11: 185–190.

Mitsui, Y. and Schneider, E. L. 1976. Relation between cell replication and volume. *Mech. Age. Dev.* 5: 45–56.

Morell, P., Greenfields, S., Costantino-Cellarine, E.,

and Wisniewski, H. 1972. Changes in the protein composition of mouse brain myelin during development. *J. Neurochem.* 19: 2545-2554.

Mosesson, M. W. and Umfleet, K. A. 1970. The cold-insoluble globulin of human plasma. I. Purification, primary characterization and relationship to fibrinogen and other cold-insoluble fraction components. *J. Biol. Chem.* 245: 5728-5736.

Naeim, F., Bergman, K., and Walford, R. L., 1981. Capping of concanavalin A receptors on lymphocytes of aged individuals and patients with Down's syndrome: enhancing effect of colchicine; possible relation to microtubular system. *Age* 4: 5-8.

Naeim, F. and Walford, R. L. 1980. Disturbance of redistribution of surface membrane receptors on peripheral mononuclear cells of patients with Down's syndrome and of aged individuals. *J. Geront.* 35: 650-655.

Ness, W. R. 1974. Role of sterols in membranes. *Lipids* 9: 596.

Nicolson, G. L. 1976a. Transmembrane control of receptors on normal and tumor cells. I. Cytoplasmic influence over cell surface components. *Biochim. Biophys. Acta* 457: 57-108.

Nicolson, G. L. 1976b. Transmembrane control of the receptors on normal and tumor cells. II. Surface changes associated with transformation and malignancy. *Biochim. Biophys. Acta.* 458: 1-72.

Nicolson, G. L. and Painter, R. G. 1973. Anionic sites of human erythrocyte membranes. II. Anispectrin-induced transmembrane aggregation of the binding sites for positively charged colloidal particles. *J. Cell Biol.* 59: 395-406.

Nicolson, G. L. and Poste, G. 1976a. The cancer cell dynamic aspects and modifications in cell-surface organization (first of two parts). *N. Engl. J. Med.* 295: 197-203.

Nicolson, G. L. and Poste. 1976b. The cancer cell dynamic aspects and modifications in cell-surface organization (second of two parts). *New Engl. J. Med.* 295: 253-258.

Novak, R., Bosze, Z., Matkovics, B., and Fachet, J., 1980. Gene affecting superoxide dismutase activity linked to the histocompatibility complex in H-2 congenic mice. *Science* 207: 86-87, 1980.

Oldfield, E. and Chapman, D. 1972. Dynamics of lipids in membranes: heterogeneity and the role of cholesterol. *FEBS Lett.* 23: 285-297.

Owicki, J. C. and McConnell, H. M. 1980. Lateral diffusion in inhomogeneous membranes. *Biophysical J.* 30: 383-398.

Packer, L., Dreamer, D. W., and Heath, R. L. 1967. Regulation and deterioration of structure in membrane. *Adv. Geront. Res.* 2: 77-120.

Patnaik, S. K. and Kanugo, M. S. 1974. Different patterns of induction of the two isozymes of alanine aminoterasferase of liver of rat as a function of age. *Biochem. Biophys. Res. Commun.* 56: 845-850.

Pieri, C., Zs-Nagy, I., Mazufferi, G., and Giuli, C. 1975. The aging of rat liver as revealed by electron microscope morphometry. I. Basic parameters. *Exp. Gerontol.* 10: 291-304.

Pieri, C., Zs-Nagy, I., Zs-Nagy, V., Guili, C., and Bertoni-Freddari, C. 1977. Energy dispersive x-ray microanalysis of the electrolytes in biological bulk specimen. II. Age-dependent alterations in the monovalent ion contents of cell nucleus and cytoplasm in rat liver and brain. *J. Ultrastructure Res.* 59: 320-331.

Platt, D. and Norwig, P. 1980. Biochemical studies of membrane glycoproteins during red cell aging. *Mech. Age. Dev.* 14: 119-126.

Popp, D. M. 1978. Use of congenic mice to study the genetic basis of degenerative disease. *In*, D. Bergsme and D. E. Harrison (eds.), *Genetic Effects on Aging*, pp. 261-280. New York: Alan R. Liss.

Popp, D. M. 1981. Genetic control of lifespan. *Fed. Proc.* 40, (part I), 789.

Portugal, F. H. 1979. Histocompatibility antigens and cytoskeletal elements. *Nature* 279: 102-103.

Prasannan, K. G. 1973. Influence of age on the total lipid, phospholipid and cholesterol contents of pancreas and liver in albino rats. *Experientia* 29: 946-947.

Puck, T. T. 1977. Cyclic AMP, the microtubule-microfilament system, and cancer. *Proc. Natl. Acad. Sci. USA* 74: 4491-4495.

Quinn, P. J. and Chapman, D. 1980. The dynamics of membrane structure. *Crit. Rev. Biochem.* 8: 1-117.

Raynolds, E. S. 1977. Liver endoplasmic reticulum target site of halocarbon metabolities. *In*, M. W. Miller and A. E. Shamoo (eds.), *Membrane Toxicity*, pp. 117-137. New York: Plenum Press.

Reiss, U. and Sackton, B. 1982. Alteration of kidney brush border membrane maltase in aging rats. *Biochim. Biophys. Acta* 704: 422-426.

Reknagel, R. O. and Glende, E. A., 1973. Carbon tetrachloride hepatotoxicity: an example of lethal cleavage. *Crit. Rev. Toxicol.* 2: 263-297.

Rivnay, B., Bergman, S., Shinitzky, M., and Globerson, A. 1980. Correlation between membrane viscosity, serum cholesterol lymphocyte activation and aging in men. *Mech. Age. Dev.* 12: 119-126.

Rivnay, B., Globerson, A., and Shinitzky, M. 1978. Perturbation of lymphocytic response to concanavalin A by exogenous cholesterol and lecithin. *Eur. J. Immunol.* 8: 185-189.

Rivnay, B., Globerson, A., and Shinitsky, M. 1979. Viscosity of lymphocyte plasma membrane in aging mice and its possible relation to serum cholesterol. *Mech. Aging Devel.* 10: 71-79.

Robbins, J. C. and Nicolson, G. L. 1975. A comprehensive treatise. *In*, F. F. Becker (ed.), *Cancer*, Vol. 4. New York: Plenum Press.

Robert, L. 1977. Membranes and aging. *Mammalian Cell Membranes* 5: 220-259.

Rouser, G., Nelson, G. J., Fleischer, S., and Simon, G. 1968. Lipid composition of animal cell membranes, organelles and organs. *In*, D. Chapman (ed.), *Biological Membranes*, pp. 5. London: Academic Press.

Rubin, M. S., Swislocki, N. I., and Sonenberg, M. 1973. Changes in rat liver plasma phospholipids during aging. *Proc. Soc. Exp. Biol. Med.* 142: 1008–1010.

Samorajski, T., Ordy, J. M., and Rady, P. 1964. The fine structure of liposfuscin in aged mice. *J. Cell Biol.* 26: 776–795.

Schmucker, D. L. 1976. Age-related changes in hepatic fine structure; a quantitative analysis. *J. Geront.* 31: 135–143.

Scribner, D. J., Weiner, H. L., and Moorhead, J. W. 1978. Anti-immunoglobulin stimulation of murine lymphocytes. V. Age-related decline in Fc receptor-mediated immunoregulation. *J. Immunol.* 121: 377–382.

Shih, J. C. and Young, H. 1978. The alteration of serotonin binding sites in aged human brain. *Life Sci.* 23: 1441–1448.

Shinitzky, M. and Barenholz, Y. 1974. Fluidity parameters of lipid regions determined by fluorescence polarization. *J. Biol. Chem.* 249: 2652–2657.

Shinitzky, M. and Barenholz, Y. 1978. Fluidity parameters of lipid regions determined by fluorescence polarization. *Biochim. Biophys. Acta* 515: 367–394.

Sinensky, M. S. 1980. The regulation of membrane lipid fluidity by membrane lipid biosynthesis. *Adv. Pathobiol.* 7: 365–376.

Singer, S. J. and Nicolson, G. L. 1972. The fluid mosaic model of the structure of cell membranes. *Science* 175: 720–731.

Siperstein, M. D., Urger, R. L., and Madison, L. L. 1968. Studies of muscle capillary basement membranes in normal subjects, diabetic and prediabetic patients. *J. Clin. Invest.* 47: 1973–1999.

Smalley, J. W. 1980a. Age-related changes in the amino acid composition of human glomerular basement membrane. *Exp. Gerontol.* 15: 43–52.

Smalley, J. W. 1980b. Age-related changes in hydroxylysyl glycosides of human glomerular basement membrane collagen. *Exp. Gerontol.* 15: 65–66.

Smith, G. S. and Walford, R. L. 1977. Influence of the main histocompatibility complex on aging in mice. *Nature* 270: 727–729.

Smith, R. J. and Hayflick, L. 1974. Variation in the life-span of clones derived from human diploid cell strains. *J. Cell. Biol.* 62: 48–53.

Stahl, W. L. 1973. Role of phospholipids in the Na$^+$, K$^+$-stimulated adenosine triphosphatase system of brain microsomes. *Arch. Biochem. Biophys.* 154: 56.

Strehler, B. L., Mark, D. D., Milovan, A. S., and Gee, M. V. 1959. Rate and magnitude of age pigment accumulation in the human myocardium. *J. Geront.* 14: 430–439.

Sulkin, N. M. and Srivary, P. 1960. The experimental production of senile pigments in the nerve cells of young rats. *J. Geront.* 15: 2–9.

Sun, G. Y. and Samorajski, T. 1972. Age changes in the lipid composition of whole homogenates and isolated myelin fractions of mouse brain. *J. Geront.* 27: 10–17.

Sun, G. Y. and Samorajski, T. 1973. Age differences in the acyl group composition of phosphoglycerides in myelin isolated from the brain of rhesus monkey. *Biochim. Biophys. Acta* 316: 19–27.

Tam, C. F. and Walford, R. L. 1978. Cyclic nucleotide levels in resting and mitogen-stimulated spleen cell suspensions from young and old mice. *Mech. Age. Dev.* 7: 309–320.

Tate, E. L. and Herbener, G. H., 1976. A morphometric study of the density of mitochondrial cristae in heart and liver of aging mice. *J. Geront.* 31: 129–134.

Tauchi, H., Sato, T., and Kobayashi, H. 1974. The effect of age on ultrastructural changes of cortisone treated mouse hepatic cells. *Mech. Age. Dev.* 3: 279–290.

Taylor, S. A. and Price, R. G. 1982. Age-related changes in rat glomerular basement membrane. *Int. J. Biochem.* 14: 201–206.

Thompson, G. A., and Nazawa, T. 1976. Tetrahymena. A system for studying dynamic membrane alterations within eukaryotic cells. *Biochem. Biophys. Acta* 431: 165–195.

Toth, S. E. 1968. The origin of lipofuscin age pigments. *Expl. Gerontol.* 3: 19–30.

Vorbeck, M. L., Michalevich, J. M., Townsend, J. F., and Martin, A. P. 1981. Effect of aging of membrane-associated properties of hepatic mitochondria. *XII International Congress of Gerontology.*

Walford, R. L. 1969. *The Immunologic Theory of Aging.* Copenhagen: Munksgaard.

Walford, R. L., 1981. A speculative proposal about the immemorial ancestry of the MHC. *AACHTion News* 5: 15–16.

Walford, R. L. 1983. Supergenes histocompatibility; immunologic and other parameters in aging. *In,* W. Regelson (ed.), *Intervention in the Aging Process, Basic Research, Pre-clinical Screening and Clinical Programs.* New York: Alan R. Liss. Pp. 53–68.

Walford, R. L., Gossett, T. C., Naeim, F., Tam, C. F., Van Lanker, J. L., Barnett, E. V., Sparkes, R. S., Fahey, J. L., Gatti, R. A., and Grossman, H. 1981. Immunological and biochemical studies of Down's syndrome as a model of accelerated aging. *In,* D. Segre and L. Smith (eds.), *Immunological Aspects of Aging,* pp. 479. New York: Marcel Dekker.

Walker, J. B. and Walker, J. P. 1973. Properties of adenylate cyclase from senescent rat brain. *Brain Res.* 54: 391–396.

Williams, R. M., Kraus, L. J., Lavin, P. T., Steele, L. L., and Yunis, E. J. 1981. Genetics of survival in mice localization of dominant effects of subregions of the major histocompatibility complex. *In,* D. Segre and L. Smith (eds.), *Immunological Aspects of Aging,* pp. 247–266. New York: Marcel Dekker.

Wilson, P. D. and Franks, L. M., 1975. The effect of age on mitochondrial ultrastructure and enzymes. *Adv. Exp. Med. Biol.* 532: 171–182.

Woda, B. A. and Feldman, J. D. 1979. Density of surface immunoglobulin and capping on rat B lymphocytes. I. Changes with aging. *J. Exp. Med.* 149: 416–423.

Woda, B. A., Yguerabide, J., and Feldman, J. D. 1979. Mobility and density of AgB, "Ia" and Fc receptors on the surface of lymphocytes from young and old rats. *J. Immunol.* 123: 2161–2166.

Wolman, M. and Zaidel, L. 1962. Hypoxia and formation of chromolipid pigments. *Experientia* 18: 323–324.

Wolosewick, J. J., and Porter, K. R. 1977. Observation on the morphological heterogeneity of WI-38 cells. *Am. J. Anat.* 149: 197–225.

Xi, Y. P., Nette, E. G., King, D. W., and Rosen, M. 1982. Age-related changes in normal human basement membrane. *Mech. Age. Dev.* 19: 315–324.

Yamada, K. M. and Olden. 1978. Fibronectin-adhesive glycoproteins of cell surface and blood. *Nature* 275: 179–184.

Zs-Nagy, I. 1978. A membrane hypothesis of ageing. *J. Theor. Biol* 75: 189–195.

Zs-Nagy, I. 1979. The role of membrane structure and function in cellular aging: a review. *Mech. Age. Dev.* 9: 237–246.

Zwaal, R. F. A., Roelofsen, B., and Colley, C. M. 1973. Localization of red cell membrane constituents. *Biochim. Biophys. Acta* 300: 159–182.

4 CELL BIOLOGY

12
THE CULTURED FIBROBLAST-LIKE CELL AS A MODEL FOR THE STUDY OF AGING

Thomas H. Norwood
University of Washington
and
James R. Smith
Baylor College of Medicine

INTRODUCTION

While the majority of aging research has utilized experimental animal models, the development of techniques for the cultivation of animal cells and tissues has had a significant impact on this area of endeavor. This technology has provided a major impetus for the study of aging at the cellular level and has provided a major experimental approach for research with human material. The modern era of tissue culture was initiated by the pioneering work of Harrison (1907) with amphibian neuronal tissue. By the 1960s mammalian cell culture had become "routine" in many laboratories throughout the world. However, despite these impressive advances, tissue culture has remained far from an exact science. Even today, the media used by the majority of laboratories require serum or other chemically undefined supplements in order to achieve sustained proliferative activity. Moreover, in the absence of specific markers, precise identification of many of the cell types utilized in tissue culture has not been possible. Until recently, classification of cell types observed in cell cultures has been based primarily upon morphologic appearance and direct microscopic observation of cell behavior (Willmer, 1965). The cell type which is most capable of sustained proliferation with the usual methods employed in tissue culture is a spindle shaped cell commonly termed a "fibroblast." Up to the present time, this cell type has been extensively used for the study of cellular senescence *in vitro*. In the absence of specific markers, the precise origin of this cultured cell type remains uncertain. Therefore, we shall use the designation "fibroblast-like cell" in this discussion.

There have been few studies attempting to directly identify the histotypic origin of the fibroblast-like cell. Based on ultrastructural morphological comparisons between tissue explants and established cultures from fetal lung, Franks and Cooper (1972) suggested that the cells that ultimately populate the cultures are derived from pericytes and endothelial cells. Although precise identification cannot be unambiguously established by morphologic analysis alone, it is not unreasonable to believe, as suggested by Franks and Cooper, that more than one cell type

291

could contribute to the population of cells that are capable of sustained proliferation *in vitro*. Indeed, this perception is supported by a number of studies showing that differences in the growth behavior (Schneider et al., 1977; Harper and Grove, 1979) and response to exogenous steroid hormones (Grove et al., 1977; Pinsky et al., 1972) in fibroblast-like cultures are mediated by the organ or region of the organ from which they were derived. In the cultures from cutaneous tissues, a variety of histologically defined cell types such as smooth muscle cells, pericytes, or myoepithelial cells could contribute to the established fibroblast-like cultures.

The lack of precise definition of cell types clearly creates problems in the interpretation of biological studies. However, it must be emphasized that, in spite of these limitations, studies carried out with the cultured fibroblast-like cell during the past two decades have had a significant impact on the present perception of the role of cellular alterations in the aging process. Recent developments in the methodology of cell culture have resulted in the extended cultivation and unambiguous identification of a variety of differentiated cell types. These advances have only recently begun to have an impact on research in cellular aging and will certainly be increasingly important. However, this discussion will deal almost exclusively with studies with the fibroblast-like cell. We will address three questions that have been central to the study of cellular aging *in vitro:* (1) Do proliferating populations of euploid cells display a finite growth potential? (2) What is the relationship between *in vitro* cellular aging and normal *in vivo* aging processes? and (3) What is the mechanism(s) that limits the growth capacity of most, if not all, euploid cell types?

GROWTH POTENTIAL OF VERTEBRATE CELLS *IN VITRO*

The question of the permanency of cultured vertebrate cells was clearly a concern of early investigators in tissue culture. Although, as pointed out by Martin (1977) in his recent review, these authors were quite conservative in their appraisal of the longevity of explanted cells, the titles of some of their publications appear to connote a preconception, as exemplified by a paper entitled "On the Permanent Life of Tissue outside the Organism," published by Carrel in 1912. Over the next several decades, Carrel (1921, 1935) and his associate Ebeling (1913) conducted a series of experiments with explanted chick heart fibroblast-like cells, which were highly publicized in both the lay and the scientific communities. By the 1930s, Carrel stated that these cells had been maintained in continuous culture for more than 20 years and concluded that vertebrate somatic cells are immortal (Carrel, 1935). These experiments had a profound influence on gerontologic thinking in the first half of this century. A general conclusion emerged that, while multicellular organisms possess a finite life span, their components (i.e., cells) are immortal when maintained under appropriate conditions outside of the body. The implication of this conclusion is that the underlying mechanism(s) of the aging process is not the result of deteriorative alterations of somatic cell function.

Until the late 1950s, little significance was attached to the cessation of growth of cultured mammalian cells, which was generally attributed to inadequacies of the existing cell culture techniques and/or other technical problems (Erlichman, 1935; Gey, 1955). Swim and Parker (1957) were the first investigators to seriously challenge this widely held assumption. They observed finite periods of active proliferation in some 51 strains of cultivated human fibroblast-like cells, and the longevity of the cultures appeared to vary as a function of the tissue from which they were derived. Hayflick and Moorhead (1961) and Hayflick (1965) greatly extended and quantitated these observations. These investigators were the first to suggest that the loss of growth potential may be an intrinsic property of euploid somatic cells, and thus *in vitro* systems may be an appropriate model for the investigation of some aspects of aging at the cellular level.

In their studies, Hayflick and Moorhead (1961) and Hayflick (1965) carried out a number of experiments designed to rule out "trivial" explanations for the finite growth potential of these cells, such as microbial contamination and nutritional depletion. These observations were rapidly confirmed by other investigators (Todaro et al., 1963; Yoshida and Makino, 1963). However, it was clear that certain cultivated mammalian cell types, such as HeLa (Gey et al., 1952) and mouse L cells (Earle, 1943), display an apparently unlimited proliferative potential. Thus, Hayflick and Moorhead (1961) proposed that two fundamental cell types can be identified *in vitro*. Various terminologies for those cell types have been proposed by Hayflick (1965) and by other authors (Martin and Sprague, 1973; Krooth, 1968). The Tissue Culture Association (1978) has suggested that these cell types be distinguished on the basis of their growth potential by the terms "finite" and "continuous" used as prefixes to the general term "cell line" which denotes a culture of multiple lineages arising from the subcultivation of a primary culture. Martin and Sprague (1973) have extensively reviewed distinguishing characteristics of these two cell types. These authors suggested that finite cell lines can be viewed as an *in vitro* model of wound healing and continuous cell lines as an *in vitro* model of neoplasia. Although considerable variation in the expression of various features attributed to these cell types is evident, this broad classification has nonetheless proven useful for predicting certain aspects of cell behavior *in vitro*.

In the last two decades, many laboratories have repeated the observations reported by Hayflick and Moorhead (1961) under a variety of culture conditions. It is interesting that only recently, a report appeared which indicated that the trauma associated with detachment with proteolytic enzymes and subcultivation does not affect the growth potential of these cultures (Hadley et al., 1979). A number of investigators have shown that maintaining human diploid (Dell'Orco et al., 1974; Goldstein and Singal, 1974a; Kaji and Matsuo, 1979) or chick embryo fibroblast-like cells (Nielsen and Ryan, 1981; Roberts and Smith, 1980) in a nondividing state for varying periods of time, up to six

months, did not decrease the number of population doublings they could achieve in culture. These results suggest that the limited *in vitro* proliferative potential of these cultures is determined by cell division rather than by calendar time in culture. It has, however, become clear that a number of environmental factors influence the proliferative behavior and growth potential of fibroblast-like cultures. Such variables as serum batch (Schneider et al., 1978) and nutrient composition of the medium (Litwin, 1972) can affect the longevity of fibroblast-like cultures. The addition of hydrocortisone to the culture medium extends the growth potential of human fibroblast-like cultures derived from some tissues (Macieira-Coelho, 1966; Cristofalo, 1975). In the presence of this hormone, responding cultures display an increased fraction of rapidly dividing cells, elevated rate of entry into DNA synthesis, and higher saturation densities (Cristofalo, 1975; Bilgin and Cristofalo, 1978). It appears that the capacity of this hormone to extend *in vitro* life span may itself be modulated by culture conditions. Didinsky and Rheinwald (1981) recently reported that they could observe no effect of hydrocortisone on the life span of embryonic fetal fibroblast-like cells when subcultivation was carried out at densities low enough to maintain the cultures in a constant state of exponential growth. With the recent advances in the development of "defined" media that will support viability and growth of a variety of cell types, there will be a continuing need to evaluate the growth potential of these cells maintained in differing culture environments (Bettger et al., 1981; Walthall and Ham, 1981; Phillips and Cristofalo, 1981; Yamane et al., 1981).

In addition to environmental conditions, intrinsic factors such as the genotype of the donor and the tissue from which the cultures are derived influence the growth potential of fibroblast-like cells. Schneider et al. (1977) reported that fetal lung cultures displayed a faster growth rate and greater life span than skin cultures from the same individuals. There is also a report indicating that cultures derived from the papillary dermis display a greater growth potential than those derived from the reticular dermis (Harper and Grove, 1979). Martin et al. (1981) have emphasized that there are human skin geographic "hot spots" containing stem cells of greater growth potential. The bases for these inter- and intraorgan differences in growth behavior are unclear. However, these observations serve to emphasize the importance of the anatomic origin of the cultures as a variable that needs to be considered in the design of experiments and the interpretation of results.

The growth potential as well as other aspects of the proliferative behavior of fibroblast-like cells from a variety of species has been examined. In contrast to Carrel's original claim (1935), it is now well established that cultured chick cells invariably exhibit a finite growth potential in culture (Hay and Strehler, 1967; Weissman-Shomer and Fry, 1975). As suggested by Hayflick (1970, 1977), it is likely that Carrel may have continuously introduced fresh, viable cells into these cultures with the crude embryo extract used in tissue culture media at that time. Unlike cultures from human and chick, cells cultivated from many species have a tendency to undergo spontaneous transformation into a cell line of unlimited growth potential. Murine and probably most rodent cells are particularly susceptible to spontaneous transformation (Macieira-Coehlo, 1980; Meek et al., 1977; Rothfels et al., 1963). In most cases, the cultures enter a crisis period, characterized by a period of depressed growth activity, prior to transformation. This is interpreted as a senescent phase of the diploid culture (Rohme, 1981). The emergence of an altered cell type in these cultures was not appreciated by early investigators, and thus the early experience with murine cultures reinforced the notion of the immortality of cultivated somatic cells.

TRANSFORMATION OF FIBROBLAST-LIKE CELLS

A prominent feature of cultured human fibroblast-like cells is their stability with respect to neoplastic transformation. With one possible exception, there is no well-documented report of spontaneous transformation. In 1976, Azzarone and his colleagues reported spontaneous transformation in their fibroblast-like cultures derived from patients with malignant neoplasms distant from biopsy site. While this observation is certainly of interest, it must be interpreted with some caution since the investigators did not exclude the possibility that the tumor cells were present in the explanted tissues. Human fibroblast-like cells also appear to be remarkably resistant to induction of transformation by chemical and physical agents. This is in contrast to cultured cells from other species, particularly rodents, which can be chemically transformed with relative ease (Mendal et al., 1975; Lasne et al., 1977; Kennedy et al., 1978). Only recently have reports begun to appear describing successful transformation of cultured human cells following exposure to mutagens and/or carcinogens (Kakunaga, 1978; Milo and DiPaolo, 1978) and to x-rays (Borek, 1980). It is of interest that in the studies by Kakunaga (1978) and Borek (1980), the strains of fibroblast-like cells (KD cells) were initiated from explanted tissues from a lip biopsy that was diagnosed as a noninvasive, venous ectasia (cited from Vincent and Haung, 1976). This is potentially important in that cells derived from certain types of lesions, such as benign neoplasms, could be more susceptible to transformation. In all of these studies, relatively prolonged subcultivation of the cultures following exposure to the oncogenic agent was required before transformation was visually evident.

Human fibroblast-like cells can be transformed following infection with both DNA tumor viruses (Koprowski, 1963; Aaronson, 1970) and RNA oncogenic viruses (Sarma et al., 1970; Klement et al., 1971; Aaronson and Todaro, 1970). The DNA virus simian virus 40 (SV-40) has been most extensively studied in this cell type. Human diploid fibroblast-like cells are semipermissive for the SV-40 virus in that infection can result in a lytic process with the production of mature virus and/or neoplastic transformation (Sack, 1981). A clearly defined alteration in the susceptibility to viral transformation with advancing donor age or passage level in fibroblast-like cultures has not been demonstrated. Lubiniecki et al. (1977) reported no differences in susceptibility to SV-40 transformation in fibroblast-like cell cultures derived from 76 donors ranging in age from the first to the seventh decade. In studies designed to examine the efficiency of SV-40 mediated transformation with respect to *in vitro* aging, Jensen et al. (1963) observed a decreased latent period in the expression of morphologic alterations in late passage cultures. However, as pointed out by Ponten (1977), an alternative interpretation is that these altered foci may become visually evident more rapidly in slowly proliferating aged cultures. Indeed, more recently, Matsumara and his colleagues (1980) were unable to demonstrate transformed foci in late passage fetal lung fibroblast-like cultures. However, several laboratories have recently reported that infection with this virus does stimulate DNA synthesis in these senescent cultures (Gorman and Cristofalo, 1982; Toshinori et al., 1983). The relevance of *in vitro* transformation studies with a mesenchymal cell type such as the fibroblast-like cell can be questioned in view of the fact that the majority of age-associated tumors are of epithelial origin. Certainly, the influence of cell age *in vivo* and *in vitro* will have to be examined with epithelial cell types when the techniques for their cultivation and propagation have been perfected.

RELEVANCE TO *IN VIVO* AGING

The suggestion by Hayflick and Moorhead (1961) that cultivated human diploid cells may be a model for the study of aging at the cellular level has not been without controversy (Kohn, 1975). However, there have been a number of observations that provide indirect but nonetheless provocative evidence supporting this hypothesis. Hayflick's hypothesis was primarily based upon the observation that fetal cells displayed a consistently greater growth potential (approximately 50 cumulative population doublings) than those derived from adult tissues (20–30 cumulative population doublings). This re-

sult has been confirmed in a number of laboratories. Martin et al. (1970) determined the growth potential of skin fibroblast-like cultures derived from 100 donors ranging from the first to the tenth decade of life and observed a regression curve of 0.2 population doubling per year of life. Critics argued that there was significant scatter of the data points and that the slope of the regression curve is reduced to questionable significance if the data from subjects in the first three decades of life are excluded. This study has been extended to include more subjects in the later decades of life (Martin et al., 1981). No significant change in the slope of the regression curve was observed. More recently, similar observations have been reported with other cell types. Bierman (1978) observed an attenuation of growth potential with advancing donor age in arterial smooth muscle cell cultures derived from a variety of sites in the vascular system. Likewise, an age-related decline in proliferative activity has also been reported in lens epithelial cell (Tassin et al., 1979) and epidermal keratinocyte cultures (Rheinwald and Green, 1975), as assessed by thymidine labeling indices and plating efficiency, respectively. Walford et al. (1981) have recently reported that T cells propagated in the presence of T-cell growth factor display a finite growth potential. This conclusion is in contrast to previous reports which suggested that in the presence of this growth factor, these cells are capable of unlimited proliferation without evidence of transformation (Gillis et al., 1978; Smith et al., 1979). These studies and those discussed earlier have included a relatively small number of donors, and will have to be extended before the results can be considered conclusive.

An obvious line of investigation was to determine if cultures from patients with genetic disorders displaying features of accelerated aging displayed an alteration of proliferative behavior and/or growth potential. Indeed, the reports by Martin et al. (1970) and Goldstein (1969) indicating that the cultures from individuals with Werner and Hutchinson-Gilford syndromes displayed a diminished growth capacity significantly increased the interest in *in vitro* systems as models for the study of cellular aging.

In an extensive review, Martin (1978) has emphasized that a number of genetic syndromes are candidates as models for the study of aging. However, none of them is an exact phenocopy of aging in the normal population; therefore, he has suggested that this heterogeneous group of disorders be referred to as "segmental progeroid syndromes." The Werner and Hutchinson-Gilford syndromes are generally considered prototypic examples of the segmental progeroid syndromes (Goldstein, 1978). The former is now generally accepted to be inherited as an autosomal recessive disorder (Epstein et al., 1966). In contrast, the mode of inheritance in Hutchinson-Gilford syndrome has not been firmly established (McKusick, 1982; DeBusk, 1972; Jones et al., 1975). A prominent feature of both of these disorders is the presence of degenerative vascular disease that is anatomically indistinguishable from that occurring in the general population. In contrast, there is a striking absence of neuro-degenerative changes in the central nervous system in these conditions, which distinguishes them from the normal aged phenotype. It is these discordant features that prompted Epstein and his colleagues (1966) to describe the Werner syndrome as a "caricature" of aging.

Cultured fibroblast-like cells from Werner patients display a reduced growth potential (Martin et al., 1970; Nienhaus et al., 1971; Holliday et al., 1974; Higashikawa and Fujiwara, 1978; Salk et al., 1981c). In the most extensive study to date with 20 strains from three patients, Salk et al. (1981c) observed a mean life span of approximately 14 cumulative population doublings versus about 54 in the normal controls.

The growth potential of fibroblast-like cultures derived from Hutchinson-Gilford patients is reduced (DeBusk, 1972; Goldstein, 1969; Danes, 1971). However, there appears to be greater variability between pedigrees, with some strains showing a growth potential within the low normal range (Goldstein and Moerman, 1975, 1976).

It is not known at the present time if the mechanism(s) that regulates the growth potential of these cultures is similar or identical to that occurring in cultures from the normal population (Brown, 1979). Indeed, there are distinctive phenotypic differences between Werner and non-Werner fibroblast-like cultures (Norwood et al., 1979a). A very distinctive feature of the Werner strains, first described by Hoehn and his colleagues (1975a), is the presence of multiple chromosomal structural rearrangements that can be detected throughout the life span of the cultures. These authors have suggested the term "variegated translocation mosaicism" (VTM) to describe this phenomenon. Salk and his associates (1981a, 1981b) demonstrated that these alterations are clonal in nature and, utilizing them as markers, have demonstrated expansion and attenuation of individual clones throughout the life span of these cultures. Recently, Salk (1982) observed the same chromosomal aberration in separate explanted fragments from a single biopsy, suggesting that those translocational events occur *in vivo*. The relationship between VTM and the regulation of proliferating cultures remains unclear. However, Salk (1981a) has observed this phenomenon in one culture from a normal individual exhibiting an *in vitro* life span within the normal range, which suggests that there is no direct causal relationship between VTM and attenuation of growth potential.

The proliferative behavior of cells from individuals with other progeroid syndromes has been less extensively studied. Cockayne syndrome, a rare autosomal recessive condition, is also included in this group of disorders (Brown, 1979). No studies of the growth capacity of cultivated Cockayne cells have been published. There is, however, some evidence that this disorder may be associated with a defect in DNA repair (Schmickel et al., 1977). This observation is of considerable theoretical interest in gerontology in view of reports indicating that DNA repair systems may be involved in the regulation of longevity (Hart and Setlow, 1974; Francis et al., 1981). These observations have heightened interest in genetic disorders that are known or strongly suspected to have an enzymatic defect in a DNA repair pathway as potential models for aging research. The so-called chromosomal instability syndromes—Fanconi's anemia, Bloom's syndrome, xeroderma pigmentosum, and ataxia-telangiectasia—are known or strongly suspected to be associated with defects in DNA repair (see Chapter 8). These autosomal recessive diseases are so named because of an increased frequency of unstable chromosomal aberrations, spontaneous and/or induced by clastogenic agents, in cultures from homozygous individuals (Hecht and McCaw, 1977). In spite of the interest in these disorders as potential models for the study of aging, there is comparatively little information regarding the *in vitro* life span of cultures derived from these individuals. The growth potential of cultures from individuals with xeroderma pigmentosum appears to be within the normal range (Goldstein, 1971). Webb et al. (1977) indicated that they observed shorter proliferative life spans in ataxia cultures as compared to normal controls. However, this was an incidental observation in their study, and no data were provided to support this claim. There are also a number of reports indicating subtle alterations in doubling time and/or the rate of DNA chain elongation as compared to controls in ataxia-telangiectasia (Elmore and Swift, 1976), Bloom's syndrome (Gianelle et al., 1977; Hand and German, 1975), and Fanconi's anemia (Elmore and Swift, 1975) cultures. These observations must be viewed with some caution since the changes in cell cycle parameters are of relatively low magnitude and may be significantly influenced by culture conditions (Ockey, 1979; Elmore and Swift, 1975).

Recently, there has been increasing interest in the study of disorders resulting from chromosomal aneuploidy as models for the study of aging (Martin, 1978; Brown, 1979). Conceptually, these disorders are appealing as models of accelerated aging because the phenotype results from altered dosage and/or regulation of multiple genes that are involved in the control of the rate and phenotype of "normal aging" (Martin, 1978). In addition, Martin (1978) has suggested that Down's syndrome (trisomy 21) may display the greatest numbers of specific features of accelerated aging among all of the segmental progeroid syndromes. A striking aspect of the phenotype of this chromosomal disorder is the presence of senile neurodegenerative changes in the CNS in virtually all subjects who survive to the fourth and fifth decades of life (Brown, 1979).

A number of earlier publications reported modest reductions of life span and of growth rate in Down's syndrome fibroblast-like cell cultures (Schneider and Epstein, 1972; Segal and McCoy, 1974). In a more extensive study, Boue et al. (1975) reported that constitutional aneuploidy in general may be associated with a reduced growth capacity. These observations contrast with those reported recently by Hoehn et al. (1980) who could demonstrate no significant differences in growth rate or proliferation between euploid cultures and a variety of aneuploid strains, including trisomy 21. These differing results serve to highlight the problem of measuring subtle changes with the relatively imprecise methods of measurement currently employed to determine proliferative life span and cell generation times. Although the bases for these apparently contrasting observations are not apparent at the present time, variations in culture conditions and interstrain variation may be responsible. The fact that alterations of proliferative behavior and/or attenuated growth potential are not expressed in many of the progeroid fibroblast-like cultures is not surprising. This is a heterogeneous group of genetic disorders defined by the premature appearance of one or more aspects of the aging that are observed in the normal aging population. Almost certainly some, if not most, of these conditions will prove to be irrelevant to the problem of aging.

Diabetes mellitus is a condition associated with advancing age. For this reason, there has been considerable interest in the proliferative behavior of cultures derived from diabetic patients. Earlier studies of the growth behavior of diabetic fibroblast-like cells revealed a moderate but significant decrease in cloning efficiency (Goldstein et al., 1969) and proliferative life span (Vracko and Benditt, 1975). More recently, Goldstein and coworkers (1978) demonstrated a striking negative regression of growth potential as a function of donor age in carefully screened diabetic and prediabetic subjects. In this study, the controls displayed only a modest negative regression that was not statistically significant. In almost direct contrast to the Goldstein study (1978), Vracko and McFarland (1980) observed a significant regression in the control cultures; however, no such correlation was evident in the diabetic cultures. The diabetic and control populations in the latter study were relatively small ($N = 10$ in both) and there was considerable scatter in the higher age ranges. In addition, the diabetic condition of one patient in the old age group may have been secondary to pancreatitis. These conflicting results serve to emphasize the need to conduct *in vitro* life span studies with carefully defined populations. With respect to studies with diabetic populations, this is particularly difficult because this condition is associated with a variety of genetically based disorders and is almost certainly of multiple etiologies. At the present time, it is safe to conclude that cultures from at least a subset of diabetics display an attenuation of growth potential. However, further elucidation of the extent of the alterations of growth activity will come when a more precise definition of this disorder is at hand.

While studies with the progeroid disorders have yielded some interesting observations, a more direct approach to the question of the relevance of the *in vitro* model to *in vivo* aging is to determine if similar decrements of cellular function occur *in vivo*. One approach has been to examine various parameters of cell function in primary and low passage cultures from donors of varying ages. The first observation relevant to this question was made by early tissue culturists who noted an increased latent period prior to migration of cells from tissue explanted

from older animals (Cohn and Murray, 1925). This observation has been confirmed in more recent studies with explanted rat (Soukupova et al., 1970), human (Waters and Walford, 1970), and chicken (Lefford, 1964) tissues. However, the interpretation of these studies is not straightforward; alterations of the extra cellular matrix, rather than intrinsic changes in cell function, could be the basis for these differences. In studies designed to address this question more directly, Macieira-Coehlo et al. (1969) observed that decrements of cell cycle function occurred relatively earlier in the life span of cultures derived from adults than in those derived from embryonic tissues. In a more extensive study, Schneider and Mitsui (1976) examined a variety of parameters previously determined to change with *in vitro* passage level in low passage cultures from old and young donors. These authors did observe a lower saturation density and longer doubling time, as well as a decreased rate of migration from the explant in cultures derived from the older donors. These changes, however, were less dramatic than those *in vitro*. These observations indicate that modest decrements of cellular function occur with age in skin fibroblast-like cells capable of migration and proliferation *in vitro*. These functional changes do not appear to be limited to this cell type. For example, several laboratories have now reported a diminished response to phytohemagglutinin in peripheral leukocyte cultures from older individuals (Tice et al., 1979; Heflon et al., 1980).

Animal studies, being less constrained by ethical considerations, provide a more direct approach to the question of the growth potential of diploid cell populations. Serial transplantation of proliferating tissues, the principal experimental approach to this question, is described in depth in Chapter 13. These studies indicate that the maximum life span of a species is not directly determined by the growth potential of proliferating cell populations in the body, a view long held by virtually all investigators in the area of cellular aging. The perceived challenges are to determine if there are decrements of proliferative activity and/or other cellular functions and if these decremental changes are of significance in the aging process (Hayflick, 1977).

Interspecific comparative studies of *in vitro* growth behavior provide another experimental avenue to examine the relevance of the *in vitro* model of cellular aging. Although conceptually attractive, this experimental approach has not been extensively exploited. Based on a review of the literature, Hayflick (1977) concluded that there is a positive correlation between life span and *in vitro* growth potential. However, conclusions derived from a series of studies of this nature carried out in different laboratories and under different experimental conditions must be considered tentative. In the first reported systematic comparative study, Stanley et al. (1975) concluded that no correlation was evident between species longevity and the growth potential of their cultured cells. The authors of this study did not rigorously rule out the possibility of spontaneous neoplastic transformation occurring in cultures displaying prolonged growth. More recently, Rohme (1981) has published a study showing a positive correlation between longevity and *in vitro* growth potential in eight mammalian species. This investigator carefully examined proliferation rates in the cultures and was able to define a growth crisis in all cultures that transformed. In an analysis of previously published data, these authors also concluded that a similar correlation exists between the length of erythrocyte survival and species life span. While this report provides the best evidence to date that a positive relationship exists between species life span and the growth potential of fibroblast-like cultures, these studies need to be extended to include more species before a final judgement on this issue can be made.

THE PHENOTYPE OF THE SENESCENT CELL

The term "senescence" is most commonly used to imply a generalized functional deterioration with aging in the whole organism. This term has also been widely used in the literature to describe the loss of proliferative capacity in human fibroblast-like cultures. This may well be a misapplication, since the loss of proliferative activity does not necessarily imply a deteriorative event. For example, loss of growth capacity in association with cellular differentiation is not generally considered to be a manifestation of senescence. In this discussion, we use this apellation to describe the postmitotic culture, with the realization that it may ultimately prove to be a misnomer.

There is now a large body of literature describing the biological, morphological, and biochemical changes that occur in cultured human fibroblast-like cells at or near the end of their proliferative life span. The descriptive phenotype of senescing cultures has been discussed in depth in a number of excellent reviews (Cristofalo and Stanulis-Praeger, 1982; Hayflick, 1977). Here we will discuss only a few of the many cytologic and biochemical changes that occur in senescent cultures.

An obvious and fundamental question regarding the phenotype of the senescent cell is whether proliferation ceases in a specific phase of the cell cycle. It is now generally accepted that the majority of cells in postmitotic cultures are in the G_1 phase of the cell cycle. The conclusion is based on quantitative measurements of DNA content (Yanishevsky et al., 1974; Schneider and Fowlkes, 1976) and analysis of the morphology of prematurely condensed chromosomes (Yanishevsky and Carrano, 1975) induced by fusion to mitotic cells (Rao and Johnson, 1972). However, it is not clear if the nondividing cells in senescent cultures enter a metabolic state identical or similar to a reversible quiescent condition (G_0) such as that induced by serum deprivation or the reduction of an essential nutrient (Baserga, 1976). Recent cell fusion studies, which show a differing response with respect to DNA synthetic activity following inhibition of protein synthesis in heterokaryons derived from the fusion of cycling cells and senescent cells on the one hand and cycling cells and serum-deprived quiescent cells on the other, suggest that these two quiescent states are metabolically distinct (Burmer et al., 1983b). In addition, Olashaw et al. (1983) have suggested that senescent cells are lodged at the G_1/S boundary. This conclusion is based on measurements of thymidine kinase activity and nucleotide pool sizes, both of which show coordinated regulation with the cell cycle. The interpretation of this observation must be viewed with some caution, since metabolic derangements associated with senescence may result in the uncoupling of cell cycle progression and enzyme activity. Indeed, it is not entirely clear whether cell cycle activity completely ceases in senescent cultures. Previous studies have demonstrated increasing cell cycle transit time in these cultures. This is primarily the result of the lengthening of the G_1 and possibly G_2 phases of the cell cycle (Macieira-Coelho, 1966; Grove et al., 1976). The presence of cycling cells in very senescent cultures is supported by the studies of Burmer and Norwood (1980) who were unable to completely eliminate S phase cells following prolonged treatment with agents that select against cells capable of synthesizing DNA. Thus, the prevailing perception at the present time is that there is increasing heterogeneity with respect to cell cycle activity in senescing fibroblast-like cultures, with a subset of cells cycling at varying rates even in "postmitotic" late passage cultures (Macieira-Coelho and Taboury, 1982).

Morphologic changes at the ultrastructural level have been examined in fibroblast-like cultures derived from fetal lung (Lipetz and Cristofalo, 1972; Brandes et al., 1972; Johnson, 1979) and adult skin (Robbins et al., 1970; Basler et al., 1979), and also in avian fibroblast-like cultures (Brock and Hay, 1971). The most consistent alterations that have been observed at advanced passage levels include an increase in the number of secondary lysosomes associated with the formation of autophagic vacuoles and residual bodies, irregular lobulation of the nuclei, and mitochondrial changes which consist principally of swollen cristae. Cristofalo et al. (1967) have shown a correlation between the alteration in lysosomal structures and

changes in enzyme activity. On the other hand, Pool et al. (1981) have recently published observations indicating that some of the nuclear and mitochondrial changes reported to occur in senescent cultures may result from fixation artifact and incomplete attachment of cells. Such alterations of cellular structure have not been demonstrated with aging *in vivo* (Robbins et al., 1970). However, as pointed out by Martin et al. (1974), expression of cell senescence *in vivo* may be apparent only under certain conditions such as in association with wound healing in aged individuals.

Few morphologic studies of the senescent cell have attempted to correlate anatomic changes with functional alterations. A notable exception is the experiments reported by Kelly and his colleagues (1979) in which they demonstrated abnormalities in the assembly of gap junctions in late passage cells, which correlate with a diminished capacity to carry out metabolic cross-feeding. These studies are also of interest because they indicate that alterations of the plasma membrane are associated with loss of proliferative activity.

The cell surface plays a vital function in the transduction and modulation of external signals that initiate and regulate a variety of cell functions including cell proliferation. It is now well established that there are receptors in the plasma membrane for a variety of mitogenic peptides (Kaplan, 1981). Analysis of a mechanism(s) of altered responsiveness to this group of effector molecules provides a well-defined experimental approach to the study of proliferative decline in fibroblast-like cultures. However, only sporadic studies in this potentially fruitful area of aging research have been reported in the literature. A diminished proliferative response has been documented in studies with epidermal growth factor (Ladda, 1979) and the insulin-like peptides (Harley et al., 1981). Most studies indicate that there are no changes in the receptor density associated with the diminished responsiveness of the cells (Ladda, 1979; Hollenberg and Schneider, 1979). However, in one study, the affinity and extent of binding of insulin was reported to be increased in cultures derived from older do-nors and from patients with the Hutchinson-Gilford and Rothmund syndromes (Rosen-bloom et al., 1976). These observations pro-vide a starting point for systematic studies of growth factors and *in vitro* senescence. This area of research will almost certainly be of increasing importance in cellular aging as the mechanisms for the intracellular transmis-sion and processing of the signals from mi-togenic factors are elucidated.

Other studies of cell surface changes with cellular aging have primarily focused on the membrane-associated glycoproteins, while relatively little effort has been devoted to possible changes in the lipid bilayer. There is one report with fetal lung fibroblast-like cells indicating that no changes occur in the phos-pholipid and neutral fat content or in flu-idity of the plasma membrane with *in vitro* age (Polgar et al., 1978). Lectin binding studies have provided the first, and to date principal, approach in the analysis of mem-brane-associated protein changes. Kelley and his associates (1978) have shown a modest decrease of concanavalin A (Con A) binding in late passage embryonic fibroblast-like cul-tures associated with increased clustering of the receptors. In a slightly different ap-proach, Aizawa and his colleagues (Aizawa and Mitsui, 1979; Aizawa and Kurimoto, 1979a, 1979b; Aizawa et al., 1980a, 1980b) examined the adsorption of human red blood cells (RBC) to the surface of cultured fibroblast-like cells throughout the *in vitro* life span after exposing either the RBCs or the cultured cells to Con A. These investi-gators observed increased RBC adsorption in late passage cells. A gradual increase in the extent of adsorption with advancing pas-sage levels occurred when the fibroblast-like cells were coated with the lectin. In contrast, this increased adsorbance occurred more ab-ruptly in late passage cultures when the RBCs were pretreated with Con A. The most im-mediate significance of these observations is that this system may provide a cytologic marker for *in vitro* senescence that is inde-pendent of the proliferative state of the cell (Aizawa et al., 1980a). These authors pre-sented some evidence that the RBC adsorp-tion is inversely correlated with the amount of a 220,000-dalton cell surface glycopro-tein, probably fibronectin. The function of this cell surface moiety is not precisely known. It appears to enhance spreading and attachment of cells (Grinnell and Feld, 1979; Hook et al., 1977), and quantitatively changes with cell density and possibly pro-liferative activity (Critchley, 1974; Haynes and Bye, 1974). Vogel et al. (1981) observed that fibronectin is significantly reduced in se-nescent fetal lung cultures as assessed by the methods of immunofluorescence. Qualita-tive changes in this molecule may also occur, as suggested by the observations of Chan-drasekhar and Millis (1980) who reported that fibronectin secreted by late passage foreskin fibroblast-like cells is less efficient in promoting adhesion of both old and young cells. The chemical basis of this functional change is unclear. However, alterations at the molecular level could reflect significant modifications of the cell membrane with *in vitro* passage levels. These could be of pri-mary significance in the proliferative behav-ior of these cells. In addition, cell surface alterations could have profound effects on cell-to-cell and cell-to-substrate interactions. As has been suggested by Martin et al. (1975a), alterations in these functions may be of greater significance in aging *in vivo* than decrements in proliferative activity.

Kinetic Analyses of the Decline in Cell Proliferation

A number of investigators, in an effort to gain some insight into the mechanism(s) of the loss of proliferative activity in human fi-broblast-like cultures, have examined var-ious aspects of the kinetics of this decline under various culture conditions. In mass culture, a gradual decline of growth rate oc-curs which has generally been assumed to be a smooth continuous decline (Figure 1, dashed line). However, Holliday et al. (1977), in studies with embryonic lung cells, interpreted their data as a biphasic curve (Figure 1, solid line).

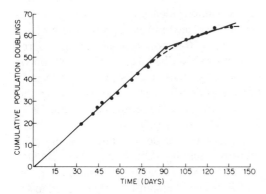

Figure 1. Growth of a mass culture of human diploid fibroblasts throughout its in vitro lifespan. Data are from a serial subcultivation series performed in one of our laboratories (JRS).

A number of laboratories have examined age-related changes in proliferative behavior at low densities in order to assess the behavior of individual cells. In the first such study, Merz and Ross (1969) observed that the proportion of individual cells incapable of division increased exponentially with culture age. These investigators also reported a considerable degree of variation in clonal growth rate among individual cells. Such heterogeneity of growth rates was also observed by Smith and Hayflick (1974). These initial observations of the clonal growth behavior have been confirmed and extended in studies by Martin et al. (1974) and Smith and Whitney (1980). Both of these groups demonstrated a bimodal distribution of intraclonal growth rates. As would be expected, the proportion of slowly growing clones increased with advancing passage levels. There may be a direct relationship between clonal growth patterns and growth potential in mass culture. Smith et al. (1977, 1978) have reported that the fraction of cells capable of generating clones of 16 or more cells is linearly related to the remaining proliferative potential of the culture. This may be of practical significance because it could provide a method for predicting maximum achievable life span in low passage cultures (Smith et al., 1977). The basis for the rapid development of intercellular heterogeneity of growth rates and doubling

potential is not entirely clear. Using the techniques of microcinematography, Absher et al. (1974) and Absher and Absher (1976) have shown considerable variation of interdivision time of individual cells descended from a single progenitor. However, Smith and Whitney (1980) concluded from their studies that the intraclonal variation of doubling potential is greater than can be accounted for by the observed variation in interdivision times as revealed by microcinematography. Clonal studies of this type have been viewed with some skepticism because of the widely held belief that fibroblast-like cells do not grow as well at clonal densities. However, Smith and Braunschweiger (1979) have shown that, given proper culture conditions, the population doubling time, fraction of dividing cells, and total *in vitro* life span are not affected by cell density.

Changes in growth rate with *in vitro* age have also been studied by determining, via autoradiography, the fraction of cells able to initiate DNA synthesis in a specified time period (generally 24 hours). The results have been somewhat variable. Cristofalo and Sharf (1973) and Matsumura et al. (1979) showed in mass culture an exponential increase in the percentage of nondividing cells similar to that observed by others in low density culture (Figure 3, line a). Other studies have shown a precipitous decline near the end of the life span of the culture (Vincent and Huang, 1976; Holliday et al., 1981; Harley and Goldstein, 1980) (Figure 3, lines b and c). These differing results are probably accounted for, in part, by the varying culture conditions, methodology, and tissue origin employed in the respective studies. A possible problem involved with this technique, as pointed out by Shall and Stein (1979), is that when cells that have been labeled divide, they give rise to two labeled cells, thereby decreasing the proportion of cells scored as nondividing. However, previous studies by Cristofalo (1976) suggest that dilution of the nondividing cell population by cell division during the labeling period is minimal. More-

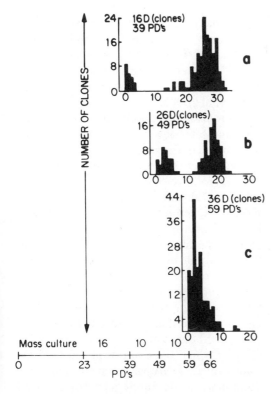

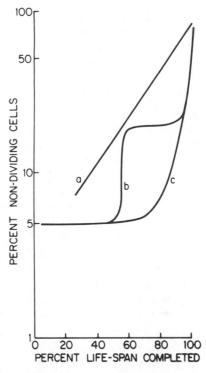

Figure 2. Intraclonal variation in proliferative potential. Frequency distribution of proliferative potential of subclones isolated from a single clone is shown at (a) 16, (b) 26, and (c) 36 PD's after initiation of the parent clone. Clones were isolated and grown as described by Smith and Hayflick (1974), (modified from Smith and Whitney, Science, 1980, by permission of the publisher) by the following procedure. Two days after subculture in Eagle's MEM supplemented with 28 mM Hepes buffer and 10 percent fetal bovine serum, a single cell suspension was prepared by trysinization of the log phase culture. The cells were cultured at low density (1000 to 5000 cells per 60mm dish) in medium 102 (16) supplemented with 10 percent fetal bovine serum in tissue culture dishes containing small cover-glass fragments (17). Clones were then isolated and grown as described in (7).

Figure 3. Schematic representation of the percentage of nondividing cells vs. percent of in vitro lifespan completed as observed by various investigators. Line (a) Merz and Ross (1969); Smith and Braunschweiger (1979); Cristofalo and Sharff (1973); Matsumura, et al. (1979); linne (b) Holliday, et al. (1981) line (c) Vinncent and Huang (1976); Harley and Goldstein (1980).

over, in the study reported by Matsumura et al. (1979), this problem was addressed.

Thus, at the present time, the precise kinetics of proliferative decline remains to be defined. However, some of the observations derived from these studies do argue against hypothetical mechanisms that have been proposed to explain the limited growth potential of fibroblast-like cultures. The extensive heterogeneity of intraclonal growth potential virtually rules out a mechanism by which the culture life span is determined by a biological clock that precisely counts number of cell divisions.

Cell Hybridization Studies

During the past decade, a number of laboratories have used the techniques of cell hybridization to probe the mechanisms controlling growth in human fibroblast-like cultures. In part, the rationale for the early cell fusion studies was based upon the studies of Harris (1967) and his colleagues (Harris et al., 1969) in which they demonstrated reactivation of nuclei from differentiated cells, such as the chick erythrocyte, after fusion to actively proliferating cells (Norwood et al., 1974). It was proposed that similar observations in parallel studies with senescent cells would support the interpretation that the mechanism(s) limiting growth in these cultures is similar, or possibly identical, to those apparent in the process of cellular differentiation. These studies involved the analysis of nuclear DNA synthesis by autoradiography in the bi- and multinucleate hybrid cells, termed heterokaryons, formed immediately following exposures to the fusogen. When senescent fibroblast-like cells were fused with proliferating cells, it was observed that DNA synthesis was not induced in the senescent nuclei and, in addition, was inhibited in the young nuclei during the 72-hour observation period (Norwood et al., 1974). More detailed analyses of this phenomenon have revealed that inhibition occurs only when the cycling parental cell is fused in the early or midportions of the G_1 phase or when it is in the G_2 phase at the time of fusion. When the cell is in late G_1 or in S phase, DNA synthesis is completed in the cycling nucleus (Yanishevsky and Stein, 1980; Rabinovitch and Norwood, 1980). Similar observations were reported in studies in which the nonreplicative state in the quiescent parental cell was induced by serum deprivation (Rabinovitch and Norwood, 1980; Stein and Yanishevsky, 1981) or by exposure to a combination of amino acid analogues (Norwood et al., 1979). These results have led to the suggestion that a variety of extrinsic or intrinsic stimuli may activate a common metabolic pathway leading to the quiescent state (Rabinovitch and Norwood, 1980). However, this interpretation must be considered tentative in view of our lack of information as regards the molecular bases of cellular growth control.

In subsequent studies, it has been shown that certain established cell lines are capable of stimulating DNA synthetic activity in postmitotic nuclei under these experimental conditions. This has been demonstrated in the case of HeLa cells and SV-40 transformed human fibroblast-like cells (Norwood et al., 1975) and with mouse L cells (Nette et al., 1982). Cytologic observation of the chromosome morphology in these hybrids indicates that complete replication of the genome of the senescent cells is occurring in these heterokaryons (Norwood and Zeigler, 1977). More recently, Stein and Yanishevsky (1979) and Stein et al., (1982) have shown that certain established cell lines are, like low passage diploid fibroblast-like cells, recessive in this assay. The cellular attributes that determine dominant or recessive behavior with respect to the capacity to initiate DNA synthesis in senescent nuclei are not known at the present time. Stein et al. (1982) have suggested that the capacity to reinitiate DNA synthesis correlates with the mechanism by which the established cell lines are transformed; DNA viral transformants are dominant, while carcinogen transformed cells are recessive with respect to the capacity to reinitiate DNA synthesis in senescent nuclei.

One criticism of these heterokaryon studies is that only the reinitiation of DNA synthesis immediately following fusion is examined and not the restoration of sequential cell cycle activity. The earlier studies that examined the proliferative behavior of hybrids (synkaryons) resulting from the fusion of proliferating cell types and senescent cultures appeared to complement the heterokaryon studies. Littlefield (1973) failed to recover proliferating hybrids following fusion of young and senescent human fibroblast-like cells. In contrast, hybrids derived from the fusion of senescent cells to established cell lines were reported to possess an apparently unlimited growth potential (Goldstein and Lin, 1972; Croce and Koprowski, 1974; Stanbridge, 1976). However, two laboratories have recently examined in greater detail the fate of proliferating hybrids recovered after fusion of young or middle-aged fibroblast-like cells and HeLa cells (Bunn and Tarrant, 1980) and SV-40 transformed human cells (Pereira-Smith and Smith, 1981). In both studies, the majority of hybrid clones exhibited a growth potential of fewer than eight population doublings, while a few displayed a more extended growth potential. In both studies, foci of rapidly dividing cells appeared in the senescent hybrid clones (one focus per approximately 10^5 cells) which gave rise to rapidly dividing cultures possessing an extended and probably infinite growth capacity. This appears to be analogous to a transformation event and indicates that the hybrids are less stable than the normal diploid parent. However, the important conclusion to be drawn from these studies is that the limited life span phenotype appears to be dominant in hybrid cultures. The observations are in apparent contrast to the heterokaryon studies in which certain transformed cell types reactivate at least one component of cellular replication, i.e., DNA synthesis, immediately following fusion. A possible explanation for these observations is that the factors involved in the initiation of DNA synthesis are elevated in the cell types which are dominant in the heterokaryon assay. This could result in a transient ablation of the action of the postulated inhibitors in senescent cells following fusion. Indeed, Pendergrass et al. (1983) have reported that there is a correlation between the levels of DNA polymerase-alpha in S phase cells and the capacity to stimulate DNA synthesis in senescent cells in heterokaryons. In the proliferating hybrids, the levels of the initiators of DNA synthetic activity would be regulated by the nontransformed or "normal" parental genome and thus exhibit a finite growth potential.

The recovery and characterization of proliferating synkaryons resulting from intraspecific hybridization of human strains are of relevance to the problem of *in vitro* senescence. In the absence of selective markers in human fibroblast-like cells, efficient isolation of such hybrids has proven to be difficult. Hoehn et al. (1975b) first reported a successful nonselective technique for the recovery of pure proliferating human-human euploid hybrid clones. These investigators

(Hoehn et al., 1978) reported that the growth potential of synkaryons recovered from the fusion of two skin fibroblast-like strains of differing proliferative life spans was intermediate to that observed in hybrids derived from the short-lived strains and the strains of longer life span. Similarly, Muggleton-Harris and Aroian (1982) reported that hybrids derived from the fusion of a neonatal foreskin strain to a shorter-lived skin fibroblast-like cell strain from a 68-year-old donor displayed a division potential intermediate to that of clones from the parental strains. However, somewhat differing observations have been reported by Pereira-Smith and Smith (1982) who observed that intraspecific hybrids isolated under selective conditions displayed a growth potential similar to that of the shorter-lived parental strain. These studies were accomplished with a clone isolated from a long-lived embryonic lung strain which contained both recessive and dominant selective markers (Duthu et al., 1982). This combination of markers permits the selective isolation of hybrids following fusion to wild-type human cell lines (Baker et al., 1974). At the present time, it is not clear if or how these differing experimental conditions may affect the results of these hybridization studies. This issue is important since, as will be discussed, these studies are of relevance to the somatic mutation hypothesis of aging.

Based primarily on the heterokaryon studies, a number of investigators have suggested that senescent cells have a diffusible factor(s) that inhibits DNA synthesis (Stein and Yanishevsky, 1979; Rabinovitch and Norwood, 1980; Smith and Lumpkin, 1980; Stein et al., 1982). Although the nature of this putative factor remains speculative, recent studies by Burmer et al. (1982) suggest that an inhibitory peptide may be present in senescent cells. These investigators observed an increased fraction of [^{3}H]-thymidine labeled nuclei in old-young heterokaryons following transient exposure to either cycloheximide or puromycin immediately following fusion. If this regulatory factor can diffuse through the cytoplasm, then its inhibitory activity should be present in anucleate senescent cytoplasms (cytoplasts). Indeed, two laboratories have recently demonstrated a depression of the [³H]-thymidine labeling index in young, dividing cells following fusion to senescent cytoplasts, an effect that was not observed following fusion of cytoplasts from low passage actively dividing cultures (Burmer et al., 1983a; Drescher-Lincoln and Smith, 1983). Another prediction of this hypothesis is that growth potential should be primarily regulated by nuclear functions. This prediction was supported in a series of studies published by Wright and Hayflick (1975a, 1975b) in which the growth potential of cells fused to senescent cytoplasts (cybrids) was observed to be no different from controls. However, in more recent cell reconstruction studies, somewhat different results were obtained (Muggleton-Harris and Hayflick, 1976). These studies entailed the enucleation of mass cultures via exposure to cytochalasin B and centrifugation, and fusion of old or young cytoplasts to old or young nuclei surrounded by small residual amounts of cytoplasm (karyoplasts) under direct microscopic visualization. Muggleton-Harris and Hayflick (1976) observed a diminished growth potential in cybrids containing cytoplasmic or nuclear components derived from senescent cells, indicating that the *in vitro* life span is in part under cytoplasmic control. Indeed the conclusion received further support in subsequent experiments by Muggleton-Harris and DeSimone (1980) in which cybrids constructed from karyoplasts from SV–40 transformed human fibroblast-like cells and cytoplasts from a nontransformed strain of embryonic lung cells (WI–38) were shown to have a finite growth potential. The nature of such cytoplasmic regulatory activities is at the present time undefined. However, this phenomenon is becoming well documented; several investigators have demonstrated sustained modulation of the activity of specific genes in cultured mammalian cells following fusion to cytoplasts (Gopalakrishnan et al., 1977; Gopalakrishnan and Anderson, 1979; Lipsich et al., 1979; Kahn et al., 1981).

Thus, while the results of the cell fusion studies can be interpreted as supporting the presence of an intrinsic inhibitor of DNA synthesis in senescent cells, the evidence is indirect and other interpretations of these studies can be envisioned (Burmer et al., 1982; Pendergrass et al., 1982; Stein et al., 1982). Future research efforts in this area will have to be directed toward isolation and biochemical characterization of these putative regulatory factors.

HYPOTHESES OF *IN VITRO* CELLULAR AGING

The explanations proposed to account for aging both *in vivo* and *in vitro* fall into two general categories: hypotheses proposing that aging is the result of the accumulation of random injurious events and those proposing that aging is the result of a developmental program. In the category of stochastic theories, random accumulation of errors in protein structure, somatic mutations, the accumulation of metabolic waste products, and free radical mediated damage have been proposed. The developmental program hypotheses have tended to focus on the possibility that aging is the result of selective gene action analogous to that which has been proposed in the process of terminal differentiation. In this section, we shall limit the discussion to studies that have tested these hypotheses with regard to the limited growth potential of cultured diploid cells.

The Error Catastrophe Hypothesis

Orgel (1963) proposed that a natural consequence of the lack of total specificity in protein synthesis would be an eventual error catastrophe. According to this hypothesis, the initial presence of errors in those enzymes involved in transcription and translation, and thus their own synthesis, leads to an exponential increase in errors and eventually to the death of the cell. The theory was later modified (Orgel, 1970) to admit the possibility that nongrowing cells need not be subject to error catastrophe provided that the rate of error production does not increase exponentially during protein synthesis. Holliday et al. (1975) argued, however, that an error catastrophe could be responsible for the loss of proliferative potential in cell cultures provided that cells could tolerate relatively large numbers of errors without a decrease in growth rate.

The error catastrophe theory of aging has attracted a great deal of attention from both experimentalists and theoreticians. Hoffmann (1974) and Goel and Ycas (1975) have presented theoretical treatments arguing that error catastrophies are very unlikely to occur in cultured mammalian cells. Kirkwood and Holliday (1975b) extended Hoffmann's treatment to include the relative activity of the translational system containing certain types of errors and concluded that if the activity of the altered translational system was high enough, then an error catastrophe could occur.

Experimental evidence derived from *in vitro* studies has been obtained that is both consistent and inconsistent with the error catastrophe hypothesis. One prediction of this hypothesis is that the level of altered enzymes, as evidenced by changes in physical properties such as heat lability, should increase during *in vitro* cellular aging. Heat-labile glucose-6-phosphate dehydrogenase (G6PD) has been detected in normal senescent human fibroblasts (Holliday and Tarrant, 1972) as well as fibroblasts from donors with the Werner and Hutchinson-Gilford syndromes (Holliday et al., 1974; Goldstein and Singal, 1974b; Goldstein and Moerman, 1975). Lewis and Tarrant (1972) found increased amounts of immunologically cross-reactive, but enzymatically inactive, lactate dehydrogenase in late passage fibroblasts from normal donors. On the other hand, a number of studies have yielded results that do not support the error hypothesis. In direct contrast to the results of Holliday and Tarrant (1972), Pendergrass et al. (1976) were unable to detect an increase in thermolabile G6PD or an increase in immunologically cross-reactive material with an increase in passage level in cultures from

normal donors. These divergent results can in part be explained by the observation that increased thermolability may be associated with the presence of this enzyme in tetrameric form (Duncan et al., 1977). Direct measurements of the accuracy of protein synthesis, assessed by the mass incorporation of [^{35}S]-methionine into histone H1 from fetal lung fibroblast-like cells, failed to detect any changes at higher passage levels (Buchanan and Stevens, 1978). Likewise, the fidelity of poly(U) directed protein synthesis in extracts from low and high passage fibroblast-like cultures and from cultures derived from progeroid patients was shown to be approximately equivalent (Wojtyk and Goldstein, 1980). Using a different approach, Harley et al. (1980) estimated the error frequency via analysis of two-dimensional gel electrophoresis of native and substituted actins. Mistranslation was induced in the proteins by histidine starvation in the presence of histidinol. These authors observed no decline in the fidelity of synthesis of these proteins with increasing *in vitro* age, but did demonstrate a three-fold increase in the rate of mistranslation in SV–40 transformed cells.

Another experimental strategy to test the error hypothesis has been to examine the capacity of aged cells to support viral replication as a probe for the fidelity of macromolecular synthesis. Holland et al. (1973) and Tomkins et al. (1974) reported that when old cells were infected with RNA or DNA viruses, the viruses were able to replicate in old cells to the same extent as in young cells. The viruses produced in the old cells were as viable as those produced in young cells, and the thermostability and mutation rate of the viruses produced in the old cells were observed to be unaltered. Pitha et al. (1975) were also unable to detect altered protein in viruses made by old cells. On the other hand, Fulder (1977) reported that the reversion frequency of two out of three temperature sensitive mutants of herpes virus was affected by the age of the host cell. For one mutant, the reversion rate was 100-fold higher in young cells than in old cells. In another, the reversion rate was 40-fold higher in the old cells. The reason for these apparently contradictory results is unknown at the present time. It is possible that certain aspects of cellular metabolism are profoundly altered as cells approach senescence and that this is reflected in the replication of certain species of viruses in the aged cells.

At the present time, it is not possible to either prove or disprove the hypothesis that an error catastrophe is the cause of *in vitro* cellular aging. However, at this time the majority of the evidence appears to argue against the error catastrophe as a major cause of *in vitro* cellular aging, since in a number of reports the major predictions of the hypothesis have not been verified by experimental results.

The Somatic Mutation Theory

It has been proposed by a number of investigators that mutations in somatic cells could be a primary cause of aging (Szilard, 1959; Burnet, 1974). While many aspects of this hypothesis are conceptually attractive, there are considerations which suggest that somatic mutations, at least in transcriptionally active genes, are not a primary cause of cellular aging. For example, Holliday and Kirkwood (1981) argued that if one assumed that the majority (approximately 95 percent) of the critical genes are located on the autosomes, then mutation rates about 100-fold higher than those known in fibroblast-like cultures would be necessary to limit the life span to 50–60 population doublings. They further pointed out that mutations on the X chromosome would result in a lower fraction of dividing cells than has been reported.

Experimental studies designed to test the somatic mutation theory have in general been nonsupportive or less than conclusive. Fulder and Holliday (1975) did report a rapid increase in the appearance of a G6PD variant in late passage cultures. However, it was not directly demonstrated that this variant was the result of gene mutations. A number of laboratories have attempted to examine the effect of an increased mutational burden induced by exposure to mutagenic agents. In

the most extensive study with chemical mutagens reported thus far, Gupta (1980) observed no attenuation of growth potential in fetal lung cultures after repeated exposure to ethyl methanesulfonate (EMS) or N-methyl-N-nitroso-N'-nitroguanidine (MNNG), although the frequency of diphtheria toxin resistant variants were observed to increase by 100-fold. Similar studies with ionizing irradiation have produced a wide spectrum of results. The response to these mutagenic agents with respect to growth potential and proliferative behavior appears to be influenced by such variables as *in vivo* and *in vitro* cell age, genotype of the donor, and species from which the cultures are derived (Macieira-Coelho et al., 1976, 1977, 1978; Diatloff and Macieira-Coelho, 1979; Lima et al., 1972). In addition, as demonstrated by Ban et al. (1980) and by Stevenson and Cremer (1981), the method of assay by which changes in growth potential are determined is an important variable in these studies. Failure to account for massive cell death following irradiation may result in an underestimation of the growth potential of the surviving cells. There is also an inherent problem of interpretation in any aging studies in which the assay involves decreases in the life span of the cell culture or an organism. Clearly, a variety of agents and environmental conditions that are of no relevance to the aging process will decrease the proliferative potential of a culture.

Experimental approaches that are relevant to the somatic mutation hypothesis of aging include studies designed to evaluate DNA damage, rate and efficiency of repair, and fidelity of DNA synthesis. Several laboratories have reported data suggesting increased damage in the DNA of late passage fibroblast-like cells. Dell'Orco and Whittle (1981) reported an increased number of sites sensitive to *Micrococcus luteus* extracts in purified chromatin preparations from late passage foreskin cultures. Evidence for increased single-strand breaks as assessed by alkaline sucrose gradients has been reported by Icard and Beaupain (1980) in fetal lung cultures (MRC5). Thus, there is some evidence for increased DNA damage in late passage fibroblast-like cultures. However, it remains to be determined if these changes are of causal significance in the loss of proliferative activity in those cultures.

The role of DNA repair in *in vitro* aging is discussed in depth in Chapter 8. In summary, no consistent defect in DNA repair has been found as a function of serial *in vitro* passage, with the possible exception of the very last passages.

Another mechanism by which mutational events could occur in DNA is by alteration of the fidelity of DNA synthesis (Loeb et al., 1979). Diminished fidelity in copying synthetic deoxyribonucleotide polymers by DNA polymerase-alpha partially purified from fetal lung fibroblasts aged *in vitro* has been reported (Linn et al., 1976). However, in later studies, Krauss and Linn (1982) observed that the fidelity of DNA polymerase-alpha is also decreased in postconfluent cultures, suggesting that this parameter may also be influenced by the proliferative state of the cells. *In vivo* studies of the fidelity of DNA synthesis have failed to detect any age-related changes. Agarwal et al. (1978) have reported that the rate of nucleotide misincorporation by DNA polymerase-alpha from human lymphocytes does not change as a function of the age. Also, Fry et al. (1981) reported no differences in fidelity of DNA polymerase-beta in chromatin preparations from liver tissue from mice of differing longevities.

The results obtained from the cell hybridization experiments discussed earlier also are inconsistent with the notion that somatic mutations are the primary cause of *in vitro* cellular senescence. In those experiments, there was no indication that young cells could complement the defects in old cells and reinitiate cell proliferation. Even in the case in which the parental cells were near the end of their *in vitro* life span but still proliferating, fusion did not yield hybrid cells with a greater proliferative potential than the parental cells (Hoehn et al., 1978; Pereira-Smith and Smith, 1982) as would be expected from the complementation of random recessive mutations. Along similar lines, it has been reported that diploid and tetraploid human fibroblasts appear to have the same *in vitro* proliferative potential (Thompson and Holliday, 1975).

The majority of experimental evidence to date does not support the hypothesis that the decline of proliferative potential in fibroblast-like cultures is the direct result of gene mutations (at least in single copy genes). However, Ohno and Nagai (1978) have argued on theoretical grounds that loss or inactivation of reiterated sequences may be of greater significance as a primary mechanism leading to the functional decline with aging. There are some experimental observations that would appear to support this proposal. Shmookler-Reis and Goldstein (1980) have reported the loss of sequences from a specific family of repeated sequences with advancing passage level in three separate strains of fibroblast-like cells. More recently, these investigators have reported amplification of extrachromosomal circular DNA, derived from sequences situated between clusters of a repeated (alu) sequence, with serial passage of fibroblast-like cultures and in lymphocytes from aged donors (Shmookler-Reiss et al, 1983). While the significance of these observations remains to be elucidated, they suggest that structural changes of the genome with age may be extensive. There is also published evidence for the loss of ribosomal sequences with age in human (Strehler et al., 1979; Strehler and Chang, 1979) and canine (Johnson and Strehler, 1972; Johnson et al., 1972) postmitotic tissues. These observations provide a rational basis for a new direction in studies of the role of mutations in aging.

Genetic Control Mechanisms

The molecular mechanisms by which a genetic control of cellular aging might operate have not in general been as well conceptualized as those pertaining to stochastic processes. The idea that fibroblast-like cells cease to proliferate as a "by-product" of their differentiation has been proposed by Martin et al. (1974, 1975b) and Bell et al. (1978). These investigators have implied that the loss of proliferative potential is a result of the cells differentiating to express a hitherto unexpressed tissue specific function. One of the major criticisms of this idea is that to date no clearly defined differentiated function has been detected in fibroblast-like cells. In certain cell types, e.g., bovine endothelial cells, it has been shown that a tissue specific function decreases dramatically with *in vitro* age. This has been shown to be true in the case of angiotensin converting enzyme in endothelial cells (Del Vecchio and Smith, 1982; Levine et al., 1983). This loss of enzyme activity is certainly not a general phenomenon because in the same cells (as in fibroblast-like cells), 5'-nucleotidase activity was found to increase dramatically as the cultures neared senescence.

Evidence has been reported indicating that senescent cells contain a diffusible inhibitor of DNA synthesis (see discussion on cell hybridization experiments). Rabinovitch and Norwood (1980) and Stein and Yanishevsky (1979) have suggested that this inhibitor of DNA synthesis may be responsible for the loss of proliferative capacity of cells aged *in vitro*. Although the evidence seems to indicate that this is possible, it still remains to provide a mechanism for the control of expression of such an inhibitor. Since the division potential of human diploid cells is probably at least 150 generations (Good, 1972), it is necessary that this control program operate during at least 150 cell divisions. Smith and Lumpkin (1980) have proposed a molecular mechanism that could control the timing of expression of this DNA synthesis inhibitor. The basis of the proposed mechanism is the gradual loss of the stringency of gene repression, which could be accomplished by a gradual loss of repeated DNA sequences involved in maintaining repression activity. As mentioned, loss of repeated sequences has been reported with aging *in vitro* (Shmookler-Reis and Goldstein, 1980) as well as *in vivo* (Strehler et al., 1979). Olovnikov (1973) has also proposed a hypothesis which involves the loss of genetic

material during replication of the genome, or so-called Marginotomy. This model is based on the idea that, during DNA replication, a certain small part of the DNA is not replicated at the ends of the replication points of the DNA molecule and that the end regions are comprised of buffer sequences or "telogenes." When all of the buffer DNA has been lost, the ends of actual structural genes can then be lost and the cell ceases division.

A number of theoretical models have been proposed to provide a conceptual framework for the observation associated with proliferative decline in fibroblast-like cultures. The commitment theory of aging of Kirkwood and Holliday (1975a) and Holliday et al. (1977) proposes that the natural condition for human embryonic lung fibroblasts is an "immortal" state. Upon division, cells can become committed to senescence at a relatively high frequency of about 0.275 per cell generation. Once the cells are committed to becoming senescent, they go through a large number of doublings (about 60) before they finally cease division. This stochastic process (commitment) and the relatively few noncommitted cells in young–middle aged cultures can account for the variability in the life span of human fibroblast cultures. Although no specific molecular mechanism is proposed, it seems likely that the probability of commitment and possibly the remaining doublings following commitment would be determined by a genetic control mechanism. It has been pointed out, however, by Harley and Goldstein (1981) and by Prothero and Gallant (1981) that the commitment theory cannot account for the commonly observed pattern of nondividing cells versus culture age (Cristofalo and Sharf, 1973; Merz and Ross, 1969; Smith and Braunschweiger, 1979) (Figure 3, line A) or for the changes in colony size distribution observed (Smith et al., 1977, 1978). More recently, Holliday et al. (1981) reported changes in the proportion of nondividing cells with age that were consistent with the commitment theory (Figure 3, line b).

Prothero and Gallant (1981) have suggested that the probability of commitment monotonically increases with increasing cell division. In their model, they propose that once a cell is committed it is then able to undergo about seven additional doublings. As a possible molecular mechanism for the increasing probability of commitment, they suggest the buildup of a protein mediated by a positive feedback mechanism. A similar control mechanism has been proposed in a simple one-parameter model suggested by Shall and Stein (1979). This model predicts a gradual buildup of a protein (called the mortalization or M protein) that competes with another (D) protein (which is produced at a constant concentration) for a binding site of an initiator gene. If the D protein binds the initiator site, the initiator is produced and the cell divides. However, if the M protein binds, it prevents the binding of the D protein, irreversibly blocks production of the initiator, and thereby inhibits cell division. Using appropriate values for the rate of increase of M, Shall and Stein were able to obtain reasonably good fit to the growth of human and mouse fibroblasts as a function of time, and also to the data of Cristofalo and Sharf (1973) on the labeling index of human fibroblasts. In addition, this model can account for the immortality of cells by mutations in the M protein or its binding site, and is consistent with the heterokaryon results of Stein and Yanishevsky (1979) and Rabinovitch and Norwood (1980). However, it is not clear that this model would give rise to the bimodal distribution of intraclonal life spans observed by Smith and Whitney (1980).

CONCLUDING REMARKS

From this discussion it should be apparent that the three questions posed in the introductory section of this chapter have been answered only to varying degrees. The question of whether euploid fibroblast-like populations possess a finite growth potential appears to have an affirmative answer. Many laboratories throughout the world have reconfirmed the original observations of Hay-

flick and Moorhead (1961). The *in vivo* studies and *in vitro* studies with other cell types indicate that probably all stem cell populations have a limited proliferative potential. However, it must be emphasized that it is very difficult to definitively exclude "trivial" causes of growth failure *in vitro*. It remains a possibility that the presently used media lack some essential nutrient or growth factor or that cells gradually accumulate toxic substance from the medium. Therefore, as we indicated above, it will be very important to continually reassess the growth behavior of cultured fibroblast-like cells and other cell types as new advances occur in the formulation of growth media and in the techniques for the cultivation of vertebrate cells.

The question of the direct relevance of the cultured fibroblast-like cell for the study of *in vivo* cellular aging remains more controversial. Certainly the evidence cited in this discussion is very suggestive, but nonetheless is indirect. In our view, the observation showing that there exists some relationship among growth behavior, donor age, and species longevity suggests that at least some cellular functions that change with age or are related to the regulation of longevity are expressed *in vitro*. Progress toward realizing a more definitive answer to this question has been hampered in part because the research with this *in vitro* system has focused primarily on proliferative functions. This narrow focus has severely limited studies in which *in vivo–in vitro* correlations can be made. Since the histiotype of the cultured fibroblast-like cell has not been identified, its precise function *in vivo* is unknown. The development of techniques for the cultivation of differentiated cell types offers the promise that a variety of cellular functions which may change with age can be examined *in vivo*. In addition, the availability of diverse cell types that can be maintained *in vitro* may permit the development of systems designed to analyze *in vitro* alterations in cell-to-cell communications which, as stressed by Martin et al. (1975a), may be a significant factor in age-related changes in cellular functional activity. It is also imperative that serious attempts be made to identify the cell type(s) that populates fibroblast-like cultures. Efforts to develop cytospecific monoclonal antibodies represent one approach to this problem that merits consideration. Also, there is a need to develop well-characterized *in vitro* models from experimental animals to facilitate studies of *in vivo–in vitro* correlations. The rodent systems are an obvious choice on the basis of cost and extent of characterization. However, the problem of spontaneous transformation in cultures from these animals will have to be considered in the selection of a specific strain or species.

The question of the mechanisms that limit the growth potential of fibroblast-like cultures remains unanswered. The extensive body of descriptive literature has made the human fibroblast-like cell one of the most extensively characterized cell types in culture. The results of studies that directly or indirectly test specific hypotheses have been generally nonsupportive or at best ambiguous. However, the extremely rapid advances in molecular biology will certainly lead to refinement of the hypotheses discussed. These hypotheses will have to be continually reassessed as advances occur in our basic understanding of the molecular biology of gene structure and function, cellular repair systems, and the biochemistry of cell cycle regulation. Many of the studies reported in the literature describe temporal relationships between proliferative decline and the parameters under study. This approach cannot definitively establish causal relationships. Greater emphasis will have to be put on the development of well-defined probes that perturb the proliferative behavior and/or growth potential of fibroblast-like cultures. The use of hydrocortisone to extend the growth potential of fibroblast-like cultures is one example of this approach that has been employed during the past decade (Cristofalo, 1975). In view of the recent impressive advances in the molecular aspects of viral oncology, tumor viruses such as a SV-40 offer the potential to study the mechanisms that alter proliferative behavior in senescent

cultures (Scott et al., 1976). It has been recently reported that a temperature sensitive strain of SV-40 (SV40TsA58) can reinitiate DNA synthesis in senescent cells at the nonpermissive temperature (Gorman and Cristofalo, 1982).

Thus, it is apparent that many questions remain regarding the use of *in vitro* systems in aging research. However, it is equally clear that new avenues of research are emerging as advances are made in cell culture and molecular biology. The observations derived from studies with cultured fibroblast-like cells have been a major factor in the increased interest in aging at the cellular level during the past several decades.

REFERENCES

Aaronson, S. A. 1970. Susceptibility of human cell strains to transformation by simian virus 40 and simian virus 40 DNA. *J. Virol.*, **6**, 470–475.

Aaronson, S. A. and Todaro, G. J. 1970. Transformation and virus growth by murine sarcoma viruses in human cells. *Nature*, **225**, 458–459.

Absher, P. M. and Absher, R. G. 1976. Clonal variation and aging of diploid fibroblasts. Cinematographic studies of cell pedigrees. *Exp. Cell Res.*, **103**, 247–255.

Absher, P. M., Absher, R. G., and Barnes, W. D. 1974. Genealogies of clones of diploid fibroblasts. Cinemicrophotographic observations of cell division patterns in relation to population age. *Exp. Cell Res.*, **88**, 95–104.

Agarwal, S. S., Tuffner, M., and Loeb, L. A. 1978. DNA replication in human lymphocytes during aging. *J. Cellular Physiol.*, **96**, 235–244.

Aizawa, S. and Kurimoto, F. 1979a. Effects of glutaraldehyde and other drugs on concanavalin A-mediated red blood cell adsorption to nonsenescent, senescent and transformed human fibroblasts. *Mech. Age. Dev.*, **11**, 237–243.

Aizawa, S. and Kurimoto, F. 1979b. Age-related cell surface changes in human diploid fibroblasts revealed by lectin-mediated red blood cell adsorption assay: a lectin survey. *Mech. Age. Dev.*, **11**, 245–252.

Aizawa, S. and Mitsui, Y. 1979. A new cell surface marker of aging in human diploid cells. *J. Cellular Physiol.*, **100**, 383–387.

Aizawa, S., Mitsui, Y., Kurimoto, F., and Matsuoka, K. 1980a. Cell surface changes accompanying aging in human diploid fibroblasts. III. Division age and senescence revealed by concanavalin A-mediated red blood cell adsorption. *Exp. Cell Res.*, **125**, 297–303.

Aizawa, S., Mitsui, Y., Kurimoto, F., and Nomura, K. 1980b. Cell surface changes accompanying aging in human diploid fibroblasts. V. Role of large major surface protein and surface negative charge in aging and transformation associated changes in concanavalin A-mediated red blood cell adsorption. *Exp. Cell Res.,* **127,** 143–157.

Azzarone, B., Pedulla, D., and Romanzi, C. A. 1976. Spontaneous transformation of human skin fibroblasts from neoplastic patients. *Nature* 262: 74–75.

Baker, R. M., Burnette, D. M., Mankovitz, R., Thompson, L. H., Whitmore, G. F., Siminovitch, L., and Till, J. E. 1974. Ouabain-resistant mutants of mouse and hamster cells in culture. *Cell* 1: 9–21.

Ban, S., Nikaido, O., and Sugahara, T. 1980. Modifications of doubling potential of cultured human diploid cells by ionizing radiation and hydrocortisone. *Exp. Geront.* 15: 539–549.

Baserga, R. 1976. Multiplication and revision in mammalian cells. *In, The Biochemistry of Disease,* Vol. 6, pp. 175–188. New York: Marcel Dekker.

Basler, J. W., David, J. D., and Agris, P. F. 1979. Deteriorating collagen synthesis and cell ultrastructure accompanying senescence of human normal and Werner's syndrome fibroblast cell strains. *Exp. Cell Res.* 118: 73–84.

Bell, E., Marek, L. F., Levinstone, D. S., Merrill, C., Sher, S., Young, I. T., and Eden, M. 1978. Loss of division potential *in vitro:* aging or differentiation? Departure of cells from cycle may not be a sign of aging, but a sign of differentiation. *Science* 202: 1158–1163.

Bettger, W. J., Boyce, S. T., Walthall, B. J., and Ham, R. G., 1981. Rapid clonal growth and serial passage of human diploid fibroblasts in a lipid-enriched synthetic medium supplemented with epidermal growth factor, insulin and dexamethasone. *Proc. Nat. Acad. Sci.* 78: 5588–5592.

Bierman, E. L., 1978. The effect of donor age on the *in vitro* life span of cultured human arterial smooth muscle cells. *In Vitro* 14: 951–955.

Bilgin, B. A. and Cristofalo, V. J. 1978. The effect of hydrocortisone on the transition probability of WI-38 cells during aging. *In Vitro* 14: 359.

Borek, C. 1980. X-ray induced *in vitro* neoplastic transformation of human diploid cells. *Nature* 282: 776–778.

Boue, A., Boue, J., Cure, S., Deluchat, C., and Perraudin, N. 1975, *In vitro* cultivation of cells from aneuploid human embryos, initiation of cell lines and longevity of the cultures. *In Vitro* 11: 409–413.

Bowman, P. D., Meek, R. L., and Daniel, C. W. 1976. Decreased unscheduled DNA synthesis in nondividing aged WI-38 cells. *Mech. Age. Dev.* 5: 251–257.

Bradley, M. O., Erickson, L. C., and Kohn, K. W. 1976. Normal DNA strand rejoining and absence of DNA crosslinking in progeroid and aging human cells. *Mutation Res.* 37: 279–292.

Brandes, D., Murphy, D. G., Anton, E. B., and Barnard, S. 1972. Ultrastructural and cytochemical changes in cultured human lung cells. *J. Ultrastruct. Res.* 39: 465–483.

Brock, M. A. and Hay, R. J. 1971. Comparative ultrastructure of chick fibroblasts *in vitro* at early and late stages during their growth span. *J. Ultrastruct. Res.* 36: 291–311.

Brown, W. T. 1979. Human mutations effecting aging—a review. *Mech. Age. Dev.* 9: 325–336.

Buchanan, J. H. and Stevens, A. 1978. Fidelity of histone synthesis in cultured human fibroblasts. *Mech. Age. Dev.* 7: 321–334.

Bunn, C. L. and Tarrant, G. M. 1980. Limited lifespan in somatic cell hybrids and cybrids. *Exp. Cell Res.* 127: 385–396.

Burmer, G. C., Motulsky, H., Zeigler, C. J., and Norwood, T. H. 1983a. Inhibition of DNA synthesis in young cycling human diploid fibroblast-like cells upon fusion to enucleate cytoplasts from senescent cells. *Exp. Cell Res.* 145: 79–84.

Burmer, G. C. and Norwood, T. H. 1980. Selective elimination of proliferating cells in human diploid cell cultures by treatment with BrdU, 33258 Hoechst, and visible light. *Mech. Age. Dev.* 12: 151–159.

Burmer, G. C., Rabinovitch, P. S., and Norwood, T. H. 1983b. Evidence for differences in the mechanism of cell cycle arrest between senescent and serum-deprived human diploid fibroblast-like cells: a comparative heterokaryon study. *J. Cellular Physiol.* 118: 97–103.

Burmer, G. C., Zeigler, C. J., and Norwood, T. H. 1982. Evidence for endogenous polypeptide-mediated inhibition of cell-cycle transit in human diploid cells. *J. Cell Biol.* 94: 187–192.

Burnet, F. M. 1974. *Intrinsic Mutagenesis: A Genetic Approach to Aging.* New York: John Wiley & Sons.

Carrel, A. 1912. On the permanent life of tissues outside of the organism. *J. Exp. Med.* 15: 516–528.

Carrel, A. 1935. *In, Man the Unknown,* pp. 172–174. New York: Halcyon House.

Carrel, A. and Ebeling, A. H. 1921. Age and multiplication of fibroblasts. *J. Exp. Med.* 34: 599–623.

Chandrasekhar, S. and Millis, A. J. T. 1980. Fibronectin from aged fibroblasts is defective in promoting cellular adhesion. *J. Cellular Physiol.* 103: 47–54.

Cohn, A. E. and Murray, H. A. 1925. Physiological ontogeny. A. Chicken embryos. VI. The negative acceleration of growth with age as demonstrated by tissue cultures. *J. Exp. Med.* 42: 275–290.

Cristofalo, V. J. 1976. Thymidine labelling index as a criterion of aging *in vitro*. *Gerontology* 22: 9–27.

Cristofalo, V. J. 1975. The effect of hydrocortisone on DNA synthesis and cell division during aging *in vitro*. *In,* V. J. Cristofalo and E. Holeckova (eds.), *Cell Impairment in Aging and Development,* pp. 7–22. New York: Plenum Press.

Cristofalo, V. J., Parris, N., and Kritchevsky, D. 1967. Enzyme activity during the growth and aging of human cells *in vitro*. *J. Cellular Physiol.* 69: 263–272.

Cristofalo, V. J. and Sharf, B. B. 1973. Cellular senescence and DNA synthesis. *Exp. Cell Res.* 76: 419–427.

Cristofalo, V. J. and Stanulis-Praeger, B. M. 1982. Cellular senescence *in vitro. In,* K. Maramorosch (ed.), *Advances in Tissue Culture,* Vol. 2, pp. 1–68. New York: Academic Press.

Critchley, D. R. 1974. Cell surface proteins of NIL 1 hamster fibroblasts labeled by a galactose oxidase tritiated borohydride method. *Cell* 3: 121–125.

Croce, C. M. and Koprowski, H. 1974. Positive control of transformed phenotype in hybrids between SV-40 transformed and normal human cells. *Science,* 184: 1288–1289.

Danes, B. S. 1971. Progeria: a cell culture study on aging. *J. Clin. Invest.* 50: 2000–2003.

Daniel, C. W., DeOme K. B., Young, J. T., Blair, P. B., and Faulken, L. J. 1968. The *in vivo* life span of normal and preneoplastic mouse mammary glands: a serial transplantation study. *Proc. Nat. Acad. Sci.* 61: 52–60.

Daniel, C. W. and Young, L. J. T. 1971. Influence of cell division on an aging process. Life span of mouse mammary epithelium during serial propagation *in vivo. Exp. Cell Res.* 65: 27–32.

DeBusk, F. L. 1972. The Hutchinson-Gilford progeria syndrome. Report of 4 cases and review of the literature. *J. Pediatr.* 80: 697–724.

Dell'Orco, R. T. and Anderson, L. E. 1981. Unscheduled DNA synthesis in human diploid cells of different donor ages. *Cell Biol. Inter. Rep.* 5: 359–364.

Dell'Orco, R. T., Mergens, J. G., and Kuse, J. F., Jr. 1974. Doubling potential calendar time and donor age of human diploid cells in culture. *Exp. Cell Res.* 84: 363–366.

Del Vecchio, P. J. and Smith, J. R. 1982. Aging of endothelium in culture: decrease in angiotensin-converting enzyme activity. *Cell Biol. Intl. Rep.* 6: 379–384.

Dell'Orco, R. T. and Whittle, W. L. 1978. Unscheduled DNA synthesis in confluent and mitotically arrested populations of aging human diploid fibroblasts. *Mech. Age. Dev.* 8: 269–279.

Dell'Orco, R. T. and Whittle, W. L. 1981. Evidence for an increased level of DNA damage in high doubling level human diploid cells in culture. *Mech. Age. Dev.* 15: 141–152.

Diatloff, C. and Macieira-Coelho, A. 1979. Effect of low-dose-rate irradiation on the division potential of cells *in vitro.* V. Human skin fibroblasts from donors with a high risk of cancer. *J. Nat. Cancer Inst.* 63: 55–59.

Didinsky, J. B. and Rheinwald, J. G. 1981. Failure of hydrocortisone or growth factors to influence the senescence of fibroblasts in a new culture system for assessing replicative life-span. *J. Cellular Physiol.* 109: 171–179.

Drescher-Lincoln, C. K. and Smith, J. L. 1983. Inhibition of DNA synthesis in proliferating human diploid fibroblasts by fusion with senescent cytoplasts. *Exp. Cell Res.* 144: 445–462.

Duncan, M. R., Dell'Orco, R. T., and Guthrie, P. L. 1977. Relationship of heat labile glucose-6-phosphate dehydrogenase and multiple molecular forms

of the enzymes in senescent human fibroblasts. *J. Cellular Physiol.* 93: 49–56.

Duthu G. S., Braunschweiger, K. I., Pereira-Smith, O. A., Norwood, T. H., and Smith, J. R. 1982, A long-lived human diploid fibroblast line for cellular aging studies: applications in cell hybridization. *Mech. Age. Dev.* 20: 243–252.

Earle, W. R. 1943. Production of malignancy *in vitro.* IV. The mouse fibroblast cultures and changes seen in living cells. *J. Nat. Cancer Inst.* 4: 165–212.

Ebeling, A. H. 1913. The permanent life of connective tissue outside of the organism. *J. Exp. Med.* 17: 273–285.

Elmore, E. and Swift, M. 1975. Growth of cultured cells from patients with Fanconi anemia. *J. Cellular Physiol.* 87: 229–234.

Elmore, E. and Swift, M. 1976. Growth of cultured cells from patients with ataxia-telangiectasia. *J. Cellular Physiol.* 89: 429–432.

Epstein, C. J., Martin, G. M., Schultz, A. L., and Motulsky, A. G. 1966. Werner's syndrome. A review of its symptomatology, natural history, pathology features, genetics and relationship to the natural aging process. *Medicine* 45: 177–221.

Erlichman, E. 1935. Human fibroblasts grown for a year in a medium of sheep plasma and two solutions of known composition. *Amer. J. Cancer* 24: 393–396.

Francis, A. A., Lee, H. W., and Regan, J. D. 1981. The relationship of DNA excision repair of ultraviolet induced lesions to the maximum life span of mammals. *Mech. Age. Dev.* 16: 181–189.

Franks, L. M. and Cooper, T. W. 1972. The origin of human embryo lung cells in culture: a comment on cell differentiation, *in vitro* growth and neoplasia. *Int. J. Cancer* 9: 19–29.

Fry, M., Loeb, L. A., and Martin, G. M. 1981. On the activity and fidelity of chromatin-associated hepatic DNA polymerase-beta in aging murine species of different life spans. *J. Cellular Physiol.* 106: 435–444.

Fulder, S. J. 1977. Spontaneous mutations in ageing human cells: studies using a herpesvirus probe. *Mech. Age. Dev.* 6: 271–282.

Fulder, S. J. and Holliday, R. 1975. A rapid rise in cell variants during the senescence of populations of human fibroblasts. *Cell* 6: 67–73.

Gey, G. O. 1955. Some aspects of the constitution and behavior of normal and malignant cells maintained in continuous culture. *Harvey Lecture Series* 50: 154–229.

Gey, G. O., Coffman, W. D., and Kubicek, M. 1952. Tissue culture studies of the proliferative capacity of cervical carcinoma and normal epithelium. *Cancer Res.* 12: 264–265.

Giannelli, F., Benson, P. F., Pawsey, S. A., and Polani, P. E. 1977. Ultraviolet light sensitivity and delayed DNA-chain maturation in Bloom's syndrome fibroblasts. *Nature* 265: 466–469.

Gillis, S., Baker, P. E., Ruscatti, F. W., and Smith, K. A. 1978. Long-term culture of human antigen-specific cytotoxic T-cell lines. *J. Exp. Med.* 148: 1093–1098.

Goel, N. S. and Ycas, M. 1975. The error catastrophe hypothesis with reference to aging and the evolution of the protein synthesizing machinery. *J. Theor. Biol.* 54: 245–282.

Goldstein, S. 1969. Lifespan of cultured cells in progeria. *Lancet* 1, 424.

Goldstein, S. 1971. The role of DNA repair in aging of cultured fibroblasts from xeroderma pigmentosum and normals (35655). *Proc. Soc. Exp. Biol. Med.* 137, 730–734.

Goldstein, S. 1978. Human genetic disorders that feature premature onset and accelerated progression of biological aging. *In,* E. L. Schneider (ed.), *The Genetics of Aging,* pp. 171–224. New York: Plenum Press.

Goldstein, S. and Lin, C. C. 1972. Rescue of senescent human fibroblasts by hybridization with hamster cells *in vitro. Exp. Cell Res.* 70: 436–439.

Goldstein, S., Littlefield, J. W., and Soeldner, J. S. 1969. Diabetes mellitus and aging: diminished plating efficiency of cultured human fibroblasts. *Proc. Nat. Acad. Sci.* 64: 155–160.

Goldstein, S. and Moerman, E. 1975. Heat-labile enzymes in skin fibroblasts from subjects with progeria. *New Engl. J. Med.* 292: 1305–1309.

Goldstein, S. and Moerman, E. J. 1976. Defective proteins in normal and abnormal human fibroblasts during aging *in vitro. Interdiscpl. Topics Geront.* 10: 24–43.

Goldstein, S., Moerman, E. L., Soeldner, J. S., Gleason, R. E., and Barnett, D. M. 1978. Chronologic and physiologic age affect replicative lifespan of fibroblasts from diabetic, prediabetic, and normal donors. *Science* 199: 781–782.

Goldstein, S. and Singal, D. P. 1974a. Senescence of cultured human fibroblasts: mitotic versus metabolic time. *Exp. Cell Res.* 88: 359–364.

Goldstein, S. and Singal, D. P. 1974b. Alteration of fibroblast gene products *in vitro* from a subject with Werner's syndrome. *Nature* 251: 719–721.

Good, P. I. 1972. Subcultivations, slits, doublings, and generations in cultures of human diploid fibroblasts. *Cell Tissue Kinet.* 5: 319–323.

Gopalakrishnan, T. V. and Anderson, W. F. 1979. Epigenetic activation of phenylalanine hydroxylase in mouse erythroleukemia cells by the cytoplast of rat hepatoma cells. *Proc. Nat. Acad. Sci.* 76: 3932–3936.

Gopalakrishnan, T. V., Thompson, E. B., and Anderson, W. F. 1977. Extinction of hemoglobin inducibility in Friend erythroleukemia cells by fusion with cytoplasm of enucleated mouse neuroblastoma or fibroblast cells. *Proc. Nat. Acad. Sci.* 74: 1642–1646.

Gorman, S. D. and Cristofalo, V. J. 1982. Reinitiation of cellular DNA replication in senescent WI-38 cells by Simian Virus 40. *J. Cell Biol.* 95: 21a.

Grinnell, F. and Feld, M. K. 1979. Initial adhesion of human fibroblasts in serum-free medium: possible role of secreted fibronectin. *Cell* 17: 117–129.

Grove, G. L., Houghton, B. A., Cochran, J. W., Kress, E. D., and Cristofalo, V. J. 1977. Hydrocortisone effects on cell proliferation: specificity of response among various cell types. *Cell Biol. Internat. Reports* 1: 147–155.

Grove, G. L., Kress, E. D., and Cristofalo, V. J. 1976. The cell cycle and thymidine incorporation during aging *in vitro. J. Cell Biol.* 70: 133a.

Gupta, R. S. 1980. Senescence of cultured human diploid fibroblasts. Are mutations responsible? *J. Cellular Physiol.* 103: 209–216.

Hadley, E. C., Kress, E. D., and Cristofalo, V. J. 1979, Trypsinization frequency and loss of proliferative capacity in WI-38 cells. *J. Geront.* 34: 170–176.

Hand, R. and German, J. 1975. A retarded rate of DNA chain growth in Bloom's syndrome. *Proc. Nat. Acad. Sci.* 72: 758–762.

Harley, C. B. and Goldstein, S. 1980. Retesting the commitment theory of cellular aging. *Science* 207: 191–193.

Harley, C. B., Goldstein, S., Posner, B. I., and Guyda, H. 1981. Decreased sensitivity of old and progeric human fibroblasts to a preparation of factors with insulin-like activity. *J. Clin. Invest.* 68: 988–994.

Harley, C. B., Pollard, J. W., Chamberlain, J. W., Stanners, C. P., and Goldstein, S. 1980. Protein synthetic errors do not increase during aging of cultured human fibroblasts. *Proc. Nat. Acad. Sci.* 77: 1885–1889.

Harper, R. A. and Grove, G. 1979. Human skin fibroblasts derived from papillary and reticular dermis: differences in growth potential *in vitro. Science* 204: 526–527.

Harris, H. 1967. The reactivation of the red cell nucleus. *J. Cellular Sci.* 2: 23–32.

Harris, H., Sidebottom, E., Grace, D. M., and Bramwell, M. E. 1969. The expression of genetic information: a study with animal cells. *J. Cell Sci.* 4: 499–525.

Harrison, D. E. 1973. Normal production of erythrocytes by mouse marrow continuous for 73 months. *Proc. Nat. Acad. Sci.* 70: 3184–3188.

Harrison, D. E. 1979. Proliferative capacity of erythropoietic stem cell lines and aging: an overview. *Mech. Age. Dev.* 9: 409–426.

Harrison, R. E. 1907. Observations on the living developing nerve fiber. *Proc. Soc. Exp. Biol.* 4: 140–143.

Hart, R. W. and Setlow, R. B. 1974. Correlation between deoxyribonucleic acid excision repair and lifespan in a number of mammalian species. *Proc. Nat. Acad. Sci.* 71: 2169–2173.

Hart, R. W. and Setlow, R. B. 1976. DNA repair in late-passage human cells. *Mech. Age. Dev.* 5: 67–77.

Hay, R. J. and Strehler, B. L. 1967. The limited growth span of cell strains isolated from the chick embryo. *Exp. Gerontol.* 2: 123–138.

Hayflick, L. 1965. The limited *in vitro* lifetime of human diploid cell strains. *Exp. Cell Res.* 37: 614–636.

Hayflick, L. 1970. Aging under glass. *Exp. Geront.* 5: 291–303.

Hayflick, L. 1977. The cellular basis for biological aging. *In*, L. Hayflick and C. E. Finch (eds.), *The Handbook of the Biology of Aging*, pp. 159–186. New York: Van Nostrand Reinhold.

Hayflick, L. and Moorhead, P. S. 1961. The serial cultivation of human diploid cell strains. *Exp. Cell Res.* 25: 585–621.

Haynes, R. O. and Bye, J. M. 1974. Density and cell cycle dependence of cell surface proteins in hamster fibroblasts. *Cell* 3: 113–120.

Hecht, F. and McCaw, B. K. 1977. Chromosome instability syndromes. *In*, J. J. Mulvihill, R. W. Miller, and J. F. Fraumeni, Jr. (eds.), *Genetics of Human Cancer*, pp. 105–123. New York: Raven Press.

Hefton, J. M., Darlington, G. J., Casazza, B. A., and Weksler, M. E. 1980. Immunologic studies of aging. V. Impaired proliferation of PHA responsive human lymphocytes in culture. *J. Immunol.* 125: 1007–1010.

Higashikawa, T. and Fujiwara, Y. 1978. Normal level of unscheduled DNA synthesis in Werner's syndrome fibroblasts in culture. *Exp. Cell Res.* 113: 438–442.

Hoehn, H., Bryant, E. M., Au, K., Norwood, T. H., Boman, H., and Martin, G. M. 1975a. Variegated translocation mosaicism in human fibroblast cultures. *Cytogenet. Cell Genet.* 15: 282–298.

Hoehn, H., Bryant, E. M., Johnston, P., Norwood, T. H., and Martin, G. M. 1975b. Non-selective isolation, stability and longevity of hybrids between normal human somatic cells. *Nature* 258: 608–610.

Hoehn, H., Bryant, E. M., and Martin, G. M. 1978. The replicative life spans of euploid hybrids derived from short-lived and long-lived human skin fibroblast cultures. *Cytogenet. Cell Genet.* 21: 282–295.

Hoehn, H., Simpson, M., Bryant, E. M., Rabinovitch, P. S., Salk, D., and Martin, G. M. 1980. Effects of chromosome constitution on growth and longevity of human skin fibroblast cultures. *Amer. J. Med. Genet.* 7: 141–154.

Hoffman, G. W. 1974. On the origin of the genetic code and the stability of translation apparatus. *J. Mol. Biol.* 86: 349–362.

Holland, J. J., Kohne, D., and Doyle, M. V. 1973. Analysis of virus replication in aging human fibroblast cultures. *Nature* 245: 316–319.

Hollenberg, M. D. and Schneider, E. L. 1979. Receptors for insulin and epidermal growth factor-urogastrone in adult human fibroblasts do not change with donor age. *Mech. Age. Dev.* 11: 37–43.

Holliday, R. 1975. Growth and death of diploid and transformed human fibroblasts. *Fed. Proc.* 34: 51–55.

Holliday, R., Huschtscha, L. I., and Kirkwood, T. B. L. 1981. Cellular aging: further evidence for the commitment theory. *Science* 213: 1505–1508.

Holliday, R., Huschtscha, L. I., Tarrant, G. M., and Kirkwood, T. B. L. 1977. Testing the commitment

theory of cellular aging. The finite lifespans of human fibroblasts may be due to the decline and loss of subpopulation of immortal cells. *Science* 198: 366–372.

Holliday, R. and Kirkwood, T. B. L. 1981. Predictions of the somatic mutation and mortalization theories of cellular ageing are contrary to experimental observations. *J. Theor. Biol.* 93: 627–642.

Holliday, R., Porterfield, J. S., and Gibbs, D. D. 1974. Premature aging and occurrence of altered enzymes in Werner's syndrome fibroblasts. *Nature* 248: 762–763.

Holliday, R. and Tarrant, G. M. 1972. Altered enzymes in ageing human fibroblasts. *Nature* 238: 26–30.

Hook, M., Rubin, K., Olberg, A., Obrink, B. and Vaheri, A. 1977. Cold-soluble lobulin mediates the adhesion of rat liver cells to plastic Petri dishes. *Biochem. Biophys. Res. Comm.* 79: 726–733.

Icard, C. and Beaupain, R. 1980. Spontaneous structural changes in DNA during fibroblast aging and the establishment process *in vitro*. *Mech. Age. Dev.* 14: 81–87.

Jenson, F., Koprowski, H., and Ponten, J. A. 1963. Rapid transformation of human fibroblast cultures by Simian Virus 40. *Proc. Nat. Acad. Sci.* 50: 343–348.

Johnson, J. E., Jr. 1979. Fine structure of IMR–90 cells in culture as examined by scanning and transmission electron microscopy. *Mech. Age. Dev.* 10: 405–443.

Johnson, R., Chrisp, C., and Strehler, B. L. 1972. Selective loss of ribosomal RNA genes during the aging of post-mitotic tissues. *Mech. Age. Dev.* 1: 183–198.

Johnson, R. and Strehler, B. L. 1972. Loss of genes coding for ribosomal RNA in aging brain cells. *Nature* 240: 412–414.

Jones, K. L., Smith, D. W., Harvey, M. A., Hall, B. D., and Quan, L. 1975. Older paternal age and fresh gene mutation: data on additional disorders. *J. Pediatr.* 86: 84–88.

Kahn, C. R., Gopalakrishnan, T. V., and Weiss, M. C. 1981. Transfer of heritable properties by cell hybridization: specificity and the role of selective pressure. *Somat. Cell Genet.* 7: 547–565.

Kaji, K. and Matsuo, M. 1979. Doubling potential and calendar time of human diploid cells *in vitro*. *Exp. Gerontol.* 14: 329–334.

Kakunaga, T. 1978. Neoplastic transformation of human diploid fibroblast cells by chemical carcinogens. *Proc. Nat. Acad. Sci.* 75: 1334–1338.

Kaplan, J. 1981, Polypeptide-binding membrane receptors: analysis and classification. *Science* 212: 14–20.

Kelley, R. O., Azad, R., Vogel, K. G. 1978. Development of the aging cell surface: concanvalin A-mediated intercellular binding and the distribution of binding sites with progressive subcultivation of human embryo fibroblasts. *Mech. Age. Dev.* 8: 203–217.

Kelley, R. O., Vogel, K. G., Crissman, H. A., Lujan, C. J., and Skipper, B. E. 1979. Development of the aging cell surface. Reduction of gap junction-mediated metabolic cooperation with progressive subcultivation of human embryo fibroblasts (IMR 90). *Exp. Cell Res.* 119: 127–143.

Kennedy, A. R., Mondal, S., Hierdelberger, C., and Little, J. B. 1978. Enhancement of X-ray transformation by 12-O-tetradecanoyl-phorbol-13-acetate in a cloned line of C3H mouse embryo cells. *Cancer Res.* 38: 439–443.

Kirkwood, T. B. L. and Holliday, R. 1975a. Commitment to senescence: a model for the finite and infinite growth of diploid and transformed human fibroblasts in culture. *J. Theor. Biol.* 53: 481–496.

Kirkwood, T. B. L. and Holliday, R. 1975b. The stability of the translation process. *J. Mol. Biol.* 97: 257–265.

Klement, V., Freedman, M. H., McAllister, R. M., Nelson-Rees, W. A., Heubner, R. J. 1971. Differences in susceptibility of human cells to mouse sarcoma virus. *J. Nat. Can. Inst.* 47: 65–71.

Kohn, R. R. 1975. Aging and cell division. *Science* 188: 203–204.

Koprowski, H. 1963. The role of SV 40 (Simian Virus 40) in the transformation of human cells. *Proc. Roy. Soc. Med.* 56: 252–253.

Krauss, S. W. and Linn, S. 1982. Changes in DNA polymerase alpha, beta, and lambda during the replicative lifespan of cultured human fibroblasts. *Biochemistry* 21: 1002–1009.

Krohn, P. L. 1966. Transplantation and aging. *In,* P. L. Krohn (ed.), *Topics in the Biology of Aging,* pp. 133–138. New York: John Wiley & Sons.

Krooth, R. S., Darlington, G. A., and Velazguez, A. A. 1968. The genetics of cultured mammalian cells. *Ann. Rev. Genet.* 2: 141–164.

Ladda, R. L. 1979. Cellular aging *in vitro:* altered responsiveness of human diploid fibroblasts to epidermal growth factor. *In,* H. Orimo, K. Shimada, M. Iriki, and D. Maeda (eds.), *Recent Advances in Gerontology.* Proceedings of the XI International Congress of Gerontology, Tokyo, Japan. *Excerpta Med. Int. Congr.* pp. 85–86.

Lasne, C., Gentil, A., and Chouroulinkov, I. 1977. Two-stage carcinogenesis with rat embryo cells in tissue culture. *Brit. J. Cancer* 35: 722–729.

Lefford, F. 1964. The effect of donor age on the emigration of cells from chick embryo explants *in vitro. Exp. Cell Res.* 35: 557–571.

Levine, E. M., Mueller, S. N., Grinspan, J. B., Noveral, J. P., and Rosen, E. M. 1983. The limited lifespan of bovine endothelial cells. *In,* F. A. Jaffe (ed.), *The Biology of Endothelial Cells.* The Hague: Martinus Nijhoff.

Lewis, C. M. and Tarrant, G. M. 1972. Error theory and ageing in human diploid fibroblasts. *Nature* 239: 316–318.

Lima, L., Malaise, E., and Macieira-Coelho. 1972. A. Aging *in vitro.* Effect of low dose rate irradiation on the division potential of chick embryonic fibroblasts. *Exp. Cell Res.* 73: 345–350.

Linn, S., Kairis, M., and Holliday, R. 1976. Decreased fidelity of DNA polymerase activity isolated from aging human fibroblasts. *Proc. Nat. Acad. Sci.* 73: 2818–2822.

Lipetz, J. and Cristofalo, V. J. 1972. Ultrastructural changes accompanying the aging of human diploid cells in culture. *J. Ultrastruct. Res.* 39: 43–56.

Lipsich, L. A., Kates, J. R., and Lucas, J. J. 1979. Expression of a liver-specific function by mouse fibroblast nuclei transplanted into rat hepatoma cytoplasts. *Nature* 281: 74–76.

Littlefield, J. W. 1973. Attempted hybridizations with senescent human fibroblasts. *J. Cellular Physiol.* 82: 129–132.

Litwin, J. 1972. Human diploid cell response to variations in relative amino acid concentrations in Eagle medium. *Exp. Cell Res.* 72: 566–568.

Loeb, L. A., Weymouth, L. A., Kunkel, T. A., Gopinathan, K. P., Beckman, R. A., and Dube, D. K. 1979. On the fidelity of DNA replication. *In, Cold Spring Harbor Symp. Quant. Biol.,* Vol. 43, pp. 921–927. Cold Spring Harbor, N.Y.: Cold Spring Harbor Laboratory.

Lubiniecki, A. S., Blattner, W. A., Dosik, H., Sun, C., and Fraumeni, Jr., J. F. 1977. SV-40 T-antigen expression in skin fibroblasts from clinically normal individuals and from ten cases of Fanconi anemia. *Amer. J. Hematol.* 2: 37–40.

Macieira-Coelho, A. 1966. Action of cortisone on human fibroblasts *in vitro. Experientia* 22: 390–391.

Macieira-Coelho, A. 1980. Implications of the reorganization of the cell genome for aging or immortalization of dividing cells *in vitro. Gerontology* 26: 276–282.

Macieira-Coelho, A., Diatloff, C., Billard, M., Fertil, B., Malaise, E., and Fries, D. 1978. Effect of low dose rate irradiation on the division potential of cells *in vitro.* IV. Embryonic and adult human lung fibroblast-like cells. *J. Cellular Physiol.* 95: 235–238.

Macieira-Coelho, A., Diatloff, C., Billardon, C., Bourgeois, C. A., and Malaise, E. 1977. Effect of low dose rate ionizing radiation on the division potential of cells *in vitro.* III. Human lung fibroblasts. *Exp. Cell Res.* 104: 215–221.

Macieira-Coelho, A., Diatloff, C., and Malaise, E. 1976. Effect of low dose rate irradiation on the division potential of cells *in vitro.* II. Mouse lung fibroblasts. *Exp. Cell Res.* 100: 228–232.

Macieira-Coelho, A. and Ponten, J. 1969. Analogy in growth between late passage human embryonic and early passage human adult fibroblasts. *J. Cell Biol.* 43: 374–377.

Macieira-Coelho, A., Ponten, J., and Philipson, L. 1966. The division cycle and RNA synthesis in diploid human cells at different passage levels *in vitro. Exp. Cell Res.* 42: 673–684.

Macieira-Coelho, A. and Taboury, F. 1982. A reevaluation of the changes in proliferation in human fibroblasts during aging *in vitro. Cell Tissue Kinet.* 15: 213–224.

MacMillan, J. R. and Wolf, N. S. 1983. Depletion of reserve in the hemopoietic system: decline in CFU-S self-renewal capacity following prolonged cell cycling. *Stem Cells* 2: 45–58.

Martin, G. M. 1977. Cellular aging—clonal senescence. *Amer. J. Path.* 89, 484–511.

Martin, G. M. 1978. Genetic syndromes in man with potential relevance to the pathobiology of aging. *In,* D. Bergsma and D. H. Harrison (eds.), *Birth Defects: Original Article Series,* Vol. 14, pp. 5–39. New York: The National Foundation—March of Dimes.

Martin, G. M., Ogburn, C. E., and Sprague, C. A. 1975a. Senescence and vascular disease. *In,* V. J. Cristofalo, J. Roberts, and R. C. Adelman (eds.), *Explorations in Aging,* pp. 163–193. New York: Plenum Press.

Martin, G. M., Ogburn, C. E., and Sprague, C. A. 1981. Effects of age on cell division capacity. *In,* D. Danon, N. W. Shock, and M. Marois (eds.), *Aging: A Challenge to Science and Society,* Vol. 1: *Biology,* pp. 124–135. Oxford: Oxford University Press.

Martin, G. M. and Sprague, C. A. 1973. Symposium on *in vitro* studies related to atherogenesis. Life histories of hyperplastoid cell lines from aorta and skin. *Exp. Molec. Path.* 18: 125–141.

Martin, G. M., Sprague, C. A., and Epstein, C. J. 1970. Replicative life-span of cultivated human cells. Effects of donor's age, tissue, and genotype. *Lab. Invest.* 23: 86–92.

Martin, G. M., Sprague, C. A., Norwood, T. H., and Pendergrass, W. R. 1974. Clonal selection, attenuation and differentiation in an *in vitro* model of hyperplasia. *Am. J. Path.* 74: 137–150.

Martin, G. M., Sprague, C. A., Norwood, T. H., Pendergrass, W. R., Bornstein, P., Hoehn, H., and Arend, W. P. 1975b. Do hyperplastoid cell lines "differentiate themselves to death"? *In,* V. J. Cristofalo and E. Holeckova (eds.), *Cell Impairment in Aging and Development,* pp. 67–90. New York: Plenum Press.

Matsumura, T., Pfendt, E. A., and Hayflick, L. 1979. Senescent human diploid cells in culture: survival, DNA synthesis and morphology. *J. Geront.* 34: 328–334.

Matsumura, T., Pfendt, E. A., Zerrudo, Z., and Hayflick, L. 1980. Senescent human diploid cells (WI-38). Attempted induction of proliferation by infection with SV–40 and by fusion with irradiated continuous cell lines. *Exp. Cell Res.* 125: 453–457.

McKusick, V. A. 1982. *Mendelian Inheritance in Man—Catalogs of Autosomal Dominant, Autosomal Recessive and X-linked Phenotypes.* Baltimore: The Johns Hopkins University Press.

Meek, R. L., Bowman, P. D., and Daniel, C. W. 1977. Establishment of mouse embryo cells *in vitro.* Relationship of DNA synthesis, senescence and malignant transformation. *Exp. Cell Res.* 125: 453–457.

Mendel, S., Boranokow, D. W., and Heidelberger, C. 1975. Two-stage chemical oncogenesis in cultures of C3H/10T1/2 cells. *Cancer Res.* 36: 2254–2260.

Merz, G. S. and Ross, J. D. 1969. Viability of human diploid cells as a function of *in vitro* age. *J. Cellular Physiol.* 74: 219–222.

Milo, G. E. and DiPaolo, J. A. 1978. Neoplastic transformation of human diploid cells *in vitro* after chemical carcinogen treatment. *Nature* 275: 130–132.

Muggleton-Harris, A. L. and Aroian, M. A. 1982. Replicative potential of individual cell hybrids derived from young and old donor human skin fibroblasts. *Somat. Cell Genet.* 8: 41–50.

Muggleton-Harris, A. L. and DeSimone, D. W. 1980. Replicative potentials of various fusion products between WI–38 and SV 40 transformed WI–38 cells and their components. *Somat. Cell Genet.* 6: 689–698.

Muggleton-Harris, A. L. and Hayflick, L. 1976. Cellular aging studied by the reconstruction of replicating cells from nuclei and cytoplasms isolated from normal human diploid cells. *Exp. Cell Res.* 103: 321–330.

Nienhaus, A. J., de Jong, B., and Tenkate, L. P. 1971. Fibroblast culture in Werner's syndrome. *Humangenetik* 13: 244–246.

Nette, E. G., Sit, H. L., and King, D. W. 1982. Reactivation of DNA synthesis in aging diploid human skin fibroblasts by fusion with mouse L karyoplasts, cytoplasts and whole L cells. *Mech. Age. Dev.* 18: 75–87.

Nielsen, P. J. and Ryan, J. M. 1981. Cumulative population doublings as the determinant of chick cell lifespan *in vitro. J. Cellular Physiol.* 107: 371–378.

Norwood, T. H., Hoehn, H., Salk, D., and Martin, G. M. 1979. Cellular aging in Werner's syndrome. A unique phenotype? *J. Invest. Dermatol.* 73: 92–96.

Norwood, T. H., Pendergrass, W., Bornstein, P., and Martin, G. M. 1979. DNA synthesis of sublethally injured cells in heterokaryons and its relevance to clonal senescence. *Exp. Cell Res.* 119: 15–21.

Norwood, T. H., Pendergrass, W. R., and Martin, G. M. 1975. Reinitiation of DNA synthesis in senescent human fibroblasts upon fusion with cells of unlimited growth potential. *J. Cell Biol.* 64: 551–556.

Norwood, T. H., Pendergrass, W. R., Sprague, C. A., and Martin, G. M. 1974. Dominance of the senescent phenotypes in heterokaryons between replicative and post-replicative human fibroblast-like cells. *Proc. Nat. Acad. Sci.* 73: 2223–2236.

Norwood, T. H. and Zeigler, C. J. 1977. Complementation between senescent human diploid cells and a thymidine kinase-deficient murine cell line. *Cytogenet. Cell Genet.* 19: 355–367.

Ockey, C. H. 1979. Quantitative replicon analysis of DNA synthesis in cancer prone conditions and the defect in Bloom's syndrome. *J. Cell Sci.* 40: 125–144.

Ohno, S. and Nagai, Y. 1978. Genes in multiple copies as the primary cause of aging. *In,* D. Bergsma and D. E. Harrison (eds.), *Genetic Effects of Aging,* pp. 501–514. New York: Alan R. Liss.

Olashaw, N. E., Kress, E. D., and Cristofalo, V. J. 1983. Thymidine triphosphate synthesis in senescent WI–38 cells: relationship to loss of replicative activity. *Exp. Cell Res.* 149: 547–554.

Olovnikov, A. M. 1973. A theory of marginotomy. The incomplete copying of template margin in enzymic synthesis of polynucleotides and biological significance of the phenomenon. *J. Theor. Biol.* 41: 181–190.

Orgel, L. E. 1963. The maintenance of the accuracy of protein synthesis and its relevance to ageing. *Proc. Nat. Acad. Sci.* 49: 517–521.

Orgel, L. E. 1970. The maintenance of the accuracy of protein synthesis and its relevance to ageing: a correction. *Proc. Nat. Acad. Sci.* 67: 1476.

Painter, R. B., Clarkson, J. M., and Young, B. R. 1973. Ultraviolet-induced repair replication in aging diploid human cells (WI–38). *Radiation Res.* 56: 560–564.

Pendergrass, W. R., Martin, G. M., and Bornstein, P. 1976. Evidence contrary to the protein error hypothesis for *in vitro* senescence. *J. Cellular Physiol.* 87: 3–13.

Pendergrass, W. R., Saulewicz, A. C., Burmer, G. C., Rabinovitch, P. S., Norwood, T. H., and Martin, G. M. 1982. Evidence that a critical threshold of DNA polymerase-alpha activity may be required for the initiation of DNA synthesis in mammalian cell heterokaryons. *J. Cellular Physiol.* 113: 141–151.

Pereira-Smith, O. M. and Smith, J. R. 1981. Expression of SV-40 T antigen infinite life-span hybrids of normal and SV-40-transformed fibroblasts. *Somat. Cell Genet.* 7: 411–421.

Pereira-Smith, O. M. and Smith, J. R. 1982. The phenotype of low proliferative potential is dominant in hybrids of normal human fibroblasts. *Somat. Cell Genet.* 6:731–742.

Phillips, P. D. and Cristofalo, V. J. 1981. Growth regulation of WI38 cells in a serum-free medium. *Exp. Cell Res.* 134: 297–302.

Pinsky, L., Finkelberg, R., Straisfeld, C., Zilahi, B., Kaufman, M., and Hall, G. 1972. Testosterone metabolism by serially subcultured fibroblasts from genital and nongenital skin of individual human donors. *Biochem. Biophys. Res. Comm.* 46: 364–369.

Pitha, J., Stork, E., and Wimmer, E. 1975. Protein synthesis during aging of human cells in culture. Direction by poliovirus. *Exp. Cell Res.* 94: 310–314.

Polgar, P., Taylor, L., and Brown, L. 1978. Plasma membrane associated metabolic parameters and the aging of human diploid fibroblasts. *Mech. Age. Dev.* 7: 151–160.

Ponten, J. 1977. Abnormal cell growth (neoplasia) and aging. *In,* C. E. Finch and L. Hayflick (eds.), *The Handbook of the Biology of Aging,* pp. 536–560. New York: Van Nostrand Reinhold.

Pool, T. B., Heitman, T. O., and Buck, M. A. 1981. Changes in nuclear shape and mitochondrial structure do not accompany the loss of division potential in human fibroblasts *in vitro*. *Amer. J. Anat.* 162: 369–382.

Prothero, J. and Gallant, J. A. 1981. A model of clonal attenuation. *Proc. Nat. Acad. Sci.* 78: 333–337.

Rabinovitch, P. S. and Norwood, T. H. 1980. Comparative heterokaryon study of cellular senescence and the serum-deprived state. *Exp. Cell Res.* 130: 101–109.

Rao, P. N. and Johnson, R. T. 1972. Cell fusion and its application to studies on the regulation of the cell cycle. *Methods Cell. Physiol.* 5: 75–126.

Reincke, U., Brookoff, D., Burlington, H., and Cronkite, E. P. 1979. Forced differentiation of CFU-S by iron-55 erythrocytocide. *Blood Cells* 5: 351–376.

Rheinwald, J. G. and Green, H. 1975. Serial cultivation of strains of human epidermal keratinocytes: the formation of keratinizing colonies from single cells. *Cell* 6: 331–344.

Robbins, E., Levine, E. M., and Eagle, H. 1970. Morphologic changes accompanying senescence of cultured human diploid cells. *J. Exp. Med.* 131: 1211–1222.

Roberts, T. W. and Smith, J. R. 1980. The proliferative potential of chick embryo fibroblasts: population doubling vs. time in culture. *Cell Biol. Int. Rep.* 4: 1057–1063.

Rohme, D. 1981. Evidence for a relationship between longevity of mammalian species and life-spans of normal fibroblasts *in vitro* and erythrocytes *in vivo*. *Proc. Nat. Acad. Sci.* 78: 5009–5013.

Rosenbloom, A. L., Goldstein, S., and Yip, C. C. 1976. Insulin binding to cultured human fibroblasts increases with normal and precocious aging. *Science* 193, 412–414.

Rothfels, F. H., Kupelweiser, E. B., and Parker, R. C. 1963. Effects of x-irradiated feeder layers on mitotic activity and development of aneuploidy in mouse embryo cells *in vitro*. *Can. Cancer Conf.* 5: 191–223.

Sack, G. H. 1981. Human cell transformation by simian virus 40—a review. *In Vitro* 17: 1–19.

Salk, D. 1982. Werner syndrome. A review of recent research with an analysis of connective tissue metabolism growth control of cultured cells and chromosomal aberrations. *Human Genet.* 62: 1–15.

Salk, D., Au, K., Hoehn, H., and Martin, G. M. 1981a. Cytogenetics of Werner's syndrome cultured skin fibroblasts: variegated translocation mosaicism. *Cytogenet. Cell Genet.* 30: 92–107.

Salk, D., Au, K., Hoehn, H., Stenchever, M. R., and Martin, G. M. 1981b. Evidence of clonal attenuation, clonal succession, and clonal expansion in mass cultures of aging Werner's syndrome skin fibroblasts. *Cytogenet. Cell Genet.* 30: 108–117.

Salk, D., Bryant, E., Au, K., Hoehn, H., and Martin, G. M. 1981c. Systematic growth studies, cocultivation, and cell hybridization studies of Werner syndrome cultured skin fibroblasts. *Hum. Genet.* 58: 310–316.

Sarma, P. S., Huebner, R. J., Basker, J. F., Vernon, L., and Gilden, R. V. 1970. Feline leukemia and sarcoma viruses: susceptibility of human cells to infection. *Science* 16: 1098–2000.

Schmickel, R. D., Chu, E. Y. H., Trosko, J. E., and Chang, C. C. 1977. Cockayne syndrome: a cellular sensitivity to ultraviolet light. *Pediatrics* 60: 135–139.

Schneider, E. L., Braunschweiger, K., and Mitsui, Y. 1978. The effect of serum batch on the *in vitro* lifespans of cell cultures derived from old and young human donors. *Exp. Cell Res.* 115: 47–52.

Schneider, E. L. and Epstein, C. J. 1972. Replication rate and lifespan of cultured fibroblasts from Down's syndrome. *Proc. Soc. Exp. Med.* 141: 1092–1094.

Schneider, E. L. and Fowlkes, B. J. 1976. Measurement of DNA content and cell volume in senescent human fibroblasts utilizing flow multiparameter single cell analysis. *Exp. Cell Res.* 98: 298–302.

Schneider, E. L. and Mitsui, Y. 1976. The relationship between *in vitro* cellular aging and *in vivo* human age. *Proc. Nat. Acad. Sci.* 73: 3584–3588.

Schneider, E. L., Mitsui, Y., Au, K. S., and Shorr, S. 1977. Tissue-specific differences in cultured human diploid fibroblasts. *Exp. Cell Res.* 108: 1–6.

Scott, W. A., Brockman, W. W., and Nathans, D. 1976. Biological activities of deletion mutants of simian virus 40. *Virology* 75: 319–334.

Segal, D. J. and McCoy, E. E. 1974. Studies on Down's syndrome in tissue culture. I. Growth rates and protein contents of fibroblast cultures. *J. Cellular Physiol.* 83: 85–90.

Shall, S. and Stein, W. D. 1979. A mortalization theory for the control of cell proliferation and for the origin of immortal cell lines. *J. Theor. Biol.* 76: 219–231.

Shmookler-Reis, R. J. and Goldstein, S. 1980. Loss of reiterated DNA sequences during serial passage of human diploid fibroblasts. *Cell* 21: 739–749.

Shmookler-Reis, R. J., Lumpkin, C. K., McGill, J. R., Riabowol, K. T., and Goldstein, S. 1983. Extrachromosomal circular copies of an inter-alu unstable sequence in human DNA are amplified during *in vitro* and *in vivo* aging. *Nature* 301: 394–398.

Smith, J. R. and Braunschweiger, K. I. 1979. Growth of human embryonic fibroblasts at clonal density: concordance with results from mass cultures. *J. Cellular Physiol.* 98: 597–602.

Smith, J. R. and Hayflick, L. 1974. Variation in the life-span of clones derived from human diploid cell strains. *J. Cell Biol.* 62: 48–53.

Smith, J. R. and Lumpkin, C. K. 1980. Loss of gene repression activity: a theory of cellular senescence. *Mech. Age. Dev.* 13: 387–392.

Smith, J. R., Pereira-Smith, O., and Good, P. I. 1977. Colony size distribution as a measure of age in cultured cells. A brief note. *Mech. Age. Dev.* 6: 283–286.

Smith, J. R., Pereira-Smith, O., and Schneider, E. L. 1978. Colony size distribution as a measure of *in vivo* and *in vitro* aging. *Proc. Nat. Acad. Sci.* 75: 1353–1356.

Smith, J. R. and Whitney, R. G. 1980. Intraclonal variation in proliferative potential of human diploid fibroblasts: stochastic mechanism for cellular aging. *Science* 207: 82–84.

Smith, K. A., Gillis, S., Baker, P. E., and McKenzie, D. T. 1979. T-cell growth factor-mediated T-cell proliferation. *Ann. N.Y. Acad. Sci.* 332: 423–432.

Soukupova, M., Holeckova, E., and Hnevkovsky, P. 1970. Changes in the latent period of explanted tissues during ontogenesis. *In,* E. Holeckova and V. J. Cristofalo (eds.), *Aging in Cell and Tissue Culture,* pp. 41–56. New York: Plenum Press.

Stanbridge, E. J. 1976. Suppression of malignancy in human cells. *Nature* 260: 17–20.

Stanley, J. F., Pye, D., and MacGregor, A. 1975. Comparison of doubling numbers attained by cultured animal cells with life span of species. *Nature* 255: 158–159.

Stein, G. H. and Yanishevsky, R. M. 1979. Entry into S phase is inhibited in two immortal cell lines fused to senescent human diploid cells. *Exp. Cell Res.* 120: 155–165.

Stein, G. H. and Yanishevsky, R. M. 1981. Quiescent human diploid cells can inhibit entry into S phase in replicative nuclei in heterodikaryons. *Proc. Nat. Acad. Sci.* 78: 3025–3029.

Stein, G. H., Yanishevsky, R. M., Gordon, L., and Beeson, M. 1982. Carcinogen-transformed human cells are inhibited from entry into S phase by fusion to senescent cells but cells transformed by DNA tumor viruses overcome the inhibition. *Proc. Nat. Acad. Sci.* 79: 5287–5291.

Stevenson, A. F. G. and Cremer, T. 1981. Senescence *in vitro* and ionising radiations—the human diploid fibroblast model. *Mech. Age. Dev.* 15: 51–63.

Strehler, B. L. and Chang, M. 1979. Loss of hybridizable ribosomal DNA from human post-mitotic tissues during aging: II. Age-dependent loss in human cerebral cortex—hippocampal and somatosensory cortex comparison. *Mech. Age. Dev.* 11: 379–382.

Strehler, B. L., Chang, M., and Johnson, L. K. 1979. Loss of hybridizable ribosomal DNA from human post-mitotic tissues during aging: I. Age-dependent loss in human myocardium. *Mech. Age. Dev.* 11: 371–378.

Suzuki, F., Watanabe, E., and Horikowa, M. 1980. Repair of x-ray-induced DNA damage in aging human diploid cells. *Exp. Cell Res.* 127: 299–307.

Swim, H. E. and Parker, R. F. 1957. Culture characteristics of human fibroblasts propagated serially. *Am. J. Hyg.* 66: 235–243.

Szilard, L. 1959. On the nature of the aging process. *Proc. Nat. Acad. Sci.* 45: 30–45.

Tassin, J., Malaise, E., and Courtois, Y. 1979. Human lens cells have an *in vitro* proliferative capacity inversely proportional to the donor age. *Exp. Cell Res.* 123: 388–392.

Thompson, K. V. A. and Holliday, R. 1975. Chromosome changes during the *in vitro* aging of MRC-5 human fibroblasts. *Exp. Cell Res.* 96: 1–6.

Tice, R. R., Schneider, E. L., Kram, D., and Thorne, P. 1979. Cytokinetic analysis of impaired proliferative response of peripheral lymphocytes from aged humans to phytohemagglutinin. *Exp. Med.* 149: 1029–1041.

Tissue Culture Association. 1978. *Manual,* Vol. 4, No. 1, pp. 779–782.

Todaro, G. J., Wolman, S. R., and Green, H. 1963. Rapid transformation of human fibroblasts with low growth potential into established cell lines by SV40. *J. Cell Comp. Physiol.* 62: 257–265.

Tomkins, G. A., Stanbridge, E. J., and Hayflick, L. 1974. Viral probes of aging in the human diploid cell strain WI-38. *Proc. Soc. Exp. Biol. Med.* 146: 385–390.

Toshinori, I., Yoshiaki, T., Ishibashi, S., and Mitsui, Y. 1983. Reinitiation of host DNA synthesis in senescent human diploid cells by infection with simian virus 40. *Exp. Cell Res.* 143: 343–349.

Vincent, R. A., Jr. and Huang, P. C. 1976. The proportion of cells labeled with tritiated thymidine as a function of population doubling level in cultures of fetal, adult, mutant, and tumor origin. *Exp. Cell Res.* 102: 31–42.

Vogel, K. G., Kelley, R. O., and Stewart, C. 1981. Loss of organized fibronectin matrix from the surface of aging diploid fibroblasts (IMR-90). *Mech. Age. Dev.* 16: 295–302.

Vracko, R. and Benditt, E. P. 1975. Restricted replicative life-span of diabetic fibroblasts *in vitro:* its relation to microangiopathy. *Proc. Fed. Amer. Soc. Exp. Biol.* 34: 68–70.

Vracko, R. and McFarland, B. H. 1980. Lifespans of diabetic and nondiabetic fibroblasts *in vitro.* Results of replicate determinations. *Exp. Cell Res.* 129: 345–350.

Walford, R. L., Jawaral, S. Q., and Naeim, F. 1981. Evidence for *in vitro* senescence of T-lymphocytes cultured from normal human peripheral blood. *Age* 4: 67–78.

Walthall, B. J. and Ham, R. G. 1981. Multiplication of human diploid fibroblasts in a synthetic medium supplemented with EGF, insulin and dexamethazone. *Exp. Cell Res.* 134: 303–311.

Waters, H. and Walford, R. L. 1970. Latent period for outgrowth of human skin explants as a function of age. *J. Gerontol.* 25: 381–383.

Weissman-Shomer, P. and Fry, M. 1975. Chick embryo fibroblast senescence *in vitro:* pattern of cell division and life span as a function of cell density. *Mech. Age. Dev.* 4: 159–166.

Willmer, E. N. 1965. Morphological problems of cell type, shape and identification. *In,* E. N. Willmer (ed.), *Cell and Tissues in Culture,* Vol. 1, pp. 143–176. New York: Academic Press.

Wojtyk, R. I. and Goldstein, S. 1980. Fidelity of protein synthesis does not decline during aging of cultured human fibroblasts. *J. Cellular Physiol.* 103: 299–303.

Wright, W. E. and Hayflick, L. 1975a. Nuclear control of cellular aging demonstrated by hybridization of anucleate and whole cultured normal human fibroblasts. *Exp. Cell Res.* 96: 113–121.

Wright, W. E. and Hayflick, L. 1975b. The regulation of cellular aging by nuclear events in cultured normal fibroblasts (WI-38). *Adv. Exp. Mol. Biol.* 61: 39–55.

Yamane, I., Kan, M., Hoshi, H., and Minamoto, Y. 1981. Primary culture of human diploid cells and its long-term transfer in a serum-free medium. *Exp. Cell Res.* 134: 470–474.

Yanishevsky, R. and Carrano, A. V. 1975. Prematurely condensed chromosomes of dividing and non-dividing cells in aging human cell cultures. *Exp. Cell Res.* 90: 169–174.

Yanishevsky, R., Mendelsohn, M. L., Mayall, B. H., and Cristofalo, V. J. 1974. Proliferative capacity and DNA content of aging human diploid cells in culture: a cytophotometric and autoradiographic analysis. *J. Cellular Physiol.* 84: 165–170.

Yanishevsky, R. M. and Stein, G. H. 1980. Ongoing DNA synthesis continues in young human diploid cells (HDC) fused to senescent HDC, but entry into S phase is inhibited. *Exp. Cell Res.* 126: 469–472.

Yoshida, M. C. and Makino, S. 1963. A chromosome study of non-treated and an irradiated human *in vitro* cell line. *Jap. J. Hum. Genet.* 8: 39–45.

13
CELL AND TISSUE TRANSPLANTATION: A MEANS OF STUDYING THE AGING PROCESS

David E. Harrison
The Jackson Laboratory

INTRODUCTION

With the sophisticated techniques now available in biomedical research, it is sometimes a shock to realize that most basic questions about mammalian aging remain unanswered. Is the loss of functional ability with time controlled by a single clock or by many independent clocks? Do different cell and tissue types in the same individual age independently or at the same rate? Can many or all of an animal's cells and tissues continue performing their normal function for time periods much greater than the life span of the species from which they came? These questions have obvious practical importance in determining how diseases that develop with age may be treated. They also have fundamental theoretical importance, and solid answers for these questions would help to guide gerontological research into the most productive areas.

Transplantation experiments can answer these basic questions on a cell and tissue level. Cells or tissues from an old donor are transplanted into a young recipient. They have not aged if they are able to perform their functions fully as well as equivalent

transplants from a young donor over the recipient's life span. When this result is confirmed for any cell or tissue type, it shows that normal function is possible beyond the donor's life span; it even suggests that cells and tissues age at different rates, and that aging is timed by independent clocks in different cell and tissue types. In addition, transplantation of old tissues simplifies mechanistic studies of aging since old tissue and young controls can be studied in identical recipients. This avoids complications from changes with age in other parts of the old animal that may affect the tissue studied.

Basically, transplantation experiments are simple, but they have several pitfalls. A severe one is immune rejection, which occurs when animals are used that are not completely inbred. Even slow rejections caused by minor histocompatibility antigens may cause severe effects on tissue functions, and these are more likely between young and old cohorts than within young cohorts of partially inbred strains. Bailey (1978) calculated that strains are not completely inbred until 40–60 generations of brother-sister mating. Fortunately, many fully inbred strains of mice and rats are readily available. Other problems can be mitigated by using the following four criteria in designing and interpreting transplantation experiments.

1. *Function.* The degree to which the tissue is aged should be measured by the degree of inability to perform its normal function. Therefore, tests that measure the maximum level of functional capacity will be the most sensitive in detecting losses with age.

2. *Identification.* The transplanted tissue must be identified as performing the functions measured. In cases where these functions involve cell proliferation, chromosome or other genetic markers are appropriate to identify the donor's cell type. By far the best means of identification is a marker that also demonstrates function. Examples are genetic markers on offspring produced by a transplanted ovary or hemoglobin markers on erythrocytes produced by transplanted stem cell lines.

3. *Control.* The degree to which functional loss with age is intrinsic within a tissue must be demonstrated by comparing old tissues transplanted into young recipients with controls: young tissues transplanted by identical procedures into identical recipients. Thus, the effect of age (a life span of normal functioning) will be the difference in functional levels between the old and the young tissues. In many cases, the process of transplantation will affect tissue function, and controls are necessary to avoid confusing a loss of function due to the transplantation procedure and the loss of function due to age. Unfortunately, it is possible that old tissues are more vulnerable to damage from the transplantation procedure, and it may be impossible to distinguish this from the loss of function with age. Under some conditions, the process increasing the vulnerability of the old tissue to transplantation may also cause it to lose function with age.

4. *Health.* The old tissue must not be damaged irreversibly by its residence in the less healthy environment of the old donor. An example of irreversible damage would be the inclusion in a marrow cell graft of metastasizing tumor cells from the old animal. In some instances, it may be impossible to distinguish such damage from intrinsically timed aging, because the damage may cause a loss of function that is not intrinsically timed within the tissue transplanted, although the tissue may be permanently damaged. An example of this is a tissue that had been damaged by autoimmune reactions in the old donor.

Although it may never be possible to satisfy these four criteria perfectly, they are useful in interpretating transplantation experiments and evaluating their results. The criteria also suggest ways to improve the accuracy of transplantation experiments. For example, the effect of transplantation can be measured independently of the effect of age by repeated serial transplantations of old and young tissues in parallel experiments. The effect of health can be taken into account through autopsies of old donors to determine whether particular pathological conditions are associated with unusually poor function of a particular transplanted tissue. In addition, donors of a range of ages should be used, including some that are not old enough to have serious afflictions. If the only apparent change with age in the tissue function occurs when the tissues are taken from donors that are extremely old and unhealthy, then it is likely that the change is not intrinsic to the tissue but results from permanent damage due to residence in a sick old host.

To illustrate how transplantation techniques are used, consider some theories that have been proposed to describe how the aging process occurs. Many theories fall into the general classes of wear and tear, programmed, and some combination of these. Wear and tear theories suggest that an organism, just as a machine, cannot be designed to be used without eventually breaking down. These types of theories can be applied to any level of biological organization, including functions of the whole individual, organs, tissues, cells, extracellular macromolecules, or molecules within the cell; any or all may fail because of accumulated damage. Over the past 20 years, the revolutionary discoveries in molecular biology and genetics have caused modern wear and tear theories to concentrate on the accumulation of damage to the molecules making up the genes, the DNA. For example, aging may be caused by accumulating somatic mutations as a result of inappropriate reactions of DNA molecules with highly reactive chemical intermediates such as free radicals formed by oxygen (Harman, 1956, 1981). Somatic mutations are also caused by radiation and by other types of mutagens, both chemical and physical in nature. If aging is caused by somatic mutation, these theories make a clearcut prediction regarding the results of transplantation experiments: cells and tissues from aged donors should not be able to function normally after transplantation into young recipients because their malfunction is due to something intrinsic or within the cells, an accumulation of somatic mutations.

This example illustrates how transplantation experiments test whole classes of theories of aging. If the loss of normal function with age in a tissue is caused by something intrinsic and irreversible such as mutations, the tissue will still malfunction after transplantation from an aged donor. On the other hand, if its malfunction is due to being in the environment of the aged donor and is not intrinsic to the transplanted old tissue, its function may improve to the young tissue level in the healthy environment of a young recipient (Figure 1). This will happen if the transplanted old tissue is undamaged or if its damage is reversed in the young recipient. Figure 1 also suggests the limitations to transplantation procedures. If transplanted tissues that malfunctioned in old donors are able to function normally in young recipients, there is no way to tell what actually caused the aging process. There might be a single tissue, or just a few tissues, in which programmed changes with time alter the internal environment of the aged donor, causing malfunction of a wide range of cell and tissue types. On the other hand, all tissues might be capable of functioning normally far beyond donor life spans; only their interactions with each other and the environment may become increasingly complex in the old donor so that their functional ability declines.

We suggested that increasingly complex tissue interactions might be an important cause of malfunctions with age in the im-

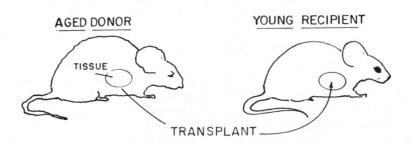

AGED DONOR   YOUNG RECIPIENT

TISSUE

TRANSPLANT

AGED ENVIRONMENT   *HEALTHY ENVIRONMENT*

POSSIBILITY	RESULT
A. AGING INTRINSIC IN ALL CELLS	DEFECT CONTINUES
B. AGING TIMED BY ONE CRUCIAL TISSUE	DEFECT CURED
C. AGING RESULTS FROM INTERACTION	DEFECT CURED

Figure 1. To determine whether or not aging in a particular tissue is intrinsically timed, that tissue is transplanted from the aged donor into a young histocompatible recipient. If aging is intrinsic (possibility A), the tissue will become defective with age, just as if it had been left in the old donor. If aging is not intrinsic (possibility B except for the key tissue, possibility C for all), the old tissue will not become defective but will function as well as transplanted young tissue. (From Harrison, 1982.)

mune system (Harrison et al., 1977). Mathematical models of the interactions between various components in complex systems have been developed by Rosen (1976), who showed that such interactions are far easier to disturb than the functions of the individual components. Rosen (1978) discusses this possibility at length in biomathematical theories interpreting cellular senescence. He concludes that experimental studies of interaction networks would require new mathematical model systems defined for the task. Transplantation *in vivo* should also be an important model system for such studies, perhaps in conjunction with the mathematical models. For the rest of this chapter, I will interpret the results of transplantation experiments as to whether or not the transplanted tissue appeared to age intrinsically, and I will leave further theoretical explanations to the interested reader.

Pioneering Studies. One of the first experiments in which transplantation was used to investigate whether changes with age were intrinsically timed was reported by Geiringer (1954, 1956). He transplanted adrenocortical tissue from middle-aged rats into young recipients and showed that this tissue could function for at least 3 years, supporting normal reproductive performances and normal growth rates in the young recipients. This was 6 months longer than the maximum life span of his rats, but still short of maximum rat longevities, which are at least 3 years under normal conditions (Masoro, 1980) and 4 years with food restriction (McKay et al., 1943). Another problem in Geiringer's work was that his rats were not fully inbred and had a series of infectious diseases, probably including mycoplasmal pneumonias. Nevertheless, he showed that old tissues were able to support normal function in much younger recipients.

Another early worker who helped define how transplantation experiments should be used to test whether tissues age intrinsically was Krohn (1962). He transplanted ovarian and skin grafts from inbred strains of mice, thus avoiding problems of histoincompatibility and tissue rejection. Ovarian transplantation has the potential to be a useful system because its function declines with age long before poor health develops. Furthermore, the number of normal offspring produced by the transplanted old ovary could provide a powerful and quantitative measure of ovarian function. The offspring could be unambiguously identified by genetic markers. In this case, both the degree of functional ability and the identification of the old donor's tissue as performing the function are provided in the same test. This is by far the best design for transplantation experiments.

Thus far, ovarian transplantation has not been used for such sophisticated experiments. Krohn (1962) showed that young ovaries or fertilized eggs functioned much less well in old than in young recipients, indicating that other factors besides the ovary were important in causing the decline with age in female reproductive ability. Fertilized eggs from old donors proved to be as viable as those from young donors when tested in young recipients, suggesting that aging did not affect the early embryo's ability to implant and develop. Transplants of old ovaries in young recipients generally failed to function as well as young ones. Krohn (1962) concluded that there was no evidence that old ovaries were rejuvenated in any way by transplantation into young recipients. Nevertheless, the generally lower success rate with transplanted old ovaries may have resulted from increased vulnerability with age to damage during grafting, intrinsically timed changes with age, or both.

Krohn (1966) reported that serially transplanted skin had functioned normally for as long as 6.7 years when skin from old CBA mice was transplanted on compatible young recipients (Table 1). There was little difference between the ability of old and young CBA donor skin to grow on young CBA or (CBA × A)F$_1$ hybrid recipients; however, old A strain skin failed to survive more than 200 days in most cases (Krohn, 1962). A critical question in interpreting these experiments is whether the cells functioning normally in the old skin transplant were

TABLE 1. The Behavior of Serial Skin Transplants.

			NUMBERS OF GRAFTS			
To Host I	Good Grafts	To Host II	Good Grafts	To Host III	Good Grafts	Total Age (years)
14	13	11	3	3	2	6.7
30	30	25	16	13	5	6.0
10	10	10	6	1[a]	1	5.3
13	11	10	9	8[a]	6	5.0
30	25	23	18	11[a]	7	4.8
26	24	20	20	2[a]	2	4.7
123	113	99	72	38[a]	23	

SOURCE: Data from Krohn (1966).

[a]More still to be transferred. In a personal communication in 1972, Krohn said that from a total of 305 transplants, 32 could still be identified at 7 years, seven at 8 years, and one survived for 10.25 years (Daniel, 1977).

those that came from the original donor, or whether they had been slowly replenished over the years by migration of cells from the several young recipients on which the transplant had been carried. The use of (CBA × A)F_1 hybrid recipients for CBA skin should have made available a variety of isoenzyme and antigenic markers in which the A and CBA strains differ. These could have been used to distinguish cells from the original donor and those from the recipients. However, use of these markers was not reported (Krohn, 1966).

Daniel (1977) refers to a personal communication from Krohn in 1972 that the longest-lived serial skin transplant survived for 10.25 years and that parental strain skin in F_1 hybrids allowed hair color to be used as a means of identification. This could not have been true for the (CBA × A)F_1 hybrid recipient of CBA skin, in which hair color in both donor and host would have been dark brown (agouti). Therefore, the interpretation of these skin transplantations remains ambiguous because it has not been clearly proven that the cells whose function was observed came from the original donor.

Proliferation versus aging. Over the past 20 years, interest in biomedical research on aging has been strongly influenced by Hayflick and Moorhead's (1962, 1965, 1968) interpretation that the loss of proliferative capacity in human embryo fibroblasts *in vitro* is a

model system for studying mammalian aging. This model system is discussed in Chapter 12, and has obvious advantages over more complicated model systems for studies at the cellular and molecular levels. Its relevance to aging processes of intact mammals can be questioned, however. Most of the loss of proliferative capacity of human fibroblasts occurs between embryonic and adult cells, not between young adult and old adult cells (Hayflick, 1965; Martin et al., 1970). Although there is a significant loss of proliferative capacity on the average when young and old adults are compared (Schneider and Mitsui, 1976), it does not occur at a rapid enough rate to be responsible for limitations in the human life span. Furthermore, some old donors have fibroblasts with proliferative capacities as high as those of young adult donors. Fibroblasts from most elderly people are able to double at least 20 times *in vitro*, while people with certain genetic defects are able to survive although their fibroblasts have much lower doubling capacities (Martin et al., 1970).

Martin (1977) has suggested that loss of fibroblast proliferative capacity with serial passage *in vitro* is not a sign of functional deficiencies but a result of terminal differentiation. The loss also may result from abnormalities in proliferative kinetics due to conditions *in vitro*: for example, unbalanced stimulation to differentiate rather than to divide (Kay, 1965). It is also possible that partially differentiated cells with less proliferative capacity outgrow earlier precursor cells with more proliferative capacity, because the former multiply more quickly under conditions of rapid continuous proliferation (Holliday et al., 1977; Good, 1976).

Despite these possibilities, the popularity of the fibroblast model has lead to a widespread belief that limitations in proliferative capacities represent the aging process. This may be true for tissues whose function requires them to proliferate, if aging is defined as a loss of ability of the tissues to carry out their normal function.

Model Systems That Will Be Considered. A wide range of model systems are discussed in this book, but in this chapter only mammalian cells and tissues transplanted *in vivo* will be considered. Transformed or precancerous cells were discussed by Daniel (1977); they will not be considered here, as their functioning is not completely normal. This restriction does not apply to malignant teratorcarcinoma cells that have an unlimited proliferative capacity but are capable of forming normal tissues when joined with preimplantation embryos (Mintz and Illmensee, 1975). Teratorcarcinoma cells behave like undifferentiated embryonic cells, able to form portions of any tissue, including germ cell lines that produce normal offspring. These cell types and germ cells demonstrate that mammalian cells capable of normal function need not age. However, this ability may be limited to undifferentiated cells of very early embryos and to germ cell lineages.

In the earlier edition of this *Handbook*, Daniel (1977) reviewed the apparently immortal transplantable cell lines in adults that can be produced from imaginal discs of *Drosophila* larva and are able to form their predetermined types of normal differentiated tissues when transplanted into larva. While these are important in illustrating biological possibilities, mammals have much less predetermined developmental processes and do not have analogous larval stages. Unless warranted by the specific case, it is probably

incorrect to consider insects to be lower organisms compared to mammals; they are not necessarily lower, just very different. Since the evolutionary separation of the lines of creatures leading to present-day insects and present-day mammals, insects have progressed at least as far along their separate pathways as mammals have. If lower organisms are considered to be simplified models for mammalian aging, I suggest that they should be as similar as possible to the evolutionary ancestors of mammals.

TRANSPLANTATION OF INTACT ORGANS AND TISSUES

Skin. As previously discussed, transplanted skin from old donors has been carried for very long periods; unfortunately, the experimental design failed to rule out the possibility of migration of host cells into the transplanted tissue (Krohn, 1962, 1966). Although skin is a complex organ, with several differentiated layers of proliferating cells, the most easily measurable function that it performs is hair growth. Whiteley and Horton (1962) and Finch (1973) reported that after plucking, mouse hair regenerates more slowly in older animals. Horton (1967) used this observation to test the functional ability of skin transplants from old and young donors. She grafted skin from donors at 30–33 months of age to 3-month-old hosts and studied them over more than 2 years. The grafted skin was identified by being rotated 90° so that its hair grew in a different direction from the host's hair. Unfortunately, this did not allow identification of cells that might have migrated in from the hosts.

In the transplanted skin, hair regrowth after plucking was similar to the patterns shown by the host (Horton, 1967). This indicates that old skin did not have an intrinsic defect in the ability of the hair follicles to increase their rate of cycling after plucking. Further support for this conclusion comes from the ability to rejuvenate hair regrowth rates in old animals by hypophysectomy and endocrine supplementation in rats (Denckla, 1980) or mice (Harrison et. al, 1982).

Although old mouse skin is capable of growing hair normally, it appears to show some intrinsic functional changes with age that make it more susceptible to tumorigenesis. Table 2 summarizes results of experiments by Ebbesen (1973, 1974) who showed that old skin was twice as likely as young skin to form papillomas on the first exposure, and three times as likely to form carcinomas on repeated exposure, to the carcinogen DMBA (dimethylbenz [a]anthracene).

When all experiments using skin are assessed by the four criteria, functional assessments are only fair: the ability to grow hair and resistance to a carcinogen. Identification is based upon the unproven assumption that the old skin grafts do not have a significant level of repopulation by normally functioning host cells. If the old cells are unable to proliferate normally, it is quite possible that cells from the young host might populate tissues, such as skin, that ordinarily would not be populated. Therefore, some sort of markers are necessary for these experiments to be unambiguously interpreted. When transplants from old donors were compared with those from young controls, old skin grew hair as well as young but had an intrinsic increase in susceptibility to the DMBA carcinogen. This latter result demonstrates a defect that was not corrected by repopulation of young cells from the host. The restoration of rapid hair growth by hypophysectomy in old animals (Denckla, 1980; Harrison et al., 1982) shows that young recipient cells are not necessary to allow rapid hair growth in the old skin.

Ebbesen's (1973, 1974) very interesting findings support theories that increased susceptibility to cancer with age results from gradual accumulation of intrinsic damages (such as somatic mutations) in the susceptible cells. However, they did not distinguish between the possibilities that the old skin was intrinsically more vulnerable to DMBA or that it had been irreversibly damaged by residence in the old donors making it more susceptible to DMBA. On the other hand, the old donors were only 14 months old, making it unlikely that the skin was populated by pretransformed cells in old but not in young donors. In such an important area, it is surprising that transplantation experiments have not been more widely utilized.

Ovaries. If there is any tissue whose aging appears to be controlled by an intrinsic clock, it is the ovary. The supply of oocytes does not increase after birth, so when the oocytes are exhausted with age, the ovary can no longer function. Thus the clock appears to have a simple control mechanism. However, transplantation studies of old and young ovaries in old and young recipients have suggested that timing of ovarian aging is more complex than this. Although their numbers are greatly reduced, there are usually enough oocytes remaining in nonfunctioning old ovaries to produce several litters. Furthermore, the endocrine changes which make it impossible for old recipients to resume normal cycling when given young ovaries, can be retarded by removing ovaries early in life. This suggests that there is a feedback mechanism by which ovarian cycling over the reproductive life span eventually exhausts the capacity of the hypothalamic-pituitary axis to support ovarian cycling.

In most strains of mice and rats, ovarian cycling becomes extremely irregular and stops before the number of oocytes in the ovaries is completely exhausted. For example, Jones and Krohn (1961a) showed that several hundred oocytes remained in the ovaries of the A, RIII, and (CBA × A)F_1 hybrid strains; only in the CBA strain were the oocytes nearly exhausted when the females became infertile. This study showed that rates of decline in oocyte numbers decrease exponentially over the reproductive period "as expected if there was a constant and not an increasing vulnerability of the population of oocytes at risk" (Krohn, 1962). Data are summarized in Figure 2.

At the time of menopause in human females, there are about 10,000 oocytes left in the ovaries (Block, 1952; Talbert, 1977) and these gradually disappear after menopause. A number of investigators used mice or rats to show that transplantation of ovaries from

TABLE 2. Papillomas and Carcinomas on DMBA-Treated Skin Grafts From Old and Young Syngeneic BALC/c Mouse Donors.

Number of Mice	Sex	Donor Age when Transplanted (months)	Graft Age when DMBA Treated (months)	Number of Grafts in Resting Growth Phase when DMBA Treated	Number of Papillomas 7 Weeks Post-DMBA	NUMBER OF CARCINOMAS (POOLED ♂ AND ♀ DATA)	
						2 Months Post-DMBA	3 Months Post-Second DMBA
24	M	14	26	12	12 (50%)		
28	F	14	26	16	18 (64%)	4/52	16/41
15	M	2	14	7	2 (16%)		
34	F	2	14	18	10 (29%)	1/49	5/41

SOURCE: Data from Ebbesen (1973, 1974).

NOTE: Two-month-old BALB/c recipients were given skin grafts from 2- or 14-month-old donors. The carcinogen DMBA (dimethylbenz[a]anthracene was applied as 25 μg in 20 μl acetone once 12 months after grafting. The 7-week and 2-month post-DMBA counts of papillomas and cracinomas were taken. DMBA was applied a second time 5 months later (17 months after grafting) in three applications; three months thereafter, the post-second DMBA numbers of carcinomas (column on far right) were counted.

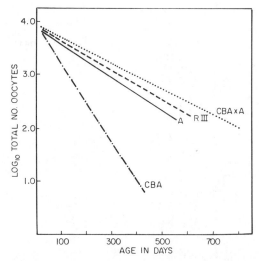

Figure 2. With age, the total numbers of oocytes decline expotentially in female mice with identical rates in both virgins and breeders. Regression lines for this relationship are shown for mice of the CBA, A, R III and (CBA × A)F₁ genotypes. (Data from Jones and Krohn, 1961a.)

old, noncycling donors to young recipients allows the old ovaries to support cycling again (Ascheim, 1976; Krohn, 1962, 1977; Peng and Huang, 1972; Zeilmaker, 1969). This is important, because regular estrous cycles cease by 16 to 20 months of age in

most strains of mice or rats, although they become increasingly long and irregular by about 12 months of age as illustrated in Figure 3 (from Nelson et al., 1980). More extensive and recent data in this area are given by Nelson et al. (1982).

Although old ovaries transplanted to young mice begin cycling again, old noncycling mice generally fail to begin cycling in response to transplanted young ovarian grafts (Ascheim, 1965; Peng and Huang, 1972; Nelson et al., 1980). Thus the cause of loss of cycling may not be intrinsic with the ovary. Further evidence that this is true comes from experiments of Ascheim (1965, 1976). He found that old rats, whose ovaries had been removed when they were young, resumed normal estrous cycling when given young ovarian transplants, even at advanced ages (24–27 months). This suggests that old females are capable of responding normally to the endocrine stimulation of the young ovaries only if their hypothalamic-pituitary system has not been exhausted by continuously responding to a normally cycling ovary over the reproductive life span in the normal fashion (Finch et al., 1980).

Ascheim's important experiment has been repeated by Nelson et al. (1980), and the re-

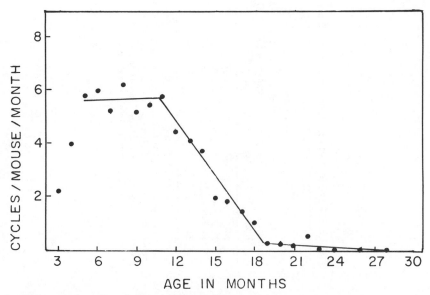

Figure 3. With age, there is a decline in the monthly frequency of estrous cycles in C57BL/6J mice, as determined by vaginal smears. (Data from Nelson et al., 1980.)

sults are shown in Table 3. Ovaries from 5-month-old donors transplanted into untreated 26-month-old B6 (C57BL/6J) mice caused cycling in only 25 percent of the cases, and cycles were abnormally long. However, if the 26-month-old recipients had been ovariectomized at 2 months of age, transplants of young ovaries caused cycling in all of the old recipients, and cycle lengths were much more nearly normal.

Finch et al. (1980) have theorized that the hypothalamus and pituitary can only respond to a limited amount of estradiol exposure. This limit is reached by the normally cycling ovaries after 16 to 20 months, and cycling ceases before the oocytes are completely exhausted from the ovary. This may explain why cycling is reactivated by a young ovarian transplant in 12-month-old noncycling CBA females (Krohn, 1962). CBA mice have an unusually early exhaustion of oocytes, and cycles usually have halted by 12 months of age or earlier (Figure 3; from Jones and Krohn, 1961a). It is likely that the loss is due to exhaustion of something in the hypothalamus or another part of the neuroendocrine system, as a young rat given old ovaries and an old pituitary is able to cycle normally (Peng and Huang, 1972). This suggests that aging is not completely timed intrinsically in either the ovary or the pituitary.

There is a rich literature describing neuroendocrine effects on ovarian aging (reviewed by Riegle and Miller, 1978; Finch, 1978; Finch et al., 1980; Meites et al., 1980). For example, Jones and Krohn (1961b) found that the rate at which oocytes were lost with age was greatly retarded by hypophysectomy. Although the pituitary and ovaries of aging female rats were less responsive than those of young rats, cycling and ovulation could be induced by various endocrine treatments in old, noncycling rats (Meites et al., 1978). However, transplantation of fertilized eggs from young donors into old recipients suggested that the old animals usually failed to support normal pregnancies (Blaha, 1975; Talbert and Krohn, 1966).

It is interesting to examine how ovarian transplants meet the four criteria for judging transplantations to study aging processes. (1) Function is measured by the ability of the old ovaries to produce normal cycling, but this is valid only when the recipient could not contribute to the cycling. It also measures only a limited part of ovarian function. A more impressive result would be the production of normal offspring from the old ovary. (2) If this was attempted, the experiment should be designed to identify the functioning of the transplanted ovary by genetic markers carried in the offspring that came from the donor rather than the host. However, this has not been accomplished with ovarian transplantations used to study aging processes. This lack leads to ambiguities; for

TABLE 3. Analysis of Ovarian Transplant Studies in Female C57BL/6J Mice.

AGE (MONTHS)				MEAN (SEM)	
Host	Ovarian Donor	No. of Mice	Mice with 2 or More Cycles[a]	Cycle Length of Responders (days)	Duration of Cycling after Transplantation[b] (Months)
5–6	5	10	100%	5.3 (0.65)	5.5 (1.2)
26	5	8	25%	8.0 (2.6)	2.4 (0.6)
26[a]	5	9	100%	6.6 (2.4)	3.0 (1.2)

SOURCE: From Nelson et al. (1980).

[a]Cycles were defined as a sequence of smears; proestrus followed by estrus or metestrus (cornified epithelial cells) and then diestrus (leukocytes), followed again by proestrus.

[b]The period of time during which cycles were observed. The termination of cycling was defined by the time after which no further cycles occurred for 10 days.

[c]Long-term ovariectomized mice, ovariectomized at 2 months of age and given ovarian transplants at 26 months of age.

example, if regeneration of host tissue is stimulated when old ovaries are transplanted, regenerating host tissue may be scored as normally functioning old ovarian tissue, causing erroneous interpretations. (3) Parallel transplantations of ovarian tissues from old and young donors have usually been done in these kinds of experiments, providing young controls for the old grafts. (4) The health of the old donors has not usually been clearly stated. Finch et al. (1980) point out that the common finding of pituitary tumors in aged female B6 mice (Felicio et al., 1980) may affect ovarian functions of old recipients. Such tumors may also cause endocrine imbalances that result in lasting damage to tissues transplanted from old donors. In any case, it is important to know what pathological lesions are present in aging individuals, whether they are used as donors or hosts.

Thymus. The thymus is the mammalian tissue that shows the earliest changes with age, in both size and structure. Maximum size and level of functional tissue in the thymus is reached soon after sexual maturity in both mice and men. Afterwards, the amounts of functional tissue gradually decline to 10 percent or less of the maximum levels (Walford, 1969; Bellamy, 1973; Adler, 1975; Kay, 1979; Tyan, 1979). Growth and development of the thymus appears to be intrinsically timed, because infant thymuses transplanted into adult or aged recipients show approximately normal growth patterns (Metcalf, 1965; Albright and Makinodan, 1966).

Only a single experiment has been reported in which old thymuses were tested in young recipients. Hirokawa and Makinodan (1975) showed that thymus grafts from 24- and 33-month-old BC3F$_1$ mice eventually restored thymic functions almost as well as grafts from 3-month-old donors in thymectomized, lethally irradiated recipients saved by marrow implants. Although the recipients of older thymus grafts recovered more slowly, Hirokawa and Makinodan (1975) concluded: "Atrophic thymus from 33-month-old mice can be rejuvenated, at least

partially, when transplanted in young adults." The longest period of time that old thymuses were left in young recipients was 12 weeks. Possibly they would have recovered more if left for longer times. Furthermore, old thymuses might recover more completely in a newborn or very young recipient rather than in an adult recipient.

Some recent results from our laboratory also suggest that thymus aging is not entirely intrinsic, as it is affected by the pituitary. When middle-aged B6 mice were hypophysectomized and given endocrine supplementation, some (but not all) T-dependent immune responses were rejuvenated, and their thymuses enlarged, especially in the cortical areas that declined the most with age (Harrison et al., 1982). Apparently, even in the thymus, changes with age are not entirely intrinsic, since they may be partially reversed by transplantation into a young recipient or by hypophysectomy. The beneficial results of hypophysectomy suggest that thymic aging, like ovarian aging, is at least partially timed via the hypothalamic-pituitary axis.

Intact Spleens. Transplants of intact spleens from old and young donors have been used to determine whether the stromal cells in the spleen, which support hemopoietic and lymphoid differentiation, age intrinsically. Harrison (1978) transplanted old and young spleens into genetically anemic Sl/Sl^d mice that have normal stem cells, but whose hemopoietic microenvironment is unable to support normal differentiation and development (reviewed by Russell, 1979). Although the spleens from old donors were less likely to cause maximum levels of improvement in the anemic recipients, some spleens from old donors functioned as well as those from young donors.

Hotta et al. (1980) grafted intact femurs and spleens into subcutaneous pockets in recipients. They transplanted tissues from donors of five different ages, 2 to 24 months old, into 2-month-old recipients. In reciprocal experiments, tissues from 2-month-old donors were transplanted into recipients of four different ages. Six weeks after implantation, Hotta et al. (1980) measured numbers of erythropoietic precursors contained in the grafts as microscopic spleen colony forming cells (CFU-S). Their results are summarized in Table 4. The numbers of CFU-S in each transplanted femur declined gradually more than ten-fold as femur donor age increased from 2 to 24 months. CFU-S numbers in each spleen declined mostly in spleens between 2 and 8 months of age. Recipient age did not affect the growth of CFU-S in femurs or spleens transplanted from 2-month-old donors. Either older femoral tissues are less able to regenerate after the initial necrosis when the tissues are first transplanted, or they have functional losses in the hemopoietic stromal cells with age, or both (Hotta et al., 1980). Between 2 and 8 months of age, the ability of donor femurs or spleens to support CFU-S declined two-to threefold (Table 4) which suggests that at least this initial loss is in the ability to regenerate after grafting, because hemopoietic function does not change by such an early age. In fact, CFU-S numbers in the femur do not decline with age in most strains of mice (reviewed by Harrison, 1979a), so aging most likely affects regenerating ability.

In similar experiments, Wolf and Arora (1982) confirmed that intact spleens and femurs transplanted from old donors had lower CFU-S contents than transplants from young donors. These authors also studied regeneration after the major vessels leading into spleens were ligated to prevent blood flow. Spleens from young mice recovered normal levels of ability to support CFU-S growth, while spleens from 12-month-old animals recovered only a third of normal levels and spleens from 24-month-old animals recovered only about one-seventh of normal levels in 90 days.

This loss with age of the ability to regenerate may result from exhausting the proliferative capacity of the splenic stromal cells, as the authors concluded from the Hayflick hypothesis (Wolf and Arora, 1982). However, there are several other equally likely explanations for these observations: it is possible that the population of cells in the spleen changes with age or that the cells in older spleens have accumulated damage as they grow older, thus becoming less able to regenerate rapidly. It is also possible that tissues from older animals store lower amounts of nutrients and, therefore, are more likely to be damaged by transplanation or ligation.

All of these experiments showed intrinsic differences between spleens and femurs from animals of different ages. However, they

TABLE 4. CFU-S Repopulation of Intact Femoral Marrow or Spleen Grafts, with Donors and Hosts of Various Ages.

AGE (MONTHS)			
Donors	Hosts	CFU-S/Femur Implant	CFU-S/Spleen Implant
2	2	1034 ± 73	86.4 ± 16.8
8	2	474 ± 56[a]	31.8 ± 4.4[b]
14	2	252 ± 15[a]	31.8 ± 3.6[b]
18	2	233 ± 14[a]	20.0 ± 2.5[a]
24	2	82 ± 12[a]	23.3 ± 6.4[a]
2	2	1108 ± 47	110 ± 13
2	8	1326 ± 72[c]	81 ± 14[c]
2	14	1328 ± 99[c]	107 ± 16[c]
2	24	1073 ± 102[c]	106 ± 12[c]

SOURCE: Data from Hotta et al. (1980).
NOTE: Values are means ±1 SE; all grafts were in hosts for 6 weeks.
[a]$P < 0.005$ different from 2-month-old donors.
[b]$P < 0.01$ different from 2-month-old donors.
[c]$P > 0.25$ different from 2-month-old hosts.

failed to show whether the reason for these differences was intrinsically timed aging. This illustrates a weakness of the transplantation technique in studying aging. It may be difficult to distinguish intrinsic functional declines with age from intrinsic increases in vulnerability to damage from the transplantation process. The fact that CFU-S numbers don't normally change with age (reviewed in Harrison, 1979a) suggests that the major effect of age is to increase the vulnerability to transplantation.

Recent results from our laboratory suggest that transplanting intact spleens causes a surprisingly high level of damage in lymphoid functions. Intact spleens from 20- to 24-month-old and 2- to 3-month-old B6D2F$_1$ donors were transplanted into healthy young recipients by surgically anastomosing the donor spleen onto the recipient spleen using Bernstein's (1970) technique. Direct antisheep red blood cell plaque forming cells were measured 3 to 4 months later. Although spleen transplants from young donors contained more plaques than those from old, the deleterious effects of transplantation were overwhelming, with the donor spleens containing less than 1 percent as many plaque forming cells as the recipients' own spleens onto which they were attached. In other experiments, donor spleens were transplanted into Sl/Sl^d recipients that had been splenectomized so that the only available splenic tissue was the transplanted spleens. In Sl/Sl^d recipients, the donor spleens reach large sizes because they perform most of the erythropoietic functions (Altus et al., 1971; Harrison and Russell, 1972). Nevertheless, the numbers of direct plaque forming cells and the responses to phytohemagglutinin from spleen cells were less than 10 percent of normal in young transplanted spleens and about 5 percent of normal in old spleens.

These results show that transplanted intact organs must be protected from transplantation damage. Otherwise intrinsic losses of function that develop with the aging process cannot be distinguished from increasing vulnerability with age to damage from transplantation.

Kidneys. Transplants of kidneys have been done in animals large enough so that veins and arteries were surgically connected to minimize damage from the transplantation process. Hollander and his colleagues transplanted kidneys from rats of different ages into young compatible animals both of whose kidneys had been removed. This rigorously tested the transplant's functional capacity. Using kidneys from 3-, 18-, and 26- to 34-month-old donors, the half-lives for recipient survival were 16, 13, and 7 months, respectively. Thus the old kidneys functioned less well on the average; however, some functioned as well as the best young ones. The maximum kidney life span was 46 months, while the longest-lived rat of the strain used was 39 months (Hollander, 1971; Van Bezooijen et al., 1974). These authors suggested that kidneys from older donors were more likely to be damaged by anoxia, despite the fact that the veins and arteries were surgically connected.

Possibly the surgical connections were not adequate, and larger animals must be used. Unfortunately, inbred strains of animals are not available for most larger mammals. Although the use of kidneys from older donors in human beings is controversial, there are data suggesting that age alone should not eliminate using older kidney donors when their kidney functions and tissue matches were good (Matus et al., 1976). Pregnancy puts a strain on kidney function, so a recent report of a successful pregnancy in a renal transplant patient with a 75-year-old kidney also suggests that an old kidney may function normally (Coulam and Zincke, 1981).

When intact large organs such as kidneys are transplanted, the first two criteria of function and identification are usually met, because the transplants usually must perform a function that is essential to the life of the recipient. Tissues from young controls (criterion 3) are available only if the experimental design included them; only such experiments meet the third criterion. The fourth criterion, health, may not be met because the less healthy internal environment of the aging donor may have made its tissues more vulnerable to transplantation, perhaps by having lower levels of stored nutrients. This possibility should be dealt with in the experimental design, in which transplanted tissues should be protected from damages associated with transplantation. For example, rat kidneys could be perfused with oxygenated, nutrient-rich blood from the time they are removed from the donor until they are perfused by the recipient's own circulation. It is also important to remember, when interpreting these experiments, that theories such as somatic mutation require intrinsic aging of all tissues in all individuals. In their simplest and most elegant form, they are not statistical and thus are contradicted if even a few old tissues remain fully functional for significantly longer than the maximum life span of the donor species. Such results would prove that damage from the accumulation of somatic mutations with age was not inevitable.

TRANSPLANTS OF SINGLE CELL SUSPENSIONS AND INDIVIDUAL CELL TYPES

One way to minimize the effects of transplantation is to transplant cells in a form that can be quickly established in a host. This would include transplanting single cell suspensions or cells in such small clumps that damage from anoxia is unlikely. Single cell suspensions are transplanted in order to study immunohemopoietic stem cell lines, and 0.5 mm pieces of mammary gland are transplanted to study mammary epithelium. In both cases, there does not seem to be an important effect of age on function of the graft, but there are limitations on the number of transplantations possible for these highly proliferative tissues.

Mammary Epithelium. Daniel and his colleagues (1968) did a series of experiments with transplanted mammary tissue that were widely interpreted as showing the Hayflick phenomena *in vivo*. The fatty stromal tissue, termed the fat pad, on which mammary epithelium grows is well developed in prepu-

bertal female mice, while the epithelial tissue is localized around the nipple and can be completely removed (DeOme et al., 1959). Transplants of mammary epithelium to be tested are transplanted in small (0.5 mm) pieces into a small incision in the fat pad, where they grow normally, filling the fat pad within 8 to 12 weeks. The transplanted tissues form glandular elements and are capable of developing, secreting, and eventually involuting as part of normal mammary gland function in hosts that become pregnant and produce milk for their offspring (Daniel, 1977).

Under favorable conditions, mammary tissues appear to survive with very few defects developing when serially transplanted at long intervals (Hoshino and Gardner, 1967). However, when mammary tissue was transplanted at intervals of 2 to 3 months, so that the gland had grown continuously, the growth rate declined to a low level after 4 to 6 serial transplantations (Daniel et al., 1968). This decline occurred more rapidly if tissue was taken for serial transplantation from the periphery rather than from the center of the mammary duct outgrowth (Daniel and Young, 1971). Growth rate, rather than mere survival, was the functional measure that Daniel used, and the loss of ability to grow was interpreted as aging at the cell and tissue level (Daniel et al., 1968; Daniel, 1972). These studies are reviewed in detail by Daniel (1977) in the first edition of this *Handbook*.

The possibility that transplantation at 2- to 3-month intervals was placing abnormal stresses on the cells and thereby exhausting their proliferative capacity was tested in the following experiment which is illustrated in Figure 5: two transplant lines were taken from a single donor, and one was transplanted at 3-month intervals while the other was transplanted every 12 months (Daniel and Young, 1971; Daniel, 1973, 1977). Transplantation at the shorter intervals caused a continuous loss of proliferative capacity with subsequent serial transplantations as previously found. Insufficient tissue remained for further transplantations after the seventh passage. However, transplantation at annual intervals not only allowed much longer times of normal function but also caused substantially less loss of function with each transplantation. Figure 4 illustrates that after 6 serial transplantations at annual intervals, the fat pads were still about 70 percent filled, while by 6 transplantations at 3-month intervals, only about 20 percent of the fat pads were filled. At last report (Daniel, 1977), this experiment was still going on and the subline of mammary epithelium transplanted at long intervals was still growing, although at a decreasing rate, after 6 years and 6 transplant generations.

These experiments show that cells of the mammary epithelium maintained by annual transplantation can function normally for at least twice as long as the life span of the donor from which they came. They also remain in excellent condition as judged by electron microscopy (Daniel, 1972). Even after mammary epithelial cells have lost their proliferative capacity, they are still capable of producing milk in lactating hosts (Daniel et al., 1971; Daniel, 1977).

In this model system, it is important to determine whether mammary epithelial cell functions alter with age. This was tested by comparing the performances of mammary duct grafts from 26-month-old donors and 3-week-old donors (Young et al., 1971). Proliferative capacities were exhausted after five serial transplantations at 2-month intervals in both cases; there was no difference between the growth of transplants from 3-week-old and 26-month-old donors during serial passage in young hosts. Since the old donors were virgins, their mammary cells had never been forced to proliferate in order to produce milk, but they had been exposed to other types of aging processes: for example, somatic mutations and the neuroendocrine factors in the aged donor. In the reverse experiment, when old and young cells were transplanted into 26-month-old hosts whose fat pads had been cleared when they were 3 weeks of age, neither young nor old trans-

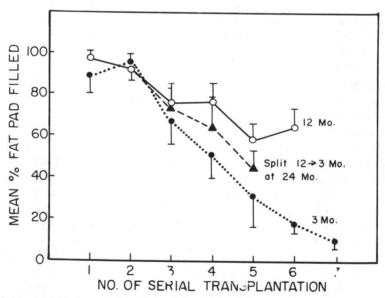

Figure 4. Serial transplantation studies of the mammary gland. Symbols show each serial transplant generation and indicate the mean percentage of fat pads filled with mammary outgrowths for successful transplants. Thirty-two fat pads were transplanted at each generation. Vertical lines give 95 percent confidence intervals. Two transplant lines were initiated from a single donor at time 0 and transplanted at intervals of 12 months (o——o) or 3 months (•···•). At 24 months, a second short-interval line (▲---▲) was split from the 12-month series. (Data from Daniel, 1977.)

plants grew very well (Young et al., 1971). This was expected because the endocrine environment of the old hosts would not be conducive to rapid growth of mammary tissue. Therefore, mammary epithelial cells do not age intrinsically over a normal mouse life span, although their proliferative capacity is limited when serially transplanted. The effects of proliferation without transplantation have not been tested.

The four criteria for judging cell transplantations were related to Daniel's experiments as follows: (1) function was measured primarily by the ability of the mammary epithelium to proliferate; (2) the transplanted cells were identified by their presence on the fat pad, which was never spontaneously populated by regenerating host tissue in control experiments; (3) when old donor tissue was compared with that from young controls, their functional abilities were identical; therefore, (4) in the single experiment using old mice, they had no health-related defect that permanently damaged their mammary duct cell functional abilities.

Although mammary epithelium cannot be transplanted at short intervals for an indefinite period, it appears to be able to function normally more than 6 years when transplanted at annual intervals; this is far longer than mice live. If proliferation occurred only under normal conditions (such as pregnancy), mammary epithelial cells may be able to function normally for even longer periods. These results can be explained by the same types of kinetic theories used to explain why hemopoietic stem cells lose their functional abilities when transplanted but are not affected by a lifetime of normal function. Cells with maximal proliferative capacities may be replaced by faster growing cells with less proliferative capacity (Good, 1976; Holliday et al., 1977). Even if transplantation eventually exhausts the proliferative capacity of mammary epithelium, the loss may be due to abnormal conditions existing as a result of the transplantation; no evidence has been reported showing that aging is intrinsically timed in this tissue. Daniel's interpretations of these experiments differ from mine and

are detailed in his published studies. He suggests that normal mammary epithelial cells *in vivo* have an intrinsically limited proliferative capacity.

Immunohemopoietic Stem Cell Lines: Background. Marrow cells contain precursor or stem cell lines that proliferate to produce more of themselves and differentiate to produce erythropoietic and lymphoid cells throughout the adult life span of an animal. Thus, at least some stem cells must continuously multiply, and their functional ability can be deduced by the production of their differentiated progeny. They can be transplanted by intravenous injections of single cell suspensions into recipients whose stem cells have been killed by lethal irradiation or are genetically defective. This provides a strong stimulus on the transplanted stem cells to repopulate the recipients and begin producing erythropoietic and lymphoid cell types. Survival of lethally irradiated recipients is a simple measure of normal function of the transplanted cells.

Figure 5 outlines how stem cells are thought to populate the immunohemopoietic systems. The earliest stem cells found in adults are generally considered to be common precursors of both lymphoid and erythropoietic cells. In Figure 5 are listed various precursor cell types as identified by specific functional assays. This figure is oversimplified, especially in the immune system and in the earliest stages of stem cell differentiation and development. Differentiation in the erythropoietic system from the macroscopic spleen colony forming cell (the CFU-S) is the best defined and has been the most studied in transplantation experiments. However, in many cases, methods to establish that differentiating cells came from the original donor rather than regenerating host cell types were not available; such experiments have been critically reviewed (Harrison, 1979a) and will not be discussed here.

The first long-term experiment with serial transplantation of stem cells was performed by workers at the Atomic Energy Research Establishment in Harwell, England (Barnes

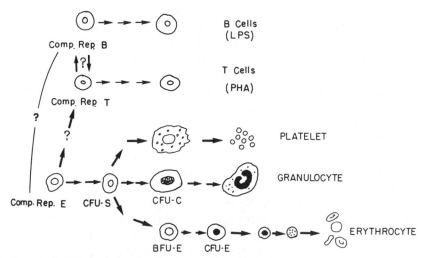

Figure 5. Stem cell differentiation in the immunohemopoietic system may begin with a single cell type, or several cell types, that multiply to replenish themselves and differentiate to populate the animal. The newly developed competitive repopulation (Comp. Rep.) assay was designed to measure the functional abilities of these earliest precursors. Comp. Rep. B, T, and E assays, respectively, test precursors of: B cells proliferating in response to lipopoly-saccharide (LPS) *in vitro*, T cells proliferating in response to phytohemagglutinin (PHA) *in vitro*, and erythropoietic cells proliferating in response to severe bleeding *in vivo*. In these assays, chromosome markers are identified in mitotic cells following procedures detailed in Harrison et al. (1978). Comp. Rep. E assays can also be performed using hemoglobin markers (Harrison, 1980). Cells that form macroscopic colonies on spleens of irradiated mice (CFU-S) are the earliest precursors detectable as single cells; they differentiate to form platelets, granulocytes, and erythrocytes. Colony forming units in semisolid agar cultures (CFU-C) produce granulocytes. Burst forming units and colony forming units that respond to erythropoietin *in vitro* (BFU-E and CFU-E) are, respectively, earlier and later precursor cells committed to form erythrocytes. (From Harrison, 1981a.)

et al., 1959; Micklem and Loutit, 1966). These workers used the easily recognizable T6 chromosome translocation (Ford, 1966) to identify donor stem cell lines after they were transplanted into lethally irradiated recipients. Once the recipients were populated by donor cells, their marrow was serially transplanted into a new set of recipients, with the primary recipients being used as donors. This process was repeated at approximately annual intervals. Unfortunately, only cells from fetal donors were used, and the stem cell lines generally began to be exhausted after 3 to 4 serial transplantations at annual intervals. Therefore, Micklem and Loutit (1966) concluded that these cells had intrinsically aged over a period comparable to a mouse's life span. Thus this early work appeared to support the conclusion that stem cells aged intrinsically. Figure 6 illustrates the serial transplantation process.

In most other early studies, the period between transplantation was very short, and the number of serial transplantations possible was as low as 2 or 3, before functional capacities declined significantly. Popp (1961) was the first to identify donor cells by differences in their hemoglobins, and found that intervals longer than 30 days between serial transplantations allowed better survival of lethally irradiated recipients. Van Bekkum and Weyzen (1961) also reported better survivals when they increased intervals between transplantations from 14 to 34 days; however, such increased intervals also increased the chances that recipient cells would regenerate, and donor cells were not identified.

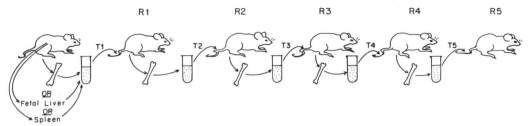

Figure 6. Marrow cells are rinsed from the femurs (and possibly also the tibias) of an adult mouse donor into a single cell suspension. Fetal livers or adult spleens are other sources of stem cells. The suspension is intravenously injected (transplant T1) into the lateral tail vein of a lethally irradiated recipient (R1). Later its marrow cells are serially transplanted (T2) into a successive recipient (R2) and so on. Spleen cells in adult mice and fetal liver cells in fetal mice may be used as a source of stem cells instead of bone marrow.

Decline in Erythrocyte Producing Ability with Age. Although old mice or rats can respond to hypoxia or bleeding by producing erythrocytes, their responses are slower than those of young animals (Garcia, 1957; Grant and LeGrande, 1964; Harrison, 1975b). Furthermore, of 16 hematologic parameters compared in old and young B6 male mice, packed cell volume of circulating erythrocytes (hematocrit) was the only one reduced with age rather than with disease (Finch and Foster, 1973). It is important to determine whether these defects are entirely or partially intrinsic to erythropoietic stem cell lines.

We tried to answer this question by testing how well stem cell lines from old or young donors produced erythrocytes after they had been transplanted to young recipients. As recipients, we used genetically anemic W/W^v mice that have defective erythropoietic stem cells (reviewed by Russell, 1979), and found that their anemias were cured equally well by marrow from old and young donors (Harrison, 1972). Furthermore, cured W/W^v recipients of old marrow responded to severe bleeding as well as recipients of young marrow and as well as young normal mice (Harrison, 1973, 1975b). This was true of cell lines that had functioned normally for as long as 73 months and 4 serial transplantations. Thus the defects in erythrocyte production that develop with age are not intrinsic to the erythropoietic stem cells. Instead, they are caused by deficiencies in the ability of the old animal to support erythroid differentiation,

perhaps in the stromal microenvironment (Trentin, 1971; Harrison, 1978; Hotta et al., 1980; Wolf and Arora, 1982).

The CFU-S Assay. Over the past 20 years, by far the most common assay for hemopoietic stem cells has depended on their ability to form macroscopically visible colonies (CFU-S) on spleens of lethally irradiated recipients. This assay was developed by Till and McCulloch (1961), who realized that the cells in these rapidly forming colonies might have proliferated from a single progenitor. Chromosome markers were used to show that this was true (Becker et al., 1963; Wu et al., 1967, 1968; Trentin, 1971). Furthermore, individual colonies sometimes contained as many as three separate lines of differentiation, with cells developing into erythrocytes, granulocytes, and platelets as shown in Figure 5 (Wu et al., 1968; Fowler et al., 1967; Curry and Trentin, 1967).

Under a variety of conditions, the ability of CFU-S to renew themselves declines with serial transplantation (Figure 7) and this decline is fastest when the interval between transplantations is short. In two cases given in Figure 7 (numbers 3 and 7), the decline in CFU-S numbers appeared to halt after the second or third serial transplantation with long intervals between transplantations. Since no genetic markers were used in these cases to distinguish donor and recipient cells, it is very likely that the serially transplanted stem cell lines were constantly replenished by

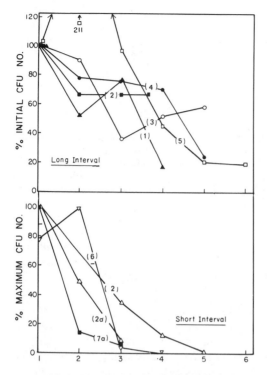

NO. OF TRANSPLANTATIONS OR TREATMENTS

Figure 7. The ability of marrow cells from young adult mice to form macroscopic spleen colonies (here called CFU, or colony forming units) in lethally irradiated recipients of the same genotype declines with serial transplantation. Long intervals are 30 days or more between transplantations, while short intervals are 7–14 days. (From Harrison, 1979a.)

The reference, symbol, number of marrow cells transplanted, transplant interval, mouse genotype, and other details of studies summarized in this figure follow:

1. (Cudkowicz et al., 1964) ▲, 5×10^5, 30 to 45 days, (BALB/c × A/He)F_1, ^{131}IUdR uptake rather than CFU;

2. (Siminovitch et al., 1964) △, 1 to 10×10^6, 14 days, (C57BL × C3H)F_1, marrow cells used in first passage and spleen cells used in following passages (individual colonies used in 2a) with CFU No./spleen measured;

3. (Lajtha and Schofield, 1971) ○, 98 to 400 CFU-S (estimate 1 to 10×10^6), 56 days, (C3H × AKR)F_1, CFU No./femur measured;

4. (Harrison, 1975a) ●, 3 to 10×10^6, 300 to 400 days, (WC/Re × C57BL/6)F_1, cells carried in genetically anemic recipients rather than irradiated recipients with CFU measured as concentrations/10^5 marrow cells;

5. (Boggs et al., 1967) □, endogenous colonies with numbers surviving similar to 1×10^5 exogenous marrow cells, 42 days, (DBA × C57BL)F_1;

recovering cell lines from the lethally irradiated recipients.

The major problem with the CFU-S as a stem cell assay is that these cells vary widely in their capacity for subsequent self-renewal. For example, when individual macroscopic spleen colonies are retransplanted, most form no subsequent colonies, but some form 10 or more. This was reported first by Till et al. (1964), who believed that this variability resulted from the stochastic nature of self-renewal rather than from variability within the CFU-S population. However, evidence has accumulated that the variations in long-term self-renewal among CFU-S result from real differences in long-term functional abilities. Cell types with widely differing amounts of long-term repopulating ability are scored as CFU-S because they all form macroscopic spleen colonies after 8 to 10 days of growth in a lethally irradiated recipient.

This conclusion is based on several types of evidence: populations of CFU-S with varying degrees of self-renewal have been separated physically (Worton et al., 1969). A number of drugs can permanently reduce, or temporarily enhance, the self-renewal capacity per CFU-S (Hellman et al., 1978; Schofield, 1978; Popp and Popp, 1979; Botnick et al., 1979; Ross et al., 1982; Hodgson et al., 1975; Rosendaal et al., 1976; Hodgson and Bradley, 1979). In addition, tests of long-term cell function do not always give results proportional to CFU-S numbers. Life-sparing abilities of marrow cells are grossly underestimated when CFU-S numbers are reduced by natural resistance (McCulloch and Till, 1963) or by the W/W^v genetic anemia (Harrison, 1972a). Life-spar-

6. (Metcalf and Moore, 1971)▽, 300 CFU (estimate 2 to 3×10^6), 14 days, CBA, marrow cells used in first passage waiting 56 days while spleen cells (1/15 of spleen) and 14-day intervals used in later passages with CFU No./spleen measured;

7. (Vos and Dolmans, 1972) ■, 4×10^6, 7 to 14 days in 7a, (C57BL × CBA) F_1, CFU No. measured/unit length of femur.

ing abilities of spleen cells are overestimated compared to marrow (Kretchmar and Conover, 1970). A recent report has suggested that macroscopic spleen colonies scored 8 days after transplantation are transient (Magli et al., 1982).

Perhaps the best evidence that the CFU-S population is heterogeneous is the fact that CFU-S numbers are not always proportional to long-term repopulating abilities. The latter are measured most accurately by competitive repopulation. This assay uses cell types distinguished by genetic markers; mixtures of the two types are allowed to compete to repopulate lethally irradiated recipients. In such experiments, CFU-S from fetal liver have much higher repopulating abilities than those from normal marrow (Micklem et al., 1972), while CFU-S from previously transplanted stem cell lines (Harrison et al., 1978; Ross et al., 1982) or circulating blood (Micklem et al., 1975) have much lower repopulating abilities.

The Competitive Repopulation Assay. As a result of this evidence, it is important to find ways to evaluate functional capacities of stem cells other than by using the CFU-S assay. This may be done by studying long-term repopulating abilities, as noted. The mixture of two genetically distinguishable stem cell types is transplanted, and they compete in repopulating the recipient under identical conditions. By use of their genetic difference, the percentage of progeny of each type is measured. The more effectively a particular stem cell type produces differentiated progeny, the more repopulating ability it has. Even slight defects are detected if they reduce the maximum rate and extent of proliferation and repopulation by the stem cell lines under the highly stimulatory conditions in the lethally irradiated recipient.

Micklem and his colleagues first used competitive repopulation techniques. They transplanted mixtures of marrow cells distinguished by a chromosome translocation and compared their abilities to repopulate lethally irradiated recipients (Micklem et al., 1972; Ogden and Micklem, 1976; Micklem et

al., 1975; Ross et al., 1982). Recipients of the same mixture were studied at different time points over as long as a year, generally showing consistent results after 25 to 50 days. We have altered this technique for two reasons: specific cell types were not identified as the chromosome markers were scored in whatever cells happened to be proliferating, and marrow cells of only two donors could be compared at a time.

Specific cell types may be identified by using genetic markers that are expressed only in cells having a particular function. For example, chromosome markers may be scored in cells proliferating in response to a specific stimulus, such as descendants of T cell precursors responding to phytohemagglutinin *in vitro* (Harrison et al., 1978; Harrison, 1981). Marrow cells from many different donors of the same genotype may be compared indirectly, by mixing cells from each donor with identical portions of pooled distinguishable cells. The repopulating abilities of cells from each donor are measured by the percentage of those cells produced in competition with the constant competitor type from the pool (Harrison et al., 1978; Harrison, 1981).

Table 5 illustrates how this system can be used. In each experiment, old and young donors of the CBA/HT6J type were used. Their cells were recognizable from the two T6 chromosome translocation markers. In some experiments, CBA/CaJ mice (with no marker chromosomes) had been lethally irradiated and used as recipients for donor cells that were previously transplanted. Marrow cells were removed from each donor and mixed with a constant portion of competitor cells containing one T6 chromosome marker from (CBA/HT6J × CBA/CaJ)F_1 hybrid mice. These mixtures were injected into lethally irradiated CBA/CaJ recipients. After 3 to 16 months, spleen cells from these recipients were stimulated *in vitro* with phytohemagglutinin (PHA) to stimulate T cells, and erythrocytes were stimulated in the recipients' marrows by severe bleeding. The percentages of cells in mitosis having the donor chromosomes were calculated to show how well cells from different types of donors

TABLE 5. Mitotic Competition: Mice Used.

Strain	Chromosomes (use)	Age
CBA/HT6J	2T6 (donor)	Old or young
CBA/HT6J × CBA/CaJ	1T6 (pooled competitor cells)	Young only
CBA/CaJ	0T6 (recipient)	Young only

NOTE: Procedure illustrated in Figure 10.

1. Mix equal number 2T6 marrow cells from each donor with a standard dose of 1T6 cells from the same pool.
2. Inject each mixture into several lethally irradiated recipients.
3. Determine percent of 2T6, 1T6, 0T6 mitoses after bleeding *in vivo* or PHA *in vitro*.

competed in repopulating the lethally irradiated recipients (Figure 8; from Harrison and Astle, 1982).

The results indicated that age made little or no difference in repopulating ability, but a single transplantation caused a large decline (Figure 8; Harrison et al., 1978; Harrison, 1981). This severe effect on functional ability is hard to understand because transplantations were performed using high cell numbers (3–10 × 10⁶ marrow cells per recipient) and remained in the original recipients from 4 to 12 months. Under these conditions marrow cells can be serially transplanted 4 to 7 times before they fail to repopulate and cure lethally irradiated or genetically anemic W/W^v recipients (Figure 7; reviewed in Harrison, 1979a).

We have studied this transplantation ef-

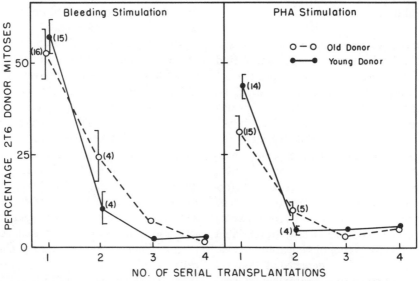

Figure 8. Old donors were 24- to 31-month-old and young donors were 3- to 6-month-old CBAT6 mice; this genotype has two T6 chromosomes. For transplantations 2, 3, and 4, their marrow was serially transplanted using 4–10 × 10⁶ marrow cells per lethally irradiated CBA carrier (see Table 5 and Figure 9 for details). These were held 4–12 months before they were used as donors. Their marrow cells were mixed with young (CBAT6 × CBA)F₁ competitor marrow (3 × 10⁶ cells each) having one T6 chromosome, and IV injected in lethally irradiated CBA recipients. A mean of 48 (range 20–65) mitoses was scored for each recipient after 2–15 months. Recipients were splenectomized to provide spleen cells for PHA stimulation *in vitro*, and bled 1–4 weeks later to stimulate marrow cells *in vivo*. Usually cells from two old and two young donors were studied in single experiments; in three experiments, donors at transplantation 2 were included, and in one experiment, donors at transplantations 3 and 4. Means for all donors are plotted, bars give ± standard error, and the number of donors is given if more than one. The value for each donor is the mean of the values for its recipients; there were an average of 2.3 recipients per donor. (From Harrison and Astle, 1982).

fect further. Different numbers of cells (from 10^5 to 10^8) were transplanted into lethally irradiated recipients, following the experimental design shown in Figure 9. Cells were also transplanted by joining recipient and donor circulations by parabiosis. In addition, donors were tested whose cells were not transplanted but were required to proliferate in order to recover from sublethal (550–600 rads) of irradiation. When chromosome markers were used to assess competitive populating ability as previously discussed, a single transplantation of 10^5–10^7 marrow cells reduced stem cell function three- to fourfold, as did recovery from sublethal irradiation or transplantation by parabiosis. In addition to stimulation by PHA *in vitro* and bleeding *in vivo*, spleen cells from recipients were stimulated by LPS (lipopolysaccharide) *in vitro*. LPS stimulates B cell classes and thus measures the repopulating ability of their precursors. All three mitogens used gave similar results (Harrison, 1981; Harrison and Astle, 1982).

The strongly deleterious effect shown by recovery from sublethal (550–600 rads) irradiation was also found using hemoglobin markers to assess effects on erythropoietic

stem cells (Harrison and Astle, 1982). This suggested that lethally irradiated recipients may be permanently damaged by the 900–1100 R that they receive, perhaps in the stromal microenvironment. This damage may prevent normal stem cell recovery and cause the deleterious effect of transplantation. This possibility was disproved by using unirradiated W/W^v mice as carriers of the first transplantation, in the experimental design shown by Figure 9. These genetically anemic mice have defective stem cells causing a macrocytic anemia that is cured when W/W^v recipients are permanently repopulated by genetically compatible stem cell lines (reviewed by Russell, 1979). No irradiation of these recipients is necessary. Cells from W/W^v carriers functioned no better than those from lethally irradiated carriers (Harrison and Astle, 1982), so irradiation damage does not explain the transplantation effect.

In addition, a much more severe reduction was apparent when erythropoietic stem cell function was measured using quantitatively distinguishable hemoglobins (Harrison, 1980) rather than chromosomes to differentiate donor and competitor cells (Harrison

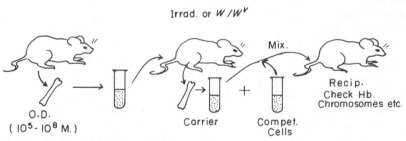

Figure 9. The competitive repopulation assay illustrated is used to study the effect of a single transplantation. Cells from the original donor (O.D.) are first transplanted into a genetically distinguishable, lethally irradiated, or W-anemic recipient, the carrier. The original donor may be young or old. Cell numbers may be varied experimentally from 10^5 to 10^8, with 3–10×10^6 marrow cells used in a standard transplantation. After several months, marrow cells from the carrier are mixed with marrow cells pooled from competitors. Usually, 1–7.5×10^6 marrow cells of each type are mixed and injected into each recipient. The competitor is often the same genotype as the carrier and the recipient; cells of these three types must be genetically distinguishable from those of the original donors. After at least 60 days, the long-term functional ability of the original donor's cells is shown by how well they repopulated the recipient and produced differentiated progeny in competition with the competitor cells in the mixture. Chromosome markers may be used to identify cells stimulated to proliferate by a specific mitogen, as in Table 5 and Figure 8. Hemoglobin markers also provide a direct, simple, and sensitive method of detecting the function of erythropoietic stem cells. (From Harrison, 1980, 1983; Harrison and Astle, 1982.)

and Astle, 1982). This does not seem to result from reduced life spans of erythrocytes produced by previously transplanted stem cells, as the ratios of freshly synthesized hemoglobins are similar to the total circulating hemoglobin ratios. In these experiments, the same genetic marker is used to identify the original donor cell type and to measure the stem cell's functional ability by its production of hemoglobin-containing cells. The fact that a single transplantation abrogated erythrocyte production much more severely than production of proliferating cells suggests that nonerythroid cells proliferating in the marrow are not affected as severely by transplantation as are erythropoietic stem cells. Nevertheless, such stem cells do not appear to be affected by age, since old cells repopulated and recovered from irradiation as well as cells from young or even fetal donors (Harrison, 1983).

Ross et al. (1982) confirmed that a single transplantation of bone marrow stem cells had severe deleterious effects on their potential for self-renewal. They also stimulated untransplanted cells to proliferate with hydroxyurea using methods of treatment that killed about 70 percent of the bone marrow CFU-S as well as more differentiated cell types (Rosendaal et al., 1976). After as many as 25 such treatments at 21-day intervals, the ability of CFU-S to self-renew was unimpaired (Ross et al., 1982). This contrasts with other studies in which much shorter treatments with various types of drugs caused permanent defects in regenerative capacity of CFU-S (Hellman et al., 1978). Since hydroxyurea only affects cells in the S phase of the cell cycle, the earliest stem cells may not have been damaged if they proliferated so slowly that they were not in the S phase. However, transplantation may have stimulated excessively rapid proliferation, causing the loss of function observed.

Transplantation experiments using erythropoietic stem cells met the four criteria (Harrison, 1973, 1975a, 1979b). (1) Function was measured by saving the lives of lethally irradiated recipients, curing genetically anemic mice with deficient stem cells, and by producing hemoglobin-containing cells, the erythrocytes. (2) Donor cells were identified by chromosome markers, by their ability to cure genetically defective recipients (that are never spontaneously cured), or by quantitative measures of genetically distinguishable hemoglobin production. Maximum precision was obtained when function was measured quantitatively by the same marker that was used to identify the donor cells. This was done by measuring the degree of repopulation of erythropoietic stem cells by the amounts of the donor's hemoglobin type. In addition, T and B cell populations were measured by the percentage of donor cells proliferating in response to specific T or B cell mitogens. (3) Donors of different ages were used, and no deleterious effects with age on erythropoietic stem cell functions were detected. (4) The health status of the donors was defined not only through studies of the donors themselves, but also through the transplanted stem cell lines. In some cases, especially with old B6 cells, all the recipients of a cell line from a particular old donor developed a characteristic leukemia-like cancer. This occurred up to two serial transplantations and a year and a half after the cells were removed from the donor, and affected about 30 percent of the old donors (Harrison, 1975a). It seems likely that transformed cells were accidentally transplanted along with the marrow stem cells from the old donors in these cases. In other cases, normal function of the old stem cells proved that they had not been deleteriously affected by the ill health in the old donor.

Lymphoid Cell Lines. Most researchers now agree that there is little or no decline with age in the functional ability of erythropoietic stem cell lines, but there is no such agreement about lymphoid stem cells. In fact the majority of workers claim that lymphoid stem cells develop intrinsic defects with age (reviewed by Makinodan and Kay, 1980). This is surprising because it is generally believed that the same early stem cell lineage in adults populates both the erythropoietic and the lymphoid systems, as is shown in Figure

6. Bone marrow has long been known to contain the precursors of cells that differentiate in the thymus to T cells (Cross et al., 1964; Tyan and Cole, 1965). However, the best evidence that the same stem cell can repopulate both the hemopoietic and immune systems was reported by Abramson et al. (1977), who extended experiments of Wu et al. (1968). Both groups induced chromosome markers by heavily irradiating marrow donors just before removing their cells, and looked for such markers in recipients of high doses of marrow cells. In a few cases, proliferating cells in a variety of lymphoid organs had the same marker, indicating that they were produced by the same precursor in which the marker had been originally induced. These experiments may be misleading if the cell lines with marker chromosomes are abnormal, perhaps transformed fully or partly to cancer cells. It is necessary to prove that they have normal functional abilities. Abramson et al. (1977) did this by showing that cell lines with marker chromosomes proliferated *in vitro* after stimulation with the T and B cell mitogens PHA and LPS. Unfortunately they did not report results for unstimulated controls. These are necessary to be sure that the cells carrying the induced chromosome marker enter mitosis specifically in response to the mitogen, as normal cells would.

Many of the conflicting results in studies of lymphoid stem cell lines result from confusion over what should be called a lymphoid stem cell. In this chapter, we will consider stem cells to be the earliest precursors; these have not been committed to specialized functions. A cell line differentiated so that it produces a specific antibody is, therefore, not considered to be a stem cell line; however, such cell lines have been shown to have remarkably high proliferative capacities. Möller (1968) showed that mouse cell lines producing a specific antibody may function for 5 to 7 serial transplantations and about 40 doublings. Williamson and Askonas (1972) confirmed this work, estimating that the maximum number of doublings could be as high as 90. These workers referred to the loss of proliferative potential of antibody forming cells as "clonal senescence" and remarked on the similar numbers of doublings in mouse antibody forming cells *in vivo* and in human fetal-derived fibroblasts studied *in vitro* (Hayflick, 1965).

This similarity is probably coincidental because the cell committed to forming a specialized antibody differs from the fetal fibroblasts in a number of ways that should reduce its proliferative potential. It is adult rather than fetal, it is from a short-lived species (mouse) rather than a long-lived one (man), and it is highly differentiated to produce only a particular type of antibody. Under these conditions, the high proliferative capacity of the antibody forming cell is remarkable. Probably lymphoid stem cells, the precursors of the antibody forming cell, have even higher proliferative capacities since they are less differentiated.

Recipients that have been repopulated by as few as four individual macroscopic spleen colonies (presumably descended from four individual CFU-S cells) responded well to three widely different types of antigens (Trentin et al., 1967). Therefore the CFU-S is an earlier precursor than the cell committed to a single antibody, because the strong responses to the different types of antigens used showed that a wide variety of differentiated antibody producing cells had been formed by the few original CFU-S (Trentin et al., 1967), as illustrated in Figure 5. Of course it is possible that the precursors of the antibody forming cells had infiltrated into the spleen colonies and were not descended from the CFU-S; nevertheless, over 90 percent of the proliferating cells in a colony are from the same precursor (Becker et al., 1963; Trentin, 1971; Wu et al., 1967).

Decline with Age in Immune Responses. Makinodan and Peterson (1962) first showed that immune responses in mice became defective with age. This work was soon confirmed and extended (Wigzell and Stjernsward, 1966; Makinodan and Peterson, 1966), and aging of immune responses has become an area of major research interest. It is central to Walford's (1969, 1974) and Burnet's (1970, 1970a) theories that many effects of age can be traced to two related changes: increasing levels of erroneous immune responses against self (auto-immunity) and decreasing abilities to react against foreign materials. Many other workers have studied how immune responses change with age, and their work has been extensively reviewed (Bellamy, 1973; Good and Yunis, 1974; Yunis and Greenberg, 1974; Adler, 1975; Kay, 1979; Tyan, 1979; Meredith and Walford, 1979; Makinodan and Kay, 1980; Kay and Makinodan, 1981; Weksler, 1981). These changes have obvious relevance for aging people. As well as reducing resistance to infectious disease, changes with age in lymphoid cells may accelerate tumor cell growth (Gozes and Trainin, 1977).

In studies of lymphoid cell types, several workers have suggested that old stem cells failed to function normally. In this case, declines with age in immune responses would be intrinsically timed in the stem cell lines that produce lymphoid cells. Marrow cells from old BC3F$_1$ mice produced half as many B lymphocytes as marrow from young donors after 4 days in lethally irradiated recipients (Farrar et al., 1974). After two doses of sublethal irradiation 5 hours apart, marrow cells from old BC3F$_1$ mice recovered significantly more slowly than young cells (Chen, 1974). In both of these experiments, there was not enough time allowed for old marrow stem cells to recover from the deleterious effects of having been in the old donors. It is important to recognize that differentiated cells may be impaired as a result of developing in the old donor; such defects are not necessarily intrinsic to the stem cells.

In longer-term studies, Tyan (1977) found that thymic regeneration was impaired 15 to 21 days after lethally irradiated recipients received marrow from donors that were more than 100 weeks old. This was true for mice of all three different F$_1$ hybrid genotypes tested. In the same study, CFU-S numbers usually did not change with age, and CFU-S from old donors formed normal sized colonies (Tyan, 1977). This disagreed with reports that CFU-S from old mice grew more slowly as measured by ^{125}IUdR uptake and by the numbers of cells in the largest dissected macroscopic spleen colonies (Albright and Makinodan, 1976). We found that old and young marrow grafts grew equally well in spleens of lethally irradiated recipients (Harrison et al., 1978), in agreement with Tyan (1977).

Tyan's long-term results also do not require intrinsic defects in stem cells, as the old marrow cells were only in the young recipients for 15 to 21 days. As previously discussed, active tissue in the thymus becomes much smaller with age, and this may have inhibited development of differentiated thymic precursor cells in the old marrow. However, if given more time in the young recipient, old stem cells might be capable of producing normal numbers of T cell precursors.

There are longer-term experiments in which old stem cells appear to be defective in producing functional lymphoid cells. Price and Makinodan (1972) transplanted spleen cells from old mice into young recipients, whose immune responses fell to the level seen in old mice by 60 days. Four to six weeks after marrow grafts from 15 to 18-month-old B6 mice were transplanted into lethally irradiated young recipients, B cell function was not as effective as in recipients of young cells (Kishimoto et al., 1976). These workers also found that 80 to 120 days after transplantation, marrow grafts from 15- to 19-month-old B6 mice had failed to populate spleens of their recipients with cells that were able to produce normal graft-versus-host (GVH) reactions (Kishimoto et al., 1973).

On the other hand, we have found that old marrow cells functioned as well as young ones in restoring immune responses of lethally irradiated recipients. We used chromosomally marked transplants to identify proliferating cells in the recipients as from the old donors and young controls (Harrison and Doubleday, 1975; Harrison et al., 1977). In the latter experiments, we measured the same immune responses in the old and young donors and, after 7 to 17 weeks, in recipients repopulated by their stem cells. Results were expressed as a ratio of old to young. The ratios for formation of direct plaques *in vivo* in response to sheep red blood cells were 0.35 ± 0.14 (6) for the original old and young donors, and 1.26 ± 0.71 (16) for recipients repopulated by their cells for 7 to 17 weeks. When responses *in vitro* to phytohemagglutinin were measured, the ratios for old and young original donors were 0.44 ± 0.17 (10) and for recipients populated by the cells from those donors 0.86 ± 0.27 (24). These data, given as mean ± S.D. (*n*), suggest that the loss of immune response with age in the old donors was not intrinsic in their stem cells. Recipients populated by old stem cells had similar immune responses to recipients populated by young stem cells, shown by the ratios of old to young approaching 1.00.

We suggested that the reason for the apparent contradiction between our results and those of Price and Makinodan (1972) is that they used BC3F$_1$ mice whose spleens contain "life shortening factors" (Albright et al., 1969). These "factors" were probably transformed reticulum cell sarcoma cells. These are commonly found in old mice of F$_1$ hybrid strains with B6, and they probably populated the recipients along with the transplanted spleen cells. Similar problems may have affected the results of Kishimoto et al. (1973, 1976) as their old B6 mice may develop transplantable cancers of similar types. Transformed cells of this kind may effect immune function long before they cause detectable cancer. Recipients of old B6 marrow sometimes appeared healthy for many months before all recipients of marrow from a particular donor died with leukemia-like symptoms within a few weeks of each other (Harrison, 1975a).

Our results have been supported by the findings of Ogden and Micklem (1976) that old stem cells were able to compete as well as young stem cells when injected in mixtures in lethally irradiated recipients. It may be significant that they used CBA mice, as did

we in studies of immune responses. We have found that CBA mice do not often develop tumor cells that would be transplanted with the marrow cells.

If old stem cells are intrinsically defective, it should be possible to improve immune responses in old mice by replacing their stem cells with young ones. This was done by Hirokawa and Makinodan (1975), who lethally irradiated old mice, and then transplanted an infant thymus and young adult bone marrow into them. This treatment improved the T cell dependent immune response to nearly normal young adult levels. We have confirmed this work and extended it with further experiments showing that old bone marrow failed to improve immune responses in old mice (Astle and Harrison, 1984). These results appear to contradict our other studies showing normal function from old stem cells tested in young recipients.

However, we suggest an alternate interpretation, because old stem cells repopulate the lymphoid systems of young recipients as rapidly as young stem cells (Ogden and Micklem, 1976; Harrison et al., 1978; Harrison, 1981; Harrison and Astle, 1982). Our recent results demonstrate that this is also true in old recipients. Therefore, the old stem cells do not appear to be defective; instead, we suggest that old marrow contains precursor cells which can produce immunosuppressive cells or factors only when in an old recipient. These suppressors are effective, however, in a young recipient, as shown by the following experiment: when the circulatory systems of old and young mice are joined in parabiosis, the immune response of the young partner declines to the level of the old partner (Harrison, 1979; Butenko and Gubrii, 1980; Astle and Harrison, 1984).

Evidence that stem cell regulation is altered with age in a complex fashion was also reported by Tyan (1980). Regulatory cells sensitive to anti-theta antisera seemed to have separate helper and suppressor functions in macroscopic spleen colony formation. Furthermore, syngeneic recipients of marrow from old B6D2F$_1$ mice had depressed hemoglobin and total lymphocyte levels 4 months after transplantation (Tyan, 1982a). This probably resulted from changes in intrinsic marrow regulatory mechanisms rather than from defects in stem cells, as precursor cell populations in old mice responded normally to the stresses of endotoxin and chronic bleeding (Tyan, 1982b). Possibly, all these defects result from defects in thymic regulatory cells as a result of the decline with age in thymus function. This hypothesis was suggested by Gozes et al. (1982) to explain a loss in T cell responses in recipients of old marrow that occurred after 8 months, but not earlier, and without any defect in erythroid stem cells. Changes with age in regulatory cells may also explain why erythropoietic stem cells from old donors had higher initial repopulating abilities than those from young or fetal donors using B6 mice (Harrison, 1983).

When stem cells from old donors produce normal functions in young recipients only after long periods of time, there are two possible explanations. (1) The stem cells are intrinsically normal but require time in the young recipient to repopulate it with the cell types that are defective in the old donor. (2) The old stem cells are intrinsically defective, differentiating and proliferating more slowly than normal, but if given enough time, they are able to reach the functional levels shown by young stem cells. To distinguish between these possibilities, we used the competitive repopulation assay previously described and analyzed lymphoid stem cell function by measuring numbers of T or B cells produced in competition with a constant pool of young cells. Figure 8 showed that old stem cells were able to repopulate recipients as well as young cells, with differentiated cell types responding to a mitogen that stimulates T cells (PHA, or phytohemagglutinin); similar results were obtained with a mitogen that stimulates B cells (LPS, or lipopolysaccharide). These results suggest that old stem cells produce these differentiated lymphoid cell types as rapidly as young stem cells. Both the ability to repopulate the lethally irradiated recipient as rapidly as possible and the ability

to maintain production of differentiated cells for several months are tested by the competitive repopulation assay (Harrison et al., 1978; Harrison, 1980, 1981; Harrison and Astle, 1982). Of course in competitive repopulation experiments, old and young stem cells are exposed to the same regulatory elements.

The criteria for transplantation experiments can be applied to lymphoid stem cells. (1) Donor cell functions were measured by standard tests of immune response, including proliferation in response to specific mitogens. (2) Donor cell types were identified using chromosome markers detectable only in proliferating cells, and proliferation was stimulated by specific mitogens. With this procedure, it is essential to determine the mitotic index (percentage of cells in mitosis) in cultures stimulated by the mitogen and in control cultures. Only if the mitogen causes at least a several fold increase in numbers of mitoses can one assume that most of the mitotic cells are proliferating in response to the specific mitogen. It is likely that a significant amount of the confusion and conflict over the functional performance of old stem cells results from ambiguities in measuring their function and identifying them. (3) Young controls are readily available and are usually tested for comparison of functional cell types. The fourth criterion, health of the old donor, is extremely important. Metastasizing tumor cells can greatly lower immune responses, even when present in as low a concentration as 1 per 2,000 normal spleen cells (Jaroslow et al., 1975). Therefore, normal looking lymphoid tissues may have greatly reduced functional abilities if transformed cells are present, even in very low numbers. For this reason, old animals should never be used if any signs of tumors are found in their lymphoid systems. Such signs include elevated white cell counts or enlarged lymphoid organs—thymus, lymph nodes, or spleens. These gross observations are not adequate to prove that no tumor cells are present. Even a complete autopsy with histological analyses of lymphoid and other important tissues may not detect early growth of tumors. If possible, the lymphoid cells to be tested should be removed without killing the animal. For example, an old mouse's spleen can be surgically removed. If no cancers develop in the tested mouse over several months, changes with age were not secondary to development of rapidly spreading tumors.

Ideally, functions of lymphoid stem cells should be evaluated when the cells are identified as donor or recipient type. Scoring the particular chromosome types in large numbers of mitotic cells is an extremely tedious procedure, so that it may not be practical to measure specific mitogen responses as described in Figure 8 and Table 5. If modern monoclonal antibody techniques are combined with cell sorters, it should be possible to measure numbers of functional cells by using fluorescent antibodies against antigens (such as Thy-1, Lyt-1, Lyt-2) that characterize these desired functions. Parent and F_1 hybrid cells differing at those antigens could be mixed in the competitive repopulation assay, or other antigenic markers, perhaps from the major histocompatibility locus, could be used to distinguish donor cells and those of the competitor or recipient. Such techniques would facilitate evaluation of lymphoid stem cell functions in transplantation experiments.

SUMMARY AND EVALUATION OF CURRENT WORK

Taken as a whole, the work in this area shows that a large number of tissue types are capable of functioning normally well beyond donor life spans when transplanted from the old donor into a young recipient. Although this has not been found in every experiment, there are many possible errors in experimental design that can cause functional losses in transplanted old tissues. These would lead to a false diagnosis of intrinsic aging, since aging is measured by the loss of normal function. The only error in design likely to lead to the false conclusion that old tissues are functioning normally is failure to distinguish old tissues from regenerating host tissues.

Thus, the critical criterion of identification must be met before concluding that old tissues function normally. The function being measured must be identified as that of the old transplanted tissue.

Tissues that have been capable of performing some of their functions for longer than donor life spans include the following: adrenal cortex, skin, pituitary glands, mammary epithelium, kidneys, and stem cell lines producing erythrocytes and lymphoid cells. There is evidence that even the thymus and the ovary may decline in function with age at least partly due to factors outside themselves. Therefore, theories predicting that all tissues age intrinsically must be modified to recognize that in many cases tissues do not age as rapidly as the animal from which they came.

A goal in the future must be to determine whether any normally functioning somatic cell types are immortal. Work on erythropoietic stem cell lines has come closest to meeting this goal, because such cell lines may be serially transplanted at least 5–6 times before they can no longer function (reviewed in Harrison, 1979a). Figure 8 shows that the effects of a single transplantation caused 3–7 times as much functional loss in PHA-responsive cell precursors as a lifetime of normal function; transplantation affected erythropoietic cell precursors at least 10–20 times as much, as no deleterious effect of age could be detected (Harrison and Astle, 1982), not even when old, young, and fetal cells were compared (Harrison, 1983). Therefore stem cell lines should be capable of functioning for at least 15–50 normal life spans, if the loss of function with transplantation results from the same mechanism that causes a loss of function with age. Hemopoietic stem cells may not age at all.

New advances in transplantation techniques will be required to transplant marrow cells without any deleterious effects. The cause of the decline in stem cell repopulating ability after a single transplantation is an object of active current research. Procedures to minimize the effects of transplantation are of obvious importance for clinical transplant recipients; they are also important in developing animal models that allow the effects of age to be unambiguously disassociated from the effects of transplantation when tissues from old donors are studied in young recipients.

IDEAS FOR THE FUTURE

The analysis of transplantation experiments as a way to study aging shows the importance of considering the criteria of function, identification, control, and health. In the most sophisticated experiments, rigorous functional measures simultaneously identify the tissues whose function is being measured. These include the following means to identify particular tissue functions: the color of hair produced by skin, the genotype of the offspring produced by an ovary, the hemoglobin type produced by erythrocytes from erythropoietic stem cells, and the karyotype of mitogen-stimulated cells from lymphoid stem cells. Possible uses of antigenic markers for both function and identification have already been outlined.

Modern molecular biology should soon make it feasible to identify a wide range of specific cell functions by production of characteristic messenger RNAs. These could be used for the functional markers, and could simultaneously distinguish donor and recipient messenger RNAs that differ even slightly in nucleic acid sequences. These differences may be detected quantitatively. For example, locations where one mRNA type fails to exactly hybridize onto a specific cloned DNA gene of the other type result in an unmatched region that is "cut" by the action of specific enzymes, causing shorter fragments to be produced (Berk and Sharp, 1978; Weaver and Weissmann, 1979). If DNA clones are available with restriction enzymes that cut in, or very near to, the area of nucleic acid difference, a rapid and quantitative means of distinguishing messenger RNAs is currently available (Ross and Donaldson, 1981). As molecular biologists clone and define more mammalian genes, more methods of measuring function and identifying donor cell types by mRNAs will become available. Although these techniques are being developed for the purpose of studying mammalian gene action on the molecular level, they will be useful in many areas, including meeting the criteria of function and identification in transplantation studies of aging.

Recent experiments suggest that nerve regeneration is possible in embryonic mammals (Gash et al., 1981). Further development of techniques to induce neural regeneration may make it possible to rejoin nerves in transplanted adult tissue. This has obvious clinical importance and also would be useful in transplantation experiments to study old neural tissues, especially neuroendocrine tissues that proliferate little over the adult life span.

The possibility of determining whether nuclei from aging cells have ultimately normal genotypes and completely normal functional capacity is suggested by experiments of Illmensee and Hoppe (1981). Nuclei from embryonic cells were transplanted into fertilized eggs, and normal mice were born that showed genetic markers characteristic of the transplanted nuclei. Of course, further development is necessary before such techniques can be applied to cells and tissues from old donors, as only embryonic tissues have thus far been successfully used. It is possible that only germ line cells or very early precursor cells from old donors will be usable.

Techniques have been developed and are constantly being improved for kidney and marrow transplants in man. Well-defined series of tests are used to assure optimal matching for histocompatibility antigens between donor and host, and both pre- and posttransplantation treatments that maximize graft success are being developed. These techniques may be applied to appropriate animal models. They should make possible long-term tissue transplantations between young and old donors from species or strains of animals that are not inbred.

It also is now theoretically possible to prepare identical old and young individuals for any species in which nuclei of early embryo cells can be successfully transplanted into fertilized eggs, as done by Illmensee and Hoppe (1981) in mice. From each single early embryo, sufficient numbers of nucleated cells could be removed for nuclear transplantations, while the remaining embryo cells were frozen. After the individuals produced by the initial procedure were old, another set of nuclear transplantations would be performed from the frozen cells, to produce genetically identical young individuals. This technique would require a reasonably high success rate from nuclear transplantation to be practical.

Relationships to Potential Therapy. Few benefits for human health have thus far been realized from research on aging, probably because the subject is so complicated, and it is so easy in studying aging to confuse causes and effects. Transplantation experiments simplify this situation, allowing functional capacities of old tissues to be studied without complications resulting from other malfunctions in the aging individual. Such experiments give us hope that in many cases tissues from old individuals are able to function normally. Further experiments should help to identify the tissues in which aging is intrinsically timed, to provide direct evidence of increasingly complex interactions of essential tissue types, and to define potential functional life spans of different tissue types. Procedures to reduce the damage from the tissues or interactions that cause the malfunctions with age can then be tested. In many cases, the test systems that will be used to develop therapies which benefit specific aging tissues will be the transplanted tissues from old donors.

REFERENCES

Abramson, S., Miller, R. G., and Phillips, R. A. 1977. The identification in adult bone marrow of pluripotent and restricted stem cells of the myeloid and lymphoid systems, *J. Exp. Med.* 145: 1567–1579.

Adler, W. H. 1975. Aging and immune function. *Bioscience* 25: 652–657.

Albright, J. F. and Makinodan, T. 1966. Growth and senescence of antibody-forming cells. *J. Cell Physiol.* 67: supp. 1, 185–206.

Albright, J. F. and Makinodan, T. 1976. Decline in the growth potential of spleen-colonizing bone marrow cells of long-lived mice. *J. Exp. Med.* 144: 1204–1213.

Albright, J. F., Makinodan, T., and Deitchman, J. W. 1969. Presence of life-shortening factors in spleens of aged mice of long lifespan and extension of life expectancy by splenectomy. *Exp. Gerontol.* 4: 267–276.

Altus, M. S., Bernstein, S. E., Russell, E. S., Carsten, A. L., and Upton, A. C. 1971. Defect extrinsic to stem cells in spleens of steel anemic mice. *Proc. Soc. Exp. Biol. Med.* 138: 985–988.

Argyris, T. S. 1970. The effect of aging on damage-induced hair growth in C57BL/6J female mice. *Anat. Rec.* 167: 371–377.

Ascheim, P. 1965. Resultats fournis per la grefe hétérochrone des ovarie dans l'etude de la regulation hypothalamus-hypophyso-ovarienne de la ratte senile. *Gerontologia* 10: 65–75.

Ascheim, P. 1976. Aging in the hypothalamic-hypophyseal-ovarian axis in the rat. *In*, A. V. Everitt and J. A. Burgess (eds.), *Hypothalamus, Pituitary, and Aging*, pp. 376–418. Springfield, Ill.: Charles C. Thomas.

Askonas, B. A., Williamson, A. R., and Wright, B. E. G. 1970. Selection of a single antibody-forming cell clone and its propagation in syngeneic mice. *Proc. Nat. Acad. Sci.* 67: 1398–1403.

Astle, C. M. and Harrison, D. E. 1984. Effects of marrow donor and recipient age on immune responses. *J. Immunol. 132:* 673–677.

Bailey, D. W. 1978. Sources of subline divergence and their relative importance for the sublines of six major inbred strains of mice. *In*, H. C. Moise III (ed.), *Origins of Inbred Strains*, pp. 197–215. New York: Academic Press.

Barnes, D. W. H., Ford, C. E., and Loutit, J. F. 1959. Greffes en série de moelle osseuse homologue chez des souris irradices. *Le Sang* 30: 762–765.

Becker, A. J., McCulloch, E. A., and Till, J. E. 1963. Cytological demonstration of the clonal nature of spleen colonies derived from transplanted mouse marrow cells. *Nature* 197: 452–454.

Bellamy, D. 1973. The thymus in relation to problem of cellular growth and aging. *Gerontologia* 19: 162–184.

Berk, A. J. and Sharp, P. A. 1978. Spliced early mRNAs of simian virus 40. *Proc. Nat. Acad. Sci.* 75: 1274–1278.

Bernstein, S. E. 1970 Tissue transplantation as an analytic and therapeutic tool in hereditary anemias. *Amer J. Surg.* 119: 448–451.

Blaha, G. C. 1975. Egg transfer between young and old mammals. *In*, R. J. Blandau (ed.), *Aging Gametes*, pp. 219–230. Basal: Karger.

Block, E. 1952. Quantitative morphological investigations of the follicular system in women. Variations at different ages. *Acta. Anat.* 14: 108–123.

Boggs, D. R., Marsh, J. C., Chervenick, P. A., Cartwright, G. E., and Wintrobe, M. M. 1967. Factors influencing hematopoietic spleen colony formation in irradiated mice. III. The effect of repetitive irradiation upon proliferative ability of colony-forming cells. *J. Exp. Med.* 126: 871–880.

Botnick, L. E., Hannon, E. C., and Hellman, S. 1979. Nature of the hemopoietic stem cell compartment and its proliferative potential. *Blood Cells* 5: 195–210.

Burnet, F. M. 1970. *Immunological Surveillance,* pp. 208–235. Sydney: Pergamon.

Burnet, M. 1970a. An immunological approach to aging. *Lancet* 2: 358–360.

Butenko, G. M. and Gubrii, I. B. 1980. Inhibition of the immune responses of young adult CBA mice due to parabiosis with their old partners. *Exp. Gerontol.* 15: 605–610.

Chen, M. G. 1974. Impaired Elkind recovery in hemopoietic colony-forming cells of aged mice. *Proc. Soc. Exp. Biol. Med.* 145: 1181–1186.

Committee. 1981. *Mammalian Models for Research on Aging.* Washington, D.C.: National Academy Press.

Coulam, C. B. and Zincke, H. 1981. Successful pregnancy in a renal transplant patient with a 75-year-old kidney. *Surg. Forum.* 32: 457–459.

Cross, A. M., Leuchars, E., and Miller, J. F. A. P. 1964. Studies on the recovery of the immune response in irradiated mice thymectomized in adult life. *J. Exp. Med.* 119: 837–850.

Cudkowicz, G., Upton, A. C., and Shearer, G. M. 1964. Lymphocyte content and proliferative capacity of serially transplanted mouse bone marrow. *Nature* 201: 165–167.

Curry, J. L. and Trentin, J. J. 1967. Hemopoietic spleen colony studies. I. Growth and differentiation. *Dev. Biol.* 15: 395–413.

Daniel, C. W. 1972. Aging of cells during serial propagation *in vivo. Adv. Gerontol. Res.* 4: 167–199.

Daniel, C. W. 1973. Finite growth span of mouse mammary gland serially propagated *in vitro. Experientia* 29: 1422–1424.

Daniel, C. W. 1977. Cell longevity *in vivo. In,* L. Hayflick and C. E. Finch (eds.), *Handbook of the Biology of Aging,* pp. 122–158. New York: Van Nostrand Reinhold.

Daniel, C. W., DeOme, K. B., Young, J. T., Blair, P. B., and Faulkin, L. J. 1968. The *in vivo* life span of normal and preneoplastic mouse mammary glands: a serial transplantation study. *Proc. Nat. Acad. Sci.* 61: 52–60.

Daniel, C. W. and Young, J. T. 1971. Life span of mouse mammary epithelium during serial propagation *in vivo*: influence of cell division on an aging process. *Exp. Cell Res.* 65: 27–32.

Daniel, C. W., Young, L. J. T., Medina, D., and DeOme, K. B. 1971. The influence of mammogenic hormones on serially transplanted mouse mammary gland. *Exp. Gerontol.* 6: 95–101.

Denckla, W. D. 1980. Personal communication.

DeOme, K. B., Faulkin, L. J., Bern, H. A., and Blair, P. B. 1959. Development of mammary tumors from hyperplastic alveolar nodules transplanted into gland-free mammary fat pads of female C3H mice. *Cancer Res.* 19: 515–520.

Ebbesen, P. 1973. Papilloma induction in different aged skin grafts to young recipients. *Nature* 241: 280–281.

Ebbesen, P. 1974. Aging increases susceptibility of mouse skin to DMBA carcino-genesis independent of general immune status. *Science* 183: 217–218.

Farrar, J. J., Loughman, B. E., and Nordin, A. A. 1974. Lymphopoietic potential of bone marrow cells from aged mice: comparison of the cellular constituents of bone marrow from young and aged mice. *J. Immunol.* 112: 1224–1249.

Felicio, L. S., Nelson, J. F., and Finch, C. E. 1980. Spontaneous pituitary tumorigenesis and plasma estradiol in aging female C57BL/5J mice. *Exp. Gerontol.* 15: 139–142.

Finch, C. E. 1973. Retardation of hair regrowth, a phenomenon of senescence in C57BL/6J male mice. *J. Gerontol.* 28(1): 13–17.

Finch, C. E. 1978. Genetic influences on female reproductive senescence in rodents. *In,* D. Bergsma and D. E. Harrison (eds.), *Genetic Effects on Aging,* pp. 335–354. New York: Alan R. Liss.

Finch, C. E., Felicio, L. S., Fluckey, K., Gee, D. M., Mobbs, C., Nelson, J. F., and Osterburg, H. H. 1980. Studies on ovarian-hypothalamic-pituitary interactions during reproductive aging in C57BL/6J mice. *Peptides* 1 (Sup. 1), 163–175.

Finch, C. E. and Foster, J. R. 1973. Hematologic and serum electrolyte values of the C57BL/6J male mouse in maturity and senescence. *Lab. Anim. Sci.* 23: 339–349.

Ford, C. E. 1966. The use of chromosome markers, *In,* H. S. Micklem and J. F. Loutit (eds.), *Appendix to Tissue Grafting and Radiation,* pp. 197–206. New York: Academic Press.

Fowler, J. H., Wu, A. M., Till, J. E., and McCulloch, E. A. 1967. The cellular composition of hemopoietic spleen colonies. *J. Cell Physiol.* 69: 65–72.

Garcia, J. F. 1957. Erythropoietic response to hypoxia as a function of age in the normal male rat. *Am. J. Physiol.* 190: 25–30.

Gash, D., Sladek, J. R., and Sladek, C. D. 1980. Functional development of grafted vasopressin neurons. *Science* 210: 1367–1369.

Geiringer, E. 1954. Homotransplantation as a method of gerontological research. *J. Gerontol.* 9: 142–149.

Geiringer, E. 1956. Young rats with adult adrenal transplants: a physiologic study. *J. Gerontol.* 11:8–17.

Good, P. I. 1976. Aging in mammalian cell populations, a review. *Mech. Age. Dev.* 5: 339–398.

Good, R. A. and Yunis, E. 1974. Association of autoimmunity, immunodeficiency, and aging in man, rabbits and mice. *Fed. Proc.* 33: 2040–2050.

Gozes, Y. and Trainin, N. 1977. Enhancement of Lewis lung carcinoma in a syngeneic host by spleen cells of C57BL/6 old mice. *Eur. J. Immunol.* 7: 159–164.

Gozes, Y., Umiel, T., and Trainin, N. 1982. Selective

decline in differentiating capacity of immunohemopoietic stem cells with aging. *Mech. Age. Dev.* 18: 251-259.

Grant, W. C. and LeGrande, M. C. 1964. The influence of age on erythropoiesis in the rat. *J. Gerontol.* 19: 505-509.

Harman, D. 1956. Aging—a theory based on free radical and radiation chemistry. *J. Gerontol.* 11: 298-300.

Harman, D. 1981. The aging process. *Proc. Nat. Acad. Sci* 78: 7124-7128.

Harrison, D. E. 1972. Normal function of transplanted mouse erythrocyte precursors for 21 months beyond donor life spans. *Nature New Biol.* 237: 220-221.

Harrison, D. E. 1972a. Lifesparing ability (in lethally irradiated mice) of W/W^v mouse marrow with no macroscopic colonies. *Rad. Res.* 52: 553-563.

Harrison, D. E. 1973. Normal production of erythrocytes by mouse marrow continuous for 73 months. *Proc. Nat. Acad. Sci.* 70(11): 3184-3188.

Harrison, D. E. 1975a. Normal function of transplanted marrow cell lines from aged mice. *J. Gerontol.* 30(3): 279-285.

Harrison, D. E. 1975b. Defective erythropoietic responses of aged mice not improved by young marrow. *J. Gerontol.* 30 (3): 286-288.

Harrison, D. E. 1978. Genetically defined animals valuable in testing aging of erythroid and lymphoid stem cells and microenvironments. *In*, D. Bergsma and D. E. Harrison (eds.), *Genetic Effects on Aging*, pp. 187-196. New York: Alan R. Liss.

Harrison, D. E. 1979a. Proliferative capacity of erythropoietic stem cell lines and aging, an overview. *Mech. Age. Dev.* 9: 409-426.

Harrison, D. E. 1979b. Mouse erythropoietic stem cell lines function normally 100 months: loss related to number of transplantations. *Mech. Age. Dev.* 9: 427-433.

Harrison, D. E. 1979c. Treatments that retard or reverse immunological losses with age. *The Gerontologist* 19: 87 (abstract).

Harrison, D. E. 1980. Competitive repopulation: a new assay for long-term stem cell functional capacity. *Blood* 55: 77-81.

Harrison, D. E. 1981. Immunopoietic stem cell lines: effects of aging and transplantation. *In*, D. Sege and L. Smith (eds.), *Immunological Aspects of Aging*, pp. 43-56. New York: Marcel Dekker.

Harrison, D. E. 1981a. Immunohemopoietic stem cell lines. In, R. T. Schimke (ed.), *Biol. Mech. in Aging*. NIH Publ. No. 81-2194.

Harrison, D. E. 1982. Must we grow old? *Biology Digest.* 8: 11-25.

Harrison, D. E. 1983. Long-term erythropoietic repopulating ability of old, young and fetal stem cells. *J. Exp. Med.* 157: 1496-1504.

Harrison, D. E., Archer, J., and Astle, C. M. 1982. The effect of hypophysectomy on thymic aging in mice. *J. Immunol.* 129: 2673-2677.

Harrison, D. E. and Astle, C. M. 1982. Loss of stem cell repopulating ability with transplantation: effects of donor age, cell number and transplant procedure. *J. Exp. Med.* 156: 1767-1779.

Harrison, D. E., Astle, C. M., and DeLaittre, J. A. 1978. Loss of proliferative capacity in immunohemopoietic stem cells caused by serial transplantation rather than aging. *J. Exp. Med.* 147: 1526-1531.

Harrison, D. E., Astle, C. M., and Doubleday, J. W. 1977. Stem cell lines from old immunodeficient donors give normal responses in young recipients. *J. Immunol.* 118: 1223-1227.

Harrison, D. E. and Doubleday, J. W. 1975. Normal function of immunological stem cells from aged mice. *J. Immunol.* 114 (4): 1314-1322.

Harrison, D. E. and Russell, E. S. 1972. The response of W/W^v and Sl/Sl^d anemic mice to haematopoietic stimuli. *Brit. J. Haematol.* 22: 155-168.

Hayflick, L. 1965. The limited *in vitro* lifetime of human diploid cell strains. *Exp. Cell Res.* 37: 614-636.

Hayflick, L. 1968. Human cells and aging. *Sci. Am.* 218: 32-37.

Hayflick, L. and Moorhead, P. S. 1961. The serial cultivation of human diploid cell strains. *Exp. Cell Res.* 25: 585-621.

Hellman, S., Botnick, L. E., Hannon, E. C., and Vigneulle, R. M. 1978. Proliferative capacity of murine hematopoietic stem cells. *Proc. Nat. Acad. Sci.* 75: 490-494.

Hirokawa, K., Albright, J. W., and Makinodan, T. 1976. Restoration of impaired immune function in aging animals. *Clin. Immunol. Immunopathol.* 5: 371-376.

Hirokawa, K. and Makinodan, T. 1975. Thymic involution: effect on T cell differentiation. *J. Immunol.* 114: 1659-1664.

Hodgson, G. S. and Bradley, T. R. 1979. Properties of haemopoietic stem cells surviving 5-fluorouracil treatment: evidence for a pre-CFU-S cell? *Nature* 281: 381-382.

Hodgson, G. S., Bradley, T. R., Martin, R. F., Sumner, M., and Fry, P. 1975. Recovery of proliferating haemopoietic progenitor cells after killing by hydroxyurea. *Cell Tissue Kinet.* 8: 51-60.

Hollander, C. F. 1971. Age limit for the use of syngeneic donor kidneys in the rat. *Transplant. Proc.* 3: 594-597.

Holliday, R., Huschtscha, L. I., Tarrant, G. M., and Kirkwood, B. L. 1977. Testing the commitment theory of cellular aging. *Science* 198: 366-372.

Horton, D. L. 1967. The effect of age on hair growth in the CBA mouse: observations on transplanted skin. *J. Gerontol.* 22: 43-46.

Hoshino, K. and Gardner, W. U. 1967. Transplantability and life span of mammary gland during serial transplantation in mice. *Nature* 213: 193-194.

Hotta, T., Hirabayashi, N., Utsumi, M., Murate, T., and Yamada, H. 1980. Age-related changes in the function of hemopoietic stroma in mice. *Exp. Hematol.* 8: 933–936.

Illmensee, K. and Hoppe, P. C. 1981. Nuclear transplantation in *Mus musculus:* developmental potential of nuclei from preimplantation embryos. *Cell* 23: 9–18.

Jaroslow, B. N., Suhrbier, K. M., Fry, R. J. M., and Tyler, S. A. 1975. *In vitro* suppression of immunocompetent cells by lymphomas from aging mice. *J. Nat. Cancer Inst.* 54: 1427–1432.

Jones, E. C. and Krohn, P. L. 1961a. The relationships between age, numbers of oocytes, and fertility in virgin and multiparous mice. *J. Endocrinol.* 21: 469–496.

Jones, E. C. and Krohn, P. L. 1961b. The effect of hypophysectomy on age changes in the ovaries of mice. *J. Endocrinol.* 20: 497–507.

Kay, H. E. M. 1965. How many cell-generations? *Lancet*, 2, 418–419.

Kay, M. M. B. 1979. A overview of immune aging. *Mech. Age. Dev.* 9: 39–59.

Kay, M. M. B. and Makinodan, T. 1981. *CRC Handbook of Immunology in Aging.* Boca Raton, Fla.: CRC Press.

Kishimoto, S., Shigemoto, S., and Yamamura, Y. 1973. Immune response in aged mice: change of cell-mediated immunity with aging. *Transplantation* 15: 455–459.

Kishimoto, S., Takahama, T., and Mizumachi, H. 1976. *In vitro* immune responses to the 2,4,6-trinitrophenyl determinant in aged C57BL/6J mice. *J. Immunol.* 116: 294–300.

Kretchmar, A. L. and Conover, W. R. 1970. A difference between spleen-derived and bone marrow-derived colony-forming units in ability to protect lethally irradiated mice. *Blood* 36: 772–776.

Krohn, P. L. 1962. Review lectures on senescence: II. Heterochronic transplantation in the study of aging. *Proc. Rov. Soc. (London) Ser. B,* 157: 128–147.

Krohn, P. L. 1966. Transplantation and aging. *In,* P. L. Krohn (ed.), *Topics of the Biology of Aging,* pp. 125–138. New York: John Wiley & Sons.

Krohn, P. L. 1977. Transplantation of the ovary. *In,* S. Zuckerman and B. J. Weir (eds.), *The Ovary,* 2nd ed., pp. 101–128. New York: Academic Press.

Lajtha, L. G. and Schofield, R. 1971. Regulation of stem cell renewal and differentiation: possible significance in aging. *In,* B. L. Strehler (ed.), *Advances in Gerontological Research,* Vol. 3, pp. 131–146. New York: Academic Press.

Magli, M. C., Iscove, N. N., and Odartchenko, N. 1982. Transient nature of early haematopoietic spleen colonies. *Nature* 295: 527–529.

Makinodan, T. 1978. Mechanism, prevention and restoration of immunologic aging. *In,* D. Bergsma and D. E. Harrison (eds.), *Genetic Effects on Aging,* pp. 197–212. New York: Alan R. Liss.

Makinodan, T. 1979. Control of immunologic abnormalities associated with aging. *Mech. Age. Dev.* 9: 7–17.

Makinodan, T. and Kay, M. M. 1980. Age influence on the immune system. *Adv. Immunol.* 29: 287–330.

Makinodan, T. and Peterson, W. J. 1962. Relative antibody-forming capacity of spleen cells as a function of age. *Proc. Nat. Acad. Sci.* 48: 234–238.

Makinodan, T. and Peterson, W. J. 1966. Further studies on the secondary antibody-forming potentials of juvenile, young adult, adult, and aged mice. *Dev. Biol.* 14: 112–129.

Martin, G. M. 1977. Cellular aging-clonal senescence. *Am. J. Pathol.* 84: 484–511.

Martin, G. M., Sprague, C. A., and Epstein, E. J. 1970. Replicative life-span of cultivated human cells: effects of donor's age, tissue, and genotype. *Lab. Invest.* 23(1): 86–92.

Masoro, E. J. 1980. Mortality and growth characteristics of rat strains commonly used in aging research. *Exp. Aging Res.* 6: 219–233.

Matus, A. J., Simmons, R. L., Kjellstrand, C. M., Buselmeier, T. J., and Najarian, J. S. 1976. Transplantation of the aging kidney. *Transplantation* 21: 160–161.

McCay, C. M., Sperling, G., and Barnes, L. L. 1943. Growth, aging, chronic diseases and lifespan in rats. *Arch. Biochem.* 2: 469–479.

McCulloch, E. A. and Till, J. E. 1963. Repression of colony-forming ability of C57BL hematopoietic cells transplanted into non-isologous hosts. *J. Cell. Comp. Physiol.* 61: 301–308.

Meites, J., Huang, H. H., and Simpkins, J. W. 1978. Recent studies on neuroendocrine control of reproductive senescence in rats. *In,* E. L. Schneider (ed.), *The Aging Reproductive System,* pp. 213–236. New York: Raven Press.

Meites, J., Steger, R. W., and Huang, H. H. H. 1980. Relation of neuroendocrine system to the reproductive decline in aging rats and human subjects. *Fed. Proc.* 39: 3168–3172.

Meredith, P. J. and Walford, R. L. 1979. Autoimmunity, histocompatibility and aging. *Mech. Age. Dev.* 9: 61–77.

Metcalf, D. 1965. Multiple thymus grafts in aging mice. *Nature,* 208: 87–88.

Metcalf, D. and Moore, M. A. S. 1971. *Haemopoietic cells. In, Frontiers of Biology,* Vol. 24, pp. 448–465. New York: Elsevier.

Micklem, H. S., Anderson, N., and Ross, E. 1975. Limited potential of circulating haemopoietic stem cells. *Nature* (London) 256: 41–43.

Micklem, H. S., Ford, C. E., Evans, E. P., Ogden, D. A., and Papworth, D. S. 1972. Competitive *in vivo* proliferation of foetal and adult haematopoietic cells in lethally irradiated mice. *J. Cell. Physiol.* 79: 293–298.

Micklem, H. S. and Loutit, J. F. 1966. *Tissue Grafting and Radiation.* New York: Academic Press.

Mintz, B. and Illmensee, K. 1975. Normal genetically mosaic mice produced from malignant teratocarcinoma cells. *Proc. Nat. Acad. Sci.* 72: 3585–3589.

Möller, G. 1968. Regulation of cellular antibody synthesis. Cellular 7S production and longevity of 7S antigen-sensitive cells in the absence of antibody feedback. *J. Exp. Med.* 127: 291–306.

Nelson, J., Felicio, L., and Finch, C. E. 1980. Ovarian hormones and the etiology of reproductive aging in mice. *In*, A. A. Dietz (ed.), *Aging—Its Chemistry*, pp. 64–81. Washington, D.C.: American Society of Clinical Chemists.

Nelson, J. F., Felicio, L. S., Randall, P. K., Sims, C., and Finch, C. E. 1982. Longitudinal study of estrous cyclicity in aging C57BL/6J mice. I. Cycle frequency, length and vaginal cytology. *Biol. Reprod.* 27: 327–329.

Ogden, D. A. and Micklem, H. S. 1976. The fate of serially transplanted bone marrow cell populations from young and old donors. *Transplantation* 22: 287–293.

Peng, M.-T. and Huang, H.-H. 1972. Aging of hypothalamic-pituitary-ovarian function in the rat. *Fert. Steril.* 23: 535–542.

Popp, R. A. 1961. Competence of retransplanted homologous marrow cells in relation to time after original transplantation into irradiated mice. *Int. J. Radiat. Biol.* 4: 155–161.

Popp, D. M. and Popp, R. A. 1979. Hemopoietic stem cell heterogeneity: use of cell cycle-specific drugs to look for age-associated alterations. *Mech. Age. Dev.* 9: 441–462.

Price, G. B. and Makinodan, T. 1972. Immunologic deficiencies in senescence. II. Characterization of extrinsic deficiencies. *J. Immunol.* 108: 413–417.

Reincke, U., Hannon, E. C., Rosenblatt, M., and Hellman, S. 1982. Proliferative capacity of murine hemopoietic stem cells *in vitro*. *Science* 215: 1619–1622.

Riegle, G. D. and Miller, A. E. 1978. Aging effects on the hypothalamic-hypophyseal-gonadal control system in the rat. *In*, E. L. Schneider (ed.), *The Aging Reproductive System*, pp. 159–192. New York: Raven Press.

Rosen, R. 1976. On the sensitivity of biodynamical interactions to parameter variations. *Math. Biosci.* 28: 237–242.

Rosen, R. 1978. Cells and senescence. *Int. Rev. Cytol.*, 54, 161–191.

Rosendaal, M., Hodgson, G. S., and Bradley, T. R. 1976. Haematopoietic stem cells are organized for use on the basis of their generation age. *Nature* (London) 264: 68–69.

Ross, E. A. M., Anderson, N., and Micklem, H. S. 1982. Serial depletion and regeneration of the murine hematopoietic system. Implications for hematopoietic organization and the study of cellular aging. *J. Exp. Med.* 155: 432–444.

Ross, J. and Donaldson, D. D. 1981. Solution hybridization using cloned 5'-³²P-labeled, double-stranded DNA to distinguish among closely related nucleic acids. *Gene* 16: 171–177.

Russell, E. S. 1979. Hereditary anemias of the mouse: a review for geneticists. *Adv. Genet.* 20: 357–459.

Schneider, E. L. and Mitsui, Y. 1976. The relationship between *in vitro* cellular aging and *in vivo* human age. *Proc. Nat. Acad. Sci.* 73: 3584–3588.

Schofield, R. 1978. The relationship between the spleen colony-forming cell and the haemopoietic stem cells. *Blood Cells* 4: 7–25.

Siminovitch, L., Till, J. E., and McCulloch, E. A. 1964. Decline in colony-forming ability of marrow cells subjected to serial transplantation into irradiated mice. *J. Cell. Comp. Physiol.* 64: 23–32.

Talbert, F. 1977. Aging of the female reproductive system. *In*, C. E. Finch and L. Hayflick (eds.), *Handbook of the Biology of Aging*, pp. 318–356. New York: Van Nostrand Reinhold.

Talbert, G. and Krohn, P. 1966. Effect of maternal age on viability of ova and uterine support of pregnancy in mice. *J. Reprod. Fert.* 11: 399–400.

Till, J. E. and McCulloch, E. A. 1961. A direct measurement of the radiation sensitivity of normal mouse bone marrow cells. *Rad. Res.* 14: 213–222.

Till, J. E., McCulloch, A., and Siminovitch, L. 1964. A stochastic model of stem cell proliferation, based on the growth of spleen colony-forming cells. *Proc. Nat. Acad. Sci.* 51: 29–36.

Trentin, J. J. 1971. Determination of bone marrow stem cell differentiation by stromal hemopoietic inductive microenvironments (HIM). *Am. J. Pathol.* 65: 621–628.

Trentin, J., Wolf, J., Cheng, V., Fahlberg, W., Weiss, D., and Bonhag R. 1967. Antibody production by mice repopulated with limited numbers of clones of lymphoid cell precursors. *J. Immunol.* 98: 1326–1337.

Tyan, M. L. 1977. Age-related decrease in mouse T-cell progenitors. *J. Immunol.* 118: 846–851.

Tyan, M. L. 1979. Development of immune competence. *Mech. Age. Dev.* 9, 79–86.

Tyan, M. L. 1980. Marrow colony-forming units: age-related changes in responses to anti-θ-sensitive helper/suppressor stimuli. *Proc. Soc. Exp. Biol. Med.* 165: 354–360.

Tyan, M. L. 1982a. Effect of age on the intrinsic regulation of murine hemopoiesis. *Mech. Age. Dev.* 19: 15–20.

Tyan, M. L. 1982b. Old mice: marrow response to endotoxin or bleeding. *Proc. Soc. Exp. Biol. Med.* 169: 295–300.

Tyan, M. L. and Cole, L. J. 1965. Bone marrow as the major source of potential immunologically competent cells in the adult mouse. *Nature* 208: 1223–1224.

Van Bekkum, D. W. and Weyzen, W. W. H. 1961. Serial transfer of isologous and homologous hematopoietic cells in irradiated hosts. *Pathol. Biol.* 9: 888–893.

Van Bezooijen, K. F. A., deLeeuw-Israel, F. R., and Hollander, C. F. 1974. Long-term functional aspects of syngeneic orthotopic rat kidney grafts of different ages. *J. Gerontol.* 29: 11–19.

Vos, O. and Dolmans, M. J. A. S. 1972. Self-renewal of colony forming units (CFU) in serial bone marrow transplantation experiments. *Cell Tissue Kinet.* 5: 371–385.

Walford, R. L. 1969. *The Immunological Theory of Aging*, pp. 21–76. Baltimore: Williams and Wilkins.

Walford, R. L. 1974. Immunological theory of aging: current status. *Fed. Proc.* 33: 2020–2027.

Weaver, R. F. and Weissmann, C. 1979. Mapping of RNA by a modification of Berk-Sharp procedure: the 5′ termini of 15S β-globin mRNA precursor and mature 10S β-globin mRNA have identical map coordinates. *Nucl. Acids Res.* 7: 1175–1193.

Weksler, M. 1982. A search for immunological markers of aging in man. *In,* M. E. Reff and E. L. Schneider (eds.), *Biological Markers of Aging*. Washington, D.C.: National Institute of Health Pub. no. 82-2221.

Whiteley, H. J. and Horton, D. L. 1962. The effect of age on the hair regrowth cycle in the CBA mouse. *J. Gerontol.* 17: 272–275.

Wigzell, H. and Stjernsward, J. 1966. Age-dependent rise and fall of immunological reactivity in the CBA mouse. *J. Natl. Cancer Inst.* 37: 513–517.

Williamson, A. R. and Askonas, B. A. 1972. Senescence of an antibody-forming cell clone. *Nature* 238: 337–339.

Wolf, N. and Arora, R. K. 1982. Senescence in the hemopoietic system: I. Self-replication by stromal cells related to chronologic age. *Mech. Age. Dev.* (20: 127–140.

Worton, R. G., McCulloch, E. A., and Till, J. E. 1969. Physical separation of hemopoietic stem cells differing in their capacity for self-renewal. *J. Exp. Med.* 130: 91–103.

Wu, A. M., Till, J. E., Siminovitch, L., and McCulloch, E. A. 1967. A cytological study of the capacity for differentiation of normal hemopoietic colony-forming cells. *J. Cell Physiol.* 69: 177–184.

Wu, A. M., Till, J. E., Siminovitch, L., and McCulloch, E. A. 1968. Cytological evidence for a relationship between normal hematopoietic colony-forming cells and cells of the lymphoid system. *J. Exp. Med.* 127: 455–463.

Young, L. J. T., Medina, D., De Ome, K. B., and Daniel, C. W. 1971. The influence of host and tissue age on life span and growth rate of serially transplanted mouse mammary gland. *Exp. Gerontol.* 6: 49–56.

Yunis, E. J. and Greenberg, L. J. 1974. Immunopathology of aging. *Fed. Proc.* 33: 2017–2019.

Zeilmaker, G. H. 1969. Effects of prolonged feeding of an ovulation inhibitor (Lyndiol) on ageing of the hypothalamic-ovarian axis and pituitary gland tumorigenesis in rats. *J. Endocrinol.* 43: 21–22.

14
CYTOGENETICS OF AGING

Edward L. Schneider, M.D.
National Institute on Aging
National Institutes of Health

INTRODUCTION

We are currently witnessing unforeseen advancements in molecular genetics related to the development of gene cloning technology. In the last two decades, less dramatic but nevertheless extremely important advances in our knowledge of cytogenetics were made possible by the development of new cytogenetic techniques.

It was not until the late 1950s that the human chromosomal number was accurately determined to be 46, rather than the 48 that had been estimated previously (Tijo and Levan, 1956). The accurate counting of chromosomes permitted the discrimination of disorders which display alterations in chromosome number, or aneuploidy. Perhaps the most common aneuploid condition is Down's syndrome, in which all the cells contain an extra chromosome 21 (Lejeune et al., 1959). Individuals with this syndrome display some features of premature aging, which suggests that gene dosage may play a role in aging processes (Martin, 1978).

The advent of specialized chromosomal staining techniques in the early 1970s finally permitted identification of each of the 23 human chromosomal pairs (22 autosomal and the two sex chromosomes) (Figure 1). Further refinements in these staining patterns permit the identification of specific bands within chromosomes and the detection of chromosomal deletions, inversions, and translocations. With somatic cell genetic techniques, and more recently with genetic cloning techniques, many human genes have been assigned to specific chromosomal bands.

Most recently, the BrdU (bromodeoxyuridine, a thymidine analogue) staining techniques differentially stain chromatids within metaphase chromosomes that replicate in the presence of BrdU (Schneider et al., 1978). This permits the detection of sister chromatid exchanges, which are sensitive indicators of cellular response to DNA damage.

In this chapter, we will examine the effect of aging on chromosomal number, chromosomal alterations, and sister chromatid exchanges. In addition, we will explore the relationship between these changes and age-related diseases such as Alzheimer disease and cancer.

CHROMOSOMAL NUMBER

Lymphocyte Studies

Most human cells contain the modal 46 chromosome complement. However, in those dividing human cell populations where analysis of metaphase chromosomes is possible, a small number of cells are found to be aneuploid (contain more or less than 46 chromosomes).

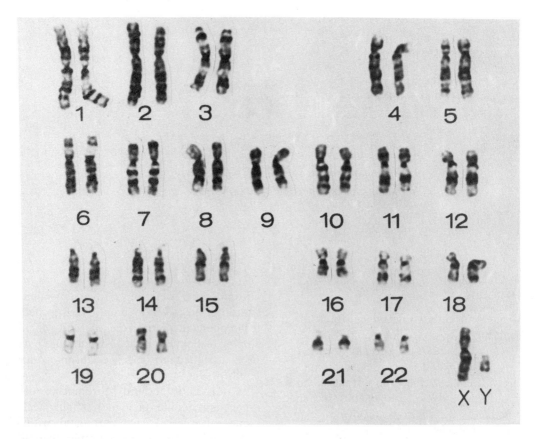

Figure 1. Human male karyotype prepared by Trypsin-Giemsa treatment to obtain chromosomal banding. With this technique, each chromosomal pair can be identified by its characteristic banding patterns. Note that the male possesses 22 pairs of autosomal chromosomes plus X and Y sex chromosomes. (Karyotype courtesy of Helen Lawce, San Francisco, California.)

Most examinations of the effect of aging on chromosomal number have involved cultured human peripheral lymphocytes because these cells (1) are easily accessible through venipuncture, (2) can be stimulated to divide by the addition of mitogens such as phytohemagglutinin, and (3) yield large numbers of metaphase cells after the addition of mitotic inhibitors.

The initial investigation of the effect of aging on human chromosomal number was performed by Dr. Patricia Jacobs and her colleagues in 1961 (Jacobs et al., 1961). These investigators found a significant increase in the number of peripheral blood lymphocytes that were hypodiploid (<46 chromosomes) and hyperdiploid (>46 chro-

mosomes) as a function of donor age. Hypodiploidy was more prominent than hyperdiploidy, with the frequency of hypodiploid cells increasing from 3 percent in the age range 5–14 years to 9 percent in the group 65 years and older (Jacobs et al., 1961). In a subsequent study, the effect of gender on hypodiploidy was found to increase with aging in male as well as female cells (Jacobs et al., 1963), and the missing chromosomes were identified as belonging to the chromosomal groups which contained the sex chromosomes.

Since these initial reports, a number of other laboratories have studied the effect of aging on chromosomal number (Hamerton et al., 1965; Sandberg et al., 1967; Bloom et al., 1967; Nielsen et al., 1970; Goodman et al., 1969; Jarvik and Kato, 1969; Neurath et al., 1970; Jarvik and Kato, 1970; Nielsen, 1970; Cadotte and Fraser, 1970; Kadontani et al., 1971; Demoise and Conrad, 1972; Mattevi and Salzano, 1975; Deknutt and Leonard, 1977; Galloway and Buckton, 1978; Martin et al., 1980). Fifteen studies are summarized in Table 1. The most consistent finding has been an increase in hypodiploidy in female cells with aging. In the hypodiploid cells of females, the most frequently lost chromosome was the C group which includes the X chromosome. The majority of cells from males yielded no significant increase in either hypo- or hyperdiploidy with aging.

The initial studies by Jacobs sampled a mixture of volunteers, hospitalized patients, and parents of patients with chromosomal disorders (Jacobs et al., 1961, 1963). To examine if age-related aneuploidy is present in a more random population, Jacobs and Court Brown (1966) as well as others performed population studies (Hamerton et al., 1965; Sandberg, et al., 1967; Bloom et al., 1967; Demoise and Conrad, 1972). In three of the four population studies, a significant increase in hypodiploidy was observed in female cells as a function of aging. The advent of the chromosomal banding techniques permitted the determination that the missing chromosome in most of the hypodiploid female cells was the X chromosome (Martin et al., 1980; Fitzgerald et al., 1975).

Since the studies described were cross-sectional in nature, several questions could be raised. (1) Is the observed aneuploidy in the older population due to the selective survival of those subjects with increased frequencies of aneuploidy? (2) Are we observing the effect of certain chemicals or drugs that were prevalent 40–70 years ago, which induced alterations in chromosome number and are not currently in use? (3) Is the increase in aneuploidy a gradual process, or does it accelerate in the last decades of life? These questions can best be addressed with longitudinal studies. However, continuing improvements in cytogenetic techniques make longitudinal studies difficult to per-

form and to analyze. Jarvik and colleagues (Jarvik et al., 1976) performed a brief longitudinal study on 11 female and 6 male subjects over a six-year period and found a significant increase in hypodiploidy and hyperdiploidy in female cells over this brief time period, with the missing chromosome belonging to the C group which includes the X chromosome.

In Vivo Bone Marrow Studies

Extrapolation of *in vitro* studies to the *in vivo* situation is often misleading. It is imperative to conduct *in vivo* studies to confirm *in vitro* observations. Unfortunately, direct examination of chromosomes *in vivo* has been extremely difficult. Cadotte and Fraser (1970) were the first to directly examine the chromosome complement of bone marrow cells as a function of aging; although they found increased aneuploidy in cultured peripheral lymphocyte cultures, their direct analysis of bone marrow cells did not reveal any significant increase in aneuploidy as a function of aging. In contrast to these studies, Pierre and Hoagland (1971), in an extensive survey of males, found a markedly increased frequency of older males possessing 45,XO cell lines in their bone marrow. In a subsequent study of females by these authors (Pierre and Hoagland, 1972), no loss of X chromosomes was found with increasing age. While the frequency of males with cells missing Y chromosomes increased with aging in their study, no correlation was observed between the degree of chromosome loss per individual and the age of the donor.

It is unlikely that population studies of bone marrow cells will be conducted, since the procedure employed to obtain marrow cells is much more complicated than the venipuncture employed to obtain blood samples. Of necessity, these studies involve subjects being screened for hematological or malignant conditions, or relatives of such subjects. Thus, conclusions based on these studies must be limited. Caution should also be exercised in interpreting the chromosome aneuploidy found in cultured peripheral

TABLE 1. Summary of Several Studies of the Frequency of Aneuploidy as a Function of Aging.[a]

Study	FEMALES[b]			MALES[b]		
	Hypodiploidy	Hyperdiploidy	C + X Group Lost	Hypodiploidy	Hyperdiploidy	G + Y Group Lost
Hamerton et al. (1965)	+	+	+	+	−	−
Sandberg et al. (1967)	+	−	NE	−	−	NE
Bloom et al. (1967)	−	−	−	−	−	+
Nielsen (1968)	+	−	+	NE	NE	NE
Goodman et al. (1969)	+	−	+	NE	NE	NE
Jarvik and Kato (1969)	+	−	NE	−	−	NE
Neurath et al. (1970)	−		−	−	−	+
Jarvik and Kato (1970)	+	−	−	−	−	+
Nielsen (1970)	+	+	+	−	−	−
Cadotte and Fraser (1970)	+	−		+	−	−
Kadontani et al. (1971)	−	−	NE	−	−	NE
Demoise and Conard (1972)	+	−	+	−	−	+
Mattevi and Salzano (1975)	+	+	+	+	−	+

[a]Following the initial studies by P. A. Jacobs et al. (1961, 1963).
[b]NE = not examined.

blood lymphocytes, until this observation can be confirmed in other cell populations *in vivo*.

Mechanisms for the Observed Hypodiploidy with Aging

There are two alternative explanations for the observed selective loss of specific chromosomes in peripheral lymphocytes with aging. (1) Loss of chromosomes is essentially random, and only those cells that have lost chromosomes that are not essential for survival remain to be examined. (2) A selective loss of specific chromosomes occurs.

Diploid cells appear to have a definitive selective advantage over aneuploid cells. In studies of human cell lines derived from patients with chromosome disorders, aneuploid cell lines had decreased replicative abilities and shortened *in vitro* life spans in comparison with diploid cell cultures (Boue et al., 1975; Schneider and Epstein, 1972). Further support for the concept of a selective disadvantage for aneuploid cells comes from the studies of cell cultures that were mosaic for diploid and aneuploid cells (Bloom et al., 1974). However, there were occasional cases where the selection appeared to be towards the aneuploid cell component of the mosaic (Bloom et al., 1974). At the level of the whole organism, selection against aneuploidy was demonstrated by Boué and Boué (1974), who found extremely high prenatal mortality for aneuploid fetuses.

Selection against aneuploid cell lines may be due to a variety of mechanisms. While trisomies for an extra dose of a chromosome may be relatively well tolerated, monosomies, with one important exception, are highly lethal (Boué and Boué, 1974). In humans, trisomies for chromosomes 13, 18, and 21 are relatively common. However, the only monosomy that is commonly observed is for the XO genotype. The phenomenon of X chromosome inactivation is probably responsible for the survival of these monosomic X (XO) infants.

The phenomenon of inactivation of one of the two X chromosomes in the female was first proposed by Lyon (1961) to explain her observations on the behavior of X-linked genes in the mouse. Subsequently, it has been demonstrated in a wide number of species, including man, that early in fetal development, one X chromosome is inactivated. Inactivation of the X chromosome appears to be random, resulting in half the cells in any tissue containing one active X while the remainder contain the other X as the active chromosome. By this mechanism, all females are chromosomal mosaics, and each of their cells contains only 45 active chromosomes. In effect, this process equalizes the amount of active genetic information in the male and female, since the Y chromosome in the male contains very little genetic information. The inactivation of one X chromosome in the female and the relative lack of genetic information on the Y chromosome could explain the survival of cells lacking these chromosomes in the face of selection against aneuploid cells. However, there is little evidence to indicate that the inactive X rather than the active X is lost in female cells. Autoradiographic studies of the chromosomes involved in the premature centromeric division reported by Fitzgerald and coworkers (1975) would suggest that the inactive X is more likely to be lost, but that conclusion was based on only three informative metaphases.

The sex chromosomes, X and Y, have other properties that might predispose them to selective loss. The X and Y chromosomes replicate later in the S phase of the cell cycle than any other chromosomes (Gilbert et al., 1965; Latt, 1973; Takagi and Sandberg, 1968). Since the G_2 period would be short in rapidly replicating cells, the late DNA replication of the X and Y chromosomes might lead to an increased frequency of missegregation of these chromosomes during mitosis.

The peripheral mitotic location of the X and Y chromosomes has also been suggested to contribute to the increased loss of the sex chromosomes. Increased fragility of cells from older persons coupled with this peripheral location might produce selective loss of X and Y chromosomes. A most intriguing finding was that the X chromosome has an increased frequency of premature centromeric division (Fitzgerald et al., 1975). Daughter cells of a cell that had premature centromeric division of an X chromosome would either lack an X chromosome or contain acentric X chromosome fragments. Fitzgerald and colleagues (Fitzgerald et al., 1975) demonstrated that with increasing age, normal females had a marked increase in cells containing these acentric fragments, as well as a specific loss of the X chromosome. The acentric fragments and the absent chromosomes in these cells were identified by the G banding technique as well as by autoradiography. This latter technique involves pulse labeling of cells with tritiated thymidine late in the S phase. Since the X is a late-replicating chromosome, it is heavily labeled and can easily be recognized by autoradiography. When the frequency of acentric fragments was examined in blood cultures derived from males, few premature centromeric divisions were observed (Fitzgerald et al., 1975).

The effect of aging on the selective loss of specific chromosomes could occur through two mechanisms: (1) increased production of aneuploidy with age, with the selection rate against aneuploid cells being unaltered; and (2) a constant rate of the production of aneuploid cells, but with a decreased selection against aneuploid cells with aging. It is difficult to distinguish between these two possibilities, since most experimental data relate to the final product of both production of aneuploidy and selection. The observed increase in aneuploidy for specific chromosomes as a function of aging supports the first mechanism.

In regard to the second mechanism, alterations in chromosomal number have important effects on gene expression. Aneuploidy can also result in altered membrane structure, which could lead the immune system to recognize aneuploid cells as foreign. Much evidence shows functional impairment of the human immune system with increasing age (Weksler and Siskind, 1976). Since immune surveillance is an important function of the immune system, aging could lead to diminished elimination of these "foreign" aneuploid cells. Unfortunately, experimental evidence for decreased removal of aneuploid cells with aging is lacking. However, Fialkow et al. (1973) demonstrated that mice with impaired immune systems have an increased frequency of aneuploid cells.

Studies of Cultured Human Fetal Lung Fibroblasts at Different Levels Of *In Vitro* Passage ("*In Vitro*" Aging)

In their original report of the limited *in vitro* life span of human fetal lung fibroblasts, Hayflick and Moorehead (1961) examined the chromosome complement of a number of fetal lung fibroblast cultures and found low levels of aneuploidy and tetraploidy. In one fetal lung fibroblast culture examined at different levels of *in vitro* passage, no significant alterations in chromosomal number were observed as a function of "*in vitro*" aging. In a more comprehensive study of two fetal lung fibroblast cultures (WI-26 and WI-38), significantly increased hypodiploidy as well as tetraploidy was observed at late passage when these cell cultures were in the senescent phase of their *in vitro* life span (Saksela and Moorehead, 1963).

Subsequent investigations of the frequency of chromosomal aneuploidy as a function of *in vitro* passage gave conflicting results. Kadanka et al. (1973) found tetraploidy without aneuploidy, while Thompson and Holliday (1975) and Benn (1976) both confirmed Saksela and Moorehead's observation of increased hypodiploidy and tetraploidy with increasing *in vitro* passage. Unfortunately, no attempt was made in these studies to identify the missing chromosomes in hypodiploidy cells.

CHROMOSOMAL ABERRATIONS

Chromosomal aberrations as a manifestation of DNA damage and repair with aging are examined in depth in Chapter 8 and will be discussed only briefly here. The initial studies of the effect of aging on chromosomal aberrations were conducted by Curtis and his coworkers in metaphase liver cells from animals recovering from either chemical or surgical hepatectomy (Stevenson and Curtis, 1961; Crowley and Curtis, 1963; Curtis et al., 1968; Curtis and Miller, 1971). This tissue was chosen because it is normally nondividing and thus might demonstrate lesions accumulated as a function of time. Studies in a variety of experimental animals, including mice, dogs, guinea pigs, and Chinese hamsters, revealed statistically significant increases in chromosomal aberrations with aging (Stevenson and Curtis, 1961; Crowley and Curtis, 1963; Curtis et al., 1968; Curtis and Miller, 1971). The majority of these studies also revealed that this age-dependent increase in chromosomal aberrations was proportional to the life span of the organism.

In other in vivo cell populations, the frequencies of chromosomal aberrations did not indicate a consistent pattern with aging. In quiescent cells such as human peripheral lymphoctyes and in continuously replicating cells such as bone marrow cells, studies have indicated either age-related increases in chromosomal aberrations or no change (Liniecki et al., 1971; Kadontani et al., 1971; Brooks et al., 1973; Bochkov, 1972; Ivanov et al., 1978).

Finally, with increasing in vitro passage ("in vitro cellular aging"), there appears to be an increase in chromosomal aberration frequencies (Thompson and Holliday, 1973); The most prominent aberration is the formation of dicentrics, chromosomes that contain two centromeres instead of the normal one.

SISTER CHROMATID EXCHANGE

A schema for the mechanisms for the detection of sister chromatid exchanges (SCE) is presented in Figure 2. After two replication cycles in the presence of BrdU, metaphase chromosomes contain two chromatids with different staining properties. Thus, exchanges between sister chromatids can be easily detected in these cells. These cytogenetic events appear to be an accurate reflection of cellular response to DNA damage. Studies of SCE have focused on background or spontaneous levels of SCE as well as on

levels on SCE induced by mutagens and carcinogens.

Measurements of spontaneous SCE levels are difficult since the agents utilized for their detection, BrdU and tritiated thymidine, are known inducers of SCE (Taylor, 1958; Stetka and Carrano, 1977). However, spontaneous SCE levels can be estimated by examining background levels of SCE at various concentrations of BrdU and extrapolating to 0 BrdU concentration (Tice et al., 1976; Kram et al., 1979).

Effect of In Vitro Passage on Background SCE Levels in Cultured Human Fetal Lung Fibroblasts

Kato and Stich (1976) found a small increase in background levels of SCE at a single concentration of 0.25 mg/ml BrdU as a function of the serial passage of cultured human fetal lung fibroblast strain He-1. Utilizing another human fetal lung strain, IMR-90, and employing a wide range of BrdU concentrations, we also noted a slight trend toward increased spontaneous SCE levels in last passage cells; however, these differences were not statistically significant (Schneider and Bickings, 1980). There are two factors which might bear on this apparent disagreement between these two laboratories. Kato and Stich (1976) utilized a different cell strain, which might have different characteristics from the IMR-90 strain used in our studies (Schneider and Bickings, 1980). In addition, only one concentration of BrdU was utilized for their SCE determinations. Slight alterations in BrdU concentrations per cell number at this concentration of BrdU could seriously affect determinations of SCE frequencies (Stetka and Carrano, 1977).

Effect of Donor Age on Background SCE Levels in Cultured Human Skin Fibroblasts and Peripheral Lymphocytes

Another approach to investigating aging cell populations in vitro is to examine cell cultures derived from young and old human subjects. These cell cultures were derived from skin biopsies obtained from the mem-

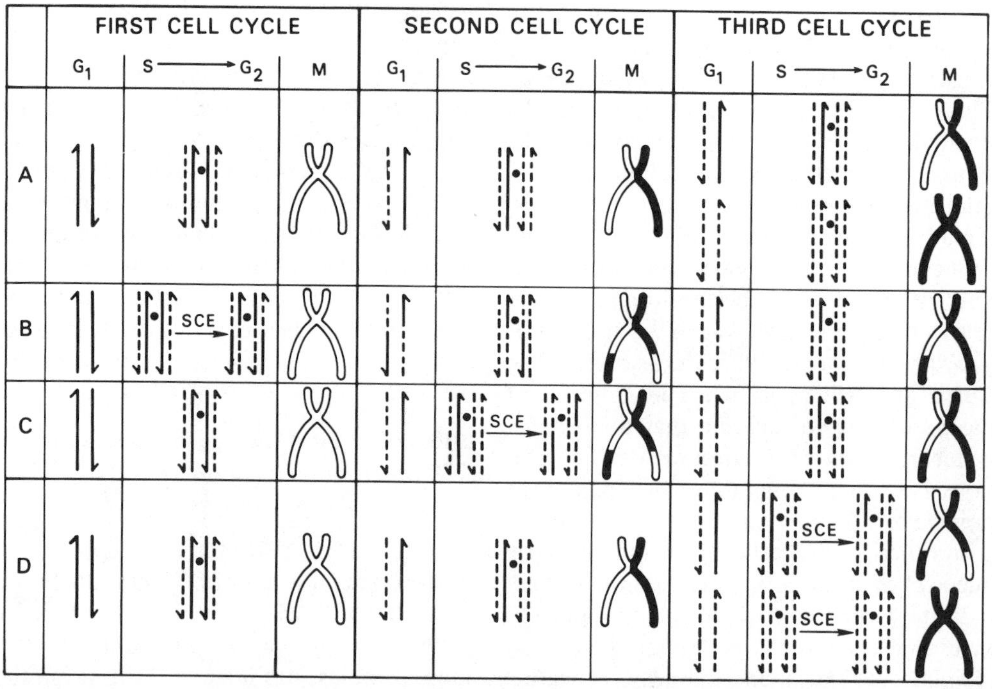

Figure 2. Schema for detection of sister chromatid exchanges in BrdU substituted chromosomes. Progression of cells through three division cycles in the presence of BrdU based on the unineme model of eukaryote chromosome structure. a-d, Appearance of chromosomes during three division cycles with (a) no SCE occurring, (b) SCE occurring in the first division cycle, (c) SCE occurring in the second division cycle, (d) SCE occurring in the third division cycle; ——————, thymidine-bearing ————————, BrdU-bearing DNA strand. Direction of arrow indicates polarity of chromatid subunits. Black chromosomal regions indicate regions which fluoresce less intensely with acridine orange. White chromosomal regions indicate regions which fluoresce more intensely with acridine orange.

bers of the Baltimore Longitudinal Study (Schneider and Mitsui, 1976).

At a single concentration of BrdU, no differences in background SCE were observed between skin fibroblast cultures derived from young and old individuals (Schneider and Gilman, 1979).

Studies of background SCE levels as a function of donor age in cultured peripheral lymphocytes gave diverse findings. Goh (1981) found slight, but significant, increased background SCE frequencies in old donors (66–88 years) when compared to his "young" (24–65 years) group. De Arce (1981) found increased background SCE levels in a group 30–40 years old when compared with a younger (0–10 years) and an older (60–70) group. Our studies of peripheral human lymphocyte cultures (Tice et al.,

unpublished results) and those of Cohen et al. (1982) found no effect of donor age on background SCE levels. All these studies were performed at only one BrdU concentration, and the range of SCE values between subjects was considerably larger than the observed age-related alterations.

Effect of *In Vivo* Aging on Background SCE Levels

Determinations of spontaneous or background SCE levels *in vitro* can be seriously affected by the tissue culture environment. Ikushima and Wolff (1974) demonstrated that brief exposures of BrdU-substituted DNA to light results in the induction of SCE. Also, components of the culture media can be activated by the fluorescent lights found in many laboratories to induce SCE (Monticone and Schneider, 1979). *In vivo* studies of SCE are, therefore, more informative since they provide an environment that simulates the natural environment of cells with minimum light exposure. In our *in vivo* studies, we have infused young and old mice and rats with increasing concentrations of BrdU, removed bone marrow cells after 26 hours of infusion, and examined the frequencies of SCE in second replication cycle metaphase cells. At the lowest BrdU concentrations where detection of SCE is accurate, background SCE frequencies in both young and old mouse and rat bone marrow cells were between 2.0 and 3.0 SCE per cell with no consistent differences observed between

young and old cell populations (Schneider et al., 1982).

The Effect of *In Vitro* Passage on Induced SCE

The effect of "*in vitro* cellular aging" on the induction of SCE was examined by exposing early, middle, and late passage IMR-90 fetal lung fibroblasts to increasing concentrations of mitomycin C (Schneider and Monticone, 1978). Our results (Figure 3) reveal a decline in SCE induction in late passage cultures when compared with early passage cells. This decline in mutagen-induced SCE was also observed with two other mutagens, ethyl methanesulfonate (EMS) and N-acetoxy-2-

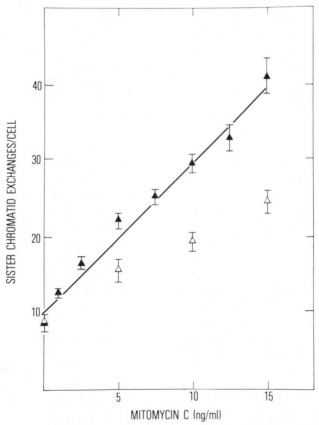

Figure 3. The frequency of sister chromatid exchanges per cell as a function of mitomycin C concentration in IMR-90 cells at early (▲, 22 PD) and late (△, 48 PD) *in vitro* passage. Values in Figures 3 through 5 represent the mean of SCE measurements of 20 second replication cycle metaphase cells; bars are the standard error of the mean. Regression line was derived by the method of least squares for values from early passage cells. From (Schneider and Monticone, 1978.)

acetylaminofluorene (AAAF). A similar decline in mutagen-induced SCE frequencies was also found in WI-38 fetal lung fibroblasts as a function of *in vitro* passage (Schneider and Monticone, 1978). Since late passage cells replicate more slowly and have lower saturation densities, we examined the effect of both cell replication rate and saturation density on SCE induction in early passage cultures and found that these factors did not affect SCE induction (Schneider and Monticone, 1978).

The Effect of the Age of the Cell Culture Donor on Induced SCE

At equal levels of early passage (before passage 10), skin fibroblast cultures from young and old human donors were examined for mitomycin C induced sister chromatid exchanges. A decline in mitomycin C induced sister chromatid exchange induction was observed in cell cultures from old donors when compared with parallel cultures obtained from young individuals (Schneider and Gilman, 1979). However, the differences between young and old donor cell cultures were not as large as those observed between early and late passage fetal lung fibroblasts. In addition, overlap was observed between individual young and old cultures in induced SCE frequencies at specific mitomycin C (MMC) concentrations. To reveal differences between young and old cell cultures, it was necessary to examine multiple young and old cell cultures at a single concentration of mitomycin C (Table 2). An age-related decline was also observed for N-acetoxy-2-acetylaminofluorene induced SCE in human skin fibroblast cultures, demonstrating that these results were not limited to mitomycin C (Table 2) (Schneider and Gilman, 1979).

The Effect of Aging on *In Vivo* Induced SCE

The *in vivo* perfusion techniques that permit continuous administration of BrdU for SCE detection also permit the administration of controlled amounts of mutagens (Schneider

TABLE 2. Mitomycin C and N-Acetoxy-2-Acetylaminofluorene (AAAF) Induced SCE in Young and Old Donor Skin Fibroblast Cultures.

Mutagen (concentration)	Young (20–33)	Old (65–80)
Mitomycin-C (7.5 ng/ml)	67.9 ± 1.4[a]	56.1 ± 1.4
AAAF (1.25 g/ml)	24.9 ± 1.7	18.6 ± 1.3

[a]Mean ± standard error of the mean of SCE determinations on 20 metaphase cells exposed to mutagens (from Schneider and Gilman, 1979).

et al., 1978). The induction of SCE by various concentrations of mitomycin C in young and old mouse and rat bone marrow metaphase cells is presented in Figure 4 (Kram et al., 1978).

SCE induction by MMC is linear in cell populations from young rodents (Kram et al., 1978). While no significant differences in SCE induction are noted at low concentrations of MMC, significant declines in SCE induction are observed in cells from old rodents at high MMC concentrations (Kram et al., 1978). Similar declines in SCE induction are found in cells from old rodents exposed to high concentrations of two other mutagens, cyclophosphamide and adriamycin (Nakanishi et al., 1979).

A decline in MMC-induced SCE was also observed in another *in vivo* cell population, spleen cells, as a function of donor aging (Table 3) (Mann et al., 1981).

In addition to examining the effect of aging on SCE induction *in vivo,* we have also investigated the effect of postnatal development (Nakanishi et al., 1980). A gradual increase in SCE induction was observed from 6 weeks to 6 months of age with several mutagens. A composite of our findings with development and aging (Figure 5) demonstrates that SCE induction increases with development (1–6 months), plateaus during early adulthood (6–12 months), and then declines with aging (12+ months).

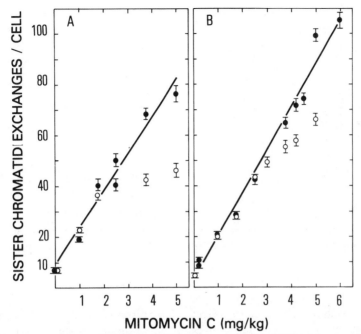

Figure 4. Induction of SCE by MMC in (A) Wistar rats and (B) C57B1/6J mice: ● = young, 6-month-old mice, 12-month-old rats; ○ = old, 24-month-old mice and rats. From (Kram et al., 1978.)

Investigations into the Contributions of Intrinsic Cellular Aging and the Old Environment to the Observed Decline in SCE Induction with Aging

The observed age-related decline in mutagen-induced SCE could be the result of an old environment, intrinsic aging of cells, or a combination of these factors. One approach to examining these possibilities is to investigate the effect of sera from humans of different ages on SCE induction. Preliminary results indicate significant differences in the induction of SCE in the indicator cell line Chinese hamster (CHO), depending upon the source of the human sera supplement (Bynum, unpublished results). The highest levels of induced SCE were found in the presence of newborn sera. There was a small decrease in SCE induction observed in cell cultures grown in the presence of sera from old human volunteers when compared with those grown with sera from young adults.

TABLE 3. Mitomycin C (MMC) Induced SCE Frequencies in Young and Old Mice.

MMC Concen-tration (mg/kg)	SCE/CELL			
	SPLEEN		BONE MARROW	
	Young	Old	Young	Old
0	6.7 ± 0.7[a]	6.8 ± 1.0	5.7 ± 0.9	5.4 ± 0.5
2.5	52.7 ± 2.0	46.1 ± 2.6	39.0 ± 3.2	44.1 ± 1.5
3.0	62.7 ± 3.2	55.7 ± 4.2	53.0 ± 1.7	53.5 ± 2.4
4.0	76.1 ± 3.6	66.8 ± 5.0	71.6 ± 2.1	60.3 ± 2.4
5.0	84.3 ± 5.3	62.6 ± 3.0	91.3 ± 4.3	61.6 ± 2.5

[a]Mean ± standard error of the mean of SCE frequencies for 15–20 second replication cells from at least three individual animals (from Mann et al., 1981).

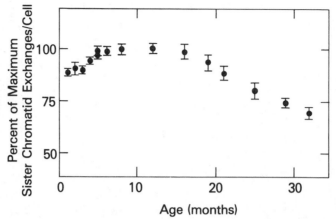

Figure 5. Percent of maximum SCE induction at one mutagen dosage as a function of aging in C57B1/6J mice. One hundred percent SCE induction occurred at age 6 to 12 months. (From Schneider and Hadley, 1982.)

Another approach to examining the effect of environment on SCE induction involves the injection of the same indicator cell line—Ehrlich ascites tumor cells—into young and old animals. These animals were then infused with BrdU and mitomycin C. While the bone marrow cells in these animals displayed the usual age-related decline in SCE induction, no significant change was noted in mitomycin C induction of SCE in the CHO cells in young and old environments (Schneider and Lewis, 1982).

The first experiment supports an environmental effect, while the second indicates that the environment may not be important. The definitive experiment, which remains to be performed, would be to examine SCE induction in young cells transplanted into old animals and in old cells transplanted into young animals.

The Mechanisms for the Diminished SCE Induction with Aging

Unfortunately, the mechanisms of SCE remain to be elucidated. If SCE reflect a yet to be defined type of cellular DNA repair, our results would suggest that this type of DNA repair is decreased with cellular aging. Since SCE are a sensitive indicator of DNA damage, we can state that this type of cel-lular response to DNA damage is affected by cellular aging. However, we must await the understanding of the mechanisms of DNA repair to be able to fully understand the effect of cellular aging on this cytogenetic event.

To examine if the observed decline in mutagen-induced SCE with aging has functional importance, we attempted to determine if a correlation exists between this decline and another well-documented, and apparently functionally important, finding—the decline in immune function (Weksler and Siskind, 1976). We, therefore, decided to compare the effect of mitomycin C on T cell response and SCE induction in young and old immune cell populations (Mann et al., 1981). Mitomycin C administered *in vivo* was found to inhibit *in vitro* mitogenic response of young and old spleen cells to phytohem-agglutinin (PHA), concanavilin A (con A), and lipopolysaccharide (LPS). At low concentrations of mitomycin C, inhibition of mitogenic response was similar in both young and old cell populations. However, at high mitomycin C concentrations, where differ-ences in SCE induction are found, a significantly increased inhibition of mitogenic response was observed in old spleen cells (Mann et al., 1981). Thus, it would appear that the age-related effect of mutagens, such as mitomycin C, on immune response parallels their effect on sister chromatid exchange induction.

CYTOGENETICS AND AGE-RELATED DISEASES

Many of the human genetic disorders which have been suggested to display features of accelerated aging have cytogenetic alterations. Down's syndrome, in which all the cells contain an additional chromosome 21, has been placed at the top of the list of disorders with the most signs and symptoms of accelerated aging (Martin, 1978). Turner's syndrome, in which all the affected individual's cells contain 45 chromosomes and only one sex chromosome, the X, is also high on this list (Martin, 1978). Human genetic diseases such as ataxia-telangiectasia, Werner's syndrome, and Fanconi's anemia, which feature cytogenetic instability as manifested by frequent chromosomal aberrations, have also been reported to have features resembling accelerated aging (Martin, 1978). Two disorders which are extremely common in the elderly, cancer and senile dementia, should be considered in more detail for their cytogenetic evaluation.

Cytogenetic Alterations with Senile Dementia

Nielsen and coworkers first examined the frequencies of chromosomal aneuploidy in peripheral blood cultures from patients with senile dementia and from young and old normal controls, and found that the age-related increase in aneuploidy seen in normal controls was accelerated in patients with senile dementia (Nielsen et al., 1968; Nielsen, 1970). The aneuploidy was chiefly hypodiploidy, and the most frequently lost chromosome was in the chromosomal group that included the X chromosome.

Other surveys confirmed this association (Ward et al., 1979). The degree of hypodiploidy was found in one study to correlate with specific tests of cognitive functioning, the Graham-Kendall Memory for Designs Test and the Stroop Color-Word Test (Jar-

vik et al., 1974). However, other reports did not find significant differences in hypodiploidy between patients with dementia and age-matched controls (Martin et al., 1981). Finally, there has been one report of increased acentric fragments, a type of chromosomal aberration, in patients with dementia of the Alzheimer type (Nordenson et al., 1980).

Examination of families of patients with Alzheimer disease, by Heston (1977), has also revealed an excessive incidence of relatives with trisomy 21 (Down's syndrome). One possible unifying hypothesis for the chromosomal and neurological abnormalities in Alzheimer disease is that this disorder involves alterations in microtubule formation and/or organization. Microtubules are crucial components of the mitotic spindle that plays the key role in chromosome separation at cell division. The paired helical filaments found in brains of patients with Alzheimer disease, however, probably are derived from intermediate filaments rather than from microtubular proteins (Anderton et al., 1982; Dahl et al., 1982).

Studies of chromosomal alterations in senile dementia must be interpreted with caution since this diagnosis includes many different disorders (Cohen, 1976). In addition, even in senile dementia of the Alzheimer type, definitive premortem diagnosis is difficult.

Cytogenetic Alterations, Malignancy, and Aging

Since the original observations by Boveri (1914), increasing evidence has accumulated demonstrating that alterations in chromosomal number and structure accompany the malignant process. The new high resolution chromosomal banding techniques have revealed that the majority of human tumors contain chromosomal alterations (Yunis, 1983). In many of these tumor cells, the chromosomal rearrangements involve chromosomal regions which contain cellular proto-oncogenes (Duesberg, 1983). The human genetic disorders which feature chromosomal instability or aneuploidy also manifest elevated incidences of cancers. Furthermore, many of the manipulations that produce transformation of a cell to the malignant phenotype also result in chromosomal alterations (Makino et al., 1964).

Many of the human genetic disorders which have features resembling accelerated aging also display chromosomal alterations and increased susceptibilities to cancers (Martin, 1978). These include Down's syndrome, Turner's syndrome, Fanconi's anemia, ataxia-telangiectasia, and Werner's syndrome. The chromosomal alterations in Werner's syndrome were recently reviewed (Salk, 1983).

The relationship between aging and cancer is also obvious on a clinical level where half of all cancers occur over age 65. There are two distinct possibilities to explain this relationship: (1) that this relationship is merely due to the long latent period for the transformation process, or (2) that aging processes may provide the mechanisms for transformation. In the latter case, the increase in aneuploidy with aging, if it occurred *in vivo,* could be related to malignant transformation. Alternatively, a decline in immune function with aging could lead to a decline in the selection process against aneuploid malignant cells.

CONCLUSIONS

Cytogenetic alterations with aging vary from the relative consistency of decreased mutagen-induced sister chromatid exchanges seen *in vitro* in human cells and *in vivo* in rodent cell populations, through the increased hypodiploidy observed in the majority of studies of female peripheral lymphocytes, to the inconsistent results of surveys of chromosomal aberration frequencies. This may reflect the technical difficulties inherent in the last two types of studies. Determinations of chromosomal aberrations depend on the quality of the cytogenetic preparations. Similarly, hypotonic swelling, which is necessary for chromosomal analysis, can result in the breakage of cells with the loss of chromo-

somes. Both aneuploidy and aberrations are unusual events, occurring in less than 5 percent of cells. By contrast, sister chromatid exchanges, particularly induced SCE, occur at sufficient frequencies that only a small number of cells need to be analyzed to obtain significant results.

One of the major limitations of the cytogenetic studies of chromosomal number described in this chapter involves the large number of metaphase cells that have to be analyzed. One of the promising approaches for large scale chromosomal analysis is flow microfluorometry (Gray et al., 1975), which has the capability of analyzing as many as 100,000 chromosomes per minute.

Another problem is the inability to conduct human cytogenetic studies *in vivo*. The practical as well as ethical limitations of human experimentation make this task extremely difficult, since bone marrow biopsy is not a routine procedure. However, it is possible that population studies of families at risk for hematopoietic cancers might yield interesting information on cytogenetic alterations with aging.

Prospective, longitudinal cytogenetic studies would be of great interest to determine if cytogenetic alterations such as chromosomal aneuploidy or sister chromatid exchanges have functional importance. Will individuals with high levels of aneuploidy or reduced inductions of SCE have increased risks of developing malignancies, immune deficiency, or other conditions which shorten life span?

REFERENCES

Anderton, B. H., Brienburg, D., Downes, M. J., Green, P. J., Tomlinson, B. E., Ulrich, J., Word, J. N., and Kahn, J. 1982. Monoclonal antibodies show that neurofibrillary tangles and neurofilaments share antigenic determinants. *Nature,* 298: 84–85.

Benn, P. A. 1976. Specific chromosome aberrations in senescent fibroblast cell lines derived from human embryos. *Am. J. Human Genetics* 28: 465–473.

Bloom, A. D., Archer, P. G., and Awa, A. A. 1967. Variation in the human chromosome number. *Nature* (London) 216: 487.

Bloom, A. D., McNeill, J. A., and Nakamura, F. T. 1974. Cytogenetics of lymphocyte cell lines. *In,* J.

German (ed.), *Chromosomes and Cancer,* pp. 111–112. New York: John Wiley & Sons.

Bochkov, N. R. 1972. Spontaneous chromosome aberrations in human somatic cells. *Humangenetik* 16: 159.

Boue, A., Boue, J., Cure, S., Deluchat, C., and Perraudin, N. 1975. *In vitro* cultivation of cells from aneuploid human embryos, initiation of cell lines and longevity of the cultures. *In Vitro* 11: 409–413.

Boue, J. G. and Boue, A. 1974. Anomalies chromosomiques dans les avortements spontanes. *In,* A. Boue and C. Thibault (eds.), *Chromosomal Errors in Relation to Reproductive Failure,* pp. 29–56. Paris: INSERM.

Boveri, T. 1914. Zur Frage der Enstehung maligner Tumoren. Jena, Germany: Gustav Fisher.

Books, A. L., Mead, D. K., and Peters, R. F. 1973. Effect of aging on the frequency of metaphase chromosome aberrations in the liver of the Chinese hamster. *J. Geront.* 28: 452–454.

Cadotte, M. and Fraser, D. 1970. Etude de l'aneuploidie observee dans les cultures de sang et de moelle en foncion du nombre et de longeur des chromosomes de chaque groupe et de l'age et du sexe des sujets. *Union Med. Can.* 99: 2003–2007.

Cohen, D. 1976. A behavioral-chromosome relationship in the elderly: a critical review of a biobehavioral hypothesis. *Exp. Aging Res.* 2: 271–287.

Cohen, M. M., Martin, A. O., Ober, C., and Simpson, S. J. 1982. A family study of spontaneous sister chromatid exchange frequency. *Am. J. Human Genetics* 34: 294–306.

Crowley, C. and Curtis, H. J. 1963. The development of somatic mutations in mice with age. *Proc. Natl. Acad. Sci.* (USA) 49: 626.

Curtis, H. J., Leith, J., and Tilley, J. 1968. Chromosome aberrations in liver cells of dogs of different ages. *J. Geront.* 21: 268.

Curtis, H. J. and Miller, K. 1971. Chromosome aberrations in liver cells of guinea pigs. *J. Geront.* 26: 292–293.

Dahl, D., Selkoe, D. J., Pero, R. T., and Bignami, A. 1982. Immunostaining of neurofibrillary tangles in Alzheimer's senile dementia with a neurofilament antiserum. *J. Neurosci.* 2: 113–119.

de Arce, M. A. 1981. The effect of donor sex and age on the number of sister chromatid exchanges on human lymphocytes growing *in vitro. Human Genetics* 57: 83–85.

Deknudt, A. and Leonard, A. 1977. Aging and radiosensitivity of human somatic chromosomes. *Exp. Geront.* 12: 237–240.

Demoise, C. F. and Conrad, R. A. 1972. Effects of age and radiation exposure on chromosomes in a Marshall Island population. *J. Geront.* 27: 197–201.

Duesberg, P. H. 1983. Retroviral transforming genes in normal cells? *Nature* 304: 219–226.

Fialkow, P. J., Paton, G. R., and East J. 1973. Chromosomal abnormalities in spleens of NZB mice, a strain characterized by autoimmunity and malignancy. *Proc. Natl. Acad. Sci.* (USA) 70: 1094–1098.

Fitzgerald, P. H., Pickering, A. F., Mercer, J. M., and Miethke, P. M. 1975. Premature centromere division: a mechanism of non-disjunction causing X chromosome aneuploidy in somatic cells of man. *Ann. Human Genetics* 38: 417–428.

Galloway, S. M. and Buckton, K. E. 1978. Aneuploidy and aging: chromosome studies on a random sample of the population using G-banding. *Cytogenet. Cell. Genet.* 20: 78–95.

Gilbert, C. W., Muldal, S., and Lathua, L. G. 1965. Rate of chromosome duplication at the end of the DNA S period in human blood cells. *Nature (London)* 208: 159–161.

Goh, K. 1981. Sister chromatid exchange in the aging population. *J. Med.,* 12: 195–198.

Goodman, R. M., Fechheimer, N. S., Miller, F., Miller, R., and Zartman, D. 1969. Chromosomal alterations in three age groups of human females. *Am. J. Med. Sci.* 258: 26–34.

Gray, J. W., Carrano, A. V., Steinmetz, L. L., Van Dilla, M. A., Moore, D. H., Mayall, B. H., and Mendelsohn, M. L. 1975. Chromosome measurement and sorting by flow systems. *Proc. Natl. Acad. Sci.* (USA) 72: 1231–1234.

Hamerton, J. L., Taylor, A. I., Angell, R., and McGuire, V. M. 1965. Chromosome investigations of a small isolated human population: chromosome abnormalities and distribution of chromosome counts according to age and sex among the population of Tristan de Cunha. *Nature (London)* 206: 1232–1234.

Hayflick, L. and Moorhead, P. S. 1961. The serial cultivation of human diploid cell cultures. *Exptl. Cell Res.* 25: 585–621.

Heston, L. L. 1977. Alzheimer's disease, trisomy 21 and myeloproliferative disorders: associations suggesting a genetic diathesis. *Science,* 196: 322–323.

Ikushima, T. and Wolff, S. 1974. Sister chromatid exchanges induced by light flashes to 5-bromodeoxyuridine and 5-iododeoxyuridine substituted Chinese hamster chromosomes. *Exptl. Cell Res.* 87: 15–19.

Ivanov, B., Praskova, L., Mileva, M., Bulanova, M., and Georgieva, I. 1978. Spontaneous chromosomal aberration levels in human peripheral lymphocytes. *Mutation Res.* 52: 421–426.

Jacobs, P. A., and Court Brown, W. M. 1966. Age and chromosomes. *Nature (London)* 212: 823.

Jacobs, P. A., Court Brown, W. M., and Doll, R. 1961. Distribution of human chromosome counts in relation to age. *Nature (London)* 191: 1178–1180.

Jacobs, P. A., Brunton, M., Court Brown, W. M., Doll, R., and Goldstein, H. 1963. Change in human chromosome count distributions with age: evidence for a sex difference. *Nature (London)* 197: 1080–1081.

Jarvik, L. F. and Kato, T. 1969. Chromosomes and mental changes in octogenarians: preliminary findings. *Br. J. Psychol.* 115: 1193–1194.

Jarvik, L. F. and Kato, T. 1970. Chromosome examinations in aged twins. *Am. J. Hum. Genet.* 22: 562–573.

Jarvik, L. F., Yen, F. S., Fu, T. K., and Matsuyaman, S. S. 1976. Chromosomes in old age: a six year longitudinal study. *Hum. Genet.* 33: 17–22.

Jarvik, L. F., Yen, F. S., and Goldstein, F. 1974. Chromosomes and mental status. *Arch. Gen. Psychiat.* 30: 186–190.

Kadanka, Z. K., Sparkes, J. D., and MacMorine, H. G. 1973. A study of the cytogenetics of the human cell strain WI-38. *In Vitro* 8: 353–361.

Kadontani, T., Ohama, K., Nakayama, T., Takahara, H., and Makino, S. 1971. Chromosome aberrations in leukocytes of normal adults from 49 couples. *Proc. Jap. Acad.* 47: 724.

Kato, H. and Stich, H. F. 1976. Sister chromatid exchanges in ageing and repair-deficient human fibroblasts. *Nature (London)* 260: 447–448.

Kram, D., Schneider, E. L., Senula, G. C., and Nakanishi, Y. 1979. Spontaneous and mitomycin-C induced sister chromatid exchanges: comparison of *in vivo* and *in vitro* systems. *Mutat. Res.* 60: 339–347.

Kram, D., Schneider, E. L., Tice, R. R., and Gianas, P. 1978. Aging and sister chromatid exchange. I. The effect of aging on mitomycin-C induced sister chromatid frequencies in mouse and rat bone marrow cells *in vivo*. *Exptl. Cell Res.* 114: 471–475.

Latt, S. 1973. Microfluorometric detection of deoxyribonucleic acid replication in human metaphase chromosomes. *Proc. Natl. Acad. Sci. (USA)* 70: 3395–3399.

Lejeune, J., Gautier, M., and Turpin, R. 1959. Etude des chromosomes somatiques de neuf enfants mongoliens. *C. R. Acad. Sci.* 248: 1721.

Liniecki, J., Bajerska, A., and Andryszek, C. 1971. Chromosomal aberrations in human lymphocytes irradiated *in vivo* from donors (male and female) of varying age. *Int. J. Radiat. Biol.* 4: 349–360.

Lyon, M. F. 1961. Gene action in the X chromosome of the mouse. *Nature (London)* 190: 372–373.

Makino, S., Sasaki, M. S., and Tonomura, A. 1964. Cytological studies of tumors. XI. Chromosome studies in fifty-two human tumors. *J. Nat. Cancer Inst.* 32: 741.

Mann, P. L., Kern, D. E., Kram, D., and Schneider, E. L. 1981. Relationship between *in vivo* mitomycin C exposure, sister chromatid exchange induction and *in vitro* mitogenic proliferation. II. Effect of aging on spleen cell mitogenesis and sister chromatid exchange induction. *Mech. Age. Devel.* 17: 203–209.

Martin, G. 1978. Genetic syndromes in man with potential relevance to pathobiology of aging. *Genetic Effects on Aging* 14: 5–39.

Martin, J. M., Kellett, J. M., and Kahn, J. 1980. Aneuploidy in cultured human lymphocytes. I. Age and sex differences. *Age and Ageing* 9: 147–153.

Mattevi, M. S., and Salzano, F. M. 1975. Senescence and human chromosome changes. *Humangenetik* 27: 1–8.

Monticone, R. F. and Schneider, E. L. 1979. Induction of sister chromatid exchanges in human cells by fluorescent light. *Mutat. Res.* 59: 215–221.

Nakanishi, Y., Dein, R., and Schneider, E. L. 1980. Aging and sister chromatid exchange. V. The effect of post-embryonic development on mutagen-induced sister chromatid exchanges in mouse and rat bone marrow cells. *Cytogenet. Cell Genet.* 27: 82–87.

Nakanishi, Y., Kram, D., and Schneider, E. L. 1979. Aging and sister chromatid exchange. IV. Reduced frequencies of mutagen-induced sister chromatid exchanges *in vivo* in mouse bone marrow cells with aging. *Cytogenet. Cell Genet.* 24: 61–67.

Neurath, P., DeRener, K., Bell, B., Jarvik, L., and Kato, T. 1970. Chromosome loss compared with chromosome size, age and sex of subjects. *Nature (London)* 225: 281–282.

Nielsen, J. 1970. Chromosomes in senile, presenile, and arteriosclerotic dementia. *J. Geront.* 25: 312–315.

Nielsen, J., Jensen, L., Lindhardt, H., Stottrup, L., and Sondergaard, A. 1968. Chromosomes in senile dementia. *Br. J. Psychiat.* 114: 303–309.

Nordenson, I., Adolfesson, R., Beckman, G., Bucht, G., and Winblad, B. 1980. Chromosomal abnormality in dementia of Alzheimer type. *Lancet* 1: 481–482.

Pierre, R. V. and Hoagland, H. C. 1971. X cell lines in adult men: loss of Y chromosome a normal aging phenomenon? *Mayo Clin. Proc.* 46: 52–55.

Pierre, R. V. and Hoagland, H. C. 1972. Age-associated aneuploidy: Loss of Y chromosome from human bone marrow cells with aging. *Cancer* 30: 889–894.

Saksela, E. and Moorhead, P. S. 1963. Aneuploidy in the degenerative phase of serial cultivation of human cell strains. *Proc. Natl. Acad. Sci. (USA)* 50: 390–395.

Salk, D. 1983. Werner syndrome: a review of recent research with an analysis of connective tissue metabolism, growth control of cultured cells, and chromosomal aberrations. *Human Genet.* (in press).

Sandberg, A. A., Cohen, M. M., Rimm, A. A., and Levin, M. L. 1967. Aneuploidy and age in a population survey. *Am. J. Hum. Genet.* 19: 633–643.

Schneider, E. L. and Bickings, C. K. 1980. Aging and sister chromatid exchange. VI. The effect of *in vitro* passage on spontaneous SCE frequencies in human fetal lung fibroblast cultures. *Cytogenet. Cell Genet.* 26: 61–64.

Schneider, E. L., Bickings, C. K., and Sternberg, H. 1982. Aging and sister chromatid exchange. VII. Effect of aging on background SCE *in vivo*. *Cytogenet. Cell Genet.*

Schneider, E. L. and Epstein, C. J. 1972. Replication rate and lifespan of cultured fibroblasts in Down's syndrome. *Proc. Soc. Exp. Biol. Med.* 141: 1092–1094.

Schneider, E. L. and Gilman, B. 1979. Sister chromatid exchanges and aging. III. The effect of donor age on mutagen-induced sister chromatid exchange in human diploid fibroblasts. *Human Genet.* 46: 57–63.

Schneider, E. L. and Hadley, E. Cytogenetic indicators of aging. *In,* E. L. Schneider and M. Reff (eds.), *Biological Markers of Aging.* DHHS, NIH, PHS, NIH Publication No. 82-2221 (1982) 252 p.

Schneider, E. L. and Lewis, J. 1982. Comparison of *in vivo* and *in vitro* sister chromatid exchange induction. Mutat. Res. 106: 85-90.

Schneider, E. L. and Mitsui, Y. 1976. The relationship between *in vitro* cellular aging and *in vivo* human age. *Proc. Natl. Acad. Sci. (USA)* 73: 3584-3588.

Schneider, E. L. and Monticone, R. E. 1978. Aging and sister chromatid exchange. II. The effect of the *in vitro* passage level of human fetal lung fibroblasts on baseline and mutagen-induced sister chromatid exchange frequencies. *Exptl. Cell Res.* 115: 269-276.

Schneider, E. L., Tice, R. R., and Kram, D. 1978. Bromodeoxyuridine differential chromatid staining technique: a new approach to examining sister chromatid exchange and cell replication kinetics. *In,* D. M. Prescott (ed.), *Methods in Cell Biology,* Vol. 20, pp. 379-409. New York, London. Academic Press.

Stetka, D. G. and Carrano, A. V. 1977. The interaction of Hoechst 33258 and BrdU substituted DNA in the formation of sister chromatid exchange. *Chromosome* 23: 21-31.

Stevenson, K. and Curtis, H. 1961. Chromosome aberrations in irradiated and nitrogen mustard treated mice. *Radiat. Res.* 15: 774-784.

Takagi, N. and Sandberg, A. A. 1968. Chronology and pattern of human chromosome replication. VII. Cellular and chromosomal DNA behavior. *Cytogenetics* 7: 118-134.

Taylor, J. H. 1958. Sister chromatid exchanges in tritium-labeled chromosomes. *Genetics* 43: 515.

Thompson, K. V. A. and Holliday, R. 1975. Chromosome changes during the *in vitro* ageing of MRC-5 human fibroblasts. *Exptl. Cell Res.* 96: 1-6.

Tice, R., Chaillet, J., and Schneider, E. L. 1976. Demonstration of spontaneous sister chromatid exchanges *in vivo. Exptl. Cell Res.* 102: 426-429.

Tijo, J. H. and Levan, A. 1956. High resolution of human chromosomes. *Science* 191: 1268.

Ward, B. E., Cook, R. H., Robinson, A., and Austin, J. H. 1979. Increased aneuploidy in Alzheimer's disease. *Am J. Med. Genet.* 3: 137-144.

Weksler, M. and Siskind, G. 1976. *In,* C. E. Finch and E. L. Schneider (eds.), *Handbook of the Biology of Aging.* New York: Van Nostrand Reinhold.

Yunis, J. J. 1983. The Chromosomal Basis of Human Neoplasia. *Science* 221: 227-236.

PART 5 PHYSIOLOGY

15
HEART AND CIRCULATION

Edward G. Lakatta

Gerontology Research Center
National Institute on Aging
National Institutes of Health

INTRODUCTION

With the passage of time over the adult age period, profound changes in appearance and function occur in all organisms. These result from the combined influences of life-style, nutrition, state of physical conditioning, and disease, all of which are superimposed on what is commonly referred to as the "aging process." While many global hypotheses have been postulated to account for aging of living tissues, none is readily testable (Shock, 1981). A different approach towards understanding aging begins with a definition of those functional aspects of a tissue that change with time and can be attributed to age *per se,* and then proceeds with attempts at elucidation of the mechanism(s) underlying the age-associated alterations by utilizing specific experimental perturbations. This chapter will consider experiments that have taken this approach to study aging of the cardiovascular system and will focus on studies in man, intact animals, and isolated tissues, both in the resting or basal state and during stress.

INTERACTION OF DISEASE AND AGING

The prevalence of specific pathological states increases with age in man. The interaction of disease and aging can be considered from multiple perspectives: (1) functional changes due to aging *per se* interfere with the assess-

ment of the extent or severity of disease; (2) aging of an organism modifies its tolerance to pathological states, thus modifying the clinical presentation and prognosis; and (3) the presence of disease interferes with studies to determine the age effect. This consideration is especially pertinent to studies of the effect of age on the cardiovascular system in man because the incidence and prevalence of cardiovascular disease increases exponentially with age (Caird and Kennedy, 1976), and a major obstacle that has retarded a true understanding of the effect of age on the heart is the high prevalence of coronary artery disease in the sixth to ninth decade. Figure 1 provides an estimate of the prevalence of this disease derived from an autopsy survey in the community of Rochester, Minnesota (White et al., 1950; Ackerman et al., 1950) in which 100 hearts were studied in men and women. It is important to note that the hearts studied were *unselected* with regard to the cause of death or antecedent disease and, specifically, that the prevalence of clinical signs and symptoms of coronary disease in the individuals prior to death did not differ from the remainder of the living population. What is striking about the data is that at least 60 percent of men who lived in the sixth decade had a major stenosis in at least one coronary artery. A similar picture emerges in women, but as depicted in the figure, the high prevalence is retarded

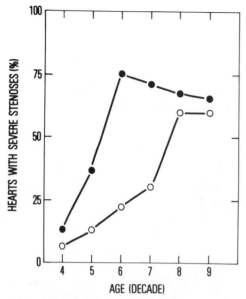

Figure 1. The effect of age on the prevalence of severe coronary stenosis (at least 60 percent narrowing) in autopsied hearts (100 hearts in each decade) from men (0) and women (0). (Redrawn from White et al., 1950; Ackerman et al., 1950.)

by two decades. This has a tremendous impact on the studies of the aging cardiovascular system in man because over half of the elderly population is not available for study on the basis of coronary artery disease alone. The most severe blow dealt to aging studies is that in nearly half of these people the disease is occult. For example, consider that by usual clinical or epidemiological screening, which utilizes history of angina or myocardial infarction, resting electrocardiographic signs, or sudden death, the prevalence of coronary artery disease runs from 2 to 30 percent, depending on the age bracketing employed, and the highest prevalence noted in an elderly population living in the community in the 75+ age bracket approximates only 30 percent (Kannel et al., 1969; Kennedy et al., 1977). Thus it seems likely that many studies which have attempted to characterize the effect of age on the cardiovascular system have not studied age *per se*, but aging as modified by occult coronary disease.

Occult coronary disease can be diagnosed during life in many individuals by employing a stress on the cardiovascular system. This approach has been taken in a population comprised of men who have participated in the Baltimore Longitudinal Study of Aging (BLSA) over the past 25 years, in whom the presence of coronary disease was screened for at repeated intervals (usually 1–2 years) over that span. The value of stress as a tool for detecting occult coronary disease can be appreciated from a consideration of the data in Table 1. In this study, an unselected subset of men in the sixth to ninth decade from the BLSA study population volunteered to undergo maximum treadmill exercise with both electrocardiographic monitoring and radionuclide imaging of the heart (Gerstenblith et al., 1980). For this latter test, radioactive thallium was injected at peak exercise, following which serial images of the heart were made with a gamma camera. The rationale used in this method is that in order to be taken up by cardiac muscle cells, thallous ion must first be delivered to the cells by the vasculature. Should coronary blood supply to an area of the heart be deficient during exercise, this area will appear as a relative cold spot on the heart images. Thus, a "defect" of this sort present during exercise, but not present at rest, indicates circulatory insufficiency to this area and is indicative of coronary artery disease. When resting criteria alone were used (i.e., history of angina pectoris or myocardial infarction, or abnormalities of the resting ECG which

TABLE 1. The Prevalence of Coronary Artery Disease (CAD) in the Elderly as Assessed by Resting[a] and Stress[b] Criteria.

	Age			
	51–60	61–70	71–80	81–90
N	70	73	36	10
% CAD by resting	13	15	22	20
% CAD by resting *and* stress	24	37	56	50

SOURCE: From Gerstenblith et al. (1980).
[a]History of angina or myocardial infarction; abnormal resting ECG, i.e., Minnesota codes 1:1, 1:2, 1:3, or 4:1.
[b]ECG positive for ischemia during maximum exercise treadmill test, i.e., Minnesota code 11:1 or abnormal thallium scan during maximum exercise but not at rest.

suggest previous infarction or ischemia, the prevalence of coronary disease ranged from 13 to 20 percent. By adding stress criteria (i.e., *either* a treadmill ECG indicative of ischemia or an abnormal exercise thallium scan), the number of subjects in whom coronary disease was diagnosed *doubled*. It is apparent, then, that cardiovascular stress is imperative when selecting a coronary artery disease-free population for studies of the effect of age on the cardiovascular system.

In assessing the effect of age on cardiovascular performance, it is also of particular importance to insure that the level of physical conditioning is similar in subjects of all ages, because heart rate, oxygen consumption, blood pressure, and a variety of other cardiorespiratory factors (Saltin and Rowell, 1980) vary substantially with the average level of physical activity. With the change in life-style that accompanies advancing age, physical activity in general decreases, and the cardiorespiratory and muscular systems become "deconditioned." Physical deconditioning will accentuate age-related declines in cardiovascular performance, particularly in response to stress. This is exemplified by the observations that maximum oxygen consumption ($V_{O_2 \text{ max}}$) in elderly subjects is not fixed but increases with exercise training (Robinson et al., 1973). In addition, in elderly subjects who have maintained a high level of physical activity, the $V_{O_2 \text{ max}}$ as compared to young physically conditioned subjects declines to only about half that observed in sedentary elderly subjects (Heath et al., 1981).

THE EFFECT OF ADULT AGE ON CARDIOVASCULAR PERFORMANCE

The overall control of cardiovascular function results from a complex interaction of modulating influences (Figure 2). A change occurring in any single factor usually effects a change in one or more of the others, and in assessing the capacity of the intact cardiovascular system, it is often difficult to determine the limiting factor. Therefore, each factor must be studied in isolation, to the extent to which this is feasible. Failure of the cardiovascular system may be manifest at rest or may be graded in response to varying stress; therefore, studies over a range of conditions, including those in which the system is stressed to capacity, must be employed. The purpose of this section will be to examine the evidence regarding age-related changes in the factors in Figure 2.

Studies at Rest

Although assessment of the effect of age on cardiac function has yielded variable results and interpretations (Gerstenblith et al., 1976), it is generally believed among many students of gerontology that age *per se* has a negative impact on cardiovascular function at rest, i.e., that some sort of predetermined obligatory decline in cardiovascular function occurs vis-à-vis advancing age. This view is particularly emphasized when attempts are made to establish "norms" or "functional indexes" of the "aging process" (Costa and McCrae, 1977). Given the interaction of disease, the level of physical conditioning, and true age-related changes in cardiovascular function, studies of a nonistitutionalized population which remains functional in the physical activities of daily living—and which has been thoroughly screened for occult coronary artery disease—are required to detect true age-related effects. Over the past decade, assessment of cardiovascular performance both at rest and during maximal exercise has been made in such a population, the participants of the BLSA, and some of the results contrast with previous notions of aging of the cardiovascular system.

Cardiac Output

The effect of age on resting cardiac output, which is determined by the total body oxygen requirements and the ability of the cardiovascular system to meet these requirements, has been the focus of many hemodynamic studies. Figure 3 compares two cross-sectional studies of the effect of advancing adult age on cardiac output normalized for body surface area, i.e., cardiac index. Brandfonbrener et al. (1955) (panel A) observed an approximate 50 percent

DETERMINANTS OF CARDIAC OUTPUT

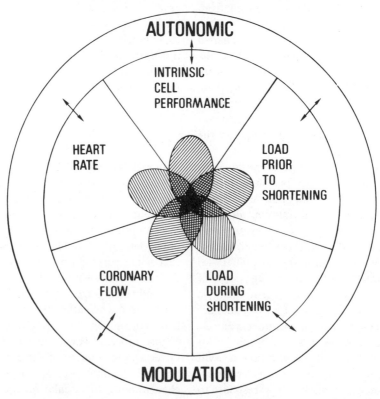

Figure 2. Factors that regulate cardiovascular performance. The ovals have been drawn to overlap each other in order to indicate the interaction among these parameters. The bidirectional arrows also indicate that each factor not only is modulated by, but also determines in part, the autonomic tone. (From La-katta, 1983.)

decrease in cardiac index measured by Direct Fick method over the 20 to 80 year age span. The subject population in that study was comprised of patients from both the acute and the chronic wards of a community hospital, none of whom had histories or physical signs compatible with cardiovascular disease and none of whom had had a surgical procedure within the previous five days. However, many were convalescing from respiratory infections or orthopedic conditions. In the study shown in panel B, cardiac index measured by radionuclide scintigraphy did not vary with age over the 30- to 80-year range. The subject population in this instance was comprised of participants of the BLSA. More specifically, this particular subset was comprised of consecutive volunteers in whom signs and symptoms of cardiovascular disease were absent; resting and stress ECGs were normal; and,

in those over the age of 40, stress thallium images were also normal (Rodeheffer et al., 1984; Fleg et al., 1982). It is important to note, however, that even in this population, estimates of physical activity as judged from the average daily caloric expenditure for activity (McGandy et al., 1966) declines with age (Rodeheffer et al., 1984). Thus, the elderly patients in this study were not "conditioned" with regard to physical activity prior to the study, but rather represented average healthy community dwellers.

The results of these two studies (Figure 3) represent the extremes regarding the effect of cardiac output at rest (Gerstenblith et al., 1976). When considered *in toto*, studies which have investigated an effect of age on cardiac performance fail to demonstrate a unique age effect on cardiac output. This indicates that such an effect is not likely to exist; rather,

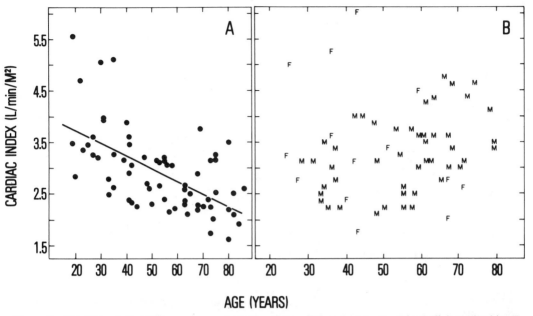

Figure 3. (A) The relation between age and cardiac index, determined by the Direct Fick method in 67 "basal" males without apparent circulatory disorders. The line indicates the simple linear regression for the points. (From Brandfonbrener et al., 1955.)

(B) The effect of age on cardiac index at rest determined by radionuclide angiography in BLSA subjects; see text for details. M and F symbols refer to males and females, respectively. (From Rodeheffer et al., 1984; Fleg et al., 1982.)

the results of a given study depend not on aging *per se* as much as on the particular population studied. Hemodynamic variables that determine cardiac output measured in the two studies in Figure 3 are summarized in Table 2. While a slight decrease in heart rate with aging was noted in the study of population A and not B, the major factors associated with the decreased cardiac index in A were an age-related decrease in stroke volume and an increased peripheral resistance; this did not occur in population B. In fact, only the increase in systolic blood pressure with age and unchanged diastolic blood pressure were common to both populations. Although the study in panel A was more heavily weighted on both age extremes than that in panel B, the marked differences between the two over the ages of 30 to 80 cannot be attributed to a different age range or to different methodologies. While this difference could be due to some unspecified cohort effect, a more attractive hypothesis is that it resulted, at least in part, from differences in the extent of occult coronary disease,

life-style (i.e., institutionalized versus community dwelling), and maintenance of a minimum level of routine daily physical activities.

Myocardial Preload and Afterload

Technological advances in relatively noninvasive methodologies over the past decade have made more detailed studies of hemodynamic variables feasible in normal human volunteers. The effects of age on some aspects of these parameters have been quantitated at rest in the BLSA population. Resting left ventricular (LV) end-diastolic diameter (Gerstenblith et al., 1977), area (VanTosh et al., 1980), and volume (Rodeheffer et al., 1984), as measured by M-mode echocardiography, two-dimensional echocardiography, and gated blood pool scans, respectively, do not decline with adult age in healthy adults. Also, the fraction of end-diastolic volume ejected with each beat at rest does not decline with age (Gerstenblith et al., 1977). Figure 4 illustrates the end-diastolic dimension and ejection fraction index

TABLE 2.   Effect of Adult Age on Resting Cardiac Function.

	Population a, Institutionalized, Unscreened for Occult CAD (2nd–9th Decade)	Population b, Active in Community Life, Screened for Occult CAD with Cardiovascular Stress (3rd–8th Decade)
Heart rate	Slight decrease	Slight decrease
Stroke volume	Decrease	Slight increase
Cardiac output	Decrease	No effect
Cardiac index	Decrease	No effect
Peripheral vascular resistance	Increase	No effect
Peak systolic blood pressure	Increase	Increase
Diastolic pressure	No effect	No effect

[a]From Brandfonbrener et al. (1955).
[b]From Rodeheffer et al. (1984) and Fleg et al. (1982).

as measured by the M-mode echocardiogram (Gerstenblith et al., 1977) over a broad age spectrum.

The effect of adult age on rates of ventricular filling and ejection has also been assessed and is depicted in Figure 5. The velocity of circumferential shortening (i.e., an ejection rate) is not age related (Figure 5A). The shortening velocity, under certain circumstances, can reflect the contractile state of the myocardium. However, because this parameter is load dependent and afterload (e.g., aortic input impedance) may vary with age (vide infra), it is best interpreted in this instance simply as a measure of chamber emptying rate. The closure rate of the anterior leaflet of the mitral valve (Figure 5B) is proportional to the rate of LV filling in early diastole (Zaky et al., 1968). The filling rate in the 65- to 80 year age group is about half that observed in the 25- to 44-year age group. This reduction in filling rate is not of sufficient magnitude to lead to a reduction in end-diastolic filling volume at rest as evidenced by Figure 4A.

The mechanism for diminished early diastolic filling may relate to one or more age-related changes in the heart: (a) the mitral valve becomes thickened and sclerosed with age (McMillan and Lev, 1964; Sell and Scully, 1965; Lev et al., 1974); (b) an age-associated decrease in compliance has been demonstrated in animal models (Templeton et al., 1975;

Spurgeon et al., 1977) and may relate in part to an increase in the amount, and/or altered properties, of collagen that occur with age in both animals and man (Gerstenblith et al., 1976; Lakatta and Yin, 1982); and (c) a prolonged isometric relaxation time has been measured in man and in many animal models (Harrison et al., 1964; Lakatta, 1979, 1980a; Lakatta and Yin, 1982).

A reduction in LV filling rate occurs in pathological states associated with cardiac hypertrophy due to an increased pressure load on the heart. Whether the myocardium hypertrophies with advancing age has until recently been a rather controversial subject. The concept that the heart undergoes atrophy in advanced age, as the result of a diminished demand for performance, has been advocated for at least three decades (Roesler, 1937; Dock, 1945; Sprague, 1954; Batsakis, 1968; Harris, 1975). This notion was by no means, however, universally held. In fact, the data accumulated in many studies indicated that in man the heart hypertrophies with advancing age (Rosahn, 1941; Strandell, 1964a; Kannel et al., 1969; Linzbach and Akuamoa-Boateng, 1973). Linzbach and Akuamoa-Boateng (1973), who reviewed autopsy data spanning 91 years in 7,112 human hearts, found that between 30 and 90 years of age, the heart increased in mass on an average of 1–1.5 grams per year. Furthermore, in quantitating mini-

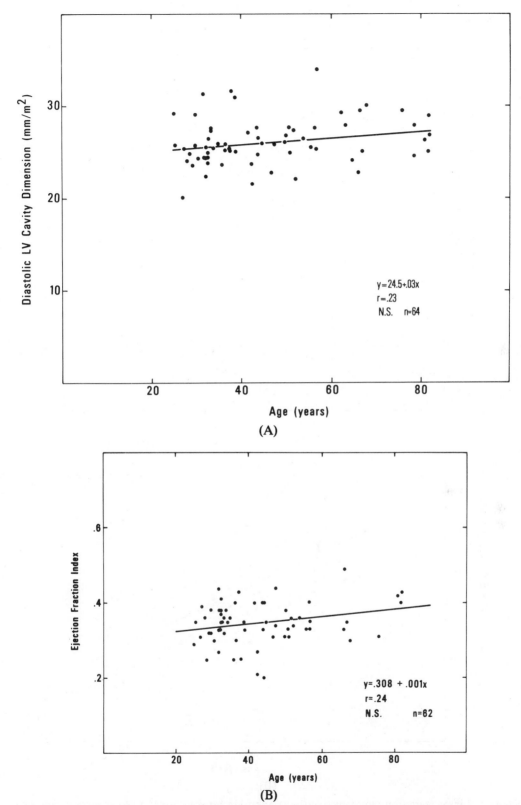

Figure 4. Linear regression plot depicting the relationship between age and (A) diastolic cavity dimension and (B) fractional shortening during systole in participants from the BLSA. (From Gerstenblith et al., 1977.)

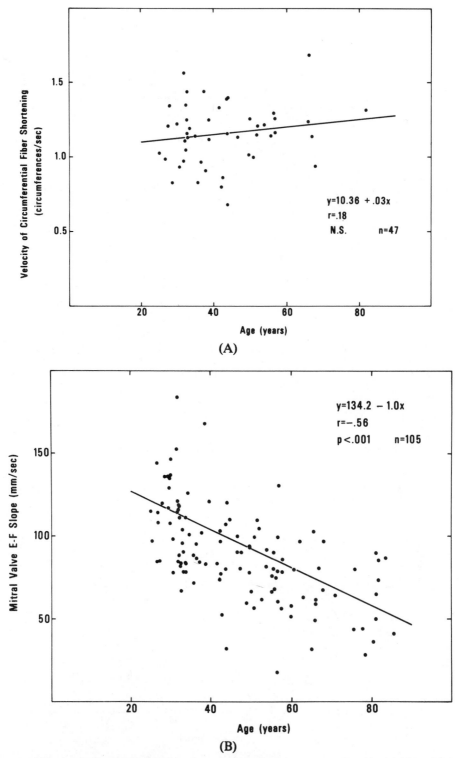

Figure 5. Linear regression plot depicting the relationship between age and (A) velocity of left ventricular shortening (circumference/sec) and (B) rate of left ventricular early diastolic filling as manifested in the closure rate of an anterior leaflet of the mitral valve (E-F) slope. (From Gerstenblith et al., 1977.)

mal heart weight, these investigators specifically failed to detect instances of cardiac atrophy in advanced age. In this study, hearts from individuals with cardiovascular disease, which as noted increases sharply with age, were included with those from normal individuals. Thus, the possibility that the observed increase in cardiac mass with age is related at least in part to cardiovascular pathology, and may not be an age-related phenomenon in normal man, must be considered.

The presence of cardiac hypertrophy has been sought noninvasively in living healthy men by echocardiography. In 100 normal men and women distributed evenly among sedentary and manual occupations, Sjogren (1972) demonstrated that the posterior LV wall thickness is increased from the second to the seventh decade. Gardin et al. (1979) also demonstrated that LV diastolic thickness is increased with age and that LV diastolic diameter remains unchanged with age in normal man. In healthy BLSA participants, Gerstenblith et al. (1977) have demonstrated an age-related increase in LV wall thickness in men over the age range of 25 to 80 years (Figure 6).

The fact that LV wall thickness increases with age in an otherwise normal population has a practical implication regarding our assessment of what constitutes "normal" aging in the cardiovascular system. The stimulus for cardiac hypertrophy is usually an increased work load. For example, in pathological conditions such as valvular disease and hypertension, cardiac hypertrophy results from an increase in either pressure or volume stroke work which requires enhanced stress (force per unit area) production by ventricular muscle. As wall thickness increases, the wall stress returns toward normal. This facilitates muscle shortening of each cardiac cell and permits normal ejection of blood during systole. The precise stimulus for the age-related cardiac hypertrophy, which is moderate compared to that observed in pathological conditions (Sjogren, 1972), is less well defined. Cardiac output (Figure 3) is not increased with age and diastolic blood pressure is not greatly altered by age (Table 2), and in healthy adults rigor-

ously screened for occult disease, calculated peripheral resistance at rest is also not altered by age (Table 2). What then constitutes the stimulus for cardiac hypertrophy? A likely candidate is the increase in systolic blood pressure with age that apparently occurs even in otherwise healthy men. Consider that even when an upper range of systolic blood pressure of 160 mm Hg is designated as normal in studies on the aging cardiovascular system, and subjects who exceed this level are excluded from the study, systolic blood pressure still increases with age in the subjects studied (Table 2 and Figure 7A).

An index of myocardial work is the product of stroke volume × systolic or mean blood pressure. Note in Figure 7B that this increases substantially with age in normal men at rest. In fact, even in studies where cardiac output was observed to fall with age (Figure 3A), stroke work was increased with age due to the elevated systolic blood pressure (Table 2). Thus, the moderate increase in wall thickness that occurs with advancing age can be interpreted as an adaptive mechanism in response to the moderately increased work load imposed by an enhanced systolic blood pressure.

Many studies have focused on the effect of age on physical characteristics of the vascular system. Both *in vitro* and *in vivo* studies have indicated that stiffness is increased in the aged aorta of man (Roy, 1880–82; Aschoff, 1924; Roach and Burton, 1959). From measurements of the change in pressure for a given change in volume in the human aorta, Learoyd and Taylor (1966) have shown that the static circumferential modulus increases with age. At 100 mm Hg, the modulus of elasticity in aortae from persons younger than 35 years of age was 7.5×10^6 dynes/cm^2, as compared with 16.6×10^6 dynes/cm^2 in aortae from persons older than 35 years of age (35–52 years). Bader (1967) also reported similar results. At 200 mm Hg, the modulus of elasticity increased from 10 kg/cm^2 at age 20 to 42.5 kg/cm^2 at age 85. Age differences found in the dynamic circumferential modulus, i.e., measurements of pressure in response to oscillations in volume at varying frequencies, have been attributed to the age changes found in

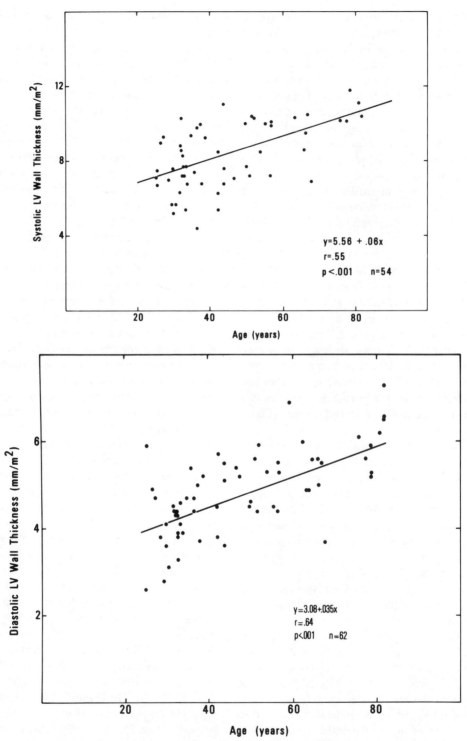

Figure 6. (*Top*) Linear regression plot depicting the relationship between age and systolic left ventricular wall thickness per square meter. Increasing age is associated with increased systolic wall thickness. (*Bottom*) Linear regression plot depicting the relationship between age and diastolic left ventricular wall thickness per square meter. Increased age is associated with increased diastolic wall thickness. (From Gerstenblith et al., 1977.)

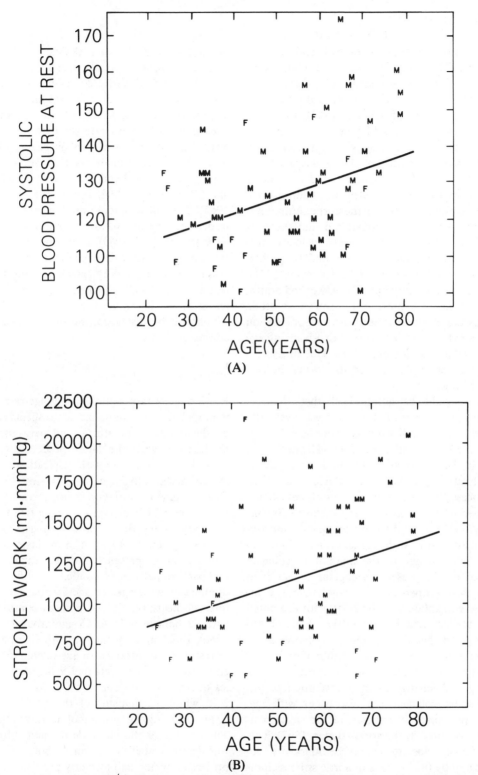

Figure 7. (A) The effect of age on systolic blood pressure at rest. Systolic pressure (mm Hg) = 105.26 + 0.41(age), r = .37, p < .003. (B) The effect of age on stroke work defined as stroke volume × systolic blood pressure at rest. Stroke work = 6451.3 + 97.61(age), r = .36, p < .004. A and B are from BLSA participants screened for occult coronary disease. The 61 subjects depicted here are the same as in Figure 3. (From Rodeheffer et al., 1984; Fleg et al., 1982.)

the static modulus (Learoyd and Taylor, 1966). The tangential elastic modulus estimated from measurements of pressure and wall thickness increases dramatically with age, so that by age 85 (Bader, 1967), the aorta becomes almost a rigid tube.

Studies *in vivo* also suggest that arterial rigidity increases with age. Gonza and associates (1974) utilized angiography and a catheter pressure transducer system to obtain a pressure-strain modulus for the aorta and pulmonary artery, and demonstrated that these increase with age. Pulse wave velocity also increases with age (Bramwell and Hill, 1922; Hallock and Benson, 1937; Yakovlev, 1971). An arterial rigidity index (Conway and Smith, 1956)—i.e., (Δ pulse pressure)/(Δ diastolic pressure) in the first beats after vasodilatation by amyl nitrate—increases with advancing age (Abboud and Huston, 1961). This likely is a manifestation of increased stiffness of the vascular tree.

It should be emphasized that the age changes in elastic moduli, pulse wave velocity, and arterial rigidity index cannot be explained on the basis of atherosclerosis (Haynes et al., 1936; Dontas et al., 1961; Freis et al., 1966) but rather are likely attributable to a diffuse process that occurs in the vessel wall. Some observers have reported frayed elastin (Wolinsky, 1972), and others, increased calcium content of elastin, with age (Lansing, 1959). An absolute change in the amount of collagen need not be present to explain a change in physical properties. In reanalyzing the increase in stiffness of the aorta with age noted by Hallock and Benson (1937), King (1946) proposed that the age changes involve a decrease in the coiling and twisting of molecular chains and a reduction in effective chain length. A change in the distribution of unstretched collagen may also occur with age.

Approximately one-half of the stroke volume is stored in the aorta (Bader, 1967). This buffering capacity would be markedly decreased by the increase in aortic stiffness indicated by the change in the elastic modulus if an increase in aortic volume which occurs with age in normal man (Gerstenblith et al., 1977) did not occur to compensate for the

loss of elasticity. However, the increased stiffness results in less diastolic recoil and, therefore, a decreased aortic contribution to forward flow, and the larger blood-filled aorta at end-diastole increases impedance by requiring the heart to accelerate the blood against larger inertial forces when systole begins. Similar age-related changes occur in the more-peripheral vessels (Landowne, 1958; Roach et al., 1959; Carter, 1964; Busby and Burton, 1965). The role of smooth muscle contraction in determining *in vivo* arterial stiffness is not clear (Remington, 1963). However, one study suggests that elastic viscous moduli of arterial vessels can be altered by catecholamines (Peterson et al., 1960). Furthermore, age differences in aortic impedance during exercise, which will be discussed, appear to have an adrenergic basis.

Autonomic Modulation

Resting heart rate, although non-age-related, is modulated by autonomic tone, specifically by the relative sympathetic and parasympathetic tone, with the latter predominating. Variation in sinus rate with respiration is diminished with advancing age (Davies, 1975). The spontaneous variation in heart rate monitored over a 24-hour period in men free from coronary artery disease also decreases with age (Kostis et al., 1982). The intrinsic sinus rate, i.e., in the presence of both sympathetic and parasympathetic blockade, is significantly diminished with age: at age 20 the average intrinsic heart rate is 104 bpm as compared with 92 bpm in a 45 to 55 age group (Jose, 1966). Blocking only the sympathetic system at rest does not produce an age-related differential effect on heart rate or LV hemodynamics in man at rest. This is depicted in Table 3 in which participants of the BLSA were given 0.15 mg/kg propranol intravenously. The efficacy of the blockade in each subject was demonstrated in that an IV bolus of isoproterenol which had formerly produced a 25 bpm increment in heart rate produced less than 2 bpm increase postblockade. While this concentration of propranolol reduced the resting heart rate, velocity of circumferential fiber

TABLE 3. Left Ventricular Performance and Dimensions in Old and Young Men at Rest.

Group	Age (yr)	N	Heart Rate min	Systolic Blood Pressure (mm Hg)	LVDD (mm)	LVSD (mm)	VCF (circumferences/sec)
				Before beta-blockade			
Old	68.5 ± 2	11	66.0 ± 2.7	129 ± 1.5	52.0 ± 1.5	31.5 ± 1.5	1.42 ± 0.05
Young	29.6 ± 1	17	69.5 ± 1.7	124 ± 2.3	50.4 ± 0.8	30.5 ± 0.9	1.48 ± 0.06
P (O vs Y)	<0.001		NS	NS	NS	NS	NS
				During beta-blockade			
Old	68.5 ± 2	11	56.0 ± 2.5 (a)	133 ± 4.7	50.7 ± 1.4	32.7 ± 1.5 (b)	1.15 ± 0.05 (a)
Young	29.6 ± 1	17	61.1 ± 1.8 (b)	122 ± 1.5	50.0 ± 1.0	33.1 ± 0.8 (a)	1.16 ± 0.04 (a)
P (O vs Y)	<0.001		NS	NS	NS	NS	NS

SOURCE: From Yin et al. (1978).
NOTE:
   LVDD = left ventricular diastolic diameter
   LVSD = left ventricular systolic diameter
   VCF = velocity of circumferential shortening.
(a) $P < 0.01$, (b) $P < 0.05$ compared with the value before beta-blockade when expressed as increments from the preblockade value. NS = Not significant.

shortening, and end-systolic dimension, no age difference in these responses was observed (Yin et al., 1978).

The Myocardium

The "contractile state" or level of excitation-contraction coupling present in the myocardium itself is difficult to ascertain in the intact circulatory system given the interaction of multiple modulators of cardiac performance (Figure 2). Thus, our understanding of the effect of age on intrinsic cardiac muscle performance has come from studies in isolated hearts or cardiac muscle isolated from hearts of animals. While numerous studies have documented that properties of muscle isolated from human hearts are very much like those from most other mammals, it remains to be documented that all species age in the same way or at the same rate. Thus, some caution is advisable when extrapolating data from animal models to link together the existing parts of the puzzle of aging in man. The prime importance of these studies in isolated animal tissue is to achieve an understanding of the nature of that tissue and how it is altered with age (or time on earth). In some cases, however, similar age-related phenomena have been observed across a wide range of species, including man, and in these instances some degree of extrapolation to the human aging model may be justified.

Force Production and Shortening in Cardiac Muscle

Several studies in isolated cardiac muscle have indicated that the capacity to develop force is not compromised in the senescent myocardium (Lakatta, 1980a), while others have suggested that the speed of shortening and myosin ATPase decline over a broad age range (Alpert et al., 1967). However, whether these changes were progressive from the maturational to the senescent period cannot be ascertained from the latter study. More recent studies have clarified this issue and have demonstrated that the age-related decline in myofilament ATPase activity occurs between the maturational and the adult periods, with virtually no further change occurring from mid-life through senescence (Chesky and Rockstein, 1977). Additional studies of the effect of age on velocity of shortening, which take into consideration age-related differences in the time course of activation, are required to determine precisely how this contractile parameter is affected by age. In relating muscle function to the ejection of blood, the *extent* of shortening would be as or more important than the velocity of shortening. The studies in isometric muscles (Lakatta, 1980a), which indicate no age difference in force production, suggest that the extent of sarcomere shortening during a contraction in isolated muscle is not age related. However, more direct measurements are required to solidify this concept, especially since noncontractile determinants of visoelasticity may change with age (Lakatta and Yin, 1982). The contractile performance of cardiac muscle is not fixed but can vary with perturbations referred to as inotropic stimuli such as stretch (Jewell, 1977), pharmacologic agents, or catecholamines. The effect of age on the *maximum* contractile response will be discussed in conjunction with studies during exercise.

Contraction Duration

One of the most widely observed characteristics of cardiac muscle from senescent rats is that isometric contraction duration is prolonged relative to that in the adult. The magnitude of this prolongation is about 20 percent (Lakatta, 1980a) and is due to increase in *both* time to peak force (Alpert et al., 1967; Froehlich et al., 1978) and relaxation time (Weisfeldt et al., 1971a; Lakatta et al., 1975a). Prolonged contraction duration with increasing age is present virtually in all species in which the cardiac contraction has been measured, i.e., in cardiac muscle isolated from guinea pigs (Rumberger and Timmermann, 1976), intact hearts isolated from dogs (Templeton et al., 1978) and rabbits (Frolkis et al., 1975), and intact man (Harrison et al., 1964) as measured noninvasively from measurements of time intervals of the cardiac cycle. Prolonged contraction may reflect an age difference in the time course of contractile activation or in the excitation-contraction process. However, age-related changes in passive viscoelastic properties might also be involved. A test of whether prolonged contraction is due to a prolonged excitation-contraction cycle can be made by determining the contractile response to premature stimuli (Lakatta et al., 1975a). The assumption made in this type of experiment is that when a test excitation occurs before

the excitation-contraction coupling mechanisms restitute, no contraction will be caused by it (Figure 8). This restitution interval was greater in senescent versus adult muscles; i.e., when the premature interval was reduced to 200 msec, a contraction could be elicited in about 50 percent of senescent muscles, and at 120 msec, a contraction could not be elicited in any senescent muscle studied. Thus, electromechanical restitution requires a longer time in the senescent versus the adult myocardium. This could result in delayed restitution of mechanisms governing the action potential or those regulating Ca^{++} loading of the site from which it is released, e.g., the sarcoplasmic reticulum.

Both action potential duration and contraction were prolonged in right ventricular isometric papillary muscles from senescent versus adult rat hearts (Wei et al., 1984). Simultaneous measurements of the isometric twitch and transmembrane action potentials made over a wide range of driving frequencies (30–440 min^{-1}) indicated that time to peak force, relaxation time, and the plateau phase of the action potential of right ventricular

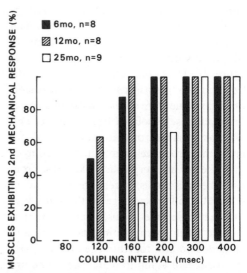

Figure 8. Effect of age on the ability of isolated rat cardiac muscles to respond to a second stimulus during paired pacing at varied coupling intervals. As the coupling interval shortens, fewer muscles in the aged group exhibit a second mechanical response, $p < 0.01(X^2)$. (From Lakatta et al., 1975a.)

muscles (Rumberger and Timmermann, 1976) were prolonged in muscles from older (26–30 months) versus younger (3–4 months) hearts. While these data seem to parallel the changes observed in contraction and action potential duration with adult aging in the rat (Wei et al., 1984), the extreme difference in heart and body weights between the 3- and 30-month guinea pigs indicates that the age comparison actually made was not between adulthood and senescence, but rather between maturation and senescence.

In unloaded rat LV endocardium studied under conditions illustrated in Figure 8, no age change in action potential duration or the electrical refractory period was observed (Lakatta et al., 1975a). In nonworking paced isolated rat atria (Fischer 344 strain), while a substantial increase in action potential repolarization time occurs from the neonatal (2 months) to the adult (6 months) period (Cavoto et al., 1974), no further changes are observed with adult aging (Roberts and Goldberg, 1975). In unloaded canine Purkinje fibers, action potential duration increased from 19 to 63 months (adult) but did not change further through 132 months (senescent) (Rosen et al., 1978). While these studies indicate that action potential duration increases during maturation and does not change with further adult aging, it need be noted that action potential duration varies substantially with loading conditions (Gulch, 1980), and therefore, measurements in the unloaded state do not necessarily reflect those in working muscle as previously noted.

The sarcoplasmic reticulum is capable of reducing myoplasmic [Ca^{++}] from systolic to diastolic levels within the time course of its measured decay following excitation (Allen and Kurihara, 1979), and the rate of Ca^{++} sequestration from the myoplasm following a given excitation may be a determinant not only of the time course of the contraction but also of the time course of restitution of the excitation-contraction cycle. The rate of Ca^{++} sequestration has been measured in microsomal preparations rich in sarcoplasmic reticulum isolated from adult (6–8 months) and senescent (24–26 months) hearts (Froehlich et al., 1978). Over the pCa which occurs upon excitation, the rate of Ca^{++} accumulation in the senescent microsomes was approximately 50 percent less than that in adult (Fig. 9). This could, at least in part, explain the prolonged active state in the senescent heart, and this hypothesis is particularly attractive since it would account for both prolonged time to peak force and prolonged relaxation time, because myoplasmic [Ca^{++}] is already reduced to low levels by the time of peak force (Allen and Kurihara, 1979). It is noteworthy that directionally similar changes in the steady state measurements of microsomal Ca^{++} accumulation and contraction duration have been observed across species (Nayler et al., 1975), in altered thyroid states (Suko, 1971; Guarnieri et al., 1980a), in experimental hypertrophy (Bing et al., 1971; Ito et al., 1974), and in response to cAMP stimulation (Kirchberger et al., 1974; Guarnieri et al., 1980a).

Tissue catecholamine content may also influence the contraction duration and electromechanical refractoriness of isolated cardiac

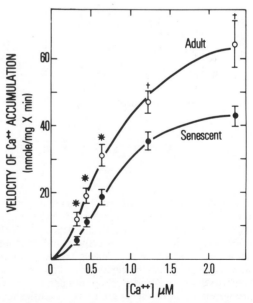

Figure 9. Velocity of calcium accumulation by sarcoplasmic reticulum isolated from adult and senescent rat hearts. The calcium accumulation velocity is significantly diminished in sarcoplasmic reticulum from senescent hearts as compared to the adult heart ($+ \ p < .01; * p < .02$). (Redrawn from Froehlich et al., 1978.)

tissue (Lakatta et al., 1975a). Subsequent to the maturational period, the catecholamine content in the heart progressively declines throughout the life span (Roberts and Goldberg, 1976), and with adult aging LV tissue catecholamines decline approximately 25 percent (Gey et al., 1965; Frolkis et al., 1970; Lakatta et al., 1975a). This results from both a diminished net synthesis and diminished reuptake into nerve endings (Gey et al., 1965; Limas, 1975). In muscles isolated from hearts in which the catecholamine content was depleted to less than 5 percent control level by 6-hydroxydopamine, the age difference in contraction duration in adult and senescent muscles persisted and was not diminished in magnitude (Lakatta et al., 1975a). Thus, the diminished catecholamine content in the senescent heart does not appear to have a major role in the prolonged contraction duration.

In both rats and humans, as noted, LV hypertrophy accompanies senescence (Lakatta, 1979). Figure 10 depicts the relationship of age, relative heart size, and contraction duration over the adult age range in Wistar rats. Heart weight indexed to tibial length is fairly constant through 15–16 months and then gradually increased approximately 15 percent by 24–26 months. Contraction duration, like relative heart mass, is constant through 16 months and by 24 months is prolonged. This raises the possibility that prolonged contraction is due to the hypertrophy rather than to aging. This hypothesis was tested by creating in 15-month animals by aortic banding (Yin et al., 1980) the same extent of hypertrophy present at 24 months. Hypertrophy of this extent prolongs contraction duration (Figure 10B) only about one-third of the extent observed in senescent hearts. This suggests

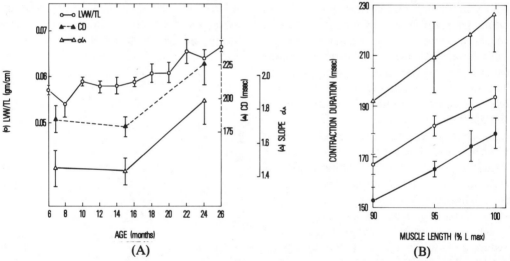

Figure 10. (A) Age-associated changes in the hypertrophy index left ventricular weight per tibial length, LVW/TL (0); contraction duration, CD (Δ); and stiffness coefficient during contraction, α_A (Δ). The bars represent ± SEM. Analysis of variance for LVW/TL across age revealed a significant variance ratio ($P < 0.001$) with differences being manifest at and above 21–22 months. The values of CD and α_A shown are those at that muscle length which is optimal for force production, L_{max}. Analysis of variance across a range of lengths demonstrated the following: $F = 5.01$, $P < 0.05$, and $F = 5.77$, $P < 0.025$, respectively, for CD and α_A. For both parameters, the differences between either of the two younger age groups versus the senescent group were significant ($P < 0.05$) by the Q test. There was no difference between the two younger age groups. (From Yin et al., 1980.)

(B) The effect of age on contraction duration measured across a range of muscle lengths in trabecular muscles isolated from hearts of adult 16-month (M), senescent 24 month (S), and adult animals in which the aorta was banded to produce moderate cardiac hypertrophy of a similar degree to that which occurs in the senescent heart (B). Contraction duration was measured as the time from onset of force to half force dissipation. Muscles were stimulated at 24 min^{-1} at 29°C in [Ca^{++}]$_e$ of 2.5 mM. Developed force and maximum rate of force development were similar in all three groups at each length. (From Yin et al., 1980.)

that the extent of hypertrophy in senescence *per se* cannot entirely account for the prolonged contraction.

Other experimental results also support this conclusion. (a) The heart can be made to atrophy when transplanted, in a nonworking mode, into the abdominal cavity of another rat. Contraction duration in cardiac muscle isolated from such chronic transplants that are 24 months or older is prolonged, even though this heart is atrophied (Korecky, 1979). (b) Right ventricular hypertrophy does not occur in 24-month rats (Yin et al., 1980), yet in right ventricular papillary muscles from senescent hearts, contraction duration is prolonged to a similar extent as that observed in LV trabeculae (Wei et al., 1984). (c) Thirty minutes of mild treadmill exercise each day for 6 months in 2- and 18-month rats (rats were 8 and 24 months at time of study) (Spurgeon et al., 1983) did not modify the extent of hypertrophy in hearts from senescent animals, but contraction duration was substantially reduced and was no longer different from that in the young group (Figure 11). This result indicates that hypertrophy *per se* is not the cause of prolonged contraction duration and, in addition, that contraction duration in muscles from senescent heart is not fixed but can be experimentally reduced.

The effect of age on additional factors that can theoretically modify the duration of contraction, e.g., the extent of velocity of myofibrillar shortening, the off rate of Ca^{++} from troponin, and the degree of asynchrony among the cells comprising multicellular muscle with respect to their contraction-relaxation cycles (Stern et al., 1983), requires further study.

Coronary Blood Flow

There are no data in man regarding the effect of age on coronary flow. In the nonworking isolated rat heart, coronary flow per gram of heart under normoxic conditions is not altered with advanced age (Weisfeldt et al., 1971b). Earlier studies have documented a decrease in the number of capillaries in the 26–27 versus the 4-month rat heart (Rakusan and Poupa, 1964). However, it is difficult to interpret this in the context that the senescent heart

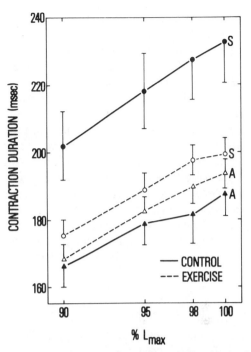

Figure 11. The effect of a moderate chronic wheel exercise protocol on contraction duration in isometric rat cardiac muscles from rats 8–9 months of age (A) and 24–26 months of age (S). Rats were run for 30–60 minutes, five days a week, for five months prior to study. Studies were performed in isolated left ventricular trabeculae across a range of muscle lengths (% L_{max}) in $[Ca^{++}]_e$ of 2.5 mM. (From Spurgeon et al., 1983.)

may be chronically hypoxic because it has been demonstrated that the capillary density is not fixed but can increase appropriately with the stimulation of chronic physical conditioning (Tomanek, 1970).

Summary

The effect of age on resting cardiac output and factors that modulate output (Figure 2) vary with the methods for selection of the study population. In subjects who are free from coronary disease and maintain the daily activities of a community existence, cardiac output [i.e., heart rate, stroke volume, and end-diastolic volume (load prior to filling)] are not markedly affected by age. Thus, the notion that an "aging process" *per se* commands a substantial *obligatory* decline in cardiovascular function at rest is not supported by these results. However, changes in aortic compliance that occur with age, and result in a progressive increase in systolic blood pressure, appear to impose a progressively increasing load on the heart. To maintain normal wall stress, mild LV hypertrophy occurs as an adaptive mechanism. A cost is paid for this, however, as stroke work is increased, and this must necessitate an age-related change in myocardial energy metabolism, probably requiring an increase in myocardial oxygen consumption. While some definite age-related changes in excitation-contraction coupling of cardiac muscle from animals have been observed, these do not appear to limit myocardial force production or extent of shortening under resting conditions.

Cardiovascular Response to Stress

That overall cardiac performance at rest is not altered by age in healthy active subjects is by no means indicative that performance during stress remains intact. Classical studies of exercise physiology have indicated that maximum exercise performance diminishes with age in apparently healthy persons (see Gerstenblith et al., 1976, for review). Specifically, age-related declines have been identified in maximum aerobic capacity, heart rate, stroke volume, cardiac output, and arteriovenous oxygen differences. A hemodynamic profile that typifies the results of such studies is given in Table 4.

One important aspect of these comparisons is that they are not made at standard exercise levels across all ages, but at the voluntary maximal exercise level in each subject. This is substantially reduced with age, as depicted in Figure 12A which illustrates stroke volume as a function of work load (level of oxygen consumption). The last recorded point in each age group was at that level reached in at least six subjects within that group. Since no plateau in the curves is evident, it cannot be ascertained whether maximum cardiac performance was achieved in the elderly or whether the limitation in work load with advanced age might be due to other factors.

Consideration of the influence of occult coronary disease is even more important in studies involving exercise than in studies of the cardiovascular system at rest. In fact, an age-dependent increase in ECG abnormalities during exercise, which in some instances may be indicative of coronary disease, has been observed in some previous studies (Strandell, 1964b; Montoye, 1975). Furthermore, the status of physical conditioning is also a major determinant of the exercise response, and a true assessment of the effect of aging *per se* on the cardiovascular exercise response thus requires strict control of both parameters (Raven and Mitchell, 1980). Although no such study has been implemented to date, the cardiovascular exercise response has been measured in BLSA participants who maintain the routine activities of daily living in a commu-

TABLE 4. Cardiovascular Performance at the Voluntary Maximal Exercise Level in 54 Normal Subjects Grouped According to Age.

| Age (yr) | O_2 Consumption (ml/min) | Pulse Rate (bpm) | ARTERIAL BLOOD PRESSURE | | Cardiac Output (liters/min) | CALCULATED | |
			Systolic (mm Hg)	Diastolic (mm Hg)		Peripheral Resistance (dynes sec cm^{-5})	A-V O_2 Difference (ml/100 ml)
18–34	2172.8 ± 128.0	169.8 ± 4.7	173.3 ± 5.22	93.2 ± 2.47	16.19 ± 1.23	620.2 ± 45.92	13.1 ± 0.72
35–49	1638.5 ± 66.7 (b)	158.7 ± 2.8 (b)	181.4 ± 4.19	94.9 ± 2.03	14.96 ± 1.02	717.5 ± 56.4	11.5 ± 0.38
50–69	1379.7 ± 89.7 (b)	139.6 ± 4.74 (c)	202.8 ± 6.34 (b)	97.1 ± 3.79	11.98 ± 0.84 (a)	977.9 ± 40.0 (a)	11.25 ± 0.80 (a)

SOURCE: From Julius et al. (1967).
NOTE: Significance values refer to differences between the youngest and other age groups: (a) $P < 0.05$; (b) $P < 0.01$; (c) $P < 0.001$.

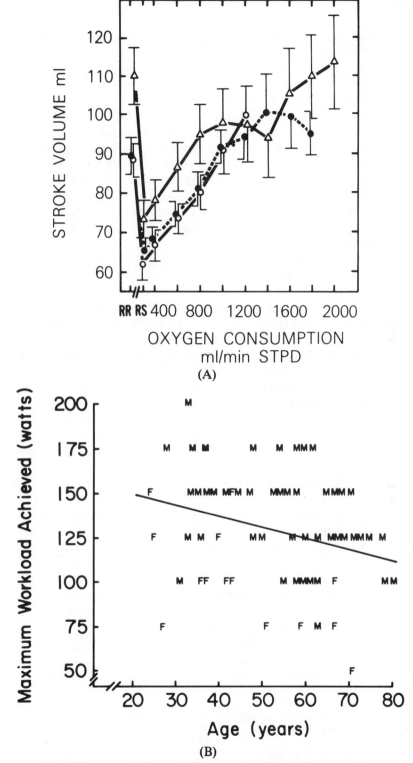

Figure 12. (A) Stroke volume as a function of oxygen consumption in three age groups of men. Subjects are the same as in Table 4. (From Julius et al., 1967.)

(B) The effect of age on the maximum work load during upright bicycle exercise in BLSA participants (same population as in Figure 3). The end point in virtually all instances was leg muscle fatigue. (From Rodeheffer et al., 1984.)

nity setting in advanced age and who had both normal ECG *and* normal thallium tests during treadmill exercise. These subjects were studied in a graded upright bicycle exercise protocol, during which cardiac volumes were measured by technetium blood pool scans (Links et al., 1982). The results obtained in the first 61 consecutive volunteers for this protocol (Rodeheffer et al., 1984) differ in many ways from previous studies that have examined the effect of age on cardiovascular response to stress. Comparison of the exercise response in these subjects with that of the population in Figure 4 will demonstrate, as in the case of studies at rest, the extremely different results that can be obtained, depending on how the population is selected. Even in these BLSA subjects, the maximum work load achieved declined with age (Figure 12B), but this decline was significantly less marked than in Figure 12A; thus, the physical endurance of the elderly in this population is apparently greater than that in some earlier studies of the effect of age on the exercise response.

Heart Rate

The heart rate increases progressively with the level of exercise. In this BLSA population, the increase in heart rate at each level of exercise was less with advancing age (Figure 13A). This contrasts with some other studies in which heart rate at submaximal exercise was

not age related (see Gerstenblith et al., 1976, for review). The maximum heart rate achieved also significantly decreased with advancing age (Table 5). It is important to note that the maximum heart rate achieved in this exercise protocol is comparable to those in other studies, including those in which the maximum work load was significantly reduced with advanced age (Robinson, 1938; Julius et al., 1967). That this result has been universally observed in virtually every population studied suggests that a diminished maximum heart rate is a true age-related phenomenon.

End-Diastolic Filling Volume (*Load Prior to Shortening*)

Blood filling the heart during diastole serves to stretch the fibers and in doing so not only alters their geometry but also results in an enhanced activation of the myofilaments (Jewell, 1977; Lakatta and Spurgeon, 1980); through these mechanisms, the heart can vary its stroke volume with changes in filling volume. This is sometimes referred to as the Frank-Starling mechanism to alter stroke volume. It has been previously hypothesized that because of changes in myocardial compliance (i.e., the heart becomes stiffer with age) and because early diastolic filling rate in this population is compromised with advancing age (Gerstenblith et al., 1977), diastolic filling volume may become reduced in elderly versus

TABLE 5. The Effect of Age on Hemodynamic Performance at Maximum Exercise in BLSA Subjects (*N* = 61).

Parameter	Linear Regression	r	p
Heart rate (bpm)	208.19 − .94 (age)	−.66	<.001
End-diastolic volume (cc)	107.56 + 0.86 (age)	.28	<.03
Stroke volume (cc)	101.6 + .34 (age)	.14	<.25
Cardiac output (liters/min)	20.36 + .05 (age)	−.14	<.26
End-systolic volume (cc)	6.51 + .51 (age)	.41	<.001
Ejection fraction	89.5 − .21 (age)	−.37	<.003
Total peripheral vascular resistance	5.84 − .04 (age)	−.24	<.06
Systolic blood pressure (mm Hg)	175.31 + .33 (age)	.17	<.19

SOURCE: From Rodeheffer et al. (1984).

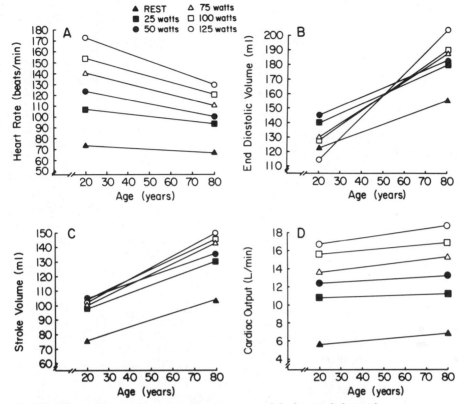

Figure 13. (A) Effect of age on heart rate (bpm) at rest and during graded exercise.

At rest (▲): heart rate = 76.88 1.12(age), $r = 1.17, p = .20, n = 61$.
At 25 watts (■): heart rate = 113.54 1.26(age), $r = 1.29, p = .02, n = 61$.
At 50 watts (●): heart rate = 130.46 1.39(age), $r = 1.39, p = .002, n = 59$.
At 75 watts (△): heart rate = 148.81 1.49(age), $r = 1.38, p = .003, n = 59$.
At 100 watts (□): heart rate = 164.25 1.54(age), $r = 1.41, p = .002, n = 55$.
At 125 watts (○): heart rate = 184.66 1.70(age), $r = 1.50, p = .002, n = 40$.

(B) Effect of age on end-diastolic volume (ml) (EDV) at rest and during graded exercise. The number of subjects is the same as in panel A.

At rest (▲): EDV = 112.64 + .53(age), $r = .20, p = .13$.
At 25 watts (■): EDV = 126.19 + .66(age), $r = .22, p = .09$.
At 50 watts (●): EDV = 132.27 + .63(age), $r = .20, p = .13$.
At 75 watts (△): EDV = 111.56 + .95(age), $r = .31, p = .02$.
At 100 watts (□): EDV = 105.95 + 1.06(age), $r = .35, p = .01$.
At 125 watts (○): EDV = 86.30 + 1.48(age), $r = .47, p = .003$.

(C) Effect of age on stroke volume (ml) (SV) at rest and during graded exercise. The number of subjects is the same as in panel A.

At rest (▲): SV = 66.05 + .47(age), $r = .26, p = .04$.
At 25 watts (■): SV = 88.01 + .52(age), $r = .24, p = .06$.
At 50 watts (●): SV = 96.30 + .50(age), $r = .22, p = .10$.
At 75 watts (△): SV = 84.76 + .73(age), $r = .32, p = .01$.
At 100 watts (□): SV = 91.25 + .66(age), $r = .29, p = .03$.
At 125 watts (○): SV = 85.52 + .80(age), $r = .37, p = .02$.

(D) Effect of age on cardiac output (liters/min) at rest and during graded exercise. The number of subjects is the same as in panel A.

At rest (▲): cardiac output = 5.3 + 0.02(age), $r = .16, p = .23$.
At 25 watts (■): cardiac output = 10.76 + 0.04(age), $r = .02, p = .86$.
At 50 watts (●): cardiac output = 11.94 + .015(age), $r = .07, p = .59$.
At 75 watts (△): cardiac output = 12.89 + .026(age), $r = .11, p = .41$.
At 100 watts (□): cardiac output = 15.23 + .018(age), $r = .07, p = .63$.
At 125 watts (○): cardiac output = 16.02 + .033(age), $r = .12, p = .46$.

It is important to note that the number of subjects able to complete the exercise period decreased with increasing work load. When the data analysis included only those who were able to achieve all work loads up to and including 125 watts, the significance, or lack thereof, of the age effect on these parameters was unchanged. (From Rodeheffer et al., 1984.)

younger adult subjects during exercise, when the filling time is reduced. However, this is not the case; rather, quite the opposite occurs: i.e., end-diastolic filling volume increases rather than decreases as a function of age during exercise response (Figure 13B and Table 5). In a previous study of another subset of the same population at submaximal work loads, i.e., during semisupine exercise at a common heart rate of 120 bpm, the measured end-diastolic area determined by two-dimensional echocardiography was also greater in older (over 65 years) than in younger (30 years) subjects (VanTosh et al., 1980). The observed increase in filling volume was a major factor through which stroke volume was maintained, and the increase was greater in the elderly during exercise than in the younger subjects (Figure 13C and Table 5). This, in part, balanced the negative effect of a decrease in heart rate on cardiac output during exercise, which in this population did not decline with age (Figure 13D and Table 5). Enhanced filling volume (or utilization of the Frank-Starling mechanism) may thus be construed as an age-related adaptive mechanism through which cardiac output is maintained during stress. A price is paid for this adaptation, however, in that generation of a given ventricular pressure requires greater wall stress (force per unit area) if the ventricular radius is increased (Laplace's law); this, in turn, requires a greater level of muscle contractility and energy production. The age-related increase in ventricular wall thickness (Figure 6) tends to reduce this stress somewhat. Furthermore, enhanced filling volume, even in the absence of diminished compliance results in an enhanced filling pressure and may explain, in part at least, the age-related increase in filling pressure observed during increased exercise in another population (Granath et al., 1964). An increase in left heart diastolic filling pressure also produces an increase in pulmonary venous pressure, which enhances the likelihood of pulmonary congestion. This may in part explain the increasing tendency for dyspnea (shortness of breath) to occur during exercise with advancing age.

Ejection Fraction

An increase in diastolic filling volume in itself not only should serve to enhance stroke volume but, all else being equal, should result in at least the same increase in the fraction of blood ejected with each beat and equal end-systolic volumes in the elderly versus young adults. However, this is not the case; rather, end-systolic volume is not reduced to the same extent during exercise in the elderly subjects as in the younger adults and, in fact, increases with age (Table 5), and the *fraction* of blood ejected is not increased but, rather, is actually decreased (Table 5). This is indicative of some additional factors operating to compromise the ejection of blood in the elderly subjects. In radionuclide studies of ejection fraction performed during exercise in another population (Port et al., 1980), it was observed that the ejection fraction *decreased* from resting levels in many apparently healthy aged subjects (Figure 14A). That study also observed a high prevalence of inhomogeneous ventricular wall motion during ejection. Both these findings are characteristic of subjects with coronary artery disease (Rerych et al., 1978). In contrast to that study, in BLSA participants, while an age-related decline in the absolute ejection fraction during exercise occurred, a pattern of a reduction in ejection fraction *below* resting levels in the elderly was not observed (Figure 14B). Note the marked difference in the response in panel A versus panel B in Figure 14.

Load during Shortening

The vascular system determines a major portion of the load on the ventricle during shortening, and age differences in vascular loading during exercise may in part explain the diminution in the elderly of ejection fraction in the presence of an increased filling volume. This load, or vascular input impedance, consists of two components: a steady component (peripheral vascular resistance) and the average pulsatile component (characteristic impedance). The former, which is governed largely by the peripheral circulation, in contrast to

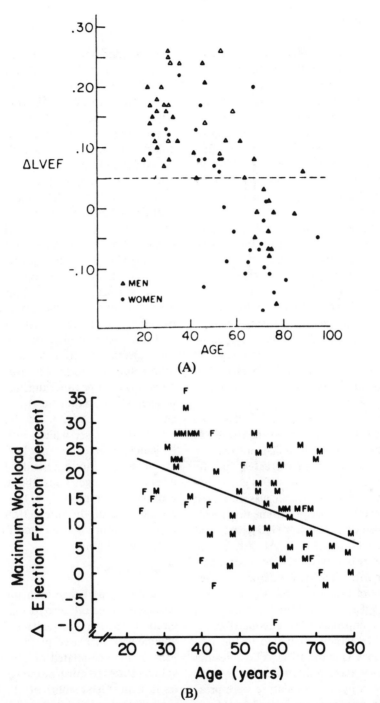

Figure 14. (A) Change in left ventricular ejection fraction (ΔLVEF) plotted against age in 46 men and 31 women. The change in ejection fraction from rest to exercise (exercise LVEF − resting LVEF) showed a decline with increase in age ($r = -0.71$). Moreover, 21 of 29 subjects over the age of 60 actually had a decrease in ejection from rest to exercise, as compared with 4 of 48 subjects under 60 ($P = 0.001$, chi square). Dashed line indicates ejection fraction of 0.05, the normal minimum increase. (From Port et al., 1980.)

(B) The change in ejection fraction (EF) at maximum upright bicycle exercise versus age in BLSA participants. Note that in contrast to panel A, while the change in ejection fraction decreases with advancing age, EF rarely decreased from the resting level. (From Rodeheffer et al., 1984.)

many previous studies (Table 4) was not markedly different with age during maximal exercise in the BLSA population (Table 5). The characteristic impedence, derived from the instantaneous relationship between pressure and pulsatile flow, and determined largely by the compliance characteristics of the aorta and pressure waves reflected from the periphery, has been less well studied than the static load component and has not been determined in normal man across a broad range. An increase in this component may be manifest in an increase in systolic blood pressure, and the age-related increase in systolic blood pressure at rest, discussed earlier, could be a manifestation of an increase in this component of impedance with advancing age. It is noteworthy, however, that during maximal exercise, the age-related difference in systolic blood pressure at rest was somewhat reduced and no significant age effect was present (Table 5). This result is also to be contrasted with that in Table 4.

Recently, in the canine model it has been demonstrated that substantial increases in characteristic aortic input impedance can occur in the absence of an increased systolic blood pressure (Yin et al., 1981). In that study, characteristic impedance was measured during treadmill exercise in chronically instrumented beagle dogs of adult (1–3 years) and senescent (10–12 years) ages. At rest, no age differences were observed in either cardiac performance or aortic impedance. However, over a wide range of exercise stress, the 10 to 12-year-old beagles demonstrated increases in characteristic impedance and a reduced increment in stroke volume compared to the 1 to 3-year-old dogs (Figure 15A). These results suggest that age-related alterations in the loading of the heart by the vasculature were present during exercise and may indeed have been a factor which limited the increase in stroke volume. Although the altered physical characteristics of the aorta in both dog (Yin et al., 1983a) and man, as noted, are an apparent cause of the altered impedance, age differences in autonomic modulation might also be a major factor because, as illustrated in Figure 15B, following propranolol, the age difference in

characteristic impedance during exercise was obliterated and the age difference in stroke volume was lessened. It is noteworthy that the response to exercise in this population of dogs differed from the BLSA human population in that maximum stroke volume was decreased in the old dogs, and the heart rate at the common levels of exercise compared was not different between the two age groups. In addition, although the change in physical characteristics of the dog aorta result in enhanced stiffness (Yin et al., 1983), the extent of dilatation of the dog aorta with age may be somewhat less than that in humans, and both factors are important determinants of aortic impedance. Thus, similar measurements of characteristic impedance are required in man to substantiate the hypothesis that diminished pump function (i.e., diminished ejection fraction or increased end-systolic volume) is in part a result of increased aortic input impedance during exercise. Such measurements require maintenance of pressure and flow catheters in the aorta during maximal exercise, which, although technologically possible, may not be feasible in otherwise healthy and physically fit men across a broad age range. Thus, the study in beagles is of particular importance to our current understanding of the interaction of the heart and vasculature and its modification due to aging during exercise.

Contractility

An age-related change in intrinsic contractile mechanisms could also explain diminished ejection fraction and enhanced end-systolic volume with increased preload in BLSA subjects or the age-related diminution in stroke volume observed during exercise in other studies in man (Gerstenblith et al., 1976) and in the beagle dog (Yin et al., 1981). As already noted, precise measurement of intrinsic contractile properties of the myocardium and their governing mechanisms cannot be determined in the intact organism, and for this purpose, studies in animal tissues are employed.

The contractile response to a stretch has been measured in cardiac muscle isolated from the LV of adult and senescent rats, and as

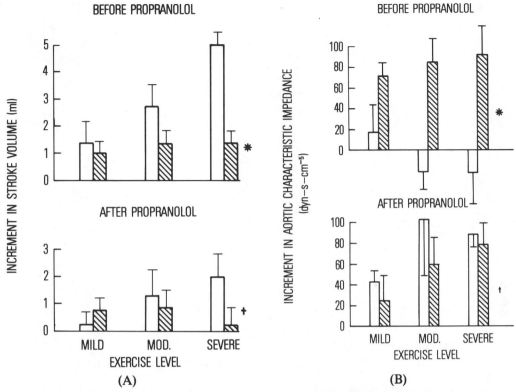

Figure 15. (A) Effect of graded exercise on left ventricular stroke volume represented as mean change from the resting values immediately preceding each exercise level in adult and senescent beagle dogs. The symbols refer to the P values for the variance ratio between age groups across the exercise levels. The progressive increases in the young group were significant before ($P = 0.005$) and after ($P = 0.006$) propranolol. The old group demonstrated an inability to increase stroke volume at all three exercise levels (□, young; ▨, old). *$P = 0.02$; †P = NS. Drug X age, P = NS.

(B) Effect of graded exercise on aortic characteristic impedance. Notation is the same as for panel A. Before propranolol, exercise caused a significant increase in aortic impedance in the old but not in the young group. After propranolol, aortic impedance was increased by exercise in both age groups to a similar extent. (From Yin et al., 1981.)

illustrated in Figure 16, no age effect was observed. An increase in muscle length, like other cardiotonic substances, alters the extent of the Ca^{++}-myofilament interaction subsequent to excitation. Figure 16B illustrates that the response to changes in $[Ca^{++}]$ in the fluid bathing these muscles is also not age related. In addition, more recent studies in "chemically skinned" muscles have not observed an age difference in the direct myofibrillar force-pCa relationship (Bhatnagar et al., 1984). Thus, there is no evidence in the rat (the only animal model in which cardiac muscle function has been extensively studied) that the *maximum* intrinsic contractility response of

force or displacement in response to Ca^{++} or stretch is altered in advanced age. During exercise, however, catecholamines, which are secreted from nerve endings, serve to augment contractility. It is indeed plausible that the response to catecholamines is altered with age (vide infra), and this would appear as a diminution in maximum muscle contractility during exercise in the intact organism.

Maximum Coronary Blood Flow

No measurements of the effect of age on maximum coronary blood flow have been made in man. Maximum coronary flow and oxygen

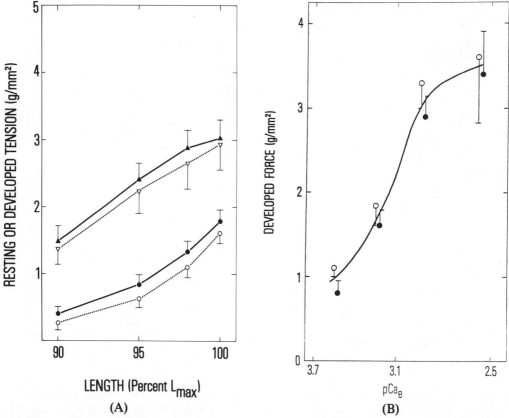

Figure 16. (A) The effect of muscle length on developed (triangles) and resting (circles) force in trabeculae isolated from hearts of adult (closed symbols) and senescent (open symbols) Wistar rats. (From Yin et al., 1980.)

(B) The effect of age and perfusate $[Ca^{++}]$ on isometric force development in trabeculae carneae isolated from adult (6–12 months, •) and senescent (25 months, o) rat hearts. Muscles were stimulated via plate electrodes at a rate of 24 min^{-1} at 29°C at the length at which force development was maximal. Figure was constructed from data from different studies from the same laboratory. (From Lakatta and Yin, 1982.)

consumption per gram heart are diminished in senescent versus adult rat hearts in both the working and the nonworking mode, and the magnitude of this decrement is approximately 15 percent (Weisfeldt et al., 1971b; Abu-Erreish et al., 1977). Since relative oxygen extraction is not age related (Weisfeldt et al., 1971b) and structural alterations in the large, medium, or small coronary vessels are not present in these hearts, the age difference for decreased maximum coronary flow and oxygen consumption likely results from a change in vascular reactivity, a failure of the coronary bed to enlarge commensurate with the increase in heart mass that occurs with senescence, or decreased mitochondrial utili-

zation. In this regard, the decrease in oxidation of palmitate observed in the senescent versus adult isolated working heart may in part be related to age-associated differences in coronary flow (Abu-Erreish et al., 1977).

Autonomic Modulation

During maximum exercise, the sympathetic component is essentially the exclusive autonomic modulator and a marked increase in catecholamine secretion occurs. An age-related alteration in sympathetic modulation of the cardiovascular response to exercise as a *single* factor could account for *all* of the age-associated changes that have been identified in the cardiovascular response to exercise: the decline in maximum heart rate; the apparent decline in maximum contractility, i.e., a diminished stroke volume, an increased end-systolic volume, or a decreased ejection fraction from a greater filling volume; the increase in aortic input impedance as observed in the dog model; and differences in the regulation of blood flow to the musculature which are suggested by the age-related diminution in arteriovenous oxygen difference in other studies (see Gerstenblith et al., 1976, for review). Several studies in both man and intact animals have suggested an age-related decrease in the efficacy of sympathetic modulation (Lakatta, 1980b). These studies of the effect of age on the adrenergic modulation of the cardiovascular system in men have taken two general approaches: infusion of catecholamines and employment of β-adrenergic blockade.

Bolus infusion of isoproterenol in healthy men aged 62–80 years produced less of an increase in heart rate than in younger adults 18–34 years of age (Yin et al., 1976). Similar results were obtained in subsequent studies (Vestal et al., 1979), while another has demonstrated less of an increase in cardiac index in response to isoproterenol in aged versus younger adult men (Figure 17) (Kuramoto et al., 1978). Although the results of these studies are clear-cut in demonstrating that the heart rate and hemodynamic response to isoproterenol decline with advancing age, the interpretation of the results is not unique, i.e., the results could be explained either by a diminished response to the adrenergic stimulation or by an enhanced vagal modulation of the heart rate with advancing age, or both. Studies of this sort in the presence of vagal blockade would clarify the interpretation somewhat.

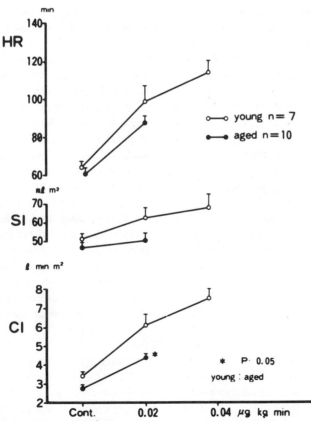

Figure 17. Hemodynamic comparison of young (21–26 years) and all subjects (63–83 years) isoproterenol infusion. HR: heart rate; SI: stroke index; CI: cardiac index. Isoproterenol was infused at a rate of 0.02 μg/kg/mm for 5 minutes. (From Kuramoto et al., 1978.)

β-Adrenergic blockade provides an additional approach toward isolating an adrenergic component of a stress response. The difference in cardiac output due to age that was observed in apparently healthy young adult and elderly men who exercised at comparable work loads during dynamic exercise was significantly less during β-adrenergic blockade (Conway et al., 1971). One interpretation of those results is that in the unblocked state the effectiveness of β-adrenergic stimulation, whether on the heart, central nervous system, or peripheral vasculature, was greater in young adult compared to the older men and permitted a greater cardiac output during exercise in the younger group. However, the results of another study indicate that in senescent men, the effect of β-adrenergic blockade may modify the non-adrenergic as well as the adrenergic components of the hemodynamic response to stress in the senescent heart (Yin et al., 1978). This study demonstrated that in response to a 30 mm Hg increase in systolic blood pressure induced by phenylephrine infusion in the presence of β-adrenergic blockade (propranolol 0.15 mg/kg IV), significant ventricular dilatation occurred in normal elderly men (aged 60 to 68), but did not occur in younger adults (aged 18 to 34). This significant dilatation was noted even in the presence of a smaller reduction of the heart rate in the elderly group. It is important to note that the efficacy of β-blockade was the same in both age groups, as demonstrated by the failure of isoproterenol to increase heart rate in either group in the presence of propranolol. Because of significant age differences in the intrinsic or non-adrenergic component of the cardiac response to an increase in afterload, the senescent heart dilated and was contracting from a greater preload than the adult heart. Thus, differential effects of β-blockade on cardiac output in young adult and elderly men could be attributable not solely to a differential effect of β-adrenergic stimulation but also to its effect on nonadrenergic determinants of cardiac output in the two age groups (Figure 2). Once again, it seems fair to conclude that complex interaction of the adrenergic and non-adrenergic components of the reflex response to stress prohibits a clear definition of the effectiveness of the adrenergic component with advancing age, even when β-adrenergic agonists and antagonists are employed to elucidate the adrenergic component.

In order to circumvent some of the limitations in studies in man, animal models have been employed to study the effect of aging on the responsiveness to catecholamines. Infusion of epinephrine and norepinephrine into intact adult and senescent rats, and into young and adult cats and rabbits, has elicited a variety of complex changes in cardiovascular function (Frolkis et al., 1970, 1975). While the specific adrenergic cardiovascular effects cannot be ascertained from such studies, the data do demonstrate a lower threshold or a supersensitivity in the total cardiovascular response in the senescent animal, while the response to high agonist concentrations is diminished with advancing age (Frolkis et al., 1970). Supersensitivity of the heart to catecholamines has been described following depletion of tissue catecholamine content (Cooper, 1966). As noted, myocardial catecholamine concentration content could explain the lower threshold for the cardiovascular response to infused catecholamines in the senescent organism. No comparable evidence for supersensitivity to catecholamines has been found in isolated cardiac muscle from the senescent rat.

The maximum heart rate response to isoproterenol infusion was diminished in senescent beagles compared to adult, and diminished response persisted in the presence of full vagal blockade with atropine (Yin et al., 1979), which suggests that age differences in cholinergic tone were not a factor contributing to the age difference response to infused catecholamines. A diminished maximum heart rate response resulting from infusion of catecholamines may be due to age-related differences in stimulation of the vasomotor center, the atrial pacemaker, or may in part result from a diminished reflex stimulation of non-adrenergic receptors such as that due to atrial stretch (Pathak, 1973). For these reasons, there is no unique interpretation regarding the precise mechanism for the diminished heart rate response to infused catecholamines in the senescent versus the adult intact dog.

A diminished sympathetic response during exercise could also result from a deficiency in the elaboration of catecholamines in aged subjects. Recently, in a subset of the BLSA population, it has been determined that both serum epinephrine and norepinephrine demonstrated a striking age-dependent *increase* during treadmill exercise (Tzankoff et al., 1980) (Figure 18). Thus, in these healthy subjects, a diminished maximum heart rate was accompanied by an increase rather than a decrease in serum catecholamines (Tzanoff et al., 1980). It has also been documented that during isometric exercise, which also elicits a diminished cardiovascular response in elderly versus younger adult men (Lakatta, 1979), serum catecholamines are elevated to greater levels in the elderly men (Palmer et al., 1978). Enhanced serum levels in the elderly in these instances result from an enhanced secretion rather than a diminished degradation rate (Rowe and Troen, 1980). Failure in the secretion of catecholamines during exercise, then, cannot be entertained as a factor which limits maximum cardiovascular performance.

To summarize the results obtained in man and intact animals, it may be concluded that while no *single* study in itself is definitively conclusive, these studies *in toto* make a strong case to suggest that a diminution in target organ responsiveness to β-adrenergic stimulation is a key mechanism for the age-related differences in many facets of the stress response.

The target organ response to catecholamines can be directly studied in animal tissues (Lakatta, 1980b) and permits elucidation of mechanisms for the age differences which are observed in the postsynaptic adrenergic response, i.e., at or distal to the level of the β-receptor. In isolated aortas and pulmonary arteries, the relaxing effect of β-adrenergic stimulation declined from the neonatal to the adult period, whereas no age differences in the maximum responsiveness to a non-adrenergic relaxant could be demonstrated (Fleisch et al., 1970; Cohen and Berkowitz, 1974; Fleisch and Hooker, 1976). Comparable studies on β-stimulation have not been performed on vessels isolated from senescent animals. However, the contractile effect of norepinephrine is diminished in the aortas from senescent compared to those from adult rats (Tuttle, 1966). The reduced direct response of smooth muscle to norepinephrine may explain in part the observation that greater voltage stimulation of the paravertebral sympathetic chain was necessary to evoke a pressor response in the leg vessels in the senescent, as compared to the adult, rat (Frolkis et al., 1975).

Recent studies have shown that catecholamines affect many cellular biochemical reactions, some of which play an integral role in mediating the contractile response (Scholz,

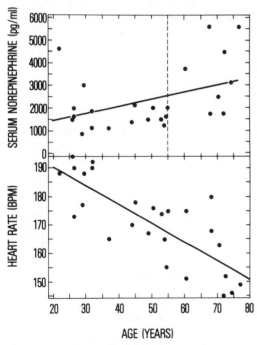

Figure 18. The effect of age on serum norepinephrine concentration and heart rate during maximum treadmill exercise in BLSA participants. The subpopulation in this protocol is different from that studied in Figure 13. Serum norepinephrine concentration at rest did not differ in these subjects. (From Tzanoff et al., 1980.)

1980). A general scheme of this β-adrenergic cascade and its purported relationship to contractility is depicted in Figure 19. Reduced to its simplest terms, β-adrenergic stimulation appears to enhance cardiac muscle performance by an increase in Ca^{++} released into the myoplasm subsequent to excitation.

In cardiac muscle isolated from the rat (Figure 20), the maximum contractile response to β-adrenergic stimulation is diminished in senescent versus adult preparations (Lakatta et al., 1975b; Guarnieri et al., 1980b).

The observed age difference in the maximum response to β-adrenergic stimulation could result from age differences in one or more steps leading to this increase of intracellular Ca^{++} upon excitation of the cardiac cell (Figure 19). Studies to date indicate that the mechanism for the age difference in contractile response does not appear to be localized to the level of the β-receptor for the following reasons: (1) the characteristics of the β-receptor, as assessed in membrane preparations, do not differ in hearts from adult and senescent

rats (Figure 21); (2) measurements of isoproterenol-induced cAMP stimulation, determined in the same hearts in which the contractile response to isoproterenol was measured, were nearly identical in both age groups (Table 6); and (3) when dibutyryl cAMP, which directly activates protein kinase and thus circumvents the receptor, rather than isoproterenol, was employed as the agonist (Figure 22B), an age difference in contractile response persisted. In addition, protein kinase activation, a step subsequent to enhanced cAMP generation, was equal in both age groups (Table 6). Thus, the age difference in contractile response must be distal to these steps in the scheme in Figure 19. Age differences in phosphodiesterase activity, although not measured in this study, cannot explain the age difference since this would be reflected in age differences in cAMP levels.

A nonspecific age difference in response to Ca^{++} cannot account for the diminished contractile response to β-stimulation, since the response to Ca^{++} added directly to the perfu-

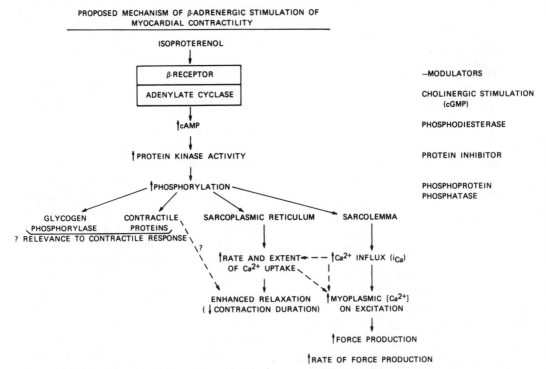

Figure 19. The proposed relationship of β-adrenergic induced changes in cellular biochemical reactions to enhancement of contractility of cardiac muscles. (From Lakatta, 1980b.)

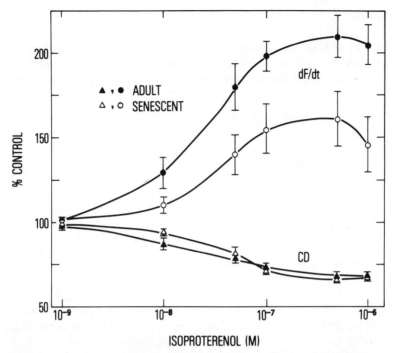

Figure 20. Effect of age on response to the maximum rate of force development (*dF/dt*) and contraction duration (CD) to isoproterenol in arterially perfused interventricular septa from adult (7–9 months) and senescent (25 months) rats. Age difference in dose-response curves of *dF/dt* is significant at $P < 0.005$ level (regression analysis of variance, $n = 6$ in each age group at each isoproterenol concentration). Prior to isoproterenol, *dF/dt* was not age related, but CD was significantly prolonged in the 25-month septa. (From Guarnieri et al., 1980b.)

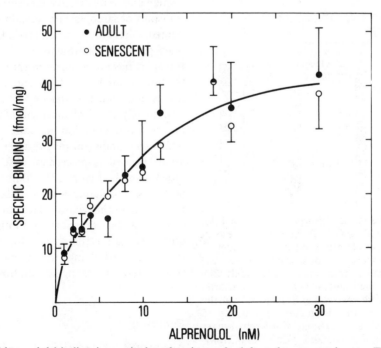

Figure 21. Alprenolol binding in particulate fractions of adult and senescent hearts. Three to eight preparations from each single heart were used at each alprenolol concentration. (From Guarnieri et al., 1980b.)

TABLE 6. **Effect of High Concentrations of Isoproterenol (5 ×10⁷m) on cAMP and Protein Kinase Activity Ratio (−cAMP/+cAMP) in Isolated Perfused Interventricular Septa from Adult (6–9 mo.) and Senescent (25 mo.) Rats.**

	cAMP pmol/mg wet wt		PKAR	
	Control	Isoproterenol	Control	Isoproterenol
Adult	0.343 ± 0.02	0.617 ± 0.03	0.191 ± 0.011	0.439 ± 0.02
	(8)	(9)	(8)	(9)
Senescent	0.356 ± 0.01	0.635 ± 0.01	0.193 ± 0.017	0.434 ± 0.02
	(9)	(6)	(8)	(6)

SOURCE: From Guarnieri et al. (1980b).
NOTE: Values are means ± S.E. Number in parenthesis is No. of septa. PKAR = protein kinase activation ratio. Absolute maximum cAMP-dependent protein kinase activity (i.e., in the presence of 2.5 uM cAMP) in homogenates, supernates, and membranes was also not age-related.

sate produced a similar enhancement of contractility in both age groups (Figure 22C) (Lakatta et al., 1975b; Guarnieri et al., 1980b). The composite results of the studies described suggest that the age difference in the contractile response to β-adrenergic stimulation observed in isolated cardiac muscle may have resulted from an age difference in phosphory-

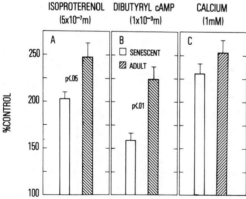

Figure 22. The effect of isoproterenol (panel A), dibutyryl cAMP (panel B), and an increase in calcium concentration in the perfusate (panel C) on the maximum rate of force production (dT/dt) in interventricular septa isolated from adult (7–9 months) and senescent (24–26 months) rat hearts. All muscles were contracting isometrically at the peak of their length-tension curve, stimulated 75 min⁻¹ at 29°C, and perfused with Krebs-Ringer bicarbonate solution containing Ca⁺⁺ of 0.3 mM. Baseline dT/dt prior to the interventions in panels A–C was not age related. (Redrawn from Guarnieri et al., 1980b.)

lation of cellular proteins and/or changes in ion transport that result from phosphorylation of organelles involved directly in excitation-contraction coupling, e.g., the sarcoplasmic reticulum, sarcolemma, or myofibrils.

That no age difference was observed in the relaxant effect of catecholamine, i.e., a reduction in contraction duration (Figure 20), suggests that the increase in cAMP-stimulated protein kinase-mediated enhancement of Ca⁺⁺ transport of sarcoplasmic reticulum is not age related. Direct measurements of cAMP-stimulated protein kinase-mediated effect on Ca⁺⁺ transport have been made in sarcoplasmic reticulum isolated from adult and senescent rat hearts, and indicate that cAMP induced approximately 25% enhancement of the velocity of Ca⁺⁺ accumulation in both age groups, which was similar in magnitude to the relaxation effect of isoproterenol observed in the intact animals (Figure 23). Additional studies of this sort isolating each cellular organelle protein phosphorylation and the resulting change in ion transport or binding are required to define the precise mechanism for the age-related change in the myocardial response to β-adrenergic stimulation.

Summary

Age-related differences in the cardiovascular response to stress in man have often been observed. The nature and the magnitude of these

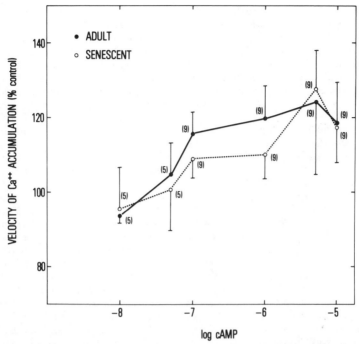

Figure 23. The effect of cAMP on the velocity of Ca^{++} accumulation in sarcoplasmic reticulum isolated from adult and senescent rat hearts. SR (crude microsomal preparations) were preincubated with protein kinase, 0.05 mg/ml. The reaction mixture contained 5 mM oxalate and free $[Ca^{++}]$ of 0.56 μm; all other conditions were as per Froehlich et al. (1978). (From Beard and Lakatta, in preparation.)

age differences have varied with the population studied. In apparently healthy populations which have not been screened for occult coronary disease, substantial decrements in maximum cardiopulmonary function and work capacity have been observed. In more selectively screened populations, although the heart rate increases less with exercise, age-related adaptations in hemodynamics occur; i.e., end-diastolic and stroke volumes increase, which serve to prevent substantial declines in cardiac output. However, end-diastolic volume is increased and ejection fraction decreased as a function of age during exercise. A common feature among many of the results of studies in both types of populations is that at least in part, the age-related alterations in hemodynamics observed may be attributed to altered responsiveness to adrenergic stimulation and/or intrinsic changes in the peripheral vasculature. Studies in animals and in cardiovascular tissues isolated from animals also demonstrate age-related differences in both these parameters.

REFERENCES

Abboud, F. M. and Huston, J. H. 1961. The effects of aging and degenerative vascular disease on the measurement of arterial rigidity in man. *J. Clin. Invest.* 40: 933–939.

Abu-Erreish, G. M., Neely, J. R., Whitmer, J. T., Whitman, V., and Sanadi, D. R. 1977. Fatty acid oxidation by isolated perfused working hearts of aged rats. *Am. J. Physiol.* 232(3): E258–E262.

Ackerman, R. F., Dry, T. J., and Edwards, J. E. 1950. Relationship of various factors to the degree of coronary atherosclerosis in women. *Circulation* 1: 1345–1354.

Allen, D. G. and Kurihara, S. 1979. Calcium transients in mammalian ventricular muscle. *In, Fifth Workshop on Contractile Behaviour of the Heart, Abstracts*, p. 2. Belgium: University of Antwerp.

Alpert, N. R., Gale, H. H., and Taylor, N. 1967. The effect of age on contractile protein ATPase activity and the velocity of shortening. *In*, K. Kavaler, R. D. Tanz, and J. Roberts (eds.), *Factors Influencing Myocardial Contractility*, pp. 127–133. New York: Academic Press.

Aschoff, L. 1924. *In, Lectures in Pathology*, pp. 131. New York: Paul Hoeber.

Bader, H. 1967. Dependence of wall stress in the human thoracic aorta on age and pressure. *Circ. Res.* 30: 354–361.

Batsakis, J. G. 1968. *In*, S. E. Gould (ed.), *Pathology of the Heart and Blood Vessels,* 3rd ed., pp. 519–526. Springfield, Ill.: Charles C. Thomas.

Bhatnagar, G. M., Walford, G. D., Beard, E. S., Humphreys, S., and Lakatta, E. G. 1984. ATPase activity and force production in myofibrils and twitch characteristics in intact muscle from neonatal, adult, and senescent ray myocardium. *J. Mol. Cell. Cardiol.* 16: 203–218.

Bing, O. H. L., Matsushita, S., Fanburg, B. L., and Levine, H. J. 1971. Mechanical properties of rat cardiac muscle during experimental hypertrophy. *Circ. Res.* 28: 234–245.

Bramwell, J. C. and Hill, A. V. 1922. The velocity of the pulse wave in man. *Proc. Roy. Soc. (Series B)* 93: 298–306.

Brandfonbrener, M., Landowne, M., and N. W. Shock. 1955. Changes in cardiac output with age. *Circulation* 12: 557–566.

Busby, D. E. and Burton, A. C. 1965. The effect of age on the elasticity of the major brain arteries. *Can. J. Physiol. Pharmacol.* 43: 185–202.

Caird, F. I. and Kennedy, R. D. 1976. Epidemiology of heart disease in old age. *In*, F. I. Caird, J. L. C. Dall, and R. D. Kennedy (eds.), *Cardiology in Old Age,* pp. 1–10. New York: Plenum Press.

Carter, S. A. 1964. *In vivo* estimation of elastic characteristics of the arteries in the lower extremities of man. *Can. J. Physiol. Pharmacol.* 42: 309–413.

Cavoto, F. V., Kelliher, G. J., and Roberts, J. 1974. Electrophysiological changes in the rat atrium with age. *Am. J. Physiol.* 226(6): 1293–1297.

Chesky, J. A. and Rockstein, M. 1977. Reduced myocardial actomyosin adenosine triphosphatase activity in the aging male Fischer rat. *Cardiovasc. Res.* 11: 242–246.

Cohen, M. L. and Berkowitz, B. A. 1974. Age-related changes in vascular responsiveness to cyclic nucleotides and contractile agonist. *J. Pharmacol. Exp. Ther.* 191: 147–155.

Conway, J. and Smith, K. S. 1956. A clinical method of studying the elasticity of large arteries. *Br. Heart J.* 18: 467–474.

Conway, J., Wheeler, R., and Sannerstedt, R. 1971. Sympathetic nervous activity during exercise in relation to age. *Cardiovasc. Res.* 5: 577–581.

Cooper, T. G. 1966. Surgical sympathectomy and adrenergic function. *Pharmacol. Rev.* 18: 611–618.

Costa, P. T. and McCrae, R. P. 1977. Functional age: a conceptual and empirical critique. *In*, S. G. Haynes, and M. Feinleib (eds.), *Second Conference on the Epidemiology of Aging,* pp. 25–50. Bethesda, Md.: U.S. Department of Health and Human Services.

Davies, H. E. F. 1975. Respiratory change in heart rate, sinus arrhythmia in the elderly. *Geront., Clin.* 17: 96–100.

Dock, W. 1945. Presbycardia, or aging of the myocardium. *N.Y. State J. Med.* 45: 983–986.

Dontas, A. S., Taylor, J. D., and Keys, A. 1961. Carotid pressure plethysmograms: effects of age, diastolic pressure, relative body weight, and physical activity. *Archiv. Kreislaufforsch.* 36: 49–58.

Fleg, J. L., Rodeheffer, R. J., Gerstenblith, G., Becker, L. C., Weisfeldt, M. L., and Lakatta, E. G. 1982. Cardiac output does not decline with age in healthy, fit subjects. *Circulation* 66: II–185.

Fleisch, J. H. and Hooker, C. S. 1976. The relationship between age and relaxation of vascular smooth muscle in the rabbit and rat. *Circ. Res.* 38: 243–249.

Fleisch, J. H., Maling, H. M., and Brodie, B. B. 1970. Beta-receptor activity in aorta. *Circ. Res.* 26: 151–162.

Freis, E. D., Heath, W. C., Luchsinger, P. C., and Snell, R. E. 1966. Changes in the carotid pulse which occur with age and hypertension. *Am. Heart J.* 71: 757–765.

Froehlich, J. P., Lakatta, E. G., Beard, E., Spurgeon, H. A., Weisfeldt, M. L., and Gerstenblith, G. 1978. Studies of sarcoplasmic reticulum function and contraction duration in young adult and aged rat myocardium. *J. Mol. Cell. Cardiol.* 10: 427–438.

Frolkis, V. V., Berzrukov, B. B., Bogatskaya, L. N., Verkhratsky, N. S., Zamostian, V. P., Shevchuk, V. G., and Shtchegoleva, I. V. 1970. Catecholamines regulation in the metabolism and functions in aging. *Gerontologia* 16: 129–140.

Frolkis, V. V., Berzrukov, B. B., and Shevchuk, V. G. 1975. Hemodynamics and its regulation in old age. *Exp. Geront.* 10: 251–271.

Gardin, J. M., Henry, W. L., Savage, D. D., Ware, J. H., Burn, C., and Borer, J. S. 1979. Echocardiographic measurements in normal subjects: evaluation of an adult population without clinically apparent heart disease. *J. Clin. Ultrasound.* 7: 439–447.

Gerstenblith, G., Fleg, J. L., Vantosh, A., Becker, L., Kallman, C., Andres, R., Weisfeldt, M., and Lakatta, E. G. 1980. Stress testing redefines the prevalence of coronary artery disease in epidemiologic studies. *Circulation* 62: Part II, III–308.

Gerstenblith, G., Frederiksen, J., Yin, F. C. P., Fortuin, N. J., Lakatta, E. G., and Weisfeldt, M. L. 1977. Echocardiographic assessment of a normal adult aging population. *Circulation* 56: 273–278.

Gerstenblith, G., Lakatta, E. G., and Weisfeldt, M. L. 1976. Age changes in myocardial function and exercise response. *Prog. Cardiovasc. Dis.* 19: 1–21.

Gey, F. K., Burkard, W. P., and Pletscher, A. 1965. Variation of the norepinephrine metabolism of the rat heart with age. *Gerontologia* 11: 1–11.

Gonza, E. R., Marble, A. E., Shaw, A., and Holland, J. G. 1974. Age-related changes in the mechanics of the aorta and pulmonary artery of man. *J. Appl. Physiol.* 36: 407–411.

Granath, A., Jonsson, B., and Strandell, T. 1964. Circulation in healthy old men studied by right heart catheterization at rest and during exercise in supine and sitting position. *Acta Med. Scand.* 176: 425–446.

Guarnieri, T., Filburn, C. R., Beard, E. S., and Lakatta, E. G. 1980a. Enhanced contractile response and protein kinase activation to threshold levels of β-adrenergic stimulation in hyperthyroid rat heart. *J. Clin. Invest.* 65: 861–868.

Guarnieri, T., Filburn, C. R., Zitnik, G., Roth, G. S., and Lakatta, E. G. 1980b. Contractile and biochemical correlates of β-adrenergic stimulation of the aged heart. *Am. J. Physiol.* 239: H501–H508.

Gulch, R. W. 1980. The effect of elevated chronic loading on the action potential of mammalian myocardium. *J. Mol. Cell. Cardiol.* 12: 415–425.

Hallock, P. and Benson, I. C. 1937. Studies on the elastic properties of human isolated aorta. *J. Clin. Invest.* 16: 595–602.

Harris, R. 1975. Cardiac changes with age. *In,* R. Goldman and M. Rockstein (eds.), *The Physiology and Pathology of Human Aging,* pp. 109–122. New York: Academic Press.

Harrison, T. R., Dixon, K., Russell, R. O., Jr., Bidwai, P. S., and Coleman, H. N. 1964. The relation of age to the duration of contraction, ejection, and relaxation of the normal human heart. *Am. Heart J.* 67: 189–199.

Haynes, F. W., Ellis, L. B., and Weiss, S. 1936. Pulse wave velocity and related conditions. *Am. Heart J.* 11: 385–401.

Heath, G. W., Hagberg, J. M., Ehsani, A. A., and Holloszy, J. O. 1981. A physiological comparison of young and older endurance athletes. *J. Appl. Physiol.: Respirat. Environ. Exercise Physiol.* 51: 634–640.

Ito, Y., Suko, J., and Chidsey, C. A. 1974. Intracellular calcium and myocardial contractility. V. Calcium uptake of sarcoplasmic reticulum fractions in hypertrophied and failing rabbit hearts. *J. Mol. Cell. Cardiol.* 6: 237–247.

Jewell, B. R. 1977. A reexamination of the influence of muscle length on myocardial performance. *Circ. Res.* 40: 221–230.

Jose, A. D. 1966. Effect of combined sympathetic and parasympathetic blockade on heart rate and cardiac function in man. *Am. J. Cardiol.* 18: 476–478.

Julius, S., Antoon, A., Whitlock, L. S., and Conway, J. 1967. Influence of age on the hemodynamic response to exercise. *Circulation* 36: 222–230.

Kannel, W. B., Gordon, T., and Offutt, D. 1969. Left ventricular hypertrophy by electrocardiogram. Prevalence, incidence, and mortality in the Framingham study. *Ann. Intern. Med.* 71: 89–105.

Kennedy, R. D., Andrews, G. R., and Caird, F. I. 1977. Ischemic heart disease in the elderly. *Brit. Heart J.* 39: 1121–1127.

King, A. L. 1946. Pressure-volume relation for cylindrical tubes with elastomeric walls: the human aorta. *J. Appl. Physics* 17: 501–505.

Kirchberger, M. A., Tada, M., and Katz, A. M. 1974. Adenosine 3′–5′ monophosphate-dependent protein kinase-catalyzed phosphorylation reaction and its relationship to calcium transport in cardiac sarcoplasmic reticulum. *J. Biol. Chem.* 249: 6166–6175.

Korecky, B. 1979. The effects of load, internal environment, and age on cardiac mechanics. *J. Mol. Cell. Cardiol.* 11: 33, Suppl. 1.

Kostis, J. B., Moreyra, A. E., Amendo, M. T., Di Pietro, J., Cosgrove, N., and Kuo, P. T. 1982. The effect of age on heart rate in subjects free of heart disease. *Circulation* 65: 141–145.

Kuramoto, K., Matsushita, S., Mifune, J., Sakai, M., and Murakami, M. 1978. Electrocardiographic and hemodynamic evaluations of isoproterenol test in elderly ischemic heart disease. *Jpn. Circ. J.* 42: 955–960.

Lakatta, E. G., 1979. Alterations in the cardiovascular system that occur in advanced age. *Fed. Proc.* 38: 163–167.

Lakatta, E. G. 1980a. Excitation-contraction. *In,* M. L. Weisfeldt (ed.), *The Aging Heart,* pp. 77–100. New York: Raven Press.

Lakatta, E. G. 1980b. Age-related alterations in the cardiovascular response to adrenergic mediated stress. *Fed. Proc.* 39: 3173–3177.

Lakatta, E. G. 1983. Determinants of cardiovascular performance: modification due to aging. *J. Chronic Dis.* 36: 15–30.

Lakatta, E. G., Gerstenblith, G., and Angell, C. S. 1975a. Prolonged contraction duration in aged myocardium. *J. Clin. Invest.,* 55: 61–68.

Lakatta, E. G., Gerstenblith, G., Angell, C. S., Shock, N. W., and Weisfeldt, M. L. 1975b. Diminished inotrophic response of aged myocardium to catecholamines. *Circ. Res.* 36: 262–269.

Lakatta, E. G. and Spurgeon, H. A. 1980. Force staircase kinetics in mammalian cardiac muscle: modulation by muscle length. *J. Physiol. (Lond.)* 299: 337–352.

Lakatta, E. G. and Yin, F. C. P., 1982. Myocardial aging: functional alterations and related cellular mechanism. *Am. J. Physiol.* 242 (Heart Circ. Physiol. 11): H927–H941.

Landowne, M. 1958. The relation between intra-arterial pressure and impact pulse wave velocity with regard to age and arteriosclerosis. *J. Gerontol.* 13: 153–161.

Lansing, A. I. 1959. Elastic tissue. *In, The Arterial Wall: Aging, Structure, and Chemistry,* pp. 136–160. Baltimore: Williams and Wilkins.

Learoyd, B. M. and Taylor, M. G. 1966. Alterations with age in the viscoelastic properties of human arterial walls. *Circ. Res.* 18: 278–292.

Lev, M., Unger, P. N., Rosen, K. M., and Bharati, S. 1974. The anatomic substrate of complete left bundle branch block. *Circulation* 50: 579–586.

Limas, C. J. 1975. Comparison of the handling of norepinephrine in the myocardium of adult and old rats. *Cardiovasc. Res.* 9: 664–668.

Links, J. M., Becker, L. C., Shindledecker, J. G., Guzman, P., Burow, R. D., Nickoloff, E. L., Alderson, P. O., and Wagner, H. N. 1982. Measurement of absolute left ventricular volume from gated blood pool studies. *Circulation* 65: 82–91.

Linzbach, A. J. and Akuamoa-Boateng, E. 1973. Altersversanderungen des menschlichen Herzens. I. Das Herzgewicht im Alter. *Klin. Wochenschr.* 51: 156–163.

McGandy, R. B., Barrows, C. H., Jr., Spanias, A., Meredith, A., Stone, J. L., and Norris, A. H. 1966. Nutrient intakes and energy expenditure in men of different ages. *J. Gerontol.* 21: 581–587.

McMillan, J. B. and Lev, M. 1964. The aging heart. II. The valves. *J. Gerontol.* 19: 1–14.

Montoye, H. J. 1957. *Physical Activity and Health: An Epidemiologic Study of an Entire Community.* Englewood Cliffs, N.J.: Prentice-Hall.

Nayler, W. G., Dunnett, J., and Burian, W. 1975. Further observations on species-determined differences in the calcium-accumulating activity of cardiac microsomal fractions. *J. Mol. Cell. Cardiol.* 7: 663–675.

Palmer, G. J., Ziegler, M. G., and Lake, C. R. 1978. Response of norepinephrine and blood pressure to stress increases with age. *J. Gerontol.* 33: 482–487.

Pathak, C. L. 1973. Autoregulation of chronotropic response of the heart through pacemaker stretch. *Cardiology* 58: 45–64.

Peterson, L. H., Roderick, E. J., and Parnell, J. 1960. Mechanical properties of arteries *in vivo. Circ. Res.* 8: 622–639.

Port, E., Cobb, F. R., Coleman, R. E., and Jones, R. H. 1980. Effect of age on the response of the left ventricular ejection fraction to exercise. *New Engl. J. Med.* 303: 1133–1137.

Rakusan, K. and Poupa, O. 1964. Capillaries and muscle fibres in the heart of old rats. *Gerontologia* 9: 107–112.

Raven, P. B. and Mitchell, J. 1980. The effect of aging on the cardiovascular response to dynamic and static exercise. *In,* M. L. Weisfeldt (ed.), *The Aging Heart,* pp. 269–296. New York: Raven Press.

Remington, J. W. 1963. The physiology of the aorta and major arteries. *In,* W. F. Hamilton, and P. Dow (eds.), *Handbook of Physiology, Circulation II,* p. 808. Washington D.C.: American Physiology Society.

Rerych, S. L., Scholz, P. M., Newman, G. E., Sabiston, D. C., Jr., and Jones, R. H. 1978. Cardiac function at rest and during exercise in normals and in patients with coronary heart disease: an evaluation by radionuclide angiocardiography. *Ann. Surg.* 187: 449–464.

Roach, M. R. and Burton, A. C. 1959. The effect of age on the elasticity of human iliac arteries. *Can. J. Biochem.* 37: 557–570.

Roberts, J. and Goldberg, P. B. 1975. Changes in cardiac membranes as a function of age with particular emphasis on reactivity to drugs. *In,* V. J. Cristofalo, J. Roberts, and R. C. Adelman (eds.), *Advances in Experimental Medicine and Biology,* Vol. 61: *Explorations in Aging,* pp. 119–148. New York: Plenum Press.

Roberts, J. and Goldberg, P. B. 1976. Changes in basic cardiovascular activities during the lifetime of the rat. *Exp. Aging Res.* 2: 487–517.

Robinson, S. 1938. Experimental studies of physical fitness in relation to age. *Arbeitsphysiologie* 10: 251–323.

Robinson, S., Dill, D. B., Ross, J. C., Robinson, R. D., Wagner, J. A., and Tzankoff, S. P. 1973. Training and physiological aging in man. *Fed. Proc.* 32: 1628–1634.

Rodeheffer, R. J., Gerstenblith, G., Becker, L. C., Fleg, J. L., Weisfeldt, M. L., and Lakatta, E. G. 1984. Exercise cardiac output is maintained with advancing age in healthy human subjects: cardiac dilatation and increased stroke volume compensate for a diminished heart rate. *Circulation* 69: 203–213.

Rosahn, P. D. 1941. Weight of the normal heart in adult males. *Am. J. Pathol.* 17: 595–596.

Roseler, H. 1937. *Clinical Roentgenology of the Cardiovascular System.* Springfield, Ill.: Charles C. Thomas.

Rosen, M. R., Reder, R. F., Hordof, A. J., Davis, M., and Danilo, P., Jr. 1978. Age-related changes in Purkinje fiber action potentials of adult dogs. *Circ. Res.* 43: 931–938.

Rowe, J. W. and Troen, B. R. 1980. Sympathetic nervous system and aging in man. *Endocr. Rev.* 1: 167–179.

Roy, C. S. 1880–1882. The elastic properties of the arterial wall. *J. Physiol.* (Lond.), 3: 125–159.

Rumberger, E. and Timmermann, J. 1976. Age-changes of the force-frequency-relationship and the duration of action potential of isolated papillary muscles of guinea pig. *Eur. J. Appl. Physiol.* 35: 277–284.

Saltin, B. and Rowell, L. B. 1980. Functional adaptation to physical activity and inactivity. *Fed. Proc.* 39: 1506–1513.

Scholz, H. 1980. Effects of beta- and alpha-adrenoceptor activators and adrenergic transmitter releasing agents on the mechanical activity of the heart. *In,* L. Szekeres (ed.), *Handbook of Experimental Pharmacology,* Vol. 54/I: *Adrenergic Activators and Inhibitors,* pp. 651–733. Berlin, Heidelberg, New York: Springer.

Sell, S. and Scully, R. E. 1965. Aging changes in the aortic and mitral valves. Histologic and histochemical studies, with observation on the pathogenesis of calcific aortic stenosis and calcification of the mitral annulus. *Am. J. Pathol.* 46: 345–365.

Shock, N. W. 1981. Biological theories of aging. *In,* J. R. Florini (ed.), *CRC Handbook of Biochemistry,* pp. 271–282. Boca Raton, Fla.: CRC Press.

Sjogren, A.-L. 1972. Left ventricular wall thickness in patients with circulatory overload of the left ventricle. *Ann. Clin. Res.* 4: 310–318.

Sprague, H. B. 1954. The normal senile heart. *In,* E. J. Stieglitz (ed.), *Geriatric Medicine,* pp. 359–371. Philadelphia: Lippincott.

Spurgeon, H. A., Steinbach, M. F., and Lakatta, E. G. 1983. Chronic exercise prevents characteristic age-related changes in rat cardiac contraction. *Am J. Physiol.* 244 (*Heart Circ. Physiol.* 13): H513–H518.

Spurgeon, H. A., Thorne, P. R., Yin, F. C. P., Shock, N. W., and Weisfeldt, M. L. 1977. Increased dynamic stiffness of trabeculae carneae from senescent rats. *Am. J. Physiol.* 232 (*Heart Circ. Physiol.* 4): H373–H380.

Stern, M. D., Kort, A. A., Bhatnagar, G. M., and Lakatta, E. G. 1983. Scattered-light intensity fluctuations in diastolic rat cardiac muscle caused by spontaneous Ca^{++}-dependent cellular mechanical oscillations. *J. Gen. Physiol.* 82: 119–153.

Strandell, T. 1964a. Heart volume and its relation to anthropometric data in old men compared with young men. *Acta Med. Scand.* 176: 205–218.

Strandell, T. 1964b. Circulatory studies on healthy old men. *Acta Med. Scand.* 175: Suppl. 414, 1–44.

Suko, J. 1971. Alterations of calcium uptake and calcium-activated ATPase of cardiac sarcoplasmic reticulum in hyper- and hypo-thyroidism. *Biochim. Biophys. Acta* 252: 324–327.

Templeton, G. H., Platt, M. R., Willerson, J. T., and Weisfeldt, M. L. 1975. Influence of aging on left ventricular stiffness. *Clin. Res.* 23: 210A.

Templeton, G. H., Willerson, J. T., Platt, M. R., and Weisfeldt, M. 1978. Contraction duration and diastolic stiffness in aged canine left ventricle. *In,* T. Kobayashi, T. Sano., and N. S. Dalla (eds.), *Recent Advances in Studies on Cardiac Structure and Metabolism,* Vol. 2, *Heart Function and Metabolism,* pp. 169–173. Baltimore: University Park Press.

Tomanek, R. J. 1970. Effects of age and exercise on the extent of the myocardial capillary bed. *Anat. Rec.* 167: 55–62.

Tuttle, R. S. 1966. Age-related changes in the sensitivity of rat aortic strips to norepinephrine and associated chemical and structural alterations. *J. Gerontol.* 21: 510–516.

Tzankoff, S. T., Fleg, J. L., Norris, A. H., and Lakatta, E. G. 1980. Age-related increase in serum catecholamine levels during exercise in healthy adult men. *The Physiologist* 23: 50.

VanTosh, A., Lakatta, E. G., Fleg, J. L. Weiss, J., Kallman, C., Weisfeldt, M., and Gerstenblith, G. 1980. Ventricular dimensional changes during submaximal exercise: effect of aging in normal man. *Circulation* 62: Part III, 129.

Vestal, R. E., Wood, A. J. J., and Shand, D. G. 1979. Reduced β-adrenoceptor sensitivity in the elderly. *Clin. Pharmacol. Ther.* 26: 181–186.

Wei, J. Y., Spurgeon, H. A., and Lakatta, E. G. 1984. Excitation-contraction in RAT myocardium: Alterations with adult aging. *Am. J. Physiol.* 246 (*Heart Circ. Physiol.* 15): H784–H791.

Weisfeldt, M. L., Loeven, W. A., and Shock, N. W. 1971a. Resting and active mechanical properties of trabeculae carneae from aged male rats. *Am. J. Physiol.* 220: 1921–1927.

Weisfeldt, M L., Wright, J. R., Shreiner, D. P., Lakatta,

E., and Shock, N. W. 1971b. Coronary flow and oxygen extraction in the perfused heart of senescent male rats. *J. Appl. Physiol.* 30: 44–49.

White, N. K., Edwards, J. E., and Dry, T. J. 1950. The relationship of the degree of coronary atherosclerosis with age, in men. *Circulation* 1: 645–654.

Wolinsky, H. 1972. Long-term effects of hypertension on the rat aortic wall and their relation to concurrent aging changes. Morphological and chemical studies. *Circ. Res.* 30: 301–309.

Yakovlev, V. M. 1971. Some data on the functional state of the arterial system in aged persons. *Kardiologiia* 11: 99–103.

Yin, F. C. P., Raizes, G. S., Guarnieri, T., Spurgeon, H. A., Lakatta, E. G., Fortuin, N. J., and Weisfeldt, M. L. 1978. Age-associated decrease in ventricular response to hemodynamic stress during beta-adrenergic blockade. *Br. Heart. J.* 40: 1349–1355.

Yin, F. C. P., Spurgeon, H. A., Greene, H. L., Lakatta, E. G., and Weisfeldt, M. L. 1979. Age-associated decrease in heart rate response to isoproterenol in dogs. *Mech. Ageing Dev.* 10: 17–25.

Yin, F. C. P., Spurgeon, H. A., and Kallman, C. H. 1983. Age-associated alterations in viscoelastic properties of canine aortic strips. *Circ. Res.* 53: 464–472.

Yin, F. C. P., Spurgeon, H. A., Raizes, G. S., Greene, H. L., Weisfeldt, M. L., and Shock, N. W. 1976. Age-associated decrease in chronotropic response to isoproterenol. *Circulation* 54: Suppl. 2, II–167.

Yin, F. C. P., Spurgeon, H. A., Weisfeldt, M. L., and Lakatta, E. G. 1980. Mechanical properties of myocardium from hypertrophied rat hearts. A comparison between hypertrophy induced by aortic banding and senescence. *Circ. Res.* 46: 292–300.

Yin, F. C. P., Weisfeldt, M. L., and Milnor, W. R. 1981. Role of aortic input impedance in the decreased cardiovascular response to exercise with aging in dogs. *J. Clin. Invest.* 68: 28–38.

Zaky, A., Nasser, W. K., and Feigenbaum, H. 1968. A study of mitral valve action recorded by reflected ultrasound and its application in the diagnosis of mitral stenosis. *Circulation* 37: 789–799.

16
CHANGES IN THE IMMUNE RESPONSE WITH AGE

Perrie B. Hausman
and
Marc E. Weksler
Division of Geriatrics and Gerontology
Department of Medicine
Cornell University Medical School

INTRODUCTION

The form and the function of all cells, tissues, and organ systems change with age. The rate of change, however, varies from individual to individual, strain to strain, and species to species. This is due to genetic influences on senescence and to environmental effects on survival. The changes in the immune system which accompany aging are summarized in this chapter.

Genes which control immune reactivity are located within the major histocompatibility complex. Genes linked to this complex not only regulate immune responses but also influence maximal life span in mice (Smith and Walford, 1977). This has been taken as evidence that not only does aging affect immune competence but also immune competence may affect aging. Important environmental influences on immunity include disease, nutrition, and exposure to ionizing radiation. Differences in inherited and acquired influences on immune function lead to the increasing heterogeneity in immune reactivity observed as individuals of a single population age. The coefficient of variation of all immunological parameters, relatively small in young populations, increases dramatically as a population ages.

Although the effects of age on every parameter of immune function may not be present in each elderly subject, nearly all immune functions in the elderly differ in comparison to young populations. Age-associated changes in the immune system have been studied in man and in experimental animals. Thymic involution and the decline in serum thymic hormone activity are universal changes in immune function found in all aging individuals and all species at the same relative age. Other changes in immune reactivity are expressed by elderly populations but may not be expressed by each elderly subject. Documenting age-associated change in immune function depends upon proper selection of subjects for study. Certain changes in immune function occur within the first quarter of the life span and can be identified only if young and adult subjects are compared. Other age-associated changes in the immune system do not occur until the last quarter of the life span and can be identified only if adult and aged subjects are compared. Finally, the increased variability of immune parameters with age frequently requires that large numbers of individuals be compared in order to obtain statistically significant results.

THYMIC INVOLUTION AND IMMUNE SENESCENCE

The involution of the thymus gland is a universal accompaniment of aging in both man and experimental animals. Long before the immune function of the thymus was recognized, careful anatomical studies documented the fact that the maximum mass of the human thymus gland is attained at sexual maturity (Boyd, 1932; Andrew, 1952). After puberty, there is a striking involution in the cellular mass of the thymus, so that humans 45 to 50 years of age retain only 5 to 10 percent of the cellular mass of the thymus gland. Studies in experimental animals have confirmed this pattern of thymic involution (Hirokawa and Makinodan, 1975). Thus, the maximal weight of the thymus in mice, approximately 70 mg, occurs at 6 weeks of age, the time of sexual maturation in this species. By 6 months of age, when the mouse has completed only one-quarter or less of its life span, the weight of the thymus has fallen to only 5 mg. Studies by (Good et al., 1962) by (Miller, 1961), and by (Jankovic et al., 1962) in the early 1960s demonstrated the crucial role of the thymus gland in the immune system. The involution of the thymus gland during the first half of life thus may explain the altered form and function of the immune system observed during the second half of life.

The thymus gland serves both as an endocrine organ and as a site of cellular differentiation. A family of thymic polypeptide hormones is synthesized in the thymus and released into the blood (Goldstein et al., 1972; Bach et al., 1975). These hormones are important in the differentiation of pre- and postthymic lymphocytes. The level of thymic hormones in the serum of man and experimental animals begins to fall soon after the morphological involution of the thymus gland (Figure 1). In man, the concentration of thymic hormone in serum begins to fall between the ages of 20 and 30, and thymic hormone can no longer be detected after 60 years of age (Lewis

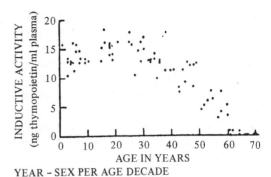

YEAR – SEX PER AGE DECADE

Figure 1. Plasma thymic hormone activity from 0–70 years of age. (From Lewis, 1978, p. 145.)

et al., 1978). Comparable studies in mice reveal that thymic hormone levels fall during young adulthood and become undetectable after 6 months of age (Goldstein et al., 1974).

The thymus gland also functions as a site of differentiation of immature lymphoid cells (Miller, 1961; Good et al., 1962). A large number of immature lymphocytes from the bone marrow enter the cortex of the thymus gland. A proportion of these lymphocytes migrate to the thymic medulla prior to leaving the gland as mature T lymphocytes. Only 5 percent of the lymphocytes which enter the thymus are released into the blood. With age, there is a decreased entry of immature lymphocytes into the thymus. Lymphoid cells of early T lineage, identified by their expression of terminal transferase activity, migrate from the bone marrow to the thymus early in the life span. By the age of 20 in man, and by 6 months in mice, the migration of terminal transferase-positive lymphocytes from the bone marrow into the thymus has declined significantly (Pahwa et al., 1981a).

Although fewer immature lymphocytes enter the thymus with age, the percentage of immature lymphocytes within the thymus gland actually increases with age. This suggests that the thymus gland loses its capacity to cause the differentiation of immature lymphocytes with age. One step in the differentiation of immature lymphocytes within the thymus is the acquisition of the surface receptor for sheep erythrocytes. The presence of this surface receptor permits mature T lymphocytes to form rosettes with sheep erythrocytes.

In humans less than 20 years of age, only 5 percent of thymic lymphocytes do not express this receptor (Figure 2). With age, however, there is a steady increase in the percentage of thymic lymphocytes which do not express the surface receptor for sheep erythrocytes. By the age of 60 or 70, nearly half the thymic lymphocytes fail to express this receptor (Singh and Singh, 1979). Thus, the increased percentage of immature lymphocytes in the thymus gland of older persons reflects the decreased capacity of the thymus gland to modulate the differentiation of immature lymphocytes.

The failure of the thymus to support the differentiation of immature lymphocytes is manifested both by an increasing number of immature lymphocytes within the gland and by the increased number of immature T lymphocytes in the peripheral blood. Immature T lymphocytes bind autologous erythrocytes forming autorosettes. With age, there is an increased number of human T lymphocytes in the blood which form autorosettes (Moody et al., 1981; Fournier and Charreire, 1977). Thus, the involution of the thymus gland is manifested by a decrease in serum thymic hormone, by an increased number of immature T lymphocytes in the thymus, and by an in-creased number of immature T lymphocytes in the peripheral blood.

The thymus gland was first recognized to be responsible for the establishment and maintainance of cell-mediated immunity. In the last decade, however, it has become clear that T lymphocytes derived from the thymus gland also influence the expression of humoral immunity mediated by B lymphocytes. Thus, thymus-dependent regulatory lymphocytes with helper or suppressor activity play an important role in humoral immunity. The effect of age on the capacity of the thymus gland to regulate lymphocyte differentiation has also been studied in considerable detail in experimental animals. Young, lethally irradiated, and thymectomized animals have been reconstituted with bone marrow cells and thymus grafts from donors of varying ages (Hirokawa and Makinodan, 1975). The rate of recovery and level of thymic-dependent immune function have been followed in these animals. Thymus grafts from neonatal animals facilitate the most rapid reconstitution of the T lymphocyte population and the most complete recovery of responsiveness to T cell mitogens and to T-dependent antigens (Figure 3). When thymus grafts are taken from older animals, the pace of recovery is delayed and in many cases the level of thymic-dependent immune function never reaches that seen in intact animals or in animals reconstituted with neonatal thymus glands. Thus, the capacity of the thymus to affect the maturation of immature T lymphocytes decreases with age. This probably explains the finding that increasing numbers of immature lymphocytes reside within the thymus of old subjects.

The thymus gland is also important in the maturation of immature B as well as T lymphocytes. Transfer studies, similar to those described, have revealed the influence of thymus gland age on the differentiation of immature B cells (Siskind et al., 1981; Szewczuk et al., 1978; Sherr et al., 1978). The capacity to generate a heterogeneous immune response with respect to affinity is one marker of B lymphocyte maturation. Thymocytes are essential for this step of B lymphocyte differentiation. Thymocytes from animals less than 2

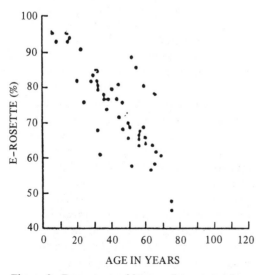

Figure 2. Percentage of human thymocytes from different age groups that form rosettes in sheep erythrocytes. (Adapted from Singh, 1979, p. 507.)

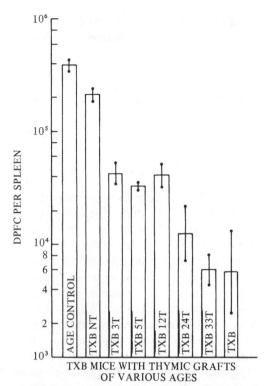

Figure 3. Influence of age on the thymic craft of the splenic T cell-dependent direct anti-sheep RBC response (DPFC) of TXB recipient mice four weeks after thymic transplantation. (From Hirokawa and Makinodan, 1975, p. 1659.)

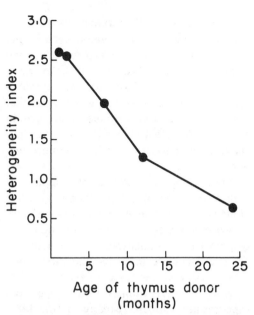

Figure 4. Effect of age of thymus donor on the heterogeneity of the B cell response

months of age have the maximal capacity to regulate this step in the maturation of B lymphocytes (Figure 4). Thymus glands from animals 6 months of age or older show a progressive loss in their capacity to cause the maturation of B lymphocytes. In summary, the involution of the thymus gland during the first half of the life span is accompanied by a decline in the concentration of thymic hormone in sera and an increase in immature T lymphocytes within the thymic gland and in the blood. Studies in experimental animals have revealed that thymus cells from mice as young as 3 to 6 months of age have already lost their capacity to differentiate immature T and B lymphocytes.

AGE-ASSOCIATED CHANGES IN LYMPHOCYTES

It may be surprising that despite the involution of the thymus gland, most studies find

that the total number of lymphocytes and the number of T or B lymphocytes in the peripheral blood of man or in lymphoid organs of animals do not change with age (Weksler and Hutteroth, 1974; Gupta and Good, 1979; Stutman, 1972). A minority of studies report that the total number of blood lymphocytes or the number of T lymphocytes is lower in older humans (MacKinney, 1978; Clot et al., 1972). Most reports find that normal strains of mice do not show a loss of splenic T cells with age although autoimmune-prone strains do. As elderly individuals have an increased frequency of autoantibodies, it is possible that these subjects, like autoimmune-prone mice, have a decreased number of one or more subpopulations of T lymphocytes (Stutman, 1972). Some reports indicate that the number of B lymphocytes is increased in elderly humans (Diaz-Jouanen et al., 1975; Augener et al., 1974). It should be emphasized that most studies have quantitated lymphocytes from a single or limited number of lymphoid compartments. This is important as there is a significant redistribution of lymphocytes with age. There is an age-associated decrease in germinal centers in lymph nodes and an increase in plasma cells and lymphocytes in the bone marrow (Benner and Haaijman, 1980). Thus, changes in the number of lymphocytes in any one compartment may not reflect the total complement of lymphocytes within the organism. Even if the total number of T lymphocytes is maintained with age, it is possible that these long-lived cells continue to circulate in a postmature state, viable but lacking the replicative capacity required for full immune function.

While it appears that the total number of T or B lymphocytes in the peripheral blood of man does not change significantly with age, evidence now exists that the proportion of T lymphocyte subpopulations changes with age. Thus, an increase in T lymphocytes which form rosettes with autologous erythrocytes is observed in elderly humans (Table 1) and old experimental animals (Moody et al., 1981; Fournier and Charreire, 1981). A significant increase in T-gamma lymphocytes in aged humans has been reported (Gupta and Good, 1979). The number of helper or inducer T lymphocytes identified by the OKT4 monoclonal antibody increases, while the number of suppressor or cytotoxic T lymphocytes identified by the monoclonal OKT5 and OKT8 antibodies decreases (Table 2) (Moody et al., 1981; Nagel et al., 1981a). The number of cells detected by an antibody present in the serum of patients with juvenile rheumatoid arthritis declines with age (Strelkauskas et al., 1981). Although the changes in the proportion of T lymphocyte subsets are modest, they may be crucial to the regulation of immune reactivity.

Cell surface determinants on lymphocytes change with age. New antigenic determinants are expressed by lymphocytes from old animals which are recognized by young syngeneic mice (Callard et al., 1979). The density of the theta determinant and of the receptor for T cell growth factor on the surface of T cells, as well as the density of surface immunoglobulin on B cells, decrease with age (Brennan and Jaroslow, 1975; Thoman and Weigle, 1981; Rosenberg et al., 1982; Woda and Feldman, 1979). Furthermore, the rate of capping of these surface determinants decreases with age. Colchicine, which increases the number of caps and the rate of capping in lymphocytes from young donors, has no effect on lymphocytes from old donors (Woda and Feldman, 1979; Gilman et al., 1981). The number of surface receptors, their affinity, and their mobility are probably important factors in immune reactivity, and changes in these functions with age may contribute to immune senescence.

These data suggest that the membrane composition and cytoskeleton are altered in lymphocytes from aged animals. Capping of membrane proteins was found to be closely related to the lateral mobility of glycoproteins in the lipid bilayer (Schreiner et al., 1977). Preliminary studies using fluorescence polarization suggest that there is a small age-related in-

TABLE 1.   Effect of Age on the Number of Human Autorosette Forming Cells.

Age of Subject (yr)	ARFC/10^3 LYMPHOCYTES	
	Male	Female
22–29	6.7 (7)	7.5 (5)
54–79	19.5 (4)	16.7 (16)

SOURCE: From Moody et al. (1981, p. 431).

TABLE 2.   Effect of Age on Distribution of Human T Cell Subsets.

Age of T Cell Donors (yr)	T CELLS IDENTIFIED (%)		
	OKT4	OKT5	OKT8
19–29 (18)	58.5	32.2	36.9
66–79 (18)	75.9	18.6	25.0

SOURCE: From Moody et al. (1981, p. 431).

crease in mocroviscosity in both murine splenic and lymph node cell membranes (Rivany et al., 1979). This change in viscosity may be due to an increase in the molar ratio of cholesterol to phospholipids with age.

Enzymes found in lymphocytes change with age. Lymphocyte adenylate cyclase has been reported to increase and guanylate cyclase to decrease with age, with a paradoxical decrease in the content of cyclic AMP and an increase in cyclic GMP (Tam and Walford, 1978; Tam and Walford, 1980). We have been unable to detect changes with age in the cyclic nucleotides in lymphocytes from humans (D. A. Mark, unpublished observations). Other enzymes, deficient in certain immunodeficiency states, are also reported to be decreased in lymphocytes from old donors. The activity of purine nucleoside phosphorylase has been reported to be decreased in spleen cells from old mice (Scholar et al., 1980). This decline in activity appeared concomitantly with the observed decline in T cell function. The activity of ecto-5-nucleotidase has also been found to be reduced in lymphocytes from old humans (Boss et al., 1980).

On the other hand, no change in the activity of adenosine deaminase was found in lymphocytes from old rodents or in the levels of superoxide dismutase and catalase in patients with Werner's syndrome, a model of premature aging (Scholar et al., 1980; Marklund et al., 1981; Nohl et al., 1979). The activity of superoxide dismutase in human lymphocytes does not change with age (P.B. Hausman, unpublished observations).

Finally, lymphocytes from both elderly experimental animals and man are more susceptible to damage induced by ionizing radiation, ultraviolet light, and mutagenic drugs (Lambert et al., 1977; Seshadri et al., 1979; Walford and Bergman, 1979). Studies with hematopoietic stem cells reveal that recovery from radiation damage is impaired in old animals as compared to young animals (Chen, 1974). For this reason, the proliferative response of aged lymphocytes to plant lectins, as measured by tritated thymidine incorporation, may reflect not only differences in proliferative potential, but an increased sensitivity to ionizing radiation (L. Staiano-Coico, unpublished observations). Such findings suggest that DNA repair enzymes may be altered with age.

Proliferation of lymphocytes is essential for the generation of a normal immune response. Normal cell surface receptor function and nucleic acid fidelity are essential for cell replication. For these reasons, changes in the number, affinity, or mobility of cell surface determinants and the increased sensitivity of nucleic acid to damage may contribute to the impaired immune reactivity of old animals.

HUMORAL IMMUNITY

The steady state of the immune system can be measured by the number of lymphocytes in blood and the concentration of immunoglobulin in serum. While there are subtle changes in lymphocyte subpopulations with age, the total number of lymphocytes does not change with age. There are also small, but statistically significant, changes in the concentration of immunoglobulins in serum. The concentration of IgA and IgG in human serum is increased in older donors, while the concentration of IgM is decreased (Radl et al., 1975; Buckley and Dorsey, 1970). In one study, humans in whom the serum concentration of IgG fell had a reduced life expectancy (Hallgren et al., 1973). It is of interest that the concentration of IgA and IgG in cerebrospinal fluid is also increased with age (Nerenberg and Prasod, 1975).

Several studies have found that there is an age-related decline in the ability of both men and mice to mount an IgE response to antigen. It has been shown that the primary IgE response of aged mice to Dinitrophenyl-*Ascaris* was significantly reduced, while the secondary response was comparable to that of young mice (Fujiwara and Kishimoto, 1979). However, the secondary antibody response declined more rapidly and was of lower avidity than that produced by young mice. When young thymocytes were added to old lymphoid cells, the IgE response was substantially restored.

A large South African study has revealed that the concentration of serum IgE declines with advancing age in healthy white subjects (Orren and Dowdle, 1975). However, this decline was not apparent in two other ethnic groups studied. In another study, old allergic patients were sensitized to fewer common allergies and also had a lower level of specific IgE antibodies when compared to young allergic patients (Hanneuse et al., 1978).

Evidence that the function of the immune system was altered during aging was first discovered more than 50 years ago. When the titer of natural antibodies was quantitated in sera from humans of different ages, it was found that the concentrations of isoagglutinins and natural antibody to sheep erythrocytes were lower in elderly humans (Paul and Bunnell, 1932; Thomsen and Kettel, 1929). Later, it was found that an increase in autoantibodies accompanies this decline in natural **antibodies** and antibodies to foreign determinants (Roberts-Thomson et al., 1974). Subsequently, autoantibodies to nucleic acids, smooth muscle, mitochondria, lymphocytes, gastric parietal cells, immunoglobulin, and thyroglobulin have all been found with increased frequency in old humans (Hallgren et al., 1973; Rowley et al., 1968; Pandey et al., 1979; Cammarata et al., 1967). When human sera were tested for antinuclear antibody, antithyroglobulin antibody, and rheumatoid factor, approximately two-thirds of humans over the age of 60 had one or more of these autoantibodies (Figure 5). Some elderly subjects have autoantibodies to a suppressor subset of T lymphocytes (Strelkauskas et al., 1981). Such autoantibodies might contribute to the deregulation of the immune system that accompanies aging. Polyclonal activation of human B lymphocytes showed that more autoantibody secreting lymphocytes were found in old as compared to young controls (Fong et al., 1981).

Although experimental animals and humans develop autoantibodies with age, autoimmune disease does not increase in fre-

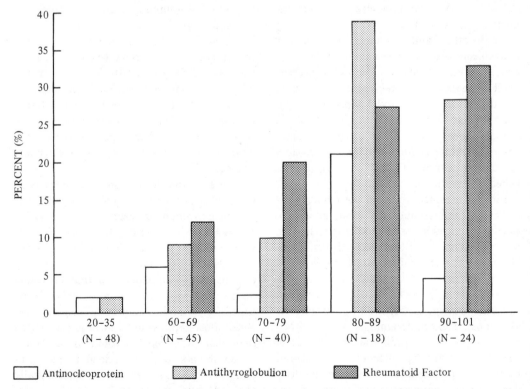

Figure 5. Incidence of autoantibodies in humans of different ages. (Adapted from Hallgren et al., 1973, p. 1101; in Weksler, 1981.)

quency. In fact, susceptibility to autoimmune disease, at least that induced by cross-reacting antigens (a common method to induce autoantibodies), is not increased in old animals. However, there is an increased number of autoantibody secreting lymphocytes in old animals (Goidl et al., 1981). An earlier study has shown that elderly mice had four times the number of autoerythrocyte antibody forming lymphocytes as did young mice (Meredith et al., 1979).

One class of autoantibodies, auto-anti-idiotypic antibodies, plays an important role in the "down" regulation of the immune response. Old animals produce excessive auto-anti-idiotypic antibody during the immune response (Goidl et al., 1980; Szewczuk and Campbell, 1980). The presence of this anti-idiotypic antibody can be demonstrated by the addition of the specific hapten which displaces anti-idiotypic antibody from the lymphocyte and thereby augments the plaque forming cell response (Figure 6). This type of autoantibody which blocks lymphocyte secretion of specific

antibody may thereby not only reflect immune senescence but also contribute to its progression.

The appearance of autoantibodies has been related to a loss of self-tolerance. Loss of self-tolerance is also suggested by the capacity of lymphocytes from old animals to induce a graft-versus-host reaction in syngeneic animals (Gozes et al., 1978). Furthermore, as has been found in autoimmune strains of mice, the induction of B lymphocyte and T lymphocyte tolerance to exogenous antigens has been shown to be very much more difficult in old mice. For example, much larger amounts of the toleragen dinitrophenyl-d-glutamic acid lysine are required to induce unresponsiveness to dinitrophenyl-bovine gamma globulin in aged mice (Dobken et al., 1980; McIntosh and Segre, 1976). As tolerance is more easily induced in high affinity B cells, resistance to tolerance with age may be related to the decrease in high affinity B cells seen with age. Lower affinity B cells require a larger amount of antigen for activation (Davie et al., 1972; DeKruyff and Siskind, 1980). The age-related defect in B cell capping and shedding of surface Ig receptors seen in rats may also be related to the decreased ease of B cell tolerance induction. It has also been reported that a higher dose of toleragen is required to induce T cell tolerance with age (DeKruyff, 1980b). Although induction of T cell tolerance is less well understood, there is some indirect evidence to suggest that there is a similar loss of high affinity T cells with age. It has been observed that the affinity of cytotoxic T cells for their target cells decreases with age (Zharhary and Gershon, 1981).

The frequency of monoclonal immunoglobulins, like autoantibodies, increases with age (Radl et al., 1975; Axelsson et al., 1966). Less than 0.1 percent of humans below the age of 50 have benign monoclonal gammopathies, while approximately 2 percent of humans over 70 have these monoclonal immunoglobulins. In one study, 19 percent of humans over the age of 95 had monoclonal immunoglobulins (Radl et al., 1975). These homogeneous proteins reflect disordered immune regulation of normal B lymphocytes and not the neoplastic

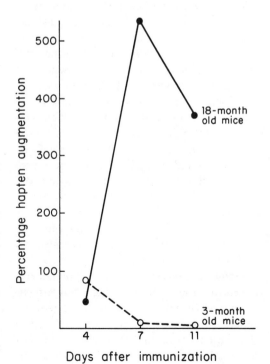

Figure 6. Effect of age on auto-anti-idiotype response as measured by hapten augmentable PFC

transformation of antibody forming cells, i.e., multiple myeloma.

Mice also show an increasing incidence of monoclonal immunoglobulins with age. By 30 months of age, 10 percent of CBA mice have monoclonal immunoglobulins in their serum. The occurrence of monoclonal immunoglobulins has been related to a loss of thymic regulation of immunoglobulin production (Radl et al., 1980). Thus, neonatally thymectomized mice not only developed monoclonal gammopathies at an earlier age, but also showed a much higher (75 percent) incidence of these homogeneous proteins at 30 months of age.

In addition to the increased incidence of autoantibodies and monoclonal immunoglobulins, and the decreased levels of natural antibodies, the response of elderly humans and experimental animals to foreign antigens decreases with age. The antibody response to the Japanese B encephalitis and parainfluenza virus vaccine was found to be lower in old as compared to young humans (Sabin et al., 1947). Similarly, the response to pneumococcal polysaccharide, salmonella flagellin, and tetanus toxoid was depressed in old humans (Roberts-Thomson et al., 1974; Ammann et al., 1980; Kishimoto et al., 1980; Whittingham et al., 1978). The character of the immune response was also altered in elderly subjects. The more thymic-dependent IgG antibody response was significantly more impaired than the IgM response, and the antibody titers were maintained for a shorter time in old as compared to young individuals.

Age-associated changes in the antibody response to foreign antigens have also been studied in experimental animals. Almost all studies revealed a decline in the antibody response with age. Peak antibody responses were observed during the first third of the life span (in mice between the ages of 2 and 12 months). Subsequently, the antibody response, usually measured as the concentration of serum antibody or as the number of splenic plaque forming cells, declined so that during the last quarter of the animal's life span the humoral response of aged mice was less than 25 percent of the maximal response (Makinodan and Peterson, 1962). In general, the primary response was more compromised than the secondary response. The dose of antigens required for a maximal antibody response was tenfold greater in old mice (Makinodan and Adler, 1975). This decline might be related to decreases in the number or affinity of surface receptors for antigen. There is a preferential loss of the IgG and high affinity antibody response in elderly mice (Goidl et al., 1976; Kishimoto et al., 1976). IgG and high affinity antibody are highly thymus dependent, and their loss in old animals probably reflects the involution of the thymus gland. The finding that thymectomy accelerates the onset of these age-associated changes, and the fact that young thymocytes or thymic hormones can augment the IgG and high affinity antibody response of old mice, support this conclusion (Goidl et al., 1976; Weksler et al., 1978). Additional support for the contribution of thymic involution to immune senescence is the greater impairment in the response of old animals to thymic-dependent as contrasted with thymic-independent antigens (Makinodan and Adler, 1975).

The age-associated changes in the immune system discussed so far do not distinguish between an immune system impaired by age and an immune system compromised by the environment within an elderly host. Evidence that changes in lymphocytes which occur with age contribute to the depressed immune response is derived from transfer studies in which lymphocytes from young or old donors are used to reconstitute syngeneic, thymectomized, lethally irradiated young mice and from *in vitro* studies of lymphocytes from young and old experimental animals and humans (Makinodan and Adler, 1975).

The transfer of lymphocytes from old mice to young syngeneic recipients revealed an intrinsic functional defect. Thus, young thymectomized recipients of old lymphocytes displayed the characteristic impairment manifested by intact old animals: a reduced immune response to foreign antigens with a preferential loss of high affinity and IgG antibodies. Mixed transfer studies in which B lymphocytes and T lymphocytes from old and young mice were combined in various combinations revealed that the predominant defect in lymphocytes from old animals resided in the T lymphocyte preparation. Thus, helper T cell activity in old spleen cells was only one-third to one-tenth that found in spleen cell preparations from young mice (Doria et al., 1980). The immune responses of recipients of old lymphocytes were, to a considerable extent, augmented if thymocytes from young animals were mixed with old lymphocytes (Goidl et al., 1976; Kishimoto et al., 1976; Weksler et al., 1978). When lymphocytes were transferred to young recipients with intact thymus glands, the immune response of these recipients was augmented. This suggests that the thymus of the young recipient was able to facilitate the development of immunologically competent lymphocytes transferred from old animals (DeKruyff et al., 1980a). Finally, it has been found that old mice treated with thymic hormone had improved immunological competence. Lymphocytes from old animals incubated in vitro with thymic hormones also had improved immunological competence when transferred to young recipients (Table 3). In addition to impaired helper T cell activity, mixed transfer studies revealed that suppressor activity in spleen cell preparations increased by 12 months of age (Goidl et al., 1976; DeKruyff et al., 1980a; Callard and Basten, 1978; Callard et al., 1980).

The humoral immune response can also be studied in vitro. Specific antibody, total antibody, and the number of antibody forming cells can be determined after incubation of human lymphocytes with polyclonal B cell activators. Lymphocytes from old humans produced significantly less specific antibody following in vivo immunization or in vitro activation with polyclonal B cell activators (Sabin et al., 1947; Czlonkowska and Korlak, 1979; Ammann et al., 1980; Kishimoto et al., 1980; Whittingham et al., 1978; Pahwa et al. 1981b; DelFraissy et al., 1980). However, there was no decrease in the total amount of immunoglobulin produced or in the total number of antibody forming cells. The major defect in specific antibody secretion in vitro by lymphocyte preparations from old humans was due to impaired T lymphocyte function. As was observed in cell transfer studies, a deficiency of helper T cells and/or an increase in suppressor T cell activity was found. B cell function appeared to be less affected by age. When human B cells were purified from young and old subjects, and specific antibody response was measured after polyclonal B cell activation, no significant difference in response was observed (Kim et al., 1982; Nagel et al., 1981b). In contrast, studies in mice, where it is possible to generate immune responses to thymic independent and thymic dependent antigens in vitro, have revealed that the immune responses to both classes of antigens were significantly reduced with age (Doria, et al., 1980; DeKruyff et al., 1980a). During the last third of the life span, significant suppressor T cell activity was detected. Suppressor activity contributes to, but does not account for, the immune deficiency of aging, since the impairment in antibody response develops before suppressor cells can be demonstrated and elimination of suppressor T cells does not reverse the impaired response of B cells to thymic-independent antigens (DeKruyff et al., 1980a).

Recently, it has been found that the decrease in T lymphocyte function in elderly

TABLE 3.   Effect of Thymopoietin Administration on the Anti-DNP PFC Response of Old Mice.

Age of Mice (mo.)	Thymopoietin Treated	Indirect Anti-DNP PFC/Spleen	Heterogeneity Index
2 (9)	No	5.916 ± 2.3	2.78 ± 0.20
24 (7)	No	385 ± 79	1.09 ± 0.05
24 (8)	Yes	977 ± 102	2.48 ± 0.33

SOURCE: From Weksler et al. (1978, p. 996).

humans and old animals can be, in part, related to their decreased capacity to produce (Figure 7) and to bind T cell growth factor (Gillis et al., 1981). Although the proliferative response of T lymphocytes from old humans was not augmented by exogenous T cell growth factor, the plaque forming cell (PFC) response of spleen cells from old animals was augmented if T cell growth factor was added to cultures (Thoman and Weigle, 1981). However, the maximal PFC response was only seen when young adult T cells were also present in the culture.

The proliferation of B lymphocytes from humans and experimental animals can be studied *in vitro*. The proliferative response induced by anti-immunoglobulin antibody does not decline with age (Weiner et al., 1978). Most reports have shown that the proliferative response of murine lymphocytes to lipopolysaccharide is modestly, if at all, impaired with age (Kishimoto et al., 1976; Abraham et al., 1977; Gerbase-Delima et al., 1975). In any case, when the proliferative responses of T cells and B cells are compared, the T cell defect is, in most reports, greater than the B cell defect.

Macrophages have been demonstrated to be required for antigen presentation, for lymphocyte proliferation, and for antibody synthesis. They are also required to phagocytize and destroy microbial agents. Several studies have reported that both the number of macrophages and their antigen processing capabilities are not altered with age (Shelton et al., 1970; Heidrick and Makinodan, 1973; Callard, 1978; Perkins, 1971). The *in vitro* phagocyte activity of peritoneal macrophages from old mice was equal to or better than that of young mice, while the activity of the lysosomal enzymes in both splenic and peritonal macrophages increased with age (Perkins, 1971; Cantrell and Elko, 1973; Heidrick and Makinodan, 1972). The ability of old and young antigen pulsed peritoneal macrophage to stimulate both primary and secondary responses was comparable (Perkins, 1971). In addition, the capability of macrophages to support lymphocyte proliferation was unaltered with age (Callard, 1978). On the other hand, one study showed that removal of macrophages by adherence to plastic restored the response of aged murine spleen to phytohemagglutinin (PHA) and concanavalin A (Con A) (Rosenstein and Strausser, 1980). Finally, the ability of human macrophages to secrete T cell replacing factor when exposed to lipopolysaccharide (LPS) or to phagocytize and kill *Candida albicans* was no different in old and young individuals (Kim et al., 1982; Gardner et al., 1981). Thus, it appears that macrophage function does not appear to be significantly compromised with age.

In summary, the humoral immune response is impaired in old subjects. This is predominantly due to a decrease in helper T cell activity, although increased suppressor activity and defects in B lymphocyte function may also play a role. It is important to note that while specific antibody responses are greatly impaired with age, the total number of antibody producing cells and the total amount of antibody formed following antigenic stimulation may be only slightly altered. These observations are reminiscent of the fact that the levels

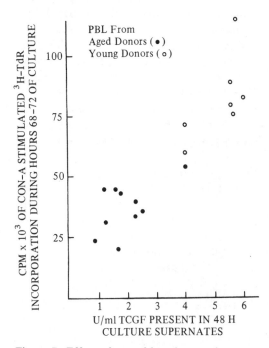

Figure 7. Effect of age of lymphocyte donor on TCGF production. (From Gillis et al., 1981, p. 937.)

of natural antibody and of antibody to foreign determinants following immunization are reduced in old animals, while the total immunoglobulin response and serum immunoglobulin concentration are little affected by age. This suggests that the production of other immunoglobulins (e.g., autoantibodies including auto-anti-idiotypic antibody) by the aged subject make up for the deficiency of specific antibody production. These observations, expressed in terms of the immunological network theory of Jerne, suggest that during the life span of the organism there is a progressive shift in balance between idiotypic and auto-anti-idiotypic reactions. In the first half of an animal's life span, idiotypic reactions dominate the immune response, but with increasing age the production of auto-anti-idiotypic antibodies and other autoantibodies becomes dominant.

CELL-MEDIATED IMMUNITY

Cell-mediated immunity depends upon the functional integrity of thymic-dependent lymphocytes. As thymic involution is a universal accompaniment of aging, many studies of immune senescence have centered on the functional capacity of T lymphocytes from individuals of different ages. Delayed hypersensitivity and graft rejection are two classic manifestations of cell-mediated immunity *in vivo*. Elderly humans have less vigorous delayed hypersensitivity reactions to common skin testing antigens such as *Candida* and mumps, than do young individuals (Roberts-Thomson et al., 1974). The impaired response of elderly people to these antigens might reflect either an altered response to antigenic challenge or the loss of immunological memory or both. Differences in the interval between sensitization and challenge can be eliminated by sensitizing individuals of different ages to a new antigen, e.g., dinitrochlorobenzene and then challenging all subjects after the same interval of time. When this protocol was used, 30 percent of humans over the age of 70 failed to respond to dinitrochlorobenzene while only 5 percent of subjects less than 70 years of age failed to respond (Walford et al., 1968).

Ethical constraints prevent the direct assessment of other indices of cell-mediated immunity, such as the graft-versus-host reaction or tissue and tumor graft rejection in humans. However, the lymphocyte transfer test, a cutaneous model of the graft-versus-host reaction, has been studied in individuals of different ages. Lymphocytes from old donors were less able to induce a positive transfer reaction than lymphocytes from young donors (Andersen, 1972).

Graft-versus-host reactivity as well as tumor and skin graft rejection have been studied in animals of different ages. Lymphocytes from old mice were less capable of eliciting a graft-versus-host reaction or of rejecting tumor or skin grafts than were lymphocytes from young mice (Menon et al., 1974; Kishimoto et al., 1973; Friedman et al., 1974). Lymphocytes from old mice are impaired in generating a graft-versus-host reaction *in vivo* and *in vitro*. However, incubation of lymphocytes from old animals with thymic hormone reconstituted their capacity to manifest a normal *in vitro* graft-versus-host reaction (Friedman et al., 1974).

Graft rejection depends upon an integrated series of immune reactions including alloantigen recognition, helper T lymphocyte proliferation, and the generation of cytotoxic T lymphocytes. Cytotoxic T lumphocytes are effector cells in graft rejection. The impaired rejection of tissue and tumor grafts reflects a defect in the generation of cytotoxic T lymphocytes. The generation of cytotoxic T lymphocytes in the allogeneic mixed lymphocyte reaction is impaired (Zharhary and Gershon, 1981; Goodman and Makinodan, 1975; Bach, 1979; Becker et al., 1979). One group has found a decrease in both the number and the affinity of functional cytotoxic cells in the murine cytotoxic response to allogeneic tumor cells (Zharhary and Gershon, 1981). In addition to cytotoxic T cells, natural killer (NK) cells also participate in tumor rejection. No significant decline in NK activity with age has been found, and interferon-inducible NK activity in lymphocytes is not diminished with age in humans (Fernandes and Gupta, 1981). However, it has been reported that both the number of NK cells and the ability of these cells to lyse NK susceptible tumors decline with age in mice (Roder, 1975).

Immunity to viral infection also depends upon the generation of cytotoxic T lymphocytes. Old mice showed a delayed generation of cytotoxic T lymphocytes with specificity for virus-infected cells, a lower peak cytotoxic response, and a shorter duration of cytotoxic activity (Doherty, 1977; Patel, 1981). Older mice are also impaired in their capacity to generate T cell-mediated immunity to *Listeria monocytogenes*. Old animals infected with *Listeria* develop only one-thousandth the level of T cell immunity found in young mice (Patel, 1981).

A syngeneic graft-versus-host reaction follows the transfer of lymphocytes from old animals to syngeneic recipients. This reaction does not occur when lymphocytes from young animals are transferred to syngeneic recipients. This observation suggests the presence of "autoimmune" T lymphocytes in old animals. Thus, the increase in autoimmune reactivity seen with age is manifested by both humoral and cell-mediated immunity.

The function of T lymphocytes has also been studied *in vitro*. The proliferative response of lymphocytes from old humans to a variety of T lymphocyte mitogens (e.g., PHA and Con A) as well as to antigens to which the lymphocyte donor had been previously sensitized is impaired (Hallgren et al., 1973; Abe et al., 1980; Inkeles et al, 1977). Elderly persons sensitized to *Mycobacterium tuberculosis* or varicella-zoster virus did not proliferate to the same degree observed with lymphocytes from young donors when cultured with these antigens (Miller, 1980; Nilsson, 1971). The proliferative defect observed in cultures from old humans could not be explained by a deficiency in the number of T lymphocytes, as the impaired proliferative response remained in purified T lymphocyte preparation from old subjects.

Prostaglandins, important cell regulatory molecules, have been shown to contribute to the impaired proliferative responses of lymphocytes from aged persons. An increased sensitivity to exogenously added prostaglandin E_2 was found in healthy human subjects over the age of 70 (Goodwin and Messner, 1979). Furthermore, the addition of indomethacin, an inhibitor of prostaglandin synthetase, resulted in an increase in tritiated thymidine incorporation by aged lymphocytes stimulated by PHA. It has also been reported that macrophages from old mice secrete more prostaglandins of the E series than do macrophages from young mice (Rosenstein and Strausser, 1980). These data suggest that the depressed mitogen response seen with age may be due in part to the down-regulation of the immune response by prostaglandins.

Calcium ions (CA^{+2}) have been shown to play an important role in cell activation. With divalent cation chelators, lymphocytes from old subjects were found to be more sensitive to increased amounts of chelating agents such as ethylenediamine tetraacetic acid and ethylenebis (oxyethylenenitrils) tetraacetic acid and they required greater amounts of CA^{+2} supplements to restore their proliferative response after inhibition (Kennes et al., 1981). Another study using verapamil, a calcium channel blocker, supported the conclusion that the CA^{+2}-dependent portion of lymphocyte activators is impaired with age (Blitstein-Willinger and Diamanstein, 1978).

The cellular basis of the impaired proliferative response of T lymphocytes of old subjects has been studied in considerable detail. No defect in the capacity of lymphocytes from old mice to bind plant lectins has been demonstrated (Hung et al., 1975). The number and affinity of receptors for PHA are the same in lymphocytes from old and young donors (J. Hefton, unpublished observations). However, lymphocyte activation following the binding of PHA is impaired in lymphocytes from old donors. A number of independent techniques have revealed that the T lymphocyte preparations from old humans contain only one-fifth to one-half as many mitogen responsive cells as do similar preparations from young humans (Inkeles et al., 1977; Pisciotta et al., 1967). Not only are there fewer mitogen responsive T lymphocytes in the blood of old humans, but their capacity to divide sequentially in culture is impaired (Inkeles et al., 1977; Hefton et al., 1980). The number of cells dividing for the second time in cultures from old subjects is only one-half that found in cultures from young subjects, although the number of cells dividing for the first time is the same in cultures of lymphocytes from old or young donors (Table 4).

Comparable studies performed in mice have produced similar results (Abraham et al., 1977; Gershon, et al., 1979; Callary and Basten, 1977). In addition to the impaired responses to plant lectins, the allogeneic and autologous mixed lymphocyte reaction has been found to be diminished both in old animals and in man (Moody et al., 1981; Fournier and Charreire, 1981; Konen et al., 1973; Nielsen, 1974; Kotch-Gutowski and Weksler, 1982; Fernandez and MacSween, 1980). Thus, a fundamental defect in cell-mediated immunity appears to result from the impaired proliferative response of T lymphocytes from old humans. This is due in part to a reduced number of responsive T lymphocytes as well as to an impaired proliferative capacity of these responsive T cells. In addition to the defects in the response of T lymphocytes, there appears to be suppressor activity present in lymphocyte preparations from old animals which depresses the proliferative response. A number of cell types have been reported to mediate suppressor activity.

CONCLUSION

There is abundant evidence that the immune system changes with age. Cell-mediated and humoral immune responses to foreign antigens are decreased, while the response to autologous antigens is increased. These defects can be related to the involution of the thymus, to an alteration in the balance among regulatory T lymphocytes, and to an altered balance between idiotypic and anti-idiotypic activity. The increased susceptibility of the elderly to infectious neoplastic disease, and perhaps to vascular injury, may be a consequence of immune senescence. The contribution of autoantibodies to the pathobiology of aging is less certain. It has been suggested that autoantibodies and circulating immune complexes, which can damage tissues and organs, contribute to the pathological changes that occur with age (Walford, 1969).

If the pathobiology of aging were related to the loss of immune competence with age, the survival of individuals with an impaired immune response would be expected to be shorter than that of individuals in whom immune competence was well maintained. Three studies have examined this thesis. In one study, more humans with severely impaired delayed hypersensitivity reactions died within a two-year period than did age-matched controls who had well-maintained delayed hypersensitivity responses (Roberts-Thomson et al., 1974). In another study, humans with autoantibodies had a shorter survival time than did age-matched individuals without autoantibodies (Mackay, 1972). A third study showed that the elderly humans with reduced suppressor cell activity had a shorter survival time than did age-matched subjects with normal suppressor activity (Hallgren and Yunis, 1980). None of these studies distinguished between an alteration in the immune response causing the shortened survival or an alteration in the immune response resulting from the

TABLE 4. Effect of Age on Proliferation of Lymphocytes in Culture.

Donor Age (yr)	LYMPHOCYTES DIVIDING FOR THE 1ST, 2ND, or 3RD TIME IN CULTURE			Thymodine Incorporation (cpm/culture ×10⁻³)
	1st	2nd	3rd	
23–32 (5)	13 (11–14)	29 (23–38)	58 (49–53)	47.7 ± 9.6
65–86 (7)	43 (25–46)	37 (27–47)	29 (22–38)	25.9 ± 6.1

Source: From Hefton et al. (1980, p. 1007).

factors which lead to reduced survival. Prospective animal studies, however, have not revealed a correlation between immune competence measured early in life and subsequent survival (Weksler, unpublished observations). However, long-lived strains generally maintain immune competence for a longer time than do short-lived strains.

In the past decade, many of the changes in the immune system that accompany aging have been defined and related to the involution of the thymus gland. The potential contribution of immune senescence to the diseases of aging has been studied. Whether immune senescence is a primary or secondary contributor to the pathology of aging, it is likely that increased knowledge of immune senescence and the increasing ability to modulate the immune defects that occur in old subjects will offer considerable promise for the control of the diseases and pathology of aging.

REFERENCES

Abe, T., Morimoto, C., Toguchi, T., Kuyotaki, M., and Homma, M. 1980. The cellular basis of impaired T lymphocyte function in the elderly. *J. Am. Ger. Soc.* 28: 265–271.

Abraham, C., Tal, Y., and Gershon, H. 1977. Reduced *in vitro* response to con A and lipopolysaccaharide in senescent mice: A function of reduced number of responding cells. *Eur. J. Immunol.* 7: 301–304.

Ammann, A. J., Schiffman, G., and Austrian, R. 1980. The antibody responses to pneumococcal capsular polysaccharides in aged individuals. *Proc. Soc. Exp. Bio. Med.* 164: 312–316.

Andersen, E. 1972. The influence of age on transplantation immunity. Reactivity to normal lymphocyte transfer at different ages. *Scand. J. Haemat.* 9: 621–624.

Andrew, W. 1952. *In,* C. C. Thomas (ed.), *Cellular Changes with Age* pp. 3–74. Springfield, Ill.: Charles C. Thomas.

Augener, W., Cohen, C., Reuter, A., and Brittinger, G. 1974. Decrease of T lymphocytes during aging. *Lancet* 1: 1164.

Axelsson, U., Bachmann, R., and Hallen, J. 1966. Frequency of pathological proteins (M-components) in 6,995 sera from an adult population. *Acta Medica Scandinavica* 179: 235–246.

Bach, J. F., Dardenne, M., Pleau, J. M., and Bach, M. A. 1975. Isolation, biochemical characteristics and biological activity of a circulating thymic hormone in the mouse and in the human. *Ann. N.Y. Acad. Sci.* 249: 186–210.

Bach, M. 1979. Influence of aging on T cell subpopula-

tions involved in the *in vitro* generation of allogeneic cytotoxicity. *Clin. Immunol. Immunopath.* 13: 220–230.

Becker, M. J., Farkas, R., Schneider, M., Drucker, I., and Klajman, A. 1979. Cell-mediated cytotoxicity in humans: age related decline as measured by a xenogeneic assay. *Clin. Immunol. Immunopath.* 14: 204–210.

Benner, R. and Haaijman, J. J. 1980. Aging of the lymphoid system at the organ level. *Exp. Comp. Immunol.* 4: 591–603.

Blitstein-Willinger, E. and Diamanstein, T. 1978. Inhibition by isoptin (a calcium antagonist) of mitogenic stimulation of lymphocytes prior to the S-phase. *Immunology* 34: 303–307.

Boss, G. R., Thompson, R. F., Speigelberg, H. L., Pichler, W. J., and Seegmiller, J. E. 1980. Age-dependency of lymphocyte ecto-5'-nucleotidase activity. *J. Immunol.* 125: 679–688.

Boyd, E. 1932. The weight of the thymus gland in health and in disease. *Amer. J. Dis. Child.* 43: 1162–1214.

Brennan, P. C. and Jaroslow, B. N. 1975. Age-associated decline in theta antigen on spleen thymus-derived lymphocytes of B6CF mice. *Cell. Immunol.* 15: 51–56.

Buckley, C. E. and Dorsey, F. C. 1970. The input of aging on human serum immunoglobulin concentrations. *J. Immunol.* 105: 964–972.

Callard, R. E. 1978. Immune function in aged mice III. *Eur. J. Immunol.* 8: 697–705.

Callard, R. E. and Basten, A. 1977. Immune function in aged mice. I. T cell responsiveness using phytohaemagglutinin as a functional probe. *Cell. Immunol.* 31: 13–25.

Callard, R. E. and Basten, A. 1978. Immune function in aged mice. IV. Loss of T cell and B cell function in thymus-dependent antibody responses. *Eur. J. Immunol.* 8: 552–558.

Callard, R. E., Basten, A., and Blanden, R. V. 1979. Loss of immune competence with age may be due to a qualitative abnormality in lymphocyte membranes. *Nature* 282: 218–219.

Callard, R. E., Fazekas De St. Groth, B., Basten, A., and McKenzie, I. F. C. 1980. Immune function in aged mice. V. Role of suppressor cells. *J. Immunol.* 124: 52–58.

Cammarata, R. J., Rodnan, G. P. and Fennell, R. H. 1967. Serum anti-gamma-globulin and antinuclear factors in the aged. *J. Am. Med. Assoc.* 199: 455–465.

Cantrell, W. and Elko, E. E. 1973. Effect of age on phagocytosis of carbon in the rat. *Exp. Parasitol.* 34:337–343.

Chen, M. G. 1974. Impaired Elkind recovery in hematopoietic colony-forming cells of aged mice. *Proc. Soc. Exp. Biol. Med.* 145: 1181–1186.

Clot, J., Charmasson, E., and Brochier, J. 1972. Age dependent changes of human blood lymphocyte subpopulations. *Clin. Exp. Immunol.* 32: 346–351.

Czlonkowska, A. and Korlak, J. 1979. The immune response during aging. *J. Geront.* 34: 9–14.

Davie, J. M., Paul, W. E., Katz, D. H., and Benacerraf, B. 1972. Hapten-specific tolerance: preferential depression of the high affinity antibody response. *J. Exp. Med.*, 136: 426–438.

Dekruyff, R. H., Kim, Y. T., Siskind, G. W., and Weksler, M. E. 1980a. Age-related chages in the *in vitro* immune response: increased suppressor activity in immature and aged mice. *J. Immunol.* 125: 142–147.

Dekruyff, R. H., Rinnooy Kan, E. A., Weksler, M. E., and Siskind, G. W. 1980b. Effect of aging on T cell tolerance induction. *Cell. Immunol.* 56: 58–67.

Dekruyff, R. H. and Siskind, G. W. 1980. Studies on the control of antibody synthesis. XVI. Effect of immunodepression on antibody affinity. *Cell. Immunol.* 49: 90–98.

DelFraissy, J. F., Galanaud, P., Dormont, J., and Wallon, C. 1980. Age-related impairment of the *in vitro* antibody response in the human. *Clin. Exp. Immunol.* 39: 208–214.

Diaz-Jouanen, E., Strickland, R. G., and Williams, R. C. 1975. Studies of human lymphocytes in the newborn and the aged. *Amer. J. Med.* 58: 620–628.

Dobken, J., Weksler, M. E., and Siskind, G. W. 1980. Effect of age on ease of B cell tolerance induction. *Cell. Immunol.* 55: 66–73.

Doherty, P. C. 1977. Diminished T cell surveillance function in old mice infected with lymphocyte choriomeningitis virus. *Immunology* 32: 751–754.

Doria, G., D'Agostaro, G., and Garavini, M. 1980. Age-dependent changes of B cell reactivity and T cell–T cell interaction in the *in vitro* antibody response. *Cell. Immunol.* 53: 195–206.

Doria, G., D'Agostaro, G., and Poretti, A. 1978. Age-dependent variations of antibody avidity. *Immunology* 35: 601–611.

Fernandes, G. and Gupta, S. 1981. Natural killing and antibody-dependent cytotoxicity by lymphocyte subpopulations in young and aging humans. *J. Clin. Immunol.* 1: 141–147.

Fernandez, L. A., and MacSween, J. M. 1980. Decreased autologous mixed lymphocyte reaction with aging. *Mech. Age. Dev.* 12: 245–248.

Fong, S., Tsoukas, C. D., Frincke, L. E., Lawrance, S. K., Holbrook, T. L., Vaughan, J. H., and Carson, D. A. 1981. Age-associated changes in Epstein-Barr virus-induced human lymphocyte autoantibody responses. *J. Immunol.* 126: 910–914.

Fournier, C. and Charreire, J. 1981. Autologous mixed lymphocyte reaction in man. I. Relationship with age and sex. *Cell. Immunol.* 60: 212–219.

Friedman, D., Keiser, V., and Globerson, A. 1974. Reactivation of immunocompetence in spleen cells of aged mice. *Nature* 251: 545–546.

Fujiwara, M., and Kishimoto, S. 1979. IgE Antibody Formation and Aging. I. Age-related changes in IgE antibody formation and avidity for the DNP determinant in mice. *J. Immunol.* 123: 263–268.

Gardner, N. D., Lim, S. T. K., and Lawton, J. W. M. 1981. Monocyte function in ageing humans. *Mech. Age. Dev.* 16: 233–239.

Gerbase-DeLima, M., Meredith, P., and Walford, R. L. 1975. Age-related changes, including synergy and suppression in the mixed lymphocyte reaction in long-lived mice. *Fed. Proc.* 34: 159–161.

Gershon, H., Merhav, S., and Abraham, C. 1979. T cell division and aging. *Mech. Age. Dev.* 9: 27–38.

Gillis, S., Kozak, R., Durante, M., and Weksler, M. E. 1981. Immunological studies of aging. Decreased production of and response to T cell growth factor by lymphocytes from aged humans. *J. Clin. Invest.* 67: 937–942.

Gilman, S. C., Woda, B. A., and Feldman, J. D. 1981. T lymphocytes of young and aged rats. I. Distribution, density, and capping of T antigens. *J. Immunol.* 127: 149–153.

Goidl, E. A., Innes, J. B., and Weksler, M. E. 1976. Immunological studies of aging. II. Loss of IgG and high avidity plaque-forming cells and increased suppressor cell activity in aging mice. *J. Exp. Med.* 144: 1037–1048.

Goidl, E. A., Michelis, M., Siskind, G. W., and Weksler, M. E. 1981. Effect of age on the induction of autoantibodies. *Clin. Exp. Immunol.* 44: 24–29.

Goidl, E. A., Thorbeck, G. J., Weksler, M. E., and Siskind, G. W. 1980. Production of auto-anti-idiotypic antibody during the normal immune response: changes in the auto-anti-idiotypic antibody response and the idiotypic repertoire associated with aging. *Proc. Natl. Acad. Sci.* 77: 6788–6792.

Goldstein.A. L., Guha, A., Zatz, M. M., Hardy, M. A., and White, A. 1972. Purification and biological activity of thymosin, a hormone of the thymus gland. *Proc. Natl. Acad. Sci.* 69: 1800–1803.

Goldstein, A. L., Hooper, J. A., Schulof, R. S., Cohen, G. H., Thurman, G. B., McDaniel, M. C., White, A., and Dardenne, M. 1974. Thymosin and the immunopathology of aging. *Fed. Proc.* 33: 2053–2056.

Good, R. A., Dalmasso, A. P., Martinez, C., Areher, D. K., Pierce, J. C., and Papermaster, B. W. 1962. The role of the thymus in development of immunologic capacity in rabbits and mice. *J. Exp. Med.* 116: 773–796.

Goodman, S. A. and Makinodan, T. 1975. Effect of age on cell-mediated immunity in long-lived mice. *Clin. Exp. Immunol.* 19: 533–542.

Goodwin, J. S. and Messner, R. P. 1979. Sensitivity of lymphocytes to prostaglandin E_2 increases in subjects over age 70. *J. Clin. Invest.* 64: 434–439.

Gozes, Y., Umiel, T., Asher, M., and Trainin, N. 1978. Syngeneic GvH induced in popliteal lymph nodes by spleen cells of old C57BL/6 mice. *J. Immunol.* 121: 2199–2204.

Gupta, S. and Good, R. A. 1979. Subpopulation of human T lymphocytes. X. Alterations in T, B, third population cells, and T cells with receptors for immunoglobulin M or G in aging humans. *J. Immunol.* 122: 1214–1219.

Hallgren, H. M., Buckley, C. E., Gilbertsen, V. A., and Yunis, E. J. 1973. Lymphocyte phytohemagglutinin responsiveness, immunoglobulins and autoantibodies in aging humans. *J. Immunol.* 111: 1101–1107.

Hallgren, H. M. and Yunis, E. J. 1980. *In*, D. Segre

and L. Smith (eds.), *Immunological Aspects of Aging,* pp. 281–293. New York: Marcel Dekker.

Hanneuse, Y., Delespesse, G., Hudson, D., De Halleux, F., and Jacques, J. M. 1978. Influence of ageing on IgE-mediated reactions in allergic patients. *Clin. Allergy.* 8: 165–174.

Hefton, J. M., Darlington, G. J., Casazza, B. A., and Weksler, M. E. 1980. Immunologic studies of aging. V. Impaired proliferation of PHA responsive Human Lymphocytes in Culture. *J. Immunol.* 125: 1007–1010.

Heidrick, M. L. and Makinodan, T. 1972. Nature of cellular deficiencies in age-related decline of the immune system. *Gerontologia* 18: 305–320.

Heidrick, M. L. and Makinodan, T. 1973. Presence of impairment of humoral immunity in non-adherent spleen cells of old mice. *J. Immunol.* 111: 1502–1506.

Hirokawa, K. and Makinodan, T. 1975. Thymic involution: effect on T cell differentiation. *J. Immunol.* 6: 1659–1664.

Hung, C., Perkins, E. H., and Yang, W. 1975. Age-related refractoriness of PHA-induced lymphocyte transformation. II. ^{125}I-PHA binding to spleen cells from young and old mice. *Mech. Age. Dev.* 4: 103–112.

Inkeles, B., Innes, J. B., Kuntz, M. M., Kadish, A. S., and Weksler, M. E. 1977. Immunological studies of aging. III. Cytokinetic basis for the impaired response of lymphocytes from aged humans to plant lectins. *J. Exp. Med.* 145: 1176–1187.

Janokovic, B. D., Waksman, B. H., and Arnason, B. G. 1962. Role of the thymus in immune reactions in rats I. The immune response to bovine serum albumin (antibody formation, arthrus reactivity, and delayed hypersensitivity) in rats thymectomized or splenectomized at various times after birth. *J. Exp. Med.* 116:159–176.

Kennes, B., Hubert, C., Brohee, D., and Neve, P. 1981. Early biochemical events associated with lymphocyte activation in ageing. I. Evidence that Ca^{2+} dependent processes induced by PHA are impaired. *Immunology* 42: 119–126.

Kim, Y. T., Siskind, G. W., and Weksler, M. E. 1982. Cellular basis of the impaired immune response of elderly humans. In, *Human B Lymphocyte Function: Activation and Immunoregulation,* (edited A. S. Fauci and R. E. Ballieux) Raven Press, N.Y. pp. 129–139.

Kishimoto, S., Shigemoto, S., and Yamamura, Y. 1973. Immune response in aged mice. *Transplant.* 15: 455–459.

Kishimoto, S., Takahama, T., and Mizumachi, H. 1976. *In vitro* immune response to the 2,4,6-trinitrophenyl determinant in aged C57BL mice: changes in the humoral response to avidity for the TNP determinant and responsiveness to LPS effect with aging. *J. Immunol.* 116: 294–300.

Kishimoto, S., Tomino, S., Mitsuya, H., Fujiwara, H., and Tsuda, H. 1980. Age-related decline in the *in vitro* and *in vivo* synthesis of anti-tetanus toxoid antibody in humans. *J. Immunol.* 125: 2347–2352.

Konen, T. G., Smith, G. S., and Walford, R. L. 1973. Decline in mixed lymphocyte reactivity of spleen cells

from aged mice of a long-lived strain. *J. Immunol.* 110: 1216–1221.

Kotch-Gutowski, J. and Weksler, M. E. 1982. Studies on the syngeneic MLR. II. Decline in the syngeneic MLR with age. *Immunol.* 46: 801–808.

Lambert, B., Ringbord, N., and Swanbert, B. 1977. Repair on UV-induced DNA lesions in peripheral lymphocytes from healthy subjects of various ages, individuals with Down's syndrome and patients with actinic keratosis. *Mut. Res.* 46: 133–134.

Lewis, V. M., Twomey, J. J., Bealmear, P., Goldstein, G., and Good, R. A. 1978. Age, thymic involution and circulating thymic hormone activity. *J. Clin. Endocrin. Metabol.* 47: 145–150.

Mackay, I. 1972. Aging and immunological function in man. *Gerontologia* 18: 285–304.

MacKinney, A. A. 1978. Effect of aging on the peripheral blood lymphocyte count. *J. Geront.* 33: 213–216.

Makinodan, T. and Adler, W. H. 1975. Effects of aging on the differentiation and proliferative potentials of cells of the immune system. *Fed. Proc.* 34: 153–158.

Makinodan, T. and Peterson, W. J. 1962. Relative antibody forming capacity of spleen cells as a function of age. *Proc. Natl. Acad. Sci.* 48: 234–241.

Marklund, S., Nordenson, I., and Back, O. 1981. Normal CuZn superoxide dismutase, Mn superoxide dismutase, catalase and glutathione peroxidase in Werner's syndrome. *J. Geront.* 36: 405–409.

McIntosh, K. R. and Segre, D. 1976. B and T cell tolerance induction in young adult and old mice. *Cell. Immunol.* 27: 230–239.

Menon, M., Jaroslow, B. N., and Koesterer, R. 1974. The decline of cell-mediated immunity in aging mice. *J. Geront.* 29: 499–505.

Meredith, P. J., Kristie, J. A., and Walford, R. L. 1979. Aging increases expression of LPS induced autoantibody-secreting B cells. *J. Immunol.* 123: 87–91.

Miller, A. E. 1980. Selective decline in cellular immune response to varicella-zoster in the elderly. *Neurology* 30: 582–587.

Miller, J. F. A. P. 1961. The immunological function of the thymus. *Lancet* 2: 748–749.

Moody, C. E., Innes, J. B., Staiano-Coico, L., Incefy, G. S., Thaler, H. T., and Weksler, M. E., 1981. Lymphocyte transformation induced by autologous cells. XI. The effect of age on the autologous mixed lymphocyte reaction. *Immunol.* 44: 341–438.

Nagel, J. A., Chrest, F. J., and Adler, W. H. 1981a. Enumeration of T lymphocyte subsets by monoclonal antibodies in young and aged humans. *J. Immunol.* 127: 2086–2088.

Nagel, J. E., Chrest, F. J., and Adler, W. H. 1981b. Human B cell function of normal individuals of various age. I. *In vitro* enumeration of pokeweed induced peripheral blood lymphocyte immunoglobulin synthesizing cells and comparison of the results with numbers of peripheral B and T cell mitogen responses, and levels of serum immunoglobulin. *Clin. Exp. Immunol.* 44: 646–653.

Nerenberg, S. T. and Prasod, R. 1975. Radioimmunoassays for Ig classes G, A, M, D and E in spinal fluids: normal values of different age groups. *J. Lab. Clin. Med.* 86: 887–898.

Nielsen, H. E. 1974. The effect of age on the response of rat lymphocytes in mixed leukocyte culture, to PHA, and in the graft-vs-host reaction. *J. Immunol.* 112: 1194–2000.

Nilsson, B. S. 1971. *In vitro* lymphocyte reactivity to PPD and phytohaemagglutinin in relation to PPD reactivity with age. *Scand. J. Resp. Dis.* 52: 39–47.

Nohl, H., Dietmar, H., and Summer, K. 1979. Responses of mitochondrial superoxide dismutase, catalase and glutathione peroxidase activities to aging. *Mech. Age. Dev.* 11: 145–151.

Orren, A. and Dowdle, E. B. 1975. The effects of sex and age on serum IgE concentrations in three ethnic groups. *Int. Archs. Allergy Appl. Immun.* 48: 824–835.

Pahwa, R. N., Modak, M. J., McMorrow, T., Pahwa, S., Fernandes, G., and Good, R. A. 1981a. Terminal deoxynucleotidyl transference (TdT) enzyme in thymus and bone marrow. *Cell. Immunol.* 58: 39–48.

Pahwa, S. G., Pahwa, R., and Good, R. A. 1981b. Decreased *in vitro* humoral immune responses in aged humans. *J. Clin. Invest.* 67: 1094–1102.

Pandey, J. P., Fudenberg, H. H., Ainsworth, S. K., and Loadholt, C. B. 1979. Autoantibodies in healthy subjects of different age groups. *Mech. Age. Dev.* 10: 399–404.

Patel, P. J. 1981. Aging and antimicrobial immunity. *J. Exp. Med.* 154: 821–831.

Paul, J. R. and Bunnell, W. W., 1932. Anti-SRBC agglutinin with age. *Am. J. Med. Sci.* 183: 90–121.

Perkins, E. H. 1971. Phagocyte activity of aged mice. *J. Reticuloendothel. Soc.* 9: 642–643.

Pisciotta, A. V., Westring, D. W., DePrey, C., and Walsh, B. 1967. Mitogenic effect of phytohaemagglutinin at different ages. *Nature* 215: 193–194.

Radl, J., DeGlopper, E., Vanderberg, P., and VanZwieten, M. J. 1980. Idiopathic paraproteinemia. III. Increased frequency of rare proteinemia in thymectomized aging C57BL/KaLwRij and CBA/BrARij mice. *J. Immunol.* 125: 31–35.

Radl, J., Spers, J. M., Skuaril, F., Morell, A., and Hijmans, W. 1975. Immunoglobulin patterns in humans over 95 years of age. *Clin. Exp. Immunol.* 22: 84–90.

Rivany, B., Globerson, A., and Shiritzky, M. 1979. Viscosity of lymphocyte plasma membrane in aging mice and the possible relation to serum cholesterol. *Mech. Age. Dev.* 10: 71–79.

Roberts-Thomson, I. C., Whittingham, S., Youngchaiyud, U., and Mackay, I. R. 1974. Ageing, immune response, and mortality. *Lancet* 2: 368–370.

Roder, J. C. 1975. Targer-effector interaction in the natural killer (NK) cell system. VI. The influence of age and genotype on NK binding characteristics. *Immunol.* 41: 483–489.

Rosenberg, J. S., Gilman, S. C., and Feldman, J. D. 1982. Activation of rat B lymphocytes. II. Functional and structural changes in "aged" rat B lymphocytes. *J. Immunol.* 128: 656–660.

Rosenstein, M. M. and Strausser, H. R. 1980. Macrophage-induced T cell mitogen suppression with age. *J. Reticuloendothel. Soc.* 27: 159–166.

Rowley, M. J., Buchanan, H., and MacKay, I. R. 1968. Reciprocal change with age in antibody to extrinisic and intrinsic antigens. *Lancet* 2: 24–26.

Sabin, A. B., Ginder, D. R., Matumoto, M., and Schlesinger, R. W. 1947. Serological response of Japanese children to Japanese B encephalitis mouse brain vaccine. *Proc. Soc. Exp. Biol. Med.* 67: 135–140.

Scholar, E. M., Rashidian, M., and Heidrick, M. L. 1980. Adenosine deaminase and purine nucleoside phosphorylase activity in spleen cells of aged mice. *Mech. Age. Dev.* 12: 323–329.

Schreiner, G. F., Fujiwara, K., Pollard, T. D., and Unanue, E. R. 1977. Redistribution of myosin accompanying capping of surface Ig. *J. Exp. Med.* 145: 1393–1398.

Seshadri, R. S., Morley, A. A., Luainor, K. J., and Sorrell, J. 1979. Sensitivity of human lymphocytes to bleomycin with age. *Experientia* 35: 233–234.

Shelton, E., Daves, S., and Hemmer, R. 1970. Quantitation of strain BALB/c mouse peritoneal cells. *Science* 168: 1232–1234.

Sherr, D. H., Szewczuk, M. R., and Siskind, G. W. 1978. Ontogeny of B lymphocyte function. V. Thymic cell involvement in the functional maturation of B lymphocytes from fetal mice transferred into adult irradiated hosts. *J. Exp. Med.* 147: 196–206.

Singh, J. and Singh, A. K. 1979. Age-related changes in human thymus. *Clin. Exp. Immunol.* 37: 507–511.

Siskind, G. W., DeKruyff, R. H., Szewczuk, M., Weksler, M. E., and Goidl, E. A. 1981. Effect of age on the capacity of thymus cells to mediate B cell differentiation. In, *B Lymphocytes in the Immune Response,* pp. 355–361. Elsevier, North Holland.

Smith, G. S. and Walford, R. L. 1977. Influence of the main histocompatibility complex on aging in mice. *Nature* 270: 727–729.

Strelkauskas, A. J., Andres, J. A., and Yunis, E. J. 1981. Autoantibodies to a regulatory T cell subset in human aging. *Clin. Exp. Immunol.* 45: 308–315.

Stutman, O. 1972. Lymphocyte subpopulations in the NZB mice: deficit of thymus-dependent lymphocytes. *J. Immunol.* 109: 602–611.

Szewczuk, M. R. and Campbell, R. J. 1980. Loss of immune competence with age may be due to auto-anti-idiotypic antibody regulation. *Nature* 286: 164–165.

Szewczuk, M. R., Sherr, D. H., and Siskind, G. W. 1978. Ontogeny of B lymphocyte function. VI. Ontogeny of thymus cell capacity to facilitate the functional maturation of B lymphocytes. *Eur. J. Immunol.* 8: 370–379.

Tam, C. F. and Walford, R. L. 1978. Cyclic nucleotide levels in resting and mitogen stimulated cell suspensions from young and old mice. *Mech. Age. Dev.* 7: 309–320.

Tam, C. F. and Walford, R. L. 1980. Alterations in cyclic nucleotides and cyclase activities in T lymphocytes of aging humans and Down's syndrome subjects. *J. Immunol.* 125:1665–1670.

Thoman, M. L. and Weigle, W. O. 1981. Lymphokines and aging: Interleukin-2 production and activity in aged animals. *J. Immunol.* 127: 2102–2106.

Thomsen, O. and Kettel, K. 1929. Die Starke der Menschlichen Isoagglutinine und Entsperchenden Blutkorperchenrezeptoren in Verschiedenen Lebensaltern. *Z. Immunitatsforsch.* 63: 67–93.

Walford, D. S., Wilkens, R. F., and Decker, J. L. 1968. Impaired delayed hypersensitivity in an aging population. Association with antinuclear reactivity and rheumatoid factor. *J. Am. Med. Assn.* 203: 832–834.

Walford, R. 1969. *The Immunologic Theory of Aging*, pp. 1–248. Baltimore: Williams and Wilkins.

Walford, R. L. and Bergman, K. 1979. Influence of genes associated with the main histocompatibility complex on deoxyribonucleic acid excision repair capacity and bleomycin sensitivity in mouse lymphocytes. *Tissue Antigens* 14: 336–342.

Weiner, H. L., Scribner, D. J., Schocket, A. L., and Moorhead, J. W. 1978. Increased proliferative response of human peripheral blood lymphocytes to anti-immunoglobulin antibodies in elderly people. *Clin. Immunol. Immunopath.* 9: 356–362.

Weksler, M. E. and Hutteroth, H. 1974. Impaired lymphocyte function in aged humans. *J. Clin. Invest.* 53: 99–104.

Weksler, M. E., Innes, J. B., and Goldstein, G. 1978. Immunological studies of aging. IV. The contribution of thymic involution to the immune deficiencies of ageing mice and reversal with thymopoietin$_{32-36}$. *J. Exp. Med.* 148: 996–1006.

Whittingham, S., Buckley, J. D., and Mackay, I. R. 1978. Factors influencing the secondary antibody response to flagellin in man. *Clin. Exp. Immunol.* 34: 170–178.

Woda, B. A. and Feldman, J. D. 1979. Density of surface immunoglobulin and capping on rat B lymphocytes. I. Changes with aging. *J. Exp. Med.* 149: 416–423.

Zharhary, D. and Gershon, H. 1981. Allogeneic T cytotoxic reactivity of senescent mice: affinity for target cells and determination of cell number. *Cell. Immunol.* 60: 470–479.

17
ENDOCRINE SYSTEMS

Kenneth L. Minaker
Graydon S. Meneilly
John W. Rowe
Harvard Medical School

As described by Andres and Tobin (1977) in the first edition of this *Handbook,* old age was at one time postulated to be a hormonal deficiency state for which replacement therapy was possible. Many current commercial approaches to restoration of vitality are rooted in this hypothesis. Endocrine systems function to maintain homeostasis. Gerontologic interest in endocrine systems has been based in part on the view that senescence is an incapacity to regulate the internal environment in response to changes in the internal or external milieu. Aspects of endocrine systems of special relevance to aging include: their broad range of sequelae, ranging from virtually no impact on life span to promoting major clincial morbidity and mortality, and the variety of factors that may be viewed as "complicating factors or contributors" to the study of endocrine aging (Table 1).

This chapter will discuss several individual endocrine systems that have received widespread attention. Readers are also referred to the chapters in this *Handbook* on reproductive physiology, neuroendocrine aging, mineral metabolism, and metabolism for completion of this treatise on endocrine aging.

The Spectrum of Morbidity of Aging Processes

Endocrine systems display a broad spectrum of effects during aging that are of major clinical relevance. This rich variety provides the opportunity to increase our understanding of specific common illnesses and evaluate general mechanisms underlying physiologic aging. At one end of the spectrum, there is no major impact of aging on some important endocrine functions. For example, reserve capacity to secrete cortisol appears unchanged with advancing age across species. Aging may, on the other hand, mimic a disorder with major morbidity, the most clear example being the carbohydrate intolerance of aging. While the progressive increase in blood glucose during aging can be distinguished from clinical diabetes mellitus, it may share certain common mechanisms or clinical complications (Blumenthal, 1983). Delineation of such common mechanisms will also provide increased understanding of the relevance of aging to clinical disease.

Aging endocrine functions may erode physi-

TABLE 1. Complicating Factors and Contributors to Endocrine Aging

1. Disease
2. Medications, including smoking and alcohol
3. Diet
4. Exercise
5. Anthropometric changes
6. Social factors
7. Study conditions

ologic reserve and lay the substrate for the expression of disease: in animals, age-related decreases in responsiveness to cold and heat stress are associated with progressive mortality and may share common mechanisms of endocrine failure (Finch et al., 1969). In humans, this erosion of physiologic reserve may underscore the increase in mortality associated with certain stresses, such as burns and surgery in advancing age (Minaker and Rowe, 1982). Finally, the endocrine changes of senescence may be so disturbing to physiologic regulation that they can be called diseases. Benign prostatic hypertrophy and the menopause are two "diseases" of physiologic endocrine aging reviewed in other sections of this *Handbook*.

"Complicating Factors" and Contributors to Endocrine Aging

While it is now agreed that endocrine systems include a spectrum of clinically relevant physiologic changes, it is also recognized that aging is associated with numerous covariables that have a major impact on the results of gerontologic endocrine studies (Table 1) (Rowe, 1977). Failure to consider these variables in study design no doubt contributes to the increased variance in physiologic performance observed in many studies of aging, and the clear variability in performance of patients with age-associated disease. At the present time, some of these factors have received widespread acceptance as being aging processes in themselves; the relationships of others to physiologic aging remains to be clarified.

The most important variable in any clinical or physiologic study of aging is the potential complication produced by disease. Considerable effort has been directed to the development of suitable animal models of aging that are acceptable for endocrine studies. A common pitfall includes studying animals who develop substantial numbers of endocrine tumors in late life. With the improvements in veterinary pathology, the use of specific pathogen-free animals, and the development of strains free of potentially confounding disease, data are more likely to reflect the aging process. In human studies, recent advancements provide additional advantages over careful history, physical, and traditional laboratory investigations in an attempt to more clearly define the subjects under study. Improvements in hormone assay, the availability of assays for many relevant regulatory hormones, and the capacity to perform assays on very small amounts of plasma have permitted a more confident characterization of subjects as being free of disease. Many early gerontologic studies were flawed by the inclusion of subjects, for example, nursing home populations, who harbored subclinical disease that influenced the conclusions of the specific endocrinologic experiments. An example of the benefits of eliminating the complicating effect of disease in studies of physiologic aging is the recent demonstration of the lack of decline in testicular hormone levels with advancing age in carefully screened subjects (Harman and Tsitouras, 1980; Sparrow et al., 1980).

The exposure of subject populations to a variety of medications is increasingly recognized as potentially deleterious to endocrine function. Many early gerontologic studies did not carefully document the intake of casual or prescription medications in their subjects, which undoubtedly led to erroneous conclusions. A surprising number of nonhormonal medications have recently been recognized as having effects on endocrine systems. Examples include cimetidine, cannabis, antihypertensives, and diuretics.

The influence of antecedent diet on assessment of physiologic hormone action has been recognized for some time. If caloric intake is not standardized, varying performance during glucose tolerance testing may result. Deficiencies of carbohydrate intake may impair carbohydrate tolerance, and hypercaloric feeding may enhance glucose uptake (Seltzer, 1970; Adelman, 1970). Endocrine evaluation, particularly for studies involving insulin action, should now employ standard diets or careful diet histories.

A fourth complicating factor during endocrine evaluations of aging that has received inadequate attention is the determination of the level of physical activity in study subjects. While it it known that inactivity provokes glucose intolerance and that increased physical activity increases insulin sensitivity, most studies have not reported activity levels in study subjects, and reliable estimates of "normal" activity levels at various ages are not available.

Anthropometric changes during the aging process have long been felt to have significant influence upon endocrine evaluations during gerontologic study. While body weight remains relatively stable through late middle life and declines subsequently, there are underlying qualitative and quantitative changes in muscle and fat (Rossman, 1977). Lean body mass decreases during aging, and there has been a consistent trend for the degree of this decline to lessen as presumably healthier subjects are evaluated (Rowe et al., 1983). This loss in lean body mass should be taken into account wherever possible when measures of total hormone production or action are being studied. The degree of fatness that occurs during aging has probably been overestimated in many studies. Some early estimates suggested that fat increases by approximately 25 percent, but more current estimates indicate that the increase is in the range of 10 percent. There is controversy regarding whether these anthropometric changes are true age changes or reflect alterations in diet, illness experience, and activity. In the last two years, concomitant with the ability to quantify regional changes in fat distribution, has come recognition that aging is associated with centripetal distribution of fat and an invasion of large central muscle groups by fat (Borkan et al., 1981, 1982). Data suggest that fat in various sites is regulated differently by steroids and catecholamines (Rudman and Girolamo, 1971; Ostman et al., 1979; Bolinder et al., 1983). The impact of anthropometric changes during aging on hormonal responsivity clearly warrants increased attention. Currently, most clinical studies include only the screening of subjects who fall within the normative range of adiposity. On occasion, more stringent anthropometric measures or 24-hour urine creatinine measures are employed.

Disturbances in the sleep-wake cycle can also influence hormonal activity. Norms for the qualitative and quantitative changes that occur in sleep patterns with age are available and indicate substantial reductions in the amount of rapid eye movement (REM), stage III, and stage IV sleep. In addition, there is an increased frequency of nocturnal arousal with advancing age. These altered patterns are associated with changes in circadian rhythm of catecholamines (Prinz et al., 1979). The state of arousal of an animal or subject during endocrine evaluation may profoundly influence results.

Recognition that the sympathoadrenal system is a modifier of many other endocrine systems has received widespread attention in recent years (Young and Landsberg, 1977). Study conditions that are not consistent and carefully controlled confound the assessment of endocrine systems. It has become increasingly recognized that aging may be associated with enhanced sympathetic responsivity, which may in turn influence other endocrine functions such as carbohydrate tolerance (Rowe and Troen, 1980). Elderly animals and humans have impaired capacity to withstand thermal stress, and the maintenance of study conditions at standard temperatures is justified in order to control for this potentially confounding influence on a variety of hormone actions.

Patterns of socialization of animals as well as man can have profound influences on endocrine function. The rationale behind considering socialization patterns is the consideration that a stimulus may be perceived differently in an older subject than in a younger subject. For example, younger subjects admitted to a clinical research center (CRC) may not perceive this experience as particularly stressful, whereas older subjects, who have different perceptions of the significance of hospitals, may perceive CRC admission as substantially stressful. This may lead to heightened sympathoadrenal activity, impaired sleep patterns, and disturbance of sympathoadrenal and cortisol secretion, which may have significant impacts on endocrine evaluation.

General Patterns of Endocrine Aging

Evaluation of endocrine systems has emphasized, until recently, the evaluations of blood hormone levels under basal conditions and during physiologically relevant stresses. The complexity of control of hormone systems now extends beyond these basic parameters to include the central nervous system control of hormone secretion and events inside the target cell initiated by hormone receptor interaction. A prototypic endocrine system (Figure 1) shows areas of current gerontologic interest and provides a framework on which to illustrate more general endocrine patterns that are emerging as a consequence of aging.

Similar normative changes occur with age in the anatomy of endocrine glands. Each gland appears to decrease in weight and to develop a patchy atrophic appearance accompanied by vascular changes and fibrosis. Most glands have a tendency to form adenomas.

Basal hormonal levels in animals and man are generally not influenced by age. Several hormones, however, clearly have reduced serum concentrations of their active form, after changes in binding hormones have been taken into account. These include renin, aldosterone, triiodothyronine (T_3) in men, and dihydroepiandrosterone (DHEA).

Secretion rates of most hormones have been inferred from excretion studies or specifically measured during infusion of unlabeled and labeled hormones. There appears to be a general decline in hormonal secretion rate with advancing age, whether lean body mass is adjusted for or not. Substantial declines in secretion of testosterone, insulin, adrenal androgens, aldosterone, and thyroid hormone appear to be established. The maintenance of near normal hormone levels in the face of decreased secretion of thse hormones necessarily implies that hormone clearance rates are decreased with advancing age. Such is the case with testosterone, insulin, adrenal androgens, aldosterone, and thyroid hormone. Clearance of norepinephrine appears to be decreased slightly with advancing age (Esler et al., 1981). The only hormone whose clearance rate appears to increase with advancing age is epinephrine (Prinz et al., 1983). It is not presently clear whether the primary defect exists in hormone secretion or in hormone clearance, but the implication is that the capacity to adjust hormone secretion in order to maintain stable levels of plasma hormones is maintained.

The generation of active metabolites, where examined, suggests that there is a decreased rate of production of these with advancing age. There is a decreased rate of generation of T_3 from thyroxine (T_4) in man and a decline in the rate of generation of active metabolites of a number of adrenal cortical hormones.

Receptor binding during aging appears to show no systematic changes. Insulin receptors are unchanged with advancing age, whereas intracellular steroid receptors appear to be decreased with advancing age. Estradiol cell surface receptors decline with advancing age as do testosterone receptors. Beta-adrenergic receptors appear to be unchanged with advancing age.

Intracellular responses to hormones (so called post-receptor) actions seem to decrease

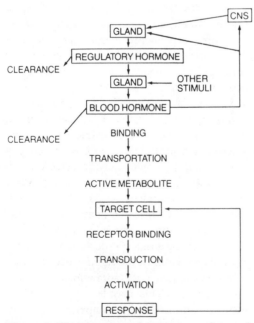

Figure 1. The sequence of hormone action and regulation. (After Korenman, 1982.)

with advancing age. This appears to be the case with somatomedins, insulin-induced glucose metabolism, catecholamines, and steroid hormone responsiveness. This frontier of gerontologic research will be only briefly addressed in this chapter.

CARBOHYDRATE METABOLISM

An age-related impairment in the capacity to maintain carbohydrate homeostasis after glucose challenge has been recognized for over 60 years (Spence, 1921). Over the past two decades, many gerontologists have focused their attention on elucidation of the mechanism underlying this age-related impairment in carbohydrate economy, and a general consensus is now emerging.

As in any gerontological study, several possible confounding factors need to be considered in an evaluation of aging and carbohydrate metabolism. In addition to avoiding the use of immature animals or individuals in order to prevent confusion between the effects of growth or development and aging, other variables which impair carbohydrate metabolism need to be taken into careful consideration. These include composition of diet with regard to both caloric adequacy and carbohydrate content, exercise, body composition with particular relevance to body fat content, and the presence of any of a broad array of pathologic states. These considerations are relevant to studies in rodents as well as in man. The two major rodent species which have been employed in studies of carbohydrate metabolism include the Sprague-Dawley rat, which is well known to develop obesity with advancing age, and the Fisher 344 rat which is susceptible to a high prevalence of renal disease. In human studies, particular attention must also be paid to the administration of any of a wide variety of medications which are known to impair glucose metabolism.

Blood Glucose Homeostasis

Many clincial studies indicate a very slight (approximately 1 mg/dl/decade) age-related increase after maturity in fasting blood glucose levels in healthy humans. This change is not affected by sex and is only slightly enhanced by cortisone administration (Davidson, 1979; Andres and Tobin, 1977). This modest age-related increase in fasting blood glucose levels is accompanied by rather striking increases in blood sugar after oral or intravenous glucose challenge. Lack of consideration of the age effect on glucose tolerance testing will result in an erroneous diagnosis of impaired carbohydrate intolerance or diabetes in many healthy elderly. In an extensive review of the English literature, Davidson (1979) found that the average post-glucose challenge increase in blood sugar with advancing age was 9.5 mg/dl/decade at one hour and 5.3 mg/dl/decade at two hours. The higher postprandial glucose levels seen with aging are also reflected in increased levels of hemoglobin A_{1c} with age (Graf et al., 1978). Alterations in glucose absorption associated with aging are unlikely to play an important role in these findings since similar results are found on both oral and intravenous glucose testing. Distribution of blood glucose levels at one and two hours after glucose challenge in the elderly is unimodal, which suggests that the change does not reflect the increasing prevalance of a second population of diabetics who are skewing the data.

It is clear that marked limitation of physical activity as well as the administration of diets low in carbohydrate content will impair glucose tolerance tests, and these factors may have played a role in many of the previous studies of aging and carbohydrate economy. Evidence that age-associated changes in body composition may play an important role in determining age effects in carbohydrate metabolism, even under basal conditions, has been developed by Elahi and his colleagues (1982) in a study of fasting levels of glucose, insulin, glucagon, and growth hormone in normal male volunteers ranging in age from 23 to 93 years. In these studies, fatness was associated with increases in basal insulin, glucagon, and fasting glucose, while basal levels of these main glucoregulatory hormones were not influenced by aging. While the apparent age-related impairment in glucose metabolism is less after this careful screening of the elderly subjects, an age-related impairment still persists (Reaven and Reaven, 1980).

Insulin Physiology and Aging

Insulin Release. A substantial literature is now available evaluating the effect of age on the molecular species of circulating insulin, the amount of insulin released from the pancreas in response to glucose or amino acid stimulation, the clearance of insulin from plasma, and insulin action on the liver and peripheral tissues.

Studies in the rat and man have evaluated the possible effect of age upon the relative amounts of proinsulin and insulin that are produced and secreted in response to glucose stimulation. Gold and colleagues (1981) studied isolated islets from the Sprague-Dawley rat and found that the ratio of proinsulin to insulin declines progressively with age. On the other hand, Duckworth and Kitabchi (1967) showed that circulating levels of proinsulin-like material were increased, relative to total immunoreactive insulin concentrations, after oral glucose challenge in individuals aged 45–54 years, when compared to younger individuals. In a more recent study, Jackson and his colleagues (1982) found similar circulating proportions of proinsulin and total insulin in elderly and younger adults after oral glucose challenge.

The past several years have seen the development of substantial interest in the effect of age on insulin release. Aging in the rat is associated with an increase in the number of large (400 μm) islets of Langerhans and a proportional decrease in the number of the smaller (50–80 μm) islets which ordinarily predominate in the younger animal. Reaven and colleagues (1979, 1980) have demonstrated an age-related decrease in glucose- or leucine-stimulated insulin secretion per beta cell of collagenase-isolated islets. This change is associated with an increase in the number of beta cells per islet in the older Sprague-Dawley rat. The authors suggest that the impaired capacity of the individual beta cell to secrete insulin with advancing age is compensated for by an increase in number of beta cells in older ani-

mals in an effort to maintain normal carbohydrate homeostasis. One characteristic of aged beta cells that may influence the decreased insulin responses, particularly at high glucose levels, is decreased levels of cyclic AMP (Lipson et al., 1981). Reaven has postulated that age-related changes in structure and function of the endocrine pancreas are not primary to the aging process itself, but rather represent a response to alterations in the sensitivity of peripheral tissues to insulin. This view is supported by the recent findings (Reaven et al., 1983) that the pancreatic changes mentioned vary in accord with the severity of peripheral insulin resistance and can be shown to be aggravated by sucrose overfeeding and largely inhibited by caloric restriction in the aging Sprague-Dawley rat.

In an interesting recent report which may shed additional light on the mechanism underlying age-related changes in pancreatic function, Chaudhuri and colleagues (1983) have shown that the somatostatin concentrations are markedly increased in islets of Langerhans of the aged Sprague-Dawley rat and that age-associated impairments of glucose-stimulated insulin release from these islets may be partly reversed by treatment of islets with anti-somatostatin antibodies.

Circulating Insulin Levels. Numerous studies have evaluated circulating insulin levels in individuals across the adult age range (Andres and Tobin, 1971; Reaven and Reaven, 1980; Davidson, 1979). Studies employing oral or intravenous glucose challenges have almost uniformly demonstrated that elderly individuals have insulin levels equivalent to, or in many cases slightly greater than, the levels found in their younger counterparts. These studies have often been criticized because the older subjects invariably have higher circulating glucose levels than the younger subjects. In response to this criticism, Andres and Tobin (1975) developed and employed the hyperglycemic glucose clamp technique in which they maintained steady-state plasma glucose levels at 140, 180, 220, and 300 mg/dl in subjects of varying ages and compared circulating insulin responses. Their results showed a decrease with age in insulin secretory capacity at all but the highest level of hyperglycemic stimulus. In similar studies employing the hyperglycemic glucose clamp technique, DeFronzo (1979) failed to detect a difference in either the early or the late phases of insulin secretion between young and old subjects in response to 140 mg/dl increases in blood glucose.

Analysis of post-stimulatory circulating levels of insulin should also take into account the possible effect of age on the removal of insulin from the circulation. Two recent studies (Minaker et al., 1982; Reaven et al., 1982) have demonstrated a clear age-related decline in insulin clearance in man and rats which may reconcile the discrepancy between the lack of an effect of age on circulating insulin levels in most studies and *in vitro* studies showing impaired pancreatic insulin release with advancing age.

Hepatic Sensitivity to Insulin

Studies in man have shown no effect of age on basal hepatic glucose production (DeFronzo, 1979; Robert et al., 1982; Fink et al., 1983). In response to high physiologic and supraphysiologic levels of hyperinsulinemia, hepatic glucose output is rapidly and almost completely suppressed in both young and old subjects (DeFronzo, 1979; Robert et al., 1982). Recently, Fink and colleagues (1983) have shown a modest decline in insulin suppression of hepatic glucose output in the elderly during steady-state insulin levels in the physiologic range (30–60 μU/ml).

Adelman and his colleagues have performed a systematic series of investigations into the effect of age on hepatic glucokinase activation after carbohydrate loading in the rat. Their early studies identified an age-related delay in enzyme adaptation from 3–4 to 10–12 hours following glucose administration as a Sprague-Dawley rat aged from 2 to 24 months (Adelman, 1970). Further studies indicated that the impaired capability for hepatic enzyme adaptation was not intrinsic to the hepatocyte, but was related to extrahepatic events, primarily

age-related sluggishness in insulin release (Adelman, 1979; Gold et al., 1976).

Sensitivity of Peripheral Tissues to Insulin

The sensitivity of peripheral tissues to insulin has been evaluated in man utilizing several techniques including insulin injection, euglycemic insulin infusions (insulin clamp technique), and studies of forearm glucose uptake in response to varying levels of hyperinsulinemia. Several studies have shown that reduction in circulating glucose level after bolus injection of insulin is impaired with advancing age. DeFronzo (1979), employing the euglycemic glucose clamp technique, demonstrated that at circulating levels of 100 μU/ml above basal, whole body glucose disposal is markedly impaired with age. In two recent studies, Rowe et al. (1983) and Fink et al. (1983) have also employed the insulin clamp technique to evaluate glucose disposal in young and old individuals over a range of circulating steady-state insulin levels varying from physiologic to supraphysiologic. Both these laboratories have demonstrated that aging, in active nonobese healthy men with normal glucose tolerance on normal diets, is associated with marked insulin resistance. Rowe and his colleagues (1983) found that maximal insulin-induced glucose disposal rates were the same in young and old, but that the dose-response curve was substantially shifted to the right in the older subjects, with the insulin level at which half-maximal glucose uptake was reached being 54 $\pm$ 14 μU/ml in the young and 113 $\pm$ 11 μU/ml in the old (Figure 2). Correction of glucose metabolism rate for lean body mass had no effect on comparisons between these groups. They interpreted these data as indicating an age-associated decline in sensitivity of peripheral tissues to insulin without a change in maximal tissue responsiveness. Employing similar techniques, Fink et al. (1983) also found a marked decrease in glucose metabolism at physiologic elevations of insulin and, in contrast to the studies of Rowe et al., found a significant decline in glucose metabolism in many elderly at supraphysiologic insulin levels. This latter effect was

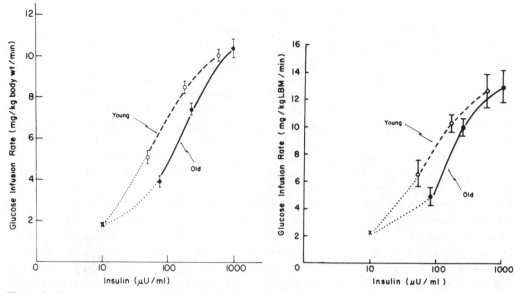

Figure 2.   Dose-response curves for insulin-medicated whole body glucose uptake in young (----) and old (———) subjects. In the panel on the left, glucose disposal is expressed as milligrams per kilogram of body weight. In the panel on the right, glucose infusion rates are normalized for lean body mass. (After Rowe et al., 1983.)

evident in elderly individuals with impaired performance on oral glucose tolerance testing, whereas comparison of maximal glucose metabolism in young and elderly individuals with normal glucose tolerance testing did not yield an age-related difference. As in the studies of Rowe et al., correction of glucose metabolism rate for lean body mass had no effect on age comparisons in these studies. In studies of the effect of age on forearm glucose uptake at similar arterial glucose levels attained by combination of oral and intravenous glucose infusion, Jackson and his colleagues (1982) also demonstrated a marked impairment in glucose disposal with advancing age. Questions that remain unanswered in this area relate to the mechanisms of insulin insensitivity during aging. Recent studies suggest that at least in the Sprague-Dawley rat, the rate limiting step in insulin-mediated glucose uptake in muscle is glucose transport (Goodman et al., 1983). However, these authors found little evidence of deterioration in glucose uptake after maturity.

Insulin Receptors in Aging

The overwhelming bulk of available data indicates that normal aging is not associated with a change in insulin receptor number or affinity in rodents or man. Sorrentino and Florini (1976) reported no effect of age on insulin receptors in mouse liver membranes. Olefsky and Reaven (1975) found no difference in insulin binding in adipocytes from young, adult, and senescent rats. Studies in human fibroblast cultures from young and old donors have shown either no change with age or an age-related increase in insulin receptors (Hollenberg and Schneider, 1979; Rosenbloom, 1976). Helderman (1980), studying insulin binding in transformed lymphocytes, was unable to detect a difference between cells from young and old subjects. Jackson, in his studies of forearm glucose uptake (1982), also evaluated monocyte insulin receptor binding in young and old subjects, and found no difference in insulin receptor binding or 50 percent inhibitory concentrations. In the studies of insulin action of Rowe et al. (1983), insulin receptors on circulating monocytes were studied and no effect of age was found. Similarly, in the recent studies of Fink et al. (1983), insulin binding to isolated adipocytes and monocytes was similar in elderly and nonelderly groups. In a lone dissenting report, Pagano (1981), studying adipocytes from surgical patients, reported a decline in insulin receptor binding in the elderly. A recent report suggests substantial heterogeneity in insulin binding and glucose uptake between muscles from different anatomic regions in young male Swiss-Weber mice (Bonen et al., 1981). The relevance of this observation to aging remains to be explored, but theoretically it may be very important as quantitative muscle changes during aging vary between anatomic regions.

Glucagon Physiology and Aging

Several studies have evaluated the influence of aging on the release and response to glucagon in man. In general, fasting levels of glucagon are not influenced by age (Dudl and Ensinck, 1977; Berger et al., 1978; Simonson and DeFronzo, 1983), nor is the post-glucose-induced suppression of glucagon release. In addition, glucagon release in response to alanine or arginine and glucagon kinetics are not impaired with aging (Dudl and Ensinck, 1977; Simonson and DeFronzo, 1983). Simonson and DeFronzo (1983) have also found that there is an increase with age in hepatic glucose production following glucagon administration. With the exception of this finding, it would appear that glucagon physiology is spared any significant changes with advancing age, despite the well-described alterations in insulin physiology that have been reviewed previously.

THE THYROID

Present data indicate that the capacity to maintain a euthyroid state continues during aging despite a number of changes in various aspects of thyroid hormone production, secretion, and action. It is likely that thyroid gland size does not change significantly with age. While autopsy studies in rats (Lansing and Wolfe, 1944) and man (Pittman, 1962; Frolkis et al., 1973) previously suggested an age-related decrease in size, a recent study in a carefully screened, healthy, community-dwelling population, using ultrasound to measure thyroid volume and correcting for body weight, suggests that the gland increases slightly in volume with age (Hegedus et al.,

1983). Microscopically, decreases in maximum follicular diameter and follicular cellularity, and increases in fibrous tissue are well established. An increase in micronodularity and cellular infiltrates in the thyroid has also been reported (Pittman et al., 1962; Frolkis et al., 1973). The prevalence of clinically palpable nodular goiter has been reported both to increase (Studer et al., 1979) and to decrease (Tunbridge et al., 1977) with age, reflecting the geographic variability in the prevalence of endemic goiter.

Basal Levels of Thyroid Hormones

The level of thyroid binding globulin (TBG) has been reported to be both unchanged (Jeffreys et al., 1972) and increased with age (Hesch et al., 1977; Burrows et al., 1975), with the increase occurring primarily in men (Braverman et al., 1967; Bigazzi et al., 1980).

Studies in rats (Klug and Adelman, 1979; Azizi, 1979; Segal et al., 1982; Eleftheriou, 1975) and hamsters (Nevé et al., 1981) suggest a decrease in total and free T_4 and T_3 during aging. Studies in man report both decreases (Herrmann et al., 1974; Chopra et al., 1978; Hesch et al., 1977) and elevations (Britton et al. 1975) in T_4 with age. The bulk of the data in man, however, indicates no change with age in total and free T_4 concentrations (Rubenstein et al., 1973; Sawin et al., 1979; Westgren et al., 1976; Caplan et al., 1981; Campbell et al., 1981; Lipson et al., 1979; Wenzel, 1976; Evered et al., 1978; Herrmann et al., 1981).

Total and free serum T_3 decreases with age in elderly euthyroid subjects, particularly males (Rubenstein et al., 1973; Sawin et al., 1979; Hesch et al., 1977; Bermudez et al., 1975; Chopra et al., 1978; Wenzel, 1976; Caplan et al., 1981; Westgren et al., 1976; Lipson et al., 1979; Evered et al., 1978; Herrmann et al., 1981). However, studies in which subjects were screened carefully, to exclude the pitfall of contamination with underlying disease, show no difference with age in serum T_3 (Olsen et al., 1978; Burrows et al., 1975). Since a variety of chronic diseases can decrease serum T_3 (Bermudez et al., 1975; Chopra et al., 1979), the decreased T_3 in some aging studies could reflect the presence of nonthyroidal illness in the study group. However, the weight of evidence suggests a decrease in T_3 with age on the order of 10–20 percent over the adult age range (Evered et al., 1978).

In addition to conversion to T_3, T_4 may also undergo peripheral mono-deiodination to reverse T_3 (RT_3), a metabolically inactive form. In most states of altered thyroid hormone economy, reductions in T_3 are associated with reciprocal increases in RT_3. Initial studies in sick elders suggested an increase in RT_3 with age (Nicod et al., 1976; Rudorff et al., 1976) compatible with observations on several disease states. Recent studies in healthy elderly subjects suggest that $R\,T_3$ does not, however, increase with normal aging (Kaplan et al., 1977; Olsen et al., 1978; Caplan et al., 1981; Herrmann et al., 1981; Lipson, 1979).

In summary, in healthy elderly patients TBG increases slightly, T_4 levels are unchanged with age, T_3 decreases slightly, and reverse T_3 is unchanged.

Metabolism and Turnover

Most studies show that the metabolic clearance (MCR) and the volume of distribution of T_4 are decreased in healthy older people by as much as 50 percent (Gregerman et al., 1962; Oddie and Fisher, 1966; Herrmann et al., 1981). It is unclear why the MCR decreases in man. Data from rats show increased (Frolkis and Valueva, 1978), normal (Herrmann et al., 1981), or decreased (Hiroshi, 1979) conversion of T_4 to T_3 in peripheral tissues. Gregerman and Davis (1978) propose that the decreased MCR may be due to decreased physical activity with age which is known to affect conversion of T_4 to T_3.

Since the serum T_4 remains constant with age in the face of decreased clearance, there is clearly a decreased production rate of T_4. Gregerman and Davis (1978) have pointed out that the decrease in T_4 production is unlikely to be due to gland failure since thyroid stimulating hormone (TSH) and T_4 are unchanged with age, T_4 turnover accelerates normally to stress in the aged, and the gland appears to respond normally to TSH (Herrmann et al.,

1981; Wenzel et al., 1974). The decreased production rate is probably a homeostatic response to decreased MCR of T_4.

In contrast to T_4, the metabolic clearance rate of T_3 does not change with age (Herrmann et al., 1981; Wenzel, 1976). If one accepts that the T_3 level is reduced in normal elderly, this implies a decreased production rate of T_3. While the decreased production of T_3 could be due to defective tissue conversion of T_4 to T_3, the data cited in this area are conflicting.

Regulation of Thyroid Hormone Levels

Little is known regarding the effect of age on thyrotropin releasing hormone (TRH) secretion. Thyroid stimulating hormone (TSH) levels have been used as an indirect measure of TRH secretion. Studies in rats suggest that pituitary content of TSH falls with age (Valueva and Verzhikovskaya, 1977; Choy et al., 1982). In contrast, however, studies of human pituitary TSH content reveal no significant change with age (Gershberg, 1957; Bakke et al., 1964).

Basal levels of TSH have been reported either not to change or to decrease with advancing age in rats (Klug and Adelman, 1979; Choy et al., 1982), and aging appears to be associated with an increase in TSH polymorphism, with normal levels on immunoassay and a fall in serum levels by bioassay (Klug and Adelman, 1977; Choy et al., 1982). TSH polymorphism has not been studied in man, and its functional significance is uncertain.

After initially conflicting results from studies on small numbers of poorly characterized subjects, recent large community studies on the relation between TSH level and aging (Tunbridge et al., 1977; Sawin et al., 1979) have shown that about 3 percent of old men and 8 percent of old women have elevated basal levels of TSH. The elevated levels are often associated with thyroid autoantibodies (Tunbridge et al., 1977) and may reflect subclinical hypothyroidism or Hashimoto's thyroiditis. Thus, supposedly normative data have been altered by subclinical illness.

In the rat, the maximal TSH response to

TRH administration appears to be unchanged with age. At low doses of TRH, TSH response is enhanced in old rats (Klug and Adelman, 1979), an effect which may reflect a decrease in T_4 and T_3 with age in rats, and thus enhanced sensitivity to TRH.

TSH response to TRH is diminished in older men, but not in women, in several studies (Snyder and Utiger, 1972; Azizi et al., 1975). Other studies have shown a decreased response to TRH with age in both sexes (Cuttelod et al., 1974; Wenzel et al., 1974; Herrmann et al., 1981), while no change (Hershman, 1978) or enhanced response (Ohara et al., 1974) has been shown by still others. The conflicting results may reflect the small numbers of patients and the complicating influences of disease.

The influence of age on the thyroid response to TSH is also uncertain. In the mouse and rat, the thyroid response to TSH is decreased (Eleftheriou, 1975) (Sartin et al., 1977). Studies in hamsters (Nevé et al., 1981) and mice (Studer et al., 1978) suggest that with age a greater number of follicles lose the capacity to phagocytize colloid droplets in response to TSH. The response in man to high doses of TSH has been variously reported to be normal or decreased (Einhorn, 1958; Herrmann et al., 1981; Lederer and Bataille, 1969; Wenzel et al., 1974), although most studies reveal a normal response. The fact that T_4 and TSH are usually normal in the aged suggests that the response is intact. In the few patients studied, TSH turnover rate in man doesn't appear to change with age (Cuttelod et al., 1974).

End-organ Responsiveness

Age-related changes in end-organ responsiveness to thyroid hormone have been studied in several systems. T_4 induction of hepatic alpha glycerophosphate dehydrogenase, which is felt to be representative of thyroid hormone effect on the liver, is not changed between maturity and senescence in the rat (Bulos et al., 1972). While T_4-induced cardiac hypertrophy occurs more slowly in aged mice (Florini, 1973), age has no effect on this response in rats (Zitnik and Roth, 1981). The response

of cardiac beta-adrenergic receptors to T_4 decreases with age.

In older rats and mice, thyroid hormone has been shown to restore certain blunted functions of the aged immune system (Piantenelli and Fabris, 1978) such as response to phytohemagglutinin (PHA) and plaque forming response to sheep erythrocytes (Fabris et al., 1982). The relevance of these observations to humans is uncertain. Denckla (1974) has shown that aged rats have a lower minimal O_2 consumption and a blunted increase in O_2 consumption in response to T_4. This age-related effect was abolished by removal of the pituitary, which suggests a potential inhibitory factor secreted by this gland. While it was initially felt that basal metabolic rate decreased with age in man, when anthropometric changes during aging are adjusted for, it is found to remain constant with age (Keys et al., 1973; Tzankoff and Norris, 1977).

In summary, at present there is uncertainty regarding the significance of changes in end-organ responsiveness to thyroid hormone with age.

ANTERIOR PITUITARY- GROWTH HORMONE

Growth hormone is an important anabolic hormone. Its direct effects include lipolysis and antagonism of insulin-induced glucose uptake. Indirectly, acting via somatomedins, it causes increased cartilage and bone growth, increased protein synthesis and lean body mass, and increase in size of liver, kidney, spleen, thymus, and red cell mass. Since aging is characterized by decreased protein synthesis (Young et al. 1975), lean body mass, and bone formation, and increased adiposity, the question can be raised as to whether growth hormone availability or influence may decline during aging.

Rat pituitary growth hormone content appears preserved with advancing age (Soloman and Greep, 1958; Bowman, 1961; Dickerman et al., 1972), although a recent study suggested a significant decline (Sonntag, 1980, 1982). Studies in man are limited but suggest a preservation of the number of pituitary growth hormone containing cells as well as total gland hormone content during aging (Gershberg, 1957; Daughday, 1968; Calderon et al., 1978). Growth hormone clearance is unchanged during aging (Taylor et al., 1969).

Basal growth hormone levels are stable during aging in rats (Sonntag et al., 1980, 1981) and mice (Finch et al., 1977). Studies in humans show conflicting results, possibly due to the confounding factor of obesity. No change in basal growth hormone levels is seen in well-screened subjects (Dudl et al., 1973; Kalk et al., 1973; Dolinska et al., 1980; Cartlidge et al., 1970; Elahi et al., 1982; Blichert-Toft, 1975) by some authors. A decrease in basal growth hormone levels during aging has been reported by others (Schramm et al., 1981; Vidalon et al., 1973; Dilman et al., 1979). Obesity is known to suppress circulating growth hormone levels in young individuals (Rabinowitz, 1970). It is well documented that the anthropometric changes which occur during aging include an increase in body fat (Myhre and Kessler, 1966). Control for obesity using currently available methodology have concluded, on one hand, that obesity is correlated with the decline in growth hormone levels with advancing age (Kalk et al., 1973; Rudman et al., 1981) and, on the other hand, that obesity is not associated with this finding (Elahi et al., 1982; Vidalon et al., 1973).

Growth Hormone Dynamics

In rats, the response of growth hormone (GH) to adrenergic stimulation, dopamine receptor agonists, and morphine is decreased during aging (Sonntag et al., 1981). Growth hormone response to hypoglycemia and arginine remains largely intact with advancing age in humans (Cartlidge et al., 1970; Kalk et al., 1973; Schramm et al., 1981; Dudl et al., 1973; Blichert-Toft, 1975). Other studies in man have demonstrated decreased growth hormone release to the sympathetic stimuli of amphetamines and surgical stress (Halbreich et al., 1980; Blichert-Toft, 1975).

Administration of synthetic growth hormone releasing factor (hpGRF 1–44) to intact rats has demonstrated a threefold increase in

growth hormone released in young rats to low dose hpGRF 1–44 and a less sensitive response in old rats. However, when growth hormone release under hpGRF stimulation from pituitary slices was measured, equal amounts of growth hormone were released from young and old animals, (Sonntag et al., 1983). This suggests that a paracrine effect is operative *in vivo* to alter GH dynamics, perhaps from somatostatin.

Biorhythms

Growth hormone is released in both young and old rats in similar pulses about every 3.3 hours. Although the troughs of the pulses are similar, the amplitudes of the pulses are significantly lower in the older male rats. Sonntag et al. (1982) have shown that chronic L-dopa therapy can restore GH pulses to normal in aged rats. Nocturnal peaks in serum hormone have been demonstrated in humans during youth in the first four hours of sleep, particularly during sleep stages III and IV (Finklestein et al., 1972; Carlson et al., 1972). Studies of older humans have shown a decrease in sleep-related and 24-hour secretion of growth hormone (Finkelstein et al., 1972; Carlson et al., 1972; Blichert-Toft, 1975; Bazzarre et al., 1976; D'Agata et al., 1974; Murri et al., 1980; Rudman et al., 1981; Dolinska et al., 1980; Prinz et al., 1983). Assessment of the total 24-hour secretion pattern indicated that the decrease in growth hormone was almost entirely confined to the first three hours of sleep (Figure 3). While there are alterations in many elderly in sleep stages III and IV (deep sleep) (Prinz, 1983), the studies noted have shown no correlation in individual patients between changes in deep sleep and GH secretion. In addition, studies have evaluated the possible confounding effect of obesity and found that age itself correlates with decreased growth hormone secretion when corrected for body fat (Rudman, 1981).

End-organ Response

The effect of aging on the cellular response to growth hormone has been examined to a

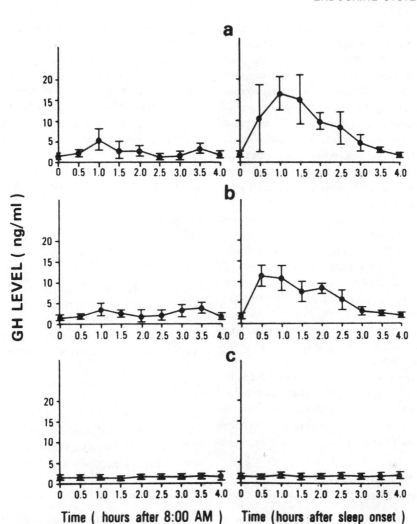

Figure 3. Average serum growth hormone concentration curves during awake (*left*) and sleeping (*right*) states for normal subjects ages (a) 20–29 years; (b) 60–79 years with somatomedin C levels $\geq$ 64 U/ml; and (c) 60–79 years with somatomedin C levels $\leq$ 64 U/ml. (After Rudman et al., 1981.)

limited degree. Declines in somatomedins have been demonstrated in old rats (Florini et al., 1980, 1981) and humans (Johanson and Blizzard, 1981; Rudman et al., 1981; Sara et al., 1982). The binding of growth hormone to mouse liver membranes is unchanged during aging (Sorrentino and Florini, 1976). In aging rats, there is a decreased skeletal response to growth hormone administration (Savostin-Asling, 1980). In mice, there appears to be enhancement of the insulin resistance producing effect of growth hormone, which results in higher insulin levels and poorer glucose tolerance in adult versus immature animals (Bailey and Flatt, 1982). Recent studies indicate that growth hormone corrects decreased protein synthesis seen during aging in rat diaphragm (Sonntag et al., 1983).

There have been only two studies addressing the end-organ responsiveness in humans. Growth hormone was administered to 12 healthy subjects in their seventies and eighties, who were compared with 6 young, healthy control subjects regarding nitrogen, phosphate, and potassium retention. The six elderly subjects with somatomedin C levels below normal had exaggerated responses to growth hormone in that they returned their somatomedin C levels to normal and retained more nitrogen, phosphate, and potassium. Those older patients with normal somatomedin C levels had virtually identical responses to the young individuals in these parameters (Rudman et al., 1981). There was a partial correlation with advancing age and degree of adiposity in those individuals with low somatomedin C levels. The other study examined the effect of daily injection of growth hormone for ten days in three hospitalized men aged 75 years of age, and it was found that there was diminished urinary hydroxyproline and calcium excretion in the elderly individuals compared to young controls. These individuals' red blood cells were resistant to growth hormone-induced inhibition of glucose consumption. Both young and old, however, did respond with nitrogen retention, decreases in blood urea nitrogen (BUN) and urinary sodium, and increases in free fatty acids (Root and Oski, 1969).

In summary, during aging, there is a decline in growth hormone release, particularly during the night. *In vivo* growth hormone response to growth hormone releasing factor is also altered with advancing age.

ANTERIOR PITUITARY— SOMATOSTATIN

Somatostatin is present in multiple areas of the central nervous system, as well as being focally distributed in the gastrointestinal tract and pancreas. Circulating levels of this hormone are negligible, and it probably acts in a paracrine fashion by effecting hormone release and tissue metabolism locally. CNS concentrations are highest in the hypothalamus where somatostatin inhibits TRH-stimulated TSH release and basal as well as stimulated growth hormone release.

The hypothalamic content of somatostatin declines with advancing age in rats (Sonntag et al., 1980, 1982). The administration of somatostatin antibody (Sonntag et al., 1981) causes a greater *rise* in growth hormone secretion in old than in young male rats. From these observations, this group has concluded that there may be heightened sensitivity during aging to somatostatin's ability to *decrease* growth hormone secretion.

Little data exist related to normative CNS changes in somatostatin in humans. In two studies, healthy elderly were found to have normal concentrations of somatostatin in several brain areas, in contrast to individuals clinically affected with Alzheimer's disease who showed decreases in somatostatin in those areas. Decrease in somatostatin in the demented group paralleled the decreases in choline acetyltransferase documented in those same patients (Davies et al., 1980, 1981).

ADRENAL GLAND

Several systematic effects of age on adrenal cortical function have been identified. Anatomically, the adrenal cortex decreases in weight in men and women during senescence. As is common with other endocrine glands, cortical nodule formation is frequent, and the senescent adrenal cortex tends to show fibrotic changes, decreases in epithelial cell number, and a decrease in steroid containing lipid. Vascular dilatation and hemorrhage are common. Subcellular alterations have been noted in mitochondria (Gregerman and Bierman, 1974).

Basal Values

There is no apparent change in plasma transcortin affinity with increasing age (DeMoor and Heyns, 1968), nor are there declines in concentrations of cortisol binding globulin (CBG) (Bernutz et al., 1979). Basal plasma glucocorticoid levels show no significant difference between maturity and old age in man (Jensen and Blichert-Toft, 1971), cows, goats, dogs, and monkeys (Riegle and Nellor, 1967; Riegle et al., 1968; Breznock and McQueen, 1973; Bowman and Wolf, 1969).

In man, resting levels of 17-hydroxycorticoids (17-OHCS) are normal from ages 23 to 92 (Samuels, 1957; Tyler et al., 1955; West et al., 1961). Plasma estrogens appear stable with aging (Kley et al., 1975).

In contrast, several other adrenal cortical steroid levels appear to decline as a consequence of aging in the basal state in man.

These are aldosterone (Flood et al., 1967) and dihydroepiandosterone sulfate (DHEA) (Yamaji and Ibayashi, 1969; Migeon et al., 1957). The declines in DHEA with advancing age are substantial, with values at age 60 being approximately one-third of those at age 30. Finally, plasma levels of androsterone are also substantially reduced during aging and, like DHEA, are almost undetectable past age 65 years (Migeon et al., 1957).

Thus, human aging has a much greater effect on adrenal androgen levels produced by the zona reticularis than on glucocorticoid levels produced by the zona fasciculata. The mechanisms for this effect are under investigation and will be discussed later in this section.

Secretion and Clearance Rates of Adrenal Hormones

As seen in other endocrine systems and accentuated in the adrenal gland, there tends to be a balanced reduction in the secretion and clearance rate of most adrenal hormones. Elderly men and women have reduced rates of adrenal cortical steroid hormone production measured indirectly by isotope dilution methods, calorimetric methods, or fluorometric methods (Romanoff et al., 1961; Samuels, 1957; Serio et al., 1969). In addition, there are decreased rates of deoxycorticosterone (Romanoff and Baxter, 1975), corticosterone, and aldosterone secretion rates during aging in man (Flood et al., 1967).

While these studies have documented decreased basal secretion of these hormones during aging in man, not all of the hormones have been found to have lowered plasma levels. This indicates an alteration in clearance rates of the hormones which may be the result of changes in hormone excretion or metabolism. The examination of which of these mechanisms is applicable has been addressed in man in a number of studies. First of all, declines in urinary adrenocorticosteroid excretion have been almost uniformly described for 17-keto-steroids (Antonini et al., 1968; Friedburg, 1954; Keutman and Mason, 1967; Moncloa et al., 1963; Pincus et al., 1954) and for 17-hydroxycorticoids (Juselius and Kenny, 1974;

Romanoff and Baxter, 1975; West et al., 1961). There has been a general trend to decreased 24-hour urine cortisol and total corticoid urinary excretion during aging (Romanoff et al., 1963; Grad et al., 1967). Progesterone and pregnanediol 24-hour urinary excretion also appears to decrease with advancing age (Romanoff et al., 1966; Pincus et al., 1954). Elderly men and women have reduced 24-hour excretions of the major urinary metabolites of cortisol including tetrahydrocortisol, tetrahydrocortisone, allotetrahydrocortisol, and cortolone (Romanoff et al., 1961).

To examine whether there was a quantitative decline in adrenocorticosteroid excretion rates related to anthropometric changes, studies expressing adrenocorticosteroid excretion in humans per gram of urinary creatinine have been performed. These studies indicate that the observed differences in excretion rates of urinary 17-hydroxycorticosteroids and production rates of cortisol expressed per unit of body weight disappear when the data are adjusted to creatinine excretion (Migeon et al., 1963; DeMoor, 1963; Juselius and Kenny, 1974; Grad et al., 1967). These same authors have also demonstrated that apparent declines in progesterone secretion and pregnanediol secretion could also be normalized for by adjusting for urinary excretion rates and expressing the data in proportion to grams of creatinine excreted.

There is some support for changes in the way adrenocorticosteroid hormones are metabolized during aging. A progressive decrease in the rate of removal of cortisol from the circulation has been demonstrated in men over age 60 years (West et al., 1961). While this decline in metabolic clearance of cortisol could well result from a decrease in blood flow to a metabolizing organ such as the liver or to the quantitative decline in liver size that occurs during aging, it is also possible that there is decreased activity of hepatic enzymes involved in cortisol metabolism. In support of the latter hypothesis, a study of hepatic cortisol sulfation and glucocorticoid sulfotransferases in young and old male rats shows decreased relative amounts of sulfotransferase with a substrate preference for glucocorticoid

(Singer and Burns, 1978). Studies in mice have shown an 80 percent decrease in liver cytosol cortisol binding fraction with a steroid specificity that suggests that it contains the enzyme steroid ring A reductase (Latham and Finch, 1976).

It is apparent that, at least for cortisol, the feedback mechanism remains intact during aging, with the body adapting to this decline in the rate of removal by decreasing production rates of this compound. For those adrenocorticosteroid hormones whose values fall dramatically with advancing age, some impairment of the feedback mechanism that regulates the levels of these hormones may be present.

Dynamic Testing

The response of adrenocorticosteroid hormones to stimulation has received intense evaluation and remains of current interest because of the recent availability of a new investi-gative tool, corticosteroid releasing factor (CRF). This newly synthesized 41 amino acid peptide has been administered to young and old rats. An age-related decrease in adrenocorticotrophic hormone (ACTH) response was seen, and a secondary decrease in cortisol production was seen in the elderly animals. Basal ACTH and cortisol were unchanged. In order to examine this observation without the need to consider factors operating *in vivo*, isolated adrenal cortical cells (Malamed and Carsia, 1983) from male Long-Evans rats underwent stimulation from various doses of alpha-1-24-corticotropin (a synthetic subunit of adrenocorticotrophic hormone) and adenosine 3':5'-cyclic monophosphate (cAMP). In this preparation, basal corticosteroid production in the absence of ACTH and cAMP decreases to 50 percent of 3-month values at 24 months. ACTH-induced corticosterone production decreased with increased age from 3 to 24 months (Figure 4). There was a similar reduction of cAMP-induced corticosterone produc-

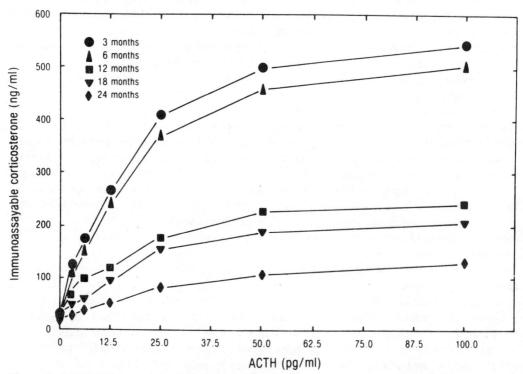

Figure 4. ACTH-induced corticosterone production by adrenocortical cells isolated from rats of different ages. (After Malamed and Carsia, 1983.)

tion with increased age of the rat. The major change was a 50 percent reduction from 3 to 12 months. Smaller decreases occurred from 12 to 24 months. Examination of these dose-response curves strongly suggests that during the period of decline between 6 and 12 months, the mechanism of impaired steroidogenesis appears to be located at an intracellular site. From the period of 12 to 24 months, the change in sensitivity observed is most consistent with a change in receptor function.

A number of animal species have been examined *in vivo* for plasma glucocorticoid response to adrenal cortical stimulation of a variety of types, including ACTH administration, ether vapor exposure, chronic restraint, Nembutal administration, and cold exposure. The *in vivo* animal literature is generally supportive of this recent observation in isolated cells. In 32 studies of the response to a variety of stimuli of corticosteroid across the age range in rats, mice, cows, goats, dogs, and monkeys, 22 show age-related declines in corticosteroid production. The majority of the remainder show no change during aging (Severson, 1981).

In man, however, there is general agreement that the increase in plasma cortisol in response to ACTH is preserved during aging (Kley, 1975; Blichert-Toft, 1975; West et al., 1961; Yamaji and Ibayashi, 1969). A few comparisons have been made of the effects of physiologic stimuli on ACTH-adrenal cortical function in y..... nd old subjects. In man, major surgery produces a normal ACTH response during aging (Blichert-Toft, 1975). The conclusions based on *in vivo* observations are clearly that, at least in man, the balance of net declines in secretion and clearance rates of cortisol during aging results in adequacy of plasma corticosterone responsiveness during aging.

The secretion of corticosteriods other than corticosterone is affected by age. Plasma aldosterone is decreased with age (Flood et al., 1967) and remains lower under conditions of sodium restriction. Age also is associated with dramatic fall in ACTH-induced serum adrenal androgen levels (Yamaji and Ibayashi,

1969). As is characteristic of this literature, however, there are several important dissenting observations. With ACTH simulation (40 U/day for two days), elderly men produce as much pregnenolone and progesterone (Romanoff et al., 1969) as young men. The dramatic declines in plasma levels of DHEA that are observed under basal conditions have been observed during ACTH stimulation in elderly subjects (Yamaji and Ibayashi, 1969; Parker, et al., 1981). In an important recent study, the coincident responses of Δ^4 and Δ^5 steroids to ACTH stimulation were compared in young and old male and female subjects. Total adrenal response was less in the elderly subjects. However, Δ^4 steroid responses (cortisol, androstenedione, 17-hydroxyprogesterone, and progesterone) were at least as great in elderly as in young groups. In contrast, Δ^5 steroid response (dehydroepiandrosterone, 17-hydroxypregnenolone, and pregnenolone) was significantly reduced (Vermeulen et al., 1982).

The circadian rhythm of plasma cortisol and 17-hydroxycorticosteroid is preserved during aging in man (Colucci et al., 1975; Silverberg et al., 1968). In response to insulin-induced hypoglycemia, the plasma cortisol response of elderly subjects has been reported to be indistinguishable from younger controls (Green and Friedman, 1968; Muggeo et al., 1975). Metyrapone-induced decreases in plasma cortisol have been shown to produce normal ACTH responses in elderly individuals (Blichert-Toft and Hummer, 1977). These data indicate that the feedback mechanism for ACTH control remains relatively preserved in old age in man and allows cortisol production to be adjusted to a decreased hormone clearance.

INTRACELLULAR CHANGES IN HORMONE ACTION

As techniques for evaluation of tissue responsiveness to hormones have become available, the boundaries between endocrinology and metabolism have become less distinct. With regard to the endocrine systems discussed in this chapter, aging's effect on intracellular hormonal mechanisms is receiving increased attention (Chang and Roth, 1979; Wolfsen, 1982). Hormone receptor concentrations in tissues or cells are decreased for corticosteroids (Roth, 1974, 1975, 1976; Roth and Livingston, 1976; Singer et al., 1973; Rosner and Cristofalo, 1978). Androgen receptor concentrations and responsiveness have been shown to be decreased in various organs of the rat during aging (Roy et al., 1974; Robinette and Mawhinney, 1977; Choukynska and Vassileva-Popova, 1977). Estrogen receptors in rat and mouse uterus decline with advancing age (Holinka et al., 1975). In several instances where examined, there has been a reduction in biologic responsiveness concurrent with the decline in receptor binding.

Further studies on the post-receptor mechanisms responsible for the insulin resistance seen during aging are needed (Rowe et al., 1983; Fink, 1983). Because of the recently demonstrated necessity for the pituitary to convert T_4 to T_3 before completion of the feedback loop, exploration of aging's effect on feedback mechanisms will increasingly require intracellular evaluation. Factors regulating the hormonal receptors within the cell have been reviewed extensively by Chang and Roth (1979).

REFERENCES

Adelman, R. C. 1970. An age-dependent modification of enzyme regulation. *J. Biol. Chem.* 245: 1032–1035.

Adelman, R. C. 1979. Loss of adaptive mechanisms during aging. *Fed. Proc.,* 38: 1968–1971.

Andres, R., and Tobin, J. D. 1975. Aging and the disposition of glucose. *Adv. Exp. Biol. Med.* 61: 239–249.

Andres, R. and Tobin, J. D. 1977. Endocrine systems. *In,* C. Finch and L. Hayflick (eds.), *Handbook of the Biology of Aging,* pp. 357–378. New York: Van Nostrand Reinhold.

Antonini, F. M., Porro, A., Serio, M., and Tinti, P. 1968. Gas chromotographic analyses of urinary 17-ketosteroids responsive to gonadotrophin and ACTH in young and old persons. *Exp. Gerontol.* 3, 181–192.

Azizi, F. 1979. Changes in pituitary and thyroid function with increasing age in young male rats. *Am. J. Physiol.* 237: E224–226.

Azizi, F., Apostolos, G., Vagenakis, K., Portnay, G. I., Rapoport, B., Ingbar, S., and Braverman, L. E. 1975. Pituitary-thyroid responsiveness to intramuscular TRH based on analysis of serum T_4, T_3, and TSH. *N. Engl. J. Med.* 292: 273–277.

Bailey, C. J. and Flatt, P. R. 1982. Hormonal control

of glucose homeostasis during development and aging in mice. *Metabolism* 31: 238–246.

Bakke, J. L., Lawrence, N., Knudtson, K. P., Roy, S., and Needham, G. H. 1964. A correlative study of the content of TSH and cell morphology of the human adenohypophysis. *Am. J. Clin. Pathol.* 41: 576–588.

Bazzarre, T. L., Johanson, A. J., Huseman, C. A., Varma, M. M., and Blizzard, R. M. 1976. Human growth hormone changes with age. *In,* Growth hormone and related peptides; proceedings of the third international symposium. *Excerpta Med. Int. Congr. Series* 381: 261–270.

Berger, D., Crowther, R., Floyd, J. C., Pelz, S., and Fajans, S. S. 1978. Effects of age on fasting levels of pancreatic hormones in man. *J. Clin. Endocrinol. Metab.* 47: 1183–1189.

Bermudez, F., Surks, M. I., and Oppenheimer, J. H. 1975. High incidence of decreased serum T_3 concentration in patients with nonthyroidal disease. *J. Clin. Endocrinol. Metab.* 41: 27–32.

Bernutz, C., Hansle, W. O., Horn, K., Pickardt, C. R., Scriba, P. C., Fink, E., Kolb, H., and Tsechesche, H. 1979. Isolation, characterization, and radioimmunoassay of corticosteroid binding globulin (CBG) in human serum—clinical significance and comparison to thyroxine binding globulin (TBG). *Acta Endocrinol. (Copenhagen)* 92: 370–384.

Bigazzi, M., Sardano, G., Martino, E., Vaudagna, G., Ronga, R., Pinchera, A., and Baschieri, L. 1980. Age and sex related variations of serum TBG. *J. Endocrinol. Invest* 4: 439–440.

Blichert-Toft, M. 1975. Secretion of corticotrophin and somatotrophin by the senescent adenohypophysis in man. *Acta Endocrinologica* 78 (Suppl. 195): 1–157.

Blichert-Toft, M. and Hummer, L. 1977. Serum immunoreactive corticotropin and response to metyrapone in old age in man. *Gerontology* 23: 236–243.

Blumenthal, H. 1983. Diabetes mellitus as a disorder of information flow. *In,* H. Blumenthal (ed.), *Handbook of the Diseases of Aging,* pp. 181–220. New York: Van Nostrand Reinhold.

Bolinder, J., Kager, L., Ostman, J., and Arner, P. 1983. Differences at the receptor and postreceptor levels between human omental and subcutaneous adipose tissue in the action of insulin on lipolysis. *Diabetes* 32: 117–123.

Bonen, A., Tan, M. H., and Watson-Wright, W. M. 1981. Insulin binding and glucose uptake differences in rodent skeletal muscles. *Diabetes* 30: 702–4.

Borkan, G., Gerzof, S., Robbins, A. H., and Hults, D. E. 1981. Computed tomography assessment of fat and muscle density in aging. *Gerontologist* 21: 126.

Borkan, G. A., Gerzof, S. G., Robbins, A. H., Hults, D. E., Silbert, C. K., and Silbert, J. E. 1982. Assessment of abdominal fat content by computerized tomography. *Amer. Jour. Clin. Nutr.* 36: 172–177.

Bowman, R. E. and Wolf, R. C. 1969. Plasma 17-hydroxycorticosteroid response to ACTH in Nomulatta: dose, age, weight, and sex. *Proc. Soc. Exp. Biol. Med.* 130: 61–64.

Bowman, R. H. 1961. Growth hormone activity of the anterior pituitary lobe of the male rat at various ages. *Nature (Lond.)* 192: 976–977.

Braverman, L. E., Foster, A. E., and Ingbar, S. H. 1967. Sex-related differences in the binding in serum of thyroid hormones. *J. Clin. Endocrinol. Metab.* 27: 227–232.

Breznock, E. M. and McQueen, R. D. 1970. Adrenocortical function during aging in the dog. *Am. J. Vet. Res.* 31: 1269–1273.

Britton, K. E., Quinn, V., Ellis, S. M., Cayley, A. C. D., Miralles, J. M., Brown, B. L., and Ekins, R. P. 1975. Is "T₄ toxicosis" a normal biochemical finding in elderly women? *Lancet* 2: 141–142.

Britton, G. W., Rotenberg, S., Freeman, C., Britton, V. J., Karoly, K., Ceci, L., Klug, T. L., Lacko, A. G., and Adelman, R. C. 1975. Regulation of corticosterone levels and liver enzyme activity in aging rats. *Adv. Exp. Med. Biol.* 61: 209–228.

Bulos, B., Shukla, S., and Sacktor, B. 1972. The rate of induction of the mitochondrial alpha glycerophosphate dehydrogenase by thyroid hormone in adult and senescent rats. *Mech. Age Dev.* 1: 227–231.

Burrows, A. W., Shakespear, R. A., Hesch, R. D., Cooper, E., Aickin, C. M., and Burke, C. W. 1975. Thyroid hormones in the elderly sick "T₄ euthyroidism," *Br. Med. J.* 4: 437–439.

Calderon, L., Ryan, N., and Kovacs, K. 1978. Human pituitary growth hormone cells in old age. *Gerontology* 24: 441–447.

Campbell, A. J., Reinken, J., and Allan, B. C. 1981. Thyroid disease in the elderly in the community. *Age and Ageing* 10: 47–52.

Caplan, R. H., Wickus, G., Glasser, J. E., Davis, K., and Wahner, H. W. 1981. Serum concentrations of the iodothyronines in elderly subjects: decreased T₃ and free T₃ index. *J. Am. Ger. Soc.* 29: 19–24.

Carlson, H. E., Gillin, J. C., Gordon, P., and Snyder, F. 1972. Absence of sleep related growth hormone peaks in aged normal subjects and in acromegaly. *J. Clin. Endocrinol. Metab.* 34: 1102–1105.

Cartlidge, N. E. F., Black, M. M., Hall, M. R. P., and Hall, R. 1970. Pituitary function in the elderly. *Gerontol. Clin.* 12: 65–70

Chang, W. and Roth, G. S. 1979. Changes in the mechanisms of steroid action during aging. *J. Steroid Biochem.* 11: 889–892.

Chaudhuri, M., Sartin, J. L., and Adelman, R. C. 1983. A role for somatostatin in the impaired insulin secretory response to glucose by islets from aging rats. *J. Gerontol.* 38: 431–435.

Chopra, I. J., Solomon, D. H., Chopra, U., Wu, S. Y., Fisher, D. A., and Nakamura, Y. 1978. Pathways of metabolism of thyroid hormones. *Recent Prog. Horm. Res.* 34: 521–567.

Chopra, I. J., Soloman, D. H., Hepner, G. W., and Morgenstern, A. A. 1979. Misleadingly low FTI and usefulness of reverse T₃ in non-thyroidal illness. *Ann. Int. Med.* 90: 905–912.

Choukynska, R. and Vassileva-Popova, J. 1977. Effect of age on the binding of H³-testosterone with receptor protein from rat brain and testes. *Compte Rendu de l'Academie Bulgare de Seances* 30: 133–135.

Choy, V. J., Klemme, W. R., and Timiras, P. S. 1982. Variant forms of immunoreactive TSH in aged rats. *Mech. Age. Dev.* 19: 273–278.

Colucci, C. F., D'Alessandro, B., Bellastella, A., and Montalbetti, N. 1975. Circadian rhythm of plasma cortisol in the aged (Cosinor method). *Gerontol. Clin.* 17: 89–95.

Cuttelod, S., Lemarchand-Beraud, T., Magenet, P., Perret, C., Poli, S., and V. Vannotti, A. 1974. Effect of age and role of kidneys and liver on TSH turnover in man. *Metabolism* 23: 101–113.

D'Agata, R., Vigneri, R., and Polosa, P. 1974. Chronobiological study on growth hormone secretion in man: its relation to sleep wake cycles and increasing age. *In,* L. E. Scheving, F. Halberg, and J. E. Pauly (eds.), *Chronobiology,* pp. 81–87. Stuttgart: G. Thieme.

Daughday, W. 1968. The adenohypophysis. *In,* R. Williams, (ed.), *Textbook of Endocrinology,* pp. 27–84. Philadelphia: Saunders.

Davidson, M. B. 1979. The effect of aging on carbohydrate metabolism: a review of the English literature and a practical approach to the diagnosis of diabetes mellitus in the elderly. *Metabolism* 28: 688–705.

Davies, P., Katzman, R., and Terry, R. D. 1980. Reduced somatostatin-like immunoreactivity in cerebral cortex from cases of Alzheimer's disease and Alzheimer's senile dementia. *Nature* 288: 279–280.

Davies, P. and Terry, R. D. 1981. Cortical somatostatin-like immunoreactivity in cases of Alzheimer's disease and senile dementia of the Alzheimer's type. *Neurobiol. Aging* 2: 9–14.

DeFronzo, R. A. 1979. Glucose intolerance and aging: evidence for tissue insensitivity to insulin. *Diabetes* 28: 1095–1101.

DeMoor, P. and Heyns, W. 1968. Cortisol binding affinity to plasma transcortin (CBA) as studied by competitive adsorption. *J. Clin. Endocrinol. Metab.* 28: 1281–1286.

DeMoor, P., Steeno, O., Meulpas, E., Hendrikx, A., Delaere K., and Ostyn, M. 1963. Influences of body size and of sex on urinary corticoid excretion in a group of normal young males and females. *J. Clin. Endocrinol. Metab.* 23: 677–683.

Denckla, W. D. 1974. Role of pituitary and thyroid glands in the decline of minimal O₂ consumption with age. *J. Clin. Invest.* 53: 572–581.

Dickerman, E., Dickerman, S., and Meites, J. 1972. Influence of age, sex and estrous cycle on pituitary and plasma GH levels in rats. *In,* Growth and growth hormones: proceedings of the second international symposium. *Excerpta Med. Int. Congr. Series* 244: 252–260.

Dilman, V. F., Bobrov, J. F., Ostroumova, M. N., Lvovich, E. G., Vishnevsky, A. S., Anisimov, V. N., and Vasiljeva, I. A. 1979. Hypothalamic mechanisms of aging and of specific age pathology. III: Sensitivity threshold of hypothalamo-pituitary complex to homeostatic stimuli in energy systems. *Exp. Gerontol* 14: 217–224.

Dolinska, G., Paradowski L., and Knapik, Z. 1980. Growth hormone secretion in elderly subjects. *Pol Tyg Lek* 35: 1421–1422.

Duckworth, W. C. and Kitabchi, A. E. 1967. The effect of age on plasma pro-insulin-like material after oral glucose. *J. Lab. Clin. Med.* 88: 359–367.

Dudl, R. J. and Ensinck, J. W. 1977. Insulin and glucose relationships during aging in man. *Metabolism* 26: 33–41.

Dudl, R. J., Ensinck, J. W., Palmer, H. E., and Williams, R. H. 1973. Effect of age on GH secretion in man. *J. Clin. Endocrinol. Metab.* 37: 11–16.

Einhorn, J. 1958. Studies on the effect of thyrotropic hormone on thyroid function in man. *Acta Radiol.* 160: 1–107.

Elahi, D., Muller, D. C., Tzankoff, S. P., Andres, R., and Tobin, J. D. 1982. Effect of age and obesity on fasting levels of glucose, insulin, glucagon, and growth hormone in man. *J. Gerontol.* 37: 385–391.

Eleftheriou, B. E. 1975. Changes with age in protein bound iodine (PBI) and body temperature in the mouse. *J. Gerontol.* 30: 417–421.

Esler, M., Skews, H., Jackman, G., Babik, A., and Korner, P. 1981. Age dependence of noradrenaline kinetics in normal subjects. *Clin. Sci.* 60: 217–219.

Evered, D. C., Tunbridge, W. M. G., Hall, R., Appleton, D., Brewis, M., Clark, F., Manuel, P., and Young, E. 1978. Thyroid hormone concentrations in a large scale community survey. Effect of age, sex, illness and medication. *Clin. Chem. Acta.* 83: 223–229.

Fabris, N., Muzzioli, M., and Mocchegiani, E. 1982. Recovery of age dependent immunological deterioration in BALB/c mice by short-term treatment with L-thyroxine. *Mech. Age. Dev.* 18: 327–330.

Finch, C. E. 1973. Monoamine metabolism in the aging male mouse. *In*, M. Rockstein and M. L. Sussman (eds.), *Development and Aging in the Nervous System*, pp. 199–213. New York: Academic Press.

Finch, C. E., Foster, J. R., and Mirsky, A. E. 1969. Aging and the regulation of all activities during exposure to cold. *J. Gen. Physiol.* 54: 690–712.

Finch, C. E., Jonec, V., Wisner, J. R., Sinha, Y. N., de Vellis, J. S., and Swerdloff, R. S. 1977. Hormone production by the pituitary and testes of male C57BL/6J mice during aging. *Endocrinology* 101: 1310–1317.

Fink, R. I., Kolterman, O. G., Griffin, J., and Olefsky, J. M. 1983. Mechanisms of insulin resistance in aging. *J. Clin. Invest.* 71: 1523–1535.

Finkelstein, J. W., Roffwarg, H. P., Boyer, R. M., Kream, J., and Hellman, L. 1972. Age related change in the 24 hour spontaneous secretion of growth hormone. *J. Clin. Endocrinol. Metab.* 35: 660–665.

Flood, C., Gherondache, C., Pincus, G., Tait, J. F., Tait, S. A. S., and Willoughby, S. 1967. The metabolism and secretion of aldosterone in elderly subjects. *J. Clin. Invest.* 46: 960–966.

Florini, J. R., Harned, J. A., Richman, R. A., and Weiss, J. P. 1981. Effect of rat age on serum levels of growth hormone and somatomedins. *Mech. Age. Dev.* 15: 165–176.

Florini, J. R., and Roberts, S. B. 1980. Effect of rat age on blood levels of somatomedin-like growth factors. *J. Gerontol.* 35: 23–30.

Florini, J. R., Saito, Y., and Manowitz, E. J. 1973. Effect of age on thyroxine induced cardiac hypertrophy in mice. *J. Gerontol.* 28: 293–297.

Friedberg, R. 1954. ACTH administration, adrenal response and age. *J. Gerontol.* 9: 429–438.

Frolkis, V. V. and Valueva, G. V. 1978. Metabolism of thyroid hormones during aging. *Gerontology* 24: 81–94.

Frolkis, V. V., Verzhikovskaya, N. V., and Valueva, G. V. 1973. The thyroid and age. *Exp. Geront.* 8: 285–296.

Gershberg, H. 1957. Growth hormone content and metabolic actions of human pituitary glands. *Endocrinology* 61: 160–165.

Gold, G., Karoly, K., Freeman, C., and Adelman, R. C. 1976. A possible role for insulin in the altered capability for hepatic enzyme adaptation during aging. *Biochem. Biophys. Res. Commun.* 73: 1003–1009.

Gold, G., Reaven, G. M., and Reaven, E. P. 1981. Effect of age on pro-insulin and insulin secretory patterns in isolated rat islets. *Diabetes* 30: 77–82.

Goodman, M. N., Dluz, S. M., McElaney, M. A., Beber, E., and Ruderman, N. B. 1983. Glucose uptake and insulin sensitivity in rat muscle: changes during 3–96 weeks of age. *Am. J. Physiol.* 244: E93–100.

Grad, B., Kral, V. A., Payne, R. C., and Berenson, J. 1967. Plasma and urinary corticoids in young and old persons. *J. Gerontol.* 22: 66–71.

Graf, R. J., Halter, J. B., and Porte, D. 1978. Glycosolated hemoglobin in normal subjects and subjects with maturity onset diabetes. Evidence for a saturable system in man. *Diabetes* 27: 834–839.

Green, M. F. and Friedman, M. 1968. Hypothalamic-pituitary-adrenal functions in the elderly. *Gerontol. Clinics* 10: 334–339.

Gregerman, R. I. and Bierman, E. L. 1974. Aging and hormones. *In*, R. H. Williams (ed.), *Textbook of Endocrinology*, pp. 1059–1070. Philadelphia: W. B. Saunders.

Gregerman, R. I. and Davis, P. J. 1978. Effects of intrinsic and extrinsic variables on thyroid hormone economy. Intrinsic physiologic variables and non-thyroidal illness. *In*, S. C. Werner and S. H. Ingbar (eds.), *The Thyroid*, pp. 223–246. New York: Harper and Row.

Gregerman, R. I., Gaffney, G. W., and Shock, N. W. 1962. Thyroxine turnover in euthyroid man with special reference to changes with age. *J. Clin. Invest.* 41: 2065–2074.

Halbreich, U., Asnis, G. M., Halpern, F., Tabrizi, M. A., and Sachar, E. J. 1980. Diurnal growth hormone responses to dextroamphetamine in normal young men and post-menopausal women. *Psychoneuroendocrinol.* 5: 339–344.

Harman, S. M. and Tsitouras, P. D. 1980. Reproductive hormones in aging men. I. Measurement of sex steroids, basal luteinizing hormone and Leydig cell response to human chorionic gonadotropin. *J. Clin. Endocrinol Metab.* 51: 35–40.

Hegedus, L., Perrild, H., Poulsen, L. R., Anderson,

J. R., Holm, B., Schnohr, P., Jensen, G., and Hansen, J. M. 1983. The determination of thyroid volume by ultrasound and its relationship to body weight, age, and sex in normal subjects. *J. Clin. Endorinol. Metab.* 56: 260–263.

Helderman, J. H. 1980. Constancy of pharmacokinetic properties of the lumphocyte insulin receptor during aging. *J. Gerontol.* 35: 329–334.

Herrmann, J., Heinen, E., Kroll, H. J., Rudorff, K. H., and Kruskemper, H. L. 1981. Thyroid function and thyroid hormone metabolism in elderly people: low T_3 syndrome in old age? *Klin. Wochenschr.* 59: 315–323.

Herrmann, J., Rusche, H. J., Kroll, H. J., Hilger, P., and Kruskemper, H. L. 1974. Free T_3 and T_4 serum levels in old age. *Hormone Metab. Res.* 6: 239–240.

Hershman, J. M. 1978. Use of thyrotropin-releasing hormone in clinical medicine. *Med. Clin. North Am.* 62: 313–325.

Hesch, R. D., Gatz, J., Juppner, H., and Stubbe, P. 1977. TBG dependency of age related variations of T_4 and T_3. *Hormone Metab. Res.* 9: 141–146.

Hiroshi, O. 1979. Changes in extra-thyroidal conversion of T_4 to T_3 *in vitro* during development and aging in the rat. *Mech. Age. Dev.* 10: 151–156.

Holinka, C. F., Nelson, J. F., and Finch, C. E. 1975. Effect of estrogen treatment on estradiol binding capacity in uteri of aged rats. *Gerontologist* 15: 30.

Hollenberg, N. D. and Schneider, E. L. 1979. Receptor for insulin in epidermal growth factor-mogastrone in adult human fibroblasts do not change with donor age. *Mech. Age. Dev.* 11: 37–43.

Jackson, R. A., Blix, P. N., Mathews, J. A., Hamling, J. B., Din, B. N., Brown, D. C., Belin, J., Rubenstein, A. H., and Nabarro, J. D. N. 1982. Influence of aging on glucose homeostasis. *J. Clin. Experimental Med.* 55: 5: 840–848.

Jefferys, P. M., Farran, H. E. A., Hoffenberg, R., Fraser, P. M., and Hodkinson, H. M. 1972. Thyroid function tests in the elderly. *Lancet* 1: 924–927.

Jensen, H. K. and Blichert-Toft, M. 1971. Serum corticotrophin, plasma cortisol, and urinary excretion of 17-ketogenic steroids. *Acta Endocrinol (Copenhagen)* 66: 25.

Johanson, A. J. and Blizzard, R. M. 1981. Low somatomedin-c levels in older men rise in response to growth hormone administration. *Johns Hopkins Med. J.* 149: 115–117.

Juselius, R. E. and Kenny, F. M. 1974. Urinary free cortisol excretion during growth and aging: correlation with cortisol production rate and 17-hydroxycorticosteroid excretion. *Metabolism* 23: 847–852.

Kalk, W. J., Vinik, A. I., Pimstone, B. L., and Jackson, W. P. U. 1973. Growth hormone response to insulin hypoglycemia in the elderly. *J. Gerontol.* 28: 431–433.

Kaplan, M. M., Schimmel, M., and Utiger, R. D. 1977. Changes in serum reverse T_3 concentrations with altered thyroid hormone secretion and metabolism. *J. Clin. Endocrinol. Metab.* 45: 447–456.

Keutman, H. E. and Mason, W. B. 1967. Individual urinary 17-ketosteroids of healthy persons determined by gas chromatography: biochemical and clinical considerations. *J. Clin. Endocrinol. Metab* 27: 406.

Keys, A., Taylor, H. L., and Grande, F. 1973. Basal metabolism and age of adult man. *Metabolism* 22: 579–587.

Kley, H. K., Nieschlag, E., and Kruskemper, H. L. 1975. Age dependence of plasma estrogen response to HCG and ACTH in men. *Acta Endocrinol. (Copenhagen)* 79: 95–101.

Klug, T. L. and Adelman, R. C. 1977. Evidence for a large thyrotropin and its accumulation during aging in rats. *Biochem. Biophys. Res. Commun.* 77: 1431–1437.

Klug, T. L. and Adelman, R. C. 1979. Altered hypothalamic-pituitary regulation of TSH in male rats during aging. *Endocrinology* 104: 1136–1142.

Korenman, S. 1982. Introduction. *In*, L. V. Avioli and S. G. Korenman (eds.), *Endocrine Aspects of Aging,* pp. 1–8. New York: Elsevier.

Lansing, W. and Wolfe, J. M. 1944. Structural changes associated with advancing age in thyroid glands of female rats with particular reference to alterations in connective tissue. *Anat. Rec.* 88: 311–322.

Laron, C., Doron, M., and Amikam, B. 1970. Plasma growth hormone in men and women over 70 years. *In, Medicine and Sport,* Vol. 4: *Physical Activity and Aging,* pp. 126–131. New York: Karger.

Latham, K. R. and Finch, C. E. 1976. Hepatic glucocorticoid binders in mature and senescent C57BL/6J male mice. *Endocrinology* 98: 1480–1489.

Lederer, J. and Bataille, J. P. 1969. Senescence et fonction thyroidienne. *Ann. Endocrinol. (Paris)* 30: 598–603.

Lipson, A., Nickoloff, E. L., Hsu, T. H., Kasecamp, W. R., Drew, H. M., Shakir, R., and Wagner, H. N. 1979. A study of age dependent changes in thyroid function tests in adults. *J. Nuc. Med.* 20: 1124–1130.

Lipson, L. G., Bobrycki, V. A., Bush, M. J., Tietjen, G. E., and Yoon, A. 1981. Insulin values in aging: studies on adenylate cyclase, phosphodiesterase, and protein kinase in isolated islets of Langerhans in rats. *Endocrinology* 108: 620–624.

Malamed, S. and Carsia, R. V. 1983. Aging of the rat adrenocortical cell: response to ACTH and cyclic AMP *in vitro. J. Gerontol.* 38: 130–136.

McConnell, J. G., Buchana, K. D., Ardill, J., and Stout, R. W. 1977. Glucose tolerance in the elderly: the role of insulin and its receptor. *European J. Clin. Invest.* 12: 55–61.

Migeon, C. J., Green, O. P., and Eckert, J. P. 1963. Study of adrenocortical function in obesity. *Metabolism* 12: 718–739.

Migeon, C., Keller, A., Lawrence, B., and Shepard, T. 1957. DHA and androsterone levels in human plasma. Effect of age and sex day to day and diurnal variation. *J. Clin. Endo. Metab.* 17: 1051–1061.

Minaker, K. L. and Rowe, J. W. 1982. Anesthesia and surgery. *In*, J. W. Rowe and R. W. Besdine (eds.), *Health and Disease in Old Age,* pp. 415–423. Boston: Little, Brown.

Minaker, K. L., Rowe, J. W., Pallotta, J., and Sparrow,

D. 1982. Clearance of insulin: influence of steady state insulin level and age. *Diabetes* 31: 132–135.

Moncloa, F., Gomez, R., and Pretell, I. 1963. Response to corticotrophin and correlation between excretion of creatinine and urinary steroids in ageing. *Steroids* 1: 437.

Muggeo, M., Fedele, D., Tiengo, A., Molinari, M., and Crepaldi, G. 1975. Human growth hormone and cortisol response to insulin stimulation in aging. *J. Gerontol.* 30: 546–551.

Murri, L., Barreca, T., Cerone, G., Massetani, R., Gallamini, A., and Baldassare, M. 1980. The 24 hour pattern of human prolactin and GH in healthy elderly subjects. *Chronobiologica* 7: 87–92.

Myhre, L. G. and Kessler, W. V. 1966. Body density and potassium-40 measurements of body composition as related to age. *J. Appl. Physiol.* 21: 1251–1256.

Nevé, P., Authelet, M., and Golstein, J. 1981. Effect of age on the morphology and function of the thyroid gland of the cream hamster. *Cell Tissue Res.* 220: 499–509.

Nicod, P., Burger, A., Staeheli, V., and Vallotton, M. B. 1976. A radioimmunoassay for reverse T_3 in unextracted serum: methods and clinical results. *J. Clin. Endocrinol. Metab.* 28: 776–782.

Oddie, T. H. and Fisher, D. 1966. An analysis of published data on thyroxine turnover in human subjects. *J. Clin. Endocrinol. Metab.* 26: 425–436.

Ohara, H. Kobayashi, T., Shiraishi, M., and Wada, T. 1974. Thyroid function of the aged as viewed from the pituitary thyroid system. *Endocrinol Jpn.* 21: 377–386.

Olefsky, J. M. and Reaven, G. M. 1975. Effects of age and obesity on insulin binding to isolated adipocytes. *Endocrinology* 96: 1486–1498.

Olsen, T., Laurberg, P., and Weeke, J. 1978. Low serum T_3 and high reverse T_3 in old age: an effect of disease not age. *J. Clin. Endocrinol. Metab.* 47: 1111–1115.

Ostman, J., Arner, P., Engfeldt, P., and Kager, L. 1979. Regional differences in the control of lipolysis in human adipose tissue. *Metabolism* 28: 12, 1198–1205.

Pagano, G. N., Casadar, N., Diana, A., Psue, E., Bozzo, C., Ferrero, F., and Lenti, G. 1981. Insulin resistance in the aged: the role of peripheral insulin receptors. *Metabolism* 30: 46–49.

Parker, L., Gral, T., Perrigo, V., and Skowsky, R. 1981. Decreased adrenal androgen sensitivity to ACTH during aging. *Metabolism* 30(6): 601–604.

Pfeiffer, M., Weinberg, C. R., Cook, D., Best, J. B., Reenan, A., and Halter, J. B. 1983. Differential changes of the autonomic nervous system function with age in man. *Am. J. Med.* 75: 249–258.

Piantanelli, L. and Fabris, W. 1978. Hypopituitary dwarf and athymic mice in the study of the relationship among thymus hormones and aging. *In,* D. Bergsma and D. Harrison (eds.), *Genetic Effects on Aging,* pp. 315–334. New York: Alan R. Liss.

Pincus, G., Romanoff, L. P., and Carlo, J. 1954. The excretion of urinary steroids by men and women of various ages. *J. Gerontol.* 9: 113–132.

Pittman, J. A. 1962. The thyroid and aging. *J. Am. Ger. Soc.* 10: 10–30.

Prinz, P. M., Halter, J., Benedetti, C., and Raskind, M. 1979. Circadian variation of plasma catecholamines in young and old men: relation to REM and slow wave sleep. *J. Clin. Endocrinol. Metab.* 40: 300–304.

Prinz, P. N., Weitzman, E. D., Cunningham, G. R., and Karacan, I. 1983. Plasma growth hormone during sleep in young and aged men. *J. Gerontol.* 38: 519–524.

Rabinowitz, P. 1970. Some endocrine and metabolic aspects of obesity. *Ann. Rev. Med.* 21: 241–258.

Reaven, E., Gold, G., and Reaven, G. 1979. Effect of age on glucose-stimulated insulin release by the β cell of the rat. *J. Clin. Invest.* 64: 591–599.

Reaven, E., Gold, G., and Reaven, G. 1980. Effect of age on leucine-induced insulin secretion by the β cell. *J. Gerontol.* 35: 324–328.

Reaven, G. M., Greenfield, M. S., Mondon, C. M., Rosenthal, M., Wright, D., and Reaven, E. 1982. Does insulin removal rate from plasma decline with age? *Diabetes* 31: 670–674.

Reaven, G. M. and Reaven, E. P. 1980. Effects of age on various aspects of glucose and insulin metabolism. *Mol. Cell Biochem.* 31: 37–47.

Reaven, E. P., Wright, E., Mondon, C. E., Solomon, R., Ho, H., and Reaven, G. M. 1983. Effect of age and diet on insulin secretion and insulin action in the rat. *Diabetes* 32: 175–180.

Riegle, G. D., Przekop, F., and Nellor, J. E. 1968. Changes in adrenocortical responsiveness in ACTH infusion in aging goats. *J. Gerontol.* 23: 187–190.

Riegle, G. D. and Nellor, J. E. 1967. Changes in adrenocortical function during aging in cattle. *J. Gerontol.* 22: 83–87.

Robert, J. J., Cummins, J. C., Wolfe, R., Durcot, M., Matthews, D. E., Zhoo, X. H., Bier, D. M., and Young, V. R. 1982. Quantitative aspects of glucose production and metabolism in healthy elderly subjects. *Diabetes* 31: 203–211.

Robinette, C. L. and Mawhinney, M. G. 1977. Cytosol binding of dihydrotestosterone in young and senile rats. *Fed. Proc.* 36: 344.

Romanoff, L. P. and Baxter, M. N. 1975. The secretion rates of deoxycorticosterone and corticosterone in young and elderly men. *J. Clin. Endocrinol. Metab.* 41: 630–633.

Romanoff, L. P., Baxter, M. N., Thomas, A. W., and Ferrechio, G. B. 1969. Effect of ACTH on the metabolism of pregnenolone-7 alpha-^{3}H and cortisol-4-^{14}C in young and elderly men. *J. Clin. Endocrinol. Metab.* 29: 819–830.

Romanoff, L. P., Grace, M. P., Baxter, M. N., and Pincus, G. 1966. Metabolism of pregnenolone-7 alpha-^{3}H and progesterone-4-^{14}C in young and elderly men. *J. Clin. Endocrinol. Metab.* 26: 1023–1031.

Romanoff, L. P., Morris, C. W., Welch, P., Grace, M. P., and Pincus, G. 1963. Metabolism of progesterone-4-C^{14} in young and elderly men. *J. Clin Endocrinol. Metab.* 23: 286–292.

Romanoff, L. P., Morris, C. W., Welch, P., Rodriguez,

R. M., and Pincus, G. 1961. The metabolism of cortisol-4-C^{14} in young and elderly men 1. Secretion rate of cortisol and daily excretion of tetrahydrocortisol, allo-tetrahydrocortisol, tetrahydrocortisone, and cortalone (20 alpha and 20 beta). *J. Clin. Endocrinol. Metab.* 21: 1413–1425.

Root, A. W. and Oski, F. A. 1969. Effects of human growth hormone in elderly males. *J. Gerontol.* 24: 97–104.

Rosenbloom, A. and Goldstein, S. 1976. Insulin binding to cultured human fibroblasts increases with normal and precocious aging. *Science* 93: 412–415.

Rosner, B. A. and Cristofalo, V. J. 1978. Specific binding of ^{3}H-dexamethasone in WI-38 cell monolayers: changes with increased *in vitro* age. *Fed. Proc.* 37: 888.

Rossman, I. 1977. Anatomic and body composition changes with aging. *In,* C. Finch and L. Hayflick (eds.), *Handbook of the Biology of Aging,* pp. 189–221. New York: Van Nostrand Reinhold.

Roth, G. S. 1974. Age-related changes in specific glucocorticoid binding by steroid responsive tissues of rats. *Endocrinology* 94: 84–90.

Roth, G. S. 1975. Reduced corticosteroid responsiveness and receptor concentration in splenic leukocytes of senescent rats. *Biochim. Biophys. Acta.* 399: 145–156.

Roth, G. S. 1976. Reduced glucocorticoid binding site concentration in cortical neuronal perikarya from senescent rats. *Brain Res.* 107: 345–354.

Roth, G. S. and Livingston, J. N. 1976. Reductions in glucocorticoid inhibition of glucose oxidation and presumptive glucocorticoid content in rat adipocytes during aging. *Endocrinology* 99: 831–839.

Rowe, J. W. 1977. Clinical research on aging: strategies and directions. *N. Eng. J. Med.* 297: 1332–1336.

Rowe, J. W., Minaker, K. L., Pallotta, J., and Flier, J. S. 1983. Characterization of the insulin resistance of aging. *J. Clin. Invest.* 71: 1581–1587.

Rowe, J. W. and Troen, B. R. 1980. Sympathetic nervous system activity and aging in man. *Endocrine Reviews* 1: 167–179.

Roy, A. K., Milin, B. S., and McMinn, D. M. 1974. Androgen receptors in rat liver: hormonal and developmental regulation of the cytoplasmic receptor and its correlation with androgen dependent synthesis of alpha 2 euglobulin. *Biochim. Biophys. Acta.* 354: 213–232.

Rubenstein, H. A., Butler, V. P., and Werner, S. C. 1973. Progressive decrease in serum T_3 concentrations with human aging: radioimmunoassay following extraction of serum. *J. Clin. Endocrinol. Metab.* 37: 247–253.

Rudman, D. D. and Girolamo, M. 1971. Effect of adrenal cortical steroids on lipid metabolism. *In,* N. P. Christy (ed.), *The Human Adrenal Cortex,* pp. 241–256. New York: Harper and Row.

Rudman, D., Kutner, M. H., Rogers, C. M., Lubin, M. F., Fleming, G. A., and Bain, R. P. 1981. Impaired growth hormone secretion in the adult population: relation to age and adiposity. *J. Clin. Invest.* 67: 1361–1369.

Rudorff, K. H., Herrmann, J., Kroll, H. J., Rusche,

H. J., and Kruskemper, H. L. 1976. T_4/T_3 turnover kinetics, TRH and TSH tests, total and free T_4 and T_3 and TBG and reverse T_3 in healthy and sick old subjects. *Acta. Endocrinol.* 82: Suppl. 204: 337–338.

Samuels, L. T. 1957. Factors affecting the metabolism and distribution of cortisol as measured by levels of 17-hydroxycorticosteroids in blood. *Cancer* 10: 746–751.

Sara, V. R., Hall, K., Enzell, K., Gardner, A., Morawski, R., and Wetterberg, L. 1982. Somatomedins in aging and dementia disorders of the Alzheimer type. *Neurbiol Aging* 3: 117–120.

Sartin, J. L., Pritchett, J. F., and Marple, D. N. 1977. TSH, theophylline and cyclic AMP. *In vitro* thyroid activity in aging rats. *Mol. Cell Endocrinol.* 9: 215–222.

Savostin-Asling, I., Nakaiye, R., and Asling, C. W. 1980. Roentgen cephalometric studies on skull development in rats. III. Gigantism versus acromegaly: age differences in response to prolonged growth hormone administration. *Anat. Rec.* 196: 9–21.

Sawin, C. T., Chopra, D., Azizi, F., Mannix, J. E., and Bachrach, P. 1979. The aging thyroid: increased prevalence of elevated TSH levels in the elderly. *J.A.M.A.* 242: 247–250.

Schramm, V. A., Pusch, H. J., Franke, H., and Haubitz, I. 1981. Hormonal adaptability in the elderly. *Fortschr. Med.* 27: 1255–1260.

Segal, J., Troen, B. R., and Ingbar, S. H. 1982. Influence of age and sex on the concentrations of thyroid hormone in serum in the rat. *J. Endocrinol.* 93: 177–181.

Seltzer, H. S. 1970. Diagnosis of diabetes. *In,* M. Ellenburg and H. Rifkin (eds.), *Diabetes Mellitus, Theory and Practice,* pp. 436–507. New York: McGraw-Hill.

Serio, M., Piolanti, P., Cappelli, G., DeMagistris, L., Ricchi, F., Anzalone, M., and Gusti, G. 1969. The miscible pool and turnover rate of cortisol with aging and variations in relation to time of day. *Exp. Gerontol* 4: 95–101.

Severson, J. A. 1981. The adrenal gland. *In,* E. J. Masoro (ed.), *Handbook of the Physiology of Aging,* pp. 295–316. Boca Raton: CRC Press.

Silverberg, A., Ruzzo, F., and Krieger, D. T. 1968. Nyctohemeral periodicity of plasma 17-OHCS levels in elderly subjects. *J. Clin. Endocrinol. Metab.* 28: 1661–1663.

Simonson, D. C. and DeFronzo, R. A. 1983. Glucagon physiology and aging: evidence for enhanced hepatic sensitivity. *Diabetologia* 25(1): 1–7.

Singer, S., Ito, H., and Litwack, G. 1973. ^{3}H-cortisol binding by young and old liver cytosol proteins *in vitro. Int. J. Biochem.* 4: 569–573.

Singer, S. S. and Burns, L. 1978. Enzymatic sulfation and glucocorticoid sulfotransferase in old and young male rats. *Exp. Gerontol.* 13: 425–429.

Snyder, P. J. and Utiger, R. D. 1972. Response to thyrotropin releasing hormone in normal man. *J. Clin. Endo. Metab.* 34: 380–384.

Snyder, P. J. and Utiger, R. D. 1972. Thyrotropin response to TRH in normal females over 40. *J. Clin. Endocrinol. Metab.* 34: 1096–1098.

Soloman, J. and Greep, R. O. 1958. Relationship between pituitary growth hormone content and age in rats. *Proc. Soc. Exp. Biol. Med.* 99: 725–727.

Sonntag, W. E., Forman, L. J., Miki, N., Steger, R. W., Ramos, T., Arimura, A., and Meites, J. 1981. Effect of CNS active drugs and somatostatin antiserum on growth hormone release in young and old male rats. *Neuroendocrinology* 33: 73–78.

Sonntag, W. E., Forman, L. J., Miki, N., Trapp, J. M., Gottschall, P. E., and Meites, J. 1982. L-Dopa restores amplitude of growth hormone pulses in old male rats to that observed in young male rats. *Neuroendocrinology* 34: 163–168.

Sonntag, W. E., Hylka, W., and Meites, J. 1983. Impaired ability of old male rats to secrete GH *in vivo* but not *in vitro* in response to hpGRF 1–44. *Endocrinology* 113(6): 2305–7.

Sonntag, W. E., Hylka, W., and Meites, J. 1983. Growth hormone increases the synthesis of protein in diaphragmatic muscle of old male rats (in press).

Sonntag, W. E., Steger, R. W., Forman, L. J., and Meites, J. 1980. Decreased pulsatile release of growth hormone in old rats. *Endocrinology* 107: 1875–1879.

Sorrentino, R. and Florini, J. R. 1976. Variations among individual mice in binding of growth hormone and insulin to membranes from animals of different ages. *Exp. Aging Res.* 2: 191–205.

Sparrow, D., Bosse, R., and Rowe, J. W. 1980. The influence of age, alcohol consumption and body build on gonadal function in men. *J. Clin. Endocrinol. Metab.* 51: 508–512.

Spence, J. C. 1921. Some observations on sugar tolerance with special reference to variations found at different ages. *Q. J. Med.* 4: 314–326.

Studer, H., Forster, A., Conti, H., Kohler, A., Haeberli, A., and Engler, H. 1978. Transformation of normal follicles into TSH refractory, cold follicles in the aging mouse thyroid. *Endocrinology* 102: 1576–1586.

Studer, H., Riek, M. M., and Greer, M. A. 1979. Multinodular goiter. *In,* L. J. De Groot, G. F. Cahill, W. D. Odell, et al. (eds.), *Endocrinology,* Vol. 1, pp. 489–499. New York: Grune and Stratton.

Taylor, A. L., Finster, J. L., and Mintz, D. H. 1969. Metabolic clearance and production rates of growth hormone. *J. Clin. Invest.* 48: 2349–2358.

Tunbridge, W. M. G., Evered, D. C., Hall, R., Appleton, D., Brewis, M., Clark, F., Evans, J. G., Young, E., Bird, T., and Smith, P. A. 1977. The spectrum of thyroid disease in a community: the Whickham survey. *Clin. Endocrinol.* 7: 481–493.

Tyler, F. H., Eik-Nes, K., Sanberg, A. A., Florentin, A. A., and Samuels, L. T. 1955. Adrenocortical capac-ity and the metabolism of cortisol in elderly patients. *J. Am. Ger. Soc.* 3: 79–84.

Tzankoff, S. P. and Norris, A. H. 1977. Effect of muscle mass decrease on age related BMR changes. *J. Appl. Physiol.* 43: 1001–1006.

Valueva, G. V. and Verzhikovskaya, N. N. 1977. Thyrotropic activity of the hypophysis during aging. *Exp. Gerontol.* 12: 97–105.

Vermeulen, J. P., Deslypere, J. P., Shelfhout, W., Verdonck, L., and Rubens, R. 1982. Adrenocortical function in old age: response to acute adrenocorticotropin stimulation. *J. Clin. Endocrinol. Metab.* 54: 187–191.

Vidalon, C., Khurana, R. C., Chae, S., Gegick, C. G., Stephan, T., Nolan, S., and Danowski, T. S. 1973. Age-related changes in growth hormone in non-diabetic women. *J. Am. Ger. Soc.* 21: 253–255.

Wenzel, K. W. 1976. T_3 and T_4 kinetics in aged man. *In,* J. Robbins and L. E. Braverman (eds.), *Thyroid Research, Excerpta Medica,* pp. 270–273. Amsterdam: Excerpta Medica; New York: American Elsevier.

Wenzel, K. W., Meinhold, H., Herpich, M., Adlkofer, F., and Schleusener, H. 1974. TRH stimulation test with age and sex specific TSH response in normal subjects. *Klin. Wochenschr.* 52: 722–727.

West, C. D., Brown, H., Simons, E. L., Carter, D. B., Kumagai, L. F., and Engelbert, E. L. 1961. Adrenocortical function and cortisol metabolism in old age. *J. Clin. Endocrinol. Metab.* 21: 1197–1207.

Westgren, U., Burger, A., Ingemansson, A., Melander, A., Tibblin, S., and Wahlin, E. 1976. Blood levels of $3,5,3'$-T_3 and thyroxine. Differences between children, adults, and elderly subjects. *Acta. Med. Scand.* 200: 493–495.

Wolfsen, A. 1982. Aging and the adrenals. *In,* L. Avioli, and S. Korenman (eds.), *Endocrinology of Aging,* pp. 55–79. New York: Elsevier.

Wolfsen, A. R. 1982. Aging and the adrenals. *In,* L. V. Avioli and S. G. Korenman (eds.), *Endocrine Aspects of Aging,* pp. 55–79. New York: Elsevier.

Yamaji, T. and Ibayashi, H. 1969. Plasma dehydroepiandrosterone sulphate in normal and pathological conditions. *J. Clin. Endocrinol. Metab.* 29: 273–278.

Young, J. B. and Landsberg, L. 1977. Catecholamines and the regulation of hormone secretion. *Clinics Endo. and Metab.* 6(3): 657–695.

Young, V. R., Steffee, W. P., Pancharz, D. B., Winterer, J. G., and Scrimshaw, N. S. 1975. Total human body protein synthesis in relation to protein requirements of various ages. *Nature (Lond.)* 253: 192–193.

Zitnik, G. and Rother, G. S. 1981. Effects of thyroid hormones on cardiac hypertrophy and β-adrenergic receptors during aging. *Mech. Age. Dev.* 15: 19–28.

18
REPRODUCTIVE AGING

S. Mitchell Harman
Gerontology Research Center
National Institute on Aging
National Institutes of Health
and
George B. Talbert
Department of Anatomy and Cell Biology
Downstate Medical Center
State University of New York

INTRODUCTION

The reproductive system does not become fully functional until about 12 to 14 years of age in the human and after varying lengths of time in other mammalian species. The dramatic transformation which occurs at this time in both sexes in the human has had considerable religious, sociological, and biomedical significance. This chapter will, however, be concerned almost exclusively with changes in this system which occur from the period when reproductive capacity begins to decline to the time when such capacity is lost. In most species which have been studied, including the human, there is a considerable sex difference in the length of reproductive life, with the female losing the ability to reproduce well before her average life span is reached while the male may carry out his part in reproduction in extreme old age.

In addition to the earlier reviews of the aging of the reproductive system which are referenced in the first edition of this *Handbook* (Talbert, 1977), the reader is also referred to Aschheim (1976) and Schneider (1978). Other reviews of specific aspects of reproductive aging will be referred to in the text.

FEMALE REPRODUCTIVE SYSTEM

Reproductive Life Span

It has not been easy to gather satisfactory data on the relation of age to fertility. The normal limit of reproductive life in the human is well documented, but the rate of decline of this function is difficult to ascertain because of socioeconomic considerations which have prompted the widespread use of contraceptive devices. Only recently has significant information become available on a few larger primates because of their very long life span and the expense of maintenance.

Primates. The average age for the advent of the menopause in the human female is 50 to 51 years (Treloar, 1981). However, because of the widespread use of contraceptive devices and the reduced frequency of intercourse in older premenopausal women (German, 1968), it is difficult to evaluate the decline in reproductive capacity in women over 40 years of age (see Talbert, 1977, for other references).

The earliest work on subhuman primates was carried out by Van Wagenen (1972) on the rhesus monkey (*Macaca mulatta*). She observed that these animals reach the menopause at 25 to 30 years of age although the average life span of this species is about 33 years (Bowden and Jones, 1979). Comparable results have been reported by Hodgen et al. (1977). Bowden and Jones (1979) have also found that baboons, with an average life span of 31 years, reach the menopause in the midtwenties.

Recently, Graham (1979) has provided the first useful data on reproductive life span of ten female chimpanzees. The mean length of menstrual cycles increased from 32.2 days in 15- to 25-year-old females to 35.6 days in animals over 35 years of age. Furthermore, in the older group only two pregnancies resulted out of 52 cycles in which the female was exposed to the male (4 percent), whereas about 20 percent of the 15- to 25-year-old animals with the same opportunity carried young into the third trimester. In spite of the evidence that chimpanzees do show ovarian cyclic function at extreme old age, Gould et al. (1981) found that urinary gonadotropin and ovarian steroid hormone patterns in one 47- and one 49-year-old champanzee were characteristic of the condition frequently observed in perimenopausal women.

In summary, there appears to be little question that reproduction is possible for a much larger proportion of the total life span in all subhuman primates which have been studied, than it is in the human.

Laboratory Rodents. Numerous studies have been carried out over a period of many years on the reproductive life span of laboratory rodents. The early work has been reviewed by Talbert (1977).

In a recent investigation, Miller et al. (1979) showed that littering ceased in the Long-Evans strain of rats at about 17 months of age, but the percentage of females which littered decreased progressively beginning at 10 months of age. In an earlier study, Huang and Meites (1975) found that estrous cycles in the rat became irregular as early as 8 months of age, and this condition became more prevalent as reproductive capacity declined for the next few months. However, a recent study has shown that regular estrous cycles in aging multiparous rats can be maintained for an extended period of time (at least up to 17 months of age) by caging with fertile males (Nass et al. 1982). This observation suggests that the cessation of regular cyclicity beginning at middle age (10–12 months) may be due in part to separation from the males.

In spite of the fact that littering ceased at about 17 months, Miller et al. (1979) found that 60 percent of the females still exhibited behavioral estrus, indicating that this aspect of reproduction is retained for a longer period of time. A similar conclusion was reached by Peng et al. (1977) who ovariectomized 20- to 32-month-old rats which were in a stage of constant estrus (CE), repetitive pseudopregnancies (RPP), or anestrus. Following administration of estrogen or estrogen plus progesterone, lordosis could still be induced in many of these old rats.

Domestic Animals. Data on reproductive decline in domestic animals are extremely sparse and, therefore, generally unreliable. The data that are available are not recent and have been summarized in the first edition of this *Handbook* (Talbert, 1977).

Ovary

The aging process of the mammalian ovary is complicated by the fact that this organ not only is the source of female gametes but also secretes female sex hormones. These two functions, although closely related to each other, do not change with age in a completely parallel manner. Earlier reviews of this process have been written by Jones (1970), Noyes (1970), and Talbert (1977, 1978).

Oocytes. No new data appear to be available on the decline in the number of oocytes in the mammalian ovary with increasing age since the papers of Block (1952, 1953) on the human, Mandl and Shelton (1959) on the rat, Jones and Krohn (1961a) on the mouse, and Erickson (1966) on the cow. Although all of these studies show that there is a rapid decline in the number of oocytes associated with advancing age, the relationship of this decline to total life span and to reproductive life span is quite variable among different species and even among different strains of the same species.

In the human, the ovary becomes virtually devoid of oocytes by the beginning of the menopause at an average age of about 50. However, Costoff and Mahesh (1975) did observe a few normal-appearing oocytes in the ovaries of postmenopausal women.

In most rodents, the picture is quite different. Although reproductive capacity ceases in most strains of these species well before the average life span has been reached, there are, with the exception of the CBA mouse, large numbers of normal-appearing oocytes still present in the ovaries into extreme old age.

Only a very small fraction of the total number of oocytes which are present in the ovary at birth are ovulated during reproductive life in all mammalian species which have been studied, so that the vast majority of oocytes appear to be lost by the process of atresia. In the human, about half of this loss appears to occur prior to puberty (Block, 1952).

Zuckerman (1956) argued convincingly that no new oogonia are produced by the germinal epithelium of the adult. Although this process has not been widely studied, it seems likely that this theory has broad application. If this concept is correct, the only way that the rate of oocyte loss can be significantly reduced is by slowing the rate of atresia.

Jones and Krohn (1961b) were the first to show that hypophysectomy would greatly reduce the rate of atresia in mice. Another method of slowing the rate of atresia was demonstrated by Huseby and Ball (1945). They placed C3H mice on a low caloric diet from weaning until 18 months of age and showed that the ovaries of these animals contained many oocytes in small follicles, whereas similar mice fed *ad libitum* had only a few oocytes. The mechanism by which either hypophy-

sectomy or low food intake results in the preservation of oocytes has not been clearly established, but it has been suggested that gonadotropins may promote atresia and that both methods create a deficiency of those hormones. Such a concept is supported by the report of Harman et al. (1975) who observed an atretogenic effect of gonadotropins in rats. However, Jones and Krohn (1961b) did point out that the decline in oocytes progresses most rapidly shortly after birth when gonadotropin stimulation is minimal. A recent short review by Ryan (1981) summarizes some of the current concepts on the process of atresia.

In addition to the marked decline in the number of oocytes associated with increasing age, there is also clear evidence that in the human, as well as in some experimental animals, there is a decline in the viability and normality of such oocytes. Several studies have been carried out to compare the viability of fertilized ova which were transplanted from the uterus of young and old donors into the uterus of pseudopregnant young adult recipients. The results which were obtained indicated considerable species difference since there was little, if any, loss of viability of ova from old mice (Talbert and Krohn, 1966; Gosden, 1975a), some loss in rabbits (Adams, 1970; Maurer and Foote, 1971), and great loss in hamsters (Blaha, 1964b). Parkening and Soderwall (1975) have suggested, however, that the timing of transfer of the ova might not have been optimal in the aged animals in the hamster study since ova obtained from old hamsters are fertilized later than those from young hamsters.

Although it is commonly accepted that women approaching the menopause are less fertile than younger women, it is not clear how much of this decline in fertility is due to loss of viability of ova or to functional deficiencies in the ovary, uterine tube, or uterus. There is conclusive evidence, however, that certain types of aneuploidy increase in the offspring of older mothers (Kram and Schneider, 1978; Tsuji and Nakano, 1978). Several studies with experimental animals have been undertaken to determine why eggs ovulated by older women are more likely to have chromosomal abnormalities than are eggs ovulated by young adults. Many etiologic agents have been proposed such as radiation, chemicals, and infectious agents, any of which might have a greater opportunity to act on eggs which have been in the ovary for up to 50 years, but none of these agents has been clearly identified as a major factor (Kram and Schneider, 1978).

The important clinical problem of Down's syndrome, which is most often associated with trisomy of chromosome 21, has directed attention toward causes for the increase in nondisjunction in eggs ovulated by older women. Henderson and Edwards (1968), in a critical study, observed that there were significantly fewer chiasmata per metaphase in 12-month-old CBA mice than in 2-month-old mice of the same strain. There was also a ten-fold increase in univalents which are due to homologous chromosomes failing to pair and to form chiasmata. These observations have been basically confirmed by Luthardt et al. (1973) and by Polani and Jagiello (1976). As an explanation for their observations, Henderson and Edwards (1968) have proposed a "production line" theory which is based on the concept that oocytes formed early in development have more chiasmata than those formed late and those that form early ovulate first. Consequently, ova ovulated by older females will typically have fewer chiasmata.

Recent studies of mice have uniformly confirmed that there is a decrease in chiasma frequency in older animals, but not all investigators have observed an increase in univalents (Speed, 1977). Jagiello and Fang (1979) observed that there were more univalents in late diplotene in old mice so that some were formed during fetal life and not during the prolonged dictyate stage. A new theory has been proposed by Crowley et al. (1979) which links the loss of chiasmata with a longer interval between the midcycle luteinizing hormone (LH) surge and ovulation. This increased interval may be due to a reduction in estradiol-induced LH receptors in follicles. The authors further suggest that as hormone levels and menstrual cycles become more erratic in women approaching the menopause, meiosis slows down and chiasma frequency declines.

Another explanation for the increase in chromosomal abnormalities with age has been proposed by Peluso et al. (1980a). In an ultrastructural study, they compared the oocytes in preovulatory follicles of 4- to 5-month-old with 10- to 11-month-old rats and observed two age changes which might cause an increase in chromosomal errors. The first change, which was observed in eggs removed from the ovary and placed in culture, was that less than one-third as many ova from old rats formed a polar body than ova from young rats. Fertilization of an oocyte which had not formed a polar body would result in triploidy. A second change, which was more frequently seen in ova from old rats, was retention of an intact nucleolus after breakdown of the germinal vesicle, and since the nucleolus is shared by bivalent pairs it might produce nondisjunction in the chromosome with which it is associated.

Other ultrastructural changes which were observed in the oocytes in older rats were increased undulation of the nuclear membrane, increased density of the nucleoplasm, deterioration of cytoplasmic rays, and a reduction in the number of cortical granules. It was proposed that the reduction in cortical granules might have been due to their premature release which could result in making the zona pellucida impenetrable to spermatozoa. Consequently, this would reduce the rate of fertilization (Peluso et al. 1980a).

In spite of the studies of possible mechanisms of nondisjunction in mice, it has proved to be a difficult task to determine if there is an increase in aneuploidy in conceptuses in older female mice. Goodlin (1965) observed no increase in trisomy at birth in 756 offspring of aged mice. However, Martin et al. (1976) did find an increase in hyperploidy in oocytes at metaphase of meiosis II which were recovered from aged CBA strain mice. Furthermore, Gosden (1973) found 6.9 percent aneuploid preimplantation embryos recovered from aged mice, compared to 2.1 percent from young females. In a much more extensive study, Maudlin and Fraser (1978) found 5.6 percent aneuploid first-cleavage mouse embryos from aged mice compared to 2.5 percent in young mice. The incidence of monosomy increased slightly but not significantly with age, but the increase in trisomy and total aneuploids was significant. Mizoguchi and Dukelow (1981) observed a decrease in fertilization rate of ova from old hamsters (84 percent compared to 91 percent) which may be associated with defective ova.

These studies support the validity of using the mouse as a model for investigating the relationship between maternal age and aneuploidy, and also demonstrate quite clearly that aneuploid embryos, particularly those that are monosomic, are much less viable than those with a normal chromosomal complement.

Follicles. Talbert (1968) and Jones (1970) have reviewed early studies of age changes in follicular development in rodents and in women. In all species which have been studied, there is a major reduction in the number of primary and preantral follicles throughout reproductive life. However, Block (1952) observed that the ratio of primary to growing follicles changed from 50 to 1 at puberty to 3 to 1 in 39- to 45-year-old women. Furthermore, there was no change in the number of graafian (preovulatory) follicles until after 39 years of age. Preservation of preovulatory follicles has also been observed in aging rodents (Faddy et al., 1976; Peluso et al., 1979, 1980b; Norris and Adams, 1982b).

The long delay in the reduction in the number of preovulatory follicles in aging mice appears to be the result of the rescuing of medium-sized follicles from atresia so that a higher percentage grow into normal-appearing preovulatory follicles. However, the exhaustion of oocytes and the reduction in the recruitment of growing follicles from the nongrowing pool ultimately lead to ovulatory failure (Gosden et al., 1983).

A recent study in aged rats (Peluso et al., 1982) has provided evidence that rescuing of atretic middle-sized follicles results in an increased number of preovulatory follicles

which have normal-appearing granulosa cells but contain nonviable oocytes which ovulate but would not be capable of normal development. Since Talbert and Krohn (1966) observed a higher percentage of abnormal-appearing oocytes in the uterine horns of aged mice than in young mice, a similar condition may exist in this species.

Although the number of preovulatory follicles tends not to decrease significantly in aging rodents, there is an increase in abnormal follicular development at this time which interferes with ovulation. Thung (1961), and Burack and Wolfe (1959), observed in mice and rats, respectively, that there is an increase in preovulatory luteinization which entraps the ova.

Another form of abnormal development of large follicles is the development of follicular cysts (see Talbert, 1977, for early references). Peluso and England-Charlesworth (1981) recently reported that over 86 percent of preovulatory follicles of both 4- to 5-month-old and 10- to 11-month-old rats appeared normal on the first day of proestrus, but 50 percent of these follicles in the older group showed morphological changes in the theca interna and secondarily in the granulosa cells which lead to follicular cyst formation by the third day of a prolonged proestrous period. A detailed description of the changes that precede cyst formation is beyond the scope of this review, but these changes include dilation of capillaries in the theca interna and the granulosa, accumulation of lipid droplets and autophagic vacuoles in the granulosa cells, and flattening of the antral layer of these cells.

The cause of cyst formation in some follicles, but not in others, is not understood, but it is known that the peak of the ovulatory LH surge is lower in middle-aged rats (Gray et al., 1980b; Cooper et al., 1980; Wise, 1982) so that it is possible that some follicles might not be able to ovulate in response to this hormone.

Corpora Lutea. There is considerable evidence that there is no significant decline in the number of corpora lutea formed during

each cycle in small rodents until after reproductive capacity has already declined due to
age changes in the uterus (Jones, 1970; Harman and Talbert, 1970). At the same time,
it is not certain whether corpora lutea of pregnancy or pseudopregnancy in aging laboratory
animals are as functional as those found in
young adults.

The initial approach to this problem was
carried out by Finn (1963) who increased the
ratio of corpora lutea to embryos by tying
off one uterine tube in aging mice. Since this
experiment failed to extend reproductive life
span, it was suggested that deficiency of luteal
tissue was not a major factor in embryonic
loss. However, Thorneycroft and Soderwall
(1969) and Gosden (1974) reported that corpora lutea of pregnancy in aging hamsters or
mice were smaller than those found in young
adults, and Harman and Talbert (1970) observed possible degenerative changes in corpora lutea of aging mice which might indicate
reduced hormone secretion. This concept was
given some support by the earlier work of
Blaha (1968) who found that ovariectomized
aged hamsters which had received ovarian
transplants from young adult donors had a
higher rate of implantation of transplanted
morulae than did aged hamsters with intact
ovaries. Further support was provided by Gosden (1975b) who improved the pregnancy rate
in aging mice by progesterone supplementation on the second to the ninth days of gestation. However, neither Parkening et al. (1978)
nor Gosden and Fowler (1979) found a significant difference in plasma progesterone between young and aging mice in the first half
of pregnancy, but Holinka et al. (1979a) reported that there is a tendency for progesterone levels to be slightly lower in old than in
young mice up to about the sixth day of pregnancy (Table 1).

Miller and Riegle (1980a) compared progesterone levels in 4 and 13- to 16-month-
old pregnant and pseudopregnant rats, and
observed no age difference in progesterone secretion by corpora lutea during early pregnancy or pseudopregnancy. However, Fayein
and Aschheim (1980) did find a significant,
but only slightly lower, level of progesterone

**TABLE 1. Serum Progesterone Levels in
Young and Old Mice During Early Pregnancy. (All values ng/ml serum.)**

Day of Pregnancy	AGE	
	Young	Old
4	26.3 ± 1.8[a]	19.4 ± 2.9[a]
	28.0 ± 2.1[b]	30.6 ± 6.5[b]
	28 ± 2[c,d]	17 ± 2[c,d]
8–9	34.1 ± 3.2[a]	26.1 ± 4.5[a]
	29.6 ± 3.1[b]	25.3 ± 3.8[b]
	28 ± 2[c,d]	34 ± 2[c,d]

[a]Parkening et al. (1978).
[b]Gosden and Fowler (1979).
[c]Holinka et al. (1979a).
[d]Data estimated from Figure 5 in Holinka et al.

in the plasma of 24-month-old rats. In summary, it does not seem likely that a major
deficiency of progesterone secretion exists in
aging rats and mice during early pregnancy.

In the human, corpora lutea cease to be
formed when ovulatory function ceases after
the menopause. However, Novak (1970) studied the ovaries of 200 women who were past
50 years of age and found 46 corpora lutea
which were judged to be less than 6 months
old. Although 21 of these corpora lutea were
associated with a secretory endometrium, the
author thought it was likely that the progestins
were coming from luteinized stromal tissue
and not from these corpora lutea.

**Epithelial, Stromal, and Interstitial Tis-
sue.** Proliferative changes have been observed
in the ovarian epithelium of postmenopausal
women. These changes consist of papilloma-
tous outgrowths or duct-like ingrowths, but
they have no known physiological or pathological significance.

The medullary portion of the aging human
ovary consists largely of corpora albicantia,
and sclerotic changes are common in the walls
of blood vessels. Hyalinization of collagen tissue was also frequently observed (Thung,
1961).

Peluso et al. (1976) demonstrated gonadotropin binding sites and 3β-hydroxysteroid
dehydrogenase activity in hyperplastic stromal and hilus cells in human postmenopausal
ovaries and suggested that these cells might

produce androgens. In a more recent study, Benkoël et al. (1980) produced ultrastructural changes *in vitro* in stromal cells from menopausal human ovaries by gonadotropin treatment. Although no steroid production was noted, the authors believe that the failure of this potential function might have been due to an incomplete physiological environment in the culture.

Proliferative activity from the epithelium has been observed in aging rodent ovaries, and a positive relationship was noted between early depletion of oocytes and follicles and the extent of this proliferation (Thung, 1961).

Crumeyrolle-Arias et al. (1976), in a light and electron microscope study of the aging rat ovary, found deficiency cells (wheel cells) in the interstitial tissue and also cord-like epithelioid structures. Administration of gonadotropin repaired the wheel cells and at the same time produced luteinization of the cords, indicating that these aging changes may be the result of gonadotropin deficiency.

Ovarian Steroidogenesis. Δ^5-3β-hydroxy-steroid dehydrogenase activity has been widely used as an indicator of steroidogenic capability of ovarian tissue. Using this tool in histochemical studies, Albrecht et al. (1975), Leathem and Murono (1975), and Steger et al. (1976) have all found that the aging rodent ovary retains considerable steroidogenic capability. These observations have been confirmed biochemically by Leathem and Shapiro (1975) and by Albrecht et al. (1977). Steger et al. (1976) and Erickson et al. (1979) have also found no evidence of reduced LH binding in the ovaries of aging rats.

Plasma Steroids. Methods for direct measurement of estrogens and progestins in the blood of laboratory rodents have now developed to the point where alterations during the estrous cycle and with increasing age can be measured with some degree of confidence. As a result, a quite complete picture of age changes in plasma steroids in the rat has emerged in recent years.

The rat has been known for many years to pass through several aging deviations of the estrous cycle (Table 2) Aschheim, 1976; Huang and Meites, 1975; Lu et al., 1979). Huang et al. (1978) demonstrated, in a radioimmunoassay study of serum levels of sex steroids in young adult and aged rats, that the principal feature in the young cycling animals was a surge of both estradiol and progesterone during proestrus followed by a rapid fall to a low point during estrus (Figure 1). Some rats continue to show estrous cycles, although typically irregular, up to at least 2 years of age. Groups of aged cycling rats were compared with young cycling animals by Miller and Riegle (1980b). These investigators observed that the older animals had lower levels of serum progesterone during the proestrous surge, estrus, and diestrus than did young adults. Van der Schoot (1976), in another study of older cycling rats, found that the LH surge was slightly delayed and its steepness reduced. Although this change did not initially result in an increase in the length of the estrous cycle, the author suggested that this might ultimately lead to loss of ovulation.

The most common condition after cycling ceases in aging rats is constant estrus (CE) (Table 2). This condition is characterized morphologically by ovaries containing many follicles of various sizes, no corpora lutea, and interstitial tissue containing some "wheel cells" which are believed to indicate LH deficiency (Aschheim, 1964–65). The most obvious feature of the serum hormone pattern in such animals is the absence of any indication of a proestrous surge of either estradiol or progesterone. Instead the estradiol level was quite constant and comparable to the moderate basal level found during diestrus in young

TABLE 2. Changes with Age in Percentage of Rats Showing Estrous Cycles, Constant Estrus (CE), and Repetitive Pseudopregnancies (RPP).[a]

Condition	Age (mo.)				
	6	12	15	20	27
Cycling	89	60	40	8	8
CE	7	20	40	64	20
RPP	4	20	20	28	72

[a]Data of Aschheim (1976).

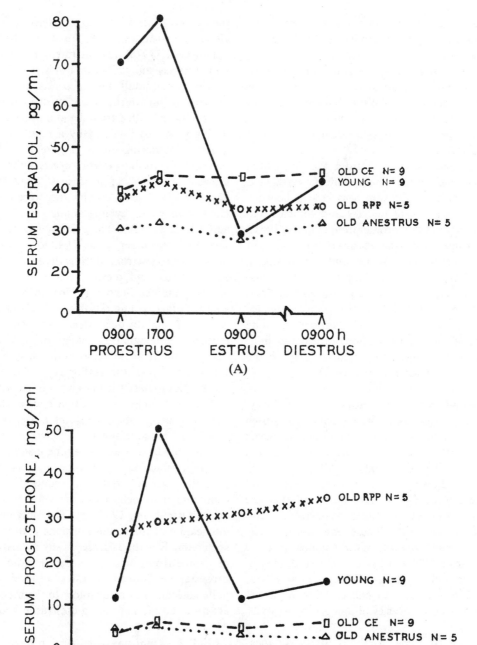

Figure 1. Serum estradiol and progesterone levels for four days in young cycling rats and in aging constant estrous, repetitive pseudopregnant, and anestrous rats. (Data of Huang et al., 1978.)

adult rats. Progesterone was found to be lower than the basal level noted in cycling animals by Huang et al. (1978) and by Miller and Riegle (1980b), but Lu et al. (1979) found little differences in the level of this hormone in young cycling and aging CE rats.

After passing through a period of CE, many rats enter a stage of repetitive pseudopregnancy (RPP). Some rats may enter this stage directly after cycling with no intervening CE. In either case, the ovaries of such animals have numerous functional-appearing corpora lutea and some follicular development. The interstitial tissue still shows evidence of LH deficiency (Aschheim, 1964–65). Lu et al. (1979) observed that RPP rats had considerably lower estradiol levels than CE rats. On the other hand, serum progesterone levels were considerably higher in RPP rats, similar to the high values seen in young females during pseudopregnancy.

A final stage of anestrus may be found in aged rats. The rats in this stage have atrophic ovaries containing only primary follicles (Huang and Meites, 1975). Rats in this condition were found by Huang et al. (1978) and by Lu et al. (1979) to have slightly lower levels of circulating estradiol than do CE or RPP rats and minimal progesterone which was comparable to the level found in CE rats. Miller and Riegle (1980b), however, observed serum progesterone levels which were only slightly lower than those found in RPP rats and considerably higher than in CE rats. Since neither of these reports mentioned any observations on ovarian morphology, it is possible that the anestrous animals were not completely comparable. Otherwise, there is no obvious explanation for the difference in the results.

It is clear that these age changes in circulating steroids may well have considerable influence on secretion of gonadotropins by the pituitary gland through positive and negative feedback. This will be discussed subsequently in the section of this chapter on the hypothalamic-pituitary axis.

Considerably less attention has been paid to age changes in the estrous cycles of the mouse than the rat, but enough information has become available in recent years about the mouse so that similarities and differences between these species can be noted. Nelson et al. (1982) have just completed the first longitudinal study of the estrous cycle of the widely used C57BL/6J mouse. Based on observations which were made in this study and their references to earlier work, these investigators concluded that the mouse estrous cycle

is more sensitive to environmental factors than the rat. As a result, irregularities in the cycle are common unless great care is taken to keep the environment uniform. Flurkey et al. (1982) have found recently that at 12 months of age, 40 percent of a colony of mice of this strain were acyclic. Four out of five of these acyclic mice were in CE, while the remainder were described as being in constant diestrus based on the vaginal smear picture. It was also observed that the condition of CE was preceded typically by an extension of the modal length of the estrous cycle from four to five days (Nelson et al., 1981). In this same study, estradiol and progesterone levels in the plasma were compared between cycling young adults and 14-month-old mice who were in CE. The pattern was found to be very similar to that reported in the rat (Lu et al., 1979) in that there was a moderate level of estradiol in the CE mice which was comparable to the basal level found in the young adults and a progesterone level comparable to that found in ovariectomized mice.

In 10- to 12½-month-old mice which are still cycling, the proestrous surge of progesterone is lower than in young adults and the estradiol surge is equal in height but typically a day late. This delay is associated with an increase in cycle length. The lower surge level of progesterone may be associated with the lower LH level which is found during the ascending and descending limbs of the LH surge (Flurkey et al., 1982). In this same investigation, it was found that preovulatory prolactin levels in the plasma of aging mice, during the time that modal length of cycles was increasing, were lower than in young adults. Acyclic mice, however, were observed to have moderately elevated prolactin levels. This differs from the results of Parkening et al. (1980) who found no increase in prolactin in acyclic mice which were several months older than those used in the study of Flurkey et al.

Human Steroidogenesis. Although it has been possible for many years to determine plasma and urinary levels of androgens, estrogens, and progestins in the human, the interpretation of the data which have been produced is frequently quite difficult. However, as new and more sensitive methods for determining hormone levels have become available, and as a better understanding of the metabolism and interconversions of these hormones has been obtained, a clearer picture is gradually developing (Table 3).

Among the factors which must be considered in interpreting plasma hormone levels are the following:

1. the effect of age and pre- and postmenopausal status on the secretion rate of androgens and estrogens by the ovary and suprarenal gland;
2. the effect of age and pre- and postmenopausal status on the peripheral interconversion of androgens and estrogens;
3. the effect of body fat on interconversion of androgens and estrogens in relation to age and pre- and postmenopausal status;
4. the effect of age and pre- and postmenopausal status on metabolic clearance of androgens and estrogens from the plasma.

Not all of these questions have been investigated completely at the present time, but some of the more recent studies, although somewhat contradictory, do provide useful information.

It has been known for some time that the plasma levels of estradiol (E_2) estrone (E_1), and androstenedione (A) drop sharply at about the time of the menopause, but there is only a small decline in testosterone (T) (Judd, 1976; Vermeulen, 1976); see data in Table 3. In a recent investigation, Studd et al. (1978a) confirmed these observations and, furthermore, pointed out that the T level did not differ after the menopause from that observed during the proliferative stage of the menstrual cycle. Since there is a major decline in plasma levels of all four of these hormones within six to eight weeks following ovariectomy in premenopausal women, it seems likely that the ovary secretes a significant amount of each prior to the menopause.

Ovariectomy of postmenopausal women has been shown quite clearly to reduce significantly T level only (Table 3). This observation suggests that E_1, E_2, and A are all produced primarily from extraovarian sources after the menopause. However, recent studies comparing hormone levels in the ovarian vein with levels of the same hormones in the general circulation have indicated that the postmenopausal human ovary, in some cases, retains some hormone production capability other than T. Longcope et al. (1980a) performed such an experiment on postmenopausal women immediately prior to hysterectomy and found that 20 percent of these women showed a concentration gradient for E_2 across the ovary, and a slightly higher percentage showed a gradient for T and A. Gronroos et al. (1980) also observed a gradient for E_1 and E_2 across the ovary in 79 postmenopausal women. There is some evidence that there is a change in hormone production rate as time passes after the menopause. Vermeulen and Verdonck (1979) showed that the ovaries of postmenopausal women secrete some estrogens for about four years, but subsequently

TABLE 3.   Plasma Levels of Estrogens, Progesterone, and Androgens Before and After the Menopause. (All values in pg/ml plasma.)

Status	E_1	E_2	P	A	T
Premenopausal	50–200[a]	100–500[a]	300–20,000[a]	1660 ± 130[c]	443 ± 23[c]
	30–200[b]	35–500[b]		1689 ± 80[e]	289 ± 12[e]
Postmenopausal	49 ± 5[c]	20 ± 1[c]	190 ± 30[c]	990 ± 130[c]	297 ± 40[c]
	38 ± 3[d]	13 ± 1[d]			
Postmenopausal	48 ± 6[c]	18 ± 4[c]	180 ± 10[c]	640 ± 90[c]	120 ± 21[c]
(ovariectomized)	44 ± 7[d]	16 ± 3[d]			

[a]Guerrero et al. (1976).
[b]Judd (1976).
[c]Vermeulen (1976).
[d]Rader et al. (1973).
[e]Judd and Yen (1973).

all estrogens are derived from peripheral conversion of androgens. Vermeulen (1980) reported, furthermore, that T and, to a minimal extent, A continue to be secreted by the ovary for many years after the menopause.

Meldrum et al. (1981) observed no difference with age in circulating levels of E_1, E_2, A, and T in women from 50 to over 80 years of age. Since Longcope et al. (1980b) found no difference in the metabolic clearance rate (MCR) for E_1, E_2, A, and T in a group of postmenopausal women whose ages ranged from 46 to 90, there is a good indication that the total production rate (PR), regardless of source, was proportional to the plasma level of these hormones. In a more recent study, Longcope et al. (1981) determined the production rate of the same four hormones in a large group of postmenopausal women and found, by linear regression analysis, that only E_2 showed a significant decline in PR with age. However, all four steroids were significantly lower in postmenopausal women than in a large group of premenopausal women.

An additional observation which was made in this study was that there is a significant correlation between PR of each of these steroids and body weight. Previous investigators have noted a correlation between plasma levels of these steroids and body weight or fat mass, but the results have not been consistent. Judd et al. (1976), Vermeulen and Verdonck (1978), Vermeulen (1980), and Frumar et al. (1980) all found a positive correlation between fat mass and plasma levels of E_1 and E_2, but the last study found no correlation between the level of androgens and body weight. Poortman et al. (1981) found a correlation between E_1 and body weight but no correlation for either E_2 or A. The consistent relationship between E_1 and body weight fits in well with the observations of MacDonald et al. (1978) and Vermeulen (1980) which showed that high body weight (fat mass) potentiates the conversion of A to E_1 and that this potentiation is greater in postmenopausal than in premenopausal women.

Hypothalamic-Pituitary-Ovarian Axis. Although the ovary is justifiably considered as the central organ in the female reproductive system, it has been recognized for many years that most of its functional capabilities are under the control of hormones secreted by the anterior lobe of the pituitary gland. In more recent years, it has become clear that the pituitary gland is heavily dependent on hormones secreted by the hypothalamus for most of its functions, including the control of secretion of gonadotropic hormones. For this reason, it is not surprising that age changes in the hypothalamus and the pituitary are of major significance in the decline in reproductive capacity.

Feedback of Ovarian Hormones. There is ample evidence that circulating levels of ovarian hormones change with age in rodents and even more dramatically in the human. There is also no doubt that the ovarian hormones exert both positive and negative feedback effects on the hypothalamic-pituitary axis throughout reproductive life. In more recent years, several laboratories have become interested in possible age changes in these feedback systems, which involves gathering data not only on circulating levels of hypothalamic, pituitary, and ovarian hormones but also on the sensitivity of the hypothalamus and the pituitary to the steroid hormones.

Negative feedback appears to be primarily concerned with controlling the level of tonic secretion of the gonadotropic hormones. Most studies of aging changes in this system have involved removal of negative feedback by ovariectomy in young and old rodents. Many investigators have shown that ovariectomy will produce a greater increase in plasma LH level in young adults than in aging rodents (Shaar et al., 1975; Gosden and Bancroft, 1976; Miller and Riegle, 1978a; Wise and Ratner, 1980a; Takahashi et al., 1980; Estes et al., 1980; Gee et al., 1983). One exception to these results was reported by Gosden et al. (1978) who found no change in plasma levels of LH after ovariectomy in either young or old CBA mice. The authors suggested that this might be due to the suprarenal glands exerting a continuing negative feedback in this strain, but proof is lacking.

More conclusive proof of age change in negative feedback was obtained by Huang et al.

(1976a) and by Gray et al. (1980b). They injected estradiol into young and aging ovariectomized rats and found that the level of circulating LH was reduced more in young than in old rats (Figure 2). However, Gosden and Bancroft (1976) found that the proportional decrease in LH in response to estrogen was the same in the old and young groups.

Less attention has been paid to the feedback control of follicle stimulating hormone (FSH) secretion than to LH; however, Steger et al. (1980a) did observe that there was a comparable increase in plasma FSH following ovariectomy in young and old rats, while Wise and Ratner (1980a) found a smaller increase in old rats.

Considerable evidence has accumulated which indicates that a preovulatory surge of LH can be elicited by injections of ovarian hormones. Since the most characteristic change in female reproductive aging is the loss of regular cyclicity and ovulation, attention has been paid in recent years to the ability of the hypothalamic-pituitary axis in aging rodents to respond to the positive feedback of ovarian steroids. Lu et al. (1977) ovariecto-

mized young adult and 11- to 12-month-old irregularly cycling rats. After 25 or 52 days, the animals were given estradiol benzoate followed 3 days later by progesterone. It was observed that there was a much smaller rise in LH in the old animals, indicating a less effective positive feedback. Similar results were obtained by Gosden and Bancroft (1976), Steger et al. (1980a), and Gray and Wexler (1980). Furthermore, Peluso et al. (1977) were not able to demonstrate positive feedback with estradiol benzoate in 18- to 19-month-old rats which had been ovariectomized for four weeks and were in CE or RPP at the time of ovariectomy. However, Lu et al. (1980) were able to obtain LH release in acutely ovariectomized RPP rats but not in similarly treated CE rats. It was suggested that the exposure of the hypothalamus to constant and elevated values of estrogen with little or no progesterone, which is characteristic of CE rats, might greatly reduce or eliminate the positive feedback response. This hypothesis was tested by Lu et al. (1981) who demonstrated that CE rats, which had been ovariectomized for five weeks, showed elevated LH levels, although less than

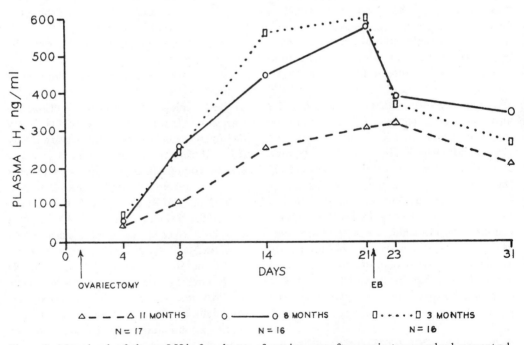

Figure 2. Mean levels of plasma LH in female rats of varying ages after ovariectomy and subsequent administration of estradiol benzoate (0.1 ug/100 g). (Data of Gray et al., 1980.)

young adults, in response to estrogen-progesterone, whereas acutely ovariectomized rats showed no response. It, therefore, appears that the lack of positive feedback response by the hypothalamus is not permanent but returns after a few weeks of exposure to low circulating levels of estrogen. Furthermore, young rats subjected to chronic estrogen treatment behaved like old CE rats. This convincing experiment strongly indicates that age *per se* is not responsible for the loss of positive feedback response, but instead the hypothalamus becomes desensitized to positive feedback by chronic exposure to elevated levels of estrogen. It is important to point out, however, that intact aging rats in CE can be induced to ovulate (Clemens et al., 1969) or to cycle temporarily (Huang et al., 1976b) by a few daily injections of progesterone so it is clear that sensitivity to positive feedback to this hormone has not been completely lost.

Serum prolactin (PRL) levels are generally higher in aged CE and RPP rats than in young adults (Shaar et al., 1975; Lu et al., 1979; Takahashi et al., 1980; Steger, 1981). By far, the highest levels are found in aged anestrous rats which invariably had tumorous pituitary glands (Huang et al., 1976a). Damassa et al. (1980) made a more detailed study of plasma levels of PRL in 20- to 26-month-old CE and RPP rats. They found that CE rats have a distinct surge of PRL at 1700 (hour) and a small surge at about 0200, whereas RPP animals had surges at the same time but the major surge was at 0200. Both CE and RPP rats which had pituitary tumors had high static plasma PRL levels.

The basal level of PRL in the plasma of young estrous and proestrous rats and aged rats in CE can be reduced by ovariectomy (Shaar et al., 1975; Wise et al., 1976; Huang et al., 1976a; Takahashi et al., 1980; Steger, 1981). The extent of the reduction tends to be greater in old than in young animals. In some of these studies, it was observed that there was no significant change in PRL levels in young rats in diestrus or old rats in RPP or anestrus following ovariectomy (Wise et al., 1976; Huang et al., 1976a; Takahashi, et al., 1980). This lack of effect is apparently due

to the low level of circulating estrogen which existed in these animals at the time of ovariectomy.

The ability of estrogen to increase the basal plasma level of PRL has been well documented in young animals as well as in old animals in CE, RPP, or anestrus, but the effect appears to be greater in the old animals (Shaar et al., 1975; Huang et al., 1976a; Steger, 1981).

In contrast to the clear evidence that estrogen administration will increase the basal level of PRL, Huang et al. (1980) were unable to induce a surge secretion of PRL in 20- to 24-month-old rats by an injection of estradiol benzoate followed three days later by progesterone, whereas young adults which were similarly treated showed a threefold increase. These data indicate that PRL surge response to ovarian steroids is lost to an even greater extent than is the LH surge. Whether this is due to age changes in the hypothalamic catecholamines or serotonin or to changes in hypothalamic or pituitary steroid receptors is not known.

It is generally accepted that estrogen has both a positive and a negative feedback influence on the hypothalamic-pituitary axis in women during their reproductive life. The 15-fold increase in the production rate of FSH (Coble et al., 1969) and the 3-fold increase in LH (Kohler et al., 1968) after the menopause provide ample evidence of the effect of reduced negative feedback on gonadotropin secretion. Further evidence has been provided by Robyn and Vekemans (1976) who observed that daily administration of 25 μg of ethinyl estradiol for three weeks to postmenopausal women reduced the circulating level of LH and FSH to less than half of the pretreatment level, and that by two weeks after estrogen administration was stopped, both gonadotropic hormones had returned to near the pretreatment level. This negative feedback influence on both FSH and LH is comparable to the earlier results obtained by Keller (1970) and Franchimont et al. (1972). However, in both of these earlier studies, low doses of estrogens had unequal effects on LH and FSH levels.

In an effort to explain the much larger increase in FSH than in LH after the menopause, Sherman and Korenman (1975) and Sherman et al. (1976) have proposed that FSH may be controlled by an inhibin which is produced in association with maturing follicles. Since such follicles decrease around the menopause, this negative feedback factor would be reduced.

There is general agreement that an increase in circulating estrogen during the late follicular phase of the cycle initiates the midcycle LH surge. Some evidence is available which indicates that estrogen levels in the plasma in the late follicular and luteal portions of the cycle decrease prior to the menopause (Judd, 1976), but there is no clear indication that the frequent increase in irregular cycles in women of this age (Treloar et al., 1967) is related to this change.

For a discussion of age changes in the hypothalamus and pituitary gland which are related to female reproductive function, see Chapter 21 and the first edition of this *Handbook* (Talbert, 1977).

Uterus

There is considerable evidence that age changes in the uterus are primarily responsible for the initial decline in reproductive capacity in the mouse and also constitute a major factor in the hamster and the rabbit. This evidence is based on several studies in which ova recovered from the uterus of young donors were transferred into the uterine lumen of young and old hosts (Blaha, 1964b; Talbert and Krohn, 1966; Adams, 1970; Maurer and Foote, 1971; Gosden, 1975a). All of these studies showed clearly that ova transferred into the uterus of young animals were much more likely to implant and be maintained than ova transferred into old hosts. More recently, data have been accumulating which indicate that the inability of the uterus to support pregnancy is probably not due to a deficiency of ovarian hormones but is more likely the result of intrinsic age changes in the uterus (see section on the ovary in this chapter).

Early studies of aging changes in the rodent uterus have shown that there is an increase in fibrous connective tissue in older animals (see Talbert, 1968, for references). This is probably due to an increase in cross-linked collagen in the aging uterus which resists degradation and turnover (Schaub, 1964–65). Maurer and Foote (1972) demonstrated that there is a reduction in collagenase activity in the uterus of aging rabbits which would slow down the rate of degradation. An increase in uterine collagen content with age has also been shown in 15- to 22-month-old hamsters which were studied on the fifth day of pregnancy (Rahima and Soderwall, 1977a).

Biggers et al. (1962b) suggested that increase in collagen might result in occlusion of some blood vessels in the uterine wall, which could have a detrimental effect on the blood supply and success of pregnancy. Such a conclusion is supported by the work of Larson and Foote (1972) who observed a decrease in uterine blood flow in 45-month-old rabbits which was not evident in animals up to 30 months of age. Similar results were obtained by Rahima and Soderwall (1978) when they compared 3- to 9-month-old with 15- to 22-month-old hamsters on the fifth day of pregnancy. Rahima (1981) observed endothelial proliferation in uterine arteries of 15- to 22-month-old pregnant hamsters so that the lumen was almost occluded. Unfortunately, the extent of the occlusion process was not studied in relation to maintenance of pregnancy.

Another possible factor which might influence the blood supply to the uterus was reported by Rahima and Soderwall (1977b). They found a larger number of mast cells in the uterus of aging hamsters. Since these cells secrete serotonin which acts as a vasoconstrictor, blood supply could also be reduced.

Lipofuscin increases with age in many tissues, including the uterus (Biggers et al., 1962a; Bal and Getty, 1973), but there is still no clear evidence that this substance interferes with cell function (Davies and Fotheringham, 1981).

Uterine Response to Ovarian Hormones. During the past several years, considerable attention has been directed toward the understanding of age changes in the ability of the uterus to respond to ovarian hormone stimulation. It is generally agreed that a prime factor in this process is the binding of these hormones to cytoplasmic receptor proteins in uterine cells after they have diffused through the cell membrane. The receptor-hormone complexes are then translocated into the nucleus (Chang and Roth, 1979).

Several studies have now shown that there is a considerable decline in estradiol (E_2) binding capacity in the uterus of aging rats (Holinka et al., 1975; Hsueh et al., 1979; Saiduddin and Zassenhaus, 1979) and in aging C57BL/6J mice (Nelson et al., 1976). In contrast to these results, Gosden (1976) found no decrease in the uptake of E_2 by 17-month-old CBA/H-T6 mice when compared with 3- to 4-month-old animals. The reason for this discrepancy is not clear.

The decline in binding capacity of E_2 in the aging rat and mouse uterus, which was demonstrated in all but one of the studies cited, is most likely related to a decline in the concentration of cytoplasmic and nuclear receptors for this hormone (Hsueh et al., 1979; Haji et al., 1981). Both of these studies showed that there was no age change in the affinity of receptor binding to E_2. Gesell and Roth (1981) have provided evidence, by immunochemical titration of cytoplasmic receptors with specific antiserum, that the apparent loss of receptor sites with age is not the result of an increase in nonfunctional although immunoreactive receptors. It seems likely, therefore, that there is a decrease with age in biosynthesis of receptor protein.

In spite of the general agreement that there is a decline with age in E_2 receptors in the uterus, Holinka et al. (1977) have demonstrated that ovariectomized 21-month-old C57BL/6J mice, which are several months past the age when reproduction is possible, are still able to exhibit a significant response to a single injection of 0.2 μg of E_2, as indicated by an increase in uterine weight and uterine contents of protein, glycogen, and alkaline phosphatase.

In addition, Soriero (1980) found that 15-month-old ovariectomized C57BL/6J mice still showed a response to E_2 as indicted by increased uptake of [^{3}H]-uridine into nuclear RNA. However, the reaction was considerably less than in 4- to 7-month-old mice.

At the present time, there does not appear to be any evidence that there is a decline in progesterone receptor sites with age, but this has not been investigated nearly as extensively as E_2 receptors. Blaha and Leavitt (1978) studied the concentration of progesterone cytoplasmic receptor in the uterus of ovariectomized young and aged hamsters following E_2 treatment, and found no change with age in either the endometrium or the myometrium. Similar results were obtained by Saiduddin and Zassenhaus (1979) in a comparison between a group of 20-month-old pseudopregnant and anestrous rats and a group of young cycling rats.

Implantation and Maintenance of Pregnancy. None of the age changes in the uterus or its hormonal support which have been discussed in this review can be identified with confidence as the primary cause of the lower rate of survival of ova in the uteri of aged laboratory animals. However, other studies of the uterus in aging rodents have dealt more specifically with changes which are related to the success or failure of pregnancy. One factor which has been considered is the possible effect of number and size of previous litters. In order to test this hypothesis, Asdell et al. (1941) and Finn (1963) reduced the number of litters in aging rats and mice by delaying breeding until the animals were 9 months of age. There was no evidence from these investigations that reproductive capacity was any better in these animals than in those which had been bred throughout their reproductive life. However, there is evidence that overcrowding of a uterine horn, which can be achieved by unilateral ovariectomy, will result in fewer litters than in animals which have had a normal number of fetuses in each horn (Jones and Krohn, 1960; Biggers et al., 1962b; Blaha, 1964a). It is likely that implantation failure in these animals is due to local changes in the uterine wall, such as blood supply (Biggers, 1969) or persistent uterine scars (Gosden, 1979). Considerable attention has been paid in the past several years to aging changes in the closure of the uterine lumen at the time of implantation. Finn and Martin (1969) observed that the lumen of aging ovariectomized mice which had been treated for three days with progesterone (P) followed by a single injection of E_2 did not close, whereas the uterus in similarly treated young animals did close. However, Thorpe et al. (1974) and Parkening (1979) observed that in aging hamsters, the lumen was eliminated in the vicinity of attaching blastocysts, so it seems unlikely that this is an important event in the decline in reproductive capacity.

Another uterine change which is essential to the implantation process in the uterus is the decidual response. Finn (1966), Blaha (1967), Shapiro and Talbert (1974), and Holinka and Finch (1977) have shown that the uterus of aging mice and hamsters is less responsive to a deciduogenic stimulus, such as intraluminal injection of oil, than is the uterus of young adults. Furthermore, Craig (1981) observed no ultramicroscopic signs of decidual changes in the uterus of 20- to 24-month-old rats. Recently, however, Finch and Holinka (1982) performed the more critical experiment of measuring the mean weight, protein, and DNA per implantation site on the sixth to the tenth days of pregnancy (Figure 3) in 3- to 7-month-old and 11- to 12-month-old mice and found no age difference. This observation indicates that use of artificial agents for producing a decidual reaction may not be a reliable indicator of the sensitivity of the uterus to an implanting blastocyst in young and old mice, and that some other, as yet unrecognized, age changes need to be identified to fully explain embryonic loss at this stage of pregnancy.

Although most studies of the effect of aging on reproductive failure have been directed toward the ova, the preimplantation embryo, and the early postimplantation period, there are significant age changes which result in increased resorptions later in pregnancy (Talbert, 1971). Gosden et al. (1981) recently observed pregnant uterine horns in 11- to 12-month-old C57BL/6J mice and found that resorbing embryos were first observed on the

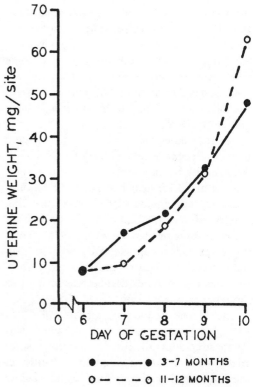

Figure 3. Change in weight of implantation sites in young and aging C57BL/6J mice during gestation. (Data of Finch and Holinka, 1982.)

tenth day of pregnancy and they increased on the following three days until they accounted for about one-third of the total number. The authors suggested that local factors in the uterine wall such as blood supply or scar tissue might account for individual resorptions, but absorption of entire litters was more likely due to some unidentified systemic factors. Fabricant et al. (1978) compared postimplantation mortality rates between the tenth and fourteenth days of pregnancy in six inbred strains of mice. Although two of the strains were chosen because of altered immunity and one because of early reproductive aging, there were no significant interstrain differences in resorptions and all strains showed a significant increase in midpregnancy losses beginning in 7-month-old animals. Parkening et al. (1978) and Holinka et al. (1979a) observed a much larger number of resorbing fetuses in old than in young C57BL/6J mice.

Since there were no significant differences in circulating ovarian hormones in the two age groups, it seems likely that the uterus *per se* and perhaps an increasing number of abnormal embryos were responsible for the greater loss of postimplantation embryos in old mice.

Length of Gestation. Soderwall et al. (1960) observed that aging hamsters had a mean increase in gestation length and also cited earlier investigations which showed comparable results. This age change in reproductive function has recently been studied in considerably greater depth by Holinka et al. (1978, 1979b). These studies show clearly that the two-day prolongation of pregnancy which is characteristic of 11- to 12-month-old C57BL/6J mice is associated with a delayed preparturitional rise in plasma E_2 and fall in P. Since a condition of high E_2 and low P has often been linked with the initiation of uterine contractions, these hormonal changes may be of considerable importance. There is no clear evidence of the cause of these aging changes in hormonal levels, although Blaha and Leavitt (1974) have suggested that prolongation of high progesterone levels may be due to delayed luteolysis.

Human Uterus. Although the human uterus undergoes aging changes which are intrinsic, by far the most notable changes are the result of age-associated modification of the hormonal environment in which this organ exists. Normally, the uterus will become atrophic in very old age and shrink to a small fraction of its premenopausal size (Lang and Aponte, 1967) because of markedly lower levels of circulating estrogens and progestins. The uterine epithelium in normal aging women consists primarily of low cuboidal cells, and there are often isolated cystic glands near the uterine lumen which are covered only by a thin layer of epithelium (Witt, 1963). Woessner (1963) reported that total collagen, elastin, and wet weight increase until about 30 years and remain the same until about the time of the menopause. After this age, wet weight and fibrous tissue decline by about 50 percent over the next 15 years. The uterine blood vessels also show sclerotic changes which will gradu-

ally narrow or occlude their lumen, and coiled arterioles, which are found in the functional layer of the endometrium in premenopausal women, are virtually absent (Speert, 1949).

The most recent anatomical studies of the postmenopausal human endometrium have been at the ultrastructural level. Deligdisch et al. (1978) have confirmed that there are a thin cuboidal epithelium and frequent dilated or cystic glands. They also observed that the endometrial cells had a paucity and random distribution of cytoplasmic organelles. Another dominant characteristic of the normal postmenopausal endometrium is the presence of a large number of vacuoles in the cytoplasm of the epithelium. An additional characteristic of these cells is the presence of short blunt microvilli. Collagen is important in the stroma which may be related to the absence of menstrual cycles.

In normally cycling premenopausal women, two estrogen binding proteins have been identified, one of which is a high affinity binding protein while the other has lower affinity. In normal postmenopausal women, the lower affinity binding protein was missing but could be restored by estrogen therapy. It, therefore, seems certain that this difference is not due to aging *per se* but probably to inadequate estrogen stimulation (Gibbons et al., 1979). Punnonen et al. (1979) found high affinity cytoplasmic estrogen receptors in the endometrium and the myometrium of postmenopausal women for several years after the menopause even in the presence of an atrophic-appearing endometrium. These results suggest that this receptor may be retained even when estrogen levels have been low for a long period.

Vagina

Very little attention has been paid to the study of age changes in the vagina of the human or laboratory animals except indirectly through the observation of vaginal smears. It has been universally recognized for some time, however, that the vagina in postmenopausal women who are not receiving estrogen treatment becomes smaller both in length and in diameter. Lang and Aponte (1967) found evidence of loss of elasticity in the vaginal wall, but Toth and Gimes (1964) found no indication of impairment of elastic fibers.

The vaginal epithelium in the human during reproductive life consists of superficial cells, intermediate cells, parabasal cells, and basal cells. These cells are sloughed off into the vaginal lumen throughout the menstrual cycle, and the relative number of each cell type is the basis for the karyopyknotic index. A major longitudinal study of menstrual cycles, including vaginal smears, was carried out by Treloar et al. (1967). More recent studies, however, have indicated that although a vaginal smear may be used with some confidence as an indicator of estrogen deficiency, it must be used with caution as an indicator of plasma level of estrogens (Benjamin and Deutsch, 1980). This limitation may be due to positive correlation of the karyopyknotic index and plasma estradiol but not estrone (Morse et al., 1971) or to possible changes in vaginal sensitivity to these hormones (Procope, 1970).

Although there are typically fewer superficial cells associated with increasing years after the menopause (Masukawa, 1960), 25 percent of women over 75 were still found to have some of these cells in their vaginal smear (McLennan and McLennan, 1971).

The principal clinical problems associated with the vagina of older women are thinning of the epithelial wall and inadequate glandular secretions, which are not due primarily to intrinsic changes in the vagina but to inadequate ovarian hormonal stimulation.

Considerable reference has already been made in this chapter to age changes in the vaginal smear in rats and mice. Thung et al. (1956) made a detailed study of changes in the vaginal smear in several strains of mice, while Mandl (1961) and Aschheim (1961) made comparable studies in rats. However, none of these investigators made a longitudinal study of the pattern of cells in the vaginal smear in the rodent throughout the reproductive life span and into the postreproductive period. Such a study has been completed recently by Nelson et al. (1982) in the C57BL/6J mouse, which demonstrates clearly that a detailed knowledge of the response of the vaginal wall to ovarian hormones in aging rodents is a valuable tool in following the pattern of reproductive decline.

Uterine Tube. In spite of its key role as the normal site of fertilization and as a passageway for the developing early embryo, there has been very little investigation of the aging uterine tube either in the human or in experimental animals. However, Komatsu and Fujita (1978) recently made an electron microscopic study of the development and aging of the mouse oviductal epithelium. They observed that the epithelium in the ampulla region of the young adult uterine tube contains two types of cells: a secretory cell and a ciliated cell. The secretory cell in particular undergoes modifications during the estrous cycle. During estrus, numerous secretory granules are distributed from the Golgi field to the apical region of the cytoplasm. The rough endoplasmic reticular (RER) and the Golgi complex are well developed. During diestrus, the granules decrease in number, and the RER and Golgi complex become reduced in size. In the ciliated cell, mitochondria are numerous in the supranuclear region, but the RER and Golgi complex are less developed than in secretory cells. Cyclic changes are less noticeable than in the secretory cell, but lipid droplets tend to increase in number during diestrus.

By 7 months of age, incipient changes are evident in both cell types although cyclicity is still present. The most obvious change which is found in both types of epithelial cells is the appearance of electron dense secondary lysosomes and large vacuoles which may be derived from the lysosomes. Both of these structures increase in number in animals between 7 and 16 months of age. By 22 months, when ovarian function has become minimal, the epithelium appears to consist of only ciliated and nonciliated cells. The ciliated cells are not too different from those in younger animals except for the occurrence of large vacuoles containing heterogeneously dense materials. Secretory granules are absent in most cells, and the cisternae of the RER are irregularly dilated. Golgi complex and mitochondria are also reduced. It has been demonstrated that the secretory cell is more sensitive to loss of ovarian hormones than is the ciliated cell since administration of sex hormones has greater influence on its structure.

Ciliated and secretory cells are also found in the tubal epithelium in the human. Novak and Everett (1928) found that these cells do not atrophy for several years after the menopause, although there is little evidence of secretion. After age 60, cilia begin to disappear in the isthmus region although they remain until very old age in the ampulla and infundibulum (Patek et al., 1972). However, Gaddum-Rosse et al. (1975) did find some loss of cilia on the fimbria and sloughing of the surface epithelium in postmenopausal women. This condition could be reversed to the premenopausal condition by estrogen treatment.

In general, age changes in the uterine tube are primarily a reflection of reduced ovarian hormone levels rather than intrinsic senile changes in this organ. At the present time, there does not appear to be any evidence that ova are damaged by exposure to the aged uterine tube, and there is also no indication of less effective tubal transport (Harman and Talbert, 1974).

Mammary Gland

The vast majority of studies of the human breast have been concerned with factors relating to the development of neoplastic disease, but normal aging patterns have also been well documented. The breast develops rapidly at puberty and remains potentially fully functional until near the age of the menopause. Similarly to other secondary sex organs, this organ is dependent on female sex hormones for its development and consequently undergoes involution when these hormones become much less prevalent.

The involutionary process involves the glandular tissue, the ducts, and the stromal tissue, but the pattern of change in these tissues may vary considerably. During involution, the basement membrane of the acini thickens and the luminal space becomes virtually eliminated. At the same time, the mucoid connective tissue of the breast lobule is converted into dense hyaline collagen. The specialized connective tissue of a lobule becomes indistinguishable from ordinary connective tissue. As a result, the outline of the lobules is lost, except that, in some cases, the specialized connective tissue becomes denser and less cellular than the adjacent interlobular stroma, so that the original position of a lobule is demarked by a ovoid hyaline mass (Azzopardi, 1978).

Occasionally, a lobule of the breast may undergo a process known as cystic lobular involution which is frequently mistaken for cystic disease. This change occurs when acini join up to form microcysts. These cysts are surrounded by the specialized connective tissue which is essential in distinguishing them from the type found in pathological cystic disease (Azzopardi, 1978).

The process involved in the disappearance of the ordinary connective tissue is not well understood, but it is clear that it is replaced to a variable degree by adipose tissue.

The major clinical problem of breast cancer is clearly related to age as well as to hormonal status. This condition is rare until the latter half of the third and during the fourth decade at which time the incidence of this neoplasm increases dramatically. In a study of 1859 reported cases, 66 percent were over the age of 50, with a median at 55 when the disease was detected (Pilnic and Leis, 1978). DeWaard et al. (1960) found some evidence of a bimodal distribution of mammary carcinoma, with a first peak occurring at about 45 years of age which was believed to be associated with ovarian dysfunction and a second peak at 65 which may be related to hypersecretion of adrenal steroids.

The proportion of estrogen receptor positive breast tumors increases steadily to a peak at 60 to 74 years of age and is unrelated to pre- or postmenopausal status (Elwood and Godolphin, 1980).

The mammary gland of rats and mice has been studied extensively as a model for the understanding of possible factors involved in the development of human breast cancer. Little attention has been paid to the effect of age on tumor development, and indeed this undoubtedly varies considerably from one strain to another.

In the widely used Charles River rat (Sprague-Dawley derivative), spontaneous mammary tumors are a common occurrence, but Durbin et al. (1966) found that ovariectomy at a young age greatly reduced the incidence of these tumors and ovariectomy plus adrenalectomy completely eliminated tumor development. However, Welsch and Nagasawa (1977) have reviewed a large number of investigations in both rats and mice which indicate that spontaneous PRL-secreting tumors or increased PRL levels produced by pituitary transplants are capable of stimulating mammary tumors in mice under 1 year of age. In mice, these tumors tend to become independent of PRL stimulation once they are established, whereas at least in some strains of rats, PRL dependence does not appear to be completely lost.

These studies suggest that the increase in plasma PRL levels, which is typical in aging rats and mice, may be a prime factor in mammary tumor development, but the susceptibility of this gland to tumors is also greatly influenced by the genetic constitution of the strain. Estrogen may also be a factor, but most of the data suggest that increased PRL levels are of greater importance (Welsch and Nagasawa, 1977).

Sex Steroid Therapy after the Menopause

Indications for postmenopausal estrogen replacement therapy include "hot flashes," atrophy of the reproductive organs, osteoporosis, and possibly increased risk of atherosclerosis. In the last ten years, a number of studies using large populations and sensitive methods of analysis have begun to clarify the extent of benefit and also to quantify the risks attendant on such therapy. The subject has recently received extensive review (Hammond and Maxson, 1982; Gambrell, 1982; Judd et al., 1981).

The vasomotor symptom complex or "hot flash" may affect from 75 to 85 percent of women undergoing natural menopause, and in up to 25 percent may persist for five years or more (Bates, 1981; Dewhurst, 1976). According to Utian (1980), as many as 10–15 percent of women are disabled by this symptom to the point that they cannot carry out their usual daily activities. The hot flash is generally described as a sensation of extreme warmth or flushing which spreads from the face and neck down the trunk. It may be accompanied by tremor, nausea, headache, and diaphoresis. Recent work has shown that the symptomatic hot flash is reproducibly accompanied by a rise in skin temperature and conductance (Meldrum et al., 1980) and that objectively recorded hot flashes are closely coordinated with pulses of LH release from the pituitary gland (Tataryn et al., 1979). This has led to the hypothesis that the hypothalamic neural excitation responsible for LH release, intensified in menopausal women by the lack of steroid feedback, spreads to the adjacent thermoregulatory neurons in the preoptic area causing vasodilation, sweating, etc. Estrogen replacement therapy provides symptomatic relief of hot flashes in over 90 percent of patients with the vasomotor syndrome (Utian, 1975; Coope, 1976; Tataryn et al., 1981).

According to Schiff and Wilson (1978), the female reproductive organs undergo striking changes at the time of the menopause. Pubic hair becomes sparse and lank and may turn gray. The labia majora lose their fullness as subcutaneous adipose is withdrawn from them and the mons veneris, thus exposing the labia minora. The vaginal lining thins to about one-third its normal height as the protective cornified layer of superficial cells is lost. Glycogen secretion is greatly reduced, resulting in an increase in pH, alteration of vaginal flora with reduction in lactobacillus and increase in coliform organisms, and increased incidence of symptomatic vaginitis. This problem may progress to ulceration and bleeding. Many women report decreased lubrication at intercourse with varying degrees of dyspareunia. The vaginal thinning and inflammation respond well to estrogen replacement, whether locally or systemically administered. Breast atrophy is another prominent result of estrogen deficiency at the menopause. Although glandular breast tissue is better maintained when estrogen is supplied, there is no reason to believe that estrogens will prevent the alteration of breast contour resulting from age-related relaxation of ligaments and loss of muscular tone.

The acceleration of calcium loss from bone at the time of the menopause and the benefits of estrogen therapy are discussed in depth in Chapter 19.

The question as to whether estrogen might help protect against atherosclerosis was initially raised by the observation that premenopausal women had only one-fifth the risk of coronary disease of age-matched men (Ober and Miller, 1980). Furthermore, from the Framingham study, it appeared that postmenopausal women have 2.4 times the risk of ischemic heart disease of menstruating women the same age (Gordon et al., 1978). It has been shown that menopause is associated with an increase in the (atherogenic) LDL cholesterol component and a decrease in the (protective) HDL cholesterol component of serum lipoprotein (Gustafson and Svanborg, 1972). Tikkanen et al. (1978) have found that treatment with natural estrogens can reverse these lipid changes. Thus it is possible, though not proven, that estrogen therapy may partially restore the female's protection against atherosclerosis. Indeed, one study (Ross et al., 1981) shows the risk of myocardial infarction to be 60 percent less in estrogen-treated women than in age-matched untreated controls, when other risk factors are taken into account.

Risks of estrogen replacement therapy have been evaluated in a number of studies. The single effect receiving the most attention has been carcinoma of the endometrium. There is little question that long-term therapy with the most commonly prescribed regimen of estrogen (Premarin, 0.625 or 1.25 mg/day) is associated with a six- to eightfold increase in the risk of endometrial cancer after five or more years of therapy (Jick et al., 1979; Weiss et al., 1979, Antunes et al., 1979; Hulka, 1980a; Mack et al., 1976; McDonald et al., 1977; Smith et al., 1975). Nonetheless, this is a rare cancer (about 1 woman per 1000 women aged 65–75 is affected per year), with

about a 95 percent cure rate (Robboy and Bradley, 1979). Furthermore, it appears that cyclically interrupted therapy (Hulka, 1980b) has less excess risk and that employment of 10 to 12 days of a progestin during each cycle eliminates precancerous hyperplastic changes (Whitehead et al., 1981) and may result in a reduced risk of endometrial cancer, even compared with untreated women of like age (Gambrell et al., 1979).

Although a few studies have shown small increases (order of 1.5- to 2.5-fold) in the risk of breast cancer with postmenopausal estrogens (Burch et al., 1975; Hoover et al., 1981; Ross et al. 1980), most other studies have not revealed any increase in this risk (Sartwell et al., 1977; Hammond et al., 1979a; Boston Collaborative Drug Surveillance Program, 1974; Fechner, 1972; Gambrell et al., 1980). Except for an increased incidence of gallbladder disease, there does not appear to be any excess risk of those chronic complications associated with birth control pills (hypertension, thrombosis, diabetes, vascular liver tumors, and atherosclerosis) in women taking estrogen replacement therapy (Boston Collaborative Drug Surveillance Program, 1974; Studd et al., 1978b; Hammond and Maxson, 1982). This is probably because lower doses of estrogen are used for replacement therapy than for contraception. Since such effects are mainly results of the effects of estrogen on hepatic protein synthesis (i.e., altered clotting factors and lipoproteins, and increased renin substrate), it seems likely that these risks could be eliminated by administration of estrogen via a parenteral route, thus avoiding pharmacologically high estrogen concentrations in the hepatic portal blood. Preliminary investigations have shown that physiologic peripheral effects cannot be achieved with oral estrogens without causing pharmacologic effects on the liver (Geola et al., 1980; Mandel et al., 1982), but that parenteral estrogen can give physiologic effects without excess secretion of hepatic proteins (Buckman et al., 1980; Lobo et al., 1980).

In summary, current evidence favors the position that benefits of estrogen replacement after the menopause probably outweigh the risks, especially when the protective effect against osteoporotic fractures is considered. Adverse effects can probably be minimized by using low doses of estrogen, cyclic therapy, and regular opposition with 10 to 12 days of a progestin. Further reduction in risk might be achieved by use of a parenteral preparation (e.g., transdermal or subcutaneous route).

MALE REPRODUCTIVE SYSTEM

In contrast to the sharp landmark provided by the menopause in aging women, reproductive senescence in men appears to be a gradual process. In fact, there is still some question as to whether a true male climacteric occurs at all in normal men. Certainly, some human males retain full reproductive function into extreme old age. For example, Seymour et al. (1935) documented successful paternity in a 94-year-old man. Nonetheless, considerable published data support the concept that males of various animal species, including man, do show reduced reproductive capacity with age. This phenomenon is of considerable importance to animal breeders and in agriculture, but seems of lesser interest in the human male, since only rarely are new offspring desired by men past the age of 50. The subject of sexual function in older men, however, arouses lively interest because, in humans, sexual activity is not necessarily associated with procreation, but rather serves deeply felt personal needs, reinforces the permanence of pair-bonding, and hence is at the root of the stability of human families and, thus, societies. It is important to remember that the same hormones which regulate reproductive function also support and modulate sexual capacity and drive. Alterations in the secretion of these hormones, whether produced by aging or disease, can produce deleterious effects on sex drive and capacity, effects which will be of concern to men of any age.

Available data demonstrate that the nature, degree, and etiology of alterations with age in male reproductive hormones vary greatly from species to species and even from individual to individual within a species. In men,

elevations of plasma luteinizing hormone (LH) and follicle stimulating hormone (FSH), and decreased serum testosterone with increased estrone and estradiol have all been reported (although not, as we shall see, in all studies). Furthermore, there is nearly universal agreement that aging in men is accompanied by reduced sexual interest, activity, and capacity, but the extent to which this phenomenon is related to the hormonal alterations (if at all) is not yet clear.

Testis

Seminiferous Tubular Function. The testes produce both germ cells and sex steroid hormones. In the testis, in contrast to the ovary, there is constant replenishment of male germ cells from puberty to old age. The length of time required for the mature male gamete to develop from a spermatogonium does not appear to be influenced by age (Talbert, 1977) but is species specific. The process typically requires several weeks, whereas the completion of oogenesis can be held in abeyance for up to 50 years. This sex difference may explain why paternal age appears to be a relatively less important factor in production of chromosomal aneuploidy than does maternal age. Nonetheless, according to Leonard and De-Knudt (1970) and to Muramatsu (1974), there is an increase with age in the number of spontaneous translocations in the chromosomes of mouse spermatogonia. Also Bynum et al. have found an increase in sperm bearing two Y chromosomes (i.e., aneuploidy) in aging men. Thus, the role of paternal age in producing chromosomal abnormalities of the embryo requires further investigation.

There have been a number of investigations of the effects of age on semen quality and fertility. Blum (1936) reported that in men, the percent of semen samples containing spermatozoa decreased from 68.5 percent in the sixth decade to 48 percent in the eighth decade. MacLeod and Gold (1953), in a study of over 1500 men ages 20–50, found rate of conception to decrease from age 25 on. They also reported that the decrease in frequency of intercourse in older men resulted in an increase in total sperm count and ejaculate volume but reduced sperm motility. Even after correcting their data for the effects of ejaculatory interval, they still found an increase in sperm concentration up to age 50, with no apparent age effect on sperm morphology. Natoli et al. (1972) found a decrease with age in the number of normal, but not in the number of total, sperm in the ejaculates of men aged 45–91. Most recently, Nieschlag et al. (1982) have found sperm number and morphology to be unaltered in healthy older men of proven fertility. Motility was somewhat decreased, which correlated with the longer interejaculatory interval in their older subjects, but ability to penetrate ova in a heterologous ovum penetration test was unimpaired.

Bishop (1970), in his review of aging changes in the reproductive system, cites several reports of severely decreased sperm production with compromised fertility in the aging bull. In contrast, Johnson and Neaves (1981) found no decrease in daily sperm production by stallions up to 20 years of age.

In the laboratory rat, Saksena et al. (1979b) reported that the maximal number of spermatozoa was present in the caput epididymidis by 72 days of age and did not change up to 500 days of age. Despite this constancy of sperm number, the number of pups per litter decreased from a high of 14 at 300 days of paternal age to an average of 8.1 sired by 500-day-old males. This change could have been due to decreased sperm quality, to altered sperm transport in the male ducts, or even to altered male sexual behavior. Franks and Payne (1970) have reported that although apparently normal spermatogenesis persisted throughout the life of the C57BL/LRF mouse, functional reproductive capacity decreased after 16 months of age, with sterility after about 24 months of age. In testis homogenates from CBF$_1$ male mice, Bronson and DesJardins (1977) documented a gradual decline from 65×10^8 sperm/testis at 6 months of age to 40×10^8 at 24 months, followed by a rapid decline to 16×10^8 by 30 months of age. These workers later confirmed a decrease in

number of spermatazoa in the caput epididymidis and in the ejaculate of aged mice in another series of experiments (Huber et al., 1980). Humphreys (1977) reported an increase in the number of degenerating undifferentiated spermatids in seminiferous tubules of old (24 months) rats. He suggested that a loss of nutritive function of Sertoli cells might be at fault. Similarly, in rabbits, Ewing et al. (1972) found decreasing daily sperm production between 24 and 36 months of age. Thus it appears that while the effects of aging on sperm production vary among species, a number of them do show decreased quantity and/or quality of spermatozoa.

Many workers have reported degenerative changes in the histologic appearance of human seminiferous tubules with age (Sniffen, 1950; Tillenger, 1957; Burgi and Hedinger, 1959; Sokal, 1964; Sasano and Ichigo, 1969; Suoranta, 1971; and Kothari and Gupta, 1974). These changes have been described in order of severity as: (a) apparent thickening of the basement membrane due to peritubular deposition of collagen, (b) decrease in spermatogenic activity with thinning of the germinal epithelium, (c) peritubular fibrosis, (d) germ cell arrest—often at the primary spermatocyte stage, (e) degeneration or total absence of germ cells with only Sertoli cells remaining, (f) narrowing of the tubular lumen, and finally (g) collapse of tubules and their obliteration by sclerotic fibrous tissue. In addition, Schulze and Schulze (1981) noted a prominent increase in the number of multinucleate Sertoli cells in testes of aged men, the nuclei having an immature appearance suggesting a reversion to mitosis by these cells (with faulty cytokinesis), possibly under the influence of increased levels of FSH. Similarly, Holstein and Hubman (1980) have described an increase in the number of multinucleate germ cells in tubules of aging men.

Most observers agree that areas of various stages of senile degeneration of tubules are typically interspersed among areas with relatively normal morphology. Engle (1952) reported that 50 percent of men aged 70 or over still had some regions of apparently normal spermatogenesis. Sasano and Ichigo (1969) found that the percentage of tubules containing spermatids fell from 90 percent to 50 percent by age 60 and decreased further to only 10 percent between ages 70 and 80.

Both Sasano and Ichigo (1969) and Suoranta (1971) observed that degenerate areas were supplied by fewer patent capillaries than areas of more normal morphology. Suoranta (1971) and Frick (1969) both commented on the presence of foci of inflammatory cells in or near areas of degenerating tubules. These observations suggest that autoimmune damage to small vessels might be involved in the pathogenesis of "senile" seminiferous tubular degeneration. Of interest in this regard is work by Fjallbrant (1975) demonstrating an increase with age in serum sperm agglutinating antibodies, a finding which he suggested might contribute to a reduction in fertility with age. In aging rats, Humphreys (1977) saw scattered areas of tubular degeneration with spermatogenic arrest, folding and thickening of the basement membranes, and collapse of tubules. By 24 months of age, only 20 percent of tubules were histologically normal. Humphrey and Ladd (1975), investigating testis morphology in aging bulls, found decreased sperm production with a pattern of tubular degeneration and fibrosis very similar to that described for humans. In addition, they noted increased numbers of plasma cells in the testes and around the efferent ductules of older animals. They raised the question whether the immunological blood-testis barrier might be breached with progressive aging, leading to an autoimmune response.

In contrast to these results, Steger et al. (1979b) reported normal seminiferous tubule morphology in old Wistar rats, and Johnson and Neaves (1981) observed normal tubular histology in stallions up to 20 years of age with progressive increase in tubular length and mass over this period.

In the rabbit, Ewing et al. (1972) showed that the blood flow through the testes slowed from 10.7 ml/min/g at 6 months to 4.3 ml/min/g at 36 months. Pirke et al. (1979a) described a similar reduction of blood flow in rat testes but showed this change to be re-versed by treatment with gonadotropin. Thus it appeared that in the rat, the decreased flow was due not to irreversible vascular damage but only to chronic understimulation of the testis by trophic hormone.

Since the seminiferous tubules make up between 60 and 70 percent of testis mass. It would be expected that their degeneration might lead to reduction in testis weight and volume. A significant decrease in human autopsy testis weights with age has been reported by Harbitz (1973a) and also Tillenger (1957), but only when those testes which also showed histologic evidence of decreased spermatogenic activity were included in the calculation. Sokal (1964) also found a decrease in testis weight, while Kaler and Neaves (1978) did not. Apparent decreases with age in testis volume, estimated in vivo, were reported by Longcope (1973), Stearns et al. (1974), and weight, while Kaler and Neaves (1978) did not. Apparent decreases with age in testis volume, estimated in vivo, were reported by Longcope (1973), Stearns et al. (1974), and Baker et al. (1976), while Kothari and Gupta (1974) and Harman et al. (1982) failed to find a significant reduction when selected healthy men were examined.

In summary, it appears that senile degeneration of seminiferous tubules is a common phenomenon but probably not a universal one. Furthermore, its relationship to aging per se versus other etiologies such as vascular and/or autoimmune disease, and possibly other changes in the health of the individual, needs to be further explored.

Leydig Cell Function. Besides germ cells, the testes also produce the sex steroid hormones, the major one being the androgen, testosterone. Pedersen-Bjergaard and Jonnesen (1948) were the first investigators to demonstrate a decrease in androgens in aging men. They found that bioassayable androgen excreted in urine decreased after age 40, reaching very low levels by the eighth decade. Hollander and Hollander (1958) found similar aging changes in testosterone concentration in testicular vein blood obtained during surgery. Investigators using chromatographic, isotope dilution, and spectrophotometric methods (Coppage and Cooner, 1965; Kent and Acone, 1965; Gandy and Petersen, 1968) all failed to confirm a decrease in peripheral serum testosterone level with age in men. Kirschner and Coffman (1968) did find a decrease in serum testosterone, and Kent and Acone (1965) reported decreases in both testosterone production and metabolic rate in older men.

More recently, a large number of investigations using radioimmunoassay to quantify testosterone have shown a decrease in plasma testosterone concentrations in men with age (Hallberg et al., 1976; Baker et al., 1976; Frick, 1969; Mazzi et al., 1974; Nieschlag et al., 1973; Rubens et al., 1974; Horton et al., 1975;

Stearns et al., 1974; Pirke and Doerr, 1973; Vermeulen et al., 1972; Lewis et al., 1976; Forti et al., 1974; Nankin et al., 1981). In general, a decline in mean serum testosterone seemed to begin at about age 50 and to progress into the eighth or ninth decades (Figure 4). It is important to note, however, that even in studies showing decrease in mean plasma testosterone, individual concentrations displayed a high degree of variation, so that although some men in their 70s to 90s had testosterone well below the lower limit of normal (in Figure 1, 230 ng/dl), many quite elderly men had normal or even high normal testosterone concentrations. Furthermore, two recent large studies of American men selected

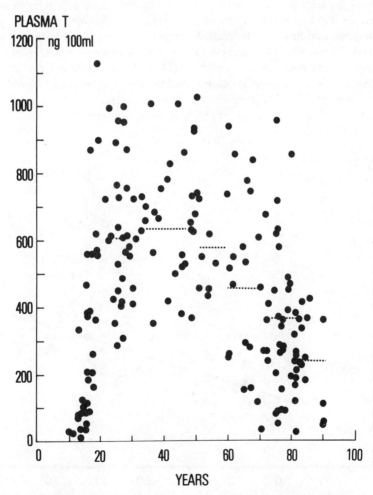

Figure 4. Effect of aging on total serum testosterone concentrations in men. (After Vermeulen et al., 1972.)

for good health, stability, and social and environmental homogeneity between younger and older subjects have not demonstrated a decrease in serum testosterone with age (Harman and Tsitouras, 1980; Sparrow et al. 1980). Nieschlag et al. (1982) now also have data from healthy fathers and grandfathers which contradict a previous finding in their laboratory of lowered testosterone levels with age.

Since testosterone availability to target tissues is modulated by its binding to a plasma protein, sex hormone binding globulin (SHBG), a number of investigators have inquired whether age-related alterations in binding might occur which would affect the free (bioavailable) testosterone fraction. These studies have generally resulted in the conclusion that SHBG capacity increases with age (Figure 5), producing a decrease in the free testosterone fraction and hence in the plasma free testosterone (Figure 6). This decrease in indices of free testosterone appears more prominent than the decrease in total plasma testosterone in some studies (Hallberg et al., 1976; Baker et al., 1976; Horst et al., 1974;

Kley et al., 1974; Pirke and Doerr, 1973, 1975a; Vermeulen and Verdonck, 1972; Vermeulen et al., 1972; Rubens, et al., 1974; Purifoy et al., 1981; Stearns et al., 1974). A number of these workers have hypothesized that the increase in SHBG might be secondary to an increase in plasma estrogenic steroids, since it is known that estrogens promote synthesis of SHBG by the liver. Increased plasma concentrations of unconjugated estradiol and estrone have indeed been demonstrated in older men in many of these same studies (Hallberg et al., 1976; Kley et al., 1974, 1975; Pirke and Doerr, 1975a; Rubens et al., 1974). Kley et al. (1975) also reported an enhanced estrogen response to human chorionic gonadotropin (hCG) stimulation of Leydig cells in older men in terms of absolute levels of estrone and estradiol, although percent response was slightly less in the elderly group. Nankin et al. (1981), however, have reported blunted late (24–48 hours) estradiol response to hCG in older men. The increase in basal plasma estrogen concentration did not appear to be simply a result of increased binding protein (SHBG

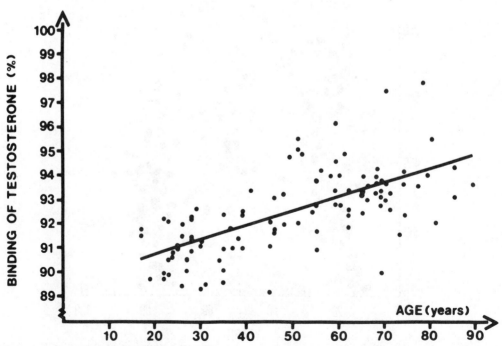

Figure 5. Effect of aging on percent binding of testosterone to sex hormone binding globulin in sera of men. (From Kley et al., 1974.)

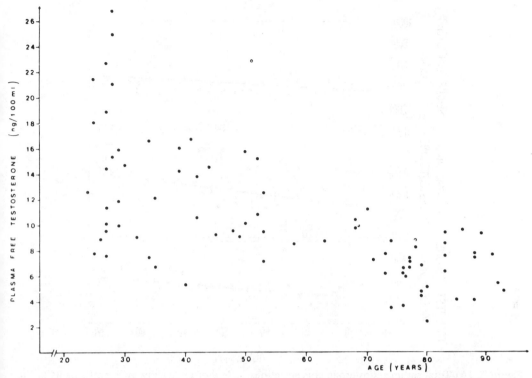

Figure 6. Effect of aging on free testosterone index in sera of men. (From Pirke and Doerr, 1975a.)

also binds estrogens), since the free estrogen concentrations were also increased (Pirke and Doerr 1975a; Rubens et al., 1974). Hemsell et al. (1974) found increased peripheral aromatization of androgens to estrogens in aging men. Since much of this conversion occurs in fatty tissue, the age-related increase in proportion of body mass which is fat may contribute to increased estrogen production in older men.

Other workers have not found altered plasma estrogen concentrations in older men (Stearns et al., 1974; Zumoff et al., 1982; Sparrow et al., 1980; Nankin et al., 1981; Nieschlag et al., 1982). In selected healthy men, Harman and Tsitouras (1980) found only a slight increase in SHBG binding of testosterone, which was insufficient to produce a significant reduction in free testosterone index with age. They also reported no alteration with age in serum estrone or estradiol (Figures 7 and 8). Similarly, Zumoff et al. (1982) found no increase in SHBG binding fraction so that measurement of free testosterone index added no inde-

pendent information beyond that obtained from the total plasma testosterone.

The estrogen question is further complicated by the fact that most estrogen circulates as glucuronide or sulfate conjugates. When urinary excretion of estrogen conjugates is examined, the total estrogen excretion actually appears to decrease in aging men, as does the major estrogen conjugate, estrone sulfate, in plasma (Skoldefors et al., 1975). Myking et al. (1980) have found that although plasma unconjugated estrone and estradiol increased with age in men, estrone sulfate decreased and estradiol sulfate increased slightly. The total estrogens (all components) showed no net change.

Most androgen target tissues have the capacity to reduce testosterone to 5α-dihydrotestosterone (DHT), which then binds to cytoplasmic androgen receptors. DHT is the intracellular active androgen and can therefore be thought of as more potent than testosterone, while plasma testosterone may be considered a circulating reservoir of precursor

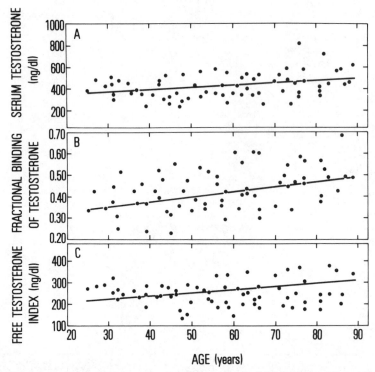

Figure 7. (A) Total serum testosterone concentrations in sera of 69 healthy male participants in the Baltimore Longitudinal Study on Aging, ages 25–80. (B) Fractional binding of testosterone to sex hormone binding globulin in these same men (C) Free testosterone indices of the same men (percent binding × total testosterone concentration). (From Harman and Tsitouras, 1980.)

androgen. DHT is also found in serum, with about 20 percent coming from direct testicular secretion and 80 percent from peripheral reduction of testosterone in cells containing 5α-reductase, followed by release from these (presumably target) cells into the circulation. Circulating DHT may thus be an indirect indicator of target tissue androgenic exposure. Giusti et al. (1975) reported reduced DHT as well as testosterone in testicular vein blood. Pirke and Doerr (1975b), Pazzagli et al. (1975), Hallberg et al. (1976), and Lewis et al. (1976) all found somewhat decreased DHT in peripheral vein blood of aging men. Pirke and Doerr (1975a) reported no significant change in total serum DHT, but decreased free DHT and an increase in DHT/testosterone ratio, suggesting more efficient reduction of testosterone to DHT with advancing age. Harman and Tsitouras (1980), Zumoff et al. (1982), and Nieschlag et al. (1982) did not see any change in DHT concentrations with age, while Horton et al. (1975) reported a significant increase in plasma DHT in a group of older men with a high incidence of benign prosratic hyperplasia, despite a decrease in the precursor testosterone.

The reasons for the wide variety of results obtained for plasma sex steroids of aging men in various studies are far from clear. It is possible that in some studies, altered sex steroid levels may represent effects of noncomparability of old and young study subjects for such variables as chronic illness, medications, obesity, alcohol intake, or environmental stress (all of which can affect plasma testosterone), rather than age *per se*. When only a single blood sample is examined, variance is increased due to the considerable minute-to-minute variation of plasma testosterone, reflecting episodic secretion. In addition, there is a pattern of diurnal variation, with a morning peak and lower afternoon plateau in plasma testosterone. A loss of the morning

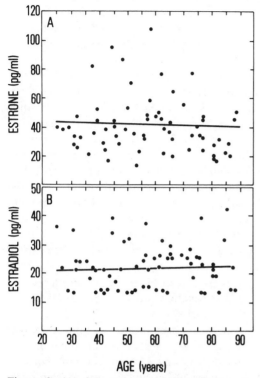

Figure 8. (A) Serum estrone concentrations in ELS men aged 25–80. (B) Serum estradiol concentrations in the same men. (From Harman and Tsitouras, 1980.)

peak in older men could result in the appearance of reduced plasma testosterone with age when morning samples are examined and no reduction when afternoon samples are compared (as by Harman and Tsitouras, 1980). Bremner and Prinz (1981) did, in fact, find a loss of diurnal testosterone peak in elderly men, so that morning but not afternoon values appeared to decrease with age. In contrast, Murono et al. (1982a) have found intact diurnal rhythm of testosterone in older men. The diurnal effect would not account for the observation of unchanged plasma testosterone in morning samples reported by Sparrow et al. (1980), Tsitouras et al. (1982), and Nieschlag et al. (1982). On the other hand, Zumoff et al. (1982) found significantly reduced 24-hour mean integrated plasma testosterone in older men, whom they described as healthy and ambulatory. The issue is not yet settled.

A number of investigators have used human chorionic gonadotropin (hCG) stimulation to compare Leydig cell reserve capacity in men of various ages. Frick (1969), Longcope (1973), and Mazzi et al. (1974) all found that although both baseline and peak testosterone levels were lower in older men, the percent response appeared to be unchanged with age. This finding is consistent with a reduced complement of normally responsive Leydig cells in older men. Rubens et al. (1974), Nieschlag et al. (1973), Nankin et al. (1981), and Nieschlag et al. (1982) all found reduced percent responses as well as absolute peak levels of testosterone after hCG stimulation. Nankin et al. (1981) state that both early (2–4 hours) and late (48–96 hours) testosterone response components were reduced in aging men and that younger men showed greater rises in 17α-hydroxyprogesterone and estradiol as well as in testosterone. When Harman and Tsitouras (1980) gave hCG to men whose baseline testosterone levels were age invariant, they also found decreased percent responses in the older men (Table 4). The results of hCG stimulation data favor the hypothesis that Leydig cell number and/or reserve secretory capacity is diminished with age in men.

Support for the concept of an androgen synthetic defect in the Leydig cells of aging men comes from experiments by Piotti et al. (1967) showing decreased activity of 3β-hydroxysteroid dehydrogenase (3β-OHSD), generally considered to be the rate-limiting enzyme in sex steroid synthesis, in testes of men over 72 years of age. Similarly, Axelrod (1965) reported a 63 percent decrease in 17–20 lyase

TABLE 4.   Serum Testosterone after Injection of hCG: Effect of Age on Response/Basal Ratio (from Harman and Tsitouras, 1980).

Group	Age	15-hr Post-hCG Mean ± S.E.	39-hr Post-hCG Mean ± S.E.
A	25–49	1.98 ± 0.13	2.20 ± 0.13
B	50–69	1.53 ± 0.09[a]	1.86 ± 0.11
C	70–89	1.55 ± 0.11[b]	1.76 ± 0.13[c]

[a]Different from group A, $p < 0.01$.
[b]Different from group A, $p < 0.02$.
[c]Different from group A, $p < 0.05$.

(desmolase) activity in testis of a 60-year-old man, compared with a 16-year-old male. Furthermore, the finding by Giusti et al. (1975) of reduced concentrations of testosterone but not androstenedione in testicular venous effluent suggests a deficiency of yet another enzyme, 17-keto reductase.

In contrast, Pirke et al. (1977) failed to find any alteration in the relative quantities of testosterone precursors in peripheral plasma with age, as would be expected if a particular enzyme were deficient. All steroids were significantly lower in the older group. The steroid ratios were not altered by stimulation with hCG. Murono et al (1982b), stimulating men with single injections of hCG, found older men to have absence of the early and late progesterone responses, which could easily be observed in young men. Older men had a small early peak of androstenedione, not detected in the young group, and both groups had a late androstenedione response which was smaller in the aged group, in both absolute and relative terms. Their study also failed to detect the alteration of precursor secretion which would be expected with a specific enzyme deficiency. Pirke et al. (1980), in another series of experiments, did find evidence of altered testicular steroid synthetic metabolism in older men. They reported an increase in testis tissue and spermatic vein blood progesterone and 17α-hydroxyprogesterone, relative to testosterone. Since incubation of testis tissue with hCG under hypoxic conditions resulted in a similar pattern of steroid secretion, they proposed that the arteriolar sclerosis previously reported by Sasano and Ichigo (1969) might be responsible for local hypoxia and hence Leydig cell dysfunction.

The metabolic fate of testosterone has also been investigated in aging men. Both Zumoff et al. (1976) and Desleypere, et al. (1981) found a lower ratio of ^{14}C-labeled urinary androsterone to etiocholanolone in aging men given ^{14}C-labeled testosterone. They suggested that this change might be an effect of higher estrogen levels on pathways of testosterone metabolism. Vermeulen et al. (1972) found a decrease in 5α-reduced testosterone metabolites, which they interpreted to reflect reduced testosterone availability to 5α-reductase con-

taining target tissues. They suggested that this might be an effect of increased plasma binding of testosterone to SHBG. Desleypere et al. (1981) confirmed the decrease with age in the ratio of 5α to 5β metabolites of both endogenous and also ^{14}C-labeled exogenous testosterone. This predominance of the 5β oxidation pathway occurred both in older men and in older women. Since, in women SHBG binding does not go up with age (estrogens decrease), the authors could not account for the metabolic alteration on the basis of increased SHBG binding and suggested that a primary decrease in the overall peripheral 5α-reductase activity might be the explanation. This work contrasts sharply with previously cited experiments in which the increased ratio of DHT/testosterone seemed to suggest an increase in the 5α reduction pathway (Pirke and Doerr, 1975a; Horton et al., 1975).

There have been various attempts to analyze the number and morphology of human Leydig cells. Sarjent and McDonald (1948) counted the number of Leydig cells per 100 seminiferous tubules in autopsy specimens and found a progressive reduction from age 20 on. Decreased Leydig cell numbers have also been reported by Tillenger (1957) and Frick (1969). Harbitz (1973b) and Kaler and Neaves (1978), using sophisticated morphometric techniques, confirmed these findings; however, Harbitz (1973b) commented that the greatest decrease in Leydig cell number was associated with protracted illness, particularly malignant neoplastic disease. In contrast to these data, Sniffen (1950) and Sokal (1964) found no decrease in number of Leydig cells with age, while Kothari and Gupta (1974) reported total Leydig cell mass to be increased in testes from their older men. It is unclear whether the reported decrease in Leydig cell mass or numbers is a true effect of age or whether it reflects a higher prevalence of debilitating disease in older men in some of the populations studied.

Another consideration with regard to androgens and their effects is whether target tissue sensitivity to these hormones may be altered with age. Although this question is difficult to answer in humans, the findings by Muta et al. (1981) that more testosterone is required to inhibit gonadotropin secretion in aged men, and by Desleypere and Vermeulen (1981) that binding of DHT to sex hormone responsive skin is reduced in older men, suggest that androgen responsiveness may be reduced with age. Shain and Axelrod (1973) and Greenstein (1979) have also reported reduced androgen receptor binding to prostate tissue of aged rats.

Use of laboratory animals to study the effects of age on Leydig cell function offers advantages in terms of the flexibility with which experiments can be designed and the availability of tissues and cells for more detailed examination. However, the investigator must be cautious not to generalize conclusions obtained from such experiments to human aging, since it appears that the patterns of hormone changes with age are very different from species to species and even from strain to strain.

The most thoroughly studied laboratory animal is the albino rat. It is clear from a large number of investigations that serum testosterone levels show a significant decrease by 15 months of age (Gray, 1978; Kaler and Neaves, 1981a) and by 20–24 months of age decline to less than half the concentration seen in mature male rats (Ghanadian et al., 1975). Simpkins et al. (1981) have found both a reduction in plasma testosterone and a loss of diurnal rhythm for testosterone in their aged Sprague-Dawley rats. At the same time, the diurnal variation of plasma progesterone was preserved and the height of the progesterone peak enhanced, leading them to speculate whether progesterone itself might be inhibiting testosterone secretion. Such a finding might also be explained by an enzymatic block in conversion of progesterone to 17α-hydroxyprogesterone in the older rats.

In contrast to humans, serum LH levels are diminished simultaneously with serum testosterone levels in the rat (Shaar et al., 1975; Riegle et al., 1977; Pirke et al., 1978, 1979b; Harman et al., 1978). Despite the hypogonadotropism, a number of investigators have questioned whether a primary defect in Leydig cell number or function might still contribute to the reduced plasma testosterone seen in the aged rat.

Although the early (<240 minutes) response of rat testis to hCG injection appears impaired (Chan et al., 1977; Miller and Riegle, 1978a; Pirke et al., 1979), stimulation *in vivo* with hCG for 3–7 days has generally resulted in restoration of plasma testosterone concentration of older rats to levels identical to those of similarly stimulated younger rats in the Wistar (Harman et al., 1978; Pirke et al., 1979a) or in the Long-Evans (Miller and Riegle, 1978b) strains. This restoration may occur as early as two hours after intravenous hCG injection (Harman et al., 1978). In contrast, using up to three weeks of hCG treatment, Lin et al. (1980) could not restore testosterone levels of their 24-month-old Sprague-Dawley rats to those seen in comparably treated controls.

Most authors are in agreement that the number of Leydig cells per testis is either unchanged or even somewhat increased in older rats (Pirke et al., 1978; Kaler and Neaves, 1981b; Lehmann et al., 1975). There is only one published report showing decreased Leydig cell mass (Bethea and Walker, 1979). Nonetheless, when teased testicular tissue (Chan et al., 1977) or suspensions of Leydig cells (Tsitouras et al., 1979; Pirke et al., 1978; Bethea and Walker, 1979; Lin et al., 1980) have been examined *in vitro,* in both unstimulated (baseline) and hCG responsive testosterone production rates per 10^6 Leydig cells appeared diminished in cells from older rats. Only Kaler and Neaves (1981) reported unchanged testosterone production by old rat Leydig cells *in vitro.* Tsitouras et al. (1980) have reported that *in vivo* pretreatment with, but not *in vitro* exposure to, hCG results in restoration of testosterone secretory responsivity of *in vitro* Leydig cells from old rats to levels comparable to Leydig cells of younger, treated rats. The effectiveness of *in vivo,* but not *in vitro,* hCG in reversing the "Leydig cell aging defect" may be related to the restoration of testicular blood flow with *in vivo* hCG treatment, noted by Pirke et al. (1979a).

Although Pirke et al. (1978) have reported a decrease in hCG binding to testis tissue, Tsitouras et al. (1979) found only a modest (30 percent) reduction in hCG binding to Leydig cell membranes. Other investigations have revealed no reduction in gonadotropin receptor binding *in vivo* (Pirke et al., 1978) or *in vitro* (Kaler and Neaves, 1981; Steger et al., 1979). Furthermore, the production rate of cAMP in response to hCG stimulation seems to be unimpaired in Leydig cells from older rats (Tsitouras et al., 1979; Chen et al., 1981), and the testosterone secretory response to cAMP analogues appears to be reduced (Lin et al., 1980; Tsitouras et al., 1980). These data suggest that the "aging" defect in the Leydig cell occurs beyond the step at which receptor-activated cyclase produces cAMP.

Total testicular 3β-OHSD activity has been reported to be decreased in old Long-Evans rats (Collins et al., 1972) but was restored to normal by *in vivo* hCG treatment (Leathem and Albrecht, 1974). In contrast, Lehmann et al. (1975) have described unaltered activities of testicular 3β-OHSD. 11β-OHSD, and 17β-OHSD in aged SPF rats. Chan et al. (1977) found that dissected testes of old Long-Evans rats, incubated with tritium-labeled progesterone, produced less testosterone and 5α-androstene-3α,17β-diol but similar amounts of 17α-hydroxyprogesterone, androstenedione, and 5α-DHT, and larger amounts of 7α-hydroxytestosterone (an inactive metabolite), when compared with young rat testes. They suggested that a shift to increased 7α hydroxylation might explain the lower testosterone production in older rats. Tsitouras, Harman, and Kowatch (unpublished observations) have data showing that the *in vitro* secretory defect for testosterone in Leydig cells of older rats resists supplementation of media with steroid intermediates, including the immediate testosterone precursor, androstenedione. This suggests that the "aging" Leydig cell defect may be a general debilitative effect rather than the lack of a particular enzyme in the steroid synthetic pathway. In contrast, Chen et al. (1981) reported that supplying either progesterone or pregnenolone reversed the impaired testosterone secretion in their *in vitro* Leydig cell system, suggesting an enzymatic defect prior to the 3β-OHSD step or precursor depletion as possible explanations for the reduced testosterone production rate.

Finally, although estrogens are known to reduce Leydig cell testosterone production by a mechanism probably involving cytoplasmic estrogen receptor, there are data to show that excess estrogen production is probably not the mechanism responsible for the reduced testosterone secretion by Leydig cells of older rats (Lin et al., 1981).

A number of studies of male reproductive aging have been carried out in laboratory mice. Eleftheriou and Lucas (1974) found no change with age in plasma testosterone or reproductive organ weights of C57BL/6J or DBA/2J mice. Finch et al. (1977) failed to demonstrate significant alterations in plasma testosterone or in testosterone response to hCG injection in C57BL/6J mice up to 28 months of age. Nelson et al. (1975) made the point that plasma testosterone and testicular weight decreased in diseased, but not in healthy, senescent C57BL/6J mice. In contrast, using the CBF_1 mouse, Bronson and Desjardins (1977) were able to demonstrate a correlation among progressive loss of mating success, decreased sperm production, and reduced serum testosterone in animals 18–30 months old. Analysis of their 24-month-old mice showed the existence of a subpopulation of sexually less robust aging males with hormone alterations not found in the more robust members of the same age cohort. As in the rat, these animals had reduced plasma LH concentrations.

In rabbits, Ewing et al. (1972) found a decrease with age in both plasma testosterone and testosterone production by isolated testes perfused with hCG containing media. In old dogs, Bondarenko et al. (1979) found reduced testicular secretion of testosterone and androstenedione into plasma, and diminished urinary excretion of androgen metabolites.

Gonadotropic Function

A modest but significant increase in excretion of urinary gonadotropins in aging men was first recorded by Pedersen-Bjergaard and Jonnesen (1948) using bioassay methods. This was confirmed by Albert (1956) and by Christiansen (1972), who reported that although both LH and FSH were elevated, the increase in FSH was more prominent. More recent studies, using radioimmunoassay methods, have nearly all demonstrated increased circulating gonadotropin concentrations in men after about age 50 (Haug et al., 1974; Mazzi et al., 1974; Rubens et al., 1974; Snyder et al., 1975; Hallberg et al., 1976; Baker et al., 1976; Stearns et al., 1974; Harman et al., 1982). Some subjects in their 80s and 90s had LH and FSH concentrations similar to those seen in postmenopausal women or castrate men. The elevations of plasma gonadotropin concentration appear to be due to increased secretion rather than diminished elimination of hormone, since the rate of clearance of LH from plasma appears to be age invariant (Kohler et al., 1968; Pepperell et al., 1975). This increase in gonadotropin secretion has been interpreted to be a secondary phenomenon due to a primary reduction in Leydig cell function with resulting decrease in sex steroid feedback

inhibition of the hypothalamic-pituitary axis. It has been suggested that the greater increase in FSH than LH may represent the independent regulation of FSH secretion by a seminiferous tubular factor (inhibin) which becomes deficient as tubular function decreases with age (Baker et al., 1976). This hypothesis is consistent with experiments showing significantly increased FSH but no increase in LH in healthy elderly men with unaltered (Sparrow et al., 1980) or even moderately decreased (Zumoff et al., 1982) plasma testosterone concentrations. In contrast, in similar subjects, Harman et al. (1982) measured increases in both serum FSH and LH levels, despite unchanged plasma sex steroid concentrations. The LH increase, they concluded, might represent compensation for a mild degree of Leydig cell failure (as demonstrated by decreased

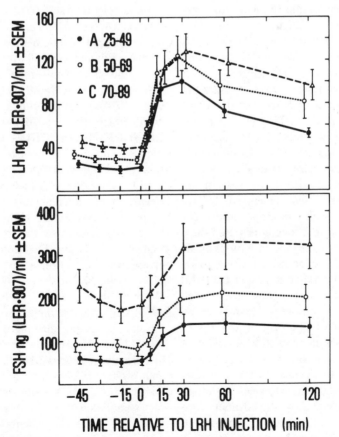

Figure 9. Mean serum gonadotropin concentrations before and up to 120 minutes after intravenous injection of a 200 μg bolus of LHRH into 69 male BLS subjects of various ages. *upper panel,* LH; *lower panel,* FSH. (From Harman et al., 1982.)

testosterone response to hCG), reduction in feedback sensitivity of the hypothalamic-pituitary axis (as suggested by Dilman and Anisimov, 1979), or a combination of both of these factors. Direct evidence for an age-related alteration in the feedback control of gonadotropin secretion comes from work by Muta et al. (1981) showing greater steroid dose requirements for inhibition of gonadotropin secretion in old versus young men.

On the other hand, the finding by Rubens et al. (1974) and others that plasma testosterone levels were decreased in their men despite demonstrated residual Leydig cell secretory capacity (in response to hCG injection) raises the question whether some limitation of gonadotropin responsiveness may develop in older men since they failed to secrete enough LH to return plasma testosterone concentrations to normal. Ryan (1962) reported increased LH content of male human pituitaries with age, eliminating exhaustion of pituitary hormone stores as an explanation for submaximal gonadotropic response. Use of luteinizing hormone releasing hormone (LHRH) to test pituitary secretory reserve for LH and FSH has given various results. Rubens et al., (1974) and Hashimoto et al. (1973) found percent, but not absolute incremental LH and FSH responses, to be diminished in older men. This was due to elevated basal levels (i.e., and increased denominator with no increase in the numerator). Since in young men, LHRH responses increase roughly in proportion to basal gonadotropin levels, they interpreted their results to mean that some diminution of pituitary LHRH responsiveness did occur with age. Haug et al. (1974) and Snyder et al. (1975) both reported decreases in absolute as well as relative LHRH responses. Harman et al. (1982), using repeated measures analysis of variance, found selected, healthy, elderly men to have smaller LH and FSH responses to LHRH than would be expected for their (elevated) basal gonadotropin levels. Although providing evidence of some impairment of pituitary gonadotropin secretory response, all of these studies document the existence of some pituitary gonadotropic reserve capacity. Therefore, the question of why, in those stud-

ies where plasma testosterone was diminished, the LH production did not increase enough to return testosterone concentrations to "normal" is still moot. That such compensation may sometimes occur is suggested by the study of Harman and Tsitouras (1980), who found normal serum testosterone with elevated basal LH levels. Its failure to occur in other studies may represent suppression of LH secretion by other plasma steroids (e.g., estrogens or DHT), a resetting of the hypothalamic "steroidostat" to accept somewhat lower levels of testosterone as normal, or disturbance of the hypothalamic-hypophyseal response to diminished steroids due to concomitant illness, general debilitation, or aging itself.

Use of clomiphene citrate (an estrogen antagonist) to block hypothalamic estrogen receptors and hence release gonadotropin secretion from steroid feedback inhibition is another way to test LH and FSH secretory reserve. Unlike LHRH infusion, clomiphene tests the hypothalamic neurosecretory as well as the pituitary secretory responses. When such tests have been done in elderly men (Mazzi et al., 1974; Natoli et al., 1972; Rubens et al., 1974), a reduction in LH response has been consistently found. However, since only LH and FSH (not LHRH) were measured, the tests did not distinguish between alterations at the hypothalamic versus the pituitary level (at the latter of which hyporesponsiveness is already documented).

Investigations in the male laboratory rat have nearly uniformly led to the conclusion that plasma LH and FSH concentrations decrease with age (Riegle and Meites, 1976; Gray, 1978; Shaar et al., 1975; Pirke et al., 1979b, Bruni et al., 1977; Bethea and Walker, 1979). Only Kaler and Neaves (1981) reported LH concentrations unchanged. Pituitary content of LH and FSH also appears to be reduced in old male rats (Pirke et al., 1979b; Bethea and Walker, 1979; Riegle and Meites, 1976; Riegle et al., 1977). Compared with young rats, stimulation of aged male rats with LHRH produced smaller incremental LH responses when a single bolus injection was given (Riegle and Meites, 1976; Bruni et al., 1977), but percent responses were about the same. When a series of nine 50 ng injections were given at 26-minute intervals (Bruni et al., 1977), older animals remained hyporesponsive; however, three 500 ng injections restored LH responsivity of old rats to normal levels (Riegle and Miller, 1978). When old male rats are castrated, the plasma LH and FSH increase less rapidly and never attain the peak levels seen in castrated young rats (Shaar et al., 1975; Gray et al., 1980a). Furthermore, in both of these studies, old castrated rats showed greater sensitivity to inhibition of LH secretion by testosterone than their younger counterparts. Experiments with isolated pituitary tissue in vitro (Riegle et al., 1977) showed an age-related reduction in LH secretion after 4 hours of LHRH stimulation. Similarly, pituitary cell suspensions from old rats with 24-hour preincubation produced less LH, FSH, and free alpha subunit both basally and after 48-hour stimulation with LHRH. Percent responses were similar. Preparations from castrate rats produced more LH, FSH, and alpha than those from intacts, but the difference between old and young rat cells was maintained (Blackman et al., 1981). All of these data are more or less consistent with the hypothesis that although hypofunction of rat pituitary gonadotrophs occurs with age, this probably results from chronically insufficient stimulation with LHRH as a result of altered hypothalamic physiology.

Further evidence for this hypothesis exists in various studies of hypothalamic function and biochemistry demonstrating reduced bioassayable (Riegle et al., 1977) and immunoassayable (Harman, Pribitkin, Wise, Blackman, unpublished) LHRH in ventral hypothalami of old male rats, altered hypothalamic content and turnover rates of dopamine, serotonin, and catecholamines (Simpkins et al., 1976; Harman, Pribitkin, Wise, and Blackman, unpublished), and partial normalization of reproductive endocrine parameters when neurotransmitters, their precursors, or blocking drugs are administered to old rats (Meites et al., 1978). There is also evidence that the binding capacity of hypothalamic steroid receptors may be reduced in aged male rats (Haji et al., 1981; Greenstein, 1979). A more complete discussion of effects of age on neuroendocrine function is found elsewhere in this volume.

Studies of hypothalamic-pituitary function in C57BL/6J mice showed no age-related changes in circulating concentrations of gonadotropins or prolactin (PRL), no alterations in LH response to LHRH in vivo or of pituitary cells after four days in vitro, but a somewhat smaller postcastration LH rise in 28- than in 12-month-old males (Finch et al., 1977). In CBF_1 mice, longitudinal cohort analysis revealed the development of a subgroup of aging animals with reduced LH levels and loss of the episodic LH release pattern (Bronson and Desjardins, 1977). When longer-lived wild mice (Peromyscus leucopus) were studied, no significant changes in circulating gonadotropins were observed, but hypothalamic LHRH content did decrease between 36 and 42 months of age (Steger et al., 1980b).

The role of altered PRL secretion as a cause and/or effect of age-related changes in reproductive hormone regulation is unclear. In men (Vekemans and Robyn, 1975; Robyn, 1975), there may be a modest rise in basal serum PRL levels with age. Hossdorf and Wagner (1980), however, found no change in basal PRL levels, but demonstrated a significantly higher and later PRL peak response to thyrotropin releasing hormone (TRH) stimulation in older men. Murri et al. (1980) have found that the diurnal rhythm for PRL, studied in 12 subjects aged 62–78, was similar to that in young men. Although clinical hyperprolactinemia is associated with hypogonadism and impotence (Carter et al., 1978), the degree of change observed in these studies of aging men is not sufficient to produce a decrease in reproductive capacity.

In aging male rats, the basal levels of plasma PRL have been shown to be elevated (Bethea and Walker, 1979; Saksena and Lau, 1979) or unchanged (Shaar et al., 1975; Riegle and Meites, 1976). The latter investigators did find prolactin secretion in aged rats to be less sensitive to inhibition by L-dopa than that of younger animals. Furthermore hypothalami of aged male rats displayed less PRL inhibiting activity *in vitro* than did those of younger animals (Riegle et al., 1977). Available data thus suggest that altered hypothalamic function in old male rats may result in a reciprocal decrease in LH secretion and increase in PRL secretion.

Accessory Organs of Reproduction

Prostate Gland. At puberty, under the influence of increasing androgen secretion, the (initially minimal) glandular component of the human prostate gland develops active secretory alveoli with a tall columnar epithelium. These alveoli contribute their secretion to the ejaculate, adding numerous enzymes, citric acid, and zinc. After about age 40, the columnar cells tend to become more cuboidal, and muscle tissue in the stroma is progressively replaced by collagen (Moore, 1952). Jahn et al. (1971) have shown progressively decreased total protein and water content, with increase in the collagen/total protein ratio in prostates of men aged 17–89. Atrophic changes are initially focal but spread to involve most of the gland by age 60–70. Accumulation of stagnant secretions in acini may lead to the formation of the laminated hyaline bodies called corpora amylaceae, commonly seen after age 65. There is prominent deposition of lipofuscin-like yellow pigment in epithelial cells (Brandes, 1966), and thickening and reduplications of the acinar basement membrane (Mao and Angrist, 1966). Biochemical and functional changes have been shown to accompany the histological alterations. The extent to which these changes are caused by androgen deprivation versus aging *per se* is unclear. In prostate nuclei, Mainwaring (1968a) has described decreased DNA primed RNA synthesis with reduction in nuclear content of nonhistone proteins and loss of template activity for RNA polymerase. He also reported an increase in cytoplasmic ribonuclease which he felt was responsible for disaggregation of polysomes and a loss of sedimentable RNA from the microsomal fraction. These changes would be expected to result in decreased protein synthesis. In fact, a decrease in human prostate protein synthesis *in vitro* has been observed

(Mainwaring, 1967) as has a reduction in enzyme-mediated citric acid production (Mainwaring, 1968b).

The issue of normal aging of the human prostate is obscured by the nearly universal occurrence of benign nodular hyperplasia (BPH) in the prostates of older men. This lesion consists of focal (adenomatous) proliferations of the stromal and glandular tissue. The primary origin of the hyperplasia has been a matter of debate, but the histological appearance of the earliest lesions favors the hypothesis that nodules begin first with stromal proliferation. The earliest hyperplastic changes tend to occur in the periurethral area (Harbitz and Haugen, 1972). The process then spreads laterally into the medial and lateral (but generally not the posterior) lobes. The parts of the gland affected are embryologically homologous to the female prostatic utricle and incorporate tissue which in the female contributes to formation of the myometrium. Furthermore, it is known that stromal fibromuscular prostate tissue responds to estrogens, while glandular tissue is more sensitive to androgens. Recently, estrogen receptors have been identified in hyperplastic human prostate tissue (Bashirelahi et al., 1976). Gasparyan and Portnoy (1970) have suggested that prostatic tumors might occur as a result of an increase of the estrogen/androgen ratio in plasma of aging men. According to this hypothesis, increased estrogen activity would stimulate stromal hyperplasia, and glandular proliferation would then follow along as acinar elements become incorporated in the expanding nodules.

The precise role of the hormonal milieu in mediating BPH is not clear; however, it is well known that the presence of functioning testes is a prerequisite for development of the lesion. Efforts to discover a definite hormone pattern associated with BPH have been disappointing. There is one report of increased plasma DHT testosterone, LH, FSH, and estrogens in the blood of men with BPH (Baranowska et al. 1980) and another of increased PRL but no change in gonadotropins and a lower serum testosterone (Ortega et al., 1979). Saroff et al. (1980) also found elevated plasma

PRL in BPH patients with lower testosterone and DHT levels than in age-matched controls. Rolandi et al. (1980) agreed that PRL secretion seemed increased in men with BPH and found no changes in LH or FSH. Hammond et al. (1979b) reported that basal LH was significantly lower in men with BPH than in age-matched controls, but that FSH and PRL did not differ. After prostatectomy, LH levels rose to values not significantly different from control. LHRH testing revealed slightly diminished LH responsiveness in men with BPH. This finding also disappeared postprostatectomy. The authors suggested that some product of hyperplastic prostate tissue, possibly DHT, might be suppressing pituitary LH secretion. Bartsch et al. (1979) were unable to demonstrate any differences in serum T, DHT, LH, or PRL in men with BPH, but reported elevated DHT levels and lower 3α, 17β-androstanediol. On the basis of these findings, they suggested that hyperplastic tissue converts testosterone preferentially to DHT and less to 3α, 17β-androstanediol, with release of the excess DHT into the circulation. Using injections of ^{14}C-labeled testosterone, and ^{3}H-labeled androstanediol (3α-diol), Morimoto et al. (1980) found that blood production rate of testosterone was reduced by nearly half in elderly men with prostate hyperplasia compared with young men. Production rate of 3α-diol was down by about one-third. Conversion of testosterone to 5α-DHT was about the same in both groups, but conversion of 5α-DHT to 3α-diol was reduced in the old group, and conversion of 3α-diol to 5α-DHT was increased. These investigators suggested that aging may favor metabolism of steroid precursors to 3α-diol which is then preferentially converted to 5α-DHT, which then stimulates prostatic hyperplasia.

Recently, Wilson (1980) proposed a hypothetical mechanism for induction of BPH based on studies of the canine prostate. According to this hypothesis, estrogen causes an increase in prostatic androgen receptor content, thus sensitizing the prostate tissue to the effects of androgens. The increase in androgen response would promote enhanced 5α-reductase activity with a resultant increase in conversion of testosterone to DHT. The DHT would then stimulate glandular hyperplasia. It is clear that estrogen is synergistic with androgen in the experimental induction of prostate hyperplasia in dogs (Walsh and Wilson, 1976; DeKlerk et al., 1979), that estrogen induces increased androgen receptor capacity in canine prostate (Moore et al., 1979), and that increased androgen receptors are also found in spontaneous canine BPH (Trachtenberg and Walsh, 1980). In contrast to the canine data, however, Trachtenberg et al. (1982) were unable to demonstrate any increase in androgen receptors in hyperplastic human prostate tissue. The idea of an increase in DHT content and production in BPH, on the other hand, is well supported by experimental evidence in both dog and human. Siiteri and Wilson (1970) have found the concentration of DHT to be increased fivefold in hypertrophic human prostate glands. Gloyna et al. (1970) reported that canine prostates with BPH also had increased DHT content, but they could not find evidence of an increase in rate of formation or metabolism of DHT. Isaacs and Coffey (1981), however, did find that canine BPH, whether spontaneous or induced by treatment with estrogens and androgens, was associated with an increase in net prostatic ability to form DHT. This finding is consistent with the results of Shain and Nitchuk (1979b) and of Bruchovsky and Lieskovsky (1979) showing increased 5α-reductase activity in hyperplastic canine and human prostates, and also with reports that plasma DHT is increased in dogs or men with BPH (Lloyd et al., 1975; Geller et al., 1976; Habib et al., 1976; Bartsch et al., 1979). Nonetheless, it is still not known whether excess DHT produces prostatic hyperplasia or is simply a product of increase in prostate tissue. The role of PRL is even less clear. Ron et al., (1981) found relatively high concentrations of PRL in hyperplastic human prostate, but whether PRL helps to mediate hyperplasia is, as yet, unknown.

Investigation of aging in the rat prostate is simplified by the fact that, unlike humans and dogs, rats do not develop hyperplasia. With increasing age, rat prostate shows a reduced uptake of testosterone (Ghanadian and Fotherby, 1975). This appears to be a result of reductions in both cytoplasmic and nuclear androgen receptors (Shain et al., 1975). At the same time, there is a shift from reductive to oxidative metabolism of steroids, leading to diminished production of DHT (Shain and Nitchuk, 1979a; Djoseland et al., 1981), and a progressive loss of RNA and DNA content (Ghanadian and Fotherby, 1975). Thus, all of the changes demonstrated appear to be involutional. The extent to which these changes are intrinsic to the prostate or are effects of the demonstrated decrease in plasma testosterone in aging rats is not yet clear, but Boesel et al. (1980) have reported that testosterone injections in senescent rats restore prostate androgen receptor content to levels comparable to those of young rats.

Epididymis. It is surprising that so little work has been done on the aging of the epididymis, when one considers its important role in sperm maturation. Clermont and Flannery (1970) studied mitotic activity in the epithelium of rats from 2½ to 12 months of age and noted a very significant decline in the thymidine labeling indices of both basal and principal cells, with a decrease in mitotic index as well. Mainwaring and Brandes (1974) have reviewed the ultrastructural changes occurring with age in epididymis. These consist of a gradual loss of columnar appearance of the principal cells, which assume a more cuboidal shape with age, and the deposition of pigment granules in epithelial cells. These granules have the morphological and histochemical properties of secondary lysosomes, autophagic vacuoles, and lipofuscin. Similar changes have been described in the epididymis of aging rats by Cran and Jones (1980). Djoseland et al. (1981) have reported that when tritiated testosterone is given, the accumulation of 5α-DHT in epididymal tissue is less in 25-month than in 3-month-old rats and that epididymal homogenates show reduced 5α-reductase activity in older animals.

Seminal Vesicle. Nilsson (1962) made a detailed study of morphological age changes in the human seminal vesicle. He found little al-

teration from childhood to puberty. In adults, the fluid capacity of the gland increases progressively from the teens (1.75 ml) to about age 60 (5 ml), then diminishes in the 70s and 80s (about 2.2 ml).

In prepubertal boys, the wall of the seminal vesicle is quite thick compared to the lumen. With age, the lumen expands and the number of mucosal folds tends to decrease. At the same time, the epithelium decreases in height and the subepithelial muscular layer is gradually replaced by connective tissue. Andrew (1971) reported that lipofuscin granules accumulate with increasing age in columnar but not in the basal epithelial cells, and Goldman (1963) observed that amyloid is frequently seen in seminal vesicle walls of men past middle age.

In the C57BL mouse, Finch and Girgis (1975) observed that the seminal vesicle became greatly enlarged with age in over 60 percent of the animals studied. This was due to cystic dilatation, the empty gland weighing no more than that of young animals. Epithelium of the dilated seminal vesicles was atrophic, and no cause of the fluid accumulation was defined. In rats, Kruszel (1967) has reported that although fructose content of seminal vesicle fluid did not appear to vary with age from puberty to 80 weeks, citric acid, a sensitive indicator of androgenic stimulation of the gland, reached a maximum at 12 to 20 weeks of age, then declined gradually thereafter. Djoseland et al. (1981) have described diminished tissue accumulation of 5α-DHT and reduced conversion of tritiated testosterone to 5α-DHT in seminal vesicles of 25-month-old rats.

Penis. Tyukov (1967) found that the first indications of involutionary changes occur in the penis of 30- to 40-year-old men. The initial alterations consist of fibroelastosis of the trabeculae in the corpus spongiosum, followed by progressive sclerosis of both small arteries and veins. Similar sclerotic changes follow in the corpora cavernosa, so that the condition becomes generalized in 55- to 60-year-old men. The author suggests that the changes he observed may be related to the high incidence of age-associated impotence.

Sexual Activity in the Male

The first reliable data on sexual activity in aging men came from Kinsey et al. (1948). They found that sexual activity, measured as mean number of reported ejaculations per week, decreased progressively after age 30 from about 3/week to less than 0.5/week by age 70 and near 0 by age 80. At the same time, the incidence of erectile impotence increased to include a majority of men by age 75. Martin (1977) has confirmed a steady decrease in reported sexual activity of middle-class white males from 600 sexual events/5 years in their 30s to less than 100 events/5 years in their late 60s. In the age range 65–79, the majority of men interviewed reported less than 100 sexual events/5 years. Martin (1981) found that in healthy elderly men, sexual frequency was not significantly correlated with a wide range of social, psychological, and biological variables such as measures of religiosity, economic class at birth, lean body mass, grip strength, alcohol use, etc. There was a strong correlation with characteristic sexual frequency in youth and weak correlations with maximal breathing capacity, chest circumference, and basal metabolic rate were found. Decline of sexual performance as well as interest with age in men has also been reported by Newman and Nichols (1960) and by Pfeiffer and Davis (1972). These investigators found the general health of their male subjects to be the first most important variable, and the health of surviving spouse to be the next most important variable, in determining the level of sexual activity of aging men. There was a lower rate of decrease of sexual activity in a selected group of healthy men (Pfeiffer et al., 1969, 1972). In all these studies, the interest in sex reported by men tended to be maintained better than actual activity. In a longitudinal study, over a period of eight years, Verwoerdt et al. (1969) found a pattern of decreasing sexual activity similar to that reported for cross-sectional studies, thus eliminating such confounding factors as the generational differences in sexual activity (at the same age) described by Hunt (1974).

Besides changes in sexual behavior, there are also age-related alterations in male sexual physiology. Masters and Johnson (1966) summarized these as: increased length of time to obtain full erection, longer plateau phase, slower and less forceful ejaculatory contractions, diminished skin flush, nipple erection, and testis enlargement (vasocongestive responses), more rapid detumescence, and a longer refractory period. Karacan et al. (1975) have shown a small, but statistically significant and progressive, decrease with age in nocturnal penile tumescence time, as a percentage both of total sleep and of REM sleep, in aging men. These findings suggest that there is some organic basis for altered sexual performance with age and that the phenomenon is not likely to be entirely due to social, psychological, or even "general health" variables.

The relationship of sexual activity in aging men to sex steroid hormone levels remains unclear. Some minimum level of testosterone is needed to maintain human male sexual activity and desire (Davidson et al., 1979). As shown in Figure 10, there does appear to be a tendency for older men with low levels of sexual activity to have lower concentrations of serum testosterone (Tsitouras et al., 1982; Vermeulen, 1979), despite the fact that there is no correlation of sexual activity and testosterone concentration (within the normal range) in younger men. Various interpretations of this relationship are possible. It may mean that higher levels of testosterone are needed to overcome a resistance to testosterone action which develops with age (possibly as a result of loss of receptors, discussed earlier). It may mean that sexual activity itself helps to increase testosterone secretion in older men. Other interpretations are also possible. Therefore, the presently available data should not be taken to suggest that administration of testosterone to elderly men will improve sexual performance. Components other than endocrine (i.e., neurologic, vascular, psychological, and constitutional factors as yet undefined) undoubtedly play a vital role in the phenomenon of decreasing male sexual performance with age. The precise contribution of these various factors remains to be elucidated.

It has been observed that sexual activity is diminished with age in male mice (Franks

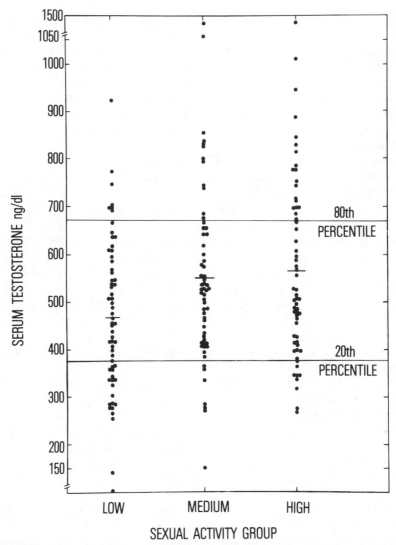

Figure 10. Individual and mean serum testosterone concentrations in 180 BLS men, aged 60–79, divided into tertiles by level of sexual activity in comparison with men in the same half-decade. (From Tsitouras et al., 1982.)

and Payne, 1970; Bronson and Desjardins, 1977; Huber et al., 1980). This decline appeared to be related to a decrease in plasma testosterone in experiments by Bronson and Desjardins (1977), but not to any general failure of neural arousal, muscular endurance, or specific pathology of the reproductive system (Huber et al., 1980). Huber and Bronson (1980) have also reported that aged mice with poor initial sexual response to estrous females will partially recover this response with repeated exposure to females. They suggested

that this phenomenon may reflect induction of increased testosterone secretion with exposure to estrous females, a mechanism known to occur in rodents. The pertinence of these findings to human studies is unknown.

CONCLUSIONS

The mammalian reproductive organs undergo many age-related changes which are similar to those occurring in other organs and tissues. However, this system is uniquely dependent on a complex interaction of hormones secreted by the hypothalamus, anterior pituitary, and gonads for its continuing function. The pattern of changes which occur in these hormones during the period of reproductive decline is not yet completely understood, but it is already obvious that there are major species differences during this period, both in the male and in the female.

During the past few years, technical advances have been made which have helped to clarify the interaction of the hypothalamus and pituitary in the control of reproduction. These advances have recently been applied to investigations of the effects of aging on the regulation of the reproductive systems of humans and animals. Highly sensitive and discriminating methods for the study of hormone levels in the blood have revealed alterations in sex hormone secretory patterns with age which are both species and sex specific and which reflect various degrees of failure of the normal secretory physiology of ovaries, testes, pituitary, and hypothalamus. Far less is known about age changes in the ability of target organs to respond to these hormones, although considerable evidence now exists that such alterations occur. In some cases, decreases in hormone receptor capacity have been documented, but alterations of post-receptor cell physiology also seems to be of great importance. Further extension of studies of the responses of target cells of aged individuals with regard to cyclic AMP formation, calcium flux, enzyme activation and synthesis, and hormone specific gene activation may prove to be extremely valuable in elucidating the mechanisms, not only of reproductive aging, but of aging in general.

It is still not possible to fully evaluate the contribution of genetic and chromosomal abnormalities in gametes to reproductive failure in the human, since many losses occur prior to, or immediately following, implantation. However, there is enough evidence from experimental animals, abortions, and births of defective infants to indicate that the aging of the mother and "microaging" of the gametes may be of considerable importance.

Only through a more thorough understanding of all aspects of the aging of the male and female reproductive systems will it be possible to improve the chances of conception and safe delivery in the later reproductive years and also to maintain better physical and mental health in the postreproductive period.

REFERENCES

Adams, C. E. 1970. Ageing and reproduction in the female mammal with particular reference to the rabbit. *J. Reprod. Fertil. Suppl.* 12: 1–16.

Albert, A. 1956. Human urinary gonadotropins. *Recent Prog.* Hormone Res. 12: 227–301.

Albrecht, E. D., Koos, R. D., and Gottleib, S. F. 1977. Pregnant mare serum and human chorionic gonadotropin stimulate ovarian Δ^5-3β-hydroxysteroid dehydrogenase in aged mice. *Fertil. Steril.* 28: 762–765.

Albrecht, E. D., Koos, R. D., and Wehrenberg, W. B. 1975. Ovarian Δ^5-3β-hydroxysteroid dehydrogenase and cholesterol in the aged mouse during pregnancy. *Biol. Reprod.* 13: 158–162.

Andrew, W. G. 1971. *The Anatomy of Aging in Man and Animals*, p. 286. New York: Grune & Stratton.

Antunes, C. M. F., Stolley, P. D., Rosenshein, N. B., Davies, J. L., Tonascia, J. A., Brown, C., Burnett, L., Rutledge, A., Pokempner, M., and Garcia, R. 1979. Endometrial cancer and estrogen use: report of a large case-control study. *N. Engl. J. Med.* 300: 9–13.

Aschheim, P. 1961. La pseudogestation a repetition chez les rattes seniles. *C. R. Acad. Sci.* 253: 1988–1993.

Aschheim, P. 1964–65. Resultats fournis par la greffeheterochrome des ovaires dans l'etude de la regulation hypothalamo-hypophyso-ovarienne de la ratte senile. *Gerontologia* 10: 65–70.

Aschheim, P. 1976. Aging in the hypothalamic-hypophyseal ovarian axis in the rat. *In*, A. V. Everett and J. A. Burgess (eds.), *Hypothalamus, Pituitary, and Aging*, pp. 376–418. Springfield, Ill.: Charles C Thomas.

Aschheim, P. 1979. Function of the aging ovary: comparative aspects. *Eur. J. Obstet. Gynecol. Reprod. Biol.* 9: 191–202.

Asdell, S. A., Bogart, R., and Sperling, G. 1941. The influence of age and rate of breeding upon the ability of the female rat to reproduce and raise young. *Mem. Cornell Univ. Agr. Exp. Sta.* No. 238.

Axelrod, L. R. 1965. Metabolic patterns of steroid biosynthesis in young and aged human testis. *Biochim. Biophys. Acta* 97: 551–556.

Azzopardi, J. G. 1978. *Problems in Breast Pathology*, pp. 17–21. London: Saunders.

Baker, H. W. G., Burger, H. G., DeKretser, D. M., Hudson, B., O'Connor, S., Wang, C., Mirovics, A., Court, J., Dunlop, M., and Rennie, G. C. 1976. Changes in the pituitary testicular system with age. *Clin. Endocrinol.* 5: 349–372.

Bal, H. S. and Getty, R. 1973. Changes in the histomorphology of the uterus of the domestic pig (*Sus scrofa domesticus*) with advancing age. *J. Geront.* 28: 160–172.

Baranowska, B., Zgliczynski, S., and Szymanski, J. 1980. Hormonal disturbances in men with prostatic adenoma. *J. Urol. (Paris)* 86: 551–558.

Bartsch, W., Becker, H., Pinkenburg, F. A., and Krieg, M. 1979. Hormone blood levels and their inter-relationships in normal men and men with benign prostatic hyperplasia (BPH). *Acta Endocrinol. (Kbh.)* 90: 727–736.

Bashirelahi, N., O'Toole, J. H., and Young, J. D. 1976. A specific 17β estradiol receptor in human benign hypertrophic prostate. *Biochem. Med.* 15: 254–261.

Bates, G. W. 1981. On the nature of the hot flash. *Clin. Obstet. Gynecol.* 24: 231–241.

Benjamin, F. and Deutsch, S. 1980. Immunoreactive plasma estrogens and vaginal hormone cytology in postmenopausal women. *Int. J. Gynaecol.* 17: 546–550.

Benköel, L., Pautrat, G., Rolland, P. H., Martin, P., Casanova, P., Donadey, C., and Laffarque, P. 1980. Stimulation by hCG of ovarian stroma cells of menopausal women—an *in vitro* study. *Cell. Mol. Biol.* 26: 515–523.

Bethea, C. L. and Walker, R. F. 1979. Age-related changes in reproductive hormones and in Leydig cell responsivity in the male Fisher 344 rat. *J. Gerontol.* 34: 21–27.

Biggers, J. D. 1969. Problems concerning the uterine causes of embryonic death with special reference to the effects of ageing on the uterus. *J. Reprod. Fertil. Suppl.* 8: 27–43.

Biggers, J. D., Finn, C. A., and McLaren, A. 1962a. Long term reproductive performance of female mice. II. Variation of litter size with parity. *J. Reprod. Fertil.* 3: 313–330.

Biggers, J. D., Finn, C. A., and McLaren, A. 1962b. Long term reproductive performance of female mice. I. Effect of removing one ovary. *J. Reprod. Fertil.* 3: 303–312.

Bishop, M. W. H. 1970. Aging and reproduction in the male. *J. Reprod. Fertil. Suppl.* 12: 65–87.

Blackman, M. R., Mukherjee, A., and Harman, S. M. 1981. Age related reduction in the *in vitro* secretion of LH, FSH, and free α subunits by pituitary cells from intact and castrate male rats. *Endocrine Society, 63rd Annual Meeting,* Abstract 810.

Blaha, G. C. 1964a. Reproductive senescence in the female golden hamster. *Anat. Record,* 150: 405–412.

Blaha, G. C. 1964b. Effect of age of the donor and recipient on the development of transferred golden hamster ova, *Anat. Record* 150: 413–416.

Blaha, G. C. 1967. Effects of age, treatment, and method of induction on deciduomata in the golden hamster. *Fertil. Steril.* 18: 477–485.

Blaha, G. C. 1968. The effect of grafted ovaries on the implantation and development of transferred ova in aged and young golden hamsters. *Anat. Record* 160: 318.

Blaha, G. C. and Leavitt, W. W. 1974. Ovarian steroid dehydrogenase histochemistry and circulating progesterone in aged golden hamsters during the estrous cycle and pregnancy. *Biol. Reprod.* 11: 153–161.

Blaha, G. C. and Leavitt, W. W. 1978. Uterine progesterone receptors in the aged golden hamster. *J. Geront.* 33: 810–814.

Block, E. 1952. Quantitative morphological investigations of the follicular system in women, Variations at different ages. *Acta. Anat.* 14: 108–123.

Block, E. 1953. A quantitative morphological investigation of follicular system in newborn female infants. *Acta. Anat.* 17: 201–206.

Blum, V. 1936. Das Problem des mannlichen Klimakteriums. *Wien. Klin. Wochnschr.* 2: 1133–1140.

Boesel, R. W., Klipper, R. W., and Shain, S. A. 1980. Androgen regulation of androgen receptor content and distribution in the ventrolateral prostates of aging AXC rats. *Steroids* 35: 157–177.

Bondarenko, L. A., Vartapetov, B. A., and Gladova, A. I. 1979. Comparative evaluation of secretion of testicular androgens and excretion of their metabolites in young and old dogs. *Probl. Endokrinol. (Mosk.)* 25: 78–80.

Boston Collaborative Drug Surveillance Program, Boston University Medical Center. 1974. Surgically confirmed gallbladder disease, venous thromboembolism, and breast tumors in relation to postmenopausal estrogen therapy. *N. Engl. J. Med.* 290: 15–19.

Bowden, D. M. and Jones, M. E. 1979. Aging research in non-human primates. *In,* D. M. Bowden (ed.), *Aging in Non-human Primates,* pp. 1–13. New York: Van Nostrand Reinhold.

Brandes, D. 1966. Lysosomes and aging pigment. *In,* P. L. Krohn (ed.), *Topics in the Biology of Aging,* pp. 149–158. New York: Interscience.

Bremner, W. J. and Prinz, P. N. 1981. The diurnal rhythm in testosterone levels is lost with aging in normal men. *Endocrine Soc. 63rd Annual Meeting,* Abstract 480, p. 202.

Bronson, F. H. and Desjardins, C. 1977. Reproductive failure in aged CBF male mice: interrelationships between pituitary gonadotropic hormones, testicular function, and mating success. *Endocrinology* 101: 939–945.

Bruchovsky, N. and Lieskovsky, G. 1979. Increased ratio of 5α-reductase∶3α-(β)-hydroxysteroid dehydrogenase activities in the hyperplastic human prostate. *J. Endocrinol,* 80: 289–301.

Bruni, J. F., Huang, H. H., Marshall, S., and Meites, J. 1977. Effects of single and multiple injections of synthetic GnRH on serum LH, FSH, and testosterone in young and old male rats. *Biol. Reprod.* 17: 309–312.

Buckman, M. T., Johnson, J., Ellis, H., Srivastava, L., and Peake, G. T. 1980. Differential lipemic and proteinemic response to oral ethinyl estradiol and parenteral estradiol cypionate. *Metabolism* 29: 803–805.

Burack, E. and Wolfe, J. M. 1959. The effect of anterior hypophyseal administration on the ovaries of old rats. *Endocrinology* 64: 676–684.

Burch, J. C., Byrd, B. F., and Vaughn, W. K. 1975.

The effects of long-term estrogen administration to women following hysterectomy. *Front. Horm. Res.* 3: 208–211.

Burgi, Von H. and Hedinger, C. 1959. Histologische Hodenveranderung im hohen Alter. *Schweiz Med. Wochschr.* 89: 1236–1239.

Bynum, G., Becker, D., and Schneider, E. Examination of the effect of paternal aging on human meiotic chromosomal nondisjunction. Personal communication.

Carter, J. N., Tyson, J. G., Tolis, G., VanVliet, S., Faiman, C., and Friesen, H. G. 1978. Prolactin secreting tumors and hypogonadism in 22 men. *N. Engl. J. Med.* 299: 847–852.

Chan, S. W. C., Leathem, J. H., and Esashi, T. 1977. Testicular metabolism and serum testosterone in aging male rats. *Endocrinology* 101: 128–133.

Chang, W. and Roth, G. S. 1979. Changes in the mechanisms of steroid action during aging. *J Steroid Biochem.* 11: 889–892.

Chen, G. C. C., Lin, T., Murono, E., Osterman, J., Cole, B. T., and Nankin, H. R. 1981. The aging Leydig cell. 2. Two distinct populations of Leydig cells and the possible site of defective steroidogenesis. *Steroids* 37: 63–72.

Christiansen, P. 1972. Urinary follicle stimulating hormone and luteinizing hormone in normal adult men. *Acta Endocrinol. (Kbh.),* 71: 1–6.

Clemens, J. A., Amenomori, Y., Jenkins, T., and Meites, J. 1969. Effects of hypothalamic stimulation, hormones, and drugs on ovarian function in old female rats. *Proc. Soc. Exp. Biol. Med.* 132: 561–563.

Clermont, Y. and Flannery, J. 1970. Mitotic activity in the epithelium of the epididymis in young and old adult rats. *Biol. Reprod.* 3: 283–292.

Coble, Y. D., Jr., Kohler, P. O., Cargille, C. M., and Ross, G. T. 1969. Production rates and metabolic clearance rates of human follicle stimulating hormone in premenopausal and postmenopausal women. *J. Clin. Invest.* 48: 359–363.

Collins, P. M., Bell, J. B., and Tsang, W. N. 1972. The effect of vasectomy on steroid metabolism by the seminiferous tubules and interstitial tissue of the rat testis—a comparison with the effects of aging. *J Endocrinol.* 55: xviii–xix.

Coope, J. 1976. Double blind crossover study of estrogen replacement therapy. *In,* S. Campbell (ed.), *The Management of the Menopause and Post-menopausal Years,* pp. 159–172. Lancaster, England: MTP Press.

Cooper, R. L., Conn, P., and Walker, R. F. 1980. Characterization of the LH surge in middle-aged female rats. *Biol. Reprod.* 23: 611–615.

Coppage, W. S. and Cooner, A. E. 1965. Testosterone in human plasma. *N. Engl. J. Med.* 273: 902–905.

Costoff, A. and Mahesh, V. B. 1975. Primordial follicles with normal oocytes in the ovaries of postmenopausal women. *J. Am. Geriatr. Soc.* 23: 193–196.

Craig, S. S. 1981. Effect of age upon uterine response to deciduogenic stimulus. *Acta Anat.* 110: 146–158.

Cran, D. G. and Jones, R. 1980. Aging male reproductive

system, changes in the epididymis. *Exp. Gerontol.* 15: 93–101.

Crowley, P. H., Gulati, D. K., Hayden, T. L., Lopez, P., and Dyer, R. 1979. A chiasma-hormonal hypothesis relating Down's syndrome and maternal age. *Nature* 280: 417–418.

Crumeyrolle-Arias, M., Scheib, D., and Aschheim, P. 1976. Light and electron microscopy of the ovarian interstitial tissue in the senile rat: normal aspect and response to hCG of deficiency cells and epithelial cords. *Gerontology* 22: 185–204.

Damassa, D. A., Gilman, D. P., Lu, K. H., Judd, H. L., and Sawyer, C. H. 1980. The twenty-four hour pattern of prolactin secretion in aging female rats. *Biol. Reprod.* 22: 571–575.

Davidson, J. M., Camargo, C. A., and Smith, E. R. 1979. Effects of androgen on sexual behavior in hypogonadal men. *J. Clin. Endocrinol. Metab* 48: 955–958.

Davies, I. and Fotheringham, A. P. 1981. Lipofuscin—does it effect cellular performance? *Exp. Geront.* 16: 119–125.

DeKlerk, D. P., Coffey, D. S., Ewing, L. L., McDermott, I. R., Reiner, W. G., Robinson, C. H., Scott, W. W., Strandberg, J. D., Talalay, P., Walsh, P. C., Wheaton, L. G., and Zirkin, B. R., 1979. Comparison of spontaneous and experimentally induced canine prostatic hyperplasia. *J. Clin. Invest.* 64: 842–849.

DeKretser, D. M., Burger, H. G., and Dumpys, R. 1978. Patterns of serum LH and FSH in response to 4-hour infusions of luteinizing hormone releasing hormone in normal women during menstrual cycle, on oral contraceptives and in postmenopausal state. *J. Clin. Endocrinol. Metab.* 46: 227–235.

Deligdisch, L., Yedwab, G., Persitz, A., and David, M. P. 1978. Ultrastructural features in normal and hyperplastic postmenopausal endometrium. *Acta Obstet. Gynecol. Scand.* 57: 439–452.

Deslypere, J. P. and Vermeulen, A. 1981. Aging and tissue androgens. *J. Clin. Endocrinol. Metab.* 53: 430–434.

Desleypere, J. P., Wiers, P. W., Sayed, A., and Vermeulen, A. 1981. Urinary excretion of androgen metabolites, comparison with excretion of radioactive metabolites after injection of ^{14}C-testosterone. Influence of age. *Acta Endocrinol. (Kbh.)* 96: 265–272.

DeWaard, R., DeLaive, J. W. J., and Baanders—VanHalewijn 1960. On the bimodal age distribution of mammary carcinoma. *Br. J. Cancer* 14: 437–448.

Dewhurst, C. J. 1976. Frequency and severity of menopausal symptoms. *In,* S. Campbell (ed.), *The Management of the Menopause and Post-menopausal Years,* pp. 25–27. Lancaster, England: MTP Press.

Dilman, V. M. and Anisimov, V. N. 1979. Hypothalamic mechanisms of aging and of specific age pathology. I. On the sensitivity threshold of hypothalamic-pituitary complex to homeostatic stimuli in the reproductive system. *Exp. Gerontol.* 14: 161–174.

Djoseland, O., Hoglo, S., Abyholm, T., and Haugen, H. N. 1981. Androgen metabolism by rat epididymis. Age dependent changes in androgen metabolizing enzymes in rat accessory sex organs. *Arch. Androl.* 6: 229–238.

Durbin, P. W., Williams, M. H., Jeung, N., and Arnold, J. S. 1966. Development of spontaneous mammary tumors over the lifespan of the female Charles River (Sprague-Dawley) rat: the influence of ovariectomy, thyroidectomy, and adrenalectomy-ovariectomy. *Cancer Res.* 26: 400–411.

Eleftheriou, B. E. and Lucas, L. A. 1974. Related changes in testes, seminal vesicles and plasma testosterone levels in male mice. *Gerontologia* 20: 231–238.

Elwood, S. M. and Godolphin, W. 1980. Oestrogen receptors in breast tumours; association with age, menopausal status, and epidemiological and clinical features in 735 patients. *Br. J. Cancer* 42: 635–644.

Engle, E. T. 1952. The male reproductive system. *In,* A. I. Lansing (ed.), *Cowdry's Problems of Aging,* 3rd ed. pp. 708–729. Baltimore: Williams and Wilkins.

Erickson, B. H. 1966. Development and senescence of the postnatal bovine ovary. *J. Anim. Sci.* 25: 800–805.

Erickson, G. F., Hsueh, A. J. W., and Lu, K. H. 1979. Gonadotropin binding and aromatase activity in granulosa cells of young proestrous and old constant estrous rats. *Biol. Reprod.* 20: 182–190.

Estes, K. S., Simpkins, J. W., and Chen, C. L. 1980. Alteration in pulsatile release of LH in aging female rats. *Proc. Soc. Exp. Biol. Med.* 163: 384–387.

Ewing, L. L., Johnson, B. H., Desjardins, C., and Clegg, R. F. 1972. Effect of age upon the spermatogenic and steroidogenic elements of rabbit testes. *Proc. Soc. Exp. Biol. Med.* 140: 907–910.

Fabricant, J. D., Dunn, G., and Schneider, E. L. 1978. Maternal age related pre- and post-implantation fetal mortality: a strain survey. *Mech. Age. Devel.* 8: 227–231.

Faddy, M. J., Jones, E. C., and Edwards, R. G. 1976. An analytical model for ovarian follicle dynamics. *J. Exp. Zool.* 197: 173–185.

Fayein, N. A. and Aschheim, P. 1980. Age related temporal changes of levels of circulating progesterone in repeatedly pseudopregnant rats. *Biol. Reprod.* 23: 616–620.

Fechner, R. E. 1972. Benign breast disease in women on estrogen therapy. A pathologic study. *Cancer* 29: 273–279.

Finch, C. E. and Girgis, F. G. 1975. Enlarged seminal vesicles of senescent C57BL/6J mice. *J. Gerontol.* 29: 134–138.

Finch, C. E. and Holinka, C. F. 1982. Aging and uterine growth during implantation in C57BL/6J mice. *Exp. Geront.* 17: 235–241.

Finch, C. E., Jones, C., Wisner, J. R., Sinha, Y. N., de Vellis, J. S., and Swerdloff, R. S. 1977. Hormone production by the pituitary and testes of male C57BL/6J mice during aging. *Endocrinology* 101: 1310–1317.

Finn, C. A. 1963. Reproductive capacity and litter size in mice: effect of age and environment. *J. Reprod. Fertil.* 6: 205–214.

Finn, C. A. 1966. Initiation of the decidual cell reaction in the uterus of the aged mouse. *J. Reprod. Fertil.* 11: 423–428.

Finn, C. A. and Martin, L. 1969. The cellular response of the uterus of the aged mouse to oestrogen and progesterone. *J. Reprod. Fertil.* 20: 545–547.

Fjallbrant, B. 1975. Autoimmune human sperm antibodies and age in males. *J. Reprod. Fertil.* 43: 145–148.

Flurkey, K., Gee, D. M., Sinha, Y. N., Wisner, J. R., Jr., and Finch, C. E. 1982. Age effects on luteinizing hormone, progesterone, and prolactin in proestrous and acyclic C57BL/6J mice. *Biol. Reprod.* 26: 835–846.

Forti, G., Pozzagli, M., Calabresi, E., Fiorelli, G., and Serio, M. 1974. Radioimmunoassay of plasma testosterone. *Clin. Endocrinol.* 3: 5–17.

Franchimont, P., Legros, J. J., and Meurice, J. 1972. Effect of several estrogens on serum gonadotropin levels in postmenopausal women. *Horm. Metab. Res.* 4: 288–292.

Franks, L. M. and Payne, J. 1970. The influence of age on reproductive capacity in C57BL/6J mice. *J. Reprod. Fertil.* 21: 563–565.

Frick, J. 1969. Darstellung eine Methode (competitive protein binding) zur Bestimmung des Testosteronspiegels in Plasma und Studie uber den Testosteronmetabolismus beim Mann uber 60 Jahre. *Urol. Int.* 24: 481–501.

Frumar, A. M., Meldrum, D. R., Geola, F., Shamonki, I. M., Tataryn, I. V., Deftos, L. J., and Judd, H. L. 1980. Relationship of fasting urinary calcium to circulating estrogen and body weight in postmenopausal women. *J. Clin. Endocrinol. Metab.* 50: 70–75.

Gaddum-Rosse, P., Rumery, R. E., Blandau, R. J., and Thiersch, J. A. 1975. Studies on mucosa of postmenopausal oviducts, surface appearance, ciliary activity, and the effect of estrogen treatment. *Fertil. Steril.* 26: 951–969.

Gambrell, R. D. 1982. The menopause: benefits and risks of estrogen-progestogen replacement therapy. *Fertil. Steril.* 37: 457–474.

Gambrell, R. D., Massey, P. M., Castaneda, T. A., and Boddie, A. W. 1980. Estrogen therapy and breast cancer in postmenopausal women. *J. Am. Geriatr. Soc.* 28: 251–257.

Gambrell, R. D., Massey, P. M., Castaneda, T. A., Ugenas, A. J., and Ricci, C. A. 1979. Reduced incidence of endometrial cancer among postmenopausal women treated with progestogens. *J. Am. Geriatr. Soc.* 27: 389–394.

Gandy, H. M. and Peterson, R. E. 1968. Measurement of testosterone and 17-KS in plasma by the double isotope dilution derivative technique. *J. Clin. Endocrinol. Metab.* 28: 949–956.

Gasparyan, A. M. and Portnoy, A. S. 1970. Reaction of the prostate to experimental endocrine disorders. *Int. Urol. Nephrol.* 23: 277–285.

Gee, D. M. Flurkey, K., and Finch, C. E. 1983. Aging and the regulation of luteinizing hormone in C57BL/6J mice: impaired elevations after ovariectomy and spontaneous elevations at advanced ages. *Biol. Reprod.* 28: 598–607.

Geller, J., Albert, J., Lopez, D., Geller, S., and Niwa-yama, G. (1976). Comparison of androgen metabolites in benign prostatic hypertrophy (BPH) and normal prostate. *J. Clin. Endocrinol. Metab.* 43: 686–688.

Geola, F. L., Frumar, A. M., Tataryn, I. V., Lu, K. H., Hershman, J. M., Efena, P., Sambhi, M. P., and Judd, H. L. 1980. Biological effects of various doses of conjugated equine estrogens in postmenopausal women. *J. Clin. Endocrinol. Metab.* 51: 620–625.

German, J. 1968. Mongolism, delayed fertilization, and human sexual behavior. *Nature* 217: 516–518.

Gesell, M. S. and Roth. G. S. 1981. Decrease in rat uterine estrogen receptors during aging; physio- and immuno-chemical properties. *Endocrinology* 109: 1502–1508.

Ghanadian, R. and Fotherby, K. 1975. Testosterone uptake by prostatic tissue from young and old rats. *Gerontologia* 21: 211–215.

Ghanadian, R., Lewis, J., and Chisholm G. 1975. Serum testosterone and dihydrotestosterone change with age in the rat. *Steroids* 25: 753–762.

Gibbons, W. B., Buttram, V. C., Besch, P. K., and Smith, R. G. 1979. Estrogen binding proteins in the human postmenopausal uterus. *Am. J. Obstet. Gynecol.* 135: 799–803.

Giusti, G., Gonelli, P., Horreli, D., Fiorelli, G., Forti, G., Pozzagli, M., and Serio, M. 1975. Age related secretion of androstenedione, testosterone, and dihydrotestosterone by the human testis. *Exp. Gerontol.* 10: 241–245.

Gloyna, R. E., Siiteri, P. K., and Wilson, J. D. 1970. Dihydrotestosterone in prostatic hypertrophy. II. The formation and content of dihydrotestosterone in the hypertrophic canine prostate and the effect of dihydro-testosterone on prostatic growth in the dog. *J. Clin. Invest.* 49: 94–98.

Goldman, H. 1963. Amyloidosis of seminal vesicles and vas deferens. Primary localized cases. *Arch. Pathol.* 75: 94–98.

Goodlin, R. C. 1965. Nondisjunction and maternal age in the mouse. *J. Reprod. Fertil.* 9: 355–356.

Gordon, T., Kannel, W. B., Hjortland, M. C., and McNamara, P. M. 1978. Menopause and coronary heart disease. *Am. J. Med.* 89: 157–161.

Gosden, R. G. 1973. Chromosomal anomalies of preimplantation mouse embryos in relation to maternal age. *J. Reprod. Fertil.* 35: 351–354.

Gosden, R. G. 1974. Corpus luteum adequacy in ageing pregnant mice. *Eur. J. Obstet. Gynaecol. Reprod. Biol. Suppl.* 4: s109–s111.

Gosden, R. G. 1975a. Survival of transferred C57BL mouse embryos. Effects of age of donor and recipient. *Fertil. Steril.* 25: 348–351.

Gosden, R. G. 1975b. Ovarian support of pregnancy in ageing inbred mice. *J. Reprod. Fertil.* 42: 423–430.

Gosden, R. G. 1976. Uptake and metabolism *in vivo* of tritiated estradiol 17β in tissues of ageing female mice. *J. Endocrinol.* 68: 153–157.

Gosden, R. G. 1979. Effects of age and parity on the breeding potential in mice with one or two ovaries. *J. Reprod. Fertil.* 57: 477–487.

Gosden, R. G. and Bancroft, L. 1976. Pituitary function in reproductively senescent female rats. *Exp. Geront.* 11: 157–160.

Gosden, R. G. and Fowler, R. E. 1979. Corpus luteum function in aging inbred mice. *Experientia* 35: 128–130.

Gosden, R. G., Holinka, C. F., and Finch, C. E. 1981. The distribution of fetal mortality in ageing C57BL/6J mice: a statistical analysis. *Exp. Geront.* 16: 127–130.

Gosden, R. G., Jones, E. C., and Jacks, F. 1978. Pituitary-ovarian relationships during the post-reproductive phase of inbred mice. *Exp. Geront.* 13: 159–166.

Gosden, R. G., Laing, S. C., Felicio, L. S., Nelson, J. F., and Finch, C. E. 1983. Imminent oocyte exhaustion and reduced follicular recruitment mark the transition to acyclicity in ageing C57BL/6J mice. *Biol. Reprod.* 28: 255–260.

Gould, K. G., Flint, M., and Graham, C. E. 1981. Chimpanzee reproductive senescence: a possible model for evolution of the menopause. *Maturitas* 3: 157–166.

Graham, C. E. 1979. Reproductive function in aged female chimpanzees. *Am J. Physical Anthropol.* 50: 291–300.

Gray, G. D. 1978. Changes in the levels of luteinizing hormone and testosterone in the circulation of ageing male rats. *J. Endocrinol.* 76: 551–552.

Gray, G. D., Smith, E. R., and Davidson, J. M. 1980a. Gonadotropin regulation in middle aged rats. *Endocrinology* 107: 2021–2026.

Gray, G. D., Tennent, E., Smith, E. R., and Davidson, J. M. 1980b. Luteinizing hormone regulation and sexual behavior in middle-aged female rats. *Endocrinology* 107: 187–194.

Gray, G. D. and Wexler, B. C. 1980. Estrogen and testosterone sensitivity of middle-aged female rats in the regulation of LH. *Exp. Geront.* 15: 201–207.

Greenstein, B. D. 1979. Androgen receptors in the rat brain, anterior pituitary gland, and ventral prostate gland: effects of orchiectomy and aging. *J. Endocrinol.* 81: 75–81.

Gronroos, M., Klemi, P., Salmi, T., Rauramo, L., and Punnonen, R. 1980. Ovarian production of estrogens in postmenopausal women. *Int. J. Gynaecol. Obstet.* 18: 93–98.

Guerrero, R., Aso, T., Brenner, P. F., Cekan, Z., Landgren, B.-M., Haganfeldt, K., and Diczfalusy, E. 1976. Studies on the pattern of circulating steroids in the normal menstrual cycle. 1. Simultaneous assays of progesterone, pregnenolone, dehydroepiandrosterone, testosterone, dihydrotestosterone, androstenedione, oestradiol, and oestrone. *Acta Endocrinol.* 81: 133–149.

Gustafson, A. and Svanborg, A. 1972. Gonadal steroid effects on plasma lippoproteins and individual plasma lipids. *J. Clin. Endocrinol. Metab.* 35: 203–207.

Habib, F. K., Lee, S. R., Stetch, S. R., and Smith, D. H. 1976. Androgen levels in the plasma and prostatic tissues of patients with benign hypertrophy and carcinoma of the prostate. *J. Endocrinol.* 71: 99–107.

Haji, M., Kato, K., Nawata, H., and Ibayashi, H. 1981.

Age related changes in the concentrations of cytosol receptors for sex steroid hormones in the hypothalamus and pituitary gland of the rat. *Brain Res.* 204: 373–386.

Hallberg, M. C., Wieland, R. G., Zoin, E. M., Furst, B. H., and Wieland, J. M. 1976. Impaired Leydig cell reserve and altered serum androgen in the aging male. *Fertil. Steril.* 27: 812–814.

Hammond, C. B., Jelovsek, F. R., Lee, K. L., Creasman, W. T., and Parker, R. T. 1979a. Effects of long-term estrogen replacement therapy. II. Neoplasia. *Am. J. Obstet. Gynecol.* 133: 537–547.

Hammond, G. L., Lukkarinen, O., Vihko, P., Kontturi, M., and Vihko, R. 1979b. The hormonal status of patients with benign prostatic hypertrophy: FSH, LH, TSH, and prolactin responses to releasing hormones. *Clin. Endocrinol.* (*Oxf.*) 10: 545–552.

Hammond, C. B. and Maxson W. S. 1982. Current status of estrogen replacement therapy for the menopause. *Fertil. Steril.* 37: 5–25.

Harbitz, T. B. 1973a. Testis weight and the histology of the prostate in elderly men. Analysis in an autopsy series. *Acta Pathol. Microbiol. Scand.* 81A: 148–158.

Harbitz, T. B. 1973b. Morphometric studies of the Leydig cells in elderly men with special reference to the histology of the prostate. *Acta Pathol. Microbiol. Scand.* 81A: 301–313.

Harbitz, T. B. and Haugen, C. A. 1972. Histology of the prostate in elderly men. *Acta Pathol. Microbiol. Scand.* 80A: 756–768.

Harman, S. M., Danner, R. L., and Roth, G. S. 1978. Testosterone secretion in the rat in response to chorionic gonadotropin: alterations with age. *Endocrinology* 102: 540–544.

Harman, S. M., Louvet, J. P., and Ross, G. T. 1975. Interaction of estrogen and gonadotropins on follicular atresia. *Endocrinology* 96: 1145–1152.

Harman, S. M. and Talbert, G. B. 1970. The effect of maternal age on ovulation, corpora lutea of pregnancy and implantation failure in mice. *J. Reprod. Fertil.* 23: 33–39.

Harman, S. M. and Talbert, G. B. 1974. Effect of maternal age on synchronization of ovulation and mating and on tubal transport of ova in mice. *J. Geront.* 29: 493–498.

Harman, S. M. and Tsitouras, P. D. 1980. Reproductive hormones in aging men. I: Measurement of sex steroids, basal LH, and Leydig cell response to hCG. *J. Clin. Endocrinol. Metab.* 51: 35–40.

Harman, S. M., Tsitouras, P. D., Costa, P. T., and Blackman, M. R. 1982. Reproductive hormones in aging men. II: Basal pituitary gonadotropins and gonadotropin responses to luteinizing hormone releasing hormone. *J. Clin. Endocrinol. Metab.* 54: 537–541.

Hashimoto, T., Miyai, K., Izumi, K., and Kumahara, Y. 1973. Gonadotropin response to synthetic LHRH in normal subjects: correlation between LH and FSH. *J. Clin. Endocrinol. Metab.* 37: 910–916.

Haug, E. A., Aakvaag, A., Sand, T., and Torjesen, P. A. 1974. The gonadotropin response to synthetic LHRH in males in relation to age, dose, and basal levels of testosterone, estradiol-17-beta, and gonadotropins. *Acta Endocrinol.* (*Kbh.*) 77: 625–635.

Hemsell, D. L., Grodin, J. M., Brenner, P. F., Siiteri, P. K., and Macdonald, P. C. 1974. Plasma precursors of estrogen. II. Correlation of extent of conversion of plasma androstenedione to estrone with age. *J. Clin. Endocrinol. Metab.* 38: 476–479.

Henderson, S. A. and Edwards, R. G. 1968. Chiasma frequency and maternal age in mammals. *Nature* 218: 22–28.

Hodgen, G. D., Goodman, A. L., O'Connor, A., and Johnson, D. K. 1977. Menopause in rhesus monkeys—model for study of disorders in human climacteric. *Am. J. Obstet. Gynecol.* 127: 581–584.

Holinka, C. F. and Finch, C. E. 1977. Age related changes in the decidual response of the C57BL/6J mouse uterus. *Biol. Reprod.* 16: 385–393.

Holinka, C. F. and Finch, C. E. 1981. Efficiency of mating in C57BL/6J female mice as a function of age and previous parity. *Exp Geront.* 16: 393–398.

Holinka, C. F., Hetland, M. D., and Finch, C. E. 1977. The responses to a single dose of estradiol in the uterus of ovariectomized C57BL/6J mice during aging. *Biol. Reprod.* 17: 262–264.

Holinka, C. F., Nelson, J. F., and Finch, C. E. 1975. Effect of estrogen treatment on estradiol binding capacity in uteri of aging rats. *Gerontologist* 15: 30.

Holinka, C. F., Tseng, Y., and Finch, C. E. 1978. Prolonged gestation, elevated preparturitional plasma progesterone and reproductive aging in C57BL/6J mice. *Biol. Reprod.* 19: 807–816.

Holinka, C. F., Tseng, Y., and Finch, C. E. 1979a. Reproductive aging in C57BL/6J mice: plasma progesterone, viable embryos, and resorption frequency during pregnancy. *Biol. Reprod.* 20: 1201–1211.

Holinka, C. F., Tseng, Y., and Finch, C. E. 1979b. Impaired preparturitional rise of plasma estradiol in aging C57BL/6J mice. *Biol. Reprod.* 21: 1009–1013.

Hollander, N. and Hollander, V. P. 1958. The microdetermination of testosterone in human spermatic vein blood. *J. Clin. Endocrinol. Metab.* 38: 966–971.

Holstein, A. F. and Hubman, R. 1980. Spermatogonia in old age. *In,* A. F. Holstein and C. Schirren (eds.), *Advances in Andrology,* Vol. 7: *Fohringer Symposium: Stem Cells in Spermatogenesis,* p. 77. Berlin: Grosse.

Hoover, R. H., Glass, A., Finkle, W. D., Azevedo, D., and Milne, K. 1981. Conjugate estrogens and breast cancer risk in women. *J. Natl. Cancer Inst.* 67: 815–820.

Horst, H. J., Becker, H., and Voigt, K. D. 1974. The determination of specific testosterone and 5-α-dihydrotestosterone binding to sex hormone binding globulin by a differential dissociation technique. *Steroids* 23: 833–846.

Horton, R., Hsieh, P., Barberia, J., Pages, L., and Cosgrove, M. 1975. Altered blood androgens in elderly men with prostate hyperplasia. *J. Clin. Endocrinol. Metab.* 41: 793–796.

Hossdorf, T. and Wagner, H. 1980. Secretion of prolactin

in healthy men and women of different age. *Aktuel Gerontol.* 10: 119–126.

Hsueh, A. J. W., Erickson, G. F., and Lu, K. H. 1979. Changes in uterine estrogen receptor and morphology in aging female rats. *Biol. Reprod.* 21: 793–800.

Huang, H. H., Marshall, S., and Meites, J. 1976a. Capacity of old vs. young female rats to secrete LH, FSH, and prolactin. *Biol. Reprod.* 14: 538–543.

Huang, H. H., Marshall, S., and Meites, J. 1976b. Induction of estrous cycles in old, non-cyclic rats by progesterone, ACTH, ether stress, or L-dopa. *Neuroendocrinology* 20: 21–34.

Huang, H. H. and Meites, J. 1975. Reproductive capacity of aging female rats. *Neuroendocrinology* 17: 289–295.

Huang, H. H., Steger, R. W., Bruni, J., and Meites, J. 1978. Patterns of sex steroid and gonadotropin secretion in aging female rats. *Endocrinology* 103: 1835–1859.

Huang, H. H., Steger, R. W., Sonntag, W. E., and Meites, J. 1980. Positive feedback by ovarian hormones on prolactin and LH in old vs. young female rats. *Neurobiol. Aging* 1: 141–143.

Huber, M. H. and Bronson, P. H. 1980. Recovery of sexual activity with experience in aged male mice. *Exp. Aging Res.* 6: 385–391.

Huber, M. H., Bronson, F. H., and Desjardins, C. 1980. Sexual activity in aged male mice: correlation with level of arousal, physical endurance, pathological status, and ejaculatory capacity. *Biol. Reprod.* 23: 304–316.

Hulka, B. S., Fowler, W. C., Kaufman, D. G., Grimson, R. C., Greenberg, B. G., Hogue, C. J., Berger, G. S., and Pulliam, C. C. 1980a. Estrogen and endometrial cancer: cases and two control groups from North Carolina. *Am J. Obstet. Gynecol.* 137: 92–101.

Hulka, B. S., Kaufman, D. G., Fowler, W. C., Grimson, R. C., and Greenberg, B. G. 1980b. Predominance of early endometrial cancers after long-term estrogen use. *JAMA* 244: 2419–2422.

Humphrey, J. D. and Ladd, P. W. 1975. A quantitative study of changes in the bovine testis and epididymis associated with age. *Res. Vet. Sci.* 19: 135–141.

Humphreys, P. N. 1977. The histology of the testis in aging and senile rats. *Exp. Gerontol.* 12: 27–34.

Hunt, M. 1974. Marital sexuality in the 40's and today: a generation of change. Lecture delivered at the Institute for Sex Research. University of Indiana, Bloomington.

Huseby, R. A. and Ball, Z. B. 1945. A study of the genesis of histological changes produced by caloric restrictions in portions of the endocrine and reproductive systems of strain A female mice. *Anat. Record.* 92: 135–155.

Isaacs, J. T. and Coffey, D. S. 1981. Changes in dihydrotestosterone metabolism associated with the development of canine benign prostatic hyperplasia. *Endocrinology* 108: 445–453.

Jagiello, G. and Fang, J. S. 1979. Analysis of diplotene chiasma frequencies in mouse oocytes and spermatocytes in relation to aging and sexual dimorphism. *Cytogenet. Cell Genet.* 23: 53–60.

Jahn, K., Leutert, G., and Rotzsch, W. 1971. Age dependent morphological and biochemical examinations of the human prostate. *Z. Alternforsch.* 23: 323–335.

Jick, H., Watkins, R. N., Hunter, J. R., Dinan, B. J., Madsen, S., Rothman, K. J., and Walker, A. M. 1979. Replacement estrogens and endometrial cancer. *N. Engl. J. Med.* 300: 218–222.

Johnson, L. and Neaves, W. B. 1981. Age-related changes in the Leydig cell population, seminiferous tubules and sperm production in stallions. *Biol. Reprod.* 24: 703–712.

Jones, E. C. 1970. The ageing ovary and its influence on reproductive capacity. *J. Reprod. Fertil., Suppl.* 12: 17–30.

Jones, E. C. and Krohn, P. L. 1960. Effect of unilateral ovariectomy on reproductive lifespan of mice. *J. Endocrinol.* 20: 129–134.

Jones, E. C. and Krohn, P. L. 1961a. The relationship between age, number of oocytes, and fertility in virgin and multiparous mice. *J. Endocrinol.* 21: 469–495.

Jones, E. C. and Krohn, P. L. 1961b. Effect of hypophysectomy on age changes in the ovaries of mice. *J. Endocrinol.* 21: 497–509.

Judd, H. L. 1976. Hormonal dynamics associated with the menopause. *Clin. Obstet. Gynecol.* 19: 775–788.

Judd, H. L., Cleary, R. E., Creasman, W. T., Figge, D. C., Kase, N., Rosenwaks, Z., and Tagatz, G. E. 1981. Estrogen replacement therapy. *Obst. and Gynecol.* 58: 267–275.

Judd, H. L., Lucas, W. E., and Yen, S. S. C. 1976. 17-Beta estradiol and estrone levels in postmenopausal women with and without endometrial cancer. *J. Clin. Endocrinol. Metab.* 43: 272–278.

Judd, H. L. and Yen, S. S. C. 1973. Serum androsterone and testosterone levels during the menstrual cycle. *J. Clin. Endocrinol. Metab.* 36: 475–481.

Kaler, L. W. and Neaves, W. B. 1978. Attrition of the human Leydig cell population with advancing age. *Anat. Rec.* 192: 513–518.

Kaler, L. W. and Neaves, W. B. 1981a. The androgen status of aging male rats. *Endocrinology* 108: 712–719.

Kaler, L. W. and Neaves, W. B. 1981b. The steroidogenic capacity of the aging rat testis. *J. Gerontol.* 36: 398–404.

Karacan, I., Williams, R. L., Thornby, J. I., and Salis, P. J. 1975. Sleep related penile tumescence as a function of age. *Am. J. Psychiatry* 132: 932–937.

Keller, P. J. 1970. Effect of natural sex steroids on the excretion of follicle-stimulating and lutenizing hormone in postmenopausal women. *Acta. Endocrinol.* 64: 479–488.

Kent, J. Z. and Acone, A. B. 1965. Plasma testosterone levels and aging in males. In A. Vermeulen and D. Exley (eds.), Androgens in Normal and Pathological Conditions, pp. 31–35. Amsterdam: Excerpta Medica Foundation, Cong. Series No. 191.

Kinsey, A. C., Pomeroy, W. E., and Martin, C. E. 1948. *Sexual Behavior in the Human Male.* Philadelphia: W. B. Saunders.

Kirschner, M. A. and Coffman, G. D. 1968. Measurement of plasma testosterone and delta-4-androstenedione using electron capture gas liquid chromatography. *J. Clin. Endocrinol. Metab.* 28: 1347–1352.

Kley, H. K., Nieschlag, E., Bidlingmaier, F., and Kruskemper, H. L. 1974. Possible age dependent influence of estrogens on the binding of testosterone in plasma of adult men. *Horm. Metab. Res.* 6: 213–215.

Kley, H. K., Nieschlag, E., and Kruskemper, H. L. 1975. Age dependence of plasma estrogen response to hCG and ACTH in men. *Acta Endocrinol. (Kbh.)* 79: 95–101.

Kohler, P. O., Ross, G. T., and Odell, W. D. 1968. Metabolic clearance and production rates of human luteinizing hormone in pre- and postmenopausal women. *J. Clin. Invest.* 47: 38–47.

Komatsu, M. and Fujita, H. 1978. Electron microscopic studies on the development and aging of the oviduct epithelium of mice. *Anat. Embryol.* 152: 243–259.

Kothari, K. L. and Gupta, A. S. 1974. Effect of aging on the volume, structure, and total Leydig cell content of the human testis. *Int. J. Fertil.* 19: 140–146.

Kram, D. and Schneider, E. L. 1978. An effect of reproductive aging: increased risk of genetically abnormal offspring. *In,* E. L. Schneider (ed.), *Aging of the Reproductive System* (Aging, Vol. 4), pp. 237–270. New York: Raven Press.

Kruszel, T. 1967. Fructose and citric acid concentrations in the seminal vesicles of rats in relationship to age. *Endokrynol. Polska* 18: 287–296.

Lang, W. R. and Aponte, G. E. 1967. Gross and microscopic anatomy of the aged female reproductive organs. *Clin. Obstet. Gynecol.* 10: 454–465.

Larson, L. L. and Foote, R. H. 1972. Uterine blood flow in young and aged rabbits. *Proc. Soc. Exp. Biol. Med.* 141: 67–69.

Leathem, J. H. and Albrecht, E. D. 1974. Effect of age on testis 3β-hydroxysteroid dehydrogenase in the rat. *Proc. Soc. Exp. Biol. Med.* 145: 1212–1214.

Leathem, J. H. and Murono, E. P. 1975. Ovarian Δ^5-3β-hydroxysteroid dehydrogenase in aging rats. *Fertil. Steril.* 26: 996–1000.

Leathem, J. H. and Shapiro, B. H. 1975. Aging and ovarian Δ^5-3β-hydroxysteroid dehydrogenase in rats. *Proc. Soc. Exp. Biol. Med.* 148: 793–794.

Lehmann, H., Lutzen, L. and Deutsch, H. 1975. Hormonal activity of testis in aged rats with Leydig cell hyperplasia: histochemical investigation of some hydroxysteroid dehydrogenases. *Beitrage zur Pathologie.* 156: 109–116.

Leonard, A. and DeKnudt, Gh. 1970. Persistence of chromosome rearrangements induced in male mice by X-irradiation on premeiotic germ cells. *Mutation Res.* 9: 127–133.

Lewis, J. G., Ghanadian, R., and Chisholm, G. D. 1976. Serum 5-α-dihydrotestosterone and testosterone, changes with age in man. *Acta Endocrinol (Kbh.)* 82: 444–449.

Lin, T., Murono, E., Osterman, J., Allen, D. O., and Nankin, H. R. 1980. The aging Leydig cell: 1. testosterone and adenosine 3',5'-monophosphate responses to gonadotropin stimulation in rats. *Steroids* 35: 653–663.

Lloyd, J. W., Thomas, J. A., and Mawhinney, M. O. 1975. Androgens and estrogens in plasma and prostatic tissue of normal dogs and dogs with benign prostatic hypertrophy. *Invest. Urol.* 13: 220–222.

Lobo, R. A., March, C. M., Goebelsmann, U., Krauss, R. M., and Mishell, D. R. 1980. Subdermal estradiol pellets following hysterectomy and oophorectomy. *Am. J. Obstet. Gynecol.* 138: 714–719.

Longcope, C. 1973. The effect of human chorionic gonadotropin on plasma steroid levels in young and old men. *Steroids* 21: 583–592.

Longcope, C., Hunter, R., and Franz, C. 1980a. Steroid secretion by the postmenopausal ovary. *Am. J. Obstet. Gynecol.* 138: 564–568.

Longcope, C., Jaffee, W., and Griffing, G. 1980b. Metabolic clearance rates of androgens and estrogens in ageing women. *Maturitas* 2: 283–299.

Longcope, C., Jaffee, W., and Griffing, G. 1981. Production rates of androgens and oestrogens in postmenopausal women. *Maturitas* 3: 215–223.

Lu, J. K., Damassa, D. A., Gilman, D. P., Judd, H. L., and Sawyer, C. H. 1980. Differential patterns of gonadotropin responses to ovarian steroids and to LH-releasing hormone between constant-estrous and pseudopregnant states in aging rats. *Biol. Reprod.* 23: 345–351.

Lu, J. K., Gilman, D. P., Meldrum, D. R., Judd, H. L., and Sawyer, C. H. 1981. Relationship between circulating estrogens and the central mechanisms by which ovarian steroids stimulate LH secretion in aged and young female rats. *Endocrinology* 108: 836–841.

Lu, K. H., Hopper, B. R., Vargo, T. M., and Yen, S. S. C. 1979. Chronological changes in sex steroid, gonadotropin, and prolactin secretion in aged female rats displaying different reproductive states. *Biol. Reprod.* 21: 193–203.

Lu, K. H., Huang, H. H., Chen, H. T., Kurcz, M., Mioduozewski, R., and Meites, J. 1977. Positive feedback by estrogen and progesterone on LH release in old and young rats. *Proc. Soc. Exp. Biol. Med.* 154: 82–85.

Luthardt, F. W., Palmer, C. G., and Yu, P-L. 1973. Chiasma and univalent frequencies in aging female mice. *Cytogenet. Cell Genet.* 12: 68–79.

MacDonald, P. C., Edman, C. D., Hemsell, D. L., Porter, J. C., and Siiteri, P. K. 1978. Effect of obesity on conversion of plasma androstenedione to estrone in postmenopausal women with and without endometrial cancer. *Am J. Obstet. Gynecol.* 130: 448–455.

Mack, T. M., Pike, M. C., Henderson, B. E., Pfeffer, R. I., Gerkins, V. R., Arthur, M., and Brown, S. E. 1976. Estrogens and endometrial cancer in a retirement community. *N. Engl. J. Med.* 294: 1262–1267.

MacLeod, J. and Gold, R. Z. 1953. The male factor in fertility and infertility. VII. Semen quality in relation to age and sexual activity. *Fertil. Steril.* 4: 194–207.

Mainwaring, W. I. P. 1967. The aging process in the mouse ventral prostate gland. A preliminary biochemical survey. *Gerontologia* 13:177–189.

Mainwaring, W. I. P. 1968a. Changes in the ribonucleic

acid metabolism of aging mouse tissues with particular reference to the prostate gland. *Biochem. J.* 110: 79–86.

Mainwaring, W. I. P., 1968b. The effect of testosterone on the age-associated changes in the ventral prostate gland of the mouse. Testosterone and aging of the prostate. *Gerontologia* 14: 133–141.

Mainwaring, W. I. P. and Brandes, D. 1974. Functional and structural changes in accessory sex organs during aging. *In,* D. Brandes (ed.), *Male Accessory Sex Organs,* pp. 469–500. New York: Academic Press.

Mandel, F. P., Geola, F., Lu, J. K., Eggena, P., Sambhi, M., Hershman, J. M., and Judd, H. L. 1982. Biologic effects of various doses of ethinyl estradiol in postmenopausal women. *Obstet. Gynecol.* 59: 673–679.

Mandl, A. M. 1961. Cyclical changes in vaginal smears of senile nulliparous and multiparous rats. *J. Endocrinol.* 22: 257–268.

Mandl, A. M. and Shelton, M. 1959. A quantitative study of oocytes in young and old nulliparous laboratory rats. *J. Endocrinol.* 18: 444–450.

Mao, P. and Angrist, A. 1966. The fine structure of the basal cell of the human prostate. *Lab. Invest.* 15: 1768–1782.

Martin, C. E. 1977. Sexual activity in the aging male. *In,* J. Money and H. Musaph (eds.), *Handbook of Sexology.* Amsterdam: ASP Biol. Med. Press.

Martin, C. E. 1981. Factors affecting sexual functioning in 60–79 year old married males. *Arch. Sex. Behav.* 10: 399–420.

Martin, R. H., Dill, F. J., and Miller, J. R. 1976. Nondisjunction in aging female mice. *Cytogenet. Cell Genet.* 17: 150–160.

Masters, W. H. and Johnson, V. E. 1966 *Human Sexual Response.* London: Churchill.

Masukawa, T. 1960. Vaginal smears in women past 40 years of age with emphasis on their remaining hormonal activity. *Obstet. Gynecol.* 16: 407–413.

Maudlin, I. and Fraser, L. R. 1978. Maternal age and the incidence of aneuploidy in first-cleavage mouse embryos. *J. Reprod. Fertil.* 54: 423–426.

Maurer, R. R. and Foote, R. H. 1971. Maternal ageing and embryonic mortality in the rabbit. I. Repeated superovulation, embryo culture and transfer. *J. Reprod. Fertil.* 25: 329–341.

Maurer, R. R. and Foote, R. H. 1972. Uterine collagenase and collagen in young and ageing rabbits. *J. Reprod. Fertil.* 30: 301–304.

Mazzi, C., Riva, L. R., and Bernasconi, D. 1974. Gonadotropins and plasma testosterone in senescence. *In,* V. H. T. James, M. Serio, and L. Martini (eds.), *The Endocrine Function of the Human Testis,* pp. 51–62. New York: Academic Press.

McDonald, T. W., Annegers, J. F., O'Fallon, W. M., Dockerty, M. B., Malkasian, G. D., and Kurland, L. T. 1977. Exogenous estrogen and endometrial carcinoma: case-control and incidence study. *Am. J. Obstet. Gynecol.* 127: 572–580.

McLennan, M. T. and McLennan, C. E. 1971. Estrogenic status of menstruating and menopausal women assessed by cervico-vaginal smears. *Obstet. Gynecol.* 37: 325–331.

Meites, J., Huang, H. H., and Simpkins, J. W. 1978. Recent studies on neuroendocrine control of reproductive senescence in rats. *In,* E. L. Schneider (ed.), *Aging of the Reproductive System,* pp. 213–235. New York: Raven Press.

Meldrum, D. R., Davidson, E. J., Tataryn, I. V., and Judd, R. L. 1981. Changes in circulating steroids with aging in postmenopausal women. *Obstet. Gynecol.* 57: 624–628.

Meldrum, D. R., Tataryn, I. V., Frumar, A. M., Erlik, Y., Lu, K. H., and Judd, H. L. 1980. Gonadotropins, estrogen, and adrenal steroids during the menopausal hot flash. *J. Clin. Endocrinol. Metab.* 50: 685–689.

Miller, A. E. and Riegle, G. D. 1978a. Hypothalamic LH-releasing activity in young and aged intact and gonadectomized rats. *Exp. Aging Res.* 4: 145–155.

Miller, A. E. and Riegle, G. D. 1978b. Serum testosterone and testicular response to hCG in young and aged male rats. *J. Gerontol.* 33: 197–203.

Miller, A. E. and Riegle, G. D. 1980a. Serum progesterone during pregnancy and pseudopregnancy and gestation length in the aging rat. *Biol. Reprod.* 22: 751–758.

Miller, A. E. and Riegle, G. D. 1980b. Temporal changes in serum progesterone in aging female rats. *Endocrinology* 106: 1579–1583.

Miller, A. E., Wood, S. M., and Riegle, G. D. 1979. Effect of age on reproduction in repeatedly mated female rats. *J. Geront.* 34: 15–20.

Mizoguchi, H. and Dukelow, W. R. 1981. Fertilizability of ova from young or old hamsters after spontaneous or induced ovulation. *Fertil. Steril.* 35: 79–83.

Moore, R. A. 1952. Male secondary sexual organs. *In,* A. I. Lansing, (ed.), *Cowdry's Problems of Ageing,* 3rd ed., pp. 686–707. Baltimore: Williams and Wilkins.

Moore, J., Gazak, J. M., and Wilson, J. D. 1979. Regulation of cytoplasmic dihydrotestosterone binding in dog prostate by 17β-estradiol. *J. Clin. Invest.,* 63: 351–357.

Morimoto, I., Edmiston, A., and Horton, R. 1980. Alteration in the metabolism of dihydrotestosterone in elderly men with prostate hyperplasia. *J. Clin. Invest.* 66: 612–615.

Morse, A. R., Hutton, J. D., Jacobs, J. S., Murray, M. A., and James, V. H. 1971. Relation between the karyopycnotic index and plasma oestrogen concentrations after the menopause. *Br. J. Obstet. Gynaecol.* 86: 981–983.

Muramatsu, S. 1974. Frequency of spontaneous translocations in mouse spermatogonia. *Mutation Research* 24: 81–82.

Murono, E. P., Nankin, H. R., Lin, T., and Osterman, J. 1982a. The aging Leydig cell. V. Diurnal rhythms in aged men. *Acta Endocrinologica* 99: 619–623.

Murono, E. P., Nankin, H. R., Lin, T., and Osterman, J. 1982b. The aging Leydig cell. VI. Response of testosterone precursors to gonadotropin in men. *Acta Endocrinol. (Kbh.)* 100: 455–461.

Murri, L., Barreca, T., Cerone, G., Massetani, R., Gallamini, A., and Baldassarre, M. 1980. The 24 hour pattern of human prolactin and growth hormone in healthy elderly subjects. *Chronobiologia* 7: 87–92.

Muta, K., Kato, K., Akamine, Y., and Ibayashi, H. 1981. Age related changes in the feedback regulation of gonadotropin secretion by sex steroids in men. *Acta Endocrinol. (Kbh.)* 96: 154–162.

Myking, O., Thorsen, T., and Stoa, K. F. 1980. Conjugated and unconjugated plasma oestrogens—oestrone, oestradiol, and oestriol—in normal human males. *J. Steroid Biochem.* 13: 1215–1220.

Nankin, H. R., Lin, T., Murono, E. R., and Osterman, J. 1981. The aging Leydig cell. III. Gonadotropin stimulation in men. *J. Androl.* 2: 181–189.

Nass, T. E., LaPolt, P. S., and Lu, J. K. H. 1982. Effects of prolonged caging with fertile males on reproductive functions in aging female rats. *Biol. Reprod.* 27: 609–615.

Natoli, A., Riondino, G., and Brancati, A. 1972. Studio della funzione gonadale ormonica e spermatogenica nel corso della senescenza maschile. *G. Gerontol.* 20: 1103–1119.

Nelson, J. F., Felicio, L. S., Osterburg, H. H., and Finch, C. E. 1981. Altered profiles of estradiol and progesterone associated with prolonged estrous cycles and persistent vaginal cornification in aging C57BL/6J mice. *Biol. Reprod.* 24: 784–792.

Nelson, J. F., Felicio, L. S., Randall, P. K., Sims, C., and Finch, C. E. 1982. A longitudinal study of estrous cyclicity in aging C57BL/6J mice: I. Cycle frequency, length, and vaginal cytology. *Biol. Reprod.* 27: 327–339.

Nelson, J. F., Holinka, C. F., and Finch, C. E. 1976. Age related changes in estradiol binding capacity of mouse uterine cytosol. *Gerontological Society, 29th Annual Scientific Meeting,* p. 34.

Nelson, J. F., Latham, K. R., and Finch, C. E., 1975. Plasma testosterone levels in C57BL/6J male mice: effects of age and disease. *Acta Endocrinol. (Kbh.)* 80: 744–752.

Newman, G. and Nichols, C. R. 1960. Sexual activities and attitudes in older persons. *JAMA* 173: 33–35.

Nieschlag, E., Kley, K. H., and Wiegelmann W. 1973. Age dependence of the endocrine testicular function in adult men. Acta Endocrinol. *(Kbh.) (Suppl.)* 177: 122 (Abstract).

Nieschlag, E., Lammers, U., Freischem, C. W., and Wickings, E. J. 1982. Reproductive functions in young fathers and grandfathers. *J. Clin. Endocrinol. Metab.* 55: 676–681.

Nilsson, S. 1962. The human seminal vesicle. A morphogenetic and gross anatomic study with special regard to changes due to age and prostatic adenoma. I, II, III. *Acta Chir. Scand. Suppl.* 296: 5–96.

Nordin, E. E. C., Gallager, J. C., Aaron, J. E., and Horsman, A. 1975. Postmenopausal osteopenia and osteoporosis. *Front. Horm. Res.* 3: 131–149.

Norris, M. L. and Adams, C. E. 1982. Effect of unilateral ovariectomy on the population of ovarian follicles relative to age in the Mongolian gerbil (*Meriones unguiculatus*). *J. Reprod. Fertil.* 66: 335–340.

Novak, E. and Everett, H. S. 1928. Cyclical and other variations in the tubal epithelium. *Am. J. Obstet. Gynecol.* 16: 499–530.

Novak, E. R. 1970. Ovulation after fifty. *Obstet. Gynecol.* 36: 903–910.

Noyes, R. W. 1970. Physiology of ovarian aging. *Ann. NY Acad. Sci.* 171: 517–525.

Ober, K. P. and Miller, F. C. 1980. Medical aspects of the menopause. *In,* B. A. Eskin (ed.), *The Menopause, Comprehensive Management,* pp. 129–150. New York: Masson Publishing.

Ortega, E., Ruiz, E., Mendoza, M. C., Martin-Andres, A., and Osorio, C. 1979. Plasma steroid and protein hormone concentrations in patients with benign prostatic hypertrophy and in normal men. *Experientia* 35: 844–845.

Parkening, T. 1979. Apposition of uterine luminal epithelium during implantation in senescent golden hamsters. *J. Geront.* 34: 335–344.

Parkening, T. A., Collins, T. J., and Smith, E. R. 1980. Plasma and pituitary concentrations of LH, FSH, and prolactin in aged female C57BL/6J mice. *J. Reprod. Fertil.* 58: 377–386.

Parkening, T. A., Lau, I. F., Saksena, S. K., and Chang, M. C. 1978. Circulating plasma levels of pregnenolone, progesterone, estrogen, luteinizing hormone, and follicle stimulating hormone in young and aged C57BL/6J mice during various stages of pregnancy. *J. Geront.* 33: 191–196.

Parkening, T. A. and Soderwall, A. L. 1975. Delayed fertilization and preimplantation loss in senescent golden hamsters. *Biol. Reprod.* 12: 618–631.

Patek, E., Nilsson, L., and Johannisson, E. 1972. Scanning electron microscopic study of the human fallopian tube. Report 2. Fetal life, reproductive life, and postmenopause. *Fertil. and Steril.* 23: 719–733.

Pazzagli, M., Forti. G., Cappellini, A., and Serio, M. 1975. Radioimmunoassay of plasma dihydrotestosterone in normal and hypogonadal men. *Clin. Endocrinol.* 4: 513–520.

Pedersen-Bjergaard, K. and Jonnesen, M. 1948. Sex hormone analysis: excretion of sexual hormones by normal males, impotent males, polyarthritics, and prostatics. *Acta Med. Scand. (Suppl.)* 213: 284–291.

Peluso, J. J. and England-Charlesworth, C. 1981. Formation of ovarian cysts in aged irregularly cycling rats. *Biol. Reprod.* 24: 1183–1190.

Peluso, J. J., England-Charlesworth, C., and Hutz, R. 1980a. Effect of age and of follicular aging on the preovulatory oocyte. *Biol. Reprod.* 22: 999–1005.

Peluso, J. J., Hutz, R., and England-Charlesworth, C. 1982. Development of preovulatory follicles and oocytes during the oestrous cycle of mature and aged rats. *Acta Endocrinol* 100: 434–443.

Peluso, J. J., Montgomery, M. K., Steger, R. W., Meites, J., and Sacher, G. 1980b. Aging and ovarian function in the white-footed mouse (*Peromyscus leucopus*) with specific reference to the development of preovulatory follicles. *Exp. Aging Res.* 6: 317–328.

Peluso, J. J., Steger, R. W., and Hafez, E. S. E. 1977. Regulation of LH secretion in aged female rats. *Biol. Reprod.* 16: 212–215.

Peluso, J. J., Steger, R. W., Huang, H., and Meites, J. 1979. Pattern of follicular growth and steroidogenesis in the ovary of older cycling rats. *Exp. Aging Res.* 5: 319–333.

Peluso, J. J., Steger, R. W., Jaszczak, S., and Hafez, E. S. E. 1976. Gonadotropin binding sites in human postmenopausal ovaries. *Fertil. Steril.* 27: 789–795.

Peng, M. T., Chuong, C. F., and Peng, Y. M. 1977. Lordosis response of senile female rats. *Neuroendocrinology* 24: 317–324.

Pepperell, R. J., deKretser, D. M., and Burger, H. G. 1975. Studies on the metabolic clearance rate and production rate of human luteinizing hormone and on the initial half-time of its subunits in man. *J. Clin. Invest.* 56: 118–126.

Pfeiffer, E. and Davis, G. C. 1972. Determinants of sexual behavior in middle and old age. J. Am Geriatric Soc. 20: 151–158.

Pfeiffer, E., Verwoerdt, A., and Davis, G. C. 1972. Sexual behavior in middle life. *Am. J. Psychiatry* 128: 1262–1264.

Pfeiffer, E., Verwoerdt, A., and Wang, H. S. 1969. The natural history of sexual behavior in a biologically advantaged group of aged individuals. *J. Gerontol.* 24: 193–198.

Pilnic, S. and Leis, H. P. 1978. Clinical diagnosis of breast lesions. *In,* H. S. Gallager, H. P. Leis, R. K. Snyderman, and J. A. Urban (eds.), *The Breast,* pp. 75–97. St. Louis: C. V. Mosby.

Piotti, L. E., Ghiringhelli, F., and Magrini, U. 1967. A propos de la fonction testiculaire du viellard: observations histochimiques et biologiques. *Revue Fr. Endocr. Clin.* 8: 479–491.

Pirke, K. M., Bofilias, B., Sintermann, R., Langhammer, H., Wolf, I., and Pabst, H. W. 1979a. Relative capillary blood flow and Leydig cell function in old rats. *Endocrinology* 105: 842–845.

Pirke, K. M. and Doerr, P. 1973. Age related changes and interrelationships between plasma testosterone, estradiol, and testosterone binding globulin in normal adult males. *Acta Endocrinol. (Kbh.)* 74: 792–800.

Pirke, K. M. and Doerr, P. 1975a. Age related changes in free plasma testosterone, dihydrotestosterone, and oestradiol. *Acta Endocrinol. (Kbh.)* 80: 171–178.

Pirke, K. M. and Doerr, P. 1975b. Plasma DHT in normal adult males and its relation to T. *Acta Endocrinol. (Kbh.)* 79: 357–362.

Pirke, K. M., Doerr, P., Sintermann, R. and Vogt, J. V. 1977. Age dependence of testosterone precursors of normal adult males. *Acta Endocrinol. (Kbh.)* 86: 415–429.

Pirke, K. M. Krings, B., and Vogt, H. J. 1979b. Further studies on hypothalamic-pituitary-testicular function in old rats. *Acta Endocrinol. (Kbh.)* 92: 358–369.

Pirke, K. M., Sintermann, R., and Vogt, H. J. 1980. Testosterone and testosterone precursors in the spermatic vein and in the testicular tissues of old men. Reduced oxygen supply may explain the relative increase of testicular progesterone and 17-alpha-hydroxy progesterone content in old age. *Gerontology* 26: 221–230.

Pirke, K. M., Vogt, H. J., and Geiss, M. 1978. *In vitro* and *in vivo* studies on Leydig cell function in old rats. *Acta Endocrinol. (Kbh.)* 89: 393–403.

Polani, P. E. and Jagiello, G. M. 1976. Chiasmata, univalents, and age in relation to aneuploid imbalance in mice. *Cytogenet. Cell Genet.* 16: 505–529.

Poortman, J., Thijssen, J. H. H., and DeWaard, F. 1981. Plasma oestrone, oestradiol, and androstenedione levels in postmenopausal women. Relation to body weight and height. *Maturitas* 3: 65–71.

Procope, E. J. 1970. Urinary excretion of oestrogens and the oestrogenic effect in vaginal smears in postmenopausal women with uterine bleeding. *Acta Obstet. Gynecol. Scand.* 49: 243–247.

Punnonen, R., Kouvonen, I., Lovgren, T., and Rauramo, L. 1979. Uterine and ovarian estrogen receptor levels in climacteric women. *Acta Obstet. Gynecol. Scand.* 58: 389–391.

Purifoy, F. E., Koopmans, L. H., and Mayes, D. M. 1981. Age differences in serum androgen levels in normal adult males. *Human Biol.* 53: 499–511.

Rader, M. D., Flickenger, G. L., deVilla, G. O., Mikuta, J. J., and Mikhail, G. 1973. Plasma estrogens in postmenopausal women. *Am. J. Obstet. Gynecol.* 116: 1069–1073.

Rahima, A. 1981. Vascular degenerative changes in the uterine arteries of senescent female golden hamsters. *Exp. Geront.* 16: 343–346.

Rahima, A. and Soderwall, A. L. 1977a. Uterine collagen content in young and senescent pregnant golden hamsters. *J. Reprod. Fertil.* 49: 161–162.

Rahima, A. and Soderwall, A. L. 1977b. Mast cells in uteri of pregnant young and senescent golden hamsters. *Biol. Reprod.* 17: 523–526.

Rahima, A. and Soderwall, A. L. 1978. Endometrial blood flow in pregnant young and senescent female golden hamsters. *Exp. Geront.* 13: 47–49.

Riegle, G. and Meites J. 1976. Effects of aging on LH and prolactin after LHRH, L-DOPA, methyl-DOPA, and stress in male rats. *Proc. Soc. Exp. Biol. (N.Y.)* 151: 507–511.

Riegle, G., Meites, J., Miller, A., and Wood, S. 1977. Effect of aging on hypothalamic LH releasing and prolactin inhibiting activities and pituitary responsiveness to LHRH in the male laboratory rat. *J. Gerontol.* 32: 13–18.

Riegle, G. D. and Miller, A. E. 1978. Aging effects on the hypothalamic-hypophyseal-gonadal control system in the rat. *In,* E. L. Schneider (ed.), *The Aging Reproductive System,* Vol. 4: *Aging,* pp. 159–192. New York: Raven Press.

Robboy, S. J. and Bradley, R. 1979. Changing trends and prognostic features in endometrial carcinoma associated with exogenous estrogen therapy. *Obstet. Gynecol.* 54: 269–277.

Robyn, C. 1975. Influence of age on serum prolactin levels in women and men. *Brit. Med. J.* 4: (Dec. 27), 738–739.

Robyn, C. 1975. Influence of age on serum prolactin levels oestrogen on circulating prolactin, LH, and FSH levels in postmenopausal women. *Acta Endocrinol.* 83: 9–14.

Rolandi, E., Pescatora, D., Milesi, G. M., Giberti, C., Sannia, A., and Barreca. T. 1980. Evaluation of LH, FSH, TSH, Prl, and GH secretion in patients suffering from prostatic neoplasms. *Acta Endocrinol. (Kbh.)* 95: 23–26.

Ron, M., Fich, A., Shapiro, A., Caine, M., and Ben-David, M. 1981. Prolactin concentration in prostates with benign hypertrophy. *Urology* 17: 235–237.

Ross, R. K., Paganini-Hill, A., Gerkins V. R., et al. 1980. A case control study of menopausal estrogen therapy and breast cancer. *JAMA* 243: 1635–1639.

Ross, R. K., Paganini-Hill, A., Mack, T. M., Arthur, M., and Henderson, B. E. 1981. Menopausal oestrogen therapy and protection from death from ischaemic heart disease. *Lancet* 1: 858–860.

Rubens, R., Dhont, M., and Vermeulen, A. 1974. Further studies on Leydig cell function in old age. *J. Clin. Endocrinol. Metab.* 39: 40–45.

Ryan, R. J. 1962. The luteinizing hormone content of human pituitaries. I. Variations with sex and age. *J. Clin. Endocrinol. Metab.* 22: 300–303.

Ryan, R. J. 1981. Follicular atresia: some speculations of biochemical markers and mechanisms. In, N. B. Schwartz and M. Hunzicker-Dunn (eds.), *Dynamics of Ovarian Function*, pp. 1–11. New York: Raven Press.

Saiduddin. S. and Zassenhaus, H. P. 1979. Estrous cycles, decidual cell response, and uterine estrogen and progesterone receptor in Fischer 344 virgin aging rats. *Proc. Soc. Exp. Biol. Med.* 161: 119–122.

Saksena, S. K. and Lau, I. F. 1979a. Variations in serum androgens, estrogens, progestins, gonadotropins, and prolactin levels in male rats from prepubertal to advanced age. *Exp. Aging Res.* 5: 179–194.

Saksena, S. K., Lau, I. F., and Chang, M. C. 1979b. Age dependent changes in sperm population and fertility in the male rat. *Exp. Aging Res.* 5: 373–381.

Sarjent, J. W. and McDonald, J. R. 1948. A method for quantitative measurement of Leydig cells in the human testis. *Mayo Clinic Proc.* 23: 249–254.

Saroff, J., Kirdani, R. Y., Chu, T. M., Wajsman, Z., and Murphy, G. P. 1980. Measurements of prolactin and androgen in patients with prostatic diseases. *Oncology* 37: 46–52.

Sartwell, P. E., Arthes, F. G., and Tonascia, J. A. 1977. Exogenous hormones, reproductive history and breast cancer. *J. Natl. Cancer Inst.* 59: 1589–1592.

Sasano, N. and Ichigo, S. 1969. Vascular patterns of the human testis with special reference to its senile changes. *Tohuku J. Exp. Med.* 99; 269–276.

Schaub, M. C. 1964–65. Changes of collagen in the aging and in the pregnant uterus of white rats. *Gerontologia* 10: 137–149.

Schiff, I. and Wilson, E. 1978. Clinical aspects of aging of the female reproductive system. In, E. L. Schneider (ed.), *The Aging Reproductive System*, pp. 9–28. New York: Raven Press.

Schneider, E. L. (ed.) 1978. *The Aging Reproductive System,* New York: Raven Press.

Schulze, W. and Schulze, C. 1981. Multinucleate Sertoli cells in aged human testis. *Cell Tissue Res.* 217: 259–266.

Seymour, F. I. Duffy, C., and Koerner, A. 1935. A case of authenticated fertility in a man of 94. *JAMA* 105: 1423–1425.

Shaar, C. J., Euker, J. S., Riegle, G. D., and Meites, J. 1975. Effects of castration and gonadal steroids on serum luteinizing hormone and prolactin in old and young rats. *J. Endocrinol.* 66: 45–51.

Shain, S. A. and Axelrod, L. R. 1973. Reduced high affinity 5α-dihydrotestosterone receptor capacity in the ventral prostate of the aging rat. *Steroids* 21: 801–812.

Shain, S. A., Boesel, R. W., and Axelrod, L. R. 1975. Aging in the rat prostate. Reduction in detectible ventral prostate androgen receptor content. *Arch. Biochem. Biophys.* 167: 247–263.

Shain, S. A. and Nitchuk, W. M. 1979a. Testosterone metabolism by the prostate of the aging AXC rat. *Mech. Ageing Dev.* 11: 9–22.

Shain, S. A. and Nitchuk, W. M. 1979b. Testosterone metabolism by the prostate of the aging canine. *Mech. Ageing Dev.* 11: 23–35.

Shapiro, M. and Talbert, G. B. 1974. The effect of maternal age on decidualization in the mouse. *J. Geront.* 29: 145–148.

Sherman, B. M. and Korenman, S. G. 1975. Hormonal characteristics of human menstrual cycle throughout reproductive life. *J. Clin. Invest.* 55: 699–706.

Sherman, B. M., West, J. H., and Korenman, S. G. 1976. The menopausal transition: analysis of LH, FSH, estradiol, and progesterone concentrations during menstrual cycles of older women. *J. Clin. Endocrinol. Metab.* 42: 629–636.

Siiteri, P. K. and Wilson, J. D. 1970. Dihydrotestosterone in prostate hypertrophy. I. The formation and content of dihydrotestosterone in the hypertrophic prostate of man. *J. Clin. Invest.* 49: 1737–1745.

Simpkins, J. W., Kalra, P. S., and Kalra, S. P. 1981. Alterations in daily rhythms of testosterone and progesterone in old male rats. *Exp. Aging Res.* 7: 25–32.

Simpkins, J. W., Mueller, G. P., Huang, H. H., and Meites, J. 1976. Changes in the metabolism of dopamine, norepinephrine, and serotonin and relation to gonadotropin secretion in the aging male rat. *The Physiologist* 19: 368.

Skoldefors, H., Carlstrom, K., and Furuhjelm, M. 1975. Aging and urinary estrogen excretion in the male. *Acta Obstet. Gynecol. Scand.* 54: 89–90.

Smith, D. C., Prentice, R., Thompson, D. J., and Herrmann, W. L. 1975. Association of exogenous estrogen and endometrial carcinoma. *N. Engl. J. Med.* 293: 1164–1167.

Sniffen, R. C. 1950. The testis. I. The normal testis. *Arch. Pathol.* 50: 259–284.

Snyder, P. J., Reitano, J. F., and Utiger, R. D. 1975. Serum LH and FSH responses to synthetic gonadotrophin releasing hormone in normal men. *J. Clin. Endocrinol. Metab.* 41: 938–945.

Soderwall, A. L., Kent, H. A., Turbyfill, C. L., and Britenbaker, A. I. 1960. Variation in gestation length and litter size of the golden hamster (*Mesocricetus auratus*). *J. Geront.* 15: 246–248.

Sokal, Z. 1964. Morphology of the human testes in various periods of life. *Folia Morphol.* 23: 102–111.

Soriero, A. 1980. Autoradiographic study of the effects of estrogen on *in vivo* incorporation of tritiated uridine into uterine smooth muscle and stromal RNA in the aging ovariectomized mouse. *J. Geront.* 35: 167–176.

Sparrow, D., Bosse, R., and Rowe, J. W. 1980. The influence of age, alcohol consumption, and body build on gonadal function in men. *J. Clin. Endocrinol. Metab.* 51: 508–512.

Speed, R. M. 1977. The effects of ageing on the meiotic chromosomes of male and female mice. *Chromosoma* 64: 241–254.

Speert, H. 1949. The endometrium of old age. *Surg. Gynacol. Obstet.* 89: 551–559.

Stearns, E. L., MacDonald, J. A., Kauffman, B. J., Lucman, T. S., Winters, J. S., and Faiman, C. 1974. Declining testis function with age: hormonal and clinical correlates. *Am. J. Med.* 57: 761–766.

Steger, R. W. 1981. Age related changes in the control of prolactin secretion in the female rat. *Neurobiol. Aging* 2: 119–123.

Steger, R. W., Huang, H. H., Chamberlain, D. S., and Meites, J. 1980a. Changes in control of gonadotropin secretion in the transition period between regular cycles and constant estrus in aging female rats. *Biol. Reprod.* 22: 595–603.

Steger, R. W., Huang, H. H., Hodson, C. A., Leung, F. C., Meites, J., and Sacher, G. A. 1980b. Effects of advancing age on hypothalamic-hypophysial-testicular functions in the male white-footed mouse (*Peromyscus leucopus*). *Biol. Reprod.* 22: 805–809.

Steger, R. W., Peluso, J. J., Bruni, J. F., Hafez, E. S. E., and Meites, J. 1979. Gonadotropin binding and testicular function in old rats. *Endokrinologie* 73: 1–5.

Steger, R. W., Peluso, J. J., Huang H., Hafez, E. S. E., and Meites, J. 1976. Gonadotrophin binding sites in the ovary of aged rats. *J. Reprod. Fertil.* 48: 205–207.

Studd, J. W. W., Chakravarti, S., and Collins, W. P. 1978a. Plasma hormone profiles after the menopause and bilateral oophorectomy. *Postgrad. Med. J.* 54 (Suppl. 2): 25–30.

Studd, J. W. W., Dubiel, M., Kakker, V. V., Thom, M., and White, P. J. 1978b. The effect of hormone replacement therapy on glucose tolerance clotting factors, fibrinolysis, and platelet behavior in postmenopausal women. *In*, I. D. Cook (ed.), *The Role of Estrogen-Progestogen in the Management of the Menopause*, pp. 41–62. Baltimore: University Park Press.

Suoranta, H. 1971. Changes in the small blood vessels of the adult human testis in relation to age and some pathological conditions. *Virchows Arch.* (*Pathol. Anat.*) 352: 165–181.

Takahashi, K., Kawashima, S., and Wakabayashi, K. 1980. Effects of gonadectomy and chlorpromazine treatment on prolactin, LH, and FSH secretion in young and old rats of both sexes. *Exp. Geront.* 15: 185–194.

Talbert, G. B. 1968. Effect of maternal age on reproductive capacity. *Am. J. Obstet. Gynecol.* 102: 451–477.

Talbert, G. B. 1971. Effect of maternal age on postimplantation reproductive failure in mice. *J. Reprod. Fertil.* 24: 449–452.

Talbert, G. B. 1977. Aging of the reproductive system. *In*, C. E. Finch and L. Hayflick (eds.), *Handbook of the Biology of Aging*, pp. 318–356. New York: Van Nostrand Reinhold.

Talbert. G. B. 1978. Effect of aging of the ovaries and female gametes on reproductive capacity. *In*, E. L. Schneider (ed.), *The Aging Reproductive System*, Vol. 4: *Aging*, pp. 59–83. New York: Raven Press.

Talbert, G. B. and Krohn, P. L. 1966. Effect of maternal age on viability of ova and uterine support of pregnancy in mice. *J. Reprod. Fertil.* 11: 399–406.

Tataryn, I. V., Lomax, P., Meldrum, D. R., Bajorek, J., Chesarek, L., and Judd, H. L. 1981. Objective techniques for the assessment of postmenopausal hot flashes. *Obstet. Gynecol.* 57: 340–344.

Tataryn, I. V., Meldrum, D. R., Lu, K. H., Frumar, A. M., and Judd, H. L. 1979. LH, FSH, and skin temperature during the menopausal hot flash. *J. Clin. Endocrinol. Metab.* 49: 152–153.

Thorneycroft, I. H. and Soderwall, A. L. 1969. Ovarian morphological and functional changes in reproductively senescent hamsters. *Anat. Record.* 165: 349–354.

Thorpe, L. W., Connors, T. J., and Soderwall, A. L. 1974. Closure of the uterine lumen at implantation in senescent golden hamsters. *J. Reprod. Fertil.* 39: 29–32.

Thung, P. J. 1961. Structural changes in the ovary. *In*, J. Bourne (ed.), *Structural Aspects of Aging*, pp. 109–142. New York: Hafner.

Thung, P. J., Boot, L. M., and Muhlbock, O. 1956. Senile changes in the oestrous cycle and in ovarian structure in some inbred strains of mice. *Acta. Endocrinol.* (Kbh) 23: 8–32.

Tikkanen, M. J., Nikkila, E. A., and Vartiainen, E. 1978. Natural oestrogen as an effective treatment for type-II hyperlipoproteinaemia in postmenopausal women. *Lancet* 2: 490–491.

Tillenger, K. G. 1957. Testicular morphology. *Acta Endocrinol.* (*Kbh.*) (*Suppl.*) 30: 28–39.

Toth, F. and Gimes, R. 1964. Senile changes in the female endocrine glands and internal sex organs. *Acta. Morph. Hung.* 12: 301–313.

Trachtenberg, J., Hicks L. L., and Walsh, P. C. (1980). Androgen and estrogen receptor content in spontaneous and experimentally induced canine prostatic hyperplasia *J. Clin. Invest.* 65: 1051–1059.

Trachtenberg, J., Bujnovszky, P., and Walsh, P. C. 1982. Androgen receptor content of normal and hyperplastic human prostate. *J. Clin. Endocrinol. Metab.* 54: 17–21.

Treloar, A. E. 1981. Menstrual activity and the pre-menopause. *Maturitas,* 3: 249–264.

Treloar, A. E., Boynton, R. E., Behn, B. G., and Brown, B. W. 1967. Variation of the human menstrual cycle through reproductive life. *Int. J. Fertil.* 12: 77–126.

Tsitouras, P. D., Kowatch, M. A., and Harman, S. M. 1979. Aged related alterations of isolated rat Leydig cell function: gonadotropin receptors, adenosine 3′,5′-monophosphate response and testosterone secretion. *Endocrinology* 105: 1400–1404.

Tsitouras, P. D., Kowatch, M. A., and Harman, S. M. 1980. HCG reverses secretory defect in Leydig cells from old rats. *Endocrine Soc. 62nd Annual Meeting.* Abstract 26, p. 81.

Tsitouras, P. D., Martin, C. E., and Harman, S. M. 1982. Relationship of serum testosterone to sexual activity in healthy elderly men. *J. Gerontol.* 37: 288–293.

Tsuji, K. and Nakano, R. 1978. Chromosome studies of embryos from induced abortions in pregnant women age 35 and over. *Obstet. Gynecol.* 52: 542–544.

Tyukov, A. I. 1967. Age changes in the vessels in the corpora cavernosa of the penis. *Arkh. Patol.* 29: 29–34.

Utian, W. H. 1975. Definitive symptoms of postmenopause—use of vaginal parabasal cell index. *Front. Horm. Res.* 3: 74–93.

Utian, W. H. 1980. *Menopause in Modern Perspective: A Guide to Clinical Practice,* p. 25. New York: Appleton-Century-Crofts.

Van der Schoot, P. 1976. Changing pro-oestrous surges of luteinizing hormone in aging 5-day cyclic rats. *J. Endocrinol.* 69: 287–288.

Van Wagenen, G. 1972. Vital statistics from a breeding colony: reproduction and pregnancy outcome in *Macaca mulatta. J. Med. Primatol.* 1: 3–28.

Vekemans, M. and Robyn, C. 1975. Influence of age on serum prolactin levels in women and men. *Br. J. Med.* 4: 738–739.

Vermeulen, A. 1976. The hormonal activity of the post-menopausal ovary. *J. Clin. Endocrinol. Metab.* 42: 247–253.

Vermeulen, A. 1979. Decline in sexual activity in ageing men: correlation with sex hormone levels and testicular changes. *J. Biosoc. Sci. (Suppl.)* 6: 5–18.

Vermeulen, A. 1980. Sex hormone status of the postmenopausal woman. *Maturitas* 2: 81–89.

Vermeulen, A., Rubens, R., and Verdonck, L. 1972. Testosterone secretion and metabolism in male senescence. *J. Clin. Endocrinol. Metab.* 34: 730–735.

Vermeulen, A. and Verdonck, L. 1972. Some studies on the biological significance of free testosterone. *J. Steroid Biochem.* 3: 421–426.

Vermeulen, A. and Verdonck, L. 1978. Sex hormone concentrations in postmenopausal women: relation to obesity, fat mass, age, and years post-menopause. *Clin. Endocrinol.* 9: 59–66.

Vermeulen, A. and Verdonck, L. 1979. Factors affecting sex hormone levels in postmenopausal women. *J. Steroid. Biochem.* 11: 899–904.

Verwoerdt, A., Pfeiffer, E., and Wang, H. S. 1969. Sexual behavior in senescence. II. Patterns of sexual activity and interest. *Geriatrics* 24: 137–154.

Walsh, P. C. and Wilson, J. D. 1976. The induction of prostatic hypertrophy in the dog with androstanediol. *J. Clin. Invest.* 57: 1093–1097.

Weiss, N. S., Szekely, D. R., English, D. R., and Schweid, A. I. 1979. Endometrial cancer in relation to patterns of menopausal estrogen use. *JAMA* 242: 261–264.

Weiss, N. S., Ure, C. L., Ballard, J. H., Williams, A. R., and Daling, J. R. 1980. Decreased risk of fractures of the hip and lower forearm with postmenopausal use of estrogen. *N. Engl. J. Med.* 303: 1195–1198.

Welsch, C. W. and Nagasawa, H. 1977. Prolactin and mammary tumorigenesis: a review. *Cancer Res.* 37: 951–963.

Whitehead, M. I., Townsend, P. T., Pryse-Davis, J., Ryder, T. A., and King, R. J. B. 1981. Effects of estrogens and progestins on the biochemistry and morphology of the postmenopausal endometrium. *N. Engl. J. Med.* 305: 1599–1605.

Wilson, J. D. 1980. The pathogenesis of benign prostatic hyperplasia. *Am. J. Med.* 68: 745–756.

Wise, P. M. 1982. Alterations in proestrous LH, FSH, and prolactin surges in middle-aged rats. *Proc. Soc. Exp. Biol. Med.* 169: 348–354.

Wise, P. M. and Ratner, A. 1980. Effect of ovariectomy on plasma LH, FSH, estradiol, and progesterone and medial-basal hypothalamic LHRH concentrations in old and young rats. *Neuroendocrinology* 30: 15–19.

Wise, P. M., Ratner, A., and Peake, G. T. 1976. Effect of ovariectomy on serum prolactin concentrations in old and young rats. *J. Reprod. Fertil.* 47: 363–365.

Witt, H-J., 1963. Structural elements and general function of the endometrium. Light microscope morphology. I. *In,* H. Schmidt-Matthiesen (ed.), *The Normal Human Endometrium,* pp. 24–64. New York: McGraw-Hill.

Woessner, J. F. 1963. Age-related changes of the human uterus and its connective tissue framework. *J. Geront.* 18: 220–226.

Yamaji, T., Shimamoto, K., Ishibashi, M., Kosaka, K., and Orimo, M., 1976. Effect of age and sex on circulating and pituitary prolactin in humans. *Acta Endocrinol. (Kbh.)* 711–719.

Zuckerman, S. 1956. The regenerative capacity of ovarian tissue. *In,* G. E. W. Wolstenholme and E. C. P. Millar (eds.), *Aging in Transient Tissues.* Vol. 2, Ciba Found. Colloq. Aging, pp. 31–58. Boston: Little, Brown.

Zumoff, B., Bradlow, H. L., Finkelstein, J., Boyar, R. M., and Hellman, L. 1976. The influence of age and sex on the metabolism of testosterone. *J. Clin. Endocrinol. Metab.* 42: 703–706.

Zumoff, B., Strain, G. W., Kream, J., O'Connor, J., Rosenfeld, R. S., Levin, J., and Fukushima, D. K. 1982. Age variation of the 24 hour mean plasma concentration of androgens, estrogens, and gonadotropins in normal adult men. *J. Clin. Endocrinol. Metab.* 54: 534–538.

19
MINERAL METABOLISM

A. N. Exton-Smith

University College London

Ionic equilibrium, which is necessary for the preservation of cell membrane potential and cell function, is maintained chiefly by potassium, sodium, calcium and magnesium among the cations and by chloride, phosphate and sulfate among the anions. The electrolytes sodium, magnesium, and potassium fall outside the scope of this chapter, leaving calcium and phosphorus preeminent. Calcium has a unique position in terms of its functional significance. Together with phosphorus, it is the only mineral present in the body in a purely organic solid form which provides the strength of the skeleton.

In this chapter, the following aspects of mineral metabolism will be discussed: the distribution of calcium and phosphorus in the body and their functions; the control mechanisms concerned with mineral homeostasis; the effects of aging on homeostasis; aging in bone and the loss of bone in the second part of life; the clinical syndrome of osteoporosis, its prevention and treatment; the change in patterns of fractures in old age and the factors involved.

DISTRIBUTION AND FUNCTION OF MINERALS

Calcium

The analyses carried out in humans by Widdowson and Dickerson (1964) have shown that calcium constitutes 0.1 to 0.2 percent of early fetal fat-free weight, rising to 2.2 percent of adult fat-free weight. In absolute terms, the calcium content of the body rises from 30 grams at birth to 1300 grams at maturity in a 70 kg individual with a fat-free weight of 60 kg. Thus during the 20 years of growth, the increment in calcium content is approximately 180 mg/day. Nearly 99 percent of the calcium is in the skeleton which represents 10 to 15 percent of body weight. The calcium content of the soft tissues and extracellular fluid amounts to about 8 grams.

About 60 percent of the skeletal calcium is contained in a highly organized crystal lattice of hydroxyapatite, and the remaining 40 percent is in the form of amorphous calcium phosphates and carbonate. Calcium in the plasma is in three main forms: ionized, protein bound, and complexed as citrate, phosphate, and proteinate. The ionized form constitutes approximately 46 percent of the total, a further 46 percent is bound to protein (and nearly 90 percent of this binding is to albumin); the

TABLE 1. Distribution of Minerals (70 kg man).

	Skeleton	Soft Tissues, Extra-cellular Fluid
Calcium	1300 g	8 g
Phosphorus	600 g	100 g
Magnesium	14 g	13 g

remaining small proportion of complexed calcium is partly diffusible as citrate and phosphate, and partly undiffusible as proteinate. Clinically, the most important fraction is the ionized calcium. The concentration of this fraction is difficult to measure accurately, although the advent of calcium ion selective electrodes has made the task easier. Total plasma calcium is usually determined, and different correction factors for protein binding have been used in order to increase the accuracy with which the measurement of total calcium reflects the ionized calcium concentration. These corrections are usually based on plasma albumin (Berry et al., 1973). Corrections are especially important in older individuals since the concentration of serum albumin falls with age and even greater decreases are to be found in a number of clinical conditions which affect the elderly.

Calcium in its ionized forms has the following functions:

1. It is required for bone formation, and calcification is controlled to a great extent by the concentration of ionic calcium in the specialized bone extracellular fluid. The calcium concentration in this fluid is appreciably lower than in the general extracellular fluid.
2. It regulates electrical transmission throughout the nervous system and at neurotransmitter junctions, and it preserves membrane potential and muscle contractility.
3. It is required for the expression of hormonal activity through cyclic adenosine monophosphate (cyclic AMP), including the actions of releasing factors, growth hormone, and thyrotrophin, the action of TSH on the thyroid and of LH on the corpus luteum, parathyroid hormone, and many other hormones (Rasmussen, 1972).
4. Many enzymes are activated by calcium ions and probably even more are inhibited.
5. Calcium ions are required for the activation of factor VIII and the conversion

of prothrombin to thrombin in the process of blood clotting.
6. Calcium ions are also required for the maintenance of the body's immune function since many antigen-antibody reactions are calcium dependent (Liberti et al., 1973).

Phosphorus

The total body phosphorus of man rises from 0.6 percent of fat-free body weight at birth to 1.2 percent in adult life (Widdowson and Dickerson, 1964). Thus the body of a 70 kg individual contains about 700 grams of phosphorus of which about 600 grams (85 percent) is in the skeleton and the rest in the soft tissues and body fluids.

Plasma inorganic phosphate is present in three forms: ionized, protein bound, and complexed. The ionized form constitutes 82 percent of the total; protein bound, 12 percent; and the remainder is complexed with calcium and magnesium. Inorganic phosphate in the plasma provides one of the major buffer systems in the regulation of acid-base balance particularly by renal excretion. The organic phosphates are present in every cell of the body, and some of them such as adenosine triphosphate (ATP) possess bonds with thermodynamic properties which are used to provide energy for cellular metabolism. Inorganic phosphate regulates calcium both within and outside the cell. It helps to control mineralization and is required for the formation of bone tissue in the ratio of 1 gram of phosphorus per 2 grams of calcium retained. Phosphorus is linked to most of the vitamins in the enzyme systems in the body and is closely allied to the metabolism of carbohydrates.

Magnesium

Total body magnesium rises from 200 to 300 mg/kg body weight at birth to nearly 400 mg/kg in adult man (Widdowson and Dickerson, 1964). In absolute terms for a 70 kg adult, the total body magnesium is 27 grams, of which 14 grams are in the skeleton and about 13 grams in the rest of the body tissues.

Although the total amount of magnesium in the body is only about one-twentieth that of calcium, in the soft tissues there is rather more magnesium than calcium. In the plasma, 70 percent of magnesium is in a diffusible ionized form. Most of the bound magnesium is associated with albumin, although the proportion found in globulin is higher than that of calcium. Magnesium in bone is not incorporated in the hydroxyapatite crystal lattice but remains in the hydration shell; only a minute fraction is diffusible with plasma magnesium. Within the cell, magnesium controls the structural integrity of the mitochondrial membrane just as calcium maintains the cellular membrane. Other important functions of magnesium ions are associated with anaerobic glycolysis and oxidative phosphorylation. Magnesium activates a number of enzyme systems including alkaline and acid phosphatases, pyrophosphatase, and ATPase. The magnesium-activated adenylate cyclase is responsible for the synthesis of AMP. In the cell nucleus, magnesium ions are required for the synthesis and stability of DNA. Magnesium controls neuromuscular excitability, and magnesium deficiency, which is rarely seen in clinical practice, produces signs similar to those of hypocalcemia. The manifestations include mental confusion, tremor, ataxia, irritability, weakness, and convulsions.

CALCIUM AND PHOSPHORUS METABOLISM

Calcium and phosphorus homeostasis is maintained by the interactions of the renal vitamin D endocrine system, parathyroid hormone (PTH), and calcitonin, and by the concentrations of calcium and phosphate ions themselves.

Vitamin D

There are two forms of vitamin D: cholecalciferol (vitamin D_3) and ergocalciferol (vitamin D_2). Deficiency of the vitamin produces rickets in childhood and osteomalacia in adult life. Man is dependent on vitamin D for adequate calcium absorption from the small intestine and for calcification of bone matrix.

Sources

Vitamin D reaches the body in two ways, by dietary ingestion and by synthesis in the skin. Skin synthesis under the influence of ultraviolet radiation acting on 7-dehydrocholesterol in the deeper layers of the epidermis is now believed to be the more important, and in the elderly, deprivation of sunlight is probably the principal cause of hypovitaminosis D (Fraser, 1983). The main dietary sources of vitamin D are oily fish (sardines, herring, mackerel, and tuna) and some dairy products such as eggs. Several foods are fortified with vitamin D, for example, margarine and some beverages used with milk. Milk itself is a poor source of vitamin D, but in the United States and Canada it is fortified and 1 U.S. quart contains 10 μg (400 I.U.) of vitamin D.

Intermediary Metabolism

Vitamin D, which has no direct action on its target organs, is converted in the body to an active hormone in two stages (Kodicek, 1974; DeLuca, 1974, 1976). In the first stage, hydroxylation takes place in the C-25 position of the steroid molecule in the liver to form 25-hydroxyvitamin D (25-OHD). This is the main circulating form of the vitamin. In the second stage, 25-OHD undergoes further hydroxylation in the renal tubule to form either 1,25-dihydroxycholecalciferol [1,25-(OH)$_2$D] or 24,25-dihydroxycholecalciferol [24,25-(OH)$_2$D]. Although there are other forms of dihydroxyvitamin D, these two forms have been most extensively studied. 1,25-(OH)$_2$D is present in minute amounts in the plasma (Kodicek, 1974; DeLuca, 1974, 1976), but it is generally believed to be the definitive hormonal form of vitamin D.

It is probable that the production of 1,25-(OH)$_2$D is regulated by intracellular calcium and/or phosphate levels and is stimulated by low calcium diets, by parathyroid hormone, and by low inorganic phosphate levels within the renal cortex.

Actions

The main action of 1,25-$(OH)_2$D is to promote calcium transport in its target organs. Thus it promotes calcium absorption from the small intestine. When calcium intake is low, an adaptation occurs with increased calcium absorption due to enhanced renal synthesis of 1,25-$(OH)_2$D at the expense of the less active 24,25-dihydroxymetabolite. In the presence of adequate concentrations of calcium and inorganic phosphate ions in the extracellular fluid surrounding bone and normal concentrations of 1,25-$(OH)_2$D, new bone formation occurs. Similarly, the maintenance of skeletal muscle contractility is dependent upon adequate calcium transport. Inadequate concentrations of 1,25-$(OH)_2$D lead to deficient bone calcification (with an increase in uncalcified osteoid) and to muscle weakness—features which are characteristic of rickets and osteomalacia. Excessive concentrations of 1,25-$(OH)_2$D promote bone resorption. There is also evidence that 1,25-$(OH)_2$D has actions on both the kidney and the parathyroid gland.

Variations in Vitamin D Status

People living in temperate zones show marked seasonal variation in their vitamin D status. This was first demonstrated by Smith et al. (1964) who compared the serum antirachitic activity of a group of elderly women living in Michigan with a group of similar age living in Puerto Rico. The Michigan group had a much lower antirachitic activity in winter than in summer, whereas for the Puerto Ricans the activity was considerably higher and showed no seasonal variation. Using the more precise index of radio-stereo assay of 25-OHD, Stamp and Round (1974) have shown seasonal variations in both young and old subjects in Britain. Mean plasma levels in healthy young white subjects were 32 nmol/liter in the early spring and rose to 55 nmol/liter in the late summer; the levels in old people showed similar sea-

sonal changes and were generally much lower than in young people. Information on any seasonal variation in the plasma concentrations of 1,25-$(OH)_2$D is lacking.

The seasonal variation in 25-OHD correlates with the daily hours of sunlight exposure (Lawson et al., 1979). Only solar radiation of a wavelength less than 313 nm is effective in vitamin D skin synthesis. The shortest wave length of UV radiation to reach the earth through the atmosphere is about 290 nm, so the effective "window" for vitamin D synthesis is very narrow. The average intensity of UV radiation declines with distance from the equator, and no radiation of less than 313 nm reaches Britain from the end of October to early March; consequently, little vitamin D can be formed during these months. Moreover, the intensity of solar ultraviolet radiation at the earth's surface varies with the time of day. Of the total available radiation in summer the proportion reaching the earth's surface between 9:30 A.M. and 3:30 P.M. is 68 percent in Dundee (latitude 56°) and 77 percent in North Dakota (latitude 47°) (Scotto and Fears, 1977; Frain-Bell, 1979). Cloud cover also reduces the intensity of solar UV radiation substantially.

In spite of the limited amounts of UV radiation of wavelengths between 290 and 313 nm reaching the earth's surface in temperate zones and the restricted sunlight exposure of certain sections of the population, including the elderly, the main determinant of vitamin D status is skin synthesis rather than dietary intake. This is supported by the experimental work of Haddad and Hahn (1973) who found that over 80 percent of the circulating 25-OHD in six Americans was present as 25-OHD_3 rather than in the D_2 form in spite of the fortification of milk with vitamin D_2 and consumption of vitamin D_2 supplements in the United States.

The studies of vitamin D status of elderly people living at home conducted by Lawson and his colleagues (1979) have shown that in summer the circulating levels of 25-OHD correlate with the amount of sunlight exposure and are independent of vitamin D content of the diet, whereas in winter the levels correlate with dietary intake and the amount of sunlight exposure the previous summer. In a study of nutrition of the elderly, Stephen and Dattani (1980) have examined the effects of increasing age on 25-OHD levels. In subjects of both sexes, there was a linear decline between the ages of 65 and 90; in the younger ages, the summer levels were higher than the winter levels (and they were higher in men than in women), but they declined more rapidly with age and by the age of 90, in each sex the summer levels equaled the winter levels. This study clearly shows the effects of limitation of sunlight exposure due to reduction in out-of-doors activity which occurs in very old people.

Housebound individuals form the largest group at risk of developing vitamin D deficiency. Not only do they lack sunlight exposure, but their dietary intakes are substantially reduced; 48 percent of housebound women aged 70–79 years had very low dietary intakes of less than 30 I.U./day compared with 13 percent of active women of similar age (Exton-Smith et al., 1972).

Parathyroid Hormone

Parathyroid hormone (PTH) plays a predominant role in the maintenance of calcium homeostasis. It is secreted in response to hypocalcemia, and it raises the concentration of plasma calcium by the following mechanisms:

1. It stimulates renal tubular calcium reabsorption.
2. It stimulates mobilization of calcium from bone by a direct action; vitamin D is required for this action which does not take place in the absence of adequate amounts of Vitamin D.
3. It increases the absorption of calcium from the small intestine by means of its control of $1,25\text{-}(OH)_2D$ synthesis by the kidney.
4. It lowers the levels of plasma inorganic phosphate by inhibition of renal tubular phosphate reabsorption.

The action of PTH on bone cells is to stimulate osteoclastic activity which causes bone resorption and the liberation of calcium into the extracellular fluid. There is also evidence that PTH may have a direct anabolic effect on bone; Reeve and his colleagues (1976) have demonstrated this action in low doses using a fragment of human PTH in patients with postmenopausal osteoporosis.

Calcitonin

Calcitonin (CT) is secreted by the C cells which in man are to be found mainly in the thyroid gland, but also in the parathyroids and in the thymus. In early studies in the dog, Copp et al. (1962) postulated that a hormone existed in the parathyroid gland which lowered plasma calcium and that its production is stimulated by hypercalcemia. Later in the pig, when bioassay techniques for CT became available, there was found to be a linear relationship between plasma calcium and CT (Care et al., 1968).

Although calcium is the main stimulus of CT secretion in the plasma of normal subjects in the basal state, there are other stimuli and chief among these are the hormones of the gastrointestinal tract. Glucagon causes an increase in CT secretion and induces hypocalcemia. Gastrin, pentagastrin, and pancreozymin are also involved, and it is probable that the control of CT secretion is mainly from the gastrointestinal tract. Although CT regulates plasma calcium, it does so indirectly by inhibiting bone resorption; following the ingestion of food, the absorbed calcium and phosphorus are taken up by bone mineralization and no change occurs in plasma calcium levels.

Homeostasis and the Effects of Age

Many studies in experimental animals have shown a decrease in the proportion of dietary calcium absorbed with increasing age. In studies using rats with everted gut sacs, the active transport of calcium was found to be greater in growing than in older animals (Schacter et al., 1960). This has been interpreted as the enhanced calcium transport needed to meet the higher calcium requirements for growth in young animals. Moreover, the adaptation in calcium absorption to a low calcium diet is more readily attained in young than in old animals.

In the human subject, a similar age-related decline in calcium absorption has been reported. In childhood and until well after puberty, there is a greater percentage of absorption of calcium from food than there is in the adult (Fourman and Royer, 1968). Since dietary calcium intake is as great or even greater in the young than in the adult, this means that in absolute terms the total calcium absorption into the body can be two to three times higher in childhood than in adult life. Balance studies and oral radiocalcium studies have shown that with increasing age, there is a progressive decline in calcium absorption (Bullamore et al., 1970). Perfusion studies following intubation of the small intestine have shown that in young subjects (average age 28 years) more calcium is absorbed for any given calcium concentration in the lumen than in elderly people (Ireland and Fordtran, 1973). This was found to be the case when the individuals had been on a high or low calcium diet prior to the study, but it was more marked on the low calcium intake, demonstrating that the old adapt less well to a low calcium diet than the young.

In both animals and man, kinetic studies of calcium absorption indicate that absorption takes place by a two-component process (Wilkinson, 1976). The first is an active process mediated by a carrier, calcium binding protein (CaBP), the formation of which is dependent upon the action of $1,25\text{-}(OH)_2D$ on the intestinal cell. With increasing age, there is a decrease in CaBP and this corresponds to the decrement in calcium absorption. The other process of calcium absorption is one of diffusion. It seems likely that the active carrier-mediated absorptive process is dominant at the lower concentrations of intraluminal calcium since it is saturable, whereas the diffusion component is relatively more important at higher concentrations.

The progressive fall in calcium absorption with age is more marked in women than in men, especially after the age of 60 years. There are several possible reasons for this decreased absorption: vitamin D deficiency which is more common in women than in men due to poor dietary intake or reduced skin synthesis, decreased hydroxylation of 25-OHD in the kidney due to the age-related impairment of renal function, and age changes in the intestine itself. Moreover in postmenopausal women, deficiency of estrogen leads to an increased sensitivity of the bone to PTH, release of calcium from bone tissue, and reduced PTH secretion (see section on osteoporosis). The reduction in PTH leads to decreased production of $1,25\text{-}(OH)_2D$ by the kidney, and this in turn results in a decrease in the carrier-mediated intestinal absorption of calcium.

It must be emphasized that the interpretation of the significance of this calcium malabsorption with increased fecal calcium excretion is open to question. An increase in fecal calcium (i.e., "calcium malabsorption") occurs in most forms of skeletal rarefaction due to a variety of causes; it is present in idiopathic juvenile osteoporosis, immobilization, corticosteroid therapy, osteomalacia, and neoplastic bone resorption (Editorial, 1976; Stamp, 1978). Stamp argues that "calcium malabsorption" thus defined is no more likely to be a primary cause of rarefaction in these conditions than in senile or postmenopausal osteoporosis. Progressive calcium malabsorption with age can equally result from progressive skeletal demineralization, or it may be an adaptation for a less metabolically active skeleton.

The concentration of calcium in plasma and extracellular fluid is regulated normally within very narrow limits. In the steady state, the plasma concentration of calcium is determined by the rate at which calcium enters the plasma and the rate at which it leaves. Entry of calcium is by absorption from the gastrointestinal tract and by resorption from bone. It leaves via the digestive juices into the feces, into the bone by mineralization, and by excretion in the urine. In normal subjects on a normal diet, the net calcium absorption is about 200 mg daily. The net excretion in the urine is also about 200 mg daily and, therefore, equals the net absorption. In healthy individuals, bone mineralization and resorption also takes place at the same rate.

With the maintenance of the constancy of

the concentration of calcium in plasma and extracellular fluid, it can be expected that plasma levels will change little in adult life. The majority of studies in healthy subjects show this to be the case. Lingarde (1972), however, found a linear decline with age. Marshall (1976) has pointed out that the data he presents are in terms of a single regression line for each sex, and he believes that this is not valid since a break occurs between the ages of 65 and 80 where the data are inadequate; he also points out that the lower values in the 80- to 95-year age group may be due to the fact that they were inhabitants of an old people's home and they may not have been healthy.

Biochemical investigations carried out in British studies of nutrition and health in old age [Department of Health and Social Security (DHSS), 1979a] showed no differences in the adjusted serum calcium (i.e., total calcium adjusted for variations in serum proteins) when the subjects were placed in two groups below and above the age of 80 years. Moreover, the concentrations were not significantly different from the reported values for younger adults. In these studies, all the old people whose ages ranged from 70 to 92 years were living at home and were medically examined.

In the DHSS studies, the mean serum phosphate concentration for men (2.87 mg/100 ml) was significantly lower ($p < 0.005$) than for women (3.38 mg/100 ml) and was also lower than that usually accepted for men in the younger age groups. The serum phosphate concentration in men up to the age of 65 years has been reported to fall with age (McPherson et al., 1978), whereas for women over the age of 50 it tends to rise (Wilding et al., 1972). The mean serum phosphate concentrations in the DHSS studies were very similar to those obtained by McPherson et al. (1978) for postmenopausal women and for men in the 55- to 65-year age group, and this suggests that little further change takes place after the age of 65 years.

The mean serum alkaline phosphatase activity of the housebound was significantly higher than that of subjects who were not housebound ($p < 0.001$). Out of 46 subjects who were housebound, 8 (17 percent) had alkaline phosphatase values above 13 King-Armstrong units compared with 14 (4 percent) of the other 319 subjects. This is a reflection of the inferior vitamin D status of the housebound due mainly to lack of sunlight exposure.

AGING IN BONE

Aging is accompanied by the loss of bone tissue from the skeleton, and this atrophy corresponds to the atrophy of other tissues which occurs with increasing age. Reduction in the amount of bone which accompanies aging is a universal phenomenon (Garn et al., 1967), but not all individuals lose bone at the same rate. Bone loss becomes manifest during the fifth decade in both sexes but proceeds more rapidly in females than in males. Before describing the patterns of bone development and bone loss, it is necessary to give a brief account of the age changes in bone structure and of the mechanisms of bone formation and resorption.

Structure

Compact cortical bone which forms the shafts of the long bones is made up of closely packed osteons or haversian systems. The thickness of the cortex increases during childhood and adolescence by subperiosteal new bone formation. In adult life, when bone turnover is low, cortical bone has a high mineral density and a uniform compact appearance. With aging, two important structural changes occur: the osteons show premature arrest and incomplete closure accompanied by a slow erosion of the haversian systems so that the porosity of the cortex increases, and those canals nearest the marrow cavity become widened leading to the conversion of the endosteal cortex into trabecular bone. Gradually, the endosteal surface becomes eroded and the rate of loss of bone at this surface exceeds the rate of subperiosteal deposition of bone so that by the time old age is reached the cortex has become thinner.

Cancellous bone, which is to be found in the axial skeleton, the majority of flat bones, and the ends of long bones, consists of a branching network of trabeculae contained within a cortical shell. The configuration of the trabeculae in a three-dimensional network is determined by the stress imposed on the bone and is such as to provide maximum strength in a light weight. In the vertebral body, with increasing age there occurs a destruction of trabeculae, first involving the horizontal and later the vertical trabeculae; the vertical trabeculae remaining show a consolidatory thickening. The loss of the horizontal struts supporting the vertical trabeculae leads to a considerable decrease in strength of the bone. Minor degrees of trauma will cause vertebral collapse with wedging or destruction of the integrity of the vertebral end-plates (see crush fractures). Comparable age changes occur in the iliac crest. Wakamatsu and Sissons (1969) found an increase in the spacing between the trabeculae, particularly in older women. Comparing the proportionate volume of bone tissue (mineralized bone + osteoid), these authors found a decrease from 23.3 percent at the age of 20 to 15.8 percent at the age of 70 years.

Bone Cells

Osteoclasts are the cells which are mainly responsible for bone resorption. Apart from the long skeletal muscle fibers, they are the largest cells in the body, with a diameter which may exceed 100 μm and with a hundred or more nuclei. Arnold and Jee (1957), who studied osteoclastic activity by means of the radioautographic distribution of plutonium, were the first to demonstrate that material from the bone surfaces is absorbed into the osteoclast. It is generally believed that the two components of this material—collagen and bone mineral—are removed simultaneously (Nordin, 1961). It appears that osteoclasts are unable to remove unmineralized bone or osteoid.

In our studies (Stewart et al., 1972) of bone resorption, histological examination was made of specimens from four sites—the ribs, skull, vertebral bodies, and the iliac crest. Particular attention was paid to changes in the ribs because at this site it was thought that there would be minimal effects of different degrees of immobility which might influence the rate

of bone resorption and formation. In general, the cortices were thin, the trabeculae reduced in thickness and number, and bone resorption was most marked at the endosteal and haversian surfaces. Occasionally, the cortex had been destroyed, and at these sites the bone marrow was in contact with the periosteum. Osteoclasis was less obvious than expected, yet the bones had lost a great deal of calcified tissue. Stewart et al. (1972) found that in the ribs, the degree of rarefaction correlated more with the number and size of osteocytic lacunae rather than with osteoclastic activity. Jowsey and her colleagues (1964), using autoradiography, reported that whereas enlarged lacunae are found in about one-fifth of normal bones, among those with osteoporosis the proportion is over 30 percent, and in those suffering from hyperparathyroidism it is over 80 percent. Bélanger et al. (1963) suggested that resorption could occur without osteoclasts and showed that under certain conditions osteocytes were capable of elaborating enzymes which could digest gelatin. Thus, in addition to the removal of bone matrix and mineral by oestoclasts, it is probable that osteocytes are capable of effecting the same process—the so-called osteocytic osteolysis. It now seems likely that while the osteoclasts are primarily associated with bone remodeling activity—a slow process in which mineral is released only after a delay period—osteocytes are responsible for the continuous exchange of calcium and phosphate between the bone and extracellular fluid. Both processes are influenced by PTH, but that mediated by the osteocytes exerts a finely controlled homeostatic mechanism for the maintenance of calcium concentration in plasma and extracellular fluid. Osteocytic osteolysis has also been observed following large doses of vitamin D, and this may account for the already mentioned bone resorption due to excessive doses of vitamin D.

In the vertebral bodies examined by Stewart et al. (1972), the osteocytes appeared to be reacting in a similar manner as in the ribs with many enlarged lacunae; in many specimens there was also a striking degree of osteoclasis. There were often areas where the osteoclasts had destroyed the outer bony shell so that the marrow was in contact with the periosteum or intervertebral disc.

It has for long been recognized that the osteoblast is the cell responsible for the production of bone matrix which subsequently becomes mineralized. Actively synthesizing osteoblasts have fine processes contacting each other and extending into the osteoid. They are able to secrete several times their own volume of osteoid before becoming embedded in the bone matrix or converted to osteocytes. The deposition of bone mineral occurs after a delay of about ten days and along a well-defined calcification front. The osteoid border, which is present outside the calcification front, varies in thickness at different sites and becomes thinner with increasing age. Except in cases of osteomalacia, osteoblastic activity is greatly reduced in older bones (Stewart et al., 1972). In the absence of vitamin D, calcification does not take place and the osteoid seams are increased in width and occupy a greater proportion of the trabecular surface.

Recent electron microscopy studies have provided indirect evidence that osteocytes are responsible for bone formation as well as osteoblasts. Aaron (1976) believes that the osteocyte plays a crucial role in bone formation and is responsible for the packaging of bone mineral into the complex structures in the Golgi apparatus before transfer to the calcification front.

Bone Remodeling

Following the cessation of growth at maturity, internal remodeling of bone continues. This process does not take place uniformly but at local sites where old or damaged tissue is replaced by new bone. In early adult life, about 10 percent of the skeleton is remodeled annually. Frost (1966) has given the name basic multicellular (metabolizing) units (BMU) to the individual sites of activity. In cortical bone, a single BMU is an osteon. Before new bone formation can occur, bone must first be resorbed; that is, the replacement of an old osteon by a new one requires the formation of a resorption cavity. The sequence is normally one of bone formation occurring one

month after bone resorption. In a transverse section of bone cortex, the resorptive phase lasts about 25 days, followed by the phase of apposition lasting about 75 days; after this, there is a "resting" phase lasting many years. With increasing age, the osteons become smaller with fewer branches than in the younger adult; moreover, the speed with which the cells complete their cycle of activity becomes slower. As a result, at the BMU level small discrete deficits in the amount of bone occur with aging, and for the whole bone the amount of bone loss corresponds to the birth rate of BMUs. Meunier and his colleagues (1979) have suggested a model to account for the increase in bone loss which occurs in various pathological conditions. In high remodeling osteoporosis induced by thyroid hormones or parathyroid hormone, although the deficit at BMU level is the same as in normal aging, the increase in birth rate of BMUs induced by these hormones leads to augmentation of bone loss in the whole bone. As would be expected in these conditions, the numbers of osteoclasts, resorption surfaces, osteoid surfaces, and osteoblast surfaces are all increased. An increase in rate of loss of bone can occur when there is a depression of osteoblastic activity without any change in activation of BMUs. The osteoblastic depression augments the deficit at the individual BMU level. Such a situation is to be found in corticosteroid-induced osteoporosis and in Cushing's syndrome. Finally, excessive bone loss can result from a combination of these two mechanisms: the summation effect brought about by an increase in the activation rate of BMUs and a decrease in collagen synthesis by the osteoblasts leads to a marked increase in bone loss. This combination occurs when corticosteroids are administered to patients with high parathyroid hormone levels. The operation of the two mechanisms is also believed to account for the acute osteoporosis induced by disuse in which there is an increase in resorption surfaces associated with a depression of osteoblastic apposition rate.

This description of the remodeling process applies to cortical bone in which resorption must always precede apposition in order to create space in which the new bone deposition can occur. A similar process probably occurs in cancellous bone with "coupling" of the processes of bone resorption and formation. However, as we have already seen, in cancellous bone some trabeculae are removed, whereas others are consolidated by the deposition of new bone on apparently inactive surfaces.

Merz and Schenk (1970) have observed that the extent of osteoblast surfaces falls with advancing age and there is an increase in the proportion of abnormally thin osteoid borders in older individuals. Moreover, aging is associated with a decreased mineralization rate (Frost, 1969). The present evidence indicates that decreased bone formation contributes to the loss of trabecular bone with age in both men and women. As the number of trabeculae becomes reduced with age, the marrow spaces increase, but many of the marrow cells are replaced by fat cells and there is a decrease in the functional marrow cell population (Meunier et al., 1971). The decreased number of osteoblasts may result from the inability of the functionally deficient marrow to provide an adequate supply of osteo-progenitor cells particularly at the endosteal surfaces in contact with the marrow.

The other important factor contributing to bone loss is increasing bone resorption with age. Jowsey and her colleagues (1965) have demonstrated the age-related increase in the surface extent of resorption cavities, and they have designated increased resorption as the underlying cause of osteoporosis. However, except in cases of secondary high remodeling osteoporoses (Meunier et al., 1979), osteoblastic activity appears to remain remarkably constant throughout life. These observations could be explained in several ways:

1. The increase in extent of resorption cavities is the result of inadequacy of bone formation and an inability to fill old cavities with osteoid.
2. The increase in bone resorption may be due to osteocytic osteolysis in the absence of increased osteoclasis.
3. The capacity of individual osteoclasts to resorb bone may be increased. This is

particularly likely to be a factor concerned in the causation of accelerated bone loss occurring in women after the menopause. The decrease or absence of the protective activity of estrogen allows the unopposed action of parathyroid hormone in promoting bone resorption.

Bone Mass

In Vitro Measurements. There have been many postmortem studies of bone mass both in the complete skeleton and in individual bones. In studies of whole bones, the properties which are most often investigated are the dry weight (W) and the external volume (V). The weight volume ratio (W/V) represents the proportion of whole bone volume occupied by bony tissue. The ratios for a number of bones have been measured over the complete age range by Trotter and her colleagues. In young skeletons, there are differences between the sexes and between races, with Negroes having higher ratios than Whites, and males having higher ratios than females (Trotter, 1971). The decrease with age in the mean W/V ratios of ten bones was found to be significant in both sexes and both races (Trotter et al., 1960). Moreover the W/V ratios of the different bones declined at about the same rate within each sex/race group.

In these studies of whole bones it is not possible to assess the relative contribution of losses in compact bone and trabecular bone to the decrease in bone mass. In healthy adults, about 80 percent of the dry weight of the skeleton is in compact bone and 20 percent in trabecular bone (Trotter et al., 1960). In absolute terms, most loss of bone tissue from the skeleton comes from cortical bone, but in proportional terms, it is the trabecular bone which is most severely affected. This is because trabecular bone, as a consequence of its open structure, has a much greater surface area (about five times) than compact bone and the surface specific resorptive processes produce a greater proportionate loss in trabecular bone weight than in cortical bone weight.

In vitro studies of trabecular bone have been

made most extensively in the vertebral bodies and the iliac crest. Arnold (1973), in postmortem studies of vertebrae, has reported a 50-percent reduction in bone tissue between youth and old age in both sexes. As already mentioned, with aging there is at first a preferential loss of horizontal trabeculae. The loss of the horizontal struts supporting the vertical trabeculae causes a considerable reduction in bone strength. The stress at failure of the vertebral bodies in relation to the amount of bone tissue has been investigated (Weaver and Chalmers, 1966; Bell et al., 1967). A reduction in the ash weight per unit volume from 0.2 to 0.1 g/cm^3 produced a fall in the stress at failure from 750 to 250 lb/in^2. Thus the loss of bone which accompanies aging from youth to old age produces a disproportionate (threefold) reduction in the failure strength.

In vitro and *in vivo* biopsy studies of trabecular bone loss in the iliac crest reveal similar findings. Iliac crest data show that women start with a slightly higher mean trabecular bone mass than men but lose bone more rapidly in middle life and have less bone than men in old age (Gallagher et al., 1973; Meunier et al., 1973). The mean trabecular bone volume in men and women below the age of 50 is 22 percent; in men over the age of 60 it is 19 percent, and in women over 60 it is 16 percent. Thus from early adult life to old age men lose 17 percent of their initial trabecular bone mass and women 29 percent (Nordin, 1980).

In Vivo Measurements. There are several methods for the quantitative investigation *in vivo* of the amount of bone in the skeleton. These procedures have been reviewed by Horsman (1976). Each method has its limitations, and there are particular difficulties in carrying out measurements of the trabecular bone content of the axial skeleton. The following are the most commonly used techniques:

1. X-ray densitometry—in this technique, the bone mineral content is measured from a radiograph by comparing the bone image with a standard (e.g., aluminum wedge) using an optical densitometer.

2. Photon absorptionometry (gamma ray densitometry) consists of the measurement of the absorption by bone of a collimated beam of gamma radiation from a low energy radioisotope source (iodine 125, americium 241). It was first introduced by Cameron and Sorenson (1963) and has been applied to a number of sites such as the distal radius and ulna, the phalanges, and the femur.

3. Neutron activation analysis measures the radioactivity of ^{49}Ca produced by neutron activation of stable calcium in the bones. This is probably the most suitable method of measuring bone mineral mass in the axial skeleton (Harrison et al., 1975, 1979).

4. Morphometry based on measurements made on hand radiographs is a simple and reliable method for assessing the amount of cortical bone. Measurements of the total and medullary widths of the midshaft of the second metacarpal were first proposed by Barnett and Nordin (1960) as a means of assessing osteoporosis. It depends on the fact that with advancing age and in osteoporosis the medullary width enlarges due to endosteal resorption of bone. The length (L) of the bone (usually the second metacarpal or the third proximal phalanx) is measured with a millimeter rule, and at the midpoint, the diameters of the medullary canal (d) and the periosteal envelope (D) are measured with a vernier caliper. It should be noted that the method does not take account of changes in the porosity of the cortex (Stewart et al., 1972), but nevertheless we have found that the transverse cross-sectional cortical area of the third proximal phalanx as well as that of the second metacarpal correlates well with the ash content as determined by incineration (Exton-Smith et al., 1969a; Gryfe et al., 1972).

Garn and his colleagues have mainly used measurements of cortical thickness ($D - d$), and they have contributed valuable information on normal developmental patterns, racial factors, and nutritional status as they relate to the skeleton (Garn et al., 1964a, 1964b, 1967); more recently derived parameters have been presented (Garn, 1970). When using morphometric methods of this kind, particularly in cross-sectional studies, it is desirable to make a correction for variations in skeletal size in order to compare the amount of bone in different individuals. It is less important to make the correction in longitudinal studies in which serial measurements are made on the same individual. Nordin (1971) has employed the ratio of cortical area to total area $[(D^2 - d^2)/D^2]$, while we have used the ratio of cortical area to surface area $[(D^2 - d^2)/DL]$ (Exton-Smith et al., 1969b; Gryfe et al., 1971), which we have shown compensates for the differences in skeletal size between individuals and between the sexes.

Patterns of Bone Development and Loss

There have been many studies using metacarpal morphometry of the loss of cortical bone with age in various populations of the world including the United States (Garn et al., 1967; Garn, 1970), South American countries (Garn et al., 1967), Britain (Nordin, 1966; Exton-Smith et al., 1969b; Gryfe et al., 1971), Finland (Halela, 1969), India (Nordin, 1966), China and Japan (Garn et al., 1964a), and South Africa (Walker, 1970, 1971).

Nordin (1966) has expressed the results as the mean ± 2 S.E. of the ratio of cortical area to total area (CA/TA) for each sex between the ages of 20 and 85 years. The mean CA/TA ratio in men falls from 0.802 in the 20- to 49-year age group to 0.706 in those aged 70–79, and in women from 0.866 in the 20- to 49-year age group (premenopausal) to 0.623 in those aged 80–89 years. The decrease in the ratio after the age of 50 is about 0.002 per year in men and about 0.006 per year in women.

In our studies of the patterns of development and loss of bone with age, the ratios of cortical area to surface area (CA/SA) or metacarpal cortical index (MCI) have been calculated, and these have been expressed in the form of percentile ranking curves for the normal population of males and females between the ages of 2 and 85 years (Exton-Smith et al., 1969b; Gryfe et al., 1971). These curves indicate the variance and distribution of values for each age (see Figure 1).

Characteristics. Some of the features of the changes in cortical bone mass with age as revealed by these curves are:

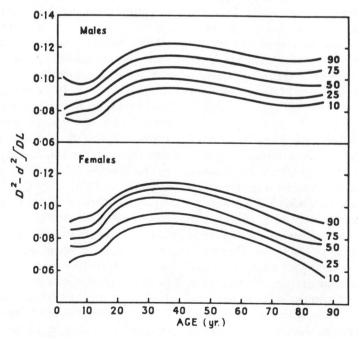

Figure 1. Percentile ranking curves for the amount of bone in the metacarpal cortex for males and females aged 3 to 85 years.

1. The curves for the percentiles (10, 25, 50, 75, and 90) remain roughly parallel with age; that is, the variance remains unchanged with age and the distribution at each age group is normal.
2. There is a rapid increase in the amount of bone during the period of growth (up to the age of 18 years), but the increase continues at a slower rate for another 12 years or so, and maturity is reached shortly after the age of 30 years.
3. The amount of bone in childhood is greater in males than in females, and this difference is apparent throughout life.
4. Loss of bone is steady after about the age of 45, occurring more rapidly in women than in men.
5. There are some individuals in old age who have more bone than others at the age of skeletal maturity.

In the study of Gryfe and his colleagues (1971), height and weight data were obtained for the children whose metacarpals were measured. There was found to be a very close correlation in each sex between height and the length of the second metacarpal; this is to be expected since height during growth and at maturity is determined largely by the length of the long bones. When, however, the amount of bone was related to body weight by calculation of the cortical area/weight ratio [$(D^2 - d^2)/W$], at the age of 18 years the mean ratio was 20 percent less in females than in males. That is, by the time growth ceases, girls have lighter skeletons in relation to body weight than boys.

Interpretation of Patterns. The interpretation of these results which are based on cross-sectional studies must be made with caution, but the following comments can be made.
1. Since the percentile ranking curves remain parallel with age, it seems likely that one of the factors determining the bone mass in old age is the amount of bone at maturity.
2. The fact that the variance and distribution remain unaltered with age indicates that bone loss is a universal phenomenon, although this does not necessarily imply that all individ-

uals lose bone at the same rate. Nor is it possible to identify a separate group of rapid bone losers, the "osteoporotics," in old age.
3. If there is a critical level for the amount of bone at which manifestations of osteoporosis occur, as suggested by Newton-John and Morgan (1968), then this level will be reached at an earlier age for those individuals with a bone mass in the lower percentile ranges than for those individuals with greater amounts of bone who can better withstand the loss of bone with age.
4. The differences in bone mass between the sexes in old age, with women having less bone than men, could be accounted for by their poorer skeletal status at maturity and more rapid bone loss after the menopause.
5. In part, the loss of bone with age may be more apparent than real due to the intrusion of cohort effects in cross-sectional studies. Thus the skeletal status of present 75 year olds at maturity may have been inferior to that of the 25 to 30 year olds today. It has been shown (Exton-Smith, 1970) that the length of the second metacarpal for men aged 75 is on average 1.5 mm less than for men aged 25–30 years. This corresponds to a difference in height of about 4 cm. Thus the present generation of 75 year olds were, in earlier life, 4 cm shorter than those aged 25 today. This estimate is close to that reported by Khosla and Lowe (1968) who have found that there has been an increase in the mean height of the adult male population in the United Kingdom of 2.5 cm per generation since the beginning of this century. It also corresponds with the accelerated growth in childhood which has occurred during the last 50 years (Tanner et al., 1966). This more rapid growth has been attributed to improvement in nutritional status generally, but Nordin (1976) has pointed out that the proportionate increase in calcium intake has been much greater than that of calories and protein, suggesting that calcium nutrition may be playing a more important role.
6. The percentile ranking curves for men show that there is an apparent increase in bone mass for men over the age of 80 compared with those aged 75 years. This reversal of a

general downward trend can be ascribed to the "survival of the fittest." Men over the age of 80 form a highly selected group and they represent a biological elite; not only do they have better developed bones, but their sustained health and physical vigor have enabled them to outlive their former contemporaries (Exton-Smith, 1970). Similar changes in other characteristics, for example, a reduced liability to fall in very old men, have been reported (Exton-Smith, 1977).

It should be noted that in most of the studies of bone loss in aging women the exact age of the menopause in each individual is not identified, and the bone loss is described as linear after the age of 45 or 50 (Newton-John and Morgan, 1968). Owing to the varying age of the menopause, the rate of loss of bone in middle age appears more uniform than it actually is; moreover, in our studies, the percentile curves are "smoothed out" and are based on the best fit of values for each percentile.

When longitudinal studies are carried out starting just before and at the time of the menopause, it is found that the rate of loss of bone is most rapid within 5–10 years after the menopause; thereafter, there is a fall in the rate of loss. Johnston and his colleagues (1979) have carried out a prospective study utilizing the photon absorption technique at two sites (the midshaft and the distal end of the radius) in Caucasian females, each of whom was followed up for a period of at least 2.5 years. The aim of the study was to ascertain at what age bone loss begins and how during the subsequent course the rate of loss changes with age. They found that before the age of 50 the rate of bone loss was low; thereafter, it increased 2½- to 3-fold, and again in old age (mean age 80.5) the rate of loss was minimal. This exponential loss of bone after age 50 implies that the rate of loss of bone is directly proportional to the initial mass of bone present at the onset of loss and is in contrast to the linear model where there is no relationship to initial mass. The rate of loss was significantly correlated with the initial mass at the midshaft ($p < 0.002$) and the distal radius ($p < 0.0001$).

As in our studies (Exton-Smith et al., 1969b and Gryfe et al., 1971), Johnston and his colleagues (1979) found in the cross-sectional data that the distribution of bone mass remained Gaussian for each decade and there was no increase in variance when the bone mass of the older groups was compared with that of the younger ones. Their longitudinal data also revealed no evidence for a bimodality in the rate of loss, again supporting the view that there is not a separate distinct group of rapid losers—the clinical "osteoporotics." Although those at the extremes of the array were separated arbitrarily into two groups of "rapid" and "slow" losers, these simply represented the extremes of a spectrum and were not distinct populations.

OSTEOPOROSIS

Osteoporosis is not a single disease entity, but it is the end result of a number of processes which become more common with increasing age and lead to a diminution in the amount of bone in the skeleton. However, in spite of its heterogeneity, there are characteristic clinical, radiological, and pathological features which enable a distinction to be made from other forms of metabolic bone disease. The condition was recognized many years ago by German anatomists, but at the clinical level the distinction from osteomalacia was only made more recently by Albright and his colleagues (1941).

Definition

The classical definition of osteoporosis by Albright is "too little bone, but what bone there is is normal," and he believed that the condition was due to a failure to make bone matrix. Now we no longer include etiology in the definition, nor do we attribute osteoporosis solely to a hormonal imbalance affecting bone formation.

The original definition can be criticized on other counts. It does not define too little bone; usually this has been taken to mean diminution in the amount of bone in comparison with the amount of bone as assessed by standards for adults at maturity. However, in the definition we ought to distinguish between the phenomenon of gradual bone loss as an accompaniment of aging and the fact that bone loss, whether normal or excessive, leads ultimately to structural failure of the skeleton or its likely risk. The normal age-related loss is sometimes called "[physiological] osteopenia" to distinguish it from "[pathological] osteoporosis" in which the clinical syndrome is characterized by collapse of the vertebral bodies and the liability to fracture of certain long bones.

Thus the cutoff point between physiological and pathological bone loss is taken to be the stage when fractures occur. This is not satisfactory from a clinical viewpoint since our aim should be to recognize the bone loss at an earlier stage and, if possible, prevent its progress to the stage of structural failure. It has already been mentioned that point of time studies show that at any given age bone mass has a Gaussian distribution, and distinct populations of "normal" and "osteoporotics" cannot be identified. Our own studies (Stewart et al., 1972) have also shown that the ash content of bones has a similar Gaussian distribution and there may be a twofold difference in ash content of bones taken from subjects of the same age.

In the original definition, the bone in osteoporosis is taken to be normal; this is true when the method of study is by histology or organic analysis. It has, however, recently been shown (Posner, 1970) that the percentage crystallinity can change and that mineral form can affect bone strength as much as mineral content. Thus, as methods improve, several diseases at present grouped as osteoporosis may be separately identified.

Etiology

One of the major obstacles in ascertaining the mechanisms responsible for the development of osteoporosis is that there have been few large scale studies on individuals while they are actually losing skeletal mass. Thomson and Frame (1976) have pointed out that evaluation of patients after bone loss has occurred may not be a valid way to ascertain the initial mechanism of loss because many of the pathogenic mechanisms may be altered with time.

Some investigators believe that osteoporosis is not a disorder which develops suddenly in middle or old age but a condition to which all people progress gradually, beginning soon after the age of 25. The limited longitudinal studies which have been undertaken (e.g., Johnston et al., 1979), however, indicate that it is possible to separate a group of "rapid bone losers." Comparison of the characteristics of this group with those of the "slow losers" should more readily provide evidence for an understanding of the mechanisms underlying the pathogenesis of osteoporosis.

Before discussing in detail the various etiological factors, it must be emphasized that histomorphometric studies reveal that primary osteoporosis exists in several forms. Thus different pathogenic mechanisms are involved, and correspondingly, the therapeutic regimens are likely to be different. Meunier et al. (1979) have demonstrated this heterogeneity. Ten percent of their patients were found to have high remodeling osteoporosis with extended active remodeling surfaces. Usually these patients have high urinary hydroxyproline excretion, indicative of increased bone resorption and elevated plasma PTH levels. The majority (90 percent) of osteoporotic patients have normal resorption and apposition surfaces, and no evidence of increased remodeling. Among these, 37 percent (that is, about 33 percent of the total osteoporotic population) have a low osteoblastic appositional rate with some of the characteristics of corticosteroid-induced osteoporosis. In over 60 percent of patients with primary osteoporosis, it was not possible to demonstrate any significant abnormality at the time of the biopsy by the methods presently used for the static and dynamic quantitative analysis of bone tissue, except for a reduced amount of bone. It is suggested that these osteoporotics could represent a population whose decreased bone mass in later life is due to the normal loss of bone with aging associated with a reduced initial bone mass at the end of the period of growth.

Although many of the factors responsible for bone loss with age have already been mentioned, it will be convenient to review these and other factors concerned in the development of osteoporosis under four headings: (1) skeletal status at maturity; (2) hormonal factors; (3) nutritional factors affecting bone loss; and (4) influence of immobilization.

Skeletal Status at Maturity. It has already been pointed out that girls at the age of 18 years have a 20 percent lower bone mass in relation to body weight than boys. This, together with more rapid bone loss after the age of 50, could be responsible for the higher prevalence of osteoporosis in women in old age. In both sexes, those individuals who have densely calcified bones at maturity may be at an advantage; the skeleton will remain adequate even when, in later life, part of the bone mineral is lost. Newton-John and Morgan (1968), from a model of bone loss in women, considered that these factors alone could be responsible for the clinical syndrome of osteoporosis and that it occurs earlier in those whose initial skeletal development is poor. The absence of longitudinal studies makes it difficult to prove that this is the case. It is equally possible that those individuals who develop osteoporosis early could have a normal bone mass at maturity but have lost bone more rapidly during middle life. The limited investigations in which serial measurements have been made indicate that variation in rate of loss occurs (Garn et al., 1964; Exton-Smith et al., 1964b; Gryfe et al., 1971; Johnston et al., 1979). On present evidence it is reasonable to assume that both these patterns exist: namely, lower than normal bone mass at maturity with a normal age-related bone loss, and adequate initial skeletal mass with accelerated loss in later life. Implicit to these hypotheses is the concept that in each population there is a critical level of bone mass which is associated with the risk of fracture, but it is just as likely that if such a level exists it varies in different individuals.

Very little is known about the factors concerned in skeletal development during the period of growth. Genetic factors are important and at maturity Negroes have a greater skeletal mass than Whites (Merz et al., 1956). Phys-ical activity may be of importance since muscle weight is significantly correlated with bone mass. Nutritional factors in early life undoubtedly play a role. Experimentally, Platt and Stewart (1962, 1968) have produced skeletal rarefaction in growing pigs and dogs fed on a low protein diet, but there is less evidence that protein nutrition is a factor in human skeletal development. The increase in height, which is an index of bone mass (Eddy, 1972), that has occurred in the British male population since the beginning of this century has already been mentioned. This more rapid growth has been attributed to a general improvement in nutritional status in childhood. According to Greaves and Hollingsworth (1966), the mean calcium intake in the U.K. population has risen from 600 mg/day in 1909 to 1150 mg/day in 1960, whereas protein intake has changed very little and the mean calorie intake by less than 10 percent. Nordin (1976) has drawn attention to this disproportionate increase in calcium intake, indicating that calcium nutrition may be exerting a dominant role in this acceleration of growth. Certainly in Japan as a result of greater milk consumption, calcium intake increased threefold from 1950 to 1970 with little change in protein and calorie intakes. Twelve-year-old schoolboys are now 10 cm taller than boys of the same age ten years ago. There is considerable experimental evidence that calcium intake is important, and skeletal rarefaction can be produced in growing rats fed on a low calcium diet (Gershon-Cohen et al., 1963, 1964; El Maraghi et al., 1965). The evidence that fluoride is related to the development of osteoporosis is inconclusive. The reduction in dental decay by fluoride administration is known to be most apparent during the period of formation of the teeth, and it is possible that the influence of fluoride in the prevention of osteoporosis in old age may be exerted maximally during the period of skeletal growth.

Hormonal Factors. Mention has already been made of the involvement of the vitamin D endocrine system in the bone loss of aging. In postmenopausal osteoporosis, the hormones which are directly concerned are believed to be parathyroid hormone, estrogen, 1,25-dihydroxy-vitamin D, calcitonin, and possibly progesterone and corticosteroids. Postmenopausal estrogen deficiency may accelerate bone loss by increasing the sensitivity of bone to the resorbing action of PTH—a hypothesis originally suggested by Heaney (1965). The resulting increase in the release of calcium from bone leads to suppression of parathyroid activity. Riggs and his colleagues (Riggs, 1979; Gallagher et al., 1979) have reported low immunoreactive parathyroid hormone (iPTH) in patients with postmenopausal osteoporosis (except for a subset of 15 percent of the total who have high iPTH levels; this subset possibly corresponds to those with high remodeling osteoporosis). Short term estrogen therapy leads to a decrease in bone resorption surfaces and in urinary hydroxyproline excretion without any change in bone formation surfaces, but with prolonged therapy bone formation is also decreased (Riggs, 1979). Serum calcium and serum iPTH increase significantly on treatment. The apparent decrease in bone resorption with no change in bone formation explains the positive calcium balance that is known to occur after short term estrogen treatment.

There are conflicting reports on the levels of circulating estrogens in postmenopausal women. Marshall and his colleagues (1977) have shown that plasma androstenedione and estrone levels are significantly lower in osteoporotic than in normal postmenopausal women, although there is considerable overlap of values. Riggs et al. (1973) failed to confirm these findings. Johnston and his coworkers (1979) in their studies of postmenopausal women who were grouped into "rapid losers" and "slow losers" were able to demonstrate only slight but insignificant differences between the groups in estrone, estradiol, and androstenedione levels; the rapid losers, however, had significantly lower ($p < 0.01$) levels of serum progesterone than the slow losers. This latter finding is of interest, and progesterone has been shown to bind to glucocorticoid receptors in bone, whereas no estrogen receptors have been found in bone cells. Moreover, progesterone has been shown to inhibit post-

menopausal bone loss (Lindsay et al., 1978). Thus it would appear that estrogen deficiency alone is not the sole determinant of osteoporosis in postmenopausal women.

There is renewed interest in the role of vitamin D and its metabolites in the pathogenesis of osteoporosis now that it is possible to measure the serum concentrations of both 1,25-$(OH)_2D$ and 25-OHD. Although in Britain low levels of 25-OHD have been reported in patients with osteoporotic fractures (Brown et al., 1976), in the United States the concentrations of 25-OHD have been found to be normal in women with postmenopausal osteoporosis (Gallagher et al., 1979). In this latter study, the serum concentrations of 1,25-$(OH)_2D$ were significantly lower in osteoporotic patients compared with age-matched women ($p < 0.005$), and in both these groups the serum 1,25-$(OH)_2D$ concentrations were significantly lower than in young subjects without osteoporosis ($p < 0.001$). Their data suggest that inadequate metabolism of 25-OHD to 1,25-$(OH)_2D$ in the kidney contributes significantly to decreased intestinal calcium absorption and adaptation in both osteoporotics and elderly normal subjects. In osteoporotic patients, this abnormality could result from a decrease in factors that normally stimulate 1,25-$(OH)_2D$ production, such as reduced PTH secretion and increased serum phosphate which were found in the osteoporotics. A third possible factor is the estrogen deficiency leading to reduced 1α-hydroxylase activity. The small group of osteoporotic women who had high serum iPTH values could have a primary (intrinsic) defect in the hydroxylation of 25-OHD to 1,25-$(OH)_2D$. Estrogen treatment of women with postmenopausal osteoporosis significantly increases both serum 1,25-$(OH)_2D$ and calcium absorption (Gallagher et al., 1978). Thus the beneficial effects of estrogen therapy in osteoporosis may be mediated via the vitamin D endocrine system, as well as by a reduction in the sensitivity of the bone to PTH.

Lindsay and his colleagues (1979) have found a significant positive correlation between the rate of bone loss and the urinary free cortisol excretion, indicating that changes in adrenal corticosteroid production could be another factor in the pathogenesis of postmenopausal osteoporosis. The studies of Meunier et al. (1979) have shown that in Cushing's disease and in osteoporosis induced by corticosteroid administration, the osteoblastic appositional rate, as measured by double labeling with tetracycline, is low. This osteblastic depression magnifies the tissue deficit at the BMU level although there is no change in the activation of BMUs. At the biochemical level, several studies have shown that corticosteroids block active calcium transport and produce a decrease in intestinal calcium absorption; this effect of corticosteroids cannot be reversed by administration of 25-OHD or of 1,25-$(OH)_2$D.

Nutritional Factors Affecting Bone Loss. As we have already seen, the two nutrients which play a major role in determining the age-related bone loss are calcium and vitamin D. Calcium absorption falls with age, and older individuals are less able to adapt to low calcium intakes. Vitamin D deficiency leads to a further decrement in calcium absorption. However, the most dramatic changes in calcium metabolism take place at the time of the menopause. Heaney and his colleagues (Heaney et al., 1978; Heaney, 1979) have investigated these changes by means of calcium balance studies in premenopausal and postmenopausal women, and in an estrogen-treated group of postmenopausal women. In the postmenopausal women untreated with estrogen, calcium balance averaged −0.043 g/day and was significantly different ($p < 0.02$) from the average of −0.0199 g/day in premenopausal women. The balance difference was due about equally to decreased absorption from the diet and to increased urinary excretion. The balance performance in the estrogen-treated postmenopausal women was indistinguishable from that of the premenopausal group. On the basis of these results, it was concluded that premenopausal women and estrogen-treated postmenopausal women have a calcium intake requirement of 0.9–1 g/day, whereas untreated postmenopausal women had an apparent requirement of 1.5 g/day.

These intake requirements are considerably greater than the Recommended Daily Allowances for the United States (National Research Council, 1974) and for the United Kingdom (Department of Health and Social Security, 1979b).

Heaney and his colleagues (Recker et al., 1977; Heaney, 1979) have shown that calcium supplementation (calcium, 1.5 grams daily, given as calcium carbonate) completely abolished the bone loss as determined by radiographic morphometry in postmenopausal women. In this respect, it is almost as effective as estrogen therapy. Similar findings have been reported by Nordin's group (Horsman et al., 1977; Nordin et al., 1979). Thus, it is concluded that inadequate calcium intake is at least part of the cause of postmenopausal bone loss and that protection against postmenopausal bone loss is provided by an increased calcium intake.

Heaney was able to confirm the observations of Linkswiler and her colleagues (Walker and Linkswiler, 1972) that a high protein intake leads to a deterioration in calcium balance and that there is a significant inverse relationship between nitrogen intake and calcium balance. This effect of increased protein is due to an increase in calcium excretion by the kidney (Heaney, 1979; Allen et al., 1979). Heaney has predicted that a 50 percent increase of protein above the mean intake for his group of perimenopausal women would lead to a deterioration in calcium balance of 0.03 g/day. This interaction between protein and calcium in the pathogenesis of osteoporosis requires further study.

Immobilization. It is well known that osteoporosis can be induced by immobilization. Immobility due to fracture, joint disease, hemiplegia (Hodkinson and Brain, 1967), and the application of splints leads to localized osteoporosis. This form of disuse atrophy can occur even when the hormonal balance is normal. Studies by Meunier et al. (1979) indicate that in the increased bone loss there is involvement of two processes which are additive: an increase in resorption surfaces associated with a depression of the osteoblastic appositional rate. Lanyon (1980, 1982) in animal experiments has demonstrated a fundamental relationship between bone mass and its load bearing requirements. Bone mass can be increased by exposing bone to strain changes which are well within the limits of normal daily activity. It appears that the frequency with which the strain is applied is a more important osteogenic stimulus than the magnitude of the peak strain.

Dietrick et al. (1948) first demonstrated the marked negative calcium balance which occurs when normal young men are immobilized in bed for three months. It has been shown that continuous bed rest is a potent stimulus to bone resorption (Donaldson et al., 1970), and restoration of bone mass can occur to a considerable degree on remobilization. A similar rapid demineralization of bone has been demonstrated in fit men subjected to prolonged weightlessness in space (Tilton et al., 1980).

Dent and Watson (1966) consider that osteoporosis due to immobilization may complicate other forms and initiate a vicious circle. In particular, many old people, mainly women, become more sedentary—a situation almost certainly contributing to their bone loss. It is also possible that osteoporotic patients are more sensitive than normal persons to increased bone resorption on immobilization.

Prevention of Postmenopausal Bone Loss

Bone loss in normal postmenopausal women can be prevented by estrogen therapy (Davis et al., 1966). Treatment is most effective when started immediately after the menopause, and it eliminates the exponential loss of bone which normally occurs during this period. Investigators in Leeds (Horsman et al., 1977) have shown the effectiveness of ethinylestradiol (25–50 μg daily) given for three weeks out of four; no loss of metacarpal bone occurred in over 60 patient-years. It is now believed (Nordin, 1980) that smaller doses in the range of 15–25 μg daily are equally effective. Recker and his colleagues (1977) have used a regimen of conjugated equine estrogen

(0.625 mg daily) and methyltestosterone (5 mg), again given for 21 days of each month to patients who were followed for two years. They concluded that postmenopausal sex hormone replacement measurably decreases bone loss by suppressing bone turnover, resorption more than accretion.

In investigations on oophorectomized women, Lindsay and his colleagues (1976, 1979) have demonstrated the effectiveness of various estrogens in preventing bone loss: mestranol (40 μg daily), conjugated equine estrogen (0.3 mg daily), and a synthetic compound Tibolone (Organon OD14, 2.5 mg daily). These investigators (Lindsay et al., 1978) have also shown that a progestogen is effective in preventing bone loss in postmenopausal women. This therapy was not accompanied by a fall in urinary hydroxyproline excretion which normally occurs with estrogen therapy.

Many of these studies have compared the effects of sex steroid therapy with that of calcium supplementation in the prevention of postmenopausal bone loss. In the study by Recker et al. (1977), calcium (1 gram daily given as calcium carbonate) produced similar results to their estrogen/androgen regimen, but was slightly less effective. In the Leeds study (Horsman et al., 1977), calcium supplementation (Sandocal 2 tablets—800 mg elemental calcium daily) substantially delayed, if not totally prevented, bone loss in 80 patient-years.

Treatment of Osteoporosis

There are many problems associated with the treatment of osteoporosis. First is the difficulty in assessing the results of treatment owing to the episodic nature of the disorder and the fact that acute episodes characterized by crush fractures are self-limiting; in these cases, spontaneous remission occurs irrespective of the drug therapy given. Second, although therapy which prevents or minimizes bone loss is encouraging, convincing proof of its effectiveness can only be obtained by assessing the effects on fracture rate in placebo-controlled studies which necessitate the cooperation of many patients over many years. Third, in the past, insufficient attention has been paid to the need for prescribing treatment which is appropriate to the type of osteoporosis in the individual patient. In this respect, Meunier et al. (1979) point out that in only about 10 percent of patients with primary osteoporosis is the mechanism due to a high remodeling activity; it is probable that treatment with estrogens, anabolic hormones, calcium, and vitamin D metabolites will prove more effective in these cases rather than in the remaining majority of osteoporotics.

It will be appropriate here to summarize some of the main forms of treatment and to pay particular attention to those regimes which appear to give more promising results.

Estrogens, Calcium and Vitamin D and Its Metabolites. In Leeds, Nordin and his colleagues (Horsman et al., 1977; Nordin et al., 1979; Nordin, 1980) have randomly allocated patients with osteoporosis to one of six different therapeutic regimes or to a no-treatment group. The long term results were assessed by means of sequential measurements of mean metacarpal cortical area (MCA) and by vertebral fracture progression using measurements of height. There was a gain in the MCA in the groups treated with estrogens and estrogens plus 1α-OHD, no significant change in MCA in the group on calcium supplementation, a significant loss of bone in the untreated cases, but an even greater loss in the groups on vitamin D and 1α-OHD; the vitamin D plus calcium group occupied an intermediate position. Similar results were obtained when change in standing height was used as the method of assessment. Thus the most effective therapy appears to be a combination of hormones with 1α-OHD. Vitamin D and 1α-OHD by themselves and in the doses used appear to do more harm than good, and this is attributed to the resorbing action of these agents; however, Nordin considers that it may be possible to find a dose level sufficient to correct calcium malabsorption but not so large as to increase bone resorption. For osteoporosis in men, the Leeds workers use a combination of 1α-OHD and testosterone proprionate (100–250 mg by injection weekly or fortnightly).

Anabolic Steroids. The use of an anabolic steroid, methandrostenolone, in the treatment of postmenopausal osteoporosis has been assessed by Chestnut et al. (1977, 1979). Determination of the total body calcium (TBC) by neutron activation analysis performed at six-monthly intervals was used as the measure of total bone mass. Those treated with methandrostenolone showed an average gain of 2 percent in TBC, while those on placebo showed an average loss of 3.1 percent during the 26-month period of the study; the differences between the two groups were significant ($p < 0.01$). Moreover, the differences in the percentage TBC between the two groups increased in a linear fashion with time, indicating a continuation of the drug effect throughout the 26 months.

Calcitonin. The use of calcitonin in the treatment of osteoporosis in postmenopausal women has also been investigated by Chestnut et al. (1979). The results were similar to those with the anabolic agent, and there were significant differences between the treated and placebo groups in the percentage TBC changes during the 18 months' study period; again the effect of calcitonin appeared to continue throughout this period. There is some evidence for a difference in response to calcitonin in osteoporotic patients. Some patients show a hypocalcemic effect following the administration of calcitonin, whereas others do not; this is at present under investigation (Hamdy, 1983).

Diphosphonates. These compounds are known to reduce bone resorption, probably by inhibiting the function, but not the formation, of osteoclasts. The use of diphosphonates in the treatment of osteoporosis has been reviewed by Fleisch (1979). In animal experiments, dichloromethane diphosphonate (Cl_2MDP), and to a lesser extent ethane-l-hydroxy-1, 1-diphosphonate (EHDP), can prevent osteoporosis induced by immobilization after nerve section. There are few investigations of their effectiveness in human osteoporosis; however, kinetic studies have shown that they reduce both bone resorption and formation, but the effect on formation is less than on resorption so that a net increase in calcium balance occurs. Fleisch points out that there is now a need for studies using diphosphonates combined with an agent which increases bone formation.

The agents which have so far been mentioned (estrogens, vitamin D and its metabolites, calcitonin, and diphosphonates), when given in appropriate dosage, have all been shown to reduce bone resorption. In prolonged therapy, however, all these drugs also reduce bone formation within a few months. Thus even in patients who have "rapid turnover" of bone, the ultimate picture is one of "low turnover." As we have seen, the majority of elderly patients with osteoporosis have the "low turnover" form of the disease. For these patients together with those who are receiving antiresorptive agents, there is a need for a therapeutic substance which will stimulate bone formation. In this context, two agents appear to be promising, parathyroid hormone and sodium fluoride.

Parathyroid Hormone. When given in small doses parathyroid hormone (PTH) has an anabolic effect by stimulation of bone formation, but when given in large doses this effect is obscured by the marked increase in bone resorption. That the balance between the anabolic and catabolic effects might be shifted favorably was indicated by the preliminary report of Reeve et al. (1976) on the beneficial effects of low doses of a fragment of human parathyroid hormone (hPTH 1–34) in osteoporosis. In further investigations, these workers have shown that in 5 out of 11 patients with osteoporosis (both male and female) treated for six months with hPTH, the proportion of trabecular surface covered with osteoid more than doubled, the mean change being 77 percent. Similar changes were seen in ^{47}Ca kinetic measurements which increased even more strikingly; the mean change in skeletal

calcium accretion was +155 percent (Parsons et al., 1979). For some patients the dose of hPTH (100 μg daily by injection) appeared to be too high, and transient hypercalcemia occurred within a few hours of each injection. Parsons and his coworkers express the view that a lower dose (less than 50 μg/day) might be more appropriate and that a better response might be obtained if a controlled release preparation were available to avoid the resorptive action of the high initial peaks.

Sodium Fluoride. Although the role of fluoride deficiency in the causation of osteoporosis is uncertain, sodium fluoride is a potent stimulator of bone formation. Rich et al. (1964) suggested that fluoride might be a useful agent for the treatment of osteoporosis on the basis of the production of osteosclerosis by excessive fluoride ingestion. Jowsey et al. (1968) have shown that fluoride causes osteoblastic stimulation, but the newly formed bone tissue is poorly mineralized. Moreover, animal experiments have shown that fluoride also produces increased bone resorption due to the development of secondary hyperparathyroidism. Both these abnormalities can be prevented by increasing the intakes of vitamin D and calcium. Jowsey et al. (1972) evaluated in patients with osteoporosis the effects of sodium fluoride (50 mg/day) administered together with supplemental calcium (900 mg/day) and vitamin D (50,000 I.U. twice a week) over a period of at least one year. In all but one of their 11 patients, bone formation was increased after treatment and the group mean was significantly higher than before treatment; the newly formed bone was normal in appearance. The degree of bone resorption was also significantly reduced, and this was significantly correlated with the amount of supplemental calcium administered.

Although these studies have shown that fluoride administration increases bone mass, the effects on bone strength have not yet been assessed; it is believed that fluoride causes an increase in crystallinity of bone structure and the bone may be more fragile than normal. Indeed in Jowsey's series, 4 out of 11 patients developed additional crush fractures during treatment, but it is considered that they may have occurred before therapy was able to change the bone mass significantly. Mitchell et al. (1975) used a similar treatment regime in 14 osteoporotic patients over a period of 12–18 months, and in this study no further fractures occurred during the period of observation. However, the most convincing evidence of the effectiveness of fluoride has come from a report of investigators at the Mayo Clinic (Riggs et al., 1982). In this study, five different treatment regimes were compared: placebo, calcium alone, fluoride and calcium, estrogen and calcium, and fluoride, estrogen, and calcium. Some of the patients in each treatment group also received vitamin D (50,000 I.U. once or twice a week). Estrogen, calcium, and calcium plus fluoride significantly reduced the vertebral fracture rate compared with no treatment. The most dramatic reduction in fracture rate was achieved when fluoride, estrogen, and calcium were given together; this was more effective than any other combination ($p < 0.001$). Although all patients received a multivitamin preparation containing 400 I.U. vitamin D daily, the addition of very large doses of vitamin D provided no extra benefit, and indeed in some patients it caused hypercalcemia and hypercalciuria. In spite of the overall remarkable results, a minority of patients failed to respond to fluoride even after 4–6 years of therapy; Riggs and his colleagues considered that these patients may have an intrinsic abnormality of osteoblast function which prevents stimulation of bone formation. This finding again emphasizes the importance of making a precise evaluation of the type of osteoporosis before treatment is commenced and before the results of different treatment regimes are assessed.

AGE-RELATED FRACTURES

The fracture patterns in the elderly differ markedly from those in the younger adult. Whereas in the younger adult (20–50 years) considerable violence—usually direct trauma—is required, in the elderly fractures result from minimal or moderate trauma. Moreover the sites of the fracture are often different, in the elderly they occur through cancellous bone next to a joint rather than through the shaft of a bone.

In younger adults, fracture incidence is lower in females than in males; in the elderly, however, sex- and age-corrected incidence of fractures is considerably higher in females than in males especially for fracture of the vertebral bodies, the lower end of the forearm, and the proximal femur. Diminution in the amount of bone with the development of osteoporosis is the main factor accounting for these differences in fracture patterns.

Vertebral Compression Fractures

The manifestations of osteoporosis typically occur earlier in the spine than in the peripheral skeleton; indeed vertebral crush fractures constitute the syndrome to which the term "osteoporosis" is commonly applied. Nordin (1980) points out that estimates of the prevalence of the crush fracture syndrome are critically dependent upon whether wedged vertebrae are accepted as indicators of osteoporosis or whether diagnosis is confined to cases where there is true vertebral compression. Use of the latter criterion yields a lower estimate of the prevalence of the syndrome than if wedging is also included in the definition: 8 percent of women and 4 percent of men develop true vertebral compression by the age of 80 years.

Nordin and his coworkers (1968), using spinal densitometry, have shown that crush fracture cases generally suffer from a more severe degree of spinal osteoporosis than other individuals of the same age. The diminished trabecular bone volume in crush fracture cases is reflected in the iliac crest where the bone volume is generally less than 6 percent compared with the normal mean value of 22 percent in young adults. Nordin (1980) has calculated that if the lower limit of the trabecular bone volume is accepted as 16 percent (mean−2 × S.D. for the young normal range) and if values of 15 percent or less are classified as osteoporotic, then 13 percent of normal young adults, 50 percent of normal old women, 20 percent of normal old men, and

80 percent of patients with crush fractures would have histological osteoporosis.

Trabecular bone volume can be most closely related to the crush fracture syndrome, and the relationship to the loss of cortical bone is less exact. Although patients with crush fractures usually have an amount of bone in the metacarpal which is less than the mean for their age, the values quite commonly fall within the normal range. Thus it is possible to have moderate to severe spinal osteoporosis with relatively normal peripheral bones; that is, loss of compact bone lags behind the trabecular bone loss in the vertebral bodies. Nevertheless, patients with the most severe degrees of osteoporosis of the spine also have low values of bone mass in the metacarpal. Indeed changes in height (due to the development of crush fractures) and changes in metacarpal cortical area are accepted indicators for assessing the efficacy of different regimens in the prevention and treatment of osteoporosis (Nordin et al., 1979). We have shown that the loss of height in old age (that is, the measured height minus the predicted height based on the length of the second metacarpal) is highly correlated with the amount of bone as determined by metacarpal morphometry (Exton-Smith, 1982). Thus elderly individuals who show the greatest reduction in height have the lowest cortical bone mass. At present it is uncertain whether this loss of height can be attributed entirely to osteoporotic vertebral collapse; in part it could be due to reduced mass of the spinal musculature which is known to correlate with the density of the vertebral bodies.

Fractures of the Lower Forearm

The effects of age and sex on the incidence of wrist fractures are also clearly seen. There is a high incidence in the young, both in boys and girls, a low incidence in adults, and a steep rise in aging women, but only a slight increase with age in men. In women, the sharp rise begins at about the age of 50 and reaches a plateau at the age of 65; thereafter, the fracture rate continues at about the same level. Nordin (1980) points out that since the distal radius where this fracture occurs is composed largely of trabecular bone and since the rise in wrist fracture incidence plateaus at about age 65 similar to the pattern of trabecular bone loss in the iliac crest, it seems reasonable to conclude that this fracture is the result of trabecular bone loss in the distal forearm. He also points out that forearm densitometry is usually performed for technical reasons at a site proximal to the actual fracture site and so a substantial proportion of the photon absorption is attributable to cortical rather than trabecular bone. This probably explains why many of the values for bone mass in the fracture cases fall within the normal range. It is also of interest that many women sustain a wrist fracture soon after the menopause when only a small amount of bone can have been lost. We do not yet know whether there is a critical level of bone mass in the population below which the risk of fracture increases, as suggested by the hypothesis of Newton-John and Morgan (1968), or if a critical level exists, whether it varies in different individuals.

Fractures of the Proximal Femur

Alffram (1964) has made an epidemiological analysis of fracture of the hip involving 1664 cases observed over a 13-year period in the population of Malmö. In both males and females, the incidence was negligible below the age of 50, and it apparently doubled for each five-year increment after the age of 60. The incidence in females was 2.4 times that in males.

Role of Osteoporosis. Nordin (1971), using his data for metacarpal cortical area/total area ratios in normal men and women, found an inverse relationship with the femoral neck fracture rate derived from the data of Knowelden et al. (1964). He suggests that the metacarpal cortex reflects the bone loss which predisposes to fractures of the proximal femur, and this is confirmed by the low CA/TA ratios found in actual hip cases. More recent data (1980) suggest that trabecular bone loss makes an important contribution to the pertrochanteric type of fracture which is about twice as common as the transcervical fracture, but Nordin admits that it is impossible to say whether low trabecular bone volume determines the fracture itself or simply the site of the fracture.

In our own studies (Exton-Smith, 1976; Cook et al., 1982), we have plotted the individual values for the metacarpal cortical index (MCI) based on the cortical area/surface area ratio, for fracture femur cases on the percentile ranking curves for the general population (Exton-Smith et al., 1969b; Gryfe et al., 1971). For female fracture patients, the regression line for the mean MCI values lies between the 25th and 50th percentiles for the general population, and for male fracture patients between the 10th and 25th percentiles. In each sex, the mean amount of bone for fracture femur cases is significantly less ($p < 0.001$) than for the general population of similar age. The absolute values for MCI in individual fracture femur cases can be expressed as percentiles of values for the general population of corresponding age, thereby eliminating the effect of age, and the resultant frequency distributions are shown in Figure 2.

The distribution of these MCI percentiles for fracture cases is skewed towards the lower values, particularly in male patients. Two-thirds of the male fracture patients and slightly more than one-third of the female patients have MCI values below the 20th percentile for the general population. Osteoporosis, therefore, appears to be a major factor in the etiology of this type of fracture, but there are some individuals who sustain fractures with MCI values in the upper percentile ranges (see Figure 2). It is difficult to interpret these findings on the basis of cross-sectional studies; it is possible that there has been an accelerated loss of bone if their skeletal status at maturity was good, that is, these individuals belong to a group of "rapid bone losers." We shall not know if this is the explanation until we have information on the rate of bone loss derived from serial measurements carried out prior to the fracture.

Role of Vitamin D. Aaron et al. (1974a) in Leeds have shown that 20–30 percent of women and about 40 percent of men with fracture of the femoral neck have histological evidence of osteomalacia. Later they showed (Aaron et al., 1974b) that the proportion with osteomalacia varied with the season of the year. The proportion of cases with decreased calcification fronts or increased osteoid-covered surfaces rose from about 15 percent

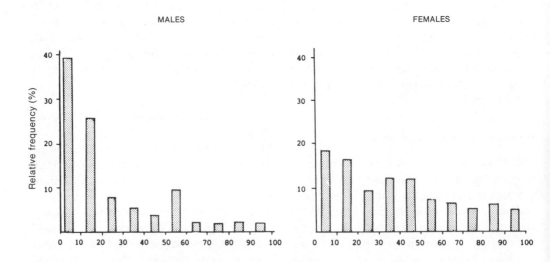

Figure 2. Metacarpal cortical indices for patients with femoral neck fractures expressed as percentiles for the normal population.

of the biopsies in the late summer to 40 percent in the spring. They conclude that seasonal variation in hours of sunshine is responsible for a seasonal change in the incidence of femoral neck fractures and possibly for osteomalacia in the elderly population as a whole.

The significance of vitamin D deficiency as an important factor in fracture of the proximal femur has been confirmed in our studies conducted in London and Manchester (Faccini et al., 1976; Cook et al., 1982). The mean value of trabecular osteoid area in the fracture group was 4 percent compared with 1 percent in a control group without fractures matched for age and sex. Thirty-eight percent of the fracture patients had histological evidence of osteomalacia based on a trabecular osteoid area of greater than 2.0 percent, and this proportion was significantly higher than in the control group ($p < 0.01$). Examination of the relationship between osteomalacia and the quantity of cortical bone expressed as MCI percentiles indicates that patients whose iliac crest biopsy specimens show osteomalacia tend to have higher MCI values than fractured femur cases without osteomalacia (Cook et al., 1982). Thus, in patients with fracture of the femoral neck, there is a trend towards an inverse relationship between osteoporosis and osteomalacia; individuals who sustain fractures but who have little or no osteoporosis may be more likely to have osteomalacia.

Although all these studies have shown the importance of changes in bone quantity and quality as factors in the pathogenesis of femoral neck fractures, there may be additional factors. The London and Manchester studies (Brocklehurst et al., 1978; Cook et al., 1982) revealed a high frequency of falls in the fracture cases. This increase in the incidence of falls in the fracture cases was highly significant ($p < 0.001$) when compared to control subjects without fractures matched for age and sex.

Thus the elucidation of "risk factors" which might identify older people who are liable to sustain a femoral neck fracture requires an examination of the contribution of a variety of factors other than changes in the quantity and quality of bone. Wootton et al. (1979,

1982) have attempted to identify such risk factors, and they point out that the need for studies of this kind has increased now that more effective regimens for the treatment of osteoporosis are becoming available. These regimens administered indiscriminately and over prolonged periods will be associated with an increased incidence of side effects. They should, therefore, be used only in those individuals in the general population who can be identified as being "at risk" of sustaining a fracture.

REFERENCES

Aaron, J. 1976. Histology and micro-anatomy of bone. In, B. E. C. Nordin (ed.), Calcium, Phosphate and Magnesium Metabolism, pp. 298–356. Edinburgh: Churchill Livingstone.

Aaron, J. E., Gallagher, J. C., Anderson, J., Stasiak, L., Longton, E. B., Nordin, B. E. C., and Nicholson, M. 1974a. Frequency of osteomalacia and osteoporosis in fractures of the proximal femur. Lancet 1: 229–233.

Aaron, J. E., Gallagher, J. C., and Nordin, B. E. C. 1974b. Seasonal variation of histological osteomalacia in femoral neck fractures. Lancet 2: 84–85.

Albright, F., Smith, P. H., and Richardson, A. M. 1941. Post-menopausal osteoporosis. J. Amer. Med. Ass., 116: 2465–2474.

Alffram, P. A. 1964. An epidemiological study of cervical and trochanteric fractures of the femur in an urban population. Acta Orthop. Scand. Supp. 65: 1–109.

Allen, L. H., Bartlett, R. S., and Block, G. D. 1979. Impairment of renal calcium reabsorption by dietary protein. In, U. S. Barzel (ed.), Osteoporosis II, p. 245. New York: Grune & Stratton.

Arnold, J. S. 1973. Amount and quality of bone in osteoporotic vertebral fractures. Clin. Endocrin Metab. 2: 221–238.

Arnold, J. S. and Jee, W. S. S. 1957. Bone growth and osteoclastic activity as indicated by radioautographic distribution of plutonium. Am. J. Anat. 101: 367–417.

Barnett, E. and Nordin, B. E. C. 1960. The radiological diagnosis of osteoporosis. Clin. Radiol. 11: 166–174.

Bélanger, L. F., Robichon, J., Migicovsky, B. B., Copp, D. H., and Vincent, J. 1963. Resorption without osteoclasts. In, R. F. Sognnaes (ed.), Mechanisms of Hard Tissue Destruction, pp. 531–556. Washington, D.C.: American Association for the Advancement of Science.

Bell, G. H., Dunbar, O., Beck, J. S., and Gibb, A. 1967. Variation in strength of vertebrae with age and their relation to osteoporosis. Calc. Tiss. Res. 1: 75–86.

Berry, E. M., Gupta, M. M., Turner, S. J., and Burns, R. R. 1973. Variation in plasma calcium with induced changes in plasma specific gravity, total protein and albumen. Br. Med. J. 4: 640–643.

Brocklehurst, J. C., Exton-Smith, A. N., Lempert-Barber,

S. M., Hunt, L. P., and Palmer, M. K. 1978. Fracture of the femur in old age: a two centre study of associated clinical factors and the cause of the fall. *Age and Ageing* 7: 7–15.

Brown, I. R. F., Bakowska, A., and Millard, P. H. 1976. Vitamin D status of patients with femoral neck fractures. *Age and Ageing* 5: 127–131.

Bullamore, J. R., Gallagher, J. C., Wilkinson, R., Nordin, B. E. C., and Marshall, D. H. 1970. The effect of age on calcium absorption. *Lancet* 2: 535–537.

Care, A. D., Cooper, C. W., Duncan, T., and Orimo, H. 1968. A study of thyrocalcitonin secretion by direct measurement of *in vivo* secretion rates in pigs. *Endocrinol.* 83: 161–169.

Chestnut, C. H., Nelp, W. B., Baylink, D. J., Denney, J. D. 1977. Effect of methandrostenolone on postmenopausal bone wasting as assessed by changes in total bone mineral mass. *Metabolism* 26: 267–277.

Chestnut, C. H., Ivey, J. L., Nelp, W. B., and Baylink, D. J. 1979. Assessment of anabolic steroids and calcitonin in the treatment of osteoporosis. *In,* U. S. Barzel (ed.), *Osteoporosis II,* pp. 135–150. New York: Grune & Stratton.

Cook, P. J., Exton-Smith, A. N., Brocklehurst, J. C., and Lempert-Barber, S. M. 1982. Fractured femurs, falls and bone disorders. *J. Roy. Coll. Physcns. Lond.* 16: 45–49.

Copp, D. H., Cameron, E. C., Cheney, B. A., Davidson, A. G. F., and Henze, K. G. 1962. Evidence for calcitonin—a new hormone from the parathyroid that lowers blood calcium. *Endocrinol.* 70: 638–649.

Davis, M. E., Strandjord, N. M., and Lanzl, L. H. 1966. Estrogens and the aging process. *J. Am. Med. Ass.* 196: 219–224.

DeLuca, H. F. 1974. Vitamin D—1973. *Am. J. Med.* 57: 1–12.

DeLuca, H. F. 1976. Recent advances in our understanding of the vitamin D endocrine system. *J. Lab. Clin. Med.* 87: 7–26.

Dent, C. E. and Watson, L. 1966. Osteoporosis. *Postgrad. Med. J. Suppl.* 42: 583–608.

Department of Health and Social Security. 1979a. *Nutrition and Health in Old Age.* Report on Health and Social Subjects No. 16. London: HMSO.

Department of Health and Social Security. 1979b. *Recommended Daily Amounts of Food Energy and Nutrients for Groups of People in the United Kingdom.* Report on Health and Social Subjects No. 15. London: HMSO.

Deitrick, J. E., Whedon, G. D., and Shorr, E. 1948. Effect of immobilization upon various metabolic and physiologic functions of normal men. *Am. J. Med.* 4: 3–36.

Donaldson, C. L., Hulky, S. B., Vogel, J. M., Hattner, R. S., Bayers, J. H., and McMillan, D. E. 1970. Effect of prolonged bed rest on bone metabolism. *Metabolism* 19: 1071–1084.

Eddy, T. P. 1972. Deaths from domestic falls and fractures. *Br. J. Prev. Soc. Med.* 26: 173–179.

Editorial. 1976. Advances in osteoporosis? *Lancet* 1: 181–182.

El-Maraghi, N. R. H., Platt, B. S., and Stewart, R. J. C. 1965. The effect of the interaction of dietary protein and calcium on the growth and the maintenance of bones of young, adult and aged rats. *Br. J. Nutr.* 19: 491–509.

Exton-Smith, A. N. 1970. Cross-sectional and longitudinal studies of aging. *Exp. Geront.* 5: 273–280.

Exton-Smith, A. N. 1976. The management of osteoporosis. *Proc. Roy. Soc. Med.* 69: 931–934.

Exton-Smith, A. N. 1977. Functional consequences of aging: clinical manifestations. *In,* A. N. Exton-Smith and J. Grimley Evans (eds.), Care of the Elderly: Meeting the Challenge of Dependency, pp. 41–53. New York: Grune & Stratton.

Exton-Smith, A. N. 1982. Nutrition and Aging. *Jap. J. Geriat.* 19: 121–129.

Exton-Smith, A. N., Millard, P. H., Payne, P. R., and Wheeler, E. F. 1969a. Method for measuring quantity of bone. *Lancet* 2: 1153–1154.

Exton-Smith, A. N., Millard, P. H., Payne, P. R., and Wheeler, E. F. 1969b. Pattern of bone development and loss of bone with age. *Lancet* 2: 1154–1157.

Exton-Smith, A. N., Stanton, B. R., and Windsor, A. C. M. 1972. *Nutrition of Housebound Old People.* London: King Edward's Hospital Fund.

Faccini, J. M., Exton-Smith, A. N., and Boyde, A. 1976. Disorders of bone and fracture of the femoral neck. *Lancet* 1: 1089–1092.

Fleisch, H. 1979. Diphosphonates and osteoporosis. *In,* U. S. Barzel (ed.), *Osteoporosis II,* pp. 205–227. New York: Grune & Stratton.

Fourman, P. and Royer, P. 1968. *Calcium Metabolism and the Bone.* Oxford: Blackwell.

Frain-Bell, W. 1979. What is that thing called light? *Clin. Exp. Dermatol.* 4: 1–33.

Fraser, D. R. 1983. The physiological economy of vitamin D. *Lancet* 1: 969–972.

Frost, H. M. 1966. *Bone Dynamics in Osteoporosis and Osteomalacia.* Springfield, Ill.: Charles C Thomas.

Frost, H. M. 1969. Tetracycline-based histological analysis of bone remodelling. *Calc. Tiss. Res.* 3: 211–239.

Gallagher, J. C., Aaron, J. E., Horsman, A., Marshall, D. H., Wilkinson, R., and Nordin, B. E. C. 1973. The crush fracture syndrome in postmenopausal women. *In,* B. E. C. Nordin (ed.), *Clinics in Endocrinology and Metabolism,* pp. 293–315. London: W. B. Saunders.

Gallagher, J. C., Riggs, B. L., Eisman, J., Hamstra, A., Arnaud, S. A., and DeLuca, H. F. 1979. Intestinal calcium absorption and serum vitamin D metabolites in normal subjects and osteoporotic patients. *J. Clin. Invest.* 64: 729–736.

Gallagher, J. C., Riggs, B. L., Hamstra, A., and DeLuca, H. F. 1978. Effect of estrogen therapy on calcium absorption and vitamin D metabolism in postmenopausal women. *Clin. Res.* 26: 415A.

Garn, S. M. 1970. *The Earlier Gain and Later Loss of Cortical Bone.* Springfield, Ill.: Charles C Thomas.

Garn, S. M., Pao, E. M., and Rihl, M. E. 1964a. Compact bone in Chinese and Japanese. *Science* 143: 1438–1439.

Garn, S. M., Rohmann, C. G., Behar, M., Viteri, F.,

and Guzman, M. A. 1964b. Compact bone deficiency in protein-calorie malnutrition. *Science* 145: 1444–1445.

Garn, S. M., Rohmann, C. G., and Wagner, P. 1967. Bone loss as a general phenomenon in man. *Fed. Proc. Fed. Am. Soc. Exp. Biol.* 26: 1729–1736.

Gershon-Cohen, J. and Jowsey, J. 1964. The relationship of dietary calcium to osteoporosis. *Metabolism* 13: 221–226.

Gershon-Cohen, J., McClendon, J. F., Jowsey, J., and Foster, W. C. 1962. Osteoporosis produced and cured in rats by low and high calcium diets. *Radiology* 78: 251–252.

Greaves, J. P. and Hollingsworth, D. H. 1966. Trends in food consumption in the United Kingdom. *Wld. Rev. Nutr. Diet.* 6: 35–89.

Gryfe, C. I., Exton-Smith, A. N., Payne, P. R., and Wheeler, E. F. 1971. Pattern of development of bone in childhood and adolescence. *Lancet* 1: 523–526.

Gryfe, C. I., Exton-Smith, A. N., and Stewart, R. J. C. 1972. Determination of the amount of bone in the metacarpal. *Age and Ageing* 1: 213–221.

Haddad, J. G. and Hahn, T. J. 1973. Natural and synthetic sources of circulating 25-hydroxyvitamin D in man. *Nature* 244: 515–517.

Hamdy, R. C. 1983. Personal communication.

Harrison, J. E., McNeill, K. G., Sturtridge, W. C., and Bayley, T. A. 1979. Bone mineral measurement of the central skeleton by IVNAA for routine investigation of osteopenia. *In,* U. S. Barzel (ed.), *Osteoporosis II,* p. 240. New York: Grune & Stratton.

Harrison, J. E., Williams, W. C., Watts, J., and McNeill, W. G. 1975. A bone calcium index based on partial-body calcium measurements by *in-vivo* activation analysis. *J. Nucl. Med.* 16: 116–122.

Heaney, R. P. 1965. A unified concept of osteoporosis. *Am. J. Med.* 39: 877–880.

Heaney, R. P. 1979. Calcium metabolic changes at the menopause. *In,* U. S. Barzel (ed.), *Osteoporosis II,* pp. 101–110. New York: Grune & Stratton.

Heaney, R. P., Recker, R. R., and Sanville, P. D. 1978. Menopausal changes in calcium balance. *J. Lab. Clin. Med.* 92: 953–963.

Helela, T. 1969. Variations in thickness of cortical bone in two populations. *Ann. Clin. Res.* 1: 227–231.

Hodkinson, H. M. and Brain, A. T. 1967. Unilateral osteoporosis in longstanding hemiplegia in the elderly. *J. Am. Geriat. Soc.* 15: 59–64.

Horsman, A. 1976. Bone mass. *In,* B. E. C. Nordin (ed.), *Calcium, Phosphate and Magnesium Metabolism,* pp. 357–404. Edinburgh: Churchill Livingstone.

Horsman, A., Gallagher, J. C., Simpson, M., and Nordin, B. E. C. 1977. Prospective trial of estrogen and calcium in postmenopausal women. *Br. Med. J.* 2: 789–792.

Ireland, P. and Fordtran, J. S. 1973. Effect of dietary calcium and age on jejunal calcium absorption in humans studied by intestinal perfusion. *J. Clin. Invest.* 52: 2672–2681.

Johnston, C. C., Norton, J. A., Khairi, R. A., and Longscope, C. 1979. Age-related bone loss. *In,* U. S. Barzel

(ed.), *Osteoporosis II,* pp. 91–100. New York: Grune & Stratton.

Jowsey, J., Kelly, P. J., Riggs, B. L., Bianco, A. J., Scholz, D. A., and Gershon-Cohen, J. 1965. Quantitative microradiographic studies of normal and osteoporotic bone. *J. Bone Jt. Surg.* 47A: 785–806.

Jowsey, J., Riggs, B. L., and Kelly, P. J. 1964. Mineral metabolism in osteocytes. *Mayo Clinic Proc.* 39: 480–484.

Jowsey, J., Riggs, B. L., Kelly, P. J., and Hoffman, D. L. 1972. Effect of combined therapy with sodium fluoride, vitamin D and calcium in osteoporosis. *Am. J. Med.* 53: 43–49.

Jowsey, J., Schenk, R. K., and Reutter, F. W. 1968. Some results of the effect of fluoride on bone tissue in osteoporosis. *J. Clin. Endocrinol. Metab.* 28: 869–874.

Khosla, T. and Lowe, C. R. 1968. Height and weight of British men. *Lancet* 1: 742–745.

Knowelden, J., Buhr, A. J., and Dunbar, O. 1964. Incidence of fractures in persons over 35 years. *J. Prev. Soc. Med.* 18: 130–141.

Kodicek, E. 1974. The story of vitamin D: from vitamin to hormone. *Lancet* 1: 325–329.

Lanyon, L. E. 1980. Bone remodeling, mechanical stress and osteoporosis. *In,* H. F. DeLuca, H. M. Frost, W. S. S. Jee, C. C. Johnston, and A. M. Parfitt (eds.), *Osteoporosis, Recent Advances in Pathogenesis and Treatment,* pp. 129–139. Baltimore: University Park Press.

Lanyon, L. E. 1982. Osteoporosis and mechanically related bone remodeling. *In,* J. Menczel, G. C. Robin, M. Makin, and R. Steinberg (eds.), *Osteoporosis,* pp. 148–156. Chichester: John Wiley.

Lawson, B. E. M., Paul, A. A., Black, A. E., Cole, T. J., Mandal, A. R., and Davie, M. 1979. Relative contributions of diet and sunlight to vitamin D state in the elderly. *Br. Med. J.* 2: 303–305.

Liberti, P. A., Callahan, H. J., and Maurer, P. H. 1973. Physiochemical studies of C^{++} controlled antigen antibody systems. *In,* M. Friedman (ed.), *Protein-Metal Interactions,* pp. 161–184. New York: Plenum Press.

Lindsay, R., Hart, D. M., Aitken, J. M., MacDonald, E. B., Anderson, J. B., and Clarke, A. C. 1976. Long-term prevention of post-menopausal osteoporosis by estrogen. *Lancet* 1: 1038–1041.

Lindsay, R., Hart, D. M., Manolagas, S., Anderson, D. C., Coutts, J. R. T., and MacLean, A. 1979. Sex steroids in pathogenesis and prevention of post-menopausal osteoporosis. *In,* U. S. Barzel (ed.), *Osteoporosis,* pp. 161–182. New York: Grune & Stratton.

Lindsay, R., Hart, D. M., Purdie, D., Ferguson, M. M., Clark, A. S., and Kraszewski, A. 1978. Comparative effects of estrogen and a progestogen on bone loss in post-menopausal women. *Clin. Sci. Mol. Med.* 54: 193–195.

Lingärde, F. 1972. Potentiometric determination of serum ionized calcium in a normal human population. *Clin. Chim. Acta* 40: 477–484.

Marshall, D. H., Crilly, R. G., and Nordin, B. E. C. 1977. Plasma androstenedione and estrone levels in normal and osteoporotic postmenopausal women. *Br. Med. J.* 2: 1177–1179.

Marshall, R. W. 1976. Plasma fractions. *In,* B. E. C. Nordin (ed.), *Calcium, Phosphate and Magnesium Metabolism,* pp. 162–185. Edinburgh: Churchill Livingstone.

McPherson, K., Healy, M. J. R., Flynn, F. V., Piper, K. A. J., and Garcia-Webb, P. 1978. The effect of age, sex and other factors on blood chemistry in health. *Clin. Chim. Acta* 84: 373–379.

Merz, A. L., Trotter, M., and Peterson, R. R. 1956. Estimation of skeletal weight in the living. *Am. J. Phys. Anthrop.* 14: 589–610.

Merz, W. A. and Schenk, R. K. 1970. A quantitative histological study on bone formation in human cancellous bone. *Acta Anat. (Basel)* 76: 1–15.

Meunier, P., Aaron, J., Edouard, C., and Vignon, G. 1971. Osteoporosis and the replacement of the cell populations of the marrow by adipose tissue. *Clin. Orthop.* 80: 147–154.

Meunier, P. J., Courpron, P., Edouard, C., Alexandre, C., Bressot, C., Lips, P., and Boyce, B. F. 1979. *In,* U. S. Barzel (ed.), *Osteoporosis II,* pp. 27–48. New York: Grune & Stratton.

Meunier, P., Courpron, P., Edouard, C., Bernard, J., Bringuier, J., and Vignon, G. 1973. Physiological senile involution and pathological rarefaction of bone: quantitative and comparative histological data. *In,* B. E. C. Nordin (ed.), *Clinics in Endocrinology and Metabolism,* pp. 239–256. London: W. B. Saunders.

Mitchell, J. C. Parsons, V., and Dische, F. 1975. The treatment of osteoporosis with sodium fluoride, vitamin D and calcium supplements. *Q. Jl. Med.* 44: 636–637.

National Research Council, Food and Nutrition Board. 1974. Recommended Dietary Allowances, 8th rev. ed. Washington, D.C.: National Academy of Sciences.

Newton-John, H. F. and Morgan, D. B. 1968. Osteoporosis: disease or senescence? *Lancet* 1: 232–233.

Nordin, B. E. C. 1961. The pathogenesis of osteoporosis. *Lancet* 1: 1011–1014.

Nordin, B. E. C. 1966. International patterns of osteoporosis. *Clin. Orthop.* 45: 17–29.

Nordin, B. E. C. 1971. Clinical significance and pathogenesis of osteoporosis. *Br. Med. J.* 1: 571–576.

Nordin, B. E. C. 1976. Nutritional considerations. *In,* B. E. C. Nordin (ed.), *Calcium, Phosphate and Magnesium Metabolism,* pp. 1–35. Edinburgh: Churchill Livingstone.

Nordin, B. E. C. 1980. Calcium metabolism and bone. *In,* A. N. Exton-Smith and F. I. Caird (eds.), *Metabolic and Nutritional Disorders in the Elderly,* pp. 123–145. Bristol: Wright.

Nordin, B. E. C., Housman, A., Marshall, D. H., Hanes, F., and Jakeman, W. 1979. The treatment of post-menopausal osteoporosis. *In,* U. S. Barzel (ed.), *Osteoporosis,* Vol. 2, pp. 183–204. New York: Grune & Stratton.

Nordin, B. E. C., Young, M. M., Bentley, B., Ormondroyd, P., and Sykes, J. 1968. Lumbar spine densitometry. *Clin. Radiol.* 19: 459–464.

Parsons, J. A., Bernat, M., Bijvoet, O. L. M., Meunier, P. J., Neer, R. M., Potts, J. T., Reeve, J., Renier, J. C., Slovik, D., and Vismans, J. 1979. Low doses of a synthetic fragment of human parathyroid hormone (hPTH 1–34) as a stimulus to bone formation. *In,* U. S. Barzel (ed.), *Osteoporosis II,* pp. 151–160. New York: Grune & Stratton.

Platt, B. S. and Stewart, R. J. C. 1962. Transverse trabeculae and osteoporosis in bones in experimental protein-calorie deficiency. *Br. J. Nutr.* 16: 483–495.

Platt, B. S. and Stewart, R. J. C. 1968. Effects of protein-calorie-deficiency on dogs. I. Reproduction, growth and behaviour. *Revl. Med. Child Neurol.* 10: 3–24.

Posner, A. S. 1970. Crystal chemistry of bone mineral. *Physiol. Rev.* 49: 760–792.

Rasmussen, H. 1972. The cellular basis of mammalian calcium homeostasis. *In,* I. MacIntyre (ed.), *Clinics in Endocrinology and Metabolism,* pp. 3–20. Philadelphia: W. B. Saunders.

Recker, R. R., Saville, P. D., and Heaney, R. P. 1977. Effect of estrogens and calcium carbonate on bone loss in postmenopausal women. *Ann. Int. Med.* 87: 649–655.

Reeve, J., Hesp, R., Williams, D., Hulme, P., Klenerman, L., Zanelli, J. M., Danby, A. J., Tregear, G. W., and Parsons, J. A. 1976. Anabolic effect of low doses of a fragment of human parathyroid hormone on the skeleton in post-menopausal osteoporosis. *Lancet* 1: 1035–1038.

Rich, C., Ensinck, J., and Ivanovich, P. 1964. The effects of sodium fluoride on calcium metabolism of subjects with metabolic bone diseases. *J. Clin. Invest.* 43: 545–555.

Riggs, B. L. 1979. Hormonal factors in the pathogenesis of osteoporosis. *In,* U. S. Barzel (ed.), *Osteoporosis II,* pp. 111–122. New York: Grune & Stratton.

Riggs, B. L., Ryan, R. J., Wahner, H. W., Jiang, N. S., and Mattox, V. R. 1973. Serum concentrations of estrogens, testosterone and gonadotrophins in osteoporotic and non-osteoporotic postmenopausal women. *J. Clin. Endocrinol. Metab.* 36: 1097–1099.

Riggs, B. L., Seeman, E., Hodgson, S. Taves, D. R., and O'Fallon, W. M. 1982. Effect of the flouride/calcium regimen on vertebral fracture occurrences in postmenopausal osteoporosis. *New Eng. J. Med.* 306: 446–450.

Robertson, W. G. 1976. Urinary excretion. *In,* B. E. C. Nordin (ed.), *Calcium, Phosphate and Magnesium Metabolism,* pp. 113–161. New York: Churchill Livingstone.

Schachter, D., Dowdle, E. B., and Schenker, H. 1960. Active transport of calcium by the small intestine of the rat. *Am. J. Physiol.* 198: 263–268.

Scotto, J. and Fears, T. R. 1977. Intensity patterns of solar utraviolet radiation. *Environ. Res.* 14: 113–127.

Smith, R. W., Rizek, J., Frame, B., and Mansour, J. 1964. Determinants of serum anti-rachitic activity. Am. J. Clin. Nutr. 14: 98–108.

Stamp, T. C. B. and Round, J. M. 1974. Seasonal changes in human plasma levels of 25-hydroxycholecalciferol. *Nature* 247: 563–565.

Stamp, T. C. B. 1978. Mineral metabolism. *In,* J. W. T.

Dickerson and H. A. Lee (eds.), *Nutrition in the Clinical Management of Disease,* pp. 246–286. London: Arnold.

Stephen, J. M. L. and Dattani, O. 1980. Unpublished observations.

Steward, R. J. C., Sheppard, H. G., Preece, R. F., and Exton-Smith, A. N. 1972. Bone resorption in the elderly. *Age and Ageing* 1:1–13.

Tanner, J. M., Whitehouse, R. H., and Tamaishi, M. 1966. Standards from birth to maturity for height, weight, height velocity and weight velocity: British children 1965. *Arch. Dis. Child.* 41:454.

Thomson, D. L. and Frame, B. 1976. Involutional osteoporosis: current concepts. *Ann. Int. Med.* 85:789–803.

Tilton, F. E., Degioanni, T. T. C., and Schneider, V. S. 1980. Long term follow-up of Skylab bone demineralization. *Aviat. Space Environ. Med.* 51:1209–1212.

Trotter, M. 1971. The density of bones in the young skeleton. *Growth* 35: 221–231.

Trotter, M., Broman, G. E., and Peterson, R. R. 1960. Densities of bones of White and Negro skeletons. *J. Bone Jr. Surg.* 42A: 50–58.

Wakamatusu, E. and Sissons, H. A. 1969. The cancellous bone of the iliac crest. *Cal. Tiss. Res.* 4: 147–161.

Walker, A. R. P., Walker, B. F., and Richardson, B. D. 1971. Metacarpal bone dimensions in young and aged South African Bantu consuming a diet low in calcium. *Postgrad. Med. J.* 47: 320–325.

Walker, A. R. P., Walker, B. F., Richardson, B. D., and Christ, H. H. 1970. Cortical thickness in underprivileged populations. *Am. J. Clin. Nutr.* 23: 244–245.

Walker, R. M. and Linkswiler, H. M. 1972. Calcium retention in the adult human male as affected by protein intake. *J. Nutr.* 100: 1297–1302.

Weaver, J. K. and Chalmers, J. 1966. Cancellous bone. Its strength and changes with aging and an evaluation of some methods of measuring its mineral content. I. Age changes in cancellous bone. *J. Bone Jt. Surg.* 48A: 239–298.

Widdowson, E. M. and Dickerson, J. W. T. 1964. Chemical composition of the body. *In,* C. L. Comar and F. Bronner (eds.), *Mineral Metabolism,* Vol. 2. New York: Academic Press.

Wilding, P. Rollason, J. G., and Robinson, D. 1972. Patterns of change for various biochemical constiutents detected in well-population screening. *Clin. Chim. Acta* 41: 375–387.

Wilkinson, R. 1976. Absorption of calcium, phosphorus and magnesium. *In,* B. E. C. Nordin (ed.), *Calcium, Phosphate and Magnesium Metabolism,* pp. 36–112. Edinburgh: Churchill Livingstone.

Wootton, R., Brereton, P. J., Clark, M. B., Hesp, R., Hodkinson, H. M., Klenerman, L., Reeve, J., Slavin, G., and Tellez-Yudilevich, M. 1979. Fractured neck of femur in the elderly: an attempt to identify patients at risk. *Clin. Sci.* 57: 93–101.

Wootton, R., Bryson, E., Elsasser, U., Freeman, R., Green, J. R., Hesp, R., Hudson, E. A., Klenerman, L., Smith, T., and Zanelli, J. 1982. Risk factors for fractured neck of the femur in the elderly. *Age and Ageing* 11: 160–168.

20
METABOLISM

E. J. Masoro

Department of Physiology
University of Texas Health Sciences Center at San Antonio

Metabolism is broadly defined as the sum of the chemical events occurring in living organisms. Since this subject area is so vast, it is necessary to select the fields of metabolism to be covered in this chapter. Fuel utilization and fuel storage are aspects of metabolism of particular significance in regard to current considerations of aging (Sacher, 1977; Harman, 1981). For this reason, this chapter will be focused on and limited to these two subjects.

AGING AND FUEL UTILIZATION

Fuel Use with Age: Assessment of Current Status

Metabolic Rate. The rate at which fuel is used to provide energy for physiologic activities including the generation of heat is called the *metabolic rate*. Since in most animals fuel utilization primarily involves aerobic metabolic processes, measurement of the rate of O_2 consumption ($\dot{V}_{O_2}$) provides a reliable measure of metabolic rate (Brown, 1973). However, energy for physiologic activities can also be obtained from anaerobic metabolic events, which for some cells (e.g., erythrocytes of mammals) provide the sole source of energy. Moreover, for short periods of time, most cells can utilize anaerobic processes for their energy needs (e.g., muscle during vigorous exercise of short duration or almost any tissue under

hypoxic conditions). The rate of fuel utilization is markedly influenced by many physiologic and environmental factors such as the level of physical activity, the environmental temperature, the body temperature, the ingestion of food, and the behavioral state. Thus, when considering metabolic rate in relation to age, all of these factors must be taken into account.

A measurement called the *basal metabolic rate* (BMR) has been developed in an attempt to standardize all of these factors when measuring the metabolic rate. The BMR is usually expressed in terms of kilocalories of energy expenditure per square meter of body surface per hour. In human subjects, it is measured under the following conditions: the subject (a) is lying quietly and is awake; (b) has not eaten for at least 12 hours; (c) is in a thermoneutral environment (i.e., the environmental temperature is not low enough to promote thermogenesis or high enough to increase heat production because of sweating and other processes involved in heat loss); (d) has normal body temperature; and (e) is not mentally excited. The BMR can be viewed to be akin to the use of fuel by an idling automobile.

Early cross-sectional studies on adult humans from different age groups (Boothby et al., 1936; Du Bois, 1936; Binet et al., 1945; Shock and Yiengst, 1955) showed that the BMR decreases with increasing age. Boothby et al. (1936) found that with men in the age range of 24 to 64 years, there is an inverse linear relationship between BMR and age, with the regression relationship in terms of kcal/m²/hr being roughly: BMR = 43 − 0.13A, where A is age in years. Shock and Yiengst (1955) obtained similar data on men aged 30 to 80 years (regression equation: BMR = 40.22 − 0.11A). In contrast, on the basis of a longitudinal study, Keys et al. (1973) concluded that the reduction in BMR attributable to aging *per se* is at most 1 to 2 percent per decade of age; they suggested that the greater decline in BMR noted in the early cross-sectional studies was due to the fact that the changes in percent body fat with age were ignored in those studies. Similarly, Gregerman (1967) found that basal O_2 consumption per liter of body water (Figure 1) is not influenced by age. Moreover, Tzankoff and Norris (1977) presented evidence that the fall in BMR with age in man primarily results from a loss of muscle mass. Thus, it appears that in humans during adult life, the BMR per unit of protoplasmic mass changes little if at all with increasing age. In line with this view, the human brain shows a small significant decrease in O_2 consumption with advancing age (Lassen et al., 1960).

Benedict and Sherman (1937) reported that basal metabolism in rats increases slightly with age, when normalized either to body weight or to surface area. Pettegrew and Ewing (1971) reported a decrease with age in oxygen consumption in resting mice. Of course, it is technically difficult to achieve basal conditions in animals, and thus other means of standardizing metabolism are needed.

Denckla (1970) developed a method for measuring the metabolic rate of rats under tightly standardized conditions. This measurement, termed the minimal oxygen consumption (MOC), is carried out at thermoneutrality while the rat is in stage III anesthesia; the data are expressed as $\dot{V}_{O_2}$ per 100 grams fat-free body weight. Although the MOC has the advantage of measuring metabolic rate under standard conditions, it has the disadvantage of being measured under conditions quite different from those normally experienced by the rat during its lifetime. Since it is not possible to standardize the BMR in rats, the relationship between MOC and BMR has not been

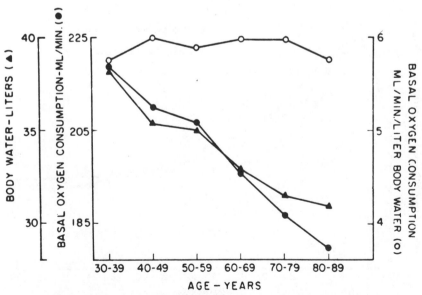

Figure 1. Relationship of age to basal oxygen consumption, total body water, and basal oxygen consumption per unit of body water; from Gregerman (1967). (From *Endocrines and Aging,* ed. by L. Gitman, 1967. Courtesy of Charles C. Thomas, Publisher, Springfield, Illinois.)

rigorously defined; the MOC is about 20 to 30 percent lower than the BMR (Denckla, 1970). Denckla (1974) reported that MOC reaches a maximum at 3 weeks of age (Figure 2) and then progressively declines with increasing age (Figures 2 and 3). Denckla proposes that a new pituitary factor (DECO), which decreases the responsiveness of tissues to thyroid hormones, is at least in part responsible for this age-related decline in MOC; DECO has not been purified.

Of course, the daily metabolic activity of men and animals is greater than the BMR or MOC. This daily metabolic activity has been measured by McGandy et al. (1966) who studied the effects of age in humans on total metabolism, basal metabolism, and the difference between total metabolism and basal metabolism (Figure 4). This difference relates to energy expenditure due to physical activity, temperature-induced thermogenesis, and food intake-induced thermogenesis. In young adult humans, the basal metabolism accounted for about 60 percent of total metabolism, and in old adults, for about 65 percent; this fractional increase with age probably relates to a decrease in physical activity. Both the basal and the total metabolism declined with age in this study; however, the data were expressed in terms of the total organism and not per liter body water. Such a decline may be generally true in many animal species; e.g., Lints and Lints (1968) reported similar findings with *Drosophila melanogaster*.

Studies have also been carried out with animal models to learn the influence of age on the metabolic activities of individual organs. For example, the cerebral metabolic rate was found to decrease with age in dogs (Michenfelder and Theye, 1969). Peng et al. (1977) reported O_2 consumption by rat brain homogenates to decrease with age, and similar changes have been noted with homogenates and slices of other tissues and organs (Ross and Ely, 1954; Wollenberger and Jehl, 1952; Barrows et al., 1962).

Electron Transport and Oxidative Phosphorylation. Since fuel utilization generates reduced nicotinamide adenine dinucleotide

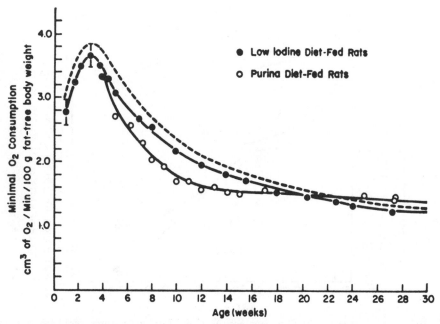

Figure 2. Change in minimal oxygen consumption from 1 to 30 weeks of age in female rats; from Denckla (1974). (Reproduced from *The Journal of Clinical Investigation,* 1974, **53,** 573 by copyright permission of The American Society for Clinical Investigation.)

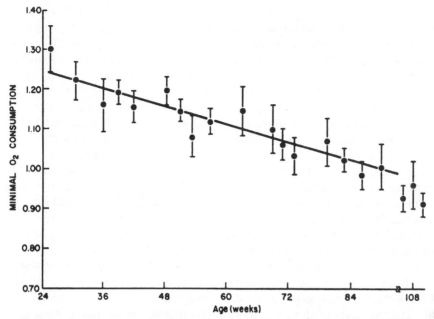

Figure 3. Change in minimal oxygen consumption from 24 to 108 weeks of age in female rats; from Denckla (1974). (Reproduced from *The Journal of Clinical Investigation*, 1974, **53**, 574 by copyright permission of The American Society for Clinical Investigation.)

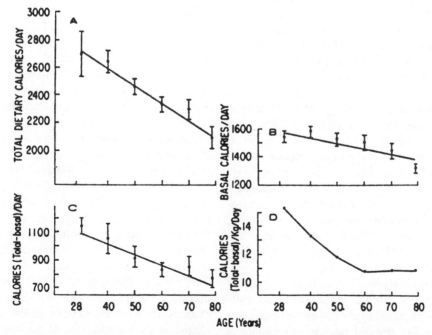

Figure 4. Energy expenditure by men: (A) total caloric intake per day; (B) basal metabolic rate; (C) energy expenditure in addition to the basal expenditure; (D) energy expenditure in addition to basal expenditure expressed as per kilogram body weight; from McGandy et al. (1966). (Reprinted by permission of *The Journal of Gerontology*, **21**, 586, 1966.)

(NADH) and reduced flavin adenine dinucleotide (FADH₂), several investigators have studied the influence of age on the enzymatic system that reoxidizes NADH and FADH₂ (i.e., the electron transport pathway). Electron transport which occurs in the mitochondria is coupled to adenosine triphosphate generation by a process called oxidative phosphorylation, and this process has also been the subject of study.

Weinbach and Garbus (1956) reported that liver mitochondria isolated from 24- to 30-month-old rats oxidize β-hydroxybutyrate at lower rates than mitochondria from 3-month-old rats. However, the efficiency of oxidative phosphorylation in fresh liver mitochondria did not change with age (Weinbach and Garbus, 1959). In this study, the efficiency of oxidative phosphorylation was measured by the P/O ratio, i.e., the moles of phosphate incorporated into ATP per atom of oxygen consumed. Gold et al. (1968) reexplored the question by using the respiratory control ratio, in addition to the P/O ratio. The respiratory control ratio, which is obtained by dividing the rate of O_2 consumption of isolated mitochondria in the presence of adenosine diphosphate (state 3 respiration) by the rate of O_2 consumption in the absence of ADP (state 4 respiration), is a more sensitive indicator of mitochondrial integrity than the P/O ratio (Hansford, 1980). Mitochondria from rat liver, heart, and kidney of 24- to 27-month-old rats had the same phosphorylation efficiency, respiratory control, and maximal ADP-stimulated oxygen consumption as mitochondria from 12- to 14-month-old rats (Gold et al., 1968). Other similar studies also found no indication of deterioration of mitochondrial functional integrity with advancing age (Chen et al., 1972); Wilson et al, 1975; Bulos et al., 1972; Inamdar et al., 1974; Chiu and Richardson, 1980).

However, this conclusion is not supported by all studies. Nohl et al. (1978) found a decrease with senescence (24-month-old compared to 3-month-old rats) in mitochondrial P/O ratio and respiratory control ratio with β-hydroxybutyrate, succinate, or glutamate plus malate as substrates; this decrease may relate to free radical production influencing mitochondrial membrane integrity, and indeed the rate of superoxide production by heart mitochondria has been found to increase with increasing age (Nohl and Hegner, 1978). Vann and Webster (1977) reported similar findings with mitochondria prepared from aging *Drosophila melanogaster,* and Weindruch et al. (1980) reported an apparently uncoupled oxidative phosphorylation in the mitochondria from spleen of aged mice. Also, Nohl and Kramer (1980) found that heart mitochondria from 30-month-old rats are less active in translocating adenine nucleotides across their inner membrane than mitochondria from 3-month-old rats.

Although the rate of state 4 respiration remains constant (Inamdar et al., 1974; Chiu and Richardson, 1980; Wohlrab, 1976), there is a decrease in the rate of state 3 respiration with age in the tissues of rodents with all substrates other than succinate (Chen et al., 1972; Deshnukh et al., 1980; Chiu and Richardson, 1980), which Murfitt and Sanadi (1978) believe relates to a decrement in the enzymatic machinery of some of the mitochondria. In addition, the number of mitochondria in tissues decreases as a function of age (Barrows et al., 1958, 1960; Tauchi and Sato, 1968; Samorajski et al., 1971; Massie et al., 1975; Herbener, 1976; Tate and Herbener, 1976; Stocco and Hutson, 1978; Burns et al., 1979; Schmucker et al., 1978). The fact that cytochrome oxidase activities of homogenates of rat muscle and heart (Hansford and Castro, 1982) and liver (Vorbeck et al., 1982), and of the liver and spleen of mice (Weindruch et al., 1980), decrease with advancing age is also in accord with this view. However, Abu-Erreish and Sanadi (1978) did report that the mitochondrial concentration of the cytochromes including cytochrome oxidase decreases with age in rat heart mitochondria. Furthermore, Bulos et al. (1975) reported a decreased electron transport activity in mitochondria from blowflies but could find no such change in partial reactions of electron transport: pyruvate dehydrogenase, pyruvate-ferri cyanide reductase, α-glycerolphosphate dehydrogenase, α-glycerolphosphate-ferricyanide reductase, cytochrome oxidase. Mitochondria from the senescent blowfly did not have decreased contents of cytochromes b, $c + c_1$, a, or a_3. Also, for mitochondria isolated from perfused hearts, Starnes et al. (1981) found that the rate of respiration decreased with age if the perfused heart had been stressed.

At odds with these findings are other data obtained on perfused hearts (Abu-Erreish et al., 1977), in which little change occurred with age in work performance. This finding indicates that ATP generation by oxidative phosphorylation is not markedly influenced by aging. In addition, the results of this investigation indicate there to be no decrease in the efficiency of energy coupling with age. Yet, Casten (1950) reported that rat heart phosphocreatine concentrations are decreased with advanced age; Steinhagen-Thiessen and Hilz (1976) obtained similar findings with human skeletal muscle. It is also of interest that physical training increases the activity of creatine kinase in skeletal muscle and heart of young and middle-aged mice but not of old mice (Steinhagen-Thiessen et al., 1980; Reznick et al., 1982).

Further insight is provided by the studies of Sylvia and Rosenthal. Although aging had no effect on the brain mitochondria energy-producing system when the rats were at rest (Sylvia and Rosenthal, 1978), an age-related decrease occurred in the capacity to respond to higher energy demands (Sylvia and Rosenthal, 1979). In addition, Ferrendelli et al. (1971) found that the use of high energy phosphate compounds by mouse brain (particularly by the striatum) decreased with age.

Tricarboxylic Acid Cycle Activity. The tricarboxylic acid cycle, which occurs in the matrix of mitochondria, catalyzes the complete oxidation of acetyl groups (major products of carbohydrate and fat metabolism) to CO_2 and H_2O. In the process, NADH and $FADH_2$ are made available to the electron transport system. The tricarboxylic acid cycle can be divided into three functional segments (Williamson, 1979) with oxaloacetate to α-ketoglutarate designated the first segment, α-ketoglutarate to malate designated the second segment, and malate to oxaloacetate designated the third segment.

Chen et al. (1972) and Hansford (1978) reported no age-related impairment in mitochondria from rats in regard to the first segment of the cycle. However, others have found citrate synthase and isocitrate dehydrogenase activity to be decreased with age in rat heart, skeletal muscle, and brain (Vitorica et al., 1981b; Hansford and Castro, 1982; Patel, 1977; Leong et al., 1981; Vitorica et al., 1981a; Lai et al., 1982).

Chen et al. (1972) reported no decrement with age of the rats in the second segment of the tricarboxylic acid cycle. In contrast, Frolkis and Bogatskaya (1968) reported a 20 percent decrease in the activity in this segment in mitochondria from 28- to 32-month-old rats compared to those from 8- to 12-month-old rats. Hansford and Castro (1982) found α-ketoglutarate dehydrogenase activity to be decreased with age in homogenates of rat skeletal muscle.

Several investigators (Chen et al., 1972; Ermini and Szelényi, 1972; Bass et al., 1975; Singh, 1973; Ermini et al., 1971; Mainwaring, 1967) have found that the activity of the third segment of the cycle decreases with age. In the case of skeletal muscle, this correlates with a decrease in respiratory capacity and the loss of red fibers (Ermini, 1976).

On the basis of findings on tricarboxylic acid cycle enzyme activities in mitochondria and homogenates, Vitorica et al. (1981b) have concluded that with advanced age there is a partial impairment of tricarboxylic acid cycle function and a decline in the energy-producing capacity of the heart. However, the studies of Abu-Erreish et al. (1977) with the perfused heart suggest that the extent of this decline with age from a physiological standpoint is small.

Use of Carbohydrate as a Fuel. The glucose tolerance test indicates that in humans there is an impaired utilization of glucose with age (Davidson, 1979). This is partly due to increase in adiposity, lack of physical activity, and the occurrence of disease, but some of the impaired glucose tolerance appears not to result from such factors. Moreover, postprandial plasma glucose levels (i.e., the levels one to two hours after a meal) rise at the rate of about 4 mg/dl/decade (O'Sullivan and Mahan, 1971). There is also a small increase in fasting plasma glucose levels (~1 mg/dl/decade) (Dudl and Ensinck, 1977; Marigo et al., 1962; Swerdloff et al., 1967).

Studies utilizing the "glucose clamp" technique (De Fronzo et al., 1979; Andres and Tobin, 1975) indicate that tissue sensitivity to secreted insulin is not impaired in aging humans. However, using the same technique, De Fronzo (1979) found the peripheral actions of endogenously secreted insulin to be impaired in aging humans. This difference in findings may be due to differences in health, adiposity, and physical fitness of the two populations studied.

Similar age-related changes in glucose tolerance also occur in other mammals (Davidson, 1979). For instance, Bailey and Flatt (1982) have recently reported that glucose tolerance deteriorates with advancing age in mice, and similar findings with rats have been reported by Bracho-Romero and Reaven (1977), Gold et al. (1976), Gommers and de Gaspara (1972), and Gommers and Genne (1975).

It has been suggested that the impaired glucose tolerance in the aged may at least in part be due to a loss of insulin receptors. Indeed, a reduced number of receptors with age has been shown to occur in adipocytes of rats (Olefsky and Reaven, 1975) and man (Pagano et al., 1981).

The effects of age on the activity of enzymes involved in carbohydrate metabolism have been studied in cell-free preparations. Phosphorylase activity has been found to decrease with age in rat heart (Frolkis and Bogatskaya, 1968) and in human aorta and coronary artery (Kirk, 1962). Hexokinase activity has been reported to decrease with age in rat heart (Frolkis and Bogatskaya, 1968) and liver (Bartoc et al., 1975), while in human aorta no change in the activity of this enzyme was noted with age (Brandstrup et al., 1957). The activities of phosphoglucomutase and phosphoglyceromutase decrease with age in human arterial tissue (Kirk, 1966). Phosphofructoki-

nase activity is reduced in homogenates prepared from brains of old compared to young people (Iwangoff et al., 1979). Triosephosphate dehydrogenase activity in fast and slow skeletal muscle and diaphragm of rats was found to decrease with increasing age (Bass et al., 1975) as did pyruvate kinase activity of rat heart (Vitorica et al., 1981a, 1981b). Lactate dehydrogenase activity of many rat tissues declines with age (Schmukler and Barrows, 1966; Singh and Kanungo, 1968; Porter et al., 1971), but there appears to be no age-related change in pyruvate dehydrogenase activity (Hansford, 1977). Recently, Leong et al. (1981) reported that the activities of aldolase and lactic dehydrogenase but not hexokinase and pyruvic dehydrogenase decline with age in rats when measured in homogenates of brain. Bartoc et al. (1975) have reported decreased aldolase activity in livers of old rats. Aldolase activity increases with physical training in muscle and heart of young and middle-aged mice but not old mice (Steinhagen-Thiessen et al., 1980; Reznick et al., 1982).

The physiological meaning of these changes in enzymatic activities is not entirely clear. Abu-Erreish, et al. (1977) found that the rate of glycolysis from exogenous glucose by perfused hearts did not decrease as the age of the donor rat increased. It is striking that glycolytic flux in heart homogenates also did not decrease with the advancing age of rats (Frolkis and Bogatskaya, 1968; Angelova-Gateva, 1969). However, Patnaik and Kanungo (1966) found that the use of glucose and galactose by skin slices declines with advancing age in rats.

The effect of age on the metabolism of glucose by brain has been an area of intensive work. In vitro studies utilizing brain homogenates (Reiner, 1947) and brain slices (Patel, 1977) of rats indicated that glucose utilization decreased with advancing age. However, in vivo studies with rats yielded a somewhat different picture. A decrease with age in the rate of glucose utilization by brain was observed during the first third of the life span, but there was no further change in glucose utilization during the last two-thirds of the life span (Sokoloff, 1979; London et al., 1981; Smith et al., 1980; Smith and Sokoloff, 1982). These *in vivo* studies with rats also showed that age-related changes in glucose metabolism are selective in regard to brain regions involved. Gibson et al. (1981) found that the total rate of glucose utilization by the brain of mice did not change with age but there were age-related changes in the regional pattern of glucose utilization. They also found that there was an increased rate of lactate production in response to hypoxia by brain of senescent mice. In the case of humans, it seems clear that there is a decline with age in the rate of glucose utilization by brain (Sokoloff, 1978; Kuhl et al., 1982). For further discussion of this issue, see Chapter 22.

Use of Fat as a Fuel. Free fatty acids (FFA) and very low density lipoprotein triglyceride (VLDL-TG) are the major forms of lipid fuel transported by the blood (Wolfe, 1982). In humans, serum FFA concentrations are elevated in old subjects, especially after an overnight fast (Metz et al., 1966; Vinik and Jackson, 1968; O'Sullivan et al., 1971; Sinha et al., 1974). In contrast, in rats, postabsorptive serum FFA levels decrease with increasing age (Liepa et al., 1980). There are no data on the effect of age on VLDL-TG levels, and the data on serum triglyceride levels are controversial, in the case of both man and rats (Porta, 1980).

The oxidation of palmitylcarnitine by rat heart mitochondria declines with the increasing age of the animal (Chen et al., 1972; Hansford, 1978). The carnitine and acylcarnitine content of rat heart decreases with age (Abu-Erreish et al., 1977) as does the carnitine content of rat heart mitochondria (Hansford, 1978). Since acylcarnitine is the form in which fatty acids are transported across the mitochondrial membrane, this transport step may be the site responsible for the age-related decrease in palmitylcarnitine oxidation by mitochondria. In this regard, it is of interest that Hansford and Castro (1982) found the carnitine palmitoyltransferase activity to be decreased with age in rat skeletal muscle homogenates. In the same study, they also found the acyl-CoA dehydrogenase and the β-hydroxyacyl-CoA dehydrogenase activities to be decreased with age. However, it is hard to know if these measurements with mitochondria and homogenates have physiological meaning since Abu-Erreish et al. (1977) found that the rate of palmitate oxidation only modestly decreases in perfused rat hearts with the advancing age of the donor.

Chen et al. (1972) reported that the rate of β-hydroxybutyrate oxidation was depressed in heart mitochondria prepared from senescent rats. Also, Patel (1977) reported a decreased rate of β-hydroxybutyrate oxidation by cerebral cortex slices of old rats. A decrease in β-hydroxybutyrate dehydrogenase activity, as well as in the activity of other β oxidation enzymes, occurs in the brain mitochondria of rats with increasing age (Deshmukh et al., 1980).

Use of Protein as Fuel. There is very little information on the effects of age on the use of protein as fuel. Body protein mass slowly declines with age in humans, due largely to a loss in skeletal muscle mass (Young et al., 1982), but the rate of this loss is so slow that it should not be taken as an indication that with age body protein stores are providing a significant amount of fuel. Indeed, the rate of tissue protein breakdown has been shown to decrease with age in rats (Yousef and Johnson, 1970), mice (Sobel and Bowman, 1971), and man (Uauy et al., 1978), which indicates that a reduced rate of protein synthesis underlies the slow loss of body protein mass. The fact that the glutamine content of tissue increases with age (Kuttner and Lorincz, 1969) has led Vitorica et al. (1981b) to suggest that amino acids may increasingly be used as fuel with advancing age. Further work is needed to provide substance for this view.

Relationship between Fuel Utilization and Aging

Rate of Living Hypothesis. Pearl (1928) proposed the rate of living hypothesis of aging. This hypothesis states that the duration of life is determined by the exhaustion of a vital substance that is consumed at a rate proportional to the metabolic rate. Economos (1981) points out that this hypothesis has fallen into disfavor because not all relevent data support it. He further points out that although the rate of living hypothesis may be an oversimplification, it still may describe an important aspect of aging which should not be viewed by itself but rather in conjunction with the fact that "counterentropic" mechanisms (e.g., DNA repair) may have developed to differing degrees in the various mammalian species.

Maximum Life Span of Mammalian Species and Metabolic Rate. Rubner (1908) described a rough inverse correlation between the life span of domestic animal species and the metabolic rate per unit body weight of that species. Indeed, in general it has been found that among mammalian species (Economos, 1981), there is a trend for maximum life span to decrease as the specific metabolic rate of the species increases (by specific metabolic rate is meant caloric expenditure per gram body weight per unit of time).

A particularly incisive study in this regard is that of Sacher and Duffy (1979) in which inbred mouse strains and their hybrids were used. They found that the life span of these mice is negatively correlated with the resting metabolism (milliliters O_2 consumed per gram body weight per hour) and average metabolism (milliliters O_2 consumed per gram body weight per hour). However, there are exceptions to this relationship. For example, sheep with a maximum life span of ~17 years, chimpanzees with a maximum life span of ~50 years, and man with a maximum life span of about ~100 years have similar specific metabolic rates (Economos, 1981).

Sacher (1978) attempted to reconcile these exceptions within a general framework developed from his analysis of the four major variables he found to influence life span, i.e., brain weight (E), body weight (S), resting metabolic rate (M), and body temperature (T_b). By multivariate analysis, the best-fit regression for life span (L) in terms of these four variables was:

$$L = 8E^{0.6} S^{-0.4} M^{-0.5} 10^{0.025 T_b}$$

This analysis agrees with the concept that life span is inversely related to metabolic rate, but

further points out that other factors can counteract this effect (note the brain weight term in the equation). Lindstedt and Calder (1981) have expressed doubt concerning the causal relationship of allometric factors, such as brain weight, to longevity. For further discussion, see Chapter 2.

To consider possible molecular mechanisms for these exceptions, the concept of Harman (1972) along with the findings of Tolmasoff et al. (1980) should be examined. Harman (1972) proposes that the rate of O_2 utilization determines the rate of accumulation of damage produced by free radical reactions and that it is this damage that underlies much of the aging process. Tolmasoff et al. (1980) found that the ratio of superoxide dismutase specific activity to specific metabolic rate of mammalian species (primarily primates) increases with increasing maximum life span. From this it seems reasonable to postulate that increasing the metabolic rate acts to decrease life span but that this action can be counteracted by protective mechanisms such as superoxide dismutase. However, the conceptual validity of the conclusions of Tolmasoff et al. (1980) has recently been challenged by Sullivan (1982).

Comparison of Homeotherms and Poikilotherms in Regard to Resting Metabolism, Metabolic Capacity, and Longevity. Like mammals, poikilothermic vertebrates exhibit an inverse correlation between the size of the animal and the standard or basal metabolic rate per gram body weight (Bennett, 1978). This relationship shows that the resting metabolic requirements are similar for the various classes of poikilothermic vertebrates (i.e., reptiles, amphibians, fish); moreover, most invertebrate groups are similar to poikilothermic vertebrates in this regard (Hemmingsen, 1960). In contrast, the basal metabolic rates of mammals and birds are six to ten times greater than those of the poikilothermic animals even at equal body temperature (Bennett, 1978; Hemmingsen, 1960; Schmidt-Nielsen, 1970).

Maximal oxygen consumption has been measured in both poikilothermic and homeothermic vertebrates. The maximal oxygen consumption of a cold-blooded vertebrate approaches that of the basal oxygen consumption of a mammal of similar size, while the maximal oxygen consumption of a mammal is greater by 5 to 15 times (Bennett, 1978). Recently, Else and Hulbert (1981) reported the results of a study of the metabolic capacity for energy production in lizards and mice of the same size. This metabolic capacity was assessed in liver, heart, brain, and kidney by the measurement of cytochrome oxidase activity and by measuring mitochondrial volume density and membrane surface area; the capacity for energy production was three- to sixfold greater in mice than in lizards. Similar findings have been reported when comparing rats and turtles (Robin and Simon, 1970).

It seems clear, therefore, that the rate of metabolic activity of poikilotherms is much less than that of mammals. Is this reflected in a marked difference in longevity between homeotherms and poikilotherms of similar size? Although some poikilotherms (e.g., turtles) have long life spans, there is not a sufficient amount of reliable data available on life span of poikilotherms of various sizes and species to permit this question to be answered (Comfort, 1979).

Environmental Temperature and Longevity.

Environmental temperature has been shown to influence the length of life of laboratory rats. Heroux and Campbell (1960) reported that the life span of rats housed at 6°C is less than that of rats housed at 30°C; Kibler et al. (1963) found that rats maintained at 28°C lived longer than those maintained at 9°C; and Carlson et al. (1957) reported that rats living at 26°C have a longer length of life than rats living at 5°C. In all three cases, the rats living at the lower temperature had a higher metabolic rate than those living at the higher temperature because of the cold-induced thermogenesis (Masoro, 1966) that occurs in homeotherms. Kibler and Johnson (1966) found that rats maintained at 34°C had a shorter length of life than rats living at 28°C. Since the rats living at 34°C had a mean body temperature more than 1°C above that of the

rats living at 28°C, it seems likely in this case that the metabolic rate of the rats living at the higher temperature was elevated.

In the first edition of this *Handbook,* Rockstein et al. (1977) stated that mammals that respond to severe winters by going into hibernation generally have shorter life spans than other mammals. However, in the same edition, Sacher (1977) stated that mammals such as bats that are capable of markedly reducing their life-time energy expenditure by hibernating have longer life spans than other mammals of similar size. A recent report by Lyman et al. (1981) has added significant new information on the effects of hibernation on length of life. In this study, the Turkish hamster (*Mesocricetus brandti*) was used. These hamsters were kept either at 25°C or at 5°C from mid-November until the end of April and at 25°C the rest of the year (this study was carried out in Massachusetts). None of the hamsters maintained at 25°C hibernated. In regard to the hamsters maintained at 5°C, there were three categories of hibernators: (a) poor hibernators (hibernated from 0 to 11 percent of their lives); (b) moderate hibernators (hibernated 12 to 18 percent of their lives); and (c) good hibernators (hibernated 19 to 33 percent of their lives). The mean life span of good hibernators was significantly greater than that of the moderate hibernators, and moderate hibernators had a significantly greater mean length of life than the poor hibernators. The mean life span of the hamsters living at 25°C was significantly less than that of the moderate or the good hibernators but significantly more than that of the poor hibernators. The data are consistent with the view that the lower the metabolic activity of the animal population, the longer is the mean life span.

Over 50 years ago, Loeb and Northrop (1917) demonstrated that the mean life span of the poikilotherm *Drosophila melanogaster* was inversely proportional to the ambient temperature, and Northrop (1926) later concluded that this was not determined by the time required to produce a limiting amount of CO_2. Alpatov and Pearl (1929), Strehler (1961, 1962), and Shaw and Bercaw (1962) provided further evidence that the aging of *D. melano-*

gaster is temperature dependent. However, on the basis of studies with *D. subobscura,* Maynard Smith (1958, 1959, 1963) and Clarke and Maynard Smith (1961a, 1961b) concluded that there is no simple relationship between aging and ambient temperature. The work of Hollingsworth (1966, 1968, 1969), of Lamb (1968), and of Nayar (1972) further attests to the complex nature of the interaction between environmental temperature and aging in *D. subobscura, D. melanogaster,* and *Aedes taeniorhynchus.* Recently, Miquel et al. (1976) not only obtained data with *D. melanogaster* which reaffirms the view that the rate of aging increases with environmental temperature but also concluded that some of the confusion in the literature relates to the fact that most of the studies used life span as the only parameter of aging. Sohal and his colleagues (Sohal et al., 1981; Buchan and Sohal, 1981; McArthur and Sohal, 1982; Sohal, 1982) have also reported that life span is inversely related to environmental temperature in *Musca domestica* and in *Oncopeltus fasciatus* (Hemiptera). It appears that the relationship between environmental temperature and the rate of aging just delineated for invertebrate animals also occurs in poikilothermic vertebrates (Liu and Walford, 1966, 1970, 1972; Walford et al., 1969). Prosser (1973) points out that increasing environmental temperature increases the rate of oxygen consumption of poikilotherms by two processes: (a) by increasing the basal metabolic rate and (b) by increasing physical activity. However, Liu and Walford (1975) point out that lowering the environmental temperature does not necessarily reduce the metabolic rate of fish. Moreover, Ragland and Sohal (1975) made it evident that raising the environmental temperature of insects does not always increase the metabolic rate and that only when the metabolic rate is increased is the length of life shortened. The same conclusion was drawn many years ago by MacArthur and Baillie (1929) on the basis of their research on *Daphnia magna.* Thus, in poikilothermic animals there appears to be a positive correlation between metabolic rate and the rate of aging.

Exercise and Longevity. Sohal and his colleagues (Sohal et al., 1981; Buchan and Sohal, 1981; Ragland and Sohal, 1973; Sohal and Buchan, 1981a, 1981b; Sohal, 1981, 1982) have extensively studied the relationship between physical activity and life span in the domestic housefly, and found an inverse correlation between physical activity and length of life; also, physical activity appears to accelerate the aging process in these animals. This provides still another example of a positive correlation between metabolic rate and the rate of aging. Further support for this view has been provided by Trout and Kaplan (1970), who concluded from studies on the short-lived shaker mutant of *D. melanogaster* that the high metabolic rate associated with a high physical activity of the animals is responsible for the short life span.

Studies on the effects of exercise on the longevity of mammals have been carried out with mice and rats. Several early studies (McCay et al., 1941; Retzlaff et al., 1966; Edington et al., 1972; Goodrick, 1974; Drori and Folman, 1976) provided data indicating that exercise increases longevity, but these studies were flawed by questionable animal maintenance procedures, by the small number of animals used, by the small effects obtained, or by a combination of these factors. The recent study of Goodrick (1980) on rats is free of these interpretational difficulties: the data show clearly that exercise caused a small but highly significant increase in mean length of life. Since energy metabolism was higher in the rats that exercised than in the control rats, in this instance an increase in metabolic rate is not associated with a decreased length of life.

Food Restriction, Fuel Utilization, and Longevity. It is almost 50 years since McCay et al. (1935) clearly demonstrated that food restriction increases the length of life of rats. This has been repeatedly confirmed and is clearly a fundamental finding in experimental gerontology (Barrows and Kokkonen, 1977; Young, 1979; Berg and Simms, 1960; Nolen, 1972; Stuchlikova et al., 1975).

The following kinds of data strongly indicate that food restriction increases longevity by decreasing the rate of aging: (a) data on specific death rates showing that food restriction alters the mortality rate constant (Sacher, 1977); (b) data showing that food restriction delays a spectrum of age-related diseases (Ross, 1976; Yu et al., 1982); and (c) data showing that food restriction delays age-related physiologic deterioration (Masoro et al., 1980; Weindruch et al., 1979; Levin et al., 1981).

There have been many hypotheses in regard to the mechanism by which food restriction has its action on the aging process. Recently, the hypothesis has gained favor that food restriction decreases the rate of aging by reducing the rate of energy metabolism per unit of protoplasmic mass (Sacher, 1977; Harman, 1981). Indeed, in the first edition of this *Hand-*

book, Sacher (1977) concluded that ". . . the decrease in rate of aging is explicable as a consequence of a decrease of the rate of energy metabolism. . . ." Sacher based this conclusion on his analysis of the work of Ross (1969) and calculated that the life span kilocaloric consumption of food per gram body weight was the same for rats fed *ad libitum* and rats fed life-prolonging restricted diets. Thus, Sacher concluded that food restriction prolongs life by reducing metabolic rate per unit body mass.

Masoro et al. (1982) recently published data that disagree with this conclusion: except for the first two postweaning months, the number of kilocalories ingested per gram lean body mass was the same for rats fed a restricted amount of food after the age of 6 weeks as for rats fed *ad libitum* (Figure 5). Calculation of the caloric intake per gram body weight

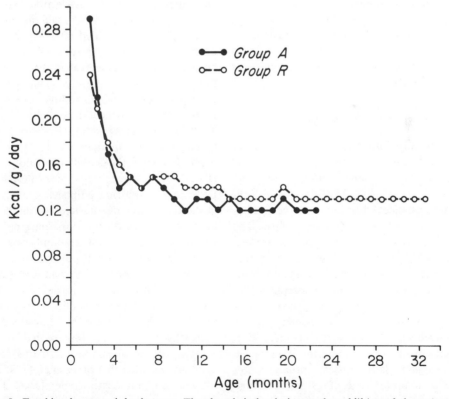

Figure 5. Food intake per unit body mass. The closed circles designate the *ad libitum* fed rats (group A) and the open circles the rats fed 60 percent of the *ad libitum* intake (group R) from 6 weeks of age on; prepared from data published by Masoro et al. (1982).

per lifetime yielded a value of 91.5 kcal for the rats fed *ad libitum* and 133.5 kcal for the rats fed a restricted amount of food.

In drawing his conclusion, Sacher (1977) assumed that most of the caloric materials ingested by the rats were absorbed and almost totally used as fuel; the validity of this assumption is difficult to establish unequivocally. In the study of Masoro et al. (1982), it appears to be sufficiently valid for this assessment to be made because: (a) calculations based on weight gain, body fat content, and food intake between 6 weeks of age and the remainder of the mean length of life indicate that less than 3 percent of the calories ingested are stored by the rats; (b) when rats are fed semi-synthetic diets with compositions like that of the diet used by Masoro et al. (1982), almost all ingested caloric materials are absorbed (Barnes et al., 1958). The findings of Masoro et al. (1982) show that food restriction can have a marked life-prolonging action (Yu et al., 1982) and delay the time of occurrence of a variety of age-related physiological deteriorations (Masoro et al., 1980) without reducing the rate of fuel utilization per gram of lean body mass.

AGING AND FUEL STORAGE

The body contains large stores of energy in the form of triglycerides (~100,000 to 200,000 kcal in the case of man) in adipose tissue depots which are made use of during postabsorptive circumstances, during prolonged moderate exercise, and during prolonged fasts. The body also contains large stores of protein (about 25,000 kcal in adult humans). Although use is made of this source of energy (e.g., during fasting), there is no known specific energy storage form of protein; thus when protein is used as fuel, the body is consuming structural elements and enzymatic machinery. Fortunately, metabolic mechanisms have developed in mammals to conserve protein stores during prolonged periods of fasting. Although the body has only small stores of carbohydrate in the form of glycogen (±1000 kcal in humans) primarily in muscle and liver, these

stores are put to daily use (e.g., during postabsorptive periods and during short bouts of physical activity). Glycogen stores are replenished during postprandial periods and when physical activity has terminated. In this section, data on age-related changes in the size of these energy reservoirs and on the ability to mobilize them will be reviewed.

Fat Stores

Age-related Changes in Fat Stores. Data from cross-sectional studies of adult human beings show that fat mass makes up an increasing fraction of total body mass with increasing age until late middle age (Brozek, 1952; Malina, 1969). However, the data are conflicting on the changes in fat mass that occur during senescence (Novak, 1972; Parizkova and Eiselt, 1971; Myhre and Kessler, 1966).

Bertrand et al. (1980a) carried out a life span longitudinal and cross-sectional study on body fat of the Fischer 344 male rat. The longitudinal study revealed that fat mass increased until about 75 percent of the rat's life span after which it decreased. The cross-sectional studies on the epididymal and perirenal fat depots yielded similar results. The increase in mass of the perirenal depot between young adulthood and late middle age occurred solely by increasing the number of adipocytes in the depot. However, the epididymal depot was enlarged during this same period, solely by hypertrophy of existing adipocytes. Moreover, in the epididymal depot there was an increase in fat cell number during senescence; paradoxically, this increase in fat cell number occurred when the mass of this depot was decreasing. The rats in the study of Bertrand et al. (1980a) were singly housed from weaning on. Since the changes in fat content of rodents with age may be sensitive to social and housing conditions, this work should be repeated utilizing a variety of such conditions. In this regard, it should be noted that Stiles et al. (1975) also showed an adipocyte hyperplasia during senescence in the epididymal depot of Fischer 344 rats housed three to five per cage for most of their lives.

Fat Mobilization and Aging. To mobilize fat from the adipose tissue, the stored triglyceride must be converted to FFA (free fatty acids) and glycerol (Masoro, 1977). This involves the action of lipolytic enzymes including the hormone-sensitive triglyceride lipase which catalyzes what appears to be the rate-limiting step. Hormones and the sympathetic nervous system in part regulate fat mobilization by their control of this rate-limiting step.

Glucagon is one of the hormones that acts at this enzymatic site to promote lipolysis. About ten years ago, Manganiello and Vaughn (1972) showed that the response of adipocytes to the lipolytic action of glucagon decreases with increasing age. This has been confirmed by Holm et al. (1976) and by Bertrand et al. (1980b). Moreover, this age-related loss in response to the fat-mobilizing action of glucagon can be delayed and partially prevented by food restriction (Bertrand et al., 1980) (Figure 6).

Livingston et al. (1974) reported that this age-related loss in response to the lipolytic action of glucagon was associated with reduced glucagon binding by the adipocytes, while Cooper and Gregerman (1976) found that glucagon could not activate adenylate cyclase in adipocyte ghosts obtained from rats 6 months of age. De Santis et al. (1974) showed that phosphodiesterase activity of adipocytes increases with increasing age. Recent evidence indicates that the age-related loss in the lipolytic response to glucagon in *ad libitum* fed rats is due either to a loss of, or a change in, glucagon receptors or to a derangement in the system coupling these receptors to adenylate cyclase; food restriction delays and partially prevents this derangement (Voss et al., 1982).

Bertrand et al. (1982) have shown that restricting food of 6-month-old rats gradually restores the lipolytic response of adipocytes to glucagon (Figure 7). Approximately 12 months of food restriction was required to attain the lipolytic response obtained with fat cells of 6-week-old rats. This finding shows

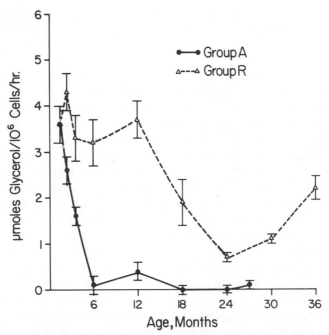

Figure 6. Lipolytic response of adipocytes to glucagon. Closed circles and solid lines refer to *ad libitum* fed rats (group A), and broken line and open triangles refer to rats restricted to 60 percent of the *ad libitum* food intake (group R) from 6 months of age on; from Masoro et al. (1980). (Reproduced by permission of *Federation Proceedings*.)

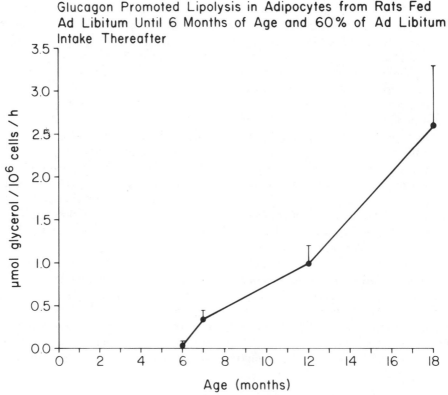

Figure 7. Lipolytic response to glucagon of adipocytes from rats fed *ad libitum* until 6 months of age and 60 percent of *ad libitum* intake thereafter; prepared from data published by Bertrand et al. (1980b, 1982.)

that not only can food restriction delay or prevent age-related physiological changes, but it can also reverse them.

Information on the effects of age on the lipolytic response of fat cells to catecholamines is contradictory. Miller and Allen (1973), Gonzales and De Martinis (1977), and Dax et al. (1981) found little effect of age on the lipolytic response of fat cells to catecholamines. In contrast, Giudicelli and Pecquery (1978) and Yu et al. (1980) reported a marked loss in the lipolytic response of adipocytes to catecholamines. This may relate to the diet fed since Yu et al. (1980) fed a 10 percent corn oil-containing diet, while most commercial laboratory chows are quite low in fat. Indeed, Yu et al. (1980) showed that there is a marked nutrition-aging interaction in the response to catecholamines, since food restriction to a great extent prevented the age-related loss in lipolytic response to catecholamines.

There is also evidence for an age-related loss in fat mobilization activity under *in vivo* conditions in Fischer 344 rats (Liepa et al., 1980) with increasing age; the postabsorptive FFA level declined with *ad libitum* fed rats, but food restriction to a great extent prevented this decline. Serum FFA concentration is a good index of the rate of fat mobilization (Masoro, 1977). An attempt to more directly measure the effect of age on fat mobilization during fasting by Roth et al. (1981) yielded equivocal data.

Relationship between Fat Stores and Length of Life. It has long been believed that increases in body fat content have a life-shortening action in humans (Van Itallie, 1979). This belief appears to have been based on the 1959 report of the Society of Actuaries. Andres (1980) has recently surveyed many studies and concluded that in the moderate ranges of adiposity, at least, there is no strong relationship between fat mass and longevity. However, there is general agreement (Van Itallie, 1979; Andres, 1980) that increases in fat mass predispose to specific diseases in humans such as coronary artery disease, hypertension, and diabetes mellitus. If the conclusion of Andres is correct concerning fat mass and longevity, moderately increased fat mass must have counterbalancing actions which are life prolonging.

Bertrand et al. (1980a) studied the relationship between length of life and body fat content in male Fischer 344 rats. They found that with *ad libitum* fed rats there was no relationship between body fat and length of life, but with rats fed a restricted food intake which prolonged life, there was a positive correlation between length of life and fat content (i.e., the fatter the rat, the longer the life).

Glycogen Stores

Remarkably little has been done on hepatic glycogen stores and their mobilization in relation to aging. About 50 years ago, Deuel et al. (1937) reported that ad libitum fed rats had little change in liver glycogen during adult life. Weigand et al. (1980) recently reported that although liver glycogen per gram liver was less in 490-day-old rats than in 72-day-old rats, the total amount of liver glycogen was greater in the old rats because of the increase in liver mass. They further showed that a three-day fast almost completely depleted the liver of glycogen in the case of both the 72-day-old rats and the 490-day-old rats. Poland et al. (1982) found that 24-month-old and older *ad libitum* fed rats had lower liver glycogen concentrations than younger rats and that in the case of rats of all ages a 24-hour fast caused a marked depletion of liver glycogen. Studies (unpublished) carried out in our laboratory show the postabsorptive concentration of liver glycogen to be similar for 6-, 12-, 18-, and 24-month-old male Fischer 344 rats. Thus, it appears that aging has little effect on hepatic glycogen content or on its mobilization to meet the challenge of fasting. However, other reports differ with these find-

ings. Ermini et al. (1971) and Szelényi et al. (1972) reported the liver glycogen concentration to be much lower in old compared to young rats, but they did not specify whether these rats were fed, fasted, or postabsorptive (i.e., the nutritional state was not defined).

The glycogen content of both white and red skeletal muscle is much less in old rats compared to young rats (Ermini et al., 1971; Szelényi et al. 1972), but again the nutritional state was not specified. In both the young and the old rats, vigorous exercise caused a marked depletion of the muscle glycogen. Frolkis and Bogatskaya (1968) state that there is a reduced cardiac glycogen content with increased age, but it is not clear whether this is true *in situ* or after some *in vitro* experimental manipulation. In contrast to these studies, Poland et al. (1982) found age to have little effect on glycogen content of heart and skeletal muscle of fed or fasted rats. There is an abundance of evidence showing that the glycogen content of insect flight muscle decreases with age (Takahashi et al., 1970; Johnson and Rowley, 1972; Butler and Nath, 1972; Rockstein et al., 1975; Simon et al., 1969; Sohal and Allison, 1971; Tribe and Ashhurst, 1972). However, in the blowfly *Phormia regina,* no decrease in muscle glycogen content with age was found (Sacktor and Shimada, 1972), while in the mosquito, there is a decreased ability during senescence to utilize muscle glycogen (Rowley and Graham, 1968).

Protein Stores

There is a loss of body protein content with age. Young et al. (1982) calculated the total body protein in young adult men to be about 9.4 kg and that of elderly men to be about 6.5 kg. They further concluded that this change occurs by means of a slow loss of protein with increasing adult age and that there is a greater percent loss of protein in muscle with age than in other tissues.

Protein is mobilized as fuel in response to trauma and during the early period of fasting. How these mobilizations are influenced by aging has not been explored. Moreover, with prolonged fasting, mechanisms for the conservation of body protein become operative, but the influence of aging on these mechanisms has not been studied. Both of these subject areas are of great importance and deserve thorough exploration.

GENERAL CONCLUSIONS

The daily metabolic activity of humans decreases with increasing age. A decrease in physical activity appears to be the main reason for this. The basal metabolic rate decreases in humans with increasing age when calculated per square meter of body surface, but not when calculated per liter of body water. Thus, it appears that there is little change with age in human basal metabolic rate per unit of protoplasmic mass.

It seems likely that the daily metabolic activity of most animals also decreases with age since in most species there is an age-related decrease in physical activity. However, there are not sufficient data involving metabolic measurements to unequivocally make this claim. In rats, a metabolic value called the minimal oxygen consumption markedly decreases with advancing age, but since this measurement is made under highly artificial conditions, it is not possible to evaluate the physiological meaning of this finding.

Much more data are needed on the effects of age on metabolic activity. In particular, the changes in daily metabolic activity with age should be defined for a spectrum of species. Also, the influence of age on temperature-induced and food-induced thermogenesis should be characterized in several species.

Most studies utilizing isolated mitochondria (primarily from rats) indicate that the efficiency of oxidative phosphorylation does not change with increasing age. However, in the case of most substrates, a decreased rate of state 3 respiration was found with mitochondria from aged rats. There is also evidence that cytochrome oxidase activity and the amount of mitochondria in tissues decrease with increasing age. Further study of electron transport and oxidative phosphorylation by isolated mitochondria will probably yield little further information of value, but work on the effects of age on the metabolic capacity of tissues and on the amount of mitochondria in tissues in a variety of species should provide important data.

Many studies have been done on the enzymatic activities of the tricarboxylic acid cycle and the Embden-Meyerhof pathway of carbohydrate metabolism in regard to aging. The activities of the different enzymes involved are variously reported to decrease, to not change, and to increase with age. Little understanding about aging can be gained by analyzing the available data on these enzymatic activities, nor is further research along this line likely to yield important information.

Further research on the basic mechanisms underlying impairment in glucose tolerance that occurs with advancing age is greatly needed. Another area that should yield important information involves studies of the influence of age on glucose utilization by individual organs under *in vivo* conditions. In humans, it seems clear that the rate of glucose utilization by brain decreases with advancing age. Similar research on fat and protein metabolism by various organs would be invaluable, but such studies must await development of the necessary technology.

There is a considerable body of data in support of the view that the life span of a species and the specific metabolic rate are inversely related. However, there are exceptions to this generalization which indicate that the specific metabolic rate is only one of the factors controlling the life span of a species. Most manipulations that increase metabolic rate (e.g., raising the environmental temperature of poikilotherms or exposing homeotherms to a cold environment) decrease the length of life of the animals. An exception to this is the effect of exercise in mammals which, under certain circumstances, can increase the length of life of the animals. Food restriction has been thought to increase the length of life of rodents by decreasing the specific metabolic rate, but a recent study indicates that this may not be so. Further work on the lifetime effects of food restriction on specific metabolic rate is needed.

Fat stores of mammals increase until late

middle age but appear to decrease with the onset of senescence. *In vitro* evidence indicates that the response of fat cells to the fat-mobilizing action of hormones and neurotransmitters decreases with age, but solid *in vivo* data in support of this view are lacking. Evidence from studies with rats and humans indicates that there is no relationship between adiposity in the moderate range and longevity. However, in the case of food-restricted, very thin rats, there is a positive correlation between adiposity and longevity; there are suggestive data that this may also be true for very thin humans.

The findings on the effects of age on the glycogen stores of muscles and liver of mammals are inconsistent, with some workers finding low levels and others reporting little or no change with age. The evidence indicates that old animals can effectively mobilize liver glycogen in response to fasting, but much more detailed studies are needed to fully define this phenomenon. There is no information on the effects of age on the use of liver glycogen during exercise. Muscle glycogen appears to be well utilized during exercise by old animals, but again more detailed studies are needed to fully characterize this.

Body protein stores and, in particular, muscle stores decline with age. Nothing has been done in regard to the effects of age on the mobilization of protein stores for fuel during trauma and fasting, nor has the ability to prevent massive protein loss during a prolonged fast been studied in old animals.

REFERENCES

Abu-Erreish, G. M., Neely, J. R., Whitman, J. T., Whitman, V., and Sanadi, D. R. 1977. Fatty acid oxidation by isolated perfused working hearts of aged rats. *Am. J. Physiol.* 232: E258–262.

Abu-Erreish, G. M. and Sanadi, D. R. 1978. Age-related changes in cytochrome concentration of myocardial mitochondria. *Mech. Age. Dev.* 7: 425–432.

Alpatov, W. W. and Pearl, R. 1929. Experimental studies on the duration of life. XII. Influence of temperature during the larval period and adult life on the duration of life of the imago of *Drosophila melanogaster. Am. Naturalist* 63: 27–66.

Andres, R. 1980. Influence of obesity on longevity in the aged. *In,* C. Borek, C. M. Fenoglio, and D. W. King (eds.), *Aging, Cancer and Cell Membranes,* pp. 238–246. Stuttgart and New York: Thieme.

Andres, R. and Tobin, J. D. 1975. Aging and the disposition of glucose. *Adv. Exp. Biol. Med.* 61: 239–249.

Angelova-Gateva, P. 1969. Tissue respiration and glycolysis in quadriceps femoris and heart of rats of different ages during hypodynamia. *Exp. Gerontol.* 4: 177–187.

Bailey, C. J. and Flatt, P. R. 1982. Hormonal control of homeostasis during development and aging in mice. *Metabolism* 31: 238–246.

Barnes, R. H., Kwong, E., and Fiala, G. 1958. Effect of the prevention of coprophagy in the rat. III. Digestibility of protein and fat. *J. Nutrition* 65: 251–258.

Barrows, C. H., Falzone, J. A., and Shock, N. W. 1960. Age difference in the succinoxidase activity of homogenate and mitochondria from the livers and kidneys of rats. *J. Geront.* 15: 130–133.

Barrows, C. H. and Kokkonen, G. C. 1977. Relationship between nutrition and aging. *Adv. Nutr. Res.* 1: 253–298.

Barrows, C. H., Roeder, L. M., and Falzone, J. A. 1962. Effect of age on the activities of enzymes and the concentration of nucleic acids in the tissues of female wild rats. *J. Geront.* 17: 144–147.

Barrows, C. H., Yiengst, M. J., and Shock, N. W. 1958. Senescence and the metabolism of various tissues. *J. Geront.* 13:351–355.

Bartoc, R., Bruhis, S., Klein, R., Moldoveanu, E., Oeriu, I., and Oeriu, S. 1975. Effect of age and —SH active groups on the activity of some enzymes involved in carbohydrate metabolism. *Exp. Geront.* 10: 161–164.

Bass, A., Gutmann, E., and Hanslikova, V. 1975. Biochemical and histochemical changes in energy supply enzyme pattern of muscles of the rat during old age. *Gerontologia* 21: 31–45.

Benedict, F. G. and Sherman, H. C. 1937. Basal metabolism of rats in relation to old age and exercise during old age. *J. Nutrition* 14: 179–198.

Bennett, A. F. 1978. Activity metabolism of the lower vertebrates. *Ann. Rev. Physiol.* 40: 447–469.

Berg, B. N. and Simms, H. S. 1960. Nutrition and longevity. II. Longevity and onset of disease with different levels of food intake. *J. Nutrition* 71: 255–263.

Bertrand, H. A., Lynd, F. T., Masoro, E. J., and Yu, B. P. 1980a. Changes in adipose mass and cellularity through the adult life of rats fed *ad libitum* or a life-prolonging restricted diet. *J. Gerontology* 35: 827–835.

Bertrand, H. A., Masoro, E. J., and Yu, B. P. 1980b. Maintenance of glucagon-promoted lipolysis in adipocytes by food restriction. *Endocrinology* 107: 591–595.

Bertrand, H. A., Masoro, E. J., and Yu, B. P. 1982. Nutritional reversal of an age-related functional deficit. *Fed. Proc.* 41: 1674.

Binet, L., Bochet, M., and Bourlière, F. 1945. Le metabolisme de base et la dépense de fond des personnes agées, leurs variations. *Bull. Acad. Natl. Med. (Paris)* 129: 447–451.

Boothby, W. M., Berkson, J., and Dunn, H. L. 1936. Studies of the energy of metabolism of normal individuals: a standard for basal metabolism with a nomogram for clinical application. *Am. J. Physiol.* 116: 468–484.

Bracho-Romero, E. and Reaven, G. M. 1977. Effect of age and weight on plasma glucose and insulin responses in the rat. *J. Am. Geriatr. Soc.* 25: 299–302.

Brandstrup, N., Kirk, J. E., and Bruni, C. 1957. The hexokinase and phosphoglucoisomerase activities of aortic and pulmonary artery tissue in individuals of various ages. *J. Geront.* 12: 166–171.

Brown, A. C. 1973. Energy metabolism. *In,* T. C. Ruch and H. D. Patton (eds.), *Physiology and Biophysics,* Vol. 3, pp. 85–104. Philadelphia: W. B. Saunders.

Brozek, J. 1952. Changes in body composition in man during maturity and their nutritional implications. *Fed. Proc.* 11: 784–795.

Buchan, P. B. and Sohal, R. S. 1981. Effect of temperature and different sex ratios on physical activity and life span in the adult housefly, *Musca domestica. Exp. Geront.* 16: 223–228.

Bulos, B., Shulka, S., and Sacktor, B. 1972. Bioenergetic properties of mitochondria from flight muscle of aging blowflies. *Arch. Biochem. Biophys.* 149: 461–469.

Bulos, B. A., Shulka, S. P., and Sacktor, B. 1975. Bioenergetics of mitochondria from flight muscles of aging blowflies: partial reactions of oxidation and phosphorylation. *Arch. Biochem. Biophys.* 166: 639–644.

Burns, E. M., Kruckeberg, T. W., Comerford, L. E., and Buschmann, T. 1979. Thinning of capillary walls and declining numbers of endothelial mitochondria in the cerebral cortex. *J. Geront.* 34: 642–650.

Butler, L. and Nath, J. 1972. Postemergence changes in ultrastructure of flight and leg muscles of the black carpet beetle. *Ann. Entomol. Soc. Am.* 65: 247–254.

Carlson, L. D., Scheyer, W. J., and Jackson, B. H. 1957. The combined effects of ionizing radiation and low temperature on the metabolism, longevity and soft tissues of the white rat. I. Metabolism and longevity. *Radiation Res.* 7: 190–197.

Casten, G. G. 1950. The effects of the aging process on acid-soluble phosphorus compounds in the myocardium of rats. *Am. Heart J.* 39: 353–360.

Chen, J. C., Warshaw, J. B., and Sanadi, D. R. 1972. Regulation of mitochondrial respiration in senescence. *J. Cell. Physiol.* 80: 141–148.

Chiu, Y. J. D. and Richardson, A. 1980. Effect of age on the function of mitochondria isolated from brain and heart tissue. *Exp. Gerontol.* 15: 511–517.

Clarke, J. M. and Maynard Smith, J. 1961a. Two phases of ageing in *Drosophila subobscura. J. Exptl. Biol.* 38: 679–684.

Clarke, J. M. and Maynard Smith, J. 1961b. Independence of temperature on the rate of aging in *Drosophila subobscura. Nature* 190: 1027–1028.

Comfort, A. 1979. *The Biology of Senescence,* 3rd ed. New York: Elsevier.

Cooper, B. and Gregerman, R. I. 1976. Hormone-sensitive fat cell adenylate cyclase in the rat: influences of growth, cell size and aging. *J. Clin. Invest.* 57: 161–168.

Davidson, M. B. 1979. The effect of aging on carbohydrate

metabolism: a review of the English literature and a practical approach to the diagnosis of diabetes mellitus in the elderly. *Metabolism* 28: 688–705.

Dax, E. M., Partillo, J. S., and Gregerman, R. I. 1981. Mechanism of age-related decrease of epinephrine-stimulated lipolysis in isolated rat adipocytes. β-Adrenergic receptor binding, adenylate cyclase activity and cyclic-AMP accumulation. *J. Lipid Res.* 23: 934–943.

De Fronzo, R. A. 1979. Glucose intolerance and aging. Evidence for tissue insensitivity to insulin. *Diabetes* 28: 1095–1101.

De Fronzo, R. A., Tobin, J. D., and Andres, R. 1979. The glucose clamp technique. A method for the quantification of beta cell sensitivity to glucose and of tissue sensitivity to insulin. *Am. J. Physiol.* 237: E214–E223.

Denckla, W. D. 1970. Minimum oxygen consumption in the female rat, some new definitions and measurements. *J. Appl. Physiol.* 29: 263–274.

Denckla, W. D. 1974. Role of the pituitary and thyroid glands in the decline of minimal O_2 consumption with age. *J. Clin. Invest.* 53: 572–581.

De Santis, R. A., Gorenstein, T., Livingston, J. N., and Lockwood, D. H. 1974. Role of phosphodiesterase in glucagon resistance of large adipocytes. *J. Lipid Res.* 15: 33–38.

Deshmukh, D. R., Owen, O. E., and Patel, M. S. 1980. Effect of aging on the metabolism of pyruvate and 3-hydroxybutyrate in nonsynaptic and synaptic mitochondria from rat brain. *J. Neurochem.* 34: 1219–1224.

Deuel, H. J., Jr., Butts, J. S., Hallman, L. F., Murray, S., and Blunden, H. 1937. The effect of age on the sex difference in the content of liver glycogen. *J. Biol. Chem.* 119: 617–620.

Drori, D. and Folman, Y. 1976. Environmental effects on longevity in the male rat: exercise, mating, castration and restricted feeding. *Exp. Geront.* 11: 25–32.

Du Bois, E. F. 1936. *Basal Metabolism in Health and Disease,* 3rd ed., p. 160. Philadelphia: Lea and Febiger.

Dudl, R. J. and Ensinck, J. W. 1977. Insulin and glucagon relationships during aging in man. *Metabolism* 26: 33–41.

Economos, A. C. 1981. Beyond rate of living. *Gerontology* 27: 258–265.

Edington, D., Cosmas, A., and McCafferty, W. 1972. Exercise and longevity. Evidence for a threshold age. *J. Gerontology* 27: 341–343.

Else, P. L. and Hulbert, A. J. 1981. Comparison of the "mammal machine" and the "reptile machine": energy production. *Am. J. Physiol.* 240: R3–R9.

Ermini, M. 1976. Ageing changes in mammalian skeletal muscle. Biochemical studies. *Gerontology* 22: 301–316.

Ermini, M. and Szelényi, I. 1972. Die Aktivität der Aldolase und der Succinatdehydrogenase (SDH) in der Weissen und roten Skelettmuskulatur Junger und Alter Ratten. *Experentia* 28: 403–404.

Ermini, M., Szelényi, I., Moser, P., and Verzar, F. 1971. The aging of skeletal (striated) muscle by changes in recovery metabolism. *Gerontology* 17: 300–311.

Ferrendelli, J. A., Sedgwick, W. G., and Suntzeff, V. 1971. Regional energy metabolism and lipofuscin accumulation in mouse brain during aging. *J. Neuropath. Exper. Neurol.* 30: 638–649.

Frolkis, V. V. and Bogatskaya, L. N. 1968. The energy metabolism of myocardium and its regulation in animals of various ages. *Exp. Gerontol.* 3: 199–210.

Gibson, G. E., Peterson, C., and Sansone, J. 1981. Neurotransmitter and carbohydrate metabolism during aging and mild hypoxia. *Neurobiol. Aging* 2: 165–172.

Giudicelli, Y. and Pecquery, R. 1978. β-Adrenergic receptors and catecholamine-sensitive adenylate cyclase in rat fat cell membranes: influence of growth, cell size and aging. *Eur. J. Biochem.* 90: 413–419.

Gold, G., Karoly, K., Freeman, C., and Adelman, R. C. 1976. A possible role for insulin in the altered capability for hepatic enzyme adaptation during aging. *Biochem. Biophys. Res. Comm.* 73: 1003–1010.

Gold, P. H., Gee, M. V., and Strehler, B. L. 1968. Effect of age on oxidative phosphorylation in the rat. *J. Geront.* 23: 509–512.

Gommers, A. and de Gaspara, M. 1972. Variation of insulinemia in relation to age in the untreated male rat. *Gerontologia* 18: 176–184.

Gommers, A. and Genne, H. 1975. Effect of aging on insulin and insulin-glucose sensitivity tests in rats. *Acta Diabetol. Lat.* 12: 303–308.

Gonzales, J. and De Martinis, F. D. 1977. Lipolytic response of rat adipocytes to epinephrine: effect of age and cell size. *Exp. Aging Res.* 4: 455–477.

Goodrick, C. L. 1974. The effects of exercise on longevity and behavior of hybrid mice which differ in coat color. *J. Gerontology* 29: 129–133.

Goodrick, C. L. 1980. Effects of long-term voluntary wheel exercise on male and female Wistar rats. I. Longevity, body weight and metabolic rate. *Gerontology* 26: 22–33.

Gregerman, R. I. 1967. The age-related alteration of thyroid function and thyroid hormone metabolism in man. *In*, L. Gitman (ed.), *Endocrines and Aging*, pp. 161–173. Springfield, Ill.: Charles C Thomas.

Hansford, R. G. 1977. Studies on inactivation of pyruvate dehydrogenase by palmitoylcarnitine oxidation in isolated rat mitochondria. *J. Biol. Chem.* 252: 1552–1560.

Hansford, R. G. 1978. Lipid oxidation by heart mitochondria from young adult and senescent rats. *Biochem. J.* 170: 285–295.

Hansford, R. G. 1980. Metabolism and energy production. *In* M. L. Weisfeld (ed.), *The Aging Heart*, pp. 25–76. New York: Raven Press.

Hansford, R. G. and Castro, F. 1982. Age-linked changes in the activity of enzymes of the tricarboxylic acid cycle and lipid oxidation, and of carnitine content in muscles of the rat. *Mech. Age. Dev.* 19: 191–201.

Harman, D. 1972. The biologic clock: the mitochondria? *J. Am. Geriat. Soc.* 20: 145–147.

Harman, D. 1981. The aging process. *Proc. Natl. Acad. Sci. USA* 78: 7124–7128.

Hemmingsen, A. M. 1960. Energy metabolism as related to body size and respiratory surfaces and its evaluation. *Rep. Steno. Mem. Hosp. Nord. Insulin-lab* 9: 1–110.

Herbener, G. H. 1976. A morphometric study of age-

dependent changes in mitochondrial populations of mouse liver and heart. *J. Geront.* 31: 8–12.

Heroux, O. and Campbell, J. S. 1960. A study of pathology and life span of 6°C- and 30°C-acclimated rats. *Lab. Invest.* 9: 305–315.

Hollingsworth, M. J. 1966. Temperature and the rate of ageing in *Drosophila subobscura. Exptl. Geront.* 1: 259–267.

Hollingsworth, M. J. 1968. Environmental temperature and life span in poikilotherms. *Nature* 218: 869–870.

Hollingsworth, M. J. 1969. The effect of fluctuating environmental temperature on the length of life of adult *Drosophila. Exptl. Geront.* 4: 159–167.

Holm, G., Jacobson, B., Bjorntorp, P., and Smith, U. 1976. Effects of age and cell size on rat adipose metabolism. *J. Lipid Res.* 16: 461–464.

Inamdar, A. R., Person, R., Kohnen, P., Duncan, H., and Mackler, B. 1974. Effect of age on oxidative phosphorylation in tissues of hamsters. *J. Geront.* 29: 638–642.

Iwangoff, P., Reichlmeir, K., Enz, A., and Meier-Ruge, W. 1979. Neurochemical findings in physiological aging of the brain. *Interdiscpl. Topics Geront.* 15: 13–33.

Johnson, B. and Rowley, W. 1972. Age-related ultrastructural changes in the flight muscle of the mosquito, *Culex tarsalis. J. Insect Physiol.* 18: 2375–2389.

Keys, A., Taylor, H. L. and Grande, F. 1973. Basal metabolism and age of adult man. *Metabolism* 22: 579–587.

Kibler, H. H. and Johnson, H. D. 1966. Temperature and longevity in male rats. *J. Geront.* 21: 52–56.

Kibler, H. H., Silsby, H. D., and Johnson, H. D. 1963. Metabolic trends and life spans of rats living at 9°C and 28°C. *J. Geront.* 18: 235–239.

Kirk, J. E. 1962. The glycogen phosphorylase activity of arterial tissue in individuals of various ages. *J. Geront.* 17: 154–157.

Kirk, J. E. 1966. The phosphoglucomutase, phosphoglyceric acid mutase and phosphomannose isomerase activities—arterial tissues of various ages. *J. Geront.* 21: 420–425.

Klimas, J. E. 1968. Oral glucose tolerance during the life span of a colony of rats. *J. Geront.* 23: 31–34.

Kuhl, D. E., Metter, E. J., Riege, W. H., and Phelps, M. E. 1982. Effects of human aging on patterns of local cerebral glucose utilization determined by the [18F] fluorodeoxyglucose method. *J. Cereb. Blood Flow and Metab.* 2: 163–171.

Kuttner, R. E. and Lorincz, A. B. 1969. The effect of catecholamines on free amino acid in rat heart and other organs. *Arch. Int. Pharmacodyn. Ther.* 182: 300–309.

Lai, J. C. K., Leong, T. K. C., and Lim, L. 1982. Activities of the mitochondrial NAD-linked isocitric dehydrogenase in different regions of the brain. *Gerontology* 28: 81–85.

Lamb, M. 1968. Temperature and life span in *Drosophila. Nature* 220: 808–809.

Lassen, W. A., Feinberg, I., and Lane, N. H. 1960. Bilateral studies of cerebral oxygen uptake in young and aged normal subjects and in patients with organic dementia. *J. Clin. Invest.* 39: 491–500.

Leong, S. F., Lai, J. C. K., Lim, L., and Clark, J. B. 1981. Energy-metabolizing enzymes in brain regions of adult and aging rats. *J. Neurochem.* 37: 1548–1556.

Levin, P., Janda, J. K., Joseph, J. A., Ingram, D. K., and Roth, G. S. 1981. Dietary restriction retards age associated loss of rat striatal dopaminergic receptors. *Science* 214: 561–562.

Liepa, G. U., Masoro, E. J., Bertrand, H. A., and Yu, B. P. 1980. Food restriction as modulator of age-related changes in serum lipids. *Am. J. Physiol.* 238: E253–E257.

Lindstedt, S. L. and Calder, W. A. III. 1981. Body size, physiological time, and longevity of homeothermic animals. *Quart. Rev. Biol.* 56: 1–16.

Lints, F. A. and Lints, C. V. 1968. Respiration in *Drosophila.* II. Respiration in relation to age by wild, inbred and hybrid *Drosophila melanogaster* imagos. *Exp. Geront.* 3: 341–349.

Liu, R. K. and Walford, R. L. 1966. Increased growth and lifespan with lowered ambient temperature in the annual fish, *Cynolebias adloffi. Nature* 212: 1277–1278.

Liu, R. K. and Walford, R. L. 1970. Observations on the lifespans of several species of annual fishes and of the world's smallest fishes. *Exper. Geront.* 5: 241–246.

Liu, R. K. and Walford, R. L. 1972. The effect of lowered body temperature on lifespan and immune and non-immune processes. *Gerontologia* 18: 363–388.

Liu, R. and Walford, R. L. 1975. Mid-life temperature-transfer effects on life-span of annual fish. *J. Geront.* 30: 129–131.

Livingston, J. N., Cuatrecasas, P., and Lockwood, D. H. 1974. Studies of glucagon resistance of large adipocytes: ^{125}I-labeled glucagon binding and lipolytic activity. *J. Lipid Res.* 15: 26–32.

Loeb, J. and Northrop, J. H. 1917. On the influence of food and temperature upon the duration of life. *J. Biol. Chem.* 32: 102–121.

London, E. D., Nespor, S. M., Ohata, M., and Rapaport, S. I. 1981. Local cerebral glucose utilization during development and aging of the Fischer-344 rat. *J. Neurochem.* 37: 217–221.

Lyman, C. P., O'Brien, R. C., Greene, G. C., and Papafrangos, E. D. 1981. Hibernation and longevity in the Turkish hamster *Mesocricetus brandti. Science* 212: 668–670.

MacArthur, J. W. and Baillie, W. H. Jr. 1929. Metabolic activity and duration of life. II. Metabolic rates and their relation to longevity in *Daphnia magna. J. Exper. Zool.* 53: 243–268.

Mainwaring, W. I. P. 1967. The ageing process in the mouse ventral prostate gland: a preliminary biochemical survey. *Gerontologia* 13: 177–189.

Malina, R. M. 1969. Quantification of fat, muscle and bone in man. *Clin. Orthoped. Relat. Res.* 65: 9–38.

Manganiello, V. and Vaughan, M. 1972. Selective loss of adipose cell responsiveness with growth in the rat. *J. Lipid. Res.* 13: 12–16.

Marigo, S., Melani, F., and Poggi, E. 1962. The tolbuta-

mide test (Rastenon test) in subjects of senile age. *G. Geront.* 10: 415–426.

Masoro, E. J. 1966. Effect of cold on metabolic use of lipids. *Physiol. Rev.* 46: 67–101.

Masoro, E. J. 1977. Lipids and lipid metabolism. *Ann. Rev. Physiol.* 39: 301–321.

Masoro, E. J., Yu, B. P., and Bertrand, H. A. 1982. Action of food restriction in delaying the aging process. *Proc. Natl. Acad. Sci. USA* 79: 4239–4241.

Masoro, E. J., Yu, B. P., Bertrand, H. A., and Lynd, F. T. 1980. Nutritional probe of the aging process. *Fed. Proc.* 39: 3178–3182.

Massie, H. R., Baird, M. B., and McMahon, M. N. 1975. Loss of mitochondrial DNA with aging in *Drosophila melanogaster. Gerontologia* 21: 231–238.

Maynard Smith, J. 1958. The effects of temperature and of egg-laying on the longevity of *Drosophila subobscura. J. Exptl. Biol.* 35: 832–842.

Maynard Smith, J. 1959. A theory of aging. *Nature,* 184: 956–957.

Maynard Smith, J. 1963. Temperature and the rate of ageing in poikilotherms. *Nature* 197: 400–402.

McArthur, M. C. and Sohal, R. S. 1982. Relationship between metabolic rates, aging, lipid peroxidation and fluorescent age pigment in milkweed bugs, *Oncopeltus fasciatus* (Hemiptera). *J. Geront.* 37: 268–274.

McCay, C. M., Crowell, M. F., and Maynard, L. A. 1935. The effect of retarded growth upon the length of life span and upon the ultimate body size. *J. Nutrition* 10: 63–79.

McCay, C., Maynard, L., Sperling, G., and Osgood, H. 1941. Nutritional requirements during the latter half of life. *J. Nutrition* 21: 45–60.

McGandy, R. B., Barrows, C. H., Jr., Spania, A., Meredith, A., Stone, J. L., and Norris, A. H. 1966. Nutrient intake and energy expenditure in men of different ages. *J. Geront.* 21: 581–587.

Metz, R., Surmaczynska, B., Berger, S., and Sobel, G. 1966. Glucose tolerance, plasma insulin and free fatty acids in elderly subjects. *Ann. Intern. Med.* 64: 1042–1048.

Michenfelder, J. P. and Theye, R. A. 1969. The relationship of age to canine cerebral metabolic rate. *J. Surg. Res.* 9: 645–648.

Miller, E. A. and Allen, D. G. 1973. Hormone stimulated lipolysis in isolated fat cells from young and old rats. *J. Lipid Res.* 14: 331–336.

Miquel, J., Lundgren, P. R., Bensch, K. G., and Atlan, H. 1976. Effects of temperature on the life span, vitality and fine structure of *Drosophila melanogaster. Mech. Age. Dev.* 5: 347–370.

Murfitt, R. R. and Sanadi, D. R. 1978. Evidence for increased degeneration of mitochondria in old rats. A brief note. *Mech. Age. Dev.* 8: 197–201.

Myhre, L. G. and Kessler, W. V. 1966. Body density and potassium 40 measurements of body composition as related to age. *J. Appl. Physiol.* 21: 1251–1255.

Nayar, K. 1972. Effects of constant and fluctuating temperature on life span of *Aedes taeniorhynchus* adult. *J. Insect Physiol.* 18: 1303–1313.

Nohl, H., Breuninger, V., and Hegner, D. 1978. Influence of mitochondrial radical formation on energy-linked respiration. *Eur. J. Biochem.* 90: 385–390.

Nohl, H. and Hegner, D. 1978. Do mitochondria produce oxygen radicals *in vivo? Eur. J. Biochem.* 82: 563–567.

Nohl, H. and Kramer, R. 1980. Molecular basis of age-dependent changes in the activity of adenine nucleotide translocase. *Mech. Age. Dev.* 14: 137–144.

Nolen, G. A. 1972. Effect of various restricted dietary regimens on the growth, health and longevity of albino rats. *J. Nutrition* 102: 1477–1494.

Northrop, J. H. 1926. Carbon dioxide production and duration of life of *Drosophila* cultures. *J. Gen. Physiol.* 9: 319–324.

Novak, L. 1972. Aging, total body potassium, fat-free mass and cell mass in males and females between the ages of 18 and 85 years. *J. Gerontol.* 27: 438–443.

Olefsky, J. M. and Reaven, G. M. 1975. Effects of age and obesity on insulin binding to isolated adipocytes. *Endocrinology* 96: 1486–1498.

O'Sullivan, J. B. and Mahan, C. M. 1971. Evaluation of age-adjusted criteria for potential diabetes. *Diabetes* 20: 811–815.

O'Sullivan, J. B., Mahan, C. M., Freedlander, A. E., and Williams, R. F. 1971. Effect of age on carbohydrate metabolism. *J. Clin. Endocrinol. Metab.* 33: 619–623.

Pagano, G., Cassader, M., Diana, A., Pisu, E., Bozzo, C., Ferrero, F., and Lenti, G. 1981. Insulin resistance in the aged: the role of the peripheral insulin receptors. *Metabolism* 30: 46–49.

Parizkova, J. and Eiselt, E. A. 1971. A further study on changes in somatic characteristics and body composition of old men followed longitudinally for 8 to 10 years. *Human Biol.* 43: 318–326.

Patel, M. S. 1977. Age-dependent changes in the oxidative metabolism in brain. *J. Geront.* 32: 643–646.

Patnaik, S. K. and Kanungo, M. S. 1966. Metabolic changes in the skin of rats of various ages; oxygen consumption and uptake of glucose. *Biochem. J.* 98: 374–377.

Pearl, R. 1928. *The Rate of Living.* New York: Alfred Knopf.

Peng, M., Peng, Y., and Chen, F. 1977. Age-dependent changes in oxygen consumption of the cerebral cortex, hypothalamus, hippocampus and amygdaloid in rats. *J. Geront.* 32: 517–522.

Pettegrew, R. K. and Ewing, K. L. 1971. Life history study of oxygen utilization in the C57 BL/6 mouse. *J. Geront.* 26: 381–385.

Poland, J. L., Poland, J. W., and Honey, R. H. 1982. Substrate changes during fasting and refeeding contrasted in old and young rats. *Gerontology* 28: 99–103.

Porta, E. A. 1980. Nutritional factors and aging. *In:* R. B. Tobin and M. A. Mehlman (eds.), *Advances in Modern Human Nutrition,* pp. 65–119. Park Forest South, Ill.: Pathotox Publishers.

Porter, H., Jr., Doty, D. H., and Bloor, C. M. 1971. Interaction of age and exercise on tissue lactate dehydrogenase activity in rats. *Lab. Invest.* 25: 572–576.

Prosser, C. L. 1973. *Comparative Animal Physiology,* 3rd ed. Philadelphia: W. B. Saunders.

Ragland, S. S. and Sohal, R. S. 1973. Mating behavior, physical activity and aging in the housefly, *Musca domestica. Exp. Geront.* 8: 135–145.

Ragland, S. S. and Sohal, R. S. 1975. Ambient temperature, physical activity and aging in the housefly, *Musca domestica. Exp. Geront.* 10: 279–289.

Reiner, J. M. 1947. The effect of age on the carbohydrate metabolism of tissue homogenates. *J. Geront.* 2: 315–320.

Retzlaff, E., Fontaine J., and Furuta, W. 1966. Effect of daily exercise on life span of albino rats. *Geriatrics* 21: 171–177.

Reznick, A. Z., Steinhagen-Thiessen, E., and Gershon, D. 1982. The effect of exercise on enzyme activities in cardiac muscles of mice of various ages. *Biochem. Med.* 28: 347–352.

Robin, E. D. and Simon, L. M. 1970. How to weigh an elephant: cytochrome oxidase as a rate-governing step in mitochondrial oxygen consumption. *Trans. Assoc. Am. Physicians* 83: 288–300.

Rockstein, M., Chesky, J., Philpott, D., Takahashi, A., Johnson, J., Jr., and Miquel, J. 1975. An electron microscopic investigation of the age-dependent changes in the flight muscle of *Musca domestica* L. *Gerontologia* 21: 216–233.

Rockstein, M., Chesky, J., and Sussman, M. 1977. Comparative biology and evaluation of aging. *In,* C. Finch and L. Hayflick (eds.), *Handbook of the Biology of Aging,* pp. 1–34. New York: Van Nostrand Reinhold.

Ross, M. H. 1969. Aging, nutrition and hepatic enzyme activity patterns in the rat. *J. Nutrition* 97 (Suppl. 1: Part II): 563–602.

Ross, M. H. 1976. Nutrition and longevity in experimental animals. *In,* M. Winick (ed.), *Nutrition and Aging,* pp. 43–57. New York: John Wiley & Sons.

Ross, M. H. and Ely, J. O. 1954. Age-related changes in respiration of sliced liver of the rat. *J. Franklin Inst.* 258: 63–66.

Roth, G. S., Tzankoff, S. P., and Elahi, D. 1981. Effects of age on control of lipolysis during fasting. *J. Gerontol.* 36: 391–397.

Rowley, W. and Graham, C. 1968. The effect of age on flight performance of females *Aedes aegypti* mosquitoes. *J. Insect. Physiol.* 14: 719–728.

Rubner, M. 1908. Das Problem der Lebensdauer und Seine Beziehungen Zun Wachstum und Ernährung. München: Oldenbourg.

Sacher, G. A. 1977. Life table modification and life prolongation. *In,* C. Finch and L. Hayflick (eds.), *Handbook of the Biology of Aging,* pp. 582–638. New York: Van Nostrand Reinhold.

Sacher, G. A. 1978. Longevity, aging and death: an evolutionary perspective. *Gerontologist* 18:112–119.

Sacher, G. A. and Duffy, P. H. 1979. Genetic relation of life span to metabolic rate for inbred mouse strains and their hybrids. *Fed. Proc.* 38: 184–188.

Sacktor, B. and Shimada, Y. 1972. Degenerative changes

in the mitochondria of flight muscle of aging blowflies. *J. Cell Biol.* 52: 465–477.

Samorajski, T., Friede, R. L., and Ordy, J. M. 1971. Age difference in the ultrastructure of axons in the pyramidal tract of the mouse. *J. Geront.* 26: 542–551.

Schmidt-Nielsen, K. 1970. Energy metabolism, body size and problems of scaling. *Fed. Proc.* 29: 1524–1532.

Schmucker, D. L., Mooney, J. S., and Jones, A. L. 1978. Stereological analysis of hepatic fine structure in the Fischer 344 rat. *J. Cell Biol.* 78: 319–337.

Schmukler, M. and Barrows, C. H. Jr. 1966. Age differences in lactic and malic dehydrogenases in the rat. *J. Geront.* 21: 109–111.

Shaw, R. F. and Bercaw, B. L. 1962. Temperature and life-span in poikilothermous animals. *Nature* 196: 454–457.

Shock, N. W. and Yiengst, M. J. 1955. Age changes in basal respiratory measurements and metabolism in males. *J. Geront.* 10: 31–40.

Simon, J., Bhatnagar, P., and Milburn, N. 1969. An electron microscopic study of changes in mitochondria of flight muscle of aging houseflies (*Musca domestica*). *J. Insect. Physiol.* 15: 135–140.

Singh, S. N. 1973. Effect of age on the activity and citrate inhibition of malate dehydrogenase of the brain and heart of rats. *Experientia* 29: 42–43.

Singh, S. N. and Kanungo, M. S. 1968. Alterations in lactate dehydrogenase of the brain, heart, skeletal muscle and liver of rats of various ages. *J. Biol. Chem.* 243: 4526–4529.

Sinha, M. K., Mondal, A. N., and Rastogi, G. K. 1974. Influence of age on glucose tolerance in normal subjects. *Acta Diabetol. Lat.* 11: 78–83.

Smith, C. B., Goochee, C., Rapaport, S. I., and Sokoloff, L. 1980. Effects of aging on local rates of cerebral glucose utilization in the rat. *Brain* 103: 351–365.

Smith, C. B. and Sokoloff, L. 1982. Age-related changes in local glucose utilization in the brain. *Exp. Brain Res. Suppl.* 5: 76–85.

Sobel, H. and Bowman, R. 1971. Protein metabolism in aging mice. *J. Geront.* 26: 558–560.

Sohal, R. S. 1981. Relationship between metabolic rate, lipofuscin accumulation and lysosomal enzyme activity during aging in the adult housefly, *Musca domestica. Exp. Geront.* 16: 347–355.

Sohal, R. S. 1982. Oxygen consumption and life span in the adult male housefly, *Musca domestica. Age* 5: 21–24.

Sohal, R. S. and Allison, V. 1971. Age-related changes in the fine structure of the flight muscle in the house fly. *Exp. Gerontol.* 6: 167–172.

Sohal, R. S. and Buchan, P. B. 1981a. Relationship between physical activity and life span in the adult housefly, *Musca domestica. Exp. Geront.* 16: 157–162.

Sohal, R. S. and Buchan, P. B. 1981b. Relationship between fluorescent age pigment, physiological age and physical activity in the housefly, *Musca domestica. Mech. Age. Dev.* 15: 243–249.

Sohal, R. S., Donato, H., and Biehl, E. R. 1981. Effect of age and metabolic rate on lipid peroxidation in the housefly, *Musca domestica* L. *Mech. Age. Dev.* 16: 159–167.

Sokoloff, L. 1978. Effects of normal aging on cerebral circulation and energy metabolism. *In* F. Hoffmeister and C. Nulbi (eds.), *Brain Function in Old Age*, pp. 367–380. Berlin: Springer-Verlag.

Starnes, J. W., Beyer, R. E., and Edington, D. W. 1981. Effects of age and cardiac work *in vitro* on mitochondrial oxidative phosphorylation and (^{3}H)-leucine incorporation. *J. Geront.* 36: 130–135.

Steinhagen-Thiessen, E. and Hilz, H. 1976. The age-dependent decrease in creatine kinase and aldolase activities in human striated muscles is not caused by an accumulation of faulty proteins. *Mech. Age. Dev.* 5: 447–457.

Steinhagen-Thiessen, E., Reznik, A., and Hilz, H. 1980. Negative adaptation to physical training in senile mice. *Mech. Age. Dev.* 12: 231–236.

Stiles, J. A., Francendese, A. A., and Masoro, E. J. 1975. Influence of age on size and number of fat cells in the epididymal depot. *Am. J. Physiol.* 229: 1561–1568.

Stocco, D. M. and Hutson, J. C. 1978. Quantitation of mitochondrial DNA and protein in the liver of Fischer 344 rats during aging. *J. Geront.* 33: 802–809.

Strehler, B. L. 1961. Studies on the comparative physiology of aging. II. On the mechanism of temperature life-shortening in *Drosophila melanogaster. J. Geront.* 16: 2–12.

Strehler, B. L. 1962. Further studies on the thermally induced aging of *Drosophila melanogaster. J. Geront.* 17: 347–352.

Stuchlikova, E., Juricova-Horokova, M., and Deyl, Z. 1975. New aspects of the dietary effects of life prolongation in rodents. What is the role of obesity in aging? *Exp. Gerontol.* 10: 141–144.

Sullivan, J. L. 1982. Superoxide dismutase, longevity and specific metabolic rate. *Gerontology* 28: 242–244.

Swerdloff, R. S., Pozefsky, T., Tobin, J. D., and Andres, R. 1967. Influence of age on intravenous tolbutamide response tests. *Diabetes* 16: 161–170.

Sylvia, A. L. and Rosenthal, M. 1978. The effect of age and lung pathology on cytochrome a,a$_3$ redox levels in the cerebral cortex. *Brain Res.* 146: 109–122.

Sylvia, A. L. and Rosenthal, M. 1979. Effects of age on brain oxidative metabolism *in vivo. Brain Res.* 165: 235–248.

Szelényi, I., Ermini, M., and Moser, P. 1972. Glycogen content in young and old rats liver and muscles. *Experientia* 15: 257–258.

Takahashi, A., Philpott, D., and Miquel, J. 1970. Electron microscope studies on aging *Drosophila melanogaster. J. Gerontology* 25: 222–228.

Tate, E. L. and Herbener, G. H. 1976. A morphometric study of the density of mitochondrial cristae in heart and liver of aging mice. *J. Geront.* 31: 129–134.

Tauchi, H. and Sato, T. 1968. Age changes in size and number of mitochondria of human hepatic cells. *J. Geront.* 23: 454–461.

Tolmasoff, J. M., Ono, T., and Cutler, R. G. 1980. Superoxide dismutase: correlation with life-span and specific metabolic rate in primate species. *Proc. Natl. Acad. Sci. USA* 77: 2777–2781.

Tribe, M. and Ashhurst, D. 1972. Biochemical and structural variations in the flight muscle of aging blowflies, *Calliphora erythrocephala. J. Cell. Sci.* 10: 443–469.

Trout, W. E. and Kaplan, W. D. 1970. A relation between longevity, metabolic rate and activity in shaker mutants of *Drosophila melanogaster. Exp. Gerontol.* 5: 83–92.

Tzankoff, S. P. and Norris, A. H. 1977. Effect of muscle mass decrease on age-related BMR changes. *J. Appl. Physiol.* 43: 1001–1006.

Uauy, R., Winterer, J. C., Bilmazes, C., Haverberg, L. N., Scrimshaw, N. S., Munro, H. N., and Young, V. R. 1978. The changing pattern of whole body protein metabolism in aging humans. *J. Geront.* 33: 663–671.

Van Itallie, T. B. 1979. Obesity: adverse effects on health and on longevity. *Am. J. Clin. Nutr.* 32: 2723–2733.

Vann, A. C. and Webster, G. C. 1977. Age-related changes in mitochondrial function in *Drosophila melanogaster. Exp. Geront.* 12: 1–5.

Vinik, A. and Jackson, W. P. U. 1968. Hyperglycemia in the elderly—is it diabetes? *Diabetes* 17: 348.

Vitorica, J., Andres, A., Satrústegui, J., and Machado, A. 1981a. Age-related quantitative changes in enzyme activities of rat brain. *Neurochem. Res.* 6: 127–136.

Vitorica, J., Cano, J., Satrústegui, J., and Machado, A. 1981b. Comparison between developmental and senescent changes in enzyme activities linked to energy metabolism in rat heart. *Mech. Age. Dev.* 16: 105–116.

Vorbeck, M. L., Martin, A. P., Park, J. K. J., and Townsend, J. F. 1982. Aging-related decrease in hepatic cytochrome oxidase of the Fischer 344 rat. *Arch. Biochem. Biophys.* 214: 67–79.

Voss, K. H., Masoro, E. J., and Anderson, W. 1982. Modulation of age-related loss of glucagon-promoted lipolysis by food restriction. *Mech. Age. Dev.* 18: 135–149.

Walford, R. L., Liu, R. K., Troup, G. M., and Hsiu, J. 1969. Alterations in soluble/insoluble collagen ratios in the annual fish, *Cynolebias bellottii,* in relation to age and environmental temperature. Exp. Geront. 4: 103–109.

Weigand, W., Hannappel, E., and Brand, K. 1980. Effect of starvation and refeeding a high protein or high carbohydrate diet on lipid composition and glycogen content of rat livers in relation to age. *J. Nutrition* 110: 669–674.

Weinbach, E. C. and Garbus, J. 1956. Age and oxidative phosphorylation in rat liver and brain. *Nature* 178: 1225–1226.

Weinbach, E. C. and Garbus, J. 1959. Oxidative phosphorylation in mitochondria from aged rats. *J. Biol. Chem.* 234: 412–417.

Weindruch, R. H., Cheung, M. K., Verity, M. A., and Walford, R. L. 1980. Modification of mitochondrial respiration by aging and dietary restriction. *Mech. Age. Dev.* 12: 375–392.

Weindruch, R. H., Kristie, J. A., Cheney, K. E., and Walford, R. L. 1979. Influence of controlled dietary restriction on immunologic function and aging. *Fed. Proc.* 38: 2007–2016.

Williamson, J. R. 1979. Mitochondrial function in the heart. *Annual Rev. Physiol.* 41: 485–506.

Wilson, P. D., Hill, B. T., and Franks, L. M. 1975. The effect of age on mitochondrial enzymes and respiration. *Gerontologia* 21: 95–101.

Wohlrab, H. 1976. Age-related changes in the flight muscle mitochondria from the blowfly *Sarcophaga bullata. J. Geront.* 31: 257–263.

Wolfe, R. R. 1982. Stable isotope approaches for study of energy substrate metabolism. *Fed. Proc.* 41: 2692–2697.

Wollenberger, A. and Jehl, J. 1952. Influence of age on rate of respiration of sliced cardiac muscle. *Am. J. Physiol.,* 170: 126–130.

Young, V. R. 1979. Diet as a modulator of aging and longevity. *Fed. Proc.* 38: 1994–2000.

Young, V. R., Gersovitz, M., and Munro, H. N. 1982. Human aging: protein and amino acid metabolism and implications for protein and amino acid requirements. *In,* G. B. Moment (ed.), *Nutritional Approaches to Aging Research,* pp. 47–81. Boca Raton, Fl: CRC Press.

Yousef, M. K. and Johnson, H. D. 1970. ^{75}Se-selenomethionine turnover rate during growth and aging in rats. *Proc. Soc. Exper. Biol. Med.* 133: 1351–1353.

Yu, B. P., Bertrand, H. A., and Masoro, E. J. 1980. Nutrition-aging influence on catecholamine-promoted lipolysis. *Metabolism* 29: 438–444.

Yu, B. P., Masoro, E. J., Murata, I., Bertrand, H. A., and Lynd, F. T. 1982. Life span study of SPF Fischer 344 male rats fed *ad libitum* or restricted diets: longevity, growth, lean body mass and disease. *J. Gerontology* 37: 130–141.

PART **6** NEUROBIOLOGY

21
NEUROENDOCRINE AND AUTONOMIC FUNCTIONS IN AGING MAMMALS

Caleb E. Finch
Department of Biological Sciences
Andrus Gerontology Center
University of Southern California
and
Philip W. Landfield
Department of Physiology and Pharmacology
Bowman-Gray School of Medicine

INTRODUCTION

Throughout postnatal development and adult life in mammals, the central and peripheral nervous systems have commanding roles in the regulation of most body functions. How the nervous system changes during aging is a subject which bears on the analysis of many aging processes, including the origins of age-correlated dysfunctions and diseases, and the exponential increase of mortality with age. This chapter will review the age-correlated changes in neuroendocrine and autonomic functions, with emphasis on the reciprocal interactions between neural and endocrine systems and their target cells, especially in regard to the limbic system. The hypothalamus and associated brain regions (including hippocampus, amygdala, septum) are often referred to as the "limbic system" and have major roles in regulating physiologic functions in target

cells throughout the body via the pituitary or via the autonomic nervous system.

The role of neural and endocrine changes in many altered cell functions during aging has been proposed in a number of theories (Everitt, 1973; Finch et al., 1969; Finch, 1976; Frolkis, 1976; Dilman and Anisimov, 1979; Dilman, 1981; Landfield et al., 1980). These theories also involve the premise that age changes are not necessarily due to intrinsic aging processes in cells or molecules. The possibility that the brain contains pacemakers for the regulation of aging processes via direct neuroendocrine cascades or via recursive cascades has attracted much attention but remains largely speculative. Nonetheless, recent evidence furthers the view that age-related changes in these higher regulatory centers are important in age-correlated alterations of some systems. Although we do not intend that this chapter be biased by an elaboration of particular theoretical views, we believe that some discussion of neuroendocrine theories of aging is appropriate.

The extent to which aging changes in particular cells of higher organisms are preprogrammed for "intrinsic" senescence may vary phylogenetically. No major generalization seems yet plausible in view of the diversity of senescent processes in multicellular animals (Finch, 1976); this diversity is illustrated by the insects which lack digestive organs as adults (Norris, 1934; Trager, 1953; Balazs et al., 1962); nematodes (see Chapter 6) and other invertebrates which lack proliferative cells in adults; and the postspawning, neuroendocrine-mediated deaths of the octopus (Wodinsky, 1977) and the Pacific salmon, the latter of which dies with cushingoid levels of adrenal steroids (see Robertson and Wexler, 1960) The range of senescent phenomena in higher plants is equally broad (see Chapter 5). Nonetheless, many characteristics of aging in multicellular organisms are clearly under genetic control at some level of the organism, as deduced from the stable, characteristic patterns of aging and the stability of the maximum life span in most species from generation to generation.

If the putative program for controls of aging involves neural and endocrine factors, among other extracellular controls, then a major prediction results: the time course of aging should be subject to extensive experimental manipulation (Finch, 1976; Finch et al., 1980). This prediction is well supported by studies of the hypothalamus and hippocampus of laboratory rodents, as we will illustrate.

FEMALE REPRODUCTIVE FUNCTIONS IN RODENTS

Basic Phenomena

The mechanisms of aging in the female reproductive system have provided many experimental approaches, including examination of the responsiveness of the ovary, hypothalamus, and pituitary to their specific hormonal stimuli and the transplantation of ovaries between different age groups (re-

viewed in Finch et al., 1980). Through such approaches, it has been possible to identify neuronal and endocrine interactions which are candidates for major mechanisms in the aging of the ovary, hypothalamus, and pituitary. The generality of age changes for different species may vary for each locus, since primates and rodents appear to differ in relation to the roles of hypothalamus, pituitary, and ovaries as pacemakers for ovulatory cycles. In mice and rats, the preovulatory gonadotropin surge is absolutely dependent on intact preoptic-hypothalamic connections and is presumably mediated by increased output of GnRH (gonadotropin-releasing hormone) into portal blood; by contrast, the hypothalamus in higher primates appears to have a lesser, perhaps passive role, in which the preovulatory gonadotropin surge can be largely accounted for by elevations of plasma estradiol acting on the pituitary and on increased pituitary responsiveness to GnRH (Fink, 1979; Knobil, 1980).

The loss of regular reproductive or ovulatory cycles occurs during mid-life in laboratory rodents and in some primates besides humans (see Chapter 18). In rodents, the loss of cycles during mid-life is usually followed by the endocrine state of "persistent vaginal cornification" in which the anovulatory ovary retains many growing follicles but lacks corpora lutea; plasma estradiol is moderately elevated (at estrous or metestrous levels), but progesterone is low, near the ovariectomized level in mice (Nelson et al., 1981) and rats (Huang et al., 1978); plasma LH (luteinizing hormone) is at basal levels (Huang et al., 1976; Gee et al., 1983). This initial postreproductive state of rodents is also known as "constant estrus" or "constant metestrus", and clearly differs from the very low, "castrate" levels of estradiol and elevated LH widely observed in women after menopause. However, plasma LH in C57BL/6J mice is eventually elevated spontaneously to ovariectomized levels after 20 months, as plasma estradiol decreases to ovariectomized levels, with the cessation of vaginal cornification and the presumed exhaustion of growing follicles (Gee et al., 1983); C57BL/GNNia mice also show spontaneous elevations of LH during aging (Parkening et al., 1982). These phenomena are very similar to those occurring at human menopause. The absence of spontaneous LH elevations in most studies of aging rats may, in part, be a consequence of their greater trend for prolactinemia.

A long-standing view holds that the ovary is the major factor in reproductive aging, since from birth onwards there is an irreversible loss of ovarian oocytes and since oogenesis is largely restricted to the embryo. The extent of the oocyte loss is under genetic influence: some rodent strains (e.g. CBA mice) undergo nearly complete ovarian exhaustion by the time cycles cease, while considerable ovarian reserve remains in other strains (see Finch, 1978). Some heterogeneity of ovarian depletion can occur between individuals, even within inbred strains: in C57BL/6J mice, aged 14 months, some individuals have less than 100 primary follicles, whereas others have a thousand (Gosden et al., 1983); this example also suggests extensive epigenetic influences on aging.

A possible role for higher (hypothalamic) centers in the loss of ovarian cycles in rodents was suggested by the transient reactivation of regular cycles in noncycling old rats by a broad range of treatments, including feeding of tyrosine or L-DOPA, injection of L-DOPA and other "adrenergic" drugs or progesterone, electrical stimulation of the hypothalamus, or stress (reviewed in Finch, 1978; Wise, 1983). A unifying theory of why these diverse treatments generally reactivate ovarian cycles is not yet available. The hypothesis that dysfunctions in hypothalamic monoaminergic neurotransmitter regulation underlie the loss of cycles is consistent with the effectiveness of catecholamine precursors (tyrosine and L-DOPA) and various adrenergic agonists (iproniazid, lergotrile) which would tend to elevate brain catecholamine levels and stimulate receptors. However, tyrosine was not effective if administered via ventricular cannulae, whereas L-

DOPA led to reactivation of cycles (Cooper and Linnoila, 1980). Such divergences may require complex explanations, such as different modes of action for L-tyrosine or L-DOPA. For example, possible reductions of serotonin levels might tend to correct negative imbalances of the catecholamine: serotonin ratio, observed in aging male (Simpkins et al., 1977) and noncycling female (Walker et al., 1980) rats. Consistent with this possibility, administration of serotonergic drugs (p-chlorophenylalanine, followed after two days by 5-hydroxytrytophan) restored the LH surge in old rats (Walker, 1982). In old female rats, the levels and turnover of hypothalamic serotonin appear to be elevated, whereas norepinephrine levels and turnover are reduced (Walker et al., 1980). Progesterone may also reactivate cycles by influencing serotonin metabolism (Franks et al., 1980). Additionally, drug and steroid effects may include peripheral mechanisms since the female reproductive tract has a rich adrenergic innervation (Bahr et al., 1974).

Age-related changes in hypothalamic catecholamine metabolism (reduced levels and turnover) are widely observed, particularly in old male rodents (see Chapter 24). Age changes of hypothalamic neurotransmitters in females are harder to interpret, because plasma steroid levels vary during the ovarian cycle and during the endocrine irregularities with approaching cycle loss. Thus, the hormonally sensitive monoamine metabolism of the hypothalamus may be influenced by endocrine fluctuations to a yet undefined extent (Wise, 1983). Reported changes in females include impaired accelerations of hypothalamic norepinephrine turnover at proestrus by one year (Wise, 1982), smaller postcastration elevations of hypothalamic catecholamine levels at two years (Wilkes and Yen, 1981), and reduced dopamine levels in the median eminence (Demarest et al., 1980, 1982) and in hypophyseal portal blood (Gudelsky et al., 1981; Reymond and Porter, 1981).

In the future, age changes of neurotransmitter turnover and synaptic functions may be mapped in detail throughout the life span, with correlations between specific structures and functions. Elucidation of such ontogenic steps with intermediate age groups might identify causal sequences in the course of reproductive aging, as rodents progress through lengthening of ovulatory cycles from the typical four-day cycles to five-day, six-day, and longer cycles (Nelson et al., 1982; Mobbs et al., 1984a.).

One intermediate stage of this putative sequence involves smaller preovulatory surges of gonadotropins (LH and FSH) (follicle stimulating hormone) at proestrus, as observed in most 8- to 14-month-old rodents (Figure 1). Reductions in the LH surge can occur during aging even in the absence of lengthened estrous cycles, as in hamsters (Chen, 1981). Similar impairments of the experimentally induced gonadotropin surge occur in middle-aged rodents after ovariectomy followed by injection of estradiol and other steroids (see Chapter 18). The smaller rise of plasma estradiol to proestrous levels in aging mice could result from a smaller pool of growing follicles (Nelson et al., 1981); nonetheless, the number of ova shed at ovulation remains remarkably constant up to 12–14 months, despite major loss of fertility (Gosden et al., 1983). The 10–50 percent smaller preovulatory gonadotropin surge in aging rodents is clearly capable of inducing ovulation since even >80 percent reductions of the normal proestrous surge still can result in ovulation (see Turgeon, 1979). However, progressive impairments of the surge are observed as rodents approach and enter acyclicity (Nass et al., 1984; Mobbs et al., 1984a.), and imply that the impaired surges are ultimately the cause of acyclicity.

The basis for the smaller gonadotropin surges at proestrus is generally believed to involve a change at the hypothalamic level, rather than the pituitary, because pituitary output of LH in response to injected GnRH is generally of normal size (e.g., in rats which had recently stopped cycling) (Wise and Ratner, 1980). Pituitary responses to GnRH in aging rodents of both sexes have yielded diverse results, with some studies showing ma-

jor changes, but others detecting none even at advanced ages (reviewed in Finch, 1979; Riegle and Miller, 1978). These heterogeneous results may derive from variations of steroidal influences in the pituitary at the time of GnRH injection, as well as longer-lasting influences from prior exposure to steroids. In one recent study, age-correlated impairments in response to GnRH were a function of hormonal status (Cooper et al., 1984).

Pituitary tumors at early stages could also be involved in the impaired gonadotropin surges. Aging female rodents, and males of some strains as well, have a high incidence of pituitary tumors after mid-life (see Duchen and Schurr, 1976; Felicio et al., 1980). The tumors are often comprised of hyperplastic mammotropes (Clayton et. al., 1984). Plasma prolactin may be very elevated, particularly in old rats (Lu et al., 1979; Huang et al., 1976). Because prolactin can inhibit gonadotropin release (Evans et al., 1982), the possibility arises that the onset of reproductive impairments observed in aging could be related to elevated plasma prolactin. However, evidence from several sources argues against this possibility. First, measurements of plasma prolactin at proestrus in aging C57BL/6J mice with lengthened cycles show a much smaller prolactin surge in mice whose proestrous LH surge is also reduced (Flurkey et al., 1982) (Figure 1). Furthermore, despite the normalization of plasma prolactin levels by administration of lergotrile (dopamine agonist), gonadotropin regulation remained impaired in aging female rats (Clemens et al., 1978). On the other hand, the transition from persistent vaginal cornification, which usually follows the loss of cycles to repetitive pseudopregnancy may involve elevations of plasma prolactin (Everett, 1980). The trend towards elevated prolactin in persistent vaginal cornification is reasonably considered to result from the sustained plasma estradiol which J. W. Everett (1980) hypothesized to eventually promote formation of corpora lutea and thence pseudopregnancy. The ability of ergot drugs (do-

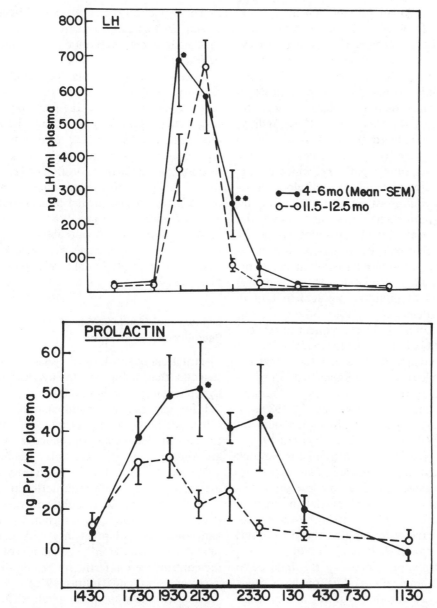

Figure 1. Plasma prolactin and luteinizing hormone (LH) at proestrus in aging mice (Flurkey et al., 1982). The dark horizontal bar denotes darkness.

paminergic agonists) to interrupt repetitive pseudopregnancy and transiently reactivate cycles is consistent with this hypothesis.

A tendency for elevated plasma prolactin is common in aging rodents of both sexes but has not yet been clearly dissociated from the presence of pituitary tumors (lactotrope ad- enomas). In male C57BL/6J mice, which have a negligible incidence of pituitary tu- mors throughout the life span (Finch, 1973), plasma prolactin is not elevated at ages up to 28 months (Finch et al., 1977). Several stud- ies indicate that elevated plasma prolactin may be associated with disturbances of hypothalamic dopamine metabolism. For example, in 2-year-old male rats with three-fold elevation of plasma prolactin, dopamine levels in pituitary stalk blood were much smaller (< 50 percent) than in the young (Gudelsky et al., 1981). Similar findings were made on aging female rats with elevated prolactin (Reymond and Porter, 1981). These findings point to a reduced feedback sensitivity to prolactin in the dopaminergic neurons of the tubero-infundibular pathway, which are the major source of pituitary stalk blood dopamine; in young rats, prolactin usually stimulates hypothalamic dopamine turnover and increases stalk blood dopamine (Gudelsky and Porter, 1980). Because dopamine in hypophyseal portal blood (hypothalamic in origin) is a major candidate for the (negative) regulation of pituitary prolactin output in rodents (Peters et al., 1981), the elevations of prolactin might be consequent to reduced availability of dopamine for the inhibition of prolactin secretion. It is of interest that hypothalamic defects are implicated in prolactin-secreting pituitary tumors in humans (Van Loon, 1978; Tucker et al., 1980). In general, plasma prolactin in humans does not increase with age (e.g. Yamaji et al., 1976).

Another factor in the trend for elevated prolactin of aging female rodents is the sustained plasma estradiol and low progesterone associated with persistent vaginal cornification (Everett, 1980). Pituitary tumors eventually appear after the onset of this ovarian state (Felicio et al., 1980) and eventually also appear in young rats induced to persistent vaginal cornification by a single injection of estradiol (Brawer and Sonnenschein, 1975; Nakagawa et al., 1980). Since progesterone can antagonize the effects of estrogens on inducing mammary tumors (e.g. Segaloff, 1973) and on prolactin secretion (Chen and Meites, 1970), the relatively unopposed estrogenic milieu of rats and mice in persistent vaginal cornification might thus favor pituitary tumorigenesis (Felicio et al., 1980; Nelson et al., 1981). Further evidence of estrogen dependency of age-related pituitary tumors is the greatly reduced incidence of pituitary tumors in long-term ovariectomized mice (Nelson et al., 1980b; Mobbs et al., 1984a). In this case, a neuroendocrine cascade leading to gross pituitary pathology can be traced back to the ovary.

Since elevations of plasma estradiol at proestrus are considered to be the major physiologic stimulus for the gonadoptropin surge, the possibility of age changes in estradiol receptors has been studied. Receptor translocation may be impaired: estradiol injections lead to the translocation of fewer estradiol receptors to the cell nucleus in the preoptic region and medial basal hypothalamus of middle-aged rats Wise and Camp, 1984). Reductions of hypothalamic estradiol receptors in aging female rats were previously suggested (Haji et al., 1981; Peng and Peng, 1973).

Experimental Manipulations of Reproductive Senescence

The transient reactivation of cycles in old rats suggests that aging in the hypothalamic-hypophyseal system has considerable potential for experimental manipulation. Some other striking manipulations of aging changes in the female reproductive system are known (for other examples see Finch, 1978 and Walker, 1983). When rats were maintained on tryptophan-deficient diets from 1 month to 23 months and then fed their "normal" diet, some regained fertility and could support pregnancy with normal fetal development at up to 26 months of age; the controls were infertile by 17 months, as expected (Segal and Timiras, 1976).

Another major approach involves chronic ovariectomy, which indicates that some age changes in the hypothalamus are dependent on exposure to ovarian steroids. If rodents are ovariectomized when young and examined at later ages, some hypothalamic functions do not show impairments, as assayed by the ability of 16- to 28-month-old, chronically ovariectomized rodents to support a series of normal estrous cycles with young ovarian grafts (Aschheim, 1965, 1976; Nelson et al., 1980a; Felicio et al., 1983) or by steroid-induced LH surges (Mobbs et al.,

1984a; Elias et al., 1979). In middle-aged, long-term ovariectomized mice, young ovarian grafts can then support nearly as many cycles as occur in young controls (Felicio et al., 1983). Hyperactivity of microglia and astroglia in the arcuate nucleus of the hypothalamus is similarly manipulated by chronic ovariectomy: increased glial activity in the arcuate nucleus of 12- to 14-month-old rats and mice is prevented by long-term ovariectomy (Schipper et al., 1981) (Figure 2). It is plausible that the microglial hyperactivity is a response to the degeneration of neuronal processes; the types of neuronal processes affected and the extent of neuronal loss, if any, are not known. These and other parameters affected by long-term ovariectomy are summarized in Table 1. The similar attenuation of age changes in some neuroendocrine structures and functions by long-term ovariectomy suggests that ovarian steroids have a

specific role in hypothalamic age changes which could indicate a cumulative impact of estradiol (Finch et al., 1980). These findings also suggest the possibility that the ovary-dependent aspects of neuroendocrine aging can be quantitated (e.g., as strength-duration relationships) for steroid-induced dysfunctions. It is important to recognize that not all sex steroid-dependent neural responses are impaired with age: for example, lordosis responses are retained in 2-year-old rats (Cooper and Walker, 1979; Peng et al., 1977). Thus, the ovarian-dependent aspects of hypothalamic aging appear to be restricted to specific circuits and cell targets. Also, ovary-independent aspects of hypothalamic-pituitary aging are clearly indicated (Felicio, et a., 1983).

Whereas long-term ovariectomy attenuates some aspects of hypothalamic aging, there is growing evidence that increased ex-

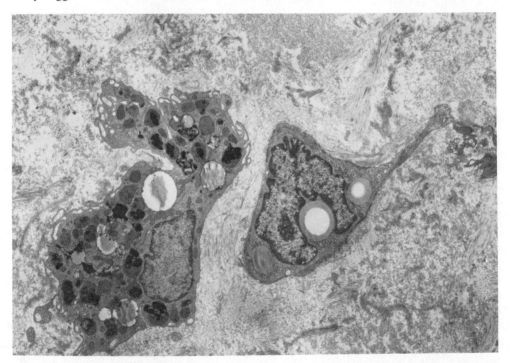

Figure 2. Glial cell morphology in the arcuate nucleus of 12 mo. old C57BL/6J mice. Left: A short-term ovariectomized mouse. The arrowhead indicates highly reactive astrocyte filled with granules; the smaller arrow indicates a reactive microglial cell filled with debris, putatively the phagocytosed remnant of a degenerating neurone or neural process. Right: Corresponding cells from a long-term ovariectomized mouse in which the glial responses are rare and equivalent to glia observed in the young mouse. Arrowhead, atrocyte; smaller arrow, microglial cell (unpublished photographs, courtesy of James R. Brawer. For details, see Shipper et al., 1981.)

TABLE 1. Manipulations of Reproductive Aging in Rodents.

Markers of Reproductive Aging	Chronic Ovariectomy Delays	Chronic E_2 Treatment Accelerates
1. Ovarian cycles lost	a	b
2. Smaller LH surge	c	c
3. Smaller postovariec-tomy LH rise	d	e
4. Glial hyperactivity in arcuate nucleus	f	g
5. Lactotrope adeno-mas (a late effect)	h	i

NOTE.

(a) = Capacity for cycles assayed with ovarian grafts (Aschheim, 1976; Nelson et al., 1980a; Felicio et al., 1983).

(b) = Kawashima (1960); Brown-Grant (1974); Brawer et al. (1978); Mobbs et al. (1984b).

(c) = LH surge induced by estradiol implants (Mobbs et al, 1984a).

(d) = Gee et al. (1983).

(e) = Mobbs et al. (1984b).

(f) = Schipper et al. (1981).

(g) = Brawer et al. (1978).

(h) = Nelson et al. (1980b); Mobbs et al., (1984a).

(i) = Brawer and Sonnenschein (1975); Casanueva et al. (1982).

Also see Finch et al., *Endo. Rev.* (1984).

posure to estrogens rapidly induces changes very much like those that occur spontaneously at later ages. For example, injections of young rats with 20 ng/day estradiol caused loss of cycles and persistent vaginal cornification after about three months, whereas progesterone or testosterone injections had no effect (Kawashima, 1960). An intriguingly similar syndrome occurs in sheep fed on types of clover which contain estrogenic isoflavones ("phytoestrogens"); such sheep may develop a permanent infertility syndrome after several years ("clover disease") with concomitant, mild glial hyperactivity in the hypothalamus (Adams, 1976) and shrinkage of hypothalamic neurons (Adams, 1977). In rats, a single large injection of estradiol rapidly produces persistent vaginal cornification (Brown-Grant, 1975; Brawer et al., 1978) as it does in mice (Mobbs et al., 1984b). The subsequent hypothalamic changes include ability to support cyclic functions with ovarian transplants (Mobbs et al., 1984b). Other changes are induced by E_2 treatment which also occur in rodents during normal aging (Table 1). Since impairments of LH regulation persist for at least two months after ovariectomy (Mobbs et al., 1981), relatively irreversible changes are induced in the hypothalamic-pituitary axis. Some effects of prolonged exposure to estradiol, however, may be reversible, as shown by the reemergence of an estradiol-progesterone-induced LH surge in old rats which were ovariectomized for one month before testing (Lu et al., 1981). Intriguingly, a single large injection of estradiol in young, *ovariectomized* rodents does not yield these long-lasting effects (Brawer et al., 1980; Mobbs et al., in prep.). The single large injection of estrogen thus probably acts by causing the initial loss of cycles. The sustained, moderate levels of plasma estradiol which continue for many months during the estrogen-rich acyche state of intact, estradiol-injected rodents are a likely cause of the subsequent hypothalamic changes. These results are consistent with the effects of chronic estrogen exposure in rats and sheep just discussed.

In addition to these effects of estradiol on the adult, estradiol and other aromatizable steroids cause permanent acyclicity if given to young rats and mice during the first postnatal week. The treated rodents, when adults, have masculinized hypothalamic functions by anatomic, physiologic, and behavioral criteria (MacLusky and Naftolin, 1981); similar effects of steroids in humans are not established (Ehrhardt and Meyer, 1981). Slightly smaller doses of estradiol given to neonatal rodents cause a "delayed anovulatory syndrome", in which adults have limited numbers of ovulatory cycles but soon enter persistent vaginal cornification, with major impairments of their LH surge mechanisms which are similar to the changes of aging (Harlan and Gorski, 1977; 1978). Thus, the hypothesis that reproductive senescence involves a cumulative impact of estradiol is consistent with these phenomena, since the neonatal rodents treated with subthreshold estradiol doses would require less additional estradiol exposure as young adults to reach the threshold (Finch et al., 1980). It is also of interest in this regard that prenatal influences can be detected; female fetuses flanked by male neighbors have higher plasma estradiol and, as adults, are more masculine and have longer cycles compared with female fetuses flanked by females (vom Saal and Bronson, 1980). Moreover, male-flanked females have an earlier loss of fertility (vom Saal, and Moyer, in prep.). Thus, it is possible to consider that estrogen exposure is a continuum during development as well as in adult phases of reproduction, in which paranatal and adult exposures are additive (Finch et al., 1980).

Although the parallels between the impairments associated with prolonged estrogen exposure of adult rodents and sheep, and those associated with aging or with paranatal steroid exposure are intriguing, it cannot yet be concluded that the cellular loci and mechanisms are identical. For example, experimental lesions at different anterior hypothalamic and preoptic loci can impair experimentally induced gonadotropin surges and can differentiate effects of estradiol and progesterone (e.g., Kawakami et al., 1978). At the least, the present observations demonstrate that adult mammals are susceptible to long-term, apparently irreversible effects of estrogens on the brain, as well as during the paranatal period when sexual differentiation of the brain occurs. The widespread usage of sex steroids as contraceptives and in treatment of postmenopausal disorders may have unexpected effects on the aging process and diseases of aging.

Thymus-Ovarian Relationships

Developmentally critical interactions between the thymus and neuroendocrine functions are shown by the permanent reductions (−40 percent) of plasma thyroxine in neonatally thymectomized mice (Pierpaolli and Besedovsky, 1975). The ability of thymic hormones (e.g., thymosin fraction 5, or thymosin B) to stimulate secretion of LHRH *in*

vitro from hypothalamic fragments (Rebar et al., 1981) indicates a direct role of the thymus on the hypothalamus and pituitary.

Another aspect is the ovarian dysgenesis which follows neonatal thymectomy in rodents (Nishizuka and Sakakura, 1971; Michael, 1979; Hattori and Brandon, 1979). The ovaries of neonatally thymectomized mice undergo major reduction of primordial follicles and growing follicles by 4 months (Michael, 1979). In many regards, this ovarian depletion resembles that of later aging, particularly that of the human ovary. Ovarian tumors are common in neonatally thymectomized mice by 20 months. As expected, the great reduction of ovarian follicles is associated with elevated gonadotropins. Such effects of thymus deprivation may not be restricted to neonates: the SL/Ni mouse strain, inbred for its small-sized thymus by Y. Nishizuka, has rapid thymic atrophy, with a loss of ovarian follicles by 7 months; ovarian tumors are common by 16 months, and gonadotropins are also elevated (Michael, 1979). Age-related alterations of thymic hormones could influence ovarian-hypothalamic-pituitary aging. The presence of receptors for estradiol (Grossman et al., 1979a, 1982) and dihydrotestosterone (Grossman et al., 1979b) in the thymus is of interest in this regard. The thymus might thus be involved in the regulation of some neuroendocrine age change functions as well as in the immune system (Piantanelli et al., 1980). The network of anti-idiotypic antibodies which appears to regulate immunological responses (Jerne, 1976) could interact at several levels with neuroendocrine factors. Eventually, it may be possible to establish linkages of immune changes with age to neuroendocrine aging.

THE HIPPOCAMPUS AND ADRENAL INTERACTIONS

The possibility that elevated glucocorticoids play an etiological role in nonneural, peripheral aging in vertebrates has generated interest for many years. Early investigators noted similarities between Cushing's syndrome and normal aging (Findlay, 1949; Solez, 1952). Moreover, Pacific salmon normally die from a cushingoid syndrome after their first spawning (Robertson and Wexler, 1960). The adrenal hyperactivity and associated histopathology can be prevented by prior castration (Robertson and Wexler, 1962); castrate salmon have a much extended life span (Robertson, 1961).

The physiology of breeder rats is viewed as a model of accelerated aging (Wexler, 1976): repeatedly bred male or female rats exhibited a spectrum of pathophysiologic lesions as early as 8–9 months of age which included diabetes-like conditions, arteriosclerotic lesions, and calcification in the cardiovascular system. Treatment with adrenal steroids or ACTH (adreno-cortico trophic hormone) accelerated these changes. The repeated breeding (or the competition associated with housing of multiple males in a single cage to enhance the success of mating) may constitute a stressful condition that increases stimulation of the hypothalamic-pituitary-adrenal axis, resulting in these cushingoid changes; these phenomena may not occur in all conditions for breeding. Since similar changes eventually occurred in 2- to 3-year-old, virgin rats, the effects of repeated breeding and hyperadrenocorticism appear to accelerate some aging processes (Wexler, 1976). Moreover, the capacity of adrenal glands from breeder rats to synthesize steroids in vitro was reduced, suggesting that the breeding-associated stimulation of neuroendocrine systems may cause adrenal exhaustion (Wexler and Kittinger, 1965). However, the effects of breeding situations on aging are not generalized, and careful definition of this model for accelerated aging is needed (Ingram et al., 1981).

In aging laboratory rats, most reports indicate that both resting and stress-induced plasma glucocorticoids increase with age (Lewis and Wexler, 1974; Landfield et al., 1978b, 1980; Chiueh et al., 1980; Tang and Phillips, 1978; Sapolsky et al., 1983). Moreover, during prolonged restraint stress, plasma corticosterone in aged Fisher 344 rats may reach levels substantially higher than those of the young (Landfield, Applegate and Kerr, unpublished). The basis for this increase appears to be an age-related increase in ACTH release and a resultant stimulation of adrenal gland mass (Landfield et al., 1980). However, increased basal corticosterone may not occur with aging in some mouse strains (Latham and Finch, 1976). Despite evidence for an age-related increase in adrenocortical output beginning around mid-life in rats, maximal adrenal steroid output may fall in the last phases of the life span. Several investigators reported a reduced maximal adrenal steroid output in response to ACTH or other stimuli in aged rats (Britton et al., 1975; Hess and Riegle, 1970; Riegle and Hess, 1972). The capacity of adrenal cortical cells to secrete steroids in vitro declined with age in rats (Malamed and Carsia, 1983). It is presently unclear, however, whether genotypic differences, the phases of the life span compared, or methodological differences account for some of the apparently inconsistent findings.

It is not resolved whether plasma glucocorticoid levels are generally increased during human aging (Andres and Tobin, 1977; Landfield, 1981). A net increase with age, however, is not a prerequisite for a role of glucocorticoids in brain aging, since normal plasma steroid levels could exert cumulative deleterious actions (Landfield, 1978).

Considerable evidence indicates that the hippocampus and the pituitary-adrenal axis have reciprocal interactions: the hippocampus modulates adrenocorticotropin (ACTH) release (Bohus, 1975); in turn, the hippocampus is rich in corticosterone receptors and appears to be a major target site for adrenal steroids (McEwen et al., 1975). The nature of hippocampal influences on the pituitary-adrenal system remains controversial, with some evidence indicating that the influence is inhibitory, some evidence suggesting that it is excitatory, and other studies failing to detect an influence (e.g., Feldman and Conforti, 1980; Lanier et al., 1975; Murphy et al., 1979). However, direct measurements of ACTH support the view that the hippocampus can be inhibitory, particularly in relation to stress-induced ACTH release (Wilson et al., 1980). The main electrophysiological effect of glucocorticoids on the hippocampus also appears to be inhibitory (Dafny et al., 1973; Pfaff et al., 1971 Urban and de Wied, 1976).

Recent evidence indicates that some aging phenomena in the hippocampus, and perhaps in other brain regions, are modulated by glucocorticoids. The hypothesis that glucocorticoids might modulate hippocampal aging (Landfield, 1978) is supported by the particular susceptibility of the hippocampus to early and severe morphologic aging changes (Ball, 1977; Tomlinson and Henderson, 1976; Wisniewski and Terry, 1973), by the high density of corticosterone receptors in the hippocampus (McEwen et al., 1975), and by possible age-like effects of glucocorticoids in the periphery (Wexler, 1976). A loss of corticosterone binding neurons occurs in the CA-3 hippocampal zone (and less elsewhere) in old rats (Sapolsky et al., 1984), suggesting that glucocorticoid-mediated age changes may be highly selective for target cells.

The converse, that hippocampal age changes may affect glucocorticoids, is supported by the hippocampal influences on ACTH regulation. The hypothesis that glucocorticoids cause aging changes in some brain regions predicts a "positive runaway feedback" interaction between pathological glucocorticoid actions on the hippocampus and decreasing hippocampal inhibition of glucocorticoid release during aging (Figure 3).

Hypotheses involving endocrine modification of brain aging lead to predictions that (1) some aspects of brain and endocrine activity should be quantitatively correlated, and (2) the experimental alteration of specific endocrine mechanisms should modulate the degree of brain aging (Landfield, 1978, 1981). To test these hypotheses, however, requires careful quantification of many brain parameters during aging. In this regard, many parameters correlated with brain aging seem well suited for quantitative assessment, although potential technical and conceptual pitfalls are associated with such measurements (reviewed in Landfield, 1982).

With regard to the prediction of quantitative relations between glucocorticoid activity and brain aging, plasma corticosterone was correlated with glial reactivity in the hippocampus of aging rats (Landfield et al., 1978b). In addition, long-term administration of glucocorticoids accelerates (Landfield et al., 1978a, and in preparation), whereas prolonged adrenalectomy retards, several quantitative indices of hippocampal aging (Landfield et al., 1979, 1981) (Figure 4). However, not all behavioral and morphological correlates of hippocampal aging are retarded by prolonged adrenalectomy. Moreover, the age-correlated decrease of hippocampal glucocorticoid receptors (Roth and Hess, 1982) remains to be investigated for effects of prolonged adrenalectomy and glucocorticoid treatment.

The specific pathways by which glucocorticoids act on the brain are not yet clarified. Alterations in plasma glucocorticoid levels, whether spontaneous or experimentally induced, might alter a wide range of other endocrine-physiological processes, with indirect effects on brain aging. The apparent restriction of neuronal loss to cells with corticosterone receptors (Sapolsky et al., 1984) suggests that adrenal steroids directly affect hippocampal aging. However, indirect effects are possible via afferent neural pathways or other hormonal systems. Prolonged adrenalectomy, for example, results in a fivefold or greater increase in circulating ACTH (Landfield et al., 1981), and ACTH is known to directly affect brain biochemical, electrophysiological, and behavioral variables (Gispen et al., 1977). Thus, elevated ACTH, which appears to stimulate hippocampal neural activity (Pfaff et al., 1971; Urban and de Wied, 1976), could be a factor in the apparent effect of prolonged adrenalectomy in retarding hippocampal changes.

The possible role of ACTH was recently examined (Landfield et al., 1981). Chronic administration of either an analogue of $ACTH_{4-9}$ (ORG 2766, which acts on brain but not on adrenal steroid production) or of

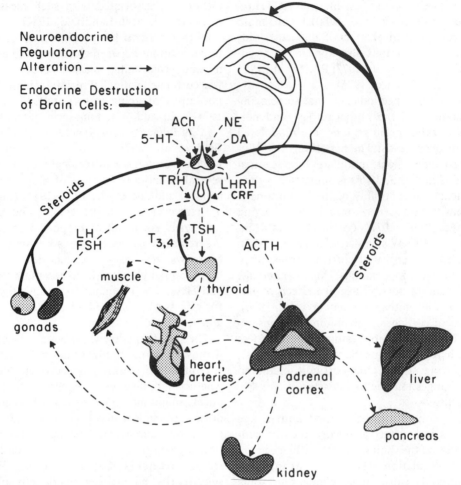

Figure 3. Schematic representation of two hypotheses of neural-endocrine interactions during aging; the neuroendocrine regulatory alteration hypothesis, in which changes in brain-endocrine control mechanisms are proposed to lead to peripheral physiological deterioration; (e.g., the neuroendocrine casade hypothesis of Finch 1976); and the hypothesis that endocrine factors may modulate brain aging. Both mechanisms could operate together in a positive feedback loop. (From Landfield, 1978, reprinted with permission of Plenum Press).

the neural stimulant pentylenetetrazol retarded some behavioral and morphological correlates of brain aging in rats. However, these effects on the brain differed from those of long-term adrenalectomy. Thus, steroids, exogenously administered peptides, and neural stimulants may all modulate aspects of brain aging. Since various exogenous peptides have stimulant actions, it is conceivable that alterations in brain peptides during ag-

ing modulate age-related brain pathology by decreasing average levels of neural stimulation; other mechanisms are possible (Landfield et al., 1981).

Much more work is needed to clarify the mechanisms and interactions of factors that influence or modulate hippocampal aging in mammals. Actions of adrenal steroids cannot account for all aspects of hippocampal aging. Peptides and ongoing levels of neural

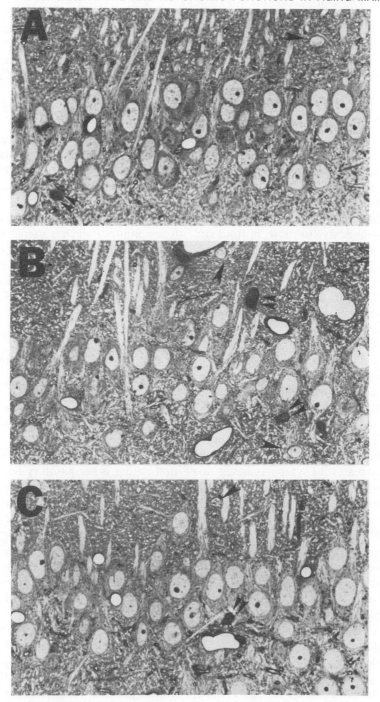

Figure 4. Examples of hippocampal pyramidal cells in the somal layer in semi-thin sections from (A) young rats. (B) aged controls, and (C) aged rats adrenalectomized 9 months earlier. Adrenalectomy appears to protect against age-related reduction in neuronal density and increases in glial reactivity. All sections are cut perpendicular to the somal layer, from CA1 region just dorsal to the tip of the dorsal limb of the dentate hyrus granule cells. Neuronal nuclei and major glial species can be recognized, astrocytes with lucent cytoplasm (arrowheads) and the darker microglia and oligodendrocytes, with chromatin clumps in the nucleus (double arrowheads) (From Landfield et al., 1981, reprinted with permission of *Science*).

activity, as well as genomically controlled cellular mechanisms, for example, may also be relevant.

HYPOTHALAMIC ASPECTS OF OSMOREGULATION

The output of arginine vasopressin by the hypothalamus is critical for rapid adjustments of fluid balance, and vasopressin output responds rapidly to changes in osmolality (reviewed in Robertson, 1980). The concept that neurohypophyseal dysfunctions underlie the age-related dysfunctions in fluid and electrolyte balances is long standing (Findlay, 1949). Detailed study showed increases with age in the osmoreceptor response to hypertonic saline infusion: in normal elderly subjects, the gain (or increase of vasopressin per unit change of osmolality) was twice that in the young (Robertson and Rowe, 1980). This increased sensitivity was not a result of altered thresholds of plasma osmolality for the release of vasopressin, nor was clearance of vasopressin altered by age. However, the elderly subjects had impaired release of vasopressin in response to sudden standing after 16 hours of bed rest: in contrast to the vigorous increases of vasopressin in the young, many of the elderly tested showed no increase of vasopressin. These data imply a lesion located distal to the baroreceptor centers, possibly between the medulla and the neurohypophysis.

Age-related abnormalities in vasopressin release were recently analyzed in aging rodents. In 2- to 3-year-old rats, the usual increase of plasma vasopressin during dehydration was greatly impaired, as was the increase of plasma renin (Sladek et al., 1981). The tissue levels of vasopressin tend to decline with age in the pituitary and hypothalamic regions (Dorsa and Bottemiller, 1982; Sladek et al., 1981), but the decrements do not parallel the major deficits in response to dehydration. Remarkably, old rats still were able to conserve urinary outflow despite these abnormalities, although less well than the young.

Altered functions with age in the neuro-hypophyseal system are suggested by microscopic studies. On one hand, neurophysin content increases with age in the rat supraoptic nucleus (by immunocytochemical techniques); the staining of catecholamine fibers in this nucleus markedly decreased (50 percent), resembling deficiencies in the vasopressin-deficient Brattleboro rat (Sladek et al., 1980). The nature of contacts between catecholaminergic fibers and the vasopressin-containing cell bodies is unknown, but could be part of the linkage between the baroreceptor and release at the lobe of the posterior pituitary which is altered with age. Age changes in the subcellular responses to dehydration include decreased rough endoplasmic reticulum in the supraoptic nucleus of mice (Davies and Fotheringham, 1980).

OTHER PHENOMENA IMPLICITLY INVOLVED IN HYPOTHALAMIC AGE CHANGES

Ultradian Release of Pituitary Hormones

Plasma levels of some pituitary hormones change in rapid episodes suggestive of pulsatile release, with a duration of about one hour, as shown for the "ultradian rhythms" of LH and other pituitary hormones (Desjardins, 1981). The prevalent view is that these secretory episodes are driven by variations in the secretion of releasing factors from hypothalamic neurons into the portal system (Knobil, 1981). Thus, effects of age (which will be described) on the fluctuations of plasma LH and GH provisionally implicate changes in hypothalamic neurosecretion.

Plasma LH ultradian rhythms also have reduced frequency and amplitude in aging CBFI mice (Coquelin and Desjardins, 1982) and rats (Karpas et al., 1983); the frequency of LH pulses is rapidly restored in middle-aged female rats by clonidine (Estes and Simkins, 1982). Disturbances in LH secretion in elderly men are probably linked to altered ultradian rhythms in plasma testosterone levels (Bremner et al., 1983), since the episodic elevation of plasma testosterone is closely coupled to that of LH in rodents (Desjardins, 1981). Thus, some change of testicular secretions with age may be secondary to altered hypothalamic-pituitary functions. Similarly, ovarian follicular growth in primates is very sensitive to the frequency of LH ultradian pulses (Pohl et al., 1983), hence some neuroendocrine contributions to cycle lengthening could be suspected in pre-menopausal women.

The pulsatile release of growth hormone with a periodicity of about three hours in rats becomes dampened with age (Sonntag et al., 1980) (Figure 5). Moreover, twice daily injections of L-DOPA restore the amplitude of plasma GH (growth hormone) fluctuations; this response implies that brain catecholamine deficits contribute to the age changes in growth hormone release (Sonntag et al., 1982). The reduced output of GH during sleep (see Chapter 25) could also involve de-

ficiencies in the regulation of central monoamines. However, the relationship of altered GH release in aging needs further evaluation for potential confounds from changes in exercise and body fat. Some age-correlated impairments of insulin regulation, for example, may be linked to body weight and locomotor activity (Reaven and Reaven, 1981). The metabolic consequences of such alterations in GH release are not known.

Other examples of neuroendocrine rhythms with major disturbances during aging include diurnal fluctuations of TSH (thyroid stimulating hormone) in rats (Klug and Adelman, 1979); pineal melatonin in hamsters (Reiter et al., 1980a), gerbils (Reiter et al., 1980a, 1980b), and rats (Reiter et al., 1981); and drinking and locomotion in female rats (Mosko et al., 1980). It is pertinent that not all diurnally varying hormones show

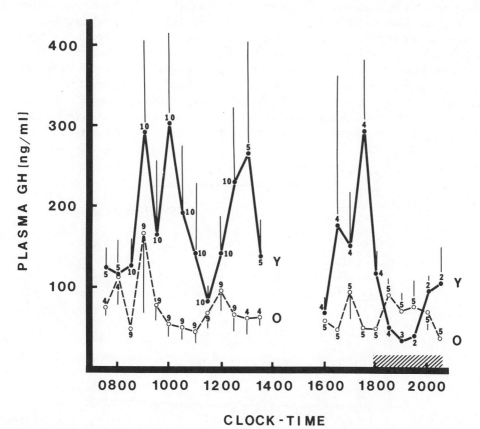

Figure 5. Plasma growth hormone (GH): pulsatile patterns determined from serial sampling in Y (6 month) and O (24 month) male rats. The dark period began at 1800h (cross-hatching on the abcissa). Courtesy of Joseph Meites.

age changes in temporal organization, for example, ACTH in humans (Jensen and Bli-chert-Toft, 1971).

Hypothalamic Influences on the Liver

Influence of the hypothalamus on liver glycogen metabolism was demonstrated by the glycogenolysis resulting rapidly from electrical stimulation of the hypothalamic ventromedial nucleus and by threefold increases of glycogen phosphorylase I within 30 seconds (Shimazu, 1967; Shimazu et al., 1968; reviewed in Shimazu, 1980). Pharmacologic studies indicate involvements of beta-adrenergic loci. Similar effects on glycogenolysis and glycogen phosphorylase resulted from stimulation of the distal ends of the sympathetic innervation to the liver. Thus, the liver can be considered as a part of the neural regulatory network in which the hypothalamus has a key role. The striking impairments with age in the response of glycogen phosphorylase to stimulation of the ventromedial hypothalamic nucleus (Figure 6) (Shimazu et al., 1978) are pertinent to the possibility that neuroendocrine cascades involving the hypothalamus have an important role in age changes of visceral and metabolic functions.

Hypothalamic Thresholds

The effects of age on the thresholds for hypothalamic responses are of much theoretical interest in relation to the role of the brain in physiological age changes (Finch, 1976; Shock, 1977; Timiras, 1978; Dilman, 1981). Unfortunately, only limited data are available. In view of the difficulties in establishing developmental changes in neuroendocrine thresholds, much effort will be required to elucidate this key issue.

THE AUTONOMIC NERVOUS SYSTEM AND AGING

The autonomic nervous system is clearly affected by age in humans and other mammals. Autonomic dysfunctions are implicated in many pathophysiologic changes of age including orthostatic hypotension, thermoregulation, gastrointestinal functions, urinary incontinence, and impaired penile erections (for general discussions see Wollner and Spalding, 1978; Collins et al., 1980; Roberts, 1981; Halter and Pfeifer, 1982). Because the central controls and relays for various autonomic pathways are still poorly understood, we cannot yet distinguish in most cases if al-

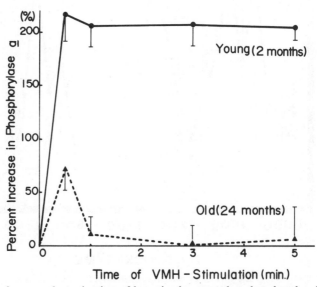

Figure 6. Effects of age on the activation of hepatic glycogen phosphorylase by electrical stimulation of the ventromedial hypothalamic nucleus in the rat (Shimazu, 1980). Courtesy of Takashi Shimazu.

tered autonomic responses are due to subspinal autonomic impairments or if central changes are also involved. Some histologic data suggest major age-correlated changes in autonomic neurotransmitter stores of old rats (e.g., Partanen et al., 1980) and humans (e.g., Hervonen et al., 1978). In the avian iris and ciliary ganglion, substantial age-correlated changes occur in cholinergic and adrenergic functions (reviewed in Giacobini, 1982). Clearly, more study is needed to identify the similarities and differences of aging in the central and peripheral nervous systems.

Sympathetic Nervous System

Numerous technical problems are associated with the measurement of sympathetic nervous system activity, and there has been little standardization in studies on aging of factors that affect sympathetic activity (e.g., fasting, time of day, behavioral activity). Nevertheless, a relatively consistent picture of sympathetic activity in human aging has begun to emerge. Although not all studies detected age effects, numerous experiments have found that plasma norepinephrine (one of the primary measures of sympathetic activity) is increased in aging humans (Pederson and Christensen, 1975; Ziegler et al., 1976; Rowe and Troen, 1980; Halter and Pfeifer, 1982).

Basal levels of plasma norepinephrine are reported to be increased with age in most studies of humans. An important variable in these studies is the duration of recumbency by the subject before sampling of peripheral blood (Saar and Gordon, 1979). The response of plasma norepinephrine to stimuli such as upright posture or exercise (Young et al., 1980; Ziegler et al., 1976) also appears to increase with age in humans. However, the release of norepinephrine may not be greater with age in response to all forms of stimuli, as shown by the smaller increase of plasma norepinephrine after insulin infusion in elderly subjects as compared with young; the generalized age-related decline in insulin sensitivity could be a factor in these results

(Minaker et al., 1982). In addition, the return of plasma norepinephrine to baseline levels during recumbency is delayed in the elderly. Interestingly, some of the age-correlated increases in sleep disturbances (Prinz et al., 1979) and blood pressure (Halter and Pfeifer, 1982) in humans were correlated with increased plasma norepinephrine levels. However, in another study, blood pressure and plasma norepinephrine were not strongly correlated in elderly humans (Rubin et al., 1982).

An unresolved issue is whether the elderly release more norepinephrine or whether the peripheral clearance of norepinephrine is reduced. No age changes were detected in plasma clearance of norepinephrine by some (Young et al., 1980; Rubin et al., 1982), whereas significant decreases of plasma clearance with age were detected by others (Esler et al., 1981). Technical problems associated with the assessment of norepinephrine clearance (Christensen, 1982) could contribute to this variability.

Although the issue of clearance is not fully resolved, other evidence suggests that the activity of sympathetic neurons increases with age, e.g., in studies of muscle nerve sympathetic activity of humans (Wallin and Sundlof, 1979). Such sympathetic activity was correlated with plasma norepinephrine levels (Wallin et al., 1981). Although plasma norepinephrine is elevated in elderly subjects during a mental stress test, plasma epinephrine is not; this suggests a specific hyperactivity of postganglionic neurons (Barnes et al., 1982).

In summary, in elderly humans, plasma norepinephrine appears to rise more readily in response to most stimuli, appears to require longer periods to return to baseline, and may well exhibit higher baseline levels.

Little is known about age effects on plasma norepinephrine in rodents. A few studies in rats, which utilized indwelling catheters to sample blood, did not obtain consistent data on subsequent stress-induced increases in plasma norepinephrine as a function of age. One reason for discrepant results could be differences among studies in the interval between catheter implantation and testing, and possible carryover effects from the stress of surgery. For example, aged rats had greater resting levels of plasma norepinephrine than did the young or middle aged, and greater increases of both norepinephrine and epinephrine to immobilization stress in comparison to middle-aged, but not to young rats (Chiueh et al., 1980); however, heart rate and blood pressure increased less in aged and young rats than in the middle aged. This pattern resembles that in aging humans, as we will indicate. On the other hand, in another study foot shock-induced elevations of plasma norepinephrine and epinephrine were diminished in aged rats compared with the young; baseline measures did not differ with age (McCarty, 1981).

In contrast to the trend for increased sympathetic activity in human aging, a variety of sympathetic end organ responses appear to be reduced with age. This observation suggests that reduced tissue responsiveness to norepinephrine may occur during aging. Hemodynamic and cardiovascular responses to stimuli such as tilting, standing, or exercise, and the increase in heart rate are reduced with aging in humans (see Chapters 15 and 30). However, not all sympathetic end organ responses are decreased with age. Basal blood pressure tends to increase with age, as does the reactive elevation of blood pressure to the stimuli already noted (Rowe and Troen, 1980). However, it is possible that altered tissue responsiveness was not a factor in the latter studies, since the greater release of norepinephrine with age might have produced the increase in response. Complex interactions could also occur between elevated plasma norepinephrine and the sensitivity of presynaptic adrenergic receptors which influence release of catecholamines and myocardial responses (Langer, 1979).

The age-related decline in cardiac responsiveness to adrenergic stimulation seems to be a primary phenomenon, rather than a secondary adaptation to such factors as peripheral resistance or a consequence of increased vagal tone. The heart rate increase induced

by infusion of adrenergic agonists is consistently reduced with age in animals and humans (Lakatta et al., 1975; Vestal et al., 1979); similar results are obtained in studies of dogs given parasympathetic blockers (Yin et al., 1979). These findings further suggest that decreased cardiac responsiveness with age is due to a primary decrease in sensitivity to adrenergic stimulation. The reduced myocardial content of norepinephrine in old rats could also be a factor (see Chapter 15).

Another physiological parameter showing a reduced response to adrenergic inputs is dark-adapted pupillary size, which appears to be decreased with age in humans (reviewed in Halter and Pfeifer, 1982).

One possible explanation for decreased tissue responsiveness is decreased receptor density. However, the evidence concerning age effects on beta-adrenergic receptor decline is not clear-cut. Some have reported an age-dependent decrease in beta-receptor density in human systems (Schoken and Roth, 1977), which others have found less evidence for changes with age (Vestal et al., 1979; Guarnieri et al., 1980). In aging rats, beta-adrenergic receptor density was reduced in adipocytes (Guidicelli and Pequery, 1978) and cerebellum (Greenberg and Weiss, 1978). Although beta receptors did not decrease with age in lung, a reduced binding affinity at the beta receptor was reported (Scarpace and Abrass, 1983), which might account for reduced adenylate cyclase stimulation by adrenergic agonists. In general, most age-correlated changes are observed in the density of binding sites, rather than in the strength or stereospecificity of binding by various ligands (Roth and Hess, 1982). The decreased tissue responsiveness to adrenergic agents may also depend upon postreceptor cellular mechanisms (Lakatta, 1980).

The causes of increased sympathetic activity with age are not yet clear. It has been hypothesized that a decline in baroreceptor sensitivity, perhaps due to altered vascular wall properties, could cause enhanced sympathetic activity (Rowe and Troen, 1980). Both age and hypertension appear to interact in the reduction of baroreceptor sensitivity associated with postprandial hypotension (Lipsitz et al., 1982). Other factors, including those more directly dependent on nerve cell function, could also contribute to enhanced norepinephrine release.

Parasympathetic Nervous System

Although less is known about the parasympathetic nervous system as a function of age, age-correlated impairments are also reported in this system. In humans, the increase in heart rate following atropine was reduced with age (Dauchot and Gravenstein, 1971). Similarly, in rats, electrical stimulation of the vagus was less effective in inhibiting heart rate with age, and 2-year-old animals may not respond at all (Frolkis et al., 1973; Kelliher and Conahan, 1980). Moreover, the heart rate decrease to methacholine was diminished, whereas the hypotensive response was not affected by age (Kelliher and Conahan, 1980). Thus, the response of the cardiac muscarinic receptor appears to decline with age, while vascular muscarinic receptors may not be substantially affected by age.

In summary, substantial alterations in autonomic function occur during aging in humans and laboratory animals. These changes are likely to play an important role in the decline of neural and endocrine control of peripheral physiological functions that occurs during aging.

THERMOREGULATION

Defects in thermoregulation commonly increase during aging (reviewed in Finch et al., 1969; Wollner and Spalding, 1978). The differential susceptibility of older humans to temperature extremes is well documented by their higher mortality during "heat waves" (Shattuck and Hilferty, 1932; Ellis, 1972; Ellis et al., 1976). Although less information is available for cold, the elderly are more susceptible to hypothermia during the winter (Wollner and Spalding, 1978). There is evidence for a subgroup of the elderly with particularly high risk for accidental hypothermia (Macmillan et al., 1967; Collins et al., 1977).

This age differential may result from diverse, independent factors related to age: cardiovascular and cerebrovascular disease; inadequate diet, clothing, and housing, which are often linked to poverty in the elderly; and age changes in physiologic responses such as shivering, piloerection, eccrine sweating, and vasomotor controls. Thus, age-related changes in thermoregulation are complex and multifactorial. The view that a multiplicity of age changes could contribute to altered thermoregulation is consistent with a recent concept of thermoregulation which proposes hierarchically arranged controls at different levels of the nervous system, rather than a single hypothalamic locus for thermoregulation (Satinoff, 1978). Some specific changes will be described.

Responses to Cold

The hypothermia during acute exposure to cold is probably not attributable to a single major cause. Age differences in acute responses to cold are well known in laboratory rodents; for example, 2-year-old animals have greater loss of core temperature (Finch et al., 1969; Huang et al., 1980) and a greater mortality (Finch et al., 1969). Impaired responses to acute cold exposure in old rodents include delayed induction of hepatic tyrosine aminotransferase (Finch et al., 1969) and smaller elevations of plasma TSH and thyroxine (Huang et al., 1980). The elevations of plasma corticosterone during cold were only slightly smaller during cold stress in old mice (Finch et al., 1969), whereas old rats had greater elevations of corticosterone which returned more slowly to baseline (Sapolsky et al., 1983a). A delayed induction of tyrosine aminotransferase in aging mice and rats during fasting (Adelman et al., 1978) may also relate to impaired thermoregulation. Defects in lipolysis, such as observed in aging rodents during other stresses (see Chapter 20), could also be a factor in the failure to maintain body temperature. In older humans, shivering is often observed to be less intense, despite greater loss of core temperature (Krag and Kountz, 1950; Collins et al., 1981a). A subgroup which had poor perceptions of changes in ambient temperature also had poorer thermoregulation (Collins et al., 1981b). It will be of much interest to learn how other aspects of neuroendocrine and autonomic regulation are impaired in this subgroup. Such global dysfunctions probably increase mortality risk (see Chapter 33).

Some age-correlated defects in thermoregulation can be experimentally manipulated. If rats are placed on a tryptophan-deficient diet when young and restored to a normal diet at middle age, then the body temperature recovery from cold stress is much more rapid than in *ad libitum* fed controls of the same age (Segall and Timiras, 1975); similar manipulations of reproductive aging have already been described.

Responses to Heat

The activities of sweat glands during controlled exposure to heat indicate significant age-correlated impairments. Older men (45–57 years) required twice as long in comparison with students (18–23 years) until the onset of sweating during moderate exercise at 38°C (Hellon and Lind, 1956). A more recent study of men and women described reduced sweating and an increased threshold for the onset of sweating; older women had the most striking impairments (Foster et al.,

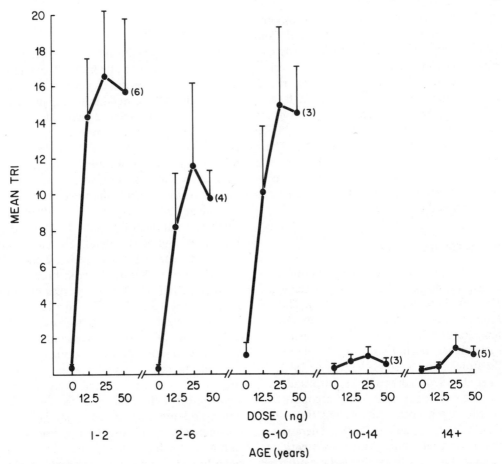

Figure 7. Effects of age in the febrile response of squirrel monkeys to varying doses of endotoxin administered to the lateral cerebral ventricle. Courtesy of James M. Lipton.

1976). The number of sweat glands is not reduced much if at all during aging according to one sample (Hellon and Lind, 1956). Further analysis of adnexal structures related to thermoregulation is needed.

Fever

The reduction of febrile responses with advanced age in humans is generally assumed (e.g., Wollner and Spalding, 1978; Petersdorf, 1980), but detailed accounts are lacking for age changes in fever during different, well-characterized diseased conditions. Recently, age-related impairments in fever induced by exogenous pyrogens (*Salmonella* endotoxins) were documented in rabbits (Lipton and Ticknor, 1979) and squirrel monkeys (Clark et al., 1980). Age-correlated differences were observed whether the pyrogens were given intravenously or injected directly into the cerebral ventricles (Figure 7). Moreover, in squirrel monkeys the fever was augmented by probenecid in the young, but not in those aged 10–14 years. These results clearly establish age changes in the febrile response and indicate age changes in central loci, presumably including the thermoregulatory centers of the hypothalamus.

CONCLUSIONS

In the seven years since the first edition of this *Handbook,* the neuroendocrinology of aging has become an established field. The complexity of physiological regulation remains great and is only dimly understood despite a century of major accomplishments; yet analysis of some aging phenomena involving the central and peripheral nervous system has already succeeded in identifying causal relationships. Many neuroendocrine changes in aging are now recognized as amenable to therapeutic approaches in clinical studies and to experimental manipulations with laboratory animals. Future research will define the developmental course of these interactions, by which age changes in various loci may reverberate and interact across the regulatory network of neural-endocrine systems.

REFERENCES

Adams, N. R. 1976. Pathological changes in the tissues of infertile ewes with clover disease. *J. Comp. Path.* 86: 29–35.

Adams, N. R. 1977. Morphological changes in the organs of ewes grazing on oestrogenic subterranean clover. *Res. Vet. Sci.* 22: 216–221.

Adelman, R. C., Britton, C. W., Rotenberg, S., Ceri, L., and Karoly, K. 1978. Endocrine regulation of enzyme activity in aging animals of different genotypes. *In,* D. Bergsma and D. E. Harrison (eds.), *Genetic Effects on Aging,* pp. 355–364. New York: Alan R. Liss.

Andres, R. and Tobin, J. D. 1977. Endocrine systems. *In,* C. E. Finch and L. Hayflick (eds.), *Handbook of the Biology of Aging,* pp. 357–378. New York: Van Nostrand Reinhold.

Aschheim, P. 1965. Resultats fournis per la greffe heterochrone des ovarie dans l'etude de la regulation hypothalamus-hypophyso-ovarienne de la ratte senile. *Gerontologia* 10: 65–75.

Aschheim, P. 1976. Aging in the hypothalamic-hypophyseal-ovarian axis in the rat. *In,* A. V. Everitt and J. A. Burgess (eds.), *Hypothalamus, Pituitary, and Aging,* pp. 376–418. Springfield, Ill.: Charles C. Thomas.

Bahr, J., Kao, L., and Nalbandov, A. V. 1974. The role of catecholamines and nerves in ovulation. *Biol. Repro.* 10: 273–290.

Balazs, A., Kovats, A., and Burg, M. 1962. Biochemical analysis of premortal involution processes in aphagous imagines. *Acta. Biol. Hung.* 13: 169–176.

Ball, M. J. 1977. Neural loss, neurofibrillary tangles and granulovascular degeneration in the hippocampus with aging and dementia: a quantitative study. *Acta Neuropath.* 37: 111–118.

Barnes, R. F., Raskind, M., Gumbrecht, G., and Halter, J. B. 1982. The effects of age on the plasma catecholamine response to mental stress in man. *J. Clin. Endocrinol. Metab.* 54: 64–69.

Bohus, B. 1975. The hippocampus and the pituitary-adrenal system hormones. *In,* R. L. Issacson and K. H. Pribram (eds.), *The Hippocampus,* pp. 323–354. New York: Plenum Press.

Brawer, J. R., Naftolin, F., Martin, J., and Sonnenschein, C. 1978. Effects of a single injection of estradiol valerate on the hypothalamic arcuate nucleus and on reproductive function in the female rat. *Endocrinology* 103: 501–512.

Brawer, J. R., Schipper, H., and Naftolin, F. 1980. Ovary-dependent degeneration in the hypothalamic arcuate nucleus. *Endocrinology* 107: 274–279.

Brawer, J. R. and Sonnenschein, C. 1975. Cytopathological effects of estradiol on the arcuate nucleus of the female rat. A possible mechanism for pituitary tumorigenesis. *Am. J. Anat.* 144: 57–87.

Bremner, W. J., Vitiello, M., and Prinz, P. N. 1983. The loss of circadian rhythmicity in blood testosterone with aging in normal men. *J. Clin. Endocrinol. and Metab.* 56: 1278–1281.

Britton, G. W., Rotenberg, S., and Adelman, R. C. 1975. Impaired regulation of corticosterone levels during fasting in aging rats. *Biochem. Biophys. Res. Commun.* 64: 184–188.

Brown-Grant, K. 1975. On "critical periods" during the postnatal development of the rat. International Symposium on Sexual Endocrinology of the Perinatal Period. *INSERM* 32: 357–376.

Chen, C. L. and Meites, J. 1970. Effect of estrogen and progesterone on serum and pituitary prolactin levels in ovariectomized rats. *Endocrinology* 86: 503–505.

Chen, H. J. 1981. Effects of aging on luteinizing hormone release in different physiological states of the female golden hamster. *Neurobiology of Aging* 2: 215–219.

Chiueh, C. C., Nespor, S. M., and Rapoport, S. I. 1980. Cardiovascular, sympathetic and adrenal cortical responsiveness of aged Fischer-344 rats to stress. *Neurobiology of Aging* 1: 157–164.

Christensen, N. J. 1982. Sympathetic nervous activity and age. *Eur. J. Clin Invest.* 12: 91–92.

Clark, S. M., Gean, J. T., and Lipton, J. M., 1980. Reduced febrile responses to peripheral and central administration of pyrogen in aged squirrel monkeys. *Neurobiology of Aging* 1: 175–180.

Clayton, C. J., Schechter. J., and Finch, C. E., 1984. The development of mammotroph adenomas in pituitaries of aging female C57BL/6J mice *Exp. Gerontol,* in press.

Clemens, J. A., Fuller, R. W., and Owen, N. V. 1978. Some neuroendocrine aspects of aging. *In,* C. E. Finch, D. E. Potter, and A. D. Kenny (eds.), *Parkinson's Disease—II. Aging and Neuroendocrine Relationships, Adv. in Exp. Biol. Med.* 113: 77–100. Plenum, New York.

Collins, K. J., Dore, C., Exton-Smith, A. N., Fox, R. H., MacDonald, I. C., and Woodward, P. M. 1977. Accidental hypothermia and impaired temperature homeostasis in the elderly. *Brit. Med. J.* 1: 353–356.

Collins, K. J., Easton, J. C., and Exton- Smith, A. N. 1981a. Shivering thermogenesis and vasomotor responses with convective cooling in the elderly. *J. Physiology* 32: 76.

Collins, K. J., Exton-Smith, A. N., and Dore, C. 1981b. Urban hypothermia: preferred temperature and thermal perception in old age. *Brit. Med. J.* 282: 175–177.

Collins, K. J., Exton-Smith, A. N., James, M. H., and Oiver, D. J. 1980. Functional changes in autonomic nervous responses with aging. *Age and Aging* 9: 17–24.

Cooper, R. L. and Linnoila, M. 1980. Effects of centrally and systemically administered L-tyrosine and L-leucine on ovarian function in the old rat. *Gerontology* 26: 270–275.

Cooper, R. L., Roberts. B., Rogers, D. C., Seay, S. G., and Conn, P. M. 1984 Endocrine status *versus* chronologic age as predictors of altered luteinizing hormone secretion in the aging rat. *Endocrinology* 114: 391–396.

Cooper, R. L. and Walker, R. F. 1979. Potential therapeutic consequence of age-dependent changes in brain physiology. *In,* W. Meer-Ruge and H. von Hahn (eds.), *Experimental and Clinical Aspects of Pharmacological Intervention of the CNS Aging Process., Interdiscipl. Topics in Gerontol.* 15: 54–72.

Coquelin, A. and Desjardins, C. 1982. Luteinizing hormone and testosterone secretion in young and old male mice. *Am. J. Physiol.* 243: E257–263.

Costoff, A. and Mahesh, V. B. 1975. Primordial follicles with normal oocytes in the ovaries of postmenopausal women. *J. Am. Geriatr. Soc.* 23: 193–196.

Dafny, M., Phillips, M. I., Taylor, A. N., and Gilman, S. 1973. Dose-effects of cortisol in single unit activity in hypothalamus, reticular formation and hippocampus of freely behaving rats correlated with plasma steroid levels. *Brain Res.* 59: 257–272.

Dauchot, P. and Gravenstein, J. S. 1971. Effects of atropine on the electrocardiogram in different age groups. *Clin. Pharmacol. Ther.* 12: 274–280.

Davies, I. and Fotheringham, A. P. 1980. The influence of age on the response of the supraoptic nucleus of the hypothalamus-neurohypophyseal system to physiological stress. II. Quantitative morphology. *Mech. Age. Dev.* 15: 367–378.

Demarest, K. T., Moore, K. E., and Riegle, G. D. 1982. Dopaminergic neuronal function, anterior pituitary dopamine content and serum concentrations of prolactin, luteinizing hormone, and progesterone in the aged female rat. *Brain Res.* 247: 347–354.

Demarest, K. T., Riegle G. D., and Moore, K. E. 1980. Characteristics of dopaminergic neurons in the aged male rat. *Neuroendocrinology* 31: 222–227.

Desjardins, C., 1981. Endocrine signaling and male reproduction. *Biol. Repro.* 24: 1–21.

Dilman, V. M. 1981. *The Law of Deviation of Homeostasis and Diseases of Aging.* Boston: John Wright.

Dilman, V. M. and Anisimov, V. N. 1979. Hypothalamic mechanisms of aging and of specific age pathology. I. sensitivity threshold of hypothalamus-pituitary complex to homeostatic stimuli in the reproductive system. *Exp. Geront.* 14: 161–174.

Dorsa, D. M. and Bottemiller 1982. Age- related changes of vasopressin content of microdissected areas of the rat form. *Brain Res.* 242: 151–156.

Duchen, L. W. and Schurr, P. H., 1976. The pathology of the pituitary gland in old age. *In,* A. V. Everitt and J. A. Burgess (eds.), *Hypothalamus, Pituitary, and Aging,* pp. 137–156. Springfield, Ill.: Charles C. Thomas.

Ehrhardt, A. A. and Meyer-Bahlburg, H. F. L. 1981. Effects of prenatal sex hormones on gender-related behavior. *Science* 211: 1312–1318.

Elias, K. A., Huffman, L. J., and Blake, C. A. 1979. Age of ovariectomy affects subsequent plasma LH responses in old age rats. *61st Annual Meeting of the Endocrine Society,* 106.

Ellis, F. P. 1972. Mortality from heat illness and heat-aggravated illness in the United States. *Environmental Res.* 5: 1–58.

Ellis, F. P., Exton-Smith, A. N., Foster, K. G., and Weiner, J. S. 1976. Eccrine sweating and mortality during heat waves in very young and very old persons. *Israel J. Med. Sci.* 12: 815–817.

Esler, M., Skews, H., Leonard, P., Jackman, G., Bobik, A., and Korner P. 1981. Age-dependence of noradrenaline kinetics in normal subjects. *Clin. Sci.* 60: 217–219.

Estes, K. S., and Simkins, J. W. 1982. Resumption of pulsatile luteinizing hormone release after beta-adrenergic stimulation in aging constant estrus rats. *Endocrinology* 111: 1778–1784.

Evans, W. F., Cronin, M. J., and Thorner, M. O. 1982. Hypogonadism in hyperprolactinemia: proposed mechanisms. *In,* W. F. Ganong and L. Martini (eds.), *Frontiers in Neuroendocrinology,* pp. 77–122. New York: Raven Press.

Everett, J. W. 1980. Reinstatement of estrous cycles in middle-aged persistent estrous rats: importance of circulating prolactin and the resulting facilitative action of progesterone. *Endocrinology* 106: 1691–1696.

Everitt, A. V. 1973. The hypothalamic- pituitary control of aging and age-related pathology. *Exp. Gerontol.* 8: 265–277.

Feldman, S. and Conforti, N. 1980. Participation of the dorsal hippocampus in the glucocorticoid feedback effect on adrenocortical activity. *Neuroendocrinology* 30: 52–55.

Felicio, L. S., Nelson, J. F., and Finch, C. E. 1980. Spontaneous pituitary tumorigenesis and plasma estradiol in aging female C57BL/6J mice. *Exp. Gerontol.* 115: 139–142.

Felicio, L. S., Nelson J. F., Gosden, R. G., and Finch, C. E. 1983. Longterm ovariectomy delays the loss of ovulating cycling potential in aging mice. *Proc. Nat. Acad. Sci (U.S.)* 80: 6076–6080.

Finch, C. E. 1973. Catecholamine metabolism in the brains of aging, male mice. *Brain Res.* 52: 261–276.

Finch, C. E. 1976. The regulation of physiological changes during mammalian aging. *Q. Rev. Biol.* 51: 49–83.

Finch, C. E. 1978. Reproductive senescence in rodents: factors in the decline of fertility and loss of regular estrous cycles. *In,* E. L. Schneider (ed.), *Aging and Reproduction,* pp. 193–212. New York: Raven Press.

Finch, C. E., Felicio, L. S., Flurkey, K., Gee, D. M., Mobbs, C., Nelson, J. F., and Osterburg, H. H. 1980. Studies in ovarian-hypothalamic-pituitary interactions during reproductive aging in C57BL/6J mice. *Peptides* 1: Suppl. 1, 163–176.

Finch, C. E., Foster, J. R., and Mirsky, A. E., 1969. Aging and the regulation of cell activities during exposure to cold. *J. Gen. Physiol.* 54: 690–712.

Finch, C. E., Jonec, V., Wisner, J. R., Jr., Sinha, Y. N., de Vellis, J. S., and Swerdloff, R. S. 1977. Hormone production by the pituitary and testes of male C57BL/6J mice during aging. *Endocrinology* 101: 1310–1318.

Finch, C. E., Marshall, J. F., and Randall, P. K. 1981. Aging and basal gangliar functions. *Ann. Rev. Gerontol. Geriatrics* 2: 49–87.

Findlay, T. 1949. Role of the neurohypophysis in the pathogenesis of hypertension and some allied disorders associated with aging. *Am. J. Med.* 7: 70–84.

Fink, G. 1979. Feedback actions of target hormones on hypothalamus with special references to gonadal steroids. *Ann. Rev. Physiol.* 41: 571–585.

Flurkey, K., Gee, D. M., Sinha, Y. N., and Finch, C. E. 1982. Age effects on luteinizing hormone, progesterone, and prolactin in proestrous and acyclic C57BL/6J mice. *Biol. Repro.* 26: 835–846.

Foster, K. G., Ellis, F. P., Dore, C., Exton-Smith, A. N., and Wiener, J. J. 1976. Sweat responses in the aged. *Age and Aging* 5: 91–101.

Franks, S., McElhone J., Young, S. N., Kraulis, I., and Ruf, K. B. 1980. Factors determining the diurnal variation in progesterone-induced gonadotropin release in the ovariectomized rat. *Endocrinology* 107: 353–358.

Frolkis, V. V., Bezrukov, V. V., Duplenko, Y. K., Stachegoleua, I. V., Shevchuk, V. G., and Verkratsky, N. S. 1973. Acetylcholine metabolism and cholinergic regulation of functions in aging. *Gerontologia* 19: 45–57.

Frolkis, W. 1976. The hypothalamic mechanism of aging. *In,* A. V. Everitt and J. A. Burgess (eds.), *Hypothalamus, Pituitary, and Aging,* pp. 614–633. Springfield, Ill.: Charles C. Thomas.

Gee, D. M., Flurkey, K., and Finch, C. E. 1983. Aging and the regulation of luteinizing hormone in C57BL/6J mice: impaired elevations after ovariectomy and spontaneous elevations at advanced ages. *Biol. Repro.* 28: 598–607.

Giacobini E. 1982. Aging of autonomic synapses. *Adv. Cell. Neurobiol.,* 3: 173–214.

Gispen, W. H., de Wied, D. Schotman, P. 1971. Brain stem polysomes and avoidance performance of hypophysectomized rats subjected to peptide treatment *Brain Res.,* 31: 341–351.

Gispen, W. H., van Ree, J. M., and de Wied, D. 1977. Lipotropin and the central nervous system. *Int. Rev. Neurobiol.* 20: 209–250.

Gosden, R. G., Liang, S. C., Felicio, L. S., Nelson, J. F., and Finch, C. E. 1983. Imminent oocyte exhaustion of reduced follicular recruitment mark the transition to acyclicity in aging C57BL/6J mice. *Biol. Repro.* 28: 255–260.

Grandison, L. J., Hodson, C. A., Chen, H. T., Advis, J., Simpkins, J., and Meites, J. 1977. Inhibition by prolactin of post-castration rise in LH. *Neuroendocrinology* 23: 312–322.

Greenberg, L. H. and Weiss, B. 1978. Beta-adrenergic receptors in aged rat brain: reduced number and capacity of pineal glands to develop supersensitivity. *Science* 201: 61–63.

Grossman, C. J., Nathan, P., Taylor, B. B., and Sholiton, L. J. 1979b. Rat thymic dihydrotestosterone receptor: preparation, location, and physiochemical properties. *Steroids* 34: 539–553.

Grossman, C. J., Sholiton, L. J., Blaha, G. G., and Nathan, P. 1979a. Rat thymic estrogen receptor. II. Physiological properties. *J. Steroid Biochem.* 11: 1241–1246.

Grossman, C. J., Sholiton, L. J., and Roselle, G. A. 1982. Estradiol regulation of thymic lymphocyte function in the rat: mediation by serum thymic factors. *J. Steroid Biochem.* 16: 683–690.

Guarnieri, T., Filburn, C., Zitnik, G., Roth, G., and Lakatta, E. 1980. Contractile and biochemical correlates of beta-adrenergic stimulation of aged heart. *Am. J. Physiol.* 230: H501–H508.

Gudelsky, G. A., Nansel, D. D., and Porter, J. C. 1981. Dopamine control of prolactin secretion in the aging male rat. *Brain Res.* 204: 446–450.

Gudelsky, G. A. and Porter, J. C. 1980. Release of dopamine from tuberoinfundibular neurons into pituitary stalk blood after prolactin or haloperidol administration. *Endocrinology* 106: 526–529.

Guidicelli, Y. and Pequery, R. 1978. Beta-adrenergic receptors and catecholamine sensitive adenylate cyclase in rat fat cell membranes: influence of growth, cell size and aging. *Eur. J. Biochem.* 90: 413–419.

Haji, M., Kato, K., Nawata, H., and Ibayashi, H. 1981. Age-related changes in the concentrations of cytosol receptors for sex steroid hormones in the hypothalamus and pituitary gland of the rat. *Brain Res.* 204: 373–386.

Halter, J. B. and Pfeifer, M. A. 1982. Aging and autonomic nervous system function in man. *In,* M. E. Reff and E. L. Schneider (eds.), *Biological Markers of Aging,* pp. 168–176. NIH Publ. No. 82-2221, Washington, D. C.

Harlan, R. E. and Gorski, R. A. 1977. Correlations between ovarian sensitivity, vaginal cyclicity and luteinizing hormone and prolactin secretion in lightly androgenized rats. *Endocrinology* 101: 750–759.

Harlan, R. E. and Gorski, R. A. 1978. Effects of postpubertal ovarian steroids on reproductive function and sexual differentiation of lightly androgenized rats. *Endocrinology* 102: 1716–1724.

Hattori, M. and Brandon, M. R. 1979. Thymus and the endocrine system: ovarian dysgenesis in neonatally thymectomized rats. *J. Endocrinol.* 83: 101–111.

Hellon, R. F. and Lind, A. R. 1956. Observations on the activity of sweat glands with special reference to the influence of aging. *J. Physiol.* 133: 132–144.

Hervonen A., Vaalasti, A., Partanen, M., Kanerva, L., and Hervonen, H. 1978. Effects of aging in the histochemically demonstratable catecholamines and acetylcholinesterase of human sympathetic ganglia. *J. Neurocytology* 7: 11–23.

Hess, G. D. and Riegle, G. D. 1970. Adrenocortical responsiveness to stress and ACTH in aging rats. *J. Gerontol.* 25: 354–358.

Huang, H. H., Marshall, S., and Meites, J. 1976. Capacity of old versus young female rats to secrete LH, FSH, and prolactin. *Biol. Reprod.* 14: 538–543.

Huang, H. H., Steger, R. W., Bruni, J., and Meites, J. 1978. Patterns of sex steroid and gonadotropin secretion in aging female rats. *Endocrinology* 103: 1855–1859.

Huang, H. H., Steger, R. W., and Meites, J. 1980. Capacity of old versus young male rats to release thyrotropin (TSH), thyroxine (T_4) and triiodo thyronine (T_3) in response to different stimuli. *Exp. Aging Res.* 6: 3–12.

Ingram, D, K., Spangler, E. L., and Vincent, G. P. 1983. Behavioral comparison of aged virgin and retired breeder mice. *Exp. Aging Res.,* 9: 111–113.

Japha J. L., Eder, T. J., and Goldsmith, E. D. 1976. Calcified inclusions in the superficial pineal gland of the Mongolian gerbil, *Meriones unguiculatus. Acta Anat.* 95: 553–544.

Jensen, H. K. and Blichert[2] Toft, M. 1971. Serum corticotrophin, plasma cortisol, and urinary excretion of 17-ketogenic steroids in the elderly (age group 66–94 years). *Acta Endocrinol.* 66: 25–34.

Jerne, N. 1976. The immune system: a web of V-domains. *The Harvey Lectures,* series 70, 93–110.

Karpas, A. E., Bremner, W. J., Clifton, D. K., Steiner, R. A., and Dorsa, D. M. 1983. Diminished luteinizing hormone pulse frequency and amplitude with aging in the male rat. *Endocrinology* 112: 788–792.

Kawakami, M., Yoshioka, E., Konda, N., Arita, J., and Visessuvan, S. 1978. Data in the sites of stimulatory feedback action of gonadal steroids indispensable for luteinizing hormone release in the rat. *Endocrinology* 102: 791–798.

Kawashima, S. 1960. Influence of continued injections of sex steroids on the estrous cycle in the adult rat. *Annot. Zool. Japon.* 33: 226–232.

Kelliher, G. J. and Conahan, S. T. 1980. Changes in vagal activity and response to muscarinic receptor agonists with age. *J. Gerontol.* 35: 842–849.

Klug, T. L. and Adelman, R. 1979. Altered hypothalamic-pituitary regulation of thyrotropin in male rats during aging. *Endocrinology* 104: 1136–1142.

Knobil, E. 1980. The neuroendocrine control of the menstrual cycle. *Rec. Prog. Horm. Res.* 36: 53–88.

Knobil, E. 1981. Patterns of hypophysiotropic signals and gonadotrophin secretion in the rhesus monkey. *Biol. Repro.* 24: 44–49.

Krag, C. L. and Kountz, W. B. 1950. Stability of body function in the aged. I. Effect of exposure of the body to cold. *J. Gerontol.* 5: 227–235.

Lakatta, E. G. 1980. Age-related alterations in the cardiovascular response to adrenergic mediated stress. *Fed. Proc.* 39: 3173–3177.

Lakatta, E. G., Gerstenblith, G., Angell, C. S., Shock, N. W., and Weisfeldt, M. L. 1975. Diminished inotropic response of aged myocardium to catecholamines. *Circ. Res.* 36: 262–269.

Landfield, P. W. 1978. An endocrine hypothesis of brain aging and studies on brain-endocrine correlations and monosynaptic neurophysiology during aging. *In*, C. E. Finch (eds.), *Parkinson's Disease, Vol. 2: Aging and Neuroendocrine Relationships,* pp. 179–199. New York: Plenum Press.

Landfield, P. W. 1981. Adrenocortical hypotheses of brain and somatic aging. *In*, R. T. Schimke. (ed.), *Biological Mechanisms of Aging, Conference Proceedings,* pp. 658–672. NIH Publ. No. 81.

Landfield, P. W. 1982. Measurement of brain aging: conceptual issues and neurobiological indices. *In*, R. Adelman and G. Roth. (eds.), *Endocrine and Neuroendocrine Mechanisms of Aging,* pp. 183–207. Boca Raton, Fla: CRC Press.

Landfield, P. W., Baskin, R. K., and Pitler, T. A. 1981. Brain aging correlates: retardation by hormonal-pharmacological treatments. *Science* 214: 581–584.

Landfield, P. W., Lindsey, J. D., and Lynch, G. 1978a. Apparent acceleration of brain aging pathology by prolonged administration of glucocorticoids. *Soc. Neurosci. Abstr.* 4: 350.

Landfield, P. W., Sundberg, D. K., Smith, M. S., Eldridge, J. C., and Morris, M. 1980. Mammalian aging: theoretical implications of changes in brain and endocrine systems during mid and late life. *Peptides* 1 (Suppl. 1): 185–196.

Landfield, P. W., Waymire, J. L., and Lynch, G. 1978b. Hippocampal aging and adrenocorticoids: quantitative correlations. *Science* 202: 1098–1102.

Landfield, P. W., Wurtz, G., Lindsey, J. D., and Lynch, G. 1979. Long-term adrenalectomy reduces some morphological correlates of brain aging. *Soc. Neurosci. Abstr.* 5: 20.

Langer, S. Z. 1979. Presynaptic receptors and the regulation of neurotransmitter release in the peripheral and central nervous system: physiological and pharmacologic significance. *In*, E. Usdin, I. J. Kopin, and J. Barchas (eds.), *Catecholamines: Basic and Clinical Frontiers,* Vol. 1, pp. 387–398. New York: Pergamon Press.

Lanier, L. P., Van Hartesveldt, C., Weiss, B. J., and Isaacson, R. L. 1975. Effects of differential hippocampal damage upon rhythmic and stress-induced corticosterone secretion in the rat. *Neuroendocrinology* 18: 154–160.

Latham, K. and Finch, C. E. 1976. Hepatic glucocorticoid binders in mature and senescent C57BL/6J male mice. *Endocrinology* 98: 1434–1443.

Lewis, B. K. and Wexler, B. C. 1974. Serum insulin changes in male rats associated with age and reproductive activity. *J. Gerontol.* 20: 204–212.

Lipsitz, L., Wei, J., and Rowe, J. 1982. Postprandial hypotension in the elderly: a risk factor for meal-related syncope. *The Gerontologist* 22: 118 (abstract).

Lipton, J. M. and Ticknor, C. B. 1979. Influences of sex and age on febrile responses to peripheral and central administration of pyrogens in the rabbit. *J. Physiol.* 295: 263–272.

Lu, J. K. H., Gilman, D. P., Meldrum, D. R., Judd, H. L., and Sawyer, C. H. 1981. Relationship between circulating estrogens and the central mechanisms by which ovarian steroids stimulates luteinizing hormone secretion in aged and young female rats. *Endocrinology* 108: 836–841.

Lu, J. K. H., Hopper, B. R. Vargo, T. M., and Yen, S. S. C. 1979. Chronological changes in sex steroid, gonadotropin, and prolactin secretion in aging female rats displaying different reproductive states. *Biol. Reprod.* 21: 193–203.

MacLusky, N. J. and Naftolin, F. 1981. Sexual differentiation of the central nervous system. *Science* 211: 1294–1302.

MacMillan, A. L., Corbett, J. L., Johnson, R. H., Smith, A. C., Spalding J. M. K., and Wollner, L. 1967. Temperature regulation in the survivors of accidental hypothermia in the elderly. *Lancet* 2: 165–169.

Malamed, S. and Carsia, R. V. 1983. Aging of the rat adrenocortical cell response to ACTH and cyclic AMP *in vitro*. *J. Gerontol.* 38: 130–136.

McCarty, R. 1981. Aged rats: diminished sympathetic-adrenal medullary responses to acute stress. *Behav. Neural Biol.* 33: 204–212.

McEwen, B. S., Gerlach, J. L., and Micco, D. J. 1975. Putative glucocorticoid receptors in hippocampus and other regions of the rat brain. *In*, R. L. Issacson and K. H. Pribram (eds.), *The Hippocampus,* pp. 285–313. New York: Plenum Press.

Meites, J. 1982. Changes in neuroendocrine control of anterior pituitary function during aging. *Neuroendocrinology* 34: 151–156.

Michael, S. D. 1979. The role of the endocrine thymus in female reproduction. *Arthrit. Rheumat.* 22: 1241–1245.

Minaker, K. L., Rowe, J. W., Young, J. B., Sparrow, D., Pallotta, J. A., and Landsberg, L. 1982. Effect of age on insulin stimulation and sympathetic nervous system activity in man. *Metabolism* 31: 1181–1184.

Mobbs, C. V., Gee, D. M., and Finch, C. E. 1984a Reproductive senescence in C57BL/6J mice: Ovarian impairments and neuroendocrine impairments that are partially reversible and delayable by ovariectomy. *Endocrinology,* in press.

Mobbs, C. V., Flurkey K., Gee, D. M., Sinha, Y. N., and Finch, C. E. 1984b. Estradiol-induced adult anovulatory syndrome in female C57BL/6J mice: Age-like neuroendocrine, but not ovarian impairments. *Biol. Repro.* 30: 556–563.

Mosko, S. S., Erickson, G. F., and Moore, R. Y. 1980. Dampened circadian rhythms in reproductivity senescent female rats. *Behav. Neural Biology* 28: 1–14.

Murphy, H. M., Wideman, C. H., and Brown, T. S. 1979. Plasma corticosterone levels and ulcer formation in rats with hippocampal lesions. *Neuroendocrinology* 28: 123–130.

Nakagawa, K., Obara, T., and Tashiro, K. 1980. Pituitary hormones of prolactin-releasing activity in rats with primary estrogen-induced pituitary tumors. *Endocrinology* 106: 1033–1039.

Nass, T. E., LaPolt, P. S., Judd, H. L. and Lu, J. H. K. 1984. Alterations in ovarian steroid and gonadotrophin secretion preceding the cessation of regular estrous cycles in aging female rats. *J. Endocr.* 100: 43–50.

Nelson, J. F., Felicio, L. S., and Finch, C. E. 1980a. Ovarian hormones and the etiology of reproductive aging in mice. *In,* A. A. Deitz (ed.), *Aging—Its Chemistry,* pp. 64–81. Washington, D.C.: American Association of Clinical Chemists.

Nelson, J. F., Felicio, L. S., Osterburg, H. H., and Finch, C. E. 1981. Altered profiles of estradiol and progesterone associated with prolonged estrous cycles and persistent vaginal cornification in aging C57BL/6J mice. *Biol. Repro.* 24: 784–794.

Nelson, J. F., Felicio, L. S., Randall, P. K., Simms, C., and Finch, C. E. 1982. A longitudinal study of estrous cyclicity in aging C57BL/6J mice. I. Cycle frequency, length, and vaginal cytology. *Biol. Repro.* 27: 327–339.

Nelson, J., Felicio, L., Sinha, Y. N., and Finch, C. E. 1980b. An ovarian role in the spontaneous pituitary tumorigenesis and hyperprolactinemia of aging female mice. *The Gerontologist* 20: (part II) abstract, 171.

Nishizuka, Y. and Sakakura, T., 1971. Effect of combined removal of thymus and pituitary on postnatal ovarian follicular development in the mouse. *Endocrinology* 89: 902–903.

Norris, M. J. 1934. Contributions towards the study of insect fertility. III. Adult nutrition, fecundity and longevity in the genus *Ephestia* (Lepidoptera, Phycitidae). *Proc. Zool. Soc. Lond.* 1: 333–366.

Osterburg, H. H., Donahue, H. G., Severson, J. A., and Finch, C. E. 1981. Catecholamine levels and turnover during aging in brain regions of male C57BL/6J mice. *Brain Res.* 213: 337–352.

Parkening, T. A., Collins, T. J., and Smith, E. R. 1982 Plasma and pituitary concentrations of LH, FSH, and prolactin in aging C57BL/6 mice at various times in the estrous cycle *Neurobiology of Aging.* 3: 31–36.

Partanen, M., Hervonen, A., and Santer, R. M. 1980. The effect of aging on the SIF cells in the hypogastric (main pelvic) ganglion of the rat. *Histochemistry* 66: 99–112.

Pederson, E. B. and Christensen, N. J. 1975. Catecholamines in plasma and urine in patients with essential hypertension determined by double-isotope derivative techniques. *Acta Med. Scand.* 198: 373–377.

Peng, M.T., Chuong, C.F., and Peng, Y. M. 1977. Lordosis response of senile female rats. *Neuroendocrinology* 24: 317–324.

Peng, M-T. and Peng, Y-M. 1973. Changes in the uptake of tritiated estradiol in the hypothalamus and adenohypophysis of old female rats. *Fertil. Steril.* 24: 534–539.

Peters, L. L., Hoefer, M. T., and Ben-Jonathan, N. 1981. The posterior pituitary: regulation of anterior pituitary prolactin secretion. *Science* 213: 659–661.

Petersdorf, R. G. 1980. Disturbances of heat regulation, and chills and fever. *In,* K. J. Isselbacker, R. D. Adams, E. Braunwald, R. G. Petersdorf, and J. D. Wilson (eds.), *Harrison's Principles of Internal Medicine,* pp. 53–67. New York: McGraw-Hill.

Pfaff, D. W., Silva, M. J. A., and Weiss, J. M. 1971. Telemetered recording of hormonal effects on hippocampal neurons. *Science* 172: 394–395.

Piantanelli, L. and Fabris, N. 1978. Hypopituitary dwarf and athymic nude mice and the study of the relationships among thymus, hormones, and aging. *In,* D. Bergsma and D. E. Harrison (eds.), *Genetic Effects on Aging. Birth Defects. Original Article Series* 14 No. 1: 315–333.

Piantanelli, L., Muzzioli, M., and Fabris, N. 1980. Thymus-endocrine interactions during aging. *Akt. Gerontol.,* 10: 199–201.

Pierpaoli, W. and Besedovsky, H. O. 1975. Role of the thymus in programming of neuroendocrine functions. *Clin. Exp. Immunol.* 20: 323–338.

Pohl, C. R., Richardson, D. W., Hutchinson, J. S., Germak, J. A., and Knobil, E. 1983. Hypophysiotrophic signal frequency and the functioning of the pituitary-ovarian system in the rhesus monkey. *Endocrinology* 112: 2076–2080.

Prinz, P. N., Halter, J., Benedetti, C., and Raskind, M. 1979. Circadian variation of plasma catecholamines in young and old men: relation to rapid eye movement and slow wave sleep. *J. Clin. Endocrinol. Metab.* 49: 300–304.

Reaven, E. and Reaven, G. M. 1981. Structure and function changes in the endocrine pancreas of aging rats with reference to the modulating effects of exercise and caloric restriction. *J. Clin. Invest.* 68: 75–84.

Rebar, R. W., Miyake, A., Low, T. L. K., and Goldstein, A. L. 1981. Thymosin stimulates secretion of luteinizing hormone-releasing factor. *Science* 214: 669–671.

Reiter, R. J., Craft, C. M., Johnson, J. E., Jr., Kings, T. S., Richardson, B. A., Vaughan, G. M., and Vaughan, M. K. 1981. Age-associated reduction in nocturnal pineal melatonin levels in female rats. *Endocrinology* 109: 1295–1297.

Reiter, R. J., Johnson, L. Y., Steger, R. W., Richardson, B. A., and Petterborg, L. J. 1980b. Pineal biosynthetic activity and neuroendocrine physiology in the aging hamster and gerbil. *Peptides* 1 Supp. 1: 69–77.

Reiter, R. J., Richardson, B. A., Johnson, L. Y., Ferguson, B. N., and Dinh, D. T. 1980a. Pineal melatonin rhythm: reduction in aging Syrian hamsters. *Science* 210: 1372–1374.

Reymond, M. J. and Porter, J. C. 1981. Secretion of hypothalamic dopamine into pituitary stalk blood of aged female rats. *Brain Res. Bull.* 7: 69–73.

Riegle, G. D. and Hess, G. D. 1972. Chronic and acute

dexamethasone suppression of stress activation of the adrenal cortex in young and aged rats. *Neuroendocrinology* 9: 175–187.

Riegle, G. D. and Miller, A. E. 1978. Aging effects on the hypothalamic-hypophyseal-gonadal control system in the rat. *In,* E. L. Schneider (ed.), *The Aging Reproductive System,* pp. 159–192. New York: Raven Press.

Roberts, J. 1981. Autonomic changes with age. *In,* R. T. Schimke (ed.), *Biological Mechanisms in Aging,* pp. 629–640. NIH Publication 81-2194.

Robertson, G. L. 1980. Control of the posterior pituitary and antidiuretic hormone secretion. *Contrib. Nephrol.* 21: pp. 33–40.

Robertson, G. L. and Rowe, J. 1980. The effects of aging on neurohypophyseal function. *Peptides* 1 (Suppl. 1): 159–162.

Robertson, O. H. 1961. Prolongation of the lifespan of Kokanee salmon (O. *nerka kennerlyi*) by castration before beginning development. *Proc. Nat. Acad. Sci.* (*U.S.*) 47: pp. 609–621.

Robertson, O. H. and Wexler, B. C. 1960. Histological changes in the organs and tissues of migrating and spawning Pacific salmon (genus *Oncorhynchus*). *Endocrinology* 66: 222–239.

Robertson, O. H. and Wexler, B. C. 1962. Histological changes in the organs and tissues of senile castrated kokanee salmon (*Oncorhynchus nerka kennerlyi*). *Gen. Comp. Endocrinol. 2,* pp. 458–472.

Roth, G. S. and Hess, G. D. 1982. Changes in the mechanisms of hormone and neurotransmitter action during aging: current status of the role of receptor and post-receptor alterations. A review. *Mech. Age. Dev.* 20: 175–194.

Rowe, J. W. and Troen, B. R. 1980. Sympathetic nervous system and aging in man. *Endocr. Rev.* 1: 167–178.

Rubin, P. C., Scott, P., McLean, K., and Reid, J. L. 1982. Noradrenaline release and clearance in relation to age and blood pressure in man. *Eur. J. Clin. Invest.* 12: 121–125.

Saar, N. and Gordon, R. D. 1979. Variability of plasma catecholamine levels: age, duration of posture and time of day. *Br. J. Clin. Pharmacol.* 8: 353–358.

Sapolsky, R. M., Krey, L. C., and McEwen, B. S. 1983. The adrenocortical stress-response in the aged male rat: impairment of recovery from stress. *Exp. Gerontol.* 18: 55–64.

Sapolsky, R. M., Krey, L. C., McEwen, B. S., and Rainbow, T. C. 1984. Do vasopressin-related peptides induce hippocampal corticosterone receptors? Implications for aging. *J. Neuroscience* 4: 1479–1485.

Satinoff, E. 1978. Neural organization and evolution of thermoregulation in mammals. *Science* 201: 16–22.

Scarpace, P. J. and Abrass, I. B. 1983. Decreased beta-adrenergic agonist affinity and adenylate cyclase activity in senescent rat lung. *J. Gerontol.* 38: 143–147.

Schipper, H., Brawer, J. R., Nelson, J. F., Felicio, L. S., and Finch, C. E. 1981. The role of gonads in the histologic aging of the hypothalamic arcuate nucleus. *Biol. Repro.* 25: 413–419.

Segall, P. E. and Timiras, P. S. 1975. Age-related changes in thermoregulatory capacity of tryptophan-deficient rats. *Fed. Proc.* 34: 83–85.

Segall, P. E. and Timiras, P. S. 1976. Pathophysiologic findings after chronic tryptophan deficiency in rats: a model for delayed growth and aging. *Mech. Age. Dev.* 5: 109–124.

Segaloff, A. 1973. Inhibition by progesterone of radiation-E$_2$ induced mammary cancer in the rat. *Canc. Res.* 33: 1136–1137.

Shattuck, G. C. and Hilferty, M. M. 1932. Sunstroke and allied conditions in the United States. *Am. J. Trop. Med.* 12: 223–245.

Shimazu, T., 1967. Glycogen synthetase activity in the liver: regulation by autonomic nerves. *Science* 156: 1256–1257.

Shimazu, T. 1980. Changes in neural regulation of liver metabolism during aging. *In,* R. C. Adelman, J. Roberts, G. T. Baker, S. I. Baskin, and V. J. Cristofalo (eds.), *Neural Regulatory Mechanisms during Aging,* pp. 159–185. New York: Alan R. Liss.

Shimazu, T. and Amakawa, A., 1968. Regulation of glycogen metabolism in liver by the autonomic nervous system. II. Neural control of glycogenolytic enzymes. *Biochim. Biophys. Acta.* 165: 335–348.

Shimazu, T., Matsushita, H., and Ishikawa, K. 1978. Hypothalamic control of liver glycogen metabolism in adult and aged rats. *Brain Res.* 144: 343–352.

Shock, N. 1977. Systems integration. *In,* C. E. Finch and L. Hayflick (eds.), *Handbook of the Biology of Aging,* pp. 639–665. New York: Van Nostrand Reinhold.

Shocken, D. and Roth, G. 1977. Reduced beta-adrenergic receptor concentrations in aging man. *Nature* **267**: 856–858.

Simpkins, J. W., Mueller, G. P., Huang, H. H., and Meites, J. 1977. Evidence for depressed catecholamine and enhanced serotonin metabolism in aging male rats: possible relation to gonadotropin secretion. *Endocrinology* 100: 1672–1678.

Sladek, J. R., Khachaturian, H. Hoffman, G. E., and Scholer, J. 1980. Aging of central endocrine neurons and their aminergic afferents. *Peptides* 1 Suppl. 1: 141–157.

Sladek, C. D., McNeill, T. H., Gregg, C. M., Blair, M. L., and Baggs, R. B. 1981. Vasopressin and renin response to dehydration in aged rats. *Neurobiology of Aging* 2: 293–302.

Smith, W. A., Cooper, R. L., and Conn, M. P. 1982. Altered pituitary responsiveness to gonadotropin-releasing hormone in middle-aged rats with 4-day estrous cycles. *Endocrinology* 111: 1843–1848.

Solez, C. 1952. Aging and adrenal cortical hormones. *Geriatrics* 7: 241–245; 290–294.

Sonntag, W. E., Forman, L. J., Miki, N. Trapp, J. M., Gottschall, P. E., and Meites, J. 1982. L-DOPA restores amplitude of growth hormone pulses in old male rats to that observed in young male rats. *Neuroendocrinology* 34: 163-168.

Sonntag, W. E., Steger, R. W., Forman, L. J., and Meites, J. 1980. Decreased pulsatile release of growth hormone in old male rats. *Endocrinology* 107: 1875-1879.

Tang, F. and Phillips, J. G. 1978. Some age-related changes in pituitary-adrenal function in the male laboratory rat. *J. Gerontol.* 33: 377-382.

Timiras, P. S. 1978. Biological perspectives on aging. *Am. Sci.* 66: 605-613.

Tomlinson, B. E. and Henderson, G. 1976. Some quantitative cerebral findings in normal and demented old people. *In,* R. D. Terry and S. Gershon (eds.), *Neurobiology of Aging,* pp. 183-204. New York: Raven Press.

Trager, W. 1953. Function of the gut in absorption, excretion and intermediary metabolism. *In,* K. D. Roeder (ed.), *Insect Physiology,* pp. 350-386. New York: John Wiley & Sons.

Tucker, H. H. G., Lankford, H. V., Gardener, D. F., and Blackard, W. G. 1980. Persistent defect in regulation of prolactin secretion after pituitary tumor removal in women with the galactorrhea- amenorrhea syndrome. *J. Clin. Endocrinol. Metab.* 51: 968-971.

Turgeon, J. L. 1979. Estradiol-luteinizing hormone relationship during the proestrous gonadotropin surge. *Endocrinology* 105: 731-736.

Urban, I. and de Wied, D. 1976. Changes in excitability of the theta activity generating substrate by ACTH 4-10 in the rat. *Exp. Brain Res.* 24: 324-344.

Van Loon, G. R. 1978. A defect in catecholamine neurons in patients with prolactin-secreting pituitary adenoma. *Lancet* 2: 868-871.

Vestal, R. E., Wood, A. J. J., and Shand, D. G. 1979. Reduced beta-adrenoreceptor sensitivity in the elderly. *Clin. Pharmacol. Ther.,* **26,** 181-186.

vom Saal, F. S. and Bronson, F. H. 1980. Variation in the length of the estrous cycle in mice due to former intrauterine proximity to male fetuses. *Biol. Reprod.* 22: 777-780.

vom Saal, F. S., and Moyer, C. L. Prenatal effects on reproductive capacity during aging in female mice. *In prep.*

Walker, R. F. 1982. Reinstatement of LH surges by serotonin neuroleptics in aging, constant estrous rats. *Neurobiology of Aging,* **3,** 253-257.

Walker, R. F. 1983. Animal models for aging in the reproductive system. In, R. F. Walker and R. L. Cooper (eds.), *Experimental and Clinical Interventions in Aging,* pp. 67-84. New York: Marcel Dekker.

Walker, R. F., Cooper, R. L., and Timiras, P. S. 1980. Constant estrus: role of rostral hypothalamic monoamines in development of reproductive dysfunction in aging rats. *Endocrinology* 107: 249-255.

Wallin, B. G. and Sundlof, G., 1979. A quantitative study of muscle nerve sympathetic activity in resting normotensive and hypertensive subjects. *Hypertension* 1: 67-77.

Wallin, B. G., Sundlof, G. Eriksson, B. M., Dominiak,

P., Grobecker, H., and Lindblad, L. E. 1981. Plasma noradrenaline correlates to sympathetic muscle nerve activity in normotensive man. *Acta Physiol. Scand* 111: 69-73.

Wexler, B. C. 1976. Comparative aspects of hyperadrenocorticism and aging. *In,* A. F. Everitt and J. A. Burgess (eds.), *Hypothalamus Pituitary and Aging,* pp. 333-361. Springfield, Ill.: Charles C. Thomas.

Wexler, B. C. and Kittinger, G. W. 1965. Steroids produced *in vitro* by adrenal glands of normal and arteriosclerotic rats during and after drug-induced myocardial necrosis. *Circ. Res.* 16: 322-331.

Wilkes, M. M. and Yen, S. S. C. 1981. Attenuation during aging of the post-ovariectomy rise in median eminence catecholamines. *Neuroendocrinology* 33: 144-147.

Wilson, M. M., Greer, S. E., Greer, M. A., and Roberts, L. 1980. Hippocampal inhibition of pituitary-adrenocortical function in female rats. *Brain Res.* 197: 433-441.

Wise, P. M. 1982. Norepinephrine and dopamine activity in microdissected brain areas of the middle-aged and young rat on proestrus. *Biol. Reprod.* 27: 562-574.

Wise, P. M. 1983. Aging of the female reproductive system. *Rev. Biol. Res. in Aging* 1: 195-222.

Wise, P. M. and Camp, C. 1984. Changes in concentrations of estradiol nuclear receptors in the preoptic area, medial basal hypothalamus, amygdala, and pituitary of middle-aged and old cycling rats. *Endocrinology* 114: 92-98.

Wise, P. M. and Ratner, A. 1980. LHRH-induced LH and FSH responses in the aged female rat. *J. Gerontology* 35: 506-511.

Wisniewski, H. M. and Terry, R. D. 1973. Morphology of the aging brain, human and animal. *In,* D. M. Ford (ed.), *Progress in Brain Research,* Vol. 40, pp. 167-186. Amsterdam: Elsevier.

Wodinsky, J. 1977. Hormonal inhibition of feeding and death in *Octopus:* control by optic gland secretion. *Science* 198: 948-951.

Wollner, L. and Spalding, J. M. K. 1978. The autonomic nervous system. *In,* J. C. Brocklehurst (ed.), *Textbook of Geriatric Medicine and Gerontology,* pp. 245-267. Edinburgh: Livingstone.

Yamaji, T., Shimamoto, K., Ishibashi, M., Kosaka, K., and Orimo, H. 1976. Effect of age and sex on circulating and pituitary prolactin levels in humans. *Acta. Endocrinol.* 83: 711-719.

Yin, F. C. P., Spurgeon, H. A., Greene, H. L., Lakatta, E. G., and Weisfeldt, M. L. 1979. Age-associated decrease in heart rate response to isoproterenol in dogs. *Mech. Age. Dev.* 10: 17-25.

Young, J. B., Rowe, J. W., Pallotta, J. A., Sparrow, D., and Landsberg, L. 1980. Enhanced plasma norepinephrine response to upright posture and oral glucose administration in elderly human subjects. *Metabolism* 29: 532-539.

Ziegler, M. G., Lake, C. R., and Kopin, I. J. 1976. Plasma noradrenaline increases with age. *Nature* 261: 333-334.

22
CHANGES IN STRUCTURE AND ENERGY METABOLISM OF THE AGING BRAIN

Ranjan Duara
Edythe D. London
Stanley I. Rapoport
Laboratory of Neurosciences
National Institute on Aging

INTRODUCTION

The brain is remarkably heterogeneous, both morphologically and functionally, and a discrete disorder involving only a small part of the brain may produce substantial disturbances. Structure and function are closely intertwined and are best understood when examined in reference to each other. This applies to studies of normal brain aging as much as it does to investigations of pathophysiological processes. This chapter reviews alterations in morphology and metabolism of the brain that occur during the aging process in animals and man.

MORPHOLOGY OF THE AGING BRAIN

Studies of morphological changes in the aging brain are fraught with difficulties. Some of the greatest problems relate to methods of fixation, the time between death and processing of tissue, and categorization of subjects. Doubts about accuracy and validity of results arise also because of the enormous complexity of the brain compared to other organs.

Brain Weight and Volume

Brain weight decreases with advancing age in man, according to many reports. Reported decrements range from 6.6 percent of the brain weight between 20 and 80 years of age (Boyd, 1860) to 11 percent between early adulthood and the tenth decade (Appel and Appel, 1942). The decrease may be linear with age (Appel and Appel, 1942; Pearl, 1905; Peress et al., 1973). In one extensive study, the reduction in brain weight between the ages of 40–50 years and 86+ years was about 10 percent of the peak brain weight at 20 years (Dekaban and Sodowsky, 1978). Nevertheless, Tomlinson (1972) found no significant decrease in brain weight of older subjects who were mentally normal prior to death.

In view of the reported correlation between body weight and brain weight (Dekaban and Sadowsky, 1978), Corsellis (1976) suggested that because the mean body weight of man has increased during the past century, cross-sectional studies show a spurious decline in brain weight with advancing age. Atrophy of gyri and widening of sulci nevertheless are apparent in the senescent human brain (Terry, 1980) although these changes may not be sufficient in intellectually normal elderly individuals to significantly decrease brain weight.

An age-related decline in brain weight has not been observed in rats; in fact, many studies show brain weight to increase (Brizzee et al., 1968; Samorajski et al., 1971). The brains of aged dogs (Wiśniewski et al., 1970) and aged monkeys (Wiśniewski et al., 1973), however, are atrophic, frequently showing neuropathologic changes closer to those seen in man than in rats (Von Braünmuhl, 1956; Ostewska, 1966; Wiśniewski et al., 1970, 1973; Pauli and Luginbahl, 1971; Mervis, 1978).

Brain volume in man usually is assessed by measuring ventricular and sulcal dimensions in autopsy specimens and, more recently, by assessing intracranial fluid volume with computed tomography (CT) scans of the brain. An increase in ventricular size with age was reported (Himwich and Himwich, 1957), as was an increase in sulcal size, particularly in the frontal lobes (Bondareff, 1959), and a widening of cortical fissures and dilation of anterior horns of the lateral ventricles with advanced age (Riggs and Wahal, 1960). However, Tomlinson et al. (1968) found no significant cerebral atrophy in nondemented elderly individuals.

Corsellis (1976) estimated gray matter and white matter volumes by means of a computerized analysis of serial sagittal slices of cerebral hemispheres from 91 men and women, and found a decline of mean hemisphere volume with increasing age. For men, the decline was 3.5 percent per decade, and for women, 2 percent per decade. There were also age-related changes in the ratio of gray matter to white matter, which was 1.28 at 20 years, fell to 1.13 at 50 years, and then increased to 1.55 at 100 years of age. Terry (1980) suggested that this temporal pattern resulted from a rapid loss of neurons after the age of 50, with resultant degeneration of heavily myelinated axons and a greater overall loss of white matter as compared to gray matter. Hubbard and Anderson (1981) showed a significant age-related increase in cerebral ventricular volume, which accelerated after 60–70 years. The mental state of the individuals was not reported.

CT scan findings show an increase in ventricular volume with age (Jacoby et al., 1980; Roberts and Caird, 1976). Zatz et al. (1982) used CT to examine 123 normal men and women between the ages of 23 and 88 years. The intracranial fluid volume increased with age, whereas brain volume decreased. The rate of increase accelerated after 60 years. Similar observations were made by Barron et al. (1976).

In summary, brain weight and volume probably decline linearly with increasing age in an average human population, where perhaps 15–35 percent of those older than 65 years have some form of mental disorder (Roth, 1980). However, in carefully screened, mentally normal older individuals, such declines may not be statistically significant. In rats, no decline or increase in brain weight is seen with aging, whereas senescent dogs and monkeys demonstrate cerebral atrophy.

Cell Counts

Various methods have been used to estimate brain cell densities. These include a technique in which cells are counted from photographic prints, a method in which suspensions of cells produced by homogenization of fixed tissue are counted in a hemocytometer (Johnson and Erner, 1972), and automated methods like the Quantimet, which counts particles such as nucleoli on the basis of individual characteristics that are programmed into a computer. However, the most reliable, although most laborious, method of brain cell counting is direct microscopic observation. The multilayered cerebral cortex makes accurate cell counting very difficult.

Detailed reviews of all the studies that examined the question of neuron loss in aging of humans, mammals, and insects are those of Hanley (1974) and Curcio et al. (1983). Hodge (1894) was the first to suggest that the decline in mental functions that accompanies old age is related to neuronal loss. This suggestion was based on cell counts in young and old honeybees as well as in man. Brody (1955, 1970) found significant decreases in neuronal numbers in the human superior frontal gyrus, superior temporal gyrus, precentral gyrus, and area striata, but not in the postcentral gyrus or the inferior temporal gyrus. The greatest neuronal loss occurred in the external and internal granular layers of the cerebral cortex, where Golgi type II neurons (which are associational and have dense synaptic connections with the pyramidal cells) are lost. These findings were confirmed by Tomlinson and Henderson (1976), who showed age-related reductions of neurons in the pre- and postcentral gyrus and the superior temporal gyrus, but no reduction in glial number. The aged human hippocampus has a decreased pyramidal and granule cell density (Ball, 1977; Mouritzen Dam, 1979). Other investigators who confirmed the loss of neurons with age in humans include Shefer (1973), who found a 20 percent decrease of cortical neurons, and Colon (1972), who found a mean neuronal loss of 44 percent for the whole cerebral cortex.

In contrast to these results, Cragg (1975a) was unable to demonstrate a reduced neuronal density in senescent human brains, and Konigsmark and Murphy (1970) were unconvinced that a reduced brain weight in humans is due to neuronal loss. Several studies of the brain stem show no cell loss with age, in the inferior olive (Monagle et al., 1974), the ventral cochlear nucleus (Konigsmark and Murphy, 1970), or the trochlear and abducens nuclei (Vijayashankar and Brody, 1971, 1973). The locus coeruleus, however, does show a significant decline in neuronal count between 14 and 87 years of age (Brody and Vijayashankar, 1977), and is the only brain stem structure in which such a decline has been demonstrated. Purkinje cells in the human cerebellum are reduced by 25 percent over a hundred-year span, but the reduction first becomes apparent at about 60 years of age (Corsellis, 1976). An age-related decrease in neuron density in the putamen has been found (Bugiani et al., 1978), contrary

to a previous study in which neuron density in the striatum was actually found to increase although the volume of this structure decreased with age (Bottcher, 1975).

Table 1 reviews findings on neuronal counts and neuronal density in aging rodents. In general, no age-related change in neuronal density was found in the cerebral cortex. Neuronal loss has been observed in canine brains (Wiśniewski et al., 1970) and in cat brains (Cragg, 1975b). Brizzee et al. (1976) showed a significant decrease in neuronal density and an increase in mean glial packing density in the motor and somatosensory areas of the rhesus monkey between 5 and 20 years of age. Glial cells can be increased in the cerebral cortex of senescent rats (Brizzee et al., 1968).

In summary, a majority of investigators have reported neuronal loss in selected layers and regions of the aging human cerebral cortex but not in most brain stem structures. The majority of studies on aging rodents do not show a decreased number of neurons in the cerebral cortex. Glial cells increase in number in animals and possibly in human brains with increasing age.

Dendritic Changes

Golgi studies have revealed significant changes with age in the anatomy of cortical neurons. In rats, the pyramidal cell and its dendritic spines have been characterized in states of health and afferent deprivation or stimulation (Globus and Scheibel, 1967; Valverde, 1967; Parnavelas et al., 1973). Because dendritic spines represent the major route for afferent impulses to reach the neuron, alterations in their number or distribution may produce functional changes. Feldman (1976) showed that the mean spine density of layer V pyramidal neurons in the visual and auditory cortices of the rat declines by about one-third from 3 to 29 months. The extent of spine loss with aging is equivalent to that produced by perinatal enucleation and consequent visual deprivation (Ryujo et al., 1975). Substantial reductions (30–50 percent) occurred in the mean

TABLE 1. Age Effects on Neuronal Populations in Rodents

Spinal Cord and Brain Stem	Cerebellum	Hypothalamus	Hippocampus and Olfactory Bulb	Neocortex
1. Motor neurons reduced in mouse spinal cord (by smear technique) (Wright and Spink, 1959).	1. Decreased density of Purkinje cells in Wistar albino rat (Inukai, 1928).	1. Decrease in neuron number in anterior hypothalamic, medial preoptic, and arcuate nuclei in Sprague-Dawley rats (Hsu and Peng, 1978).	1. No change in density of granule cells in F-344 rat (Geinisman et al., 1978).	1. No change in density of neurons in cortical area 2 of Long-Evans rat (Brizzee et al., 1968).
2. No change in neuron number in F-344 rat locus coeruleus (Goldman and Coleman, 1981).	2. Decreased density of Purkinje cells in Sprague-Dawley rat (Rogers et al., 1980).	2. No change in neuron density in medial preoptic and arcuate nuclei in senescent hamsters (Lamperti and Blaha, 1980).	2. Decreased density of pyramidal cells in CA1 sector (Brizzee and Ordy, 1979).	2. No change in neuron density in secondary visual area of Long-Evans rat (Diamond et al., 1977).
3. No change in neuron number in Long-Evans rat brain stem (counted by dispersion of sonicated fixed tissue) (Peng and Lee, 1979).	3. Decrease in neuron number in Long-Evans rat (counted by dispersion of sonicated tissue) (Peng and Lee, 1979).		3. Decrease in neuron count in indusium griseum of male ASH/TO mice (Sturrock, 1979).	3. No change in fraction of neurons to all other cells in frontal and occipital cortex of Wistar rats (Klein and Michel, 1977).
			4. Decrease in mitral cell number in olfactory bulb of Sprague-Dawley rats (Hinds and McNelly, 1977).	4. No change in neuron number in primary somatosensory cortex of C57BL/6 mice (Curcio, 1981).
			5. No change in mitral cell number in olfactory bulb of Charles River strain (Hinds and McNelly, 1980).	5. Decrease in neuron number in cerebrum in Long-Evans rat (counted by dispersion of sonicated tissue) (Peng and Lee, 1979).

dendritic length in layer V basal dendrites, in layer IV oblique dendrites, and in layer III basal dendrites after 12 months of age in the rat (Feldman, 1976). In cingulate and hippocampal neurons in brains of subjects with Alzheimer's disease, spine density was reduced (Mehraein et al., 1975) compared to controls, whose ages, unfortunately, were unspecified.

Scheibel and Scheibel (1976) demonstrated a progressive age-related loss of horizontal (basilar) dendrites, particularly of pyramidal cells, in the frontal, entorhinal, and hippocampal cortices of the human brain. These changes preceded degeneration of the apical dendrite, and atrophy and pyknosis of the cell body. A similar sequence of events occurred in frontal cortical neurons of the aging canine brain (Mervis, 1978). Scheibel and Scheibel (1976) suggested that the dendritic changes in man are correlated more closely with psychomotor capacity than with calendar age.

Although there is an age-related regression of the dendritic field, dendritic growth and arborization occur as well during aging. For example, as the number of mitral receptor cells in the rat olfactory bulb declines between 24 and 33 months of age, synaptic arborization increases in the remaining receptor cells (Hinds and McNelly, 1980). Similarly, a simplification of the dendritic tree with loss of spines occurs during aging of the rat occipital cortex, whereas the arborization of superficial pyramidal neurons increase (Connor et al., 1980). In humans, Buell and Coleman (1979 and 1981) reported continuing growth from adulthood to old age of the terminal dendritic branches of pyramidal cells in the parahippocampal gyrus. However in very old animals, as in the prefrontal cortex of 28-year-old *Macaca mulatta,* there is a dendritic regression, even though dendritic growth continues until 20 years of age (Cupp and Uemura, 1980).

In summary, there is a significant decline in dendritic spine density in aged animals and a characteristic shrinkage of the dendritic arbor, which involves basilar dendrites earliest and most severely. This regressive pattern also has been shown in human brains, but age differences in dendritic spine counts have not yet been demonstrated for man. Concurrently with such changes, neurons in brains of aged animals and man retain a capacity for dendritic growth and arborization, possibly in compensation for some neuronal loss.

Lipofuscin

The term "lipofuscin" is derived from *lipo-* (i.e., fat) and *fuscus* (i.e., dark); it represents a dark, pigmented lipid. Lipofuscin occurs typically in postmitotic aging cells of many organs of different species, including man (Nandy and Schneider, 1976; Brody and Vijayashankar, 1977). The distinction of lipo-

fuscin from ceroid, another intraneuronal pigment, may be only historical because careful comparisons have failed to demonstrate any differences between the two pigments (Nishioka et al., 1968). Lipofuscin is chemically and ultrastructurally heterogeneous (Beregi, 1982; Brody and Vijayashankar, 1977).

Most investigators believe that lipofuscin is of lysosomal origin (Beregi, 1982), but mitochondria also have been implicated (Hasan and Glees, 1973). Excessive lipofuscin accumulates in cells following exposure to acetanilid or to hypoxia, and in vitamin E deficiency (Sulkin, 1958). Peroxidation of polyunsaturated lipids may mediate lipofuscin formation, which is inhibited by biological antioxidants such as vitamin E (Tappel, 1970). Age pigment accumulates more rapidly in houseflies that are short-lived and highly active than in those that are long-lived with low activity (Sohal and Donato, 1978). This suggests that factors such as metabolic rate as well as chronological age determine lipofuscin accumulation.

Although some authors suggest that lipofuscin accumulation may result in cell death (Mann and Yates, 1974), it is striking that neurons of the inferior olive, where the largest intracellular accumulation occurs in man, are not lost during aging (Monagle and Brody, 1974). The effect of lipofuscin on cell function is unknown.

Intraneuronal Organelles

The size of the neuronal perikaryon decreases with age (Feldman, 1976). Furthermore, there is a loss of the characteristic perinuclear distribution and fragmentation of the Golgi complex in neurons (Andrew, 1939; Sulkin and Srivanij, 1960). An alteration in mitochondrial structure of the optic nerves of aging mice has been noted, involving enlargement and abnormal cristae (dystrophic mitochondria) (Johnson et al., 1978). Mitochondrial numbers decline (Samorajski et al., 1971), and the quantities of endoplasmic reticulum and Nissl substance decrease with age (Hasan and Glees, 1973). In regard to the nucleus and nucleolus, Brody and Vijayashankar (1977) concluded that "decreased cytoplasmic basophilia, diminution of Feulgen-reactive chromatin, and infolding of the nuclear membrane are some features observed in aging nerve cells."

Neurofibrillary Tangles

These structures within neuronal cytoplasm consist of masses of silver-staining fibers which are composed of paired helical filaments (Wiśniewski et al., 1976). Some neurofibrillary tangles occur in hippocampal pyramidal neurons in the majority of normal old people (Tomlinson et al., 1968). Occasional tangles may be found in the neocortex of nondemented senescent individuals, but very rarely in the basal ganglia, cerebellum, or spinal cord. Heavy tangle formation throughout the cortex occurs in patients with Alzheimer's disease and a variety of other dementing and neurodegenerative disorders.

The paired helical filaments of the tangles are biochemically and immunologically unlike neurofilaments of healthy neurons (Iqbal et al., 1980). Paired helical filaments in human brains consist of 10 nm filaments wound in a helix with a half turn period of approximately 80 nm, and lack side arms which are found in normal neurofilaments (Terry, 1982). Paired helical filaments with a different periodicity have been reported in the neuron terminals of the aged rhesus monkey (Wiśniewski et al., 1973). Although exposure of cultured human fetal neurons to an extract of Alzheimer brain tissue was reported to induce paired helical filaments (DeBoni and Crapper, 1978), the same authors subsequently reported paired helical filaments in unexposed tissue, possibly because of cross-contamination (Crapper-McLachlan and DeBoni, 1982).

Neurofibrillary degeneration in some species (e.g., cats and rabbits) can be induced by injecting aluminum salts into the brain. Neurons can develop large numbers of 10 nm single filaments that resemble normal neurofilaments, but not paired helical filaments (Selkoe et al., 1979).

In summary, neurofibrillary tangles are seen in normal aged human brains, particularly in the hippocampus; however, they occur more diffusely and in much greater quantities in various neuropathological states. In animals neurofibrillary tangles have been reported to occur naturally only in the aged monkey.

Neuritic (Senile) Plaques

Plaques occur in great numbers in brains of subjects with Alzheimer's and other dementing diseases but are less common in the normal elderly. They are typically composed of degenerating neuronal processes, reactive astrocytes, and amyloid. The neuronal processes or neurites are mainly presynaptic terminals (Gonatas et al., 1967) which are filled with argentophilic material (found to be clusters of paired helical filaments) and degenerating cellular organelles (Terry, 1982). The amyloid material which forms the core of the plaque is chemically different from systemic secondary amyloid, and may arise in part from local factors (Crapper-McLachlan and DeBoni, 1982).

Neuritic plaques are seen most frequently in brains of normal senescent individuals in the hippocampus, amygdala, and hippocampal gyrus and in the neocortex, in the depths of the sulci. They are not seen in the cerebellum or spinal cord and rarely in basal ganglia. Ninety percent of normal elderly subjects have less than 10 plaques per high power field, and 70 percent have less than 5 plaques per field (Tomlinson and Henderson, 1976). Plaque counts have been correlated with scores for dementia in elderly normal subjects and patients with Alzheimer's disease (Roth et al., 1966). Furthermore, a positive correlation has been noted between the number of neuritic plaques and the decrease in choline acetyltransferase in demented patients (Perry et al., 1978).

Neuritic plaques have been reported in brains of aged dogs (Von Braünmuhl, 1956; Ostewska, 1966; Wiśniewski et al., 1970) and monkeys (Wiśniewski et al., 1973). Plaques lacking amyloid cores have been induced in animals by large intrathecal doses of aluminum phosphate (Wiśniewski and Terry, 1970). Wiśniewski et al. (1975) also induced amyloid-containing plaques by injecting the scrapie agent intracranially in mice. However, these plaques lacked neurofibrillary tangles.

In summary, neuritic plaques are seen in brains of aged normal man and of patients with Alzheimer's disease. Plaque density is related roughly to the extent of decline in mental function in Alzheimer's subjects. Brains of apparently normal, aged dogs and monkeys show these plaques; plaques have been induced in brains of other species by aluminum salts or the scrapie agent.

Conclusion

Aging human and animal brains show some common morphological changes, which include reduced neuronal numbers in selected cortical regions, shrinkage of the dendritic arbor (although compensatory growth may occur as well), an increase in neuronal lipofuscin, and altered numbers of intracellular organelles. Reductions in human brain weight and volume have been quantified and occur more rapidly after 60 years of age in man. Like the senescent human brain, brains of aged monkeys and dogs demonstrate senile plaques. Human and monkey brains have neurofibrillary tangles.

CEREBRAL METABOLISM

Relationships between Function, Metabolic Rates for Glucose and Oxygen, and Blood Flow in the Brain

Animal experiments have confirmed earlier findings in man that glucose is the main substrate for cerebral metabolism in fed adults and that most of the glucose extracted by the brain is oxidized (Siesjö, 1978). Under physiological conditions, glucose oxidation is tightly coupled to adenosine triphosphate (ATP) formation and is stoichiometrically related to oxygen consumption. Therefore,

measurements of the cerebral metabolic rate for glucose (CMR_{glc}) provide information on the cerebral metabolic rate for oxygen (CMR_{O_2}) and thereby on cerebral energy metabolism and functional activity. Accordingly, various studies of CMR_{glc} show the relation between cerebral functional activity and CMR_{glc} (Sokoloff, 1977a).

Cerebral blood flow (CBF) also provides information on brain functional activity. Roy and Sherrington's (1890) proposal that CBF is regulated to meet the requirements of cerebral metabolism was confirmed in animals, in normal human subjects, and in subjects with chronic, stable brain disease (Nilsson et al., 1978). In this regard, a close relation was observed between regional CMR_{glc} ($rCMR_{glc}$) and regional CBF (rCBF) in the rat in the conscious state as well as during anesthesia (Des Rosiers et al., 1974). Similarly rCBF is coupled to the regional cerebral metabolic rate for oxygen ($rCMR_{O_2}$) in the human cortex during hand exercise (Raichle, 1975).

Methods to Measure CBF, CMR_{O_2} and CMR_{glc}

The first measurement of CBF was performed in man by the inert gas method (Kety and Schmidt, 1945, 1948). This method applies the Fick principle to a non–steady state situation, in which a subject inhales nitrous oxide. The saturation of the brain by N_2O is followed in an artery and one internal jugular vein, which carries mixed venous blood with a concentration of N_2O proportional to that of brain.

The Fick principle was also applied to isotope clearance methods, as introduced by Lassen and Ingvar (1961). This approach required the injection of an inert isotope (e.g., ^{133}Xe) into the internal carotid artery, with extracranial monitoring. Subsequently, Mallett and Veall (1963) introduced an inhalation method for administering the ^{133}Xe, allowing simultaneous bilateral measurements of CBF. Modifications of this method allow accurate determination of CBF by a three-compartment model to provide separate estimates of blood flow for "gray" and "white" matter and extracerebral tissue (Obrist et al., 1967).

An autoradiographic inert gas technique for the determination of rCBF in conscious laboratory animals was originally designed for use with [^{131}I]trifluoroiodomethane (Landau et al., 1955). If the Kety principles are applied to analyze brain-blood exchange (Kety, 1951, 1960), rCBF could be measured simultaneously in all structures of the brain visible on autoradiographs. Studies using the nonvolatile tracer [^{14}C]antipyrine and, more recently, [^{14}C]iodoantipyrine gave essentially the same values as those obtained with [^{131}I]trifluoroiodomethane (Sakurada et al., 1978; Ohno et al., 1979).

Combining the inert gas method for measuring CBF (Kety and Schmidt, 1945, 1948) with measurements of arteriovenous (A-V) differences for metabolic substrates allows calculation of global cerebral metabolic rates as the products of A-V differences and CBF.

CMR_{glc} also can be determined without measuring CBF. By 1977, a method was available for quantitative estimation of regional cerebral metabolic rates for glucose ($rCMR_{glc}$) in animals (Sokoloff et al., 1977b). This technique uses an intravenous tracer pulse of 2-deoxy-D[1-^{14}C]glucose ([^{14}C]DG), a tracer for glucose utilization. Whereas the labeled products of radioactive glucose are lost rapidly from cerebral tissue, [^{14}C]DG-6-phosphate, which is formed from [^{14}C]DG, is a poor substrate for enzymes which occur in appreciable concentrations in the brain; it accumulates as it is formed and is effectively trapped in the cerebral tissue. In this procedure, the tissue radioactivity, which can be measured by quantitative autoradiography, is proportional to the rate of glucose utilization.

Advances in computer technology and the development of a positron emitting tracer analogue of glucose, [^{18}F]2-fluoro-2-deoxy-D-glucose (FDG), have allowed the measurement of $rCMR_{glc}$ in man by positron emission tomography (PET). The Sokoloff model was applied to man, with in vivo autoradiography by PET scanning after injec-

tion of FDG (Reivich et al., 1979; Phelps et al., 1979).

CBF and CMR_{O2} also have been studied using PET. Three-dimensional reconstructions of brain slices are obtained following the injection of a positron emitting isotope of oxygen (^{15}O) attached to hemoglobin or following inhalation of $^{15}O_2$ or $C^{15}O_2$ (Ter-Pogossian et al., 1969; Alpert et al., 1979).

Cerebral Metabolism in Aging Experimental Animals

In vivo studies of indices of cerebral metabolism in aging animals include studies of whole brain and regional CMR_{glc} in rodents and dogs and rCBF in rats. They indicate that age-related reductions in metabolic rate are regional and vary widely among animal species.

Two studies with the [^{14}C]DG technique to assess effects of aging per se on $rCMR_{glc}$ in conscious, resting rats indicate major changes by mid-life. The $rCMR_{glc}$ in Sprague-Dawley rats was lower at 14–16 months than at 4–6 months (Smith et al, 1980). Significant differences in $rCMR_{glc}$ occurred in the sensory-motor and parietal cortices, the visual, auditory, and extrapyramidal motor systems, and the inferior olivary, gracile, and cuneate nuclei. Interestingly, the limbic system in general was relatively unaffected by age except for the supragranular zone of the dentate gyrus. In general, no differences were seen in rats 26–36 months of age compared with 14 to 16-month-old rats.

London et al. (1981) extended these findings to include developing (1- and 3-month-old) as well as mature (12-month-old) and senescent (24- and 34-month old) Fischer 344 rats (Table 2). They noted that $rCMR_{glc}$ was higher at 3 months than at 1 month. This was consistent with an increased flux through the tricarboxylic acid cycle and increased glycolysis in rat cerebral hemispheres between 20 days and 3 months of age (Hothersall et al., 1979). $rCMR_{glc}$ apparently decreased during the first year of life, between 3 and 12 months. Whereas some regions showed no

TABLE 2. rCMR$_{glc}$ in Fischer-344 Rats of Different Ages.[a]

Brain region	Age				
	1 Month	3 Months	12 Months	24 Months	34 Months
	rCMR$_{glc}$ (μmol glucose/100 g tissue/min)[b]				
Frontal lobe	69 ± 5	77 ± 4	59 ± 2[c]	61 ± 4	63 ± 5
Sensory-motor cortex	61 ± 4	74 ± 4[c]	60 ± 3[c]	59 ± 3	61 ± 5
Hypothalamus and thalamus	42 ± 4	53 ± 4	41 ± 3	42 ± 4	39 ± 3
Striatum	68 ± 5	73 ± 4	55 ± 3[c]	52 ± 4	58 ± 4
Hippocampus	44 ± 4	56 ± 3[c]	46 ± 3[c]	43 ± 3	46 ± 4
Inferior colliculus	71 ± 5	94 ± 5[c]	68 ± 3[c]	57 ± 4	56 ± 4
Superior colliculus	46 ± 3	64 ± 3[c]	50 ± 3[c]	47 ± 4	46 ± 4
Midbrain basis and tegmentum	44 ± 4	56 ± 3[c]	43 ± 2[c]	39 ± 3	40 ± 4
Medulla	40 ± 3	46 ± 2[c]	36 ± 3[c]	34 ± 3	32 ± 3
Pons	42 ± 3	48 ± 3	33 ± 2[c]	33 ± 2	33 ± 2

[a]Data from London et al. (1981).
[b]Each value is the mean ± S.E. for 7–10 rats.
[c]Significant difference from rCMR$_{glc}$ at previous age, $p \leq 0.05$.

differences in rCMR$_{glc}$ at 12 months compared with 3 months, others, notably the striatum, inferior colliculus, and pons, showed decrements of 25–31 percent. No differences in rCMR$_{glc}$ were noted between rats aged 12, 24, and 34 months. Generally the findings agreed with those of Smith et al. (1980); however, in the study by London et al. (1981), a significant age-related decrement was noted in rCMR$_{glc}$ of the frontal cortex.

It is possible that resting rCMR$_{glc}$ does not reflect the morphological, neurochemical, and functional sequelae of aging in the brain. Other parameters change with aging in the rat brain after the first and even after the second year, as described in morphological studies already noted. Examples of later onset changes in the rat brain after the first year are described in Chapter 24.

It seems reasonable that discrete sequelae of aging in a particular brain region may not affect overall resting metabolism because any brain region comprises various cell types and neurotransmitter systems. Whereas an age-related decline in any of these components may be insufficient to affect regional metabolism in the resting state, it may alter the

metabolic responses to physiological or pharmacologic stress. Therefore, London et al. (1982) tested the effect of age on the stimulation of rCMR$_{glc}$ by oxotremorine, a cholinergic muscarinic agonist drug (Cho et al., 1962; Levy and Michel-Ber, 1965) which stimulates rCMR$_{glc}$ in motor system regions (Dow-Edwards et al., 1981) as well as in the cerebral cortex (Dam et al., 1982) and Papez circuit of the rat brain (Dam and London, 1984). Data from two representative brain regions are shown in Table 3.

Treatment of 12-month-old rats with 0.1 mg/kg of oxotremorine elevated rCMR$_{glc}$ to the same levels as in 3-month-old rats given 0.1 mg/kg of oxotremorine. This was not true of 24-month-old rats, which generally showed no significant response to this dose of oxotremorine. Thus, while decrements in resting rCMR$_{glc}$ do not occur after 12 months in the Fischer-344 rat, decreases in rCMR$_{glc}$ responses to oxotremorine do occur between 12 and 24 months. These decrements may reflect age-related muscarinic receptor defects (Freund, 1980; Morin and Wasterlain, 1980).

Because rCBF and rCMR$_{glc}$ are coupled when local function increases or decreases (Lassen et al., 1978; Siesjö, 1978; Sokoloff,

TABLE 3. rCMR$_{glc}$ Responses to Oxotremorine in Fischer-344 Rats of Different Ages.[a]

Brain Region	Age	Control	Oxotremorine (0.1 mg/ kg, i.p.)
		rCMR$_{glc}$ (μmol/100 g/min)[b]	
Visual cortex	3 months	92 ± 3	101 ± 6
	12 months	77 ± 7	110 ± 9[c]
	24 months	74 ± 3[d]	84 ± 7
Striatum	3 months	73 ± 5	77 ± 5
	12 months	53 ± 5[d]	78 ± 7[d]
	24 months	47 ± 4[d]	63 ± 6

[a]Data from London, E. D., Rapoport, S. I., and Dam, M. (unpublished results).
[b]Each value is the mean ± S.E. for 6–8 rats.
[c]Significant difference from rCMR$_{glc}$ in control rats, $p \leq 0.05$.
[d]Significant difference from rCMR$_{glc}$ in 3-month-old rats given the same treatment, $p \leq 0.05$

1977, 1978), it was of interest to examine rCBF in the conscious Fischer-344 rat in relation to age. Although rCBF was not different in posterior regions at 12 months compared with 3 months, rCBF in anterior brain regions (e.g., frontal lobe) was higher at 12 months than at 3 months. The anatomic distribution of differences in rCBF in anterior and posterior regions of the rat brain corresponds qualitatively to the capillary growth patterns in these same regions and may reflect earlier maturation of the posterior brain (Craigie, 1924; Himwich, 1970; Kennedy et al., 1972; Zeman and Innes, 1963). The rCBF declined significantly between 12 and 24 months (17–30 percent) in the inferior colliculus, thalamus and hypothalamus, midbrain, pons, and medulla. However, no differences in any of the regions occurred between 24- and 34-month-old rats.

Tables 2 and 4 display values of rCBF and rCMR$_{glc}$ in representative brain regions. More extensive lists appear elsewhere (Ohata et al., 1981; London et al., 1981). It is apparent that rCBF and rCMR$_{glc}$ do not follow the same time course during aging of the rat brain. Between 3 and 12 months, rCMR$_{glc}$ falls while rCBF remains unchanged or increases. The significant declines in rCBF between 12 and 24 months of age do not correlate with the constancy of rCMR$_{glc}$. The reason for this dissociation between rCBF and rCMR$_{glc}$ is not known.

The constancy in resting rCMR$_{glc}$ of Fischer 344 rats after 12 months of age and

TABLE 4. rCBF in Fischer-344 Rats of Different Ages.[a]

Brain region	Age				
	1 Month	3 Months	12 Months	24 Months	34 Months
	rCBF (ml/100 g/min)[b]				
Frontal lobe	104 ± 6	127 ± 4	155 ± 10[c]	141 ± 8	149 ± 7
Parietal lobe	115 ± 8	166 ± 8[c]	188 ± 11	179 ± 15	213 ± 18
Striatum	84 ± 5	123 ± 5[c]	115 ± 8	97 ± 7	105 ± 5
Hypothalamus and thalamus	86 ± 4	103 ± 3[c]	117 ± 6	97 ± 6[c]	107 ± 5
Hippocampus	80 ± 4	108 ± 4[c]	118 ± 7	103 ± 6	117 ± 6
Inferior colliculus	99 ± 6	118 ± 5[c]	131 ± 8	97 ± 6[c]	115 ± 6
Superior colliculus	85 ± 6	105 ± 4[c]	109 ± 5	94 ± 7	103 ± 5
Midbrain basis and tegmentum	77 ± 4	85 ± 3	91 ± 4	71 ± 5[c]	80 ± 4
Medulla	77 ± 4	82 ± 2	84 ± 3	67 ± 4[c]	74 ± 3
Pons	79 ± 4	86 ± 3	89 ± 4	70 ± 4[c]	78 ± 3

[a]Data from Ohata et al. (1981).
[b]Each value is the mean ± S.E. for 21–22 rats.
[c]Significant difference from rCBF at previous age, $p \leq 0.05$.

in resting rCBF after 24 months, despite senescence-associated morphological and neurochemical sequelae (Feldman and Dowd, 1975; Greenburg and Weiss, 1978; Inukai, 1928; McGeer et al., 1971), may reflect compensation, such as dendritic arborization, that occurs in the aged rat brain. However, because the senescent canine brain has more severe age-related neuropathology than is seen in rodents, the age-related structural changes in the aged canine brain might exceed a threshold beyond which compensation would be inadequate to sustain the adult level of $rCMR_{glc}$. Therefore, $rCMR_{glc}$ was studied as a function of age in beagle dogs (London et al., 1983). Mean rates of $rCMR_{glc}$ for ten brain regions at four ages are presented in Table 5. A more detailed account appears elsewhere (London et al., 1983). Most gray matter regions had age-related decrements between 3 and 14 years. The greatest decrements (ca. 40 percent) occurred in the superior frontal gyrus, geniculate bodies, and inferior colliculus. Some regions, for example, the head of the caudate nucleus and the hippocampus, showed decreases between 3 and 6 years, with no subsequent decrements between 6 and 14–16 years. Other regions, such as the superior frontal gyrus, the genic-

ulate bodies, and the superior and inferior colliculi, decreased between 3 and 6 years with further decreases between 6 and 14–16 years. In most cases, the significant decrements after 6 years occurred between 10–12 and 14–16 years. In the temporal cortex, there were no significant decreases between 3 and 10–12 years, but $rCMR_{glc}$ was significantly reduced between 10–12 and 14–16 years.

The relative absence of light microscopic neuropathology and the lack of change in $rCMR_{glc}$ during senescence of the rat suggest that compensation for age-related sequelae is adequate to maintain normal resting $rCMR_{glc}$ in the senescent rat brain. Because some age-related neuropathologic changes are more extensive in the canine brain than in the rat brain (Wiśniewski et al., 1970; Pauli and Luginbahl, 1971; Mervis, 1978) and because $rCMR_{glc}$ in the canine brain continues to decline during senescence, it appears that a threshold of age-related neuropathology is exceeded and compensation is inadequate to maintain the young-adult level of $rCMR_{glc}$ (Rapoport and London, 1982). This hypothesis warrants further testing involving quantitative neuropathologic analyses.

TABLE 5. $rCMR_{glc}$ in Beagle Dogs of Different Ages.[a]

Brain Region	AGE			
	3 Years (5)	6 Years (4)	10–12 Years (6)	14–16 Years (3)
	$rCMR_{glc}$ (μmol glucose/100 g/min)[b]			
Cerebral cortex:				
Superior frontal gyrus	44 ± 3	34 ± 0.9[c]	37 ± 2	28 ± 2[c]
Temporal pole	30 ± 2	26 ± 0.7	29 ± 1	23 ± 2[c]
Caudate nucleus, head	37 ± 0.7	32 ± 1[c]	29 ± 1	28 ± 2
Hippocampus	20 ± 0.6	15 ± 1[c]	17 ± 0.8	17 ± 0.9
Hypothalamus	20 ± 0.9	17 ± 1	18 ± 1	16 ± 1
Geniculate bodies	28 ± 2	27 ± 1	24 ± 1	20 ± 3[c]
Superior colliculus	34 ± 2	28 ± 1[c]	32 ± 1	25 ± 2[c]
Inferior colliculus	57 ± 2	43 ± 0.5[c]	39 ± 2	34 ± 3[d]
Pons	15 ± 0.9	12 ± 0.4	13 ± 0.9	11 ± 1
Medulla	16 ± 0.6	14 ± 0.6	14 ± 0.5	13 ± 1
Cerebellar flocculus	23 ± 1	13 ± 10	24 ± 2	23 ± 2

[a]Data from London et al., 1983.
[b]Each value is the mean ± S.E. for the number of dogs indicated in parentheses.
[c]Significant difference from previous age, $p \leq 0.05$.
[d]Significant difference from 6 years but not from 10–12 years.

CBF and Metabolism in Aging Man

Following the pioneering work of Kety and Schmidt in 1948, there have been numerous studies of CBF, CMR_{O_2} and CMR_{glc} in various human disease states. Kety (1956) reviewed the data from the four studies which had been conducted on CBF, CMR_{O_2} and aging *per se*. To this, he added three studies on young subjects. The absolute values for CBF and CMR_{O_2} by seven different laboratories were pooled after adjustments were made to compensate for a slight difference in methodology between two laboratories. Kety derived a curve from these data showing a rapid decline in CBF and CMR_{O_2} from the first to the third decade of life and a more gradual decline to the tenth decade. A frequent criticism of this conclusion (Obrist, 1979; Sokoloff, 1979) was that the health status of the subjects in several of the studies was too variable to allow distinction between the effects of age *per se* and assorted diseases in these patients. Another disadvantage was that the results of many different laboratories were combined and were not amenable to statistical methods.

In order to eliminate vascular disease as a variable in aging, Dastur et al. (1961) carefully selected a healthy group of aged men (mean age 71 years) and compared them with a group of young men (mean age 21 years). There was no significant difference in CBF and CMR_{O_2}, but CMR_{glc} was lower in the aged group. It was postulated (Sokoloff, 1979) that the older subjects had higher levels of ketone bodies, which could partially replace glucose as metabolic substrates. Although Owen et al. (1967) demonstrated that ketone bodies can serve as substrates for brain metabolism, no available data show that ketone bodies are present in sufficiently high levels in old subjects to explain the lower than expected CMR_{glc} found in old subjects by Dastur et al. (1963).

To date, 14 studies have examined one or more indices of cerebral metabolism with respect to aging (Table 6). In 8 of 13 studies of CBF, 3 of 7 studies of CMR_{O_2}, and 2 of 3 studies of CMR_{glc}, significant age-related declines occurred. When the health status of the subjects along with the results of each study is examined, it is apparent that in four of the eight studies in which CBF declined with age the subjects were carefully screened healthy individuals. Furthermore, in the five studies in which CBF showed no change with age two studies had perhaps the least healthy subjects, including cases of hypertension, diabetes, "arteriosclerosis," and strokes, and two studies had very healthy subjects.

Observations made on studies of CMR_{O_2} in aging reveal that in seven studies showing no change of CMR_{O_2} with age, three included only very healthy subjects, and three included subjects with a variety of medical disorders. Three studies showed a decline of CMR_{O2} with age. Of these, one included only healthy subjects, and two included subjects with various health disorders.

Of the three studies of CMR_{glc} in aging, two studies showed a decline; of these two, one had very carefully screened normal subjects, and the other had subjects with hypertension and diabetes. The single study showing no change of CMR_{glc} with age included only very healthy subjects.

Several studies have examined the effects of aging and hypertension on CBF (Shenkin et al., 1953; Aizawa et al., 1961; Fazekas et al., 1955). Shenkin et al. (1953) pointed out that the combination of aging and arteriosclerosis without hypertension caused no reduction in CBF and CMR_{O_2}. However, when hypertension was superimposed on aging and arteriosclerosis, CBF and CMR_{O_2} decreased with age. This finding was supported by Aizawa et al. (1961). Fazekas et al. (1955) also reported that elderly subjects with hypertension alone had no reduction of CBF or CMR_{O_2}, but the occurrence of cerebrovascular disease in the form of strokes in elderly or young subjects with or without hypertension caused a significant reduction in CBF.

The question still remains as to why so many studies in which the subjects were carefully selected for the absence of hypertension, neurological, and other disease, the CBF, CMR_{O_2}, or CMR_{glc} showed a decline with advancing age. One factor in physiological

TABLE 6. Indices of Cerebral Metabolism as a Function of Age in Man.

Reference	Number of Subjects	Ages Tested (years; group means or ranges)	Method	Health Status	Physiological State during Study	AGE EFFECT			Comments
						CBF	$CMRO_2$	CMR_{glc}	
Heyman et al. (1953)	48	29 vs 56	Nitrous oxide	All convalescent from acute non-neurological disease. Nine were hypertensive.	Not Stated	Decline	Decline	Not Measured	Comparison of older group with a group that showed acute or chronic cerebrovascular disease showed higher CBF and CMR_{O_2} in the former.
Fazekas et al. (1952)	42	23 to 102	Nitrous oxide	All age groups had some hypertensives; 1/3 of old subjects were demented.	Not stated	Decline	Decline	Not measured	There was no correlation of CBF or CMR_{O_2} with mental state.
Shenkin et al. (1953)	35	18 to 86	Nitrous oxide	All normotensive. Older group had arteriosclerosis and 4 had strokes.	"Post-absorptive state"	No change	No change	Not measured	Comparison with hypertensive subjects showed that older but not younger hypertensives had reductions in CBF and CMR_{O_2}.
Scheinberg et al. (1953)	51	18 to 79	Nitrous oxide	Carefully screened. Normal mental state. Normotensive.	Fasting, without sedation	Decline	No change	Not measured	The older group had CBF similar to age-matched subjects with cerebrovascular disease.

(Continued)

TABLE 6. (*Cont.*)

Reference	Number of Subjects	Ages Tested (years; group means or ranges)	Method	Health Status	Physiological State during Study	AGE EFFECT CBF	AGE EFFECT CMRO$_2$	AGE EFFECT CMR$_{glc}$	Comments
Schieve et al. (1953)	29	21 to 76	Nitrous oxide	Normotensive. Young and middle-age groups had many schizophrenics. Older groups were normal.	Not stated	No change	No change	Not measured	No statistics were provided.
Gordan (1956)	123	13 to 91	Nitrous oxide	Not known.	Not stated	No change	No change	Not measured	
Dastur et al. (1963)	41	20 vs 71	Nitrous oxide	Normotensive. Carefully screened. No arteriosclerosis. Devoid of even minor health disorders.	Eyes open, ears unplugged	No change	No change	Decline	A different age group with minor helath disorders showed significant reductions in CBF and CMR$_{O_2}$ as compared with young normals.
Aizawa et al. (1961)	72	13 to 83	Nitrous oxide	Normotensive.	Not stated	No change	No change	Not measured	A significant decline in CBF occurred only between third and fourth decades.
Wang et al. (1970)	39	20 vs 79	^{133}Xe clearance	Many in aged group had cardiopulmonary, neurological disease.	Not stated	Decline	Not measured	Not measured	Only the left parietal region was studied.

Study	N	Age	Method	Subjects	Condition				Comments
Gottstein (1979)	137	20s to 80s	Nitrous oxide	Mild to moderate hypertensives and diabetics included.	Not stated	Decline	Decline	Decline	No statistics were provided. A graph indicates decline of all parameters, particularly CMR$_{glc}$.
Naritomi et al. (1979)	46	21 to 63	^{133}Xe clearance	Normotensive. Negative history of cerebrovascular disease.	Not stated	Decline	Not measured	Not measured	The greatest decline occurred in the middle cerebral artery territory. Further reductions were noted in arteriosclerotic older subjects.
Frackowiak et al. (1980)	14	26 to 74	PET scan ^{15}O	Normotensive. No neurological or medical disease.	Not stated	Decline	Decline	Not measured	Temporal gray matter and white matter were analyzed. A decline occurred in gray matter only.
Melamed et al. (1980)	44	19 to 76	^{133}Xe clearance	Normotensive. No neurological, pulmonary, or vascular disease.	Eyes closed, ears closed	Decline	Not measured	Not measured	
Duara et al. (1982)	21	21 to 83	PET scan ^{18}FDG	Normotensive. No medical disease. Carefully screened.	Eyes closed, ears closed	Not measured	Not measured	No change	

studies on aging is the sensory state in which the examination is done. Mazziotta et al. (1982) showed reduction in $rCMR_{glc}$ in young adult men when in the eyes-closed, ears-open state and further in the eyes-closed, ears-closed state when compared with the eyes-open, ears-open state. Although $rCMR_{glc}$ was lower in both hemispheres, the reduction was greatest in the inferior frontal and temporal regions of the right hemisphere. Thus, age-related declines in auditory (Pickett et al., 1979) and visual acuity (Ordy and Brizzee, 1979) may of themselves cause reductions in CBF and metabolism in old subjects when young subjects with eyes and ears open are compared with old subjects in a similar state. Although ear and eye closure in young as well as old groups would eliminate the effects of the age-related differences hearing and vision, they would not correct for differences in other sensory inputs such as proprioception, vibration, and pressure on the skin surface.

The issue of intrinsic brain metabolism and aging, without the influence of input from the sense organs, needs to be addressed. In most studies of CBF and CMR_{O_2}, information is not available about the sensory state of the subjects. It is highly unlikely that the ears were plugged in most of these studies, and the frequency of eye closure probably varied considerably. The majority of these studies may be regarded as having been conducted under conditions of sensory stimulation and, therefore, as more likely to show a decline in metabolism with age. Only in the study of Melamed et al. (1980), which utilized eye closure and plugging of ears, did CBF decline with age.

It also may be noted that animal studies show perhaps the most impressive age-associated cerebral metabolic changes in sensory-related brain structures, such as the visual, auditory, and parietal cortices, the inferior colliculus, and cuneate and gracile nuclei. The well-described age-related deficits in sensory end-organs in animals (Ordy and Brizzee, 1979; Ordy et al., 1979), therefore, may have a bearing on regional metabolic decrements. This possibility further supports the hypothesis that the observed decline in human brain metabolism with aging is related, at least in part, to reductions in sensory input that accompany the aging process.

Duara et al. (1983) examined 21 carefully screened, healthy men between the ages of 21 and 83 years, and measured cerebral glucose metabolism by positron emission tomography using FDG. The studies were performed using uniform sensory deprivation (see Table 6). They concluded that hemispheric and regional cerebral glucose metabolism did not change with age. Recent studies by Frackowiak (see Duara et al., 1983) show CMR_{O_2} to remain unchanged but CBF to decline with age. Therefore, CMR_{O_2} and CMR_{glc} appear to be constant, although CBF—perhaps due to arteriosclerosis—declines with age.

Conclusion

Several parameters of cerebral energy metabolism such as CBF, CMR_{O_2} and CMR_{glc} have been examined in animals and human subjects of different ages. These parameters have been shown to be coupled in the normal brain and in chronic brain disease. In aged rats, which have only few age-related neuropathologic changes, there is little if any decline in indices of energy metabolism, and declines are mainly in sensory-related areas. In the dog, where more extensive neuropathologic changes with age have been reported, significant reductions in $rCMR_{glc}$ are seen in sensory-related structures and in the frontal and temporal cortices. Finally, in man, where clear age-related neuropathology is seen, a decline in cerebral energy metabolism with age was shown in many, but not in all, studies. The results of human studies require larger samples before definitive statements can be made. Closer attention to the health status of the subjects and the sensory environment during the studies is needed to resolve these subtle issues.

ACKNOWLEDGMENTS

We wish to thank Dr. Ronald Mervis, Department of Pathology, Ohio State University, College of Medicine, Columbus, Ohio, for providing the figures.

REFERENCES

Aizawa, T., Tazaki, Y., and Gotoh, F. 1961. Cerebral circulation in cerebrovascular disease. *World Neurol. Minn.* 2: 635–648.

Alpert, N. M., Ackerman, R. H., Correia, J. A., Grotta, J. C., Chang, J. Y., and Taveras, J. M. 1979. Measurement of cerebral blood flow and oxygen metabolism in transverse section—preliminary results *Acta Neurol. Scand. Suppl.* 72: (60), 196–197.

Andrew, W. 1939. The Golgi apparatus in the nerve cells of the mouse from youth to senility. *Am. J. Anat.* 64: 351–376.

Appel, F. W. and Appel, E. M. 1942. Intracranial variation in the weight of the human brain. *Human Biology*, 14: 48–68, 235–250.

Ball, M. J. 1977. Neuron loss, neurofibrillary tangles, and granulovacuolar degeneration in the hippocampus with aging and dementia. *Acta Neuropathol.* 37: 111–118.

Ball, M. J. 1978. Topographic distribution of neurofibrillary tangles and granulovacuolar degeneration in hippocampal cortex of aging and demented patients. A quantitative study. *Acta Neuropathol. (Berl.)* 42: 73–80.

Barron, S. A., Jacobs, L., and Kinkel, W. R. 1976. Changes in size of normal lateral ventricles during aging determined by computerized tomography. *Neurology*, 26: 1011–1013.

Beregi, E. 1982. The significance of lipofuscin in the aging process, especially in the neurons. *In*, R. D. Terry, C. L. Bolis, and G. Toffano (eds.) *Aging, Vol. 18: Neural Aging and Its Implications in Human Neurological Pathology*, pp. 15–21. New York: Raven Press.

Berlet, H. H. 1976. Hypoxic survival of normoglycaemic young adult and adult mice in relation to cerebral metabolic rates. *J. Neurochem.* 26: 1267–1274.

Bondareff, W. 1959. Morphology of the aging nervous system. *In*, James E. Birren (ed.), *Handbook of Aging and the Individual*, pp. 136–172. Chicago: University of Chicago Press.

Bottcher, J. 1975. Morphology of the basal ganglia in parkinson's disease. *Acta Neurol. Scand.* 52: (Suppl. 62).

Boyd, R. 1860. The average weights of human body and brain. Philosophical transactions. *In*, Schafer and Thane (eds.), *Reference in Quain's Anatomy*, p. 219. London: Longmans and Green, 1895.

Brizzee, K. R. and Ordy, J. M. 1979. Age pigments, cell loss and hippocampal function. *Mech. Age. Devl.* 9: 143–162.

Brizzee, K. R., Ordy, J. M., Hansche, J., and Kaack, B. 1976. Quantitative assessment of changes in neuron and glial cell packing density and lipofuscin accumulation with age in the cerebral cortex of nonhuman primate (*Macaca mulatta*). *In*, R. D. Terry and S. Gershon (eds.), *Neurobiology of Aging*, Vol. 3, pp. 229–244. New York: Raven Press.

Brizzee, K. R., Sherwood, N., and Timiras, P. S. 1968. A comparison of cell populations at various depth levels in cerebral cortex of young adult and aged Long-Evans rats. *J. Gerontol.* 23: 289–297.

Brody, H. 1955. Organization of the cerebral cortex. III. A study of aging in cerebral cortex. *J. Comp. Neurol.* 102: 511–556.

Brody, H. 1970. Structural changes in the aging nervous system. *In*, H. Blumenthal (ed.), *Interdisciplinary Topics in Gerontology* Vol. 7, pp. 9–21. Basel/Munchen: Karger.

Brody, H. and Vijayashankar, N. 1977a. Cell loss with aging. *In*, K. Nandy and I. Sherwin (eds.), *The Aging Brain and Senile Dementia. Advances in Behavioral Biology*, Vol. 23, pp. 15–21. New York: Plenum Press.

Brody, H. and Vijayashankar, N. 1977b. Anatomical changes in the nervous system. *In*, C. E. Finch and L. Hayflick (eds.), *Handbook of the Biology of Aging*, pp. 241–261. New York: Von Nostrand Reinhold.

Buell, S. J. and Coleman, P. D. 1979. Dendritic growth in the aged human brain and failure of growth in senile dementia. *Science (Wash.)* 206: 854–856.

Buell, S. J. and Coleman, P. D. 1981. Quantitative evidence for selective dendritic growth in normal human aging but not in senile dementia. *Brain Res.* 214: 23–41.

Bugiani, D., Salvarania, S., Perdelli, F., Mancardi, G. L., Leonardi, A. 1978. Nerve cell loss with aging in the putamen. *Eur. Neurol.* 17: 286–291.

Cho, A. K., Haslett, W. L., and Jenden, D. J. 1962. The peripheral actions of oxotremorine, a metabolite of tremorine. *J. Pharmacol. Exp. Ther.* 138: 249–257.

Coleman, G. L., Barthold, S. W., Osbaldiston, G. W., Foster, S. J., and Jones, A. M. 1977. Pathological changes during aging in barrier-reared Fischer-344 male rats. *J. Gerontol.* 32: 258–278.

Colon, E. J. 1972. The elderly brain. A quantitative analysis of cerebral cortex in two cases. *Psychiat. Neurol. Neurochir. (Amst.)* 75: 261–270.

Connor, J. R., Beban, S. E., Hansen, B., Hopper, P., and Diamond, M. C. 1980. Dendritic increases in the aged rat somatosensory cortex. *Abstr. Soc. Neurosci.* 6: 739.

Corsellis, J. A. N. 1976. Some observations on the Purkinje cell population and on brain volume in human aging. *In*, R. D. Terry and S. Gershon (eds.), *Aging*, Vol. 3: *Neurobiology of Aging*, pp. 205–210. New York: Raven Press.

Cragg, B. G. 1975a. The density of synapses and neurons in normal, mentally defective and ageing human brains. *Brain* 98: 81–90.

Cragg, B. G. 1975b. The development of synapses in the visual system of the cat. *J. Comp. Neurol.* 160: 147–166.

Craigie, E. H. 1924. Changes in the vascularity in the brain stem and cerebellum of the albino rat between birth and maturity. *J. Comp. Neurol.* 38: 27–48.

Crapper-McLachlan, D. R. and DeBoni, U. 1982. Models for the study of pathological neural aging. *In,* R. D. Terry, C. L. Bollis, and G. Toffano (eds.), *Aging,* Vol. 18: *Neural Aging and Its Implications in Human Neurological Pathology,* pp. 61–71. New York: Raven Press.

Cubells, J. F., Filburn, C. R., Roth, G., Engel, B. T., and Joseph, J. A. 1980. Specificity of age-related changes in striatal DA receptors: plasticity in the face of a deficit. *Abstr. Soc. Neurosci.* 6: 739.

Cupp, C. G. and Uemura, E. 1980. Age related changes in prefrontal cortex in *Macaca mulatta:* quantitative analyses of dendritic branching patterns. *Exp. Neurol.* 69: 143–163.

Curcio, C. A., Buell, S. J., and Coleman, P. D. (in press). Morphology of the aging central nervous system: not all downhill. *In,* J. A. Mortimer, F. J. Preozzolo, and J. G. Maletta (eds.), *The Aging Motor System. Advances in Neurogerontology,* Vol. 3, pp. 7–35. Praeger.

Dam, M. and London, E. D. 1984. Glucose utilization in the Papez circuit: Effects of oxotremorine and scopalamine. *Brain Res.,* 295: 137–144.

Dam, M., Wamsley, J. K., Rapoport, S. I., and London, E. D. 1982. Effect of oxotremorine on local glucose utilization in the rat cerebral cortex. *J. Neurosci.* 2: 1072–1078.

Dastur, D. K., Lane, M. H., Hansen, D. B., Kety, S. S., Butler, R. N., Perlin, S., and Sokoloff, L. 1963. Effects of aging on cerebral circulation and metabolism in man. *In, Human Aging: A Biological and Behavioral Study,* pp. 59–76, P.H.S. Publication No. 986. Washington D. C.: U.S. Government Printing Office.

Dekaban, A. S. and Sadowsky, D. 1978. Changes in brain weights during the span of human life: relation of brain weights to body heights and body weights. *Ann. Neurol.* 4: 345–356.

Des Rosiers, M. H., Kennedy, C., Patlak, C. S., Pettigrew, K. D., Sokoloff, L., and Reivich, M. 1974. Relationship between local cerebral blood flow and glucose utilization in the rat. *Neurology* 24: 389.

Diamond, M. C., Johnson, R. E., and Gold, M. W. 1977. Changes in neuron number and size in glial number in the young, adult and aging medial occipital cortex. *Behav. Biol.* 20: 409–418.

Dow-Edwards, D., Dam, M., Peterson, J. M., Rapoport, S. I., and London, E. D. 1981. Effect of oxotremorine on local cerebral glucose utilization in motor system regions of the rat brain. *Brain Res.* 226: 281–289.

Duara, R., Margolin, R. A., Robertson-Tchabo, E. A., London, E. D., Schwartz, M., Renfrew, J. W., Kessler, R., Sokoloff, L., Ingvar, D. H., and Rapoport, S. I. 1982. Regional cerebral glucose utilization in healthy men at different ages. *Neurology* 32: A166–A167.

Duara, R., Margolin, R. A., Robertson-Tchabo, E. A., London, E. D., Schwartz, M., Renfrew, J. W., Koziarz, B. J., Sundaram, M., Grady, C., Moore, A. M., Ingvar, D. H., Sokoloff, L., Weingartner, H., Kessler, R. M., Manning, R. G., Channing, M. A., Cutler, N. R., and Rapoport, S. I. 1983. Cerebral glucose utilization, as measured with positron emission tomography in 21 resting healthy men between the ages of 21 and 83 years. *Brain* 106: 761–775.

Fazekas, J. F., Alman, R. W., and Bessman, A. N. 1952. Cerebral physiology of the aged. *Am. J. Med. Sci.* 223: 245–257.

Fazekas, J. H., Kleh, J., and Finnerty, F. A. 1955. Influence of age and vascular disease on cerebral hemodynamics and metabolism. *Am. J. Med.* 18: 477–484.

Feldman, M. 1976a. Aging changes in the morphology of cortical dendrites. *In,* R. D. Terry and S. Gershon (eds.), *Neurobiology of Aging,* (Vol. 3), pp. 211–227. New York: Raven Press.

Feldman, M. L. 1976b. Dendritic changes in aging rat brain: pyramidal cell dendrite length and ultrastructure. *In,* K. Nandy and I. Sherwin (eds.), *The Aging Brain and Senile Dementia. Advances in Behavioral Biology,* Vol. 23, pp. 23–38. New York: Plenum Press.

Feldman, M. L. and Dowd, C. 1975. Loss of dendritic spines in aging cerebral cortex. *Anat. Embryol. (Berl.)* 148: 279–301.

Frackowiak, R. S. J., Lenzi, G.-L., Jones, T., and Heather, J. D. 1980. Quantitative measurement of regional cerebral blood flow and oxygen metabolism in man using ^{15}O and positron emission tomography: theory, procedure and normal values. *J. Comput. Assist. Tomogr.* 4: (6), 727–736.

Freund, G. 1980 *Cholinergic receptors loss in brain of aging mice. Life Sciences* 26: 371–375.

Geinisman, Y., Bondareff, W., and Dodge, J. T. 1977. Dendritic atrophy in the dentate gyrus of the senescent rat. *Am. J. Anat.* 152: 321–330.

Globus, A. and Scheibel, A. B. 1967. Synaptic loci on visual cortical neurons of the rabbit. The specific afferent radiation. *Exp. Neurol.* 18: 116–131.

Goldman, G. and Coleman, P. D. 1981. Neuron numbers in locus coerulus do not change with age in Fischer-344 rat. *Neurobiol. Aging* 2: 33–36.

Gonatas, N. K., Anderson, W., and Evangelista, I. 1967. The contribution of altered synapses in the senile plaque: and electron microscopic study in Alzheimer's disease. *J. Neuropathol. Exp. Neurol.* 26: 25–39.

Gordan, G. S. 1956. Hormones and metabolism: influence of steroids on cerebral metabolism in man. *Rec. Prog. Horm. Res.* 12: 153–174.

Gottstein, U. and Held, K. 1979. Effects of aging on cerebral circulation and metabolism in man. *Acta Neurol. Scand. Suppl. 72:* (60), 54–55.

Greenberg, L. H. and Weiss, B. 1978. β-Adrenergic receptors in aged rat brain: reduced number and capacity of pineal gland to develop supersensitivity. *Science (Wash.)* 201: 61–63.

Hägerdal, M., Harp, J., Nilsson, L., and Siesjö, B. K. 1975. The effect of induced hypothermia upon oxygen consumption in the rat brain. *J. Neurochem.* 24: 311–316.

Hanley, T. 1974. "Neuronal fall-out" in the aging brain: critical review of the quantitative data. *Age and Ageing.* 3: 133–151.

Hasan, M. and Glees, P. 1973. Ultrastructural age changes in hippocampal neurons, synapses and neuroglia. *Exp. Gerontol.,* 8, 75–83.

Heyman, A., Patterson, J. L., Dube, T. W., and Battey, L. L. 1953. The cerebral circulation and metabolism in arteriosclerotic and hypertensive cerebrovascular disease. *N. Engl. J. Med.* 249: 223–229.

Himwich, H. E. 1970. Historical review. *In,* W. A. Himwich (ed.), *Developmental Neurobiology,* pp. 22–44. Springfield, Ill.: Charles C. Thomas.

Himwich, W. A. and Himwich, H. E. 1957. Brain composition during whole life. *Geriatrics* 12: 1927.

Hinds, J. W. and McNelly, N. A. 1977. Aging of the rat olfactory bulb: growth and atrophy of constituent layers and changes in size and number of mitral cells. *J. Comp. Neurol.* 171: 345–348.

Hinds, J. W. and McNelly, N. A. 1980. Correlation of aging changes in the olfactory epithelium and olfactory bulb of the rat. *Abstr. Soc. Neurosci.* 6: 739.

Hodge, C. F. 1894. Changes in ganglion cells from birth to senile death. Observations on man and honeybee. *J. Physiol. (London)* 17: 129–134.

Hodgkin, A. L. and Keynes, R. D. 1955. Active transport of cations in giant axons from Sepia and Loligo. *J. Physiol. (London)* 128: 28–60.

Hothersall, J. S., Baquer, N., Greenbaum, A. L., and McLean, P. 1979. Alternative pathways of glucose utilization in brain. Changes in the pattern of glucose utilization in brain during development and the effect of phenazine methosulfate on the integration of metabolic routes. *Arch. Biochem. Biophys.* 198: 478–492.

Hsu, H. K. and Peng, M. T. 1978. Hypothalamic neuron number of old female rats. *Gerontology* 24: 434–440.

Hubbard, B. M. and Anderson, J. M. 1981. Age, senile dementia and ventricular enlargement. *J. Neurol. Neurosurg. Psychiatry* 44: 631–635.

Inukai, T. 1928. On the loss of Purkinje cells with advancing age, from the cerebellar cortex of the albino rat. *J. Comp. Neurol.* 45: 1–31.

Iqbal, K., Grundke-Iqbal, I., Johnson, A. B., and Wiśiewski, H. M. 1980. Neurofibrous proteins in aging and dementia. *In,* L. Amaducci, A. N. Davison, and P. Antuono (eds.), *Aging of the Brain and Dementia,* pp. 39–48. New York: Raven Press.

Jacoby, R. J., Levy, R., and Dawson, J. M. 1980. Computed tomography in the elderly. 1. The normal population. *Br. J. Psychiatry* 136: 249–255.

Johnson, H. A. and Erner, S. 1972. Neuron survival in the aging mouse. *Exp. Gerontology* 7: 111–117.

Johnson, J. E., Philpott, D. E., and Miquel, J. 1978.

A study of axonal degeneration in the optic nerves, of aging mice. *Age* 1: 50–55.

Kennedy,C., Grave, G. D., Jehle, J. W., and Sokoloff, L. 1972. Changes in blood flow in the component structures of the dog brain during postnatal maturation. *J. Neurochem.* 19: 2423–2433.

Kety, S. S. 1951. The theory and application of the exchange of inert gas at the lungs and tissues. *Pharmacol. Rev.* 3: 1–41.

Kety, S. S. 1956. Human cerebral blood flow and oxygen consumption as related to aging. *J. Chron. Dis.* 3: 478–486.

Kety, S. S. 1960. Measurement of local blood flow by the exchange of an inert, diffusible substance. *Methods Med. Res.* 8: 228–236.

Kety, S. S. and Schmidt, C. 1945. The determination of cerebral blood flow in man by the use of nitrous oxide in low concentrations. *Amer. J. Physiol.* 143: 53–66.

Kety, S. S. and Schmidt, C. F. 1948. The nitrous oxide method for the quantitative determination of cerebral blood flow in man: theory, procedure and normal values. *J. Clin. Invest.* 27: 476–483.

Klein, A. W. and Michel, M. E. 1977. A morphometric study of the neocortex of young adult and old maze-differentiated rats. *Mech. Age Dev.* 6: 441–452.

Konigsmark, B. W. and Murphy, E. A. 1970. Neuronal populations in the human brain. *Nature (Lond.)* 228: 1335–1336.

Lamperti, A. and Blaha, G. 1980. The number of neurons in the hypothalamic nuclei of young and reproductively senescent female golden hamsters. *J. Gerontol.* 35: 335–338.

Landau, W. M., Freygang W. H., Rowland, L. P., Sokoloff, L., and Kety, S. S. 1955. The local circulation of the living brain; values in the unanesthetized and anesthetized rat. *Trans. Am. Neurol. Assoc.* 80: 125–129.

Lassen, N. A. and Ingvar, D. H. 1961. Blood flow of the cerebral cortex determined by radioactive krypton 85. *Experientia (Basl)* 17: 42–43.

Lassen, N. A., Ingvar, D. H., and Skinhøj, E. 1978. Brain function and blood flow. *Sci. Am.* 239: 62–71.

Lévy, J. and Michel-Ber, E. 1965. Sur le metabolite de la tremorine, l'oxotrémorine. *Therapie* 20: 265–267.

London, E. D., Mahone, P., Rapoport, S. I., and Dam, M. 1982. Effect of age on oxotremorine-induced stimulation of local cerebral glucose utilization. *Fed. Proc.* 41: 1323.

London, E. D., Nespor, S. M., Ohata, M., and Rapoport, S. I. 1981. Local cerebral glucose utilization during development and aging of the Fischer-344 rat. *J. Neurochem.* 37: 217–221.

London, E. D., Ohata, M., Takei, H., French, A. W. and Rapoport, S. I. 1983. Regional cerebral metabolic rate for glucose in Beagle dogs of different ages. *Neurobiol. Aging* 4: 121–126.

Mallett, B. L. and Veall, N. 1963. Investigation of cerebral blood flow in hypertension, using radioactive-xenon inhalation and extracranial recording. *Lancet* 1: 1081–1082.

Mann, D.M. and Yates, P. O. 1974. Lipoprotein pigments—their relationship to ageing in the human nervous sytstem. I. The lipofuscin content of nerve cells. *Brain* 97: 481–488.

Mazziotta, J. C., Phelps, M. E., Carson, R. E., and Kuhl, D. E. 1982. Tomographic mapping of human cerebral metabolism: sensory deprivation. *Ann. Neurol.* 12: 435–444.

McGeer, E. G., Fibiger, H. C., McGeer, P. L., and Wickson, V. 1971. Aging and brain enzymes. *Exp. Gerontol.* 6: 391–396.

Mehraein, P., Yamada, M., and Tarnowska-Dzidusko, E. 1975. Quantitative studies on dendrites and dendritic spines in Alzheimer's disease and senile dementia. *In,* G. W. Krentzberg (ed.), *Advances in Neurology,* Vol. 12, pp. 453–458. New York: Raven Press.

Melamed, E., Lavy, S., Bentin, S., Cooper, G., and Rinot, Y. 1980. Reduction in regional cerebral blood flow during normal aging in man. *Stroke* 11: 31–35.

Mervis, R. F. 1978. Structural alterations in neurons of aged canine neocortex: a Golgi study. *Exp. Neurol.* 62: 417–432.

Monagle, R. D. and Brody, H. 1974. The effects of age upon the main nucleus of the inferior olive in the human. *J. Comp. Neurol.* 155: 61–66.

Morin, A. M. and Wasterlain, C. G. 1980. Aging and rat brain muscarinic receptors as measured by quinuclidinyl benzilate binding. *Neurochem. Res.* 5 (3), 301–308.

Mouritzen Dam, A. 1979. The density of neurons in the human hippocampus. *Neuropath. Appl. Neurobiol.* 5: 249–264.

Nandy, K. and Schneider, H. 1976. Lipofuscin pigment formation in neuroblastoma cells in culture. *In,* R. D. Terry and S. Gershon (eds.), *Neurobiology of Aging,* pp. 245–264. New York: Raven Press.

Naritomi, H., Meyer, J. S., Sakai, F., Yamaguchi, F., and Shaw, T. 1979. Effects of advancing age on regional cerebral blood flow. Studies in normal subjects and subjects with risk factors for atherothrombotic stroke. *Archiv. Neurol.* 36: 410–416.

Nilsson, B., Rehncrona, S., and Siesjö, B. K. 1978. Coupling of cerebral metabolism and blood flow in epileptic seizures, hypoxia and hypoglycaemia. *Ciba Found. Symp.* 56: 199–218. Amsterdam: Elsevier-Excerpta Medica-North Holland.

Nishioka, N., Takahata, N., and Iizuka, R. 1968. Histochemical studies on the lipo-pigments in the nerve cells. A comparison with lipofuscin and ceroid pigment. *Acta. Neuropath. (Berlin)* 11: 174–181.

Obrist, W. D. 1979. Cerebral circulatory changes in normal aging and dementia. *In,* F. Hoffmeister, C. Müller, and H. P. Krause (eds.), *Bayer-Symposium VII: Brain Function in Old Age,* pp. 278–287. Berlin: Springer-Verlag.

Obrist, W. D., Thompson, H. K., King, C. H., and Wang, H. S. 1967. Determination of regional cerebral blood flow by inhalation of 133-xenon. *Circ. Res.* 20: 124–135.

Ohata, M., Sundaram, U., Fredericks, W. R., London, E. D., and Rapoport, S. I. 1981. Regional cerebral blood flow during development and ageing of the rat brain. *Brain* 104: 319–332.

Ohno, K., Pettigrew, K. D., and Rapoport, S. I. 1979. Local cerebral blood flow in the conscious rat as measured with ^{14}C-antipyrine, ^{14}C-iodoantipyrine and ^{3}H-nicotine. *Stroke* 10: 62–67.

Ordy, J. M. and Brizzee, K. R. 1979. Functional and structural age differences in the visual system of man and nonhuman primate models. *In,* J. M. Ordy and K. Brizzee (eds.), *Aging* Vol. 10: *Sensory Systems and Communication in the Elderly,* pp. 13–50. New York: Raven Press.

Ordy, J. M., Brizzee, K. R., Beavers, T., and Medart, P. 1979. Age differences in the functional and structural organization of the auditory system in man. *In,* J. M. Ordy and K. R. Brizzee (eds.), *Aging* Vol. 10: *Sensory Systems and Communication in the Elderly,* pp. 153–166. New York: Raven Press.

Ostewska, E. 1966. Étude anatomorphathologique sur le cerveau de chiens seniles. *In, Proceedings of the Fifth International Congress of Neuropathology,* pp. 497–502. Amsterdam: Excerpta Medica Foundation.

Owen, O. E., Morgan, A. P., Kemp, H. G., Sullivan, J. M., Herrera, M. G., and Cahill, G. F. 1967. Brain metabolism during fasting. *J. Clin. Inv.* 46: 1589–1595.

Parnavelas, J. G., Globus, A., and Kaups, P. 1973. Continuous illumination from birth affects spine density of neurons in the visual cortex of the rat. *Exp. Neurol.* 40: 742–747.

Pauli, B. and Luginbahl, H. 1971. Fluorescenzmikroskopische Untersuchungen bei der cerebralen Amyloidose bei alten Hunden und senilen Menschen. *Acta Neuropathol. (Berlin)* 19: 121–128.

Pearl, R. 1905. Biometrical studies on man. I. Variation and correlation in brain weight. *Biometrika* (4): 13–104.

Peng, M. T. and Lee, L. R. 1979. Regional differences of neuron loss of rat brain in old age. *Gerontology* 25: 205–211.

Peress, N. S., Kane, W. C., and Aronson, S. M. 1973. Central nervous system findings in a tenth decade autopsy population. *Prog. Brain Res.* 40: 473–483.

Perry, E. K., Tomlinson, B. E., Blessed, G., Bergmann, K., Gibson, P. H., and Perry, R. H. 1978. Correlation of cholinergic abnormalities with senile plaques and mental test scores in senile dementia. *Br. Med. J.* 2: 1457–1459.

Phelps, M. E., Huang, S. C., Hoffman, E. J., Selin, C., Sokoloff, L., and Kuhl, D. E. 1979. Tomographic measurement of local cerebral glucose metabolic rate in humans with [F-18]2-fluoro-2-deoxy-D-glucose: validation of method. *Ann. Neurol.* 6: 371–388.

Pickett, J. M., Bergman, M., and Levitt, H. 1979. Aging and speech understanding. *In,* J. M. Ordy and

K. Brizzee (eds.), *Aging* Vol. 10: *Sensory Systems and Communication in the Elderly,* pp. 167-186. New York: Raven Press.

Puri, S. K. and Volicer, L. 1977. Effects of aging on cyclic AMP levels and adenylate cyclase and phosphodiesterase activities in the rat corpus striatum. *Mech. Age. Dev.* 6 (1), 53-58.

Raichle, M. E. 1981. Measurement of local cerebral blood flow and metabolism in man with positron emission tomography. *Fed. Proc.* 40: 2331-2334.

Raichle, M. E., Grubb, R. L., Jr., Gado, M. H., Eichling, J. O., and Ter-Pogossian, M. M. 1976. Correlation between regional cerebral blood flow and oxidative metabolism. *In vivo* studies in man. *Arch Neurol.* 33: 523-526.

Rapoport, S. I., and London, E. D. 1982. Brain metabolism during aging of the dog. Implication for brain function in man during aging and in dementia. *In,* R. D. Terry, C. L. Bolis, and G. Toffano (eds.), *Aging,* Vol. 18: *Neural Aging and Its Implication in Human Neurological Pathology,* pp. 79-88. New York: Raven Press.

Reivich, M., Kuhl, D., Wolf, A., Greenberg, J., Phelps, M., Ido, T., Casella, V., Fowler, J., Hoffman, E., Alavi, A., Som, P., and Sokoloff, L. 1979. The [18F]fluorodeoxyglucose method for the measurement of local cerebral glucose utilization in man. *Circ. Res.* 44: 127-137.

Riggs, H. E. and Wahal, K. M. 1960. Changes in the brain associated with senility. *Arch. Neurol. (Chic.)* 2: 151-159.

Ritchie, J. M. 1967. The oxygen consumption of mammalian non-myelinated nerve fibres at rest and during activity. *J. Physiol. (London)* 188: 309-329.

Roberts, M. A. and Caird, F. I. 1976. Computerized tomography and intellectual impairment in the elderly. *J. Neurol. Neurosurg. Psychiatry* 39: 986-989.

Rogers, J., Silver, M. A., Shoemaker, W. J., and Bloom, F. E. 1980. Senescent changes in a neurobiological model system: cerebellar Purkinje cell electrophysiology and correlative anatomy. *Neurobiol. Aging* 1: 3-12.

Roth, M. 1980. Aging of the brain and dementia: an overview. *In,* L. Amaducci, A. N. Davison, and P. Antuono (eds.), *Aging,* Vol. 13: *Aging of the Brain and Dementia,* pp. 1-21. New York: Raven Press.

Roth, M., Tomlinson, B. E., and Blessed, G. 1966. Correlation between scores for dementia and counts of "senile plaques" in cerebral grey matter of elderly subjects. *Nature (Lond.)* 209: 109.

Roy, C. S. and Sherrington, C. S. 1890. On the regulation of the blood supply of the brain. *J. Physiol. (London)* 11: 85-108.

Ryugo, R., Ryugo, D. K., and Killackey, H. 1975. Differential effect of enucleation on two populations of layer V pyramidal cells. *Brain Res.* 88: 554-559.

Sakurada, O., Kennedy, C., Jehle, J., Brown, J. D., Carbin, G. L., and Sokoloff, L. 1978. Measurement of local cerebral blood flow with iodo[14C]antipyrine. *Am. J. Physiol.* 234: (1), H59-H66.

Samorajski, T., Friede, R. L., and Ordy, J. M. 1971. Age differences in the ultrastructure of axons in the pyramidal tract of mouse. *J. Gerontol.* 26: 542-551.

Scheibel, M. E. and Scheibel, A. B. 1976. Differential changes in old and new cortices. *In,* K. Nandy and I. Sherwin (eds.), *The Aging Brain and Senile Dementia. Advances in Behavioral Biology,* Vol. 23, pp. 39-58. New York: Plenum Press.

Scheinberg, P., Blackburn, I., Rich, M., and Saslaw, M. 1953. Effects of aging on cerebral circulation and metabolism. *Arch. Neurol. Psych.* 70 77-85.

Schieve, J. F. and Wilson, W. P. 1953. The influence of age, anaesthesia and cerebral arteriosclerosis on cerebral vascular activity to CO_2. *Am. J. Med.* 15: 171-174.

Selkoe, D. J., Liem, R. K., Yen, S. H., and Shelanski, M. L. 1979. Biochemical and immunological characterization of neurofilaments in experimental neurofibrillary degeneration induced by aluminum. *Brain Res.* 163: 235-252.

Shefer, V. F. 1973. Absolute number of neurons and thickness of cerebral cortex during aging, senile and vascular dementia and Pick's and Alzheimer's diseases. *Neurosci. Behav. Physiol.* 6: 319-324.

Shenkin, H. A., Novak, P., Goluboff, B., Soffe, A. M., and Bortin, L. 1953. The effects of aging, arteriosclerosis and hypertension upon cerebral circulation. *J. Clin. Inv.* 32: 459-465.

Siesjö, B. K. 1978. *Brain Energy Metabolism.* Chichester: John Wiley & Sons.

Smith, C. B., Goochee, C., Rapoport, S. I., and Sokoloff, L. 1980. Effects of ageing on local rates of cerebral glucose utilization in the rat. *Brain* 103: 351-365.

Sohal, R. S. and Donato, H., Jr. 1978. Effects of experimentally altered lifespans on the accumulation of fluorescent age pigment in the house-fly, *Musca domestica. Exp. Gerontol.* 13: 335-341.

Sokoloff, L. 1972. Circulation and energy metabolism of the brain. *In,* G. J. Siegel, R. W. Albers, R. Katzman, and B. W. Agranoff (eds.), *Basic Neurochemistry,* 2nd ed., pp. 388-413. Boston: Little Brown.

Sokoloff, L. 1977. Relation between physiological function and energy metabolism in the central nervous system. *J. Neurochem.* 29: 13-26.

Sokoloff, L. 1978. Local cerebral energy metabolism: its relationships to local functional activity and blood flow. *In, Cerebral Vascular Smooth Muscle and Its Control. Ciba Found. Symp.* 56: 171-197. Amsterdam: Elsevier-Excerpta Medica-North Holland.

Sokoloff, L. 1979. Effects of normal aging on cerebral circulation and energy metabolism. *In,* F. Hoffmeister, C. Muller, and H. P. Krause (eds.), *Bayer Symposium,* Vol. 7: *Brain Function in Old Age,* pp. 367-380. Berlin: Springer Verlag.

Sokoloff, L., Reivich, M., Kennedy, C., Des Rosiers, M. H., Patlak, C. S., Pettigrew, K. D., Sakurada, O., and Shinohara, M. 1977b. The 14C-deoxy-glucose method for the measurement of local cerebral glucose utilization: theory, procedure, and normal values in the conscious and anesthetized albino rat. *J. Neurochem.* 28: 897–916.

Sturrock, R. R. 1979. A quantitative life span study of cell number, cell division and cell death in various regions of the mouse forebrain. *Neuropath. Appl. Neurobiol.* 5: 433–456.

Sulkin, N. M. 1958. The occurrence and reduction of senile pigments experimentally induced in the nerve cells of young rats. *Anat. Record* 130: 377–378.

Sulkin, N. M. and Srivanij, P. 1960. The experimental production of senile pigments in the nerve cells of young rats. *J. Geront.* 15: 2–9.

Tappel, A. L. 1970. Biological antioxidant-protection against lipid peroxidation damage. *Am. J. Clin. Nutr.,* 23: 1137–1139.

Ter-Pogossian, M. M., Eichling, J. O., Davis, D. O., Welch, M. J., and Metzger, J. M. 1969. The determination of regional cerebral blood flow by means of water labeled with radioactive oxygen-15. *Radiology,* 93: 31–40.

Terry, R. D. 1980. Structural changes in senile dementia of the Alzheimer type. *In,* L. Amaducci, A. N. Davison, and P. Antuono (eds.), *Aging of the Brain and Dementia,* pp. 23–32. New York: Raven Press.

Terry, R. D. 1982. Brain disease in aging, especially senile dementia. *In,* R. D. Terry, C. L. Bollis, and G. Toffano (eds.), *Aging,* Vol. 18: *Neural Aging and Its Implications in Human Neurological Pathology,* pp. 43–52. New York: Raven Press.

Tomlinson, B. E. 1972. Morphological brain changes in non-demented old people. *In,* H. M. van Praag and A. F. Kalverboer (eds.), *Aging of the Central Nervous System: Biological and Psychological Aspects.* pp. 38–57. Haarlem, The Netherlands: De Ervin F. Bohn N. V.

Tomlinson, B. E., Blessed, G., and Roth, M. 1968. Observations on the brains of non-demented old people. *J. Neurol. Sci.* 7: 331–356.

Tomlinson, B. E., Blessed, G., and Roth, M. 1970. Observations on the brains of demented old people. *J. Neurol. Sci.,* 11, 205–242.

Tomlinson, B. E. and Henderson, G. 1976. Some quantitative cerebral findings in normal and demented old people. *In,* R. D. Terry and S. Gershon (eds.), *Neurobiology of Aging,* Vol. 3, pp. 183–204. New York: Raven Press.

Valverde, F. 1967. Apical dendritic spines of the visual cortex and light deprivation in the mouse. *Exp. Brain Res.* 3: 337–352.

Vaughan, D. and Peters, A. 1974. Neuroglial cells in the cerebral cortex of rats from young adulthood to old age: an electron microscope study. *J. Neurocytol.* 3: 405–429.

Vijayshankar, N. and Brody, H. 1971. Neuronal population of human abducens nucleus. *Anat. Record* 169: (2), 447.

Vijayashankar, N. and Brody, H. 1973. The neuronal population of the nuclei of the trochlear nerve and locus coeruleus in the human. *Anat. Record* 172: (2), 421–422.

Von Braunmihl, A. 1956. Kongophile Angiopathie und "Senile Plaques" bei greisen Hauden. *Arch. Psychiatr. Nervenkr.* 194: 396–414.

Wang, H. S., Obrist, W. D., and Busse, E. W. 1970. Neurophysiological correlates of the intellectual function of elderly persons living in the community. *Amer. J. Psychiat.* 126 (9): 1205–1212.

Weiss, B., Greenberg, L., and Cantor, E. 1979. Age-related alterations in the development of adrenergic denervation supersensitivity. *Fed. Proc.* 38: 1915–1921.

Wiśniewski, H. M., Bruce, M. E., and Fraser, H. 1975. Infectious etiology of neuritic (senile) plaques in mice. *Science* 190: 1108–1110.

Wiśniewski, H. M., Ghetti, B., and Terry, R. D. 1973. Neuritic (senile) plaques and filamentous changes in aged rhesus monkeys. *J. Neuropathol. Exp. Neurol.* 32: 566–584.

Wiśniewski, H., Johnson, A. B., Raine, C. S., Kay, W. J., and Terry, R. D. 1970. Senile plaques and cerebral amyloidosis in aged dogs. A histochemical and ultrastructural study. *Lab. Invest.* 23: 287–296.

Wiśniewski, H. M., Narang, H. K., and Terry, R. D. 1976. Neurofibrillary tangles of paired helical filaments. *J. Neurol. Sci.* 27: 173–181.

Wiśniewski, H. and Terry, R. D. 1970. An experimental approach to the morphogenesis of neurofibrillary degeneration and the argyrophilic plaque. *In,* G. Wolstenholme and M. O'Connor (eds.), *Alzheimer's Disease and Related Conditions, Ciba Foundation Symposium,* pp. 223–250. London: Churchill.

Wiśniewski, H. M. and Terry, R. D. 1976. Neuropathology of the aging brain. *In,* R. D. Terry and S. Gershon (eds.), *Aging* Vol. 3: *Neurobiology of Aging,* pp. 265–280. New York: Raven Press.

Wright, E. A. and Spink, J. J. 1959. A study of the loss of nerve cells in the central nervous system in relation to age. *Gerontologia* 3: 277–287.

Zatz, L. M., Jernigan, T. L., and Ahumada, A. J., Jr. 1982. Changes on computed cranial tomography with aging: intracranial fluid volume. *A.J.N.R.* 3: 1–11.

Zeman, W. and Innes, J. R. M. 1963. *Craigie's Neuroanatomy of the Rat,* p. 37. New York: Academic Press.

23
STRUCTURAL CHANGES AT SYNAPSES WITH AGE: PLASTICITY AND REGENERATION*

Carl W. Cotman
and
Vicky R. Holets
Department of Psychobiology
University of California

INTRODUCTION

The purpose of this chapter is to survey and anaiyze current knowledge on the structure and plasticity of central nervous system (CNS) circuits in the aged brain, particularly with reference to synapses. Knowledge of the structural state of the aged nervous system will aid in understanding CNS functions which change with age. It is important to document those parts of the CNS where there are changes, as well as to identify those areas where there are none. Inasmuch as aging brings about cell loss, metabolism changes, and a variety of new external and internal influences, it would be surprising if there were no significant circuitry changes with age.

We have organized this review according to areas of the brain and spinal cord in order to determine how selective aging is to particular regions and systems. This is in line with the finding that aging affects only certain

functions. First, we describe changes with aging in the synaptic circuitry and neuronal morphology of various brain areas. The question of whether synaptic connections in particular pathways change with age, and the possible alteration of the distribution of synapses along the neuronal surface, are dealt with in the first section. In the second and third sections, synaptic plasticity in the aged CNS is examined. Is circuitry fixed in the aged brain, and if not, to what extent is it altered by injury (cell loss), diet, or experience? At the outset, we should note that the available data on all of these issues are quite incomplete at this stage, and one of the messages of this review is to point out the major gaps. Previous chapters in this volume have reviewed the influence of age on neuronal loss and the age-dependent changes in neurotransmitters and specific synthetic enzymes.

SYNAPTIC ABUNDANCE AND STRUCTURE IN THE AGED CNS: A REGIONAL SURVEY

Most studies on the aged nervous system have centered upon the cerebral cortex, hippocampus, and olfactory bulb. Limited data

* The authors would like to thank Dr. Steven F. Hoff for valuable discussions and Susie Bathgate for assistance in preparation of the manuscript. The authors are supported in part by NIA Grant AG00538 (C.W.C.) and NIH Fellowship NS07007 (V.R.H.).

are available on hypothalamus, brain stem, spinal cord, and cerebellum. It is startling that little if any data have been reported on synapses in other regions.

Dendrites and dendritic spines have been studied in more detail than other synaptic indices because they can be examined at the light microscopic level by Golgi methods. Since most synapses terminate on dendritic spines, this provides an index of synapse abundance and distribution. The majority of studies report a loss of dendritic spines and even dendritic branches, but gains have also been described as a function of age. Tables 1 through 4 summarize the regional data on changes in dendrites and synapses in the mammalian CNS.

Cerebral Cortex

Over the past few years, the cerebral cortex has been the focus of relatively extensive Golgi and electron microscopic studies in a variety of species.

Auditory Cortex. Qualitative examination of Golgi-impregnated pyramidal cells in the auditory cortex (area 4) of 3- to 29.5-month-old rats reveals a progressive loss of dendritic spines with advancing age (Feldman and Dowd, 1975). Select dendritic areas in 29.5-month-old animals appeared to be particularly denuded. Dendrites in the older animals have spines belonging to all of the morphological types present in young adults (stubby,

TABLE 1. Structural Changes at Synapses: Cerebral Cortex.

Subject, Strain	Age	Brain Area	Change with Aging	Reference
Rat, SD	2–29.5 mo.	Auditory cortex, layer V pyramidal cells	−36% apical dendrites −24% terminal tuft dendrites −32% basal dendrites −40% oblique dendrites	Feldman and Dowd, 1975
Rat, SD	2–29.5 mo.	Auditory cortex	−20% thick dendrites −36% medium dendrites −31% thin dendrites	Feldman, 1976
Rat, SD	34–36 mo.	Auditory cortex, layer V pyramidal cells	−Dendrites, −Mean No. 1° dendrites +No. 3° dendrites	Vaughan, 1977 Vaughan and Vaughan 1977
Rat, SD	34–36 mo.	Auditory cortex	−37% spine loss − Mean No. 1° dendrites + Mean No. 3° dendrites	Vaughan, 1977
Rat, SD	3–29.5 mo.	Auditory and visual cortex	Loss of dendritic spines, patchy loss	Feldman and Dowd, 1975
Dog, mixed breeds	13–18 yr	Cerebral cortex, frontal pyramidal cells	Shrinkage of both vertical and particularly horizontal branches; apical branches almost totally denuded of spines; occasional kinks, swelling along dendritic shafts	Mervis, 1978
Monkey, *Macaca mulatta*	16–18, 22–23 yr	Cerebral cortex, frontal, temporal, hippocampal, parietal, occipital	1. Watery type of degeneration, proliferation of smooth membranes, aggregation of floccular material 2. Electron-dense laminated profiles, excessive number of mvb's	Wisniewski, et al., 1973

NOTE:

In this and other tables (Tables 2 through 4): + = increase; − = decrease; 0 = no change; No. = number; mo. = month; yr = year. For rat strains: F344 = Fischer 344; LE = Long-Evans; SD = Sprague-Dawley; W = Wistar.

TABLE 1. (*Cont.*)

Subject, Strain	Age	Brain Area	Change with Aging	Reference
Monkey, *Macaca mulatta*	7–28 yr (7–12, group I) (18–20, II) (27–28, III)	Prefrontal cortex	Preferential loss of whole branches on apical dendrites −Length of terminal dendrites of basal dendrites +Total dendritic length of apical dendrites/cell (I to II) −Total dendritic length of apical dendrites/cell (II–III)	Cupp and Uemura, 1980
Monkey, *Macaca mulatta*	7–20 yr	Prefrontal cortex	0 Basal dendritic branch orders/cell (I–II) −(I,II–III)	Cupp and Uemura, 1980
Monkey, *Macaca mulatta*	7–20 yr	Prefrontal cortex	0 (mean synaptic density 8.77 × 10^8 synapses/mm^3)	Uemura, 1980
Monkey, *Macaca mulatta*	7–28 yr (7–12, I) (18–20, II) (27–28, III)	Prefrontal cortex	+Group I–II total dendritic length of apical dendrites/cell −Group II–II (same as above) 0 Group I–II basal dendritic branch orders/cell −Group I, II–III (same as above) 0 Group I–II No. basal dendritic branches/neuron −Group I,II–III (same as above) +Group I–II mean total dendritic length/cell of basilar dendrites −Group II–III (same as above)	Cupp and Uemura, 1980
Human	74–102 yr	Cerebral cortex, precentral gyrus, esp. Betz cells	Swelling, varicosities on principal shafts; shortening disruption; loss of basilar dendrites; loss of spines	Scheibel et al., 1977
Human	58–96 yr	Cerebral cortex, prefrontal and superior temporal areas	Progressive loss of horizontal shafts and other dendrites 0 No. of branch and end points of basal dendrites +Total dendritic length (more segments/tree; greater average length of segments) 0 No. of basal dendritic branches/neurons	Scheibel et al., 1977
Human	24–93 yr	Frontal, temporal cortex, hippocampus	Slightly enlarged presynaptic terminals; clear limiting membrane; distended structures	Gibson et al., 1976

(*Continued*)

TABLE 1. (Cont.)

Subject, Strain	Age	Brain Area	Change with Aging	Reference
Human	70–76 yr	Cerebral cortex, frontal, temporal cortex	Profiles with abnormal shape and size mitochondria; membranous whorls	Rees, 1976
Human	16–90 yr	Frontal cortex, layer III pyramidal cells	$-(9.56 \times 10^8$ synapses/ mm^3 in 74–90 yr; from 11×10^8 synapses/mm^3 in 16–72 yr	Huttenlocher, 1979
Human	15–54, 68–84 yr	Cerebral cortex, frontal and temporal areas	0 Synaptic density	Cragg, 1975
Rat	6, 12, 18, 24, 28, 52 mo.	Motor and visual cortex	Thinning of synaptic membranes; shortened synaptic contacts −No. of synaptic vesicles; flattening of spines (axodendritic); appearance of mvb's, ribosomes in spines near presynaptic membrane; penetration of glia into synaptic cleft −No. of axosomatic and axodendritic synapses	Artjukhina, 1968
Rat, SD	3–36 mo.	Visual cortex	Loss of dendritic spines; spine-free proximal areas	Feldman, 1976
Rat, LE	90, 414, 630 days	Occipital cortex	−(90–414 days) then +(414–630 days) L-type spines −(90–414 days) then 0 (414–630 days) N-type spines	Connors et al., 1980b
Rat, LE	90, 414, 630 days	Cerebral cortex, layer II, III pyramidal cells	+Basal dendrites	Connors et al., 1980a
47 vertebrate species	Aged	Cerebral cortex, cerebellum, basal ganglia, brain stem, medulla	0 Change	Dayan, 1971

pedunculated, and those with or without terminal bulbous expansions). The aging process does not appear to lead selectively to the loss of dendritic spines of one particular form (Feldman and Dowd, 1975).

The dendritic loss shows a large cell-to-cell variability ranging from a 24 percent to a 40 percent decrease in dendritic spine numbers (Feldman and Dowd, 1975). The apical dendrites of relatively large diameter dendrites (3 µm or more) appeared to have more spines than those of relatively small diameter dendrites (1 µm), regardless of the age of the an-

imal. In old animals (29 months), the largest spine loss occurs on the medium diameter (2 µm) dendrites, whereas both the thicker and thinner dendrites lose fewer spines, 20 and 30 percent, respectively. In this case, the loss of spines on apical dendritic shafts appears to be related to the diameter of the shafts.

Vaughan (1977) also reported that the mean number of primary dendrites in the auditory cortex of old rats was less than in young animals. In the young animals, the third order branches are more frequent than the second order branches (Figure 1). How-

TABLE 2. Structural Changes at Synapses: Olfactory Bulb.

Subject, Strain	Age	Brain Area	Change with Aging	Reference
Rat, SD	3–30 mo.	Olfactory bulb, mitral cells	Swelling of dendrites, loss of dendrites +Mitochondria (% volume fraction in mitral cells)	Hinds and McNelly, 1977
	27–30 mo.	Olfactory bulb, mitral cells	−Volume mitochondria/cell (after + between 24 and 27 mo.)	
Rat, SD	3, 12, 24, 27, 30 mo.	Olfactory bulb	+No. mitral to granule cell synapses (3–27 mo.) −No. synapses (27–30 mo.) +No. of mitral to granule cell synapses/olfactory bulb (3–24 mo.) −No. synapses/olfactory bulb (27–30 mo.)	Hinds and McNelly, 1979
			+98% volume of large dendrites (3–24 mo.) −50% volume of large dendrites (24–30 mo.) (esp. 27–30 mo.) +Relative density of mitral to granule cell synapses (3–12 mo.) −Slight (12–27 mo.), +Slight (27–30 mo.) relative density of mitral to granule cell synapses	Hinds and McNelly, 1977
Mouse, C57BL/6J	1–35 mo.	Olfactory bulb, mitral cells	Lumpy, nodal appearance; dendritic areas without spines; patchy loss	Machado-Salas and Scheibel, 1979

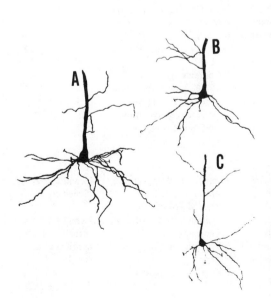

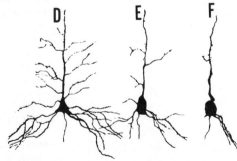

Figure 1. A comparison of Golgi-impregnated neurons from aged rat and human. Note the decrease in dendritic domain in B, C, E, and F. (A–C) Layer V pyramidal cells from the auditory cortex of 3-month-old rat (A), 34-month-old rat (B), and 36-month-old rat (C). (D–F) Summary of progression of senile changes in human cortical pyramidal cells. (A–C from Vaughan, 1977; D–F from Scheibel, 1978.)

TABLE 3. Structural Changes at Synapses: Dentate Gyrus and Hippocampus.

Subject, Strain	Age	Brain Area	Change with Aging	Reference
Rat, F344	3, 25 mo.	Dentate gyrus, granule cells	Loss of dendrites, decreased volume fraction and surface area	Geinisman et al., 1978a
Rat, F344	3, 25 mo.	Dentate gyrus, middle 1/3 ml	0 General anatomy	Cotman and Scheff, 1979
Rat, F344	3, 25 mo.	Dentate gyrus, middle 1/3 ml	0 Postsynaptic density length	Geinisman et al., 1976
Rat, F344	3, 25 mo.	Dentate gyrus, molecular layer	−15% synapses/length of plasma membrane −27% No. of synapses/ unit area of square area of neuropil (axodendritic)	Bondareff, 1979, 1980; Geinisman et al., 1977
		Middle 1/3 ml	−35% mean No. synapses on shafts	Bondareff, 1979
		Granule cell layer	−22% granule cell surface covered by synapses −15% No. of axosomatic synapses/unit length of neuronal soma −10% mean length of synaptic apposition	Geinisman, 1979
		Supragranular zone	−35% synapses/square area of synapses on dendritic shafts −24% synapses/square area of synapses on dendritic spines	Geinisman et al., 1977
Rat, F344	3, 25 mo.	Dentate gyrus supragranular zone	−39.6% synapses/dendritic unit length on shafts −39.7% synapses/dendritic unit length on spines	Geinisman et al., 1977
Rat, SD	2–30 mo.	Dentate gyrus, molecular layer	0 General anatomy	Scheff et al., 1980
Rat, SD	2, 2.5 yr	Outer molecular layer	−19.7% synapses (2 yr) −22.7% synapses (2.5 yr)	Hoff et al., 1982a
		Supragranular zone	−31.4% synapses (2.5 yr)	
		Middle and inner molecular layer	0 (2 yr) 0	
Rat, SD	2, 2.5 yr	Dentate gyrus Supragranular zone	+26.7% complex synapses (2 yr)	Hoff et al., 1982
		Dentate molecular layer	0 Complex synapses −19.6% noncomplex synapses (2, 2.5 yr)	
		Outer 2/3 molecular layer	0 Noncomplex synapses	
		Middle molecular layer	−22.5% noncomplex synapses	
		Outer molecular layer		
Mouse, C57BL/6J	1–35 mo.	Dentate gyrus, granule cells	Lumpy, nodal appearance, apical dendrites, decreased arborization	Machado-Salas and Scheibel, 1979
Human	69–102 yr	Dentate gyrus, granule cells	Proximal portions of CA1 dendrites	Machado-Salas and Scheibel, 1979
Rat, F344	4–12, 24–28 mo.	Hippocampus, CA1 pyramidal cells	0 Synaptic terminal number 0 Synaptic terminal area	Landfield et al., 1979

TABLE 3. (Cont.)

Subject, Strain	Age	Brain Area	Change with Aging	Reference
Rat, W	4–12, 24–40 mo.	Hippocampus	− Axosomatic synapses + Dendrodendritic contacts	Hasan and Glees, 1973
Mouse, C57BL/6J	1–35 mo.	Hippocampus, pyramidal cells	Lumpy, nodal appearance; loss of dendrites; fragmentation and distortion of basilar dendrites; scattered loss of spines − No. of apical dendrites	Machado-Salas and Scheibel, 1979
Human	69–102 yr	Hippocampus, pyramidal cells	Swelling of proximal bifurcations; thinning of dendritic spines; large areas of spine-free dendrites	Scheibel et al., 1976; Scheibel, 1978
Human	69–102 yr	Entorhinal cortex	Swollen varicosities; spindle-shaped enlargements along apical shafts; spines appeared normal	Scheibel et al., 1977
Human	44–55 yr (normal), 68–92 yr (aged)	Parahippocampal gyrus	+ No. of intersections of dendrites of average apical tree with successively larger concentric spheres in aged 0 No. of branch and end points of apical dendrites + No. of intersections of basil dendrites with successively larger concentric spheres in aged	Buell and Coleman, 1981

ever, in the old animals, the number of third order branches is less than second order branches. This difference is interpreted as reflecting a dying back process in the distal dendritic branches. Quantitative counts of the number of synapses are not available.

Frontal/Prefrontal Cortex. Wisniewski and coworkers (1973) reported that in the frontal cortex and other cortical areas of the aged *Macaca mulatta* monkey, some dendrites appeared watery with a proliferation of smooth membranes and aggregations of floccular proteinaceous material. Another type of dendrite was characterized by electron-dense laminated profiles and excessive numbers of multivesicular bodies. Both dendritic types appeared to be degenerating and form synaptic contacts with normal terminals, as well as with degenerating ones.

In the prefrontal cortex of old dogs, dis-tortion of the soma of neocortical pyramidal cells with a loss of dendritic spines, dendritic swelling (varicosities), and shrinkage of primarily the horizontal, but also the vertical, dendritic branches has been described (Mervis, 1978). The loss of dendritic spines correlated with the development of occasional kinking, constrictions, and swellings, particularly along the shafts of the apical dendrites. It was suggested that the additional membrane absorbed from the spines shifted to the main shaft. Dendritic spine remnants appearing as small nub-like protuberances along the swellings are seen in more advanced stages. Also, apical branches were frequently found almost totally denuded of spines and lacking dendritic swellings (Mervis, 1978). Normal appearing neurons were found in close proximity to aged looking cells. Mervis (1978) also described two dogs in which filament-like tufting was observed

TABLE 4. Structural Changes at Synapses: Spinal Cord, Brain Stem, Medulla, and Hypothalamus.

Subject, Strain	Age	Brain Area	Change with Aging	Reference
Rat, WI	93–804 days	Gracile nucleus	− Volume fraction − No. of dendrites − Synaptic terminal number	Fujisawa et al., 1970
		Cuneate nucleus	− Volume fraction − No. of dendrites	
Monkey, *Macaca mulatta*	16–18, 22–23 yr	Gracile nucleus	Dystrophic endings; degenerating cytoplasmic organelles	Wisniewski et al., 1973
Rat, SD	1–2, 6–8, 18–20 mo.	Lateral vestibular nucleus	+ 5% flat terminals − 5% spherical terminals (6–8 mo.) + 35% flat terminals − 35% spherical terminals (18–20 mo.)	Johnson and Miquel, 1974
Rat, SD	18 mo.	Lateral vestibular nucleus	+ No. of mitochondria in dendritic processes which formed contacts	Johnson and Miquel, 1974
	8 mo.	Lateral vestibular nucleus	Axons with altered mitochondria, in or near synaptic terminal	
Rat, SD, vitamin E deficient	3–23 mo.	Dorsal column nuclei	Altered axons at synapses	Johnson et al., 1975
Mouse, C57BL/6J	26–30 mo.	Spinal cord and lower brain stem	Lumpy, swollen dendrites; loss of distal dendrites; shrinkage of proximal dendrites; breakage of dendrites; loss of small projections	Machado-Salas et al., 1977b
Mouse, C57BL/6J	1–9, 26–34 mo.	Hypothalamus	Progressive dendritic surface loss; swelling of dendritic shaft; decrease in dendritic arborization; thinning and shortening of dendrites	Machado-Salas et al., 1977a

along the apical dendrites. He suggested that the tufting appeared to be the formation of spines. The author conceded that these structures are rare but may represent a form of plastic response by an occasional neuron in the aged brain. Possible dendritic growth has also been reported in the brains of patients with Alzheimer's disease (Scheibel and Tomiyasu, 1978).

It is worthwhile noting that dogs (Von Braunmuhl, 1956; Ostewska, 1966; Wisniewski et al., 1970) and rats (Vaughan and Peters, 1981) are the only nonprimates in which age-related neuritic (senile) plaques have been observed. Vaughan and Peters (1981) point out that the neuritic plaques observed in the rat cerebral cortex contain the same three components found in neuritic plaques in humans: degenerating neuronal processes, neuroglial cells, and amyloid filaments. Aggregates of helical filaments are observed in the neuritic (senile) plaques in dendrites and axons in both normal and demented elderly people (Tomlinson et al., 1968), as well as in individuals with Alzheimer's disease (Kidd et al., 1964; Terry et al., 1964). These helical filaments may be species specific, since they are not found in the neuritic (senile) plaques in aged dogs and monkeys. Neuritic (senile) plaques were not thought to occur in the brains of other aging mammals, for example, rats and mice (Dayan, 1971; Wisniewski et al., 1975), but recent reports indicate their presence in rodents (Vaughan and Peters, 1981). The presence of neuritic (senile) plaques in aged rats (Vaughan and Peters, 1981) and dogs (Von Braunmuhl, 1956; Ostewska, 1966; Wisniewski et al., 1970) serves to support the use of these animals as suitable experimental models in aging studies, particularly those related to normal aging. Structural studies of the aged rat brain are extensive, but morphological studies of the aged canine brain are, at present, quite rare.

In the prefrontal cortex of the *M. mulatta* monkey, the frequency distributions of dendritic length in the 7- and 28-year-old animals were different (Cupp and Uemura, 1980). Loss of apical dendritic branches was observed in the oldest animals, particularly those terminal branches of short length. However, the number of longer peripheral dendritic branches remained the same or even increased. These authors suggested that in advanced age, certain branch segments in the peripheral part of the dendritic tree are lost, resulting in an increased length of the remaining terminal branches. In the prefrontal cortex of *M. mulatta* brains, Uemura (1980) also found a loss of dendritic spines, as well as a loss of synapses, with increasing age. In these old animals, the dendritic spines decrease at several dendritic levels, i.e., terminal tuft (25 percent decrease), apical shaft (25 percent), oblique branches (26 percent), and basal dendrites (29 percent). A significant decrease in the mean synaptic density was also observed (8.6×10^8 synapses/mm³ in animals 7 to 12 years old; 8.8×10^8 synapses/mm³ in animals 18 to 20 years old; 6.9×10^8 synapses/mm³ in animals 27 to 28 years old). This decrease corresponded in general with the loss of dendritic spines.

In autopsy material from the human cerebral cortex (16- to 90-year-old subjects), a slight decrease (13 percent) in the synaptic density was observed in the middle frontal gyrus layer III cells (9.56×10^8 synapses/mm³ in 74 to 90 year olds) compared to the relatively constant synaptic density throughout adult life (11×10^8 synapses/mm³ in 16 to 72 year olds) (Huttenlocher, 1979). Previously, Cragg (1975) found no significant decrease in synaptic density in the cerebral cortex. However, he reported a mean synaptic density of 6×10^8 synapses/mm³ which is lower than that reported by Huttenlocher (1979). It is possible that the different methodologies used by the two investigators to determine synaptic density resulted in different mean synaptic densities. Cragg's (1975) observations were based on counts in various cortical areas (frontal, temporal, and parietal; humans, 13 to 89 years old). It is likely that differences in synaptic density exist in different cortical layers, as well as in different areas of the cerebral cortex, and that one area of the cortex may be affected more than another area during aging. More study is necessary to determine if these differences exist in different areas of the cortex and to determine if the slight drop in synaptic density with age reported by Huttenlocher (1979) is significant.

Visual Cortex. Feldman and Dowd (1975), using Golgi-impregnated tissue, described a progressive loss of dendritic spines with age in the pyramidal cell layer of the rat cerebral cortex. In the pyramidal cells of 29.5-month-old animals, about one-third of the spines are lost relative to 2-month-old animals (36 percent of the spines on apical dendrites, 24 percent on terminal tuft dendrites, 32 percent on basal dendrites, and 40 percent on oblique dendrites). Connor and coworkers (1980a) reported that the type L (lollipop) dendritic spine density per unit length was nearly the same in the 90- and 630-day-old animals. A loss in the type L spines in 414-day-old animals with a subsequent increase in type L spines from 444 to 630 days of age has also been observed (Connor et al., 1980a). The density of type N (nubbin) spines increased from 3 months to 12 months and did not change thereafter. The basal and apical segments of the dendritic tree responded differently with age. Terminal dendritic segments in the apical tree appeared to grow and branch, whereas terminal segments in the basal tree showed a net growth but not a net branching. Sixth order dendritic segments were found to be 86 percent longer in aged animals which had spent their final 30 days in an enriched environment (Connor et al., 1981).

The results of Connor and coworkers (1980a, 1980b, 1981) are not consistent with the work of Feldman and Dowd (1975). The total number of synapses in 36-month-old rats was 20 percent of that in 3-month-old animals. A 26 percent decrease in axosomatic synapses and a 10 percent increase in axodendritic synapses were also reported (Feldman, 1976). A slight shift in the relative proportions of spine and shaft synaptic densities with age was noted as well. In young animals, 81 percent of the synapses are on dendritic spines and 19 percent on dendritic shafts, whereas in old animals, 74 percent are on spines and 26 percent on shafts (Feldman, 1976). The studies of both Feldman (1976) and Connor and coworkers (1980a) appear to be carefully done. The disagreement between them may be that different cortical layers were examined and different strains of rats were used. More data are necessary to clarify these differences.

In summary, it is difficult to draw decisive conclusions on the effects of aging on the structure of the cerebral cortex. Some neurons lose segments of their dendrites, and dendrites shed and/or rearrange their spines. Such injured neurons may lie adjacent to normal appearing ones, so the deficit, whenever it occurs, is not general even in the same locus.

Differences in the strains of some species and in the exact site of sampling probably account for some of the discrepancies in the literature. Recent enzyme studies serve to underscore this possibility. For example, in Sprague-Dawley rats, Strong and coworkers (1980) reported large losses of choline acetyltransferase (CAT) and glutamic acid decarboxylase (GAD) in cortex, but in C57BL/6J mice these enzymes were essentially unchanged. Strain differences have also been described to occur with age between two strains of mice (A/J and B6) tested for their motor abilities and upper body strength (Ingram et al., 1981). Trachimowicz and coworkers (1981) have also observed that the retinas of the pigmented mouse strain (C57BL/6J) maintain their full neuronal complement during aging and only show shrinkage at the latest time point studied (1000 days). These findings are inconsistent with retinal aging studies using albino rats (Weisse and Stotzer, 1974; Seitz et al., 1977; Lai et al., 1978; Glatt et al., 1979; Shinowara et al., 1980). Thus, it is important to consider that the strain, or even the particular animal (mouse versus rat), used in aging studies may result in variable conclusions which should not be generalized across strains or species. It is also important to be aware of the differences between albino and pigmented animals within a species when choosing an appropriate animal for aging studies.

Synaptic changes in particular types of synapses have not been reported, but they can be anticipated. In the frontal cortex of the human brain, substance P (SP) and neurotensin (NT) levels are unchanged (Buck et al., 1981), whereas GAD levels (McGeer and McGeer, 1976) and CAT levels (McGeer and McGeer, 1979) decline with age. One of the areas which is presently unexplored is the correlation between structural changes and those of a neurochemical nature.

Olfactory Bulb

The olfactory bulb is interesting because it shows continual neurogenesis and synaptic growth throughout life (Graziadei and Graziadei, 1978). In the rat olfactory bulb, mitral cells gain approximately 270 percent more granule cell synapses between 3 and 27 months, and then lose approximately 26 percent between the ages of 27 and 30 months (Hinds and McNelly, 1979). Generally, the ratio of perikaryal mitral to granule cell synapses changes in parallel with the growth of the mitral cells. The pattern of change with age in synapses per mitral cell and per olfactory bulb resembles that of the volume of mitral cell bodies. The number of synaptic junctions per square micrometer from 12 to 30 months remains the same. The loss of synapses between 27 and 30 months reflects the loss of mitral cells in the rat olfactory bulb during this time period (Hinds and McNelly, 1979). Additional synaptic growth on residual neurons apparently does not occur to compensate for the lost connections.

Sequential dilations in the apical, or primary, dendrites, as well as a distortion of the mitral cell bodies, have been reported in the olfactory bulb of aged mice (Machado-Salas and Scheibel, 1979). The dendrites appear progressively more irregular, and the dendritic tufts of the olfactory glomeruli become more nodular and show a decrease in the total number of branches (Machado-Salas and Scheibel, 1979). Horizontal, or secondary, branches also appear beaded and irregular. Spineless dendritic branches are characteristic of aging olfactory granule cells, and sometimes these cells exhibit swollen dendritic spines.

Patchy and uneven changes in dendrites as a function of age are characteristic of various brain areas in several species (see Tables 1 through 4). However, the frequency of abnormal appearing cells is usually unclear. For example, in the Feldman and Dowd (1975) study, a large variability in the loss of dendrites in the auditory cortex was reported, and Wisniewski and coworkers (1973) and Mervis (1978) reported that normal neurons were located in proximity to those with abnormal dendrites. Machado-Salas and Scheibel (1979) discuss the patchy and uneven distribution of changes which take place with aging not only in an individual system but throughout the range of several fields making up the limbic complex in both humans and mice. The question remains: Are the extremes observed with age the exception or a general response? Do the aging changes vary extensively from one area of the brain to another and between animals in a given strain or species? Comprehensive quantitative studies are necessary to clarify these points

in most areas of the brain and spinal cord, and in different species.

Hippocampus and Limbic Areas

In the hippocampus of the aged mouse, pyramidal cells showed fragmented and distorted basal dendrites, a decrease in the number of apical branches, and a scattered loss of dendritic spines (Machado-Salas and Scheibel, 1979). The same type of degeneration has been reported in granule cells of the human dentate gyrus (Scheibel et al., 1976). Differences in aging in the human versus the rodent hippocampus can be expected. CAT levels decrease by over 50 percent in human hippocampus (Davies, 1979; Bartus et al., 1982a), and such large decreases have not been reported in the rodent. This is one of the best examples showing structural differences between species in a specific neuronal projection.

Although dendritic atrophy is often described in the CNS, in some cases dendrites may continue to grow from mid-life to old age. An increase in both the number and the average length of terminal dendritic segments is observed in the human layer II pyramidal cells in the parahippocampal gyrus (Figure 2) (Buell and Coleman, 1979, 1981). This report may be the first evidence for morphological plasticity in the adult human brain. Grossly atrophied neurons are also observed both in the adult rat and in senile dementia brains. Buell and Coleman (1979) suggest that there are two populations of neurons in normal aging of the cortex: one that is dying and has a shrinking dendritic tree, another that is healthy and has an expanding dendritic tree. In the normal aged human brain, the latter group appears to prevail. There may be growth by healthy neurons to compensate for the loss of dendrites on the dying neurons. This same phenomenon may also occur in the rat pyramidal cells of layers II and III of the visual cortex. Connor and coworkers (1980b) reported that in aged rats a significant increase occurs in the number of basal dendrites, primarily at the intermediate segments.

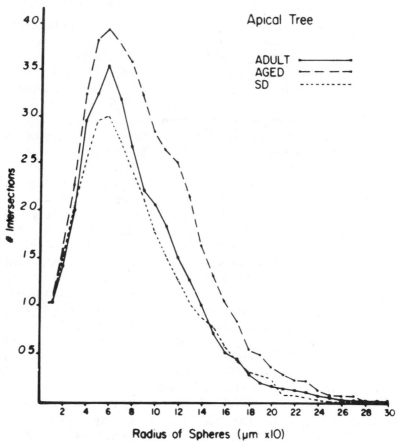

Figure 2. (A) Number of dendritic (apical) intersections per cell with concentric spheres centered around the cell body and spaced 10 μm apart. Points represent averages of the 75 cells in each group. (B) Dendritic length per apical tree as a function of centrifugal orders. Points are means of 75 cells in each group. (From Buell and Coleman, 1979.)

With respect to changes in synapse number with age, the rat hippocampal formation and dentate gyrus present a controversy. In a semiquantitative study of the rat hippocampus, axosomatic synapses were observed less frequently in the brains of old versus young rats (Hasan and Glees, 1973). These investigators also describe an increase in the incidence of dendritic profiles and dendro-dendritic contacts without intervening glial fibers in old animals (24 to 40 months), compared to young rats (4 to 12 months; Hasan and Glees, 1973).

More recent studies also show a moderate loss of synapses (about 20 percent) in the rodent dentate gyrus. However, the details are still uncertain, particularly with respect to the position where synaptic loss is maximal. The dentate gyrus molecular layer, where granule cell dendrites arborize, is commonly divided into three sectors corresponding to the lamination pattern of input (see Cotman and Nadler, 1978). In 3- versus 25-month-old Fischer 344 rats (Bondaroff, 1979, 1980; Geinisman et al., 1977) and in 3- versus 24-month-old Sprague-Dawley rats (Hoff et al.,

B

AVERAGE TOTAL DENDRITIC LENGTH / ORDER / CELL

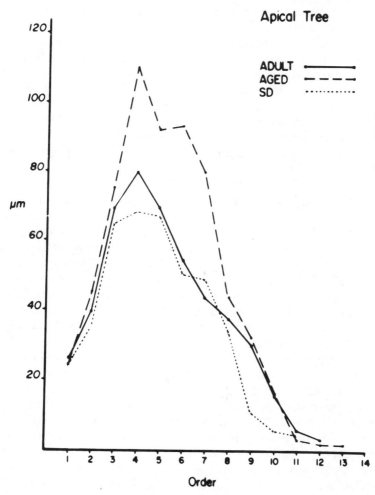

Figure 2. (*Cont.*)

1982a), the number of synapses decreases in the supragranular zone (the zone immediately above the granule cell bodies). In the old Fischer 344 rats, synapses per length of plasma membrane decrease by 15 percent; the number of synapses per square area of synapses involving dendritic shafts decreases by 35 percent, and the number of synapses per square area of synapses involving dendritic spines declines 24 percent (Geinisman et al., 1977). Hoff and coworkers (1982a) likewise found a significant decrease in the synaptic density in the outer molecular layer (the zone furthest from granule cell bodies) of 2-year-old rats (20 percent decrease). Within the supragranular zone, only the 2.5-year-old rats demonstrated a significant loss of synapses (31 percent decrease) when compared to young adults. The older animals in general show more animal-to-animal variability. Recently, the rodent dentate gyrus granular layer has been reported to increase 35 percent in total volume, with a net gain of granule cells (43 percent increase) between 1 and 12 months (Bayer et al., 1982). Bayer and coworkers have not extended their studies to include 24-month-old rats, so it is difficult to make a correlation between the net gain of granule cells and a net loss of synapses with age in the dentate gyrus.

The loss of synaptic density in the dentate gyrus appeared to originate primarily from one type of synapse. Synapses in the dentate gyrus can be categorized as simple or complex on the basis of their synapse junction and spine shape. Simple synapses (i.e., those with smaller synaptic junctions and noninvoluted spine heads) appear to be solely responsible for the loss of synapses in aged animals. In the outer two-thirds of the molecular layer, 20 percent of these synapses are lost in 2- and 2.5-year-old rats. No significant changes are observed in the middle molecular layer, and 26 percent decrease in the outer molecular layer is seen when compared to young adults (Hoff et al., 1982a).

Spinal Cord and Brain Stem

Only limited studies have been carried out on the spinal cord and brain stem. Machado Salas and coworkers (1977a) reported progressive dendritic changes throughout life. With the exception of a few sensory nuclear zones, such as the substantia gelatinosa and the nucleus of the trigeminal nerve (CN V), the neurons of most brain stem and spinal cord nuclei are relatively spineless in young mature animals, except for small projections along the shafts of the dendrites. In the aged mouse (26 to 30 months old), these projections disappear, and the dendritic surface appears featureless except for irregular swellings along the length of the dendrite. Some of the dendrites also appear shorter and thinner, and show constrictions; portions of the dendritic shaft are lost (Machado-Salas et al., 1977b).

The extent of the degenerative changes varies with age in the different brain stem and brain nuclear areas. For example, in the nucleus of the hypoglossal nerve (CN XII), less than 5 percent of the neurons appear atrophied (neuronal retraction, basophilic cytoplasm loaded with lipofuscin, pyknotic nucleus) compared to over 30 percent of the neurons in the same nucleus in mice (Machado-Salas and Scheibel, 1977a). However,

in the substantia nigra, up to 80 percent of the neurons show this kind of atrophy in the aged mice (Machado-Salas and Scheibel, 1977b).

In the rat lateral vestibular nucleus, dendritic swellings containing large numbers of mitochondria are more frequent in the 18- to 20-month-old rat than in young animals (Sotelo and Palay, 1971; Johnson and Miquel, 1974). These dendritic swellings also occur in the human brain (Terry and Wisniewski, 1972). A large increase (40 percent) in axonal terminals containing flattened vesicles which formed axosomatic contacts is observed in 18- to 20-month-old rat lateral vestibular nucleus, compared to 1- to 2-month-old animals. A 30 percent decrease in the number of axonal terminals with spherical vesicles which form axosomatic contacts has also been reported (Johnson and Miquel, 1974).

GAD levels, indicative of the status of many intrinsic and extrinsic connections in the brain stem, have been reported to remain unchanged between 2 and 26 months in the rat brain stem (Epstein and Barrows, 1969). The GAD levels appear to remain constant with age in the gamma-aminobutyric acid (GABA) systems in the brain stem. However, morphological changes in the GABA system may occur with age and could reflect a functional change with age which is not observed when measuring enzyme (GAD) levels.

Decreased levels of serotonin (5-hydroxytryptamine, 5HT) (Bucht et al., 1981) have been reported in discrete brain areas of both rats (Meek et al., 1977) and humans (Bucht et al., 1981). The findings of Meek and coworkers (1977) suggest that destruction of 5HT secreting neurons with aging is occurring. To date, quantitative cell counts of the raphe nuclear area (the location of the majority of 5HT neurons in the brain) in aged animals have not been done. A major loss of norepinephrine (NE) containing cells in the human locus coeruleus was observed in a subgroup of elderly Alzheimer's patients (Bondareff, 1982). Findings in laboratory rodents are divergent (see Chapters 22 and 24).

In a recent study, Ponzio and coworkers (1982) reported a significant decrease in NE concentration in the spinal cord of Sprague-Dawley rats, as well as a decrease in the activity of tyrosine hydroxylase (TH) in the brain stem. The levels of 5HT and 5-hydroxyindoleacetic acid (a 5HT metabolite) are unchanged with age in the spinal cord. However, Simpkins and coworkers (1977) report that the turnover of 5HT increases in the aged brain, a finding also confirmed by Ponzio and coworkers (in press). Dopamine (DA) levels decrease in all areas studied in the aged brain, whereas 5HT levels and turnover increase. An imbalance between DA and 5HT has been suggested to occur in the aging brain (Ponzio et al., 1982).

Hypothalamus

In the hypothalamus of aged mice, severe changes have been reported in neuronal and dendritic morphology. In the suprachiasmatic nucleus, enhanced swelling of the dendritic shaft and a decrease in dendritic arborization are observed (Machado-Salas et al., 1977a). In several hypothalamic nuclei, dendrites appear thin, irregular, and shortened, and they have no spines (Machado-Salas et al., 1977b). The anterior hypothalamus, particularly the preoptic area, shows a moderate loss of dendrites.

Hoffman and Sladek (1980) report that in the rat median eminence the density and intensity of LHRH and somatostatin (SOM) immunoreactive fibers decreased (Figure 3). DA fluorescent fibers also decrease, whereas the staining intensity and the number of DA neurons in the arcuate nucleus (the origin of the DA fibers in the median eminence) appear to increase with advancing age (Hoffman and Sladek, 1980). These authors suggest that this increase in DA intensity may indicate an age-dependent deficit in axonal transport or site of storage of the transmitter within the neurons. It is also possible that a higher turnover of catecholamines occurs (Lichtensteiger, 1971) resulting in an increase in cell body fluorescence and a decrease in the catecholamine terminal areas.

The study by Hoffman and Sladek (1980) is interesting and is one of the first to employ a semiquantitative immunochemical approach to the study of the aged brain. Partanen and coworkers (1982) have used microspectrofluorimetry of formaldehyde-induced catecholamine fluorescence to study regions which are known to contain dopamine (areas A8–10, 12) and norepinephrine (areas A1–2, 6–7) neurons. Significant decreases in catecholamine fluorescence were detected only in A12 dopamine containing neurons between 24- and 32-month-old animals. The discrepancy between the work of Partanen and coworkers (1982) and Hoffman and Sladek (1980) may be due to differences between the age of the animals used by the two groups or to the use of microspectrofluorimetric quantitation of catecholamine fluorescence by Partanen and coworkers (1982) and not by Hoffman and Sladek (1980). Quantitative studies are needed on other brain areas and other transmitter systems in young and aged animals in order to determine the changes in specific transmitter systems and specific nuclei with age.

In the hypothalamus of the rat, a significant decrease with age in the concentration of DA is observed in the Sprague-Dawley strain (Ponzio et al., 1982) but not in the Wistar strain (Algeri et al., 1978; Ponzio et al., 1978). However, a decrease in the synthesis of this amine is observed in the hypothalamus and striatum of Wistar rats (Algeri et al., 1978; Ponzio et al., 1978). DA histofluorescence is also reduced in the perikarya of old Fischer 344 rats (Sladek and Blanchard, 1981) and old monkeys (Sladek and Sladek, 1979).

Measurements of other transmitter-related markers further support relatively selective restructuring of the hypothalamus. For example, in rodents, TH (Cote and Kremzner, 1974; Reis et al., 1977) and beta-endorphin (B-END) (Gambert et al., 1980) show little, if any, change. It would appear that the hypothalamus shows a major remodeling of its circuitry, and more work is needed to identify these changes.

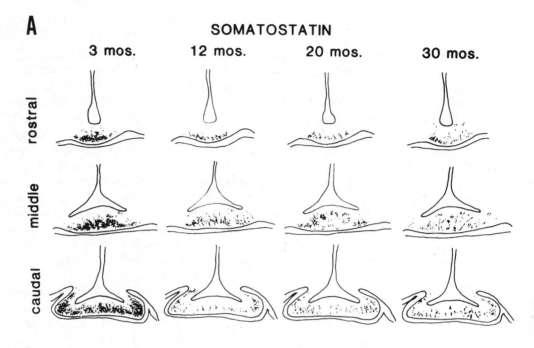

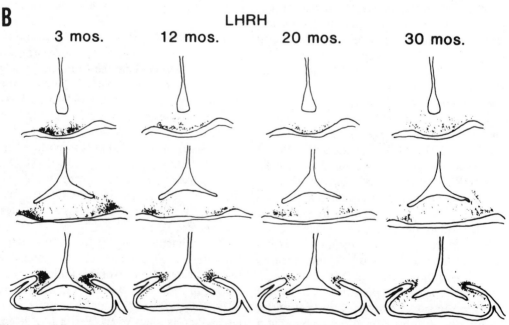

Figure 3. Schematic illustrating somatostatin (A) and LHRH (B) fiber staining within the rostral, middle, and caudal median eminence at four different ages. A generalized decrease in fiber density is seen at all levels of the median eminence during the aging process. (From Hoffman and Sladek, 1980.)

Cerebellum

In the 12- and 25-month-old rat cerebellar cortex, a 33 percent decrease in synaptic contacts on dendritic spines, but not on dentritic shafts, has been reported (Glick and Bondareff, 1979). A significant decrease in the surface density of the synaptic contact zones (S_V), the total length of the synaptic contact zones per unit area (L_A), and the numerical density (N_V) of the synapses in the cerebellar glomeruli of rats has been reported (Bertoni Freddari and Giuli, 1980). S_V, L_A, and N_V showed significant decreases between the adult (18 months) and the old (28 months) animals: 80, 81, and 58 percent, respectively. The authors (Bertoni Freddari and Giuli, 1980) suggest that the age-dependent decrease in synaptic parameters observed in the cerebellar glomerulus may be a morphological basis for the known decline in integration of complex motor activities performed by the cerebellum which had previously been attributed to an increased synaptic delay (Wayner and Emmers, 1958). A decrease in the numerical density of synapses within the glomerulus may have the same influence as an increased synaptic delay, resulting in a disruption of the processing of information coming from the periphery which is required for complete motor coordination (Bertoni Freddari and Giuli, 1980). It is surprising that more work has not been done on this well-defined structure (see, however, Chapter 24). Perhaps just as surprising is the absence of light or electron microscopic analysis on the basal ganglia despite their extensive enzymatic characterization with age.

In summary, age-dependent changes in synapses and dendrites are widespread in the CNS. Most studies report aging losses in synapses, dendrites, and spines. However, recent studies have also reported significant dendritic growth with age. It is likely that such changes, more subtle in nature, escaped earlier detection because quantitative methods are necessary for their detection. Probably, structural changes in the aged brain will consist of selective remodeling (increases and decreases) laid upon a background of age-

dependent disorders. At this time, only a minimal amount of data are available, and little has been done to relate gross structural changes to specific neurochemical ones.

Intracellular Changes

While this review is intended to focus primarily on neuronal circuits and their structure, it is worthwhile noting briefly intracellular changes in neuronal soma, terminals, and dendrites which may relate to synapses. In small diameter dendrites, large whorled membranous bodies have been described in the aged rat brain with increased frequency. These membranous whorls would seem to be a factor in the blockage and subsequent dying back of dendrites, but this has been questioned because they are not sufficiently widespread to serve this function (Vaughan, 1976). In some manner, the normal cytoplasmic transport along dendrites is probably disrupted, leading eventually to a loss of dendrites. Scheibel and coworkers (1975a, 1975b) have suggested that neurofibrillary tangles within the perikaryon at the base of the dendrites in the human cortex occlude the flow of material and cause dendritic remodeling. A severe loss of dendritic branches probably results in further loss as trophic balances or other disturbances occur.

Among the cytoplasmic changes which have been observed in neurons in aged animals are changes in the Golgi apparatus (Weiss and Lansings, 1953; Sosa and de-Zorrilla, 1966; Barden, 1971; Johnson and Miquel, 1974; Sekhon and Maxwell, 1974; Hinds and McNelly, 1979), fusion of the granules in catecholamine containing structures (Masuoka and Chase, 1980), changes in filaments and microtubules (Samorajski et al., 1971; Suzuki et al., 1978), and changes in free ribosomes (Nosal, 1979). A number of the mitochondrial changes have been reported to occur in aging animals (see also Wisniewski et al., 1973; Brizzee and Knox, 1980). These include granulated or fragmented mitochondria in the dorsal column nuclei in mice (Johnson et al., 1975), a decrease in the number of mitochondria in axons of the mouse pyramidal tract (Samorajski et al., 1971), an increase in the number of mitochondria in the neurons of the rat lateral vestibular nucleus (Johnson and Miquel, 1974), an increase in the diameter of the mitochondria in the mouse anterior pituitary cells (Weiss and Lansings, 1953), unusual shape and size of mitochondria (Rees, 1976), and a loss of the outer unit membrane of the mitochondria, accompanied by vesiculation of the cristae and formation of multivesicular bodies (Kaneta, 1966). Alterations in the mitochondria of the axon terminal (Wisniewski and Terry, 1973) are the first changes observed in the development of senile plaques.

Some studies report a decrease in Nissl substance (Cammermeyer, 1963; Johnson and Miquel, 1974; Sekhon and Maxwell, 1974; Nosal, 1979) or more dispersed Nissl substance (Hinds and McNelly, 1978; Hasan and Glees, 1973); however other investigators have not found changes in the Nissl substance in certain areas of the central nervous system in aged animals (Hinds and McNelly, 1978, 1979; Wilcox, 1951; Brizzee, 1973). Neuronal inclusions (other than lipofuscin) such as neuromelanin in the substantia nigra and locus coeruleus (Barden, 1971; Mann and Yates, 1974b), crystalline bodies (Fraser et al., 1970), rod-like paracrystalline bodies (Wisniewski et al., 1973), membrane-bound inclusions (Sekhon and Maxwell, 1974). complex membranous bodies (Vaughan, 1976), dense bodies (Johnson et al., 1975), eosin bodies (Fraser et al., 1970), calcium deposits (Fraser et al., 1968), spheroids and Lafora-like bodies (Suzuki et al., 1979) occur in the CNS of various species. Fibrillar or filamentous tangles or bundles are present in increasing numbers in the aged human hippocampus (Tomlinson et al., 1968; Morimatsu et al., 1975; Ball, 1977), rat gracile nucleus (Fujisawa et al., 1970), and lateral vestibular nucleus (Johnson and Miquel, 1974). (For review, see Brizzee and Knox, 1980; Mervis, 1981.)

SYNAPTIC GROWTH AND REMODELING

It is now well known that new synapses can form in the adult brain. Their growth can be elicited by partial denervation or various manipulations of the external environment. In the first section that follows, we shall discuss the capacity of the aged neurons to sprout and replace synapses lost when other cells are destroyed. These data may bear on whether or not residual neurons can replace connections lost upon natural cell death as well as after stroke and other forms of injury. In the second section, we shall discuss the remodeling and growth of synapses provoked by environmental manipulations. These capabilities are particularly relevant in that use or related stimuli may cause changes in the number and distribution of synapses which are a function of the environmental history of the animal or person rather than aging *per se.*

In the CNS, partial denervation elicits synapse replacement by the sprouting of residual fibers. Most, but not all, lesions cause sprouting. At present, it appears that age has no influence on the specificity of sprouting; that is, the same connection will form at any time. However, age can influence the rate of sprouting after partial denervation and, in certain cases, its magnitude.

In 2- to 2.5-year-old male Sprague-Dawley rats, the sprouting response declines with age in the hippocampus after an entorhinal lesion (Scheff et al., 1980a) and in the septum and hippocampus after a fimbria transection (Scheff et al., 1978). Electron microscopic analysis of synapse number has been carried out in the hippocampus after partial denervation. The data show clearly that synapse replacement is initially delayed and then proceeds at the same rate as in young adult animals (Figure 4) (Hoff et al., 1981).

The removal of degenerating boutons after lesion is also slower in aged animals. In both young and old animals, there appears to be a good correlation between the rate of reinnervation and the rate at which degeneration is cleared. This suggests that the slower re-

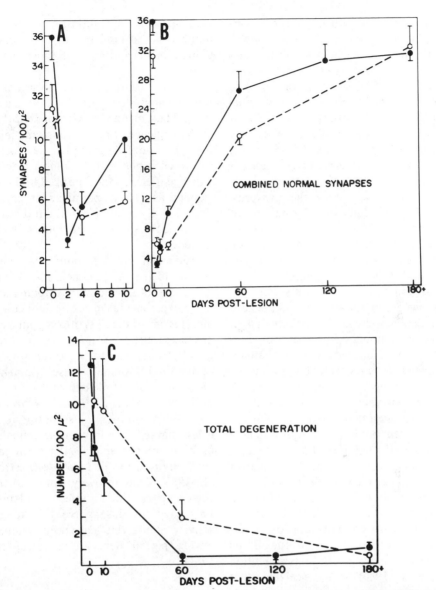

Figure 4. Time course for synapse reappearance in the ipsilateral outer two-thirds of the molecular layer after an entorhinal lesion in young adult (•) compared to aged rats (○). (A) Initial time course. (B) Complete time course. Note the nearly equal rate of synapse reappearance after ten days postlesion and the equal synaptic density at the end of the time course. (C) Time course showing the removal of the degeneration products from the ipsilateral outer two-thirds of the molecular layer in young adults (•) and aged rats (○). Note the more rapid removal in young adult animals. (From Hoff et al., 1982a, 1982b.)

pair rate in the aged brain after injury may be due in part to an age-related malfunction of the maintenance or cleanup capabilities of the brain. It has been proposed that this may involve endocrine mechanisms which stabi-lize lysosomes (Scheff et al., 1980b; Hoff et al., 1981).

The finding that synapse growth occurs in the aged brain, albeit more slowly, indicates that small injuries or "nicks" in brain circuitry such as occur with neuron loss, vascular insult, etc., may be repaired. In this way, sprouting may participate in the maintenance and stabilization of brain function. Sprouting in the CNS has been proposed to mediate recovery after certain types of spinal cord, hippocampal, cortical, and cerebellar injury (see Cotman et al., 1981). The exact consequence of the process can vary widely, however, and in most cases its significance is not understood. Sprouting can facilitate recovery or it can reduce the prospects of recovery through the formation of inappropriate connections. The return and/or maintenance of function depends on which connections form and how they relate to the total functional assembly. If the growth is homotypical (i.e., only fibers of like neurons grow), the system could benefit by the maintained circuit. On the other hand, replacement by a mixture of fibers could increase the noise along information channels and contribute to brain dysfunction with age.

Most sprouting responses are examined within the denervated zone. However, several reports suggest that synaptic growth and remodeling can occur at locations remote from the site of the injury. For example, it appears as if cross-union of motor nerves produces synapse remodeling in brain stem nuclei (red nucleus; Tsukahara, 1981) and amputation of a digit produces rearrangements in the sensory homunculus of the somatosensory cortex so that the digits remaining gain more cortical representation (Nelson et al., 1980). It is conceivable that this form of plasticity participates in the improvement of function. The influence of age on these forms of plasticity is unknown.

We recently described a related phenomenon in the hippocampus, and in this case the influence of age is known (Hoff et al., 1981). Unilateral lesions of certain hippocampal inputs can be made which produce essentially only unilateral injury. Synapse replacement occurs within the denervated zone on the injured side. However, in addition, synapse loss and reacquisition occur bilaterally in nondenervated zones. This effect is slow in onset and slow to return to normal.

It appears that such adjustments in synapse number at various levels of the circuit participate in reacquisition of functional symmetry.

Synapse turnover at distal locations in the hippocampus does not occur in aged animals. Thus, there is a qualitative difference in the sequence of events following injury in the aged brain. Apparently, the most difficult to elicit plasticities are most readily lost with age. Perhaps too, the aged brain cannot respond as fully to peripheral injury. Most likely it will be possible in the future to correlate recovery of CNS function with biological age.

Studies at the neuromuscular junction support in general the conclusion obtained in the CNS. Botulinum toxin is frequently used as an experimental means to induce sprouting. It is one of the class of compounds which produces sufficient inactivity to promote growth. Botulinum toxin treatment in young (2-month-old) animals causes a marked increase in end-plate length and terminal arborization. In older (10- and 18-month-old) animals, in contrast, the sprouting response is less marked than in younger animals, and in 28-month-old animals the toxin fails to elicit any measurable response (Pestronk et al., 1980). Thus recovery would not be expected in the oldest subjects, and presumably they are insensitive to changes in activity. Similar data have been obtained following partial denervation (Fagg et al., 1981).

ENDOGENOUS INFLUENCES ON SYNAPTIC GROWTH AND REMODELING

In the previous section, we described data showing that synaptic formation can actively occur in the adult brain after cell loss. The next question is whether or not the brain is also capable of responding to endogenous and/or naturally occurring influences with new synaptic growth and remodeling. If the brain is capable of this type of remodeling, what are the influences which cause or initiate this process in normal aging?

Environment

It has been established that dendritic spines are influenced by both age and environment (Coss and Globus, 1978, 1979; Globus et al., 1973). Connor and coworkers were the first to investigate the interaction between the environment and old age. Recently, Connor and coworkers (1980a, 1980b) described their initial experiments on the influence of environment on dendritic branching and spines in young and old rats. Animals placed into an enriched condition (EC) relative to the standard condition (SC) (animals housed individually) show slight increases (nonsignificant) in the number of dendritic branches and spines compared to the SC animals. It has been reported that dendritic spines decrease in density when a young animal has been isolated (Globus et al., 1973; Coss and Globus, 1978) and that there are morphological effects of environmental stimulation (Diamond et al., 1964; Volkmar and Greenough, 1972; Globus et al., 1973). In an early study, Connor and coworkers did not find a significant effect of the environment on either dendritic branching (Connor et al., 1980b) or dendritic spines (1980a). They suggested that the environment may be an important factor in changes which were observed in the CNS. More recent studies indicate that sixth order dendritic segments are 86 percent longer in aged animals (630 days old) which have spent their final 30 days in an enriched environment compared with their littermates which were housed individually (Connor et al., 1981). The total spine density of pyramidal cells from layers II, III, Va, and Vb of the visual cortex was not influenced by the two housing conditions (Connor and Diamond, 1982). The type L spine density was not effected by the different housing conditions. In contrast, the density of the type N spines was usually greater on neurons from rats which had been living alone irrespective of the cortical layer or the dendritic segment counted. The investigators suggest that type N spines are more responsive to environmental conditions in aging animals than are the type L spines (Connor and Diamond, 1982). Feldman and Dowd (1975) counted all spines and did not differentiate between them in their studies. Mervis (1978) suggested that the type N spine is a degenerating spine or a spine remnant. The results of the Connor and Diamond (1982) study indicate that the number of type N spines increases under conditions which may reflect a decreased amount of sensory input to the cortex. The decrease and then increase in type L spines may be a compensatory hypertrophy for spine degeneration. Another explanation might be the loss of a genetic repressor mechanism or the removal of some other inhibitory influence on the neurons. It is possible, in fact likely, that the aged brain can respond to an altered environment and that morphological changes due to cage experience can be observed throughout life.

Diet

It has been suggested that diet may effect aging and changes which occur in the brain and CNS (Bartus, 1979; Weindruch and Walford, 1982). Recent evidence shows that neuronal plasticity in the adult brain may be enhanced by dietary manipulation. The cholinergic precursors choline and lecithin have been studied since the availability of these substances in adequate amounts is normally a major rate limiting factor in the synthesis of acetylcholine (ACH). Thus, additional amounts of the precursor might be expected to stimulate the synthesis of ACH in aged subjects (Growden, 1979; Growden and Wurtman, 1979). However, these attempts have not yet produced convincing evidence of efficacy (Ferris et al., 1980; Bartus et al., 1982b).

After adult (8-month-old) mice are fed a choline-enriched diet for 4.5 months, tests show that they improve retention of a passive-avoidance measure and perform like younger mice in comparison to age-matched controls and that age-matched animals fed a choline-deficient diet perform as poorly as senescent (23-month-old) mice (Bartus et al., 1980). Mice maintained on either a choline-enriched or a choline-deficient diet for an additional 6 months were examined for morphological changes in the layer IV and V neocortical pyramidal cell dendritic spine population (Mervis and Bartus, 1981, Mervis, 1982). In all areas, except along the apical trunk of the dendrites, the choline-enriched mice have a significantly greater spine density than the controls. Along most lengths of the dendrites, the choline-deprived mice had significantly fewer spines than the control animals. This provides the first structural-functional evidence that dietary choline can apparently influence behavior concomitant with a corresponding enhancement or diminution of interneuronal communication (Mervis and Bartus, 1981). This further implies that not only may dietary choline change cholinergic mechanisms, but by increasing phospholipid synthesis, it may affect the production of dendritic membranes.

Recently, Bartus and coworkers (1980) suggested that although choline may be the rate limiting factor in ACH synthesis in young subjects, certain age-related problems in neural function, such as decreases in other apsects of cholinergic metabolism and transmission, may make the increased amount of precursor a necesary, but insufficient, condition for increased ACH synthesis and release.

Transmitters

To date, insufficient evidence exists to demonstrate definitive cause-effect relationships between neurochemical defects and the cognitive losses seen in the elderly. The cholinergic hypothesis is one suggestion for some of the cognitive deficits with age (Bartus et al., 1982b). Changes in some aspect of neuropeptide function may also play a role, either independently or in concert with other neurochemical defects (Bartus et al., 1982a). The neuropeptides of mainly hypothalamic and pituitary origin have been implicated in roles that influence behavior, independent of their neuroendocrine effects (Rigter and Crabbe, 1979). Measures of several neuro-

peptides show that they decrease in the brains of aged and demented subjects (Davies et al., 1980; Rossor et al., 1980a, 1980b; Davies and Terry, 1981). Quantitative measures of somatostatin (SOM) using radioimmunoassay techinques show a decrease in the brain of Alzheimer's patients (Davies et al., 1980; Rossor et al., 1980; Davies and Terry, 1981). Morphological studies using immunohistochemical techniques have also revealed a decrease in SOM in the aged rodent brain (Hoffman and Sladek, 1980). In a recent study by Bartus and coworkers (1982), several neuropeptides were tested in aged monkeys for their effects on a memory task which is normally impaired in aging animals. In no case are consistent group effects obtained with any single dose of any neuropeptides tested (ACTH, arginine-vasopressin, lysine-vasopressin, oxytocin, and SOM). Although reliable improvement in some monkeys is achieved, in absolute terms, these effects must be considered subtle.

In summary, effects of the environment, diet, and the addition of precursors or the transmitters themselves on brain morphology and behavior in aged animals have only begun to be examined. Neurochemical defects exist in the aged brain, and it remains to be seen if dietary supplements or other manipulations are capable of either decreasing or abolishing these deficits.

CONCLUSION

On the basis of the current literature, there are examples which can support almost any type of age-dependent change in CNS circuitry. In some CNS regions, dendritic spines and synapses are lost; in others, they appear to increase; while in still others, changes appear to be minimal. Few overall changes in structure exceed 25 percent (Tables 1 through 4) except in disease states and perhaps the terminal one or two months of life. Selective populations can be affected more, however, as evidenced by enzyme losses in excess of 25 percent. Some abnormal appearing neurons occur, but these seem to be the exception rather than the rule. Normal appearing cells often exist adjacent to abnormal neurons, indicating that the disturbance is not general. Some select neurons show a loss of fine dendritic branching and appear to have segments of dendrites where the spines have been lost. It is possible that these effects are compensated for elsewhere on adjacent or even distal neurons, or on the individual neuron itself.

Synaptic growth and remodeling probably occurs well into old age. Lesion-induced synaptogenesis has been demonstrated in the aged CNS indicating that this potential exists. Some neurons show more complex dendrites with age. This natural growth of dendrites, the gain of fibers, and the influence of diet on dendritic structure point toward a continued role of synaptic plasticity in old age. Some of the structural changes reported in the aged CNS may, in fact, be a form of plasticity. For example, losses or decrements in structure may, in fact, be an age-dependent decline in the need (use) of certain circuits.

Inconsistencies in the literature are most problematic and point toward a serious need for a better data base. There are disagreements between studies even in the same brain area. Rarely are more than two studies focused on the same issue, and it is difficult to draw conclusions when two studies disagree. It is our impression that much of the disagreement reflects subtle sampling problems. (e.g., exact lamina, subfield, etc.) and in some cases the strain of animal. Differences may also arise from the previous history of the animals used (caging conditions, diet, etc.). An additional inconsistency may result from the use of two-point studies, i.e., young versus old animals. Few studies also include animal groups between the young and the old animal, and important information may be overlooked because of this. For example, the work of Hinds and McNelly (1977, 1978, 1979) includes intermediate time points which add very important data to their studies that would have been missed if they had done two-point studies. It is necessary to de-

fine the conditions used exactly and to use animals at all ages from young to old in order to develop trends in aging rather than to look at only two time points.

Early studies are hard to evaluate because nonstandard strains were used and other conditions were not clearly stated. These types of pitfalls emphasize the difficulty, and even in some cases the futility, of poorly defined structural studies. Future studies need to take these considerations into account. At present, little information is available whereby structural changes can be related to particular pathways in which the transmitter type is known. Few studies have succeeded in relating structure to function in aged individuals. Nevertheless, progress is being made, and past work on CNS structures helps to provide a foundation for understanding the CNS and the changes which occur with aging.

REFERENCES

Algeri, S., Bonati, M., Brunello, N., Ponzio, F., Stramentinoli, G., and Gualano, M. 1978. Biochemical changes in central catecholaminergic neurons of the senscent rat. In, P. Deniker, C. Radouco-Thomas, and A. Villeneuve (eds.), Neuropsychopharmacology, pp. 1647–1654. Oxford: Pergammon Press.

Andrew, W. and Winston-Salem, N. C. 1956. Structural alterations with aging in the nervous system. J. Chronic Dis. 3: 575–596.

Artjukhina, N. I. 1968. An electron microscopic study of ageing changes of the synapses of the cerebral cortex of rats. Tsitologiya 10: 1505–1513.

Ball, M. J. 1977. Neuronal loss, neurofibrillary tangles and granulovacuolar degeneration in the hippocampus with ageing and dementia. Acta Neuropath. (Berl.) 37: 111–118.

Barden, H. 1971. The histochemical distribution and localization of copper, iron, neuromelanin and lysosomal enzyme activity in the brain of aging rhesus monkey and the dog. J. Neuropath. Exp. Neurol. 30: 650.

Bartus, R. T. 1979. Physostigmine and recent memory: effects in young and aged non-human primates. Science 206: 1087–1089.

Bartus, R. T., Dean, R. L., and Beer, B. 1980. Memory deficits of aged cebus monkeys and facilitation with central cholinomimetics. Neurobiol. Aging 1: 145–152.

Bartus, R. T., Dean, R. L., and Beer, B. 1982a. Neuropeptide effects on memory in aged monkeys. *Neurobiol. Aging* 3: 61–68.

Bartus, R. T., Dean, R. L., Beer, B., and Lippa, A. S. 1982b. The cholinergic hypothesis of geriatric memory dysfunction: a critical review. *Science* 217: 408–417.

Bayer, S. A., Yackel, J. W., and Puri, P. S. 1982. Neurons in the rat dentate gyrus granular layer substantially increase during juvenile and adult life. *Science* 216: 890–892.

Bertoni Freddari, C. and Giuli, C. 1980. A quantitative morphometric study of rat cerebellar glomeruli during aging. *Mech. Age. Dev.* 12: 127–136.

Bondareff, W. 1979. Synaptic atrophy in the senescent hippocampus. *Mech. Age. Dev.* 9:163–171.

Bondareff, W. 1980. Changes in synaptic structure affecting neural transmission in the senescent brain. *Adv. Exp. Med. Biol.* 129: 201–211.

Bondareff, W., Mountjoy, C. Q., and Roth, M. 1982. Loss of neurons of origin of the adrenergic projection to cerebral cortex (N. locus ceruleus) in senile dementia. *Neurology* 32: 164–168.

Brizzee, K. R. 1973. Neurobiological aspects of maturation and aging. *In,* D. H. Ford (ed.), *Progress in Brain Research,* Vol. 40. Amsterdam: Elsevier.

Brizzee, K. R. and Knox, C. 1980. The aging process in the neuron. *Adv. Exp. Med. Biol.* 129: 71–98.

Bucht, G., Adolfsson, R., Gottfries, C. G., Roos, B.-E., and Winblad, B. 1981. Distribution of 5-hydroxytryptamine and 5-hydroxyindolacetic acid in human brain in relation to age, drug influence, agonal status and circadian variation. *J. Neural. Trans.* 51: 185–203.

Buck, S. H., Deshmukh, P. P., Burks, T. F., and Yamamura, H. I. 1981. A survey of substance P, somatostatin, and neurotensin levels in aging in the rat and human central nervous system. *Neurobiol. Aging* 2: 257–264.

Buell, S. J. and Coleman, P. D. 1979. Dendritic growth in the aged human brain and failure of growth in senile dementia. *Science* 206: 854–856.

Buell, S. J. and Coleman, P. D. 1981. Quantitative evidence for selective dendritic growth in normal human aging but not in senile dementia. *Brain Res.* 214: 23–41.

Cammermeyer, J. 1963. Cytological manifestations of aging in rabbit and chinchilla brains. *J. Geront.* 18: 41.

Connor, J. R. and Diamond, M. C. 1982. A comparison of dendritic spine number and type on pyramidal neurons of the visual cortex of old adult rats from social or isolated environments. *J. Comp. Neurol.* 210: 99–106.

Connor, J. R., Jr., Diamond, M. C., and Johnson, R. E. 1980a. Aging and environmental influences on two types of dendritic spines in the rat occipital cortex. *Exptl. Neurol.* 70: 371–379.

Conner, J. R., Jr., Diamond, M. C., and Johnson, R. E. 1980b. Occipital cortical morphology of the rat: alterations with age and environment. *Exptl. Neurol.* **68,** 158–170.

Connor, J. R., Jr., Melone, J. H., Yuen, A. R., and Diamond, M. C. 1981. Dendritic length in aged rats' occipital cortex: an environmentally induced response. *Exptl. Neurol.* 73: 827–830.

Coss, R. G. and Globus, A. 1978. Spine stems on tectal interneurons in jewel fish are shortened by social stimulation. *Science* 200: 787–789.

Coss, R. G. and Globus, A. 1979. Social experience affects the development of dendritic spines and branches on tectal interneurons in the jewel fish. *Devel. Psychobiol.* 12: 347–358.

Cote, L. J. and Kremzner, L. T. 1974. Changes in neurotransmitter systems with increasing age in human brain. *Trans. Am. Soc. Neurochem.* 5: 83.

Cotman, C. W. and Nadler, J. V. 1978. Reactive synaptogenesis in the hippocampus. *In,* C. W. Cotman, (ed.), *Neuronal Plasticity* pp. 227–271. New York: Raven Press.

Cotman, C. W., Nieto-Sampedro, M., and Harris, E. W. 1981. Synapse replacement in the nervous system of adult vertebrates. *Physiol. Rev.* 61: 684–784.

Cotman, C. W. and Scheff, S. W. 1979. Compensatory synapse growth in aged animals after neuronal death. *Mech. Age. Dev.* 9: 103–117.

Cragg, B. G. 1975. The density of synapses and neurons in normal mentally defective and ageing human brains. *Brain* 98: 81–90.

Cupp, C. J. and Uemura, E. 1980. Age-related changes in prefrontal cortex of *Macaca mulatta:* quantitative analysis of dendritic branching patterns. *Exptl. Neurol.* 69: 143–163.

Davies, P. 1979. Loss of choline acetyltransferase activity in normal aging and in senile dementia. *In,* C. E. Finch, D. E. Potter, and A. D. Kenny (eds.), *Parkinson's Disease—II. Advances Experimental Med. Biol.* 113: 251–256.

Davies, P., Katzman, R., and Terry, R.D. 1980. Reduced somatostatin-like immunoreactivity in cerebral cortex from cases of Alzheimer disease and Alzheimer senile dementia. *Nature* 288: 279–280.

Davies, P. and Terry, R. D. 1981. Cortical somatostatin-like immunoreactivity in cases of Alzheimer's disease and senile dementia of the Alzheimer type. *Neurobiol. Aging* 2: 9–14.

Dayan, A. D. 1971. Comparative neuropathology of ageing. Studies on the brains of 47 species of vertebrates. *Brain* 94: 31–42.

Diamond, M. C., Krech, S., and Rosenzweig, M. R. 1964. The effects of an enriched environment on the histology of the rat cerebral cortex. *J. Comp. Neurol.* 123: 111–120.

Epstein, M. H. and Barrows, C. H., Jr. 1969. The effects of age on the activity of glutamic acid decarboxylase in various regions of the brains of rats. *J. Geront.* 24: 136–139.

Fagg, G. E., Scheff, S. W., and Cotman, C. W. 1981. Axonal sprouting at the neuromuscular junction of adult and aged rats. *Exptl. Neurol.* 74: 847–854.

Feldman, M. L. 1976. Aging changes in the morphology of cortical dendrites. *In,* R. D. Terry and S. Gershon (eds.), *Neurobiology of Aging* pp. 211–227. New York: Raven Press.

Feldman, M. L. and Dowd, C. 1975. Loss of dendritic spines in aging cerebral cortex. *Anat. Embryol.* 148: 279–301.

Ferris, S. H., Reisberg, B., and Gershon, S. 1980. Neuropeptide modulation of cognition and memory in humans. *In,* L. W. Poon (ed.), *Aging in the 1980's* pp. 212–220. Washington D.C.: American Psychological Association.

Fraser, H. 1968. Bilateral thalamic calcification in aging mice. *J. Path. Bact.* 96: 220–224.

Fraser, H. 1969. Eosinophilic bodies in some neurons in the thalamus of aging mice. *J. Path. Bact.* 98: 201–204.

Fraser, H., Smith, W., and Gray, E. W. 1970. Ultrastructural morphology of cytoplasmic inclusions within neurons of ageing mice. *J. Neurol. Sci.* 11: 123–127.

Fujisawa, K., Shiraki, H., and Katsui, G. 1970. Early phase of axonal dystrophy in vitamin E-deficient rats. *Proceedings of the 5th International Congress of Neuropathology.* Paris: Masson et Cie.

Gambert, S. R., Garthwaite, T. L., Pontzer, C. H., and Hagen, T. C. 1980. Age-related changes in central nervous system beta-endorphin and ACTH. *Neuroendocr.* 31: 252–255.

Geinisman, Y. 1979. Loss of axosomatic synapses in the dentate gyrus of aged rats. *Brain Res.* 168: 485–492.

Geinisman, Y. and Bondareff, W. 1976. Decrease in the number of synapses in the senescent brain: a quantitative electron microscopic analysis of the dentate gyrus molecular layer in the rat. *Mech. Age. Dev.* 5: 11–23.

Geinisman, Y., Bondareff, W., and Dodge, J. T. 1977. Partial deafferentation of neurons in the dentate gyrus of the senescent rat. *Brain Res.* 134: 541–545.

Geinisman, Y., Bondareff, W., and Dodge, J. T. 1978. Dendritic atrophy in the dentate gyrus of the senescent rat. *Amer. J. Anat.* 152: 321–329.

Gibson, P. H., Stones, M., and Tomlinson, B. E. 1976. Senile chanes in the human neocortex and hippocampus compared by the use of the electron and light microscopes. *J. Neurol. Sci.* 27: 389–405.

Glatt, H. J., Henkind, P., and Levine, H. 1979. Aging changes in the retina of the rat. *Invest. Opthal.* **18**, Suppl. 82.

Glick, R. and Bondareff, W. 1979. Loss of synapses in the cerebellar cortex of the senescent rat. *J. Gerontol.* 34: 818–822.

Globus, A., Rosenzweig, M., Bennet, E., and Diamond, M. C. 1973. Effects of differential experience on dendritic spine counts in rat cerebral cortex. *J. Comp. Physiol. Psych.* 82: 175–181.

Graziade, P. P. C. and Graziadei, M. 1978. The olfactory system: a model for the study of neurogenesis and axon regeneration in mammals. *In,* C. W. Cotman (ed.), *Neuronal Plasticity,* pp. 131–153. New York: Raven Press.

Growdon, J. H. 1979. Neurotransmitter precursors in the diet: their use in the treatment of brain disease. *In,* R. J. Wurtman and J. J. Wurtman (eds.), *Nutrients in Treatment of Brain Disease,* pp. 117–181. New York: Raven Press.

Growdon, J. H. and Wurtman, R. J. 1979. Dietary influences on the synthesis of neurotransmitters in the brain. *Nutr. Rev.* 37: 129–136.

Hasan, M. and Glees, P. 1973. Ultrastructural age changes in hippocampal neurons, synapses and neuroglia. *Exp. Geront.* 8: 75–83.

Hinds, J. W. and McNelly, N. A. 1977. Aging in the rat olfactory bulb: growth and atrophy of constituent layers and changes in size and number of mitral cells. *J. Comp. Neurol.* 171: 345–368.

Hinds, J. W. and McNelly, N. A. 1978. Dispersion of cisternae of rough endoplasmic reticulum in aging CNS neurons: a strictly linear trend. *Am. J. Anat.* 152: 433–439.

Hinds, J. W. and McNelly, N. W. 1979. Aging in the rat olfactory bulb: quantitative changes in mitral cell organelles and somato-dendritic synapses. *J. Comp. Neurol.* 184: 811–820.

Hoff, S. F., Scheff, S. W., Bernardo, L. S., and Cotman, C. W. 1982a. Lesion-induced synaptogenesis in the dentate gyrus of aged rats. I. Loss and reacquisition of normal synaptic density. *J. Comp. Neurol.* 205: 246–252.

Hoff, S. F., Scheff, S. W., and Cotman, C. W. 1982b. Lesion-induced synaptogenesis in the dentate gyrus of aged rats. II. Demonstration of an impaired degeneration clearing response. *J. Comp. Neurol.* 205: 253–259.

Hoff, S. F., Scheff, S. W., Kwan, A. Y., and Cotman, C. W. 1981. A new type of lesion-induced synaptogenesis. II. The effects of aging on synaptic turnover in non-denervated zones. *Brain Res.* 222: 15–29.

Hoffman, G. E. and Sladek, J. R., Jr. 1980. Age-related changes in dopamine, LHRH and somatostatin in the rat hypothalamus. *Neurobiol. Aging* 1: 27–37.

Huttenlocher, P. R. 1979. Synaptic density in human frontal cortex—developmental changes and effects of aging. *Brain Res.* 163: 195–205.

Ingram, D. K., London, E. D., Reynolds, M. A., Waller, S. B., and Goodrick, C. L. 1981. Differential effects of age on motor performance in two mouse strains. *Neurobiol. Aging* 2: 221–227.

Johnson, J. E., Jr., Mehler, W. R., and Miquel, J. 1975. A fine structural study of degenerative changes in the dorsal column nuclei of aging mice. Lack of protection by vitamin E. *J. Gerontol.* 30: 395–411.

Johnson, J. E., Jr., and Miquel, J. 1974. Fine structural changes in the lateral vestibular nucleus of aging rats. *Mech. Age. Dev.* 3: 203–224.

Kaneta, N. 1966. Histochemical studies on the diencephalon of senescent rats. *Tohoku J. Exp. Med.* 90: 249–254.

Kidd, M. 1964. Alzheimer's disease—an electron microscopical study. *Brain* 87: 307–321.

Lai, Y. L., Jacoby, R. O., and Jonas, A. M. 1978. Age-related and light-associated retinal changes in Fischer rats. *Invest. Opthal.* 17:634–639.

Landfield, P. W. 1979. An endocrine hypothesis of brain aging and studies on brain-endocrine correlations and monosynaptic neurophysiology during aging. *In*, C. E. Finch, D. E. Potter, and A. D. Kenney (eds.), *Parkinson's Disease—II. Advances Experimental Med. Biol.* 179–199.

Lichtensteiger, W. 1971. Effect of electrical stimulation of the fluorescence intensity of catecholamine-containing tuberal nerve cells. *J. Physiol.* 218: 63–84.

Machado-Salas, J. P. and Scheibel, A. B. 1979. Limbic system of the aged mouse. *Exptl. Neurol.* 63, 347–355.

Machado-Salas, J. P., Scheibel, M. E., and Scheibel, A. B. 1977a. Morphological changes in the hypothalamus of the old mouse. *Exptl. Neurol.* 57: 102–111.

Machado-Salas, J. R., Scheibel, M. E., and Scheibel, A. B. 1977b. Neuronal changes in the aging mouse: spinal cord and lower brainstem. *Exptl. Neurol.* 54: 504–512.

Mann, D. M. A. and Yates, P. O. 1974. Motor neurone disease: the nature of the pathogenic mechanism. *J. Neurol. Neurosurg. Psych.* 37: 1036–1046.

Masuoka, D. T. and Chase, D. 1980. The fine structure of large intensely fluorescent catecholamine-containing bodies in aged mouse brain. *Brain Res.* 182: 167–171.

McGeer, P. L. and McGeer, E. G. 1976. Enzymes associated with the metabolism of catecholamines, acetylcholine and GABA in human controls and patients with Parkinson's disease and Huntington's chorea. *J Neurochem.* 26: 65–76.

McGeer, P. L. and McGeer, E. G. 1979. Aging and neurotransmitter systems. *In*, C. E. Finch, D. E. Potter, and A. D. Kenney (eds.), *Parkinson's Disease-II. Advances in Experimental Med. and Biol.*, 41–57.

Mervis, R. 1978. Structural alterations in neurons of aged canine neocortex: a Golgi study. *Exptl. Neurol.* 62: 417–432.

Mervis, R. 1981. Cytomorphological alterations in the aging animal brain with emphasis on Golgi studies. *In*, J. E. Johnson, Jr. (ed.), *Aging and Cell Structure*, Vol. 1, pp. 143–186. New York: Plenum.

Mervis, R. 1982. Chronic dietary choline represses age-related loss of dendritic spines in mouse neocortical pyramidal cells. *J. Neuropathol. Exptl. Neurol.* 41: 363.

Mervis, R. and Bartus, R. T. 1981. Modulation of pyramidal cell dendritic spine population in aging mouse neocortex: role of dietary choline. *J. Neuropath. Exptl. Neurol.* 40: 313–320.

Morimatsu, M., Hirai, S., Muramatsu, A., and Yoshikawa, M. 1975. Senile degenerative brain lesions and dementia. *J. Amer. Geriat. Soc.* 23: 390–406.

Nelson, R. J., Merzenich, M. M., Wall, J., Sur, M.,

Felleman, D. J., and Kaas, J. H. 1980. Variability in the proportional representations of the hand in somatosensory cortex of primates. *Soc. Neurosci. Abstr.* 6: 651.

Nosal, G. 1979. Neuronal involution during ageing, ultrastructural study in rat cerebellum. *Mech. Age. Dev.* 10: 295–314.

Ostewska, E. 1966. Etude anatomorphopathologique sur le cerveau des chiens seniles. *In*, F. Luthy and A. Brechoff (eds.), *Proceedings of the Fifth International Congress of Neuropathology*, pp. 497–502. Amsterdam: Excerpta Medica.

Partanen, M., Hervonen, A., and Rappoport, S. I. 1982. Microspectrofluorimetric quantitation of histochemically demonstrable catecholamines in peripheral and brain catecholamine containing neurons in male Fischer 344 rats at different ages. *In*, E. Giacobini, G. Giacobini, G. Filogamo, and A. Vernadakis (eds.), *The Aging Brain: Cellular and Molecular Mechanisms of Aging in the Nervous System*, Vol. 20, pp. 161–171. New York: Raven Press.

Pestronk, A., Drachman, D. B., and Griffin, J. W. 1980. Effects of aging on nerve sprouting and regeneration. *Exptl. Neurol.* 70: 65–82.

Ponzio, F., Brunello, N., and Algeri, S. 1978. Catecholamine synthesis in brain of ageing rat. *J. Neurochem.* 30: 1617–1620.

Ponzio, F., Calderini, G., Lomuscio, G., Vantini, G., Toffano, G., and Algeri, S. 1982. Changes in monoamines and their metabolite levels in some brain regions of aged rats. *Neurobiol. Aging* 3: 23–29.

Rees, S. 1976. A quantitative electron microscopic study of the aging human cerebral cortex. *Acta Neuropath. (Berl.)* 36: 347–362.

Reis, D. J., Ross, R. A., and Joh, T. H. 1977. Changes in the activity and amounts of enzymes synthesizing catecholamines and acetylcholine in brain, adrenal medulla and sympathetic ganglia of aged rat and mouse. *Brain Res.* 136: 465–474.

Rigter, H. and Crabbe, J. C. 1979. Modulation of memory by pituitary hormones and related peptides. *Vitam. Horm.* 37: 153–241.

Rossor, M. N., Emson, P. C., Mountjoy, C. Q., Roth, M., and Iversen, L. L. 1980a. Reduced amounts of immunoreactive somatostatin in the temporal cortex in senile dementia of the Alzheimer type. *Neurosci. Letts.* 20: 373–377.

Rossor, M. N., Iversen, L. L., Mountjoy, C. Q., Roth, M., Hawthorn, J., Ang, V. Y., and Jenkins, J. S. 1980b. Arginine vasopressin and choline acetyltransferase in brains of patients with Alzheimer type senile dementia. *Lancet* 2: 1367–1370.

Samorajski, T., Friede, R. L., and Ordy, J. M. 1971. Age differences in the ultrastructure of axons in the pyramidal tract of the mouse. *J. Geront.* 26: 542–551.

Scheff, S. W., Bernardo, L. S., and Cotman, C. W. 1978. Decrease in adrenergic axon sprouting in the senescent rat. *Science* 202: 775–778.

Scheff, S. W., Bernardo, L. S., and Cotman, C. W.

1980a. Decline in reactive fiber growth in the dentate gyrus of aged rats compared to young rats following entorhinal cortex removal. *Brain Res.* 199: 21–28.

Scheff, S. W., Bernardo, L. S., and Cotman, C. W. 1980b. Hydrocortisone administration retards axon sprouting in the rat dentate gyrus. *Exptl. Neurol.* 68: 195–201.

Scheibel, A. B. 1978. Structural aspects of the aging brain: spine systems and the dendritic arbor. *In,* R. Katzman, R. D. Terry, and K. L. Bick (eds.), *Aging,* Vol. 1: *Alzheimer's Disease: Senile Dementia and Related Disorders* pp. 353–373. New York: Raven Press.

Scheibel, A. B. 1979. The hippocampus: organizational patterns in health and senescence. *Mech. Age. Dev.* 9: 89–102.

Scheibel, M. E., Lindsay, R. D., Tomiyasu, U., and Scheibel, A. B. 1975a. Progressive changes in aging human cortex. *Exptl. Neurol.* 47: 392–403.

Scheibel, M. E., Lindsay, R. D., Tomiyasu, U., and Scheibel, A. B. 1975b. Structural changes in the aging brain. *In,* H. Brody, D. Harman, and J. M. Ordy (eds.), *Aging,* Vol. 1, pp. 11–37. New York: Raven Press.

Scheibel, M. E., Lindsay, R. D., Tomiyasu, U., and Scheibel, A. B. 1976. Progressive dendritic changes in the aging human limbic system. *Exptl. Neurol.* 53: 420–430.

Scheibel, A. B. and Tomiyasu, U. 1978. Dendritic sprouting in Alzheimer's presenile dementia. *Exptl. Neurol.* 60: 1–8.

Seitz, R., Weisse, I., and Stotzer, H. 1977. Altersbedingte und lichtabhangige netzhautveranderungen. *Klin. Mbl. Augenheilk.* 171: 431–442.

Sekhon, S. S. and Maxwell, D. S. 1974. Ultrastructural changes in neurons of the spinal anterior horn of ageing mice with particular reference to the accumulation of lipofuscin pigment. *J. Neurocytol.* 3: 59–66.

Shinowara, N. L., Rapoport, S. I., Hoover, M. J., and London, E. D. 1980. Changes in retinal morphology and local glucose utilization (LGU) in 1 to 34 month old Fischer-344 rats. *Soc. Neurosci. Abstr.* 6: 346.

Simpkins, J. W., Mueller, G. P., Huang, H. H., and Meites, J. J. 1977. Evidence for depressed catecholamines and enhanced serotonin metabolism in aging male rats: possible relation to gonadotropin secretion. *Endocrinology* 100: 1672–1678.

Sladek, J. R., Jr. and Blanchard, B. C. 1981. Age-related declines in perikaryal monoamine histofluorescence in the Fischer 344 rat. *In,* S. Enna, T. Samorajski, and B. Beer (eds.), *Brain Neurotransmitters and Receptors in Aging and Age-related Disorders* pp. 13–21. New York: Raven Press.

Sladek, J. R., Jr. and Sladek, C. D. 1979. Relative quantitation of monoamine histofluorescence in young and old non-human primates. *Adv. Exp. Med. Biol.* 113: 231–240.

Sosa, J. M. and de Zorrilla, N. B. 1966. Morphological variations of Golgi apparatus in spinal ganglion nerve cells, related to ageing. *Acta Anat.* 64: 475–497.

Sotelo, C. and Palay, S. L. 1971. Altered axons and axon terminals in the lateral vestibular nucleus of the rat: possible example of axonal remodeling. *Lab. Invest.* 25: 653–671.

Strong, R., Hicks, P., Hsu, L., Bartus, R. T., and Enna, S. J. 1980. Age-related alterations in the rodent brain cholinergic system and behavior. *Neurobiol. Aging* 1: 59–63.

Suzuki, Y., Ohta, K., and Sun, S. 1979. Correlative studies of axonal spheroids and Lafora-like bodies in aged dogs. *Acta Neuropathol. (Berl.)* 48: 77–81.

Terry, R. D., Gonatas, N. K., and Weiss, M. 1964. Ultrastructural studies in Alzheimer's presenile dementia. *Am. J. Pathol.* 44: 269–297.

Terry, R. D. and Wisniewski, H. M. 1972. Ultrastructure of senile dementia and of experimental analogs. *In,* C. M. Gaitz (ed.), *Aging and the Brain* pp. 89–116. New York: Plenum Press.

Tomlinson, B. E., Blessed, G., and Roth, M. 1968. Observations on the brains of demented old people. *J. Neurol. Sci.* 11: 205–242.

Trachimowicz, R. A. 1981. Preservation of retinal structure in aged pigmented mice. *Neurobiol. Aging* 2: 133–141.

Tsukahara, N. 1981. Synaptic plasticity in the mammalian central nervous system. *Annual Rev. Neurosci.* 4: 351–379.

Uemura, E. 1980. Age-related changes in prefrontal cortex of *Macaca Mulatta:* synaptic density. *Exptl. Neurol.* 69: 164–172.

Vaughan, D. W. 1976. Membranous bodies in the cerebral cortex of aging rats: an electron microscopic study. *J. Neuropath. Exp. Neurol.* 35: 152–166.

Vaughan, D. W. 1977. Age-related deteriorations of pyramidal cell basal dendrites in rat auditory cortex. *J. Comp. Neurol.* 171: 501–516.

Vaughan, D. W. and Peters, A. 1981. The structure of neuritic plaques in the cerebral cortex of aged rats. *J. Neuropathol. Exptl. Neurol.* 40: 472–487.

Volkmar, F. R. and Greenough, W. T. 1972. Rearing complexity affects branching of dendrites in the visual cortex of the rat. *Science* 176: 1445–1447.

Von Braunmuhl, A. 1956. Kongophile Angiopathie and "senile plaques" bei greisen Hunden. *Arch. Psychiatr. Nervenkr.* 194: 396–414.

Wayner, M. J. and Emmers, R. 1958. Spinal synaptic delay in young and aged rats. *Am. J. Physiol.* 194: 403–405.

Weindruch, R. H. and Walford, R. L. 1982. Dietary restriction in mice beginning at one year of age: effect on life-span and spontaneous cancer incidence. *Science* 215: 1415–1417.

Weiss, J. and Lansings, A. J. 1953. Age changes in the fine structure of anterior pituitary of the mouse. *Proc. Soc. Exp. Biol. Med.* 82: 460–466.

Weisse, I. and Stotzer, H. 1974. Age- and light-dependent changes in the rat eye. *Virchows Arch. Path. Anat. Histol.* 362: 145–156.

Wilcox, H. H. 1951. Changes accomaning aging in the

brains of guinea pigs. *J. Gerontol.* 6: (Suppl. to No. 3), 168.

Wisniewski, H., Bruce, M. E., and Fraser, H. 1975. Infectious etiology of neuritic (senile) plaques in mice. *Science* 190: 1108–1110.

Wisniewski, H. M., Ghetti, B., and Terry, R. D. 1973. Neuritic (senile) plaques and filamentous changes in aged rhesus monkeys. *J. Neuropath. Exp. Neurol.* 32: 566–584.

Wisniewski, H., Johnson, A. B., Raine, C. S., Kay, W. J., and Terry, R. D. 1970. Senile plaques and amyloidosis in aged dogs. *Lab. Invest.* 23: 287–296.

Wisniewski, H. M. and Terry, R. D. 1973. Re-examination of the pathogenesis of the senile plaque. *In,* H. M. Zimmerman (ed), *Progress in Neuropathology,* Vol. II, pp. 1–26. New York: Grune & Stratton.

24
Neurotransmitter Metabolism and Function in the Aging Central Nervous System

Joseph Rogers
Department of Neurology
University of Massachusetts Medical School
and
Floyd E. Bloom
A.V. Davis Center for Behavioral Neurobiology
The Salk Institute

INTRODUCTION

Of all the infirmities of age, the deterioration of brain function may have the greatest human consequence. Senile cognitive dysfunction strikes the source of what makes us so uniquely human, our ability to reason and to remember. It already afflicts nearly two million Americans, a figure which will steadily increase through this century as population demographics shift (Ostfeld and Gibson, 1972; Miller and Cohen, 1981). Yet even if one is spared senile dementia, there remains the prospect of retaining a vigorous mind in a body that no longer responds properly, because of some age-related motor disorder such as Parkinson's disease. To be unable to act on the accumulated wisdom of many decades is a terrible loss, both for the individual and for society.

Brain biochemistry is at the center of most current efforts to ameliorate the difficulties of advanced age. Many of the anatomic changes characteristic of neural aging appear relatively irreversible. Not only are new brain cells not regenerated to replace old ones, it would probably be disastrous if they were. The precise synaptic organization laid down by a lifetime of memory and learned motor skills would be impossible to retain in the face of constant turnover of neurons. Because the brain is an organ perilously inaccessible to physical, anatomic intervention, it is natural that pharmacologic strategies play a major role in treatment of central nervous system disorders. This will be no less true for disorders of the aging central nervous system. The basis for modern neuropharmacology follows from an understanding of neurotransmitter metabolism and function; how neurotransmitter metabolism and function change with age is the subject of this chapter.

AGING OF NEUROTRANSMITTER SYSTEMS

The list of putative neurotransmitters grows almost daily, with reports of senescent alterations in each not far behind. In this section, we cover acetylcholine, dopamine, norepinephrine, serotonin, γ-aminobutyric acid, other putative amino acid neurotransmitters, opioid peptides, and other possible peptide neurotransmitter systems.

Acetylcholine

Acetylcholine (ACh) is widely distrubuted throughout the central and peripheral nervous systems. Until recently, physicochemical methods for determining ACh levels have been so insensitive as to be nearly worthless. Perhaps for this reason, investigations of age changes in ACh have been based primarily on evaluating changes in ACh metabolism.

Synthesis. ACh is synthesized from choline (taken up at presynaptic terminals) and acetyl coenzyme A (synthesized in mitochondria). The reaction is catalyzed by the enzyme choline acetyltransferase (CAT). Choline uptake appears to be the rate limiting factor and shows significant decline with age in several areas of rat brain (Hicks et al., 1979), particularly hippocampus (Sherman et al., 1980). The latter group of experimenters stress that their results are on V_{max} of the Na^+-dependent, high affinity choline uptake system; prior depolarization with K^+ stimulates choline uptake to similar levels in old and young rats, and there is no age change in K_m of the Na^+-dependent system (Sherman et al., 1981). V_{max} typically reflects the number of sites available for a particular biochemical process (here, choline uptake), whereas K_m reflects the affinity or activity of those sites with respect to some given ligand. Thus, the changes described for choline uptake may relate more to changes in number or activity of septal or hippocampal neurons (both of which can alter V_{max}) than to specific biochemical defects (e.g., changes in the structure-activity of binding site proteins).

Results on age changes in CAT activity are inconsistent. Significant decreases were reported in rodent (Strong et al., 1980; Unsworth, et al., 1980) and human (McGeer and McGeer, 1975; Perry et al., 1977b, 1977c, 1981; Perry, 1980) cortex, rodent (McGeer, et al., 1971; Enna and Strong, 1981; Strong et al., 1980; Noda et al., 1982) and human (McGeer and McGeer, 1975, 1976) striatum, rodent (Vijayan, 1977; Noda et al., 1982) and human (Perry et al., 1977c) hippocampus, and rodent cerebellum (Morin and Wasterlain, 1980; Unsworth et al., 1980). In every case, other studies of these same brain structures in the same species did not reveal age changes in CAT. Negative results include assays of rodent (Timiras and Vernadakis, 1971; Meek et al., 1977; Reis et al., 1977; Strong et al., 1980; Ingram et al., 1981; Makman et al., 1980; Noda et al., 1982) and human (Bowen et al., 1976; White et al., 1977; Spokes, 1979; Carlsson et al., 1980; Yates et al., 1980) cortex, rodent (Reis et al., 1977; Makman et al., 1980) and human (Bowen et al., 1976; Perry et al., 1977b, 1977c; Davies, 1978; Carlsson et al., 1980; Yates et al., 1980; Bird and Iversen, 1974) striatum or caudate, rodent (Meek et al., 1977; Lippa et al., 1980; Strong et al., 1980; Ingram et al., 1981; Sherman et al., 1981) and human (Carlsson et al., 1980) hippocampus, and rodent cerebellum (Timiras and Vernadakis, 1972; Vijayan, 1977; Noda et al., 1982). Waller et al. (1981) reported increases in CAT from 4 to 24 months of age in A/J and C57BL/6J mouse cortex, A/J cerebellum, and C57BL/6J striatum and hippocampus.

Ingram et al. (1981) made outstanding use of a within-subjects design to get around the heterogeneity of their data for CAT activity in old subjects. Although young and old rat hippocampal CAT did not differ when traditional between-group comparisons were used (i.e., analysis of variance), there was a correlation between the poor maze recall of old subjects and the CAT activity. Thus, old rats with normal to high CAT comparable to young controls performed relatively well in the maze, like the young controls, whereas old rats with low CAT performed poorly in the maze.

Bartus et al. (1982) have made the important observation that whereas CAT measures have not produced altogether consistent findings in normal aging, major CAT losses are almost universally obtained in cases of senile dementia (reviewed in Bartus et al., 1982). Decreases in CAT activity are typically small with normal aging, and so may be difficult reliably to detect. Senile dementia may occasion more extreme cholinergic changes, resulting in more consistently detectable differences. It should also be kept in mind that CAT has primarily been used as a marker for cholinergic neurons, not as an index of cholinergic synthetic capacity. Since CAT is not rate limiting in ACh formation, decreases in CAT would probably have to be substantial for any effect on synthesis to be evident. On the other hand, choline uptake is rate limiting in ACh formation. In view of the decline in choline uptake with age in several recent studies mentioned earlier, one might predict a senescent decline in ACh synthesis. Gibson and his colleagues (Gibson and Peterson, 1981; Gibson et al., 1981a, 1981b) have, in fact, suggested this result by showing that [^{14}C] glucose and choline incorporation into ACh decreases significantly with age in whole brain, cortex, hippocampus, and striatum of the mouse. Sherman et al. (1981), however, found no age change in ACh synthesis by rat hippocampal or cortical slices under basal or K^+-stimulated conditions.

Content. Only recently have data begun to emerge on central nervous system ACh levels in aging. Although it is tempting to infer that ACh levels would be lower given decreases in choline uptake and CAT, this could be balanced by concurrent decreases in ACh release and catabolism. For example, in the study of Gibson and Peterson (1981) the significant senescent decrease in [^{14}C] glucose incorporation into ACh was not paralleled by changes in ACh levels. Likewise, Meek et al. (1977) and Sherman et al. (1981) report no age-related differences in concentrations of either ACh or choline in rat hippocampus, cortex, and striatum. In rat cerebrum, Sastry et al. (1981) report 50–60 percent decreases with age in spontaneous and electrically stimulated ACh release. This decreased release could balance decreased ACh synthe-sis and may explain why ACh levels do not appear to change with age.

Inactivation and Catabolism. The synaptic actions of ACh are terminated by acetylcholinesterase (AChE), which hydrolyzes ACh to choline and acetate at prodigious rates. Data on age changes in AChE are even more contradictory than those for CAT. For example, decreases in human cortical AChE in one study (McGeer and McGeer, 1975) stand in contrast to other reports on human and rat cortex showing no change (Perry, 1980; Noda et al., 1982), and reports on avian cerebral material of a significant increase from 12 to 36 months of age (Vernadakis, 1973). AChE is also reportedly increased in human brain material containing senile plaques (Friede and Magee, 1962; Friede, 1965). Decreases (Morin and Wasterlain, 1980; Noda et al., 1982), as well as no observable age changes (McGeer et al., 1971), are given for rodent striatum and caudate. Rodent cerebellar AChE decreases (Meier-Ruge et al., 1976; Morin and Wasterlain, 1980; Unsworth et al., 1980) or remains the same (Vijayan, 1977), whereas avian cerebellar AChE rises dramatically (Vernadakis, 1973). Rat cerebral AChE is reported to decrease from 3 to 33 months of age, with concurrent increases in butyrylcholinesterase (Sastry et al., 1981). Three published assays on whole brain homogenates have shown a significant decline in AChE (Meier-Ruge et al., 1976; McGeer and McGeer, 1976; Ordy and Schjeide, 1973); earlier papers by some of these investigators reported no age change in total brain AChE (caudate plus rest of brain samples) (McGeer et al., 1971; Samorajski et al., 1971).

Receptors. There is better general concordance that cholinergic receptor binding declines with normal aging in both human and rodent tissues. Almost without exception, the alteration is in B_{max} (an estimate of the number of binding sites) rather than K_d (the affinity of the receptor for its ligand). Brain areas for which decreases in muscarinic binding have been reported (typically using the ligand quinuclininyl benzilate, QNB) include cortex (Perry, 1980; White et al., 1977; James and Kanungo, 1976; Strong et al., 1980; Enna and Strong, 1981; Noda et al., 1982) (but see also Morin and Wasterlain, 1980; Makman et al., 1980), cerebellum (Morin and Wasterlain, 1980) (but see also James and Kanungo, 1976), hippocampus (Lippa et al., 1980; Noda et al., 1982) (but see also Morin and Wasterlain, 1980; Enna and Strong, 1981), striatum (Morin and Wasterlain, 1980; Strong et al., 1979; Enna and Strong, 1981; Smith et al., 1981; Noda et al., 1982) (but see also Makman et al., 1980), and whole brain (Briggs et al., 1982). Curiously, these changes do not appear to occur in Alzheimer's disease patients (Perry, 1980; White et al., 1977; Davies and Verth, 1977) (but see also Yamamura, 1981). In their excellent review, Kubanis and Zornetzer (1981) point out that this suggests a different etiology—presynaptic as opposed to postsynaptic degeneration—in Alzheimer's disease. On the other hand, unless some compensatory mechanism in response to afferent loss is invoked, one wonders why Alzheimer's patients, who are themselves middle aged to elderly, would not also show the postsynaptic deterioration characteristic of normal aging. One telling explanation, offered in a comprehensive review of cholinergic mechanisms and aging by Bartus et al. (1982), is that comparisons are made to young subjects in studies of normal aging, whereas in studies of Alzheimer's disease, old people with Alzheimer's are most often compared to unafflicted old people. Thus, it is probably more accurate to state that Alzheimer's disease does not exacerbate the loss of cholinergic receptors typical of old animals (Bartus et al., 1982).

Although the extent of brain nicotinic ACh innervation remains unsettled, one report has suggested cortical decline of nicotinic ACh receptors with age (Davies and Fiesullin, 1981).

Function. The response of individual hippocampal pyramidal cells to iontophoretic ACh is decreased in old rats (Lippa et al., 1980; Enna and Bartus, 1981; Segal, 1982).

Behaviorally, a cholinergic link in mnemonic function has long been suspected (for reviews, see Deutsch, 1973; Moss and Deutsch, 1975; Davis and Yamamura, 1978; Davis and Berger, 1979). Since aged humans and other animals exhibit well-documented changes in memory, particularly that for relatively recent events, numerous investigators have sought a cholinergic basis (Drachman and Leavitt, 1974) and therapy (Barbeau et al., 1979) for age-related mnemonic dysfunction. Young adult humans (Drachman and Leavitt, 1974; Drachman et al., 1980) and monkeys (Bartus and Johnson, 1976) receiving cholinergic blocking agents (e.g., scopolamine) show recall and cognitive deficits similar in character to those exhibited by aged cohorts. In addition, these drug-induced deficits are reduced by the cholinesterase inhibitor physostigmine in both the human (Drachman, 1977) and the monkey (Bartus, 1978). As the next logical step in this work, facilitation of cholinergic neurotransmission was tested as a means for improving senile mnemonic losses. Recall of old monkeys with demonstrable delayed-response deficits is improved after administration of the cholinesterase inhibitor physostigmine (Bartus, 1979) or the cholinergic agonist arecoline (Bartus et al., 1980a). Both these agents have subsequently shown some efficacy in studies with old people (Drachman and Sahakian, 1980; Muramoto et al., 1979; Smith and Swash, 1979; Peters and Leving, 1978) and Alzheimer's disease patients (Sitaram et al., 1978; Christe et al., 1981). In the human and animal studies, finding a "best dose" for each subject appears to be important for physostigmine, but not for arecoline efficacy (cf. Bartus, 1979; Davis et al., 1979).

Long-term dietary manipulations of choline produce significant improvements in recall of middle-aged mice when the diet is choline enriched and significant memory deficits when the diet is choline deficient (Bartus et al., 1980b). The fact that choline therapy for senile cognitive deficits has so far not been successful in at least ten human studies (reviewed in Bartus et al., 1982) raises several important considerations about pharmacologic treatment strategies for aging. First, it is possible to begin choline enrichment at a relatively early age in animal studies and to carry that therapy through until such time as normal (i.e., unenriched) control groups begin to show aging deficits. This is not generally true in human studies where chronic treatment, even for several months (cf. Mohs et al., 1979, 1980), constitutes a very limited portion of the human life span and where drug therapy is initiated only at advanced ages when irreparable damage to cholinergic systems may already have occurred. The best pharmacologic strategy for aging may be a prophylactic regimen instituted before senescent deterioration begins. In this light, it is also worth noting that choline is an important structural component of cells and that any demonstrable "antigeriatric" effect it may have could owe more to the latter than to an effect on cholinergic neurotransmission. Results of treatment with lecithin (a dietary source high in phosphatidylcholine), like the results with choline, have also been somewhat disappointing up to this point, perhaps for the same reasons. However, a study in which choline plus piracetam (a GABA analogue) was given to rats produced significant recall improvements in the old subjects (Bartus et al., 1981), and this drug combination has shown some efficacy in limited trials with Alzheimer's disease patients (Friedman et al., 1981). An excellent short review of these and other data, particularly as they relate to cholinergic mechanisms in Alzheimer's disease, is provided by Corkin (1981). Bartus et al. (1982) also provide a detailed survey of cholinergic mechanisms and senile cognitive dysfunction.

Dopamine

Dopamine (DA) is widely distributed in the central nervous system, primarily through medium-length projections (tuberoinfundibular, incerto-hypothalamic, and medullary periventricular systems) and the long projections of the ventral tegmental and substantia nigra DA cell groups to neostriatal and limbic targets. Technical advances in anatomic and biochemical assays of DA and other catecholamines (CAs) have helped avoid some of the limitations of research on ACh.

Synthesis. The synthesis of brain DA requires tissue uptake of dietary tyrosine from the circulation. The initial and rate limiting step in conversion of tyrosine to DA is the hydroxylation of tyrosine to dihydroxyphenylalanine (DOPA). This reaction is catalyzed by the enzyme tyrosine hydroxylase (TH). DOPA is then decarboxylated to DA by aromatic amino acid decarboxylase (DOPA decarboxylase). Changes in tyrosine hydroxylase may also influence norepinephrine, a subsequent product found in pathways containing dopamine β-hydroxylase.

Activity of tyrosine hydroxylase is reported to decrease with age in a number of human and rat brain structures. These include striatum (McGeer et al., 1971; Cote and Kremzner, 1974; Algeri et al., 1977), caudate (Reis et al., 1977; McGeer and McGeer, 1976), putamen (McGeer and McGeer, 1976), substantia nigra (Cote and Kremzner, 1974), accumbens (McGeer and McGeer, 1976), olfactory tubercle (Reis et al. 1977), cortex (Algeri et al., 1977), diencephalon (Algeri et al., 1977), and brain stem (Algeri et al., 1977, 1982). The locus coeruleus and cerebellum of chickens show 50 and 86 percent decreases, respectively, from 8 to 60 months of age (Yurkewicz et al., 1981). Reis et al. (1977) find no change in tyrosine hydroxylase in several regions of aged mouse brain, despite observing significant alterations in similar regions of aged rat brain.

No change (Cote and Kremzner, 1974) in human and even increases (Reis et al., 1977) in rat hypothalamic tyrosine hydroxylase have been reported (but see also Algeri et al., 1982). Waller et al. (1981) report increases in tyrosine hydroxylase activity with age in A/J and C57BL/6J mouse cortex and cerebellum, no change in striatum, and increases in A/J hippocampus. Ingram et al. (1981) also find age-dependent increases in rat hippocampal tyrosine hydroxylase.

Many of the negative results on age changes in tyrosine hydroxylase reflect serious interpretational difficulties. For example, whole brain assays generally do not provide significant results (McGeer et al., 1971; Grote et al., 1977), but this does not at all mean that significant changes in specific catecholamine-rich structures would not have been found had those structures been assayed separately. A second interpretive difficulty in some studies lies in the designation of certain age groups as "young" or "old." For example, the lack of TH aging decline in men reported by Grote et al. (1974) may be due to the fact that comparisons were made to a 30- to 40-year-old "young" group. For humans, it may not, in fact, be correct to speak of senescent changes in caudate and putamen tyrosine hydroxylase, since the far greatest decline in the enzyme occurs before 20 years of age (McGeer and McGeer, 1978). For rats, on the other hand, neostriatal tyrosine hydroxylase decreases from around 10 months of age to the end of the life span (McGeer and McGeer, 1978). Finally, several investigators note the difficulties imposed by postmortem delay in their assays (McGeer and McGeer, 1976; Bird and Iversen, 1974; Grote et al., 1974). Human postmortem studies showing no age change in tyrosine hydroxylase include work by Robinson et al. (1977) and Grote et al. (1974).

In human brain samples from subjects 5–50 years old, DOPA decarboxylase activity declined with age in amygdala, putamen, caudate, substantia nigra, septum, and accumbens, but not hypothalamus (McGeer and McGeer, 1976). The decline in human substantia nigra was confirmed (Cote and Kremzner, 1974), but other results are less clear. Both Finch (1973) and Reis et al. (1977) report being unable to find any changed DOPA decarboxylase activity in mouse striatum or caudate, and Cote and Kremzner (1974) do find declines in human hypothalamus. Rat and mouse adrenal and superior cervical ganglion DOPA decarboxylase increases significantly with age (Reis et al., 1977), but no change is reported for whole brain samples from mice (Papavasiliou et al., 1981).

As with synthesis of ACh, where age changes in CAT may be less important than those in choline uptake (because the latter is rate limiting), so also alterations in DOPA decarboxylase may be less important than those in tyrosine hydroxylase. Brain DOPA decarboxylase occurs in 4 to 5 fold greater concentrations than brain tyrosine hydroxylase, and the latter is rate limiting in DA synthesis. Concurrent losses of both enzymes probably suggest a loss of DA neurons, not a biochemical defect. Alternatively, the maintenance of one enzyme with senescent loss of the other suggests a relative preservation of DA neurons and some hope that DA functional changes with age are treatable by pharmacologic means.

A dynamic means for measuring DA synthesis is by administration of radiolabeled precursors. When this is done, impairments are seen in senescent mouse cerebellum, brain stem, hypothalamus, and striatum (Finch, 1973), as well as rat hypothalamus and striatum (Ponzio et al., 1978).

Synthesis of DA has also recently been tested in old rats by measuring accumulation of DOPA after inhibition of DOPA decarboxylase. Decreases are found in median eminence, but not striatum, of old male rats (Demarest et al., 1980) and old, anestrous, female rats (Demarest et al., 1982).

Content. In general, there is consensus that DA levels are decreased after mid-life in the striatum. Subject species include mice (Finch, 1973; Osterburg et al., 1981) (but see also Papavasiliou et al., 1981), rats (Joseph et al., 1978; Demarest et al., 1980), and man (Bertler, 1961; Hornykiewicz, 1974; Carlsson and Winblad, 1976; Carlsson et al., 1980; Riederer and Wuketich, 1976; Adolfsson et al., 1979). Parkinson's disease, which has an age-related onset, is also characterized by severe nigrostriatal DA deficiencies (Hornykiewicz, 1974; Lee et al., 1978). However, Bird and Iversen (1974) and Adolfsson et al. (1979) report no change in human putamen DA levels (nonparkinsonian patients), and Makman et al. (1980) fail to find an age change in rabbit striatal DA.

The striatum is an obvious, DA-rich area to assay for DA age changes; more varied results have been found in other brain structures. DA concentrations are unchanged with age in mouse olfactory bulbs (Osterburg et al., 1981). Hippocampal DA—a minute fraction of total catecholamine there—is unchanged in old rats (Roubein et al., 1981) but declines with age in humans (Adolfsson et al., 1979). Several reports on hypothalamic DA show an aging decline (Miller et al., 1976; Simpkins et al., 1977; Austin et al., 1978), but other studies have not always replicated these results (Huang et al., 1979; Ponzio et al., 1978; Carlsson et al., 1980; Adolfsson et al., 1979). One explanation may be differences in dissection: significant DA losses are found in mouse (Osterburg et al., 1981) and rat (Estes and Simpkins, 1980; Demarest et al., 1980) median eminence, a DA-rich area that, in our experience, is easy to lose in a whole hypothalamus dissection. Such regional differences, in fact, may occur throughout the hypothalamus. For example, Estes and Simpkins (1980) have assayed discrete regions of the structure in rats and found that whereas some mediobasal hypothalamic nuclei lose DA with age, several other regions of the preoptic area gain DA with age. Similar regional differences in age changes of mouse hypothalamic DA are also evident in the data of Osterburg et al. (1981). In this light, perhaps it is not surprising that results on whole hypothalamus show no major senescent alteration. The same caveat probably also applies to whole brain assays of DA, which have shown near universal negative results in mice (Finch, 1973; Papavisiliou et al., 1981) and rats (McGeer et al., 1971). No age change is observed in nucleus accumbens or posterior pituitary DA content of old male rats (Demarest et al., 1980), although these authors do find decreases in these structures in old female rats (Demarest et al., 1982).

Another basis for differences in experimental results on DA concentrations with age may be due to differences in the ages of subject groups. Osterburg et al. (1981) have provided evidence that losses of DA are not progressive through the life span of the mouse, but rather are a relatively late change.

Inactivation and Catabolism. The synaptic actions of DA are terminated by presynaptic reuptake and by actions of the enzymes monoamine oxidase (MAO) and, possibly, catechol O-methyltransferase (COMT). DA uptake by synaptosomes from mouse striatum, hypothalamus (Jonec and Finch, 1975), and forebrain (Haycock et al., 1977) is reduced with age. However, DA uptake from striatal slices in rats shows no consistent aging trend (Thompson et al., 1981), nor does amphetamine or KCl-stimulated DA release (Thompson et al., 1981).

MAO increases in senescent human brain and serum (Grote et al., 1974; Robinson et al., 1972, 1977; Robinson, 1975; Carlsson et al., 1980), and in rat caudate-putamen (Noda et al., 1982). COMT may (Algeri et al., 1976; Stramentinoli et al., 1977) or may not (Prange et al., 1967) show similar increases with age in rat brain. Mouse brain MAO activity (assayed with DA as substrate) increases with age, but COMT does not (Papavasiliou et al., 1981). The results showing MAO and COMT elevation are consistent with increases of monoamine catabolites in cerebrospinal fluid (CSF) of elderly patients (Robinson et al., 1972; Gottfries et al., 1971) (but see also Bowers and Gerbode, 1968). However, the approximately 25 percent decreased levels of homovanillic acid (HVA, a DA catabolite) in aged rat striatum, limbic area, and substantia nigra (Algeri et al., 1982) further complicate simple predictions about DA metabolism based on senescent alterations in MAO.

DA turnover rates, which provide a dynamic measure of both levels and metabolism, show senescent decline in mouse rostral striatum (Osterburg et al., 1981) and rat striatum (Ponzio et al., 1978; Algeri et al., 1982). The findings in hypothalamus are mixed, depending on the region assayed. DA turnover in whole hypothalamus exhibits no age change according to Huang et al. (1977). In a subsequent study, however, this group observed losses in mediobasal, but not other hypothalamic areas (Simpkins et al., 1977). Osterburg et al. (1981) find little change in DA turnover in medial preoptic, suprachiasmatic, zona incerta, and retrochiasmatic regions of old mouse hypothalamus, but a significant decrease in the median eminence-arcuate area. This variability for hypothalamic DA turnover parallels that for hypothalamic DA levels—probably for similar reasons (e.g., differences in dissections, discreteness of dissections).

Receptors. As with synthetic mechanisms and levels, DA-related ligand displacement binding (often considered to quantify total receptors) exhibits its most consistent change in striatum. This aging decline apparently holds true over a wide range of species, including rabbits (Thal et al., 1980), mice (Severson and Finch, 1980b), rats (Govoni et al., 1980; Joseph et al., 1978; Makman et al., 1978; Misra et al., 1980; Severson and Finch, 1980b; Smith et al., 1981) and man (caudate, substantia nigra, accumbens) (Severson and Finch, 1980a).

Parkinson's disease, with its attendant striatal DA deficits, can result in significant increases in postsynaptic DA receptors (Lee et al., 1978). This result is really not so surprising when the facility of DA systems for up- and down-regulation is considered. Consistent with this, DA receptor binding decreases (Yamamura, 1981) to normal (Lee et al., 1978) in Parkinson's patients after chronic L-DOPA therapy. On the other hand, if plasticity of DA systems explains increased DA binding in Parkinson's disease (in response to decreased DA levels), then it becomes difficult to reconcile consistent findings of both decreased DA binding and decreased DA levels in normal aging. One explanation could be that senescent animals lose much of their capacity for compensatory receptor increases (Greenberg and Weiss, 1978, 1979; Randall et al., 1981) (but see also Joseph et al., 1981; Smith et al., 1981). Parkinson's disease frequently strikes in middle age and, thus, the deficiency in DA levels could occur before the senescent loss in ability to up-regulate receptors. In normal aging, however, both DA up-regulation and DA levels could concurrently be lost. Such an explanation is parsimonious, but altogether speculative (for other attempts to reconcile Parkinson's and Huntington's disease with normal DA aging, see Finch, 1980).

Function. In several DA systems (e.g., nigrostriatal), the DA receptor is functionally linked to a cAMP second messenger. As would be expected, there is a good match between the decreased receptor binding in these systems and a decreased ability of exogenously applied DA to stimulate cAMP accumulation. Thus, rat and rabbit caudate, substantia nigra, and striatal samples exhibit aging declines in cAMP after incubation with DA (Govoni et al., 1977; Makman et al., 1978, 1980; Puri and Volicer, 1977; Walker and Walker 1973). Cortex, hypothalamus, hippocampus, and cerebellum also may show this change (Makman et al., 1980; Walker and Walker, 1973).

Basal (i.e., nonstimulated) cAMP activity does not so consistently show senescent DA decline. Schmidt (1981) reviews studies reporting no basal cAMP age change (Joseph et al., 1978; Govoni et al., 1977; Puri and Volicer, 1977; Makman et al., 1978), including unpublished data of his own; use of a new microwave apparatus for killing rats revealed decreased basal cAMP from 12 to 24 months of age in rat striatum, hippocampus, and hypothalamus (Schmidt, 1981). Basal adenylate cyclase activity also declines significantly in whole brain samples from old mice (Papavasiliou et al., 1981), as does basal cAMP in cerebellar samples from old rats (Austin et al., 1978). On the other hand, Zimmerman and Berg (1975) find no change in old rat cortical adenylate cyclase, despite a significant decrease in basal cAMP concentrations, and Walker and Walker (1973) report significantly elevated basal adenylate cyclase activity in caudate and cerebellum of old rats.

The fact that DA stimulation of adenylate cyclase consistently exhibits an aging decline, but there remain disparities in the results on basal adenylate cyclase, should not necessarily be troublesome and, in fact, may be suggestive. Neurotransmitters other than DA, particularly norepinephrine, may also employ a cAMP second messenger, and cAMP plays an important role in many cellular processes not specifically related to neurons or neurotransmission. Relative stability of these latter processes could easily obscure aging deficits in the functional link between DA and adenylate cyclase. Indeed, the coɪ sistency of results obtained when the enzyme is incubated with DA (and the inconsistency of results when only basal, nonstimulated activity is measured) suggests a specific deficit in the coupling of DA receptors with cAMP-producing mechanisms.

The tuberoinfundibular DA system is believed to help regulate anterior pituitary release of prolactin and, possibly, luteinizing hormone (LH) (Weiner and Ganong, 1978). In their study showing decreased median eminence DA synthesis and concentrations in old male rats, Demarest et al. (1980) also observed a significant increase in serum prolactin and a significant decrease in serum LH with age. The data on prolactin were replicated by Barden et al. (1981). These results on prolactin are consistent with the hypothesis, from other studies, that DA inhibits pituitary prolactin release (Weiner and Ganong, 1978). Thus, an aging decline in tuberoinfundibular DA might be expected to lead to increased release of prolactin into the circulation.

Age changes in hypothalamic DA systems, perhaps acting through changes in prolactin secretion (Estes et al., 1982), are widely implicated in senescent disruption of estrous cycling (cf. Meites, 1981; see also Chapter 21). L-DOPA and tyrosine administration, for example, can reinitiate estrous cycling in old, acyclic rodents (Meites et al., 1978). Alternatively, there are few hypothalamic neurotransmitters that have not been suggested to play a role in female reproductive senescence (see the sections on norepinephrine, serotonin, and enkephkalin). Which, if any, neurotransmitter plays the primary role remains to be determined.

Behavioral results are also generally consistent with a decline in DA systems during the life span. Typical responses (e.g., increased locomotor activity, stereotypy) to

high doses of DA agonists (e.g., apomorphine) are blunted in old rodents (Lal et al., 1979; Bhattacharyya and Pradhan, 1980; Verzar, 1961) (but see also Smith et al., 1981).

Old rats appear deficient in their ability to thermoregulate in response to a cold stress challenge (Algeri et al., 1982; see Chapter 21). Likewise, these same aged subjects are deficient in their ability to increase hypothalamic TH in response to cold stress (Algeri et al., 1982). The causal relationship between impaired thermoregulatory and TH responses suggested in the report, however, remains to be tested.

Papavasiliou et al. (1981) report that chronic dietary supplementation with L-DOPA protects mice from the age-related decreases in motor activity observed in non-supplemented cohorts. Moreover, L-DOPA supplementation in this study (Papavasiliou et al., 1981) and an earlier one (Cotzias et al., 1977) appears to have exerted perhaps the ultimate functional effect on aging: it prolonged the mean life span of treated mice by 50 percent. Unfortunately, these potentially important results will require further confirmation since the maximum life span for the control group ($N = 100$) in the later study (Papavasiliou et al., 1981) was only 23 months, a period nearly a third shorter than usual for most mouse strains (Storer, 1969), and the purported 50 percent extension of *mean* life span for the L-DOPA supplemented mice actually amounted to a mean longevity of only about 650 days (Cotzias et al., 1977; Papavasiliou et al., 1981), which is fairly typical for untreated mice in other studies (cf. Abbey, 1979).

Joseph and his colleagues (Joseph et al., 1978, 1980, 1981; Thompson et al., 1981; Cubells and Joseph, 1981) have systematically attempted to develop behavioral correlates of senescent striatal DA deficiencies. Using lesion-induced rotational behavior as a paradigm, these workers have demonstrated that old rats exhibit denervation supersensitivity, an approximately 50 percent DA receptor increase. This ability of old rats to up-regulate DA receptors after denervation is equivalent to the 50 percent increase in young rats (Joseph et al., 1981). However, the old rats start from a baseline 40 percent lower. The rotational response of unilaterally lesioned rats to contralateral DA injection is, therefore, blunted in old rats (Cubells and Joseph, 1981). Interestingly, whereas L-DOPA administration potentiates rotation in lesioned young animals, it does not do so in old animals, which suggests presynaptic defects in DA metabolism in addition to changes in DA receptors (Joseph et al., 1980).

Finally, some note must be taken of DA augmentation therapy in Parkinson's disease, for it provides an excellent example of the practical, human usefulness of biochemical studies of aging. Once basic research had revealed the severe nigrostriatal loss of DA and DA-containing cells characteristic of this pathology (Ehringer and Hornykiewicz, 1960; Hornykiewicz, 1974), a pharmacologic rationale for clinical treatment became apparent. Although DA itself does not readily cross the blood-brain barrier, L-DOPA, its immediate precursor, does (Franz, 1975). On reaching the brain (but also in the peripheral circulation), L-DOPA is rapidly decarboxylated to DA, thus increasing brain DA levels. This augmentation of brain DA presumably helps restore more normal balance of DA and ACh tone, although other mechanisms of action are possible (discussed in Franz, 1975). In any case, the functional effects of L-DOPA therapy (especially in combination with drugs which inhibit peripheral decarboxylase activity) can be dramatic, and the success of this treatment has largely eliminated the need for surgical intervention even in the most severe cases of Parkinson's disease (Adams and Victor, 1977).

Norepinephrine

Norepinephrine (NE) shares with DA several enzymes of synthesis and catabolism. Thus, many of the age changes described earlier for DA metabolic systems are equally applicable to NE. For example, decreased levels of tyrosine hydroxylase will result in decreased synthesis of both DA and NE. Central NE systems are derived mainly from the locus coeruleus, a prominent nucleus located in the brain stem reticular formation at the level of the isthmus. NE-containing locus coeruleus cell bodies are highly collateralized, projecting to virtually all areas of the central nervous system, including the telencephalon, diencephalon, brain stem, cerebellum, and spinal cord.

Synthesis. NE is synthesized by the action of dopamine β-hydroxylase (DBH) on DA. Age changes in tyrosine hydroxylase, DOPA decarboxylase, and DA have been described in the previous section. Given the widespread overlap in general regional distribution of NE and DA in brain (although not in specific target nuclei), and their parallel synthetic mechanisms, it is possible that the changes described for DA metabolism actually derive more from changes in NE systems (which contain, up to the point of DBH, the same enzymes and precursors). This is especially true, for example, in the work of Yurkewicz et al. (1981) who report a 50 percent drop in locus coeruleus tyrosine hydroxylase activity in very old chickens (60 months). As mentioned above, the locus coeruleus is a primary source for central NE. Senescent decreases in DBH were described for rat hypothalamus (Reis et al., 1977), but not for the NE-rich locus coeruleus (Reis et al., 1977) or the DA-rich mouse caudate (Reis et al., 1977), human striatum, or human substantia nigra (Grote et al., 1977).

Content. As with assays on DA, NE levels do not change with age in whole brain preparations (Finch 1973; Austin et al., 1978; Papavasiliou et al., 1981; Samorajski et al., McGeer et al., 1971). However, when some consideration is paid to the anatomy of the system, the biochemical results are both more useful and more sensitive. Thus, brain stem assays, which incorporate the locus coeruleus, almost universally show aging declines in man (Robinson, 1975; Robinson et al., 1972; Rolsten, 1973; Nies et al., 1973) monkeys (Samorajski and Rolsten, 1973), mice (Sun, 1976) (but see also Finch, 1973), and rats (Ponzio et al., 1978; Ida et al., 1982).

When the area to be assayed contains only NE projection fibers rather than cell bodies, the biochemical results become more inconsistent. Finch (1973, 1978), Rogers et al. (1980), and Austin et al. (1978) report no NE age change in rodent cerebellum. Ponzio et al. (1978) and Finch (1973, 1978) also see no age change in rat hypothalamic NE. However, Miller et al. (1976), Simpkins et al. (1977), Huang et al. (1977), Austin et al. (1978), and Ida et al. (1982) observed an age-related decline in rat hypothalamus, a result replicated in mice (Sun, 1976), in monkeys (Samorajski and Rolsten, 1973) and more recently, in a human postmortem study (Carlsson et al., 1980). Estes and Simpkins (1980) report both increases and no change in old rat hypothalamus, depending on the particular hypothalamic area assayed. Likewise, Demarest et al. (1980) find a significant decrease in old rat median eminence NE concentrations, but no change in the rest of the hypothalamus. A similar result is observed in mice: arcuate–median eminence and suprachiasmatic areas show significant NE aging decline, but other hypothalamic nuclei do not (Osterburg et al., 1981). No senescent change in NE levels is found in rat hippocampus by Roubein et al. (1981) or in nucleus accumbens and posterior pituitary by Demarest et al. (1980). However, Ida et al. (1982) find significant increases in rat hippocampus, amygdala, and thalamus NE from 2 to 15 months of age in the rat; this limited age range probably makes the study more relevant to maturational than senescent processes. Human cortex, striatum, hypothalamus, and thalamus NE (Carlsson et al., 1980) does not appear remarkably altered with age. Likewise, rabbits exhibit little change in cortical or striatal NE content as they grow old (Makman et al., 1980). Spokes (1979) observes a 64 percent loss of septal NE and a 50 percent loss of substantia nigra NE in postmortem tissues from 25 to 85-year-old humans.

Inactivation and Catabolism. The synaptic inactivation of NE is primarily accomplished by reuptake. One study reports no age change in hypothalamic synaptosome NE uptake, but a significant striatal decrease (Jonec and Finch, 1975). Although Haycock et al. (1977) do find "aging" decreases in mouse forebrain synaptosome uptake of NE, it is difficult to put their data into the framework of aging research since the "old" mice in their study were approximately the same age as the "young" mice in the other investigations of NE uptake. Sun (1976) sees a slight, but significant, 15 percent decline in NE uptake from 4 to 24 months of age in mice.

The catabolism of NE is accomplished mainly by MAO, age changes which are covered in the preceding section on DA. NE turnover overall is decreased in mouse brain stem and hypothalamus (Finch, 1978), and in rat hypothalamus (Ponzio et al., 1978; Huang et al., 1977; Simpkins et al., 1977; Ida et al., 1982) and brain stem (Ponzio et al., 1978; Ida et al., 1982). The finding that cortical NE turnover increases from 2 to 15 months in the rat (Ida et al., 1982) should be considered in light of the limited age range of the subjects and the fact that these workers also report increased cortical NE levels in the same animals (Ida et al., 1982).

Receptors. NE β-receptors generally decrease with age in cerebellum in rats (Maggi et al., 1979; Greenberg and Weiss, 1978), mice (Enna and Strong, 1981), and man (Maggi et al., 1979; Enna and Strong, 1981). It is worth noting that cerebellar Purkinje cells contain β-adrenergic receptors and that senescent loss of Purkinje cells is also a consistent finding (Corsellis, 1976; Rogers et al., 1980; Porta et al., 1980; Zornetzer et al., 1981). Decreases with age in β-adrenergic binding are also reported for rat striatum, pineal gland (Greenberg and Weiss, 1978), and brain stem (Enna and Strong, 1981). One study shows a significant loss of cortical β-receptors (Misra et al., 1980), with a partial replication (Maggi et al., 1979; Noda et al., 1982) and a lack of replication (Pittman et al., 1980) in three others. In addition, in rat cortex there is a senescent decrease in α-adrenergic binding (Misra et al., 1980).

β-Adrenergic receptors are also localized in nonneural tissues, and senescent decline of β-adrenergic binding in lymphocytes (Schocken and Roth, 1977) and adipocytes (Giudicelli and Pequery, 1978) can be demonstrated.

Function. β-Adrenergic receptors are functionally linked to a cAMP second messenger, as in the D_1 form of the DA receptor. Thus, the measures of resting or basal cAMP in young and old animals described in the section on DA are, in general, equally relevant for NE. More specific data are provided by experiments that use NE or NE agonists to stimulate adenyl cyclase and cAMP accumulation. Where this has been done, aging losses have been reported in rat cerebellum (Walker and Walker, 1973; Schmidt and Thornberry, 1978; Schmidt, 1981), hippocampus (Walker and Walker, 1973), cortex (Berg and Zimmerman, 1975; Walker and Walker, 1973), and caudate (Govoni et al., 1977; Walker and Walker, 1973). Schmidt (1981) replicated the cerebellar decline but saw no change in rat brain stem, hypothalamus, limbic forebrain, or hippocampus; he also observed an increase with age in NE-stimulated cAMP production by cortical slices, a result opposite to that obtained in cortical homogenates by Berg and Zimmerman (1975) and Walker and Walker (1973).

The consistency of biochemical findings on β-receptors and cAMP in the aging cerebellum is paralleled by significant physiological results. For example, Marwaha and coworkers observe decreased Purkinje cell response (inhibition) to locus coeruleus electrical stimulation (Marwaha, et al., 1980), iontophoretic NE, and iontophoretic cAMP (Marwaha et al., 1981).

Finally, a possibly overlooked factor in reconciling experimental results on NE systems and aging is the chronology of NE age changes. In rat cerebellum, at almost every level of analysis, the biggest drop is between 3 and 12 months of age, with much less change thereafter. For example, cerebellar $β_2$-adrenergic receptors decrease 33 percent from 3 to 10 months of age, with no further change observed at later ages (Pittman et al., 1980). Binding of dihydroalprenolol (an NE

antagonist with high β-receptor affinity) in rat cerebellum decreases approximately twice as much from 6 to 12 months of age as from 12 to 24 months of age (Greenberg and Weiss, 1978). Rat cerebellar basal and NE-stimulated cAMP levels drop three times more from 3 to 12 months that from 12 to 24 months in one study (Schmidt and Thornberry, 1978) and over two times more in another (Austin et al., 1978). The significantly altered electrophysiological responses of rat Purkinje cells to NE agents and locus coeruleus stimulation are fully evident at 12 months of age, with little discernible change thereafter (Marwaha et al., 1980). Goldman and Coleman (1981) report no change in locus coeruleus neuron numbers with age in the rat, and emphasize the difference in their results and those showing significant decline in human postmortem samples (Vijayashankar and Brody, 1979; Wree et al., 1980). However, Goldman and Coleman only examine rats from 12 to 32 months of age, a time span in which the other indices of NE systems reveal little age-dependent alteration. It would be interesting to know if rat locus coeruleus cells are lost between 3 and 12 months of age, as are postsynaptic NE mechanisms.

Hypothalamic NE is thought by some investigators to play a role in regulating gonadotropin secretion (cf. Lofstrom et al., 1977; Weiner and Ganong, 1978). Demarest et al. (1980) have suggested a possible relationship between the significant losses of median eminence NE and serum LH they observe in the same old rats (also see Sawyer et al., 1974; Meites, 1981).

Serotonin

Cell bodies of origin for serotonin (5-HT) lie in nine clusters in or near the raphe regions of the pons and upper brain stem. Projections are widespread throughout the nervous system, including descending tracts which innervate medulla and spinal cord, and ascending tracts which reach the telencephalon and diencephalon. The pineal gland, lying on the dorsal surface of the thalamus, is also rich in 5-HT.

Synthesis. 5-HT is synthesized in brain from plasma tryptophan. The latter is hydroxylated by tryptophan hydroxylase to form 5-hydroxytryptophan (5-HTP), then decarboxylated to yield 5-HT. The hydroxylation step is rate limiting and is apparently quite sensitive to oxygen levels (Diaz et al., 1968), a point that might be of some interest for aging studies. Age changes in uptake of tryptophan have not been studied. Meek et al. (1977) describe senescent decreases in raphe (and hippocampus) tryptophan hydroxylase activity, but Reis et al. (1977) did not confirm this result.

Originally it was thought that the enzyme for 5-HTP decarboxylation was identical to DOPA decarboxylase. If so, then age changes described for this enzyme in the sections on DA and NE would be equally relevant to 5-HT metabolism. On the other hand, when assays are run to select for optimal conditions for these neurotransmitters, more recent evidence suggests a separate 5-HTP decarboxylating enzyme (cf. Sims and Bloom, 1973; Costa and Meek, 1974). In this case, little can presently be said regarding age changes at this step of 5-HT synthesis.

By inhibiting monoamine oxidase (MAO) with pargyline, blocking the primary 5-HT catabolic step, Simpkins et al. (1977) demonstrated significant increases in 5-HT synthesis in hypothalamus of old rats.

Content. The results on senescent alterations in 5-HT levels are mixed. Whole brain assays show a small decline (Samorajski et al., 1971) or no change (Finch, 1973) in mice, and an increase (Segal, et al., 1975) or no change (Simpkins et al., 1977) in rats. Monkey hypothalamus exhibits both a significant maturational and a significant senescent decline (Samorajski and Rolsten, 1973). Rat hypothalamic 5-HT is unaltered from 3 to 21 months of age (Simpkins et al., 1977). Raphe nucleus 5-HT is lower in old rats (Meek et al., 1977), whereas 5-HT in hindbrain samples from old humans remains unchanged in one study (Robinson et al., 1972) and is significantly elevated with age in another (medullary samples) (Carlsson et al., 1980). Rat

hippocampal 5-HT either is unchanged with age (Brennan et al., 1981; Roubein et al., 1981) or declines 42 percent (Meek et al., 1977).

Inactivation and Catabolism. 5-HT shares with DA and NE a common mode of synaptic inactivation, presynaptic reuptake, and (possibly) a common catabolic enzyme, MAO. Uptake of [^{3}H] 5-HT into mouse hypothalamic synaptosomes does not change with age (Jonec and Finch, 1975). This lack of age change in hypothalamus has been confirmed and extended to the cortex and septal-preoptic area (Azmitia et al., 1979). However, a significant reduction in hippocampal reuptake was observed in the latter study.

In general, most studies report increases in MAO activity with age (cf. Robinson et al., 1977). These data are covered in the sections on DA and NE. However, another form of MAO—one more specific for 5-HT than for DA or NE—may exist (Neff et al., 1974). Thus, MAO A, the possibly 5-HT specific form of the enzyme, is reportedly decreased or unaltered with age (Benedetti and Keane, 1980; Brennan et al., 1981; Carlsson et al., 1980 (but see also Papavasiliou et al., 1981; Noda et al., 1982), whereas the preponderance of evidence for the nonspecific form favors age-related increases (cf. Carlsson et al., 1980). If this differentiation of MAO A and MAO B continues to hold up, a number of theories on 5-HT metabolic changes with age will have to be discarded.

The most consistent change observed in 5-HT metabolism is an age-dependent increase in 5-hydroxyindoleacetic acid (5-HIAA). This catabolite results from the further oxidation of 5-hydroxyindoleacetaldehyde, the MAO-deaminated product of 5-HT. Blood, brain, or CSF 5-HIAA is reportedly increased in old humans (Gottfries et al., 1971; Nies et al., 1973) (but see also Bowers and Gerbode, 1968) and old rats (Simpkins et al., 1977; Brennan et al., 1981) (but see also Algeri et al., 1982). Many investigators attribute this senescent rise in 5-HIAA to the generally consistent finding of increased

MAO activity with age. For example, although Robinson et al. (1972) did not observe age changes in human hindbrain 5-HIAA, they did observe a positive correlation of 5-HIAA and MAO. On the other hand, several gaps need to be filled in for the hypothesis that increased MAO activity causes the senescent rise in 5-HIAA. First it is unclear whether or not the MAO being discussed in many of these reports is, in fact, the MAO that deaminates 5-HT (Neff et al., 1974). Indeed, MAO A (the more likely 5-HT specific form) shows senescent decreases in many brain areas (Benedetti and Keane, 1980). Second, brain levels of MAO are already manyfold higher in young animals than necessary to catabolize brain monoamine content. Thus, increasing MAO in old brains does not necessarily predict increased monoamine catabolites. Alternative mechanisms to increase MAO activity could as well account for the senescent rise in 5-HIAA; for example, it could be that 5-HIAA is poorly cleared or excreted in old animals.

Receptors. Assays for receptors in 5-HT systems may be somewhat more problematic than for DA or NE. At least two receptor types, 5-HT$_1$ and 5-HT$_2$, appear to exist; they are differentially distributed in brain and have different ligand specificities. Spiroperidol binds well to both receptors, but unfortunately this ligand also binds well to DA recognition sites. 5-HT itself is actually a relatively poor 5-HT$_2$ ligand compared to spiroperidol. LSD, a frequently employed 5-HT ligand, also has differential binding depending on the brain region assayed and the distribution of 5-HT receptor types therein. Perhaps for these reasons, there are scant data yet on age changes in 5-HT binding. Shih and Young (1978) do find decreased [³H] 5-HT binding in cortical samples from aged humans; Huntington's disease patients also reportedly exhibit lower binding in basal ganglia (Enna et al., 1976). Old rabbits have a decreased number of spiroperidol binding sites in cortex according to Thal et al. (1980); these authors further demonstrate, by pharmacological characterization, that spiroper-

idol binds primarily to a 5-HT receptor in their cortical samples.

Further study of 5-HT receptor binding could help resolve mechanisms of altered 5-HT turnover in aging, as well as help explain why data on 5-HT levels are so inconsistent. For example, Aghajanian and his colleagues (Aghajanian et al., 1967) have demonstrated postsynaptic feedback modulation of 5-HT turnover. This provides still another alternative to increased MAO as an explanation for age changes in 5-HT metabolism. The loss of recurrent collateral inhibition of 5-HT neurons would increase their activity, increase 5-HT turnover, and elevate 5-HIAA/5-HT ratios.

Finally, Heron et al. (1980a) have presented data on membrane fluidity and 5-HT binding that could have wide and important implications for studies of age changes in binding of nearly all neurotransmitters. Noting that alterations in synaptic membrane viscosity can modulate ligand binding, these investigators have generated and linked four sets of data. First, they demonstrate microviscosity-dependent shifts in 5-HT and opiate binding to rat forebrain synaptosomes (Heron et al., 1980). Second, they show age-dependent decreases in 5-HT receptor affinity and number in rat forebrain synaptosomes (Heron et al., 1982). Third, they show age-dependent hyperviscosity of membrane preparations from mouse brain (Heron et al., 1980b). Fourth, they demonstrate that fluidization of aged hyperviscous synaptosomes (by an "Active Lipid" preparation derived from egg yolk) can restore normal 5-HT binding parameters to values equivalent to those for young rats (Heron et al., 1982). (For further discussion of age changes in membrane properties, see Chapter 11.)

Function. The hyperpolarizing response of hippocampal CA1 pyramidal cells to applications of 5-HT is decreased 71 percent in senescent rats (Segal, 1982).

Serotonergic and hippocampal functions have both been associated with exploratory behavior in rodents. Exploratory behavior is known to decrease with age. Putting these facts together, Brennan et al. (1981) found correlations between the elevated 5-HIAA/5-HT ratios in hippocampus of old mice and the altered responses of these same old mice to novel stimuli in an explored environment.

Like several other neurotransmitter age changes (see sections on DA, NE, and enkephalin), senescent alterations of 5-HT have been suggested as a basis for the disruption of estrous cycling in old rodents. Walker (1981), the chief exponent of this view, has, for example, demonstrated reinstatement of LH surges in old rats by administration of 5-HTP and pCPA (Walker, 1982).

γ-Aminobutyric Acid

It is ironic that we know much more about aging of ACh, DA, NE, and 5-HT than we do about putative amino acid neurotransmitters such as γ-aminobutyric acid (GABA). The latter is so much more abundant in CNS as to make the monoamines and ACh appear quantitatively trivial. However, most amino acid neurotransmitter candidates (e.g., glutamate, glycine, aspartate, but not GABA) are also the building blocks of protein. Thus, so far it has proven nearly impossible separately to assay amino acids only for their neurotransmitter role. The structural and metabolic pools for most amino acids greatly outweigh the neurotransmitter pool, and the techniques for distinguishing one pool from the others remain quite limited.

GABA is probably the major inhibitory neurotransmitter in brain, occurring in micromole per gram concentrations (as opposed to nanomole per gram concentrations for monoamines). Distribution is widespread, with highest concentrations in substantia nigra, globus pallidus, hypothalamus, inferior and superior colliculi, periaqueductal gray, and dentate nucleus (of the hippocampus).

In the following review of age changes in GABA metabolism, particular caution should be exercised in evaluating results of studies using postmortem material: GABA levels in rat brain have been shown to rise nearly 50 percent within two minutes of death (see Cooper et al., 1978).

Synthesis. GABA is synthesized from glutamate in a reaction catalyzed by the CNS specific enzyme glutamic acid decarboxylase (GAD). Although many studies have described age-related GAD decline, the most conclusive of these are limited to the striatum—and even here there are notable exceptions and inconsistencies. GAD losses in the basal ganglia of humans are observed by McGeer and McGeer (1978), Cote and Kremzner (1974), and Bowen et al. (1976), but not (in putamen) by Bird and Iversen (1974). Rodent striatal GAD activity exhibits senescent loss in most cases (Waller et al., 1981; Strong et al., 1980; McGeer et al., 1971).

Cortical GAD changes are very inconsistent. For rats, one study reports an aging decline (Strong et al., 1980), and another study does not (Ingram et al., 1981). For humans, McGeer and McGeer (1976) note that cortical GAD losses are usually much greater in human development and maturation (5–20 years old) than at more advanced ages (20–50 years old), a result partially confirmed by Bowen et al. (1976). Other areas with age-related GAD losses include human hypothalamus (McGeer and McGeer, 1976), cerebellum, substantia nigra, hippocampus (McGeer and McGeer, 1976; Spokes, 1979), inferior olive, locus coeruleus (McGeer and McGeer, 1976), amygdala, and red nucleus (Spokes, 1979). The hippocampal change is not replicable in rats (Strong et al., 1980) or mice (Ingram et al., 1981; Strong et al., 1980), nor is there a senescent loss in mouse cerebellar GAD (Unsworth et al., 1980). Finally, mouse whole brain GAD activity is stated to decline 20 percent by 37 months of age (Fonda et al., 1973).

Gibson et al. (1981a) have compared the synthesis of labeled GABA from [^{14}C] glucose in whole brain samples from 3- to 30-month-old mice, finding consistent age-related decreases in both C57BL/6J and BALB/c strains.

In contrast to studies on normal aging,

there are clear and consistent findings on degenerative changes in GABA (and ACh) systems in Huntington's disease, a hereditary disorder with age-related onset. These changes include reductions in GAD (Bird et al., 1973; McGeer et al., 1973) and GABA binding (Lloyd et al., 1977; Reisine et al., 1979). However, these biochemical changes may be secondary to morphologic changes. Huntington's disease is known to involve neuronal degeneration, particularly in cerebral cortex and basal ganglia (see Barbeau et al., 1973). It is these areas which most strikingly show GABAergic decline. Moreover, instead of being limited to a single neurotransmitter system, as might be expected if biochemical changes were the primary event, almost all neurotransmitter systems prominent in basal ganglia show decline, including ACh (Enna et al., 1976; Wastek et al., 1976; Yamamura, 1978; Yamamura et al., 1979), 5-HT (Enna et al., 1976), and DA (Reisine et al., 1979). Such results suggest a primary morphologic degeneration, rather than altered biochemical activity, in Huntington's disease (for a somewhat contrasting view, see Finch, 1981).

Content. To our knowledge there are only two reports on brain GABA levels and aging: one described a significant, but very small (12 percent), senescent decline (Fonda et al., 1973), and the other observed no alteration (Gibson et al., 1981a). GABA levels are elevated in CSF of patients with multiple infarct dementia (but not Alzheimer's disease). However, this could be a secondary effect unrelated to neurotransmitter metabolism *per se*. GABA does not readily penetrate the blood-brain barrier and under normal circumstances is detected in 1000-fold lower concentrations in CSF than in brain. It could be that multiple infarction simply permits more endogenous GABA to enter the CSF, rather than increasing GABA synthesis.

Inactivation and Catabolism. Although it remains to be demonstrated conclusively, the active and efficient uptake of GABA by brain slices and synaptosomes suggests that, at least in part, GABA synaptic inactivation, like NE and DA, may be accomplished by reuptake. No difference in GABA uptake is observed in young (2 months) versus early middle-aged (12 months) mice (Haycock et al., 1977). However, when sufficiently old rodents are examined (30-month-old rats), several parameters of GABA transport exhibit senescent decline (Wheeler, 1982). GABA is degraded to succinic semialdehyde by GABA transaminase (GABA-T). There have been two aging studies to date on this step of GABA metabolism: Fonda et al. (1973) describe a significant increase in whole brain GABA-T in very old (37 month) mice, and Noda et al. (1982) find significant GABA-T increases in rat cortex, caudate-putamen, and globus pallidus.

Receptors. GABA receptor binding does not change with age in rat cerebellum, brain stem, cerebral cortex, striatum, accumbens (Maggi et al., 1979; Govoni et al., 1980), or hippocampus (Lippa et al., 1981), but it does decline significantly in substantia nigra and hypothalamus (Govoni et al., 1980). A nearly opposite pattern of results occurs in Huntington's disease, where GABA binding is decreased in basal ganglia (Lloyd et al., 1977; Reisine et al., 1979), unchanged in cortex (Enna et al., 1976), and increased in cerebellum (Lloyd et al., 1977).

Function. In old rats, the ability of iontophoretically applied GABA to inhibit hippocampal pyramidal cells is increased, despite no change in GABA receptor binding (Lippa et al., 1981). Segal (1982) adds to these data by showing that the duration of CA1 pyramidal cell depolarization after GABA administration is significantly lengthened in old rats. Inhibition of rat cerebellar Purkinje cells by iontophoretic GABA is stable from 4 through 22 months of age (Marwaha et al., 1981).

Behaviorally, Ingram et al. (1981) showed a correlation in young and old rats between cortical GAD activity and radial arm maze performance—the latter exhibiting significant senescent decline.

Clinical studies have noted an increased sensitivity of elderly patients to side effects of the benzodiazepines (Boston Collaborative Drug Surveillance Program Report, 1973). This was once thought to be due to changes with age in GABAergic systems, since GABA has been shown to enhance benzodiazepine binding (cf. Karobath et al., 1980). However, neither benzodiazepine binding (Pedigo et al., 1981; Reisine et al., 1980) nor the functional allosteric interaction of GABA with benzodiazepine binding (Pedigo et al., 1981) is altered with age.

Other Putative Amino Acid Neurotransmitters

In addition to GABA, several other amino acids have been proposed as candidates for neurotransmitter status. Foremost among these are glycine, as a (quantitatively) major inhibitory neurotransmitter, and glutamate, as an excitatory neurotransmitter. Taurine and aspartate are also possible neurotransmitters. Although techniques for assaying these substances have become more and more feasible, normative—much less aging—data remain scant.

Synthesis. To our knowledge there presently are no data on age changes in synthesis of amino acids that are specific to their neurotransmitter role. However, the overall synthesis of labeled glutamate and aspartate from [^{14}C] glucose decreased from 3 to 30 months in both C57BL/6J and BALB/c mice (Gibson et al., 1981a). These findings are not replicated in 3- to 30-month-old rats (De-Koning-Verest, 1980).

Content. Whole brain levels of aspartate decrease in old rats (Dekoning-Verest, 1980), a finding in keeping with earlier work by Timeras et al. (1973) who observed 15 to 52 percent declines in rat cortex, cerebellum, brain stem, and spinal cord aspartate. On the other hand, two studies on whole mouse brain failed to detect an aspartate age change (Fonda et al., 1973; Gibson et al., 1981a).

Taurine, in the only study done to our knowledge, declines with age in rat cortex, cerebellum, brain stem, and spinal cord, whereas glycine does not exhibit any consistent aging trend (Timeras et al., 1973).

More extensive data are available for glutamate and indicate relatively consistent age changes. Striatal (Price et al., 1981), cortical, cerebellar (Timeras et al., 1973), and whole brain (DeKonig-Verest, 1980) levels of this powerful neural excitant exhibit aging decline in rats. Striatal glutamate levels are stable from 3 to 6 months of age, then fall significantly through 19 months (the oldest age group in the study) (Price et al., 1981). Whole brain glutamate levels are lower through 30 months of age in the rat (De-Konig-Verest, 1980). However, both Fonda et al. (1973) and Gibson et al. (1981a) report little age change in whole brain glutamate concentrations, even in very old (37 and 30 months, respectively) mice.

Inactivation and Catabolism. Although there are no conclusive data, it seems likely that synaptic inactivation of amino acid neurotransmitters is at least partially accomplished by reuptake. The striatal loss of glutamate is chronologically well paralleled by significant drops in high affinity synaptosomal uptake (Price et al., 1981). Interestingly both V_{max} and K_m of the uptake system are reduced with age, suggesting a loss in transport sites and a compensatory, increased affinity of remaining sites (Price et al., 1981). Wheeler (1980) also reports senescent decreases in glutamate uptake by cortical synaptosomes.

Glutamate may be catabolized by glutamate dehydrogenase. Patients with adult-onset spinocerebellar degeneration exhibit impaired oxidative deamination of glutamate, glutamic acidemia, and decreased activity of glutamate dehydrogenase (Plaitakis et al., 1982).

Receptors. Basal glutamate receptor binding increases from 3 to 24 months of age in rat hippocampus, but the maximal stimulatory effect of Ca^{++} to stimulate glutamate receptor binding is concurrently decreased (Baudry et al., 1981).

Function. Several functional correlates to the biochemical findings on glutamate are suggested. Following brief high frequency electrical stimulation, synapses in rat hippocampus undergo a long-term potentiation (LTP) to subsequent stimulation. This phenomenon is believed to occur at glutamate synapses (Storm-Mathisen, 1976, 1977) and to be mediated by Ca^{++}-stimulated glutamate binding (Baudry and Lynch, 1980). The latter declines in old age (Baudry et al., 1981), as does LTP (Barnes, 1979; Landfield and Lynch, 1977; Landfield et al., 1978). Moreover, the senescent decline in hippocampal LTP is highly correlated (within subjects) with senescent impairments of maze recall (Barnes, 1979).

Olney has made the interesting speculation that if glutamate synaptic inactivation is largely accomplished by reuptake, then the decreased synaptosomal glutamate uptake he (Price et al., 1981) and others (Wheeler, 1980) have observed in old rats could have toxic effects on postsynaptic elements, much like kianate lesions. Such an idea is consistent with the axospinous degeneration in the upper cerebellar molecular layer of aged rats (Zornetzer et al., 1981), where there is a high probability that these synapses are glutamatergic parallel fiber–Purkinje cell contacts. Our finding that cerebellar Purkinje cells are less responsive to parallel fiber stimulation (Rogers et al., 1981) is consistent both with this hypothesis and with the senescent decrease in glutamate levels seen in other brain areas. Moreover, glutamate deamination, another possible mechanism for synaptic inactivation of the amino acid, is impaired in an adult-onset disorder characterized by spinocerebellar degeneration (Plaitakis et al., 1982).

The hypothermia produced by central administration of taurine appears to be blunted in old squirrel monkeys (Clark and Lipton, 1981), and the ability of histamine to activate adenylate cyclase is 50 percent lower in hypothalamus and cortex of old rabbits (Makman et al., 1980).

Opioid Peptides

Several types of opioid peptide, primarily β-endorphin, met-enkephalin, and leu-enkephalin, appear to act as neurotransmitters in brain. A 31,000 molecular weight pro-opiocortin has been isolated that contains the sequences for endorphin, lipotropin, melanocyte stimulating hormone (MSH), adrenocorticotropic hormone (ACTH), and met-enkephalin. Originally it was thought that all these peptides were derived from the pro-opiocortin precursor. However, much evidence suggests that endorphin and enkephalin represent distinct, separate systems in CNS (despite the fact that the sequence for met-enkephalin is also the NH_2-terminal pentapeptide in β-endorphin). Thus, immunoreactive (IR) β-endorphin cell bodies are found in the tuberal zone of the hypothalamus, with projections innervating the lateral hypothalamus, preoptic area, medial amygdala, and midline of the thalamus and brain stem (periventricular system) as far caudal as the locus coeruleus. In general, areas such as these, rich in IR β-endorphin, also contain IR MSH and ACTH, and treatments that alter levels of one alter levels of the others. By contrast, areas rich in IR enkephalin have little or no IR β-endorphin. This is particularly true for the striatum, where IR β-endorphin is nearly absent, but enkephalin imunoreactivity is among the highest in brain. IR enkephalin cell bodies are found in caudate and putamen (innervating the globus pallidus), amygdala (innervating the bed nucleus of the stria terminalis), and paraventricular and supraoptic hypothalamus (innervating the neurohypophysis). Levels of IR met-enkephalin are generally 5–10 times higher than those for IR leu-enkephalin. These and other details of endorphin and enkephalin systems are thoroughly reviewed elsewhere (cf. Bloom and McGinty, 1981).

Synthesis. As indicated, there remain many unanswered questions concerning the synthetic origin or brain endorphins and enkephalins in young animals. It is, therefore, appropriate that there are no aging data on this step of opioid peptide metabolism.

Content. IR β-endorphin is reported to decline significantly in rat striatum, but not pituitary, whole hypothalamus, or frontal lobe from 6 to 20–24 months of age (Gambert et al., 1980). Extremely high variability may account for the latter, negative results: despite failing to achieve statistical significance, hypothalamic IR β-endorphin dropped 67 percent, pituitary IR β-endorphin dropped 17 percent, and frontal cortex IR β-endorphin increased 200 percent from 6 to 24 months of age (Gambert et al., 1980)

As for several other neurotransmitters, data on hypothalamic β-endorphin become more sensitive when anatomic organization is taken into account. Thus, whereas Gambert et al. (1980) observe a nonsignificant trend to lower IR β-endorphin levels in whole 20- to 24-month rat hypothalami, Barden et al. (1981) do find significant IR β-endorphin losses in discrete hypothalamic nuclei of similar strain rats. Not surprisingly, the decline is most pronounced in arcuate nucleus, an area containing cell bodies of origin for brain β-endorphin. Forman et al. (1981) find significantly decreased concentrations (nanograms per milligram protein) but not content (nanograms per sample) of IR β-endorphin in old rat hypothalamus. These authors also report increases in pituitary and plasma IR β-endorphin with age. By contrast, periaqueductal gray, a major projection area for β-endorphin fibers, exhibits a senescent decline in concentration of this peptide (Barden et al., 1981).

From an anatomic perspective, the senescent decrease in rat striatal IR β-endorphin reported by Gambert (Gambert et al., 1980), and replicated by him in a subsequent study (Gambert, 1981), is perplexing since there is both immunocytochemical and biochemical evidence (reviewed in Bloom and McGinty, 1981) that rat striatum contains little β-endorphin at any age, much less the nanogram per milligram protein concentrations observed in these two aging studies (Gambert et al., 1980; Gambert, 1981). This, perhaps, raises another biochemical caveat: most antisera to enzyme and neurotransmitter peptides cross-react to one degree or another with peptides other than the one they are intended to measure. Although the antiserum used by Gambert (Gambert et al., 1980; Gambert, 1981) is stated to have no cross-reactivity with enkephalin, it is nonetheless true that rat striatum in other studies appears devoid of IR β-endorphin but contains the highest levels in brain of enkephalin. It is also true that a structure near striatum, the endorphin-containing amygdala, could easily be inadvertently dissected with striatal samples.

The separateness of endorphin and enkephalin systems may be exemplified by differences in the effects of age on them. Whereas hypothalamic IR β-endorphin appears to decline with age in male rats (Gambert, 1981; Barden et al., 1981), IR met-enkephalin appears to rise (Steger et al., 1980). Old female rats may also show elevated mediobasal hypothalamic IR met-enkephalin, although comparisons are difficult because levels of the pentapeptide may fluctuate with estrous cycling in females. Thus, when young females in estrus are compared to old females in constant estrus, there appears to be a significant senescent IR met-enkephalin increase (0.48 ± 0.08 ng/mg versus 0.82 ± 0.20 ng/mg; $N = 9$ and 11, respectively), but this becomes only a nonsignificant trend when the data from old, irregularly cycling and pseudopregnant females are included in the analysis (Kumar et al., 1980). Anterior pituitary IR met-enkephalin is also significantly elevated with age in the latter study, regardless of estrous state (Kumar et al., 1980).

Inactivation and Catabolism. There are no aging data, to our knowledge, on this step of opioid peptide metabolism.

Receptors. Significant decreases in B_{max}, but not K_d, for [^{3}H] etorphine binding are observed in 24-month-old rat frontal pole, hippocampus, and striatum, with no aging changes in anterior cortex or amygdala (Hess et al., 1981). These results are replicable in frontal pole and striatum, and can be extended to thalamus and midbrain, using a [^{3}H] dihydromorphine ligand (Messing et al., 1980, 1981). However, a significant age-related reduction in anterior cortex binding is also reported with this ligand (Messing et al., 1981). Anatomically, the significance of most of these findings awaits further study, since there is little IR β-endorphin in cerebral cortex.

Function. Opiates, particularly met-enkephalin, can inhibit pituitary release of luteinizing hormone (LH) and depress serum levels of testosterone. These effects are reversible by naloxone (an opiate antagonist), but they are less so in old rats (Steger et al., 1980). Moreover, blood LH and testosterone levels are lower in old male rats (Steger et al., 1980), a result consistent with the increased hypothalamic met-enkephalin levels described earlier (Steger et al., 1980; Kumar et al., 1980). Thus, Steger et al. (1980) proposed that senescent increases in hypothalamic met-enkephalin may play a role in senescent disruption of reproductive function. Similar statements, however, have been made about several other neurotransmitters, as noted in previous sections of this chapter.

Endogenous opiate systems are alleged to play a role in almost every conceivable behavior, including control of dietary intake, temperature regulation, reproductive function, and memory. Many of these behaviors do exhibit age changes, and a few of those may even have some relation to age changes in endogenous opiates. For example, old rats exhibit a reduced ability to develop thermal tolerance to morphine (McDougal et al., 1980). Considerable effort will be necessary, however, to demonstrate a primary role of opioid peptides in these behaviors in young animals, much less senescent ones.

Other Putative Peptide Neurotransmitters

In addition to the opioid peptides, several other peptides have been proposed as neurotransmitter candidates. Foremost among these are somatostatin, substance P, vasoactive intestinal peptide (VIP), vasopressin, and neurotensin. What little aging data there are for these peptides primarily concern radioimmunoassayable levels.

Somatostatin. In a study on rats, no age-related change in IR somatostatin was observed in the nucleus accumbens, olfactory tubercle, striatum, frontal cortex, septum, substantia nigra, or hypothalamus (Burks et al., 1981). Hoffman and Sladek (1980), however, report a decline of somatostatin immunofluorescence in rat mediobasal hypothalamus. In one human postmortem study (Buck et al., 1981), no age change in IR somatostatin was found in caudate, putamen, frontal cortex, or substantia nigra, in general agreement with the results on rat. This lack of change in somatostatin with normal aging may distinguish normal aging from Alzheimer's disease: Davies and Terry (1981) recently found significant losses of IR somatostatin in several cortical regions and hippocampus of Alzheimer's disease patients. Moreover, a correlation between the IR somatostatin losses and losses in CAT activity was also obtained. Behaviorally, somatostatin administration to aged monkeys had little ability to reverse their deficits on a memory task (Bartus et al., 1982).

Substance P. Burks et al. (1981) find losses of substance P in rat putamen, but not caudate, frontal cortex, hypothalamus, thalamus, nucleus accumbens, septum, substantia nigra, or olfactory tubercle. These results are generally consistent with those from another study by this group (Buck et al., 1981) using human postmortem tissue.

VIP. A recent report (Perry et al., 1981) shows significantly increased IR VIP from 61 to 92 years of age in human temporal lobe (postmortem).

Neurotensin. In both rats (Burks et al., 1981) and humans at autopsy (Buck et al., 1981), no age change in neurotensin concentration is observed in caudate, putamen, or frontal cortex. A decline is seen in human (Buck et al., 1981), but not rat (Burks et al., 1981), substantia nigra. The rat data have also been extended to the nucleus accumbens, olfactory tubercle, septum, and hypothalamus, none of which exhibit senescent decline.

Vasopressin. Rat hypothalamic vasopressin appears to decline in old rats (Turkington and Everitt, 1976), a change suggested to underlie the decreased ability of these subjects to maintain conditioned taste aversions (McNamara and Cooper, 1979; Cooper et al., 1980). There is also an aging decline in rat neural lobe IR vasopressin that may relate to alterations in fluid and electrolyte balance in old animals (Sladek et al., 1981).

Behaviorally, vasopressin administration to old monkeys significantly improves their performance on a memory task in three out of five cases; the authors note, however, that in no case is the improvement great enough to match the level of performance of young monkeys on the same task (Bartus et al., 1982). Clinical trials of vasopressin therapy for dementia of the elderly have been equally equivocal. Weingartner et al. (1981) report reliable improvement in one study of progressive dementia, but confirmation and agreement on the utility of vasopressin therapy remain open questions (cf. Branconnier, 1981; Ferris et al., 1980; Prange et al., 1979).

SUMMARY AND CONCLUSIONS

At first sight, a review of age changes in neurotransmitter metabolism and function appears to reveal almost as many problems as progress. There is virtually no metabolic step for any of the neurotransmitter systems where at least two conflicting reports on the effects of age cannot be cited. What can account for this apparent diversity, and is there some perspective that may help unify the potential wealth of present data?

We will next consider some of the problems unique to aging research, particularly brain aging, that have been constantly in evidence throughout the review. These difficulties do, in fact, provide good reasons why a consensus is difficult to achieve for age-related neurochemical results, and they suggest ways in which to evaluate the significance of discrepant results (see also Himwich, 1973).

Research Issues

Every aging study makes tacit assumptions about proper methods, subject groups, species, and the process of aging itself. Differences in these assumptions, frequently unaddressed in individual reports, may better account for why investigators obtain different results than simple differences in their skill at the bench. The following caveats and questions should suggest how uniquely difficult studies of brain aging can be and how disparities in individual findings may yet prove reconcilable.

How Old Is Old? Many differences of opinion about senescent change for a particular neurotransmitter system are almost wholly attributable to differences in age of the subjects employed in experiments. It is discouraging to find instances in which one group of experimenters used 12-month-old rats as the "old" subjects, whereas another set of workers used 12-month-old rats as the "young" subjects. Indeed, a computer search for the neurobiology of aging invariably turns up hundreds of papers on juvenile development. Journals on aging might require authors both to cite published life span curves for their subjects and to identify experimental groups based on such curves.

Localization of Changes. Part of the difference between results on age changes in neurotransmitters is due to which brain regions are studied. Whole brain homogenates may provide ample tissue and maximum sensitivity for the assay; however, a big decline in a small area may be swamped by lack of change in the remaining large mass of tissue. Moreover, whole brain assays, even when they do produce significant results, tell us little about where the alteration occurs. In general, the more attention is paid to the specific anatomic localization of a neurotransmitter system, the more consistent are the findings. This can be seen for the neurotransmitter norepinephrine, for example. Assays of brain stem, which contains the cell bodies of origin for central norepinephrine, almost universally show a significant decline. Assays of brain structures that have heavy noradrenergic projections also tend to show decline, but the results are less consistent from experimenter to experimenter. Assays of structures moderately innervated by norepinephrine fibers give variable results. Assays of whole brain homogenates fail to detect any change at all. In general, arranging the neurochemical data by neuroanatomic structure tends to reveal more coherence than is otherwise apparent in a straight transmitter-by-transmitter arrangement. For example, of the 82 recent papers we have reviewed on changes in brain DA synthesis or content, 47 percent report senescent decline, 44 percent report no age change, and 9 percent report a significant elevation in old subjects. This discouraging picture can be brightened considerably once it is accepted that senescent neuropharmacologic change is importantly linked to region-specific neuroanatomic change. Thus, if one looks only at the striatum, the vast majority of papers consistently show senescent DA decline; other structures are the ones that contribute the negative results. In fact, taken regionally, even the negative results tend to achieve some consistency. For example, the majority of cortical DA assays show little effect of age.

Secondary Pathology as Effect. Correlations with changes in anatomy and physiology are required to make many neurochemical results about aging interpretable. The pharmacologist may report senescent decline in levels of a transmitter, but without correlative anatomy, it cannot be specified whether the decline is due to changes in biochemical machinery or to loss of the cells which contain it. Indeed, in many cases the biochemical data actually suggest a primary anatomic change, with neurotransmitter-related alterations more likely to be epiphenomena. For example, age changes in the enzymes of neurotransmitter metabolism are almost universally changes only in V_{max}, not K_m. Similarly, age changes in neurotransmitter receptor binding are almost universally changes only in B_{max}, not K_d. Since K_m and K_d reflect affinities of enyzmes and receptors for substrates and ligands, whereas V_{max} and B_{max} reflect amounts of enzymes or receptors, these data suggest that the enzymes and receptors produced by aged animals are not qualitatively and biochemically dissimilar from those produced by young animals. An underlying morphologic degeneration (e.g., dendrite or cell loss) would be one of the more parsimonious explanations for unaltered K_m and K_d, with concurrent decreases of V_{max} and B_{max}, in old age. This same explanation should also be preferred when not one, but many, neurotransmitter systems all show decline in the same brain structure. Facilitating this kind of global view is another reason for arranging the summary table data (see Tables 1 through 7) by neuroanatomic region rather than by neurotransmitter system: one can see at a glance whether changes are centered more around a specific neurotransmitter substance (suggesting a specific biochemical deficit) or are general for most of the neurotransmitters in a structure (suggesting atrophy of anatomic elements). Defects in receptor binding for nearly every neurotransmitter even remotely speculated to exist in a structure, as in the striatum, strongly suggest general deterioration of all neuronal elements there, not just neurotransmitter specific elements.

Secondary Pathology as Cause. Many investigators feel obliged to remove obviously unhealthy aged animals from their studies before experiments are begun. The most frequently proffered rationale for this is the desire to study "normal aging." Other investigators probably do not eliminate such animals so conscientiously, and this can be a source of variation between their data and those of others. Under these circumstances, changes obtained with age, particularly for some of the neuropeptides, could owe more to secondary disease states correlated with aging than to aging itself. On the other hand, if it is true that many secondary disease states are characteristic of aging (cf. Coleman et al., 1977), it could be equally argued that animals suffering these states should be included in aging studies so as to provide a more typical sample population. Probably the best solution to this dilemma is to include all subjects in the assay, but to make special note of those with obvious illness (e.g., rapid weight loss) and to report such data separately (cf. Nelson et al., 1975). Finally, certain disease states, because of their clear age-related incidence (e.g., Huntington's disease, Parkinson's disease, Alzheimer's disease), can even become the focus of aging research. To the extent that these pathologies incorporate many of the neurotransmitter changes characteristic of normal aging, they have been partially covered here. For greater detail, the reader is referred to specific treatises such as *Parkinson's Disease* (Finch et al., 1978) or *Alzheimer's Disease: Senile Dementia and Related Disorders* (Katzman et al., 1978).

Species, Strains, and Members of a Population. It is a commonplace that humans, monkeys, and rats age at different rates. The distinctions, however, go deeper. Different strains of the same species also often age at different rates (Gibson et al., 1978). Moreover, different members of the same strain of the same species may age at different rates. The difference between chronological age and biological age can produce subject groups that are more heterogeneous than homogeneous despite a common birthday. Under such conditions, the variability of data collected from the group will likely be increased, as will the probability of failing to find a significant difference when one actually exists (Type II statistical error). Thus, with aging research perhaps more than other fields, results which show no change in a system should not necessarily be regarded as incontrovertible proof of stability.

The Study of Survivors. It is perhaps an ultimate irony that most studies searching for the roots of senile dysfunction and death must do so using healthy, living animals. It should be recognized that subjects may live to be in our experiments precisely because they have not yet contracted the particular age pathology we are investigating. This is another good reason for not clinging too firmly to negative results showing a lack of pharmacological age change.

Postmortem Change. On the other side of the coin from the study of survivors is the study of dead subjects. Although the latter neatly sidesteps problems of the former, postmortem analyses have their own special caveats (cf. Spokes, 1979). Degradation of tissue and the biochemical substances it contains may occur after death, creating a floor effect where values have dropped so low that the original differences between age groups are no longer detectable. Biochemical mechanisms dependent on active metabolism or the integrity of membranes may behave abnormally. Moreover, postmortem assays are usually based on materials from human subjects where it is difficult to control for prior environment, disease history, and drug treatment. Most investigators are careful to note these and other issues (cf. Adolfsson et al., 1979).

Standards for Comparison. It is customary and wise in most experiments to normalize biochemical data for each subject (e.g., by dividing by protein content) so as to account for differences in the amount of tissue being assayed. For aging studies, however, this practice has several pitfalls that do not normally obtain in other areas of research (cf. Benedetti and Keane, 1980). One experimenter may report failure to replicate a decline in pituitary endorphin, for example, because he divided significantly reduced pituitary endorphin content by a concurrent, significant, and equally important reduction in pituitary wet weight. Estimates based on milligrams of protein or RNA/DNA content also have their problems because neither measure discriminates between neural and nonneural elements. Glial proliferation and hypertrophy in the senescent nervous system (cf. Adams and Jones, 1982) are especially troublesome in this respect. Moreover, glia often contain the very same neurotransmitter-related substances (e.g., cAMP) that are being assayed for "specific" neuronal change with age. Hence, a lack of age change in cAMP could actually reflect a loss of neuronal cAMP balanced by an increase of glial cAMP or vice-versa. The same is equally true for many other substances related to neurotransmission: for example, glutamate reuptake probably occurs both in neurons and in glia (Koelle, 1975). It would be helpful, therefore, if experimenters would provide separate estimates of the weights and/or protein for the tissues assayed, in addition to weight- or protein-corrected biochemical data.

Key to Tables

Summary Tables

Tables 1 through 7 summarize the major findings in the reports we have reviewed. These data are current through 1982, when our review was completed. As suggested earlier, the data are organized by anatomic region rather than by neurotransmitter type for several reasons. One is that organization by anatomic region tends to reveal a greater concordance of results than is appreciable when comparisons are lumped together across many brain structures. Secondly, organization by anatomic region may aid in the discrimination between age changes that have a more specific biochemical basis and those that are more likely secondary to wholesale morphologic deterioration of the structure. Abbreviations and symbols used in the tables are provided in the following key:

[a]Caudate
[c]Median eminence
[e]Retrochiasmatic nucleus
[g]Preoptic hypothalamus
[i]Brain stem
[k]Locus coeruleus
[s]Slice preparations
[A/J]A/J mouse
[HC]Huntington's chorea
↑ Significant increase
△Trend to increase
0% No change
Haldol Haloperidol
Dihymorph Dihydromorphine
α-Toxin α-Bungarotoxin
cis-MDOX cis-Methyldioxide
B_1 B_1-adrenergic receptor
B_2 B_2-adrenergic receptor
Scop Scopolamine
Smstatin Somatostatin
β-Endo β-Endorphin
HIS Histamine
GLU Glutamate
DDC DOPA decarboxylase
ADTN 2-Amino-6,7-dihydroxyl-1,2,3,4-tetrahydronaphthalene HCl
QNB Quinuclininyl benzilate or other muscarinic ligand
Spk Rate Neuronal firing rate
Membrane Potential[m] Depolarizing or hyperpolarizing response to transmitter application
Membrane Potential[n] Duration of depolarizing response to transmitter application
Age range Range of subject ages used to calculate percentage change. Ages are in years for primates, and in mos for all other species

[ct]Cerebral cortex
[b]Putamen
[th]Thalamus
[d]Arcuate nucleus
[f]Mediobasal hypothalamus
[h]Substantia nigra
[j]Inferior olive
[l]Raphe nucleus
[C57]C57BL/6J mouse
[PD]Parkinson's disease
[AD]Alzheimer's disease
↓ Significant decrease
▽Trend to decrease
Spdol Spiroperidol or other DA ligand
Apomorph Apomorphine
Etorph Etorphine
WB4101 An α-adrenergic ligand
Ch Choline
Sub P Substance P
Vaso Vasopressin
m-Enk met-Enkephalin
ASP Aspartate
Glu Glucose
TRY HYD Tryptophan hydroxylase
DHA Dihydroalprenolol or other β-adrenergic ligand
LTP Long-term potentiation
Explor Exploratory behavior

(Text continued on p. 682)

TABLE 1. Striatum and Basal Ganglia.

Trans-mitter	Substrate Measured	Age Change		Species	Age Range	Reference
			SYNTHESIS			
ACh	Ch		0%	Rat	6–26	Sherman et al., 1981
ACh	Glu to ACh	↓	69%	Mouse	3–30	Gibson and Peterson, 1981
ACh	CAT	↓	13%	Rat	10–26	Enna and Strong, 1981
ACh	CAT	↓	26%	Rat	4–18	Noda et al., 1981
ACh	CAT		0%	Human	25–93	Carlsson et al., 1980
ACh	CAT	↓	27%	Rat	1–24	Meek et al., 1977
ACh	CAT		0%	Rat	4–22	Morin and Wasterlain, 1980
ACh	CAT		0%	Rat	4–26	Reis et al., 1977
ACh	CAT	↓	19%	Rat	2–29	McGeer et al., 1971
ACh	CAT	↓	%	Mouse	4–24	Waller et al., 1981
ACh	CAT	↓	19%	Mouse	6–30	Strong et al., 1980
ACh	CAT		0%	Rabbit	5–66	Makman et al., 1980
ACh	CAT	↓	40%	Human[a]	5–80	McGeer and McGeer, 1978
ACh	CAT		0%	Human[a]	61–92	Perry et al., 1977c
ACh	CAT		0%	Human[b]	5–80	McGeer and McGeer, 1978
ACh	CAT		0%	Human[b]	12–85	Bird and Iversen, 1974
ACh	CAT	↓	37%	Human[AD,a]	—	Perry et al., 1971a
ACh	CAT	↓	50%	Human[HC]	—	Enna et al., 1976
ACh	CAT	↓	63%	Human[HC]	—	Wastek et al., 1980
ACh	CAT	↓	50%	Human[HC]	—	Bird and Iversen, 1974
DA,NE	DOPA to DA	↓	30%	Mouse	10–30	Finch, 1973
DA,NE	TYR to DA	↓	25%	Rat	3–36	Ponzio et al., 1978
DA,NE	TH		0%	Mouse	4–24	Waller et al., 1981
DA,NE	TH	↓	32%	Rat	2–29	McGeer et al., 1971
DA,NE	TH	↓	31%	Rat	3–30	Algeri et al., 1977
DA,NE	TH	↓	25%	Rat[a]	4–26	Reis et al., 1977
DA,NE	TH		0%	Mouse[a]	4–28	Reis et al., 1977
DA,NE	TH	↓	%	Human	15–60	Cote and Kremzner, 1974
DA,NE	TH	↓	88%	Human	5–80	McGeer and McGeer, 1976
DA,NE	TH		0%	Human	4–83	Robinson et al., 1977
DA,NE	DDC	↓	66%	Human	5–80	McGeer and McGeer, 1976
DA,NE	DDC	↓	%	Human	15–60	Cote and Kremzner, 1974
DA,NE	DDC	▽	14%	Mouse	10–30	Finch, 1973
DA,NE	DDC		0%	Mouse	4–28	Reis et al., 1977
GABA	GAD	↓	%	Mouse[A/J]	4–24	Waller et al., 1981
GABA	GAD	↑	%	Mouse[C57]	4–24	Waller et al., 1981
GABA	GAD	↓	85%	Human[HC]	—	Enna et al., 1976
GABA	GAD	↓	52%	Rat	10–26	Strong et al., 1980
GABA	GAD	▽	18%	Mouse	6–30	Strong et al., 1980
GABA	GAD		0%	Human	12–85	Bird and Iversen, 1974
GABA	GAD	↓	%	Human	15–60	Cote and Kremzner, 1974
GABA	GAD	↓	17%	Rat	2–29	McGeer et al., 1971
GABA	GAD	↓	50%	Human	5–80	McGeer and McGeer, 1978
GABA	GAD	↓	50%	Human	45–85	Bowen et al., 1976
GABA	GAD	↓	75%	Human[HC]	—	Bird and Iversen, 1974
			CONTENT			
ACh	ACh		0%	Rat	6–26	Sherman et al., 1981
ACh	ACh		0%	Mouse	3–30	Gibson and Peterson, 1981

(Continued)

TABLE 1. (Cont.)

Trans-mitter	Substrate Measured	Age Change		Species	Age Range	Reference
DA	DA	↓	27%	Mouse	10–30	Finch, 1973
DA	DA	↓	14%	Mouse	4–24	Osterburg et al., 1981
DA	DA		0%	Mouse	2–21	Papavasiliou et al., 1981
DA	DA	↓	55%	Rat	6–25	Joseph et al., 1978
DA	DA	↓	23%	Rat	5–24	Demarest et al., 1980
DA	DA	↓	%	Human	25–93	Carlsson et al., 1980
DA	DA	↓	93%	Human[PD]	—	Lee et al., 1980
DA	DA	↓	49%	Human[b]	28–90	Carlsson and Winblad, 1976
DA	DA		0%	Human[b]	24–92	Adolfsson et al., 1979
DA	DA		0%	Human[b]	12–85	Bird and Iversen, 1974
DA	DA	↓	13%	Human	45–95	Riederer and Wuketich, 1976
DA	DA	↓	80%	Human	24–92	Adolfsson et al., 1979
DA	DA		0%	Rabbit	5–66	Makman et al., 1978
NE	NE		0%	Rat	2–15	Ida et al., 1982
NE	NE		0%	Human	25–93	Carlsson et al., 1980
NE	NE		0%	Rabbit	5–66	Makman et al., 1980
GABA	GABA	↓	43%	Human[HC]	—	Bird and Iversen, 1974
Smstatin	Smstatin	↓	42%	Rat	4–28	Buck et al., 1981
Smstatin	Smstatin	∇	%	Human	15–105	Buck et al., 1981
Ntnsin	Ntnsin		0%	Rat	4–28	Buck et al., 1981
Ntnsin	Ntnsin		0%	Human	15–105	Buck et al., 1981
Sub P	Sub P		0%	Rat	4–28	Buck et al., 1981
GLU	GLU	↓	20%	Rat	3–19	Price et al., 1981

TURNOVER

Trans-mitter	Substrate Measured	Age Change		Species	Age Range	Reference
DA	HVA	∇	20%	Rat	4–29	Algeri et al., 1982
DA	DA	↓	13%	Mouse	4–24	Osterburg et al., 1981
NE	MHPG-SO$_4$		0%	Rat	2–15	Ida et al., 1982

UPTAKE

Trans-mitter	Substrate Measured	Age Change		Species	Age Range	Reference
DA	DA	↓	31%	Mouse	8–26	Jonec and Finch, 1975
DA	DA		0%	Rat	7–24	Thompson et al., 1981
NE	NE	↓	23%	Mouse	8–26	Jonec and Finch, 1975
5-HT	5-HT		0%	Mouse	8–26	Jonec and Finch, 1975
GLU	GLU (V_{max})	↓	44%	Rat	3–19	Price et al., 1981
GLU	GLU (K_M)	↓	38%	Rat	3–19	Price et al., 1981

CATABOLISM

Trans-mitter	Substrate Measured	Age Change		Species	Age Range	Reference
ACh	AChE	↓	37%	Rat	4–22	Morin and Wasterlain, 1980
ACh	AChE	↓	25%	Rat	4–18	Noda et al., 1982
ACh	AChE	∇	20%	Human	5–50	McGeer and McGeer, 1976
DA,NE,5-HT	MAO	↑	33%	Human	12–70	Robinson et al., 1977
DA,NE	MAO B	↑	40%	Rat	2–26	Benedetti and Keane, 1980
DA,NE	MAO B	↑	14%	Rat	4–18	Noda et al., 1982
DA,NE	MAO B	↑	%	Human	25–93	Carlsson et al., 1980
DA,NE	COMT		0%	Human	4–83	Robinson et al., 1977
5-HT	MAO A	↑	18%	Rat	4–18	Noda et al., 1982

TABLE 1. (Cont.)

Trans-mitter	Substrate Measured	Age Change	Species	Age Range	Reference
5-HT	MAO A	0%	Rat	2–26	Benedetti and Keane, 1980
GABA	GABA-T	↑ 20%	Rat	4–18	Noda et al., 1982

RECEPTORS

ACh	QNB	↓ 29%	Rat	4–22	Morin and Wasterlain, 1980
ACh	QNB	0%	Rat	4–18	Noda et al., 1982
ACh	QNB	↓ 22%	Rat	10–26	Enna and Strong, 1981
ACh	QNB	↓ %	Rat	7–25	Smith et al., 1976
ACh	QNB	↓ 23%	Mouse	6–30	Strong et al., 1980
ACh	QNB	0%	Rabbit	5–66	Makman et al., 1980
ACh	QNB	↓ 64%	Human[HC]	—	Wastek et al., 1980
ACh	QNB	↓ 50%	Human[HC]	—	Enna et al., 1976
ACh	Soop	0%	Human[AD,a]	—	Perry et al., 1977a
ACh	QNB	0%	Human	—	Perry, 1980
ACh	QNB	0%	Human	—	White et al., 1977
ACh	QNB	0%	Human	—	Yamamura, 1981
DA	Spdol	↓ 83%	Rat	3–30	Govoni et al., 1980
DA	Spdol	↓ 36%	Rat	6–26	Joseph et al., 1978
DA	Spdol	↓ 50%	Rat	12–30	Makman et al., 1978
DA	Spdol	↓ 36%	Rat	5–25	Misra et al., 1980
DA	Spdol	↓ 66%	Rat	7–27	Severson and Finch, 1980b
DA	Spdol	↓ 45%	Mouse	3–28	Severson and Finch, 1980b
DA	Spdol	↓ %	Rat	7–25	Smith et al., 1981
DA	ADTN	↓ 58%	Rabbit	5–66	Thal et al., 1980
DA	Spdol	↓ 28%	Rabbit	5–66	Thal et al., 1980
DA	Apomorph	↓ 63%	Human[PD]	—	Lee et al., 1980
DA	Haldol	↑ 68%	Human[PD]	—	Lee et al., 1980
DA	Spdol	↓ 25%	Human	2–94	Severson and Finch, 1980a
NE	DHA	↓ 33%	Rat	6–24	Greenberg and Weiss, 1978
NE	DHA	0%	Human[HC]	—	Enna et al., 1976
5-HT	LSD	↑ 50%	Human[HC]	—	Enna et al., 1976
GABA	GABA	0%	Rat	3–24	Maggi et al., 1979
GABA	GABA	0%	Rat	3–30	Govoni et al., 1980
GABA	GABA	0%	Human[HC]	—	Enna et al., 1976
GABA	GABA	↓ 25%	Human[HC]	—	Lloyd et al., 1977
GABA	GABA	↓ %	Human	—	Reisine et al., 1979
Opiate	Etorph	↓ 43%	Rat	2–25	Hess et al., 1981
Opiate	Dihymorph	↓ 34%	Rat[ct]	5–26	Messing et al., 1981
Opiate	Dihymorph	0%	Rat[f]	5–26	Messing et al., 1980

FUNCTION

DA	cAMP	↓ 24%	Rat	2–24	Govoni et al., 1977
DA	cAMP	↓ 32%	Rat	3–24	Schmidt and Thornberry, 1978
DA	cAMP	↓ 21%	Rat	4–30	Puri and Volicer, 1977
DA	cAMP	↓ 40%	Rat[a]	3–24	Walker and Walker, 1973
DA	cAMP	↓ 50%	Rat	12–30	Makman et al., 1978
DA	cAMP	↓ 50%	Rabbit	5–66	Makman et al., 1978
DA	Rotation	↓ 54%	Rat	6–26	Cubells and Joseph, 1981
NE	cAMP	↓ 30%	Rat	3–24	Walker and Walker, 1973

TABLE 2. Cerebellum

Trans-mitter	Substrate Measured	Age Change	Species	Age Range	Reference
		SYNTHESIS			
ACh	CAT	↓ 44%	Rat	4–22	Morin and Wasterlain, 1980
ACh	CAT	0%	Rat	4–18	Noda et al., 1982
ACh	CAT	0%	Rat	2–30	Timiras and Vernadakis, 1972
ACh	CAT	0%	Mouse	3–24	Vijayan, 1977
ACh	CAT	↓ 53%	Mouse	12–30	Unsworth et al., 1980
ACh	CAT	↑ %	Mouse	4–24	Waller et al., 1981
DA,NE	DOPA to DA	↓ 39%	Mouse	10–30	Finch, 1973
DA,NE	TH	↑ %	Mouse	4–24	Waller et al., 1981
DA,NE	TH	0%	Rat	3–30	Algeri et al., 1977
DA,NE	TH	↓ 83%	Chicken	8–60	Yurkewicz et al., 1981
GABA	GAD	↑ 67%	Rat	2–24	Epstein and Barrows, 1969
GABA	GAD	↓ 70%	Human	5–80	McGeer and McGeer, 1978
GABA	GAD	↓ 58%	Human	25–85	Spokes, 1979
		CONTENT			
NE	NE	0%	Rat	3–18	Austin et al., 1978
NE	NE	0%	Mouse	10–30	Finch, 1973, 1978
NE	NE	0%	Mouse	11–28	Osterburg et al., 1981
ASP	ASP	↓ 24%	Rat	2–30	Timiras et al., 1973
GLU	GLU	↓ 16%	Rat	2–30	Timiras et al., 1973
GLY	GLY	0%	Rat	2–30	Timiras et al., 1973
TAU	TAU	↓ 31%	Rat	2–30	Timiras et al., 1973
		CATABOLISM			
ACh	AChE	↓ 13%	Rat	5–30	Meier-Ruge et al., 1976
ACh	AChE	↓ 36%	Rat	4–22	Morin and Wasterlain, 1980
ACh	AChE	0%	Mouse	3–24	Vijayan, 1977
ACh	AChE	↓ 33%	Mouse	1–30	Unsworth et al., 1980
ACh	AChE	∇ 10%	Human	5–50	McGeer and McGeer, 1976
DA,NE	COMT	0%	Rat	3–30	Stramentinoli et al., 1977
DA,NE	MAO B	↑ 25%	Rat	2–26	Benedetti and Keane, 1980
5-HT	MAO A	↑ 18%	Rat	2–26	Benedetti and Keane, 1980
		TURNOVER			
5-HT	5-HIAA	0%	Rat	4–29	Algeri et al., 1982
		RECEPTORS			
ACh	QNB	∇ 27%	Rat	4–22	Morin and Wasterlain, 1980
ACh	Atropine	0%	Rat	2–20	James and Kanungo, 1976
NE	DHA	↓ 30%	Rat	3–24	Maggi et al., 1979
NE	DHA	↓ 53%	Rat	6–24	Greenberg and Weiss, 1978
NE	β_1	↑ 350%	Rat	3–14	Pittman et al., 1980
NE	β_2	↓ 25%	Rat	3–14	Pittman et al., 1980
NE	DHA	↓ 30%	Rat	3–24	Enna and Strong, 1981
NE	DHA	↓ 24%	Mouse	6–30	Enna and Strong, 1981
NE	DHA	↓ 50%	Human	2–80	Maggi et al., 1979
GABA	Muscimol	0%	Rat	3–24	Maggi et al., 1979
GABA	GABA	0%	Rat	3–30	Govoni et al., 1979
GABA	GABA	↑ 193%	Human[HC]	—	Lloyd et al., 1977

TABLE 2. (*Cont.*)

Trans-mitter	Substrate Measured	Age Change		Species	Age Range	Reference
			FUNCTION			
NE	Spk Rate	↓	%	Rat	3–20	Marwaha et al., 1980, 1981
NE	cAMP	↓	90%	Rat	3–20	Walker and Walker, 1973
NE	cAMP	↓	77%	Rat	1–18	Austin et al., 1978
NE	cAMP	↓	58%	Rat	3–24	Schmidt and Thornberry, 1978
GABA	Spk Rate		0%	Rat	3–20	Marwaha et al., 1981

TABLE 3. Hypothalamus.

Trans-mitter	Substrate Measured	Age Change		Species	Age Range	Reference
			SYNTHESIS			
ACh	CAT	▽	15%	Human	5–50	McGeer and McGeer, 1976
DA,NE	TYR to DA	↓	27%	Rat	3–36	Ponzio et al., 1978
DA,NE	DOPA to DA	↓	50%	Mouse	10–30	Finch, 1973
DA,NE	TH	↑	19%	Rat	4–26	Reis et al., 1977
DA,NE	TH		0%	Rat	4–29	Algeri et al., 1982
DA,NE	TH		0%	Mouse	4–28	Reis et al., 1977
DA,NE	TH		0%	Human	5–50	McGeer and McGeer, 1976
DA,NE	TH		0%	Human	4–83	Robinson et al., 1977
DA,NE	TH		0%	Human	15–60	Cote and Kremzner, 1974
DA,NE	DDC		0%	Mouse	4–28	Reis et al., 1977
DA,NE	DDC		0%	Human	5–50	McGeer and McGeer, 1976
DA,NE	DDC	↓	94%	Human	15–60	Cote and Kremzner, 1974
NE	TYR to NE	↓	52%	Rat	3–36	Ponzio et al., 1978
NE	DOPA to NE	↓	43%	Mouse	10–30	Finch, 1973
NE	DBH	↓	20%	Rat	4–26	Reis et al., 1977
NE	DBH		0%	Mouse	4–28	Reis et al., 1977
GABA	GAD	↓	50%	Human	5–80	McGeer and McGeer, 1978
GABA	GAD	↓	66%	Human	15–60	Cote and Kremzner, 1974
5-HT	5-HT	↑	14%	Rat	3–21	Simpkins et al., 1977
			CONTENT			
DA	DA	↓	52%	Rat	4–26	Miller et al., 1976
DA	DA	↓	60%	Rat	1–18	Austin et al., 1978
DA	DA	↓	13%	Rat	5–24	Demarest et al., 1980
DA	DA	↓	27%	Rat[c]	5–24	Demarest et al., 1980
DA	DA	↓	33%	Rat	3–21	Simpkins et al., 1977
DA	DA	↓	46%	Rat[c]	3–25	Estes and Simpkins, 1980
DA	DA	↓	33%	Rat[d]	3–25	Estes and Simpkins, 1980
DA	DA	↓	50%	Rat[e]	3–25	Estes and Simpkins, 1980
DA	DA		0%	Rat	4–20	Huang et al., 1977
DA	DA	↓	28%	Mouse[c,d]	3–30	Osterburg et al., 1981
DA	DA		0%	Human	24–92	Adolfsson et al., 1979
DA	DA	↑	293%	Rat[g]	3–25	Estes and Simpkins
DA	DA	△	19%	Mouse[g]	3–30	Osterburg et al., 1981
DA	DA	↓	29%	Mouse[e]	3–30	Osterburg et al., 1981

(*Continued*)

TABLE 3. (Cont.)

Trans-mitter	Substrate Measured	Age Change	Species	Age Range	Reference
NE	NE	0%	Rat	3–36	Ponzio et al., 1978
NE	NE	∇ 19%	Rat	12–25	Sun, 1976
NE	NE	0%	Rat	5–24	Demarešt et al., 1980
NE	NE	↓ 21%	Rat[c]	5–24	Demarest et al., 1980
NE	NE	↓ 9%	Rat	2–15	Ida et al., 1982
NE	NE	↓ 52%	Rat	4–26	Miller et al., 1976
NE	NE	↓ 47%	Rat	1–18	Austin et al., 1978
NE	NE	↓ 13%	Rat[f]	3–21	Simpkins et al., 1977
NE	NE	↓ %	Rat	4–20	Huang et al., 1977
NE	NE	↓ 30%	Rat	3–25	Estes and Simpkins, 1980
NE	NE	0%	Mouse	10–30	Finch, 1973, 1978
NE	NE	↓ 25%	Mouse	3–30	Osterburg et al., 1981
NE	NE	0%	Human	25–93	Carlsson et al., 1980
NE	NE	↓ 54%	Monkey	4–15	Samorajski and Rolsten, 1973
5-HT	5-HT	0%	Rat	3–21	Simpkins et al., 1977
5-HT	5-HT	↓ 19%	Monkey	4–15	Samorajski and Rolsten, 1973
5-HT	5-HT	0%	Human	5–93	Carlsson et al., 1980
β-Endo	β-Endo	∇ 67%	Rat	6–24	Gambert et al., 1980
β-Endo	β-Endo	↓ 56%	Rat	6–24	Gambert, 1981
β-Endo	β-Endo	↓ 50%	Rat	3–24	Barden et al., 1981
β-Endo	β-Endo	↓ 50%	Rat	3–23	Forman et al., 1981
m-Enk	m-Enk	↑ 71%	Rat	4–20	Steger et al., 1980
m-Enk	m-Enk	↑ 200%	Rat[f]	4–24	Kumar et al., 1980
Sub P	Sub P	∇ 26%	Rat	4–28	Buck et al., 1981
Sub P	Sub P	∇ %	Human	15–105	Buck et al., 1981
Smstatin	Smstatin	0%	Rat	4–28	Buck et al., 1981
Ntnsin	Ntnsin	0%	Rat	4–28	Buck et al., 1981
Vaso	Vaso	0%	Rat	4–28	Sladek et al., 1981
			TURNOVER		
DA	DA	0%	Rat	4–20	Huang et al., 1977
DA	DA	↓ 14%	Rat[f]	3–21	Simpkins et al., 1977
DA	DA	↓ 28%	Mouse[c,d]	4–30	Osterburg et al., 1981
NE	NE	↓ %	Rat	4–20	Huang et al., 1977
NE	MHPG-SO$_4$	↓ 15%	Rat	2–15	Ida et al., 1982
NE	NE	↓ 24%	Rat	3–21	Simpkins et al., 1977
NE	NE	↓ 46%	Mouse	10–30	Finch, 1978
NE	NE	↓ 13%	Mouse[c,d]	4–30	Osterburg et al., 1981
			UPTAKE		
DA	DA	↓ 27%	Mouse	8–26	Jonec and Finch, 1975
NE	NE	0%	Mouse	8–26	Jonec and Finch, 1975
5-HT	5-HT	0%	Mouse	8–26	Jonec and Finch, 1975
5-HT	5-HT	0%	Mouse	6–28	Azmitia et al., 1979
			CATABOLISM		
DA,NE,5-HT	MAO	↑ 33%	Human	12–70	Robinson et al., 1977
DA,NE	COMT	0%	Human	4–83	Robinson et al., 1977
DA,NE	MAO B	↑ 24%	Rat	2–26	Benedetti and Keane, 1980
DA,NE	MAO B	↑ %	Human	25–93	Carlsson et al., 1980
5-HT	MAO A	0%	Rat	2–26	Benedetti and Keane, 1980

TABLE 3. (Cont.)

Trans-mitter	Substrate Measured	Age Change	Species	Age Range	Reference
		RECEPTORS			
ACh	QNB	0%	Rat	4–22	Morin and Wasterlain, 1980
GABA	GABA	↓ 39%	Rat	3–30	Govoni et al., 1980
		FUNCTION			
DA	Prolactin	↓ 33%	Rat	3–24	Barden et al., 1981
DA	Cold Stress (TH)	↓ 27%	Rat	4–29	Algeri et al., 1982
DA	cAMP	↓ 50%	Rabbit	5–66	Makman et al., 1980
NE	cAMP	0%	Rat	3–24	Schmidt, 1981
DA,NE	cAMP	∇ 33%	Rat	1–18	Austin et al., 1978
m-Enk	LH	↓ 56%	Rat	4–20	Steger et al., 1980
HIS	cAMP	↓ 50%	Rabbit	5–66	Makman et al., 1980

TABLE 4. Midbrain and Hindbrain.

Transmitter	Substrate Measured	Age Change	Species	Age Range	Reference
		SYNTHESIS			
ACh	CAT	0%	Rat[h]	4–18	Noda et al., 1982
ACh	CAT	∇ 20%	Human[h]	5–50	McGeer and McGeer, 1976
ACh	CAT	↓ 38%	Mouse[i]	18–30	Unsworth et al., 1980
DA	DOPA to DA	↓ 53%	Mouse	10–30	Finch, 1973
DA,NE	TH	0%	Rat[k]	4–26	Reis et al., 1977
DA,NE	TH	0%	Mouse[h,l]	4–28	Reis et al., 1977
DA,NE	TH	∇ 29%	Rat[i]	3–30	Algeri et al., 1977
DA,NE	TH	↓ 30%	Rat[i]	4–29	Algeri et al., 1982
DA,NE	TH	∇ 19%	Rat[h]	4–26	Reis et al., 1977
DA,NE	TH	↓ 48%	Chicken	8–60	Yurkewicz et al., 1981
DA,NE	TH	↓ 96%	Human[h]	15–60	Cote and Kremzner, 1974
DA,NE	TH	0%	Human[h]	4–83	Robinson et al., 1977
DA,NE	DDC	0%	Mouse[h,l]	4–28	Reis et al., 1977
DA,NE	DDC	↓ 71%	Human	20–50	McGeer and McGeer, 1976
DA,NE	DDC	↓ 95%	Human[h]	15–60	Cote and Kremzner, 1974
NE	DOPA to NE	↓ 29%	Mouse	10–30	Finch, 1973
NE	TYR to NE	↓ 58%	Rat	3–36	Ponzio et al., 1978
NE	DBH	0%	Rat[k]	4–26	Reis et al., 1977
NE	DBH	0%	Mouse[h,l]	4–28	Reis et al., 1977
5-HT	TRY HYD	↓ 39%	Rat[l]	1–24	Meek et al., 1977
5-HT	TRY HYD	0%	Rat[l]	4–26	Reis et al., 1977
GABA	GAD	↑ 55%	Rat[i]	2–24	Epstein and Barrows, 1969
GABA	GAD	0%	Mouse[i]	1–24	Unsworth et al., 1980
GABA	GAD	↓ 90%	Human[h]	15–60	Cote and Kremzner, 1974
GABA	GAD	↓ 54%	Human[h]	25–85	Spokes, 1979
GABA	GAD	↓ 55%	Human[h]	5–80	McGeer and McGeer, 1978

(Continued)

TABLE 4. (*Cont.*)

Transmitter	Substrate Measured	Age Change	Species	Age Range	Reference
GABA	GAD	↓ 78%	Human[j]	20–50	McGeer and McGeer, 1976
GABA	GAD	↓ 57%	Human[k]	20–50	McGeer and McGeer, 1976

CONTENT

Transmitter	Substrate Measured	Age Change	Species	Age Range	Reference
DA	DA	0%	Mouse[h]	4–30	Osterburg et al., 1981
DA	DA	0%	Human	24–92	Adolfsson et al., 1979
NE	NE	↓ 35%	Rat	3–36	Ponzio et al., 1978
NE	NE	↓ 11%	Rat	2–15	Ida et al., 1982
NE	NE	0%	Mouse	10–30	Finch, 1973
NE	NE	0%	Rat	12–25	Sun, 1976
NE	NE	↓ 67%	Monkey	4–15	Samorajski and Rolsten, 1973
NE	NE	↓ 33%	Human	25–70	Robinson, 1975
NE	NE	↓ 50%	Human[h]	25–85	Spokes, 1979
NE	NE	↓ 39%	Human	25–70	Nies et al., 1973
5-HT	5-HT	↓ 40%	Rat	1–24	Meek et al., 1977
5-HT	5-HT	0%	Human	25–70	Robinson et al., 1972
Sub P	Sub P	0%	Rat[h]	4–28	Buck et al., 1981
Ntnsin	Ntnsin	0%	Rat[h]	4–28	Buck et al., 1981
Ntnsin	Ntnsin	↓ %	Human[h]	15–105	Buck et al., 1981
ASP	ASP	0%	Rat[h]	2–30	Timiras et al., 1973
GLU	GLU	↓ 15%	Rat[h]	2–30	Timiras et al., 1973
GLY	GLY	0%	Rat[h]	2–30	Timiras et al., 1973
TAU	TAU	↓ 26%	Rat[h]	2–30	Timiras et al., 1973

TURNOVER

Transmitter	Substrate Measured	Age Change	Species	Age Range	Reference
DA	HVA	▽ 25%	Rat[h]	4–29	Algeri et al., 1982
NE	NE	↓ 32%	Rat	3–36	Ponzio et al., 1978
NE	MHPG–SO$_4$	↓ 8%	Rat	2–15	Ida et al., 1982
5-HT	5-HIAA	0%	Rat[h]	4–29	Algeri et al., 1982
5-HT	5-HIAA	0%	Human	25–70	Robinson et al., 1972

CATABOLISM

Transmitter	Substrate Measured	Age Change	Species	Age Range	Reference
ACh	AChE	↓ 33%	Mouse[i]	4–30	Unsworth et al., 1980
ACh	AChE	↓ 36%	Human[h]	20–50	McGeer and McGeer, 1976
DA,NE,5-HT	MAO	↑ 60%	Human	25–70	Robinson, 1975
DA,NE,5-HT	MAO	↑ %	Human	4–83	Robinson et al., 1977
DA,NE	MAO B	0%	Rat	2–26	Benedetti and Keane, 1980
5-HT	MAO A	↓ 15%	Rat	2–26	Benedetti and Keane, 1980

RECEPTORS

Transmitter	Substrate Measured	Age Change	Species	Age Range	Reference
NE	DHA	↓ 55%	Rat	3–24	Enna and Strong, 1981
GABA	GABA	↓ 55%	Rat[h]	3–30	Govoni et al., 1980
GABA	GABA	0%	Rat[i]	3–24	Maggi et al., 1979

FUNCTION

Transmitter	Substrate Measured	Age Change	Species	Age Range	Reference
DA	cAMP	↓ 37%	Rat	2–24	Govoni et al., 1977
NE	cAMP	0%	Rat	3–24	Schmidt, 1981

TABLE 5. Cortex

Transmitter	Substrate Measured	Age Change		Species	Age Range	Reference
			SYNTHESIS			
ACh	Glu to ACh	↓	51%	Mouse	3–30	Gibson and Peterson, 1981
ACh	CAT	↓	50%	Rat	10–26	Enna and Strong, 1981
ACh	CAT		0%	Rat	4–18	Noda et al., 1982
ACh	CAT		0%	Rat	8–26	Ingram et al., 1981
ACh	CAT		0%	Rat	1–24	Meek et al., 1977
ACh	CAT		0%	Rat	2–30	Timiras and Vernadakis, 1972
ACh	CAT	↑	%	Mouse	4–24	Waller et al., 1981
ACh	CAT	▽	22%	Mouse	6–30	Strong et al., 1980
ACh	CAT		0%	Rabbit	5–66	Makman et al., 1980
ACh	CAT	↓	66%	Chicken	12–36	Vernadakis, 1973
ACh	CAT	↓	80%	Human	5–80	McGeer and McGeer, 1978
ACh	CAT	↓	63%	Human	61–92	Perry et al., 1977c,1981
ACh	CAT		0%	Human	65–93	White et al., 1977
ACh	CAT		0%	Human	41–85	Bowen et al., 1976
ACh	CAT		0%	Human	25–93	Carlsson et al., 1980
ACh	CAT	↓	70%	Human[AD]	—	Perry et al., 1977a,1977c
ACh	CAT	↓	87%	Human[AD]	—	Davies and Feisullin, 1981
ACh	CAT	↓	24%	Human[AD]	—	White et al., 1977
ACh	α-Toxin	↓	39%	Human[AD]	—	Davies and Feisullin, 1981
ACh	Ch		0%	Rat	6–26	Sherman et al., 1981
DA,NE	TH	▽	31%	Rat	3–30	Algeri et al., 1977
DA,NE	TH		0%	Rat	8–26	Ingram et al., 1981
DA,NE	TH	↑	%	Mouse	4–24	Waller et al., 1981
DA,NE	TH		0%	Human	4–83	Robinson et al., 1977
GABA	GAD	↓	52%	Rat	10–26	Strong et al., 1980
GABA	GAD		0%	Rat	8–26	Ingram et al., 1981
GABA	GAD		0%	Mouse	6–30	Strong et al., 1980
GABA	GAD	↓	53%	Human	20–50	McGeer and McGeer, 1976
GABA	GAD		0%	Human	45–85	Bowen et al., 1976
			CONTENT			
ACh	ACh		0%	Rat	6–26	Sherman et al., 1981
ACh	ACh		0%	Rat	1–24	Meek et al., 1977
DA	DA		0%	Rabbit	5–66	Makman et al., 1980
DA	DA		0%	Human	24–92	Adolfsson et al., 1979
NE	NE	↑	56%	Rat	2–15	Ida et al., 1982
NE	NE		0%	Rabbit	5–66	Makman et al., 1980
NE	NE		0%	Human	25–93	Carlsson et al., 1980
5-HT	5-HT		0%	Human	25–93	Carlsson et al., 1980
Sub P	Sub P		0%	Rat	4–28	Buck et al., 1981
Sub P	Sub P		0%	Human	15–105	Buck et al., 1981
Sub P	Sub P	▽	%	Human	61–92	Perry et al., 1981
Smstatin	Smstatin		0%	Rat	4–28	Buck et al., 1981
Smstatin	Smstatin		0%	Human	15–105	Buck et al., 1981
Smstatin	Smstatin	↓	60%	Human[AD]	—	Davies and Terry, 1981
Ntnsin	Ntnsin		43%	Rat	4–28	Buck et al., 1981
Ntnsin	Ntnsin		0%	Human	15–105	Buck et al., 1981
ASP	ASP	↓	29%	Rat	2–30	Timiras et al., 1973
GLU	GLU	↓	25%	Rat	2–30	Timiras et al., 1973
GLY	GLY		0%	Rat	2–30	Timiras et al., 1973
TAU	TAU	↓	31%	Rat	2–30	Timiras et al., 1973

(Continued)

TABLE 5. (Cont.)

Transmitter	Substrate Measured		Age Change	Species	Age Range	Reference
β-Endo	β-Endo	△	200%	Rat	6–24	Gambert et al., 1980
VIP	VIP	△	%	Human	61–92	Perry et al., 1981
				RELEASE		
ACh	ACh	↓	50%	Rat	3–33	Sastry et al., 1981
				UPTAKE		
DA	DA	↓	16%	Mouse	2–12	Haycock et al., 1977
NE	NE	↓	21%	Mouse	2–12	Haycock et al., 1977
GABA	GABA		0%	Mouse	2–12	Haycock et al., 1977
5-HT	5-HT		0%	Mouse	6–28	Azmitia et al., 1979
GLU	GLU	↓	80%	Rat	2–30	Wheeler, 1980
				TURNOVER		
NE	MGPG–SO_4	↑	17%	Rat	2–15	Ida et al., 1982
				CATABOLISM		
ACh	AChE		0%	Rat	4–18	Noda et al., 1982
ACh	AChE	↓	%	Rat	3–33	Sastry et al., 1981
ACh	AChE	↑	114%	Chicken	12–36	Vernadakis, 1973
ACh	AChE	▽	20%	Human	5–50	McGeer and McGeer, 1976
ACh	AChE		0%	Human	—	Perry, 1980
DA,NE	MAO	↑	%	Human	4–83	Robinson et al., 1977
DA,NE	MAO B	↑	42%	Rat	2–26	Benedetti and Keane, 1980
DA,NE	MAO B	↑	%	Human	25–93	Carlsson et al., 1980
5-HT	MAO A	↓	5%	Rat	2–26	Benedetti and Keane, 1980
GABA	GABA–T	↑	9%	Rat	4–18	Noda et al., 1982
				RECEPTORS		
ACh	Atropine	↓	67%	Rat	2–20	James and Kanungo, 1976
ACh	Atropine	↓	30%	Human	65–93	White et al., 1977
ACh	Scop		0%	Human[AD]	—	Perry et al., 1977a
ACh	QNB	↓	18%	Rat	10–26	Enna and Strong, 1981
ACh	QNB	↓	18%	Rat	4–18	Noda et al., 1982
ACh	QNB		0%	Rat	4–22	Morin and Wasterlain, 1980
ACh	QNB	↓	34%	Mouse	6–30	Strong et al., 1980
ACh	QNB		0%	Rabbit	5–66	Makman et al., 1980
ACh	QNB		0%	Human[HC]	—	Enna et al., 1976
NE	β_1		0%	Rat	3–14	Pittman et al., 1980
NE	β_2		0%	Rat	3–14	Pittman et al., 1980
NE	DHA	↓	37%	Rat	5–25	Misra et al., 1980
NE	DHA	▽	12%	Rat	4–18	Noda et al., 1982
NE	DHA		0%	Rat	7–25	Smith et al., 1981
NE	DHA		0%	Rat	3–24	Enna and Strong, 1981
NE	DHA		0%	Human	2–80	Maggi et al., 1979
NE	DHA		0%	Human[HC]	—	Enna et al., 1976
NE	WB4101	↓	35%	Rat	5–25	Misra et al., 1980
NE	WB4101	▽	%	Rat	7–25	Smith et al., 1981
5-HT	Spdol	↓	30%	Rabbit	5–66	Thal et al., 1980
5-HT	5-HT	↓	30%	Human	23–70	Shih and Young, 1978
5-HT	LSD		0%	Human[HC]	—	Enna et al., 1976
GABA	GABA	▽	29%	Rat	3–24	Maggi et al., 1979

TABLE 5. (*Cont.*)

Transmitter	Substrate Measured	Age Change		Species	Age Range	Reference
GABA	GABA		0%	Rat	3–30	Govoni et al., 1980
GABA	GABA		0%	Human[HC]	—	Enna et al., 1976
GABA	GABA		0%	Human[HC]	—	Lloyd et al., 1977
Opiate	Etorph	↓	27%	Rat	2–25	Hess et al., 1981
Opiate	Dihymorph	↓	43%	Rat[th]	5–26	Messing et al., 1981
		FUNCTION				
DA	cAMP	↓	20%	Rat	3–24	Walker and Walker, 1973
DA	cAMP	↓	50%	Rabbit	5–66	Makman et al., 1980
NE	cAMP	↓	68%	Rat	2–24	Berg and Zimmerman, 1975
NE	cAMP	↓	20%	Rat	3–24	Walker and Walker, 1973
NE	cAMP	↑	36%	Rat	3–24	Schmidt and Thornberry, 1981
HIS	cAMP	↓	50%	Rabbit	5–66	Makman et al., 1980

TABLE 6. Hippocampus.

Transmitter	Substrate Measured	Age Change		Species	Age Range	Reference
		SYNTHESIS				
ACh	Glu to ACh	↓	56%	Mouse	3–30	Gibson and Peterson, 1981
ACh	CAT	↓	26%	Rat	4–18	Noda et al., 1982
ACh	CAT		0%	Rat	6–26	Sherman et al., 1980,1981
ACh	CAT		0%	Rat	10–26	Strong et al., 1980
ACh	CAT		0%	Rat	6–28	Lippa et al., 1980
ACh	CAT		0%	Rat	1–24	Meek et al., 1977
ACh	CAT	↓	33%	Mouse	3–24	Vijayan, 1977
ACh	CAT		0%	Mouse	6–30	Strong et al., 1980
ACh	CAT	↑	%	Mouse	4–24	Waller et al., 1981
ACh	CAT		0%	Human	25–93	Carlsson et al., 1980
ACh	CAT	↓	88%	Human	61–92	Perry et al., 1977c
ACh	CAT	∇	20%	Human	5–50	McGeer and McGeer, 1976
ACh	CAT	↓	80%	Human[AD]	—	Perry et al., 1977c
ACh	Ch Uptake	↓	32%	Rat	6–26	Sherman et al., 1980,1981
ACh	Ch Levels		0%	Rat	6–26	Sherman et al., 1981
DA,NE	TH	↑	29%	Rat	8–26	Ingram et al., 1981
DA,NE	TH	↑	%	Mouse	4–24	Waller et al., 1981
DA,NE	TH		0%	Human	5–50	McGeer and McGeer, 1976
DA,NE	TH		0%	Human	4–83	Robinson et al., 1977
5-HT	TRY HYD	↓	29%	Rat	1–24	Meek et al., 1977
GABA	GAD		0%	Rat	10–26	Strong et al., 1980
GABA	GAD		0%	Rat	6–26	Ingram et al., 1981
GABA	GAD		0%	Mouse	6–30	Strong et al., 1980
GABA	GAD	↓	56%	Human	20–50	McGeer and McGeer, 1976
GABA	GAD	↓	60%	Human	25–85	Spokes, 1979
		CONTENT				
ACh	ACh		0%	Rat	6–26	Sherman et al., 1981
ACh	ACh		0%	Rat	1–24	Meek et al., 1977

(*Continued*)

TABLE 6. (Cont.)

Transmitter	Substrate Measured	Age Change	Species	Age Range	Reference
ACh	ACh	0%	Mouse	3–30	Gibson and Peterson, 1981
DA	DA	0%	Rat	3–33	Roubein et al., 1981
DA	DA	↓ 92%	Human	24–92	Adolfsson et al., 1979
NE	NE	↑ 37%	Rat	2–15	Ida et al., 1982
NE	NE	0%	Rat	3–33	Roubein et al., 1981
NE	NE	↓ %	Human	25–93	Carlsson et al., 1980
5–HT	5–HT	↓ 42%	Rat	1–24	Meek et al., 1977
5–HT	5–HT	0%	Rat	3–33	Roubein et al., 1981
5–HT	5–HT	0%	Mouse	5–28	Brennan et al., 1981
5–HT	5–HT	0%	Human	25–93	Carlsson et al., 1980

UPTAKE

Transmitter	Substrate Measured	Age Change	Species	Age Range	Reference
5–HT	5–HT	↑ %	Mouse	6–28	Azmitia et al., 1979

CATABOLISM

Transmitter	Substrate Measured	Age Change	Species	Age Range	Reference
ACh	AChE	0%	Mouse	3–24	Vijayan, 1977
ACh	AChE	↓ 11%	Rat	4–18	Noda et al., 1982
ACh	AChE	▽ 20%	Human	5–50	McGeer and McGeer, 1976
DA,NE,5–HT	MAO	↑ %	Human	4–83	Robinson et al., 1977
DA,NE	MAO B	↑ 38%	Rat	2–26	Benedetti and Keane, 1980
DA,NE	MAO B	↓ %	Human	25–93	Carlsson et al., 1980
5–HT	MAO A	↓ 8%	Rat	2–26	Benedetti and Keane, 1980

TURNOVER

Transmitter	Substrate Measured	Age Change	Species	Age Range	Reference
NE	MHPG-SO$_4$	▽ 5%	Rat	2–15	Ida et al., 1982
5–HT	5–HIAA	0%	Rat	4–29	Algeri et al., 1982

RECEPTORS

Transmitter	Substrate Measured	Age Change	Species	Age Range	Reference
ACh	QNB	↓ 22%	Rat	6–28	Lippa et al., 1980,1981
ACh	QNB	0%	Rat	4–18	Noda et al., 1982
ACh	QNB	0%	Rat	4–22	Morin and Wasterlain, 1980
ACh	QNB	0%	Rat	10–26	Enna and Strong, 1981
ACh	QNB	▽ 27%	Mouse	6–30	Strong et al., 1980
ACh	cis-MDOX	↓ 17%	Rat	6–28	Lippa et al., 1980,1981
GLU	GLU plus Ca^{++}	0%	Rat	3–24	Baudry et al., 1981
GLU	GLU minus Ca^{++}	↑ 21%	Rat	3–24	Baudry et al., 1981
GABA	Muscimol	0%	Rat	6–28	Lippa et al., 1981
Opiate	Etorph	↓ 29%	Rat	2–25	Hess et al., 1981
Opiate	Dihymorph	0%	Rat	5–26	Messing et al., 1980

FUNCTION

Transmitter	Substrate Measured	Age Change	Species	Age Range	Reference
ACh	Spk Rate	↓ 53%	Rat	6–28	Lippa et al., 1980,1981
ACh	Membrane Potential[m]	↓ 93%	Rat	3–30	Segal, 1982
NE	cAMP	↓ %	Rat	3–24	Walker and Walker, 1973
NE	cAMP	0%	Rat	3–24	Schmidt, 1981
5–HT	Membrane Potential[m]	↓ 71%	Rat	3–30	Segal, 1982

TABLE 6. (*Cont.*)

Transmitter	Substrate Measured	Age Change		Species	Age Range	Reference
5-HT	Explor	↓	38%	Mouse	5–28	Brennan et al., 1979
GABA	Spk Rate	↑	33%	Mouse	5–28	Brennan et al., 1979
GABA	Spk Rate	↑	33%	Rat	6–28	Lippa et al., 1981
GABA	Membrane Potential[m]	↑	450%	Rat	3–30	Segal, 1982
GLU	Spk Rate		0%	Rat	6–28	Lippa et al., 1980,1981
GLU	LTP	↓	%	Rat	10–34	Barnes, 1979
GLU	LTP	↓	%	Rat[s]	4–27	Landfield and Lynch, 1977
GLU	LTP	↓	%	Rat	4–27	Landfield et al., 1978

TABLE 7. Whole Brain.

Transmitter	Substrate Measured	Age Change		Species	Age Range	Reference
				SYNTHESIS		
ACh	Glu to ACh	↓	58%	Mouse	3–30	Gibson et al., 1981a, 1981b
ACh	Ch to ACh	↓	73%	Mouse	3–30	Gibson et al., 1981b
ACh	CAT	↓	11%	Rat	6–24	Briggs et al., 1982
ACh	CAT		0%	Rat	2–29	McGeer et al., 1971
DA,NE	TH		0%	Rat	2–28	McGeer et al., 1971
DA,NE	TH		0%	Human	33–74	Grote et al., 1977
DA,NE	DDC		0%	Mouse	2–21	Papavasiliou et al., 1981
NE	DBH		0%	Human	33–74	Grote et al., 1977
GABA	Glu to GABA	↓	39%	Mouse	3–30	Gibson et al., 1981a
GABA	GAD	▽	13%	Rat	2–29	McGeer et al., 1971
GABA	GAD	↓	21%	Mouse	10–37	Fonda et al., 1973
GLU	Glu to GLU	↓	23%	Mouse	3–30	Gibson et al., 1981a
GLU	Glu to GLU		0%	Rat	3–30	DeKoning-Verest, 1980
ASP	Glu to ASP	↓	20%	Mouse	3–30	Gibson et al., 1981a
ASP	Glu to ASP		0%	Rat	3–30	DeKoning-Verest, 1980
				CONTENT		
ACh	ACh	▽	15%	Rat	3–30	DeKoning-Verest, 1980
DA	DA		0%	Rat	2–29	McGeer et al., 1971
DA	DA		0%	Rat	1–18	Austin et al., 1978
DA	DA		0%	Mouse	10–30	Finch, 1973
DA	DA		0%	Mouse	2–21	Papavasiliou et al., 1981
NE	NE		0%	Rat	2–29	McGeer et al., 1971
NE	NE		0%	Rat	1–18	Austin et al., 1978
NE	NE		0%	Mouse	3–28	Samorajski et al., 1971
NE	NE		0%	Mouse	10–30	Finch, 1973
NE	NE		0%	Mouse	2–21	Papavasiliou et al., 1981
5-HT	5-HT		0%	Rat	3–21	Simpkins et al., 1977
5-HT	5-HT		0%	Mouse	3–28	Samorajski et al., 1971
5-HT	5-HT		0%	Mouse	10–30	Finch, 1973
GABA	GABA	↓	12%	Mouse	10–37	Fonda et al., 1973
GABA	GABA		0%	Mouse	3–30	Gibson et al., 1981a

(*Continued*)

TABLE 7. (Cont.)

Transmitter	Substrate Measured	Age Change	Species	Age Range	Reference
GLU	GLU	↓ 13%	Rat	3–30	DeKoning-Verest, 1980
GLU	GLU	0%	Mouse	3–30	Gibson et al., 1981a
GLU	GLU	0%	Mouse	10–37	Fonda et al., 1973
ASP	ASP	↓ 12%	Rat	3–30	DeKoning-Verest, 1980
ASP	ASP	0%	Mouse	3–30	Gibson et al., 1981a
ASP	ASP	0%	Mouse	10–37	Fonda et al., 1973
			UPTAKE		
NE	NE	↓ 15%	Mouse	4–24	Sun, 1976
			CATABOLISM		
ACh	AChE	↓ 35%	Rat	5–30	Meier-Ruge et al., 1976
ACh	AChE	0%	Rat	2–29	McGeer et al., 1971
ACh	AChE	0%	Mouse	3–28	Samorajski et al., 1971
ACh	AChE	↓ %	Mouse	4–24	Ordy and Schjeide, 1973
DA,NE	MAO B	↑ 33%	Rat	2–26	Benedetti and Keane, 1980
DA,NE	MAO B	↑ 37%	Mouse	2–21	Papavasiliou et al., 1981
DA,NE	COMT	↑ 25%	Rat	3–30	Algeri et al., 1976
DA,NE	COMT	↑ 25%	Rat	3–30	Stramentinoli et al., 1977
DA,NE	COMT	0%	Rat	1–35	Prange et al., 1967
DA,NE	COMT	0%	Mouse	2–21	Papavasiliou et al., 1981
DA,NE	COMT	0%	Human	33–74	Grote et al., 1977
DA,NE,5-HT	MAO	0%	Rat	1–35	Prange et al., 1967
DA,NE,5-HT	MAO	↑ 34%	Human	33–74	Grote et al., 1974
5-HT	MAO A	0%	Rat	2–26	Benedetti and Keane, 1980
5-HT	MAO A	↑ 35%	Mouse	2–21	Papavasiliou et al., 1981
GABA	GABA-T	↑ 41%	Mouse	10–37	Fonda et al., 1973
			RECEPTORS		
ACh	QNB	↓ 16%	Rat	6–24	Briggs et al., 1982
			FUNCTION		
DA,NE	cAMP	0%	Rat	1–18	Austin et al., 1978

The condensation of an entire research report into a single line of a summary table has both vices and virtues; the careful reader is directed to primary sources. In particular, the subject species, experimental parameters, and assessment techniques employed in the various reports differ so widely as sometimes to make necessary a somewhat subjective judgment about whether or not an age change should be listed. Moreover, the percent changes given in the tables most often had to be extrapolated from curves and so should only be regarded as convenient estimates. These estimates represent comparisons between the youngest and oldest groups listed under "Age Range." That is, if the age range for a particular study is given as 3–30 months, then the percent change is calculated from the data for 3-month and 30-month groups only. Occasionally, some of the subject groups in a study were so young that we felt it necessary to estimate the percent change based on data from more mature groups in the experiment. In these cases, the very young groups are not included in "Age Range." Some studies provided only qualitative conclusions rather than numerical data; percent changes were, therefore, not always calculable, and in such cases the percent change has been left blank. All ages reported for primates are expressed in years; ages for all other species are expressed in months. No age ranges are given for studies on Alzheimer's disease, Parkinson's disease, or Huntington's disease because these experiments typically compare afflicted patients to age-matched healthy subjects.

ACKNOWLEDGMENTS

We thank Raymond Bartus, Caleb Finch, and Kenneth Moore for their generous consideration and helpful comments on this manuscript.

REFERENCES

Abbey, H. 1979. Survival characteristics of mouse strains. In, D. C. Gibson, R. E. Adelman, and C. E. Finch (eds.), Development of the Rodent as a Model System of Aging. Washington, D. C.: U.S. Government Printing Office, DHEW Publication No. (NIH) 79-161.

Adams, I. and Jones, D. G. 1982. Synaptic remodelling and astrocytic hypertrophy in rat cerebral cortex from early to late adulthood. Neurobiol: Aging 3: 179-186.

Adams, R. D. and Victor, M. 1977. Principles of Neurology, pp. 827-832. New York: McGraw-Hill.

Adolfsson, R., Gottfries, C. G., Roos, B. E., and Winblad, B. 1979. Postmortem distribution of dopamine and homovanillic acid in human brain, variations related to age, and a review of the literature. J. Neural Transmission 45: 81-105.

Aghajanian, G. K., Rosecrans, J. A., and Sheard, M. H. 1967. Serotonin: release in the forebrain by stimulation of the midbrain raphe. Science 156: 402-404.

Algeri, S., Bonati, M., Brunello, N., and Ponzio. 1977. Dihydropteridine reductase and tyrosine hydroxylase activities in rat brain during development and senescence: a comparative study. Brain Res. 132: 569-574.

Algeri, S., Calderini, G., Lomuscio, G., Vantini, G., Toffano, G., and Ponzio, F. 1982. Changes with age in rat central monoaminergic system responses to cold stress. Neurobiol. Aging 3: 237-242.

Algeri, S., Ponzio, F., Bonati, M., and Brunello, N. 1976. Biochemical changes in monoaminergic nerves in the CNS of the senescent rat. Paper presented at 10th CINP meeting, Quebec, Canada.

Austin, J. H., Connole, E., Kett, D., and Collins, J. 1978. Studies in aging of the brain. V. Reduced norepinephrine, dopamine, and cyclic AMP in rat brain with advancing age. Age 1: 121-124.

Azmitia, E. C., Quartermain, D., and Brennan, M. J. 1979. Hippocampal 3H-5HT uptake and behavioral change in young and aged mice. Expl. Brain Res. 36: No. 3 (Supplement), R4.

Barbeau, A., Chase, T., and Paulson, G. W. 1973. In, A. Barbeau, T. Chase, and G. W. Paulson (eds.), Advances in Neurology, Vol. 1: Huntington's Chorea, 1872-1972. New York: Raven Press.

Barbeau, A., Growdon, J. H., and Wurtman, R. J. 1979. Nutrition and the Brain, Vol. 5: Choline and Lecithin in Brain Disorders. New York: Raven Press.

Barden, N., Dupont, A., Labrie, F., Merand, Y., Rouleu, D., H. Vaudry, and Boissier, J. R. 1981. Age-dependent changes in the beta-endorphin content of discrete rat brain nuclei. Brain Res. 208: 209-212.

Barnes, C. A. 1979. Memory deficits associated with senescence: a neurophysiological and behavioral study in the rat. Journal of Comparative and Physiological Psychology 93: 74-101.

Bartus, R. T. 1979. Physostigmine and recent memory: effects in young and aged nonhuman primates. Science 206: 1087-1088.

Bartus, R. T. 1978. Evidence for a direct cholinergic involvement in the scopolamine-induced amnesia in monkeys: effects of concurrent administration of physostigmine and methylphenidate with scopolamine. Pharm. Biochem. Behav. 9: 833-836.

Bartus, R. T., Dean, R. L., and Beer, B. 1980a. Memory deficits in aged cerebus monkeys and facilitation with central cholinomimetics. Neurobiol: Aging, 1, 145-152.

Bartus, R. T., Dean, R. L., and Beer, B. 1982. Neuropeptide effects on memory in aged monkeys. Neurobiol. Aging 3: 61-68.

Bartus, R. T., Dean, R. L., Beer, B., and Lippa, A. S. 1982. The cholinergic hypothesis of geriatric memory disfunction: a critical review. Science, 217: 408-471.

Bartus, R. T., Dean, R. L., Goas, J. A., and Lippa, A. S. 1980b. Age-related changes in passive avoidance retention:modulation with dietary choice. Science 209: 301-303.

Bartus, R. T., Dean, R. L. III, Sherman, K. A., Friedman, E., and Beer, B. 1981. Profound effects of combining choline and piracetam on memory enhancement and cholinergic function in aged rats. Neurobiol. Aging 2: 105-112.

Bartus, R. T. and Johnson, H. R. 1976. Short-term memory in the rhesus monkey: disruption from the anti-cholinergic scopolamine. Pharm. Biochem. Behav. 5: 39-46.

Baudry, M., Arst, D. S., and Lynch, G. 1981. Increased [3H] glutamate receptor binding in aged rats. Brain Res. 223: 195-198.

Baudry, M. and Lynch, G. 1980. Hypothesis regarding the cellular mechanisms responsible for long-term synaptic potentiation in the hippocampus. Exp. Neurol. 68: 202-204.

Baudry, M. and Lynch, G. 1982. Hippocampal glutamate receptors. *Mol. Cell. Biochem.* 38: 5–15.

Benedetti, M. S. and Keane, P. E. 1980. Differential changes in monoamine oxidase A and B activity in the aging rat brain. *J. Neurochem.* 35: 1026–1032.

Berg, A. and Zimmerman, I. D. 1975. Effects of electrical stimulation and norepinephrine on cyclic-AMP levels in the cerebral cortex of the aging rat. *Mech. Age. Dev.* 4: 377–383.

Bertler, A. 1961. Occurrence and localization of catecholamines in the human brain. *Acta Physiol. Scand.* 51: 97–107.

Bhattacharyya, A. K. and Pradhan, S. N. 1980. Comparative effects of dopamine agonists in young and old rats. *Fed. Proceedings* 39: 508.

Bird, E. D. and Iversen, L. L. 1974. Huntington's chorea: post-mortem measurement of glutamic acid decarboxylase, choline acetyltransferase and dopamine in basal ganglia. *Brain* 97: 457–472.

Bird, E. D., Mackay, A. V. P., Rayner, C. N., and Iversen, L. L. 1973. Reduced glutamic-acid-decarboxylase activity of post-mortem brain in Huntington's chorea. *Lancet* 1: 1090–1092.

Bloom, F. E. and McGinty, J. F. 1981. Cellular distribution and function of endorphins. In, *Endogenous Peptides and Learning and Memory Processes,* pp. 199–223. New York: Academic Press.

Boston Collaborative Drug Surveillance Program Report. 1973. Clinical depression of the central nervous system due to diazepam and chlordiazepoxide in relation to cigarette smoking and age. *New Engl. J. Med.* 288: 277–280.

Bowen, D. M., Smith, C. B., White, P., and Davison, A. N. 1976. Neurotransmitter-related indices of hypoxia in senile dementia and other abiotrophies. *Brain* 99: 459–496.

Bowers, M. B. and Gerbode, F. A. 1968. Relationship of monoamine metabolites in human cerebrospinal fluid to age. *Nature,* 219: 1256–1257.

Branconnier, R. J. 1981. The human behavioral pharmacology of the common core heptapeptides. *Pharmacol. Ther.* 14: 161–175.

Brennan, M. J., Dallob, A., and Friedman, E. 1981. Involvement of hippocampal serotonergic activity in age-related changes in exploratory behavior. *Neurobiol. Aging.* 2: 199–204.

Briggs, R. S., Peterson, M. M., and Cook, P. J. 1982. Muscarinic agonist receptor subtypes in aging rat brain. *Neurobiol. Aging.* 3: 259–261.

Buck, S. H., Deshmukh, P. P., Burks, T. F., and Yamamura, H. I. 1981. A survey of substance P., somatostatin, and neurotensin levels in aging in the rat and human central nervous system. *Neurobiol. Aging* 2: 257–264.

Burks, T. F., Buck, S. H. Yamamura, H. I., and Deshmukh, P. P. 1981. Level of Substance P, somatostatin, and neurotensin in rodent and human CNS in aging. *Age* 4: 143.

Carlsson, A., Adolfsson, R., Aquilonius, S. M., Gottfries, C. G., Oreland, L., Svennerholm, L., and Winblad, B. 1980. In, M. Goldstein, A. Lieberman, D. Calne, and M. Thorner (eds.), *Ergot Compounds and Brain Function,* pp. 295–304. New York: Raven Press.

Carlsson, A. and Winblad, B. 1976. The influence of age and time interval between death and autopsy on dopamine and 3-methoxyltyramine levels in human basal ganglia. *J. Neural Transmission* 38: 271–276.

Christie, J. E., Shering, A., Ferguson, J., and Glen, A. I. M. 1981. Physostigmine and arecholine: effects of intravenous infusions in Alzheimer presenile dementia. *Brit. J. Psychiat.* 138: 46–50.

Clark, S. M. and Lipton, J. M. 1981. Hypothermia produced in aged squirrel monkeys by central administration of taurine. *Exp. Aging Res.* 7: 17–24.

Coleman, G. L., Barthold, S. W., Osbaldiston, G. W., Foster, S. J., and Jonas, A. M. 1977. Pathological changes during aging in barrier-related Fischer 344 male rats. *J. Geront.* 32: 258–278.

Cooper, J. R., Bloom, F. E., and Roth, R. H. 1978. *The Biochemical Basis of Neuropharmacology,* p. 225. New York: Oxford University Press.

Cooper, R. L., McNamara, M. C., and Thompson, W. G. 1980. Vasopressin and conditioned flavor aversion in aged rats. *Neurobiol. Aging.* 1: 53–57.

Corkin, S. 1981. Acetylcholine, aging and Alzheimer's disease. *TINS* 42: 287–290.

Corsellis, J. A. N. 1976. Some observations on the Purkinje cell population and on brain volume in human aging. *In,* R. D. Terry and S. Gershon (eds.), *Aging: Neurobiology of Aging,* pp. 205–209. New York: Raven Press.

Costa, E. and Meek, J. 1974. Regulation of the biosynthesis of catecholamines and serotonin in the CNS. *Ann. Rev. Pharmacol.* 14: 491–550.

Cote, L. J. and Kebabian, T. W. 1978. Beta-adrenergic receptor in brain: comparison of 3H dihydroalprenolol binding sites and a beta-adrenergic receptor regulating the adenyl cyclase activity in cell free homogenates. *Life Sci.* 23: 1703–1714.

Cote, L. J. and Kremzner, L. T. 1974. Changes in neurotransmitter systems with increasing age in human brain. *In, Transactions of the American Society for Neurochemistry* 5: 83.

Cotzias, G. E., Miller, S. T., Tang, L. C., and Papavasiliou, P. S. 1981. Levodopa, fertility, and longevity. *Science* 196: 549–551.

Crook, T. and Gershon, S. 1981. *Strategies for the Development of an Effective Treatment for Senile Dementia:* New Canaan, Conn.: Mark Powley Associates. 322 p.

Cubells, J. F. and Joseph, J. A. 1981. Neostriatal dopamine receptor loss and behavioral deficits in the senescent rat. *Life Sci.* 28: 1215–1218.

Davies, P. 1978. *In,* R. Katzman, R. D. Terry, and K. L. Bick, (eds.), *Aging,* Vol. 7: *Alzheimer's Disease: Senile Dementia and Related Disorders.* New York: Raven Press.

Davies, P. and Fiesullin, S. 1981. Postmortem stability

of α-bungarotoxin binding sites in mouse and human brain. *Brain Res.* 216: 449–454.

Davies, P. and Verth, A. H. 1977. Regional distribution of muscarinic acetylcholine receptor in normal and Alzheimer's type dementia brains. *Brain Res.* 138: 385–392.

Davies, P. and Terry, R. D. 1981. Cortical somatostatin-like immunoreactivity in cases of Alzheimer's disease and senile dementia of the Alzheimer type. *Neurobiol. Aging* 2: 9–14.

Davis, K. L. and Berger, P. A. 1979. *Brain Acetylcholine and Neuropsychiatric Disease.* New York: Plenum Press.

Davis, K. L., Mohs, R. C., and Tinklenberg, J. R. 1979. Enhancement of memory by physostigmine. *N. Eng. J. Med.* 301: 946.

Davis, K. L. and Yamamura, H. I. 1978. Cholinergic underactivity in human memory disorders. *Life Sci.* 23: 1729–1734.

Dekoning-Verest, I. F. 1980. Glutamate metabolism in aging rat brain. *Mech. Age. Dev.* 13: 83–92.

Demarest, K. T., Moore, K. E., and Riegle, G. D. 1982. Dopaminergic neuronal function, anterior pituitary dopamine content, and serum concentrations of prolactin, luteinizing hormone and progesterone in the aged female rat. *Brain Research* 247: 347–354.

Demarest, K. T., Riegle, G. D., and Moore, K. E. 1980. Characteristices of dopaminergic neurons in the aged male rat. *Neuroendocrinology* 31: 222–227.

Dutsch, J. A. 1973. The cholinergic synapse and the site of memory. *In,* J. A. Deutsch (ed.), *The Physiological Basis of Memory,* pp. 59–76. New York: Academic Press.

Diaz, P. M., Ngai, S. H., and Costa, E. 1968. Factors modulating brain serotonin turnover. *In,* E. Costa and M. Sandler (eds.), *Advances in Pharmacology;* Vol. 6, Part B, pp. 75–95 New York: Academic Press.

Drachman, D. A. 1977. Memory and cognitive function in man: does the cholinergic system have a specific role? *Neurol.* 27: 783–790.

Drachman, D. A. and Leavitt, J. L. 1974. Human memory and the cholinergic system. A relationship to aging? *Archives of Neurobiology* 30: 113–121.

Drachman, D. A., Noffsinger, D., Sahakian, B. J., Kurdzeil, S., and Fleming, P., 1980. Aging, memory, and the cholinergic system: a study of dichotic listening. *Neurobiol. Aging* 1: 39–44.

Drachman, D. A. and Sahakian, B. J. 1980. Memory and cognitive function in the elderly: a preliminary trial of physostigmines. *Arch. Neurol.* 37: 674–675.

Ehringer, H. and Hornykiewicz, O. 1960. Verteilung von Noradrenalin und Dopamin im Gehirn des Menschen und ihr Verhalten bei Erkoankungen des extrapyramidalon Systems. *Klin. Wschr.* 38: 1236–1239.

Enna, S. J., Bird, E. D., Bennet, J. P., Bylund, D. B., Yamamura, H. I., Iversen, L. L., and Snyder, S. H. 1976. Huntington's chorea: changes in neurotransmitter receptors in the brain. *N. Eng. J. Med.* 294: 1305–1309.

Enna, S. J. and Strong, R., 1981. Age related alterations in central nervous system neurotransmitter receptor binding. *In,* S. Enna, T. Samorajski, and B. Beer (eds.), *Brain Neurotransmitters and Receptors in Aging and Age-related Disorders,* pp. 133–142, New York: Raven Press.

Epstein, M. H. and Barrows, C. H., Jr. 1969. The effects of age on the activity of glutamic acid decarboxylase in various regions of the brains of rats. *J. Gerontology* 24: 136–139.

Estes, K. S. and Simpkins, J. W. 1980. Age-related alterations in catecholamine concentrations in discrete preoptic area and hypothalamic regions in the male rat. *Brain Res.* 194: 556–560.

Estes, K. S., Simpkins, J. W., and Kalra, S. P. 1982. Normal LHRH neuronal function and hyperprolactinemia in old pseudopregnant Fischer 344 rats. *Neurobiol. Aging* 3: 247–252.

Ferris, S. H., Reisberg, B., and Gershon, S. 1980. Neuropeptide modulation of cognition and memory in humans. In, L. W. Poon (ed.), *Aging in the 1980s,* pp. 212–220. Washington: American Psychological Association.

Finch, C. E. 1973. Catecholamine metabolism in the brains of aging male mice. *Brain Res.* 52: 261–276.

Finch, C. E. 1976. The regulation of physiological changes during mammalian aging. *The Quarterly Review of Biol.* 51: 49–83.

Finch, C. E. 1977. Neuroendocrine and autonomic aspects of aging. *In,* C. E. Finch and L. Hayflick (eds.), *Handbook of the Biology of Aging,* pp. 262–280. New York: Van Nostrand Reinhold.

Finch, C. E. 1978. Age-related changes in brain catecholamines: a synopsis of findings in C57BL/6J mice and the rodent models. *In,* C. E. Finch, D. E. Potter, and A. D. Kenny (eds.), *Advances in Experimental Medicine and Biology,* Vol. 113: *Parkinson's Disease—II,* pp. 15–39. New York: Plenum Press.

Finch, C. E. 1980. The relationships of aging changes in the basal ganglia to manifestations of Huntington's chorea. *Ann. Neurol.* 7: 406–411.

Finch, C. E., Potter, D. E., and Kenny, A. D. (eds.) 1978. *Advances in Experimental Medicine and Biology,* Vol: 113: *Parkinson's Disease—II.* New York: Plenum Press.

Fonda, M. L., Acree, D. W., and Auerbach, S. B. 1973. The relationships of gamma-aminobutyrate levels and its metabolism to age in brains of mice. *Arch. Biochem. Biophys.* 159: 622–628.

Forman, L. J., Sonntag, W. E., Van Vugt, D. A., and Meites, J. 1981. Immunoreactive β-endorphin in the plasma, pituitary and hypothalamus of young and old male rats. *Neurobiol. Aging* 2: 281–284.

Franz, D. N. 1975. Drugs for Parkinson's disease. *In,* L. S. Goodman and A. Gilman (eds.), *The Pharmacological Basis of Therapeutics,* pp. 227–244. New York: MacMillan.

Friede, R. L. and Magee, K. R. 1962. Alzheimer's disease. *Neurology* 12: 213–222.

Friede, R. L. 1965. Enzyme histochemical studies of senile plaques. *J. Neuropathol. Exp. Neurol.* 24: 477–491.

Friedman, E., Sherman, K. A., Ferris, S. H., Reisberg, B., Bartus, R. T., and Schneck, M. K. 1981. Clinical response to choline plus piracetam in senile dementia: relation to red-cell choline levels. *New Engl. J. Med.* 304: 1490–1491.

Gambert, S. R. 1981. Interaction of age and thyroid hormone status on beta-endorphin content in rat corpus striatum and hypothalamus. *Neuroendocrin.* 32: 114–117.

Gambert, S. R., Garthwaite, T. L., Pontzer, C. H., and Hagen, T. C. 1980. Age-related changes in central nervous system beta-endorphin and ACTH. *Neuroendocrinology* 31: 252–255.

Gibson, D. C., Adelman, R. C., and Finch, C. E. 1978. *Development of the Rodent as a Model System of Aging.* Washington, D. C.: U. S. Government Printing Office, DHEW Publication No. (NIH) 79-161.

Gibson, G. E. and Peterson, C. 1981. Regional acetylcholine metabolism in senescent mice. *Age* 4: 143.

Gibson, G. E., Peterson, C., and Jenden, D. J. 1981b. Brain acetylcholine synthesis declines with senescence. *Science* 213: 674–678.

Gibson, G. E., Peterson, C., and Sansone, J. 1981a. Neurotransmitter and carbohydrate metabolism during aging and mild hypoxia. *Neurobiol. Aging* 2: 165–172.

Giudicelli, Y. and Pequery, R. 1978. *Eur. J. Biochem.,* 90: 413–419.

Goldman, G. and Coleman, P. D. 1981. Neuron numbers in locus coeruleus do not change with age in Fischer 344 rat. *Neurobiol. Aging* 2: 33–36.

Gottfries, C. S., Gottfries, I., Johansson, B., Olsson, R., Persson, T., Roos, B. E., and Sjostrom, R. 1971. Acid monoamine metabolites in human cerebrospinal fluid and their relations to age and sex. *Neuropharm.* 10: 665–672.

Govoni, S., Loddo, P., Spano, P. F., and Trabucchi, M. 1977. Dopamine receptor sensitivity in brain and retina of rats during aging. *Brain Res.* 138: 565–570.

Govoni, S., Memo, M., Saiani, L., Spano, P. F., and Trabucchi, M. 1980. Impairment of brain neurotransmitter receptors in aged rats. *Mech. Age. Dev.* 12: 39–46.

Greenberg, L. H. and Weiss, B. 1978. Beta-adrenergic receptors in aged rat brain: reduced number and capacity of pineal gland to develop supersensitivity. *Science* 201: 61–63.

Greenberg, L. H. and Weiss, B. 1979. Ability of aged rats to alter beta-adrenergic receptors of brain in response to repeated administration of reserpine and desmethylimipramine. *J. Pharmacol. Experimental Therap.* 211: 309–316.

Grote, S. S., Moses, S. G., Robins, E., Hudgens, R. W., and Croninger, A. B. 1974. A study of selected catecholamine metabolizing enzymes: a comparison of depressive suicides and alcoholic suicides with controls. *J. Neurochem.* 23: 791–802.

Haycock, J. W., White, W. F., McGaugh, J. L., and

Cotman, C. W. 1977. Enhanced stimulus-secretion coupling from brains of aged mice. *Experimental Neurol.* 57: 873–882.

Heron, D. S., Hershkowitz, M., Shinitzky, M., and Samuel, D. 1980a. The lipid fluidity of synaptic membranes and the binding of serotonin and opiate ligands. *In,* U. Z. Littaner, Y. Dudai, I. Silman, V. I. Teichberg, and Z. Vogel (eds.), *Neurotransmitters and Their Receptors,* pp. 125–137. New York: John Wiley & Sons.

Heron, D., Shinitzky, M., Herskowitz, M., Israeli, M., and Samuel, D. 1982. Membrane hyperviscosity and serotonin receptors in the senescent mouse brain—restoration by *in vivo* lipid treatment. *Abstracts of the Tenth Ahavon Katzir-Katchalsky Conference* 10: 31.

Heron, D. S., Shinitzky, M., Hershkowitz, M., and Samuel, D. 1980b. Lipid fluidity markedly modulates the binding of serotonin to mouse brain membranes. *Proc. Natl. Acad. Sci. U.S.A.* 77: 7463–7467.

Hess, G. D., Joseph, J. A., and Roth, G. S. 1981. Effect of age on sensitivity to pain and brain opiate receptors. *Neurobiol. Aging* 2: 49–56.

Hicks, P., Rolsten, C., Hsu, L., Schoolar, J., and Samorajski, T. 1979. Brain uptake index for choline in aged rats. *Soc. Neurosci. Abstr.* 5: 6.

Himwich, W. A. 1973. Problems in interpreting neurochemical changes occurring in developing and aging animals. *In,* D. H. Ford (ed.), *Progress in Brain Research,* Vol. 40: *Neurobiological Aspects of Maturation and Aging,* pp. 13–23. Amsterdam: Elsevier.

Hoffman, G. E. and Sladek, J. R., Jr. 1980. Age-related changes in dopamine, LHRH and somatostatin in the rat hypothalamus. *Neurobiol. Aging* 1: 27–38.

Hornykiewicz, O. 1974. Abnormalities of nigrostriatal dopamine metabolism: neurochemical, morphological and clinical correlations. *J. Pharmacol.* 5 (Suppl.): 64.

Huang, H. H., Simpkins, J. W., and Meites, J. 1977. Hypothalamic norepinephrine (NE) dopamine (DA) turnover and relation to LH, FSH, and prolactin release in old female rats. *Endocrin. (Suppl.)* 100: 331.

Ida, Y., Tanaka, M., Kohno, Y., Nakagawa, R., Imori, K., Tsuda, A., Hoaki, Y., and Nagasaki, N. 1982. Effects of age and stress on regional noradrenaline metabolism in the rat brain. *Neurobiol. Aging* 3: 233–236.

Ingram, D. K., London, E. D., and Goodrick, C. L. 1981. Age and neurochemical correlates of radial maze performance in rats. *Neurobiol. Aging* 2: 41–48.

James, T. C. and Kanungo, M. S. 1976. Alterations in atropine sites of the brain of rats as a function of age. *Biochem. Biophys. Res. Commun.* 72: 170–175.

Jonec, V. J. and Finch, C. E. 1975. Senescence and dopamine uptake by subcellular fractions of the C57BL/6J male mouse brain. *Brain Res.* 91: 197–215.

Joseph, J. A., Berger, R. E., Engel, B. T., and Roth, G. S. 1978. Age-related changes in the nigrostriatum:

a behavioral and biochemical analysis. *J. Gerontology* 33: 643–649.

Joseph, J. A., Filburn, C. R., and Roth, G. S. 1981. Development of dopamine receptor denervation supersensitivity in the neostriatum of the senescent rat. *Life Sci.* 29: 575–584.

Joseph, J. A., Filburn, C., Tzankoff, S. P., Thompson, J. M., and Engel, B. T. 1980. Age-related neostriatal alterations in the rat: failure of L-DOPA to alter behavior. *Neurobiol. Aging* 1: 119–125.

Karnaukhov, V. N. 1973. The role of carotenoids in the formation of lipofuscin and the adaptation of animal cells to oxygen insufficiency. *Tsitologica* 15: 538–542.

Karobath, M., Placheta, P., Lippitsch, M., and Krogsgaard-Larsen, P. 1980. Characterization of GABA-stimulated benzodiazepine receptor binding. *In*, G. Pepeu, M. J. Kuhar, and S. J. Enna (eds.), *Receptors for Neurotransmitters and Peptide Hormones*, pp. 313–320. New York: Raven Press.

Katzman, R., Terry, R. D., and Bick, K. L. (eds.), 1978. *Alzheimer's Disease: Senile Dementia and Related Disorders.* New York: Raven Press.

Koelle, G. B. 1975. Neurohumoral transmission and the autonomic nervous system. *In*, L. S. Goodman and A. Gilman (eds.), *The Pharmacological Basis of Therapeutics*, p. 432. New York: Macmillan.

Kubanis, P. and Zornetzer, S. F. 1981. Age-related behavioral and neurobiological changes: a review with emphasis on memory. *Behav. Neurol. Biol.* 31: 115–172.

Kumar, M. S. A., Chen, C. L., and Huang, H. H. 1980. Pituitary and hypothalamic concentration of met-enkephalin in young and old rats. *Neurobiol. Aging* 1: 153–156.

Lal, H., Gianforcano, R., and Nandy, K. 1979. Marked alterations in responsivity to psycho-stimulation and cholinergic drugs associated with senescence in the female mouse. *Soc. Neurosci. Abstr.* 5: 7.

Landfield, P. W. and Lynch, G. 1977. Impaired monosynaptic potentation in *in vitro* hippocampal slices from aged, memory deficient rats. *J. Gerontology* 32: 523–533.

Landfield, P. W., McGaugh, J. L., and Lynch, G. 1978. Impaired synaptic potentation processes in the hippocampus of aged, memory-deficient rats. *Brain Res.* 150: 85–101.

Lee, T., Seeman, P., Rajput, A., Farley, I. J., and Hornykiewicz, O. 1978. Receptor basis for dopaminergic supersensitivity in Parkinson's disease. *Nature* 273: 59–61.

Lippa, A. S., Critchett, D. J., Ehlert, F., Yamamura, H. I., Enna, S. J., and Bartus, R. T. 1981. Age-related alterations in neurotransmitter receptors: an electrophysiological and biochemical analysis. *Neurobiol. Aging* 2: 3–8.

Lippa, A. S., Pelham, R. W., Beer, B., Critchett, D. J., Dean, R. L., and Bartus, R. T. 1980. Brain cholinergic dysfunction and memory in aged rats. *Neurobiol. Aging* 1: 13–20.

Lloyd, K. G., Drekser, S., and Bird, E. D. 1977. Alterations in 3H-GABA binding in Huntington's chorea. *Life Sci.* 21: 747–754.

Lofstrom, A. P., Eneroth, J. A., Gustafsson, J. A., and Skett, P. 1977. Effect of estradiol benzoate on catecholamine levels and turnover in discrete areas of the median eminence and the limbic forebrain, and on serum luteinizing hormone, follicle stimulating hormone, and prolactin concentrations in the oveariectomized female rat. *Endocrinol.*, 101: 1559–1569.

Maggi, A., Schmidt, M. J., Shetti, B., and Enna, S. J. 1979. Effect of aging on neurotransmitter receptor binding in rat and human brain. *Life Sci.* 24: 367–374.

Makman, M. H., Ahn, H. S., Thal, L., Dvorkin, B., Horowitz, S. G., Sharpless, N., and Rosenfeld, M. 1978. Decreased brain biogenic amine-stimulated adenylate cyclase and spiroperidol-binding sites with aging. *Fed. Proc.* 37: 548.

Makman, M. H., Ahn, H. S., Thal, L. J., Sharpless, N. S., Dvorkin, B., Horowitz, S. G., and Rosenfeld, M. 1980. Evidence for selective loss of brain dopamine and histamine-stimulated adenylate cyclase activities in rabbits with aging. *Brain Res.* 192: 177–184.

Marwaha, J., Hoffer, B. J., and Freedman, R. 1981. Changes in noradrenergic neurotransmission in rat cerebellum during aging. *Neurobiol. Aging* 2: 95–98.

Marwaha, J., Hoffer, B., Pittman, R., and Freedman, R. 1980. Age-related electrophysiological changes in rat cerebellum. *Brain Res.* 201: 85–97.

McDougal, J. N., Marques, P. R., and Burks, T. F. 1980. Age-related changes in body temperature responses to morphine in rats. *Life Sci.* 27: 2679–2685.

McGeer, E. G., Fibiger, H. C., McGeer, P. L., and Wickson, V. 1971. Aging and brain enzymes. *Experimental Gerontol.* 6: 391–396.

McGeer, E. G. and McGeer, P. L. 1975. Age changes in the human for some enzymes associated with metabolism of catecholamines, GABA, and acetylcholine. *In*, J. M. Ordy and K. R. Brizzee (eds.), *Neurobiology of Aging*, pp. 287–305. New York: Plenum Press.

McGeer, E. G. and McGeer, P. L. 1976. Neurotransmitter metabolism and the aging brain. *In*, R. D. Terry and S. Gershon (eds.), *Aging*, Vol. 3: *Neurobiology of Aging*, pp. 389–404. New York: Raven Press.

McGeer, P. L. and McGeer, E. G. 1976. Enzymes associated with the metabolism of catecholamines, acetylcholine and GABA in human controls and patients with Parkinson's disease and Huntington's chorea. *J. Neurochem.* 26: 65–76.

McGeer, P. L. and McGeer, E. G. 1978. Aging and neurotransmitter systems. *In*, C. E. Finch, D. E. Potter, and A. D. Kenny (eds.), *Parkinson's Disease* Vol. 2: *Aging and Neuroendocrine Relationships*, pp. 41–58. New York: Plenum Press.

McGeer, P. L., McGeer, E. G., and Fibiger, H. C. 1973. Glutamic acid decarboxylase and choline acetylase in

Huntington's chorea and Parkinson's disease. *Lancet* 2: 623-624.

McNamara, M. C. and Cooper, R. L. 1979. Age differences in conditioned taste aversion: possible role of vasopressin. *Soc. Neurosci. Abstr.* 5: 8.

Meek, J. L., Bertilsson, L., Cheney, D. L., Zsilla, G., and Costa, E. 1977. Aging-induced changes in acetylcholine and serotonin content of discrete brain nuclei. *J. Gerontology* 32: 129-131.

Meier-Ruge, W., Reichlmeier, K., and Iwangoff, P. 1976. Enzymatic and enzyme histochemical changes of the aging animal brain and consequences for experimental pharmacology on aging. *In,* R. D. Terry and S. Gershon (eds.), *Aging,* Vol. 3: *Neurobiology of Aging,* pp. 379-388. New York: Raven Press.

Messing, R. B., Vasquez, B. J., Samaniego, B., Jensen, R. A., Martinez, J., and McGaugh, J. L. 1981. Alterations in dihydromorphine binding in cerebral hemispheres of aged male rats. *J. Neurochem.* 36: 784-790.

Messing, R. B., Vasquez, B. J., Spiehler, V. R., Martinez, J. L., Jensen, R. A., Rigter, H., and McGaugh, J. L. 1980. 3H-Dihydromorphine binding in brain regions of young and aged rats. *Life Sci.* 26: 921-927.

Mietes, J. 1981. Changes in hypothalamic regulation of pituitary function in aging rats. *In,* S. J. Enna, T. Samorajski, and B. Beer (eds.), *Aging,* Vol. 17: *Brain Neurotransmitters and Receptors in Aging and Age-Related Disorders,* pp. 107-116. New York: Raven Press.

Mietes, J., Huang, H., and Simpkins, J. W. 1978. Recent studies on neuroendocrine control of reproductive senescence in rats. *In,* E. L. Schneider (ed.), *The Aging Reproductive System,* pp. 213-235. New York: Raven Press.

Miller, N. E. and Cohen, G. D. 1981. *In,* N. E. Miller and G. D. Cohen (eds.), *Aging,* Vol. 15: *Clinical Aspects of Alzheimer's Disease and Senile Dementia.* New York: Raven Press.

Miller, A. E., Shaar, C. J., and Riegle, G. D. 1976. Aging effects on hypothalamic dopamine and norepinephrine content in the male rat. *Experimental Aging Research* 2: 475-480.

Misra, C. H., Shelat, H. S., and Smith, R. C. 1980. Effect of age on adrenergic and dopaminergic receptor binding in rat brain. *Life Sci.* 27: 521-526.

Mohs, R. C., Davis, K. L., Tinklenberg, J. R., and Hollister, L. E. 1980. Choline chloride effects on memory in the elderly. *Neurobiol. Aging,* 1: 21-26.

Mohs, R. C., Davis, K. L., Tinklenberg, J. R., Hollister, L. E., Yesavage, J. A., and Kopell, B. S. 1979. Choline chloride treatment of memory deficits in the elderly. *Amer. J. Psychiatry* 136: 1275-1277.

Morin, A. M. and Wasterlain, C. G. 1980. Aging and rat brain muscarinic receptors as measured by quinulininyl benzilate binding. *Neurochem. Res.* 5: 301-308.

Moss, D. E. and Deutsch, J. A. 1975. Cholinergic mechanisms and memory. *In,* P. G. Waser (ed.), *Cholinergic Mechanisms,* pp. 483-492. New York: Raven Press.

Muramoto, O., Sugishita, M., Sugota, H., and Toyokura, Y. 1979. Effect of physostigmine on constructional and memory tasks in Alzheimer's disease. *Arch. Neurol.* 36: 501-503.

Nandy, K. 1981. Morphological changes in the cerebellar cortex of aging *Macaca nemestrina. Neurobiol. Aging* 2: 61-64.

Neff, N. H., Yang, H.-L. T., and Fuentes, J. A. 1974. The use of selective monoamine oxidase inhibitory drugs to modify amine metabolism in brain. *In,* E. Usdin (ed.), *Neuropsychopharmacology of the Monoamines and Their Regulatory Enzymes.* New York: Raven Press.

Nelson, F. J., Latham, K. R., and Finch, C. E. 1975. Plasma testosterone levels in C57BL/6J mice: effects of age and disease. *Acta Endocrinol.* 80: 744-752.

Nies, A., Robinson, D. S., and Davis, J. M. 1973. *In,* C. Eisdorfer and W. E. Fann (eds.), *Psychopharmacology and Aging,* pp. 41-54. New York: Plenum Press.

Noda, Y., McGeer, P. L., and McGeer, E. G. 1982. Lipid peroxidases in brain during aging and vitamin E deficiency: possible relations to changes in neurotransmitter indices. *Neurobiol. Aging* 3: 173-178.

Ordy, J. M. and Scheide, O. A. 1973. Univariate and multivariate models for evaluating long-term changes in neurobiological development, maturity, and aging. *In,* D. H. Ford (ed.), *Progress in brain Research,* Vol. 40: *Neurobiological Aspects of Maturation and Aging,* pp. 25-31. Amsterdam: Elsevier.

Osterburg, H. H., Donahue, H. G., Severson, I. A., and Finch, C. E. 1981. Catecholamine levels and turnover during aging in brain regions of male C57BL/6J mice. *Brain Res.* 224: 337-352.

Ostfeld, A. M. and Gibson, D. C. 1972. *Epidemiology of Aging.* Washington, D.C.: U.S. Government Printing Office.

Papavasiliou, P. S., Miller, S. T., Thal, L. J., Nerder, L. J., Houlihan, G., Rao, S. N., and Stevens, J. M. 1981. Age-related motor and catecholamine alterations in mice on levodopa supplemented diet. *Life Sci.* 28: 2947-2952.

Pedigo, N. W., Schoemaker, H., Morelli, M., McDougal, J. N., Malick, J. B., Burks, T. F., and Yamamura, H. I. 1981. Benzodiazepine receptor binding in young mature and senescent rat brain and kidney. *Neurobiol. Aging* 2: 83-88.

Perry, E. K. 1980. The cholinergic system in old age and Alzheimer's disease. *Age and Aging,* 9: 1-8.

Perry, E. K., Blessed, G., Tomlinson, B. E., Perry, R. H., Crow, T. J., Cross, A. J., Dockray, G. J., Dimaline, R., and Aggregui, A. 1981. Neurochemical activities in human temporal lobe related to aging and Alzheimer-type changes. *Neurobiol. Aging* 2: 251-256.

Perry, E. K., Perry, R. H., Blessed, G., and Tomlinson, B. E. 1977a. Necropsy evidence of central cholinergic deficits in senile dementia. *Lancet* 1: 189.

Perry, E. K., Perry, R. H., Blessed, G., and Tomlinson, B. E. 1977b. *J. Neurol. Sci.* 34: 247.

Perry, E. K., Perry, R. H., Gibson, P. H., Blessed, G., and Tomlinson, B. E. 1977c. A cholinergic connection between normal aging and senile dementia in the human hippocampus. *Neurosci. Lett.* 6: 85–89.

Peters, B. H. and Leving, H. S. 1978. Effects of physostigmine and lecithin on memory in Alzheimer's disease. *Ann. Neurol.* 6: 219–221.

Pittman, R. N., Minneman, K., and Molinoff, P. B. 1980. Alterations in β_1- and β_2-adrenergic receptor density in the cerebellum of aging rats. *J. Neurochem.* 35: 273–275.

Plaitakis, A., Berl, S., and Yahr, M. D. 1982. Abnormal glutamate metabolism in an adult-onset degenerative neurological disorder. *Science* 216: 193–196.

Ponzio, F., Brunello, N., and Algeri, S. 1978. Catecholamine synthesis in brain of aging rats. *J. Neurochem.* 30: 1617–1620.

Porta, E. A., Nitta, R. T., and Nguyen, L. 1980. Effects of dietary fat, vitamin E, and aging on cerebellar Purkinje cells of the rat. *Fed. Proc.* 39: 500.

Prange, A. J., Loosen, P. T., and Nemeroff, C. B. 1979. Peptides: applications to research in nervous and mental disorders. *In,* S. Fielding and R. C. Effland (eds.), *New Frontiers in Psychotropic Drug Research,* pp. 117–189. Mt. Kisco, N.Y.: Future Publishing Co.

Prange, A. J., White, J. E., Lipton, M. A., and Kindead, M. A. 1967. Influence of age on monamine oxidase and catechol-O-methyl transferase in rat tissues. *Life Sch.* 6: 581–586.

Price, M. T., Olney, J. W., and Haft, R. 1981. Age-related changes in glutamate concentration and synaptosomal glutamate uptake in adult rat striatum. *Life Sci.* 28: 1365–1370.

Puri, S. K. and Volicer, L. 1977. Effects of aging on cyclic AMP levels and adenylate cyclase and phosphodiesterase activities in the rat corpus striatum. *Mech. Age. Dev.* 6: 53–58.

Randall, P. K., Severson, J. A., and Finch, C. E. 1981. *J. Pharm. Exp. Ther.* 219: 695–700.

Reis, D. J., Rosse, R. A., and Joh, T. H. 1977. Changes in the activity and amounts of enzymes synthesizing catecholamines and acetylcholine in brain, adrenal medullar, and sympathetic ganglia of aged rat and mouse. *Brain Res.* 136: 465–474.

Reisine, T. D., Beaumont, K., Bird, E. D., Spokes, E., and Yamamura, H. I. 1979. Huntington's disease: alterations in neurotransmitter receptor binding in the human brain. *In* A. Barbeau, T. Chase, and G. W. Paulson (eds.), *Advances in Neurology,* Vol. 23: *Huntington's Disease,* pp. 717–726. New York: Raven Press.

Reisine, T. D., Pedigo, N. W., Meiners, C., Igbal, K., and Yamamura, H. I. 1980. Alzheimer's disease: studies on neurochemical alterations in the brain. *In,* L. Amaducci, A. N. Davison, and P. Antuono (eds.), *Aging of the Brain and Dementia,* pp. 147–150. New York: Raven Press.

Riederer, P. and Wuketich, S. T. 1976. Time course of nigrostriatal degeneration in Parkinson's disease. *J. Neural Transmission* 38: 277–301.

Robinson, D. S. 1975. Changes in monoamine oxidase and monoamines with human development and aging. *Fed. Proc.* 34: 103–107.

Robinson, D. S., Nies, A., Davis, J. N., Bunney, W. E., Davis, J. M., Colburn, R. W., Bourne, H. R., Shaw, D. M., and Coppen, A. J. 1972. Aging, monoamines and monoamine oxidase levels. *Lancet* 1: 290–291.

Robinson, D. S., Sourkes, R. L., Nies, A., Harris, L. S., Spector, S., Bartlett, D. L., and Kaye, I. S. 1977. Monoamine metabolism in human brain. *Arch. Gen. Psychiatr.* 34: 89–92.

Rogers, J., Silver, M. A., Shoemaker, W. J., and Bloom, F. E. 1980. Senescent changes in a neurobiological model system: cerebellar Purkinje cell electrophysiology and correlative anatomy. *Neurobiol. Aging* 1: 3–11.

Rogers, J., Zornetzer, S. F., and Bloom, F. E. 1981. Senescent pathology of cerebellum: Purkinje neurons and their parallel fiber afferents. *Neurobiol. Aging,* 2: 15–26.

Rogers, J., Zornetzer, S., Shoemaker, W. J., and Bloom, F. E. 1981. Electrophysiology of aging brain: senescent pathology of cerebellum. *In,* S. J. Enna and T. Samorajski (eds.), *Brain Neurotransmitters and Receptors in Aging and Age-related Disorders.* pp. 81–94. New York: Raven Press.

Roubein, I. F., Embree, L. J., Kay, D., and Jackson, D. J. 1981. Aging effect on biogenic amines in rat hippocampus. *Age* 4: 144.

Samorajski, T. and Rolsten, C. 1973. Age and regional differences in the chemical composition of brains of mice, monkeys, and humans. *In,* D. H. Ford (ed.), *Neurobiological Aspects of Maturation and Aging, Progress in Brain Research,* Vol. 40, pp. 251–265. Amsterdam: Elsevier.

Samorajski, T., Rolsten, C., and Ordy, J. M. 1971. Changes in behavior, brain, and neuroendocrine chemistry with age and stress in C57BL/10 male mice. *J. Gerontology* 26: 168–175.

Sastry, B. V., Janson, V. E., Jaiswal, N., and Tayeb, O.S. 1981. Deficiencies in the cholinergic nervous system of the rat cerebrum as a function of age. *Age* 4: 142.

Sawyer, C. H., Hilliard, J., Kanematsu, S., Scaramuzzi, R., and Blake, C. A. 1974. Effects of intraventricular infusions of norepinephrine and dopamine on LH release and ovulation in the rabbit. *Neuroendocrinol.* 15: 328–337.

Schmidt, M. J. 1981. The cyclic nucleotide system in the brain during aging. *In,* S. J. Enna, T. Samorajski, and B. Beer (eds.), *Brain Neurotransmitters and Receptors in Aging and Age-related Disorders.* pp. 171–193. New York: Raven Press.

Schmidt, M. J. and Thornberry, J. F. 1978. Cyclic AMP and cyclic GMP accumulation *in vitro* in brain regions of young, old, and aged rats. *Brain Res.* 139: 159–177.

Schocken, D. D. and Roth, G. S. 1977. Reduced beta-adrenergic receptor concentrations in aging man. *Nature (London)* 267: 856–858.

Segal, M. 1982. Changes in neurotransmitter actions in the aged rat hippocampus. *Neurobiol. Aging* 3: 121–124.

Segal, P. E., Miller, C., and Timiras, P. S. 1975. *Abstr. 10th Int. Cong. Gerontol.* 2: 33.

Severson, J. A. and Finch, C. E. 1980a. Age changes in human basal ganglion dopamine receptors. *Fed. Proc.* 39: 508.

Severson, J. A. and Finch, C. E. 1980b. Reduced dopaminergic binding during aging in the rodent striatum. *Brain Res.* 192: 147–162.

Sherman, K., Dallob, A., Dean, R. L., Bartus, R. T., and Friedman, E. 1980. Neurochemical and behavioral deficit in aging rats. *Fed. Proc.* 39: 508

Sherman, K. A., Friedman, E., and Bartus, R. T. 1981. Presynaptic cholinergic mechanisms in brains of aged, memory impaired Fischer 344 rats. *Age* 4: 142.

Shih, J. C. and Young, H. 1978. The alteration of serotonin binding sites in aged human brain. *Life Sci.* 23: 1441–1448.

Siakatos, A. N. and Armstrong, D. 1976. *In,* J. M. Ordy and K. R. Brizzee (eds.), *Advances in Behavioral Biology,* Vol. 16, pp. 369. New York: Plenum Press.

Simpkins, J. W., Mueller, G. P., Huang, H. H., and Meites, J. 1977. Evidence for depressed catecholamine and enhanced serotonin metabolism in aging male rats: possible relation to gonadotropin secretion. *Endocrinol.* 100: 1672–1678.

Sims, L. and Bloom, F. E. 1973. Rat brain 3, 4-dihydroxyphenylalanine and 5-hydroxytryptophan decarboxylase activities: differential effects of 6-hydroxydopamine. *Brain Res.* 49: 165–173.

Sitaram, N., Weingartner, H., and Gillin, J. C. 1978. Human serial learning: enhancement with arecoline and choline and impairment with scopolamine. *Science* 201: 274–275.

Sladek, C. D., McNeill, T. H., Gregg, C. M., Blair, M. L., and Baggs, R. B. 1981. Vasopressin and renin response to dehydration in aged rats. *Neurobiol. Aging* 2: 293–302.

Smith, A. M. and Swash, M. 1979. Physostigmines in Alzheimer's disease. *Lancet* 1: 42.

Smith, R. C., Shelat, H. S., Sammeta, J., and Misra, C. H. 1981. Aging, receptors and neuroleptic drugs. *In,* S. J. Enna, T. Samorajski, and B. Beer (eds.), *Aging,* Vol. 17: *Brain Neurotransmitters and Receptors in Aging and Age-related Disorders,* pp. 231–243. New York: Raven Press.

Spokes, G. S. 1979. An analysis of factors influencing measurements of dopamine, noradrenaline, glutamate decarboxylase and choline acetylase in human post-mortem brain tissue. *Brain* 102: 333–346.

Steger, R. W., Sonntag, W. E., Van Vugt, D. A., Forman, L. J., and Meites, J. 1980. Reduced ability of naloxone to stimulate LH and testosterone release in aging male rats; possible relation to increase in hypothalamic met^5-enkephalin. *Life Sci.* 27: 747–753.

Storer, J. B. 1969. Longevity and gross pathology at death in 22 inbred mouse strains. *J. Gerontology* 21: 404–409.

Storm-Mathisen, J. 1976. Distribution of the components of the GABA system in neuronal tissue: cerebellum and hippocampus. *In,* E. Roberts, T. N. Chase, and D. B. Tower (eds.), *GABA in Nervous System Function,* pp. 149–168. New York: Raven Press.

Storm-Mathisen, J. 1977. Localization of transmitter candidates in the brain: the hippocampal formation as a model. *Prog. Neurobiol.,* 8: 119–181.

Stramentinoli, G., Gualano, M., Catto, E., and Algeri, S. 1977. Tissue levels of S-adenosylmethionine in aging rats. *J. Gerontology* 32: 392–394.

Strong, R., Hicks, P., Hsu, L., Bartus, R. T., and Enna, S. J. 1980. Age-related alterations in the rodent brain cholinergic system and behavior. *Neurobiol. Aging* 1: 59–64.

Strong, R., Hsu, L., Hicks, P., and Enna, S. J. 1979. Age-related decrease in mouse brain cholinergic muscarinic receptor binding. *Soc. Neurosci. Abstr.* 5: 11.

Sun, A. Y. 1976. Aging and *in vivo* norepinephrine-uptake in mammalian brain. *Expl. Aging Res.* 2: 207–219.

Thal, L. J., Horowitz, S. G., Dvorkin, B., and Makman, M. H. 1980. Evidence for loss of brain [3H]spiroperidol and [3H]ADTN binding sites in rabbit brain with aging. *Brain Res.* 192: 185–194.

Thompson, J. M., Witaker, J. R., and Joseph, J. A. 1981. [³H] Dopamine accumulation and release from striatal slices in young, mature and senescent rats. *Brain Res.* 224: 436–440.

Timiras, P. S., Hudson, D. B., and Oklund, S. 1973. Changes in central nervous system free amino acids with development and aging. *In,* D. H. Ford (ed.), *Neurobiological Aspects of Maturation and Aging; Progress in Brain Research,* Vol. 40, pp. 267–275. Amsterdam: Elsevier.

Timiras, P. S. and Vernadakis, A. 1972. Structural, biochemical, and functional aging of the nervous system. *In,* P. S. Timiras (ed.), *Developmental Physiology and Aging,* pp. 502–526. New York: Macmillan.

Turkington, M. R. and Everitt, A. V. 1976. The neurohypophysis and aging with special reference to the antidiuretic hormone. *In,* A. V. Everitt and J. A. Burgess (eds.), *Hypothalamus, Pituitary, and Aging,* pp. 123–136. Springfield, Ill.: Charles C. Thomas.

Unsworth, B. R., Fleming, L. H., and Caron, P. C. 1980. Neurotransmitter enzymes in telencephalon, brain stem, and cerebellum during the entire life span of the mouse. *Mech. Age. Dev.* 13: 205–217.

Vernadakis, A. 1973. Comparative studies of neurotransmitter substances in the maturing and aging central nervous system of the chicken. *In,* D. H. Ford (ed.), *Progress in Brain Research,* Vol. 40: *Neuro-*

biological Aspects of Maturation and Aging. pp. 341–354. Amsterdam: Elsevier.

Verzar, F. 1961. The age of the individual as one of the parameters of pharmacological action. *Acta Physiol. Acad. Sci. Hungary* 19: 313–318.

Vijayan, V. K. 1977. Cholinergic enzymes in the cerebellum and the hippocampus of the senescent mouse. *Experimental Gerontology* 12: 7–11.

Vijayashankar, N. and Brody, H. 1979. A quantitative study of the pigmented neurons in the nuclei locus coeruleus and subcoeruleus in man as related to aging. *J. Neuropathol. Experimental Neurology* 38: 490–497.

Walker, J. B. and Walker, J. P. 1973. Properties of adenylate cyclase from senescent rat brain. *Brain Res.* 54: 391–396.

Walker, R. 1981. Reproductive senescence and the dynamics of hypothalamic serotonin metabolism in the femal rat. *In,* S. J. Enna, T. Samorajski, and B. Beer (eds.), *Aging,* Vol. 17: *Brain Neurotransmitters and Receptors in Aging and Age-Related Disorders.* pp. 95–106. New York: Raven Press.

Walker, R. 1982. Reinstatement of LH surges by serotonin neuroleptics in aging, constant estrous rats. *Neurobiol. Aging* 3: 253–257.

Waller, S. B., Ingram, D. K., Reynolds, M. A., and London, E. D. 1981. Changes in neurotransmitter synthetic enzymes as a function of genotype and age. *Age* 4: 143.

Wastek, G. J., Stern, L. Z., Johnson, P. C., and Yamamura, H. I. 1976. Huntington's disease: regional alteration in muscarinic cholinergic receptor binding in human brain. *Life Sci.* 19: 1033–1040.

Weiner, R. I. and Ganong, W. F. 1978. Role of brain monoamines and histamine in regulation of anterior pituitary secretion. *Physiol. Rev.* 58: 905–976.

Weingartner, H., Kay, W., Gold, P., Smallberg, S., Peterson, R., Gillin, J. C., and Ebert, M. 1981. Vasopressin treatment of cognitive dysfunction in progressive dementia. *Life Sci.* 29: 2721–2726.

Wheeler, D. D. 1980. Aging of membrane transport mechanisms in the central nervous system—high affinity glutamic acid transport in rat cortical synaptosomes. *Exp. Gerontol.* 15: 269–284.

Wheeler, D. D. 1982. Aging of membrane transport mechanisms in the central nervous system—GABA transport in rat cortical synaptosomes. *Exp. Gerontol.* 17: 71–85.

White, P., Hiley, C. R., Goodhardt, M. J., Carrasco, L. H., Keet, J. P., Wiliams, I. E. I., and Bowen, D. M. 1977. Neocortical cholinergic neurons in elderly people. *Lancet* 1: 668–671.

Wree, A., Braak, H., Schleicher, A., and Zilles, K. 1980. Biomathematical analysis of the neuronal loss in the aging human brain of both sexes, demonstrated in pigment preparations of the pars cerebellaris locus coerulei. *Anat. Embryol.* 160: 105–119.

Yamamura, H. I. 1981. Neurotransmitter receptor alterations in age-related disorders. *In,* S. . Enna, T. Samorajski, and B. Beer (eds.), *Brain Neurotransmitters and Receptors in Aging and Age-related Disorders,* pp. 143–147. New York: Raven Press.

Yates, C. M., Simpson, J., Maloney, A. F. J., Gordon, A., and Reid, A. H. 1980. Alzheimer-like cholinergic deficiency in Down syndrome. *Lancet* 2: 979.

Yurkewicz, L., Marchi, M., Lauder, J. M., and Giacobini, E. 1981. Development and aging of noradrenergic cell bodies and axon terminals in the chicken. *J. Neurosci. Res.* 6: 621–641.

Zimmerman, I. D. and Berg, A. P. 1975. Phosphodiesterase and adenyl-cyclase activities in the cerebral cortex of the aging rat. *Mech. Age. Dev.* 4: 89–96.

Zornetzer, S. F., Bloom, F. E., Mervis, R., and Rogers, J. 1981. Senescent changes in balance, coordination, and cerebellar microanatomy. *Neurosci. Abstr.* 7: 690.

25
CHANGES OF SLEEP AND WAKEFULNESS WITH AGE

William Dement,[1] Gary Richardson,[1] Patricia Prinz,[2]
Mary Carskadon,[1], Daniel Kripke,[3] Charles Czeisler[4]

[1]*Sleep Disorders and Research Center, Stanford University
School of Medicine.*
[2]*Department of Psychiatry and Behavioral Science, University
of Washington.*
[3]*Department of Psychiatry, University of California.*
[4]*Center for Health Policy, J.F. Kennedy School of Government.
Harvard University.*

INTRODUCTION

A key question in geriatric medicine and research concerns the nature of changes during aging in sleep/wakefulness. The issue perhaps most in need of clarification is whether observed changes in sleep are an intrinsic part of normal aging or, rather, are a consequence of age-related increases in pathological processes. We have not yet, however, achieved a precise delineation of those sleep-related changes that may be intrinsic to "normal aging." Furthermore, recent investigations show that specific sleep-related processes unequivocally designated pathological in the young become increasingly prevalent with age. Indeed, their pervasiveness suggests that a high percentage of senior citizens may benefit from the diagnosis and treatment of sleeping/waking disorders.

One caveat is necessary. The literature may give undue emphasis to observations in humans. This is simply because the bulk of the scientific work on sleep and aging has utilized human subjects and patients, and because a widely accepted animal model of sleep and aging is not currently available. On the other hand, studies of the formal properties of the circadian systems have been carried out largely in animals.

SLEEP STATES AND STAGES

Definitions and Standard Conditions for Sleep/Wakefulness Parameters

The quantitative description of an entire night of sleep in a human being poses problems roughly akin to describing all the nuances of human behavior throughout the daytime. The comparative quiescence of the sleeping organism reduces certain difficulties and complexities of descriptive measurement; however, the fragility of sleep and the necessity to monitor in a "naturalistic" setting increase other problems. For example, several experiments suggest that the first night of laboratory-recorded sleep differs from subsequent nights (Agnew et al., 1966; Mendels and Hawkins, 1967; Schmidt and Kaelbling, 1971; Webb and Campbell, 1979); therefore, a period of adaptation to laboratory procedures is required. The length of the adaptation period or the number of nights required for an adequate description of night-to-night variability has not been standardized for any age group. Common usage, however, has established a one-night adaptation, followed by a basal period of one or two subsequent nights. This concept of measurement also presupposes that nocturnal sleep is the single or major episode of sleep each day. However, measurement of sleep at night alone may not provide an optimal description—especially for the very young or the old; continual (24-hour) observations are suggested.

In general, the characterization of a night of sleep is based upon continuous recording of just three physiological parameters, which then serve for the assessment of many other parameters. Thus the evaluation of human sleep is launched by the standard recording of electroencephalogram (EEG), electrooculogram (EOG), and electromyogram (EMG). By and large, these measures are taken while the individual is sleeping in a laboratory bedroom. Although standards have been developed for the documentation of sleep states and stages in the young adult (Rechtschaffen and Kales, 1968), no separate standards for older human have been established; most assessments of sleep in the elderly are based on rules developed for younger persons.

According to standard practice, a sleep record is analyzed by a human scorer with resolution to a scoring epoch size of 20, 30, or 60 seconds. The scorer classifies each epoch by state—as waking, NREM (non–rapid eye movement) sleep, or REM (rapid eye movement) sleep—and within NREM sleep, classifying into four stages. The NREM sleep stages are defined by changes in the EEG (Figure 1). NREM Stage 1 sleep is defined as a "relatively low voltage, mixed frequency" EEG and, as a transition stage, is easily distinguished from the rhythmic alpha activity

of relaxed wakefulness. Stage 2 NREM sleep is characterized by two well-delineated EEG wave forms, the K complex (a high amplitude negative wave followed immediately by a slower positive component) and the sleep spindle (a waxing/waning burst of 12–14 cps activity), which are easily seen above the low voltage, mixed frequency background. Stages 3 and 4 NREM sleep show a relative predominance (Stage 3 = 20 to 50 percent; Stage 4 = >50 percent) of high amplitude (>75 μV), slow frequency (<2 cps) activity. Stages 3 and 4 are often called slow wave or delta sleep. The EOG in NREM sleep is generally quiescent, although slow eye movements may occur, particularly in Stage 1. EMG activity is low throughout NREM sleep, but muscles continue to show electrical activity and reflex excitability is maintained.

By contrast, REM sleep is characterized by an active brain wave pattern, similar in many ways to the EEG of the waking brain. Rapid, binocularly synchronous eye movements occur in bursts during REM sleep. In addition, there is a complete subsidence of tonic EMG activity, and spinal reflexes can no longer be elicited. Waking from REM sleep is typically associated with a dream report, while NREM awakenings show a dearth of mental activity.

The sequence of states and stages in normal adult humans shows a characteristic pattern (Figure 2). The onset of nocturnal sleep is through the NREM state, which is maintained for about 80 minutes or more before REM sleep ensues. The two states alternate throughout the night with an average period of 90–100 minutes in the mature human. Many age-related changes are found in the amount of sleep and the specific sleep stage distributions.

Changes with Age

Among the earliest publications describing the states and stages of sleep in elderly subjects were those of Kales et al. (1966) and Feinberg et al. (1967). In 1974, Williams and colleagues gave a detailed description of sleep patterns across the entire human life span

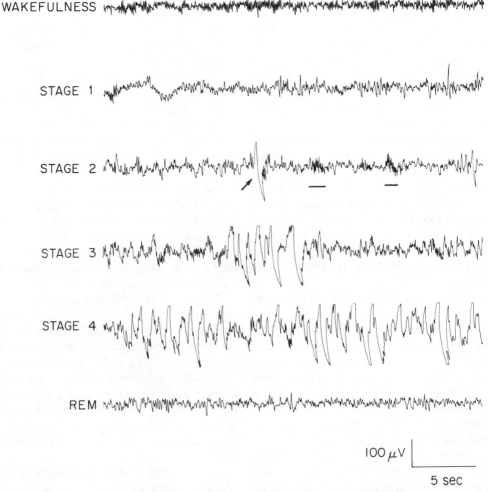

Figure 1. EEG patterns in wakefulness and sleep, recorded from referential central lead (C3/A2) in a 23-year-old male subject at a paper speed of 10 mm/sec. The first EEG pattern shows a rhythmic alpha (8–10 Hz) activity characteristic of relaxed wakefulness with eyes closed. The EEG of Stage 1 sleep is mixed frequency activity of relatively low voltage; a vertex sharp wave can be seen toward the latter part of the Stage 1 tracing. Stage 2 sleep is characterized by K complexes (arrow) and sleep spindles (underscored) in the EEG. The EEGs of Stages 3 and 4 sleep show progressively greater amounts of high amplitude (>75 μV), slow wave (<2 cps) activity. The REM sleep EEG is similar to Stage 1, with mixed frequencies at relatively low amplitude.

based on 10–12 male and female subjects in various age groups: the elderly had greatly diminished NREM Stages 3 and 4 (slow wave sleep, SWS), increased nocturnal wakefulness, and a consistent increase in the intraindividual variability of many sleep parameters. These findings are widely confirmed. The following discussion will emphasize those parameters that show a substantial change with aging. Figure 3 gives a sense of the absolute amounts of sleep at various ages. A more complete review may be found in the monograph of Miles and Dement (1980).

Time in Bed (TIB). The amount of time spent in bed is highly variable, even in sleep laboratory studies, where investigators may establish an arbitrary bedtime, set the sleeping hours according to sleep diary information,

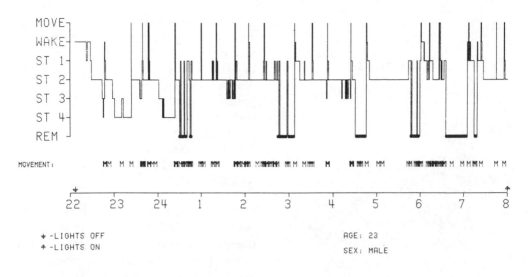

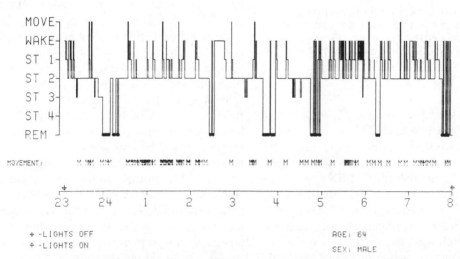

Figure 2. Nocturnal sleep stage profiles of a 23-year-old male (top) and a 64-year-old male (bottom) volunteer. While both profiles show a characteristic alternation of REM and NREM sleep, the older subject has more frequent and longer awakenings, a greater amount of Stage 1 sleep, and much less Stage 4 sleep than the young man.

or permit subjects to sleep *ad libitum*. In the general population, this important variable is subject to countless personal whims, social pressures, and other influences in addition to the desire to sleep and to comply with a regular daily schedule. Generally, elderly people seem to spend more time in bed at night without attempting to sleep, in bed at night unsuccessfully trying to sleep, and in bed resting or napping during the day, than do younger subjects.

Total Sleep Time (TST = TNREM + TREM). Since the elderly tend to have increased nocturnal wakefulness, their total sleep time (TST) is especially vulnerable to a limited time in bed (TIB), and polygraphic studies of their TST have yielded inconsistent data.

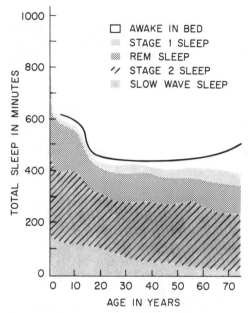

Figure 3. Nocturnal sleep in humans from birth to old age shows a characteristic pattern of declining total sleep and slow wave (Stages 3 and 4) sleep, and increased time awake in bed with advanced age.

Although usually wakefulness after sleep onset (WASO) is excluded from TST, brief (e.g., 2–15 second) arousals are not. The Williams et al. (1974) data showed a slight (nonsignificant) reduction of TST in the elderly subjects; however, the variability of sleep time in middle-aged and elderly subjects increases significantly over that of younger subjects, particularly in males. A nonsignificant reduction in TST of aged volunteers was also observed in the Prinz (1977) study both for nighttime and 24-hour observation periods. Feinberg et al. (1967) reported an average TST in their normal-aged subjects that was slightly but not significantly less than younger people. Campbell and Webb (1980) investigated the length of the major sleep period, by allowing 50–60 year olds to sleep as long as they could until sleep terminated in the morning with an awakening of more than 10 minutes. The mean sleep length of their older subjects was shorter and less variable than for younger adults. In contrast to these polygraphic stud-

ies, nursing home subjects had much longer average nightly sleep times in the aged (Webb and Swinburne, 1971). Large survey studies by Hammond (1964) and O'Connor (1962) (but not McGhie and Russell, 1962) also reported longer TST in the aged (as summarized in Miles and Dement, 1980). In general, polygraphically measured TST at night is reduced; however, subjective survey data indicate that the TST per 24 hours increases with age.

Wake after Sleep Onset (WASO) Increases in the Elderly. WASO refers to the amount of time spent awake between the onset of nocturnal sleep and the final awakening of the night. The aged have greatly increased amounts of WASO (Figures 2 and 3), and the number of midsleep awakenings is much higher for men than for women. Brief arousals which escape observation may be quite significant; preliminary evidence suggests that the number of brief wakes (2–15 seconds) may closely parallel changes in daytime function (Carskadon et al., 1982).

Most authors consider changes in the efficiency of sleep to be a "weakening" of basic sleep mechanisms. In recent years, however, it has become apparent that many overt or occult sleep pathologies associated with repeated arousal from sleep are more common in the elderly. The prevalence of these disorders in elderly volunteers is so high that many elderly persons would show increased interruption of sleep even if the sleep process *per se* did not deteriorate.

An hypothesis recently explored by Zepelin's group is that the increased tendency for disturbed sleep in aged individuals may simply reflect a lower threshold for arousal (Zepelin et al., 1980; McDonald et al., 1981; Zepelin and McDonald, in press). Using auditory arousal threshold as the dependent variables, these authors have examined arousal thresholds in young (18–25 years), middle-aged (40–48 years), and older (52–71 years) subjects during Stage 2, Stage 4, and REM sleep. In general, their findings showed a nearly linear decline by age in arousal threshold during all three sleep stages in both men and women. Arousal thresholds were consistently highest in Stage 4 sleep across age groups (with the exception of REM sleep in middle-aged females). Collins and Iampietro (1973) found a similar age response to the effects of simulated sonic booms presented during sleep, while Thiessen (1978) found that young and old adults appeared to be less sensitive than the middle aged to traffic noise occurring during sleep. While not conclusive, these findings, combined with the overall reduction in Stage 4 sleep in older adults, suggest a somewhat greater tendency for arousal from sleep by auditory stimuli in the aged; other sensory modalities remain to be tested.

Rapid Eye Movement Sleep State (REM) Remains Constant until Extreme Old Age. In general, absolute amounts of REM sleep fall slightly in parallel with the change in nocturnal TST, but relative amounts of REM are well maintained until extreme old age, when they do show some decline. This reduction in the percentage of REM sleep may be due to the fact that the elderly tend to be awake in the latter part of the night when REM is usually most prevalent. Latency to the first REM episode may decrease with age (Feinberg et al., 1967; Gillin et al., 1981) or may remain stable after the second decade (Williams et al., 1974). The REM-NREM cycle length remains constant across adulthood (Figure 2), although the variability increases in the eighth decade (Williams et al., 1974). The REM sleep decline also appears to follow the trend of reduced intellectual function and is implicated in the presence of organic brain syndrome, changes in cerebral blood flow, and alpha frequency decline. When the amount of REM sleep decreases, there is also a decrease in the physiological concomitants of REM (muscular twitches, penile tumescence, rapid irregular respiration and heart rate, and increased cerebral blood flow).

NREM Stage 1 Sleep Increases in the Elderly. An excessive total duration of Stage 1 sleep and an increase in the number of shifts into Stage 1 sleep are both indicative of sleep disturbance. The amount of TST spent in Stage 1 sleep appears to increase steadily throughout life. Kales et al. (1967) found a fairly high percentage of TST spent in Stage 1 sleep in their elderly subjects on the first laboratory night (11.7 percent), with a substantial decline by night four (6.5 percent). Agnew et al. (1967) reported that an average of 10.9 percent of TST was spent in Stage 1 by elderly subjects.

NREM Stage 2 Sleep Decreases in the Elderly. When scored by standard criteria, the mean percentage of TST spent in Stage 2 sleep approximates an inverted U-shaped curve throughout life. The levels in old age are similar to those seen in early adult life, and there is little sex difference. The decrease of Stage 2 seen in the elderly may reflect the fact that sleep spindles tend to be poorly formed and appear to occur less often with age (Kales et al., 1967). Furthermore, sleep spindles or true episodes of Stage 2 tend to interrupt and fragment REM sleep. This is yet another example of the difficulty of fitting the sleep of the elderly into the standardized classification schema developed largely from recordings of young adults. Using an automated analysis system, Principe and Smith (1982) found that sleep spindles were higher in frequency and lower in amplitude in subjects aged 67–79 years than in several younger groups.

Slow Wave Sleep (SWS)—NREM Sleep Stages 3 and 4 Decrease in the Elderly. The aged show an absolute and relative reduction in the time spent in Stage 4 sleep, as assessed using the Rechtschaffen and Kales (1968) criteria. This is one of the most consistent age-related changes found to date. In general, Stage 3 sleep tends to be normal or even elevated in elderly females, and normal or reduced in males. These changes are apparently due to the fact that the amplitude of the delta waves is noticeably reduced from that in the young adult (Figure 4). In the sixth decade, one may find little or no Stage 4 sleep in one-fourth of the population. A study in the So-

STAGE 4 SLEEP EEG

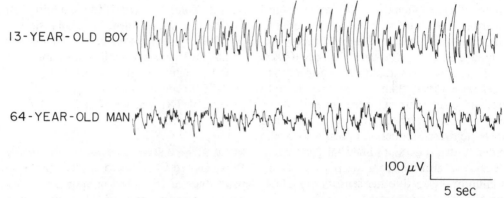

Figure 4. EEG recorded from referential central (C3/A2) leads in an adolescent and an elderly male subject during Stage 4 sleep. Recording parameters and calibrations were identical for both subjects. Amplitude of the slow wave activity is 3–4 times greater in the 13-year-old versus the 64-year-old. (Paper speed = 10 mm/sec.)

viet Union of 15 healthy men aged 90–110 showed negligible amounts of SWS (Saradzhishvil et al., 1974).

Feinberg et al. (1967) reported greater Stage 3 sleep as a percentage of TST in aged normals (17 percent) than in young normals (10 percent). Stage 4 sleep in the elderly (7 percent), while significantly lower than in young normals (13 percent), was nonetheless greater than reported elsewhere. One explanation for this difference may be that the investigators utilized a 50 μV amplitude criterion in scoring slow waves. Webb (1982), using no amplitude criterion for scoring Stages 3 and 4 sleep, found no difference in SWS percentage between 50- to 60-year-old and 20- to 30-year-old subjects. Recently, Smith et al. (1977) and Feinberg et al. (1978; 1980) applied sophisticated computer techniques to analyzing delta activity of slow wave sleep by frequency, amplitude, and incidence of individual waves; these variables do not always follow identical patterns. Age-related declines in delta activity amplitudes during the middle years are suggested by the data of Smith et al., though changes in frequency and incidence were less compelling. In Feinberg's reports, nearly all computer-derived measures of delta activity showed an age-related decline as early as the twenties.

NREM Stages 3 and 4 may be the sleep variables most well suited as noninvasive biological age markers. They are highly reliable from night to night in the absence of daytime napping, with reliability as high as .90 having been reported (Bliwise, 1982). The age-related decline in SWS amplitude is unquestioned and has been confirmed in many studies. Recent work showing a decline in delta activity across the decade of the twenties (Bliwise, 1982) suggests that slow wave sleep decline may be a close correlate of the aging process in the human central nervous system (CNS) across the entire human adult life span. Growth hormone (GH) release, highly correlated with SWS onset in young adults, is greatly diminished in old age (Prinz et al., in press). It is not possible to conclude, however, that growth hormone and SWS measurements are essentially interchangeable, since the GH-SWS correlation becomes weak when age is parcelled out (Prinz and Haeter, 1983).

In addition to the foregoing, SWS may be intimately related to other possible influences on longevity. Physical exercise, for example, has been linked to increases in SWS in several studies (Baekland, 1970; Horne and Porter, 1975), though this finding remains controversial (Walker et al., 1978); several recent studies (Shapiro and Verschoor, 1979; Shapiro et al., 1981; Griffin and Trinder, 1978) suggest that fitness may be a mediating variable. Several studies have also suggested that fasting may increase SWS (Parker et al., 1972; MacFyden et al., 1973; Karacan et al., 1973), but again these results are tentative.

One might wonder what consequences, if any, could arise from age-related changes in total sleep and/or SWS. Human and animal experiments have revealed that sleep deprivation that is partial (e.g., REM sleep only) or short term has few neurobiological consequences (Horne, 1978). Total, prolonged sleep deprivation, however, results in the following neurological deficits and neuropathological changes: vacuolization and degenerative change in neurons, and loss of neural ribosomal apparatus (Nissl substance) (Daddi, 1898; Manaceine, 1894; Crile, 1921; Bast and Bloemendal, 1927; Leake et al., 1927); changes in neurotransmitters (Bowers et al., 1966); altered brain electrolytes (Heiner et al., 1968); and modification in brain energy metabolism (Van den Noort and Brine, 1970; Karadzic and Mrsulja, 1969). If forced wakefulness continues long enough, the animal dies. In spite of the methodological problem that sleep deprivation may be confounded by stress effects (Karnofsky and Reich, 1977), it is tempting to speculate that some aspect of sleep is biologically important in the maintenance of CNS integrity.

With regard to SWS, one hypothesis is that the slow waves occurring during sleep (which in man correspond to a 1–2 μV oscillating potential across the cortical neuroplexus) are involved in some aspect of the restorative functions that sleep serves. It is known that transport phenomena across neuronal membranes can be altered by potential gradients in the 1–2 μV range. Phylogenetically, slow wave amplitudes are greatest in those species with the better developed cortical neurophils. Further work in this area would be very

fruitful in elucidating the biological function of slow wave sleep, an important first step for understanding the role (if any) of sleep in maintaining the structure and function of the brain across the life span.

Gender Differences in All-night Polygraphic Sleep Parameters

Elderly men appear to have more "abnormal" objective sleep parameters than elderly women, but these changes appear to be but an accentuation of preexisting differences between the sexes apparent in data from young adults. For example, males have a higher percentage of Stage 1 sleep than females from puberty onward. The most obvious gender differences in elderly volunteers are in SWS and intercurrent arousals. A small but significant number of elderly females continue to display sustained periods of Stage 4 sleep (Spiegel, 1981), but most males over age 60 have only negligible amounts of slow wave sleep that meets the Rechtschaffen and Kales criteria. Intercurrent awakenings are generally greater in number in males than in females from puberty until the eighth decade, at which time the male/female difference is no longer apparent (Williams et al., 1974).

Comparative Age-related Sleep Data in Other Species

Relatively few experiments have examined the effects of aging on the sleep patterns of animals. An increase in overall waking time in aged animals is reported for cats (Chase, 1981) and rats (Rosenberg et al., 1976, 1979; Zepelin et al., 1972). Reduced length of sleep bouts has also been noted with increasing age in cats (Chase, 1981) and rats (Rosenberg et al., 1979; Zepelin et al., 1972).

Several studies have shown a marked change in REM sleep during old age in other species. Chase et al. (1976) noted a reduction in REM in aged cats as did Bowersox et al. (in press). Eleftheriou et al. (1975) found a REM percentage decrement in old mice, particularly the DBA/2J strain, in which no

REM sleep was recorded at age 23.5 months. The percentage of time spent in REM sleep was found to be stable during aging in rats (Rosenberg et al., 1976; Zepelin et al., 1972), although a later study showed an age-related reduction of REM percentage in this species (Rosenberg et al., 1979).

NREM sleep percentage decreased in aged cats (Chase, 1981), rats (Rosenberg et al., 1979), and mice (Eleftheriou et al., 1975). In other studies, however, slow wave sleep was observed as remaining stable in aged rats (Rosenberg et al., 1979; Zepelin et al., 1972), although the amplitude of the circadian rhythm of slow wave sleep was reported to be reduced with advancing age (Rosenberg and Rechtschaffen, 1978).

Although the interspecies data on age-related changes of specific sleep stages are somewhat contradictory, a general pattern of disrupted sleep, paralleling the findings in humans, is apparent. Certain of the interspecies differences may be accounted for by differences in methodologies and the generally small sample sizes that have been evaluated (Ingram et al., 1982).

PHYSIOLOGY DURING SLEEP

The scientific basis of clinical medicine has rested almost exclusively on the physiology of wakefulness. The notion that regulatory processes might be qualitatively different during sleep is quite recent. Indeed, essentially all physiological data were obtained from waking or anesthetized animal models and generalized to all states of vigilance, including REM and NREM sleep.

New findings in the field of respiration, temperature regulation, and motor function during sleep necessitate further examination of what happens to sleep-related regulatory processes as a function of aging. In addition, age-related structural changes impact upon physiological processes in ways that may vary either quantitatively or qualitatively, again as a function of the states of sleep. For example, vital capacity decreases with age, presumably due to a loss of elasticity of pulmonary tissues, chronic changes in bron-

chi and alveoli, loss of muscle strength in the thorax, and so on. These changes may not reach threshold in the waking state, but in the sleeping state could produce serious decompensation when interacting with normal sleep processes.

An excellent example of this general tendency is seen in chronic obstructive pulmonary disease. Though ventilation may remain marginally adequate all through wakefulness and during NREM sleep, it is not uncommon to see precipitous drops in oxygen saturation during REM episodes. Each REM episode thus offers the possibility of acute respiratory failure. The ventilatory changes are almost certainly related to the inhibition of intercostal muscles and partial inhibition of the diaphragm during REM sleep. Thus, the diminution or complete loss of function in these respiratory muscles can interact with structurally impaired lung parenchyma to create a respiratory crisis each time there is REM sleep. Similar crises may take place with temperature regulation, cardiovascular regulation, and so on. Unfortunately, at the present time there is very little work on physiology during sleep in elderly subjects.

Respiration and Cardiovascular Physiology during Sleep in the Elderly

Respiration during Sleep in Healthy Elderly Volunteers. In the elderly, the absence of a sleep/wake complaint does not mean the absence of sleep disturbance. Nowhere is this more apparent than in the area of respiratory function. Recent reviews (Orem, 1980; Phillipson, 1978; Sullivan, 1980) cite convincing evidence that respiratory regulation proceeds differently during sleep as opposed to wakefulness. This difference makes it possible to account for the coexistence in sleep disorders of normal breathing during wakefulness and pathological breathing during sleep.

The first observations on older individuals were made by Webb (1974) and Webb and Hiestand (1975) who continuously measured oxygen consumption in 20 normal volunteers aged 19 to 63. They found that respiration during sleep was very irregular in 9 of 11 subjects who were 45 years or older. Subsequently, Block et al. (1979) described sleep apneas, hypopneas, and episodes of oxygen desaturation in normal subjects, of whom seven males and one female were in their sixth or seventh decade. Carskadon and Dement (1981a) conducted systematic observations on breathing during sleep in the elderly. In these studies, elderly volunteers were selected on the basis of having no complaint about their sleep and no serious health problem. They were, therefore, felt to be the elderly segment most likely to have good (undisturbed) sleep and normal respiration during sleep. Table 1 shows data from 40 elderly subjects compared to 24 middle-aged subjects.

Since each apneic pause or hypopnea was terminated by an arousal (Figure 5), we may conclude that one-third of the elderly subjects experienced five or more interruptions of their sleep per hour. These findings suggest that age-related respiratory impairment may account for a great deal of the well-known sleep fragmentation observed in the elderly. Thirty percent of the aged volunteers

TABLE 1. Apneas during Sleep in Noncomplaining Healthy Volunteers.

	Middle Age	Elderly
N	24 (12M, 12F)	40 (18M, 22F)
Mean age	49.9	73.8
Age range	48–60	62–86
Mean respiration disturbances/ night	4.7	50.0
Range respiration disturbances/ night	0–12	0–216
Number with RDI > 5	0	15

NOTE:

Respiration disturbances = apnea or hypopnea.
Hypopnea = 50% reduction of breathing >10 seconds, terminating in arousal.
Apnea = respiratory pause >10 seconds.
RDI = respiration distrubance index (number of respiration disturbances per hour of sleep).

had ten or more respiration disturbances per hour, with no significant differences between males and females.

Ancoli-Israel et al. (1981) studied 24 healthy elderly volunteers selected because of sleep complaints. Of these subjects, one-third had in excess of 30 apneic episodes per night, most commonly of the upper airway type. McGinty and Arand (1980) have reported work on elderly V.A. patients who were asymptomatic with regard to sleep. They found that one-half of a small sample had severe oxygen desaturation during sleep. Krieger et al. (1980) and Smallwood et al. (1983) also observed that among healthy aged volunteers, apnea or hypopnea episodes exceeded 5 per hour of sleep or 80 apneas per night in 50 percent of male and 0 percent of female subjects.

We note that none of the above data are from patients in sleep disorders centers. Most specialists in sleep disorders regard 5–8 apneas per hour of sleep as the upper limit of normal. Application of this criterion leads one to conclude that about one-third of all elderly individuals who are judged to be in good health when awake would receive a clinical diagnosis of the sleep apnea syndrome. This raises the issue of what level of sleep apnea should be considered abnormal in the elderly. The physiological significance of this level of respiratory dysfunction in otherwise asymptomatic older individuals is not understood, and the possible long term medical sequelae have not been assessed.

Snoring in the Elderly. The presence of snoring almost always indicates some degree of impairment of upper airway function and, in some cases, a very serious impairment. Lugaresi and his colleagues (1975) made pioneering observations of blood pressure during sleep in normal adult males who were heavy snorers. *All* subjects showed hemodynamic abnormalities during sleep. In a subsequent study, Lugaresi et al. (1978, 1980) concluded that lifelong nonapneic snoring may be a very important risk factor in the development of cardiovascular disease. A similar relationship to hypertension was re-

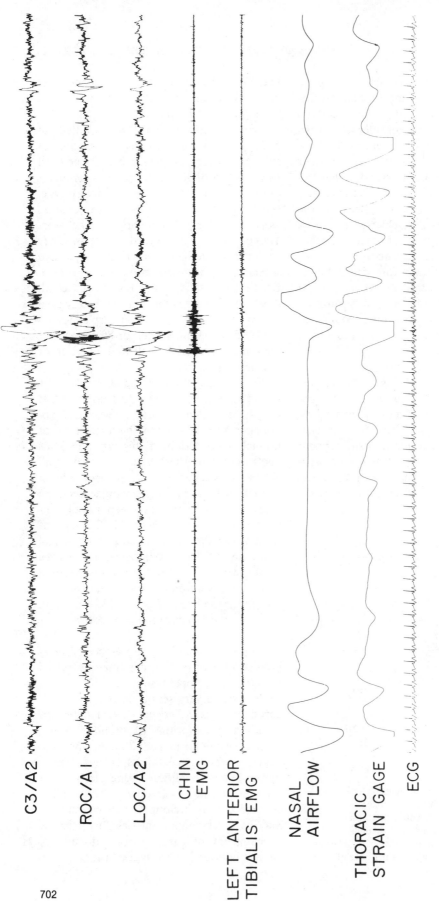

C3/A2

ROC/A1

LOC/A2

CHIN
EMG

LEFT ANTERIOR
TIBIALIS EMG

NASAL
AIRFLOW

THORACIC
STRAIN GAGE

ECG

100 μV

5 sec

Figure 5. Sleep apnea associated with a transient arousal in a 74-year-old female volunteer with no sleep complaints. This tracing, excerpted from a series of apneic events, shows the characteristic transient arousal accompanying the termination of an apnea followed by an immediate return to sleep. (Abbreviations: C3/A2 = referential central EEG; ROC/A1 and LOC/A2 = referential electro-oculogram from right and left outer canthi; chin EMG = electromyogram from surface electrodes below the chin; left anterior tibialis EMG = electromyogram from surface electrodes over the left anterior tibialis muscle; nasal airflow was recorded using a thermistor; ECG = electrocardiogram. Paper speed = 10 mm/sec.)

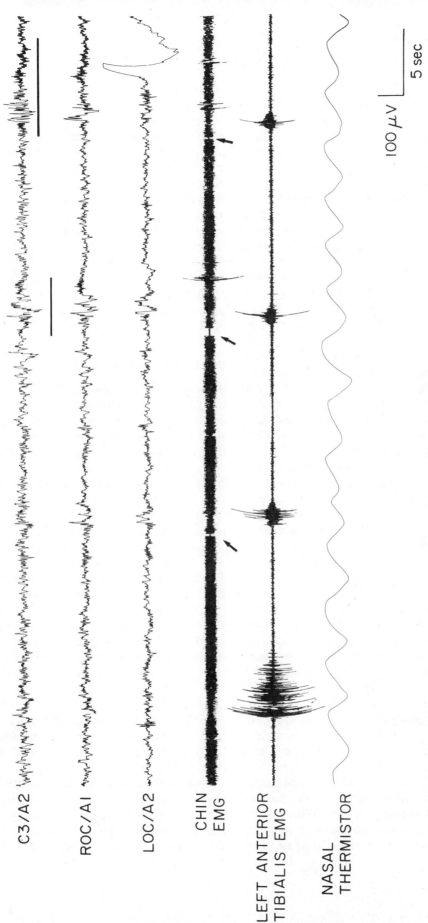

C3/A2

ROC/A1

LOC/A2

CHIN EMG

LEFT ANTERIOR TIBIALIS EMG

NASAL THERMISTOR

5 sec

100 μV

Figure 6. Periodic leg movements during sleep in a 67-year-old female, excerpted from a series of over 150 movements. The movements are very rhythmic, with a period of about 16 seconds in this woman. The movements are often accompanied by a transient arousal (underscored) and may be preceded by a phasic suppression of chin EMG activity (arrows). (Abbreviations: see Figure 5.)

703

cently reported by Pollak et al. (1978). Lu-garesi and his colleagues also found that the prevalence of snoring increases with age. It seems that almost 60 percent of males in their sixties and 45 percent of females are habitual snorers.

Sleep Apnea Syndromes in Patients with Sleep/Wake Complaints Referred to Sleep Centers.

Of the three types of sleep apneas—upper airway, central, and mixed—the former is most often found in patients complaining of excessive daytime sleepiness. Other clinical symptoms include inordinately loud snoring, abnormal behavior, and choking attacks during sleep (which are mainly the result of the struggle to breathe), morning headache, and personality changes. Cardiac arrhythmias and pulmonary hypertension are common during the apneic episodes, and many patients have systemic hypertension. The anoxia, cardiac arrhythmias, and duration of apneas tend to be worst during REM sleep and to be associated with a large release of norepinephrine from sympathetic nerve terminals in the vasculature (Vitiello et al., 1982). Central apnea appears to be more often associated with multiple arousals from sleep and overt insomnia (Guilleminault et al., 1973, 1976).

Periodic Movement in Sleep

Periodic movement during sleep, or nocturnal myoclonus, was first described in the 1950s (Symonds, 1953), but it was only in the late 1970s that the high prevalence of this disorder became known (Coleman, 1979). The sleep-related leg movements have a marked stereotypy, the hallmark of which is a regular periodicity—they occur every 20–40 seconds during large parts of the night—and frequently each movement is associated with a brief arousal (Figure 6). It is difficult to determine if the movements and associated arousals arise from central nervous system or peripheral processes. Whatever the etiology, it is now clear that in a subgroup of older individuals, periodic movements are responsible for frequent arousals during sleep.

Little is known concerning the nature and etiology of periodic movement in sleep, although it apparently involves a defect in motor excitation and inhibition. In one sleep disorders clinic case series, the prevalence of periodic movements rose steadily with age up to about 30 percent in groups over 60 (Coleman et al., 1982). Similarly, among 24 senior citizen volunteers who complained of sleep disorders, 37 percent had periodic movements in sleep (Ancoli-Israel et al., 1981). A random sample of San Diego citizens 65 and older also suggests that about 30 percent may have this disorder (Kripke et al., 1982).

DAYTIME ALERTNESS/SLEEPINESS

Although sleepiness and drowsiness are typically related to inadequate sleep on the preceding night, this phenomenon is little studied. Yet, it is likely that most of the daytime consequences of sleep deprivation can be explained by the generation of a state of extreme sleepiness. Naitoh (1976) suggested that "we should use some physiological (or other) non-performance measures, most probably they would be those variables which reflect a varying degree of sleepiness."

In recent years, an objective measure of daytime sleepiness called the Multiple Sleep Latency Test (MSLT) has been developed and applied (Carskadon and Dement, 1982a). This test relies upon the principle that sleepiness is a physiological state predisposing to sleep. Because the exact time of transition from wakefulness to sleep is relatively easy to specify in polygraphic recordings (Rechtschaffen and Kales, 1968), it has been possible to design a standard situation in which the momentary sleep tendency (sleepiness) of an individual can be measured as the speed of falling asleep.

Many studies in young adult volunteers have shown a relationship between nocturnal sleep time and daytime sleep tendency. For example, volunteers given the opportunity to sleep eight hours each night for a week

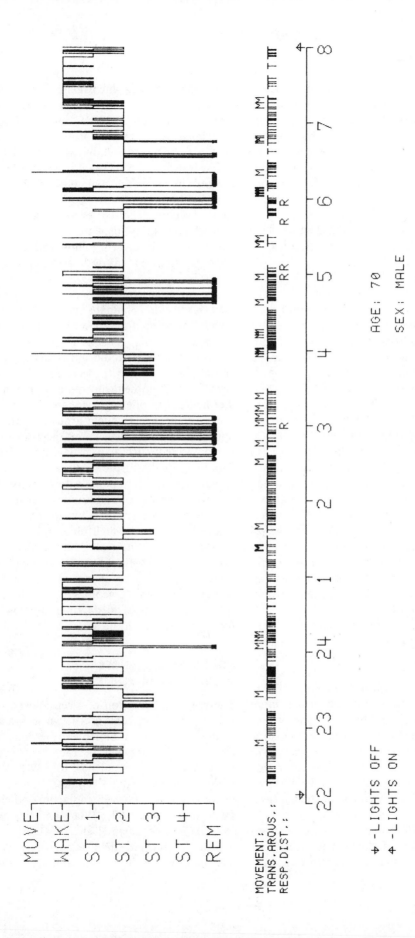

Figure 7. Nocturnal sleep profile in a 70-year-old man who had 373 transient arousals in 461 minutes of sleep. His mean MSLT score on the following day was 6.8 minutes, indicating severe sleepiness. (From Carskadon et al., 1982.)

showed a very stable intraindividual pattern of MSLT scores from day to day (Carskadon and Dement, 1982b). Minor day-to-day variations in MSLT scores were uncorrelated with total sleep time but were related to the amount of Stage 1 sleep: the greater the Stage 1 sleep, the lower were the sleep latencies (indicating greater sleepiness). Across several groups of young subjects with a variety of nocturnal sleep schedules, MSLT scores were clearly related to total sleep time (Carskadon and Dement, 1982b).

The data on elderly volunteers are less numerous and the results less clearcut. Initial data in aged humans showed them to have a significantly higher sleep tendency on the MSLT than adolescents or young adults studied under identical conditions (Carskadon et al., 1980); in this experiment, the increased sleepiness of the elderly group was related to increased sleep-related respiratory disturbance. However, a subsequent study, in which elderly volunteers were screened for sleep-related respiratory disturbances and periodic movements, showed no differences in the MSLT profiles as compared to young adults (Richardson et al., 1982). In addition, when the MSLT was given to these subjects in a modified format throughout the 24 hours, there were no differences in sleep tendency between elderly and young adult subjects, even though the young adults slept an average of 40 minutes longer at night (Richardson et al., 1982).

If we assume that daytime alertness/sleepiness is an important criterion for judging the quality of nocturnal sleep, it appears that the elderly may have a slightly reduced "need" for sleep. That is, their MSLTs did not differ from young adults sleeping somewhat more at night. On the other hand, in elderly subjects not screened for nocturnal sleep disturbance, daytime sleepiness was greater than in young adults (Carskadon et al., 1980), which suggests that factors other than the absolute sleep time may be involved in nocturnal sleep quality. To investigate this possibility, Carskadon et al. (1982) evaluated the relationship of MSLT in 24 elderly volunteers to a number of nocturnal sleep parameters: day-

time sleepiness was uncorrelated with total sleep time or the amount of any sleep stage or wakefulness during sleep, but MSLT was correlated with the number of very brief arousals (2–15 seconds) during sleep. Figure 7 illustrates the pattern of such transient arousals in one elderly male subject who had over 7.5 hours of sleep. The MSLT profile in this volunteer showed severe daytime sleepiness. This study also indicated the relationship of respiratory disturbances to daytime sleepiness, as well as to transient arousals.

The causes or consequences of diminished alertness in elderly humans are poorly understood. Several studies support the notion that observable events, such as respiratory disturbances and periodic movements, are causally associated with decreased sleep efficiency and consequent reduced daytime alertness in the elderly. There are also, however, instances of frequent arousals with no apparent cause, though many factors could be considered, such as gastroesophageal reflux, nocturnal arthritic pain, or occult nocturnal cardiac symptoms. Alternatively, in the evolution of social primates, nocturnal restlessness among older adults may have developed to promote watchfulness in those individuals for whom peak daytime alertness was no longer required as younger members assumed the waking chores. Thus, in the context of a primeval ecology, frequent nocturnal awakenings and daytime napping in older primates could be adaptive.

AGE-RELATED CHANGES IN CIRCADIAN RHYTHMS

The regular alternation of sleep and wakefulness is perhaps one of the most fundamental endogenous biological rhythms in man. Each component of the sleep/wake cycle (such as the tendency for SWS and REM sleep, subjective sleepiness, and sleep latency) varies with a circadian periodicity (Mills and Hume, 1977; Webb and Agnew, 1971, 1974; Weitzman et al., 1974). Abnormalities of the circadian sleep/wake cycle and changes in its relationship to other rhythms may well be responsible for some of the difficulties of old age.

As in the study of changes in sleep during development, the study of age-related changes in circadian rhythms is hampered by the incomplete understanding of their normal function at any age. Fortunately, the field has recently entered a stage of significant progress (for comprehensive review see Moore-Ede et al., 1982), which should soon provide answers to questions of the relevance of age-related changes in circadian rhythms to health and to the process of aging itself. In some respects, this period of progress might be considered late in arriving. The fundamental endogenous property of circadian rhythms was first recognized over 250 years ago with the remarkable experiments of De Mairan (1729).

Formal Properties of Circadian Rhythms: Changes with Age

Rodents continue to show regular rhythms of activity when placed in chambers isolated from potential exogenous time cues such as light and temperature. Further, these rhythms no longer have a cycle-length or period of precisely 24 hours, but instead "free-run" with a period slightly but consistently different from that of the environment. This non-24-hour free-running period of the endogenous biological oscillator is found in almost all organisms and is the source of the descriptive term "circadian," meaning approximately a day (Halberg, 1959).

Age-related changes in the free-running period of circadian rhythms in a variety of organisms are widely found. Unfortunately, no consensus exists about the nature of these changes. Pittendrigh and Daan (1974) performed the most rigorous analysis of this effect, demonstrating a reduction of circadian period in the hamster and two species of deer mouse as a continuous function of age. By contrast, Wax and Goodrick (1975) demonstrated an age-related lengthening of period in the house mouse. In three other rodent species, such age changes were found (Kenagy, 1978; Gander, 1980). Data on human

subjects are no less confusing. Wever (1970) saw no change in the period of the body temperature rhythm with age, whereas Weitzman et al. (1982) reported age-dependent shortening in the periods of both the body temperature and the sleep-wake rhythms.

These discrepant findings could represent real differences in the age-dependent changes of the endogenous period, or they could be a consequence of differences in the experimental design. Significantly, only Pittendrigh and Daan (1974) used a longitudinal paradigm in which individual animals were observed at both "young" and "old" ages; most other studies were cross-sectional, comparing distinct groups of young to a distinct group of older animals. The risk with this latter approach is the tendency for large intragroup variability in the quantity being measured to obscure small intergroup effects. On the other hand, longitudinal paradigms are obviously impractical for species with even moderately long life spans. It seems likely, however, that until more longitudinal data are collected, the question of a consistent age effect on endogenous circadian period will remain unanswered.

The entrainment of the endogenous circadian rhythm to the normal environmental period requires the capacity to sense and respond to periodic environmental events, termed *zeitgebers*, such as the light-dark transitions at dawn and dusk. In response to the zeitgeber, the endogenous oscillator makes the necessary small adjustment in phase to achieve stable entrainment and a stable phase relationship of the internal rhythms to the outside environment. This mechanism also appears to be changed with age. In the elderly human, the phase relationship of the entrained sleep-wake cycle (Webb, 1978), the body temperature rhythm (Weitzman et al., 1982), and a number of neuroendocrine rhythms to the environment appears to advance to an earlier phase. Also, in rats (Ehret et al., 1978; Quay, 1972) and mice (Rosenberg et al., 1980), older animals require a longer reentrainment period after abrupt alterations in the phase orientation of the exogenous environment (the equivalent of air travel across time zones). This evidence corroborates the primarily subjective data available in humans, suggesting a decreased tolerance with age to abrupt phase shifts (Solberger, 1965; Preston, 1973).

In addition to synchronizing physiological functions to the environment, the circadian system must also maintain internal synchrony and coordinate mutually dependent functions while maintaining temporal segregation of mutually exclusive ones. The potential independence of the components of the circadian system is best appreciated during "internal desynchronization," which is occasionally seen in the free-running rhythms of human subjects living in environments without time cues (Aschoff et al., 1967; Czeisler et al., 1980). Under such conditions, individual rhythms cluster into two groups represented by body temperature and rest-activity which free-run with significantly different periods (24.7 and 32.6 hours, respectively). A similar phenonemon has recently been recognized in hamsters treated with agents such as imipramine and clorgyline that are known to lengthen the circadian period (Wirz-Justice et al., 1980). These animals show dissociation of two components of the rest-activity rhythm which free-run with markedly different periods. This potential independence illustrates the requirement for the maintenance of internal synchrony and may provide an explanation for the assertion that the aged circadian system is less capable of maintaining "internal temporal order" (Halberg and Nelson, 1978; Samis, 1968). Evidence for this point is incomplete, but a few studies have documented dissociation of rhythms under normal entrained conditions in aged animals (Sachar and Duffy, 1978) and in humans (Cahn et al., 1968).

Another possible consequence of a breakdown in internal phase relationships is the common finding of reduced amplitude of circadian rhythms in the aged. Age-related reductions in rhythm amplitude have been documented in mouse and rat body temperature rhythms (Yunis et al., 1974), in mouse seizure threshold (Halberg et al., 1955), in mouse oxygen consumption (Sachar and

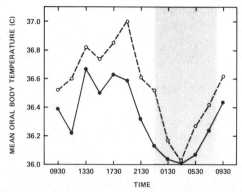

Figure 8. Mean oral temperature in degrees Celsius for young (open circles, N = 8) and old (filled circles, N = 10) subjects as a function of time of day. Subjects and conditions same as in Figure 9. (From Richardson et al., 1982.)

Duffy, 1978), and in human rhythms of body temperature (Weitzman et al., 1982) and potassium excretion (Lobban and Tredre, 1967). In addition, a number of neuroendocrine rhythms show similar age-dependent changes.

Age-related Changes in Neuroendocrine Rhythms

Neuroendocrine rhythms may in some cases undergo changes with age. Recent reviews by Halberg (1982) and Cole et al. (1982) summarize this complex and expanding field. Not all neuroendocrine rhythms are altered; e.g., the adrenocortical hormones in man include an unaltered basal ACTH or ACTH periodicity (Blichert-Toft, 1971, 1975; Jensen and Blichert-Toft, 1971). In general, basal cortisol level and circadian corticosteroid rhythmicity are unaltered (Blichert-Toft, 1975; Friedman et al., 1969; Serio et al., 1970; Krieger et al., 1971; Grad et al., 1971; Halberg et al., 1981); the timing of the cortisol peak in the aged may be slightly delayed (Serio et al., 1970) and reach a higher midnight level (Friedman et al., 1969). The minor age effect on rhythms of adrenocortical hormones can be contrasted with the more pronounced age effects on cortisol secretion rate and half-life, which are both increased (West et al., 1961; Serio et al., 1969; Romanoff et al., 1961), and 17-hydroxycorti-costerone secretion rate, which is markedly decreased (Romanoff et al., 1961; Grad et al., 1967). In general, these findings suggest that there is adequate homeostatic regulation of circadian rhythms in spite of appreciable age effects on rates of secretion and degradation of adrenocortical hormones.

Other neuroendocrine rhythms may change to a greater extent with age. In males, testosterone rhythms are similar to cortisol, with a nadir that occurs during nighttime sleep and becomes shifted when rest/activity cycles are shifted (Lincoln et al., 1974). Elderly men have smaller mean 24-hour plasma testosterone levels as well as reduced rhythm amplitudes (Bremner et al., in press). In women, hormones related to reproductive function (prolactin, estrone, estradiol, and 17-hydroxyprogesterone) may also show age reductions in mean 24-hour levels and in amplitudes of the rhythm (Halberg, 1982). Age changes in the timing of reproductive hormonal rhythms were not noted in any of these studies. (See chapter 18 for discussion of menstrual cycle changes with aging).

Growth hormone secretion does not occur with a true circadian rhythm but, rather, in pulses in response to specific stimuli, including the appearance of Stage 3 and 4 sleep (SWS). Both SWS and nighttime growth hormone secretion are minimal in the elderly (Carlson et al., 1972; Finkelstein et al., 1972; Prinz and Halter, 1983). Cole et al. (1982) note that age effects are minimal on GH releasing stimuli other than sleep. Somatomedins, peptides that do not vary diurnally and are known to mediate the actions of GH at the cellular level (including brain), are reduced with aging in both rat (Florini and Roberts, 1978) and man (Prinz and Hintz, unpublished observations).

Another interesting neurohormonal rhythm that undergoes an age-related change is the plasma level of norepinephrine (NE), which is elevated both day and night in healthy aged subjects, without any significant change in the timing of the rhythm (Prinz et al., 1979; Prinz and Halter, 1983; also see Chapter 21). Experimental manip-

ulations of sleep (reversal of sleep-wake rhythm, periodic nighttime awakenings) did not induce changes in plasma NE. Endogenous differences in plasma NE level, however, were correlated with sleep quality, such that poorer sleep was associated with higher basal mean nighttime NE levels. Similarly, endogenously elevated plasma NE levels (achieved experimentally via low salt diets) resulted in significant impairment of sleep, i.e., increased wakefulness, and decreased slow wave sleep and REM sleep (Vitiello et al., 1983). Thus, increased basal nighttime plasma NE is associated with impaired sleep, but the converse in not necessarily true.

Physiologically or pharmacologically induced increases in sympathetic tonus are accompanied by increased arousal, as indicated by an electroencephalograph arousal pattern and behavioral attentiveness (Gellhorn, 1957; Baust et al., 1963). Therefore, if higher plasma NE levels reflect a heightened sympathetic activation at night in older individuals, this heightened sympathetic tonus could interfere with sleep by promoting nighttime wakefulness. It is possible that new pharmacologic approaches to age-related insomnia may develop from a better understanding of nighttime sympathetic activity levels.

The Sleep-Wake Cycle as a Circadian Rhythm

The regular alternation of sleep and wakefulness may be the most obvious circadian rhythm in mammals. A free-running circadian rhythm of polygraphically defined sleep is documented in many species, including rodents (Mitler et al., 1977), monkeys (McNew et al., 1972), and man (Czeisler et al., 1980a). In addition, the various components of sleep have also been shown to be timed by the circadian clock. The normal distribution of REM sleep exhibits a circadian pattern (Maron et al., 1964; Weitzman et al., 1974; Carskadon and Dement, 1980; Czeisler et al., 1980b; Zulley, 1980; Hume, 1980; Weitzman et al., 1980). In addition, the timing of REM sleep is linked to changes in body temperature (Carskadon and Dement, 1980; Czeisler et al., 1980a, 1980b; Zulley, 1980). There are also documented circadian rhythms in objective sleep tendency and subjective sleepiness (Richardson et al., 1982).

These rhythms which comprise the sleep-wake rhythm are markedly sensitive to disruptions in the circadian system. Current models of its normal physiology suggest two categories of pathologies of the circadian system: disorders of the oscillator itself in which normally rhythmic variables are arrhythmic or rhythmic with an abnormal period, and disorders of entrainment to the environment or disorders of mutual entrainment within the multioscillator circadian system. In practice, the effect of such pathologies on the majority of physiological variables may be very subtle. It is difficult, for example, to predict the effect of an isolated error in timing on the otherwise normal expression of adrenal cortex steroid hormone excretion. In the case of rhythms of sleep and wakefulness, however, the proper timing and temporal segregation of these mutually exclusive behaviors are obviously fundamental to their normal expression. In the clinical setting, abnormalities in sleep-wake expression are readily recognized by the patient. It is thus logical to expect that disorders of the circadian timing system may first present as sleep-wake pathologies.

A number of sleep-wake disorders appear to have disordered function of the circadian system as their etiologic basis (see Association of Sleep Disorders Centers, 1979). Certainly the most common such disorders are a consequence of exogenous disruptions of the circadian system such as jet lag (McFarland, 1975) and shift work dyssomnia (Conroy et al., 1970; Halberg and Nelson, 1976; Walsh et al., 1978). Other sleep-wake disorders, however, may be a consequence of endogenous pathology; delayed sleep phase syndrome (Czeisler et al., 1981; Weitzman et al., 1981) was suggested to reflect an abnormality in the mechanism which allows resetting of the circadian clock after transient shifts of phase; and there is a converse disorder, advanced sleep phase syndrome (Kamei et al., 1979). Complete failure of the mechanisms of entrainment would be expected to produce a sleep-wake disorder characterized by free-running sleep times despite the presence of adequate environmental zeitgebers. Individuals with this disorder have also been identified (Miles et al., 1977; Kokkoris et al., 1978).

Age-related Changes in the Sleep-Wake Cycle. The disrupted sleep-wake pattern common in the elderly may also be a consequence of abnormalities in the circadian timing system. Aged humans show a breakdown of the normal monophasic pattern of sleep and wakefulness, with increased fragmentation of nocturnal sleep (Feinberg, 1969; Smith et al., 1977) and increased napping during the day (Tune, 1969; Webb and Swinburne, 1971). The polyphasic sleep-wake pattern of the rat also becomes increasingly fragmented as a function of age (Rosenberg et al., 1979). These changes can be thought of as a reduction in the "amplitude" of the circadian rhythms of sleep and wakefulness analogous to the reduced amplitude in the body temperature and neuroendocrine rhythms mentioned earlier.

Although there is no consensus regarding the precise nature of the age-related change in the circadian clock, there is also no evidence that the sleep-wake patterns of the elderly are a consequence of complete arrhythmicity of the circadian oscillator. The fragmented sleep-wake pattern is more likely due to abnormal phase relationships between the component rhythms and perhaps between their distinct driving oscillators. Wever (1979) reported that aged subjects free-running in constant conditions are more likely to show "internal desynchronization" than younger subjects. This finding raises the possibility that the individual oscillators of the complex circadian system in the aged are less tightly coupled to each other, perhaps as a consequence of greater disparity in their endogenous periods. Evidence suggesting abnormal entrained conditions comes from the demonstration of an age-related increase in the phase variability in the maxima of circadian rhythms of heart rate, temperature, and urinary constituents (Cahn et al., 1968).

Clinical Significance

The age-dependent changes in the multiple components of the circadian system have several consequences of varying significance. Disruptions of the circadian control of sleep and wakefulness may be causally related to the previously mentioned increase in sleep-related complaints among the aged. Additionally, the increased incidence of early morning wakefulness reported in the aged is presumably a consequence of the abnormally advanced position of the circadian oscillator relative to the environment. This particular abnormality, however, is apparently benign and seems compatible with normal life-style in most elderly.

Of more concern is the possibility that changes in the circadian timing system may be causally related to the increase of psychiatric pathology in the elderly. An underlying rhythm disturbance has long been postulated as a cause of primary depression (Georgi, 1947). Recent studies document a specific disruption of the circadian system in depression—an advanced position relative to the environment—that can reasonably explain the abnormalities in circadian rhythms observed in primary depressives, such as early morning waking, disrupted nocturnal sleep, decreased REM latency, increased length of first REM period, and advanced positions of body temperature and a variety of neuroendocrine rhythms (Hawkins and Mendels, 1966; Hartmann, 1968; Snyder, 1968; Kupfer et al., 1973; Pflug and Tolle, 1971; Sachar et al., 1973a, 1973b; Sachar, 1975; Vogel et al., 1973; Wehr et al., 1980; also see the review of Wehr and Goodwin, 1981).

There is a striking similarity between the characteristic circadian disruption of depression and that seen in normal aged individuals. The incidence of depression is commonly accepted to increase with age and is the most prevalent psychiatric diagnosis in the elderly

(Duckworth and Ross, 1975; Roth, 1955; Varsamis et al., 1972). Thus it appears plausible, given the validity of the circadian model for primary depression, that the abnormalities of circadian organization in the aged may contribute to an increase in psychiatric pathology.

A central issue in gerontology research is the discrimination between normal aging processes and pathologic deterioration. When age-related processes are identified as pathogenic, strategies for intervention require determining the extent to which the change is separable from the aging process *per se*.

For example, the age-related decrease in amplitude of the body temperature and neuroendocrine rhythms has unknown significance. Whether such changes reflect pathologic deterioration can be addressed using the method suggested by Sacher and Duffy (1978) in their longitudinal study of declining rates of energy metabolism in mice. By demonstrating that the rate of this decline was a better predictor of longevity than age itself, the authors proved that this decline was not a benign consequence of aging but instead represented significant pathologic deterioration, the reversal of which could be expected to increase life expectancy. Such assessments clearly require significant experimental effort because longitudinal studies are an absolute requirement: nonetheless, if the central issues of gerontology are to be successfully addressed, such experimental approaches are necessary.

CONCLUSION

When the various aspects of sleep and wakefulness are compared in old and young organisms, many differences are apparent, although there are major gaps in knowledge. The paucity of longitudinal studies of sleep and aging is noteworthy.

Nonetheless, certain tendencies seem well established. Advancing age is associated with increasing interruption of sleep, decreasing amount and percentage of SWS, deterioration of circadian organization, increasing prevalence of disordered breathing during sleep, and increasing prevalence of periodic leg movements. With regard to the latter two conditions, we would like to know when they begin, why, and the details of their natural history.

A critical issue in the area of sleep, biological rhythms, and aging is the distinction between processes intrinsic to aging and those representing pathophysiology. To some extent, this is a matter of definition, and sleep research will follow the lead of other gerontological research areas. Certainly, some changes seem to have little consequence for health and well-being, while others, at least when severe, might even be fatal.

ACKNOWLEDGMENTS

Supported in part by National Institute on Aging Grant AG 02504 and Research Scientist Award MH 05804 to W. Dement.

REFERENCES

Agnew, H. W., Webb, W. B., and Williams, R. L. 1966. The first night effect: an EEG study of sleep. *Psychophysiology* 2: 263–266.

Agnew, H. W., Webb, W. B., and Williams, R. L. 1967. Sleep patterns in late middle aged males: an EEG study. *Electroencephalogr. Clin. Neurophysiol.* 23: 168–171.

Ancoli-Israel, S., Kripke, D., Mason, W., and Messin, S. 1981. Sleep apnea and nocturnal myoclonus in a senior population. *Sleep* 4: 349–358.

Aschoff, J., Gerecke, U., and Wever, R. 1967. Desynchronization of human circadian rhythms. *Japanese Journal of Physiology* 17: 450–457.

Association of Sleep Disorders Centers. 1979. Diagnostic classification of sleep and arousal disorders, 1st ed. Prepared by Sleep Disorders Classification Committee, H. Roffwarg, Chairman. *Sleep* 2: 1–137.

Baekeland, F. 1970. Exercise deprivation, sleep and physiological reactions. *Arch. Gen. Psychiatry* 22: 365–369.

Bast, T. H. and Bloemendal, W. B. 1927. Studies in experimental exhaustion due to lack of sleep. IV. Effects on the nerve cells in the medulla. *Am. J. Physiol.* 82: 140–146.

Baust, W., Niemczyk, H., and Vieth, J. 1963. The action of blood pressure on the ascending reticular activating system with special reference to adrenaline-induced EEG arousal. *Electroencephalogr. Clin. Neurophysiol.* 15: 63–72.

Blichert-Toft, M. 1971. Assessment of serum corticotrophin concentration and its nyctohemeral rhythm in the aging. *Clin. Gerontol.* 13: 215–220.

Blichert-Toft, M. 1975. Secretion of corticotrophin and somatotrophin by the senescent adenohypophysis in man. *Acta Endrocrinol.* 78: 1–157.

Bliwise, D. L. 1982. Individual differences in EEG delta activity during sleep. Doctoral dissertation, University of Chicago.

Block, J., Boysen, P., Wynne, J., and Hunt, L. 1979. Sleep apnea, hypopnea and oxygen desaturation in normal subjects. *N. Engl. J. Med.* 300: 513–517.

Bowers, M. B., Hartman, G. L., and Freedman, D. X. 1966. Sleep deprivation and brain acetylcholine. *Science* 153: 1416–1417.

Bowersox, S. S., Baker, T. L., and Dement, W. C. Circadian sleep and waking patterns in the aged cat. *Sleep Res.* (in press).

Bremner, W. J., Vitiello, M. V., and Prinz, P. N. A loss of circadian rhythmicity in blood testosterone levels with aging in normal men. *J. Clin. Endocrin. Metab.* (in press).

Cahn, H. A., Folk, G. E., Jr., and Huston, P. E. 1968. Age comparison of human day-night physiological differences. *Aerospace Med.* 39: 608–610.

Campbell, S. S. and Webb, W. B. 1980. Sleep length and sleep termination in an aging population. *Sleep Res.* 9: 122.

Carlson, H. E., Gillin, J. C., Gordon, P., and Snyder, F. 1972. Absence of sleep-related growth hormone peaks in aged normal subjects and in acromegaly. *J. Clin. Endocrin.* 34: 1102–1105.

Carskadon, M. A., Brown, E. D., and Dement, W. C. 1982. Sleep fragmentation in the elderly, relationship to daytime sleep tendency. *Neurobiol. Aging* 3: 321–327.

Carskadon, M. A. and Dement, W. C. 1980. Distribution of REM sleep on a 90-minute sleep-wake schedule. *Sleep* 2: 309–317.

Carskadon, M. A. and Dement, W. C. 1981a. Respiration during sleep in the aging human. *J. Gerontol.* 36: 420–423.

Carskadon, M. A. and Dement, W. C. 1981b. Cumulative effects of sleep restriction on daytime sleepiness. *Psychophysiology* 18: 107–113.

Carskadon, M. A. and Dement, W. C. 1982a. The multiple sleep latency test: What does it measure? *Sleep* 5: S67–S72.

Carskadon, M. A. and Dement, W. C. 1982b. Nocturnal determinants of daytime sleepiness. *Sleep* 5: S73–S81.

Carskadon, M. A., van den Hoed, J. and Dement, W. C. 1980. Sleep and daytime sleepiness in the elderly. *J. Geriatr. Psychiatry* 13: 135–151.

Chase, M. H. 1981. Sleep patterns in old cats. Unpublished MS read at the 1981 Intra-Science Symposium, Santa Monica.

Chase, M., Babb, M., Stone, M., and Rich, S. 1976. Active sleep patterns in the old cat. *Sleep Res.* 5: 20.

Coccagna, G. and Lugaresi, E. 1978. Arterial blood

gases and pulmonary and systemic arterial pressure during sleep in chronic obstructive pulmonary disease. *Sleep* 1: 117–124.

Cole, G. M., Segall, P. E., and Timiras, P. S. 1982. Hormones during aging. *In,* A. Vernandakis (ed.), *Hormones in Development and Aging,* pp. 447–550. New York: Spectrum Publications.

Coleman, R. 1979. Periodic nocturnal myoclonus in disorders of sleep and wakefulness. Doctoral dissertation, Yeshiva University.

Coleman, R. M., Roffwarg, H. P., Kennedy, S. J., Guilleminault, C., Cinque, J., Cohn, M. A., Karacan, I., Kupfer, D. J., Lemmi, H., Miles, L. E., Orr, W. C., Phillips, E. R., Roth, T., Sassin, J. F., Schmidt, H. S., Weitzman, E. D., and Dement, W. C. 1982. Sleep-wake disorders based on a polysomnographic diagnosis, a national cooperative study. *JAMA* 247: 997–1003.

Collins, W. E. and Iampietro, P. F. 1973. Effects of repeated simulated sonic booms of 1.0 PSF on the sleep behavior of young and old subjects. *Aerosp. Med.* 44: 987–995.

Conroy, R., Elliot, A., and Mills, J. 1970. Circadian excretory rhythms in night workers. *Br. J. Int. Med.* 27: 356–363.

Crile, G. W. 1921. Studies in exhaustion. *Arch. Surg.* 2: 196–220.

Czeisler, C. A., Richardson, G. S., Coleman, R. M., Zimmerman, J. C., Moore-Ede, M. C., Dement, W. C., and Weitzman, E. D. 1981. Chronotherapy, resetting the circadian clocks of patients with delayed sleep phase insomnia. *Sleep* 4: 1–21.

Czeisler, C. A., Weitzman, E. D., Moore-Ede, M. C., Zimmerman, J. C., and Knauer, R. S. 1980a. Human sleep: its duration and organization depend on its circadian phase. *Science* 210: 1264–1267.

Czeisler, C. A., Zimmerman, J. C., Ronda, J. M., Moore-Ede, M. C., and Weitzman, E. D. 1980b. Timing of REM sleep is coupled to the circadian rhythm of body temperature in man. *Sleep* 2: 329–346.

Daddi, L. 1898. Sulle alterazioni degli elementi del sistema nervosa centrale nell'insomnia sperimentale. *Riv. Pat. Nerv. Ment.* 3: 1–72.

De Mairan, J. 1979. Observation botanique. *Histoire de L'Academie Royal des Sciences* 35: 36.

Duckworth, G. S. and Ross, H. 1975. Diagnostic differences in psychogeriatric patients in Toronto, New York and London, England. *Canad. M. A. J.* 112: 847–851.

Ehret, C. F., Gron, K. R., and Mernert, J. C. 1978. Circadian dyschronism and chronotypic ecophilia as factors in aging and longevity. *In,* H. V. Samis, Jr. and S. Copabianco (eds.), *Aging and Biological Rhythms* pp. 185–213. New York: Plenum Press.

Eleftheriou, B. E., Zolovick, A. J., and Elias, M. F. 1975. Electroencephalographic changes with age in male mice. *Gerontologia* 21: 21–30.

Feinberg, I. 1969. Effects of age on human sleep patterns. *In,* A. Kales (ed.), *Sleep: Physiology and Pathology* pp. 39–52. Philadelphia: Lippincott.

Feinberg, I., Fein, G., and Floyd, T. C. 1980. Period and amplitude analysis of NREM EEG in sleep, repeatability of results in young adults. *Electroencephalogr. Clin. Neurophysiol.* 48: 212–221.

Feinberg, I., Koresko, R. L., and Heller, N. 1967. EEG sleep patterns as a function of normal and pathological aging in man. *J. Psychiat. Res.* 5: 107–144.

Feinberg, I., March, J. D., Fein, G., Floyd, T. C., Walker, J. M., and Price, L. 1978. Period and amplitude analysis of 0.5–3 c/sec activity in NREM sleep. *Electroencephalogr. Clin. Neurophysiol.* 44: 202–213.

Finkelstein, J. W., Roffwarg, H. P., Boyar, R. M., Kream, J., and Hellman, L. 1972. Age-related change in the twenty-four-hour spontaneous secretion of growth hormone. *J. Clin. Endocrinol.,* 35: 660–665.

Flick, M. and Block, A. 1977. Continuous *in vivo* monitoring of arterial oxygenation in chronic obstructive lung disease. *Ann. Int. Med.* 86: 725–730.

Florini, J. R. and Roberts, S. B. 1978. Age-related changes in somatomedin levels. *Gerontol.* 18: A172.

Friedman, M., Green, M. F., and Sharland, D. E. 1969. Assessment of hypothalamic-pituitary-adrenal function in the geriatric age group. *J. Gerontol.* 24: 292–297.

Gander, P. H. 1980. Circadian organization in the regulation of locomotor activity and reproduction in Rattus exulans. Ph.D. thesis, University of Auckland, New Zealand.

Gellhorn, E. 1957. *Autonomic Imbalance and the Hyptothalamus.* New York: University of Minnesota Press.

Georgi, F. 1947. Psychophysiologische korrelationen. Psychiatrische probleme im licht der rhythmusfiorschung. *Schweiz. Med. Wochenschr.* 49: 1267–1280.

Gillin, J. C., Duncan, W. C., Murphy, D. L., Post, R. M., Wehr, T. A., Goodwin, F. K., Wyatt, R. J., and Bunney, W. E. 1981. Age-related changes in sleep in depressed and normal subjects. *Psychiatry Res.* 4: 73–78.

Grad, B., Kral, V. A., Payne, R. C., and Berenson, J. 1967. Plasma and urinary corticoids in young and old persons. *J. Gerontol.* 22: 66–71.

Grad, B., Rosenberg, G. M., Liberman, H., Trachtenberg, D., and Kral, V. A. 1971. Diurnal variation in serum cortisol level of geriatric subjects. *J. Gerontol.* 26: 351–357.

Griffin, S. J. and Trinder, J. 1978. Physical fitness, exercise, and human sleep. *Psychophysiology* 15: 447–450.

Guilleminault, C., Cummiskey, J., and Motta, J. 1980. Chronic obstructive airflow disease and sleep studies. *Am. Rev. Resp. Dis.* 122: 397–406.

Guilleminault, C., Eldridge, F., and Dement, W. C. 1973. Insomnia with sleep apnea, a new syndrome. *Science* 181: 856–858.

Guilleminault, C., Eldridge, F., Phillips, J. and Dement, W. 1976. Two occult causes of insomnia and their therapeutic problems. *Arch. Gen. Psychiatry* 33: 1241–1245.

Halberg, F. 1959. Physiologic 24-hour periodicity in human beings and mice, the lighting regimen and daily routine. *In,* R. B. Withrow (ed.), *Photoperiodism and Related Phenomena in Plants and Animals* pp. 803–878. Washington, D.C.: American Association for the Advancement of Science.

Halberg, F., 1982. Biological rhythms, hormones, and aging. *In,* A. Vernandakis (ed.), *Hormones in Development and Aging* pp. 451–476. New York: Spectrum Publications.

Halberg, F., Bittner, J. J., Gully, R. J., Albrecht, P. G., and Brackney, E. L. 1955. Twenty-four-hour periodicity and audiogenic seizure thresholds in mice of various ages. *Proceedings of the Society for Experimental Biology and Medicine* 88: 169–173.

Halberg, J., Halberg, E., Regal, P., and Halberg, F. 1981. Changes with age characterize circadian rhythm in telemetered core temperature of stroke-prone rats. *J. Gerontol.* 36: 28–30.

Halberg, F. and Nelson, W. 1976. Some aspects of chronobiology relating to the optimization of shift work. *In, Shift Work and Health* pp. 13–47. HEW Publication No. (NIOSH) 76–203.

Halberg, F. and Nelson, W. 1978. Chronobiologic optimization of aging. *In,* H. V. Samis, Jr. and S. Capobianco (eds.), *Aging and Biological Rhythms* pp. 5–56. New York: Plenum Press.

Hammond, E. 1964. Some preliminary findings on physical complaints from a prospective study of 1,064,000 men and women. *Am. J. Public Health* 54: 11–23.

Hartmann, E. 1968. Longitudinal studies of sleep and dream patterns in manic-depressive patients. *Arch. Gen. Psychiatry* 19: 312–329.

Hawkins, D. R. and Mendels, J. 1966. Sleep disturbances in depressive syndromes. *Am. J. Psychiatry* 123: 682–690.

Heiner, L., Godin, Y., Mark, J., and Mandel, P. 1978. Electrolyte content of brain and blood after deprivation of paradoxical sleep. *J. Neurochem.* 15: 150–151.

Hensley, M. and Read, D. 1976. Intermittent obstruction of the upper airway during sleep causing profound hypoxemia, a neglected mechanism exacerbating chronic respiratory failure. *N. Z. J. Med.* 6: 481–486.

Horne, J. A. 1978. A review of the biological effects of total sleep deprivation in man. *Biol. Psychol.* 7: 55–102.

Horne, J. A. and Porter, J. M. 1975. Exercise and human sleep. *Nature* 256: 573–575.

Hume, K. I. 1980. Sleep adaptation after phase shifts of the sleep-wakefulness rhythm in man. *Sleep* 2: 417–435.

Ingram, D. K., London, E. D., and Reynolds, M. A. 1982. Circadian rhythmicity and sleep, effects of aging in laboratory animals. *Neurobiol. Aging* 3: 287–297.

Jensen, H. K. and Blichert-Toft, M. 1971. Serum corticotrophin, plasma cortisol and urinary excretion of 17-ketogenic steroids in the elderly age group, 66–94. *Acta Endocrinol.* 74: 511–523.

Kales, A., Kales, J., Jacobson, A., Weissbach, R., Walter, R. D., and Wilson, T. 1966. All night EEG studies, children and elderly. *Electroencephalogr. Clin. Neurophysiol.* 21: 415.

Kales, A., Wilson, T., Kales, J., Jacobson, A., Paulson, M., Kollar, E., and Walter, R. D. 1967. Measurements of all-night sleep in normal elderly persons, effects of aging. *J. Am. Geriatr. Soc.* 15: 405–414.

Kamei, R., Hughes, L., Miles, L., and Dement, W. 1979. Advanced sleep phase syndrome studied in a time isolation facility. *Chronobiologica* 16: 115.

Karacan, I., Rosenbloom, A. L., London, J. H., Salis, P. J., Thornby, J. I., and Williams, R. L. 1973. The effects of acute fasting on sleep and sleep growth hormone response. *Psychosomatics* 14: 33–37.

Karadzic, V. and Mrsulja, B. 1969. Deprivation of paradoxical sleep and brain glycogen. *J. Neurochem.,* 16: 29–34.

Karnovsky, M. L. and Reich, P. 1977. Biochemistry of sleep. *Adv. Neurochem.* 2: 213–275.

Kenagy, G. J. 1978. Seasonality of endogenous circadian rhythms in a diurnal rodent *Ammospermophilus leucurus* and a nocturnal rodent *Dipodomys merriami. J. Comp. Physiol.* 128: 21–36.

Koella, W. P. 1967. *Sleep: Its Nature and Physiological Organization.* Springfield, Ill.: Charles C. Thomas.

Kokkoris, C., Weitzman, E., Pollak, C., Spielman, A., Czeisler, C., and Bradlow, H. 1978. Long-term ambulatory temperature monitoring in a subject with hypernychthemeral sleep-wake cycle disturbance. *Sleep* 1: 177–190.

Krieger, D., Allen, W., Rizzo, F., and Krieger, H. 1971. Characterization of the normal pattern of plasma corticosteroid levels. *J. Clin. Endocrinol. Metab.* 32: 266–284.

Krieger, J., Mangin, P., and Kurtz, D. 1980. Les modifications respiratoires au cours du sommeil du sujet age normal. *Rev. EEG Neurophysiol.* 10: 177–185.

Kripke, D. F., Ancoli-Israel, S., and Okudaira, N. 1982. Sleep apnea and nocturnal myoclonus in the elderly. *Neurobiol. Aging* 3: 329–336.

Kupfer, D. J., Foster, F. G., and Detre, T. P. 1973. Sleep continuity changes in depression. *Dis. Nerv. Syst.* 34: 192–195.

Leake, C., Grab, J. A., and Senn, M. J. 1927. Studies in exhaustion due to lack of sleep. II. Symptomatology in rabbits. *Am. J. Physiol.* 92: 127–130.

Lincoln, G. A., Rowe, P. H., and Racey, R. A. 1974. The circadian rhythm in plasma testosterone concentration in man. *In,* J. Aschoff, F. Ceresa, and F. Halberg (eds.), *Chronobiological Aspects of Endocrinology* pp. 137–150. Stuttgart: F. K. Schattauer Verlag.

Lobban, M. C. and Tredre, B. E. 1967. Diurnal rhythms of renal excretion and of body temperature in aged subjects. *Journal of Physiology (London)* 188: 48P–49P.

Lugaresi, E., Cirignotta, F., Coccagna, G., and Piana, C. 1980. Some epidemiological data on snoring and cardiocirculatory disturbances. *Sleep* 3: 221–224.

Lugaresi, E., Coccagna, G., and Cirignotta, F. 1978. Snoring and its clinical implications. *In,* C. Guilleminault and W. Dement (eds.), *Sleep Apnea Syndromes* pp. 13–21. New York: Alan R. Liss.

Lugaresi, E., Coccagna, G., Farneti, P., Mantovani, M., and Cirignotta, F. 1975. Snoring. *Electroencephalogr. Clin. Neurophysiol.* 39: 59–64.

MacFayden, U. M., Oswald, I., and Lewis, S. A. 1973. Starvation and human slow wave sleep. *J. Appl. Physiol.* 35: 391–394.

Manaceine, M. 1894. Quelques observations experimentales sur l'influence de l'insomnie absolue. *Arch. Ital. Biol.* 21: 322–325.

Maron, L., Rechtschaffen, A., and Wolpert, E. A. 1964. Sleep cycle during napping. *Arch. Gen. Psychiatry* 11: 503–508.

McDonald, C. S., Zepelin, H., and Zammit, G. K. 1981. Age and sex patterns in auditory awakening thresholds. *Sleep Res.* 10: 115.

McFarland, R. A. 1975. Air travel across time zones. *Am. Sci.* 63: 23–30.

McGhie, A. and Russell, S. 1962. The subjective assessment of normal sleep patterns. *J. Ment. Sci.* 108: 642–654.

McGinty, D. and Arand, D. 1980. Unpublished MS presented at the 33rd Annual Meeting of the Gerontological Society of America, San Diego.

McNew, J. J., Burson, R. C., Hoshizaki, T., and Adey, W. R. 1972. Sleep-wake cycle of an unrestrained isolated chimpanzee under entrained and free-running conditions. *Aviat. Space Environ Med.* 43: 155–161.

Mendels, J. and Hawkins, D. R. 1967. Sleep laboratory adaptation in normal subjects and depressed patients, first night effect. *Electroencephalogr. Clin. Neurophysiol.* 22: 556–558.

Miles, L. E. and Dement, W. C. 1980. Sleep and aging. *Sleep* 3: 119–220.

Miles, L. E., Raynal, D., and Wilson, M. 1977. Blind man living in normal society has circadian rhythm of 24.9 hours. *Science* 198: 421–422.

Mills, J. and Hume, K. 1977. The circadian rhythm of sleep stages. *Chronobiologia* 4: 132.

Mitler, M. M., Lund, R., Sokolove, P. G., Pittendrigh, C. S., and Dement, W. C. 1977. Sleep and activity rhythms in mice: a description of circadian patterns and unexpected disruptions in sleep. *Brain Research* 131: 129–145.

Moore-Ede, M. C., Sulzman, F. M., and Fuller, C. A. 1982. *The Clocks That Time Us: Physiology of the Circadian Timing System.* Cambridge, Mass.: Harvard University Press.

Naitoh, P. 1976. Sleep deprivation in human subjects, a reappraisal. *Waking Sleep* 1: 53–60.

National Institute on Aging. 1979. Special report: re-search planning workshop on sleep and aging (W. Dement, Chairman). *Sleep* 1: 221–230.

O'Connor, A. 1962. Sleep questionnaire responses related to age. Unpublished M. A. Thesis, University of Florida.

Orem, J. 1980. Neuronal mechanisms of respiration in REM sleep. *Sleep* 3: 251–267.

Parker, D. C., Rossman, L. G., and Vanderlaan, E. F. 1972. Persistence of rhythmic human growth hormone release during sleep in fasted and nonisocalorically fed normal subjects. *Metabolism* 21: 241–252.

Pflug, B. and Tolle, R. 1971. Disturbance of the 24-hr rhythm in endogenous depression by sleep deprivation. *Int. J. Pharmacopsychiat.* 6: 187–196.

Phillipson, E. 1978. Respiratory adaptations in sleep. *Ann. Rev. Physiol.* 40: 133–156.

Pittendrigh, C. and Daan, S. 1974. Circadian oscillations in rodents, systematic increase of their frequency with age. *Science* 186: 548–550.

Pollak, C., Brodlow, H., Spielman, A., and Weitzman, E. 1978. A pilot survey of the symptoms of hypersomnia-sleep apnea syndrome as possible risk factors for hypertension. Unpublished MS presented at the 18th Annual Meeting of the Association of the Psychophysiological Study of Sleep, Stanford, Calif.

Preston, F. 1973. Further sleep problems in airline pilots on world-wide schedules. *Aerosp. Med.* 44: 775–782.

Principe, J. C. and Smith, J. R. 1982. Sleep spindle characteristics as a function of age. *Sleep* 5: 73–84.

Prinz, P. N. 1977. Sleep patterns in the healthy aged, interrelationships with intellectual function. *J. Gerontol.* 32: 179–186.

Prinz, P. N. and Halter, J. B. 1983. Sleep disturbances in the elderly, neurohormonal correlates. *In,* M. Chase (ed.), *Sleep Disorders: Basic and Clinical Research* pp. 463–488. New York: Spectrum Publications.

Prinz, P. N., Halter, J., Benedetti, C., and Raskind, M. 1979. Circadian variation of plasma catecholamines in young and old men, relation to rapid eye movement and slow wave sleep. *J. Clin. Endocrinol. Metab.* 49: 300–304.

Prinz, P. N., Weitzman, E. D., Cunningham, G. R. and Karacan, I. Plasma growth hormone during sleep in young and aged men. *J. Gerontol.* (in press).

Quay, W. B. 1972. Pineal homeostatic regulation of shifts in the circadian activity rhythm during maturation and aging. *Trans. N. Y. Acad. Sci.* 34: 239–254.

Rechtschaffen, A. and Kales, A. (eds.) 1968. *A Manual of Standardized Terminology, Techniques and Scoring System for Sleep Stages of Human Subjects.* Los Angeles: UCLA BIS/BRI.

Richardson, G. S., Carskadon, M. A., Orav, E. J., and Dement, W. C. 1982. Circadian variation of sleep tendency in elderly and young adult subjects. *Sleep* 5: S82–S94.

Romanoff, L. P., Morris, C. W., Welch, P., Rodriguez, R. M., and Pineus, G. 1961. The metabolism of cortisol-4-14C in young and elderly men. I. Secretion rate of cortisol and daily excretion of tetrahydrocortisol, allotetrahydrocortisol, tetrahydrocortisone and coratolone 20a and 20B. *J. Clin. Endocrinol.* 21: 1413–1425.

Rosenberg, R. S. and Rechtschaffen, A. 1978. Lifespan changes in the diurnal sleep pattern of rats. *Soc. Neurosci. Abs.* 4: 125.

Rosenberg, R. S., Winter, J. B., and Rechtschaffen, A. 1980. Effects of light cycle phase reversal on sleep rhythms in young and old rats. *Sleep Research* 9: 105.

Rosenberg, R. S., Zepelin, H., and Rechtschaffen, A. 1976. EEG comparisons of young and old rats. *Sleep Res.* 5: 88.

Rosenberg, R. S., Zepelin, H., and Rechtschaffen, A. 1979. Sleep in young and old rats. *J. Geront.* 34: 525–532.

Roth, M. 1955. The natural history of mental disorder in old age. *J. Ment. Sci.* 101: 281–301.

Sachar, E. 1975. Hormonal changes in stress and mental illness. *Hosp. Pract.* 10: 49–55.

Sachar, E. J., Halpern, F., Rosenfeld, R., Gallagher, T., and Hellman, L. 1973a. Plasma and urinary testosterone levels in depressed men. *Arch. Gen. Psychiatry* 28: 15–18.

Sachar, E., Hellman, L., Roffwarg, H., Halpern, F., Fukushima, D., and Gallagher, T. 1973b. Disrupted 24-hour patterns of cortisol secretion in psychotic depression. *Arch. Gen. Psychiatry* 288: 19–24.

Sachar, G. A. and Duffy, P. H. 1978. Age changes in rhythms of energy metabolism, activity, and body temperature in *Mus* and *Peromyscus. In,* H. B. Samis, Jr. and S. Copabianco (eds.), *Aging and Biological Rhythms* pp. 105–124. New York: Plenum.

Samis, H. V. 1968. Aging: the loss of temporal organization. *Perspectives in Biology and Medicine* 12: 95–102.

Saradzhishvil, P., Geladze, T. Sh., Bibileishvili, Sh. T., Shubladze, G., and Toidze, O. 1974. [Clinical sleep patterns of long living males.] *Soobshenheniva Akademii Nauk Gruzinskoy SSR (Tbilisi)* 75: 693–695.

Schmidt, H. S. and Kaelbling, R. 1971. The differential laboratory adaptation of sleep parameters. *Biol. Psychiatry* 33: 33–45.

Serio, M., Piolanti, P., Cappelli, G., DeMagistris, L., Ricci, F., Anzalone, M., and Guisti, G. 1969. The miscible pool and turnover rate of cortisol in the aged, and variations in relation to time of day. *Exp. Gerontol.* 4: 95–101.

Serio, M., Piolanti, P., Romano, S., DeMagistris, L., and Guisti, G. 1970. The circadian rhythm of plasma cortisol in subjects over 70 years of age. *J. Gerontol.* 4: 95–97.

Shapiro, C. M., Bortz, R., Mitchell, D., Bartel, P., and Jooste, P. 1981. Slow wave sleep, a recovery period after exercise. *Science* 214: 1253–1254.

Shapiro, C. M. and Vershcoor, G. J. 1979. Sleep patterns after a marathon. *S. Af. J. Sci.* 75: 415–416.

Smallwood, R. G., Vitiello, M. V., Giblin, E. C., and Prinz, P. N. 1983. Sleep apnea, relationship to age, sex, and Alzheimer's dementia. *Sleep* 6: 16–22.

Smith, J. R., Karacan, I., and Yang, M. 1977. Ontogeny of delta activity during human sleep. *Electroencephalogr. Clin. Neurophysiol.* 43: 229–237.

Snyder, F. 1968. Electroencephalographic studies of sleep in depression. *In,* N. S. Kline and E. Lasha (eds.), *Computers and Electronic Devices in Psychiatry* pp. 272–301. New York: Grune & Stratton.

Solberger, A. 1965. *Biological Rhythm Research.* Amsterdam: Elsevier.

Spiegel, R. 1981. *Sleep and Sleeplessness in Advanced Age.* New York: S. P. Medical and Scientific Books.

Sullivan, C. E. 1980. Breathing in sleep. *In,* J. Orem and C. D. Barnes (eds.), *Physiology in Sleep* pp. 214–272. New York: Academic Press.

Symonds, C. 1953. Nocturnal myoclonus. *J. Neurol. Neurosurg. Psychiatry* 16: 166–177.

Thiessen, G. J. 1978. Distrubance of sleep by noise. *J. Acoust. Soc. Am.* 64: 216–222.

Tune, G. 1969. The influence of age and temperament on the adult human sleep-wakefulness pattern. *Br. J. Psychol.* 60: 431–441.

van den Noort, S. and Brine, K. 1970. Effect of sleep on brain labile phosphates and metabolic rate. *Am. J. Physiol.* 218: 1434–1439.

Varsamis, J., Zuchowski, T., and Maini, K. K. 1972. Survival rates and causes of death in geriatric psychiatry patients. *Canad. Psychiat. S. J.* 17: 17–22.

Vitiello, M. V., Giblin, E. C., Schoene, R. B., Halter, J. B., and Prinz, P. N. 1982. Obstructive apnea, sympathetic activity, respiration and sleep, a case report. *Neurobiol. Aging* 3: 263–266.

Vitiello, M. V., Prinz, P. N., and Halter, J. B. 1983. Sodium-restricted diet increases nighttime plasma norepinephrine and impairs sleep patterns in man. *J. Clin. Endocrinol. Matab.* 56: 553–556.

Vogel, G., Thompson, F., Thurmond, F., and Rivers, E. 1973. The effect of REM deprivation on depression. *Psychosomatics* 14: 104–107.

Walker, J. M., Floyd, T. C., Fein, G., Cavness, C., Lualhati, R., and Feinberg, I. 1978. Effects of exercise on sleep. *J. Appl. Physiol.* 44: 945–951.

Walsh, J., Stock, C., and Tepas, D. 1978. The EEG sleep of workers frequently changing shifts. *Sleep Res.* 7: 314.

Wax, T. M. and Goodrick, C. L. 1975. Voluntary exposure to light by young and aged albino and pigmented inbred mice as a function of light intensity. *Dev. Psychobiol.* 8: 297–303.

Webb, P. 1974. Periodic breathing during sleep. *J. Appl. Physiol.* 37: 889–903.

Webb, P. and Hiestand, M. 1975. Sleep, metabolism, and age. *J. Appl. Physiol.* 38: 257–262.

Webb, W. B. 1972. Sleep deprivation, total, partial, and selective. *In,* M. Chase (ed.), *The Sleeping Brain* pp. 323–361. Los Angeles: UCLA BIS/BRI.

Webb, W. B. 1978. Sleep, biological rhythms and aging. *In,* H. V. Samis, Jr. and S. Capobianco (eds.), *Aging and Biological Rhythms.* pp. 309–323. New York: Plenum Press.

Webb, W. B. 1982. The measurement and characteristics of sleep in older persons. *Neurobiol. Aging* 3: 311–319.

Webb, W. B. and Agnew, H. 1971. Stage 4 sleep, influence of time course variables. *Science* 174: 1354–1356.

Webb, W. B. and Agnew, H. 1974. Sleep and waking in a time-free environment. *Aerosp. Med.* 45: 617–622.

Webb, W. B. and Campbell, S. S. 1979. The first night effect revisited with age as a variable. *Waking Sleep* 3: 319–324.

Webb, W. B. and Swinburne, H. 1971. An observational study of sleep in the aged. *Percept. Mot. Skills* 32: 895–898.

Wehr, T. A. and Goodwin, F. K. 1981. Biological rhythms and psychiatry. *In,* S. Arieti and H. Brodie (eds.), *American Handbook of Psychiatry,* 2nd ed., Vol. 7, pp. 46–74. New York: Basic Books.

Wehr, T. A., Muscettola, G., and Goodwin, F. K. 1980. Urinary 3-methoxy-4-hydroxyphenylglycol circadian rhythm, early timing phase advance in manic-depressives compared with normal subjects. *Arch. Gen. Psychiatry* 37: 257–263.

Weitzman, E. D., Czeisler, C. A., Coleman, R. M., Spielman, A. J., Zimmerman, J. C., and Dement, W. C. 1981. Delayed sleep phase syndrome, a chronobiological disorder with sleep-onset insomnia. *Arch. Gen. Psychiatry* 38: 737–746.

Weitzman, E. D., Czeisler, C. A., Zimmerman, J. C., and Ronda, J. M. 1980. Timing of REM and stages 3 + 4 sleep during temporal isolation in man. *Sleep* 2: 391–407.

Weitzman, E. D., Moline, M. L., Czeisler, C. A., and Zimmerman, J. C. 1982. Chronobiology of aging: temperature, sleep-wake rhythms and entrainment. *Neurobiol. Aging* 3: 299–309.

Weitzman, E. D., Nogiere, C., Perlow, M. Fukushima, D., Sassin, J., McGregor, P., Gallagher, T. F., and Hellman, L. 1974. Effects of a prolonged 3-hour sleep-wake cycle on sleep stage, plasma cortisol, growth hormone and body temperature in man. *J. Clin. Endocrinol. Metab.* 38: 1018–1030.

West, C. D., Brown, H., Simons, E. L., Carter, D. B., Kumagai, L. F., and Englert, C. 1961. Adrenocortical function and cortisol metabolism in old age. *J. Clin. Endocrinol. Metab.* 21: 1197–1207.

Wever, A. 1979. *The Circadian System of Man. Results of Experiments under Temporal Isolation.* New York: Springer-Verlag.

Williams, R., Karacan, I., and Hursch, C. 1974. *Electroencephalography EEG of Human Sleep: Clinical Applications.* New York: John Wiley & Sons.

Wirz-Justice, A., Wehr, T. A., Goodwin, F. K., Kafka, M. S., Naber, D., Marangos, P. J., and Campbell, I. C. 1980. Antidepressant drugs slow circadian rhythms in behavior and brain neurotransmitter receptors. *Psychopharmacology Bulletin* 16: 45–47.

Wynne, J., Block, A., Hemenway, J., Hunt, L., and Flick, M. 1979. Disordered breathing and oxygen desaturation during sleep in patients with chronic obstructive lung disease. *Am. J. Med.* 66: 573–579.

Yunis, G. J., Fernandes, G., Nelson, W., and Halberg, F. 1974. Circadian temperature rhythms and aging in rodents. *In,* L. E. Schering, F. Halberg, and J. E. Pauly (eds.), *Chronobiology.* Tokyo: Iguku Shoin.

Zepelin, H. and McDonald, C. Age differences in adaptation to auditory stimuli during sleep. *Sleep Res.* (in press).

Zepelin, H., McDonald, C., Wanzie, F., and Zammit, G. 1980. Age differences in auditory awakening thresholds. *Sleep Res.* 9: 109.

Zepelin, H., Whitehead, W. E., and Rechtschaffen, A. 1972. Aging and sleep in the albino rat. *Behav. Biol.* 7: 65–74.

Zulley, J. 1980. Distribution of REM sleep in entrained 24 hour and free-running sleep-wake cycles. *Sleep* 2: 377–389.

PART 7 HUMAN BIOLOGY AND PATHOLOGY

26
LONGITUDINAL STUDIES OF AGING IN HUMANS

Nathan W. Shock
National Institute on Aging

METHODS FOR THE STUDY OF AGING

Traditionally, age changes have been inferred from the average differences observed between measurements made on groups of subjects of different ages or from the regression on age of observations made on subjects distributed over the total age span who are measured at about the same time. This cross-sectional method does not provide a direct measurement of age changes in individuals, since differences between age groups may be due to age-cohort effects. The age changes can only be inferred.

In order to assess age changes directly, it is necessary to make repeated measurements on the same individual as he ages. This is the longitudinal method, which eliminates the effects of birth-cohort differences present in cross-sectional findings.

The goal of this chapter is to describe the longitudinal method and to indicate some of the unique advantages (and disadvantages) it brings to the study of aging.

LIMITATIONS OF CROSS-SECTIONAL STUDIES OF AGING

The cross-sectional method, which had been used for most studies of growth and development in children, was adopted by geron-tologists to study aging in adults. The chief advantages of the method are its ease of application and the speed with which potential age effects on a variable can be assessed, since subjects of all ages are measured at about the same time.

The primary limitation of the cross-sectional method is that the differences between age groups confound the effects of birth cohort with the effects of age. Subjects from different age decades (birth cohorts) have lived through common environmental events, such as disasters, wars, and economic depressions, at different ages. If such factors affect test performance, differences in average values may be erroneously ascribed to aging. For example, subjects 70 years of age tested in 1980 may obtain lower scores than 40 year olds on tests of mental performance simply because of differences in their levels of schooling. Practically all the 40-year-old subjects, but fewer than half the 70 year olds, will have graduated from high school.

Cross-sectional studies also suffer from the effects of selective mortality. Since mortality rates increase logarithmically with age, the older groups are more highly selected for potential longevity than the young and middle-aged ones. This selection will have an indeterminate effect on the mean values for each age decade.

Another limitation of the cross-sectional method is that the values produced permit comparisons only between groups of subjects of different ages. The cross-sectional method cannot indicate the rate of change in a variable within an individual.

Neither can the cross-sectional method detect the effect of specific events on subsequent performance in individual subjects. For example, although cross-sectional studies have shown that lung function is poorer on the average in smokers than in nonsmokers at any age (Edelman et al., 1966), they cannot provide evidence of the amount of improvement that can be expected in individual smokers when they stop smoking. Longitudinal observations made while the subject was smoking and for a period after he has stopped are required for this analysis.

LONGITUDINAL STUDIES

Some of the limitations of cross-sectional studies can be overcome by the longitudinal design, in which measurements are repeated on the same subjects as they age. Although longitudinal studies avoid the confounding of birth-cohort differences with age changes, since all subjects in each group studied are drawn from the same birth cohort, other effects may now be confounded with age. Changes observed in serial measurements may be due to period effects as well as to aging. These effects may be confounded in a longitudinal study which has eliminated age-cohort effects. Period effects are for the most part either cultural changes that have influenced measurements on subjects of all ages or undetected shifts in methodology. A change in eating habits that affects adults at all ages, e.g., a reduction in fat intake, is an example of a period effect that might influence serial observations of blood cholesterol levels.

Some period effects, such as changes in methodology, can be controlled by repeating analyses on aliquots of blood or urine samples taken in the early stages of the study that have been frozen or lyophilized. When improved methods become available during the

course of a study, they can be introduced after determinations have been made on the same sample by both the old and the new methods to assure comparability of results. Constant vigilance during a longitudinal study is essential to maintain quality control of all methods.

Performances on some tests may improve on subsequent testing because of practice effects. Tests of mental and motor skills are especially susceptible to this cohort effect which must be controlled in longitudinal studies. The effects of practice can be detected by cross-sequential analysis, which compares results from a group of subjects who have never before been tested with results obtained in subjects of the same age who have been tested several times previously.

Changes in longitudinal observations may thus include both age and period effects, while cross-sectional differences may include age and cohort effects. Each set of differences may thus be influenced by two of the primary effects, i.e., those of age, period, and birth cohort. In order to separate the effects of period and cohort from age effects, two variations of the longitudinal design have been proposed, namely, the cross-sequential and the time-sequential designs (Schaie, 1977). In the cross-sequential design, independent samples of individuals from the same birth cohort are compared at different times of measurement and thus at different ages. Since each individual is tested only once, practice effects are eliminated. In the time-sequential design, independent samples of individuals of a specified age are compared at different times of measurement. Age and time of measurement are separated, but both are confounded with birth cohort.

Unfortunately, there are no statistical methods that can clearly separate the effects of birth cohort and period from the effects of aging, although many attempts have been made and much has been written on the subject (Schaie, 1965; Baltes, 1968; Riley et al., 1972; Mason and Mason, 1973; Palmore, 1978; Nesselroade and Baltes, 1979; Schulsinger et al., 1981). In the final analysis, reliable interpretation of the effect of aging on a variable requires the simultaneous accumulation of both cross-sectional and multiple longitudinal data, and the interpretations of an astute investigator (Costa and McCrae, 1982).

Although studies made on the same subjects at two times will meet the definition of a longitudinal study, the value of a two-point difference score as an index of aging is limited by the fact that no estimate of its reliability can be calculated. The reliability of the estimate of the change that occurs with time can be improved if the slope based on a linear* regression of the measurement on age is calculated from three or more serial observations on each subject. Both the reliability and the significance of a longitudinal study increase with its duration and the frequency of testing. The relations among the reliability of the test, the average rate of change in the variable with age, the period covered by the study, and the number of testings carried out on each subject have been analyzed so that an investigator designing a longitudinal study may choose from a variety of designs the one that will yield the desired level of reliability (Schlesselman, 1973a, 1973b). In some studies, such as the Framingham study (Dawber et al., 1963; Framingham, 1968, 1974, 1978), the Duke studies (Busse and Maddox, 1980; Palmore, 1981), and the Baltimore Longitudinal Study of Aging (BLSA) (Shock et al., 1984), measurements have been made at intervals of 1, 2, or 6 years for 15 to 22 years. However the BLSA is the only study in which regressions on age of specific variables have been calculated for individual subjects (Shock et al., 1979).

Since longitudinal studies usually require long-term commitments from the subjects, they are seldom based on randomly selected subjects. Most studies have used highly selected populations that are apt to have more education, higher incomes, better health care, and better health habits than the average. Furthermore, ethnic groups other than Caucasian are usually underrepresented. As a result, findings from such studies can be generalized only with caution.

Longitudinal studies that continue for long periods of time are also plagued by subjects who drop out, often for reasons related to age. Among the oldest subjects (75 and over), the primary causes are illness and death, while the younger subjects are more likely to drop out because of changes in residence. Studies have shown that the effect of dropouts on final results of a longitudinal study depends on the variable being studied as well as on the differences in characteristics between the dropouts and the loyal subjects (Schaie et al., 1973). Each study must assess the effects of dropouts on the variables under consideration (Shock et al., 1984).

In spite of such difficulties, it is essential to carry out longitudinal studies, since they represent the only design that can answer the following questions about aging in humans:

1. Does the average curve of age differences based on cross-sectional data represent the progression of aging in individual subjects?
2. What is the rate of change with age in specific variables in individual subjects?
3. Is there a general aging factor for an individual that coordinates aging in different organs and functions, and is related to longevity, or is aging a specific characteristic for each tissue and organ system? How are age changes in different variables related in an individual subject?
4. Do critical events in the life cycle of an individual affect aging?
5. Can patterns or levels of performance at a given age predict longevity or performance at a later age?
6. Can aging be distinguished from disease?
7. Does age influence the progression of disease processes?

It is obvious that data collected in longitudinal studies may also be analyzed cross-

*Only linear regressions can be calculated because of the relatively small number of serial observations that are available.

sectionally. Such analyses may be of great importance to the understanding of aging, since the repetition of measurements may greatly enhance their reliability and increase the probability of detecting occult diseases.

Events or processes experienced at various times during adulthood may affect not only health or function later in life but also survival. Longitudinal observations greatly enhance the probability that the long-term effects of specific events will be detected. The longitudinal approach, with frequent evaluations over periods of ten or more years, decreases memory errors in subjects' reports of historical events; it may also provide objective evidence for the presence of an event, as well as more accurate identification of the time when both the event and its effects occur.

In addition to such events as illness, accidents, "life cycle" events (loss of job, change in work, retirement, death of spouse, separation), changes in life-style (cessation of smoking, changes in dietary habits, initiation of exercise programs), and other stresses, another class of predictors may be related to continuing biological and behavioral characteristics. The prediction of future outcomes may depend not only on the level of a variable at a given time, but also on how it changes over a span of years. Investigations of these questions require longitudinal observations.

Longitudinal observations also provide an opportunity to identify the effects of physiological events on other variables, an opportunity not offered by cross-sectional analyses. For example, cross-sectional observations of basal heat production of boys and girls aged 12 to 17.5 years led to the conclusion that basal metabolic rate (BMR) falls gradually from age 12 to 16. Figure 1 shows the average values for basal heat production in 50 males and 50 females tested at six-month intervals between the ages of 12 and 18 years. In males, the values fell gradually between the ages of 12 and 15 1/2 years and remained stable between the ages of 16 and 17 1/2. In females, the average value for basal heat production showed an increase at 16 1/2 years. Since none of these differences was statistically significant, it was concluded

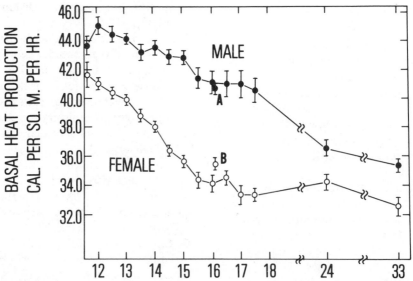

Figure 1. Average basal heat production in males (•——•) and females (○——○). Measurements were made every 6 months from age 11.5 to 17.5 years in the same individuals. Other subjects were recruited at ages 24 and 33 years. (A and B) Average values for 50 boys and 50 girls aged 16 years, measured for the first time. (From Shock, 1942.)

that during adolescence, basal heat production fell at a gradual rate in both boys and girls (Shock, 1942).

However, when the data for girls were replotted so that each girl's age of menarche represented the zero point and serial observations taken at six-month intervals were plotted as deviations from age of menarche (Figure 2), it became apparent that a physiological event (menarche) is more important than chronological age in determining the timing of the adolescent fall in BMR in girls (Shock, 1943).

Some clues to the way a variable is related to life span can be derived from longitudinal data. If mean values found at the first testing in individuals who died within a relatively short time are compared with the mean values of survivors, subjects who died are usually found to have shown poorer performance at the original testing than the survivors. Higher blood pressure levels (Tobin, 1981), poorer pulmonary performance ($FEV_{1.0}$) (Tobin, 1981), and poorer creatinine clearance (Tobin, 1981; Shock et al., 1979) were found in subjects of all ages who died within ten years of testing than in survivors who had been the same age at the first testing. No differences were found in carbohydrate metabolism as measured by blood glucose levels after fasting or two hours after

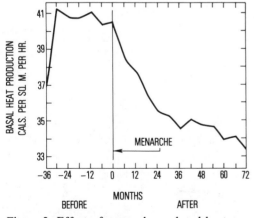

Figure 2. Effect of menarche on basal heat production. Average values calculated for six-month intervals before and after menarche for each of 50 girls. Zero time is taken for each girl at the age of menarche. (From Shock, 1943.)

ingestion of a standard dose of glucose (Tobin, 1981). Thus, poor performance in a number of physiological tests at any age may be associated with shorter life spans.

Measurements made on participants in longitudinal studies offer a rich resource for the study of aging. The repeated measurements, including the physical examinations, greatly enhance the probability that occult diseases will be detected so that only healthy subjects will be included in studies on aging. Since the subjects are apt to be better educated and to have higher incomes and better health habits than the general population, the serial changes observed are less apt to have been influenced by factors other than age. The probability that observed differences can be ascribed to aging rather than to disease or socioeconomic factors such as educational levels or income is thus materially enhanced.

LONGITUDINAL STUDIES IN ADULTS

Although a number of longitudinal studies of growth and development of children had been carried out before 1940 [Harvard Growth Study (Shuttleworth, 1937, 1939); Berkeley growth studies (Jones et al., 1971); Terman-Stanford Study of Gifted Children (Terman and Oden, 1947, 1959); Iowa growth studies (Baldwin, 1921)], no such studies had been done in adults. In the late 1940s, however, interest in determining specific risk factors for cardiovascular diseases stimulated longitudinal studies of middle-aged subjects designed to identify the factors associated with increased risk of cardiovascular disease. In 1947, Dr. Ancel Keys and his associates recruited a group of 281 Minneapolis and St. Paul businessmen, aged 45–54, whom they tested at annual intervals until 1977 (Keys et al., 1963). Primary emphasis was placed on comparison of the characteristics of subjects who developed cardiovascular disease with those of subjects who did not. Cardiovascular function was thus the major focus of this study.

About a year later, in 1948, the Framingham study was initiated with the examination of 5209 men and women aged 30

TABLE 1. Selected Longitudinal Studies of Adults Performed in The United States.

Study	Began	Ended	Nature of Sample	N	Sex and Ages at Entry	Test Interval	Test Period	N Repeat Cycles	Variables Measured
Minnesota (Keys et al., 1963, 1971)	1947	1977	Professional and businessmen—Minneapolis and St. Paul	281	M 45–54	1 yr	1 day	?	Anthropometry Behavior and personality
Duke I (Palmore, 1970, 1974)	1955	1976	Community residents.—Durham, N.C., and vicinity	260	M and F 60–94	2 yr	2 days	11	Psychiatric Psychology Physiology Anthropometry Blood chemistry Social history
Duke II (Palmore, 1981)	1968	1976	Community residents selected from register of Health Insurance Plan—Raleigh, N.C.	502	M and F 45–69	2 yr	1 day	4	Psychology Social history Personality
Normative Aging (Bell et al., 1966, 1972)	1963	Continuing	Veterans living in the Boston area	2,032	M 25–75	5 yr	3 half-days over 5-year period	3	Biochemistry Special senses Anthropometry Psychology Sociology
1000 Aviator (Oberman et al., 1965a, 1965b)	1940	1970	Cadets and officers in flight training at Pensacola, Fla.	1,056	M 20–30	Irregular	—	4	Physiology Psychomotor Psychology
NIMH (Birren et al., 1963)	1955	1967	Community residents in Philadelphia area	47	M 65–91	5 yr	2 weeks	3	Psychiatric interview Cerebral physiology Psychological tests Social history

Study	Started	Ended	Population	N	Sex and age	Interval	Duration	No.	Variables
Framingham (Dawber et al., 1963; the Framingham Study, 1968)	1948	Con-tin-uing	Community resi-dents—Fra-mingham, Mass.	5,209	M and F 30–59	2 yr	1 day	10	Blood chemistry End points—CV disease
Tecumseh (Montoye, 1975)	1959	1969	Total commu-nity—Tecum-seh, Mich.	8,641	M and F Birth to 70 + (45% under age 20)	3 yr	—	3	Anthropometry Physiology Blood chemistry Activity ques-tionnaire.
BLSA (Shock et al., 1984)	1958	Con-tin-uing	Community resi-dents—Balti-more-Washington	1,142	M 17–96	1–2 yr	2½ days	21 (as of 6/81)	Anthropometry Blood chemistry Physiology Psychology Social character-istics
Owens (Ow-ens, 1953, 1966)	1919	1961	University of Iowa fresh-men	96	M	Irreg-ular	—	3	Army Alpha test of intelli-gence
Terman (Ter-man et al., 1947, 1959)	1922	1952	Intellectually gifted chil-dren—Cali-fornia	1,525	M and F 13–19	12 yr	—	3	Intelligence tests Personality questionnaire
Schaie (Schaie et al., 1973; Schaie and Labouvie-Vief, 1974)	1956	1970	Patients from pre-paid medical plan—Seattle area	18,000	M and F 21–70	7 yr	—	3	Intelligence tests (Thurstone) Behavioral rigid-ity (Schaie)

to 59 years (Framingham, 1968, 1974, 1978; Kannel, 1978). In addition to clinical histories and physical examinations, a number of laboratory tests such as blood cholesterol, vital capacity, and electrocardiogram were administered at two-year intervals. Examinations of the same subjects are still (1982) repeated at two-year intervals among survivors. This study also sought to identify early characteristics of subjects who subsequently developed cardiovascular disease.

Over the following ten years, a number of other longitudinal studies were initiated and continued for varying periods of time with a variety of testing schedules and instruments [Duke I and II (Palmore, 1981); Normative Aging (Bell et al., 1966, 1972); National Institute of Mental Health study (NIMH) (Birren et al., 1963; Granick and Patterson, 1971); BLSA (Shock et al., 1984)]. Table 1 summarizes some of the characteristics of some of the longitudinal studies that have been carried out on adults.*

Although most of the studies listed were based on normal subjects living in the community, the characteristics and age span of the subjects, methods of selection, test interval, duration of the study, clinical histories and physical examinations, and tests administered varied widely. Some placed primary emphasis on mental tests and behavioral characteristics (Owens, 1953, 1966; Terman and Oden, 1947, 1959; Schaie and Strother, 1968; Schaie and Labouvie-Vief, 1974), while others provided observations on both physiological and psychological variables on the same subjects [the Minnesota study (Keys et al., 1963); the Duke studies (Palmore, 1981); NIMH (Birren et al., 1963; Granick and Patterson, 1971); the Normative Aging Study—Boston (Bell et al., 1966, 1972); and the BLSA (Shock et al., 1984)].

Since most of the studies limited testing procedures to a single day's visit, physiological measurements could not be made under basal conditions, and testing procedures were usually limited to determining current status

*Table 1 reviews only studies that can be compared with the BLSA. Other longitudinal studies are described by Mednick et al. (1981) and Migdel et al. (1981).

of the variable rather than its rate of return to normal levels after experimental displacement.

Difficulties in financing long-term studies also took their toll; only a few survived for 20 years or more (Berkeley growth studies, Framingham, Minnesota, Duke, Normative Aging, BLSA). These studies provide the basis for most of our knowledge about the effects of aging on physiological and psychological performance in normal human subjects residing in their communities.

The diversity of subjects, experimental designs, and methods illustrated in Table 1 indicates the difficulties in summarizing and comparing results from different studies. Each study must be examined in detail. Although it is seldom possible to regard results from one study as a replication of another because of differences in subject selection, design, tests, and methods, the studies can be compared with respect to their general conclusions. For example, although the actual level of resting blood pressure varied considerably among different longitudinal studies (Rose, 1976), all agreed that systolic blood pressure increased with age and that measurements made on the first visit were higher than those made on later visits.

THE BALTIMORE LONGITUDINAL STUDY OF AGING

Rather than offering a detailed description of each longitudinal study, this section describes the design and operation of the BLSA as a prototype. Since the study is still in progress at the Gerontology Research Center (GRC) as part of the intramural research program of the National Institute on Aging, only preliminary results illustrating some methods used in the analysis of longitudinal data can be presented. Specific variables have been chosen to illustrate methodologic strengths and pitfalls of the longitudinal method, rather than to summarize the major changes found in human aging. The Baltimore study was chosen as the prototype for the following reasons:

1. At the time of their entry into the study,

all subjects were regarded as healthy and were leading successful lives in the community.

2. Subjects are, for the most part, recruited by one another from a population with better than average educational backgrounds and socioeconomic status.

3. Subjects are highly motivated, and most are interested in the scientific aspects of the study as well as in their own aging.

4. The test battery includes a broad spectrum of clinical, anthropometric, physiological, and psychological tests and observations collected during 2 1/2 days at intervals of one to six years.

5. From 3 to 18 observations taken over a period of 22 years are available on a substantial number of subjects (about 650 for many of the variables). This characteristic, unique among longitudinal studies, makes it possible to calculate linear age regressions for a number of variables in individual subjects. This type of analysis of such physiological indicators as basal oxygen uptake and kidney function (creatinine clearance) has not previously been possible.

6. Repeated physical examinations make it possible to define the health status of each subject each time he is tested. Detailed screening for a number of specific diseases identifies subgroups of healthy subjects at each age decade.

7. I know more about the Baltimore study than any of the other studies.

The primary goal of the BLSA is to examine the effects of aging in healthy successful people (aged 20–100+) who have not suffered the disadvantages of poor education and low or marginal incomes. The first phase of the study, initiated in 1958, was limited to males because of restricted facilities; since 1978, women have also been included. Most of the subjects were recruited by other participants, many of whom had homes or summer cottages at Scientists' Cliffs, a residential community on the western shore of the Chesapeake Bay about 60 miles southeast of Baltimore. Dr. W. W. Peter, a retired Public Health Service Officer who lived at Scientists' Cliffs, firmly believed that studies of aging should be conducted on normal healthy volunteers living in the community and became an enthusiastic recruiter.

The method of recruitment generated a sample of an upper-middle-class segment of the population. An analysis completed in 1981 indicated that 84 percent of the subjects, at initial visit, were identified with professional, technical, and managerial occupations; 71 percent had bachelors' or higher academic degrees; and 73 percent (82 percent of those reporting) rated their financial situations as comfortable or better. In addition, the sample includes a high proportion of government employees: 56 percent were or had been in municipal, state, or federal positions, exclusive of public school teaching and military service. Eighty-four percent of the population (93 percent of those reporting) rated their health as good or excellent.

Test Schedule. In the early days of the study, only four subjects could be tested each week. As resources expanded, more subjects were admitted, and by 1968, the weekly capacity had risen to 12. Subjects 18 to 96 years of age were recruited. Each provided his own transportation to the Baltimore city hospitals, where for 2 1/2 days he was given an extensive series of clinical, physiological, biochemical, and psychological tests, and personality questionnaires. Each subject returned for retesting after 1 1/2–2 years.* Some of the tests (such as medical history and physical examinations, anthropometric measurements, basal oxygen uptake, creatinine clearance, and pulmonary function) were repeated at each visit. Others (psychological tests of problem-solving ability, for example) were administered at six-year intervals. A total of about 650 men, aged 18 to 96, have been tested from 3 to 18 times over the past 24 years.

Subjects—Recruitment. Although no health criteria were applied for admission to the

---

*Subjects aged 70 years and over were tested annually.

study, subjects were carefully screened for diabetes, coronary artery disease, pulmonary disease, and renal disease. From his physical examination, history, and laboratory tests, each subject was assigned to one of the following categories with respect to specific diseases: (1) disease definitely present, (2) no evidence for the presence of the disease, and (3) disease may or may not be present. Only subjects assigned to category (2) were used in the analysis of data for age differences and trends.

The application of rigorous objective criteria for the presence of specific diseases excluded an increasing proportion of the subjects as they aged. Only about 50 percent of those over the age of 80 were deemed free of coronary artery disease when they were tested under conditions of exercise stress (Shock et al., 1984) as well as under resting conditions.

As of June 30, 1977, 1088 subjects had been tested at least once. Of these, 150 were known to have died and 280 had failed to return within three years after their last visit. All but 5 of the 280 were located. Of the 275 subjects located, 56 had died. Seventy-six (35 percent) of those alive were persuaded to return to the GRC for testing, and 80 subjects (37 percent) returned a written questionnaire or were interviewed by telephone. Only two subjects refused further cooperation. Thus, of 1088 subjects who were examined at least once, the alive/dead status is known in 99.5 percent, and health and social information is available in 97.6 percent (Shock et al., 1984).

Tests. The battery of tests used in the study is designed to evaluate the association with aging of a broad spectrum of genetic, anthropometric, clinical, physiological, psychological, personality, and social variables. As Table 2 shows, they include evaluation of the performance of such organ systems as heart, kidneys, lungs, and muscles, as well as of the ability to integrate the activities of a number of organ systems in adapting to physiological stresses such as exercise and glucose loading. Age changes in body dimensions, body composition, bone density, and body fatness were also measured.

Many other functions with potential value for the understanding of aging have been studied in relatively small selected subsamples of the population. An example is the response of old and young subjects to the intravenous administration of alcohol (Vestal et al., 1977).

Data Management. The data-management system provides a flexible facility for the collection, storage, and analysis of a variety of medical, biochemical, physiological, nutritional, anthropological, psychological, and sociological observations.

The data base comprises 600,000 records, of which 400,000 are in fixed-field format (data in identifiable locations that remain the same for all persons and times). Fixed-field records include numerical results as well as numerical encoded data from medical histories and physical examinations.

Facilities available at the GRC include a Digital Equipment Corporation (DEC) PDP 11/70 computer, which utilizes MUMPS (Massachusetts General Hospital Utility Multi-Programming System) as an operating and programming system, and serves as a secure repository for the BLSA data. Scientists and managers gain access to this system through remote terminals in the laboratories and offices for the entry, review, editing, and retrieval of single record data.

Batch-processing support for computation and analysis of the data includes a local DEC VAX 11/780 computer and the NIH Bethesda computer facilities, via a Remote Job Entry System (Data General Eclipse C-150).

Software is available to extract subsets of the data from the data base system in forms suitable for analyses by standard packaged statistical programs (SAS, BMDP, SPSS, etc.) or by specific programs developed for the BLSA (Shock et al., 1984).

Thus far, only a small part of the accumulated data has been analyzed. GRC investigators welcome the collaboration of other scientists interested in longitudinal studies of aging in adults.

TABLE 2. Tests and Observations Administered to Subjects of the BLSA. (Tests Repeated Three or More Times at 1½- to 6-year Intervals.)

	Test Interval in Years
I. Clinical Evaluation—History and Physical Examination	1½ to 2
1. Clinical urinalysis	1½ to 2
2. Hemogram (Hb, V_c, white cells, differential count)	1½ to 2
3. Serological test for syphilis	6
4. Cornell Medical Index Health Questionnaire (195 questions)	6
II. Genetic Characteristics	
1. Family history (updated at each visit)	1½ to 2
2. Taste test (phenylthiocarbamate)	One visit only
3. Blood types (ABO, MN, Rh; Kell, Kidd, and Duffy factors)	One visit only
4. Dermatoglyphics of hand	One visit only
5. Handedness—hand, foot, eye preference	One visit only
III. Clinical Chemistry Tests	
1. Total serum protein, albumin, and globulin	1½ to 2
2. Serum cholesterol	1½ to 2
3. Serum triglycerides	1½ to 2
IV. Body Structure and Composition	
1. Anthropometry (height and weight, 8 diameters, 12 circumferences, 8 lengths, 9 measurements of skin-fold thickness)	1½ to 2
2. Bone density (hand x-ray, photon scan)	1½ to 2
3. Behenke index of components of body mass (fat, muscle, bone)	1½ to 2
4. Basal oxygen uptake	1½ to 2
V. Nutrition	
1. Dietary habits	6
2. Diet diaries	6
VI. Neuromotor Function and Exercise	
1. Tapping test	1½ to 2
2. Reaction time	
a. Touch	Irregular
b. Auditory	Irregular
3. Reflex time	2 to 4
4. Nerve conduction velocity	2 to 4
5. Physical work—O_2 consumption	Irregular
a. Strength tests	1½ to 2
b. Maximum work rate (cranking)	Irregular
c. Maximum O_2 uptake during exercise	Irregular
VII. Renal Function	
1. 24-hour creatinine clearance	1½ to 2
VIII. Pulmonary Function[a]	
1. Vital capacity	1½ to 2
2. Pulmonary subdivisions	1½ to 2
3. Maximum breathing capacity	1½ to 2
4. Smoking history	Updated at each visit
5. Chest x-ray	5 to 6
IX. Cardiovascular Function[a]	
1. 12-lead resting ECG	1½ to 2
2. Exercise ECG	1½ to 2
a. Double Master test (1960–1968)	1½ to 2
b. Treadmill test (1968–present)	1½ to 2
3. Echocardiograms[a] (two dimensional)	7
X. Carbohydrate Metabolism	
1. Intravenous glucose tolerance test	6
2. Cortisone glucose tolerance test	6

(*Continued*)

TABLE 2. (*Cont.*)

	Test Interval in Years
3. Oral glucose tolerance test	
1.75 g/kg body wt	6
40 g/m² surface area	6
4. Intravenous tolbutamide response test	6
5. Glucose clamp test[a]	6
XI. Sense Organs and Perception	
1. Eye tonography	1½ to 2
2. Visual screening test (acuity, depth vision, color discrimination, phoria)	3 to 4
3. Audiometry	2 to 4
XII. Cognitive Functions	
1. Verbal learning (serial learning; paired associates)	6
2. Southern California tests of mental ability	6
3. Army Alpha examination (forms A and B)	6 to 8
4. Vocabulary test (Wechsler)	6 to 8
5. Benton Visual Retention Test	6 to 8
6. Logical problem solving (reasoning)	6 to 8
7. Concept identification	6 to 8
XIII. Personality Characteristics	
1. Guilford-Zimmerman Temperament Survey	6 to 12
2. Activities and Attitudes Questionnaire (Burgess-Caven-Havighurst)	8 to 10
3. Marital and sexual experience (retrospective)	One visit only

[a]Other tests were administered to selected subjects.

RESULTS FROM THE BALTIMORE LONGITUDINAL STUDY OF AGING

During the early years of the BLSA, when repeated observations were not yet available for longitudinal analysis, many cross-sectional studies of age differences in a variety of physiological and psychological functions were published. These studies, conducted on healthy community-residing subjects carefully screened to eliminate data from subjects with evidence of specific diseases (heart, pulmonary, renal, or metabolic), have been useful contributions to gerontology (Shock et al., 1984). However, only those studies in which longitudinal analyses have also been made will be discussed here.

A unique characteristic of the BLSA is the possibility of calculating age regressions of specific variables for individual subjects. Figure 3 provides plots of 6–9 serial observations of creatinine clearance in four subjects, to illustrate the method. Although discontinuities in the progressive changes with time may be present in some individuals, the linear regression of the measure-

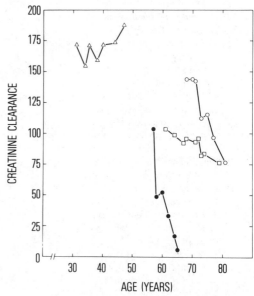

Figure 3. Serial measurements of creatinine clearance (milliliters per minute) in four individual men. △, subject 199, age regression: +1.006 ml/min/yr; □, subject 101, age regression: −1.425 ml/min/yr; o——o, subject 554, age regression: −6.179 ml/min/yr; •——•, subject 123—subject showed clinical evidence of renal disease at second testing, age regression −11.233 ml/min/yr.

ments on time was selected as the best estimate of aging in each individual subject. The nine measurements made on subject 101 closely approximate the age regression in creatinine clearance derived from cross-sectional observations. The measurements made on this subject between the ages of 61 and 79 gave a regression on age of -1.425 ml/min/yr. In contrast, subject 199 showed a linear increase in creatinine clearance (regression coefficient of $+1.006$ ml/min/yr) over the interval of 31 to 48 years. Subject 554 shows a stable creatinine clearance from age 68 to 72 years, followed by a period of rapid fall (age regression of -6.179 ml/min/yr) from age 72 to 81. Subject 123 developed renal disease at age 57, shortly after joining the study. His rate of decline (age 57 to 65) was -11.233 ml/min/yr.

Longitudinal analyses were carried out by calculating the age regression for each individual for whom five or more observations were available. This value was used as the index of aging in the individual, and mean values for subjects at each decade were calculated. In some analyses, the mean of the individual regression was plotted as the slope of a line at the average age for the decade under consideration, as in Figure 5.

Serial observations on height and weight in adults illustrate the importance of longitudinal analyses in determining age changes in contrast to age differences. Figure 4 shows the average values for height and weight of subjects from the BLSA. These cross-sectional results indicate a gradual reduction in both height and body weight over the age span of 30 to 85 years. However, when serial observations on the same subject are analyzed, it is found that the pattern of aging in individual subjects does not follow that of the average curve. The longitudinal analysis was performed by calculating the regression of each variable (height and weight) on age for each individual subject on whom three or more observations had been made. Figure 5 summarizes the results of this analysis by plotting the average for regression slopes of age against height and weight determined in

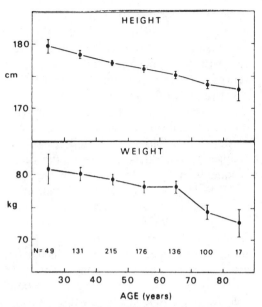

Figure 4. Regression of height and weight on age in normal males. The vertical line represents ± 1 standard deviation of the mean value. (From Shock, 1972.)

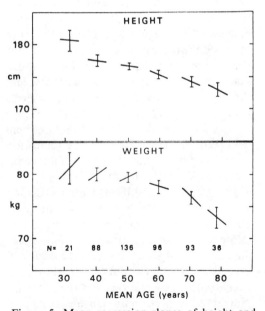

Figure 5. Mean regression slopes of height and weight on age determined from serial measurements on the same subjects (normal males) over a period of eight years. The vertical line represents ± 1 standard deviation of the mean value. (From Shock, 1972.)

individual subjects within an age decade at the mean value for the age group.

As can be seen from Figure 5, body height falls with advancing age from 30 on, and the rate of fall determined in individual subjects corresponds to the average decrement determined from average values calculated from cross-sectional observations. That is, cross-sectional and longitudinal analyses of age changes in body height agree in showing a gradual reduction in height over the age span of 20 to 90 years. In contrast, longitudinal analysis of serial observations of body weight shows that individual subjects 50 years of age or younger are gaining body weight even though the average value determined from cross-sectional analysis is falling. Subjects 55 years and older show an average loss in body weight; i.e., individuals follow the same pattern of age change as that indicated by cross-sectional data (Shock, 1972).

This method of calculating age regressions for serial observations made on a single subject was also applied to tests of kidney function (Rowe et al., 1976) and blood-cholesterol levels (Hershcopf et al., 1982). Figure 6, plotted like Figure 5, shows the average regression of creatinine clearance on age when calculated from serial observations made on the same subject. It is apparent that the age regression for individual subjects agrees reasonably well with the overall age regression determined from cross-sectional data, except that the slope of the regression determined in individual subjects tends to increase with age, as shown in Table 3.

In a group of 398 subjects from the BLSA, 8 were found to have statistically significant positive regression coefficients of creatinine clearance on age; i.e., their creatinine clearance over a ten-year interval improved with age, while average values were declining. Longitudinal observations can thus identify individual subjects who deviate markedly from the average pattern of age changes predicted from cross-sectional data (Shock et al., 1979).

Cross-sectional studies have indicated that average values for blood cholesterol rise from early adulthood to age 60–65 and then

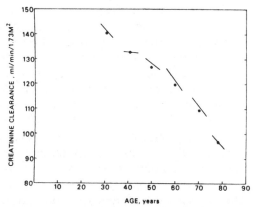

Figure 6. Comparison of cross-sectional age differences and longitudinal age changes in creatinine clearance. The dots represent the mean values for each age decade obtained from cross-sectional data. Longitudinal results are represented by line segments which indicate the mean slope of changes in creatinine clearance for each decade. Lines are drawn with the midpoints at the mean clearance for each age decade, and with their lengths, along the abscissa, representing the mean time span over which the longitudinal data were collected for each age group. (From Rowe et al., 1976.)

fall (Hershcopf et al., 1982). From cross-sectional data, it is impossible to decide whether this phenomenon is due to the effect of differential mortality (i.e., selective death of individuals with high blood-cholesterol levels) or whether the levels begin to fall in individual subjects after age 65.

Regression slopes of serum cholesterol against age were calculated for individual subjects as before. In subjects aged 30 to 50 years, the regression slopes were positive;

TABLE 3. Mean Values of Individual Regression Slopes for Creatinine Clearance on Age.[a]

Age (yr)	N (Subjects)	Mean slope ($\bar{b}$ ± S.E.) (ml/min/1.73 m²/yr)
20–39	33	−.26 ± .331
40–59	201	−.40 ± .145
60–79	149	−.92 ± .193
80–100	15	−1.51 ± .504
20–100	398	−.627 ± .109

[a]From Shock et al. (1979).

i.e., blood-cholesterol values were increasing. In subjects aged 50 to 60, the average individual regression of blood cholesterol on age was zero, whereas subjects aged 60 to 70 and 70 to 80 showed negative regressions. The data thus show clearly that blood-cholesterol values fall systematically in individual subjects over the age of 60 (Figure 7).

An unidentified environmental change that occurred in 1971–1972 induced a drop in blood-cholesterol levels of about 6 percent in all BLSA subjects of all ages. Analysis of aliquots of the original blood samples, which had been lyophilized or frozen and stored at $-20°C$, found values identical with those originally obtained when the samples were drawn. The conclusion was that the 6 percent drop could not be attributed to changes in methodology. Again, longitudinal observations made it possible to detect period changes that would otherwise have been missed.

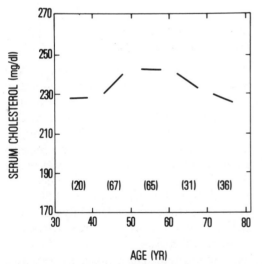

AGE (YR)

Figure 7. Longitudinal changes in serum cholesterol concentration (1963–1971). Longitudinal results are represented by line segments which indicate the mean slope of changes in serum cholesterol for individual subjects in each age decade. Each line is drawn with the midpoint at the mean cholesterol value for the decade, with the length along the abscissa representing the mean time span over which the longitudinal data were collected. Number of subjects used to compute each mean slope is given in parentheses. (From Hershcopf et al., 1982.)

These analyses are only a sample of the results that are being obtained from the longitudinal observations. The examination of the relationships between rates of change with age in different variables is also a challenge that can be met from analysis of longitudinal observations. The power of this method of analysis increases greatly with the number of observations of each variable available on each subject. Continuation of data collection and new data evolving from the women's program initiated in 1978 will make the BLSA a continuing resource for the study of human aging.

Longitudinal analysis of tests of learning, problem solving, memory, and mental performance, which were given at intervals of six years to minimize the effects of learning and practice, took a somewhat different approach. Since subjects entered the study at different times and aged as the study progressed, it was possible to analyze data from subgroups who had been born in different epochs and subjected to different environmental regimes. The methods estimated the relative effects of birth cohort, period, and age. Although no experimental design can statistically isolate the three effects that influence longitudinal observations, "educated guesses" can be made about their relative importance (Costa and McCrae, 1982).

The basic data for analysis of age changes in psychological and behavioral characteristics consisted of scores on the Guilford Zimmerman Temperament Survey (GZTS), the Benton Visual Retention Test, the Wechsler Vocabulary Test, the Army Alpha Test, and the Southern California Test of Mental Abilities. In addition, special procedures were designed to test learning ability (paired associate and serial), logical problem-solving ability, and concept identification.

Some of the findings resulting from the longitudinal analysis of these observations included the following:

1. Young and middle-aged subjects performed equally well on a vigilance task, while individuals over age 70 showed a decline over a six-year interval. [The vigilance task consisted of detecting and reporting instances

when the pointer attached to a large blank circular clock face progressed for two intervals (in 100) instead of the usual single interval.]

2. Reaction time to infrequent auditory stimuli did not slow progressively over the entire age span. The slowing occurred primarily after the age of 70.

3. Cross-sectional results showed that with increasing age, the proportion of subjects who were able to solve the logical problems included in the test battery decreased and uninformative trial solutions increased. In contrast, longitudinal measures of changes in successful solutions showed a decline in performance only for subjects who were 70 or over at the first testing. Although a significant mean decline was found for the 70+ group, the performance of some of the subjects (then 76 years and over) had not declined from that observed six years earlier (Arenberg, 1974).

4. For both paired-associate and serial learning of verbal material, age decrements were found in the oldest groups (over age 70) when serial observations were made on the same subjects (Arenberg, 1967; Arenberg and Robertson-Tchabo, 1977).

5. From age 20 to age 70, memory for visual designs, as measured by the number of errors, showed only slight impairment. However, the increase in errors became substantial in subjects who were 70 or older at the first testing (Arenberg, 1978).

6. In every age group, even among the oldest, individuals were found whose performance on mental tasks did not decline with age but was indistinguishable from that of younger adults (Arenberg, 1982).

7. No relationship was found between blood-pressure level and intellectual performance as measured by the Army Alpha Test (Costa and Shock, 1980).

8. Personality characteristics indicated by the GZTS remained remarkably stable over adult ages (Douglas and Arenberg, 1978). Only two scales (General Activity and Masculinity) showed any effects of aging in tests administered to the same subjects after a six-year average interval. Preference for fast-paced activities started to decline at age 50. Masculine interests showed a decline over the total age span (30 to 85). The results offered strong evidence for the stability of adult personality characteristics. At all ages, individual differences in personality traits were far more pronounced than age differences (Costa et al., 1980).

9. Factor analysis produced no evidence for changes in personality structure with age (McCrae et al., 1980).

10. No evidence was found to support the claim that old people become hypochondriacs (Costa and McCrae, 1980).

11. Enduring personality dispositions preceded and predicted measures of personal adjustment to aging (Costa et al., 1980).

12. The frequency of self-reported problems related to sensory, cardiovascular, musculoskeletal, and genitourinary systems increased with age, while health habits (smoking, hours of sleep, diet) improved (Costa and McCrae, 1980).

RESULTS FROM OTHER LONGITUDINAL STUDIES

Risk Factors for Cardiovascular Disease. As I have indicated, a number of longitudinal studies were originally designed to identify risk factors for the development of cardiovascular disease. The Framingham study, initiated in 1948, was based on measurements made on 5209 male and female residents of Framingham, Massachusetts, selected at random from the population aged 30 to 59 years. The study was designed to reexamine each subject every two years over a period of 20 years. Each examination included a physical examination and history, as well as a number of laboratory tests (fasting blood glucose, cholesterol, phospholipids), ECG, chest x-ray, and vital capacity.

The outstanding achievements of the study include the identification of significant risk factors for the development of coronary artery disease and the demonstration that they may be additive in their effects. The risk factors that were identified included cigarette smoking, elevated serum cholesterol and low-density lipoproteins, low vital capacity, diabetes, and obesity. In addition, certain ECG abnormalities and x-ray evidence of cardiac enlargement were predictive. These findings, which are convincing because of the longitudinal or prospective design of the study, have had a significant impact on public health programs designed to reduce the development of cardiovascular disease in the population (Kannel, 1978).

Other community-based studies such as the Tecumseh study were less successful than the Framingham study in identifying risk factors because the differences between the repeated testings were small and of questionable significance, and only three cycles of testing were carried out between 1960 and 1969 (Montoye, 1975). Major emphasis was placed on the clinical examinations of the subjects, anthropometric measurements, and physiological tests such as the cardiovascular responses to standardized exercise, pulmonary function, glucose tolerance, and measurements of blood lipids.

Even though the number of subjects was relatively small (281 businessmen), the Minneapolis study (Keys et al., 1971), which continued annual testings for 30 years (1947–1977), indicated that below the age of 65, high blood-cholesterol levels, high blood pressure, and obesity (more than 25 percent overweight for height) increased the probability of heart disease in men. Beyond age 65, however, these factors ceased to be important predictors.

The Duke Studies. Two longitudinal studies have been carried out at Duke University (Palmore, 1981). The first made observations on 276 men and women aged 60–90 years who lived in the community. Each subject was reexamined every two to four years between 1955 and 1976, when the eleventh series of tests was conducted on 43 survivors ($\bar{x} = 85.25$ years). Each subject was admitted to the Duke Medical Center for two days of medical, neurological, psychiatric, physiological, psychological, and sociological tests and examinations.

A second longitudinal study, based on 261 men and 241 women aged 45–70 years, selected at random from the participants in a major health insurance plan in the Durham, N.C., area, was initiated in 1968. Four cycles of testing were completed between 1968 and 1976, when 375 of the original 502 subjects were tested. The medical data are similar to the first study. The psychological test data included four of the subtests of the Wechsler Adult Intelligence Scale (WAIS), personality as assessed by Cattell's 16 PF (Form C), and a continuous performance task with concomitant psychophysiological measures. The sociological data included social psychological attitude scales; estimates of self-concept; questions on activities, work, and retirement; and self-evaluations of health status.

The Duke studies were unique in that they were designed to identify the physical, mental, and social processes of normal aging, so that the prediction of the occurrence of disease was not a primary concern. The Duke studies have had an important impact on gerontology since they included measurements of physiological, psychological, and social variables made on presumably healthy subjects. The design and results, summarized by Palmore (1970, 1974, 1981), emphasize the advantages of multidisciplinary longitudinal studies for the study of aging.

The inference, drawn from averages based on cross-sectional observations, that functions gradually decline over the entire adult life span was contradicted by the longitudinal finding that a substantial number of subjects aged 65 and over showed no decline in health status or intellectual function, and that some actually showed improvement in health (Maddox and Douglass, 1973, 1974) over a number of years. Even subjects who showed substantial impairment of physical functioning, EEG abnormalities, cardiovascular diseases, or impairments in vision and hearing often remained active in the community, living fairly mobile and independent lives.

The range of individual differences was very large for all measurements made in these studies. It was clear that many factors in addition to age had great influence on both physiological and psychological performance. It was also found that adults showed little change with age in personality characteristics.

The major goals of the BLSA and the first Duke study were strikingly similar—the description of age changes that occur in presumably healthy adults. The results of the two studies are also in agreement: average age changes identified by cross-sectional studies do not offer a very good prediction of the pattern of aging that may occur in an individual subject. The conclusion that aging is a highly individualized process that differs greatly among individuals and among functions is common to both.

The BLSA differs from the Duke studies primarily in the larger number of subjects studied, the broader spectrum of tests applied, and the larger number of repeated testings of the same individual. The educational level of the BLSA subjects was probably more advanced than that of the Duke subjects. The Duke studies included both men and women, whereas the BLSA included only men until 1978.

The BLSA is the only study in which the number of repetitions of a test is large enough to permit calculation of the regression of the test score on age in individual subjects. It also includes a broader spectrum of physiological and psychological tests than any of the other longitudinal studies. Thus the BLSA offers the most extensive data bank available for longitudinal analyses.

Other Longitudinal Studies. In 1963, the Veterans Administration Outpatient Clinic in Boston began the Normative Aging Study (Bell et al., 1966, 1972). Subjects were 2032 men, aged 25–75 years, living in the Boston area. All were screened for a high level of health at entry, and only four of each ten applicants were accepted after the first physical examination. Subjects came to the laboratory for three nonconsecutive half-days in each five-year cycle. First-cycle tests were administered to approximately 2000 subjects from 1963 to 1968. Cycle II covered the period 1969–1973, and Cycle III, 1974–1978.

Tests included biochemical determinations (cholesterol, glucose, etc.), clinical observation, oral medicine, neurology, the special senses, anthropometry, psychology, and sociology.

With the completion of the second cycle of testing, the differences in anthropometric measurements made after an interval of five years were analyzed. Friedlaender et al. (1977) showed that most of the temporal trends in anthropometric measurements that had been observed in previous cross-sectional analysis (Damon et al., 1972) were due not to aging but to a combination of aging and secular trends (period effects). In general, subjects of any given age measured in 1970 were bigger (taller, greater circumferences, heavier, etc.) than subjects of the same age measured 10 or 20 years earlier.

Some longitudinal studies focused their attention on young adults. Thus a group of 1000 cadets and young officers (aged 20–30 years) enrolled in flight training at Pensacola, Fla., were administered a battery of physiological and psychological tests for the first time in 1941 (Oberman et al., 1965a, 1965b). The original goal of the study was to devise a test for prediction of success in flight training. The first retests were conducted in 1951. Survivors were reexamined in 1957–58, 1963–64, and 1969–70.

To date, only the blood pressure and ECG observations from this study have been analyzed longitudinally. Although the mean blood pressure for the group showed a slight increase over the 24-year interval, blood pressure did not increase in every subject. Most subjects showed random variations over the 24 years.

Longitudinal analyses of resting ECG (Harlan et al., 1965) indicated that of 90 men entering flight training in 1940 with ECGs that by today's standards would indicate frank or borderline abnormalities, 59 had reverted to normal by 1952. Of individuals with persistent ECG abnormalities, none had developed clinically apparent heart disease at the time of the 1963–64 examinations. This important finding was made possible only by longitudinal observations.

Other longitudinal studies have emphasized the important role of general health status and physical fitness in determining performance on physiological and psychological tests. In 1955, a multidisciplinary study of aging was organized and carried out by Dr. J. E. Birren at the National Institute of Mental Health (Birren et al., 1963). The subjects were 47 male volunteers, aged 65–91 years (median age 71), who were living in the community. Subjects were admitted to the Clinical Center, NIH, for a period of two weeks during which an extensive battery of physiological and psychological tests was administered. When survivors were retested 5 and 11 years later, significantly greater decrements in intellectual performance with advancing age were found in subjects who had also developed cardiovascular disease than in those who had remained healthy (Granick and Patterson, 1971). This study emphasized the importance of disease in inducing impairments in performance in old people.

Longitudinal Studies of Physiological Variables. A number of studies have included longitudinal analyses of blood-pressure measurements made on the same subjects over periods of 20 or more years (Dock and Fukushima, 1978; Jenss, 1934; Engel and Malmstrom, 1967). All reported a small rise in systolic blood pressure from age 20 to age 60, after which there was little change.

Longitudinal studies of physiological responses to physical exercise have been made on only a few subjects. Most of these subjects have maintained an interest in the physiology of exercise over their entire lifetimes and have continued to participate in sports and regular exercise regimes. Good examples are Dr. David Bruce Dill and Dr. Sidney Robinson (Horvath, 1981). Both participated in many studies of physiological responses to maximum exercise at different times during their lives so that their physical fitness was considerably better than that of most of their age peers. The results of these tests were assembled by Dr. Horvath and are shown in Figure 8. It is clear that in the case of Dr. Dill, aging had little effect on either

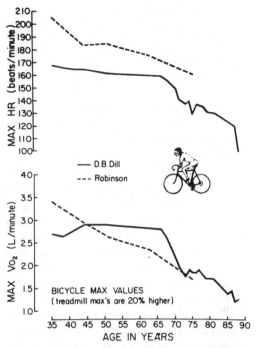

Figure 8. A comparison of values for maximum heart rate and maximum oxygen uptake during exercise obtained on David Bruce Dill (——) and Sid Robinson (---) over the age span of 35 to 87 years. (From Horvath, 1981.)

maximum heart rate or maximum oxygen uptake during exercise until after the age of 65 years. In contrast, aging with respect to these variables followed a gradual decrement over Dr. Robinson's entire life span. While no test of statistical significance can be applied, it is interesting to note the differences in the paths of aging exhibited by the two men, each of whom maintained a high level of physical training throughout his lifetime. Although oxygen consumption at moderate levels of exercise increased in proportion to the gain in body weight, efficiency did not change with age. In both, the amount of oxygen consumed per unit of work was the same at age 50 as at age 20.

WHAT HAS BEEN LEARNED ABOUT AGING FROM LONGITUDINAL STUDIES?

Although relatively few longitudinal studies of aging in adults have been completed, results lead to a number of general conclusions. The first is that relatively few individuals follow the pattern of age changes predicted from averages based on measurements made on different subjects. Aging is so highly individual that average curves give only a rough approximation of the pattern of aging followed by individuals.

There is little evidence for the existence of a single factor that regulates the rate of aging in different functions in a specific individual. Because of the large range in the performance of most physiological variables among subjects of the same chronological age, it appears that age alone is a poor predictor of performance. Subjects who perform well on physiological tests when they are first tested, however, are more likely to be alive ten years later than subjects who perform poorly.

It has also been demonstrated that age regressions can be calculated for individual subjects with respect to many measurements, provided they are repeated at short enough intervals over sufficiently long periods of time. The time required and the interval between testings depend on (a) the rate at which the variable is changing with age, (b) the variability of the measurement among different subjects, and (c) the precision with which it can be made, i.e., the instrumental error inherent in the method and the biological variability (the fluctuation in the measurement when it is repeated on the same subject at short intervals).

Longitudinal observations have shown that the rate of change with age for some variables observed in individual subjects did not differ significantly from the mean rates derived from analysis of cross-sectional observations. On the other hand, many individuals followed patterns of aging that could never have been identified from cross-sectional data alone. For example, many subjects experienced periods of 5–10 years during which their kidney function showed no significant change while the average curve was declining. In a few, kidney function actually improved over the ten-year interval when average values were falling.

Longitudinal observations have also iden-

tified subjects who showed an increasing rate of change with age in contrast to the linear decrement predicted from cross-sectional studies. In short, longitudinal observations can identify individuals who deviate markedly from aging patterns derived from cross-sectional data.

Such observations have also shown that the highly selected BLSA subjects suffered little impairment in performance on psychological tests (learning, memory, problem solving) up to the age of 70, after which small but significant decrements appeared.

These studies have also demonstrated their usefulness in predicting future effects of changes in life-style. The impairment in lung function observed among cigarette smokers at all ages disappeared within a year after the subjects stopped smoking (Edelman et al., 1966).

THE FUTURE OF LONGITUDINAL STUDIES

Gerontologists are now beginning to recognize the importance of life-styles such as diet, exercise, smoking habits, etc., in influencing health status and life span. In order to explore these effects, longitudinal observations will be required to relate such critical events as retirement, the onset of a disease state, the loss of mobility, and the death of a spouse to subsequent performance levels. Studies on women will be of special importance in view of their changing role in society and the fact that their life span is longer than that of men.

Longitudinal studies on subjects from well-defined ethnic and national groups are essential for the understanding of aging as a factor in determining health status and longevity. Determination of the long- and short-term consequences of specific events requires longitudinal observations under controlled experimental conditions.

Only three longitudinal studies are still operating in the United States—the Framingham study, the Normative Aging Study, and the BLSA—although some others may be reactivated. Future longitudinal studies must thus look to the recruitment of new groups of subjects selected for specific purposes. For example, studies of the effect of the menopause on health and behavior might be carried out by following groups of women over the age span of 45 to 55 years, the period during which most will experience this physiological event.

Similar longitudinal studies of the impact of retirement are badly needed. The effects of such differences in life-style as smoking habits, exercise regimes to maintain physical fitness, regular physical and mental activities, participation in community activities, and dietary habits may play a primary role in determining the effects of aging; they deserve intensive investigation in the future. Only longitudinal observations can identify the effects of changing environmental conditions on aging in an individual.

Above all, longitudinal observations emphasize the individuality of aging and the difficulty of projecting the future course of aging in individual subjects. Aging is a highly individual process that can be interpreted only by the longitudinal method broadened and deepened by cross-sectional and multiple-functional analysis.

REFERENCES

Arenberg, D. 1967. Regression analyses of verbal learning on adult age at two anticipation intervals. *J. Geront.* 22: 411–414.

Arenberg, D. 1974. A longitudinal study of problem solving in adults. *J. Geront.* 29: 650–658.

Arenberg, D. 1978. Differences and changes with age in the Benton Visual Retention Test. *J. Geront.* 33: 534–540.

Arenberg, D. 1982. Estimates of age changes on the Benton Visual Retention Test. *J. Geront.* 37: 87–90.

Arenberg, D. and Robertson-Tchabo, E. A. 1977. Learning and aging. *In,* J. E. Birren and K. W. Schaie (eds.), *Handbook of the Psychology of Aging,* Ch. 18, pp. 421–449. New York: Van Nostrand Reinhold.

Baldwin, B. T. 1921. The physical growth of children from birth to maturity. *Univ. Iowa Studies Child Welfare* 1: 1.

Baltes, P. B. 1968. Longitudinal and cross-sectional sequences in the study of age and generation effects. *Hum. Develop.* 11: 145–171.

Bell, B., Rose, C. L., and Damon, A. 1966. The Veterans Administration longitudinal study of healthy aging. *Gerontologist* 6: 179–184.

Bell, B., Rose, C. L., and Damon, A. 1972. The normative aging study: an interdisciplinary and longitudinal study of health and aging. *Aging Hum. Develop.* 3: 5–17.

Birren, J. E., Butler, R. N., Greenhouse, S. W., Sokoloff, L., and Yarrow, M. R. 1963. *Human Aging.* Washington, D. C.: U.S. Government Printing Office, Publ. No. 986.

Busse, E. W. and Maddox, G. L. 1980. Final report. *The Duke Longitudinal Studies. An Integrated Investigation of Aging and the Aged, Ancillary Studies, and Research Support Services, 1955–1980.* Durham, N.C.: Duke University Medical Center, Center for the Study of Aging and Human Development.

Costa, P. T. and McCrae, R. R. 1980. Somatic complaints in males as a function of age and neuroticism: a longitudinal analysis. *J. Behav. Med.* 3: 245–255.

Costa, P. T. and McCrae, R. R. 1982. An approach to the attribution of aging, period, and cohort effects. *Psychol. Bull.* 92: 238–250.

Costa, P. T., McCrae, R. R., and Arenberg, D. 1980. Enduring dispositions in adult males. *J. Personality Soc. Psychol.* 38: 793–800.

Costa, P. T. and Shock, N. W. 1980. New longitudinal data on the question of whether hypertension influences intellectual performance. *In,* M. F. Elias and D. H. P. Streeten (eds.), *Hypertension and Cognitive Processes,* pp. 83–93. Mt. Desert, Me.: Beech Hill.

Damon, A., Seltzer, H., Stoudt, H. W., and Bell, B. 1972. Age and physique in healthy white veterans at Boston. *J. Geront.* 27: 202–208.

Dawber, T. R., Kannel, W. B., and Lyell, L. P. 1963. An approach to longitudinal studies in a community: the Framingham study. *Ann. N.Y. Acad. Sci.* 107: 539–556.

Dock, D. S. and Fukushima, K. 1978. A longitudinal study of blood pressure in the Japanese, 1958–1972. *J. Chronic Dis.* 31: 669–689.

Douglas, K. and Arenberg, D. 1978. Age changes, cohort differences, and cultural change on the Guilford-Zimmerman Temperament Survey. *J. Geront.* 33: 737–747.

Edelman, N. H., Mittman, C., Norris, A. H., Cohen, B. H., and Shock, N. W. 1966. The effects of cigarette smoking upon spirometric performance of community dwelling men. *Amer. Rev. Resp. Dis.* 94: 421–429.

Engel, B. T. and Malmstrom, E. J. 1967. An analysis of blood pressure trends based on annual observations of the same subjects. *J. Chronic Dis.* 20: 29–43.

The Framingham Study: An Epidemiological Investigation of Cardiovascular Disease. 1968. Bethesda, Md.: NIH, National Heart Institute, Sects. 1 and 2; 1974. Washington, D. C.: U.S. Government Printing Office, Sect. 30, DHEW Publ. No. (NIH) 74–599; 1978. Washington, D.C.: U.S. Government Printing Office, Sect. 33, DHEW Publ. No. (NIH) 79–1671.

Friedlaender, J. D., Costa, P. T., Bosse, R., Ellis, E.,

Rhoads, J. G., and Stoudt, H. W. 1977. Longitudinal physique changes among healthy white veterans at Boston. *Hum. Biol.* 49: 541–558.

Granick, S. and Patterson, R. D. (eds.) 1971. *Human Aging II*. Washington, D.C.: U.S. Government Printing Office, DHEW Publ. No. (HSM) 71–9037.

Harlan, W. R., Graybiel, A., and Osborne, R. K. 1965. Determinants of cardiovascular disease in a young population. *Amer. J. Cardiol.* 15: 1–12.

Hershcopf, R. J., Elahi, D., Andres, R., Baldwin, H. L., Raizes, G. S., Schocken, D. D., and Tobin, J. D. 1982. Longitudinal changes in serum cholesterol in man: an epidemiologic search for an etiology. *J. Chronic Dis.* 35: 101–114.

Horvath, S. M. 1981. Aging and adaptation to stressors. *In*, S. M. Horvath and M. K. Yousef (eds.), *Environmental Physiology; Aging, Heat and Altitude*, pp. 437–451. New York: Elsevier North Holland.

Jenss, R. 1934. Age variations of systolic blood pressure in United States Army officers. *Amer. J. Hygiene* 20: 574–603.

Jones, M. C., Bayley, N., McFarlane, J. W., and Honzik, M. P. (eds.) 1971. *The Course of Human Development*. Waltham, Mass.: Xerox.

Kannel, W. B. 1978. Recent findings of the Framingham study. *Resident and Staff Physician* 24: 56–61; 64–66; 71.

Keys, A., Taylor, H. D., Blackburn, H., Brozek, J., Anderson, J. T., and Simonson, E. 1963. Coronary heart disease among Minnesota business and professional men followed fifteen years. *Circulation* 28: 381–395.

Keys, A., Taylor, H. L., Blackburn, H., Brozek, J., Anderson, J. T., and Simonson, E. 1971. Mortality and coronary heart disease among men studied for 23 years. *Arch. Intern. Med.* 128: 201–214.

Maddox, G. L. and Douglass, E. B. 1973. Self-assessment of health: a longitudinal study of elderly subjects. *J. Hlth. Soc. Behav.* 14: 87–93.

Maddox, G. L. and Douglass, E. B. 1974. Aging and individual differences; a longitudinal analysis of social, psychological and physiological indicators. *J. Geront.* 29: 555–563.

Mason, K. and Mason, W. 1973. Some methodological issues in cohort analysis of archival data. *Amer. Sociol. Rev.* 38: 242–258.

McCrae, R. R., Costa, P. T., and Arenberg, D. 1980. Constancy of adult personality structure in males: longitudinal, cross-sectional, and times-of-measurement analyses. *J. Geront.* 35: 877–883.

Mednick, S. A., Baert, A. E., and Bachmann, B. P. (eds.) 1981. *Prospective Longitudinal Research. An Empirical Basis for the Primary Prevention of Psychosocial Disorders*. New York: Oxford University Press.

Migdel, S., Abeles, R. P., and Sherrod, L. R. 1981. *An Inventory of Longitudinal Studies of Middle and Old Age*. New York: Social Science Research Council.

Montoye, H. J. 1975. *Physical Activity and Health: An Epidemiologic Study of an Entire Community*. Englewood Cliffs, N.J.: Prentice Hall.

Nesselroade, J. R. and Baltes, P. B. 1979. *Longitudinal Research in the Study of Behavior and Development*. New York: Academic Press.

Oberman, A., Lane, N. E., Mitchell, R. E., and Graybiel, A. 1965a. *The Thousand Aviator Study. Distributions and Inter-correlations of Selected Variables*. Pensacola, Fla.: U.S. Naval School of Aviation Medicine, Monogr. 12.

Oberman, A., Mitchell, R. E., and Graybiel, A. 1965b. *The Thousand Aviator Study. Methodology*. Pensacola, Fla.: U.S. Naval School of Aviation Medicine, Monogr. 11.

Owens, W. A. 1953. Age and mental abilities; a longitudinal study. *Genetic Psychol. Monogr.* 48: 3–54.

Owens, W. A. 1966. Age and mental abilities: a second adult follow-up. *J. Educ. Psychol.* 57: 311–325.

Palmore, E. (ed.) 1970. *Normal Aging*. Durham, N.C.: Duke University Press.

Palmore, E. (ed.) 1974. *Normal aging II*. Durham, N.C.: Duke University Press.

Palmore, E. 1978. When can age, period, and cohort be separated? *Soc. Forces* 57: 282–295.

Palmore, E. 1981. *Social Patterns in Normal Aging: Findings from the Duke Longitudinal Study*. Durham, N.C.: Duke University Press.

Riley, M., Johnson, M., and Foner, A. 1972. *Aging and Society*, Vol. III. New York: Russell Sage Foundation.

Rose, C. L. (ed.) 1976. *Collaboration among Longitudinal Aging Studies*. Boston, Mass.: V.A. Outpatient Clinic, Publ. No. 8.

Rowe, J. W., Andres, R., Tobin, J. D., Norris, A. H., and Shock, N. W. 1976. The effect of age on creatinine clearance in men: a cross-sectional and longitudinal study. *J. Geront.* 31: 155–163.

Schaie, K. W. 1965. A general model for the study of developmental problems. *Psychol. Bull.* 64: 92–107.

Schaie, K. W. 1977. Quasi-experimental research designs in the psychology of aging. *In*, J. E. Birren and K. W. Schaie (eds.), *Handbook of the Psychology of Aging*, Ch. 2, pp. 39–58. New York: Van Nostrand Reinhold.

Schaie, K. W. and Labouvie-Vief, G. 1974. Generational versus ontogenetic components of change in adult cognitive functioning; a fourteen-year cross-sequential study. *Develop. Psychol.* 10: 305–320.

Schaie, K. W., Labouvie, G. V., and Barrett, T. J. 1973. Selective attrition effects in a fourteen-year study of adult intelligence. *J. Geront.* 28: 328–334.

Schaie, K. W. and Strother, C. R. 1968. A cross-sequential study of age changes in cognitive behavior. *Psychol. Bull.* 70: 671–680.

Schlesselman, J. J. 1973a. Planning a longitudinal study. I. Sample size determination. *J. Chronic Dis.* 26: 553–560.

Schlesselman, J. J. 1973b. Planning a longitudinal study. II. Frequency of measurement and study duration. *J. Chronic Dis.* 26: 561–570.

Schulsinger, F., Knop, J., and Mednick, S. A. 1981. *Longitudinal Research*. Hingham, Mass.: Kluwer-Nijhoff.

Shock, N. W. 1942. Standard values for basal oxygen consumption in adolescents. *Amer. J. Dis. Child*. 64: 19–32.

Shock, N. W. 1943. The effect of menarche on basal physiological functions in girls. *Amer. J. Physiol*. 139: 288–292.

Shock, N. W. 1972. Energy metabolism, caloric intake and physical activity of the aging. *In*, L. A. Carlson (ed.), *Nutrition in Old Age*. Uppsala: Almqvist & Wiksell.

Shock, N. W., Andres, R., Norris, A. H., and Tobin, J. D. 1979. Patterns of longitudinal changes in renal function. *In*, H. Orimo, K. Shimada, M. Iriki, and D. Maeda (eds.), *Recent Advances in Gerontology*, pp. 525–527. Amsterdam: Excerpta Medica.

Shock, N. W., Greulich, R. C., Andres, R., Arenberg, D., Costa, P. T., Jr., Lakatta, E. G., and Tobin, J. D. 1984. *Normal Human Aging: The Baltimore Longitudinal Study of Aging*. Washington, D.C.: U.S. Government Printing Office, NIH Publ. No. 84–2450.

Shuttleworth, F. K. 1937. Sexual maturation and the physical growth of girls age six to nineteen. *Monogr. Soc. Res. Child Develop*. 2: No. 5.

Shuttleworth, F. K. 1939. The physical and mental growth of girls and boys age six to nineteen in relation to age at maximum growth. *Monogr. Soc. Res. Child Develop*. 4: No. 3.

Terman, L. M. and Oden, M. H. 1947. *Genetic Studies of Genius*, Vol. 4: *The Gifted Child Grows up*. Stanford, Calif.: Stanford University Press.

Terman, L. M. and Oden, M. H. 1959. *Genetic Studies of Genius*, Vol. 5: *The Gifted Group at Mid-life*. Stanford, Calif.: Stanford University Press.

Tobin, J. D. 1981. Physiological indices of aging. *In*, M. Marois (ed.), *Aging: A Challenge to Science and Society*, Vol. 1, pp. 286–295. London: Oxford University Press.

Vestal, R. E., McGuire, E. A., Tobin, J. D., Andres, R., Norris, A. H., and Mezey, E. 1977. Aging and ethanol metabolism. *Clin. Pharmacol. Therap*. 21: 343–354.

27
PHARMACOLOGY AND AGING*

Robert E. Vestal
Veterans Administration Medical Center
Boise, Idaho
University of Washington School of Medicine
Seattle, Washington
and
Gary W. Dawson
Idaho State University College of Pharmacy
Pocatello, Idaho
Veterans Administration Medical Center
Boise, Idaho

INTRODUCTION

The elderly are a more heterogeneous group than the young in many ways. Physiological aging does not necessarily parallel chronological aging. Aside from overt pathology, which often plays the dominant role, it is physiological aging which seems to underlie age differences in the fate and action of drugs. Statistically valid age differences or correlations with age can be demonstrated; however, biological variation precludes broad generalizations regarding the effects of age on drug disposition and drug response. It should be emphasized that all currently available studies in gerontological pharmacology in both man and experimental animals are cross-sectional rather than longitudinal in design. As such, they can only provide information about age *differences* as opposed to *changes* with age or the effects of *aging* (Rowe, 1977). Although Lasagna's appeal (1956) for "the systematic collection of data" on the effects of age on the fate and action of drugs was largely unheeded for more than a decade, there is now a rapidly expanding clinical and basic science literature in the field of gerontological pharmacology (Triggs and Nation, 1975a; Crooks et al., 1976; Richey and Bender, 1977; Vestal, 1978; Schmucker, 1979; O'Malley et al., 1980; Plein and Plein, 1981; Ouslander, 1981; Greenblatt et al., 1982; Thompson et al., 1983), including several monographs (Crooks and Stevenson, 1979; Petersen et al., 1979; Lamy, 1980; Jarvik et al., 1981; Conrad and Bressler, 1982; Vestal, 1984). The purpose of this chapter is to review the general aspects (epidemiology, adverse drug reactions, compliance) and the physiological, pharmacokinetic (the time course of

*The authors are grateful to Louise Leary, Gayle Cory, and Patricia Martinez for their assistance with manuscript preparation. We also wish to acknowledge that some of the tabular material in this chapter was expanded and updated based on material presented in the excellent review of Plein and Plein (1981). Supported in part by the Veterans Administration and by a grant (AG 2901) from the National Institutes of Health.

drug absorption, distribution, and elimination), and pharmacodynamic (drug response) aspects of drug use in the elderly.

GENERAL ASPECTS OF DRUG USE IN THE ELDERLY

Demographic Trends

In developed countries, trends show that the proportion of elderly in the population has been rising steadily over the past several decades. This is due to a combination of falling birth rate and medical, economic, and social factors which favor longevity. Although 11 percent of the American population, more than 23 million people, is over 65 years of age, this older age group spends more than three billion dollars per year on prescription and nonprescription drugs (Fisher, 1980). This expenditure represents 20 to 25 percent of the total national expenditure for drugs. It is projected that by the year 2030 this age group will nearly double in size, which means that expenditures for drugs by the elderly may make up over 40 percent of the national total. In the United Kingdom, where the elderly represent only 12 percent of the population, they are already responsible for approximately 30 percent of the expenditures for drugs (O'Malley et al., 1980). Such figures emphasize that the needs of geriatric patients will constitute an increasingly important aspect of medical care for the future.

Patterns of Drug Use and Drug Prescribing

In a study of an ambulatory, community-dwelling population over 60 years of age in Albany, New York, Chien et al. (1978) found that the most commonly used prescribed and nonprescribed medications were analgesics (67 percent), cardiovascular preparations (34 percent), laxatives (31 percent), vitamins (29 percent), antacids (26 percent), and antianxiety agents (22 percent). Of the 244 individuals interviewed, 83 percent were taking two or more preparations. Over-the-counter (OTC) and prescription drugs, respectively, accounted for 40 and 60 percent of the medications used. In a similar study conducted in Washington, D.C., Guttman (1978) found that the most frequently used classes of prescribed medications were cardiovascular agents (61 percent), sedatives and tranquilizers (17 percent), antiarthritic agents (12 percent), and gastrointestinal agents (11 percent). Over-the-counter drugs were used by 69 percent of this sample of 447 subjects. Of these, 52 percent were using analgesics, 8 percent were using vitamins, and 7 percent were using laxatives. These two studies indicate that nonnarcotic analgesics are the most commonly consumed nonprescription drugs, and that cardiovascular agents and psychoactive substances are the most commonly prescribed medications. Data for ambulatory patients in other countries are similar (World Health Organization, 1981). For example, among the oldest patients (76 years of age and older) in one London practice, 87 percent were receiving prescribed drug therapy, and 34 percent were taking three or more different drugs each day (Law and Chalmers, 1976).

In long term care facilities, the pattern is somewhat different. In one 200-bed nursing home, psychotropics were shown to be prescribed to 61 percent of the patients, followed by diuretics and antihypertensives to 46 percent, analgesics to 44 percent, other cardiovascular agents such as digoxin and nitroglycerin to 39 percent, and antimicrobials to 31 percent (Kalchthaler et al., 1977). Of the psychotropics, haloperidol was the most frequently prescribed major tranquilizer (86 percent), diazepam the most frequently prescribed minor tranquilizer (82 percent), and flurazepam and most frequently prescribed hypnotic (80 percent). A study suggesting misuse of antipsychotic drugs in nursing homes (Ray et al., 1980) matched each resident with an ambulatory person enrolled in Medicaid throughout the study year. Among nursing home patients, central nervous system (CNS) drugs were the most frequently prescribed medications (74 percent of patients). In contrast, only 36 percent of the ambulatory comparison group received CNS drugs. Nursing home patients often received prescriptions for drugs from multiple categories of CNS drugs: 34 percent from two or more different categories, 9 percent from three or more, and 1.6 percent from four categories. The most frequent combination was an antipsychotic and a hypnotic, most commonly thioridazine and flurazepam. The next most frequent combination was a minor tranquilizer and a hypnotic, usually diazepam and chloral hydrate. The three most frequently prescribed antipsychotic drugs were thioridazine, chlorpromazine, and haloperidol. The authors suggest that these drugs may be used to mold patients into the institutional routine. Another study suggested that psychoactive drugs may be prescribed more often to patients with superior mentation and minimal physical disabilities than to those who are more severely disabled (Ingman et al., 1975).

Data for acute care hospitals suggest that drug prescribing varies widely in different countries. A study by the Boston Collaborative Drug Surveillance Program (Lawson and Jick, 1976) showed that on the average, medical inpatients (including geriatric patients) in the United States received 9.1 drugs per hospital admission compared to 7.1 in Canada, 6.3 in Israel, 5.8 in New Zealand, and 4.6 in Scotland. American patients were discharged with 2.1 drugs in comparison to 1.3 in Scotland. The explanation for such differences is not clear. Unfortunately, epidemiological data are often difficult to evaluate because of the absence of uniform methodology. Since drug consumption varies widely in different countries, the Nordic countries have used the defined daily dose (DDD) to make comparisons within and between countries (Bergman et al., 1980). This approach should be adopted for general use by epidemiologists comparing drug utilization in large populations or age groups.

Adverse Drug Reactions

Although statistics vary considerably, a number of studies from different countries (Table 1) seem to indicate that adverse drug reactions are a common problem among the elderly. The incidence of adverse drug reactions is increased by two- or threefold in older patients (age $\geq$ 60 years) compared to younger patients (age $\leq$ 30 years). Most studies have been conducted in a hospital setting. However, adverse drug reactions leading to hospital admissions have been documented for outpatients as well. Of 236 consecutive patients admitted to a psychogeriatric unit, 37 (16 percent) were experiencing direct adverse effects of psychotherapeutic medications (Learoyd, 1972): 7

TABLE 1. Relationship of Age to Incidence of Adverse Drug Reactions.

Patient Age Group (yr)	UNITED STATES[a] Number of Patients		NORTHERN IRELAND[b] Number of Patients		ISRAEL[c] Number of Patients	
	Receiving Drugs	Experiencing Reactions	Receiving Drugs	Experiencing Reactions	Receiving Drugs	Experiencing Reactions
<20	62	7 (11.3%)			72	3 (4.2%)
20–29	71	7 (9.9%)	100	3 (3.0%)	224	11 (4.9%)
30–39	107	12 (11.2%)	122	7 (5.7%)	351	9 (2.6%)
40–49	136	16 (11.8%)	159	12 (7.5%)	352	10 (2.8%)
50–59	126	18 (14.3%)	222	18 (8.1%)	376	22 (5.9%)
60–69	127	20 (15.7%)	252	27 (10.7%)	703	34 (4.8%)
70–79	60	11 (18.3%)	178	38 (21.3%)	645	56 (8.7%)
>80	25	6 (24%)			210	22 (10.5%)
TOTALS	714	97 (13.6%)	1033	105 (10.2%)	2933	167 (5.7%)

[a]Baltimore (from Seidl et al., 1966).
[b]Belfast (from Hurwitz, 1969).
[c]Jerusalem (from Levy et al., 1980).

patients were excessively sedated or confused; 14 patients had disinhibition reactions with restlessness, agitation, paranoia, and aggression; and 16 patients had psychic disturbances associated with respiratory depression, hypotensive syncope, urinary retention, and gastrointestinal ileus. All improved and were discharged from the hospital when their medication was significantly reduced or stopped. In another study, 3 percent of 6063 consecutive admissions were necessitated by drug-induced illness (Caranasos et al., 1974). Forty-one percent of these 177 patients were over age 60.

Predisposing factors to adverse drug reactions include advanced age, female sex, small body size, hepatic or renal insufficiency, multiple drug therapy, and previous drug reactions (Jue, 1984). Although the epidemiological data certainly suggest that the elderly are more vulnerable than the young to adverse drug reactions, the magnitude of the problem is difficult to evaluate because many of the studies either have methodological weaknesses or are prone to misinterpretation (Klein et al., 1981; Jue, 1984). For example, control for disease severity has not been considered in the data analysis. The true population at risk is not the total number of patients admitted to the hospital but the total number of persons in the immediate community who are taking drugs (Klein et al., 1981). Until studies are performed which are designed to control for disease severity, prevalence of drug use, and type of drug consumed as well as age, the relationship between age and adverse drug reactions will be limited to an apparent association.

Compliance with Drug Therapy

In his review of more than 50 studies of patient compliance, Blackwell (1972) found that complete failure to take medication occurred in 25 to 50 percent of outpatients. Based on a careful review of drug histories in 178 chronically ill, ambulatory patients aged 60 or older in a general medical clinic in New York, Schwartz et al. (1962) found that 59 percent made medication errors and

26 percent made potentially serious errors. Patients who made errors were more likely to make multiple mistakes than single mistakes. These patients were also more likely to be older than 75 years, to live alone, to have several different diagnoses, and to be having difficulty coping with their environment. The average number of errors was 2.6 per error-making patient. Omission of medication (47 percent) was the most frequent error, followed by inaccurate knowledge about medications (20 percent), use of medications not prescribed by a clinician (17 percent), errors of dosage (10 percent), and improper sequence or timing (6 percent). Almost identical data were obtained by similar techniques in a Seattle area clinic (Neely and Patrick, 1968). In a study of geriatric patients ten days after hospitalization, Parkin et al. (1976) found that 66 of 130 patients deviated from the drug regimen prescribed at discharge. Noncomprehension or lack of a clear understanding of a regimen (in 46 patients) was actually a greater problem than noncompliance or failure to follow instructions (in 20 patients). A Swedish study has shown that in patients over age 65, the rate of noncompliance doubles (32 percent versus 69 percent) when more than three drugs are prescribed, whereas in patients under age 65, the rates are similar (28 percent versus 33 percent) (Bergman and Wilholm, 1981).

Although medication errors are prevalent among elderly patients, studies using objective measures of compliance indicate that they are not necessarily more prone to noncompliance than younger patients. When studies of compliance are performed in large heterogeneous groups, the rates for different age groups are almost always similar, and in several studies the highest compliance rate was in patients over age 70 (Weintraub, 1981). Recalculation of the data from a study of compliance with antacid therapy on the basis of age revealed that 62 percent of patients over age 60 were adherent to the prescribed regimen, compared to only 34 percent of patients under 45 and 54 percent in the middle age group (Weintraub, 1981). Patient compliance with digoxin therapy was ascertained in 101 outpatients by asking the patients how often they missed taking digoxin and correlating the response with serum digoxin concentrations. Of the patients 60 years of age or older, 70 percent were compliant and had a mean serum level of 1.1 ng/ml. Similar results were found in younger patients (Weintraub et al., 1973).

Noncompliance or nonadherence to drug therapy does not always result in adverse consequences. The concept of intelligent noncompliance has been proposed to account for the fact that some patients alter prescribed therapy, usually by decreasing the prescribed dose or by not taking their medication at all, in order to minimize adverse effects (Weintraub, 1976). Studies in Finland and the United States have found that many elderly patients adjust their medications according to their symptoms. In the digoxin study, about 10 percent of patients were judged to be intelligently noncompliant (Weintraub et al., 1973), but a more complete understanding of the prevalence and the factors influencing this interesting aspect of patient behavior awaits further investigation.

EFFECTS OF AGE ON DRUG METABOLISM AND PHARMACOKINETICS

Sometimes subtle but important physiological changes occur with "normal" aging, which are independent of the multiple disease states so often present in geriatric patients. Such age-related changes might be expected to alter the response to drugs by influencing drug disposition. Although it is certainly not true for all drugs, older patients seem to be more susceptible to both the therapeutic and the toxic effects of many drugs. However, except for drugs predominantly eliminated from the body by the kidney, it is not possible to generalize on the type, magnitude, or importance of the age differences in pharmacokinetics which have been reported in the literature. Indeed, some studies of the same drug have produced conflicting data. This is probably due to the relatively small numbers of subjects studied, and to

differences in subject selection criteria and protocol design. Apparent age differences in drug disposition are multifactorial and influenced by environmental and genetic, as well as physiological and pathological, factors. Some of these are summarized in Table 2 and are discussed in more detail in the sections which follow.

General Concepts of Pharmacokinetics and Drug Metabolism

Since some readers will not be familiar with the terminology used to describe various aspects of drug disposition and metabolism, this section is intended to be a brief primer. Several excellent references should be consulted for a more comprehensive discussion of this topic (LaDu et al., 1971; Goldstein et al., 1974; Greenblatt and Koch-Weser, 1975; Gibaldi and Levy, 1976). Pharmacokinetics is the study of the time course of the absorption, distribution, metabolism, and excretion of drugs and their metabolites from the body, and the relationship of drug disposition to the intensity and duration of therapeutic effect. Mathematical relationships are often used to delineate models which help describe and interpret physiological and pharmacological observations. Such pharmacokinetic models vary considerably in complexity from the simple "one-compartment" model, which assumes that a drug is instantaneously distributed throughout the fluids and tissues of the body, to more complex multicompartmental models, which usually include a central compartment of small apparent volume and one or more peripheral compartments into which drugs seem to distribute more slowly. The central compartment probably consists of total blood or plasma volume and the extracellular fluid of highly perfused organs such as heart, lungs, liver, kidneys, endocrine organs, and brain. Drugs distribute throughout this compartment within a few minutes. The peripheral compartments are composed of less highly perfused organs, such as fat, muscle, skin, and bone, into which drugs distribute more slowly. The characteristics of

TABLE 2. Summary of Factors Affecting Drug Disposition in the Elderly.

Pharmacokinetic Parameter	Age-related Physiological Changes	Pathological Conditions	Environmental Factors
Absorption	Increased gastric pH Decreased absorptive surface Decreased splanchnic blood flow Decreased gastrointestinal motility	Achlorhydria Diarrhea Gastrectomy Malabsorption syndromes Pancreatitis	Antacids Anticholinergics Cholestyramine Drug interactions Food or meals
Distribution	Decreased cardiac output Decreased total body water Decreased lean body mass Decreased serum albumin Increased body fat	Congestive heart failure Dehydration Edema or ascites Hepatic failure Malnutrition Renal failure	Drug interactions Protein binding displacement
Metabolism	Decreased hepatic mass Decreased enzyme activity Decreased hepatic blood flow	Congestive heart failure Fever Hepatic insufficiency Malignancy Malnutrition Thyroid disease Viral infection or immunization	Dietary composition Drug interactions Induction of metabolism Inhibition of metabolism Insecticides Tobacco (smoking)
Excretion	Decreased renal blood flow Decreased glomerular filtration rate Decreased tubular secretion	Hypovolemia Renal insufficiency	Drug interactions

blood flow and the physical-chemical properties of a particular drug determine its rate of entry and affinity for the tissues and fluids comprising these compartments. The time course of plasma or blood concentrations after bolus or even slow intravenous administration is generally described by a two-compartment system. In the case of intramuscular or oral administration, a third compartment (the injection site or the gastrointestinal tract) is sometimes added. However, the simple one-compartment model is often sufficient for analysis of absorption data.

In general, either drugs are metabolized by the liver to less active or inactive compounds prior to elimination by the kidney, or they are excreted by the kidney unchanged. The process of drug metabolism by the liver and excretion by the kidney occurs in the central compartment and usually proceeds via "first-order" processes, meaning that the rate of elimination is proportional to the amount of drug in the compartment. Rates of transfer between compartments are also usually assumed to be first order. The enzymatic systems in the liver may become saturated at plasma levels typically achieved in clinical practice. Phenytoin, salicylates, and ethanol are good examples. When this occurs, "zero-order" kinetics predominate, and the amount of drug removed per unit time approaches or becomes a fixed amount (as opposed to a fractional amount or percentage) until concentrations decline to levels where the elimination process again becomes first order. Thus, biotransformation (drug metabolism) follows classical Michaelis-Menten kinetics. Enzyme activity, affinity for the drug (substrate), and drug concentration determine its rate of conversion to metabolite(s) or conjugated form(s). Other factors which influence metabolism include cofactor availability and product inhibition. The enzyme reactions have been classified into Phase I and Phase II reactions. Phase I reactions include oxidation, reduction, and hydrolysis. Phase II reactions include glycine, sulfate, and glucuronide conjugation and acetylation. Oxidation reactions of many drugs take place in the microsomal fraction of liver homogenates, consisting of fragments of endoplasmic reticulum. This microsome fraction contains a hemoprotein (or family of hemoproteins) known as cytochrome P-450, which acts as the terminal oxidase for a variety of oxidative reactions that drugs undergo. Measurements of the levels of microsomal protein and cytochrome P-450, the activity of the major flavoproteins such as NADPH–cytochrome c reductase, and rates of metabolism of various model substrates have been used to assess the influence of age on hepatic drug metabolism. Oxidation of some compounds, such as the alcohols, occurs in the soluble fraction of liver. Reduction, hydrolysis, and conjugation reactions also occur in this fraction.

The most commonly used pharmacokinetic terms should also be defined. *Absorption* is the passage of drug from its site of administration into the circulation. It should be distinguished from *bioavailability* (F) which refers to the relative amount of drug from an administered dosage form which actually enters the systemic circulation. After intravenous administration, the bioavailability is 100 percent, but it may be significantly less after oral administration due to first-pass metabolism by the liver and, to a much lesser extent, the intestine. Measures of the rate of absorption include the rate constant of absorption (k_{abs} or k_a), the half-life of absorption ($t_{1/2abs}$), and the time to peak concentration (t_{Cmax}). The *volume of distribution* (Vd) is the hypothetical volume of body fluid that would be required to dissolve the total amount of drug at the same concentration as that found in the blood. For most drugs, it is an apparent rather than a real volume. It is small for a drug which is highly bound to plasma proteins and not widely distributed in the tissues, but large for drugs which diffuse easily into peripheral tissues. The *biological* or *elimination half-life* ($t_{1/2}$) is the time interval required for elimination of one-half of the amount of drug in the body after distribution has been achieved. It takes five half-lives for a drug to accumulate to 97 percent of its plateau or steady state plasma concentration after initiation of chronic drug administration. After discontinuation of the drug it takes the same amount of time for its plasma level to fall to 3 percent of its plateau value. *Clearance* (Cl) is a more direct index of drug elimination from the systemic circulation and represents the volume of blood or plasma from which the drug is completely eliminated per unit of time. It is directly proportional to the volume of distribution and inversely proportional to the half-life. Total clearance is the sum of hepatic and extrahepatic, such as renal or gastrointestinal, clearance. With these general concepts in mind, let us turn now to a discussion of what is known about the effect of old age on the disposition of drugs.

Drug Absorption

The effect of aging on intestinal drug absorption has not been exhaustively studied in man. As reviewed by Bender (1968), Crooks et al. (1976), Vestal (1978), and Stevenson et al. (1979), alterations in gastric pH, gastric emptying, gastrointestinal absorptive surface, and motility would be expected to influence drug absorption (Table 2). There is relatively little evidence, however, for an overall age-related decline in absorption, despite conjecture that drug absorption may be impaired or delayed in the elderly. Recently, studies have appeared in the literature which suggest that there may be age-related differences in the extent and rate of absorption, but only with selected drugs (Table 3).

A number of age-associated changes may take place in the gastrointestinal tract which might be expected to modify drug absorption (Bender, 1968; Bhanthumnavin and Schuster, 1977). Gastric pH is increased, and

TABLE 3. Effect of Age on Drug Absorption Following Oral Administration.

					EXTENT OF ABSORPTION			RATE OF ABSORPTION			
Drug	Age Group	Mean Age (yr)	Range (yr)	N(sex)	$AUC_{0\to\infty}$ ($\mu g \cdot$ min/ml)	Bioavailability	Dose Excreted in Urine (%)	k_{abs} (hr^{-1})	$t_{1/2abs}$ (min)	t_{cmax} (hr)	Reference
Acetaminophen	Young	24.0	22–27	6			73			0.67	Triggs et al., 1975b
	Old	88.9	73–91	7			60			0.74	Fulton et al., 1979
	Young	23.9		11		0.98					
	Old	75.8		12		0.95					
	Young	28.4	22–39	16		0.79 (tablet)			12.6	0.79	Divoll et al., 1982b
						0.87 (elixir)			8.6	0.52	
	Old	70.7	61–78	12		0.72 (tablet)			8.2	0.69	
						0.80 (elixir)			6.1	0.54	
Ampicillin	Young	28.0	22–46	6	983.4			0.61		2.08	Triggs et al., 1980
	Old	74.2	68–76	5	3463.8[a]			0.72		3.07	
Antipyrine (in combination with acetylsalicylic acid and d-propoxyphene)	Young		24–37	8	4.5×10^3					1.17	Melander et al., 1978
	Old		74–75	6	6.1×10^3					1.0	
Aspirin	Young	29		6				4.3		0.7	Castleden et al., 1977b
	Old	84		11				3.4		0.7	
	Young	21	Not stated	7	55.0×10^3				1.29 hr		Cuny et al., 1979
	Old	77	>65	15	57.8×10^3				1.51		
	Young		20–40	6	8.2×10^3			13.8		0.8	Stevenson et al., 1979
	Old		>65	5	17.2×10^{3a}			12.5		1.2	
Aspirin (in combination with antipyrine and d-propoxyphene)	Young		24–37	8	6.8×10^3					2.3	Melander et al., 1978
	Old		74–75	6	7.8×10^3					2.4	

(Continued)

TABLE 3. (*Cont.*)

Drug	Age Group	Mean Age (yr)	Range (yr)	N(sex)	EXTENT OF ABSORPTION AUC$_{0\to\infty}$ ($\mu g \cdot$ min/ml)	Bioavailability	Dose Excreted in Urine (%)	RATE OF ABSORPTION k_{abs} (hr^{-1})	$t_{1/2abs}$ (min)	t_{Cmax} (hr)	Reference
Atenolol	Young		23–53	6	150.4					2.5	Barber et al., 1981
	Old		66–72	5	301.5[a]					2.6	
	Young		23–32	7		0.56					Rubin et al., 1982
	Old		66–78	7		0.55					
Azapropazone	Young	26	19–37	6	19.1					43.4	Ritch et al., 1982
	Old	85	76–96	12	39.5[a]					51.5	
Chlordiazepoxide	Young	24.5	21–30	28				7.6	5.5		Shader et al., 1977
	Old	68.8	63–74	8				2.12	19.6		
Chlormethiazole	Young	26.7	25–28	3	56.3					0.68	Nation et al., 1977b
	Old	69.7	68–71	3	457.1					1.09	
Cimetidine	Age as a continuous variable		22–84	20	Increased with age ($r = 0.81$, $p < 0.001$)						Redolfi et al., 1979
	Age as a continuous variable		28–64	12		No significant effect of age					Somogyi et al., 1980
Clobazam	Young	27.5	20–37	8 (M)					24	1.6	Greenblatt et al., 1981b
		21.3	18–26	8 (F)					22	1.3	
	Old	63.3	60–69	7 (M)					13	1.6	
		64.5	60–72	6 (F)					20	1.5	
Desmethyldiazepam (from clorazepate)	Young	30.1	22–39	9 (M)					24.5	1.42	Shader et al., 1981
		33.5	26–38	6 (F)					24.5	0.88	
	Old	68.4	64–76	7 (M)					29.5	2.14	
		67.6	56–85	10 (F)					22.5	1.48	
Desmethyldiazepam (from prazepam)	Young	31.0	22–42	8 (M)					65.8	16.6	Allen et al., 1980
		27.9	22–31	7 (F)					75.0	15.9	
	Old	68.4	62–76	8 (M)					181.3[b]	11.7	
		72.7	65–85	6 (F)					292.0	20.0	

Drug	Group		Age range	n						Reference
Diclofenac	Young	19.4	18-21	8 (M)	87.3 (0→ 8hr)				1.5	Willis and Kendall, 1978
				8 (F)	112.6					
Digoxin	Old	68.1	>62						2.0	Cusack et al., 1979
	Young	47	34-61	6		0.76			0.75	
	Old	81	72-91	7		0.84			1.75[a]	Kelly et al., 1982
Labetalol	Age as a continuous variable		28-75	10		35 = 0.29 70 = 0.57 ($r = 0.70$, $p < 0.05$)				
Levodopa	Young		22-34	6	82.3				0.6	Evans et al., 1980
	Old (parkinsonian)		71-86	5	243.7[a]				1.4	
	Young		22-31	6	116.4				0.6	Evans et al., 1981a
	Old		73-86	5	341.9[a]				1.6	
	Old (parkinsonian)		72-83	6	328.7[a]				0.7	
Lidocaine	Young		20-34	6		0.13			1.0	Cusack et al., 1980
	Old		73-87	6		0.27[a]			0.75	
Lormetazepam	Young	24.2		6	3.66 (1 mg p.o.)	0.73	30		2.2	Hümpel et al., 1980
					11.88 (3 mg p.o.)	0.80	48		3.0	
Mecillinam	Old	65.8		6	5.10	0.82	54			Ball et al., 1978
					13.92	0.78	30			
	Young	Not stated		6	384			0.83	1.75	
Metoprolol	Old	>65						0.55	2.3	Quarterman et al., 1981
	Young	21	18-25	6	750[a] (day 1)				2.4	
				8	48.7 (day 1)				2.3	
					89.3 (day 8)					
	Old	69	63-74	7	27.9 (day 1)				1.2[a]	
					59.2 (day 8)				1.3[a]	

(Continued)

TABLE 3. (*Cont.*)

Drug	Age Group	Mean Age (yr)	Range (yr)	N(sex)	EXTENT OF ABSORPTION AUC$_{0\to\infty}$ (μg·min/ml)	Bioavailability	Dose Excreted in Urine (%)	RATE OF ABSORPTION k_{abs} (hr^{-1})	$t_{1/2abs}$ (min)	t_{Cmax} (hr)	Reference
Oxazepam	Age as a continuous variable		22–76 / 28–84	18 (M) / 20 (F)			No significant effects of age		41.7 / 34.5	2.18 / 3.10	Greenblatt et al., 1980c
Practolol	Young / Old	27 / 80		13 / 8				0.8 / 0.7		2.8 / 2.5	Castleden et al., 1977b
Prazosin	Young / Old		22–32 / 66–78	7 / 7		0.68 / 0.48[a]					Rubin et al., 1981
Propicillin K	Young / Old		20–30 / 60–80	10 / 16			53.4 / 51.8	1.54 / 1.50			Simon et al., 1972
Propoxyphene (in combination with antipyrine and acetylsalicylic acid)	Young / Old		24–32 / 74–75	8 / 6	26.8 / 31.5					1.7 / 1.7	Melander et al., 1978
Propranolol	Young / Old	29 / 78		7 / 8		Increased with age[a]				1.6 / 2.4	Castleden and George, 1979
	Younger / Older		21–37 / 46–73	13 / 14		No effect of age					Vestal and Wood, 1980 (after Vestal et al., 1979)
	Young / Old		23–33 / 66–72	6 / 5	22.8 / 45.6					2.2 / 3.0	Barber et al., 1981
Propylthiouracil	Young		Not stated	6		0.83		0.024 min^{-1}			Kampman et al., 1979
	Old	81	74–86	9		0.71		0.007			

Drug	Group	Mean age	Age range	n	AUC$_{0\to\infty}$	k_{abs}	$t_{1/2\,abs}$	t_{cmax}	Reference
Quinine	Young		20-40	6	600		1.29	2.1	Stevenson et al., 1979
	Old		>65	5	1542[a]		1.83	6.0	
Ranitidine	Young		Not stated	10		0.51			Young et al., 1982
	Old					0.48			
Sotalol	Young	23.9	19-35	12	626.8		2.5	87.6	Ishizaki et al., 1980
	Old	65.7	60-74	9	875.0[a]		2.9	78.5	
Sulfamethizole	Young	24.0	22-27	6			1.2	91	Triggs et al., 1975b
	Old	88.9	73-91	7			2.1	83	
Temazepam	Young	24.7	21-31	10 (F)			1.75		Briggs et al., 1980
	Old	72.9	67-77	10 (F)			0.3[b]		
	Young	29.0	24-30	7 (M)			2.18		Divoll et al., 1981
	Young	29.7	28-33	7 (F)			2.75		
	Old	69.1	60-76	8 (M)			1.84		
	Old	69.8	62-84	10 (F)			4.65		
Tetracycline	Young	26	21-34	5			0.65 (capsule) 0.82 (solution)		Kramer et al., 1978
	Old	69	61-75	5			0.58 (capsule) 0.70 (solution)		
Theophylline	Young	26	21-30	5	34.8		1.8	1.5	Cusack et al., 1980
	Old	75	67-81	6	25.8		2.2	2.1	
	Young	35.6	26-51	8	150.60	0.94	1.09		Fox et al., 1983
	Old	66.9	60-81	30	114.99[a]	0.87	1.12		

NOTE:

AUC$_{0\to\infty}$ = area under the curve (plasma concentration vs time curve) from 0 to infinity

k_{abs} = absorption rate constant

$t_{1/2\,abs}$ = absorption half-life

t_{cmax} = time from drug administration to maximum concentration in plasma

M = male

F = female

[a]Significant difference between old and young age group ($p < 0.05$).

[b]Significant difference between old and young age group of same sex ($p < 0.05$).

this may effect the ionization and solubility of certain drugs. In a small study, however, absorption of tetracycline by elderly patients with achlorhydria was similar to that of young healthy controls (Kramer et al., 1978). Unfortunately, there are few specific data in man on the effects of elevated pH on the bioavailability of drugs or the range of pH values which may be encountered in the elderly population.

If, in fact, reduced gastric emptying rates prevail in the elderly patient, the resultant effects on drug absorption may be clinically significant for drugs normally expected to have a rapid onset of action after oral dosing. Additionally, drugs which are eliminated at a rapid rate may not achieve therapeutic plasma concentrations (Nimmo, 1976). Evans et al. (1981) studied the effect of age on gastric emptying in 11 elderly subjects (average age, 77 years) and in 7 young healthy volunteers. Using a radioisotopic technique, they found that the gastric emptying time in the older subjects was more than twice that of the younger group. This finding was contrary to that observed by other investigators (Halvorsen et al., 1973; Van Liere and Northup, 1941) but could be explained by differences in protocol and patient exclusion criteria. Heading et al. (1973) observed that the rate of gastric emptying could be correlated with the rate of acetaminophen absorption. Divoll et al. (1982b), however, studied the absorption of acetaminophen with age as a primary variable. They found no significant age-related changes in absorption and, by inference, no decline in gastric emptying.

There may also be a reduction in the number of absorbing cells in the gastrointestinal tract. Surface area of the small intestine has been calculated from measurements of length and volume of male Sprague-Dawley rats ranging in age from 2.5 to 92 weeks (Meshkinpour et al., 1981). The intestinal surface area varied from 82 to 171 cm and increased linearly with age during the first 6 weeks of life. No further increase was noted up to age 92 weeks. This study assumes, however, a constant villus architecture. Loss of villus architecture with age has been reported in mice, rats, and man (Warren et al., 1978). Based on microscopic examination of upper jejunal biopsy specimens from well-nourished elderly (age 60–73) and control (age 16–30) patients without malabsorption, mucosal surface area was found to be reduced by about 20 percent in the older age group (Warren et al., 1978).

While passive transport out of the lumen of the gastrointestinal tract has not been shown to be markedly altered with aging, active transport mechanisms may be more susceptible. The urinary excretion of D-xylose, which has been used clinically to assess the active absorptive capacity of the upper small intestine, decreases with age (Guth, 1968), but this is probably due to reduced renal function rather than impaired absorption (Bhanthumnavin and Schuster, 1977; Mayersohn, 1982). The absorption of calcium, iron, thiamine, and vitamin B_{12} is also by active transport and is decreased (Bhanthumnavin and Schuster, 1977). Applying this knowledge to the absorption of drugs in the aging patient, however, is tenuous since most drugs are absorbed by passive diffusion.

Data from studies that have included evaluation of absorption are shown in Table 3. Unfortunately, the studies summarized here utilize a wide variety of methodologies and criteria, which makes direct comparisons and identification of age-related changes difficult. Except for drugs with high first-pass metabolism, such as prazosin (Rubin et al., 1981) and propranolol (Castleden et al., 1977b; Castleden and George, 1979; Vestal et al., 1979a), bioavailability tends to be equivalent in young and old subjects or patients. Shader et al. (1977) observed a delay in the apparent first-order absorption half-life of chlordiazepoxide in 8 elderly subjects compared to 28 young subjects, but the difference did not reach statistical significance because of the larger standard error for k_{abs} in the young individuals. Cusack et al. (1979) observed a delay of 60 minutes in the time to peak concentration of digoxin after oral administration in elderly subjects compared to young, but there was no difference in overall bioavailability. It is worthy to note that although careful studies of drug absorption are few, higher—rather than lower—plasma levels after oral administration of several drugs have been found in elderly as compared to young subjects. These differences may be explained by decreased hepatic elimination or by alterations in drug distribution rather than differences in drug absorption (Crooks et al., 1976; Vestal, 1978).

Drug Distribution

A variety of factors (Table 2) may produce altered distribution of drugs in the elderly (Crooks et al., 1976; Vestal, 1978; Schmucker, 1979). Among these, body composition is one of the most important and correlates with age. Total body water, both in absolute terms (Shock et al., 1963) and as a percentage of body weight (Edelman and Leibman, 1959; Vestal et al., 1975), has been shown to be reduced by 10 to 15 percent between ages 20 and 80. It should be noted, however, that body composition data may be dependent upon the population under investigation, and studies by the same group of investigators in two different populations gave differing results (Shock et al., 1963; Norris et al., 1963). Lean body mass in proportion to body weight also is diminished with age (Forbes and Reina, 1970; Novak, 1972). This seems to be due to a relative increase in body fat with age. Comparing the age groups 18–25 and 65–85 years, Novak (1972) found that body fat increased from 18 to 36 percent of body weight in men and from 33 to 45 percent in women. In the very elderly, even fat tends to be reduced (Norris et al., 1963).

The effect of these changes in total body water and body fat is a reduction in the proportion of actual lean body mass per unit of total body weight. Longitudinal data in a small group of subjects support this generalization (Forbes and Reina, 1970). Thus, one may predict that drugs that are distributed mainly in body water or lean body mass will have higher blood levels in the elderly, particularly if the dose is based on total body weight or surface area. This is true for ethanol, which distributes in body water (Vestal et al., 1977). Higher peak ethanol levels were observed in older subjects without a difference in rates of metabolism. Digoxin is mainly distributed to lean body mass (Ewy et al., 1971), and it could be hypothesized that the loss of lean body mass with aging might lead to higher plasma levels. Cusack et al. (1979) studied digoxin kinetics in the elderly and found that the apparent volume of distribution of digoxin was significantly reduced in older patients (Table 9). It has also been suggested that reduced tissue binding in the elderly may contribute to an altered volume of distribution (Aronson and Grahame-Smith, 1977). Highly lipid-soluble drugs may also undergo alterations in their pharmacokinetics because of increases in body fat with age. This is at least a partial explanation for the marked increase in the volume of distribution of thiopental (Table 7) observed in older patients and may account in part for similar observations with some of the benzodiazepines (Table 8).

Since free drug concentration is an important determinant of drug distribution and elimination, alterations in the binding of drugs to plasma proteins, red blood cells, and other body tissues may be important causes of altered pharmacokinetics in aged patients. Although conflicting data have been published (Bender et al., 1975), serum albumin is reduced by 10–20 percent in old age (Woodford-Williams et al., 1964; Cammarata et al., 1967; Greenblatt, 1979; Adir et al., 1982). One study compared serum protein concentrations in 50 young normal adults (average age 27 years) with 90 elderly subjects ranging in age from 65 to 103 years. There was essentially no difference in total serum protein. Young subjects, however, had a mean albumin concentration of 4.7 g/dl as compared with 3.8 g/dl in the elderly subjects. This 19 percent reduction was accompanied by an increase in the globulin fraction (Cammarata et al., 1967). Data suggest that disease and immobility may be more important than age *per se* (Woodford-Williams et al., 1964). A disturbance of the normal metabolic response to the stimulus of a reduced albumin pool seems to be present in some elderly individuals (Misera et al., 1975). Although the numbers of subjects were small, Gersovitz et al. (1980) have reported an elegant study utilizing stable isotope techniques, which indicates that the fractional synthesis rate of albumin is reduced in the elderly and is controlled at a lower set point, which prevents its response to higher protein intakes in that age group.

Many drugs bind reversibly to serum albumin to varying degrees. The albumin concentrations, the number of available binding sites, and the binding affinity, or tightness of binding, will be important determinants of the free or unbound plasma drug concentration. The less albumin available for drug binding, the more free drug that is available for diffusion into body tissues where sites of action may be located or, in the case of liver and kidney, where drug elimination can take place. Drugs such as phenytoin, warfarin, phenylbutazone, and tolbutamide are highly protein bound (Table 4), and only slight changes in the amount of free drug can produce significant changes in the proportion of free drug. For other drugs with a lesser degree of protein binding, such as chlormethiazole, meperidine, theophylline, and penicillin, slight changes in protein binding may not be clinically significant. Although some studies have yielded conflicting results, drugs which have shown age-related reductions in protein binding include carbenoxolone, chlormethiazole, meperidine, furosemide, phenylbutazone, phenytoin, salicyclic acid, warfarin, and tolbutamide (Table 4).

The binding of drugs by red cells has also been investigated. Chan et al. (1975) demonstrated that red cell binding of pethidine in young patients was greater than that in elderly patients. However, interpretation of these results is clouded by technical considerations (Wilkinson and Schenker, 1976), and except for chlormethiazole (Nation et al., 1977b), thus far age-related differences in the proportion of erythrocyte-bound drug have not been shown for other drugs. Only a small number of drugs, however, have been studied.

Drug Metabolism

Animal Studies. Studies in experimental animals have generally shown that after maturity, hepatic drug metabolism declines with increasing age (reviewed by Schmucker, 1979) (Tables 5 and 6). Several early investigators observed that "old" animals required smaller doses of barbiturates to induce anesthesia than young animals and suggested that this might be due to an age-dependent decline in hepatic drug metabolism (Streicher and Garbus, 1953; Farner and Verzar, 1961). In a series of classic studies, however, Kato and his colleagues were the first to actually demonstrate the relationship between chronological age and hepatic drug metabolizing activity. Although the oldest rats were only 8 months of age and would be considered mature rather than senescent, Kato et al. (1962) found a significant age dependence in the capacity of rat liver microsomes to metabolize strychnine *in vitro*. A subsequent study (Kato et al., 1964) extended these observations to hexobarbital, pentobarbital, meprobamate, and carisoprodol as well as strychnine. Drug metabolism increased to a maximum level at 30 days and then fell progressively. This correlated with a progressive increase in the *in vivo* half-lives of pentobarbital and carisoprodol, and with the duration of pentobarbital hypnosis and carisoprodol paralysis. *In vitro* mixing experiments, in which microsomes from animals of different ages were combined, failed to demonstrate either an activator or an inhibitor of microsomal drug metabolism. These findings were later confirmed in animals 20 months of age and were shown to be influenced by sex (Kato and Takanaka, 1968a, 1968b). Drug metabolizing enzyme activity was somewhat higher in male than in female rats of the Wistar strain regardless of age. Furthermore, the activities of microsomal enzymes and electron transport system following phenobarbital treatment were markedly higher in 40-day-old-rats than in

TABLE 4. Age and Plasma Protein Binding of Drugs.

Drug	Age Group	Mean Age (yr)	Range (yr)	N	Percent Bound	Reference
Carbenoxolone	Young		<40	9	798 μmol/liter	Hayes et al., 1977
	Old		>65	10	640[a]	
Chlormethiazole	Young	26	25–28	6	69.2	Nation et al., 1977b
	Old	76	71–86	6	59.7[a]	
Etomidate	Young	27	20–35	10	75.1	Carlos et al., 1981
	Old	77	71–90	17	56.4	
Furosemide	Young		20–45	14	97.7	Andreasen and Husted, 1980
	Old		60–84	7	96.5[a]	
Haloperidol	Age as a continuous variable		22–79	14	87.5	Rowell et al., 1981
					(No correlation with age)	Tedeschi et al., 1981
	Young			18	90.5	
	Old			10	91.5	
Lidocaine	Young		20–34	6	48.1	Cusack et al., 1980
	Old		73–87	6	69.5[a]	
Meperidine	Young	24	22–26	5	No significant age difference	Chan et al., 1975
	Old	78	67–87	4		
	Age as a continuous variable		18–73	19	Age 35 = 60.8 $70 = 39.1^a$ $(r = -0.58, p < 0.001)$	Mather et al., 1975
Penicillin G	Young	24		10	55 ± 15.2	Mitchard, 1979
	Old	78		10	40 ± 12.1	
	Younger		<50	5	42.4 ± 3.0	Bender et al., 1975
	Older		>50	4	45.1 ± 3.6	
Phenobarbital	Younger		<50	5	41.8 ± 1.3	Bender et al., 1975
	Older		>50	3	41.9 ± 2.1	
Phenylbutazone	Young	27	19–40	16[c]	96[b]	Wallace et al., 1976
	Young	30	14–39	15[d]	90[b,c]	
	Old	79	69–85	16[c]	94[b,c]	
	Old	84	74–92	22[f]	92[b,c]	
Phenytoin	Young		<50	6	82.4 ± 0.8	Bender et al., 1975
	Old		>50	3	83.6 ± 0.4	
	Young		20–38		727 μmol/liter	Hayes et al., 1975b
	Old		65–90		595[a]	
	Young	28.8		14	91.4	Bach et al., 1981
	Old	82.5		14	87.1[a]	
	Young	25	18–33	24	88.9	Patterson et al., 1982
	Old	75	62–87	22	87.5[a]	

(*Continued*)

TABLE 4. (Cont.)

Drug	Age Group	Mean Age (yr)	Range (yr)	N	Percent Bound	Reference
Quinidine	Young	28.9	23–24	14	75.4	Ochs et al., 1978
	Old	65.5	60–69	8	71.8	
Salicylic acid (salicylate)	Young	27	19–40	16[c]	74[b]	Wallace et al., 1976
	Young	30	14–39	15[d]	72[b]	
	Old	79	69–85	16[c]	74[b]	
	Old	84	74–92	22[f]	58[b,c]	
Sulfadiazine	Young	27	19–40	16[c]	50[b]	Wallace et al., 1976
	Young	30	14–39	15[d]	48[b]	
	Old	79	69–85	16[c]	47[b]	
	Old	84	74–92	22[f]	34[b,c]	
Theophylline	Young	23.1	19–31	14	68.8	Antal et al., 1981
	Old	76.2	70–85	14	62.5[a]	
Thiopental	Age as a continuous variable		25–83	22	Decreased with age (range 83.2–72.4)	Jung et al., 1982
Tolbutamide	Young	38.7	23–46	24	96.8	Miller et al., 1978
	Old	72.1	61–87	19	96.0[a]	
	Age as a continuous variable		23–87	44	Percent bound decreased with age at total plasma concentrations of tolbutamide of 25, 100, 200, and 300 μg/ml	Adir et al., 1982
Warfarin	Young	25	17–37	13	98.6	Shepherd et al., 1977
	Old	78	68–94	15	98.5	
	Young		20–45	9	561 μmol/liter	Hayes et al., 1975a
	Old		65–90	12	451[a]	
	Age as a continuous variable	58.5	33–78	15	97.4–98.3 (No correlation with age)	Routledge et al., 1979

[a]Significant difference between old and young age group ($p < 0.05$)
[b]Estimated from graph.
[c]Taking no drugs.
[d]Healthy, surgical patients taking sedatives, analgesics, and antibiotics.
[e]Significant difference when compared with young (19–40) group taking no drugs.
[f]Taking one or more drugs.

TABLE 5. Effect of Age on *In Vitro* Hepatic Microsomal Enzyme Activity in Rodent Species.

Species	Strain	Sex	Age	Control[a]	TREATED/CONTROL			Reference
					Phenobarbital	Polycyclic Hydrocarbon	Steroid	
Liver wt %/Body wt								
Rat	Sprague-Dawley	Female	30 days	4.65 ± 0.06				Kato et al., 1964
			100	4.15 ± 0.09				
			250	3.51 ± 0.08				
Rat	Wistar	Female	40 days	4.87 ± 0.15	1.24			Kato and Tak-anaka, 1968c
			100	4.24 ± 0.17	1.11			
			300	3.57 ± 0.19	1.09			
			600	3.22 ± 0.15	1.04			
Rat	Wistar	Male	4 months	2.96 ± 0.17 (S.D.)	1.18			McMartin et al., 1980
			12	3.07 ± 0.40	1.12			
			36	3.01 ± 0.26	1.11			
			7	2.66 ± 0.39		1.19 (BNF)		
			31	2.61 ± 0.28		1.26		
Rat	Fischer 344	Male	1 month	3.8	1.29			Schmucker and Wang, 1980
			16	2.6	1.31			
			27	3.2	1.19			
Mouse	ICR	Male	5 weeks	6.08 ± 0.15	1.20			Kato et al., 1970
			15	5.24 ± 0.20	1.21			
			50	4.69 ± 0.20	1.24			
Microsomal protein, mg/g liver								
Rat	Wistar	Female	40 days	27.5 ± 0.6	1.23			Kato and Taka-naka, 1968c
			100	27.8 ± 0.5	1.12			
			300	26.4 ± 0.8	1.08			
			600	25.8 ± 0.4	1.06			
Rat	Fischer	Male	3 months	41.4 ± 5.5 (S.D.)	1.15		0.70 (TAM)	Gold and Wid-nell, 1974
			24	39.2 ± 5.3	1.23		0.77	
Rat	Fischer 344	Male	10 weeks	16.4 ± 1.2	1.28	1.06 (BNF)		Kao and Hud-son, 1980
			100	11.4 ± 1.1	1.68	1.19		
Rat	Fischer 344	Male	3–5 months	29.0 ± 0.9				Rikans and Not-ley, 1982
			14	30.2 ± 0.7				
			24	31.7 ± 1.2				
Mouse	ICR	Male	5 weeks	29.3 ± 0.4	1.21			Kato et al., 1970
			15	30.2 ± 0.3	1.17			
			50	29.9 ± 0.2	1.20			

(Continued)

TABLE 5. *(Cont.)*

Species	Strain	Sex	Age	Control[a]	TREATED/CONTROL Phenobarbital	Polycyclic Hydrocarbon	Steroid	Reference
Cytochrome P-450, nmol/mg protein								
Rat	Wistar	Female	40 days	0.98 ± 0.06	3.59			Kato and Takanaka, 1968c
			100	0.83 ± 0.06	2.31			
			300	0.67 ± 0.04	1.60			
			600	0.58 ± 0.05	1.36			
Rat	CFN (Wistar)	Male	3 months	1.26 ± 0.02	2.5	1.75 (3MC)		Birnbaum and Baird, 1978
			28–30	1.01 ± 0.08	2.5	2.1		
Rat	Fischer 344	Male	1 month	0.8 ± 0.1	2.88		1.5 (PCN)	Schmucker and Wang, 1980
			16	0.7 ± 0.1	3.00		1.6	
			27	0.3 ± 0.1	4.00			
Rat	Fischer 344	Male	10 weeks	1.22 ± 0.07	2.16	1.81 (BNF)		Kao and Hudson, 1980
			100	0.89 ± 0.04	2.28	2.37		
Rat	Wistar	Male	4 months	1.03 ± 0.13 (S.D.)	2.05			McMartin et al., 1980
			12	1.16 ± 0.12	2.01			
			36	0.94 ± 0.17	1.72			
Rat	Wistar	Male	7 months	1.15 ± 0.13 (S.D.)		1.37 (BNF)		McMartin et al., 1980
			31	0.97 ± 0.09		1.36		
Rat	Fischer 344	Male	3–5 months	0.79 ± 0.01	1.68	1.62 (BNF)	1.29 (MT)	Rikans and Nottley, 1981, 1982
			14–15	0.54 ± 0.03	2.20	2.30	1.30	
			24	0.55 ± 0.03				
Mouse	ICR	Male	5 weeks	1.08 ± 0.05	2.51			Kato et al., 1970
			15	1.14 ± 0.04	2.40			
			50	1.18 ± 0.05	2.22			
Mouse	Swiss-Webster	Female	1 month	0.59 ± 0.07 (S.D.)				Stohs et al., 1980
			3	0.83 ± 0.05				
			6	0.78 ± 0.04				
			12	0.64 ± 0.03				
			18	0.63 ± 0.04				
Mouse	C57BL/6J	Male	3 months	1.04 ± 0.05		3.47 (PCB)		Birnbaum, 1980
			12	1.26 ± 0.15		2.48		
			25–27	1.05 ± 0.21		3.12		
NADPH–cytochrome c reductase, nmol/mg protein/min								
Rat	Wistar	Female	40 days	119 ± 6.3	3.49			Kato and Takanaka, 1968c
			100	105 ± 4.7	2.16			
			300	89 ± 5.7	1.52			
			600	78 ± 6.0	1.22			

	Strain	Sex	Age	Value				Reference
Rat	Fischer	Male	3 months	137 ± 30 (S.D.)	1.27		1.12 (TAM)	Gold and Widnell, 1974
			24	106 ± 20	1.41		1.18	
Rat	CFN (Wistar)	Male	3 months	58.6 ± 2.3	2.25	1.0 (3MC)	1.75 (PCN)	Birnbaum and Baird, 1978
			28–30	58.4 ± 1.8	1.9	1.0	1.9	
Rat	Fischer 344	Male	1 month	77 ± 7	1.95			Schmucker and Wang, 1980
			16	112 ± 10	2.50			
			27	36 ± 10	2.11			
Rat	Fischer 344	Male	10 weeks	265.7 ± 19.6	1.36	0.82 (BNF)		Kao and Hudson, 1980
			100	178.3 ± 14.0	1.57	0.89		
Rat	Fischer 344	Male	3–5 months	240 ± 10	1.21	0.88 (BNF)	0.96 (MT)	Rikans and Notley, 1981, 1982
			14–15	140 ± 10	1.21	0.79	0.86	
			24	120 ± 10				
Mouse	ICR	Female	5 weeks	146 ± 8	1.79			Kato et al., 1970
			15	152 ± 7	1.65			
			50	143 ± 10	1.73			
Mouse	C57BL/6J	Male	3 months	51.0 ± 1.0		2.30 (PCB)		Birnbaum, 1980
			12	39.7 ± 2.0		2.60		
			25–27	40.8 ± 2.1		3.37		
Cytochrome b_5 nmol/mg protein								
Rat	CFN (Wistar)	Male	3 months	0.75 ± 0.02	1.5	1.2 (3MC)	1.0 (PCN)	Birnbaum and Baird, 1978
			28–30	0.85 ± 0.03	1.25	1.25	1.0	
Rat	Wistar	Male	4 months	0.053 ± 0.007 (S.D.)	1.14			McMartin et al., 1980
			12	0.066 ± 0.007	0.99			
			36	0.062 ± 0.006	1.07			
Rat	Wistar	Male	7 months	0.057 ± 0.005 (S.D.)		1.26 (BNF)		McMartin et al., 1980
			31	0.061 ± 0.008		0.87 (BNF)		
Rat	Fischer 344	Male	3–5 months	0.46 ± 0.01				Rikans and Notley, 1982
			14	0.36 ± 0.01				
			24	0.41 ± 0.01				
Mouse	C57BL/6J	Male	3 months	0.37 ± 0.01				Birnbaum, 1980
			12	0.36 ± 0.02				
			25–27	0.40 ± 0.03				

NOTE:

BNF = β-naphthoflavone
TAM = triamcinolone
3MC = 3-methylcholanthrene
PCN = pregnenolone-16α-carbonitrile
MT = methyltestosterone
PCB = polychlorinated biphenyls

[a]Values are mean ± S.E. unless otherwise indicated.

TABLE 6. Effect of Age on Rates of *In Vitro* Hepatic Microsomal Metabolism of Model Substrates in Rodent Species.

| | | | | | TREATED/CONTROL | | | |
Species	Strain	Sex	Age	Control[a]	Phenobarbital	Polycyclic Hydrocarbon	Steroid	Reference
Hexobarbital hydroxylation								
μg/g/hr								
Rat	Sprague-Dawley	Male	5 days	21 ± 3.8				Kato et al., 1964
				272 ± 10.3				
				250 ± 8.7				
nmol/mg protein/30 min	Rat	Wistar	Female	40 days	46.4 ± 2.5	5.92			Kato and Taka-naka, 1968c
				100	40.9 ± 1.9	3.93			
				300	32.0 ± 2.7	2.34			
				600	27.1 ± 2.1	1.34			
nmol/g/30 min	Mouse	ICR	Male	5 weeks	1252 ± 68	1.93			Kato et al., 1970
				15	1240 ± 103	1.71			
				50	1221 ± 89	1.82			
Aniline hydroxylation								
nmol/mg protein/30 min	Rat	Wistar	Female	40 days	18.9 ± 1.2	2.65			Kato and Taka-naka, 1968c
				100	15.1 ± 1.3	1.94			
				300	11.9 ± 1.4	1.40			
				600	10.5 ± 1.0	1.31			
nmol/nmol P-450/min	Rat	Fischer 344	Male	3–5 months	0.90 ± 0.03				Rikans and No-tley, 1982
				14	0.89 ± 0.03				
				24	0.67 ± 0.04				
nmol/g/30 min	Mouse	ICR	Male	5 weeks	1752 ± 69	1.65			Kato et al., 1970
				15	1798 ± 88	1.67			
				50	1858 ± 105	1.49			
nmol/mg protein/min	Mouse	Swiss-Web-ster	Female	1 month	0.27 ± 0.03 (S.D.)				Stohs et al., 1980
				3	0.59 ± 0.05				
				6	1.92 ± 0.24				
				12	1.56 ± 0.25				
				18	0.97 ± 0.06				

	Species	Strain	Sex	Age/Dose	Value ± S.D.				Reference
Aminopyrine N-demethylation									
nmol/mg protein/30 min	Rat	Wistar	Female	40 days 100 300 600	6.4 ± 0.5 5.3 ± 0.4 3.9 ± 0.3 3.4 ± 0.4	8.13 4.95 2.73 1.36			Kato and Takanaka, 1968c
nmol/g/30 min	Mouse	ICR	Male	5 weeks 15 50	428 ± 35 458 ± 26 472 ± 31	1.83 1.95 1.64			Kato et al., 1970
Ethoxycoumarin de-ethylation									
nmoles product/mg protein/min	Rat	Fischer 344	Male	10 weeks 100	2.42 ± 0.32 1.87 ± 0.21	1.70 1.69	3.70 (BNF) 4.35		Kao and Hudson, 1980
	Mouse	C57BL/6J	Male	3 months 12 25–27	4.89 ± 0.22 6.25 ± 0.27 9.46 ± 1.58		2.22 (PCB) 1.60 0.99		Birnbaum, 1980
Units not specified	Mouse	Swiss-Webster	Female	1 months 3 6 12 18	226.5 ± 38.6 (S.D.) 516.3 ± 35.4 568.5 ± 72.3 451.5 ± 46.9 413.4 ± 38.1				Stohs et al., 1980
Benzphetamine N-demethylation									
nmol product/mg protein/min	Rat	CNF (Wistar)	Male	3 months 28–30	5.64 ± 0.31 2.94 ± 0.49	1.0 3.0	1.0 (3MC) 1.0	1.0 (PCN) 2.5	Birnbaum and Baird, 1978
nmol product/nmol P-450/min	Rat	Fischer 344	Male	10 weeks 100	4.48 ± 0.32 1.45 ± 0.20	1.50 4.55	0.35 (BNF) 0.53		Kao and Hudson, 1980
	Rat	Fischer 344	Male	3–5 months 14 24	6.08 ± 0.10 10.06 ± 0.33 2.26 ± 0.16				Rikans and Notley, 1982

(Continued)

TABLE 6. (*Cont.*)

	Species	Strain	Sex	Age	Control[a]	TREATED/CONTROL Phenobarbital	TREATED/CONTROL Polycyclic Hydrocarbon	TREATED/CONTROL Steroid	Reference
nmol product/mg protein/min	Mouse	C57BL/6J	Male	3 months 12 25–27	4.56 ± 0.26 4.79 ± 0.65 1.46 ± 0.13				Birnbaum, 1980
Zoxazolamine hydroxylation									
nmol metabolized/30 min/mg 17,000 × g supernatant	Mouse	C57BL/6J	Male	3 months 12 25–27	19.81 ± 2.14 14.06 ± 0.18 12.57 ± 1.36				Birnbaum, 1980
Ethylmorphine N-demethylation									
nmol product/mg protein/min	Rat	CNF (Wistar)	Male	3 months 28–30	3.90 ± 0.45 1.29 ± 0.11	2.0 4.6	1.7 (3MC) 1.8	2.3 (PCN) 5.5	Birnbaum and Baird, 1978
	Mouse	C57BL/6J	Male	3 months 12 25–27	6.88 ± 0.21 5.13 ± 0.42 4.56 ± 0.40				Birnbaum, 1980

Benzo[a]pyrene hydroxylation

units/mg protein/15 min	Rat	CNF (Wistar)	Male	3 months 28–30	138.5 ± 10.5 91.8 ± 23.4	1.0 1.5	23.2 (3MC) 39.0	1.5 (PCN) 1.8	Birnbaum and Baird, 1978
nmoles product/mg protein/min	Mouse	C57BL/6J	Male	3 months 25–27	1.04 ± 0.21 1.71 ± 0.14 3.29 ± 0.36		7.48 (PCB) 5.03 2.53		Birnbaum, 1980
Units not specified	Mouse	Swiss-Webster	Male	1 month 3 6 12 18	0.78 ± 0.14 (S.D.) 0.90 ± 0.09 1.46 ± 0.13 1.20 ± 0.27 1.13 ± 0.10				Stohs et al., 1980

Nitrosoanisole O-demethylation

nmol product/nmol P-450/min	Rat	Fischer 344	Male	3–5 months 14 24	1.28 ± 0.03 2.68 ± 0.11 3.38 ± 0.36				Rikans and Notley, 1982

NOTE:

For abbreviations, see Table 5.

[a]Values are mean ± S.E. unless otherwise indicated.

600-day-old rats (Kato and Takanaka, 1968c).

The observations of other investigators also support the conclusions of Kato and his colleagues that the capacity of the liver to metabolize drugs is reduced in old rats (Klinger, 1969; Kuhlman et al., 1970; Gold and Widnell, 1974; Birnbaum and Baird, 1978; Kao and Hudson, 1980; McMartin et al., 1980; Schmucker and Wang, 1980, 1981; Rikans and Notley, 1981, 1982). The effect of age may be substrate specific (Table 6). For example, in mice, Birnbaum (1980) observed decreases in the rate of benzphetamine N-demethylation, ethylmorphine N-demethylation, and zoxazolamine hydroxylation with age but an increase in benzo[a]pyrene hydroxylation. Rikans and Notley (1982) found decreases in the rates of benzphetamine N-demethylation and aniline hydroxylation with increases in nitroanisole O-demethylation in old as compared to young rats. There is controversy, however, regarding the effect of age and the character of the response following administration of various inducers of hepatic drug metabolism, such as phenobarbital and polycyclic hydrocarbons. Although Kato and Takanaka (1968c) reported lower concentrations of cytochrome P-450 and lower activities of NADPH–cytochrome c reductase in older animals as late as 72 hours after phenobarbital stimulation, others (Adelman, 1971; Gold and Widnell, 1974; Birnbaum and Baird, 1978; Kao and Hudson, 1980; Rit-kans and Notley, 1981) have found similar maximal responses relative to control values. In addition, the total response achieved was usually comparable to that in younger animals despite lower control values. Adelman (1971, 1972) performed studies with parabiotic pairs of rats (2-month-old and 2-year-old) in order to explore the possibility that humoral factors were slowing the rate of enzyme induction and with partial hepatectomy (to induce synchronous division of liver cells and regeneration) in order to determine if newly created rat liver cells were biochemically similar to those of young or old rats. He found that livers of the 2-year-old ani-mals still required 96 hours of phenobarbital treatment to achieve the same level of NADPH–cytochrome c reductase activity as achieved in livers of 2-month-old animals at 72 hours. In a subsequent study, young and old rats were pulse labeled with radioactive leucine and sacrificed at intervals following the administration of phenobarbital. The rate of leucine incorporation into NADPH–cytochrome c reductase was determined in each group and was indicative of an age-dependent lag in the *de novo* synthesis of the enzyme (Adelman, 1975).

In an attempt to resolve this controversy, Schmucker and Wang (1980, 1981) treated 1-, 16-, and 27-month-old Fischer 344 rats with phenobarbital or saline for six days and then permitted them to recover for an additional four days. The amount of cytochrome P-450, the activity of microsomal NADPH–cytochrome c reductase, and the rate of ethylmorphine N-demethylation were measured at various intervals, including preinduction, induction, and postinduction. Liver weights and microsomal protein increased more in the young and mature animals than in the senescent animals. Both parameters returned to or near the noninduced values by four days postinduction. There were no age-related differences between the young and mature animals, but the noninduced concentration of cytochrome P-450, the activity of NADPH–cytochrome c reductase, and the rate of ethylmorphine N-demethylation were significantly less in the senescent animals. The chronic administration of phenobarbital increased all three parameters, but the maximal induced levels achieved after six days of treatment and the rates of induction and postinduction recovery were significantly greater in the young and mature animals than in the senescent rats (Figure 1).

The effect of enzyme inducers may vary with age, depending upon the specific inducer being used and the substrates being metabolized. McMartin et al. (1980) have recently shown that based upon the pattern of warfarin metabolites, the major form of cytochrome P-450 induced by β-naphtho-

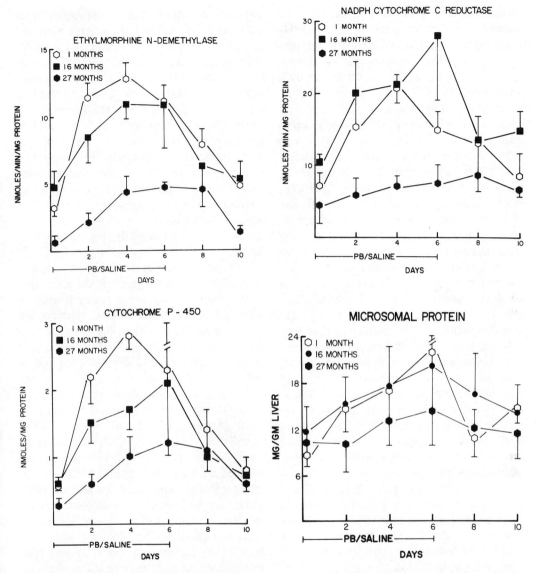

Figure 1. Effect of age and phenobarbital administration on selected components of the hepatic microsomal drug metabolizing system of the rat. Since there were no differences between the saline-treated control rats, the 0-day values represent untreated animals and subsequent points reflect only those animals treated with phenobarbital. Each point represents the mean of five animals ± S.D. (From Schmucker and Wang, 1981.)

flavone was not altered in old rats, while one of the forms induced by phenobarbital showed reduced activity in old rats relative to young rats. Strain differences are also important. Thus, Gold and Widnell (1975) found marked differences in control and phenobarbital-induced activity of NADPH–cytochrome c reductase and in levels of cy-

tochrome P-450 in mature Fischer rats compared to mature Sprague-Dawley rats.

Species differences have also been reported. The results of some studies in mice conflict with those in rats. Although hexobarbital anesthesia and zoxazolamine paralysis were longer in the older animals, Kato and Takanaka (1970) observed no age differences in control and phenobarbital-induced levels of cytochrome P-450, NADPH–cytochrome c reductase activity, hexobarbital hydroxylation, aminopyrine N-demethylation, or aniline hydroxylation in ICR strain mice aged 5, 15, and 50 weeks. An absence of an effect of age on nicotine metabolism has also been reported in mice (Slanina and Stalhandski, 1977). Similarly, Birnbaum (1980) found no effect of age on cytochrome P-450 levels, cytochrome b, or NADPH–cytochrome c reductase in male C57BL/6J mice. However, she did find a reduction in NADPH–cytochrome c reductase, ethylmorphine N-demethylation, benzphetamine N-demethylation, and zoxazolamine hydroxylation, and an increase in benzo[a]pyrene hydroxylation and ethoxycoumarin deethylation in senescent (25–27 months) compared to young (3 months) or mature (12 months) animals. It is interesting that Pardon and Jones (1978) reported that senescent mice (24 months old) eliminated pentobarbital more rapidly than young mice (3 months old), but manifested a longer duration of narcosis. Brain concentrations were not statistically different. The data of Stohs et al. (1980), however, in Swiss-Webster mice are more consistent with the findings in rats and emphasize that strain differences also exist in mice. It is not possible to conclude, as seemed to be the implication of Kato and Takanaka's earlier study (1970), that aging does not decrease the activities of the mouse liver mixed-function oxidase system in contrast to those in the rat.

In addition to effects of age on hepatic microsomal drug metabolism, there is limited evidence to suggest that biliary excretion of drugs may also be impaired with aging. Varga and Discher (1978) have reported that in Sprague-Dawley rats aged 2–20 months, biliary excretion of eosine decreased at a greater rate than either bile flow or hepatic uptake. They suggested that the concomitant reduction of hepatic blood flow, mainly portal venous blood flow (> 50 percent), might play a role in reduced hepatobiliary function, perhaps due to diminished oxygen supply to the hepatocytes. Ouabain is also rapidly excreted into the bile, probably by an active process, without appreciable biotransformation in the liver. Kitani et al. (1978) have shown age-dependent declines in both the plasma clearance and the biliary excretion rates of this drug in 24-month-old rats compared to 2-month-old rats. Pretreatment with spironolactone enhanced the plasma clearance and biliary excretion of ouabain in both young and old animals, which seems to indicate that the age-related changes were due to reduced rates of hepatic uptake and excretion. The effect of age on the relationship of hepatobiliary function to drug elimination will undoubtedly be clarified by future studies.

The mechanisms responsible for the age-dependent changes in hepatic drug metabolism demonstrated in experimental animals have not been fully elucidated. Reduced hepatic blood flow, which has been demonstrated in rats (Kitani, 1977; Varga and Fischer, 1978), might explain impaired *in vivo* hepatic metabolism of some drugs with age, but would not explain the *in vitro* data. Other extrahepatic or humoral factors have been proposed (Gold and Widnell, 1974; Baird et al., 1975, 1976). However, the altered fine structure in newly regenerated liver of aged animals (Pieri et al., 1975a, 1975b) and parabiosis experiments (Adelman, 1971, 1972) seem to favor quantitative and perhaps qualitative changes in the aging liver rather than extrahepatic physiological factors. At least in some studies, the ratio of liver mass to body weight and the proportion of microsomal protein decline with age (Table 5). In addition, a variety of morphological changes have been described. Although somewhat different results have been reported in female Wistar rats (Pieri et al., 1975a, 1975b), in male Fischer 344 rats these include a significant decrease in average liver cell volume, ground substance volumes, and the surface density of hepatic smooth endoplasmic reticulum between ages 20 and 30 months (Schmucker et al., 1977). Such data suggest that reduced drug metabolism in old animals may be due to reduced liver mass, with an age-dependent loss of smooth endoplasmic reticulum and its associated microsomal enzymes. Some biochemical studies have failed to demonstrate alterations in the electrophoretic patterns of cytochrome P-450 peptides or the lipid composition of microsomes (Birnbaum and Baird, 1978; Birnbaum, 1980). However, a recent study demonstrated a significant increase in the ratio of saturated to unsaturated fatty acids in microsomes with increasing age (Rikans and Notley, 1982). Nevertheless, the evidence for qualitative changes is largely indirect and limited to the studies with enzyme inducers.

Human Studies. Despite an increasing body of knowledge regarding age-related changes in drug metabolism, the effects are not yet sufficiently described to allow generalizations. Since there are no studies of the effects of age on *in vitro* drug metabolism in man, the evidence of altered hepatic drug metabolism is indirect. From autopsy studies, it is known that liver mass bears a relatively constant relationship to body weight (2.5 percent) until middle age, when it becomes relatively and progressively smaller with age (1.6 percent of body weight by the tenth decade of life) (Geokas and Haverback, 1969). Regional blood flow to the liver also decreases with advancing age. Estimates of the decline in the liver blood flow range from 0.3 to 1.5 percent per year based on indirect measurements (Geokas and Haverback, 1969). Thus, in a person aged 65, the hepatic blood flow is reduced by 40 to 45 percent compared with a person aged 25. This decline in liver blood flow is partially the result of the decline in cardiac output which occurs with aging (Bender, 1965). For drugs with high hepatic extraction ratios, such as lidocaine and propranolol whose metabolism is highly dependent upon liver blood flow, one might predict an effect of age on hepatic drug clearance (Nies et al., 1976).

The evidence suggests that in man, the aging process may result in alteration of the intrinsic metabolic capacity of the liver for some drugs. Several drugs that are eliminated primarily by hepatic metabolism have

consistently longer half-lives and reduced clearances in the elderly compared to the young, but some studies have yielded conflicting results (Table 7 and 8). The conflicting data are probably a reflection of differences in the populations studied and the failure to adequately control for environmental influences.

O'Malley et al. (1971) were the first to suggest an alteration in the intrinsic drug metabolizing capacity of the liver in aged human subjects. Their study revealed a 45 percent prolongation of the half-life of antipyrine in elderly subjects when compared to young controls. Further analysis of their data revealed an age-related reduction in total plasma clearance of antipyrine. Antipyrine is a useful model compound for the study of factors influencing drug metabolism. It is rapidly absorbed and distributes in total body water. It is metabolized almost entirely in the liver prior to excretion and has a low hepatic extraction ratio. Because of these characteristics and its minimal protein binding, its metabolism is considered to be capacity limited and binding insensitive. Thus, its hepatic clearance is limited only by the activity of the drug metabolizing enzymes. Although most studies with antipyrine subsequent to those of O'Malley have reported a prolonged half-life and reduced metabolic clearance in older subjects (Liddell et al., 1975; Vestal et al., 1975; Swift et al., 1978; Wood et al., 1979; Bach et al., 1981; Greenblatt et al., 1982a), conflicting data have been reported recently (Mucklow and Fraser, 1980). Data also suggest that reduced antipyrine metabolism correlates with a reduction in liver volume in elderly subjects (Swift et al., 1978; Bach et al., 1981). The largest available study of antipyrine metabolism (Figure 2), however, showed that interindividual variation (sixfold) exceeded the effect of age, and only 3 percent of the variance in metabolic clearance could be explained by age alone (Vestal et al., 1975). Most of this interindividual variation in drug metabolism is undoubtedly due to a variety of genetic and environmental factors, including cigarette smoking which accounted for 12 percent of

TABLE 7. Effect of Age on Disposition of Drugs Eliminated Primarily by Hepatic Metabolism.

Drug	Age Group	Mean Age (yr)	Range (yr)	N (sex)	Mean $t_{1/2}$ (hr)	Mean Volume of Distribution	Mean Clearance	Reference
Analgesic-Antipyretics, Anti-inflammatory Agents								
Acetaminophen	Young	24.0	22–27	6	1.8	1.03 liters/kg	477 ml/min/1.73 m²	Triggs et al., 1975b
	Old	88.9	73–91	7	2.2[a]	1.05	379	
	Young	28.2		14 (M)	1.77	0.927 liters/kg	370 ml/kg/hr	Briant et al., 1976
		28.1		14 (M)	1.74	0.802	307	
			20–40	28	1.75	0.863	340	
	Old	77.4		14 (M)	2.19	0.803	254	
		76.5		14 (F)	2.15	0.740	254	
			>65	28	2.17[a]	0.771	254[a]	
	Young	23.9		11	1.24	0.96 liters/kg	363.5 ml/min	Fulton et al., 1979
	Old	75.8		12	1.39	0.90	240.8[a]	
	Young	30.8	24–37	8 (M)	2.6	1.09 liters/kg	5.07 ml/kg/min	Divoll et al., 1982a
		27.3	23–33	8 (F)	2.7	0.94	4.08	
	Old	70.3	61–77	8 (M)	2.7	0.89[b]	3.90	
		69.1	64–78	8 (F)	2.8	0.79[b]	3.36	
	Young	28.4	22–39	16	2.6	1.02	4.64 ml/kg/min	Divoll et al., 1982b
	Old	70.7	61–78	12	2.8	0.86[a]	3.74[a]	
Acetanilide	Young		<35	19	1.45			Farah et al., 1977
	Old		>65	24	2.1[a]			
Aminopyrine	Young	23		15	1.57	48.0 liters	0.35 liters/kg/hr	Playfer et al., 1978
	Old	81		15	1.75	44.4	0.33	
	Young	26.0	25–30	8	4.3			Jori et al., 1972
	Old	77.6	65–85	10	7.7[a]			
Antipyrine	Young	26.0	20–50	61	12.0			O'Malley et al., 1971
	Old	77.6	70–100	19	17.4			
	Young	28.2	25–33	13 (M)	12.2	0.61 liters/kg		Liddell et al., 1975
		26.2	21–40	12 (F)	12.2	0.59		
			21–40	26	12.5	0.60		
	Old	77.9	65–89	13 (M)	17.5	0.63		
		79.8	68–92	13 (F)	16.1	0.48[b]		
			65–92	26	16.8[a]	0.56		

Drug	Group	Mean	Age	n		Volume	Clearance	Reference
	Young	32.9		73 (M)	12.7	0.573 liters/kg	34.6 ml/kg/hr	Vestal et al., 1975
	Middle	49.9		15 (M)	13.8	0.537[a]	30.9[a]	
	Old	68.7		84 (M)	14.8[a]	0.536[a]	28.2[a]	
	All	51.0	18–92	307 (M)	13.8	0.545	31.0	
	Young		20–29	15	11.8	0.624 liters/kg	41.8 ml/min	Swift et al., 1978
	Old—normal		75–86	11	16.7[a]	0.566[a]	24.1[a]	
	Old—hospitalized		70–89	10	10.4[c]	0.500[a]	33.7[c]	
	Young		24–37	8	16.8			Melander et al., 1978
	Old		74–75	6	22.3			
	Younger		21–37	11	11.3	0.72 liters/kg	48.7	Vestal and Wood, 1980 (after Wood et al., 1979)
	Older		46–68	9	13.0	0.52[a]	29.7[a]	
	Young	28.8		14	7.8	40.4 liters	61.9 ml/min	Bach et al., 1981
	Old	82.5		14	12.6[a]	29.5[a]	29.6[a]	
	Young	29.4	23–43	14 (M)	10.0	0.66 liters/kg	0.81 ml/kg/min	Greenblatt et al., 1982
		27.9	22–33	15 (F)	11.5	0.58	0.64	
	Old	68.9	60–76	10 (M)	15.5[b]	0.55[b]	0.49[b]	
		69.1	62–84	12 (F)	11.6	0.47[b]	0.49[b]	
Aspirin	Young		20–20	6	2.3	0.078 liters/kg	24 ml/kg/hr	Stevenson et al., 1979
	Old		>65	5	5.2[a]	0.106	17	
	Younger	21		7	2.38	3.83 liters	1.61 liters/hr	Cuny et al., 1979
	Older	77	>65	15	3.71[a]	5.51[a]	1.68	
Indomethacin	Young	33.3	20–50	7 (M)	1.53			Traeger et al., 1973 (after Triggs and Nation, 1975a)
	Old	75.8	71–83	7 (M)	1.73			
Phenylbutazone	Young		20–50	18	81.2			O'Malley et al., 1971
	Old		70–100	19	104.6			
	Young	24.0	22–30	8	110	172 liters/kg		Triggs et al., 1975b
	Old	88.9	73–91	7	87	165		
Anesthetics								
Thiopental	Young		20–40	8 (M)	5.45	12.6 liters (V_2); 31.6 (V_3)	0.164 liters/min	Christensen et al., 1981
				8 (F)	8.92[c]	12.4; 92.8[c]	0.131	
	Old		60–79	8 (M)	13.18[b]	28.3[b] (V_2); 125.0[b] (V_3)	0.220[b]	
				8 (F)	16.50[b]	20.9[b]; 161.3[b]	0.190	

(Continued)

TABLE 7. (Cont.)

Drug	Age Group	Mean Age (yr)	Range (yr)	N (sex)	Mean $t_{1/2}$ (hr)	Mean Volume of Distribution	Mean Clearance	Reference
Anticoagulants								
Heparin	Age as a continuous variable		25–83	22 (F)	Increased with age ($r = 0.80$, $p < 0.001$)	Increased with age (Vd_β: $r = 0.64$ and Vd_{ss}: $r = 0.70$; both $p < 0.001$)	No significant correlation with age	Jung et al., 1982
	Age as a continuous variable		18–68	20	0.88	50.4 ml/kg LBW (only minor influence of age)	41.8 ml/kg LBW/hr	Cipolle et al., 1982
Warfarin	Young	25	27–40	13	37	193 ml/kg	3.80 ml/kg/hr	Shepherd et al., 1977
	Old	82	65–94	13	44	200	3.26	
	Young	24		18	34	160 ml/kg	3.45 ml/kg/hr	Shepherd et al., 1979
	Old	82		20	41	190	3.4	
	Young		44–69	25			3.0 ml/kg/hr	Hotraphinyo et al., 1978
	Old		66–82	14			2.8	
	Age as a continuous variable	58.5	33–78	15			2.56–6.37 ml/kg/hr (No correlation with age)	Routledge et al., 1979
Anticonvulsants								
Phenytoin	Young	28.8	20–43	10			26.1 ml/kg/hr (500 mg p.o.)	Hayes et al., 1975b
		28.6	20–38	10			44.3 (250 mg i.v.)	
		25.5	20–35	10 (F)			47.3 (250 mg i.v.)	
	Old	79.2	67–95	11			42.2[a]	
		78.7	65–86	10			67.3[a]	
		80.7	66–90	15 (F)			71.7[a]	
	Young	28.8		14	10.6	40.91	48.4 ml/min	Bach et al., 1981
						486.8 (free)	569 (free)	
	Old	82.5		14	11.8	44.4	50.5	
						296.3[a]	309[a]	

Antimicrobials

Drug / Group		Mean age	Age range	N	$t_{1/2}$	V_d	Clearance	Reference
Isoniazid	Young		<35	23	1.4 (fast acetylators) 3.7 (slow acetylators)[c]			Farah et al., 1977
	Old		>65	27	1.5 4.2[c]			
	Young	39		3	1.06 (fast acetylators) 3.05 (slow acetylators)[c]	0.67 liters/kg ($V_1 + V_2$) 0.68	7.36 ml/kg/min 3.68[e]	Advenier et al., 1980
		36		7				
	Old	89		5	1.35 3.13[e]	0.54 0.69	8.36 3.63[e]	
		80		6				

Bronchodilators

Drug / Group		Mean age	Age range	N	$t_{1/2}$	V_d	Clearance	Reference
Theophylline	Young	44.5		18			63.4 ml/kg/hr	Jusko et al., 1977
	Old	60.2		40			48.6[a]	
	Young		<20	23			91.9 ml/kg/hr	Jusko et al., 1979
			20–39.9	79			64.2	
	Middle		40–59.9	37			47.8	
	Old		>60	61			43.1	
	All			200			57.9 ($r = -0.49, p < 0.01$)	
	Young	26	21–30	5	7.6	0.30 liters/kg	0.46 ml/kg/min	Cusack et al., 1980
		21	20–23	8 (smokers)	5.9[f]	0.36	0.72[f]	
	Old	75	67–81	6	8.0	0.36	0.51	
		75	67–79	6 (smokers)	5.9[f]	0.36	0.71	
	Age as a continuous variable	43.9	22–79	36 (smokers with COPD)			62.6 ml/kg/hr (No correlation with age)	Bauer and Blouin, 1981a
		61.9	41–81	23 (smokers with COPD and CHF)			28.1 (No correlation with age)	
	Young	23.1	19–31	14	8.51	0.43 liters/kg 1.38 (unbound)	34.9 ml/min 113.5 (unbound) 17.79 (renal)	Antal et al., 1981

(Continued)

TABLE 7. (*Cont.*)

Drug	Age Group	Mean Age (yr)	Range (yr)	N (sex)	Mean $t_{1/2}$ (hr)	Mean Volume of Distribution	Mean Clearance	Reference
	Old	76.2	70–85	14	9.81	0.32 / 0.86[a]	29.4 / 79.8[a] / 9.35[a]	Fox et al., 1983
	Young	35.6	26–51	8	8.14	0.36 liters/kg	32.97 ml/kg/hr	Fox et al., 1983
	Old	69.3	62–81	19	7.27	0.56	43.65[a]	
	Old	62.7	60–69	11 (smokers)	6.44[a]	0.54[a]	44.74[a]	
Cardiovascular Agents								
Digitoxin	Young	26	25–30	6	10.0 days	0.64 liters/kg	0.045 liters/kg/day	Donovan et al., 1981
	Old	71	69–79	6	8.3	0.62	0.054	
Labetalol	Age as a continuous variable		28–75	10	Age 35 = 3.53 Age 70 = 4.44 ($r = 0.73, p < 0.02$)	7.7 liters/kg (No correlation with age)	22.4 ml/kg/min (No correlation with age)	Kelly et al., 1982
Lidocaine	Young	24	22–26	4	1.34	0.895 liters/kg	7.60 ml/kg/min	Nation et al., 1977a
	Old	65	61–71	6	2.33[a]	1.586[a]	8.12	
	Young		20–34	6	1.5	0.69	5.3 ml/kg/min	Cusack et al., 1980
	Old		73–87	6	2.1[a]	0.85[a]	5.0	
Metoprolol	Old		61–88	12	3.7 (20 mg dose) 3.0 (50 mg dose, $n = 5$) Values are comparable to data in younger subjects			Lundborg and Steen, 1976
	Young	21	18–25	8	4.1 (day 1) 4.0 (day 8)			Quarterman et al., 1981
	Old	69	63–74	7	2.8[a] 3.7			

Prazosin	Young		22–32	7	2.05	0.63 liters/kg (Vd_{ss})	3.94 ml/kg/min	Rubin et al., 1981
	Old		66–78	7	3.23[a]	0.89[a]	3.53	
Propranolol	Young	29		7 (40 mg p.o.) (0.15 mg/kg i.v.)	3.6	2.7 liters/kg	13.2 ml/kg/min	Castleden and George, 1979
	Old	78		8	2.5	3.0	7.8[a]	
	Younger			6 (80 mg p.o. q8hr)	3.6	3.82 liters/kg	10.6 ml/kg/min (systemic)	Vestal and Wood, 1980 (after Vestal et al., 1979)
							24.4 (intrinsic)	
				7 (smokers)	4.2	4.43	14.9	
							65.5[f]	
				13 (total)	4.5	4.18	12.9	
							46.5	
	Older			6	3.6	4.24	9.0	
							26.8	
				8 (smokers)	4.0	4.22	10.4[a]	
							35.3[a]	
				14 (total)	5.6	4.23	9.8[a]	
							31.6	
	Young	27		6 (20 mg p.o.)			515 liters/hr	Schneck et al., 1980
				(40 mg p.o.)			459	
				(160 mg p.o.)			232	
	Old	71		4			244[a]	
							323	
							178	
	Young		23–33	6 (80 mg p.o. daily)			266 liters/hr	Barber et al., 1981
	Old		66–72	5			130	
Quinidine	Young	28.9	23–24	14	7.25	2.39 liters/kg	4.04 ml/kg/min (total)	Ochs et al., 1978
							1.43 (renal)	
	Old	65.5	60–69	8	9.70[a]	2.18	2.64[a]	
							0.99[a]	

TABLE 7. (*Cont.*)

Drug	Age Group	Mean Age (yr)	Range (yr)	N (sex)	Mean $t_{1/2}$ (hr)	Mean Volume of Distribution	Mean Clearance	Reference
Hypoglycemic Agents								
Chlorpropamide	Young		23–28	11	No effect of age on half-life			Sartor et al., 1980
	Old		62–77	12				
Tolbutamide	Age as a continuous variable	54.3	16–86	219	5.8 (No effect of age on half-life)			Sotaniemi and Huhti, 1974
	Age as a continuous variable	36.8	15–72	50	5.3 (No correlation with age)		14.2 ml/min (No correlation with age)	Scott and Poffenbarger, 1979
Narcotic Analgesics								
Meperidine	Young	24.6	18–29	6	4.18	5.38 liters/kg	16.18 ml/min/kg	Holmberg et al., 1982
	Old	74.4	67–86	9	7.59[a]	5.69	9.13[a]	
Morphine	Age as a continuous variable	49	23–75	20	No correlation of either initial or terminal half-life with age			Berkowitz et al., 1975
Psychoactive Drugs (excluding Benzodiazipines)								
Amobarbital	Young		20–40	8	22.8			Ritschel, 1978 (data of Irvine et al., 1974)
	Old		>65	8	86.6			
Chlormethiazole (i.v.)	Young	22.7	20–27	6	4.05	7.93 liters/kg	22.92 ml/kg/min	Nation et al., 1976 (and Moore et al., 1975)
	Old	75.3	69–91	6	8.49[a]		16.14[a]	
(p.o.)	Young	27	25–28	3	6.15	11.20[a]	14.13 liters/min 221.9 ml/kg/min 1.76[a]	Nation et al., 1977b
	Old	70	68–71	3	6.34		35.3[a]	
Desipramine	Young } Old		21–68	35	34.2 75.8 ($r = 0.62$, $p < 0.01$)			Nies et al., 1977
Ethanol	Young	38.7	21–56	25		34.9 liters	73.7 mg/kg/hr	Vestal et al., 1977
	Old	68.0	57–81	25		31.8 ($r = 0.28$, $p < 0.05$)	76.4 (No correlation with age)	
	(Age as a continuous variable)							

Imipramine	Young		21-68	35	19.0			Nies et al., 1977
	Old				23.8 (No correlation with age)			
Nortriptyline	Age as a continuous variable		20-74	66	18.1-93.3 ($r = 0.40$, $p < 0.05$)		10.1-113.9 liters/hr (No correlation with age)	Braithwaite et al., 1979
	Young	25.5	20-35	17	26		52 liters/hr	Dawling et al., 1980
	Old	81.0	68-100	20	45[a]		20	
Phenobarbital	Young		20-40	6 (M)	75			Traeger et al., 1974
				6 (F)	70			
	Middle		50-60	3 (M)	74			
				4 (F)	89			
	Old		>70	7 (M)	110[b]			
				4 (F)	105[b]			
Other Drugs								
Carbenoxolone	Young		<40	9	16.3	105 ml/kg	4.72 ml/kg/hr	Hayes et al., 1977
	Old		>65	15	22.9[a]	98	3.28[a]	
Diphenhydramine	Young		20-26	5 (4M)	4.1	292 liters/70 kg	51 liters/70 kg/hr	Berlinger et al., 1982
						295	42	
Propylthiouracil	Old		65-81	6 (F)	4.9	0.35 liters/kg	122 ml/m²/min	Kampmann et al., 1979
	Younger		Not stated	6				
Quinine	Old	80	74-86	9		0.37	105	Stevenson et al., 1979
	Young		20-40	6	5.7	3.17 liters/kg	0.397 liters/kg/hr	
	Old		>65	5	6.6	1.74[a]	0.193[a]	

NOTE:

CHF = congestive heart failure
COPD = chronic obstructive pulmonary disease
LBW = lean body weight
Vd_β = apparent volume of distribution
Vd_{ss} = volume of distribution at steady state

[a] Significant difference between old and young age group ($p < 0.05$).
[b] Significant difference between old and young age group of same sex ($p < 0.05$)
[c] Significant difference between hospitalized and normals in same age group ($p < 0.05$).
[d] Significant difference between male and female in same age group ($p < 0.05$).
[e] Significant difference between fast and slow acetylators in same age group ($p < 0.05$).
[f] Significant difference between smokers and nonsmokers in same age group ($p < 0.05$).

TABLE 8. Effect of Age on Disposition of Benzodiazepines.

Drug	Age Group	Mean Age (yr)	Age Range (yr)	N (sex)	Mean $t_{1/2}$ (hr)	Mean Volume of Distribution	Mean Clearance	Mean Percent Bound	Reference
Chlordiazepoxide	Young	24.5	21–30	28	10.1	0.42 liters/kg	46 ml/min 0.606 liters/kg/min		Shader et al., 1977
	Old	68.8	63–74	8	18.2[a]	0.52[a]	27[a] 0.345[a]		Roberts et al., 1978
	Age as a continuous variable		16–86	27	Age 20: 3.8 Age 80: 39.2 (r = 0.67, p p < 0.001)	0.26 liters/kg (Vd_{ss}) 0.38 (r = 0.60, p < 0.05)	30.8 ml/min 8.0 (r = −0.71, p < 0.001)	96.5 (No correlation with age)	
Clobazam	Young	27.5	20–37	8 (M)	16.6	0.87 liters/kg	0.63 ml/kg/min	88.8	Greenblatt et al., 1981b
		21.3	18–26	8 (F)	30.7	1.37	0.56	89.1	
	Old	63.3	60–69	7 (M)	47.7[b]	1.40[b]	0.36[b]	88.1	
		64.5	60–72	6 (F)	48.6[b]	1.83[b]	0.48	87.7	
Desalkylflura- zepam (from flurazepam)	Young	25.3	19–34	7 (M)	74			96.6	Greenblatt et al., 1981a
		28.0	20–33	7 (F)	90			96.9	
	Old	68,3	66–72	6 (M)	160[b]			96.3	
		71.3	61–85	6 (F)	120			96.3	
Desmethyldiaz- epam (20 mg p.o.)	Young	31.0	29–34	4	51	0.64 liters/kg	11.3 ml/min		Klotz and Müller- Seydlitz, 1979
	Old		65–85	4	151[a]	0.85	4.3[a]		
(from praze- pam)	Young	31.0	22–42	8 (M)	61.8	1.60 liters/kg	0.35 ml/kg/min		Allen et al., 1980
		27.9	22–31	7 (F)	84.2	2.11	0.39	97.3	
	Old	68.4	62–76	8 (M)	127.8[b]	2.56[b]	0.27	97.1	
		72.7	65–85	6 (F)	75.4	3.01	0.46	96.9	

Drug / Group	Mean age	Age range	N (sex)	Half-life	V_d	Clearance	Protein binding (%)	Reference
Young	56.1	22–33	5 (M)	64.5	1.05 liters/kg	0.22 ml/kg/min	97.4	Shadel et al., 1981
Old	33.5	26–38	6 (F)	83.2	1.28	0.21	96.6	
	68.4	64–76	7 (M)	120.1[b]	1.24	0.15	96.7[b]	
	67.5	56–85	10 (F)	71.6	1.54	0.27	96.9	
(from diazepam) Age as a continuous variable		15–82	33				97.6 (No correlation with age)	Klotz et al., 1975
Diazepam Age as a continuous variable		15–82	33	Age 20: 23.7 Age 80: 88.8 ($r = 0.83$, $p < 0.001$)	0.76 liters/kg($V_{d_{ss}}$) 1.80 ($r = 0.74$, $p < 0.001$)	28.8 ml/min 17.6 ($r = -0.39$, $p < 0.089$)	97.4 (No correlation with age)	Klotz et al., 1975
Young	24.3	21–29	4 (M)	24.0	1.00 liters/kg	34.5 ml/min		MacLeod et al., 1979
Old	25.6	21–30	5 (F)	43.9[c]	1.28[c]	20.7		
	25.0	21–30	9	35.0	1.15	26.9		
	80.0	73–88	5 (M)	35.8	1.58	32.8		
	79.2	70–85	5 (F)	56.6[c]	1.87	25.5		
	79.6	70–88	10	41.7	1.71	29.1		
Age as a continuous variable	57	32–78	14	Age 35: 9.8 Age 75: 44.6 ($r = 0.57$, $p < 0.05$)	0.39 liters/kg ($V_{d_{ss}}$) 1.99 ($r = 0.64$, $p < 0.05$)	84.7 ml/min 23.5 ($r = -0.58$, $p < 0.05$)		Kanto et al., 1979
Young	27.7	23–37	11 (M)	36.0	1.11 liters/kg	0.39 ml/kg/min 29.90 (free)	98.7	Greenblatt et al., 1980b
	28.3	21–32	11 (F)	42.4	1.73	0.51 43.60 (free)	98.8	
Old	68.9	63–76	11 (M)	98.5[b]	1.83[b]	0.24[b] 14.90[b]	98.3	
	68.9	61–84	11 (F)	71.8[b]	2.64[b]	0.48 28.00[b]	98.3[b]	

(Continued)

TABLE 8. (*Cont.*)

Drug	Age Group	Mean Age (yr)	Age Range (yr)	N (sex)	Mean $t_{1/2}$ (hr)	Mean Volume of Distribution	Mean Clearance	Mean Percent Bound	Reference
	Age as a continuous variable	56.9	18–95	19	Age 20: 27.6 Age 80: 84.0 ($r = 0.80$, $p < 0.001$)	0.45 liters/kg 2.85 ($r = 0.78$, $p < 0.001$)	19.68 ml/min 19.48 (No correlation with age) Age 20: 1270 ml/min (free) Age 80: 641 ($r = -0.72$, $p < 0.001$)	99.2 94.4 (Correlated log linearly with age: $r = -0.93$, $p < 0.001$)	Macklon et al., 1980
Flunitrazepam	Age as a continuous variable	52.1	19–79	20	28.7 (No correlation with age)	3.72 liters/kg (No correlation with age)	135 ml/min (No correlation with age)		Kanto et al., 1981
Lorazepam	Age as a continuous variable		15–73	11	21.7 (No correlation with age)	1.28 liters/kg (No correlation with age)	0.75 ml/kg/min (No correlation with age)	93.2 (No correlation with age)	Kraus et al., 1978
	Young	27.3	19–38	16	14.1	1.11 liters/kg	0.99 ml/kg/min		Greenblatt et al., 1979
	Old	69.8	60–85	16	15.9	0.99	0.77[a]		

Lormetazepam	Young	24.2		6	10.6 (0.5 mg i.v.) 9.9 (1.0 mg p.o.) 10.7 (1.0 mg p.o.)	289 liters	227 ml/min 311 272		Hümpel et al., 1980
	Old	65.8		6	11.5 14.2 15.2	204	182 210 244		
Midazolam	Young		20–40	10	2.8	1.71 liters/kg (Vd_{ss})	0.45 liters/kg/hr		Collier et al., 1982
	Old		>60	10	4.3	2.46[a]	0.43		
Nitrazepam	Young	25.3	<40	10	33.0	2.9 liters/kg			Castleden et al., 1977a
	Old	74.7	>69		32.5	2.7			
	Young	24.2	18–38	25	28.9	2.4 liters/kg	4.1 liters/hr		Kangas et al.,
	Old	77.4	66–89	12	40.4[a]	4.8[a]	4.7		
Oxazepam	Young	25.0	14–30	8	7.1	47.7 liters (Vd_β) 52.5 (Vd_{extrap})	113.5 ml/min	86.7	Shull et al., 1976
	Old	53.6	45–84	8	6.4	61.2[a] 70.6	136.0	89.3	
	Age as a continuous variable	49.9	22–76	18 (M)	7.8	0.73 liters/kg	1.15 ml/kg/min	95.7	Greenblatt et al., 1980c
		47.3	28–84	20 (F)	9.7 (M vs F, $p < 0.05$; no correlation with age)	0.65 (No correlation with age)	0.82 (M vs F, $p < 0.02$; no correlation with age)	95.6	

(Continued)

TABLE 8. (*Cont.*)

Drug	Age Group	Mean Age (yr)	Age Range (yr)	N (sex)	Mean $t_{1/2}$ (hr)	Mean Volume of Distribution	Mean Clearance	Mean Percent Bound	Reference
	Age as a continuous	46	21–72	13	10 (No correlation with age)	1.0 liters/kg (Vd_{ss}) (No correlation with age)	90 ml/kg/hr (No correlation with age)		Murray et al., 1981
	Age as a continuous variable	50.7	24–86	22 (M)	7.5	0.96 liters/kg	1.48 ml/kg/min		Ochs et al., 1981
		43.7	20–76	9 (M)	8.5 (No correlation with age)	1.17 (No correlation with age)	1.70 (No correlation with age)		
Temazepam	Young	29.0	24–39	7 (M)	12.8	1.53 liters/kg	1.36 ml/kg/min	97.5	Divoll et al., 1981
	Old	29.7	28–33	7 (F)	16.2	1.40	1.10	97.7	
		69.1	60–76	8 (M)	11.9	1.32	1.35	96.9	
		69.8	62–84	10 (F)	17.2	1.39	0.97	97.25	

NOTE:

For abbreviations, see Table 7.

[a]Significant difference between old and young age group ($p < 0.05$).

[b]Significant difference between old and young age group of same sex ($p < 0.05$).

[c]Significant difference between males and females in same age group ($p < 0.05$).

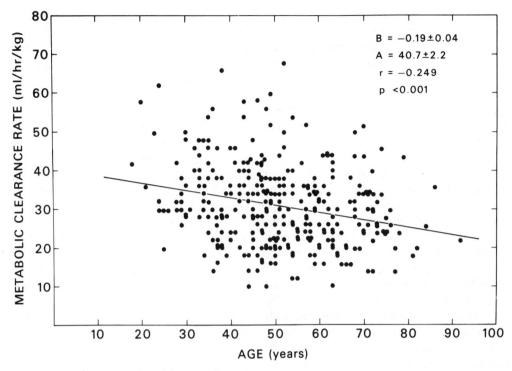

Figure 2. Decline in the metabolic clearance rate of antipyrine with age in 307 healthy male subjects. (From Vestal et al., 1975.)

the variance. Thus, age itself probably has only a minor influence on rates of metabolism of antipyrine in adults. Interestingly, a study comparing the effects of age on the oxidation of acetanilide and the acetylation of isoniazid found a significant prolongation of the plasma half-life of acetanilide in the elderly subjects but no age difference in the half-life of isoniazid (Farah et al., 1977). Whatever the mechanisms of the effect of aging on hepatic drug metabolism, this study emphasizes that nonmicrosomal enzyme pathways of biotransformation may be unaffected. This is true for the oxidation of ethanol by alcohol dehydrogenase, an enzyme present in the soluble fraction of liver cell homogenates (Vestal et al., 1977).

Alterations in blood flow to the liver may influence drug metabolism. Indocyanine green and propranolol have been used to estimate liver blood flow. In contrast to antipyrine, the hepatic extraction of indocyanine green is very efficient and results in a high clearance which is largely dependent upon the rate of delivery of the compound to the liver and is considered flow limited. Wood et al. (1979) reported a 40 percent increase in indocyanine green half-life and a 24 percent reduction in clearance in older subjects when compared to young subjects without a difference in volume of distribution. A comparison study (Vestal et al., 1979a) demonstrated that propranolol, which has an intermediate hepatic extraction ratio and has both blood flow and enzyme activity as major determinants of hepatic clearance, had a 28 percent longer half-life in the elderly as compared to the younger subjects. Systemic clearance for the younger subjects was 32 percent higher than for the older subjects without a difference in volume of distribution. Apparent liver blood flow was 24 percent lower in the older group compared to the younger group and decreased in both smokers and nonsmokers. Intrinsic clearance after oral administration, which most closely reflects drug metabolizing enzyme activity, seemed to be more influenced by smoking than by age. Thus, Vestal and Wood (1980) concluded from their data with model compounds that advanced age is associated with two distinct alterations which effect drug elimination: (1) an age-related reduction in liver blood flow, possibly reflecting an age-related decline in cardiac output, and (2) an age-related reduction in the effect of environmental influences, such as smoking, on intrinsic clearance.

The degree of plasma protein binding may also influence hepatic clearance. For example, total plasma clearance of phenytoin was negatively correlated with serum albumin concentration and was greater in old than in young subjects (Figure 3) (Hayes et al., 1975b). The same relationship seems to hold for tolbutamide. Miller et al. (1977) reported that total plasma clearance and volume of distribution were positively correlated with age. These parameters were both correlated with the unbound fraction of tolbutamide which was itself positively correlated with age. Both phenytoin and tolbutamide are highly bound to plasma protein, but they are slowly metabolized by the liver (capacity limited or low extraction and binding sensitive). Thus, it should be apparent that the ultimate effect of age on drug elimination will depend on the pharmacokinetic characteristics of the drug. These include the extent to which metabolism is limited by hepatic blood flow or enzyme activity, the degree of protein binding, and in some cases, the route of drug administration (oral or intravenous).

Renal Excretion

Studies of the effect of age on renal physiology indicate that both glomerular and tubular functions are affected. Glomerular filtration rate (GFR), as measured by inulin or creatinine clearance, may fall as much as 50 percent, with an average decline of about 35 percent between ages 20 and 90 (Rowe et al., 1976). Renal plasma flow declines approximately 1.9 percent per year (Bender, 1965). In contrast to intrinsic hepatic drug metabolism for which the effects of old age are less certain and probably less important

than interindividual variation, diminished renal function is common and easily measured in the elderly. The extent of impairment may vary from individual to individual, but a simple clinical test of renal function, such as the creatinine clearance, can be used along with plasma level determinations in adjusting doses and dosage schedules of drugs which are primarily excreted by the kidney. Drugs excreted by the kidney which show age-related changes in the rate of elimination include those listed in Table 9. In general, drugs which are significantly excreted by the kidney can be assumed to have diminished plasma clearance in the elderly. However, if renal function is normal (>80 ml/min/1.73 m^2), then age differences in pharmacokinetics are unlikely. This has been clearly shown for amikacin, gentamicin, and tobramycin (Bauer and Blouin, 1981b, 1982a, 1983).

Nutritional and Environmental Factors

Dietary composition is an important environmental determinant of drug metabolism and drug toxicity (Campbell and Hayes, 1974). Most studies have been conducted in experimental animals. Recent studies in man, however, have shown that a low carbohydrate–high protein diet (Kappas et al., 1976), charcoal-broiled beef (Kappas et al., 1978), and dietary brussel sprouts and cabbage (Pantuck et al., 1979) stimulate the metabolism of antipyrine, theophylline, and phenacetin. The extent to which the elderly may respond to dietary manipulations is not known, but overt protein calorie malnutrition is associated with impaired drug metabolism in undernourished children and adults (Krishnaswamy, 1978). In the elderly, vitamin deficiency, particularly of ascorbic acid, is associated with reduced antipyrine metabolism which is increased after vitamin supplementation (Smithard and Langman, 1977, 1978). Changes in dietary ascorbic acid did not affect caffeine metabolism in the elderly (Trang et al., 1982).

Cigarette smoking has an important influence on drug metabolism (Jusko, 1978; Ves-

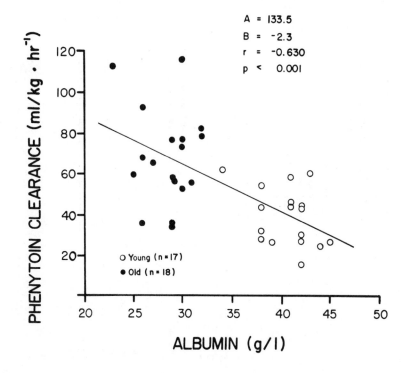

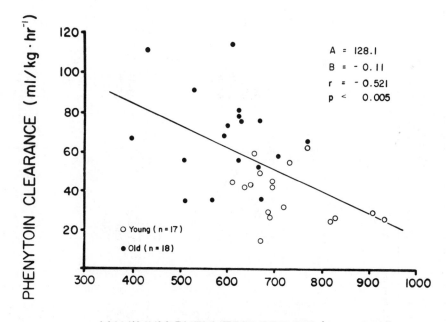

Figure 3. Correlation of phenytoin clearance with serum albumin (upper panel) and with phenytoin binding (lower panel) in young (aged 20–38 years) and old (aged 65–90 years) subjects. Total plasma clearance of phenytoin was determined after 250 mg phenytoin. Maximum plasma binding was determined from measurements of free and bound drug at four different drug concentrations. (From the data of Hayes et al., 1975b.)

TABLE 9. Effect of Age on the Disposition of Drugs Eliminated Primarily as Unchanged Drugs by the Kidney.

Drug	Age Group	Mean Age (yr)	Age Range (yr)	N (sex)	Mean $t_{1/2}$ (hr)	Mean Volume of Distribution	Mean Clearance	Reference
Acetylprocainamide	Age as a continuous variable	57	8–90	32			Age 35 = 2.25 Age 70 = 1.79 (Ratio of acetyl-procainamide clearance to creatinine clearance; $r = -0.32$, $p < 0.1$)	Reidenberg et al., 1980
Amikacin	Young	31.2	20–39	31[a]	2.3	0.27	1.32 ml/min/kg	Bauer and Blouin, 1983
	Middle	49.1	40–59	27[a]	2.1	0.24	1.27	
	Old	71.2	60–79	29[a]	2.5	0.22	1.23	
Ampicillin	Young		21–30		1.0			Simon et al., 1975 (cited in Richey and Bender, 1978)
	Old		60–76		1.2			
Atenolol	Young		22–46	6	1.88 p.o. 1.27 i.v.	0.28 liters/kg (Vd_{ss})	0.25 liters/hr/kg	Triggs et al., 1980
	Old		68–84	5	4.89 6.70	0.30	0.08[b]	
	Young		23–33	6			364 ml/min	Barber et al., 1981
	Old		66–72	5			183[a]	
	Young		23–32	7	4.7 p.o. 3.3 i.v.	0.55 liters/kg (Vd_{ss})	203 ml/min	Rubin et al., 1982
	Old		66–78	7	5.8 3.5	0.75	163	
Azapropazone	Young		19–37	6	18	0.22 liters/kg	0.551	Ritch et al., 1982
	Old		79–96	12	31	0.21	0.292[a]	
Cefazolin[c]	Young		24–33	17	1.57		83 ml/min	Simon et al., 1976
	Old		66–88	13	3.15[d]		43[d]	
Cephadrine[c]	Young		24–33	17	0.53		378 ml/min	Simon et al., 1976
	Old		66–88	13	1.20[d]		152[d]	

Drug	Group	n	Age range	Mean age	$t_{1/2}$	V_d	Clearance	Reference
Cimetidine	Young	5	28–45				702 ml/min	Gugler and Somogyi, 1979
	Old	7	53–64				347[d]	
	Age as a continuous variable	20	22–84		Age 36.6 = 125 min; Age 74.2 = 156	Age 36.6 = 1.63 liters/kg; Age 74.2 = 1.37 ($r = -0.45$, $p < 0.05$)	Age 36.6 = 551 ml/kg/hr; Age 74.2 = 339[b] ($r = 0.75$, $p < 0.001$)	Redolfi et al., 1979
	Age as a continuous variable	12	28–64		Age 35 = 1.8; Age 60 = 2.2 ($r = 0.69$, $p < 0.05$)	Age 35 = 74 liters (Vd_{ss}); Age 60 = 41 ($r = -0.87$, $p < 0.005$)	Age 35 = 680 ml/min; Age 60 = 310[b] ($r = -0.89$, $p < 0.001$)	Somogyi et al., 1980[c]
	Age as a continuous variable	35	20–86				Age 35 = 458 ml/min; Age 70 = 213 ($r = -0.63$, $p < 0.001$)	Drayer et al., 1982
Digoxin	Young	9	20–30	27	51		83 ml/min/1.73 m²	Ewy et al., 1969
	Old	5	73–81	77	73[c]		53[e]	
	Young	6	34–61	47	37 p.o. 38 i.v.	339 liters; 5.3 liters/kg	1.7 ml/kg/min	Cusack et al., 1979
	Old	7	72–91	81	70[b] 69[b]	194[b] 4.1	0.8[b]	
Dihydrostreptomycin	Young	16	18–33	24.8	5.2			Vartia and Leikola, 1960 (cited in Richey and Bender, 1977)
	Old	15	63–87	76.7	8.4			
Gentamicin	Young	12	20–50		1.5	15.2% body wt		Lumholtz et al., 1974
	Middle	12	51–70		2.0[d]	16.2		
	Old	25	>70		3.6[d]	24.2[f]		
	Young	51[a]	20–39	28.8	2.2	0.23 liters/kg	1.29 ml/kg/min	Bauer and Blouin, 1982
	Middle	59[a]	40–59	51.2	2.1	0.27	1.35	
	Old	63[a]	60–79	70.5	2.4	0.26	1.31	

(Continued)

TABLE 9. (*Cont.*)

Drug	Age Group	Mean Age (yr)	Age Range (yr)	N (sex)	Mean $t_{1/2}$ (hr)	Mean Volume of Distribution	Mean Clearance	Reference
Kanamycin	Young		20–50	13	1.8			Kristensen et al., 1974
	Middle		50–70	21	2.5			
	Old		70–90	27	4.7			
	Young		20–50	13	1.8			Lumholtz et al., 1974
	Middle		51–70	21	2.5	16.7% body wt		
	Old		<70	33	5.5	16.0		
						23.1^f		
Lithium[g]	Young	25					41.5 ml/min	Lehmann and Merten, 1974 (cited in Richey and Bender, 1977)
	Middle	58					16.8	
	Old	63					7.7	Ball et al., 1978
Mecillinam	Young		Not stated	6	0.88			
	Old		>65	6	3.97^b			
Pancuronium	Age as a continuous variable		20–86	19		No significant difference with increasing age	Decreased with increasing age	McLeod et al., 1979
Penicillin G	Control	35	25–60	18	1.78	275 ml/kg	1.81 ml/kg/min	Duvaldestin et al., 1982
	Old	79	>75	15	3.40	320	1.18^b	
	Young	30		9	0.4			Kampmann et al., 1972
	Old	80		13	0.9^b			
	Young	24.8	15–33	19	0.55 (sodium) 10.0 (procaine)			Leikola and Vartia, 1957 (cited in Richey and Bender, 1977)
	Old	76.7	71–86	19	1.0 18.0			
	Young		<30	7 (M)	0.35			Hansen et al., 1970
			<50	9 (F)	0.40			
	Old		>65	8 (M)	0.65^b			
			>70	18 (F)	0.93^b			
Practolol	Young	27		13	7.1			Castelden et al., 1975
	Old	80		8	8.6			

Drug	Age group	Age	Age range	N				Reference
Procainamide	Age as a continuous variable	57	8–90	32			Age 35 = 4.05 Age 70 = 2.65 (Ratio of procainamide clearance to creatinine clearance; $r = -0.49$ $p < 0.01$)	Reidenberg et al., 1980
Propicillin K	Young		20–30	10	0.57		29.1 liters	Simon et al., 1972
	Old		60–80	16	0.66	0.43 liters/kg	18.4[b] 0.26[b]	
Sotalol	Young	23.9	19–35	12	7.1	3.55 liters/kg	5.93 ml/kg/min (total) 4.10 (renal)	Ishizaki et al., 1980
	Old	65.7	60–74	9	11.4[a]	2.22[a]	3.32[a] 1.93[a]	
Sulfamethizole	Young	24	22–30	6	1.75	0.345 liters/kg	167 ml/min/1.73 m²	Triggs et al., 1975
	Old	81	73–91	7	3.0[b]		90[b]	
Tetracycline	Young	26	21–34	5	6.3 (capsules) 5.8 (solution)	0.338	64 ml/min/1.73 m² 69	Kramer et al., 1978
	Old	69	61–75	5	9.2[b] 9.4[b]		37[a] 42[a]	
	Young	27	18–33	10	3.5			Vartia and Leikola, 1960 (cited in Richey and Bender, 1977)
	Old	75	63–87	11	4.5			
Tobramycin	Young	30.1	20–39	25[a]	2.3	0.25 liters/kg	1.34 ml/kg/min	Bauer and Blouin, 1981b
	Middle	50.5	40–59	23[a]	2.2	0.26	1.44	
	Old	69.6	60–79	29[a]	2.4	0.25	1.25	

[a] Subjects with normal renal function.

[b] Significant difference between old and young age group ($p < 0.05$).

[c] Data also indicate that other cephalosporins such as cephalothin and cefuroxime have decreased clearance and prolonged half-life in elderly persons with impaired renal function (Broekhuysen et al., 1981; Ouslander, 1981).

[d] Statistical analysis of age-related differences not reported.

[e] The values shown for the Somogyi et al. (1980) study were estimated from figures presented in the study and appear to present a complete analysis of the preliminary report presented earlier (Gugler and Somogyi, 1979).

[f] Significant difference between >70 and two younger groups.

[g] Data of Hewick et al. (1977) indicate that in patients age 70–79 years, the dose required to achieve a therapeutic plasma concentration is 31% lower than in patients under age 50.

tal and Wood, 1980), but the enzyme inducing effects of polycyclic hydrocarbons produced by combustion of tobacco seem to be different in the elderly compared to the young (Vestal et al., 1975; Wood et al., 1979; Vestal et al., 1979a). The association of cigarette smoking with enhanced metabolism of antipyrine and propranolol was limited to young and middle-aged subjects. Other data for the effects of age and smoking on antipyrine metabolism (Mucklow and Fraser, 1980) and theophylline metabolism (Cusack et al., 1980) do not confirm these earlier studies. Salem and his associates (1978) showed a significant increase in plasma clearance of antipyrine and quinine in young subjects following enzyme induction by dichloralphenazone treatment, but no significant alteration in the elderly group. While elderly patients may show a reduced response to enzyme induction, additional studies are needed to confirm these observations and elucidate the mechanism. In contrast, since cimetidine reduced the clearance of antipyrine and desmethyldiazepam to a similar extent in both young and elderly subjects (Divoll et al., 1982c), old age may not be associated with an altered response to the effect of inhibitors of drug metabolism.

PHARMACOKINETICS AND PHARMACODYNAMICS OF SELECTED DRUGS IN RELATION TO AGE

The effects of age on pharmacokinetics are of interest primarily because they may provide insight into the mechanisms of altered pharmacodynamics in geriatric patients. The term pharmacodynamics refers to the physiological or psychological response to a drug or combination of drugs. Pharmacodynamics in the elderly has received relatively less attention than pharmacokinetics (Table 10), but increasingly, clinical investigators are attempting to examine drug response as well as drug disposition. Because data are not available for all drugs, however, the effects of age on pharmacokinetics and pharmacodynamics for only a few selected drugs are discussed in the following sections.

Analgesics, Antipyretics, and Anti-inflammatory Drugs

The metabolism and disposition of salicylates have been studied extensively and shown to be dose dependent (Levy, 1965). Aspirin (acetylsalicylic acid) is absorbed from the stomach and hydrolyzed to salicylic acid in the gut wall, liver, and kidneys, and by serum hydrolases. It is extensively protein bound. The major metabolite is salicyluric acid formed as a result of conjugation with glycine. Salicylic acid is also hydroxylated to gentisic acid. Glucuronides have also been identified.

Several studies have suggested that there is a significant difference in salicylate metabolism between young and old subjects (Stevenson et al., 1979; Cuny et al., 1979). However, at least one study (Melander et al., 1978) failed to find any differences. In those studies in which age-related differences have been noted, the data show that while absorption and total clearance of aspirin are unaffected with age, there is an increase in both the half-life and the volume of distribution. Despite this apparent age-related alteration in aspirin disposition, evidence is lacking to suggest that there is a relationship among age, kinetic changes, and altered pharmacodynamics.

Montgomery and Sitar (1981) found increased serum concentrations of salicyluric acid and gentisic acid in older subjects when compared to younger subjects. Unfortunately, their data did not provide insight into the possible mechanisms of this observation which might include decreased renal excretion, increased production, or altered distribution. None of their patients had any evidence of salicylism.

Acetaminophen has gained acceptance as an aspirin substitute, and as a result, its use has increased. Because of its widespread use and potential for serious hepatotoxicity, acetaminophen kinetics in the elderly are of obvious interest. The major metabolites of acetaminophen in man are the glucuronide and sulfate conjugates, both of which are formed in the liver (Ameer and Greenblatt, 1977; Koch-Weser, 1976; Levy, 1981; Mitch-

TABLE 10. Age and Drug Sensitivity in Man.

Drug	Effect of Age	Reference
Anesthetics		
Epidural anesthesia (lidocaine, mepivacaine, bupivacaine, xylidide)	Exaggerated spread and decline in dose requirement with age.	Bromage et al., 1962; Bromage, 1969; Sharrock, 1978
	Constant epidural dose requirement above age 40; no correlation between age and recovery time in adults.	Park et al., 1980; Dohi et al., 1979; Park et al., 1982
Halothane	Decreased mean alveolar halothane concentration with age indicates decreased anesthetic requirement.	Gregory et al., 1969
Anticoagulants		
Heparin	Increased risk of bleeding in women over age 60.	Jick et al., 1968
	No correlation between age and anticoagulant effect (activated PTT) in plasma.	Whitfield et al., 1982
Warfarin	No significant effect of age on dosage requirement.	Hotraphinyo et al., 1978; Jones et al., 1980
	Dosage requirement reduced in older patients.	O'Malley et al., 1977; Shepherd et al., 1977; Husted and Andreasen, 1977; Joly et al., 1977; Routledge et al., 1979
Bronchodilators		
Theophylline	No significant association between age and toxic effects of theophylline.	Pfeifer and Greenblatt, 1978
Cardiovascular Agents		
Angiotension II	Decreased pressor dose requirement in older subjects and decreased reflex bradycardia in response to blood pressure elevation.	Randall et al., 1978; Meier et al., 1980
Atropine	Decreased tachycardic response in older patients.	Dauchot and Gravenstein, 1971
Deslanoside C	No age difference in cardiac inotropic response.	Cokkinos et al., 1980
Diuretics	Increased prevalence of diuretic-associated hypokalemia in elderly females compared to elderly males.	Krakuer and Lauritzen, 1978; Clark et al., 1982
	No apparent increase in frequency of postural hypotension (ages 50–79 vs 80–99).	Myers et al., 1978
Isoproterenol	Reduced chronotropic and peripheral vascular responsiveness with age.	London et al., 1976; Vestal et al., 1979; Bertel et al., 1980; Brummelen et al., 1981; Kendall et al., 1982
	Decreased cyclic AMP and adenylate cyclase response in lymphocytes from elderly subjects.	Dillon et al., 1980; Krall et al., 1981
	No difference in cyclic AMP response in lymphocytes from young and old subjects.	Kraft and Castleden, 1981
Methyldopa	Patients over age of 60 years more responsive.	Dollery and Harington, 1962
	Frequency of hypotension decreases with age, while frequency of other reactions is unchanged.	Lawson et al., 1978

(*Continued*)

TABLE 10. (*Cont.*)

Drug	Effect of Age	Reference
Norepinephrine	Norepinephrine pressor dose not correlated with age.	Meier et al., 1980
	Vascular α-adrenoceptor sensitivity in isolated human arteries and veins unchanged with age.	Scott and Reid, 1982; Stevens et al., 1982
Phenylephrine	Decreased reflex bradycardia in response to acute elevation of blood pressure.	Gribbin et al., 1971
	Greater increase in left ventricular end-diastolic dimension during beta-blockade in elderly compared to young subjects.	Yin et al., 1978
Procainamide	Toxicity directly related to total daily dose but not to age.	Lawson and Jick, 1977
Propranolol	Adverse reactions more common with increasing age, but not statistically significant.	Greenblatt and Koch-Weser, 1973
	Reduced effect during exercise; effectiveness of free concentration decreased with age.	Conway et al., 1973; Vestal et al., 1979
Hypoglycemic Agents		
Tolbutamide	Decreased hypoglycemic response to acute intravenous administration in older subjects.	Swerdloff et al., 1967
Muscle Relaxants		
d-Tubocurarine	Recovery times from neuromuscular blockade and following reversal by neostigmine are similar in young and elderly patients.	Chmielewski et al., 1978
Pancuronium	Slower recovery in the elderly from neuromuscular blockade induced by this agent, but same dose-response relationship.	Marsh et al., 1980; Duvaldestin et al., 1982
Narcotic Analgesics		
Morphine	Increased extent and duration of postoperative pain relief in older compared to younger cancer patients.	Bellville et al., 1971; Kaiko et al., 1980
Pentazocine	Increased pain relief in older postoperative patients.	Bellville et al., 1971
Psychoactive Drugs (including Benzodiazepines)		
Antidepressants	No effect of age on systolic time intervals.	Burckhardt et al., 1978
Chlordiazepoxide	Increased sedation in older patients.	Boston Collaborative Drug Surveillance Program, 1973
Chlormethiazole	No change in psychomotor function, postural sway, or EEG.	Briggs et al., 1980
	Increased postural sway and psychomotor impairment in elderly.	Hockings et al., 1982
Diazepam	Increased sedation in older patients.	Boston Collaborative Drug Surveillance Program, 1973
	Elderly patients require lower doses as premedication for endoscopy and cardioversion.	Giles et al., 1978; Reidenberg et al., 1978
Dichloralphenazone	Increased postural sway without other changes in psychomotor performance.	Hockings et al., 1982

TABLE 10. (*Cont.*)

Drug	Effect of Age	Reference
Ethanol	Increased impairment of cognitive and psychomotor function with age.	Robertson-Tchabo et al., 1975
Flunitrazepam	Increased sedative and amnestic effect in older patients	Korttila et al., 1978; Kanto et al., 1981
Flurazepam	Increased side effects at high doses (greater than 15 mg per day).	Greenblatt et al., 1977a
	No increase in sensitivity with chronic dose of 15 mg nightly for 15 consecutive nights.	Greenblatt et al., 1981a
Nitrazepam	Elderly patients susceptible to mistakes in psychomotor testing and excessive CNS depression at high dose (daily dose 10 mg or more).	Castleden et al., 1977a; Greenblatt and Allen, 1978a
Temazepam	No change in pyschomotor function, postural sway, or EEG.	Briggs et al., 1980
	Increased sensitivity to psychomotor impairment in elderly (single 20 mg dose).	Swift et al., 1981
Other Drugs		
Bleomycin	Progressive reduction of dose required to inhibit phytohemagglutinin-stimulated lymphocyte proliferation with age.	Seshadri et al., 1979
Diphenhydramine	No effect of age on psychomotor function.	Berlinger et al., 1982
Levodopa	Smaller doses required to avoid side effects.	Grad et al., 1974
Lithium	Dose requirement lower in older patients.	Hewick et al., 1977
Prostaglandin E_1	Decreased cyclic AMP response in human lymphocytes from older subjects.	Doyle et al., 1981a
Sodium fluoride	Decreased cyclic AMP response in human lymphocytes from older subjects.	Doyle et al., 1982

ell et al., 1974). The studies to date (Triggs et al., 1975b; Briant et al., 1976; Fulton et al., 1979; Divoll et al., 1982a; Divoll et al., 1982b) all suggest that the kinetics of acetaminophen are altered only slightly with age. The volume of distribution, with or without correction for body weight, is somewhat smaller in women than in men but declines with age in both sexes. This may be the result of a greater proportion of total body weight comprised of fat in the elderly and in women, together with incomplete distribution of acetaminophen into body fat (Abernathy et al., 1982). Total clearance of acetaminophen, a major determinant of drug accumulation during chronic dosing, is lower in both sexes with age. Since the drug is nontoxic at the usual therapeutic doses, however, no alterations in acetaminophen dosage are required for the elderly. Whether the elderly are more susceptible to hepatotoxicity from overdosage or excessive chronic use of acetaminophen is unknown.

Acetanilide, which is metabolized to acetaminophen by the liver, has been suggested as a "model" substrate to study age-related changes in drug disposition (Playfer et al., 1978). It is possible to measure its conversion to acetaminophen and thus assess the activity of the hepatic microsomal enzymes. Acetaminophen is further conjugated with glucuronic acid or sulfate and then excreted via the kidney. This permits evaluation of the influence of age-related differences in renal function. In contrast to the observations of earlier investigators (Farah et al., 1977), Playfer et al. (1978) reported that half-life, clearance, and volume of distribution of acetanilide were the same in young and old subjects. Levels of acetaminophen and its two conjugates were significantly elevated, however, in the older group. It was concluded that higher levels of unconjugated acetaminophen reflect a reduced ability of the liver to form conjugates, while higher levels of the conjugates in the plasma reflect reduced renal clearance.

Age has been shown to be an important variable in determining the degree of pain relief following the administration of a potent analgesic (Bellville et al., 1971). Under double-blind conditions, there was a progressive age-related increase in relief of pain intensity in postoperative patients receiving 10 mg of morphine or 20 mg pentazocine by the intramuscular route. There were no differences in the frequency of side effects with age. Kaiko (1980) also found that the duration of pain relief after 8 mg and 16 mg morphine intramuscularly increased with age (Figure 4). Pharmacokinetic age differences have been reported following intravenous administration of morphine (0.14 mg/kg). Serum levels at two minutes correlated directly with patient age and averaged 70 percent higher in the older age group (Berkowitz et al., 1975). The serum half-life, however, was independent of age.

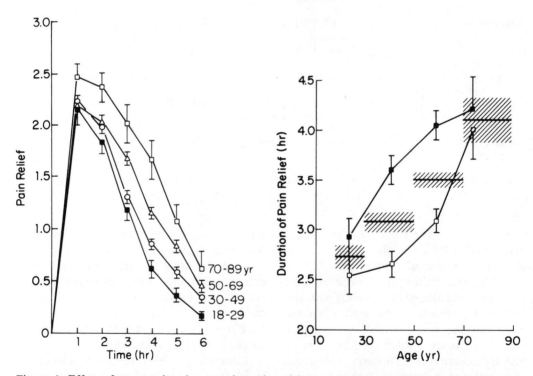

Figure 4. Effect of age on the pharmacodynamics of intramuscular morphine. (*Left*) Time-effect curves for morphine according to age of patient. Each point represents the mean hourly effect of the combined 8 mg and 16 mg doses. (*Right*) Duration (mean ± S.E.) of pain relief in relation to age after 8 mg (lower curve) and 16 mg (upper curve) morphine administered intramuscularly. The duration of pain relief is the hour after drug administration that the patient reports the last positive pain relief score. Shaded areas define age range of each group. (From Kaiko, 1980.)

Anticoagulants

There is evidence to suggest that elderly individuals are more sensitive to the effects of both heparin (Jick et al., 1968) and warfarin (O'Malley et al., 1977; Routledge et al., 1979; Shepherd et al., 1977). The increased risk of hemorrhagic complications may be due in part to diminished mechanical homeostatic response in the presence of degenerative vascular disease. With warfarin, at concentrations much above therapeutic plasma levels, a decrease in the binding capacity of the elderly has been demonstrated which correlated with a reduction in plasma albumin (Hayes et al., 1975a). At therapeutic concentrations, however, no effect of age was seen, nor were any other kinetic age-related differences noted (Shepherd et al., 1977). However, at similar plasma warfarin concentrations, there was greater inhibition of vitamin K-dependent clotting factor synthesis in the elderly than in the young, without a difference in the rate of clotting factor degradation. Possible explanations for these observations are that the elderly have a decreased affinity for vitamin K and are relatively deficient in vitamin K due to reduced dietary intake, defective absorption, or altered pharmacokinetics of the vitamin itself. It should be noted that not all investigators agree that sensitivity to warfarin is increased in the elderly (Hotraphinyo et al., 1978; Jones et al., 1980). Unfortunately, little information is available regarding the kinetics of heparin in the elderly. One study showed a small effect of age on volume of distribution, without other significant age differences in pharmacokinetic parameters (Cipolle et al., 1982).

Anticonvulsants

Age-related increases in plasma phenytoin levels have been observed. Bauer and Blouin (1982b) reported a decline in V_{max} with age in the absence of an effect of age on K_m. Based on these age differences, it was estimated that elderly patients would require 21 percent less phenytoin per day than younger patients. The marked interindividual variation suggests, however, that genetic differences and the effect of saturation (dose-dependent) elimination kinetics may be more important determinants of steady state serum phenytoin concentrations than are age, weight, height, or sex (Houghton et al., 1975). In one study, total plasma clearance of phenytoin after single dose administration (Figure 3) was shown to increase with age (Hayes et al., 1975b). This somewhat paradoxical finding was attributed to decreased plasma albumin and an increase in unbound (free) phenytoin concentration. Reduced protein binding with age has been reported in several studies (Hooper et al., 1974; Hayes et al., 1975b; Patterson et al., 1982; Bach et al., 1981. In contrast to total plasma clearance, another study revealed an age-dependent reduction in clearance of unbound phenytoin, which may be due to reduced liver volume and reduced microsomal enzyme activity per unit of liver volume in the elderly (Bach et al., 1981). The possible clinical significance of these findings in terms of drug sensitivity has yet to be defined. Systematic studies of the kinetics of other anticonvulsants in the elderly are lacking.

Bronchodilators

The results of studies on the effects of aging on the pharmacokinetics of theophylline in man are conflicting. From a clinical standpoint, published nomograms (Jusko et al., 1977; Talseth et al., 1981) suggest reductions in usual infusion rates and oral doses for older patients and for patients with congestive heart failure or liver disease. This suggests that age or age-related factors influence the disposition of theophylline and produce a reduction in total body clearance. Data in support of the age-related effects (Ramsay et al., 1980; Nielsen-Kudsk et al., 1978) suggest that the mean half-life of theophylline is almost twice, and the clearance approximately half, that reported for younger subjects (Mitenko and Ogilvie, 1973; Jenne et al., 1972). Contradictory evidence has been published (Cusack et al., 1980; Bauer and Blouin,

1981a; Fox et al., 1983), which suggests that factors other than aging must be considered before it is accepted that old age is associated with reduced clearance of theophylline.

Cardiovascular Drugs

The elderly are frequently afflicted by cardiovascular disease requiring the use of digitalis preparations often in combination with diuretics. There is only limited evidence, however, that the elderly are more sensitive to the therapeutic and toxic effects of digitalis. Chamberlain et al. (1970) studied 166 patients with atrial fibrillation who were taking digoxin on a long term basis. Mean plasma levels in both the young (32 to 59 years of age) and the old group (60 to 84 years of age) were 1.5 ng/ml. All patients had well-controlled ventricular rates between 60 and 80 beats per minute, with slightly greater variance in the elderly. The plasma levels in the older group were attained with a mean dose of 0.32 mg per day, whereas the younger group averaged 0.42 mg per day. This difference was explained on the basis of reduced renal function in the elderly.

Studies which have evaluated digoxin kinetics in some detail have revealed an age-dependent change in kinetics. Ewy et al. (1969) and Cusack et al. (1979) found that digoxin half-life in the elderly may increase by as much as 40 percent compared to younger patients. Both absolute and weight-corrected clearances decrease, while volume of distribution and extent of absorption do not change with age. It is suggested that in the elderly patient with reduced lean body mass and reduced renal function, both the loading dose and the maintenance dose should be reduced.

In addition to the typical manifestations of digitalis toxicity such as fatigue, anorexia, visual complaints, and nausea, one should be alert to central nervous system effects which may be attributed to organic brain disease. Portnoi (1979) described four elderly patients with psychiatric complications which were shown to be early, or the only, signs of digoxin intoxication. This phenomenon has been reported previously (Church and Marriott, 1959; Shear and Sacks, 1978) and may represent a digitalis side effect which is predominately characteristic of the elderly.

It should also be remembered that not all patients taking digitalis require maintenance therapy. Dall (1970) showed that almost 75 percent of elderly patients in sinus rhythm on maintenance digoxin therapy could be safely withdrawn from treatment. Another study revealed that only one-third of the elderly patients receiving digoxin were getting an ideal dose, and withdrawal of the drug or revision of the dosage, where appropriate, resulted in clinical benefit (Whiting et al., 1978).

β-Adrenergic antagonists also have received considerable attention. Several groups of investigators have studied the effect of age on the pharmacokinetics of propranolol, with relatively similar findings (Castleden et al., 1975; Castleden and George, 1979; Vestal et al., 1979a; Schneck et al., 1980; Feely et al., 1981). In both single-dose and multiple-dose studies, propranolol blood levels in the elderly tend to be higher than in younger patients given the same dosage. While the volume of distribution is not altered following intravenous administration of propranolol, clearance is decreased in the elderly when compared to young subjects (Castleden and George, 1979). The results of one study indicate that age differences may be dose related (Schneck et al., 1980). After a single 20 mg oral dose, the older subjects had a 53 percent lower clearance than the young. Their clearance values were also less than those in the young after the 40 and 160 mg doses, but the differences were not statistically significant. These observations, together with those indicating that the age-related reduction in propranolol metabolism can be demonstrated only in the presence of hepatic enzyme inducing agents such as smoking or in hyperthyroidism (Vestal et al., 1979a; Feely et al., 1981), probably account for the absence of age effects noted in other studies (Schneider et al., 1980). With the observation that metabolites of propranolol accumulate in the plasma of patients with reduced renal function (Stone and Walle, 1980), the kinetics of these active metabolites must also be studied in the elderly.

It is possible that age-related pharmacokinetic differences for propranolol may contribute to the higher incidence of propranolol toxicity (such as bradycardia, pulmonary edema, and hypotension) in patients 60 years or older (Greenblatt and Koch-Weser, 1973), but it is more likely that this age group is predisposed to toxicity because of underlying cardiovascular disease, diminished renal function with azotemia, and use of multiple cardiovascular drug therapy.

Conway et al. (1973) showed that propranolol reduces the heart rate and cardiac output during exercise, but to a lesser extent in older subjects aged 50 to 64 years than in younger subjects aged 20 to 35. It was concluded that the sympathetic drive to the heart elicited by the stimulus of exercise declines with age. There is evidence, however, that the sensitivity to propranolol itself in elderly subjects is reduced. Utilizing dose response curves to isoproterenol before and after a continuous infusion of propranolol (Figure 5), Vestal et al. (1979b) found that resistance to β-adrenergic blockade increased linearly with age. The chronotropic and peripheral vascular response to β-adrenergic stimulation with isoproterenol is also reduced in the elderly (London et al., 1976; Vestal et al., 1979b; Bertel et al., 1980; Brummelen et al., 1981). One study indicates that the effects of age are cardioselective and involve only β_1-adrenoceptor mediated functions (Kendall et al., 1982). Although initially the number of β-adrenergic receptors in membrane fractions of human lymphocytes was found to correlate negatively with age, without apparent alteration in receptor affinity (Schocken and Roth, 1977), more recent studies indicate that neither β-receptor affinity nor receptor density is altered in this tissue (Abrass and Scarpace, 1981; Landeman et al., 1981; Doyle et al., 1981b). In the human lymphocyte system, it has been shown that the response of adenylate cyclase and cyclic AMP to isoproterenol stimulation is reduced (Dillon et al., 1980; Krall et al.,

1981a; Krall et al., 1981b). Whether the lymphocyte can provide information about myocardial tissue is open to question. Although reduced isoproterenol-stimulated myocardial contractile performance has been demonstrated in isolated perfused septa from adult and senescent rats, β-receptor number and affinity, cyclic AMP levels, and cyclic AMP-dependent protein kinase activity are not different in the two age groups (Guarnieri et al., 1980).

The age-related changes in the pharmacokinetics of metoprolol are not as well defined as those with propranolol. Kendall et al. (1977), Lundborg and Steen (1976), and Lundborg et al. (1982) examined plasma concentrations of metoprolol following oral doses and found no significant differences between young and old subjects. However, greater interindividual variation was noted in the old subjects (Lundborg and Steen, 1976). Quarterman et al. (1981), in a more detailed study, investigated the effects of age on the pharmacokinetics of metoprolol after single and multiple doses, and assayed metabolites along with the parent compound. Interestingly, they found that plasma concentrations of metoprolol were the same in the young and the old subjects, but concentrations of the major active metabolite were greater in the older subjects. This observation was recently substantiated by Lundborg et al. (1982). The active metabolite, designated H119/66, is excreted by the kidney, and it is assumed that the elevated plasma levels of this metabolite are the result of reduced renal function which occurs with advancing age (Friedman et al., 1972; Rowe et al., 1976). Quarterman et al. (1981) concluded that when volunteers who are otherwise healthy, ambulatory, nonsmoking, and drug naive are studied, the plasma concentrations of drugs which are metabolized by the liver may not be influenced by advancing age. On the other hand, pharmacologically active metabolites excreted by the kidney may accumulate in the face of age-related reductions in renal function and subsequently assume a role in altered pharmacodynamics.

In contrast to propranolol, practolol is ex-

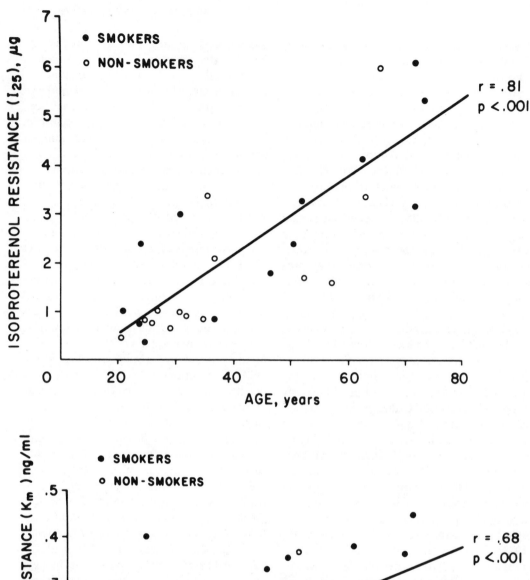

Figure 5. Relationship between age and isoproterenol resistance (upper panel) and between age and propranolol resistance (lower panel). Subjects were 27 normal male volunteers, aged 21 to 73, years whose heart rate response to increasing doses of isoproterenol was measured before and during a continuous infusion of propranolol. (From Vestal et al., 1979b.)

creted primarily via the kidney (Bodem and Chidsey, 1973). When the metabolism of practolol was compared in young and elderly subjects (Castleden et al., 1975), there was no significant difference between the two age groups two hours after dosing. Subsequent levels in the elderly, however, were greater than in the younger group. This was attributed to age-related reductions in renal function. Castelden et al. (1975) concluded that in the absence of reduced renal function, reductions in practolol maintenance doses are not warranted in the elderly. Because of serious toxicity involving epithelial tissues, practolol was never released for clinical use in the United States and has been largely replaced by other β-adrenergic blocking agents in other countries.

Like practolol, atenolol is poorly protein bound and eliminated largely unchanged in the kidney. In a single-dose study using both oral and intravenous atenolol, Rubin et al. (1982) found no age-related changes in clearance, volume of distribution, or bioavailability when young and old subjects were compared. These findings differ with those of Barber et al. (1981) who observed an age-related reduction in atenolol clearance after chronic (eight-day) dosing. To date, there are insufficient data available to determine whether or not clearance of atenolol changes with continued dosing.

Prazosin is the only α-adrenergic blocking agent which has been studied for an effect of age on its disposition. This drug is subject to extensive first-pass metabolism in man, with only 40–60 percent of an oral dose reaching systemic circulation unchanged (Bateman et al., 1979). In a study of the effects of age on the disposition of prazosin, Rubin et al. (1981) compared the pharmacokinetics of prazosin in healthy young and elderly men. The half-life was increased in the elderly (123 ± 19 minutes versus 194 ± 36 minutes) along with the volume of distribution (0.63 ± 0.14 liters/kg versus 0.89 ± 0.26 liters/kg). There was a corresponding reduction of clearance in the elderly (3.94 ± 0.73 ml/min/kg versus 3.53 ± 1.0 ml/min/kg). Surprisingly, the absolute bioavailability of orally administered prazosin was reduced in the elderly (0.68 ± 0.17 versus 0.48 ± 0.16). This finding is in contrast to that discussed earlier with propranolol. It was concluded that the lower absorption of prazosin in older subjects may reflect physiological changes in the gastrointestinal tract associated with age.

Among the antiarrhythmic agents, lidocaine, quinidine, and procainamide have been studied. Toxicity to lidocaine has been reported to be twice as common among elderly patients (4 percent under age 50 and 8 percent age 70 or older) (Pfeifer et al., 1976). Again, this probably reflects the tendency of adverse drug reactions to occur more commonly in patients with serious underlying disease, including congestive heart failure. In a study of young (age 22–26 years) and elderly (age 61–71 years) subjects, Nation et al. (1977a) found a prolonged half-life in the elderly (139.6 ± 64 minutes) when compared to the young (80.6 ± 9.4 minutes). The elderly had a larger volume of distribution, but no difference was noted in clearance. Since total plasma clearance of lidocaine remained unchanged, it was concluded that the increase in half-life was not a reflection of a reduction in hepatic drug metabolizing enzyme activity. These results were confirmed in a report by Cusack et al. (1980).

Ochs et al. (1978) studied the influence of age on the pharmacokinetics of quinidine. Their subjects received quinidine by constant rate infusion over 10–15 minutes, followed by multiple serum samples and urine collection for determination of quinidine. The elimination half-life was longer in the elderly (7.3 hours versus 9.7 hours), and total quinidine clearance was significantly less in the older subjects when compared to the younger subjects (4.04 ml/min/kg versus 2.64 ml/min/kg). It was concluded that hepatic and renal clearance of quinidine decreases with age and that this decrease could predispose to excessive accumulation and possible toxicity. A recent report (Drayer et al., 1980) supports these findings. Procainamide clearance declines with age in proportion to the decline in renal function (Reidenberg et al., 1980).

Sedative-Hypnotic and Anxiolytic Agents

The increased sensitivity and paradoxical response of the elderly to barbiturates is well known anecdotally (Bender, 1964) but not well documented by careful clinical studies. In a significant proportion of elderly patients, the response to barbiturates may vary from mild restlessness to frank psychosis. For this reason, barbiturates have little if any role in geriatric therapy. Traeger et al. (1974) have shown that the half-life of phenobarbital increased from 71 hours in young subjects to 107 hours in subjects over age 70. Amobarbital has also been shown to achieve higher plasma levels in an elderly patient group (Irvine et al., 1974; Ritschel 1978). There was also a marked reduction in excretion of the 3-hydroxy metabolite. These pharmacokinetic differences were attributed to impaired metabolism in the older subjects, but an effect of age on renal excretion cannot be excluded. Animal studies (Jones and Beaney, 1980; Jones and Pardon, 1980) have shown that while protein binding of pentobarbital is unchanged relative to age, higher brain-plasma ratios suggest that there may be an age-related increase in the permeability of the blood-brain barrier.

A prolonged half-life with both a reduced clearance and a reduced volume of distribution has been found in elderly subjects given intravenous chlormethiazole (Nation et al., 1976). After oral administration, peak plasma levels were markedly elevated in elderly subjects compared with young, which may reflect decreased presystemic clearance of the drug by the liver (Nation et al., 1977b). These findings, together with the reduced plasma and red cell binding, suggest that older patients would be predisposed to adverse effects from standard doses of chlormethiazole. In a comparative study of temazepam and chlormethiazole, however, Briggs et al. (1980) reported both subjective and objective parameters which suggest that chlormethiazole was not more prone to producing side effects, particularly hangover, in elderly female subjects.

Considerable information has accumu-lated on the pharmacokinetics and pharmacodynamics of the benzodiazepines in the elderly. An early study revealed a four- to fivefold increase in the plasma half-life of diazepam with increasing age (Klotz et al., 1975). The data suggested that rather than reduced clearance, a markedly increased volume of distribution was the cause of the long half-life. Similar results have been obtained in rats (Klotz, 1979). Thus, although it may take longer for diazepam to reach steady state, accumulation to excessive plasma levels is unlikely. Studies of diazepam disposition in patients with cirrhosis (Andreasen et al., 1976; Greenblatt et al., 1978b) also emphasized the importance of age, sex, and body size as independent variables in pharmacokinetic studies. Stepwise multiple regression analysis indicated that age and liver disease were equally important determinants of elimination half-life and together accounted for 34 percent of the variance. Age and sex collectively accounted for 33 percent of the variance in the volume of distribution. Liver disease, however, was the single most important determinant of weight-corrected diazepam clearance. Greenblatt et al. (1980a) and Macklon et al. (1980) independently investigated the pharmacokinetics of free (unbound) diazepam in relation to age. In addition to confirming an age-related increase in half-life together with a slight increase in volume of distribution, they also demonstrated that the clearance of free drug in plasma was decreased in the elderly. It was concluded that on the average, the extent of accumulation of unbound, pharmacologically active diazepam in elderly persons during multiple-dose therapy would be greater than in young persons of the same sex and weight receiving the same daily dose. The precise importance of these pharmacokinetic differences to the pharmacodynamics of diazepam in the elderly has not been completely evaluated. There is evidence for an age-related decline in the dose of diazepam required to produce central nervous system depression (Boston Collaborative Drug Surveillance Program, 1973; Reidenberg et al., 1978; Giles et al., 1978; Kanto et al., 1979).

Desmethyldiazepam is an extremely important benzodiazepine derivative. It is a metabolite of diazepam (Schwartz et al., 1965), prazepam (Allen et al., 1979), clorazepate (Shader et al., 1981), and medazepam (Viukari and Linnoila, 1979). Although understanding the age-related changes of desmethyldiazapam kinetics is of clinical importance, there has been little investigation. Using young and elderly subjects, Klotz and Müller-Seydlitz (1979) evaluated the effects of age on the kinetics of desmethyldiazepam. Older age was associated with increased half-life and volume of distribution, and reduced clearance, of desmethyldiazepam. Greenblatt and Shader (1980) have also reported similar results, with the additional finding that females are less noticeably affected than males. These studies suggest that there is a need for separate assessment of gender with respect to benzodiazepine metabolism and the effects of age.

Chlordiazepoxide kinetics were the subject of a study by Shader et al. (1977) in a series of healthy young and elderly male volunteers. There was a significant increase in half-life from 10 hours to 18 hours in the elderly group compared to the young group. The volume of distribution was also increased, while the total clearance was reduced in the elderly. The reduced clearance of chlordiazepoxide has been associated with a reduced formation of the major active metabolite, desmethylchlordiazepoxide (Greenblatt et al., 1977b). Roberts et al. (1978) confirmed this observation using an intravenous technique in males. Furthermore, since age did not appear to influence plasma protein binding of chlordiazepoxide, these findings which—in contrast to those for diazepam—are based upon total (free plus bound) chlordiazepoxide concentration are unlikely to be confounded by age-related differences in protein binding. As with diazepam, however, there appears to be an age-related increase in side effects associated with chlordiazepoxide therapy in the elderly (Boston Collaborative Drug Surveillance Program, 1973).

Oxazepam kinetics are affected more by gender and smoking than by age alone (Shull et al., 1976; Greenblatt et al., 1980b; Ochs et al., 1981). When healthy young and elderly males were compared, there was no difference in oxazepam volume of distribution, half-life, clearance, or protein binding. When males and females were compared, however, total oxazepam clearance was greater in men than in women. The free fraction of oxazepam tended to increase with age and was associated with a reduction in plasma albumin concentration. Smoking accelerated oxazepam clearance. Goldstein et al. (1978) compared the effectiveness and hangover from oxazepam, flurazepam, and chloral hydrate. They found that while morning drowsiness was the most common side effect, it was least frequent with oxazepam. This led them to conclude that oxazepam was safer and more efficacious for short term management of insomnia in the elderly.

Temazepam and lorazepam, like oxazepam, are principally metabolized via glucuronidation. Available information on these two compounds suggests that they do not demonstrate age-related changes in their kinetics either (Kraus et al., 1978; Greenblatt et al., 1979; Swift et al., 1981; Divoll et al., 1981). An apparent age-associated increased sensitivity to temazepam, however, has been reported (Swift et al., 1981).

Flurazepam is the most commonly prescribed hypnotic among hospitalized medical patients in the United States and Canada (Greenblatt et al., 1977a). It has generally been considered safe and efficacious for both short term and long term use (Greenblatt et al., 1975). The major metabolite, desalkylflurazepam, has a long elimination half-life approaching 70–100 hours, which results in accumulation during chronic dosing (Schwartz and Postma, 1970; Kaplan et al., 1973). Studies have shown performance impairment and daytime sedation, and have raised questions about the potential hazards of its long term use (Church and Johnson, 1979; Oswald, 1979; Solomon et al., 1979).

The pharmacokinetics of flurazepam and desalkylflurazepam in the elderly have been studied (Greenblatt et al., 1981a). Flurazepam itself was detectable in trace amounts only after oral dosage, whereas numerous active metabolites were identified. Of these metabolites, desalkylflurazpam is the most abundant and the most persistent. When the half-life of desalklflurazepam in young subjects was compared to that observed in the elderly, a marked increase was seen with advancing age (74 hours versus 160 hours). Furthermore, after multiple dosing, the steady state concentration of desalkylflurazepam and the amount of unbound desalkylflurazepam were significantly higher. While this study, using 15 mg oral doses of flurazepam, provided no evidence of increased sensitivity to flurazepam among elderly subjects, other studies suggest that higher doses are more toxic (Greenblatt et al., 1977a; Marttila et al., 1977). When the dose of flurazepam is increased to over 15 mg per day, there is a dramatic increase in the frequency and severity of side effects in the elderly (Figure 6). In fact, nearly 40 percent of pa-

tients over 70 years of age receiving 30 mg of flurazepam will experience unwanted effects.

The kinetics of oral nitrazepam have been studied in young and old subjects (Kangas et al., 1979). After a single dose of nitrazepam, the half-life in the elderly was longer than in the young (40 hours versus 29 hours), and the volume of distribution was larger (4.8 liters/kg versus 2.4 liters/kg). Total plasma clearance and the average steady state levels in both groups were similar. Unfortunately, the subject groups were not well matched. The young group was healthy and drug free, whereas the elderly group was hospitalized, generally debilitated, and receiving other drug therapy. Castleden et al. (1977a), in a limited study of nitrazepam kinetics, reported that while age *per se* had no effect on nitrazepam kinetics, the elderly patients appeared more sensitive to the sedative and depressant effects. A similar observation by Greenblatt and Allen (1978) suggests that while low doses (5 mg) are safe for the el-

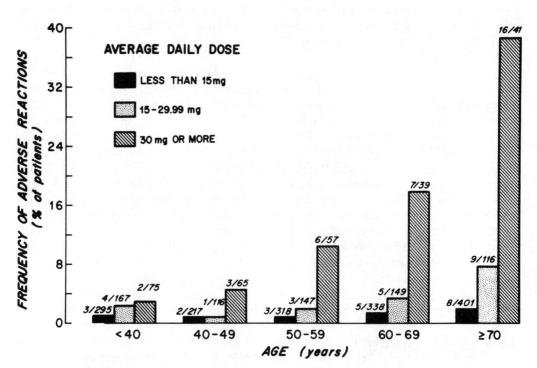

Figure 6. Effect of age and average daily dose on the frequency of adverse reactions to flurazepam. (From Greenblatt et al., 1977a.)

derly, doses of 10 mg or more are associated with a high (55 percent) incidence of adverse reactions in patients over 80 years of age. These observations suggest that alterations in kinetics are not necessarily the cause of increased sensitivity. Neither the study of Kangas nor that of Castleden assessed age-dependent changes in protein binding. In contrast to the lack of an effect of age on benzodiazepine receptor binding characteristics (Pedigo et al., 1981; Tsang et al., 1982), age differences in the distribution of benzodiazepines in brain tissue may be important. Studies in rats showed that brain concentrations were higher in 540-day-old animals than in 100-day-old animals in the absence of pharmacokinetic differences (Hewick and Shaw, 1978). Analogous to the situation in man, the older animals were more sedated than the young at equivalent doses.

Tricyclic Antidepressants

Elderly patients are more prone to adverse effects from tricyclic antidepressants. These include cardiotoxicity (mainly higher degrees of heart block in patients with preexisting bundle-branch block), orthostatic hypotension, confusional states, and urinary retention. Aggravation of glaucoma, dryness of mouth, and other confounding side effects are related to the atropine-like properties of these drugs. These drugs should be used with caution, and attention should be given to the increased possibility of adverse reactions (Fann, 1976; Salzman and Shader, 1978; Rodstein and Oei, 1979).

Nies et al. (1977) evaluated the effect of age on the metabolism of imipramine and amitriptyline. Steady state plasma levels of imipramine and amitriptyline correlated in a positive fashion with age. In the case of the demethylated metabolites of these two compounds, only desipramine levels correlated with age. It is of interest to note that two of the subjects over age 70 required dosage reduction subsequent to substantial orthostatic hypotension. The half-life of desipramine showed significant correlation with age and

was increased by 50 percent, while imipramine half-life showed a trend but was not significant. Neither amitriptyline nor nortriptyline showed a correlation. This is consistent with other reports (Vandel et al., 1978; Ziegler and Biggs, 1977).

Hrdina et al. (1980) compared the pharmacokinetics of imipramine and maprotiline. After single oral doses to elderly subjects, these investigators found that imipramine half-life and plasma clearance were markedly reduced in the elderly when compared to literature values for young normals. They claimed that maprotiline kinetics in the elderly were similar to those reported for young subjects. By comparison, Cutler et al. (1981) found no differences in desipramine kinetics in elderly women after oral doses of 25–50 mg of desipramine.

It is of interest that hydroxylated metabolites of the tricyclics may possess appreciable activity (Potter et al., 1979; Potter et al., 1980). Kitanaka et al. (1982) investigated the kinetics of 2-hydroxydesipramine in elderly depressed patients given desipramine. The ratio of the hydroxydesipramine to desipramine at steady state was significantly higher (0.86) in the elderly patients than in younger patients (0.38). The renal clearance of unconjungated hydroxydesipramine was also evaluated. A negative correlation between clearance and age was found. Similar observations have been noted with a hydroxylated metabolite of nortriptyline (Bertilsson et al., 1979). It may be that the increased sensitivity of the elderly to tricyclics is partly a response to elevated levels of these hydroxy metabolites which previously have been undetected. It is clear that considerable work remains to be done before the pharmacokinetics of this group of drugs are fully understood.

Antipsychotic Drugs

Like the tricyclic antidepressants, the antipsychotic drugs have prominent sedative, cardiovascular, and anticholinergic side effects. Extrapyramidal side effects are also common in the elderly. The peak incidence of akathisia occurs between the ages of 40 and 50, and that of akinetic disorders around 80 years. Choreiform side effects from long term phenothiazine treatment are five times more frequent in the aged than in the younger population (Salzman et al., 1976). Thus, it is important to carefully establish a diagnosis before using these agents and to use them conservatively when indicated. It is also critical to ascertain that an underlying medical illness has not caused or exacerbated psychiatric symptoms. Along with drugs, undiagnosed medical conditions have been found to be the cause of cognitive dysfunction, paranoia, and depression in 25 percent of patients seen by a crisis intervention team (Raskind et al., 1976).

Haloperidol and other high potency antipsychotics have been suggested as drugs of choice in elderly schizophrenic patients (Branchey et al., 1978). This recommendation, however, is based upon pharmacodynamic studies as opposed to kinetic studies. While complete studies of haloperidol kinetics in the aged are lacking, some basic information is available. Rowell et al. (1981) investigated the effects of age on the serum levels and protein binding of haloperidol. Utilizing data from an earlir study (Forsman and Ohman, 1977), they found no correlation between age and serum levels. Their data on protein binding revealed considerable interindividual variation. A significant negative correlation between age and percentage of free haloperidol was observed *in vitro* but could not be substantiated with serum samples from aged patients taking haloperidol. The authors concluded that the age-binding relationship may be altered by schizophrenia or that metabolites of haloperidol, which were not coincubated in the *in vitro* experiments, obscured the relationship *in vivo*. Systematic studies of haloperidol pharmacokinetics and the kinetics of other antipsychotics in the elderly are lacking and are required in the face of the widespread use of these drugs in the elderly.

CONCLUSION

Although much progress has been made in understanding the effects of age on pharmacology, much research is still needed. The elderly use more drugs than younger people and often require multiple drugs, with the potential for drug interactions and adverse drug reactions. It is not known to what extent age *per se* may predispose to drug interactions. The toxicology of drugs in the elderly has received almost no systematic investigation. For example, it is not known whether the elderly are more susceptible than the young to the hepatotoxic effects of acetaminophen. Although compliance with therapeutic regimens is not necessarily worse in the elderly than in younger age groups, the consequences of errors in self-medication may be more severe. Thus, further efforts are needed to develop ways of enhancing the comprehension and compliance of geriatric patients. Future epidemiologic studies on drug use patterns in the elderly should employ a standard methodology, such as the defined daily dose, in order that comparisons can be made between different population groups, institutions, and even regions or countries. This will provide the basis for the evaluation of the effects of educational programs aimed at promoting rational drug therapy in the elderly. Analysis of the differences in drug use and drug prescribing patterns in various countries may yield insight into the determinants of those patterns and suggest optimal educational approaches.

Available evidence indicates that age-related alterations in the physiology of drug distribution, drug elimination, and drug action constitute the substrate upon which disease-related alterations in drug disposition and drug response are superimposed. Continued efforts to characterize these age-related and disease-related effects are needed. For some classes of drugs, generalizations are difficult because of conflicting data. Attention to subject selection, environmental factors such as smoking and diet, and protocol design is necessary. As much as possible, research protocols should attempt to simulate the actual clinical use of the drug under study. Depending upon the characteristics of the drug under investigation, this may mean conducting studies at steady state after multiple dosing rather than only after a single dose. A longitudinal study using model compounds would be of great interest to help distinguish the effects of aging *per se* from those of disease, environmental influence, and selective mortality. Wherever possible, pharmacodynamic studies should be combined with studies of pharmacokinetics. Gaps in our knowledge exist for all drug classes. Continued basic research in pharmacology and physiology is required to elucidate the mechanisms for the age differences observed in clinical studies. This research depends on the use of animal and *in vitro* model systems. Efforts to define the optimal animal or *in vitro* model(s) for human geriatric pharmacology are obviously important components of this basic research.

REFERENCES

Abernathy, D. R., Divoll, M., Greenblatt, D. J., and Ameer, B. 1981. Obesity, sex, and acetaminophen disposition. *Clin. Pharmacol. Ther.* 31: 783–790.

Abrass, I. B. and Scarpace, P. J. 1981. Human lymphocyte beta-adrenergic receptors are unaltered with age. *J. Gerontol* 36: 298–301.

Adelman, R. C. 1971. Age-dependent effects in enzyme induction—a biochemical expression of aging. *Exp. Gerontol.* 6: 75–87.

Adelman, R. C. 1972. Age-dependent control of enzyme adaptation. *Adv. Gerontol. Res.* 4: 1–23.

Adelman, R. 1975. Impaired hormonal regulation of enzyme activity during aging. *Fed. Proc.* 34: 179–182.

Adir, J., Miller, A. K., and Vestal, R. E. 1982. Effects of total plasma concentration and age on tolbutamide plasma protein binding. *Clin. Pharmacol. Ther.* 31: 488–493.

Advenier, C., Saint-Aubin, A., Gobert, C., Houin, G., Albengres, J. P., and Tillement, J. P. 1980. Pharmacokinetics of isoniazid in the elderly. *Brit. J. Clin. Pharmacol.* 10: 167–168.

Allen, M. D., Greenblatt, D. J., Harmatz, J. S., and Shader, R. I. 1979. Single-dose kinetics of prazepam, a precursor of desmethyldiazepam. *J. Clin. Pharmacol.* 19: 445–450.

Allen, M. D., Greenblatt, D. J., Harmatz, J. S., and Shader, R. I. 1980. Desmethyldiazepam kinetics in the elderly after oral prazepam. *Clin. Pharmacol. Ther.* 28: 196–202.

Ameer, B. and Greenblatt, D. J. 1977. Acetaminophen. *Ann. Intern. Med.* 87: 202–209.

Andreasen, P. B., Hendel, J., Greisen, G., and Hvidberg, E. F. 1976. Pharmacokinetics of diazepam in disordered liver function. *Eur. J. Clin. Pharmacol.* 10: 115–120.

Andreasen, F. and Husted, S. 1980. The bindings of furosemide to serum proteins in elderly patients: dis-

placing effect of phenprocoumon. *Acta Pharmacol. Toxicol.* 47: 202–207.

Antal, E. J., Kramer, P. A., Mercik, S. A., Chapron, D. J., and Lawson, I. R., 1981. Theophylline pharmacokinetics in advanced age. *Brit. J. Clin. Pharmacol.* 12: 637–645.

Aronson, J. K. and Grahame-Smith, D. G. 1977. Monitoring digoxin therapy. II. Determinants of the apparent volume of distribution. *Brit. J. Clin. Pharmacol.* 4: 223–227.

Bach, B., Hansen, J. M., Kampmann, J. P., Rasmussen, S. N., and Skovsted, L. 1981. Disposition of antipyrine and phenytoin correlated with age and liver volume in man. *Clin. Pharmacokinet.* 6: 389–396.

Baird, M., Nicolosi, R., Massie, H., and Samis, H. 1975. Microsomal mixed-function oxidase activity and senescence. I. Hexobarbital sleep time and induction of components of the hepatic microsomal enzyme system in rats of different ages. *Exp. Gerontol.* 10: 89–99.

Baird, M., Zimmerman, J., Massie, H., and Pacilio, L. 1976. Microsomal mixed function oxidase activity and senescence. II. *In vivo* and *in vitro* hepatic drug metabolism in rats of different ages following partial hepatectomy. *Exp. Gerontol.* 11: 161–165.

Ball, A. P., Viswan, A. K., Mitchard, M., and Wise, R. 1978. Plasma concentrations and excretion of mecillinam after oral administration of pivmecillinam in elderly patients. *J. Antimicrob. Chemother.* 4: 241–246.

Barber, M. E., Hawksworth, G. M., Petre, J. C., Rigby, J. W., Robb, O. J., and Scott, A. K. 1981. Pharmacokinetics of atenolol and propranolol in young and elderly subjects (abst.). *Brit. J. Clin. Pharmacol.* 11: 118P–119P.

Bateman, D. N., Hobbs, D. C., Twomey, T. M., Stevens, E. A., and Rawlins, M. D. 1979. Prazosin, pharmacokinetics and concentration effect. *Eur. J. Clin. Pharmacol.* 16: 177–181.

Bauer, L. and Blouin, R. A. 1981a. Influence of age on theophylline clearance in patients with chronic obstructive pulmonary disease. *Clin. Pharmacokinet.* 6: 469–474.

Bauer, L. A. and Blouin, R. A. 1981b. Influence of age on tobramycin in pharmacokinetics in patients with normal renal function. *Antimicrob. Agents Chemother.* 9: 587–589.

Bauer, L. A. and Blouin, R. A. 1982a. Gentamicin pharmacokinetics: the effect of age in patients with normal renal function. *J. Am. Geriatr. Soc.* 30: 309–311.

Bauer, L. A. and Blouin, R. A. 1982b. Age and phenytoin kinetics in adult epileptics. *Clin. Pharmacol. Ther.* 31: 301–304.

Bauer, L. A. and Blouin, R. A. 1983. Influence of age on amikacin pharmacokinetics in patients with normal renal function. Comparison with gentamicin and tobramycin. Eur. J. Clin. Pharmacol. 24:639–642.

Bellville, J. W., Forrest, W. H., Miller, E., and Brown, B. W. 1971. Influence of age on pain relief from analgesics. A study of postoperative patients. *J. Am. Med. Assoc.* 217: 1835–1841.

Bender, A. D. 1964. Pharmacological aspects of aging. A survey of the effect of increasing age on drug activity in adults. *J. Am. Geriatr. Soc.* 12: 114–134.

Bender, A. D. 1965. The effect of increasing age on the distribution of peripheral blood flow in man. *J. Am. Geriatr. Soc.* 13: 192–198.

Bender, A. D. 1968. Effect of age on intestinal absorption: implications for drug absorption in the elderly. *J. Am. Geriatr. Soc.* 16: 1331–1339.

Bender, A. D., Post, A., Meier, J. P., Higson, J. E., and Richard, G. 1975. Plasma protein binding of drugs as a function of age in adult human subjects. *J. Pharm. Sci.* 64: 1711–1713.

Bergman, U., Christenson, I., Jansson, B., and Wiholm, B.-E. 1980. Auditing hospital drug utilization by means of defined daily doses per bed-day: a methodological study. *Eur. J. Clin. Pharmacol.* 17: 183–187.

Bergman, U. and Wilholm, B.-E. 1981. Patient medication on admission to a medical clinic. *Eur. J. Clin. Pharmacol.* 20: 185–191.

Berkowitz, B. A., Ngai, S. H., Yang, J. C., Hempstead, J., and Spector, S. 1975. The disposition of morphine in surgical patients. *Clin. Pharmacol. Ther.* 17: 629–635.

Berlinger, W. G., Goldberg, M. J., Spector, R., Chiang, C.-K., and Ghoneim, M. M. 1982. Diphenhydramine: kinetics and psychomotor effects in elderly women. *Clin. Pharmacol. Ther.* 32: 387–391.

Bertel, O., Bühler, F. R., Kiowski, W., and Lutold, B. E. 1980. Decreased beta-adrenoceptor responsiveness as related to age, blood pressure, and plasma catecholamines in patients with essential hypertension. *Hypertension* 2: 130–138.

Bertilsson, L., Mellstrom, B., and Sjoqvist, F. 1979. Pronounced inhibition of noradrenaline uptake by 10-hydroxy-metabolites of nortriptyline. *Life Sci.* 25: 1285–1292.

Bhanthumnavin, K. and Schuster, M. M. 1977. Aging and gastrointestinal function. *In,* C. E. Finch and L. Hayflick (eds.), *Handbook of the Biology of Aging,* pp. 709–723. New York: Van Nostrand Reinhold.

Birnbaum, L. S. 1980. Altered hepatic drug metabolism in senescent mice. *Exp. Gerontol.* 15: 259–267.

Birnbaum, L. S. and Baird, M. B. 1978. Induction of hepatic mixed function oxidases in senescent rodents. *Exp. Gerontol.* 13: 299–303.

Blackwell, B. 1972. The drug defaulter. *Clin. Pharmacol. Ther.* 13: 841–848.

Bodem, G. and Chidsey, C. A. 1973. Pharmacokinetic studies of practolol, a beta adrenergic antagonist in man. *Clin. Pharmacol. Ther.* 14: 26–29.

Boston Collaborative Drug Surveillance Program. 1973. Clinical depression of the central nervous system due to diazepam and chlordiazepoxide in relation to cigarette smoking and age. *New Engl. J. Med.* 288: 277–280.

Braithwaite, R., Montgomery, S., and Dawling, S. 1979.

Age, depression and tricyclic antidepressant levels. *In,* J. Crooks and I. H. Stevenson (eds.), *Drugs and the Elderly,* pp. 133–144. Baltimore: University Park Press.

Branchey, M. H., Lee, J. H. L., Amin, R., and Simpson, G. M. 1978. High- and low-potency neuroleptics in elderly psychiatric patients. *J. Am. Med. Assoc.* 239: 1860–1862.

Briant, R. H., Dorrington, R. E., Cleal, J., and Williams, F. M. 1976. The rate of acetaminophen metabolism in the elderly and the young. *J. Am. Geriatr. Soc.* 24: 359–361.

Briggs, R. S., Castleden, C. M., and Kraft, C. A. 1980. Improved hypnotic treatment using chlormethiazole and temazepam. *Brit. Med. J.* 280: 601–604.

Broekhuysen, J., Deger, F., Douchamps, J., Freschi, E., Mal, N., Neve, P., Parafait, R., Siska, G., and Winand, M. 1981. Pharmacokinetic study of cefuroxime in the elderly. *Brit. J. Clin. Pharmacol.* 12: 801–805.

Bromage, P. R. 1962. Exaggerated spread of epidural analgesia in arteriosclerotic patients: dosage in relation to biological and chronological ageing. *Brit. Med. J.* 2: 1634–1638.

Bromage, P. R. 1969. Ageing and epidural dose requirements. *Brit. J. Anaesth.* 41: 1016–1022.

Brummelen, P. van, Bühler, F. R., Kiowski, W., and Amann, F. W. 1981. Age-related decrease in cardiac and peripheral vascular responsiveness to isoprenaline: studies in normal subjects. *Clin. Sci.* 60: 571–577.

Burkhardt, D., Raeder, E., Müller, V., Imhof, P., and Neubauer, H. 1978. Cardiovascular effects of tricyclic and tetracyclic antidepressants. *J. Am. Med. Assoc.* 239: 213–216.

Cammarata, R. J., Rodnan, G. P., and Fennell, R. M. 1967. Serum anti-gamma-globulin and anti-nuclear factors in the aged. *J. Am. Med. Assoc.* 199: 115–118.

Campbell, T. C. and Hayes, J. R. 1974. Role of nutrition in the drug-metabolizing enzyme system. *Pharmacol. Rev.* 26: 171–197.

Caranasos, G. J., Stewart, R. B., and Cluff, L. E. 1974. Drug-induced illness leading to hospitalization. *J. Am. Med. Assoc.* 228: 713–717.

Carlos, R., Calvo, R., and Erill, S. 1981. Plasma protein binding of etiomidate in different age groups and in patients with chronic respiratory insufficiency. *Int. J. Clin. Pharmacol. Toxicol.* 19: 171–174.

Castleden, C. M. and George, C. F. 1979. The effect of ageing on the hepatic clearance of propranolol. *Brit. J. Clin. Pharmacol.* 7: 49–54.

Castleden, C. M., George, C. F., Marcer, D., and Hallett, C. 1977a. Increased sensitivity to nitrazepam in old age. *Brit. Med. J.* 1: 10–12.

Castleden, C. M., Kaye, C. M., and Parsons, R. L. 1975. The effect of age on plasma levels of propranolol and practolol in man. *Brit. J. Clin. Pharmacol.* 2: 303–306.

Castleden, C. M., Volans, C. N., and Raymond, K.

1977b. The effect of ageing on drug absorption from the gut. *Age Ageing* 6: 138–143.

Chamberlain, D. A., White, R. J., Howard, M. R., and Smith, T. W. 1970. Plasma digoxin concentrations in patients with atrial fibrillation. *Brit. Med. J.* 3: 429–432.

Chan, K., Kendall, J. J., Mitchard, M., Wells, W. D. E., and Vickers, M. D. 1975. The effect of ageing on plasma pethidine concentration. *Brit. J. Clin. Pharmacol.* 2: 297–302.

Chien, C.-P., Townsend, E. J., and Ross-Townsend, A. 1978. Substance use and abuse among the community elderly: the medical aspect. *Addict. Dis.* 3: 357–372.

Chmielewski, A. T., Pybus, D. A., Leach, A. B., and Goat, V. A. 1978. Recovery from neuromuscular blockade. A comparison between old and young patients. *Anesthesia* 33: 539–542.

Christensen, J. H., Andreasen, F., and Jansen, J. A., 1981. Influence of age and sex on the pharmacokinetics of thiopentone. *Brit. J. Anaesth.* 53: 1189–1195.

Church, G. and Marriott, H. J. L. 1959. Digitalis delirium. *Circulation* 20: 549–553.

Church, M. W. and Johnson, L. C. 1979. Mood and performance of poor sleepers during repeated use of flurazepam. *Psychopharmacology* 61: 309–316.

Cipolle, R. J., Seifert, R. D., Neilan, B. A., Zaske, D. E., and Haus, E. 1982. Heparin kinetics: variables related to disposition and dosage. *Clin. Pharmacol. Ther.* 29: 387–393.

Clark, B. G., Wheatley, R., Rawlings, J. L., and Vestal, R. E. 1982. Female preponderance in diruetic-associated hypokalemia: a retrospective study in seven long-term care facilities. *J. Am. Geriatr. Soc.* 30: 316–322.

Cokkinos, D. V., Tsartsalis, G. D., Heimonas, E. T., and Gardikas, C. D. 1980. Comparison of the inotropic action of digitalis and isoproterenol in younger and older individuals. *Am. Heart. J.* 100: 802–806.

Collier, P. S., Kawar, P., Gamble, J. A. S., and Dundee, J. W. 1982. Influence of age on pharmacokinetics of midazolam (abst.). *Brit. J. Clin. Pharmacol.* 13: 602P.

Conrad, K. A. and Bressler, R. (eds.) 1982. *Drug Therapy for the Elderly Patient.* St. Louis: C. V. Mosby.

Conway, J., Whealer, R., and Sannerstedt, R. 1973. Sympathetic nervous activity during exercise in relation to age. *Cardiovasc. Res.* 5: 577–581.

Crooks, J., O'Malley, K., and Stevenson, I. H. 1976. Pharmacokinetics in the elderly. *Clin. Pharmacokinet.* 1: 280–296.

Cuny, G., Royer, R. J., Mur, J. M., Serot, J. M., Faure, G., Netter, P., Maillard, A., and Penin, F. 1979. Pharmacokinetics of salicylates in elderly. *Gerontology* 25: 49–55.

Cusack, B., Kelly, J. G., Lavan, J., Noel, J., and O'Malley, K. 1980. Theophylline kinetics in relation to age: the importance of smoking. *Brit. J. Clin. Pharmacol.* 10: 109–114.

Cusack, B., Kelly, J. G., Lavan, J., Noel, J., and O'Malley, K. 1980. Pharmacokinetics of lignocaine in the elderly (abst.). *Brit. J. Clin. Pharmacol.* 9: 293P–294P.

Cusack, B., Kelly, J., O'Malley, K., Noel, J., Lavan, J., and Horgan, J. 1979. Digoxin in the elderly: pharmacokinetic consequences of old age. *Clin. Pharmacol. Ther.* 25: 772–776.

Cutler, N. R., Zavadil, A. P., Eisdorfer, C., Ross, R. J., and Potter, W. Z. 1981. Concentrations of desipramine in elderly women. *Am. J. Psych.* 138: 1235–1237.

Dall, J. L. C. 1970. Maintenance digoxin therapy in elderly patients. *Brit. Med. J.* 2: 705–706.

Dauchot, P. and Gravenstein, J. S. 1971. Effects of atropine on the electrocardiogram in different age groups. *Clin. Pharmacol. Ther.* 12: 274–280.

Dawling, S., Crome, P., and Braithwaite, R. 1980. Pharmacokinetics of single oral doses of nortriptyline in depressed elderly hospital patients and young healthy volunteers. *Clin. Pharmacol. Ther.* 5: 394–401.

Dillon, N., Chung, S., Kelly, J., and O'Malley, K. 1980. Age and beta-adrenoceptor-mediated function. *Clin. Pharmacol. Ther.* 27: 769–772.

Divoll, M., Abernathy, D. R., Ameer, B., and Greenblatt, D. J. 1982a. Acetaminophen kinetics in the elderly. *Clin. Pharmacol. Ther.* 31: 151–156.

Divoll, M., Ameer, B., Abernathy, D. R., and Greenblatt, D. J. 1982b. Age does not alter acetaminophen absorption. *J. Am. Geriatr. Soc.* 30: 240–244.

Divoll, M., Greenblatt, D. J., Abernathy, D. R., and Shader, R. I. 1982c. Cimetidine impairs clearance of antipyrine and desmethyldiazepam in the elderly. *J. Am. Geriatr. Soc.* 30: 684–689.

Divoll, M., Greenblatt, D. J., Harmatz, J. S., and Shader, R. I. 1981. Effect of age and gender on disposition of temazepam. *J. Pharm. Sci.* 70: 1104–1107.

Dohi, S., Naito, H., and Takahashi, T. 1979. Age-related changes in blood pressure and duration of motor block in spinal anesthesia. *Anesthesiology* 50: 319–323.

Dollery, C. T. and Harington, M. 1962. Methyldopa in hypertension: clinical and pharmacological studies. *Lancet* 1: 759–763.

Donovan, M. A., Castleden, C. M., Pohl, J. E. F., and Kraft, C. A. 1981. The effect of age on digitoxin pharmacokinetics. *Brit. J. Clin. Pharmacol.* 11: 401–402.

Doyle, V. M., Kelly, J. G., and O'Malley, K. 1981b. Lymphocyte β-adrenoceptors in the elderly. *Brit. J. Clin. Pharmacol.* 12: 265P–266P.

Doyle, V. M., O'Malley, K., and Kelly, J. G. 1981a. Lymphocytic cyclic AMP production in the elderly: the effects of prostaglandin E_1. *Brit. J. Clin. Pharmacol.* 12: 597–598.

Drayer, D. E., Hughes, M., Lorenzo, B., and Reidenberg, M. M. 1980. Prevalence of high (3S) 3-hydroxyquinidine/quinidine ratios in serum, and clearance of quinidine in cardiac patients with age. *Clin. Pharmacol. Ther.* 27: 72–75.

Drayer, D. E., Romankiewicz, J., Lorenzo, B., and Reidenberg, M. M. 1982. Age and renal clearance of cimetidine. *Clin. Pharmacol. Ther.* 31: 45–50.

Duvaldestin, P., Saada, J., Berger, J. L., D'Hollander, A., and Desmonts, J. M. 1982. Pharmacokinetics, pharmacodynamics, and dose-response relationships of pancuronium in control and elderly subjects. *Anesthesiology* 56: 36–40.

Edelman, I. S. and Leibman, J. 1959. Anatomy of body water and electrolytes. *Am. J. Med.* 27: 256–277.

Evans, M. A., Broe, G. A., Triggs, E. J., Cheung, M., Creasey, H., and Paull, P. D. 1981a. Gastric emptying rate and the systemic availability of levodopa in the elderly parkinsonian patient. *Neurology* 31: 1288–1294.

Evans, M. A., Triggs, E. J., Broe, G. A., and Saines, N. 1980. Systemic availability of orally administered L-dopa in the elderly parkinsonian patient. *Eur. J. Clin. Pharmacol.* 17: 215–221.

Evans, M. A., Triggs, E. J., Cheung, M., Broe, G. A., and Creasey, H. 1981b. Gastric emptying rate in the elderly: implications for drug therapy. *J. Am. Geriatr. Soc.* 29: 201–205.

Ewy, G. A., Kapadia, G. G., Yao, L., Lullin, M., and Marcus, F. I. 1969. Digoxin metabolism in the elderly. *Circulation* 34: 449–453.

Ewy, G. A., Bertron, M. G., Ball, M. F., Nimmo, L., Jackson, B., and Marcus, F. 1971. Digoxin metabolism in obesity. *Circulation* 44: 810–814.

Fann, W. E. 1976. Pharmacotherapy in older depressed patients. *J. Gerontol.* 31: 304–310.

Farah, F., Taylor, W., Rawlins, M. D., and James, O. 1977. Hepatic drug acetylation and oxidation: effects of aging in man. *Brit. Med. J.* 2: 155–156.

Farner, O. and Verzar, F. 1961. The age parameter of pharmacological activity. *Experientia (Basel)* 18: 421–422.

Feely, J., Crooks, J., and Stevenson, I. H. 1981. The influence of age, smoking and hyperthyroidism on plasma propranolol steady state concentration. *Brit. J. Clin. Pharmacol.* 12: 73–78.

Fisher, C. R. 1980. Differences by age groups in health care spending. *Health Care Financing Review* 1: 65–90.

Forbes, G. B. and Reina, J. C. 1970. Adult lean body mass declines with age: some longitudinal observations. *Metabolism* 19: 653–663.

Forsman, A. and Ohman, R. 1977. Applied pharmacokinetics of haloperidol in man. *Curr. Ther. Res.* 21: 396–411.

Fox, R. W., Samaan, S., Bukantz, S. C., and Lockey, R. F. 1983. Theophylline kinetics in a geriatric group. *Clin. Pharmacol. Ther.* 34: 60–67.

Freidman, S. A., Raizner, A. E., Rosen, H., Soloman, N. A., and Sy, W. 1972. Functional defects in the ageing kidney. *Ann. Intern. Med.* 76: 41–45.

Fulton, B., James, O., and Rawlins, M. D. 1979. The influence of age on the pharmacokinetics of paracetamol (abst.). *Brit. J. Clin. Pharmacol* 7: 418P.

Gardner, P., Goodner, C. J., and Dowling, J. T., 1963. Severe hypoglycemia in elderly patients receiving therapeutic doses of tolbutamide. *J. Am. Med. Assoc.* 186: 991–993.

Geokas, M. C. and Haverback, B. J. 1969. The aging gastrointestinal tract. *Am. J. Surg.* 117: 881–892.

Gersovitz, M., Munro, H. N., Udall, J., and Young, V. R. 1980. Albumin synthesis in young and elderly subjects using a new stable isotope methodology: response to level of protein intake. *Metabolism* 29: 1075–1086.

Gibaldi, M. and Levy, G. 1976. Pharmacokinetics in clinical practice: 1. concepts and 2. applications. *J. Am. Med. Assoc.* 235: 1864–1867; 1987–1992.

Giles, H. G., MacLeod, S. M., Wright, J. R., and Sellers, E. M. 1978. Influence of age and previous use on diazepam dosage required for endoscopy. *Can. Med. Assoc. J.* 118: 513–514.

Gold, G. and Widnell, C. C. 1974. Reversal of age-related changes in microsomal enzyme activities following the administration of triamcinolone, triiodothyronine and phenobarbital. *Biochim. Biophys. Acta.* 334: 75–85.

Gold, G. and Widnell, C. C. 1975. Response of NADPH cytochrome c reductase and cytochrome P-450 in hepatic microsomes to treatment with phenobarbital—differences in rat strain. *Biochem. Pharmacol.* 24: 2105–2106.

Goldstein, A., Aronow, L., and Kalman, S. M. 1974. *Principles of Drug Action: The Basis of Pharmacology,* 2nd ed. New York: John Wiley & Sons.

Goldstein, S. W., Birnbom, F., Lancee, W. J., and Darke, A. C. 1978. Comparison of oxazepam, flurazepam, and chloral hydrate as hypnotic sedatives in geriatric patients. *J. Am. Geriatr. Soc.* 26: 36–371.

Grad, B., Wener, J., Rosenberg, G., and Wener, S. W. 1974. Effects of levodopa therapy in patients with Parkinson's disease: statistical evidence for reduced tolerance to levodopa in the elderly. *J. Am. Geriatr. Sco.* 22: 489–494.

Greenblatt, D. J. 1979. Reduced serum albumin concentration in the elderly: report from the Boston Collaborative Drug Surveillance Program. *J. Am. Geriatr. Soc.* 27: 20–22.

Greenblatt, D. J. and Allen, M. D. 1978. Toxicity of nitrazepam in the elderly: a report from the Boston Collaborative Drug Surveillance Program. *Brit. J. Clin. Pharmacol.* 5: 407–413.

Greenblatt, D. J., Allen, M. D., Harmatz, J. S., and Shader, R. I. 1980a. Diazepam disposition determinants. *Clin. Pharmacol. Ther.* 27: 301–312.

Greenblatt, D. J., Allen, M. D., Locniskar, A., Harmatz, J. S., and Shader, R. I. 1979. Lorazepam kinetics in the elderly. *Clin. Pharmacol. Ther.* 26: 103–113.

Greenblatt, D. J., Allen, M. D., and Shader, R. I. 1977a. Toxicity of high-dose flurazepam in the elderly. *Clin. Pharmacol. Ther.* 21: 355–361.

Greenblatt, D. J., Divoll, M., Abernathy, D. R., Harmatz, J. S., and Shader, R. I. 1982a. Antipyrine kinetics in the elderly: prediction of age-related changes in benzodiazepine oxidizing capacity. *J. Pharmacol. Exp. Ther.* 220: 120–126.

Greenblatt, D. J., Divoll, M., Harmatz, J. S., MacLaughlin, D. S., and Shader, R. I. 1981a. Kinetics and clinical effects of flurazepam in young and elderly noninsomniacs. *Clin. Pharmacol. Ther.* 30: 475–486.

Greenblatt, D. J., Divoll, M., Harmatz, J. S., and Shader, R. I. 1980b. Oxazepam kinetics: effects of age and sex. *J. Pharmacol. Exp. Ther.* 215: 86–91.

Greenblatt, D. J., Divoll, M., Puri, S. K., Ho, I. Zinny, M. A., and Shader, R. I. 1981b. Clobazam kinetics in the elderly. *Brit. J. Clin. Pharmacol.* 12: 631–636.

Greenblatt, D. J., Harmatz, J. S., and Shader, R. I. 1978. Factors influencing diazepam pharmacokinetics: age, sex and liver disease. *Int. J. Clin. Pharmacol.* 16: 177–179.

Greenblatt, D. J., Harmatz, J. S., Stanski, D. R., Shader, R. I., Franke, K., and Koch-Weser, J. 1977b. Factors influencing blood concentrations of chlordiazepoxide: a use of multiple regression analysis. *Psychopharmacology,* 54: 277–282.

Greenblatt, D. J. and Koch-Weser, J. 1973. Adverse reactions to propranolol in hospitalized medical patients: a report from the Boston Collaborative Drug Surveillance Program. *Am. Heart J.* 86: 478–484.

Greenblatt, D. J. and Koch-Weser, J. 1975. Clinical pharmacokinetics. *New Engl. J. Med.* 293: 702–705; 964–970.

Greenblatt, D. J., Sellers, E. M., and Shader, R. I. 1982b. Drug disposition in old age. *New Engl. J. Med.* 306: 1081–1088.

Greenblatt, D. J. and Shader, R. I. 1980. Effects of age and other drugs on benzodiazepine kinetics. *Arzn. Forsch.* 30: 886–890.

Greenblatt, D. J., Shader, R. I., and Koch-Weser, J. 1975. Flurazepam hydrochloride. *Clin. Pharmacol. Ther.* 17: 1–14.

Gregory, G. A., Eger, E. I., and Munson, E. S. 1969. The relationship between age and halothane requirements in man. *Anesthesiology* 30: 488–491.

Gribbin, B., Pickering, T. G., Sleight, P., and Peto, R. 1971. Effect of age and high blood pressure on baroreflex sensitivity in man. *Circ. Res.* 29: 424–431.

Guarnieri, T., Filburn, C. R., Zitnik, G., Roth, G. S., and Lakatta, E. G. 1980. Contractile and biochemical correlates of β-adrenergic stimulation of the aged heart. *Am. J. Physiol.* 239: H501–H508.

Gugler, R. and Somogyi, A. 1979. Reduced cimetidine clearance with age (letter). *New Engl. J. Med.* 301: 435.

Guth, P. H. 1968. Physiologic alteration in small bowel function with age. The absorption of D-xylose. *Am. J. Digest. Dis.* 13: 365–372.

Guttman, D. 1978. Patterns of legal drug use by older Americans. *Addict. Dis.* 3: 337–356.

Halvorsen, L., Dotevall, G., and Walan, A. 1973. Gastric emptying in patients with achlorhydria or hyposecretion of hydrochloric acid. *Scand. J. Gastroenterol.* 8: 395–399.

Hansen, J. M., Kampann, J., and Laursen, H. 1970. Renal excretion of drugs in the elderly. *Lancet* 1: 1170.

Hayes, M. J., Langman, M. J. S., and Short, A. H. 1975a. Changes in drug metabolism with increasing age. 1. Warfarin binding and plasma proteins. *Brit. J. Clin. Pharmacol.* 2: 69–72.

Hayes, M. J., Langman, M. J. S., and Short, A. H. 1975b. Changes in drug metabolism with increasing age. 2. Phenytoin clearance and protein binding. *Brit. J. Clin. Pharmacol.* 2: 73–79.

Hayes, M. J., Sprackling, M., and Langman, M. J. S. 1977. Changes in the plasma clearance and protein binding of carbenoxolone with age, and their possible relationship with adverse drug effects. *Gut* 18: 1054–1058.

Heading, R. C., Nimmo, J., and Prescott, L. F. 1973. The dependence of paracetamol absorption on the rate of gastric emptying. *Brit. J. Pharmacol.* 47: 415–421.

Hewick, D. S., Newbury, P., Hopwood, S., Naylor, G., and Moody, J. 1977. Age as a factor effecting lithium therapy. *Brit. J. Clin. Pharmacol.* 4: 201–205.

Hewick, D. S. and Shaw, V., 1978. Tissue distribution of radioactivity after injection of [^{14}C] nitrazepam in young and old rats. *J. Pharm. Pharmacol.* 30: 318–319.

Hockings, N., Stevenson, I. H., and Swift, C. G. 1982. Hypnotic response in the elderly—single dose effects of chlormethiazole and dichloralphenazone (abst.). *Brit. J. Clin. Pharmacol.* 14: 143P.

Holmberg, L., Odar-Cederlöf, I., Boreus, L. O., Heyner, L., and Ehrnebo, M., 1982. Comparative disposition of pethidine and norpethidine in old and young patients. *Eur. J. Clin. Pharmacol.* 22: 175–179.

Hooper, W. D., Bochner, F., Eadie, M. J., and Tyrer, J. H. 1974. Plasma protein binding of diphenylhydantoin: effect of sex hormones, renal and hepatic disease. *Clin. Pharmacol. Ther.* 15: 276–282.

Hotraphinyo, K., Triggs, E. J., Maybloom, B., and Maclaine-Cross, A. 1978. Warfarin sodium: steady-state plasma levels and patient age. *Clin. Exp. Pharmacol. Ther.* 5: 143–149.

Houghton, G. W., Richens, A., and Leighton, M. 1975. Effects of age, height, weight, and sex on serum phenytoin concentration in epileptic patients. *Brit. J. Clin. Pharmacol.* 2: 251–256.

Hrdina, P. D., Rovei, V., Henry, J. F., Gomeni, R., Forette, F., and Morselli, P. L. 1980. Comparison of single-dose pharmacokinetics in imipramine and maprotiline in the elderly. *Psychopharmacology* 70: 29–34.

Hümpel, M., Nieuweboer, B., Milius, W., Hanke, H., and Wendt, H. 1980. Kinetics and biotransformation of lormetazepam. II. Radioimmunologic determinations in plasma and urine of young and elderly subjects: first-pass effect. *Clin. Pharmacol. Ther.* 28: 673–679.

Hurwitz, N. 1969. Predisposing factors in adverse reactions to drugs. *Brit. Med. J.* 1: 536–539.

Husted, S. and Andreasen, F. 1977. The influence of age on the response to anticoagulants. *Brit. J. Clin. Pharmacol.* 4: 559–565.

Ingman, S. R., Lawson, K. R., Pierpaoli, P. G., and Blake, P. 1975. A survey of the prescribing and administration of drugs in a long-term care institution for the elderly. *J. Am. Geriatr. Soc.* 23: 309–316.

Irvine, R. E., Grove, J., Toseland, P. A., and Trounce, J. R. 1974. The effect of age on the hydroxylation of amylobarbitone sodium in man. *Brit. J. Clin. Pharmacol.* 1: 41–43.

Ishizaki, T., Hirayama, H., Tawara, K. Nakaya, H., Sato, M., and Sato, K. 1980. Pharmacokinetics and pharmacodynamics in young normal and elderly hypertensive subjects: a study using sotalol as a model drug. *J. Pharmacol. Exp. Ther.* 212: 173–181.

Jarvik, L. F., Greenblatt, D. J., and Harman, D., 1981. *Clinical Pharmacology and the Aged Patient.* New York: Raven Press.

Jenne, J. W., Wyze, E., Rood, F. S., and McDonald, F. M. 1972. Pharmacokinetics of theophylline: application to the adjustment of the clinical dose of aminophylline. *Clin. Pharmacol. Ther.* 13: 349–360.

Jick, H., Slone D, Borda, I. T., Shapiro, S. 1968. Efficacy and toxicity of heparin in relation to age and sex. *New Engl. J. Med.* 279: 284–286.

Joly, F., Valty, J., and Emar, A. 1977. Traitement anticoagulant au long cours chez les sujets âgés de plus de 75 ans. *Arch. Mal. Coeur* 70: 521–529.

Jones, B. R., Baran, A., and Reidenberg, M. M. 1980. Evaluating patients' warfarin requirements. *J. Am. Geriatr. Soc.* 28: 10–12.

Jones, T. W. G. and Beaney, J. 1980. The effect of age and pentobarbitone tolerance on pentobarbitone depression of calcium-45 uptake by mouse brain synaptosomes. *Mech. Age. Dev.* 14: 417–426.

Jones, T. W. G. and Pardon, I. S., 1980. The effect of age on the plasma protein binding of pentobarbitone in the mouse. A brief note. *Mech. Age. Dev.* 14: 409–415.

Jori, A., DiSalle, E., and Quadri, A. 1972. Rate of aminopyrine disappearance from plasma in young and aged humans. *Pharmacology* 8: 273–279.

Jue, S. G. 1984. Adverse drug reactions in the elderly. *In,* R. E. Vestal (ed.), *Drug Treatment in the Elderly,* pp. 29–42. Sydney: Adis Health Science Press.

Jung, D., Mayersohn, M., Perrier, D., Calkins, J., and Saunders, R. 1982. Thiopental disposition as a function of age in female patients undergoing surgery. *Anesthesiology* 56: 263–268.

Jusko, W. J. 1980. Role of tobacco smoking in pharmacokinetics. *J. Pharmacokinet. Biopharm.* 6: 7–39.

Jusko, W. J., Gardner, M. J., Mangione, A., Schentag, J., Koup, J., and Vance, J. W. 1979. Factors affecting theophylline clearances: age, tobacco, mari-

juana, cirrhosis, congestive heart failure, obesity, oral contraceptives, benzodiazepines, barbiturates, and ethanol. *J. Pharm. Sci.* 68: 1358–1365.

Jusko, W. J., Koup, J. R., Vance, J. W., Schentag, J. J., and Kuritzky, P. 1977. Intravenous theophylline therapy: nomogram guidelines. *Ann. Intern. Med.* 86: 400–404.

Kaiko, R. F. 1980. Age and morphine analgesia in cancer patients with postoperative pain. *Clin. Pharmacol. Ther.* 28: 823–826.

Kalchthaler, T., Coccaro, E., and Lichtiger, S. 1977. Incidence of polypharmacy in a long-term care facility. *J. Am. Geriatr. Soc.* 25: 308–313.

Kampmann, J., Hansen, J. M., Siersbaek-Nielsen, K., and Laursen, J. 1972. Effect of some drugs on penicillin half-life in blood. *Clin. Pharmacol. Ther.* 13: 516–519.

Kampmann, J. P., Mortensen, H. B., Bach, B., Waldorff, S., Kristensen, M. B., and Hansen, J. M., 1979. Kinetics of propylthiouracil in elderly. *Acta. Med. Scand., Suppl.* 624: 93–98.

Kangas, L., Iisalo, E., Kanto, J., Lehtinen, V., Pynnönen, S., Ruikka, I., Salminen, J., Silanpää, M., and Syvälahti, E. 1979. Human pharmacokinetics of nitrazepam: effect of age and diseases. *Eur. J. Clin. Pharmacol.* 15: 163–170.

Kanto, J., Kangas, L., Aaltonen, L., and Hilke, H. 1981. Effect of age on the pharmacokinetics and sedative effect of flunitrazepam. *Int. J. Clin. Pharmacol. Ther. Toxicol.* 19: 400–404.

Kanto, J., Mäenpää, M., Mäntylä, R., Sellman, R., and Valovirta, E. 1979. Effect of age on the pharmacokinetics of diazepam given in conjunction with spinal anesthesia. *Anesthesiology* 51: 154–159.

Kao, J. and Hudson, P. 1980. Induction of the hepatic cytochrome P-450-dependent mono-oxygenase system in young and geriatric rats. *Biochem. Pharmacol.* 29: 1191–1194.

Kaplan, S. A., DeSilva, J. A. F., Jack, M. L., Alexander, K., Strojny, N., Weinfield, R. E., Puglisi, C. V., and Weissman, L. 1973. Blood level profile in man following chronic oral administration of flunitrazepam hydrochloride. *J. Pharm. Sci.* 62: 1932–1935.

Kappas, A., Alvares, A. P., Anderson, K. E., Pantuck, E. J., Pantuck, C. B., Chang, R., and Conney, A. H. 1978. Effect of charcoal-broiled beef on antipyrine and theophylline metabolism. *Clin. Pharmacol. Ther.* 23: 445–450.

Kappas, A., Anderson, K. E., Conney, A. H., and Alvares, A. P. 1976. Influence of dietary protein and carbohydrate on antipyrine and theophylline metabolism in man. *Clin. Pharmacol. Ther.* 20: 643–653.

Kato, R., Chiesara, E., and Vassanelli, P. 1962. Increased activity of microsomal strychnine-metabolizing enzymes induced by phenobarbital and other drugs. *Biochem. Pharmacol.* 11: 913–922.

Kato, R. and Takanaka, A. 1968a. Metabolism of drugs in old rats (I): activities of NADPH-linked electron transport and drug-metabolizing enzyme systems in liver microsomes in old rats. *Jap. J. Pharmacol.* 18: 381–388.

Kato, R. and Takanaka, A. 1968b. Metabolism of drugs in old rats. II. Metabolism *in vivo* and effect of drugs in old rats. *Jap. J. Pharmacol.* 18: 389–396.

Kato, R. and Takanaka, A. 1968c. Effect of phenobarbital on electron transport system, oxidation and reduction of drugs in liver microsomes of rats of different age. *J. Biochem. (Tokyo)* 63: 406–408.

Kato, R., Takanaka, A., and Onoda, K.-I. 1970. Studies on age differences in mice for the activity of drug-metabolizing enzymes of liver microsomes. *Jap. J. Pharmacol.* 20: 572–576.

Kato, R., Vassanelli, P., Frontino, G., and Chiesara, E. 1964. Variation in the activity of liver microsomal drug-metabolizing enzymes in rats in relation to age. *Biochem. Pharmacol.* 13: 1037–1051.

Kelly, J. G., McGarry, K., O'Malley, K., and O'Brien, E. T. 1982. Bioavailability of labetalol increases with age. *Brit. J. Clin. Pharmacol.* 14: 304–305.

Kendall, M. J., Brown, D., and Yates, R. A. 1977. Plasma metoprolol concentrations in young, old and hypertensive subjects. *Brit. J. Clin. Pharmacol.* 4: 497–499.

Kendall, M. J., Woods, K. L., Wilkins, M. R., and Worthington, D. J. 1982. Responsiveness to β-adrenergic receptor stimulation: the effects of age are cardioselective. *Brit. J. Clin. Pharmacol.* 14: 821–826.

Kitanaka, I., Ross, R. J., Cutler, N. R., Zavadil, A. P., and Potter, W. Z. 1982. Altered hydroxydesipramine concentrations in elderly depressed patients. *Clin. Pharmacol. Ther.* 31: 51–55.

Kitani, K. 1977. Functional aspects of the ageing liver. *In,* D. Platt (ed.), *Liver and Aging,* pp. 5–17. Stuttgart: F. K. Schattauer Verlag.

Kitani, K., Kanai, S., Miura, P., Morita, Y., and Kisahara, M. 1978. The effect of ageing on the biliary excretion of ouabain in the rat. *Exp. Gerontol.* 13: 9–17.

Klein, L. E., German, P. S., and Levine, D. M. 1981. Adverse drug reactions among the elderly: a reassessment. *J. Am. Geriatr. Soc.* 29: 525–530.

Klinger, W. 1969. Zur pharmacokinetik von dimethylaminophenazon, 4-aminophenazon und phenazon bei ratten verschidenen alters. *Arch. Int. Pharmacodyn. Ther.* 180: 309–322.

Klotz, U. 1979. Effect of age on levels of diazepam in plasma and brain of rats. *Naunyn-Schmiedeberg's Arch. Pharmacol.* 307: 167–169.

Klotz, U., Avant, G. R., Hoyumpa, A., Schenker, S., and Wilkinson, G. R. 1975. The effects of age and liver disease on the disposition and elimination of diazepam in adult man. *J. Clin. Invest.* 55: 347–359.

Klotz, U. and Müller-Seydlitz, P. 1979. Altered elimination of desmethyldiazepam in the elderly. *Brit. J. Clin Pharmacol.* 7: 119–120.

Koch-Weser, J. 1976. Acetaminophen. *New Engl. J. Med.* 295: 1297–1300.

Kortilla, K., Saarnivaara, L., Tarkkanen, J., Himberg, J.-J., and Hytönen, M. 1978. Effect of age on amnesia and sedation induced by flunitrazepam during local anaesthesia for bronchoscopy. *Brit. J. Anaesth.* 50: 1211–1218.

Kraft, C. A. and Castleden, C. M. 1981. The effect of age on β-adrenoceptor-stimulated cyclic AMP formation in human lymphocytes. *Clin. Sci.* 60: 587–589.

Krakauer, R. and Lauritzen, M. 1978. Diuretic therapy and hypokalemia in geriatric out-patients. *Dan. Med. Bull.* 25: 126–129.

Krall, J. F., Connelly, M., and Tuck, M. L. 1981b. Evidence for reversibility of age-related decrease in human lymphocyte adenylate cyclase activity. *Biochem. Biophys. Res. Comm.* 99: 1028–1034.

Krall, J. F., Connelly, M., Weisbart, R., and Tuck, M. L. 1981a. Age-related elevation of plasma catecholamine concentration and reduced responsiveness of lymphocyte adenylate cyclase. *J. Clin. Endocrinol. Metab.* 52: 863–867.

Kramer, P. A., Chapron, D. J., Benson, J., and Mercik, S. A. 1978. Tetracycline absorption in elderly patients with achlorhydria. *Clin. Pharmacol. Ther.* 23: 467–472.

Kraus, J. W., Desmond, P. V., Marshall, J. P., Johnson, R. F., Schenker, S., and Wilkinson, G. R. 1978. Effects of aging and liver disease on disposition of lorazepam. *Clin. Pharmacol. Ther.* 24: 411–419.

Krishnaswamy, K. 1978. Drug metabolism and pharmacokinetics in malnutrition. *Clin. Pharmacokinet.* 3: 216–240.

Kristensen, M., Hansen, J. M., Kampmann, J., Lumholtz, B., and Siersbaek-Nielsen, K. 1974. Drug elimination and renal function. *J. Clin. Pharmacol.* 14: 307–308.

Kuhlmann, J., Odouah, M., and Coper, H. 1970. The effects of barbiturates on rats of different ages. *Naunyn-Schmiedeberg's Arch. Pharmacol.* 265: 310–320.

LaDu, D. N., Mandell, H. G., and Way, E. L. 1971. *Fundamentals of Drug Metabolism and Drug Disposition.* Baltimore: Williams and Wilkins.

Lamy, P. P., 1980. *Prescribing for the Elderly.* Littleton, Mass.: PSG Publishing Co.

Landmann, R., Bittiger, H., and Bühler, F. R. 1981. High affinity beta-2-adrenergic receptors in mononuclear leucocytes: similar density in young and old normal subjects. *Life Sci.* 29: 1761–1771.

Lasagna, L. 1956. Drug effects as modified by aging. *J. Chronic Dis.* 3: 567–574.

Law, R. and Chalmers, C. 1976. Medicines and elderly people: a general practice survey. *Brit. Med. J.* 1: 565–568.

Lawson, D. H., Gloss, D., and Jick, H. 1978. Adverse reactions to methyldopa with particular reference to hypotension. *Am. Heart J.* 96: 572–579.

Lawson, D. H. and Juck, H. 1976. Drug prescribing in hospitals: an international comparison. *Am. J. Public Health* 66: 644–648.

Lawson, D. H. and Jick, H. 1977. Adverse reactions to procainamide. *Brit. J. Clin. Pharmacol.* 4: 507–511.

Learoyd, B. M. 1972. Psychotropic drugs and the elderly patient. *Med. J. Aust.* 1: 1131–1133.

Lehmann, K. and Merten, K. 1974. Die elimination von lithium in abhangigkeit vom lebensalter bei gesunden und niereninsuffizienten. *Int. J. Clin. Pharmacol.* 10: 292–298.

Leikola, E. and Vartia, K. O. 1957. On penicillin levels in young and geriatric subjects. *J. Gerontol.* 12: 48–52.

Levy, G. 1965. Pharmacokinetics of salicylate elimination in man. *J. Pharm. Sci.* 54: 959–967.

Levy, G. 1981. Comparative pharmacokinetics of aspirin and acetaminophen. *Arch. Intern. Med.* 141: 279–281.

Levy, M., Kewitz, H., Altwein, W., Hillebrand, J., and Eliakim, M. 1980. Hospital admissions due to adverse drug reactions: a comparative study from Jerusalem and Berlin. *Eur. J. Clin. Pharmacol.* 17: 25–31.

Liddell, D. E., Williams, F. M., and Briant, R. H. 1975. Phenazone (antipyrine) metabolism and distribution in young and elderly adults. *Clin. Exp. Pharmacol. Physiol.* 2: 481–487.

London, G. M., Safar, M. E., Weiss, Y. A., and Milliez, P. L. 1976. Isoproterenol sensitivity and total body clearance of propranolol in hypertensive patients. *J. Clin. Pharmacol.* 16: 174–182.

Lumholtz, B., Kampmann, J., Siersbaek-Nielsen, K., and Hansen, J. M. 1974. Dose regimen of kanamycin and gentamicin. *Acta Med. Scand.* 196: 521–524.

Lundborg, P., Regardh, C. G., and Landahl, S. 1982. The pharmacokinetics of metoprolol in healthy elderly individuals (abst.). *Clin. Pharmacol. Ther.* 31: 246.

Lundborg, P. and Steen, B. 1976. Plasma levels and effect on heart rate and blood pressure of metoprolol after acute oral administration in 12 geriatric patients. *Acta Med. Scand.* 200: 397–400.

Macklon, A. F., Barton, M., James, O., and Rawlins, M. D. 1980. The effect of age on the pharmacokinetics of diazepam. *Clin. Sci.* 59: 479–483.

MacLeod, S. M., Giles, H. G., Bengert, B., Liu, F. F., and Sellers, E. M. 1979. Age- and gender-related differences in diazepam pharmacokinetics. *J. Clin. Pharmacol.* 19: 15–19.

Marsh, R. H. K., Chmielewski, A. T., and Goat, V. A. 1980. Recovery from pancuronium: a comparison between old and young patients. *Anesthesia,* 35: 1193–1196.

Marttila, J. K., Hammel, R. J., Alexander, B., and Zustiak, R. 1977. Potential untoward effects of long-term use of flurazepam in geriatric patients. *J. Am. Pharm. Assoc.* 17: 692–695.

Mather, L. E., Tucker, G. T., Pflug, A. E., Lindop, M. J., and Wilkerson, C. 1975. Meperidine kinetics: intravenous injection in surgical patients and volunteers. *Clin. Pharmacol. Ther.* 17: 21–30.

Mayersohn, M. 1982. The "xylose test" to assess gastrointestinal absorption in the elderly: a pharmacokinetic evaluation of the literature. *J. Gerontol.* 37: 300–305.

McLeod, K., Hull, C. J., and Watson, M. J. 1979. Effects of ageing on the pharmacokinetics of pancuronium. *Brit. J. Anaest.* 51: 435–538.

McMartin, D. N., O'Connor, J. A. Jr., Fasco, M. J., and Kaminsky, L. S. 1980. Influence of aging and induction on rat liver and kidney microsomal mixed function oxidase systems. *Toxicol. Appl. Pharmacol.* 54: 411–419.

Meier, A., Gübelin, U., Weidmann, P., Grimm, M., Keusch, G., Glück, A., Minder, I., and Beretta-Piccoli, C. 1980. Age-related profile of cardiovascular reactivity to norepinephrine and angiotensin II in normal and hypertensive man. *Klin. Wochenschur.* 58: 1183–1188.

Melander, A., Bodin, N.-O., Danielson, K., Gustafsson, B., Haglund, G., and Westerlund, D. 1978. Absorption and elimination of *d*-propoxyphene, acetylsalicylic acid, and phenazone in a combination tablet (Doleron®): comparison between young and elderly subjects. *Acta Med. Scand.* 203: 121–124.

Meshkinpour, H., Smith, M., and Hollander, D. 1981. Influence of age on the surface area of the small intestine in the rat. *Exp. Gerontol.* 16: 399–404.

Miller, A. K., Adir, J., and Vestal, R. E. 1977. Effect of age on the pharmacokinetics of tolbutamide in man (abst.). *Pharmacologist* 19: 128.

Miller, A. K., Adir, J., and Vestal, R. E. 1978. Tolbutamide binding in plasma proteins of young and old human subjects. *J. Pharm. Sci.* 67: 1192–1193.

Misera, D. P., London, J. M., and Staddon, G. E. 1975. Albumin metabolism in elderly patients. *J. Gerontol.* 30: 304–306.

Mitchard, M. 1979. Drug distribution in the elderly. *In,* J. Crooks and I. M. Stevenson (eds.), *Drugs and the Elderly,* 65–76. Baltimore: University Park Press.

Mitchell, J. R., Thorgeirsson, S. S., Potter, W. Z., Jollow, D. J., and Keiser, H. 1974. Acetaminophen-induced injury: protective role of glutathione in man and rationale for therapy. *Clin. Pharmacol. Ther.* 16: 676–684.

Mitenko, P. A. and Ogilvie, M. D. 1973. Pharmacokinetics of intravenous theophylline. *Clin. Pharmacol. Ther.* 14: 509–513.

Montgomery, P. R. and Sitar, D. S. 1981. Increased serum salicylate metabolites with age in patients receiving chronic acetylsalicylic acid therapy. *Gerontology* 27: 329–333.

Moore, R. G., Triggs, E. J., Shanks, C. A., and Thomas, J. 1975. Pharmacokinetics of chlormethiazole in humans. *Eur. J. Clin. Pharmacol.* 8: 353–357.

Mucklow, J. C. and Fraser, H. S. 1980. The effects of age and smoking upon antipyrine metabolism. *Brit. J. Clin. Pharmacol.* 9: 613–614.

Murray, T. G., Chiang, S. T., Koepke, H. H., and Walker, B. R. 1981. Renal disease, age, and oxazepam kinetics. *Clin. Pharmacol. Ther.* 30: 805–809.

Myers, M. G., Kearns, P. M., Kennedy, D. S., and

Fisher, R. H. 1978. Postural hypotension and diuretic therapy in the elderly. *Canad. Med. Assoc. J.* 119: 581–585.

Nation, R. L., Learoyd, B., Barber, J., and Triggs, E. J. 1976. The pharmacokinetics of chlormethiazole following intravenous administration in the aged. *Eur. J. Clin. Pharmacol.* 10: 407–415.

Nation, R. L., Triggs, E. J., and Selig, M. 1977a. Lignocaine kinetics in cardiac patients and aged subjects. *Brit. J. Clin. Pharmacol.* 4: 439–448.

Nation, R. L., Vine, J., Triggs, E. J., and Learoyd, B. 1977b. Plasma level of chlormethiazole and two metabolites after oral administration to young and aged human subjects. *Eur. J. Clin. Pharmacol.* 12: 137–145.

Neely, E. and Patrick, M. L. 1968. Problems of aged persons taking medications at home. *Nursing Res.* 17: 52–55.

Nielsen-Kudsk, F., Magnussen, I., and Jakobsen, P. 1978. Pharmacokinetics of theophylline in ten elderly patients. *Acta Pharmacol. Toxicol.* 42: 226–234.

Nies, A., Robinson, D. S., Friedman, M. J., Green, R., Cooper, T. B., Ravaris, C. L., and Ives, J. O. 1977. Relationship between age and tricyclic antidepressant plasma levels. *Am. J. Psychiat.* 134: 790–793.

Nies, A. S., Shand, D. G., and Wilkinson, G. R. 1976. Altered hepatic blood flow and drug disposition. *Clin. Pharmacokinet.* 1: 125–155.

Nimmo, W. S. 1976. Drugs, diseases and altered gastric emptying. *Clin. Pharmacokinet.* 1: 189–203.

Norris, A. H., Lundy, T., and Shock, N. W. 1963. Trends in selected indices of body composition in men between the ages of 30 and 80 years. *Ann. N.Y. Acad. Sci.* 110: 623–639.

Novak, L. P. 1972. Aging, total body potassium, fat-free mass, and cell mass in males and females between the ages of 18 and 85 years. *J. Gerontol.* 27: 438–443.

Ochs, H. R., Greenblatt, D. J. and Otten, H., 1981. Disposition of oxazepam in relation to age, sex, and cigarette smoking. *Klin. Wochenschr.* 59: 899–903.

Ochs, H. R., Greenblatt, D. J., Wood, E., and Smith, T. W. 1978. Reduced quinidine clearance in elderly persons. *Am. J. Cardiol.* 42: 481–485.

O'Malley, K., Crooks, J., Duke, E., and Stevenson, I. H. 1971. Effect of age and sex on human drug metabolism. *Brit. Med. J.* 3: 607–609.

O'Malley, K., Judge, T. G., and Crooks, J. 1980. Geriatric clinical pharmacology and therapeutics, *In,* G. Avery (ed.), *Drug Treatment* 2nd ed, pp. 158–181. Syndey and New York: Adis Press.

O'Malley, K., Stevenson, I. H., Ward, C. A., Wood, A. J. J., and Crooks, J. 1977. Determinants of anticoagulant control in patients receiving warfarin. *Brit. J. Clin. Pharmacol.* 4: 309–314.

Oswald, I. 1979. The why and how of hypnotic drugs. *Brit. Med. J.* 1: 1167–1168.

Ouslander, J. G. 1981. Drug therapy in the elderly. *Ann. Intern. Med.* 95: 711–722.

Pantuck, E. J., Pantuck, C. B., Garland, W. A., Min, B. J., Wattenberg, L. W., Anderson, K. E., Kappas, A., and Conney, A. H. 1979. Stimulatory effect of dietary brussels sprouts and cabbage on human drug metabolism. *Clin. Pharmacol. Ther.* 25: 88–95.

Pardon, I., and Jones, T. 1978. Barbiturate pharmacokinetics in aging tolerant and non-tolerant mice. *In,* K. Kitani (ed.), *Liver and Ageing—1978,* pp. 301–311. Amsterdam: Elsevier-North Holland.

Park, W. Y., Hagins, F. M., Rivat, E. L., and MacNamara, T. E. 1982. Age and epidural dose response in adult men. *Anesthesiology* 56: 318–320.

Park, W. Y., Massengale, M., Kim, S. I., Poon, K. C., and MacNamara, T. E. 1980. Age and the spread of local anesthetic solutions in the epidural space. *Anesth. Analg.* 59: 768–771.

Parkin, D. M., Henney, C. R., Quirk, J., and Crooks, J. 1976. Deviation from prescribed drug treatment after discharge from hospital. *Brit. Med. J.* 2: 686–688.

Pedigo, N. W., Schoemaker, H., Morelli, M., McDougal, J. N., Malick, J. B., Burks, T. F., and Yamamura, M. I., 1981. Benzodiazepine receptor binding in young, mature and senescent rat brain and kidney. *Neurobiol. Aging* 2: 83–88.

Peterson, D. M., Whittington, F. J., and Payne, B. P. (eds.) 1979. *Drugs and the Elderly: Social and Pharmacological Issues.* Springfield, Ill.: Charles C. Thomas.

Petterson, M., Heazelwood, R., Smithurst, B., and Eadie, M. J. 1982. Plasma protein binding of phenytoin in the aged: *in vivo* studies. *Brit. J. Clin. Pharmacol.* 13: 423–425.

Pfeifer, H. J. and Greenblatt, D. J. 1978. Clinical toxicity of theophylline in relation to cigarette smoking: a report from the Boston Collaborative Drug Surveillance Program. *Chest* 73: 455–459.

Pfeifer, H. J., Greenblatt, D. J., and Koch-Weser, J. 1976. Clinical use and toxicity of intravenous lidocaine. *Am. Heart J.* 92: 168–173.

Pieri, C., Zs.-Nagy, I., Giuli, C., and Mazzufferi, G. 1975a. The aging of rat liver as revealed by electron microscopic morphometry. I. Basic parameters. *Exp. Gerontol.* 10: 291–304.

Pieri, C., Zs.-Nagy, I., Giuli, C., and Mazzufferi, G. 1975b. The aging of rat liver as revealed by electron microscopic morphometry. II. Parameters of regenerated old liver. *Exp. Gerontol.* 10: 341–349.

Playfer, J. R., Baty, J. D., Lamb, J., Powell, C., and Price-Evans, D. A. 1978. Age related differences in the disposition of acetanilide. *Brit. J. Clin. Pharmacol.* 6: 529–533.

Portnoi, V. A. 1979. Digitalis delirium in elderly patients. *J. Clin. Pharmacol.* 19: 747–750.

Potter, W. Z., Calil, H. M., Manian, A. A., Zavadil, A. P., and Goodwin, F. K. 1979. Hydroxylated metabolites of tricyclic antidepressants—preclinical assessment of activity. *Biol. Psychiat.* 14: 601–613.

Potter, W. Z., Calil, H. M., Zavadil, A. P., Jusko, W.

J., Sutfin, T. A., Rapoport, J., and Goodwin, F. K. 1980. Steady-state concentrations of hydroxylated metabolites of tricyclic antidepressants in patients: relationship to clinical effect. *Psychopharmacol. Bull.* 16: 32–34.

Quarterman, C. P., Kendall, M. J., and Jack, D. B. 1981. The effect of age on the pharmacokinetics of metoprolol and its metabolites. *Brit. J. Pharmacol.* 11: 287–294.

Ramsay, L. E., Mackay, A., Eppel, M. L., and Oliver, J. S. 1980. Oral sustained-release aminophylline in medical inpatients: factors related to toxicity and plasma theophylline concentration. *Brit. J. Clin. Pharmacol.* 10: 101–107.

Randall, O., Esler, M., Culp, B., Julius, S., and Zweifler, A. 1978. Determinants of baroreflex sensitivity in man. *J. Lab. Clin. Med.* 91: 514–519.

Raskind, M. A., Alvarez, C., Pietrzyk, M., Westerlund, K., and Herlin, S. 1976. Helping the elderly psychiatric patient in crisis. *Geriatrics* 31: 51–56.

Ray, W. A., Federspiel, C. F., and Schaffner, W. 1980. A study of antipsychotic use in nursing homes: epidemiologic evidence suggesting misuse. *Am. J. Public Health* 70: 485–491.

Redolfi, A., Borgogelli, E., and Lodola, E. 1979. Blood level of cimetidine in relation to age. *Eur. J. Clin. Pharmacol.* 15: 257–261.

Reidenberg, M., Camacho, M., Kluger, J., and Drayer, D. 1980. Aging and renal clearance of procainamide and acetylprocainamide. *Clin. Pharmacol. Ther.* 28: 732–735.

Reidenberg, M. M., Levy, M., Warner, H., Coutinho, C. B., Schwartz, M. A., Yu, G., and Cheripko, J. 1978. Relationship between diazepam dose, plasma level, age, and central nervous system depression. *Clin. Pharmacol. Ther.* 23: 371–374.

Richey, D. P. and Bender, D. 1977. Pharmacokinetic consequences of aging. *Ann. Rev. Pharmacol. Toxicol.* 17: 49–65.

Rikans, L. E. and Notley, B. A. 1981. Substrate specificity of age-related changes in the inducibility of hepatic microsomal mono-oxygenases in middle-aged rats. *Mech. Age. Dev.* 16: 371–378.

Rikans, L. E. and Notley, B. A. 1982. Age-related changes in hepatic microsomal drug metabolism are substrate dependent. *J. Pharmacol. Exp. Ther.* 220: 574–578.

Ritch, A. E. S., Perera, W. N. R., and Jones, C. J. 1982. Pharmacokinetics of azapropazone in the elderly. *Brit. J. Clin. Pharmacol.* 14: 116–119.

Ritschel, W. A. 1978. Age-dependent distribution of amobarbital: analog computer evaluation. *J. Am. Geriatr. Soc.* 26: 540–543.

Roberts, R. K., Wilkinson, G. R., Branch, R. A., and Schenker, S. 1978. Effect of age and parenchymal liver disease on the disposition and elimination of chlordiazepoxide (Librium). *Gastroenterology* 75: 479–485.

Robertson-Tchabo, E. A., Arenberg, D., and Vestal, R. E. 1975. Age differences in memory performance

following ethanol infusion (Abst. 455). *Proc. 10th Internat. Congr. Gerontol.* 2: 62.

Rodstein, M. and Oei, L. S. 1979. Cardiovascular side effects of long-term therapy with tricyclic antidepressants in the aged. *J. Am. Geriatr. Soc.* 27: 231–234.

Routledge, P. A., Chapman, P. H., Davis, D. M., and Rawlins, M. D. 1979. Pharmacokinetics and pharmacodynamics of warfarin at steady state. *Brit. J. Clin. Pharmacol.* 8: 243–247.

Routledge, P. A. and Shand, D. G., 1979. Clinical pharmacokinetics of propranolol. *Clin. Pharmacokinet.* 4: 73–90.

Rowe, J. W. 1977. Clinical research on aging: strategies and directions. *New Engl. J. Med.* 297: 1332–1336.

Rowe, J. W., Andres, R., Tobin, J. D., Norris, A. H., and Shock, N. W. 1976. The effect of age on creatinine clearance in man: a cross-sectional and longitudinal study. *J. Gerontol.* 31: 155–163.

Rowell, F. J., Hui, S. M., Fairbairn, A. F., and Eccleston, D. 1981. Total and free serum haloperidol levels in schizophrenic patients and the effect of age, thioridazine and fatty acid on haloperidol-serum protein binding *in vitro. Brit. J. Clin. Pharmacol.* 11: 377–382.

Rubin, P. C., Scott, P. J. W., McLean, K. Pearson, A., Ross, D., and Reid, J. L. 1982. Atenolol disposition in young and elderly subjects. *Brit. J. Clin. Pharmacol.* 13: 235–237.

Rubin, P. C., Scott, P. J. W., and Reid, J. L. 1981. Prazosin disposition in young and elderly subjects. *Brit. J. Clin. Pharmacol.* 12: 401–404.

Salem, S. A. M., Rajjayabun, P., Shepherd, A. M. M., and Stevenson, I. H. 1978. Reduced induction of drug metabolism in the elderly. *Age Aging* 7: 68–73.

Salzman, C. and Shader, R. I. 1978. Depression in the elderly. II. Possible drug etiologies; differential diagnostic criteria. *J. Am. Geriatr. Soc.* 26: 303–308.

Salzman, C., Shader, R. I., and Vander Kolk, B. A. 1976. Clinical psychopharmacology and the elderly patient. *N.Y. State J. Med.* 76: 71–77.

Sartor, G., Melander, A., Scherstén, B., and Wåhlin-Boll, E. 1980. Influence of food and age on the single-dose kinetics and effects of tolbutamide and chlorpropamide. *Eur. J. Clin. Pharmacol.* 17: 285–293.

Schmucker, D. L. 1979. Age-related changes in drug disposition. *Pharmacol. Rev.* 30: 445–456.

Schmucker, D. L., Mooney, J. S., and Jones, A. L. 1977. Age-related changes in the hepatic endoplasmic reticulum: a quantitative analysis. *Science* 197: 1005–1008.

Schmucker, D. L. and Wang, R. K. 1980. Age-related changes in liver drug-metabolizing enzymes. *Exp. Gerontol.* 15: 321–329.

Schmucker, D. L. and Wang, R. K. 1981. Effects of aging and phenobarbital on the rat liver microsomal drug-metabolizing system. *Mech. Age. Dev.* 15: 189–202.

Schneck, D. W., Luderer, J. R., Pritchard, J. F., Vary

J. E., DeWitt, F. O., Bew, J. C., and Hayes, A. H. 1980. A comparison of the intrinsic clearance of propranolol in young and elderly subjects (abst.). *Clin. Pharmacol. Ther.* 27: 284–285.

Schneider, R. E., Bishop, H., Yates, R. A., Quarterman, C. P., and Kendall, M. J. 1980. Effect of age on plasma propranolol levels. *Brit. J. Clin. Pharmacol.* 10: 169–171.

Schocken, D. D. and Roth, G. S. 1977. Reduced beta-adrenergic receptor concentrations in aging man. *Nature* 267: 856–858.

Schwartz, D., Wang, M., Feitz, L., and Goss, M. E. W. 1962. Medication errors made by elderly, chronically ill patients. *Am. J. Public Health* 52: 2018–2029.

Schwartz, M. A., Koechlin, B. A., Postma, E., Palmer, S., and Krol, G. 1965. Metabolism of diazepam in rat, dog and man. *J. Pharmacol. Exp. Ther.* 149: 423–435.

Schwartz, M. A. and Postma, E. 1970. Metabolism of flurazepam, a benzodiazepine, in man and dog. *J. Pharm. Sci.* 59: 1800–1806.

Scott, J. and Poffenbarger, P. L. 1979. Pharmacogenetics of tolbutamide metabolism in humans. *Diabetes* 28: 41–51.

Scott, P. J. W. and Reid, J. 1982. The effect of age on the responses of human isolated arteries to noradrenaline. *Brit. J. Clin. Pharmacol.* 13: 237–239.

Seidl, L. G., Thornton, G. F., Smith, J. W., and Cluff, L. E. 1966. Studies on the epidemiology of adverse drug reactions. III. Reactions in patients on a general medical service. *Bull. Johns Hopkins Hosp.* 119: 299–315.

Seshadri, R. S., Morley, A. A., Trainor, K. J., and Sorrell, J. 1979. Sensitivity of human lymphocytes to bleomycin increases with age. *Experientia* 35: 233–234.

Shader, R. I., Greenblatt, D. J., Ciraulo, D. A., Divoll, M., Harmatz, J. S., and Georgotas, A. 1981. Effect of age and sex on disposition of desmethyldiazepam formed from its precursor clorazepate. *Psychopharmacology* 75: 193–197.

Shader, R. I., Greenblatt, D. J., Harmatz, J. S., Franke, K., and Koch-Weser, J. 1977. Absorption and disposition of chlordiazepoxide in young and elderly male volunteers. *J. Clin. Pharmacol.* 17: 709–718.

Sharrock, N. E. 1978. Epidural anesthetic dose responses in patients 20 to 80 years old. *Anesthesiology* 49: 425–428.

Shear, M. K. and Sacks, M. H. 1978. Digitalis delirium: report of two cases. *Am. J. Psychiat.* 135: 109–110.

Shepherd, A. M. M., Hewick, D. S., Moreland, T. A., and Stevenson, I. H. 1977. Age as a determinant of sensitivity to warfarin. *Brit. J. Clin. Pharmacol.* 4: 315–320.

Shepherd, A. M. M., Wilson, N., Stevenson, I. H. 1979. Warfarin sensitivity in the elderly. *In,* J. Crooks, and I. H. Stevenson (eds.), *Drugs and the Elderly,* pp. 199–209. Baltimore: University Park Press.

Shock, N. W., Watkin, D. M., Yiengst, B. S., Norris,

A. H., Gaffney, G. W., Gregerman, R. E., and Falzone, J. A. 1963. Age differences in the water content of the body as related to basal oxygen consumption in males. *J. Gerontol.* 18: 1–8.

Shull, H. J., Wilkinson, G. R., Johnson, R., and Schenker, S. 1976. Normal disposition of oxazepam in acute viral hepatitis and cirrhosis. *Ann. Intern. Med.* 84: 420–425.

Simon, C., Malerczyk, V., Engelke, H., Preuss, I., Grahmann, H., and Schmidt, K. 1975. Die pharmacokinetik von doxycyclin bei niereninsuffizienz und geriatrischen patienten im vergleich zu jungeren erwachsenen. *Schweiz. Med. Wochenschur.* 105: 1615–1620.

Simon, C., Malerczyk, V., Müller, U., and Müller, G. 1972. Zur pharmakokinetik von propicillin bei geriatrischen patienten im vergleich zu jügeren erwachsen. *Dtsch. Med. Wochen.* 97: 1999–2003.

Simon, C., Malerczyk, V., Tenschert, B., and Möhlenbeck, F. 1976. Die geriatrische pharmakologie von cefazolin, cefradin und sulfisomidin. *Arzneim. Forsch.* 26: 1377–1382.

Simon, C., Malerczyk, V., Zierott, G., Lehmann, K., and Thiesen, U. 1975. Blut-, harn-, und gallespiegel von ampicillin bei intravenoser dauerinfuson. *Arzneim. Forsch.* 25: 654–656.

Slanina, P. and Stålhandske, T. 1977. *In vitro* metabolism of nicotine in liver of ageing mice. *Arch. Int. Pharmacodyn. Ther.* 226: 258–262.

Smithard, D. J. and Langman, M. J. S. 1977. Drug metabolism in the elderly. *Brit. Med. J.* 3: 520–521.

Smithard, D. J. and Langman, M. J. S. 1978. The effect of vitamin supplementation upon antipyrine metabolism in the elderly. *Brit. J. Clin. Pharmacol.* 5: 181–185.

Solomon, F., White, C. C., Parron, D. L., and Mendelson, W. B. 1980. Sleeping pills, insomnia, and medical practice. *New Engl. J. Med.* 300: 803–808.

Somogyi, A., Rohner, H.-G., and Gugler, R. 1980. Pharmacokinetics and bioavailability of cimetidine in gastric and duodenal ulcer patients. *Clin. Pharmacokinet.* 5: 84–94.

Sotaniemi, E. A. and Huhti, E. 1974. Half-life of intravenous tolbutamide in the serum of patients in medical wards. *Ann. Clin. Res.* 6: 146–154.

Stevens, M. J., Lipe, S., and Moulds, R. F. W. 1982. The effects of age on the responses of human isolated arteries and veins to noradrenaline. *Brit. J. Clin. Pharmacol.* 14: 750–752.

Stevenson, I. H., Salem, S. A. M., and Shepherd, A. M. M. 1979. Studies on drug absorption and metabolism in the elderly. *In,* J. Crooks and I. H. Stevenson (eds.), *Drugs and the Elderly,* pp. 51–63. Baltimore: University Park Press.

Stohs, S. J., Al-Turk, W. A., and Hassing, J. M. 1980. Altered drug metabolism in hepatic and extrahepatic tissues in mice as a function of age. *Age* 3: 88–92.

Stone, W. J. and Walle, T. 1980. Massive propranolol metabolite retention during maintenance hemodialysis. *Clin. Pharmacol. Ther.* 28: 449–455.

Streicher, E. and Garbus, J. 1953. The effect of age and sex on the duration of hexobarbital anesthesia in rats. *J. Gerontol.* 10: 441–444.

Swerdloff, R. S., Pozefsky, T., Tobin, J. D., and Andres, R. 1967. Influence of age on the intravenous tolbutamide response test. *Diabetes* 16: 161–170.

Swift, C. G., Haythorne, J. M., Clarke, P., and Stevenson, I. H. 1981. The effect of ageing on measured responses to single doses of oral temazepam (abst.) *Brit. J. Clin. Pharmacol.* 11: 413P–414P.

Swift, L. G., Homeida, M., Halliwell, M., and Roberts, C. J. C. 1978. Antipyrine disposition and liver size in the elderly. *Eur. J. Clin. Pharmacol.* 14: 149–152.

Talseth, T., Kornstad, S., Boye, N. P., and Bredesen, J. E. 1981. Individualization of oral theophylline dosage in elderly patients. *Acta Med. Scand.* 210: 489–492.

Tedeschi, G., Bianchetti, G., Henry, J. F., Braithwaite, R. A., Mikulic, E., Dugas, M., and Morselli, P. L. 1981. Influence of age and disease states on the plasma protein binding of haloperidol (abst.). *Brit. J. Clin. Pharmacol.* 11: 430P.

Thompson, T. L., Moran, M. G., and Nies, A. S. 1983. Psychotropic drug use in the elderly. *New Engl. J. Med.* 308: 134–138; 194–199.

Traeger, A., Kiesewetter, R., and Kunze, M. 1974. Zur pharmakokinetik von phenobarbital bei erwachsenen und greisen. *Dtsch. Ges. Wesen.* 29: 1040–1042.

Traeger, A., Kunze, M., Stein, G., and Ankerman, H. 1973. Zur pharmakokinetik von indomethazin bei alten menschen. *L. Alternsforsch.* 27: 151–155.

Trang, J. M., Blanchard, J., Conrad, K. A., and Harrison, G. G. 1982. The effect of vitamin C on the pharmacokinetics of caffeine in elderly men. *Am. J. Clin. Nutr.* 35: 487–494.

Triggs, E. J., Johnson, J. M., and Learoyd, B. 1980. Absorption and disposition of ampicillin in the elderly. *Eur. J. Clin. Pharmacol.* 18: 195–198.

Triggs, E. J. and Nation, R. L. 1975a. Pharmacokinetics in the aged: a review. *J. Pharmacokinet. Biopharm.* 3: 387–418.

Triggs, E. J., Nation, R. L., Long, A., and Ashley, J. J. 1975b. Pharmacokinetics in the elderly. *Eur. J. Clin. Pharmacol.* 8: 55–62.

Tsang, C. C., Speeg, K. V., and Wilkinson, G. R., 1982. Aging and benzodiazepine binding in rat cerebral cortex. *Life Sci.* 30: 343–346.

Vandel, S., Vandel, B., Sandoz, B., Allers, G., Bechtel, P., and Volmat, T. 1978. Clinical response and plasma concentration on amitriptyline and its metabolite nortriptyline. *Eur. J. Clin. Pharmacol.* 14: 185–190.

Van Liere, E. J. and Northrup, D. W. 1941. The emptying time of the stomach of old people. *Am. J. Physiol.* 134: 719–722.

Varga, F. and Fischer, E. 1978. Age-dependent changes in blood supply of the liver and in the biliary excretion of eosin in rats. *In,* K. Kitani (ed.), *Liver and Aging—1978,* pp. 327–340. Amsterdam: Elsevier-North Holland.

Vartia, K. O. and Leikola, E. 1960. Serum levels of antibiotics in young and old subjects following administration of dihydrostreptomycin and tetracycline. *J. Gerontol.* 15: 392–394.

Vestal, R. E. 1978. Drug use in the elderly: a review of problems and special considerations. *Drugs* 16: 358–382.

Vestal, R. E. (ed.) 1984. *Drug Treatment in the Elderly.* Sydney: Adis Health Science Press.

Vestal, R. E., McGuire, E. A., Tobin, J. D., Andres, R., Norris, A. H., and Mezey, E. 1977. Aging and ethanol metabolism. *Clin. Pharmacol. Ther.* 21: 343–354.

Vestal, R. E., Norris, A. H., Tobin, J. D., Cohen, B. H., Shock, N. W., and Andres, R. 1975. Antipyrine metabolism in man: influence of age, alcohol, caffeine and smoking. *Clin. Pharmacol. Ther.* 18: 425–432.

Vestal, R. E. and Wood, A. J. J. 1980. Influence of age and smoking on drug kinetics in man: studies using model compounds. *Clin. Pharmacokinet.* 5: 309–319.

Vestal, R. E., Wood, A. J. J., Branch, R. A., Shand, D. G., and Wilkinson, G. R. 1979a. Effects of age and cigarette smoking on propranolol disposition. *Clin. Pharmacol. Ther.* 26: 8–15.

Vestal, R. E., Wood, A. J. J., and Shand, D. G. 1979b. Reduced β-adrenoceptor sensitivity in the elderly. *Clin. Pharmacol. Ther.* 26: 181–186.

Viukari, M. and Linnoila, M. 1979. Serum medazepam, diazepam, and N-desmethyldiazepam levels after single and multiple oral doses of medazepam. *Ann. Clin. Res.* 9: 284–286.

Wallace, S., Whiting, B., and Runcie, J. 1976. Factors affecting drug binding in plasma of elderly patients. *Brit. J. Clin. Pharmacol.* 3: 327–330.

Warren, P. M., Pepperman, M. A., and Montgomery, R. D. 1978. Age changes in small-intestinal mucosa. *Lancet* 2: 849–850.

Weintraub, M. 1976. Intelligent and capricious noncompliance. *In,* L. Lasagna (ed.), *Compliance,* pp. 39–47. Mt. Kisco: Futura.

Weintraub, M. 1981. Intelligent noncompliance with special emphasis on the elderly. *Contemp. Pharm. Pract.* 4: 8–11.

Weintraub, M., Au, W. Y. W., and Lasagna, L. 1973. Compliance as a determinant of serum digoxin concentration. *J. Am. Med. Assoc.* 244: 481–485.

Whitfield, L. R., Schentag, J. J., and Levy, G. 1982. Relationship between concentration and anticoagulant effect of heparin in plasma of hospitalized patients: magnitude of predictability of interindividual differences. *Clin. Pharmacol. Ther.* 32: 503–516.

Whiting, B., Wandless, I., Sumner, D. J., and Goldkey, A. 1978. A computer-assisted review of digoxin therapy in the elderly. *Brit. Heart J.* 40: 8–13.

Wilkinson, G. R. and Schenker, S. 1976. Pharmacokinetics of meperidine in man (letter). *Clin. Pharmacol. Ther.* 19: 486–488.

Willis, J. V. and Kendall, M. J. 1978. Pharmacokinetic studies on diclofenac sodium in young and old volunteers. *Scand. J. Rheumatol. Suppl.* 22: 36–41.

Wood, A. J. J., Vestal, R. E., Wilkinson, G. R.,

Branch, R. A., and Shand, D. G. 1979. Effect of aging and cigarette smoking on antipyrine and indocyanine green elimination. *Clin. Pharmacol. Ther.* 26: 16–20.

Woodford-Williams, E., Alvarez, A. S., Webster, D., Landless, B., and Dixon, M. P. 1964/65. Serum protein patterns in "normal" and pathological aging. *Gerontologia* 10: 86–99.

World Health Organization. 1981. Health care in the elderly: report of the technical group on use of medicaments by the elderly. *Drugs* 22: 279–294.

Yin, F. C. P., Raizes, G. S., Guarnieri, T., Spurgeon, H. A., Lakatta, E. G., Fortuin, N. J., and Weisfeldt, M. 1978. Age-associated decrease in ventricular response to haemodynamic stress during beta-adrenergic blockade. *Brit. Heart J.* 40: 1349–1355.

Young, C. J., Daneshmend, T. K., and Roberts, C. J. C. 1982. Pharmacokinetics of ranitidine in hepatic cirrhosis and in the elderly (abst.). *Brit. J. Clin. Pharmacol.* 14: 152P.

Ziegler, V. E. and Biggs, J. T. 1977. Tricyclic plasma levels: effect of age, race, sex, and smoking. *J. Am. Med. Assoc.* 238: 2167–2169.

28
AGING OF HUMAN SKIN

Albert M. Kligman
University of Pennsylvania
School of Medicine
Gary L. Grove
Simon Greenberg Foundation
and
Arthur K. Balin
The Rockefeller University

OVERVIEW AND CLINICAL CONSIDERATIONS

Architecturally, the skin is probably the most complex body organ. As shown in Figure 1, it is not only stratified horizontally into three compartments, the epidermis, dermis and subcutis, but also perforated vertically by a variety of appendages, which produce different products: sebum, hair, and eccrine and apocrine sweat. The epidermis alone is a mixture of five cell types of which three are of major importance: the keratinocyte, which creates the keratinized horny layer; the melanocyte, which makes melanin, and the Langerhans' cell, which performs peripheral immune surveillance as part of the macrophage system.

Inevitably, all these tissues undergo regressive structural changes with age. It is a fundamental task to show how this structural decadence affects functional capabilities. Clinically, it is important to assess the extent to which such physiologic losses predispose to disease. Unfortunately, until recently very little effort has been expended in these endeavors. One proposed explanation

for this lack of activity has been that it is not clear why one should bother to study cutaneous aging. After all, no one dies of old skin! The skin never really wears out or falls off. There is heart failure but no skin failure. We are well packaged to the very end.

In addition, skin diseases in the elderly are rarely lethal. The commonest skin cancers—squamous and basal cell carcinomas—are rather benign since they usually do not metastasize. This contrasts starkly with the traditional concerns of gerontology, namely, death and disability, and may help to explain why textbooks of gerontology give the skin such short shrift. Usually there is a chapter on every organ except the skin.

This is not to say that either the severity or the prevalence of skin disorders among the elderly should be considered insignificant. As regards the magnitude of skin disorders among the U.S. elderly, the most complete data derive from a health and nutritional survey by the U.S. Public Health Service between 1971 and 1974. More than 20,000 non-institutionalized persons, 1 to 74 years of age, selected by the U.S. Census Bureau as representative of the population, were ex-

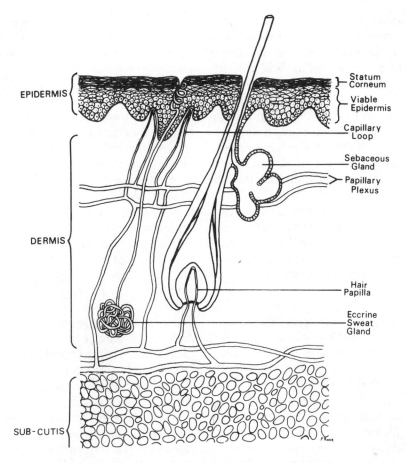

EPIDERMIS {

DERMIS {

SUB-CUTIS {

Statum Corneum

Viable Epidermis

Capillary Loop

Sebaceous Gland

Papillary Plexus

Hair Papilla

Eccrine Sweat Gland

Figure 1. Schematic diagram of various units of human skin.

amined by dermatologists (Johnson and Roberts, 1977). A skin condition was judged to be significant if it was serious enough to require treatment by a doctor. The staggering burden of skin conditions in persons over 70 years of age is reflected in a prevalence rate of 66 percent. About a third of these had more than one skin problem. Multiple skin conditions were characteristic of the very old, and the common ones were different from those which affect the young.

Other surveys in private practices and in various institutions bear out the high incidence of skin abnormalities in the elderly. Tindell and Smith (1963) examined 163 community volunteers over 64 years of age in North Carolina. Almost all had lax skin, certainly an undisputed characteristic of aged skin. Benign tumors, angiomas, skin tags,

nevi, lentigines, and seborrheic keratoses were exceedingly common. Almost four out of five had fungus infections of the feet, and a similar percentage had dry skin. Almost a third had actinic keratoses and premalignant lesions. There were 16 separate conditions which occurred together in at least 10 percent of this sample. Typically, most had more than one skin problem, including varicosities. It is also noteworthy that in the course of one year in a chronic care facility in New York, Young (1965) found that over 65 percent of its geriatric patients developed a skin disorder and 50 percent had two.

It should not be supposed that we have a complete or accurate picture of the skin afflictions of the elderly. Of the few surveys available in different parts of the world, the samples are small and often peculiar to one socioeconomic group. The data in any given study are strongly influenced by such factors as race, social and economic status, ethnicity, climate, availability of medical care, etc. (Droller, 1953; Waisman, 1979). The skin records life's hardships in strong surface etchings (Verbov, 1975). The integument of the rural poor is often ruined at an early age. Poverty and poor skin usually go together.

It should also be mentioned that dermatologists are fond of pointing out that the skin often provides important clues to the presence of systemic diseases. Since aging is ineluctably accompanied by an increased risk of internal diseases which are life threatening and disabling, the skin's role as a diagnostic window becomes even more worthy of attention.

A cautionary note must be introduced regarding purely statistical associations. Correlations will be found among all conditions whose prevalence increases with age. Thus, trichostasis spinulosa, in which many vellus hairs are retained in sagging follicles of facial skin, increases steadily with advancing age. This has been spuriously linked to nephropathy. Similarly, a high sounding syndrome (Favre-Racouchot), which is nothing more than huge comedones in severely sun-damaged skin, has been speciously linked to kidney disease. It has also been claimed, falsely, that premature graying of the hair indicates predisposition to artherosclerosis and hypertension (Stoughton, 1962). Persons with early graying are not known to be at any greater risk for any internal disease.

On the other hand, the association between transparent skin and osteoporosis or rheumatoid arthritis is no doubt valid (McConkey et al., 1963). Transparent skin is not simply thin skin; the latter is very common in aged women, but the skin is still opaque and its collagen content is fairly normal. McConkey et al. (1967) found that the water content of transparent skin was generally over 95 percent and collagen was not organized into bundles. The importance of these observations is that the same mechanisms which underlie osteoporosis and rheumatoid arthritis may be operative in producing transparent skin. Indeed, Horan et al. (1982) have described the "white nails of old age" which they also associate with osteosporosis and thin skin in the institutionalized elderly. They, too, suspect a collagen disorder.

It is also true that the Leser-Trélat sign, a sudden outcropping of numerous, rapidly growing seborrheic keratoses, is unequivocally associated with internal malignancy, although a tumor is not found in every case (Bravin, 1966). The keratoses seem to have a growth dependency on the tumor for they sometimes regress after surgical removal.

Some other associations are intriguing but provoke skepticism. Skin tags around the neck and shoulders are common in older women but are rather rare in men. According to Margolis (1976), their presence in males raises a suspicion of diabetes. He examined 500 admissions to a veterans' hospital in Texas of whom only 20 were female. Of 47 males with skin tags, 34 had chemical diabetes. He also observed 62 diabetics who did not have skin tags.

It is quite clear that old skin does not end life, but it can certainly spoil its quality. Aged skin can be a major vexation with its many pesky problems. For example, dryness with its accompanying pruritis is ruinous to well-being and equanimity. Itching becomes an exclusive preoccupation, denying sleep, while scratching may induce bacterial infections that go unrecognized and hence untreated.

One should always have a proper regard for the emotional impact of skin aging. No one watches the disfigurements, discolorations, and deteriorations of aging skin without anxiety. We read our mortality in the skin's decadence. The psychologic distress can be unnerving. Moreover, the skin is a powerful organ of nonverbal communication. We estimate age, personality, status, race, and health merely by looking. A positive self-image and a sense of worth are related to a good appearance. A recent psychological study at the University of Pennsylvania found that the aged who are physically attractive are more optimistic and more social, have better personalities, and feel that they are in better health than the unattractive (Graham, 1983).

It cannot be overstressed that a considerable number of skin lesions afflicting the elderly are preventable. They are not the result of the passage of time but rather the consequences of cumulative environmental insults. Chemical, physical, and mechanical trauma impinge continuously on the skin. Unless protective steps are taken, these will prematurely damage the fabric. Sunlight, owing mainly to its ultraviolet component abetted by infrared radiation, is a notorious enemy of good skin (Kligman, 1969). Practically all of the dreary stigmata registered on the "old" face, are sunshine induced, namely, precancers (actinic keratoses); cancers (basal and squamous); lentigo maligna (which become invasive and lethal), a half-dozen benign growths (seborrheic keratoses, skin tags, sebaceous nevi, etc); blotches and splotches (senile lentigines, freckles, etc.); saggy, stretchable, redundant, inelastic, coarse, wrinkled, and yellowed skin. The proper use of high strength sunscreens would prevent most, if not all, of these changes (Kligman et al., 1982). However, although most of the age-associated changes observed in sun-exposed areas are a reflection of chronic actinic damage, as we will catalog in later sections, anatomical alterations and physiological impairments have been observed in nonexposed, protected areas as well.

Some state that photoaging of sun-exposed areas merely represents an accentuation or acceleration of normal aging, differing only in degree (Montagna and Carlisle, 1979). This is simply untrue. In actinically damaged skin, there is a great increase in glycosaminoglycans (ground substance), whereas there is little or no change in protected skin (Smith et al., 1962). The massive outgrowth of deranged elastic fibers is never observed in unexposed skin (Kligman, 1969). There is massive resorption of collagen in actinically damaged skin, while in protected skin, the density of collagen merely decreases. Histologists long ago noted that in sun-damaged skin, a subepidermal zone seemed to be spared. This so-called Grenz zone is sometimes regarded as a scar. The fact is that it represents a repair zone in which new, entirely normal collagen is being laid down continuously by numerous hyperactive fibroblasts (Lavker, 1979). In protected skin, the fibroblasts are sparse and there is no Grenz zone. Braverman and Fonferko (1982A) have also described two types of elastic fiber abnormalities—one related to actinic damage and the other to chronological aging.

Unfortunately, many investigators have not properly distinguished between photoaging and normalative aging changes, which has led to confusing and sometimes contradictory reports in the literature. Moreover, every organ function that has been reported in the gerontology literature shows increased variability with aging. This is especially true for skin where rates of aging among individuals are so vastly different. This increased variability imposes strict criteria for proving that some parameters are significantly different in the aged. We found, for example, that the mean size of horny cells from aged individuals was considerably increased (Grove, 1979). However, as seen in Figure 2, the values were dispersed over a huge range, with large standard deviations. It is noteworthy that a few had values below the mean of the young. Small numbers can never be conclusive when the variance is so great.

We would also like to point out that there are many instances in which sweeping generalizations have been made from paltry sample sizes. One example will suffice. Quevedo et al. (1969) found that the density of melanocytes in unexposed buttock skin decreased 20 percent every decade past young adulthood. This neat linear decline now passes for dogma. However, the total sample size was 12 individuals of whom one was 60 and the oldest 65! This same linear decline was also noted in a study of the protected skin of the upper arms. This time the decrease was 6 to 8 percent per decade (Gilchrest et al., 1979). The sample comprised eight persons of whom four were over 60.

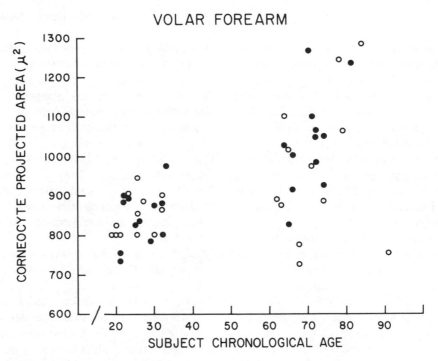

Figure 2. Scatter plot of cross-sectional data on projected area of corneocytes obtained from two age cohorts. (See Grove, 1979, for details.)

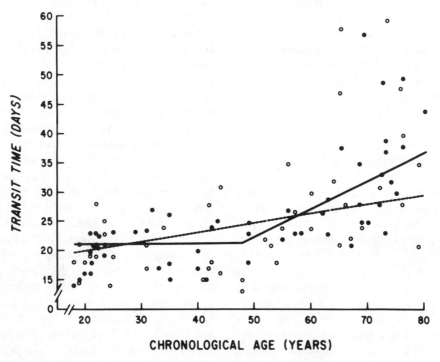

Figure 3. Stratum corneum transit times for approximately 100 healthy white volunteers as a function of chronologic age. Transit time was estimated as the time required for dansyl chloride fluorescence to disappear completely from fully stained site on mid-upper inner arm. Best fit was determined using least residual mean squares as an indication of unexplained variability for linear regression model (---) or hinged linear spline model (———); women (○) men (●). (See Grove and Kligman, 1983, for details.)

Linearity seems to be a fundamental bias of those who study age-dependent skin functions. However, our own investigations do not confirm a continuous decrease for any of the functions we have studied. For example, in Figure 3, which is a plot of proliferative activity with age, a true decrease does not become evident till after age 50. The pattern of skin aging seems to be different from most other organs (Grove and Kligman, 1983) in which function declines linearly after peaking in young adulthood.

Thus, although a rather extensive literature exists with regard to cutaneous aging, the findings reported are of varied quality. Because the basic knowledge is so limited, many statements in the synopsis which follows in this text are derived from our personal experiences and are accordingly not referenced.

ANATOMICAL ALTERATIONS

The Epidermis

It is frequently stated that the epidermis thins and becomes atrophic in old age (Selmanowitz et al., 1977). This is one of those easy generalizations which turn out to be incomplete and misleading. Evans et al. (1943) showed that epidermal thickness in routine sections was appreciably less in the aged. Still, they concluded that the epidermis of individuals over 80 was not significantly thinner than young adults. They explained this paradox by showing that excised aged skin shrinks slightly or not at all, while specimens from young persons were reduced in area by as much as 50 percent. In young tissue, the dermis contracts, causing the epidermal cells to crowd together—a shrinkage artifact. Whitton and Everall (1973) thoroughly appreciated this difficulty and avoided it by first separating the epidermis in sodium bromide and weighing it after drying. They, too, thought that age had little if any effect on epidermal thickness. There were no sex differences.

A cursory glance at a histologic section indicates that the epidermal area is lessened in the aged. The explanation lies in the fact that the rete pegs disappear and the lower surface of the epidermis loses its undulating contour. The epidermis flattens because of loss of the papillae (Figure 4). The contact arc between the dermis and epidermis thus diminishes. Consequently, a shearing force will more readily peel off the epidermis. Also, there will be fewer mitotically active basal cells per unit of surface.

Lavker (1979) found no important age-associated changes in the fine structure of cells of viable epidermis and the stratum corneum. Light microscopy readily identifies a pattern which is typical of aged tissue, namely cellular-heterogeneity. There are marked disparities in the size, shape, and staining qualities of epidermal cells (Montagna, 1965). The orderly differentiation from cuboidal basal cells to spheroidal malpighian cells and flattened granular cells is disrupted in older epidermis; polarity is lost.

Langerhans' cells, derived from the bone marrow, comprise about 5 percent of the cells of the epidermis. In old skin, their density may be decreased by more than 50 percent (Gilchrest et al., 1982a). These cells are now classified as macrophages and play an important role in antigen processing, contributing to diminished cell-mediated immunity in aged skin.

Sweat Glands

There is clinical evidence that the aged sweat less; recruitment of sweat glands by thermal stimulation takes longer. Measurements are sparse. On the fingertips, it has been found that there are fewer active glands and the amount secreted per gland is less (Silver et al., 1965). Responsiveness to pharmacologic stimuli is also diminished. Palmar sweating is a continuous process; yet McKinnon (1954) found that beginning in adult life, the density of actively secreting glands on the palmar digits of unstimulated persons decreases sharply with age. This may reflect decreased cortical activity in less active, older individuals.

Histologic studies are compatible with de-

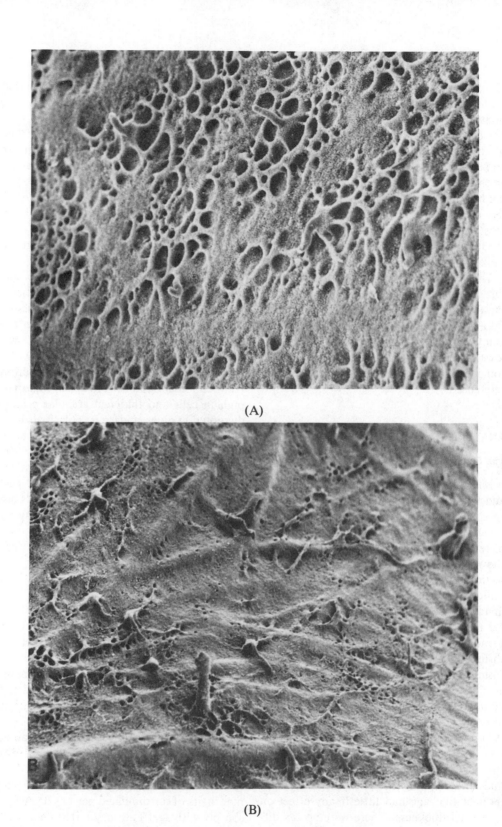

Figure 4. Undersurface of separated epidermis (SEM × 100) · (a) Abdominal specimen from 29-year-old male showing numerous variable cavities formerly occupied by dermal papillae. (b) Abdominal specimen from 71-year-old female. The undersculpting has been effaced. The cavities are small and sparse. This corresponds to the flat dermo-epidermal junction in transverse sections.

826

creased function. Juniper and Dykman (1967) observed fewer intact glands in sections of exposed and unexposed skin. Montagna (1965) observed disarray and shrinkage of the secretory coil, sometimes with complete involution, along with luminal dilatation. The adventitial connective tissue around the sweat gland was excessively "fibrotic" with fewer vessels.

The elderly are at increased risk of heat stroke during spells of exceedingly hot weather (see Chapter 21). This is probably linked to impairment of evaporative heat loss through sweating. An attenuated vasculature would also decrease heat loss.

Apocrine Sweat Glands

These glands are best developed in the axilla, being vestigial or absent over most of the body surface. They are under androgen control, coming into secretory activity at puberty. Apocrine sweat is the sole source of the pungent acrid body odor so typical of humans, a result of bacterial action. Decreased apocrine sweating is likely in old age, especially in females, since androgen production decreases after menopause. Indeed, Hurley and Shelley (1960) found that intradermally injected epinephrine produced droplets of apocrine sweat in all young persons but in only 6 of 11 elderly individuals. The elderly have less body odor and consequently can give up using deodorants. This is one of the unsung benefits of growing old. There is a suggestion of greater disorganization of the secretory tubules in the aged (Montagna, 1965).

Sebaceous Glands

These oil-producing glands are androgen dependent. Their activity throughout the life span correlates well with testosterone production by the ovary and adrenal glands. Sebum production increases sharply at puberty, peaks in late adolescence, and remains steady throughout adult life. It falters first in postmenopausal women, declining steadily thereafter (Pochi et al., 1979). In aged females,

sebum production may be half that of young adults. In men, the output does not begin to decline until about the early seventies. In the sixth decade, sebum output in men is about twice that of women.

In the young, sebum output parallels gland size. Highly oily persons have large sebaceous glands. However, in the elderly this relationship does not hold. Plewig and Kligman (1978) compared the sebaceous glands of young and old persons in regard to several parameters. The average mean size was almost twofold greater in the old cohort. There was an impressive proliferation of sebaceous lobules; the sebaceous tissue sometimes comprised 70 percent of the total area. The transit time of thymidine-labeled cells decreased greatly. In the young, labeled nuclei were well within the fundus in one week, whereas in the old, they were still in or near the basal layer.

The sebaceous glands of the elderly are still able to respond to hormonal stimuli. Pochi et al. (1979) administered the androgen fluoxymesterone, 20 mg per day, to postmenopausal women, increasing the sebum output from 1.65 to 2.12 mg/10 cm/3 hrs.

It is noteworthy that Miles (1958), studying sebaceous glands of the human cheek, found that these increased in number and size with increasing age, sometimes reaching huge proportions. Whereas sunlight may contribute to sebaceous hyperplasia of the face, the enormous development of multilobulated, exuberant sebaceous glands in the mouth may represent a true age-dependent change.

On the glabrous skin of humans, sebum has no clear-cut function. In some mammals, it serves as a sexual attractant and territorial marker, as well as protecting the fur from overwetting and trauma. Perhaps the frequent complaint of dry skin of the face of older females may be partially due to a decreased supply of sebum.

Hair

Those unfamiliar with the literature will be surprised to learn that knowledge about age-related hair changes is not much advanced over that possessed by the average hairdresser. Of course, scalp hair growth decreases, with noticeable thinning past 65. The rate of growth declines, and the diameter diminishes. Most people over 40 have some graying of scalp hair. The tendency to graying is inherited, as is baldness. Beyond that, substantive data are scanty. The most informative review is by Giacometti (1965).

It is technically troublesome to secure quantitative data. Efforts have been made to popularize the trichogram, which involves determination of the ratio of growing (androgen) to resting (telogen) hairs (Barman et al., 1965). The hair population in any region is extremely heterogenous; individual hairs grow at independent rates, are of variable thickness, and follow different cyclical patterns. Density varies greatly from person to person. Blondes have more hairs than brunettes. Determining hair mass by shaving and weighing is burdensome and imprecise.

Without a quantitative data base, the outcome of therapeutic interventions is burdened by uncertainty. The media are replete with seductive, but generally specious, advertisements guaranteeing to grow or to remove hair permanently. There is a vast, billion dollar business centered on improving appearance by various attentions to the hair.

There are intriguing paradoxes which await scientific inquiry. For example, hair growth does not uniformly decrease after adult life. The opposite may occur. Most women past 65, especially those of Mediterranean origin, have excess growth of darker, thicker, longer hairs over the lip and chin. This localized hirsutism cannot be explained. These same women may stop shaving their axillae, and the pubic pelage may be very thin. Often, there is an accompanying thinning, even baldness, at the center of the scalp. Alopecia and hirsutism unaccountably exist side by side. Despite age decrements in hair growth, the follicles themselves remain responsive to the appropriate hormonal stimulus. Chieffi (1950), for example, promoted the beard growth of elderly men by administering testosterone. Tufts of stout hairs could be elicited on the face of aged

females at sites repeatedly injected with testosterone (Maguire, 1964).

Old men have contrasting problems. They lose their proud beard hair in old age but grow an unsightly crop of coarse hairs over the rim of the ears and out of the nostrils; the eyebrows often become bushier. These events await serious study.

Dermis

The main function of the dermis is to provide a tough matrix to support the many structures embedded in it, namely, vessels, nerves, and various appendages. It is mainly composed of highly stable fibers, predominantly collagen and about 5 percent elastin. Collagen has high tensile strength and prevents the skin from being torn by overstretching. Elastin is a springy material which maintains normal skin tension but is readily extensible to accomodate movement of the joints and muscles. When young skin is stretched and let go, it snaps back swiftly to ground level. A number of devices have been used to evaluate these biomechanical properties (Daly and Odlund, 1979); these are not routine instruments. The fibroblast is the cell which synthesizes all the components of the matrix—collagen, elastin, and ground substance. Mast cells and macrophages comprise the other permanent cells of the dermis.

Despite substantial anatomic, biochemical, and biomechanical studies, we are still far from a consensus regarding age-associated alterations in the dermis. There are many areas of dispute. The wrinkle, the most telltale sign of aging, is still unexplained! Its anatomy does not distinguish it from surrounding tissue.

Dermal components of man and animals have received much attention in the hope of identifying markers of biologic aging (Hall, 1976). Collagen has been the object of much study since it seems to undergo characteristic changes with time. There is general agreement that it becomes less soluble and stiffer with age, shows greater thermal contractibility, and becomes more resistant to enzymatic digestion. These changes are supposedly due to progressive cross-linking (Bentley, 1979). However, clinical inspection shows that old skin is loose, not stiff and tight.

Langer's lines, familiar to every medical student, are thought to come about as a result of preferential orientation of collagen fibers. This has never been demonstrated, though it would explain the skin's anisotropy, that is, its direction-dependent behavior. We do not, and Langer did not, understand why holes punched into the skin with a round instrument become oval. Had Langer done his studies on very old skin, he would never have discovered his lines. In the aged, round holes simply gape and do not contract to an oval shape.

Preoccupation with molecular events may have delayed appreciation of important architectural changes in the collagen network (Prockop and Kisirikko, 1967). Perhaps old collagen is not so very different, molecularly speaking. The most important change may be in the loosened weaving of the fabric; the three-dimensional meshwork may become distorted by lifelong mechanical stresses.

Our scrutiny of the dermis by scanning electron microscopy indicates marked architectural rearrangements (Figure 5). The fibers are disposed in coarser, rope-like bundles which are in disarray, in contrast to their more ordered organization in young dermis. Progressive derangement of the fibrous network could account for laxity.

The dermis definitely thins in old age. There is less collagen per surface area, and it is less dense (Shuster and Black, 1975). Males have a thicker dermis (Tan et al., 1982). This may help to explain why female facial skin seems to deteriorate more readily with aging. Thinner skin is more easily damaged by actinic radiation, trauma, and mechanical stress.

Changes in elastin with age have provoked much interest and, as usual, controversy. Elastic tissue is vastly increased in sun-damaged skin (Kligman, 1969). By light microscopy, the vertical, subepidermal fine skeins of elastic fibers, often in verticillate patterns as in Figure 6, are invariably lost in old skin

(Montagna and Carlisle, 1979). Electron microscopy shows enhanced arrays of tubular elastic microfibrils inserting into the basement membrane, a futile restorative effort (Lavker, 1979). The ablation of these fine fibers unquestionably contributes to the superficial laxity of old skin and its finely wrinkled surface. The regression of the subepidermal elastic network occurs in all body regions and is a clear, age-dependent change. At low loads, old skin can be stretched over quite a distance before a resistance develops.

The elastic network in the underlying reticular dermis shows an opposite change—the fibers become thicker, more numerous, and more branched and disarrayed (Tsuji and Hamada, 1981). Contrary to common belief, they do not become more fragmented; shorter segments and an artifact from sectioning highly coiled fibers. Despite a greater abundance of elastic tissue, it is structurally abnormal, with consequent loss of resiliency and recuperability after stretching. Untrastructural studies show that degenerative changes begin as early as age 30 with loss of microfibrils and appearances of cavities (Stadler and Orfanos, 1978). Moreover, Braverman and Fonferko (1982a) have shown that one of the features of cutaneous aging is a slow, spontaneous, progressive degradative process inherent in the elastic fiber which can be artificially accelerated from decades to hours by elastase and chymotrypsin. These are highly characteristic changes which may provide more reliable indicators of biologic aging.

It is generally said that the ground substance, composed mainly of glycosaminoglycans and glycoproteins, diminishes in aged skin (Fleishmajer et al., 1973). This is disputed territory; the changes are slight in any case (Bentley, 1979). The ground substance comprises less than 0.2 percent of the dry weight of the dermis. It is only recently that methods exist for accurately quantifying individual glycosaminoglycans. Hyaluronic acid is an important constituent and has provoked a lot of commentary in relation to aging. Nonetheless, the roles assigned to the ground substance are speculative. Its con-

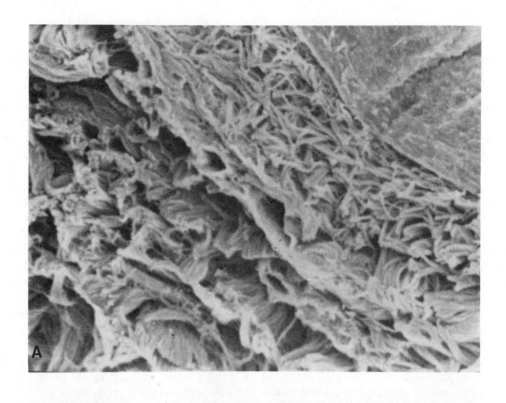

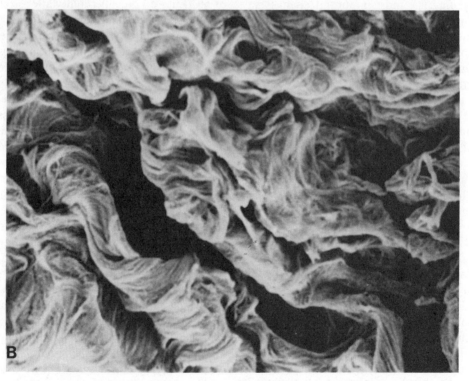

Figure 5. Three-dimensional view of dermal collagen of abdomen (SEM × 345). (a) Specimen from 20-year-old female. The collagen bundles tend to be horizontal tiers and are rather delicate. (b) Specimen from 71-year-old female. The bundles are thick, coarse, and tangled with large interspaces.

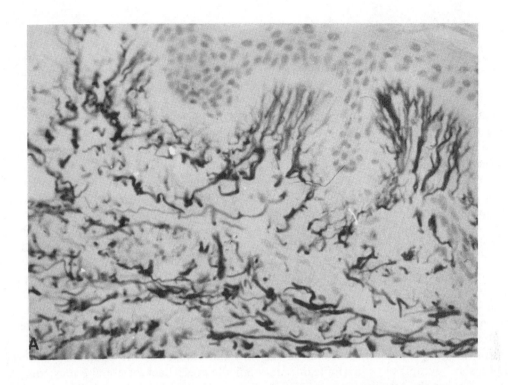

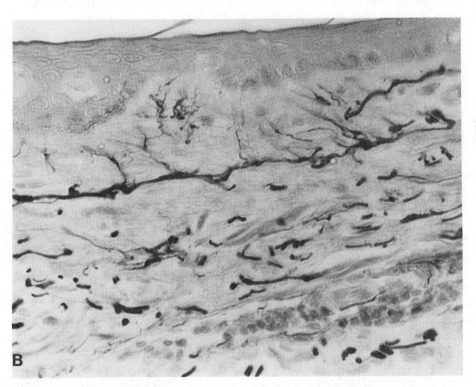

Figure 6. Architecture of subepidermal elastic fibers (Luna Stain × 225). (a) Buttock skin of 23-year-old female. Note vertical skins of fine fibers almost inserting into the basement membrane. (b) Buttock skin of 80-year-old female. The subepidermal network was collapsed, leaving a few straggly fibers.

stituents undoubtedly contribute to the rheo-logical properties of the skin. Presumably they function as lubricants, allowing colla-gen fibers to slide past each other. They cer-tainly provide a pathway for diffusion of nutrients through the interstices of the der-mis. Many think that hyaluronic acid is re-sponsible for the normal turgor of the dermis because of its extraordinary water-holding capacity, at least a thousand times its dry weight. We cannot go much beyond saying that the dermis would probably be nonfunc-tional without the ground substance, but its exact role is unknown.

Anatomists are agreed that the population of dermal cells diminishes with age (Andrew et al., 1964; Gilchrest, 1982). In addition to this hypocellularity, the master cell—the fi-broblast—takes the form of a shrunken fi-brocyte, being narrower with a much diminished cytoplasm with indicates de-creased metabolic activity (Papa and Klig-man, 1967). From this appearance, we would expect the turnover of matrix components, especially the ground substance, to be de-creased in aged dermis. This appears to be the case (Prockop and Kisirikko, 1967).

Depletion of macrophages inevitably af-fects numerous maintenance functions, namely secretion of proteases, mediation of inflammation, phagocytosis, clearing of for-eign material, etc. However, the clinical con-sequences of fewer macrophages have not been clearly delineated.

Hellstrom and Holmgren (1950) noted a great decrease in mast cells of the dermis and the heart of aged subjects. Gilchrest (1982) observed at least a 50 percent reduction in aged skin. Fewer mast cells would explain why it is more difficult in aged skin to raise wheals by histamine-releasing drugs and why urticaria is uncommon in the aged.

The Subcutaneous Tissue

The subcutis serves as a shock absorber against trauma. It is a high calorie storage depot and also modulates conductive heat loss. The subcutis is said to undergo atrophy with age. This certainly holds for unpro-tected areas such as the back of the hands and generally the face. Loss of subcutaneous fat of the soles of aged persons increases the trauma of walking and magnifies the many foot problems of the aged. However, resorp-tion of subcutaneous tissue is not the rule in all regions.

Nutritionists routinely make skin-fold measurements to estimate the fat content of the body, usually at 8 to 12 body sites. It turns out that the proportion of body fat after puberty steadily increases with age at least up to 70 years, more so in women than in men (Shephard et al., 1969). However, re-gional differences are great. For example, the triceps fold remains more or less constant during aging. The greatest increases occur in the abdomen, waist, and supra-iliac areas, especially in postmenopausal women. Every layman recognizes the paunchiness of the middle aged. Lack of exercise may contrib-ute to spreading of the waistline, but thin-ning of the subcutis of the hands, soles, and pretibial area must reflect other influences, perhaps pressure, trauma, or sunlight. This area is wide open for investigation.

Cutaneous Nerves

In their study of aged skin from various body regions, Montagna and Carlisle (1979) con-cluded that free nerve endings are little af-fected by age. On the other hand, Meissner's corpuscles have been shown to decrease con-tinuously with age, accompanied by various degenerative changes (Cauna, 1965; Winkle-man, 1965). Selmanowitz et al. (1977) assert that these changes are "sufficiently typical to enable approximate prediction of the bearer's age." This seems an overly optimis-tic proposal in view of the great individual differences among similarly aged persons. Histologic variability plagues all anatomical studies of skin. Free nerve endings are prob-ably reforming continuously. Even around the dwarfed follicles of the bald scalp, the sensory nerve unit simply condenses to a structure resembling the mucocutaneous end-organ but is well preserved nonetheless (Montagna and Carlisle, 1979).

Physiologic tests tell another story. Clinical observations suggest that the elderly have far less acuity in the perception of pain: we have sometimes been startled to find that elderly persons who were fearful of needle injections could endure a shave biopsy with virtually no pain. This is one reason why burns tend to be more serious and widespread in the aged (Linn, 1980): the elderly are less capable of sensing danger and reacting appropriately.

Pain perception can be accurately measured by the Hardy dolorimeter. This instrument applies radiant energy in a controlled fashion, enabling determination of the pain threshold, the smallest amount of heat causing a sharp, jabbing sensation. Sherman and Robillard (1960) compared pain thresholds on the foreheads of young and old persons. They also determined the pain reaction threshold, the smallest stimulus causing wincing. Both values were sharply increased in the old group, indicating decreased sensitivity. Procacci et al. (1970) also determined pain thresholds in two large age cohorts. Between 50 and 90 years, there was a progressive loss of sensitivity. Typically, the values were more variable in the aged. Of course, the reaction to pain is modified by higher cognitive functions, and depends on both past experiences and one's outlook on life. The aged are often resigned to distress. Such attitudes increase the risk of being harmed.

Tactile sensitivity doubtless diminishes in old age as well. This has been shown clearly for the cornea where there are only free nerve endings (Salavisto et al., 1951).

The Microcirculation

Humans have an unusually rich superficial microvasculature; this underlies the extraordinary repertoire of inflammatory dermatoses. The distribution and quality of the small vessels are not well displayed in routine H & E sections. Visualization is best secured in thick, alkaline phosphatase-stained specimens providing a three-dimensional view (Figure 7). One-micron plastic sections provide intimate details of the endothelium and vessel walls.

Observers are in agreement that in advanced age, regression and disorganization of small vessels are invariant changes. Many capillaries and vessels seem to be deleted altogether (Montagna and Carlisle, 1979). With resorption of the papillae, the capillary loops necessarily disappear. In aged, protected skin, it was found that the number of venular cross-sections per 3 mm of surface was reduced by at least 30 percent (Gilchrest et al., 1982). The rarefaction of the microvasculature is especially prominent in actinically damaged skin where only a few scraggly, dilated, tortuous, blurred vessels may remain.

Small vessels around the appendages also diminish in density with age. Decreased sweating and thinning hair may partly reflect an attenuated vasculature. Ellis (1958) noted involution of the perifollicular venular network in the haired scalp of older persons. The degeneration of small vessels is almost certainly an intrinsic age change and progresses relentlessly, even in protected skin.

Braverman and Fonferko (1982b) have also shown that in actinically damaged skin, the vascular walls of postcapillary venules and of arterial and venous capillaries were thickened by the peripheral addition of a layer of basement membrane-like material. Increased numbers of veil cells displaying dilated cisternae of rough endoplasmic reticulum containing electron dense material, indicative of synthetic activity, were seen in intimate association with these thickened walls. Thickened vessels with prominent veil cells were also seen in the sun-protected buttock skin of three individuals in their early 70s, suggesting that this abnormality might be a feature of chronologic aging as well. In four older subjects 80–93 years old, these workers found abnormally thinned vessels which were associated with a decreased number of veil cells, as well as a marked decrease or absence of metabolic activity. This seems to indicate that as aging progresses, the functions of the veil cell begin to decrease, so that the basement membrane material of the ves-

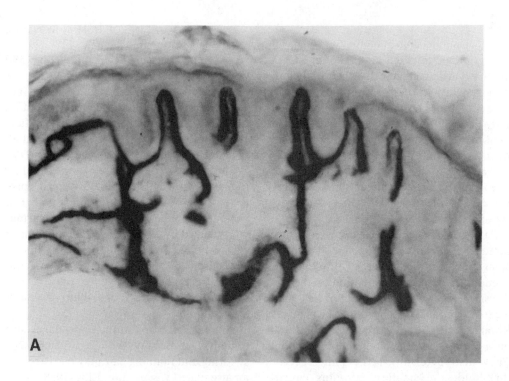

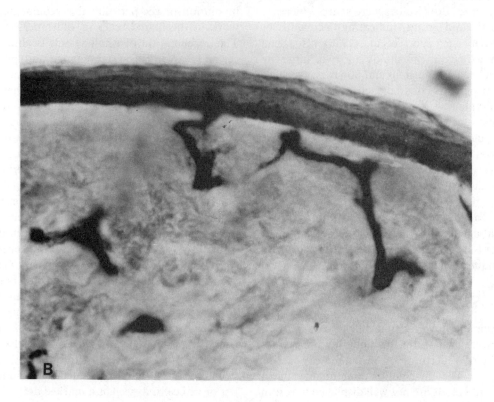

Figure 7. The microvasculature (alkaline phosphatase × 125). (a) Dorsal forearm of 24-year-old male. Capillary loops are prominent, and the venules below are sharply defined. (b) Dorsal forearm of 63-year-old male with severe actinic damage. The venules are blurred, sparse, and irregularly widened. The capillaries have disappeared.

sel wall is not replaced during normal metabolic turnover, which causes the vessel wall to become thinner.

Clinical observations support the rarefaction of the microvasculature in the aged. Protected skin often shows pallor. Moreover, when the temperature falls, the elderly quickly experience coldness. A comfortable temperature for old people is often 10–15° higher than the level recommended for public institutions (about 65°F).

By thermography, Horikawa and Yuasa (1981) showed that facial skin temperature of Japanese females decreased with aging. Lower skin temperature had previously been demonstrated for the extremities (King, 1937). Recently, Howell (1982) evaluated the temperature gradient between the groin and the toes of 104 women, 61 to 100 years of age. At room temperature, there was a mean difference of 8.8°C; some actually showed a drop of 16°C. This gradient is much larger than in young subjects. Everyone over 65 readily appreciates coldness of the feet at low ambient temperatures.

It is well-known that even brief exposure to cold can precipitate hypothermia in the aged; this may be lethal (Shock, 1977). Exposure to 5–15°C produces a 1.0° loss in core temperature; the young are not affected. This is an age-dependent failure in thermoregulatory hemeostasis. The young vasoconstrict more, shiver more, and generate more metabolic heat. Also, in bitter cold, the aged may fail to take appropriate corrective action because of diminished pain perception, another age-dependent decrement.

Quantitative estimates of micro-blood flow are presently beyond the reach of modern technology. Available methods are indirect and relatively crude, such as disappearance of radiolabeled xenon, capillary plethysmography, and Doppler monitoring. Still, useful comparative information may be obtained by estimating the rate of removal of intradermally injected water soluble substances. This is dependent on interstitial fluid movement which indirectly reflects blood supply. Christophers and Kligman (1965) showed that the time to clear 50 percent of

injected radiolabeled sodium ion was 13.3 minutes in the aged and 8.7 minutes in the young. Tagami's results were similar, using the same methodology (Tagami, 1972). On the forearms, Aschner (1960) found that the resorption times of saline wheals in the young ranged from 50 to 90 minutes. In subjects over 65, the mean was 122 minutes, about double. Kligman (1979) also found that it took about twice as long for the wheals to flatten in people over 70.

A reduced blood supply has both therapeutic and toxicologic applications for the aged. It seems likely that with topical drugs such as corticosteroids, fewer applications might have the same therapeutic effect owing to reduced clearance. Conversely, the customary t.i.d. schedule might enhance adverse effects. Topical therapy has to be reevaluated in the aged. This is another serious "gap" area.

PHYSIOLOGICAL IMPAIRMENTS

In addition to these anatomical derangements, various age-associated changes in skin function have been observed.

Inflammatory Responses

The literature is contradictory regarding whether aged persons have altered inflammatory responses to chemical and physical stresses. Lorincz (1960) remarked that the aged react more readily to formalin and adhesive tape. Others found that patch test reactions to soaps and detergents increased with age (Nilzen and Voss-Lagerland, 1962). By contrast, Coenraads et al. (1975) patch tested 600 patients to various irritants and concluded that the reaction rate was not age dependent.

We have established beyond reasonable doubt that acute inflammatory reactions of all kinds are muted and reduced in the aged. The elderly respond far less sharply to croton oil, cationic and anionic surfactants, weak acids, solvents (DMSO, kerosene). Higher concentrations produce weaker reactions, whether the end points are wheals, bullae, vesicles, pustules, dermatitis, redness, etc. (Grove et al., 1981).

Carlizza and Bologna (1965) recorded fewer inflammatory cells in cantharidin blisters from older subjects. Reduced responses are not limited to chemical irritants. Gilchrest and her associates irradiated buttock skin with 3 minimal erythema doses (3 MED's) from a mercury vapor lamp (Gilchrest et al., 1982b). In comparison to young subjects, individuals between 62 and 81 years of age showed diminished erythema, edema, microscopic sunburn cells, and histamine levels. Thus, the total response was attenuated and evolved more slowly. This pattern is characteristic of the aged and is partly explained by fewer mast cells.

The failure to react promptly to a toxic stimulus carries with it the danger of continued exposure to noxious agents. The elderly have a deficient early warning detection system. Redness appearing shortly after exposure signals a young person to desist. In the aged, because of a long latent period, applications may continue until suddenly the tissue collapses, sometimes with ulceration. The elderly should be cautioned regarding self-treatment with home remedies so abundantly at hand, many of which are more suitable for cleaning toilet bowls!

Immunologic Alterations

Immunology is discussed in detail in Chapter 16. Both cell-mediated and humoral immunity decrease in old age (Weksler, 1982). Impairment of cell-mediated immunity has many adverse cutaneous effects. For example, herpes zoster and the dreaded neuralgia it induces are practically limited to the aged. With regard to humoral immunity, it is curious that the titer of antinuclear antibodies goes up in almost all aged persons, and autoimmune antibodies to various tissues also increase (Hallgren et al., 1973). Thus, serious autoimmune dermatological disorders such as pemphigus and bullous pemphigoid have their highest prevalence among the elderly.

One may think of the aged as having a mild to moderate cell-mediated immunodeficiency. The intradermal reaction to ubiquitous antigens such as tuberculin, *Candida*, and mumps declines (Grossman et al., 1975). It is important to take into account the suppressive effect of disease, especially malignancy and febrile illnesses (Novick et al., 1972). Clinicians sense that contact allergy is less frequent in the aged, and experiments have shown that the aged are more resistant to contact sensitization with potent allergens such as dinitrochlorobenzene (Catalona et al., 1972). Also, immunologic testing is beginning to assume importance in assessing biologic age: Hallgren et al. (1973) found that aged individuals who were anergic to five recall antigens had decreased survival over a two-year follow-up period.

It has been established that older cancer patients with T-cell deficiencies are more likely to have recurrences and shorter life expectancy. Depressed cellular immunity has been correlated with aggressive tumors which lack a rigorous lymphocytic response, a sign of impaired immune surveillance (Cutler et al., 1969). A failure in immune surveillance is the logical explanation for the tendency of immunosuppressed patients to develop various tumors which also behave more aggressively (Harville and Aaron, 1973). About half the malignancies in immunosuppressed patients, mainly renal transplants, develop in sun-exposed skin (Penn, 1980). Actinically damaged skin is less reactive to contact and recall antigens indicating that contact sensitization is also impaired. Finally, the new science of photoimmunology has convincingly demonstrated that the effects of sunlight are systemic and not merely local (Granstein and Morrison, 1982). Kripke and Fisher (1976) have demonstrated that ultraviolet light induces suppressor T-cells which prevent contact sensitization of irradiated mice, as well as allowing the survival of malignant skin tumors. This new knowledge emphasizes the great importance of a consistent program of protection against excessive sunlight exposures.

Permeability

There is a widespread belief that elderly skin is more permeable. This seems natural, but the evidence is not convincing. The stratum corneum is the rate limiting barrier to the diffusion of substances across the skin. In normal skin, its diffusional resistance is directly proportional to the number of cell layers. Years ago, Christophers and Kligman (1965) found that the numbers of cell layers in cantharidin blister roofs of the back were the same for old and young subjects, about 15. In our studies, we could find no age-related difference in the number of horny cell layers at two protected sites, the mean being about 16 (Grove et al., 1982). The most convenient way to assess barrier function is to determine transepidermal water loss; this is entirely controlled by the stratum corneum. Measurement of diffusional water loss through isolated sheets of horny layer has not shown any increase in the aged (Christophers and Kligman, 1965).

Thus, the stratum corneum of the aged is not thinner and its barrier function is not impaired, even though exfoliated horny cells show cytologic irregularities and great variability (Grove, 1979). No matter how battered the viable epidermis becomes after a lifetime of environmental insults, it still manages to produce a horny layer which suffers very little functional loss.

It must be understood that the term percutaneous absorption involves more than flux, the amount which diffuses across the horny layer in a given time. The net effect will also be influenced by blood flow. Substances that diffuse at the same rate might not be equivalently absorbed. The attenuated microvasculature of the aged will diminish the rate at which substances are removed from the dermis. Malkinson (1958), monitoring the surface disappearance of [^{14}C]-testosterone, found that absorption in men over 75 was about one-third that of young males.

Decreased clearance may have dire consequences. A case in point is the elderly woman who extensively applied calamine lotion containing 1 percent phenol to the entire body twice daily. She suffered convulsions in ten days, reproduced by reexposure (Light, 1935). The combination of a large area of application and decreased dermal (and probably renal) clearance led to elevated blood levels.

Wound Healing

It is always assumed that healing is delayed in the aged, but quantitative information is unsatisfactory. The studies of DuNuoy (1936), a surgeon in World War I, are brought forth to show impaired wound healing with aging. It was found that 30-year-old men healed more slowly than 20-year olds; the same decrement was noted in the comparison between 40- and 30-year-old individuals (Carrel and DuNuoy, 1921). We find it exceedingly difficult to put much stock in this work in view of the fact that no two wounds could have been alike under the exigencies of warfare in the preantibiotic era. The variables in depth and size of the wounds, degree of contamination, and source of injury, together with low standards of medical care, all conspire to nullify the relevance of DuNuoy's findings. Orentreich and Selmanowitz (1969) reexamined these data and found that the age differences were even more striking than originally reported. The central question is whether the undoubted loss in reparative ability begins to decline after age 20 and in a continuous linear fashion.

Surgical experience clearly demonstrates that even the old-old (beyond 85) can effectively repair extensive wounds. Surgeons are not the least bit daunted in performing major operations on the elderly, including head and neck dissections, cardiac surgery, abdominal aneurysmectomy, etc. (Yung et al., 1979). The predictably high success rate has tended to obscure substantial differences in wound repair (Claus and Gotham, 1966). Most dehiscences of abdominal surgical wounds occur in older subjects (Halasz,

1968). In a cooperative study at 19 Veterans Administration hospitals, wound dehiscence after surgery for duodenal ulcer increased from one percent in patients 30 to 39 years old to five percent in those over 70 (Halasz et al., 1960). The time required for postsurgical care is also increased in old age.

Sandblum et al. (1953) measured the force required to disrupt incisions in humans; they found that tensile strength of five-day wounds was considerably less in the elderly. Likewise, in implanted sponges left in human incisions, Viljanto (1969) found that the collagen deposited in seven days decreased with increasing age of the patients.

With regard to more superficial wounds, Orentreich has done more than 12,000 dermabrasions on the face using a rotating wire brush on frozen skin. He estimates that re-epithelialization takes about ten days for 25 year olds and twice that long for patients over 75 years (Orentreich and Salmanowitz, 1969). Grove (1982) has conducted the most rigorous study on the healing of superficial wounds in humans. He raised up ammonium hydroxide blisters and determined the time for the surface markings to be completely restored in two age cohorts, 18–25 years and 65–75 years. He found that the elderly lagged behind the young cohort at every stage of repair. As usual, restoration times were more variable in the elderly.

It should never be forgotten that after surgery, medical complications are more numerous and serious in the elderly (McGuirt et al., 1977).

BIOLOGIC VERSUS CHRONOLOGIC AGING

It is obvious that there may be a wide gap between chronologic and biologic age. Some elderly people seem to be more youthful in appearance and physiologic capacities. The measurement of physiologic aging is one of the central concerns of gerontology. For this purpose, no tissue can be more convenient than the skin. Still, in a recent publication by the National Institute of Aging, which deals with biologic markers of aging, the in-tegument was not even mentioned (Reff and Scheider, 1982).

The extensive studies of the Atomic Bomb Casualty Commission in Hiroshima and Nagasaki, Japan, constitute a prototype of the utilization of skin as an age marker. Hollingsworth et al. (1965) initially employed 17 physiologic aging tests, encompassing simple measurements of hand strength, vital capacity, blood pressure, etc. The two parameters which showed the highest correlation coefficients with chronologic age were hair graying and skin elasticity. Despite crude methods such as estimating the time for a pinch of dorsal hand skin to flatten, useful information was obtained. It was observed that appreciable changes in elasticity did not occur until after about the age of 50; this is concordant with our data.

Hollingsworth et al. (1961) designed a simple, multipurpose spring pincer-caliper to measure skin elasticity, skin-fold thickness, and skin looseness of the forearm, along with 0 to 4 grading of hair graying. They concluded that radiation did not accelerate aging in atomic bomb survivors. Survivors did not look older to a trained nurse.

A powerful longitudinal study which assesses biologic age has been conducted since 1958 in more than 1000 adult males at the Gerontology Research Center in Baltimore, Maryland. Twenty-four tests of physiologic age have been employed (Borkan and Norris, 1980). Biologic age was calculated by a linear regression of each variable on age, and the data were plotted by the pattern profile technique. When this is done, it is immediately noticeable that within the same individual, some tissues are "older" than others; i.e., organs do not age at the same rate. No single clock synchronizes the timing of age changes in different tissues.

In this study, a visual estimate of chronologic age was also made. Thus, it could be ascertained whether individuals who looked older than their years were physiologically older. Borkan and Norris (1980) compared men who were judged to be most old for their age with those who appeared youngest. In 19 of 24 tests, members of the subgroup that looked oldest for their age were indeed biologically older as well. Even more important, subjects who had died since the start of the study were biologically older in 19 of 24 variables. Thus, rather surprisingly, visual estimates seem to be fairly reliable indicators of biologic age.

We, too, found in various measurements, such as wound healing, that the laggards were invariably the ones who looked the oldest (Grove et al., 1982). Moreover, healing has been found to be correlated with epidermal proliferative activity. Soon it will be practical to use the skin to assess biologic age.

REFERENCES

Andrew, W., Behake, R., and Sato, T. 1964. Changes with advancing age in the cell population of human dermis. *Gerontologica* 10: 1–19.

Aschner, B. M. 1960. Intradermal salt solution test in elderly patients. *Exp. Med. Surg.* 18: 17–20.

Barman, J. M., Astorie, I., and Pecoraro, V. 1965. The normal trichogram of the adult. *J. Invest. Derm.* 44: 233–238.

Bentley, J. P. 1979. Aging of collagen. *J. Invest. Derm.,* 73: 80–83.

Borkan, G. A. and Norris, A. H. 1980. Assessment of biological age using a profile of physical parameters. *J. Gerontol.* 35: 177–184.

Braverman, I. M. and Fonferko, E. 1982a. Studies in cutaneous aging. I. The elastic fiber network. *J.I.D.* 78: 434–443.

Braverman, I. M. and Fonferko, E. 1982b. Studies in cutaneous aging. II. The microvasculature. *J.I.D.* 78: 444–448.

Bravin, T. B. 1966. The Lesar-Trélat sign. *Br. Med. J.* 2: 437–440.

Carlizza, L. and Bologna, E. 1965. Variazioni della reattivata, cutanea in rapporto con l'eta. *Bull. Soc. Ital. Biol. Sper.* 41: 344–348.

Carrel, A. and DuNuoy, P. 1921. Cicatrization of wounds. *J. Exp. Biol.* 34: 339–348.

Catalona, W. J., Taylor, P. T., Rabson, A. S., and Chretein, P. B. 1972. A method of dinitrochlorobenzene sensitization: a clinicopathologic study. *New Eng. J. Med.* 286: 399–406.

Cauna, N. 1965. The effect of aging on the receptor organs of the human dermis. *In,* W. Montagna (ed.), *Advances in Biology of Skin,* Vol. 11: 97–118, 1965 Oxford: Pergamon Press.

Chieffi, M. 1950. Effect of testosterone on the beard growth of elderly males. *J. Gerontol.* 5:200–205.

Christophers, E. and Kligman, A. M. 1965. Percutaneous absorption in aged skin. *In,* W. Montagna (ed.), *Advances in Biology of the Skin.,* Vol. 11: 163–175, 1965 Oxford: Pergamon Press.

Claus, G. and Gotham, B. 1966. Results of geriatric surgery. *Acta Chir. Scand.* 357: 85–90.

Coenraads, P. J., Bleumink, E., and Nofer, J. P. 1975. Susceptibility to primary irritants. Age dependence. *Contact Dermatitis* 1: 377–381.

Confort, A. 1972. Measuring the human aging rate. *Mechanisms of Ageing and Development* 1: 101–110.

Cutler, S. J., Black, M. M., Mork, T., Harvei, S., and Freeman, C. 1969. Further observations on prognostic factors in cancer of the female breast. *Cancer* 24: 653–657.

Daly, C. H. and Odlund, G. F. 1979. Age-related changes in the mechanical properties of human skin. *J. Invest. Derm.* 73: 84–87.

Droller, H. 1953. Dermatologic findings in a random sample of old persons. *Geriatrics* 10: 421–424.

DuNuoy, P. 1936. *Biological Time.* New York: Macmillan.

Evans, R., Cowdry, E., and Nielson, P. 1943. Aging of human skin. *Anat. Rec.* 86: 545–550.

Fleishmajer, R., Perlish, J. J., and Bashey, R. I. 1973. Aging of human dermis. *In,* Frontiers of Matrix Biology C. L. Robert (ed.), Vol. 1 pp. 90–106. Basel: Karger.

Giacometti, L. Hair growth and aging. 1965. *In,* W. Montagna (ed.), *Advances in Biology of the Skin.* pp. 97–118. Oxford: Pergamon Press.

Gilchrest, B. A. 1982b. Age-associated changes in the skin. *J. Am. Geriatric Soc.* 30: 139–143.

Gilchrest, B. A., Blog, F., and Szabo, G. 1979. Effects of aging and chronic sun exposure on melanocytes in human skin. *J.I.D.* 73: 141–143.

Gilchrest, B. A., Murphy, G., and Soter, N. A. 1982a. Effect of chronologic aging and ultraviolet light on Langerhans cells in human epidermis. *J. Invest. Derm.* 85–88.

Gilchrest, B. A., Stoff, J. S., and Soter, N. A. 1982. Chronologic aging alters the response to UV-induced inflammation in human skin. *J. Invest. Derm.* 79: 11–16.

Graham, J. A. 1983. The psychotherapeutic value of cosmetics. *Cosmetic Technology* 5: No. 1, 25–26.

Grossman, J., Baum, J., Gluckman, J., Fosner, J., and Condemi, J. 1975. The effect of aging and acute illness in delayed hypersensitivity. *J. All. Clin. Immunol.* 55: 268–275.

Grove, G. L. 1979. Exfoliative cytological procedures as a nonintrusive method for dermatogerontological studies. *J. Invest. Derm.* 73: 67–69.

Grove, G. L. 1982. Age-related differences in healing of superficial skin wounds in humans. *Arch. Dermatol. Res.* 272: 381–385.

Grove, G. L., Duncan, S., and Kligman, A. M. 1982. Effect of aging on the blistering of human skin with ammonium hydroxide. *Brit. J. Derm.* 107: 393–400.

Grove, G. L. and Kligman, A. M. 1983. Age-associated changes in human epidermal cell renewal. *J. Geront.* 38: No. 2 137–142.

Grove, G. L., Lavker, R. M., Holzle, E., and Kligman, A. M. Use of nonintrusive tests to monitor age-associated changes in human skin. *J. Soc. Cosm. Chem.* 32: 15–26.

Halasz, N. A. 1968. Dehiscence of laparotomy wounds. *Am. J. Surg.* 116: 210–214.

Halasz, N. A., Leaming, D. B., Walter, D. N., and Braithwaite, F. 1960. The treatment of hands. *Br. J. Surg.* 48: 247–270.

Hall, D. A. 1976. The Aging of Connective Tissue. New York: Academic Press.

Hallgren, H. M., Kersey, J. H., Dubey, D. P., and Yunis, E. J. 1978. Lymphocyte subsets and integrated immune function in aging humans. *Clin. Immunol. Immunopathol.* 10: 65–78.

Hallgren, H. M., Kersey, J. H., Greenberg, L. J., and Yunis, E. J. 1973. T and B cells in aging humans. *Fed. Proc.* 33: 646–647.

Harville, D. and Aaron, J. 1973. Cutaneous oncogenesis and immunosuppression. *Cutis* 11: 188–191.

Hollingsworth, J. W., Hashizume, A., and Jablon, S. 1965. Correlations between tests of aging on Hiroshima subjects, an attempt to define "physiological age." *Yale Journal of Biology and Medicine* 38: 11–26.

Hollingswoth, J. W., Ishi, G., and Conrad, R. A. 1961. Skin aging and hair graying in Hiroshima. *Geriatrics* 6: 27–36.

Horan, M. A., Poxty, J. A., and Fox, R. A. 1982. The white nails of old age. *J. Am. Geriatric. Soc.* 30: 734–737.

Horikawa, H. and Yuasa, S. 1981. Character of skin temperature distribution of the facial surface of Japanese women. *J. Jap. Cosm. Sci. Soc.* 5: 22–25.

Howell, T. H. 1982. Skin temprature gradient in the lower limbs of old women. *Exper. Gerontol.* 17: 65–67.

Hurley, J. H. and Shelley, W. B. 1960. *The Apocrine Sweat Gland in Health and Disease.* Springfield, Ill.: Charles C. Thomas.

Johnson, M. L. T. and Roberts, J. 1977. Prevalence of dermatologic disease among persons 1–74 years of age. *Advance Data.* Washington, D.C.: U.S. Department of Health, Education and Welfare.

Juniper, K. and Dykman, R. A. 1967. Skin resistance, sweat glands counts and salivary flow. Age, race and sex differences. *Phycophysiology* 4: 216–222.

King, F. 1937. Haut temperatormessungen an Mannern von uber 60 Jahren. *Z. Ges. Exp. Med.* 107: 98–105.

Kligman, A. M. 1969. Early destructive effect of sunlight in human skin. *JAMA* 210: 2377–2380.

Kligman, A. M. 1979. Perspectives and problems in cutaneous gerontology. *J. Invest. Derm.* 73: 39–46.

Kligman, L. H., Aiken, F. J., and Kligman, A. M. 1982. Prevention of ultraviolet damage to the dermis of hairless mice by sunscreens. *J. Invest. Derm.* 78: 181–189.

Kripke, M. L. and Fisher, M. S. 1976. Immunologic parameters of ultraviolet light carcinogenesis. *J. Natl. Cancer Inst.* 57: 211–215.

Lavker, R. 1979. Structural alterations in exposed and unexposed skin. *J. Invest. Derm.* 73: 59–66.

Light, S. E. 1935. Convulsive seizures following the application of phenol to the skin. *Northeast Med.* 30: 232–237.

Linn, B. S. 1980. Age differences in the severity and outcome of burns. *J. Am. Geriatric Soc.* 28: 118–130.

Lorincz, A. B. 1960. Physiology of aging skin. *Ill. Med. J.* 117: 59–62.

MacKinnon, P. C. B. 1954. Variations with age in the number of active palmar digital sweat glands. *J. Neurol. Neurosurg. Psychiat.* 17: 124–126.

Maguire, H. C. 1964. Facial hair growth over sites of testosterone injection in women. *Lancet* 1: 864–865.

Malkinson, F. D. 1958. Studies on the percutaneous absorption of C14 labelled steroid by use of the gas flow cell. *J. Invest. Derm.* 31: 19–28.

Margolis, J. 1976. Skin tags—a frequent sign of diabetes mellitus. *N. Eng. Med.* 294: 1184.

McConkey, B., Fraser, G. M., Bligh, A. S., and Whitely, H. 1963. Transparent skin and osteoporosis. *Lancet* 1: 693–694.

McConkey, B., Walton, K. W., Carney, S. A., Lawrence, J. C., and Ricketts, C. R. 1967. Significance of the occurrence of transparent skin. *Ann. Rheum. Dis.* 26: 219–225.

McGuirt, W. F., Loery, S., McCabe, B. F., and Kruse, C. J. 1977. The risks of major head and neck surgery in the aged population. *Laryngoscope* 87: 1378–1382.

Miles, A. E. W. 1958. Sebaceous glands on the lip and cheek mucosa of man. *Brit. Dermatol. J.* 105: 205–210.

Montagna, W. 1965. Morphology of aging skin. In, W. Montagna (ed.), *Advances in the Biology of the Skin.* Vol. 11: 1–15.

Montagna, W. and Carlisle, K. 1979. Structural changes in aging human skin. *J. Invest. Derm.* 73: 47–53.

Nilzen, A. and Voss-Lagerand, K. 1962. Epicutaneous tests with detergents and a number of other common allergens. *Dermatologica* 174: 42–57.

Novick, A., Novick, I., and Putoker, J. 1972. Tuberculin skin testing in a chronically sick population. *J. Am. Geriatric Soc.* 20: 455–460.

Orentreich, N. and Selmanowitz, V. J. 1969. Levels of biological functions with aging. *Trans. Acad. Sci. Series B* 31: 992–1012.

Papa, C. M. and Kligman, A. M. 1967. Effect of topical hormones on aging human skin. *J. Soc. Cosm. Chem.* 18: 549–562.

Parrish, J. A. 1983. The effect of ultraviolet radiation on the immune system. Sponsored by New Mexico Health Coalition and Johnson & Johnson Baby Product Co.

Penn, I. 1980. Immunosuppression and skin cancer. *Clinics in Plastic Surgery* 7: 361–368.

Plewig, G. and Kligman, A. M. 1978. Proliferative activity of the sebaceous glands of the aged. *J. Invest. Derm.* 70: 314–318.

Pochi, P. E., Strauss, J. S., and Downing, D. T. 1979. Age related changes in sebaceous gland activity. *J. Invest. Derm.* 73: 108–111.

Procacci, P., Bozza, G., Buzzelli, G., and Cortz, M. D. 1970. The cutaneous pricking pain threshold in old age. *Geront. Clin.* 12: 213–218.

Prockop, D. J. and Kisirikko, K. I. 1967. Relationship of hydroxyproline excretion in urine to collagen metabolism. *Ann. Int. Med.* 66: 1243–1266.

Quevedo, W. C., Szabo, G., and Vicks, J. 1969. Influence of age and ultraviolet on the populations of dopa-positive melanocytes in human skin. *J.I.D.* 52: 287–290.

Reff, M. E. and Schneider, E. L. 1982. Biological markers of aging. *NIH Publication* 82: 2221.

Salavisto, E., Orma, E., and Tawast, M. 1951. Aging and relation between stimulus intensity and duration in corneal sensibility. *Acta Physiol. Scand.* 23: 224–230.

Sandblum, P. H., Peterson, P., and Muren, A. 1953. Determination of the tensile strength of healing wounds as a clinical test. *Acta Chir. Scand.* 105: 252–257.

Selmanowitz, V. J., Rizer, R. L., and Orentreich, N. 1977. Aging of the skin and its appendages. *In,* C. E. Finch and L. Hayflick (eds.), *Handbook of the Biology of Aging,* pp. 496–507. New York: Van Nostrand Reinhold.

Shephard, R. J., Jones, G., Ishi, K., Kaneko, M. and Ulbrecht, H. J. 1969. Factors affecting body density and thickness of subcutaneous fat. *Am. J. Clin. Nutrit.* 22: 1175–1189.

Sherman, E. D. and Robillard, E. 1960. Sensitivity to pain in the aged. *Canad. Med. Assoc. J.* 83: 944–947.

Shock, N. 1977. System integration. *In,* C. E. Finch and L. Hayflick (eds.), *Handbook of the Biology of Aging,* pp. 639–661. New York: Van Nostrand Reinhold.

Shuster, S. and Black, M. M. 1975. The influence of age and sex on skin thickness, skin collagen and density. *Brit. J. Derm.* 93: 639–643.

Silver, A., Montagna, W., and Karacan, I. 1965. The effect of age on human eccrine sweating. *In,* W. Montagna (ed.) *Advances in Biology of Skin,* pp. 129–149. Oxford: Pergamon Press.

Smith, J. G., Davidson, E. A., Sams, W. M., and Clark, R. D. 1962. Alterations in human dermal connective tissue with age and chronic sun damage. *J. Invest. Derm.* 39: 345–350.

Stadler, R. and Orfanos, C. E. 1978. Reifung und Alterung der elastischen Fasern. *Arch. Dermatol. Res.* 262: 97–102.

Stoughton, R. B. 1962. Physiological changes from maturity through senescence. *JAMA* 179: 636–638.

Tagami, H. 1972. Functional characteristics of aged skin. *Acta. Dermatol.—Kyoto* 66: 19–21.

Tan, C. Y., Statham, B., Marks, R., and Payne, P. A. 1982. Skin thickness measurement by pulsed ultrasound: its reproducibility and validation. *Brit. J. Derm.* 106: 657.

Tindall, J. P. and Smith, J. G. 1963. Skin lesions of the aged and their association with internal changes. *JAMA* 186: 1039–1042.

Tsuji, T. and Hamada, T. 1981. Age related changes in human dermal elastic fibers. *Brit. J. Derm.* 105: 57–63.

Verbov, J. 1975. Skin problems in the older patient. *Practitioner* 215: 612–614.

Viljanto, J. A. 1969. A sponge implant method for testing connective tissue regeneration in surgical patients. *Acta. Chir. Scand.* 136: 297–300.

Waisman, M. 1979. A clinical look at the aging skin. *Post-graduate Medicine* 66: 87–96.

Weksler, M. E. 1982. Age-associated changes in the immune response. *J. Am. Geriatrics Soc.* 30: 718–723.

Whitton, J. and Everall, J. D. 1973. The thickness of the epidermis. *Brit. J. Derm.* 89: 467–476.

Winklemann, R. K. 1965. Nerve changes in aging skin. *In,* W. Montagna (ed.), *Advances in Biology of the Skin.* Vol. 11: 51–62. Oxford: Pergamon Press.

Young, A. W. 1965. Dermatogeriatric problems in the chronic disease hospital. *N.Y. State J. Med.* 63: 1748–1752.

Yung, G. W., Goodson, W. A., and Hunt, T. K. 1979. Wound healing and aging. *J. Invest. Derm.* 73: 88–91.

29
ARTERIOSCLEROSIS AND AGING

Edwin L. Bierman
Department of Medicine
University of Washington

Atherosclerosis, a distinctly age-related disorder, is responsible for the majority of deaths in most westernized societies and is by far the leading cause of death in the United States above age 65 (*Arteriosclerosis,* 1981). It is the most common disorder included under the rubric of arteriosclerosis, a generic term for thickening and hardening of the arterial wall. Atherosclerosis is a disorder of the larger arteries that underlies most coronary artery disease and peripheral arterial disease of the lower extremities, and also plays a major role in cerebrovascular disease. Nonatheromatous forms of arteriosclerosis include focal calcific arteriosclerosis (Mönckeberg's sclerosis) and arteriosclerosis.

NATURAL HISTORY

Atherosclerosis in humans appears to begin very early in life and develops progressively over the years, resulting in an exponential increase in the incidence of clinical atherosclerotic events (myocardial infarction, angina pectoris, cerebrovascular accidents, gangrene) with age (Figure 1). A high prevalence of atherosclerotic changes in the arteries of American males as early as the second and third decades of life has been documented from autopsies of casualties of war in Korea and Vietnam (McNamara et al., 1971; Enos et al., 1953). Despite differences

in prevalence rates of atherosclerosis among various countries, there is a progressively increasing mortality with age from atherosclerosis-related diseases (Eggen and Solberg, 1968). In the United States, more than 80 percent of cases of atherosclerotic cardiovascular disease occur in individuals over age 65 (*Arteriosclerosis,* 1981).

Thus atherosclerosis is almost a universal age-related phenomenon in human populations and is thereby closely linked to aging. It is also apparent that atherosclerosis is a multifactorial disease. The hypothesis presented in this chapter and earlier reviews (Bierman and Ross, 1977; Bierman, 1978a) is that both intrinsic aging processes and environmental factors (such as diet) operate over many years, and are superimposed on unknown genetic factors, to produce the disorder. Clearly, atherosclerosis is not simply the result of unmodified intrinsic biological aging processes, since most mammalian species age without spontaneously developing atherosclerosis (Roberts and Strauss, 1965). Furthermore, there are populations in the world that age to the life span appropriate to the human species without developing clinical evidence of atherosclerosis (Goldrick et al., 1970). Therefore, although there may be almost universal prevalence of atherosclerosis, there is considerable difference in the prevalence rate in various parts of the world, probably related to factors other than age *per*

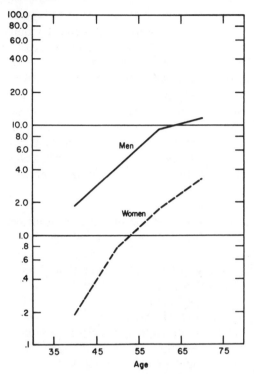

Figure 1. Average annual incidence rate of the first myocardial infarction in the Framingham population during a 16-year follow-up.

se (*Arteriosclerosis,* 1981). The dramatically increased prevalence of atherosclerosis during the last century, albeit partly related to improved diagnosis, presumably largely reflects both the marked increase in human life span and changes in environment and lifestyle.

NONATHEROMATOUS ARTERIOSCLEROSIS

Focal calcific arteriosclerosis (Mönckenberg's sclerosis), a disorder of the medial layer of medium-sized muscular arteries, is also related to aging. It is rare in individuals below age 50 and affects both sexes indiscriminately. The process involves degeneration of medial smooth muscle cells, followed by calcium deposition, which gives a characteristic radiological appearance consisting of regular concentric calcifications com-

monly seen in pelvic and femoral arteries. These changes are common in the elderly but, alone, do not narrow the arterial lumen, have little effect on the circulation, and may have little functional significance. However, in the lower extremities, medial sclerosis is often associated with atherosclerosis, contributing to arterial occlusion. In individuals with diabetes mellitus or those who are receiving long-term corticosteroid drugs, focal calcification may be accelerated and severe. Focal calcification also is responsible for the arteriosclerotic aortic valve in the elderly which may progress to the severe calcific aortic stenosis of the aged.

Since little is known of the pathogenesis of either focal calcification or arteriosclerosis (a degenerative disorder of arterioles in visceral organs related to hypertension) in relation to aging or otherwise, the remainder of the chapter will be devoted to a discussion of atherosclerosis, one of the scourges of modern industrialized civilizations.

RISK FACTORS FOR ATHEROSCLEROSIS IN RELATION TO AGING

A number of conditions and habits are present more frequently in individuals who develop atherosclerosis than in the general poulation ("risk factors"). Most people below age 65 with atherosclerosis have one or more identifiable risk factors other than aging *per se* (Table 1). The presence of multiple risk factors makes a person more likely to develop a clinical atherosclerotic event and to do so earlier than a person with no risk factors. Thus there is a lower prevalence of the major risk factors among the elderly afflicted with their first clinical manifestation.

Among the risk factors, aging, male sex, and genetic factors are currently considered to be nonreversible, whereas there is continually emerging evidence that elimination of cigarette smoking, treatment of hypertension, and reduction of marked obesity reverse the high risk for atherosclerosis attributable to those factors (*Arteriosclerosis,* 1981). Potentially reversible factors currently under study include hyperglycemia and the various forms of hyperlipidemia.

TABLE 1. Risk Factors for Atherosclerosis.

Not reversible
  Aging
  Male sex
  Genetic traits—positive family history of premature atherosclerosis
Reversible
  Cigarette smoking
  Hypertension
  Obesity
Potentially or partially reversible
  Hyperlipidemia—hypercholesterolemia and/or hypertriglyceridemia
  Hyperglycemia and diabetes mellitus
  Low levels of high density lipoproteins (HDL)
Other possible factors
  Physical inactivity
  Emotional stress and/or personality type

These factors are not mutually exclusive since they clearly interact. For example, obesity appears to be causally associated with hypertension, hyperglycemia, hypercholesterolemia, and hypertriglyceridemia. Genetic factors may play a role by exerting direct effects on arterial wall structure and metabolism, or they may act indirectly via such factors as hypertension, hyperlipidemia, diabetes, and obesity. Aging appears to be one of the more complex factors associated with the development of atherosclerosis, since many of the risk factors in themselves are related to age, e.g., elevated blood pressure, hyperglycemia, and hyperlipidemia. Thus, in addition to possible involvement of intrinsic aging in atherogenesis (perhaps through effects on arterial wall metabolism), a variety of associated metabolic factors are also time and age dependent.

Obesity. There is both an inexorable and a preventable increase in adiposity with aging. Even if body weight remains constant throughout life, there are changes in body composition with a decline in lean body mass (muscle and bone) and a reciprocal increase in the proportion of fat tissue, resulting in an increase in relative adiposity (Bierman, 1973). This results in a decrease in caloric requirements with age (Ahrens, 1970). Ac-

tually, in most westernized populations, body weight does not remain constant with age, perhaps because caloric intake is not decreased in harmony with reduced requirements, resulting in an absolute increase in adiposity as well (Montoye et al., 1965). Obesity, defined as being more than 30 percent above the average weight, appears to be important in atherogenesis since, in general, morbidity and mortality from atherosclerotic heart disease are higher in direct relation to the degree of overweight, particularly that apparent before age 50 (Kannel et al., 1967).

Hypertension. Blood pressure levels also appear to increase inexorably with age, and the risk of atherosclerosis appears to increase progressively with increasing blood pressure (it can also be diminished by therapeutic reduction of blood pressure) (Dawber, 1975). The nature of this age relation, however, varies among populations since there are remote populations that appear to age without any changes in blood pressure levels, perhaps related to physical activity or salt intake (Oliver et al., 1975). In contrast to other age-related risk factors, hypertension appears to increase the development of atherosclerosis throughout the age span (Kannel, 1974). It is an especially strong risk factor for cerebrovascular lesions resulting in stroke.

Hyperglycemia. Blood glucose levels increase progressively with age in most population studies (Hayner et al., 1965), and hyperglycemia in turn appears to play a significant role in the development of atherosclerosis (Stout, 1981). There is a high prevalence of diabetes and hyperglycemia associated with clinically evident atherosclerosis (Ostrander et al., 1967; Goldstein et al., 1973a). Increasing adiposity and decreasing physical activity probably play some role in the progressive increase in circulating glucose levels with age (DeFronzo, 1981) since there are primitive populations which remain active and thin that show minimal age-related changes (Goldrick et al., 1970). This suggests that intrinsic aging effects on glucose metabolism and glucoregulatory hormone homeostasis are present and contributory, but superimposed environmental factors, such as caloric excess, amplify the age-related effect.

Hyperlipidemia. Both hypercholesterolemia and hypertriglyceridemia appear to be important age-related risk factors for the development of atherosclerosis. While genetic factors are important for emergence of premature atherosclerosis in affected individuals from families with one of the familial hyperlipidemias (Motulsky, 1976; Goldstein et al., 1973b), triglyceride and cholesterol levels in whole populations are also important, since they appear to increase with age (U.S. Department of Health and Human Services, 1980). Adiposity may play a critical role in the age-associated increase in triglyceride and cholesterol levels since curves for the increase in plasma triglyceride with age and comparable curves for plasma cholesterol with age are superimposable on the obesity-age curve in populations (Bierman and Ross, 1977). Again, in primitive people who remain thin throughout adulthood, serum lipids do not increase with age (Goldrick et al., 1970). Metabolic mechanisms have been postulated whereby obesity, which is associated with insulin resistance of peripheral tissues and compensatory hyperinsulinemia, promotes enhanced production of triglyceride- and cholesterol-rich lipoproteins from the liver (Olefsky et al., 1974). Studies in man have shown that overweight individuals have higher production rates of both triglyceride and cholesterol (Grundy et al., 1979; Nestel et al., 1969). Current concepts of plasma lipoprotein transport suggest that high plasma levels of cholesterol may in part be secondary to excessive production of triglyceride-rich lipoproteins (Bierman and Glomset, 1981). Furthermore, progressive accumulation of cholesterol in extrahepatic tissues of man occurs during the lifetime, particularly in connective and adipose tissues (Crouse et al., 1972). Thus, aging is associated with an expansion of both circulating and tissue pools of cholesterol.

The importance of hyperlipidemia as a risk factor for atherosclerosis varies in relation to age. Serum cholesterol levels appear to relate to the development of coronary heart disease in males, predominantly below the age of 40, much less so in older individuals (Dawber, 1975). In a study in Seattle of the role of genetic forms of hyperlipidemia in clinical atherosclerosis in which 500 consecutive survivors of myocardial infarction were tested (Goldstein et al., 1973a), hyperlipidemia was present in about one-third of the group. Approximately one-half of the males and two-thirds of the females below age 50 had either hypertriglyceridemia, hypercholesterolemia, or both. In contrast, in individuals over age 70, the prevalence of atherosclerotic coronary disease was very high, yet very few males had hyperlipidemia and only about one-fourth of the females had elevated lipid levels. Thus, in both sexes there appeared to be a progressive decline with age in association of hyperlipidemia with this disorder.

More than half of the hyperlipidemic-atherosclerotic survivors appeared to have simple, monogenic, familial disorders inherited as an autosomal dominant trait (familial combined hyperlipidemia, familial hypertriglyceridemia, and familial hypercholesterolemia, in descending order of frequency) (Goldstein et al., 1973b). These simply inherited hyperlipidemias (particularly familial hypercholesterolemia) were more frequent in myocardial infarction survivors below age 60 than in those who were older. In contrast, nonmonogenic forms of hyperlipidemia occurred with equal frequency above and below age 60 (Bierman, 1978). Thus, it appears that genes associated with the simply inherited hyperlipidemias accelerate changes seen with age leading to atherosclerosis prematurely.

Several lipoprotein fractions transport cholesterol. Low density lipoproteins (LDL) carry most of the plasma cholesterol, LDL cholesterol levels thus usually parallel plasma cholesterol concentrations and are directly related to the risk of atherosclerosis. In contrast, high density lipoproteins (HDL), which carry about 20 percent of the plasma cholesterol, are inversely related to the risk of atherosclerosis (Castelli et al., 1977; Tyroler, 1980). Thus, high HDL cholesterol levels are considered to be protective. HDL cholesterol levels do not appear to change with age after puberty (Heiss et al., 1980), but other age-related factors, such as obesity and hypertriglyceridemia, are associated with low HDL cholesterol levels.

THE NORMAL ARTERY WALL

Structure

The normal artery wall consists of three fairly well-defined layers: the intima, the media, and the adventitia.

Intima. A single continuous layer of *endothelial cells* lines the lumen of all arteries. The intima is delimited on its outer aspect by a perforated tube of elastic tissue, the *internal elastic lamina,* which is particularly prominent in the large elastic arteries and the medium-caliber muscular arteries but disappears in capillaries. The endothelial cells are attached to one another by a series of junctional complexes and are also attached to an underlying meshwork of loose connective tissue, the *basal lamina*. These lining endothelial cells normally form a barrier that controls the entry of substances from the blood into the artery wall. Such substances usually enter the cells by specific transport systems. Normally, no other cell type is present in the intima of most arteries.

Media. The media consists of only one cell type, the *smooth muscle cell,* arranged in either a single layer (as in small muscular arteries) or multiple layers (as in elastic arteries). These cells are surrounded by small amounts of collagen and elastic fibers, which they elaborate, and usually take the pattern of diagonal concentric spirals through the vessel wall. They are closely apposed to one another and may be attached by junctional complexes. The smooth muscle cell appears to be the major connective tissue-forming cell

of the artery wall; it produces collagen, elastic fibers, and proteoglycans. In that sense, it is analogous to the fibroblast in skin, the osteoblast in bone, and the chondroblast in cartilage. The media is bounded on the luminal side by the internal elastic lamina and on the abluminal side by a less continuous sheet of elastic tissue, the *external elastic lamina*. Located about midway through the media of most arteries is a "nutritional watershed." The outer portion is nourished from the small blood vessels (vasa vasorum) in the adventitia; the inner layers receive their nutrients from the lumen.

Adventitia. The outermost layer of the artery is the adventitia, which is delimited on the luminal aspect by the external elastic lamina. This external coat consists of a loose interwoven admixture of collagen bundles, elastic fibers, smooth muscle cells, and fibroblasts. This layer also contains the vasa vasorum and nerves.

Function

The artery wall is a metabolically active organ that must meet a steady demand for energy to maintain smooth muscle tension and endothelial cell function, and to repair and replenish tissue constituents. The mechanical forces on the arterial wall are complex, and considerable tensile stresses are imposed on it, mainly by hydraulic force. Shear or frictional stresses are especially prominent near the entrance regions of branches. Arteries are also permeable pipes, which constantly exchange fluid and solutes with the blood they carry.

Maintenance of the endothelial cell lining is critical. Endothelial cell turnover occurs at a slow rate but may be accelerated in focal areas by changing patterns of flow along the vessel wall (Schwartz et al., 1981). When intact, these cells selectively control the passage of circulating substances by active transport (endocytosis and exocytosis) through their cytoplasm and elaborate connective tissue components to form their own substratum. In addition, intact endothelial cells function to prevent clotting partly by elaboration of a particular prostaglandin (prostacyclin or PGI_2) that inhibits platelet function, thereby enhancing unimpeded flow of blood. When the lining is damaged, platelets adhere to it, in part as the result of production of a different class of prostaglandins, the thromboxanes, and form a clot; endothelial cells function in the clotting process by elaboration of key substances including factor VIII.

The metabolism of arteries reflects the biochemistry of smooth muscle cells. Recent studies of these cells in tissue culture under conditions in which they retain their differentiated phenotype have helped elucidate their metabolism and function (Ross and Glomset, 1976; Ross, 1981). Arterial smooth muscle cells form abundant collagen, elastic fibers, soluble and insoluble elastin, and glycosaminoglycans (mainly dermatan sulfate). Multiple anabolic and catabolic pathways are present. These cells metabolize glucose by both anaerobic and aerobic glycolysis. A variety of catabolic enzymes are present including fibrinolysins, mixed function oxidases, and lysosomal hydrolases. Because of the prominence of lipids in atherosclerotic lesions, much attention has been directed to lipid metabolism in arteries. Arterial wall cells can synthesize fatty acids, cholesterol, phospholipids, and triglycerides from endogenous substrates to satisfy their structural needs (membrane replenishment), but smooth muscle cells appear preferentially to utilize lipids from plasma lipoproteins transported into the wall. Circulating lipoproteins traverse endothelial cells in pinocytotic vesicles. Smooth muscle cells possess specific high affinity surface receptors for certain apoproteins on the surface of lipid-rich lipoproteins, thus facilitating the entry of lipoproteins into the cell by adsorptive endocytosis. As has been shown for cultured skin fibroblasts, in arterial smooth muscle cells these vesicles fuse with lysosomes, which results in catabolism of lipoprotein components (Bierman and Albers, 1975). Free cholesterol entering the cell in this manner inhibits endogenous cholesterol synthesis,

facilitates its own esterification, and partially limits further entry of cholesterol by regulating the number of lipoprotein receptors (Goldstein and Brown, 1977).

Thus, many complex and interrelated metabolic processes are present in arterial wall cells. Although some of these may play a role in the production of arteriosclerosis, no one biochemical reaction can be singled out as culpable. Physiological factors, such as transfer processes across the endothelial lining, the flux of oxygen and substrates from both the luminal and the adventitial sides of the wall, and the reverse flow of catabolic products, need to be considered as well. The ability of the arterial wall to maintain the integrity of its endothelium, prevent platelet aggregation, and ensure the nutrition of its middle portion may be the critical determinant of the arteriosclerotic process.

Changes with Aging

The major change that occurs with normal aging in the arterial wall in humans is a slow, apparently continuous, symmetrical increase in the thickness of the intima. This intimal thickening results from a gradual accumulation of smooth muscle cells (presumably resulting from migration of these cells from the media and their subsequent proliferation), surrounded by additional connective tissue. In the nondiseased artery wall, lipid content, mainly cholesterol ester and phospholipid (particularly sphingomyelin), also progressively increases with age (Eisenberg et al., 1969). Phospholipid synthesis rises with aging (perhaps in response to the need for more membrane formation for plasma membranes, vesicles, lysosomes, and other intracellular organelles) followed by a compensatory increase in activity of all phospholipases except sphingomyelinase. While most of the phospholipid in the normal artery wall appears to be derived from *in situ* synthesis, the cholesterol ester that accumulates with aging appears to be derived from plasma, since it contains principally linoleic acid, the major plasma cholesterol ester fatty acid. Furthermore, low density lipoproteins (LDL) are immunologically detectable in the intima of normal arteries in direct relation to their concentration in plasma (Smith and Slater, 1972). It has been estimated that between the second and sixth decade, the normal intima accumulates approximately 10 mg cholesterol per gram of tissue (Stein and Stein, 1973). Thus, as the normal artery ages, smooth muscle cells and connective tissue accumulate diffusely in the intima, leading to progressive thickening of this layer, coupled with progressive accumulation of sphingomyelin and cholesterol linoleate. This diffuse age-related intimal thickening is to be distinguished from focal discrete raised fibromuscular plaques, a characteristic feature of atherosclerosis.

Functionally, these changes with aging result in gradually increasing rigidity of vessels. The larger arteries may become dilated, elongated, and tortuous, and aneurysms may form in areas of an encroaching degenerating arteriosclerotic plaque. Such "wear-and-tear" changes are frequently proportional to the vessel diameter and correlated with branching, curvature, and anatomic points of attachment. The amount of external support also determines ability of vessels, weakened by loss of elasticity, to withstand hydrostatic pressure. The unsupported cerebral arteries may be particularly vulnerable in this regard. Although senescence is accompanied by the intimal thickening that is a feature of localized atheromatosis, the changes of aging and arteriosclerosis appear to be separate and distinct processes.

LESIONS OF ATHEROSCLEROSIS

Humans. Lesions are commonly classified as *fatty streaks, fibrous plaques,* and *complicated lesions.* Fatty streaks may be the earliest lesions of atherosclerosis, but the evidence is very uncertain. They are characterized by an accumulation of lipid-filled smooth muscle cells and macrophages (foam cells), and fibrous tissue in focal areas of the intima. They are stained distinctly by fat-soluble dyes but may be visible without staining as yellowish or whitish patches on the intimal surface. The lipid is mainly cholesterol

oleate, partly derived from synthesis *in situ.* The fatty streak is usually sessile, and causes little obstruction and no symptoms. The lesion is universal, appearing in various segments of the arterial tree at different ages beginning in the aorta in infancy. In all children, regardless of race, sex, or environment, fatty streaks are present in the aorta by age 10 and increase to occupy as much as 30 to 50 percent of the aortic surface by age 25, but they do not appear to extend further with aging (Bierman and Ross, 1977). Despite a presumed relation between fatty streaks and fibrous atherosclerotic plaques, aortic fatty streaks are not correlated with the location and extent of fibrous lesions. In the coronary arteries, the extent of fatty streaks may be a better indicator of the development of clinically significant raised lesions later in life. They are usually observed by age 15 and continue to involve more surface area with increasing age. Fatty streaks in the cerebral arteries are also present in all populations, develop during the third and fourth decade, and are more extensive in those populations having a higher incidence of cerebrovascular disease. It is generally believed that fatty streaks may be reversible, but the evidence is inconclusive.

Fibrous plaques, also called raised lesions, are palpably elevated areas of intimal thickening and represent the most characteristic lesion of advancing atherosclerosis. They do not share with fatty streaks the ubiquitous distribution among populations. These plaques first appear in the abdominal aorta, coronary arteries, and carotid arteries in the third decade, and increase progressively with age. They appear in men before women, in the aorta before the coronary arteries, and much later in the vertebral and intracranial cerebral arteries. Reasons for the difference in susceptibility of various segments of the arterial tree and for the nonuniform distribution of lesions are not known. Typically, the fibrous plaque is firm, elevated, and dome shaped, with an opaque glistening surface that bulges into the lumen. It consists of a central core of extracellular lipid and necrotic cell debris ("gruel") covered by a fibromuscular layer or cap containing large numbers of smooth muscle cells, macrophages, and collagen (Figure 2). Thus the plaque is much thicker than normal intima. Although the lipid, like that of fatty streaks, is mainly cholesterol ester, linoleic acid, rather than oleic, is the principal esterified fatty acid. Thus plaque cholesterol ester composition differs from fatty streaks but resembles plasma lipoproteins.

The *complicated lesion* is a calcified fibrous plaque containing various degrees of necrosis, thrombosis, and ulceration. These are the lesions frequently associated with symptoms. With increasing necrosis and accumulation of gruel, the arterial wall progressively weakens, and rupture of the intima

can occur, causing aneurysm and hemorrhage. Arterial emboli can form when fragments of plaque dislodge into the lumen. Stenosis and impaired organ function result from gradual occlusion as plaques thicken and thrombi form.

Animal Models. Most animals in the wild do not develop atherosclerosis. Historically, atherosclerosis was first produced experimentally about 70 years ago by feeding cholesterol to rabbits (Anitschkow, 1933). This animal has remained the most popular, easiest, and best-established model for human atherosclerosis. However, there are difficulties with the use of the rabbit as a model for

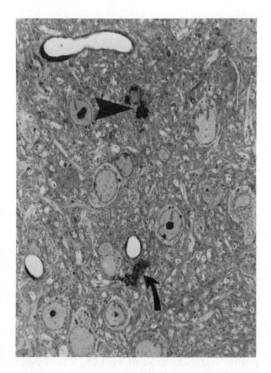
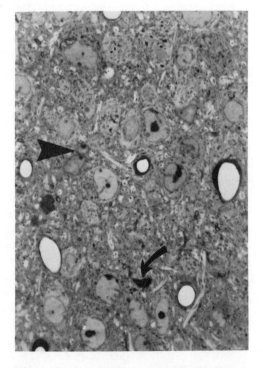

Figure 2. Electron micrograph demonstrating two "foam cells" from a human atherosclerotic lesion, obtained and fixed at the time of surgery. The cell on the left is a macrophage, recognized by its fimbriated cytoplasm and nuclear morphology. It contains numerous membrane-bounded secondary lysosomes, as well as nonmembrane-bounded lipid droplets. The cell on the right is a smooth muscle cell, recognized by its surrounding basement membrane, nuclear morphology, and cytoplasmic myofilaments. This cell also contains lipid droplets ($\times$ 8000). (From Ross, 1981; reproduced with permission.)

the human disease. The distribution of lipids among plasma lipoproteins differs from the human. Perhaps more important, the pathogenesis of the lesions at the cellular level appears to differ. Much of the deposited arterial lipid appears in blood monocyte-derived macrophages rather than in arterial smooth muscle cells. Also, human atherosclerosis is a multifactorial disease (see section on risk factors) and not simply the consequence of dietary-induced hypercholesterolemia.

Rats and dogs have been notoriously resistant to cholesterol feeding (presumably reflecting marked differences in lipoprotein transport) and have been used as models of resistance to atherosclerosis (Mahley, 1978). The induction of hypothyroidism needs to be added to produce lesions in these species, which then bear some similarity to the human disease. Inbred mice can exhibit either susceptibility or resistance to cholesterol feeding depending on the genetic strain (Roberts and Thompson, 1976).

Recent work has focused on swine and nonhuman primate species as models. Severe raised plaques have been produced in swine by a combination of balloon catheter injury (scraping of the endothelial lining) and the feeding of a fat-rich diet with sodium cholate (Daoud et al., 1976). Plasma lipoproteins of swine closely resemble those of humans. A similar potential advantage pertains to nonhuman primates. Several investigators have produced lesions, resembling those of humans, by dietary, drug, and/or mechanical manipulations in rhesus and other primates (Wissler, 1978). The feeding of typical American diets can produce aortic and coronary atherosclerosis. Studies of reversibility and regression, which will be discussed, have made use of this model extensively.

PATHOGENESIS OF ATHEROSCLEROSIS

The Cell Biology of the Arterial Wall and Theories of Atherogenesis. One generally accepted theory for the pathogenesis of atherosclerosis consistent with a variety of experimental evidence is the *reaction to injury* hypothesis (Ross, 1981). According to this idea, the endothelial cells lining the intima are exposed to repeated or continuing insults to their integrity. The injury to the endothelium may be subtle or gross, resulting in a loss of the ability of the cells to attach to one another and to the underlying connective tissue. The cells then become susceptible to the shearing stress of the blood flow and they may desquamate. Examples of types of "injury" to the endothelium include chemical injury, as in chronic hypercholesterolemia or homocystinemia, mechanical stress associated with hypertension, and immunologic injury, which may be seen after cardiac or renal transplantation. Loss of endothelial cells at susceptible sites in the arterial tree would lead to exposure of the subendothelial tissue to increased concentrations of plasma constituents; to a sequence of events including platelet adherence, platelet aggregation, and formation of microthrombi; and to the release of platelet granular components, including a potent mitogenic factor. This "platelet-derived growth factor," in conjunction with other plasma constituents including lipoproteins and hormones such as insulin, could stimulate both the migration of medial smooth muscle cells into the intima and their proliferation at these sites of injury. These proliferating smooth muscle cells would deposit a connective tissue matrix and accumulate lipid, a process that would be particularly enhanced with hyperlipidemia. Macrophages derived from circulating blood monocytes might enter the arterial wall and also accumulate lipid (Figure 2).

Thus repeated or chronic injury could lead to a slowly progressing lesion involving a gradual increase in smooth muscle cells, macrophages, connective tissue, and lipid. Areas where the shearing stress on endothelial cells is increased, such as branch points or bifurcation of vessels, would be at greater risk. As the lesions progress and the intima becomes thicker, blood flow over the sites will be altered and potentially place the lining endothelial cells at even greater risk for further injury, leading to an inexorable cycle of events culminating in the complicated lesion. However, a single or a few injurious episodes may lead to a proliferative response that could regress, in contrast to continued or chronic injury. This reaction to injury hypothesis thus is consistent with the known intimal thickening observed during normal aging, would explain how many of the etiologic factors implicated in atherogenesis might enhance lesion formation, might explain how inhibitors of platelet aggregation could interfere with lesion formation, and fosters some optimism regarding the possibility of interrupting progression, or even producing regression, of these lesions.

Potential Role of Aging Processes in Atherogenesis. Other theories of atherogenesis are not mutually exclusive and relate to aging processes as well. The *monoclonal hypothesis* suggests, on the basis of single isoenzyme types found in lesions (Benditt and Benditt, 1973), that the intimal proliferative lesions result from the multiplication of single individual smooth muscle cells, as do benign tumors. In this manner, mitogenic, and possibly mutagenic, factors that might stimulate smooth muscle cell proliferation would act on single cells. Focal *clonal senescence* may explain how intrinsic aging processes contribute to atherosclerosis. According to this theory (Martin et al., 1975), the intimal smooth muscle cells that proliferate to form an atheroma are normally under feedback control by diffusible agents (mitosis inhibitors) formed by the smooth muscle cells in the contiguous media, and this feedback control system tends to fail with age as these controlling cells die and are not adequately replaced. This idea is consistent with the recent observation that cultured human arterial smooth muscle cells, like fibroblasts, show a decline in their ability to replicate as a function of donor age (Figure 3) (Bierman, 1978b). If this loss of replicative potential applies to a controlling population of smooth muscle cells, then cells that are usually suppressed would be able to proliferate.

This intrinsic aging and loss of replicative potential, if it occurs in endothelial cells,

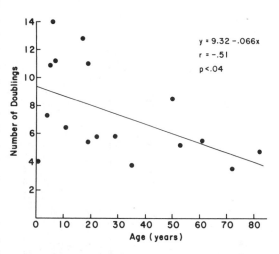

Figure 3. Cumulative number of cell population doublings of cultured human arterial smooth muscle cells as a function of age of the donor (From Bierman, 1978b; reproduced with permission.)

could be critical, since it would lead to loss of integrity of the endothelial lining of the artery wall—the initial step leading to the progression of events in the reaction to injury hypothesis.

The *lysosomal theory* suggests that altered lysosomal function might contribute to atherogenesis. Since lysosomal enzymes can accomplish the generalized degradation of cellular components required for continuing renewal, this system has been implicated in cellular aging and the accumulation of lipofuscin or "age pigment." It has been suggested that increased deposition of lipids in arterial smooth muscle cells may be related in part to a relative deficiency in the activity of lysosomal cholesterol ester hydrolase (Wolinsky, 1976). This decreased enzyme activity would result in increased accumulation of cholesterol esters within the cells, perhaps accentuated by lipid overloading of lysosomes, eventually leading to cell death and extracellular lipid deposition. Consonant with this idea, impaired degradation of ^{125}I-labeled LDL by human arterial smooth muscle cells cultured from older donors has been

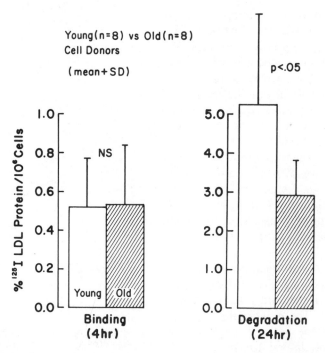

Figure 4. Low density lipoprotein binding and degradation by human arterial smooth muscle cells obtained from younger (age 5–17) and older (age 47–71) donors.

observed (Bierman et al., 1979) (Figure 4). Since LDL binding to the specific high affinity receptors on arterial smooth muscle cells does not appear to decrease with donor age, smooth muscle cells are not protected from the increasing LDL concentrations associated with aging. These observations may be relevant to the enhanced accumulation of cellular cholesterol and LDL observed in atherosclerotic lesions *in vivo* (Smith and Slater, 1972).

AGE-ASSOCIATED RISK FACTORS AND THE PATHOBIOLOGY OF ATHEROSCLEROSIS

Obesity. Adiposity produces insulin resistance in peripheral tissues (mainly muscle and adipose), which leads to compensatory hyperinsulinemia. The liver is not resistant to some effects of insulin, and enhanced production of triglyceride-rich lipoproteins results, which in turn leads to elevated plasma triglyceride and cholesterol levels. Thus it has been demonstrated that body weight is re-

lated not only to triglyceride levels but also to cholesterol levels. Concomitantly, obesity is associated with increased total body cholesterol synthesis. Obesity produces higher circulating levels of insulin, both in the basal state and after stimulation with glucose or other secretagogues. Since obesity is related to atherosclerosis—both directly and via hypertension, hypertriglyceridemia, hypercholesterolemia, and hyperglycemia—it is not surprising that many studies show a relationship between serum insulin levels, particularly after oral glucose intake, and atherosclerotic disease of the coronary and peripheral arteries (Stout, 1981). A few studies, however, suggest that this association between insulin and artherosclerosis occurs independently of obesity (Stout et al., 1974). It has been postulated that insulin may directly affect arterial wall metabolism, leading to increased endogenous lipid synthesis and thus predisposing to atherosclerosis. Insulin has been shown in physiological concentrations to stimulate proliferation of arterial smooth muscle cells (Stout et al., 1975) and to enhance binding of LDL and VLDL to fibroblasts (Chait et al., 1978; Chait et al., 1979); it, therefore, may be one of the plasma factors gaining increased access to the intima and media after endothelial injury, and thus may be an additional factor in atheroma formation.

Hypertension. High mean arterial pressures may enhance atherogenesis by directly producing injury via mechanical stress on endothelial cells at specific high pressure sites in the arterial tree. This would allow the sequence of events in the chronic injury hypothesis of atherogenesis to take place. In addition, hypertension might allow more lipoproteins to be transported through intact endothelial lining cells by altering permeability. Hypertension markedly increases lysosomal enzyme activity, presumably owing to stimulation of the cellular disposal system by the internalization of increased amounts of plasma substances (Wolinsky, 1976). This might lead to increased cell degeneration and release of the highly destructive enzymes (within the lysosomes) into the arterial wall. Experimental hypertension also increases the thickness of the intimal smooth muscle layer in the arterial wall and increases connective tissue elements (Wolinsky, 1972). It is possible that continued high pressure within the artery *in vivo* produces changes in the ability of smooth muscle cells or stem cells to proliferate. Recent studies using human aortic coarctation as a model have shown that smooth muscle cells cultured from tissue proximal to the site of coarctation had fewer population doublings and a slower replication rate than cells grown from a distal site (Bierman et al., 1981) (Figure 5). Since the proximal cells presumably had been stimulated to divide excessively *in vivo* by chronic exposure to elevated intra-arterial pressure, these results suggest that the number of prior smooth muscle cell divisions limits their further replicative potential. Thus characteristics of accelerated aging, which may be relevant to atherogenesis, can be induced by chronic exposure to hypertension.

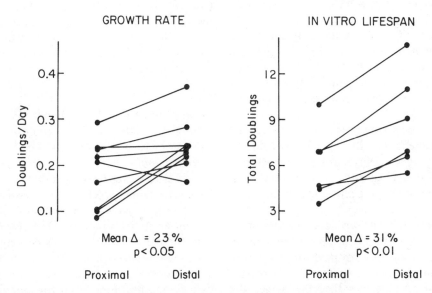

Figure 5. Growth rate and life span of human arterial smooth muscle cells cultured from proximal (hypertensive) and distal (control) sides of aortic coarctations removed at surgery. The replication rate during the logarithmic growth phase was calculated by the least squares method. The number of cell doublings was calculated by previously described methods (Bierman, 1978b). Donor age for growth rate data ranged from 4.9 to 32 years and for life span data from 6.4 to 19.2 years. (Adapted from Bierman et al., 1981.)

Diabetes and Hyperglycemia. In addition to obesity and hyperlipidemia which are closely associated with the non–insulin dependent diabetic state in humans, diabetes *per se* could provide a unique contribution to atherogenesis. Although the fundamental genetic abnormality in human diabetes mellitus remains unknown, it has been suggested that one type of genetic diabetes in humans is associated with a primary cellular abnormality intrinsic to all cells, resulting in a decreased life span of individual cells, which in turn results in increased cell turnover in tissues (Goldstein, 1971; Vracko and Benditt, 1974). If arterial endothelial and smooth muscle cells are intrinsically defective in diabetes, accelerated atherogenesis can be readily postulated on the basis of any one of the current theories of pathogenesis. Platelet dysfunction in diabetes might also play a role.

The role of glucose in atheroma formation, if any, is poorly understood. Hyperglycemia is known to affect aortic wall metabolism. Sorbitol, a product of the insulin-independent aldose reductase pathway of glucose metabolism (the polyol pathway), accumulates in the arterial wall in the presence of high glucose concentrations, resulting in osmotic effects including increased cell water content and decreased oxygenation (Morrison et al., 1972). Increased glucose also appears to stimulate proliferation of cultured arterial smooth muscle cells (Turner and Bierman, 1978).

Thus there are a variety of factors related to the diabetic state that potentially could be involved in the pathogenesis of athersclerosis by diverse mechanisms. There is little basis at present to support any single mechanism.

Hyperlipidemia. The development of atherosclerosis accelerates in an approximately quantitative relation to the degree of hyperlipidemia (Dawber, 1975). A long-established theory suggests that the higher the circulating levels of lipoprotein, the more likely they are to gain entry into the arterial wall. By an acceleration of the usual transendothelial transport, large concentrations of cholesterol-rich lipoproteins within the ar-

terial wall could overwhelm the ability of smooth muscle cells to metabolize them. Low density lipoproteins have been immunologically identified in atheroma, and in humans there is a direct relationship between plasma cholesterol and arterial lipoprotein cholesterol concentration. High density lipoproteins may be protective by virtue of their ability to promote cholesterol removal from artery wall cells (Oram et al., 1981). Chemically modified lipoproteins, possibly produced in hyperlipidemic disorders, could gain access to the scavenger arterial wall macrophages, leading to formation of foam cells (Goldstein et al., 1979) as in xanthomas. It is possible that the lipid that accumulates in the arterial wall with increasing age results from infiltration of plasma cholesterol-rich lipoproteins. However, atheromatous lesions are associated with a more marked increase in arterial wall lipids than that associated with increasing age. This excess accumulation of lipids may result in part from injury to the endothelium, possibly produced by chronic hyperlipidemia, as demonstrated in cholesterol-fed monkeys (Ross and Harker, 1976). A further possible mechanism for accelerated atherogenesis in hyperlipidemia is related to the ability of LDL to stimulate proliferation of arterial smooth muscle cells (Ross and Glomset, 1973).

Cigarette Smoking. Although not directly age related, cigarette smoking is too powerful a risk factor to be overlooked. The effect of *chronic smoke inhalation* from cigarettes could result in repetitive injury to endothelial cells, thereby accelerating atherogenesis. Hypoxia stimulates proliferation of cultured human arterial smooth muscle cells (Albers and Bierman, 1976); thus, since cigarette smoking is associated with high levels of carboxyhemoglobin and low oxygen delivery to tissues, another mechanism for atherogenesis is suggested. Hypoxia could produce diminished lysosomal enzyme degradative ability, as evidenced by impaired degradation of LDL by smooth muscle cells (Albers and Bierman, 1976), causing LDL to accumulate in the cells. Consistent with this suggestion is the fact that aortic lesions that resemble atheroma have been produced in experimental animals by systemic hypoxia (Helin and Lorenzen, 1969), and lipid accumulation in the arterial wall of cholesterol-fed rabbits and monkeys appears to be increased by hypoxia (Webster et al., 1968; Astrup and Kjeldsen, 1973).

REVERSIBILITY AND REGRESSION IN RELATION TO AGING

Animal Models. Anitschkow (1933) observed that lesions induced in cholesterol-fed rabbits appear to regress when the animals are placed on a normal diet. More recent extension of this type of study to cholesterol-fed nonhuman primates (Wissler, 1978) has provided firm evidence for reversibility and regression. The usual protocol has been to induce lesions of varying severity by feeding the atherogenic diet to young monkeys for several years, then to switch diets to a chow or low fat diet, and sacrifice the animals at intervals. Aortic and coronary lesions have been shown to decrease in size and content of lipid, cells and connective tissue. The relevance of these studies lasting a few years to the human lesions evolving over decades is open to some question, however. The mechanisms of regression are under study. In general, it appears that lower circulating levels of cholesterol and LDL lead to a healing endothelium, decreased ingress of LDL into the artery wall, less cell proliferation and collagen synthesis, and more egress of cholesterol from cells and wall. These studies have not yet approached the question of repeated insults (or repeated induction and regression cycles) which may be more relevant to the question of aging and atherosclerosis in humans.

Humans. Both retrospective and prospective human epidemiological studies support the concepts of reversibility and regression. Clinical and autopsy studies during the world wars showed less severe atherosclerosis in malnourished subjects, which provided circumstantial evidence (Vartiainen and Kanerva, 1947). Recent studies of plaque regression in living human subjects are providing some evidence of regression of advanced atherosclerosis based on functional effects and on evaluation of plaque size by sequential arteriographs taken before and after a period of treatment (Brown et al., 1982). Treatments now under study include ileal bypass operations, drug treatment of hyperlipidemias, and combinations of diet, exercise, and drug therapy. Advanced atherosclerotic lesions appear to respond more favorably when serum cholesterol levels are reduced to the low levels that prevail in animals or humans consuming a low fat, low cholesterol diet. The effect of age has not been studied directly since most of the subjects have been hyperlipidemic and relatively young.

PREVENTION

The steps taken to delay or prevent atheroma formation ("primary prevention") must begin early in life, long before there is a suspicion of the existence of clinical disease. Steps taken to prevent recurrence of disease ("secondary prevention") later in life will not necessarily be the same. Although an effective program has not been defined with certainty, enough is known to guide both in identification of those individuals with a higher risk and in development of measures that probably will reduce that risk. Thus prevention currently is equated with risk factor reduction.

Whole communities can be influenced to reduce smoking, change diet, and lower blood pressure levels by mass-media educational efforts (Farquhar et al., 1977). There has been a trend toward lower cholesterol and saturated fat consumption in the United States, coupled with increasing attention to reducing overweight and the use of exercise programs. Concomitantly, and perhaps as a result of these trends, there has been a decline in mortality from atherosclerotic disease almost uniquely in the United States during the past 15 years (*Arteriosclerosis,*

1981). Treatment of hyperlipidemia in some instances has been shown to reduce atherosclerotic involvement of peripheral vessels by both invasive and noninvasive measurement (Blankenhorn et al., 1978). Therefore, efforts to prevent atherogenesis and to interrupt progression by risk factor reduction seem warranted.

CONCLUSION

Atherosclerosis, the most prevalent form of arteriosclerosis, occurs so commonly with aging in industrialized populations that the disorder can be mistaken for a natural consequence of intrinsic aging rather than a superimposed disease. In this multifactorial disorder, environmental factors (such as diet) appear to operate over many years ("age related"), in concert with intrinsic cellular aging processes and genetic determinants, to generate the disease. Since alteration of intrinsic aging processes and genetic manipulation remain only theoretical possibilities, efforts should be directed at understanding and reversing the age-related environmental factors that act over time and accelerate atherogenesis throughout the life span.

REFERENCES

Ahrens, E. H., Jr. 1970. Liquid formula diets in metabolic studies. *Adv. Metab. Disord.* 4: 297.

Albers, J. J. and Bierman, E. L. 1976. The effect of hypoxia on uptake and degradation of low density lipoproteins by cultured human arterial muscle cells. *Biochim. Biophys. Acta* 424: 422–429.

Anitschkow, N. 1933. Experimental arteriosclerosis in animals. *In,* E. V. Cowdry, (ed.), *Arteriosclerosis, A Survey of the Problem,* pp. 271–322. New York: Macmillan.

Arteriosclerosis 1981. 1981. Report of the Working Group on Arteriosclerosis of the NHLBI. Washington, D.C.: U.S. Department of Health and Human Services, NIH Publication No. 81-2034.

Astrup, P. and Kjeldsen, K. 1973. Carbon monoxide, smoking, and atherosclerosis. *Med. Clin. No. Am.* 58: 323.

Benditt, E. P. and Benditt, J. M. 1973. Evidence for a monoclonal origin of human atherosclerotic plaques. *Proc. Nat. Acad. Sci. USA* 70: 1753–1756.

Bierman, E. L. 1973. Fat metabolism, atherosclerosis and aging in man: a review. *Mech. Ageing Dev.* 2: 315–332.

Bierman, E. L. 1978a. Atherosclerosis and aging. *Fed. Proc.* 37: 2832–2836.

Bierman, E. L. 1978b. The effect of donor age on the *in vitro* lifespan of cultured human arterial smooth muscle cells. *In Vitro* 14: 951–955.

Bierman, E. L. and Albers, J. J. 1975. Lipoprotein uptake by cultured human arterial smooth muscle cells. *Biochim. Biophys. Acta* 388: 198.

Bierman, E. L., Albers, J. J., and Chait, A. 1979. Effect of donor age on the binding and degradation of low density lipoproteins by cultured human arterial smooth muscle cells. *J. Gerontol.* 34: 483–488.

Bierman, E. L., Brewer, C., and Baum, D. 1981. Hypertension decreases replication potential of arterial smooth muscle cells: aortic coarctation in humans as a model. *Proc. Soc. Exp. Biol. Med.* 166: 335–338.

Bierman, E. L. and Glomset, J. A. 1981. Disorders of lipid metabolism. *In,* R. H. Williams (ed.), *Textbook of Endocrinology,* pp. 876–906. Philadelphia: W. B. Saunders.

Bierman, E. L. and Ross, R. 1977. Aging and atherosclerosis. *In,* R. Paoletti and A. M. Gotto, Jr. (eds.), *Atherosclerosis Reviews,* p. 79. New York: Raven Press.

Blankenhorn, D. H., Brooks, S. H., Selzer, R. H., and Barndt, R. J. 1978. The rate of atherosclerosis change during treatment of hyperlipoproteinemia. *Circulation* 57: 355–361.

Brown, G., Bolson, E. L., and Dodge, H. 1982. Arteriographic assessment of coronary atherosclerosis. Review of current methods, their limitations and clinical applications. *Arteriosclerosis* 2: 2–15.

Castelli, W. P., Doyle, J. T., Gordon, T., Hames, C. G., Hjortland, M. C., Hulley, S. B., Kagan, A., and Zukel, W. J. 1977. HDL cholesterol and other lipids in coronary heart disease: the cooperative lipoprotein phenotyping study. *Circulation* 55: 767–772.

Chait, A., Bierman, E. L., and Albers, J. J. 1978. Regulatory role of insulin in the degradation of low density lipoprotein by cultured human skin fibroblasts. *Biochim. Biophys. Acta* 529: 292–299.

Chait, A., Bierman, E. L., and Albers, J. J. 1979. Low density lipoprotein receptor activity in cultured human skin fibroblasts: mechanism of insulin-induced stimulation. *J. Clin. Invest.* 64: 1309–1319.

Crouse, J. R., Grundy, S. M., and Ahrens, E. H., Jr. 1972. Cholesterol distribution in the bulk tissues of man: variation with age. *J. Clin. Invest.* 51: 1292–1296.

Daoud, A. S., Jarmolych, J., Augustyn, J. M., Fritz, K. E., Singh, J. K., and Lee, K. T. 1976. Regression of advanced swine atherosclerosis. *Arch. Pathol. Lab. Med.* 100: 372–379.

Dawber, T. R. 1975. Risk factors for atherosclerotic disease. *In, Current Concepts.* Kalamazoo, Mich.: Upjohn.

DeFronzo, R. A. 1981. Glucose intolerance and aging. *Diabetes Care,* 4: 493–501.

Eggen, D. A. and Solberg, L. A. 1968. Variation of atherosclerosis with age. *Lab. Invest.* 18: 571–579.

Eisenberg, S., Stein, Y., and Stein, O. 1969. Phospolipases in arterial tissue. IV. The role of phosphatide acyl hydrolase, lysophosphatide acyl hydrolase, and sphingomyelin choline phosphohydrolase in the regulation of phospholipid composition in the normal human aorta with age. *J. Clin. Invest.* 48: 2320–2329.

Enos, W. F., Holmes, R. H., and Beyer, J. 1953. Coronary disease among United States soldiers killed in action in Korea. *JAMA* 152: 1090–1093.

Farquhar, J. W., Maccoby, N., Wood, P. D., et al. 1977. Community education for cardiovascular health. *Lancet* 1: 1192–1195.

Goldrick, R. B., Sinnett, P. F., and Whyte, H. M. 1970. An assessment of coronary heart disease and coronary risk factors in a New Guinea highland population. *In,* R. J. Jones (ed.), *Atherosclerosis, Proceedings of the Second International Symposium,* pp. 366–368. New York: Springer-Verlag.

Goldstein, J. L. and Brown, M. S. 1977. The LDL pathway and its relation to atherosclerosis. *Ann. Rev. Biochem.* 46: 897–930.

Goldstein, J. L., Hazzard, W. R., Schrott, H. G., Bierman, E. L., and Motulsky, A. G. 1973a. Hyperlipidemia in coronary heart disease. I. Lipid levels in 500 survivors of myocardial infarction. *J. Clin. Invest.* 52: 1533–1543.

Goldstein, J. L., Ho, Y. K., Basu, S. K., and Brown, M. S. 1979. Binding site on macrophages that mediate uptake and degradation of acetylated LDL, producing massive cholesterol deposition. *Proc. Nat. Acad. Sci. USA* 76: 333–337.

Goldstein, J. L., Schrott, H. G., Hazzard, W. R., Bierman, E. L., and Motulsky, A. G. 1973b. Hyperlipidemia in coronary heart disease. II. Genetic analysis of lipid levels in 176 families and delineation of a new inherited disorder, combined hyperlipidemia. *J. Clin. Invest.* 52: 1544–1568.

Goldstein, S. 1971. The pathogenesis of diabetes mellitus and its relationship to biological aging. *Humangenetik* 12: 83–100.

Grundy, S. M., Mok, H. Y. I., Zech, L., Steinberg, D., and Berman, M. 1979. Transport of very low density triglycerides in varying degrees of obesity and hypertriglyceridemia. *J. Clin. Invest.* 63: 1274–1283.

Hayner, N. S., Kjelsberg, M. O., Epstein, F. H., and Francis, T. Jr. 1965. Carbohydrate tolerance and diabetes in a total community, Tecumseh, Michigan. *Diabetes* 14: 413.

Heiss, G., Johnson, J. J., Reiland, S., Davis, C. E., and Tyroler, H. A. 1980. The epidemiolgoy of plasma HDL cholesterol levels: the Lipid Research Clinics Prevalence Study. Summary. *Circulation* 62 (Suppl. IV): 116–135.

Helin, P. and Lorenzen, I. B. 1969. Arteriosclerosis in rabbit aorta induced by systemic hypoxia. *Angiology* 20: 1–12.

Kannel, W. B. 1974. Role of blood pressure in cardiovascular morbidity and mortality. *Prog. Cardiov. Dis.* 17: 5.

Kannel, W. B., LeBauer, E. J., Dawber, T. R., and

McNamara, P. M. 1967. Relation of body weight to development of coronary heart disease: the Framingham study. *Circulation* 35: 734–744.

Mahley, R. W. 1978. Alterations in plasma lipoproteins induced by cholesterol feeding in animals including man. *In,* J. M. Dietschy, A. M. Gotto, and J. A. Ontko (eds.), *Disturbances in Lipid and Lipoprotein Metabolism,* pp. 181–197. Washington: American Physiological Society.

Martin, G., Ogburn, C., and Sprague, C. 1975. Senescence and vascular disease. *In,* V. J. Cristofalo, J. Roberts, and R. C. Adelmann (eds.), *Explorations in Aging* pp. 163–193. New York: Plenum Press.

McNamara, J. J., Malot, M. A., Stremple, J. F., and Cutting, R. T. 1971. Coronary artery disease in combat casualties in Vietnam. *JAMA* 216: 1185–1187.

Montoye, H. J., Epstein, F. H., and Kjelsberg, M. O. 1965. The measurement of body fatness: a study in a total community. *Am. J. Clin. Nutr.* 16: 417–427.

Morrison, A. D., Clements, R. S., Jr., and Winegrad, A. I. 1972. Effects of elevated glucose concentrations on the metabolism of the aortic wall. *J. Clin. Invest.* 51: 3114–3123.

Motulsky, A. G. 1976. The genetic hyperlipidemias. *N. Engl. J. Med.* 294: 823–827.

Nestel, P. J., Whyte, H. M., and Goodman, D. S. 1969. Distribution and turnover of cholesterol in humans. *J. Clin. Invest.* 48: 982.

Olefsky, J. M., Farquhar, J. W., and Reaven, G. M. 1974. Reappraisal of the role of insulin in hypertriglyceridemia. *Am. J. Med.* 57: 551–560.

Oliver, W. J., Cohen, E. L., and Neel, J. V. 1975. Blood pressure, sodium intake, and sodium related hormones in the Yanomamo Indians, a "no-salt" culture. *Circulation* 52: 146–151.

Oram, J. F., Albers, J. J., Cheung, M. C., and Bierman, E. L. 1981. The effects of subfractions of high density lipoprotein on cholesterol efflux from cultured fibroblasts: regulation of low density lipoprotein receptor activity. *J. Biol. Chem.* 255: 8348–8356.

Ostrander, L. D., Jr., Neff, B. J., Block, W. D., Francis, T., Jr., and Epstein, F. H. 1967. Hyperglycemia and hypertriglyceridemia among persons with coronary heart disease. *Ann. Intern. Med.* 67: 34.

Roberts, A. and Thompson, J. S. 1976. Inbred mice and their hybrids as an animal model for atherosclerosis research. *Adv. Exp. Med. Biol.* 67: 313–326.

Roberts, J. C., Jr. and Strauss, R. (eds.) 1965. *Comparative Atherosclerosis.* New York: Harper & Row.

Ross, R. 1981. Atherosclerosis: a problem of the biology of arterial wall cells and their interactions with blood components. *Arteriosclerosis* 1: 293–311.

Ross, R. and Glomset, J. 1973. Atherosclerosis and the arterial smooth muscle cell. *Science* 180: 1332–1339.

Ross, R. and Glomset, J. 1976. The pathogenesis of atherosclerosis. *N. Engl. J. Med.* 295: 369; 420.

Ross, R. and Harker, L. 1976. Hyperlipidemia and atherosclerosis. *Science* 193: 1094–1098.

Schwartz, S. M., Gajdusek, C. M., and Selden, S. C.

III 1981. Vascular wall growth control: the role of the endothelium. *Arteriosclerosis* 1: 107–126.

Smith, E. B. an dSlater, R. S. 1972. Relationship between low-density lipoprotein in aortic intima and serum-lipid levels. *Lancet* 1: 463–469.

Stein, Y. and Stein, O. 1973. Lipid synthesis and degradation and lipoprotein transport in mammalian aorta. *In,* Ciba Foundation Symposium 12, *Atherogenesis: Initiating Factors* pp. 165–179. Amsterdam: Elsevier.

Stout, R. W. 1981. Blood glucose and atherosclerosis. *Arteriosclerosis* 1: 227–234.

Stout, R. W., Bierman, E. L., and Ross, R. 1975. Effect of insulin on the proliferation of cultured primate arterial smooth muscle cells. *Circ. Res.* 36: 319.

Stout, R. W., Brunzell, J. D., and Bierman, E. L. 1974. Atherosclerosis and disorders of lipid metabolism in diabetes. *In,* J. Vallance-Owen (ed.), *Diabetes: Its Physiological and Biochemical Basis.* Lancaster: MTP Press Ltd.

Turner, J. L. and Bierman, E. L. 1978. Effects of glucose and sorbitol on proliferation of cultured human skin fibroblasts and arterial smooth-muscle cells. *Diabetes* 27: 583–588.

Tyroler, H. A. (ed.) 1980. Epidemiology of plasma HDL cholesterol levels: the Lipid Research Clinics Program Prevalence Study. *Circulation* 62 (Suppl. 4).

U.S. Department of Health and Human Services. 1980. *The Lipid Research Clinics Population Studies Data Book,* Vol. 1: *The Prevalence Study.* Washington, D.C.: PHS NIH Publication No. 80–1527.

Vartiainen, T. and Kanerva, K. 1947. Arteriosclerosis and wartime. *Ann. Med. Int. Fenn.* 36: 748–758.

Vracko, R. and Benditt, E. P. 1974. Manifestations of diabetes mellitus—their possible relationships to an underlying cell defect. *Am. J. Pathol.* 75: 204–222.

Webster, W. S., Clarkson, T. B., and Lofland, H. B. 1968. Carbon monoxide-aggravated atherosclerosis in the squirrel monkey. *Exp. Mol. Pathol.* 13: 36–50.

Wissler, R. W. 1978. Current status of regression studies. *In,* R. Paoletti and A. M. Gotto, Jr. (eds.), *Atherosclerosis Reviews,* Vol. 3: pp. 213–229. New York: Raven Press.

Wolinsky, H. 1972. Long-term effects of hypertension on the rat aortic wall and their relation to concurrent aging changes. *Circ. Res.* 30: 301–309.

Wolinsky, H. 1976. The role of lysosomes in vascular disease: a unifying theme. *Ann. N.Y. Acad. Sci.* 275: 238.

30
HYPERTENSION AND AGING

William B. Kannel, M.D.

Boston University School of Medicine

With an expanding elderly population in the United States, the importance of hypertension as it relates to morbidity and mortality is assuming greater importance. As the number of older people increases from the current 27 million to the estimated 55 million in 2050, the sequelae of hypertension will assume huge dimensions (Niarchos and Laragh, 1980). Disease, disability, and death from cardiovascular disease are major public health concerns in the elderly. Among the various risk factors which predispose to cardiovascular disease in the elderly, hypertension predominates. Unlike the risks associated with serum total cholesterol, diabetes, and cigarette smoking, the cardiovascular risk associated with hypertension is undiminished in the elderly (Kannel and Gordon, 1978).

There has been an accelerated decline in cardiovascular mortality in the United States since 1968 (Thom and Kannel, 1981). This decline has occurred in both sexes, in blacks as well as whites, and has included the elderly as well as the young (Table 1). Stroke mortality in particular, which has been declining for decades, has exhibited a recent, accelerated decline. These declines, at least in part, appear to be attributable to earlier detection and better control of hypertension at all ages.

The Framingham Study has clearly demonstrated that cardiovascular diseases are the major cause of mortality and disabling mor-

TABLE 1. Decline in Age-Specific Coronary and Cerebrovascular Mortality, U.S., 1963–1979.

Age	Percent Decline in Age-Specific Mortality[a]	
	Coronary Mortality	Cerebrovascular Mortality
35–44	42.8	38.8
45–54	34.5	40.8
55–64	33.1	50.3
65–74	34.3	49.2
75–84	22.2	38.8
85+	31.5	44.7

[a]Figures for calculating percentage changes obtained from National Center for Health Statistics. Declines calculated after multiplying rates before 1968 (7th revision of ICD) by 1.1457 to make them comparable to 8th revision (1968–1978). The 9th revision (1979) multiplied by 1.138.

bidity in the elderly. These diseases are inevitable consequences not of senescence but rather of identified risk factors, most prominently, hypertension (Kannel and Gordon, 1978).

DIAGNOSTIC EVALUATION

Blood pressure must be measured with special care in the elderly. Because of changes in weight, muscle tone, and skin texture, it is important to position the cuff carefully around the arm and to use a large enough cuff. In addition to the routine seated blood pressure, it is advisable to perform blood pressure measurements with the patient supine and then in the standing position two and five minutes after assuming an upright position. Evaluation of the postural blood pressure response is helpful in characterizing and treating hypertension in the elderly. The heart rate should also be noted after upright posture as this is helpful in detecting baroreceptor defects.

Indirect measurement of arterial pressure by the usual cuff method may give 15–30 mm Hg falsely high diastolic pressure readings compared to direct intra-arterial pressure recordings (Niarchos and Laragh, 1980; Spence et al., 1978). Systolic pressure, on the other hand, may be underestimated by the indirect method. Another source of error is failure to take into account the auscultatory gap which occurs more often in the elderly. This may result in as much as a 50 mm Hg underestimation of systolic pressure (Niarchos and Laragh, 1980). This error can be avoided if the cuff is inflated to greater than 250 mm Hg and then deflated slowly.

Because of these considerations and the more variable blood pressure measurements found in the elderly, it is important to base judgments on the average of a series of office blood pressure determinations. This increased variability encountered in the elderly is attributable to increased arterial rigidity, decreased cardiovascular response via the sympathetic nervous system, inaccuracy in the indirect method of measurement, and the generally higher pressures in the elderly. Continuous 24-hour blood pressure recordings have shown that, as in the young, the elderly exhibit diurnal variation in blood pressure (Niarchos and Laragh, 1980).

Several types of hypertension may be distinguished in the elderly, aside from the usual forms of secondary hypertension. Three varieties can be identified: isolated systolic hypertension, predominant systolic hypertension, and combined systolic-diastolic hypertension.

Isolated systolic hypertension is present when the systolic pressure exceeds 160 mm Hg, while the diastolic pressure is persistently below 95 mm Hg. Thus, the pulse pressure is increased and the mean arterial pressure is elevated (Niarchos and Laragh, 1980). When mild, the total peripheral resistance is generally increased moderately. When isolated systolic hypertension is accompanied by very low diastolic pressures (e.g., <70 mm Hg), this generally not only signifies loss of aortic and large vessel elasticity, but indicates concurrent insufficiency of the aortic valve due either to a dilated aortic root or to calcific degeneration of the aortic valve. The mean arterial pressure is apt to be normal, and diastolic aortic murmurs should be sought (Niarchos and Laragh, 1980).

Predominant systolic hypertension is characterized by a disproportionately high systolic pressure compared to diastolic which is also slightly elevated. In this variety, the pulse pressure, mean arterial pressure, and ratio of mean arterial pressure to cardiac output are increased (Niarchos and Laragh, 1980). There are two formulas which express the expected relationship between systolic and diastolic pressure: expected systolic pressure = 3/2 × diastolic pressure; expected systolic pressure = (diastolic pressure − 15) × 2. The former is more applicable when there is isolated systolic hypertension present. The latter defines undue systolic elevation when there is concurrent diastolic hypertension (Niarchos and Laragh, 1980). This may provide an early clue to conditions such as hyperthyroidism, aortic regurgitation, arteriovenous fistula, and arterial rigidity.

Combined systolic and diastolic hypertension is the characteristic pattern of essential hypertension, consisting of a proportional increase in both systolic and diastolic pressure which continues into old age. The pulse pressure is normal or increased, whereas mean arterial pressure is markedly increased as is peripheral resistance. Systolic-diastolic hypertension pretreatment evaluation can usually be kept simple in most cases. Extensive studies are indicated only if the hypertension is newly acquired late in life, has abruptly exacerbated from a stable, well-controlled status, or is not responding to treatment. Malignant hypertension in patients over age 65 is almost always secondary to some identifiable cause, usually vascular diseases involving the kidneys.

In all elderly patients with hypertension, the evaluation should emphasize the status of those organs most affected by this disorder such as the heart, kidneys, brain, and eyes. The evaluation should always include, in addition to a history and physical examination, a blood count, urinalysis (including microscopic), BUN (or creatinine), serum potassium, chest x-ray, and an electrocardiogram.

PREVALENCE

Hypertension, however defined, is very common in the elderly except for some primitive societies where the usual rise in blood pressure with age does not occur. Estimates of the prevalence of hypertension in older persons vary widely depending on the definition of the upper limits of "normal" and the methods by which the pressures were obtained (Koch-Weser, 1978; Alderman and Yano, 1976). Hypertension in the elderly has been variously defined as systolic pressures exceeding anywhere between 130 and 200 mm Hg or diastolic pressures between 90 and 120 mm Hg. The Framingham Study defined hypertension at all ages as above 160 mm Hg systolic and over 95 mm Hg diastolic (Kannel, 1974). By this definition, about 22 percent of men and 34 percent of women aged 65–74 were found to be hypertensive. Others have estimated a prevalence as high as 65 percent in 70-year-old men (Chrysant et al., 1976; Master, 1952). National health survey data indicate that over the age of 65, the prevalence of hypertension remains about 50 percent higher in blacks than whites, much as it is at younger ages (Niarchos and Laragh, 1980; Ostfeld, 1978). The Health and Nutrition Examination Survey (1971–1974) indicated that 40 percent of whites and more than 50 percent of blacks between ages 65 and 74 have either isolated systolic hyperten-

TABLE 2. Prevalence of Hypertension Among Men and Women, Black and White, Ages 65–74.[a]

Black women	58.8%
White women	42.3%
Black men	50.1%
White men	35.3%

[a]From HANES, 1977. Health and nutrition exam survey 1971–1974. *Vital and Health Statistics,* Series 11, No. 203.

sion or combined systolic-diastolic hypertension (Table 2).

Owing to a disproportionate rise in systolic pressure relative to diastolic with aging, the prevalence of isolated systolic hypertension increases to a high rate in the elderly. Using commonly accepted definitions (e.g., systolic pressures over 160 and diastolic pressures consistently below 95 mm Hg), the Framingham Study showed that 30 percent of women and 18 percent of men have this condition at ages 70 to 74 (Figure 1). The prevalence of systolic hypertension increases sharply with age beyond age 45, being distinctly uncommon prior to that age in both sexes. Beyond age 50, the prevalence in women rises more steeply with age than in men.

AGE TRENDS IN BLOOD PRESSURE

Although blood pressure rises with age in most population samples studied, and particularly in affluent societies, this is not inevitable and should not be considered a normal or desirable aging phenomenon. There are some isolated, primitive populations in which a rise in pressure with age evidently does not occur (Maddocks, 1961; Page et al., 1974). Within Western societies, longitudinal studies suggest that increases in blood pressure over time are more related to the initial blood pressure level and to subsequent weight gain than to age itself (Harlan et al., 1973).

In Western and industrialized societies, blood pressure characteristically rises with

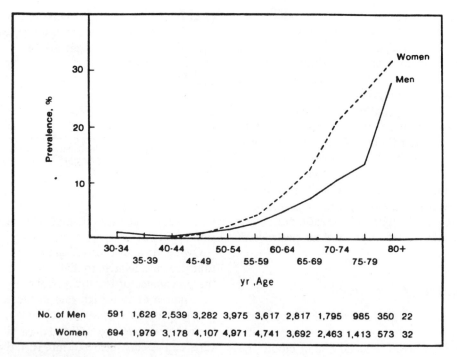

Figure 1. Prevalence of isolated systolic hypertension by age and sex in 24-year follow-up in Framingham study.

age in adults. Longitudinal observation of trends in blood pressure in the Framingham Study indicates a magnitude of rise with age of about 20 mm Hg systolic and 10 mm Hg diastolic from age 30 to 64 (Figure 2). Longitudinal biennial monitoring of pressures, reflecting changes as persons actually age, indicates that diastolic pressures in the two sexes are parallel over time, with women's pressures persistently lower than those of men the same age. These diastolic pressures rise with age until the mid-50s and then plateau until about age 65, after which they decline in both sexes. Even at this time in life, diastolic pressures remain parallel in the two sexes, with women's diastolic pressures persistently lower than those of men.

Systolic pressures present a distinctly different age trend. Those of women are initially lower than those of men but rise more steeply so that they converge at about age 60 (Figure 2). The rise in systolic pressure continues unabated, in contrast to diastolic pressure, at least until age 75. Thus, there is a

disproportionate rise in systolic pressure with advancing age, attributed to a progressive loss of arterial elasticity.

Cross-sectional, or prevalence-based, inferences about age trends in blood pressure appear to be misleading. In the same Framingham cohort, cross-sectional data show an apparent crossover in pressures in the two sexes for both systolic and diastolic pressure, with women's pressures initially lower than those of men but higher beyond middle age (Figure 2).

Thus, there is good evidence that blood pressure rises with age in Western cultures. However, it is not all certain that the observed rise is *caused* by aging *per se*. Even in these populations, not all persons exhibit a rise in pressure with age in adult life.

Because blood pressure usually rises with age, it is often considered a "normal" phenomenon. The statistical definition of "normal" is based on what is usual, and what is common is—unfortunately—not necessarily optimal in terms of function (Severe et al.,

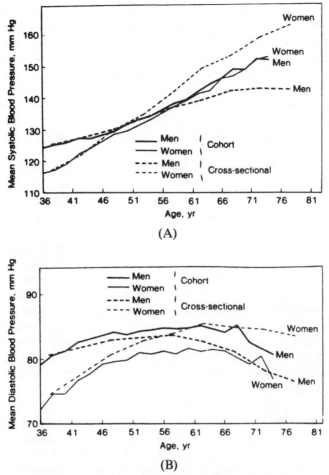

Figure 2. Average age trends in systolic (a) and diastolic (b) blood pressure levels for cross-sectional and cohort data, examinations 3 to 10, Framingham study.

1977). Impaired function, though common in the elderly, is undesirable and pathological. The elderly with lower blood pressures suffer less morbidity and mortality for their age than those with blood pressures closer to the mean in Western or affluent societies. Debate about what is "normal" pressure in the elderly is pointless unless it is based on morbidity and mortality.

PATHOPHYSIOLOGY

It is difficult to distinguish the increase in blood pressure which results directly from growth and aging *per se* from those influences which reflect the intrusion of a disease process. It appears that the increase in pressure during aging may to some extent reflect a continuum of hemodynamic phenomena observed during normal growth (Niarchos and Laragh, 1980). However, aging is often associated with increased rigidity of the aorta and peripheral arteries because of loss of elastic fibers in the arterial media, accompanied by increased collagen and calcium deposition, and intimal atherosclerosis. The aorta is no longer able to dampen the peaks of arterial pressure generated by left ventricular systole. Thus, the widened pulse pressure characteristic of aging is largely due to impaired distensibility of the large arterial vessels. Even in normotensive persons, aging tends to displace the arterial pressure-volume curve downward and decrease its slope or arterial capacitance (Niarchos and Laragh, 1980; Tarazi et al., 1975). In hypertensive persons, the ratio of pulse pressure to stroke volume, which is a useful index of arterial rigidity, correlates significantly with age (Tarazi et al., 1975). The higher pressure generated in the large arteries is transmitted to the smaller peripheral arteries and arterioles which also reflect this pressure back, further increasing the pressure in the aorta and large vessels.

Changes in the precapillary arterioles are believed to be fundamental to the maintenance of essential hypertension (Niarchos and Laragh, 1980). It is not known how aging *per se* affects these structures. It is believed that long-standing hypertension, by producing arteriolar sclerosis, enhances the resistance of these vessels, and their responsiveness to physiological nervous and humoral stimuli (Folkow et al., 1973). It is not known if aging itself has a similar effect.

The effects of aging on the veins, the capacitance vessels of the circulation, are unknown. It is not known whether hypertension affects venous tone in humans. Long-term effects of gravity may affect the integrity of venous valves, leading to a tendency to decreased venous return.

Cardiac performance under a load is often diminished in older persons, compared to those age 25. The fall in stroke volume and myocardial contractibility makes heart rate a more important determinant of cardiac output in the elderly than in the young. It is not clear how much of the decrease in cardiac function is an age-related biochemical aberration and how much is attributable to disease of the coronary arteries and to aortic valvular calcification. Because of the decreased cardiac reserve in the elderly, hypertension is likely to have more serious consequences in this group.

After the age of 40–50 years, there is usually a decrease in renal cortical blood flow associated with 15 percent decreases in renal cortical mass and glomerular filtration rate (Hollenberg et al., 1974). A decline in both the number of functioning glomeruli and their functional capacity occurs (Darmady et al., 1973). Hence, reabsorption, secretion, and concentration of urine may be impaired, and the remaining nephrons may not excrete or conserve sodium normally under a load or restriction (Epstein and Hollenberg, 1976). The vascular changes in the arterioles and small arteries in the aged kidney are distinct from those of nephrosclerosis, and they may occur even in the absence of hypertension (Niarchos and Laragh, 1980; Takazaiwra, 1972; Lungquist, 1962). These changes are more severe and occur earlier if hypertension is present. The role of these alterations in the kidney in sustaining hypertension in the elderly is not well understood.

Blood volume generally decreases with age, and small decreases in volume may result in a larger fall in pressure, particularly in systolic pressure. This may explain the greater sensitivity of the blood pressure of the elderly to antihypertensive drugs and to sodium administration (Niarchos and Laragh, 1980). Local vascular stenosis in the elderly cerebral vessels may decrease the ability of the central circulation to autoregulate to accommodate wide fluctuations in arterial pressure. Atherosclerosis in the renal arteries of the elderly may initiate or aggravate hypertension (Dustan, 1974).

Renin and aldosterone values decline gradually throughout life in inverse relationship to the blood pressure rise with advancing age (Niarchos and Laragh, 1980). The low renin values of elderly patients can still stimulate the adrenal cortex which has become more sensitive to angiotensin so that aldosterone is still produced. The contribution of these changes in the renin-angiotensin system to the progressive rise in pressure in the elderly is not well understood.

Plasma norepinephrine increases progressively with age (Severe et al., 1977), and hypertensive patients appear to be more sensitive to circulating catecholamines. In later life, this increased sensitivity may be secondary to structural changes in the arterioles. The cause of the increase in catecholamines with age is uncertain and apparently not a response to a decreased number or sensitivity of beta receptors (Niarchos and Laragh, 1980; Guannieri et al., 1980).

As a consequence of decreased aortic elasticity and atheromatous involvement, the barorecepter area of the aorta may become more rigid, thereby dampening reactive baroreceptor function. Hence, an acute increase in blood pressure may not elicit much bradycardia or vasodilatation. This could be responsible for the increased variability of blood pressure with advancing age and may play a role in sustaining hypertension. Compensatory tachycardia and vasoconstriction in response to decreases in blood pressure are often even more impaired because of accompanying sinus node dysfunction and reduced sensitivity to circulating catecholamines.

To what extent vasoactive substances such as the prostaglandins and the kallikrein-kinin systems are involved in the hypertension in the elderly is not known. It is not even clear whether their function or concentration changes with aging.

In the elderly subject, the loss of distensibility of the aorta often results in a disproportionate rise in systolic pressure which can result in isolated systolic hypertension. Cardiac hypertrophy occurs with this type of hypertension because cardiac work is mainly a function of systolic pressure. In the elderly, the impedance to left ventricular ejection is further aggravated by a high total peripheral resistance. Resistance to flow in systolic hypertension is reflected better by the ratio of systolic pressure to systolic flow than by the ratio of mean arterial pressure to cardiac output (total arterial resistance), since in isolated systolic hypertension, mean arterial pressure may not be greatly altered (Niarchos and Laragh, 1980). Recent evidence suggests a possible relationship between hypertension and calcium metabolism. Persons with essential hypertension tend to have lower calcium intakes, reduced ionized serum calcium levels, higher parathyroid hormone, and elevated urinary calcium compared to normotensive persons (McCarron, 1982). Administration of calcium to the spontaneously hypertensive rat tends to blunt development of hypertension. Whether this applies to hypertension in the elderly is worthy of investigation.

DETERMINANTS

Elevation of systolic and diastolic pressure in the elderly usually represents primary hypertension as it does in the young. Only a small proportion is secondary to some identifiable cause. When hypertension involving both components of the blood pressure appears for the first time after age 55, there is a good chance that it is not essential hypertension. Longitudinal studies of hypertension in Framingham indicate that if hypertension of both components of the blood pressure is to develop, it will happen before age 55. Hence, newly developing hypertension in persons over age 55 deserves an investigation for some underlying cause, particularly renovascular disease.

Isolated systolic hypertension is to a great extent intrinsic to a progressive loss of arterial elasticity accompanying aging. This is attributable to *arteriosclerosis* but not necessarily *atherosclerosis*. However, this type of hypertension is not a homogenous entity, and other causes include aortic valve insufficiency, atrioventricular conduction disturbance, hyperthyroidism, Paget's disease, and severe anemia. However, these etiologies, which can also cause cardiac failure or other sequelae of hypertension, account for only a small proportion of systolic hypertension in the elderly.

Secondary forms of hypertension occur in the elderly as well as in the younger hypertensive person and include undiagnosed renovascular disease, primary aldosteronism, and pheochromocytoma. However, *de novo* hypertension in the elderly most often is caused by progressive atherosclerosis occluding one or both renal arteries. This renovascular disease may also produce an acceleration of diastolic pressure increase in patients with isolated systolic hypertension, or it may cause resistance to treatment in a previously well-controlled subject with essential hypertension. Obstructive uropathy is common in the elderly male. It is not known how often this leads to development of new hypertension in elderly men.

The determinants of most hypertension, including that in the elderly, are unknown. However, in the elderly as well as in the young, hypertension occurs more commonly in those who are obese (Kannel and Sorlie, 1974). Weight gains and losses are generally mirrored by corresponding changes in blood pressure (Ashley and Kannel, 1974), and this occurs independent of salt intake (Reisen et al., 1978). Alcohol intake is also related to hypertension, and it is likely that this too applies in the elderly (Kannel and Sorlie, 1974). The Framingham Study has found that those in the upper end of the normal distribution of blood hematocrit have about twice as much hypertension as those at the lower end (Kannel and Sorlie, 1974). Diabetes and gout are more common in the elderly, and those who develop these metabolic problems have more hypertension. There is a tendency for higher pressures as cholesterol values and heart rates rise (Kannel and Sorlie, 1974).

High salt intake is believed to play a role in the development of hypertension and very likely in its persistence into advanced age. A high prevalence of hypertension is found in cultures subsisting on more than 4 grams of salt per day or those excreting more than 70 mg of sodium (Freis, 1976). The elderly raised in primitive isolated societies tend to escape hypertension. This protection tends to be lost on migration to more "advanced" civilization (Freis, 1976).

There is undoubtedly a strong familial and inherent susceptibility to hypertension, which very likely applies in the elderly as in the young. However, this is only permissive, requiring some environmental cofactor for the hypertension to be expressed. Blacks seem more susceptible than whites at all ages. Families share more than genes, as indicated by the observation that spouses of hypertensive subjects tend to have higher blood pressures (Sackett, 1975).

HAZARDS OF HYPERTENSION

Hypertension is a prominent contributor to overall mortality, doubling the risk of death, and to cardiovascular mortality in particular, where the risk in the elderly is tripled compared to normotensive persons of the same age (Table 3). In fact, it takes on added significance in the elderly where the absolute risk of dying is greater than in the young. While the long-term risk is greater over a lifetime in the young hypertensive, the short-term risk of cardiovascular catastrophes in the hypertensive elderly is formidable.

The risk of every major cardiovascular sequela of hypertension is increased in the elderly hypertenisve subject (Table 4). The impact of hypertension is greatest for the risk of stroke and least for occulsive peripheral arterial disease, but it is substantial even for the latter. This conclusion is based on a comparison of risk ratios in elderly hypertensives compared to normotensives of the same age and sex. In terms of the absolute incidence,

TABLE 3. Mortality Experience According to Hypertensive Status, Elderly Subjects (Age 65-74)—The Framingham Study, 20-Year Follow-Up.

| Hypertensive Status | Average Annual Mortality Per 1000 | | | |
| | Overall | | Cardiovascular | |
	Men	Women	Men	Women
Normal	23.6	14.5	9.6	3.8
Borderline	37.7	17.8	20.2	9.8
Definite	42.6	24.7	24.5	18.6

TABLE 4. Risk of Specified Cardiovascular Events According to Hypertensive Status (Persons Aged 65–74)—The Framingham Study, 20-Year Follow-Up.

Blood Pressure Status	Coronary Disease		Stroke		Peripheral Arterial Disease		Cardiac Failure	
	Men	Women	Men	Women	Men	Women	Men	Women
Normotensive	12.4	5.4	2.7	0.6	6.2	2.6	3.9	3.2
Borderline	24.0	13.7	8.1	6.4	5.9	2.6	6.8	6.3
Hypertensive	28.4	22.1	18.9	16.4	7.0	5.9	18.1	9.7

[a]All trends significant $P < .01$ except for peripheral arterial disease.

coronary heart disease is still the most common sequela or hypertension in the elderly as in the young.

Although elevated blood pressure is highly prevalent in the elderly, there is no evidence to suggest that the associated danger is any less than in the younger hypertensive. The absolute risk is certainly greater (Table 5). Relative risks, when normotensives are compared with hypertensives within each sex, give no indication of a diminishing impact with advancing age. Likewise, risk gradients, reflected by coefficients for the regression of incidence of cardiovascular events on blood pressure, also do not diminish with advancing age. Attributable risk, which takes into account the high prevalence of hypertension in the elderly and the relative risk, is also as great in the elderly as in the young. Thus, there is nothing to suggest a lesser hazard of hypertension in the elderly.

There is also no evidence that elderly women tolerate hypertension better than men. Relative risks and risk gradients are just as large for women as for men, and the attributable risks in women are even larger than for men in those over age 65 (Table 5). With regard to risk of strokes and cardiac failure, even the absolute risks are no lower in women than in men.

ISOLATED SYSTOLIC HYPERTENSION

Isolated systolic hypertension is a common variety of hypertension in the aged. Because this is usually a reflection of diminished distensibility of the aorta, it is too often considered an innocuous, normal accompaniment of advanced age. There is little to suggest that such hypertension is well tolerated.

As in the young, the risk of cardiovascular sequelae is no more closely related to the diastolic than to the systolic pressure (Table 6). An examination of logistic regression coefficients standardized to place each compo-

TABLE 5. Risk of Cardiovascular Disease According to Age in Hypertensives (Persons Aged 45–74)—The Framingham Study, 20-Year Follow-Up.

Age	Incidence Per 1000		Risk Ratio[a]		Regression Coefficient		Attributable Risk	
	Men	Women	Men	Women	Men	Women	Men	Women
45–54	23.6	9.7	2.7	3.6	.521	.654	16.4	17.4
55–64	43.9	23.7	2.8	3.9	.544	.668	17.9	25.5
65–74	51.0	35.6	3.0	4.1	.575	.654	18.8	25.9
All ages	35.7	20.6	2.8	3.5	.537	.643		

[a]Risk Ratio $= \dfrac{\text{Rate in HBPs}}{\text{Rate in Normotensives}}$.

TABLE 6. Gradients of Risk of Brain Infarction According to Component of Blood Pressure (Subjects Aged 45–84)—The Framingham Study, 24-Year Follow-Up.

Component of Blood Pressure	Ave. Standardized Regression Coefficients		Z Values	
	Men	Women	Men	Women
Pulse pressure	.5346	.5696	7.22	8.36
Mean arterial pressure	.6059	.7562	7.49	10.56
Isolated systolic HBP	.2676	.2106	3.44	2.48
Systolic BP	.6335	.7223	8.27	10.49
Diastolic BP	.5060	.6833	5.83	9.02

nent of the pressure on an equal footing for the different units of measurement gives no indication of a greater impact of diastolic than systolic pressure for any of the cardiovascular sequelae of hypertension. In fact, analysis of every component of blood pressure, including pulse pressure, suggests that nothing is clearly superior to the systolic pressure in predicting cardiovascular events in general and stroke, the most closely related hypertensive event, in particular (Table 6).

Criteria for defining hypertension have traditionally been based on diastolic pressure, which reflects the belief that diastolic pressure elevation is more pathological than systolic. Recent multicenter clinical trials testing the efficacy of antihypertensive treatment have tended to foster this misconception by basing the indication for treatment on the diastolic pressure regardless of the systolic pressure. Hence, subjects with isolated systolic pressure elevations have been largely ignored.

There is clinical evidence which suggests that isolated systolic hypertension is a distinct clinical syndrome (Niarchos and Laragh, 1980; Koch-Weser, 1978). It also has a different population distribution than essential hypertension by age, race, and sex. Systolic pressure is to a large extent a reflection of the compliance of the aorta and major arteries. Hence, if the aorta is rigid, ejection of the stroke output of the left ventricle during systole results in a higher systolic pressure than if it can expand. When the aorta is less compliant, the pressure wave of sys-

tole is more directly transmitted to the periphery and this may be damaging to vital organs. Also, during diastole, the compliant aorta contracts, sustaining arterial blood flow, and this is impaired in systolic hypertension.

Data from the Framingham Study have shown not only that systolic pressure is a better predictor of cardiovascular disease than diastolic pressure but that the predictive value of systolic pressure relative to diastolic increases with age (Koch-Weser, 1978; Alderman and Yano, 1976).

Systolic pressure increases continuously with age, while diastolic pressure falls after age 60 when cardiovascular morbidity and mortality are rapidly escalating (Figure 2). This suggests the epidemiologic importance of systolic pressure even in the presence of low diastolic pressure. The longitudinal epidemiologic data from the Framingham Study bear this out. In subjects with diastolic pressures that have never exceeded 95 mm Hg, risk is strikingly related to systolic pressure (Figure 3). There is no indication that the risk gradients are any less steep with advancing age.

The physiologic model of a disproportionately elevated systolic pressure as an indicator of arteriosclerotic change in the major arteries is supported by epidemiologic data which indicate a low incidence of isolated systolic hypertension through middle age and a rapid escalation thereafter (Figure 1). In contrast to blood pressure trends after age 50, the prevalence of isolated systolic hypertension is greater in women than in men, and

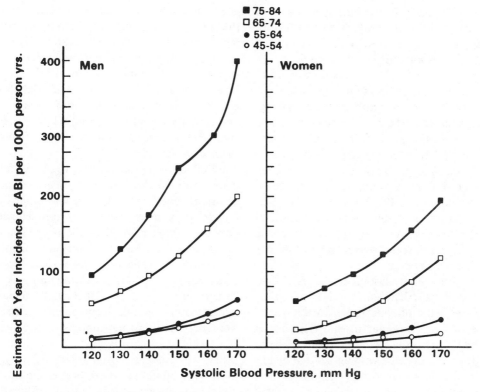

Figure 3. Incidence of ABI according to systolic blood pressure in subjects 45–84 years whose diastolic pressure is < 95 mm Hg Framingham study, 24 year follow-up

the relative risk of cardiovascular mortality associated with this type of hypertension is also greater in women.

There appears to be some connection between essential hypertension and isolated systolic hypertension in that a high prevalence of affected individuals have had prior diastolic blood pressure elevation and the proportion increases with age (Table 7).

Among elderly subjects with systolic hypertension, it is not particularly helpful to know the diastolic pressure to assess risk, and use of the diastolic pressure may actually be misleading. Thus, not only does systolic pressure improve as a predictor with advancing age, but it is associated with an increased risk even when the diastolic pressure is not elevated.

It is conceivable that systolic hypertension is only a sign of arteriosclerosis which is actually responsible for the associated in-

creased incidence of cardiovascular sequelae. Multivariate analysis in the Framingham Study, using the depth of the dicrotic notch in pulse wave recordings to reflect the elastic

TABLE 7. **Percent of Persons with Isolated Systolic Hypertension Who Were Previously Diagnosed as Having Elevated Diastolic Pressure—The Framingham Study, 20-Year Follow-Up.**

	PERCENT WITH PREVIOUSLY ELEVATED DIASTOLIC PRESSURE[a]	
Age	Men	Women
35–44	37.5	24.4
45–54	50.0	46.0
55–64	62.1	52.0
65–74	57.7	62.0

[a] < 95 mm Hg.

recoil of the arterial circulation, would seem to indicate that the isolated systolic pressure elevation is not merely a sign of rigid, diseased arteries but a direct contributor to risk Kannel et al., 1981). However this conclusion depends on the credibility of the pulse wave recording as a valid indicator of arterial rigidity. Although the dicrotic notch reflects the rebound elastic recoil after aortic valve closure, peripheral factors such as the tone and resistance of the peripheral vessels have been shown to influence the appearance of the incisura (Hamilton, 1974; Feinberg and Lax, 1958). However, in the absence of peripheral vasoconstriction, cardiac failure, or aortic valve disease, it seems reasonable to consider the depth of the dicrotic notch as an indicator of arteriolar elasticity. Studies at Framingham have shown a relationship of absence of the dicrotic notch to the occurrence of cardiovascular disease (Dawber et al., 1973). Also the loss the dicrotic incisura was found to increase with age so that by age 65–74, less than 10 percent of the elderly have a normal pulse wave tracing and 11 percent exhibit a complete absence of the incisura (Dawber et al., 1973; Kannel et al., 1981). In the elderly, the prevalence of systolic hypertension and the pulse pressure were found to increase with the degree of blunting of the dicrotic notch. These findings lend support to the claim that the dicrotic notch reflects arterial rigidity, albeit imperfectly (Kannel et al., 1981).

Thus, it is not likely that isolated systolic hypertension is only an innocent accompaniment of aged rigid arteries. The pulse wave data strongly suggest that systolic hypertension *per se* is associated with hypertensive as well as atherosclerotic cardiovascular sequelae whether the vessel is rigid or not (Kannel et al., 1981). Multivariate analysis taking age, pulse wave findings, and systolic pressure into account indicates that it is the systolic pressure that determines the risk.

LABILE HYPERTENSION

Labile hypertension is usually regarded as an innocuous antecedent of "fixed" hypertension and hence unworthy of treatment. This is an especially important consideration in the elderly because lability of blood pressure increases with age. To a large extent, this increased lability is a result of the higher pressures generally observed in the elderly. Higher pressures are more labile than low ones so that what has been termed "fixed hypertension" actually has more labile pressures than so-called labile hypertension (Kannel et al., 1980).

Blood pressure fluctuates physiologically in response to changes in physical activity, emotion, mood, wakefulness, and other demands for greater tissue perfusion. Hence, pressures under office conditions are sometimes variable. This had engendered skepticism about the value of a single office blood pressure reading. In the Framingham Study, 35 percent of male and 27 percent of female hypertensives on one biennial examination were borderline or normotensive the next (Kannel et al., 1980). By this criterion, those found to be normotensive might be judged to be very labile and those borderline moderately so. However, this concept of lability is confounded by the statistical phenomenon of regression toward the mean and is invalid.

A better indication of the lability of the blood pressure is the standard deviation about the mean of a series of pressures obtained over an hour on a particular examination. The variation in pressure by this criterion in the Framingham Study did not appear to be a repeatable characteristic of subjects from one examination to another, although the blood pressures themselves were highly correlated (Kannel and Sorlie, 1980). Thus, there is little evidence to support the contention that there are actually identifiable persons in a population who characteristically have unusually labile pressures on multiple examinations.

"Basal" pressures have been considered the best basis for judging the need for treatment so that those pressures not elevated under bed-rest conditions were often thought to be innocuous. As a dangerous extension of this concept, physicians have tended to use the lowest pressure recorded on a patient as the most valid for evaluating risk. It is not safe to disregard patients whose pressures fail to be persistently elevated on every determination if the average pressure is high.

The risk of caridovascular disease is best judged from the average of a series of pressures. Patients whose pressures are more "labile" have no lower risk of cardiovascular events than those whose pressures are less variable. In fact, taken alone, the risk of cardiovascular disease actually increases with the degree of variability in pressure (Kannel et al., 1980). However, this only reflects the higher average values of those with more variable values, and when adjusted for the mean level of pressure, there is no relation of variability to risk. This is confirmed in multivariate analysis which has indicated that for any given average pressure, the risk of cardiovascular events is unaffected by the degree of variability of the pressure (Table 8).

Labile hypertension has no distinguishing features which make it unique, and almost all normotensive persons occasionally have pressures above the arbitrary normal limits. Likewise, almost all patients with so-called fixed hypertension occasionally exhibit pressures below conventional hypertensive limits. Casual pressures obtained in the clinic predict cardiovascular events surprisingly well. The only reason that fixed or basal pressure elevations are associated with a higher risk than "labile" hypertension is that the average pressure is higher. It is, therefore, more logical to rely on the average pressure rather than on these more ambiguous indicators.

TABLE 8. Cardiovascular Disease vs Systolic Level, Lability, and Age (Persons Aged 45–74)—The Framingham Study, 20-Year Follow-Up.

	STANDARDIZED MULTIPLE LOGISTIC COEFFICIENTS	
	Men	Women
SBP lability	0.027	0.080
SBP level	0.357[a]	0.420[a]
Age	0.303[a]	0.458[a]

[a] $P < 0.001$.

It is unwise to label a patient hypertensive on the basis of a single office blood pressure. It does not appear good practice to place patients who may have been transiently emotionally upset on antihypertensive therapy for the remainder of their lifetime on the basis of one office blood pressure reading. However, it is equally unwise to conclude that a patient who occasionally has a normotensive pressure is in no jeopardy. It is recommended that the average of a series of pressures be used to determine risk, preferably over more than one examination.

PATTERNS OF CARDIOVASCULAR DISEASE

Patterns of cardiovascular disease incidence vary among hypertensives depending on age. Also, in the elderly hypertensive subject, the patterns of cardiovascular disease vary with the severity of the blood pressure.

Over 24 years of follow-up in the Framingham Study cohort, there were 552 cardiovascular events in men and 405 in women who achieved age 56–74, allowing an examination of the patterns of cardiovascular events in this age group. For all grades of hypertension, coronary heart disease incidence exceeded that of any other cardiovascular sequela (Table 9). However, the proportion of cardiovascular events presenting as a stroke increased sharply with the severity of hypertension, particularly in elderly women. This was not true for any other cardiovascular event, including coronary heart disease, cardiac failure, or occlusive peripheral arterial disease (Table 9). Among the strokes, the proportion of brain infarctions *increased* with the severity of blood pressure elevation.

Among hypertensive subjects, there appears to be an increasing tendency for cardiovascular events to occur as strokes with advancing age in women, but not men. The same is true for cardiac failure (Table 10). Coronary heart disease and occlusive peripheral arterial disease did not vary among hypertensives of different ages. Manifestations of coronary heart disease in hypertensives showed a tendency to present as myocardial infarction more often in the elderly, than in

TABLE 9. Pattern of Cardiovascular Disease in the Elderly According to Severity of Hypertension (Subjects Aged 65–74)—The Framingham Study, 20-Year Follow-Up.

Severity of Hypertension	Percent of Cardiovascular Events Manifested as:							
	Stroke		Coronary Disease		Cardiac Failure		Peripheral Vascular Disease	
	Men	Women	Men	Women	Men	Women	Men	Women
Normal	15.8	7.0	72.5	62.8	22.8	37.2	36.3	30.2
Mild	24.8	28.4	73.4	60.9	20.8	28.0	18.0	16.0
Severe	37.1	46.1	55.7	62.1	35.8	27.2	13.7	16.6

TABLE 10. Pattern of Cardiovascular Disease Among Hypertensives According to Age and Sex—The Framingham Study, 20-Year Follow-Up.

Age	Percent of Cardiovascular Disease Occurring as:							
	Stroke		Coronary Disease		Cardiac Failure		Peripheral Vascular Disease	
	Men	Women	Men	Women	Men	Women	Men	Women
45–54	18.1	22.6	67.1	69.1	26.1	15.5	13.1	18.6
55–64	18.0	25.3	70.2	62.0	20.5	24.1	20.7	15.2
65–74	17.5	46.1	55.7	62.1	35.5	27.2	13.7	16.6

the younger, female. There was also a greater tendency for coronary attacks to be fatal in both sexes with advancing age. The proportion of sudden deaths, in particular, increased sharply with age in women.

The preponderance of deaths among hypertensives is due to cardiovascular diseases at all ages. In the hypertensive elderly female, the proportion of deaths due to cardiovascular disease also increased substantially with age. This tendency was not noted in hypertensive men.

CARDIOVASCULAR RISK FACTORS

Because the risk of hypertension is not uniform, it is useful to consider hypertension as an ingredient of a cardiovascular risk profile. Risk associated with any degree of hypertension varies widely depending on the number and level of the cardiovascular risk factors (Kannel, 1974). Despite the fact that the impact of cholesterol, glucose tolerance, and cigarettes diminishes with advancing age, multivariate risk profiles made up of these variables, blood pressure, and ECG-LVH have been found to predict as well in the elderly as in the young (Table 11). Fractionation of the serum total cholesterol into its Low Density Lipoprotein (LDL) and High Density Lipoprotein (HDL) components restores its ability to predict coronary heart disease in the elderly (Kannel and Castelli, 1979). A total cholesterol to HDL cholesterol ratio provides a good approximation of the joint effect of the two-way traffic of cholesterol in the atherogenic LDL and protective HDL fractions (Kannel and Castelli, 1979).

Most important in assessing the gravity of hypertension in the elderly, as in the young, are the height of the systolic pressure, the

TABLE 11. Percentage of Cases of Cardiovascular Disease in Upper Decile of Multivariate Risk[a] According to Age—The Framingham Study, 16-Year Follow-Up.

Age	Coronary Disease		Brain Infarction	
	Men	Women	Men	Women
45–54	26	20	55	44
55–64	27	26	52	43
65–74	21	41	57	46

[a]Based on systolic pressure, serum cholesterol, glucose tolerance, number of cigarettes smoked, and ECG-LVH.

number of associated cardiovascular risk factors, and whether or not there is target organ involvement (Kannel, 1974; Kannel and Castelli, 1979).

PREVENTIVE AND THERAPEUTIC IMPLICATIONS

In Western and affluent societies, a rise in blood pressure with age is usual, but it does not appear to be inevitable as many individuals do not have elevated pressures despite advanced age. In some isolated primitive societies, a rise in blood pressure with age does not occur, which suggests that hypertension can be prevented. Although the determinants of essential hypertension in general, and hypertension in the elderly in particular, are not well established, evidence to date suggests that some hypertension can be prevented. Thus, in subjects with a family history of hypertension, the avoidance of obesity, excessive alcohol intake, and too much salt might well prevent some hypertension in advanced age. It is clear that hypertension is as great a contributor to cardiovascular mortality in the elderly as it is in the young. Life insurance and epidemiologic data have shown consistently that the impact of blood pressure does not diminish as a cause of cardiovascular morbidity and mortality with advancing age. Since the cost of hypertension to the community

in terms of cardiovascular mortality and illness rises with age in both sexes, there is no justification for neglecting hypertension in the elderly. Systolic hypertension in particular appears to have been sorely neglected. Because a given degree of elevation of either component of the blood pressure carries the same relative risk and a higher absolute risk than in the young, it seems pointless to use the usual level of pressure encountered in the elderly as a normal standard. What is common is not necessarily optimal. The fact that hypertension in the elderly is predominantly systolic does not make it an innocuous condition. There is no reason why the damage caused to the arterial system by hypertension should derive more from the diastolic than the systolic component.

There are, however, legitimate questions as to whether the risk associated with hypertension in the elderly is reversible with treatment, and at what cost in side effects and inconvenience. In advanced age, the effort and the expense of treating asymptomatic hypertension are justified only if the quality, as well as the length, of life can be improved. Therapeutic misadventures are more likely in the elderly because of inappropriate dosage, diminished homeostatic capacity, erratic pill taking, and the often associated polypharmacy for multiple diseases. It is not clear whether producing a subnormal diastolic arterial pressure in an attempt to reduce isolated systolic elevations is safe. It seems unlikely that drug therapy can restore the reduced arterial capacitance of isolated systolic hypertension to normal. Because of decreases in cardiac output, glomerular filtration rates, renal blood flow and tubular function, and some hepatic metabolic functions, it is likely that the half-life of many drugs is increased and clearance slowed in the elderly, which means that adjustment of dosage is required.

Pharmacotherapeutic reduction of blood pressure appears to reduce the excess cardiovascular morbidity and mortality associated with hypertension as effectively in the elderly as in the young. However, the benefits and risks of drug therapy in those of advanced age and those with isolated systolic hypertension require further study.

The Veterans Administration Cooperative Study, which included some subjects over age 60, and the European Working Party on High Blood Pressure in the Elderly indicate that both the systolic and the diastolic pressure can be safely lowered in the elderly (Veterans Administration Cooperative Study Group, 1972; Amery et al., 1978). The Hypertension Detection and Follow-up Program has demonstrated the value of antihypertensive therapy in reducing total mortality in patients aged 30–69 years with diastolic blood pressures greater than 89 mm Hg. Although only 22 percent of patients included in the study were 60–69 years of age, the benefit to those in the advanced age group was as great as to the younger patients.

No prospective double-blind trial of the value of treatment of isolated systolic hypertension is available. This makes it difficult to provide definitive recommendations regarding treatment. In the completed trials on the effectiveness of antihypertensive therapy to date, elderly subjects have been grossly underrepresented. Trials of antihypertensive therapy in the elderly have indicated that prudent therapy with diuretics and methyldopa can be safely carried out.

A lingering concern over the past quarter century is that reduction of blood pressure in the elderly will dangerously reduce perfusion of vital organs such as the heart, brain, or kidney (Freis, 1972). Although there has been no indication that this occurs in clinical trials to date, these trials have not included the elderly who may have a lesser ability to autoregulate blood flow. It seems likely that elderly hypertensives have more irreversible structural arterial disease than younger patients (Dustan, 1974). However, there is no evidence that elderly hypertensive patients are unable to maintain the necessary perfusion of vital organs when blood pressure is gradually reduced (Koch-Weser, 1978). Readaptation of distorted cerebral autoregulation towards normal occurs with effective antihypertensive treatment at all

ages. In many patients, reduction in blood pressure ultimately decreases cerebral vascular resistance and increases blood flow (Meyer, 1968). Although creatinine may initially rise, hypertensives are also generally able to maintain adequate cardiac and renal perfusion when pressure is prudently reduced by the use of appropriate drugs (Dustan, 1974; Koch-Weser, 1974).

Inadvertent excessive precipitous blood pressure reduction may be more common because of inefficient homeostatic mechanisms, inappropriate choice of drug dosages, drug interactions, or medication errors (Koch-Weser, 1978). With care, a significant reduction of pressure can be safely achieved without major side effects in most elderly hypertensive subjects (Koch-Weser, 1978; Amery and DeSchaepdrijver, 1975; Richey and Bender, 1977).

Although there are no completed trials specifically directed at the treatment of isolated systolic hypertension, the trials showing the efficacy of lowering diastolic pressure may well apply to systolic pressure. They certainly must reflect the decrease in pressure throughout the cardiac cycle. However, treatment of diastolic hypertension succeeds more often than does treatment of isolated systolic hypertension (Richey and Bender, 1977). In the absence of controlled trials, it would appear prudent to reduce diastolic pressures only to normal values and accept a certain degree of residual systolic elevation, rather than risk decreased perfusion of vital organs.

Although recommendations abound (Chrysant et al., 1976; Harris, 1970; Fishback, 1976), there are no controlled trial data comparing the safety and efficacy of the various antihypertensive drugs. It has been found that stepwise progression from a diuretic to a beta blocker to a vasodilator is as effective and well-tolerated in the elderly as in younger hypertensive subjects (Koch-Weser, 1978).

Although extensive experience from controlled therapeutic trials is lacking, it would appear that most elderly patients can be treated with tolerable side effects if proper precautions are taken in selecting drugs on an individual response basis and if dosage is increased gradually over weeks. The low blood volume and reduced baroreceptor reflex sensitivity in the elderly may increase responsiveness to antihypertensive treatment. Appropriate dietary advice needs emphasis to ensure potassium supplementation and weight control.

While older patients may not tolerate orthostatic changes induced by antihypertensive treatment as well as younger patients, it is often possible to achieve acceptable reductions in pressure without inducing intolerable orthostatic responses or too great a reduction in diastolic pressure. The goal in isolated systolic hypertension may have to be between 140 and 160 mm Hg rather than normal values. The National High Blood Pressure Education Program Coordinating Committee recommends oral diuretics initially as they may be effective as the sole agent in controlling systolic hypertension. The addition of methyldopa or clonidine is recommended when diuretics alone are inadequate. Hydralazine may be added as a third agent since it usually does not cause reflex tachycardia in elderly patients because of the sluggish baroreceptor activity. It has been reported that beta-adrenergic blockers are not as effective in elderly patients with isolated systolic hypertension. Dietary management, such as salt and caloric restriction, may reduce dependence on drugs in some patients.

Complications such as cardiac failure, angina pectoris, or cerebrovascular disease may indicate one or another antihypertensive agent but, in general, make the indications for reducing pressure more, not less, urgent. Diabetes, which is common in the elderly, should not be a contraindication to antihypertensive treatment, including oral diuretics, dietary management, and adjustment of hypoglycemic agent dosage. Likewise, gout is not a contraindication if properly managed. Diminished renal function must be considered.

Compliance may be a problem, particularly for elderly patients with poor eyesight,

mental confusion, or difficulty in opening safety caps on medications. Absence of family reinforcement and fixed limited income may hinder adherence or keeping of appointments. The number of medications and schedule of administration should be kept as simple as possible. Where appropriate, community or public health services, senior citizens programs, or home nursing services should be utilized to assist in the endeavor.

SUMMARY

Disease, disability, and death from cardiovascular disease are major public health problems in the elderly. Among the predisposing cardiovascular risk factors, hypertension predominates since its impact does not decrease with advancing age. Unlike serum cholesterol, diabetes, and cigarette smoking, the risk associated with hypertension is undiminished in the elderly.

Except for some primitive societies, hypertension, however defined, is very common in the elderly. A disproportionate rise in systolic pressure occurs with age so that isolated systolic hypertension is particularly frequent, occurring in about 30 percent of women and 18 percent of men. The rise in pressure which is commonly observed with advancing age is not inevitable and does not occur in some unacculturated isolated populations.

Whether predominantly systolic or diastolic, labile or fixed, casually or basally elevated, hypertension in the elderly of either sex is clearly dangerous. Any degree or type of hypertension in the elderly is associated with a higher absolute risk of cardiovascular morbidity and mortality than in the young. Also, the relative risk, risk gradients, and attributable risks are just as large in the elderly as in the young and as great for women as for men.

Cardiovascular mortality is tripled in the hypertensive elderly compared to normotensives the same age. In the elderly, the relative impact is greatest for stroke and least for occlusive peripheral arterial disease, but coronary heart disease is still the most common sequela.

Isolated systolic hypertension, especially prevalent in the elderly, predisposes to cardiovascular disease in general and to stroke in particular, independent of arterial rigidity determined by pulse wave configuration. Elderly subjects with isolated systolic hypertension have been found to develop two to four times as many strokes as normotensive persons and to exhibit a two- to fivefold excess of cardiovascular mortality. There is no indication that risk is more closely linked to the diastolic than to the systolic pressure in the elderly. In the elderly with systolic hypertension, diastolic pressure is not a good indicator of risk and may actually be misleading. Factors responsible for systolic hypertension are not well defined, although decreased arterial capacitance, which results from arterial calcification and elastic tissue degeneration, undoubtedly plays a role. Many with systolic hypertension have had prior long-standing essential hypertension, and about 60 percent have had prior diastolic hypertension. Reduced baroreceptor sensitivity has been suggested as etiologic on scanty evidence.

Lability of pressure increases with age and also with the level of pressure. At a given average pressure in the elderly, the risk is unaffected by the degree of lability. It is not safe to judge the cardiovascular risk based on the lowest pressure recorded for the patient.

Because a given elevation of pressure carries the same relative risk and a higher absolute risk in the elderly than in the young, it seems pointless to accept the usual pressures encountered in the aged as "normal." There is no justification for neglect of hypertension in the elderly. Controlled trials to better determine the indications, contraindications, best drugs, side effects, benefits, and hazards of treatment of hypertension in the elderly in general, and systolic hypertension in particular, are long overdue. Hypertension is the chief remediable contributor to cardiovascular morbidity and mortality in the elderly, which is available for correction by prevention-minded physicians. Correction of hypertension in the elderly has great potential for improving their length and quality of life.

REFERENCES

Alderman, M. H. and Yano, K. 1976. How prevalence of hypertension varies as diagnostic criteria change. *Amer. J. Med. Sci.* 271: 343.

Amery, A., Berthaux, P., and Birkenhager, W. 1978. Antihypertensive therapy in patients above 60 years (4th Interim Report of the European Working Party on High Blood Presure in the Elderly). *Clin. Sci. Mol. Med.* 55: 263–270.

Amery, A. and DeSchaepdrijver, A. 1975. Should elderly hypertensives be treated? *Lancet* 1: 272.

Ashley, F. and Kannel, W. B. 1974. Relation of weight change to changes in atherogenic trends: the Framingham Study. *J. Chronic Dis.* 27: 103.

Beevers, D. G., Johnson, J., Devine, B. L., Dunn, F. G., Larkin, H., Titterington, T. M. 1978. Relation between prognosis and the blood pressure before and during treatment of hypertensive patients. *Clin. Sci. Mol. Med.* 55: 333–336.

Chrysant, S. G., Frohlich, E. D., and Papper, S. C. 1976. Why hypertension is so prevalent in the elderly—and how to treat it. *Geriatrics* 31: 101.

Darmady, E. M., Offer, J., and Woodhouse, M. A. 1973. The parameters of the aging kidney. *J. Pathol.* 109: 182–195.

Dawber, T. R., Thomas, H. E., Jr., and McNamara, P. M. Characteristics of the dicrotic notch of the arterial pulse wave in corornary heart disease. *Angiology* 24: 244.

Dustan, H. P. 1974. Atherosclerosis complicating chronic hypertension. *Circ.* 80: 871–879.

Epstein, M. and Hollenberg, N. K. 1976. Age as a determinant of renal sodium conservation in normal men. *J. Lab. Clin. Med.* 87: 411–417.

Feinberg, A. W. and Lax, H. 1958. Studies of the arterial pulse wave. *Circ.* 18: 1125.

Fishback, D. B. 1976. An approach to the treatment of hypertension in the aged. *Angiology* 27: 212.

Folkow, B., Hallback, M., Lundgren, Y., Silvertsson, R., and Weiss, L. 1973. Importance of adaptive change in vascular design for establishment of primary hypertension studied in man and in spontaneously hypertensive rats. *Circ. Res.* (Suppl. 1): 2–9.

Freis, E. D. 1972. Hypertension: a controllable disease. *Clin. Pharmacol. Ther.* 3: 627.

Guarnieri T., Filburn, C. R., Litnik, G., Roth, G. S., Lakatta, E. G. *Am. J. Physiol.* 239. Lontractile and Biochemical Correlates of β-Adrenergic Stimulation of the Aged Heart.

Hamilton, W. F. 1944. The patterns of the arterial pressure pulse. *Am. J. Physiol.* 141: 235.

Harlan, W., Oberman, A., Mitchell, R. E., Graybiel,

A. 1973. A 30-year study of blood pressure in a white male cohort. *In,* Onesti, G., Kwan, K. E., Moyer, J. H. (eds.), *Hypertension: Mechanisms in Management.* New York: Grune & Stratton.

Harris, R. 1970. *The Management of Geriatric Cardiovascular Disease.* Philadelphia: Lippincott.

Hollenberg, N. K., Adams, D. F, Solomon, H. A., Rashid, A., Abrams, H. L., and Morrill, J. P. 1974. Senescence of the renal vasculature in normal man. *Circ. Res.* 34: 309–316.

Kannel, W. B. 1974. Role of blood pressure in cardiovascular morbidity and mortality. *Prog. Cardiov. Dis.* 17: 5.

Kannel, W. B. and Castelli, W. P. 1979. Cholesterol in the prediction of atherosclerotic disease. *Ann. Intern. Med.* 90: 85–91.

Kannel, W. B. and Gordon, T. 1978. Evaluation of cardiovascular risk in the elderly: the Framingham Study. *Bull N.Y. Acad. Med.* 54: 573–591.

Kannel, W. B. and Sorlie, P. D. 1974. Hypertension in Framingham. *In,* O. Paul (ed.), *Proceedings of Second International Symposium on the Epidemiology of Hypertension, Chicago.* Symposia Specialists. Miami.

Kannel, W. B. and Sorlie, P. D. 1981. Left ventricular hypertrophy in hypertension: prognostic and pathogenetic implications. The Framingham Study. *In,* B. E. Strauer (ed.), *The Heart and Hypertension,* pp. 223–242: Springer-Verlag.

Kannel, W. B., Sorlie, P. D., and Gordon, T. 1980. Labile hypertension: a faulty concept? The Framingham Study. *Circ.* 61: 1183–1187.

Kannel, W. B., Wolf, P. A., McGee, D. L., Dawber, T. R., McNamara, P. M., and Castelli, W. P. 1981. Systolic blood pressure, arterial rigidity and risk of stroke: the Framingham Study. *JAMA* 245: 1225–1229.

Koch-Weser, J. 1974. Vasodilator drugs in the treatment of hypertension. *Arch. Inter. Med.* 133: 1017.

Koch-Weser, J. 1978. Arterial hypertension in old age. *Herz* 3: 235–244.

Maddocks, I. 1961. Possible absence of essential hypertension in two complete Pacific Island populations. *Lancet* 2: 396–399.

Master, A. M. 1982. *Normal Blood Pressure and Hypertension.* Philadelphia: Lea & Febiger.

McCarron, D. 1982. Low serum concentrations of ionized calcium in patients with hypertension. *N. Eng. J. Med.* 307: 226–228.

Meerson, F. Z. 1962. Compensatory hyperfunction of the heart and cardiac insufficiency. *Circ. Res.* 10: 256–258.

Meyer, J. S., Sawada, R., Kitamura, A., and Toyoda, M. 1968. Cerebral blood flow after control of hypertension in stroke. *Neurol.* 18: 772.

Niarchos, A. P. and Laragh, J. H. 1980. Hypertension in the elderly. *Modern Conc. Cardiov. Dis.* 49: 43–54.

Ostfeld, A. M. 1978. Elderly hypertensive patient. Epidemiologic review. *N.Y. State J. Med.* 78: 1125–1129.

Page, L. B., Damon, A., and Moellering, R. C., Jr. 1974. Antecendents of cardiovascular disease in six Solomon Island societies. *Circ.* 49: 1132.

Reisen, E., Abel, R., Modan, M., Silverberg, D. S., Eliahoulfe, Modan, B. 1978. Effect of weight loss without salt restriction on the reduction of blood pressure in overweight hypertensive patients. *N. Engl. J. Med.* 298: 106.

Richey, D. P. and Bender, A. D. 1977. Pharmacokinetic consequences of aging. *Ann. Rev. Pharmacol. Toxicol.* 17: 49.

Sackett, D. L. 1975. Studies of blood pressure in spouses. *In,* O. Paul (ed.), *Epidemiology and Control of Hypertension.* pp. 21–35. Symposia Specialists. Miami.

Severe, P. S., Osikava, B., Birch, M., and Tumbridge, R. D. C. 1977. Plasma noradrenaline in essential hypertension. *Lancet* 1: 1078–1081.

Spence, J. D., Sibbald, W. J., and Cape, R. D. 1978. Pseudohypertension in the elderly. *Clin. Sci. Mol. Med.* 55: 399–402.

Tarazi, R. C., Magrini, F., and Dustan, H. P. 1975. The role of aortic distensibility in hypertension. *In,* P. Milhriz and M. Safar (eds.), *Advances in Hypertension,* Vol. 2, p. 133. Boehringer-Ingelheim.

Thom, T. J. and Kannel, W. B. 1981. Downward trend in cardiovascular mortality. *Ann. Rev. Med.* 32: 427–434.

Veterans Administration Cooperative Study Group on Antihypertensive Agents. 1972. Effect of treatment on morbidity in hypertension. III. Influence of age, diastolic pressure and prior cardiovascular disease. *Circ.* 45: 991–1004.

31
NUTRITION AND AGING

Yves Guigoz
and
Hamish N. Munro

Department of Nutrition and Food Science
Massachusetts Institute of Technology
and
USDA Human Nutrition Research Center on Aging,
Tufts University

INTRODUCTION

Animals are distinguished from other forms of life by their need for external sources of half of the 20 primary amino acids found in proteins, for organic carbon sources of energy, and for vitamins. Dependence on supplies of these nutritional factors from the environment has been a potent force in shaping the evolution of animals from single-celled forms up to man (Munro, 1969). This role of nutrition in allowing full expression of the genetic potential of animals is recognized in relation to growth and development, but less attention has been paid to the role of nutrition in maintaining optimum tissue function in aging of the adult animal. If we accept that aging includes genetically determined components, then it is plausible to consider whether nutrition plays a part also by interacting with genetic factors in the process of senescence.

The relationship of nutrition to the aging process in man presents considerable complexities, some of which can be recognized and studied in other mammals, some of which are peculiar to the societal conditions of human populations and individuals. As pointed out elsewhere (Munro, 1981), three main themes can be recognized when we ask the question, What is the role of nutrition in the aging process of man? *First,* there is a progressive decline throughout adult life in many physiological functions, accompanied by changes in body composition and in metabolism of nutrients. There is little evidence relating nutrition of man to such functional changes, the most extensive being the role of diet in the bone salt loss of osteoporosis. *Second,* nutrition is one of the prime candidates among etiological factors in the genesis of age-related diseases such as atherosclerosis, cancer, etc. *Third,* it is well-established that the food intake of man diminishes with age, but little is directly known about the nutrient requirements of elderly human subjects and whether the reduced intakes of the elderly fall below such desirable levels. This chapter will deal with the first and third of these topics; aspects of the nutritional factors in degenerative diseases of aging are dealt with in Chapters 29 and 30.

NUTRITION AND TISSUE IMPAIRMENT

As several chapters of this book demonstrate, the body of the mammal undergoes progressive changes in composition and in function throughout adult life. Using whole-body potassium measured by ^{40}K, both cross-sectional measurements (Forbes and Reina, 1970; Parizkova et al., 1971; Cohn et al., 1980) and longitudinal studies (Forbes and Reina, 1970; Forbes, 1976; Steen et al., 1979) agree in showing a reduction in body protein content (lean body mass) over the adult life span. By combining ^{40}K measurements with *in vivo* neutron activation of N atoms, Cohn et al. (1980) were able to compare loss of N with loss of K (the latter more concentrated in muscle) and concluded that the reduction in muscle mass accounts for most of the age-related change in lean body mass, thus agreeing with autopsy measurements of individual tissues by Korenchevsky (1961) and with the much lower urinary output of the muscle-specific metabolites creatinine and 3-methylhistidine by old people (Munro, 1981). Another important tissue that loses substance during aging is bone, which results in osteoporosis. Many dietary factors (calcium, phosphorus, and vitamin D from the diet and from the skin, protein, fluoride, fiber) are implicated in determining the extent of osteoporotic bone loss. The effect of nutritional factors on bone mineral metabolism is discussed in Chapter 19. In addition to these changes in tissue mass and composition, aging leads to diminished function and metabolism in many tissues, some of them very extensive over the life span of adult men and women (see Chapter 26).

Animal Models

The most extensive evidence suggesting a relationship between long-term nutrition and aging comes from studies of animal models of aging.

Dietary Restriction and Life Span. Many studies testify to the influence of nutrition on the life span and disease pattern of experimental animals, notably rodents (for review, see Everitt and Porter, 1976; Barrows and Kokkonen, 1978; Young, 1979). In the first systematic studies, McCay (McCay et al., 1935, 1939, 1943) showed that rats whose growth was severely impaired by restricting caloric intake from weaning onwards survived significantly longer than animals fed *ad libitum*. Prolongation of life by early food restriction was confirmed by Berg and Simms (Berg, 1960; Berg and Simms, 1960, 1961; Berg et al., 1962) who also found a reduced incidence of glomerulonephritis, periarteritis, myocardial degeneration, and tumor incidence when survivors from restricted and control groups were killed at 800 days of age. Production of dietary restriction by reducing protein intake was first reported by McCay et al. (1941). The most comprehensive studies are those of Ross and Bras (Ross, 1959, 1961, 1972, 1976; Ross and Bras, 1971, 1973; Ross et al., 1970; Bras and Ross, 1964). They varied intake of protein in combination with different levels of caloric restriction and demonstrated that caloric restriction prolonged life span, while within the restricted groups, protein levels were directly correlated to life expectancy. Masoro et al. (1982) provide evidence that the prolongation of life in calorically restricted rats is not due to a decrease in metabolic rate.

Regarding the duration and timing of the dietary restriction, it is not essential to institute this process at weaning. Nolen (1972) has found that maximal prolongation of life is still achieved if restriction is begun at 12 weeks of age. On the other hand, limitation of restriction to the period between weaning and 3.5 months of age has been found to have little effect on the life expectancy of the rat (Ross, 1972; Ross and Bras, 1971; Nolen, 1972), while maximum survival is obtained by extending the restriction until 1 year of age for rats, mice, and golden hamsters (Stuchlikova et al., 1975). Severe calorie restriction initiated at middle age or later was at first reported to decrease the life span of rats (Barrows and Roeder, 1965), but later experiments initiating restriction at a some-what younger adult age (Nolen, 1972) or even at middle age (Stuchlikova et al., 1975; Friend et al., 1978; Weindruch and Walford, 1982) have prolonged life. The severity of re-striction of adult animals may affect the re-sponse (Ross, 1972), and gradual imposition of restriction is probably more effective in obtaining prolongation of life (Weindruch and Walford, 1982). Restriction of protein intake has also been shown to prolong lon-gevity of the rat when started at a young adult age (Miller and Payne, 1968) or at mid-dle age (16 months) (Barrows and Kokko-nen, 1975), but in the latter study, this only occurred by reducing protein from 24 per-cent to 12 percent but not below. Dietary re-striction initiated at an adult age, rather than restriction in early life, should permit a bet-ter model of true aging changes under die-tary conditions that are relevant to the human situation.

It is also important to note the patterns of disease that are associated with *ad libitum,* compared with restricted, feeding. Dietary restriction from weaning delayed the onset and reduced the severity of chronic ne-phrosis, periarteritis, and myocardial degen-eration and of muscular dystrophy in very old animals (for review, see Berg, 1976). Chronic restriction has also been shown to inhibit certain types of tumors, to decrease the frequency of neoplasm, and to delay the time of tumor appearance (Tannenbaum, 1959; Ross, 1976; Cheney et al., 1980; Yu et al., 1982). The pattern of tumor is also mod-ified by the dietary carbohydrate-protein ra-tio, a lower tumor incidence being observed in chronically restricted rats fed a low pro-tein diet (Ross, 1976; Ross and Bras, 1973). Recently, Weindruch and Walford (1982) and Weindruch et al. (1982) reported that in mice restricted from middle adult age, there was a decreased incidence of spontaneous lymphomas; fewer animals had multiple tu-mors, and more animals had no tumors.

Dietary Restriction and Physiological Func-tion. Fewer studies have focused on the ef-fect of restriction on physiological changes

associated with aging. Nevertheless, there is evidence to show that dietary restriction can delay many age-dependent physiological changes. A chronic reduction in food intake has been shown to retard aging of the tail tendon collagen fibers of rats (Everitt and Porter, 1976) and to modulate the age-re-lated losses in muscle mass and muscle func-tion (Herlihy and Yu, 1980; Yu, et al., 1982; McCarter et al., 1982). Kidney function has also been reported to be better retained by dietary restriction, probably due to the re-duction of protein intake, as judged by the beneficial effects of lowering only protein in-take (Tucker et al., 1976; Johnson and Bar-rows, 1980). The increase in body fat associated with aging can also be controlled by dietary restriction of total food intake (Berg, 1960; Nolen, 1972; Bertrand et al., 1980a). Changes in fat metabolism also oc-cur; dietary restriction delays the age-depen-dent loss of adipocyte responsiveness to hormones, prevents the decline in serum free fatty acid level, delays the increase in serum cholesterol, and reduces the increasing tri-glyceride level of aging rats (Cooper et al., 1977; Masoro et al., 1980; Yu et al., 1980; Bertrand et al., 1980b; Liepa et al., 1980; Voss et al., 1982).

Other aspects of tissue function in re-stricted rats have been observed. Restriction in weight gain, either through exercise or chronic food restriction, is equally effective in preventing the age-related increase in plasma insulin levels and triglyceride concen-tration observed in sedentary rats fed *ad li-bitum.* These benefits were associated with retention of normal function and morphol-ogy of the endocrine pancreas (Reaven and Reaven, 1981a, 1981b). Chronic dietary re-striction decreases brain serotonin levels (Se-gall et al., 1978) and retards the loss of striatal dopamine receptors in senescent rats (Levin et al., 1981), and the maze learning ability of old restricted rats was found to be similar to that of young *ad libitum* fed rats (Goodrick, 1984). The delayed aging process in rats chronically restricted from weaning has been suggested to be due to diminished pituitary hormone secretion (Everitt and

Porter, 1976). Much more data, however, are necessary before the effect of chronic restriction on neuroendocrine functions can be clearly described, and no study has been reported with restriction initiated at an adult age.

The immunological system is an important one that undergoes extensive changes over the life span. Immune functions decline with age, especially T-cell mediated cellular immunity and the regulatory function of T cells (Makinodan, 1977). Investigation of the interrelationship between diet, immunity, and aging has been undertaken mainly on two different mouse models: an autoimmune-prone mouse strain and normal mice (for reviews, see Good et al., 1979; Makinodan and Kay, 1980; Watson and Safranski, 1981; Weindruch and Makinodan, 1981).

In normal mice, chronic restriction from weaning delayed thymus involution and the decline in T-cell immune response to mitogens, whereas it did not affect the B-cell response to mitogen (Gerbase-Delima et al., 1975; Mann, 1978; Weindruch et al., 1979). Also, a thymus morphology similar to younger animals was reported in chronically restricted adult mice (Weindruch and Suffin, 1980). Dietary restriction from weaning delayed immunological maturation, but immunological functions were maintained at a higher level in old mice (Walford et al., 1974, 1975; Gerbase-Delima et al., 1975; Mann, 1978; Watson and Safranski, 1981).

In autoimmune disease-prone mice, dietary restriction involving either energy, protein, or amino acid restriction delayed the onset and reduced the severity of the specific autoimmune diseases, hemolytic anemia or nephropathy (Fernandes et al., 1976a, 1976b, 1978; Dubois and Strain, 1973; Gardner et al., 1977). Autoantibodies to DNA (Gardner et al., 1977; Fernandes et al., 1978; Friend et al., 1978) and brain-reactive antibodies (Nandy, 1982) were lower in the serum of restricted mice.

Thus, there is ample evidence of better maintenance of T-cell-dependent immunological responses in aging mice chronically restricted from weaning. However, recently, it has been reported that restriction initiated at an adult age can also delay the age-specific decrease in immune function (Fernandes et al., 1977; Friend et al., 1978; Mann, 1978; Weindruch et al., 1979, 1982).

Dietary Fat and Antioxidants. High dietary fat levels induce obesity (Lemonnier, 1967; Mickelson et al., 1955). The effect on longevity is related to the level of dietary fat and the age at which it is initiated. Generally, increasing the dietary fat level results in a shortened life span (French et al., 1953; Silberberg and Silberberg, 1955a, 1955b). High levels of fat resulted also in earlier appearance and increased incidence of specific types of tumors, such as skin and mammary tumors (Carroll, 1975; Clayson, 1975; Reddy et al., 1976). Others report that increasing the dietary fat level decreased cell-mediated immunity, promoted autoimmune disease, improved breeding performance of NZB mice (Fernandes et al., 1972; Fernandes et al., 1973), and accelerated the aging of collagen fibers (Hruza and Chvapil, 1962; Everitt et al., 1981). The influence of different dietary fats fed at the same level was reported by Kaunitz and Johnson (1975): tumor and disease incidences, as well as life span, were affected by different dietary fats, but not in a way related to their fatty acid composition; they concluded that the differences were due to minor constituents in the nontriglyceride fraction of the fats. Minor constituents of dietary fats and oils were also reported to have a possible effect on tumorigenesis, e.g., the effect of cyclopropene fatty acid in cottonseed oil on spontaneous mammary tumors in mice (Tinsley et al., 1982).

The influence of dietary antioxidants on aging has been studied in order to test the free radical theory proposed by Harman (1956), which suggests that age-related deleterious changes are due to lipid peroxidation by free radicals and their subsequent reactions with other cellular macromolecules (for reviews, see Chow, 1979; Leibovitz and Siegel, 1980; Harman, 1981). From the published data, life prolongation specific to antioxidants is not unequivocal: thus in some studies, the longevity of the control group was inexplicably low; in others, food intake was not measured and could have been reduced by the addition of the antioxidants to the diet. In a recent study, chronic vitamin E supplementation of diets with different degrees of fat unsaturation prolonged the life span of rats fed high levels of unsaturated fat, and reduced the incidence of malignant neoplasms. However, their food intake was significantly lower between 3 and 9 months of age (Porta et al., 1980). Until now, no pair-feeding experiments, to control for the effect of food restriction as such, have been reported. Lower production of free radicals in rats restricted in total food intake is suggested, however, by reduced lipofuscin accumulation in brain and heart (Enesco and Kruk, 1981) and by the increased efficiency of electron transport and oxidative phosphorylation by their liver mitochondria (Weindruch et al., 1980). Sun and Sun (1982) have reported increased *in vitro* peroxidation of membrane lipids taken from the brains of rats on a diet deficient in vitamin E and selenium. This effect disappeared on adding vitamin E and selenium to the diet, but not when the synthetic antioxidant butylated hydroxytoluene was added.

Other Specific Deficiencies. Restriction of specific nutrients, other than protein, can also prolong life span. Vitamin restriction lengthened the life span in rats (Kayser et al., 1972). Diets deficient in essential fatty acids prevented autoimmune glomerulonephritis and prolonged the life span of NZB mice (Hurd et al., 1981). Protection against autoimmune disease was also reported in mice fed zinc-deficient diets from weaning or from an adult age (Beach et al., 1981, 1982). However, since vitamin restriction, essential fatty acid deficiency, and zinc deprivation may result in reduced food intake, we cannot dissociate effects of this reduction from a more specific nutrient action on longevity.

Conclusion. This review of the literature on animal models of aging provides extensive and impressive evidence that restriction in total food intake or in the intake of some specific nutrients can increase the life duration of rodents, due apparently to delayed onset of chronic diseases and accompanied by better retention of many physiological functions. The time of initiation of restriction seems not to be critical and can occur in adulthood. While the comparison of *ad libitum* fed control adults and restricted adult rodents may appear to come closest to a model for human aging that can be applied after human growth has ceased, it should be pointed out that the control *ad libitum* fed rat confined to a cage bears little resemblance to the natural rat hunting for food and having to exercise. Indeed, the food-restricted rat comes nearer to the natural control, while the typical *ad libitum* fed caged rat is a model for human indolence and overindulgence, which in man also leads to premature death from obesity and related ills. In this context, the beneficial effects of exercise on the aging rat (Reaven and Reaven, 1981a, 1981b) are particularly relevant. Everitt (1982) suggests that dietary restriction prolongs life by reducing pituitary hormone secretion, since hypophysectomy produces similar effects to reduction in food intake.

NUTRIENT NEEDS OF THE ELDERLY

Various countries have developed standard intakes (allowances) of nutrients that are set high enough to protect almost all of the population against deficiency. The ninth edition of the U.S. Recommended Dietary Allowances (RDA), published in 1980, provides allowances of this kind for all essential nutrients except energy, for which *average* needs (with a range) are given. Since the nutrient needs of adults are based mainly on studies made on young adults, many of the allowances for older adults are largely estimated by extrapolation. It is thus not surprising that the RDA are restricted to two categories of adults, namely, 23 through 50 years and 51 years upwards. Since the latter category covers a lengthy period of continuous bodily change, the single allowance for each nutrient can only be a gross approximation. In addition, many older people have some chronic ailment for which the Recommended Dietary Allowances make no provision.

Energy

The energy needs and intakes of adults of various ages were examined most extensively in a cross-sectional study of male executives ranging in age from 20 to 93 years and attending the NIA Gerontology Research Center at Baltimore (McGandy et al., 1966). The energy intakes of this group declined linearly from 2700 kcal/day at age 30 to 2100 kcal at 80 years (Figure 1). This reduction was partly

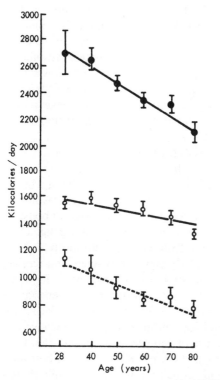

Shock (1972)
by permission of
Almqvist & Wiksell

KEY:
●————● total intake
○————○ basal expenditure
○———○ expenditure for activity
Vertical lines represent ± 1 standard error of the mean

Figure 1. Daily intake of energy in normal males.

accounted for by a decline in basal metabolism (200 kcal) which paralleled the reduction in lean body mass, but the major reduction in energy expenditures (400 kcal) was due to a larger decline with age in physical activity. This picture is confirmed by data collected on young and old men and women in Scotland (Munro, 1964).

The rate of reduction in energy intake shown in Figure 1 may not be true for subjects in their late 70s and older. Exton-Smith (1980a) describes a longitudinal study on subjects from 70 to 80 years of age; during this decade, their energy intake fell 19 percent. According to Exton-Smith, the more rapid reduction in energy intake in the later years is due to disabilities limiting the physical activity of the aging person. Studies of the energy intakes of nursing home patients, whose immobility is often considerable, confirm this. Stiedemann et al. (1978) report from Colorado that men in nursing homes averaged 1729 kcal/day and women 1330 kcal, little more than the energy needs for basal metabolism. The importance of activity is underlined by a comparison of elderly women living in French towns and in the countryside; Debry et al. (1977) found that energy intake was considerably greater for the latter group, presumably because of the greater physical demands of life in the country.

Because of the reduction in energy intake throughout adult life, nutrients present in the energy source are liable to be eaten in smaller amounts by the aging person. In the Baltimore study (McGandy et al., 1966), only slight decreases in intakes of iron, thiamine, riboflavin, and niacin, and no reduction in intake of calcium, vitamin A, and ascorbic acid, were observed as age increased. However, this group was likely to have been better able financially to select foods with a high nutrient density. Less privileged groups, such as the low income elderly reported in the Ten-State Survey (1972), had unsatisfactory intakes of some nutrients. In a survey of nursing homes in Colorado, Stiedemann et al. (1978) found that the average intakes of thiamine, calcium, and iron were below the recommended allowances. In an English study of old people living at home, Exton-Smith and Stanton (1965) found that intakes of all nutrients underwent extensive reductions during the period 70–80 years of age. It is thus important to ask whether the reduced nutrient intakes of old people bring them below the levels of adequacy. This reflects our lack of knowledge of whether the needs of the elderly for individual nutrients become less with the aging process, remain the same, or possibly even increase from factors such as malabsorption. This underlines the desirability of remaining physically active into old age, with the double advantage of maintaining energy expenditure and also physical fitness.

Protein

The FAO/WHO (1973) recommendations for the elderly allow 0.57 gram of high quality (e.g., whole egg) protein per kilogram of body weight, or 0.8 g/kg when mixed dietary protein of good quality is consumed. Direct assessment of requirements of protein is mostly based on determinations of the minimum amount of protein or essential amino acids needed to bring the subject into nitrogen (N) equilibrium. The difficulties of using N balance are discussed by Munro and Young (1981). Errors in measurement of N intake and of urinary N output will generally favor an apparent N balance that is more favorable than the true N balance. Most investigators do not directly estimate cutaneous and other N losses from the body, although these losses may vary considerably. In addition, the state of the subject affects the N balance obtained. This includes previous nutritional status; subjects who are protein depleted respond to an increase in protein intake with a larger N retention. Finally and importantly, the energy intake of the subject is a major factor in determining a positive or negative N balance (Munro, 1964, 1979). Since energy balance and energy requirements are not easily determined, the amount of protein needed to achieve N equilibrium for a given subject remains less than precise. Despite these criticisms, N balance remains

our major resource in assessing the protein needs of the elderly.

Four recent N balance studies form the basis on which to arrive at a decision on the protein allowances for people over 60 years of age. First, Cheng et al. (1978) studied young and old prisoners in Chile who received different levels of protein intake, along with an energy intake of 40 kcal/kg. Both age groups achieved N balance on 0.8 gram of protein per kilogram of body weight. However, older people have a lower caloric need, and the provision of the same caloric intake for them as for the younger subjects could lead to a more favorable energy balance for the older group, thus allowing them to retain dietary protein better and masking their greater protein needs at a more appropriate caloric intake. Second, Zanni et al. (1979) concluded from N balance studies that the RDA allowance for older men of 0.59 gram high quality protein per kilogram of body weight was adequate to sustain N equilibrium. However, their administration of a protein-free diet just prior to the critical N balance study is likely to have resulted in more favorable utilization of the dietary protein.

In contrast to this study, Uauy et al. (1978) found that the nitrogen requirement of elderly men and women receiving a high quality food protein (whole egg) was not met by 0.59 gram protein per kilogram body weight, and only marginally at 0.8 g/kg. Gersovitz et al. (1982) report a continuous 30-day study on elderly men and women who received 0.8 gram whole egg protein per kilogram body weight, with an appropriate energy intake. By days 26–30, three out of the seven men and four out of the eight women were still in negative balance. This implies that 0.8 gram egg protein per kilogram is at best marginal and probably inadequate. While these studies suggest that the elderly do not need less protein than younger subjects and may even need more to maintain N balance, they do not address the question of whether the progressive loss of lean body mass throughout adult life is affected by the level of protein intake or what the critical level may be. Using [40]K measurements, Steen et al. (1979)

found that their elderly subjects lost 1 kg lean body mass between age 70 and 75 years, equivalent to a daily negative N balance of 0.02 gram N per 70 kg man. Regimens that caused this to double would still be far below the level of detection by N balance. Nevertheless, it is improbable that high intakes of protein can prevent the loss of lean body mass in aging, since measurements showing loss of lean body mass and of tissue function with age have been made in Western countries in which the consumption of protein by adults is customarily about twice that of the estimated allowance for protein of 0.8 g/kg body weight. What we need is evidence that populations living at 0.8 g/kg or even lower levels of dietary protein show accelerated losses of lean body mass and of tissue function, information which appears to be lacking.

Vitamins

Recommended intakes of vitamins are very similar for young and old adults (RDA, 1980). In some cases where the vitamin functions directly in energy metabolism, the recommended level is slightly less for older people because of their reduced energy needs. One such vitamin is thiamine, for which the intake recommended should exceed 0.5 mg per 1000 kcal. In a recent survey of the literature on the thiamine status of the elderly, Iber et al. (1982) concluded that most North American elderly receive more than this level. The major cause of gross thiamine deficiency is chronic alcoholism, which impedes thiamine absorption from the diet. The activity in red cells of the enzyme transketolase, which requires thiamine pyrophosphate as a cofactor, can be used to screen the population for inadequacy of thiamine status, especially when used in conjunction with assays of blood or urine thiamine levels. Thus Dibble et al. (1967) found that up to 30 percent of hospitalized elderly and 17 percent of free-living elderly were thiamine deficient by this criterion, a smaller proportion of whom were severely deficient. Our own data on Boston elderly (unpublished) show that about 10 percent of the elderly on ordinary diets have mild to moderate deficiency by transketolase assay, whereas essentially no low enzyme levels were encountered in the elderly taking vitamin supplements. The frequency of mild thiamine deficiency in the elderly is confirmed by surveys in the United States and Europe (Table 1). The sensitivity of some elderly subjects to thiamine deficiency may be increased by a genetic defect in the transketolase enzyme (Blass and Gibson, 1977), which is claimed to make the enzyme more sensitive to thiamine deficiency. When body thiamine levels are reduced, as

TABLE 1. Proportion of Subnormal Values for Four Selected Vitamins Tested on the Blood of Elderly Populations in Northern Ireland and in New Jersey.

| | PERCENT OF POPULATION WITH SUBNORMAL VALUES | | | |
Population	Thiamine	Vitamin B_6	Folate	Vitamin C
Northern Ireland[a]				
Free living	13	43	48	23
Nursing home	11	63	28	56
Hospitalized	11	29	37	41
New Jersey[b]				
Free living	25	18	9	24
Nursing home	4	37	20	4

[a]From data of Baker et al. (1979).
[b]From data of Vir and Love (1979).

in alcoholism, this could result in psychiatric manifestations. More evidence for this genetic defect is needed.

Deficiency of other B vitamins in some elderly can be demonstrated by application of appropriate biochemical tests to populations in this age category, but these data can only occasionally be related to functional impairment. According to Fleming (1982), who has published an exhaustive summary of the literature on the vitamin status of the elderly, there is little evidence of deficiency of riboflavin, niacin, or vitamin B_{12} among populations of elderly. A recent review by Rosenberg et al. (1982) of the folate status of the elderly reports a number of studies in which intakes below the RDA and low blood levels were seen in a variable proportion of subjects. Low serum and red cell folate levels were also not uncommonly seen in surveys of British elderly [Department of Health and Social Security (DHSS), 1979], and this was also reported in surveys in Belfast (Vir and Love, 1979) and in New Jersey (Baker et al., 1979). In a survey of old people in Sweden (Borgstrom et al., 1979), the major deficit revealed by blood analysis was folate deficiency. Despite these findings, Rosenberg et al. (1982) concluded that in no instance were low levels of folate associated with tissue dysfunction, as indicated by the absence of megalocytic anemia. An exception is the occurrence of anemia with low serum folate levels due to alcoholism. A recent interesting concept relating aging to folate malabsorption has been proposed by Baker et al. (1978), who found that polyglutamate folate but not free folate is poorly absorbed. They conclude that folate conjugase is less active in the intestinal mucosa of the elderly, so that conjugated forms of folate become unavailable.

The recommended intake of vitamin C (ascorbic acid) for older people is 60 mg daily (RDA, 1980). For elderly men, the Baltimore study averaged more than 100 mg/day. However, much lower intakes were reported along with unacceptably low levels of ascorbic acid in the plasma of 10 percent of old men examined in the Ten-State Survey (1972). Ascorbic acid levels in the white blood cells of nursing home cases in Britain (Andrews et al. 1969) averaged half those found in young adults, and large supplements (80 mg) of ascorbic acid had to be added to the nursing home diet to restore the white cell levels to those of young people. Either the absorption of ascorbic acid or its retention in the cells is less efficient in older people. In a subsequent study (Burr et al., 1975), no clinical benefit was obtained when nursing home cases received supplementary ascorbic acid over a two-year period. In another study (Schorah et al., 1981), in which a series of hospitalized elderly were given 1 gram of vitamin C per day for two months, plasma albumin and pre-albumin levels rose. However, this may have been secondary to an increased food intake, since there was an accompanying gain in weight by the treated group.

Among fat-soluble vitamins, the most recent edition of the RDA (1980) recommends vitamin D intake for adults, who were excluded in previous editions. This emphasizes the possible role of vitamin D in the genesis of osteoporosis, as discussed in an exhaustive review (Parfitt et al., 1982); these authors conclude that lack of exposure of the elderly to sunshine, especially those who are house bound or institutionalized, can cause inadequacy of vitamin D nutriture, with osteomalacia as a clinical consequence, and probably also contributes to hip fractures from osteoporosis of the femoral bone. The recent RDA handbook also includes for the first time recommendations for intakes of vitamin K. Using a test for incompletely carboxylated prothrombin in order to identify insufficiency of vitamin K status (Blanchard et al., 1981), the presence of this abnormal prothrombin was demonstrated in the plasma of a small number of free-living elderly people in the Boston area.

Minerals

Calcium is an important mineral for the aging adult because of its involvement in osteoporosis. Heaney et al. (1982) exhaustively summarized the literature on calcium nutrition and bone health in the elderly and concluded that inadequacy of calcium intake is a major factor in causing skeletal loss of minerals. They suggested that the RDA for calcium intake for adults, especially postmenopausal women, should be raised from 800 mg to 1200–1500mg daily. This requirement is determined not only by the need for calcium but also by other dietary and physiological factors in its utilization, notably intake of protein and fiber, estrogen status in women, and mechanical loading. Aspects of calcium metabolism are discussed in more detail in Chapter 19.

Anemia due to iron deficiency is encountered in certain groups in every country and is common in many underdeveloped countries. In developed countries, adult women during their reproductive years have low stores of iron, but like men at a younger age, their iron stores start to increase after the age of 50, when the U.S. allowance for both men and women is 10 mg of iron daily (RDA, 1980). Although iron deficiency anemia is *not* common in the elderly of either sex (Cook et al., 1976), nevertheless the Ten-State Survey (1972) and a survey in Syracuse, New York (Dibble et al., 1967) both showed that the *average* iron intake of elderly women was below the recommended allowance of 10 mg, implying that some in each population must have been well below the recommended intake. A recent reassessment of the iron status of older Americans (Lynch et al., 1982) concludes that while there is little direct evidence of inadequacy of iron intake by the elderly up to age 75, the sources of dietary iron change from meat to the less available iron of cereals. The consequence in terms of bioavailability of iron has not been studied in the elderly.

Among trace elements, the most extensively investigated in the elderly has been zinc. Sandstead et al. (1982) recently reviewed the literature on zinc nutriture in the elderly. Their report emphasizes the contradictory evidence on whether plasma zinc levels change with age. However, plasma levels that are normal according to standards for young adults do not necessarily mean that tissue concentrations remain adequate in the elderly. Thus, zinc uptake by fibroblasts fell 40 percent as they aged in tissue culture (Sugarman and Munro, 1980a), while fat cells taken from rats of increasing age also showed a reduced capacity to take up zinc *in vitro* (Sugarman and Munro, 1980b). The alleged relation of zinc nutriture to taste acuity has not produced evidence that impaired taste (hypogeusia) in the elderly is often due to zinc deficiency (Greger and Geissler, 1978). Interestingly, night blindness in alcoholics is often relieved by vitamin A administration but sometimes only yields to zinc (Morrison et al., 1978), presumably because the vitamin A derivative retinol must first be oxidized to retinaldehyde by the zinc metalloenzyme alcohol dehydrogenase. It is not known whether night blindness in nonalcoholic elderly is ever due to zinc deficiency.

Smith and Hsu (1982) reviewed the scanty literature on the status of other trace elements in the elderly and concluded that plasma copper levels may decline slightly with aging. However, since copper is transported in plasma in various forms (as ceruloplasmin, bound to albumin or to amino acids) which perform different functions as copper donors to the tissues, we must await more sophisticated studies in order to evaluate the status of the elderly. In the same review, Smith and Hsu concluded that data on chromium status with aging are confusingly contradictory, but that there appears to be an age-related reduction in plasma selenium levels.

THE NUTRITIONAL STATUS OF ELDERLY POPULATIONS

Evidence from Dietary and Biochemical Studies

The determination that elderly people suffer from nutrient deficiencies should include clinical examination and biochemical indices, as well as a dietary history. Using these approaches to study representative samples of the elderly population in Great Britain, periodic government surveys (DHSS, 1979) have demonstrated malnutrition in 6 percent of men and 5 percent of women between 70 and 80 years of age, and in 12 percent of men and 8 percent of women over the age of 80. The most common deficiency states were protein-calorie malnutrition and iron deficiency, while the dietary studies showed evidence of inadequate intakes of iron, thiamine, folate, vitamin C, and vitamin D. Study of the nutritional status of old people living in the Swedish town of Dalby (Borgstrom et al., 1979) showed a reduced intake of all nutrients, with especially low intakes of energy, folate, potassium, zinc, calcium, and magnesium. The major deficiency found on blood analysis was a low level of folate.

Studies have also been made of special subgroups of the elderly. Table 1 summarizes data obtained from specific groups in New Jersey and in Belfast, Northern Ireland. The New Jersey study (Baker et al., 1979) compares the blood vitamin profiles of elderly living at home and in nursing homes with the levels found in a younger control population. Acceptable blood levels of vitamins A and E, riboflavin, biotin, and pantothenate were obtained, but the levels of vitamin C, thiamine, folate, and vitamin B_{12} were frequently lower among the free-living elderly than in young people. Among the institutionalized elderly, low levels of niacin and vitamin B_6 occurred in one-third of the subjects, while less frequent deficiencies of vitamin B_{12}, folate, thiamine, and ascorbate were observed. In Belfast (Vir and Love, 1979), nutrient intakes as well as blood levels were assessed. The largest deficits in dietary nutrients were potassium, magnesium, vitamin B_6, and vitamin D. Regarding blood levels, there was subclinical deficiency of iron, ascorbic acid, thiamine, riboflavin, vitamin B_6, and vitamin D, the data displaying wide differences between free-living and institutionalized subjects (Table 1). This underlines the greater nutritional vulnerability of certain target groups of elderly.

It is important to determine whether these biochemical deficiencies are associated with functional changes. Exton-Smith (1980b) considers that marginal nutrient deficiencies make the elderly vulnerable to acute deficiency under stress. Thus, acute infections can precipitate Wernicke's encephalopathy in elderly people on marginal thiamine intakes. Acute encephalopathy can also be precipitated by infection in old people suffering from niacin deficiency, and low folic acid levels in the blood are common in the elderly with dementia. It has also been observed that certain deficiencies in the elderly are associated with early mortality. Chope (1954) studied elderly subjects in California on two occasions separated by three to four years, and found that dietary deficiencies of vitamins A and C and niacin were associated with an excess of deaths before the second visit. In Britain, Exton-Smith (1977) reports that low vitamin C intakes by men and low serum pyridoxine levels in old women predict early mortality. These findings do not necessarily indicate a direct relationship of specific nutrients to survival, but may only mean that the physically less fit eat less well.

Factors Affecting Nutritional Status

Exton-Smith (1980a) has identified the causes of malnutrition in the elderly as belonging to primary or secondary classes. The primary causes include (1) ignorance regarding the need for a balanced diet; (2) poverty, which determines the range of foods available to the elderly; (3) social isolation, which causes loss of interest in food, which results in a higher frequency of anemia and of low leucocyte ascorbic acid levels in men living alone; (4) restriction by physical disability of the capacity to go out to purchase varied foods, as shown by a survey of nutrient intakes by such house-bound elderly (Exton-Smith, 1980a); and finally, (5) mental disorders, including confusion and depression, which make for unplanned nutrition.

Secondary causes of malnutrition include: malabsorption due to a variety of intestinal conditions, the major nutrients affected being the fat-soluble vitamins, as well as folic acid and vitamin B_{12}; alcoholism, which causes malnutrition by substituting alcohol for energy sources from ordinary dietary constituents and also affecting nutrient absorption (e.g., folic acid); and extensive use of therapeutic drugs by the elderly, some of which can interfere with nutrient utilization.

CONCLUSION

Aging is a phenomenon involving the whole of adult life, with progressive loss of tissue function and eventual accumulation of degenerative diseases. Discerning the role of nutrition in moderating these processes involves more than determining the levels of essential nutrients to be consumed; it also requires information about desirable levels of other nonessential food constituents (e.g., dietary fiber) and about the role of interactions between various nutrients. We are only at the beginning of understanding how long-term nutritional habits, in combination with other life-style factors such as regular exercise, may conspire to minimize age-related loss of tissue function and to limit the development of chronic ailments. Nevertheless, evidence from animal studies and from the role of nutritional factors in one major age-related degenerative condition—osteoporosis—shows that nutrition has a part to play in the maintenance of structure and function. In this context, animal models of aging should be evaluated for relevance.

The second aspect of nutrition and aging is the practical problem of providing adequate levels of nutrients for those who are already old. Here also, the objective should be to preserve function, but there is little solid evidence on which to base allowances for nutrients in successive decades of later life. Since intakes of many nutrients decline with the diminishing appetite of increasing age, we must ask whether a significant number of the elderly consume less than their needs of essential nutrients. In the context of determining the nutritional status of elderly people, an unanswered but important question is whether standards for plasma nutrient concentrations appropriate for the young are also relevant for the elderly. Our own preliminary observations (Sugarman and Munro, 1980a, 1980b) suggest that the capacity of aging cells to concentrate nutrients from the environment may be considerably impaired. This suggests that we must examine the relationship of tissue to plasma nutrient concentrations in elderly as compared to young subjects in order to evaluate the significance of plasma levels of nutrients. In the last analysis, we need well-authenticated dietary allowances for elderly people, divided into decades of age. The levels chosen must have relevance to benefits for maintenance of tissue function and performance, and not just represent intakes that normalize biochemical values of nutrients in body fluids.

REFERENCES

Andrews, J., Letcher, M., and Brook, M. 1969. Vitamin C supplementation in the elderly: 17 month trial in an old persons' home. *Brit. Med. J.* 2: 416.

Baker, H., Frank, O., Thind, S., Jaslow, J. P., and Louria, D. B. 1979. Vitamin profiles in elderly persons living at home or in nursing homes versus profiles in healthy young subjects. *J. Am. Geriatr. Soc.* 27: 444–450.

Baker, H., Jaslow, S. P., and Frank O. 1978. Severe impairment of dietary folate utilization in the elderly. *J. Am. Geriatr. Soc.* 26: 218–221.

Barrows, C. H. and Kokkonen, G. 1975. Protein synthesis, development, growth and lifespan. *Growth* 39: 525–533.

Barrows, C. H. and Kokkonen, G. C. 1978. Diet and life extension in animal model systems. *Age* 1: 131–143.

Barrows, C. H. and Roeder, L. M. 1965. The effect of reduced dietary intake on enzymatic activities and lifespan of rats. *J. Gerontol.* 20: 69–71.

Beach, R. S., Gershwin, M. E., and Hurley, L. S. 1981. Nutritional factors and autoimmunity. I. Immunology of zinc deprivation in New Zealand mice. *J. Immunol.* 126: 1999–2006.

Beach, R. S., Gershwin, M. E., and Hurley, L. S. 1982. Nutritional factors and autoimmunity. II. Prolongation of survival in zinc-deprived NZB/W mice. *J. Immunol.* 128: 308–313.

Berg, B. N. 1960. Nutrition and longevity in the rat. I. Food intake in relation to size, health and longevity. *J. Nutr.* 71: 242–254.

Berg, B. N. 1976. Pathology and aging. *In,* Everitt, A. V. and Burgess, J. A., (eds.), *Hypothalamus, Pituitary and Aging* pp. 43–67. Springfield, Ill.: Charles C. Thomas.

Berg, B. and Simms, H. S. 1960. Nutrition and longevity in the rat. II. Longevity and onset of disease with different levels of food intake. *J. Nutr.* 71: 255–263.

Berg, B. N. and Simms, H. S. 1961. Nutrition and longevity in the rat. III. Food restriction beyond 800 days. *J. Nutr.* 74: 23–37.

Berg, B. N., Wolf, A., and Simms, H. S. 1962. Nutrition and longevity in the rat. IV. Food restriction and radiculoneuropathy of aging rats. *J. Nutr.* 77: 439–447.

Bertrand, H. A., Lynd, F. T., Masoro, E. J., and Yu, B. D. 1980a. Changes in adipose mass and cellularity through the adult life of rats fed *ad libitum* or a life-prolonging restricted diet. *J. Gerontol.* 35: 827–835.

Bertrand, H. A., Masoro, E. J., and Yu, B. P. 1980b. Maintenance of glucagon-promoted lipolysis in adipocytes by food restriction. *Endocrinol.* 107: 591–595.

Blanchard, R. A., Furie, B. C., Jorgensen, M., Kruger, S. F., and Furie, N. 1981. Acquired vitamin K-dependent carboxylation deficiency in acquired liver disease. *New Engl. J. Med.* 305: 242–248.

Blass, J. P. and Gibson, G. E. 1977. Abnormality of a thiamine-requiring enzyme in patients with Wernicke-Korsakoff syndrome. *N. Engl. J. Med.* 297: 1367–70.

Borgstrom, B., Norden, A., Akesson, B., Abdullah, M., and Jagerstrom, M. 1979. Nutrition and old age. *Scand. J. Gastroenterol.* 14(suppl.), 52.

Bras, G. and Ross, M. H. 1964. Kidney disease and nutrition in the rat. *Toxicol. Appl. Pharmacol.* 6: 247–262.

Burr, M. L., Hurley, R. J., and Sweetman, P. M. 1975. Vitamin C supplementation of old people with low blood levels. *Gerontol. Clin.* 17: 236.

Carroll, K. K. 1975. Experimental evidence of dietary factors and hormone dependent cancers. *Cancer Res.* 35: 3374–3383.

Cheney, K. E., Liu, R. K., Smith, G. S., Leung, R. E., Mickey, M. R., and Walford, R. L. 1980. Survival and disease patterns in C57BL/6 mice subjected to undernutrition. *Exp. Gerontol.* 15: 237–258.

Cheng, A. H. R., Gomez, A., Gergan, J. G., Lee, T. C., Monckeberg, F., and Chichester, C. O. 1978. Comparative nitrogen balance study between young and aged adults using three levels of protein intake from a combination of wheat-soy-milk-mixture. *Am. J. Clin. Nutr.* 31: 12–22.

Chow, C. K. 1979. Nutritional influence on cellular antioxidant defense systems. *Am. J. Clin. Nutr.* 32: 1066–1081.

Clayson, D. B. 1975. Nutrition and experimental carcinogenesis: a review. *Cancer Res.* 35: 3292–3300.

Cohn, S. H., Vartsky, D., Yasumura, S., Sawitsky, A., Zanzi, I., Vaswani, A., and Ellis, K. J. 1980. Compartmental body composition based on total body nitrogen, potassium and calcium. *Am. J. Physiol.* 239: E524–530.

Cook, J. D., Finch, C. A., and Smith, N. J. 1976. Evaluation of the iron status of a population. *Blood* 48: 449–455.

Cooper, B., Weinblatt, F., and Gregerman, R. I. 1977. Enhanced activity of hormone-sensitive adenylated cyclase during dietary restriction in the rat. *J. Clin. Invest.* 39: 467–474.

Debry, G., Bleyer, R., and Martin, J. M. 1977. Nutrition of the elderly. *J. Human Nutr.* 31: 195–204.

Department of Health and Social Security (DHSS). 1979. A nutrition survey of the elderly. *Rep. Public Health Soc. Subj. No. 16,* London: H. M. Stationery Office.

Dibble, M. V., Brin, M., Thiele, V. F., Peel, A., Chen, N., and McMullen, E. 1967. Evaluation of the nutritional status of elderly subjects with a comparison between fall and spring. *J. Am. Geriatr. Soc.* 15: 1031–1061.

Dubois, E. L. and Strain, L. 1973. Effect of diet on survival and nephropathy of NZB/NZW hybrid mice. *Biochem. Med.* 7: 336–347.

Enesco, E. H. and Kruk, P. 1981. Dietary restriction reduces fluorescent age pigment accumulation in mice. *Exp. Gerontol.* 16: 357–361.

Everitt, A. V. 1982. Nutrition and the hypothalamic-pituitary influence on aging. *In,* G. B. Moment (ed.), *Nutritional Approaches to Aging Research,* pp. 245–256. Boca Raton, Fla.: CRC Press.

Everitt, A. V. and Porter, B. 1976. Nutrition and aging. *In,* A. V. Everitt and J. A. Burgess (eds.), *Hypothalamus, Pituitary and Aging* pp. 570–613. Springfield, Ill.: Charles C. Thomas.

Everitt, A. V., Porter, B. D., and Steele, M. 1981. Dietary, caging and temperature factors in the aging of collagen fibers in rat-tail tendon. *Gerontol.* 27: 37–41.

Exton-Smith, A. N. 1980a. Nutritional status: diagnosis and prevention of malnutrition. *In,* A. N. Exton-Smith and F. I. Caird (eds.), *Metabolic and Nutritional Disorders in the Elderly,* pp. 66–76. Bristol: John Wright and Sons.

Exton-Smith, A. N. 1980b. Vitamins. *In,* A. N. Exton-Smith and F. I. Caird (eds.), *Metabolic and Nutritional Disorders in the Elderly,* pp. 26–38. Bristol: John Wright and Sons.

Exton-Smith, A. N. and Stanton, B. R. 1965. *Report of an Investigation into the Diets of Elderly Women Living Alone.* London: King Edward's Hospital Fund.

FAO/WHO Ad Hoc Expert Committee. 1973. *Energy and Protein Requirements: Report,* World Health Organization Technical Report Series No. 522. Geneva: WHO.

Fernandes, G., Friend, P., and Yunis, E. J. 1977. Influence of calorie restriction on autoimmune disease. *Fed. Proc.* 36: 1313.

Fernandes, G., Friend, P., Yunis, E. J., and Good, R. A. 1978. Influence of dietary restriction on immunological function and renal disease in (NZB × NZW)F mice. *Proc. Natl. Acad. Sci. USA* 75: 1500–1504.

Fernandes, G., Yunis, E. J., and Good, R. A. 1976a.

Influence of protein restriction on immune functions in NZB Mice. *J. Immunol.* 116: 782–790.

Fernandes, G., Yunis, E. J., and Good, R. A. 1976b. Influence of diet on survival of mice. *Proc. Natl. Acad. Sci. USA* 73: 1279–1283.

Fernandes, G., Yunis, E. J., Jose, D. G., and Good, R. A. 1973. Dietary influence on antinuclear antibodies and cell-mediated immunity in NZB mice. *Int. J. Allergy* 44: 770–782.

Fernandes, G., Yunis, E. R., Smith, J., and Good, R. A. 1972. Dietary influence on breeding behavior, hemolytic anemia and longevity in NZB mice. *Proc. Soc. Exp. Biol. Med.* 139: 1189–1196.

Fleming, B. 1982. The vitamin status and requirements of the elderly. *In*, G. B. Moment (ed.), *Nutritional Approaches to Aging Research*, pp. 83–117. Boca Raton, Fla.: CRC Press.

Forbes, G. B. 1976. The adult decline in lean body mass. *Hum. Biol.* 48: 161–173.

Forbes, G. B. and Reina, J. C. 1970. Adult lean body mass declines with age: some longitudinal observations. *Metabolism* 19: 653–663.

French, C. E., Ingram, R. H., Unram, J. A., Barron, G. P., and Swift, R. W. 1953. The influence of dietary fat and carbohydrate on growth and longevity in rats. *J. Nutr.* 51: 329–339.

Friend, P. S., Fernandes, G., Good, R. A., Michael, A. F., and Yunis, E. J. 1978. Dietary restrictions early and late. Effects on nephropathy of the NZB and NZW mouse. *Lab. Invest.* 38: 629–632.

Gardner, M. B., Ihle, J. N., Pillarisetty, R. J., Talal, N., Dubois, E. L., and Levy, J. A. 1977. Type C virus expression and host response in diet-cured NZB/NZW mice. *Nature* 268: 341–344.

Gerbase-Delima, M., Liu, R. K., Cheney, K. E., Mickey, M. R., and Walford, R. L. 1975. Immune function and survival in a long-lived mouse strain subjected to undernutrition. *Gerontologia* 21: 184–202.

Gersovitz, M., Motil, K., Munro, H. N., Scrimshaw, N. S., and Young, V. R. 1982. Human protein requirements: assessment of the adequacy of the current Recommended Dietary Allowance for dietary protein in elderly men and women. *Am. J. Clin. Nutr.* 35: 6–14.

Good, R. A., Fernandes, G., and West A. 1979. Nutrition, immunologic aging and disease. *In*, S. K. Singhal, N. R. Sinclair, and R. S. Stiller (eds.), *Aging and Immunity* pp. 141–163. New York: Elsevier/North Holland.

Goodrick, C. L. 1984. Effect of life-long restricted feeding on complex maze performance in rats. *Age* 7, 1–2.

Greger, J. L. and Geissler, A. H. 1978. Effect of zinc supplementation on taste acuity of the aged. *Am. J. Clin. Nutr.* 31: 633–637.

Harman, D. 1956. Aging: a theory based on free radical and radiation chemistry. *J. Gerontol.* 11: 298–300.

Harman, D. 1981. The aging process. *Proc. Natl. Acad. Sci. USA*, 78: 7124–7128.

Heaney, R. P., Gallagher, J. C., Johnston, C. C., Neer, R., Parfitt, A. M., and Whedon, G. D. 1982. Calcium nutrition and bone health in the elderly. *Am. J. Clin. Nutr.* 36: 987–1013.

Herlihy, J. T. and Yu, B. P. 1980. Dietary manipulation of age-related decline in vascular smooth muscle function. *Am. J. Physiol.* 238: H652–H655.

Hruza, Z. and Chvapil, M. 1962. Collagen characteristics in the skin, tail tendon and lungs in experimental atherosclerosis in the rat. *Physiol. Bohemoslav.* 11: 423–429.

Hurd, E. R., Johnston, J. M., Okita, J. R., MacDonald, P. C., Ziff, M., and Gilliam, J. N. 1981. Prevention of glomerulonephritis and prolonged survival in New Zealand black/New Zealand white F_1 hybrid mice fed on essential fatty acid-deficient diet. *J. Clin. Invest.* 67: 476–485.

Iber, F. L., Blass, J. P., Brin, M., and Leevy, C. M. 1982. Thiamine in the elderly—relation to alcoholism and to neurological degenerative disease. *Am. J. Clin. Nutr.* 36: 1067.

Johnson, J. E. and Barrow, C. H., Jr. 1980. Effects of age and dietary restrictions on the kidney glomeruli of mice: observations by scanning electron microscopy. *Anatom. Rec.* 196: 145–151.

Kaunitz, H. and Johnson, R. E. 1975. Influence of dietary fats on disease and longevity. *In*, A. Chavez, H. Bourges, and S. Basta (eds.), *Proceedings of the Ninth International Congress on Nutrition*, pp. 362–373. Basel: Karger.

Kayser, J., Neumann, J., and Lavolley, J. 1972. Effets favorables exercés sur la longévité du rat Wistar par divers types de restrictions vitaminiques. *C. R. Acad. Sci. Paris, Serie D* 274: 3593–3596.

Korenchevsky, V. 1961. *Physiological and Pathological Aging*. New York: Hafner.

Leibovitz, B. E. and Siegel, B. V. 1980. Aspects of free radical reactions in biological systems: aging. *J. Gerontol.* 35: 45–56.

Lemmonier, D. 1967. Obesite par des regimés hyperlipidiques chez le rat et le souris. *Nutr. Dieta.* 9: 27–42.

Levin, P., Janda, J. K., Joseph, J. A., Ingram, D. K., and Roth, G. S. 1981. Dietary restriction retards the age-associated loss of rat striatal dopaminergic receptors. *Science* 214: 561–562.

Liepa, G. U., Masoro, E. J., Bertrand, H. A., and Yu, B. P. 1980. Food restriction as a modulation of age-related changes in serum lipids. *Am. J. Physiol.* 238: E253–E257.

Lynch, S. R., Finch, C. A., Monsen, E. R., and Cook, J. D. 1982. Iron status of elderly Americans. *Am. J. Clin. Nutr.* 35: (suppl.).

Makinodan, T. 1977. Immunity and aging. *In*, C. E. Finch and L. Hayflick (eds.), *Handbook of the Biology of Aging* pp. 379–408. New York: Van Nostrand Reinhold.

Makinodan, T. and Kay, M. M. B. 1980. Age influence on the immune system. *In*, H. Kunkel and F. Dixon (eds.), *Advances in Immunology*, Vol. 29, pp. 287–330. New York: Academic Press.

Mann, P. L. 1978. The effect of various dietary restricted regimes on some immunological parameters of mice. *Growth* 42: 87–103.

Masoro, E. J., Yu, B. P., and Bertrand, H. A. 1982. Action of food restriction in delaying the aging process. *Proc. Natl. Acad. Sci. USA* 79: 4239–4241.

Masoro, E. J., Yu, B. P., Bertrand, H. A., and Lynd, F. T. 1980. Nutritional probe of the aging process. *Fed. Proc.* 39: 3178–3182.

McCarter, R. J. M., Masoro, E. J., and Yu, B. P. 1981. Rat muscle structure and metabolism in relation to age and food intake. *Am. J. Physiol.* 242: R89–R93.

McCay, C. M., Crowell, M. F., and Maynard, L. A. 1935. The effect of retarded growth upon the length of the life-span and upon ultimate body size. *J. Nutr.* 10: 63–79.

McCay, C. M., Maynard, L. H., Sperling, G., and Barnes, L. L. 1939. Retarded growth, life-span, ultimate body size and age changes in the albino rat after feeding diets restricted in calories. *J. Nutr.* 18: 1–13.

McCay, C. M., Maynard, L. A., Sperling, G., and Osgood, H. S. 1941. Nutritional requirements during the latter half of life. *J. Nutr.* 21: 45–60.

McCay, C. M., Sperling, G., and Barnes, L. L. 1943. Growth, ageing, chronic diseases and life-span in rats. *Arch. Biochem.* 2: 469–479.

McGandy, R. B., Barrows, C. H., Spanias, A., Meredith, A., Stone, J. L., and Norris, A. H. 1966. Nutrient intakes and energy expenditure in men of different ages. *J. Gerontol.* 21: 551–558.

Mickelson, O., Takahashi, S., and Craig, S. 1955. Experimental obesity. I. Production of obesity in rats by feeding high fat diets. *J. Nutr.* 57: 541–554.

Miller, D. S. and Payne, P. R. 1968. Longevity and protein intake. *Exp. Gerontol.* 3: 231–234.

Morrison, S. A., Russell, R. M., Carney, E. A., and Oaks, E. V. 1978. Zinc deficiency: a cause of abnormal dark adaptation in cirrhotics. *Am. J. Clin. Nutr.* 31: 276–281.

Munro, H. N. 1964. An introduction to nutritional aspects of protein metabolism. *In,* H. N. Munro, and J. B. Allison (eds.), *Mammalian Protein Metabolism* Vol. 2, pp. 3–38. New York: Academic Press.

Munro, H. N. 1969. An introduction to protein metabolism during the evolution and development of mammals. *In,* H. N. Munro (ed.), *Mammalian Protein Metabolism,* Vol. 3, pp. 3–19. New York: Academic Press.

Munro, H. N. (1979) Energy intake and nitrogen metabolism. *In,* J. M. Kinney, E. R. R. Buskirk, and H. N. Munro (eds.), *Assessment of Energy Metabolism in Health and Disease, Ross Conference on Medical Research, pp. 105–110. Columbus Ohio.*

Munro, H. N. 1981. Nutrition and aging. *Brit. Med. Bull.* 37: 83–88.

Munro, H. N. and Young, V. R. 1981. New approaches to the assessment of protein status in man. *In,* A. N.

Howard and I. M. Baird, (eds.), *Recent Advances in Clinical Nutrition,* pp. 33–41. London: Libby.

Nandy, K. 1982. Effects of controlled dietary restriction on brain reactive antibodies in sera of aging mice. *Mech. Age. Dev.* 18: 97–102.

Nolen, G. A. 1972. Effect of various restricted dietary regimens on the growth, health and longevity of albino rats. *J. Nutr.* 102: 1477–1494.

Parfitt, A. M., Gallagher, J. C., Heaney, R. P., Johnston, C. C., Neer, R., and Whedon, G. D. 1982. Vitamin D and bone health in the elderly. *Am. J. Clin. Nutr.* 36: 1014–1031.

Parizkova, J., Eiselt, E., Sprynorova, S., and Wachtlova, M. 1971. Body composition, aerobic capacity and density of muscle capillaries in young and old men. *J. Appl. Physiol.* 31: 323–325.

Porta, E. A., Joun, N. S., and Nitta, R. T. 1980. Effects of the type of dietary fat at two levels of vitamin E in Wistar male rats during development and aging. I. Lifespan, serum biochemical parameters and pathological changes. *Mech. Age. Dev.* 13: 1–39.

Reaven, E. P. and Reaven, G. M. 1981a. Structure and function changes in the endocrine pancreas of aging rats with reference to the modulating effects of exercise and calorie restriction. *J. Clin. Invest.* 68: 75–84.

Reaven, G. M. and Reaven, E. P. 1981b. Prevention of age-related hypertriglyceridemia by calorie restriction and exercise training in the rat. *Metabolism* 30: 982–986.

Recommended Dietary Allowances, 9th ed. 1980. Washington, D.C.: National Academy of Sciences.

Reddy, B. S., Narisawa, T., Vakusich, D., Weisburger, J. H., and Wynder, E. 1976. Effect of quality and quantity of dietary fat and dimethyl-hydrazine in colon carcinogenesis in rats. *Proc. Soc. Exp. Biol. Med.* 151: 237–239.

Rosenberg, I. H., Cooper, B., Halsted, C., and Lindenbaum, J. 1982. Dietary intake of folate in the elderly. *Am. J. Clin. Nutr.* 36: 1060–1067.

Ross, M. H. 1959. Protein, calories and life expectancy. *Fed. Proc.* 18: 1190–1207.

Ross, M. H. 1961. Length of life and nutrition in the rat. *J. Nutr.* 75: 197–210.

Ross, M. H. 1972. Length of life and caloric intake. *Am. J. Clin. Nutr.* 25: 834–838.

Ross, M. H. 1976. Nutrition and longevity in experimental animals. *In,* M. Winick (ed.), *Nutrition and Aging,* pp. 23–41. New York: John Wiley & Sons.

Ross, M. H. and Bras, G. 1971. Lasting influence of early caloric restriction on prevalence of neoplasms in the rat. *J. Nat. Cancer Inst.* 47: 1095–1113.

Ross, M. H. and Bras, G. 1973. Influence of protein under- and over-nutrition on spontaneous tumor prevalence in the rat. *J. Nutr.* 103: 944–963.

Ross, M. H., Bras, G., and Ragbeer, M. S. 1970. Influence of protein and caloric intake upon spontaneous tumor incidence of the anterior pituitary gland of the rat. *J. Nutr.* 100: 177–189.

Sandstead, H. H., Henriksen, L. K., Greger, J. L., Prasad, A. S., and Good, R. A. 1982. Zinc nutrition in the elderly *Am. J. Clin. Nutr.* 36: 1046–1059.

Schorah, C. J., Romey, W. P., Brooks, G. H., Robertshaw, A. M., Young, G. A., Talukder, R., and Kelly, J. F. 1981. The effect of vitamin C supplements on body weight, serum proteins, and general health of an elderly population. *Am. J. Clin. Nutr.* 34: 871–876.

Segall, P. E., Ooka, H., Rose, K., And Timiras, P. S. 1978. Neural and endocrine development after chronic tryptophan deficiency in rats. I. Brain monamine and pituitary responses. *Mech. Age. Dev.* 7: 1–7.

Silberberg, R. and Silberberg, M. 1955a. Lifespan of mice fed high fat diet at various ages. *Can. J. Biochem. Physiol.* 33: 167–173.

Silberberg, M. and Silberberg, R. 1955b. Diet and lifespan. *Physiol. Rev.* 35: 347–362.

Smith, J. C., Jr. and Hsu, J. M. 1982. Trace elements in aging research: emphasis on zinc, copper, chromium and selenium. *In,* G. B. Moment (ed.), *Nutritional Approaches to Aging Research,* pp. 119–134. Boca Raton, Fla.: CRC Press.

Steen, G. B., Isaksson, B., and Svanberg, A. 1979. Body composition at 70 and 75 years of age: a longitudinal population study. *J. Clin. Exp. Gerontol.* 1: 185–200.

Stiedemann, M., Jansen, C., and Harrill, I. 1978. Nutritional status of elderly men and women. *J. Am. Diet. Assoc.* 73: 132–139.

Stuchlikova, E., Juricova-Horakova, M., and Deyl, Z. 1975. New aspects of dietary effects of life prolongation in rodents. What is the role of obesity in aging? *Exp. Gerontol.* 10: 141–144.

Sugarman, B. and Munro, H. N. 1980a. Altered ^{64}Zn chloride accumulation by aged rats' adipocytes *in vitro. J. Nutr.* 110: 2317–2320.

Sugarman, B. and Munro, H. N. 1980b. Altered accumulation of zinc by aging human fibroblasts in culture. *Life Sci.* 26: 915–920.

Sun, A. Y. and Sun, G. Y. 1982. Dietary antioxidants and aging on membrane functions. *In,* G. B. Moment (ed.), *Nutritional Approaches to Aging Research,* pp. 135–156. Boca Raton, Fla.: CRC Press.

Tannenbaum, A. 1959. Nutrition and cancer. *In,* F. Homberger (ed.), *The Physiopathology of Cancer,* 2nd ed., pp. 517–562. New York: Holber-Harper.

Ten-State Survey: Highlights. 1972. DHEW publication No. (HSM) 72-8134. Washington D.C.: U.S. Department of Health, Education and Welfare.

Tinsley, I. J., Wilson, G., and Lowry, R. R. 1982. Tissue fatty acid changes and tumor incidence in CZH mice ingesting cottonseed oil. *Lipids* 17: 115–117.

Tucker, S. M., Mason, R. L., and Beauchene, R. E. 1976. Influence of diet and feed restriction on kidney function of aging male rats. *J. Gerontol.* 31: 264–270.

Uauy, R., Scrimshaw, N. S., and Young, V. R. 1978. Human protein requirements: nitrogen balance response to graded levels of egg protein in elderly men and women. *Am. J. Clin. Nutr.* 31: 779–785.

Vir, S. C. and Love, A. H. G. 1979. Nutritional status of institutionalized and non-institutionalized aged in Belfast, Northern Ireland. *Am. J. Clin. Nutr.* 32: 1934–1947.

Voss, K. H., Masoro, E. J., and Anderson, W. 1982. Modulation of age-related loss of glucagon-promoted lipolysis by food restriction. *Mech. Age. Dev.* 18: 135–149.

Walford, R. L., Liu, R. K., Gerbase-Delima, M., Mathies, M., and Smith, G. S. 1974. Long term dietary restriction and immune function in mice: response to sheep red blood cells and to mitogenic agents. *Mech. Age. Dev.* 2: 447–451.

Walford, R. L., Liu, R. K., Mathies, M., Lipps, L. and Konen, T. 1975. Influence of caloric restriction on immune function: relevance for an immunologic theory of aging. *Proceedings of the 9th International Congress on Nutrition* 1: 374–381.

Watson, R. R. and Safranski, D. V. 1981. Dietary restrictions and immune responses in the aged. *In,* M. M. B. Kay and T. Makinodan (eds.), *CRC Handbook of Immunology in Aging,* pp. 125–139. Boca Raton, Fla.: CRC Press.

Weindruch, R. H., Cheung, M. K., Verity, M. A., and Walford, R. L. 1980. Modification of mitochondrial respiration by aging and dietary restriction. *Mech. Age. Dev.* 12: 375–397.

Weindruch, R., Gottesman, S. R., and Walford, R. L. 1982. Modification of age-related immune decline in mice dietarily restricted from or after mid-adulthood. *Proc. Natl. Acad. Sci. USA* 79: 898–902.

Weindruch, R. H., Kristie, J. A., Cheney, K. E., and Walford, R. L. 1979. Influence of controlled dietary restriction on immunologic function and aging. *Fed. Proc.* 38: 2007–2106.

Weindruch, R. H. and Makinodan, T. (1981). Dietary restriction and its effects on immunity and aging. *In,* M. Salvey and P. L. White (eds.) *Nutrition in the 1980's: Constraints on Our Knowledge.* pp. 319–325 Alan Liss, New York.

Weindruch, R. H. and Suffin, S. C. 1980. Quantitative histologic effects on mouse thymus of controlled dietary restriction. *J. Gerontol.* 35: 525–531.

Weindruch, R. and Walford, R. L. 1982. Dietary restriction in mice beginning at 1 year of age: effect on life-span and spontaneous cancer incidence. *Science* 215: 1415–1418.

Young, V. R. 1979. Diet as a modulator of aging and longevity. *Fed. Proc.* 38: 1994–2000.

Yu, B. P., Bertrand, H. A., and Masoro, E. J. 1980. Nutrition-aging influence of catecholamine-promoted lipolysis. *Metabolism* 29: 438–444.

Yu, B. P., Masoro, E. J., Murata, I., Bertrand, H. A., and Lynd, F. T. 1982. Lifespan study of SPF Fischer 344 male rats fed *ad libitum* on restricted diets: longevity, growth, lean body mass and disease. *J. Gerontol.* 37: 130–141.

Zanni, E., Calloway, D. H., and Zezulka, A. Y. 1979. Protein requirements of elderly men. *J. Nutr.* 109: 513–524.

32
HEALTH MAINTENANCE AND LONGEVITY: EXERCISE

Elsworth R. Buskirk

Laboratory for Human Performance Research
Intercollege Research Programs
and
College of Health, Physical Education and Recreation
The Pennsylvania State University

INTRODUCTION

In this chapter, focus is on those physiological responses that are altered when elderly subjects participate in exercise on an acute or chronic basis. Hopefully, the information is presented in such a way so as to complement the chapter by Shock (1977) that appeared in the first edition of this *Handbook*. Particular attention has been given to literature published subsequent to that time. An exception has been made for some relevant areas of research not previously covered. A variety of pertinent reviews have appeared in recent years, and the interested reader would be well advised to peruse them. An alphabetical listing follows: Bassey (1978); Bolduan and Horvath (1981); Bruce (1981); Cantu (1982); Fries and Crapo (1981); Goldman and Rockstein (1975); Harris and Frankel (1977); Haynes and Feinleib (1980); Hodgson and Buskirk (1977, 1981); Horvath (1981); Masaro (1981); Ostfeld and Gibson (1972); Polednak (1979); President's Council on Physical Fitness and Sports (1981); Rockstein and Sussman (1979); Serfass (1980); Shephard (1978, 1982); Smith and Serfass

(1981); Taylor and Montoye (1972); and Weisfeldt (1980a).

Shock (1982), who has spent a considerable portion of his career thinking about aging and its effects, had the following to say about exercise and aging:

> In general the greatest age decrements are found in performances such as maximum work output that require the coordinated responses of a number of different organ systems. The age decrement is much greater in the maximum work output that can be achieved by turning a crank than is found in measurements of static strength of the same muscles involved in turning the crank. The neuromuscular responses involved in producing an integrated response are less effective in the old than in the young subjects.
>
> With increasing age, the time required to readjust experimentally induced displacements in physiological characteristics is increased.

He goes on to say that "a primary factor in aging is a reduced sensitivity to control mechanisms"; i.e., reaction time is increased.

From data collected in the Baltimore Longitudinal Study of Aging, Shock drew the following conclusions:

The calories required for each subject to maintain his activities were calculated in accordance with his activity records. With the experimentally determined basal oxygen uptake, it was possible to show that the age decrement in total dietary caloric intake could be accounted for by the age-associated decrease in basal metabolism plus the decline in physical activity and the calories required for the activity.

There are several practical problems that influence a discussion of exercise and aging. For example, there are few longitudinal data collected from individuals or groups studied over many years. The relatively sedentary nature of most older people makes comparison with younger more active people speculative because subtle cross-sectional differences in physical activity habitus no doubt exist. Disease processes may go unrecognized, and the physiological changes associated with disease may be inadvertently interpreted as changes due to aging. Finally, it is difficult to separate the effects of disuse from those of aging, but many investigators are making the effort as the subsequent discussion will demonstrate.

HABITUAL ACTIVITY

Since the population of elderly citizens in the United States is increasing, efforts are needed to keep them as physically fit as possible so that they can retain greater independence. Nevertheless, at least 45 percent of U.S. adults do not engage in significant non-job-related physical activity, according to a physical fitness survey conducted for the President's Council on Physical Fitness and Sports (1973). Incidentally, about 71 percent of the interviewed people over age 60 thought that they engaged in enough exercise. Serfass (1980) has cited evidence provided by Conrad and by McAvoy that older people underestimate their exercise abilities. Sidney and Shephard (1977a) arrived at a similar conclusion. Thus, an educational effort would appear necessary to counter the rather negative perception among many elderly people of the desirability of physical activity.

Physical activity in the elderly can be low for a variety of reasons including: disability, disease, lack of knowledge about exercise, lack of knowledge about conditioning principles, lack of knowledge of availability of facilities, lack of facilities, inclement weather, lack of exercise leadership, and lack of companionship for exercise. In a study of activity patterns in relation to aging, Montoye (1975) found that in Tecumseh, Michigan, there was a small but significant decrease in hours worked per week and in the strenuousness of the work that was undertaken. It was concluded that these small changes occurred because many occupations were relatively sedentary so that little change could take place with aging for the person tended to stay on the same job. There was also a decrease in all leisure activities with age, except walking and gardening, with participation in the more strenuous activities declining the most.

The total energy turnover is known to be reduced among the elderly as is the basal metabolic rate (BMR). The former is also influenced by disablement, lessened physical work, and otherwise modified life-style. In an experiment to determine the energy requirements of six elderly men, aged 63 to 77 years, Calloway and Zanni (1980) found that their total body potassium was 12 percent less than that of younger men ($\bar{x} = 28$ years) of similar height, whereas their body weights were 8 to 19 kg greater. Their BMR averaged 1622 ± 189 kcal/day or 13 percent less than that for the younger men. BMR per unit potassium was equal in the two groups. It was concluded that the minimum maintenance energy requirement of healthy older men appears to be about $1.5 \times$ BMR or the same as that in other age groups. No significant difference between groups in the energy expenditure associated with the performance of usual activities was observed.

Serfass (1980) has pointed out that any decreases in fitness can catalyze further inactivity, thereby producing a cyclic phenomenon. It is not inevitable for the elderly to be physically inactive, for Leaf (1973), in his observations of several more rural populations around the world, found those in agrarian pursuits to be quite active. Athletes who remain physically active maintain relatively high fitness (Pollock, 1974; Pollock et al., 1974; Robinson et al., 1976; Shephard and Kavanagh, 1978; Heath et al., 1981).

The physical activity patterns of elderly men and women over the age of 60, many of whom were retired, were examined (Sidney and Shephard, 1977a). It was found that both activity measurements and assessment of fitness indicated an inactive life-style even though the people thought they were active. Based on diaries, ECG recordings, and electrochemical pulse integrators, commonly accepted physical conditioning thresholds were seldom obtained. On weekdays, the women engaged in 90 minutes more physical activity than men. On weekends, the men added an average of 100 minutes of physical activity, whereas the women had 30 minutes less. The modest addition of a physical activity class lasting one hour a day, four days per week, to their lives increased their daily energy expenditure by 150 to 200 kcal/day, or to 2500 kcal/day in the men and 2200 kcal/day in the women. Aerobic capacity was increased by the 12-month regimen, and diary data indicated that life-style modifications had accrued such that less time was spent driving a car by the men.

In studies of the inverse relationship of physical activity and heart attack risk, Paffenbarger et al. (1978) investigated the physical activity habits of 36,500 Harvard University alumni—men who entered college from 1916 to 1950. They observed physical activity records from student days and from middle age, the latter by questionnaire. A six- to ten-year follow-up was conducted during the periods 1966–1972 and 1962–1972 that totaled 117,680 man-years of observation. The goal was to provide expressions of quantity and quality of exercise that would produce a meaningful measure of higher and lower levels of energy output. A brief summary of findings in relation to physical activity is provided in Table 1. Entries are by man-years of observation. Most of the men climbed

TABLE 1. Summary of Physical Activity Assessment in Follow-up of Harvard Alumni.[a,b]

Physical Activity in 1962 or 1966	Man-years of Observation	Ratio Less Active / More Active
Stairs climbed daily		
<50	37,946	0.50
50+	76,064	
	114,010	
City blocks walked		
<5	24,996	0.29
5+	85,345	
Light sports play		
No	50,606	3.16
Yes	16,032	
Strenuous sports play		
No	66,638	1.46
Yes	45,724	
Physical activity index		
<2000 kcal·wk^{-1}	56,459	1.48
2000+ kcal·wk^{-1}	38,027	
Undetermined	23,194[c]	

[a]Adapted from Paffenbarger et al. (1978).
[b]Contributions by age class to observation pool: age 35–44, 43%; 45–54, 30%; 55–64, 20%; 65–74, 8%.
[c]Not included in ratio calculation.

some stairs daily or walked more than five blocks, but the ratios contrasting the less active to the more active shifted substantially when focus was on either sports activity or the total physical activity index. It is apparent that many men were not actively participating in sports, and lack of such participation may well have meant that their weekly caloric turnover associated with physical activity fell below the arbitrary dividing value of 2000 kcal/week (Physical Activity Index) that Paffenbarger et al. (1978) established. Using this criterion, the authors concluded that men with an index below 2000 kcal/week were at 64 percent higher risk of a first heart attack than classmates with a higher index. They also concluded that varsity athletic status implies selective cardiovascular fitness, but these athletes retained lower risk only if they maintained a high physical activity index as alumni.

PHYSICAL DISABILITY

Frequently, old age is considered synonymous with disability, but evidence exists to counter this view, particularly when the elderly outside of institutions are studied. Thus, Jette and Branch (1981) have concluded that life after 60 is not a period inexorably marked with exceptional physical disability (see Table 2). Their appraisal involved elderly citizens in the Framingham Study who were 55 to 84 years of age. Among their subjects there was a consistent increase in physical disability with advancing age,

with women relatively more disabled than men, although the women were no more likely than the men to report functional disabilities such as those noted to affect bathing, dressing, transferring, etc. (see Table 3). The relatively greater disability among women was not attributable to an artifact resulting from an increased proportion of women living into older ages. Whether the gender difference reflected a variance in perception of disability or an actual difference in disability could not be checked. Comparison with earlier work, which was referred to by Jette and Branch (1981) as Branch's 1976 "Massachusetts Elders Survey of Noninstitutionalized Elders Living in Massachusetts," suggested similar disability appraisals. The Framingham cohort was regarded as somewhat less physically disabled than the Massachusetts sample.

Shanas (1980) established an incapacity index based on answers to six self-care questions. A score of 3 or more was approximately equivalent to the Framingham summary index which assessed the use of assistance to perform one or more activities associated with daily living. Shanas estimated that 12 of every 100 persons, 65 years of age or older, would achieve a score of 3 or more on her incapacity index. In the Framingham Study, 7 of every 100 persons reported use of assistance to perform one or more usual daily activities. This comparison suggested to Jette and Branch (1981) that the Framingham cohort was less physically disabled than the U.S. aged population. Such

TABLE 2. Percentage of Elderly Persons Able to Perform Gross Mobility Activities by Gender and Age.[a]

Age	HEAVY HOUSEHOLD WORK		WALK HALF MILE		CLIMB STAIRS	
	Men	Women	Men	Women	Men	Women
55–64	87	73[b]	97	96	98	96[c]
65–74	78	67[b]	95	90[c]	97	95
75–84	66	42[b]	87	72[b]	93	80[b]
Total	80	63[b]	95	88[b]	97	92[b]

[a]Adapted from Jette and Branch (1981).
[b]$p < 0.01$.
[c]$p < 0.05$.

TABLE 3. Prevalence Summary in Percentage of Physical Disability by Gender and Age: Additive Index.[a]

Age	USES ASSISTANCE IN ONE OR MORE ACTIVITIES		DIFFICULTY IN ONE OR MORE ACTIVITIES	
	Men	Women	Men	Women
55–64	2	3	55	74
65–74	5	4	62	78
75–84	8	14	74	91

[a]Adapted from Jette and Branch (1981).

analysis indicates, however, that most of the noninstitutionalized elderly can care for themselves.

BODY COMPOSITION INCLUDING BONE MINERAL

Body Composition

The aging process has been associated with several changes in body composition including loss of fat-free body weight and tissue mass, a reduction in bone mineral, and a gain in body fat (Sidney et al., 1977). The latter occurs probably into the 60s, but the gain may not be pronounced, as reflected by different increases in skin-fold thicknesses (see Table 4). Thereafter, body fatness may de-

TABLE 4. Percentage Increase in the Thickness of Selected Skin Folds from Age 25–65 Years.[a]

Skin Fold	INCREASE IN THICKNESS (%)	
	Men	Women
Chin	39	67
Subscapular	31	77
Triceps	12	26
Suprailiac	8	59
Waist	62	101
Suprapubic	111	68
Chest	49	106
Knee	37	90

[a]From Shephard (1978, 1982).

crease. Physical inactivity no doubt plays a role, for when sedentary people become active or active people remain active, their body composition tends to resemble that of younger people (Sidney et al., 1977; Heath et al., 1981).

Study of body protein loss with aging as measured by 24-hour creatinine excretion suggested that men in their 70s have about 9 kg less muscle mass and 3.4 kg more fat and connective tissue than men in their 40s (Tzankoff and Norris, 1977). Preservation of muscle mass as a result of participation in regular physical activity may only be partial.

Increases in lean body mass and bone mineral, and reductions in body fatness with regular exercise, have been found in young and middle-aged subjects (Oscai, 1973), but few comparable data are available for the elderly. DeVries (1970) found a small but significant decrease in the body fatness of elderly men, following six weeks of regular exercise involving calisthenics, stretching, walk-jogging, and some aquatics. Continuation of the program for 42 weeks produced no further change. Sidney et al. (1977b) found that a walk-jog regimen lasting 52 weeks for men and women in their 60s produced a significant reduction in skin-fold thickness, but body weight did not change, which suggested an increase in lean body mass.

Cross-sectional studies have indicated that body fatness increases through middle age but frequently decreases at older ages. In contrast, metabolically active cells continue to be lost during the aging process. A longitudinal study of one man throughout more than four decades of adult life substantiated the cross-sectional observations. Body fat and lean body mass (LBM) were calculated from body density determined by underwater weighing or from body volume measurements obtained either by water displacement or by helium dilution procedures. Total body potassium (TBK) was calculated from ^{40}K measurements using a 4π whole-body liquid scintillation counter. Total body water (TBW) was measured using antipyrine, tritiated water, or ethanol dilution. It was observed that fluctuations in body weight left the relationship of TBW to LBM relatively unaltered. LBM decreased gradually at a rate of about 3.6 percent per decade from age 30 to 70 years. After age 70, the decrease was about 9 percent per decade. TBK similarly decreased through age 55, but decreased more markedly than LBM after age 70. It was concluded that in older age, the degenerative loss of lean tissue was in part replaced by other tissue that was likely low in potassium (Behnke and Myhre, 1982).

The role played by physical activity in controlling body fatness is no doubt complicated, and involves appetite and satiety control as well as mechanisms related to caloric turnover. Nevertheless, a number of studies have clearly demonstrated that regular hard muscular work leads to relatively low stores of body fat. An example has been provided by Skrobak-Kaczynski and Andersen (1975) who examined 312 forest workers (lumberjacks) in Norway. The cross-sectional study involved men from 20 to 70 years of age. The principal differences from studies on more sedentary populations were that body weight, sum of three skin folds, and percent body fat were essentially the same for the men in each decade. Body fatness averaged about 13 percent. It was pointed out that the forest workers came from areas without other occupational possibilities, where they were firmly integrated into the social structure of their communities. Dilution of the work force via emigration was deemed negligible. On an average, the men consumed about 3750 kcal/day.

Since total body potassium is related to the fat-free body mass and to skeletal muscle mass, it could be assumed that strength and total body potassium (as an indicator of skeletal muscle mass) would be related. Bahemuka and Hodkinson (1976) investigated this possibility by measuring red blood cell potassium (presumably proportional to total body potassium) and grip strength; 6 men and 43 women over the age of 65 took part in the study. Red blood cell potassium was unrelated to grip strength, and there was no evidence of a hypokalemic subpopulation among the elderly subjects. Age was inversely related to grip strength as was female sex. A single normal distribution of red blood cell potassium was found. They concluded that handgrip strength cannot be recommended as an index of potassium status among relatively healthy elderly subjects. They did, however, recommend red blood cell potassium as a better index of potassium status than serum potassium concentration.

The body composition of 16 masters athletes, all men, who ranged in age from 50 to 75 years was compared to that of younger athletes and untrained men (Heath et al., 1981). There were 1 cyclist and 15 runners in the group of masters athletes. The masters athletes were quite lean, with comparable body composition to the younger athletes. The recruitment of lean older men who were a visual match for the masters athletes revealed different body composition; i.e., the untrained lean men were fatter (see Table 5). The conclusion was that training for competition in cycling and running has a marked effect on body composition.

Bone Mineral

Reviews of the relationship of osteoporosis to physical activity in relation to aging have been prepared by Smith (1973, 1981). The reduction in cortical bone and bone strength with osteoporosis among the elderly makes them susceptible to broken bones and victims of the hypoactivity of the attendant immobilization and bed rest during rehabilitation.

Body calcium content as measured by neutron activation analysis remained relatively constant when elderly men and women engaged in an endurance training program for one year. In contrast, those who exercised less showed a 9 percent loss in body calcium (Sidney et al., 1977b). Montoye (1975) reported a significant decrease in cortical bone area as measured by hand and wrist x-ray among those aged 45 to 54 and restudied at ages 55 to 64. There was no detectable difference in loss between the most and least active men. It was postulated that only a

TABLE 5. Mean Values for Age, Height, Weight, and Body Composition for Athletes and Untrained Men.[a]

Group	N	Age (yr)	Height (cm)	Weight (kg)	Fat (%)	Fat-free Weight (kg)
Young athletes	16	22	175.8	65.2	9.3	59.2
Masters athletes	16	59	173.0	63.3	9.8	57.1
Untrained	9	50	175.3	85.0[b]	20.4[b]	67.7
Lean, untrained	9	52	174.8	69.1[c]	14.2[b,c]	59.3[c]

[a]From Heath et al. (1981).
[b]$p < 0.01$ significant difference from masters athletes.
[c]$p < 0.05$ significant difference from untrained.

minimal amount of regular physical activity may maintain a normal-for-age amount of cortical bone through the mechanical stress exercise imposes on bone.

There is evidence that bone responds to increased physical stress with mineral accretion, at least among younger people, but whether such a process remains viable among the elderly has not been clearly demonstrated. Smith and Reddan (1976) observed that the bone mineral content of the distal one-third of the radius, as determined by photon absorptiometry of 40 women aged 69 to 95 years, increased among those who were physically active over a three-year period. Twenty of the women participated in exercise sessions scheduled three times per week at an intensity of 3 Mets or less. The nonexercise or control women lost 2.5 percent of their bone density, whereas those who exercised regularly gained 4.2 percent. When neutron activation analysis was employed as well as photon absorptiometry, Aloia et al. (1978) also showed that exercise reduced bone mineral loss in postmenopausal women.

In a study of the effects of regular exercise on the status of bone mineralization, the bone mineral content of the radii of experienced tennis players was measured. The 35 men played in the 70-, 75-, and 80-year age groups of the U.S. Tennis Association. The bone mineral content was measured with a collimated ^{125}I source using an aluminum standard. The bone mineral content of the

radius in the playing arm was greater than that in the nonplaying arm (1.37 versus 1.23 g/cm) in all but one player. In general, the values for the playing arm exceeded those from the dominant arm of a control group of normal men—rather direct evidence that regular exercise influences bone mass (Huddleston et al., 1980). Jones et al. (1977) had previously shown that professional tennis players all showed hypertrophy of bone on the playing side. There is also evidence from earlier work that increased bone mineralization may be expected in the active lower extremities of athletes (Nilsson and Westlin, 1971).

BLOOD LIPIDS

A similar increase in plasma triglycerides (TG) with age has been found in both rats and men. Reaven and Reaven (1981) cite data suggesting that aging rats have both an increase in TG production and a decrease in the efficiency of TG removal from plasma. In an effort to study means of lowering TG secretion, they subjected Sprague-Dawley rats to wheel running exercise or caloric restriction (cellulose-diluted standard chow mixture) as they grew from 1 1/2 to 12 months of age. The exercised and calorically restricted rats gained less weight than control animals, and no age-related increase in plasma TG concentration was observed with either treatment. Both exercise and caloric restriction inhibited the increase in plasma insulin concentration noted to occur in control animals. There is other evidence (Brownell et al., 1982) that exercise may reduce plasma TG by virtue of an increased capacity to lower the very low density lipoprotein-TG secretion rate, which is perhaps related to an increase in insulin sensitivity and a fall in plasma insulin concentration. Bjorntorp et al. (1972) observed previously, as have others, that exercise can lower plasma TG concentration in man.

Considerable research has evolved in recent years in regard to serum lipid and lipoprotein changes in middle-aged and elderly subjects with regular exercise. These studies are too numerous to be treated in detail so representative studies have been selected in order to describe the general trends observed. Twenty middle-aged men ($\bar{x} = 39$ years, normolipidemic) underwent a 15-week program of regular exercise involving walking, jogging, cycling, cross-country skiing, and swimming. Although no change in body weight was observed, there was a measurable improvement in physical fitness (about 15 percent) as assessed at a heart rate of 150 beats/min on a cycle ergometer. Total cholesterol (TC) decreased slightly, high density lipoproteins (HDL_c) increased by about 7 percent, low density lipoproteins (LDL_c) decreased, and the HDL_c/TC ratio increased by 11 percent. Fasting serum insulin concentration also decreased. Postheparin hepatic lipase (HL) was negatively related to HDL_c concentration. Postheparin plasma and adipose tissue lipoprotein lipase (LPL) activity increased by 33 and 56 percent, respectively. A control group of seven nonexercising subjects was utilized (Peltonen et al., 1981). LPL is apparently located in the capillary endothelium in several tissues and is thought to mediate the increase in HDL_c with regular exercise (Nikkila et al., 1978) by producing precursors of HDL_c. The role of hepatic lipase in lipoprotein metabolism is not fully understood, but may involve activity in the hepatic endothelial cells with uptake of part of the cholesterol content of HDL_c and LDL_c taken up by the liver.

"In the Collaborative Lipid Research Clinic Studies, after adjustment for age, relative ponderosity, alcohol, cigarettes, and geographical location, active men had a mean HDL_c concentration that was 2 mg·dl^{-1} higher than inactive men with similar findings in women. Although this difference seems quantitatively small, a difference of as little as 4 mg·dl^{-1} in the Framingham studies was very strongly associated with differential risk for coronary heart disease" (Glueck, 1982, from Haskell et al., 1980). It is apparent that controversial data and interpretations appear in the literature. The following two quotations illustrate the diversity.

Consistent, high level, aerobic exercise is associated with high HDL_c levels in men but probably not in women, particularly when compared to the preexercised, nonconditioned state. (Wynne et al., 1980)
Octogenarian subjects also often have remarkably elevated HDL_c levels or low LDL_c, or both. (Glueck et al., 1977)

In a study of middle-aged men who differed significantly in habitual physical activity, the relative cardiovascular fitness of marathoners and joggers was significantly greater than that of sedentary man. Higher HDL_c was associated with running and jogging, although qualitative dietary habits (food selection) were no different. Based on consideration of risk for the development of coronary heart disease, both the runners and the joggers were deemed to be a lower risk than the inactive men (see Table 6). In terms of a regular physical activity threshold for lowering risk, it was assumed to be between the caloric turnover associated with regular jogging, about 300 kcal/day (2100 kcal/week), and that for the inactive men, about 140 kcal/day (1000 kcal/week) (Hartung et al., 1981). Paffenbarger et al. (1978) established their arbitrary physical activity threshold for comparison of Harvard alumni at 2000 kcal/week. Hartung et al. (1981) reiterated the opinion that active people may adopt a life-style that promotes overall health through proper sleeping habits, regular

TABLE 6. Mean Values for Middle-aged Men Who Differed Significantly in Habitual Physical Activity (N = 22 in each group).[a]

Variable	Marathoners (M)	Joggers (J)	Inactive (I)	p
Age, yr	78.2	48.7	48.3	NS
Weight, kg	72.4	76.2	86.0	<0.001 M, J, I
Triceps skin fold, mm	8.4	9.5	12.5	<0.01 M, J, I
Distance run per year, km	2644	1488	—	<0.001 M, J
$\dot{V}_{O_2 max}$ ml·kg^{-1}·min^{-1}	57.2	49.2	42.5	<0.05 M, J, I
Total cholesterol, mg·dl^{-1}	195.6	204.3	213.4	NS
Triglycerides, mg·dl^{-1}	87.4	103.6	146.6	<0.01 M, I
HDL$_c$ mg·dl^{-1}	69.3	61.5	38.4	<0.001 M, J, I
HDL$_c$/total cholesterol	0.36	0.31	0.18	<0.001 M, J, I

[a]From Hartung et al. (1981).

meals, moderate alcohol consumption, maintenance of normal weight, and no smoking. Such a life-style has been associated with increased longevity (Belloc, 1973).

CENTRAL NERVOUS SYSTEM

Whether endurance training prevents the age-related central nervous system (CNS) deterioration observed in older persons is unclear, but it remains an intriguing and unresolved question. Brenner and Appenzeller (1981), as cited in Appenzeller and Atkinson (1981), in assessing brain stem auditory evoked responses (BAER) as measurements of electrical transmission through the brain stem from the cochlear hair cells to the upper midbrain, found decreased latencies to BAER in ten runners after a 24.2 km run. Latencies of visual evoked potentials (VEPO) normally increase with age. They are electrical responses of the brain to visual stimuli that reflect CNS transmission from the retina to the occipital cortex. VEPO before and after endurance efforts by runners revealed shorter latencies following running and shorter latencies in the endurance trained compared to age-matched nontrained persons. "These VEPO changes could reflect an enhanced CNS transmission in endurance trained subjects" (Appenzeller and Atkinson, 1981, p. 43). (Also see Carlow et al., 1978.) The possibilities of shorter latency for spinal cord transmission in the endurance

trained person have not been reported, but should probably be investigated.

MOTOR CONTROL—REACTION TIME

Carlow and Appenzeller (1978, 1981) have surmised that pre-exercise warm-up may increase motor nerve conduction velocity, thus facilitating motor activity. Marathon runners and other highly conditioned athletes may have motor nerve conduction velocities that are faster than normal for their age. Observations on a 50-year-old marathoner revealed a peroneal nerve conduction velocity of 61 m/sec (well above normal for age 50) that did not change after a ten-mile run. A more sedentary person would have been expected to have an increased postrun nerve conduction velocity. Carlow and Appenzeller suspect that regular running may delay the usual decline in motor nerve conduction velocity seen with advancing age. This possibility remains to be determined, as does confirmation of greater nerve conduction velocity among runners.

Only a few studies of reaction and movement time have included elderly athletic or other active groups. Most groups for the study of neuromuscular variables among the elderly have involved institutionalized subjects with inactive life-styles. Spirduso (1975) reported reaction and movement times for four groups of men: OA, older active sportsmen of mean age 57.2 years; ONA, older nonactive men, 56.3 years; YA, young active, 23.6 years; and YNA, young nonactive, 25.4 years. The active groups reacted and moved faster than the nonactive. The ONA group was significantly slower for all variables studied, i.e., simple reaction time, discrimination reaction time, and movement time. The OA group had slower movement times than the YA group, but faster than the YNA group. Simple reaction time and discrimination reaction time in the OA group were about the same as those for the YNA group. The results suggested that regular physical activity preserves reaction and movement times. The average decrement in these variables attributable to age was about 8 percent when the young and old active groups were compared, whereas between the nonactive groups the decrement was about 22 percent.

DeVries et al. (1981) have studied that "tranquilizer effect" of exercise using a test consisting of electrical stimulation of the tibial nerve to elicit Hofmann reflexes in the calf muscles. The first muscle action potential (M wave) results from direct stimulation of the motor nerve fibers. The second muscle action potential (H wave) results from a monosynaptic reflex that is propagated in afferents from the muscle and back through the efferents of the same muscle. The H wave provides a measure of motoneuron excitability (Angel and Hofmann, 1963). Following a 20-minute exercise bout on a cycle ergometer at 40 percent of the difference between the resting and maximal heart rate, all subjects showed a fall in the H/M ratio ($\bar{x}$ = 18 percent; range = 6 to 44 percent) which the authors contend provides strong evidence for an exercise-induced "tranquilizer effect." Earlier electromyographic data from the elbow flexors following leg exercise suggested a similar conclusion (deVries and Adams, 1972a). Two elderly subjects aged 66 and 80 years showed H/M responses comparable to the younger subjects.

A significant relationship appears to exist between physical fitness and psychomotor speed. This area of research was reviewed by Spirduso (1980) who pointed out that reac-

tion and movement times were fastest in highly fit subjects whether or not they were athletes. In general, reaction time is decreased with physical conditioning. Spirduso also pointed out that aerobic power has only infrequently been assessed as a yardstick for physical fitness in psychomotor studies and that other important modifying factors have not routinely been controlled or investigated, e.g., alcohol consumption, smoking habits, drug usage, state of anxiety, motivation, and instructional set. Thus, the specific focus for neuromuscular change with exercise is unclear. Nor has clear delineation usually been between the known effects of learning and practice on the decrease in reaction and movement times, and those decreases associated with enhanced physical condition. An important question remains as to whether chronic exercise can change or preserve oxidative capacity in the brain and, thereby, preserve time-limited psychomotor processing throughout aging. The potential benefits to the individual and society are indeed great if the question can be answered affirmatively. Perhaps the chronic effects of regular exercise will be related to more optimal circulatory concentrations and turnover of catecholamines, and to optimal functioning of transmitter systems both centrally and peripherally, as well as to better autoregulation of cerebral blood flow. Encouraging in this perspective is the fact that transmitter synthesis, speed of muscular contraction, plus weight and size of the diaphragm (and possibly other respiratory muscles) do not show a substantial age-related decline, perhaps because of constant neural stimulation and activity (Vyckocil and Gutmann, 1972).

Differential proportions of cardiovascular disease by age decade no doubt contribute to a substantial sampling bias in psychomotor studies and are associated with the rather large interindividual differences found in older groups. Ingvar et al. (1976) have reported that cortical blood flow (CBF) is coupled to the synaptic activity of the cortical neurons; i.e., an increased CBF follows a variety of stimuli. The observation that CBF remains constant despite the intensity or duration of exercise (Fixler et al., 1976) does not preclude the importance of regional shifts associated with metabolic demands or chronic changes brought about by exercise. Spirduso (1980) has postulated that "exercise may prevent or postpone a commonly existing cycle: disuse decreases metabolic demands in motor and somatosensory brain tissue, which decreases the need for circulatory flow, which may result in neuronal destruction, leading to disuse of brain tissue." Spirduso calls for studies of EEG variables, behavioral and psychomotor performance, and regional CBF in those who are elderly and physically fit or unfit. Comparative results to date are regarded as largely descriptive and incomplete.

The intellectual differences among adult men who varied in age has been reviewed by Elsayed et al. (1980). These authors found that "fluid intelligence," as measured by the Cattell Culture Fair Intelligence Test, was higher in older men and who were more physically fit than in more unfit men. The same was true for younger men, with the younger men scoring higher than the older men. No differences were found for "crystallized intelligence." Reasons for the age- and exercise-induced differences were not proposed, other than the usually recognized physiological and biochemical changes commonly attributable to participation in regular exercise.

The effects of regular exercise therapy were tested among a group of elderly geriatric patients with psychological problems ($\bar{x}$ = 82 years) (Diesfeldt and Diesfeldt-Groenendijk, 1977). All of the patients were inmates in a geriatric nursing home. There were 34 women and 6 men who were divided into two groups—an experimental group and a control. Main symptoms included: disorientation, decreased ability to dress themselves, apathy and inertia, stereotyped movements, grasp impairment, and impairment of expression ability. All were able, however, to take part in the exercise therapy and psychological-motor testing. The four-week exercise program consisted of group activities, most of which were conducted while sitting in a chair, and involved light bending and stretching supplemented by kicking, throwing a large ball, and knocking down skittles (bowling). A free-recall task, a test for visumotor coordination, and a recognition task were administered before and after the exercise program. Analysis suggested greater retrieval activity, as well as improved cognitive performance, among those who exercised.

In tests of changed range of motion of different functional joints, Lesser (1978) concluded that regular rhythmic exercise designed to flex and extend the respective joints produced significantly greater flexibility in 8 of the 12 joints measured. A peripheral benefit of the program was the gaining of a feeling of enhanced physical independence in performing life's usual tasks.

SKELETAL MUSCLE

A variety of changes in mammalian skeletal muscle with exercise have been reported by Ermini (1976), but a review of specific papers should complement his review. In an examination of skeletal muscle changes with regular exercise among elderly men and women, Suominen et al. (1977b) studied 26 men and women who were 69-year-old pensioners in Finland. The subjects engaged in five one-hour exercise periods per week for eight weeks. Activities included walking, jogging, swimming, gymnastics, and ball games. Biopsies were taken from the vastus lateralis muscle before and after the eight weeks of exercise. Malate dehydrogenase activity (related to oxidative capacity) was increased, whereas lactate dehydrogenase activity (related to glycolytic capacity) decreased or remained the same, with higher values in the men than in the women. The percentage of slow twitch fibers (about 50 percent) was comparable among the men and women. These enzyme changes suggested an enhanced capacity for aerobic metabolism in skeletal muscle following the exercise regimen. Similarly, collagen metabolism (biosynthesis) may have been enhanced because prolyl-hydroxylase activity was also increased, particularly in the women.

Age-related muscle fiber atrophy was observed in biopsies from the vastus lateralis muscles from 18 sedentary men, aged 25 to 65 years (Larsson, 1982). Following an initial biopsy, they participated in a low resistance, high repetition training program designed to develop strength. The exercise sessions were scheduled twice per week for 15 weeks. Fiber size increased with strength development, particularly in the older subjects. An independent effect of age was observed when the influence of fiber size on strength was eliminated through statistical treatment of the data. The anthropometric characteristics and distribution of fiber types did not change with training. The data reported, compared to those in an earlier study (Larsson et al., 1978), suggested progressive disuse as the primary cause of muscle atrophy during aging, i.e., a slow adaptation to a more sedentary life-style. Since the fiber size of both type I and type II fibers increased, this was taken as evidence that both phasic and tonic motor units were activated in the elderly subjects.

Larsson (1982) concluded that "muscle strength is proportional to the active cross-sectional area of muscle, which can be expressed as a function of the total number of muscle fibers, mean fiber area, fiber tension, and percent activated muscle fibers, an impaired excitation-contraction coupling, and/or a decreased activation of high threshold motor units appear to be the most plausible cause(s) of the lower peak strength in old age." Although the thigh cross-section was unaltered by the strength training, the number of muscle fibers could have been reduced with area replacement by fat and connective tissue. Perhaps there is selective degeneration with age of the largest and fastest motoneurons that innervate the high threshold type II fibers or there is decreased activation of such units (Burke and Edgerton, 1975).

Orlander and Aniansson (1980) found an increased oxidative capacity after 12 weeks of regular exercise in 70- to 75-year-old men. In contrast, decreased oxidative capacity per gram of muscle has been implicated in the decline in aerobic power with age (Souminen et al., 1975, 1977a, 1977c). Although the role of reduced oxidative capacity in muscle is probably small relative to that of the respiratory cardiovascular delivery systems in explaining the decline with age in aerobic power, it is important to try to understand the oxidative events associated with the mitochondria in skeletal muscle. One approach has involved fractionation of the mitochondrial population in the fibers of the gastrocnemius plantaris muscle in endurance trained rats (Farrar et al., 1981). There was a decrease in mitochondrial protein with age, i.e., in 300- compared to 720-day-old animals. The decrease occurred primarily in the intermyofibrillar area rather than the subsarcolemmal area. It was suggested that the subsarcolemmal mitochondria are primarily involved in providing energy for nuclear protein synthesis and the production of ATP for the phosphorylation of glucose. It was concluded that the ability of the skeletal muscle to respond to aerobic training (endurance running) was unimpaired in the older animals for an increase was found in mitochondrial protein in both populations of mitochondria. There was, however, a significant decrease in muscle weight in the older animals, indicating either a decrease in protein synthesis or an increase in degradation (Farrar et al., 1981). Perhaps the protein loss was selective in that it came from fibers not used in endurance running, e.g., fast glycolytic fibers.

In contrast to the observations of Farrar et al. (1981), Goodrick (1980) suggested that free-running animals maintained their muscle mass, and hence their resting metabolic rate, throughout their lifetimes. This supposition does not appear to agree with the usual impression of the gradual loss of lean body mass in man (Tzankoff and Norris, 1977), with probable acceleration of the process with the onset of senility. Nevertheless, the common observation of an increase in oxidative capacity of skeletal muscle in response to regular high aerobic demands (Holloszy and Booth, 1976) suggests that muscular changes with physical conditioning should be more rigorously studied among the elderly.

The effect of a 12-week program of regular exercise on characteristics of the vastus lateralis muscle was investigated in five men aged 70 to 75 years. The intensity of the exercise program was established at about 70 percent of the predicted aerobic power and remained unchanged during the program. Exercise consisted of walking, jogging, and other calisthenic-type exercises, without use of ancillary equipment. Sessions were scheduled three times a week for 45 minutes per session. No medical complications resulted from participation in the exercise. Along with the usual reduction of heart rate during submaximal work and an increase in predicted aerobic power, it was concluded that these old men responded much the same as younger men to regular exercise. Lactate dehydrogenase increased 49 percent with regular exercise, which suggests an elevated anaerobic capacity. The 31 percent increase in cytochrome oxidase indicated that the mitochondrial oxidative capacity was augmented. Phosphofructokinase tended to be increased with regular exercise, which agreed with an earlier observation of Orlander et al. (1978) in a group of active old men and suggested an increased glycolytic capacity. No enzymatic evidence was found suggesting that fatty acid oxidative capacity was altered by the regular exercise (i.e., citrate synthase or 3-hydroxyacyl-CoA dehydrogenase). Nor were there changes in lipid droplets. There was no change in the volume fraction of mitochondria. Thus, any increase in oxidative capacity must have taken place within the existing mitochondrial volume—a finding in contrast to that among younger men (Orlander et al., 1977; Bylund et al., 1977).

Strenuous exercise has been shown to cause skeletal muscle fiber injury with focal fiber necrosis and invasion of inflammatory phagocytes (Vihko et al., 1978). Such injury may be reversed, but an increase in acid hydrolytic capacity two to seven days after strenuous exercise suggested enhanced autolytic breakdown. The question is whether such processes are enhanced in older animals. In a study of NMRI mice, aged 3, 6, 9, and 12 months, that were made to run at a speed of 13.5 m/min on a treadmill, Salminen and Vihko (1980) found that the alkaline and myofibrillar proteases increased considerably in skeletal muscles with age. Running increased acid hydrolytic capacity more in the younger than in the older mice. The authors suggested that the increased acid proteolytic capacity is involved in subcellular regenerative processes of skeletal muscle fibers. The smaller lysosomal response of older mice was thought to indicate a reduced capacity for cellular repair, i.e., a loss in adaptive capacity.

Presumably, acid hydrolases in skeletal muscle originate either in muscle fibers or in interstitial cells such as fibroblasts, endothelial cells, or invaded macrophages (Vihko et al., 1978). Since no signs of muscle inflammation were found by Salminen and Vihko (1980), they contended that the increase in acid hydrolase activity with strenuous exercise originated in the fibers, particularly the red oxidative fibers. Earlier, Gollnick and King (1969) had found transient mitochondrial swelling plus intracellular edema after heavy exercise. Salminen and Vihko (1980) found an increased number of autophagic vacuoles in skeletal muscle fibers after prolonged running—a response that coincides with the increased acid hydrolase activity. Reduced lysosomal response after strenuous exertion plus decreased protein biosynthesis in older animals (Britton and Sherman, 1975) may lengthen the time for subcellular regeneration. Interestingly, Salminen and Vihko (1980) did not find that exhaustive exercise induced changes in cardiac muscle comparable to those found in skeletal muscle.

In a study of isometric and dynamic strength and endurance associated with knee extension, Larsson and Karlsson (1978) found that strength decreased with increasing age among relatively sedentary men, aged 20 to 65 years. When corrected for the decrease in maximum strength with age, endurance tended to increase slightly. Similar

TABLE 7. Fiber-type Distribution, Area Ratio, and M-Lactate Dehydrogenase Activity in Relatively Sedentary Men, Aged 22–65 Years.[a,b]

Age Group	n	Mean Age	Mean Percent Type I Fibers	Mean Type II/I Ratio	Mean M-LDH ($\mu m \cdot g^{-1} \cdot min^{-1}$)
20–29	10	26.1	43.0	1.30	34
30–39	10	35.3	36.8	1.24	46
40–49	8	42.6	48.2	1.08	30
50–59	12	54.5	51.7	0.99	20
60–65	10	61.6	55.0	0.99	23

[a]From Larsson and Karlsson (1978).
[b]Biopsies from the vastus lateralis muscle.

results in terms of endurance had previously been observed by Petrofsky and Lind (1975). There was a negative correlation between isometric endurance and type II fiber area. There was greater relative dynamic endurance with larger relative area of type I fibers. A decline with age was found in muscle-lactate dehydrogenase activity and in the proportion of type II fibers (see Table 7). Larsson and Karlsson (1978) postulated lactate translocation from type II to type I fibers as a limiting factor in dynamic endurance.

There is evidence that the muscles of senile mice (27 months of age) show a negative adaptation to nonexhaustive exercise. Such a phenomenon was not observed in 22-month-old animals (Steinhagen-Thiessen et al., 1980). The 22-month-old mice reacted to a challenge of five weeks of wheel running with

an adaptive increase in creatine kinase, protein, and total hind leg muscle weight (see Table 8). Adaptation in the 22-month-old mice proceeded more slowly and to a lesser extent than in the 6-month-old mice. Thus, support was found for the concept of reduced but still functioning adaptation in aged individuals, whereas in very old animals, a paradoxical adaptation results in a reduction of vital enzymes and of muscle mass and structure.

Shephard (1982), in reviewing the literature, has concluded that the elderly are vulnerable to muscle and tendon rupture. He lists as possible contributory factors: (1) muscle stiffness due to fatigue, (2) slow relaxation of antagonists, (3) loss of elastic tissue and alterations in collagen structure, (4) loss of joint flexibility, and (5) decrease in blood supply to tendons.

TABLE 8. Relative Changes of Various Hind Leg Muscle Variables after Five Weeks of Wheel Running. Change with Respect to Unexercised Control Mice (100%).[a]

Variable	AGE		
	6 Months	22 Months	27 Months
Muscle wet weight	115 ± 4^b	104 ± 5	79 ± 4^b
Soluble protein	110 ± 2	101 ± 2	84 ± 9
Total protein	92 ± 2^b	111 ± 2	84 ± 8
DNA	103 ± 4	—	93 ± 4^b
Creatine kinase	122 ± 2^b	112 ± 4^b	67 ± 5^b

[a]From Steinhagen-Thiessen et al. (1980).
[b]$p \leq 0.05$ compared to unexercised animals.

STRENGTH

Lind and Petrofsky (1978) have conducted a variety of investigations of handgrip strength and endurance, and the associated changes in cardiovascular variables. These investigations have shown that men are stronger than women, but that women could sustain longer a contraction at 40 percent of their maximal voluntary contraction (MVC). In both men and women, when body bulk and fatness were taken into account, there was reduction in handgrip strength with aging. In contrast, aging was associated with a small increase in endurance, i.e., the maintenance of a 40 percent MVC. Older subjects displayed a smaller increase in exercising heart rate than younger subjects. Not only was aging associated with an increase in resting systolic blood pressure, but aging increased the slope of the rise in systolic blood pressure during the handgrip exercise. The authors speculated about the mechanisms for the increase in endurance and the decrease in strength with age. The reduction in absolute tension at 40 percent MVC was cited as a factor; i.e., the lower absolute tension may be easier to maintain. They also cited possible conversion of fast twitch to slow twitch fibers and the reduction in the number of active muscle fibers.

Both isometric strength and dynamic strength decrease with age, particularly beyond age 50 (Larson et al., 1979); e.g., both types of knee extension strength decreased after age 50, and this decrease was associated with a decrease in type II fiber (fast twitch) area (see Table 9). Kroll and Clarkson (1978) added a resistance comparable to 10 percent of maximum strength to a reaction time test; older subjects developed a relative force as well as younger subjects. The older subjects generated a lower absolute force faster than the younger subjects developed a higher absolute force. Kroll and Clarkson's results agreed with the general observation in the literature that aging is associated with a decrease in absolute tension development. In an extension of this work, Clarkson et al. (1981) tested 15 older subjects ($\bar{x} = 64.5$ years) and 9 younger subjects ($\bar{x} = 23.2$ years). They found that maximal voluntary contraction (MVC), fast maximal voluntary contraction (FMVC), and the fast twitch to slow twitch muscle fiber ratio in the vastus lateralis were significantly lower in the older group, but that the rate of relative tension development was similar between groups. They also found that the older subjects produced a FMVC that was 19 percent greater than their MVC. The authors suggested that the type of test utilized is important in assessing strength changes with age since the rapid strength development test (FMVC) was performed quite well by the older subjects as was the relative tension development test.

TABLE 9. Selected Regression Analyses of Strength in Relatively Sedentary Men, Aged 22-65 Years.[a]

Strength Variable	Independent Variable	REGRESSION COEFFICIENTS		
		Single	Partial	Multiple
Maximum isometric	Type II fiber area	0.17[b]	0.18[b]	0.51[b]
Maximum dynamic	Type II fiber area	0.014[b]	0.001	0.59[c]
Isometric endurance	Type II fiber area	−0.01[d]	−0.01[d]	0.34[d]
Absolute force decline	M-LDH activity	50.7[c]	42.0[c]	0.51[c]
	Type I fiber area	−0.004	−0.006[d]	0.65[c]
Relative force decline	% type II fibers	0.21[d]	0.29[c]	0.38[c]

[a]From Larsson and Karlsson (1978).
[b]$p < 0.001$.
[c]$p < 0.01$.
[d]$p < 0.05$.

Grip and arm strength tests were given to more than 6000 participants in a community project in Tecumseh, Michigan (Montoye and Lamphiear, 1977). The authors contend that since the population on which their data are based is a well-defined population and self-selection was minimized, the data reported probably are more representative of healthy men and women in the United States than are other published values. In keeping with earlier results, a gradual small decrease in strength was observed after early adulthood. From about age 20 to age 50, there was really not much change in absolute grip strength, arm strength, or strength index. A decrease in strength per unit weight was more apparent and was greater among men than among women. The concomitant gain in weight and fatness accounted for the relative strength differences.

Bosco and Komi (1980) subjected men and women of different ages to power tests involving the mechanical behavior of the leg extensors. Although the men were invariably stronger than the women, total force calculated per unit body weight appreciably reduced the sex-related differences. Peak forces were observed in both sexes at about age 20 to 30 years when they performed vertical jumps with and without a stretch-shortening cycle on a force platform. The results suggested that not only is the performance utilizing concentric contractions modified by aging, but also modified are elastic behavior and reflex potentiation, for the ability to tolerate high stretch loads declines after age 20 to 25. Similarly, Larsson et al. (1978) found the torque-velocity relationship sensitive to aging.

Bosco and Komi (1980) provide a possible explanation for the decrease in performance among the older subjects. From earlier work (Bosco and Komi, 1979), they associated vertical jump performance with fast twitch fiber percentage in the vastus lateralis muscle. Larsson et al. (1978) noted a reduction in the number of fast twitch fibers with older age. A greater decline in power output relative to muscular strength perhaps indicated poorer coordination in the older subjects.

AEROBIC AND ANAEROBIC METABOLISM

The progressive decline in the functional cardiovascular oxygen delivery system with age, following maturity, has been amply demonstrated. A thorough review was recently presented by Shephard (1982) and by many others, including investigators in our laboratory (Hodgson and Buskirk, 1977, 1981). A survey of the literature of cross-sectional studies indicates a decline of aerobic power (aerobic capacity and maximal oxygen intake are terms used interchangeably) ($\dot{V}O_{2max}$) of approximately 0.45 ml $O_2 \cdot kg^{-1} \cdot min^{-1} \cdot yr^{-1}$, regardless of habitual activity. Most data from longitudinal studies indicate a more rapid decline than do the cross-sectional studies. Among sedentary women the decline in $\dot{V}O_2$ appears to be less than for men, i.e., about 0.3 ml $O_2 \cdot kg^{-1} \cdot min^{-1} \cdot yr^{-1}$ (Drinkwater et al., 1975).

The principal reason for the reduction in aerobic power with age is unknown, although lower cardiac output and particularly lower arteriovenous oxygen differences have been implicated. The decreased arteriovenous oxygen difference among active adults was largely explained on the basis of increased mixed venous oxygen content in 13 men and women studied over a 13-year period. In four men studied in various states of physical fitness over an 11-year period, the reduction in aerobic power was largely due to a reduced cardiac output brought about by a reduced stroke volume while the arteriovenous oxygen difference remained relatively unchanged (Kanstrup and Ekblom, 1978). These results tend to support the concept that lessened physical condition or detraining plays a role in the age-related reduction in aerobic power—a concept supported by the data of Kasch and Wallace (1976) and Heath et al. (1981).

Among groups of average physical fitness, women attain an aerobic power per kilogram of body weight about 80 to 85 percent of that for men (Astrand and Astrand, 1978). The sex differences are further reduced when aerobic power is related to fat-free body weight. Since skeletal muscle fiber composition is comparable among men and women, it cannot account for the sex difference in aerobic power. The difference in aerobic power between men and women remains as aging proceeds and appears to be associated with the reduction in maximal cardiac output which, in turn, is associated with a reduction in maximal heart rate.

The concept that longitudinal data are more appropriate for the evaluation of changes in aerobic capacity with age is persuasive because of the minimization of genetic differences as well as those associated with survivorship (Hodgson and Buskirk, 1977; Plowman et al., 1979). The latter investigators attempted to gain some information from 36 women who were studied 6.1 years apart. The age range was 20 to 70 years, but only three subjects were in their seventh decade. The changes from age 30 or older yielded age decrements in $\dot{V}O_{2max}$ that resembled those obtained during an earlier cross-sectional study (Drinkwater et al., 1975); i.e., the regression equation for those 20 years and older was:

$$\dot{V}O_{2max} \, (ml \cdot kg^{-1} \cdot min^{-1}) = 44.86 - 0.29 \, age$$
$$in \ years$$

On retesting, the respective regression line for the physically more active women was:

$$\dot{V}O_{2max} = 54.62 - 0.38 \, age$$

and for those who were less active:

$$\dot{V}O_{2max} = 44.71 - 0.37 \, age$$

The question was raised by Plowman et al. as to whether the use of linear regression analysis is appropriate, particularly for older subjects. The answer is probably no because of the likelihood of more rapid deterioration in aerobic capacity beyond age 70. A further observation was that aerobic capacity per kilogram of lean body mass did not change appreciably with age, which indicates that the loss of muscle tissue is important in the decline in aerobic capacity. The similarity in the downward slopes of the regression lines for the active and sedentary women agrees with the cross-sectional studies reviewed by Hodgson and Buskirk (1977) revealing per-

haps a true aging effect when comparable exercise programs are maintained. The slope of the regression line for women can no doubt be lessened if physical condition is improved during the interval between tests and women follow the same trend as men (Kasch and Wallace, 1976; Shephard, 1982). The active women retained higher aerobic capacities at all ages, thereby confirming previous data.

The issue of appropriate test procedures for assessing aerobic capacity in elderly subjects has been addressed by Sidney and Shephard (1977b). They described the limitation of physical effort as different among the elderly than among younger people; it involves such factors as dyspnea, fear, muscular weakness, poor motivation, and perception of premature fatigue. Many of their elderly subjects failed to reach a recognized plateau in oxygen consumption at their highest work loads. Their data support the view that valid aerobic capacity data cannot be obtained without working subjects to near exhaustion since $\dot{V}O_{2max}$ was consistently higher in subjects who made a good effort and whose blood lactate concentrations were high, i.e., > 8 mmol/liter. They concluded that practical options for the assessment of cardiovascular fitness in elderly subjects are: (1) establishment of an oxygen plateau through progressive work load testing and (2) reporting physiological data at a target heart rate corresponding to a fixed percentage of a maximum oxygen intake. They suggest that the plateau method is acceptable for about 67 percent of an elderly population who pass a preliminary medical examination. Half of the remaining 33 percent could reach a plateau during a second test, after adjustment of work loads based on experience gained during the first test. Thus, it was estimated that only about 16 percent would have to be tested at a fixed submaximal work load. Such an analysis assumes the participation of "healthy" subjects.

An interesting cross-sectional analysis of wheelchair exercise performance was made by Sawka et al. (1981). They found that aerobic capacity decreased with age when their data for arm exercise were combined with those in the literature. The combined regression equation was:

$$\text{peak } \dot{V}O_2 \ (ml \cdot kg^{-1} \cdot min^{-1}) = 31.9 - 0.29$$
$$\text{age in years}$$

Their own data, based on studies using a wheelchair ergometer for subjects from age 20 to 85 years, yielded:

$$\text{peak } \dot{V}O_2 \ (ml \cdot kg^{-1} \cdot min^{-1}) = 28.3 - 0.26$$
$$\text{age in years}$$

In other words, the aerobic capacity values decreased at the rate of about 2 to 3 $ml \cdot kg^{-1} \cdot min^{-1}$ per decade after age 20. They found relatively low values at age 80, i.e., about 10 $ml \cdot kg^{-1} \cdot min^{-1}$. The subjects studied had been confined to wheelchairs for an average of about 12 years and were generally healthy other than for their disability. In seeking such subjects from among those at a Veterans Administration hospital, it is interesting that 56 percent of the interviewed patients were deemed ineligible to participate in the study because of cardiovascular disease.

In a program in which Japanese housewives participated regularly in recreational sports two hours per day, twice a week, those over age 50 did not change their aerobic capacity over a two-year period of observation. No age-related decline was observed, and the values for aerobic capacity remained above those for sedentary women (Atomi and Miyashita, 1976).

Few studies of the effect of physical conditioning on aerobic power for those over age 60 have appeared in the literature. Benestad (1965) was unable to produce changes in aerobic power among 70- to 81-year-old subjects who exercised for 30+ minutes three times per week for six weeks at intensities as high as 50 percent or more of aerobic power.

Kasch and Wallace (1976) demonstrated that it is possible to maintain aerobic power at about the same value over a span of ten years (from about age 45 to 55) by one-hour bouts of running or swimming three times per week. Kasch (personal communication) indicated that some loss in aerobic power has

been observed in several of the subjects who have continued the exercise program at San Diego State, but it is unknown whether this effect is accelerated past the seventh decade. Hodgson (1971), in a survey of the literature on the effects of physical conditioning on aerobic power, suggests that 60-year-old men can possibly increase aerobic power by about 10 percent with appropriate regular exercise.

Detraining or deconditioning among the elderly has not been well studied, although the debilitating effects of bed rest are obvious to most everyone. Miyashita et al. (1978) evaluated the effects of 15-weeks of physical conditioning and the deconditioning that subsequently resulted from reversion to a sedentary life-style. Their results appear in Table 10. The close relationship of changes in aerobic capacity ($\dot{V}O_{2max}$) to maximal cardiac output was apparent. Very little change was observed in the arteriovenous difference in oxygen content.

Work performance tests have seldom been carried out in epidemiological surveys, but investigators in Göteborg decided to obtain baseline exercise data for their program of study on ischemic heart disease (Bengtsson et al., 1978). Of the 239 women sampled, 194 (81 percent) participated in a progressive cycle ergometer test up to a maximum work load. Presumably, these women were representative of those in comparable age strata in the general Swedish population. Women

TABLE 10. Percentage Changes in Several Variables with Physical Conditioning for 15 Weeks and Deconditioning for 26 Weeks in Men Aged 35 to 54 Years.[a]

Variable	With Conditioning	With Deconditioning
$\dot{V}O_{2max}$	+11.7	−7.2
$\dot{V}_{E2\ max}$	+15.1	−13.9
$\dot{Q}_{max}$	+9.9	−6.9
HR_{max}	+2.7	−3.5
SV_{max}	+7.1	−3.9
$C(a - \bar{v})\,O_2$	+2.0	−1.0

[a]From Miyashita et al. (1978).

in the upper age groups had reduced work capacities and reached their capacities at lower maximal heart rates (see Table 11). At the same work load, however, heart rate, respiratory frequency, and rating of perceived effort were unaffected by age. Two minutes after cessation of maximum exercise, systolic blood pressure increased significantly more in relation to age. Table 12 shows that only 8 percent of the women had their exercise tolerance test interrupted. Interruption of the exercise occurred for a variety of reasons, the most common of which were significant electrocardiographic changes and clinically worrisome elevated blood pressures.

An interesting metabolic feature of aging associated with anaerobic metabolism has been found as a response to continuous multistage treadmill walking up to a maximal intensity. Postexercise blood lactate concentrations were elevated, but comparable, at three, five, and seven minutes of recovery in men aged 20 to 40 years. For men in their 50s and 60s, blood lactate concentrations continued to rise through the seventh minute. The authors suggested that there is a progressive, age-related diminution of the ability of lactate to diffuse from muscle to the extracellular fluid. They also suggested that the intracellular retention of lactate could be associated with decreased work capacity and endurance plus a prolongation of recovery (Tzankoff and Norris, 1979). As a practical matter, they suggested that when lactate metabolism is assessed in older subjects, single blood samples should be obtained no sooner than five minutes postexercise for men up to age 50, and up to seven minutes for those between 50 and 70. For those over age 70, the obtaining of multiple samples is advisable, with some sampling beyond seven minutes.

The capacity for involvement of anaerobic metabolism as reflected by different variables appears to be decreased among the elderly. Shephard (1982) indicated that the equivalent oxygen delivery for performing a staircase sprint decreases from 165 $ml \cdot kg^{-1} \cdot min^{-1}$ in a young adult to about 90 $ml \cdot kg^{-1} \cdot min^{-1}$ in a 65-year-old person. Increased creatinuria has been found by Hall (1973) in the elderly, with the inference that they may have difficulty resynthesizing creatine phosphate after vigorous physical activity. Blood lactate concentrations, respiratory exchange ratios, and oxygen debts have been found to be low after exhausting exercise (Adams et al., 1972). Sidney and Shephard (1977b) contend, however, that lack of motivation to perform hard exercise may be a factor among the elderly since they have found blood lactate concentrations of 10 to 12 mmol/liter in highly motivated elderly subjects in contrast to 7 mmol/liter among those probably not so highly motivated. Of importance is consideration of the fact that the extracellular fluid/muscle mass ratio may be greater in the elderly. This means that lactate produced in the muscle and diffusing into the extracellular pool, including blood, will probably be at lower concentration in the elderly, if one assumes an equal quantity of lactate production in the muscles of older as compared to younger subjects. Lactate may also diffuse less readily from the muscles of the elderly, but lactate kinetics have not been studied.

Physiological characteristics of a "good" maximal effort as viewed by Shephard (1982) are presented in Table 13. The reasons for not attaining a "good" effort are: dyspnea, fear of overexertion, muscular weakness, poor motivation, and the appearance of electrocardiographic abnormalities.

Shephard (1978) has raised an important issue with respect to the comparison of cross-sectional to longitudinal effects of exercise. If the assumption is made that our U.S. and Canadian populations have become less active, a regression line calculated for aerobic power from people of different ages would fall below that for a similar study performed 20 or 30 years ago. Longitudinal analysis of data from subjects who were studied on both occasions would probably show a greater age-related decrement in aerobic power because of the probable reduction in habitual

TABLE 11. Mean Maximal Loads on a Cycle Ergometer and Cumulative Frequencies (%) of Women Who Managed Various Maximum Loads.[a]

Mean Age	N	Maximum Load (Watts)	Maximum Heart Rate (beats·min⁻¹)	Systolic Blood Pressure (mm Hg)[b]	Watts ≥160	≥130	≥100	≥70	≥30
38	27	113	172	169	21.5	43.0	85.8	100.0	100.0
46	40	105	173	171	19.4	34.0	85.2	97.3	100.0
50	32	102	173	182	2.7	27.0	72.9	100.0	100.0
54	45	103	166	195	2.1	12.5	81.2	95.8	100.0
60	31	98	158	196	0.0	15.8	58.0	97.5	100.0

[a]From Bengtsson et al. (1978).
[b]Systolic blood pressure measured 2 minutes after cessation of maximum work.

TABLE 12. Number of Women in Whom a Progressive Cycle Ergometer Test Was Interrupted and the Cause for the Interruption.[a,b]

Mean Age	N	Insufficient Cooperation	Chest Pain	ECG Changes	Claudication	Uremia	Exhaustion	Arterial Hypertension
38	28							1
46	41							1
50	37		1	2		1		
54	48	1		2			1	1
60	40	1		2	2			
Total	194	2	1	6	2	1	1	3

(MAIN CAUSE OF INTERRUPTION)

[a]From Bengtsson et al. (1978).
[b]Test interrupted in 16 of 194 women tested or 8%.

TABLE 13. Characteristics Associated with Maximum Effort in 65-year-old Subjects Who Made a "Good" Effort.[a]

Variable	Men (N = 19)	Women (N = 20)
$\dot{V}O_{2max}$, liters·min^{-1}	2.35 ± 0.35	1.64 ± 0.21
$\dot{V}O_{2max}$, ml·kg^{-1}·min^{-1}	31.4 ± 4.4	26.8 ± 2.9
Plateau, % of subjects (<2 ml·kg^{-1}·min^{-1})	79	75
HR_{max} beats·min^{-1}	172 ± 12	161 ± 12
R	1.11 ± 0.08	1.07 ± 0.09
HLa, mmol·liter^{-1}	11.1 ± 3.3	9.1 ± 2.0
SBP, mm Hg	210 ± 31	192 ± 27

[a]Based on data from Sidney and Shephard, (1977) and Shephard (1982).

physical activity. By and large, comparative analyses that appear in the literature conform to this possibility.

CARDIOVASCULAR FUNCTION

The effects of exercise in relation to age-related alterations in cardiovascular function are summarized in Chapter 15.

RESPIRATORY FUNCTION

Aging is associated with a variety of structural changes in the thorax and lung, and these changes have been summarized by Reddan (1981) (see Table 14). He draws our attention to the fact that the degree and the rate of change in structure are variable and dependent on the habits of the individual (particularly physical activity) and his/her involvement with disease. Nevertheless, structural changes in the chest are pronounced in senescence.

Changes in lung volumes and ventilatory variables have also been reviewed by Reddan (1981), and his summary appears in Table 15. Age-related differences are readily apparent. Of consequence is the fact that the inability to sustain high ventilation at rest is directly related to the maximal ventilation achievable during exercise.

Maximal ventilation during exercise (i.e., during maximal effort) is reduced but appears to be coupled to, rather than limiting, aerobic capacity. The expiratory minute volume ($\dot{V}_E$) responds in roughly similar fashion; however, there appears to be an earlier onset and rapid increase in anaerobic metabolism, resulting in a greater relative hyperventilation and a reduction in $\dot{V}_{Emax}$ among the elderly (Shephard, 1978; Reddan, 1981). Both the time required to achieve a steady state $\dot{V}_E$ during exercise and the time for return to pre-exercise $\dot{V}_E$ during rest following exercise are prolonged in the older person (Reddan, 1981). With advanced age, there occur a loss in distensibility and elastic recoil of the lung, and an increased functional residual capacity. Early airway closure may inhibit expiratory flow (deVries and Adams, 1972c; Reddan, 1981). As tidal volume may increase more in the elderly during light and moderate work than would occur in younger people (deVries and Adams, 1972c), if it exceeds about 60 percent of vital capacity then dyspnea or shortness of breath may ensue (Reddan, 1981). The reduction in achievable tidal volume in the elderly would reduce V_{Emax} (Jammes et al., 1979). With increasing age, the maximum flow-volume loop is reduced during performance of heavy exercise; particularly, expiratory flow achieved may be quite limited (Grimby, 1976; Reddan, 1981).

Dyspnea during prolonged exercise may well be associated with respiratory muscle fatigue resulting from sustained relatively high ventilation or an increased muscle weakness with age (Roussas and Macklem, 1977). As the rib cage stiffens with age, an

TABLE 14. Morphological Changes in the Thorax and Lung with Age.[a]

Morphological Change	Functional Significance
Thorax	
Calcification of bronchial and costal cartilage	↑resistance to deformation of chest wall (elastic work)
↑stiffness in costovertebral joints	↑use of diaphragm in ventilation
↑rigidity of chest wall	
↑anterior-posterior diameter (kyphosis)	↓tidal volume response to exercise hyperpnea
Wasting of respiratory muscles	↓maximal voluntary ventilation
Lung	
Enlarged alveolar ducts	↓surface area for gas exchange
↓supporting duct framework, enlarged alveoli	↓pulmonary diffusing capacity
Thinning, separation of alveolar membrane	↑physiological dead space
↑mucous gland	
↓number, thickness of elastic fibers (?)	↓lung elastic recoil
	↓VC, RV/TLC %
	↓ventilatory flow rate
	↓ventilation distribution
	↑resistance to flow in small airways
↓pulmonary capacity network	↓ventilation: blood flow equality
↑fibrosis of pulmonary capillary intima	
↑fibrosis of pulmonary capillary intima	

[a]From Reddan (1981).

increased proportion of the ventilatory power generated during exercise may be handled by the diaphragm (Rizzato and Marrazini, 1970; Reddan, 1981). Thus, the source of fatigue remains unknown for the diaphragm is not easily fatigued; it may well be that the coordination of accessory muscles is compromised or that these muscles fatigue earlier because of chest wall stiffness. Exertional dyspnea among the elderly is a commonly observed problem when work to aerobic capacity is performed (Grimby and Stiksa, 1970; Shephard, 1978; Reddan, 1981).

In summary, Reddan (1981) has speculated:

More information is needed on the mechanisms that underlie the coupling of ventilation to exercise intensity. The integrated role of the dia-

TABLE 15. Lung Volumes and Ventilation Variables in 20- and 60-year-old Individuals Matched for Height and Weight.[a]

Variable	MEN		WOMEN	
	20 Years	60 Years	20 Years	60 Years
Total lung capacity, liter	7.20	6.90	5.10	4.70
Vital capacity, liters	5.20	4.00	4.17	3.29
Functional residual capacity, liters	2.20	3.50	2.40	2.50
Residual volume, % TLC	25	40	28	40
Forced expiratory volume in one second				
(a) liters (BTPS)	4.45	3.17	3.26	2.26
(b) % (VC)	81	71	80	70
Maximum voluntary ventilation, liters/min	150	99	110	77
Maximal expiratory flow @ 50% VC, liters·sec^{-1}	5.00	3.80	4.40	2.70
Closing volume, % VC	8	25	8	25
Recoil pressure of lung @ 60% TLC, cm H_2O	7.8	4.4	7.8	4.4
Recoil pressure of chest wall @ 60% TLC, cm H_2O	−6.0	−4.0	−6.0	−4.0

[a]From Reddan (1981).

phragm, chest wall, and abdominal muscles in producing an adequate alveolar ventilation at minimal cost with a loss of lung compliance and an increase in rigidity of the rib cage needs to be elucidated. In addition, the integrated role of the rib cage and abdomen and subsequent choice of breathing frequency and tidal volume in exertional dyspnea need to be studied.

Changes in pulmonary function to be anticipated with age include a reduction in alveolar ventilation due to structural changes in the lungs, such as modification of the alveolar surface and the capillary bed, and an increase in functional dead space. Although the ventilatory equivalent for oxygen is much the same in younger and older people, the reduction in alveolar ventilation must be small. Fortunately, the elevated pulmonary pressure in the elderly would assist in the maintenance of a relatively better ventilation/perfusion ratio in their upper lung lobes (Shephard, 1982). Another change brought about by age is a loss of elastic fibers so that by age 65, about 25 percent of the vital capacity range is affected by airway closure (LeBlanc et al., 1970). Aging may increase the work of breathing due to the stiffening of rib and other "respiratory" joints such that diaphragmatic breathing is increased. In the small airways, the number and size of the radial elastic fibers are reduced, and these fibers maintain patency. Shephard (1982) contends that the effort-independent portion of the flow-volume curve is likely to be reached sooner during exercise by the elderly. Slowing of rapid expiration, where there is demand for high respiratory frequency, may result in dyspnea at ventilation rates of 60 to 65 liters/min in men and 50 liters/min in women.

Shephard (1978, 1982) has concluded that the reduction of static lung volumes, stiffening of the joints of the thoracic cage, and increase of airway resistance (often exacerbated by chronic bronchitis or emphysema) reduces the maximum voluntary ventilation from 200 to 120 liters/min. The elderly appear to generate ventilation during exercise at a faster respiratory rate and smaller tidal volume (deVries, 1978), a conclusion in disagreement with earlier findings (deVries and Adams, 1972c). Despite the equivocality, Shephard (1982) contends that maximum exercise ventilation remains about 50 percent of the maximal voluntary ventilation in the elderly—a value comparable among younger and older subjects in the absence of pulmonary disease. Shephard (1982) cites seven studies of elderly men in which maximum exercise ventilation averaged about 63 liters/min (STPD); in three studies of elderly women, the average was about 47 liters/min. Niinimaa and Shephard (1978) found the age-related loss in respiratory function to be substantially greater in smokers than nonsmokers.

An approximation of the efficiency of pulmonary ventilation can be obtained from the ventilatory equivalent ($\dot{V}E/\dot{V}O_2 \times 100$) which is the number of liters of ventilation ($\dot{V}_E$, BTPS) required to supply each liter of oxygen consumed ($\dot{V}O_2$, STPD). Under resting conditions, the ventilatory equivalent tends to have a value of about 25 to 28 and remains there until the anaerobic threshold is surpassed at a relative exercise intensity of about 60 percent of aerobic capacity. Little effect of aging on the ventilatory equivalent during either rest or exercise has been noted (see Table 16), but extensive investigations of age-related effects have not been undertaken.

Although the resting pulmonary diffusing capacity is reduced in the elderly (Niinimaa and Shephard, 1978), there is a relatively

TABLE 16. Ventilatory Equivalent ($\dot{V}E/\dot{V}O_2 \times 100$) at 100% of Aerobic Capacity for Selected Groups.[a,b]

Group	($\dot{V}E/\dot{V}O_2$) $\times$ 100
Young men	35.4
Old men	39.0
Young women	41.8
Old women	37.2

[a]From Sidney and Shephard, (1977) and Shephard (1982).
[b]$\dot{V}E$ = liters of pulmonary ventilation (BTPS); $\dot{V}O_2$ = liters of oxygen consumption (STPD).

TABLE 17. Diffusing Capacity (DLCO) in Relation to Oxygen Intake ($\dot{V}O_2$) among 65-year-old Adults.[a]

Variable[b]	Men			Women		
$\dot{V}O_2$, liters/min	0.30	0.93	1.44	0.25	0.73	1.01
DLCO,mM·min^{-1}·kPa^{-1}	3.8	7.6	12.5	2.8	5.7	9.1

[a]From Shephard (1978).
[b]kPa = kilopascals.

greater increase of diffusing capacity in the elderly with increments in exercise intensity (Shephard, 1978). Presumably, the pulmonary diffusing capacity increases by about 4 mmol·min^{-1}·kPa^{-1} (where kPa = kilopascals) for each liter per minute oxygen intake. In 65-year-old people, the slope increased about twofold (see Table 17). Shephard (1978) postulated that the increased slope is due to the fact that uneven ventilation among lung lobes is corrected as is the relatively poor distribution of blood flow. Shephard (1982) offers the somewhat contradictory statement: "The estimated maximum diffusing capacity of a healthy 65-year-old person (~ 18.7 mmol·min^{-1}·mPa^{-1} in a man, 13.8 mmol·min^{-1}·kPa^{-1} in a woman) is therefore not much poorer than in a young adult." Because of the high aerobic capacities found in older athletes by Heath et al. (1981), it appears that their diffusing capacities should be comparable to those of younger men. Nevertheless, it would appear that further studies of diffusing capacity in relation to age, sex, and physical condition are merited.

ENDOCRINOLOGY

Exercise and caloric restriction appear to affect the age-related structural and functional changes in the pancreas. Specific age-related alterations that are affected include an increase in islet size (volume) and number of endocrine cells, an increase in beta granules per beta cell, and more insulin storage per islet. Isolated islets from 18-month-old rats secreted insulin less efficiently in response to stimulation by glucose or leucine than islets from younger animals. There was impair-

ment in insulin secretion per beta cell that worsened with each 6 months of age (Reaven et al., 1979, 1980). Extension of this work, to ascertain whether aging was responsible for the changes observed or whether there were age-related changes such as a tendency toward obesity or inactivity, involved study of weight-restricted (reduced caloric intake) rats and rats that ran several miles daily in exercise wheels over a one-year period on their specific regimens. Control rats became hyperinsulinemic with enlarged, multilobulated, fibrotic islets. Their normal-appearing islets showed significantly reduced glucose-induced insulin release. The exercised and weight-restricted rats did not show increased serum insulin or pancreatic pathology. Nevertheless, islets from the weight-restricted rats functioned *in vitro* like those from the sedentary control animals. Islets from the exercised rats functioned slightly better (see Table 18). Reaven and Reaven (1981b) concluded that exercise and weight control diminished an animal's need for insulin. Although pancreatic islets appeared more youthful, the age-related decline in beta cell function was not modified by weight restriction and only slightly improved by regular exercise.

The insulin-like effect of regular exercise is relatively well known, at least among some diabetics. An attempt has been made to relate glucose tolerance in nondiabetic subjects to habitual physical activity, while controlling for age and body fatness. As part of the Tecumseh, Michigan, Community Health Study, this assessment was made on a sample of 1300 boys and men aged 16 to 65 years (Montoye et al., 1977). The subjects were classified into three groups on the basis of

TABLE 18. Mean Values for Sprague-Dawley Rats Growing to 12 Months of Age on Different Diet and Exercise Programs.[a]

Treatment	N	Serum Glucose (mg·dl⁻¹)	Serum Insulin (μU·ml⁻¹)	Islet Volume (× 10⁶ μ³)	IN VITRO ISLET INSULIN SECRETION AFTER GLUCOSE (μU insulin·islet vol⁻¹·min⁻¹) 8.3 mM	16.7 mM	25 mM
2 mo. controls	7	99[b]	22[b]	2.3	0.79	1.50	1.79
12 mo. controls	12	102	61	3.7	0.48[c]	0.90[c]	0.83[c]
12 mo. exercised	12	101	21	2.6	0.48[c]	1.28	1.50
12 mo., kcal restricted	12	87	20	2.7	0.37[c]	1.02[c]	1.12[c]

[a]From Reaven and Reaven (1981).
[b]Twenty animals involved.
[c]$p < 0.01$ as compared to 2 mo. control animals.

their habitual, occupational, and leisure physical activity through use of a questionnaire and interview procedure. A blood sample was obtained by venipuncture one hour after a glucose challenge for determination of glucose concentration. Body fatness was assessed from skinfolds. One significant finding was a lower glucose concentration among those who were both relatively lean and most active. It was concluded, however, that when habitually active normal people are compared with sedentary normal people, the differences in blood glucose concentration or glucose tolerance are not impressive.

Exercise training in rats produced age-related variability in the plasma corticosterone increase observed in response to acute swimming. Presumably less ACTH was released in the older animals. Perhaps, the need for glucocorticoids for stimulation of gluconeogenesis was reduced, but in any event, there was reduced stimulation of the pituitary-adrenal axis among older, exercise trained rats, perhaps because of a reduced response to epinephrine or a central inhibition of epinephrine secretion from the adrenal medulla (Severson et al., 1977). Buguet et al. (1980) suggested that adrenal cortical activity after exercise differs among fit and unfit subjects.

Exercising to an intensity of 80 to 90 percent of aerobic capacity produced no increase in plasma cortisol concentration (Sidney and Shephard, 1978). With isometric exercise, standing, and cold exposure, catecholamine concentrations (particularly norepinephrine) in blood tended to be higher in the elderly than in younger subjects (Ziegler et al., 1976; Palmer et al., 1978). McDermott et al. (1974) saw no significant increase in plasma catecholamine concentrations during performance of isometric handgrip exercise at 33 percent of maximal voluntary contraction in young men, but they saw a significant increase in older men that was largely accounted for by epinephrine. McDermott et al. concluded that adrenal medullary responses to static exercise are affected by aging. Although norepinephrine concentrations in plasma in subjects at rest were not affected by physical conditioning, plasma norepinephrine was lower at the same absolute

work load following a conditioning regimen, but not when expressed relative to aerobic capacity. No effect of physical conditioning has been observed for plasma epinephrine concentration (Hartley et al., 1972; Hartley, 1975; Cousineau et al., 1977).

SLEEP

Physical activity is thought to increase the need for slow-wave sleep (Oswald, 1976), and those who sustain a higher level of physical fitness probably require less slow-wave sleep. Nevertheless, slow-wave sleep increases in the fit person and does not change appreciably in the relatively unfit person after unaccustomed exercise (Griffin and Trinder, 1978).

In a study of paradoxical sleep in rats, it was found that the onset of paradoxical sleep was significantly delayed in older animals that had been exercised compared to younger animals exercised the same way. Thus, paradoxical sleep was inhibited by exercise in the older animals. Following treadmill running for four hours, the animals were placed in a control cage for observation. The older rats tended to be inactive, whereas the younger rats remained active. The implication was that the older rats were relatively more fatigued than the younger rats. The experiments were complicated by the inclusion of both sleep and food deprivation as variables, although each of these treatments failed to depress paradoxical sleep. Administration of DOPA blocked the exercise-exhaustion effect in that paradoxical sleep occurred at about 100 minutes, i.e., at a time equal to that of younger animals. Matsumoto et al. (1968) suggest from these results that the inhibition of paradoxical sleep in the relatively exhausted older animals resulted from a decrease in norepinephrine in the brain. It is interesting that slow-wave sleep was accentuated; i.e., it appeared earlier after treadmill exercise.

REGULAR PHYSICAL ACTIVITY—TRAINING

The results from studies involving participation in regular exercise, physical conditioning, or training (preparation for competition) programs have been presented in other sections of this chapter, but other studies are also of consequence and the results from several have been selected for inclusion here. Twenty-four elderly people (15 women and 9 men), of average age 77 years, participated regularly in exercise programs at a drop-in center. The group participated in light exercise, with gradually increased intensity, three times per week for 12 weeks. Significant weight loss occurred, with the men losing more weight than the women. Both resting and exercise heart rates declined, as did both systolic and diastolic blood pressure. Balance while standing on one foot was improved (Emes, 1979).

Seventeen women, aged 52 to 79 years, participated in a three-month exercise program that involved calisthenics, jogging, and stretching exercises for one hour three times per week. The physical working capacity, aerobic capacity, and oxygen pulse when riding a cycle ergometer increased significantly, and a modest bradycardia during rest was achieved postconditioning. The responses to regular exercise were approximately the same for these women as for elderly men. In contrast, no changes in pulmonary ventilatory variables were observed among the women as had been found for the men (Adams and deVries, 1973). The older men had higher tidal volumes and lower respiratory frequencies at all submaximal work loads. The older men increased their tidal volume more at relatively low exercise intensities, with smaller increments than occurred among the younger men as exercise intensity increased further. The older men had greater expiratory minute volumes, both per unit work and per unit oxygen consumption, than the younger men. The reasons for the ventilatory differences between men and women with respect to aging are not readily apparent.

In an attempt to ascertain the least stressful physical activities for older men, deVries and Adams (1977) subjected 12 men, aged 60 to 75 years, to five intensities of exercise during the separate activities of crawling, cycling, and walking. These activities were selected to stress the cardiovascular system

in different ways. The rate of increase of systolic blood pressure with increasing work load was the most important variable with regard to the rate of increase in cardiac effort. It was suggested that it is important to minimize sympathetic-adrenergic vasoconstrictor-related effects in exercise programs for older men by maximizing rhythmic activity and involvement of a large muscle mass, such as takes place in walking. The minimization of static contractions and superimposition of ancillary small muscle masses would also appear to be important.

Suominen et al. (1977c) carried out a study of functional aging by examining a group of 22 habitually active men and an age-matched group of 22 sedentary men. The age range was 33 to 70 years. Compared to the sedentary group, the active men (runners and cross-country skiers, i.e., endurance-type activity) had significantly higher aerobic power, generated greater vertical velocity, and had higher maximal voluntary ventilation. The active men had lower values for body weight, systolic and diastolic blood pressure, patellar reflex time, and serum triglycerides. Determinations on biopsy samples from the vastus lateralis muscle revealed a greater percentage of slow twitch fibers (type I) and fast twitch (type IIA), and a lower percentage of fast twitch fibers (particularly glycolytic fibers, type IIB) among the active men. The isocitrate dehydrogenase concentration in muscle was also greater in the active men. Various regression lines were plotted, and in general, the changes with age were parallel in the two groups. An exception was aerobic power, for the respective regression lines were:

Active men: $\dot{V}O_{2max}$, ml·kg^{-1}·min^{-1} = 91.0 − 0.70 age in years

Sedentary men: $\dot{V}O_{2max}$, ml·kg^{-1}·min^{-1} = 51.7 − 0.24 age in years

In other words, the suggested loss in aerobic power with age was greater among the active than the sedentary men. The differences in muscle fiber composition between the groups suggested to the authors the importance of an inherited selection of the active life-style. The shift toward increased muscle concentrations of aerobic enzymes with age remains unexplained.

Both longitudinal observations and numerous cross-sectional studies (see review by Shephard, 1982) show that aerobic power declines steadily with age. In contrast, Kasch and Wallace (1976) have indicated that aerobic power can be maintained with endurance types of regular exercise. The results of Souminen et al. (1977c) appear to support an age-related decline since the active men they studied had substantially similar activity regimens through the represented four decades of life. The weekly hours of exercise were comparable to those of Kasch and Wallace (1976), as was the relative intensity of exercise.

Frekany and Leslie (1975) found that a seven-month program of biweekly 30-minute exercise sessions that emphasized flexibility, balance, and muscle toning improved the flexibility of 71- to 90-year-old women. Ankle and knee joint, as well as lower back, flexibility was assessed. Similarly, Buccola and Stone (1975) found that a 14-week exercise program, involving 10 minutes of warm-up followed by 25 to 50 minutes of walk-jogging biweekly, produced greater trunk flexibility in men aged 60 to 70 years.

Chapman et al. (1972) reported the effects of exercise on strength and joint stiffness in boys and old men (boys, 15–19 years old; older men, 63–88 years). Values for strength and stiffness of both right and left index fingers were obtained, with one side as a control for half the subjects and the opposite side for the other half. Joint stiffness was measured by the torque and energy requirements necessary to oscillate the index finger passively about its metacarpophalangeal joint. Measured finger strength was comparable across age, but there was greater joint stiffness in the old men. Following six weeks of regular index finger weight training, increases in finger strength and decreases in joint stiffness were observed in both groups. The investigators concluded that joint stiffness is a somewhat reversible phenomenon in

the absence of arthritis or other joint disease.

DeVries (1970, 1971a, 1979) has emphasized that older people can be physically conditioned in relatively the same way as younger people, but that the hazards of regular exercise are somewhat greater so that a physical conditioning regimen must be initiated slowly and carefully. Such programs can result in substantial physiological improvement and can reverse or delay functional losses commonly associated with aging. Walking, walk-jog, and jogging regimens were employed. Over a 42-week period, oxygen transport increased 29 percent and arm strength increased 12 percent. Weight loss, reduction in skinfold thickness, and a small decrease in systolic and diastolic blood pressures were commonly observed. Exercise also produced a "tranquilizer" effect on resting action potentials from muscle that was greater than that of meprobamate. DeVries advised medical screening and individual assessment of exercise responses before any conditioning program is undertaken that exceeds vigorous walking. He also concluded that trainability of older men can be significant and does not depend upon having trained vigorously in youth. Improvement in muscular function was thought more related to changes in neural activation than to muscular hypertrophy. The latter tended to be small.

In an evaluation of the product of heart rate × systolic blood pressure (HR·SBP) resulting from cycle ergometer exercise that was progressively increased in intensity, it was found that older men had consistently higher values (deVries and Adams, 1972b). The difference between old ($\bar{x} = 69.2$ years) and young ($\bar{x} = 16.7$ years) men arose primarily because of the initial differences in systolic blood pressure, which imply greater peripheral resistance. The slope of the increase in HR·SBP was comparable for the older ($\bar{x} = 69.2$ years) and younger ($\bar{x} = 16.7$ years) men. When this investigation was extended to different types of rhythmic exercise deemed suitable for use by older men ($\bar{x} = 69.2$ years), it was found that HR·SBP increased less per unit increase in exercise intensity as assessed by oxygen consumption (deVries and Adams, 1977). Cycling and crawling produced higher HR•SBPs, particularly at the higher work loads. Crawling produced higher values than cycling. The differences between cycling and walking were accounted for by relative increases in SBP. With static muscular involvement, a greater SBP response is expected, and DeVries and Adams (1972a) have shown static involvement during cycling with integrated electromyographic techniques. Activation levels in wrist flexor, elbow extensor, pectoral, and latissimus dorsi muscles were greater in cycling than in the free swinging activity of walking. The differences in crawling compared to cycling and walking involved a relative increase in both HR and SBP. It was concluded that since walking showed the least increase in HR•SBP, and particularly since SBP was least affected, walking constituted the recommended exercise. Multiple regression analysis revealed that SBP response was largely determined by the relative muscle loading factor (i.e., the specific muscle groups used during a particular exercise), whereas HR and pulmonary ventilation were better related to the total muscle mass activated (deVries and Adams, 1972c).

In an investigation of the exercise intensity required to achieve improved physical fitness among older men in their 60s and 70s, it was found that the exercise intensity threshold was about 40 percent of the heart rate range (maximum HR–resting HR), compared to about 60 percent in younger subjects. It was concluded that for all but the more highly conditioned older men, vigorous walking (which raised the heart rate to between 100 and 120 beats/min) for 30 to 60 minutes daily constituted a sufficient stimulus for improvement in cardiovascular function (deVries, 1971a, 1972d). Hodgson and Buskirk (1977) arrived at a similar conclusion based on an analysis of walking as a physical conditioning stimulus in relation to aerobic capacity. DeVries (1971b) extended his analysis to other types of exercise, together with the provision of a nomogram for heart rate es-

timation of exercise intensity for exercise prescription of walk-jog regimens. He concluded that static-stretching exercises and selected calisthenics can be used safely with normal older men if performed at the slow cadences described. Since jogging is more strenuous, careful subject monitoring during jogging was suggested as well as use of the nomogram for exercise planning after a medical examination and cycle ergometer testing to maximal tolerance. Subsequent to these studies, deVries (1979) suggested that appropriate heart rate guidelines for older men might well be:

Minimum heart rate	40 percent of heart rate range
Target heart rate	60 percent of heart rate range
Heart rate not to exceed	75 percent of heart rate range

A program involving walking-jogging was outlined to help stay within these limits.

One year of physical conditioning in the seventh decade of life produced a variety of changes among 13 men and 25 women. The individualized physical conditioning involved about one hour per day, four days a week, of vigorous walking progressing to jogging that turned over about 150–200 kcal per session. Skinfold thicknesses were significantly reduced as was body fatness calculated from total body ^{40}K. Total body potassium (^{40}K) increased by 4 percent. Arm circumference, right handgrip strength, and knee extension force all increased. No calcium loss was found with neutron activation analysis over the year of regular exercise, except in those taking the least exercise. Thus, in addition to improved cardiorespiratory fitness, a loss in body fat and a gain in lean mass were observed (Sidney et al., 1977).

In a study of former champion middle-distance runners, 25 to 43 years of age, after their competitive careers, it was found that they performed an aerobic walk with less strain, as indicated by lower blood lactates, ventilatory equivalents, and heart rates, than nonathletes of corresponding age. Mean

$\dot{V}O_{2max}$ declined from 71.4 to 41.8 ml·kg^{-1}·min^{-1}at mean age 56.6 years. The nonathletes had respective values of 50.6 and 36.5 ml·kg^{-1}·min^{-1}. Mean maximal heart rate declined from 186 to 180 beats/min in the runners and from 199 to 186 in the nonathletes (Robinson et al., 1976).

Training usually results in increased functional capacity, and retention of such capacity has been demonstrated in a competitive cyclist by Faria and Frankel (1977). The cyclist was a moderately successful half-mile runner in college. He did not train for 37 years but did jog some. After starting to cycle, he began training and, at age 70, was cycling 6 miles a day at high intensity. The combination of training miles totaled about 2380 miles per year. He dominated the 65-year and older racing class in the annual Senior Sports International Road Race and competed successfully elsewhere. His physiological data relative to aerobic capacity appear in Table 19 along with those for distance runners and more sedentary men of comparable age. He weighed 79 kg, was 177.5 cm tall, and was 13 percent fat. His aerobic capacity has since been measured about 44 ml·kg^{-1}·min^{-1}, or approximately 55 percent of that reported for young national champion road racing cyclists. It is apparent that a high level of cardiovascular, pulmonary, and skeletal muscle function was retained by this elderly cyclist, but the relative contributions of heredity, residual effects of early training, maintenance of physical condition through the middle years, and impact of later training remain unresolved.

In order to ascertain whether the relative trainability of various physiological systems deteriorates with age, the effects of an eight-week (3–5 one-hour sessions per week) exercise program on the skeletal muscle metabolism of 56- to 70-year-old sedentary men were examined. Aerobic capacity was increased by 11 percent. Muscle glycogen stores determined from muscle biopsy samples were increased about 10 percent. Enzymes associated with aerobic metabolism (malate dehydrogenase and succinate dehydrogenase) were increased, as were the anaerobic enzymes creatine phosphokinase and lactate dehydrogenase. Blood lactate concentrations during submaximal work decreased (Suominen et al., 1977a). These results are similar to those reported by Kiessling et al. (1974), who found an 8 percent increase in the aerobic capacity of 46- to 62-year-old men during a program of regular exercise twice a week for 10 to 13 weeks. Others have found comparable increases in enzymes associated with aerobic metabolism in younger subjects (cf. Gollnick et al., 1973; Holm and Schersten, 1974). In contrast, the enzymes associated with anaerobic metabolism are usually in low concentration in endurance trained athletes (Karlsson et al., 1975; Suominen and Heikkinen, 1975). Thus, the increased concentration of anaerobic enzymes in skeletal muscle in the elderly, although small, was cited by Suominen et al. (1977a) as a possible specific

TABLE 19. Comparison of Cardiovascular Variables Related to Aerobic Capacity of a Competitive Cyclist Compared to Distance Runners and More Sedentary Men All in Their Eighth Decade.

Variable	Cyclist[a]	Distance Runners[b]	Normal Men
HR$_{max}$, beat·min^{-1}	166.0	162.8	155.0
$\dot{V}E_{max}$, liters·min^{-1} (BTPS)	159.0	96.4	79.8
$\dot{V}O_{2max}$, liters·min^{-1}	4.7	2.7	2.2
$\dot{V}O_{2max}$, ml·kg^{-1}·min^{-1}	44.0	42.3	27.7
O$_2$ pulse, ml·kg^{-1}·beat^{-1})	0.36	0.26	0.18

[a]Data from Faria and Frankel (1977) (with subsequently determined $\dot{V}O_{2max}$.
[b]Data from Wilmore et al. (1974).

metabolic activation brought about by regular exercise among formerly sedentary older people. Differences in muscle fiber types and their adaptation to exercise could also be important. A further factor could have been the difference in the type of regular exercise, for the elderly subjects engaged in some anaerobic physical activity, since they participated in ball games and other forms of games that involved multiple starts and stops. Finally, Kiessling et al. (1974) found lactate dehydrogenase activity to be increased after a short period of endurance training among sedentary men as contrasted to the decreased enzyme activity in habitually training athletes. This suggests a specific time course for skeletal muscle anaerobic enzyme adaptation to regular exercise that may be uninfluenced by age. Further research should clarify the issue.

SUMMARY

The chapter provides an update to the contribution prepared for the first edition of this *Handbook* by N. W. Shock (1977). In the current offering, more attention is paid to regulatory mechanisms as modified by aging among physically active men and women. In general, a variety of regulatory mechanisms are modified by participation in regular exercise, with an associated enhancement of physical performance. Thus, a general adaptation occurs with regular exercise that is somewhat age dependent (i.e., relatively greater effects at younger age), but the fact appears to remain that results of participation in a physical conditioning regimen are measurable in the healthy person at any age or at least up until the time that senescence makes exercise most difficult. Thus, functional alterations wrought by regular exercise blunt the downward trends commonly associated with aging.

ACKNOWLEDGMENTS

The assistance of Larry Barlett and Vincent Rabatin with the literature search is gratefully acknowledged as is the assistance of Becky Nilson in typing the manuscript.

REFERENCES

Adams, G. M. and deVries, H. A. 1973. Physiological effects of an exercise training regimen upon women aged 52 to 79. *J. Gerontol.* 28: 50–55.

Adams, W. C., McHenry, M. M., and Bernauer, E. M. 1972. Multistage treadmill walking performance and associated cardiovascular responses of middle-aged men. *Clin. Sci.* 42: 355–370.

Aloia, J. F., Cohn, S. H., Ostuni, J. A., Cane, R., and Ellis, K. 1978. Prevention of involutional bone loss by exercise. *Ann. Intern. Med.* 89: 356–358.

Angel, R. W. and Hofmann, W. W. 1963. The H reflex in normal, spastic and rigid subjects. *Arch. Neurol.* 8: 591–596.

Appenzeller, O. and Atkinson, R. 1981. *Sports Medicine.* Baltimore: Urban and Schwarzenberg, 395pp.

Appenzeller, O., Standefer, J., Appenzeller, J., and Atkinson, R. 1980. Neurology of endurance training. V. Endorphins. *Neurology* 30: 418–419.

Astrand, I. and Astrand, P. O. 1978. Aerobic work performance, a review. *In,* L. J. Folinsbee et al. (eds.), *Environmental Stress,* pp. 149–163. New York: Academic Press.

Atomi, Y. and Miyashita, M. Effects of moderate recreational activities on the aerobic work capacity of middle-aged women. *J. Sports Med.* 16: 261–266.

Bahemuka, M. and Hodkinson, H. M. 1976. Red-blood-cell potassium and hand-grip strength in healthy elderly people. *Age and Aging* 5: 116–118.

Bassey, E. J. 1978. Age, inactivity and some physiological responses to exercise. *Gerontology* 24: 66–77.

Behnke, A. R. and Myhre, L. G. 1982. Body composition and aging: a longitudinal study spanning four decades. *Abstract in,* J. A. Loeppky and M. L. Riedesel (eds.), *Oxygen Transport to Human Tissues,* p. 359. New York: Elsevier.

Belloc, N. D. 1973. Relationship of health practices and mortality. *Prev. Med.* 2: 67–81.

Benestad, A. M. 1965. Trainability of old men. *Acta Med. Scand.* 178: 321–327.

Bengtsson, C., Vedin, J. A., Grimby, G., and Tibblin, G. 1978. Maximal work performance test in middle-aged women: results from a population study. *Scand. J. Clin. Lab. Invest.* 38: 181–188.

Bittel, J. and Henane, R. 1975. Comparison of thermal exchanges in men and women under neutral and hot conditions. *J. Physiol.* 250: 475–489.

Bjorntorp, P., Fahlen, M., Grimby, G., Gustafson, A., Holm, J., Renstrom, R., and Schersten, T. 1972. Carbohydrate and lipid metabolism in middle-aged physically well-trained men. *Metabolism* 21: 1037–1044.

Bolduan, N. W. and Horvath, S. M. 1981. Survey of exercise and aging. *In,* E. J. Masoro (ed.), *Hand-*

book of Physiology in Aging, pp. 443–455. Boca Raton, Fl.: CRC Press.

Bosco, C. and Komi, P. V. 1979. Potentiation of the mechanical behavior of the human skeletal muscle through prestretching. Acta Physiol. Scand. 106: 467–472.

Bosco, C. and Komi, P. V. 1980. Influence of aging on the mechanical behavior of leg extensor muscles. Eur. J. Appl. Physiol. 43: 209–219.

Britton, G. W. and Sherman, F. G. 1975. Altered regulation of protein synthesis during aging as determined by in vitro ribosomal assays. Exp. Geront. 10: 67–77.

Brownell, K. D., Bachorik, P. S., and Ayerle, R. S. 1982. Changes in plasma lipid and lipoprotein levels in men and women after a program of moderate exercise. Circulation 65: 477–484.

Bruce, R. A. 1981. Human data from Seattle Heart Watch and Network Registries, 1971–1977. In, E. J. Masoro (ed.), Handbook of Physiology in Aging, pp. 457–472. Boca Raton, Fla.: CRC Press.

Buccola, D. and Stone, W. J. 1975. Effects of jogging and cycling programs on physiological and personality variables in aged men. Res. Quart. 46: 134–139.

Buguet, A., Roussel, B., Angus, R., Sabistou, B., and Radomski, M. 1980. Human sleep and adrenal individual reactions to exercise. Electroenceph. Clin. Neurophysiol. 49: 515–523.

Burke, R. E. and Edgerton, V. R. 1975. Motor unit properties and selective involvement in movement. In, Exercise and Sport Sciences Reviews, Vol. 3, pp. 31–83. New York: Academic Press.

Buskirk, E. R. 1977. Temperature regulation with exercise. In, R. S. Hutton (ed.), Exercise and Sports Sciences Reviews, Vol. 5, pp. 45–88. Santa Barbara: Journal Publishing Affiliates.

Bylund, A. C., Bjuro, T., Cederblad, G., Halm, J., Lundholm, Sjostrom, M., Angquist, K. A., and Schersten, T. 1977. Physical training in man. Skeletal muscle metabolism in relation to muscle morphology and running ability. Eur. J. Appl. Physiol. 36: 151–170.

Calloway, D. H. and Zanni, E. 1980. Energy requirements and energy expenditure of elderly men. Am. J. Clin. Nutr. 33: 2088–2092.

Cantu, R. C. 1982. The Exercising Adult. Lexington, Mass.: Collamore Press, D. C. Heath. 171 pp.

Carey, R., Natarajan, G., Bove, A., Coulson, R., and Spann, J. 1979. Myosin adenosine triphosphate activity in the volume-overloaded hypertrophied feline right ventricle. Circ. Res. 45: 81–87.

Carlow, T. J. and Appenzeller, O. 1978. Endurance training and the nervous system. In, O. Appenzeller and R. Atkinson (eds.), Medicine and Sport, Vol. 12: Health Aspects of Endurance Training, pp. 18–25. New York: Karger.

Carlow, T. J. and Appenzeller, O. 1981. Neurology of endurance training. In, O. Appenzeller and R. Atkinson (eds.), Sports Medicine: Fitness•

Training•Injuries, pp. 41–49. Baltimore: Urban and Schwarzenberg.

Carlow, T. J., Appenzeller, O., and Rodriquez, M. 1978. Neurology of endurance training: visual evoked potentials before and after a run. Neurology 28: 390.

Chapman, E. A., deVries, H. A., and Swezey, R. 1972. Joint stiffness: effects of exercise on young and old men. J. Gerontol. 27: 218–221.

Clarkson, P. M., Kroll, W., and Melchionda, A. M. 1981. Age, isometric strength, rate of tension development and fiber type composition. J. Gerontol. 36: 648–653.

Collins, K. J., Dore, C., Exton-Smith, A. N., Fox, R. H., MacDonald, I. C., and Woodward, P. M. 1977. Accidental hypothermia and impaired temperature homeostasis in the elderly. Brit. Med. J. 1: 353–356.

Corre, K. A., Cho, H., and Barnard, R. J. 1976. Maximum exercise heart rate reduction with maturation in the rat. J. Appl. Physiol. 40: 741–744.

Cousineau, D., Ferguson, R. J., deChamplain, J., Gauthier, P., Cote, P., and Bourassa, M. Catecholamines in coronary sinus during exercise in man before and after training. J. Appl. Physiol.: Respirat. Environ. Exer. Physiol. 43: 801–806.

Cumming, G. R., Dufresne, C., and Samm, J. 1973. Exercise ECG changes in normal women. Can. Med. Assoc. J. 109: 108–111.

Davies, C. T. M. 1979. Thermoregulation during exercise in relation to sex and age. Eur. J. Appl. Physiol. 42: 71–79.

deVries, H. A. 1970. Physiological effects of an exercise training regimen upon men aged 52 to 88. J. Gerontol. 25: 325–336.

deVries, H. A. 1971a. Exercise intensity threshold for improvement of cardiovascular-respiratory function in older men. Geriatrics 26: 94–101.

deVries, H. A. 1971b. Prescription of exercise for older men from telemetered exercise heart rate data. Geriatrics 26: 102–111.

deVries, H. A. 1978. Physiology of exercise and aging. In, F. Landry and W. A. R. Orban (eds.), Physical Activity and Human Well Being, pp. 79–94. Miami: Symposia Specialists.

deVries, H. A. 1979. Tips on prescribing exercise regimens for your older patient. Geriatrics 34: 75–81.

deVries, H. A. and Adams, G. M. 1972a. Electromyographic comparison of single doses of exercise and meprobamate as to effects on muscular relaxation. Am. J. Phys. Med. 51: 130–141.

deVries, H. A. and Adams, G. M. 1972b. Comparison of exercise responses in old and young men. I. The cardiac effort/total body effort relationship. J. Gerontol. 27: 344–348.

deVries, H. A. and Adams, G. M. 1972c. Comparison of exercise responses in old and young men. II. Ventilatory mechanics. J. Gerontol. 27: 349–352.

deVries, H. A. and Adams, G. M. 1972d. Total muscle mass activation vs relative loading of individual muscle as determinants of exercise response in older men. *Med. Sci. Spts.* 4: 146–154.

deVries, H. A. and Adams, G. M. 1977. Effect of the type of exercise upon the work of the heart in older men. *J. Spts. Med.* 17: 41–47.

deVries, H. A., Wiswell, R. A., Bulbulian, R., and Maritani, T. 1981. Tranquilizer effect of exercise: acute effects of moderate aerobic exercise on spinal reflex activation level. *Am. J. Phys. Med.* 60: 57–66.

Diesfeldt, H. F. A. and Diesfeldt-Groenendijk, H. 1977. Improving cognitive performance in psychogeriatric patients: the influence of physical exercise. *Age and Aging* 6: 58–64.

Dill, D. B. and Consolazio, C. F. 1962. Response to exercise as related to age and environmental temperature. *J. Appl. Physiol.* 17: 645–648.

Dill, D. B., Hall, F. G., and Van Beaumont, W. 1966. Sweat chloride concentration, sweat rate, metabolic rate, skin temperature and age. *J. Appl. Physiol.* 21: 99–106.

Dill, D. B., Hillyard, S. D., and Miller, J. 1980. Vital capacity, exercise performance, and blood gases at altitude as related to age. *J. Appl. Physiol.: Environ. Respirat. Exer. Physiol.* 48: 6–9.

Dill, D. B., Horvath, S. M., Dahms, T. E., Parker, R. E., and Lynch, J. R. 1969. Hemoconcentration at altitude. *J. Appl. Physiol.* 27: 514–518.

Dill, D. B., Horvath, S. M., Van Beaumont, W., Gehlsen, W., and Burrus, K. 1967. Sweat electrolytes in desert walks. *J. Appl. Physiol.* 23: 746–751.

Dill, D. B., Robinson, S., Balke, B., and Newton, J. L. 1964. Work tolerance: age and attitude. *J. Appl. Physiol.* 19: 483–488.

Dill, D. B., Terman, J. W., and Hall, F. G. 1963. Hemoglobin at high altitude as related to age. *Clin. Chem.* 9: 711–716.

Dill, D. B., Yousef, M. K., and Nelson, J. D. 1973. Responses of men and women to two hour walks in desert heat. *J. Appl. Physiol.* 35: 231–235.

Drinkwater, B. L., Horvath, S. M., and Wells, C. L. 1975. Aerobic power of females ages 10 to 68. *J. Gerontology* 30: 385–394.

Drori, D. and Folman, Y. 1976. Environmental effects of longevity in the male rat: exercise, mating, castration and restricted feeding. *Exp. Gerontol.* 11: 25–32.

Edington, D. W., Cosmos, A. C., and McCafferty, W. B. 1972. Exercise and longevity: evidence for a threshold age. *J. Gerontol.* 27: 341–343.

Ekblom, B., Kilbom, A., and Soltysiak, J. 1973. Physical training bradycardia and autonomic nervous system. *Scand. J. Clin. Lab. Invest.* 32: 251–256.

Ellis, F. P., Exton-Smith, A. N., Foster, K. G., and Weiner, J. S. 1976. Eccrine sweating and mortality during heat waves in very young and very old persons. *Isr. J. Med. Sci.* 12: 815–817.

Elsayed, M., Ismail, A. H., and Young, R. J. 1980. Intellectual differences of adult men related to age and physical fitness before and after an exercise program. *J. Gerontol.* 35: 383–387.

Emes, C. G. 1979. The effects of a regular program of light exercise on seniors. *J. Spts. Med.* 19: 185–190.

Ermini, M. 1976. Ageing changes in mammalian skeletal muscle. Biochemical studies. *Gerontol.* 22: 301–316.

Faria, I. and Frankel, M. 1977. Anthropometric and physiologic profile of a cyclist—age 70. *Med. Sci. Spts.* 9: 118–121.

Farrar, R. P., Martin, T. P., and Ardies, C. M. 1981. The interaction of aging and endurance exercise upon the mitochondrial function of skeletal muscle. *J. Gerontol.* 36: 642–647.

Fixler, D. E., Atkins, J. M., Mitchell, J. H., and Horwitz, L. D. 1976. Blood flow to respiratory, cardiac and limb muscles in dogs during graded exercise. *Am. J. Physiol.* 231: 1515–1519.

Frekany, G. A. and Leslie, D. K. 1975. Effects of an exercise program on selected flexibility measurements of senior citizens. *Gerontol.* 15: 182–183.

Fries, J. F. and Crapo, L. M. 1981. *Vitality and Aging.* San Francisco: W. H. Freeman. 172pp.

Gerstenblith, G., Spurgeon, H. A., Froehlich, J. P., Weisfeldt, M. L., and Lakatta, E. G. 1979. Diminished inotropic responsiveness to ouabain in aged rat myocardium. *Circ. Res.* 44: 517–523.

Glueck, C. J. 1982. Cradle to grave atherosclerosis: high density lipoprotein cholesterol. *J. Am. Coll. Nutr.* 1: 41–48.

Glueck, C. J., Gartside, P. S., Steiner, P. M., Miller, L., Todhunter, T., Haaf, J., Pucke, M., Terrana, M., Fallat, R. W., and Kashyap, M. L. 1977. Hyperalpha- and hypobetalipoproteinemia in octogenarian kindreds. *Atherosclerosis* 27: 387–406.

Golden, F. 1974. Notes on survival at sea. *J. Royal Naval Med. Serv.* 60: 8–19.

Goldman, R. and Rockstein, M. 1975. *The Physiology and Pathology of Human Aging.* New York: Academic Press. 232pp.

Gollnick, P. D., Armstrong, R. B., Saltin, B., Saubert, C. V., Sembrowich, W. L., and Shepherd, R. E. 1973. Effect of training on enzyme activity and fiber composition of human skeletal muscle. *J. Appl. Physiol.* 34: 107–111.

Gollnick, P. D. and King, D. W. 1969. Effect of exercise and training on mitochondria of rat skeletal muscle. *Am. J. Physiol.* 216: 1502–1509.

Goodrick, C. L. 1980. Effects of long term wheel exercise on male and female Wistar rats. I. Longevity, body weight and metabolic rate. *Gerontol.* 26: 22–23.

Granath, A., Jonsson, B., and Strandell, T. 1964. Circulation of healthy old men, studied by right heart catheterization at rest and during exercise in supine and sitting position. *Acta Medica Scand.* 176: 425–446.

Granath, A. and Strandell, T. 1964. Relationship between cardiac output, stroke volume and intracardiac pressures at rest and during exercise in supine position and some anthropometric data in healthy old men. *Acta Medica Scand.* 176: 447–466.

Griffin, S. J. and Trinder, J. 1978. Physical fitness, exercise and human sleep. *Psychophysiol.* 15: 447–450.

Grimby, G. 1976. Pulmonary mechanics: the load. *In,* J. A. Dempsey and C. Reed (eds.), *Muscular Exercise and the Lung,* pp. 17–24. Madison: University of Wisconsin Press.

Grimby, G. and Stiksa, J. 1970. Flow-volume curves and breathing patterns during exercise in patients with obstructive lung disease. *Scand. J. Clin. Lab. Invest.* 24: 303–313.

Hall, D. A. 1973. Metabolic and structural aspects of aging. *In,* J. C. Brocklehurst (ed.), *Textbook of Geriatric Medicine and Gerontology.* Edinburgh: Churchill-Livingstone.

Harris, R. and Frankel, L. J. 1977. *Guide to Fitness after Fifty.* New York: Plenum Press, 356pp.

Hartley, L. H. 1975. Growth hormone and catecholamine response to exercise in relation to physical training. *Med. Sci. Spts.* 7: 34–36.

Hartley, L. H., Mason, J. W., Hagan, R. P., Jones, L. G., Katchen, T. A., Mougey, E. H., Wherry, F. E., Pennington, L. L., and Ricketts, P. T. 1972. Multiple hormonal responses to graded exercise in relation to physical training. *J. Appl. Physiol.* 33: 602–606.

Hartung, G. H., Farge, E. J., and Mitchell, R. E. 1981. Effects of marathon running, jogging and diet on coronary risk factors in middle-aged men. *Prev. Med.* 10: 316–323.

Haskell, W. L., Taylor, H. L., Wood, P. D., Schrott, H., and Heiss, G. 1980. Strenuous physical activity, treadmill exercise test-performance and plasma high-density lipoprotein cholesterol. *Circ.* 62: (Suppl. 4), 53–61.

Haynes, S. G. and Feinleib, M. (eds.) 1980. *Second Conference on the Epidemiology of Aging.* Bethesda, Md.: U.S. Department of Health and Human Services, National Institute on Aging, NIH Publ. No. 80–969, 387pp.

Heath, G. W., Hagberg, J. M., Ehsani, A. A., and Holloszy, J. O. 1981. A physiological comparison of young and old endurance athletes. *J. Appl. Physiol.: Respirat. Environ. Exer. Physiol.* 51: 634–640.

Hodgson, J. L. 1971. Age and aerobic capacity of urban midwestern males. Ph.D. thesis. Minneapolis: University of Minneasota. 351pp.

Hodgson, J. L. and Buskirk, E. R. 1977. Physical fitness and age with emphasis on cardiovascular function in the elderly. *J. Am. Geriatr. Soc.* 25: 385–392.

Hodgson, J. L. and Buskirk, E. R. 1981. Role of exercise in aging. *In,* D. Danon and N. W. Shock (eds.), *Aging: A Challenge to Science and Social Policy,* Vol. 1, pp. 189–196. Oxford: Oxford University Press.

Holloszy, J. O. and Booth, F. W. 1976. Biochemical adaptations to endurance exercise in muscle. *Ann. Rev. Physiol.* 38: 273–291.

Holm, J. and Schersten, T. 1974. Metabolic changes in skeletal muscles after physical conditioning and in peripheral arterial insufficiency. *Forsvarsmedicin* 10: 71–82.

Horvath, S. M. 1981. Aging and adaptation to stresses. *In,* S. M. Horvath and M. Yousef (eds.), *Environmental Physiology: Aging, Heat and Altitude,* pp. 437–452. New York: Elsevier North Holland.

Horvath, S. M. 1982. Exercise in a cold environment. *In,* D. I. Miller (ed.), *Exercise and Sports Science Reviews* Vol. 9, pp. 221–263. Philadelphia: The Franklin Institute Press.

Horvath, S. M. and Rochelle, R. D. 1977. Hypothermia in the aged. *Env. Hlth. Perspectives* 20: 127–130.

Huddleston, A. L., Rockwell, D., Kulund, D. N., and Harrison, R. B. 1980. Bone mass in lifetime tennis athletes. *JAMA* 244: 1107–1109.

Ingvar, D. H., Sjolund, B., and Ardo, A. 1976. Correlation between dominant EEG frequency, cerebral oxygen uptake and blood flow. *Electroencephalgraphy Clin. Neurol.* 41: 268–276.

Jammes, Y., Auran, Y., Gouvernet, J., Delpierre, S., and Grimaud, C. 1979. The ventilatory pattern of conscious man according to age and morphology. *Bull. Europ. Physiopath. Resp.* 15: 527–540.

Jette, A. M. and Branch, L. G. 1981. The Framingham disability study. II. Physical disability among the aging. *Am. J. Pub. Hlth.* 71: 1211–1216.

Jones, H. H., Nabel, D. A., Priest, J. D., Hayes, W. C., Tichenor, C. C., and Nagel, D. A. 1977. Humeral hypertrophy in response to exercise. *J. Bone Joint Surg. Am.* 59: 204–208.

Jose, A. D. and Collison, D. 1970. The normal range and determinants of the intrinsic heart rate in man. *Card. Res.* 4: 160.

Kanstrup, I. and Ekblom, B. 1978. Influence of age and physical activity on central hemodynamics and lung function in active adults. *J. Appl. Physiol.: Respirat. Environ. Exer. Physiol.* 45: 709–717.

Karlsson, J., Sjodin, B., Thorstensson, A., Hulten, B., and Frith, K. 1975. LDH isozymes in skeletal muscles of endurance and strength trained athletes. *Acta Physiol. Scand.* 93: 150–156.

Kasch, F. W. and Wallace, J. P. 1976. Physiological variables during 10 years of endurance exercise. *Med. Sci. Spts.* 8: 5–8.

Keatinge, W. R. 1969. *Survival in Cold Water.* Oxford: Blackwell Scientific Publications. 131pp.

Keatinge, W. R. 1978. Body fat and cooling rates in relation to age. *In,* L. J. Folinsbee et al. (eds.), *Environmental Stress,* pp. 299–302. New York: Academic Press.

Kersheim, H. R. 1976. Systemic arterial baroreceptor reflexes. *Physiol. Rev.* 56: 100–112.

Kiessling, K. H., Pilstrom, L., Bylund, A. C., Saltin, B., and Piehl, K. 1974. Enzyme activities and morphometry in skeletal muscle of middle-aged men after training. *Scand. J. Clin. Lab. Invest.* 33: 63–69.

Knip, A. S. 1977. Ethnic studies of sweat gland counts. *In,* J. S. Weiner (ed.), *Physiological Variation and Its Genetic Basis,* pp. 113–123. New York: Halstead Press.

Kollias, J., Barlett, L., Bergsteinova, V., Skinner, J. S., Buskirk, E. R., and Nicholas, W. C. 1974. Metabolic and thermal response of women during cooling in water. *J. Appl. Physiol.* 36: 577–580.

Kostis, J. B., Moreyra, A. E., Amendo, M. T., Di-Pietro, J., Cosgrove, N., and Kuo, P. T. 1982. The effect of age on heart rate in subjects free of heart disease: studies by ambulatory electrocardiography and maximal exercise stress test. *Circ.* 65: 141–146.

Kroll, W. and Clarkson, P. M. 1978. Age, isometric knee extension strength, and fractionated resistance response time. *Exper. Aging Res.* 4: 389–409.

Kusumi, F., Bruce, R. A., Ross, M. A., Trimble, S., and Voigt, A. E. 1976. Elevated arterial pressure and postexertional ST-segment depression in middle-aged women. *Am. Heart J.* 92: 576–583.

Lakatta, E. G. 1980. Age related alterations in the cardiovascular response to adrenergic mediated stress. *Fed. Proc.* 39: 3173–3177.

Lakatta, E. G., Gerstenblith, G., Angell, C. S., Shock, N. W., and Weisfeldt, M. L. 1975. Diminished inotropic response of aged myocardium to catecholamines. *Circ. Res.* 36: 262–269.

Lakatta, E. G. and Yin, F. C. P. 1982. Myocardial aging: functional alterations and related cellular mechanisms. *Am. J. Physiol.* 242: (Heart Circ. Physiol. 11), H927–H941.

Larsson, L. 1982. Physical training effects on muscle morphology in sedentary males at different ages. *Med. Sci. Spts. Exer.* 14: 203–206.

Larsson, L., Grimby, G., and Karlsson, J. 1979. Muscle strength and speed of movement in relation to age and muscle morphology. *J. Appl. Physiol.: Respirat. Environ. Exer. Physiol.* 46: 451–456.

Larsson, L. and Karlsson, J. 1978. Isometric and dynamic endurance as a function of age and skeletal muscle characteristics. *Acta Physiol. Scand.* 104: 129–136.

Larsson, L., Sjodin, B., and Karlsson, K. 1978. Histochemical and biomechanical changes in human skeletal muscle with age in sedentary males, age 22–65 years. *Acta Physiol. Scand.* 103: 31–39.

Leaf, A. 1973. Observations of a peripatetic gerontologist. *Nutr. Today* 8: 4–12.

LeBlanc, J., Cote, J., Dulac, J., and Turcot, F. 1978. Age, sex and fitness and the response to local cooling. *In,* L. J. Folinsbee et al. (eds.), *Environmental Stress: Individual Human Adaptation* pp. 267–277. New York: Academic Press.

LeBlanc, P., Ruff, F., and Milic-Emili, J. 1970. Effects of age and body position in "airway closure" in man. *J. Appl. Physiol.* 28: 448–451.

Lenapert, P. and Cooper, K. 1967. The effect of exercise on intraocular pressure. *Am. J. Opthalmol.* 63: 1673–1976.

Leon, A. S. and Bloor, C. M. 1970. Exercise effects on the heart of different ages (abstract). *Circ.* 41–42: (Suppl. 3), 50.

Lesser, M. 1978. The effects of rhythmic exercise on the range of motion in older adults. *Am. Corr. Ther. J.* 32: 118–122.

Lind, A. R., Humphreys, P. W., Collins, K. J., Foster,

K., and Sweetland, K. F. 1970. Influence of age and daily duration of exposure on responses of men to work in heat. *J. Appl. Physiol.* 28: 50–56.

Lind, A. R. and Petrofsky, J. S. 1978. The influences of age, sex and body fat content on isometric strength and endurance. *In,* L. J. Folinsbee et al. (eds.), *Environmental Stress,* pp. 195–204. New York: Academic Press.

MacMillan, A. L., Corbett, J. L., Johnson, R. H., Crampton-Smith, A., Spalding, J. M. K., and Wallner, L. 1967. Temperature regulation in survivors of accidental hypothermia of the elderly. *Lancet* 2: 165–169.

Masoro, E. J. (ed.) 1981. *CRC Handbook of Physiology in Aging.* Boca Raton, Fla.: CRC Press. 502pp.

Matsumato, J., Nishisho, T., Suto, T., Sadahiro, T., and Miyoshi, M. 1968. Influence of fatigue on sleep. *Nature* 218: 177–178.

McCormick, R. J. 1973. Heat tolerance of exercising lean and obese middle-aged men. Ph.D. thesis. University Park, Pa.: The Pennsylvania State University, 116pp.

McCormick, R. J. and Buskirk, E. R. 1974. Heat tolerance of exercising lean and obese middle-aged men. *Fed. Proc.* 33: 441 (Abstract).

McDermott, D. J., Stekiel, W. J., Barbariak, J. J., Kloth, L. C., and Smith, J. J. 1974. Effect of age on hemodynamic and metabolic response to static exercise. *J. Appl. Physiol.* 37: 923–926.

McFarland, R. A. 1972. Psychophysiological implications of life at altitude and including the role of oxygen in the process of aging. *In,* M. K. Yousef, S. M. Horvath, and R. W. Bullard (eds.), *Physiological Adaptations,* pp. 157–181. New York: Academic Press.

Milvy, P. 1977. Statistical analysis of deaths from coronary heart disease anticipated in a cohort of marathon runners. *Ann. N.Y. Acad. Sci.* 301: 620–626.

Miyashita, M., Haga, S., and Mizuta, T. 1978. Training and detraining effects on aerobic power in middle-aged and older men. *J. Spts. Med.* 18: 131–137.

Montoye, H. J. 1974. Health and longevity of former athletes. *In,* W. R. Johnson and E. R. Buskirk (eds.), *Science and Medicine of Exercise and Sport,* 2nd ed., pp. 366–376. New York: Harper & Row.

Montoye, H. J. 1975. *Physical Activity and Health: An Epidemiologic Study of an Entire Community.* Englewood Cliffs, N.J.: Prentice Hall, 131pp.

Montoye, H. J., Block, W. D., Metzner, H., and Keller, J. B. 1977. Habitual physical activity and glucose tolerance. *Diabetes* 26: 172–176.

Montoye, H. J. and Lamphiear, D. E. 1977. Grip and arm strength in males and females, age 10 to 69. *Res. Qrtly.* 48: 109–120.

Murphy, E. and Faul, P. J. 1963. Accidental hypothermia in the elderly. *J. Irish Med. Assoc.* 53: 4.

Niinimaa, V. and Shephard, R. J. 1978. Training and oxygen conductance in the elderly. (1) The respiratory system. *J. Gerontol.* 33: 354–361.

Nikkila, E. A., Taskinen, M. R., and Kekki, M. 1978.

Relation of plasma high-density lipoprotein cholesterol to lipoprotein-lipase activity in adipose tissue and skeletal muscle of man. *Atherosclerosis* 29: 497–501.

Nilsson, B. E. R. and Westlin, N. E. 1971. Bone density in athletes. *Clin. Orthop.* 77: 179–182.

Olson, H. W., Teitelbaum, H., Van Huss, W. D., and Montoye, H. J. 1977. Years of sports participation and mortality in college athletes. *J. Spts. Med.* 17: 321–326.

Orlander, J. and Aniansson, A. 1980. Effects of physical training on skeletal muscle metabolism and ultrastructure in 70 to 75 year old men. *Acta Physiol. Scand.* 109: 149–154.

Orlander, J., Kiessling, K. H., Karlsson, J., and Ekblom, B. 1977. Low intensity training, inactivity and resumed training in sedentary men. *Acta. Physiol. Scand.* 101: 351–362.

Orlander, J., Kiessling, K. H., Larsson, L., Karlsson, J., and Aniansson, A. 1978. Skeletal muscle metabolism and ultrastructure in relation to age in sedentary men. *Acta Physiol. Scand.* 104: 249–261.

Oscai, L. B. 1973. The role of exercise in weight control. *In,* J. H. Wilmore (ed.), *Exercise and Sports Science Reviews* Vol. 1, pp. 103–123. New York: Academic Press.

Ostfeld, A. M. and Gibson, D. C. (eds.) 1972. *Epidemiology of Aging.* Bethesda, Md.: U.S. Department of Health, Education and Welfare, National Institute on Aging, DHEW Publ. No. NIH 75-711, 286pp.

Oswald, I. 1976. The function of sleep. *Postgrad. Med. J.* 52: 15–18.

Paffenbarger, R. S., Wing, A. L., and Hyde, R. T. 1978. Physical activity as an index of heart attack risk in college alumni. *Am. J. Epidemiol.* 108: 161–175.

Palmer, G. J., Ziegler, M. G., and Lake, C. R. 1978. Response of norepinephrine and blood pressure to stress increases with age. *J. Gerontol.* 33: 482–487.

Palmore, E. 1980. Predictors of longevity. *In,* S. G. Haynes and M. Feinleib (eds.), *Second Conference on the Epidemiology of Aging,* pp. 57–64. Washington, D.C.: U.S. Department of Health and Human Services, NIH Publ. No. 80-969.

Peltonen, P., Marniemi, J., Hietanen, E., Vvori, I., and Ehnholm, C. 1981. Changes in serum lipids, lipoproteins, and heparin releasable lipolytic enzymes during moderate physical training in man: a longitudinal study. *Metabol.* 30: 518–526.

Petrofsky, J. S. and Lind, A. R. 1975. Isometric strength, endurance, and the blood pressure and heart rate responses during isometric exercise in healthy men and women, with special reference to age and body fat content. *Pflügers Arch. Ges. Physiol.* 360: 49–61.

Plowman, S. A., Drinkwater, B. L., and Horvath, S. M. 1979. Age and aerobic power in women: a longitudinal study. *J. Gerontol.* 34: 512–520.

Polednak, A. P. (ed.) 1979. *The Longevity of Athletes.* Springfield, Ill.: Charles C. Thomas. 255pp.

Pollock, M. L. 1974. Physiological characteristics of older champion track athletes. *Res. Quart.* 45: 363–373.

Pollock, M. L., Miller, H. S., and Wilmore, J. 1974. Physiological characteristics of champion American track athletes 40 to 75 years of age. *J. Gerontol.* 29: 645–649.

Port, S., Cobb, F. R., Coleman, R. E., and Jones, R. H. 1980. The effect of age on the response of the left ventricular ejection fraction to exercise. *N. Engl. J. Med.* 303: 1133–1137.

President's Council on Physical Fitness and Sports. 1973. National adult physical fitness survey. *Newsletter* Special Edition, Washington, D.C.

President's Council on Physical Fitness and Sports 1981. *A Synopsis of the National Conference on Fitness and Aging.* Washington, D.C., 48pp.

Profant, G. R., Early, R. G., Nilson, K. L., Kusumi, F., Hofer, V., and Bruce, R. A. 1972. Responses to maximal exercise in healthy middle-aged women. *J. Appl. Physiol.* 33: 595–599.

Prout, C. 1972. Life expectancy of college oarsmen. *JAMA* 220: 1709–1711.

Rakusan, K. and Poupa, O. 1964. Capillaries and muscle fibers in the hearts of old rats. *Gerontologia* 9: 107–112.

Reaven, E. P., Gold, G., and Reaven, G. M. 1979. Effect of age on glucose-stimulated insulin release by the beta cell of the rat. *J. Clin. Invest.* 64: 591–599.

Reaven, E. P., Gold, G., and Reaven, G. M. 1980. Effect of age on leucine-induced insulin secretion by the beta cell. *J. Gerontol.* 35: 324–328.

Reaven, E. P. and Reaven, G. M. 1981b. Structure and function changes in the endocrine pancreas of aging rats with reference to the modulating effects of exercise and caloric restriction. *J. Clin. Invest.* 68: 75–84.

Reaven, G. M. and Reaven, E. P. 1981a. Prevention of age related hypertriglyceridemia by caloric restriction and exercise training in the rat. *Metabol.* 30: 982–986.

Reddan, W. G. 1981. Respiratory system and aging. *In,* E. L. Smith and R. C. Serfass (eds.), *Exercise and Aging: The Scientific Basis,* pp. 89–107. Hillside, N.J.: Enslow.

Richardson, D. and Shewchuk, R. 1980. Comparison of calf muscle blood flow responses to rhythmic exercise between mean age 25- and 74-year-old men. *Proc. Soc. Exptl. Biol. Med.* 164: 550–555.

Rizzato, G. and Marrazini, L. 1970. Thoracoabdominal mechanics in elderly men. *J. Appl. Physiol.* 28: 457–460.

Robinson, S., Belding, H. S., Consolazio, F. C., Horvath, S. M., and Turrell, E. S. 1965. Acclimatization of older men to work in the heat. *J. Appl. Physiol.* 20: 583–586.

Robinson, S., Dill, D. B., Robinson, R. D., Tzankoff,

S. P., and Wagner, J. A. 1976. Physiological aging of champion runners. *J. Appl. Physiol.* 41: 46–51.

Rockstein, M., Chesky, J. A., and Lopez, T. 1981. Effects of exercise on the biochemical aging of mammalian myocardium. I. Actomyosin ATPase. *J. Gerontol.* 36: 294–297.

Rockstein, M. and Sussman, M. 1979. *Biology of Aging*. Belmont, Calif.: Wadsworth, 203pp.

Rodenheffer, R., Gerstenblith, G., Fleg, J. L., Lakatta, E. G., Clulow, J., Kallman, C. H., Weisfeldt, M. L., and Becker, L. C. 1981. The impact of age on gated blood pool scan (GBPS) measurements of LV volumes during exercise. *Circ.* 64: IV243.

Roussos, C. S. and Macklem, D. T. 1977. Diaphragmatic fatigue in man. *J. Appl. Physiol.* 43: 189–197.

Salminen, A. and Vihko, V. 1980. Effects of age and prolonged running on proteolytic capacity in mouse cardiac and skeletal muscles. *Acta Physiol. Scand.* 112: 89–95.

Sato, I., Hasegawa, Y., Takahashi, N., Hirata, Y., Shimonura, K., and Hotta, K. 1981. Age-related changes of cardiac control function in man. *J. Gerontol.* 36: 564–572.

Sawka, M. N., Glaser, R. M., Laubach, L. L., Al-Samkari, O., and Suryaprasad, A. G. 1981. Wheelchair exercise performance of the young, middleaged, and elderly. *J. Appl. Physiol.: Respirat. Environ. Exer. Physiol.* 50: 824–828.

Scheuer, J. and Bhan, A. 1979. Cardiac contractile proteins—adenosine triphosphate activity and physiological function. *Circ. Res.* 45: 1–12.

Schocken, D. D., Blumenthal, J. A., Coleman, R. E., Hindle, P., Needels, T., Koisch, F. P., Part, S., and Wallace, A. G. 1981. Physical conditioning and ventricular function in the elderly. *Circ.* 64: IV12.

Sebban, C., Berthaux, P., Lenoir, H., Eugene, M., Venet, R., Menin, Y., de la Fuente, X., and Reisner, C. 1981. Arterial compliance, systolic pressure and heart rate in elderly women at rest and on exercise. *Gerontol.* 27: 271–280.

Serfass, R. C. 1980. Physical exercise and the elderly. *In,* G. A. Stull and T. K. Cureton, Jr. (eds.), *Encyclopedia of Physical Education, Fitness and Sports: Training, Environment, Nutrition and Fitness,* pp. 575–594. Salt Lake City: Brighton.

Severson, J. A., Fell, R. D., Vander Tuig, J. G., and Griffith, D. R. 1977. Adrenocortical function in aging exercise-trained rats. *J. Appl. Physiol.* 43: 839–843.

Shanas, E. 1980. Self-assessment of physical function: white and black elderly of the United States. *In,* S. G. Haynes et al. (eds.), *Second Conference on the Epidemiology of Aging* pp. 269–285. Bethesda, Md.: U.S. Department of Health and Human Services, NIH Publ. No. 80-969.

Shephard, J., Donovan, W., and Mundle, P. 1975. *Age Records 1975 Revision.* Los Altos, Calif.: Track and Field News, 31pp.

Shephard, R. J. 1978. *Physical Activity and Aging.* Chicago: Year Book.

Shephard, R. J. 1982. *Physiology and Biochemistry of Exercise.* New York: Praeger, 672pp.

Shephard, R. J. and Kavanagh, T. 1978. The effects of training on the aging process. *Phys. Spts. Med.* 6: 32–40.

Shock, N. W. 1977. Systems integration. *In,* C. E. Finch and L. Hayflick (eds.), *Handbook of the Biology of Aging,* pp. 639–661. New York: Van Nostrand Reinhold.

Shock, N. W. 1982. The role of nutrition in aging. *J. Am. Coll. Nutr.* 1: 3–9.

Sidney, K. H. and Shephard, R. J. 1977a. Activity patterns of elderly men and women. *J. Gerontol.* 32: 25–32.

Sidney, K. H. and Shephard, R. J. 1977b. Maximum and submaximum exercise tests in men and women in the seventh, eighth and ninth decades of life. *J. Appl. Physiol.: Respirat. Environ. Exer. Physiol.* 43: 280–287.

Sidney, K. H., Shephard, R. J., and Harrison, J. E. 1977. Endurance training and body composition of the elderly. *Am. J. Clin. Nutr.* 30: 326–333.

Skrobak-Kaczynski, J. and Andersen, K. L. 1975. The effect of a high level of habitual physical activity in the regulation of fatness during aging. *Int. Arch. Occup. Environ. Hlth.* 36: 41–46.

Smith, E. L. 1973. Effects of physical activity on bone in the aged. *In,* R. B. Mazess (ed.), *International Conference on Bone Mineral Measurement.* Washington, D.C.: U.S. Department of Health, Education and Welfare, DHEW Publ. No. (NIH) 75-683.

Smith, E. L. 1981. Physical activity: a preventive and maintenance modality for bone loss with age. *In,* F. J. Nagle and H. J. Montoye (eds.), *Exercise in Health and Disease,* pp. 196–202. Springfield, Ill.: Charles C. Thomas.

Smith, E. L. and Reddan, W. 1976. Physical activity—a modality for bone accretion in the aged. *Am. J. Roentgenol.* 126: 1297.

Smith, E. L. and Serfass, R. C. (eds.) 1981. *Exercise and Aging: The Scientific Basis.* Hillside, N.J.: Enslow Publishers, 191pp.

Spirduso, W. W., 1974. Reaction and movement times as a function of age and physical activity level. *J. Gerontol.* 30: 435–440.

Spirduso, W. W. 1980. Physical fitness, aging, and psychomotor speed: a review. *J. Gerontol.* 35: 850–865.

Steinhagen-Thiessen, E., Reznik, A., and Hilz, H. 1980. Negative adaptation to physical training in senile mice. *Mech. Age. Dev.* 12: 231–236.

Stewart, R. H., LeBlanc, R., and Becker, B. 1970. Effects of exercise on aqueous dynamics. *Am. J. Opthalmol.* 69: 245–248.

Suominen, H. and Heikkinen, E. 1975. Enzyme activities in muscle and connective tissue of m. vastus lateralis in habitually training and sedentary 33 to 70-year-old-men. *Eur. J. Appl. Physiol.* 34: 249–254.

Suominen, H., Heikkinen, E., Liesen, H., Michel, D., and Hollmann, W. 1977a. Effects of 8 weeks' endurance training on skeletal muscle metabolism in 56–

70 year old sedentary men. *Eur. J. Appl. Physiol.* 37: 173–180.

Suominen, H., Heikkinen, E., and Parkatti, T. 1977b. Effects of eight weeks' physical training on muscle and connective tissue of the m. vastus lateralis in 69-year-old men and women. *J. Gerontol.* 32: 33–37.

Suominen, H., Heikkinen, E., Parkatti, T., Forsberg, S., and Kiiskinen, A. 1977c. Effects of "lifelong" physical training on functional aging in men. *Scand. J. Soc. Med.* 14: (Suppl. 5), 225–240.

Taylor, H. L., Buskirk, E. R., and Remington, R. D. 1973. Exercise in controlled trials of the prevention of coronary heart disease. *Fed. Proc.* 32: 1623–1627.

Taylor, H. L. and Montoye, H. J. 1972. Physical fitness, cardiovascular function and age. *In*, A. M. Ostfeld and D. C. Gibson (eds.), *Epidemiology of Aging* pp. 223–241. Washington, D.C.: U.S. Department of Health, Education and Welfare, DHEW Publ. No. (NIH) 75–711.

Tomanek, R. J. 1970. Effects of age and exercise on the extent of the myocardial capillary bed. *Anat. Rec.* 167: 55–62.

Tzankoff, S. P. and Norris, A. H. 1977. Effect of muscle mass decrease on age related BMR changes. *J. Appl. Physiol.* 43: 1000–1006.

Tzankoff, S. P. and Norris, H. H. 1979. Age-related differences in lactate distribution kinetics following maximal exercise. *Eur. J. Appl. Physiol.* 42: 35–40.

Van Huss, W. D. 1979. Physical activity and aging. *In*, R. H. Strauss (ed.), *Sports Medicine and Physiology* pp. 373–385. Philadelphia: W. B. Saunders.

Van Tosh, A., Lakatta, E. G., Fleg, J. L., Weiss, J., Kallman, C., Weisfeldt, M., and Gerstenblith, G. 1980. Ventricular dimension changes during submaximal exercise: effects of aging in normal man. *Circ.* 62: III–483.

Vihko, V., Rantamaki, J., and Salminen, A. 1978. Exhaustive physical exercise and acid hydrolase activity in mouse skeletal muscle. A histochemical study. *Histochemistry* 57: 237–249.

Vyckocil, F. and Gutmann, E. 1972. Spontaneous transmitter release from nerve endings and contractile properties in the soleus and diaphragm muscles of senile rats. *Experientia,* 28, 280–281.

Wagner, J. A., Robinson, S., and Marino, R. P. 1974. Age and temperature regulation of humans in neutral and cold environments. *J. Appl. Physiol.* 37: 562–565.

Wagner, J. A. Robinson, S., Tzankoff, S. P., and Marino, R. P. 1972. Heat tolerance and acclimatization to work in the heat in relation to age. *J. Appl. Physiol.* 33: 616–622.

Weisfeldt, M. L. (ed.) 1980a. *The Aging Heart, Its Function and Response to Stress (Aging* Vol. 12). New York: Raven Press, 335pp.

Weisfeldt, M. L. 1980b. Aging of the cardiovascular system. *New Eng. J. Med.* 303: 1172–1173.

Wilmore, J. H., Miller, H. L., and Pollock, M. L. 1974. Body composition and physiological characteristics of active endurance athletes in their eighth decade of life. *Med. Sci. Spts.* 6: 44–48.

Wynne, T. P., Frey, M. A., Laubach, L. L., and Glueck, C. J. 1980. Effect of a controlled exercise program on serum lipoprotein levels in women on oral contraceptives. *Metabol.* 29: 1267–1272.

Yin, F. C. P., Raizes, G. S., Guarnieri, T., Spurgeon, H. A., Lakatta, E. G., Fortuin, N. J., and Weisfeldt, M. L. 1978. Age associated decrease in ventricular response to hemodynamic stress during beta-adrenergic blockade. *Br. Heart J.* 40: 1349–1355.

Yin, F. C. P., Weisfeldt, M. L., and Milnor, W. R. 1981. Role of aortic input impedance in the decreased cardiovascular response to exercise with aging in dogs. *J. Clin. Invest.* 68: 28–38.

Ziegler, M. G., Lake, C. R., and Kopin, I. J. 1976. Plasma noradrenaline increases with age. *Nature* 261: 333–335.

33
GERIATRIC MEDICINE

John W. Rowe
and
Kenneth L. Minaker
Harvard Medical School

INTRODUCTION

Geriatrics is the branch of medicine concerned with the preventive, remedial, social, educational, and research aspects of illness in old age (Sherman, 1980). While much of this *Handbook* deals with the factors influencing the "quantity" of life span, geriatric medicine has as its main goal the promoting of the highest "quality" of life, that is, the optimum of maximal personal function in a population with the dual afflictions of the effects of the aging process and the accumulation of chronic diseases (Cluff, 1981). While a solid data base now exists with which to approach geriatric patients, substantial gaps in knowledge and service delivery continue. Recent demographic changes indicate that geriatrics will dominate the internal medicine of the 21st century (Hazzard, 1982; Institute of Medicine, 1978), and considerable improvements in data base and health care delivery skills relevant to the elderly can be anticipated over the next decades (Rogers, 1982).

DEVELOPMENT OF HEALTH CARE POLICIES FOR THE ELDERLY IN THE UNITED STATES

The initiation of scientific inquiry into disease in the elderly is often credited to Sir Francis Bacon whose *History of Life and Death* was published in 1645. However, it was not until 1909 that principles central to the practice of medicine in late life were clarified by Nasher who coined the term "geriatrics" and emphasized the impact of social factors on illness patterns in old age. Following the formation of freestanding academic and service departments of geriatric medicine in Great Britain in 1948 (Brocklehurst, 1980), significant improvements were made in health care delivery based on a continuum of care model. The recognition of clinical syndromes common to geriatric medical patients and the development of multidisciplinary treatments necessary to create functional improvements resulted, in part, from the creation of this area of special interest. In the United States, the elderly have long been recognized as having special needs, but little systematic attention was given to geriatrics in medical education or health services research until the 1970s (Besdine, 1980). In 1935, the Social Security Act represented a major response to the special financial needs of the elderly. The need for special aid in financing health care in old age was first recognized by the 1960 Kerr-Mills Amendment to the Social Security Act which provided payments for medical care to the "medically indigent aged." In 1965, more comprehensive health care financing, in the form of amendments to the Social Security Act, was enacted: health insurance for the aged (Title VIII; Medicare) and grants to the states for Medical Assistance Program (Title XIX; Medicaid).

Medicare, available to all people over age 65, has two parts. Part A is an insurance program that provides protection against the costs of hospital and related posthospital services. Medicare Part B is an optional insurance program that covers certain physician and health services fees. Both are third party payment systems, and are subject to deductible and coinsurance payments by the beneficiary. Medicare does not cover costs of long term care in nursing homes. Medicaid provides complete third party payments for some services within five categories (in-hospital services, outpatient hospital services, laboratory and x-ray services, skilled nursing home services, and physician services) for those, including elders, who meet an income eligibility criterion.

The Older Americans Act of 1965 expressed general goals for the elderly which included, among others, "the best possible physical and mental health which science can make available and without regard to economic status" and "full restorative services for those who require institutional care." To achieve these goals, state units on aging and local area agencies on aging were established. Advocacy and service programs are provided by this network, most notable of which is the nutrition program; this provides hot meals at a community location at least once a day, five days a week. The Veterans Administration independently addresses all these needs for the population eligible for its benefits.

While financial, health insurance, and some service needs of the elderly have been addressed, the Congressional Budget Office estimates that substantial areas remain unaddressed. Less than 60 percent of the need for personal care, homes, sheltered living arrangements, and congregate housing, and less than 20 percent of the need for home health and day care, are being met.

HEALTH AND THE ELDERLY

In general, as we age, we accumulate disease, disability, and physician visits. As is well known, this century has been characterized by an exchange of acute infectious illnesses for chronic incremental illness such as cancer, diabetes, arthritis, and atherosclerosis (Fries, 1980); Fries and Crapo, 1981). Eighty percent of health care resources in the United States, including facilities, services, and biomedical research, are now devoted to chronic disease (Somers, 1971). Thirty million Americans have dysfunction due to chronic disease, and 33 percent of them are over age 65, a disproportionate burden relative to their numbers (11 percent of the population) (Rice and Hodgson, 1978). Chronic disease accounts for 60 percent of patient days for hospitalization and 52 percent of physician visits, and contributes to the major limitation in function that half of those with chronic disease possess. Because we accumulate disease over time, the elderly are likely to suffer from several coincident ailments, a condition reflected in their needs for services and their functional incapacity. Physician visits per year per capita increase from 4.4 (age 17–44) to 5.5 (age 45–64), and peak at 6.6 (over age 64) (Health, 1981). Persons with a hospital episode in the previous year increase from 13.4 percent (age 17–44) to 21.9 percent (age 45–64), and peak at 30.4 percent (over age 64) (Health, 1981). Surprisingly, the portion of our population which enjoys excellent health (13–15 percent) remains stable through the life span (Health, 1981).

Reports of the percentage of noninstitutionalized elderly with activity limitation due to chronic conditions in the United States in 1978 (Health, 1981) reveal the functional impact of age-associated illness (Figure 1). Most geriatricians view the degree of improvement of functional capacity rather than the elimination of a specific disease process, as the measure of success in managing the elderly patient.

The goal of improving *function* for elderly

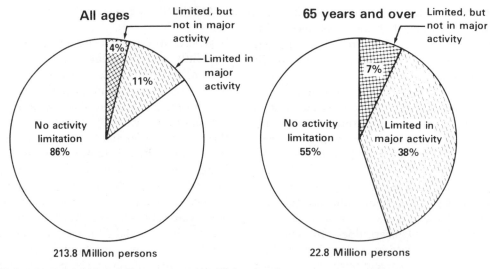

Figure 1. Percent of elderly with activity limitation due to chronic conditions: United States, 1978.

individuals forms the basis for the determination of medical resources and crucial "nonmedical" supports. The recognition that function depends on emotional tone and personality structure, including lifelong habits and coping strategies, has prompted very comprehensive geriatric assessments.

The translation of indirect measures of functional capacity and physician visits into health care utilization patterns confirms the staggering need for health care among the elderly. Figure 2 illustrates the use of health services by the elderly, and Figure 3 shows the per capita health expenditures for the elderly by type of care and source of payment in the United States for 1978. It can be seen that there is disproportionate use of these services by the elderly. The $2026 per capita per year expenditure for the elderly individual is approximately three times that of a younger individual.

The recognition of the increased vulnerability of individuals over 75 years old has, among geriatricians, earned that group the title of "old-old," while those between 65 and 75—who differ more in economic, social, and psychological than medical characteristics from those under 65—are termed

"young-old." Over age 65, there is also a progressive increase in the use of health care services with increased age. Whereas those aged 65–69 averaged three acute hospital days in 1975–76, those over age 85 averaged 8.3 days. In 1973 for every 1000 people aged 65–74, 12 resided in nursing homes. This contrasted with 237 nursing home residents per 1000 individuals aged 85 years and over (Kovar, 1978). Examination of the nursing home population over 85 reveals a material increase in functional impairment. In 1977, of the 1,303,100 individuals in nursing homes, 449,900 were over the age of 85 (Division of Health Care Statistics, 1977). Functional status assessments revealed that between ages 65–74 years and over-84 years, independence in feeding fell from 73 percent to 64 percent, satisfactory vision fell from 75 percent to 57 percent, and good hearing fell from 81 percent to 55 percent. The functional capacity of the noninstitutionalized elderly is better than the institutionalized, but Figure 4 indicates the dramatic falloff in independent function after age 85 which this group also experiences.

Present and future expenditures for health services used by the elderly are illustrated in

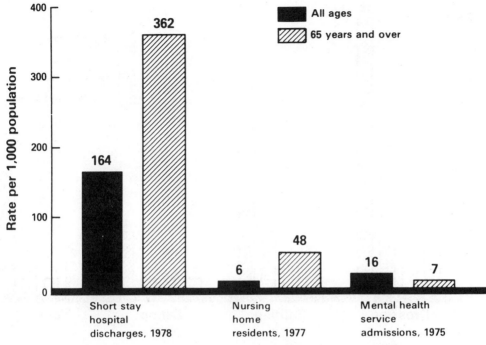

NOTE: Mental health services include state, county and private psychiatric hospitals,
        psychiatric units of general hospitals, community mental health centers, and
        outpatient psychiatric services
SOURCE: National Center for Health Statistics and National Institute of Mental Health

Figure 2. Use of health services by the elderly.

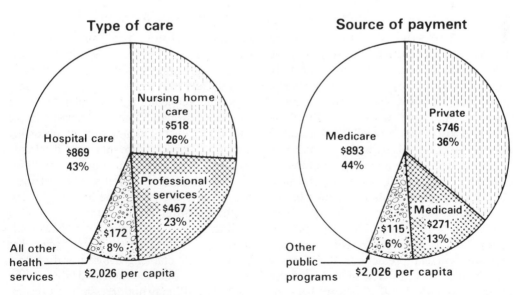

SOURCE: Health Care Financing Administration

NOTE: Other health services include drugs and drug sundries, eyeglasses and appliances, and other health services

Figure 3. Per capita health care expenditures for the elderly by type of care and source of payment:
United States, 1978.

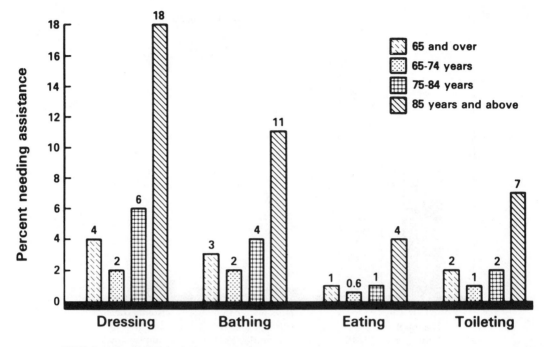

NOTE: Excludes elderly in institutions.
SOURCE: National Center for Health Statistics.

Figure 4. Percent of elderly needing assistance in four activities of daily living by age groups: United States, 1978.

Figure 5. The elderly will continue to require services at a rate higher than their relative numbers would initially suggest. The elderly population will increase in size dramatically in the next 20 years, and this is the major factor accounting for the projected increase in service costs. Not only will there be more elderly, but there will be increased numbers of extremely old individuals, as indicated in Figure 6. These data indicate that the most rapidly enlarging population group in the United States today is the over-85 age group.

It is hard to be confident of these projections in the face of several recent trends that may alter present predictions significantly over the next 20 years. The mortality of the extreme aged, which fell 10 percent between 1933 and 1966, declined 26 percent between 1966 and 1977 (Rosenwaike et al., 1980). During this latter period, the over-85 group had the greatest reduction in mortality of any

population group. The causes of death among persons 85 years and above closely parallel those among populations of all ages. Numerically the greatest reduction comes from the decline in cardiovascular deaths. It has been postulated that modification in the length of functional impairment occurring during an individual life span may also lessen the impact of increased numbers of "old-old" persons by the "compression of morbidity" into the end of the life span (Fries, 1980). The resultant claim that as mortality declines due to treating chronic disease successfully, the morbidity will also decline has been recently challenged by several authors who suggest that the increased life span of the "old-old" may not necessarily be accompanied by decreased morbidity but may, on the other hand, result in even more dramatic increases in the need for long term care services (Siegel, 1980; Manton, 1982).

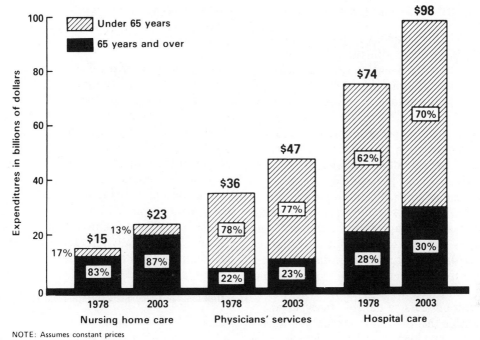

NOTE: Assumes constant prices
SOURCE: National Center for Health Statistics

Figure 5. Projected expenditures for health services used by the elderly, by age group and type of service: United States, 1978 and 2003.

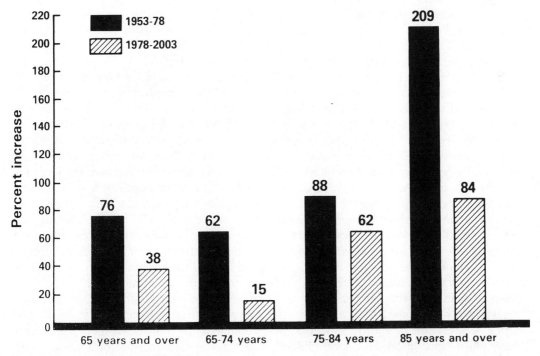

SOURCE: National Center for Health Statistics

Figure 6. Percent increase in elderly population by age group: United States, 1953–1978 and 1978–2003.

INTERACTION OF AGING AND DISEASE

The preceding chapters in this volume have dealt, in general, with the normal changes that occur with advancing age in a variety of organisms, including man. In the biomedical sciences, these studies form the data base of what is generally called *Gerontology,* whereas the term *geriatrics* or *geriatric medicine* is most often applied to the clinical aspects of the care of the elderly. A thorough knowledge of age-related physiologic changes that occur in man, in the absence of disease, is critical to a proper understanding of disease in old age since these physiologic changes form the substrate for the influence of age on the presentation of disease, its reponse to treatment, and the complications that ensue (Rowe and Besdine, 1982).

Before discussing the specific types of relationship that exist, it is appropriate to emphasize two major factors which play dominant roles in the expression of disease in the elderly. One principle relevant to both geriatric medicine and gerontological physiology is the marked *variability* that accompanies advanced age (Freis and Crapo, 1981). Decades of study of normal and abnormal aging have shown, perhaps more clearly than anything else, that the older people become, the less like each other they become. The marked variability in the clinical manifestations of a given illness in the elderly is due in part to: (1) variability in the underlying physiological changes, (2) the other diseases that the individual has accumulated over time, (3) the pattern of response to illness and the interaction with health care professionals that are characteristic of the individual, and (4) the varying degrees of severity of pathophysiologic processes. A second major principle has to do with the *critical importance of nonbiomedical factors* in the determination of the clinical manifestations of disease late in life. More than any other segment of our society, the elderly manifest differing degrees of disability and loss of function, depending on behavioral and sociological factors (Besdine, 1980).

THE CONTINUUM OF INTERACTION BETWEEN PHYSIOLOGY AND PATHOLOGY IN THE ELDERLY

A robust understanding of the varying interaction of the normal aging process with different stresses and pathologic mechanisms is required to provide the proper framework for evaluation of the elderly patient. The interaction of age and disease varies from a lack of interaction on one end of the spectrum to the extreme example in which the changes that occur with age actually represent disease inasmuch as they have direct, predictable, adverse clinical sequelae. Several specific, clinically relevant points along the continuum can be identified.

Variables That Do Not Change with Age

Perhaps the most important type of change that occurs with age, from a clinical standpoint, is no change at all. Too frequently, clinicians are apt to ascribe a disability or an abnormal physical or laboratory finding to "old age" when the actual cause is a specific disease process. Several examples of this category can be identified. In the first subset, there is no effect of age on the variable under study. An example of this lack of change may be seen in hematocrit or packed red cell volume. This measurement is routinely obtained in many clinical settings since a significant lowering of hematocrit defines the presence of anemia, a common and important medical illness of varying cause. Very frequently, elderly individuals will be found to have low hematocrit levels and the clinician will categorize the patient as having "anemia of old age." The physician may fail to pursue the underlying basis of the anemia in his belief that the normal aging process has induced the anemia and no investigation or treatment is warranted. However, data from several sources, including the Framingham Study, indicate that in healthy community-dwelling elders there is no change with age in hematocrit (Gordon and Shurtleff, 1973) (Figure 7). Thus a lower hema-

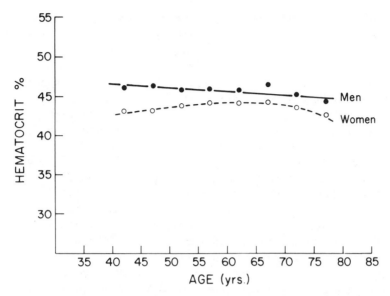

Figure 7. Age trend in hematocrit (cross-sectional data from the Framingham Study).

tocrit in an elderly individual cannot be ascribed to "anemia of old age" but deserves proper investigation and treatment. Three common, often treatable, causes of anemia in the elderly include: (1) nutritional deficits, particularly iron deficiency; (2) pernicious anemia or vitamin B 12 deficiency which develops as levels of intrinsic factor fall in advanced old age as a consequence of atrophy of the gastric mucosa; and (3) iron deficiency anemia secondary to blood loss, often from intestinal malignancies. Anemia and gastrointestinal blood loss are frequently the initial clinical evidences of an otherwise asymptomatic colonic carcinoma which, if detected early, can be very effectively treated surgically.

A second circumstance in which there is no change in a clinical variable with age relates to factors in which a balanced physiological change results in a lack of measurable change. An example of such a circumstance might be seen in the circulatory levels of many hormones, including testosterone. While the circulating level in blood of testosterone appears not to decline in healthy community-dwelling elderly men

(Sparrow et al., 1980); Harman and Tsitouras, 1980), studies indicate that this is the result of a balanced 25–30 percent decline in both testosterone production and testosterone catabolism rates (Vermeulen et al., 1972). Similar changes have been identified with regard to cortisol (West et al., 1961), thyroxine (Gregerman et al., 1962); Oddi et al., 1968), and aldosterone (Flood, 1967) and probably also exist for insulin (Minaker et al., 1982); Reaven et al., 1982). The clinically relevant fact remains that the variable most frequently measured does not change with age, and deviation from the normal range for all adults should be viewed as clearly abnormal, independent of age.

Diseases Associated with Passage of Time

Some variables that are not influenced by the aging process *per se* include abnormalities that occur in the elderly, not because of the biological or physiological changes of aging, but because of the increased *time* that elderly individuals have been alive. Several specific examples can be cited. Elderly individuals, by virtue of their greater life experience, have a greater likelihood of exposure to certain infectious diseases. Thus they may be found to have a greater prevalence of antibody levels against one or another infectious agent, while aging *per se* has no influence on their likelihood of contracting the specific infectious diseases reflected in the elevated antibody levels. A second change that occurs over time, and thus might be seen more commonly in the elderly, relates to the development of certain abnormalities in organs in which there is an inherited disease that is generally not manifest until late in life. Polycystic kidney disease represents an inherited condition in which the clinical manifestations are frequently not expressed until the sixth decade of life (Brenner and Rector, 1981). As far as we know, time, rather than the aging process itself, is the main influence on the development of cysts in kidneys; thus, clearly, some individuals must live until at least the sixth decade of life before they show manifestations of this inherited disease. A third type of abnormality which appears to be more related to the passage of time than to changes associated with age might be seen in those disorders that are related to the accumulation of exposure to environmental or dietary toxin. Thus, development of a cutaneous cancer secondary to sun exposure in individuals with fair skin is much more likely in older individuals than younger individuals because older individuals have accumulated greater exposure to ultraviolet radiation via sunlight (Gilchrest, 1979). Similarly, individuals who smoke cigarettes are more likely to develop pulmonary carcinoma in middle to late life than during younger adulthood because of the time required to accumulate exposure to a carcinogenic dose of cigarette tobacco (Peto, 1976; Doll and Peto, 1980).

Physiologic Changes by Which Specific Diseases Become Less Likely or Severe with Age

While aging is characteristically considered to be associated with a greater prevalence or severity of disease, it is quite possible that the physiologic changes associated with normal aging result in many diseases being less likely or less severe in advanced age. Clearly some disorders that appear to be based in altered immune system response, such as systemic lupus erythematosis, myasthenia gravis, and multiple sclerosis, are seen much more commonly in younger individuals than in older individuals. It is feasible that the changes which occur in the immune system with age, with marked decrease of function of T-lymphocytes and other aspects of immune competence, might result in a less robust immunological response to the inciting agent or event in these disorders (Gillis et al., 1981).

Similarly, some diseases which occur in old age as well as in younger adults clearly run a less virulent natural history in the elderly. One example may be carcinoma of the breast. Many cancer specialists feel that carcinoma of the breast runs a more virulent and more aggressive course in premenopausal than postmenopausal women. In addition, the likelihood of breast carcinoma responding well to hormonal therapy increases with the number of years after menopause. Thus, elderly individuals with this disease might be expected, on the average, to enjoy a more favorable clinical course than their younger counterparts.

Physiologic Changes That Alter the Presentation of a Disease

The existence of physiologic changes which alter the presentation of disease has long been recognized as of major importance to the practice of geriatric medicine. Many diseases that occur in both young and old adults have manifestly different clinical presentations and natural histories in the two age groups. Unlike the example of breast cancer just discussed, these disorders should not necessarily be looked upon as being less severe or more severe in the elderly, just *different*. One example of such a disorder is hyperthyroidism. Younger individuals with hyperthyroidism often present as agitated, anxious, and hyperkinetic with a palpable goiter (enlarged thyroid gland), elevated heart rate and blood pressure, hyperactive deep tendon reflexes, and almost ubiquitous complaints of irritability. Conversely, it is well recognized that many elderly individuals with hyperthyroidism, manifested by elevations of circulating thyroid hormone to levels equivalent to those seen in younger individuals, will have a strikingly different clinical presentation. In these individuals, irritability and hyperkinesis are infrequent, and goiter is very rare (Davis and Davis, 1974). Deep tendon reflexes may be normal or even hypoactive, and the patient generally presents a deactivated or "apathetic," as opposed to activated, clinical picture. The treatment of hyperthyroidism with generally the same modalities available to younger individuals results in the same generally excellent prognosis in both young and old individuals. The major clinical importance of this difference relates to the education of physicians in the recognition of hyperthyroidism in the elderly. Many physicians not familiar with the special presentation of thyroid hormone excess in the elderly will not detect the disease, and thus will allow its adverse physiologic and pathologic sequelae to continue untreated, thereby permitting continued morbidity and, perhaps, mortality.

A second example of a common disorder which presents much differently in the elderly than in young adults is the uncontrolled hyperglycemia of diabetes mellitus. In children and in young adults, uncontrolled diabetes is generally manifested by a syndrome termed diabetic ketoacidosis. This is characterized by limitations of elevations of blood glucose to levels between 300 and 500 mg/dl because of the low renal threshold for glucose. Conversely, elderly individuals with uncontrolled diabetes will frequently present with a syndrome termed hyperosmolar nonketotic coma, which is characterized by striking elevations of blood glucose, often to levels over 1000 mg/dl, due to a high renal threshold for glucose. The elderly present with obtundation and coma secondary

to the marked hyperosmolality induced by the elevated glucose levels, while younger individuals are more likely to present with manifestation of symptoms related to the volume of urine produced and the compensatory thirst that results.

Other disorders in which the presentation is strongly influenced by age, without necessarily making the disorder more or less severe, include depression, acute glomerulonephritis, and rheumatoid arthritis.

Physiologic Changes That Increase the Likelihood or Severity of a Disease

A large and important category encompasses those abnormalities which are most commonly recognized as resulting from an interaction of age and disease, and which account for the increasing morbidity and mortality of disease in old age. Age-related reductions in the function of numerous organs place the elderly individual at special risk for enhanced morbidity from diseases in those organs.

Finch has recently proposed a mechanism whereby normal age-related changes in brain neurotransmitters may influence the onset or severity of a variety of degenerative central nervous system diseases (Finch, 1980; Finch and Morgan, in press). In the case of Parkinson's disease, he points out that normal human aging has been associated with progressive reductions in basal ganglia levels of dopamine, as well as dopamine receptors and key enzymes required for dopamine synthesis (Finch and Morgan, 1984; Severson, et al., 1977; McGeer and McGeer, 1978). These decreases may interact with pathophysiologic changes to account for the increasing prevalence of Parkinson's disease in late life, whether secondary to viral encephalitis or associated with a genetic predisposition. While several models may be postulated for the interaction of aging and Parkinson's disease, Finch notes that the onset of the disease many years after acute encephalitis (Schwab et al., 1976) and the enhanced susceptibility of old individuals to extrapyramidal side effects of neuroleptic agents (Ayd, 1961) are consistent with the development of age-related subclinical dopaminergic deficits which become manifest is the presence of a preexisting subclinical pathologic lesion or when the dopaminergic tone is impaired pharmacologically.

Normal aging is associated with a marked reduction in pulmonary function as reflected in the forced vital capacity and other measures of lung function (Weiss, 1982). Healthy individuals in the ninth decade of life frequently will have lung function equal to only one-half of that of their 30-year-old counterparts. Thus, an acute pulmonary disease such as bacterial pneumonia, of equal initial severity, will be much more likely to induce a serious clinical manifestation in the elderly because of the markedly lessened pulmonary functional reserve. Over the past decade, very significant advances have been made in our understanding of the marked reduction in immune competence that occurs with age. Immunosenescence is likely responsible, in some ways, for the increased incidence of certain infections and perhaps cancers in the elderly, as well as for the increased severity of infections in the elderly. Thus, an elderly individual with pneumonia may be less likely to contain and control that infection in his respiratory tract than a young individual. Failure of an immune function may result in dissemination of that infection to many organs, and a much more serious—if not lifethreatening—clinical illness may develop.

A similar argument holds for function in many other organs including the kidneys. Normal renal function in the elderly is approximately 40 percent less than in young healthy adults (Rowe, 1976). Thus the loss of one kidney due to obstruction, vascular occlusion, or trauma in the elderly would be much more likely to result in a clinically significant reduction in glomerular filtration rate and overall renal function than the loss of function of one kidney in a healthy young individual.

In elderly individuals, multiple pathology, or the simultaneous presence of diseases in several organs or organ systems, is often the rule rather than the exception. In many cases, physiologic changes that occur with age interact with multiple pathology to induce specifically geriatric syndromes. The high prevalence in the elderly of falls may be viewed as such a case. Several studies have demonstrated a marked increase in postural sway or decrease in the capacity to maintain upright posture with advancing age, particularly in women (Sheldon, 1963; Hasselkus and Shambes, 1975; Exton-Smith, 1976). Recent evidence suggests this may be related to age-associated changes in the mechanoreceptors in the cervical spine (Wyke, 1979). Regardless of the mechanism of this age-related effect, elderly individuals, by virtue of their decreased capacity to maintain upright posture, are at particular risk for the development of falling under a variety of circumstances which would not result in falls in younger individuals. Thus, ice on the front step, a poorly lit stairway at home, or a moist bathtub without a rubber mat may all result in a near fall in a young individual and a serious fall in the elderly. The risk of the elderly to develop a serious consequence of this fall is enhanced by another age-related change, which is also particularly common in elderly women, loss of bone mass or osteopenia. Thus hip fracture is essentially a disease of elderly women and, in most instances, is induced by a fall under circumstances which would not have induced a fall or fracture in younger individuals.

A final example of a mechanism whereby age-related alterations in function increase the prevalence of a disease relates to the development of accidental hypothermia in frail elderly. This disorder has a high mortality rate and can be seen not only in individuals exposed to unheated rooms in the winter, but in individuals in heated rooms who appear to spontaneously develop marked lowering of body temperature. This disorder is essentially absent in healthy young individuals and occurs with increasing frequency with advancing old age. While the mechanisms of accidental hypothermia are poorly understood, alterations in sympathetic nervous system responsiveness seem likely to be major contributors.

Physiologic Changes Which Mimic Specific Diseases

Some changes that occur with aging may be seen to mimic specific clinical entities, thus causing confusion regarding the diagnosis of specific diseases in the elderly. Perhaps the best and most widely recognized instance of this is the decrease in carbohydrate economy that occurs with advancing age in the absence of diabetes mellitus (Davidson, 1979). Normal aging appears to be associated with a decrease in the sensitivity of peripheral tissues to the effects of insulin (Defronzo, 1979; Rowe et al., 1983). This change is reflected by decreased performance on oral or intravenous glucose tolerance tests.

The oral glucose tolerance test (OGTT) is frequently employed clinically as a means of diagnosing the presence of chemical diabetes mellitus. In this test, fasting individuals are given a standard oral dose of glucose and the plasma glucose level is checked at regular intervals over the next two hours. The level of blood sugar two hours after ingestion of a glucose challenge can be used to determine whether an individual is normal or has impaired glucose tolerance. Very high blood glucose is diagnostic of diabetes mellitus. Many medical textbooks include criteria for the diagnosis of diabetes mellitus on the oral glucose tolerance test which are based solely on studies of healthy young populations. The changes in glucose tolerance with age, independent of diabetes or other confounding diseases, are so dramatic that more than 50 percent of individuals over 60 years of age would be diagnosed as diabetic if age-adjusted criteria were not employed (Davidson, 1979). Unfortunately, physicians and other health professionals are frequently unaware of the need for age adjustment in this as well as other types of clinical tests, which results in a tendency for the overdiagnosis of diabetes in the elderly. The present criteria from the Diabetes Study Group include an age adjustment which has partially resolved the difficulties in interpretation of the OGTT.

Physiologic Changes Which Have a Direct Clinical Impact

For many decades gerontologists and geriatricians have drawn a very clear line between the changes that occur with age and those that are associated with specific disease states. We have staunchly defended the view that age is not a disease but a normal process which must be clearly understood in order to adequately diagnose and treat the increasing burden of illness that will befall a rapidly enlarging population. Substantial data in several different areas suggest that this approach is no longer tenable. There is no question that some physiologic changes that are aspects of normal aging itself have clearly adverse clinical sequelae. While a change may represent "normal aging" inasmuch as it is present in the entire population and cannot be avoided, one should not assume that this "normal" change is necessarily harmless.

While one can argue about the specific criteria for the definition of a "disease," a generally acceptable definition would include any process that results in clear, adverse clinical sequelae measured as either morbidity or mortality. Under this definition, there are clear changes that occur with advancing age which appear to be normal characteristics of the aging process and which would also qualify as diseases. Of the potentially very long list of such processes, four will be briefly reviewed.

More than any other biological change, menopause seems clearly to be accepted as age related. While menopause is thus clearly "normal," it has become abundantly clear that this normal change is associated with increased risk for certain diseases such as osteoporosis and atherosclerosis, as well as symptomatic clinical manifestations such as hot flashes which are associated with sleep disturbances and are so frequent and severe as to be disabling in many individuals (Hannon, 1927; McKinlay, 1974).

A second change that occurs with normal aging which has direct, adverse clinical consequences is cataract formation. Posttranslational modifications of central lens proteins with advancing age result in increasing opacity as well as decreasing flexibility of the lens, which is manifested in decreasing capacity to accommodate to near vision (Weale, 1963). While the reasons for the development of cataracts in some individuals and not others are not clearly understood, they probably lie in the marked physiological variability that was previously commented on as being characteristic of most if not all changes that occur with advancing age. Lens opacification or cataract is a common cause of blindness in older Americans. Thus, this normal age-related change, in its most extreme form, would seem to clearly represent a disease.

A third set of age-related changes with clear potential for classification as a "disease" consists of the endocrine changes that underlie the development of benign prostatic hypertrophy (BPH), which is present to some extent in all elderly men. Systematic investigations over the past decade have clarified the underlying endocrine mechanisms operative in the development of this age-related hyperplasia of the prostate (Swyer, 1944; Hammond, 1978; Geller and Albert, 1982). Present understanding would indicate that BPH is the result of the accumulation of dihydrotestosterone in the prostate. Dihydrotestosterone, a growth factor for prostatic tissue, is a normal metabolite of testosterone, but it is found in markedly elevated levels in hyperplastic tissue. The accumulation of dihydrotestosterone in the prostate of elderly men would seem to be the consequence of an age-related reduction in the catabolism of dihydrotestosterone to 5-androstenediol as well as an increase in the conversion of 5-androstenediol to dihydrotestosterone. BPH is an important cause of urinary tract obstruction in elderly men, and has major costs both in economic and in health terms. Most cases are treated surgically for the relief of symptoms of urinary obstruction such as urinary frequency and urgency. A considerable number of cases, however, go undetected until the degree of urinary obstruction is so great as to result in significant loss of renal function. This important and costly disease would appear, at the present time, to be largely a normal, age-related phenomenon.

A fourth characteristic type of change with advancing age that would appear to have direct clinical consequences is arteriosclerosis. This thickening of the walls of major arteries must be distinguished from atherosclerosis, which represents the development of plaques on the vessel intima that encroach on the lumen. Arteriosclerosis appears to be a normal consequence of age-related changes in the extracellular material in arterial walls; it is reflected in decreased compliance and increased stiffening of vessels with advancing age (O'Rourke, 1970). This is manifested in increased systolic blood pressure. Epidemiological studies, including the Framingham Study, have identified increases in systolic blood pressure as major risk factors for several types of vascular disorders, most notably cerebrovascular disease or stroke (Kannel et al., 1970, 1981). Thus, increases in systolic pressure, which appear to be consequences of normal age-related changes in vessel walls, carry with them an increased risk for serious morbidity or mortality.

It can thus be seen that increased understanding of the physiologic changes that occur with age, as well as the risk associated with the many changes which are considered "normal," leads to a consideration that aging can, in some ways, represent a disease state.

Pharmacology and Aging

Some changes with age have the greatest impact not on the presentation or recognition of a disease, but on its treatment. In this regard, the changes that occur in hepatic oxidation systems and in renal function with advancing age have their major clinical impact on alterations in the pharmacokinetics of many medications (Vestal, 1978; see Chapter 27). Several very commonly used medications, such as digitalis, are excreted via renal mechanisms and thus have prolonged half-lives in elderly individuals when compared to younger counterparts. This necessitates an adjustment in the treatment schedule of these medications in elderly individuals. These pharmacokinetic considerations are compounded by parallel changes in pharmacodynamics inasmuch as the tissues of elderly individuals, especially the central nervous system, become more sensitive to some agents with advancing age. The elderly are more sensitive than younger adults to the sedative or analgesic effects of tranquilizers such as diazepam or narcotics such as morphine (Vestal, 1978). The combination of alterations in pharmacokinetics and pharmacodynamics is often further aggravated by changes in body composition in the elderly. The average old individual has more fat and less lean body mass per kilogram of body weight than the younger adult. Thus the volumes of distribution of many agents will be altered in the elderly (Forbes and Reina, 1970). Similarly, circulating levels of serum albumin fall moderately with age and influence the free circulating level of medications that are highly protein bound (Gibaldi, 1977).

The combination of all of these factors is reflected in the clear-cut increase in the number and severity of adverse medication effects in the elderly. Thus, even if a physician correctly diagnoses a disease in the elderly, he is often confronted with the difficult therapeutic decision of designing a medication regimen which will be effective against the underlying disease process without inducing serious adverse effects.

ILLNESS BEHAVIOR IN THE ELDERLY

In the physician's quest to treat illness and minimize its recurrence and sequelae, maximal effectiveness depends on understanding the underlying social, psychological, and biological factors (Mechanic, 1966). In addition, as noted, physiologic changes with age in many organs influence the presentation of disease, its response to treatment, and the complications that ensue. The cultural, social, and psychological factors which influence an elder's recognition of illness, his decision to seek medical care, his choice of health care professional, his compliance with therapy, and his capacity to maintain appropriate follow-up are different from those of the younger patient (Besdine, 1982). The result of these combined age-related changes is a marked difference between young and old adults in illness behavior. Important characteristics of illness behavior in the elderly include underreporting of illness, delayed presentation, multiple pathology, altered presentation, and variable performance.

Underreporting of Illness/Delayed Presentation

Delayed presentation as a consequence of failure to report illness in its early stages is a characteristic common to geriatric patients (Anderson and Cowan, 1955; Anderson, 1966; Williamson, 1964). In several studies in Great Britain, in spite of a system of convenient and affordable care, many elderly individuals were identified by an aggressive outreach team to be harboring illnesses unknown to the responsible physician. These illnesses were serious, symptom producing, and often treatable conditions such as pernicious anemia, iron deficiency anemia, congestive heart failure, gastrointestinal bleeding, uncontrolled diabetes, active tuberculosis, foot disease interfering with mobility, oral pathology interfering with eating, correctable hearing and visual defects, and a high prevalence of depression. This underreporting appears to be most prevalent for serious illnesses, with some studies showing that the elderly may actually be more likely than their younger counterparts to seek medical care for mild or "trivial" symptoms or complaints which are felt to be "functional" rather than "organic" in nature (Haug, 1981).

Our medical care system, based on the principle that illness would produce symptoms which would provoke entry into a waiting health care delivery system, seems to fail the elderly. Examination of this failure to report illness has revealed multiple reasons for nonreporting. Foremost among these reasons is ageism (Butler, 1975). The attitude that old age is a time of pain, and that disability is to be expected and not questioned, is prevalent in society at large as well as in the elderly themselves. With this basic orientation, it is understandable that symptomatic illness is not reported. A second reason is that the high incidence of depression, estimated at between 15 percent (Blazer and Williams, 1980) and 33 percent (Anderson, 1966), coupled with the cumulative losses of old age, reduces interest in gaining health. An almost unique aspect of depression in old age is its tendency to produce memory failure (Wells, 1976; Ron et al., 1980). When judgment and insight are thus clouded, the ability to be a skilled health consumer declines, and failure to report disease occurs. The third major factor causing delayed presentation is that of impaired cognition. Normative changes in cognitive function during aging would not, of themselves, be a major contributor to delayed reporting of illness (Eisdorfer, 1975). Significant cognitive impairment is increasingly prevalent with advancing age however, due to brain disorders (NIA Task Force Report, 1980) which affect 10 percent of all those over age 65, half of whom are severely affected. The prevalence of significant cognitive impairment is striking in some select locations such as nursing homes where chronic brain disease affects up to 63 percent of the patients (Kovar, 1977).

The cognitively impaired elderly patient is unable to act as his or her own advocate in the process of identifying a symptom as something requiring medical attention and seeking out the appropriate health care provider. Clearly then, attitudinal and illness factors promote delayed entry into the health care system, with the consequence that illnesses are far advanced and less likely to be fully remediable.

Multiple Pathology

Multiple pathology, a phenomenon first described by Williamson (1964), indicates that numerous other social, psychological, and medical problems will be found when an illness occurs in an older individual. This observation is a natural extension of the phenomenon of the increasing accumulation of chronic diseases during aging. The resulting interference of these illnesses with the diagnosis and treatment of the presenting disease leads to disproportionately longer hospital stays, increased frequency of complications (both in the natural history of the illness and in treatment complications), and the increased likelihood of death or incomplete recovery (Korenchevsky, 1961). It is common in the elderly to have five or six major diagnoses in as many organ systems, each of which can act as the substrate for a new clinical event.

Altered Presentation of Illness

Presentation of illness in the elderly is often misleadingly different from that in younger age groups, and in particular, it may be entirely nonspecific (Hodkinson, 1973). Altered presentation may take the form of a change in the severity or type of symptom in the affected organ, symptoms in an organ distant from the site of acute illness, or a generalized nonspecific feeling of ill health without organ-specific symptoms. Classic examples of altered presentation are the painless myocardial infarction (Konu, 1977), apathetic hyperthyroidism (Thomas et al. 1970), depression presenting as a dementia syndrome (Wells, 1976), hypothyroidism presenting as nonspecific deterioration without focal signs (Jeffreys, 1972), and lobar pneumonia presenting with confusion, unsteadiness, and only slight breathlessness.

Physiologic changes with age may be responsible, in part, for the altered presentation of disease in old age. For instance, age-related alterations in pain perception may account for the increase in "painless" myocardial infarction in the elderly, and age-related blunting of the cardiovascular response to sympathetic stimulation may play a major role in the relative lack of "classical" cardiovascular symptoms. Similarly, multiple pathology—the simultaneous existence of impaired function in several organs—doubtless influences disease presentation. Anemia may precipitate heart failure in individuals with preexisting cardiac disease, while similar reductions in blood count would not be associated with cardiovascular symptoms in otherwise healthy younger patients. The vulnerability of the elderly to develop acute confusion in the face of disease outside the central nervous system is perhaps the classical nonspecific presentation encountered in geriatric medicine. The aged brain may be a victim of enhanced "sensitivity" due to preexisting disease as well as being at the center of a complex set of integrated functions. Conversely, one organ may not fail, but a basic function of daily living may become impaired. In general, the common syndromes seen in geriatric medicine are failures in complex, multisystem function or activities that are vulnerable to disruption from multiple insults. These syndromes such as falling (a failure in postural control function) and incontinence (failure in excretory control function) are also contributors to the nonspecific presentation of illness.

Variable Performance

For most physiologic parameters influenced by age, declines occur in median performance in a linear fashion after maturity. The result for the individual who remains at the median performance level on all these measures is a loss of homeostatic reserve capacity without specific symptom production. A characteristic of studies across the age span is the increased variability between individuals in physiologic performance, which indicates different rates of progression of aging processes. Marathon running times, in which the variance can be seen to be an exponential function of age, illustrates this fact. Indeed, in an analysis of record performances (Stones and Kozma, 1980), the standard deviations for record performances at ages 75–79 were 365 percent greater than the values for younger ages. Measures of basal physiologic function such as urea clearance, pulmonary function, and carbohydrate tolerance also show this age-related increased variation between individuals.

Chronic disease is at least as variable as aging in causing loss of functional reserve. Coronary artery disease does not develop at an equal pace in every individual, nor does it progress at the same rate in each segment of the vessel. Personal health choices, as well, can be seen as modifiers of the rate of progression of chronic disease (Belloc, 1973) and, in this context, can be seen as adding to the variability of the rate at which end-organ reserve deteriorates.

This variability in the rates of progression of aging processes and associated chronic diseases is translated at the patient level into the unpredictable behavior that characterizes the elderly. Clinically, this concept contributes to the unpredictability of response to therapeutic endeavors such as drug administration (Hurwitz and Wode, 1969; Williamson and Chopin, 1969) and surgical interventions (Stahlgren, 1961). In order to defend against this unpredictability, individualization of therapy is indicated in the elderly, and in general, the best approach to most interventions is to perform them slowly and incrementally, and to assess the response to the therapeutic stress before further therapy is undertaken. Clearly, decisions should be based on the patient's clinical condition and *not on the patient's age.*

ASSESSMENT OF THE ELDERLY PATIENT

Comprehensive assessment of the geriatric patient is designed to identify a patient's difficulties and quantify their impact on functional capacity (Williams, 1982). After assessment, the health care team serves the patient and his family by treating illness, identifying and arranging needed services, and reinforcing the existing support system. In teaching settings, geriatric assessment has also served as a training vehicle in interdisciplinary consultation (Steele and Hays, 1981).

Implicit in any comprehensive assessment is the presupposition that the best result in health care delivery occurs with services are closely matched with needs, and that thorough multidisciplinary assessment facilitates the congruence between services and needs. Geriatric assessment requires systematic consideration of function in three dimensions: physical/medical, mental/psychiatric, and social/financial. While the physical/medical evaluation is most familiar to health providers, special care and knowledge are necessary even in this area when assessing frail elderly.

Physical/Medical Assessment

Barriers to physical assessment of the elderly present themselves early due to the high prevalence of hearing disorders (22 percent), visual handicaps (15 percent), and communication problems secondary to mental and nervous disorders (10 percent). Effective communication, therefore, demands increased skill and time in history taking and in reviewing medical records, and reliance on "significant others" to put the patient's complaints in perspective. "Significant others" may include family, friends, or caring neighbors. The high prevalence of multiple, chronic, symptomatic disorders (Gotz and Gotz, 1978) frequently requires review of extensive records before the physical assessment can be considered complete. As discussed in detail elsewhere in this chapter, the physician assessing medical conditions in the elderly must be equipped with a working knowledge of the data base of geriatrics. First, he must be familiar with the impact that the process of aging has on normal values and their ranges. For example, one must know the impact of aging on carbohydrate tolerance and renal, cardiac, or pulmonary function in order to determine whether a given test result represents normal aging or the presence of a disease state. Similarly, knowing that hematocrit does not change with advancing age in normal individuals helps one to avoid making the diagnosis of "anemia of old age." More complex, but equally important in medical recommendations, is an awareness of dynamic capacity changes during aging. An example is the age-related decline in maximal power output and oxygen consumption that is possible during upper body skeletal exercise. This decline in capacity makes common wheelchair maneuvers stressful for the 80–90 year old (i.e., by using 100 percent of power output to propel a wheelchair at 3 km/hr) (Sawka et al., 1981). Although the choice of a wheelchair existence may be well founded, it is crucial to appreciate the disproportionate stress that wheelchair activity causes in the elderly.

In another chapter, the pharmacokinetic and pharmacodynamic changes which occur during aging and influence drug therapy are described in detail (see Chapter 27). Failure to approach the elderly patient with an awareness of basal and dynamic changes that occur during aging is at the root of much iatrogenic disease. The increased availability of cross-sectional and longitudinal data sets on normal aging individuals provides a substantial compilation of reference values for many physiologic functions of direct clinical relevance. The second type of specific data required by the physician assessing the elderly is awareness of illness behavior patterns, clinical syndromes, and specific diseases that are most common to the elderly. These are discussed in other parts of this chapter and other parts of this volume.

An essential component of clinical assessment of ill elderly is that of measurement of the functional impact of an unweighted list of diagnoses. This is necessary since diagnoses or physical findings, by themselves, present an inadequate index of health because the range of severity within a diagnosis is often greater than among diagnoses and the interaction of diagnoses is equally unpredictable (Lawton et al., 1967). The aim of therapy in the elderly is to improve function by modifying (more often than curing) chronic illness. There is little consensus about the operational guidelines for such assessments, and many assessment tools exist (Kane and Kane, 1981). The purposes common to all such measures are a description of the population group under study, a screen to indicate the need for specific further information, a formal assessment leading to diagnosis of functional capacity and recommendation for therapy, a monitoring component designed to sensitively detect changes in function brought about by specific interventions, and a predictive capacity that strengthens the overall clinical impression.

In general, physical assessment methodologies are concerned with understanding physical health capacities for personal care (activities of daily living) and capacities that permit independent living (instrumental activities of daily living). Self-reporting methodologies seem to be useful in general screening (Linn and Linn, 1980); Ferraro, 1980), but specific measurement is clearly superior (Brocklehurst et al., 1978). With the demonstration that paraprofessionals are capable of reliable questioning and examination (Milne et al., 1972), many tools have been developed. Each tool varies in reliability and its emphasis on the three components of physical assessment. These components are measures of general physical health, the ability to perform activities of daily living,

and the ability to perform those complex activities associated with independent living called instrumental activities of daily living. A summary of the common tools available, their strengths and weaknesses, is presented in Table 1 (Kane and Kane, 1981).

The use of these tools and awareness of their specific attributes will become more important as multidisciplinary assessment is more widely employed for geriatric patients and as research in clinical geriatrics makes more extensive use of functional outcome measures in documenting the benefits of specific treatment strategies.

Mental/Psychiatric Assessment

By and large, generalists and geriatricians who may have had little training in psychiatry have been leading the management teams for the elderly with psychiatric problems. The incidence of psychopathology increases

TABLE 1. Selected Measures of Physical Functioning by User, Purpose, and Recommendations.[a]

Measure	User[b]	Purpose[c]	Recommendations
Cornell Medical Index	n,r	d,s	Not recommended
Health Index	r	d,a,m	Promising self-report on health
PACE II and Patient Classification Form (relevant sections)	g	d,a	Record-keeping system only
OARS (relevant sections)	n,g,c,r	d,a	Community-based assessment when observation is impractical
Cumulative Illness Rating Scale	n,g	d,a,p	Not recommended
PULSES	g,c	d,a,p	Not recommended
Katz Index of ADL	n,g	d,a,m,p	Useful general tool
Barthel Index	n,g	d,a,m,p	Useful when sensitive tool needed
Disability Rating Scale	n,r	d,p	Not recommended
Kenny Self-Care Evaluation[d]	g	d,a,m,p	Useful in rehabilitation settings
Granger Range of Motion	n,g	d,a,m	Useful in rehabilitation settings
Rosow Functional Health Scale	r	d	For group information only
PGC IADL	g,c	d,s,a	Promising tool, best for women
PGC Instrumental Role Maintenance	g,c	d,s,a	Promising tool, best for women
Caro Functioning for Independent Living Scale	c	d,s	Promising tool, practical
Performance ADL	n,g,e	d,m,a,p	Promising tool, depends on demonstration
PGAP Functional Assessment Instrument	g	d,m,a	Promising tool, offers added dimensions of ADL and IADL

[a]From Kane and Kane (1981).
[b]User: n = nongeriatric provider; g = geriatric provider; c = case manager; r = researcher.
[c]Purpose: d = description; s = screening; a = assessment; m = monitoring; p = prognosis.
[d]As refined by Schoening et al. (1965).

with advancing age (Butler and Lewis, 1973). Suicide rates are highest in elderly white males (Hellon and Solomon, 1980; Miller, 1978). According to the Biometry Branch of the National Institute of Mental Health, about 80 percent of elderly people who need psychiatric assistance are not currently being served (U.S. Senate Special Committee on Aging, 1971). Perhaps 2 percent of psychiatrists' time in private practice is spent with older patients (Butler, 1973). The interplay of physical, mental, and social function (Weinstock and Bennett, 1971) justifies mental/psychiatric assessment for its own sake as well as for its influence on other realms of function.

The measurement of mental function in old age can be performed in a variety of ways, but the major domains of cognitive performance, affective state, and general mental health must be assessed. Experience with the utility of most of the psychiatric assessment tools in the elderly is limited. This restricts their prognostic capacity. Some general comments on each of the major mental/psychiatric measures have been made (Kane and Kane, 1981). Most of these tools have clinical and research utility and, as with measures of health, will find increasing use.

Social/Financial Assessment

An individual's quality of life has been suggested to be composed of four elements: life satisfaction measures, self-esteem measures, general health and functional status measures, and socioeconomic measures (George and Bearson, 1980). Social function (relationships with family and friends, and community interactions) is viewed as an important creator of self-esteem. While social assessment tools exist, there is a general lack of support for specific measurements (Kane and Kane, 1981). It is important to recognize that 80 percent of the long term care needs of elderly individuals are provided by family and friends. The practical elements of social assessment are focused clearly, then, on the quality of support that family members are able to provide and their ability to satisfy the usually increasing needs of the elderly home-bound patient. Growing out of this interaction, and crucial to the treatment plan, is consideration of the morale of the relatives and any services that might be designed to provide them with respite and education.

The impact of social forces on the physical well-being of an individual has been best described for the loss of a spouse—the clearest social support of all. The link between bereavement and mortality due to suicide was first stressed in British studies (Durkheim, 1952; Fainsbury, 1955). In early studies on overall mortality during widowhood, widowers suffered increased mortality during the six months following the death of a spouse (Young et al., 1963; Parkes et al., 1968). Widows experience a less dramatic early mortality and have their peak mortality in the second year after bereavement (McNeill, 1973). Even when the effects of homogamy (the sick marrying the sick), common infections (i.e., tuberculosis), and joint unfavorable environment were considered as causes for this excess mortality, other factors seem more causally attractive. As the causes of death seem to parallel the usual causes of death for the respective age groups, it is conceptually consistent that grief acts as a stress which can unmask established disease. The pathophysiologic mechanism may be bound in neuroendocrine or immune changes (Hofer et al., 1972; Mason, 1968).

The management of the grief reaction is based on awareness of bereavement's capacity to induce morbid events and the recognition that 25 to 50 percent of recently widowed individuals will visit their physician early on with nonspecific symptoms (Lipowski, 1975). This presents to the physician an opportunity to practice a preventive approach. Few data exist presently, however, on the type of intervention that would be most successful, and fruitful research in this area can be anticipated.

In summary, geriatric assessment involves a multidisciplinary approach, often extending over several patient visits, in order to make a complex clinical situation understandable and thus therapeutically approachable.

GERIATRIC SYNDROMES

Elderly individuals commonly demonstrate one or more well-defined clinical syndromes which are generally not seen in younger adults and which account for much of the morbidity associated with old age. Mnemonics have been developed in recognition of the contribution they make to clinical geriatrics. They include the O complex (Cape, 1978) (Figure 8), the 5 I's (immobility, incontinence, impaired homeostasis, iatrogenic disease, impairment—mental), and 3 M's (micturition, mobility, mentation). Emphasis here will be placed on illustrating two syndromes—urinary incontinence and acute confusion—to demonstrate that the differential diagnosis of these syndromes has characteristics unique to the elderly, and when they are approached systematically, there is considerable potential for successful treatment.

Incontinence

So prevalent is this disorder in old age that at the outset it must be emphasized that it is not an inherent part of the aging process. Urinary incontinence, the often unexpected, uncontrollable loss of urine, affects 5 to 15 percent of the community-dwelling elderly (Holson and Pemberton, 1955; Williams and Pannill, 1982) and 50 to 60 percent of those living in nursing homes (Milne, 1976). The development of incontinence, often not assessed beyond an uninformative urine culture, is a major cause for institutionalization. The reasons for this include the doubling in nursing time that this condition creates (Adams and McIlcorath, 1963) and the stigma that this malodorous "loss of control" represents. Urinary incontinence in the elderly represents an excellent example of a geriatric disorder which is very common and very costly, highly morbid, frequently treatable, and almost totally neglected by the medical research community.

The physiology of continence is well characterized (Freed, 1982), and the high prevalence of multiple factors known to interfere at one or several control sites due to aging or age-related disease forms the basis for the frequency of urinary dysfunction in old age. The approach to this clinical syndrome involves first identifying the presence of causes of temporary incontinence that may be simply treated (Resnick and Rowe, 1982). Sec-

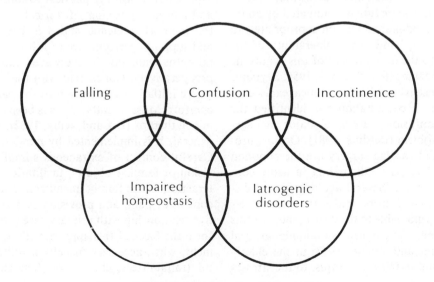

Figure 8. The O complex of geriatric medicine.

ondly, fixed forms of incontinence, such as urge, reflex, stress, and overflow, require a pathologic categorization by a clinical evaluation including cystometrography, urine flow studies, and electromyography of the urethral sphincter.

Specific therapy should follow correction of any identified precipitating event and should be guided by other etiologies discovered after evaluation. Therapies may include surgery for benign prostatic hypertrophy or severe stress incontinence (Stamey, 1980), psychotherapy or behavioral modification (Frewen, 1978), several effective, specific pharmacologic therapies (Khanna, 1976), or frequent toileting. In summary, a diagnostic appraisal is warranted for the elderly incontinent individual, and if it is carefully performed, symptomatic relief is a real possibility.

Acute Confusional States

Although it has many features, the syndrome of acute confusion has been recognized as an important cause of morbidity since the first clear description of postoperative disturbances of mental status by Duypuytren in 1834. The basic feature of this syndrome is a potentially reversible inability to maintain a coherent stream of thought and behavior (Mesulam and Geschwind, 1976).

The clinical picture is dominated by an inability to maintain attention appropriately to the tasks at hand. The vulnerability of the elderly to the development of this syndrome is well documented (Bedford, 1955; Seymour and Henschke, 1977), and clinical experience in geriatric consultation has identified the acute confusion state as a major management problem (Besdine, 1981). Ocular, urologic, and cardiac surgery are the common types of surgery culminating in acute confusional states. Several age-related and disease-related factors make the elderly especially vulnerable to the development of this syndrome. Heightened autonomic arousal (Eisdorfer and Wilkie, 1977) in the elderly may result in failure to adjust to the stresses

of acute illness. The decline during aging of the ability to handle new information or to sustain attention to multiple tasks limits adaptive capacity. Added to these changes, which are considered normal facets of aging, is the high prevalence of cognitive and mental disorders in the elderly, and the common administration of medications with potent psychotropic effects. Preexisting dementia almost certainly predisposes to the development of acute confusion during the stress of an illness (Bedford, 1955).

The differential diagnosis of acute confusion is broad, with the majority of precipitating causes originating outside of the central nervous system. Pneumonia, cardiac failure, fever, hypoxemia, and depression appear to be the most common causes (Hodkinson, 1973). Hyponatremia, a not uncommon complication of many severe acute illnesses in hospitalized elderly, is a clear contributing cause for acute confusion (Minaker and Rowe, 1981). Patients who exhibit postoperative confusional states clearly have received more medications than nonconfused patients (Morse, 1969), and the elderly are particularly sensitive to developing drug toxicity (Chapter 25).

The therapeutic approach is multidisciplinary. The first responsibility is to diagnose and treat any underlying medical problem after careful history, physical examination, and laboratory testing. Historical review of the premorbid mental status is imperative and supports performance of a formal mental status evaluation on every aged individual preoperatively. Concurrent with the investigative initiatives is attention to the patient's comfort. Most recently, this has been termed milieu therapy (Dix and Reilly, 1982), and in general, it is implemented by nursing staff. Careful control of extraneous stimuli, provision of familiar objects, facilitation of interaction with family members, adequate control of pain, and provision of a supportive relationship with primary care providers form the basis of this approach. Drug treatment, when necessary, usually involves major tranquilizers, chosen for their capacity not to alter level of consciousness and for their ability to control agitation. Choices within the group are dictated by the type of side effects desired (i.e., sedation) or to be avoided (i.e., hypotension) (Saltzman, 1982). Drug holidays, properly supervised, occasionally are necessary.

The prognosis of acute confusional states in the elderly depends on the underlying cause but, in general, is less optomistic than in younger populations. In one British study (Hodkinson, 1973), 25 percent of cases died within one month and 35 percent recovered to be discharged, with the rest remaining in hospital at the study's termination. The genuine reversibility of a significant proportion of acute confusional states justifies a thorough investigation of this common geriatric syndrome (NIA Task Force, 1980).

LONG TERM CARE

Long term care refers to the range of medical, social, and personal care for persons with chronic physical or medical conditions who are functionally limited in that they require assistance in activities of daily living. This care, whether continuous or intermittent, is required for an extended period of time and can be provided in institutional settings or at home, either through formal organizations, informal supports (family/ friends), or commonly a combination of both.

Past/Future

During the past few decades, there has been a dramatic increase in both the demand for and the cost of long term care. Although only 5 percent of the 25 million Americans currently over the age of 65 reside in nursing homes, 25 percent of all those over age 80 currently reside in nursing homes (Division of Health Care Statistics, 1978). As the over-80 group increases in number to nearly three million by the year 2000, the demand for long

term care will continue to increase dramatically.

The cost of long term care services has increased dramatically, from 0.5 billion dollars in 1960 to 21.6 billion dollars in 1978, and is expected to reach 76 billion dollars by the end of this present decade. Despite these massive increases, there exist unmet needs of considerable proportions. On both sides of the Atlantic Ocean, great concerns have also been raised about the quality of what is available (Vladek, 1980; Sherwood, 1975; Special Committee on Aging, 1974) as well as the inadequacy of financial coverage for care (Loeser et al., 1981).

Various Settings

Historically, public financing for long term care has emphasized institutional care, with less than 1 percent of the Medicaid long term care budget devoted to home-based care. Even though 1.3 million individuals are presently housed in institutions, at least two times as many individuals are in the community with similar needs. It has been estimated that between 10 and 40 percent of institutionalized elderly could be housed in less expensive settings if they were available. Hospice care, home care, congregate housing, day care, and family homes may be more cost effective and preserve a higher quality of life than an institution. HMO's (Health Maintenance Organizations) (Meyers, 1981), specifically organized primary care practices (Master et al., 1980), and local initiatives for providing long term care, such as the ACCESS (Assessment for Community Care Services) model in New York State (Eggert et al., 1980); Price et al., 1980) and the On Lok model in California (Zawadski and Ansak, 1981), have all proven successful in providing alternatives to institutionalized care. They have done so by emphasizing home-based care and centralizing the responsibility for managing the home care system. Most of these models also provide a continuum of care, as well as ongoing assessment and surveillance—the former helping to build an appropriate mix of services, the latter lessening the delay between the onset of symptoms and treatment. Geriatric evaluation settings have recently been analytically reviewed (Rubenstein et al., 1982).

Placement Decisions

Making long term care decisions is a complex process even when a balance of accessible services is available. One approach that has proven useful in simplifying this process is use of an algorithm with branch points directed toward the various long term care services available (Williams et al., 1973, 1982). Implicit in any program which is to enjoy long term success would be that (1) the arrows are bidirectional (i.e., individuals can return to a lower level of care should their status change) and (2) the surveillance mechanisms extend into "end points" where most individuals remain for six months to a year. Evidence that such an approach is useful can be inferred from the success of the ACCESS program, where only 35 percent of those originally awaiting nursing home placement ended up in nursing homes. Independent evaluations confirmed that these alternate arrangements were highly appropriate, and spending for long term care was decreased from 8 billion to 5 million dollars in three years.

The complexity of assessment dictates that several visits are often necessary and that a team of health care professionals is involved in the assessment process. The presence of family members who care and are capable of providing support clearly creates the opportunity for noninstitutional care. The future may pose some increased difficulties for noninstitutional care because social and demographic trends indicate decreasing informal supports. These trends include: increased divorce rates which weaken family ties and increase the number of elders without spouses (the progressively smaller remarriage rates with advancing age compound this); the entry into the labor market of increasing numbers of women who have been traditional care providers; and the growth of Social Security and other pension programs which permit independence in early old age, making transitions by elders into their children's homes less necessary and, therefore, more difficult as needs grow.

The Academic Nursing Home

The recognition of the necessity to expand medical and allied professional school curricula to encompass the needs of the geriatric patient has been caused, in part, by the demographic imperative, the cost of health service financing, particularly from the public sector, and the recognition of the special knowledge required to care for the elderly (Dans and Kerr, 1979). Realization that the acute care hospital, which serves as the primary clinical training ground for health professionals (Kane and Kane, 1978), is not the most suitable vehicle for developing skills necessary to practice long term care, led to the development of the concept of the "teaching nursing home" (Butler, 1981).

The purpose of the creation of such facilities would be to provide a high level of care, to engage in the vigorous training of health care professionals from all disciplines, and to foster new clinical research relevant to the geriatric population. The secondary effects conceivably would include improvement of the quality of institutional care, as well as diminished patient suffering and health care costs.

Several prerequisites must be met before exposure of trainees to long term care occurs. The institution must be adequately prepared to teach. This would necessitate the development of affiliations between long term care centers and teaching hospitals, and the recruitment of teachers who are competitive role models for students. It would be preferable that the teachers be primary care providers in the institutional setting. This would lessen the anxiety of the institution in relinquishing "turf" and also increase comfort regarding the experience of the home residents with trainees. An in-house teacher is clearly in the best position to demonstrate the gratification that genuine caring interaction with patients produces (Besdine, 1980).

The curriculum to be emphasized in such a setting will vary according to the available resources. Ideally, experience in day care, home care, and various levels of institutional care would be available (Sherman, 1980). Regardless of the mix, however, the principles of geriatric medicine as outlined here should be emphasized.

REFERENCES

Adams, G. E. and McIlwrath, P. M. 1963 *Geriatric Nursing.* Oxford: Oxford University Press.

Anderson, W. F. 1966. *The Prevention of Illness in the Elderly: The Rutherglen Experiment in Medicine in Old Age;* proceedings of a conference held at the Royal College of Physicians of London. London: Pittman.

Anderson, W. F. and Cowan, N. R. 1955. A consultative health center for people. *Lancet* 1: 1117–1120.

Ayd, F. J. 1961. A survey of drug-induced extra-pyramidal reactions. *J. Amer. Med. Assoc.* 175: 1054–1060.

Bedford, P. D. 1955. Adverse cerebral effects of anaesthesia on old people. *Lancet* 2: 259–263.

Belloc, N. B. 1973. Relationship of health practices and mortality. *Prev. Med.* 2: 67–81.

Besdine, R. 1980. Geriatric medicine. *In,* C. Eisdorfer (ed.), *Annual Review of Gerontology and Geriatrics* Vol. 1, pp. 135–153. New York: Springer Verlag.

Besdine, R. W. 1982. The data base of geriatric medicine. *In,* J. W. Rowe and R. W. Besdine (eds.), *Health and Disease in Old Age,* pp. 1–14. Boston: Little, Brown.

Besdine, R. W., Dix, G., Kravitz, L., and Minaker, K. L. 1982. Interdisciplinary geriatric consultation: consensus development. *Gerontologist* 22(5): 157.

Blazer, J. T. and Williams, C. D. 1980. Epidemiology of dysphoria and depression in the elderly population. *Am. J. Psychiatry* 137: 439–444.

Brenner, B. M. and Rector, F. C. 1981. *The Kidney.* Philadelphia: W. B. Saunders.

Brice, L. C., Ripps, H. M., and Piltz, D. M. 1980. *Third Year Evaluation of the Monroe County Long Term Care Program.* Silver Spring, Md.: Macro Systems.

Brocklehurst, J. C. 1975. *Geriatric Care in Advanced Societies.* Lancaster: Blackburn Times Press.

Brocklehurst, J. C., Carthy, M. H., Leeming, J. T., and Robinson, J. M. 1978. Medical screening of old people accepted for residential care. *Lancet* 1: 141–143.

Butler, R. N. 1975. *Why Survive? Being Old in America.* New York: Harper & Row.

Butler, R. N. 1981. The teaching nursing home. *J.A.M.A.* 245: 1435–1437.

Butler, R. N. and Lewis, M. I. 1973. *Aging and Mental Health.* St. Louis: C.V. Mosby.

Cape, R. 1978. Brain failure. *In, Aging, Its Complex Management,* p. 82. Hagerstown, Md.: Harper & Row.

Cluff, L. 1981. Chronic disease, function, and the quality of care. *J. Chron. Disease* 34: 299–304.

Dans, P. E. and Kerr, M. R. 1979. Gerontology and geriatrics in medical education. *N. Engl. J. Med.* 300(5): 228–232.

Davidson, M. B. 1979. The effect of aging on carbohydrate metabolism: a review of the English literature and a practical approach to the diagnosis of diabetes mellitus in the elderly. *Metabolism* 28: 688–705.

Davis, P. J. and Dvis, F. G. 1974. Hyperthyroidism in patients over the age of 60 years. Clinical features in 85 patients. *Medicine* 53: 161.

Defronzo, R. A. 1979. Glucose intolerance and aging: evidence for tissue insensitivity to insulin. *Diabetes* 28: 1095–1101.

Division of Health Care Statistics. 1978. National nursing home survey. Washington, D.C. Government Printing Office DHEW publication no. (PHS78-1250).

Dix, G., and Reilly, K. 1982. Milieu therapy and geriatric nurse consultation. *Gerontologist* 22(5): 183.

Doll, R., Gray, R., Hafner, B., and Peto, R. 1980. Mortality in relation to smoking: 22 years' observations on female British doctors. *Br. Med. J.* 280(6219): 967–71.

Doll, R. and Peto, R. 1976. Mortality in relation to smoking: 20 years' observations on male British doctors. *Br. Med. J.* 2(6051): 1525–36.

Durkheim, E. 1951. *Suicide, a Study in Sociology* (translated by J. A. Spaulding and G. Simpson). Glencoe, Ill.: Free Press.

Duypuytren, B. G. 1834. On nervous delirium (traumatic delirium). Successful employment of laudanum lavements. *Lancet* 1: 919–923.

Eggert, G. M., Borolyow, J. E., and Nichols, C. W. 1980. Gaining control of the long term care system: first returns from the ACCESS experiment. *Gerontologist* 20: 356–63.

Eisdorfer, C. 1975. Intelligence and cognition in the aged. *In,* E. Busse and E. Pfeiffer (eds.), *Behavior and Adaptation in Late Life,* 2nd ed. Chicago: Little, Brown.

Eisdorfer, C. and Wilkie, F. 1977. Stress, disease, aging, and behavior. *In,* J. F. Birren and K. W. Schaie (eds.), *Handbook of the Psychology of Aging.* New York: Van Nostrand Reinhold.

Exton-Smith, A. N. 1976. Lecture to conference on geriatric medicine. University of Western Ontario, Canada.

Exton-Smith, A. N. 1977. Clinical manifestations. *In,* A. N. Exton-Smith and J. G. Evans (eds.), *Care of the Elderly,* pp. 41–52. London: Academic Press.

Ferraro, K. F. 1980. Self ratings of health among the

old and the old-old. *J. Health Soc. Behavior* 21: 377–383.

Finch, C. E. 1980. Relationships of aging changes in the basal ganglia to manifestations of Huntington's chorea. *Ann. Neurology* 7: 406–411.

Finch, C. E. and Morgan, D. 1984. Aging and schizophrenia: a hypothesis relating asynchrony in neural aging processes to the manifestations of schizophrenia and other neurologic diseases with age. *In, NIMH Symposium on Aging and Schizophrenia* (in press).

Flood, C. et al. 1967. The metabolism and secretion of aldosterone in elderly subjects. *J. Clin. Invest.* 46: 960.

Flood, C., Gherondache C., Pincus, G., Tait, J. F., Tait, S. A. S., and Willoughby, S. In Schizophrenia, Paranoia and Schizophreniform disorders in late life (Miller, N. E., and Cohen, G. N., eds.) NIMH Washington, D.C. (in press).

Freed, S. Z. 1982. Urinary incontinence in the elderly. *Hospital Practice* 81–94.

Frewen, W. K. 1978. An objective assessment of the unstable bladder of psychosomatic origin. *Br. J. Urol.* 50: 246.

Fries, J. F. 1980. Aging, natural death, and the compression of morbidity. *New Engl. J. Med.* 303(3): 130–135.

Fries, J. F. and Crap, L. M. 1981. The emergence of chronic, universal disease. *In, Vitality and Aging*, pp. 79–96. San Francisco: W. H. Freeman.

Geller, J. and Albert, J. 1982. The effect of aging on the prostate. *In,* S. G. Korenman, (ed.), *Endocrine Aspects of Aging*, pp. 137–163. New York, Amsterdam, Oxford: Elsevier Biomedical.

George, L. K. and Bearon, L. B. 1980. *Quality of Life in Older Persons: Meaning and Measurement.* New York: Human Sciences Press.

Gibaldi, M. 1977. *Biopharmaceutics and Clinical Pharmacokinetics.* Philadelphia: Lea and Febiger.

Gilchrest, B. A., Blog, F. B., and Szabo, G. 1979. Effects of aging and chronic sun exposure on melanocytes in human skin. *J. Invest. Dermatol.* 73: 219.

Gillis, S., Kozak, R., Durante, M., and Weksler, M. E. 1981. Immunological studies of aging. Decreased production of and response to T cell growth factor by lymphocytes from aged humans. *J. Clin. Invest.* 67(4): 937–42.

Gordon, T. and Shurtleff, D. 1973. Means at each examination and inter-examination variation of specific characteristics: Framingham study—exams 1–10. *In,* W. B. Kannel (ed.), *The Framingham Study: An Epidemiological Investigation of Cardiovascular Disease,* DHEW Publication No-NIH74-478. Washington, D.C.: U.S. Government Printing Office.

Gotz, B. E. and Gotz, U. P. 1978. Drugs and the elderly. *Am. J. Nurs.* 78: 1347–1351.

Gregerman, R. I., Gaffney, G. W., and Shock, N. W. 1962. Thyroxine turnover in euthyroid man with special reference to changes with age. *J. Clin. Invest.* 41: 2065–2074.

Hammond, G. L. 1978. Endogenous steroid levels in the human prostate from birth to old age—a comparison of normal and diseased tissues. *J. Endocrinol.* 78: 7–19.

Hannan, J. H. 1927. *The Flushings of the Menopause,* pp. 1–22. London: Bailliere, Tindall and Cox.

Harman, S. M. and Tsitouras, P. D. 1980. Reproductive hormones in aging men. Measurement of sex steroids, basal luteinizing hormone and Leydig cell response to human chorionic gonadotropin. *J. Clin. Endocrinol. Metab.* 51: 35–40.

Hasselkus, B. R. and Shambes, G. M. 1975. Aging and postural sway in women. *J. Gerontol.* 30: 661–667.

Haug, M. R. 1981. Age and medical care utilization patterns. *J. Gerontol.* 36(1): 103–111.

Hazzard, W. R. 1983. Geriatric medicine—leading the health care team of the elderly. *In,* E. Braunwald (ed.), *Harrison's Textbook of Internal Medicine,* Ch. 75. New York: McGraw-Hill.

Health 1981. U.S. Department of Health and Human Services, Public Health Service, Office of Health Research, Statistics, and Technology.

Hellon, C. P. and Solomon, M. I. 1980. Suicide and age in Alberta, Canada, 1951–1977: the changing profile. *Arch. Gen. Psych.* 37: 505–513.

Hobot, B. and Libow, L. S. 1980. The interrelationship of mental and physical status and its assessment in the older adult: mind-body interaction. *In,* J. E. Birren and R. B. Sloane (eds.), *Handbook of Mental Health and Aging.* Englewood Cliffs, N.J.: Prentice Hall.

Hodkinson, H. M. 1973a. Mental impairment in the elderly. *J. R. Coll. Phys. London* 7: 305–317.

Hodkinson, H. M. 1973b. Nonspecific presentation of illness. *Brit. Med. Journal.* 4: 94–96.

Hofer, M. A., Wolff, C. T., Friedman, S. B., Mason, J. W. 1972. A psychoendocrine study of bereavement. II. Observations on the process of mourning in relation to adrenocortical functioning. *Psychosom. Med.* 34: 6 492–504.

Holson, W. and Pemberton, J. 1955. *The Health of the Elderly at Home* pp. 39–44. London: Butterworth.

Hurwitz, N. and Wade, O. L. 1969. Intensive hospital monitoring of adverse reactions to drugs. *Br. Med. J.* 1: 531–536.

Institute of Medicine. 1978. Report of a study: aging and medical education. National Academy of Sciences, Washington, D.C. Publication 10M-78-04.

Jacobs, S. and Ostfeld, A. 1977. An epidemiologic review of the mortality of bereavement. *Psychosom. Med.* 39(5): 344–357.

Jarvik, L. F. 1980. Diagnosis of dementia in the elderly: a 1980 perspective *In,* C. Eisdorfer (ed.), *Annual Review of Gerontology and Geriatrics* Vol. 1, pp. 180–203. New York, New York: Springer.

Jefferys, P. M. 1972. Prevalence of thyroid disease in patients admitted to a geriatric department. *Age Ageing* 1: 33–37.

Kane, R. A. and Kane, R. L. 1981. *Assessing the Elderly: a Practical Guide to Measurement.* Lexington, Mass.: Lexington Books.

Kane, R. L. and Kane, R. A. 1978. Care of the aged: old problems in need of new solutions. *Science* 200: 913-919.

Kannel, W. B., Wolf, P. A., Verter, J., and McNamara, P. M. 1970. Epidemiologic assessment of the role of blood pressure in stroke—the Framingham study. *J.A.M.A.* 214: 301-310.

Kannel, W. B., Wolf, P. A., McGee, D. L., Dawber, T. R., McNamara, P. M., and Castelli, W. P. 1981. Systolic blood pressure, arterial rigidity, and the risk of stroke. *J.A.M.A.* 245: 12, 1225-1229.

Korenchevsky, V. 1961. *Physiologic and Pathological Aging.* New York: Basel/Karger.

Kornu, U. 1977. Myocardial infarction in the elderly. *Acta Med. Scand.* (suppl.), 604: 3-68.

Kovar, M. G. 1977. Elderly people: the population 65 years and over. *In, Health United States 1976-77,* DHEW Pub. No. (HRA) 77-1232. National Center for Health Statistics, United States Department of Health, Education, and Welfare.

Kovar, M. G. 1978. Testimony before the Select Committee on Aging and the Select Committee on Population, United States House of Representatives.

Lawton, M. P., Ward, M., and Yaffe, S. 1967. Indices of health in an aging population. *J. Gerontol.* 22: 332-342.

Linn, B. S. and Linn, M. W. 1980. Objective and self assessed health in the young and the very old. *Soc. Sci. Med.* 14: 311-315.

Lipowski, Z. J. 1975. Psychiatry of somatic diseases: epidemiology, pathogenesis, classification. *Comp. Psych.* 16: 105.

Loeser, W. D., Dickstein, E. S., and Schiavone, L. D. 1981. Medicare coverage in nursing homes: a broken promise. *N. Engl. J. Med.* 304(6): 353-355.

Manton, K. G. 1982. Changing concepts of morbidity in the elderly population. *Millbank Memorial Fund Quarterly* 60(2): 183-244.

Mason, J. W. 1968. A review of psychoendocrine research on the sympathetic-adrenal medullary system. *Psychosom. Med.* 30(suppl.): 631-658.

Master, R. J., Feltin, M., Jainchill, J., Mark, R., Kavesh, W. N., Rabkin, M. T., Turner, B., Bachrach, S., and Lennox, P. A. 1980. A continuum of care for the inner city. *N. Engl. J. Med.* 302(20): 1434-1440.

Mechanic, D. 1966. Response factors in illness: the study of illness behavior. *Social Psychiatry* 1: 11-20.

Mesulam, M. and Geschwind, N. 1976. Disordered mental states in the post partum period. *Urol. Clin. N.A.* 3(2): 199-215.

Meyers, S. M. 1981. *Growth in Health Maintenance Organizations.* Washington, D.C.: National Center for Health Services Research.

McGeer, P. L. and McGeer, E. G. 1978. Aging and neurotransmitter systems. *In,* C. E. Finch, D. E. Poster, and A. D. Kenny (eds.), *Parkinson's Disease* Vol. 2: *Aging and Neuroendocrine Relationships.* pp. 41-58. New York: Plenum Press.

McGeer, P. L., McGeer, E. G., and Suzuki, G. S. 1977.

Aging and extrapyramidal function. *Arch. Neurol. (Chicago)* 34: 33-35.

McKinlay, S. and Jefferys, P. M. 1974. The menopausal syndrome. *Br. J. Prev. Soc. Med.* 28: 108-115.

McNeill, D. N. 1973. Mortality among the widowed in Connecticut. M. P. H. essay, Yale University, New Haven, Conn.

Miller, M. 1978. Geriatric suicide: the Arizona study. The Gerontologist 18: 488-495.

Milne, J. S. 1976. Prevalence of incontinence in the elderly age group. *In,* F. L. Wilington (ed.), *Incontinence in the Elderly* pp. 9-21. New York: Academic Press.

Milne, J. S., Mawle, M. M., Cormack, S., and Williamson, J. 1972. The design and testing of a questionnaire and examination to assess physical and mental health in older people using a staff nurse as observer. *J. Chronic Disease.* 25: 385-405.

Minaker, K. L. and Rowe, J. W. 1981. Behavioral manifestations of renal disease in the elderly. *In,* A. Levenson (ed.), *Somatopsychiatry in the Elderly.* New York: Raven Press.

Minaker, K. L., Rowe, J. W., Pallotta, J., and Sparrow, D. 1982. Clearance of insulin: influence of steady state insulin level and age. *Diabetes* 31: 132-135.

Morse, R. M. and Litkin, E. M. 1969. Postoperative delirium: a study of etiologic factors. *Am. J. Psych.* 126: 388-395.

NIA Task Force Report. 1980. Senility reconsidered: treatment possibilities for mental impairment in the elderly. *J.A.M.A.* 244(3): 259-263.

Oddie, T. H., Myhill, J., Pirnique, F. G., and Fisher, D. A. 1968. Effect of age and sex on the radioiodine uptake in euthyroid subjects. *J. Clin. Endocrinol.* 28: 776-782.

O'Rourke, M. F. 1970. Arterial hemodynamics in hypertension. *Circ. Res.* 6 (suppl 2): 123.

Parkes, C. M., Benjamin, B., and Fitzgerald, R. G. 1969. Broken heart: a statistical study of increased mortality among widowers. *Brit. Med. J.* 1: 740-743.

Reaven, G. M., Greenfield, M. S., Mondon, C. M., Rosenthal, M., Wright, D., and Reaven, E. 1982. Does insulin removal rate from plasma decline with age? *Diabetes* 31: 670-674.

Resnick, N. M. and Rowe, J. W. 1982. Urinary incontinence. *In,* J. W. Rowe and R. W. Besdine (eds.), *Health and Disease in Old Age* pp. 399-414. Boston: Little, Brown.

Rice, D. P. and Hodgson, R. 1978. *Scope and Impact of Chronic Disease in the United States.* National Arthritis Advances Board Forum on Public Policy and Chronic Disease.

Rogers, D. E. 1974. The doctor himself must become the treatment. *Pharos* 37: 124.

Rogers, D. E. 1982. Ambulatory care: a new research frontier. *Clin. Res.* 30(2): 109-111.

Ron, M. A., Toone, B. K., Garrolda, M. E., and Lishman, W. A. 1979. Diagnostic accuracy in presenile dementia. *Brit. J. Psych.* 134: 161-168.

Rosenwaike, I., Yaffe, N., and Sagi, P. C. 1980. The recent decline in mortality of the extreme aged. *A.J.P.H.* 70(10): 1074–1080.

Rowe, J. W. 1977. Clinical research on aging: strategies and new directions. *New Engl. J. Med.* 297: 1332–1336.

Rowe, J. W. and Besdine, R. W. 1982. Preface. *In,* J. W. Rowe and R. W. Besdine (eds.), *Health and Disease in Old Age.* Boston: Little, Brown.

Rowe, J. W., Minaker, K. L., Pallotta, J., and Flier, J. S. 1983. Characterization of the insulin resistance of aging. *J. Clin. Invest.* 71: 1581–1587.

Rowe, J. W., Tobin, J. D., Andres, R. A., Norris, A., and Shock, N. W. 1976. The effect of age on creatinine clearance in man. *J. Gerontol.* 31: 155–163.

Rubenstein, L. Z., Rhee, L., and Kane, R. L. 1982. The role of geriatric assessment units in caring for the elderly: an analytic review. *J. Gerontol.* 37: 513–521.

Sainsbury, P. 1955. *Suicide in London* p. 81. London: Chapman and Hall.

Saltzman, C. 1982. A primer on geriatric psychopharmacology. *Am. J. Psych.* 131(1): 67–74.

Sawka, M. N., Glaser, R. M., Louback, L. L., Al-Samkari, O., Suryaprasad, A. G. 1981. Wheelchair exercise performance in the young, middle-aged, and elderly. *J. Appl. Physiol. Resp. Environ. Exercise Physiol.* 50(4): 824–828.

Schoening, H. A., Anderegg, L., Bergstrom, D., Fonda, M., Steinke, N., and Ulrich, P. 1965. Numerical scoring of self-care status of patients. *Arch. Phys. Med. Rehab.* 46: 689–697.

Schwab, R. S., Doshay, L. J., Garland, H., Bradshaw, P., Garvey, E., and Crawford, B. 1956. Shift to older age distribution in parkinsonism. *Neurology* 6: 783–790.

Severson, J. A., Marcussen, J., Windblod, B., and Finch, C. E. 1982. Age-related loss of dopaminergic binding sites in human basal ganglia. *J. Neurochem.* (in press).

Seymour, D. C. and Henschke, P. J. 1977. Unpublished data.

Sheldon, J. H. 1963. The effect of age on the control of sway. *Gerontol. Clin.* 5: 129–138.

Sherman, F. T. 1980. A medical school curriculum in gerontology and geriatric medicine. *The Mount Sinai Journal of Medicine* 47(2): 99–103.

Sherwood, S. (ed.) *Long Term Care: A Handbook for Researchers, Planners, and Providers* pp. 3–79. New York: Spectrum.

Siegel, J. S. 1980. Recent and prospective demographic trends for the elderly population and some implications for health care. *In,* S. G. Haynes, and M. Feinleib (eds.), *Epidemiology of Aging.* Washington, D.C.: U.S. Government Printing Office.

Somers, A. M. 1971. Health Care in Transition: Directions for the Future. Chicago Hospital and Education Trust.

Sparrow, D., Bosse, R., and Rowe, J. W. 1980. The influence of age, alcohol consumption, and body build on gonadal function in men. *J. Clin. Endocrinol. Metab.* 51: 508–512.

Stahlgren, L. 1961. An analysis of factors which influence mortality following extensive abdominal operations upon geriatric patients. *Surg. Obstet. Gynecol.* 113: 283.

Stamey, T. A. 1980. Endoscopic suspension of the vesical neck for urinary incontinence in females. Report on 203 consecutive patients. *Ann. Surg.* 192: 465–471.

Steel, K. and Hays, A. 1981. The teaching of geriatrics in an acute teaching hospital. *In,* K. Steel (ed.), *Geriatric Education* pp. 35–40. Lexington: The Collamore Press.

Stones, M. J. and Kozma, A. 1980. Adult age trends in record running performances. *Exp. Aging Res.* 6(5): 407–416.

Swyer, G. I. M. 1944. Postnatal growth changes in the human prostate. *J. Anat.* 78: 130–145.

Thomas, F. B., Mazzaferri, L., and Skillman, T. G. 1970. Apathetic thyrotoxicosis: a distinct clinical and laboratory entity. *Ann. Int. Med.* 72: 679.

United States Senate Special Committee on Aging. 1971. *Mental Health Care and the Elderly: Shortcomings in Public Policy* (R. N. Butler, consultant). Washington, D.C.: U.S. Government Printing Office.

United States Senate Special Committee on Aging. 1974. *Nursing Home Care in the United States: Failure in Public Policy,* 93rd Congress, 2nd Session. Washington, D.C.: U.S. Government Printing Office.

Vermeulen, A., Rubens, R. and Verdonck, L. 1972. Testosterone secretion and metabolism in male senescence. *J. Clin. Endocrinol. Metabl.* 34: 730–735.

Vestal, R. E. 1978. Drug use in the elderly: a review of problems and special considerations. *Drugs* 16: 358–382.

Vladek, B. 1980. *Unloving Care: The Nursing Home Tragedy.* New York: Basic Books.

Weale, R. A. 1963. *The Aging Eye.* New York: Harper & Row.

Weinstock, C. and Bennett, R. 1971. From "waiting on the list" to "becoming a newcomer" and an "oldtimer in a home for the aged": two studies of socialization and its impact on cognitive functioning. *International Journal of Aging and Human Development* 2: 46–58.

Weiss, S. T. 1982. Pulmonary system. *In,* J. W. Rowe and R. W. Besdine (eds.), *Health and Disease in Old Age.* Boston: Little, Brown.

Wells, C. E. 1978. Geriatric organic psychoses. *Psychiatric Annals* 8(9): 466–479.

West, C. D., Brown, H., Simons, E. L., Carter, D. B., Kumagai, L. F., and Engelbert, E. L. 1961. Adrenocortical function and cortisol metabolism in old age. *J. Clin. Endocrinol. Metab.* 21: 1197–1207.

Williams, M. E. and Pannill, F. C., 1982. Urinary incontinence in the elderly. *Ann Int. Med.* 97: 895–907.

Williams, T. F., Hill, J. G., Fairbank, M. E., and Knox, K. G. 1973. Appropriate placement of the chronically ill and aged: a successful approach by evaluation. *J.A.M.A.* 226: 11, 1332–1335.

Williams, T. F., Williams, M. E., and Butley, D. W. 1982. Clinical conference: assessment of the elderly for long term care. *J. Am. Ger. Soc.* 30(1): 71–75.

Williamson, J. 1964. Old people at home: their unreported needs. *Lancet* 1: 1117–1120.

Williamson, J. and Chopin, J. M. 1980. Adverse reactions to prescribed drugs in the elderly: a multivariate investigation. *Age and Ageing* 9(2): 73–80.

Wyke, B. 1979. Cervical articular contributions to posture and gait: their relation to senile disequilibrium. *Age and Aging* 8: 251–258.

Young, M., Benjamin, B., and Wallis, C. 1963. The mortality of widowers. *Lancet* 2: 454–456.

Zawadski, R. T. and Ansak, M. L. 1981. *On Lok: Community Care Organization for Dependent Adults—the First Two Years.* San Francisco: On Lok Senior Health Services.

AUTHOR INDEX

Venet, R., *930*
Verbov, J., 822, *841*
Verdonck, L., 449, *456,* 466, 467, 481, 482, 486, *510*
Verdone-Smith, C., 56, 66, *70*
Verity, M. A., 544, *563,* 882, *893*
Verkhratsky, N. S., 276, *285,* 392, 404, *410,* 585, *589*
Verma, I. M., 259, *271*
Vermeulen, A., 466, 467, 481, 482, 483, 485, 486, 487, 489, 490, 495, *499, 508, 510*
Vermeulen, J. P., 449, *456*
Vernadakis, A., 646, 647, 672, 677, 678, *692*
Verni, F., 88, *104*
Vernon, L., 294, *319*
Vershcoor, G. J., 699, *716*
Verter, J., 944, *957*
Verth, A. H., 648, *685*
Verwoerdt, A., 495, *507, 510*
Verzar, F., 61, *76,* 545, 555, *558,* 653, *691,* 758, *810*
Verzhikovskaya, N. V., 441, 442, *452, 456*
Veselovska, L. D., 229, 230, 246, 253
Vestal, R. E., 403, *413,* 584, *594,* 730, *743,* 744, 750, 754, 756, 757, 760, 771, 773, 777, 778, 785, 786, 792, 793, 794, 795, 798, 799, 800, *807, 809, 814, 816, 818,* 944, 945, *958*
Veterans Administration Cooperative Study Group on Antihypertensive Agents, 874, *877*
Vibert, M., 247, *254*
Vickers, M. D., 758, 759, *809*
Vicks, J., 823, *841*
Victor, M., 654, *683*
Vidali, G., 235, *250*
Vidalon, C., 444, *456*
Vieth, J., 709, *712*
Vigneri, R., 444, *451*
Vigneulle, R. M., 340, 344, *353*
Vignon, G., 520, 521, *538*
Vihko, P., 493, *502*
Vihko, R., 493, *502*
Vihko, V., 906, *930, 931*
Vijayan, V. K., 646, 647, 672, 679, 680, *691*
Vijayashankar, N., 656, *691*
Viljanto, J. A., 838, *841*
Villers, T. A., 106, *126*
Vincent, J., 518, *535*
Vincent, R. A., Jr., 183, 184, 197, 199, *219, 224,* 294, 303, *321*
Vine, J., 752, 758, 759, 778, 802, *815*
Vinik, A. I., 444, *453,* 547, *563*
Vir, S. C., 885, 886, 888, *893*
Virkajarvi, J., 52, *72*
Visessuvan, S., 575, *590*
Vishnevsky, A. S., 444, *451*
Vismans, J., 531, *538*
Visscher, M. B., 47, *68*
Viswan, A. K., 753, 790, *807*
Viteri, F., 521, *536*

Vitiello, M. V., 580, *588,* 701, 704, 709, *716*
Vitorica, J., 545, 546, 547, *563*
Viukari, M., 803, *818*
Vlachou, K., 99, *101*
Vladek, B., 953, *958*
Vochitu, E., 56, 6, *73*
Vogel, G., 711, *716*
Vogel, J. M., 529, *536*
Vogel, K. G., 132, *144,* 300, 301, *316, 321*
Vogler, N., 278, *286*
Vogt, H. J., 486, 487, 490, *507*
Vogt, J. V., 486, *507*
Vogt, P. K., 263, *269*
Voigt, A. E., *928*
Voigt, K. D., 482, *502*
Voisin, G. A., 99, *104*
Volans, C. N., 751, 754, 756, *808*
Volicer, L., *615,* 652, 671, *689*
Volkmar, F. R., *643*
Volmat, T., 805, *818*
vom Saal, F. S., 575, *594*
von Abrams, G. J., 119, *126*
vonBahr, C., 204, *221*
Von Braunmuhl, A., 624, 625, *643*
von Ehrenstein, G., 129, *142, 143,* 144
von Hahn, H. P., 190, 191, *224*
von Hahn, 160
Vorbeck, M. L., 277, *288,* 544, *563*
Vos, O., 340, *355*
Voss, K. H., 553, *563,* 880, *893*
Voss-Lagerland, K., 835, *840*
Vrabiescu, A., 64, *68*
Vracko, R., 298, *321,* 854, *858*
V, Vannotti, A., 443, *451*
Vvori, I., 901, *929*
Vyckocil, F., 903, *931*

Wachtlova, M., 879, *892*
Wada, T., 443, *454*
Waddington, C. H., 160, *169*
Wade, D. L., 113, *124*
Wade, O. L., 947, *956*
Wagner, D. J., 242, *251*
Wagner, H., 491, *502*
Wagner, H. N., 396, *411,* 441, 442, *453*
Wagner, J. A., 379, *412,* 896, 923, *929, 931*
Wagner, P., 517, 521, 522, *537*
Wahlin, E., 441, *456*
Wahlin-Boll, E., 778, *816*
Wahner, H. W., 441, 442, *451,* 527, *538*
Waisman, M., 822, *841*
Wajsman, Z., 492, *508*
Wakabayashi, K., 467, 469, *509*
Wakamatusu, E., 518, *539*
Waksman, B. H., 415, *430*
Walan, A., 756, *811*
Walburg, H. E., Jr., 199, 200, 213, *219, 224*
Waldorff, S., 754, 779, *812*
Waldstein, E. A., 175, 197, 199, *224*
Walford, D. S., 425, *432*

Walford, G. D., 401, *410*
Walford, R. L., 36, *43,* 69, 70, 72, *76, 145,* 202, 214, *218,* 234, *254,* 274, 276, 280, 281, 282, 283, *285, 286, 287, 288,* 295, 298, *321,* 346, *354, 356,* 414, 419, 421, 424, 427, *429, 430, 431, 432,* 544, 550, 551, *560, 563,* 637, *643,* 880, 881, 882, *890, 891, 893*
Walker, A. M., 477, *503*
Walker, A. R. P., 522, *539*
Walker, B. F., 522, *539*
Walker, B. R., 784, *814*
Walker, I. G., 185, 187, 212, *216*
Walker, J. B., 276, *288,* 652, 656, 671, 673, 679, 680, *691*
Walker, J. M., 698, 699, *713, 716*
Walker, J. P., 276, *288,* 652, 656, 671, 673, 679, 680, *691*
Walker, P. L., 179, *216*
Walker, R. F., 461, 487, 490, 491, *499,* 569, 572, 573, *588, 594,* 659, *691*
Walker, R. M., 528, *539*
Wall, J., 636, *642*
Wallace, A. G., *930*
Wallace, B., 154, *169*
Wallace, J. P., 909, 910, 911, 921, *927*
Wallace, S., 759, 760, *818*
Wallach, Z., 238, 239, *254*
Walle, T., 799, *817*
Waller, H., 208, 209, *219*
Waller, M., 208, 209, *219*
Waller, S. B., *641,* 646, 649, 659, 669, 672, 677, 679, *691*
Wallin, B. G., 583, *594*
Wallis, C., 950, *959*
Wallner, L., *928*
Wallon, C., 423, *429*
Walne, P. L., 82, *101*
Walsh, B., 208, *222,* 426, *431*
Walsh, J., 710, *716*
Walsh, P. C., 493, *499, 509, 510*
Walter, D. N., 838, *840*
Walter, R. D., 693, 697, 714, *714*
Walthall, B. J., 293, *313, 321*
Walton, D. C., 112, *126*
Walton, K. W., 822, *840*
Wamsley, J. K., *612*
Wandless, I., 798, *818*
Wang, C., 480, 481, 482, 489, *497*
Wang, C. Y., 120, *122*
Wang, H. S., 64, *76,* 495, *507, 510,* 616
Wang, J. C., *100*
Wang, J. L., 273, *285*
Wang, M., 747, *817*
Wang, R. K., 761, 763, 768, 769, *816*
Wangermann, E., 107, *126,* 166, *166*
Wanzie, F., 696, *717*
Wara, M. D., 63, *76*
Ward, B. E., 369, *373*
Ward, C. A., 793, 797, *815*
Ward, M., 948, *957*
Ward, R. L., 256, *271*
Ward, S., 130, *141*

SUBJECT INDEX